MAJOR 20th-CENTURY WRITERS

◆

◆

◆

◆

MAJOR 20th-CENTURY WRITERS

A Selection of Sketches from
Contemporary Authors

Contains more than one thousand entries on the most widely studied twentieth-century writers, all originally written or updated for this set.

Second Edition

Kathleen Wilson, Editor

Volume 2: Ch-G

GALE

DETROIT · LONDON

STAFF

Kathleen Wilson, *Project Manager*

James E. Person, Jr., *Senior Editor*
Kathy D. Darrow, *Manuscript Editor*
Craig E. Hutchinson, *Assistant Manuscript Editor*
Aarti D. Stephens, *Managing Editor*

Bonnie E. Burns, Edith S. Davis, Carol Dell'Amico, George Delury, Sarah Madsen Hardy,
Katherine Hasal, Blaine Howard, Erik Huber, Jean Leverich, Maarten Reilingh,
Judith C. Reveal, Kathleen Savory, Robert E. Schnakenberg,
Kelly Winters, Robert E. Winters, *Sketchwriters*

Nicholas Assendelft, Karen C. Branstetter, Rebecca C. Condit, Karen J. Hansen,
Daniel J. Harvey, Wyn A. Hilty, John Kane, Jill Kushner, Patricia A. Onorato, Carol Page,
Debra M. Reilly, Bohdan R. Romaniuk, Molly C. Stephanou, Lisa A. Wroble, *Proofreaders*

Victoria Cariappa, *Research Manager*
Tamara C. Nott, Tracie A. Richardson, Norma Sawaya, Cheryl Warnock, *Research Associates*

Mary Beth Trimper, *Production Director*
Deborah Milliken, *Production Assistant*
Gary Leach, *Graphic Artist*

Contents

Introduction

An Important Information Source on Twentieth-Century Literature and Culture

Major Twentieth-Century Authors (*MTCW*) provides students, educators, librarians, researchers, and general readers with a concise yet comprehensive source of biographical and bibliographical information on more than 1,000 of the most influential authors of the century. Based on Gale's award-winning *Contemporary Authors* series, *MTCW* gives users a one-stop resource for information on the figures who have shaped literature in the past 100 years.

New to This Edition

MTCW, second edition, includes sketches on over 1,000 authors. Over 20 percent of these authors are new to this edition, evidencing Gale's commitment to identifying emerging and important writers of recent eras and of many cultures. In addition, sketches on authors who appeared in the first edition of *MTCW* have been updated to include information on their lives and works through 1998.

Who Is a "Major" Author?

In the interests of winnowing the massive list of published world authors to a number that could fit within these five volumes, the editors enlisted the expert guidance of ten advisers, professionals in library science and literature, whose input resulted in informal inclusion criteria. Of no doubt was that *MTCW* would need to include prominent novelists, poets, short story writers, and playwrights who have had at least part of their oeuvre published in English. It was also evident that *MTCW* would have to include writers of all nationalities, ethnicities, and genres, including children's literature and literary criticism. Perhaps not as obvious, advisors believed that authors must have had a significant portion of their writings first published in the twentieth century. This eliminates writers like Mark Twain, who lived until 1910, but includes the French Symbolist Remy de Gourmont, who lived until 1915. Secondly, the editors decided to focus on those who have made writing literature their primary occupation. Therefore, figures such as Adolf Hitler, well known as the author of *Mein Kampf,* have been excluded. Journalists, screenwriters, reporters, and television writers have also been excluded unless their work has been collected into significant, book-length publications. The most spirited debate between the editors and advisors involved choosing between writers who are popular and those whose popularity may not be as broad but whose critical reputations cannot be denied. Although it is hard to determine the eventual reputation of many of today's popular writers, there can be no doubt that their works are known and appreciated by millions, thus conferring upon them the status of "major" author. Lastly, though the primary focus of *MTCW* is writers of fiction, the editors and advisors agreed that authors of the major nonfiction works of the twentieth century should be represented. Therefore, *MTCW* includes writers such as Sigmund Freud, whose writings have had a profound influence on both science and art during the twentieth century, and Martin Luther King, Jr., whose essays and speeches have had a major impact on society and politics over the course of the last several decades.

How Authors Were Chosen for *MTCW*

A preliminary list of authors was sent to an advisory board of librarians, teaching professionals, and writers in both the United States and Great Britain. In consultation with the editors, the list was narrowed to 1,000 authors. Writers who were in the first edition of *MTCW* were not automatically chosen for the second edition. For information about our advisory board for the second edition of *MTCW,* please see p. ix.

Broad Coverage in a Single Source

MTCW provides coverage of the most influential writers of our time, including:

- *Novelists and short story writers:* James Baldwin, Saul Bellow, William Faulkner, Ellen Glasgow, James Joyce, Franz Kafka, C. S. Lewis, Flannery O'Connor, Carlos Fuentes, George Orwell, Eudora Welty, and Edith Wharton, among many others.

- *Dramatists:* Samuel Beckett, Tony Kushner, Bertolt Brecht, Eugene O'Neill, Wendy Wasserstein, and Tennessee Williams, and many more.

- *Poets:* W. H. Auden, Joseph Brodsky, T. S. Eliot, Robert Frost, Howard Nemerov, Charles Simic, Rainer Maria Rilke, and William Butler Yeats, among many others.

- *Contemporary literary figures:* Martin Amis, Maya Angelou, Wendell Berry, Amy Tan, Don DeLillo, Laura Esquivel, Gabriel Garcia Marquez, Nadine Gordimer, Leslie Marmon Silko, Maxine Hong Silko, Tony Kushner, Madeleine L'Engle, Toni Morrison, V. S. Naipaul, Jeanette Winterson, Joyce Carol Oates, and Thomas Pynchon, among many more.

- *Genre writers:* Ray Bradbury, Agatha Christie, Tom Clancy, Stephen King, Anne Rice, Anne Rivers Siddons, Georges Simenon, J. R. R. Tolkien, and P. G. Wodehouse, among many others.

- *Twentieth-century thinkers:* Hannah Arendt, Bruno Bettelheim, Albert Einstein, Mohandas Gandhi, Russell Kirk, Margaret Mead, Jean-Paul Sartre, and Aleksandr Solzhenitsyn, among many more.

How Entries Are Organized

Each entry begins with a series of rubrics that outline the writer's personal history, including information on the author's birth, death, family life, education, career, memberships, and awards. The *Writings* section lists all known first editions of the author's works, along with the publisher and year published. In some cases, this section may be further divided with helpful subheadings, such as *Plays* or *Mysteries,* in an effort to group like publications together for the user's convenience. The *Sidelights* section provides a critical overview of the author's reception among critics and readers, and the *Biographical/Critical Sources* section provides a useful list of books, feature articles, and reviews in which the writer's work has been treated. This section includes citations for all material quoted in the *Sidelights* essay.

Other helpful sections include *Adaptations,* listing film and television versions of an author's works and information on collections of the author's papers.

Using the Indexes

MTCW includes a Nationality/Ethnicity index as well as a Subject/Genre index. More than 60 nations are represented in the Nationality index, reflecting the international scope of this set and the multinational status of many authors. The Subject/ Genre index covers over 25 genres and subject areas of fiction and nonfiction frequently referenced by educators and students, including Holocaust literature, environmental issues, and science fiction/science fantasy literature.

Citing *MTCW*

Students writing papers who wish to include references to information found in *MTCW* may cite sources in their bibliographies using the following format. Teachers adhering to other bibliographic formats may request that their students alter the citation below, which should serve only as a guide:

"Margaret Atwood." *Major Twentieth-Century Writers,* 2nd edition. Ed. Kathleen Wilson. Vol. 1. Detroit: Gale, 1999, pp. 159-64.

Comments are Appreciated

Major Twentieth-Century Writers is intended to serve as a useful reference tool for a wide audience, so your comments about this work are encouraged. Suggestions of authors to include in future editions of *MTCW* are also welcome. Send comments and suggestions to The Editor, *Major Twentieth-Century Writers,* Gale Research, 27500 Drake Road, Farmington Hills, MI 48331-3535. Or, call toll-free at 1-800-347-GALE.

Advisory Board

In preparation for the first edition of *Major Twentieth-Century Writers* (*MTCW*), the editors of *Contemporary Authors* conducted a telephone survey of librarians and mailed a print survey to more than four thousand libraries to help determine the kind of reference resource libraries wanted. Once it was clear that a comprehensive, yet affordable source of information on twentieth-century writers was needed to serve small and medium-sized libraries, a wide range of resources was consulted: national surveys of books taught in American high schools and universities; British secondary school syllabi; reference works such as the *New York Public Library Desk Reference, Reading Lists for College-Bound Students: The Books Most Recommended by America's Top Colleges, The List of Books,* E. D. Hirsch's *Cultural Literacy,* and volumes in Gale's Literary Criticism Series and *Dictionary of Literary Biography.* From these resources and with the advice of an international advisory board, the author list for the first edition of *MTCW* was finalized, the sketches edited, and the volume published.

For the second edition, the editors submitted a preliminary author list based largely upon a list of authors included in the first edition. This list was sent to an advisory board of librarians, authors, and teaching professionals in both the United States and Great Britain. In addition to vetting the existing list, the advisors suggested other writers who had not appeared in the first edition. Recommendations made by the advisors ensure that authors from all nations and genres are represented. The ten-member advisory board includes the following individuals, whom the editors wish to thank for sharing their expertise:

- **Robert Bibbee,** Chief of the Literature and Language Division, Chicago Public Library, Harold Washington Library Center, Chicago, Illinois.

- **Michael Burgess,** Head of Technical Services and Collection Development, John M. Pfau Library, California State University, San Bernardino, California.

- **Mary Ann Capan,** Associate Professor and Young Adult and Children's Literature Specialist in the Elementary Reading Department, Western Illinois University, Macomb, Illinois.

- **Eleanor Dore,** Chief of the Language and Literature Division, District of Columbia Public Library, Washington, D.C.

- **Rebecca Havenstein-Coughlin,** Department Head, Adult Services, Canton Public Library, Canton, Michigan.

- **Marcia Pankake,** Professor and Bibliographer in English and American Literature, Meredith Wilson Library, University of Minnesota, Minneapolis, Minnesota.

- **Janice Schuster,** Head of Public Services, Phillips Memorial Library, Providence College, Providence, Rhode Island.

- **Brian Stableford,** literary critic and writer of speculative fiction, Reading, England.

- **Darlene Ursel,** reference librarian at the Plymouth District Library, Plymouth, Michigan.

- **Hope Yelich,** reference librarian at the Earl Gregg Swem Library, The College of William and Mary, Williamsburg, Virginia.

Major 20th-Century Authors

VOLUME 1: A-Ce

Abbey, Edward 1927-1989
Abe, Kobo 1924-1993
Abrahams, Peter 1919-
Abse, Dannie 1923-
Achebe, Chinua 1930-
Ackroyd, Peter 1949-
Adams, Alice 1926-
Adams, Douglas 1952-
Adams, Henry 1838-1918
Adams, Richard 1920-
Adler, Mortimer J. 1902-
Agee, James 1909-1955
Agnon, S. Y. 1888-1970
Aiken, Conrad 1889-1973
Akhmatova, Anna 1888-1966
Albee, Edward 1928-
Aldiss, Brian W. 1925-
Alegria, Claribel 1924-
Aleixandre, Vicente 1898-1984
Alexie, Sherman 1966-
Algren, Nelson 1909-1981
Allen, Paula Gunn 1939-
Allende, Isabel 1942-
Allingham, Margery 1904-1966
Allison, Dorothy E. 1949-
Alvarez, Julia 1950-
Amado, Jorge 1912-
Ambler, Eric 1909-
Amichai, Yehuda 1924-
Amichai, Yehudah
    See Amichai, Yehuda
Amis, Kingsley 1922-1995
Amis, Martin 1949-
Ammons, A. R. 1926-
Anand, Mulk Raj 1905-
Anaya, Rudolfo A. 1937-
Anderson, Maxwell 1888-1959
Anderson, Poul 1926-
Anderson, Sherwood 1876-1941
Angelou, Maya 1928-

Anouilh, Jean 1910-1987
Anthony, Piers 1934-
Apollinaire, Guillaume 1880-1918
Aragon, Louis 1897-1982
Arenas, Reinaldo 1943-1990
Arendt, Hannah 1906-1975
Arias, Ron 1941-
Arnow, Harriette Simpson 1908-1986
Artaud, Antonin 1896-1948
Ashbery, John 1927-
Ashton-Warner, Sylvia 1908-1984
Asimov, Isaac 1920-1992
Asturias, Miguel Angel 1899-1974
Atwood, Margaret 1939-
Auden, W. H. 1907-1973
Auster, Paul 1947-
Ayckbourn, Alan 1939-
Ayer, A. J. 1910-1989
Azuela, Mariano 1873-1952
Babel, Isaak 1894-1941
Bachman, Richard
    See King, Stephen
Bainbridge, Beryl 1933-
Baker, Russell 1925-
Baldwin, James 1924-1987
Ballard, J. G. 1930-
Bambara, Toni Cade 1939-
Banks, Russell 1940-
Baraka, Amiri 1934-
Barker, Clive 1952-
Barnes, Djuna 1892-1982
Barnes, Julian 1946-
Barrie, J. M. 1860-1937
Barthelme, Donald 1931-1989
Barthes, Roland 1915-1980
Bates, H. E. 1905-1974
Baum, L. Frank 1856-1919
Baxter, Charles 1947-
Beagle, Peter S. 1939-
Beattie, Ann 1947-

Beauchamp, Kathleen Mansfield 1888-1923
Beauvoir, Simone de 1908-1986
Beckett, Samuel 1906-1989
Beerbohm, Max 1872-1956
Behan, Brendan 1923-1964
Bell, Madison Smartt 1957-
Belloc, Hilaire 1870-1953
Bellow, Saul 1915-
Bely, Andrey
    See Bugayev, Boris Nikolayevich
Benavente, Jacinto 1866-1954
Benchley, Peter 1940-
Benet, Stephen Vincent 1898-1943
Bennett, Alan 1934-
Bennett, Arnold 1867-1931
Berendt, John 1939-
Berger, Thomas 1924-
Bergman, Ingmar 1918-
Berry, Wendell 1934-
Berryman, John 1914-1972
Betjeman, John 1906-1984
Bettelheim, Bruno 1903-1990
Binchy, Maeve 1940-
Bioy Casares, Adolfo 1914-
Bishop, Elizabeth 1911-1979
Biyidi, Alexandre 1932-
Black Elk 1863-1950
Blair, Eric 1903-1950
Blais, Marie-Claire 1939-
Bland, Edith Nesbit
    See Nesbit, E.
Blixen, Karen 1885-1962
Bloch, Robert 1917-1994
Block, Lawrence 1938-
Bloom, Harold 1930-
Blount, Roy, Jr. 1941-
Blume, Judy 1938-
Bly, Robert 1926-
Boell, Heinrich 1917-1985

Bogan, Louise 1897-1970
Boland, Eavan 1944-
Bonnefoy, Yves 1923-
Bontemps, Arna 1902-1973
Borges, Jorge Luis 1899-1986
Bowen, Elizabeth 1899-1973
Bowles, Paul 1910-
Boyle, Kay 1902-1992
Boyle, T. Coraghessan 1948-
Bradbury, Edward P.
Bradbury, Malcolm 1932-
Bradbury, Ray 1920-
Bradley, Marion Zimmer 1930-
Brecht, Bertolt 1898-1956
Breslin, James 1930-
Breslin, Jimmy
    See Breslin, James
Breton, Andre 1896-1966
Brink, Andre 1935-
Brittain, Vera 1893(?)-1970
Brodsky, Iosif
    Alexandrovich 1940-1996
Brodsky, Joseph
    See Brodsky, Iosif Alexandrovich
Brooke, Rupert 1887-1915
Brookner, Anita 1928-
Brooks, Cleanth 1906-1994
Brooks, Gwendolyn 1917-
Brophy, Brigid 1929-1995
Brown, Dee 1908-
Brown, Rita Mae 1944-

Brown, Sterling Allen 1901-1989
Brownmiller, Susan 1935-
Bruchac, Joseph III 1942-
Brunner, John 1934-1995
Bryher
    See Ellerman, Annie Winifred
Buber, Martin 1878-1965
Buchan, John 1875-1940
Buchwald, Art 1925-
Buck, Pearl S. 1892-1973
Buckley, William F., Jr. 1925-
Buechner, Frederick 1926-
Buero Vallejo, Antonio 1916-
Bugayev, Boris
    Nikolayevich, 1880-1934
Bukowski, Charles 1920-1994
Bulgakov, Mikhail 1891-1940
Bullins, Ed 1935-
Burgess, Anthony
    See Wilson, John Burgess
Burke, Kenneth 1897-1993
Burroughs, Edgar Rice 1875-1950
Burroughs, William S. 1914-1997
Butler, Octavia E. 1947-
Butler, Robert Olen 1945-
Butor, Michel 1926-
Byatt, A. S. 1936-
Cabell, James Branch 1879-1958
Cabrera Infante, G. 1929-
Caldicott, Helen 1938-
Caldwell, Erskine 1903-1987

Caldwell, Taylor 1900-1985
Calisher, Hortense 1911-
Callaghan, Morley
    Edward 1903-1990
Calvino, Italo 1923-1985
Campbell, Bebe Moore 1950-
Campbell, Joseph 1904-1987
Campbell, Roy 1901-1957
Camus, Albert 1913-1960
Canetti, Elias 1905-1994
Capek, Karel 1890-1938
Capote, Truman 1924-1984
Card, Orson Scott 1951-
Cardenal, Ernesto 1925-
Carey, Peter 1943-
Carr, John Dickson 1906-1977
Carroll, James P. 1943-
Carruth, Hayden 1921-
Carson, Rachel 1907-1964
Carter, Angela 1940-1992
Cartland, Barbara 1901-
Carver, Raymond 1938-1988
Cary, Joyce 1888-1957
Casares, Adolfo Bioy
    See Bioy Casares, Adolfo
Castellanos, Rosario 1925-1974
Cather, Willa Sibert 1873-1947
Catton, Bruce 1899-1978
Cavafy, C. P. 1863-1933
Cela, Camilo Jose 1916-
Cesaire, Aime 1913-

VOLUME 2: Ch-G

Challans, Mary 1905-1983
Chandler, Raymond 1886-1959
Char, Rene 1907-1988
Chase-Riboud, Barbara 1939-
Chavez, Denise 1948-
Cheever, John 1912-1982
Chesnutt, Charles W. 1858-1932
Chesterton, G. K. 1874-1936
Ch'ien, Chung-shu 1910-
Childress, Alice 1920-1994
Chomsky, Noam 1928-
Christie, Agatha 1890-1976
Churchill, Winston 1874-1965
Ciardi, John 1916-1986
Cisneros, Sandra 1954-
Cixous, Helene 1937-
Clancy, Thomas L. 1947-
Clancy, Tom

    See Clancy, Thomas L.
Clark, John Pepper 1935-
Clark, Kenneth 1903-1983
Clark, Mary Higgins 1929-
Clarke, Arthur C. 1917-
Clarke, Austin C. 1934-
Clavell, James 1925-1994
Cleary, Beverly 1916-
Cleaver, Eldridge 1935-1998
Clifton, Lucille 1936-
Clutha, Janet Paterson Frame 1924-
Cocteau, Jean 1889-1963
Codrescu, Andrei 1946-
Coetzee, J. M. 1940-
Colette 1873-1954
Comfort, Alex 1920-
Commager, Henry Steele 1902-
Commoner, Barry 1917-

Compton-Burnett, I. 1884-1969
Conan Doyle, Arthur
    See Doyle, Arthur Conan
Conde, Maryse 1937-
Condon, Richard 1915-1996
Connell, Evan S., Jr. 1924-
Connolly, Cyril 1903-1974
Conrad, Joseph 1857-1924
Conroy, Pat 1945-
Cookson, Catherine 1906-
Cooper, Susan 1935-
Coover, Robert 1932-
Cormier, Robert 1925-
Cornwell, David 1931-
Cornwell, Patricia 1956-
Corso, Gregory 1930-
Cortazar, Julio 1914-1984
Cousins, Norman 1915-1990

Coward, Noel 1899-1973
Cowley, Malcolm 1898-1989
Cox, William Trevor 1928-
Cozzens, James Gould 1903-1978
Crane, Hart 1899-1932
Creeley, Robert 1926-
Crews, Harry 1935-
Crichton, Michael 1942-
Cruz, Victor Hernandez 1949-
Cullen, Countee 1903-1946
Cummings, E. E. 1894-1962
Dahl, Roald 1916-1990
Danticat, Edwidge 1969-
Dario, Ruben 1867-1916
Darwish, Mahmud 1942-
Davies, Robertson 1913-1995
Davis, Ossie 1917-
Day Lewis, C. 1904-1972
de Beauvoir, Simone
    See Beauvoir, Simone de
de Gourmont, Remy
    See Gourmont, Remy de
Deighton, Len
    See Deighton, Leonard Cyril
Deighton, Leonard Cyril 1929-
de la Mare, Walter 1873-1956
Delany, Samuel R. 1942-
DeLillo, Don 1936-
de Man, Paul 1919-1983
Derrida, Jacques 1930-
Desai, Anita 1937-
de Vries, Peter 1910-1993
Dexter, Colin 1930-
Dick, Philip K. 1928-1982
Dickey, James 1923-1997
Didion, Joan 1934-
Dillard, Annie 1945-
Dinesen, Isak
    See Blixen, Karen
Disch, Thomas M. 1940-
Disch, Tom
    See Disch, Thomas M.
Doctorow, E. L. 1931-
Donleavy, J. P. 1926-
Donoso, Jose 1924-1996
Doolittle, Hilda 1886-1961
Dorris, Michael 1945-1997
Dos Passos, John 1896-1970
Dove, Rita 1952-
Doyle, Arthur Conan 1859-1930
Doyle, Conan
    See Doyle, Arthur Conan
Doyle, Roddy 1958-
Drabble, Margaret 1939-

Dreiser, Theodore 1871-1945
D'Souza, Dinesh 1961-
Du Bois, W. E. B. 1868-1963
Duerrenmatt, Friedrich 1921-1990
du Maurier, Daphne 1907-1989
Duncan, Robert 1919-1988
Dunn, Katherine 1945-
Dunsany, Edward John Moreton
    Drax Plunkett 1878-1957
Dunsany, Lord
    See Dunsany, Edward John
    Moreton Drax Plunkett
Durang, Christopher 1949-
Durant, Will 1885-1981
Duras, Marguerite 1914-1996
Durrell, Lawrence 1912-1990
Dworkin, Andrea 1946-
Eagleton, Terence 1943-
Eagleton, Terry
    See Eagleton, Terence
Eco, Umberto 1932-
Ehrenreich, Barbara 1941-
Einstein, Albert 1879-1955
Ekwensi, Cyprian 1921-
Eliot, T. S. 1888-1965
Elkin, Stanley L. 1930-1995
Ellerman, Annie Winifred
    1894-1983
Ellis, Alice Thomas
    See Haycraft, Anna
Ellis, Bret Easton 1964-
Ellison, Harlan 1934-
Ellison, Ralph 1914-1994
Ellmann, Richard 1918-1987
Ellroy, James 1948-
El-Shabazz, El-Hajj Malik
    See Little, Malcolm
Elytis, Odysseus 1911-1996
Emecheta, Buchi 1944-
Empson, William 1906-1984
Endo, Shusaku 1923-1996
Erdrich, Louise 1954-
Erikson, Erik H. 1902-1994
Esquivel, Laura 1951(?)-
Esslin, Martin 1918-
Estleman, Loren D. 1952-
Fair, A. A.
    See Gardner, Erle Stanley
Faludi, Susan 1959(?)-
Farrell, James T. 1904-1979
Fast, Howard 1914-
Faulkner, William 1897-1962
Ferber, Edna 1887-1968
Ferlinghetti, Lawrence 1919(?)-

Ferre, Rosario 1942-
Fiedler, Leslie A. 1917-
Fisher, M. F. K. 1908-1992
Fitzgerald, F. Scott 1896-1940
Fitzgerald, Penelope 1916-
Fleming, Ian 1908-1964
Fo, Dario 1926-
Foote, Shelby 1916-
Forche, Carolyn 1950-
Ford, Ford Madox 1873-1939
Ford, Richard 1944-
Forster, E. M. 1879-1970
Forsyth, Frederick 1938-
Foucault, Michel 1926-1984
Fowles, John 1926-
France, Anatole
    See Thibault, Jacques Anatole
    Francois
Francis, Dick 1920-
Frank, Anne 1929-1945
Franklin, Miles 1879-1954
Fraser, Antonia 1932-
Fraser, George MacDonald 1925-
Frayn, Michael 1933-
French, Marilyn 1929-
Freud, Sigmund 1856-1939
Friedan, Betty 1921-
Friedman, Milton 1912-
Frisch, Max 1911-1991
Frost, Robert 1874-1963
Fry, Christopher 1907-
Frye, Northrop 1912-1991
Fuentes, Carlos 1928-
Fuller, R. Buckminster 1895-1983
Fussell, Paul 1924-
Gaddis, William 1922-
Gaines, Ernest J. 1933-
Galbraith, John Kenneth 1908-
Gallant, Mavis 1922-
Galsworthy, John 1867-1933
Gandhi, Mahatma
    See Gandhi, Mohandas
    Karamchand
Gandhi, Mohandas Karamchand
    1869-1948
Garcia Lorca, Federico 1898-1936
Garcia Marquez, Gabriel 1928-
Gardner, Erle Stanley 1889-1970
Gardner, John, Jr. 1933-1982
Garner, Alan 1934-
Garnett, David 1892-1981
Gass, William H. 1924-
Gasset, Jose Ortega y
    See Ortega y Gasset, Jose

Gates, Henry Louis, Jr. 1950-
Geisel, Theodor Seuss 1904-1991
Genet, Jean 1910-1986
Gibbons, Kaye 1960-
Gibran, Kahlil 1883-1931
Gibson, William 1948-
Gibson, William 1914-
Gide, Andre 1869-1951
Gilchrist, Ellen 1935-
Gill, Brendan 1914-1997
Gilman, Charlotte Perkins
    1860-1935
Ginsberg, Allen 1926-1997
Ginzburg, Natalia 1916-1991
Giovanni, Nikki 1943-

Glasgow, Ellen, 1873-1945
Gluck, Louise 1943-
Godoy Alcayaga, Lucila 1889-1957
Godwin, Gail 1937-
Golding, William 1911-1993
Gordimer, Nadine 1923-
Gordon, Caroline 1895-1981
Gorky, Maxim
    See Peshkov, Alexei Maximovich
Gould, Stephen Jay 1941-
Gourmont, Remy de 1858-1915
Goytisolo, Juan 1931-
Grahame, Kenneth 1859-1932
Grass, Guenter 1927-
Graves, Robert 1895-1985

Gray, Alasdair 1934-
Gray, Francine du Plessix 1930-
Gray, Spalding 1941-
Greeley, Andrew M. 1928-
Green, Julien 1900-1998
Greene, Graham 1904-1991
Greer, Germaine 1939-
Grey, Zane 1872-1939
Grigson, Geoffrey 1905-1985
Grisham, John 1955-
Grumbach, Doris 1918-
Guare, John 1938-
Guest, Judith 1936-
Guterson, David 1956-

VOLUME 3: H-Ma

Haggard, H. Rider 1856-1925
Hailey, Arthur 1920-
Halberstam, David 1934-
Hale, Janet Campbell 1947-
Haley, Alex 1921-1992
Hall, Donald 1928-
Hall, Radclyffe 1886-1943
Hamilton, Clive
    See Lewis, C. S.
Hamilton, Virginia 1936-
Hammett, Dashiell 1894-1961
Handke, Peter 1942-
Hansberry, Lorraine 1930-1965
Hardwick, Elizabeth 1916-
Hardy, Thomas 1840-1928
Hamson, Knut
    See Pedersen, Knut
Harjo, Joy 1951-
Hartley, L. P. 1895-1972
Hasek, Jaroslav 1883-1923
Havel, Vaclav 1936-
Hawkes, John 1925-
Hawking, S. W.
    See Hawking, Stephen W.
Hawking, Stephen W. 1942-
Haycraft, Anna
Hayden, Robert E. 1913-1980
Hayek, F. A. 1899-1992
H. D.
    See Doolittle, Hilda
Head, Bessie 1937-1986
Heaney, Seamus 1939-
Hebert, Anne 1916-
Heidegger, Martin 1889-1976

Heinlein, Robert A. 1907-1988
Heller, Joseph 1923-
Hellman, Lillian 1906-1984
Helprin, Mark 1947-
Hemingway, Ernest 1899-1961
Hempel, Amy 1951-
Henley, Elizabeth Becker 1952-
Henry, O.
    See Porter, William Sydney
Herbert, Frank 1920-1986
Herriot, James 1916-1995
Hersey, John 1914-1993
Hesse, Hermann 1877-1962
Heyer, Georgette 1902-1974
Heyerdahl, Thor 1914-
Hiassen, Carl 1953-
Hibbert, Eleanor Alice Burford
    1906-1993
Highsmith, Patricia 1921-1995
Highway, Tomson 1951-
Hijuelos, Oscar 1951-
Hillerman, Tony 1925-
Himes, Chester 1909-1984
Hinojosa, Rolando 1929-
Hinton, S. E. 1950-
Hiraoka, Kimitake 1925-1970
Hoban, Russell 1925-
Hochhuth, Rolf 1931-
Hodgson, William Hope 1877-1918
Hoeg, Peter 1957-
Hoffman, Alice 1952-
Holroyd, Michael 1935-
Hooks, Bell
    See Watkins, Gloria

Hope, A. D. 1907-
Hopley-Woolrich, Cornell George
    1903-1968
Horgan, Paul 1903-1995
Housman, A. E. 1859-1936
Howard, Maureen 1930-
Howe, Irving 1920-1993
Howells, W. D.
    See Howells, William Dean
Howells, William Dean 1837-1920
Hoyle, Fred 1915-
Hubbard, L. Ron 1911-1986
Hueffer, Ford Madox
    See Ford, Ford Madox
Hughes, Langston 1902-1967
Hughes, Ted 1930-
Hurston, Zora Neale 1903-1960
Huxley, Aldous 1894-1963
Hwang, David Henry 1957-
Infante, G. Cabrera
    See Cabrera Infante, G.
Inge, William 1913-1973
Ionesco, Eugene 1912-1994
Irving, John 1942-
Isaacs, Susan 1943-
Isherwood, Christopher 1904-1986
Ishiguro, Kazuo 1954-
Jackson, Shirley 1919-1965
Jakes, John 1932-
James, Henry 1843-1916
James, P. D.
    See White, Phyllis Dorothy James
Jarrell, Randall 1914-1965
Jeffers, Robinson 1887-1962

Jhabvala, Ruth Prawer 1927-
Jimenez, Juan Ramon 1881-1958
Johnson, Charles 1948-
Johnson, James Weldon 1871-1938
Johnson, Pamela Hansford
    1912-1981
Jones, Gayl 1949-
Jones, LeRoi
    See Baraka, Amiri
Jong, Erica 1942-
Joyce, James 1882-1941
Jung, C. G. 1875-1961
Justice, Donald 1925-
Kael, Pauline 1919-
Kafka, Franz 1883-1924
Kantor, MacKinlay 1904-1977
Kaufman, George S. 1889-1961
Kawabata, Yasunari 1899-1972
Kaye, M. M. 1909-
Kazantzakis, Nikos 1883(?)-1957
Keillor, Garrison
    See Keillor, Gary
Keillor, Gary 1942-
Keneally, Thomas 1935-
Kennedy, William 1928-
Kerouac, Jack
    See Kerouac, Jean-Lous Lebris de
Kerouac, Jean-Louis Lebris de
    1922-1969
Kesey, Ken 1935-
Keyes, Daniel 1927-
Keynes, John Maynard 1883-1946
Kienzle, William X. 1928-
Kincaid, Jamaica 1949-
King, Martin Luther Jr. 1929-1968
King, Stephen 1947-
Kingsolver, Barbara 1955-
Kingston, Maxine Hong 1940-
Kinnell, Galway 1927-
Kinsella, Thomas 1928-
Kinsella, W. P. 1935-
Kinsey, Alfred 1894-1956
Kipling, Rudyard 1865-1936
Kirk, Russell 1918-1994
Kizer, Carolyn 1925-
Knight, Etheridge 1931(?)-1991
Knowles, John 1926-
Koch, Kenneth 1925-
Koestler, Arthur 1905-1983
Kogawa, Joy Nozomi 1935-
Kosinski, Jerzy 1933-1991
Kueng, Hans 1928-
Kumin, Maxine 1925-
Kundera, Milan 1929-

Kung, Hans
    See Kueng, Hans
Kunitz, Stanley 1905-
Kushner, Tony 1956-
Lagerkvist, Paer 1891-1974
Lagerkvist, Par
    See Lagerkvist, Paer
Lagerloef, Selma 1858-1940
La Guma, Alex 1925-1985
Lamming, George 1927-
L'Amour, Louis 1908-1988
Lampedusa, Giuseppe Tomassi di
    1896-
Lardner, Ring W. 1885-1933
Larkin, Philip 1922-1985
Lasch, Christopher 1932-1994
Laurence, Margaret 1926-1987
Lawrence, D. H. 1885-1930
Laye, Camara 1928-1980
Layton, Irving 1912-
Leacock, Stephen 1869-1944
Leavis, F. R. 1895-1978
Leavitt, David 1961-
Le Carre, John
    See Cornwell, David
Lee, Harper 1926-
Le Guin, Ursula K. 1929-
Lehmann, Rosamond 1901-
Leiber, Fritz 1910-1992
L'Engle, Madeleine 1918-
Leonard, Elmore 1925-
Leonov, Leonid 1899-1994
Leseig, Theo.
    See Geisel, Theodore Seuss
Lessing, Doris 1919-
Levertov, Denise 1923-1997
Levi, Primo 1919-1987
Levin, Ira 1929-
Levi-Strauss, Claude 1908-
Lewis, C. Day
    See Day Lewis, C.
Lewis, C. S. 1898-1963
Lewis, Sinclair 1885-1951
Lewis, Wyndham 1882(?)-1957
Leyner, Mark 1956-
Liebling, A. J. 1904-1963
Lindbergh, Anne Morrow 1906-
Lippmann, Walter 1889-1974
Little, Malcolm 1925-1965
Lively, Penelope 1933-
Llosa, Mario Vargas
    See Vargas Llosa, Mario
Lodge, David 1935-
London, Jack

    See London, John Griffith
London, John Griffith 1876-1916
Loos, Anita 1893-1981
Lorca, Federico Garcia
    See Garcia Lorca, Federico
Lorde, Audre 1934-1992
Lorenz, Konrad Zacharias
    1903-1989
Lovecraft, H. P. 1890-1937
Lowell, Amy 1874-1925
Lowell, Robert 1917-1977
Lowry, Lois 1937-
Lowry, Malcolm 1909-1957
Ludlum, Robert 1927-
Lukacs, George
    See Lukacs, Gyorgy
Lukacs, Gyorgy 1885-1971
Lustbader, Eric Van 1946-
Maas, Peter 1929-
MacDonald, John D. 1916-1986
MacInnes, Colin 1914-1976
MacInnes, Helen 1907-1985
MacKinnon, Catharine A. 1946-
MacLeish, Archibald 1892-1982
MacLennan, Hugh 1907-1990
MacLeod, Alistair 1936-
MacNeice, Louis 1907-1963
Madhubuti, Haki R. 1942-
Mahfouz, Naguib 1911(?)-
Mailer, Norman 1923-
Maillet, Antonine 1929-
Malamud, Bernard 1914-1986
Malcolm X
    See Little, Malcolm
Malouf, David 1934-
Malraux, Andre 1901-1976
Mamet, David 1947-
Manchester, William 1922-
Mandelstam, Osip 1891(?)-1938(?)
Mann, Thomas 1875-1955
Mansfield, Katherine
    See Beauchamp, Kathleen
    Mansfield
Mao Tse-tung 1893-1976
Marcel, Gabriel Honore
    1889-1973
Marquand, John P. 1893-1960
Marquez, Gabriel Garcia
    See Garcia Marquez, Gabriel
Marsh, Ngaio 1899-1982
Marshall, Paule 1929-
Martinez, Jacinto Benavente y
    See Benavente, Jacinto
Masefield, John 1878-1967

Maslow, Abraham H. 1908-1970
Mason, Bobbie Ann 1940-
Masters, Edgar Lee 1868-1950
Mathabane, Mark 1960-

Matthiessen, Peter 1927-
Maugham, W. Somerset 1874-1965
Maupin, Armistead 1944-
Mauriac, Francois 1885-1970

Maurois, Andre 1885-1967
Mayakovsky, Vladimir 1893-1930

VOLUME 4: Mc-Se

McCaffrey, Anne 1926-
McCarthy, Charles, Jr. 1933-
McCarthy, Cormac
    See McCarthy, Charles, Jr.
McCarthy, Mary 1912-1989
McCullers, Carson 1917-1967
McCullough, Colleen 1938-
McEwan, Ian 1948-
McInerney, Jay 1955-
McKay, Claude
    See McKay, Festus Claudius
McKay, Festus Claudius 1889-1948
McLuhan, Marshall 1911-1980
McMillan, Terry 1951-
McMurtry, Larry 1936-
McNally, Terrence 1939-
McPhee, John 1931-
McPherson, James Alan 1943-
Mead, Margaret 1901-1978
Mencken, H. L. 1880-1956
Mendez, Miguel 1930-
Menninger, Karl 1893-1990
Merrill, James 1926-1995
Merton, Thomas 1915-1968
Merwin, W. S. 1927-
Metalious, Grace 1924-1964
Michener, James A. 1907(?)-1997
Millar, Kenneth 1915-1983
Millay, Edna St. Vincent 1892-1950
Miller, Arthur 1915-
Miller, Henry 1891-1980
Millett, Kate 1934-
Millhauser, Steven 1943-
Milne, A. A. 1882-1956
Milosz, Czeslaw 1911-
Mishima, Yukio
    See Hiraoka, Kimitake
Mistral, Gabriela
    See Godoy Alcayaga, Lucila
Mitchell, Margaret 1900-1949
Mofolo, Thomas 1875(?)-1948
Momaday, N. Scott 1934-
Montgomery, L. M. 1874-1942
Moorcock, Michael 1939-
Moore, Brian 1921-

Moore, Marianne 1887-1972
Morante, Elsa 1918-1985
Moravia, Alberto 1907-1990
Morris, Wright 1910-
Morrison, Toni 1931-
Morrow, James 1947-
Mortimer, John 1923-
Mosley, Walter 1952-
Mowat, Farley 1921-
Mphahlele, Ezekiel 1919-
Muggeridge, Malcolm 1903-1990
Mukherjee, Bharati 1940-
Munro, Alice 1931-
Munro, H. H. 1870-1916
Murdoch, Iris 1919-
Musil, Robert 1880-1942
Myers, Walter Dean 1937-
Nabokov, Vladimir 1899-1977
Naipaul, Shiva 1945-1985
Naipaul, V. S. 1932-
Narayan, R. K. 1906-
Nash, Ogden 1902-1971
Naylor, Gloria 1950-
Nemerov, Howard 1920-1991
Neruda, Pablo 1904-1973
Nesbit, E. 1858-1924
Ngugi Wa Thiong'o 1938-
Nin, Anais 1903-1977
Niven, Laurence Van Cott 1938-
Norway, Nevil Shute 1899-1960
Oates, Joyce Carol 1938-
Oates, Stephen B. 1936-
O'Brian, Patrick 1914-
O'Brien, Edna 1936-
O'Brien, Tim 1946-
O'Casey, Sean 1880-1964
O'Connor, Flannery 1925-1964
Odets, Clifford 1906-1963
Oe, Kenzaburo 1935-
O'Faolain, Sean 1900-1991
O'Flaherty, Liam 1896-1984
O'Hara, Frank 1926-1966
O'Hara, John 1905-1970
Okigbo, Christopher 1932-1967
Okri, Ben 1959-

Olds, Sharon 1942-
Olsen, Tillie 1912-
Olson, Charles 1910-1970
Ondaatje, Michael 1943-
O'Neill, Eugene 1888-1953
Onetti, Juan Carlos 1909-1994
Ortega y Gasset, Jose 1883-1955
Orton, Joe
    See Orton, John Kingsley
Orton, John Kingsley 1933-1967
Orwell, George
    See Blair, Eric
Osborne, John 1929-1994
Owen, Wilfred 1893-1918
Oz, Amos 1939-
Ozick, Cynthia 1928-
Paglia, Camille 1947-
Paley, Grace 1922-
Parker, Dorothy 1893-1967
Parks, Gordon 1912-
Pasternak, Boris 1890-1960
Paton, Alan 1903-1988
Pauling, Linus 1901-1994
Paz, Octavio 1914-1998
p'Bitek, Okot 1931-1982
Pedersen, Knut 1859-1952
Percy, Walker 1916-1990
Percy, William Alexander
    1885-1942
Perelman, S. J. 1904-1979
Peretti, Frank E. 1951-
Peshkov, Alexei Maximovich
    1868-1936
Phillips, Caryl 1958-
Phillips, Jayne Anne 1952-
Piaget, Jean 1896-1980
Piercy, Marge 1936-
Pinsky, Robert 1940-
Pinter, Harold 1930-
Pirandello, Luigi 1867-1936
Pirsig, Robert M. 1928-
Plath, Sylvia 1932-1963
Plimpton, George 1927-
Pohl, Frederik 1919-
Pollitt, Katha 1949-

Popper, Karl R. 1902-1994
Porter, Katherine Anne 1890-1980
Porter, William Sydney 1862-1910
Potok, Chaim 1929-
Potter, Beatrix 1866-1943
Pound, Ezra 1885-1972
Powell, Anthony 1905-
Powys, John Cowper 1872-1963
Priestley, J. B. 1894-1984
Pritchett, V. S. 1900-1997
Prokosch, Frederic 1908-
Proulx, E. Annie 1935-
Proust, Marcel 1871-1922
Puig, Manuel 1932-1990
Puzo, Mario 1920-
Pyle, Ernie 1900-1945
Pym, Barbara 1913-1980
Pynchon, Thomas 1937-
Queneau, Raymond 1903-1976
Quindlen, Anna 1953-
Quoirez, Francoise 1935-
Rand, Ayn 1905-1982
Ransom, John Crowe 1888-1974
Rao, Raja 1909-
Rattigan, Terence 1911-1977
Rawlings, Marjorie Kinnan
    1896-1953
Reed, Ishmael 1938-
Remarque, Erich Maria
    1898-1970
Renault, Mary
    See Challans, Mary

Rendell, Ruth 1930-
Rexroth, Kenneth 1905-1982
Rhys, Jean 1890(?)-1979
Rice, Anne 1941-
Rice, Elmer 1892-1967
Rich, Adrienne 1929-
Richards, I. A. 1893-1979
Richler, Mordecai 1931-
Richter, Conrad 1890-1968
Rilke, Rainer Maria 1875-1926
Robbe-Grillet, Alain 1922-
Robbins, Harold 1916-1997
Robbins, Thomas Eugene 1936-
Robbins, Tom
    See Robbins, Thomas Eugene
Robinson, Edwin Arlington
    1869-1935
Roethke, Theodore 1908-1963
Rogers, Will 1879-1935
Rossner, Judith 1935-
Roth, Henry 1906-1995
Roth, Philip 1933-
Rozewicz, Tadeusz 1921-
Rukeyser, Muriel 1913-1980
Rule, Ann 1935-
Rulfo, Juan 1918-1986
Runyon, Damon 1884(?)-1946
Rushdie, Salman 1947-
Russell, Bertrand 1872-1970
Sabato, Ernesto 1911-
Sachs, Nelly 1891-1970
Sacks, Oliver 1933-

Sackville-West, V. 1892-1962
Sagan, Carl 1934-1996
Sagan, Francoise
    See Quoirez, Francoise
Said, Edward W. 1935-
Saint-Exupery, Antoine de
    1900-1944
Saki
    See Munro, H. H.
Salas, Floyd Francis 1931-
Salinger, J. D. 1919-
Sanchez, Sonia 1934-
Sandburg, Carl 1878-1967
Sandoz, Mari 1896-1966
Saroyan, William 1908-1981
Sarraute, Nathalie 1900-
Sarton, May 1912-1995
Sartre, Jean-Paul 1905-1980
Sassoon, Siegfried 1886-1967
Sayers, Dorothy L. 1893-1957
Schaeffer, Susan Fromberg 1941-
Schlesinger, Arthur M., Jr. 1917-
Schulz, Bruno 1892-1942
Schwartz, Delmore 1913-1966
Schwartz, Lynne Sharon 1939-
Seifert, Jaroslav 1901-1986
Sendak, Maurice 1928-
Senghor, Leopold Sedar 1906-
Seth, Vikram 1952-
Seuss, Dr.
    See Geisel, Theodore Seuss
Sexton, Anne 1928-1974

VOLUME 5: Sh-Z

Shaffer, Peter 1926-
Shange, Ntozake 1948-
Shapiro, Karl 1913-
Shaw, Bernard
    See Shaw, George Bernard
Shaw, George Bernard 1856-1950
Shaw, Irwin 1913-1984
Sheed, Wilfrid 1930-
Sheldon, Sidney 1917-
Shepard, Sam 1943-
Shiel, M. P. 1865-1947
Shields, Carol 1935-
Shilts, Randy 1951-1994
Shirer, William L. 1904-1993
Sholokhov, Mikhail 1905-1984
Shute, Nevil
    See Norway, Nevil Shute

Siddons, Anne Rivers 1936-
Silko, Leslie Marmon 1948-
Sillitoe, Alan 1928-
Silverberg, Robert 1935-
Silverstein, Shel 1932-
Simenon, Georges 1903-1989
Simic, Charles 1938-
Simon, Neil 1927-
Simpson, Louis 1923-
Sinclair, Upton 1878-1968
Singer, Isaac Bashevis 1904-1991
Sitwell, Dame Edith 1887-1964
Skinner, B. F. 1904-1990
Skvorecky, Josef 1924-
Smith, Clark Ashton 1893-1961
Smith, Florence Margaret
    1902-1971

Smith, Martin Cruz 1942-
Smith, Rolando Hinojosa
    See Hinojosa-Smith, Rolando
Smith, Stevie
    See Smith, Florence Margaret
Smith, Wilbur 1933-
Snodgrass, W. D. 1926-
Snow, C. P. 1905-1980
Snyder, Gary 1930-
Solzhenitsyn, Aleksandr 1918-
Sontag, Susan 1933-
Soto, Gary 1952-
Soyinka, Wole 1934-
Spark, Muriel 1918-
Spender, Stephen 1909-1995
Spiegelman, Art 1948-
Spillane, Frank Morrison 1918-

Spillane, Mickey
    See Spillane, Frank Morrison
Spock, Benjamin 1903-1998
Stafford, Jean 1915-1979
Stead, Christina 1902-1983
Steel, Danielle 1947-
Stegner, Wallace 1909-1993
Stein, Gertrude 1874-1946
Steinbeck, John 1902-1968
Steinem, Gloria 1934-
Steiner, George 1929-
Stephen, Virginia
    See Woolf, Virginia
Stevens, Wallace 1879-1955
Stewart, J. I. M. 1906-1994
Stine, Jovial Bob
    See Stine, R. L.
Stine, R. L. 1943-
Stone, Irving 1903-1989
Stoppard, Tom 1937-
Strachey, Lytton 1880-1932
Straub, Peter 1943-
Strindberg, August 1849-1912
Sturgeon, Theodore 1918-1985
Styron, William 1925-
Susann, Jacqueline 1921-1974
Suzuki, Daisetz Teitaro 1870-1966
Swenson, May 1919-1989
Swift, Graham 1949-
Szymborska, Wislawa 1923-
Tagore, Rabindranath 1861-1941
Talese, Gay 1932-
Tan, Amy 1952-
Tanizaki, Jun'ichiro 1886-1965
Tarkington, Booth 1869-1946
Tate, Allen 1899-1979
Taylor, A. J. P. 1906-1990
Taylor, Peter 1917-1994
Terkel, Louis 1912-
Terkel, Studs
    See Terkel, Louis
Theroux, Paul 1941-
Thibault, Jacques Anatole Francois
    1844-1924
Thomas, D. M. 1935-
Thomas, Dylan 1914-1953
Thomas, Joyce Carol 1938-
Thomas, Lewis 1913-1993
Thompson, Francis Clegg
Thompson, Hunter S. 1939-
Thurber, James 1894-1961
Tillich, Paul 1886-1965
Toffler, Alvin 1928-

Toland, John 1912-
Tolkien, J. R. R. 1892-1973
Tonson, Jacob
    See Bennett, Arnold
Toole, John Kennedy 1937-1969
Toomer, Jean 1894-1967
Tournier, Michel 1924-
Trakl, Georg 1887-1914
Tremblay, Michel 1942-
Trevor, William
    See Cox, William Trevor
Trillin, Calvin 1935-
Trilling, Diana 1905-1996
Trilling, Lionel 1905-1975
Tsvetaeva, Marina 1892-1941
Tuchman, Barbara W. 1912-1989
Turow, Scott 1949-
Tutuola, Amos 1920-1997
Tyler, Anne 1941-
Tynan, Kenneth 1927-1980
Tzara, Tristan 1896-1963
Uchida, Yoshiko 1921-1992
Unamuno, Miguel de 1864-1936
Undset, Sigrid 1882-1949
Updike, John 1932-
Uris, Leon 1924-
Ustinov, Peter 1921-
Valery, Paul 1871-1945
Van Doren, Mark 1894-1972
Vargas Llosa, Mario 1936-
Vendler, Helen 1933-
Vian, Boris 1920-1959
Vidal, Gore 1925-
Vizenor, Gerald 1934-
Vollmann, William T. 1959-
Vonnegut, Kurt 1922-
Wain, John 1925-1994
Wakoski, Diane 1937-
Walcott, Derek 1930-
Walker, Alice 1944-
Walker, Margaret 1915-
Wallace, David Foster 1962-
Wallace, Irving 1916-1990
Wallant, Edward Lewis 1926-1962
Walpole, Hugh 1884-1941
Wambaugh, Joseph 1937-
Warner, Sylvia Ashton
    See Ashton-Warner, Sylvia
Warner, Sylvia Townsend
    1893-1978
Warren, Robert Penn 1905-1989
Wasserstein, Wendy 1950-
Waterhouse, Keith 1929-

Watkins, Gloria 1952-
Waugh, Evelyn 1903-1966
Weil, Simone 1909-1943
Weldon, Fay 1931-
Wells, H. G. 1866-1946
Welty, Eudora 1909-
West, Jessamyn 1902-1984
West, Morris L. 1916-
West, Nathanael 1903-1940
West, Paul 1930-
West, Rebecca 1892-1983
West, V. Sackville
    See Sackville-West, V.
Westlake, Donald E. 1933-
Wharton, Edith 1862-1937
White, E. B. 1899-1985
White, Edmund 1940-
White, Phyllis Dorothy James 1920-
White, Theodore H. 1915-1986
Whitney, Phyllis A. 1903-
Wideman, John Edgar 1941-
Wiesel, Elie 1928-
Wilbur, Richard 1921-
Wilder, Laura Ingalls 1867-1957
Wilder, Thornton 1897-1975
Williams, Tennessee 1911-1983
Williams, William Carlos 1883-1963
Wilson, A. N. 1950-
Wilson, Angus 1913-1991
Wilson, August 1945-
Wilson, Edmund 1895-1972
Wilson, Edward O. 1929-
Wilson, John Burgess 1917-1993
Winterson, Jeanette 1959-
Wittgenstein, Ludwig 1889-1951
Wodehouse, P. G. 1881-1975
Wolfe, Gene 1931-
Wolfe, Thomas 1900-1938
Wolfe, Thomas Kennerly, Jr. 1930-
Wolfe, Tom
    See Wolfe, Thomas Kennerly, Jr.
Wolff, Tobias 1945-
Woodiwiss, Kathleen E. 1939-
Woolf, Virginia 1882-1941
Wouk, Herman 1915-
Wright, Charles 1935-
Wright, James 1927-1980
Wright, Judith 1915-
Wright, Richard 1908-1960
Yeats, William Butler 1865-1939
Yourcenar, Marguerite 1903-1987
Zelazny, Roger 1937-1995
Zindel, Paul 1936-

Ch–Cz

CHALLANS, Mary 1905-1983
(Mary Renault)

PERSONAL: Born September 4, 1905, in London, England; died of bronchial pneumonia, December 13, 1983, in Cape Town, South Africa; emigrated to South Africa in 1948; daughter of Frank (a doctor) and Clementine Mary (Baxter) Challans. 3 Atholl Rd., Camps Bay, Cape Town 8001, South Africa. *Education:* St. Hugh's College, Oxford, M.A.; Radcliffe Infirmary, Oxford, S.R.N., 1936. *Politics:* Progressive.

CAREER: Writer, 1938–. Worked as a nurse in England.

MEMBER: PEN Club of South Africa (past president), Royal Society of Literature (fellow).

AWARDS, HONORS: MGM award, 1946, for *Return to Night*; National Association of Independent Schools Award, 1963; Silver Pen Award, 1971, for *Five From Heaven*.

WRITINGS:

NOVELS, ALL UNDER PSEUDONYM MARY RENAULT

Promise of Love, Morrow, 1939, published in England as *Purposes of Love*, Longmans, Green, 1939.
Kind Are Her Answers, Morrow, 1940.
The Friendly Young Ladies, Longmans, Green, 1944, published as *The Middle Mist*, Morrow, 1945.
Return to Night, Morrow, 1947.
North Face, Morrow, 1948.
The Charioteer, Longmans, Green, 1953.
The Last of the Wine, Pantheon, 1956.
The King Must Die (Book-of-the-Month-Club selection), Pantheon, 1958.
The Bull From the Sea, Pantheon, 1962.
The Mask of Apollo, Pantheon, 1966.
Fire From Heaven, Pantheon, 1969.
The Persian Boy, Pantheon, 1972.
The Praise Singer, Pantheon, 1978.

OTHER, UNDER PSEUDONYM MARY RENAULT

The Lion in the Gateway: Heroic Battles of the Greeks and Persians at Marathon, Salamis, and Thermopylae (juvenile; illustrated by C. Walter Hodges), Harper, 1964.
The Nature of Alexander, Pantheon, 1975.

SIDELIGHTS: Mary Challans decided at an early age that she wanted to be a writer. Because Challans felt that a writer must participate actively in life, she enrolled in a nursing school. Her experiences as a nurse provided material for her first novel, *Promise of Love*, which she wrote under the pseudonym Mary Renault. *Promise of Love* was well received by critics. A reviewer for the *New York Times* stated: "On a double count *Promise of Love* strikes me as an unusually excellent first novel. There is a fusion between background and personal drama, between inner and outer reality, which enriches and dignifies both. The story of Mic and Vivian would not be nearly so arresting as it is if one were not so sharply aware of the pressure of their environment . . . . When one adds to this that Mary Renault's style has a sure, fluid quality, that she possesses humor as well as sensitiveness, that even her minor characters are shrewdly drawn—the sum total is quite impressive."

Buoyed by the success of her first novel, Challans planned to become a full-time writer, but World War II interfered with her plans. She continued her nursing career and wrote in her spare time. A novel that appeared after the war, *Return to Night,* brought her name to the attention of the American reading public because it received the MGM prize, the largest financial award in the field of literature. Echoing the enthusiasm of many other critics, a *New Yorker* reviewer described *Return to Night* as "an expert, vivid novel," explaining that "Miss Renault sets forth the characters of three extremely complex people with a penetrating lucidity and a certain moderate reasonableness, making this not just an impassioned love story but a novel of considerable depth."

Following the end of World War II, Mary Challans traveled extensively in France, Italy, Africa, Greece, and the Aegean Islands. She was most impressed with Greece, and it became the setting for many of her historical novels. The first of these novels, *The Last of the Wine,* concerns the Theseus myth and takes place during the Third Peloponnesian War. "To read *The Last of the Wine,*" wrote a critic in *New York Herald Tribune Book Review,* "is to walk for a while in the shadow of the Acropolis with Plato and his friends." Observed the *Times Literary Supplement:* "*The Last of the Wine* is a superb historical novel. The writing is Attic in quality, unforced, clear, delicate. The characterization is uniformly successful and, most difficult of all, the atmosphere of Athens is realized in masterly fashion. Miss Renault is not only obviously familiar with the principal sources. She has disciplined her imagination so that the reader ceases to question the authenticity of her fiction."

Challans discovered her metier in the historical novel. *The Bull From the Sea,* a sequel to *The King Must Die,* also earned accolades from critics. Moses Hadas wrote that *The King Must Die* "is brilliantly and convincingly imagined, artistically presented, at once mind-stretching and deeply moving." In *The Mask of Apollo,* Challans describes Syracuse and Athens in the fourth century B.C. A trilogy comprised of *Fire From Heaven, The Persian Boy,* and Challan's last novel, *Funeral Games,* thoroughly examines the life of Alexander the Great. The appearance of each book helped enhance her reputation as the foremost historical novelist of our time.

Striving to explain why Challans's work is so highly esteemed, a commentator for *New York Herald Tribune Book Review* stated: "Miss Renault's historical novels are excellent. They hold their own as artistically wrought and moving stories and they are rich in the adult entertainment which is the special province of historical fiction. They are particularly welcome because they illuminate uncharted but essential passages and epochs in the formative stages of our civilization . . . . Her narrative is not, nor does it claim to be, history; but it is a well-considered suggestion of how things may have happened, and for the personality and culture with which she deals we have nothing more plausible."

BIOGRAPHICAL/CRITICAL SOURCES:

BOOKS

Dick, Bernard F., *The Hellenism of Mary Renault,* Southern Illinois Press, 1972.
Sweetman, David, *Mary Renault: A Biography,* Harcourt Brace (New York), 1993.
Wolfe, Peter, *Mary Renault,* Twayne, 1969.

PERIODICALS

Atlantic, December, 1972.
Best Sellers, December 15, 1969.
Booklist, June 15, 1958.
Books, March 12, 1939.
Book Week, November 6, 1966.
Catholic World, September, 1970.
Christian Science Monitor, July 17, 1958; November 6, 1975.
Commonweal, August 1, 1958.
Contemporary Literary Criticism, Volume 3, Gale, 1975.
Economist, October 4, 1975.
New Republic, November 19, 1966.
New Yorker, April 19, 1947.
New York Herald Tribune Book Review, October 14, 1956; July 13, 1958; February 18, 1962.
New York Times, March 12, 1939; April 20, 1947; July 13, 1958.
New York Times Book Review, February 18, 1962; October 30, 1966; December 14, 1969; December 31, 1979.
Saturday Review, July 12, 1958; February 17, 1962; October 1, 1966; December 9, 1972.
Sewanee Review, autumn, 1973.
Times Literary Supplement, February 25, 1939; June 29, 1956; September 19, 1958; March 16, 1962; December 15, 1966; December 11, 1970; November 3, 1972.
Virginia Quarterly Review, summer, 1973.
Washington Post Book World, November 23, 1969.

CHAMBERS, Jessie
See LAWRENCE, D(avid) H(erbert Richards)

*   *   *

CHANDLER, Raymond (Thornton) 1886-1959

PERSONAL: Born July 23, 1888, in Chicago, IL; died March 26, 1959, in La Jolla, CA; buried at Mount Hope Cemetery, San Diego, CA; son of Maurice Benjamin and Florence Dart (Thornton) Chandler; married Pearl Cecily (some sources say Eugenia or Eugenie) Hurlburt, 1924 (died, 1954). *Education:* Educated in England, France, and Germany.

CAREER: The Admiralty, London, worker in supplies and accounting departments, 1907; reporter for *Daily Express,* London, and *Western Gazette,* Bristol, England, both 1908-12; worked as menial laborer in St. Louis, MO, c. 1912; worked at sporting goods company in California; Los Angeles Creamery, Los Angeles, CA, accountant and bookkeeper, 1912-17; worked at bank in San Francisco, CA, 1919; *Daily Express,* Los Angeles, reporter, 1919; Dabney Oil Syndicate, Los Angeles, 1922-32, began as bookkeeper, became auditor; writer, 1933-59. *Military service:* Served in Canadian Army, 1917-18, and in Royal Air Force, 1918-19.

MEMBER: Mystery Writers of America (president, 1959).

AWARDS, HONORS: Nomination for Academy Award for best screenplay from Academy of Motion Picture Arts and Sciences, 1944, for *Double Indemnity;* Edgar Allan Poe Award from Mystery Writers of America and nomination for Academy Award for best original screenplay, both 1946, both for *The Blue Dahlia;* Edgar Allan Poe Award from Mystery Writers of America, 1954, for *The Long Goodbye.*

WRITINGS:

The Big Sleep (novel), Knopf, 1939.
Farewell, My Lovely (novel), Knopf, 1940.
The High Window (novel), Knopf, 1942.
The Lady in the Lake (novel), Knopf, 1943.
Five Murders (short stories), Avon, 1944.
Five Sinister Characters (short stories), Avon, 1945.
Red Wind: A Collection of Short Stories, World, 1946.
Spanish Blood (short stories), World, 1946.
The Blue Dahlia (screenplay; released by Paramount, 1946), edited by Bruccoli, Southern Illinois University Press, 1976.
Finger Man, and Other Stories, Avon, 1947.
The Little Sister (novel), Houghton, 1949, reprinted as *Marlowe,* Pocket Books, 1969.
The Simple Art of Murder (includes the stories "Trouble Is My Business" and "Pick-Up on Noon Street," and the essay "The Simple Art of Murder"; also see below), Houghton, 1950, "The Simple Art of Murder" published separately, Pocket Books, 1953.
Trouble Is My Business: Four Stories From "The Simple Art of Murder," Pocket Books, 1951.
Pick-Up on Noon Street (short stories), Pocket Books, 1952.
The Long Good-Bye (novel), Hamish Hamilton, 1953, published as *The Long Goodbye,* Houghton, 1954.
Pearls Are a Nuisance (short stories), Hamish Hamilton, 1953.
Playback (novel), Houghton, 1958.

Raymond Chandler Speaking (letters, criticism, and fiction), edited by Dorothy Gardiner and Kathrine Sorley Walker, Houghton, 1962.

Killer in the Rain (short stories), edited by Philip Durham, Houghton, 1964.

The Smell of Fear (short stories), Hamish Hamilton, 1965.

The Midnight Raymond Chandler (omnibus), edited by Joan Kahn, Houghton, 1971.

Chandler Before Marlowe: Raymond Chandler's Early Prose and Poetry, 1908-1912, edited by Matthew J. Bruccoli, introduction by Jacques Barzun, University of South Carolina Press, 1973.

The Smell of Fear (short stories), Hamish Hamilton, 1973.

The Notebooks of Raymond Chandler, and "English Summer: A Gothic Romance," edited by Frank McShane, Ecco Press, 1976.

Smart-Aleck Kill (short stories), Penguin, 1976.

(With James M. Fox) *Raymond Chandler and James M. Fox: Letters,* privately printed, 1979.

Selected Letters of Raymond Chandler, edited by McShane, Columbia University Press, 1981.

Raymond Chandler's Unknown Thriller: The Screenplay of "Playback," Mysterious Press, 1985.

(With Robert B. Parker) *Poodle Springs* (novel), Putnam, 1989.

(With Byron Preiss) *Raymond Chandler's Philip Marlowe: A Centennial Celebration,* Perigee Books (New York City), 1990.

"The Big Sleep" and "Farewell, My Lovely," Modern Library (New York City), 1995.

Raymond Chandler: Later Novels and Other Writings, Library of America (New York City), 1995.

Raymond Chandler: Stories and Early Novels, Library of America (New York City), 1995.

The Australian Love Letters of Raymond Chandler, edited by Alan Close, McPhee Gribble Publishers, 1995.

Contributor to periodicals, including *Academy, Atlantic Monthly, Black Mask, Detection Fiction Weekly, Detective Story, Dime Detective, Spectator, Unknown,* and *Westminster Gazette.*

OTHER SCREENPLAYS

(With Billy Wilder) *Double Indemnity* (adapted from James M. Cain's novel of the same title), Paramount, 1944.

(With Frank Partos) *And Now Tomorrow* (adapted from Rachel Field's novel of the same title), Paramount, 1944.

(With Hagar Wilde) *The Unseen* (adapted from Ethel Lina White's book *Her Heart in Her Throat*), Paramount, 1945.

(With Czenzi Ormonde) *Strangers on a Train* (adapted from Patricia Highsmith's novel of the same title), Warner Bros., 1951.

MEDIA ADAPTATIONS: Farewell, My Lovely was filmed as *Murder, My Sweet* with Dick Powell in 1945, and, under its original title, with Robert Mitchum in 1975; *The Big Sleep* was filmed—by director Howard Hawks from an adaptation by William Faulkner, among others—with Humphrey Bogart and Lauren Bacall in 1946, and with Robert Mitchum in 1978; *The Lady in the Lake* was filmed in 1946 by actor-director Robert Montgomery; *The High Window* inspired the 1942 film *Time to Kill* and was filmed as *The Brasher Dubloon* with George Montgomery in 1947; *The Little Sister* was filmed as *Marlowe* with James Garner in 1969; *The Long Goodbye* was filmed—by director Robert Altman—with Elliott Gould in 1973.

SIDELIGHTS: Raymond Chandler has been acclaimed as American literature's finest writer of hard-boiled detective fiction. Despite a romantic nature and genteel tastes, he was drawn to contemporary society's venal underside, and he captured its rough idiom with acuity and imaginative power. His fictional milieu was the mean streets of urban America, a country he described in *Trouble Is My Business* (1951) as "a world gone wrong." He was particularly drawn to southern California, with its image as a modern paradise blighted by corruption, and better than any other writer of his time he captured the area's seamy glamour. For Chandler, the Golden State, bathed in the mystique of the American Dream but vitiated by sham and plunder, symbolized the dark side of success. Indeed his entire fictional canon may be understood as a sustained indictment of a nation obsessed with the pursuit of money and power. As his admirer and literary heir Ross Macdonald declared in his introduction to Matthew J. Bruccoli's *Kenneth Millar/Ross Macdonald: A Checklist,* Chandler was a "slumming angel" who transformed the detective story into a critique of American culture's more base aspects.

Chandler's fiction was propelled by a complex morality, one that biographer Jerry Speir described as an "essential dualism of mind . . . which perpetually balanced an innate romanticism against a very self-conscious cynicism." This dualism was rooted in Chandler's English upbringing. Though born in midwest America, he was transplanted in early youth to England, where he studied the classics and embraced the public school's traditional code of manly virtue through honor and personal sacrifice. At home in his maternal grandmother's household, he was sequestered in what Natasha Spender has described—in an essay collected in editor Miriam Gross's *The World of Raymond Chandler*—as an atmosphere of "high Victorian rectitude," prompting in the adolescent boy both a fussy puritanism and an exaggerated attraction to things masculine and tough.

In his twenties, he worked as a freelance writer, publishing reviews, poetry, and essays. Although realizing his literary aspirations, Chandler soon grew discontented with life in England. "America seemed to call me in some mysterious way," he recalled in a July 1958 letter to English mystery writer Michael Gilbert. Seeking more lucrative prospects, Chandler repatriated to the United States, and he eventually settled in southern California. After a series of false starts he took an executive position with an oil company. Around this time—the mid-1920s—he also married a socially prominent woman who was his elder by eighteen years. But despite his prosperity, Chandler harbored acute inner conflicts. Alcohol, profligacy, and the impending economic catastrophe of the Depression compounded his turmoil, and at the age of forty-four Chandler lost his job. He then decided to fulfill his long-thwarted literary ambitions.

Taking inspiration from his precursors in what has come to be called "tough guy" fiction, Chandler published the deftly executed "Blackmailers Don't Shoot" in the April 1933 issue of *Black Mask.* This dark tale of extortion and racketeering contains all the hard-boiled genre's convention: violence, corrupt officials, gangsters and gun molls, and a detective with a fast gun and a code of ethics.

Black Mask was a fitting forum for Chandler and other writers who practiced cynicism while adhering to a romantic ethos. Joseph T. Shaw, chief editor of the magazine, had described its typical reader as "a . . . stalwart, rugged specimen of humanity—hard as nails, swift of hand and foot, clear-eyed, unprovocative but ready to tackle anything that gets in the way." Such readers,

Shaw contended, despise "injustice, cowardly underhandedness" and cheer "for the right guy to come out on top." This profile became a model for Chandler's own literary hero: a latter-day knight driven by romantic quests in a seamy world of crime and compromise.

In addition Chandler developed his own literary style. More verbally adventurous than Hammett, Chandler produced a narrative pattern blending underworld vernacular with poetic diction. This pattern relied on pungent imagery, including startling similes, for dramatic effect and figurative meaning. As Peter Wolfe wrote in *Something More Than Night: The Case of Raymond Chandler,* Chandler created a darkly lyrical prose that turned his stories into "metaphors of the urban nightmare."

Chandler set most of these "urban nightmares" in Los Angeles, and its portrait is among the most salient feature of his novels. A latecomer to southern California, Chandler was at once attracted and repulsed by "its paradox of beauty and tawdriness," as Robert Kirsch asserted in the *Los Angeles Times Book Review.* Chandler knew of California's appeal as a mecca of opportunity—a holdover from the gold rush days of easy money—and its image as a pastoral haven. But Los Angeles at mid-century hardly lived up to its advertised allurements, and Chandler was struck by the disparity. Pilgrims to the city found there a sprawling town that had grown explosively and erratically. Irresponsible development, fueled by the discovery of oil in the southern basin in 1892, despoiled the landscape; scandal marred local government; and the movie industry nurtured a subculture of artifice and excess.

In 1939, Chandler vividly depicted Los Angeles in his first novel, *The Big Sleep,* which showed the city as a squalid hotbed of blackmail, gambling, flesh-peddling, and drug-dealing. The hero is Philip Marlowe, a private detective whose investigation into an apparently routine extortion scheme sucks him into a cycle of progressively more menacing events. In the beginning, Marlowe conceives of his task in relatively simple terms: free the daughter of his employer, the tycoon Sternwood, from extortionists. But like Dante in Hell, Marlowe undertakes a dark and disgusting journey, one that reveals the consequences of ghastly transgressions. The childlike Carmen Sternwood, pampered and indulged from birth, is initially seen as the victim of crime. Marlowe, however, discovers that the Sternwood family's veneer of gentility masks perversion and treachery, and in uncovering the blackmailers he exposes Carmen Sternwood as a murderer. As Peter J. Rabinowitz observed in *Texas Studies in Literature and Language,* "the novel ends not with the soothing conservative affirmation of order, but with something more politically unsettling: . . . a pervasive sense of individual despair, social chaos, and the triumph of evil." Indeed, some critics found *The Big Sleep* so hard-boiled as to make other crime writers seem totally innocuous by comparison.

In Marlowe, the consummate detective, Chandler created his most enduring hero. Like Chandler's earlier heroes, Marlowe is an idealist at heart, and he is embittered by the decadence of contemporary life. He too is cast as a would-be knight, but his chivalry, though admirable to his author, is now seen as "hopelessly anachronistic," according to William H. Marling in his study *Raymond Chandler.*

Throughout *The Big Sleep* and Chandler's subsequent novels, allusions to Marlowe's heroic bravura are pointedly ironic, and he frequently mocks his own gallantry or conceals it behind a caustic wit and tough-guy banter. E. M. Beekman describes the sleuth in the *Massachusetts Review* as "an outsider, a loner, a man who will

not fit the pattern" and "must not tow the line." Rootless, friendless, without family bonds, and devoid of personal history, Marlowe is the archetypal modern man, struggling to preserve his integrity in a profligate society of debased values. His self-proclaimed mission—futile but no less implacably pursued—is to cleanse the modern world of its venality.

Chandler followed *The Big Sleep* with *Farewell, My Lovely* (1940), his personal favorite of the Marlowe novels. This work features all the characteristic Chandler elements and entwines themes of female duplicity, affluent criminality, and police corruption. The story's locale is Bay City, a fictional town—based loosely on Santa Monica—whose resplendent surface belies its corrupt core. As Frank MacShane asserted in *The Life of Raymond Chandler,* "For Chandler, Bay City was a symbol of hypocrisy: he hated the pretense of uprightness in a place virtually owned by a few people with money." Focusing on what Gavin Lambert described in *The Dangerous Edge* as "Chandler's favorite mystery pattern, the secret alliances between wealth and the underworld," *Farewell, My Lovely* concerns a wealthy socialite who commits murder to conceal her lowly show-girl background. Marlowe, seeking to uncover the woman's past, delves into the workings of Bay City law enforcement, which has conspired to guard her secret. He discovers corruption spanning from street police to high-ranking city officials.

The theme of corruption as a massive chain of crime and cover-up is reworked in variant fashion in Chandler's subsequent novels. *The High Window* traces the private vices of a high-born Pasadena clan whose misdeeds have recoiled upon them, blighting the entire family and engendering a pattern of violent retribution that destroys them all before ending. *The Lady in the Lake,* reviving *Farewell, My Lovely*'s motif of disguised identity, features an ambitious and amoral social climber who repeatedly sheds aliases as she ensnares others into her ruthless scheme of self-advancement. *The Little Sister,* set in the Hollywood "dream factory," uses the movie industry, with its cynical propagation of illusion and staged sex, to diagnose the deeper social ills that befall a culture smitten with pretense. Philip Marlowe, sentimental but more case-hardened with each new foray into evil, provides the moral and visual sensibility that knits these novels into a cohesive design.

The Long Goodbye (1953), another Marlowe novel, signals some subtle evolutions in Chandler's work. The recurrent story of the woman who schemes her way into high society undergirds this novel, but here the emphasis has shifted from the perfidy of the *femme fatale* to the plight of the men who have been her victims: Roger Wade, a sullen writer drowning in alcohol and self-pity, and Terry Lennox, a self-aggrandizing American with a British background. Both have been viewed by critics as autobiographical portraits of Chandler, for he shared both Wade's acrimonious personality—his writer's angst—and Terry Lennox's British past and flair for self-dramatization. Jerry Speir, in his *Raymond Chandler,* called *The Long Goodbye* Chandler's "most personal novel and his most . . . autobiographical work," and he added that it is Chandler's "boldest attempt to exceed the confines of the detective mystery."

The Long Goodbye also marks a modification in the character of Marlowe, whose tough exterior is here more easily and deeply penetrated, and whose repressed yearnings for both male friendship and romantic love are acted out. Though *The Long Goodbye* reprises the hard-boiled elements that defined Chandler's previous works, some critics complained that its more poignant tone lacked the sparkle of its predecessors. Other critics, however, have admired the novel's sensitive and subtly layered portrait of Marlowe and its more rounded vision of humanity. In *The Black Mask Boys* William F. Nolan expressed the favorable judgment, praising *The Long Goodbye* as Chandler's "finest, most mature writing achievement."

Following the publication of *The Long Goodbye,* Chandler's productivity dissipated markedly. The death of his wife in 1954 after a long illness hurried the decline. Chandler, who had idealized his wife while simultaneously committing repeated infidelities, surrendered increasingly to bouts of guilt and alcoholic depression. His work habits, which had never been stable, degenerated accordingly, and his creativity atrophied.

Playback, published in 1958, represented Chandler's last substantial endeavor. It is a disappointing and relatively uninspired work derived from an unproduced film script. The novel's title calls attention to the recurrent theme of the inescapable past. Marlowe is again faced with an enigmatic woman whose impersonation conceals a string of crimes, but his unraveling of that mystery is overshadowed by an ending that has him accepting a marriage proposal. Most critics share Peter Wolfe's judgment in *Something More Than Night,* where he wrote that *Playback* is "tired and flawed," relying on both cliched plot devices and a banal, unconvincingly romantic resolution.

At the time of his death in 1959, Chandler was at work on a novel in which Marlowe is married and living in Palm Springs. That work, left incomplete by Chandler, was finished by a later crime writer, Robert B. Parker, and published in 1989 as *Poodle Springs.*

Although Chandler will be remembered for his Marlowe novels, he had also proved a successful screenwriter before he began his decline. It is not difficult to understand why Paramount sought out Chandler in 1943 to collaborate with director Billy Wilder on a movie version of James M. Cain's thriller *Double Indemnity.* Cain's grim novel, in which a wife plots with an insurance agent to murder her husband and claim a big payoff, replicates Chandler's own corrupt California world. Chandler's contribution to the film was substantial. Writing most of the film's charged dialogue and restructuring the narrative by layering flashbacks, he produced a deft fusion of the eroticism and danger that characterized the *film noir* genre.

With the success of *Double Indemnity,* which earned Chandler an Academy Award nomination, came more film projects. One such project, *Playback,* was scrapped in 1947 and emerged later as the novel; the other, *The Blue Dahlia,* was completed in 1946 as a vehicle for actor Alan Ladd. Chandler's original story, in which a faithless wife is murdered by a disturbed veteran friend of her husband's, reflected the plot ingenuity and psychological resonance that had been hallmarks of Chandler's best work. But various circumstances, including a hectic production schedule, wartime censorship imposed by the Navy, and Chandler's heavy drinking, resulted in a hurried final script. Though the film proved commercially and critically successful, earning Chandler another Academy Award nomination, it nonetheless served to indicate his growing dissatisfaction with film work. His final filmed script, an adaptation of Patricia Highsmith's thriller *Strangers on a Train,* was disdained by director Alfred Hitchcock, and in the early 1950s Chandler withdrew from Hollywood.

Despite the creative decline and personal dislocation of Chandler's final years, his ample literary legacy was consequential enough to sustain his stature as one of America's most original literary voices. He had demonstrated, better than any other writer

of his day or since, the imaginative possibilities of the detective story, and he had transformed the genre from formulaic puzzlement to cultural inquiry. What was perfunctory violence in the hands of less gifted and less visionary writers was, for Chandler, a kind of poetry of the streets. He invested the regional literature of southern California with evocative power and metaphoric energy, making it stand as an emblem of the latent pathologies of American life. He created enduring images of the dark forces of contemporary experience. Biographer Frank MacShane aptly summarized Chandler's achievement by calling him "a prophet of modern America," one whose vision "has become increasingly fulfilled."

BIOGRAPHICAL/CRITICAL SOURCES:

BOOKS

Benstock, Bernard, editor, *Art in Crime Writing: Essays on Detective Fiction,* St. Martin's, 1983.

Brewer, Gary, *A Detective in Distress: Philip Marlowe's Domestic Dream,* Brownstone Books (Madison, IN), 1989.

Bruccoli, Matthew J., *Kenneth Millar/Ross Macdonald: A Checklist,* Gale (Detroit) 1971.

Clark, Al, *Raymond Chandler in Hollywood,* Silman-James Press (Los Angeles), 1996.

Close, Alan, and Deirdre Gartrell, editors, *The Australian Love Letters of Raymond Chandler,* McPhee Gribble Publishers (Ringwood, Victoria), 1995.

Dictionary of Literary Biography Documentary Series, Volume 6, Gale, 1989.

Fine, David, editor, *Los Angeles in Fiction,* University of New Mexico Press, 1984.

Gross, Miriam, editor, *The World of Raymond Chandler,* A & W Publishers, 1978.

Hamilton, Cynthia S., *Western and Hard-Boiled Detective Fiction in America: From High Noon to Midnight,* University of Iowa Press, 1987.

Hiney, Tom, *Raymond Chandler: A Biography,* Atlantic Monthly Press, 1997.

Knight, Stephen, *Form and Ideology in Crime Fiction,* Macmillan, 1980.

Luhr, William, *Raymond Chandler and Film,* Ungar, 1982, second edition, Florida State University Press (Tallahassee), 1991.

MacShane, Frank, *The Life of Raymond Chandler,* Dutton, 1976.

Marling, William, *The American Roman Noir: Hammett, Cain, and Chandler,* University of Georgia Press (Athens), 1995.

Most, Glenn W., and William W. Stowe, editors, *The Poetics of Murder: Detective Fiction and Literary Theory,* Harcourt, 1983.

Newlin, Keith, *Hardboiled Burlesque: Raymond Chandler's Comic Style,* Brownstone, 1984.

Nolan, William F., *The Black Mask Boys,* Morrow, 1985.

Nolan, William F., *The Black Mask Murders: A Novel Featuring the Black Mask Boys, Dashiell Hammett, Raymond Chandler, and Erle Stanley Gardner,* St. Martin's Press (New York City), 1994.

Nolan, William F., *The Marble Orchard: A Black Mask Boys Mystery Featuring Dashiell Hammett, Raymond Chandler, and Erle Stanley Gardner,* St. Marin's Press (New York City), 1996.

Pendo, Stephen, *Raymond Chandler on Screen: His Novels Into Film,* Scarecrow, 1976.

Porter, Dennis, *The Pursuit of Crime: Art and Ideology in Detective Fiction,* Yale University Press, 1981.

Speir, Jerry, *Raymond Chandler,* Ungar, 1981.

Thorpe, Edward, *Chandlertown: The Los Angeles of Philip Marlowe,* Vermilion, 1983.
Twentieth-Century Literary Criticism, Gale, Volume 1, 1978, Volume 7, 1982.
Van Dover, J. Kenneth, *The Critical Response to Raymond Chandler,* Greenwood Press (Westport, CT), 1995.
Wolfe, Peter, *Something More Than Night: The Case of Raymond Chandler,* Bowling Green State University Press, 1985.

PERIODICALS

American Heritage, February-March, 1996, p. 106.
Antaeus, spring-summer, 1977.
Atlantic Monthly, November, 1945; October, 1989, p. 113.
Black Mask, April, 1933.
Clues: A Journal of Detection, fall-winter, 1980.
Commentary, February, 1963.
Economist, April 28, 1990, p. 96.
Entertainment Weekly, October 27, 1995, p. 86.
Gentleman's Quarterly, December, 1994, p. 114.
Kenyon Review, spring, 1979.
London Magazine, December, 1959.
Los Angeles Magazine, March, 1989, p. 134.
Los Angeles Times Book Review, June 27, 1976.
Massachusetts Review, winter, 1973.
Nation, April 23, 1960; September 4, 1960.
New Republic, May 7, 1962.
New Statesman, April 9, 1949.
Newsweek, May 14, 1945; October 31, 1949.
New York, July 1, 1991, p. 127.
New Yorker, March 11, 1962; September 25, 1995, pp. 32-8.
New York Review of Books, December 21, 1995, p. 32.
New York Times, May 9, 1946; April 13, 1996, p. 13.
New York Times Book Review, September 27, 1949; October 15, 1989, p. 35; October 14, 1990, p. 1; October 8, 1995, p. 22.
New York Times Magazine, December 23, 1973; December 4, 1994, p. 104.
Partisan Review, May-June, 1947.
Southern Review, summer, 1970.
Texas Studies in Literature and Language, summer, 1980.
Time, October 3, 1949.
Tribune Books (Chicago), October 12, 1989; November 12, 1995, p. 3.
Voice Literary Supplement, November, 1995, p. 4.

*   *   *

CHAPMAN, Lee
See BRADLEY, Marion Zimmer

*   *   *

CHAPMAN, Walker
See SILVERBERG, Robert

*   *   *

CHAR, Rene (-Emile) 1907-1988

PERSONAL: Born June 14, 1907, in L'Isle-sur-la-Sorgue, Vaucluse, France; died, February 19, 1988, in the military hospital Val-de-Grace, Paris, France; buried in L'Isle-sur-la-Sorgue; son of Emile (an industrialist) and Marie-Therese-Armande (Rouget)

Char; married Georgette Goldstein, 1933 (divorced, 1949). *Education:* Baccalaureate degree from Lycee d'Avignon; attended Ecole de Commerce a Marseille, 1925. *Religion:* No religious convictions.

CAREER: Poet. Sojourn in Tunisia, 1924; first went to Paris in 1929, where he met Louis Aragon, Paul Eluard, and Andre Breton; was a companion of the Surrealists, 1930-34, during the second period of the movement; in L'Isle-sur-Sorgue in 1940 the Vichy police searched his home, leading to his denunciation as a communist as a result of his association with the Surrealists before the war; between 1940 and 1945, he was regional head of a partisan group in the Alpes-de-Provence for the Armee Secrete, working for the Resistance in France and North Africa, using the name Capitain Alexandre; in 1944, he was wounded by the Germans; a month later he was ordered to Algiers on an advisory mission to Supreme Allied Headquarters. *Military service:* French Artillery, Nimes, 1927-28; served again, 1939-40, in Alsace.

MEMBER: Academie de Baviere (Germany), Modern Language Association of America (honorary fellow).

AWARDS, HONORS: Prix des Critiques, 1966, for *Retour amont.* *Military*—Chevalier de la Legion d'Honneur; Medaille de la Resistance; Croix de Guerre.

WRITINGS:

Les Cloches sur le coeur, Le Rouge et le noir, 1928.
Arsenal, Meridiens (Nimes), 1929, new edition published as *De la Main a la Main,* 1930.
(With Andre Breton and Paul Eluard) *Ralentir Travaux,* Editions Surrealistes, 1930.
Le Tombeau des secrets, [Nimes], 1930.
Artine, Editions Surrealistes, 1930, new edition published as *Artine et autres poemes,* Tchou, 1967.
L'Action de la justice est eteinte, Editions Surrealistes, 1931.
Le Marteau sans maitre (also see below), Editions Surrealistes, 1934.
Dependence de l'adieu, G.L.M., 1936.
Moulin premiere (also see below), G.L.M., 1936.
Placard pour un chemin des ecoliers (also see below), G.L.M., 1937.
Dehors la nuit est gouvernee (also see below), G.L.M., 1938.
Seuls demeurent, Gallimard, 1945.
Le Marteau sans maitre [and] *Moulin Premier, 1927-1935,* J. Corti, 1945.
Feuillets d'Hypnos (war journal), Gallimard, 1946, translation by Cid Corman published as *Leaves of Hypnos,* Grossman, 1973.
Le Poeme pulverise (also see below), Fontaine, 1947.
Fureur et Mystere, Gallimard, 1948, new edition, 1962.
Fete des arbres et du chasseur, G.L.M., 1948.
Dehors la nuit est gouvernee [and] *Placard pour un Chemin des Ecoliers,* G.L.M., 1949.
Claire: Theatre de Verdure, Gallimard, 1949.
Le soleil des eaux, etchings by Georges Braque, H. Matarasso, 1949, new edition, Gallimard, 1951.
Les Matinaux, Gallimard, 1950, new edition, 1962, new edition published as *The Dawn Breakers: Les Matinaux,* translated by Michael Worton, Bloodaxe Books, 1992.
Art bref [and] *Premieres alluvions,* G.L.M., 1950.
Quatre fascinants: La Minutieuse, S.N. (Paris), 1951.
A une serenite crispee, Gallimard, 1951.
Poemes, woodcuts by Nicolas de Stael, S.N., 1951.
La Paroi et la prairie, G.L.M., 1952.

Lettera amorosa, Gallimard, 1953, 2nd edition, 1962, lithographs by Braque, E. Engelberts (Geneva), 1963.

Arriere-histoire du "Poeme pulverise" (the nineteen texts of *Le Poeme pulverise* with the author's comments on each), lithographs by de Stael, J. Hugues, 1953, 2nd edition, 1972.

Choix de poemes, Brigadas Liricas (Mendoza, Argentina), 1953.

Le Rempart de brindilles, etchings by Wifredo Lam, L. Broder, 1953.

A la sante du serpent, G.L.M., 1954.

Le Deuil des Nevons, etchings by Louis Fernandez, Le Cormier (Brussels), 1954.

Recherche de la Base et du Sommet [and] *Pauvrete et privilege* (also see below), Gallimard, 1955, new edition, 1965.

Poemes des deux annees, 1953-1954, G.L.M., 1955.

Chanson des etages, P.A.B. (Ales), 1955.

La Bibliotheque est en feu (also see below), etchings by Braque, L. Broder, 1956.

Hypnos Waking (poems and prose), selected and translated by Jackson Mathews, with the collaboration of William Carlos Williams, Richard Wilbur, William Jay Smith, Barbara Howes, W. S. Merwin, and James Wright, Random House, 1956.

Pour nous, Rimbaud, G.L.M., 1956.

En trente-trois morceaux (aphorisms), G.L.M., 1956.

Jeanne qu'on brula verte, illustration by Braque, P.A.B., 1956.

La Bibliotheque est en feu, et autres poemes, G.L.M., 1957.

L'Abominable homme des neiges, Librairie L.D.F. (Cairo), 1957.

L'Une et l'autre, P.A.B., 1957.

De moment en moment, engravings by Joan Miro, P.A.B., 1957.

Les Compagnons dans le jardin, engravings by Zao Wou-Ki, L. Broder, 1957.

Poemes et prose choisis (also see below), Gallimard, 1957.

Elisabeth, petite fille, P.A.B., 1958.

Sur la poesie, G.L.M., 1958, new edition, 1967.

Cinq poesies en hommage a Georges Braque, lithographs by Braque, S.N. (Geneva), 1958.

L'Escalier de Flore, engravings by Pablo Picasso, P.A.B., 1958.

La Faux relevee, P.A.B., 1959.

Nous avons (prose poem), engravings by Miro, L. Broder, 1959.

Pourquoi la journee vole, engraving by Picasso, P.A.B., 1960.

Le Rebanque, P.A.B., 1960.

Anthologie, G.L.M., 1960, new edition published as *Anthologie, 1934-1969,* 1970.

Les Dentelles de Montmirail, P.A.B., 1960.

L'Allegresse, engraving by Madeleine Grenier, P.A.B., 1960.

(With Paul Eluard) *Deux Poemes* (also see below) J. Hugues, 1960.

L'Inclemence lointaine, engravings by Vieira da Silva, P. Beres, 1961.

L'Issue, P.A.B., 1961.

La Montee de la nuit, P.A.B., 1961.

La Parole en archipel, Gallimard, 1962.

Deux Poemes, engraving by da Silva, P.A.B., 1963.

Poemes et prose choisis, Gallimard, 1963.

Impressions anciennes, G.L.M., 1964.

Commune presence, Gallimard, 1964.

L'An 1964, P.A.B., 1964.

L'Age cassant, J. Corti, 1965.

Flux de l'aimant, 2nd edition, G. P. Tarn (Veilhes), 1965.

La Provence, Point Omega, [Paris], 1965.

(With Albert Camus) *La Posterite du soleil,* E. Engelberts, 1965.

Retour amont, illustrations by Alberto Giacometti, G.L.M., 1966.

Le Terme epars, Imprimerie Union, 1966.

Trois coups sous les arbres: Theatre Saisonnier (collection of six plays), Gallimard, 1967.

Dans la pluie giboyeuse, Gallimard, 1968.

(With Martin Heidegger and others) *L'Endurance de la pensee: Pour Saleur Jean Beaufret,* Plon, 1968.

(With Andre Frenaud and others) *Bazaine,* Maeght, 1968.

Le Chien de coeur, G.L.M., 1969.

L'Effroi, la joie, Au vent d'Arles (Saint-Paul), 1969.

Le Nu perdu (also see below), Gallimard, 1971.

La Nuit talismanique, A. Skira (Geneva), 1972.

Picasso sous les ventes Etesiens, French & European, 1973.

Se recontrer paysage avec Joseph Sema, French & European, 1974.

Aromates chasseurs, Gallimard, 1975.

Poems of Rene Char, translated with notes by Mary Ann Caws and Jonathan Griffin, Princeton University Press, 1976.

Recherche de la Base et du Sommet, Schoenhof, 1977.

Chants de la Balandrane: Poemes, Gallimard, 1977.

Le Nu perdu et autres poemes, Gallimard, 1978.

Fenetres dormantes et porte sur le toit, Gallimard, 1979.

Oeuvres completes, Gallimard, 1983.

No Seige Is Absolute, translation by Frank Wright, Lost Roads, 1983. *Les voisinages de Van Gogh,* Gallimard, 1985.

Eloge d'une soupconnee, Gallimard, 1990.

Selected Poems of Rene Char, edited by Mary Ann Caws and Tina Jolas, New Directions, 1992.

Also author of *Le gisant mis en lumiere.*

CONTRIBUTOR

Violette nozieres, N. Flamel (Brussels), 1933.

Reves d'encre, J. Corti, 1945.

Les Miroirs profonds, Editions Pierre a Feu, 1947.

Cinq parmi d'autres, Editions de Minuit, 1947.

A Braque, P.A.B., 1955.

Le Ruisseau de ble, P.A.B., 1960.

Poetes, Peintres, Sculpteurs, Maeght, 1960.

Un Jour entier, P.A.B., 1960.

25 octobre 1961, P.A.B., 1961.

13 mai 1962, P.A.B., 1962.

20 avril 1963, P.A.B., 1963.

OTHER

Also translator from the English of Tiggie Ghika's *Le Bleu de l'aile,* Cahiers d'Art, 1948, Theodore Roethke's "Le Reveil," and "Les Orchidees," published in *Preuves,* June, 1959, and (with Tina Jolas) *La Planche de vivre,* poems from the English, Italian, Spanish, and Russian, Gallimard, 1981. Author of numerous prefaces, forewords, introductions, and catalogs, and of surrealism tracts (1930-34). Also author of numerous pamphlets and leaflets, some decorated with his own engravings. Contributor to *Le Revue Nouvelle, Sagesse, La Revolution Surrealiste, L'Impossible, Cahiers d'Art, Les Lettres Francaises, Les Quatre Vents, Fontaine, Cahiers du Sud, Combat, Mercure de France, Botteghe Oscure, Le Figaro Litteraire, Le Journal des Poetes, Temoins, Carrefour, Action, Realities Secretes, Poetry* (Chicago), *Miscellaneous Man, Western Review, Quarterly Review of Literature, Chelsea, Tiger's Eye, Minnesota Review,* and other publications.

Translations of Char's poems have appeared in Germany, Italy, Spain, South America, Poland, Sweden, the U.S.S.R., Yugoslavia, Japan, and other countries.

SIDELIGHTS: In 1952 France's most prominent novelist, the late Albert Camus, wrote: "I consider Rene Char to be our greatest living poet, and *Fureur et Mystere* to be the most astonishing

product of French poetry since *Les Illuminations* and *Alcools*."
Gabriel Bounoure notes a typical reaction to Char's work: "I
remember when I first read Char's poetry I was drawn by its
evident greatness, repelled by the asperities, the challenge, and the
seismic violence of its inner meaning. . . . Nothing more salutary
had appeared since Nietzsche. Cruel and devouring, this work,
enclosing us like a single diamond, yet with all the sting of
immense spaces of air. Char's universe is the kingdom of the open
air." Camus called this poetry "strange and rigorous," emanating
from "a poet of all time who speaks for our time in particular."

In the early thirties Char became a follower of Andre Breton's
surrealist movement (an artistic style that uses surprising, fantastical imagery) and though he broke with the surrealists shortly
thereafter, the novelty of his imagery and his liberated imagination remain. He was his own master; Camus wrote: "No doubt he
did take part in Surrealism, but rather as an ally than as an
adherent, and just long enough to discover that he could walk
alone with more conviction." Gaetan Picon added: "Char's work
is great, in so far as it both confirms and transcends Surrealism,
both fulfills and exposes the poetry of today, inherits the past and
opens up the future."

During the political turmoil of the late thirties, Char began
producing poems that dealt with Europe's increasingly political
facism. During World War II, after participating in the French
defeat at Alsace, he became a target of investigation by France's
pro-Nazi Vichy government, which considered anyone with
surrealist connections as a likely communist and thus an enemy of
the state. Char fled into the Alps, where he assumed command of
a Free French Forces' parachute division. Although wounded in
1944, he remained active in the Resistance, and he eventually
fought in the battles leading to the liberation of Provence. For his
actions he received the Medal of the Resistance and the Cross of
War. After the war Char resumed his writing career to great
acclaim, and he was subsequently named to the French Legion of
Honor.

Many of Char's poems are aphoristic—stabbing distillations of
language. Emile Snyder writes: "A poem by Rene Char is an act
of violence within which serenity awaits the end of violence." The
concentrated lucidity he attains is, in Char's words "the wound
closest to the sun," and, he might have added, closest to the
essence of poetry, so simple that it is most commonly considered
difficult. Camus remarked that this poetry "carries daytime and
night on the same impulse. . . . And so, when Char's poetry
appears to be obscure, it is because a furious condensation of
imagery, an intensification of light removes it from that degree of
abstract transparency which we all too often demand only because
it makes no demands on us."

Char's concern was with human experience and with beauty amid
struggle and chaos. He said: "Nothing obsesses me but life." And,
"In our darkness, there is no one place for beauty. The whole
place is for beauty." Ralph J. Mills, Jr., notes Char's concern with
the primacy of the poet: "In a world 'faced with the destroyed
god,' as he believes, the solitary figure of the poet is transformed
into the last priest, the final proprietor of value." Char believed
that "to every collapse of the proofs, the poet replies with a salvo
of futurity." And, though he called himself a humanist, the
meaning of the poem, James Wright observes, "is not to be found
in a prose commentary. It is somehow to be found in the
lightning's weeping face."

"An air of pomp hangs over a number of Char poems, early and
late; he seems to be trying too hard to keep the right company and

to strike the right, the philosophically approved, sententious note,"
remarks *Times Literary Supplement* reviewer Malcolm Bowie in a
review of *The Dawn Breakers: Les Matinaux*, first published in
1950. However, Bowie notes, Char was occasionally able to
transcend the philosophical rigor of his poetry by focusing on
"everyday things seen and touched." His language, most frequently compared to fireworks, is "a contained violence," according to
Picon, and bears "the tranquil solidity of a mine which the
slightest nudge will detonate." He "surprised the secret of atomic
energy in language," identifying "poetry with the word." He
sought in language "cruel tools," and Picon believes this language
is lethal, "possessing something of the feeling of weapons set
beneath a glass case." Menard believes it to be a language "unique
in present-day Letters. It is neither prose nor poem. . . . Char
appears to me the first writer of that future in which, as Being is to
be known directly without the cheats of myths and theologies,
language will be truly, in the image of Heidegger, 'the house of
Being' and will reflect its unity."

Char's philosophical master was Heraclitus whom he called that
"vision of a solar eagle" reconciling opposites. Char believed that
"the poem is always married to someone," and the technique of
his poetry can be expressed in the Heraclitian saying, "The Lord
whose oracle is at Delphi neither expresses nor conceals, but
indicates." "I am torn," writes Char, "by all the fragments there
are." Yet his mind could "polarize the most neutral objects,"
writes Bounoure. His inspiration was ancient. Camus noted Char's
right to "lay claim to the tragic optimism of pre-Socratic Greece.
From Empedocles to Nietzsche, a secret had been passed on from
summit to summit, an austere and rare tradition which Char has
revived after prolonged eclipse. . . . What he has called 'Wisdom, her eyes filled with tears,' is brought to life again, on the
very heights of our disasters."

BIOGRAPHICAL/CRITICAL SOURCES:

BOOKS

Benoit, P. A., *Bibliographie des oeuvres de Rene Char de 1928 a
    1963,* Demi-Jour, 1964.
Berger, Pierre, *Rene Char,* Segher, 1951.
Caws, Mary Ann, *The Presence of Rene Char,* Princeton
    University Press, 1976.
Caws, *Rene Char,* Twayne, 1977.
Contemporary Literary Criticism, Gale, Volume 9, 1981; Volume
    11, 1982; Volume 14, 1983; Volume 55, 1989.
Eichbauer, Mary E., *Poetry's Self-Portrait: The Visual Arts as
    Mirror and Muse in Rene Char and John Ashbery,* Peter
    Lang Publishing, 1992.
Fowlie, Wallace, *A Guide to Contemporary French Literature,*
    Meridian Books, 1957.
Lawler, James R., *Rene Char, The Myth and the Poetry,* Princeton
    University Press, 1978.
Minahen, Charles D., *Figuring Things: Char, Ponge, and Poetry
    in the Twentieth Century,* French Forum (Lexington, KY),
    1994.
Mounin, Georges, *Avez-vous la Char?,* Gallimard, 1946.
Piore, Nancy Kline, *Lightning, The Poetry of Rene Char,*
    Northeastern University Press, Boston, 1981.
Rau, Greta, *Rene Char ou la Poesie accrue,* Corti, 1957.
Rene Char's Poetry, Editions de Luca (Italy), 1956.

PERIODICALS

Booklist, March 15, 1992, p. 1331.
Chicago Review, autumn, 1961.
Fifties, third issue, 1959.

French Review, February, 1990, p. 574.
L'Arc, Number 22 (special Char issue), 1963.
L'Herne, Number 18 (special Char issue), 1971.
Liberte, July, 1968.
Library Journal, March 15, 1992, p. 92.
Publishers Weekly, February 17, 1992, p. 59.
Times Literary Supplement, October 14, 1983; January 27, 1995, p. 11.
Western Review, autumn, 1953.
World Literature Today, summer (special Char issue), 1977; summer, 1989, p. 452.

* * *

CHARBY, Jay
See ELLISON, Harlan (Jay)

* * *

CHASE-RIBOUD, Barbara (Dewayne Tosi) 1939-

PERSONAL: Surname is pronounced Chase-ri-boo; born June 26, 1939, in Philadelphia, PA; daughter of Charles Edward (a building contractor) and Vivian May (a medical assistant; maiden name, West) Chase; married Marc Eugene Riboud (a photojournalist), December 25, 1961 (divorced, 1981); married Sergio Tosi (an art expert, publisher, and historian), July 4, 1981; children: (first marriage) David Charles, Alexei Karol. *Education:* Temple University, B.F.A., 1957; Yale University, M.F.A., 1960.

ADDRESSES: Home—3 rue Auguste Comte, 75006 Paris, France. *Agent*—Mitch Douglas and Herb Chayette, International Creative Management, 40 West 57th St., New York, NY 10019.

CAREER: Sculptor, poet, and novelist. State Department lecturer in Senegal, Mali, Ghana, Tunisia, and Sierra Leone, 1975. Chairman of the board, Hessmayling Corporation, Brussels, Belgium, 1983-1990; boardmember, La Napoule Art Foundation, La Napoule, France.

Work represented in permanent collections including those at the Centre Pompidou, Paris, Museum of Modern Art, New York City, Metropolitan Museum of Art, New York City, University Museum, Berkeley, CA, Newark Museum, Newark, NJ, Lannon Foundation, Palm Springs, FL, Centre National des Arts Contemporains, Paris, Geigy Foundation, New York City, Philadelphia Art Alliance, Philadelphia, PA, and Schoenburg Collection, New York Public Library, New York City. Has appeared in documentaries and interviews for film and television, including the television show *Sixty Minutes,* Columbia Broadcasting System (CBS), May 1979.

MEMBER: American Center (NY), Century Association, PEN, Yale Alumni Association.

AWARDS, HONORS: John Hay Whitney Foundation fellowship, 1957-58, for study at the American Academy in Rome; National Endowment for the Arts fellowship, 1973; first prize in the New York City Subway Competition, 1973, for architecture; U.S. State Department traveling grant, 1975; named Academic of Italy with gold medal, 1978, for sculpture and drawing; Janet Heidinger Kafka Prize, 1979, for best novel by an American woman; Carl Sandberg Poetry Prize for best poet, 1988; Van Der Zee Sculpture Prize, 1995; honorary doctorate from Temple University, 1981, and from Muhlenberg College, 1993.

WRITINGS:

POETRY

From Memphis and Peking, Random House, 1974.
Portrait of a Nude Woman as Cleopatra, Morrow, 1987, published as *Nu, comme Cleopatra,* Editions Felin (Paris), 1994.

NOVELS

Sally Hemings, Viking, 1979, revised edition, Random House, 1994.
Valide: A Novel of the Harem, Morrow, 1986.
Echo of Lions, Morrow, 1989.
The President's Daughter, Random House, 1994.

SIDELIGHTS: Fascinated by Fawn Brodie's biography *Thomas Jefferson: An Intimate History,* which touches on the relationship between the U.S. president and his alleged mistress Sally Hemings, a quadroon slave, internationally known sculptor Barbara Chase-Riboud decided to research the couple herself. The result of Chase-Riboud's efforts is her 1979 best-selling historical novel, *Sally Hemings.* Although little information on Hemings's life and her relationship with Jefferson exists, Chase-Riboud's findings reaffirmed the suspicion that Jefferson was Hemings's lover and the father of her seven children.

In *Sally Hemings,* Chase-Riboud endeavored to present the Hemings-Jefferson relationship from various angles, exploring some of its sociological, political, and emotional implications for all races, both sexes, and the United States as a whole. Although Marcy Heidish of the *Washington Post* noted that *Sally Hemings*'s narrative thread is "uneven [and its] recurring changes in voice and chronology tend to blur the book's focus and power, disrupting the narrative flow and the reader's empathy with the characters," the consensus of reviewers was positive. The *New York Times*'s John Russell, for example, lauded Chase-Riboud's ability to portray life in Hemings's time from different points of view. "The slave world," Russell explained, "is made vivid to us in terms of physical and psychic hardship alike. The scenes of high life, whether in Monticello or in Paris, are as succinct as they are deft. . . . [Chase-Riboud] is everywhere on top of her material."

The Hemings-Jefferson story intrigued Chase-Riboud because of its complexity and because she saw in it a union of black and white American history. As Chase-Riboud explained to Susan McHenry of *Ms.,* "what struck me were the very complicated and convoluted relationships between those two families—the 'black' Hemingses and the 'white' Jeffersons. That's typically American." Yet, according to Chase-Riboud, "America perceives itself as a white man's country, and this has nothing to do with reality. . . . There *has* to be a kind of synthesis between 'black' experience and 'white' experience in America, because they are the same."

In addition to garnering critical praise, *Sally Hemings* became the focus of a precedent-setting legal battle. In 1991 the playwright Granville Burgess wrote *Dusky Sally,* a dramatization of the relationship between Hemings and Jefferson. Chase-Riboud, however, felt that much of Burgess's story was based not upon history but upon her own interpretation of the story, as related in her novel. Hemings sued Burgess for copyright infringement. She explained in the *New York Times*: "When you make a big leap of imagination based on historical events, it's not fair that this kind of imaginative effort pass into the public domain just because historical figures are involved." Though Burgess argued that he used historical sources—not Chase-Riboud's novel—as the basis for his play, a Pennsylvania judge upheld Chase-Riboud's claim that her interpretation of history was copyrighted. "The copyright laws were not enacted to inhibit creativity," the judge, as quoted in the *New York Times,* said. "But it is one thing to inhibit creativity and another thing . . . to maintain that the protection of copyright law is negated by any small amount of tinkering with another writer's idea that results in a different expression."

Chase-Riboud further explored the black slave's experience in America in her historical novel *Echo of Lions.* Based on the true story of a rebellion staged by a group of Africans brought to America on a slave ship known as the *Amistad,* the novel recounts the experiences the group's leader, a Mende warrior later given the name of Joseph Cinque, who, along with several others, attempted to sail the slave ship back to Africa. Unintentionally, the crew landed the vessel in Long Island, New York, where the mutineers were captured and forced to spend the next two years imprisoned while a controversial court battle ensued; eventually the men were allowed to return to Africa. Chase-Riboud's depiction of the event received mixed reviews. While most critics found her subject matter of interest and her descriptions of the slave ships and trade vivid and convincing, some argued that the characters lack adequate development and that the narrative's structure is disjointed. Martha Southgate, in the *New York Times Book Review,* observed that Chase-Riboud "partially succeeds in conveying the unrelenting horror of the Middle Passage, but as the story proceeds [her] attempts to give the story an epic feel too often result in overblown and awkward prose." Gary Nash, on the other hand, in a review for the *Los Angeles Times Book Review,* praised Chase-Riboud for her re-creation, finding it "as personal and vividly horrific as words have been able to render this dark chapter in human history."

In her 1986 novel *Valide: A Novel of the Harem,* Chase-Riboud turned her attention to the Ottoman Empire. The story involves a young woman from the French Caribbean island of Martinique who is captured by pirates in 1781 and sold into slavery—specifically into the harem of the sultan of the Ottoman Empire. While the young woman eventually becomes a wife of the sultan, bears him a son, and rises to the exalted status of "Valide" when that son becomes sultan, she remains bound by the slavery and lack of women's rights that characterize the empire. The novel thus explores how slavery "poisons all personal relationships and eliminates the possibility of free choice that is at the root of all real love," remarked Wendy Smith in the *New York Times Book Review.* In telling her story, Chase-Riboud offers numerous details of life inside the insular Ottoman Empire, both for the hundreds of women enslaved in the sultan's harem and for the rulers themselves, imprisoned as well in the decadent court culture. Many reviewers praised Chase-Riboud for creating a provocative historical novel of ideas but felt that the scattered narrative and strained prose kept the novel from living up to "its exceptional promise," in the words of a *Publishers Weekly* reviewer. *Ms.* reviewer Marcia Gillespie commended the author, noting that Chase-Riboud "weaves an incredibly rich and complex tapestry, a panoply of history as grand march beside the intimate life of a woman." Smith concluded that Chase-Riboud failed to create "a successful fictional context" for her ideas but declared that the author "has large ambitions and an important subject, both fine things for a novelist."

Chase-Riboud returned to the era of Thomas Jefferson and Sally Hemings in *The President's Daughter,* published in 1994. The novel focuses on Harriet Hemings, whom the author presents as the illegitimate daughter of Jefferson and Hemings. At the age of twenty-one, Harriet decides to leave Monticello to live in Philadelphia. Changing her name and passing for white, Harriet falls in love with a wealthy white man and becomes active in the local abolitionist movement. Against the backdrop of the momentous events of the mid-nineteenth century, Chase-Riboud once again offers a story about the meaning of love and friendship in the midst of the institution of slavery. While a *Kirkus Reviews* contributor felt that the narrative "lack[s] literary finesse," *New York Times Book Review* commentator Kiki Olson remarked that the author "vividly . . . illuminates the brutal politics of slavery."

In addition to her novels, Chase-Riboud has also written and published poetry. Her 1987 work, *Portrait of a Nude Woman as Cleopatra,* is a "verse novel" that explores the life of Cleopatra. Inspired by a Rembrandt sketch, the work presents the Egyptian queen as a lustful, powerful woman living through important historical events.

The issues and concerns Chase-Riboud raises in her writings and political views are often reflected in her artwork. For instance, in her drawing and her metal and textile sculpture, Chase-Riboud is attracted to what she calls the theme of the couple, the combination of opposites. She is drawn to it, she explained to McHenry, because it is "banal and impossible, the need to join opposing forces: male/female, negative/positive, black/white." Despite the impossibility of merging these forces, Chase-Riboud feels there are harmonious ways for races, sexes, and individuals to influence each other, much as colors and materials influence one another in her art. As McHenry noted, what Chase-Riboud calls "'the metaphysics of color' gives the lie to the myth of race and to the destructive reality of racism through an essentially feminist and humanist acceptance of human diversity." "There are differences," Chase-Riboud commented to McHenry, concerning the races' experiences, "but there is no escape from the influence of one to the other, from their interrelation and interlocking," much as, in the prismatic scale, "one color relates to another, takes on its attributes as they touch." Indeed, Chase-Riboud remarked in an *International Herald Tribune* article, "white and black mean nothing by themselves, only in relation to each other."

In late 1997, Chase-Riboud sued movie mogul Steven Spielberg, alleging unfair use of elements of her *Echo of Lions* in his movie, *Amistad.* The suit was settled out of court on undisclosed terms in February 1998.

BIOGRAPHICAL/CRITICAL SOURCES:

PERIODICALS

Booklist, July, 1987, p. 1644.
Chicago Tribune, July 3, 1979.
Christian Science Monitor, March 22, 1989, p. 13.
Contemporary Literature, spring, 1994, p. 100.
Critique, summer, 1995, p. 258.
Emerge, October, 1994, p. 70.
Essence, December, 1994, p. 56; May, 1995, p. 59.
International Herald Tribune, October 26, 1979.
Kirkus Reviews, July 15, 1994, p. 930.
Los Angeles Times Book Review, June 18, 1989, p. 12.
Ms., October, 1980; September, 1986, p. 20; November, 1989, p. 40.
National Review, December 21, 1979.
New Republic, July 7, 1979.
New York Times, September 5, 1979; August 15, 1991.
New York Times Book Review, October 28, 1979; August 10, 1986, p. 22; May 14, 1989, p. 22; November 6, 1994, p. 24.

People, October 8, 1979.
Publishers Weekly, May 23, 1986, p. 90; May 8, 1987, p. 66.
Virginia Quarterly Review, spring, 1995, p. 60.
Washington Post, June 15, 1979.
Washington Post Book World, February 26, 1989, p. 8.

*   *   *

CHAUCER, Daniel
See FORD, Ford Madox

*   *   *

CHAVEZ, Denise (Elia) 1948-

PERSONAL: Born August 15, 1948, in Las Cruces, NM; daughter of Ernesto E. (an attorney) and Delfina (a teacher; maiden name, Rede) Chavez; married Daniel Zolinsky (a photographer and sculptor), December 29, 1984. *Education:* New Mexico State University, B.A., 1971; Trinity University, San Antonio, TX, M.F.A., 1974; University of New Mexico, M.A., 1982. *Politics:* Democrat. *Religion:* Roman Catholic. *Avocation:* Swimming, bowling, movies.

ADDRESSES: Home—480 La Colonia, Las Cruces, NM 88005.

CAREER: Northern New Mexico Community College, Espanola, instructor in English, 1975-77, professor of English and Theatre, 1977-80; playwright, 1977–; New Mexico Arts Division, Santa Fe, artist in the schools, 1977-83; University of Houston, Houston, TX, visiting scholar, 1988, assistant professor of drama, 1988-91; New Mexico State University, Las Cruces, assistant professor of creative writing, playwrighting, and Chicano literature, 1996–. Instructor at American School of Paris, 1975-77; visiting professor of creative writing at New Mexico State University, 1992-93 and 1995-96; artistic director of the Border Book Festival, 1994–; past member of faculty at College of Santa Fe; teacher at Radium Springs Center for Women (medium-security prison); gives lectures, readings, and workshops throughout the United States and Europe; has given performances of the one woman show *Women in the State of Grace* throughout the United States. Writer in residence at La Compania de Teatro, Albuquerque, NM, and Theatre-in-the-Red, Santa Fe, NM; artist-in-residence at Arts with Elders Program, Santa Fe and Las Cruces; co-director of senior citizen workshop in creative writing and puppetry at Community Action Agency, Las Cruces, 1986-89.

MEMBER: National Institute of Chicana Writers (founding member), PEN USA, PEN USA West, Author's Guild, Western Writers of America, Women Writing the West, Santa Fe Writers Cooperative.

AWARDS, HONORS: Best Play Award, New Mexico State University, 1970, for *The Wait;* grants from New Mexico Arts Division, 1979-80, 1981, and 1988; award for citizen advocacy, Dona Ana County Human Services Consortium, 1981; grants from National Endowment for the Arts, 1981 and 1982, Rockefeller Foundation, 1984, and University of Houston, 1989; creative writing fellowship, University of New Mexico, 1982; Steele Jones Fiction Award, New Mexico State University, 1986, for short story "The Last of the Menu Girls"; Puerto del Sol Fiction award, 1986, for *The Last of the Menu Girls;* creative artist fellowship, Cultural Arts Council of Houston, 1990; Favorite Teacher Award, University of Houston, 1991; Premio Aztlan Award, American

Book Award, and Mesilla Valley Writer of the Year Award, all 1995, all for *Face of an Angel;* New Mexico Governor's Award in literature and *El Paso Herald Post* Writers of the Pass distinction, both 1995; Luminaria Award for Community Service, New Mexico Community Foundation, 1996.

WRITINGS:

PLAYS

The Wait (one-act), 1970, also produced as *Novitiates,* Dallas Theater Center, Dallas, TX, 1971.
Elevators (one-act), produced in Santa Fe, NM, 1972.
The Flying Tortilla Man (one-act), produced in Espanola, NM, 1975.
The Mask of November (one-act), produced in Espanola, NM, 1977.
Nacimiento (one-act; title means "Birth"), produced in Albuquerque, NM, 1979.
The Adobe Rabbit (one-act), produced in Taos, NM, 1979.
Santa Fe Charm (one-act), produced in Santa Fe, NM, 1980.
Si, hay posada (one-act; title means "Yes, There Is Shelter"), produced in Albuquerque, NM, 1980.
El santero de Cordova (one-act; title means "The Woodcarver of Cordova"), produced in Albuquerque, NM, 1981.
How Junior Got Throwed in the Joint (one-act), produced in Santa Fe at Penitentiary of New Mexico, 1981.
(With Nita Luna) *Hecho en Mexico* (one-act; title means "Made in Mexico"), produced in Santa Fe, NM, 1982.
The Green Madonna (one-act), produced in Santa Fe, NM, 1982.
La morenita (one-act; title means "The Dark Virgin"), produced in Las Cruces, NM, 1983.
Francis! (one-act), produced in Las Cruces, NM, 1983.
El mas pequeno de mis hijos (one-act; title means "The Smallest of My Children"), produced in Albuquerque, NM, 1983.
Plaza (one-act), produced in Albuquerque, NM, 1984, also produced in Edinburgh, Scotland, and at the Festival Latino, New York City.
Plague-Time, 1985.
Novena narrativas (one-woman show; title means "The Novena Narratives"), produced in Taos, NM, 1986.
The Step (one-act), produced in Houston at Museum of Fine Arts, 1987.
Language of Vision (one-act), produced in Albuquerque, NM, 1987.
Women in the State of Grace (one-woman show), produced in Grinnell, IA, 1989; produced nationally since 1993.
The Last of the Menu Girls (one-act; adapted from Chavez's short story of the same title), produced in Houston, TX, 1990.

Author of unproduced plays *Mario and the Room Maria,* 1974, *Rainy Day Waterloo,* 1976, *The Third Door* (trilogy), 1979, and *Cruz Blanca, Story of a Town.*

OTHER

(Editor) *Life Is a Two-Way Street* (poetry anthology), Rosetta Press (Las Cruces, NM), 1980.
The Last of the Menu Girls (stories), Arte Publico (Houston, TX), 1986.
The Woman Who Knew the Language of Animals (juvenile), Houghton (Boston), 1992.
(Selector) *Shattering the Myth: Plays by Hispanic Women,* edited by Linda Feyder, Arte Publico, 1992.
Face of an Angel (novel), Farrar, Straus (New York City), 1994.

Work represented in numerous anthologies, including *An Anthology of Southwestern Literature,* University of New Mexico Press,

1977; *An Anthology: The Indian Rio Grande,* San Marcos Press, 1977; *Voces: An Anthology of Nuevo Mexicano Writers,* El Norte Publications, 1987; *Iguana Dreams: New Latino Fiction,* Harper Collins, 1992; *Mirrors Beneath the Earth,* Curbstone Press, 1992; *Growing Up Latino: Memories and Stories,* Houghton, 1993; *New Mexico Poetry Renaissance,* Red Crane Books, 1994; *Modern Fiction about Schoolteaching,* Allyn and Bacon, 1996; *Mother of the America,* Riverhead Books, 1996; *Chicana Creativity and Criticism: New Frontiers in American Literature,* edited by Maraia Herrera-Sobek and Helena Maraia Viramontes, University of New Mexico Press, 1996; *Walking the Twilight II: Women Writers of the Southwest,* edited by Kathryn Wilder, Northland, 1996. Contributor to periodicals, including *Americas Review, New Mexico, Journal of Ethnic Studies,* and *Revista Chicano-Riquena.*

SIDELIGHTS: Denise Chavez is widely regarded as one of the leading Chicana playwrights and novelists of the U.S. Southwest. She has written and produced numerous one-act plays since the 1970s; however, she is best known for her fiction, including *The Last of the Menu Girls,* a poignant and sensitive short story collection about an adolescent girl's passage into womanhood, and *Face of an Angel,* an exploration of a woman's life in a small New Mexico town. With the publication of *Face of an Angel*—and its selection as a Book-of-the-Month Club title in 1994—Chavez gained a national readership for her portraits of Chicanos living in the Mexican-American borderlands.

Born in Las Cruces, New Mexico, Chavez was reared in a family that particularly valued education and self-improvement. The divorce of her father, an attorney, and her mother, a teacher, when Chavez was ten was a painful experience. She spent the rest of her childhood in a household of women that included her mother, a sister, and a half-sister, and has acknowledged that the dominant influences in her life—as well as in her work—have been female. From an early age Chavez was an avid reader and writer. She kept a diary in which she recorded her observations on life and the personal fluctuations in her own life. During high school she became interested in drama and performed in productions. Chavez recalled her discovery of the theater to *Journal North* interviewer Jim Sagel as a revelation: "I can extend myself, be more than myself." She wrote her first play while a senior in college at New Mexico State University: originally entitled *The Wait,* it was renamed *Novitiates* when it was produced in 1971. A story about several persons in transitional periods in their lives, her play won a prize in a New Mexico literary contest.

Critics have noted that Chavez's plays typically focus on the characters' self-revelation and developing sense of their personal place within their community. *Mario and the Room Maria,* for example, is a play about personal growth: its protagonist, Mundo Reyes, is unable to develop emotionally due to his refusal to confront painful experiences from his past. Likewise, *Si, hay posada* depicts the agony of Johnny Briones, whose rejection of love during the Christmas season is the result of emotional difficulties experienced as a child. While Chavez's plays often concentrate on her characters' inner lives, some deal with external and cultural elements that impede social interaction. Set in Santa Fe, New Mexico, her well-known 1984 play *Plaza* contrasts characters who have different impressions of life in the town square. According to *Dictionary of Literary Biography* contributor Rowena A. Rivera, the theme of *Plaza* "emphasizes the importance of family and friendship bonds as a means by which individuals can recover their personal and cultural heritage."

Many of the themes pervading Chavez's plays are echoed and drawn together in her short story collection *The Last of the Menu Girls.* Composed of seven related stories, the work explores the coming of age of Rocio Esquibel through high school and college. In the opening story, Rocio goes to work handing out menus in a hospital, where she is exposed to many different people and experiences. Her impressions are shaped, in large part, by the ordinary individuals whom she daily encounters: the local repairman, the grandmother, and the hospital staff, among others.

Reviewers have argued that Chavez interweaves the seven stories that comprise *The Last of the Menu Girls* in order to emphasize the human need for *comunidad,* or community. Although some scholars find her style to be disjointed and flawed, many laud her lively dialogue, revealing characterization, and ability to write with insight. Chavez does not look upon *The Last of the Menu Girls* as a novel, but as a series of dramatic vignettes that explore the mysteries of womanhood. In fact, she envisions all her work as a chronicle of the changing relationships between men and women as women continue to avow their independence. This assertion has led to the creation of non-stereotypical Chicana heroines like Rocio, who *Women's Studies Review* contributor Maria C. Gonzalez described as "an individual who fights the traditional boundaries of identity that society has set up and expects her to follow."

Chavez's ambitious first novel, *Face of an Angel,* centers on the life of Soveida Dosamantes and her relations with her family, coworkers, former husbands, and lovers in the small New Mexico town of Agua Oscura. Soveida has worked as a waitress for more than thirty years and is deeply involved in preparing a handbook, *The Book of Service,* that she hopes will aid other would-be waitresses. *Face of an Angel* received far wide attention for a first novel; it was chosen as a Book-of-the-Month Club selection and slated as a major paperback release as well. Groundbreaking in the Chicana fiction genre due to its nontraditional heroines and frank discussion of sexual matters, the book was generally hailed as the debut of an important new voice in Hispanic American letters. *Belles Lettres* correspondent Irene Campos Carr called *Face of an Angel* "engrossing, amusing, and definitely one to be savored," adding: "The author's mordant wit is pervasive, the language is pithy, blunt, and explicit." Campos Carr concluded: "Chavez has become a fine writer and a great storyteller. With *Face of an Angel,* her second book, her name can be added to the growing list of Chicana authors making their mark in contemporary American fiction."

Chavez once told *Contemporary Authors*: "I consider myself a performance writer. My training in theater has helped me to write roles that I myself would enjoy acting. My characters are survivors, and many of them are women. I feel, as a Chicana writer, that I am capturing the voice of so many who have been voiceless for years. I write about the neighborhood handymen, the waitresses, the bag ladies, the elevator operators. They all have something in common: they know what it is to love and to be merciful. My work as a playwright is to capture as best as I can the small gestures of the forgotten people, the old men sitting on park benches, the lonely spinsters inside their corner store. My work is rooted in the Southwest, in heat and dust, and reflects a world where love is as real as the land. In this dry and seemingly harsh and empty world there is much beauty to be found. That hope of the heart is what feeds me, my characters."

BIOGRAPHICAL/CRITICAL SOURCES:

BOOKS

Balassi, William, John Crawford, and Annie Eysturoy, editors, *This Is about Vision: Interviews with Southwestern Writers,* University of New Mexico Press (Albuquerque), 1990.
Contemporary Authors New Revision Series, Volume 56, Gale, 1997.
Dictionary of Literary Biography, Volume 122: *Chicano Writers, Second Series,* Gale (Detroit), 1992, pp. 70-6.
Kester-Shelton, Pamela, editor, *Feminist Writers,* St. James Press (Detroit), 1996, pp. 94-6.
Saldivar, Jose-David, and Rolando Hinojosa, editors, *Criticism in the Borderlands: Studies in Chicano Literature, Culture, and Ideology,* Duke University Press (Durham, NC), 1991.

PERIODICALS

American Studies International, April, 1990, p. 48.
Americas Review, Volume 16, number 2, 1988.
Belles Lettres, spring 1995, p. 35.
Bloomsbury Review, September/October 1993; May/June 1995.
Boston Globe, September 30, 1994, p. 61.
Journal North, August 14, 1982, p. E4.
Journal of Semiotic and Cultural Studies, 1991, pp. 29-43.
Los Angeles Times, November 9, 1994, pp. E1, E4.
New York Times Book Review, October 12, 1986, p. 28; September 25, 1994, p. 20.
Performance, April 8, 1983, p. 6.
Publishers Weekly, August 15, 1994, pp. 77-8.
Village Voice, November 8, 1994, p. 18.
Women's Studies Review, September/October 1986.
World Literature Today, autumn, 1995, p. 792.

*   *   *

CHEEVER, John 1912-1982

PERSONAL: Born May 27, 1912, in Quincy, MA; died June 18, 1982, of cancer in Ossining, New York; buried in Norwell, MA; son of Frederick (a shoe salesman and manufacturer) and Mary (Liley) Cheever (a gift shop owner); married Mary M. Winternitz (a poet and teacher), March 22, 1941; children: Susan, Benjamin Hale, Frederico. *Education:* Attended Thayer Academy. *Religion:* Episcopal. *Avocation:* Sailing and skiing.

CAREER: Novelist and short story writer. Instructor, Barnard College, 1956-57, Ossining (NY) Correctional Facility, 1971-72, and University of Iowa Writers Workshop, 1973; visiting professor of creative writing, Boston University, 1974-75. Member of cultural exchange program to the U.S.S.R., 1964. *Military service:* U.S. Army Signal Corps, 1943-45; became sergeant.

MEMBER: National Institute of Arts and Letters, Century Club (New York).

AWARDS, HONORS: Guggenheim fellowship, 1951; Benjamin Franklin Award, 1955, for "The Five Forty-Eight"; American Academy of Arts and Letters award in literature, 1956; O. Henry Award, 1956, for "The Country Husband," and 1964, for "The Embarkment for Cythera"; National Book Award in fiction, 1958, for *The Wapshot Chronicle;* Howells Medal, American Academy of Arts and Letters, 1965, for *The Wapshot Scandal;* Editorial Award, *Playboy,* 1969, for "The Yellow Room"; honorary doctorate, Harvard University, 1978; Edward MacDowell Medal, MacDowell Colony, 1979, for outstanding contributions to the arts; Pulitzer prize in fiction, 1979, National Book Critics Circle Award in fiction, 1979, and American Book Award in fiction, 1981, all for *The Stories of John Cheever;* National Medal for Literature, 1982.

WRITINGS:

NOVELS

The Wapshot Chronicle (also see below), Harper, 1957.
The Wapshot Scandal (also see below), Harper, 1964.
Bullet Park (Book-of-the-Month Club selection), Knopf, 1969.
Falconer, Knopf, 1977.
The Wapshot Chronicle [and] *The Wapshot Scandal,* Harper, 1979.
Oh, What a Paradise It Seems, Knopf, 1982.

SHORT STORIES

The Way Some People Live: A Book of Stories, Random House, 1943, Random House, 1994.
The Enormous Radio and Other Stories, Funk, 1953.
(With others) *Stories,* Farrar, Straus, 1956 (published in England as *A Book of Stories,* Gollancz, 1957).
The Housebreaker of Shady Hill and Other Stories, Harper, 1958.
Some People, Places and Things That Will Not Appear in My Next Novel, Harper, 1961.
The Brigadier and the Golf Widow, Harper, 1964.
Homage to Shakespeare, Country Squire Books, 1965.
The World of Apples, Knopf, 1973.
The Day the Pig Fell into the Well (originally published in the *New Yorker,* October 23, 1954), Lord John Press, 1978.
The Stories of John Cheever, Knopf, 1978.
The Leaves, the Lion-Fish and the Bear, Sylvester and Orphanos, 1980.
Angel of the Bridge, Redpath Press, 1987.
Thirteen Uncollected Stories by John Cheever, Academy Chicago Publishers, 1994.

Also author of *Depression Stories by John Cheever: The Apprentice Years, 1931-1945,* Academy Chicago Publishers.

OTHER

Benjamin Cheever, editor, *The Letters of John Cheever,* Simon & Schuster, 1988.
The Journals of John Cheever, Knopf, 1991.
(With John D. Weaver) *Glad Tidings: A Friendship in Letters,* HarperCollins, 1993.

Also author of television scripts, including *Life with Father.* Contributor to numerous anthologies, including *O. Henry Prize Stories,* 1941, 1951, 1956, 1964. Contributor to the *New Yorker, Collier's, Story, Yale Review, New Republic, Atlantic,* and other publications.

MEDIA ADAPTATIONS: Several of Cheever's short stories have been adapted for motion pictures and television. "The Swimmer" was produced by Columbia in 1968 and PBS-TV broadcast "The Sorrows of Gin," "The Five Forty-Eight," and "O Youth and Beauty!" all in 1979. The film rights to Cheever's novels *The Wapshot Chronicle, The Wapshot Scandal, Bullet Park,* and *Falconer* have been sold. A. R. Gurney has published *A Cheever Evening: A New Play Based on the Stories of John Cheever,* Dramatists Play Service (New York City), 1995.

SIDELIGHTS: John Cheever has come to be considered among the finest American writers of the twentieth century, a master of the short story and a competent novelist. Best known as a chronicler of suburbia, Cheever won critical acclaim for his humorous, yet compassionate, accounts of privileged communities populated by affluent people living spiritually impoverished lives. A rehabilitated alcoholic and a suburban dweller himself, "Cheever knew," eulogized Peter S. Prescott in *Newsweek,* "that in a world that most people envy there are people who are bravely enduring."

Cheever's long career as a short story writer began at the age of seventeen when he sold his first story to the *New Republic.* He became a regular contributor to the *New Yorker* five years later, a relationship that would last for decades and account for the publication of a majority of his stories. Cheever's short work, at times discounted because it was categorized as *New Yorker* style, earned a wider audience and greater recognition when his collection, *The Stories of John Cheever,* was awarded the Pulitzer prize in fiction in 1979. The publication of this volume of sixty-one stories, including such titles as "The Enormous Radio," "The Country Husband," "The Chimera," and "The Swimmer," "revived singlehanded publishers' and readers' interest in the American short story," according to *Time*'s Paul Gray. Commenting on the author's place in American literature, John Leonard wrote in a 1973 *Atlantic* article, "I happen to believe that John Cheever is our best living writer of short stories: a[n Anton] Chekhov of the exurbs."

Cheever, the novelist, was not as widely praised, but even in this role he had his champions. In 1977, fellow author John Gardner maintained that "Cheever is one of the few living American novelists who might qualify as true artists. His work ranges from competent to awesome on all the grounds I would count: formal and technical mastery; educated intelligence; what I would call 'artistic sincerity' . . . ; and last, validity." His novels—most notably *The Wapshot Chronicle, Bullet Park,* and *Falconer*—display "a remarkable sensitivity and a grimly humorous assessment of human behavior that capture[s] the anguish of modern man," commented Robert D. Spector in *World Literature Today,* "as much imprisoned by his mind as by the conventions of society."

Cheever drew on the same confined milieu—geographical and social—in creating his five novels and numerous stories. "There is by now a recognizable landscape that can be called Cheever country," Walter Clemons observed in an article in *Newsweek.* It comprises "the rich suburban communities of Westchester and Connecticut," explained Richard Locke in the *New York Times Book Review,* "the towns [the author] calls Shady Hill, St. Botolphs and Bullet Park." In this country, Cheever found the source for his fiction, the lives of upwardly mobile Americans, both urban and suburban, lives lacking purpose and direction. His fictional representation of these lives captured what a *Time* reviewer termed the "social perceptions that seem superficial but somehow manage to reveal (and devastate or exalt) the subjects of his suburban scrutiny." Fashioned from the author's observations and presented in this manner, Cheever's stories have become, in the opinion of Jesse Kornbluth, "a precise dissection of the ascending middle class and the declining American aristocracy."

For the most part, the characters represented in Cheever's short stories and novels are white and Protestant; they are bored with their jobs, trapped in their lifestyles, and out of touch with their families. "Mr. Cheever's account of life in suburbia makes one's soul ache," Guy Davenport remarked in the *National Review.* Added the reviewer: "Here is human energy that once pushed plows and stormed the walls of Jerusalem . . . spent daily in getting up hung over, staggering drugged with tranquilizers to

wait for a train to . . . Manhattan. There eight hours are given to the writing of advertisements about halitosis and mouthwash. Then the train back, a cocktail party, and drunk to bed." According to Richard Boeth of *Newsweek,* "what is missing in these people is not the virtue of their forebears . . . but the passion, zest, originality and underlying stoicism that fueled the Wasps' domination of the world for two . . . centuries. Now they're fat and bored and scared and whiny."

A recurring theme in Cheever's work is nostalgia, "the particular melancholia induced by long absence from one's country or home," Joan Didion explained in the *New York Times Book Review.* In her estimation, Cheever's characters have "yearned always after some abstraction symbolized by the word 'home,' after 'tenderness,' after 'gentleness,' after remembered houses where the fires were laid and the silver was polished and everything could be 'decent' and 'radiant' and 'clear.'" Even so, Didion added: "Such houses were hard to find in prime condition. To approach one was to hear the quarreling inside. . . . There was some gap between what these Cheever people searching for home had been led to expect and what they got." What they got, the critic elaborated, was the world of the suburbs, where "jobs and children got lost." As Locke put it, Cheever's character's nostalgia grows out of "their excruciating experience of present incivility, loneliness and moral disarray."

Throughout his tales of despair and nostalgia, Cheever offered an optimistic vision of hope and salvation. His main characters struggled to establish an identity and a set of values "in relation to an essentially meaningless—even absurd—world," Stephen C. Moore commented in the *Western Humanities Review.* Kornbluth found that "Cheever's stories and early novels are not really about people scrapping for social position and money, but about people rising toward grace." In his *Dictionary of Literary Biography* essay, Robert A. Morace came to a similar conclusion. Morace maintained that "while he clearly recognizes those aspects of modern life which might lead to pessimism, his comic vision remains basically optimistic. . . . Many of his characters go down to defeat, usually by their own hand. Those who survive,. . . discover the personal and social virtues of compromise. Having learned of their own and their world's limitations, they can, paradoxically, learn to celebrate the wonder and possibility of life."

Critics have also been impressed by Cheever's episodic style. In a discussion of the author's first published work, "Expelled," Morace commented: "The opening paragraph lures the reader into a story which, like many of the later works, is a series of sketches rather than a linear narrative. The narrator, who remains detached even while recognizing his own expulsion, focuses on apparently disparate events which, taken together, create a single impression of what life at prep school is like." And in a review of *Bullet Park,* a *Time* critic notes that most of the novel "is composed of Cheever's customary skillful vignettes in which apparent slickness masks real feeling."

Some reviewers did find, however, that although this episodic structure worked well in Cheever's short fiction, his novels "flounder under the weight of too many capricious, inspired, zany images," as Joyce Carol Oates remarked in the *Ontario Review.* John Updike once offered a similar appraisal: "In the coining of images and incidents, John Cheever has no peer among contemporary American fiction writers. His short stories dance, skid, twirl, and soar on the strength of his abundant invention; his novels fly apart under its impact." Moreover, Oates contended that though "there are certainly a number of powerful passages in *Falconer,* as in *Bullet Park* and the Wapshot novels, . . . in general the whimsical impulse undercuts and to some extent damages the more serious intentions of the works."

Clemons, among others, drew a different conclusion. He noted that "the accusation that Cheever 'is not a novelist' persists," despite the prestigious awards, such as the Howells Medal and the National Book Award, his novels have received. Clemons suggested that this lack of reviewer appreciation was due to Cheever's long affiliation with the *New Yorker.* "The recognition of Cheever's [work] has . . . been hindered by its steady appearance in a debonair magazine that is believed to publish something familiarly called 'the *New Yorker* story,'" he wrote, "and we think we know what *that* is." Clemons added: "Randall Jarrell once usefully [defined the novel] as prose fiction of some length that has something wrong with it. What is clearly 'wrong' with Cheever's . . . novels is that they contain separable stretches of exhilarating narrative that might easily have been published as stories. They are loosely knit. But so what?"

Over the years, the critical and popular response to Cheever's work has been decidedly favorable. Although some have argued that his characters are unimportant and peripheral and that the problems and crises experienced by the upper middle class are trivial, others, such as *Time*'s Gray, contended that the "fortunate few [who inhabit Cheever's fiction] are much more significant than critics seeking raw social realism will admit." Gray explained: "Well outside the mainstream, the Cheever people nonetheless reflect it admirably. What they do with themselves is what millions upon millions would do, given enough money and time. And their creator is less interested in his characters as rounded individuals than in the awful, comic and occasionally joyous ways they bungle their opportunities." John Leonard of the *New York Times* found the same merits, concluding that "by writing about any of us, Mr. Cheever writes about all of us, our ethical concerns and our failures of nerve, our experience of the discrepancies and our shred of honor."

In 1991 Cheever's son Benjamin published an edited version of Cheever's journals. Written over a period of thirty-five years, and composing twenty-nine looseleaf notebooks when unedited, the journals were distilled to a hefty 399-page book by Robert Gottlieb titled *The Journals of John Cheever.* The book is marked by Cheever's woeful reminiscences about life—in particular his addiction to alcohol and his growing dissatisfaction with his marriage.

Cheever's alcoholism grew slowly. He began as a social drinker during the 1950s, and over the years progressed to a full-blown alcoholic. In 1975 he checked himself into a rehabilitation clinic and managed to end his addiction. Unlike many other authors, he was able to continue writing successfully after giving up drinking. During this same period, Cheever found much to complain about in his marriage. He found his wife angry, mean, and unsupportive, even after he gave up alcohol.

Cheever also delves into his awakening sexual identity. As a child, he was considered effeminate by others, and friends and family members speculated that he might be gay. Cheever, himself, hid the fact from others and himself for many years. It was not until he had been with several male lovers that he became more open about his bisexuality.

Critical reaction to the book was mixed. Scott Donaldson, writing in the Chicago *Tribune Books,* felt that the volume was "exquisite-ly written" but depressing: "the story these . . . journals tell is almost unrelievedly one of woe." He concludes that "troubled though the story of [his] life may be, it is told in the same luminous prose that characterized his stories and novels. He takes us on a journey to the depths, but we could not want a better guide." While Jonathan Yardley of the *Washington Post Book World* also characterized the writing in the book as exceptional, he pondered the need for the publication of the volume: "it is difficult to see how it contributes anything of genuine importance to our understanding of Cheever's work."

After Cheever's death, his widow signed a contract with small publisher Academy Chicago to publish some of his previously uncollected short stories. However, when the family realized the publisher was going to print all sixty-eight of Cheever's uncollected stories, they balked and took legal action against the publisher. After a long and expensive battle, Academy Chicago lost the right to publish all the works but were allowed to publish thirteen of the stories. Oddly, Cheever had chosen not to publish these early stories in a collection form during his lifetime because he did not believe they measured up to his later works.

The stories tread on familiar Cheever ground—the troubles of the East Coast middle class. In "His Young Wife," an older man is upset by the fact that his wife is slipping away from him. He turns to gambling to ruin his rival and win back the love of his wife. "In Passing" visits Saratoga, New York, during its famed racing season. Against that capitalistic backdrop, a Marxist organizer is upset over the bank's repossession of his family house and finds himself in turmoil over his family's reaction to the tragedy. "Family Dinner" looks at the devices a husband and wife use to fool themselves and each other in an unhappy marriage. "Cheever's sympathetic feelings are liberal, generous and extensive," commented Mark Harris in the Chicago *Tribune Books,* "His command of his craft, on the other hand, had yet to be fully developed."

Sven Birkerts, writing in the *New York Times Book Review,* found that "the stories are competent, solid," yet he believed that "such a collection would not see the light if it did not have the Cheever name on the cover." John B. Breslin of *America* concluded that "immature some of these stories may be, but not embarrassingly so, and certainly much less 'naked' in their revelations of the writer than the letters and journals that have been published with the approval and participation of his family. [Editor] Franklin Dennis has done Cheever no disservice with this collection and has done his admirers a favor."

Cheever's name is often raised by critics alongside the names of such highly regarded contemporaries as John O'Hara, Saul Bellow, Thomas Pynchon, and Philip Roth. Yet, as Peter S. Prescott noted in a *Newsweek* tribute on the occasion of Cheever's death, "His prose, unmatched in complexity and precision by that of any of his contemporaries . . . is simply beautiful to read, to hear in the inner ear—and it got better all the time." "More precisely than his fellow writers," added Prescott, "he observed and gave voice to the inarticulate agonies that lie just beneath the surface of ordinary lives." In the words of Gray, recorded in a *Time* tribute, Cheever "won fame as a chronicler of mid-century manners, but his deeper subject was always the matter of life and death."

BIOGRAPHICAL/CRITICAL SOURCES:

BOOKS

Aldridge, John W., *Time to Murder and Create: The Contemporary Novel in Crisis,* McKay, 1966.

Bosha, Francis J., *John Cheever: A Reference Guide,* G. K. Hall, 1981.

Bosha, Francis J., editor, *The Critical Response to John Cheever,* Greenwood Publishing Group, 1994.

Byrne, Michael, *Dragons and Martinis: The Skewed Realism of John Cheever,* Borgo Press, 1993.

Cheever, Susan, *Home before Dark,* Houghton, 1984.

Concise Dictionary of American Literary Biography, 1941-1968, Gale, 1987.

Contemporary Authors Bibliographical Series, Volume 1, Gale, 1986.

Contemporary Literary Criticism, Gale, Volume 3, 1975; Volume 7, 1977; Volume 8, 1978; Volume 11, 1979; Volume 15, 1980; Volume 25, 1983; Volume 64, 1991.

Dictionary of Literary Biography, Gale, Volume 2: *American Novelists since World War II,* 1978; Volume 102: *American Short-Story Writers, 1910-1945, Second Series,* 1991.

Dictionary of Literary Biography Yearbook, Gale, 1980, 1982.

Donaldson, Scott, editor, *Conversations with John Cheever,* University Press of Mississippi, 1987.

Donaldson, Scott, *John Cheever: A Biography,* Random House, 1988.

Hassan, Ihab, *Radical Innocence,* Princeton University Press, 1961.

Kazin, Alfred, *Bright Book of Life,* Atlantic-Little, Brown, 1973.

Meanor, Patrick, *John Cheever Revisited,* Twayne (New York City), 1995.

Short Story Criticism, Volume 1, Gale, 1988.

Updike, John, *Picked-Up Pieces,* Knopf, 1976.

Waldeland, L., *John Cheever,* G. K. Hall, 1979.

PERIODICALS

America, October 1, 1994, pp. 28, 30-1.
Atlantic, May, 1969; June, 1973; November, 1993, p. 159.
Book Week, January 5, 1964.
Chicago Tribune, February 27, 1989.
Chicago Tribune Magazine, April 22, 1979.
Christian Century, May 21, 1969.
Christian Science Monitor, October 22, 1964.
Commonweal, May 9, 1969.
Critique, spring, 1963.
Detroit News, November 28, 1978.
Life, April 18, 1969.
Manchester Guardian, January 30, 1959.
Ms., April, 1977.
Nation, December 5, 1988, p. 606.
National Review, June 3, 1969.
New Leader, May 26, 1969.
New Republic, May 25, 1953; June 3, 1957; May 15, 1961; January 25, 1964; April 26, 1969; March 6, 1989, p. 35; December 2, 1991, p. 46.
Newsweek, March 14, 1977; October 30, 1978; June 28, 1982.
New York, April 28, 1969; October 7, 1991, p. 109.
New Yorker, August 19, 1991, p. 26; May 30, 1994, p. 107-110.
New York Herald Tribune Lively Arts, April 30, 1961.
New York Times, March 24, 1965; August 2, 1965; December 18, 1966; April 29, 1969; March 3, 1977; November 7, 1978.
New York Times Book Review, May 10, 1953; September 7, 1958; January 5, 1964; April 27, 1969; May 20, 1973; March 6,

1977; December 3, 1978; January 28, 1979; December 18, 1988; October 6, 1991, p. 1, 21-2; March 13, 1994, p. 17.
New York Times Magazine, October 21, 1979.
Ontario Review, fall/winter, 1977-78.
Playboy, December, 1993, p. 36.
Publishers Weekly, November 6, 1987; August 26, 1988.
Ramparts, September, 1969.
San Francisco Chronicle, May 24, 1953; March 25, 1957; April 28, 1961.
Saturday Review, May 27, 1961; April 26, 1969; April 2, 1977.
Time, March 27, 1964; April 25, 1969; February 28, 1977; October 16, 1978; June 28, 1982; November 28, 1988, p. 98; October 17, 1994, p. 78.
Times Literary Supplement, October 9, 1953; October 18, 1957; August 4, 1961; December 6, 1991, p. 6.
Tribune Books (Chicago), September 22, 1991, p. 5; March 20, 1994, p. 3.
Twentieth Century Literature, January, 1969.
Variety, October 10, 1994, p. 93.
Washington Post, April 29, 1969; October 8, 1979.
Washington Post Book World, March 30, 1980; September 22, 1991, p. 3.
World Literature Today, autumn, 1977.

*   *   *

CHESNUTT, Charles W(addell) 1858-1932

PERSONAL: Born June 20, 1858, in Cleveland, OH; died November 15, 1932, in Cleveland, OH; son of Andrew Jackson (in grocery business) and Ann (one source says Anne) Maria (Sampson) Chesnutt; married Susan Utley Perry (a teacher), June 6, 1878; children: Ethel, Helen Maria, Edwin, Dorothy. *Education:* Educated at schools in Cleveland, OH, and Fayetteville, NC.

CAREER: Teacher, lawyer, businessman, and writer. Taught at public schools in Spartanburg, SC, Charlotte, NC, and Fayetteville, NC, 1872-77; New State Normal School, Fayetteville, assistant principal, 1877-80, principal, 1880-83; worked as a reporter for Dow Jones & Co., 1883; *New York Mail and Express,* New York, NY, stenographer, reporter, and author of daily column "Wall Street Gossip," 1883; Nickel Plate Railroad Co., Cleveland, OH, 1884-89, began as clerk, became stenographer for the firm's legal counsel; admitted to the Bar of Ohio, 1887; private practice of court reporting, beginning in 1890. Active in community affairs and social causes; served on General Committee of National Association for the Advancement of Colored People (NAACP).

AWARDS, HONORS: Spingarn Medal from NAACP, 1928.

WRITINGS:

The Conjure Woman (short stories; contains "The Goophered Grapevine," "Po' Sandy," "Mars Jeems's Nightmare," "The Conjurer's Revenge," "Sis' Becky's Pickaninny," "The Gray Wolf's Ha'nt," and "Hot-Foot Hannibal"), Houghton, 1899, deluxe edition with a foreword by Joel Elias Spingarn, 1929, retold for young readers by Ray Anthony Shepard as *Conjure Tales,* with illustrations by John Ross and Clare Romano, Dutton, 1973.

The Wife of His Youth, and Other Stories of the Color Line (short stories; contains "The Wife of His Youth," "Her Virginia Mammy," "The Sheriff's Children," "A Matter of Principle," "Cicely's Dream," "The Passing of Grandison," "Uncle

Wellington's Wives," "The Bouquet," and "The Web of Circumstance"), Houghton, 1899, reprinted with illustrations by Clyde O. DeLand, Gregg, 1967.
Frederick Douglass (biography), Small, Maynard, 1899.
The House behind the Cedars (novel), Houghton, 1900, reprinted with an introduction by Darwin Turner, P. F. Collier, 1969.
The Marrow of Tradition (novel), Houghton, 1901.
The Colonel's Dream (novel), Doubleday, Page, 1905.
The Short Fiction of Charles W. Chesnutt, edited with an introduction by Sylvia Lyons Render, Howard University Press, 1974.
The Journals of Charles W. Chesnutt, Duke University Press, 1993.
Collected Stories of Charles Chesnutt, Amereon Ltd., 1996.

Contributor to periodicals, including *Alexander's Magazine, Boston Evening Transcript, Family Fiction, Puck, Youth's Companion, Cleveland News and Herald, Atlantic Monthly, Crisis, Overland Monthly, Chicago Ledger, Century, New Haven Register, New York Independent, Outlook,* and *Southern Workman.*

SIDELIGHTS: In her biography, *Charles W. Chesnutt: Pioneer of the Color Line,* Helen M. Chesnutt describes her father as "a pioneer Negro author, the first to exploit in fiction the complex lives of men and women of mixed blood." Similarly, Sylvia Lyons Render writes admiringly in her introduction to *The Short Fiction of Charles W. Chesnutt* of his "extraordinary ability to blend his African and European heritages into distinctly American forms." Because of his fair complexion, Render pointed out, Chesnutt could have "passed" for white; instead "he chose to remain identified as an Afro-American and sought to remove rather than to avoid various forms of discrimination." Chesnutt also merits recognition as one of the first black American fiction writers to receive serious critical attention and acclaim for portraying blacks realistically and sensitively, shunning condescending characterizations and nostalgia for antebellum days of slavery in the South.

Chesnutt was born in 1858 in Cleveland, Ohio, the son of free Negro parents who had moved from Fayetteville, North Carolina, before the Civil War in flight from increasingly severe restrictions imposed on the free colored population of North Carolina. In 1866 the family returned to Fayetteville, and Chesnutt's father started a grocery store there. When young Charles wasn't working in the store, he attended the Howard School for blacks, founded by the Freedman's Bureau in 1865. Pressed to help support his family, Chesnutt was forced to end his formal education when he was only fourteen. However, Robert Harris, the school's principal, prevailed upon Charles's father to let his son stay at the school as a pupil-teacher and turn his modest salary over to his father. At sixteen Chesnutt went to Charlotte as a full-time teacher, and in 1877 he returned to Fayetteville as assistant principal of Howard School, becoming upon Harris's death three years later its principal. Concomitantly Chesnutt commenced a vigorous program of reading and study that led to his proficiency in Latin, German, French, mathematics, and stenography. In 1883 Chesnutt resigned his school administrator post and struck out alone in search of more lucrative employment in the North. He found a job in New York City as a stenographer and journalist on Wall Street, then later returned to Cleveland, where he was hired as a railway clerk and, in 1884, settled with his family.

Chesnutt eventually became a stenographer for the railway company's lawyer, Judge Samuel E. Williamson, in whose office he studied law, and in 1887 he passed the Ohio Bar at the top of his class. Judge Williamson offered to finance a law practice for

Chesnutt in Europe, which was less racist than the United States, but Chesnutt declined the offer. He also turned down the invitation of George Washington Cable, a prominent American writer, to become his private secretary.

Instead, in 1890 Chesnutt chose to support his growing family by establishing a court reporting business and devoting his evenings to his longtime avocation, writing fiction. His first stories were generally light in tone and dealt with conventional subjects of appeal to lesser magazines ranging from *Puck* to *Youth's Companion* and to newspaper syndicates such as S. S. McClure's. These early efforts were crowned by *Atlantic Monthly*'s acceptance of his stories "The Goophered Grapevine" in 1887 and "Po' Sandy" in 1888. At Cable's urging he also contributed commentary to the *New York Independent* and other liberal publications, and by 1889 Chesnutt had completed his first novel, eventually published in 1900 as *The House Behind the Cedars.*

Chesnutt's first published volume, *The Conjure Woman*—issued in 1899 by Houghton Mifflin—was a collection of dialect stories told by an old Negro gardener, "Uncle" Julius McAdoo, to his Northern employer. Ostensibly simple tales of metamorphosis, voodoo, and conjuring, they nonetheless illuminate the dynamics of master-slave relationships and the injustices of slavery. One slaveholder, for instance, resorts to conjuring his grapevine to protect his grapes from thieving slaves. That idea misfires when a new slave mistakenly eats some of the "goophered" grapes. Even after he has tried a magic antidote, the unlucky slave has strange tendrils of grapes growing all over his head—grapes that appear every spring and die down in the winter along with his strength and youth, which also wax and wane with the seasons. Yet his owner profits from this, selling the slave in the spring, when he is young and vigorous, and buying him back cheaply in the fall, when he looks about to die. As several critics noted, these stories convey a very different picture of Southern society from those in the Uncle Remus stories of Joel Chandler Harris, in which happy slaves cheerfully tell animal fables about mischievous Brer Rabbit.

In *The Wife of His Youth, and Other Stories of the Color Line,* a second collection of short stories also published in 1899, Chesnutt portrays the dilemma of mulattoes who felt alien in the black community and excluded from the white. Chesnutt satirized the race-conscious Blue Veins of Cleveland—people of Negro descent with skin light enough to show the blueness of their veins—for snubbing their darker-skinned relatives and mimicking middle-class whites. A third 1899 Chesnutt publication was *Frederick Douglass,* a biography of the prominent abolitionist, for the series "Beacon Biographies of Eminent Americans."

In September, 1900, buoyed by the favorable initial reception given *The Conjure Woman, The Wife of His Youth,* and *Frederick Douglass,* Chesnutt closed down his stenography business so that he could write and lecture full time. Financial success, however, did not match critical acclaim and recognition. His first two novels, *The House Behind the Cedars* and *The Marrow of Tradition,* published in 1900 and 1901 respectively, attracted more controversy than sales. Reviewers who had applauded *The Conjure Woman* became disenchanted with Chesnutt when he began to treat taboo themes such as miscegenation and racial hatred. His sympathetic treatment of erotic love in *The House Behind the Cedars* and his pessimism toward the likelihood of racial harmony in *The Marrow of Tradition* outraged critics. Even William Dean Howells, the distinguished American novelist and critic who in 1900 had praised Chesnutt for "sound[ing] a fresh note, boldly, not blatantly" and placed him in the top rank of American short story writers, declared in a 1901 issue of *North American Review* that "at his worst, [Chesnutt] is no worse than the higher average of the ordinary novelists, but he ought always to be very much better, for he began better."

Chesnutt's earnings from the sales of his two novels and from his freelance journalism and speaking engagements proved inadequate to the financial needs of his family. Consequently in 1902 he reopened the stenography firm he had closed two years earlier. Chesnutt continued writing, however, and in 1905 he published *The Colonel's Dream,* a novel examining the futility of amoral schemes for the economic regeneration of the South. *The Colonel's Dream* received less attention than *The Marrow of Tradition* and garnered even fewer sales. It was to be Chesnutt's last book-length work to appear during his lifetime.

Chesnutt's last published work was an article titled "Post-Bellum—Pre-Harlem" that appeared in *Colophon* a year before his death in 1932. In the article Chesnutt reflected on his literary life and on the history of Afro-American writing in general. He summarized his various books and commented on the ambivalence of his publishers toward revealing his racial identity during the early years of his career. He accepted the fact that literary fashion had passed him by, but he proudly noted that Afro-American literature and the attitude of the white literary world had advanced considerably since the days of his earliest publications. Once possibly the only black American to write serious fiction about Negroes, Chesnutt had devoted his art to reorienting his readers toward what he considered the real issues of race in America.

BIOGRAPHICAL/CRITICAL SOURCES:

BOOKS

Andrews, William L., *The Literary Career of Charles W. Chesnutt,* Louisiana State University Press, 1980.
Bigsby, C. W. E., editor, *The Black American Writer,* Everett/ Edwards, 1969.
Chesnutt, Helen M., *Charles Waddell Chesnutt: Pioneer of the Color Line,* University of North Carolina Press, 1952.
Dictionary of Literary Biography, Volume 12: *American Realists and Naturalists,* Gale, 1982; Volume 50: *Afro-American Writers Before the Harlem Renaissance,* Gale, 1986.
Ellison, Curtis W. and E. W. Metcalf, Jr., *Charles W. Chesnutt: A Reference Guide,* G. K. Hall, 1977.
Keller, Frances Richardson, *An American Crusade: The Life of Charles Waddell Chesnutt,* Brigham Young University Press, 1978.
McElrath, Jr., Joseph R., and Robert C. Leitz III, *"To Be an Author": Letters of Charles W. Chesnutt, 1889-1905,* Princeton University Press (Princeton, NJ), 1996.
Pickens, Ernestine Williams, *Charles W. Chesnutt and the Progressive Movement,* Pace University Press (New York City), 1994.
Render, Sylvia Lyons, editor, *The Short Fiction of Charles W. Chesnutt,* Howard University Press, 1974.
Twentieth-Century Literary Criticism, Gale, Volume 5, 1981.
Wonham, Henry B., *Charles W. Chesnutt: A Study of the Short Fiction,* Twayne Publishers, 1998.

PERIODICALS

American Literature, May, 1975.
American Scholar, winter, 1972.
American Visions, April-May, 1994, p. 30.
Atlantic Monthly, May, 1900.
Books and Bookmen, December, 1975.
CLA Journal, March, 1972; December, 1974.
Colophon, Volume II, number 5, 1931.
Crisis, January, 1933.
Growing Point, January, 1976.
Kirkus Reviews, September 15, 1973; December 15, 1973.
Kliatt, winter, 1979.
New Republic, March 1, 1975.
New York Times Book Review, November 4, 1973; January 17, 1974.
Observer, December 7, 1975.
Phylon, spring, 1971.
Saturday Review, June 21, 1969; October 25, 1969.
Southern Literary Journal, fall, 1982.
Spectator, March 21, 1969; August 16, 1979.
Times Literary Supplement, December 5, 1975.

*   *   *

CHESTERTON, G(ilbert) K(eith) 1874-1936

PERSONAL: Born May 28, 1874, in London, Campden Hill, Kensington, England; died of complications resulting from an edematous condition, aggravated by heart and kidney trouble, June 14, 1936, in Beaconsfield, Buckinghamshire, England; son of Edward (a house agent) and Mary Louise (Grosjean) Chesterton; married Francis Blogg, June 28, 1901. *Education:* Attended Colet Court School, London; St. Paul's School, London, 1887-92; Slade School of Art, London, 1893-96. *Religion:* Converted to Roman Catholicism, 1922.

CAREER: Author, social and literary critic, poet and illustrator. Worked for Redway (publisher), 1896, and T. Fisher Unwin, 1896-1902. Leader of the Distributist movement, and president of Distributist League. Lecturer at Notre Dame University, 1930; radio broadcaster during the 1930s.

MEMBER: Royal Society of Literature (fellow), Detection Club (president, 1928-36).

AWARDS, HONORS: Knight Commander with Star, Order of St. Gregory the Great, 1934.

WRITINGS:

NOVELS

The Napoleon of Notting Hill (also see below) John Lane/Bodley Head, 1904.
The Man Who Was Thursday: A Nightmare (also see below) Dodd, Mead, 1908.
The Ball and the Cross, John Lane, 1909, Dover (New York City), 1995.
Manalive, Nelson, 1912.
The Flying Inn (also see below) John Lane, 1914.
The Return of Don Quixote, Dodd, Mead, 1926.
A G. K. Chesterton Omnibus (includes *The Napoleon of Notting Hill, The Man Who Was Thursday,* and *The Flying Inn*), Methuen, 1936.

SHORT STORIES

The Tremendous Adventures of Major Brown, Shurmer Sibthorp, 1903.
The Club of Queer Trades, Harper, 1905.
The Innocence of Father Brown, Cassell, 1911, annotated edition published as *The Annotated Innocence of Father Brown,* edited by Martin Gardner, Oxford University Press, 1987.

The Wisdom of Father Brown, Cassell, 1914.

The Perishing of the Pendragons, Paget, 1914.

The Man Who Knew Too Much and Other Stories, Cassell, 1922, abridged edition published as *The Man Who Knew Too Much,* Harper, 1922.

Tales of the Long Bow, Cassell, 1925, selections published as *The Exclusive Luxury of Enoch Oates* [and] *The Unthinkable Theory of Professor Green,* Dodd, Mead, 1925, and *The Unprecedented Architecture of Commander Blair,* Dodd, Mead, 1925.

The Incredulity of Father Brown, Cassell, 1926.

The Secret of Father Brown, Cassell, 1927.

The Sword of Wood, Elkin Mathews, 1928.

Stories, Harrap, 1928.

The Poet and the Lunatics: Episodes in the Life of Gabriel Gale, Dodd, Mead, 1929.

The Moderate Murderer [and] *The Honest Quack* (also see below), Dodd, Mead, 1929.

The Father Brown Stories, Cassell, 1929, 12th edition, 1974, published as *The Father Brown Omnibus,* Dodd, Mead, 1933, new and revised edition, 1951.

The Ecstatic Thief (also see below), Dodd, Mead, 1930.

Four Faultless Felons (includes *The Moderate Murderer, The Honest Quack, The Ecstatic Thief,* and *The Loyal Traitor*), Dodd, Mead, 1930.

The Scandal of Father Brown, Dodd, Mead, 1935.

The Paradoxes of Mr. Pond, Dodd, Mead, 1937.

The Pocket Book of Father Brown, Pocket Books, 1943.

The Vampire of the Village, privately published, 1947.

Father Brown: Selected Stories, edited and with an introduction by Ronald Knox, Oxford University Press, 1955.

The Amazing Adventures of Father Brown, Dell, 1961.

Father Brown Mystery Stories, selected and edited by Raymond T. Bond, Dodd, Mead, 1962.

G. K. Chesterton: Selected Stories, edited by Kingsley Amis, Faber, 1972.

Daylight and Nightmare: Uncollected Stories and Fables, edited by Marie Smith, Xanadu, 1987.

Thirteen Detectives: Classic Mystery Stories, edited by Marie Smith, Xanadu, 1987.

(W. W. Robson, editor), *Father Brown—a Selection,* Oxford University Press (New York City), 1995.

Father Brown of the Church of Rome: Selected Mystery Stories, Ignatius Press (San Francisco), 1996.

VERSE

Greybeards at Play: Literature and Art for Old Gentlemen, Rhymes and Sketches (also see below), Johnson, 1900.

The Wild Knight and Other Poems, Richards, 1900, 4th revised edition, Dutton, 1914.

The Ballad of the White Horse, John Lane, 1911.

Poems, John Lane, 1915.

Wine, Water and Song, Methuen, 1915.

A Poem, privately published, 1915.

Old King Cole, privately published, 1920.

The Ballad of St. Barbara and Other Verses, Palmer, 1922.

Poems, Dodd, Mead, 1922.

G. K. Chesterton (collected verse), E. Benn, 1925.

The Queen of Seven Swords, Sheed & Ward, 1926.

The Collected Poems of G. K. Chesterton, Palmer, 1927, Dodd, Mead, 1932, revised edition, Methuen, 1933, Dodd, Mead, 1966.

Gloria in Profundis, Rudge, 1927.

Ubi Ecclesia, Faber, 1929.

Lepanto, Federal Advertising Agency, Inc., 1929.

The Grave of Arthur, Faber, 1930.

Graybeards at Play and Other Comic Verse, edited by John Sullivan, Elek, 1974.

Poems for All Purposes: The Selected Poems of G. K. Chesterton, edited by Stephen Medcalf, Trafalgar Square, 1994.

LITERARY CRITICISM AND ESSAYS

The Defendant (essays), Johnson, 1901, Dodd, Mead, 1902.

(With J. E. Hodder Williams) *Thomas Carlyle,* Hodder & Stoughton, 1902.

Twelve Types, Humphreys, 1902, enlarged edition published as *Varied Types,* Dodd, Mead, 1908, abridged edition published as *Five Types: A Book of Essays,* Humphreys, 1910, Holt, 1911, new abridged edition published as *Simplicity and Tolstoy,* Humphreys, 1912.

(With W. Robertson Nicoll) *Robert Louis Stevenson* (also see below) Pott, 1903.

(With G. H. Perris and Edward Garnett) *Leo Tolstoy,* Pott, 1903.

(With F. G. Kitton) *Charles Dickens,* Pott, 1903.

Robert Browning, Macmillan, 1903.

(With Richard Garnett) *Tennyson,* Hodder & Stoughton, 1903.

(With Lewis Melville) *Thackeray,* Pott, 1903.

G. F. Watts, Dutton, 1904.

Heretics (essays), John Lane, 1905.

Charles Dickens: A Critical Study, Dodd, Mead, 1906, new edition, with a foreword by Alexander Woolcott, published as *Charles Dickens: The Last of the Great Men,* Readers Club Press, 1942.

All Things Considered (essays), John Lane, 1908.

George Bernard Shaw, John Lane/Bodley Head, 1909, revised edition, Devin-Adair, 1950.

Orthodoxy (essays), John Lane/Bodley Head, 1909.

Alarms and Discussions (essays), Methuen, 1910, enlarged edition, Dodd, Mead, 1911.

William Blake, Dutton, 1910.

What's Wrong with the World (essays), Cassell, 1910.

Appreciations and Criticisms of the Works of Charles Dickens, Dutton, 1911.

A Defence of Nonsense and Other Essays, Dodd, Mead, 1911.

The Victorian Age in Literature, Williams & Norgate, 1913.

Utopia of Usurers and Other Essays, Boni & Liveright, 1917.

Charles Dickens Fifty Years After, privately published, 1920.

The Uses of Diversity: A Book of Essays, Methuen, 1920, Dodd, Mead, 1921.

Eugenics and Other Evils (essays), Cassell, 1922.

William Cobbett, Dodd, Mead, 1925.

The Everlasting Man (essays), Dodd, Mead, 1925.

Robert Louis Stevenson, Hodder & Stoughton, 1927, Dodd, Mead, 1928.

Generally Speaking: A Book of Essays, Methuen, 1928.

Essays, Harrap, 1928.

Come to Think of It . . . : A Collection of Essays, Methuen, 1930.

All Is Grist: A Book of Essays, Methuen, 1931, Dodd, Mead, 1932.

Chaucer, Farrar & Rinehart, 1932.

Sidelights on London and Newer York and Other Essays, Sheed & Ward, 1932.

All I Survey: A Book of Essays, Methuen, 1933.

Avowals and Denials: A Book of Essays, Methuen, 1934, Dodd, Mead, 1935.

The Well and the Shallows (essays), Sheed & Ward, 1935.

As I Was Saying: A Book of Essays, Dodd, Mead, 1936.

Essays, edited by John Guest, Collins, 1939.

Selected Essays, edited by Dorothy Collins, Methuen, 1949.

Essays, edited by K. E. Whitehorn, Methuen, 1953.

A Handful of Authors: Essays on Books and Writers, edited by Dorothy Collins, Sheed & Ward, 1953.

The Glass Walking-Stick and Other Essays from the Illustrated London News, 1905-1936, edited by Dorothy Collins, Methuen, 1955.

Lunacy and Letters (essays) edited by Dorothy Collins, Sheed & Ward, 1958.

The Spice of Life and Other Essays, edited by Dorothy Collins, Finlayson, 1964, Dufour, 1966.

Chesterton on Shakespeare, edited by Dorothy Collins, Dufour, 1971.

The Apostle and the Wild Ducks and Other Essays, edited by Dorothy Collins, Elek, 1975.

OTHER

Tremendous Trifles, Dodd, Mead, 1909.

(Editor) *Thackeray* (selections), Bell, 1909.

The Ultimate Lie, privately published, 1910.

(Editor with Alice Meynell) *Samuel Johnson* (selections), Herbert & Daniel, 1911.

A Chesterton Calendar, Kegan Paul, 1911, published as *Wit and Wisdom of G. K. Chesterton,* Dodd, Mead, 1911, published as *Chesterton Day by Day,* Kegan Paul, 1912.

The Future of Religion: Mr. G. K. Chesterton's Reply to Mr. Bernard Shaw, privately published, 1911.

The Conversion of an Anarchist, Paget, 1912.

A Miscellany of Men, Methuen, 1912, enlarged edition, Dodd, Mead, 1912.

Magic: A Fantastic Comedy (play; first produced November 7, 1913, at Little Theatre, London; produced in New York, 1917), Putnam, 1913.

Thoughts from Chesterton, edited by Elsie E. Morton, Harrap, 1913.

The Barbarism of Berlin, Cassell, 1914, published as *The Appetite of Tyranny, Including Letters to an Old Garibaldian,* Dodd, Mead, 1915.

London, photographs by Alvin Langdon Coburn, privately published, 1914.

Prussian versus Belgian Culture, Belgian Relief and Reconstruction Fund, 1914.

Letters to an Old Garibaldian, John Lane, 1915.

The So-Called Belgian Bargain, National War Aims Committee, 1915.

The Crimes of England, Palmer & Hayward, 1915, John Lane, 1916.

Divorce versus Democracy, Society of SS. Peter and Paul, 1916.

Temperance and the Great Alliance, True Temperance Association, 1916.

The G. K. Chesterton Calendar, edited by H. Cecil Palmer, Palmer & Hayward, 1916.

A Shilling for My Thoughts, edited by E. V. Lucas, Methuen, 1916.

A Short History of England, John Lane, 1917.

Lord Kitchener, privately published, 1917.

How to Help Annexation, Hayman Christy & Lilly, 1918.

Irish Impressions, Collins, 1919, John Lane, 1920.

(Editor with Holbrook Jackson and R. Brimley Johnson) Charles Dickens, *The Personal History of David Copperfield,* C. Chivers, 1919.

The Superstition of Divorce, Chatto & Windus, 1920.

The New Jerusalem, Hodder & Stoughton, 1920, Doran, 1921.

What I Saw in America, Hodder & Stoughton, 1922.

Fancies versus Fads, Dodd, Mead, 1923.

St. Francis of Assisi (biography), Hodder & Stoughton, 1923, Doran, 1924.

The End of the Roman Road: A Pageant of Wayfarers, Classic Press, 1924.

The Superstitions of the Sceptic (lecture), Herder, 1925.

A Gleaming Cohort, Being Selections from the Works of G. K. Chesterton, edited by Lucas, Methuen, 1926.

(Editor) *Essays by Divers Hands 6,* Oxford University Press, 1926.

The Outline of Sanity, Sheed & Ward, 1926.

The Catholic Church and Conversion, Macmillan, 1926.

Selected Works, nine volumes, Methuen, 1926.

Social Reform versus Birth Control, Simpkin Marshall, 1927.

The Judgement of Dr. Johnson: A Comedy in Three Acts (play; first produced January 20, 1932, at Arts Theatre Club, London), Sheed & Ward, 1927, Putnam, 1928.

Culture and the Coming Peril (lecture), University of London Press, 1927.

(With George Bernard Shaw) *Do We Agree? A Debate between G. K. Chesterton and Bernard Shaw, with Hilaire Belloc in the Chair,* Mitchell, 1928.

A Chesterton Catholic Anthology, edited by Patrick Braybrooke, Kenedy, 1928.

The Thing, Sheed & Ward, 1929, published as *The Thing: Why I Am a Catholic,* Dodd, Mead, 1930.

G. K. C. as M. C., Being a Collection of Thirty-Seven Introductions, selected and edited by J. P. de Foneska, Methuen, 1929.

The Turkey and the Turk, St. Dominic's Press, 1930.

At the Sign of the World's End, Harvest Press, 1930.

The Resurrection of Rome, Dodd, Mead, 1930.

(With E. Haldeman-Julius) *Is There a Return to Religion?* Haldeman-Julius, 1931.

(Contributor) *The Floating Admiral,* Hodder & Stoughton, 1931, Doubleday, Doran, 1932.

Christendom in Dublin, Sheed & Ward, 1932.

St. Thomas Aquinas (biography), Sheed & Ward, 1933.

G. K. Chesterton (selected humor), edited by E. V. Knox, Methuen, 1933, published as *Running after One's Hat and Other Whimsies,* McBride, 1933.

(Editor) *G. K.'s* (miscellany from *G. K.'s Weekly*), Rich & Cowan, 1934.

Explaining the English, British Council, 1935.

Stories, Essays, and Poems, Dent, 1935, Dutton, 1957.

Autobiography, Hutchinson, 1936, published as *The Autobiography of G. K. Chesterton,* Sheed & Ward, 1936.

The Man Who Was Chesterton: The Best Essays, Stories, Poems and Other Writings of G. K. Chesterton, compiled and edited by Raymond T. Bond, Dodd, Mead, 1937.

The Coloured Lands, Sheed & Ward, 1938.

The End of the Armistice, compiled by F. J. Sheed, Sheed & Ward, 1940.

(Contributor) Ellery Queen, editor, *To the Queen's Taste,* Little, Brown, 1946.

The Common Man, compiled by F. J. Sheed, Sheed & Ward, 1950.

The Surprise (play; first produced June 5, 1953, at University College Assembly Hall, Hull, England), preface by Dorothy L. Sayers, Sheed & Ward, 1952.

G. K. Chesterton: An Anthology, edited and with an introduction by D. B. Wyndham Lewis, Oxford University Press, 1957.

Essays and Poems, edited by Wilfrid Sheed, Penguin Books, 1958.

Where All Roads Lead, Catholic Truth Society, 1961.

The Man Who Was Orthodox: A Selection from the Uncollected Writings of G. K. Chesterton, edited by A. L. Maycock, Dobson, 1963.

G. K. Chesterton: A Selection from His Non-Fictional Prose, edited by W. H. Auden, Faber, 1970.

G. K.'s Weekly: A Sampler, edited by Lyle W. Dorsett, Loyola University Press, 1986.

Collected Nonsense and Light Verse, edited by Smith, Dodd, Mead, 1987.

As I Was Saying . . . : A Chesterton Reader, edited by Robert Knille, Eerdmans, 1987.

The Essential G. K. Chesterton, edited by P. J. Kavanagh, Oxford University Press, 1987.

Contributor to *Daily News* (London), 1901-13, *Illustrated London News,* 1905-36, and *Daily Herald* (London), 1913-14. Editor, *The Debater* (St. Paul's School publication), 1891-93; co-editor, *Eye Witness,* 1911-12; editor, *New Witness,* 1912-23; editor, *G. K.'s Weekly,* 1925-36. Editor, with H. Jackson and R. B. Johnson, "Readers' Classics" series, 1922. Many of Chesterton's papers are held in the Robert John Bayer Memorial Chesterton Collection, John Carroll University Library, Cleveland, Ohio; other materials are at Columbia University, Marquette University, and the British Library.

SIDELIGHTS: "G. K. Chesterton," declared William B. Furlong in the *Dictionary of Literary Biography,* "was a legend in London literary circles even during his lifetime. George Bernard Shaw called him 'a man of colossal genius,' and as a young man Chesterton was hailed as Fleet Street's reincarnation of Samuel Johnson." Dabbling in genres including journalism, social activism, politics, literary criticism, poetry, drama, and mystery fiction, this huge (over three hundred pounds) genial man dominated British letters during the first decades of the twentieth century. Ian Boyd explained in the *Dictionary of Literary Biography,* "He belonged to that category of writer which used to be called the man of letters, and like the typical man of letters he wrote journalism which included a wide variety of literary forms and literature which possessed many of the characteristics of journalism."

Chesterton, Boyd stated, was "very much in the tradition of the Victorian sage"—a *litterateur* prepared to comment on almost any subject. Thomas M. Leitch asserted in the *Dictionary of Literary Biography* that Chesterton "seemed from his early years to combine the disposition of a determined amateur, the imagination of a fantasist, and the temperament of a gadfly." "His pride in his amateur status," Leitch continued, "as philosopher, historian, and economist; his willingness to debate the most unlikely opponents on the most trivial subjects—gave him a reputation as a heroic crank." He was renowned for his wit, having a special aptitude for the *bon mot*; Furlong reported, "There was the famous telegram to his wife: 'Am in Manchester. Where should I be?' Her rejoinder: 'Home.' Asked on Fleet Street which single book he would want if stranded on a desert island he replied without breaking stride, '*Robertson's Guide to Practical Shipbuilding.*' Always though the repartee sparkled best between Shaw and Chesterton. To a rather gaunt Shaw: 'I see there's been a famine in the land.' Reply to a less than gaunt Chesterton: 'Yes, and now I see what caused it.'"

Although best known nowadays for his detective fiction, Chesterton first gained public attention as a journalist and social philosopher. "Like his close friends G. B. Shaw and H. G. Wells," Boyd explained, "he preferred the role of teacher and prophet to

that of literary man, but unlike them his vision of life was fundamentally Christian and even mystical, and the influence he sought to exercise through his writings was directed toward a social change which would be thoroughly religious." His book *What's Wrong with the World* advocated distributism, a social philosophy that divided property holders into small communities, trying to foster neighborliness. Chesterton viewed distributism as a counter to socialism and capitalism, ideologies that, he felt, reduced people to inhumane units. Stephen Metcalf, writing in the *Times Literary Supplement,* pointed out that this philosophy, also expounded in the 1904 novel *The Napoleon of Notting Hill,* more accurately reflects modern society's problems than does George Orwell's classic *1984*; "It is not only . . . that Chesterton cared passionately for what ordinary humanity feels and thinks," Metcalf stated. "It is also that he had particular convictions about how one should understand humanity."

Didacticism has alienated modern readers from some of Chesterton's fiction. His detective stories, however, remain popular. Chesterton himself was very fond of the detective story: "Virtually all of his fiction," Leitch stated, "contains such typical detective elements as the posing of a riddle and its logical solution; many of his stories have the structure of formal detective stories without the presence of a detective; and in his novel *The Man Who Was Thursday* (1908) detectives appear in wild profusion." The author himself recognized that much of his writing was pedantic and would probably not survive him. "Chesterton assumed that he would never be considered a novelist of enormous importance," asserted Brian Murray in the *Dictionary of Literary Biography,* "that, as a writer of fiction, he would always remain best known for the long series of Father Brown stories he began with *The Innocence of Father Brown* in 1911—stories he sometimes tossed off in a day or two."

Loosely based upon Chesterton's friend, the Roman Catholic priest John O'Connor, Father Brown "drops typical Chestertonian quips as he solves ghastly transgressions not with Holmes-sharp logic but by 'getting inside' the criminal mind," according to Murray. Rather than using deductive methods to discover the perpetrator of a crime, Father Brown—whom Chesterton depicted in his *Autobiography* as "shabby and shapeless [in appearance], his face round and expressionless, his manners clumsy"—bases his conclusions on his knowledge of human nature. This knowledge is drawn in part from his experience in the confessional box, but also from his recognition of his own capacity for evil. "The little priest could see," stated Ronald Knox in his introduction to *Father Brown: Selected Stories,* "not as a psychologist, but as a moralist, into the dark places of the human heart; could guess, therefore, at what point envy, or fear, or resentment would pass the bounds of the normal, and the cords of convention would snap, so that a man was hurried into crime." "To Father Brown," wrote Eric Routley in *The Puritan Pleasures of the Detective Story: A Personal Monograph,* "any criminal is a good man gone wrong. He is not an evil man who has cut himself off from the comprehension or sympathy of those who labour to be good."

Father Brown remains, in the minds of most readers, Chesterton's greatest creation, although his contribution to the art of mystery writing is also recognized. "If Chesterton had not created Father Brown," Leitch declared, "his detective fiction would rarely be read today, but his place in the historical development of the genre would still be secure." "Long before he published his last Father Brown stories," the contributor continued, "Chesterton was widely regarded as the father of the modern English detective story. When Anthony Berkeley founded the Detection Club in 1928, it was Chesterton, not Conan Doyle [creator of Sherlock Holmes], who became its first president and served in this capacity until his death." In addition, Leitch asserted, Chesterton "was the first habitual writer of detective stories . . . to insist on the conceptual unity of the form, a criterion he expounded at length in several essays on the subject."

Under the influence of Chesterton's Father Brown, the mystery story became less a portrait of the detective's personality, and more a puzzle that the detective and the reader could both solve. "Chesterton's determination to provide his audience with all the clues available to his detectives," stated Leitch, "has been so widely imitated as to become the defining characteristic of the formal or golden age period (roughly 1920-1940) in detective fiction. . . . Modern readers, for whom the term *whodunit* has become synonymous with *detective story,* forget that the concealment of the criminal's identity as the central mystery of the story is a relatively modern convention." He continued, "Chesterton's Father Brown stories, many of which present murder puzzles in which the murderer's identity constitutes the climactic revelation, are the most orthodox of his stories in the context of the succeeding golden age, whose conventions they so largely established." In the end, H. R. F. Keating (himself a prominent mystery writer) concluded in *Twentieth-Century Crime and Mystery Writers,* "Chesterton's fame rests on the priest with 'the harmless, human name of Brown' and it will endure."

BIOGRAPHICAL/CRITICAL SOURCES:

BOOKS

Barker, Dudley, *G. K. Chesterton: A Biography,* Stein & Day, 1973.

Canovan, Margaret, *G. K. Chesterton: Radical Populist,* Harcourt, 1977.

Carol, Sister M., *G. K. Chesterton: The Dynamic Classicist,* Morilal Banarsidass, 1971.

Coates, John, *Chesterton and the Edwardian Cultural Crisis,* Hull University Press, 1984.

Conlon, D. J., editor, *G. K. Chesterton: A Half Century of Views,* Oxford University Press, 1987.

Dale, Alzina Stone, *The Outline of Sanity: A Life of G. K. Chesterton,* Eerdmans, 1982.

Dictionary of Literary Biography, Gale, Volume 10: *Modern British Dramatists, 1900-1945,* 1982; Volume 19: *British Poets, 1880-1914,* 1983; Volume 34: *British Novelists, 1890-1929: Traditionalists,* 1985; Volume 70: *British Mystery Writers, 1860-1919,* 1988.

Kenner, Hugh, *Paradox in Chesterton,* Sheed & Ward, 1947.

Knox, Ronald, editor and author of introduction, *Father Brown: Selected Stories* by G. K. Chesterton, Oxford University Press, 1955.

O'Connor, John, *Father Brown on Chesterton,* Muller/Burns, Oates, 1937.

Pearce, Joseph, *Wisdom and Innocence: A Life of G. K. Chesterton,* Ignatius Press, 1997.

Peters, Thomas C., *Battling for the Modern Mind: A Beginner's Chesterton,* CPH (St. Louis), 1994.

Rauch, Rufus William, *A Chesterton Celebration,* Notre Dame University Press, 1983.

Routley, Eric, *The Puritan Pleasures of the Detective Story: A Personal Monograph,* Gollancz, 1972.

Short Story Criticism, Volume 1, Gale, 1988.

Sprug, Joseph W., editor, *An Index to G. K. Chesterton,* Catholic University of America Press, 1966.

Sullivan, John, *G. K. Chesterton: A Bibliography,* University of London Press, 1958.

Sullivan, John, *Chesterton Continued: A Bibliographic Supplement,* University of London Press, 1968.

Tadie, Andrew A. and Michael H. MacDonald, *Permanent Things: Toward the Recovery of a More Human Scale at the End of the Twentieth Century,* William B. Eerdmans (Grand Rapids, MI), 1995.

Titterton, W. R., *G. K. Chesterton: A Portrait,* Organ, 1936.

Twentieth-Century Crime and Mystery Writers, 2nd edition, St. James Press/St. Martin's, 1985.

Twentieth-Century Literary Criticism, Volume 6, Gale, 1982.

PERIODICALS

Chesterton Review, fall/winter, 1974–.

Times Literary Supplement, December 25-31, 1987.

*   *   *

CH'IEN, Chung-shu 1910-
(Qian Zhongshu)

PERSONAL: Born November 21, 1910, in Wuhsi, Kiangsu, China; married Yang Jiang (a writer), 1935; children: Qian Yuan. *Education:* Attended Qinghua University, 1929-33; Oxford University, B.Litt., 1937; further study in Paris, France, 1937-38.

ADDRESSES: Office—c/o Chinese Academy of Social Sciences, 5 Jianguomen Nei Da Jie 5 Hao, Beijing, People's Republic of China.

CAREER: Writer, 1932–. Teacher at various schools in China, including Guanghua University, Shanghai, 1933-1935; Southwest Associated University, Yunnan (now Kun-ming), 1938-39; Lantian Normal College, Baoqing, Hunan, 1939-41; Aurora Women's College, Shanghai, 1941-45; National Jinan University, Shanghai, 1946-1948; and Qinghua University, Peking, 1949-52; senior fellow of the Institute of Chinese Literature of the Chinese Academy of Social Sciences, 1952–.

MEMBER: Chinese Academy of Social Sciences (vice president, 1982–).

WRITINGS:

UNDER NAME CH'IEN CHUNG-SHU

Xie zai rensheng bianshang (essays; title means "Written on the Margin of Life"), Shanghai, 1941.

Ren, Shou, Gui (short stories; title means "Humans, Beasts, and Ghosts"; contains "God's Dream," "The Cat," "Inspiration," and "Souvenir"), Kaiming (Shanghai), 1946.

Wei cheng (novel), Chenguang (Shanghai), 1947, translation by Jeanne Kelly and Nathan K. Mao published as *Fortress Besieged,* Indiana University Press, 1979.

Tan yi lu (essays; title means "On Poetry and Poetics"), Kaiming (Shanghai), 1948, revised edition, Zhonghua (Peking), 1984.

Song shi xuan zhu (title means "Annotated Anthology of Song Poetry"), Renmin Wenxue (Peking), 1958, revised, 1979.

Jiu wen sipian (title means "Four Old Essays"), Guji (Shanghai), 1979.

Guanzhui pian (title means "Partial Views on Ideas and Letters"), four volumes, Zhonghua (Peking), 1979-80.

Qizhui ji (title means "Seven Essays: A Miscellany"), Guji, 1985.

Works have also been published under name variation Qian Zhongshu. Also author of an essay on Chinese literature, included in *Chinese Year Book,* 1944-45. Works represented in anthologies, such as *Modern Chinese Stories and Novellas, 1919-1949.* Author of monograph *Limited Views: Essays on Ideas and Letters,* Harvard-Yenching Monograph Series, 1998. Editor of *Philobiblon.* Contributor of reviews and literary criticism to periodicals, including *T'ien Hsia Monthly, Wenxue Yanjiu,* and *Renditions.*

SIDELIGHTS: Though largely unknown in the West, Ch'ien Chung-shu is one of China's most distinguished literary figures. The author of numerous essays, a significant body of literary criticism, and several short stories, he is probably best known for *Fortress Besieged,* his only novel. Originally published in Shanghai as *Wei cheng* in 1947, the controversial satire did not appear in English translation until more than thirty years later. The novel is now regarded as one of the greatest Chinese literary works of the twentieth century.

Ch'ien was born into a scholarly family that fostered an appreciation of culture and the arts. A gifted student, Ch'ien soon established himself as an outspoken member of the Chinese intelligentsia, publishing his first articles of literary criticism by the age of twenty. His early reviews of works by Chinese writers Zhou Zuoren, Cao Baohua, and Shen Qiwu argue for a break from the traditional forms of Chinese literature and an infusion of renewed passion into modern writings. According to Theodore Huters in *Qian Zhongshu,* the author's criticism is pervaded by "ambivalence," that contrasts "the need for Chinese literature to break new ground" with "the complaisance toward and sense of continuity with tradition."

Ch'ien wrote only a small body of short fiction. Huters contended that these works are marked by "a pronounced thinness of texture" and reflect the difficulty the author faced in shifting from the expository style of the essay to the narrative voice of fiction. Four of Ch'ien's stories were collected in the 1946 volume *Ren, Shou, Gui* ("Humans, Beasts, and Ghosts"). One story, "God's Dream," chronicles the creation of humans and their subsequent degeneration into a virtueless species. Faulted for its contrived and digressive nature and limited plot and character development, the story was nevertheless praised for its strong images and original ideas. "Inspiration," another story in the collection, employs complex word plays in a satire of literary culture, but several critics were again disappointed by the stilted evolution of plot and character.

The other two stories in *Ren, Shou, Gui* received a more enthusiastic critical reception. "Souvenir," about the ramifications of a woman's affair with her husband's cousin, and "The Cat," a chronicle of jealousy and revenge between husband and wife, both achieve "more control over the various elements of fiction . . . , [making] real progress toward the harmonization of narrative devices that [would] reach fruition in *Fortress Besieged,*" noted Huters.

Fortress Besieged takes its title from a French proverb: "Marriage is like a fortress besieged; those who are outside want to get in; those who are inside want to get out." Set mainly in Japanese-occupied China from 1937 to 1939, the satirically comical novel centers on a weak-willed protagonist, Fang Hongjian, returning to Shanghai by boat following a four-year stay in Europe. Fang had traveled to the continent to obtain a doctorate but, devoting little time to his studies, he eventually runs low on money. Having procured a fraudulent degree, he boards a boat to Shanghai and becomes embroiled in a love triangle: after a brief affair and rejection, Fang misleads another woman into believing he loves her. He eventually marries a third woman, but the match proves

unsuitable and soon dissolves. *Fortress Besieged* was lauded for its wry wit, penetrating insights into human nature, and provocative use of language. Angela Jung Palanduri, writing in the *Journal of Asian Studies,* declared that the novel's "rich verbal texture . . . makes this prose narrative border on poetry."

In his preface to *Fortress Besieged,* Ch'ien implies that Fang is the satirical embodiment of all westernized pseudointellectuals, a segment of the Chinese population for which the author holds little regard. An evocation of the moral and cultural dissolution of a society from within, the novel is generally regarded as a testament to the futile human pursuit of the unattainable and, noted Francis B. Randall in *National Review,* "the desperate peril and likely fall of the great Chinese culture that once was." In an article for *World Literature Today,* Robert E. Hegel commented on the novel's power: "It's wit aside, *Fortress Besieged* is a disturbing book, leaving the reader exposed in the existential isolation that remains when both laughter and tears finally subside. Certainly this is one of the finest works of contemporary Chinese fiction."

Fortress Besieged is Ch'ien's only lengthy work of fiction. The Chinese civil war and the spread of communism in the years following the novel's original 1947 publication served to stifle reactionary writing in China. Ch'ien chose to abandon fiction writing, publishing essays—including the 1948 collection *Tan yi lu,* a notable volume concerning traditional poetry—and his annotated anthology of Song dynasty poetry during the late 1940s and 1950s. He withdrew from the literary scene in the 1960s but reemerged after a change in China's political regime in 1978. The next year Ch'ien toured the United States as a delegate of the Chinese Academy of Social Sciences. *Guanzhui pian,* a four-volume examination of classic Chinese works, was composed by Ch'ien during his silence and published in Peking between 1979 and 1980. While acknowledging Ch'ien's contribution to Chinese literature and criticism, David Hawkes, writing in the *Times Literary Supplement,* lamented that the country's "most intellectually distinguished" twentieth-century writer did not follow his masterful novel *Fortress Besieged* with another work of fiction: "So brilliant a beginning if it had been made almost anywhere else in the world would almost certainly have been followed by other equally brilliant and more mature successors."

BIOGRAPHICAL/CRITICAL SOURCES:

BOOKS

Contemporary Literary Criticism, Volume 22, Gale, 1982.
Huters, Theodore, *Qian Zhongshu,* Twayne, 1982.

PERIODICALS

Journal of Asian Studies, November, 1980.
National Review, June 13, 1980.
Spectator, July 12, 1980.
Times Literary Supplement, June 27, 1980.
World Literature Today, autumn, 1980.

*   *   *

CHILDRESS, Alice 1920-1994

PERSONAL: Surname is pronounced "*Chil*-dress"; born October 12, 1920, in Charleston, SC; died of cancer, August 14, 1994, in Queens, NY; first husband unknown; married second husband, Nathan Woodard (a musician), July 17, 1957; children: (first marriage) Jean (Mrs. Richard Lee). *Education:* Attended public schools in New York, NY.

ADDRESSES: Office—Beacon Press, 25 Beacon St., Boston, MA 02108-2824. *Agent*—c/o Flora Roberts Inc., 157 W. 57th St, New York, NY 10019.

CAREER: Playwright, novelist, actress, and director. Began career in theater as an actress, with her first appearance in *On Strivers Row,* 1940; actress and director with American Negro Theatre, New York City, for eleven years, featured in the plays *Natural Man,* 1941, *Anna Lucasta,* 1944, and *Florence,* which she also wrote and directed, 1949; also performed on Broadway and television; made her film appearance in *Uptight,* in 1968. Lecturer at universities and schools; member of panel discussions and conferences on Black American theater at numerous institutions, including New School for Social Research, 1965, and Fisk University, 1966; visiting scholar at Radcliffe Institute for Independent Study (now Mary Ingraham Bunting Institute), Cambridge, MA, 1966-68. Member of governing board of Frances Delafield Hospital.

MEMBER: PEN, Dramatists Guild (member of council), American Federation of Television and Radio Artists, Writers Guild of America East (member of council), Harlem Writers Guild.

AWARDS, HONORS: Obie Award for best original off-Broadway play, *Village Voice,* 1956, for *Trouble in Mind;* John Golden Fund for Playwrights grant, 1957; Rockefeller grant, 1967; Outstanding Book of the Year, *New York Times Book Review,* Best Young Adult Book of 1975, Woodward School Book Award, 1974, Jane Addams Children's Book Honor Award for young adult novel, 1974, National Book Award nomination, 1974, and Lewis Carroll Shelf Award, University of Wisconsin, 1975, all for *A Hero Ain't Nothin' but a Sandwich;* Sojourner Truth Award, National Association of Negro Business and Professional Women's Clubs, 1975; Virgin Islands film festival award for best screenplay, and first Paul Robeson Award for Outstanding Contributions to the Performing Arts, Black Filmmakers Hall of Fame, both 1977, both for *A Hero Ain't Nothin' but a Sandwich;* "Alice Childress Week" officially observed in Charleston and Columbia, SC, 1977, to celebrate opening of *Sea Island Song;* Paul Robeson Award, 1980; Best Book, *School Library Journal,* 1981, one of the Outstanding Books of the Year, *New York Times,* 1982, notable children's trade book in social studies, National Council for the Social Studies and Children's Book Council, 1982, and honorable mention, Coretta Scott King Award, 1982, all for *Rainbow Jordan;* Radcliffe Graduate Society Medal, 1984; Audelco Pioneer Award, 1986; Lifetime Achievement Award, Association for Theatre in Higher Education, 1993.

WRITINGS:

Like One of the Family: Conversations from a Domestic's Life, Independence Publishers, 1956, reprinted with an introduction by Trudier Harris, Beacon Press (Boston), 1986.
(Editor) *Black Scenes* (collection of scenes from plays written by African Americans), Doubleday (New York City), 1971.
A Hero Ain't Nothin' but a Sandwich (novel; also see below), Coward (London), 1973.
A Short Walk (novel), Coward, 1979.
Rainbow Jordan (novel), Coward, 1981.
Many Closets, Coward, 1987.
Those Other People, Putnam (New York City), 1989.

PLAYS

Florence (one-act), first produced in New York City at American Negro Theatre, 1949.
Just a Little Simple (based on Langston Hughes's short story collection *Simple Speaks His Mind*), first produced in New York City at Club Baron Theatre, September, 1950.
Gold through the Trees, first produced at Club Baron Theatre, 1952.
Trouble in Mind, first produced off-Broadway at Greenwich Mews Theatre, November 3, 1955, revised version published in *Black Theatre: A Twentieth-Century Collection of the Work of Its Best Playwrights,* edited by Lindsay Patterson, Dodd (New York City), 1971.
Wedding Band: A Love/Hate Story in Black and White (first produced in Ann Arbor, MI, at University of Michigan, December 7, 1966; produced off-Broadway at New York Shakespeare Festival Theatre, September 26, 1972; also see below), Samuel French (New York City), 1973.
String (one-act; based on Guy de Maupassant's story "A Piece of String"; also see below), first produced off-Broadway at St. Mark's Playhouse, March 25, 1969.
Mojo: A Black Love Story (one-act; also see below), produced in New York City at New Heritage Theatre, November, 1970.
Mojo [and] *String,* Dramatists Play Service (New York City), 1971.
When the Rattlesnake Sounds: A Play (juvenile), illustrated by Charles Lilly, Coward, 1975.
Let's Hear It for the Queen: A Play (juvenile), Coward, 1976.
Sea Island Song, produced in Charleston, SC, 1977, produced as *Gullah* in Amherst, MA, at University of Massachusetts, Amherst, 1984.
Moms: A Praise Play for a Black Comedienne (based on the life of Jackie "Moms" Mabley), music and lyrics by Childress and her husband, Nathan Woodard, first produced by Green Plays at Art Awareness, 1986, produced off-Broadway at Hudson Guild Theatre, February 4, 1987.

Also author of *Martin Luther King at Montgomery, Alabama,* music by Woodard, 1969; *A Man Bearing a Pitcher,* 1969; *The Freedom Drum,* music by Woodard, produced as *Young Man Martin Luther King* by Performing Arts Repertory Theatre, 1969-71; *The African Garden,* music by Woodard, 1971; and *Vashti's Magic Mirror.*

SCREENPLAYS

Wine in the Wilderness: A Comedy-Drama (first produced in Boston by WGBH-TV, March 4, 1969), Dramatists Play Service, 1969.
Wedding Band (based on her play of the same title), American Broadcasting Companies (ABC-TV), 1973.
A Hero Ain't Nothin' but a Sandwich (based on her novel of the same title), New World Pictures, 1978.
String (based on her play of the same title), Public Broadcasting Service (PBS-TV), 1979.

Author of "Here's Mildred" column in *Baltimore Afro-American,* 1956-58. Contributor of plays, articles, and reviews to *Masses and Mainstream, Black World, Freedomways, Essence, Negro Digest, New York Times,* and other publications.

SIDELIGHTS: Alice Childress's work is noted for its frank treatment of racial issues, its compassionate yet discerning characterizations, and its universal appeal. Because her books and plays often deal with such controversial subjects as interracial relationships and teenage drug addiction, her work has been banned in certain locations. She recalled that some affiliate stations refused to carry the nationally televised broadcasts of *Wedding Band* and *Wine in the Wilderness,* and in the case of the latter play, the entire state of Alabama banned the telecast. In addition, Childress noted that as late as 1973 the novel *A Hero Ain't Nothin' but a Sandwich* "was the first book banned in a Savannah, Georgia school library since *Catcher in the Rye.*" Despite such regional resistance, Childress won praise and respect for writings that a *Variety* reviewer termed "powerful and poetic."

A talented writer and performer in several media, Childress began her career in the theater, initially as an actress and later as a director and playwright. Although "theater histories make only passing mention of her, . . . she was in the forefront of important developments in that medium," wrote *Dictionary of Literary Biography* contributor Trudier Harris. Rosemary Curb pointed out in another *Dictionary of Literary Biography* essay that Childress's 1952 drama *Gold through the Trees* was "the first play by a black woman professionally produced on the American stage." Moreover, Curb added, "As a result of successful performances of [*Just a Little Simple* and *Gold through the Trees*], Childress initiated Harlem's first all-union off-Broadway contracts recognizing the Actors Equity Association and the Harlem Stage Hand Local."

Partly because of her pioneering efforts, Childress is considered a crusader by many. But she is also known as "a writer who resists compromise," explained Doris E. Abramson in *Negro Playwrights in the American Theatre: 1925-1959.* "She tries to write about [black] problems as honestly as she can," thus, the problems Childress addressed most often were racism and its effects. Her *Trouble in Mind,* for example, is a play within a play that focuses on the anger and frustration experienced by a troupe of black actors as they try to perform stereotyped roles in a play that has been written, produced, and directed by whites. As Sally R. Sommer explained in the *Village Voice,* "The plot is about an emerging rebellion begun as the heroine, Wiletta, refuses to enact a namby-Mammy, either in the play or for her director." In the *New York Times,* Arthur Gelb stated that Childress "has some witty and penetrating things to say about the dearth of roles for [black] actors in the contemporary theatre, the cutthroat competition for these parts and the fact that [black] actors often find themselves playing stereotyped roles in which they cannot bring themselves to believe." And of *Wedding Band,* a play about an interracial relationship that takes place in South Carolina during World War I, Clive Barnes wrote in the *New York Times,* "Childress very carefully suggests the stirrings of black consciousness, as well as the strength of white bigotry."

Both Sommer and the *New York Times*'s Richard Eder found that Childress's treatment of the themes and issues in *Trouble in Mind* and *Wedding Band* gives these plays a timeless quality. "Writing in 1955, . . . Alice Childress used the concentric circles of the play-within-the-play to examine the multiple roles blacks enact in order to survive," Sommer remarked. She found that viewing *Trouble in Mind* years later enables one to see "its double cutting edge: It predicts not only the course of social history but the course of black playwriting." Eder stated: "The question [in *Wedding Band*] is whether race is a category of humanity or a division of it. The question is old by now, and was in 1965, but it takes the freshness of new life in the marvelous characters that Miss Childress has created to ask it."

The strength and insight of Childress's characterizations have been widely commented upon; critics contend that the characters who populate her plays and novels are believable and memorable.

Eder called the characterizations of *Wedding Band: A Love/Hate Story in Black and White* "rich and lively." Similarly impressed, Harold Clurman wrote in the *Nation* that "there is an honest pathos in the telling of this simple story, and some humorous and touching thumbnail sketches reveal knowledge and understanding of the people dealt with." In the novel *A Short Walk,* Childress chronicled the life of a fictitious black woman, Cora James, from her birth in 1900 to her death in the middle of the century, illustrating, as *Washington Post* critic Joseph McLellan described it, "a transitional generation in black American society." McLellan noted that the story "wanders considerably" and that "the reader is left with no firm conclusion that can be put into a neat sentence or two." What is more important, he asserted, is that "the wandering has been through some interesting scenery, and instead of a conclusion the reader has come to know a human being— complex, struggling valiantly and totally believable." In her play *Moms,* Childress drew a portrait of real-life comic Jackie "Moms" Mabley, a popular black comedienne of the 1960s and 1970s. Dressed as a stereotypical shopping-bag lady, Moms Mabley was a television staple with her stand-up routine as a feisty woman with a sharp tongue. Childress, Mel Gussow writes in the *New York Times,* "shrewdly gives Moms center stage and lets her comic sensibility speak for itself."

In several novels aimed at a young adult audience, Childress displayed her talent for believable characterization. In the novel *A Hero Ain't Nothin' but a Sandwich,* the author creates a portrait of a teenaged heroin addict by giving us his story not only from his point of view but from several of his friends and family as well. The *Lion and the Unicorn*'s Miguel Oritz stated, "The portrait of whites is more realistic in this book, more compassionate, and at the same time, because it is believable, more scathing." In *Those Other People,* Childress tells of a group of young friends who are all outsiders: a homosexual, a wealthy black sister and brother, a teacher who has molested one of his students, and a psychiatric patient who was sexually abused as a girl. Each character tells his or her story in separate chapters. The result is a multifaceted look at a pivotal incident at their school which calls into question matters of race and sexual preference. Kathryn Havris, writing in the *School Library Journal,* called *Those Other People* "a disturbing, disquieting novel that reflects another side to life." A *Publishers Weekly* critic concluded that the novel was "a penetrating examination of bigotry and racism."

Many have acclaimed Childress's work for its honesty, insight, and compassion. In his review of *A Hero Ain't Nothin' but a Sandwich,* Oritz wrote: "The book conveys very strongly the message that we are all human, even when we are acting in ways that we are somewhat ashamed of. The structure of the book grows out of the personalities of the characters, and the author makes us aware of how much the economic and social circumstances dictate a character's actions." Loften Mitchell concluded in *Crisis:* "Childress writes with a sharp, satiric touch. Character seems to interest her more than plot. Her characterizations are piercing, her observations devastating."

BIOGRAPHICAL/CRITICAL SOURCES:

BOOKS

Abramson, Doris E., *Negro Playwrights in the American Theatre, 1925-1959,* Columbia University Press (New York City), 1969.
Betsko, Kathleen, and Rachel Koenig, *Interviews with Contemporary Women Playwrights,* Beech Tree Books (Taylors, SC), 1987.

Children's Literature Review, Volume 14, Gale (Detroit), 1988.

Contemporary Literary Criticism, Gale, Volume 12, 1980; Volume 15, 1980.

Dictionary of Literary Biography, Gale, Volume 7: *Twentieth-Century American Dramatists,* 1981; Volume 38: *Afro-American Writers after 1955: Dramatists and Prose Writers,* 1985.

Donelson, Kenneth L., and Alleen Pace Nilson, *Literature for Today's Young Adults,* Scott, Foresman (Glenview, IL), 1980, 2nd edition, 1985.

Evans, Mari, editor, *Black Women Writers (1950-1980): A Critical Evaluation,* Doubleday-Anchor (New York City), 1984.

Hatch, James V., *Black Theater, U.S.A.: Forty-five Plays by Black Americans,* Free Press (New York City), 1974.

Jennings, La Vinia Delois, *Alice Childress,* Twayne (New York City), 1995.

Mitchell, Loften, editor, *Voices of the Black Theatre,* James White (Clifton, NJ), 1975.

Street, Douglas, editor, *Children's Novels and the Movies,* Ungar (New York City), 1983.

PERIODICALS

Atlanta Constitution, March 27, 1986, p. 1.
Crisis, April, 1965.
Freedomways, Volume 14, number 1, 1974.
Horn Book Magazine, May-June, 1989, p. 374.
Interracial Books for Children Bulletin, Volume 12, numbers 7-8, 1981.
Lion and the Unicorn, fall, 1978.
Los Angeles Times, November 13, 1978; February 25, 1983.
Los Angeles Times Book Review, July 25, 1982.
Ms., December, 1979.
Nation, November 13, 1972.
Negro Digest, April, 1967; January, 1968.
Newsweek, August 31, 1987.
New Yorker, November 4, 1972; November 19, 1979.
New York Times, November 5, 1955; February 2, 1969; April 2, 1969; October 27, 1972; November 5, 1972; February 3, 1978; January 11, 1979; January 23, 1987; February 10, 1987, p. 16; March 6, 1987; August 18, 1987; October 22, 1987.
New York Times Book Review, November 4, 1973; November 11, 1979; April 25, 1981.
Publishers Weekly, November 25, 1988, p. 67.
School Library Journal, February, 1989, p. 99.
Show Business, April 12, 1969.
Variety, December 20, 1972.
Village Voice, January 15, 1979.
Washington Post, May 18, 1971; December 28, 1979.
Wilson Library Bulletin, September, 1989, p. 14.

*   *   *

CHLAMYDA, Jehudil
See PESHKOV, Alexei Maximovich

*   *   *

CHOMSKY, (Avram) Noam 1928-

PERSONAL: Born December 7, 1928, in Philadelphia, PA; son of William (a Hebrew scholar) and Elsie (Simonofsky) Chomsky; married Carol Schatz (a linguist and specialist on educational technology), December 24, 1949; children: Aviva, Diane, Harry Alan. *Education:* University of Pennsylvania, B.A., 1949, M.A., 1951, Ph.D., 1955. *Politics:* Libertarian socialist.

ADDRESSES: Home—15 Suzanne Rd., Lexington, MA 02173. *Office*—Room E39-219, Massachusetts Institute of Technology, 77 Massachusetts Ave., Cambridge, MA 02139.

CAREER: Massachusetts Institute of Technology, Cambridge, assistant professor, 1955-58, associate professor, 1958-62, professor, 1962-65, Ferrari P. Ward Professor of Modern Languages and Linguistics, 1966-76, Institute Professor, 1976–. Visiting professor of linguistics, Columbia University, 1957-58, University of California, Los Angeles, 1966, University of California, Berkeley, 1966-67, and Syracuse University, 1982. Member, Institute of Advanced Study, Princeton University, 1958-59. John Locke lecturer, Oxford University, 1969; Bertrand Russell Memorial Lecturer, Cambridge University, 1971; Nehru Memorial Lecturer, University of New Delhi, 1972; Huizinga Lecturer, University of Leiden, 1977; Woodbridge Lecturer, Columbia University, 1978; Kant Lecturer, Stanford University, 1979.

MEMBER: National Academy of Sciences, American Academy of Arts and Sciences, Linguistic Society of America, American Philosophical Association, American Association for the Advancement of Science (fellow), British Academy (corresponding fellow), British Psychological Society (honorary member), Deutsche Akademie der Naturforscher Leopoldina, Gesellschaft fur Sprachwissenschaft (honorary member), Linguistic Society of America, Royal Anthropological Institute of Great Britain, Royal Anthropological Institute of Ireland, Utrecht Society of Arts and Sciences (honorary member).

AWARDS, HONORS: Junior fellow, Harvard Society of Fellows, 1951-55; research fellow at Harvard Cognitive Studies Center, 1964-67; named one of the "makers of the twentieth century" by the London *Times,* 1970; Guggenheim fellowship, 1971-72; distinguished scientific contribution from American Psychological Association, 1984; Gustavus Myers Center Award, 1986 and 1988; George Orwell Award, National Council of Teachers of English, 1987, 1989; Kyoto Prize in Basic Sciences, 1988; Professional Excellence Award, Association for Education in Journalism and Mass Communication, 1991; James Killian Faculty Award, MIT, 1992; Lannan Literary Award for Nonfiction, 1992; Joel Seldin Peace Award, Psychologists for Social Responsibility, 1993; Homer Smith Award, New York University School of Medicine, 1994; Loyola Mellon Humanities Award, Loyola University, 1994; Helmholtz Medal, Berlin-Brandenburgische Akademie Wissenschaften, 1996. Honorary degrees include D.H.L., University of Chicago, 1967, Loyola University of Chicago and Swarthmore College, 1970, Bard College, 1971, University of Massachusetts, 1973, University of Pennsylvania, 1984, Gettysburg College and University of Maine, 1992, and Amherst College, 1995; D.Litt., University of London, 1967, Delhi University, 1972, Visva-Bharati University (West Bengal), 1980, and Cambridge University, 1995.

WRITINGS:

Syntactic Structures, Mouton & Co., 1957.
Current Issues in Linguistic Theory, Mouton & Co., 1964.
Aspects of the Theory of Syntax, MIT Press (Cambridge, MA), 1965.
Cartesian Linguistics: A Chapter in the History of Rationalist Thought, Harper (New York City), 1966.

Topics in the Theory of Generative Grammar, Mouton & Co., 1966.

(With Morris Halle) *Sound Patterns of English,* Harper, 1968.

Language and Mind, Harcourt, 1968, enlarged edition, 1972.

American Power and the New Mandarins, Pantheon (New York City), 1969.

At War with Asia, Pantheon, 1970.

Problems of Knowledge and Freedom: The Russell Lectures, Pantheon, 1971.

(With George A. Miller) *Analyse formelle des langues naturelles,* Mouton & Co., 1971.

Studies on Semantics in Generative Grammar, Mouton & Co., 1972.

(Editor with Howard Zinn) *The Pentagon Papers, Volume 5: Critical Essays,* Beacon Press (Boston), 1972.

(With Edward Herman) *Counterrevolutionary Violence,* Warner Modular, Inc., 1974.

Peace in the Middle East? Pantheon, 1974.

The Logical Structure of Linguistic Theory, Plenum (New York City), 1975.

Reflections on Language, Pantheon, 1975.

Essays on Form and Interpretation, North-Holland (New York City), 1977.

Dialogues avec Mitsou Ronat, Flammarion, 1977, translation published as *Language and Responsibility,* Pantheon, 1979.

Human Rights and American Foreign Policy, Spokesman, 1978.

(With Herman) *The Political Economy of Human Rights,* Volume I: *The Washington Connection and Third World Fascism,* Volume II: *After the Cataclysm: Postwar Indochina and the Construction of Imperial Ideology,* South End (Boston), 1979.

Rules and Representations, Columbia University Press (New York City), 1980.

Lectures on Government and Binding, Foris, 1981.

Radical Priorities, Black Rose Books (New York City), 1982.

Towards a New Cold War: Essays on the Current Crisis and How We Got There, Pantheon, 1982.

Noam Chomsky on the Generative Enterprise: A Discussion with Riny Huybregts and Henk van Riemsdijk, Foris, 1982.

(With Jonathan Steele and John Gittings) *Superpowers in Collision: The Cold War Now,* Penguin (New York City), 1982.

Some Concepts and Consequences of the Theory of Government and Binding, MIT Press, 1982.

The Fateful Triangle: The United States, Israel, and the Palestinians, South End, 1983.

Turning the Tide: U.S. Intervention in Central America and the Struggle for Peace, South End, 1985.

Barriers, MIT Press, 1986.

Knowledge of Language: Its Nature, Origins, and Use, Praeger (New York City), 1986.

Pirates and Emperors: International Terrorism in the Real World, Claremont, 1986.

On Power and Ideology: The Managua Lectures, South End, 1987.

James Peck, editor, *The Chomsky Reader,* Pantheon, 1987.

Language and Problems of Knowledge: The Managua Lectures, MIT Press, 1987

Language in a Psychological Setting, Sophia University (Tokyo), 1987.

Generative Grammar: Its Basis, Development, and Prospects, Kyoto University of Foreign Studies, 1988.

The Culture of Terrorism, South End, 1988.

(With Edward Herman) *Manufacturing Consent,* Pantheon, 1988.

(With C. P. Otero) *Language and Politics,* Black Rose Books, 1988.

Necessary Illusions: Thought Control in a Democratic Society, South End, 1989.

Deterring Democracy, Verso (New York City), 1991.

Terrorizing the Neighborhood: American Foreign Policy in the Post-Cold War Era, Pressure Drop Press (San Francisco), 1991.

Chronicles of Dissent: Interviews with David Barsamian, Common Courage Press (Monroe, ME), 1992.

What Uncle Sam Really Wants, Odonian Press (Berkeley, CA), 1992.

Letters from Lexington: Reflections on Propaganda, Common Courage Press, 1993.

(With David Barsamian) *The Prosperous Few and the Restless Many,* Odonian Press, 1993.

Rethinking Camelot: JFK, the Vietnam War, and U.S. Political Culture, South End, 1993.

Year 501: The Conquest Continues, South End, 1993.

World Orders, Old and New, Columbia University Press, 1994, revised and expanded edition, 1996.

Language and Thought, Moyer Bell (Wakefield, RI), 1994.

Keeping the Rabble in Line: Interviews with David Barsamian, Common Courage Press, 1994.

Secrets, Lies, and Democracy: Interviews with David Barsamian, Odonian Press, 1994.

The Minimalist Program, MIT Press, 1995.

Class Warfare: Interviews with David Barsamian, Common Courage Press, 1996.

Power and Prospects: Reflections on Human Nature and the Social Order, South End, 1996.

SIDELIGHTS: "Judged in terms of the power, range, novelty and influence of his thought, Noam Chomsky is arguably the most important intellectual alive today," writes Paul Robinson in the *New York Times Book Review.* Chomsky, a professor of linguistics at the Massachusetts Institute of Technology, has attracted worldwide attention with his ground-breaking research into the nature of human language and communication. As the founder of the "Chomskyan Revolution," the scholar has become the center of a debate that transcends formal linguistics to embrace psychology, philosophy, and even genetics. *New York Times Magazine* contributor Daniel Yergin maintains that Chomsky's "formulation of 'transformational grammar' has been acclaimed as one of the major achievements of the century. Where others heard only a Babel of fragments, he found a linguistic order. His work has been compared to the unraveling of the genetic code of the DNA molecule." Yergin further contends that Chomsky's discoveries have had an impact "on everything from the way children are taught foreign languages to what it means when we say that we are human." Chomsky is also an impassioned critic of American foreign policy, especially as it affects ordinary citizens of Third World nations. Many of his books since 1969 concern themselves with "the perfidy of American influence overseas," to quote *Atlantic* essayist James Fallows. In *America,* Kenneth J. Gavin finds a unifying strain in all of Chomsky's various writings. The author's goal, says Gavin, is "to highlight principles of human knowledge and indicate the priority of these principles in the reconstruction of a society. His efforts leave us with more than enough to think about."

Chomsky was born in Philadelphia on December 7, 1928. His father was a Hebrew scholar of considerable repute, so even as a youngster Chomsky "picked up a body of informal knowledge about the structure and history of the Semitic languages," according to David Cohen in *Psychologists on Psychology*. While still in high school Chomsky proofread the manuscript of his father's edition of a medieval Hebrew grammar. Yergin notes: "This backdoor introduction to 'historical linguistics' had considerable impact in the future; it helped fuel his later conviction that the explanation of how language worked, rather than categories and description, was the business of linguistic study." The young Chomsky was more interested in politics than grammar, however. He was especially passionate about the rebirth of a Jewish culture and society in what later became the state of Israel, and for a time he entertained the idea of moving there. In 1945 he enrolled at the University of Pennsylvania, where he came under the influence of Zellig Harris, a noted professor of linguistics. John Lyons observes in *Noam Chomsky* that it was the student's "sympathies with Harris's political views that led him to work as an undergraduate in linguistics. There is a sense, therefore, in which politics brought him into linguistics."

Chomsky began to develop in the 1950s a mathematically precise description of some of human language's most striking features. Yergin contends that the scholar was "particularly fascinated by 'generative systems'—the procedures by which a mathematician, starting with postulates and utilizing principles and inferences, can generate an infinite number of proofs. He thought that perhaps language was 'generated' from a few principles as well." Yergin claims that this line of reasoning led Chomsky to another salient question, namely: *"How is it possible that, if language is only a learned habit, one can be continually creative and innovative in its use?"* This question—and its explication—would provide a novel and compelling critique of two established fields, traditional structural linguistics and behavioral psychology. Justin Leiber concludes that Chomsky's new theory "explained many features of language that were beyond structuralist linguistics and placed the specific data, and many lower-level generalizations, of the structuralists within a richer theory."

Many of Chomsky's new ideas were published in his first book, *Syntactic Structures,* in 1957. Yergin calls the work "the pale blue book . . . which heralded the Chomskyan Revolution." He adds that the volume "demonstrated that important facts about language could not be explained by either structural linguistics or by computer theory, which was then becoming fashionable in the field. In *Syntactic Structures,* Chomsky departed from his mentors in stressing the importance of explaining creativity in language and introduces his own transformational grammar as a more 'powerful' explanation of how we make sentences." Webster Schott offers a similar assessment in the *Washington Post Book World*. In *Syntactic Structures,* writes Schott, "Chomsky [presents] and [seems] to demonstrate the proposition that every human being has an innate ability to acquire language, and this ability to learn language is called into use when one hears, at the right age, language for the first time. He also [offers] a concept— it came to be known as 'generative' or 'transformational-generative' grammar—which [has] made it possible to predict ('generate') the sentence combinations in a language and to describe their structure." Lyons states that the short and relatively nontechnical *Syntactic Structures* "revolutionized the scientific study of language."

Chomsky has argued that all natural human languages possess deep and surface structures and cycles of transformations between them. In the *Nation*, Gilbert Harman writes: "These built-in aspects of grammar will be parts of the grammar of every language. They are, in other words, aspects of 'universal grammar.' We must therefore suppose that people have a specific faculty of language, a kind of 'mental organ' which develops in the appropriate way, given appropriate experience, yielding a knowledge of whatever language is spoken in their community." John Sturrock elaborates in the *New York Times Book Review*: "Chomskyism starts with grammar and finishes in genetics. Drill deep enough into the structure of our sentences, he maintains, and you will come to those ultimate abstractions with which we were born, the grammar of any given language being originally determined by the fairly restricted grammatical possibilities programmed in the brain. . . . DNA sets up to master a syntax, the accident of birth determines which one." Needless to say, not everyone agrees with Chomsky's view. *Psychology Today* contributor Howard Gardner calls the human being in Chomsky's formulation "a totally preprogrammed computer, one that needs merely to be plugged into the appropriate outlet." Lyons, conversely, states that Chomsky "was surely right to challenge 'the belief that the mind must be simpler in its structure than any known physical organ and that the most primitive of assumptions must be adequate to explain whatever phenomena can be observed.'"

While establishing his academic reputation, Chomsky continued to be concerned about the direction of American politics and ideology. His moral indignation was excited in the 1960s and he became "one of the most articulate spokesmen of the resistance against the Vietnam war," to quote Jan G. Deutsche in the *New York Times Book Review*. Chomsky attacked the war in articles, in books, and from the podium; in the process he became better known for his political views than for his linguistic scholarship. In a *New York Times* piece written during that era, Thomas Lask observes: "Unlike many others, even those who oppose the war, Noam Chomsky can't stand it and his hatred of what we are doing there and his shame, as well as his loathing for the men who defend and give it countenance are tangible enough to touch." *Nation* essayist Brian Morton finds "nothing exotic about his critique of the U.S. role in Vietnam: He attempted no analysis of arcane economic or political structures. All he did was evaluate our government's actions by the same standards that we apply when we evaluate the actions of other governments."

Chomsky's first book-length work on Vietnam, *American Power and the New Mandarins,* offers "a searing criticism of the system of values and decision-making that drove the United States to the jungles of Southeast Asia," according to Michael R. Beschloss in the *Washington Post Book World*. The book's strongest vitriol is directed toward those so-called "New Mandarins"—the technocrats, bureaucrats, and university-trained scholars who defend America's right to dominate the globe. Deutsch states that Chomsky's concern "is not simply that social scientists have participated widely in designing and executing war-related projects. What he finds disturbing are the consequences of access to power by intellectuals; the difficulties involved in retaining a critical stance toward a society that makes the reward of power available as well as the need to be 'constructive,' the recognition as problems of only those difficulties that are soluble by the means at hand." Inevitably, Chomsky's volume has drawn scathing criticism from those who oppose his views and high praise from those who agree with him. *Chicago Tribune Book World* reviewer Arthur Schlesinger, Jr., claims: "Judging by *American Power and the New Mandarins,* one can only conclude that Chomsky's idea of the responsibility of an intellectual is to forswear reasoned analysis, indulge in moralistic declamation, fabricate evidence when necessary and shout always at the top of one's voice. It need hardly be said that, should the intellectual community follow the Chomsky example, it would betray its own traditions and hasten society along the road to unreason and disaster."

Subsequent Chomsky books on American foreign policy have explored other political hotbeds around the world, drawing the conclusion that U.S. interests in human rights, justice, and morality are inevitably subordinated to the needs of big business. Critics point out that a good introduction to Chomsky's views and main themes is provided by *Chronicles of Dissent: Interviews with David Barsamian,* which collects interviews conducted in a variety of settings from 1984 through 1991. As a *Publishers Weekly* reviewer summarizes them, the interviews "range all over world history," but focus on standard Chomsky themes, such as American imperialism and the corruption of the media and academic elite. Several of the conversations also touch on autobiographical topics, with Chomsky discussing his childhood and the development of his thought. In Chomsky's and Edward S. Herman's book *Manufacturing Consent: The Political Economy of the Mass Media,* they examine the various ways news organizations ultimately serve the ideological aims of the government. Chomsky and Herman propose a "propaganda model" of the mass media in the United States; countering the commonly held belief that the mass media tend to respond to rather than create public opinion, the two authors argue that the major American news organizations actively misinform the public about the activities of the United States government. As Philip Green of *The Nation* puts it, Chomsky and Herman seek to discover how it is "that the major American mass media manage so often to produce accounts of the world that are largely indistinguishable from what a commissar [of information and cultural affairs] would have commanded." The bulk of the book tests the "propaganda model" against events in recent North and South American history, including the reporting of elections in El Salvador and the coverage given to the murders of Polish priest Jerzy Popieluszko and Salvadoran Archbishop Oscar Romero.

The very narrowness of public discussion is the subject of *Deterring Democracy,* a book in which Chomsky examines how, regardless of the facts, the American mass media and the United States government conspire to limit the range of opinions that can be widely expressed. Chomsky discusses, for example, the fact that mainstream public opinion embraced only specific kinds of debates regarding the Sandanista government and the Contras in Nicaragua; he shows that the vast majority of lawmakers and reporters disagreed only as to which methods should be employed to rid that country of its communist leaders—no serious attention was given to the debate about whether the Sandanistas or the U.S.-backed Contras would best serve the people of Nicaragua. Also, regarding the "war on drugs," Chomsky examines the government's propaganda campaign supporting its various "successes" and describes the positive news coverage these victories receive; the facts that 1) drug use was declining in the United States before President George Bush announced the start of the "war" and that 2) drug use has increased in the meantime receive very little attention. He concludes that no substantial discussion arises about the effects of this war on the countries involved, and he bitterly denounces the ironic policy of the United States government of threatening trade sanctions against those East Asian countries that block the importing of U.S. tobacco, a product that is proven to be deadly. Chomsky himself transcends that narrow spectrum of debate, however, adducing "example after example to illuminate how American policies have led knowingly to large scale human suffering," to quote Beschloss. In the *New York Times Book Review,* Sheldon S. Wolin suggests that the author "is relentless in tracking down official lies and exposing hypocrisy and moral indifference in the high places. . . . Yet the passion of Chomsky's indictment is always controlled, and while he is harsh toward his opponents, he is never unfair or arrogant."

In *Year 501: The Conquest Continues,* Chomsky examines what he sees as the U.S. government's shabby behavior toward its neighbors in the hemisphere. His strident denunciations of U.S. imperialism are often conveyed through striking comparisons, however; *Kirkus Reviews* offers as an example Chomsky's realization that "the logic of [the United States government's] annexation of Texas was essentially [the same as] that attributed to Saddam Hussein by US propaganda after his conquest of Kuwait."

Leiber finds an overriding commitment to freedom in the Chomsky's work—"the freedom of the individual to produce and create as he will without the goad of external force, economic competition for survival, or legal and economic restraint on social, intellectual, or artistic experiment; and the freedom of ethnic and national groups to work out their own destinies without the intervention of one or another Big Brother." "From his earliest writings to his latest, Chomsky has looked with astonishment at what the powerful do to the powerless," Morton declares. "He has never let his sense of outrage become dulled. If his voice has grown hoarse over twenty years, who can blame him? And who can feel superior? No one has given himself more deeply to the struggle against the horrors of our time. His hoarseness is a better thing than our suavity."

In 1970, the London *Times* named Chomsky one of the thousand "makers of the twentieth century." According to Yergin, his theory "remains the foundation of linguistics today," and "his vision of a complex universe within the mind, governed by myriad rules and prohibitions and yet infinite in its creative potential, opens up vistas possibly as important as Einstein's theories." Yergin adds: "The impact of Chomsky's work may not be felt for years. . . . Yet this beginning has revolutionized the study of language and has redirected and redefined the broad inquiry into intelligence and how it works." Robinson calls the scholar's work "a prolonged celebration of the enormous gulf that separates man from the rest of nature. He seems overwhelmed by the intellectual powers that man contains within himself. Certainly nobody ever stated the case for those powers more emphatically, nor exemplified them more impressively in his own work. Reading Chomsky on linguistics, one repeatedly has the impression of attending to one of the more powerful thinkers who ever lived."

BIOGRAPHICAL/CRITICAL SOURCES:

BOOKS

Achbar, Mark and the Institute of Policy Alternatives, *Manufacturing Consent: Noam Chomsky and the Media: The Companion Book to the Award-Winning Film by Peter Wintonick and Mark Achbar,* Black Rose Books, 1994.
Botha, Rudolf P., *Challenging Chomsky: The Generative Garden Game,* B. Blackwell (New York City), 1989.
Cohen, David, *Psychologists on Psychology,* Taplinger, 1977.
Cohn, Werner, *Partners in Hate: Noam Chomsky and the Holocaust Deniers,* Avukah Press (Cambridge, MA), 1995.
Contemporary Issues Criticism, Volume 1, Gale, 1982.
Cook, V. J. and Mark Newson, *Chomsky's Universal Grammar,* Basil Blackwell, 1996.
Haley, Michael C. and Ronald F. Lunsford, *Noam Chomsky,* Twayne (New York City), 1994.
Harris, Randy Allen, *The Linguistics Wars,* Oxford University Press (New York City), 1993.

Huck, Geoffrey J. and John A. Goldsmith, *Ideology and Linguistic Theory: Noam Chomsky and the Deep Structure Debates,* Routledge (New York City), 1995.

Kasher, Asa, *The Chomskyan Turn,* Basil Blackwell, 1991.

Kim-Renaud, Young-Key, *Studies in Korean Linguistics,* Hanshin Publishing, 1986.

Leiber, Justin, *Noam Chomsky: A Philosophical Overview,* Twayne, 1975.

Lyons, John, *Noam Chomsky,* 2nd edition, Penguin Books, 1977, 3rd edition, Fontana Press (London), 1991.

Newmeyer, Frederick J., *Generative Linguistics,* Routledge (New York City), 1994.

Osiatynski, Wiktor, *Contrasts: Soviet and American Thinkers Discuss the Future,* Macmillan, 1984.

Otero, Carlos Peregrin, *Noam Chomsky: Critical Assessments,* Routledge, 1994.

Rai, Milan, *Chomsky's Politics,* Verso (New York City), 1995.

Rieber, Robert W., editor, *Dialogues on the Psychology of Language and Thought: Conversations with Noam Chomsky, Charles Osgood, Jean Piaget, Ulric Neisser, and Marcel Kinsbourne,* Plenum, 1983.

Salkie, Raphael, *The Chomsky Update: Linguistics and Politics,* Unwin Hyman (Boston), 1990.

Sen Gupta, Kalyan and Jadavpur University, *Mentalistic Turn, A Critical Evaluation of Chomsky,* K. P. Bagchi & Co. (Calcutta) and Jadavpur University, 1990.

Smith, N. V. and Deirdre Wilson, *Modern Linguistics: The Results of Chomsky's Revolution,* Penguin Books (New York City), 1990.

Thinkers of the Twentieth Century, Gale, 1983.

Williams, T. C., *Kant's Philosophy of Language: Chomskyan Linguistics and Its Kantian Roots,* E. Mellen Press (Lewiston, NY), 1993.

PERIODICALS

America, December 11, 1971; July 15, 1989, p. 42; August 27, 1994, p. 30.

Atlantic, July, 1973; February, 1982.

Bloomsbury Review, September, 1993.

Book World, March 23, 1969.

Christian Century, July 23, 1969.

Christian Science Monitor, April 3, 1969; May 14, 1970.

Chronicle of Higher Education, May 12, 1982.

Commentary, May, 1969.

Current Biography, August, 1995, p. 15.

Dissent, January-February, 1970.

Economist, November 29, 1969.

Globe and Mail (Toronto), June 16, 1984; July 5, 1986.

Harvard Education Review, winter, 1969.

Horizon, spring, 1971.

Humanist, November-December, 1990, p. 8.

International Affairs, January, 1971.

London Review of Books, August 20, 1992.

Los Angeles Times Book Review, December 27, 1981; June 8, 1986; August 30, 1987.

Maclean's, August 18, 1980; March 22, 1993.

Nation, September 9, 1968; March 24, 1969; May 17, 1971; May 8, 1976; March 31, 1979; February 16, 1980; December 22, 1984; December 26, 1987; January 2, 1988; May 7, 1988; May 15, 1989, p. 670.

National Review, June 17, 1969; July 8, 1991, p. 40.

New Republic, April 19, 1969; October 26, 1974; March 13, 1976; February 17, 1979; September 6-13, 1980; March 24, 1982; March 23, 1987; January 9, 1989, p. 34.

New Statesman, November 28, 1969; August 17, 1979; April 25, 1980; July 17, 1981; August 14, 1981; September 11, 1981; January 21, 1983.

New Statesman & Society, July 5, 1991, p. 35; November 27, 1992, p. 43; March 12, 1993, p. 14; April 16, 1993, p. 38; June 3, 1994, p. 22.

Newsweek, March 24, 1969.

New Yorker, November 11, 1969; May 8, 1971.

New York Review of Books, August 9, 1973; January 23, 1975; November 11, 1976; October 23, 1980; February 1, 1996, p. 41.

New York Times, March 18, 1969; August 2, 1973; February 5, 1979; March 8, 1982.

New York Times Book Review, March 16, 1969; January 17, 1971; January 9, 1972; September 30, 1973; October 6, 1974; February 15, 1976; February 25, 1979; October 19, 1980; March 21, 1982; April 13, 1986.

New York Times Magazine, May 6, 1968; December 3, 1972.

Observer, June 23, 1991.

Progressive, December, 1982; October, 1991, p. 39; October, 1993, p. 41; January, 1995, p. 39.

Psychology Today, July, 1979.

Rolling Stone, May 28, 1992, p. 42.

Saturday Review, May 31, 1969.

Science and Society, spring, 1970.

Scientific American, May, 1990, p. 40.

Sewanee Review, winter, 1977.

Times Literary Supplement, March 27, 1969; March 31, 1972; December 21, 1973; December 12, 1975; September 10, 1976; November 21, 1980; February 27, 1981; July 23, 1982; July 15-21, 1988.

Utne Reader, November-December, 1993, p. 120.

Village Voice, June 18, 1980; June 23, 1980; July 13, 1982.

Virginia Quarterly Review, summer, 1969.

Washington Post Book World, March 11, 1979; March 7, 1982; February 21, 1988.

*   *   *

CHRISTIE, Agatha (Mary Clarissa) 1890-1976
(Agatha Christie Mallowan; Mary Westmacott)

PERSONAL: Born September 15, 1890, in Torquay, Devon, England; died January 12, 1976, in Wallingford, England; daughter of Frederick Alvah and Clarissa Miller; married Archibald Christie (a colonel in Royal Air Corps), December 24, 1914 (divorced, 1928); married Max Edgar Lucien Mallowan (an archaeologist), September 11, 1930 (died, 1978); children: (first marriage) Rosalind. *Education:* Tutored at home by her mother until age 16; later studied singing and piano in Paris.

CAREER: Writer. During World War I, served as Voluntary Aid Detachment (V.A.D.) nurse in a Red Cross Hospital, Torquay, South Devon, England; after divorce in 1928, traveled for several years; after marriage to Max Mallowan, 1930, helped him with tabulations and photography at his excavations in Iraq and Syria; during World War II, worked in dispensary for University College Hospital, London, England; during postwar 1940s, helped her husband with excavation of Assyrian ruins.

MEMBER: Royal Society of Literature (fellow), Detection Club (president).

AWARDS, HONORS: Grand Master Award, Mystery Writers of America, 1954; New York Drama Critics' Circle Award, 1955, for

Witness for the Prosecution; Commander of the British Empire, 1956; D.Litt., University of Exeter, 1961; Dame Commander, Order of the British Empire, 1971.

WRITINGS:

MYSTERY NOVELS

The Secret Adversary, Dodd, 1922.
The Man in the Brown Suit, Dodd, 1924.
The Secret of Chimneys, Dodd, 1925.
The Seven Dials Mystery, Dodd, 1929.
The Murder at Hazelmoor, Dodd, 1931 (published in England as *The Sittaford Mystery,* Collins, 1931).
(With others) *The Floating Admiral,* Hodder & Stoughton, 1931, Doubleday, 1932.
Why Didn't They Ask Evans?, Collins, 1934, published as *The Boomerang Clue,* Dodd, 1935.
Easy to Kill, Dodd, 1939 (published in England as *Murder Is Easy,* Collins, 1939).
Ten Little Niggers (also see below), Collins, 1939, published as *And Then There Were None,* Dodd, 1940, published as *Ten Little Indians,* Pocket Books, 1965.
N or M?, Dodd, 1941.
Death Comes as the End, Dodd, 1944.
Towards Zero (also see below), Dodd, 1944.
Remembered Death, Dodd, 1945 (published in England as *Sparkling Cyanide,* Collins, 1945).
The Crooked House, Dodd, 1949.
They Came to Baghdad, Dodd, 1951.
Destination Unknown, Collins, 1954, published as *So Many Steps to Death,* Dodd, 1955.
Ordeal by Innocence, Collins, 1958, Dodd, 1959.
The Pale Horse, Collins, 1961, Dodd, 1962.
Endless Night, Collins, 1967, Dodd, 1968.
By the Pricking of My Thumbs, Dodd, 1968.
Passenger to Frankfurt, Dodd, 1970.
Postern of Fate, Dodd, 1973.
Murder on Board, Dodd, 1974.
(With others) *The Scoop, and Behind the Scenes,* Gollancz, 1983.

NOVELS FEATURING HERCULE POIROT

The Mysterious Affair at Styles, Lane, 1920, Dodd, 1927.
The Murder on the Links, Dodd, 1923.
The Murder of Roger Ackroyd, Dodd, 1926.
The Big Four, Dodd, 1927.
The Mystery of the Blue Train, Dodd, 1928.
Peril at End House, Dodd, 1932.
Thirteen at Dinner, Dodd, 1933 (published in England as *Lord Edgware Dies,* Collins, 1933).
Murder in Three Acts, Dodd, 1934 (published in England as *Three Act Tragedy,* Collins, 1935).
Murder on the Calais Coach, Dodd, 1934 (published in England as *Murder on the Orient Express,* Collins, 1934).
Death in the Air, Dodd, 1935 (published in England as *Death in the Clouds,* Collins, 1935).
The A. B. C. Murders, Dodd, 1936, published as *The Alphabet Murders,* Pocket Books, 1966.
Cards on the Table, Collins, 1936, Dodd, 1937.
Murder in Mesopotamia, Dodd, 1936.
Poirot Loses a Client, Dodd, 1937 (published in England as *Dumb Witness,* Collins, 1937).
Death on the Nile (also see below), Collins, 1937, Dodd, 1938.
Appointment with Death, Peril at End House (also see below), Dodd, 1938.

Hercule Poirot's Christmas, Collins, 1938, published as *Murder for Christmas,* Dodd, 1939, published as *A Holiday for Murder,* Avon, 1947.
One, Two, Buckle My Shoe, Collins, 1940, published as *The Patriotic Murders,* Dodd, 1941, published as *An Overdose of Death,* Dell, 1953, reprinted as *The Patriotic Murders,* edited by Roger Cooper, Berkley, 1988.
Sad Cypress, Dodd, 1940.
Evil Under the Sun, Dodd, 1941.
Murder in Retrospect, Dodd, 1942 (published in England as *Five Little Pigs* [also see below], Collins, 1942).
The Hollow (also see below), Dodd, 1946, published as *Murder After Hours,* Dell, 1954.
There Is a Tide . . . , Dodd, 1948 (published in England as *Taken at the Flood,* Collins, 1948).
Mrs. McGinty's Dead, Dodd, 1952, published as *Blood Will Tell,* Detective Book Club, 1952.
Funerals Are Fatal, Dodd, 1953 (published in England as *After the Funeral,* Collins, 1953; published as *Murder at the Gallop,* Fontana, 1963).
Hickory, Dickory, Death, Dodd, 1955 (published in England as *Hickory, Dickory, Dock,* Collins, 1955).
Dead Man's Folly, Dodd, 1956.
Cat Among the Pigeons, Collins, 1959, Dodd, 1960.
The Clocks, Collins, 1963, Dodd, 1964.
Third Girl, Collins, 1966, Dodd, 1967.
Hallowe'en Party, Dodd, 1969.
Elephants Can Remember, Dodd, 1972.
Curtain: Hercule Poirot's Last Case, Dodd, 1975.

Hercule Poirot novels also published in various omnibus volumes (see below).

NOVELS FEATURING MISS JANE MARPLE

The Murder at the Vicarage, Dodd, 1930.
The Body in the Library, Dodd, 1942.
The Moving Finger, Dodd, 1942.
A Murder Is Announced, Dodd, 1950.
Murder with Mirrors, Dodd, 1952 (published in England as *They Do It with Mirrors,* Collins, 1952).
A Pocket Full of Rye, Collins, 1953, Dodd, 1954.
What Mrs. McGillicudy Saw!, Dodd, 1957 (published in England as *4:50 from Paddington,* Collins, 1957), published as *Murder She Said,* Pocket Books, 1961.
The Mirror Crack'd from Side to Side, Collins, 1962, published as *The Mirror Crack'd,* Dodd, 1963.
A Caribbean Mystery, Collins, 1964, Dodd, 1965.
At Bertram's Hotel, Collins, 1965, Dodd, 1966, revised edition, Pocket Books, 1984.
Nemesis, Dodd, 1971.
Sleeping Murder, Dodd, 1976.

Miss Jane Marple novels also published in various omnibus volumes (see below).

SHORT STORY COLLECTIONS

Poirot Investigates, Lane, 1924, Dodd, 1925.
Partners in Crime, Dodd, 1929 (abridged edition published in England as *The Sunningdale Mystery,* Collins, 1933).
The Under Dog, and Other Stories, Readers Library, 1929, Dodd, 1951.
The Mysterious Mr. Quin (also published as *The Passing of Mr. Quin*), Dodd, 1930.
The Thirteen Problems, Collins, 1932, published as *The Tuesday Club Murders,* Dodd, 1933, abridged edition published as

The Mystery of the Blue Geraniums, and Other Tuesday Club Murders, Bantam, 1940.

The Hound of Death, and Other Stories, Odhams Press, 1933.

Mr. Parker Pyne, Detective, Dodd, 1934 (published in England as *Parker Pyne Investigates,* Collins, 1934).

The Listerdale Mystery, and Other Stories, Collins, 1934.

Dead Man's Mirror, and Other Stories, Dodd, 1937 (published in England as *Murder in the Mews, and Three Other Poirot Stories,* Collins, 1937).

The Regatta Mystery, and Other Stories, Dodd, 1939.

The Mystery of the Baghdad Chest (also see below), Bantam, 1943.

The Mystery of the Crime in Cabin 66, Bantam, 1943 (published in England as *The Crime in Cabin 66,* Vallencey, 1944).

Poirot and the Regatta Mystery, Bantam, 1943.

Poirot on Holiday, Todd, 1943.

Problem at Pollensa Bay [and] *Christmas Adventure,* Todd, 1943.

The Veiled Lady [and] *The Mystery of the Baghdad Chest,* Todd, 1944.

Poirot Knows the Murderer, Todd, 1946.

Poirot Lends a Hand, Todd, 1946.

The Labours of Hercules: New Adventures in Crime by Hercule Poirot, Dodd, 1947 (published in England as *Labours of Hercules: Short Stories,* Collins, 1947), published as *The Labors of Hercules,* Putnam, 1993.

Witness for the Prosecution, and Other Stories (also see below), Dodd, 1948.

The Mousetrap, and Other Stories (also see below), Dell, 1949, published as *Three Blind Mice, and Other Stories,* Dodd, 1950.

The Adventure of the Christmas Pudding, and Selection of Entrees, Collins, 1960.

Double Sin, and Other Stories, Dodd, 1961.

13 for Luck!: A Selection of Mystery Stories for Young Readers, Dodd, 1961.

Surprise! Surprise!: A Collection of Mystery Stories with Unexpected Endings, Dodd, 1965.

(Under name Agatha Christie Mallowan) *Star Over Bethlehem, and Other Stories,* Dodd, 1965.

13 Clues for Miss Marple, Dodd, 1966.

Selected Stories, Progress Publishers (Moscow), 1969.

The Golden Ball, and Other Stories, Dodd, 1971.

Hercule Poirot's Early Cases, Dodd, 1974 (published in England as *Poirot's Early Cases,* Collins, 1974).

Miss Marple's Final Cases, and Two Other Stories, Collins, 1979.

Hercule Poirot's Casebook: Fifty Stories, Putnam, 1984.

The Agatha Christie Hour, Collins, 1982.

Miss Marple: The Complete Short Stories, Putnam, 1985.

(Contributor) *More Murder Most Cozy: More Mysteries in the Classic Tradition,* NAL/Dutton, 1993.

Short stories also collected in various other volumes.

OMNIBUS VOLUMES

Agatha Christie Omnibus (contains *The Mysterious Affair at Styles, The Murder on the Links,* and *Poirot Investigates*), Lane, 1931.

The Agatha Christie Omnibus of Crime (contains *The Sittaford Mystery, The Seven Dials Mystery, The Mystery of the Blue Train,* and *The Murder of Roger Ackroyd*), Collins, 1932.

Hercule Poirot, Master Detective (contains *The Murder of Roger Ackroyd, Murder on the Calais Coach,* and *Thirteen at Dinner*), Dodd, 1936, published as *Three Christie Crimes,* Grosset, 1937.

Two Detective Stories in One Volume: The Mysterious Affair at Styles [and] *The Murder on the Links,* Dodd, 1940.

Triple Threat: Exploits of Three Famous Detectives, Hercule Poirot, Harley Quin and Tuppence (contains *Poirot Investigates, The Mysterious Mr. Quin,* and *Partners in Crime*), Dodd, 1943.

Crime Reader (contains selections from *Poirot Investigates, The Mysterious Mr. Quin,* and *Partners in Crime*), World, 1944.

Perilous Journeys of Hercule Poirot (contains *The Mystery of the Blue Train, Death on the Nile,* and *Murder in Mesopotamia*), Dodd, 1954.

Surprise Ending by Hercule Poirot (contains *The A. B. C. Murders, Murder in Three Acts,* and *Cards on the Table*), Dodd, 1956.

Christie Classics (contains *The Murder of Roger Ackroyd, And Then There Were None, Witness for the Prosecution, Philomel Cottage,* and *Three Blind Mice*), Dodd, 1957.

Murder Preferred (contains *The Patriotic Murders, A Murder Is Announced,* and *Murder in Retrospect*), Dodd, 1960.

Make Mine Murder! (contains *Appointment with Death, Peril at End House,* and *Sad Cypress*), Dodd, 1962.

A Holiday for Murder, Bantam, 1962.

Murder International (contains *So Many Steps to Death, Death Comes as the End,* and *Evil Under the Sun*), Dodd, 1965.

Murder in Our Midst (contains *The Body in the Library, Murder at the Vicarage,* and *The Moving Finger*), Dodd, 1967.

Spies Among Us (contains *They Came to Baghdad, N or M?,* and *Murder in Mesopotamia*), Dodd, 1968.

The Nursery Rhyme Murders (contains *A Pocket Full of Rye, Hickory, Dickory, Death,* and *The Crooked House*), Dodd, 1970.

Murder-Go-Round (contains *Thirteen at Dinner, The A. B. C. Murders,* and *Funerals Are Fatal*), Dodd, 1972.

Murder on Board (contains *Death in the Air, The Mystery of the Blue Train,* and *What Mrs. McGillicudy Saw!*), Dodd, 1974.

Five Complete Novels of Mystery and Detection, Outlet Book Co., 1986.

Best Detective Stories of Agatha Christie, Longman, 1986.

Agatha Christie: Six Mary Westmacott Novels, Outlet Book Co., 1988.

Agatha Christie: Best Loved Sleuths (contains *The Moving Finger, Murder in Three Acts, Murder on the Links,* and *There Is a Tide*), Berkley, 1988.

Agatha Christie: Murder by the Box (includes *The Secret of Chimneys, The Man in the Brown Suit,* and *Partners in Crime*), Berkley, 1988.

Three Puzzles for Poirot, Putnam, 1989.

Murderers Abroad: Five Complete Novels—Twenty-Six Tales of Seasonal Malice, Outlet Book Co., 1989.

Agatha Christie: Five Complete Hercule Poirot Novels, Outlet Book Co., 1990.

Agatha Christie: Five Classic Murder Mysteries, Outlet Book Co., 1990.

Agatha Christie: Five Complete Miss Marple Novels, Outlet Book Co., 1990.

Agatha Christie Detectives: Five Complete Novels, Outlet Book Co., 1990.

Agatha Christie's Murderers Abroad: Complete Novels, Outlet Book Co., 1991.

Agatha Christie: Five Complete Novels of Murder and Detection, Outlet Book Co., 1991.

Agatha Christie's Detectives: Five Complete Novels (contains *The Murder at the Vicarage, Sad Cypress, N or M?, Towards*

Zero, and *Dead Man's Folly*), G. P. Putnam's Sons (New York City), 1995.
The Harlequin Tea Set and Other Stories, G. P. Putnam's Sons (New York City), 1997.

Works also published in numerous other omnibus volumes.

PLAYS

Black Coffee (first produced on the West End, December 8, 1930), Baker, 1934.
Ten Little Niggers (based on novel of the same title; first produced in London, October 17, 1943; produced as *Ten Little Indians* on Broadway at Broadhurst Theatre, June 27, 1944), Samuel French (London), 1944, published as *Ten Little Indians,* Samuel French (New York), 1946.
Appointment with Death (based on the novel of the same title; first produced on the West End at Piccadilly Theatre, March 31, 1945; also see below), Samuel French, 1945.
Little Horizon (based on the novel *Death on the Nile;* first produced in London at Wimbledon Theatre, 1945), revised version entitled *Murder on the Nile* (first produced on the West End at Ambassadors' Theatre, March 19, 1946; produced on Broadway at Plymouth Theatre, September 19, 1946), Samuel French, 1948.
The Hollow (based on the novel of the same title; first produced on the West End at Fortune Theatre, 1951; produced in Princeton, NJ, 1952; produced in New York City, 1978), Samuel French, 1952.
The Mousetrap (based on the radio script *Three Blind Mice;* first produced on the West End at Ambassadors' Theatre, November 25, 1952; produced off-Broadway at Maidman Playhouse, 1960; also see below), Samuel French, 1954.
Witness for the Prosecution (based on the short story of the same title; first produced in London, October 28, 1953; produced in New York City, December 16, 1954), Samuel French, 1954.
Spider's Web (first produced on the West End at Savoy Theatre, December 14, 1954; produced in New York City, January 15, 1974), Samuel French, 1957.
(With Gerald Verner) *Towards Zero* (based on the novel of the same title; first produced in London, September 4, 1956; produced on Broadway at the St. James Theatre, 1956), Dramatists Play Service, 1957.
The Unexpected Guest (first produced on the West End at Duchess Theatre, August 12, 1958), Samuel French, 1958.
Verdict (first produced on the West End at Strand Theatre, 1958), Samuel French, 1958.
Go Back for Murder (based on the novel *Five Little Pigs*; first produced on the West End at Duchess Theatre, March 23, 1960), Samuel French, 1960.
Rule of Three (contains *Afternoon at the Sea-side, The Patient,* and *The Rats,* all of which have been produced separately; first produced on the West End, December 20, 1962), Samuel French, 1963.
Fiddlers Three, first produced in Southsea at Kings Theatre, June 7, 1971; produced in London, 1972.
Akhnaton (first produced under title *Akhnaton and Nefertiti* in New York City, 1979), Dodd, 1973.
The Mousetrap, and Other Plays (contains *Witness for the Prosecution, Ten Little Indians, Appointment with Death, The Hollow, Towards Zero, Verdict,* and *Go Back for Murder*), with introduction by Ira Levin, Dodd, 1978.

RADIO PLAYS

The Mousetrap (originally broadcast as *Three Blind Mice*), British Broadcasting Corporation (BBC-Radio), 1952.
Personal Call, BBC-Radio, 1960.

NOVELS UNDER PSEUDONYM MARY WESTMACOTT

Giant's Bread, Doubleday, 1930.
Unfinished Portrait, Doubleday, 1934.
Absent in the Spring, Farrar & Rinehart, 1944.
The Rose and the Yew Tree, Rinehart, 1948.
A Daughter's a Daughter, Heinemann, 1952.
The Burden, Heinemann, 1956.

OTHER

The Road of Dreams (poems), Bles, 1925.
Come, Tell Me How You Live (autobiographical travel book), Dodd, 1946.
Poems, Dodd, 1973.
(Editor with others) *The Times of London Anthology of Detective Stories,* John Day, 1973.
Agatha Christie: An Autobiography, Dodd, 1977.

MEDIA ADAPTATIONS: The Murder of Roger Ackroyd was adapted for the stage by Michael Morton and first produced under the title *Alibi* on the West End at Prince of Wales Theatre in 1928; the short story "Philomel Cottage" was adapted for the stage by Frank Vosper and first produced under the title *Love from a Stranger* on the West End at Wyndham's Theatre in 1936; *Peril at End House* was adapted for the stage by Arnold Ridley and first produced on the West End at the Vaudeville Theatre in 1940; *Murder at the Vicarage* was adapted for the stage by Moie Charles and Barbara Toy and first produced in London at the Playhouse Theatre in 1949; *Towards Zero* was adapted for the stage by Gerald Verner and first produced on Broadway at the St. James Theatre in 1956.

The short story "Philomel Cottage" was filmed under the title *Love from a Stranger* by United Artists in 1937, and by Eagle Lion in 1947; *And Then There Were None* was filmed by Twentieth Century-Fox in 1945; *Witness for the Prosecution* was filmed for theatrical release by United Artists in 1957 and for television by Columbia Broadcasting System in 1982; *The Spider's Web* was filmed by United Artists in 1960; *Murder She Said* was filmed by Metro-Goldwyn-Mayer in 1962; *Murder at the Gallop* was filmed by Metro-Goldwyn-Mayer in 1963; *Mrs. McGinty's Dead* was filmed under the title *Murder Most Foul* by Metro-Goldwyn-Mayer in 1965; *Ten Little Indians* was filmed by Associated British & Pathe Film in 1965; *The Alphabet Murders* was filmed by Metro-Goldwyn-Mayer in 1967; *Endless Night* was filmed by British Lion Films in 1971; *Murder on the Orient Express* was filmed by EMI in 1974; *Death on the Nile* was filmed by Paramount in 1978; *The Mirror Crack'd* was filmed by EMI in 1980; *The Seven Dials Mystery* and *Why Didn't They Ask Evans?* were filmed by London Weekend Television in 1980; *Evil Under the Sun* was filmed by Universal in 1982. *Murder Ahoy,* filmed by Metro-Goldwyn-Mayer in 1964, features the character Miss Jane Marple in a story not written by Christie. Many of Christie's works have been adapted for television.

SIDELIGHTS: "Oh, I'm an incredible sausage machine," the late mystery writer Agatha Christie once jokingly claimed, speaking of her prolific output of novels, stories, and plays. Christie's many works have sold a phenomenal 2 billion copies—a record topped only by the Bible and William Shakespeare—and have been translated into 103 languages; her books still sell a reported 25 million copies a year. Her play *The Mousetrap,* originally written as a birthday gift for Queen Mary, is the longest-running play in history. These staggering statistics testify to the enduring popularity of Christie's work. She remains, according to H. R. F. Keating in his article for the *Dictionary of Literary Biography,* "a towering figure in the history of crime literature."

"I don't enjoy writing detective stories," Christie once told an interviewer. "I enjoy thinking of a detective story, planning it, but when the time comes to write it, it is like going to work every day, like having a job." Christie only began writing on a dare from her sister, who challenged her to "write a good detective story." Christie wrote one, *The Mysterious Affair at Styles,* and in 1920 it was published by the English firm of Lane. Although the book only sold some two thousand copies and earned Christie seventy dollars, the publication encouraged her to continue writing mysteries. Throughout the 1920s she wrote them steadily, building a loyal following among mystery aficionados for her unfailingly clever plots.

It wasn't until the publication of *The Murder of Roger Ackroyd* in 1926 that Christie's talent for deceptive mystery plotting caught the attention of the general reading public. The sheer audacity of the novel's plot resolution—the murderer is revealed as a character traditionally above suspicion in mystery novels—outraged, surprised, and delighted readers everywhere. "*The Murder of Roger Ackroyd,*" wrote a *New York Times* reviewer, "cannot be too highly praised for its clean-cut construction, its unusually plausible explanation at the end, and its ability to stimulate the analytical faculties of the reader." "The secret [of this novel] is more than usually original and ingenious," a *Nation* reviewer thought, "and is a device which no other writer could have employed without mishap." William Rose Benet of *Saturday Review* recommended that *The Murder of Roger Ackroyd* "should go on the shelf with the books of first rank in its field. The detective story pure and simple has as definite limitations of form as the sonnet in poetry. Within these limitations, with admirable structured art, Miss Christie has genuinely achieved." Writing in *Murder for Pleasure: The Life and Times of the Detective Story,* Howard Haycraft judged the book "a tour de force in every sense of the word and one of the true classics of the literature."

The Murder of Roger Ackroyd proved to be the first in a long string of superlative and highly original mystery novels that made Christie's name synonymous with the mystery story. Such books as *The A. B. C. Murders, Ten Little Indians,* and *Murder on the Orient Express* have been especially singled out by critics as among the best of Christie's work and, indeed, among the finest novels to have been written in the mystery genre. "These books," Anthony Lejeune of *Spectator* believed, "are famous because each of them turns on a piece of misdirection and a solution which, in their day, were startlingly innovatory."

Christie's ability to construct a baffling puzzle was, Emma Lathen wrote in *Agatha Christie: First Lady of Crime,* the strongest aspect of her writing. "Friend and foe alike," Lathen stated, "bow to the queen of the puzzle. Every Christie plot resolution had been hailed as a masterpiece of sleight-of-hand; she herself as a virtuoso of subterfuge." Julian Symons echoed this judgment in his contribution to *Agatha Christie: First Lady of Crime:* "Agatha Christie's claim to supremacy among the classical detective story writers of her time rests on her originality in constructing puzzles. This was her supreme skill. . . . Although the detective story is ephemeral literature, the puzzle which it embodies has a permanent appeal. . . . If her work survives it will be because she was

the supreme mistress of a magical skill that is a permanent, although often secret, concern of humanity: the construction and the solution of puzzles."

Another important factor in Christie's popularity must lie in her ability to create charming and enduring detective characters. Undoubtedly her most popular detective has been Hercule Poirot, an eccentric and amusingly pompous Belgian detective who Christie described in *The Mysterious Affair at Styles* as "an extraordinary-looking little man. He was hardly more than five feet, four inches, but carried himself with great dignity. His head was exactly the shape of an egg. His moustache was very still and military. The neatness of his attire was almost incredible. I believe a speck of dust would have caused him more pain than a bullet wound."

According to David J. Grossvogel in *Mystery and Its Fictions: From Oedipus to Agatha Christie,* Christie "was aware of the faintly ridiculous figure cut by Poirot when she baptized him. She named him after a vegetable—the leek (*poireau,* which also means a wart, in French)—to which she opposed the (barely) Christian name Hercule, in such a way that each name would cast ridicule on the other." Grossvogel saw this bit of absurdity as essential to Poirot's success as a character. He believed that, in order to maintain the tension in a mystery story, there must be some doubt as to the detective's ability to solve the crime. Because Poirot is often "patronizingly dismissed" by other characters, his eventual solution of the crime is that much more entertaining. "Part of the artificial surprise of the detective story," Grossvogel observed, "is contained within the detective who triumphs, as he brings the action to a close, even over his own shortcomings."

"Few fictional sleuths," wrote Howard Haycraft, "can surpass the amazing little Belgian—with his waxed moustache and egg-shaped head, his inflated confidence in the infallibility of his 'little grey cells,' his murderous attacks on the English language—either for individuality or ingenuity." "Poirot," Lejeune explained, "like a survivor from an almost extinct race of giants, is one of the last of the Great Detectives: and the mention of his name should be enough to remind us of how much pleasure Agatha Christie gave millions of people over the past fifty years."

Poirot's illustrious career came to an end in *Curtain: Hercule Poirot's Last Case,* published shortly before Christie's death. Written just after World War II and secreted in a bank vault, the book was originally intended to be posthumously published, but Christie decided to enjoy the ending of Poirot's career herself and published the book early. "*Curtain,*" wrote Peter Prescott of *Newsweek,* "is one of Christie's most ingenious stories, a tour de force in which the lady who had bent all the rules of the genre before bends them yet again." John Heideury of *Commonweal* expressed the usual bafflement when confronted with a Christie mystery: "On page 35 I had guessed the identity of the murderer, by the next page knew the victim, and on page 112 deduced the motive. (On page 41 I had changed my mind and reversed murderer and victim, but on page 69 returned steadfast to my original position.) . . . I was wrong on all counts at book's end."

Christie's own favorite among her detectives was Miss Jane Marple, a spinster who lives in a small town in the English countryside. "Both Poirot and Miss Marple," wrote Ralph Tyler in *Saturday Review,* "are made a little bit absurd, so that we do not begrudge them their astuteness." In *Agatha Christie: First Lady of Crime,* Julian Symons gave Christie's own views of her two famous detectives: "Miss Marple, she said, was more fun [than

Poirot], and like many aunts and grandmothers was 'a splendid natural detective when it comes to observing human nature.' " In contrast to Poirot, a professional detective who attributes his successes to the use of his "little grey cells," Miss Marple is an amateur crime solver who often "owes her success," Margot Peters and Agate Nesaule Krouse wrote in *Southwest Review,* "to intuition and nosiness. Operating on the theory that human nature is universal, she ferrets out the criminal by his resemblance to someone she has known in her native village of St. Mary Mead, since her knowledge of life extends little farther."

While her mystery novels featuring Hercule Poirot and Miss Marple have enjoyed tremendous success and established Christie as the most widely read mystery writer of all time, her relatively small output of plays has set equally impressive records. She is the only playwright to have had three plays running simultaneously on London's West End while another of her plays was running on Broadway. Christie's *The Mousetrap* holds the singular distinction of being the longest-running play in theatrical history. It has been translated into twenty-two languages, performed in forty-four countries, and seen by an estimated eight million people. Despite the success of the work, Christie received no royalties for it. She gave the rights to her nine-year-old grandson when the play first opened in 1952. The grandson, it is estimated, has since earned well over fifteen million pounds from his grandmother's gift.

Upon Christie's death in 1976, Max Lowenthal of the *New York Times* offered this summary of her work: "Dame Agatha's forte was supremely adroit plotting and sharp, believable characterization (even the names she used usually rang true). Her style and rhetoric were not remarkable; her writing was almost invariably sound and workmanlike, without pretense or flourish. Her characters were likely to be of the middle-middle class or upper-middle class, and there were certain archetypes, such as the crass American or the stuffy retired army officer now in his anecdotage. However familiar all this might be, the reader would turn the pages mesmerized as unexpected twist piled on unexpected twist until, in the end, he was taken by surprise. There was simply no outguessing Poirot or Miss Marple—or Agatha Christie."

BIOGRAPHICAL/CRITICAL SOURCES:

BOOKS

Bargainnier, Earl F., *The Gentle Art of Murder: The Detective Fiction of Agatha Christie,* Bowling Green University Press, 1981.

Contemporary Literary Criticism, Gale, Volume 1, 1973; Volume 6, 1976; Volume 8, 1978; Volume 12, 1980; Volume 39, 1986; Volume 48, 1988.

Dictionary of Literary Biography, Gale, Volume 13: *British Dramatists Since World War II,* Gale, 1982; Volume 77: *British Mystery Writers, 1920-1939,* 1989.

Dommermuth-Costa, Carol, *Agatha Christie: Writer of Mystery,* Lerner Publications, 1997.

Feinman, Jeffrey, *The Mysterious World of Agatha Christie,* Award Books, 1975.

Gill, Gillian, *Agatha Christie: The Woman and Her Mysteries,* Free Press, 1990.

Grossvogel, David I., *Mystery and Its Fictions: From Oedipus to Agatha Christie,* Johns Hopkins University Press, 1979.

Hart, Anne, *The Life and Times of Miss Jane Marple: An Entertaining and Definitive Study of Agatha Christie's Famous Amateur Sleuth,* Dodd, 1985.

Haycraft, Howard, *Murder for Pleasure: The Life and Times of the Detective Story,* Biblo & Tannen, 1969.

Kaska, Kathleen, *What's Your Agatha Christie I. Q.? 1,101 Puzzling Questions About the World's Most Beloved Mystery Writer,* Carol Publishing Group (Secaucus, NJ), 1996.

Keating, H. R. F., editor, *Agatha Christie: First Lady of Crime,* Holt, 1977.

Maida, Patricia D. and Nicholas B. Spornick, *Murder She Wrote: A Study of Agatha Christie's Detective Fiction,* Bowling Green University, 1982.

Mallowan, Max, *Mallowan's Memoirs,* Dodd, 1977.

Morgan, Janet, *Agatha Christie: A Biography,* J. Cape, 1984.

Morselt, Ben, *An A to Z of the Novels and Short Stories of Agatha Christie,* David & Charles, 1985.

Osborne, Charles, *The Life and Crimes of Agatha Christie,* Holt, 1983.

Riley, Dick, and Pam McAllister, editors, *The Bedside, Bathtub, and Armchair Companion to Agatha Christie,* Ungar, 1979.

Riviere, Francois, *In the Foosteps of Agatha Christie,* English translation by Alexandra Campbell, photographs by Jean-Bernard Naudin, Trafalgar Square Pub., 1997.

Robyns, Gwen, *The Mystery of Agatha Christie,* Doubleday, 1978.

Sanders, Dennis and Len Lovalio, *The Agatha Christie Companion: The Complete Guide to Agatha Christie's Life and Work,* Delacorte, 1984.

Sova, Dawn B., *Agatha Christie A to Z: The Essential Reference to Her Life and Writings,* Facts on File (New York City), 1996.

Symons, Julian, *Mortal Consequences: A History—From the Detective Story to the Crime Novel,* Harper, 1972.

Symons, Julian, and Tom Adams, *Agatha Christie: The Art of Her Crimes, the Paintings of Tom Adams,* Everest House, 1982.

Toye, Randall, *The Agatha Christie Who's Who,* Holt, 1980.

Wagoner, Mary S., *Agatha Christie,* Twayne, 1986.

Wynne, Nancy Blue, *An Agatha Christie Chronology,* Ace Books, 1976.

PERIODICALS

Armchair Detective, April, 1978; summer, 1981.
Christian Science Monitor, December 20, 1967.
Commonweal, February 13, 1976.
Detroit News, November 13, 1977.
Globe and Mail (Toronto), September 15, 1990.
Harvard Magazine, October, 1975.
Life, December 1, 1967.
Los Angeles Times, March 8, 1970; December 15, 1974; April 20, 1975; September 13, 1990; November 1, 1990.
McCall's, February, 1969.
Milwaukee Journal, February 1, 1976.
Nation, July 3, 1926.
New Republic, July 31, 1976.
New Statesman, May 10, 1930; December 18, 1937; November 18, 1939.
Newsweek, October 6, 1975.
New Yorker, October 14, 1944; January 30, 1978.
New York Herald Tribune Book Review, March 4, 1934.
New York Review of Books, December 21, 1978.
New York Times, July 18, 1926; January 13, 1976; November 10, 1977; December 24, 1985.
New York Times Book Review, March 25, 1923; April 20, 1924; September 22, 1929; February 25, 1940; September 25, 1966; March 17, 1968; October 14, 1990.
Pittsburgh Press, March 28, 1976.
Saturday Review, July 24, 1926; October 4, 1975.
Seattle Post-Intelligencer, December 23, 1973.
Southwest Review, spring, 1974.

Spectator, May 31, 1930; February 14, 1936; September 19, 1970.
Times (London), September 19, 1984; September 5, 1990.
Times Literary Supplement, April 3, 1924; June 10, 1926; December 2, 1965; September 26, 1975.

*　　　*　　　*

CHUBB, Elmer
See MASTERS, Edgar Lee

*　　　*　　　*

CHURCHILL, Winston (Leonard Spencer) 1874-1965

PERSONAL: Born November 30, 1874, at Blenheim Palace, Oxfordshire, England; died of a cerebral thrombosis, January 24, 1965, in London, England; son of Lord Randolph Henry Spencer (a politician) and Jennie (Jerome) Churchill; married Clementine Ogilvy Hozier, September, 1908; children: Randolph, Sarah, Diana, Mary, and another daughter (died in infancy). *Education:* Royal Military Academy at Sandhurst, received degree, 1894. *Avocation:* Painting, gardening.

CAREER: Soldier, statesman, historian, journalist. Correspondent for the *London Daily Telegraph* and *Morning Post* covering the South African Boer War, 1899; member of British Parliament from Oldham, beginning 1900; undersecretary for the colonies, 1905-08; member of Parliament from Northwest Manchester, 1906-08, from Dundee, 1908-18; president of the board of trade, 1908-10; home secretary, 1910-11; first lord of the admiralty, 1911-15; minister of munitions, 1916-18; secretary of state for war and for air, 1918-21; secretary of state for air and colonies, 1921-22; painter and writer, 1922-24; member of Parliament from Epping, 1922-45; chancellor of the exchequer, 1924-29; writer, 1929-39; first lord of the admiralty, 1939-40; prime minister of Great Britain, 1940-45; member of Parliament from Woodford, 1945-65; leader of opposition in Parliament, 1945-51; prime minister, 1951-55; minister of defense, beginning 1951. Lord rector at University of Edinburgh, 1929-31; chancellor of Bristol University, 1930; lord warden of the Cinque Ports, beginning 1941. *Military service:* Royal Army, 1895-99, served in Cuba, India, and the Sudan; commanded Sixth Royal Scots Fusiliers as lieutenant-colonel, 1916.

AWARDS, HONORS: Albert Gold Medal of the Royal Society, 1945; Order of Merit, 1946; elected Royal Academician Extraordinary, 1948; Grotius Medal (Netherlands), 1949; London *Times* literary award, 1949; created Knight of the Garter by Queen Elizabeth II, 1953; Nobel prize for literature, 1953; Williamsburg Award, 1955; Charlemagne Prize (West Germany), 1956; made honorary U.S. citizen by act of Congress, 1963; recipient of numerous others awards, including more than eighteen honorary degrees from British and foreign universities.

WRITINGS:

The Story of the Malakand Field Force: An Episode of Frontier War (also see below), Longmans, Green, 1898.
The River War: An Historical Account of the Reconquest of the Soudan (also see below), two volumes, Longmans, Green, 1899, revised single-volume edition, 1902.

Ian Hamilton's March; Together with Extracts from the Diary of Lieutenant H. Frankland (also see below), Longmans, Green, 1900.
London to Ladysmith via Pretoria (also see below), Longmans, Green, 1900.
Savrola: A Tale of the Revolution in Laurania (novel), Longmans, Green, 1900.
Lord Randolph Churchill, two volumes, Macmillan, 1906, new edition, Odhams Press, 1952.
My African Journey, Hodder & Stoughton, 1908.
The World Crisis, Scribner, Volume I: *1911-1914,* 1923, Volume II: *1915,* 1923, Volumes III and IV: *1916-1918,* 1927, Volume V: *The Aftermath,* 1929, Volume VI: *The Unknown War: The Eastern Front,* 1931, revised and abridged edition of original four volumes, 1931.
A Roving Commission: My Early Life, Scribner, 1930 (published in England as *My Early Life: A Roving Commission,* Butterworth, 1930), published as *My Early Life, 1874-1904,* Simon & Schuster (New York City), 1996.
Amid These Storms: Thoughts and Adventures, Scribner, 1932, published as *Thoughts and Adventures,* Macmillan, 1942.
Marlborough: His Life and Times, six volumes, Scribner, 1933-38, abridged edition published as *Marlborough and His Times,* 1968.
Great Contemporaries, Putnam, 1937, revised edition, Butterworth, 1938.
Ten Chapters, 1942 to 1945, Hutchinson, 1945.
The Second World War, Houghton, Volume I: *The Gathering Storm,* 1948, Volume II: *Their Finest Hour,* 1949, Volume III: *The Grand Alliance,* 1950, Volume IV: *The Hinge of Fate,* 1951, Volume V: *Closing the Ring,* 1951, Volume VI: *Triumph and Tragedy,* 1954, abridged edition of original six volumes, with epilogue, 1959, published as *Memoirs of the Second World War,* Bonanza Books, 1978, abridgement of complete set published as *Memoirs of the Second World War: An Abridgement of the Six Volumes of The Second World War with an Epilogue by the Author on the Postwar Years Written for This Volume,* Houghton Mifflin (Boston), 1990, selections from these volumes published as *The Great Battles and Leaders of the Second World War: An Illustrated History,* Houghton Mifflin (Boston), 1995.
A History of the English-speaking Peoples, Dodd, Volume I: *The Birth of Britain to 1485,* 1956, Volume II: *The New World, 1485-1688,* 1956, Volume III: *The Age of Revolution, 1688-1815,* 1957, Volume IV: *The Great Democracies, 1815-1901,* 1958 (published as *The American Civil War,* 1961), abridged edition of original four volumes published as *The Island Race,* Dodd, 1964.
Winston Churchill and Emery Reves: Correspondence, 1937-1964, University of Texas Press (Austin, TX), 1997.

SPEECHES

Mr. Broderick's Army, A. L. Humphreys, 1903.
For Free Trade, A. L. Humphreys, 1906.
Liberalism and the Social Problem, Hodder & Stoughton, 1909.
The People's Rights, Hodder & Stoughton, 1910.
India: Speeches and an Introduction, Butterworth, 1931.
While England Slept: A Survey of World Affairs 1932-1938, Putnam, 1938, published in England as *Arms and the Covenant,* Harrap, 1938.
Step by Step: 1936-1939, Putnam, 1939.
Blood, Sweat, and Tears, Putnam, 1941 (published in England as *Into Battle,* Cassell, 1941), published as *Churchill in His*

Own Words: Years of Greatness; Memorable Speeches of the Man of the Century, Capricorn Books, 1966.

Broadcast Addresses to the People of Great Britain, Italy, Poland, Russia, and the United States, Ransohoffs, 1941.

The Unrelenting Struggle, Little, Brown, 1942.

The End of the Beginning, Little, Brown, 1943.

Winston Churchill, Prime Minister: A Selection from Speeches Made by Winston Churchill during the Four Years That Britain Has Been at War, British Information Services, 1943.

Onwards to Victory, Little, Brown, 1944.

The Dawn of Liberation, Little, Brown, 1945.

Victory, Little, Brown, 1946.

Winston Churchill's Secret Session Speeches, Simon & Schuster, 1946 (published in England as *Secret Session Speeches,* Cassell, 1946).

The Sinews of Peace: Post-War Speeches, Houghton, 1948.

Europe Unite: Speeches 1947 and 1948, Houghton, 1950.

War Speeches, Cassell, 1951-52, Houghton, 1953.

In the Balance: Speeches 1949 and 1950, Houghton, 1952.

Stemming the Tide: Speeches 1951 and 1952, Cassell, 1953, Houghton, 1954.

The Unwritten Alliance: Speeches 1953 to 1959, Cassell, 1963.

(David Cannadine, editor) *Blood, Toil, Tears, and Sweat: The Speeches of Winston Churchill,* Houghton Mifflin (Boston), 1989.

COLLECTIONS

Maxims and Reflections, Eyre & Spottiswoode, 1948, Houghton, 1949, revised and enlarged edition published as *Sir Winston Churchill: A Self-Portrait,* Eyre & Spottiswoode, 1954.

A Churchill Reader: The Wit and Wisdom of Sir Winston Churchill, Houghton, 1954.

The Wisdom of Sir Winston Churchill (selections from speeches, 1900-55), Allen & Unwin, 1956.

The Eloquence of Winston Churchill, New American Library, 1957.

Great War Speeches, Transworld, 1959.

Frontiers and Wars (contains abridged editions of *The Story of the Malakand Field Force, The River War, Ian Hamilton's March,* and *London to Ladysmith via Pretoria*), Harcourt, 1962.

A Churchill Anthology (selected writings and speeches), Odhams, 1962.

First Journey, Heinemann, 1964, Random House, 1965.

The Churchill Wit, Coward, 1965.

Great Destiny: Sixty Years of the Memorable Events in the Life of the Man of the Century, Recounted in His Own Incomparable Words, Putnam, 1965, published as *Churchill in His Own Words: Years of Adventure, Memorable Events in the Life of the Man of the Century,* Capricorn Books, 1966.

The Wit of Sir Winston, Frewin, 1965.

Churchill on Men and Events (selections from *Thoughts and Adventures* and *Great Contemporaries*), Ginn, 1965.

Irrepressible Churchill: A Treasury of Winston Churchill's Wit, World Publishing, 1966.

Never Give In! The Challenging Words of Winston Churchill, introduction by Dwight D. Eisenhower, Hallmark, 1967.

Heroes of History (selections from *A History of the English-speaking Peoples* and other works), Dodd, 1968.

The Roar of the Lion, Wingate, 1969.

Winston Churchill on America and Britain: A Selection of His Thoughts on America and Britain, foreword by wife, Lady Churchill, Walker, 1970.

If I Live My Life Again, W. H. Allen, 1974.

Immortal Jester: A Treasury of the Great Good Humor of Sir Winston Churchill, 1874-1965, Frewin, 1974.

Young Winston's Wars: The Original Dispatches of Winston S. Churchill, War Correspondent, 1897-1900, Cooper, 1972, Viking, 1973, new revised edition published as *Winston S. Churchill, War Correspondent,* Brassey's (Washington), 1992.

Winston S. Churchill: His Complete Speeches, 1897-1963, eight volumes, Chelsea House, 1974.

The Collected Works of Winston Churchill, a centenary limited edition, Library of Imperial History, Volume I: *My Early Life; My African Journey,* 1973; Volume II: *The Story of the Malakand Field Force,* 1974; Volume III: *The River War,* 1974; Volume IV: *The Boer War; London to Ladysmith via Pretoria; Ian Hamilton's March,* 1974; Volume V: *Savrola,* 1974, Volume VI: *Lord Randolph Churchill,* 1974; Volume VII: *Mr. Broderick's Army and Other Early Speeches* (includes *For Free Trade, Liberalism and the Social Problem, The People's Rights,* and *India*), 1974; Volumes VIII-XII: *The World Crisis,* 1974; Volume XIII: *Thoughts and Adventures,* 1974; Volumes XIV-XV: *Marlborough: His Life and Times,* 1974; Volume XVI: *Great Contemporaries,* 1974; Volume XVII: *Arms and the Covenant,* 1975; Volume XVIII: *Step by Step, 1936-1939,* 1975; Volumes XIX-XXI: *The War Speeches,* 1975; Volumes XXII-XXVII: *The Second World War,* 1975; Volumes XXVIII-XXX: *Post-War Speeches,* 1975; Volumes XXXI-XXXIV: *A History of the English-speaking Peoples,* 1976.

OTHER

Painting as a Pastime, Whittlesey House, 1950.

(With others) *The Eagle Book of Adventure Stories,* Hulton, 1950.

Churchill: His Paintings, foreword by Lady Churchill, World Publishing, 1967.

(With John Glubb) *Great Issues 71: A Forum on Important Questions Facing the American Public,* Troy State University, 1972.

Memories and Adventures, Weidenfeld, 1989.

J. L. Lane, editor, *The Sayings of Winston Churchill,* Duckworth (London), 1992.

James C. Humes, editor, *The Wit & Wisdom of Winston Churchill: A Treasury of More than 1,000 Quotations and Anecdotes,* HarperCollins (New York City), 1994.

Also author of *Coniston,* 1906.

SIDELIGHTS: Winston Churchill led an impressive life. His parliamentary career spanned the reigns of six monarchs, from Queen Victoria to her great-great-granddaughter, Elizabeth II. His early military service included hand-to-hand combat in the Sudan, and he lived to see the use of atomic weapons as a means to end World War II.

Evaluating Churchill's legacy, both as a historian and a world leader, John Kenneth Galbraith noted the enormous importance of his "fearsome certainty that he was completely right." But Galbraith added that "the greater element in Churchill's power was his use of language as a weapon." Not only could Churchill amass and organize huge quantities of information; he could also communicate it with an air of excitement and vitality. This in turn depended, Galbraith believed, "on inventive, if often extravagant and sometimes reckless, use of adjective and metaphor . . . [and] on the power, resource, and flow of the language itself."

Churchill's military career began almost immediately upon his graduation with honors from Sandhurst, the West Point of Great

Britain. In March, 1895, he was appointed to the Fourth (Queen's Own) Hussars as a sub-lieutenant, assigned to duty at the Aldershop camp in Hampshire. After attachment as an "observer" to an anti-insurrectionary Spanish force in Cuba, he served in Bangalore, India. His next assignments included the Tirah Expeditionary Force in 1898 and the Nile Expeditionary Force, where he participated in the famous cavalry charge at Omdurman.

Churchill also saw battle as a journalist. In 1897, as a war correspondent for the *London Daily Telegraph,* he joined General Sir Benden Blood's expedition against the Pathams in the area of the Malakand Pass. In a similar capacity for the *London Morning Post,* he went to South Africa after the outbreak of the Boer War; there, on November 15, 1899, he was taken prisoner by Louis Botha, who later became the first prime minister of the Union of South Africa and a close friend of Sir Winston's. Churchill's subsequent dramatic escape from a Pretoria prison, which brought him immediate world fame, is detailed in his autobiography, *A Roving Commission.*

In 1911 Churchill became first lord of the admiralty, readying the British fleet for war with Germany. By the start of World War I in 1914, the Royal Navy was so well prepared, having changed over from coal to oil-fueled vessels, that it quickly confined the German fleet to its home ports. The Germans refrained from an all-out naval confrontation, relying instead upon the submarine. Churchill's other major accomplishment at this time was the establishment of the Royal Air Force, first called the Royal Flying Corps. But after encountering loud criticism for the British landings on Gallipoli (the Dardanelles campaign), which resulted in heavy casualties, Churchill was demoted. He resigned his office in 1916 to go to the front as a lieutenant-colonel in command of the Sixth Royal Fusiliers. Nevertheless, he was soon recalled by Prime Minister Lloyd George to become minister of munitions.

After World War I Churchill introduced a number of military reforms as secretary of state for war and for air (1918-21). As secretary for the colonies (1921-22), he worked toward the establishment of new Arab states, toward a Jewish homeland in the Middle East, and toward an Irish free state. At this time Churchill was growing increasingly anti-socialist, setting himself at odds with the pro-labor segment of the Liberal party. His use of British troops to suppress the Bolshevist regime in the Soviet Union lost him the favor of Lloyd George, who appointed Sir Robert Horne chancellor of the exchequer over Churchill. But in 1924 Churchill rejoined the Conservatives and was immediately named chancellor of the exchequer.

Churchill was out of office during the 1930s until the outbreak of World War II. Then, as a result of public pressure, he was reappointed first lord of the admiralty in September, 1939. Upon the resignation of Neville Chamberlain in May, 1940, Churchill became prime minister, a position he held almost unchallenged till the end of the war. In his first speech as prime minister in the House of Commons, after the fall of France to the Nazis, he made clear Britain's uncompromising ambition: "You ask, what is our aim? I can answer in one word: Victory—victory at all costs, victory in spite of all terror; victory, however long and hard the road maybe."

Churchill's specialty was probably military history. "He learned of wars by fighting in them," Henry Steele Commager noted, and it was a subject central to most of his writings. He covered wars that ranged from India, Cuba, and the Sudan to South Africa, Western Europe, and eventually the entire globe. He observed them as a cavalryman and a journalist, then as the lord of the

admiralty and the supreme commander of the Allied forces. He was, Commager said, "in all likelihood, the greatest of military historians who wrote in English." Even his least characteristic book, the autobiographical novel *Savrola,* is "a testament to Churchill's early sophistication in military and political matters," wrote Manfred Weidhorn.

Churchill's early military experience resulted in several volumes, notably those published collectively as *Frontiers and Wars.* His journalism, which at the time provided a needed source of income, has also been collected as *Young Winston's Wars.* But his first major literary undertaking began in 1902 when the family trustees gave him his father's papers. The project was, according to Weidhorn, "not only an homage to the father never fully known or confronted on equal terms and a revelation to the world of the greatness of the prematurely dead statesman . . . but also a discovery of and dedication to the father's values, a study of a political program handed down from one generation to the next within the same family." Commager described the two-volume *Life of Lord Randolph Churchill* as "judicious, comprehensive, and mature, penetrating not only to the realities of politics in those turbulent years, but to the realities of character."

Churchill worked on his other biography, *Marlborough,* for five years. Of this study he wrote: "It is my hope to recall this great shade from the past, and not only invest him with the panoply, but make him living and ultimate to modern eyes. I hope to show that he was not only the foremost of English soldiers, but in the first rank among the statesmen of our history; not only that he was a Titan . . . but that he was a virtuous and benevolent being, eminently serviceable to his age and country, capable of drawing harmony and design from chaos." Commager remarked: "Rarely in the history of historical writing have author and subject seemed so made for each other as were Churchill and the Duke of Marlborough."

In *The World Crisis,* Churchill presented himself as a participant in history. Lord Balfour called it "Winston's brilliant autobiography disguised as a history of the universe." It outlines his career against a background of international affairs, and it records not only the events of World War II, but also of the years preceding it. While some critics considered these six volumes among Churchill's best, Weidhorn felt the balance between history and memoir was not successfully maintained: "Uneven, at times naive, bombastic, dated, it is, finally, a personal account, an 'entertainment,' a piece of storytelling or fine journalism that often masquerades as a formal analytic history."

The Second World War was also autobiographical, but to Weidhorn it was more successful than *The World Crisis.* It is "the usual Churchillian melange of autobiography, apologia, general history, and selected documents; of impersonal autobiography and personal history. But it is much more unified because Churchill was in a central position continuously and could observe events from a higher vantage point." As a result, continued Weidhorn, it benefits from a dramatic narrative flow as well as convincing evocation of setting, mood, and character.

In Churchill's later years, *The Second World War* and *History of the English-speaking Peoples* were outsold only by the Bible. *History of the English-speaking Peoples,* his last major work, was written for the most part in the late 1930s, but not published until 1956. It chronicles the rise of the British Empire and the English-speaking world, but it is also a vehicle for Churchill's ideas about politics, history, and tradition. "As Churchill saw it, the welfare of mankind was inextricably bound up with that of the English-speaking peoples," Commager explained. "It was, above all else, the English character which had lighted up the corridors of time." "The impact Churchill had on the lives of his contemporaries will never be forgotten. When he died he was acclaimed a citizen of the world and given a state funeral in St. Paul's Cathedral, an honor previously bestowed on only two other men of war—Admiral Lord Nelson, victor at Trafalgar, and the Duke of Wellington, victor at Waterloo." Such were his honors because, as Taylor noted, to men of the time "he was the savior of his country, the first Englishman to be so hailed since King Alfred the Great."

BIOGRAPHICAL/CRITICAL SOURCES:

BOOKS

Addison, Paul, *Churchill on the Home Front, 1900-1955,* Pimlico (London), 1993.

Alberg, Victor Lincoln, *Winston Churchill,* Twayne, 1973.

Ben-Moshe, Tuvia, *Churchill, Strategy and History,* Lynne Rienner Publishers (Boulder, CO), 1992.

Blake, Robert and William Roger, editors, *Churchill,* Oxford University Press (New York City), 1992.

Boyle, Peter G., editor, *The Churchill-Eisenhower Correspondence, 1953-1955,* University of North Carolina Press (Chapel Hill), 1990.

Bradley, John, *Churchill,* Gloucester Press (New York City), 1990.

Broad, Lewis, *Winston Churchill: A Biography,* two volumes, Greenwood, 1972.

Charmley, John, *Churchill, the End of Glory: A Political Biography,* Harcourt Brace (San Diego), 1994.

Churchill, Randolph Spencer, and Martin Gilbert, *Winston S. Churchill,* eight volumes, Heinemann, 1967-88.

David, Saul, *Churchill's Sacrifice of the Highland Division: France 1940,* Brassey's (Washington), 1994.

Day, David, *Menzies & Churchill at War: A Controversial New Account of the 1941 Struggle for Power,* Paragon House (New York City), 1988.

Driemen, J. E., *Winston Churchill, an Unbreakable Spirit,* Dillon Press (Minneapolis, MN), 1990.

(Edited by Martin Gilbert) *Winston Curchill and Emery Reves: Correspondence, 1937-1964,* University of Texas Press (Austin, TX), 1997.

Edmonds, Robin, *The Big Three: Churchill, Roosevelt, and Stalin in Peace & War,* Norton (New York City), 1991.

Feske, Victor, *From Belloc to Churchill: Private Scholars, Public Culture, and the Crisis of British Liberalism, 1900-1939,* University of North Carolina Press (Chapel Hill), 1996.

Gilbert, Martin, *Never Despair: Winston S. Churchill, 1945-1965,* Heinemann (London), 1988.

Gilbert, Martin, *Churchill: A Life,* Holt (New York City), 1991.

Gilbert, Martin, *Churchill: A Photographic Portrait,* Wings Books (New York City), 1993.

Hough, Richard Alexander, *Winston & Clementine: The Triumphs and Tragedies of the Churchills,* Bantam (New York City), 1991.

Humes, James C., *The Sir Winston Method: The Five Secrets of Speaking the Language of Leadership,* Quill/William Morrow (New York City), 1993.

Hunt, John Gabriel, editor, *The Essential Winston Churchill,* Gramercy Books (New York City), 1995.

Italia, Bob and Rosemary Wallner, *The Story of Winston Churchill,* Abdo & Daughters (Edina, MN), 1990.

Jablonsky, David, *Churchill, the Making of a Grand Strategist,* Strategic Studies Institute, U.S. Army War College (Carlisle Barracks, PA), 1990.

Jablonsky, David, *Churchill, the Great Game and Total War,* F. Cass (Portland, OR), 1991.

Jablonsky, David, *Churchill and Hitler: Essays on the Political-Military Direction of Total War,* F. Cass (Portland, OR), 1994.

Jefferys, Kevin, *The Churchill Coalition and Wartime Politics, 1940-1945,* Manchester University Press (New York City), 1991.

Jordan, Anthony J., *Churchill, a Founder of Modern Ireland,* Westport Books (Dublin), 1995.

Kemper, R. Crosby, III, *Winston Churchill: Resolution, Defiance, Magnanimity, Good Will,* University of Missouri Press (Columbia), 1996.

Kilzer, Louis C., *Churchill's Deception: The Dark Secret That Destroyed Nazi Germany,* Simon & Schuster (New York City), 1994.

Lace, William W., *Winston Churchill,* Lucent Books (San Diego), 1995.

Lamb, Richard, *Churchill as War Leader,* Carroll & Graf (New York City), 1993.

Lambakis, Steven James, *Winston Churchill, Architect of Peace: A Study of Statesmanship and the Cold War,* Greenwood Press (Westport, CT), 1993.

Lawlor, Sheila, *Churchill and the Politics of War, 1940-1941,* Cambridge University Press (Cambridge, MA), 1994.

Lukacs, John, *The Duel: 10 May-31 July 1940: The Eighty-Day Struggle Between Churchill and Hitler,* Ticknor & Fields (New York City), 1991.

Mansfield, Stephen, *Never Give In,* Highland Books (Elkton, MD), 1995.

Martin, David, *The Web of Disinformation: Churchill's Yugoslav Blunder,* Harcourt Brace Jovanovich (San Diego), 1990.

Mason, David, *Churchill,* Ballantine, 1972.

Mayer, Frank A., *The Opposition Years: Winston S. Churchill and the Conservative Party, 1945-1951,* P. Lang (New York City), 1992.

Mieder, Wolfgang, editor, *The Proverbial Winston S. Churchill: An Index to Proverbs in the Works of Sir Winston Churchill,* Greenwood Press (Westport, CT), 1995.

Moran, Charles McMoran Wilson, Baron, *Churchill: The Struggle for Survival, 1940-1965,* Cherokee Publishing Co. (Atlanta), 1990.

Nadeau, Remi A., *Stalin, Churchill, and Roosevelt Divide Europe,* Praeger (New York City), 1990.

Newfield, Dalton, *Young Winston: 1874-1898: A Biography Using Stamps,* International Churchill Society (Hopkinton, NH), 1990.

Parker, Robert Alexander Clarke with Correlli Barnett and Churchill College, *Winston Churchill: Studies in Statesmanship,* Brassey's (London), 1995.

Pearson, John, *Citadel of the Heart: Winston and the Churchill Dynasty,* Macmillan (London), 1991.

Pelling, Henry, *Winston Churchill,* Dutton, 1974, second edition, Macmillan (Hampshire), 1989.

Pitt, Barrie, *Churchill and the Generals: Their Finest Hour,* Borgo Press (San Bernadino, CA), 1989.

Ponting, Clive, *Churchill,* Sinclair-Stevenson (London), 1994.

Robbins, Keith, *Churchill,* Longman (New York City), 1992.

Rose, Norman, *Churchill: The Unruly Giant,* Free Press (New York City), 1995.

Rushbridger, James and Eric Nave, *Betrayal at Pearl Harbor: How Churchill Lured Roosevelt into World War II,* Summit Books (New York City), 1991.

Sainsbury, Keith, *Churchill and Roosevelt at War: The War They Fought and the Peace They Hoped to Make,* New York University Press (Washington Square, NY), 1994.

Sandys, Celia, *The Young Churchill: The Early Years of Winston Churchill,* Dutton (New York City), 1995.

Severance, John B., *Winston Churchill: Soldier, Statesman, Artist,* Clarion Books (New York City), 1996.

Thomas, David Arthur, *Churchill: The Member for Woodford,* F. Cass (Portland, OR), 1995.

Thompson, Kenneth W., *Foreign Policy and Arms Control: Churchill's Legacy,* University Press of America (Lanham, MD), 1990.

Waszak, Leon J., *Agreement in Principle: The Wartime Partnership of General Wladyslaw Sikorski and Winston Churchill,* P. Lang (New York City), 1996.

Weidhorn, Manfred, *A Harmony of Interests: Explorations in the Mind of Sir Winston Churchill,* Farleigh Dickinson University Press (Rutherford, NJ), 1992.

Whatney, John Basil, *Churchills: Portrait of a Great Family,* Gordon Cremonesi, 1977.

Wilson, Theodore A., *The First Summit: Roosevelt and Churchill at Placentia Bay, 1941,* University Press of Kansas (Lawrence), 1991.

Woods, Frederick, *Artillery of Words: The Writings of Sir Winston Churchill,* L. Cooper (London), 1992.

PERIODICALS

American Mercury, October, 1949.

American Spectator, April, 1991, p. 19.

Atlantic Monthly, July, 1948; September, 1949; January, 1951; November, 1991, p. 141.

Nation, May 6, 1950; March 19, 1956; December 1, 1956; July 5, 1958; September 21, 1974.

National Review, October 13, 1989, p. 52; May 20, 1996, p. 63.

Newsweek, January 21, 1946; January 28, 1946; March 18, 1946; March 25, 1946; April 8, 1946; August 26, 1946; April 8, 1946; August 18, 1947; October 31, 1947; June 21, 1948; April 4, 1949; March 6, 1950; May 4, 1953; October 20, 1953; December 6, 1954; March 4, 1957; May 13, 1957; March 17, 1958; May 5, 1958; September 8, 1958; February 16, 1959; March 24, 1961; September 3, 1962; April 22, 1963; May 18, 1970; May 15, 1973; November 18, 1974; November 13, 1978.

New Yorker, March 26, 1990, p. 95.

New York Times, March 6, 1927; March 17, 1929; November 20, 1930; November 29, 1931; December 4, 1932; November 12, 1933; March 17, 1935; March 28, 1937; November 14, 1937; October 9, 1938; October 23, 1938; September 3, 1939; April 13, 1941; October 25, 1942; August 22, 1943; July 23, 1944; August 5, 1945; August 25, 1946; June 20, 1948; March, 13, 1949; April 3, 1949; June 12, 1949; February 12, 1950; April 23, 1950; June 11, 1950; November 26, 1950; November 25, 1951; November 29, 1953; April 15, 1956; August 22, 1956; November 25, 1956; February 22, 1959.

New York Times Book Review, March 20, 1955; November 24, 1974; February 10, 1991, p. 3.

New York Times Magazine, February 9, 1947; November 21, 1948; January 2, 1949; November 2, 1949; November 26, 1950; October 14, 1951; November 11, 1951; January 4, 1953; October 25, 1953; November 28, 1954; April 1, 1956; January 19, 1958; February 16, 1958; November 1, 1964; October 5, 1969; April 28, 1974.

Publishers Weekly, May 24, 1993, p. 46.

Saturday Evening Post, May-June, p. 86.

Saturday Review, March 16, 1929; October 31, 1953; November 28, 1953; December 4, 1954; April 21, 1956; February 6, 1965; May 18, 1968.

Saturday Review of Literature, April 30, 1927; June 19, 1948; March 4, 1950; November 25, 1950.

Time, January 21, 1946; March 18, 1946; April 1, 1946; June 10, 1946; May 19, 1947; December 20, 1948; May 10, 1948; January 2, 1950; November 5, 1951; December 15, 1952; February 1, 1954; June 21, 1954; December 13, 1954; March 28, 1955; June 10, 1958; July 6, 1962; December 4, 1964; February 25, 1966; April 22, 1966; May 6, 1966; November 24, 1967; May 31, 1968.

Times Literary Supplement, March 3, 1927; October 23, 1950; November 5, 1931; October 12, 1933; October 9, 1937; June 25, 1938; July 1, 1939; October 3, 1942; July 31, 1943; July 1, 1944; July 27, 1946; September 28, 1946; August 14, 1948; July 1, 1949; July 21, 1950; April 27, 1956; November 30, 1956; October 26, 1967; September 15, 1972.

*   *   *

CIARDI, John (Anthony) 1916-1986
(John Anthony)

PERSONAL: Surname pronounced *Char*-dee; born June 24, 1916, in Boston, MA; died of a heart attack, March 30, 1986, in Edison, NJ; son of Carminantonia (an insurance agent) and Concetta (De Benedictus) Ciardi; married Myra Judith Hostetter, July 28, 1946; children: Myra Judith, John Lyle Pritchett, Benn Anthony. *Education:* Attended Bates College, 1934-36; Tufts College (now University), A.B. (magna cum laude), 1938; University of Michigan, M.A., 1939. *Politics:* Democrat. *Avocation:* "Indifferent golf and neglected gardening."

CAREER: Poet and critic. University of Kansas City, Kansas City, MO, instructor in English, 1940-42, 1946; Harvard University, Cambridge, MA, Briggs-Copeland Instructor in English, 1946-48, Briggs-Copeland Assistant Professor of English, 1948-53; Rutgers University, New Brunswick, NJ, lecturer, 1953-54, associate professor, 1954-56, professor of English, 1956-61; *Saturday Review,* New York, NY, poetry editor, 1956-72. Bread Loaf Writers' Conference, lecturer in poetry, 1947-73, director, 1955-72; lecturer in American poetry, Salzburg Seminar in American Studies, 1951. Editor with Twayne Publishers, 1949; served as a judge in Children's Literature Section of National Book Awards, 1969. Host of *Accent,* a weekly educational program presented by Columbia Broadcasting System-Television, 1961-62. Has given public poetry readings. *Military service:* U.S. Army Air Forces, 1942-45; served as gunner on B-29 in air offensive against Japan; became technical sergeant; received Air Medal with Oak Leaf Cluster.

MEMBER: American Academy of Arts and Sciences (fellow), National Institute of Arts and Letters (fellow), National College English Association (director, 1955-57; president, 1958-59), Northeast College English Association (past president), Phi Beta Kappa.

AWARDS, HONORS: Avery Hopwood Award for poetry, University of Michigan, 1939; Oscar Blumenthal Prize, Poetry, 1943; Eunice Tietjens Award, 1945; Levinson Prize, 1946; Golden Rose trophy of New England Poetry Club, 1948; Fund for the Advancement of Education grant, 1952; Harriet Monroe Memorial Prize, 1955; Prix de Rome, American Academy of Arts and Letters, 1956-57; Litt.D., Tufts University, 1960; Junior Book

Award, Boys' Clubs of America, 1962, for *The Man Who Sang the Sillies*; D.Hum., Wayne State University, 1963, and Keane College of New Jersey, 1976; LL.D., Ursinus College, 1964; L.H.D., Kalamazoo College, 1964, Bates College, 1970, Washington University, 1971, Ohio Wesleyan University, 1971; D.H.L., Kean University, 1975, University of Missouri, Kansas City, 1983.

WRITINGS:

POETRY

Homeward to America, Holt, 1940.
Other Skies, Atlantic Monthly Press, 1947.
Live Another Day: Poems, Twayne, 1949.
From Time to Time, Twayne, 1951.
As If: Poems New and Selected, Rutgers University Press, 1955.
I Marry You: A Sheaf of Love Poems, Rutgers University Press, 1958.
Thirty-Nine Poems, Rutgers University Press, 1959.
In the Stoneworks, Rutgers University Press, 1961.
In Fact, Rutgers University Press, 1962.
Person to Person, Rutgers University Press, 1964.
This Strangest Everything, Rutgers University Press, 1966.
An Alphabestiary, Lippincott, 1967.
A Genesis, Touchstone Publishers (New York), 1967.
The Achievement of John Ciardi: A Comprehensive Selection of his Poems with a Critical Introduction (poetry textbook), edited by Miller Williams, Scott, Foresman, 1969.
Lives of X (autobiographical poetry), Rutgers University Press, 1971.
The Little That Is All, Rutgers University Press, 1974.
For Instance, Norton, 1979.
Selected Poems, University of Arkansas Press, 1984.
The Birds of Pompeii, University of Arkansas Press, 1985.
Echoes: Poems Left Behind, University of Arkansas Press, 1989.
Poems of Love and Marriage, University of Arkansas Press, 1989.
Stations on the Air, Bookmark Press of the University of Missouri-Kansas City, 1993.
The Collected Poems of John Ciardi, University of Arkansas Press (Fayetteville, AK), 1997.

JUVENILE

The Reason for the Pelican (poetry), Lippincott, 1959, new edition, Wordsong/Boyds Mills Press (Honesdale, PA), 1994.
Scrappy the Pup (poetry), Lippincott, 1960.
The Man Who Sang the Sillies (poetry), Lippincott, 1961.
I Met a Man (poetry), Houghton, 1961.
You Read to Me, I'll Read to You (poetry), Lippincott, 1962.
The Wish-Tree (fiction), Crowell-Collier, 1962.
John J. Plenty and Fiddler Dan: A New Fable of the Grasshopper and the Ant (poetry), Lippincott, 1963.
You Know Who (poetry), Lippincott, 1964.
The King Who Saved Himself from Being Saved (poetry), Lippincott, 1965.
The Monster Den; or, Look What Happened at My House—and to It (poetry), Lippincott, 1966.
Someone Could Win a Polar Bear (poetry), Lippincott, 1970.
Fast and Slow: Poems for Advanced Children and Beginning Parents (poetry), Houghton, 1975.
Doodle Soup, Houghton, 1986.

TRANSLATOR

Dante Alighieri, *The Inferno* (poetry; also see below), Rutgers University Press, 1954, Modern Library (New York City), 1996.

Dante, *The Purgatorio* (poetry; also see below), New American Library, 1961, 1996.
Dante, *The Paradiso* (poetry; also see below), New American Library, 1970.
Dante, *The Divine Comedy* (includes *The Inferno, The Purgatorio, and The Paradiso*), Norton, 1977.

RECORDINGS

About Eskimos and Other Poems (cassette phonotape), Spoken Arts, 1974.
What Do You Know about Poetry?: An Introduction to Poetry for Children (cassette phonotape), Spoken Arts, 1974.
What Is a Poem?: A Discussion of How Poems Are Made (phonodisc), Spoken Arts, 1974.
Why Noah Praised the Whale and Other Poems (cassette phonotape), Spoken Arts, 1974.

OTHER

(Editor) *Mid-Century American Poets*, Twayne, 1950.
(Author of introduction) Fritz Leiber and others, *Witches Three* (prose), Twayne, 1952.
(Contributor) William White, *John Ciardi: A Bibliography*, Wayne State University Press, 1959.
(Editor and contributor) *How Does a Poem Mean?* (prose), Houghton, 1960, 2nd edition (with Miller Williams), 1975.
Dialogue with an Audience (collection of *Saturday Review* essays), Lippincott, 1963.
(Editor with James M. Reid and Laurence Perrine) *Poetry: A Closer Look* (prose), Harcourt, 1963.
(Contributor) A. L. Bader, editor, *To the Young Writer* (prose), University of Michigan Press, 1965.
(Contributor) *Dante Alighieri: Three Lectures* (prose), Library of Congress, 1965.
(Author of introduction) John A. Holmes, *The Selected Poems*, Beacon Press, 1965.
(With Joseph B. Roberts) *On Poetry and the Poetic Process* (prose), Troy State University Press, 1971.
Manner of Speaking (selected *Saturday Review* columns), Rutgers University Press, 1972.
(With Isaac Asimov) *Limericks, Too Gross*, Norton, 1978.
A Browser's Dictionary and Native's Guide to the Unknown American Language, Harper, 1980.
(With Laurence Urdang and Frederick Dickerson) *Plain English in a Complex Society*, Poynter Center, Indiana University, 1980.
(With Asimov) *A Grossery of Limericks*, Norton, 1981.
A Second Browser's Dictionary and Native's Guide to the Unknown American Language, Harper, 1983.
Good Words to You: An All-New Browser's Dictionary and Native's Guide to the Unknown American Language, Harper, 1987.
The Complete Browser's Dictionary: The Best of John Ciardi's Two Browser's Dictionaries in a Single Compendium of Curious Expressions and Intriguing Facts, Harper, 1988.
Saipan: The War Diary of John Ciardi, University of Arkansas Press, 1988.
Ciardi Himself: Fifteen Essays in the Reading, Writing, and Teaching of Poetry, University of Arkansas Press, 1989.
The Hopeful Trout and Other Limericks, Houghton, 1989.
The Selected Letters of John Ciardi, University of Arkansas Press, 1991.

Also contributor of short story, under name John Anthony, to science fiction anthology *A Decade of Fantasy and Science Fiction: Out of This World Masterworks by Masterminds of the*

Near and the Far Out. Contributor of articles and essays to periodicals. Contributing editor, *Saturday Review,* 1955-1986, and *World Magazine,* 1970-72.

SIDELIGHTS: To millions of Americans, the late John Ciardi was "Mr. Poet, the one who has written, talked, taught, edited, translated, anthologized, criticized, and propelled poetry into a popular, lively art," according to Peter Comer of the *Chicago Tribune.* Although recognized primarily as a poet and critic, Ciardi's literary endeavors encompassed a vast range of material. From juvenile nonsense poetry to scholarly verse translations, Ciardi made an impact upon the general public. His poetry received popular approval while his academic research attracted critical kudos. Driven by his love of words and language, John Ciardi provided lively and frequently controversial offerings to the literary scene.

The son of Italian immigrants, Ciardi, at age three, lost his father in an automobile accident. Ciardi recalls a peaceful youth, enlivened by the addition of Irish and Italian families to the neighborhood. His tranquil life developed into a series of bruises and black eyes as the neighborhood children clashed frequently. Perhaps due to his heritage, Ciardi's interest in Italian literature has resulted in translations of Dante's *Inferno* that many authorities consider classics.

Once a denizen of the English faculties at Harvard and Rutgers, Ciardi, in 1961, broke with formalized education in favor of pursuing his own literary endeavors full time. He remained a part of the academic community through countless lectures and poetry readings each year, in addition to numerous appearances on educational television. Influenced by poet John Holmes, his favorite teacher at Tufts University, Ciardi decided early in his college career to devote time to writing verse. He turned to composing juvenile poetry as a means of playing and reading with his own children. His juvenile selections have been enormously successful, especially *I Met a Man.* Ciardi's position as a poetry critic with *Saturday Review* developed from his own verse publications, but he told Comer that "it was a hobby job," adding, "I think at most it earned me $4,000 a year."

Ciardi was strongly in favor of exposing poetry to mass audiences. Aware of the linguistic and allusive complexities inherent in "good" verse and acknowledging the public's general aversion to poems, he consciously attempted to address the average reader through much of his work. While not sacrificing his message for popularity and renown, Ciardi nevertheless gained a large public following. While critics acclaimed the intellectual elements in his work, the reading public derived equal meaning and relevance from his poetry. In his preface to *Dialogue with an Audience,* Ciardi expressed the hope that some readers "can be brought to a more than merely general interest in poetry."

Ciardi's work has inspired both praise and criticism from reviewers. Edward Cifelli writes in the *CEA Critic:* "Ciardi's verse is intensely personal, introspective, and self-revealing. His poems reflect the quiet considerations of a thoughtful, sensitive man. They are not white-hot representations of emotion: Ciardi more often thinks about passion. His diction is less emotionally charged than it is intricately patterned. Frequently passion emerges in Ciardi 'imagery' only after it has been filtered through the poet's sense of the ironic or comic." Cifelli also believes that "[Ciardi] focuses with remarkable clarity on the elements upon which one builds a theme into a poem," adding, "The theme that exemplifies the great diversity of Ciardi's talent is poetry itself." In the *Dictionary of Literary Biography,* Alice Smith Haynes

analyzes the totality of the poet's verse and its connected relativity: "Just as [Ciardi] maintains that Dante must be experienced as a whole, so his poetry, more than that of most poets, must be seen as an interrelated body of parts." In the *Chicago Tribune,* Reed Whittemore, also a poet and essayist, observes: "If [Ciardi's] poetry has any persistent theme, it is probably that human nonsense and folly are persistent. He is a cynic all right. . . . But he is not all cynic. The positive feelings do slop pleasantly through." Comer illustrates Ciardi's literary success: "John Ciardi long has been the rare American who could walk into a bank, declare his occupation as 'poet,' and emerge with a mortgage."

As a critic, Ciardi frequently provoked controversy with his frank and often candidly honest reviews. Known for promoting poetry, he nonetheless never shied away from denigrating what he considers unworthy verse. The first major disturbance surrounding his assessment of poetry stemmed from his unfavorable *Saturday Review* article about Anne Morrow Lindbergh's *The Unicorn.* Such forthright criticism in 1957 shocked readers and prompted voluminous mail protest. Ciardi defended his position in later issues of the magazine, arguing that a critic's role is to examine the work itself, not the popularity of the artist. He also maintained that the primary responsibility of good poetry lies to itself, and that the publishing arena should not serve simply to enhance any particular individual's reputation. Ciardi's fresh approach to criticism set the mood for later evaluative standards not yet accepted in the late 1950s.

One of Ciardi's late passions emerged in his conversation with Corner: "I'm not a complicated man, and I don't have any gripping internal problems. But I get interested in things. Words have become a happy obsession." His linguistic research culminated in a multi-volume work, *The Browser's Dictionary.* In the first volume, Ciardi indulged his interest in etymology, word derivations, and linguistic development throughout the entries. Concentrating on precision, the tome reflected Ciardi's commitment to bringing the intricacies of language closer to the reading public.

Reassessing his writing career, John Ciardi told Corner that perhaps his first works exhibit indiscriminate editing: "Early on I was offered more chances to publish than was really good for me, and I lacked the character to say no. . . . I need to go back over everything and take only the ones that stay memorable for me, probably less than half I've published. And I'd like to signalize that the other ones are fakes. . . . I denounce them. . . . I did not write them." Despite his concern over quality, Ciardi remained immersed in literary pursuits. His opinion in the *Writer* that "what passes as our poetry has too largely been taken over by loud illiterates and by officiously important editors" belies his constant quest for self-improvement. He wrote "as an alcoholic drinks, compulsively." This "tough-guy poet, the art's Edward C. Robinson, with his feelings leaking out unexpectedly in the midst of flat, machine-gun commentary," in Whittemore's words, explained to Corner: "I find I like what I do . . . and enjoy working at the things I enjoy. To me that's a description of blessedness." Perhaps to ensure the perpetuation of his poetic dominion even in death, John Ciardi created his own epitaph: "Here, time concurring (and it does); / Lies Ciardi. If no kingdom come, / A kingdom was. Such as it was / This one beside it is a slum."

BIOGRAPHICAL/CRITICAL SOURCES:

BOOKS

Cifelli, Edward M., *John Ciardi: A Biography,* University of Arkansas Press, 1997.
Contemporary Literary Criticism, Gale, Volume 10, 1979; Volume 40, 1986; Volume 44, 1987.
Dictionary of Literary Biography, Volume 5: *American Poets since World War II,* Gale, 1980.
Dictionary of Literary Biography Yearbook: 1986, Gale, 1987.
Hopkins, Lee Bennett, *Books Are by People,* Citation Press, 1969.
John Ciardi, Twayne, 1980.
White, William, *John Ciardi: A Bibliography,* Wayne State University Press, 1959.

PERIODICALS

America, July 27, 1957; April 4, 1987.
Book Week, September 29, 1963; November 1, 1964; November 8, 1970; September 24, 1972; September 28, 1980.
Booklist, December 1, 1972; February 1, 1975; October 15, 1979; July 15, 1980.
CEA Critic, November, 1973.
Chicago Review, autumn-winter, 1956; summer, 1957.
Chicago Tribune, December 16, 1979; September 8, 1980; April 3, 1986.
Choice, October, 1967; February, 1972; February, 1975; June, 1979.
Christian Science Monitor, December 24, 1964; May 7, 1975; October 23, 1978; January 2, 1980.
Contemporary Literature, winter, 1968.
Critic, December, 1963-January, 1964.
Detroit Free Press, February 28, 1964.
Detroit News, April 2, 1986.
Explicator, December, 1968; May, 1970.
Horn Book Magazine, September-October, 1989.
Library Journal, March 1, 1989.
Milwaukee Sentinel, April 1, 1986.
Nation, September 13, 1958.
National Observer, November 30, 1970.
New York Times, April 2, 1986.
New York Times Book Review, April 16, 1950; July 4, 1954; August 3, 1958; November 11, 1962; May 12, 1963; November 10, 1963; October 4, 1964; November 1, 1964; November 8, 1970; May 4, 1975; November 16, 1975; August 17, 1980.
New York Herald Tribune, November 11, 1962; August 11, 1963.
Newsweek, April 14, 1986.
Poetry, September, 1940; May, 1948; July, 1956; October, 1958; December, 1962; July, 1963; December, 1967; July, 1975.
Prairie Schooner, winter, 1972-73.
Publishers Weekly, June 12, 1987; January 27, 1989.
Saturday Review, January 28, 1956; November 10, 1962; March 23, 1963; December 14, 1963; June 3, 1967; February 6, 1971; May 22, 1971; November 27, 1971; May 31, 1975.
Time, February 18, 1957; February 26, 1979; April 14, 1986.
University of Kansas City Review, autumn, 1949.
Virginia Quarterly Review, winter, 1964; spring, 1965.
Wall Street Journal, May 28, 1971.
Washington Post, April 2, 1986.
Whole Earth Review, spring, 1993.
Woodbridge News Tribune (Woodbridge, NJ), September 25, 1986.
Writer, March, 1964; August, 1976; June, 1980.
Yale Review, March, 1956.

CISNEROS, Sandra 1954-

PERSONAL: Born December 20, 1954, Chicago IL. *Education:* Loyola University, B.A., 1976; University of Iowa Writers' Workshop, M.F.A., 1978.

ADDRESSES: Office—Alfred A. Knopf Books, 201 E. 50th St., New York, NY 10022. *Agent*—Susan Bergholz Literary Services, 17 West 10th St. #5, New York, NY 10011.

CAREER: Writer. Latino Youth Alternative High School, Chicago IL, teacher, 1978-80; Loyala University of Chicago, Chicago, IL, college recruiter and counselor for minority students, 1981-82; Foundation Michael Karolyi, Vence, France, artist in residence, 1983; Guadalupe Cultural Arts Center, San Antonio, TX, literature director, 1984-85; guest professor, California State University, Chico, 1987-88, University of California, Berkeley, 1988, University of California, Irvine, 1990, University of Michigan, Ann Arbor, 1990, and the University of New Mexico, Albuquerque, 1991.

MEMBER: PEN, Mujeres por la paz (member and organizer; a women's peace group).

AWARDS, HONORS: National Endowment for the Arts fellow, 1982, 1988; American Book Award from Before Columbus Foundation, 1985, for *The House on Mango Street*; Paisano Dobie Fellowship, 1986. First and second prize in Segundo Concurso Nacional del Cuento Chicano, sponsored by University of Arizona; Lannan Foundation Literary Award, 1991; H.D.L, State University of New York at Purchase, 1993; MacArthur fellow, 1995.

WRITINGS:

Bad Boys (poems), Mango Publications, 1980.
The House on Mango Street, Arte Publico, 1984.
My Wicked, Wicked Ways (poems), Third Woman Press, 1987.
Woman Hollering Creek and Other Stories (stories), Random House, 1991.
Hairs: Pelitos (juvenile; bilingual), illustrated by Terry Ybanez, Knopf, 1994.
Loose Woman (poems), Knopf, 1994.

Contributor to various periodicals, including *Imagine, Contact II, Glamour, New York Times, Los Angeles Times, Village Voice* and *Revista Chicano-Riquena.*

SIDELIGHTS: With only a handful of poetry and short story collections, Sandra Cisneros has garnered wide critical acclaim as well as popular success. Drawing heavily upon her childhood experiences and ethnic heritage as the daughter of a Mexican father and Chicana mother, Cisneros addresses poverty, cultural suppression, self-identity, and gender roles in her fiction and poetry. She creates characters who are distinctly Latina/o and often isolated from mainstream American culture by emphasizing dialogue and sensory imagery over traditional narrative structures. Best known for *The House on Mango Street,* a volume of loosely structured vignettes that has been classified as both a short story collection and a series of prose poems, Cisneros seeks to create an idiom that integrates both prosaic and poetic syntax. "Cisneros is a quintessentially American writer, unafraid of the sentimental; avoiding the cliches of magical realism, her work bridges the gap between Anglo and Hispanic," remarked Aamer Hussein in the *Times Literary Supplement.*

Born in Chicago, Cisneros was the only daughter among seven children. Concerning her childhood, Cisneros recalled that because her brothers attempted to control her and expected her to assume a traditional female role, she often felt like she had "seven fathers." The family frequently moved between the United States and Mexico because of her father's homesickness for his native country and his devotion to his mother who lived there. Consequently, Cisneros often felt homeless and displaced. She began to read extensively, finding comfort in such works as Virginia Lee Burton's *The Little House* and Lewis Carroll's *Alice's Adventures in Wonderland.* Cisneros periodically wrote poems and stories throughout her childhood and adolescence, but it was not until she attended the University of Iowa's Writers Workshop in the late 1970s that she realized her experiences as a Latina woman were unique and outside the realm of dominant American culture.

Following this realization, Cisneros decided to write about conflicts directly related to her upbringing, including divided cultural loyalties, feelings of alienation, and the degradation associated with poverty. Incorporating these concerns into *The House on Mango Street,* a work that took nearly five years to complete, Cisneros created the character Esperanza, a poor, Latina adolescent who longs for a room of her own and a house of which she can be proud. Esperanza ponders the disadvantages of choosing marriage over education, the importance of writing as an emotional release, and the sense of confusion associated with growing up. In the story "Hips," for example, Esperanza agonizes over the repercussions of her body's physical changes: "One day you wake up and there they are. Ready and waiting like a new Buick with the key in the ignition. Ready to take you where?" Written in what *Booklist* contributor Penelope Mesic called "a loose and deliberately simple style, halfway between a prose poem and the awkwardness of semiliteracy," the pieces in *The House on Mango Street* won praise for their lyrical narratives, vivid dialogue, and powerful descriptions.

Woman Hollering Creek and Other Stories is a collection of twenty-two narratives revolving around numerous Mexican-American characters living near San Antonio, Texas. Ranging from a few paragraphs to several pages, the stories in this volume contain the interior monologues of individuals who have been assimilated into American culture despite their sense of loyalty to Mexico. In "Never Marry a Mexican," for example, a young Latina begins to feel contempt for her white lover because of her emerging feelings of inadequacy and cultural guilt. And in the title story, a Mexican woman deluded by fantasies of a life similar to that found on American soap operas ventures into Texas to marry an American. When she discovers that her husband and marriage share little in common with her dreams, she is forced to reappraise her life.

Reviewers praised the author's vivid characters and distinctive prose. Noting Cisneros's background as a poet, *Los Angeles Times Book Review* contributor Barbara Kingsolver remarked that "Cisneros has added length and dialogue and a hint of plot to her poems and published them in a stunning collection." Kingsolver further stated that "nearly every sentence contains an explosive sensory image," and concludes that Cisneros "takes no prisoners and has not made a single compromise in her language." Writing in *The Nation,* Patricia Hart exclaimed, "Cisneros breathes narrative life into her adroit, poetic descriptions, making them mature, fully formed works of fiction." Hart also commended Cisneros's "range of characters" as "broad and lively." *Time* reviewers Peter S. Prescott and Karen Springen averred, "Noisily, wittily, always compassionately, Cisneros surveys woman's condition—a condition that is both precisely Latina and general to

women everywhere." Similarly, Bebe Moore Campbell, discussing the work in the *New York Times Book Review,* felt that "the author seduces with precise, spare prose and creates unforgettable characters we want to lift off the page and hang out with for a little while." Prescott and Springen agreed that *Woman Hollering Creek* "should make Cisneros's reputation as a major author."

Although Cisneros is noted primarily for her fiction, her poetry has also garnered attention. In *My Wicked Wicked Ways,* published in 1987, Cisneros writes about her native Chicago, her travels in Europe, and, as reflected in the title, sexual guilt resulting from her strict Catholic upbringing. A collection of sixty poems, each of which resemble a short story, this work further evidences Cisneros's penchant for merging various genres. *Bloomsbury Review* critic Gary Soto explained: "Cisneros's poems are intrinsically narrative, but not large, meandering paragraphs. She writes deftly with skill and idea, in the 'show-me-don't-tell-me' vein, and her points leave valuable impressions." Writing in *Belles Lettres,* Andrea Lockett commented, "Particularly alluring here are the daring, perceptive, and sometimes rough-hewn expressions about being a modern woman." In her 1994 poetry collection, *Loose Woman,* Cisneros offers a portrait of a fiercely proud, independent woman of Mexican heritage. "Cisneros probes the extremes of perceptions and negotiates the boundary regions that define the self," remarked Susan Smith Nash in a *World Literature Today* review of the collection. Discussing her poetry with David Mehegan of the *Boston Globe,* Cisneros stated that her poetry "is almost a journal of daily life as woman and writer. I'm always aware of being on the frontier. Even if I'm writing about Paris or Sarajevo, I'm still writing about it from this border position that I was raised in."

In her poetry, as in all her works, Cisneros incorporates Latino dialect, impressionistic metaphors, and social commentary in ways that reveal the fears and doubts unique to Latinas and women in general. She told Mary B. W. Tabor in a *New York Times* interview: "I am a woman and I am a Latina. Those are the things that make my writing distinctive. Those are the things that give my writing power. They are the things that give it *sabor* [flavor], the things that give it *picante* [spice]."

BIOGRAPHICAL/CRITICAL SOURCES:

BOOKS

Chesla, Elizabeth L., *Sandra Cisneros' "The House on Mango Street,"* Research & Education Association (Piscataway, NJ), 1996.
Contemporary Literary Criticism, Volume 69, Gale, 1992.
Dictionary of Literary Biography, Volume 152: *American Novelists Since World War II, Fourth Series,* Gale, 1995.

PERIODICALS

America, July 18, 1992, p. 39.
Americas Review, spring, 1987, pp. 69-76.
Belles Lettres, summer, 1993, p. 51; spring, 1995, p. 62.
Bloomsbury Review, July-August, 1988, p. 21.
Boston Globe, May 17, 1994, p. 73.
Chicago Tribune, November 19, 1992, section 5, p. 8; December 20, 1992, section 2, p. 1.
Christian Science Monitor, March 12, 1993, p. 12.
Glamour, November, 1990, pp. 256-57.
Horn Book, November-December, 1994, p. 716.
Library Journal, May 15, 1994, p. 76.
Los Angeles Times, May 7, 1991, p. F1.
Los Angeles Times Book Review, April 28, 1991, p. 3.
Mirabella, April, 1991, p. 46.

Nation, May 6, 1991, p. 597.
Newsweek, June 3, 1991, p. 60.
New York Times, January 7, 1993, p. C10.
New York Times Book Review, May 26, 1991, p. 6.
Publishers Weekly, March 29, 1991, pp. 74-5; April 25, 1994, p. 61.
Quill & Quire, May, 1991, p. 30.
Revista Chicano-Riquena, fall-winter, 1985, pp. 109-19.
School Library Journal, August, 1994, p. 181.
Times Literary Supplement, August 13, 1993, p. 18.
Washington Post Book World, June 9, 1991, p. 3.
World Literature Today, winter, 1995, p. 145.

*   *   *

CIXOUS, Helene 1937-

PERSONAL: Surname is pronounced "Seek-sue"; born June 5, 1937, in Oran, Algeria; daughter of Georges (a physician) and Eva (a midwife; maiden name, Klein) Cixous; married, 1955 (divorced, 1964); children: Anne Berger, Pierre- Francois Berger. *Education:* Received Agregation d'Anglais, 1959, and Docteur es Lettres, 1968.

ADDRESSES: Office—Universite de Paris VIII, 2 rue de la Liberte, 93526 St. Denis Cedex 02, France; Editions des Femmes, 6 rue de Mezieres, 75006, Paris, France.

CAREER: University of Bordeaux, Bordeaux, France, assistante, 1962-65; University of Paris (Sorbonne), Paris, France, maitre assistante, 1965-67; University of Paris X (Nanterre), Nanterre, France, maitre de conference, 1967-68; helped found the university's experimental University of Paris VIII (Vincennes, then St. Denis), France, 1968, professor of English literature, 1968–, founder and director of Centre de Recherches en Etudes Feminines and doctoral program in women's studies, 1974–; cofounder of *Revue de Theorie et d'Analyse Litteraire: Poetique* in 1969. Visiting professor and lecturer at numerous universities, including Columbia University, Cornell University, Dartmouth College, Harvard University, New York University, Northwestern University, State University of New York at Binghamton and Buffalo, Swarthmore Universitiy, University of Wisconsin at Madison, University of California at Berkeley, and universities in Austria, Canada, Denmark, England, Greece, India, Italy, Japan, Norway, Tunisia, and Spain.

AWARDS, HONORS: Prix Medicis, 1969, for *Dedans*; Southern Cross of Brazil, 1989; Legion d'Honneur, 1994; Prix des Critiques for best theatrical work, 1994, for *La Ville parjure, ou le reveil des Erinyes*; Doctor Honoris Causa, Queen's University, Canada, 1991, Edmonton University, Canada, 1992, York University, England, 1993, Georgetown University, 1995, and Northwestern University, 1996.

WRITINGS:

FICTION

Le Prenom de Dieu (stories), Grasset et Fasquelle (Paris), 1967.
Dedans, Grasset et Fasquelle, 1969, 2nd edition, Des Femmes, 1986, translation by Carol Barko published as *Inside,* Schocken (New York City), 1986.
Le Troisieme Corps, Grasset et Fasquelle, 1970.
Les Commencements, Grasset et Fasquelle, 1970.
Un Vrai Jardin (poetic short story), L'Herne, 1971.
Neutre, Grasset et Fasquelle, 1972, translated by Lorene M. Birden in M.A. thesis, "Making English Clairielle: An Introduction and Translation for Helene Cixous' 'Neutre,'" University of Massachusetts Press, 1988.
Portrait du soleil, Denoel, 1973.
Tombe, Seuil, 1973.
Revolutions pour plus d'un Faust, Seuil, 1975.
Souffles, Femmes (Paris), 1975.
La, Gallimard (Paris), 1976, 2nd edition, Des Femmes, 1979.
Partie, Femmes, 1976.
Angst, Femmes, 1977, translation by Jo Levy published as *Angst,* Riverrun Press (New York City), 1985.
Preparatifs de noces au dela de l'abime, Femmes, 1978.
Ananke, Femmes, c. 1979.
Vivre l'orange/To Live the Orange (bilingual edition), English translation by Ann Liddle and Sarah Cornell, Femmes, 1979.
Illa, Femmes, 1980.
With ou, L'Art de l'innocence, Femmes, 1981.
Limonade tout etait si infini, Femmes, 1982.
Le Livre de Promethea, Gallimard, 1983, translation by Betsy Wing published as *The Book of Promethea,* University of Nebraska Press (Lincoln), 1991.
La Bataille d'Arcachon (tale), Trois (Laval, Quebec), 1986.
Manne aux Mandelstams aux Mandelas, Femmes, 1988, translation by Catherine A. F. MacGillivray published as *Manna: For the Mandelstams for the Mandelas,* University of Minnesota Press, 1993.
Jours de l'an, Femmes, 1990, translated by Catherine A. F. MacGillivray as *First Days of the Year,* University of Minnesota Press (Minneapolis), 1997.
L'ange au secret, Femmes, 1991.
Deluge, Femmes, 1992.
Beethoven a jamais, ou, L'existence de Dieu, Femmes, 1993.
La Fiancee juive ou de la tentation Femmes, 1995.
Messie, Femmes, 1996.

Author of manifesto "Le Rida de la Meduse" (title means "The Laugh of the Medusa"). Work represented in anthologies, including *New French Feminisms,* edited by Elaine Marks and Isabelle de Courtivron, University of Massachusetts Press (Amherst), 1980, and *The Future of Literary Theory,* edited by Ralph Cohen, 1987, *The Helene Cixous Reader,* Routledge (New York City), 1994. Contributor to numerous periodicals.

ESSAYS

L'Exil de James Joyce; ou, L'Art du remplacement (doctoral thesis), Grasset et Fasquelle, 1968, translation by Sally A. J. Purcell published as *The Exile of James Joyce,* D. Lewis (New York City), 1972.
Prenoms de personne (essays), Seuil, 1974.
(With Catherine Clement) *La Jeune Nee* (essay), Union Generale d'Editions, 1975, translation by Betsy Wing published as *The Newly Born Woman,* with introduction by Sandra M. Gilbert, University of Minnesota Press, 1986.
Un K incomprehensible: Pierre Goldman, Bourgois, 1975.
(With Madeleine Gagnon and Annie Leclerc) *La Venue a l'ecriture* (essay), Union Generale d'Editions, c. 1977.
Entre l'ecriture (essays) Femmes, c. 1986.
L'heure de Clarice Lispector: Precede de Vivre l'orange (literary criticism), Femmes, 1989.
Reading with Clarice Lispector, translated, edited, and with an introduction by Verena Andermatt Conley, University of Minnesota Press, 1990.
"Coming to Writing" and Other Essays, translated by Sarah Cornell and others, Harvard University Press (Cambridge, MA), 1991.

Readings: The Poetics of Blanchot, Joyce, Kafka, Kleist, Lispector, and Tsvetaeva (literary criticism), translated, edited, and with an introduction by Verena Andermatt Conley, University of Minnesota Press, 1992.

Three Steps on the Ladder of Writing (lectures), translation by Sarah Cornell and Susan Sellers, Columbia University Press (New York City), 1993.

(With Mireille Calle-Gruber) *Helene Cixous, Photos de racines,* Femmes, 1994, translation by Eric Prenowitz published as *Helene Cixous, Rootprints,* Routledge (London), 1997.

PLAYS

La Pupille, Gallimard, 1972.

Portrait de Dora, produced in Paris, 1976, Femmes, 1976, translation by Anita Barrow published as *Portrait of Dora,* in *Benmussa Directs,* Riverrun Press, 1979.

La Prise de l'Ecole de Madhubai, produced in Paris, 1983, translation by Deborah Carpenter as *The Conquest of the School at Madhubai* in *Women and Performance 3,* 1986.

L'Histoire terrible mais inachevee de Norodom Sihanouk, roi du Cambodge, first produced at Theatre du Soleil, 1985, translation by Juliet Flower MacCannell and others published as *The Terrible but Unfinished Story of Norodom Sihanouk, King of Cambodia,* University of Nebraska Press, 1994.

L'Indiade; ou, L'Inde de leurs reves, first produced at Theatre du Soleil, September, 1987.

On ne part pas, on ne revient pas, Femmes, 1991.

Translation and introduction, *Les Eumenides d'Eschyle,* produced in Paris, 1992, Theatre du Soleil, 1992.

La Ville parjure ou le reveil des Erinyes, produced in Paris, 1994), Theatre du Soleil, 1994, translation by Bernadette Fort.

Voile Noir Voile Blanche/Black Sail White Sail (bilingual; English translation by Catherine A. F. MacGillivray), produced in London, 1994, New Literary History (Minnesota), 1994.

L'histoire qu'on ne connaitra jamis, produced in Paris, Femmes, 1994.

Also author of teleplay with Ariane Mnouchkine, *La Nuit miraculeuse,* 1989, and author of radio play *Amour d'une delicatesse,* 1982.

OTHER

Le Nom d'Oedipe: Chant du corps interdit (libretto), music by Andre Boucourechliev, Femmes, 1978, translation by Christiane Makward and Judith Miller as *The Name of Oedipus* in *Out of Bounds: Women's Theatre in French* University of Michigan Press, 1991.

Theatre (collection), Femmes, 1986.

SIDELIGHTS: Helene Cixous, a professor at the University of Paris and the founder and director of France's only doctoral program in women's studies, was the winner of the 1969 Prix Medicis for her first novel, *Dedans,* translated in 1986 as *Inside. La Jeune Nee,* which she wrote in 1976 with Catherine Clement and which was translated ten years later as *The Newly Born Woman,* was deemed a "ground-breaking feminist tract" by the *New York Times Book Review.* Cixous also received wide acclaim for her doctoral thesis, published in 1968 as *L'Exil de James Joyce; ou, L'Art du remplacement* and translated in 1972 as *The Exile of James Joyce.* Although she supports and writes women's literature, Cixous told *Contemporary Authors* she does not use the label "feminist" because of the politically restrictive and unanalyzed overtones the term has taken on within the French context. She related to Stella Hughes, contributor to *Times Higher Education Supplement,* "'Feminist' has an extremely precise

meaning: It is a reformist demand in terms of equality and not at all in terms of difference." Cixous prefers the concept and the practice of what she calls the "poetics of sexual difference," and is one of the best-known and most influential advocates of *ecriture feminine,* or feminine writing—a form that she stresses may include works by both male and female writers. "This writing is dedicated to exploding the binary oppositions on which Western thinking rests," explained Marianne Hirsch in the *New York Times Book Review,* "which relegate woman to the side of silence, of otherness."

Cixous, like other French feminist writers, emphasizes "the place of 'woman' in language and the question of a feminine relation to language that [has] relatively little currency within Anglophone feminist thought," explained translator Annette Kuhn in *Signs.* Some critics find Cixous's writings an attempt to negate the male/female distinction through puns and word manipulations. But Cixous explained to *Contemporary Authors* that her aim is to defuse the violence of fixed sexual hierachy, without negating the infinite richness of sexual difference, by engaging all the resources of language, subverting standard usages or pushing them further than their conventionally fixed forms allow. Cixous contends she plays with the apparent rigidity of the grammatical gender that marks the French language, which, unlike English, has "masculine" and "feminine" words. Her aim is not to replace one rigid linguistic system with another, in a reformist shuffle, but rather to use the possibilities of language to take us beyond our own self-imposed boundaries.

The English translation of Cixous's award-winning first novel, *Dedans,* was published as *Inside* in 1986, seventeen years after the original French edition appeared. The highly metaphoric work is commonly regarded as an autobiography, although the author did not introduce the book as such. The main character, like Cixous, was born of a North African Jewish father and a German Jewish mother and was raised in Algeria. The novel depicts the daughter's intense love for her father and the grief she suffers when he dies young, as Cixous's father had. "It dwells on a sense of enclosure and entrapment," Hirsch described. "The nameless narrator . . . is inside a family romance where her father is God, the owner of all the words, and where her German-speaking mother offers no access to knowledge." After her father dies, the daughter imagines his death ceaselessly, trying to understand it. Finally, related Hirsch, "she gains the means to write from [her father's] overwhelming bodily closeness and from his empowering mental gifts in life."

Some feminists have decried the importance of the father's role in *Inside* as defeating the purpose of feminism, and a *Kirkus Reviews* critic deemed the "densely compact philosophical narrative" simply "intellectual passion from the school of radical French narrative, by turns brilliant and boring." Hirsch, however, offered high praise for the "series of reflections on identity, death and writing." The reviewer noted that *Inside* was timely as well as poignant, calling it a "moving and disturbing experimental work written at the moment of emergence of feminist consciousness— both for the author herself and for a broader intellectual and political movement whose important representative she would become."

Cixous maintains her "special and elusive style" in *Angst,* according to Lorna Sage in the *Observer.* The novel, first published in 1977, was translated into English in 1985. "The writing is dense, direct, often lurid with metaphor as it records a woman's reflections on her life and her attempt to create mental order out of the chaos she finds," wrote Sage. Nicole Irving in *Times Literary Supplement* praised Cixous's innovative prose style as well as the "loving" translation by Jo Levy, despite calling much of the book "incomprehensible": "[Cixous's] text has a rhythmic pattern, moving from obscurity to relative clarity, from the bodily (erotic and otherwise) to the sometimes punning metaphysical, from violence to calm and occasional tenderness, and at the end, 'she' [the main character] reaches a wholeness." As Sage observed: "The writing is alive even at its oddest."

Like Hirsch and Schneider, Olga Prjevalinskaya Ferrer observed in her *World Literature Today* review of *Partie* that "Helene Cixous's works most certainly voice a protest against the very strict rules of French intellectual thought and its expression through speech and writing." Perhaps as a protest against even the traditional appearance of books, Ferrer speculated, Cixous presented the work as a wide book divided into two sections, each upside down in relation to the other, with pages meeting in the middle of the volume. Commenting on the difficulty of classifying *Partie* in terms of genre, Ferrer stated: "Though [Cixous's] writings are, most of the time, poetic, her originality and freedom have surpassed any poetic thought, any poetic trends." The author's freedom of expression, the reviewer asserted, provides *Partie* "an enchanting depth."

With ou, L'Art de l'innocence is likewise about woman's multiplicity. "Cixous's sinuous prose poem is a conversation between various aspects of her person," explained Rosette C. Lamont in *World Literature Today*. Although the author's various selves are disparate, Lamont observed, "the many voices of Cixous's novel-poem blend into a single interrogation about freedom, a multilingual existence in *l'ecriture* and the mystery of being woman."

Even though the feminist movement that brought Cixous to the fore lost momentum through the late 1980s and into the 1990s, she continued to strengthen her reputation as a highly inventive writer. Her publications included literary criticism, dramas, essays, and books that many reviewers consider unclassifiable. *Modern Language Review* contributor Clare Hanson commented on Cixous's *Reading with Clarice Lispector,* an analysis of the Latin American author: "Cixous's approach to Lispector mirrors that capacity to mark difference without recourse to binary, hierarchical oppositions which distinguishes Lispector's texts. . . . What emerges is a reading . . . which is both powerful and delicate, in which Cixous holds in balance her own theoretical sophistication and the different economies, drives, and trajectories of Lispector's texts." Cixous discussed her own writing, and more, in her 1991 publication *L'ange au secret.* Patricia M. Gathercole stated in *World Literature Today* that the book contained "observations about human life and [Cixous's] own struggles in writing a book. . . . The volume is . . . written in a highly imaginative style . . . [and] offers a powerful account of her own feelings and thoughts, her reflections on her identity as a writer."

On ne part pas, on ne revient pas was also published in 1991. *World Literature Today* reviewer Bettina L. Knapp believed that it was "perhaps one of Helen Cixous's finest and most powerful works. . . . [It] deals with death, love, sorrow, escape, violence—and music. As is true of many of Cixous's writings, it may be read on many levels. The work is a drama written in free verse, cadenced and stressed in keeping with the magma of sought-for meanings." *Three Steps on the Ladder of Writing* was yet another book published by Cixous in 1991; it contained the text of a lecture series she delivered at the University of California at

Irvine. In an introduction to one of these lectures, Jacques Derrida comments: "Helene Cixous is today, in my view, the greatest writer in what I will call my language, the French language if you like. And I am weighing my words as I say that. For a great writer must be a poet-thinker, very much a poet and a very thinking poet."

In 1993, Cixous reached a new level of creativity, according to Pamela A. Genova. Reviewing *Beethoven a jamais, ou, L'existence de Dieu* for *World Literature Today,* Genova marvelled at Cixous's skill in weaving together many styles of writing. ". . . *Beethoven a jamais* combines elements from several styles of writing, weaving together such forms as free verse, interior monologue, spoken dialogue, and third-person narrative prose. . . . This experimentation seems appropriate in a book whose central personality is that of Beethoven, present in all his forms: the man, the musical genius, the lover. Instead of merely describing the life or work of Beethoven, Cixous constructs a textual framework that reflects his talent and stands as a hymn to Beethoven and his music."

"Cixous tells us that she always wished she were a painter, and that this accounts for the way she writes," mused Peter Baker in an *American Book Review* piece on Cixous's *"Coming to Writing" and Other Essays.* "Somehow she manages to paint with words in such a way as actually to bring about an insight into what this might mean. Like the mimosa, which overwhelms the senses but recedes, sensitive to the touch, Cixous overwhelms the written word with layers of thought and sense-description, while withdrawing any possible center or point. As she says: 'And the lesson is: one does not paint ideas. One does not paint "a subject." And in the same way: no writing ideas. There is no subject. There are only mysteries.'"

BIOGRAPHICAL/CRITICAL SOURCES:

BOOKS

Calle-Gruber, Mireille, editor, *On the Feminine,* Humanities Press (Atlantic Highlands, NJ), 1996.
Conley, Verena Andermatt, *Writing the Feminine,* University of Nebraska Press (Lincoln), 1984, expanded edition, 1991.
Conley, *Helene Cixous,* University of Toronto Press (Toronto), 1992.
Contemporary Authors, Volume 126, Gale, 1989.
Dictionary of Literary Biography, Volume 83: *French Novelists since 1960,* Gale (Detroit), 1989, pp. 52-61.
Gelfland, Elissa, and Virginia Hules, editors, *French Feminist Criticism: Women, Language, and Literature,* Garland Publishing (New York City), 1985.
Kim, C. W. Maggie, and others, editors, *Transfigurations: Theology and the French Feminists,* Fortress Press (Minneapolis), 1993.
Moi, Toril, *Sexual/Textual Politics: Feminist Literary Theory,* Methuen (New York City), 1985.
Nordquist, Joan, *French Feminist Theory: Luce Irigaray and Helene Cixous: A Bibliography,* Reference and Research Services (Santa Cruz, CA), 1990.
Penrod, Lynn, *Helene Cixous,* Twayne (New York City), 1996.
Sellers, Susan, *Helene Cixous: Authorship, Autobiography, and Love,* Blackwell (Cambridge, MA), 1996.
Shiach, Morag, *Helene Cixous: A Politics of Writing,* Routledge (London), 1991.
Stambolian, George, and Elaine Marks, editors, *Homosexuality and French Literature,* Cornell University Press (Ithaca, NY), 1979.

Wilcox, Helen, editor, *The Body and the Text: Helene Cixous*, St. Martin's (New York City), 1990.

PERIODICALS

American Book Review, June-July, 1992, pp. 16, 18-19.
Contemporary Literature, summer, 1983.
Kirkus Reviews, September 1, 1986.
Library Journal, June 15, 1993, p. 19; June 1, 1994, p. 106.
Modern Language Review, October, 1993, pp. 934-36.
New York Times, June 8, 1994, p. C13.
New York Times Book Review, February 11, 1973; August 24, 1986; December 7, 1986.
Observer, January 12, 1986; April 3, 1994, p. 22.
Publishers Weekly, March 21, 1994, pp. 55-6.
Signs, autumn, 1981.
Theatre Journal, March, 1994, pp. 31-44.
Times Literary Supplement, April 24, 1969; February 12, 1971; March 21, 1986; January 31, 1992, p. 24; December 24, 1993, p. 18.
Triquarterly, fall, 1997, pp. 259-79.
Women's Review, May, 1985.
World Literature Today, winter, 1977; spring, 1977; summer, 1977; spring, 1981; summer, 1982; winter, 1984; summer, 1992, p. 482; winter, 1993, pp. 148-49; winter, 1994, p. 76.

*   *   *

CLANCY, Thomas L. 1947-
(Tom Clancy)

PERSONAL: Born in 1947 in Baltimore, MD; son of a mail carrier and a credit employee; married Wanda Thomas (an insurance agency manager) in August, 1969; children: Michelle, Christine, Tom, Kathleen. *Education:* Graduated from Loyola College, Baltimore, MD, 1969. *Politics:* Conservative. *Religion:* Roman Catholic.

ADDRESSES: Home—P.O. Box 800, Huntingtown, MD 20639-0800. *Agent*—c/o Putnam, 200 Madison Ave., New York, NY 10016.

CAREER: Insurance agent in Baltimore, MD, and Hartford, CT, until 1973; O. F. Bowen Agency (insurance company), Owings, MD, agent, beginning in 1973, owner, beginning in 1980; writer. *Military service:* U.S. Army Reserve Officers Training Corps.

WRITINGS:

NOVELS; UNDER NAME TOM CLANCY

The Hunt for Red October, Naval Institute Press, 1984.
Red Storm Rising, Putnam (New York City), 1986.
Patriot Games, Putnam, 1987.
The Cardinal of the Kremlin, Putnam, 1988.
Clear and Present Danger, Putnam, 1989.
The Sum of All Fears, Putnam, 1991.
Patriot Games (film version), Berkley (New York City), 1992.
Red Storm Rising; The Cardinal of the Kremlin: Two Complete Novels, Putnam, 1993.
Submarine, Berkley, 1993.
Without Remorse, Putnam, 1994.
Debt of Honor, Putnam, 1994.
Three Complete Novels: Patriot Games, Clear and Present Danger, The Sum of All Fears, Putnam, 1994.
Executive Orders, Putnam, 1996.

NONFICTION

Armed Cav: A Guided Tour of an Armored Calvary Regiment, Putnam, 1994.
Fighter Wing: A Guided Tour of an Air Force Combat Wing, Berkley, 1995.
Marine: A Guided Tour of a Marine Expeditionary Unit, Berkley, 1996.
Into the Storm: A Study in Command, Putnam, 1997.
Reality Check: What's Going on Out There? Putnam, 1997.
(With Martin Harry Greenberg and Roland J. Green, editors) *The Tom Clancy Companion,* Berkley Books (New York City), 1992.

Also author of foreword to *Silent Chase: Submarines of the U.S. Navy,* by Steve Kaufman, Thomasson-Grant, 1989.

MEDIA ADAPTATIONS: The Hunt for Red October was adapted as a film for Paramount, directed by John McTiernan and starring Sean Connery and Alec Baldwin, 1990; *Patriot Games* was adapted as a film for Paramount, directed by Phillip Noyce and starring Harrison Ford and Anne Archer, 1992; *Clear and Present Danger* was adapted as a film for Paramount, directed by Phillip Noyce and starring Harrison Ford and Willem Dafoe, 1994.

SIDELIGHTS: Known for hugely successful, detailed novels about espionage, the military, and advanced military technology, Tom Clancy was proclaimed "king of the techno-thriller" by Patrick Anderson in the *New York Times Magazine.* Since the 1984 publication of his first novel, the acclaimed *Hunt for Red October,* all of his books have become best-sellers. Rich Cohen wrote in *Rolling Stone,* "Indeed, Clancy seems to have saturated the national consciousness, creating a new American style, a hybrid of rugged individualism and high technology." Popular with armed forces personnel as well as the public, they have garnered praise from such prominent figures as former President Ronald Reagan and Secretary of Defense Caspar Weinberger. Clancy's work has also received more negative attention from officials who found his extrapolations from declassified information uncomfortably close to the top-secret reality and from reviewers who criticized his characterizations and too-perfect weaponry. Still, sales in the millions and constant best-seller status attest to his continued popularity as "novelist laureate of the military-industrial complex," as Ross Thomas described him in the *Washington Post Book World.*

The Hunt for Red October, which describes the race between U.S. and Soviet forces to get their hands on a defecting Russian submarine captain and his state-of-the-art vessel, marked a number of firsts. It was a first novel for both its author and its publisher, Naval Institute Press, whose catalogue had previously consisted of scholarly and strategic works and the occasional collection of short stories or poems about the sea. It was the first best-seller for both parties as well, and it became the first of Clancy's books to be made into a motion picture. Conceived before the author, an insurance agent, had ever set foot on a submarine, it is "a tremendously enjoyable and gripping novel of naval derring-do," according to *Washington Post Book World* critic Reid Beddow. The book contains descriptions of high-tech military hardware so advanced that former Navy Secretary John Lehman, quoted in *Time,* joked that he "would have had [Clancy] court-martialed: the book revealed that much that had been classified about antisubmarine warfare. Of course, nobody for a moment suspected him of getting access to classified information." The details were actually based on unclassified books and naval documents, Clancy's interviews with submariners, and his own educated guesses, the author asserts. Admitting that "neither characterization nor dialogue are strong weapons in Clancy's literary arsenal," Richard Setlowe in the *Los Angeles Times Book Review* nonetheless expressed an opinion shared by other reviewers: "At his best, Clancy has a terrific talent for taking the arcana of U.S. and Soviet submarine warfare, the subtleties of sonar and the techno-babble of nuclear power plants and transforming them into taut drama."

In Clancy's second novel, *Red Storm Rising,* U.S.-Soviet conflict escalates to a non-nuclear World War III. Crippled by a Moslem terrorist attack on a major Siberian oil refinery, the Soviet Union plots to defeat the countries in the North Atlantic Treaty Organization (NATO) so that it can dominate oil-rich Arab nations unhindered. The novel covers military action on land and in the air as well as on submarines; its complicated narrative prompted *Chicago Tribune Book World* reviewer Douglas Balz to note that Clancy's "skill with the plot . . . is his real strength." Balz and other critics faulted Clancy's characterization, although in the *New York Times Book Review* Robert Lekachman deemed the problem irrelevant to the book's merits as a "rattling good yarn" with "lots of action" and the "comforting certainty that our side will win." John Keegan, writing in the *Washington Post Book World,* called *Red Storm Rising* "a brilliant military fantasy—and far too close to reality for comfort."

Patriot Games, Clancy's third book, tells how former Marine officer Jack Ryan, a key figure in *The Hunt for Red October,* places himself between a particularly fanatical branch of the Irish Republican Army and the British royal family. Several reviewers criticized it for lack of credibility, lags in the action, simplistic moral lines, and, again, poor characterization, conceding nevertheless that it should appeal to fans of the earlier books. Anderson voiced another perspective: "*Patriot Games* is a powerful piece of popular fiction; its plot, if implausible, is irresistible, and its emotions are universal." Pointing out Clancy's authentic detail, powerful suspense, and relevance to current history, James Idema suggested in a *Tribune Books* review that "most readers [will] find the story preposterous yet thoroughly enjoyable."

Ryan appears again in *The Cardinal of the Kremlin,* which returns to the theme of conflict between the United States and the Soviet Union. In this episode, regarded by critics such as Lekachman as "by far the best of the Jack Ryan series" to date, Clancy focuses on the controversial laser-satellite "strategic defense systems" also known as "Star Wars." According to Lekachman: "The adventure . . . is of high quality. And while [Clancy's] prose is no better than workmanlike . . . , the unmasking of the title's secret agent, the Cardinal, is as sophisticated an exercise in the craft of espionage as I have yet to encounter." Remarked *Fortune* contributor Andrew Ferguson, Clancy "aims not only to entertain but also to let his readers in on the 'inside story,' meanwhile discussing with relish the strategic and technological issues of war and peace." Concluded Ferguson, "It is refreshing to find a member of the literati who is willing to deal with [defense policy] in a manner more sophisticated than signing the latest disarmament petition in the *New York Times.*"

In *Clear and Present Danger* Ryan, in league with the Central Intelligence Agency (CIA), joins the fight against the powerful South American organizations that supply illegal drugs to the U.S. market. After the director of the Federal Bureau of Investigation (FBI) is murdered on a trip to Colombia, the fight becomes a covert war, with foot soldiers and fighter planes unleashed on virtually any target suspected of drug involvement. Reviewing the

novel in the *Wall Street Journal,* former Assistant Secretary of State Elliott Abrams wrote, "What helps to make *Clear and Present Danger* such compelling reading is a fairly sophisticated view of Latin politics combined with Mr. Clancy's patented, tautly shaped scenes, fleshed out with colorful technical data and tough talk." Abrams commended Clancy's awareness of the ethical dilemmas that complicate such covert military operations. Some reviewers echoed earlier criticisms of Clancy's characterizations, his focus on technology, and his prose style, but, noted Evan Thomas in *Newsweek,* "it doesn't really matter if his characters are two dimensional and his machines are too perfect. He whirls them through a half dozen converging subplots until they collide in a satisfyingly slam-bang finale." Thomas called the book "Clancy's best thriller since his first" and "a surprisingly successful cautionary tale."

Patrick O'Brian commented in the *Washington Post Book World* that *The Sum of All Fears* "is about four times the length of the usual novel and deals with at least four times the usual number of themes." In the novel, Jack Ryan is deputy director of the CIA, a Middle East peacemaker, and out of favor with the White House. Not all of the factions accept the peace he negotiates. Palestinian terrorists and other radicals obtain a nuclear weapon that they explode at the Super Bowl, hoping to cause an all-out war between the United States and the Soviet Union. "The scenes of deployment and nuclear hell at the Super Bowl are truly chilling," wrote Les Standford in his review of the novel in the Chicago *Tribune Books.* Standford added, "And Ryan's subsequent attempts to calm a crackpot president and avert a global nuclear war are harrowing. It's just a shame we couldn't get to the plot a bit sooner." Morton Kondracke remarked in *The New York Times Book Review* that "it's [one] of Mr. Clancy's gifts that he can keep several sub-plots and sub-sub-plots in the air at the same time. In this book he has outdone himself."

In *Without Remorse,* former Navy SEAL John Kelly becomes somewhat of a vigilante, tracking down and killing the drug-smuggling pimps who are after the prostitute he has befriended following the deaths of his wife and unborn child. In addition, the U.S. government dispatches him on a special mission to Vietnam to liberate POWs. In *Washington Post Book World* Marie Arana-Ward declared, "What Clancy manages to deliver to us armchair warriors . . . is a different kind of virtuosity: a meticulous chronicle of military hardware, a confident stride through corridors of power, an honest-to-God global war game, and a vertiginous plot that dutifully tracks dozens of seemingly disparate strands to a pyrotechnic finish." Gene Lyons, writing in *Entertainment Weekly,* commented, "given his turgid style and psychological absurdities, Clancy still knows how to tell a tale, and millions of would-be warriors who make up his loyal readership will no doubt find themselves thrilled to their toes."

The plot of *Debt of Honor* emanates from a Japanese financier who blames the United States for his parents' deaths during World War II and seeks revenge in the economic markets and through military means. Jack Ryan, White House national security adviser, becomes vice president as a result of the way he handles the crisis, and ascends to the presidency when a Japanese airman hits the Capitol with a Boeing 747. *Los Angeles Times Book Review* contributor John Calvin Batchelor remarked, "Clancy's passion is overwhelming. His sense of cliffhanging is state of the art. The close of this book is a five-run homer." *Executive Orders* picks up where *Debt of Honor* concludes—with Jack Ryan facing the burden of running a government whose power holders are now dead. He also is being assailed by domestic and foreign political and military challenges. "Clancy stacks up the enemies and would-be assassins like thrill-seekers waiting to ride the next roller coaster," noted Jason Zappa in *The Weekly Tribune Plus*. Of the weighty ninth Clancy novel, Gina Bellafante said in *Time* that it "is another doozy of laborious plot, bombastic jingoism and tedious detail."

Op-Center is a briefer yet still complex Clancy novel. In the novel, Paul Hood is the director of a new U.S. intelligence agency that must investigate the implications of a terrorist bombing at a celebration in Seoul, South Korea.

Unprecedented knowledge of military technology, plots of rousing adventure and taut suspense, and themes that address current international concerns have combined to make Clancy "one of the most popular authors in the country," in the estimation of *Washington Post Book World* writer David Streitfeld. He is so well liked by military personnel, in particular, that he has been invited to military bases and given tours of ships; reported Evan Thomas in *Newsweek*, "Bluntly put, the Navy realized that Clancy was good for business." Cohen drew the similarities between Clancy and his popular character Jack Ryan. He wrote, "In a way, Tom Clancy has become Jack Ryan: He lectures at the FBI; he dines at the White House; he has been asked on numerous occasions to run for public office; he gives his thoughts on world affairs; he hosts fund-raisers for his friend Oliver North; he attends meetings at the CIA; and like his friends there, he seems almost comically obsessed with leaks and the flow of information." Some critics even credit the author with helping to banish the negative opinion of the military that arose after the United States's controversial involvement in the Vietnam War.

As for criticism of his work, Clancy admitted in a *Washington Post* article: "I'm not that good a writer. I do a good action scene. I handle technology well. I like to think that I do a fair—fairer—job of representing the kind of people we have in the Navy . . . portraying them the way they really are. Beyond that, I'll try to . . . improve what needs improving." The secrets of his success as an entertainer, concluded Anderson, are "a genius for big, compelling plots, a passion for research, a natural narrative gift, a solid prose style, a hyperactive . . . imagination and a blissfully uncomplicated view of human nature and international affairs."

BIOGRAPHICAL/CRITICAL SOURCES:

BOOKS

Contemporary Literary Criticism, Volume 45, Gale, 1987.
Garson, Helen S., *Tom Clancy: A Critical Companion*, Greenwood Press (Westport, CT), 1996.

PERIODICALS

American Legion, December, 1991, p. 16.
Chicago Tribune Book World, September 7, 1986.
Detroit News, January 20, 1985.
Economist, March 17, 1990, p. 87.
Entertainment Weekly, August 6, 1993, pp. 50-1.
Fortune, July 18, 1988; August 26, 1991.
Globe and Mail (Toronto), September 2, 1989.
Kliatt, November, 1995, p. 6.
Los Angeles Times, July 16, 1989.
Los Angeles Times Book Review, December 9, 1984; July 26, 1987; August 21, 1994, pp. 1, 9.
Magazine of Fantasy and Science Fiction, December, 1991, p. 73.
National Review, April 29, 1988.
Newsweek, August 17, 1987; August 8, 1988; August 21, 1989.
New Yorker, September 16, 1991, p. 91.

New York Times, July 17, 1986; August 12, 1986; February 25, 1990; March 1, 1990.
New York Times Book Review, July 27, 1986; August 2, 1987; July 31, 1988; August 13, 1989; July 28, 1991, pp. 9-10; August 22, 1993, pp. 13-14; October 2, 1994, pp. 28-9.
New York Times Magazine, May 1, 1988.
People, September 8, 1986; September 12, 1988; September 5, 1994, p. 34.
Publishers Weekly, August 8, 1986; July 1, 1988; July 25, 1994, pp. 34-5; August 5, 1996, p. 433.
Rolling Stone, December 1, 1994, p. 114.
School Library Journal, June, 1995, p. 143.
Saturday Evening Post, September-October, 1991, p. 16.
Time, March 4, 1985; August 11, 1986; August 24, 1987; July 25, 1988; August 21, 1989; March 5, 1990; March 12, 1990; September 2, 1996, p. 61.
Tribune Books (Chicago), July 5, 1987; August 11, 1991, p. 7.
Wall Street Journal, October 22, 1984; August 16, 1989.
Washington Post, January 29, 1985; March 17, 1989; March 2, 1990; August 8, 1993, pp. 1, 14.
Washington Post Book World, October 21, 1984; July 27, 1986; May 14, 1989; August 13, 1989; July 28, 1991, pp. 1-2.
Weekly Tribune Plus, September 16, 1994, p. 8.
West Coast Review of Books, November-December, 1984.
Writer's Digest, October, 1987.

*   *   *

CLANCY, Tom
See CLANCY, Thomas L.

*   *   *

CLARK, Curt
See WESTLAKE, Donald E(dwin)

*   *   *

CLARK (BEKEDEREMO), J(ohn) P(epper) 1935-

PERSONAL: Real name John Pepper Clark Bekederemo. Born April 6, 1935, in Kiagbodo, Nigeria; son of Clark Fuludu and Poro Clark Bekederemo. *Education:* University of Ibadan, B.A. (with honors), 1960.

ADDRESSES: Office—PEC Repertory Theatre, J. K. Randle Hall, King George V Rd., Onikan, Lagos, Nigeria. *Agent*—Andrew Best, Curtis Brown Ltd., 162-168 Regent St., London W1R 5TB, England.

CAREER: Nigerian federal government, information officer, 1960-61; *Daily Express*, Lagos, Nigeria, head of features and editorial writer, 1961-62; University of Lagos, Lagos, research fellow, 1964-66, professor of African literature and instructor in English, 1966-. Poet, playwright, and filmmaker; founding editor of *Horn* magazine, Ibadan, Nigeria.

MEMBER: Society of Nigerian Authors (founding member).

AWARDS, HONORS: Institute of African Studies research fellow, 1961-62, 1963-64; Parvin fellow at Princeton University, 1962-63.

WRITINGS:

Song of a Goat (also see below; play; first produced at Ibadan University, 1961), Mbari Writers Club, 1961.
Poems, Mbari Press (Ibadan), 1962.
(Contributor) Gerald Moore, editor, *Seven African Writers,* Oxford University Press, 1962.
Three Plays: Song of a Goat, The Masquerade, The Raft, Oxford University Press, 1964.
(Contributor) John Reed and Clive Wake, editors, *A Book of African Verse,* Heinemann, 1964.
America, Their America (nonfiction), Deutsch, 1964, Africana Publishing, 1969.
A Reed in the Tide, Longmans, Green, 1965, 2nd edition published as *A Reed in the Tide: A Selection of Poems,* Humanities, 1970.
Ozidi: A Play, Oxford University Press, 1966.
(Contributor) *West African Verse: An Anthology,* Longmans, Green, 1967.
Casualties: Poems, 1966-68, Africana Publishing, 1970.
The Example of Shakespeare: Critical Essays on African Literature, Northwestern University Press, 1970.
(Translator) *The Ozidi Saga* by Okabou Ojobolo, Ibajan University Press, 1977.
A Decade of Tongues: Selected Poems 1958-1968, Longman, 1981.
The Bikoroa Plays: Boats, The Return Home, Full Circle, Oxford University Press, 1995.
Mandela and Other Poems, Longman, 1988.
Collected Plays and Poems, 1958-1988, Howard University Press, 1991.

Author of screenplays, director, and producer of two documentary films, *The Ozidi of Atazi* and *The Ghost Town.* Founder and editor, *The Horn* (literary magazine; Ibadan); co-editor of *Black Orpheus,* 1968–. Contributor of literary criticism to *Presence Africaine, Nigeria, Transition, African Forum, Black Orpheus,* and other journals.

SIDELIGHTS: Along with Wole Soyinka, John Pepper Clark is one of Nigeria's foremost anglophone dramatists and poets. He writes in English in order to reach the widest possible audience in a country where many different languages are spoken. However, African images, themes, settings, and speech patterns are central to Clark's writing. Having been raised in the Niger delta and educated in English literature at Ibadan University, Clark describes himself as "that fashionable cultural phenomenon they call 'mulatto'—not in flesh but in mind!" Critics note a wide range of influences in Clark's work, from ancient and modern Western sources to the myths and legends of Clark's people, the Ijaw.

Clark's first two plays, *Song of a Goat* (1961) and *The Masquerade* (1965), contain elements of classical Greek and Shakespearean drama, the poetic plays of T. S. Eliot, and the folk literature of the Ijaw people, which, according to Clark, has much in common with classical drama. In the first play, a barren woman consults with a masseur and conceives a child by her husband's brother. Unable to accept this situation, both the husband and his brother commit suicide. The child, grown to manhood and oblivious of the circumstances of his birth, is the tragic hero of *The Masquerade.* He travels to a strange village and becomes engaged to a beautiful, strong-willed girl. When the young man's background is revealed, the girl's father forbids her to marry, but she refuses to abide by his decision. In the violent denouement, all die. Both plays are written in verse and share a relentless aura of doom; neighbors function as a chorus, commenting on the tragic

happenings. *Song of a Goat, The Masquerade,* and *The Raft* (1966) were first published in the volume *Three Plays* (1964). *The Raft* concerns the misadventures of four men on a raft who attempt to bring logs downstream to be sold. Critics generally view the play as an exploration of the human condition or as a character study. It has also been interpreted as an allegory of the political division of Nigeria and as a critique of society based on economic determinism.

Ozidi (1966), Clark's first full-length play, was adapted from an Ijaw saga, the performance of which traditionally took seven days and involved mime, music, and dance. Clark retains many of these elements in his version and also uses masks and drums for the first time in his work. *Ozidi* is a revenge drama which, like Clark's earlier plays, involves a family curse and a series of violent actions. Clark also satirizes political corruption in this work.

A Reed in the Tide (1965) was Clark's first volume of poetry to be published internationally. Besides new poems, the volume also includes many pieces from Clark's first poetry collection, *Poems* (1962), which was published in Nigeria, and some from *America, Their America* (1964), a prose and poetry impression of the United States based on Clark's year in a postgraduate fellowship at Princeton University. Most of the poems are "occasional verse," inspired by something in the poet's immediate surroundings. Such poems as "Agbor Dancer," "Fulani Cattle," and "Girl Bathing" are based on Nigerian scenes; others based on Clark's trip to the United States reveal his impression of the country as harsh and unfeeling. Two of Clark's most famous poems, "Ibadan" and "Night Rain," simply describe the Nigerian landscape. Many of his poems, however, go beyond concrete description to take on symbolic value. For example, in "Agbor Dancer," Clark reflects on how he as a writer has moved away from his native culture in his art, in contrast to the dancer. Folk beliefs dominate many of Clark's poems, including "Abiku" and "The Imprisonment of Obatala."

Stylistically, Clark's early verse reflects his study of English poetry, with Gerard Manley Hopkins being the most obvious influence; one of Clark's poems is entitled "Variations on Hopkins." Like Hopkins, Clark uses complicated metrical patterns and rich, sensuous language. Critics note that Clark begins to move away from this style in the later poems of *A Reed in the Tide.* They applaud this simpler style and contend that his most beautiful and effective lines are those filled with nature imagery. *Casualties: Poems 1966-1968* (1970) is almost journalistic in its concentration on the Nigerian-Biafran conflict, during which Clark supported the Nigerian government. Because of the detailed and intimate knowledge of the war that Clark imparts to the poems, the volume is heavily annotated. The role of the artist during war, an emotional issue of the civil war in which many writers actually fought, is also an underlying theme. Clark contends that an artist is valuable both as a healer and as a reporter of war.

Besides his poetry and drama, Clark has also written literary criticism. He has published *The Example of Shakespeare: Critical Essays on African Literature* (1970) and *The Philosophical Anarchism of William Godwin* (1977) and has contributed to such prestigious literary journals as *Black Orpheus* and *Presence Africaine.* He is a professor of English at Lagos University and a founding member of The Society of Nigerian Authors.

BIOGRAPHICAL/CRITICAL SOURCES:

BOOKS

Black Literature Criticism, Gale, 1992.
Contemporary Literary Criticism, Gale, Volume 38, 1986.
Dictionary of Literary Biography, Volume 117, Gale, 1992.
Elimimian, Isaac I, *The Poetry of J. P. Clark Bekederemo,* Longman, 1988.

PERIODICALS

African Studies Review, September, 1993, pp. 121-23.
Concerning Poetry, fall, 1984.
Ibadan, June, 1966.
Research in African Literatures, spring, 1994, pp. 1-21.
World Literature Written in English, autumn, 1987; spring, 1988.

* * *

CLARK, Kenneth (Mackenzie) 1903-1983

PERSONAL: Born July 13, 1903, in London, England; died after a short illness, May 21, 1983, in Hythe, England; son of Kenneth Mackenzie (an industrial tycoon) and Margaret Alice (McArthur) Clark; married Elizabeth Martin, 1927 (died, 1976); married Nolwen de Janze-Rice, 1977; children: Alan, Rolin, Colette. *Education:* Trinity College, Oxford, received A.B., M.A., Ph.D.

CAREER: Worked with Bernard Berenson in England, Italy, and France, 1926-28; Ashmolean Museum, Oxford, England, keeper of department of fine art, 1931-33; National Gallery, London, England, director, 1934-45; surveyor of king's pictures, Hampton Court, Buckingham Palace, and Windsor Palace, England, 1934-44; U.K. Ministry of Information, controller of home publicity and director of films division, 1939-41; Oxford University, Oxford, Slade Professor of Fine Arts, 1946-50 and 1961-62; University of York, Heslington, York, England, chancellor, beginning in 1969. Chairman of Arts Council of Great Britain, 1953-60, and Independent Television Authority, 1954-57.

MEMBER: British Academy (fellow), Royal College of Art (fellow), National Art Collection Fund, Contemporary Art Society, Covent Garden Opera Trust, Victoria and Albert Museum (member of advisory council). Committee member of numerous organizations, including National Theatre Board, Conseil Artistique des Musees Nationaux, and Art Collection Fund. Honorary member of many organizations, including Royal Scottish Academy, Swedish Academy, American Academy of Arts and Letters, Commendatore della Corona d'Italia, Commendatore al Ordine de Merito, Florentine Academy, American Institute of Architects, and fellow of the Royal Institute of British Architects.

AWARDS, HONORS: Created Knight Commander of the Bath, 1938; knighted by Queen Elizabeth II, 1953; Serena Medal from British Academy for Italian Studies, 1955; Companion of Honor, 1959; fellow at University of Oxford, 1968; created Baron of Saltwood (life peerage), 1969; U.S. National Gallery of Art Award for distinguished services, 1970, for *Civilisation;* named Companion of Literature by Royal Society of Literature, 1974; Order of Merit, 1976; gold medal from New York University; commander of French Legion of Honor; Knight of the Lion of Finland. Honorary degrees from more than ten universities and colleges.

WRITINGS:

The Gothic Revival: An Essay in the History of Taste, Constable, 1929.
(With David Lindsay) *A Commemorative Catalogue of the Exhibition of Italian Art,* [London], 1931.
A Catalogue of the Drawings of Leonardo da Vinci in the Collection of His Majesty the King, at Windsor Castle, three volumes, Macmillan, 1935, 2nd edition, Phaidon Press, 1968-69.
Leonardo da Vinci: An Account of His Development as an Artist, Macmillan, 1939, 2nd edition, Cambridge University Press, 1952.
(Editor) *The Penguin Modern Painters,* Penguin, 1943.
(Author of introduction) *Paintings of Graham Bell,* Lund Humphries, 1947.
Landscape into Art, John Murray, 1949, Penguin, 1956, revised and enlarged edition, Harper, 1979.
Landscape Painting, Scribner, 1950.
Piero della Francesca, Phaidon Press, 1951.
Moments of Vision, Oxford University Press, 1954, variant edition, John Murray, 1975.
Selected Drawings from Windsor Castle: Leonardo da Vinci, three volumes, Phaidon Press, 1955.
The Nude: A Study in Ideal Form, Pantheon Books, 1956, Penguin, 1960.
Looking at Pictures, Holt, 1960.
(Author of introduction and notes) Walter H. Pater, *The Renaissance: Studies in Art and Poetry,* Collins, 1961.
Sidney Nolan, Thames & Hudson, 1961.
Provincialism, Oxford University Press, 1963.
(Author of introduction) Douglas Cooper, editor, *Great Private Collections,* Macmillan, 1963.
(Editor) *Ruskin Today* (anthology), John Murray, 1964, published as *Selected Writings,* Penguin (New York City), 1991.
Rembrandt and the Italian Renaissance, John Murray, 1966.
(Editor) R. M. Slyth, *Guides to the Published Work of Art Historians,* Bournemouth, 1968.
(With others) *Civilisation* (television series; also see below), British Broadcasting Corp. (BBC), 1969.
Civilisation: A Personal View, John Murray, 1969, Harper, 1970, 2nd edition, John Murray, 1971.
The Artist Grows Old, Cambridge University Press, 1972.
Studies in the History of the Renaissance, Fontana, 1973.
Blake and Visionary Art, University of Glasgow, 1973.
Romantic versus Classic Art (television series; also see below), BBC, 1973.
The Romantic Rebellion: Romantic versus Classic Art, John Murray, 1973.
Another Part of the Wood: A Self-Portrait, John Murray, 1974, Harper, 1975.
(Editor) *Henry Moore Drawings,* Thames & Hudson, 1974.
Concept of Universal Man, Ditchley Foundation, 1976.
The Drawings by Sandro Botticelli for Dante's "Divine Comedy": After the Originals in the Berlin Museums and the Vatican, Thames & Hudson, 1976.
Animals and Men: Their Relationship as Reflected in Western Art from Prehistory to the Present Day, Thames & Hudson, 1977.
The Other Half: A Self-Portrait, John Murray, 1977.
An Introduction to Rembrandt, John Murray, 1978.
The Best of Aubrey Beardsley, John Murray, 1979.
Happiness, University of Birmingham, 1979.
Feminine Beauty, Rizzoli, 1980.

(With David Finn) *The Florence Baptistry Doors,* Thames & Hudson, 1980.

What Is a Masterpiece?, Thames & Hudson, 1981.

Moments of Vision and Other Essays, Harper, 1982.

(With National Gallery) *100 Details from Pictures in the National Gallery,* Harvard University Press (Cambridge, MA), 1990.

Also author of *A Failure of Nerve,* 1967.

SIDELIGHTS: Sir Kenneth Clark, English art authority and historian, has been called a "Renaissance grandee," the "picture of patrician grace," and the "quintessential English gentleman." Heir to a vast fortune amassed by his tycoon grandfather, he described his parents as belonging "to a section of society known as the 'idle rich,' and although, in that golden age, many people were richer, there can be few who were idler. . . . They were two of the most irresponsible people I have ever known." His father, though he encouraged young Kenneth in his passion for art, spent his days with drink, and his mother, whose harsh indifference left him frequently in the care of servants who mistreated him, revealed to him early the cruel injustices of life. "Kenneth Clark was left in no doubt," stated John Russell, "that life has its vicissitudes. He developed two lines of defense: a lifelong passion for works of art and a highly developed sense for the ridiculous."

After completing his studies at Oxford University, Clark journeyed to Florence with renowned art authority Bernard Berenson to work on a revision of the latter's *Florentine Drawings.* Upon returning to England, Clark published his first book, *The Gothic Revival,* at the age of twenty-six. A year later he was named keeper of the fine art department of the Ashmolean Museum at Oxford, and by the time he reached thirty, he was appointed to the prestigious post of director of London's National Gallery, the youngest ever so honored.

Clark is perhaps best remembered for *Civilisation,* the highly successful thirteen-part television series on art and culture that he wrote and narrated for the British Broadcasting Corporation (BBC-TV). The series, which contained Clark's personal commentary on thirteen hundred years of Western culture, was broadcast in the United States by the Public Broadcasting System (PBS-TV). In discussing the enterprise with one of the directors, the word "civilisation" was mentioned. "I had no clear idea what he meant, but I thought it was preferable to barbarism and fancied that this was the moment to say so," recalled Clark in the foreword to *Civilisation.* He went on to express that he "would like to think that these programmes have done two things: they have made people feel that they are part of a great human achievement, and be proud of it; and they have made them feel humble in thinking of the great men and women of the past. Also, I like to think that they are entertaining." While the televised version of *Civilisation* was praised highly, the book version, for some, was disappointing. Oswell Blakeston felt that the "idea of presenting a selection of crucial civilising episodes from the Fall of the Roman Empire to the present day was a serious one—for TV; but when a book raises such profound issues as the nature of civilisation, it needs backbone, an all-over philosophy which is fully reasoned and unclouded. . . . I'm not impressed with the book as book, which is another way of saying that I'm not impressed with the trivialisation of the TV medium."

The Romantic Rebellion was another book derived from a televised series, though not so well received as was *Civilisation.* "On the whole," claimed Ruth Berenson, "it offers the neophyte a well written, if incomplete, introduction to some of the great artists of the late eighteenth and nineteenth centuries. For readers with more than a passing acquaintance with the subject, however, Lord Clark hasn't much new to say—though he does say it very well indeed." Comprised of essays on thirteen artists of the classic and romantic periods, Clark presented *The Romantic Rebellion* as a broad survey of the age. "'The Romantic Rebellion,'" assessed Peter Conrad, "is remarkable in dealing not only in great confident arcs of generalisation about cultural history but in those small, unique apprehensions of detail which are Kenneth Clark's signature."

In *Animals and Men,* Clark took the reader on a "delightful romp" through the animal kingdom as depicted by the Lascaux cave drawings of preliterate man and into the abstract world of Pablo Picasso. The book was written at the urgings of Fleur Cowles, the international trustee of the World Wildlife Fund (which, incidentally, receives a percentage of the royalties). Howard Fox related that Clark "pursues his thesis that a dual relationship of love and worship, enmity and fear, has persisted between men and animals since prehistory." Jan Morris, however, suggested that it is an "irony that a book professing to examine the immemorial relationship between man and beast should disregard the very territories where they have come closest to understanding one another." Fox disagreed, stating that "it is very much to Clark's credit that in his brevity he piques the reader's curiosity rather than lays it to rest. For lovers of animals and art, the book is a delight; for those who like one but not the other, the book could provide just enough substance for a second look."

Clark's two autobiographies, *Another Part of the Wood* and *The Other Half,* have received contrasting reviews. The latter, for example, has been deemed by Christopher Booker "one of the most unconsciously self-revealing books ever written," but was also referred to by Rene Kuhn Bryant as one that details a life "without revealing more than the merest minimum of the man who has written it." Clark's style of writing is another aspect that invites opposing opinions. Robert Melville flatly stated that part of the fascination is "his attempt to find a style in which to present himself to the general reader as an ordinary chap who happens to be a wealthy aesthete, and one of the most sensitive and stylish writers we have ever had. He makes a glorious hash of it. His false modesty is excruciating." On the other hand, Bryant asserted that "Clark marries substance with style, links wit to criticism, and demonstrates yet again his extraordinary ability to convey complex conceptions to a diverse and random audience with clarity and concision."

Another Part of the Wood, which recalls Clark's life until his late thirties, confirms that he was "brought face to face at a very early age with the fragility and instability of our human lot," observed John Russell. Though he was the product of a wealthy family and had tremendous success in his career, Clark himself conceded that he learned from playwright Henrik Ibsen "how full of cruel surprises life can be, how mixed are all motives, how under each layer of deception lies a still deeper layer of self-deception." He saw his life as one long string of good luck and felt somewhat awed by it all: "How my small talents came to arouse this kind of mass hysteria I shall never understand." In fact, he admitted to being almost bullied by his own phenomenal rise and reputation as the foremost authority on art and culture, and revealed that he was afflicted by "that subtle corruption that attacks almost everyone when he can no longer be contradicted or prevented from doing things, and when everyone except a few old friends kow-tows him."

Robert Hughes, writing in *Time* magazine, called Clark the "Leonard Bernstein of the visual arts," whose appearance on the small screen gave a generation of Americans (and Britons) starved for culture a taste of "continuity, authority, and masterpieces." The very things that helped give Clark his celebrity status—an enigmatic personality married to an urbane style—hurt his standing in the academic community. He was not a deeply profound scholar, a fact reflected in his tendency to gloss over certain periods in art history in favor of others. Despite this shortcoming, Clark was an enthusiastic and sympathetic interpreter of the visual arts and their relationship to other art forms. As Hughes noted: "No critic can make people see, but he can encourage them to look, and that was Clark's mission."

BIOGRAPHICAL/CRITICAL SOURCES:

BOOKS

Secrest, Meryle, *Kenneth Clark: A Biography,* Weidenfeld and Nicolson (London), 1984.

PERIODICALS

Books and Bookmen, September, 1971.
Chicago Tribune Book World, December 7, 1980.
Los Angeles Times Book Review, June 27, 1982.
National Review, April 26, 1974.
New Statesman, November 30, 1973; October 11, 1974.
New York Times, September 17, 1976; May 29, 1978; April 14, 1982.
New York Times Book Review, March 30, 1975; July 2, 1978; November 29, 1980.
Saturday Review, August 28, 1971.
Spectator, November 12, 1977.
Times Literary Supplement, November 14, 1980.
Washington Post, May 17, 1978.
Washington Post Book World, November 13, 1977; May 11, 1980; November 30, 1980.

* * *

CLARK, Mary Higgins 1929-

PERSONAL: Born December 24, 1929 (some sources say 1931), in New York City; daughter of Luke Joseph (a restaurant owner) and Nora C. (a buyer; maiden name, Durkin) Higgins; married Warren F. Clark (an airline executive), December 26, 1949 (died September 26, 1964); married Raymond Charles Ploetz (an attorney), August 8, 1978 (marriage annulled); children: Marilyn, Warren, David, Carol, Patricia. *Education:* Attended Villa Maria Academy, Ward Secretarial School, and New York University; Fordham University, B.A. (summa cum laude), 1979. *Politics:* Republican. *Religion:* Roman Catholic. *Avocation:* Traveling, skiing, tennis, playing piano.

ADDRESSES: Home—2508 Cleveland Ave., Washington Township, NJ 07675; and 210 Central Park S., New York, NY 10019. *Agent*—Eugene H. Winick, McIntosh & Otis, Inc., 475 Fifth Ave., New York, NY 10017.

CAREER: Writer. Remington Rand, New York City, advertising assistant, 1946; Pan American Airlines, flight attendant, 1949-50; Robert G. Jennings, radio scriptwriter and producer, 1965-70; Aerial Communications, New York City, vice president, partner, creative director, and producer of radio programming, 1970-80; David J. Clark Enterprises, New York City, chairman of the board

and creative director, 1980–. Chairman, International Crime Writers Congress, 1988.

MEMBER: Mystery Writers of America (president, 1987; member of board of directors), Authors Guild, Authors League of America, American Academy of Arts and Sciences, American Society of Journalists and Authors, American Irish Historical Society (member of executive council).

AWARDS, HONORS: New Jersey Author Award, 1969, for *Aspire to the Heavens,* 1977, for *Where Are the Children?* and 1978, for *A Stranger Is Watching*; Grand Prix de Litterature Policiere (France), 1980; honorary doctorates, Villanova University, 1983, Rider College, 1986, Stonehill College and Marymount Manhattan College, 1992, Chestnut Hill, Manhattan College, and St. Peter's College, 1993.

WRITINGS:

Aspire to the Heavens: A Biography of George Washington, Meredith Press, 1969.
Where Are the Children?, Simon & Schuster, 1975.
A Stranger Is Watching, Simon & Schuster, 1978.
(Contributor) *I, Witness,* Times Books, 1978.
The Cradle Will Fall (Literary Guild selection), Simon & Schuster, 1980.
A Cry in the Night, Simon & Schuster, 1982.
Stillwatch, Simon & Schuster, 1984.
(With Thomas Chastain and others) *Murder in Manhattan,* Morrow, 1986.
Weep No More, My Lady, Simon & Schuster, 1987.
(Editor) *Murder on the Aisle: The 1987 Mystery Writers of America Anthology,* Simon & Schuster, 1987.
While My Pretty One Sleeps, Simon & Schuster, 1989.
The Anastasia Syndrome and Other Stories, Simon & Schuster, 1989.
Loves Music, Loves to Dance, Simon & Schuster, 1991.
All Around the Town, Simon & Schuster, 1992.
Missing in Manhattan: The Adams Round Table, Longmeadow Press, 1992.
Mists from Beyond: Twenty-two Ghost Stories and Tales from the Other Side, New American Library/Dutton, 1993.
I'll Be Seeing You, Simon & Schuster, 1993.
Remember Me, Simon & Schuster (New York City), 1994.
The Lottery Winner: Alvirah and Willy Stories, Simon & Schuster (New York City), 1994.
Silent Night: A Novel, Simon & Schuster (New York City), 1995.
Mary Higgins Clark: Three Complete Novels (includes *A Stranger Is Watching, The Cradle Will Fall,* and *Where Are the Children?*), Wings Books (New York City), 1995.
(Contributor) *The International Association of Crime Writers Presents Bad Behavior,* Harcourt Brace (San Diego), 1995.
Let Me Call You Sweetheart, Simon & Schuster, 1995.
Moonlight Becomes You: A Novel, Simon & Schuster (New York City), 1996.
Mary Higgins Clark, Three New York Times Bestsellers (includes *While My Pretty One Sleeps, Loves Music, Loves to Dance,* and *All Around the Town*) Wings Books (New York City), 1996.
My Gal Sunday, Simon and Schuster (New York), 1996.
Mary Higgins Clark, Three New York Times Bestselling Novels, Wings Books (New York City), 1996.
Pretend You Don't See Her, Simon and Schuster (New York City), 1997.
(Editor) *The Plot Thickens,* Pocket Books, 1997.

Work anthologized in *The Best "Saturday Evening Post" Stories,* 1962. Also author of syndicated radio dramas. Contributor of stories to periodicals, including *Saturday Evening Post, Redbook, McCall's,* and *Family Circle.*

MEDIA ADAPTATIONS: A Stranger Is Watching was filmed by Metro-Goldwyn-Mayer in 1982; *The Cradle Will Fall* was shown on CBS as a "Movie of the Week" in 1984; *A Cry in the Night* was filmed by Rosten productions in 1985; *Where Are the Children?* was filmed by Columbia in 1986; *Stillwatch* was broadcast on CBS in 1987; Ellipse, a French production company, produced *Weep No More My Lady, A Cry in the Night* (starring Clark's daughter Carol), and two stories from *The Anastasia Syndrome.*

SIDELIGHTS: Mary Higgins Clark began her writing career as a newly widowed mother of five, and has instilled her passion for suspense stories in her children, including daughter Carol, also a best-selling novelist. Clark's stories "about nice people confronting the forces of evil and vanquishing them," as Patti Doten noted in the *Boston Globe,* have proven so popular that her publisher, Simon & Schuster, signed her to a record-breaking $11.4 million contract in 1989 to produce four novels and a short story collection, and a $35 million contract for five novels and a memoir in 1992.

Clark's success began with her first novel, *Where Are the Children?,* a best seller in 1975 that earned over $100,000 in paperback royalties. She followed that with another thriller, *A Stranger Is Watching,* which earned more than $1 million in paperback rights and was filmed by Metro-Goldwyn-Mayer in 1982. For Clark, this meant financial security. "[The money] changed my life in the nicest way," she told Bina Bernard in *People.* "It took all the choking sensation out of paying for the kids' schools."

The key to Clark's popularity, according to several critics, is her technique. Jean M. White of the *Washington Post* maintains that Clark "is a master storyteller who builds her taut suspense in a limited time frame," noting that *Where Are the Children?* takes place in one day and *A Stranger Is Watching* in three. Carolyn Banks, moreover, points out in the *Washington Post* that there is a kind of "Mary Higgins Clark formula" that readers both expect and enjoy: "There are no ambiguities in any Clark book. We know whom and what to root for, and we do. Similarly, we boo and hiss or gasp when the author wants us to. Clark is a master manipulator." Although Clark wants to provide her readers with entertainment and romance, she once told *Contemporary Authors*: "I feel a good suspense novel can and should hold a mirror up to society and make a social comment."

Clark's style is to write about "terror lurking beneath the surface of everyday life," observes White. "[She] writes about ordinary people suddenly caught up in frightening situations as they ride a bus or vacuum the living room," as are characters of *Loves Music, Loves to Dance,* who encounter a murderer when they agree to participate in an experiment involving newspaper personal ads. Other stories play on readers' fears of unfamiliar or undesirable situations. For example, Clark explored mental illness in both *Loves Music, Loves to Dance,* in which the killer's behavior is caused by a personality disorder, and *All Around the Town,* in which the main character is afflicted with multiple personality disorder attributed to severe sexual abuse in her childhood. In *I'll Be Seeing You,* Clark's characters find themselves victimized by villains more knowledgeable than they in the issues of genetic manipulation and in-vitro fertilization. Many of the events and details of Clark's stories come from the lives of her friends and

family, news events, and even her own experiences. Clark told *New York Times* interviewer Shirley Horner that the burglary which the heroine comes home to in *Stillwatch* was based on break-ins Clark herself has endured. "Everything that a writer experiences goes up in the mental attic," she told Horner.

In her most recent series of novels, nice people have been vanquishing the powers of darkness with great flair. In *Moonlight Becomes You,* Maggie Holloway, a young photographer and amateur sculptor, visits her deceased stepmother's home in Newport, Rhode Island, in order to investigate the woman's mysterious death. Maggie's search leads her to a nursing home plagued by a series of sudden deaths, and she begins to suspect that she, too, is being targeted by the killer, who does not want her to expose his diabolical plot. A reviewer from *Booklist* acknowledged that "though this is not her finest book, Clark's popularity will surely put *Moonlight* on the lists."

In her latest collection of short stories, *My Gal Sunday,* Clark gives us a new detective team positively brimming with niceness. Henry Parker Britland IV is a former U.S. president enjoying an early retirement, and his wife, Sandra (Sunday), has just been elected to Congress and appointed the darling of the media. Henry and Sunday specialize in solving the crimes that occur among their friends in political society. In one story, when Henry's former secretary of state is indicted for the murder of his mistress, Henry and Sunday determine that he is willing to take the fall for a crime of passion he did not commit. Henry and Sunday's niceness on occasion ventures into blandness, observes Justine Elias of the *New York Times,* who finds that "the most vivid characterizaitons . . . exist on the fringes of the action, reminders that Ms. Clark can be a far more engaging writer than she's letting on here."

In Pretend You Don't See Her, Clark takes on the federal witness protection program. While working as a real estate agent in Manhattan, Lacey Farrell witnesses a client's murder and has been given a new name and a new life by the government. However, merely changing her name does not protect her from the web of danger and deceit that surrounds the crime. As new clues emerge, Lacey realizes that a link exists between her family and the murder. In the meantime, romance enters her life and leads her to embark on a perilous journey to reclaim her old identity. *Booklist* finds the story "briskly paced" though with few surprises. Kimberly Marlowe of the *New York Times Book Review* notes that in the author's fifteenth novel, Clark covers "a lot of ground. . . . Life, death threats and the perfect date."

Writing has become a family affair for the Clarks. Carol Higgins Clark's first novel, *Decked,* appeared on the paperback bestseller list as her mother's *I'll Be Seeing You* was departing the hardcover list after seventeen weeks. Carol's second book, *Snagged,* debuted in hardcover in 1993, and a third, to be titled *Iced,* is in progress. To critics who suggest that Clark may have contributed to the writing of her daughter's books, the elder author's response is, "Not so, we have very different voices," Sarah Booth Conroy noted in the *Washington Post.* Conroy observed that Mary "writes deadly serious novels about the sort of chilling fears that come to women in the middle of the night," while Carol "spoons in a bit of bawdy, a soupcon of slapstick." Carol did, however, exert some influence in her mother's writing: she is responsible for saving two of Clark's most popular characters, Alvirah, a cleaning woman who wins the lottery, and her husband, Willy. When they first appeared in a short story, Alvirah was poisoned and Clark planned to finish her off, but Carol convinced her mother to allow

Alvirah to recover. The two have since become recurring characters and are featured in *The Lottery Winner: Alvirah and Willy Stories,* published in 1994.

BIOGRAPHICAL/CRITICAL SOURCES:

BOOKS

Bestsellers 89, Issue 4, Gale, 1989.
Contemporary Authors New Revision Series, Volume 36, 1992.
Pelzer, Linda Claycomb, *Mary Higgins Clark: A Critical Companion,* Greenwood Press (Westport, CT), 1995.

PERIODICALS

Best Sellers, December, 1984.
Booklist, October 15, 1994, p. 371; April 15, 1996.
Chicago Tribune, September 20, 1987; July 31, 1989.
Chicago Tribune Book World, June 8, 1980.
Cosmopolitan, May, 1989.
Current Biography, January, 1994, p. 6.
English Journal, volume 68, number 9, December, 1979, p. 80.
Good Housekeeping, November, 1996, pp. 23-4.
Newsweek, June 30, 1980.
New Yorker, August 4, 1980; June 27, 1994, p. 91.
New York Times, January 22, 1982; December 6, 1989; May 18, 1997.
New York Times Book Review, May 14, 1978; November 14, 1982; May 2, 1993, p. 22; December 15, 1996; May 5, 1996; June 29, 1997.
Observer, May 7, 1978, p. 34.
People, March 6, 1978; May 9, 1994, p. 35; December 16, 1996, pp. 54-6.
Progressive, volume 42, number 5, May, 1978, p. 45.
Publishers Weekly, May 19, 1989; October 14, 1996, pp. 28-9.
Wall Street Journal, May 29, 1996, p. A16.
Washington Post, May 19, 1980; July 17, 1980; October 18, 1982; August 10, 1987.

*   *   *

CLARKE, Arthur C(harles) 1917-
(E. G. O'Brien, Charles Willis)

PERSONAL: Born December 16, 1917, in Minehead, Somersetshire, England; son of Charles Wright (a farmer) and Nora (Willis) Clarke; married Marilyn Mayfield, June 15, 1953 (divorced, 1964). *Education:* King's College, University of London, B.Sc. (first class honors), 1948. *Avocation:* "Observing the equatorial skies with a fourteen-inch telescope," table-tennis, scuba diving, and "playing with his Rhodesian Ridgeback and his six computers."

ADDRESSES: Agent—Scott Meredith Literary Agency, Inc., 845 Third Ave., New York, NY 10022; David Higham Associates, 5-8 Lower John St., Golden Square, London W1R 4HA, England.

CAREER: British Civil Service, His Majesty's Exchequer and Audit Department, London, England, auditor, 1936-41; Institution of Electrical Engineers, *Science Abstracts,* London, assistant editor, 1949-50; freelance writer, 1951–. Underwater explorer and photographer, in partnership with Mike Wilson, on Great Barrier Reef of Australia and coast of Sri Lanka, 1954-64. Has appeared on television and radio numerous times, including as commentator with Walter Cronkite on Apollo missions, CBS-TV, 1968-70, and as host of television series *Arthur C. Clarke's Mysterious World,* 1980, and *Arthur C. Clarke's World of Strange Powers,* 1984.

Acted role of Leonard Woolf in Lester James Peries's film *Beddagama* (based on Woolf's *The Village in the Jungle*), 1979.

Director of Rocket Publishing Co., United Kingdom; founder, director, and owner, with Hector Ekanayake, of Underwater Safaris (a scuba-diving business), Sri Lanka; founder and patron, Arthur C. Clarke Centre for Modern Technologies, Sri Lanka, 1984–. Chancellor of University of Moratuwa, Sri Lanka, 1979–; Vikram Sarabhai Professor, Physical Research Laboratory, Ahmedabad, India, 1980; trustee, Institute of Integral Education, Sri Lanka. Fellow, Franklin Institute, 1971, King's College, 1977, Institute of Robotics, Carnegie-Mellon University, 1981. Lecturer, touring United States and Britain, 1957-74. Board member of National Space Institute, United States, Space Generation Foundation, United States, International Astronomical Union (Search for ExtraTerrestrial Intelligence) Commission 51, International Space University, Institute of Fundamental Studies, Sri Lanka, and Planetary Society, United States. Chairperson, Second International Astronautics Congress, London, 1951; moderator, "Space Flight Report to the Nation," New York, 1961. *Military service:* Royal Air Force, radar instructor, 1941-46; became flight lieutenant.

MEMBER: International Academy of Astronautics (honorary fellow), International Science Writers Association, International Council for Integrative Studies, World Academy of Art and Science (academician), British Interplanetary Society (honorary fellow; chairperson, 1946-47, 1950-53), Royal Astronomical Society (fellow), British Astronomical Association, Association of British Science Writers (life member), British Science Fiction Association (patron), Royal Society of Arts (fellow), Society of Authors (council member), American Institute of Aeronautics and Astronautics (honorary fellow), American Astronautical Society (honorary fellow), American Association for the Advancement of Science, National Academy of Engineering (United States; foreign associate), Science Fiction Writers of America, Science Fiction Foundation, H. G. Wells Society (honorary vice president), Third World Academy of Sciences (associate fellow), Sri Lanka Astronomical Society (patron), Institute of Engineers (Sri Lanka; honorary fellow), Sri Lanka Animal Welfare Association (patron), British Sub-Aqua Club.

AWARDS, HONORS: International Fantasy Award, 1952, for *The Exploration of Space;* Hugo Award, World Science Fiction Convention, 1956, for "The Star"; Kalinga Prize, UNESCO, 1961, for science writing; Junior Book Award, Boy's Club of America, 1961; Stuart Ballantine Gold Medal, Franklin Institute, 1963, for originating concept of communications satellites; Robert Ball Award, Aviation-Space Writers Association, 1965, for best aerospace reporting of the year in any medium; Westinghouse Science Writing Award, American Association for the Advancement of Science, 1969; Second International Film Festival special award, and Academy Award nomination for best screenplay with Stanley Kubrick, Academy of Motion Picture Arts and Sciences, both 1969, both for *2001: A Space Odyssey; Playboy* editorial award, 1971, 1982; D.Sc., Beaver College, 1971, and University of Moratuwa, 1979; Nebula Award, Science Fiction Writers of America, 1972, for "A Meeting with Medusa"; Nebula Award, 1973, Hugo Award, 1974, John W. Campbell Memorial Award, Science Fiction Research Association, 1974, and Jupiter Award, Instructors of Science Fiction in Higher Education, 1974, all for *Rendezvous with Rama;* Aerospace Communications Award, American Institute of Aeronautics and Astronautics, 1974; Bradford Washburn Award, Boston Museum of Science, 1977, for "contributions to the public understanding of science"; GALAXY

Award, 1979; Nebula and Hugo Awards, both 1980, both for *The Fountains of Paradise;* special Emmy Award for engineering, National Academy of Television Arts and Sciences, 1981, for contributions to satellite broadcasting; "Lensman" Award, 1982; Marconi International Fellowship, 1982; Centennial Medal, Institute of Electrical and Electronics Engineers, 1984; E. M. Emme Astronautical Literature Award, American Astronautical Society, 1984; Grand Master Award, Science Fiction Writers of America, 1986; Vidya Jyoti Medal (Presidential Science Award), 1986; Charles A. Lindbergh Award, 1987; named to Society of Satellite Professionals Hall of Fame, 1987; named to Aerospace Hall of Fame, 1988; Special Achievement Award, Space Explorers Association, 1989; Lord Perry Award, 1992; Nobel peace prize nomination, 1994; Distinguished Public Service Medal, NASA, 1995; Space Achievement Medal and Trophy, BIS, 1995; Mohamed Sabeen Award for Science, 1996; Von Karman Award, IAA, 1996. D. Sc., Beaver College, 1971, and University of Moratuwa, 1979; D.Litt., University of Bath, 1988.

WRITINGS:

NONFICTION

Interplanetary Flight: An Introduction to Astronautics, Temple, 1950, Harper (New York City), 1951, 2nd edition, 1960.
The Exploration of Space (U.S. Book-of-the-Month Club selection), Harper, 1951, revised edition, Pocket Books (New York City), 1979.
The Young Traveller in Space, Phoenix, 1953, published as *Going into Space,* Harper, 1954, revised edition (with Robert Silverberg) published as *Into Space: A Young Person's Guide to Space,* Harper, 1971.
The Exploration of the Moon, illustrated by R. A. Smith, Harper, 1954.
The Coast of Coral, Harper, 1956.
The Reefs of Taprobane: Underwater Adventures around Ceylon, Harper, 1957.
The Scottie Book of Space Travel, Transworld Publishers, 1957.
The Making of a Moon: The Story of the Earth Satellite Program, Harper, 1957, revised edition, 1958.
Voice across the Sea, Harper, 1958, revised edition, 1974.
(With Mike Wilson) *Boy beneath the Sea,* Harper, 1958.
The Challenge of the Spaceship: Previews of Tomorrow's World, Harper, 1959.
(With Wilson) *The First Five Fathoms: A Guide to Underwater Adventure,* Harper, 1960.
The Challenge of the Sea, Holt (New York City), 1960.
(With Wilson) *Indian Ocean Adventure,* Harper, 1961.
Profiles of the Future: An Inquiry into the Limits of the Possible, Harper, 1962, revised edition, Holt, 1984.
The Treasure of the Great Reef, Harper, 1964, new edition, Ballantine (New York City), 1974.
(With Wilson) *Indian Ocean Treasure,* Harper, 1964.
(With the editors of *Life*) *Man and Space,* Time-Life (Alexandria, VA), 1964.
Voices from the Sky: Previews of the Coming Space Age, Harper, 1965.
(Editor) *The Coming of the Space Age: Famous Accounts of Man's Probing of the Universe,* Meredith, 1967.
The Promise of Space, Harper, 1968.
(With Neil Armstrong, Michael Collins, Edwin E. Aldrin, Jr., Gene Farmer, and Dora Jane Hamblin) *First on the Moon,* Little, Brown (Boston), 1970.
Report on Planet Three and Other Speculations, Harper, 1972.
(With Chesley Bonestell) *Beyond Jupiter,* Little, Brown, 1972.

The View from Serendip (autobiography), Random House (New York City), 1977.
Arthur C. Clarke's Mysterious World (also see below; television series), Yorkshire Television, 1980.
(With Simon Welfare and John Fairley) *Arthur C. Clarke's Mysterious World* (based on television series), A&W Publishers, 1980.
Ascent to Orbit, a Scientific Autobiography: The Technical Writings of Arthur C. Clarke, Wiley (New York City), 1984.
1984: Spring—A Choice of Futures, Del Rey, 1984.
(With Welfare and Fairley) *Arthur C. Clarke's World of Strange Powers* (also see below; based on television series of same title), Putnam (New York City), 1984.
(With Peter Hyams) *The Odyssey File,* Fawcett (New York City), 1985.
Arthur C. Clarke's July 20, 2019: Life in the 21st Century, Macmillan (New York City), 1986.
Arthur C. Clarke's Chronicles of the Strange and Mysterious, edited by Welfare and Fairley, Collins, 1987.
Astounding Days: A Science Fictional Autobiography, Bantam (New York City), 1989.
How the World Was One: Beyond the Global Village, Bantam, 1992.
By Space Possessed, Gollancz (London), 1993.
The Snows of Olympus: A Garden on Mars, Norton (New York City), 1995.

Also author of introduction to *Inmarsat History.* Contributor to books, including *Mars and the Mind of Man,* Harper, 1973; and *Frontline of Discovery: Science on the Brink of Tomorrow,* National Geographic Society (Washington, DC), 1994.

FICTION

The Sands of Mars (also see below), Sidgwick & Jackson, 1951.
Prelude to Space (also see below), World Editions, 1951, published as *Master of Space,* Lancer Books, 1961, published as *The Space Dreamers,* Lancer Books, 1969.
Islands in the Sky, Winston, 1952, new edition, Penguin Books, 1972.
Childhood's End (also see below), Ballantine, 1953.
Against the Fall of Night (also see below), Gnome Press, 1953.
Expedition to Earth (also see below; short stories), Ballantine, 1953.
Earthlight (also see below), Ballantine, 1955.
Reach for Tomorrow (short stories), Ballantine, 1956.
The City and the Stars (also see below; based on novel *Against the Fall of Night*), Harcourt, 1956.
The Deep Range (also see below), Harcourt, 1957.
Tales from the White Hart, Ballantine, 1957.
The Other Side of the Sky (short stories), Harcourt, 1958.
Across the Sea of Stars (anthology; includes *Childhood's End* and *Earthlight*), Harcourt, 1959.
A Fall of Moondust (also see below), Harcourt, 1961, abridged edition, University of London Press, 1964.
From the Oceans, from the Stars (anthology; includes *The Deep Range* and *The City and the Stars*), Harcourt, 1962.
Tales of Ten Worlds (short stories), Harcourt, 1962.
Dolphin Island: A Story of the People of the Sea, Holt, 1963.
Glide Path, Harcourt, 1963.
Prelude to Mars (anthology; includes *Prelude to Space* and *The Sands of Mars*), Harcourt, 1965.
An Arthur C. Clarke Omnibus (contains *Childhood's End, Prelude to Space,* and *Expedition to Earth*), Sidgwick & Jackson, 1965.

(Editor) *Time Probe: The Science in Science Fiction,* Dial (New York City), 1966.

The Nine Billion Names of God (short stories), Harcourt, 1967.

A Second Arthur C. Clarke Omnibus (contains *A Fall of Moondust, Earthlight,* and *The Sands of Mars*), Sidgwick & Jackson, 1968.

(With Stanley Kubrick) *2001: A Space Odyssey* (screenplay; also see below), Metro-Goldwyn-Mayer, 1968.

2001: A Space Odyssey (based on screenplay), New American Library, 1968, published with a new introduction by Clarke, ROC (New York City), 1994.

The Lion of Comarre; and, Against the Fall of Night, Harcourt, 1968.

The Lost Worlds of 2001, New American Library, 1972.

The Wind from the Sun (short stories), Harcourt, 1972.

(Editor) *Three for Tomorrow,* Sphere Books, 1972.

Of Time and Stars: The Worlds of Arthur C. Clarke (short stories), Gollancz, 1972.

Rendezvous with Rama (also see below), Harcourt, 1973, adapted edition, Oxford University Press, 1979.

The Best of Arthur C. Clarke, edited by Angus Wells, Sidgwick & Jackson, 1973, published as two volumes, Volume 1: *The Best of Arthur C. Clarke: 1937-1955,* Volume 2: *The Best of Arthur C. Clarke: 1956-1972,* 1977.

Imperial Earth: A Fantasy of Love and Discord, Gollancz, 1975, Harcourt, 1976.

Four Great Science Fiction Novels (contains *The City and the Stars, The Deep Range, A Fall of Moondust,* and *Rendezvous with Rama*), Gollancz, 1978.

The Fountains of Paradise, Harcourt, 1979.

(Editor with George Proctor) *The Science Fiction Hall of Fame,* Volume 3: *The Nebula Winners,* Avon (New York City), 1982.

2010: Odyssey Two, Del Rey, 1982.

The Sentinel: Masterworks of Science Fiction and Fantasy (short stories), Berkeley Publishing, 1983.

Selected Works, Heinemann, 1985.

The Songs of Distant Earth, Del Rey, 1986.

2061: Odyssey Three, Del Rey, 1988.

(With Gentry Lee) *Cradle,* Warner Books (New York City), 1988.

A Meeting with Medusa (bound with *Green Mars* by Kim Stanley Robinson), Tor Books (New York City), 1988.

(With Lee) *Rama II,* Bantam, 1989.

(With Gregory Benford) *Beyond the Fall of Night,* Putnam, 1990.

The Ghost from the Grand Banks, Bantam, 1990.

Tales from the Planet Earth, illustrated by Michael Whelan, Bantam, 1990.

(With Gentry Lee) *The Garden of Rama,* Bantam, 1991.

The Hammer of God, Bantam, 1993.

(With Lee) *Rama Revealed,* Bantam, 1994.

(With Mike McQuay) *Richter 10,* Bantam, 1996.

3001: The Final Odyssey, Ballantine, 1997.

OTHER

(Author of afterword) Paul Preuss, *Breaking Strain,* Avon, 1987; and Preuss, *Maelstrom,* Avon, 1988.

Opus 700, Gollancz, 1990.

Rama: The Official Strategy Guide, Prima Pub. (Rocklin, CA), 1996.

Also author of television series *Arthur C. Clarke's World of Strange Powers* and a movie treatment based on *Cradle.* Contributor of more than six hundred articles and short stories, occasionally under pseudonyms E. G. O'Brien and Charles Willis,

to numerous magazines, including *Harper's, Playboy, New York Times Magazine, Vogue, Holiday,* and *Horizon.*

Clarke's works have been translated into Polish, Russian, French, German, Spanish, Serbo-Croatian, Greek, Hebrew, Dutch, and over twenty other languages.

MEDIA ADAPTATIONS: 2010: Odyssey Two was filmed in 1984 by Metro-Goldwyn-Mayer (Clarke has a cameo in the film); the short story "The Star" was adapted for an episode of *The New Twilight Zone* by CBS-TV in 1985. The following works have been optioned for movies: *Childhood's End,* by Universal; *The Songs of Distant Earth,* by Michael Phillips; *The Fountains of Paradise,* by Robert Swarthe; and *Cradle,* by Peter Guber. Arthur C. Clarke has made the following sound recordings of his works for Caedmon: *Arthur C. Clarke Reads from his 2001: A Space Odyssey,* 1976; *Transit of Earth*; *The Nine Billion Names of God*; and *The Star,* 1978; *The Fountains of Paradise,* 1979; *Childhood's End,* 1979; and *2010: Odyssey Two.* A full-length recording of *A Fall of Moondust* was made by Harcourt in 1976.

SIDELIGHTS: Renowned not only for his science fiction, which has earned him the title of Grand Master from the Science Fiction Writers of America, Arthur C. Clarke also has a reputation for first-rate scientific and technical writing. Perhaps best known in this field for "Extraterrestrial Relays," the 1945 article in which he first proposed the idea of communications satellites, Clarke has also published works on such diverse topics as underwater diving, space exploration, and scientific extrapolation. Nevertheless, it is Clarke's science fiction which has secured him his reputation, with such novels as *Childhood's End* and *Rendezvous with Rama* acknowledged as classics in their field. In addition, his story "The Nine Billion Names of God" was named to the science fiction "Hall of Fame," while the movie *2001: A Space Odyssey,* written with director Stanley Kubrick, has been called the most important science fiction film ever made.

Often dealing with themes of exploration and discovery, Clarke's fiction almost always conveys to the reader a sense of wonder about the universe. Some critics, seeing the author's detailed descriptions of possible futures, have accused Clarke of ignoring the human element for the sake of science in his work. But while the development of scientific ideas and speculations plays a large role in Clarke's narratives, "what distinguishes Clarke's fictions from the usually more ephemeral examples of science fiction is his vision," asserts Eric S. Rabkin in his study *Arthur C. Clarke.* This vision, writes Rabkin, is "a humane and open and fundamentally optimistic view of humankind and its potential in a universe which dwarfs us in physical size but which we may hope some day to match in spirit."

Born in 1917 in an English seaside town, Clarke first discovered science fiction at the age of twelve, when he encountered the pulp magazine *Amazing Stories.* The encounter soon became an "addiction," as Clarke describes in the *New York Times Book Review*: "During my lunch hour away from school I used to haunt the local Woolworth's in search of my fix, which cost threepence a shot, roughly a quarter today." The young Clarke then began nurturing his love for the genre through the books of such English writers as H. G. Wells and Olaf Stapledon. He started writing his own stories for a school magazine while in his teens, but was unable to continue his schooling for lack of funds. He consequently secured a civil service job as an auditor, which left him plenty of free time to pursue his "hobby." Alone in London, Clarke joined an association of several science fiction and space enthusiasts, and as he relates in *The View from Serendip,* "my life was dominated by the infant British Interplanetary Society [BIS], of which I was treasurer and general propagandist." As part of his involvement with the BIS, Clarke wrote several scientific articles on the feasibility of space travel for the organization's journal; the BIS also gained him contacts with several science fiction editors and writers, which led to the publication of some of his short stories.

In 1941, although his auditor's position was still a reserved occupation, Clarke engaged in "what was probably the single most decisive act of my entire life," as he describes in *Ascent to Orbit, a Scientific Autobiography: The Technical Writings of Arthur C. Clarke*; he voluntarily enlisted in the Royal Air Force. En route to becoming a radar instructor in a new system called Ground Controlled Approach, Clarke taught himself mathematical and electronics theory. After World War II ended, Clarke entered college and obtained a degree in physics as well as pure and applied mathematics; after graduation he spent two years as an assistant editor for a technical journal. But with publication of the novel *Childhood's End* (1953) and *The Exploration of Space,* which in 1952 was the first science book ever chosen as a Book-of-the-Month Club selection, Clarke began earning enough money to pursue writing full-time.

The Exploration of Space, besides allowing Clarke to leave his job, also broke ground in explaining scientific ideas to a popular audience. As H. H. Holmes describes in the *New York Herald Tribune Book Review,* in "the realm of speculative factual writing . . . Mr. Clarke's new book will serve as the most important yet in its field. Not that it says much that is new," explains Holmes, but because "it is precisely calculated to bring our present knowledge of space travel before a whole new public." What enables the book to reach such an audience is a "charm and magnetism" that is due to "Clarke's ability to reduce complex subjects to simple language and his steadfast avoidance of fantasy as a substitute for factual narration," observes Roy Gibbons in the *Chicago Sunday Tribune.*

Clarke applied the same speculative techniques to other areas in the 1962 book *Profiles of the Future: An Inquiry into the Limits of the Possible.* The author "has a thorough grounding in science, and, in addition has a nimble and most receptive mind," states Isaac Asimov in the *New York Times Book Review.* "Nothing reasonable frightens him simply because it seems fantastic, and—equally important—nothing foolish attracts him simply because it seems fantastic." As his previous books have been, *Profiles of the Future* "is highly entertaining reading," remarks R. C. Cowen in the *Christian Science Monitor.* "It also is informative, for the author is careful to adhere to the yardstick of natural laws that set the bounds of the possible." The critic concludes that Clarke "thus helps a layman to learn the difference between rational speculation and . . . wholly baseless imaginings." Asimov concurs, writing that "this book offers all of us a chance to raise our eyes from the ground and to contemplate the scenery ahead. It is marvelous scenery indeed, and there could scarcely be a better guide to its landmarks than Arthur Clarke."

Although most speculative science texts are soon outdated, Clarke's work has withstood years of technical progress. In *The Promise of Space,* published in 1968 to "replace" *The Exploration of Space,* Clarke "is able to show the manner in which many of his predictions have been fulfilled," notes a *Times Literary Supplement* contributor. But rather than simply cataloging recent discoveries, Clarke's work incorporates them into new ideas: "All through the book Clarke not only recounts what has been done

during the last two decades," describes Willy Ley in the *New York Times Book Review,* "but has his eye on both the immediate results and the future." Similarly, *Science* contributor Eugene M. Emme asserts that the book contains "the best available summary of scientific and imaginative theory regarding space potentials. . . . Collectively they offer a most persuasive rationale." A 1984 revision of *Profiles of the Future* also withstands years of advancement: "Testing the limits of technological progress," observes David N. Samuelson in the *Los Angeles Times Book Review,* "it has remained remarkably current since its 1962 book publication." Gregory Benford, who calls Clarke "a vindicated sage in his own time," theorizes in the *Washington Post Book World* that while "books on futurology date notoriously, this one has not, principally because Clarke was unafraid of being adventurous." And *New York Times Book Review* writer Gerald Jonas offers this reason for Clarke's success: "What makes Clarke such an effective popularizer of science is that, without bobbling a decimal point or fudging a complex concept, he gives voice to the romantic side of scientific inquiry."

Although much of Clarke's early fiction reinforced the idea that space travel was an eventuality, *Childhood's End,* his first successful novel, is "Clarke's only work—fiction or nonfiction—in which 'The stars are not for Man,'" suggests Thomas D. Clareson in *Voices for the Future: Essays on Major Science Fiction Writers.* The novel relates the appearance of the Overlords, a race of devil-shaped aliens who have come to guide Earth to peace and prosperity. Beginning by eliminating all individual governments and thus ending war, the Overlords use their superior technology to solve the problems of poverty, hunger, and oppression. The cost of this utopia is that most scientific research is set aside as unnecessary, and the exploration of space is forbidden. The motives of the Overlords become clear as the youngest generation of humans develops extrasensory powers; the children of Earth are to join the Overmind, a collective galactic "spirit" that transcends physical form. The need for science, technology, and space is eliminated with humanity's maturation, and the Earth itself is destroyed as her children join the Overmind.

Some critics view *Childhood's End* as the first manifestation of the theme of spiritual evolution that appears throughout Clarke's fiction. John Huntington, writing in the critical anthology *Arthur C. Clarke,* believes the novel to be Clarke's solution to one of the problems posed by technological progress: how spiritual development can keep pace with scientific development when by making man comfortable, science often takes away man's curiosity and drive.

Childhood's End solves the problem with a stage of "transcendent evolution," and Huntington proposes that "it is its elegant solution to the problem of progress that has rightly earned *Childhood's End* that 'classic' status it now enjoys." Donald A. Wollheim, however, considers this solution a negative one; writing in *The Universe Makers* he comments that the work "has always seemed to me to be a novel of despair. Others may see it as offering hope, but this tampering with humanity always struck me as being synthetic." But other critics reaffirm the novel as hopeful: *Childhood's End* "becomes a magnificently desperate attempt to continue to hope for a future for the race in the face of mounting evidence to the contrary," writes John Hollow in *Against the Night, the Stars: The Science Fiction of Arthur C. Clarke.* Written in 1953 in the midst of the Cold War, "it becomes, in fact, a sometimes brilliant attempt to turn the contrary evidence to the positive," adds Hollow. "It becomes nothing less than an effort to make positive the destruction of the race."

Perhaps Clarke's best-known work, *2001: A Space Odyssey* was the result of four years work on both the film version and the subsequent novel. The collaboration between Clarke and director Stanley Kubrick began when the filmmaker sought a suitable basis for making the "proverbial good science fiction movie," as he has frequently described it. The two finally settled upon Clarke's 1951 short story "The Sentinel," and developed it "not [into] a script, which in [Kubrick's] view does not contain enough of the visual and emotional information necessary for filming, but a prose version, rather like a novel," relates Michel Ciment in *Focus on the Science Fiction Film.* The result "was of more help to him in creating the right atmosphere because it was more generous in its descriptions," adds Ciment.

The film and the novel have the same basic premise: a large black monolith has been sent to Earth to encourage the development of man. First shown assisting in the "dawn of man" four million years ago, a monolith is next uncovered on the moon, and upon its unveiling sends a strong radio signal toward the outer planets. As a result the spaceship *Discovery,* operated by the intelligent computer HAL 9000, is sent in the direction of the signal to investigate. However, while the human crew is kept ignorant of the ship's true assignment, the HAL 9000 begins to eliminate what it sees as obstacles in the way of the mission—including all of the crew. First captain Dave Bowman manages to survive, however, and upon his arrival at a moon of Saturn (Jupiter in the film) encounters yet a third monolith which precipitates a journey through the infinite, "into a world where time and space are relative in ways beyond Einstein," describes Penelope Gilliatt in the *New Yorker.* Bowman is transformed during this journey, and subsequently arrives at a higher plane of evolution as the Star Child. "In the final transfiguration," notes Tim Hunter in *Film Heritage,* "director Kubrick and coauthor Arthur Clarke . . . suggest that evolutionary progress may in fact be cyclical, perhaps in the shape of a helix formation." The critic explains: "Man progresses to a certain point in evolution, then begins again from scratch on a higher level."

"Clarke's *2001: A Space Odyssey* was an extraordinary development in fiction, a novel written in collaboration with the director who was simultaneously filming it," writes Colin Greenland of the *Times Literary Supplement.* Clarke himself explains in the epilogue to the 1982 edition of *2001* that during the project he "often had the strange experience of revising the manuscript *after* viewing rushes based upon an earlier version of the story—a stimulating but rather expensive way of writing a novel." Because the book appeared three months after the movie's premiere, it was inevitable that critics would draw comparisons between the two. *New Statesman* contributor Brenda Maddox finds the book lacking beside the movie; the novel "has all the faults of the film and none of its virtues." The critic elaborates: "The characters still have the subtlety of comic-strip men and, lacking the film's spectacular visual gimmickry . . . the story must propel itself with little gusts of scientific explanation." In contrast, Eliot Fremont-Smith asserts in the *New York Times* that "the immense and moving fantasy-idea of '2001' . . . is an idea that can be *dramatically* envisioned only in the free oscillations of the delicately cued and stretched mind." The critic adds that the film "is too direct for this, its wonders too unsubtle and, for all their majesty, too confining." And where the movie may have been obscure, "all of it becomes clear and convincing in the novel. It is indeed an odyssey, this story, this exhilarating and rather chilling science fiction fantasy." Nevertheless, in comparing the visual genius of the film with the clarity of the book, Clarke himself

admits in *Focus on the Science Fiction Film* that both versions "did something that the other couldn't have done."

"Although it lacks some of the metaphysical fireworks and haunting visionary poetry of [his earlier work]," Clarke's *Rendezvous with Rama* is nevertheless "essentially an expression of wonder in the presence of Mystery," comments a *Virginia Quarterly Review* contributor. Written in 1973, the novel is the only work to win all four major awards in its genre; Disch calls it "probably [Clarke's] most considerable work of art." The book follows the appearance of an asteroid-like object which is hurtling directly towards the inner solar system—and which turns out to be a cylindrical, obviously unnatural artifact. An Earth ship is dispatched to the object, labelled "Rama," and a team led by commander Bill Norton enters to investigate. The exploration of the many mysterious aspects of Rama is interrupted by several distractions—including the emergence of what appears to be generated life forms and the arrival of a nuclear warhead sent by paranoid colonists from nearby Mercury. The study of Rama is concluded safely, however, although Norton's team has not gathered enough information to discern a purpose to the craft. Seemingly indifferent to a meeting with intelligent life, Rama then exits the solar system and continues its journey. "This is story-telling of the highest order," notes Theodore Sturgeon in the *New York Times Book Review.* "There are perpetual surprise, constant evocation of the sense of wonder, and occasions of the most breathless suspense."

Although classic works such as *Childhood's End* and *Rendezvous with Rama* focus on the effects of extraterrestrial visitation, Clarke's next two works concentrate more on the achievements of humanity. *Imperial Earth: A Fantasy of Love and Discord,* which takes place in the quincentennial year of 2276, most directly "shows Clarke at the height of his [extrapolative] powers," remarks Jonas. The novel includes demonstrations of outer planet mining operations, cloning, and spaceship propulsion systems, all woven into the story of Titan native Duncan Makenzie's visit to Earth. Duncan's trip serves many purposes; ostensibly it is to deliver an address at the quincentennial celebration, but it is also to investigate political and scientific intrigues, as well as to procure, through cloning, an heir for the sterile Duncan. Through Duncan's eyes "Clarke not only supplies us with a fair number of technological wonders," observes Mark Rose in the *New Republic,* but the author also "makes much of such human matters as the political and psychological isolation of a distant colonial world such as Titan." Nevertheless, "one problem with the full-blown novel of extrapolation is that the author may neglect plot and character," states Jonas. But while he notes some of these faults, *National Review* contributor Steve Ownbey calls *Imperial Earth* "a book nobody should miss. It's an utterly delightful tale, suspenseful and moving, full of unexpected chuckles and stunning surprises." And Rose comments that the novel is "a literary performance conducted with genuine intelligence and grace."

Clarke's Hugo and Nebula-winning *The Fountains of Paradise* is even more technical in its basic premise: the construction of an orbital "space elevator" designed to make escaping the Earth's gravity a simple process. Based on actual scientific treatises, Clarke once again develops his idea "with sufficient technical detail to lend plausibility" says Jonas, "and the more plausible it sounds, the more stupendous it becomes." The novel also concerns Vannevar Morgan, the engineer obsessed with realizing the creation of his space elevator. Providing a "curious backdrop" to Morgan's enterprise is "a highly advanced galactic civilization [which] has already communicated with the human race through a robot probe," summarizes Jonas. In addition, Morgan's story is paralleled by the account of Prince Kalidasa, who two thousand years earlier challenged the gods by attempting to build a garden tower into heaven—on Taprobane, the same island that Morgan wants for his elevator. But while critics commend this parallel, they fault Clarke for not sustaining it: "the direct interweaving of Kalidasa's story should have extended throughout the entire work rather than petering out," comments Paul Granahan in *Best Sellers*. Similarly, *New Republic* contributor Tim Myers criticizes Clarke for ending the parallel: "The Indian king, the only character with nobility, is taken from us. We are left with Morgan, a pathetic egotist who is also hopelessly stereotyped."

Although for several years Clarke (and others) insisted that a sequel to *2001* would be impossible, in 1982 Clarke published *2010: Odyssey Two*. Incorporating elements of both the film and novel versions, as well as new information from the *Voyager* probes of Jupiter, in *2010* "Clarke sensibly steps back down to our level to tell the story of a combined Russian and American expedition to salvage Bowman's deserted ship, the *Discovery*, and find out what happened," relates Greenland. Although the expedition finds the remains of the ship and repairs the HAL 9000, the purpose of the black monolith mystifies them. While some critics find this an adequate approach to a sequel, others criticize Clarke for even attempting to follow up a "classic." *Science Fiction Review* writer Gene DeWeese believes a large problem is that *2010* "is not so much a sequel to the original book, which was in many ways superior to the movie, but a sequel to and an explanation of the movie. Unfortunately, many of these explanations already existed [in the novel of *2001*]." *Washington Post Book World* contributor Michael Bishop similarly notes a tendency to over-explain: "Ponderous expository dialogue alternates with straightforward expository passages in which Heywood Floyd . . . or the author himself lectures the reader." And Jonas complains that *2010* "violates the mystery [of the original] at every turn."

Despite the various criticisms, *2010* still "has its share of that same sense of wonder, which means that it is one of the dozen or so most enjoyable SF books of the year," says DeWeese. "Clarke deftly blends discovery, philosophy, and a newly acquired sense of play," states *Time* contributor Peter Stoler, creating a work that will "entertain" readers. Cary Neeper presents a similar assessment in the *Christian Science Monitor*, noting that "Clarke's story drives on to an exciting finish in which the mix of fantasy and fact leaves the reader well satisfied with a book masterfully written." And in contrast to the criticisms of the sequel's worthiness, Bud Foote claims in the *Detroit News* that with "the book's penultimate triumph [of] a new, awesome and terrifying world transformation," Clarke has created "a fine book." The critic concludes that *2010* "is better than the original book, and it illuminates and completes the original movie. It is so good, in fact, that even Clarke couldn't write a sequel to it."

Despite this assertion and Clarke's own remarks to the *Washington Post*'s Curt Suplee that "if I ever do write 'Odyssey III'—allowing for the fact that my energies are declining—it won't be before the year 2001," 1988 brought *2061: Odyssey Three*, the next chapter in the saga of the black monolith. 2061 is the year of the next appearance of Halley's comet; *Odyssey Three* follows Heywood Floyd on a survey of the object. While en route, the survey party is redirected to rescue a ship that has crashed on the Jovian moon of Europa—the one celestial object the monoliths have warned humans against visiting. Some critics have been skeptical of a second sequel, such as the *Time* reviewer who finds

that "the mix of imagination and anachronism is wearing as thin as the oxygen layer on Mars." Although Jonas also observes that "Mr. Clarke's heart is obviously not in the obligatory action scenes that advance the plot," he concedes that the author "remains a master at describing the wonders of the universe in sentences that combine a respect for scientific accuracy with an often startling lyricism." Clarke "is not to be measured by the same standards we apply to a mundane plot-smith," asserts David Brin in the *Los Angeles Times*. "He is, after all, the poet laureate of the Space Age. He is at his best making the reader feel, along with Heywood Floyd," continues Brin, "how fine it might be to stand upon an ancient comet, out under the stars, knowing that it is those dreams that finally come true that are the best dreams of all."

Between the publication of the two *Odyssey* sequels Clarke finished *The Songs of Distant Earth*, an elaborate revision and extension of a short story first published in 1958. The novel takes place on the ocean world of Thalassa, where the few habitable islands there have been populated by descendants of an Earth "seedship," sent to perpetuate humanity even after the nova explosion of the Earth's sun. The Thalassan society is a type of utopia, for superstition, prejudice, and extreme violence no longer exist; the robots who raised the first generations eliminated all religion and art which might encourage these elements. The Thalassans are seemingly content with their world when the starship *Magellan* lands, bringing with it the last survivors (and witnesses) of the Earth's destruction. Although the ship is not permitted to colonize a world that has already been settled, the idyllic setting tempts the crew to a possible mutiny. Further complicating the situation is the emergence of a marine life form that appears to be intelligent, creating a possible conflict on two different fronts.

Although this dilemma "makes for an interesting novel," *Science Fiction Review* contributor Richard E. Geis still faults Clarke's plot as improbable, decrying the lack of individual conflict. Echoing previous criticisms, Geis comments that the "characters are uncomplicated, non-neurotic, with only minor problems to be solved. . . . Clarke has written a story of plausible high-tech future science and peopled it with implausible, idealized, 'nice' humans." In contrast, Dan K. Moran of the *West Coast Review of Books* believes that "how Clarke deals with the mutiny is interesting; and his characters come alive throughout." Nevertheless, the critic finds that "the great flaw is the lack of sense-of-wonder. Nothing herein is really new, neither science nor Clarke's synthesis," concludes Moran.

The "grand theme" that runs throughout Clarke's fiction "can be stated only in the form of a paradox," suggests Jonas: "Man is most himself when he strives greatly, when he challenges the very laws of the universe; yet man is small and the universe is large, and anything he creates must, in the long run, be dwarfed by the works of others." The science in Clarke's fiction provides a good backdrop for this theme; Benford writes that Clarke "prefers a pure, dispassionate statement of facts and relationships, yet the result is not cold. Instead, he achieves a rendering of the scientific esthetic, with its respect for the universal qualities of intelligence, its tenacity and curiosity. His fiction neglects conflict and the broad spectrum of emotion, which gives it a curiously refreshing honesty." Although Clarke's fiction "may appear to be about science, appear to be about numbers, appear to be about ideas," Rabkin feels that "in fact at bottom whatever Clarke writes is about people and that means it is about the human spirit."

Clarke's faith in the human spirit is evident in his nonfiction book *The Snows of Olympus: A Garden on Mars*. Published in 1995, at a time when NASA struggled with massive budget cutbacks, this book nevertheless looks optimistically toward a future when humans will visit and colonize the planet Mars. Clarke asserts that if money were no object, human beings could walk on Mars early in the twenty-first century. He outlines a three-part mission to Mars, beginning with robot probes, which would locate needed resources on the planet and choose suitable landing sites. Unmanned space freighters would follow with equipment and supplies, intended to support the third part of the mission: the landing of a human crew. Clarke predicts that once a human colony is established, work will begin to alter the environment of Mars to make it habitable by unprotected human beings. He even believes that it is possible to create oceans and large-scale agricultural projects there. *The Snows of Olympus* is illustrated with computer-generated art depicting the transformation of Mars. Clarke created the pictures himself, beginning with maps of the planet generated by NASA's *Voyager* probe. In addition to his speculations on the years to come, Clarke's book also takes a look at past conceptions of Mars, beginning with the late nineteenth-century idea that the planet was populated by a race of intelligent beings who specialized in building canals.

Known as a futurist, Clarke turned to the past in *Astounding Days: A Science Fictional Autobiography*. Focusing on Clarke's youth and early days as a writer, the memoir is divided into three sections, each dedicated to one of the three editors who created the magazine *Astounding Science Fiction* (renamed *Analog* in the 1960s). Writing for *Wilson Library Bulletin*, Gene LaFaille describes *Astounding Days* as a "rambling paean to the glory years of early science fiction." *Astounding Days* provides "a sweeping view of popular science and popular fiction," states *Library Journal* reviewer Katherine Thorp.

As an octogenarian, Clarke turns once again toward the future, both immediate and distant. In *Richter 10*, written in collaborations with Mike McQuay, Clarke combines earthquakes, politics, and environmental disaster to produce a futuristic disaster novel. By the near-future year 2030, the Nation of Islam is orchestrating a civil war in California and demanding a state of its own, China is the dominant world power, southern Europe and the Middle East have been destroyed by Israel's nuclear weapons, and the ozone layer has vanished. The book's hero, Lewis Crane, is a leading authority on earth tremors and is able to predict earthquakes, but no one believes him when he predicts a giant earthquake that might wipe out the central United States. When the earthquake does not occur on time, the Nation of Islam attacks and the earth disintegrates into chaos. Crane, who has lost all credibility and support from his Chinese business sponsor, buys real estate on the moon and starts a space colony. *Booklist* calls *Richter 10* "a taut, well-written thriller that should satisfy both Clarke's fans and the many devotees of disaster novels." *Kirkus Reviews* finds it long-winded, but remarks that "while improbable," the novel is "never dull."

Clarke told John F. Burns of the *New York Times Book Review* that in the years when he was not writing, he felt like Frank Poole after he had his air supply cut off by HAL. Thus, Clarke has done what he long insisted was impossible: write the fourth installment of his Odyssey series, *3001: The Final Odyssey*. In *3001*, another manned space voyage finds the deep-frozen Frank Poole, long presumed dead, and revives him with fourth-millenium technology. Poole masters the use of the "braincap" and other gadgets, learns about Star City, and studies a thousand years of history he

has slept through. During his long sleep, a monolith has exploded Jupiter, turning it and its moons into a secondary solar system. One moon, Europa, has been colonized by a monolith that monitors human behavior and influences the plantlike beings beneath the surface to grow. Poole is alarmed to learn that his old colleague, Dave Bowman, and HAL have both become absorbed by the monolith and that the black slab's superiors are intent on doing something unthinkable to the humans that they have enslaved. Writing in the *New York Times Book Review*, John Allen Paulos finds that while the plot hangs together "reasonably well," much of the enjoyment comes from Clarke's ruminations on high technology, Freudian therapy, computer security, terrorism, and religious mania. Ian Watson of the *Times Literary Supplement* suggests that what makes *3001* compelling reading is the way in which he "retrofits" earlier episodes "so that they blend with the new future and the now ex-future." Eric Korn of the *Economist* argues that the novel begs its most interesting question: What if the monolith's part in human evolution were a bad thing? Korn writes, "In *2001*, the monoliths were doors of transcendent perception; in *3001*, they become banal and easily dealt-with alien threats." Korn finds *3001* a "disappointing end" to the Odyssey series. Watson agrees that there are not many surprises to be had in the novel, but praises Clarke for having "the unnerving habit of proving that whatever it is, he imagined it first."

"Science fiction is often called escapism—always in a negative sense," Clarke told Alice K. Turner in a *Publishers Weekly* interview. "Of course it's not true. Science fiction is virtually the only kind of writing that's dealing with real problems and possibilities; it's a concerned fiction." Clarke added that "we know so much more now that we don't have to waste time on the petty things of the past. We can use the enormous technological advances in our work. Vision is wider now, and interest has never been deeper." Although he has been involved with the genre for over half a century, Clarke has not greatly changed his style of writing and the themes he writes about over the years. "I guess I'm just an old conservative," the author told Charles Platt in *Dream Makers: The Uncommon Men and Women Who Write Science Fiction*. "Although, really, if I have stayed true to the original form of my writing that's simply because I have a constant commitment to science." Clarke also remarked to Platt that he is proud of retaining the "sense of wonder" in his writing: "I regard it as something of an achievement not to have become cynical. . . . I do remain an optimist, especially in my fiction, because I hope it may operate as a self-fulfilling prophecy."

BIOGRAPHICAL/CRITICAL SOURCES:

BOOKS

Agel, Jerome, editor, *The Making of Kubrick's 2001*, New American Library, 1970.

Aldiss, Brian W., *Trillion Year Spree: The History of Science Fiction*, Atheneum (New York City), 1986.

Bleiler, E. F., editor, *Science Fiction Writers: Critical Studies of the Major Authors from the Early Nineteenth Century to the Present Day*, Scribners (New York City), 1982.

Clareson, Thomas D., editor, *Voices for the Future: Essays on Major Science Fiction Writers*, Bowling Green University Press (Bowling Green, OH), 1976.

Contemporary Literary Criticism, Gale (Detroit), Volume 1, 1973; Volume 4, 1975; Volume 13, 1980; Volume 16, 1981; Volume 18, 1981; Volume 35, 1985.

Hollow, John, *Against the Night, the Stars: The Science Fiction of Arthur C. Clarke*, Harcourt, 1983, expanded edition, Ohio University Press (Athens, OH), 1987.

Johnson, William, editor, *Focus on the Science Fiction Film,* Prentice-Hall (Englewood Cliffs, NJ), 1972.

Ketterer, David, *New Worlds for Old: The Apocalyptic Imagination, Science Fiction, and American Literature,* Indiana University Press (Bloomington), 1974, pp. 43-9.

Knight, Damon, *In Search of Wonder: Essays on Modern Science Fiction,* Advent (Chicago), 1967, pp. 177-205.

Magill, Frank N., editor, *Survey of Science Fiction Literature,* Volumes 1-5, Salem Press (Englewood Cliffs, NJ), 1979.

Malik, Rex, editor, *Future Imperfect,* Pinter, 1980.

McAleer, Neil, *Arthur C. Clarke: The Authorized Biography,* Contemporary Books (Chicago), 1992.

Moskowitz, Sam, *Seekers of Tomorrow: Masters of Science Fiction,* World Publishing, 1966.

Of Time and Stars: The Worlds of Arthur C. Clarke, Gollancz, 1972, pp. 7-10.

Olander, Joseph D., and Martin Harry Greenburg, editors, *Arthur C. Clarke,* Taplinger (New York City), 1977.

Platt, Charles, *Dream Makers: The Uncommon Men and Women Who Write Science Fiction,* Volume II, Berkeley Publishing, 1983.

Rabkin, Eric S., *Arthur C. Clarke,* Starmont House, 1979.

Reid, Robin Anne, *Arthur C. Clarke: A Critical Companion,* Greenwood Press, 1997.

Samuelson, David N., *Arthur C. Clarke: A Primary and Secondary Bibliography,* G. K. Hall (Boston), 1984.

Short Story Criticism, Volume 3, Gale, 1989.

Slusser, George Edgar, *The Space Odysseys of Arthur C. Clarke,* Borgo (San Bernadino, CA), 1978.

Wollheim, Donald A., *The Universe Makers,* Harper, 1971.

PERIODICALS

Algol, November, 1974.
Atlantic, July, 1952; April, 1963, p. 152.
Best Sellers, October 1, 1973; May, 1979; May, 1984, p. 75-76; December 24, 1953, p. 13.
Booklist, October 1, 1995, pp. 239-40; January 1-15, 1997, p. 778.
Book World, June 30, 1968, pp. 1, 3; December 19, 1971, p. 6.
Chicago Sunday Tribune, July 13, 1952.
Chicago Sunday Tribune Magazine of Books, February 16, 1958, p. 7.
Chicago Tribune, December 30, 1990, section 14, p. 6; January 30, 1994, section 14, p. 6.
Christian Science Monitor, February 26, 1963; February 10, 1972, p. 10; August 8, 1973, p. 9; December 3, 1982, p. B3; November 26, 1993, p. 15.
Commonweal, May 3, 1968.
Detroit News, November 28, 1982.
Discover, May, 1997, p. 68-69.
Economist, April 12, 1997, p. 85.
Extrapolation, winter, 1980, pp. 348-60; summer, 1987, pp. 105-29; spring, 1989, pp. 53-69.
Kirkus Reviews, November 1, 1987.
Library Journal, March 1, 1990, p. 98; November 1, 1995, pp. 101-02; February 15, 1997, p. 164.
Locus, February, 1994, p. 75; November, 1993, p. 27.
Los Angeles Times, December 1, 1982; January 24, 1992, pp. E1, E4; February 12, 1995, p. M4; January 29, 1996.
Los Angeles Times Book Review, December 19, 1982; March 4, 1984; December 6, 1987; December 9, 1990, p. 10; February 3, 1991, p. 10; January 24, 1992, p. E1; August 8, 1993, p. 11; March 10, 1996.
Magazine of Fantasy and Science Fiction, September, 1979, pp. 25-6.

Nation, March 5, 1983.
National Review, November 20, 1962, pp. 403-04; May 14, 1976.
New Republic, May 4, 1968; March 20, 1976; March 24, 1979.
New Scientist, April 12, 1997, pp. 44.
Newsday, April 4, 1968; April 20, 1968.
New Statesman, December 20, 1968, pp. 877-78; January 26, 1979.
Newsweek, October 30, 1961.
New Yorker, April 24, 1965; May 27, 1967; April 13, 1968; September 21, 1968; August 9, 1969, pp. 40-65; December 13, 1982; December 20, 1982.
New York Herald Tribune Book Review, July 13, 1952; August 10, 1952; August 23, 1953; March 2, 1958, p. 6.
New York Times, May 29, 1968; July 5, 1968; August 22, 1973, p. 35; February 26, 1985; April 7, 1993, p. C13, C19; November 28, 1994, p. A4; April 1, 1997; April 11, 1997.
New York Times Book Review, March 14, 1954; July 15, 1956, p. 20; April 14, 1963, pp. 22, 24; August 25, 1968, p. 10; September 23, 1973; January 18, 1976; October 30, 1977, p. 12; March 18, 1979; January 23, 1983, p. 24; March 6, 1983; May 11, 1986; December 20, 1987; May 6, 1990, p. 22; July 8, 1990, p. 22; February 3, 1991, p. 33; September 1, 1991, p. 13; June 13, 1993, p. 22; March 13, 1994, p. 30; January 28, 1996; March 9, 1997.
New York Times Magazine, March 6, 1966.
Omni, March, 1979.
People, December 20, 1982.
Playboy, July, 1986.
Publishers Weekly, September 10, 1973; June 14, 1976; January 6, 1984, p. 75; January 27, 1984, p. 72; September 18, 1995, p. 121-22; January 22, 1996, p. 61.
Reader's Digest, April, 1969.
Saturday Review, July 5, 1952; April 20, 1968.
Science, August 30, 1968, pp. 874-75.
Science Fiction Review, March/April, 1979; August, 1981; February, 1983, p. 15; May, 1984; fall, 1984, p. 26; summer, 1986.
Science-Fiction Studies, July, 1979, pp. 230-31; November, 1997, pp. 441-58.
Time, July 19, 1968; November 15, 1982; January 11, 1988.
Times (London), November 25, 1982.
Times Literary Supplement, July 15, 1968; January 2, 1969; December 5, 1975; June 16, 1978, p. 662; January 21, 1983; October 31, 1986; March 21, 1997.
Tribune Books (Chicago), January 30, 1994, section 14, p. 6.
Virginia Quarterly Review, winter, 1974.
Voice Literary Supplement, November, 1982, pp. 8-9.
Washington Post, February 16, 1982; November 16, 1982.
Washington Post Book World, December 26, 1982, p. 6; March 25, 1984, p. 6; November 25, 1990, p. 8; March 9, 1992, p. B1.
West Coast Review of Books, Number 1, 1986.
Western Folklore, Number 28, 1969, pp. 230-37.
Wilson Library Bulletin, March, 1990, pp. 110-11.
World Press Review, April, 1985.

*   *   *

CLARKE, Austin C(hesterfield) 1934-

PERSONAL: Born July 26, 1934, in Barbados, West Indies; son of Kenneth Trothan (an artist) and Gladys Clarke; married Trinity College; children: Janice, Loretta, Jordan. *Education:* Harrison

College, Barbados, West Indies, Oxford and Cambridge Higher certificate, 1950; additional study at University of Toronto.

ADDRESSES: Agent—Harold Ober Associates, 40 East 49th St., New York, NY 10017.

CAREER: Canadian Broadcasting Corp., Toronto, Ontario, producer and freelance broadcaster, beginning 1963; Brandeis University, Waltham, MA, Jacob Ziskind Professor of Literature, 1968-69; Williams College, Williamstown, MA, Margaret Bundy Scott Professor of Literature, 1971-72; Barbados Embassy, Washington, DC, cultural and press attache, 1974-75; Caribbean Braodcasting Corp., St. Michael, Barbados, general manager, 1976. Visiting professor of Afro-American literature and creative writing, Yale University, 1968-71. Writer-in-residence, Concordia University, Monreal, 1977, University of Western Ontario, London, Ontario, 1978. Member of Board of trustees, Rhode Island School of Design, Providence, 1970-75; member, Immigrations and Refugees Board of Canada, 1989. Vice-chairman, Ontario Board of Censors, 1983-85.

MEMBER: Writers Guild, Writers' Union of Canada (founding member), Yale Club (New Haven).

AWARDS, HONORS: Canada Council senior arts fellowships, 1968, 1970, 1974; University of Western Ontario President's medal for best story, 1965; Belmont Short Story Award, for "Four Stations in His Circle"; Casa de las Americas Literary Prize, 1980.

WRITINGS:

NOVELS

The Survivors of the Crossing, McClelland & Stewart, 1964.
Amongst Thistles and Thorns, McClelland & Stewart, 1965.
The Meeting Point, Macmillan, 1967.
Storm of Fortune, Little, Brown, 1973.
The Bigger Light, Little, Brown, 1975.
The Prime Minister, General Publishing, 1977.
Growing up Stupid under the Union Jack (autobiographical novel), McClelland & Stewart, 1980.
Proud Empires, Viking, 1986.
There Are No Elders, Exile, 1993.
The Austin Clarke Reader, Exile Editions (Toronto), 1996.
The Origin of Waves, McClelland and Stewart (Toronto), 1997.

SHORT STORIES

When He Was Free and Young and He Used to Wear Silks, Anansi, 1971, Little, Brown, 1974.
When Women Rule, McClelland and Stewart, 1985.
Nine Men Who Laughed, Penguin, 1986.

Author of *Short Stories of Austin Clark,* 1984.

OTHER

A Passage Back Home: A Personal Reminiscence of Samuel Selvon, Exile Editions (Toronto), 1994.

Also author of *Myths and Memories, African Literature,* and other filmscripts for Educational Television (ETV), Toronto, 1968–.

SIDELIGHTS: Austin C. Clarke's childhood in colonial Barbados and his experiences as a black immigrant to Canada have provided him with the background for most of his fiction. His writing is almost exclusively concerned with the cultural contradictions that arise when blacks struggle for success in a predominantly white society. Clarke's "one very great gift," in the words of a *New Yorker* critic, is the ability to see "unerringly into his characters' hearts," and this ability is what makes his stories memorable.

Martin Levin writes in the *New York Times Book Review,* "Mr. Clarke is plugged into the fixations, hopes, loves and dreams of his characters. He converts them into stories that are charged with life."

Clarke's autobiographical novel, *Growing Up Stupid under the Union Jack,* is an example of the author's typical theme and style. The narrator, Tom, is a young man from a poor Barbadan village. Everyone in the village is proud that Tom is able to attend the Combermere School, for it is run by a "real, true-true Englishman"—an ex-British army officer who calls his students "boy" and "darky" and who flogs them publicly. The students eagerly imitate this headmaster's morals and manners, for to them, he represents "Mother England"; they are unaware that in England he would be looked down upon as a mere working-class soldier. The book is "a personal, captivating, provoking, and often humorous record of ignorance, inhumanity and lowly existence under colonial imperialism in World War II Barbados. . . . With its major emphasis on education and childhood, *Growing Up Stupid under the Union Jack* continues to draw attention to one of the chief preoccupations of the anti-colonial Anglo-Caribbean novel," writes Robert P. Smith in *World Literature Today.* The theme is well rendered in what Darryl Pinckney calls in the *New York Review of Books* Clarke's "tender, funny, unpolemical style."

Clarke's best known work is a trilogy detailing the lives of the Barbadan blacks who immigrate to Toronto hoping to better their lot. In these novels, *The Meeting Point, Storm of Fortune,* and *The Bigger Light,* "it is as if the flat characters of a Dickensian world have come into their own at last, playing their tragicomic roles in a manner which owes much to Clarke's extraordinary facility with the Barbadian dialect," writes Diane Bessai in *Canadian Literature.* Bessai also expresses eagerness for Clarke to "continue to create his Brueghel-like canvasses with their rich and contrasting detail and mood." "The sense of defeat among the poor islanders is enlivened by the humour of the characters and their glowing fantasies about the presumed wealth of relatives and friends who make it big in the fatlands of the United States or Canada," writes John Ayre in *Saturday Night.*

The first two novels dwell mostly on Bernice Leach, a live-in maid at a wealthy Toronto home, and her small circle of fellow immigrants. Levin writes: "Mr. Clarke is masterful at delineating the oppressive insecurities of Bernice and her friends, and the claustrophobic atmosphere that envelops such a mini-minority" as the Caribbean blacks in Toronto. The third novel, *The Bigger Light,* explores the life of Boysie, the most successful of this immigrant group, and his wife, Dots. Boysie has at last realized the dream that compelled him to leave Barbados; he owns a prosperous business and his own home. However, in the process of realizing his goals, he has become alienated from his wife and his community. Now he searches for a greater meaning to his life—a "bigger light." "*The Bigger Light* is a painful book to read," writes David Rosenthal in the *Nation.* It is "a story of two people with many things to say and no one to say them to, who hate themselves and bitterly resent the society around them. . . . Certain African novelists have also dealt with the isolation of self-made blacks, but none with Clarke's bleak intensity." A *New Yorker* writer praises the book further, citing Clarke's strong writing skill as the element that lifts the book beyond social comment: "the universal longings or ordinary human beings are depicted with a simplicity and power that make us grateful for all three volumes of this long and honest record."

In *The Origin of Waves,* Clarke continues to explore the Caribbean-immigrant experience in Canada. Set in Toronto, the novel begins with a snowstorm that shuts down the city, leaving Tim, a black immigrant from Barbados, more than usually isolated as he walks down the city's strangely empty Yonge Street. By chance he meets an old boyhood friend, John, and the two find a bar where they settle down to reminisce. Tim suffers over the loss of his lover Lang, who died fifteen years earlier, and John, visiting from the United States, struggles to define an identity for himself beyond material success. Although the dominant mood of Clarke's novel is melancholy, it still manages to suggest that Tim and John's "travails need not end in unmitigated bitterness," writes John Bemrose in *Maclean's.* Bemrose admires Clarke's ability to weave seamlessly in and out of memory, and contends that the author's fiction is "a strong rebuke to the naturalism that still dominates so much Canadian fiction."

BIOGRAPHICAL/CRITICAL SOURCES:

BOOKS

Algoo-Kaksh, Stella, *Austin C. Clarke: A Biography,* Press of the University of the West Indies/ECW Press, c. 1994.
Brown, Lloyd, *El Dorado and Paradise; A Critical Study of the Works of Austin Clarke,* Center for Social and Humanistic Studies, University of Western Ontario, 1989.
Contemporary Authors Autobiography Series, Volume 16, Gale, 1992.
Contemporary Literary Criticism, Volume 8, Gale, 1978; Volume 53, 1989.
Dictionary of Literary Biography, Volume 53: *Canadian Writers since 1960, First Series,* Gale, 1986; Volume 125: *Twentieth-Century Caribbean and Black African Writers,* 1993.
Gibson, Graeme, *Eleven Canadian Novelists,* Anansi, 1973, pp. 33-54.

PERIODICALS

Books in Canada, October, 1986, pp. 20-1.
Canadian Literature, summer, 1974; autumn, 1981, pp. 136-38; winter, 1982, pp. 181-85.
CLA Journal, September, 1985, pp. 9-32.
College Language Association Journal, December, 1992, pp. 123-33.
Listener, June 15, 1978.
Maclean's, April 21, 1997, p. 62; June 23, 1997, p. 23.
Nation, November 1, 1975.
New Yorker, February 24, 1975.
New York Review of Books, May 27, 1982.
New York Times Book Review, April 9, 1972; December 9, 1973; February 16, 1975; August 23, 1987.
Quill & Quire, fall, 1997, p. 47.
Saturday Night, October, 1971; June, 1975.
Times Literary Supplement, May 11, 1967, p. 404.
World Literature Today, winter, 1982.

* * *

CLAVELL, James (duMaresq) 1925-1994

PERSONAL: Born October 10, 1925, in Australia; came to the United States, 1953; naturalized, 1963; died of complications from cancer, September 6, 1994, in Vevey, Switzerland; son of Richard Charles (a captain in the British Royal Navy) and Eileen (Collis) Clavell; married April Stride, February 20, 1951; children: Michaela, Holly. *Education:* Attended University of Birmingham, 1946-47. *Avocation:* Sailing, flying helicopters.

ADDRESSES: Agent—Foreign Rights, Inc., 400 East 58th St., #17D, New York, NY 10022; Contemporary Artists, 132 Lasky Dr., Beverly Hills, CA 90212.

CAREER: Worked as a carpenter, 1953; screenwriter, director, and producer, 1954-94; director of television programs, beginning 1958; novelist, 1962-94. *Military service:* Served as captain with the Royal Artillery, 1940-46; taken prisoner of war by Japanese.

MEMBER: Writers Guild, Authors League of America, Producers Guild, Dramatists Guild, Directors Guild.

AWARDS, HONORS: Writers Guild Best Screenplay Award, 1963, for *The Great Escape;* honorary doctorates from the University of Maryland and the University of Bradford.

WRITINGS:

NOVELS

King Rat, Little, Brown (Boston), 1962, reprinted as *James Clavell's "King Rat,"* Delacorte (New York City), 1983.
Tai-Pan: A Novel of Hong Kong, Atheneum (New York City), 1966.
Shogun: A Novel of Japan, Atheneum, 1975.
Noble House: A Novel of Contemporary Hong Kong, Delacorte, 1981.
The Children's Story, Delacorte, 1981.
James Clavell's "Whirlwind," Morrow (New York City), 1986.
James Clavell's "Thrump-o-moto," illustrated by George Sharp, Delacorte, 1986.
James Clavell's Gai-Jin: A Novel of Japan, Delacorte, 1993.
Two Complete Novels (includes *Tai-Pan* and *King Rat*), Wings Books (New York City), 1995.

SCREENPLAYS

The Fly, Twentieth Century-Fox, 1958.
Watusi, Metro-Goldwyn-Mayer, 1959.
(And producer and director) *Five Gates to Hell,* Twentieth Century-Fox, 1959.
(And producer and director) *Walk Like a Dragon,* Paramount, 1960.
(And producer and director) *The Great Escape,* United Artists, 1963.
633 Squadron, United Artists, 1964.
The Satan Bug, United Artists, 1965.
(And producer and director) *Where's Jack?* Paramount, 1968.
(And producer and director) *To Sir with Love,* Columbia, 1969.
(And producer and director) *The Last Valley,* ABC Pictures, 1969.

OTHER

Countdown to Armageddon: E=mc2 (play), produced in Vancouver, British Columbia, at Vancouver Playhouse Theatre, 1966.
(Author of introduction) *The Making of James Clavell's "Shogun,"* Dell (New York City), 1980.
(Editor and author of foreword) Sun Tzu, *The Art of War,* Hodder & Stoughton (London), 1981, Delacorte, 1983.

Also author of poetry ("published and paid, by God").

MEDIA ADAPTATIONS: King Rat was produced by Columbia, 1965; *Tai-Pan* was produced by DeLaurentiis Entertainment Group, 1986. *Shogun* was produced as a television miniseries, 1980 (Clavell was executive producer); *The Children's Story* was produced as a Mobile Showcase television special, 1982; *Noble House* was produced as a television miniseries under the title *James Clavell's "Noble House",* 1988; a television miniseries based on *King Rat* and one based on *Whirlwind* are planned. *Shogun* was produced for the stage at the Kennedy Center in Washington, DC, and on Broadway in 1990.

SIDELIGHTS: James Clavell, who called himself an "old-fashioned storyteller," is one of the twentieth century's most widely read novelists. His sagas of the Far East—*Tai-Pan: A Novel of Hong Kong, Shogun: A Novel of Japan,* and *Noble House: A Novel of Contemporary Hong Kong*—have each sold millions of copies and dominated bestseller lists for months, while his Iran-based adventure, *James Clavell's "Whirlwind,"* commanded a record-setting $5,000,000 advance from its publisher. In the *Los Angeles Times,* an industry insider described Clavell as "one of the very few writers . . . whose names have marquee value. Clavell's name on the cover sells enormous quantities of books." As James Vesely noted in the *Detroit News,* the author "always does one thing right: he is never boring." Indeed, Clavell combined action, intrigue, cultural conflicts, and romance to produce "event-packed books with the addictive appeal of popcorn," asserted *Detroit News* correspondent Helen Dudar. Although critics agreed that Clavell's blockbusters do not aspire to literary greatness, they also concurred that his works possess the sort of research and detail rarely found in so-called "popular novels." In the *National Review,* Terry Teachout called Clavell a "first-rate novelist of the second rank," the kind of writer "who provides genuinely stimulating literary entertainment without insulting the sensibilities."

Clavell's life was almost as eventful as one of his books. He was born in Australia in 1925, the son of a British Royal Navy captain who traveled to ports all over the world. As a child, Clavell relished the swashbuckling sea tales—most of them fictional—recounted by his father and grandfather, both career military men. A career in the service seemed a natural choice for Clavell, too, and after his secondary schooling was completed, he joined the Royal Artillery in 1940. A year later, he was sent to fight in the Far East and was wounded by machine-gun fire in the jungles of Malaysia. For several months he hid in a Malay village, but he was eventually captured by the Japanese and sent to the notorious Changi prison near Singapore. The conditions at Changi were so severe that only 10,000 of its 150,000 inmates survived incarceration—and Clavell was there three and a half years. He told the *Guardian*: "Changi was a school for survivors. It gave me a strength most people don't have. I have an awareness of life others lack. Changi was my university. . . . Those who were supposed to survive didn't." The experience invested Clavell with some of the same verve and intensity which characterize his fictional protagonists. Calling Changi "the rock" on which he put his life, he said: "So long as I remember Changi, I know I'm living forty borrowed lifetimes."

Released from captivity after the war, Clavell returned to Great Britain to continue his military career. A motorcycle accident left him lame in one leg, however, and he was discharged in 1946. He attended Birmingham University briefly, considering law or engineering as a profession, but when he began to visit movie sets with his future wife, an aspiring actress, he became fascinated with directing and writing for films. He entered the movie industry on the ground floor as a distributor, gradually moving into production work. In 1953 he and his wife immigrated to the United States, where, after a period of television production in New York, they moved to Hollywood. There Clavell bluffed his way into a screenwriting contract ("They liked my accent, I suppose," he told the *Washington Post*) and set to work in the field that would bring him his first success. His first produced

screenplay, *The Fly,* was based on a science fiction story about an atomic scientist whose experiments cause an exchange of heads with a housefly. The movie made a $4,000,000 profit in two years and has since become a classic genre film in its own right and the source of several sequels and remakes. Clavell won a Writers Guild Best Screenplay Award for the 1963 film *The Great Escape,* also a box-office success. Of the films the author produced, directed, and wrote, perhaps the most notable remains the 1969 hit *To Sir with Love,* starring Sidney Poitier. Created with a budget of $625,000, the movie about a black teacher's efforts to mold a class of tough British delinquents grossed $15,000,000. Both Clavell and Poitier had contracted for percentages of the profits, so the project proved lucrative.

A Hollywood screenwriters' strike brought a fortuitous change to Clavell's career in 1960. Simultaneously sidelined from his regular employment and haunted by returning memories of Changi, he began to work on a novel about his prison experiences. The process of writing released many suppressed emotions for Clavell; in twelve weeks he had completed the first draft of *King Rat.* Set in Changi, the novel follows the fortunes of an English prisoner of war and his ruthless American comrade in their struggles to survive the brutal conditions. *New York Times Book Review* contributor Martin Levin observed, "All personal relationships [in the work] pale beside the impersonal, soul-disintegrating evil of Changi itself which Mr. Clavell, himself a Japanese P.O.W. for three years, renders with stunning authority." Some critics have maintained that the book loses some impact because it is aimed at a popular audience, but Paul King of *Maclean's* called *King Rat* the work of "a sensitive craftsman." A *New York Herald Tribune Books* reviewer concluded that *King Rat* is "at once fascinating in narrative detail, penetrating in observation of human nature under survival stress, and provoking in its analysis of right and wrong." In the *Christian Science Monitor,* R. R. Bruun also noted that by virtue of his careful plotting, "Mr. Clavell manages to keep the tension wound up to the snapping point through much of the book." A bestseller, *King Rat* was adapted for film in 1965.

Clavell was still primarily a screenwriter when he penned *Tai-Pan,* a sweeping fictional account of the founding of Hong Kong. A historical novel set in 1841, the story recounts the adventures of Dirk Struan, first *tai-pan,* or merchant overlord, of the Noble House trading company. Struan builds his empire on the nearly deserted peninsula of Hong Kong, convinced that a British colony there would provide a power base for the growing empire. *New York Times* reviewer Orville Prescott claimed that in *Tai-Pan,* Clavell "holds attention with a relentless grip. *Tai-Pan* frequently is crude. It is grossly exaggerated much of the time. But seldom does a novel appear so stuffed with imaginative invention, so packed with melodramatic action, so gaudy and flamboyant with blood and sin, treachery and conspiracy, sex and murder." A *Time* critic labeled the work "a belly-gutting, god-rotting typhoon of a book" and added: "Its narrative pace is numbing, its style deafening, its language penny dreadful. . . . It isn't art and it isn't truth. But its very energy and scope command the eye." Since its publication in 1966 and its forty-four-week stay on the bestseller lists, it has sold more than 2,000,000 copies. It too has been made into a motion picture that was released in 1986.

According to the *Washington Post*'s Cynthia Gorney, Clavell's best-known novel, *Shogun,* had an inauspicious beginning in the author's mind. She wrote, "James Clavell, his imagination awash with plans for the modern-day Asian chronicle that was to be his third novel, picked up one of his 9-year-old daughter's school books one afternoon in London, and came upon an intriguing bit of history." He read the following sentence from the text: "In 1600, an Englishman went to Japan and became a Samurai." Fascinated by that possibility, Clavell began to read everything he could find about medieval Japan and Will Adams, the historical figure in question. The research led Clavell into the story of *Shogun,* but it also gave him a new understanding of the culture that had kept him in captivity during the Second World War. "I started reading about Japan's history and characteristics," he told the *New York Times,* "and then the way the Japanese treated me and my brothers became clearer to me." After a year of research in the British Museum and several visits to Japan, Clavell created the tale of John Blackthorne, an Elizabethan sailor cast upon the shores of Japan during a period of internal conflict between rival warlords. Spanning all the elements of seventeenth-century Japanese society, the adventure recounts Blackthorne's transformation from a European "barbarian" into a trusted adviser to the powerful Shogun Toranaga.

Most critics have praised *Shogun* for its historical detail as well as for its riveting plot. "Clavell offers a wide-ranging view of feudal Japan at a time of crisis," stated Bruce Cook in the *Washington Post Book World,* adding, "Scene after scene is given, conversation after conversation reported, with the point not merely of advancing the narrative (which does somehow grind inexorably forward), but also of imparting to us the peculiar flavor of life in feudal Japan and the unique code of conduct (*bushido*) which dominated life there and then." Other reviewers have cited the story itself as the source of *Shogun*'s appeal. Gorney of the *Washington Post* described it as "one of those books that blots up vacations and imperils marriages, because it simply will not let the reader go," and *Library Journal* contributor Mitsu Yamamoto deemed it "a wonderful churning brew of adventure, intrigue, love, philosophy, and history."

Critics have also praised *Noble House,* Clavell's 1981 bestseller about financial power struggles in modern Hong Kong. *Washington Post* correspondent Sandy Rovner informed readers of the mass of the novel—"1,207 pages long, 2 1/2 inches (not counting covers) thick and 3 pounds and 13 ounces"—because *Noble House* must be carried with you since "you can't put it down." Henry S. Hayward commented on the book's mass as well in the *Christian Science Monitor.* "James Clavell is a master yarn-spinner and an expert on detail," Hayward asserted. "Indeed, one sometimes feels overwhelmed with the masses of information and wishes a firmer editing pencil had been applied. But the author, nevertheless, is in a class with James Michener and Robert Elegant in his ability to handle a massive cast and hold your attention through the intricacies of a 1,200 page plot." The *National Review*'s Teachout remarked that one "races through *Noble House* like a fire engine, torn between savoring each tasty bit of local color and wanting to find out as soon as possible what new outrage [the hero] will put down next." In the *New York Times Book Review,* Webster Schott concluded that the novel "isn't primarily about any particular story or character or set of characters. It's about a condition that's a place, Hong Kong. Mr. Clavell perceives that city to be a unique setting for extremes of greed and vengefulness, international intrigue and silky romance." Commenting on Clavell's plotting, *New York Times* columnist Christopher Lehmann-Haupt opined: "Curiously enough, its staggering complexity is one of the things that the novel has going for it. Not only is *Noble House* as long as life, it's also as rich with possibilities. . . . There are so many irons in the fire that almost anything can plausibly happen."

Noble House, the Far East trading company featured in *Tai-Pan* and *Noble House,* is also a part of *James Clavell's Gai-Jin.* Set in Japan in the 1860s, *Gai-Jin* offers a fictional chronicle concentrating on early Yokohama and its turbulent history, based on events which actually happened in the late 1800s. *Gai-Jin* introduces Malcolm Struan, twenty-year-old heir to the Far East English shipping firm Noble House. The novel received mixed reviews. Lehmann-Haupt observed, "At the start of *Gai-Jin,* which means foreigner in Japanese, *Tai-Pan* crashes into *Shogun,*" referring in part to the intermixing of characters and action between the three novels. Lehmann-Haupt added, "At its best, *Gai-Jin* achieves a grand historical perspective that makes us feel we're understanding how today's Japan came into being with its ambivalence toward outsiders." The critic questions the inclusion of Japanese dialogue, complete with its stereotypical English pronunciations, comparing it to a "World War I comic book." Lehmann-Haupt concluded that the thousand-page tome "is in the mainstream of a great and enduring storytelling tradition, full of rich characters and complicated action. It's just that modernism makes such fiction seem unreal."

The publishing industry knows that Clavell's name alone is quite appealing to book buyers. An auction of his 1986 novel *Whirlwind* brought Clavell an unprecedented $5,000,000 advance from the William Morrow Company, which had based its bid on a preview of only 10 percent of the manuscript. Morrow also ordered a first printing of 950,000 hardcover copies, another unprecedented move. Set in Iran during the hectic weeks after the overthrow of the Shah, *Whirlwind* charts the activities of a group of helicopter pilots trying to move their precious machinery out of the country before the government can seize it. Dorothy Allison described the work as "1147 pages of violence, passion, cutthroat business, religious obsession, and martyrdom—exactly what his readers expect and want along with their exotic settings." Although *Whirlwind* received mixed reviews, it was also a bestseller; a miniseries based on it has been planned.

In various interviews, Clavell discussed both his aims as a writer and his methods of putting a book together. He told the *Los Angeles Times:* "I look at storytelling in picture form," he explained. "I watch the story happen, and I describe what I see. When you write a screenplay, you write only what you can photograph and what you can hear. As a result, my books have no fat, no purple prose, and they're very visual." Writing a lengthy novel, he told the *Washington Post,* "is pertinacity, you know, grim determination. And a marvelous selfishness to finish, to exclude everything. I begrudge the time spent away from my novel. . . . I've got this need to finish, to find the last page." Clavell mentioned in the *National Review* that his basic goal was entertainment—for himself as well as his readers. "I'm not a novelist, I'm a storyteller," he contended. "I'm not a literary figure at all. I work very hard and try to do the best I can; and I try and write for myself, thinking that what I like, other people may like."

BIOGRAPHICAL/CRITICAL SOURCES:

BOOKS

Contemporary Literary Criticism, Gale (Detroit), Volume 6, 1976; Volume 25, 1983; Volume 87, 1995.
MacDonald, Gina, *James Clavell: A Critical Companion,* Greenwood Press (Westport, CT), 1996.
The Making of James Clavell's "Shogun," Dell, 1980.

PERIODICALS

Best Sellers, July 15, 1966; October, 1981.

Chicago Tribune, April 12, 1981; February 18, 1982; November 21, 1986.

Christian Science Monitor, August 9, 1962; June 24, 1981, May 12, 1993, p. 13; May 13, 1994, p. 12.

Detroit News, May 3, 1981; May 12, 1993, p. 13.

Fantasy Review, June, 1987, p. 42.

Far Eastern Economic Review, May 20, 1993, p. 46.

Globe and Mail (Toronto), January 4, 1986.

Guardian, October 4, 1975.

History Today, October, 1981, pp. 39-42.

Los Angeles Times, November 7, 1986; December 11, 1986.

Maclean's, May 11, 1981; November 24, 1986.

National Review, October 12, 1982, pp. 23-4; November 12, 1982, pp. 14, 20-2.

New Republic, July 4, 1981.

New Statesman, November 21, 1975.

Newsweek, November 10, 1986, p. 84.

New York Herald Tribune Books, August 5, 1962.

New York Review of Books, September 18, 1975; December 18, 1986, pp. 58-60.

New York Times, May 4, 1966; April 28, 1981; May 17, 1981; February 18, 1982; December 28, 1985; January 7, 1986; January 11, 1986; November 1, 1986; November 7, 1986; November 17, 1986; May 24, 1993, p. C16.

New York Times Book Review, August 12, 1962; May 22, 1966; June 22, 1975; May 3, 1981; April 18, 1993, p. 13.

New York Times Magazine, September 13, 1981.

Observer, July 4, 1993, p. 62.

People, May 10, 1993, pp. 27, 29.

Poe Studies, June, 1983, p. 13.

Publishers Weekly, October 24, 1986; March 22, 1993, p. 69.

Saturday Review, August 11, 1962.

Time, June 17, 1966; July 7, 1975; July 6, 1981.

Times (London), November 2, 1986, pp. 41, 43-4.

Times Literary Supplement, December 5, 1986; December 26, 1986.

Village Voice, September 2, 1981, p. 37; December 16, 1986.

Wall Street Journal, October 7, 1986, p. 30.

Washington Post, February 4, 1979; May 5, 1981; November 11, 1986.

Washington Post Book World, July 13, 1975; October 26, 1986; December 7, 1986, p. 4.

*   *   *

CLEARY, Beverly (Atlee Bunn) 1916-

PERSONAL: Born in 1916, in McMinnville, OR; daughter of Chester Lloyd and Mable (Atlee) Bunn; married Clarence T. Cleary, October 6, 1940; children: Marianne Elisabeth, Malcolm James (twins). *Education:* University of California, Berkeley, B.A., 1938; University of Washington, Seattle, B.A. in librarianship, 1939. *Avocational interests:* Travel, needlework.

ADDRESSES: Home—California. *Office*—c/o William Morrow & Co., 1350 Avenue of the Americas, New York, NY 10019.

CAREER: Public Library, Yakima, WA, children's librarian, 1939-40; U.S. Army Hospital, Oakland, CA, post librarian, 1942-45; writer, 1950–.

MEMBER: Authors Guild, Authors League of America.

AWARDS, HONORS: Young Readers' Choice Award from Pacific Northwest Library Association, 1957, for *Henry and*

Ribsy, 1960, for *Henry and the Paper Route,* 1968, for *The Mouse and the Motorcycle,* 1971, for *Ramona the Pest,* and 1980, for *Ramona and Her Father;* Dorothy Canfield Fisher Memorial Children's Book Award, 1958, for *Fifteen,* 1961, for *Ribsy,* and 1985, for *Dear Mr. Henshaw;* Notable Book citation from American Library Association, 1961, for *Jean and Johnny,* 1966, for *The Mouse and the Motorcycle,* 1978, for *Ramona and Her Father,* and 1984, for *Dear Mr. Henshaw.*

Distinguished Alumna Award from University of Washington, 1975; Laura Ingalls Wilder Award from American Library Association (ALA), 1975, for substantial and lasting contributions to children's literature; Mark Twain Award from Missouri Library Association and Missouri Association of School Librarians, 1978, for *Ramona the Brave;* Newbery Honor Book Award from ALA and *Boston Globe-Horn Book* Honor Award, both 1978, for *Ramona and Her Father.*

International Board on Books for Young People Honor Book Award, 1980, for *Ramona and Her Father;* Regina Medal from Catholic Library Association, 1980, for "continued distinguished contributions to literature"; American Book Award, 1981, for *Ramona and Her Mother;* Newbery Honor Book Award, ALA and American Book Award nomination, both 1982, for *Ramona Quimby, Age Eight.*

Christopher Award, 1983, for *Dear Mr. Henshaw;* Newbery Medal from ALA, Commonwealth Silver Medal from Commonwealth Club of California, and *New York Times* notable book citation, all 1984, all for *Dear Mr. Henshaw.*

WRITINGS:

Henry Huggins, Morrow (New York City), 1950.

Ellen Tebbits, Morrow, 1951.

Henry and Beezus, Morrow, 1952.

Otis Spofford, Morrow, 1953.

Henry and Ribsy, Morrow, 1954.

Beezus and Ramona, Morrow, 1955.

Fifteen, Morrow, 1956.

Henry and the Paper Route, Morrow, 1957.

The Luckiest Girl, Morrow, 1958.

Jean and Johnny, Morrow, 1959.

The Real Hole (preschool), Morrow, 1960, revised edition, 1986.

Hullabaloo ABC (preschool) Parnassus, 1960.

Two Dog Biscuits (preschool), Morrow, 1961, revised edition, 1986.

Emily's Runaway Imagination, Morrow, 1961.

Henry and the Clubhouse, Morrow, 1962.

Sister of the Bride, Morrow, 1963.

Ribsy, Morrow, 1964.

The Mouse and the Motorcycle, Morrow, 1965.

Mitch and Amy, Morrow, 1967, with illustrations by Bob Marstall, Morrow, 1991.

Ramona the Pest (also see below), Morrow, 1968.

Runaway Ralph, Morrow, 1970.

Socks, Morrow, 1973.

The Sausage at the End of the Nose (play), Children's Book Council, 1974.

Ramona the Brave, Morrow, 1975.

Ramona and Her Father (also see below), Morrow, 1977.

Ramona and Her Mother (also see below), Morrow, 1979.

Ramona Quimby, Age Eight (also see below), Morrow, 1981.

Ralph S. Mouse, Morrow, 1982.

Young Love, Dell, 1982.

Dear Mr. Henshaw, Morrow, 1983.

Cutting Up with Ramona! Dell, 1983.
Ramona Forever (also see below), Morrow, 1984.
The Ramona Quimby Diary, Morrow, 1984.
Lucky Chuck, Morrow, 1984.
Beezus and Ramona Diary, Morrow, 1986.
The Growing-Up Feet, Morrow, 1987.
Janet's Thingamajigs, Morrow, 1987.
A Girl from Yamhill: A Memoir, Morrow, 1988.
Ramona Quimby: The Making of a Television Film, Dell, 1988.
Meet Ramona Quimby (includes *Ramona and Her Father, Ramona and Her Mother, Ramona Forever, Ramona Quimby, Age Eight,* and *Ramona the Pest*), Dell, 1989.
Muggie Maggie, Morrow, 1990.
Strider, Morrow, 1991.
Petey's Bedtime Story, illustrated by David Small, Morrow (New York City), 1993.
My Own Two Feet: A Memoir, Morrow (New York City), 1995.

Also author of *Ramona and Her Friends* (an omnibus edition), and *Leave It to Beaver* (adapted from television scripts). Contributor of an adult short story to *Women's Day.*

MEDIA ADAPTATIONS: Pied Piper produced recordings and filmstrips of *Henry and the Clubhouse,* 1962, and *Ribsy,* 1964. Miller-Brody produced recordings, some with accompanying filmstrips, of *Ramona and Her Father,* 1979, *Beezus and Ramona,* 1980, *Henry Huggins,* 1980, *Henry and Ribsy,* 1980, *Ramona and Her Mother,* 1980, *Ramona the Brave,* 1980, *Ramona Quimby, Age Eight,* 1981, *Henry and Beezus,* 1981, *Ralph S. Mouse,* 1983, and *Dear Mr. Henshaw,* 1984. A six-episode series based on *The Mouse and the Motorcycle, Runaway Ralph,* and *Ralph S. Mouse* was produced by Churchill Films for American Broadcasting Companies, Inc. (ABC-TV); *Ramona,* a ten-part series based on Cleary's character Ramona Quimby was broadcast on the Public Broadcasting Service (PBS) in 1988; television programs based on the "Henry Huggins" books have appeared in Japan, Sweden, and Denmark.

SIDELIGHTS: Beverly Cleary's humorous, realistic portrayal of American children's lives has made her a favorite of young readers and their parents for more than thirty years. Books were important to Cleary from an early age; her mother established the first lending library in the small town where the author was born. "It was in this dingy room filled with shabby leather-covered chairs and smelling of stale cigar smoke that I made the most magic of discoveries," she recalls in *Top of the News.* "There were books for children!"

Cleary looked eagerly forward to school and learning to read. Once there, however, she found herself stifled by the rigid teaching methods of that time. "We had no bright beckoning book with such words as 'fun,' 'adventure,' or 'horizon' to tempt us on. . . . Our primer looked grim," she remembers in a *Horn Book* article. "Its olive-green cover with its austere black lettering bore the symbol of a beacon light, presumably to guide us and to warn us of the dangers that lay within. . . . The first grade was soon sorted into three reading groups: Bluebirds, Redbirds, and Blackbirds. I was a Blackbird, the only girl Blackbird among the boy Blackbirds who had to sit in the row by the blackboard. . . . To be a Blackbird was to be disgraced. I wanted to read, but somehow I could not. I wept at home while my puzzled mother tried to drill me on the dreaded word charts."

Under the guidance of a teacher in the second grade, Cleary learned "to plod through [the] reader a step or two ahead of disgrace" and eventually regained her original enthusiasm for

books. She found, however, that the books available were ultimately unsatisfactory, for they bore no relation to the life she knew as a middle-class child in Portland, Oregon. Instead, they were about "wealthy English children who had nannies and pony carts or books about poor children whose problems were solved by a long-lost rich relative turning up in the last chapter," she explained in a speech reprinted in *Horn Book.* "I had had enough. . . . I wanted to read funny stories about the sort of children I knew and decided that someday when I grew up I would write them."

Cleary did just that, setting most of her books on or around Klickitat Street, a real street near her childhood home. The children in her books face situations common in real children's lives—finding a stray dog, forgetting to deliver newspapers, the horror of having to kiss in a school play. They discover that adults are not always fair; they misbehave. Cleary recalled in a speech reprinted in *Catholic Library World* that "*Otis Spofford* was considered controversial when it was published in 1953, and some school libraries did not buy it because Otis threw spitballs and did not repent."

Perhaps the most endearing and popular of Cleary's characters is Ramona Quimby, a spunky little girl who would make fairly regular appearances in her books after the Henry Huggins stories of the 1950s. It was not until 1968, however, with the publication of *Ramona the Pest,* that Ramona had a book to herself. Critics as well as readers responded enthusiastically to this expansion of Ramona's character, and each successive book would be met with almost unqualified praise. A critic in *Young Readers' Review* comments: "As in all her books about the boys and girls of Klickitat Street, Mrs. Cleary invests [*Ramona the Pest*] with charm, humor, and complete honesty. There are some adults who can remember many incidents from their early childhood; there are few who can remember how they felt about things and why; there are fewer who can communicate these feelings. And fewer still who can retain the humorous aspects. Mrs. Cleary is one of those rare ones. . . . Even boys and girls who dislike stories about children younger than themselves enjoy the incidents in which Ramona makes a pest of herself. . . . Ramona has never been funnier and has never been so sympathetic a character. . . . As usual, this is standard Cleary first rate entertainment." Polly Goodwin of *Book World* calls Ramona "a wonderfully real little girl trying hard to express herself, to understand and be understood in a bewildering world."

The sequel to *Ramona the Pest,* titled *Ramona the Brave,* was equally well received. A reviewer in the *Bulletin of the Center for Children's Books* writes that it is "diverting [and] written with the ebullient humor and sympathy that distinguish Cleary's stories. Ramona is as convincing a first-grader as a fictional character can be." *Growing Point* calls it "straight domestic writing at its liveliest and most skilful."

Cleary told *Contemporary Authors* that the books about Ramona reflect a "child's relationship with adults." This is evident in *Ramona and Her Father,* in which Mr. Quimby loses his job and begins to smoke too much, prompting Ramona to start a ferocious no-smoking campaign in order to save her father's life. A critic in *Booklist* writes: "With her uncanny gift for pinpointing the thoughts and feelings of children right down to their own phraseology—while honoring the boundaries of clean, simple writing—the author catches a family situation that puts strain on each of its members, despite their intrinsic strength and invincible humor. . . . [The resulting story is] true, warm-hearted, and funny."

The ability to portray the world of adults through a child's perspective is a strength of Cleary's nonfiction as well as her fiction. In her two volumes of autobiographical writing—1988's *A Girl from Yamhill: A Memoir* and *My Own Two Feet: A Memoir,* the latter published in 1995—Cleary "immediately makes one understand why [her] books are perennial favorites," according to Mary M. Burns in *Horn Book.* Recounting her childhood in Portland, Oregon, during the Great Depression, *A Girl from Yamhill* reveals the real Klickitat Street, and shows that the roots of many of the fictional episodes of Ramona Quimby were based on her creator's own life. Praising Cleary's choice of topics, which include the emotional difficulties in moving to a new town, dealing with an overly demonstrative male relative, an undemonstrative mother whose affection was channeled into molding her children to her own designs, and dealing with the pangs of adolescent first love, Lillian N. Gerhardt writes in *School Library Journal* that, "As with her fiction, readers are likely to want her memoir to go on when they read her last page."

A Girl from Yamhill ends in 1934, as Cleary begins her college education in Southern California. *My Own Two Feet* takes up the story where its predecessor left off: the soon-to-be author on a Greyhound bus bound from Oregon to California, ready to begin her life as an independent adult. *My Own Two Feet* "is a Depression story and then a World War II home-front story," explains Perri Klass in the *New York Times Book Review,* "but most remarkably it is a story about craving independence and craving education." From college, where she studied library science, Cleary got a job as a children's librarian in Washington. The children she met there would inspire her early attempts at fulfilling her childhood dream of becoming a writer of books for young readers. In between college and her first published book in 1950 were courtship and marriage, the financial stresses caused by making a living during the Depression years, and an emotional confrontation with a strong-willed, controlling mother. Cleary's "vivid recollections" of the many small events that figured in her journey as a student and young wife "are continued evidence of this author's ability to convince readers," maintains Ruth K. MacDonald in *School Library Journal.* "It's all in the details."

While her autobiographies reveal that many of her books had their basis in her own life, Cleary has also written on topics with which she has not had firsthand experience. Publication of *Dear Mr. Henshaw* in 1983, for example, marked Cleary's response to many letters asking for a book about a child of divorce. In this book, Leigh Botts's letters to his favorite author reveal his loneliness and confusion following his parents' separation. While the typical Cleary humor is still present, *Dear Mr. Henshaw* represents a change in style and tone for Cleary; it is the author's most serious work. She remarked in a speech reprinted in *Horn Book*: "When I wrote *Dear Mr. Henshaw,* I did not expect every reader to like Leigh as much as Ramona. Although I am deeply touched that my books have reached two generations of children, popularity has never been my goal. If it had been, I would have written *Ramona Solves the Mystery of the Haunted House and Finds a Baby Brother* or something like *Henry and Beezus Play Doctor,* instead of a book about the feelings of a lonely child of divorce."

Critics and children alike responded enthusiastically to Cleary's efforts. Natalie Babbitt declares in the *New York Times Book Review*: "Beverly Cleary has written many very good books over the years. This one is the best. It is a first-rate, poignant story."

My Own Two Feet is Beverly Cleary's sequel to the autobiographical reminisces of her childhood that began in *A Girl from Yamhill* and traces the author's journey through college, marriage, and the publication of her first book—in short, it traces Cleary's growth into an adult woman capable of standing on her own two feet. The memoir begins in the 1930s, when Cleary left home to attend junior college in California, because, as her mother told her, "We want to leave you prepared to take care of yourself and any children you might have. Widows so often have to run boarding-houses." Cleary softens her account of the difficulties of the Depression with anecdotes like the one about an admirer from her hometown who traveled hundreds of miles to visit her at college only to turn around and go home when he thought she might not like to see him. Mary M. Burns, writing for *Horn Book Magazine,* says that the memoir "is a marvelously sensitive, often funny portrayal of a young woman's progress to adulthood and to independence. It is also the story of a writer-in-the-making, for the geneses of her novels are rooted deep in her own experiences." *Publishers Weekly* says that "the author's unsentimental recollections of herself as a student in the Depression, a librarian and a newlywed are told humorously and candidly." Although Cleary's memoir might seem directed toward adult audiences rather than her usual fans, young writers like Susanna C. Berger find Cleary's memoir particularly engaging and inspiring. Reporting for *Stone Soup,* Berger writes, "I have long wondered how one could make it as a writer. . . . This memoir traces clearly the road to becoming a good writer."

BIOGRAPHICAL/CRITICAL SOURCES:

BOOKS

Berg, Julie, *Beverly Cleary,* Abdo & Daughters (Edina, MN), 1993.

Chambers, Mary, editor, *The Signal Review I: A Selective Guide to Children's Literature,* Thimble Press, 1983.

Children's Literature Review, Gale (Detroit), Volume 2, 1976, Volume 8, 1985.

Contemporary Authors New Revision Series, Volume 19, 1987.

Cullinan, Bernice E., and others, *Literature and the Child,* Harcourt, 1981.

Dictionary of Literary Biography, Volume 52: *American Writers for Children since 1960: Fiction,* Gale, 1986.

Egoff, Sheila A., *Thursday's Child: Trends and Patterns in Contemporary Children's Literature,* American Library Association, 1981.

Kelly, Joanne, *The Beverly Cleary Handbook,* Teacher Ideas Press (Englewood, CO), 1996.

Pflieger, Pat, *Beverly Cleary,* Twayne (Boston), 1991.

Rees, David, *The Marble in the Water: Essays on Contemporary Writers of Fiction for Children and Young Adults,* Horn Book, 1980.

Sebesta, Sam Keaton, and William J. Iverson, *Literature for Thursday's Child,* Science Research Associates, 1975.

Something about the Author, Gale, Volume 2, 1971; Volume 43, 1986; Volume 79, 1995.

Something about the Author Autobiography Series, Volume 20, Gale, 1995.

Sutherland, Zena, and others, *Children and Books,* 6th edition, Scott, Foresman, 1981.

PERIODICALS

Atlantic Monthly, December, 1953; December, 1964.

Booklist, September 1, 1953; September 1, 1954; October 1, 1977; May 1, 1979; September 1, 1981; September 1, 1983; September 1, 1984; August, 1995, p. 1948.

Book World, September 8, 1968.
Bulletin of the Center for Children's Books, September, 1959; September, 1961; October, 1963; May, 1967; July, 1975; December, 1977; June, 1979; September, 1982; May, 1984; September, 1984.
Catholic Library World, February, 1980; July-August, 1981.
Children's Book Review, spring, 1975.
Christian Science Monitor, September 6, 1951; November 27, 1957; November 15, 1962; October 15, 1979; May 14, 1982; June 6, 1983.
Detroit News, August 10, 1983.
Early Years, August-September, 1982.
Entertainment Weekly, May 7, 1993, p. 66; August 20, 1993, p. 73.
Five Owls, July/August 1990, p. 106-07; September/October, 1991, p. 18; February, 1994, p. 58.
Growing Point, March, 1963; January, 1976; September, 1978; July, 1980; January, 1983; May, 1983.
Horn Book, December, 1951; December 1959; October, 1962; October, 1963; December, 1964; June, 1969; August, 1970; August, 1975; December, 1977; October, 1982; December, 1982; October, 1983; August, 1984; September, 1984; May/June, 1988, pp. 369-70; November/December, 1990, p. 738; September-October, 1991, p. 595; May-June, 1995, p. 297; December, 1995, p. 775.
Language Arts, January, 1979.
Library Journal, September 15, 1950; October 15, 1952; September 15, 1957; September 15, 1962.
Los Angeles Times Book Review, May 22, 1988, p. 11.
New York Herald Tribune Book Review, October 14, 1951; October 12, 1952; September 27, 1953; November 6, 1955; November 18, 1956; November, 1959.
New York Times Book Review, September 14, 1952; October 4, 1953; September 26, 1954; September 16, 1956; October 9, 1960; December 26, 1965; October 14, 1979; November 1, 1981; October 23, 1983; November 11, 1984; November 10, 1985; September 9, 1990, p. 17; November 10, 1991, p. 33; November 12, 1995, p. 40.
Pacific Sun Literary Quarterly, May 14, 1975.
Parenting, October, 1995, p. 130.
Publishers Weekly, August 4, 1951; August 15, 1953; July 10, 1954; August 13, 1955; September 1961; April 3, 1967; April 15, 1968; May 14, 1970; March 31, 1975; February 23, 1976; October 1, 1977; July 30, 1979; July 10, 1981; March 2, 1984; July 12, 1993, p. 80; July 17, 1995, p. 138; July 31, 1995, p. 31; September 16, 1996, p. 29; February 16, 1998.
St. Louis Globe-Democrat, February 13, 1984.
Saturday Review, November 17, 1956; October 28, 1961; March 18, 1967; May 9, 1970.
Saturday Review of Literature, November 1950; November 10, 1951.
School Librarian, June, 1974; June, 1981.
School Library Journal, May, 1988, p. 115; June, 1990, p. 98; February, 1994, p. 78; September, 1995, pp. 222-23.
Signal, January, 1981.
Southeastern Librarian, fall, 1968.
Stone Soup, September-October 1997, p. 18.
Times Literary Supplement, July 7, 1978; July 2, 1980; January 13, 1984; November 20, 1984; February 1985.
Top of the News, December, 1957; April, 1975; winter, 1977.
Tribune Books (Chicago), September 13, 1987.
Washington Post, May 31, 1983; January 10, 1984.

Washington Post Book World, October 9, 1977; July 12, 1981; September 12, 1982; August 14, 1983; September 9, 1984; May 8, 1988; December 10, 1995, p. 20.
Wilson Library Bulletin, October, 1961.
Writers Digest, January, 1983.
Young Readers' Review, November, 1965; February, 1966; May, 1968.

OTHER

Meet the Newbery Author: Beverly Cleary (filmstrip), Random House/Miller Brody.

*   *   *

CLEAVER, (Leroy) Eldridge 1935-1998

PERSONAL: Born August 31, 1935, in Wabbaseka (some sources say June 5, 1935), AR; died May 1, 1998; son of Leroy (a dining-car waiter) and Thelma (a janitor) Cleaver; married Kathleen Neal, December, 1967; children: Maceo (son), Joju (daughter). *Education:* Attended junior college; also educated in Soledad Prison.

ADDRESSES: Office—c/o Random House, 201 East 50th St., New York, NY 10022.

CAREER: Prisoner at Soledad Prison, 1954-57, 1958-66; *Ramparts* (magazine), San Francisco, CA, assistant editor and contributing writer, 1966-68; Black Panther Party, Oakland, CA, minister of information, 1967-71; presidential candidate, Peace and Freedom Party, 1968; in exile in Cuba, Algeria, and France, 1968-75; owner of boutique in Hollywood, CA, 1978-79; founder of Eldridge Cleaver Crusades, 1979; independent candidate for Congress in 8th Congressional District, CA, 1984. Lecturer at universities.

AWARDS, HONORS: Martin Luther King Memorial Prize, 1970, for *Soul on Ice.*

WRITINGS:

Soul on Ice, introduction by Maxwell Geismar, McGraw, 1968.
Eldridge Cleaver: Post-Prison Writings and Speeches, edited by Robert Scheer, Random House, 1969.
Eldridge Cleaver's Black Papers, McGraw, 1969.
(Author of introduction) Jerry Rubin, *Do It!* Simon & Schuster, 1970.
(With others) *Revolution in the Congo, Stage 1 for the Revolutionary Peoples' Newtwork,* 1971.
(Contributor) G. Louis Heath, editor, *The Black Panther Leaders Speak: Huey P. Newton, Bobby Seale, Eldridge Cleaver, and Company Speak Out through the Black Panther Party's Official Newspaper,* Scarecrow, 1976.
Soul on Fire, Word Inc., 1978.

Also author, with others, of *War Within: Violence or Non-violence in Black Revolution,* 1971, of *Education and Revolution,* Center for Educational Reform, and of pamphlets for the Black Panther Party and People's Communication Network. Work appears in anthologies, including *Prize Stories, 1971: The O. Henry Awards.* Contributor to *Ramparts, Commonweal, National Review,* and other periodicals.

SIDELIGHTS: Speaking of his days as a leader of the revolutionary Black Panther Party, Eldridge Cleaver told Lynne Baranski and Richard Lemon of *People* that at that time he felt "there was no hope of effecting real freedom within the capitalistic system. I was the guy who demanded we go down shooting." Cleaver's radical exhortations endeared him to the militant nationalists who made up the Black Panthers. During the Party's short and turbulent history, nineteen Panthers were killed in gun battles with the police. "It was exhilarating. . . ," Cleaver's wife Kathleen told Baranski and Lemon about that period. "But it was also terrible—people getting killed."

Cleaver joined the Black Panther Party shortly after his release from prison in 1966. He had served nine years for drug dealing and rape and was only released on parole after a number of literary figures petitioned the government on his behalf. *Soul on Ice,* a book Cleaver wrote while in prison, was the catalyst for the literary campaign. A collection of essays about the situation of black people in America and about Cleaver's own life, *Soul on Ice* is "an original and disturbing report on what a black man, reacting to a society he detests, reacting to life behind bars for nine years, finally becomes," as Gertrude Samuels writes in *Saturday Review.* Charlayne Hunter of the *New York Times Book Review* judges Cleaver to be "not a nihilist like so many of his contemporaries who share his revolutionary zeal more than his sense of history. He can tear the system apart, but, unlike them, he has a few ideas about how to put it back together again." In *Soul on Ice,* Jervis Anderson of *Commentary* believes, Cleaver expresses "the profound alienation from America which black nationalists feel and the extreme political and cultural view of its future which they take."

The inspiration for *Soul on Ice* comes from a number of writers Cleaver read while in prison, including Thomas Paine, Karl Marx, Nikolai Lenin, and James Baldwin. The most important influence, however, was Malcolm X, a leader of the Black Muslims. Cleaver joined the Muslims in the early 1960s and, when Malcolm X broke away from Elijah Muhammad's leadership of the group, Cleaver followed. Shortly after this break, Malcolm X was assassinated. "I have, so to speak," Cleaver writes in *Soul on Ice,* "washed my hands in the blood of the martyr, Malcolm X, whose retreat from the precipice of madness created new room for others to turn about in, and I am now caught up in that tiny space, attempting a maneuver of my own."

Shortly after his release from prison, Cleaver became the minister of information for the Black Panther Party. Calling for an armed insurrection to overthrow the United States government and establish a black socialist government in its place, the Panthers were described by F.B.I. director J. Edgar Hoover, *People* notes, as the nation's "greatest threat." The Panthers ran free lunch programs for poor children and operated other service-oriented programs in several cities. But they were also heavily armed for "self-defense" and had frequent problems with the police, including a number of gun battles. *Playboy* noted at the time that Cleaver "has been called the first black leader since Malcolm X with the potential to organize a militant mass movement of 'black liberation.' Whether he will succeed in forging it, whether he will remain free—or even alive—to lead it, and whether, if he does, it will be a force for racial reconciliation or division remains to be seen."

The extent of support Cleaver and the Panthers enjoyed in the white liberal and black communities became clear when Cleaver's parole was revoked in 1968 after he was involved in a gun battle with the police in Oakland, California. One Panther was killed and a police officer and Cleaver were wounded in the battle. He was charged with assault and attempted murder. Support for Cleaver came from throughout the world. A demonstration in New York

City on his behalf included participants such as writer Susan Sontag and actor Gary Merrill. In Europe, French film director Jean-Luc Godard urged his audience to donate to Cleaver's defense fund. Later that same year, while he was still fighting these charges, his wide liberal support became even more clear when Cleaver was chosen as the presidential candidate of the Peace and Freedom Party, an organization of both black and white radicals. "I never exactly dreamed of waking up in the White House after the November election," Cleaver tells Nat Hentoff in a *Playboy* interview, "but I took part in that campaign because I think it's necessary to pull a lot of people together, black and white."

Rather than face charges over the gun battle with police, Cleaver fled the country in late 1968. Over the next seven years he lived in Cuba, Algeria, and France and was warmly welcomed on his visits to the Soviet Union, China, North Vietnam, and North Korea. During this time, writes Richard Gilman in the *New Republic,* "Cleaver played a complicated role from afar in the troubled internal politics of the Black Panthers, served as an unofficial emissary of American radicalism to various communist regimes . . . , fathered two children with his wife Kathleen and found himself growing more and more disenchanted with both his life as an expatriate and his former political beliefs."

This disenchantment stemmed from his realization, after actually visiting and living in many communist countries, that communism did not work as well as he had thought. "I had heard," Cleaver writes in *Soul on Fire,* "so much rhetoric about their glorious leaders and their incredible revolutionary spirit that even to this very angry and disgruntled American, it was absurd and unreal." Cleaver now "derides Cuba's system as 'voodoo socialism,'" Baranski and Lemon report, "and says North Korea and Algeria are 'even worse, because they have been doing it longer.'" Parallel to this political awakening was Cleaver's conversion to Christianity, the result of a mystical vision. Cleaver saw his own face on the moon, then the faces of "my former heroes . . . Fidel Castro, Mao Tsetung, Karl Marx, Friedrich Engels. . . . Finally, at the end of the procession, in dazzling, shimmering light, the image of Jesus Christ appeared . . . ," Cleaver explains in *Soul on Fire.* "I fell to my knees."

In 1975, Cleaver returned to the United States and surrendered to the F.B.I. Although he faced up to seventy-two years in prison, Cleaver struck a deal with the government. By pleading guilty to the assault charge, he had the attempted murder charge dropped and was sentenced to 1,200 hours of community service. One reason for the lenient treatment was the feeling that Cleaver's religious conversion had changed him. Baranski and Leon quote Earl Anthony, an ex-Panther, who believes: "Eldridge changed from one of the most vicious dudes against the system into a person who is reaching out. He's become a nice human being."

Cleaver was involved in a number of ventures after returning to the United States. In 1978, he opened a boutique in Hollywood featuring men's trousers with a codpiece, his own design. The following year he founded the Eldridge Cleaver Crusades, an evangelical organization with plans to open a headquarters in the Nevada desert. Cleaver returned to politics in 1984 as an independent conservative candidate for Congress; his bid for election was unsuccessful. Denying charges that he has somehow mellowed since his return, Cleaver told Baranski and Lemon: "That implies your ideas have changed because of age. I've changed because of new conclusions."

BIOGRAPHICAL/CRITICAL SOURCES:

BOOKS

Contemporary Literary Criticism, Volume 30, Gale, 1984.
Cranston, Maurice, editor, *The New Left,* Library Press, 1971.
Hemenway, Robert, editor, *Black Novelist,* Merrill, 1970.
Lockwood, Lee, *Conversation with Eldridge Cleaver: Algiers,* McGraw, 1970.
Oliver, John A., *Eldridge Cleaver: Ice and Fire!* Bible Voice, 1977.
Parks, Gordon, *Born Black,* Lippincott, 1971.

PERIODICALS

Antioch Review, fall, 1968.
Atlantic, June, 1968.
Best Sellers, February, 1979.
Christianity Today, March 23, 1977; July 8, 1977; December 7, 1979; April 20, 1984.
Commentary, December, 1968.
Communication Quarterly, winter, 1986, pp. 24-40.
Critic, June-July, 1969.
Detroit Free Press, August 30, 1976.
Dissent, July/August, 1969.
Economist, November 22, 1975.
Evergreen Review, October, 1968.
Humanist, September/October, 1976.
Jet, August 20, 1984; September 3, 1984; March 21, 1994, p. 37; April 4, 1994, p. 36.
Life, February 6, 1970.
Look, January, 1969.
Nation, May 13, 1968; January 20, 1969; August 11, 1969; December 6, 1975.
National Review, December 5, 1975; February 10, 1984.
Negro American Literature Forum, March, 1970.
Negro Digest, June, 1968; October, 1969.
New Leader, March 25, 1968.
New Letters, winter, 1971.
New Republic, March 9, 1968; March 13, 1968; November 30, 1968; January 20, 1979.
Newsweek, December 9, 1968; December 1, 1975; September 11, 1978; August 13, 1979; December 3, 1979.
New York Review of Books, December 19, 1968; May 8, 1969.
New York Times, March 13, 1968; November 27, 1968; December 1, 1968; October 7, 1969; November 1, 1970; September 9, 1972.
New York Times Book Review, March 24, 1968; April 27, 1969.
New York Times Magazine, September 7, 1969; January 16, 1977.
People Weekly, March 22, 1982; April 15, 1996, p. 79.
Playboy, May, 1968; December, 1968.
Progressive, May, 1968; July, 1969.
Ramparts, May, 1968; June, 1968; December, 1968; September, 1969.
Reader's Digest, September, 1976.
Saturday Evening Post, November 16, 1968.
Saturday Review, March 9, 1968; March 1, 1969.
Spectator, February 2, 1969; September 13, 1969.
Time, April 5, 1968; September 20, 1968.
Times Literary Supplement, February 27, 1969.
Village Voice, April 11, 1968; March 6, 1969.
Washington Post, December 11, 1968.
Yale Review, October, 1968.

CLERK, N. W.
See LEWIS, C(live) S(taples)

*   *   *

CLIFTON, (Thelma) Lucille 1936-

PERSONAL: Born June 27, 1936, in Depew, NY; daughter of Samuel Louis, Sr. (a laborer) and Thelma (a laborer; maiden name, Moore) Sayles; married Fred James Clifton (an educator, writer, and artist), May 10, 1958 (died November 10, 1984); children: Sidney, Fredrica, Channing, Gillian, Graham, Alexia. *Education:* Attended Howard University, 1953-55, and Fredonia State Teachers College (now State University of New York College at Fredonia), 1955.

ADDRESSES: Office—Distinguished Professor of Humanities, St. Mary's College of Maryland, St. Mary's City, MD 20686. *Agent*—Marilyn Marlow, Curtis Brown Ltd., 10 Astor Pl., New York, NY 10003.

CAREER: New York State Division of Employment, Buffalo, claims clerk, 1958-60; U.S. Office of Education, Washington, DC, literature assistant for CAREL (Central Atlantic Regional Educational Laboratory), 1969-71; Coppin State College, Baltimore, MD, poet in residence, 1971-74; University of California, Santa Cruz, professor of literature and creative writing, 1985-89; St. Mary's College of Maryland, St. Mary's City, MD, distinguished professor of humanities, 1989–; Columbia University, professor of writing, 1994–; Visiting writer, Columbia University School of the Arts; Jerry Moore Visiting Writer, George Washington University, 1982-83; Trustee, Enoch Pratt Free Library, Baltimore.

MEMBER: International PEN, Authors Guild, Authors League of America.

AWARDS, HONORS: Discovery Award, New York YW-YMHA Poetry Center, 1969; *Good Times: Poems* was cited as one of the year's ten best books by the *New York Times,* 1969; National Endowment for the Arts awards, 1969, 1970, and 1972; Poet Laureate of the State of Maryland, 1979-82; Juniper Prize, University of Massachusetts, 1980; Pulitzer prize nominations for poetry, 1980, 1988; Coretta Scott King Award, American Library Association, 1984, for *Everett Anderson's Goodbye;* honorary degrees from University of Maryland and Towson State University; Lannan Literary Award for poetry, 1996, for *The Terrible Stories.*

WRITINGS:

ADULT

Good Times: Poems, Random House, 1969.
Good News about the Earth: New Poems, Random House, 1972.
An Ordinary Woman (poetry), Random House, 1974.
Generations: A Memoir (prose), Random House, 1976.
Two-Headed Woman (poetry), University of Massachusetts Press, 1980.
Good Woman: Poems and a Memoir, 1969-1980, Boa Editions, 1987.
Next: New Poems, Boa Editions, 1987.
Ten Oxherding Pictures, Moving Parts Press, 1988.
Quilting: Poems 1987-1990, Boa Editions, 1991.
The Book of Light, Copper Canyon Press, 1993.

Also author of *The Terrible Stories,* BOA Editions, Ltd.

JUVENILE

The Black BCs (alphabet poems), illustrations by Don Milller, Dutton, 1970.

Good, Says Jerome, illustrations by Stephanie Douglas, Dutton, 1973.

All Us Come Cross the Water, pictures by John Steptoe, Holt, 1973.

Don't You Remember?, illustrations by Evaline Ness, Dutton, 1973.

The Boy Who Didn't Believe in Spring, pictures by Brinton Turkle, Dutton, 1973, translation into Spanish by Alma Flor Ada, E. P. Dutton, 1976.

The Times They Used to Be, illustrations by Susan Jeschke, Holt, 1974.

My Brother Fine with Me, illustrations by Moneta Barnett, Holt, 1975.

Three Wishes, illustrations by Douglas, Viking, 1976, illustrations by Michael Hays, Delacorte, 1992.

Amifika, illustrations by Thomas DiGrazia, Dutton, 1977.

The Lucky Stone, illustrations by Dale Payson, Delacorte, 1979.

My Friend Jacob, illustrations by DiGrazia, Dutton, 1980.

Sonora Beautiful, illustrations by Michael Garland, Dutton, 1981.

Dear Creator: A Week of Poems for Young People and Their Teachers, illustrations by Gail Gordon Carter, Doubleday (New York City), 1997.

"EVERETT ANDERSON" SERIES; JUVENILE

Some of the Days of Everett Anderson, illustrations by Ness, Holt, 1970.

Everett Anderson's Christmas Coming, illustrations by Ness, Holt, 1971, illustrations by Jan Spivey Gilchrist, Holt, 1991.

Everett Anderson's Year, illustrations by Ann Grifalconi, Holt, 1974.

Everett Anderson's Friend, illustrations by Grifalconi, Holt, 1976.

Everett Anderson's 1 2 3, illustrations by Grifalconi, Holt, 1977.

Everett Anderson's Nine Month Long, illustrations by Grifalconi, Holt, 1978.

Everett Anderson's Goodbye, illustrations by Grifalconi, Holt, 1983.

OTHER

(Compiler with Alexander MacGibbon) *Composition: An Approach through Reading,* Harcourt, 1968.

(Contributor) Langston Hughes and Arna Bontemps, *Poetry of the Negro, 1746-1970,* Doubleday, 1970.

(Contributor) Marlo Thomas and others, *Free to Be . . . You and Me,* McGraw-Hill, 1974.

Also contributor to *Free to Be a Family,* 1987, *Norton Anthology of Literature by Women, Coming into the Light,* and *Stealing the Language.* Contributor of poetry to the *New York Times.* Contributor of fiction to *Negro Digest, Redbook, House and Garden,* and *Atlantic.* Contributor of nonfiction to *Ms.* and *Essence.*

SIDELIGHTS: Lucille Clifton "began composing and writing stories at an early age and has been much encouraged by an ever-growing reading audience and a fine critical reputation," writes Wallace R. Peppers in a *Dictionary of Literary Biography* essay. "In many ways her themes are traditional: she writes of her family because she is greatly interested in making sense of their lives and relationships; she writes of adversity and success in the ghetto community; and she writes of her role as a poet." Clifton's work emphasizes endurance and strength through adversity. Ronald Baughman suggests in his *Dictionary of Literary Biography* essay

that "Clifton's pride in being black and in being a woman helps her transform difficult circumstances into a qualified affirmation about the black urban world she portrays."

Clifton's first volume of poetry, *Good Times: Poems,* which was cited by the *New York Times* as one of 1969's ten best books, is described by Peppers as a "varied collection of character sketches written with third person narrative voices." Baughman notes that "these poems attain power not only through their subject matter but also through their careful techniques; among Clifton's most successful poetic devices . . . are the precise evocative images that give substance to her rhetorical statements and a frequent duality of vision that lends complexity to her portraits of place and character." Calling the book's title "ironic," Baughman indicates, "Although the urban ghetto can, through its many hardships, create figures who are tough enough to survive and triumph, the overriding concern of this book is with the horrors of the location, with the human carnage that results from such problems as poverty, unemployment, substandard housing, and inadequate education."

In Clifton's second volume of poetry, *Good News about the Earth: New Poems,* "the elusive good times seem more attainable," remarks Baughman, who summarizes the three sections into which the book is divided: the first section "focuses on the sterility and destruction of 'white ways,' newly perceived through the social upheavals of the early 1970s"; the second section "presents a series of homages to black leaders of the late 1960s and early 1970s"; and the third section "deals with biblical characters powerfully rendered in terms of the black experience." Harriet Jackson Scarupa notes in *Ms.* that after having read what Clifton says about blackness and black pride, some critics "have concluded that Clifton hates whites. [Clifton] considers this a misreading. When she equates whiteness with death, blackness with life, she says: 'What I'm talking about is a certain kind of white arrogance—and not all white people have it—that is not good. I think airs of superiority are very dangerous. I believe in justice. I try not to be about hatred.'" Writing in *Poetry,* Ralph J. Mills, Jr., says that Clifton's poetic scope transcends the black experience "to embrace the entire world, human and non-human, in the deep affirmation she makes in the teeth of negative evidence."

An Ordinary Woman, Clifton's third collection of poems, "abandons many of the broad racial issues examined in the two preceding books and focuses instead on the narrower but equally complex issues of the writer's roles as woman and poet," says Baughman. Peppers notes that "the poems take as their theme a historical, social, and spiritual assessment of the current generation in the genealogical line" of Clifton's great-great-grandmother, who had been taken from her home in Dahomey, West Africa, and brought to America in slavery in 1830. Peppers notes that by taking an ordinary experience and personalizing it, "Clifton has elevated the experience into a public confession" which may be shared, and "it is this shared sense of situation, an easy identification between speaker and reader, that heightens the notion of ordinariness and gives . . . the collection an added dimension." Helen Vendler writes in the *New York Times Book Review* that "Clifton recalls for us those bare places we have all waited as 'ordinary women,' with no choices but yes or no, no art, no grace, no words, no reprieve." "Written in the same ironic, yet cautiously optimistic spirit as her earlier published work," observes Peppers, the book is "lively, full of vigor, passion, and an all-consuming honesty."

In *Generations: A Memoir,* "it is as if [Clifton] were showing us a cherished family album and telling us the story about each person which seemed to sum him or her up best," says a *New Yorker* contributor. Calling the book an "eloquent eulogy of [Clifton's] parents," Reynolds Price writes in the *New York Times Book Review* that, "as with most elegists, her purpose is perpetuation and celebration, not judgment. There is no attempt to see either parent whole; no attempt at the recovery of history not witnessed by or told to the author. There is no sustained chronological narrative. Instead, clusters of brief anecdotes gather round two poles, the deaths of father and mother." Price, however, believes that *Generations* stands "worthily" among the other modern elegies that assert that "we may survive, some lively few, if we've troubled to *be* alive and loved." However, a contributor to *Virginia Quarterly Review* thinks that the book is "more than an elegy or a personal memoir. It is an attempt on the part of one woman to retrieve, and lyrically to celebrate, her Afro-American heritage."

Clifton's books for children are designed to help them understand their world. *My Friend Jacob,* for instance, is a story "in which a black child speaks with affection and patience of his friendship with a white adolescent neighbor . . . who is retarded," writes Zena Sutherland in *Bulletin of the Center for Children's Books.* "Jacob is Sam's 'very very best friend' and all of his best qualities are appreciated by Sam, just as all of his limitations are accepted. . . . It is strong in the simplicity and warmth with which a handicapped person is loved rather than pitied, enjoyed rather than tolerated." Critics find that Clifton's characters and their relationships are accurately and positively drawn. Ismat Abdal-Haqq notes in *Interracial Books for Children Bulletin* that "the two boys have a strong relationship filled with trust and affection. The author depicts this relationship and their everyday adventures in a way that is unmarred by the mawkish sentimentality that often characterizes tales of the mentally disabled." And a contributor to *Reading Teacher* states that "in a matter-of-fact, low-keyed style, we discover how [Sam and Jacob] help one another grow and understand the world."

Clifton's children's books also facilitate an understanding of black heritage specifically, which in turn fosters an important link with the past generally. *All Us Come Cross the Water,* for example, "in a very straight-forward way . . . shows the relationship of Africa to Blacks in the U.S. without getting into a heavy rap about 'Pan-Africanism,'" states Judy Richardson in the *Journal of Negro Education,* adding that Clifton "seems able to get inside a little boy's head, and knows how to represent that on paper." An awareness of one's origins figures also in *The Times They Used to Be.* Called a "short and impeccable vignette—laced with idiom and humor of rural Black folk," by Rosalind K. Goddard in *School Library Journal,* it is further described by Lee A. Daniels in the *Washington Post* as a "story in which a young girl catches her first glimpse of the new technological era in a hardware store window, and learns of death and life." "Most books that awaken adult nostalgia are not as appealing to young readers," says Sutherland in *Bulletin of the Center for Children's Books,* "but this brief story has enough warmth and vitality and humor for any reader."

In addition to quickening an awareness of black heritage, Clifton's books for children frequently include an element of fantasy as well. Writing about *Three Wishes,* in which a young girl finds a lucky penny on New Year's Day and makes three wishes upon it, Christopher Lehmann-Haupt in the *New York Times Book Review* calls it "an urbanized version of the traditional tale in which the first wish reveals the power of the magic object . . . the second wish is a mistake, and the third undoes the second." Lehmann-Haupt adds that "too few children's books for blacks justify their ethnicity, but this one is a winning blend of black English and bright illustration." And *The Lucky Stone,* in which a lucky stone provides good fortune for all of its owners, is described by Ruth K. MacDonald in *School Library Journal* as: "Four short stories about four generations of Black women and their dealings with a lucky stone. . . . Clifton uses as a frame device a grandmother telling the history of the stone to her granddaughter; by the end, the granddaughter has inherited the stone herself."

Barbara Walker writes in *Interracial Books for Children Bulletin* that "Clifton is a gifted poet with the greater gift of being able to write poetry for children." But in a *Language Arts* interview with Rudine Sims, Clifton indicated that she doesn't think of it as poetry especially for children, though. "It seems to me that if you write poetry for children, you have to keep too many things in mind other than the poem. So I'm just writing a poem." *Some of the Days of Everett Anderson* is a book of nine poems, about which Marjorie Lewis observes in *School Library Journal,* "Some of the days of six-year-old 'ebony Everett Anderson' are happy; some lonely—but all of them are special, reflecting the author's own pride in being black." In the *New York Times Book Review,* Hoyt W. Fuller thinks that Clifton has "a profoundly simple way of saying all that is important to say, and we know that the struggle is worth it, that the all-important battle of image is being won, and that the future of all those beautiful black children out there need not be twisted and broken." *Everett Anderson's Christmas Coming* concerns Christmas preparations in which "each of the five days before Everett's Christmas is described by a verse," says Anita Silvey in *Horn Book,* observing that "the overall richness of Everett's experiences dominates the text." Jane O'Reilly suggests in the *New York Times Book Review* that "Everett Anderson, black and boyish, is glimpsed, rather than explained through poems about him." *Everett Anderson's Year* celebrates "a year in the life of a city child . . . in appealing verses," says Beryl Robinson in *Horn Book,* adding that "mischief, fun, gaiety, and poignancy are a part of his days as the year progresses. The portrayals of child and mother are lively and solid, executed with both strength and tenderness."

Language is important in Clifton's writing. In answer to Sim's question about the presence of both black and white children in her work, Clifton responds specifically about *Sonora Beautiful,* which is about the insecurities and dissatisfaction of an adolescent girl and which has only white characters: "In this book, I *heard* the characters as white. I have a tendency to *hear* the language of the characters, and then I know something about who the people are." However, regarding objections to the black vernacular she often uses, Clifton tells Sims: "I do not write out of weakness. That is to say, I do not write the language I write because I don't know any other. . . . But I have a certain integrity about my art, and in *my* art you have to be honest and you have to have people talking the way they really talk. So all of my books are not in the same language." Asked by Sims whether or not she feels any special pressures or special opportunities as a black author, Clifton responds: "I do feel a responsibility. . . . First, I'm going to write books that tend to celebrate life. I'm about that. And I wish to have children see people like themselves in books. . . . I also take seriously the responsibility of not lying. . . . I'm not going to say that life is wretched if circumstance is wretched, because that's not true. So I take that responsibility, but it's a responsibility to the truth, and to my art as much as anything. I owe everybody that. . . . It's the truth as I see it, and that's what my responsibility is."

In Clifton's 1991 title, *Quilting: Poems 1987-1990,* the author uses a quilt as a poetic metaphor for life. Each poem is a story, bound together through the chronicles of history and figuratively sewn with the thread of experience. The result is, as Roger Mitchell in *American Book Review* describes it, a quilt "made by and for people." Each section of the book is divided by a conventional quilt design name such as "Eight-Pointed Star" and "Tree of Life," which provides a framework within which Clifton crafts her poetic quilt. Clifton's main focus is on women's history; however, according to Mitchell her poetry has a far broader range: "Her heroes include nameless slaves buried on old plantations, Hector Peterson (the first child killed in the Soweto riot), Fannie Lou Hamer (founder of the Mississippi Peace and Freedom Party), Nelson and Winnie Mandela, W. E. B. DuBois, Huey P. Newton, and many other people who gave their lives to Black people from slavery and prejudice."

Enthusiasts of *Quilting* include critic Bruce Bennett in the *New York Times Book Review,* who praises Clifton as a "passionate, mercurial writer, by turns angry, prophetic, compassionate, shrewd, sensuous, vulnerable and funny. . . . The movement and effect of the whole book communicate the sense of a journey" through which the poet achieves an understanding of "something new." Pat Monaghan in *Booklist* admires Clifton's "terse, uncomplicated" verse, and judges the poet "a fierce and original voice in American letters." Mitchell finds energy and hope in her poems, referring to them as "visionary." He concludes that they are "the poems of a strong woman, strong enough to . . . look the impending crises of our time in the eye, as well as our customary limitations, and go ahead and hope anyway."

Clifton's 1993 poetry collection, *The Book of Light,* examines "life through light in its various manifestations," comments Andrea Lockett in a *Belles Lettres* review of the collection. Among the poetic subjects of the collection are bigotry and intolerance, epitomized by a poem about notorious U.S. Senator Jesse Helms; destruction, including a poem about the tragic bombing by police of a MOVE compound in Philadelphia in 1985; religion, characterized by a sequence of poems featuring a dialogue between God and the Devil; and mythology, rendered by poems about figures such as Atlas and Superman. "If this poet's art has deepened since . . . *Good Times,* it's in an increased capacity for quiet delicacy and fresh generalization," remarks *Poetry*'s Calvin Bedient. Bedient criticizes the poems in the collection that take an overtly political tone, taking issue with "Clifton's politics of championing difference—except, of course, where the difference opposes her politics." However, Bedient commends the more personal poems in *The Book of Light,* declaring that when Clifton writes without "anger and sentimentality, she writes at her remarkable best." Lockett concludes that the collection is "a gift of joy, a truly illuminated manuscript by a writer whose powers have been visited by grace."

BIOGRAPHICAL/CRITICAL SOURCES:

BOOKS

Beckles, Frances N., *20 Black Women,* Gateway Press, 1978.
Black Literature Criticism, Gale, 1992.
Children's Literature Review, Volume 5, Gale, 1983.
Contemporary Literary Criticism, Gale, Volume 9, 1981; Volume 66, 1991.
Dictionary of Literary Biography, Gale, Volume 5: *American Poets since World War II,* 1980; Volume 41: *Afro-American Poets since 1955,* 1985.

Dreyer, Sharon Spredemann, *The Bookfinder: A Guide to Children's Literature about the Needs and Problems of Youth Aged 2-15,* Volume 1, American Guidance Service, 1977.
Evans, Mari, editor, *Black Women Writers (1950-1980): A Critical Evaluation,* Doubleday-Anchor, 1984.

PERIODICALS

America, May 1, 1976.
American Book Review, June, 1992, p. 21.
Belles Lettres, summer, 1993, p. 51.
Black Scholar, March, 1981.
Black World, July, 1970; February, 1973.
Booklist, June 15, 1991, p. 1926; May 1, 1997, p. 1506; August, 1996, p. 187.
Book World, March 8, 1970; November 8, 1970; November 11, 1973; November 10, 1974; December 8, 1974; December 11, 1977; September 14, 1980; July 20, 1986; May 10, 1987.
Bulletin of the Center for Children's Books, March, 1971; November, 1974; March, 1976; September, 1980.
Christian Science Monitor, February 5, 1988, p. B3; January 17, 1992, p. 14.
Horn Book, December, 1971; August, 1973; February, 1975; December, 1975; October, 1977; March, 1993, p. 229.
Interracial Books for Children Bulletin, Volume 5, numbers 7 and 8, 1975; Volume 7, number 1, 1976; Volume 8, number 1, 1977; Volume 10, number 5, 1979; Volume 11, numbers 1 and 2, 1980; Volume 12, number 2, 1981.
Journal of Negro Education, summer, 1974.
Journal of Reading, February, 1977; December, 1986.
Kirkus Reviews, April 15, 1970; October 1, 1970; December 15, 1974; April 15, 1976; February 15, 1982.
Language Arts, January, 1978; February 2, 1982.
Ms., October, 1976.
New Yorker, April 5, 1976.
New York Times, December 20, 1976.
New York Times Book Review, September 6, 1970; December 6, 1970; December 5, 1971; November 4, 1973; April 6, 1975; March 14, 1976; May 15, 1977; February 19, 1989, p. 24; March 1, 1992; April 18, 1993, p. 15.
Poetry, May, 1973; March, 1994, p. 344.
Reading Teacher, October, 1978; March, 1981.
Redbook, November, 1969.
Saturday Review, December 11, 1971; August 12, 1972; December 4, 1973.
School Library Journal, May, 1970; December, 1970; September, 1974; December, 1977; February, 1979; March, 1980.
Tribune Books (Chicago), August 30, 1987.
Virginia Quarterly Review, fall, 1976; winter, 1997, p. 41.
Voice of Youth Advocates, April, 1982.
Washington Post, November 10, 1974; August 9, 1979.
Washington Post Book World, February 10, 1980; February 13, 1994, p. 8.
Western Humanities Review, summer, 1970.

*   *   *

CLINTON, Dirk
See SILVERBERG, Robert

CLUTHA, Janet Paterson Frame 1924-
(Janet Frame)

PERSONAL: Original name Janet Paterson Frame; surname legally changed; born August 28, 1924, in Dunedin, New Zealand; daughter of George Samuel (a railway engineer) and Lottie Clarice (Godfrey) Frame. *Education:* Attended Dunedin Teachers Training College and Otago University.

ADDRESSES: Agent—Brandt & Brandt, 1501 Broadway, New York, NY 10036.

CAREER: Writer.

AWARDS, HONORS: Hubert Church Prose Awards for *The Lagoon: Stories, Scented Gardens for the Blind, A State of Siege,* and *Intensive Care*; New Zealand Literary Fund Award, 1960, for *Owls Do Cry*; New Zealand Scholarship in Letters, 1964, and Award for Achievement, 1969; Robert Burns fellowship, 1965, and H.D.L., 1978, both from Otago University; Menton fellowship, 1974; Commander, Order of the British Empire, 1983; Wattie Book of the Year from the Book Publishers Association of New Zealand, 1984, for *To the Is-Land: An Autobiography,* and 1986, for *The Envoy from Mirror City;* Commonwealth Writers Prize, 1989, for *The Carpathians.*

WRITINGS:

ALL UNDER NAME JANET FRAME
NOVELS

Owls Do Cry, Pegasus Press, 1957, Braziller, 1960.
Faces in the Water, Braziller, 1961.
The Edge of the Alphabet, Braziller, 1962.
Scented Gardens for the Blind, Pegasus Press, 1963, Braziller, 1964.
The Adaptable Man, Braziller, 1965.
A State of Siege, Braziller, 1966.
The Rainbirds, W. H. Allen, 1968, published as *Yellow Flowers in the Antipodean Room,* Braziller, 1969.
Intensive Care, Braziller, 1970.
Daughter Buffalo, Braziller, 1972.
Living in the Maniototo, Braziller, 1979, 2nd edition, 1980.
The Carpathians, Braziller, 1988.

SHORT STORIES

The Lagoon: Stories, Pegasus Press, 1951, revised edition published as *The Lagoon and Other Stories,* 1961.
The Reservoir: Stories and Sketches, Braziller, 1963.
Snowman, Snowman: Fables and Fantasies, Braziller, 1963.
The Reservoir and Other Stories, Pegasus Press, 1966.
You Are Now Entering the Human Heart, Victoria University Press, 1983.

OTHER

The Pocket Mirror (poems), Braziller, 1967.
Mona Minim and the Smell of the Sun (juvenile), illustrations by Robin Jacques, Braziller, 1969.
To the Is-Land: An Autobiography (also see below), Braziller, 1983.
An Angel at My Table: An Autobiography (also see below), Braziller, 1984.
The Envoy from Mirror City: An Autobiography (also see below), Braziller, 1985.
An Autobiography, Women's Press, Volume 1: *To the Is-Land,* Volume 2: *An Angel at My Table,* Volume 3: *The Envoy from Mirror City,* 1987.

The Janet Frame Reader, edited by Carole Ferrier, Women's Press, 1995.

Contributor of short stories to *Harper's Bazaar* and *New Yorker.*

MEDIA ADAPTATIONS: A State of Siege was adapted as a film of the same title, directed by Costa-Gavras, released by Cinema 5, 1973. *An Angel at My Table* was filmed by Jane Campion in 1989, starring Kerry Fox. The film won over twenty national and international film awards.

SIDELIGHTS: Considered one of New Zealand's most important writers, Janet Frame has authored several collections of stories, three volumes of autobiography, plus a book of poetry; but it is as a novelist that she is most admired. Calling her "a most distinguished and disturbing writer," Elizabeth Ward explains in the *Washington Post Book World* that "all her novels combine or juxtapose satirical social observation with a visionary dimension bordering perhaps on the morbid in its fascination with death and mental illness." In Carole Cooke's estimation, Frame "writes novels like spiders make lace—almost instinctively, without looking back," and, continues Cooke in the *Saturday Review,* "her books are so unlike what we expect a novel to be that they almost evanesce into their own mysticism." In *Contemporary Novelists,* W. H. New observes that "she has an uncanny ability to arouse the diverse sensibilities of shifting moods and to entangle in language the wordless truths of her inner eye."

Born in Dunedin, she grew up on the coast of South Island in the small town of Oamaru, characterized by Susan Wood in the *Washington Post Book World* as "physically, emotionally and culturally deprived." Her father worked for the railroad and her mother, who once served as a maid in the home of writer Katherine Mansfield, wrote poems that she sold door-to-door. Poor and painfully shy, Frame escaped the austerity of her childhood in literature and nurtured dreams of becoming a poet. As a young woman, however, she lacked self-esteem as well as a sense of her own identity. Eventually, she completed a teacher training course but, rather than face evaluation by her superiors, she fled from the classroom and never returned. This perceived failure resulted in her attempted suicide; and after confiding the incident to a psychology professor, she found herself confined to a hospital's psychiatric ward. Mistakenly diagnosed as a schizophrenic, Frame endured years of hospitalizations and hundreds of shock treatments. She continued to write, though, and published her first book of stories, *The Lagoon,* while she was still a patient. When a hospital official happened to read about a literary award that the stories had won—an award about which even Frame was unaware—he released her from the hospital, and she thereby escaped the frontal lobotomy she was scheduled to undergo.

"Things began to change dramatically for Janet Frame after that," writes Wood. "She was befriended by one of her heroes, the New Zealand writer Frank Sargeson, who gave her a place to live and helped arrange a small stipend so that she could work on her first novel, *Owls Do Cry*." The novel probes the memory of its mentally disturbed protagonist and reveals the deterioration of a financially and intellectually impoverished New Zealand family. It summoned much critical praise and, according to Robert Pick in the *New York Times Book Review,* it "was hailed as the first important novel to come out of New Zealand." One *New Yorker* critic calls Frame "a very sharp judge of character and a writer with a real narrative gift," and in the *New York Herald Tribune Book Review,* F. H. Bullock proposes that because of her "compassion" as a narrator, "and her poet's temperament," the novel "glows with the inner light of her human awareness." In a

Times Literary Supplement review, Kevin Brown refers to the novel as a "tale of metamorphosis" and a "kind of personal archaeology, painstaking and intensely felt." In light of Frame's own years in psychiatric wards and the attendant "shock treatments that left her past in ashes," says Brown, "it is moving to watch her torchlit wandering in the labyrinth of memory."

Drawing again from personal experience, Frame's second novel, *Faces in the Water,* records one woman's years in a New Zealand asylum; or, in the words of Frances Hope in *Spectator,* it presents the reader with "a view into the madwoman's view out." A *Time* contributor finds Frame's writing "sensitive, and her evocation of madness unforgettable." And although Patrick Cruttwell wishes the novel had delved into why the character suffers, he acknowledges in the *Guardian* that it "is a piece of writing whose honesty and power are never in doubt." Considering it Frame's best book, Joyce Carol Oates explains in the *New York Times Book Review* that Frame deals with "the fluid boundary between sanity and madness, the watery depths of madness in which the normal 'see' their own faces." Oates thinks that "her novels exist for the purpose of illuminating certain mysteries for us—Miss Frame is obsessed with the mysteries of madness and death—the illumination is attempted through language, not through dramatic tension of one kind or another."

Frame's surrealistic next novel, *The Edge of the Alphabet,* presents a protagonist who, "in an effort to achieve her own identity . . . narrowly observes the lives of half a dozen persons and finds them perpetually baffled, dogged by loneliness and a sense of ineffectuality, and all variously aware that communication between the living is impossible," writes a contributor to the *New York Herald Tribune Book Review.* According to William Peden in the *Saturday Review,* all the characters are "adrift in a limbo between illusion and reality which [the protagonist] calls 'the edge of the alphabet,' where 'words crumble' and communication is useless." Neal Ascherson suggests, though, in *New Statesman* that "Frame launches at intervals into formidable harangues addressed over the reader's head." However, a *Times Literary Supplement* reviewer regards the narrative as "beautifully economical and told in a mixture of realism and fantasy, through interior monologue, snatches of dialogue, and flights of brilliant description."

Scented Gardens for the Blind presents, through interior monologue, three characters—a New Zealand genealogist working in England, his wife, and his daughter, who becomes mute upon leaving school. Calling it "the most remarkable novel that I have read in many years," Stanley Edgar Hyman proposes in his *Standards: A Chronicle of Books for Our Time,* "If it is not a work of genius . . . it is surely a brilliant and overwhelming tour de force." The novel proved less successful for other critics. In the *New York Times Book Review,* for example, Peter Buitenhuis suggests that if "Frame intended this novel as a study in isolation and madness she has failed . . . for there are clearly passages that have so strong a flavor of autobiography that she seems to have discharged the contents of her notebooks straight on to her pages." However, a contributor to the *Times Literary Supplement* believes that "any failure in communication on the part of the book as a whole, however, is redeemed by the beauty of the lyric style," adding that "there is no mistaking the power of Miss Frame's imagination and the anguish of her concern for suffering and beauty."

In *A State of Siege,* the unmarried protagonist tries to start a new life by leaving her native New Zealand for an isolated island after years of teaching art and nursing her ailing mother; but, while on the island she endures a night of terror and dies. In the *New York Times Book Review,* Millicent Bell calls the novel "a study of the isolated and stagnant spirit struggling unsuccessfully for definition and expression," and relates it to Frame's "earlier explorations of lives cut off from outer relationship." Although Bell thinks that "Frame sets herself no easy task in seeking out interest in the drab stuff of a spinster's dreams and gropings," she adds that "Frame's gifts are unquestionably poetic—the description of personal mood and of nature. These, and a verbal wit are at her command." Finding it "an extraordinary novel," H. T. Anderson comments in *Best Sellers* that it "is worth the experience just for the richness and color of the prose alone." The New Zealand Film Commission assisted in adapting the book into a successful Golden Globe Award-winning film.

In *Yellow Flowers in the Antipodean Room,* published as *The Rainbirds* in England, Frame writes about an English emigrant to New Zealand who dies in an automobile accident only to return to life. "Life, however, rejects his resurrection," writes a *Time* reviewer. "He is fired from his job . . . branded an anathema by society . . . resented by his family for the inconvenience of his miracle." New calls it Frame's "gentlest, most comic (however hauntingly, macabrely, relentlessly discommoding) book"; and, according to J. A. May in the *Christian Science Monitor,* the novel "has all the inevitability and awfulness of a Greek tragedy." For some critics, such as Oates, though, the novel did not quite achieve its potential. "One simply does not believe," says Oates in her *New York Times Book Review* piece, remarking that "this is a pity, for much of the novel is finely written, in a peculiar limpid style that seems a cross between Virginia Woolf and Samuel Beckett."

Intensive Care is the chronicle of two families living in Waipori, New Zealand, and includes several tragic elements and a futuristic era in which social problems are met by a computer that marks people for death. A critic for *Time* writes that *Intensive Care* continues Frame's preoccupation with history as "a hereditary malignancy that engulfs the present and dooms the future to madness, loneliness and death." While L. J. Davis, in *Book World,* compares the novel to "spending an evening in the company of a compulsively talkative, brilliant, neurotic woman obsessed with blood, disease, death, and the suffering of lonely people whose lives have gone all wrong," Arthur Edelstein finds it "a tangle of prose, verse, ballad, imaginary letters, and an enormous leap in the end to something like lyric allegory." Continuing in the *Southern Review,* Edelstein describes it as "bewildering yet powerful, an experience in which it cannot be determined how many layers of dream one has descended into, in which the characters dreaming seem themselves to be dreamed, as though all were the fevered conjurings of a patient in one of the novel's 'Recovery Units.'"

With the bizarrely plotted *Daughter Buffalo,* Frame concentrates again on death and insanity. According to J. A. Avant in *Library Journal,* the novel is "a strange, visionary work, as much a poem as a novel, with images of insanity, mutation, and death, and perceptions of how language changes reality." The book alternately tells the stories of its two protagonists; and in the words of Barbara Harte in *Best Sellers,* Frame's technique "is virtually a novel within a novel, or a dual novel, and within this perilous framework, anathema to the insensitive amateur." Josephine Hendin, who labels it "a poem to the union of the living dead," continues in the *New York Times Book Review,* "Pathetic and ugly, sad and destructive, it has the grim power of life drawn up as a suicide pact. . . . But she writes with a beauty that confers a morbid grandeur, that makes poetry of the particular, the private, the enclosed."

"Language, in everyday use and in fiction, and its relation to experience—of self and others, nature and the denaturing effects of modern life—is the theme of *The Carpathians*," writes Jayne Pilling in the *Times Literary Supplement*. Related by Nancy Wartik in the *New York Times Book Review* as a "small masterpiece of literary craftsmanship, the work of an original thinker with a poet's ear for the sound and cadence of language," the story centers on a rich American whose author wife, in an attempt to end a long writing block, travels to exotic places "in search of contact with other people's experience," remarks Pilling. During a stay in New Zealand, a new galaxy is discovered that is simultaneously close and far away. Observing a frequent and "curious, combustible mix of modes at work" in Frame's novels, Pilling thinks that in *The Carpathians,* the "possibilities are so rich that Frame needs several different narratives, Chinese box-style, to contain them." Moreover, Frame's autobiographical works illumine her fictional ones, says Pilling: "Frame has already given us the opportunity to see how a creative imagination works with felt and observed experience, since her autobiographical works can be read alongside her fiction, and it is richly rewarding to do so."

"Her fictional and autobiographical writings are so closely interrelated that to read one work creates an appetite for the others; her various treatments of any subject enhance, rather than diminish, each other," notes Fleur Adcock in the *Times Literary Supplement.* "Everything she presents is illuminated and thrown into sharp focus by the limpid clarity of a highly individual vision; she can be detached and passionate at the same time." Frame's *To the Is-Land* recalls her early childhood and is described by Helen Bevington in the *New York Times Book Review* as "a wistful tale, honestly and believably told, of the puzzling encounters of childhood, the recognitions, the gain and the loss." The book's title originated from what Ward says was Frame's "mispronunciation of the word 'island,' but eventually elevated into a kind of ideal state, neither the 'Was-Land' nor the Future, but the everlasting literal-minded here and now of the young." Ward indicates that while *Owls Do Cry* contains the same information as *To the Is-Land,* the latter is "much simpler and more lighthearted." Bevington suggests that "if one is to know Janet Frame better, hear the rest of it, one must consent to follow her on her journey to as many Is-Lands as there are."

An Angel at My Table continues Frame's personal story through her travels abroad, made possible by a government grant; and, according to Bevington in the *New York Times Book Review,* it "gives further evidence she has an arresting story to tell." Describing it as "fascinating, moving, and sometimes blackly humorous," Susan Wood writes in the *Washington Post Book World* that the book details her misdiagnosis as schizophrenic and her long ordeal in and out of mental hospitals. "Simply living on her own, proving to herself that she was capable of existing in the world, seems to have been just what Frame and her writing needed. . . . What she has done," observes Wood, "is quite amazing and that she has done it with a sense of humor and without self-pity is more amazing still."

The Envoy from Mirror City, which continues the autobiographical trilogy, is regarded as "a memoir of travel and imagination" by Carol Sternhell in the *New York Times Book Review.* It begins with Frame's arrival in London at the age of 32 and ends eight years later with her journey home to New Zealand. Ward suggests

in the *Washington Post Book World* that while "some readers will value the book for . . . literary insights; others will appreciate more easily Janet Frame's comic spirit, her courage and honesty. For all these things, the entire trilogy is a work to treasure." While Sternhell suggests that the book is "less compelling than the earlier volumes," she concludes that "it's impossible not to be moved by this extraordinary portrait of a woman for whom art is life, a life well worth living."

BIOGRAPHICAL/CRITICAL SOURCES:

BOOKS

Alley, Elizabeth, editor, *The Inward Sun: Celebrating the Life and Work of Janet Frame,* Daphne Brasell Associates Press (Wellington, NZ), 1994.
Baisnaee, Valaerie, *The Autobiographies of Simone de Beauvoir, Maya Angelou, Janet Frame, and Marguerite Duras,* Rodopi, 1997.
Contemporary Literary Criticism, Gale, Volume 2, 1974; Volume 3, 1975; Volume 6, 1976; Volume 22, 1982.
Contemporary Novelists, St. James, 1986.
Dalziel, Margaret, *Janet Frame,* Oxford University Press, 1981.
Evans, Patrick, *An Inward Sun: The Novels of Janet Frame,* New Zealand University Press, 1971.
Evans, P., *Janet Frame,* Twayne, 1977.
Hyman, Stanley Edgar, *Standards: A Chronicle of Books for Our Time,* Horizon Press, 1966.
Irvine, Lorna, *Critical Spaces: Margaret Laurence and Janet Frame,* Camden House (Columbia, SC), 1995.
Mercer, Gina, *Janet Frame: Subversive Fictions,* University of Queensland Press (St. Lucia, Queensland), 1994.
Panny, Judith Dell, *I Have What I Gave: The Fiction of Janet Frame,* G. Braziller (New York City), 1993.
The Ring of Fire: Essays on Janet Frame, Dangaroo Press (Sydney), 1992.

PERIODICALS

Atlantic, October, 1961.
Best Sellers, July 15, 1966; June 15, 1970; October 1, 1972.
Books Abroad, spring, 1967; summer, 1967.
Books and Bookmen, June, 1967; July, 1973.
Book Week, August 16, 1964.
Book World, May 3, 1970.
Christian Science Monitor, September 2, 1965; February 8, 1969.
Commonweal, October 19, 1962.
Guardian, January 19, 1962.
Harvard Advocate, winter, 1973.
Journal of Commonwealth Literature, August, 1977.
Library Journal, August, 1972; July, 1992, p. 132.
Ms., January-February, 1991, p. 67.
New Leader, August 13, 1960; August 14, 1967.
New Republic, September 11, 1965; May 31, 1975.
New Statesman, November 23, 1962.
New Yorker, August 13, 1960; May 17, 1969; September 30, 1972.
New York Herald Tribune Book Review, August 14, 1960; September 23, 1962.
New York Review, February 27, 1969.
New York Times, February 3, 1969; December 13, 1989.
New York Times Book Review, July 31, 1960; October 8, 1961; August 18, 1963; August 16, 1964; July 18, 1966; September 11, 1966; November 11, 1966; February 9, 1969; May 3, 1970; August 27, 1972; September 16, 1979; November 21, 1982; October 7, 1984; October 6, 1985; January 22, 1989.
Observer Review, October 13, 1968.

Punch, February 7, 1968.
Saturday Review, September 9, 1961; September 29, 1962; April 19, 1969; October 27, 1979.
Southern Review, summer, 1973.
Spectator, January 19, 1962.
Time, September 22, 1961; August 6, 1965; March 21, 1969; May 18, 1970; August 6, 1979.
Times Literary Supplement, January 26, 1962; November 23, 1962; August 2, 1963; October 21, 1965; April 27, 1967; February 15, 1968; January 26, 1973; November 9, 1984; November 15, 1985; December 2, 1988.
Washington Post Book World, August 26, 1979; January 2, 1983; September 16, 1984; October 27, 1985.
World Literature Written in English, April, 1975; November, 1978.

* * *

COCTEAU, Jean (Maurice Eugene Clement) 1889-1963

PERSONAL: Born July 5, 1889, in Maisons-Lafitte, Yvelines, France; died October 11, 1963; buried at Milly-la-Foret, Essone, France, in the garden of the chapel Saint-Blaise-des Simples, which he designed himself; son of Georges (a lawyer) and Eugenie (Lecomte) Cocteau. *Education:* Studied at Lycee Condorcet, Paris; attended private classes.

CAREER: Poet, playwright, novelist, essayist, painter, and director. Founder, with Blaise Cendrars, of Editions de la Sirene, 1918. *Military service:* During World War I, Cocteau went to Rheims as a civilian ambulance driver, and then to Belgium, where he joined a group of marine-riflemen, until it was discovered that his presence was unauthorized; also served for a time with an auxiliary corps in Paris.

MEMBER: Academie Francaise, Academie Royale de Belgique, Academie Mallarme, American Academy, German Academy (Berlin), Academie de Jazz (president), Academie du Disque, Association France-Hongrie, National Institute of Arts and Letters (New York, honorary member).

AWARDS, HONORS: Prix Louions-Delluc, 1946; Grand Prix de la Critique Internationale, 1950; Grand Prix du Film Avant-garde, 1950, for *Orphee;* D.Litt., Oxford University, 1956; Commandeur de la Legion d'Honneur, 1961.

WRITINGS:

POETRY

La Lampe d'Aladin, Societe d'Editions, 1909.
Le Prince frivole, Mercure de France, 1910.
La Danse de Sophocle, Mercure de France, 1912.
Le Cap de Bonne-Esperance, Editions de la Sirene, 1919.
L'Ode a Picasso, Francois Bernouard, 1919.
(With Andre Lhote) *Escales,* Editions de la Sirene, 1920.
Poesies: 1917-20, Editions de la Sirene, 1920.
Vocabulaire, Editions de la Sirene, 1922.
Plain-Chant, Stock, 1923.
Poesie, 1916-23, Gallimard, 1924.
La Rose de Francois, Francois Bernouard, 1924.
Cri ecrit, Imprimerie de Montane (Montpellier), 1925.
Pierre Mutilee, Editions des Cahiers Libres, 1925.
L'Ange heurtebise, Stock, 1925.

Opera: Oeuvres poetiques 1925-27, Stock, 1927, revised edition, 1959, published as *Oeuvres poetiques: 1925-27,* Dutilleul, 1959.
Morceaux choisis, Gallimard, 1932, published as *Poemes,* H. Kaeser (Lausanne), 1945.
Mythologie (poems written on lithographic stones; contains 10 original lithographs by Giorgio di Chirico), Editions de Quatre-Chemins, 1934.
Allegories, Gallimard, 1941.
Leone, Nouvelle Revue Francaise, 1945, translation by Alan Neame, published as *Leoun,* [London], 1960.
La Crucifixion, Morihien, 1946.
Le Chiffre sept, Seghers, 1952.
Appogiatures (with a portrait of Cocteau by Modigliani), Editions du Rocher (Monaco), 1953.
Dentelle d'eternite, Seghers, 1953.
Clair-Obscur, Editions du Rocher, 1954.
Poemes: 1916-55, Gallimard, 1956.
(Contributor) Paul Eluard, *Corps memorabiles,* Seghers, 1958.
De la Brouille, Editions Dynamo (Liege), 1960.
Ceremonial espagnol du Phoenix [suivi de] *La Partie d'echecs,* Gallimard, 1961.
Le Requiem, Gallimard, 1962.
Faire-Part (ninety-one previously unpublished poems), foreword by Jean Marais and Claude-Michel Cluny, Librairie Saint-Germain des Pres, 1968.
Vocabulaire, Plain-Chant et autre poemes, Gallimard, 1983.
Poemes (contains *Appogiatures, Clair-Obscur,* and *Paraprosodies*), Editions du Rocher, 1984.

NOVELS

Le Potomak, Societe Litteraire de France, 1919, definitive edition, Stock, 1924.
(Self-illustrated) *Le Grand Ecart,* Stock, 1923, translation by Lewis Galantiere published as *The Grand Ecart,* Putnam, 1925, translation by Dorothy Williams published as *The Miscreant,* P. Owen, 1958.
Thomas l'imposteur, Nouvelle Revue Francaise, 1923, revised edition, edited by Bernard Garniez, Macmillan, 1964, translation and introduction by Galantiere published as *Thomas the Impostor,* Appleton, 1925, translation by Williams published as *The Impostor,* Noonday Press, 1957.
Les Enfants terribles (also see below), Grasset, 1929, revised edition, edited by Jacques Hardre, Blaisdell, 1969, translation by Samuel Putnam published as *Enfants Terribles,* Harcourt, 1930, translation by Rosamund Lehmann published in England as *The Children of the Game,* Harvill, 1955, same translation published as *The Holy Terrors* (not the same as translation of *Les Monstres sacres,* below), New Directions, 1957.
La Fin du Potomak, Gallimard, 1940.
Deux travestis (contains lithographs by Cocteau), Fournier, 1947.

PLAYS

(With Frederic de Madrazo) *Le Dieu bleu* (ballet), first produced in Paris at the Theatre du Chatelet, June, 1912.
(With Pablo Picasso, Erik Satie, Leonide Massine, and Sergei Pavlovich Diaghilev) *Parade* (ballet), first produced in Paris at the Theatre du Chatelet, May 18, 1917.
(Author of scenario) *Le Boeuf sur le toit ou, The Do Nothing Bar,* with music by Darius Milhaud, first produced in Paris at the Comedie des Champs-Elysees, February 21, 1920.
Les Maries de la tour Eiffel (ballet; first produced in Paris at the Theatre des Champs-Elysses, June 18, 1921), Nouvelle

Revue Francaise, 1924, translation by Dudley Fitts published as *The Eiffel Tower Wedding Party,* in *The Infernal Machine, and Other Plays,* New Directions, 1963, translation by Michael Benedikt published as *The Wedding on the Eiffel Tower,* in *Modern French Plays,* Faber, 1964.

Antigone (based on the play by Sophocles), with music by Arthur Honegger (first produced in Paris at the Theatre de l'Atelier, December 20, 1922), Nouvelle Revue Francaise, 1928, translation by Carl Wildman published in *Four Plays,* MacGibbon & Kee, 1961.

Romeo et Juliette (five-acts and twenty-three tableaux), first produced in Paris at the Theatre de la Cigale, June 2, 1924.

Orphee (one-act tragedy; first produced in Paris at the Theatre des Arts, June 15, 1926), Stock, 1927, translation by Carl Wildman published as *Orphee: A Tragedy in One Act* (first produced in New York at the Living Theatre as *Orpheus,* September 30, 1954), Oxford University Press, 1933, translation by John Savacool published as *Orphee,* New Directions, 1963.

La Voix humaine (also see below; one-act; first produced in Paris at the Comedie-Francaise, February 17, 1930), Stock, 1930, translation by Wildman published as *The Human Voice,* Vision Press, 1951 (produced in New York, 1980).

La Machine infernale (four-act tragedy; first produced in Paris at the Theatre Louis Jouvet, April 10, 1934), Grasset, 1934, published in England in French, under the original title, with an introduction and notes by W. M. Landers, Harrap, 1957, translation and introduction by Wildman published as *The Infernal Machine,* Oxford University Press, 1936, translation by Albert Bermel published as *The Infernal Machine,* New Directions, 1963.

Oedipe-Roi (based on the play by Sophocles), first produced in 1937.

Les Chevaliers de la table ronde (four-act; first produced in Paris at the Theatre de l'Oeuvre, October 14, 1937), Gallimard, 1937, translation by W. H. Auden published as *The Knights of the Round Table,* New Directions, 1963.

Les Parents terribles (also see below; three-act; first produced in Paris at the Theatre des Ambassadeurs, November 14, 1938), Gallimard, 1938, revised edition, edited by R. K. Totton, Methuen, 1972, translation by Charles Frank published as *Intimate Relations,* MacGibbon & Kee, 1962.

Les Monstres sacres (three-act; first produced in Paris at the Theatre Michel, February 17, 1940), Gallimard, 1940, translation by Edward O. Marsh published as *The Holy Terrors,* MacGibbon & Kee, 1962.

La Machine a ecrire (three-act; first produced in Paris at the Theatre Hebertot, April 29, 1941), Gallimard, 1941, translation by Ronald Duncan published as *The Typewriter,* Dobson, 1957.

Renaud et Armide (three-act tragedy; first produced in Paris at the Comedie-Francaise, April 13, 1943), Gallimard, 1943.

L'Aigle a deux tetes (also see below; three-act; first produced in Paris at the Theatre Hebertot, November, 1946), Gallimard, 1946, translation by Duncan published as *The Eagle Has Two Heads,* Funk, 1948, translation by Wildman published as *The Eagle with Two Heads,* MacGibbon & Kee, 1962.

(Adaptor) Tennessee Williams, *Un Tramway nomme desir* (first produced in Paris at the Theatre Edouard VII, October 17, 1949), Bordas, 1949.

Bacchus (three-act; first produced in Paris at the Theatre Marigny, December 20, 1951), Gallimard, 1952, translation by Mary C. Hoeck published as *Bacchus: A Play,* New Directions, 1963.

(Translator and adaptor) Jerome Kilty, *Cher menteur* (first produced in Paris at Theatre de l'Athenee, October 4, 1960), Paris-Theatre, 1960.

L'Impromptu du Palais-Royal (first produced in Tokyo, May 1, 1962), Gallimard, 1962.

OPERA

Oedipus rex: Opera-oratorio en deux actes d'apres Sophocle, Boosey & Hawkes, 1949.

FILMS

(And director) *Le Sang d'un Poete* (produced, 1932), Editions du Rocher, 1948, augmented edition, 1957, translation by Lily Pons published as *The Blood of a Poet,* Bodley Press, 1949.

La Comedie du bonheur, produced, 1940.

Le Baron fantome (appeared also as actor), produced, 1942.

L'Eternel retour (produced, 1944), Nouvelles Editions Francaises, 1948.

Les Dames du Bois du Boulogne, produced, 1944.

(And director) *La Belle et la bete* (based on a fairy tale by Mme. Leprince de Beaumont; produced, 1945), Editions du Rocher, 1958, bilingual edition, New York University Press, 1970.

Ruy Blas (adaptation of the play by Victor Hugo; produced, 1947), Editions du Rocher, 1947.

La Voix humaine (adaptation of the play), produced, 1947.

(And director) *L'Aigle a deux tetes* (adaptation of the play), produced, 1947.

Noces de sable, produced 1948.

(And director) *Les Parents terribles* (adaptation of the play; produced, 1948), Le Monde Illustre, 1949, translation and adaptation by Charles Frank produced under title *Intimate Relations* (also known as *Disobedient*), 1952.

Les Enfants terribles (adaptation of the novel), produced, 1948.

(And director) *Orphee* (Cocteau speaks a few lines as *author;* produced, 1949), Andre Bonne, 1951.

(And director) *Santo Sospiro* (short film), produced, 1951.

Ce Siecle a cinquante ans (short film), produced, 1952.

La Coronna nagra, produced, 1952.

(And director) *Le Rouge est mis* (short film), produced, 1952.

(And director) *Le Testament d'Orphee* (produced, 1959), Editions du Rocher, 1959.

NONFICTION

Le Coq et l'arlequin (with a portrait of Cocteau by Picasso), Editions de la Sirene, 1918, translation by Rollo H. Myers published as *Cock and Harlequin: Notes Concerning Music,* Egoist Press (London), 1921.

Dans le ciel de la patrie, Societe Spad, 1918.

Le Secret professionnel, Stock, 1922.

Dessins, Stock, 1923, translation published as *Drawings,* Dover, 1972.

Picasso, Stock, 1923.

Lettre a Jacques Maritain, Stock, 1926, published as *Lettre a Maritain: Reponse a Jean Cocteau* (including response by Maritain), Stock, 1964.

Le Rappel a l'ordre, Stock, 1926, translation by Myers published as *A Call to Order,* Faber & Gwyer, 1926.

Romeo et Juliette: Pretexte a mise en scene d'apres le drame de William Shakespeare, Se Vend au Sans Pareil, 1926.

Le Mystere laic (an essay on indirect study), Editions de Quatre Chemins, 1928, published as *Essai de critique indirecte: Le mystere laic-Des beaux arts consideres comme un assassinat,* introduction by Bernard Grasset, Grasset, 1932.

(Published anonymously) *Le Livre blanc,* Les Quatre Chemins (Paris), 1928, translation published as *The White Paper,*

Olympia Press (Paris), 1957, Macaulay, 1958, translation with an introduction by Margaret Crosland, containing woodcuts by Cocteau, published as *Le Livre blanc,* P. Owen, 1969, revised edition published as *Le Livre blanc suivi de quatorze textes erotiques inedits; illustre de dix-huit dessins,* Persona (Paris), 1981.

(Self-illustrated) *Opium: Journal d'une desintoxication,* Stock, 1930, translation by Ernest Boyd published as *Opium: The Diary of an Addict* (contains twenty-seven illustrations by Cocteau), Longmans, Green, 1932, translation by Margaret Crosland and Sinclair Road published as *Opium: The Diary of a Cure,* P. Owen, 1957, revised edition, 1968, Grove, 1958.

(Self-illustrated) *Portraits-Souvenir, 1900-1914,* Grasset, 1935, translation by Crosland published as *Paris Album, 1900-1914,* W. H. Allen, 1956.

(Contributor) Gea Augsbourg, *La Vie de Darius Milhaud,* Correa, 1935.

60 dessins pour "Les Enfants terribles," Grasset, 1935.

Mon premier voyage: Tour du monde en 80 jours, Gallimard, 1936, translation by Stuart Gilbert published as *Round the World Again in Eighty Days,* G. Routledge, 1937, translation by W. J. Strachan published as *My Journey Round the World,* P. Owen, 1958.

Dessins en marge du texte des "Chevaliers de la table ronde," Gallimard, 1941.

Le Greco, Le Divan, 1943.

Portrait de Mounet-Sully (contains sixteen drawings by Cocteau), F. Bernouard (Paris), 1945.

La Belle et la bete: Journal d'un film, Janin, 1946, translation by Ronald Duncan published as *Diary of a Film,* Roy, 1950, revised edition published as *Beauty and the Beast: Diary of a Film,* Dover, 1972.

Poesie critique (poetry criticism), edited by Henri Parisot, Editions des Quatre Vents, 1946, published in two volumes, Gallimard, 1959.

(With Paul Claudel, Paul Eluard, and Stephane Mallarme) *De la musique encore et toujours!,* preface by Paul Valery, Editions du Tambourinaire, 1946.

La Difficulte d'etre, P. Morihien, 1947, translation by Elizabeth Sprigge published as *The Difficulty of Being,* introduction by Ned Rorem, P. Owen, 1966, Coward, 1967.

Le Foyer des artistes, Plon, 1947.

L'Eternel retour, Nouvelles Editions Francaises, 1947.

Art and Faith: Letters between Jacques Maritain and Jean Cocteau, Philosophical Library, 1948.

(Self-illustrated) *Drole de menage,* P. Morihien, 1948.

Lettre aux Americains, Grasset, 1949.

(Editor) *Almanach du theatre et du cinema,* Editions de Flore, 1949.

Maalesh: Journal d'une tournee de theatre, Gallimard, 1949, translation by Mary C. Hoeck published as *Maalesh: Theatrical Tour in the Middle East,* P. Owen, 1956.

(Editor) *Choix de lettres de Max Jacob a Jean Cocteau: 1919-1944,* P. Morihien, 1949.

Dufy, Flammarion, 1950.

(With Andre Bazin) *Orson Welles,* Chavane, 1950.

Modigliani, F. Hazin (Paris), 1950.

(With others) *Portrait de famille,* Fini, 1950.

Jean Marais, Calmann-Levy, 1951.

Entretiens autour de cinematographe, recueillis par Andre Fraigneau, A. Bonne, 1951, translation by Vera Traill published as *Cocteau on Film: A Conversation Recorded by Andre Fraigneau,* Roy, 1954.

Journal d'un inconnu, Grasset, 1952, translation by Alec Brown published as *The Hand of a Stranger,* Elek Books (London), 1956, Horizon, 1959, translation by Jese Browner published as *Diary of an Unknown,* Paragon House, 1988.

Reines de la France, Grasset, 1952.

(With Julien Green) *Gide vivant* (includes commentary by Cocteau and excerpts from the diary of Green), Amiot-Dumont, 1952.

Carte blanche (prose sketches with drawings, watercolors and photographs by Cocteau), Mermod (Lausanne), 1953.

(With others) *Prestige de la danse,* Clamart, 1953.

Discours de reception de M. Jean Cocteau a l'Academie francaise et reponse de M. Andre Maurois, Gallimard, 1955.

Look to the Glory of Your Firm and the Excellence of Your Merchandise, for If You Deem These Good, Your Welfare Becomes the Welfare of All, translated by Lewis Galantiere, Draeger (Montrouge), c. 1955.

Aux confins de la Chine, Edition Caracteres, 1955.

Colette: Discours de reception a l'Academie Royale de Belgique, Grasset, 1955 (extracts in English published in *My Contemporaries,* 1967; also see below).

Lettre sur la poesie, Dutilleul, 1955.

Le Dragon des mers, Georges Guillot, 1955.

(Contributor) *Marbre et decoration,* Federation Marbriere de France, c. 1955.

Journals (contains sixteen drawings by Cocteau), edited and translated with an introduction by Wallace Fowlie, Criterion Books, 1956.

Adieu a Mistinguett, Editions Dynamo, 1956.

Art et sport, Savonnet (Limoges), 1956.

Impression: Arts de la rue, Editions Dynamo, 1956.

(Author of introduction and notes) Jean Dauven, compiler, *Jean Cocteau chez les sirens: Une experience de linguistic sur le discours de reception a l'Academie francaise de M. Jean Cocteau* (illustrations by Picasso), Editions du Rocher, 1956.

Temoignage (with portrait and engraving by Picasso), P. Bertrand, 1956.

Le Discours de Strasbourg, Societe Messine d'Editions et d'Impressions (Metz), 1956.

Le Discours d'Oxford, Gallimard, 1956, translation by Jean Stewart published as *Poetry and Invisibility,* in *London Magazine,* January, 1957.

(With Louis Aragon) *Entretiens sur le Musee de Dresde,* Cercle d'Art, 1957, translation published as *Conversations on the Dresden Gallery,* Holmes, 1983.

Erik Satie, Editions Dynamo, 1957.

La Chapelle Saint Pierre, Villefranche sur Mer, Editions du Rocher, 1957.

La Corrida du premier mai, Grasset, 1957.

Comme un miel noir (in French and English), L'Ecole Estienne, 1958.

(With Roloff Beny and others) *Merveilles de la Mediterranee,* Arthaud, 1958.

Paraprosodies precedees de 7 dialogues, Editions Du Rocher, 1958.

(Contributor) G. Coanet, *De bas en haut,* La Societe Messine d'Editions et d'Impressions (Metz), 1958.

La Salle des mariages, Hotel de ville de Menton, Editions du Rocher, 1958.

La Canne blanche, Editions Estienne, 1959.

Gondole des morts, All'Insegne del Pesce d'Oro (Milan), 1959.

Guide a l'usage des visiteurs de la Chapelle Saint Blaise des Simples, Editions du Rocher, 1960.

De la brouille, Editions Dynamo, 1960.

Notes sur "Le Testament d'Orphee," Editions Dynamo, 1960.
(Editor) *Amedeo Modigilani: Quinze dessins,* Leda, 1960.
Decentralisation, (Paris), 1961.
Du Serieux, (Paris), 1961.
(With others) *Insania pingens,* Ciba (Basle), 1961, published as *Petits maitres de la folies,* Clairfontaines (Lausanne), 1961.
Le Cordon ombilical, Plon, 1962.
Picasso: 1916-1961 (with twenty-four original lithographs by Picasso), Editions du Rocher, 1962.
Discours a l'Academie royale de langue et de litterature francaises, Editions Dynamo, 1962.
Hommage, Editions Dynamo, 1962.
Interview par Jean Breton (preceded by two poems by Cocteau, Malediction au laurier, and Hommage a Igor Stravinsky), (Paris), 1963.
Adieu d'Antonio Ordonez, Editions Forces Vives, 1963.
(Contributor) *La Comtesse de Noailles,* Librairie Academique Perrin, 1963.
(Contributor) *Exposition les peintres temoins de leur temps* (catalog), Musee Galliera (Paris), 1963.
(Contributor) *Toros muertos,* Editions Forces Vives, 1963.
La Mesangere, De Tartas, 1963.
Jean Cocteau: Entretien avec Roger Stephane (interview), J. Tallandier, 1964.
(Contributor) *Exposition Lucien Clergue* (catalog), Le Musee (Luneville), 1964.
Entretien avec Andre Fraigneau (interview), preface by Pierre de Boisdeffre, Union Generale d'Editions, 1965.
Pegase, Nouveau Cercle Parisien du Livre, 1965.
My Contemporaries, translated, edited, and introduced by Crosland, P. Owen, 1967, Chilton, 1968.
Entre Radiguet et Picasso, Editions Hermann, 1967.
Professional Secrets: The Autobiography of Jean Cocteau (not related to 1922 book), translated by Richard Howard, edited by Robert Phelps, Farrar, Straus, 1970.
Lettres a Andre Gide avec quelques reponses d'Andre Gide, La Table Ronde, 1970.
(With Raymond Radiguet) *Paul et Virginie,* Edition Speciale, 1973.
Lettres a Milorad, 1955-1963, Editions Saint-Germain-des-Pres, 1975.
Correspondence avec Jean-Marie Magnan, Belfond, 1981.
Le Passe defini I, 1951-1952, journal, edited by Pierre Chanel, Gallimard, 1983, translation by Richard Howard published as *Past Tense: The Diaries of Jean Cocteau,* Volume 1, Harcourt, 1986.
Lettres a Jacques Maritain, Stock, 1984.
Le Passe defini II, 1953, journal, edited by Chanel, Gallimard, 1985.

OMNIBUS VOLUMES

Call to Order (contains *Cock and Harlequin, Professional Secrets,* and other critical essays), translated by Rollo H. Myers, Holt, 1923.
Oedipe-Roi [and] *Romeo et Juliette,* Plon, 1928.
Jean Cocteau (contains a study of Roger Lannes, poems, and a bibliography), Seghers, 1945.
Oeuvres completes, 11 volumes, Marguerat, 1947-51.
Theatre, 2 volumes, Gallimard, 1948, augmented edition, 2 volumes, Grasset, 1957.
Poemes (contains *Leone, Allegories, La Crucifixion,* and *Neige*), Gallimard, 1948.
Theatre de Poche, P. Morihien, 1949, published as *Nouveau theatre de poche,* Editions du Rocher, 1960.

Anthologie poetique de Jean Cocteau, Le Club Francais du Livre, 1951.
Venise images par Ferruccio Leiss [and] *L'Autre face de Venise par Jean Cocteau,* D. Guarnati (Milan), 1953.
Le Grand ecart [and] *La Voix humaine,* Club des Editeurs, 1957.
Impression [with] *Arts de la rue* [and] *Eloge de l'imprimerie,* Editions Dynamo, 1957.
Cocteau par Lui-meme, edited by Andre Fraigneau, Editions du Seuil, 1957.
Five Plays (contains *Orphee, Antigone, Intimate Relations, The Holy Terrors,* and *The Eagle with Two Heads*), Hill & Wang, 1961.
Orpheus, Oedipus Rex, [and] *The Infernal Machine,* translated with a foreword and introductory essay by Wildman, Oxford University Press, 1962.
Four Plays (contains *Antigone, Intimate Relations, The Holy Terrors,* and *The Eagle with Two Heads*), MacGibbon Kee, 1962.
Les Enfants terribles [and] *Les Parents terribles,* Club des Librairies de France, 1962.
Special Cocteau: Les Maries de la Tour Eiffel [and] *Les Chevaliers de la table ronde,* (Paris), 1966.
Opera [with] *Le Discours du grand sommeil,* preface by Jacques Brosse, Gallimard, 1967.
The Infernal Machine, and Other Plays, New Directions, 1967.
Opera [with] *Plain-Chant,* Livre de Poche, 1967.
Le Cap de Bonne-Esperance [with] *Le Discours du grand sommeil,* Gallimard, 1967.
Pages choisies, edited by Robert Prat, Hachette, 1967.
Opera [with] *Des mots, De mon style,* Tchou, 1967.
Two Screenplays: The Blood of a Poet [and] *The Testament of Orpheus,* translated by Carol Martin-Sperry, Orion Press, 1968.
Screenplays and Other Writings on the Cinema (contains *The Blood of a Poet, Beauty and the Beast,* and *Testament of Orpheus*), Orion Press, 1968.
White Paper [with] *The Naked Beast at Heaven's Gate,* the latter by P. Angelique, Greenleaf Classics, 1968.
Three Screenplays: L'Eternal retour, Orphee, La Belle et la bete, translated by Carol Martin-Sperry, Orion Press, 1968.
Cocteau's World: An Anthology of Writings by Jean Cocteau, translated and edited by Margaret Crosland, P. Owen, 1971, Dodd, 1973.
Du cinematographie (collected works), edited by Andre Bernard and Claude Gauteur, P. Belfond, 1973.
Entretiens sur le cinematographie, edited by Bernard and Gauteur, P. Belfond, 1973.
Mon Premier voyage, Des beaux-arts consideres comme un assassinat, Lettre a Maritan, Vialetay, 1973.
Orphee: Extraits de la tragedie d'Orphee ainsi que des films Orphee et Le Testament d'Orphee, Bordas, 1973.
Poesie de journalism, 1935-1938, P. Belfond, 1973.

Also author of *Sept dialogues avec le Seigneur qui est en nous,* Editions du Rocher.

OTHER

Contributor on the arts to *Paris-Midi,* March to August, 1919; wrote a regular series for *Ce Soir,* 1937-38; founder, with Maurice Rostand and others, of the review *Scheherazade.*

Some of Cocteau's manuscripts are housed at the Archives Jean Cocteau, Milly-la-Foret, Essonne, France.

MEDIA ADAPTATIONS: There are several recordings of Cocteau's works in French; *Opium: Journal of a Cure* has been dramatized by Roc Brynner and produced in Dublin and London, 1969, and in New York, 1970.

SIDELIGHTS: Jean Cocteau had a wide-ranging career as a poet, dramatist, screenwriter, and novelist. "Cocteau's willingness and ability to turn his hand to the most disparate creative ventures," James P. Mc Nab wrote in the *Dictionary of Literary Biography,* "do not fit the stereotypical image of the priestlike—or Proust-like—writer single-mindedly sacrificing his life on the altar of an all-consuming art. But the best of his efforts, in each of the genres that he took up, enriched that genre." Among Cocteau's most influential works are *Parade,* a seminal work of the modern ballet, *La Machine infernale,* a play that is still performed some sixty years after it was written, such films as *La Belle et le bete* and *Le Sang d'un Poete (The Blood of a Poet),* and his novel *Les Enfants terrible,* a study of adolescent alienation. A *National Observer* writer suggested that, "of the artistic generation whose daring gave birth to Twentieth Century Art, Cocteau came closest to being a Renaissance man." Cocteau, according to Annette Insdorf in the *New York Times,* "left behind a body of work unequalled for its variety of artistic expression."

Cocteau's first early success was the ballet *Parade,* written with composer Erik Satie, painter Pablo Picasso, choreographer Leonide Massine, and Sergei Pavlovich Diaghilev of the Russian Ballet. Telling of a group of mysterious promoters trying unsuccessfully to entice spectators into a circus tent where an undefined spectacle is taking place, *Parade* is generally considered to be the first of the modern ballets. It was also Cocteau's "first public attempt," Alan G. Artner explained in the *Chicago Tribune,* "to express the mysterious and eternal in the everyday." Jacques Guicharnaud and June Beckelman wrote in *Modern French Theatre from Giraudoux to Beckett* that *Parade* "has a theme that might serve as a symbol for the whole of Cocteau's works: Cocteau keeps his public outside. The true spectacle of the inner circus remains forbidden, despite the poet's innumerable invitations to enter. And perhaps that inner circus is no more than an absolute vacuum."

Cocteau's involvement with the ballet and theater brought him in the early 1920s into contact with a group of six young composers. Acting as their spokesman, Cocteau brought "Les Six," as they became known, into prominence throughout Europe. Wallace Fowlie in *The Journals of Jean Cocteau* remarked: "The group of *Les Six*—Honegger, Poulenc, Milhaud, Taillefer, Auric and Durey—owes [Cocteau] its name and the early support it received in Paris." In addition, Fowlie related, Cocteau served as an "impresario and interpreter" for such other artists as Satie, Braque, Picasso and Stravinsky, all of whom "owe some of their glory to Cocteau."

During this time Cocteau also began a homosexual relationship with Raymond Radiguet, the young author of several novels. When Radiguet died of typhoid in 1923, Cocteau was distraught. He turned to opium, then a brief reconciliation with the Catholic Church, and finally to a series of young lovers. One of these lovers, Jean Desbordes, inspired a novella entitled *Le Livre blanc.* Published anonymously because Cocteau wished to avoid embarrassing his mother, the book is a frank, first-person account of a homosexual's life in 1920s France, ending with the narrator leaving the country to seek freedom and love. "Although the aesthetic interest of *Le Livre blanc* is quite slim," Mc Nab admitted, "it is as rich a compendium of Cocteau's obsessions as any single work he ever wrote."

Opium: The Diary of an Addict recounted the facts of Cocteau's opium addiction, for which he twice required hospitalization before being cured. The book is based on Cocteau's notes of a three-month hospital stay in late 1928 and early 1929. It is, as Mc Nab described it, "a fascinating account of the stages of withdrawal." Cocteau also wrote several poems, collected in *Opera,* in which the opium experience figured prominently. These poems, according to Bettina Liebowitz Knapp in her study *Jean Cocteau,* "are chiseled in incisive strokes. The feelings of lightness and giddiness are conveyed in harmonious tonalities, a blend of sharp consonants and free-flowing vowels, very nearly concretizing his drug-induced euphoria. During these periods he seemed to attain a kind of second sight that enabled him to discern the invisible from the visible, the inhuman from the human, and to express these visions in dramatic and poignant terms."

During the 1920s Cocteau also devoted his time to writing several novels, a new genre for him. These novels are usually concerned with protagonists who cannot leave their childhoods behind them. In *Le Grand Ecart,* for example, Jacques Forestier finds that beauty always brings him pain, a pattern established when he was a child. As a young man, the pattern continues when he loses his first love to another man, leading Jacques to attempt suicide. Germaine Bree and Margaret Guiton note in *The French Novel from Gide to Camus* that Jacques is "the most directly autobiographical of Cocteau's fictional characters." In addition, as Mc Nab pointed out, the novel anticipates Cocteau's later obsession with childhood.

In *Thomas l'Imposteur,* a novel released only days after *Le Grand Ecart,* Cocteau tells the story of a young boy of sixteen who finds stability and purpose in his life only by joining the French Army during World War I. To enlist in the army, Guillaume Thomas has lied about his age and borrowed a friend's uniform. Soon he is even posing as the nephew of a military hero. "Cocteau hastens to add, however, that this is not an ordinary imposture, a vulgar means of 'getting ahead,'" as Bree and Guiton explained. "Guillaume, floating on the edges of a dream, is more at home, more himself, in a fictional than in a real existence." As Mc Nab noted, for Guillaume, "the enemy soldiers are merely a kind of catalyst, allowing his game to go on."

Les Enfants terribles (The Children of the Game) was begun while Cocteau was in the clinic recovering from his opium addiction. It was first published in 1929. The novel focuses on the doomed relationship between a brother and sister whose isolated existence is threatened and eventually destroyed by the outside world. To escape the loss of their isolation, the two siblings commit a double suicide. "On the one hand," wrote Leon S. Roudiez in *MOSAIC,* "the text extols the impossible values of a lost paradise of childhood; on the other hand, it condemns the contemporary world on account of its ugliness and evil. But Elizabeth and Paul demonstrate that the lost paradise is a myth. . . . The choice between total rejection, which can only be achieved in death, and total compromise, which means corruption of the individual, represents the truth that the text proclaims." Speaking of the book's structure, Bree and Guiton wrote: "*Les Enfants terribles* . . . has the rigorous economy of means, the geometrical construction, the almost claustrophobic *unite de lieu* of a classical tragedy. . . . This most ordered of Cocteau's novels also has the strongest poetic impact."

Les Enfants terribles has won lasting critical acclaim for its haunting evocation of childhood. Knapp praised "the manner in which Cocteau catches and describes with such accuracy the protagonists' innermost thoughts and sensations. . . . The frequent omissions of rational plot sequences, the starkly drawn portraits of the children, the flavor of mystery and excitement which comes with the introduction of the unknown . . . , and the march of Fate . . . lend an enduring haunting quality to the book."

During the 1930s Cocteau devoted his time to the theater, writing two of his most accomplished dramatic works at this time: *La Machine infernale* and *Les Parents terribles*. *La Machine infernale* is an update of the Oedipus legend from ancient Greece. But Cocteau transforms the story into a kind of "Parisian drawing-room comedy," as Joseph Chiari wrote in *The Contemporary French Theatre: The Flight from Naturalism*. This was accomplished by having the characters live in ancient Greece and modern France at the same time, a "time simultaneity," according to Knapp. She explained: Cocteau "succeeded in bringing about such a feat by scenic manipulation. . . . The characters, who lived in the contemporary world, performed on a brightly lit daislike structure placed in the center of the stage; the rest of the area, symbolizing the ancient mythological, inexorable aspect of existence, was clothed in darkness." Characters speak in contemporary slang, jazz music can be heard in the background, and talk of war and revolution is common. All of these factors successfully mingle the present and the past. "This realism," Knapp believed, "makes disturbingly actual the plight of the entire family—a whole society—which is at the mercy of an inescapable fate." In addition, the blending of present and past was specifically designed to appeal to the Parisian audience. Speaking of the play in *Literary Criticism—Idea and Act: The English Institute, Selected Essays, 1939-1972*, Francis Fergusson found that Cocteau "presents a very ancient myth, the myth of Oedipus, not as a joke, but as a perennial source of insight into human destiny. Yet at the same time the play is addressed to the most advanced, cynical, and even *fashionable* mind of contemporary Paris. It is at one and the same time chic and timeless." Neal Oxenhandler, writing in *Jean Cocteau and the French Scene*, declared that *La Machine infernale* "has always been considered Cocteau's greatest work for the theater."

With *Les Parents terribles* Cocteau adopted a Naturalist approach to the theater. "The characters," Guicharnaud and Beckelman explained, "constantly remind us that they are acting out a play—vaudeville, drama, or tragedy, depending on the moment and situation." The plot revolves around a troubled marriage and a mother's obsessive love for her son. When the son falls in love with a young girl, his mother is distraught. Unknown to both of them, however, is that the girl is also the mistress to the boy's father. The play ends with the mother's suicide. As Oxenhandler noted in his *Scandal and Parade: The Theater of Jean Cocteau*, the play "possesses the chief virtues of good naturalistic theater: psychological depth and insight coupled with a generally liberal and humanitarian view. . . . It is one of the peaks of Cocteau's achievement. . . . But in renouncing the world of myth and poetry where he situates his earlier works [Cocteau] has diminished himself."

Cocteau also filmed his plays *Les Parents terribles* and *Les Enfants terribles*, as well as *Orphee* and *Le Testament d'Orphee*, both adaptations of ancient Greek myths. The best of his films, Alan G. Artner wrote in the *Chicago Tribune*, "are masterpieces that equal if not surpass his work in poetry and the theater. Their

visions have haunted spectators the world over." "Cocteau," Insdorf stated, "was a boldly personal, stylistically innovative and internationally influential filmmaker. His legacy of elegantly crafted fantasy and dark poetry can be felt in such diverse films as those of Vincent Minnelli and Jacques Demy, as well as David Lynch's 'Elephant Man.'"

Evaluations of Cocteau's career note the variety of his work and his prolific creation. Tom Bishop wrote in *Saturday Review*: "Cocteau's output is staggering in quantity and diversity, encompassing novels, plays, poems, films, essays, autobiographical writings, journalism, painting, and a voluminous correspondence. Much of this *oeuvre* is minor and some is frankly bad, but enough of it is outstanding, either intrinsically or as pure invention. . . . His failures do not diminish his major accomplishments." "One overlooks a lot in the case of Cocteau," Artner stated, "from narcissism and opium addiction to some less than sterling behavior during the Occupation. One overlooks it because he worked so very hard at becoming a poet and achieved it so irresistibly in film and in the ballet theater." Bree, writing in *Contemporary Literature*, called Cocteau "one of the most versatile and talented personalities France has produced in our own time, a poet, essayist, novelist, playwright, film-maker, draftsman, and animator whose accomplishments have yet to be assessed."

BIOGRAPHICAL/CRITICAL SOURCES:

BOOKS

Anderson, Alexandra, and Carol Saltus, editors, *Jean Cocteau and the French Scene*, Abbeville Press, 1984.
Bree, Germaine, and Margaret Guiton, *The French Novel from Gide to Camus*, Harcourt, 1962.
Brown, Frederick, *An Impersonation of Angels: A Biography of Jean Cocteau*, Viking, 1968.
Chiari, Joseph, *The Contemporary French Theatre: The Flight from Naturalism*, Rockcliff, 1958.
Contemporary Literary Criticism, Gale, Volume 1, 1973; Volume 8, 1978; Volume 15, 1980; Volume 16, 1981; Volume 43, 1987.
Crowson, Lydia, *The Esthetic of Jean Cocteau*, University Press of New England, 1978.
Dictionary of Literary Biography, Volume 65: *French Novelists, 1900-1930*, Gale, 1988.
Evans, Arthur B., *Jean Cocteau and His Films of Orphic Identity*, Art Alliance, 1975.
Fifield, William, *Jean Cocteau*, Columbia University Press, 1974.
Fowlie, Wallace, editor and translator, *The Journals of Jean Cocteau*, Criterion, 1956.
Guicharnaud, Jacques and June Beckelman, *Modern French Theatre from Giraudoux to Beckett*, Yale University Press, 1961.
Kihm, Jean-Jacques and Elizabeth Sprigge, *Jean Cocteau: The Man and the Mirror*, Coward-McCann, 1968.
Oxenhandler, Neal, *Scandal and Parade: The Theatre of Jean Cocteau*, Rutgers University Press, 1957.
Peters, Arthur King, *Jean Cocteau and Andre Gide: An Abrasive Friendship*, Rutgers University Press, 1973.
Sprigge, Elizabeth and Jean-Jacques Kihm, *Jean Cocteau: The Man and the Mirror*, Gollancz, 1968.
Steegmuller, Francis, *Cocteau: A Biography*, Little, Brown, 1970.

PERIODICALS

American Imago, summer, 1976.
Cahiers Jean Cocteau, Numbers 1-10, 1969-1985.

Chicago Tribune, May 17, 1988; July 2, 1989.
Choice, November, 1973.
Commentary, April, 1971.
Commonweal, November 17, 1967.
Contemporary Literature, Volume 9, number 2, 1968, p. 251.
Dance Scope, fall-winter, 1976-77, pp. 52-67.
Empreintes (Brussels), May, 1950; June, 1950; July, 1950.
Films and Filming, July, 1960, p. 21.
French Review, spring, 1974, pp. 162-70.
Interview, December, 1994, p. 66.
Kenyon Review, winter, 1944, pp. 24-42.
London Magazine, March, 1967.
Los Angeles Times, February 12, 1989.
Modern Drama, March, 1976, pp. 79-87.
MOSAIC, spring, 1972, pp. 159-66.
Nation, October 19, 1970, p. 379.
National Observer, June 12, 1967.
New Yorker, September 27, 1969.
New York Times, December 24, 1947, p. 12; May 13, 1984; April 17, 1988; September 22, 1989.
New York Times Book Review, December 25, 1966.
Paris Review, summer-fall, 1964, pp. 13-37.
Saturday Review, September 19, 1970.
La Table Ronde, October, 1955.
Time, September 28, 1970, p. 77.
Times (London), November 28, 1984; April 4, 1985; April 2, 1987.
Times Literary Supplement, October 6-12, 1989.
Variety, May 16, 1994, p. 48.
Yale French Studies, Number 5, 1950; Number 17, 1956, pp. 14-20.

*　　*　　*

CODRESCU, Andrei 1946-
(Betty Laredo, Maria Parfenie, Urmuz)

PERSONAL: Born December 20, 1946, in Sibiu, Romania; son of Julius and Eva (Mantel) Codrescu; immigrated to the United States, 1966; married Alice Henderson, 1968; naturalized U.S. citizen, 1981; children: Luciah, Tristan.

ADDRESSES: Agent—Jonathan Lazear, 930 First Ave. N., Suite 416, Minneapolis, MN 55401.

CAREER: Writer, journalist, editor, and translator. Johns Hopkins University, Baltimore, visiting assistant professor, 1979-80; Naropa Institute, Boulder, Colorado, visiting professor; Louisiana State University, Baton Rouge, LA, professor of English, 1984–. Regular commentator on NPR's *All Things Considered,* and for Radio Free Europe's *The American Scene.* Appeared in documentary film *Road Scholar,* directed by Roger Weisberg, Metro-Goldwyn-Mayer, 1993.

MEMBER: American-Romanian Academy of Arts and Sciences, Modern Language Association of America, American Association of University Professors, Authors League of America, PEN American Chapter.

AWARDS, HONORS: Big Table Younger Poets Award, 1970, for *License to Carry a Gun;* National Endowment for the Arts fellowships, 1973, 1983; Pushcart Prize, 1980, for "Poet's Encyclopedia," and 1983, for novella *Samba de Los Agentes;* A. D. Emmart Humanities Award, 1982; National Public Radio fellowship, 1983; Towson University prize for literature, 1983, for

Selected Poems: 1970-1980; National Endowment for the Arts grants, 1985, 1988; General Electric/CCLM Poetry Award, 1985, for "On Chicago Buildings"; American-Romanian Academy of Arts and Sciences Book Award, 1988; George Foster Peabody Award, Best Documentary Film, San Francisco Film Festival, Best Documentary Film, Seattle Film Festival, Cine Award, and Golden Eagle Award, all for *Road Scholar;* ACLU Civil Liberties Award, 1995; Romanian National Foundation Literature Award, 1996.

WRITINGS:

POETRY

License to Carry a Gun, Big Table/Follett (Chicago), 1970.
A Serious Morning, Capra Press (Santa Barbara, CA), 1973.
The History of the Growth of Heaven, George Braziller (New York City), 1973, originally published in limited edition chapbook, Kingdom Kum Press (San Francisco), 1973.
For the Love of a Coat, Four Zoas Press (Boston), 1978.
The Lady Painter, Four Zoas Press, 1979.
Necrocorrida, Panjandrum (Los Angeles), 1982.
Selected Poems: 1970-1980, Sun Books (New York City), 1983.
Comrade Past and Mister Present, Coffee House Press (Minneapolis), 1986, second edition, 1991.
Belligerence, Coffee House Press, 1991.
Alien Candor: Selected Poems, 1970-1995, Black Sparrow Press (Santa Rosa, CA), 1996.

NOVELS

The Repentance of Lorraine, Pocket Books (New York City), 1976.
Monsieur Teste in America and Other Instances of Realism, Coffee House Press, 1987, Romanian edition translated by Traian Gardus and Lacrimioara Stoie, published as *Domnul Teste in America,* Editura Dacia (Cluj, Romania), 1993.
The Blood Countess, Simon & Schuster (New York City), 1995.

ESSAYS

A Craving for Swan, Ohio State University Press (Columbus), 1986.
Raised by Puppets Only to Be Killed by Research, Addison-Wesley (Reading, MA), 1988.
The Disappearance of the Outside: A Manifesto for Escape, Addison-Wesley, 1990, Romanian edition translated by Ruxandra Vasilescu, published as *Disparitia Lui Afara,* Editura Univers (Bucharest), 1995.
The Muse Is Always Half-Dressed in New Orleans and Other Essays, St. Martin's Press (New York City), 1993.
Zombification: Stories from NPR, St. Martin's Press, 1994.
The Dog with the Chip in His Neck: Essays from NPR and Elsewhere, St. Martin's Press, 1996.
Hail Babylon!: In Search of the American City at the End of the Millennium, St. Martin's Press, 1998.

CHAPBOOKS; LIMITED EDITION

Why I Can't Talk on the Telephone (stories), Kingdom Kum Press, 1972.
The Here What Where (poetry), Isthmus Press (San Francisco), 1972.
Grammar and Money (poetry), Arif Press (Berkeley, CA), 1973.
A Mote Suite for Jan and Anselm (poetry), Stone Pose Art (San Francisco), 1976.
Diapers On the Snow (poetry), Crowfoot Press (Ann Arbor, MI), 1981.

RADIO/AUDIO RECORDINGS

Traffic Au Bout Du Temps (poetry reading), Watershed Intermedia (Washington, DC), 1980.

American Life with Andrei Codrescu, National Public Radio (Washington, DC), 1984.

New Letters on the Air: Andrei Codrescu (poetry reading and interview), KSUR Radio (Kansas City), 1987.

An Exile's Return, National Public Radio, 1990.

Common Ground (radio series on world affairs), Stanley Foundation, 1991.

(With Spalding Grey, Linda Barry, Tom Bodett, and others) *First Words* (tape and compact disc; introductory recording to "Gang of Seven" spoken word series), BMG Distribution, 1992.

No Tacos for Saddam (tape and compact disc; "Gang of Seven" spoken word series), BMG Distribution, 1992.

Fax Your Prayers, Dove Audio (Los Angeles), 1995.

Plato Sucks, Dove Audio, 1996.

Valley of Christmas, Gert Town, 1997.

OTHER

(Editor with Pat Nolan) *The End over End,* privately printed, 1974.

(Translator) *For Max Jacob* (poetry), Tree Books (Berkeley, CA), 1974.

The Life and Times of an Involuntary Genius (autobiography), George Braziller, 1975.

In America's Shoes (autobiography), City Lights (San Francisco), 1975.

(Editor and contributor) *American Poetry since 1970: Up Late* (anthology), Four Walls Eight Windows (New York City), 1987, second edition, 1990.

(Editor) *The Stiffest of the Corpse: An Exquisite Corpse Reader,* City Lights, 1988.

(Translator) Lucian Blaga, *At the Court of Yearning: Poems by Lucian Blaga,* Ohio State University Press, 1989.

The Hole in the Flag: A Romanian Exile's Story of Return and Revolution (reportage), Morrow (New York City), 1991.

Road Scholar (film; also see below), directed by Roger Weisberg, Metro-Goldwyn-Mayer, 1993.

Road Scholar: Coast to Coast Late in the Century (reportage), with photographs by David Graham, Hyperion (New York City), 1994.

(Editor) *Reframing America: Alexander Alland, Otto Hagel & Hansel Mieth, John Gutmann, Lisette Model, Marion Palfi, Robert Frank,* University of New Mexico Press, 1995.

(Editor with Laura Rosenthal) *American Poets Say Goodbye to the Twentieth Century,* Four Walls Eight Windows, 1996.

Also author, under pseudonym Betty Laredo, of *Meat from the Goldrush* and *36 Poems by Betty Laredo.* Author of novella *Samba de Los Agentes.* Contributor to anthologies, including *The World Anthology,* Bobbs-Merrill, 1969; *Another World,* Bobbs-Merrill, 1973; *The Fiction Collective Anthology,* Braziller, 1975; *Kaidmeon: An International Anthology,* Athens, 1976; *The Penguin Anthology of British and American Surrealism,* Penguin, 1978; *The Random House Anthology of British and American Surrealism,* Random House, 1979; *Longman Poetry Anthology,* Longman, 1985. Author of columns "La Vie Boheme," 1979-82, and "The Last Word," 1981-85, and a bi-weekly editorial column, "The Penny Post," all for the Baltimore *Sun*; author of monthly book column "The Last Word," for *Sunday Sun* and *Philadelphia Inquirer,* 1982–; author of weekly column "Caveman Cry," for *Soho Arts Weekly,* 1985-86; author of weekly book column

"Melville & Frisby," for the *City Paper* in Baltimore and Washington, DC; author of the column "Actual Size," for *Organica,* and of weekly book review for National Public Radio's *Performance Today.*

Contributor of poetry, sometimes under pseudonyms Urmuz and Marie Parfenie, to periodicals, including *Poetry, Poetry Review, Chicago Review, World, Antaeus, Sun, Confrontation, Isthmus,* and *Editions Change;* also contributor of short stories and book reviews to periodicals, including *Washington Post Book World, New York Times Book Review, American Book Review, Chicago Review, Playboy, Tri-Quarterly, Paris Review, World Press Review, Co-Evolution Quarterly,* and *New Directions Annual.* Poetry editor, *City Paper,* 1978-80, and Baltimore *Sun,* 1979-83; contributing editor, *San Francisco Review of Books,* 1978-83, and *American Book Review,* 1983–; editor, *Exquisite Corpse: A Journal of Books and Ideas,* 1983–; contributing editor, *Cover: The Arts,* 1986-88; editor, *American Poetry,* 1970–. Member of advisory board, *Performance Today* and *ARA: Journal of the American Romanian Academy of Arts and Sciences.*

Codrescu's writing has been translated into six languages. A collection of Codrescu's manuscripts is kept at the Hill Memorial Library, Louisiana State University.

MEDIA ADAPTATIONS: The Blood Countess has been recorded by Simon & Schuster Audio, read by Codrescu and Suzanne Bartish, 1995.

SIDELIGHTS: A Romanian-born poet, fiction writer, editor, and journalist, Andrei Codrescu was expelled from the University of Bucharest for his criticism of the communist government and fled his homeland before he was conscripted into the army. Traveling to Rome, the young writer learned to speak fluent Italian; he then went to Paris and finally to the United States. Arriving in the U.S. in 1966 without any money or knowledge of English, Codrescu was nonetheless impressed with the social revolution that was occurring around the country. As *Village Voice* contributor M. G. Stephens relates, Codrescu quickly "hooked up with John Sinclair's Artist Workshop, and learned, as on a tabula rasa, the American language via the street, hippies, radical poets, rock records, and later from runaway girls he picked up on 8th Street." Within four years he had learned to speak colloquial English colorfully and fluently enough to write and publish his first poetry collection, *License to Carry a Gun.* The collection was hailed by many critics who recognized Codrescu to be a promising young poet, and, according to Thomas A. Wassmer in *Best Sellers,* he is now "considered by many writers to be one of this country's most imaginative poets, with talents similar to those of Walt Whitman and William Carlos Williams."

Although Codrescu enjoys the artistic freedoms that exist in the United States, he is still as critical of bureaucracy in his adopted country as he was in his native Romania—a skepticism that is made evident in his poetry and his autobiographies, *The Life and Times of an Involuntary Genius* and *In America's Shoes.* "In Mr. Codrescu's native Transylvania," Bruce Schlain observes in a *New York Times Book Review* article on the author's poetry collection, *Comrade Past and Mister Present,* "poets are social spokesmen, and that perhaps explains his fearlessness of treading on the languages of philosophy, religion, politics, science or popular culture. His focus on a pet theme, oppression, is as much concerned with the private as with the public."

Just as *Comrade Past and Mister Present* compares East and West through poetry, in *The Disappearance of the Outside: A Manifesto for Escape* Codrescu discusses the matter in direct prose. He addresses here such subjects as the mind-numbing effects of television and mass marketing, the sexual and political implications that are a part of language, and the use of drugs and alcohol. "In line with his literary modernism," writes Josephine Woll in the *Washington Post Book World,* "[Codrescu's] tastes run to the whimsical, the surreal (about which he writes with great understanding), even the perverse. He means to provoke, and he does. His ideas are worth thinking about." Codrescu's skill as an observant commentator about life in America has led critics like Wassmer to conclude that Codrescu has given his audience "a clearer penetration into the soul of America by a foreigner than any by a native American poet."

Codrescu returned to Romania after twenty-five years to observe firsthand the 1989 revolution which shook dictator Nicolai Ceausescu from power. The range of emotions Codrescu experienced during this time, from exhilaration to cynicism, are described in the volume *The Hole in the Flag: A Romanian Exile's Story of Return and Revolution.* Initially enthusiastic over the prospects of a new political system to replace Ceausescu's repressive police state, Codrescu became disheartened as neo-communists, led by Ion Iliescu, co-opted the revolution. Iliescu himself exhorted gangs of miners to beat student activists "who represented to Codrescu the most authentic part of the revolution in Bucharest," according to Alfred Stepan in the *Times Literary Supplement.* "It seemed to him the whole revolution had been a fake, a film scripted by the Romanian communists."

In preparation for the 1993 book and documentary film *Road Scholar: Coast to Coast Late in the Century,* Codrescu drove across the United States in a red Cadillac accompanied by photographer David Graham and a video crew. Encountering various aspects of the American persona in such cities as Detroit and Las Vegas, Codrescu filters his experiences through a distinctively wry point of view. "Codrescu is the sort of writer who feels obliged to satirize and interplay with reality and not just catalogue impressions," observes Francis X. Clines in the *New York Times Book Review,* who compares Codrescu's journey to the inspired traveling of "road novelist" Jack Kerouac and poet Walt Whitman.

The title of Codrescu's 1995 novel, *The Blood Countess,* refers to Elizabeth Bathory, a sixteenth-century Hungarian noblewoman notorious for bathing in the blood of hundreds of murdered girls. "While during the day she functions as administrator for her and her husband's estates . . . at night, in her private quarters, she rages at, tortures, and frequently kills the endless supply of peasant maidens. . . . Convinced that blood restores the youth of her skin, she installs a cage over her bath, in which young girls are pierced to death," informs Robert L. McLaughlin in the *American Book Review.*

Codrescu tells Bathory's gruesome story in tandem with a contemporary narrative about the countess's descendant, Drake Bathory-Kereshtur, an American reporter working in Budapest. Of royal lineage, Drake is called upon by Hungarian monarchists to become the next king (although the true goal of this group, which Drake soon suspects, is to install a fascist government). During the course of Drake's travels in Hungary, he meets up with various manifestations of Elizabeth and eventually is seduced by her spirit to commit murder. "Pleating the sixteenth century with the twentieth, Codrescu is nervously alert for recurrent patterns of evil and its handmaiden, absolute authority," points out *Time* contributor R. Z. Sheppard. "Both Elizabeth's and Drake's Hungarys are

emerging from long periods of totalitarian culture," comments McLaughlin in the *American Book Review.* The critic further states, "These monolithic systems, by tolerating no heresy, were able to establish virtually unquestioned order and stability for a period of time. But when these periods end, the societies are thrown into chaos." During the era of communist repression in Hungary, the violence inextricably linked to the land was dormant. But in the words of Nina Auerbach in the *New York Times Book Review,* "ancient agents of savagery" are roused from sleep in *The Blood Countess* after the fall of communism and during the resultant political upheaval—these evil forces "overwhelm modernity and its representative, the bemused Drake."

While some reviewers comment on the horrific aspects of *The Blood Countess,* Bettina Drew points out in the *Washington Post Book World* that "Codrescu has done more than tap into a Western fascination, whipped up by Hollywood Draculas and vampires. . . . He has written a vivid narrative of the sixteenth century . . . [and] has made the history of Hungary and its shifting contemporary situation entertaining and compelling." Although McLaughlin observes in the *American Book Review* that *The Blood Countess*'s "historical foundation is interesting; the incidents of its parallel plots keep one turning the pages; it has much to say about our world." Sheppard observes in *Time* that "*The Blood Countess* offers stylish entertainment" while *Entertainment Weekly* contributor Margot Mifflin finds the book "beautifully written and meticulously researched."

Like *Zombification,* the volume of essays that precedes it, *The Dog with the Chip in His Neck: Essays from NPR and Elsewhere* collects Codrescu's commentaries for National Public Radio's "All Things Considered" along with other essays and addresses that Codrescu has published or presented, as the title suggests, elsewhere. In an interview with *New Orleans Magazine,* Codrescu commented on the experience of writing poetry and fiction and of writing prose: "I write poetry and fiction for pleasure, and nonfiction for money. [Nonfiction] is plenty of fun; it's just slowed-down poetry." In this collection, Codrescu attempts to slow down the motion of mass culture in America. Joanne Wilkinson, writing for *Booklist,* notes that "Codrescu is a very distinctive writer, displaying a formidable command of the language, heady opinions, and a mordant sense of humor. This potent combination makes him perfectly suited to address America's strange brew of high culture and low."

BIOGRAPHICAL/CRITICAL SOURCES:

PERIODICALS

American Book Review, July-August, 1990; September-October, 1995, pp. 16, 23.
Best Sellers, June, 1975.
Booklist, July, 1994, p. 1915; July, 1996, p. 1796.
Chicago Tribune, July 12, 1990.
Choice, June, 1988, p. 1552; November, 1991, p. 514.
Entertainment Weekly, September 8, 1995, p. 76; July 26, 1996, p. 51; December 5, 1997, p. 94.
Kirkus Reviews, May 1, 1990.
Library Journal, July, 1970; May 11, 1990; May 15, 1990; July, 1996, p. 129; August 1996, p. 72; October 15, 1996.
Los Angeles Times Book Review, August 21, 1983; November 15, 1987.
New Orleans Magazine, October, 1996, p. 13.
New Republic, August 16, 1993, p. 24.
New York Review of Books, March 5, 1992, p. 43.
New York Times, July 11, 1993, sec. 2, p. 22.

New York Times Book Review, January 25, 1987; January 10, 1988; May 9, 1993, pp. 1, 22-3; June 30, 1993, p. 16; July 30, 1995, p. 7; October 20, 1996, p. 23.
Poetry, December, 1974.
Publishers Weekly, May 4, 1990; May 10, 1991, p. 265; March 1, 1993, p. 97; June 21, 1993, p. 97; June 13, 1994, p. 58; May 27, 1996, p. 57.
San Francisco Review of Books, winter, 1983-84; September/October, 1995.
Time, August 14, 1995, p. 70.
Times Literary Supplement, August 5, 1988; October 9, 1992, p. 26.
Variety, July 19, 1993, p. 72.
Village Voice, December 31, 1970; September 22, 1975.
Voice Literary Supplement, July, 1993, p. 10.
Washington Post, August 10, 1993, sec. B, pp. 1, 4.
Washington Post Book World, July 29, 1990; August 6, 1995, pp. 3, 10; December 8, 1996, p. 8.

* * *

COE, Tucker
See WESTLAKE, Donald E(dwin)

* * *

COETZEE, J(ohn) M(ichael) 1940-

PERSONAL: Born February 9, 1940, in Cape Town, South Africa; son of an attorney (father) and a schoolteacher (mother); married, 1963 (divorced, 1980); children: Nicholas, Gisela. *Education:* University of Cape Town, B.A., 1960, M.A., 1963; University of Texas, Austin, Ph.D., 1969.

ADDRESSES: Home—P.O. Box 92, Rondebosch, Cape Province 7700, South Africa. *Agent*—Peter Lampack, 551 Fifth Ave., New York, NY 10017.

CAREER: International Business Machines (IBM), London, England, applications programmer, 1962-63; International Computers, Bracknell, Berkshire, England, systems programmer, 1964-65; State University of New York at Buffalo, assistant professor, 1968-71, Butler Professor of English, 1984, 1986; University of Cape Town, Cape Town, South Africa, lecturer in English, 1972-82, professor of general literature, 1983–; Johns Hopkins University, Hinkley Professor of English, 1986, 1989; Harvard University, visiting professor of English, 1991.

MEMBER: International Comparative Literature Association, Modern Language Association of America.

AWARDS, HONORS: CNA Literary Award, 1977, for *In the Heart of the Country*; CNA Literary Award, James Tait Black Memorial Prize, and Geoffrey Faber Award, all 1980, all for *Waiting for the Barbarians*; CNA Literary Award, Booker-McConnell Prize, and Prix Femina Etranger, all 1984, all for *The Life and Times of Michael K*; D. Litt., University of Strathclyde, Glasgow, 1985; Jerusalem Prize for the Freedom of the Individual in Society, 1987; *Irish Times* International Fiction Prize, 1995, for *The Master of Petersburg*; Life Fellow, University of Cape Town.

WRITINGS:

NOVELS

Dusklands (contains two novellas, *The Vietnam Project* and *The Narrative of Jacobus Coetzee*), Ravan Press (Johannesburg), 1974, Penguin Books (New York City), 1985.
From the Heart of the Country, Harper (New York City), 1977, published in England as *In the Heart of the Country,* Secker & Warburg, 1977.
Waiting for the Barbarians, Secker & Warburg, 1980, Penguin Books, 1982.
The Life and Times of Michael K., Secker & Warburg, 1983, Viking (New York City), 1984.
Foe, Viking, 1987.
Age of Iron, Random House (New York City), 1990.
The Master of Petersburg, Viking, 1994.

OTHER

(Translator) Marcellus Emants, *A Posthumous Confession,* Twayne (Boston), 1976.
(Translator) Wilma Stockenstroem, *The Expedition to the Baobab Tree,* Faber, 1983.
(Editor with Andre Brink) *A Land Apart: A Contemporary South African Reader,* Viking, 1987.
White Writing: On the Culture of Letters in South Africa (essays), Yale University Press (New Haven, CT), 1988.
Doubling the Point: Essays and Interviews, edited by David Attwell, Harvard University Press (Cambridge, MA), 1992.
(With Graham Swift, John Lanchester, and Ian Jack) *Food: The Vital Stuff,* Penguin, 1995.
Giving Offense: Essays on Censorship, University of Chicago Press (Chicago), 1996.
Boyhood: Scenes from Provincial Life, Viking (New York City), 1997.
(With Bill Reichblum) *What is Realism?* Bennington College, 1997.

Contributor of reviews to *New York Review of Books.*

MEDIA ADAPTATIONS: An adaptation of *In the Heart of the Country* was filmed as *Dust,* by ICA (Great Britain), 1986.

SIDELIGHTS: Often using his native South Africa as a backdrop, J. M. Coetzee explores the implications of oppressive societies on the lives of their inhabitants. As a South African, however, Coetzee is "too intelligent a novelist to cater for moralistic voyeurs," Peter Lewis declared in *Times Literary Supplement.* "This does not mean that he avoids the social and political crises edging his country towards catastrophe. But he chooses not to handle such themes in the direct, realistic way that writers of older generations, such as Alan Paton, preferred to employ. Instead, Coetzee has developed a symbolic and even allegorical mode of fiction—not to escape the living nightmare of South Africa but to define the psychopathological underlying the sociological, and in doing so to locate the archetypal in the particular."

Though many of his stories are set in South Africa, Coetzee's lessons are relevant to all countries, as *Books Abroad*'s Ursula A. Barnett wrote of *Dusklands,* which contains the novellas *The Vietnam Project* and *The Narrative of Jacobus Coetzee.* "By publishing the two stories side by side," Barnett remarked, "Coetzee has deliberately given a wider horizon to his South African subject. Left on its own, *The Narrative of Jacobus Coetzee* would immediately have suggested yet another tale of African black-white confrontation to the reader." Although each is a complete story, "their nature and design are such that the book can and should be read as a single work," Roger Owen commented in *Times Literary Supplement*. *Dusklands* "is a kind of diptych, carefully hinged and aligned, and of a texture so glassy and mirror-like that each story throws light on the other." Together the tales present two very different outcomes in confrontations between the individual and society.

The Vietnam Project introduces Eugene Dawn, employed to help the Americans win the Vietnam War through psychological warfare. The assignment eventually costs Dawn his sanity. The title character of *The Narrative of Jacobus Coetzee*, a fictionalized ancestor of the author, is an explorer and conqueror in the 1760s who destroys an entire South African tribe over his perception that the people have humiliated him through their indifference and lack of fear. H. M. Tiffin, writing in *Contemporary Novelists*, found that the novellas in *Dusklands* are "juxtaposed to offer a scarifying account of the fear and paranoia of imperialists and aggressors and the horrifying ways in which dominant regimes, 'empires,' commit violence against 'the other' through repression, torture, and genocide."

Coetzee's second novel, *In the Heart of the Country*, also explores racial conflict and mental deterioration. A spinster daughter, Magda, tells the story in diary form, recalling the consequences of her father's seduction of his African workman's wife. Both jealous of and repulsed by the relationship, Magda murders her father, then begins her own affair with the workman. The integrity of Magda's story eventually proves questionable. "The reader soon realizes that these are the untrustworthy ravings of a hysterical, demented individual consumed by loneliness and her love/hate relationship with her patriarchal father," Barend J. Toerien reported in *World Literature Today*. Magda's "thoughts range widely, merging reality with fantasy, composing and recomposing domestic dramas for herself to act in and, eventually introducing voices . . . to speak to her from the skies," Sheila Roberts noted in *World Literature Written in English*. "She imagines that the voices accuse her, among other things, of transforming her uneventful life into a fiction." *World Literature Today*'s Charles R. Larson found *In the Heart of the Country* "a perplexing novel, to be sure, but also a fascinating novelistic exercise in the use of cinematic techniques in prose fiction," describing the book as reminiscent of an overlapping "series of stills extracted from a motion picture."

Coetzee followed *In the Heart of the Country* with *Waiting for the Barbarians*, in which the author, "with laconic brilliance, articulates one of the basic problems of our time—how to *understand* . . . mentality behind the brutality and injustice," Anthony Burgess wrote in *New York*. In the novel, a magistrate attempting to protect the peaceful nomadic people of his district is imprisoned and tortured by the army that arrives at the frontier town to destroy the "barbarians" on behalf of the Empire. The horror of what he has seen and experienced affects the magistrate in inalterable ways, bringing changes in his personality that he cannot understand. Doris Grumbach, writing in the *Los Angeles Times Book Review*, found *Waiting for the Barbarians* a book with "universal reference," an allegory which can be applied to innumerable historical and contemporary situations. "Very soon it is apparent that the story, terrifying and unforgettable, is about injustice and barbarism inflicted everywhere by 'civilized' people upon those it invades, occupies, governs." "The intelligence Coetzee brings us in *Waiting for the Barbarians* comes straight from Scripture and Dostoevsky," Webster Schott asserted in the *Washington Post Book World*. "We possess the devil. We are all barbarians."

Foe, a retelling of Daniel Defoe's *Robinson Crusoe*, marked a transitional stage for Coetzee, according to Maureen Nicholson in *West Coast Review*. Nicholson found many areas in which *Foe* differs from Coetzee's previous work. "Coetzee initially appeared to me to have all but abandoned his usual concerns and literary techniques" in *Foe*, Nicholson commented. "I was mistaken. More importantly, though, I was worried about why he has chosen *now* to write this kind of book; I found his shift of focus and technique ominous. Could he no longer sustain the courage he had demonstrated [in *Waiting for the Barbarians* and *The Life and Times of Michael K.*], turning instead to a radically interiorized narrative?" Nicholson concluded, "Perhaps *Foe* is best viewed as a pause for recapitulation and evaluation, transitional in Coetzee's development as a writer." Ashton Nichols, however, writing in *Southern Humanities Review*, found that Coetzee had not strayed far from his usual topics. "Like all of Coetzee's earlier works, *Foe* retains a strong sense of its specifically South African origins, a sociopolitical subtext that runs along just below the surface of the narrative," Nichols remarked. The reviewer emphasized Coetzee's role as "an archeologist of the imagination, an excavator of language who testifies to the powers and weaknesses of the words he discovers," a role Coetzee has performed in each of his novels, including *Foe*. Central to this idea are the mute Friday, whose tongue was cut out by slavers, and Susan Barton, the castaway who struggles to communicate with him. Daniel Foe, the author who endeavors to tell Barton's story, is also affected by Friday's speechlessness. Both recognize their duty to provide a means by which Friday can relate the story of his escape from the fate of his fellow slaves who drowned, still shackled, when their ship sank, but also question their right to speak for him. "The author, whether Foe or Coetzee, . . . wonders if he has any right to speak for the one person whose story most needs to be told," Nichols noted. "Friday is . . . the tongueless voice of millions."

In *Age of Iron* Coetzee addresses the crisis of South Africa in direct rather than allegorical form. The story of Mrs. Curren, a retired professor dying of cancer and attempting to deal with the realities of apartheid in Cape Town, *Age of Iron* is "an unrelenting yet gorgeously written parable of modern South Africa, . . . a story filled with foreboding and violence about a land where even the ability of children to love is too great a luxury," Michael Dorris wrote in *Tribune Books*. As her disease and the chaos of her homeland progress, Mrs. Curren feels the effects her society has had on its black members; her realization that "now my eyes are open and I can never close them again" forms the basis for her growing rage against the system. After her housekeeper's son and his friend are murdered in her home, Mrs. Curren runs away and hides beneath an overpass, leaving her vulnerable to attack by a gang. She is rescued by Vercueil, a street person she has gradually allowed into her house and her life, who returns her to her home and tends to her needs as the cancer continues its destruction. The book takes the form of a letter from Mrs. Curren to her daughter, living in the United States because she cannot tolerate apartheid. "Dying is traditionally a process of withdrawal from the world," Sean French commented in *New Statesman and Society*. "Coetzee tellingly reverses this and it is in her last weeks that [Mrs. Curren] first truly goes out in the baffling society she has lived in." As her life ends, Mrs. Curren's urgency to correct the wrongs she never before questioned intensifies. "In this chronicle of an aged white woman coming to understand, and of the unavoidable claims of her country's black youth, Mr. Coetzee has created a superbly realized novel whose truths cut to the bone," Lawrence Thornton declared in the *New York Times Book Review*.

Reviewers voiced mixed opinions of Coetzee's next novel, *The Master of Petersburg.* The central character in the book is the Russian novelist Fyodor Dostoevsky, but the plot is only loosely based on his real life. In Coetzee's story, the novelist goes to St. Petersburg upon the death of his stepson, Pavel. He is devastated by grief for the young man, and begins an inquiry into his death. He discovers that Pavel was involved with a group of nihilists and was probably murdered either by their leader or by the police. During the course of his anguished investigation, Dostoevsky's creative processes are exposed; Coetzee shows him beginning work on his novel *The Possessed.*

In real life, Dostoevsky did have a stepson named Pavel; but he was a foppish idler, a constant source of annoyance and embarrassment to the writer. The younger man outlived his stepfather by some twenty years, and as Dostoevsky died, he would not allow Pavel near his deathbed. Some reviewers were untroubled by Coetzee's manipulation of the facts. "This is not, after all, a book about the real Dostoevsky; his name, and some facts connected to it, form a mask behind which Coetzee enacts a drama of parenthood, politics and authorship," Harriett Gilbert explained in *New Statesman and Society.* She went on to praise Coetzee's depiction of "the barbed-wire coils of grief and anger, of guilt, of sexual rivalry and envy, that Fyodor Mikhailovich negotiates as he enters Pavel's hidden life. From the moment he presses his face to the lad's white suit to inhale his smell, to when he sits down, picks up his pen and commits a paternal novelist's betrayal, his pain is depicted with such harsh clarity that pity is burnt away. If the novel begins uncertainly, it ends with scorching self-confidence."

Coetzee's nonfiction works include *White Writing: On the Culture of Letters in South Africa, Doubling the Point: Essays and Interviews,* and *Giving Offense: Essays on Censorship.* In *White Writing,* the author "collects his critical reflections on the mixed fortunes of 'white writing' in South Africa, 'a body of writing [not] different in nature from black writing,' but 'generated by the concerns of people no longer European, yet not African,'" Shaun Irlam observed in *MLN.* The seven essays included in the book discuss writings from the late seventeenth century to the present, through which Coetzee examines the foundations of modern South African writers' attitudes. Irlam described the strength of *White Writing* as its ability "to interrogate succinctly and lucidly the presuppositions inhabiting the language with which 'white writers' have addressed and presumed to ventriloquize Africa." In the *Rocky Mountain Review of Language and Literature,* Barbara Temple-Thurston noted, "Coetzee's book reiterates impressively how cultural ideas and language bind and limit the way in which we interpret our world." In *Doubling the Point: Essays and Interviews,* a collection of critical essays on Samuel Beckett, Franz Kafka, D. H. Lawrence, Nadine Gordimer, and others, Coetzee presents a "literary autobiography," according to Ann Irvine in a *Library Journal* review. Discussions of issues including censorship and popular culture and interviews with the author preceding each section round out the collection.

Giving Offense: Essays on Censorship is Coetzee's first collection of essays in ten years, since *White Writing* appeared. In these more recent essays, written over a period of about six years, Coetzee, a writer quite familiar with the varying forms of censorship and the writer's response to them, attempts to complicate what he calls "the two tired images of the writer under censorship: the moral giant under attack from hordes of moral pygmies and the helpless innocent persecuted by a mighty state apparatus." Coetzee discusses three tyrannical regimes: Nazism, Communism, and apartheid; and, drawing upon his training as an academic scholar as well as his experiences as a fiction writer, argues that the censor and the writer have often been "brother-enemies, mirror images one of the other" in their struggle to claim the truth of their position.

In *Boyhood: Scenes from Provincial Life,* Coetzee experiments with autobiography, a surprising turn for a writer, as Caryl Phillips in the *New Republic* notes, "whose literary output has successfully resisted an autobiographical reading." Written in the third person, *Boyhood,* claims Denise S. Sticha in *Library Journal,* "reads more like a novella than a true autobiography. Coetzee develops his character, a young boy on the verge of adolescence, through a richly detailed interior monolog." He recounts his life growing up in Worcester, South Africa, where he moved with his family from Cape Town after his father's latest business failure. There, he observes the contradictions of apartheid and the subtle distinctions of class and ethnicity with a precociously writerly eye. Rand Richards Cooper, writing for the *New York Times Book Review,* states that "Coetzee's themes lie where the political, the spiritual, the psychological and the physical converge: the nightmare of bureaucratic violence; or forlorn estrangement from the land; a Shakespearean anxiety about nature put out of its order; and the insistent neediness of the body." Coetzee, an Afrikaaner whose parents chose to speak English, finds himself between worlds, neither properly Afrikaaner nor English. Throughout his boyhood, he encounters the stupid brutalities inflicted by arbitrary divisions between white and black, Native and Coloured, Afrikaaner and English. Phillips speculates that "as a boy Coetzee feels compelled to learn how to negotiate the falsehoods that white South Africa offers up to those who wish to belong. In short, he develops the mentality of the writer. He fills his world with doubt, he rejects authority in all its forms—political, social, persona—and he cultivates the ability to resign himself to the overwhelming insecurity of the heart."

In addition to his writing, Coetzee produces translations of works in Dutch, German, French, and Afrikaans, serves as editor for others' work, and teaches at the University of Cape Town. "He's a rare phenomenon, a writer-scholar," Ian Glenn, a colleague of Coetzee's, told the *Washington Post's* Allister Sparks. "Even if he hadn't had a career as a novelist he would have had a very considerable one as an academic." Coetzee told Sparks that he finds writing burdensome. "I don't like writing so I have to push myself," he said. "It's bad if I write but it's worse if I don't." Coetzee hesitates to discuss his works in progress, and views his opinion of his published works as no more important than that of anyone else. "The writer is simply another reader when it is a matter of discussing the books he has already written," he told Sparks. "They don't belong to him anymore and he has nothing privileged to say about them—while the book he is engaged in writing is far too private and important a matter to be talked about."

BIOGRAPHICAL/CRITICAL SOURCES:

BOOKS

Attwell, David, *J. M. Coetzee: South Africa and the Politics of Writing,* University of California Press, 1993.

Gallagher, Susan V., *A Story of South Africa: J. M. Coetzee's Fiction in Context,* Harvard University Press, 1991.

Goddard, Kevin, *J. M. Coetzee: A Bibliography,* National English Literary Museum, 1990.

Head, Dominic, *J. M. Coetzee,* Cambridge University Press, 1998.

Huggan, Graham, and Stephen Watson, editors, *Critical Perspectives on J. M. Coetzee,* introduction by Nadine Gordimer, St. Martin's Press, 1996.

Jolly, Rosemary Jane, *Colonization, Violence, and Narration in White South African Writing: Andre Brink, Breyten Breytenbach, and J. M. Coetzee,* Ohio University Press, 1996.

Kossew, Sue, *Pen and Power: A Post-Colonial Reading of J. M. Coetzee and Andre Brink,* Rodopi, 1996.

Kossew, Sue, ed, *Critical Essays on J. M. Coetzee,* G. K. Hall, 1998.

Moses, Michael Valdez, ed., *The Writings of J. M. Coetzee,* Duke University Press, 1994.

Penner, Dick, *Countries of the Mind: The Fiction of J. M. Coetzee,* Greenwood Publishing Group, 1989.

PERIODICALS

Africa Today, third quarter, 1980.

America, September 25, 1982.

Ariel: A Review of International English Literature, April, 1985, pp. 47-56; July, 1986, pp. 3-21; October, 1988, pp. 55-72.

Booklist, November 1, 1994, p. 477; April 1, 1996, p. 1328; August, 1997, p. 1869.

Books Abroad, spring, 1976.

Books and Culture, March, 1997, p. 30.

Books in Canada, August/September, 1982.

Boston Globe, November 20, 1994, p. B16.

British Book News, April, 1981.

Chicago Tribune Book World, April 25, 1982; January 22, 1984, section 14, p. 27; November 27, 1994, p. 3.

Christian Science Monitor, December 12, 1983; May 18, 1988, pp. 503-05.

Contemporary Literature, summer, 1988, pp. 277-85; fall, 1992, pp. 419-31.

Critique: Studies in Modern Fiction, winter, 1986, pp. 67-77; spring, 1989, pp. 143-54.

Encounter, October, 1977; January, 1984.

English Journal, March, 1994, p. 97.

Globe and Mail (Toronto), August 30, 1986.

Library Journal, June 1, 1992, p. 124; September 1, 1994, p. 213; March 15, 1996, p. 70; September 1, 1997, p. 181.

Listener, August 18, 1977.

London Review of Books, September 13, 1990, pp. 17-18.

Los Angeles Times Book Review, May 23, 1982, p. 4; January 15, 1984; February 22, 1987; November 20, 1994, p. 3.

Maclean's, January 30, 1984, p. 49.

MLN, December, 1988, pp. 1147-50; December 17, 1990, pp. 777-80.

Nation, March 28, 1987, pp. 402-05.

New Republic, December 19, 1983; February 6, 1995, pp. 170-72; October 16, 1995, p. 53; November 18, 1996, p. 30; February 9, 1998, p. 37.

New Statesman and Society, September 21, 1990, p. 40; February 25, 1994, p. 41; November 21, 1997, p. 50.

Newsweek, May 31, 1982; January 2, 1984; February 23, 1987.

New York, April 26, 1982, pp. 88, 90.

New Yorker, July 12, 1982.

New York Review of Books, December 2, 1982; February 2, 1984; November 8, 1990, pp. 8-10; November 17, 1994, p. 35.

New York Times, December 6, 1983, p. C22; February 11, 1987; April 11, 1987; November 18, 1994, p. C35; October 7, 1997, p. B7.

New York Times Book Review, April 18, 1982; December 11, 1983, pp. 1, 26; February 22, 1987; September 23, 1990, p. 7;

November 20, 1994, p. 9; September 22, 1996, p. 33; November 2, 1997, p. 7.

Publishers Weekly, September 5, 1994, p. 88; January 22, 1996, p. 52; July 28, 1997, p. 59.

Research in African Literatures, fall, 1986, pp. 370-92.

Sewanee Review, winter, 1990, pp. 152-59; April, 1995, p. R48.

South Atlantic Quarterly, winter, 1994, pp. 1-9, 33-58, 83-110.

Southern Humanities Review, fall, 1987, pp. 384-86.

Spectator, December 13, 1980; September 20, 1986.

Time, March 23, 1987; November 28, 1994, pp. 89-90.

Times (London), September 29, 1983; September 11, 1986; May 28, 1988.

Times Literary Supplement, July 22, 1977; November 7, 1980, p. 1270; January 14, 1983; September 30, 1983; September 23, 1988, p. 1043; September 28, 1990, p. 1037; March 4, 1994, p. 19.

Tribune Books (Chicago), February 15, 1987, pp. 3, 11; September 16, 1990, p. 3.

Tri-Quarterly, spring-summer, 1987, pp. 454-64.

Village Voice, March 20, 1984.

Voice Literary Supplement, April, 1982.

Wall Street Journal, November 3, 1994, p. A16.

Washington Post, October 29, 1983.

Washington Post Book World, May 2, 1982, pp. 1-2, 12; December 11, 1983; March 8, 1987; September 23, 1990, pp. 1, 10; November 27, 1994, p. 6.

West Coast Review, spring, 1987, pp. 52-8.

World Literature Today, spring, 1978, pp. 245-47; summer, 1978, p. 510; autumn, 1981; autumn, 1988, pp. 718-19; winter, 1990, pp. 54-7; winter, 1995, p. 207; autumn, 1996, p. 1038.

World Literature Written in English, spring, 1980, pp. 19-36; spring, 1986, pp. 34-45; autumn, 1987, pp. 153-61, 174-84, 207-15.

*   *   *

COLEMAN, Emmett
See REED, Ishmael

*   *   *

COLETTE, (Sidonie-Gabrielle) 1873-1954 (Willy, Colette Willy)

PERSONAL: Born January 28, 1873, in Burgundy, France; died August 3, 1954, in Paris, France; daughter of Jules and Sidonie Colette; married Henry Gauthier-Villars (music critic, journalist, and novelist), 1893 (separated, 1906; divorced, 1910); married Baron Henri de Jouvenel des Ursins (politician and editor), December 19, 1912 (divorced, c. 1925); married Maurice Goudeket, April, 1935; children: (second marriage) Colette de Jouvenel ("Bel-Gazou").

CAREER: Novelist and short story writer; music hall dancer and mime, 1906-11; columnist for *Le Matin,* beginning in 1911.

AWARDS, HONORS: Elected to Royal Belgian Academy and Goncourt Academy (president); grand officer of the Legion of Honor; received state funeral, France's highest posthumous honor.

WRITINGS:

(Under pseudonym Willy) *Claudine a l'ecole,* Ollendorff, 1900, translation by Janet Flanner published as *Claudine at School,*

Gollancz, 1930, also translated by H. Mirande, A. & C. Boni, 1930.

(Under pseudonym Willy) *Claudine a Paris,* Mercure de France, 1901, published as *Claudine amoureuse,* Ollendorff, 1902, translation by James Whitall published as *Young Lady of Paris,* A. & C. Boni, 1931.

(Under pseudonym Willy) *Claudine en menage,* Mercure de France, 1902, translation by Frederick A. Blossom published as *The Indulgent Husband,* Farrar & Rinehart, 1935.

(Under pseudonym Willy) *Claudine s'en va: Journal d'Annie,* Ollendorff, 1903, translation by Blossom published as *The Innocent Wife,* Farrar & Rinehart, 1935, translation by Antonia White published as *Claudine and Annie,* Secker & Warburg, 1962.

(Under pseudonym Willy), *Minne,* Ollendorff, 1904, revised and published with *Les Egarements de Minne* (also see below) as *L'Ingenue libertine,* under name Colette Willy, 1909 (also see below).

(Under name Colette Willy) *Dialogues de betes,* Mercure de France, 1904, enlarged edition published as *Douze Dialogues de betes,* 1930 (also see below).

(Under pseudonym Willy) *Les Egarements de Minne,* Ollendorff, 1905, revised and published with *Minne* as *L'Igenue libertine,* under name Colette Willy, 1909 (also see below).

(Under name Colette Willy) *La Retraite sentimentale,* Mercure de France, 1907, translation by Margaret Crosland published as *Retreat From Love,* Indiana University Press, 1974.

(Under name Colette Willy) *Les Vrilles de la vigne* (title means "The Tendrils of the Vine"), Editions de la Vie Parisienne, 1908.

(Under name Colette Willy) *L'Igenue libertine* (contains *Minne* and *Les Egarements de Minne*), Ollendorff, 1909, translation by Rosemary Carr Benet published as *The Gentle Libertine,* Farrar & Rinehart, 1931.

(Under name Colette Willy) *La Vagabonde,* Ollendorff, 1910 (also see below), translation by Charlotte Remfry-Kidd published as *Renee la vagabonde,* Doubleday, 1931, translation by Enid McLeod published as *The Vagabond,* Secker & Warburg, 1954, Wings (New York City), 1995.

L'Envers du music-hall, Flammarion, 1913, translation by Anne-Marie Callimachi published as *Music-Hall Sidelights* with Helen Beauclerk's translation of *Mes Apprentissages* (also see below), Secker & Warburg, 1957.

L'Entrave, Librairie des Lettres, 1913, translation by Viola Gerard Garvin published as *Recaptured,* Gollancz, 1931, Doubleday, 1932, translation by White published as *The Shackle,* Secker & Warburg, 1964.

Prrou, Poucette et quelques autres, Librairie des Lettres, 1913.

La Paix chez les betes, Georges Cres, 1916 (also see below).

Les Heures longues, 1914-1917, Fayard, 1917.

Les Enfants dans les ruines, Editions de la Maison du Livre, 1917.

Dans la foule, Georges Cres, 1918.

Mitsou; ou, Comment l'esprit vient aux filles (includes *En Camarades, piece en deux actes*), Fayard, 1919, translation by Jane Terry published as *Mitsou; or, How Girls Grow Wise,* A. & C. Boni, 1930.

La Chambre eclairee, Edouard Joseph, 1920.

Cheri, Fayard, 1920 (also see below), translation by Flanner published under same title, A. & C. Boni, 1930, Wings Books (New York City), 1995.

La Maison de Claudine, Ferenczi, 1922, revised, 1930, translation by McLeod and Una Vicenzo Troubridge published as *My Mother's House* (also see below) with McLeod's translation of *Sido* (also see below), Farrar, 1953.

Le Voyage egoiste, Editions d'Art Edouard Pelletan, 1922.

(With Leopold Marchand) *Cheri, comedie en quatre actes* (adapted from Colette's novel), Librairie Theatrale, 1922.

La Vagabonde (four-act comedy adapted from Colette's novel of the same title; first produced in Paris at the Theatre de la Renaissance), Impr. de l'Illustration, 1923.

Le Ble en herbe, Flammarion, 1923, translation by Ida Zeitlin published as *The Ripening,* Farrar, 1932, translation by Roger Senhouse published as *Ripening Seed,* Secker & Warburg, 1955, Farrar, 1956.

Reverie du nouvel an, Stock, 1923.

La Femme cachee, Flammarion, 1924, translation by Crosland published as *The Other Woman,* Owen, 1971.

Aventures quotidiennes, Flammarion, 1924.

Quatre Saisons, Philippe Ortiz, 1925.

L'Enfant et les sortileges, Durand, 1925.

La Fin de Cheri, Flammarion, 1926, translation published as *The Last of Cheri,* Putnam, 1932.

La Naissance du jour, Flammarion, 1928, translation by Benet published as *A Lesson in Love,* Farrar, 1932, translation by McLeod published as *Break of Day,* Farrar, 1961.

Renee Vivien, Edouard Champion, 1928.

La Seconde, Ferenczi, 1929, translation by Garvin published as *The Other One,* Cosmopolitan Book Corp., 1931.

Sido; ou, Les Pointes cardinaux, Editions Kra, 1929, revised, Ferenczi, 1930, translation by McLeod published as *Sido* with McLeod and Troubridge's translation of *La Maison de Claudine,* Farrar, 1953.

Histoires pour Bel-Gazou, Stock, 1930.

Prisons et paradis, Ferenczi, 1932, revised, 1935.

Ces Plaisirs, Ferenczi, 1932, translation by Edith Dally published as *The Pure and the Impure,* Ferrar, 1933, translation also published as *These Pleasures,* White Owl, 1934.

La Chatte, Grasset, 1933, translation by Morris Bentinck published as *Saha the Cat,* Farrar, 1936.

Duo, Ferenczi, 1934, translation by Blossom published under same title, Farrar, 1935.

La Jumelle noire, four volumes, Ferenczi, 1934-38.

Discours de reception a l'Academie Royale de Langue et de Litterature Francaises de Belgique, Grasset, 1936.

Mes Apprentissages: Ce que Claudine n'a pas dit, Ferenczi, 1936, translation by Helen Beauclerk published as *My Apprenticeships* with Callimachi's translation of *L'Envers du music-hall,* Secker & Warburg, 1957.

Bella-Vista, Ferenczi, 1937, translation by Antonia White, The Modern Library (New York City), 1996.

Le Toutounier, Ferenczi, 1939.

Chambre d'hotel, Fayard, 1940, translation by Patrick Leigh Fermor published as *Chance Acquaintances* with his translation of *Julie de Carneilhan* (also see below), Secker & Warburg, 1952, and with his translations of *Gigi* (also see below) and *Julie de Carneilhan,* Farrar, 1952.

Mes Cahiers, Armes de France, 1941.

Journal a rebours, Fayard, 1941, translation by David Le Vay published with his translation of *Paris de ma fenetre* (also see below) as *Looking Backwards* (also see below).

Julie de Carneilhan, Fayard, 1941, translation by Fermor published with *Chambre d'hotel,* Secker & Warburg, 1952, and with *Gigi* and *Chambre d'hotel,* Farrar, 1952.

De ma fenetre, Armes de France, 1942, enlarged edition published as *Paris de ma fenetre,* translation by Le Vay published with his translation of *Journal a rebours* as *Looking Backwards* (also see below).

De la patte a l'aile, Correa, 1943.

Flore et Pomone, Galerie Charpentier, 1943.

Nudite, Mappemonde, 1943.

Le Kepi, Fayard, 1943.

Broderie ancienne, Editions du Rocher, 1944.

Gigi et autres nouvelles, La Guilde du Livre, 1944 (also see below), translation by Fermor of title story published with his translations of *Julie de Carneilhan* and *Chambre d'hotel,* Farrar, 1952.

Trois . . . six . . . neuf, Correa, 1944.

Belles Saisons, Galerie Charpentier, 1945.

L'Etoile vesper, Milieu du Monde, 1946, translation by Le Vay published as *The Evening Star,* Owen, 1973, Bobbs-Merrill, 1974.

Pour un herbier, Mermod, 1948, translation by Senhouse published as *For a Flower Album,* McKay, 1959.

Trait pour trait, Fleuron, 1949.

Journal intermittent, Fleuron, 1949 (also see below).

Le Fanal bleu, Ferenczi, 1949, translation by Senhouse published as *The Blue Lantern,* Farrar, 1963.

La Fleur de l'age, Fleuron, 1949.

En Pays connu, Manuel Bruker, 1949.

Chats de Colette, A. Michel, 1950.

(With Anita Loos) *Gigi* (play; adapted from Colette's novel of the same title), France-Illustration, 1954.

Creatures Great and Small: Creature Conversations; Other Creatures; Creature Comforts (includes *Dialogues de betes* and *La Paix chez les betes*), translated by McLeod, Farrar, 1957.

Paysages et portraits, Flammarion, 1958.

Notes marocaines, Mermod, 1958.

The Stories of Colette, translated by White, Secker & Warburg, 1958, published as *The Tender Shoot and Other Stories,* Farrar, 1959.

Decouvertes, Mermod, 1961.

Earthly Paradise: An Autobiography Drawn From Her Lifelong Writings, edited by Robert Phelps, translated by Beauclerk and others, Farrar, 1966.

Contes des mille et un matins, Flammarion, 1970, translation by Le Vay and Crosland published as *The Thousand and One Mornings,* Bobbs-Merrill, 1973.

Places (includes *Journal intermittent*), translated by Le Vay, Owen, 1970, Bobbs-Merrill, 1971.

Journey for Myself: Selfish Memories, translated by Le Vay, Owen, 1971.

Looking Backwards (contains Le Vay's translations of *De ma fenetre* and *Journal a rebours*), Indiana University Press, 1975.

Ralph Gibson, editor, *The Spirit of Burgundy* (includes selections from *My Mother's House* and *Sido,* translated by Una Vicenzo Troubridge and Enid McLeod), Aperture (New York City), 1994.

Gigi and *The Cat (La Chatte),* Penguin (New York City), 1995.

CORRESPONDENCE

Lettres a Helene Picard, Flammarion, 1958 (also see below).

Lettres a Marguerite Moreno, Flammarion, 1959 (also see below).

Lettres de la vagabonde, Flammarion, 1961 (also see below).

Lettres au petit corsaire, Flammarion, 1963 (also see below).

Lettres a ses pairs, Flammarion, 1973 (also see below).

Letters From Colette (contains excerpts from *Lettres a Helene Picard, Lettres a Marguerite Moreno, Lettres de la vagabonde, Lettres au petit corsaire,* and *Lettres a ses pairs*), translated by Phelps, Farrar, 1980.

COLLECTED WORKS

Oeuvres completes, fifteen volumes, compiled with an introduction by Colette and Maurice Goudeket, Flammarion, 1948-50, enlarged edition published as *Oeuvres completes de Colette,* sixteen volumes, with illustrations and previously unpublished pieces, Editions du Club de l'Honnete Homme, 1973-76.

The Collected Stories of Colette, edited with an introduction by Phelps, translated by Matthew Ward, Farrar, 1983.

Colette: Oeuvres, edited by Claude Pichois, Gallimard, 1984-86.

MEDIA ADAPTATIONS: Claudine at School was adapted for stage; *Cheri* was adapted for both stage and film; *Gigi* was adapted for an Academy Award-winning film of the same title by Alan Jay Lerner, directed by Vincente Minnelli, Metro-Goldwyn-Mayer, 1958.

SIDELIGHTS: Sidonie-Gabrielle Colette, better known as Colette, was an important figure in early twentieth-century French literature. Her impressive series of novels, stories, plays, and newspaper articles include chronicles of backstage life in turn-of-the-century music halls, novels of love and betrayal from the early 1900s through World War II, and nostalgic reminiscences of her childhood. All of Colette's works are marked by sensitive descriptions of nature, sexual frankness, and a flair for the theatrical. Robert Cottrell noted in an essay collected in *Women, the Arts, and the 1920s in Paris and New York* that Colette's 1920 novel *Cheri,* "firmly established her reputation in France as a popular novelist" and as one of the best women writers of her day. Elected to Belgium's Royal Academy of French Language and Literature in 1935, Colette was the first woman to serve as president of France's prestigious literary jury, the Goncourt Academy, and the first woman to attain the rank of Grand Officer of the Legion of Honor.

"We suspect that something new in women's writing begins with Colette," wrote Erica Mendelson Eisinger and Mari Ward McCarty in their introduction to *Colette: The Woman, The Writer.* "The androcentric [male-centered] optic is displaced," they continued, and "a new subject appears: the woman who desires." Some critics have complained, however, that Colette's male characters appear wooden, one-dimensional, and far less interesting than her women. Nevertheless, as Marcelle Biolley-Godino argued in *L'Homme-objet chez Colette,* it is precisely by this reversal of the traditional novelistic point of view, by this objectification of the male under the dominant gaze of the desiring female, that Colette strikes a new chord in the French novel.

Colette would most likely have remained silent, as she herself recognized, without the partnership of her first husband. In 1893, a country girl barely twenty years of age, Colette married the socially prominent journalist and music critic Henry Gauthier-Villars, better known in Parisian circles simply as "Willy." Fourteen years her senior, Willy dominated his young wife and introduced her to Parisian high life. In her 1936 work *Mes Apprentissages* (translated as *My Apprenticeships*), Colette recalls her thirteen years as Madame Colette Willy: "It is true that, at first, ridden by youth and ignorance, I had known intoxication—a guilty rapture, an atrocious, impure, adolescent impulse. There are many scarcely nubile girls who dream of becoming the show, the plaything, the licentious masterpiece of some middle-aged man. It is an ugly dream that is punished by its fulfillment. . . . So I was punished, quickly and thoroughly." Willy was not only openly unfaithful to his wife, but he apparently exploited the talent for literature he discovered in her.

Ostensibly a prolific novelist and journalist, Willy operated on the simple principle of signing his name to works actually penned by others. It was perhaps only a matter of time before Willy brought his wife into his underground workshop of ghost writers. In the late 1890s, as Colette told the story in *My Apprenticeships,* Willy asked her to write a memoir of her school years in the Burgundian town of Saint-Sauveur. However, he judged the finished manuscript worthless and consigned it to a desk drawer. Some two years later, Willy rediscovered it, swore roundly at his lack of foresight, and set his wife to work spicing up the manuscript that he now recognized as having commercial potential. The fruit of this uneven collaboration between husband and wife, *Claudine a l'ecole* (translated as *Claudine at School*) was published in 1900. It bore only Willy's signature.

The book was an immediate success, and thus Colette, who would protest all her life that she had no writer's "vocation," became a novelist. She produced, one after another, the sequels to *Claudine at School* that Willy also claimed as his own: *Claudine a Paris* (title means "Claudine in Paris") in 1901, *Claudine en menage* (title means "Claudine Married") in 1902, *Claudine s'en va* (later translated as *Claudine and Annie*) in 1903. The series turned Willy and Colette into indisputable Parisian celebrities.

The 1907 novel *La Retraite sentimentale* (translated as *Retreat From Love*), was published shortly after Colette and Willy separated. The last of the Claudine novels, it ends the cycle with both an indictment and a panegyric of marriage. In contrast with both Colette and Annie, Claudine finally obtains her independence through widowhood and is given over to a peaceful retirement with her dog, her cats, and her tender memories in the tranquil confines of her childhood home.

The signature "Colette Willy" first appeared on the 1904 *Dialogues de betes,* written while Colette was still married to and living with Willy. The work is a collection of short dialogues featuring the bull terrier Toby-Chien and the angora cat Kiki-la-Doucette. In *Colette Free and Fettered,* Michele Sarde speculated that Willy allowed Colette to sign her own name to these short writings, since he judged them to be women's pieces and of scant commercial value compared to the "Claudines." He was apparently unimpressed with this aspect of his wife's talent; as Colette recalled in *My Apprenticeships,* he remarked that he hadn't known he had married "the last of the lyric poets." In the preface to *Dialogues de betes,* however, as reprinted in Colette's *Complete Works,* the Belgian Symbolist poet Francis Jammes lavishly praised both Colette's bourgeois domestic sense and her poetic gifts: "It pleased Mme. Colette Willy," he wrote "to concentrate in two charming little animals all the fragrance of the gardens, all the freshness of the prairies, all the heat of the departmental road, all the emotions of man. . . ."

The short novel *Minne,* published the same year as *Dialogue de betes,* was cast in the mold of the "Claudines." The work depicts a young girl's obsession with the mysterious leader of a band of delinquents; their petty criminal exploits in the no-man's-land of the Paris fortifications stimulate Minne's romantic imagination and lead her on a nightmarish odyssey through the nighttime city. Colette recounted in a later preface to the work that she had hoped to publish *Minne* under her own name, and so "it was necessary, to keep away from it a [husband's] greediness that usually addressed itself to works the size of a novel, that my story should be kept rather brief." But Willy again foresaw the success of his wife's literary endeavors and published *Minne* under his name. A

sequel to the work, which appeared in 1905 as *Les Egarements de Minne* ("Minne's Misconduct"), was again signed "Willy."

Colette's first divorce forced her to tap her own resources for her financial and professional survival. In an essay collected in *Colette: The Woman, The Writer,* Janet Whatley described how the ability to survive reversals of romantic or domestic fortune is a trait uniquely ascribed to the female characters in Colette's work. "Most of Colette's heroines place a certain value on unhappiness," Whatley observed; "They do not wallow in it: they use it as a source of energy. To be unhappy is to make one's own acquaintance." The 1908 collection of reflective pieces *Les Vrilles de la vigne* ("The Tendrils of the Vine") shows how quickly Colette arrived at this parallel of unhappiness and self-knowledge. Certain of the short narrative pieces in the work suggest the genteel retreat of the disabused ex-wife into a countryside solitude shared only with her dog, her cat, and the selected women friends who remain in discreet relations with the "disgraced" divorcee. In reality, however, Colette's postdivorce period was much more public than this, much noisier and more scandalous. She was openly cohabitating with a new mentor, the well-known lesbian Missy de Belbeuf, the Marquise de Morny; their love scene in the pantomime "Reve d'Egypte" ("Egyptian Dream") performed at the Moulin Rouge in January 1903 had created a city-wide scandal. De Belbeuf is widely considered to be the tender lover celebrated in *Les Vrilles de la vigne.* Colette's bisexuality, of which her affair with de Belbeuf was perhaps the most flagrant example, contributed to her reputation for sensuality, if not questionable morality.

Another major cycle of Colette's narrative works deals with her career between 1906 and 1911 as a music-hall dancer and mime. The 1913 *L'Envers du music-hall* (*Music-Hall Sidelights*) and *Mitsou* (1919), as well as her earlier work *La Vagabonde* (*The Vagabond,* 1910) have as their setting the behind-the-scenes world of the traveling song, dance, pantomime, and animal acts that made up the popular French theater of the music hall and the cafe-concert during the first decades of the twentieth century. *The Vagabond* and *Mitsou* are both novels of rejection. In the former, protagonist Renee turns down a marriage proposal, fearing that acceptance will cost her her freedom. In the latter, set during the First World War, music-hall performer Mitsou falls in love by correspondence with the young man who signs himself the "Blue Lieutenant" after the color of his uniform. Their first night together, however, proves disastrous and Mitsou's new lover feigns an early end to his leave in order to break their next date. Mitsou responds with the distinctive wisdom of Colette's heroines, writing to her lieutenant, "You say: 'Madame, I am charmed to be with you. I must just slip out to get some cigarettes; I won't be a minute,' and you leave her there for the rest of her life."

Sarde has traced connections between the decisions of these two music-hall heroines and those that determined Colette's own relationships with men in the period following her first divorce. Around 1910 she received an offer of marriage from department store heir Auguste Heriot but, according to Sarde, "countered her friends' attempts at her [marital] rehabilitation with a stubborn and active resistance . . . reflected in *La Vagabonde.*" *Mitsou* might also be read as a reflection of this continuing fear of commitment, of this suspicion that however strong the initial attraction between the couple, faithfulness on the part of the male is pure fantasy. By the time *Mitsou* appeared in 1919, however, Colette had already accepted her own return to domesticity. In December 1912 she married her second husband, the Baron Henri de Jouvenel des Ursins, an up-and-coming French political figure who was also one of the chief editors of the Paris daily *Le Matin,* for which Colette had been writing a weekly column since December 1911. In July 1913, at forty years of age, she gave birth to her only child, Colette de Jouvenel, nicknamed as Colette herself had been as a child, "Bel-Gazou."

In *L'Entrave* (translated as *The Shackle*), the 1916 sequel to *The Vagabond,* Renee allows herself to be seduced by the much younger Jean, with whom she has little in common beyond their physical attraction. Jean betrays her, and the ending of the novel thus casts Jean, rather than Renee, in the privileged role of wanderer: "It seems to me," Renee concludes, "as I watch him launch out enthusiastically into life, that he has changed places with me; that he is the eager vagabond and that I am the one who gazes after him, anchored forever." If this exchange of female for male independence appears strikingly unfair, Colette herself expressed considerable dissatisfaction with the conclusion to *L'Entrave.* In *L'Etoile vesper* (*The Evening Star,* 1936) she recalled that, interrupted by the birth of her daughter, the novel, "did not recover from the blows inflicted by the feeble and triumphant creature. Consider, hypothetical readers, consider the scamped ending, the inadequate corridor through which I desired my diminished heroes to pass. Consider the fine but empty tone of an ending in which they do not believe, and the modal chord, as a musician might say, so hurriedly sounded. . . . I have, since, tried to rewrite the ending of *L'Entrave.* I have not succeeded."

Colette's shorter pieces from 1911 to 1924 appear in collections published between 1916 and 1924 (available in translation in *Creatures Great and Small* and *Journey for Myself: Selfish Memories*). In these short pieces, often produced under newspaper deadline, she proved equally at ease describing the cozy retreat of a corner by the hearth or observing the tumult of a political meeting. The beauties of nature, the change of seasons, the wisdom of animals, and the comfort of home are all favorite themes. Into these pieces she poured her receptivity to what Joan Hinde Stewart, writing in *Colette,* called the "fleeting encounters [that] enriched her as woman and as writer," as well as her professional discipline.

Colette's marriage to Henri de Jouvenel ended in divorce in 1925. The union had foundered on two crises in particular: Jouvenel's affair with the Rumanian princess Marthe Bibesco begun in 1923, and Colette's affair with the adolescent Bertrand de Jouvenel, Henri's second oldest son by his former lover Isabelle de Comminges, and thus Colette's stepson. Colette's situation at the end of this second marriage, however, was far better assured than it had been at the end of her first: touring as an actress and lecturer, writing drama criticism in addition to her stories and novels, she was now an established artist in her own right.

Prior to her divorce, Colette completed the 1920 novel *Cheri,* a vehicle for two of her most memorable characters. In this story the aging courtesan Lea de Lonval discovers to what depths of devotion and renunciation she has been inspired by her love for the much younger Cheri, the spoiled and remarkably beautiful son of her friend Charlotte Peloux. Although Colette paints a compelling portrait of Lea as a woman coming to terms with her age, it was the character of Cheri himself, an indisputably dominant male, god-like and childishly selfish in his need for love and admiration, that guaranteed the novel's success. In *The Evening Star,* Colette recalled with amusement the question a young journalist still saw fit to ask her twenty-five years after the novel's publication: "Madame, did Cheri . . . did Cheri ever exist?" She assured her readers that he had, but not in flesh and

blood: "I could not wholeheartedly affirm that the Cheri . . . of my novel resembled anyone," she continued. "But I should lie if I said that he resembled no one. But that everyone should model Cheri in their own fashion, isn't that just what I wanted?" Colette made no secret of the just pride she took in *Cheri:* "For the first time in my life," she wrote in *The Evening Star,* "I felt morally certain of having written a novel for which I needed neither blush nor doubt, a novel whose appearance massed partisans and critics round it. . . . I know where my best work as a writer is to be found."

In *La Maison de Claudine* (*My Mother's House,* 1922) Colette turned her considerable scenic talents—the ability to evoke in a few brief pages a precise atmosphere, a moral lesson, or a psychological insight—to the service of her nostalgia for her childhood home—indeed, for the entire lost world of childhood. But Colette's most vivid example of nostalgic writing is the 1929 memoir *Sido.* In the joint preface to *Sido* and *My Mother's House* in her *Complete Works,* Colette credited her mother, Sidonie Colette, known as Sido, with both the happiness of her childhood and the wisdom of her adult years: "As a child I was poor and happy, like many children who need neither money nor comfort to achieve an active sort of happiness. But my felicity knew another and less commonplace secret: the presence of her who, instead of receding far from me through the gates of death, has revealed herself more vividly to me as I grow older."

As a theme of Colette's work, homosexuality is but one part of the overriding attention she gives to the senses in all their pleasures and pitfalls; one may just as easily accuse her of indiscretion for her rhapsodic descriptions of nature as for her descriptions of sexual experience. The work most explicitly devoted to homosexuality, the 1932 *Le Pur et l'impur* (*The Pure and the Impure,* originally entitled *Ces Plaisirs* (*These Pleasures*), is in fact a curious memoir describing people she had known or known of, including Missy de Belbeuf (appearing in the guise of the virile La Chevaliere); the suicidal lesbian poet Renee Vivien; and the couple known as the Ladies of Llangollen, celebrated for their lifelong devotion to each other.

In 1935 Colette married her third and last husband, Maurice Goudeket, who was sixteen years her junior. The two had been a couple since 1925, and her later writings refer to Goudeket as her best friend and companion. He undertook in 1939 the first edition of Colette's *Complete Works* and nursed her faithfully through her long bout with arthritis that set in following a fracture of her fibula in September 1931 and that by the end of her life had almost completely immobilized her. Goudeket, a Jew, was arrested in December of 1941 and detained in a prison camp outside of Paris for two months.

The novella *Gigi* is probably Colette's best known postwar work, partially because of its successful screen adaptation. *Gigi* tells the story of a young girl who is destined for a career as a modern-day courtesan, but who opts instead for a love match, which has a double-edged verve to it. Colette once again builds a love story around a disproportioned couple (Gaston is considerably older than Gigi and enjoys much higher social status) and attributes a precocious, prematurely disillusioned wisdom to her adolescent heroine. Certain, as are all of Colette's women, that Gaston will eventually betray her, Gigi confesses her love for him as the lesser of two evils: she would, she tells him in Colette's parody of the romantic happy ending, rather be unhappy with him than unhappy without him.

Some observers have noted that many of Colette's later works of fiction and nonfiction can seem rambling and anecdotal; these writings lack the incisiveness, clean pacing, and crisp insight of her earlier works. The author's various journals and memoirs—the 1942 *De ma fenetre* and the 1949 *Journal intermittent,* in addition to *The Evening Star* and *The Blue Lantern,*—are, by her own admission, less chronological accounts of her life or philosophical reflections on her experiences than they are scattered collections of anecdotes, observations, character portraits, reminiscences, and comments. "I do not possess the knack of writing a proper journal," she declared at the beginning of *The Blue Lantern.* "The art of selection, of noting things of mark, retaining the unusual while discarding the commonplace, has never been mine, since most of the time I am stimulated and quickened by the ordinary." The increasing immobility imposed upon her by her arthritis is a dominant theme of *The Blue Lantern.* Its title refers to the blue shade of the lamp in her window by which, confined to her sofa-bed, she continued to write. Colette died in Paris on August 3, 1954; her funeral on August 7 was the first state funeral accorded to a woman in France.

BIOGRAPHICAL/CRITICAL SOURCES:

BOOKS

Biolley-Godino, Marcelle, *L'Homme-objet chez Colette,* Klinck-sieck, 1972.
Corbin, Laurie, *The Mother-Mirror: Self-Representation and the Mother-Daughter Relation in Colette, Simone de Beauvoir, and Marguerite Duras,* P. Lang (New York City), 1996.
Cottrell, Robert D., *Colette,* Ungar, 1974.
Crosland, Margaret, *Colette—The Difficulty of Loving: A Biography,* Dell, 1973.
Dictionary of Literary Biography, Volume 65: *French Novelists, 1930-1960,* Gale, 1988.
Eisinger, Erica Mendelson and Mari Ward McCarty, editors, *Colette: The Woman, the Writer,* Pennsylvania State University Press, 1981.
Perry, R. and M. W. Brownley, editors, *Mothering the Mind: Twelve Studies of Writers and Their Silent Partners,* Holmes & Meier, 1984.
Richardson, Joanna, *Colette,* F. Watts, 1984.
Sarde, Michele, *Colette Free and Fettered,* translated by R. Miller, Morrow, 1980.
Stewart, Joan Hinde, *Colette,* Twayne (New York City), 1983.
Strand, Dana, *Colette: A Study of the Short Fiction,* Twayne, 1995.
Twentieth-Century Literary Criticism, Gale, Volume 1, 1978; Volume 5, 1981; Volume 16, 1985.
Wheeler, K. W. and V. L. Lussier, editors, *Women, the Arts, and the 1920s in Paris and New York,* Transaction Books, 1982.

PERIODICALS

Centerpoint: A Journal of Interdisciplinary Studies, fall-spring, 1981.
Contemporary Literature, summer, 1983.
Modern Language Studies, spring, 1981; summer, 1983.
New Republic, September 6, 1954.
Times Literary Supplement, August 22, 1968.

*   *   *

COLT, Winchester Remington
See HUBBARD, L(afayette) Ron(ald)

COLVIN, James
See MOORCOCK, Michael (John)

*   *   *

COMFORT, Alex(ander) 1920-

PERSONAL: Born February 10, 1920, in London, England; son of Alexander Charles and Daisy Elizabeth (Fenner) Comfort; married Ruth Muriel Harris, 1943 (divorced, 1973); married Jane Tristram Henderson, 1973 (died, 1991); children: (first marriage) Nicholas Alfred Fenner. *Education:* Cambridge University, B.A., 1943, M.B., B.Ch., 1944, M.A., 1945; London Hospital, M.R.C.S., L.R.C.P., 1944; University of London, D.C.H., 1946, Ph.D. (biochemistry), 1949, D.Sc. (gerontology), 1963. *Politics:* "Anarchist."

ADDRESSES: Home—Fitzwarren House, Hornsey Lane, London N6 5LX, England.

CAREER: London Hospital, London, house physician, 1944; Royal Waterloo Hospital, London, resident medical officer, 1944-45; London Hospital Medical College, London, lecturer in physiology, 1945-51; University of London, University College, London, Nuffield research fellow in gerontology, 1952-64, director of Medical Research Council Group on Aging, 1965-73; Stanford University, Stanford, CA, clinical lecturer in psychiatry, 1974-83; Institute for Higher Studies, Santa Barbara, CA, fellow, 1975-85; University of California, School of Medicine, Irvine, professor of pathology, 1976-79; University of California, Los Angeles, Neuropsychiatric Institute, adjunct professor, 1979–. Consultant psychiatrist, Brentwood VA Hospital, 1977-81. *Wartime service:* Conscientious objector during World War II.

MEMBER: British Society for Research on Aging (past president), Royal Society of Medicine, American Medical Association, American Psychiatric Association, Gerontological Society, American Association of Sex Educators, Counselors, and Therapists, Conchological Society, Malacological Society, Peace Pledge Union (sponsor).

AWARDS, HONORS: Ciba Foundation prize for research in gerontology, 1958; Borestone poetry award, second prize, 1962; Karger Memorial Prize in gerentology, 1969.

WRITINGS:

NONFICTION

Art and Social Responsibility: Lectures on the Ideology of Romanticism, Falcon Press, 1946.
The Novel and Our Time, Phoenix House, 1948.
Barbarism and Sexual Freedom: Lectures on the Sociology of Sex from the Standpoint of Anarchism, Freedom Press, 1948.
First Year Physiological Technique, Staples, 1948.
Sexual Behavior in Society, Viking, 1950, published as *Sex in Society,* Duckworth, 1963.
Authority and Delinquency in the Modern State: A Criminological Approach to the Problem of Power, Routledge & Kegan Paul, 1950, published as *Authority and Delinquency,* Sphere, 1970.
The Biology of Senescence, Rinehart, 1956, published as *Ageing: The Biology of Senescence,* Holt, 1964.
Darwin and the Naked Lady: Discursive Essays on Biology and Art, Routledge & Kegan Paul, 1961.
The Process of Ageing, New American Library, 1964.

The Nature of Human Nature, Harper, 1966, published in England as *Nature and Human Nature,* Weidenfeld & Nicolson, 1966.

The Anxiety Makers: Some Curious Preoccupations of the Medical Profession, Thomas Nelson, 1967, Dell, 1969.

The Joy of Sex: A Cordon Bleu Guide to Lovemaking, illustrated by Charles Raymond and Christopher Foss, Simon & Schuster, 1972, revised edition published as *The Joy of Sex: A Gourmet Guide to Lovemaking,* Crown, 1972, additional revision published as *The New Joy of Sex: A Gourmet Guide to Lovemaking in the Nineties,* Crown, 1991.

More Joy: A Lovemaking Companion to "The Joy of Sex," illustrated by Raymond and Foss, Crown, 1974.

A Good Age, Crown, 1975.

Sexual Consequences of Disability, George Stickley, 1978.

I and That: Notes on the Biology of Religion, Crown, 1979.

(With wife, Jane Comfort) *The Facts of Love,* Crown, 1979.

A Practice of Geriatric Psychiatry, American Elsevier, 1980.

What Is a Doctor?, George Stickley, 1980.

Reality and Empathy: Physics, Mind, and Science in the 21st Century, State University of New York Press, 1984.

Say Yes to Old Age: Developing a Positive Attitude Toward Aging, Crown, 1990.

The New Joy of Sex, illustrated by John Raynes with photographs by Clare Park, Crown, 1991.

Sexual Foreplay, Crown, 1997.

Sexual Positions, Crown, 1997.

(Translation and introduction by) *The Illustrated Koka Shastra: Medieval Indian Writings on Love Based on the Kama Sutra,* Simon and Schuster Editions (New York City), 1997.

NOVELS

The Silver River, Chapman & Hall, 1937.

No Such Liberty, Chapman & Hall, 1941.

The Almond Tree, Chapman & Hall, 1943.

The Powerhouse, Viking, 1945.

On This Side of Nothing, Routledge & Kegan Paul, 1948, Viking, 1949.

A Giant's Strength, Routledge & Kegan Paul, 1952.

Come Out to Play, Eyre & Spottiswoode, 1961, Crown, 1975.

Tetrarch, Shambhala, 1980.

Imperial Patient: The Memoirs of Nero's Doctor, Duckworth, 1987.

The Philosophers, Duckworth, 1989.

POETRY

France and Other Poems, Favil Press, 1942.

A Wreath for the Living, Routledge & Kegan Paul, 1942.

(Contributor) *Three New Poets: Roy McFadden, Alex Comfort, Ian Serrailler,* Grey Walls Press, 1942.

Elegies, Routledge & Kegan Paul, 1944.

The Song of Lazarus, Viking, 1945.

The Signal to Engage, Routledge & Kegan Paul, 1946.

And All but He Departed, Routledge & Kegan Paul, 1951.

Haste to the Wedding, Eyre & Spottiswoode, 1962.

All but a Rib: Poems Chiefly of Women, Mitchell Beazley, 1973.

Poems for Jane, Crown, 1979.

Mikrokosmos, Sinclair Stevenson, 1994.

PLAYS

Into Egypt, Grey Walls Press, 1942.

Cities of the Plain, A Democratic Melodrama, Grey Walls Press, 1943.

OTHER

Letters from an Outpost (stories), Routledge & Kegan Paul, 1947.

The Pattern of the Future (radio programs), Routledge & Kegan Paul, 1949.

Are You Sitting Comfortably? (political songs), Sing Magazine, 1962.

(Editor and translator) *The Koka Shastra and Other Mediaeval Writings on Love,* Allen & Unwin, 1964, Stein & Day, 1965.

(Editor) Inge and Sten Hegeler, *An Abz of Love,* Nevill Spearman, 1969.

Contributor of articles to literary and professional journals; editor with Peter Wells of *Poetry Folios,* 1942-44; editor of *New Road,* 1943-44.

SIDELIGHTS: Though well known and highly respected in professional circles for his pioneering work in gerontological research, Alex Comfort is perhaps best known to readers as the author of *The Joy of Sex: A Cordon Bleu Guide to Lovemaking* and its sequels, *More Joy* and *The New Joy of Sex.* A conscientious objector in World War II who was once arrested at an anti-nuclear demonstration with English author Bertrand Russell, Comfort has been a physician, political activist, and writer since the early 1940s with published works that include collections of poetry, travelogues, novels, and plays. Wayne Burns summarized Comfort's approach in the *Humanist:* "He realizes that science is not opposed to art, that, rather, the two modes of knowledge complement one another."

A best-seller for years, Comfort's *Joy of Sex* has been called "the only self-help book ever worth a dang" by William Cole of *Saturday Review,* a "Kamasutra for the coffee table" by David Gelman of *Newsweek,* but "educational pornography" by others, noted Gelman. The explicitness of the book's drawings and text created controversy upon its publication in 1972. Pen and ink illustrations depicted various sexual practices, and chapters were provocatively titled "Main Courses" and "Sauces." Comfort's reason for writing the book, according to Dennis Breo in the *Chicago Tribune,* was to put forth the idea "that human sexuality should always be a liberating counterpoint to . . . man's unrelenting struggle against an always hostile environment." Breo also quoted Comfort as saying: "There's nothing new in the book. It's just reassurance, telling people its OK."

The book's sequel, *More Joy,* continued in the same vein, promoting the changing mores of the 1970s in which attitudes toward sex, according to Comfort, should be "based on nonanxiety, noncompulsion and recognition of personhood," quoted Benjamin DeMott in the *Atlantic.* However, DeMott warned, "some will contend that this second volume . . . [is] a fresh exploitation of the middle-class porn markets." The 1991 version, *The New Joy of Sex,* reflected a newly conservative sexual ethic with its sober warnings concerning AIDS, cautioning that some practices highlighted in previous volumes could now have disastrous consequences. To update the book's look, the Japanese etchings from the first volume were replaced with a series of photographs. In addition, new illustrations portrayed a couple "whose trim looks and complaisant expressions seem to suggest their energetic lovemaking is designed to take inches off your tummy," stated Gelman.

Many of Comfort's other nonfiction books encompass ideas regarding sexuality as they relate to politics and sociology. *The Nature of Human Nature* is a broad study of the evolution of humankind from sociological, psychological, and anthropological viewpoints. Influenced by the teachings of Austrian neurologist Sigmund Freud and English naturalist Charles Darwin, Comfort "lays at least as much emphasis on man's emotional life, his religion and his art as upon his genetic constitution," according to a reviewer for the *Times Literary Supplement.* True to Comfort's later writings, sexuality is discussed as a factor that motivates human beings in all types of relationships, "even our relationship with things," claimed the *Times Literary Supplement* reviewer. Comfort narrowed his focus in *The Process of Ageing,* which outlines the various methods of maintaining youth that have gained popularity through the years and discusses changing societal attitudes toward the aged. Again, Comfort notes the effect of mating habits on longevity—he says that marriage and similar relationships tend to increase it. Despite Comfort's thorough observations, however, a *Times Literary Supplement* writer commented that "it is clear . . . that we know now very little about the causes of ageing and can do little, in consequence, to prevent it."

In his novels as well, Comfort frequently employs sexual themes as integral parts of his plots. Topics range from the life of the Roman emperor Nero in *Imperial Patient: The Memoirs of Nero's Doctor* to a science fictional allegory in *Tetrarch.* Comfort's early fiction received comparisons to American writer Henry David Thoreau in terms of philosophy and caught the attention of literary luminaries of the day, including George Orwell, who called Comfort's 1941 anti-war novel *No Such Liberty* "a good novel as novels go." The novel helped establish Comfort's reputation; Burns in the *Humanist* recognized that Comfort "has combined scientific knowledge with artistic insight and understanding to produce some of the most vital social-political studies of recent years." *On This Side of Nothing,* written in 1948, brought comparisons to Austrian writer Franz Kafka's work and was declared to "embod[y] significant philosophical ideas in a significant form of pictorial realism . . . and therefore [is] a novel-of-ideas equal to all but the masterpieces in this genre," by Burns in *Arizona Quarterly.*

Comfort's 1961 novel, *Come Out to Play,* was considered risque enough to have its U.S. publication postponed until 1975, several years after *The Joy of Sex* had made him a popular author. Though the novel concerns an unemployed doctor who, along with his mistress, opens a sex clinic for couples, it "is no great shakes either as a manifesto or as a comic novel," wrote Anatole Broyard in the *New York Times.* The doctor's treatment successfully transforms belligerent men into sexually-charged romantics who no longer need weapons or other forms of violence in their lives. Although Broyard's 1975 review claimed that "Dr. Comfort's sexual expertise has led him into the hubristic error of assuming that he knows all about other people's intimate lives," Paul Gray of *Time* called the publication of the novel "a ho-hum incident at the time but noteworthy in hindsight . . . a tame reminder of how things have changed since 1961."

In *Imperial Patient,* Comfort takes readers back to the waning days of the Roman Empire through his portrait of one of history's more notorious rulers. As witnessed through the eyes of Callimachus, the Greek physician hired to treat Nero's wife for infertility, the emperor "turns out to be Elvis Presley *manque,* a frustrated entertainer, but with a hunger for spiritual enlightenment," according to Kirsty Milne of the London *Observer.* Peter Howell of the *Times Literary Supplement* faulted the book for its arcane humor but conceded that it contains "some wonderfully bizarre ideas" when Comfort uses the narrative to expound upon his "esoteric expertise" in mysticism and technology.

Comfort applied his philosophy to the genre of science fiction in *Tetrarch,* an allegorical novel about a sexually and politically utopian society that is forced to battle the technological evils of a rival planet. Earthlings Edward and Rosanna wander through a door to the time-bending land of Los where they join the search to recover a crystal that holds magical secrets. William Fadiman of the *Los Angeles Times Book Review* faulted the book for its use of science fiction conventions, claiming that "Comfort couches his narrative of derring-do in prose that is a gallimaufry of contemporary slang [and] scientific jargon." Influenced by the poet William Blake as well as Eastern mysticism, the moral of the novel, according to Gerald Jonas of the *New York Times Book Review,* is that "our secularized, dehumanized society had better find a gate of its own before it perishes in a cloud of intellectual pollution."

Comfort's research and writing on gerontology and sexuality is fundamentally concerned with tapping the potential of humanity. "Comfort's art is an art of protest," stated Breo. Through his fiction, nonfiction, short stories, and plays, Comfort has put forth a philosophy that prizes peace and anarchy above warfare and organized politics. In *The Nature of Human Nature* Comfort wrote that "Man is the only animal which is inherently able, corporately and individually, to be his own worst enemy."

BIOGRAPHICAL/CRITICAL SOURCES:

PERIODICALS

Atlantic, April, 1975, pp. 88-91.
Arizona Quarterly, summer, 1952.
Chicago Tribune, February 24, 1979.
Humanist, November/December, 1951, pp. 269-74.
Los Angeles Times Book Review, June 22, 1980, p. 8.
Newsweek, October 21, 1991, p. 69.
New York Times, April 30, 1975.
New York Times Book Review, September 14, 1980, p. 38.
Observer (London), July 7, 1987.
Saturday Review, September 9, 1974.
Time, May 19, 1975.
Times Literary Supplement, October 28, 1965; January 12, 1967; July 20, 1967; September 18, 1987.

*   *   *

COMMAGER, Henry Steele 1902-

PERSONAL: Born October 25, 1902, in Pittsburgh, PA; son of James Williams and Anna Elizabeth (Dan) Commager; married Evan Carroll, July 3, 1928; married Mary E. Powlesland, July 14, 1979; children: (first marriage) Henry Steele (deceased), Nellie Thomas McColl, Elisabeth Carroll. *Education:* University of Chicago, Ph.B., 1923, M.A., 1924, Ph.D., 1928; attended University of Copenhagen; Cambridge University, M.A.; Oxford University, M.A. *Politics:* Independent Democrat.

ADDRESSES: Home—405 South Pleasant St., Amherst, MA 01002. *Office*—Department of history, Amherst College, Amherst, MA 01002.

CAREER: New York University, New York City, instructor in history, 1926-29, assistant professor, 1929-30, associate professor, 1930-31, professor, 1931-38; Columbia University, New York City, professor of American history, 1939-56, adjunct professor, 1956-59, Sperenza Lecturer, 1960; Amherst College, Amherst, MA, Smith Professor of History, 1956-72, Simpson Lecturer, beginning 1972, then professor emeritus. Pitt Professor of American History, Cambridge University, 1941, 1947-48; Bacon Lecturer, Boston University, 1943; Richards Lecturer, University of Virginia, 1944; Harmsworth Professor of American History,

Oxford University, 1952-53; Gottesman Lecturer, Uppsala University, 1953; Ziskind Professor, Brandeis University, 1955; Commonwealth Lecturer, University of London, 1963; Harris Lecturer, Northwestern University, 1964; Patton Lecturer, Indiana University, 1977. Visiting professor or lecturer at several universities in the United States and abroad. Member of War Department Commission on History of the War; travelled to Britain for War Department, Office of War Information, summer, 1943, and to France and Belgium, 1945. *Military service:* Served with U.S. Army Information and Education Division, 1945.

MEMBER: American Academy of Arts and Letters, American Scandinavian Society (fellow), American Antiquarian Society, Massachusetts Historical Society, Phi Beta Kappa, Century Association, St. Botolph's (Boston), Athenaeum Club (London).

AWARDS, HONORS: Herbert B. Adams Award of the American Historical Association, 1929; special award from Hillman Foundation, 1954, for *Freedom, Loyalty, Dissent*; Guggenheim fellowship, 1960-61; Gold Medal Award for history from American Academy and Institute of Arts and Letters, 1972; Sarah Josepha Hale Award, 1973; decorated Knight, Order of Dannebrog. Honorary degrees from numerous colleges and universities.

WRITINGS:

The Literature of the Pioneer West, Saint Paul, 1927.
(With Samuel Eliot Morison) *The Growth of the American Republic,* Oxford University Press, 1931, 7th edition, 1980, abbreviated and newly revised edition published as *A Concise History of the American Republic,* 1977.
Our Nation's Development, Harper, 1934.
Theodore Parker, Little, Brown, 1936, reissued with a new introduction, Beacon Press, 1960.
(With Allan Nevins) *America: The Story of a Free People,* Little, Brown, 1942, Oxford University Press, 1976, reissued in paperback as *The Pocket History of the United States,* Pocket Books, 1943, revised edition, 1982.
Majority Rule and Minority Rights, Oxford University Press, 1943.
(With Nevins) *A Short History of the United States,* Modern Library, 1945, 6th edition, Knopf, 1976.
The American Mind: An Interpretation of American Thought and Character since the 1880s, Yale University Press, 1950.
(With others) *Civil Liberties under Attack,* University of Pennsylvania Press, 1951.
(Contributor) Courtlandt Canby, editor, *The World of History,* New American Library, 1954.
(With Geoffrey Brunn) *Europe and America since 1492,* Houghton, 1954.
Freedom, Loyalty, Dissent, Oxford University Press, 1954.
Federal Centralization and the Press, University of Minnesota, 1956.
(Contributor) *Conference on the American High School,* University of Chicago Press, 1958.
(With Robert W. McEwen and Brand Blanshard) *Education in a Free Society,* University of Pittsburgh Press, 1961.
The Nature and the Study of History, C. E. Merrill, 1965.
The Role of Scholarship in an Age of Science, Laramie, 1965.
Freedom and Order: A Commentary on the American Political Scene, Braziller, 1966.
The Study of History, C. E. Merrill, 1966.
(With Elmo Giordonetti) *Was America a Mistake?: An Eighteenth-Century Controversy,* Harper, 1967.
The Search for a Usable Past, and Other Essays in Historiography, Knopf, 1967.

(With Richard B. Morris) *Colonies in Transition,* Harper, 1968.
The Commonwealth of Learning, Harper, 1968.
The Defeat of America: Presidential Power and the National Character, Simon & Schuster, 1974.
Britain through American Eyes, McGraw, 1974.
Jefferson, Nationalism, and the Enlightenment, Braziller, 1974.
The Empire of Reason: How Europe Imagined and America Realized the Enlightenment, Doubleday, 1977.
(Author of text) *Mort Kuenstler's Fifty Epic Paintings of America,* Abbeville Press, 1979.
(With Raymond H. Muessig) *The Study and Teaching of History,* Merrill, 1980.
(Author of introduction) *The Civil War Almanac,* Facts on File, 1983.
(Author of introduction) *Of America East and West: From the Writings of Paul Horgan,* Farrar, Straus, 1984.
(Contributor) John Grafton, editor, *America: A History of the First 500 Years,* Crescent Books (New York City), 1992.
Commager on Tocqueville, University of Missouri Press (Columbia), 1993.
The Odes of Horace: A Critical Study, University of Oklahoma Press (Norman), 1995.

EDITOR

Documents of American History (Volume 1, to 1898; Volume 2, from 1865), F. S. Crofts, 1934, 10th edition, Prentice-Hall, 1988.
(With Nevins) *The Heritage of America,* Little, Brown, 1939, revised and enlarged edition, 1949.
(And author of historical narrative) *The Story of the Second World War,* Little, Brown, 1945, Brassey's (Washington), 1991.
(And author of introduction and notes) *America in Perspective: The United States through Foreign Eyes,* Random House 1947, abridged edition, New American Library, 1959.
Alexis de Tocqueville, *Democracy in America,* translated by Henry Reeve, Oxford University Press, 1947.
Selections from "The Federalist," Appleton, 1949.
(With others) *Years of the Modern: An American Appraisal,* Longmans, Green, 1949.
The Blue and the Gray: The Story of the Civil War as Told by Participants, two volumes, Bobbs-Merrill, 1950, revised and abridged, Meridian (New York City), 1994.
William Dean Howells, *Selected Writings,* Random House 1950.
(And author of commentary) *Living Ideas in America,* Harper, 1951, enlarged edition, 1967.
(With Morris) *The Spirit of '76: The Story of the American Revolution as Told by the Participants,* two volumes, Bobbs-Merrill, 1958, bicentennial edition, Harper, 1975.
Official Atlas of the Civil War, Yoseloff, 1958.
Living Documents of American History, (Washington), 1960.
The Era of Reform, 1830-1860, Van Nostrand, 1960.
Theodore Parker: An Anthology, Beacon Press, 1960.
James Bryce, *Reflections on American Institutions: Selections from "The American Commonwealth,"* Fawcett, 1961.
Immigration and American History: Essays in Honor of Theodore C. Blegen, University of Minnesota Press, 1961.
Chester Bowles, *The Conscience of a Liberal,* Harper, 1962.
Winston Churchill, *History of the English-Speaking Peoples* (one volume of a four volume series), Bantam, 1963.
Noah Webster's American Spelling Book, Teachers College Press, 1963.
The Defeat of the Confederacy: A Documentary Survey, Van Nostrand, 1964.
Fifty Basic Civil War Documents, Van Nostrand, 1965.

(Consulting editor) *Encyclopedia of American History,* Harper, 1965.

Lester Ward and the Welfare State, Bobbs-Merrill, 1966.

The Struggle for Racial Equality: A Documentary Record, Harper, 1967.

Churchill, *Marlborough: His Life and Times,* Scribner, 1968.

(With others) *The West: An Illustrated History,* Promotory Press, 1976.

Edward M. Kennedy, *Our Day and Generation: The Words of Edward M. Kennedy,* Simon & Schuster, 1979.

(With others) *Illustrated History of the American Civil War,* Orbis, 1979.

Also editor with Morris of the "New American Nation" series, published by Harper; editor-in-chief of *The American Destiny: An Illustrated Bicentennial History of the United States,* twenty volumes, published by Danbury Press.

FOR CHILDREN

(With Eugene Campbell Barker) *Our Nation,* Row, Peterson, 1941.

(Editor) *St. Nicholas Anthology,* Random House, 1948.

(Editor) *Second St. Nicholas Anthology,* Random House, 1950.

America's Robert E. Lee, Houghton, 1951, Marshall Cavendish Corporation (North Bellmore, NY), 1991.

Chestnut Squirrel, Houghton, 1952.

The First Book of American History, illustrated by Leonard Everett Fisher, F. Watts, 1957.

The Great Declaration, Bobbs-Merrill, 1958.

A Picture History of the United States of America, F. Watts, 1958.

The Great Proclamation, Bobbs-Merrill, 1960.

The Great Constitution, Bobbs-Merrill, 1961.

Crusaders for Freedom, Doubleday, 1962.

OTHER

Contributor of essays to scholarly and popular journals, including *Book Week, New York Times Book Review, New Republic, Saturday Review, New York Review of Books,* and *American Scholar.*

SIDELIGHTS: Henry Steele Commager is revered by many as among America's most preeminent historians of the twentieth century. His writings include textbooks for children and college students, edited compilations of historical source material, original studies of the nature of U.S. democracy, and biographies of prominent U.S. citizens. As Lawrence Wells Cobb explains in the *Dictionary of Literary Biography,* Commager "has devoted his energies to making it easier for scholars and lay readers both to 'get at' the sources of the American historical record and to understand their heritage more fully. He has undertaken these tasks so that his readers might become more informed and responsible participants in the great experiment launched in the eighteenth century to make a free, democratic, and bountiful society a reality on the North American continent." *New Republic* contributor Alexander R. Butler calls Commager "one of America's most distinguished historians," an educator and scholar whose "excellent reputation" stems from his "simple, straightforward, and assertive" style.

Commager's best known book is *The Growth of the American Republic,* a title he co-authored with Samuel Eliot Morison. First published in 1931, the work continues to be read by students of U.S. history. According to *New York Times Book Review* correspondent Esmond Wright, the "limpidly clear style and the easy marshaling of arguments . . . have made '*The Growth of the American Republic*' one of the most unusual and certainly one of the most readable of textbooks." Commager's other books for lay readers include 1941's *Our Nation* for high school students, and the popular study *America: The Story of a Free People,* co-authored by Allan Nevins in 1942. Commager's aim, in Cobb's words, has been "always to provide the facts within the matrix of an unobtrusive liberal interpretation and to provoke thought on the part of the reader." As early as 1934 Commager also began the editing duties for which he has become well known; his *Documents of American History* collects in two volumes the important primary sources on the creation and development of the United States. Cobb calls the work "the best single-volume source book in its field." Throughout the following forty years Commager has continued to publish anthologies of historical source material; his efforts have produced, among others, *The Blue and the Gray: The Story of the Civil War as Told by Participants, The Era of Reform, 1830-1860,* and *The Struggle for Racial Equality: A Documentary Record.*

As a scholar Commager has sought to define the strengths of democracy. Cobb suggests that the historian's theses "always revolved around Jeffersonian liberalism: give the public the maximum amount of information and the people can be trusted to make the right decisions in the long run." Such a view stresses the importance of education as well as the necessity for free speech and dissent; not surprisingly, Commager became one of the strongest opponents of the intellectual purges of the communist-fearing McCarthy Era conformity of the 1950s. His comment in the 1951 volume *Civil Liberties under Attack* has since become famous: "The great danger that threatens us is neither heterodox thought nor orthodox thought, but the absence of thought." Throughout the following decade, as the Vietnam War and social unrest escalated, Commager continued to argue for the preservation of free speech and inquiry. According to Cobb, the historian "reminded visitors, distressed to see all the unrest in America, . . . that the idealism of the 1960s was a reassertion, not a repudiation, of our Revolutionary ideals of liberty and equality."

Commager's 1993 work, *Commager on Tocqueville,* provides another link with the past that has much to teach modern America. Based on the classic *Democracy in America,* a political study of the young American republic written by French historian Alexis de Tocqueville in 1835 and translated by Commager in 1947, *Commager on Tocqueville* focuses on several areas of concern in the historic nineteenth-century critique of early democracy. While the French historian evinced concern by what he perceived as the potential for a tyranny of the majority, the difficulty of finding an equilibrium between individuality and equality, the role of a military arm of government within a democratic state, and the advocacy of personal liberty by a central ruling body, Commager contends that many of these concerns have been proven to be unfounded. However, he warns, such things as the overly large federal and state governmental bureaucracies and the extreme economic inequity that have manifested themselves in the United States over the past century may be symptomatic of some of de Tocqueville's concerns. While D. J. Maletz dubs *Commager on Tocqueville* "an ardent defense of all the institutions of the contemporary liberal welfare state," Commager maintains throughout the work that the problems facing the United States at the close of the millennia—including environmental depredations, overpopulation over much of the earth's inhabitable surface, and chronic political upheavals—call for a revisioning of democratic government along global rather than nationalistic boundaries.

A prolific writer, Commager has continued to edit and compile historical texts that reveal both the benefits and the challenges of democratic government since retiring from his professorial duties at Amherst College. In the *New York Times Book Review,* Arthur Schlesinger Jr. concludes that in Henry Steele Commager, "learning and reason are at the service of a mind whose understanding of democracy gains brilliance and power from a passion for democratic freedom."

BIOGRAPHICAL/CRITICAL SOURCES:

BOOKS

Civil Liberties under Attack, University of Pennsylvania Press, 1951.
Dictionary of Literary Biography, Volume 17: *Twentieth Century American Historians,* Gale, 1983.
Garraty, John, *Interpreting American History: Conversations with Historians,* Macmillan, 1970.
Hyman, Harold M. and Leonard W. Levy, editors, *Freedom and Reform: Essays in Honor of Henry Steele Commager,* Harper, 1967.

PERIODICALS

Atlantic, May, 1950.
Choice, November, 1993, p. 535.
Christian Century, July 5, 1950; October 24, 1962.
Christian Science Monitor, April 6, 1936; March 18, 1950.
Commonweal, May 5, 1950.
Library Journal, May 15, 1993, p. 81; October 15, 1995, p. 96.
Nation, April 22, 1950; December 23, 1950.
New Republic, April 24, 1950; May 24, 1954; May 20, 1967; December 21, 1974.
New Statesman, June 2, 1967.
Newsweek, November 15, 1948.
New York Herald Tribune Book Review, March 12, 1950; November 19, 1950; May 30, 1954.
New York Times, March 12, 1950; November 12, 1950; June 7, 1977.
New York Times Book Review, March 12, 1950; October 23, 1966; June 25, 1967; November 26, 1967; August 14, 1977; November 4, 1979; April 8, 1984.
San Francisco Chronicle, March 24, 1950; November 26, 1950.
Saturday Review, March 11, 1950; December 2, 1950; May 1, 1954; January 28, 1967; May 14, 1977.
Survey, April, 1950.
Time, December 11, 1950.
Times Literary Supplement, November 17, 1950; July 23, 1954; September 27, 1974; August 4, 1978.
Yale Review, summer, 1950.

*   *   *

COMMONER, Barry 1917-

PERSONAL: Born May 28, 1917, in Brooklyn, NY; son of Isidore (a tailor) and Goldie (Yarmolinsky) Commoner; married Gloria C. Gordon (a psychologist), December 1, 1946 (marriage ended); married Lisa Feiner, 1980; children (first marriage): Lucy Alison, Fredric Gordon. *Education:* Columbia University, A.B. (with honors), 1937; Harvard University, M.A., 1938, Ph.D., 1941. *Religion:* Humanist.

ADDRESSES: Office—Queens College Center for the Biology of Natural Systems, Flushing, NY 11367.

CAREER: Harvard University, assistant in biology, 1938-40; Queens College (now of the City University of New York),

Flushing, instructor in biology, 1940-42; *Science Illustrated* magazine, New York City, associate editor, 1946-47; Washington University, St. Louis, MO, associate professor, 1947-53, professor of plant physiology, 1953-76, chairman of department of botany, 1965-69, director of Center for the Biology of Natural Systems, 1965-81, professor of environmental science, 1976-81; Queens College, Flushing, professor of geology, 1981-81, director, Center for the Biology of Natural Systems, 1981–, professor of earth and environmental science, 1981-87, professor emeritus, 1987–. *Military service:* U.S. Naval Reserve, 1942-54; served in Naval Air Force and as liaison officer with Senate committee on military affairs; became lieutenant.

MEMBER: American Association for the Advancement of Science (fellow; member of board of directors, 1967–), American Institute of Biological Sciences (member of governing board, 1965-67), Society of General Physiologists (member of council, 1961), American Society of Plant Physiologists, American Society of Biological Chemists, Institute for Environmental Education (trustee), American Association of University Professors, National Parks Association (member of board of directors, 1968–), Sierra Club, American Chemical Society, American School Health Association, Ecological Society of America, Federation of American Scientists, British Soil Association (honorary life vice president, 1968–), Sigma Xi, Phi Beta Kappa.

AWARDS, HONORS: Newcomb Cleveland Prize, American Association for the Advancement of Science, 1953; First International Humanist Award, International Humanist and Ethical Union, 1970; Phi Beta Kappa Award, 1972, and International Prize for Safeguarding the Environment, City of Cervia, Italy, 1973, both for *The Closing Circle;* commander in the Order of the Merit (Italy), 1977; Premio Iglesias (Sardinia, Italy), 1978, for *The Poverty of Power,* and 1982, for *The Politics of Energy;* American Institute of Architects Medal, 1979; D.Sc., Hahnemann Medical College, 1963, Clark University, 1967, Grinnell College, 1968, Lehigh University, 1969, Williams College, 1970, Ripon College, 1971, Colgate University, 1972, Cleveland State University, 1980, St. Lawrence University, 1988, and Connecticut College, 1992; LL.D., University of California, 1967 and 1974, Grinnell College, 1981; D.HL., Lowell University, 1990.

WRITINGS:

Science and Survival, Viking, 1966.
(With others) *Balance and Biosphere: A Radio Symposium on the Environmental Crisis,* Canadian Broadcasting Corp., 1971.
The Closing Circle: Nature, Man, and Technology, Knopf, 1971, second edition, Bantam, 1974, published as *The Closing Circle: Confronting the Environmental Crisis,* Cape (London), 1972.
(Contributor) *Electric Power Consumption and Human Welfare: The Social Consequences of the Environmental Effects of Electric Power Use,* Washington University, 1972.
(Editor) Virginia Brodine, *Air Pollution,* Harcourt, 1973.
(With others) *The Effect of Recent Energy Price Increases on Field Crop Production Costs,* Center for the Biology of Natural Systems, Washington University, 1974.
(Editor) Julian McCaull and Janice Crossland, *Water Pollution,* Harcourt, 1974.
(Editor, with Howard Boksenbaum and Michael Corr) *Energy and Human Welfare,* Volume 1: *The Social Costs of Power Production,* Volume 2: *Alternative Technologies for Power Production,* Volume 3: *Human Welfare: The End Use for Power,* Macmillan Information, 1976.

The Poverty of Power: Energy and the Economic Crisis, Random House, 1976.

Energy (essays; originally published in *New Yorker*), New Yorker, 1976.

Reliability of Bacterial Mutagenesis Techniques to Distinguish Carcinogenic and Noncarcinogenic Chemicals, Environmental Protection Agency, 1976.

The Politics of Energy, Knopf, 1979.

Making Peace with the Planet, Pantheon, 1990.

OTHER

Power to the Person (sound recording), Big Sur Recordings, 1971.

The Destruction of Our Environment (sound recording), Pacifica Tape Library, 1972.

The Human Meaning of the Environmental Crisis (sound recording), Big Sur Recordings, 1973.

The Environment and the Energy Crisis (sound recording), Encyclopedia Americana/CBS News Audio Resource Library, 1973.

Freedom and the Environment (sound recording), Pennsylvania State Library, 1976.

Contributor of more than two hundred articles to journals in his field. Author of "If I Were President," in *Environmental Action,* spring, 1992, p. 31. Member of editorial board, *International Review of Cytology,* 1957-65, *Problems of Virology,* 1956-60, *American Naturalist,* 1959-63, *Theoretical Biology,* 1960-64, *Science Year,* 1967-72, *World Book Encyclopedia,* 1968-73, *Environmental Pollution,* 1969-79, *National Wildlife,* 1970–, and *Environment Magazine,* 1977–; honorary member of editorial advisory board, *Chemosphere,* 1972–; member, board of sponsors, *In These Times,* 1976–.

SIDELIGHTS: Biologist and environmental activist Barry Commoner first rose to national prominence in the late 1950s when he and other academic colleagues led a protest against the atmospheric testing of the U.S. arsenal of nuclear weapons. Basing his opposition to the testing on a deep knowledge of free radicals, fossil fuels, and other chemical-based pollutants, Commoner expanded his public image during the following decades, speaking out and writing on such wide-ranging environmental issues as pollution, the petrochemical industry and alternative energy sources, as well as social issues from population control to Third World debt. In 1980 he augmented his unrelenting social activism by making a failed bid for the U.S. presidency on the ecological advocative Citizen's Party ticket, winning a total of 200,000 votes. Works by Commoner include 1971's *The Closing Circle,* 1979's *The Politics of Power,* and *Making Peace with the Planet,* published in 1991.

The Closing Circle outlines Commoner's four rules of ecology, the most central of which is "Everything has to go somewhere," an expression of what its author calls "the fundamental importance of cycles in the ecosphere." Despite the sobering nature of Commoner's message, in a *New York Times* review of *The Closing Circle,* Christopher Lehmann-Haupt wrote that the work "is not a Doomsday book at all. . . . Dr. Commoner presents as lucid a description of ecology and its laws as I have yet come across. In between, he illustrates how those laws have been broken with disastrous consequences. . . . He weighs the impacts on the environment of our population explosion and in particular our shockingly high per capita consumption of natural resources."

In *Making Peace with the Planet,* Commoner restates his four rules of ecology and continues his discussion of the changes wrought upon the earth's atmosphere by the post-industrial, technological age. Citing population growth as a secondary issue to humanity's recklessness in not refining technological advances to their most environmentally sound, he maintains that the Americanization of the world—through wasteful, polluting products such as cars, pesticides, and nitrogen-based fertilization methods—should be curtailed in favor of a technology based upon solar power, recycling, and other prevention—rather than control-based strategies.

As Commoner once explained, "Human beings have broken out of the circle of life, driven not by biological need, but by the social organization which they have devised to 'conquer' nature; means of gaining wealth that are governed by requirements conflicting with those which govern nature. The end result is the environmental crisis, a crisis of survival. Once more, to survive, we must close the circle. We must learn how to restore to nature the wealth that we borrow from it."

BIOGRAPHICAL/CRITICAL SOURCES:

BOOKS

Chisholm, Anne, *Philosophers of the Earth,* Dutton, 1972.
Contemporary Literary Criticism, Volume 1, Gale (Detroit), 1982.
Rubin, Charles T., *The Green Crusade: Rethinking the Roots of Environmentalism,* Macmillan, 1994.
Taylor, Bob Pepperman, *Our Limits Transgressed: Environmental Political Thought in America,* University Press of Kansas (Lawrence), 1992.

PERIODICALS

America, May 13, 1995, p. 3.
Los Angeles Times, May 2, 1990.
Los Angeles Times Book Review, April 22, 1990, p. 15.
Mother Earth News, March-April, 1990, p. 116.
Mother Jones, March-April, 1991, p. 35.
Nation, September 22, 1979.
New Republic, November 6, 1971; August 18, 1979; April 30, 1990, pp. 30-9.
Newsweek, November 1, 1971; December 27, 1971; May 31, 1976.
New York Review of Books, August 5, 1976.
New York Times, April 22, 1970; January 15, 1988.
New York Times Book Review, November 6, 1966; October 17, 1971; May 23, 1976; June 5, 1977; July 29, 1979; April 22, 1990, pp. 15-16.
Saturday Review, May 15, 1976; September 1, 1979.
Spectator, January 22, 1977.
Time, February 2, 1970; May 31, 1976.
Village Voice, May 3, 1976.
Washington Post Book World, October 10, 1971; May 9, 1976; December 12, 1976; June 24, 1979; April 1, 1990, p. 8.
Wilderness, fall, 1990, p. 62.

* * *

COMPTON-BURNETT, I(vy) 1884-1969

PERSONAL: Born 1884 (some sources say 1892), in Middlesex, England; died of bronchitis on August 27, 1969, in London, England; daughter of James and Katherine (Rees) Compton-Burnett. Lived with Margaret Jourdain, 1919-51. *Education:* Howard College; University of London, Royal Holloway College, B.A. in classics, 1907.

CAREER: Novelist.

AWARDS, HONORS: Commander of the Order of the British Empire, 1951; James Tait Black Memorial Prize, 1956, for *Mother and Son*; D.Litt., University of Leeds, 1960; Dame Commander of the Order of the British Empire, 1967.

WRITINGS:

Dolores, Blackwood, 1911.
Pastors and Masters, Heath Cranton, 1925.
Brothers and Sisters, Harcourt, 1930.
Men and Wives, Heinemann, 1931.
More Women Than Men, Heinemann, 1933.
A House and Its Head, Heinemann, 1935.
Daughters and Sons, Gollancz, 1937.
A Family and a Fortune, Gollancz, 1939.
Parents and Children, Gollancz, 1941.
Elders and Betters, Gollancz, 1944.
Manservant and Maidservant, Gollancz, 1947.
Two Worlds and Their Ways, Knopf, 1949.
Darkness and Day, Knopf, 1951.
The Present and the Past, Messner, 1954.
Mother and Son, Messner, 1956.
A Father and His Fate, Messner, 1958.
A Heritage and Its History, Simon & Schuster, 1960.
The Mighty and Their Fall, Simon & Schuster, 1962.
A God and His Gifts, Gollancz, 1963.
The Last and the First, Knopf, 1971.
Collected Works, nineteen volumes, Gollancz, 1972.

MEDIA ADAPTATIONS: A Heritage and Its History was adapted by Julia Mitchell for British television in 1968. Mitchell has also adapted *A Family and a Fortune.*

SIDELIGHTS: British novelist Ivy Compton-Burnett wrote of the upper-class, seemingly genteel world that existed in England before the First World War, a world Edward Sackville-West once compared to that of "Jane Austen, of George Eliot, of Mrs. Gaskell. But with this difference—that the plots which involve that outwardly quiet and orderly world are violent and dramatic in the extreme."

Choosing to regard Victorian and Edwardian family life as a model of civilization as a whole, Compton-Burnett explored the "swamp of discontent, mixed motives, and deception" that exist just below the surface of normal social behavior, according to Frederick R. Karl. Family members snipe at and tyrannize each other while maintaining an appropriate veneer of politeness and wit. Her plots, in which lost objects, suppressed wills, overheard conversations, and concealed identities figure prominently, are of only secondary concern; the real focus is the manner in which relatives proceed to destroy themselves when faced with the sudden emergence of certain skeletons from the family closet— among them such "universal sins" as murder, incest, adultery, suicide, and theft.

Despite the limited social and chronological context of her novels, Compton-Burnett managed to convey the sense of "a timeless present," observed critic Blake Nevius. A. C. Ward attributed her contemporary appeal to the fact that she combined "a Victorian stuffiness of atmosphere and a Victorian appetite for melodrama with a twentieth-century ruthlessness in stripping off conventional veils of pretence in order to expose make-believers, hypocrites, and petty tyrants naked to their souls." Like the author's plots, however, these assorted "make-believers, hypocrites, and petty tyrants" vary little from book to book; Compton-Burnett's

women, for example, are nearly always domineering and evil, her men are either overly effete or obsessed with power, and her children and young adults are lonely and pitiably mistreated. Yet it would be incorrect, insisted Robert Liddell, to label them as mere "types": "They are in fact very subtly differentiated. They are limited on the whole to certain broad categories, because the plot is to deal with certain kinds of happenings. Since the happenings come out of the people, that entails certain kinds of people." At any rate, noted Pamela Hansford Johnson, all of them "exemplify the real horror of human frailty. . . . [They live in] a world where everyone says what he thinks and where deadly words are spoken. Her people are Mr. and Mrs. Darling gone sour."

"Deadly spoken words," in fact, provide the main narrative thrust of Compton-Burnett's novels, for each one consists of approximately ninety-five percent conversation. Though each character is described in detail at the time of his or her first appearance, after that there are few, if any, references to physical traits; landscapes, houses, and rooms are not described at all. Because these brief and infrequent passages serve as little more than stage directions, many critics maintained that her novels had more in common with plays than they did with other novels. But as Nevius pointed out, in Compton-Burnett's case the dialogue "is made to bear a greater burden than in either the drama or the conventional novel. It has usurped almost completely the functions of exposition, narrative and description."

Another burden Compton-Burnett forced her dialogue to bear was the highly stylized tone of her characters' speech. Deliberately artificial, bland, and sententious, it requires the reader to concentrate fully on what is being said and who is saying it. Explained Julian Mitchell of *Plays and Players:* "The conversations are so full of nuance and subtlety that it takes a new reader several chapters to get the hang of them, and sometimes he gives up in despair. There is no internalisation, no 'he thought' and 'she wondered,' to help him understand what's going on or what the characters' motives are. . . . And, greatest difficulty of all, the characters seem at first reading, and sometimes at second, all to talk alike. This is an illusion: once one's ear is trained to Compton-Burnett one can hear that everyone speaks quite differently and individually."

Ruth Blackman of the *Christian Science Monitor* agreed that straightening out who said what in a Compton-Burnett novel can be exasperating at times, but she emphasized that making the effort to keep track is the only way a reader can become familiar with each character. Wrote Blackman: "[Compton-Burnett] works very little from the interior of a character. Once she has placed him in his family relationship, and sketched in his outward aspect, she leaves him to reveal himself through conversation. And what conversation! Brilliant, incisive, subtle, ironic (and, the unenchanted might say, endless), it is absolutely plausible but like nothing ever heard."

In the eyes of several critics, including Arnold Kettle, both humor and dramatic tension in Compton-Burnett's novels originate in the contrast the author set up "between what is actually said [in the dialogues] and what is expressed but only thought and the consequent ruthlessness in the exposure of the underlying issues and implications of a scene." In short, Compton-Burnett's technique was to devise a situation in which there is a marked difference between appearance and reality, then examine that difference with a wit, said Kettle, that "is not a matter of superficial smartness or a cunning ornamentation of style. It springs from deep in her observation of life, from her critical consideration of the standards and values of the society she is presenting." But because of what those acidic observations implied about human nature, some readers and critics found her type of wit more "frightening" than funny. Quite often, wrote Milton Crane in the *Saturday Review,* the cumulative effect of such grim irony is one of "an ultimately distressing, though unfailingly interesting, exercise in savage comedy." Commented an *Outlook* critic, "Not everybody can stand to be dashed with ice water."

Malcolm Bradbury, though, felt that Compton-Burnett's books "were, and remain, ambiguous. One could see in them a kind of essential artlessness, or else a very high kind of artistic management, a precision of control both moral and technical of the most eminent sort. One could read them as an elegant camp game played with life, or as a harsh and cruel, almost a tragic, vision of experience. And one could find them either basically reassuring novels, nostalgic under the wit and malice, or else profoundly disturbing works."

Johnson agreed with this assessment. Compton-Burnett, she concluded, "is not to be mildly liked or disliked. She is a writer to be left alone, or else to be made into an addiction. . . . Yet readers who come to know her fascination will discern one startling fact; that this piercingly wise, discreet, mannered Victoriana conceals abysses of the human personality."

As the author herself once commented: "My writing does not seem to me 'stylised.' I do not feel that I have any real or organic knowledge of life later than about 1910—I should not write of later times with enough grasp or confidence. . . . I think that actual life supplies a writer with characters less than is thought. . . . As regards plots, I find real life no help at all. Real life seems to have no plots. And as I think a plot desirable and almost necessary I have this extra grudge against life. But I do think there are signs that strange things happen, though they do not emerge."

BIOGRAPHICAL/CRITICAL SOURCES:

BOOKS

Asoka Rani, T., *Ivy Compton-Burnett and English Domestic Novel,* Prestige Books, 1995.

Burkhart, Charles, editor, *The Art of I. Compton-Burnett: A Collection of Critical Essays,* Gollancz, 1972.

Burkhart, *Herman and Nancy and Ivy: Three Lives in Art,* Gollancz, 1977, pp. 74-108.

Contemporary Literary Criticism, Gale, Volume 1, 1973; Volume 3, 1975; Volume 10, 1979; Volume 15, 1980; Volume 34, 1985.

Greig, Cicely, *Ivy Compton-Burnett: A Memoir,* Garnestone Press, 1972.

Grylls, R. Glynn, *I. Compton-Burnett,* Longman, 1971.

Johnson, Pamela Hansford, *I. Compton-Burnett,* Longman, Green, 1951.

Karl, Frederick R., *A Reader's Guide to the Contemporary English Novel,* Farrar, Straus, 1962.

Kettle, Arnold, *An Introduction to the English Novel,* Volume II, Hutchinson, 1960.

Liddell, Robert, *A Treatise on the Novel,* J. Cape, 1947.

Liddell, *The Novels of I. Compton-Burnett,* Gollancz, 1955.

McCarthy, Mary, *The Writing on the Wall and Other Essays,* Harcourt, 1970.

Nevius, Blake, *Ivy Compton-Burnett,* Columbia University Press, 1970.

Powell, Violet, *A Compton-Burnett Compendium,* Heinemann, 1973.

Sackville-West, Edward, *Living Writers,* Sylvan Press, 1947.

Sprigge, Elizabeth, *The Life of Ivy Compton-Burnett,* Braziller, 1973.

Spurling, Hilary, *Ivy When Young: The Early Life of I. Compton-Burnett, 1884-1919,* Gollancz, 1974.

Spurling, *Secrets of a Woman's Heart: The later Life of Compton-Burnett,* 1984.

PERIODICALS

Atlantic, June, 1949; March, 1962; March, 1964.

Books, April 24, 1938.

Book Week, February 2, 1964.

Boston Transcript, December 4, 1929.

Chicago Sunday Tribune, February 25, 1962.

Christian Science Monitor, September 7, 1929; June 16, 1949; January 28, 1960.

Commonweal, November 13, 1953; April 17, 1964.

Encounter, July, 1973.

English Studies, Volume LI, number 1, 1970.

Guardian, September 18, 1959; September 22, 1961.

Hudson Review, winter, 1971-72.

London Times, August 28, 1969.

Manchester Guardian, March 16, 1937; June 17, 1949; March 27, 1953; February 8, 1955; August 20, 1957.

Nation, April 30, 1955.

New Republic, June 14, 1948; April 1, 1955; March 4, 1957.

New Statesman, June 1, 1929; August 10, 1957; September 19, 1959; September 22, 1961; December 6, 1963.

New Statesman and Nation, April 11, 1931; March 20, 1937; April 28, 1951; April 4, 1953; March 5, 1955.

Newsweek, April 23, 1973.

New Yorker, June 19, 1948; June 11, 1949; March 24, 1951; January 19, 1957; May 5, 1962; May 2, 1964.

New York Evening Post, November 23, 1929.

New York Herald Tribune Book Review, October 18, 1953; March 20, 1955; February 3, 1957; March 30, 1958; February 7, 1960; March 11, 1962.

New York Herald Tribune Books, November 10, 1929; March 11, 1962.

New York Herald Tribune Weekly Book Review, June 13, 1948; June 5, 1949.

New York Times, October 6, 1929; May 3, 1931; April 24, 1938; June 20, 1948; June 5, 1949; March 18, 1951; October 4, 1953; March 20, 1955; November 18, 1956; March 23, 1958; May 20, 1965; August 28, 1969.

New York Times Book Review, January 31, 1960; February 11, 1962; February 2, 1964; August 15, 1971.

Observer Review, September 7, 1969.

Outlook, April 29, 1931.

Partisan Review, winter, 1965.

Plays and Players, April, 1975.

San Francisco Chronicle, March 24, 1951.

Saturday Review, March 26, 1955; March 2, 1957; April 19, 1958; February 10, 1962; February 1, 1964; February 20, 1965.

Saturday Review of Literature, November 30, 1929; July 25, 1931; April 23, 1938; June 26, 1948; June 4, 1949.

Spectator, March 19, 1937; March 7, 1947; June 24, 1949; February 18, 1955; August 16, 1957; September 18, 1959; September 22, 1961; September 6, 1969.

Springfield Republican, May 22, 1938; January 31, 1960.

Time, April 4, 1955; January 28, 1957; February 15, 1960; March 2, 1962; August 16, 1971.

Times Literary Supplement, April 10, 1937; March 22, 1947; June 17, 1949; April 20, 1951; February 11, 1955; August 16, 1957; September 18, 1959; September 22, 1961; November 21, 1963; November 11, 1965; February 5, 1971.

Twentieth Century Literature (special Compton-Burnett issue), summer, 1979.

*   *   *

CONAN DOYLE, Arthur
See DOYLE, Arthur Conan

*   *   *

CONDE, Maryse 1937-
(Maryse Boucolon)

PERSONAL: Born February 11, 1937, in Guadeloupe, West Indies; daughter of Auguste and Jeanne (Quidal) Boucolon; married Mamadou Conde, 1958 (divorced, 1981); married Richard Philcox (a translator), 1982; children: (first marriage) Leila, Sylvie, Aicha. *Education:* Sorbonne, University of Paris, Ph.D., 1976.

ADDRESSES: Home—Montebello, 97170 Petit Bourg, Guadeloupe, French West Indies. *Agent*—Rosalie Siegel, Act III Productions, 711 Fifth St., New York, NY 10022.

CAREER: Ecole Normale Superieure, Conakry, Guinea, instructor, 1960-64; Ghana Institute of Languages, Accra, Ghana, 1964-66; Lycee Charles de Gaulle, Saint Louis, Senegal, instructor, 1966-68; French Services of the BBC, London, England, program producer, 1968-70; University of Paris, Paris, France, assistant at Jussieu, 1970-72, lecturer at Nanterre, 1973-80, charge de cours at Sorbonne, 1980-85; program producer, Radio France Internationale, France Culture, 1980–. Bellagio Writer in Residence, Rockefeller Foundation, 1986; visiting professor, University of Virginia and University of Maryland, 1992–; lecturer in the United States, Africa, and the West Indies. Presenter of a literary program for Africa on Radio-France.

AWARDS, HONORS: Fulbright Scholar, 1985-86; Prix litteraire de la Femme, Prix Alain Boucheron, 1986, for *Moi, Tituba, Sorciere Noire de Salem;* Guggenheim fellow, 1987-88; Puterbaugh fellow, University of Oklahoma, Norman, 1993.

WRITINGS:

(Editor) *Anthologie de la litterature africaine d'expression francaise,* Ghana Institute of Languages, 1966.

Dieu nous l'a donne (four-act play; title means "God Given"; first produced in Martinique, West Indies, at Fort de France, 1973), Oswald, 1972.

Mort d'Oluwemi d'Ajumako (four-act play; title means "Death of a King"; first produced in Haiti at Theatre d'Alliance Francaise, 1975), Oswald, 1973.

Heremakhonon (novel), Union Generale d'Editions, 1976, translation by husband, Richard Philcox, published under same title, Three Continents Press, 1982.

(Translator into French with Philcox) Eric Williams, *From Columbus to Castro: The History of the Caribbean,* Presence Africaine, 1977.

(Editor) *La Poesie antillaise* (also see below), Nathan (Paris), 1977.

(Editor) *Le Roman antillais* (also see below), Nathan, 1977.

La Civilisation du bossale (criticism), Harmattan (Paris), 1978.

Le profil d'une oeuvre: Cahier d'un retour au pays natal (criticism), Hatier (Paris), 1978.

La Parole des femmes (criticism), Harmattan, 1979.

Tim tim? Bois sec! Bloemlezing uit de Franstalige Caribsche Literatuur (contains revised and translated editions of *Le Roman antillais* and *La Poesie antillaise*), edited by Andries van der Wal, In de Knipscheer, 1980.

Une Saison a Rihata (novel), Robert Laffont (Paris), 1981, translation by Philcox published as *A Season in Rihata,* Heinemann, 1988.

Segou: Les murailles de terre (novel), Robert Laffont, 1984, translation by Barbara Bray published as *Segu,* Viking, 1987.

Segou II: La terre en miettes (novel), Robert Laffont, 1985, translation by Linda Coverdale published as *The Children of Segu,* Viking, 1989.

Pays Mele (short stories), Hatier, 1985.

Moi, Tituba, sorciere noire de Salem (novel), Mercure de France (Paris), 1986, translation by Philcox published as *I, Tituba, Black Witch of Salem,* University Press of Virginia, 1992.

La Vie scelerate (novel), Seghers, 1987, translation by Victoria Reiter published as *Tree of Life,* Ballantine, 1992.

Haiti Cherie (juvenile), Bayard Presse, 1987.

Pension les Alizes (play), Mercure de France, 1988.

The Children of Nya, Viking, 1989.

Victor et les barricades (juvenile), Bayard Presse, 1989.

Traversee de la mangrove (novel), Mercure de France, 1990, translation by Richard Philcox published as *Crossing the Mangrove,* Doubleday, 1995.

Les derniers rois mages (novel), Mercure de France, 1992.

Tree of Life: A Novel of the Caribbean, Ballantine, 1992.

La colonie du nouveau monde (novel), Robert Laffont, 1993.

The Tropical Breeze Hotel (play), Ubu Repertory Theater Publications, 1994.

Last of the African Kings, translated by Richard Philcox, University of Nebraska Press, 1998.

OTHER

(With Francoise Pfaff) *Conversations with Maryse Conde,* University of Nebraska Press, 1996.

Also author of recordings for Record CLEF and Radio France Internationale. Contributor to anthologies; contributor to journals, including *Presence Africaine* and *Recherche Pedagogique.*

SIDELIGHTS: West Indian author Maryse Conde "deals with characters in domestic situations and employs fictitious narratives as a means of elaborating large-scale activities," assert *World Literature Today* writers Charlotte and David Bruner. Drawing on her experiences in Paris, West Africa, and her native Guadeloupe, Conde has created several novels which "attempt to make credible on an increasingly larger scale the personal human complexities involved in holy wars, national rivalries, and migrations of peoples," the Bruners state. *Heremakhonon,* for example, relates the journey of Veronica, an Antillean student searching for her roots in a newly liberated West African country. During her stay Veronica becomes involved with both a powerful government official and a young school director opposed to the new regime; "to her dismay," David Bruner summarizes, "she is unable to stay out of the political struggle, and yet she is aware that she does not know enough to understand what is happening."

The result of Veronica's exploration, which is told with an "insinuating prose [that] has a surreal, airless quality," as Carole Bovoso relates in the *Voice Literary Supplement,* is that "there were times I longed to rush in and break the spell, to shout at this black woman and shake her. But no one can rescue Veronica," the critic continues, "least of all herself; Conde conveys the seriousness of her plight by means of a tone of relentless irony and reproach." "Justly or not," write the Bruners, "one gains a comprehension of what a revolution is like, what new African nations are like, yet one is aware that this comprehension is nothing more than a feeling. The wise reader will go home as Veronica does," the critics conclude, "to continue more calmly to reflect, and to observe."

Conde expands her scope in *Segu,* "a wondrous novel about a period of African history few other writers have addressed," notes *New York Times Book Review* contributor Charles R. Larson. In tracing three generations of a West African family during the early and mid-1800s, "Conde has chosen for her subject . . . [a] chaotic stage, when the animism (which she calls fetishism) native to the region began to yield to Islam," the critic describes. "The result is the most significant historical novel about black Africa published in many a year." Beginning with Dousika, a Bambara nobleman caught up in court intrigue, *Segu* trails the exploits of his family, from one son's conversion to Islam to another's enslavement to a third's successful career in commerce, connected with stories of their wives and concubines and servants. In addition, Conde's "knowledge of African history is prodigious, and she is equally versed in the continent's folklore," remarks Larson. "The unseen world haunts her characters and vibrates with the spirits of the dead."

Some critics, however, fault the author for an excess of detail; *Washington Post* contributor Harold Courlander, for example, comments that "the plethora of happenings in the book does not always make for easy reading." The critic explains that "the reader is sometimes uncertain whether history and culture are being used to illuminate the fiction or the novel exists to tell us about the culture and its history." While Howard Kaplan concurs with this assessment, he adds in the *Los Angeles Times Book Review* that *Segu* "glitters with nuggets of cultural fascination. . . . For those willing to make their way through this dense saga, genuine rewards will be reaped." "With such an overwhelming mass of data and with so extensive a literary objective, the risks of . . . producing a heavy, didactic treatise are, of course, great," the Bruners maintain. "The main reason that Conde has done neither is, perhaps, because she has written here essentially as she did in her two earlier novels: she has followed the lives of the fictional characters as individuals dominated by interests and concerns which are very personal and often selfish and petty, even when those characters are perceived by other characters as powerful leaders in significant national or religious movements." Because of this, the critics conclude, *Segu* is "a truly remarkable book. . . . To know [the subjects of her work] better, as well as to know Maryse Conde even better, would be a good thing."

BIOGRAPHICAL/CRITICAL SOURCES:

PERIODICALS

Library Journal, March 15, 1995, p. 96.
Los Angeles Times Book Review, March 8, 1987.
New York Times, February 22, 1995, p. C15.
New York Times Book Review, May 31, 1987; October 25, 1992, p. 11.
Washington Post, March 3, 1987.
World Literature Today, winter, 1982; winter, 1985, pp. 9-13; spring, 1985; summer, 1986; spring, 1987; summer, 1988; autumn 1993, pp. 1-768.

CONDON, Richard (Thomas) 1915-1996

PERSONAL: Born March 18, 1915, in New York, NY; died April 9, 1996; son of Richard Aloysius and Martha Irene (Pickering) Condon; married Evelyn Rose Hunt, January 14, 1938; children: Deborah Weldon, Wendy Jackson. *Education:* Graduated from high school in New York City.

ADDRESSES: Home—3436 Asbury, Dallas, TX 75205. *Agent*—Harold Matson, 276 Fifth Ave., New York, NY 10001.

CAREER: Publicist in New York, NY, and Hollywood, CA, for Walt Disney Productions, 1936-41, Twentieth Century-Fox Film Corp., 1941-45, Richard Condon, Inc., 1945-48, and Paramount Pictures Corp., 1948-53, and in Europe and Great Britain for United Artists Corp., 1953-57; novelist. Producer, with Jose Ferrer, of Broadway shows *Twentieth Century* and *Stalag 17,* 1951-52.

MEMBER: International Confederation of Book Actors (honorary life president), Dramatists Guild, Authors Guild, Authors League of America.

AWARDS, HONORS: Writers Guild of America award, Bafta Award from British Academy of Film and Television Sciences, and Academy Award nomination, all 1986 for screen adaptation of *Prizzi's Honor.*

WRITINGS:

And Then We Moved to Rossenarra; or, The Art of Emigrating, Dial, 1973.
(With daughter, Wendy Jackson) *The Mexican Stove: What to Put on It and in It,* Doubleday, 1973.

NOVELS

The Oldest Confession (Book-of-the-Month Club alternate selection), Appleton-Century-Crofts, 1958.
The Manchurian Candidate, McGraw, 1959.
Some Angry Angel: A Mid-Century Faerie Tale, McGraw, 1960.
A Talent for Loving; or, The Great Cowboy Race, McGraw, 1961.
An Infinity of Mirrors, Random House, 1964.
Any God Will Do, Random House, 1965.
The Ecstasy Business, Dial, 1967.
Mile High (Literary Guild alternate selection), Dial, 1968.
The Vertical Smile (Literary Guild selection), Dial, 1971.
Arigato, Dial, 1972.
Winter Kills, Dial, 1974.
The Star Spangled Crunch, Bantam, 1974.
Money Is Love, Dial, 1975.
The Whisper of the Axe, Dial, 1976.
The Abandoned Woman: A Tragedy of Manners, Dial, 1977.
Bandicoot, Dial, 1978.
Death of a Politician, Richard Marek, 1978.
The Entwining, Richard Marek, 1980.
Prizzi's Honor (second novel in trilogy; Book-of-the-Month Club joint main selection; also see below), Coward, McCann & Geoghegan, 1982.
A Trembling upon Rome, Putnam, 1983.
Prizzi's Family (first novel in trilogy; Literary Guild joint main selection), Putnam, 1986.
Prizzi's Glory (third novel in trilogy), Dutton, 1988.
The Final Addiction, Saint Martin's Press, 1991.
Prizzi's Money, Crown Publishing, 1994.

SCREENPLAYS

(With Janet Roach) *Prizzi's Honor* (adaptation), Twentieth Century-Fox Film Corp., 1985.

Also author of *The Summer Music.*

OTHER

Also author of a play *Men of Distinction,* produced on Broadway, 1953. Contributor to *Holiday, Nation, Vogue, Harper's, Gourmet, Esquire, Travel and Leisure,* and *Sunday Times Magazine.* Condon's novels have been published in twenty-two languages and in braille.

MEDIA ADAPTATIONS: The Manchurian Candidate was filmed by MGM studios in 1962, directed by John Frankenheimer, and starred Frank Sinatra and Angela Lansbury. The film was nominated for several Academy Awards and won for Best Supporting Actress. *Winter Kills* was filmed in 1979, directed by William Richert, and starred Jeff Bridges, John Huston, and Anthony Perkins. *Prizzi's Honor* was filmed in 1985, starring Jack Nicholson, Kathleen Turner, and Angelica Huston. It was nominated for several Academy Awards, including Best Picture.

SIDELIGHTS: Since he began writing at age forty-two, following a successful career as a movie publicist, novelist Richard Condon "has proved original, prolific, and profitable, possibly in that order," writes *Los Angeles Times* arts editor Charles Champlin. Condon's reputation as a writer of what Richard Lingeman describes in the *New York Times* as "cynical, hip political thrillers that contain [a unique] extravagance of invention" was secured with his first two novels, *The Oldest Confession* and *The Manchurian Candidate.* Condon's body of work includes over twenty novels, two nonfiction books, a handful of plays and screenplays, and numerous articles on his twin passions, food and travel. This output has netted him an income of about two and a half million dollars, which Condon told *Publishers Weekly* interviewer John F. Baker "sounds like a lot, but it's only about what someone in middle management would have made over the same period in salary. The difference—and it's an important one—is that I've lived wherever I wanted to, and I didn't have to drive to the office every day."

Condon's preoccupation with examining abuses of power has made him into a cult figure of sorts to readers who share his convictions. *New York Times Book Review* contributor Leo Braudy describes Condon's writing as "paranoid surrealism," fiction that draws "equally on the facts of national life and the cliches of popular fiction to create a world where technology, politics and history [have] run wild and the only possible humanism [is] gallows humor." Other novelists who have written in this genre include Joseph Heller, William Burroughs, Norman Mailer, Thomas Berger, Ken Kesey, and Thomas Pynchon. Braudy declares that Condon is "one of the most distinguished members of this group and through the controlled corrosiveness of his two great early novels—*The Manchurian Candidate* (1959) and *Some Angry Angel* (1960)—has some claim to being a founder."

The "mythologized fact" of Condon's second novel, *The Manchurian Candidate,* "touched a nerve that made America jump," according to a *Newsweek* reviewer. Published in 1959, *The Manchurian Candidate* remains Condon's most highly acclaimed novel, one that critics frequently cite as a basis of comparison to his later works. The title of the book refers to the main character, Raymond Shaw, a soldier who becomes a prisoner of war in Korea and is unknowingly brainwashed into committing crimes

for his former captors *after* he returns to the United States. Commenting on this novel as well as on Condon's first novel, *The Oldest Confession, New Yorker* critic Whitney Baillett writes that they both "are brilliant, highly individualistic, and hopelessly unfashionable demonstrations of how to write stylishly, tell fascinating stories, assemble plots that suggest the peerless mazes of Wilkie Collins, be very funny, make acute social observations, and ram home digestible morals. They demonstrate, in short, a good many of the things that were expected of the novel before the creative-writing courses got its practitioners brooding in their mirrors." A *Chicago Sunday Tribune* reviewer describes *The Manchurian Candidate* as "a novel of today, crammed with suspense, humor, horror, satire, sex, and intrigue. . . . Fitting all [the] sidelines of the plot into a whole was a monumental writing task, and few authors could have succeeded as admirably as Condon. The result is an exciting, brilliantly told story, peopled with characters symbolic of our times."

Although other reviewers express similarly enthusiastic opinions about the novel, they distinguish carefully between Condon's novel and literature. A *New Statesman* critic, for example, comments that *The Manchurian Candidate* is "so well written, and so ingeniously constructed, that [it] command[s] the highest admiration without ever being considered, or even asking to be considered, as 'literature.'" A *New York Herald Tribune Book Review* critic calls the novel "a smooth and palatable pousse-cafe of political satire, psychological speculation, pleasantly risque antics a la Thorne Smith, and espionage maneuvering. . . . The basic assumptions of the plot do not withstand close examination. Happily, however, such examination is not necessary: this is a diversion, and a good one." After recommending a place for it on a "Ten Best Bad Novels" list—"books whose artistic flaws are mountainous but whose merits, like Loreleis on the rocks above, keep on luring readers"—a *Time* reviewer notes: "The book carries a superstructure of plot that would capsize Hawaii, and badly insufficient philosophical ballast. Yet Condon distributes his sour, malicious humor with such vigor and impartiality that the novel is certain to be read and enjoyed."

Reviews of *An Infinity of Mirrors* (1964), and *The Vertical Smile* (1971) revealed disillusioned opinions. In a review of *The Vertical Smile,* a *Time* critic declares: "Since the foaming manias of [his first two novels], Condon's fine, random wrath has aged until it is nothing more than irritability. Once he could have picked up the Republican and Democratic parties by their tails and swung them around his head like a couple of dead cats. . . . Now he can't manage it." Reed Whittemore speculates in the *New Republic:* "My guess is that Condon has had it with the genre itself, and this is his way of moving on—to what and where I wouldn't know. A large talent in limbo." Reviewing *An Infinity of Mirrors* in *Newsweek,* the critic concludes: "Condon, who seems to be equipped to write sound, pertinent, appealing stories in the almost vacant territory between the literary drive-ins of Robbins and Wallace and the transcendental realm of pure literature, has suffered here, one hopes, a temporary setback."

Critics' hopes for Condon's recovery were realized with the publication of his 1974 novel *Winter Kills.* Condon's most enthusiastically received novel since *The Manchurian Candidate, Winter Kills* closely parallels the lives of members of the Kennedy family. The main character, Nick Thirkield, is the half brother of John F. Kennedy analogue Tim Kegan, a young, liberal Irish president who is assassinated by a lone maniac. The assassin is caught and charged with the murder, but when Thirkield learns that another man may also have been involved, he has the case reopened.

Several reviewers found themselves pleasantly surprised by *Winter Kills*. *New York Times Book Review* contributor Leo Braudy, for example, comments that *Winter Kills* is "a triumph of satire and knowledge, with a delicacy of style and a command of tone that puts Condon once again into the first rank of American novelists." Braudy explains, "*Winter Kills* succeeds so brilliantly because the Kennedy assassination furnished Condon with a familiar mythic landscape through which his Gulliver-like hero can wander, simultaneously prey to Lilliputian politics, Brobdingnagian physicality, Laputan science, and Houyhnhnm moralism." Christopher Lehmann-Haupt expresses a like opinion in the *New York Times*. "By the time I reached the end of the novel's incredibly complex plot and had followed Nick Thirkield through the many blind alleys and trapdoors that eventually bring him face to face with the person behind his brother's assassination, I was a Richard Condon fan once more."

Winter Kills was made into a critically acclaimed but briefly run film of the same title. In a lengthy article for *Harper's* magazine entitled "Who Killed *Winter Kills?*," in which he discusses the novel and its transformation into film, Condon writes: "I wrote *Winter Kills* to reflect, in parable form, on the confusing trail of events that had followed the murder of John Kennedy. . . . The novel worked outward from the core of the real event—the assassination—advancing through mazes of American myth and nightmare, and using the motley cast this country provided: a blinkered presidential commission, the media, . . . revealed oligarchs, and labor leaders. The trail led . . . [to] that small community of people who run the United States and who had decided that the president should be murdered because he was not 'cooperating' with them. The father, an active member of the group, was chosen to carry out the deed, because only he could get close enough."

After two years of filming for which most of the cast and crew were never paid, "Winter Kills" opened in New York in 1979 to favorable reviews. The film's three-week run in showcase theaters was followed by what Condon calls "the Great and Mysterious Disappearance." This disappearance, Condon adds in *Harper's,* "began to offer a feast for the paranoid among us." Condon's paranoia was further incited by the murder of one of the producers shortly after the film's opening; two years later the second producer was sentenced to forty years in prison on a drug charge.

Condon's novel *Prizzi's Honor* deals with a similarly sensitive milieu: organized crime. Although this setting has been exploited by several other authors, notably Mario Puzo, reviewers believe that Condon's novel offers a fresh outlook. Champlin observes in the *Los Angeles Times Book Review*: "Condon, once again accepting the perceived reality as police leaks, newspaper exposes and Puzo have given it to us—complete with Sicilian litany of *consiglieri, capiregimes, sottocapos, soldati,* and a godfather with a lethal wheeze and a mind Machiavelli might envy—steps over it to present an outrageous and original love story. . . ." *New York Times Book Review* editor Robert Asahina notes: "Richard Condon is not Mario Puzo; suspense, not the family saga, is his forte. And he winds the mainspring of the plot so tight that the surprise ending will knock your reading glasses off. Yet *Prizzi's Honor* is also a sendup of the prevailing sentimental picture of the underworld. To Mr. Condon, there *is* honor among these thieves—but it is precisely in the name of *omerta* that the *fratellanza* has been willing to 'cheat, corrupt, scam, and murder anybody who stands between them and a buck.'"

According to several reviewers, Condon's exploration of the seamier side of organized crime is distressing. *Best Sellers* contributor Tony Bednarczyk writes: "There is solid storytelling, but the subject raises disturbing questions about morals, and-or the lack thereof. It is a fast-paced, very readable story, but one feels a bit guilty for being interested in what comes next." A *Washington Post Book World* reviewer finds it unrealistic for Condon to expect readers to care about his psychopathic characters simply because he gives them "a few homey attributes." The reviewer adds that Charley's cooking and cleaning compulsions are "supposed to endear him to us, despite the fact that he goes for the slow kill, described in lavish detail. We're to laugh while his wife [Irene], plotting kidnapping and murder, at the same time dazzles as a hostess."

While *Time* critic Michael Demarest also believes that *Prizzi's Honor,* "like most of [Condon's] books, comes sometimes too close to the truth for comfort," he nevertheless concludes: "Condon's stylish prose and rich comedic gift once again spice a moral sensibility that has animated 16 novels since *The Manchurian Candidate* appeared in 1962. If wit and irony could somehow neutralize villainy, the novelist would make a fine FBI director."

Prizzi's Honor was also made into a successful film of the same title, with Jack Nicholson and Kathleen Turner playing the roles of Charley Partanna and Irene Walker. The film was nominated for several Academy Awards, and the screenplay, adapted by Condon and coauthor Janet Roach, received awards from the Writers Guild of America and the British Academy of Film and Television Sciences. The project was initiated and eventually directed by John Huston, who was attracted to the material by "that wonderful hyperbole and extravagance mixed with grandeur that Richard [Condon] has in all his best books—I thought this one epitomized that," he told *New York Times* reporter Janet Maslin. Huston added that he was also drawn to the book's "outstandingly jaundiced view of American enterprise and the ethics of the business world."

BIOGRAPHICAL/CRITICAL SOURCES:

BOOKS

Contemporary Authors Autobiography Series, Volume 1, Gale, 1984.
Contemporary Literary Criticism, Gale, Volume 4, 1975; Volume 6, 1976; Volume 8, 1978; Volume 10, 1979; Volume 44, 1987.
Newquist, Roy, *Conversations,* Volume 1, Rand McNally, 1967.

PERIODICALS

America, September 12, 1964.
Atlantic, September, 1969.
Best Sellers, September 15, 1964; September 1, 1969; June, 1982; December, 1986.
Booklist, September 15, 1992; January 1, 1994.
Books and Bookmen, December, 1969; August, 1982.
Book Week, September 13, 1964.
Book World, October 24, 1967; August 17, 1969; October 31, 1971.
Chicago Sunday Tribune, March 1, 1958; May 31, 1959.
Chicago Tribune, June 14, 1985.
Chicago Tribune Book World, June 6, 1982.
Christian Century, September 16, 1964; February 21, 1968; October 1, 1969.

Christian Science Monitor, September 11, 1969.
Detroit News, October 9, 1983.
Extrapolation, summer, 1984.
Globe & Mail (Toronto), December 6, 1986.
Harper's, September, 1977; May, 1983.
Los Angeles Times, February 19, 1983; June 14, 1985; August 16, 1987.
Los Angeles Times Book Review, April 25, 1982.
Nation, February 3, 1962.
New Republic, October 16, 1971.
New Statesman, November 8, 1968; October 10, 1969; September 5, 1975; August 13, 1976.
Newsweek, September 14, 1964; June 9, 1975.
New Yorker, June 21, 1958; May 30, 1959; April 2, 1960; July 22, 1961; August 25, 1975; December 11, 1978; October 28, 1991.
New York Herald Tribune Book Review, June 1, 1958; June 28, 1959; May 1, 1960.
New York Herald Tribune Books, August 27, 1961.
New York Review of Books, February 8, 1979.
New York Times, June 22, 1958; April 26, 1959; May 24, 1974; May 21, 1976; April 20, 1982; June 9, 1985; June 14, 1985; October 29, 1986.
New York Times Book Review, March 20, 1960; July 23, 1961; September 13, 1964; October 29, 1967; August 31, 1969; October 10, 1971; May 26, 1974; May 25, 1975; May 23, 1976; April 18, 1982; September 4, 1983; September 28, 1986; October 9, 1988; February 11, 1990; November 17, 1991; December 13, 1992; February 6, 1994.
New York Times Magazine, September 2, 1979.
People, December 8, 1986.
Publishers Weekly, June 24, 1983; July 19, 1991; September 7, 1992; November 15, 1993.
Saturday Review, June 14, 1958; April 2, 1960; November 28, 1964; September 6, 1969.
Spectator, April 22, 1972; September 21, 1974.
Time, July 6, 1959; July 21, 1961; March 22, 1968; September 5, 1969; October 4, 1971; June 24, 1974; June 2, 1975; May 17, 1982; June 10, 1985; September 22, 1986; September 19, 1988.
Times (London), October 25, 1985; January 15, 1987.
Times Literary Supplement, October 5, 1967; October 16, 1969; April 28, 1972; September 20, 1974; June 11, 1982.
Village Voice, October 9, 1969.
Washington Post, November 10, 1978; May 10, 1979; September 13, 1980.
Washington Post Book World, May 30, 1976; April 4, 1982; June 14, 1985; August 24, 1986.

*   *   *

CONNELL, Evan S(helby), Jr. 1924-

PERSONAL: Born August 17, 1924, in Kansas City, MO; son of Evan Shelby (a surgeon) and Elton (Williamson) Connell. *Education:* Attended Dartmouth College, 1941-43; University of Kansas, A.B., 1947; graduate study at Stanford University, 1947-48, Columbia University, 1948-49, and San Francisco State College (now University).

ADDRESSES: Home—Fort Marcy 13, 320 Artist Rd., Santa Fe, NM 87501. *Agent*—Elizabeth McKee, 22 East 40th St., New York, NY 10016.

CAREER: Writer. Editor, *Contact* magazine, Sausalito, CA, 1960-65. *Military service:* U.S. Navy, pilot, 1943-45; served as flight instructor.

AWARDS, HONORS: Eugene F. Saxton fellow, 1953; Guggenheim fellow, 1963; Rockefeller Foundation grant, 1967; California Literature silver medal, 1974, for *The Connoisseur;* nomination for award for general nonfiction from National Book Critics Circle, 1984, and *Los Angeles Times* Book Award, 1985, both for *Son of the Morning Star: Custer and the Little Bighorn;* American Academy and Institute of Arts and Letters award, 1987.

WRITINGS:

The Anatomy Lesson, and Other Stories, Viking, 1957.
Mrs. Bridge (novel), Viking, 1959.
The Patriot (novel), Viking, 1960.
(Editor) Jerry Stoll, *I Am a Lover,* Angel Island Publications, 1961.
Notes from a Bottle Found on the Beach at Carmel (epic poem), Viking, 1963.
At the Crossroads: Stories, Simon & Schuster, 1965.
The Diary of a Rapist (novel), Simon & Schuster, 1966.
Mr. Bridge (novel), Knopf, 1969.
(Editor) *Woman by Three,* Pacific Coast Publishers, 1969.
Points for a Compass Rose (epic poem), Knopf, 1973.
The Connoisseur (novel), Knopf, 1974.
Double Honeymoon (novel), Putnam, 1976.
A Long Desire (nonfiction), Holt, 1979.
The White Lantern (nonfiction), Holt, 1980.
St. Augustine's Pigeon (stories), North Point Press, 1980.
Son of the Morning Star: Custer and the Little Bighorn (nonfiction), North Point Press, 1984.
The Alchymist's Journal (novel), North Point Press, 1991.
The Collected Stories of Evan S. Connell, Counterpoint (Washington, DC), 1995.

Contributor of short stories and reviews to periodicals, including *New York Times, Washington Post, Chicago Sun-Times, New York, San Francisco Chronicle, Carolina Quarterly, Paris Review,* and *Esquire.* Editor of *Contact* (literary magazine), 1959-65.

MEDIA ADAPTATIONS: The novels *Mrs. Bridge* and *Mr. Bridge* were adapted as the film *Mr. and Mrs. Bridge* by Merchant Ivory Productions in 1990, and starred Paul Newman and Joanne Woodward.

SIDELIGHTS: The works of Evan S. Connell, Jr., have been widely reviewed and highly praised. According to William H. Nolte in the *Dictionary of Literary Biography,* Connell "would probably rank today as the most important American novelist if critical reception were the sole criterion for determining the reputation of a writer." Brooks Landon in the *Dictionary of Literary Biography Yearbook 1981* explains that "Connell's works have been successful with critics and have enjoyed respectable sales, but his impressive writing still remains one of America's best-kept literary secrets." While his novels and stories have brought him much critical acclaim, Connell has also made a reputation for himself as a successful writer of nonfiction. His *Son of the Morning Star,* an account of General George Armstrong Custer's Battle of the Little Bighorn, was a bestseller.

The critical acclaim for Connell's work began with his first collection, *The Anatomy Lesson, and Other Stories.* At the time of the book's publication in 1957, Anne Chamberlain wrote that "with a virtuoso's dexterity [Connell] explores theme and treatment, subject matter and attack, darting from the precious and the esoteric to almost legendary folk tales, laid in his native Midwest and in distant corners of America. This is a many-faceted writer." Siegfried Mandel called him a "craftsman who can evoke, sustain and dignify the 'small' tragedy that is often hidden from view." And William Hogan said that the stories in *The Anatomy Lesson* are "well-observed, well-worked slices of life that exhibit craftsmanship, discipline and maturity. Connell is obviously a serious writer of promise and I look forward with great expectations to the publication of his first novel."

That first novel, *Mrs. Bridge,* published in 1959, is probably Connell's best-known work as well as the one to which his subsequent books are most often compared. In it the author tells the story of India Bridge, an upper-class Midwestern woman, wife of a lawyer, mother of three children, who comes to personify Connell's concept of the idle rich: She is easily confused; she is bored with her leisure-class existence; and she is dominated by materialism and the need to be "socially correct." India Bridge, according to some critics, may be the most fully developed character in any post-World War II American novel. Anne Chamberlain says that Connell has achieved "a triumph of ironic characterization. In his heroine, who appears at first meeting the acme of mediocrity, he manages to create an interesting, a pathetically comic, a tragically lonely figure. . . . It is sad, somewhat terrifying to reflect upon the numberless Mrs. Bridges trotting befuddledly through this urgent age."

In the decade following the publication of *Mrs. Bridge,* Connell published two more novels, *The Patriot* and *The Diary of a Rapist,* one book-length poem, *Notes from a Bottle Found on the Beach at Carmel,* and a collection of short stories, *At the Crossroads*; most of these were generously accepted by reviewers. He then returned to the Bridge family for his fourth novel, *Mr. Bridge,* which tells the story from the husband's point of view. A *Playboy* critic calls the book "a brilliant dissection of the quintessential small-town WASP—performed under the light of high art, with irony, insight, and a bleak pity." Webster Schott writes in *Washington Post Book World*: "Had Sinclair Lewis possessed compassion equal to his anger, discipline to complement his energy, he might have written *Mr. Bridge.* Evan Connell looks at his world straight. No artifice. But with full awareness of the quiet comedy, tenderness and tight-lipped waste. This job need not be done again. *Mr. Bridge* is a tour de force of contemporary American realism, a beautiful work of fiction." One or two reviewers feel that the novel doesn't quite live up to Connell's work in *Mrs. Bridge*; some believe that the characterization is somewhat weaker in the newer book. However, as John Gross explains: "If *Mr. Bridge* is a less engaging work than its predecessor, it is chiefly because Walter Bridge himself has little of his wife's pathos. Where she was vulnerable in her innocence, funny and touching in her hapless cultural aspirations, he is rigid, efficient, proud of knowing his own mind. Not an especially likable man; but then Mr. Connell's purpose in writing about him is not to draw up a brief for the defense, but simply to restore a cliche-figure to humanity."

Connell's 1991 novel, *The Alchymist's Journal,* is a demanding work that features the journal entries of seven sixteenth-century men, all of them attempting alchemy—the transformation of basic metals into gold. Only one of the men is named—Paracelsus, based on the actual physician who experimented with new methods of treatment in the 1500s. The other men reflect readily identifiable types, such as a skeptic, a revolutionary, and a philosopher. As with many other Connell works, reviewers of this novel expressed admiration for the author's obvious painstaking

research, experimental form, and intellectual daring. Bettina L. Knapp, writing in *World Literature Today,* calls the "highly cerebral and wisdom-filled work" a "tour de force." *Hudson Review* critic William H. Pritchard, while calling the novel "erudite," admits that "most of the entries were impenetrable to this uninformed sensibility." In an interview with Melody Sumner for the *San Francisco Review of Books,* Connell brushed aside questions about the inaccessibility of *The Alchymist's Journal,* commenting, "I don't write to an audience. . . . I wanted all seven of the journals to create a unity, but I was trying to avoid repetition. I went over it several times, just to make sure I wasn't using the same words again and again."

In 1995 many of Connell's short stories were collected and published as *The Collected Stories of Evan S. Connell.* Many of the collection's fifty-six stories were written in the fifties and sixties, while most of the remainder were products of the 1990s. All of the stories feature Connell's trademark minimalist prose; many offer wry commentaries on contemporary American life. The character of Koerner, a writer who in some ways resembles Connell, reappears in several of the stories, searching San Francisco for a prostitute he once knew or enduring the absurd banter of a dinner party. Concludes a *Kirkus Reviews* contributor, "the whole sparkles with Connell's learnedness, sharp wit, and spare, concise prose."

Aside from his works of fiction, Connell's most notable work is *Son of the Morning Star,* his account of the Battle of the Little Bighorn, where Sioux Indian Sitting Bull's warriors overwhelmed and slaughtered General George Armstrong Custer's band of American troops. A classic story of American history, "Custer's Last Stand" has been the subject of numerous books and articles since the 1880s. But despite the story's familiarity, Connell's account of the battle became a bestseller as well as a critical success. Besides winning a National Book Critics Circle nomination and the *Los Angeles Times* Book Award in history, *Son of the Morning Star* sold over 80,000 copies in hardcover, and paperback rights were sold for over $200,000. The book's success did not surprise Connell. He tells the *New York Times*: "I always thought it was a pretty wild story. I had a feeling that since I found it so intensely interesting, other people would, too."

Research and writing for the book took Connell four years and involved reading dozens of books on the battle, the diaries of soldiers who participated in the campaign, and accounts by the Indians themselves. He visited the battle site in Montana on four occasions. The resulting manuscript was difficult to sell. Holt, publisher of some of his earlier fiction, declined *Son of the Morning Star.* They wanted Connell to rewrite the book as a straight biography of Custer or as an overview of the Indian Wars. Connell refused. Eventually North Point Press, a relatively small publisher in California, accepted the book as it was written.

Critical reception to *Son of the Morning Star* was enthusiastic. Ralph E. Sipper of the *Los Angeles Times* calls the book "a monumental study of the philosophical and cultural differences between red and white men that instigated so much mutual animosity and destruction. . . . In a masterly display of literary structure, Connell has drawn from hundreds of pertinent historical accounts and created the modern equivalent of a biblical work of witness." Writing in the *New York Times Book Review,* Page Stegner states that "Connell's narrative of the life and times of General Custer becomes a narrative of the conflict between two cultures, and the battle Custer fought at the Little Bighorn [becomes] a metaphor for all the self-righteous hypocrisy that characterizes Indian-white negotiations to this day." Kenneth Turan in *Time* concludes that *Son of the Morning Star* is "a new American classic."

When asked by interviewer Lawrence Bensky for his critical opinion of modern American literature, Connell replied: "I seldom like anything I read; most contemporary fiction is so bad. I look through things in bookstores, read the first few pages, and I see what the writer is getting at. Usually it's like looking through a piece of pipe—there's nothing at the other end. There are two or three books a year that people call masterpieces [a word that is used not infrequently in reviews of his own work]. I wait a few years, and if they're still around, I might read them." Connell said that he has observed an ongoing trend toward romanticism in this country, and "what I've tried to do as a writer is get behind this romanticism and into people's fantasies—and show them as they are."

BIOGRAPHICAL/CRITICAL SOURCES:

BOOKS

Contemporary Authors Autobiography Series, Volume 2, Gale, 1985.
Contemporary Literary Criticism, Gale, Volume 4, 1975; Volume 6, 1976; Volume 45, 1987.
Dictionary of Literary Biography, Volume 2: *American Novelists since World War II,* Gale, 1978.
Dictionary of Literary Biography Yearbook: 1981, Gale, 1982.

PERIODICALS

Best Sellers, April 15, 1969; June 15, 1973.
Bloomsbury Review, June, 1991.
Boston Review, June, 1991.
Catholic World, March, 1959.
Chicago Tribune Book World, April 5, 1981; October 14, 1984.
Christian Science Monitor, May 22, 1969.
Commentary, March, 1985.
Commonweal, February 13, 1959; August 23, 1963.
Detroit News, March 10, 1985.
Harper's, January, 1974.
Hudson Review, summer, 1986; autumn, 1991, p. 507.
Interview, November, 1990.
Kenyon Review, September, 1966.
Kirkus Reviews, March 1, 1957; July 15, 1960; August 15, 1995, p. 1126.
Library Journal, April 15, 1957; January 1, 1959; September 1, 1960; March 15, 1973; August, 1974; April 15, 1991; November 1, 1991; October 1, 1995, p. 122.
Life, April 25, 1969.
Los Angeles Times, November 21, 1980; October 3, 1984.
Los Angeles Times Book Review, August 3, 1986; April 19, 1987; July 14, 1991.
Nation, June 15, 1963; June 30, 1969.
National Review, February 28, 1975; August 9, 1985.
New Mexico Quarterly, summer, 1966.
New Republic, October 14, 1957; June 7, 1969; October 22, 1990.
New Statesman, February 13, 1960.
Newsweek, May 12, 1969; February 4, 1991.
New Yorker, October 14, 1974; June 3, 1985; July 1, 1991.
New York Herald Tribune Book Review, May 26, 1957; January 18, 1959; September 25, 1960; May 26, 1963.
New York Review, April 24, 1969.
New York Review of Books, June 23, 1966; May 17, 1973; November 28, 1974.

New York Times, May 19, 1957; February 1, 1959; April 23, 1969; February 13, 1985; February 18, 1990; May 13, 1990.
New York Times Book Review, February 1, 1959; September 25, 1960; April 20, 1969; April 29, 1973; September 1, 1974; May 23, 1976; June 24, 1979; July 20, 1980; December 7, 1980; March 29, 1981; May 30, 1982; January 20, 1985; April 30, 1989; May 12, 1991; September 13, 1992, p. 40.
People Weekly, December 10, 1990.
Playboy, June, 1969.
Publishers Weekly, November 20, 1981; February 22, 1991; August 21, 1995, p. 47.
San Francisco Chronicle, May 28, 1957; January 19, 1959; September 19, 1960.
San Francisco Review of Books, February, 1991, p. 26.
Saturday Review, May 18, 1957; January 31, 1959; September 24, 1960; July 17, 1965; May 3, 1969; April 17, 1976.
Time, May 27, 1957; January 19, 1959; June 20, 1969; September 2, 1974; June 21, 1976; November 5, 1984.
Times Literary Supplement, July 29, 1983.
Village Voice, June 18, 1991.
Village Voice Literary Supplement, March, 1985; November, 1991.
Virginia Quarterly Review, autumn, 1965; summer, 1969; spring, 1991; winter, 1992, p. 23.
Washington Post, July 17, 1979; November 11, 1981.
Washington Post Book World, April 20, 1969; May 27, 1973; September 1, 1974; July 13, 1980; March 15, 1981; November 18, 1984; September 22, 1985; October 27, 1985; May 3, 1987; September 4, 1988; May 7, 1989; May 19, 1991.
Wisconsin Studies in Contemporary Literature, summer, 1967.
World Literature Today, summer, 1992, p. 526.
Yale Review, winter, 1985.

*   *   *

CONNOLLY, Cyril (Vernon) 1903-1974 (Palinurus)

PERSONAL: Born September 10, 1903, in Coventry, England; died November 26, 1974; son of Matthew (an army major) and Muriel (Vernon) Connolly; married Jean Bakewell; Barbara Skelton, 1950; Deirdre Craig, 1959; children: one son, one daughter. *Education:* Attended Balliol College, Oxford.

CAREER: Writer for the *New Statesman* and other periodicals, 1927-74; *Horizon,* London, England, founder, editor, and writer, 1939-50; *Observer,* London, literary editor, 1942-43; weekly contributor to the *Sunday Times,* 1951-74.

MEMBER: Royal Society of Literature (fellow), White's, Pratt's, Beefsteak Clubs.

AWARDS, HONORS: Chevalier de la Legion d'Honneur; Brackenbury scholar; D.Litt., Trinity College, Dublin; Companion of Honour, L'Academie Francaise; knighted; Commander of the Order of the British Empire, 1972.

WRITINGS:

The Rock Pool (fiction), Scribner, 1936.
Enemies of Promise, Routledge & Kegan Paul, 1938, Little, Brown, 1939, revised edition, Macmillan, 1948.
(Editor) *Horizon Stories,* Faber, 1943, Vanguard, 1946.

(Translator) Jean Bruller (writing under pseudonym Vercors), *Silence of the Sea,* Macmillan, 1944, published in England as *Put Out the Light,* Macmillan, 1944.

(Under pseudonym Palinurus) *The Unquiet Grave: A Word Cycle,* Horizon (London), 1944, Harper, 1945, revised edition, Hamish Hamilton, 1945.

The Condemned Playground (essays), Routledge & Kegan Paul, 1945, Macmillan, 1946.

The Missing Diplomats, Queen Anne Press, 1952.

Ideas and Places, Harper, 1953.

The Golden Horizon, Weidenfeld & Nicolson, 1953, University Books, 1955.

(Editor and author of introduction) *Great English Short Novels,* Dial, 1953.

(With Jerome Zerbe) *Les Pavillons: French Pavilions of the Eighteenth Century,* Macmillan, 1962.

Previous Convictions: Selected Writings of a Decade, Harper, 1963.

The Modern Movement: 100 Key Books from England, France, and America, Deutsch, 1965, Atheneum, 1966.

(Translator with Simon W. Taylor) Alfred Jarry, *The Ubu Plays* (contains *Ubu Rex, Ubu Cuckolded,* and *Ubu Enchained*), Grove, 1969.

The Evening Colonnade, Harcourt, 1975.

The Selected Essays of Cyril Connolly, edited by Peter Quennell, Persea Books, 1984.

(With Peter Levi) *Shade Those Laurels,* Pantheon (New York City), 1990.

Contributor of article to *Art and Literature.*

SIDELIGHTS: Cyril Connolly was a respected literary critic and essayist who was at the center of the English literary scene for much of his life. He related his "Georgian boyhood" in Eton College in the last part of his formidable work *Enemies of Promise.* He believed that he was a spoiled child who suffered all the miseries of the English public school caste system while managing to acquire an excellent education. With a sharp tongue he wasn't afraid to use, he was at times a critic of the literary world, at times a self-critic. Remembering a "very nasty review" he had written on Ernest Hemingway's *Green Hills of Africa,* Connolly remarked that "the first time I met Hemingway I was introduced to him, just after I had reviewed this book, in Sylvia Beach's bookshop in Paris. When he realised who I was, he turned to Sylvia Beach and he said: 'This is a very bad moment for both of us.' That, I think, is a lovely remark: you see, he forgave me, because I was minding terribly the tactlessness of being introduced to him after writing this review, and he showed that he minded the review. We had dinner together and we became great friends, because after all I had liked his earlier books and said so."

The *New Yorker* critic found *Enemies of Promise* to be "a collection of searching and idea-packed literary essays, precisely noting the temper of current writing and pointing out the pitfalls that beset the beginning or the successful author." To Geoffrey Grigson, the complete book was most interesting, sociologically, "as a specimen [and] as a piece from the war between the ninety per cent art-gentlemen and his gentility. It is good to see conscience at work in an art-gentleman." James Stern reflected that "had I a son, whether destined for Eton, Dalton or the dogs, I would place a copy of *Enemies of Promise* in his hands at an early age. For this book is an education, a warning, an encouragement, a preparation for the literary life."

Connolly wrote one complete novel, *The Rock Pool,* published in 1936. After Connolly's death, Peter Levi, a longtime friend and admirer, completed *Shade Those Laurels,* a second novel that Connolly had worked on for nearly forty years before he died; three early parts of the novel, a murder mystery, were included in the magazine *Encounter* in the 1950s. Frank Kermode wrote in the *London Review of Books* that Connolly left "it unfinished for what must have come to seem good reasons—for example, that his talents were for silvery prose and high-spirited parody rather than for sustained narrative." He stated that "Peter Levi has a good try at keeping up the tone," but indicated the book should have been left uncompleted. Charlotte Innes gave a similar opinion in the *New York Times Book Review*: "Mr. Levi does a stylish job of rounding out a flimsily structured novel that at times threatens to keel over under the weight of its literary and gastronomic obsessions."

BIOGRAPHICAL/CRITICAL SOURCES:

BOOKS

Enright, D. J., *Conspirators and Poets,* Dufour, 1966.

Fisher, Clive, *Cyril Connolly: The Life and Times of England's Most Controversial Literary Critic,* St. Martin's Press (New York City), 1996.

Lewis, Jeremy, *Cyril Connolly: A Life,* Jonathan Cape (London), 1997.

Martin, Kingsley, editor, *New Statesman Profiles,* Phoenix House, 1958.

Shelden, Michael, *Friends of Promise: Cyril Connolly and the World of Horizon,* Harper & Row (New York City), 1989.

PERIODICALS

Boston Transcript, October 10, 1936.

Encounter, February, 1964.

Listener, April 11, 1968.

London Review of Books, January 24, 1991, p. 20.

Manchester Guardian, December 13, 1938.

New Republic, July 15, 1946; January 31, 1948.

New Statesman and Nation, May 30, 1953.

New Yorker, April 8, 1939; October 27, 1945; January 29, 1996, p. 84.

New York Herald Tribune Weekly Book Review, February 27, 1949.

New York Times Book Review, October 11, 1936; October 7, 1945; October 20, 1991, p. 36.

Spectator, November 12, 1938.

Time, March 25, 1966.

Times Literary Supplement, December 7-13, 1990, p. 1325.

*   *   *

CONRAD, Joseph 1857-1924

PERSONAL: Birth name Jozef Teodor Konrad Nalecz Korzeniowski; name legally changed; born December 3, 1857, in Berdiczew, Podolia, Russia (now Poland); naturalized British citizen, 1886; died of a heart attack, August 3, 1924, in Bishopsbourne, Kent, England; buried in Canterbury, England; son of Apollo Nalecz (a poet, writer, and political activist) and Ewa (Bobrowski) Korzeniowski; married Jessie George, March 24, 1896; children: Alfred Borys, John Alexander. *Education:* Studied at schools in Poland and under tutors in Europe. *Religion:* Roman Catholic.

CAREER: Joined French Merchant Marine, 1874, sailed to Martinique and to West Indies as apprentice and then steward, 1875; British Merchant Service, 1878-94, traveled to Africa, Australia, India, Indonesia, and the Orient; full-time writer, 1894-1924.

MEMBER: Athenaeum Club.

WRITINGS:

FICTION

Almayer's Folly: A Story of an Eastern River (novel), Macmillan, 1895, published as *Almayer's Folly,* Doubleday, Page, 1921.

An Outcast of the Islands (novel), D. Appleton, 1896.

The Children of the Sea: A Tale of the Forecastle (novel), Dodd, Mead, 1897, published in England as *The Nigger of the "Narcissus": A Tale of the Sea,* Heinemann, 1898, published with new preface by Conrad as *The Nigger of the "Narcissus": A Tale of the Forecastle,* Doubleday, Page, 1914, published under English title, Doubleday, Page, 1926, recent edition, Norton, 1979.

Tales of Unrest (stories; includes "The Idiots," "An Outpost of Progress," and "The Lagoon"), Scribner, 1898.

Lord Jim: A Romance (novel), Doubleday, McClure, 1900 published in England as *Lord Jim: A Tale,* W. Blackwood, 1900, published under English title, Doubleday, Page, 1927, published as *Lord Jim,* introduction by J. Donald Adams, Modern Library, 1931, enlarged edition, F. Watts, 1966, recent edition, Oxford University Press, 1983.

(With Ford Madox Heuffer [later Ford Madox Ford]) *The Inheritors: An Extravagant Story* (novel), McClure, Phillips, 1901.

"Youth: A Narrative," and Two Other Stories (contains "Youth, A Narrative," "Heart of Darkness" [also see below], and "The End of the Tether"), W. Blackwood, 1902, published as *"Youth" and Two Other Stories,* McClure, Phillips, 1903, recent edition published as *"Youth," "Heart of Darkness," and "The End of the Tether,"* Oxford University Press, 1984.

Typhoon, illustrations by Maurice Grieffenhagen, Putnam, 1902 (also see below).

Typhoon, and Other Stories (includes "To-Morrow" [also see below] and "Falk"), Heinemann, 1903, Doubleday, Page, 1926.

(With Ford) *Romance* (novel), Smith, Elder, 1903, McClure, Phillips, 1904.

Nostromo: A Tale of the Seaboard (novel), Harper & Brothers, 1904, recent edition, Oxford University Press, 1984.

The Secret Agent: A Simple Tale (novel), Harper & Brothers, 1907, recent edition, Viking, 1985 (also see below).

The Point of Honor: A Military Tale, illustrations by Dan Sayre Broesbeck, McClure, 1908.

"Falk," "Amy Foster," "To-Morrow": Three Stories by Joseph Conrad, McClure, Phillips, 1908.

A Set of Six (stories), Methuen, 1908, Doubleday, Page, 1915.

Under Western Eyes (novel), Harper & Brothers, 1911, recent edition, Viking, 1985.

'Twixt Land and Sea (stories; includes "The Secret Sharer" [also see below], "A Smile of Fortune," and "Freya of the Seven Isles"), Hodder & Stoughton, 1912.

Chance: A Tale in Two Parts (novel), Doubleday, Page, 1913, recent edition, Hogarth Press, 1984.

Victory: An Island Tale (novel), Doubleday, Page, 1915.

Within the Tides: Tales (includes "Because of the Dollars" [also see below] and "The Planter of Malata"), Dent, 1915, Doubleday, Page, 1916.

The Shadow Line: A Confession (novel), Doubleday, Page, 1917, recent edition, Oxford University Press, 1985.

The Arrow of Gold: A Story Between Two Notes (novel), Doubleday, Page, 1919.

The Rescue: A Romance of the Shallows (novel), Doubleday, Page, 1920.

The Rover (novella), Doubleday, Page, 1923.

(With Heuffer) *The Nature of a Crime,* Doubleday, Page, 1924.

Suspense: A Napoleonic Novel (unfinished), Doubleday, Page, 1925.

Tales of Hearsay, preface by R. B. Cunninghame Graham, Doubleday, Page, 1925.

The Sisters (unfinished), introduction by Ford, C. Gaige, 1928.

"Heart of Darkness" and "The Secret Sharer," introduction by Albert J. Guerard, New American Library, 1950.

"Lord Jim," "Heart of Darkness," "Nostromo," Oxford University Press (New York City), 1994.

"Heart of Darkness" with "The Congo Diary", Penguin (New York City), 1995.

"The Secret Agent" and "Almayer's Folly," Bantam (New York City), 1995.

Ross C. Murfin, editor, *"Heart of Darkness": Complete, Authoritative Text with Biographical and Historical Contexts, Critical History, and Essays from Five Contemporary Critical Perspectives,* Bedford Books of St. Martin's Press (Boston), 1996.

Thomas C. Moser, editor, *"Lord Jim": Authoritative Text, Backgrounds, Sources, Criticism,* Norton (New York City), 1996.

Stories and novels also in other multi-titled volumes.

PLAYS

One Day More: A Play in One Act (adaptation of Conrad's story "To-Morrow;" first performed June 25, 1905), Clement Shorter, 1917, Doubleday, Page, 1920 (also see below).

The Secret Agent: A Drama in Four Acts (adaptation of Conrad's novel of the same title), H. J. Goulden, 1921 (also see below).

Laughing Anne: A Play (adaptation of Conrad's story "Because of the Dollars"), Morland Press, 1923 (also see below).

Laughing Anne [and] *One Day More,* introduction by John Galsworthy, J. Castle, 1924, Doubleday, Page, 1925.

Three Plays: Laughing Anne, One Day More, [and] *The Secret Agent,* Methuen, 1934.

CORRESPONDENCE

Lettres Francaises, introduction and notes by Georges Jean-Aubry, Gallimard, 1920.

Joseph Conrad's Letters to His Wife, Bookman's Journal, 1927.

Letters From Joseph Conrad, 1895-1924, edited with introduction and notes by Edward Garnett, Bobbs-Merrill, 1928.

Conrad to a Friend: One Hundred Fifty Selected Letters From Joseph Conrad to Richard Curle, edited with introduction and notes by Richard Curle, Bobbs-Merrill, 1928.

Letters of Joseph Conrad to Marguerite Poradowska, 1890-1920, translated from the French and edited with introduction and notes by John A. Gee and Paul J. Sturm, Yale University Press, 1940.

Joseph Conrad: Letters to William Blackwood and David S. Meldrum, edited by William Blackburn, Duke University Press, 1958.

Conrad's Polish Background: Letters to and From Polish Friends, translated by Halina Carroll, edited by Zdzislaw Najder, Oxford University Press, 1964.

Joseph Conrad and Warrington Dawson: The Record of a Friendship, edited by Dale B. J. Randall, Duke University Press, 1968.
Joseph Conrad's Letters to Cunninghame Graham, edited by C. T. Watts, Cambridge University Press, 1969.
The Collected Letters of Joseph Conrad, edited by Frederick R. Karl and Laurence Davies, Cambridge University Press, Volume I: *1861-1897,* 1983; Volume II: *1898-1902,* 1988; Volume III: *1903-1907,* 1988; Volume IV: *1908-1911,* 1990.

OTHER

The Mirror of the Sea: Memories and Impressions (autobiographical essays), Harper & Brothers, 1906 (also see below).
A Personal Record (autobiography), Harper & Brothers, 1912, published in England as *Some Reminiscences,* Eveleigh Nash, 1912 (also see below).
Notes on Life and Letters (essays), Doubleday, Page, 1921.
Notes on My Books, Doubleday, Page, 1921.
(Contributor) *Hugh Walpole: Appreciations,* Doran, 1923.
(Contributor) Charles Kenneth Scott-Moncrief, editor, *Marcel Proust: An English Tribute,* Chatto & Windus, 1923.
Last Essays (includes "Geography and Some Explorers"), introduction by Richard Curle, Doubleday, Page, 1926.
Joseph Conrad's Diary of His Journey up the Valley of the Congo in 1890, Strangeways, 1926 (also see below).
Joseph Conrad's Prefaces to His Works, introduction by Edward Garnett, Dent, 1937.
Joseph Conrad on Fiction, edited by Walter F. Wright, University of Nebraska Press, 1964.
Congo Diary and Other Uncollected Pieces, edited by Najder, Doubleday, 1978.
The Mirror of the Sea [and] *A Personal Record,* Oxford University Press, 1988.

Contributor to periodicals, including *Oxford and Cambridge Review,* London *Times, Fortnightly Review,* and the *Daily Mail.*

OMNIBUS VOLUMES

Wisdom and Beauty From Conrad, selected and arranged by M. Harriet M. Capes, Melrose, 1915, Doubleday, 1922.
The Shorter Tales of Joseph Conrad, Doubleday, 1924.
The Complete Short Stories of Joseph Conrad, Hutchinson, 1933.
The Famous Stories of Joseph Conrad, Doubleday, 1938.
A Conrad Argosy, Doubleday, 1942.
The Portable Conrad, edited with introduction and notes by Zabel, Viking, 1947.
Tales of Land and Sea, illustrated by Richard M. Powers, introduction by William McFee, Hanover House, 1953.
Tales of the East and West, edited with introduction by Zabel, Doubleday, 1958.
Tales of Heroes and History, edited by Zabel, Doubleday, 1960.
Tales of the East, edited with introduction by Zabel, Doubleday, 1961.
Great Short Works of Joseph Conrad, Harper, 1967.
Stories and Tales of Joseph Conrad, Funk & Wagnalls, 1968.
Sea Stories, Granada, 1984.
The Complete Short Fiction of Joseph Conrad, edited by Samuel Hynes, Volumes I and II: *The Stories;* Volume III and IV: *The Tales,* 1992.
Joseph Conrad, Selected Works, Gramercy Books (New York City), 1994.
Selected Works of Joseph Conrad, Barnes & Noble Books (New York City), 1994.

Stories and novels also published together in other collections; works widely represented in anthologies.

COLLECTED WORKS

The Works of Joseph Conrad, twenty-one volumes, Dent, 1923-38, reprinted and enlarged, twenty-six volumes, 1946-55.
The Collected Works of Joseph Conrad, twenty-one volumes, Doubleday, 1925.

MEDIA ADAPTATIONS: Lord Jim was released as a movie starring Peter O'Toole by Columbia in 1965; Conrad's short story "The Secret Sharer" was adapted into a one-act play of the same title by C. R. Wobbe in 1969; the award-winning 1979 United Artists film *Apocalypse Now,* starring Marlon Brando and Martin Sheen, is an adaptation of Conrad's "Heart of Darkness."

SIDELIGHTS: Joseph Conrad was a Polish-born British novelist and short story writer whose major works appeared between 1895 and 1924. Conrad's work marks a shift from the novel as popular entertainment to the novel as high art, an art as carefully crafted as poetry. His experiments in fictional form and narrative prepared the way for the technical innovations of novelists Virginia Woolf, William Faulkner, and John Fowles; his characteristic themes of alienation and thwarted heroism and his preoccupation with individuals in remote places have had continuing impact on writers throughout this century.

Conrad was born in Russian-occupied Poland on December 3, 1857. Although Poland had been a major power in central Europe from the fourteenth through seventeenth centuries, the country had been partitioned into German, Austrian, and Russian sectors, and, by the time of Conrad's birth, only Warsaw remained under Polish control. The Poles fought partition and occupation, particularly Russian occupation, with patriotic and religious fervor. Conrad's family on both sides had a history of commitment to the cause of a free Poland; his parents, Apollo and Ewa Korzeniowski, were active in the insurrection of 1863. The Russian authorities sentenced the family to exile in Vologda, Russia, then, after two years, to Chernikhov in the Ukraine. When Conrad was five, his mother died from illness worsened by the privations of their exile. Ewa's death plunged Apollo into depression and illness, despite his having gained permission to return to Warsaw. When he died in May of 1869, he was given a public funeral befitting a hero.

Conrad, twelve years old, was put in the care of his mother's younger brother, Tadeusz Bobrowski, a lawyer. Conrad remained under Tadeusz's care until the age of seventeen, when, after two years of importuning his uncle, he was allowed to attend a maritime school in Marseilles. Conrad's four years in Marseilles have received considerable scrutiny because of evidence of his attempted suicide. Conrad himself told his son and friends that he had been shot in the chest during a duel. But Bobrowski, who went to his nephew's rescue, seems plainly to say in a letter to a friend that Conrad had tried to kill himself, as Zdzislaw Najder in *Joseph Conrad: A Chronicle* and Frederick R. Karl in *Joseph Conrad: The Three Lives* point out. Biographers speculate that the suicide attempt may have been the result of debts, a foiled love relationship, or disappointed expectations. When Conrad recovered from his injury, he fulfilled his ambition to sail on an English ship, the *Mavis,* bound for Constantinople.

Conrad spent the next fifteen years on English ships, where he was known among sailors as "Polish Joe." Conrad rose steadily in his profession, passing the required examinations for second mate in 1880, first mate in 1883, and then, on his second try, captain in 1886, the same year he became a naturalized British citizen. In

1890 Conrad accepted a job as commander of a Congo River steamboat owned by a Belgian firm. Once in Africa, he saw extreme examples of imperialistic exploitation, which he described in "Geography and Some Explorers" (included in the collection *Last Essays*) as "the vilest scramble for loot that ever disfigured the history of human conscience and geographical exploration." When he arrived at the town of Kinshasa after a thirty-six day overland trek, he found his command had been sunk, but he was given another steamboat and ordered to proceed immediately up the Congo River to rescue Georges Antoine Klein, a valuable company agent who had taken ill. On the return trip the agent died, and Conrad was stalled in Kinshasa, perhaps, as some have theorized, because he did not get on with his superiors. After months fighting fever and dysentery, he returned to Europe, his health wrecked.

During the next five years, Conrad spent less time at sea and committed himself to the life of a writer. In 1894 his guardian, Bobrowski, died. A year later, Conrad published his first novel, *Almayer's Folly: A Story of an Eastern River,* and dedicated it to his uncle. His second novel, *An Outcast of the Islands,* derived in plot and theme from the first, followed quickly in 1898, a productivity stimulated, perhaps, by Conrad's marriage in 1896 to Jessie George, with whom he had two sons, Borys and John.

Much of the fiction in Conrad's early phase arose from his experiences as mate on the trading vessel *Vidar,* on which he sailed from Singapore on several voyages throughout the Malay Archipelago beginning in 1887. The works based on Conrad's life on the *Vidar* include his first novel, *Almayer's Folly,* many short stories, and four other novels: *An Outcast of the Islands, Lord Jim, Victory,* and *The Rescue.* Recognized for its experiments in narrative technique, evocation of place, characterization, and profound exploration of alienation, *Almayer's Folly* is considered a remarkable first novel.

Almayer's Folly centers on Kaspar Almayer, a Dutch trader at the port of Sambir, holding what had been a very profitable post until Arabs found their way through the thirty miles of the Pantai River channels to the town. Almayer dreams of returning, with his beloved half-caste daughter Nina, to the native land that he has never seen. A third major figure in the tale, Dain Waris, is a Malay chieftain from Bali, sent out by his father, the Rajah, to secure gunpowder to fight the Dutch. The fourth actor is Tom Lingard, an aging British trader-adventurer. All intensely isolated, these figures are bound together in a "community of hopes and fears."

The work was well received by critics; an anonymous reviewer for *Bookman* termed it "a remarkable novel where wild nature and strange humanity [are] powerfully portrayed." Conrad's second work, *An Outcast of the Islands* (1896), which recounts how the Arabs traveled up the Pantai and ruined Lingard's monopoly, received even better press than *Almayer's Folly.* Both novels, however, are considered minor works.

After he had finished *An Outcast of the Islands,* Conrad wrote three short stories ("The Idiots," "The Lagoon," "An Outpost of Progress"), and then began *The Nigger of the "Narcissus"* (1898; originally published as *The Children of the Sea,* 1897). Whereas the earlier novels and tales are derivative, solidly in a tradition of what Conrad called in the work's preface stories of the "white man in the tropics," *The Nigger of the "Narcissus"* transcends and transforms the sea tale as told by such nineteenth-century writers as James Fenimore Cooper, Frederick Marryat, Richard Henry Dana, and Herman Melville. Conrad combined his intimate

understanding of life at sea with his vision of "the truth of life," which he also explains in the novel's preface. "Truth," he wrote, is "what is enduring and essential," yet it is also an "appeal of one temperament to all the other innumerable temperaments." Both absolute and changing, truth is "the stress and passion within the core of each convincing moment"; it is "the feeling of unavoidable solidarity. . . which binds men to each other and all mankind to the visible world." Thus, in Conrad's view, art is an intimation of solidarity forged despite each person's individual loneliness.

Another work based on Conrad's life as a sailor, "Heart of Darkness" (1899, in serial form), is the first of three great works produced by Conrad between 1897 and 1902. The novella is a fictional version of Conrad's Congo experience. An indictment of European imperialism, the work takes much of its descriptive material from a diary Conrad kept during his service in the African interior. The story is told by Marlow, who narrates the events of his journey up the Congo to four companions on a boat on London's Thames River. In the employ of the Belgian government, Marlow is charged with finding and relieving Kurtz, one of Belgium's most profitable ivory traders. Through Marlow's narration, Conrad exposes the brutal exploitation and destruction wreaked by the Belgians on the African country and its people and satirizes such bourgeois European ideals as the work ethic, efficiency, faith, home and family, community, progress, self-restraint, and the processes of law. Small incidents in each stage of Marlow's journey dramatize the corruption of these ideals: a French man-of-war firing into the bush like a toy ship at a continent; black workers left to die in a grove; and an accountant who keeps his books "in apple-pie order" despite the groans of a man dying nearby.

Lord Jim (1900), perhaps Conrad's greatest novel and certainly his best known, is also narrated by Marlow. The first four chapters are told by an anonymous narrator who relates the early life and career of the titular figure. After the initial chapters, the narrative presents Marlow watching the proceedings of a maritime Board of Inquiry, which is probing the conduct of the captain and officers of the *Patna.* Believing the ship to be sinking, the crew had abandoned the ship and left the eight hundred pilgrims on board to drown. Jim is one of the deserters, and Marlow befriends him. Jim, who never admits guilt, appeals deeply to Marlow as the embodiment of hopeful youth. After the court pronounces Jim's guilt, Marlow obtains several jobs for Jim, each one ending when his involvement in the *Patna* affair is revealed. Finally Marlow seeks the advice of an old trader and explorer, Stein, who gives Jim charge of a remote but prosperous trading post, Patusan.

There Jim rises to a place of honor. The natives call him "Tuan Jim"—Lord Jim. But Jim fails again with the arrival of the renegade, Gentleman Brown. An escaped convict, Brown intends to ravage the village, but he and his men are trapped by the villagers, who have united under Jim's leadership. Brown, however, makes an instinctive and devastating reference to Jim's past, asking him if he agrees that when "it came to saving one's own life in the dark, one didn't care who else went—three, thirty, three hundred people." Jim lets Brown and his men have an open road back to sea, but the white trader whom Jim has supplanted shows Brown how to ambush a contingent of men led by Jim's best friend, Dain Maroola. When his friend is murdered by Brown, Jim presents himself to Dain's father to be shot.

Using chronological juxtapositions, sudden and rapid jumps in time, and incidents placed within incidents, Conrad designed *Lord Jim* to sustain pervasive ironies and ambiguities. Thus the telling of the tale is just as much the subject of *Lord Jim* as are heroism, courage, self-understanding, or the impingement of European ideals upon native peoples. The novel's unresolved ambiguities still fascinate readers.

Typhoon (1902), the last work of Conrad's early period, focuses on the responses of officers to a natural and human crisis. The natural crisis is a typhoon; the human crisis is occasioned by the cargo, a load of coolies returning home with their wages of several years kept in small wooden chests. During the gale, the chests smash and the coolies start a free-for-all. Captain MacWhirr sends in an officer to quell the riot, then devises a way to distribute the cash among the laborers. *Typhoon* is considered Conrad's best piece of direct, idiomatic prose. In contrast to *Lord Jim* and "Heart of Darkness," it has a simple, linear narrative structure, each of its five chapters marking off a distinct segment of the tale.

While Conrad's early work typed him as a writer of the sea, the major works of his middle period—*Nostromo* (1904), *The Secret Agent* (1907), and *Under Western Eyes* (1911)—turn resolutely away from the sea to cities and to the development of political themes that had been implicit but secondary in the early work. Among Conrad scholars, the first two of these novels are rated very highly, and the last also has devoted admirers. But these novels diverged from Conrad's earlier concerns, eliciting criticism from some of his contemporaries. British novelist D. H. Lawrence, for example, thought *Under Western Eyes* incomprehensible and boring, although he liked Conrad's previous works very much. *Nostromo* received negative reviews, except in American newspapers; fourteen years after its publication, Virginia Woolf, in the *Times Literary Supplement,* called the novel a "rare and magnificent wreck." The judgment would be echoed forty years later by Albert J. Guerard in *Conrad the Novelist*; for him, *Nostromo* was "a great but radically defective novel." Not until the 1960s were *Nostromo, The Secret Agent,* and *Under Western Eyes* accorded the esteem they now have among Conrad scholars. Among critics in general, *The Secret Agent* is greatly admired for the ferocity of its plot and the sustained irony of its tone.

The Secret Agent is austere, ironic fiction. Set in London, the novel uses as its central incident the death of an idiot boy named Stevie. Stevie's brother-in-law, Verloc, is a triple agent—working for the police, for the anarchists, and for an unnamed central European power; he uses the code name Agent Delta. As a cover Verloc sells cheap stationery and petty pornography; in this way he has lived for several years, happily married to Stevie's sister, Winnie. But his European paymaster suddenly demands real action from him—a bombing—in order to stir up popular resentment against the anarchists and thus abolish the haven England provides for them. Verloc is outraged at this intrusion into his placid, bourgeois existence, but he has no choice. He obtains the bomb and gives it to Stevie to carry. On the way to the target the boy trips over a root and is blown to bits. When Winnie learns how her brother died, she stabs Verloc, runs off with an anarchist, and commits suicide on the crossing to France.

The final work of Conrad's political phase, *Under Western Eyes,* is set in Russia and Geneva. Protagonist Razumov, a student who is the illegitimate and unacknowledged son of a Russian official, is implicated in an assassination. He turns over one assassin to the authorities and is sent off to Geneva to act as a double agent, since the revolutionaries believe him to have been an accomplice of the real assassin, Victor Haldin. In Geneva he meets Haldin's sister, falls in love with her, confesses his guilt, and, deafened by a revolutionary who is also a double agent, is run over and maimed

for life. The tale's narrator is an English professor of languages who lives in Geneva. His sustained incomprehension of events is interpreted as a study of the differences between the traditions of autocracy and democracy.

The work of Conrad's third and last period is much less thematically unified than the work of the earlier phases. Marlow appears again in the 1913 novel *Chance* and tells the tale of Flora DeBarral, daughter of a ruined financier, and her lover, Captain Anthony. *Victory* (1915) relates the story of another pair of lovers, Axel Heyst and Lena. *Chance* ends happily for the lovers, while *Victory,* set in the East of *Lord Jim,* ends with Lena's death from a gun shot and Heyst's suicide. In 1920, Conrad published a novel that he had begun in 1897 as a sequel to *Almayer's Folly* and *An Outcast of the Islands.* Originally titled "The Rescuer," *The Rescue* portrays Lingard's love for a married woman, Edith Travers, a love that destroys his plans to help a native friend regain his land.

All of the work in Conrad's third phase looks, in part, to the past. In 1919 Conrad looked back even farther, to his days in Marseilles, for material for *The Arrow of Gold,* in which love is found and lost amid intrigue, duels, and gunrunning. Conrad set his last two novels, *The Rover* (1923) and the incomplete *Suspense* (1925), during the Napoleonic Wars. He had wanted to write a historical novel for many years, a desire that was perhaps an outgrowth of his lifelong preoccupation with the individual's relationship to history. In *The Rover* Conrad creates an optimistic tale, with an elderly seaman as its protagonist.

The publication of *The Collected Short Fiction of Joseph Conrad,* conscientiously edited and introduced by Samuel Hynes, brings together thirty-one chronologically arranged stories and tales in four volumes, including minor works alongside such masterpieces as "Heart of Darkness." David Grylls writes in the *Times Literary Supplement,* "Together, these volumes demonstrate Conrad's remarkable versatility and range." Referring to the first volume of the series, Wendy Lesser notes in the *Yale Review,* "What you will find, in his collection of such widely reprinted stories such as 'Youth' and 'An Outpost of Progress' as well as incredible neglected works like 'The Idiots,' 'The Return,' and 'To-morrow,' is that Conrad was a man of many faces, many hearts."

According to Walter Sullivan, who comments on the collection in *Sewanee Review,* "Joseph Conrad was gloomy by nature and was made more so by the circumstances of his early life—his father's exile and premature death, his own disordered young manhood—and few of his fictions come to happy endings. Reading his novels and his long stories, one encounters the workings of an antagonistic fate, a cosmic scheme devised in irony to bring men and women ultimately to grief. In most of Conrad's novels, you know things are going to end badly, but the characters are so fully developed and the plots are built with such compelling causality that most of us remain unaware that, should it be required, the author's hand is poised to nudge the story further still into bleakness."

BIOGRAPHICAL/CRITICAL SOURCES:

BOOKS

Bachelor, John, *The Life of Joseph Conrad: A Critical Biography,* Blackwell (Cambridge, MA), 1994.
Billy, Ted, *A Wilderness of Words: Closure and Disclosure in Conrad's Short Fiction,* Texas Tech University Press, 1997.
Bloom, Harold, *Joseph Conrad's "Heart of Darkness" and "The Secret Sharer,"* Chelsea House (New York City), 1995.

Dictionary of Literary Biography, Gale, Volume 10: *Modern British Dramatists, 1940-1945,* 1982; Volume 34: *British Novelists, 1890-1920: Traditionalists,* 1985; Volume 156: *British Short-Fiction Writers, 1880-1914: The Romantic Tradition,* 1995.

Ford, Ford Madox, *Joseph Conrad: A Personal Remembrance,* Little, Brown, 1924.

Gillon, Adam and Raymond Breibach, *Joseph Conrad—Comparative Essays,* Texas Tech University Press (Lubbock), 1994.

GoGwilt, Christopher Lloyd, *The Invention of the West: Joseph Conrad and the Double-Mapping of Europe and Empire,* Stanford University Press (Stanford, CA), 1995.

Griffith, John W., *Joseph Conrad and the Anthropological Dilemma: "Bewildered Traveller,"* Oxford University Press (New York City), 1995.

Guerard, Albert J., *Conrad the Novelist,* Harvard University Press, 1958.

Harpham, Geoffrey Galt, *One of Us: The Mastery of Joseph Conrad,* University of Chicago Press, 1996.

Jackson, Tony E., *The Subject of Modernism: Narrative Alterations in the Fiction of Eliot, Conrad, Woolf, and Joyce,* University of Michigan Press (Ann Arbor), 1994.

Jordan, Elaine, *Joseph Conrad,* St. Martin's Press (New York City), 1996.

Karl, Frederick R., *Joseph Conrad: The Three Lives,* Farrar, Straus, 1979.

Moore, Gene M., *Conrad on Film,* Cambridge University Press, 1998.

Morzinski, Mary, *Linguistic Influence of Polish on Joseph Conrad's Style,* East European Monographs (Boulder), 1994.

Moses, Michael Valdez, *The Novel and the Globalization of Culture,* Oxford University Press (New York City), 1995.

Murfin, Ross C., editor, *Conrad Revisited: Essays for the Eighties,* University of Alabama Press, 1985.

Najder, Zdzislaw, *Joseph Conrad: A Chronicle,* Rutgers University Press, 1983.

Najder, Zdzislaw, *Conrad in Perspective: Essays on Art and Fidelity,* Cambridge University Press, 1997.

Navarette, Susan J., *The Shape of Fear: Horror and the Fin de Siecle Culture of Decadence,* University Press of Kentucky, 1998.

North, Michael, *The Dialect of Modernism: Race, Language, and Twentieth-Century Literature,* Oxford University Press (New York City), 1994.

Pendleton, Robert, *Graham Greene's Conradian Masterplot: The Arabesques of Influence,* Macmillan (New York City), 1996.

Phillips, Gene D., *Conrad and Cinema: The Art of Adaptation,* P. Lang (New York City), 1995.

Stape, J. H., *The Cambridge Companion to Conrad,* Cambridge University Press (New York City), 1996.

Twentieth-Century Literary Criticism, Gale, Volume 1, 1978; Volume 6, 1982; Volume 13, 1984; Volume 25, 1988.

Wilson, Robert, *Joseph Conrad, Sources and Traditions,* Weir Press (Rogers, AR), 1995.

PERIODICALS

Bookman, May, 1896.
Choice, June, 1992, p. 1539.
Modern Fiction Studies, winter, 1989, p. 786; summer, 1992, p. 507.
Modern Language Review, January, 1990, p. 159.
New York Times Book Review, January 25, 1987.
Review of English Studies, May, 1990, p. 282; November, 1993, p. 606.

Sewanee Review, January, 1994, p. 171.
Times Literary Supplement, March 15, 1918; August 6, 1993, p. 22.
Washington Post Book World, March 1, 1992.
Yale Review, July, 1992, p. 205.

*   *   *

CONROY, (Donald) Pat(rick) 1945-

PERSONAL: Born October 26, 1945, in Atlanta, GA; son of Donald (a military officer) and Frances Dorothy "Peg" (Peek) Conroy; married Barbara Bolling, 1969 (divorced, 1977); married Lenore Gurewitz, March 21, 1981; children: (first marriage) Megan; Jessica, Melissa (stepdaughters); (second marriage) Susannah; Gregory, Emily (stepchildren). *Education:* The Citadel, B.A., 1967. *Politics:* Democrat.

ADDRESSES: Office—Old New York Book Shop, 1069 Juniper St. N.E., Atlanta, GA 30309. *Agent*—IMG-Bach Literary Agency, 22 E. 71 St., New York, NY 10021-4911.

CAREER: Writer. Worked as a high school teacher in Beaufort, SC, 1967-69, and as an elementary schoolteacher in Daufuskie, SC, 1969.

MEMBER: Authors Guild, Authors League of America, Writers Guild, PEN.

AWARDS, HONORS: Leadership Development grant, Ford Foundation, 1971; Anisfield-Wolf Award, Cleveland Foundation, 1972, for *The Water Is Wide*; National Endowment for the Arts award for achievement in education, 1974; Georgia Governor's Award for Arts, 1978; Lillian Smith Award for fiction, Southern Regional Council, 1981; *The Lords of Discipline* was nominated for the Robert Kennedy Book Award, Robert F. Kennedy Memorial, 1981; inducted into the South Carolina Hall of Fame, Academy of Authors, 1988; Thomas Cooper Society Literary Award, Thomas Cooper Library, University of South Carolina, 1995; South Carolina Governor's Award in the Humanities for Distinguished Achievement, South Carolina Humanities Council, 1996; Humanitarian Award, Georgia Commission on the Holocaust, 1996; The Lotos Medal of Merit in Recognition of Outstanding Literary Achievement, 1996.

WRITINGS:

The Boo, McClure Press (Verona, VA), 1970.
The Water Is Wide, Houghton (Boston), 1972.
The Great Santini, Houghton, 1976.
The Lords of Discipline, Houghton, 1980.
The Prince of Tides, Houghton, 1986.
Beach Music, Nan A. Talese/Doubleday (New York City), 1995.

Author of screenplay for television movie *Invictus,* 1988; also author with Becky Johnson of the Academy Award-nominated screenplay for the movie version of *The Prince of Tides.* Coauthor, with Doug Marlett, of the screenplay *Ex.*

MEDIA ADAPTATIONS: The film *Conrack,* based on *The Water Is Wide,* was produced by Twentieth-Century Fox in 1974; the musical *Conrack* was adapted for the stage by Granville Burgess, and was first produced off-off Broadway at AMAS Repertory Theater, November, 1987; *The Great Santini* was produced by Warner Brothers in 1979; *The Lords of Discipline* was produced by Paramount in 1983; Barbra Streisand produced, directed, and starred in *The Prince of Tides,* a motion picture released in 1991.

SIDELIGHTS: Best-selling novelist Pat Conroy has worked some of his bitterest experiences into stories that present ironic, often jarring, yet humorous views of life and relationships in the contemporary South. Garry Abrams in the *Los Angeles Times* reports that "misfortune has been good to novelist Pat Conroy. It gave him a family of disciplinarians, misfits, eccentrics, liars and loudmouths. It gave him a Southern childhood in which the bizarre competed with the merely strange. It gave him a military school education apparently imported from Sparta by way of Prussia. It gave him a divorce and a breakdown followed by intensive therapy. It gave him everything he needed to write best sellers, make millions and live in Rome." Brigitte Weeks touches on Conroy's appeal in the *Washington Post*: "With his feet set firmly on his native earth, Conroy is, above all, a storyteller. His tales are full of the exaggeration and wild humor of stories told around a camp fire."

Conroy's first work to receive national attention was openly autobiographical. After graduation, Conroy taught English in public high schools, but unsatisfied, he looked for a new challenge. When a desired position in the Peace Corps did not surface, he took a job teaching nearly illiterate black children on Daufuskie Island, a small, isolated area off the South Carolina coast. But he was not prepared for his new students. They did not know the name of their country, that they lived on the Atlantic Ocean, or that the world was round. On the other hand, Conroy found his pupils expected him to know how to set a trap, skin a muskrat, and plant okra.

Conroy came to enjoy his unusual class, but eventually his unorthodox teaching methods, such as his unwillingness to allow corporal punishment of his students, and disregard for the school's administration turned numerous school officials against him and cost him his job. As a way of coping with his fury at the dismissal, Conroy wrote *The Water Is Wide,* an account of his experiences. The process of writing did more than cool him down however; he also gained a new perspective on his reasons for choosing Daufuskie (Yamacraw Island in the book) and on his own responses to racism. Anatole Broyard describes Conroy in the *New York Times Book Review* as "a former redneck and self-proclaimed racist, [who] brought to Yamacraw the supererogatory fervor of the recently converted."

After the successful publication of *The Water Is Wide,* Conroy began writing full-time. Although his following book, *The Great Santini,* was a novel, many critics think it represents his adolescence. An article in the *Virginia Quarterly Review* states that "the dialogue, anecdotes, and family atmosphere are pure Marine and probably autobiographical." Conroy did draw heavily on his family background to write the story of a tough Marine, Bull Meecham, his long-suffering wife, Lillian, and the eldest son Ben, who is striving for independence outside his father's control. Robert E. Burkholder writes in *Critique: Studies in Modern Fiction* that *The Great Santini* "is a curious blend of lurid reality and fantastic comedy, which deals with approximately one year in the life of Ben Meecham and his family. It is primarily a novel of initiation, but central to the concept of Ben's initiation into manhood and to the meaning of the whole novel is the idea that individual myths must be stripped away from Ben and the other major characters before Ben can approach reality with objectivity and maturity."

Bull Meecham is modeled on Conroy's father, Colonel Donald Conroy, who "would make John Wayne look like a pansy," as Conroy told Bill McDonald for the South Carolina *State.* Conroy reports that his father initially disliked *The Great Santini.* The author tells *Chicago Tribune* contributor Peer Gorner that "Dad could only read the book halfway through before throwing it across the room. Then people started telling him he actually was lovable. Now, he signs Christmas cards *The Great Santini,* and goes around talking about childrearing and how we need to have more discipline in the home—a sort of Nazi Dr. Spock." The movie created from the novel helped to change the Colonel's attitude. *The Great Santini* starred Robert Duvall, and the Colonel liked the way "his" character came across.

Another period of Conroy's life appeared in his next book, *The Lords of Discipline.* According to his father's wishes, Conroy attended the Citadel, South Carolina's venerable military academy. "Quirky, eccentric, and unforgettable," Conroy describes the academy in the preface to *The Boo,* his first book, which gave a nostalgic look at the Citadel and its Commander of Cadets during the 1960s. But Willingham describes the Citadel in another way: "It is also an anachronism of the 1960s with a general disregard for the existence of the outside world." *The Lords of Discipline* paints an even bleaker picture of its fictionalized institution, the Carolina Military Institute. This school, says Frank Rose in the *Washington Post Book World,* "combines some of the more quaint and murderous aspects of the Citadel, West Point, and Virginia Military Institute."

The Lords of Discipline concerns Will, the narrator, and his three roommates. Will is a senior cadet assigned to watch over the Institute's first black student. The novel's tension lies in the conflict between group loyalty and personal responsibility. Will eventually discovers the Ten, "a secret mafia whose existence has long been rumored but never proven, a silent and malevolent force dedicated . . . to maintain the purity of the Institute—racial purity included," comments Rose. He continues, "What Conroy has achieved is twofold; his book is at once a suspense-ridden duel between conflicting ideals of manhood and a paean to brother love that ends in betrayal and death. Out of the shards of broken friendship a blunted triumph emerges, and it is here, when the duel is won, that the reader finally comprehends the terrible price that any form of manhood can exact."

Conroy's wildest tale is *The Prince of Tides,* which follows Tom Wingo, an unemployed high school English teacher and football coach on a journey from coastal South Carolina to New York City to help his twin sister Savannah. Savannah, a well-known poet, is recovering from a nervous breakdown and suicide attempt. In an attempt to help Savannah's psychiatrist understand her patient, Tom relates the Wingo family's bizarre history. Despite the horrors the Wingos have suffered, including several rapes and the death of their brother, a sense of optimism prevails. Writes Judy Bass in Chicago *Tribune Books,* "Pat Conroy has fashioned a brilliant novel that ultimately affirms life, hope and the belief that one's future need not be contaminated by a monstrous past. In addition, Conroy . . . deals with the most prostrating crises in human experience—death of a loved one, parental brutality, injustice, insanity—without lapsing into pedantry or oppressive gloom."

The Prince of Tides's style drew more attention than that of Conroy's other books. Some critics felt the novel was overblown: Richard Eder in the *Los Angeles Times Book Review* claims that "inflation is the order of the day. The characters do too much, feel too much, suffer too much, eat too much, signify too much, and above all, talk too much. And, as with the classical American tomato, quantity is at the expense of quality." Gail Godwin in the

New York Times Book Review says that while "the ambition, invention and sheer irony in this book are admirable . . . , many readers will be put off by the turgid, high-flown rhetoric that the author must have decided would best match his grandiose designs. And as the bizarre, hyperbolic episodes of Wingo family life mount up, other readers are likely to feel they are being bombarded by whoppers told by an overwrought boy eager to impress or shock."

In his long-awaited next novel, *Beach Music,* Conroy continues to mine his personal and family experience for the characters, events, and themes of his fiction. He weaves into this novel the difficulties of family relationships, the pain of a mother's death, changing friendships, and the personal impact of global events such as the Holocaust, Vietnam, and present-day terrorism. What Conroy creates is a story of family, betrayal, and place. As Don Paul writes in the *San Francisco Review of Books,* "In *Beach Music* Pat Conroy takes the theme of betrayal and fashions from it a story rambling and uneven and, like the family it portrays, erratic and flawed and magnificent. South Carolina overflows from his pages, sentimental and unforgiving, soft as sleepy pears and hard as turtle shells."

Beach Music is the story of Jack McCall. After his wife commits suicide, McCall leaves South Carolina and takes his young daughter to Italy to escape his memories and his strained relationships with his own and his wife's family. He returns to South Carolina when his mother becomes ill with leukemia. There, he finds himself caught up in the lives and intrigues of family and close friends. McCall and his friends are forced by current events to revisit the Vietnam era in their small South Carolina community. Some joined the military, some joined the anti-war movement, and some struggled with both. But, as Paul explains, "Central to the plot is the betrayal of the anti-war movement by a friend who turns out to be an FBI informer." The effect of this act continue to ripple into the novel's present.

Because of the autobiographical nature of Conroy's work, his family often judges his novels more harshly than do reviewers. Although Conroy's mother is the inspiration for shrimper's wife Lila Wingo in *The Prince of Tides,* she died before he finished the novel and never read it. Conroy's sister, who did see the book, was offended. As Conroy told Rick Groen for the Toronto *Globe and Mail,* "Yes, my sister is also a poet in New York who has also had serious breakdowns. We were very close, but she has not spoken to me . . . since the book. I'm saddened, but when you write autobiography, this is one of the consequences. They're allowed to be mad at you. They have the right." This, however, was not the first time a family member reacted negatively to one of Conroy's books. *The Great Santini* infuriated his Chicago relatives: "My grandmother and grandfather told me they never wanted to see me or my children again," Conroy told Sam Staggs for *Publishers Weekly.* Conroy's Southern relatives have also responded to the sex scenes and "immodest" language in his books. Staggs relates, "After *The Lords of Discipline* was published, Conroy's Aunt Helen telephoned him and said, 'Pat, I hope someday you'll write a book a Christian can read.' 'How far did you get?' her nephew asked. 'Page four, and I declare, I've never been so embarrassed.'" Perhaps the most sobering moment for Conroy's autobiographical impulse was when a tragic event from his writing came true. In early manuscripts of *Beach Music,* Conroy had included a scene where one of the characters, based on one of his younger brothers, Tom, committed suicide. Tom Conroy, a paranoid schizophrenic, committed suicide in August of 1994. Devastated, Pat removed the scene from *Beach Music.*

BIOGRAPHICAL/CRITICAL SOURCES:

BOOKS

Burns, Landon, *Pat Conroy: A Critical Companion,* Greenwood, 1996.

PERIODICALS

Atlanta Journal-Constitution, March 27, 1988, p. J1.
Book-of-the-Month Club News, December, 1986.
Chicago Tribune, November 25, 1986.
Chicago Tribune Book World, October 19, 1980; September 14, 1986; October 19, 1986.
Cincinnati Enquirer, March 25, 1974.
Critique: Studies in Modern Fiction, Volume 21, number 1, 1979.
Detroit Free Press, July 9, 1995, p. 7G.
Detroit News, October 12, 1986; December 20, 1987.
Globe and Mail (Toronto), February 28, 1987; November 28, 1987.
Los Angeles Times, February 19, 1983; October 12, 1986; October 19, 1986; December 12, 1986.
Los Angeles Times Book Review, October 19, 1986, p. 3.
New York Times, January 10, 1987.
New York Times Book Review, July 13, 1972; September 24, 1972; December 7, 1980; October 12, 1986, p. 14.
Oregonian, April 28, 1974.
People, February 2, 1981, p. 67.
Publishers Weekly, May 15, 1972; September 5, 1986; May 8, 1995, p. 286; July 10, 1995, p. 16; July 31, 1995, p. 17.
San Francisco Review of Books, July-August, 1995, p. 24.
State (Columbia, South Carolina), March 31, 1974.
Time, October 13, 1986, p. 97; June 26, 1995, p. 77.
Tribune Books (Chicago), September 14, 1986, p. 23; October 19, 1986, p. 3; January 3, 1988, p. 3.
Vanity Fair, July, 1995, p. 108.
Virginia Quarterly Review, autumn, 1976.
Washington Post, October 23, 1980; March 9, 1992, p. B3.
Washington Post Book World, October 19, 1980; October 12, 1986.

*　　*　　*

CONYBEARE, Charles Augustus
  See ELIOT, T(homas) S(tearns)

*　　*　　*

COOK, Roy
  See SILVERBERG, Robert

*　　*　　*

COOKE, John Estes
  See BAUM, L(yman) Frank

*　　*　　*

COOKSON, Catherine (McMullen) 1906-
  (Catherine Marchant)

PERSONAL: Born June 20, 1906, in Tyne Dock, South Shields, England; mother's name, Catherine Fawcett; married Thomas H. Cookson (a schoolmaster), June 1, 1940.

ADDRESSES: Home—Bristol Lodge, Langley on Tyne, Northumberland, England. *Agent*—Anthony Sheil Associates Ltd., 43 Doughty St., London WC1N 2LF, England.

CAREER: Writer. Lecturer for women's groups and other organizations.

MEMBER: Society of Authors, PEN (England), Authors Guild (U.S.A.), Authors League of America, Women's Press Club (London).

AWARDS, HONORS: Winifred Holtby Award for best regional novel from Royal Society of Literature, 1968, for *The Round Tower*; Order of the British Empire, 1985; recipient of Freedom of the County Borough of South Shields in recognition of her services to the city; honorary Master's and Doctorate degrees from the University of Newcastle, England, 1983.

WRITINGS:

Kate Hannigan, Macdonald & Co., 1950.
Fifteen Streets (also see below), Macdonald & Co., 1952.
Colour Blind, Macdonald & Co., 1953, published as *Color Blind,* New American Library, 1977.
Maggie Rowan, Macdonald & Co., 1954, New American Library, 1975.
Rooney, Macdonald & Co., 1957.
The Menagerie, Macdonald & Co., 1958.
Slinky Jane, Macdonald & Co., 1959.
Fenwick Houses, Macdonald & Co., 1960.
The Garment, Macdonald & Co., 1962, New American Library, 1974.
The Blind Miller (also see below), Macdonald & Co., 1963.
Hannah Massey, Macdonald & Co., 1964, New American Library, 1973.
The Long Corridor, Macdonald & Co., 1965, New American Library, 1976.
The Unbaited Trap, Macdonald & Co., 1966, New American Library, 1974.
Katie Mulholland, Macdonald & Co., 1967.
The Round Tower (also see below), Macdonald & Co., 1968, New American Library, 1975.
The Nice Bloke, Macdonald & Co., 1969, published as *The Husband,* New American Library, 1976.
Our Kate: An Autobiography, Macdonald & Co., 1969, Bobbs-Merrill, 1971, published as *Our Kate: Catherine Cookson—Her Personal Story,* Macdonald & Jane's, 1974.
The Glass Virgin, Macdonald & Co., 1970, Bantam, 1981.
The Invitation, Macdonald & Co., 1970, New American Library, 1974.
The Dwelling Place, Macdonald & Jane's, 1971.
Fanny McBride, Corgi Books, 1971.
Feathers in the Fire (also see below), Macdonald & Co., 1971, Bobbs-Merrill, 1972.
Pure as the Lily, Macdonald & Co., 1972, Bobbs-Merrill, 1973.
The Invisible Cord (also see below), Dutton, 1975.
The Gambling Man (also see below), Morrow, 1975.
The Tide of Life, Morrow, 1976.
The Girl (also see below), Morrow, 1977.
The Cinder Path (also see below), Morrow, 1978.
Tilly Trotter, Heinemann, 1978, published as *Tilly,* Morrow, 1980.
Selected Works, Heinemann/Octopus, Volume 1 (contains *Fifteen Streets, The Blind Miller, The Round Tower, Feathers in the Fire,* and *A Grand Man* [also see below]), 1978; Volume 2 (contains *The Mallen Streak* [also see below], *The Invisible*

Cord, The Gambling Man, The Girl, and *The Cinder Path*), 1980.
The Man Who Cried, Morrow, 1979.
Tilly Wed, Morrow, 1981 (published in England as *Tilly Trotter Wed,* Heinemann, 1981).
Tilly Alone, Morrow, 1982 (published in England as *Tilly Widowed,* Heinemann, 1982).
The Whip, Summit Books, 1982.
Hamilton (comic), Heinemann, 1983.
The Black Velvet Gown, Summit Books, 1984.
Goodbye Hamilton, Heinemann, 1984.
The Bannaman Legacy, Summit Books, 1985 (published in England as *A Dinner of Herbs,* Heinemann, 1985).
Harold, Heinemann, 1985.
The Moth, Summit Books, 1986, also published as *The Thorman Inheritance: A Novel,* Summit Books, 1986.
Bill Bailey, Heinemann, 1986.
Catherine Cookson Country, Heinemann, 1986.
The Parson's Daughter, Summit Books, 1987.
The Baily Chronicles, Summit Books, 1988.
The Harrogate Secret, Summit Books, 1988.
Let Me Make Myself Plain, Bantam, 1988.
The Black Candle: A Novel, Summit Books, 1989.
The Spaniard's Gift: A Novel, Summit Books, 1989.
The Gillyvors, Bantam, 1990.
The Wingless Bird, Summit, 1990.
Bill Bailey's Lot, G. K. Hall (Boston), 1990.
Bill Bailey's Daughter, G. K. Hall, 1990.
The Love Child: A Novel, Summit Books, 1990.
My Beloved Son, Bantam, 1991.
The Iron Facade, Bantam, 1991.
The Rag Nymph, Bantam, 1991.
The House of Women, Bantam, 1992.
The Maltese Angel: A Novel, Simon & Schuster, 1992.
The Forester Girl: A Novel, Simon & Schuster, 1993.
The Golden Straw: A Novel, Simon & Schuster, 1993.
The Year of the Virgins: A Novel, Simon & Schuster, 1993.
Justice Is a Woman, Bantam, 1995.
The Obsession, Bantam, 1995.
Plainer Still: A New Personal Anthology, Bantam, 1995.
A Ruthless Need, Bantam, 1995.
Three Complete Novels (includes *The Love Child, The Maltese Angel,* and *The Year of the Virgins*), Wings (New York City), 1996.
Tinker's Girl, Bantam, 1996.
The Upstart, Bantam, 1996.

"MARY ANN" SERIES

A Grand Man, Macdonald & Co., 1954.
The Lord and Mary Ann, Macdonald & Co., 1956, Morrow, 1975.
The Devil and Mary Ann, Macdonald & Co., 1958, Morrow, 1976.
Love and Mary Ann, Macdonald & Co., 1961, Morrow, 1976.
Life and Mary Ann, Macdonald & Co., 1962, Morrow, 1977.
Marriage and Mary Ann, Macdonald & Co., 1964, Morrow, 1978.
Mary Ann's Angels, Macdonald & Co., 1965, Morrow, 1978.
Mary Ann and Bill, Macdonald & Co., 1966, MOrrow, 1979.
Mary Ann Omnibus (contains all novels in "Mary Ann" series), Macdonald & Jane's, 1981.

"MALLEN NOVELS" TRILOGY

The Mallen Streak (also see below), Heinemann, 1973.
The Mallen Girl (also see below), Heinemann, 1974.
The Mallen Lot, Dutton, 1974, published in England as *The Mallen Litter* (also see below), Heinemann, 1974.

The Mallen Novels (contains *The Mallen Streak, The Mallen Girl,* and *The Mallen Litter*), Heinemann, 1979.

JUVENILE NOVELS

Matty Doolin, Macdonald & Co., 1965, New American Library, 1976.
Joe and the Gladiator, Macdonald & Co., 1968.
The Nipper, Bobbs-Merrill, 1970.
Blue Baccy, Macdonald & Jane's, 1972, Bobbs-Merrill, 1973.
Our John Willie, Morrow, 1974.
Mrs. Flanagan's Trumpet, Macdonald & Jane's, 1977, Lothrop, 1980.
Go Tell It to Mrs. Golightly, Macdonald & Jane's, 1977, Lothrop, 1980.
Lanky Jones, Lothrop, 1981.

UNDER PSEUDONYM CATHERINE MARCHANT

Heritage of Folly, Macdonald & Co., 1963.
The Fen Tiger, Macdonald & Co., 1963, Morrow, 1979.
House of Men, Macdonald & Co., 1964, Macdonald & Jane's, 1980.
Evil at Roger's Cross, Lancer Books, 1965, revised edition published as *The Iron Facade,* Heinemann, 1976, Morrow, 1980.
Miss Martha Mary Crawford, Heinemann, 1975, Morrow, 1976.
The Slow Awakening, Heinemann, 1976, Morrow, 1977.

Other titles include: *The Cultured Handmaiden,* 1988, and the children's books *Rory's Fortune, Nancy Nutall and the Mongrel,* and *Bill and the Mary Ann Shaughnessy.*

SIDELIGHTS: Catherine Cookson is a prolific British author with a large following. Her family sagas, for which she is most noted, are read in some thirty countries. A frequent name on the bestseller list, in the early 1980s Cookson was commemorated by Corgi Books for exceeding the 27 million mark in paperback sales alone. According to Anne Duchene in the *Times Literary Supplement,* "these days there are never fewer than fifty Cookson titles in print in English at any time; they are translated into fifteen languages; and new books are still readily produced." In a London *Times* interview with Caroline Moorehead, Cookson emphasizes that she never has trouble coming up with ideas for her historical novels: "I've always been a jabberer. I just talked. I see everything in images. The plot sort of unfolds. Even the dialogue. In the morning, it's all there to put down." As Duchene observes: "[Cookson] writes stories in which her readers can gratefully recognize experiences and emotions of their own—heightened, to be sure, by greater comedy or greater violence than their own lives normally vouchsafe, but based on all their own affections, furies, aspirations and reactions."

Born the illegitimate daughter of an alcoholic mother, Cookson lived with her mother in her grandparents' strict, Catholic household during most of her childhood. By the age of eighteen, Cookson had been working as a laundry checker, although she longed for an education. Cookson's success in overcoming her disadvantaged childhood, critics note, is one source of her broad appeal. Anita Brookner of *Observer* comments: "[Cookson] brings comfort to millions and one can see the reason why: she represents the strong woman of various mythologies, a Mother Courage with no children but [more than 57] titles. She is an entirely remarkable person." Published in 1969, Cookson's autobiography *Our Kate* documented the difficulties she experienced during her childhood, and became a popular and critical success. A later autobiographical work, *Let Me Make Myself*

Plain, presents essays, poetry, and paintings, each of which draw upon the author's personal reflections and experiences.

Cookson's experience of life in the working-class, industrial environment of Tyneside has also provided material for her numerous novels. Autobiographical elements strongly inform the narrative of *The Love Child,* for example, which portrays a nineteenth-century girl who is tormented by the hostility of villagers and the disapproval of the church pastor due to her illegitimate status. An example of Cookson's use of the "family saga" form, *The House of Women,* focuses on four generations of women living in the same house in Tyneside and chronicles their experience of hypochondria, an unhappy marriage, and teenaged pregnancy, among other trials. Along with their treatment of northern English settings and British class structures, Cookson's novels are noted for their portrayal of appealing female characters. *The Wingless Bird,* for instance, depicts Agnes Conway, the daughter of an English shop-keeper, who must choose between an unhappy marriage or spinsterhood. Her life changes unexpectedly, however, when she falls in love with an upper-class man and subsequently finds the courage and the means to escape her family's oppressive treatment.

The character Mary Ann Shaughnessy has reappeared in eight of Cookson's novels, which have been published together in a single volume titled *The Mary Ann Omnibus.* Mary Ann is eight years old in *A Grand Man,* the first novel of the series, and the twenty-seven-year-old mother of twins in *Mary Ann and Bill,* the final story. "In the earlier books Mary Ann bounces through her own and other people's lives like a cross between a deus (or dea) ex machina and a gremlin, interfering in situations and people with blithe impartiality, generally for the benefit of her beloved, drunken father Mike Shaughnessy," notes Judith Rhodes in *Romance and Historical Writers.* "Few of Cookson's other novels demonstrate her capacity for comedy as this series does; not only does Mary Ann herself create a number of amusing situations, but her grannie McMullen . . . is a wonderful comic character."

Cookson is also well-established as an author of children's books, several of which draw upon historical and autobiographical themes. Set in England during the 1850s, her juvenile novel *Our John Willie,* for example, portrays two brothers who manage to survive poverty and exploitation at the hands of mine-owners. While some objected to the extreme sentimentality of the story, others commented favorably on Cookson's treatment of her historical subject. Like many of her novels for adults, Cookson's children's stories often draw upon her experience of the English community of Tyneside. *Joe and the Gladiator,* for example, is set in the Tyneside shipyards and depicts a hard-working young man who is plagued with financial and family problems that grow worse when an elderly man dies, leaving an old horse in Joe's care.

BIOGRAPHICAL/CRITICAL SOURCES:

PERIODICALS

Booklist, February 1, 1984, p. 769; January 15, 1991, p. 979; September 1, 1991, p. 28; November 1, 1992, p. 466.
Books, November, 1990; July 1991, p. 10.
Catholic World, June, 1955.
Chicago Tribune, November 27, 1994, p. 9.
Kirkus Reviews, August 1, 1969, p. 793; May 15, 1978, p. 562; February 1, 1981, p. 140; October 1, 1992, p. 1203; October 1, 1993, p. 1219; September 1, 1994, p. 1148; February 1, 1995, p. 86.
Kliatt, September, 1990, p. 6.

Library Journal, June 1, 1975, p. 1152; May 15, 1985, p. 78; March 15, 1987, p. 400; April 15, 1987, p. 96; April 15, 1990, p. 141; September 1, 1991; October 1, 1994, pp. 112, 228.

London Review of Books, June 27, 1991, p. 22.

New York Times, January 7, 1955.

New York Times Book Review, October 20, 1974, p. 41; April 2, 1984, p. 25; June 30, 1985, p. 20.

Observer, April 1, 1984; November 27, 1988.

Publishers Weekly, July 21, 1969, p. 53; November 17, 1975, p. 95; August 16, 1976, p. 118; March 22, 1985, p. 51; March 28, 1986, p. 52; March 27, 1987, p. 37; February 10, 1989, p. 53; March 16, 1990, p. 60; January 25, 1991, p. 48; August 9, 1991, p. 44; October 12, 1992, p. 64; October 11, 1993, p. 70; October 3, 1994, p. 52; February 20, 1995, p. 195.

School Library Journal, August, 1990, p. 174.

Spectator, July 6, 1991, p. 26; October 12, 1991, p. 39.

Times (London), August 15, 1983.

Times Literary Supplement, January 7, 1955; June 6, 1968; June 19, 1969; March 29, 1974; July 24, 1981, p. 830.

Washington Post Book World, April 1, 1990.

*   *   *

COOPER, Susan (Mary) 1935-

PERSONAL: Born May 23, 1935, in Burnham, Buckinghamshire, England; came to United States in 1963; daughter of John Richard and Ethel May (Field) Cooper; married Nicholas J. Grant, August 3, 1963 (divorced, 1983); children: Jonathan, Katharine; stepchildren: Anne, Bill (died, 1986), Peter. *Education:* Somerville College, Oxford, M.A., 1956. *Avocational interests:* Music, islands.

ADDRESSES: Office—c/o Margaret J. McElderry, Macmillan, 866 Third Ave., New York, NY 10022.

CAREER: Writer. *Sunday Times,* London, England, reporter and feature writer, 1956-63.

MEMBER: Society of Authors (United Kingdom), Authors League of America, Authors Guild, Writers Guild of America.

AWARDS, HONORS: Horn Book Honor List citation for *Over Sea, under Stone; Horn Book* Honor List and American Library Association Notable Book citations, both 1970, both for *Dawn of Fear; Boston Globe-Horn Book* award, American Library Association Notable Book citation, Carnegie Medal runner-up, all 1973, and Newbery Award Honor Book, 1974, all for *The Dark Is Rising;* American Library Notable Book citation, for *Greenwitch; Horn Book* Honor List and American Library Association Notable Book citation, Newbery Medal, Tir na N'og Award (Wales), and commendation for Carnegie Medal, all 1976, for *The Grey King;* Tir na N'og Award for *Silver on the Tree;* Christopher Award, Humanitas Prize, Writers Guild of America Award, and Emmy Award nomination from Academy of Television Arts and Sciences, all 1984, all for *The Dollmaker;* Emmy Award nomination, 1987, and Writers Guild of America Award, 1988, for teleplay *Foxfire; Horn Book* Honor List citation, 1987, for *The Selkie Girl;* B'nai B'rith Janusz Korczak Award, 1989, for *Seaward.*

WRITINGS:

"THE DARK IS RISING" SEQUENCE; JUVENILE NOVELS

Over Sea, under Stone, illustrated by Margery Gill, J. Cape, 1965, Harcourt, 1966.

The Dark Is Rising, illustrated by Alan E. Cober, Atheneum, 1973.

Greenwitch, Atheneum, 1974.

The Grey King, illustrated by Michael Heslop, Atheneum, 1975.

Silver on the Tree, Chatto & Windus (London), 1975, Atheneum, 1977.

OTHER

(Contributor) Michael Sissons and Philip French, editors, *The Age of Austerity: 1945-51,* Hodder & Stoughton (London), 1963, Penguin (New York City), 1965.

Mandrake (science-fiction novel), J. Cape (London), 1964, Penguin, 1966.

Behind the Golden Curtain: A View of the U.S.A. (Book Society Alternative Choice), Hodder & Stoughton, 1965, Scribner (New York City), 1966.

(Editor and author of preface) J. B. Priestley, *Essays of Five Decades,* Little, Brown (Boston), 1968.

J. B. Priestley: Portrait of an Author, Heinemann (London), 1970, Harper (New York City), 1971.

Dawn of Fear, illustrated by Margery Gill, Harcourt (New York City), 1970.

Jethro and the Jumbie, illustrated by Ashley Bryan, Atheneum (New York City), 1979.

(With Hume Cronyn) *Foxfire* (play), first produced at Stratford, Ontario, 1980; produced on Broadway at Ethel Barrymore Theatre, November 11, 1982 (also see below), Samuel French (New York City), 1983.

(Reteller) *The Silver Cow: A Welsh Tale,* illustrated by Warwick Hutton, Atheneum, 1983.

Seaward, Atheneum, 1983.

(With Cronyn) *The Dollmaker* (teleplay) adaptation of novel of the same title by Harriette Arnow, produced by American Broadcasting Companies, Inc. (ABC), May 13, 1984.

(Author of introduction) John and Nancy Langstaff, editors, *The Christmas Revels Songbook: In Celebration of the Winter Solstice,* David R. Godine (Boston), 1985.

(Reteller) *The Selkie Girl,* illustrated by Warwick Hutton, Margaret McElderry Books/Macmillan (New York City), 1986.

Foxfire (teleplay), produced by Columbia Broadcasting System, Inc. (CBS), December 13, 1987.

Tam Lin, illustrated by Warwick Hutton, Margaret McElderry Books/Macmillan, 1991.

Matthew's Dragon, illustrated by Jos. A. Smith, Margaret McElderry Books/Macmillan, 1991.

The Boggart, Margaret McElderry Books/Macmillan, 1993.

Dreams and Wishes: Essays on Writing for Children, Margaret McElderry Books/Macmillan, 1996.

Also author of teleplay *Dark Encounter,* 1976; author of teleplay version of Anne Tyler's novel *Dinner at the Homesick Restaurant.* Cooper's manuscripts are held in the Lillian H. Smith collection, Toronto Public Library, Toronto, Ontario, Canada.

MEDIA ADAPTATIONS: The Dark Is Rising (two-cassette recording), Miller-Brody, 1979; *The Silver Cow* (filmstrip), Weston Woods, 1985; *The Silver Cow* (recording), Weston Woods, 1986.

SIDELIGHTS: "Susan Cooper is one of the small and very select company of writers who—somehow, somewhere—have been touched by magic; the gift of creation is theirs, the power to bring to life for ordinary mortals 'the best of symbolic high fantasy,'" cites Margaret K. McElderry in *Horn Book Magazine.* In her works for children, Cooper mixes elements of her own life with myth, legend, and folklore from the Caribbean, Wales, and the English countryside where she grew up. "Music and song, old tales and legends, prose and poetry, theater and reality, imagination and intellect, power and control, a strong sense of place and people both past and present—all are part of the magic that has touched Susan Cooper," McElderry states. "Her journeys add great luster to the world of literature."

Over Sea, under Stone traces the adventures of three English siblings—Simon, Jane, and Barnabas Drew—who discover in the attic of their old Cornish vacation home a clue to an ancient hidden treasure endowed with mystic powers against the Dark, an evil force that has warred with its counterpart, the Light, throughout history. With the help of Merriman Lyon, a college professor and family friend who is in fact a strong agent of the Light, the three Drews recover the treasure and defeat the forces of the Dark. The story, published in 1965, eventually became the first part of a quintet called "The Dark Is Rising," a series of fantasy novels based in part on Arthurian legend. "My sequence belongs to the vanished rural Buckinghamshire in which I lived my first eighteen years; to the Cornwall of childhood holidays; to the part of North Wales in which my grandmother was born and my parents lived their last twenty-five years," Cooper writes in her publicity release. "Haunted places all, true springs of the Matter of Britain. Bronze Age barrows littered our landscapes; Celt and Anglo-Saxon merged in our faces; Arthur filled our daydreams, the Welsh legends our darker dreams at night."

Cooper published several more books—a biography of her personal friend, the British writer J. B. Priestley, and *Dawn of Fear,* a fictionalized account of her childhood war experiences— and married an American college professor and moved to the United States before she continued the quintet. The second volume, *The Dark Is Rising*—a Newbery Honor Book in 1974—is the story of Will Stanton, youngest son of a Buckinghamshire family, who awakes one morning shortly before the winter solstice to discover that he is no longer entirely human. He is the last of the Old Ones, the agents of the Light, and he is coming into his power. Merriman Lyon, of *Over Sea, under Stone,* reappears in *The Dark Is Rising* as Will's tutor, and he, with the help of the other Old Ones, struggles to prevent the Dark from overwhelming Will as Will learns to control his new powers. *Dictionary of Literary Biography* contributor Joel D. Chaston finds *The Dark Is Rising* "a powerful book" that "contains some of the most suspenseful moments in the series." He continues that "the reader is drawn into an intense struggle between good and evil that never lets up."

Greenwitch, the third volume of the sequence, brings the Drews and Will to Cornwall. The treasure the Drews had uncovered in *Over Sea, under Stone* has been stolen by an agent of the Dark, and Will, Merriman, and the three children work together to recover it. *The Grey King,* Cooper's Newbery Award-winning fourth volume, takes Will to Wales, where he discovers Bran Davies, the Pendragon—the lost heir of Arthur—and combats the evil mountain spirit called the Grey King. In the final volume, *Silver on the Tree,* Will, Bran, and the Drews unite to combat the final rising of the Dark. "The underlying theme of my 'Dark Is Rising' sequence, and particularly of its fourth volume *The Grey King,*" Cooper explained in her Newbery acceptance speech, reprinted in *Horn Book Magazine,* "is, I suppose, the ancient problem of the duality of human nature. The endless coexistence of kindness and cruelty, love and hate, forgiveness and revenge—

as inescapable as the cycle of life and death, day and night, the Light and the Dark."

Since completing the "Dark Is Rising" sequence, Cooper has begun working in other genres. "All my life," she writes in *Horn Book,* "I had been rooted in libraries, both as a reader of other people's books and writer of my own. All my life I had been stagestruck, haunted by the theater. Within a year of finishing *Silver on the Tree,* and my sequence of novels," she continues, she had begun working on stage pieces, including a play called *Foxfire,* coauthored with Hume Cronyn, that played on Broadway with Cronyn and his wife Jessica Tandy in the lead roles. Later Cooper wrote a television adaptation of Harriette Arnow's novel *The Dollmaker,* which was presented on ABC in 1984. Jane Fonda played the lead role and was awarded an Emmy for her performance.

In addition to her stage works, Cooper has continued to publish fantasy stories for children and young adults. *Jethro and the Jumbie* is the story of an encounter between a young boy and a ghost, set in the West Indies, where Cooper and her husband had a vacation home. *Seaward,* a young adult novel, was written just after Cooper's parents died and her marriage broke up, and intertwines themes of love, life, death, and hate. Cally and Westerly are two young people who have lost their parents and are thrown into an ambiguous myth-haunted other world. *Seaward* reintroduces the dualism theme that predominates in the "Dark Is Rising" novels, showing how Cally and Westerly are manipulated by the Old Gods in their journey together. Joel D. Chaston observes that "*Seaward,* although not as popular as the Dark is Rising series, has been praised by critics who describe it as dreamlike, allegorical, and poignant." And Paul Heins concludes in a *Horn Book* review that in this book, Cooper "has endowed the concept of human responsibility—of human choice—with the face of fantasy."

Cooper followed *Seaward* with a series of folktales retold. In the first, *The Silver Cow: A Welsh Tale,* the magic cow of the title appears to a Welsh lad, Huw, forced by his father to tend the herd while other children are at school. Huw's father rejects the idea that the cow has been sent by the magic people of the Welsh countryside, but he reaps the benefits of the cow's abundant milk. The father grows rich because of the cow, but he shows it no mercy when it ages and he plans to slaughter it. When the cow disappears with her calves, so does the father's money. In the second folktale, Cooper draws upon the selkie legends. Selkies are seals that can transform themselves into humans. *The Selkie Girl* tells the tale of a man who falls in love with a selkie. In order to marry her, he hides her sealskin, robbing her of her ability to return to the sea and to her seal babies. In her human form, the selkie has human children, one of whom tells her where to find her sealskin. She returns to the sea but continues to protect her human family. In *Tam Lin,* Cooper brings a modern sensibility to a Scottish folk ballad. Margaret, a young princess, goes in search of adventure and a man to share it with. She finds the Elfin knight Tam Lin and finds herself in a struggle to save him from the Elfin queen. All three books earned praise for Cooper's poetic language and her ability to bring old tales to a modern audience; they were also praised for the watercolors of English illustrator Warwick Hutton.

In 1993, Cooper published *The Boggart,* a story for children that brings together an ancient spirit from the Scottish highlands and a thoroughly modern family living in Toronto. After inheriting a decaying Scottish castle that they cannot afford to keep, the

Volnik family sells the estate but brings some of the antiques home with them. Hidden in the antiques is a boggart, an ancient trickster now transported into the twentieth century. "In Cooper's hands," writes Michelle Landsberg in the *Washington Post Book World,* "those ancient forces sweep into the lives of the Volnik family to create alarming chaos, as well as dazzling enchantment." For *New York Times Book Review* contributor Rafael Yglesias, *The Boggart* demonstrates Cooper's "gift for rubbing fantasy and reality together, to make storytelling fire." But as Landsberg points out, the author does more than tell a fine story here. She manages to infect the reader with the plausibility of boggarts. "One of the delights of this novel," writes Landsberg, "is the way it teases the reader with a Boggarty explanation for all the maddening bewitchments of daily life." Landsberg also notes that the boggart allows Cooper to make some humorous observations about modern culture. "The flip side of the fun is the way the Boggart reacts to urban North America. With goggle-eyed glee, he discovers pizza, peanut butter and infinite varieties of ice cream." Yglesias concludes that "the inevitable failure of a spirit to coexist with our dreary practical world isn't a new theme, although in 'The Boggart' it seems fresher than ever. . . . As long as writers with Susan Cooper's skill continue to publish, magic is always available."

"Every book is a voyage of discovery," Cooper writes in *Celebrating Children's Books.* "Perhaps I speak only for myself, perhaps it's different for other writers; but for me the making of a fantasy is quite unlike the relatively ordered procedure of writing any other kind of book. . . . Each time, I am striking out into a strange land, listening for the music that will tell me which way to go. And I am always overcome by wonder, and a kind of unfocused gratitude, when I arrive." The author describes herself as "a writer whose work sometimes turns out to belong on the children's list, and sometimes elsewhere. To tell the truth," she concludes, "I don't write for you, whoever you are; I write for me. And 'me' is a complicated word; perhaps I know less about its meaning now than when I was that busy ten-year-old."

BIOGRAPHICAL/CRITICAL SOURCES:

BOOKS

Children's Literature Review, Volume 4, Gale, 1982.
de Montreville, Doris, and Elizabeth D. Crawford, editors, *Fourth Book of Junior Authors and Illustrators,* H. W. Wilson (Bronx, NY), 1978, pp. 98-9.
Dictionary of Literary Biography, Volume 161: *British Children's Writers since 1960, First Series,* Gale, 1996.
Hearne, Betsy, and Marilyn Kaye, *Celebrating Children's Books: Essays on Children's Literature in Honor of Zena Sutherland,* Lothrop (New York City), 1981.
Something about the Author Autobiography Series, Volume 6, Gale, 1988.
Sutherland, Zena, and others, *Children and Books,* Scott, Foresman (Glenview, IL), 1981.
The Voice of the Narrator in Children's Literature: Insights from Writers and Critics, Greenwood Press (New York City), 1989.

PERIODICALS

American Libraries, December, 1974.
Atlanta Constitution, December 15, 1993, p. B3.
Best Sellers, May 15, 1971.
Booklist, February 15, 1991, p. 1191; April 15, 1996, p. 1448.
Books, November, 1970.
Books and Bookmen, October, 1973; January, 1975.

Bookseller, September 19, 1970.
Books for Your Children, spring, 1976.
Children's Book Review, September, 1973; autumn, 1974.
Children's Literature in Education, September, 1973, p. 10; summer, 1977; spring, 1982, p. 95; March, 1987, p. 34.
Christian Science Monitor, November 2, 1977; November 7, 1986, p. B2.
Globe and Mail (Toronto), May 12, 1984.
Growing Point, September, 1965; January, 1975; December, 1975; March, 1978.
Horn Book Magazine, October, 1975; February, 1976, pp. 367, 443, 522; August, 1976, pp. 367-72; October, 1976; December, 1977, p. 660; February, 1982, p. 436; February, 1984, p. 59; May/June, 1990; February, 1993, p. 330.
Junior Bookshelf, August, 1965; August, 1972; April, 1978.
Kirkus Reviews, January 1, 1991, p. 43; July 15, 1991, p. 929.
Locus, April, 1993, p. 30.
Los Angeles Times, February 18, 1983.
Los Angeles Times Book Review, June 16, 1996, p.15.
New Statesman, June 2, 1972.
New York Times, November 12, 1982; May 11, 1984.
New York Times Book Review, October 27, 1968; November 8, 1970; May 22, 1973; May 5, 1974; September 28, 1975, p. 10; November 10, 1991, p. 53; May 16, 1993, p. 23.
School Librarian and School Library Review, December, 1965.
School Library Journal, October, 1975; December, 1977; February, 1980; April, 1988, p. 99; May, 1991, p. 88.
Time, November 22, 1982, p. 176.
Times Educational Supplement, June 20, 1980; December 7, 1984, p. 24; May 10, 1985, p. 24; July 12, 1985, p. 21; June 4, 1993, p. A11.
Times Literary Supplement, September 18, 1970; July 14, 1972; June 15, 1973; July 5, 1974; December 5, 1975; December 2, 1977; November 25, 1983; March 29, 1985, p. 348.
Tribune Books (Chicago), November 16, 1986, p. 4; April 11, 1993, p. 6.
Wall Street Journal, November 16, 1982, p. 32.
Washington Post Book World, July 8, 1973, p. 13; May 9, 1993, p. 14; July 7, 1996, p. 15.
World of Children's Books, fall, 1978.

*   *   *

COOVER, Robert (Lowell) 1932-

PERSONAL: Born February 4, 1932, in Charles City, IA; son of Grant Marion and Maxine (Sweet) Coover; married Maria del Pilar Sans-Mallafre, June 3, 1959; children: Diana Nin, Sara Chapin, Roderick Luis. *Education:* Attended Southern Illinois University at Carbondale, 1949-51; Indiana University at Bloomington, B.A., 1953; University of Chicago, M.A., 1965.

ADDRESSES: Home—Providence, RI. *Office*—Linden Press, 49 George St., Providence, RI 02912. *Agent*—Georges Borchardt, Inc., 136 East 57th St., New York, NY 10022.

CAREER: Writer of fiction, plays, essays, and poetry. Instructor, Bard College, Annandale-on-Hudson, NY, 1966-67, University of Iowa, Iowa City, 1967-69, Princeton University, Princeton, NJ, 1972-73, Columbia University, New York City, 1972, Virginia Military Institute, Lexington, 1976, and Brandeis University, Waltham, MA, 1981; Brown University, Providence, RI, distinguished professor, 1979–. Producer and director of film *On a Confrontation in Iowa City,* 1969. Organized conference on literature, "Unspeakable Practices: A Three-Day Celebration of Iconoclastic American Fiction," Brown University, 1988. *Military service:* U.S. Naval Reserve, 1953-57; became lieutenant.

MEMBER: American Academy of Arts and Letters.

AWARDS, HONORS: William Faulkner Award for best first novel, 1966, for *The Origin of the Brunists*; Rockefeller Foundation grant, 1969; Guggenheim fellowships, 1971 and 1974; citation in fiction from Brandeis University, 1971; Academy of Arts and Letters award, 1975; National Book Award nomination, 1977, for *The Public Burning*; National Endowment for the Humanities award, 1985; Rea Award, Dungannan Foundation, 1987, for *A Night at the Movies*; DAAD fellowship, 1991.

WRITINGS:

NOVELS

The Origin of the Brunists, Putnam (New York City), 1966.
The Universal Baseball Association, Inc., J. Henry Waugh, Prop., Random House (New York City), 1968.
The Public Burning, Viking (New York City), 1977.
Gerald's Party, Simon & Schuster (New York City), 1986.
Whatever Happened to Gloomy Gus of the Chicago Bears?, Simon & Schuster, 1987.
Pinocchio in Venice, Simon & Schuster, 1991.
John's Wife, Simon & Schuster, 1996.
Ghost Town, Holt, 1998.

SHORT FICTION

Pricksongs & Descants, Dutton (New York City), 1969.
The Water Power, Bruccoli-Clark (Bloomfield Hills, MI), 1972.
The Hair o' the Chine, Bruccoli-Clark, 1979.
A Political Fable, Viking, 1980.
Charlie in the House of Rue, Penmaen Press (Great Barrington, MA), 1980.
The Convention, Lord John (Northridge, CA), 1981.
Spanking the Maid, Bruccoli-Clark, 1981.
In Bed One Night and Other Brief Encounters, Burning Deck (Providence, RI), 1983.
Aesop's Forest (bound with *The Plot of the Mice and Other Stories* by Brian Swann), Capra Press (Santa Barbara, CA), 1986.
A Night at the Movies; or, You Must Remember This, Simon & Schuster, 1987.
Briar Rose, Grove Press (New York City), 1996.

PLAYS

A Theological Position (contains *A Theological Position* and *Rip Awake* [both produced in Los Angeles, 1975], *The Kid* [produced off-Broadway, 1972], *Love Scene* [produced in Paris as *Scene d'amour,* 1973, produced in New York City, 1974]), Dutton, 1972.
After Lazarus: A Filmscript, Bruccoli-Clark, 1980.
Bridge Hound, produced in Providence, RI, 1981.

OTHER

(Editor with Kent Dixon) *The Stone Wall Book of Short Fiction,* Stone Wall Press (Washington, DC), 1973.
(Editor with Elliott Anderson) *Minute Stories,* Braziller (New York City), 1976.

Work represented in anthologies, including *New American Review 4,* New American Library, 1968, *New American Review 14,* Simon & Schuster, 1972, and *American Review,* Bantam, 1974. Author of introduction, *Statements Two,* edited by Jonathan Baumbach, Fiction Collective Two, 1977, and Wilfrido D.

Nolledo, *But for the Lovers,* Dalkey Archive Press, 1994. Contributor of short stories, poems, essays, reviews, and translations to numerous periodicals, including *Noble Savage, Saturday Review, New York Times Book Review, Granta, Fiction International,* and *Fiddlehead.* Fiction editor, *Iowa Review,* 1975-77.

MEDIA ADAPTATIONS: Theater adaptations of Coover's stories include *The Baby Sitter* and *Spanking the Maid.* "Pedestrian Accident" has been made into an opera and "The Leper's Helix" into a chamberwork. *The Babysitter* was filmed by Guy Ferland in 1995 and starred Alicia Silverstone and George Segal.

SIDELIGHTS: In a literary career that has spanned over three decades, Robert Coover has emerged as one of the leading American postmodern writers. As is true of his peers—John Barth, Donald Barthelme, William Gass, and Thomas Pynchon—Coover experiments with traditional fictional forms and familiar stories, twisting them in ways that challenge society's assumptions. Coover often mixes actuality with illusion, creating an alternative world. Amazing, fantastic, and magic are among the words used by critics to describe the effect of his fiction. *Time*'s Paul Gray notes that Coover has won a "reputation as an avant-gardist who can do with reality what a magician does with a pack of cards: Shuffle the familiar into unexpected patterns."

The Origin of the Brunists, Coover's first and most conventional novel, chronicles the rise and fall of a fictitious religious cult. This cult arises when the sole survivor of a mining disaster, Giovanni Bruno, claims to have been visited by the Virgin Mary and rescued via divine intervention. As the cult gains followers and generates hysteria, the furor is fueled by a local newspaper editor until the situation reaches what Philip Callow of *Books & Bookmen* terms "apocalyptic proportions." Although some critics, such as Callow, find the novel's conclusion disappointing and anticlimactic, others, such as *New Statesman*'s Miles Burrows, describe the book as being "a major work in the sense that it is long, dense, and alive to a degree that makes life outside the covers almost pallid."

In a *New Republic* review of Coover's second novel, *The Universal Baseball Association, Inc., J. Henry Waugh, Prop.,* Richard Gilman writes, "What this novel summons to action is our sense . . . of the possible substitution of one world for another, of the way reality implies alternatives." The book's protagonist, Henry Waugh, is bored with his job and his life. To alleviate his boredom, he creates, within his imagination, an entire baseball league, complete with statistics and team and player names and histories. Plays, players, and fates are determined by dice, and Waugh, according to Gilman, presides "over this world of chance with a creator's calm dignity." When the dice rule that a favored player must die during a game, both Waugh's imaginary and real worlds fall apart. Waugh could, of course, choose to ignore the dice's decision, but to do so would be in violation of "the necessary laws that hold the cosmos together," a *Time* reviewer explains. At the novel's end, Waugh disappears from the story, leaving his players to fashion their own existence, myths, and rituals.

Pricksongs & Descants, Coover's collection of short fiction pieces, has been widely praised. The author's experimental forms and techniques produce "extreme verbal magic," according to Christopher Lehmann-Haupt in the *New York Times.* "Nothing in Mr. Coover's writing is quite what it seems to be," the critic continues. "In the pattern of the leaves there is always the smile of the Cheshire Cat." And Marni Jackson explains in *Critique:* "An innocent situation develops a dozen sinister possibilities, sprouting in the readers imagination while they are suspended, open-ended, on the page. . . . Every disturbing twist the story might take is explored; all of them could have happened, or none. . . . Like a good conjurer, even when you recognize his gimmicks, the illusion continues to work."

With *The Public Burning,* Coover returns to longer fiction and pushes his exploration of alternative realities to new levels, further blurring the distinction between fact and fiction. The book can be called a "factional" account of the 1953 conviction and execution of alleged spies Julius and Ethel Rosenberg. A satire on the mood and mentality of the nation at the time of the Rosenbergs' execution, the novel loosely combines events from both history and its author's imagination. Coover sets the site of the electrocutions in New York City's Times Square, adds surrealistic parodies of various personalities and events of the era, and provides then-Vice President Richard M. Nixon as the narrator-commentator. Reaction to the book has included admiration for Coover's creative efforts as well as criticism that those efforts go too far. Piers Brendon of *Books & Bookmen* describes the novel as a "literary photo-montage" and "a paean of American self-hatred, a torrid indictment of the morally bankrupt society where for so long Nixon was the one." Lehmann-Haupt, in a *New York Times* review, states that he was "shocked and amazed" by the book; "*The Public Burning,*" he explains, "is an astonishing spectacle. It does not invite us to participate. . . . It merely allows us to watch, somewhat warily, as its author performs."

Coover's 1987 novel *Whatever Happened to Gloomy Gus of the Chicago Bears?* is another alternative reality involving former president Richard Nixon. This time, a young Nixon follows his success on the football fields of Whittier, California, with a career, not in politics, but in professional football. His rise and fall comes not in Washington, but in Chicago. In the late 1930s, Nixon—known here as Gloomy Gus—falls in with several Chicago labor activists, including the book's narrator, Meyer, a sculptor. On Memorial Day of 1937, in a crowd of demonstrators picketing Republic Steel, Gus catches a police bullet and dies. Meyer looks back to tell this story—a story that challenges the reader by warping historical events—and as Christopher Walker comments in the *New Statesman and Society,* "At [Nixon's] expense Coover reveals 'the inherent contradictions in the American dream' in a book which is both touching and hilariously funny."

While Coover often manipulates historical events for his artistic purposes, he does so with a solid knowledge of the facts. As Sara Paretsky notes in Chicago *Tribune Books,* "Coover obviously knows Richard Nixon's life well. He displays the same careful research into events of the '30s on the streets of Chicago and the battlefields of Spain." And *New York Times Book Review* contributor Richard Kelly finds that Coover's fictionalized Nixon captures the essence of the man Americans came to know through his political ups and downs. The reviewer writes, "Gloomy Gus is Richard Nixon, in all his awkward triumphs, in all the plodding determination every act takes, in the harsh light of the will that makes every act equal to every other." Still, Kelly believes, "Mr. Coover's Richard Nixon is a nobler, stupider character than history's." Through this character, he concludes, "Coover shows us the madness of the will as it operates without intelligence, and makes us think about that most secret of all our transgressions, the deep sin of being innocent."

In 1991's *Pinocchio in Venice,* Coover updates the story originated by the Italian writer Carlo Collodi in 1883 about the puppet who became a boy. "Robert Coover's adult fable . . .

comes closer to the stern morality of the early Italian story than Disney's saccharine film ever did," observes Constance Markey in Chicago *Tribune Books. Times Literary Supplement*'s Lorna Sage characterizes Coover's update as "a hilariously phallic riposte, a carnivalesque reprise all about the agonies and delights of turning back to wood. His Pinocchio, after a century of humanity, opts for the dry rot and the unstrung joints, follows his nose and looks to his roots." Coover's Pinocchio has grown up and grown old, one hundred years old. After a long career as a renowned professor and philosopher in U.S. universities, he decides to return to his native Italy. In Venice he encounters all the characters from his past—the fox, the cat, the puppets in the traveling show, and the blue fairy—all in new guises. "One ecstatic disaster follows on another," notes Sage. As she points out, "Fun, Coover-style, is perfectly nightmarish—murderous in its intensity, chilling in the thoroughness with which it scatters and splinters the remnants of 'character.'" In the end, Pinocchio's updated story "requires that the reader take a new hard look at his own wooden-headed ways, mulish choices and false blue fantasies," comments Markey.

Coover's 1996 novel, *John's Wife,* is a complex, convoluted work that, according to Michael Harris in the *Los Angeles Times,* offers its reader many layers. He suggests that the novel is "on one level a bawdy and deadly satire of good-ol'-boy mores; on another level a complex portrait of the townspeople . . . on still another, a philosophical inquiry into the relationship between life and art." John is a builder whose money, ambition, and works are the heart of a small Midwestern town. He is an object of both love and hatred for his fellow townspeople, but his wife is an object of obsession. Each of the townspeople has his or her own image of John's wife; she stands at the center of each character's imagination while, in reality, she remains elusive. The result, as Jennifer Howard observes in the *Washington Post Book World,* is that "the town . . . lives in a frenzy of desire, much of it unwholesome."

Brad Leithauser, writing in the *New York Times Book Review,* finds *John's Wife* "a rambling, reiterated and squalid affair." He calls Coover's writing "overworked: too much fuss, not enough fineness." Yet a reviewer for *Publishers Weekly* writes of the author, "His prose is, as always, biting and suggestive, a spicy blend of erudition and scatology, epic and farce."

In a retelling of the Sleeping Beauty tale, Coover's *Briar Rose* reinterprets the conventions of a fairy tale. Infusing his version with more sexuality than traditional version of the story, Coover's *Briar Rose* is about storytelling itself. Using humor to unfold the traditional tale, the author structures it so that, in the words of the *New York Times Book Review*'s Michael Gorra, "this short and almost perfect book seems—paradoxically, blissfully—to go on forever."

Because of his interest in experimenting with form, Coover has explored not only the novel and short story, but also poetry, plays, and filmscripts. "Coover's interest in film has been evident in his fiction, which often relies blatantly on cinematic techniques," notes Larry McCaffery and Sinda J. Gregory in *Dictionary of Literary Biography Yearbook: 1981.* "He finds interesting the notion of cinematic montage or juxtaposition, the ability of cinema to manipulate time, its great sense of immediacy, its mixture of what he calls 'magic and documentary power'—all of which have potential applications in fiction." More recently, Coover has been intrigued by the possibilities of hypertext—the branching, multiplex, interactive writing made possible by computers and the internet. In a *New York Times Book Review* article on the growing presence of hypertext literature, he admits that he is not "likely to engage in any major hypertext fictions of my own. But, interested as ever in the subversion of the traditional bourgeois novel and in fictions that challenge linearity, I felt that something was happening out (or in) there and that I ought to know what it was." To this end, Coover has not only begun reading and reviewing hypertext writing; he has also launched a university course to introduce students to its possibilities and has publicized both hypertext fictions and the software that makes them possible.

Coover is often compared to his contemporaries in the experimental branch of literature labeled postmodern fiction. As Joyce Carol Oates comments in the *Southern Review*: "Coover . . . exists blatantly and brilliantly in his fiction as an authorial consciousness. . . . He will remind readers of William Gass, of John Barth, of Samuel Beckett. He is as surprising as any of these writers, and as funny as Donald Barthelme; both crude and intellectual, predictable and alarming, he gives the impression of thoroughly enjoying his craft." Still, as Lois G. Gordon writes in *Robert Coover: The Universal Fictionmaking Process*, "Coover has developed a style unique among his contemporaries, mixing so-called fact and fiction with realism and surrealism, merging narrative line with adjacent and 'descanting' poetic or fragmentary evocations of moral, mythic, historical, philosophical, and psychological dimensions." In his review of *Pricksongs & Descants* in the *New York Times*, Lehmann-Haupt dubs Coover simply "among the best we now have writing."

BIOGRAPHICAL/CRITICAL SOURCES:

BOOKS

Anderson, Richard, *Robert Coover,* Twayne (Boston), 1981.
Contemporary Literary Criticism, Gale, Volume 3, 1975; Volume 7, 1977; Volume 15, 1980; Volume 32, 1985; Volume 46, 1988; Volume 87, 1995.
Cope, Jackson I., *Robert Coover's Fictions,* Johns Hopkins University Press (Baltimore), 1986.
Dictionary of Literary Biography, Volume 2: *American Novelists since World War II,* Gale, 1978.
Dictionary of Literary Biography Yearbook: 1981, Gale, 1982.
Gordon, Lois G., *Robert Coover: The Universal Fictionmaking Process,* Southern Illinois University Press (Carbondale), 1983.
Kennedy, Thomas E., *Robert Coover: A Study of the Short Fiction,* Twayne (New York City), 1992.
LeClair, Thomas, and Larry McCaffery, *Interviews with Contemporary American Novelists,* University of Illinois Press (Urbana), 1982.
Maltby, Paul, *Dissident Postmodernists: Barthelme, Coover, Pynchon,* University of Pennsylvania Press (Philadelphia), 1991.
McCaffery, Larry, *The Metafictional Muse: The Works of Robert Coover, Donald Barthelme, and William Gass,* University of Pittsburgh Press (Pittsburgh), 1982.
Pughe, Thomas, *Comic Sense: Reading Robert Coover, Stanley Elkin, Philip Roth,* Birkhauser Verlag (Basel, Switzerland), 1994.
Semrau, Janusz, *American Self-Conscious Fiction of the 1960s and 1970s: Donald Barthelme, Robert Coover, Ronald Sukenick,* Poznan, 1986.
Sorkin, Adam J., editor, *Politics and the Muse: Studies in the Politics of Recent American Literature,* Bowling Green State University Popular Press (Bowling Green, OH), 1989.

PERIODICALS

Atlanta Journal & Constitution, March 1, 1987.
Atlantic Monthly, November, 1977; February, 1991, p. 92.
Booklist, October 1, 1992.
Books and Bookmen, May, 1967; August, 1978.
Book World, July 7, 1968; November 2, 1969.
Critique, Volume 11, number 3, 1969, pp. 11-29; Volume 17, number 1, p. 78; Volume 31, number 2, 1990, p. 85; Volume 33, number 3, p. 29; Volume 34, number 4, 1993, p. 220; Volume 35, number 2, 1994, p. 67.
Esquire, December, 1970.
Essays in Literature, fall, 1981, pp. 203-17.
Film Comment, May/June, 1987.
Harvard Advocate, Volume CCXXX, number IV, 1996.
Hollins Critic, April, 1970.
Library Journal, February 15, 1987; October 1, 1987; January 1991; March 1, 1996, p. 104.
London Review of Books, April 17, 1986, p. 18; September 17, 1987, p. 19.
Los Angeles Times, February 6, 1987; April 22, 1996, p. E3; April 22, 1996.
Los Angeles Times Book Review, February 2, 1986, p. 2; October 25, 1987, p. 9; May 29, 1988, p. 14; January 27, 1991, p. 3.
Maclean's, April 13, 1987.
Modern Fiction Studies, spring, 1987, p. 161.
Nation, December 8, 1969.
National Observer, July 29, 1968.
New Republic, August, 17, 1967; March 24, 1986, p. 28.
New Statesman, April 13, 1967; June 16, 1978; May 16, 1986, p. 28; February 13, 1987; November 27, 1987, p. 33; July 1, 1988, p. 44.
Newsweek, December 1, 1969; January 5, 1987, p. 58.
New York Review, March 13, 1969.
New York Review of Books, April 24, 1986, p. 38.
New York Times, June 13, 1968; October 22, 1969; November 18, 1972; September 7, 1977; December 19, 1985; January 7, 1987; August 22, 1987; January 15, 1991; April 1, 1996, p. B2; February 6, 1997.
New York Times Book Review, July 7, 1968; August 14, 1977, p. 9; June 27, 1982; December 29, 1985, p. 1; February 1, 1987, p. 15; September 27, 1987, p. 9; July 30, 1989, p. 28; January 27, 1991, pp. 3, 31; June 21, 1992, p. 1; January 3, 1993, p. 20; August 29, 1993, p. 1; April 7, 1996, p. 7; February 16, 1997.
Notes on Contemporary Literature, November, 1995, p. 5.
Novel: A Forum on Fiction, spring, 1974, pp. 210-19; winter, 1979, pp. 127-48; fall, 1993, pp. 85-101.
Observer (London), April 13, 1986, p. 25; August 16, 1987, p. 23; June 25, 1989, p. 45; April 21, 1991, p. 59.
Publishers Weekly, December 26, 1986; July 10, 1987; July 1, 1988; February 5, 1996, p. 75.
Quill and Quire, May 1986, p. 29.
Review of Contemporary Fiction, fall, 1986, p. 143; fall, 1991, p. 267; fall, 1994, p. 9.
Saturday Review, August 31, 1968.
Short Story, fall, 1993, p. 89.
Southern Review, winter, 1971.
Studies in Short Fiction, spring, 1994, p. 217.
Studies in the Novel, fall, 1993, p. 332.
Time, June 28, 1968; August 8, 1977.
Times (London), February 5, 1987; May 2, 1991.
Times Literary Supplement, June 16, 1978; May 2, 1986, p. 478; February 13, 1987; August 14, 1987, p. 873; July 1, 1988, p. 730; May 31, 1991, p. 19.

Tribune Books (Chicago), January 18, 1987, p. 3; August 16, 1987, p. 3; January 6, 1991, p. 1; January 27, 1991, p. 1.
Village Voice, July 30, 1970.
Voice Literary Supplement, April, 1986, p. 7.
Wall Street Journal, April 5, 1996, p. A6.
Washington Post Book World, May 11, 1982; January 18, 1986, p. 5; March 1, 1987, p. 9; May 21, 1989, p. 12; January 6, 1991, p. 1; March 31, 1996, p. 6.
Yearbook of Comparative and General Literature, 1992, pp. 40, 83-9.

*   *   *

CORMIER, Robert (Edmund) 1925-
(John Fitch IV)

PERSONAL: Born January 17, 1925, in Leominster, MA; son of Lucien Joseph (a factory worker) and Irma Margaret (Collins) Cormier; married Constance B. Senay, November 6, 1948; children: Roberta Susan, Peter Jude, Christine Judith, Renee Elizabeth. *Education:* Attended Fitchburg State College, 1944. *Religion:* Roman Catholic.

ADDRESSES: Home—1177 Main St., Leominster, MA 01453.

CAREER: Radio WTAG, Worcester, MA, writer, 1946-48; *Telegram and Gazette,* Worcester, reporter, 1948-55, writing consultant 1980-83; *Fitchburg Sentinel* (became *Fitchburg-Leominster Sentinel and Enterprise*), Fitchburg, MA, reporter, 1955-59, wire editor, 1959-66, associate editor, 1966-78; freelance writer, 1978–. Member of board of trustees of Leominster (MA) Public Library, 1978–.

MEMBER: L'Union St. Jean Baptiste d'Amerique, PEN.

AWARDS, HONORS: Best human interest story of the year award, Associated Press in New England, 1959 and 1973; Bread Loaf Writers' Conference fellow, 1968; best newspaper column award, K. R. Thomson Newspapers, Inc., 1974; outstanding book of the year awards, *New York Times,* 1974, for *The Chocolate War,* 1977, for *I Am the Cheese,* and 1979, for *After the First Death*; "Best Book for Young Adults" citations, American Library Association, 1974, for *The Chocolate War,* 1977, for *I Am the Cheese,* 1979, for *After the First Death,* and 1983, for *The Bumblebee Flies Anyway;* Maxi Award, *Media and Methods,* 1976; Doctor of Letters, Fitchburg State College, 1977; Woodward School Annual Book Award, 1978, for *I Am the Cheese*; Lewis Carroll Shelf Award, 1979, for *The Chocolate War;* "Notable Children's Trade Book in the Field of Social Studies" citation, National Council for Social Studies and Children's Book Council, 1980, for *Eight Plus One*; Assembly on Literature for Adolescents (ALAN) Award, National Council of Teachers of English, 1982; "Best of the Best Books, 1970-1983" citations, American Library Association, for *The Chocolate War, I Am the Cheese,* and *After the First Death*; "Best Books of 1983" citation, *School Library Journal,* for *The Bumblebee Flies Anyway*; Carnegie Medal nomination, 1983, for *The Bumblebee Flies Anyway*; Reader's Choice Award, 1983, for the *Eight Plus One* short story "President Cleveland, Where Are You?"; "Honor List" citation from *Horn Book,* 1986, for *Beyond the Chocolate War*; Young Adult Services Division "Best Book for Young Adults" citation, American Library Association, 1988, for *Fade*; World Fantasy Award nomination, 1989, for *Fade*; Margaret A. Edwards Award, American Library Association, 1991, for *The Chocolate War, I Am the Cheese,* and *After the First Death*; named

Massachusetts Author of the Year, Massachusetts Library Association, 1985; finalist for Best Young Adult award, Mystery Writers of America, 1996, for *In the Middle of the Night.*

WRITINGS:

YOUNG ADULT NOVELS, EXCEPT AS NOTED

The Chocolate War, Pantheon, 1974.
I Am the Cheese, Pantheon, 1977.
After the First Death, Pantheon, 1979.
Eight Plus One (short stories), Pantheon, 1980.
The Bumblebee Flies Anyway, Pantheon, 1983.
Beyond the Chocolate War, Knopf, 1985.
Fade, Delacorte, 1988.
Other Bells for Us to Ring, Delacorte, 1990.
I Have Words to Spend: Reflections of a Small Town Editor (autobiography), Doubleday, 1991.
We All Fall Down, Delacorte, 1991.
Tunes for Bears to Dance To, Delacorte, 1992.
In the Middle of the Night, Delacorte, 1995.
Tenderness, Delacorte, 1997.

Also author of *The Rumple Country* and *In the Midst of Winter,* both unpublished novels.

ADULT NOVELS

Now and at the Hour, Coward, 1960.
A Little Raw on Monday Mornings, Sheed, 1963.
Take Me Where the Good Times Are, Macmillan, 1965.
Heroes, Delacorte Press, 1998.

CONTRIBUTOR

Betsy Hearne and Marilyn Kay, editors, *Celebrating Children's Books: Essays in Honor of Zena Sutherland,* Lothrop, 1981.
Sixteen: Short Stories by Outstanding Writers for Young Adults, Delacorte, 1984.
Mark I. West, editor, *Trust Your Children: Voices against Censorship in Children's Literature,* Neal-Schuman, 1987.

OTHER

(With Malcolm Knopp) *Mayflies: An Angler's Study of Trout Water Ephemeroptera,* Greycliff, 1997.

Fitchburg Sentinel, author of book review column "The Sentinel Bookmark," 1964-78, and of human interest column under pseudonym John Fitch IV, 1969-78; also author of monthly human interest column "1177 Main Street," for *St. Anthony Messenger,* 1972-82. Contributor of articles and short stories to periodicals, including *Catholic Library World, McCall's, Redbook, Saturday Evening Post, Sign,* and *Woman's Day. The Chocolate War, I Am the Cheese,* and *After the First Death* were all released as records and cassettes by Random House/Miller Brody in 1982.

Several of Cormier's novels have been translated into French, Spanish, Italian, Swedish, Japanese, Danish, Hungarian, German, and other languages.

MEDIA ADAPTATIONS: I Am the Cheese, a motion picture adapted from Cormier's novel of the same name, was released in 1983 by the Almi Group, starring Robert Wagner, Hope Lange, Robert Macnaughton, and featuring Cormier in the role of Mr. Hertz; *The Chocolate War* was released as a movie of the same title by Management Company Entertainment Group in 1989, directed by Keith Gordon and starring John Glover, Ilan Mitchell-Smith, and Wally Ward.

SIDELIGHTS: Robert Cormier is widely acclaimed for his powerful and disturbing novels for young adult readers, though his realistic subject matter—including murder, sex, and terminal illness—has at times made his work controversial. His novels, which include *The Chocolate War* and *I Am the Cheese,* often involve teenage protagonists faced with difficult, uncompromising situations. "A lot of people underestimate that intelligent teenager out there," Cormier noted in an interview for *Authors and Artists for Young Adults.* "These kids today, I'm talking about the sensitive, intelligent kid, are really far ahead of a lot of adults. They have been exposed to so much. Anybody who writes down to these people is making a mistake."

Cormier wrote and published three adult novels before writing *The Chocolate War* in 1974. Young adult readers received *The Chocolate War* with great enthusiasm, as they have all Cormier's young adult offerings. "Cormier seems to believe that teenagers are more idealistic today than in years past," Joe Stines observed in *Dictionary of Literary Biography,* "and he affords them respect and responsibility in his writing while simultaneously awakening them to the harsh realities of life in contemporary America." Cormier does this only incidentally, though, for what is first and foremost his intent is to tell a gripping story based on emotions, character, and plot. Cormier wrote *The Chocolate War* because of a true life experience, as he described in his Random House/Miller Brody interview: "My son was going to a high school much like the school in the book. They were having a chocolate sale, and Peter refused to sell the chocolates. It was a family decision, a matter of principle. . . . He was the only kid in the place who didn't sell the chocolates. Nothing happened to him but something happened to me. I used the thing all writers use: 'What if? What if there had been peer pressure; what if there had been faculty pressure?' The emotional content was there. When Peter brought those chocolates back the next day, I was apprehensive for him, I was fearful. I felt guilty that we allowed him to do this. He was fourteen years old, a freshman in a new school, in a different city—these emotions got me to the typewriter. Then I saw a chance to explore themes, the individual against society, manipulation. That's how *The Chocolate War* began."

His other books have also been written to find answers to that "what if?" question. *I Am the Cheese,* for example, was written after Cormier read about the U.S. Witness Relocation Program. It tells the story of a boy whose father testified against organized crime figures, but even new identities do not protect the family from harm. News of terrorist hijackings drove Cormier to write *After the First Death.* So important is his need to be interested that if Cormier does not become emotionally engaged by the subject, he finds himself unable to continue writing about it.

In *We All Fall Down,* Cormier tackles teenage violence firsthand with the story of a group of boys who vandalize a suburban home and attack a young girl. As is typical of a Cormier novel, he goes on to further explore good and evil when one of the attackers falls in love with the girl's older sister. Clouding the arena further is the existence of a voyeur, known only as The Avenger. Nancy Vsilakis, writing for *Horn Book Magazine,* called the novel "a gripping page-turner," noting "The black hole down which the novelist draws the reader is both repellant and enthralling." "Most of us forget the aching awfulness of adolescence when we become adults. It's Cormier's special burden to remember," wrote Michael Cart in the *Los Angeles Times Book Review.* It is also Cormier's gift, Cart continued, "to be able to translate that memory into novels of intensity, immediacy and empathy." Citing Cormier's manipulation of the reader through "artificial" techniques, Mike

Hayhoe of *School Librarian* admitted, "As an admirer of Cormier, I had an uneasy feeling that this [manipulation] sometimes moved towards the artifice of Stephen King; but I am confident that many readers will disagree strongly with me on that point!"

Cormier's 1995 novel, *In the Middle of the Night,* is based on a true event in which 500 people died in a fire in an overcrowded nightclub. An usher was initially blamed for lighting a match but was eventually exonerated. Cormier's story twists the nightclub into a cinema and the victims to children. He then picks up twenty-five years later with the usher receiving midnight phone calls from parents of the children while his sixteen-year-old son listens. "Unnerving and piercingly honest," noted Lois Metzger in the *New York Times Book Review.* While Elizabeth Hand in her review for *Washington Post Book World* called the plot "brazenly manipulative, the characterization unpleasant and dank," Patty Campbell, critic for *Horn Book Magazine,* called the tale "pure Cormier, a tight and spare construction of amazing complexity worthy of a place among his best works."

Cormier also wrote several books for a younger audience than the intended readers of *The Chocolate War.* Set during World War II, *Other Bells for Us to Ring* tells the story of eleven-year-old Darcy, who has just moved to Frenchtown, Massachusetts. In an article for *Horn Book Magazine,* Mary M. Burns, comparing the book to Cormier's previous books for older children, called it "no less thought-provoking, no less intense in its emotional impact, no less remarkable for carefully honed phrases and an unfailing sense of the right detail to convey an idea." Burns concluded her praise by calling *Other Bells for Us to Ring* "one of those rare and brilliant gems for all seasons and for all those who would be possessed by its honest poignancy and superb craftsmanship." Janice M. Del Negro, reviewer for *School Library Journal,* was less impressed. While Del Negro praised Cormier's "effective evoking" of a bygone time and place, she called the characters "flat and two-dimensional."

Tunes for Bears to Dance To, published in 1992, is also aimed at younger children, although it retains Cormier's "enormous capacity for evoking the positive force of evil," as a reviewer for the *Junior Bookshelf* noted. Eleven-year-old Henry is the surviving child in a house where his older brother's death has traumatized his parents. After his family moves to a different home to banish these memories, Henry befriends a concentration camp survivor who spends his hours recreating the village he lived in before it was devastated by Nazis. In the *Washington Post Book World,* Anne Scott wrote that in the novel Cormier "stacks the deck of trouble and darkness more absolutely and less effectively than he has in his previous work," but a *Kirkus Reviews* critic felt that the tale was "ultimately less grim" than Cormier's previous work and called it a "thought-provoking story."

Tenderness, the story of a cat-and-mouse game between a clean-cut, handsome eighteen-year-old serial killer and a veteran cop, involving a sexually precocious 15-year-old female runaway, is one of Cormier's most notably dark novels. According to *Booklist,* "the sexual component here is far stronger than in Cormier's earlier books." Lori, a victim of sexual harassment and abuse, uses her sexuality to get what she wants; and, like Eric (the serial killer) she searches for genuine tenderness. "It is the idea of Eric's humanity that is the most disquieting aspect of the novel," maintains the critic for *Booklist,* adding that the killer's humanity is also what "makes the book so seductive." *Kirkus Reviews* praises the "devastatingly ironic climax," while *Horn Book* praises the style as "vintage Cormier: short pithy sentences and bends in the text that take the reader along startling paths." The *Horn Book* reviewer goes on to praise Cormier as a "master of irony," but laments that "the basic premise—that there will be a serious exploration of tenderness—is unfulfilled."

Cormier does not include explicit scenes or controversial subject matter for their market value. "All that controversial stuff, all that stuff that upsets people, is almost secondary in my mind as I write it," Cormier stated to Roger Sutton in *School Library Journal.* "And yet there's always the qualifier there, you know the readers are out there. When I was writing *Fade,* I was conscious of the audience when I wrote a couple of scenes that the boy witnesses. As I wrote them, I knew that people would be upset about them. I modified, and I made sure that I wasn't being titillating or exploitive, that I didn't make the acts sound attractive. I wanted to make them sound sordid, and I tried to make them brief. So there is that consciousness there as you're writing all the time. But again it's all bent on the altar of storytelling."

Whatever objections people have to Robert Cormier's books, they are commercially successful: avid fans in many countries have purchased millions of copies. "Cormier has acquired these fans," wrote Sylvia Patterson Iskander in *Concise Dictionary of American Literary Biography,* "because of his sensitive awareness about what actually occurs in the lives of teenagers today and his abundant talent for conveying that awareness through fiction. He has brought controversy and, simultaneously, a new dimension to the field of young-adult literature. He has earned the respect of his readers, regardless of their age, because of his refusal to compromise the truth as he sees it. His superb craftsmanship, his ability to create suspense and to shock the reader repeatedly, and his forcing the reader to think are all qualities which make Cormier's works entertaining, unique, and, indeed, unforgettable."

BIOGRAPHICAL/CRITICAL SOURCES:

BOOKS

Authors and Artists for Young Adults, Volume 3, Gale, 1990, pp. 65-76.
Campbell, Patricia J., *Presenting Robert Cormier,* Twayne, 1985.
Children's Literature Review, Volume 12, Gale, 1987.
Concise Dictionary of American Literary Biography: Broadening Views, 1968-1988, Gale, 1989, pp. 34-51.
Contemporary Authors New Revision Series, Volume 23, Gale, 1988.
Contemporary Literary Criticism, Volume 17, 1980; Volume 30, 1984.
Dictionary of Literary Biography, Volume 52: *American Writers for Children since 1960,* Gale, 1986, pp. 107-14.
Fifth Book of Junior Authors and Illustrators, H. W. Wilson, 1983.
Inglis, Fred, *The Promise of Happiness: Value and Meaning in Children's Fiction,* Cambridge University Press, 1981.
Rees, David, *The Marble in the Water: Essays on Contemporary Writers of Fiction for Children and Young Adults,* Horn Books, 1980.
Twentieth-Century Children's Writers, 3rd edition, St. James Press, 1989.

PERIODICALS

English Journal, November, 1989; January, 1990; April, 1992; November, 1992.
Horn Book Magazine, March-April, 1985; May-June, 1985, pp. 289-96; March-April, 1989; November-December, 1990; November-December, 1991, p. 742; May-June, 1995, p. 365; February, 1997.

Junior Bookshelf, August, 1992, p. 161.
Kirkus Reviews, October 1, 1992, p. 1252; January 1, 1997.
Lion and the Unicorn: A Critical Journal of Children's Literature, June 12, 1988, pp. 12-18.
Los Angeles Times Book Review, October 27, 1991, p. 7.
New Statesman, April 17, 1987.
New York Times Book Review, February 12, 1989; July 16, 1995, p. 27.
Publishers Weekly, July 29, 1988; November 16, 1990, p. 57; October 25, 1991, p. 69; September 7, 1992, p. 97.
School Librarian, August, 1992, p. 112.
School Library Journal, November, 1990; June, 1991, pp. 28-33; September, 1991, p. 277; September, 1992, p. 97.
Tribune Books (Chicago), January 12, 1992, p. 6.
Voice of Youth Advocates, August, 1988, pp. 122-24.
Washington Post Book World, December 6, 1992, p. 20; May 7, 1995.

*   *   *

CORNWELL, David (John Moore) 1931- (John le Carre)

PERSONAL: Born October 19, 1931, in Poole, Dorsetshire, England; son of Ronald Thomas Archibald and Olive (Glassy) Cornwell; married Alison Ann Veronica Sharp, November 27, 1954 (divorced, 1971); married Valerie Jane Eustace, 1972; children: (first marriage) Simon, Stephen, Timothy; (second marriage) Nicholas. *Education:* Attended Bern University, Switzerland, 1948-49; Lincoln College, Oxford, B.A. (with honours), 1956.

ADDRESSES: Agent—Bruce Hunter, David Higham Ltd., 5-8 Lower John St., Golden Sq., London W1R 4HA, England.

CAREER: Writer. Millfield Junior School, Galstonbury, Somerset, England, teacher, 1954-55; Eton College, Buckinghamshire, England, tutor, 1956-58; British Foreign Office, second secretary in Bonn, West Germany (now Germany), 1960-63, consul in Hamburg, West Germany (now Germany), 1963-64. *Military service:* British Army Intelligence Corps, beginning 1949.

AWARDS, HONORS: Gold Dagger, Crime Writers Association, 1963, Somerset Maugham Award, 1964, and Edgar Allan Poe Award, Mystery Writers of America, 1965, all for *The Spy Who Came in from the Cold;* James Tait Black Memorial Prize, 1977, and Gold Dagger, 1978, both for *The Honourable Schoolboy;* Gold Dagger, 1980; honorary fellow, Lincoln College, Oxford, 1984; Grand Master Award, Mystery Writers of America, 1986; Malparte prize, 1987; Diamond Dagger, Crime Writers Association, 1988; honorary doctorates, University of Exeter, 1990, University of St. Andrews, 1996, and University of Southampton, 1997.

WRITINGS:

NOVELS; ALL WRITTEN UNDER THE PSEUDONYM JOHN LE CARRE

Call for the Dead, Gollancz (London), 1960, Walker (London), 1962, published as *The Deadly Affair,* Penguin (New York City), 1966.
A Murder of Quality, Gollancz, 1962, Walker, 1963.
The Spy Who Came in from the Cold, Gollancz, 1963, Coward, 1964.
The Incongruous Spy: Two Novels of Suspense (contains *Call for the Dead* and *A Murder of Quality*), Walker, 1964.

The Looking Glass War, Coward, 1965.

A Small Town in Germany, Coward, 1968.

The Naive and Sentimental Lover, Knopf (New York City), 1971.

Tinker, Tailor, Soldier, Spy, Knopf, 1974.

The Honourable Schoolboy, Knopf, 1977.

Smiley's People, Knopf, 1980.

The Quest for Karla (contains *Tinker, Tailor, Soldier, Spy*; *The Honourable Schoolboy*; and *Smiley's People*), Knopf, 1982.

The Little Drummer Girl, Knopf, 1983.

A Perfect Spy, Knopf, 1986.

The Russia House, Knopf, 1989.

The Secret Pilgrim, Knopf, 1991.

The Night Manager, Knopf, 1993.

Our Game, Knopf, 1995.

John Le Carre: Three Complete Novels (includes *Tinker, Tailor, Soldier, Spy*; *The Honourable Schoolboy*; and *Smiley's People*), Wings (Avenel, NY), 1995.

The Tailor of Panama, Knopf, 1996.

OTHER; ALL WRITTEN UNDER THE PSEUDONYM JOHN LE CARRE

Dare I Weep, Dare I Mourn (teleplay), produced on *Stage 66,* American Broadcasting Corp. (ABC), 1966.

(Author of introduction) Bruce Page, Phillip Knightley, and David Leitch, *The Philby Conspiracy,* Doubleday (New York City), 1968.

(With John Hopkins) *Smiley's People* (teleplay; based on his novel), British Broadcasting Corp. (BBC), 1982.

The Clandestine Muse, Seluzicki (Portland, OR), 1986.

(With Gareth H. Davies) *Vanishing England,* Salem House, 1987.

A Murder of Quality (made for television film; directed by Gavin Miller), parts 1 and 2, Thames Television, WETA-TV, 1991.

Contributor to periodicals, including *Saturday Evening Post.*

MEDIA ADAPTATIONS: The Spy Who Came in from the Cold was filmed by Paramount in 1965; *Call for the Dead* was filmed as *The Deadly Affair* by Columbia in 1967; *The Looking Glass War* was filmed by Columbia in 1970; *Tinker, Tailor, Soldier, Spy* was filmed for television by the BBC in 1980; *The Little Drummer Girl* was filmed by Warner Brothers; *A Perfect Spy* was a seven-hour BBC-TV series and was shown on public television's *Masterpiece Theatre* in the United States; a film version of *The Russia House,* written by Tom Stoppard, directed by Fred Schepisi, and starring Sean Connery and Michelle Pfeiffer, was released in 1990.

SIDELIGHTS: The novels of David Cornwell, written under the pseudonym John le Carre, depict the clandestine world of Cold War espionage as a morally ambiguous realm where treachery, deceit, fear, and betrayal are the norm. The atmosphere in a le Carre novel, writes a reviewer for the *Times Literary Supplement,* is one of "grubby realism and moral squalor, the frazzled, fatigued sensitivity of decent men obliged to betray or kill others no worse than themselves." Le Carre uses his fiction to dramatize what he sees as the moral bankruptcy of the Cold War. In an open letter published in *Encounter,* le Carre writes: "There is no victory and no virtue in the Cold War, only a condition of human illness and a political misery." Leonard Downie, Jr., quotes le Carre in a *Washington Post* article as saying, "We are in the process of doing things in defense of our society which may very well produce a society which is not worth defending." It is this paradox, and the moral ambiguity which accompanies it, that informs le Carre's espionage novels and makes them, many critics believe, among the finest works of their genre. Le Carre's novels are believed by some critics to have raised the entire espionage genre to a more respectable and serious level of literature. "The espionage novel," writes Joseph McClellan in the *Washington Post Book World,* for example, "has become a characteristic expression of our time . . . and John le Carre is one of the handful of writers who have made it so." "More than any other writer," George Grella states in the *New Republic,* "[le Carre] has established the spy as an appropriate figure and espionage as an appropriate activity for our time, providing both symbol and metaphor to explain contemporary history."

Le Carre began writing espionage fiction in the early 1960s while working as a diplomat with the British Foreign Office in London. He had earlier worked for an undisclosed length of time with the British Secret Service, and there is some speculation among reviewers that le Carre's work as a diplomat was also espionage-related, a speculation le Carre dismisses as untrue. Nevertheless, his novels reveal an intimate knowledge of the workings of the British government's espionage bureaucracy. "Le Carre's contribution to the fiction of espionage," writes Anthony Burgess in the *New York Times Book Review,* "has its roots in the truth of how a spy system works. . . . The people who run Intelligence totally lack glamour, their service is short of money, [and] they are up against the crassness of politicians. Their men in the field are frightened, make blunders, grow sick of a trade in which the opposed sides too often seem to interpenetrate and wear the same face."

Le Carre wrote his first two novels, *Call for the Dead* and *A Murder of Quality,* while working for the Foreign Office, first in London and then in Bonn. At that time, the German capital was a center for intelligence operations. "You couldn't have been [in Germany] at that period," le Carre tells Miriam Gross of the *Chicago Tribune Magazine,* "without being aware of the shadow of an enormous intelligence apparatus." Le Carre introduced George Smiley, an intelligence agent featured in many of his later novels, in *Call for the Dead.* Smiley is an "improbable spy master," writes Richard W. Noland in *Clues: A Journal of Detection.* "[He is] short, fat, quiet and wears 'really bad clothes, which hung about his squat frame like skin on a shrunken toad,'" Noland quotes from *Call for the Dead.* Though physically unimposing, Smiley is a brilliant espionage agent who has served in the British Secret Service for more than thirty years. In *Call for the Dead,* Smiley investigates the suicide of a Foreign Office clerk who had just been given a security clearance, while in *A Murder of Quality* he tracks down the murderer of a schoolmaster's wife.

It wasn't until the publication of *The Spy Who Came In from the Cold* in 1963 that le Carre's work attracted widespread critical and popular acclaim. An immediate world-wide best-seller (the book has sold over twenty million copies since it first appeared), *Spy* enabled le Carre to leave his position with the Foreign Office to write full time. The novel tells the story of Alec Leamas, a fifty-year old British intelligence agent who wishes to retire from active duty and "come in from the cold," as he describes it. He is persuaded to take on one last assignment before leaving the Secret Service: a pretended defection behind the Iron Curtain to give false information to the East Germans implicating one of their high-ranking intelligence officers as a British agent. It is thought that the officer will then be imprisoned, thereby removing him from effective espionage work against the British. Leamas's real mission, and the treachery of his superiors, only gradually becomes clear to him as the plot unfolds.

Le Carre's pessimism about East-West relations is clearly evident in *Spy,* where both sides in the Cold War conflict are depicted as amoral and murderous. "The bureaucracies of East and West," writes Noland, describing the situation as related in *Spy,* "wage the Cold War by one simple rule—operational convenience. . . . In the name of operational convenience and alliances of expediency, any and all human values—including love and life itself—are expendable." In *Spy,* writes a *Times Literary Supplement* critic, le Carre puts forth the ideas that "the spy is generally a weak man, the tool of bureaucrats who are neither scrupulous nor particularly efficient, and that there is nothing to choose between 'us' and 'them' in an ethical sense." This is underlined when Leamas and his girlfriend are pitted against the intelligence agencies of both Britain and East Germany, "the two apparently opposed organizations on one side and helpless human beings . . . on the other," as Julian Symons writes in *Mortal Consequences: A History from the Detective Story to the Crime Novel.* Symons believes that *Spy* is the best of le Carre's novels because in *Spy* "the story is most bitterly and clearly told, the lesson of human degradation involved in spying most faithfully read."

Graham Greene sets the tone for most critical commentary about *The Spy Who Came In from the Cold* when he calls it, as K. G. Jackson of *Harper* quotes Greene, "the best spy novel I have ever read." D. B. Hughes of *Book Week* also praises *Spy* as "a beautifully written, understated and immensely perilous story. . . . Only rarely does a book of this quality appear—an inspired work and one in which the author's own inner excitement kindles the page." Several critics feel that with this novel le Carre transcends the espionage genre entirely, writing not category fiction but literature. Noland finds, for example, that with *The Spy Who Came In from the Cold* le Carre's "spy fiction became something more than most conventional spy fiction. It became, in fact, a political statement about the moral confusion and bankruptcy of the Cold War." Anthony Boucher in the *New York Times Book Review* also sees something more to le Carre's novel. "The author develops his story superbly," he writes, "both as a compelling and dazzlingly plotted thriller, and as a substantial and penetrating novel of our time. [Le Carre is one of] the small rank of [espionage] writers who can create a novel of significance, while losing none of the excitement of the tale of sheer adventure."

This high critical praise has continued with each succeeding espionage novel le Carre has published. *The Looking Glass War,* for example, is described by Hughes as "a superb spy story, unflawed, a bitter, cruel, dispassionate—yet passionate—study of an unimportant piece of espionage and the unimportant little men who are involved in it." A group of British agents mount an operation into East Germany that is doomed to failure under present political conditions, a fact which the agents refuse to see. Symons argues in *New Review* that in both *Spy* and *The Looking Glass War,* betrayal is the primary theme. In the first, an agent is betrayed to further the career of a more highly placed agent. In the second, an entire operation is abandoned and the people involved in it are left to die. It is possible, Symons writes, "to see espionage activities as brave and patriotic. . . , and yet to view them also as basically disgusting, outrages to the human personality. From such a point of view these two books seem to say an ultimate word about the nature of spying."

Le Carre draws heavily upon his time at the British Foreign Office in writing *A Small Town in Germany,* a novel set in Bonn, West Germany. The novel relates the story of a British diplomat who disappears with very sensitive documents which may damage Britain's chances of joining the Common Market. Speaking of the novel in a *Nation* review, John Gliedman states that le Carre "has long been a master of the essential machinery of the spy and detective novel. He has also shown himself to be a sensitive observer of character and manner, within the limits of the genre. But nothing which has come before quite prepares us for the literary distinction of this effort—the quality of its prose, the complexity of its construction, the cunning of some of its dialogue. . . . It represents something of a breakthrough in the use of the spy genre for serious purposes. *A Small Town in Germany* is that rarest of all things in contemporary fiction—good art which is also popular art." Robert Ostermann, writing in *National Observer,* agrees that *A Small Town in Germany* is better than le Carre's previous fiction. He calls it "broader in scope and more confidently crafted; tuned with exquisite fineness to the sliding nuances of its characters; shot through with the physical presence of Bonn, . . .and conveyed in a tough, precise prose that matches the novel's mordant tone down to the smallest metaphor."

Tinker, Tailor, Soldier, Spy, le Carre's next espionage novel, begins a loosely connected trilogy in which George Smiley is pitted against the Russian master spy "Karla." Writing in *Newsweek,* Alexis Gelber and Edward Behr report that "with *Tinker, Tailor* and Smiley, [le Carre] hit his stride." *Tinker, Tailor* is a fictionalized treatment of the Kim Philby spy case in which Smiley goes after a Soviet mole in British intelligence, a mole placed and directed by Karla. The novel's structure "derives from the action of Smiley's search," writes Noland. "[Smiley] must pursue his man through the maze of official documents." Knowing that the mole must be a highly placed agent, Smiley goes back through the records of intelligence operations, seeking a pattern of failure which might be attributed to the machinations of a particular agent. His investigation finally becomes, Noland believes, "a moral search . . . a quest for some kind of truth about England."

As in previous novels, le Carre examines the ramifications of betrayal, but this time in greater depth than he had previously attempted. The mole Smiley uncovers has not only betrayed his country and friends but has seduced Smiley's wife as well. The critic for the *Times Literary Supplement* sees a "moral dilemma" at the center of the book: "Smiley gets his man. In doing so he removes from another man his last illusions about friendship, loyalty and love, and he himself is left drained in much the same way. It is a sombre and tragic theme, memorably presented." Similarly, Richard Locke writes in the *New York Times Book Review* of the "interlocking themes of sexual and political betrayal" to be found in *Tinker, Tailor.*

Smiley's running battle with the Soviet spy master Karla continues in *The Honourable Schoolboy,* a novel set in Hong Kong, where British intelligence is investigating a prosperous businessman who seems to be working for the Soviets. Several critics point out a similarity between le Carre's novel and Joseph Conrad's novel, *Lord Jim.* The character Jerry Westerby, a British intelligence officer and friend of Smiley, is very similar to Conrad's character Jim. "Le Carre," Noland states, "obviously has Conrad's romantic protagonist in mind in his portrait of Westerby and in many of the events of the story." This "huge and hugely engrossing new thriller. . . ," writes David Ansen in *Newsweek,* "keeps opening out, like a Conrad adventure, into ever-widening pools of moral and emotional complexity."

Again concerned with one of Karla's moles, this one working inside Communist China, *The Honourable Schoolboy* traces Smiley's diligent efforts to discover and capture the agent for the West. As in previous novels, *Schoolboy* depicts an agent, this time Westerby, who is at odds with the amorality of espionage work and who, because of his belief in human values, loses his life in the course of an espionage operation. "The point, surely," writes Noland, "is that such romantic heroism is not very useful in the world of Cold War espionage." "It is difficult not to overpraise [*The Honourable Schoolboy*]," Mollie Panter-Downes writes in her *New Yorker* review. Although believing the novel too long, the plot "essentially thin," and le Carre's "fondness for stylistic mocking" embarrassing, Panter-Downes nonetheless praises *The Honourable Schoolboy*. "It has a compelling pace," she states, "a depth beyond its genre, a feeling for even the least of its characters, a horrifying vision of the doomed and embattled Southeast Asian left in the wake of the Vietnam War, and a dozen set pieces—following, fleeing, interrogating—that are awesomely fine."

Le Carre brings his trilogy to a close with *Smiley's People,* the last confrontation between George Smiley and the Soviet master spy Karla. No longer content to thwart Karla's agents, Smiley works in this novel to force Karla himself to defect to the West. This operation is done off the record because the British Secret Service, due to political pressure, cannot engage in an offensive intelligence operation. It becomes instead a personal mission involving the retired Smiley and the friends and espionage contacts he has gathered over the years. "Smiley and his people," Noland states, "carry it out by personal choice and commitment, not for the British (or American) establishment. The whole operation is a victory for personal human loyalty and skill."

Despite the success of the operation, there is an ambiguity about it which brings into question the morality of espionage. "Smiley and his people are fighting for decency," writes Michael Wood in the *New York Times Book Review,* "but there is more blood on their hands than they or anyone else care to contemplate." Julian Moynihan clarifies this in *New Republic.* "We know," Moynihan writes, "that Smiley has ruined many lives, some innocent, in his tenacious pursuit of Karla; . . . and we just don't believe that the dirty tricks of one side are OK because they were ordered up by a decent little English guy with a disarming name." "If this is the end of the Smiley stories. . . ," writes Joseph McClellan in the *Washington Post Book World,* "it is an appropriately ambiguous conclusion to a series that has dealt splendidly in ambiguities from the beginning."

In *The Little Drummer Girl,* le Carre turns to a different world arena for his setting—the Middle East refugee camps of the Palestinians. "It is as if Mr. le Carre," writes Anatole Broyard of the *New York Times,* "has had enough of British politics, as if he feels that neither Britain nor the Soviet Union is at the hot center of things anymore." Le Carre had originally planned to write a Smiley story set in the Middle East but could not find a convincing plot for his character. Because the espionage activity in this novel is of an active and open variety, unusual for le Carre, there is a great deal more action in *Drummer Girl* than is usual for a le Carre novel. There is also a female protagonist, le Carre's first, who is recruited by the Israelis to infiltrate a Palestinian terrorist group and set up its leader for assassination. "The Israelis triumph in the novel," William F. Buckley, Jr., writes in *National Review,* "even as they do in life. But Mr. le Carre is careful to even up the moral odds. . . . He permits the Palestinian point to be made with rare and convincing eloquence." Writing in *Esquire,*

Martin Cruz Smith gives the opinion that *The Little Drummer Girl* is "the most balanced novel about Jews and Arabs, outrage for outrage and tear for tear, I've read." "Without condoning terrorism," Gelber and Behr write, "the book makes the reasons for it understandable—perhaps the first popular novel to do so."

Some reviewers, however, see le Carre as an apologist for the Palestine Liberation Organization (PLO) and *The Little Drummer Girl* as lacking the moral ambiguity that characterizes his earlier books. "Here, one might have thought, is an ideal subject for moral ambiguity," David Pryce-Jones writes in the *New Republic.* "Le Carre finds it clear-cut. To him, the Palestinians are good, the Israelis bad." In their review of the book for *Chronicles of Culture,* Rael Jean Isaac and Erich Isaac acknowledge that le Carre does introduce the kind of moral ambiguities and correspondences between adversaries that he uses in other novels, "but these suggestions of ambiguity and correspondence are deceptive, for le Carre sets Israel up as the villain of this novel. . . . Le Carre employs meretricious techniques to make Israel appear guilty of the vicious practices that the PLO has made famous."

In his novels since *The Little Drummer Girl,* le Carre has featured stories that reflect the dissolution of the former Soviet Union and the end of the Cold War while continuing to portray flawed protagonists caught up in sinister circumstances. In *The Russia House,* which is set in a decaying Soviet Union, an aging publisher is recruited by British Intelligence to secure a top-secret manuscript from a Soviet engineer. After falling in love with the engineer's former girlfriend, however, the publisher must use his wits to keep himself and the woman alive while British and American spies pursue national interests not concerned with such individual freedoms. The novel was made into a movie starring Sean Connery and Michelle Pfeiffer.

The Night Manager, on the other hand, leaves behind Cold War settings altogether as a hotel manager in Switzerland struggles against international arms dealers funded by wealthy British businessmen. And *Our Game,* which is set in the warring republics of the former Soviet Union-Ossetia, Ingushetia, and Chechnia—again features a troubled central character caught up in socio-political forces beyond his control.

In *The Tailor of Panama,* published in 1996, le Carre explores his usual terrain of spy games and intrigue, this time against the tropical backdrop of Panama. Harry Pendel, a clothes tailor to the powerful and wealthy of Panama, is coerced into spying for British Intelligence in the midst of a plot to undo the Panama Treaty that will give control of the Panama Canal back to Panama in 1999. Although he does his duty by supplying information to his British recruiter, Pendel finds his life—and the lives of his family—in jeopardy in part because of the falsehoods he makes up to embellish his information. Writing in the *New York Times,* Michiko Kakutani praises le Carre's refined storytelling prowess and his "colorful and deft" depiction of Panama. Kakutani, however, avers that the author is less successful in creating a plausible story line. *Times Literary Supplement* reviewer Frederic Raphael concurs, remarking that le Carre "does not seem to finish his button-holes, or fashion his concealed pockets, with quite the old finesse." Still, Kakutani notes, "the result is a riotous, readable novel."

Speaking of the relationship between his life and writings to Fred Hauptfuhrer of *People,* le Carre reveals: "If I write knowledgeably about gothic conspiracies, it's because I had knowledge of them from earliest childhood." In several published interviews, le Carre has spoken of his personal life and how the business dealings and political ambitions of his father colored his own views of the world. Because his father often found himself in legal or financial trouble due to his sometimes questionable business deals, the family found itself, le Carre tells Gross, "often living in the style of millionaire paupers. . . . And so we arrived in educated, middle-class society feeling almost like spies, knowing that we had no social hinterland, that we had a great deal to conceal and a lot of pretending to do." In an interview with Melvyn Bragg in the *New York Times Book Review,* le Carre states: "From early on, I was extremely secretive and began to think that I was, so to speak, born into occupied territory." He tells *Newsweek* that "there is a correlation, I suppose, between the secret life of my father and the secret life I entered at a formative age." Le Carre fictionalized his relationship with his father in the 1986 novel, *A Perfect Spy.*

"As for my own writing," le Carre tells Gross, "the real fun is the fun of finding that you've enchanted people, enchanted them in the sense that you've admitted them to a world they didn't know about. And also that you've given them a great deal of relief, in a strange way, because they've discovered a bit of life interpreted for them in ways that, after all, they find they understand."

BIOGRAPHICAL/CRITICAL SOURCES:

BOOKS

Barley, Tony, *Taking Sides: The Fiction of John le Carre,* Open University Press, 1986.
Cobbs, John, *Understanding John le Carre,* University of South Carolina Press, 1998.
Contemporary Literary Criticism, Gale, Volume 3, 1975; Volume 5, 1976; Volume 9, 1978; Volume 15, 1980; Volume 28, 1984.
Dictionary of Literary Biography, Volume 87: *British Mystery and Thriller Writers since 1940, First Series,* Gale, 1989.
Harper, Ralph, *The World of the Thriller,* Press of Case Western University (Cleveland, OH), 1969.
Homberger, Eric, *John le Carre,* Ungar (New York City), 1985.
Monaghan, David, *The Novels of John le Carre: The Art of Survival,* Blackwell (Oxford), 1985.
Monaghan, David, *Smiley's Circus: A Guide to the Secret World of John le Carre,* Orbis (London), 1986.
Palmer, Jerry, *Thrillers: Genesis and Structure of a Popular Genre,* St. Martin's (New York City), 1979.
Symons, Julian, *Mortal Consequences: A History from the Detective Story to the Crime Novel,* Harper (New York City), 1972.
Wolfe, Peter, *Corridors of Deceit: The World of John le Carre,* Bowling Green University Popular Press (Bowling Green, OH), 1987.

PERIODICALS

Armchair Detective, spring, 1980.
Booklist, January 1, 1998, p. 835.
Book Week, January 26, 1964.
Chicago Tribune, June 19, 1989.
Chicago Tribune Book World, March 6, 1983.
Chicago Tribune Magazine, March 23, 1980.
Christian Science Monitor, January 14, 1980.
Chronicles of Culture, August, 1983.
Clues: A Journal of Detection, fall/winter, 1980; fall/winter, 1982.
Commentary, June, 1983.
Detroit News, August 29, 1982.
Economist, July 1, 1989, p. 75.
Entertainment Weekly, November 15, 1996, p. 66.
Esquire, April, 1983.

Globe and Mail (Toronto), June 10, 1989.
Harper's, January, 1964; November, 1965; December, 1968; February, 1998, p. 18.
Life, February 28, 1964.
Listener, July 4, 1974.
Los Angeles Times, May 31, 1989; October 16, 1989.
Los Angeles Times Book Review, June 18, 1989.
Maclean's, March 7, 1983; November 25, 1996, p. 17.
Nation, December 30, 1968.
National Observer, October 28, 1968.
National Review, March 13, 1983.
New Leader, June 24, 1974; March 7, 1983.
New Republic, July 31, 1976; January 19, 1980; April 18, 1983; August 21, 1989, p. 30; August 9, 1993.
New Review, July, 1974.
New Statesman, July 12, 1974; September 23, 1977.
Newsweek, October 28, 1968; June 17, 1974; September 26, 1977; March 7, 1983; June 5, 1989, p. 52; July 5, 1993, p. 54.
New York, December 24, 1979; October 25, 1982.
New Yorker, October 3, 1977; August 23, 1993, p. 165; December 8, 1997, p. 37.
New York Review of Books, October 27, 1977; February 7, 1980; April 14, 1983; September 28, 1989, p. 9; March 28, 1991, p. 8; August 12, 1993, p. 20; November 28, 1996, p. 16.
New York Times, January 28, 1969; September 22, 1977; February 25, 1983; May 18, 1989, p. C28; December 1, 1991; July 8, 1993; October 18, 1996, p. B16.
New York Times Book Review, January 12, 1964; June 5, 1965; March 11, 1966; January 27, 1967; June 30, 1974; September 25, 1977; January 6, 1980; March 13, 1983; June 7, 1987, p. 34; May 21, 1989, p. 3; January 6, 1991, p. 3; June 27, 1993.
New York Times Magazine, September 8, 1974.
People, August 19, 1974; September 13, 1993, p. 63; November 18, 1996, p. 33.
Publishers Weekly, September 19, 1977.
Quest/80, January, 1980.
Salmagundi, summer, 1970.
Saturday Review, July 24, 1965.
Spectator, July 6, 1974.
Time, January 17, 1964; May 29, 1964; September 29, 1980; January 14, 1991, p. 61.
Times (London), September 6, 1982; June 24, 1989.
Times Literary Supplement, September 13, 1963; June 24, 1965; September 24, 1971; July 19, 1974; September 9, 1977; August 4, 1989; October 18, 1996, p. 22.
Tribune Books (Chicago), May 21, 1989.
U.S. News and World Report, June 19, 1989, p. 59.
Village Voice, October 24, 1977; January 14, 1980.
Washington Post, September 29, 1980; November 29, 1982; May 25, 1989; October 14, 1989.
Washington Post Book World, December 8, 1974; December 23, 1979; June 4, 1989.
Yale Review, January, 1994, p. 150.

*　　　*　　　*

CORNWELL, Patricia (Daniels) 1956-

PERSONAL: Born June 9, 1956, in Miami, FL; daughter of Sam (an attorney) and Marilyn (a secretary; maiden name, Zenner) Daniels; married Charles Cornwell (a college professor), June 14, 1980 (divorced, 1990). *Education:* Davidson College, North Carolina, B.A. in English, 1979. *Religion:* Presbyterian. *Avocation:* Tennis.

ADDRESSES: Agent—International Creative Management, 40 W. 57th St., New York, NY 10019.

CAREER: Charlotte Observer, Charlotte, NC, police reporter, 1979-81; Office of the Chief Medical Examiner, Richmond, VA, computer analyst, 1985-91. Volunteer police officer. Bell Vision Productions (film production company), president.

MEMBER: International Crime Writers Association, International Association of Chiefs of Police, International Association of Identification, National Association of Medical Examiners, Authors Guild, Mystery Writers of America, Virginia Writers Club.

AWARDS, HONORS: Investigative reporting award, North Carolina Press Association, 1980, for a series on prostitution; Gold Medallion Book Award for biography, Evangelical Christian Publishers Association, 1985, for *A Time for Remembering: The Story of Ruth Bell Graham*; John Creasy Award, British Crime Writers Association, Edgar Award, Mystery Writers of America, Anthony Award, Boucheron, World Mystery Convention, and Macavity Award, Mystery Readers International, all for best first crime novel, all 1990, and French Prix du Roman d'Aventure, 1991, all for *Postmortem*; Gold Dagger award, for *Cruel and Unusual*.

WRITINGS:

CRIME NOVELS

Postmortem, Scribner (New York City), 1990.
Body of Evidence, Scribner, 1991.
All That Remains, Scribner, 1992.
Cruel and Unusual, Scribner, 1993.
The Body Farm, Scribner, 1994.
From Potter's Field, Scribner, 1995.
Cause of Death, Putnam (New York City), 1996.
Hornet's Nest, Putnam, 1997.
Unnatural Exposure, Putnam, 1997.
Point of Origin, Putnum, 1998.

OTHER

A Time for Remembering: The Story of Ruth Bell Graham (biography), Harper (New York City), 1983, published as *Ruth, A Portrait: The Story of Ruth Bell Graham,* Doubleday, 1997.

MEDIA ADAPTATIONS: Brilliance Corp. released a sound recording of *Body of Evidence* in 1992; sound recordings are also available for *Postmortem, All That Remains, Cruel and Unusual, The Body Farm,* and *From Potter's Field.* Negotiations are in progress for the film rights to *From Potter's Field.*

SIDELIGHTS: Since 1990, Patricia Cornwell's novels have followed Dr. Kay Scarpetta, a medical examiner called upon to solve murders with forensic sleuthing. The novels are praised for their accurate detail based upon research Cornwell did in the Virginia medical examiner's office, witnessing scores of autopsies. In addition to this, Cornwell also went out on police homicide runs. "I'm not sure I could have read my last book if I hadn't written it," Cornwell told Sandra McElwaine in *Harper's Bazaar.* "The violence is so real, I think it would have scared me to death."

Cornwell began her book-writing career in 1983 with a biography of Ruth Graham, wife of evangelist Billy Graham. It was Graham who encouraged her to pursue writing. "I felt she had real ability," Graham told Joe Treen in *People.* "I've kept every note I ever got from her." With Graham's encouragement, Cornwell went back to

school at Davidson College in North Carolina, majoring in English. Right after graduation she married Charles Cornwell, one of her former professors, and began working as a crime reporter for the *Charlotte Observer.*

Cornwell, prompted by friends who knew of her longing to write crime fiction, eventually became a regular visitor at a forensic center and also took on technical writing projects for the morgue to absorb more of the forensic knowledge she craved. The result was *Postmortem,* the first in a series of mysteries chronicling Cornwell's fictional investigative forensic pathologist, Dr. Kay Scarpetta.

Postmortem focuses on the rape and murder of several Richmond women by a serial killer. The book charts the work of Scarpetta, the chief medical examiner of Virginia, as she attempts to uncover the killer's identity. Frequently faced with sexism regarding her ability to handle a "man's job," Scarpetta aptly displays her knowledge of the innovative technologies of today's forensic medicine to crack the case. "Dr. Scarpetta has a terrible time with the chauvinists around her, one of whom in particular is malevolently eager for her to fail," writes Charles Champlin in the *Los Angeles Times Book Review.* "These passages have the ring of truth as experienced, and so does the portrait of an investigative reporter who abets the solving."

"*Postmortem* . . . won just about every mystery fiction award," declares *New York Times Book Review* contributor Bill Kent. "The follow-up novel, *Body of Evidence,* proved that Ms. Cornwell's success wasn't mere beginner's luck." *Body of Evidence* centers on Beryl Madison, a young woman who is writing a controversial book for which she has received death threats. Shortly after she reports these events she is murdered—apparently after allowing the killer to enter her home. Scarpetta must once again use tiny bits of evidence to track down the murderer.

In later novels, Cornwell introduces Temple Gault, a serial killer with intelligence to match Scarpetta's. Gault, who specializes in the murder of children, only narrowly escapes being captured by Scarpetta herself in *Cruel and Unusual.* "With his pale blue eyes and his ability to anticipate the best minds of law enforcement," writes Elise O'Shaughnessy in the *New York Times Book Review,* "Gault is a 'malignant genius' in the tradition of Hannibal Lecter," the cannibalistic character in Thomas Harris's *The Silence of the Lambs.* "Like Lecter's bond with Clarice Starling," O'Shaughnessy concludes, "Gault's relationship with Scarpetta is *personal.*"

In a column for *Mystery Scene* magazine, Cornwell shed some light on the nature of her heroine, Dr. Scarpetta. "Violence is filtered through her intellectual sophistication and inbred civility, meaning that the senseless cruelty of what she sees is all the more horrific," the author explained. She added that Dr. Scarpetta "approaches the cases with the sensitivity of a physician, the rational thinking of a scientist, and the outrage of a humane woman who values, above all else, the sanctity of life. Through Dr. Scarpetta's character I began to struggle with an irony that had eluded me before: the more expert one gets in dismantling death, the less he understands it."

Scarpetta faces Temple Gault again in Cornwell's 1995 novel, *From Potter's Field,* set in New York City. Critics again note the research involved in the novel, as Mary B. W. Tabor comments in the *New York Times:* "There is something especially savory about novels set in real places, with real street names, real shops, real sights and smells that ring true for those who know the territory." Scarpetta is called in after Gault murders a young homeless woman on Christmas Eve in Central Park. *Booklist* reviewer Emily Melton compares reading *From Potter's Field* to "riding one of those amusement-park roller coasters . . . [that leave] the rider gasping and breathless." Melton lauds Cornwell's "magnificent plotting, masterful writing, and marvelous suspense," rating her among the top crime fiction writers.

BIOGRAPHICAL/CRITICAL SOURCES:

PERIODICALS

Armchair Detective, winter, 1991, p. 32.
Booklist, May 1, 1995.
Entertainment Weekly, June 26, 1992, p. 73.
Harper's Bazaar, August, 1992, pp. 46, 148.
Kirkus Reviews, June 1, 1995.
Library Journal, September 1, 1994, p. 213.
Los Angeles Times, March 28, 1991, p. F12.
Los Angeles Times Book Review, February 11, 1990, p. 5; February 10, 1991, p. 9; September 20, 1992, p. 8.
Mystery Scene, January, 1990, pp. 56-7.
Newsweek, August 3, 1992; July 5, 1993.
New York Times Book Review, January 7, 1990; February 24, 1991; August 23, 1992; April 4, 1993, p. 19; July 4, 1993; September 16, 1994, p. 38-9.
People, August 24, 1992, pp. 71-2; October 3, 1994, pp. 37-8.
Publisher's Weekly, December 7, 1990, p. 76; February 15, 1991, pp. 71-2; June 15, 1992, p. 89; September 12, 1994.
School Library Journal, December, 1992, pp. 146-47.
Time, September 14, 1992; October 3, 1994.
Times Literary Supplement, July 16, 1993, p. 22.
Washington Post Book World, January 21, 1990, p. 6.
Wilson Library Bulletin, December, 1993.

*　　*　　*

CORSO, (Nunzio) Gregory 1930-

PERSONAL: Born March 26, 1930, in New York, NY; son of Fortunato Samuel and Michelina (Colonni) Corso; married Sally November (a teacher), May 7, 1963 (divorced); married Belle Carpenter, 1968; married Jocelyn Stern; children: (first marriage) Mirandia; (second marriage) Cybelle Nuncia, Max-Orphe. *Education:* Attended grammar school. *Politics:* "Individualism and freedom." *Religion:* "God."

ADDRESSES: Home—100 Sullivan St., New York, NY. *Agent*—c/o New Directions, 80 Eighth Ave., New York, NY 10011.

CAREER: Writer. Manual laborer in New York City, 1950-51; employee of *Los Angeles Examiner,* Los Angeles, CA, 1951-52; merchant seaman on Norwegian vessels, 1952-53. English department, State University of New York at Buffalo, 1965-70. Appeared in Peter Whitehead's film, *Wholly Communion,* and in Andy Warhol's *Couch.*

AWARDS, HONORS: Longview Award for poem, "Marriage"; $1,000 Poetry Foundation award; Jean Stein Award for Poetry, American Academy and Institute of Arts and Letters, 1986.

WRITINGS:

The Vestal Lady on Brattle, and Other Poems, R. Brukenfeld (Cambridge, MA), 1955.
This Hung-Up Age (play) produced at Harvard University, 1955.
Bomb (poem; broadside), [San Francisco], 1958.

Gasoline (poems), introduction by Allen Ginsberg, City Lights, 1958, new edition, 1992.
(With Henk Marsman) *A Pulp Magazine for the Dead Generation: Poems,* Dead Language, 1959.
(With William S. Burroughs, Brion Gysin, and Sinclair Beiles) *Minutes to Go,* Two Cities Editions (Paris, France), 1960.
Happy Birthday of Death (poems), New Directions, 1960.
(Editor with Walter Hollerer) *Junge Amerikanische Lyrik* (anthology), Carl Hansen Verlag, 1961.
The American Express (novel), Olympia Press, 1961.
(With Anselm Hollo and Tom Raworth) *The Minicab War,* Matrix Press, 1961.
Find It So Hard to Write the How Why & What . . . , Paterson Society, 1961.
Long Live Man (poems), New Directions, 1962.
Selected Poems, Eyre & Spottiswoode, 1962.
(With Lawrence Ferlinghetti and Allen Ginsberg) *Penguin Modern Poets 5,* Penguin, 1963.
The Mutation of the Spirit: A Shuffle Poem, Death Press, 1964.
There Is Yet Time to Run Back through Life and Expiate All That's Been Sadly Done (poems), New Directions, 1965.
(Contributor) Paris Leary and Robert Kelly, editors, *A Controversy of Poets,* Doubleday Anchor, 1965.
The Geometric Poem: A Long Experimental Poem, Composite of Many Lines and Angles Selective, [Milan, Italy], 1966.
(Contributor) Bob Booker and George Foster, editors, *Pardon Me, Sir, But Is My Eye Hurting Your Elbow?* (screenplays), Bernard Geis, 1967.
10 Times a Poem: Collected at Random From 2 Suitcases Filled With Poems—the Gathering of 5 Years, Poets Press, 1967.
Elegiac Feelings American, New Directions, 1970.
Gregory Corso, Phoenix Book Shop, 1971.
Egyptian Cross, Phoenix Book Shop, 1971.
The Night Last Night Was at Its Nightest . . . , Phoenix Book Shop, 1972.
Earth Egg, Unmuzzled Ox, 1974.
Way Out: A Poem in Discord (play), Bardo Matrix (Kathmandu, Nepal), 1974.
The Japanese Notebook Ox, Unmuzzled Ox, 1974.
Collected Plays, City Lights, 1980.
Writings from Ox, edited by Michael Andre, Unmuzzled Ox, 1981.
Herald of the Autochthonic Spirit, New Directions, 1981.
Mindfield: New and Selected Poems, Thunder's Mouth, 1989.

Also coauthor of screenplay *Happy Death,* 1965; contributor to periodicals, including *Evergreen Review* and *Litterair Paspoort.*

SIDELIGHTS: Gregory Corso is a key member of the Beat movement, a group of convention-breaking writers who are generally credited with sparking much of the social and political change that transformed America in the 1960s. Corso's spontaneous, insightful, and inspirational verse once prompted fellow Beat poet Allen Ginsberg to describe him as an "awakener of youth." Although Corso enjoyed his greatest level of popularity during the 1960s and 1970s, he continues to influence contemporary readers and critics today. Writing in the *American Book Review,* Dennis Barone remarked that Corso's 1990 volume of new and selected poems was a sign that "despite doubt, uncertainty, the American way, death all around, Gregory Corso will continue, and I am glad he will."

Born in 1930 to teenaged parents who separated a year after his birth, Corso spent his early childhood in foster homes and orphanages. At the age of eleven, he went to live with his natural father, who had remarried. A troubled youth, Corso repeatedly ran away and was eventually sent to a boys' home. One year later, he was caught selling a stolen radio and was forced to testify in court against the dealer who purchased the illegal merchandise. While he was held as a material witness in the trial, the twelve-year-old boy spent several months in prison where, as he wrote in a biographical sketch for *The New American Poetry,* the other prisoners "abused me terribly, and I was indeed like an angel then because when they stole my food and beat me up and threw pee in my cell, I . . . would come out and tell them my beautiful dream about a floating girl who landed before a deep pit and just stared." He later spent three months under observation at Bellevue Hospital.

When Corso was sixteen, he returned to jail to serve a three-year sentence for theft. There he read widely in the classics, including Fyodor Dostoevsky, Stendahl, Percy Bysshe Shelley, Thomas Chatterton, and Christopher Marlowe.

After his release in 1950, Corso worked as a laborer in New York City, a newspaper reporter in Los Angeles, and a sailor on a boat to Africa and South America. It was in New York City that he first met Allen Ginsberg, the Beat poet with whom he is most closely associated. The pair met in a Greenwich Village bar in 1950 while Corso was working on his first poems. Until then he had read only traditional poetry, and Ginsberg introduced him to contemporary, experimental work. Within a few years Corso was writing in long Whitmanesque lines similar to those Ginsberg had developed in his own work. The surreal word combinations that began to appear in Ginsberg's work about the same time may in turn suggest Corso's reciprocal influence.

In 1954, Corso moved to Boston, where several important poets, including Edward Marshall and John Wieners, were experimenting with the poetics of voice. But the center for Corso's life there was not "the School of Boston," as these poets were called, but Harvard and particularly the Harvard library, where he spent his days reading the great works of poetry. His first published poems appeared in the *Harvard Advocate* in 1954, and his play, *In This Hung-Up Age* (concerning a group of Americans who, after their bus breaks down midway across the continent, are trampled by buffalo), was performed by students at the university the following year.

Harvard and Radcliffe students also underwrote the expenses of Corso's first book, *The Vestal Lady on Brattle, and Other Poems.* The poems featured in the volume are usually considered apprentice works heavily indebted to Corso's reading. They are, however, unique in their innovative use of jazz rhythms (notably in "Requiem for 'Bird' Parker, Musician," which many call the strongest poem in the book), cadences of spoken English, and hipster jargon. Corso explained his use of rhythm and meter in an interview with Gavin Salerie for *Riverside Interviews*: "My music is built in—it's already natural. I don't play with the meter." In other words, Corso believes the meter must arise naturally from the poet's voice; it is never consciously chosen.

In a review of Corso's first book for *Poetry,* Reuel Denney asked whether "a small group jargon" such as bop language would "sound interesting" to those who were not part of that culture. Corso, he concluded, "cannot balance the richness of the bebop group jargon . . . with the clarity he needs to make his work meaningful to a wider-than-clique audience." Ironically, within a few years, that "small group jargon" became, of course, a national idiom.

Despite Corso's reliance on traditional forms and archaic diction, he remains a street-wise poet, described by Bruce Cook in *The Beat Generation* as "an urchin Shelley." Gaiser suggested that Corso adopts "the mask of the sophisticated child whose every display of mad spontaneity and bizarre perception is consciously and effectively designed"—as if he is in some way deceiving his audience. But the poems at their best are controlled by an authentic, distinctive, and enormously effective voice that can range from sentimental affection and pathos to exuberance and dadaist irreverence toward almost anything except poetry itself.

When Corso moved to San Francisco in 1956, he was too late to participate in the famous reading at the Six Gallery, at which Ginsberg read "Howl" and which, since it was widely noted in newspapers and popular magazines, is conventionally cited as the first major public event in the rise of the Beat movement. However, Corso was soon identified as one of the major figures of the movement and that celebrity status or notoriety undoubtedly contributed much to the fame of his poetry in the late 1950s and early 1960s. With Ginsberg, he also coauthored "The Literary Revolution in America" (originally published in *Litterair Paspoort*), an article in which they declared that America now had poets who "have taken it upon themselves, with angelic clarions in hand, to announce their discontent, their demands, their hope, their final wondrous unimaginable dream."

From 1957 to 1958, Corso lived in Paris, where, he told Michael Andre in an *Unmuzzled Ox* interview, "things burst and opened, and I said, 'I will just let the lines go. . . .'" Poems that resulted were published in *Gasoline,* his first major book. *Gasoline* also contains poems written while Corso was traveling with Ginsberg in Mexico, and Ginsberg's influence is evident in much of the work. Here Whitman's long poetic line has become Corso's much as it had become Ginsberg's, and the diction is occasionally reminiscent of Ginsberg as well. "Ode to Coit Tower," for example, echoes "In the Baggage Room at Greyhound," on which Ginsberg recently had been working, and "Sun" utilizes structural devices and incantatory effects used in "Howl." But however influential Ginsberg may have been, Corso always maintained his own distinctive voice. In an essay collected in *The Beats: Essays in Criticism,* Geoffrey Thurley summarized some of the principal characteristics that differentiate Corso from Ginsberg: "Where Ginsberg is all expression and voice, Corso is calm and quick, whimsical often, witty rather than humourous, semantically swift rather than prophetically incantatory."

The influence of bop is far more evident in *Gasoline* than in *The Vestal Lady on Brattle.* In his introduction, Ginsberg quotes Corso as saying that his poems were written the way Charlie Parker and Miles Davis played music. He would start with standard diction and rhythm but then be "intentionally distracted diversed [sic] into my own sound." The result is an intricate linguistic pattern involving extremely subtle modulations of sound and rhythm. "For Corso," Neeli Cherkovski wrote in *Whitman's Wild Children: Profiles of Ten Contemporary American Poets,* "poetry is at its best when it can create a totally unexpected expression," and many of these linguistic fusions suggest the pleasure in invention for its own sake.

Corso shaped his poems from 1970 to 1974 into a book that he planned to call *Who Am I—Who I Am,* but the manuscript was stolen, and there were no other copies. Aside from chapbooks and a few miscellaneous publications, he did not issue other work until 1981 when *Herald of the Autochthonic Spirit* appeared. Shorter than any of his major books since *Gasoline,* it contains some critically acclaimed poems, many of them written in clipped, almost prosaic lines more reminiscent of William Carlos Williams than of Whitman. "Return" deals with barren times in which there had been no poems but also asserts that the poet can now write again and that "the past [is] my future." The new poems, however, are generally more subdued than the earlier ones, though there are surreal flights, as in "The Whole Mess . . . Almost," in which the poet cleans his apartment of Truth, God, Beauty, Death, and essentially everything but Humor.

By the early 1980s, when Corso's *Herald of the Autochthonic Spirit* was published, language-centered writing, in which the conventions of language themselves become the subjects of poems, had long since surpassed the poetics of voice as the center of attention for many younger poets working outside academic traditions. Thus the book was not widely reviewed, even though it contains some of Corso's best work. But if the voice that shaped these poems is often quieter than it had been a generation before, it nonetheless continues to affirm Kenneth Rexroth's characterization of Corso as "a real wildman." "At his worst," Rexroth added, "he is an amusing literary curiosity; at his best, his poems are metaphysical hotfoots and poetic cannon crackers."

In 1991, Corso published a volume entitled *Mindfield: New and Selected Poems.* The book consists of selections from five previously published books and close to sixty pages of previously unpublished poems, including one almost thirty pages long. Barone declared that the volume "provides for new readers the opportunity to be awakened and for those familiar with Corso's work a chance to be reawakened."

Although Corso has greatly reduced the number of poems he publishes in recent years, he continues to believe in the power of poetry to bring about change. He once explained his Utopian vision in a letter to *Contemporary Authors*: "I feel that in the future many many poets will blossom forth—the poetic spirit will spread and reach toward all; it will show itself not in words—the written poem—but rather in man's being and in the deeds he enacts. . . . A handful of poets in every country in the world can and have always been able to live in the world as well as in their own world; . . . [and] when such humankind becomes manifold, when all are embraced by the poetic spirit, by a world of poets, not by the written word but by deed and thought and beauty, then society will have no recourse but to become suitable for them and for itself. I feel man is headed in such a direction; he is fated and due to become aware of and knowledgeable about his time; his good intelligence and compassion will enable him to cope with almost all the bothersome, distracting difficulties that may arise— and when he becomes so, 'poet' will not be his name, but it will be his victory."

BIOGRAPHICAL/CRITICAL SOURCES:

BOOKS

Bartlett, Lee, *The Beats: Essays in Criticism,* McFarland, 1981.
Chassman, Neil A., editor, *Poets of the Cities: New York and San Francisco, 1950-1965,* Dutton, 1974.
Cherkovski, Neeli, *Whitman's Wild Children: Profiles of Ten Contemporary American Poets,* Lapis Press, 1988.
Contemporary Authors New Revision Series, Volume 41, Gale, 1994.
Contemporary Literary Criticism, Gale, Volume 1, 1973; Volume 11, 1979.
Cook, Bruce, *The Beat Generation,* Scribner, 1971.
Dictionary of Literary Biography, Gale, Volume 5: *American Poets since World War II,* 1980; Volume 16: *The Beats: Literary Bohemianism in Postwar America,* 1983.
Gifford, Barry, and Lawrence Lee, *Jack's Book: An Oral Biography of Jack Kerouac,* St. Martin's, 1978.
Knight, Arthur, and Kit Knight, editors, *The Beat Vision: A Primary Sourcebook,* Paragon House, 1987.
Leary, Paris, and Robert Kelly, editors, *A Controversy of Poets,* Doubleday Anchor, 1965.
Nemerov, Howard, editor, *Poets on Poetry,* Basic Books, 1966.
Parkinson, Thomas, editor, *A Casebook on the Beat,* Crowell, 1961.
Rexroth, Kenneth, *Assays,* New Directions, 1961.
Selerie, Gavin, *Riverside Interviews 3: Gregory Corso,* Binnacle Press, 1982.
Tytell, John, *Naked Angels: The Lives and Literature of the Beat Generation,* McGraw, 1976.
Wilson, Robert A., *A Bibliography of Works by Gregory Corso, 1954-1965,* Phoenix Book Shop, 1966.

PERIODICALS

American Book Review, September, 1990, p. 17.
Hudson Review, spring, 1963.
Kenyon Review, spring, 1963.
New York Times, April 13, 1997.
North Dakota Quarterly, spring, 1982.
Partisan Review, fall, 1960.
Poetry, October, 1956.
Thoth, winter, 1971.
Unmuzzled Ox, winter, 1981.

*   *   *

CORTAZAR, Julio 1914-1984
(Julio Denis)

PERSONAL: Born August 26, 1914, in Brussels, Belgium; held dual citizenship in Argentina and (beginning 1981) France; died of a heart attack February 12, 1984, in Paris, France; son of Julio Jose and Maria Herminia (Descotte) Cortazar; married former spouse Aurora Bernardez, August 23, 1953. *Education:* Received degrees in teaching and public translating; attended Buenos Aires University. *Avocation:* Jazz, movies.

CAREER: Writer. High school teacher in Bolivar and Chivilcoy, both in Argentina, 1937-44; teacher of French literature, University of Cuyo, Mendoza, Argentina, 1944-45; manager, Argentine Publishing Association (Camara Argentina del Libro), Buenos Aires, Argentina, 1946-48; public translator in Argentina, 1948-51; freelance translator for UNESCO, Paris, 1952-84. Member of jury, Casa de las Americas Award.

AWARDS, HONORS: Prix Medicis, 1974, for *Libro de Manuel;* Ruben Dario Order of Cultural Independence awarded by Government of Nicaragua, 1983.

WRITINGS:

FICTION

Bestiario (short stories; also see below), Sudamericana (Buenos Aires), 1951.
Final del juego (short stories; also see below), Los Presentes (Mexico), 1956, expanded edition, Sudamericana, 1964.
Las armas secretas (short stories; title means "The Secret Weapons"; also see below), Sudamericana, 1959.

Los premios (novel), Sudamericana, 1960, translation by Elaine Kerrigan published as *The Winners,* Pantheon, 1965.

Historias de cronopios y de famas (novel), Minotauro (Buenos Aires), 1962, translation by Paul Blackburn published as *Cronopios and Famas,* Pantheon, 1969.

Rayuela (novel), Sudamericana, 1963, translation by Gregory Rabassa published as *Hopscotch,* Pantheon, 1966.

Cuentos (collection), Casa de las Americas (Havana), 1964.

Todos los fuegos el fuego (short stories), Sudamericana, 1966, translation by Suzanne Jill Levine published as *All Fires the Fire, and Other Stories,* Pantheon, 1973.

La vuelta al dia en ochenta mundos (essays, poetry, and short stories), Siglo Veintiuno (Mexico), 1967, translation by Thomas Christensen published as *Around the Day in Eighty Worlds,* North Point Press, 1986.

El perseguidor y otros cuentos (short stories), Centro Editor para America Latina (Buenos Aires), 1967.

End of the Game, and Other Stories, translated by Blackburn (includes stories from *Final del juego, Bestiario,* and *Las armas secretas*), Pantheon, 1967, published as *Blow-Up, and Other Stories,* Collier, 1968.

Ceremonias (collection), Seix Barral, 1968.

62: Modelo para armar (novel), Sudamericana, 1968, translation by Rabassa published as *62: A Model Kit,* Pantheon, 1972.

Ultimo round (essays, poetry, and stories; title means "Last Round"), Siglo Veintiuno, 1969.

Relatos (collection), Sudamericana, 1970.

La isla a mediodia y otros relatos (contains twelve previously published stories), Salvat, 1971.

Libro de Manuel (novel), Sudamericana, 1973, translation by Rabassa published as *A Manual for Manuel,* Pantheon, 1978.

Octaedro (stories; title means "Octahedron"; also see below), Sudamericana, 1974.

Antologia (collection), La Libreria, 1975.

Fantomas contra los vampiros multinacionales (title means "Fantomas Takes on the Multinational Vampires"), Excelsior (Mexico), 1975.

Los relatos (collection), four volumes, Alianza, 1976-1985.

Alguien que anda por ahi y otros relatos (short stories), Alfaguara (Madrid), 1977, translation by Rabassa published as *A Change of Light, and Other Stories* (includes *Octaedro;* also see below), Knopf, 1980.

Territorios, Siglo Veintiuno, 1978.

Un tal Lucas, Alfaguara, 1979, translation by Rabassa published as *A Certain Lucas,* Knopf, 1984.

Queremos tanto a Glenda, Alfaguara, 1980, translation by Rabassa published as *We Love Glenda So Much, and Other Tales* (also see below), Knopf, 1983.

Deshoras (short stories), Alfaguara, 1982, translation by Alberto Manguel published as *Unreasonable Hours,* Coach House Press (Toronto), 1995.

We Love Glenda So Much and *A Change of Light,* Vintage, 1984.

Salvo el Crepusculo, translated by Stephen Kessler, published as *Save Twilight,* City Lights Books (San Francisco, CA), 1997.

TRANSLATOR

Alfred Stern, *Filosofia de la risa y del llanto,* Iman (Buenos Aires), 1950.

Lord Houghton, *Vida y cartas de John Keats,* Iman, 1955.

Marguerite Yourcenar, *Memorias de Adriano,* Sudamericana, 1955.

Edgar Allan Poe, *Obras en prosa,* two volumes, Revista de Occidente, 1956.

Poe, *Cuentos,* Editorial Nacional de Cuba, 1963.

Poe, *Aventuras de Arthur Gordon Pym,* Instituto del Libro (Havana), 1968.

Poe, *Eureka,* Alianza (Madrid), 1972.

Daniel Defoe, *Robinson Crusoe,* Bruguera, 1981.

Also translator of works by G. K. Chesterton, Andre Gide, and Jean Giono, published in Argentina between 1948 and 1951.

OTHER

(Under pseudonym Julio Denis) *Presencia* (poems; title means "Presence"), El Bibliofilo (Buenos Aires), 1938.

Los reyes (play; title means "The Monarchs"), Gulab y Aldabahor (Buenos Aires), 1949.

(Contributor) *Buenos Aires de la fundacion a la angustia,* Ediciones de la Flor (Buenos Aires), 1967.

(With others) *Cuba por argentinos,* Merlin (Buenos Aires), 1968.

Buenos Aires, Buenos Aires (includes French and English translations), Sudamericana, 1968.

Viaje alrededor de una mesa (title means "Trip around a Table"), Cuadernos de Rayuela (Buenos Aires), 1970.

(With Oscar Collazos and Mario Vargas Llosa) *Literatura en la revolucion y revolucion en la literatura,* Siglo Veintiuno, 1970.

(Contributor) *Literatura y arte nuevo en Cuba,* Estela (Barcelona), 1971.

Pameos y meopas (poetry), Editorial Libre de Sivera (Barcelona), 1971.

Prosa del observatorio, Lumen (Barcelona), 1972.

La casilla de los Morelli (essays), edited by Jose Julio Ortega, Tusquets, 1973.

Convergencias, divergencias, incidencias, edited by Ortega, Tusquets, 1973.

(Author of text) *Humanario,* La Azotea (Buenos Aires), 1976.

(Author of text) *Paris: Ritmos de una ciudad,* Edhasa (Barcelona), 1981.

Paris: The Essence of an Image, Norton, 1981.

(With Carol Dunlop) *Los autonautas de la cosmopista,* Muchnik (Buenos Aires), 1983.

Nicaragua tan violentamente dulce (essays), Nueva Nicaragua, 1983.

Argentina: Anos de almabradas culturales (essays), edited by Saul Yurkievich, Muchnik, 1984.

Nada a pehuajo: Un acto; Adios, Robinson (plays), Katun, 1984.

Salvo el crepusculo (poems), Nueva Imagen, 1984.

Textos politicos, Plaza y Janes, 1985.

Divertimento, Sudamericana/Planeta, 1986.

El examen, Sudamericana/Planeta, 1986.

Nicaraguan Sketches, Norton, 1989.

Contributor to numerous periodicals, including *Revista Iberoamericana, Cuadernos Hispanoamericanos, Books Abroad,* and *Casa de las Americas.*

MEDIA ADAPTATIONS: The story *Las babas del diablo,* from the collection *Las armas secretas* was the basis for Michaelangelo Antonioni's 1966 film *Blow Up.*

SIDELIGHTS: Argentine author Julio Cortazar was "one of the world's greatest writers," according to novelist Stephen Dobyns. "His range of styles," Dobyns wrote in the *Washington Post Book World,* "his ability to paint a scene, his humor, his endlessly peculiar mind makes many of his stories wonderful. His novel *Hopscotch* is considered one of the best novels written by a South American."

A popular as well as a critical success, *Hopscotch* not only established Cortazar's reputation as a novelist of international merit but also, according to David W. Foster in *Currents in the Contemporary Argentine Novel*, prompted wider acceptance in the United States of novels written by other Latin Americans. For this reason many critics, such as Jaime Alazraki in *The Final Island*, viewed the book as "a turning point for Latin American literature." A *Times Literary Supplement* reviewer, for example, called *Hopscotch* "the first great novel of Spanish America."

Hopscotch is one such novel. In *Into the Mainstream: Conversations with Latin-America Writers*, Luis Harss and Barbara Dohmann wrote that *Hopscotch* "is the first Latin American novel which takes itself as its own central topic or, in other words, is essentially about the writing of itself. It lives in constant metamorphoses, as an unfinished process that invents itself as it goes, involving the reader in such a way to make him part of the creative impulse." Thus, *Hopscotch* begins with a "Table of Instructions" that tells the reader that there are at least two ways to read the novel. The first is reading chapters one to fifty-six in numerical order. When the reader finishes chapter fifty-six he can, according to the instructions, stop reading and "ignore what follows [nearly one hundred more short chapters] with a clean conscience." The other way of reading suggested by the instructions is to start with chapter seventy-two and then skip from chapter to chapter (hence, the title of the book), following the sequence indicated at the end of each chapter by a number which tells the reader which chapter is next. Read the second way, the reader finds that chapter 131 refers him to chapter fifty-eight, and chapter fifty-eight to chapter 131, so that he is confronted with a novel that has no end. With his "Table of Instructions" Cortazar forces the reader to write the novel while he is reading it.

Cortazar's other experimental works include *62: A Model Kit* (considered a sequel to *Hopscotch*), *A Manual for Manuel*, *Ultimo round* ("Last Round"), and *Fantomas contra los vampiros multinacionales* ("Fantomas Takes on the Multinacional Vampires"). *62: A Model Kit* is based on chapter sixty-two of *Hopscotch* in which a character, Morelli, expresses his desire to write a new type of novel. "If I were to write this book," Morelli states, "standard behavior would be inexplicable by means of current instrumental psychology. Everything would be a kind of disquiet, a continuous uprooting, a territory where psychological causality would yield disconcertedly."

In *62: A Model Kit* Cortazar attempted to put these ideas into action. Time and space have no meaning in the novel: although it takes place in Paris, London, and Vienna, the characters move and interact as if they are in one single space. The characters themselves are sketchily presented in fragments that must be assembled by the readers; chapters are replaced by short scenes separated by blank spaces on the pages of the novel. Cortazar noted in the book's introduction that once again the reader must help create the novel: "The reader's option, his personal montage of the elements in the tale, will in each case be the book he has chosen to read."

A Manual for Manuel continues in the experimental vein. Megan Marshall described the book in *New Republic* as "a novel that merges story and history, a supposed scrapbook of news clippings, journal entries, diagrams, transcripts of conversations, and much more." The book, about the kidnapping of a Latin American diplomat by a group of guerillas in Paris, is told from the double perspective of an unnamed member of the group, who takes notes on the plans for the kidnapping, and a nonmember of the group,

Andres, who reads the notes. Periodically, these two narrations are interrupted by the inclusion of English-, French-, and Spanish-language texts reproduced in the pages of the novel. These texts, actual articles collected by Cortazar from various sources, form part of a scrapbook being assembled for Manuel, the child of two of the members of the group. On one page, for example, Cortazar reprinted a statistical table originally published in 1969 by the U.S. Department of Defense that shows how many Latin Americans have received military training in the United States. The reader reads about the compilation of the scrapbook for Manuel, while at the same time reading the scrapbook and reacting to the historical truth it contains.

Other such experimentation is found in *Ultimo round*, a collection of essays, stories, and poetry. William L. Siemens noted in the *International Fiction Review* that this book, like *Hopscotch* and *62: A Model Kit*, "is a good example of audience-participation art." In *Ultimo round*, he declared, "it is impossible for the reader to proceed in a conventional manner. Upon opening the book the reader notes that there are two sets of pages within the binding, and he must immediately decide which of them to read first, and even whether he will go through by reading the top and then the bottom of page one, and so on."

Cortazar's brief narrative *Fantomas contra los vampiros multinacionales* is yet another experiment with new forms of fiction. It presents, in comic book form, the story of a "superhero," Fantomas, who gathers together "the greatest contemporary writers" to fight the destructive powers of the multinational corporations. Chilean Octavio Paz, Italian Alberto Moravia, and American Susan Sontag, along with Cortazar himself, appear as characters in the comic book. Although short, the work embodies several constants in Cortazar's fiction: the comic (the comic book form itself), the interplay of fantasy and reality (the appearance of historical figures in a fictional work), and a commitment to social activism (the portrayal of the writer as a politically involved individual). These three elements, together with Cortazar's experiments with the novelistic form, are the basic components of his fiction.

Cortazar explained how these elements function together in his essay "Algunos aspectos del cuento" ("Some Aspects of the Story"), which Alazraki quoted in *The Final Island*. His work, Cortazar claimed, was "an alternative to that false realism which assumed that everything can be neatly described as was upheld by the philosophic and scientific optimism of the eighteenth century, that is, within a world ruled more or less harmoniously by a system of laws, of principles, of causal relations, of well defined psychologies, of well mapped geographies. . . . In my case, the suspicion of another order, more secret and less communicable [was one of the principles guiding] my personal search for a literature beyond overly naive forms of realism." Whatever the method, whether new narrative forms, unexpected humor, incursions into fantasy, or pleas for a more humane society, Cortazar strove to shake the reader out of traditional ways of thinking and seeing the world and to replace them with new and more viable models. Dobyns explained in the *Washington Post Book World*, "Cortazar wants to jolt people out of their self-complacency, to make them doubt their own definition of the world."

Cortazar's last full-length work of fiction, *A Certain Lucas*, for example, "is a kind of sampler of narrative ideas, a playful anthology of form, including everything from parables to parodies, folk tales to metafictions," as Robert Coover describes it in the *New York Times Book Review*. Including chapters with such titles as "Lucas, His Shopping," "Lucas, His Battles with the Hydra," and "Lucas, His Pianists," the book "builds a portrait, montage-like, through a succession of short sketches (humorous set-pieces, really) full of outrageous inventions, leaping and dream-like associations and funny turns of phrase," states *Los Angeles Times Book Review* critic Charles Champlin. "Lucas is not Cortazar," Dobyns suggests in the *Washington Post Book World,* "but occasionally he seems to stand for him and so the book takes on an autobiographical quality as we read about Lucas' friends, his struggles with himself, his dreams, his tastes, his view of writing." The result, writes Champlin, might appear to be "no more than a series of extravagant jokes, [and] it would be an exceptional passing entertainment but no more than that. Yet under the cover of raillery, self-indicting foolishness and extreme-ly tall tales," the critic continues, "Cortazar is discovered to be a thoughtful, deep-feeling man, impassioned, sentimental, angry, complicated, a philosopher exploring appearances vs. realities is the way of philosophers ever." "What we see in Lucas and in much of Cortazar's work is a fierce love of this earth, despite the awfulness, and a fierce respect for life's ridiculousness," concludes Dobyns. "And in the midst of this ridiculousness, Cortazar dances . . . and that dance comforts and eases our own course through the world."

Hopscotch is filled with humorous elements, some of which Saul Yurkievich listed in *The Final Island.* He included "references to the ridiculous, . . . recourse to the outlandish, . . . absurd associations, . . . juxtaposition of the majestic with the popular or vulgar," as well as "puns, . . . [and] polyglot insults." *New York Times* writer John Leonard called absurdity "obligatory" in a work by Cortazar and gave examples of the absurd found in *A Manual for Manuel,* such as "a turquoise penguin [is] flown by jet to Argentina; the stealing of 9,000 wigs . . . and obsessive puns." In an interview with Evelyn Picon Garfield, quoted in *Books Abroad,* Cortazar called *Cronopios and Famas* his "most playful book." It is, he continued, "really a game, a very fascinating game, lots of fun, almost like a tennis match."

"Extraordinary elements" enter into the lives of Cortazar's characters in the form of fantastic episodes which interrupt their otherwise normal existences. Alexander Coleman observed in *Cinco maestros: Cuentos modernos de Hispanoamerica (Five Masters: Modern Spanish-American Stories):* "Cortazar's stories start in a disarmingly conversational way, with plenty of local touches. But something always seems to go awry just when we least expect it." "Axolotl," a short story described by novelist Joyce Carol Oates in the *New York Times Book Review* as her favorite Cortazar tale, begins innocently: a man describes his trips to the Parisian botanical gardens to watch a certain type of salamander called an axolotl. But the serenity ends when the narrator admits, "Now I am an axolotl." In another story, a woman has a dream about a beggar who lives in Budapest (a city the woman has never visited). The woman ends up actually going to Budapest where she finds herself walking across a bridge as the beggar woman from her dream approaches from the opposite side. The two women embrace in the middle of the bridge and the first woman is transformed into the beggar woman—she can feel the snow seeping through the holes in her shoes—while she sees her former self walk away. In yet another story, a motorcyclist is involved in a minor traffic accident and suddenly finds himself thrown back in time where he becomes the victim of Aztec ritual sacrifice. Daniel Stern noted in *Nation* that with these stories and others like them "it is as if Cortazar is showing us that it is essential for us to reimagine the reality in which we live and which we can no longer take for granted."

Although during the last years of his life Cortazar was so involved with political activism that Jason Weiss described him in the *Los Angeles Times* as a writer with hardly any time to write, the Argentine had early in his career been criticized "for his apparent indifference to the brutish situation" of his fellow Latin Americans, according to Leonard. Evidence of his growing political preoccupation is found in his later stories and novels. Leonard observed, for instance, that *A Manual for Manuel* "is a primer on the necessity of revolutionary action," and William Kennedy in the *Washington Post Book World* noted that the newspaper clippings included in the novel "touch[ed] the open nerve of political oppression in Latin America." Many of the narratives in *A Change of Light, and Other Stories* are also politically oriented. Oates described the impact of one story in the *New York Times Book Review.* In "Apocalypse at Solentiname," a photographer develops his vacation photographs of happy, smiling people only to discover pictures of people being tortured. Oates commented, "The narrator . . . contemplates in despair the impotence of art to deal with in any significant way, the 'life of permanent uncertain-ty . . . [in] almost all of Latin America, a life surrounded by fear and death.'"

Cortazar's fictional world, according to Alazraki in *The Final Island,* "represents a challenge to culture." This challenge is embedded in the author's belief in a reality that reaches beyond our everyday existence. Alazraki noted that Cortazar once declared, "Our daily reality masks a second reality which is neither mysterious nor theological, but profoundly human. Yet, due to a long series of mistakes, it has remained concealed under a reality prefabricated by many centuries of culture, a culture in which there are great achievements but also profound aberrations, profound distortions." Novelist C. D. B. Bryan further explained these ideas in the *New York Times Book Review:* Cortazar's "surrealistic treatment of the most pedestrian acts suggest[ed] that one way to combat alienation is to return to the original receptiveness of childhood, to recapture this original innocence, by returning to the concept of life as a game."

Cortazar confronted his reader with unexpected forms, with humor, fantasy, and unseemly reality in order to challenge him to live a more meaningful life. He summarized his theory of fiction (and of life) in an essay, "The Present State of Fiction in Latin America," which appeared in *Books Abroad.* The Argentine concluded: "The fantastic is something that one must never say good-bye to lightly. The man of the future . . . will have to find the bases of a reality which is truly his and, at the same time, maintain the capacity of dreaming and playing which I have tried to show you . . . , since it is through those doors that the Other, the fantastic dimension, and the unexpected will always slip, as will all that will save us from that obedient robot into which so many technocrats would like to convert us and which we will not accept—ever."

BIOGRAPHICAL/CRITICAL SOURCES:

BOOKS

Alazraki, Jaime and Ivar Ivask, editors, *The Final Island: The Fiction of Julio Cortazar,* University of Oklahoma Press, 1978.

Alonso, Carlos J., editor, *Julio Cortazar: New Readings,* Cambridge University Press, 1998.

Boldy, Steven, *The Novels of Cortazar,* Cambridge University Press, 1980.

Colas, Santiago, *Postmodernity in Latin America: The Argentine Paradigm,* Duke University Press (Durham, NC), 1994.

Coleman, Alexander, editor, *Cinco maestros: Cuentos modernos de Hispanoamerica,* Harcourt, Brace & World, 1969.

Contemporary Literary Criticism, Gale, Volume 2, 1974; Volume 3, 1975; Volume 5, 1976; Volume 10, 1979; Volume 13, 1980; Volume 15, 1980; Volume 33, 1985; Volume 34, 1985.

Donoso, Jose, *Historia personal del "boom,"* Anagrama (Barcelona), 1972, translation by Gregory Kolovakos published as *The Boom in Spanish American Literature: A Personal History,* Columbia University Press, 1977.

Foster, David W., *Currents in the Contemporary Argentine Novel,* University of Missouri Press, 1975.

Garfield, Evelyn Picon, *Julio Cortazar,* Ungar, 1975.

Garfield, Evelyn Picon, *Cortazar por Cortazar* (interviews), Universidad Veracruzana, 1981.

Giacoman, Helmy F., editor, *Homenaje a Julio Cortazar,* Anaya, 1972.

Harss, Luis and Barbara Dohmann, *Into the Mainstream: Conversations with Latin-American Writers,* Harper, 1967.

Prego, Omar, *La fascinacion de las palabras* (interviews), Muchnik, 1985.

Ramirez, Sergio, *Hatful of Tigers: Reflections on Art, Culture, and Politics,* Curbstone Press (Willimantic, CT), 1995.

Stavans, Ilan, *Julio Cortazar: A Study of the Short Fiction,* Twayne (New York City), 1996.

Vasquez Amaral, Jose, *The Contemporary Latin American Narrative,* Las Americas, 1970.

PERIODICALS

America, April 17, 1965; July 9, 1966; December 22, 1973.

Atlantic, June, 1969; October, 1973.

Books Abroad, fall, 1965; winter, 1968; summer, 1969; winter, 1970; summer, 1976.

Book World, August 17, 1969.

Chicago Tribune, September 24, 1978; February 14, 1984.

Chicago Tribune Book World, November 16, 1980; May 8, 1983.

Christian Science Monitor, August 15, 1967; July 3, 1969; December 4, 1978; July 17, 1984, p. 24.

Commentary, October, 1966.

Hispania, December, 1973.

Hispanic Journal, spring, 1984, pp. 172-73.

Hudson Review, spring, 1974; autumn, 1983, pp. 549-62.

International Fiction Review, January, 1974; January, 1975.

Library Journal, July, 1967; September, 1969; September 15, 1980.

Listener, December 20, 1979.

Los Angeles Times, August 28, 1983; February 14, 1984.

Los Angeles Times Book Review, December 28, 1980; June 12, 1983; May 27, 1984; June 24, 1984, pp. 4, 14.

Nation, September 18, 1967.

National Review, July 25, 1967.

New Republic, April 23, 1966; July 15, 1967; October 21, 1978; October 25, 1980.

Newsweek, September 17, 1984, p. 82.

New Yorker, May 18, 1965; February 25, 1974.

New York Review of Books, March 25, 1965; April 28, 1966; April 19, 1973; October 12, 1978.

New York Times, November 13, 1978; March 24, 1983; February 13, 1984.

New York Times Book Review, March 21, 1965; April 10, 1966; June 15, 1969; November 26, 1972; September 9, 1973; November 19, 1978; November 9, 1980; March 27, 1983, pp. 1, 37-8; March 4, 1984; May 20, 1984.

Review of Contemporary Fiction (special Cortazar issue), fall, 1983.

Saturday Review, March 27, 1965; April 9, 1966; July 22, 1967; September 27, 1969.

Symposium, spring, 1983, pp. 17-47.

Time, April 29, 1966; June 13, 1969; October 1, 1973.

Times Literary Supplement, October 12, 1973; December 7, 1979.

Virginia Quarterly Review, spring, 1973.

Washington Post Book World, November 18, 1973; November 5, 1978; November 23, 1980; May 1, 1983; June 24, 1984.

World Literature Today, winter, 1977; winter, 1980.

*   *   *

COURTNEY, Robert
See ELLISON, Harlan (Jay)

*   *   *

COUSINS, Norman 1915-1990

PERSONAL: Born June 24, 1915, in Union Hill, NJ; died November 30, 1990; son of Samuel and Sara Barry (Miller) Cousins; married Ellen Kopf, June 23, 1939; children: Andrea, Amy Loveman, Candis Hitzig, Sara Kit. *Education:* Attended Teachers College, Columbia University.

ADDRESSES: Home—2644 Eden Pl., Beverly Hills, CA 90201. *Office*—Department of Psychiatry and Biobehavioral Sciences, 2859 Slichter Hall, University of California, Los Angeles, CA 90024.

CAREER: New York Evening Post, New York City, educational editor, 1934-35; *Current History,* New York City, 1935-40, began as book critic, became literary editor and managing editor; *Saturday Review of Literature* (now *Saturday Review*), New York City, executive editor, 1940-42, editor, 1942-71, editor emeritus, 1980-82; *World,* New York City, editor, 1972-73; *Saturday Review/World,* New York City, editor, 1973-74; *Saturday Review,* New York City, editor, 1975-78; University of California, Los Angeles, professor of medical humanities and affiliated with Brain Research Institute. McCall's Corp., New York City, vice-president and director, 1961-90.

Office of War Information, Overseas Bureau, member of editorial board, 1943-45; co-chairman of national campaign board of 1943 Victory Book Campaign. U. S. Government diplomat and lecturer in India, Pakistan, and Ceylon, 1951; Japan-America exchange lecturer, Japan, 1953. Chairman of board of directors of National Educational Television, 1969-70; member of Commission to Study Organized Peace; member of board of directors of Freedom House and Willkie Memorial Foundation; member of board of directors of Columbia University Conference on Science, Philosophy, and Religion. Chairman of Connecticut Fact Finding Commission on Education, 1948-52; founder and president of United World Federalists, 1952-54, honorary president, 1954-56; co-chairman of National Committee for a Sane Nuclear Policy, 1957-63; served on Mayor's Task Force on Air Pollution, New York City, from 1966.

MEMBER: American Council of Learned Societies (member-at-large), National Planning Association, National Academy of Sciences (member of committee on international relations), Hiroshima Peace Center Association, Menninger Foundation,

Ruth Mott Foundation, Charles F. Kettering Foundation (trustee), United Nations Association (director of U.S. Division), World Association of World Federalists, Council on Foreign Relations, National Press Club, Overseas Press Club (member of board of governors), PEN (vice-president of American Center, 1952-55), Century Club, Coffee House (New York).

AWARDS, HONORS: Thomas Jefferson Award for the Advancement of Democracy in Journalism, 1948; Tuition Plan award for outstanding service to American education, 1951; Benjamin Franklin citation in magazine journalism, 1956; Wayne State University award for national service to education, 1958; New York State Citizens Education Commission award, 1959; John Dewey Award for Education, 1959; New York State Citizens Education Community award, 1959; Eleanor Roosevelt Peace award, 1963; Publius award, United World Federalists, 1964; Overseas Press Club award, 1965; Distinguished Citizen award, Connecticut Bar Association, 1965; New York Academy of Public Education award, 1966; Family of Man award, 1968; Annual award, Aquinas College, 1968; national magazine award, Association of Deans of Journalism Schools, 1969.

Peace medal, United Nations, 1971; Sarah Josepha Hale award, 1971; Carr Van Anda award for contributions to journalism, Ohio State University, 1971; Henry Johnson Fisher award as magazine publisher of the year, Magazine Publishers Association, 1971; Gold medal for literature, National Arts Club, 1972; Journalism Honor award, University of Missouri School of Journalism, 1972; Irita Van Doren book award, 1972; award for service to the environment, Government of Canada, 1972; Human Resources award, 1977; Convocation medal, American College of Cardiology, 1978; Author of the Year award, American Society of Journalists and Authors, 1981; American Book Award nomination in paperback nonfiction, 1982, for *Anatomy of an Illness as Perceived by the Patient;* Niwano Peace Award (Japan), 1990; Physicians for Social Responsibility Award, 1990; Albert Schweitzer Peace Prize, John Hopkins University, 1990.

Also recipient of nearly fifty honorary doctorate degrees, including: Litt.D., American University, 1948, Syracuse University, 1956, Temple University, 1961, Michigan State University, 1969; L.H.D. from Colgate University, 1959, Brandeis University, 1969; L.L.D. from Washington and Jefferson College, 1956 and George Washington University, 1982; honorary M. D. from New Haven County Medical Association/Connecticut State Medical Society, 1984.

WRITINGS:

The Good Inheritance: The Democratic Chance, Coward, 1942.
(Editor) *A Treasury of Democracy,* Coward 1942.
Modern Man Is Obsolete, Viking, 1945.
(Editor with William Rose Benet) *An Anthology of the Poetry of Liberty,* Modern Library, 1945.
(Editor) *Writing for Love or Money: Thirty-Five Essays Reprinted from the Saturday Review of Literature,* Longmans, Green, 1949.
(Contributor) John W. Chase, editor, *Years of the Modern,* Longmans, Green, 1949.
(With Jawaharlal Nehru) *Talks with Nehru,* Day, 1951.
Who Speaks for Man? Macmillan, 1953.
Amy Loveman, 1881-1955, A Eulogy (pamphlet), Overbrook Press, 1956.
The Religious Beliefs of the Founding Fathers, 1958.
(Editor) *In God We Trust,* Harper, 1958.
(Editor) Francis March, *Thesaurus Dictionary,* Doubleday, 1958.

The Rejection of Nothingness (pamphlet), Pacific School of Religion, 1959.
Dr. Schweitzer of Lambarene, Harper, 1960.
In Place of Folly, Harper, 1961, revised edition, Washington Square Press, 1962.
Can Cultures Co-Exist? (symposium), Ministry of Scientific Research & Cultural Affairs (New Delhi), 1963.
(With others) *". . . Therefore Choose Life, That Thou Mayest Live, Thou and Thy Seed,"* Center for the Study of Democratic Institutions, 1965.
(Editor) *Profiles of Nehru: America Remembers a World Leader,* Indian Book Co., 1966.
(Editor) *Great American Essays,* Dell, 1967.
Present Tense: An American Editors Odyssey, McGraw, 1967.
(With others) *Issues: 1968,* University Press of Kansas, 1968.
Profiles of Gandhi: America Remembers a World Leader, Indian Book Co., 1969.
The Improbable Triumvirate: John F. Kennedy, Pope Paul, Nikita Khruschev: An Asterisk to the History of a Hopeful Year, 1962-1963, Norton, 1972.
The Celebration of Life: A Dialogue on Immortality and Infinity, Harper, 1974, published as *The Celebration of Life: A Dialogue on Hope, Spirit, and the Immortality of the Soul,* Bantam (New York City), 1991.
The Quest for Immortality, Harper, 1974.
(Editor with Mary L. Dimond) *Memoirs of a Man: Grenville Clark,* Norton, 1975.
Anatomy of an Illness as Perceived by the Patient: Reflections on Healing and Regeneration, G. K. Hall, 1979, published as *Anatomy of an Illness as Perceived by the Patient,* Bantam, 1981.
Reflections on Healing and Regeneration, G. K. Hall, 1980.
Human Options: An Autobiographical Notebook, Norton, 1981.
The Physician in Literature, Saunders, 1981.
Healing and Belief, Mosaic Press, 1982.
The Healing Heart: Antidotes to Panic and Helplessness, Norton, 1983.
The Trial of Dr. Mesmer: A Play, Norton, 1984.
Albert Schweitzer's Mission: Healing and Peace, Norton, 1985.
The Human Adventure: A Camera Chronicle, Saybrook, 1986.
The Pathology of Power, Norton, 1987.
(Editor) *The Republic of Reason: The Personal Philosophies of the Founding Fathers,* Harper, 1988.
(Author of commentary) *Jason Sitwell's Book of Spoofs,* Dutton, 1989.
Head First: The Biology of Hope, Dutton, 1989, published as *Head First: The Biology of Hope and the Healing Power of the Human Spirit,* Penguin (New York City), 1990.
The Words of Albert Schweitzer: Selected by Norman Cousins, Newmarket Press, 1990.

Also author of *The Last Defense in a Nuclear Age,* 1960. Also featured in sound recording "Betting One's Life on the Future of Print," Development Digest, 1973. Editor *U. S. A.,* 1943-45; member of board of editors, *Encyclopaedia Britannica;* editorial supervisor, *March's Dictionary-Thesaurus,* 1980.

MEDIA ADAPTATIONS: Anatomy of an Illness as Perceived by the Patient: Reflections on Healing and Regeneration was adapted into a television movie for Columbia Broadcasting System. Titled "Anatomy of an Illness," the film starred Ed Asner as Cousins and was broadcast on May 15, 1984.

SIDELIGHTS: "I get a kick out of challenging the odds," Norman Cousins told *Publishers Weekly* interviewer Lisa See. His life and career gave him ample opportunity to do just that. As longtime editor of *Saturday Review,* Cousins bolstered that magazine's circulation to 650,000. He also served as a diplomat during three presidential administrations, became a professor of medical humanities, and produced numerous books on political and social issues. In the process, Cousins fended off a life-threatening disease and a massive coronary, both times using his own regimen of nutritional and emotional support systems as opposed to traditional methods of treatment (and he chronicled his experiences in two books, *Anatomy of an Illness as Perceived by the Patient: Reflections on Healing and Regeneration* and *The Healing Heart: Antidotes to Panic and Helplessness*). "Cousins has led a wonderful, if strangely related, series of overlapping lives," comments See. "He is a complex meshing of science and letters. He is serious and silly, intellectual and maniacal."

Cousins has often been described as the man who laughed his way to health, a simplified explanation of the controversial healing method the author/editor employed when he was diagnosed in the mid-1960s as having ankylosing spondylitis. The degenerative disease causes the breakdown of collagen, the fiberous tissue that binds together the body's cells. Almost completely paralyzed, given only a few months to live, Cousins ordered himself checked out of the hospital where he had spent weeks undergoing tests. He moved into a hotel room and began taking extremely high doses of vitamin C, counting on the ascorbic acid to oxygenate his bloodstream, counteracting the effects of the illness. At the same time, intent on maintaining a positive mental outlook, Cousins exposed himself to equally high doses of humor—old "Candid Camera" tapes, Marx Brothers movies, and books by P. G. Wodehouse, Robert Benchley, and James Thurber. This unusual regimen started to work: "I made the joyous discovery that ten minutes of genuine belly laughter had an anesthetic effect and would give me at least two hours of pain-free sleep," writes Cousins in *Anatomy of an Illness.* Slowly, the patient regained use of his limbs. As his condition steadily improved over the following months, Cousins resumed his busy life, eventually returning to work full-time at the *Saturday Review.*

As Cousins notes in his book, "the will to live is not a theoretical abstraction, but a physiologic reality with therapeutic characteristics." While not denying that the right attitude can certainly help a patient through his illness, some of his critics have questioned the nature of Cousins's ailment and the healing methods he swore by. In a *Commentary* article Florence A. Ruderman takes exception to the author's case history as related in *Anatomy of an Illness.* Ruderman emphasizes that she does believe that "'positive emotions' play a role in health. But the 'positive emotions' that are a force in maintaining life, well-being, resistance to disease, or recuperative or regenerative capacity, are those that stem from deep, relatively constant levels of one's psychological nature, one's inner being. They are affected by long-term circumstances of life and by major life events."

The critic also questions whether Cousins's treatment can be adapted by the general public—and if it should be at all. "Should *all* patients have the same rights and freedom that Cousins had?" she writes. "If not, why is it inspiring that such rights and deference were accorded to Cousins? Under what circumstances should doctors allow patients to choose their own drugs, invent their own routines and regimens—in effect, direct their doctors? . . . How was it possible for so many doctors to greet [the author's] account with enthusiasm, and ignore every substantive and ethical issue in it?" Cousins responded to Ruderman's charge, claiming in the *Publishers Weekly* article that "she didn't see the

medical reports and didn't interview the doctors." Another criticism, he added, "in the *Mt. Sinai Journal of Medicine,* . . . said that I might have had a nominal remission. That may be right, but the doctors didn't think so at the time."

In December, 1980, some fifteen years after winning his bout with ankylosing spondylitis, Cousins suffered a near-fatal heart attack while on a teaching assignment in California. Again faced with the challenge of restoring his health, Cousins responded by telling his doctors at the UCLA Intensive Care unit that they were "looking at what is probably the darndest healing machine that has ever been wheeled into the hospital," according to Joel Elkes's *Saturday Review* article on *The Healing Heart.* "As before," Elkes continues, "Cousins makes his body a personal laboratory and befriends the society within his skin. He refuses morphine; he asks for a change in the visiting routine to ensure rest. Gradually he improves."

One major obstacle Cousins faced in his recovery was the treadmill test, designed to chart the progress of his heart rate. The patient was "scared stiff at *being* exercised, at an accelerating pace, on a moving band over which he had no control," explains Elkes. "He tries to suppress his fear, but fails and has to stop. He tries again and cannot manage." Realizing his fear was the factor in slowing his progress, Cousins adopted a more relaxed life style, changing his diet and avoiding stressful situations. "As his health improves, Cousins repeats the treadmill examination," Fred Rosenfelt reports in the *Los Angeles Times.* "This time, he controls the machine while listening to classical music and comedy tapes. His test is better."

In publishing these findings in *The Healing Heart,* Cousins again met with mixed reaction. Rosenfelt, for instance, while acknowledging that the author's "opinion of the salutary effects of positive emotion is widely accepted," nevertheless wonders "how many patients have the fortitude to disagree with their physicians and follow an alternative recovery program after a major heart attack? Furthermore, if a large number of individuals do so, how many will improve or worsen?" Elkes, on the other hand, argues that *The Healing Heart* is not a medical textbook, but a study of "awareness, listening, trust, choice, and intention, and about the intelligent use of a benevolent, centering will. It is about communication and partnership between the healer and the healed. It addresses as complementary the art of medicine and the science of medicine, the person and the institution, and freedom of choice and professional responsibility. [The book] affirms hope and belief as biologically constructive forces: not as blind faith, but as belief guided by knowledge and tempered by reason. It asserts that the quality of a person's life is the sum of the quality of his days."

Despite his bouts with near-fatal ailments, Cousins remained an active literary force. His most popular book of the late 1980s was almost certainly *Head First,* a further elucidation of his beliefs and concerns regarding medicine and doctor-patient relations. Another key work, 1987's *The Pathology of Power,* addressed the issue of world peace. Wray Herbert, writing in the *Washington Post Book World,* hailed this volume as "an important and disturbing document."

BIOGRAPHICAL/CRITICAL SOURCES:

PERIODICALS

American Health, January-February, 1990, p. 106.
Chicago Tribune, December 26, 1979.
Commentary, May, 1980.
Detroit News, June 22, 1980.

Esquire, February, 1980.
Journal of the American Medical Association, April 17, 1996, p. 1209.
Los Angeles Times, September 29, 1983.
Los Angeles Times Book Review, December 13, 1981; October 24, 1982; December 3, 1989.
National Review, April 30, 1982; December 9, 1983.
New England Journal of Medicine, April 26, 1990, p. 1240.
New Republic, September 29, 1979; December 10, 1990, p. 10.
New Statesman, October 3, 1980.
New York Times, June 22, 1972; September 15, 1979; May 8, 1984; May 15, 1984.
New York Times Book Review, January 1, 1984.
People, June 1, 1979.
Publishers Weekly, September 23, 1983.
Saturday Review, September-October, 1983.
Time, August 30, 1982.
Times Literary Supplement, March 30, 1984.
Washington Post, October 9, 1979; November 9, 1981.
Washington Post Book World, April 12, 1987; November 5, 1989.

*   *   *

COWARD, Noel (Peirce) 1899-1973
(Hernia Whittlebot)

PERSONAL: Some sources spell middle name "Pierce"; born December 16, 1899, in Teddington-on-Thames, Middlesex, England; suffered a fatal heart attack, March 26, 1973, in Blue Harbour, Jamaica; son of Arthur Sabin (a clerk in a music publishing house and piano salesman) and Violet Agnes (Veitch) Coward. *Education:* Attended Chapel Royal School, Clapham.

CAREER: Playwright, author, composer, songwriter, actor, singer, director, producer, and nightclub entertainer. First appearance on stage as Prince Mussel in a children's play, *The Goldfish,* Little Theatre (London), 1911. Other roles include (all London productions except as indicated): Cannard in *The Great Name,* Prince of Wales Theatre, 1911; William in *Where the Rainbow Ends,* Savoy Theatre, 1911; dancer in ballet, *An Autumn Idyll,* Savoy Theatre, 1911; one of the Angels of Light in *Hannele,* Liverpool Repertory Theatre, 1913; Tommy in *War in the Air,* Palladium Theatre, 1913; the Boy in *A Little Fowl Play,* Coliseum, 1913; Slightly in *Peter Pan,* Duke of York's Theatre, 1913; toured as Charley Wykeham in *Charley's Aunt,* 1916; Basil Pyecroft in *The Light Blues,* Shaftesbury Theatre, 1916; Jack Morrison in *The Happy Family,* Prince of Wales Theatre, 1916; Ripley Guildford in *The Saving Grace,* Garrick Theatre, 1917; Courtney Borner in *Scandal,* Strand Theatre, 1918; Ralph in *The Knight of the Burning Pestle,* Birmingham Repertory Theatre, 1919; Clay Collins in *Polly with a Past,* St. James Theatre, 1921; Lewis Dodd in *The Constant Nymph,* New Theatre, 1926; Clark Storey in *The Second Man,* Playhouse, 1928; Captain Stanhope in *Journey's End* (three performances), Victoria Theatre (Singapore, China), ca. 1930; King Magnus in *The Apple Cart,* Haymarket Theatre, 1953; narrator of *Carnival of the Animals,* Carnegie Hall (New York), 1956.

Film roles include: *Hearts of the World,* Comstock World, 1918; *The Scoundrel,* Paramount, 1935; *Around the World in 80 Days,* United Artists, 1956; *Our Man in Havana,* Columbia, 1960; *Surprise Package,* Columbia, 1960; *Paris When It Sizzles,* Paramount, 1964; *Bunny Lake Is Missing,* Columbia, 1965; *Boom!* Universal, 1968; *The Italian Job,* Paramount, 1968. Producer of

Blithe Spirit, United Artists, 1945, and *This Happy Breed,* Universal, 1946. President of Actors' Orphanage, 1934-56. *Military service:* British Army, Artists' Rifles, 1918; entertained troops during World War II.

MEMBER: Royal Society of Literature (fellow).

AWARDS, HONORS: New York Drama Critics Circle Award for Best Foreign Play, 1942, for *Blithe Spirit;* Special Academy Award of Merit (Oscar) for Outstanding Production Achievement from the Academy of Motion Picture Arts and Sciences, 1942, for *In Which We Serve;* Special Antoinette Perry Award (Tony) from the League of American Theatres and Producers, 1970; knighted, 1970; D.Litt., University of Sussex, 1972; memorialized in Westminster Abbey, 1984.

WRITINGS:

PUBLISHED PLAYS

I'll Leave It to You (first produced in London at New Theatre, 1920), S. French, 1920.
The Young Idea (first produced in London at Savoy Theatre, 1923), S. French, 1924.
The Rat Trap, Benn, 1924.
The Vortex (first produced in London at Everyman Theatre, 1924; director, with Basil Dean, of Broadway production at Henry Miller's Theater, 1925), Harper, 1925.
Fallen Angels (first produced in London at Globe Theatre, 1925; produced in New York at Playhouse, 1956), Benn, 1925, French (New York), 1958.
Hay Fever (first produced in London at Ambassador's Theatre, 1925; produced in New York at Maxine Elliot's Theatre, 1925), Harper, 1925, revised edition, S. French, 1927, with an introduction by author, Heinemann, 1965.
Easy Virtue (first produced in London at St. Martin's Theatre, 1926), Benn, 1926.
This Was a Man (first produced in London), Harper, 1926.
The Marquise (first produced in London at Criterion Theatre, 1927; produced in New York at Biltmore Theatre, 1927), Benn, 1927.
Home Chat (first produced in London at Duke of York's Theatre, 1927), M. Secker, 1927.
Sirocco (first produced in London at Daly's Theatre, 1927), M. Secker, 1927.
(And composer and lyricist) *Charles B. Cochran's Revue* (first produced in London at London Pavilion, 1931), Chappell, 1928.
(And composer) *This Year of Grace* (revue; first produced in New York at Selwyn Theater, 1928; also see below), published in *Second Play Parade,* Heinemann, 1939.
(And director) *Bitter Sweet* (operetta; first produced in London at His Majesty's Theatre, 1929; Broadway production directed by Coward at Times Square Theatre, 1931; also see below), Heinemann, 1930, Doubleday, 1931.
Private Lives (first produced in London at Phoenix Theatre, 1930), Doubleday, 1968.
Post-Mortem, Doubleday, 1931.
(And director) *Cavalcade* (first produced in London at Drury Lane Theatre, 1931), Heinemann, 1932, Doubleday, 1933.
(And composer and lyricist) *Words and Music* (revue; first production directed and conducted by Coward in London at Adelphi Theatre, 1932; also see below), published in *Second Play Parade,* Heinemann, 1939.

(And producer with Alfred Lunt and Lynn Fontanne) *Design for Living* (first produced in New York at Ethel Barrymore Theatre, 1933), Doubleday, 1933.

Conversation Piece (first produced in London at His Majesty's Theatre, 1934; Broadway production directed by Coward at 44th Street Theatre, 1934), Doubleday, 1934.

(And director) *Point Valaine* (first produced in New York at Ethel Barrymore Theater, 1935), Doubleday, 1935.

(And director) *Tonight at Eight-Thirty* (series of plays consisting of *The Astonished Heart, Family Album, Fumed Oak, Hands Across the Sea, Red Peppers, Shadow Play, Still Life, Ways and Means,* and *We Were Dancing*; first six plays originally produced in London at Phoenix Theatre, 1936; entire series produced in New York at National Theater, 1936; also see below), Doubleday, 1936.

The Astonished Heart (part of *Tonight at Eight-Thirty* series), S. French, 1938.

Family Album (part of *Tonight at Eight-Thirty* series), S. French, 1938.

Fumed Oak (part of *Tonight at Eight-Thirty* series), S. French, 1938.

Hands Across the Sea (part of *Tonight at Eight-Thirty* series), S. French, 1938.

Red Peppers (musical interlude; part of *Tonight at Eight-Thirty* series), S. French, 1938.

Shadow Play (musical; part of *Tonight at Eight-Thirty* series), S. French, 1938.

Still Life (part of *Tonight at Eight-Thirty* series), S. French, 1938.

We Were Dancing (part of *Tonight at Eight-Thirty* series), S. French, 1938.

(And composer and lyricist) *Operette* (first produced in London at His Majesty's Theatre, 1938), Heinemann, 1938.

Blithe Spirit (first produced in London at Piccadilly Theatre, 1941; produced in New York at Morosco Theater, 1941), Doubleday, 1941.

(And director) *Relative Values* (first produced in London at Savoy Theatre, 1951), Heinemann, 1942.

(And director) *Present Laughter* (first produced in England, 1942; produced in London at Haymarket Theatre, 1943; produced in Paris at Theatre Edouard VII, 1948, with title *Joyeux Chagrins*), Heinemann, 1943, Doubleday, 1947.

(And director) *This Happy Breed* (first produced in London at Haymarket Theater, 1943), Heinemann, 1943, Doubleday, 1947.

Peace in Our Time, Heinemann, 1947, Doubleday, 1948.

(And director) *Quadrille* (first produced in London at Phoenix Theatre, 1952; produced in New York at Coronet Theater, 1954), Heinemann, 1952, Doubleday, 1955.

(And composer and lyricist) *After the Ball* (operetta based on Oscar Wilde's *Lady Windermere's Fan*; first produced in London at Globe Theatre, 1954), Chappell, 1954.

South Sea Bubble (first produced in London at Lyric Theatre, 1956), Heinemann, 1956.

(And director with John Gielgud) *Nude with Violin* (first produced in New York at Belasco Theater, 1957), Heinemann, 1957, Doubleday, 1958, revised acting edition, S. French, 1958.

Look after Lulu (based on Georges Feydeau's *Occupe-toi d'Amelie;* first produced in London at Royal Court Theatre, 1959; produced in New York at Henry Miller's Theatre, 1959), Heinemann, 1959.

Waiting in the Wings (first produced in London at Duke of York's Theatre, 1960), Heinemann, 1960, Doubleday, 1961.

(And composer, lyricist, and director) *Sail Away* (libretto; first produced in New York at Broadhurst Theater, 1961), Bonard Productions, 1961.

Suite in Three Keys (includes *A Song at Twilight, Shadows of the Evening,* and *Come into the Garden, Maud*; first produced in London at Queens Theatre, 1966; also see below), Heinemann, 1966, Doubleday, 1967.

Shadows of the Evening, S. French, 1967.

Come into the Garden, Maud, S. French, 1967.

A Song at Twilight, S. French, 1967.

UNPUBLISHED PLAYS

(And composer and lyricist with Ronald Jeans) *London Calling,* first produced in London at Duke of York's Theatre, 1923.

(With others) *Charlot's Revue,* first produced in London at Prince of Wales Theatre, 1924.

(And composer with others) *On with the Dance* (revue), first produced in London, 1925.

Biography, first produced in London at Globe Theatre, 1934.

(Composer and lyricist) *Set to Music* (revue), first production directed by Coward in New York at Music Box, 1939.

Sigh No More (revue), first produced in London at Piccadilly Theatre, 1945.

(And director) *Pacific 1860* (musical), first produced in London at Drury Lane Theatre, 1946.

(And director) *Ace of Clubs* (musical), first produced in London at Cambridge Theatre, 1950.

(And director) *Island Fling,* first produced in 1951.

(Author of scenario and score) *London Morning* (ballet), 1959.

(Composer and lyricist) *The Girl Who Came to Supper* (based on *The Sleeping Prince,* by Terence M. Rattigan), first produced in New York at Broadway Theater, 1963.

(And director) *High Spirits* (musical adaptation of Coward's *Blithe Spirit*), first produced in New York at Alvin Theater, 1964.

(Contributor of material) *Carol Channing with 10 Stout-Hearted Men* (revue), first produced in London at Drury Lane Theatre, 1970.

OMNIBUS VOLUMES

Three Plays: The Rat Trap, The Vortex [and] *Fallen Angels* (also contains Coward's reply to his critics), Benn, 1925.

The Plays of Noel Coward, first series (contains *Sirocco, Home Chat,* and *The Queen Was in the Parlour*), Doubleday, 1928.

Bitter Sweet, and Other Plays (contains *Bitter Sweet, Easy Virtue,* and *Hay Fever*), notes by W. Somerset Maugham, Doubleday, 1929.

Collected Sketches and Lyrics, Hutchinson, 1931, Doubleday, 1932.

Play Parade (contains *Design for Living, Cavalcade, Private Lives, Bitter Sweet, Post-Mortem, The Vortex,* and *Hay Fever*), Doubleday, 1933, revised edition, Heinemann, 1949.

Tonight at Eight-Thirty, three volumes, Doubleday, 1936.

Second Play Parade (contains *This Year of Grace Words and Music Operette,* and *Conversation Piece*), Heinemann, 1939, 2nd edition published as *Play Parade, Volume II,* with addition of *Fallen Angels* and *Easy Virtue,* 1950.

Curtain Calls (includes *Tonight at Eight-Thirty, Ways and Means, Still Life, Family Album, Conversation Piece, Easy Virtue, Point Valaine,* and *This Was a Man*), Doubleday, 1940.

Play Parade, Volume III (contains *The Queen Was in the Parlour, I'll Leave It to You, The Young Idea, Sirocco, The Rat Trap, This Was a Man, Home Chat,* and *The Marquise*), Heinemann, 1950.

Play Parade, Volume IV (contains *Tonight at Eight-Thirty, Present Laughter,* and *This Happy Breed*), Heinemann, 1952.
Play Parade, Volume V, Heinemann, 1958.
Play Parade, Volume VI, Heinemann, 1962.
Three Plays by Noel Coward: Blithe Spirit, Hay Fever, [and] *Private Lives,* with an introduction by Edward Albee, Dell, 1965.

FICTION

To Step Aside (seven short stories), Doubleday, 1939.
Star Quality (six short stories; also see below), Doubleday, 1951.
Short Stories, Short Plays, and Songs, Dell, 1955.
Pomp and Circumstance (novel), Doubleday, 1960.
Collected Short Stories, Heinemann, 1962, new edition published as *The Collected Short Stories of Noel Coward,* 1969.
Seven Stories, Doubleday, 1963.
Pretty Polly Barlow, and Other Stories, Heinemann, 1964, published as *Pretty Polly, and Other Stories,* Doubleday, 1965.
Bon Voyage and Other Stories, Heinemann, 1967, published as *Bon Voyage,* Doubleday, 1968.
The Collected Stories of Noel Coward, Dutton, 1983.

OTHER

(Compiler) *Terribly Intimate Portraits,* Boni & Liveright, 1922.
A Withered Nosegay (imaginary biographies), Christophers, 1922.
(Under pseudonym Hernia Whittlebot; real name cited as editor) *Chelsea Buns* (poems), Hutchinson, 1925.
(Editor) *Spangled Unicorn* (anthology), Hutchinson, 1932, Doubleday, 1933.
Present Indicative (autobiography; also see below), Doubleday, 1937.
Australia Visited, 1940 (broadcast series), Heinemann, 1941.
Middle East Diary, Doubleday, 1944.
Noel Coward Song Book, Simon & Schuster, 1953.
Future Indefinite (autobiography; sequel to *Present Indicative;* also see below), Doubleday, 1954.
(Editor) Frederick Thomas Bason, *Last Bassoon,* Parrish, 1960.
(Translator) J. Dramese, *Les Folies du Music-hall,* Blond, 1962.
The Lyrics of Noel Coward, Heinemann, 1965, Doubleday, 1967.
Not Yet the Dodo and Other Verses, Heinemann, 1967, Doubleday, 1968.
Dick Richards, compiler, *The Wit of Noel Coward,* Frewin, 1968.
(Author of introduction) Michael Arlen, *The London Venture,* Cassell, 1968.
(Author of foreword) Raymond Mander and Joe Mitchenson, *Musical Comedy: A Story in Pictures,* P. Davies, 1969, Taplinger, 1970.
(Author of text) John Hadfield, editor, *A Last Encore* (pictures), Little, Brown, 1973.
Collected Verse of Noel Coward, edited by Graham Payn and Martin Tickner, Routledge, Chapman & Hall, 1985.
Autobiography, Volume 1: *Present Indicative,* Volume 2: *Past Conditional,* Volume 3: *Future Indicative,* Methuen, 1986.
(Author of introduction) *The Penguin Complete Saki,* Penguin, 1988.

FILMS

Private Lives, starring Norma Shearer and Robert Montgomery, Metro-Goldwyn-Mayer, 1931.
Bitter Sweet, starring Anna Neagle, British & Dominion, 1933.
Design for Living, starring Fredric March and Gary Cooper, Paramount, 1933.
Cavalcade, starring Diana Wynyard and Clive Brook, Fox, 1933.

Tonight Is Ours (based on the play *The Queen Was in the Parlour*), starring Claudette Colbert and Fredric March, Paramount, 1933.
Bitter Sweet, starring Jeanette MacDonald and Nelson Eddy, Metro-Goldwyn-Mayer, 1940.
We Were Dancing (based in part on *Tonight at Eight-Thirty*), starring Norma Shearer and Melvyn Douglas, Metro-Goldwyn-Mayer, 1942.
(Also co-producer) *This Happy Breed,* starring Robert Newton and Celia Johnson, Universal, 1944.
Brief Encounter (based on the play *Still Life*), starring Celia Johnson and Trevor Howard, Cineguild, 1945.
(Also co-producer) *Blithe Spirit,* starring Rex Harrison and Constance Cummings, United Artists, 1945 (television), Compass Productions, 1966.
The Astonished Heart, starring Noel Coward and Celia Johnson, Universal, 1950.
Tonight at Eight-Thirty (based on three playlets, *Ways and Means, Red Peppers,* and *Fumed Oak*), starring Valerie Hobson and Nigel Patrick, British Film Makers, 1953.
A Matter of Innocence (based on short story Pretty Polly Barlow), starring Hayley Mills and Trevor Howard, Universal, 1968.
Star Quality (based on short stories from collection of same title), Masterpiece Theatre, PBS-TV, first aired 1987.

MUSICALS

Mr. and Mrs. (based on *Still Life* and *Fumed Oak*), produced in London, 1968.

REVUES BASED ON EXCERPTS FROM COWARD'S WORKS

And Now Noel Coward, retitled *Noel Coward's Sweet Potato,* both produced in New York, 1968.
Cowardy Custard, produced in New York, 1972, published as *Cowardy Custard: The World of Noel Coward,* Heinemann, 1973.
Oh Coward! produced in New York, 1972, published as *Oh Coward! A Musical Comedy Revue,* Doubleday, 1974.

RECORDINGS

Noel and Gertie (based on *Private Lives*), RCA Victor, 1954.
Noel Coward's Theatre, Argo Eclipse, 1973.

Noel Coward Dialogues and *Noel Coward Reading His Poems* have both been recorded by Caedmon.

SIDELIGHTS: "No one of this or any age," declared Alan Jay Lerner in his *The Musical Theatre: A Celebration,* "has ever been crowned with adulation and acclaim as Noel Coward." Born on December 16, 1899, in the middle-class London suburb of Teddington, Coward began his lengthy career in the theater as a child actor. By the time he died in 1973, Coward was world-famous, not only as an actor, but also as a playwright, director, producer, composer, lyricist, screenwriter, nightclub entertainer, novelist, memoirist, and poet. He numbered among his close friends some of the greatest talents of the twentieth-century stage, including Fred and Adele Astaire, John Gielgud, Gertrude Lawrence, Beatrice Lilly, Alfred Lunt and Lynne Fontanne, and Laurence Olivier.

The moderate success of *I'll Leave It to You* in 1920 launched Coward's career as a playwright. Over the next few years he wrote a great deal but was not able to get his work performed, partly because he was not well-known. In 1923 he contributed songs and playlets to *London Calling!* a revue show consisting of unrelated playlets and songs. The show is chiefly remembered today for the song *Parisian Pierrot,* performed by Gertrude Lawrence, which became a Coward favorite. Contemporary audiences also noted one of Coward's playlets, "The Swiss Family Whittlebot," which was "an accurate if uncharitable send-up of a family of contemporary poets called Hernia, Gob and Sago," explained Sheridan Morley in *A Talent to Amuse: A Biography of Noel Coward.* Critics thought that the Whittlebots were parodies of the Sitwells—Edith, Osbert, and Sacheverell—one of England's premier literary families. Coward later used the name "Hernia Whittlebot" on a volume of poetry and read some of "her" poetry on radio.

In 1924, Coward's first great critical and financial success, *"The Vortex,"* was produced. It tells the story of a drug-addicted son's obsession with his nymphomaniacal mother, and it was considered extremely risque. Crowds flocked to see it, bringing Coward the prosperity that had eluded him for so long.

The success of *The Vortex* caused a great demand for Coward's plays. 1925 marked the debut of *Fallen Angels.* This three-act comedy both shocked and entertained theater-goers with its portrayal of two middle-aged women slowly getting drunk while awaiting the arrival of a mutual lover. *Hay Fever,* produced the same year, tells the story of four obnoxious members of an artistic family who invite company to their estate for the weekend. They then proceed to revile each other's guests. Other works produced in the mid-to-late 1920s included the revues *On with the Dance!* and *This Year of Grace!* (which introduced "A Room with a View," one of Coward's most popular numbers), and the plays *Easy Virtue, The Queen Was in the Parlour, This Was a Man,* and *Home Chat.* The constant pressure exerted on Coward by the demand for his work—he performed in starring roles in his own plays—caused a nervous breakdown in 1926. He began to travel, mostly by ship, to regain his health, and soon developed a passion for voyaging and ships that lasted the rest of his life.

In 1929, believing that the British theater was ready for a romantic revival, Coward wrote and directed *Bitter Sweet,* which became one of his most successful works. Unlike the earlier *London Calling!, Bitter Sweet* had a plot: it tells the story (in flashback) of young, strong-willed Londoner Sarah Millick, who in 1875 deserts her fiancee and runs off to Vienna with her music teacher, Carl Linden. Tragically, Carl is killed in a duel only five years later. Sarah, however, lives on to become an opera star and eventually marries the Marquis of Shayne. *Bitter Sweet* featured some of Coward's best-loved songs, including "If Love Were All" and "I'll See You Again." Coward later claimed that the tune for "I'll See You Again" "dropped into my head, whole and complete" during a taxi ride in New York.

Coward repeated the success of *Bitter Sweet* on the New York stage late in 1929. With the American production well underway, he began to travel again. But he could not escape the theater entirely. While awaiting the arrival of a friend in a Tokyo hotel, he literally dreamed up what would become his most successful play. "The moment I switched out the lights," Coward recalled, "Gertie [Lawrence] appeared in a white Molyneux dress on a terrace in the South of France and refused to go again until four in the morning, by which time *Private Lives,* title and all, had constructed itself." Somewhat later on the same trip, while motoring from Hanoi to Saigon in what is now Vietnam, Coward composed his most famous song: "Mad Dogs and Englishmen," a satiric paean to British imperialism in the tropics. In 1931 *Private Lives* moved to New York, where it played to capacity crowds.

Many of the leading roles in Coward's works were written for the author to perform himself. He often wrote other roles with his actor friends in mind. In 1933, he appeared on Broadway with his American actor friends Alfred Lunt and Lynne Fontanne in the comedy *Design for Living.* This play tells the story of three artistic people—Leo, a playwright, Otto, a painter, and Gilda, an interior decorator—each devoted to the other two, who decide that they must live together in order to be truly happy. "As if to ward off the accusations of immorality that he knew would come," Morley writes, "Coward makes it clear that his characters are artists . . . living in a world of their own that has little in common with, and cannot be invaded by, ordinary mortals. . . . Above all else, this vehicle for three players, all known intimately to the author and all cast by him long before the actual play was written, is simply about three people who happen to love each other very much."

Coward continued to produce, direct, write, compose, and star in his own plays, revues, operettas and musicals throughout the 1930s. In the 1935-36 theater season, he appeared with Gertrude Lawrence in a series of one-act plays entitled *Tonight at Eight-Thirty.* "To both Coward and Gertrude Lawrence the plays offered countless opportunities for virtuoso solos and duets which they clutched with both hands," remarks Morley, "but for Coward as author and director and composer and lyricist as well as actor it was beyond doubt the best showcase for his varied talents that he [had] ever managed to build. *Tonight at Eight-Thirty* seemed dedicated to the idea that there was nothing in the theatre that Coward couldn't do."

Coward wrote *Blithe Spirit,* the play that became the fourth longest-running production in the history of the English theater, during a six-day stay in a holiday resort in North Wales in 1941. The story of an author henpecked by his second wife, and Madame Arcati, the eccentric medium who raises his first wife's spirit, the play was greeted enthusiastically by wartime audiences. "Not for the first time in his career," states Morley, "though perhaps for the last, Noel had written a play which was exactly what the theatre-going public wanted at precisely the moment they wanted it most."

After Great Britain became involved in World War II, Coward was enlisted to act as an unofficial ambassador to the United States, Europe and Australia. Soon, inspired by love of the sea and admiration for the Royal Navy, he conceived the idea for a film loosely based on the career of Lord Admiral Mountbatten called *In Which We Serve.* The film traced the history of HMS *Torrin* from its commissioning until its sinking in battle. Although some government censors questioned the effect a movie about the sinking of a friendly ship would have on Allied morale, Coward, supported by Mountbatten and King George VI, released it in 1942. The picture proved extremely popular and became one of Great Britain's most successful pieces of propaganda. Coward advanced his own popularity through the many morale-boosting tours he made to Allied troops in combat zones all over the world.

By the mid-fifties, Coward had added a new dimension to his varied career: that of a cabaret entertainer. In June, 1955, he opened at the Desert Inn in Las Vegas, and played consistently to capacity crowds. "I have made one of the most sensational successes of my career and to pretend that I am not absolutely delighted would be idiotic," Coward wrote in his diary. "I have had screaming rave notices and the news has flashed round the world. I am told continually, verbally and in print, that I am the greatest attraction that Las Vegas has ever had and that I am the greatest performer in the world, etc., etc. It is all very, very exciting and generous, and when I look back at the grudging dreariness of the English newspaper gentlemen announcing, when

I first opened at the Cafe de Paris, that I massacred my own songs, I really feel that I don't want to appear at home much more."

Theater audiences used to the social criticism of Harold Pinter and Kenneth Tynan found new relevance in Coward's witty comedies of the 1920s when they were successfully revived in the 1960s. At the same time, this era plagued him, for it was a time of revolution in the theater, and for the rejection of entertainment for its own sake. The new artists wrote "message plays," and rejected the emphasis on style that characterized much of Coward's work.

The "Coward Renaissance" continued through the sixties with productions of his plays all over the world, a number of distinguished film and television appearances and honors such as few theatre artists enjoy. Coward himself was revered as one of the greatest playwrights of the twentieth century. "I remember one of the last parties given for him in London in the early seventies to celebrate the successful revival of *Private Lives*," Lerner reminiscences. "The full roster of the giants of the British theatre were on hand, as well as a few fortunate foreigners such as myself. Noel was not well, but upon inducement falteringly made his way to the piano, and with an uncertain touch and with a slight tremble in his voice sang two of his songs, and ended with 'If Love Were All.'" As Coward concluded the song, which ends with the lines 'But I believe that since my life began/The most I've had is just/A talent to amuse/Heigh-o, if love were all,' the entire room burst into tears. The playwright was knighted in 1970.

BIOGRAPHICAL/CRITICAL SOURCES:

BOOKS

Castle, Terry, *Noel Coward and Radclyffe Hall: Kindred Spirits,* Columbia University Press (New York City), 1996.
Contemporary Literary Criticism, Gale (Detroit), Volume 1, 1973; Volume 9, 1978; Volume 29, 1984; Volume 51, 1989.
Dictionary of Literary Biography, Volume 10: *Modern British Dramatists, 1900-1945,* Gale, 1982.
Hoare, Philip, *Noel Coward: A Biography,* Simon & Schuster (New York City), 1995.
Lahr, John, *Coward the Playwright,* Methuen, 1983.
Lerner, Alan Jay, *The Musical Theater: A Celebration,* McGraw-Hill, 1986, pp. 109-14.
Lesley, Cole, Graham Payn, and Sheridan Morley, *Noel Coward and His Friends,* Morrow, 1979.
Morella, Joe and George Mazzei, *Genius and Lust: The Creative and Sexual Lives of Noel Coward and Cole Porter,* Carroll & Graf Publishers (New York City), 1995.
Morley, Sheridan, *A Talent to Amuse: A Biography of Noel Coward,* Doubleday, 1969, revised edition, 1985.
O'Connor, Sean, *Straight Acting: Popular Gay Drama from Wilde to Rattigan,* Cassell, 1997.
Payn, Graham, and Sheridan Morley, editors, *The Noel Coward Diaries,* Little, Brown, 1982.
Payn, Graham and Barry Day, *My Life with Noel Coward,* Applause (New York City), 1994.

PERIODICALS

Chicago Tribune Book World, December 11, 1983.
Encounter, July, 1966.
Listener, April 7, 1966.
Los Angeles Times Book Review, September 29, 1985.
New York Times Book Review, December 18, 1983.
Times (London), May 1, 1986.
Times Literary Supplement, March 25, 1983; May 9, 1986.

COWLEY, Malcolm 1898-1989

PERSONAL: Born August 24, 1898, in Belsano, PA; died of a heart attack, March 27 (one source says March 28), 1989, in New Milford, CT; son of William (a homeopathic physician) and Josephine (Hutmacher) Cowley; married Marguerite Frances Baird, August 1919 (divorced, June 1932); married Muriel Maurer, June 18, 1932; children: Robert William. *Education:* Harvard University, B.A. (cum laude), 1920; Universite de Montpellier, diplome, 1922. *Politics:* Democrat. *Avocation:* Gardening, pine trees.

CAREER: Writer, editor, lecturer. Worked for Sweet's Architectural Service, New York City; freelance writer and translator, 1925-29; *New Republic,* New York City, literary editor, 1929-40; Office of Facts and Figures, Washington, DC, member of staff, 1942; Viking Press, New York City, literary adviser, 1948-85. Visiting professor, University of Washington, 1950-51; Stanford University, 1956-57, 1959-61, and 1965; University of Michigan, 1957-58; University of California, 1962-63; Cornell University, 1964-65; Hollins College, 1968-69 and 1970-71; University of Minnesota, 1971-72; and University of Warwick, 1973. Helped organize first American Writers Congress in 1935, and co-founder of resultant League of American Writers; director of Corporation of Yaddo. Chairman of zoning board, Sherman, CT, 1945-68. *Military service:* American Field Service, 1917; served in France. U.S. Army, artillery officers' training school, 1918.

MEMBER: National Institute of Arts and Letters (president, 1956-59 and 1962-65), American Academy of Arts and Letters (chancellor, 1967-76), Club des Bibliophages, Phi Beta Kappa, Century Association and Harvard Club (both New York).

AWARDS, HONORS: Levinson Prize, 1928, and Harriet Monroe Memorial Prize, 1939, both for verse published in *Poetry;* National Institute of Arts and Letters grant in literature, 1946; National Endowment for the Arts grant, 1967; Signet Society Medal, 1976; Hubbell Medal for service to the study of American letters, 1979; National Institute Gold Medal, 1981; Who's Who in America Achievement Award, 1984; Elmer Holmes Bobst Award for Arts and Letters, New York University, 1985, for literary criticism. Litt.D. from Franklin and Marshall College, 1961, Colby College, 1962, University of Warwick, 1975, University of New Haven, 1976, Monmouth College, 1978, and Indiana University of Pennsylvania, 1985.

WRITINGS:

Exile's Return: A Narrative of Ideas (literary history), Norton (New York City), 1934, revised edition published as *Exile's Return: A Literary Odyssey of the 1920s,* Viking (New York City), 1951.
The Literary Situation (literary history), Viking, 1954.
(With Daniel Pratt Mannix) *Black Cargoes: A History of the Atlantic Slave Trade, 1518-1865,* Viking, 1962.
The Faulkner-Cowley File: Letters and Memoirs, 1944-1962, Viking, 1966.
Think Back on Us: A Contemporary Chronicle of the 1930s (literary history), edited and with an introduction by Henry Dan Piper, Southern Illinois University Press (Carbondale), 1969.
A Many-Windowed House: Collected Essays on American Writers and American Writing, edited by H. D. Piper, Southern Illinois University Press, 1970.
(With Howard Hugo) *The Lesson of the Masters* (criticism), Scribner (New York City), 1971.

A Second Flowering: Works and Days of the Lost Generation (literary history), Viking, 1973.

And I Worked at the Writer's Trade (memoirs), Viking, 1978.

The Faulkner-Cowley File: Letters and Memories, 1944-1962, Viking, 1978.

The Dream of the Golden Mountains: Remembering the 1930s (memoirs), Viking, 1980.

The View from Eighty (essay), Viking, 1980.

The Flower and the Leaf (selected essays), edited by Donald W. Faulkner, Viking, 1985.

Unshaken Friend (profile of Maxwell Perkins), Roberts Rinehart (Boulder, CO), 1985.

Conversations with Malcolm Cowley, edited by Thomas Daniel Young, University Press of Mississippi (Jackson), 1986.

The Selected Correspondence of Kenneth Burke and Malcolm Cowley, 1915-1981, edited by Paul Jay, Viking, 1988.

The Portable Malcolm Cowley, edited by Donald W. Faulkner, Penguin (New York City), 1990.

New England Writers and Writing, edited by Donald W. Faulkner, University Press of New England (Hanover, NH), 1996.

POETRY

Blue Juniata, Cape & Smith, 1929, revised and expanded as *Blue Juniata: Collected Poems,* Viking, 1968.

The Dry Season, New Directions Publishing (New York City), 1941.

Blue Juniata: A Life: Collected and New Poems, Viking, 1985.

Poetry anthologized in *Eight More Harvard Poets,* edited by S. Foster Damon and Robert Hillyer, Brentano's (New York City), 1923, and *The Harvard Advocate Anthology,* edited by Donald Hall, Twayne (Boston), 1950.

EDITOR

Brantz Mayer, *Adventures of an African Slaver; Being a True Account of the Life of Captain Theodore Canot, Trader in Gold, Ivory & Slaves on the Coast of Guinea: His Own Story as Told in the Year 1854 to Brantz Mayer* Boni (New York City), 1928.

(And contributor) *After the Genteel Tradition: American Writers since 1910,* Norton, 1937, revised edition, Southern Illinois University Press, 1964.

(With Bernard Smith) *Books That Changed Our Minds,* Doubleday (Garden City, NY), 1940.

(And author of introduction) *The Viking Portable Hemingway,* Viking, 1944.

(With Hannah Josephson) *Aragon, Poet of the French Resistance,* Duell, Sloan & Pearce, 1945, published as *Aragon, Poet of Resurgent France,* Pilot Press (London), 1946.

(And author of introduction) *The Portable Faulkner,* Viking, 1946, published as *The Essential Faulkner,* Chatto & Windus (London), 1967.

(And author of introduction and notes) *The Portable Hawthorne,* Viking, 1948, published as *Nathaniel Hawthorne: The Selected Works,* Chatto & Windus, 1971.

(And author of introduction) *The Complete Poetry and Prose of Walt Whitman,* two volumes, Pellegrini, 1948, published with new introduction as *The Works of Walt Whitman,* two volumes, Funk (New York City), 1968.

(And author of introduction) *The Stories of F. Scott Fitzgerald: A Selection of Twenty-Eight Stories,* Scribner, 1951.

(And author of preface) F. Scott Fitzgerald, *Tender Is the Night: A Romance . . . with the Author's Final Revisions,* Scribner, 1951.

(And author of introduction, with Edmund Wilson) *Three Novels of F. Scott Fitzgerald: The Great Gatsby, Tender Is the Night (with the Author's Final Revisions), The Last Tycoon,* Scribner, 1953.

Great Tales of the Deep South, Lion Press, 1955.

Writers at Work: The "Paris Review" Interviews, Viking, 1958.

(And author of introduction) Walt Whitman, *Leaves of Grass: The First (1855) Edition,* Viking, 1959.

Sherwood Anderson, *Winesburg, Ohio,* Viking, 1960.

(And author of introduction) Ernest Hemingway, *Three Novels of Ernest Hemingway,* Scribner, 1962.

(And author of introduction) *The Bodley Head F. Scott Fitzgerald . . . Short Stories,* two volumes, Bodley Head (London), 1963.

(With son, Robert Cowley) *Fitzgerald and the Jazz Age,* Scribner, 1966.

(With Howard Hugo) *The Lessons of the Masters: An Anthology of the Novel from Cervantes to Hemingway,* Scribner, 1971.

TRANSLATOR FROM THE FRENCH

Pierre MacOrlan, *On Board the Morning Star,* A. & C. Boni, 1924.

Joseph Delteil, *Joan of Arc,* Minton, 1926.

(And author of introduction) Paul Valery, *Variety,* Harcourt (San Diego), 1927.

(And author of introduction) Marthe Lucie Bibesco, *Catherine-Paris,* Harcourt, 1928.

M. L. Bibesco, *The Green Parrot,* Harcourt, 1929.

(And author of introduction) Maurice Barres, *The Sacred Hill,* Macaulay, 1929.

Raymond Radiguet, *The Count's Ball,* Norton, 1929.

(And author of introduction) Andre Gide, *Imaginary Interviews,* Knopf (New York City), 1944.

(With James R. Lawler) P. Valery, *Leonardo, Poe, Mallarme,* Princeton University Press (Princeton, NJ), 1972.

Also author with R. D. Oakes of *Van Wyck Brooks,* 1963. Contributor to *Gargoyle,* 1922. Also contributor to *Horizon* and *Sewanee Review.* Associate editor, *Broom,* 1928, and *Secession*; associate editor and book critic, *New Republic,* 1929-44. Cowley's papers are housed at the Newberry Library, Chicago.

SIDELIGHTS: In 1934 Malcolm Cowley published an autobiographical literary history, *Exile's Return: A Narrative of Ideas,* and established himself as an important writer. Three decades later in 1965 the editor of *Literary Times* would write, "Malcolm Cowley is, next to Edmund Wilson, the finest literary historian and critic . . . in America today."

While in the early 1930s Cowley's name was often associated with Communism and the political left, reviewers frequently noted that his most important achievement as a critic was his treatment of William Faulkner's fiction. The *Literary Times* editor wrote: "Probably more than any single person, Cowley is responsible for the entrenchment of . . . Faulkner as a major American writer with his brilliant introduction and presentation of *The Portable Faulkner* in 1946."

Cowley is also recognized as one of the major literary historians of the twentieth century, and his *Exile's Return,* if not the definitive chronicle of the 1920s, is certainly one of the most widely read. At the time the book was first published in 1934, J. D. Adams of the *New York Times* noted: "As the sincere attempt of a writer of our time to explain himself and his generation, to trace the flux of ideas and other influences to which he was subjected during his formative years, Mr. Cowley's book is a valuable document. It should interest the literary historian of the future no less than it must interest Mr. Cowley's contemporaries, however hard some of them may find it to grant him all his premises and to agree with all his deductions from them." When *Exile's Return* was revised in 1951, the new edition sparked further critical commentary. Lloyd Morris, in a *New York Herald Tribune Book Review* article, called it "the most vivacious of all accounts of literary life during the fabulous 1920s" and said that the book "offers an intimate realistic portrait of the era that produced a renaissance in American fiction and poetry." J. W. Krutch of the *Saturday Review of Literature* noted that "Mr. Cowley's estimate of his most successful elder contemporaries, including Joyce, Eliot, and Proust, is cool and on the whole rather remarkably far this side of idolatry. But these evaluations do not seem unjust, and his picture of life on the Left Bank and in Greenwich Village is highly colored without being exaggerated."

Another literary history for which Cowley received considerable praise was *A Second Flowering: Works and Days of the Lost Generation,* which deals with the works of F. Scott Fitzgerald, Ernest Hemingway, John Dos Passos, e. e. cummings, Thornton Wilder, William Faulkner, Thomas Wolfe, and Hart Crane. William Styron, in a *New York Times Book Review* article, wrote: "It is testimony to Cowley's gifts both as a critic and a literary chronicler that the angle of vision seems new; that is, not only are his insights into these writers' works almost consistently arresting, but so are his portraits of the men themselves."

Writing in the *Sewanee Review,* Lewis P. Simpson explained that Cowley dedicated a portion of his career "to redeem[ing] the American writer from his condition of alienation." According to Simpson, the theme of alienation ran throughout Cowley's entire body of work, including his poetry. "As both a creator and an interpreter of the literature of the lost generation," continued the critic, "Cowley is a contributor to one of its leading aspects: a myth or a legend of creativity which is definable as a poetics of exile. He apprehended first the American writer's exile from childhood, second his exile from society, and finally his exile from what may be termed the sense of being in the wholeness of the self." In works such as *Exile's Return* these first two "stages" may be seen; in *Blue Juniata: Collected Poems* the third—the exile from self—is in evidence.

In an interview with Allen Geller, Cowley compared the literature of the 1960s and 1970s to the work produced earlier in the century. "I think there is a very interesting group of writers today," he said, mentioning Saul Bellow and John Cheever among those he considered most important. "[Literary taste] has become more sophisticated. Whether it's better or not is always the question, but it has more knowledge, more points of reference." He added, "The great change from the 1930s is that nobody any longer believes in his duty or ability to any extent or in any manner whatever to reshape or alter conditions."

Regarding his own career, Cowley explained to *Southern Review* interviewer Diane U. Eisenberg: "I didn't drive myself to write some big work that was really expected of me. I had chances, too, but I didn't drive myself to finish it. And the fact that I didn't drive myself hard enough in my twenties is the big error I made. I should have been looking much more at the big overall pattern . . . keeping at producing bigger books." Still, he remained content that his life was spent in the field of literature. "The writer's trade is a laborious, tedious but lovely occupation of putting words into patterns," he told Eisenberg. "I love that trade,

profession, vocation. And that is something that persists over time."

BIOGRAPHICAL/CRITICAL SOURCES:

BOOKS

Bak, Hans, *Malcolm Cowley: The Formative Years,* University of Georgia Press, 1993

Eisenburg, Diane U., *Malcolm Cowley, a Checklist of His Writings, 1916-1973,* Southern Illinois University Press, 1975.

PERIODICALS

Booklist, June 15, 1951.
Bookman, October, 1930.
Books, May 27, 1934.
Canadian Forum, January, 1968.
Chicago Tribune, March 3, 1985.
Choice, September, 1973.
Detroit News, April 21, 1985.
Globe and Mail (Toronto), June 15, 1985.
Literary Review, autumn, 1968.
Literary Times, April, 1965.
Los Angeles Times, September 7, 1980; August 4, 1985.
Nation, July 4, 1934; June 5, 1967.
New Republic, March 11, 1967.
New Yorker, June 30, 1951; June 23, 1973.
New York Herald Tribune Book Review, May 28, 1934; June 24, 1951; October 7, 1951.
New York Post, June 2, 1934.
New York Times, May 27, 1934; June 10, 1951; February 13, 1962; August 17, 1977; April 28, 1978; March 26, 1980; October 1, 1980; December 11, 1985.
New York Times Book Review, July 8, 1951; February 12, 1967; November 17, 1968; May 6, 1973.
Saturday Review, March 11, 1967.
Saturday Review of Literature, January 16, 1934; June 30, 1951.
Sewanee Review, January/March, 1932; spring, 1976.
Southern Review, autumn, 1973; spring, 1977; spring, 1979.
Washington Post Book World, September 7, 1980; January 20, 1985; January 26, 1986.

*   *   *

COX, William Trevor 1928-
(William Trevor)

PERSONAL: Born May 24, 1928, in Mitchelstown, County Cork, Ireland; son of James William (a bank official) and Gertrude (Davison) Cox; married Jane Ryan, August 26, 1952; children: Patrick, Dominic. *Education:* Attended St. Columba's College, Dublin, Ireland, 1941-46; Trinity College, Dublin, B.A., 1950. *Politics:* Liberal.

ADDRESSES: Office—c/o Sterling Lord Literistic Ltd.,1 Madison Ave, New York, NY 10010; and c/o Peters, Fraser, and Dunlop Group, 503-504 The Chambers, Chelsea Harbour, Lots Road, London SW10 0FX, England.

CAREER: Teacher in County Armagh, Northern Ireland, 1952-53; art teacher at prep school near Rugby, England, 1953-55, and in Somerset, England, 1956-59; while teaching, worked as a church sculptor; advertising copywriter for Notley's, London, England, 1960-65; writer, 1965–. Has had one-man exhibitions of his artwork in Dublin, Ireland, and Bath, England.

MEMBER: Irish Academy of Letters.

AWARDS, HONORS: Winner of Irish section, "Unknown Political Prisoner" sculpture competition, 1953; second prize, *Transatlantic Review* short story competition, 1964; Hawthornden Prize, Royal Society of Literature, 1965, for *The Old Boys*; Society of Authors' traveling scholarship, 1972; Benson Medal, Royal Society of Literature, 1975, for *Angels at the Ritz, and Other Stories*; Allied Irish Bank Prize for literature, 1976; Heinemann Award for fiction, 1976; Whitbread Prize, 1978, for *The Children of Dynmouth*, and 1983, for *Fools of Fortune*; honorary Commander, Order of the British Empire, 1979; Irish Community Prize, 1979; Giles Cooper Award for radio play, 1980, for *Beyond the Pale*, and 1982, for *Autumn Sunshine*; Jacob Award for television play, 1983; D.Litt., University of Exeter, 1984, Trinity College, Dublin, 1986, University of Belfast, 1989, and National University of Ireland, Cork, 1990; *Sunday Express* Book of the Year Award, 1994, for *Felicia's Journey*.

WRITINGS:

NOVELS; UNDER NAME WILLIAM TREVOR

A Standard of Behavior, Hutchinson (London), 1958.
The Old Boys (also see below), Viking (New York City), 1964.
The Boarding-House, Viking, 1965.
The Love Department, Bodley Head (London), 1966, Viking, 1967.
Mrs. Eckdorf in O'Neill's Hotel, Bodley Head, 1969, Viking, 1970.
Miss Gomez and the Brethren, Bodley Head, 1971.
Elizabeth Alone, Bodley Head, 1973, Viking, 1974.
The Children of Dynmouth, Bodley Head, 1976, Viking, 1977.
Other People's Worlds, Bodley Head, 1980, Viking, 1981.
Fools of Fortune, Viking, 1983.
Nights at the Alexandra, Harper (New York City), 1987.
The Silence in the Garden, Viking, 1988.
Two Lives (contains the novels *Reading Turgenev* and *My House in Umbria*), Viking, 1991.
Felicia's Journey, Viking, 1994.
Juliet's Story, Simon & Schuster (New York City), 1994.
After Rain, Viking, 1996.
Death in Summer, Viking, 1998.

STORIES; UNDER NAME WILLIAM TREVOR

The Day We Got Drunk on Cake, and Other Stories, Bodley Head, 1967, Viking, 1968.
The Ballroom of Romance, and Other Stories (includes "The Mark-2 Wife," "The Grass Widows," and "O Fat White Woman"; also see below), Viking, 1972.
Angels at the Ritz, and Other Stories, Bodley Head, 1975, Viking, 1976.
Lovers of Their Time, and Other Stories (includes "Matilda's England" and "Attracta"), Viking, 1978.
The Distant Past, and Other Stories, Poolbeg Press, 1979.
Beyond the Pale, and Other Stories, Bodley Head, 1981, Viking, 1982.
The Stories of William Trevor (includes "The Penthouse Apartment," "Broken Homes," "A Complicated Nature," "In at the Birth," "The Hotel of the Idle Moon," "Another Christmas," "Being Stolen From," and "Teresa's Wedding,") Penguin (Hammondsmith, Middlesex, U.K.), 1983.
The News from Ireland, and Other Stories, Viking, 1986.
Family Sins, and Other Stories (includes "Kathleen's Field," "Events at Drimaghleen," "Coffee with Oliver," "The Third Party," "A Trinity," "A Husband's Return," "In Love with Ariadne," "August Saturday," and "Family Sins"), Viking, 1989.
William Trevor: Collected Stories, Viking, 1992.
Outside Ireland: Selected Stories, Penguin, 1995.
Cocktails at Doney's and Other Stories, Bloomsbury, 1996.
Ireland: Selected Stories, Penguin, 1998.

Also author of other stories, including "The Wedding in the Garden," "Mulvihill's Memorial," "Miss Smith," "The Bedroom Eyes of Mrs. Vansittart," and "The Time of Year." Stories anthologized in numerous collections, including *The Bedside Guardian*, edited by W. L. Webb, Collins, 1969, *The Bodley Head Book of Longer Short Stories*, edited by James Michie, Bodley Head, 1974, *Best for Winter*, edited by A. D. Maclean, Macmillan, 1979, *The Bodley Head Book of Irish Short Stories*, edited by Marcus, Bodley Head, 1980, and *Seven Deadly Sins*, Severn House, 1983.

PLAYS; UNDER NAME WILLIAM TREVOR

The Elephant's Foot, produced in Nottingham, England, 1966.
The Girl, French (London), 1968.
The Old Boys (adapted from his novel; produced on the West End, 1971), Davis-Poynter, 1971.
Going Home (one-act; produced in London at King's Head Islington, February 29, 1972), French, 1972.
A Night with Mrs. da Tanka (one-act; produced in London, 1972), French, 1972.
A Perfect Relationship (one-act), produced in London, 1973.
The 57th Saturday (one-act), produced in London, 1973.
Marriages (one-act; produced in London, 1973), French, 1974.
Beyond the Pale (radio play), broadcast in England, 1980, televised, 1989.
Scenes from an Album, produced in Dublin at the Abbey Theatre, 1981.

Also author of television and radio plays for British Broadcasting Corp. (BBC) and ITV, including *The Mark-2 Wife, O Fat White Woman, The Grass Widows, The General's Day, Love Affair, Last Wishes, Matilda's England, Secret Orchards, Autumn Sunshine, The Penthouse Apartment, Travellers*, and *Events at Drimaghleen*.

OTHER; UNDER NAME WILLIAM TREVOR

Old School Ties (memoir), Lemon Tree Press (London), 1976.
A Writer's Ireland: Landscape in Literature (nonfiction), Viking, 1984.
(Editor) *The Oxford Book of Irish Short Stories*, Oxford University Press, 1989.
Excursions in the Real World: Autobiographical Essays, Knopf (New York City), 1994.

A collection of Trevor's manuscripts is housed at the University of Tulsa.

MEDIA ADAPTATIONS: *The Old Boys* was adapted as a BBC television play, 1965; *The Ballroom of Romance* was broadcast on BBC-TV, 1982; *The Children of Dynmouth* was aired on BBC-TV, 1987; a screenplay by Michael Hirst was based on *Fools of Fortune* and directed by Pat O'Connor, 1990; *Elizabeth Alone* was also produced for BBC-TV.

SIDELIGHTS: Short-story writer, novelist, and playwright William Trevor Cox is an Irish-born English writer better known to his readers as William Trevor. Highly acclaimed for his short fiction, Trevor has been called "one of the finest living short-story writers in English" by such critics as *Washington Post Book World* contributor Jonathan Yardley. However, he is also a two-time recipient of the Whitbread Prize for his novels and is widely known in England for the British television productions of his novels. Having lived in both Ireland and England, Trevor has written about people in both countries and is especially concerned with the many ordinary people in the world who lead tragic, lonely lives. "I don't really have any heroes or heroines," Trevor remarks in a *Publishers Weekly* interview with Amanda Smith. "I don't seem to go in for them. I think I am interested in people who are not necessarily the victims of other people, but simply the victims of circumstances. . . . I'm very interested in the sadness of fate, the things that just happen to people." Originally working as a sculptor, Trevor became displeased with the increasingly abstract turn his art was taking, and so he took up writing as a means of better expressing his concern for the human condition. "I think the humanity that isn't in abstract art began to go into [my] short stories," Trevor tells Smith.

In many of Trevor's novels and stories, the events or situations that most affect his characters occur offstage and often years in the past. This interest in the importance of the past is evident from as early as his first successful novel, *The Old Boys,* a tale of how the public school reunion of eight octogenarians causes them to revert back to childish competitive behavior by reminding them of old grudges and rivalries. "For Trevor," observes *Encounter* critic Tom Paulin in a later review of *Lovers of Their Time,* "an obsession with the past is a kind of madness," a notion that is invested in many of the author's stories and novels. But the novel's situation also provides Trevor plenty of opportunities to demonstrate his characteristic use of understated humor.

Satire is also prominent in such early Trevor books as *The Boarding House* and *The Love Department,* although the situations in which his characters find themselves are often lamentable. However, *New York Times Book Review* critic Robert Towers writes, since "the mid-1970's there has been . . . a subtle change of tone in the stories. The harsh comedy—the gleeful misanthropy—is less in evidence, as is the stance of impartiality; in the later work one can guess rather clearly where the author's sympathies lie."

In what one *Times Literary Supplement* reviewer declares to be "a collection that is never disappointing," *The Ballroom of Romance, and Other Stories* portrays a series of characters who are caught in dreary, barren lives, but are not self-confident enough to change. Instead, they can only reflect upon what might have been, their memories and dreams leaving them isolated and alone. "The stories may be sad, but they have about them the unmistakable ring of truth." It is with these sad stories of ordinary people that the author finds himself repeatedly concerned. They may live unhappy lives because of their unwillingness or inability to give up the past or their illusions of reality, or, as with Trevor's *Elizabeth Alone,* because they are simply victims of fate.

With *Elizabeth Alone* Trevor first proposes a possible reason for human suffering. Set in a hospital, the author presents a series of ostensibly comic situations while simultaneously probing deeper issues through his sympathetic character portrayals. The title character, Elizabeth Aidallbery, has in one way or another lost everyone in her life that was important to her, and has even begun to lose her sense of identity. She finds the strength to overcome her loneliness and carry on through one of her hospital mates, Miss Samson, whose religious faith has recently been shaken. Miss Samson convinces Elizabeth that the importance of caring for others, even—or perhaps especially—if the world has no God, gives people a purpose in life. A *Times Literary Supplement* critic

compliments Trevor on his ability to execute this conclusion convincingly in a seriocomic novel, attributing this success to "the authority he has built up, as a writer, out of the sheer, detailed understanding of the characters he creates. . . . The stance of compassion which is adopted finally in *Elizabeth Alone* can now be seen to be implicit in all Mr. Trevor's best work. It gives him a place as a writer capable of handling the human comedy instead of merely manipulating comic human beings."

Collections such as *Angels at the Ritz, and Other Stories* and *Lovers of Their Time, and Other Stories* that followed *Elizabeth Alone* continue to illustrate Trevor's concern for average people and the importance of the effects of time. "Trevor is especially adept at making the presence of the past, the presence of people offstage, lean upon his characters," says Peter S. Prescott in a *Newsweek* review of *Angels at the Ritz.* Similarly, *New York Times Book Review* contributor Victoria Glendinning comments on the stories in *Lovers of Their Time,* "Nothing very extraordinary happens to [Trevor's] teachers, tradesmen, farmers and shop-assistants; the action is all off-stage, and they are caught and thrown off course by the wash of great and passionate events that happened in another time, another place."

With Trevor's *The Children of Dynmouth,* his first Whitbread Prize-winning book, the author takes a different approach to his theme of personal suffering by focusing on an unsympathetic boy named Timothy Gedge. Abandoned by his father and ignored by the rest of his family, Timothy has become a despicable character who has a crude sense of humor and is fascinated by death. Desperate for attention, he becomes convinced that he can find fame by doing an act for the variety television show, "Opportunity Knocks." But to get the props he needs, Timothy blackmails several of the respectable citizens of Dynmouth and "by the novel's end he has come close to destroying several people," writes Joyce Carol Oates in the *New York Times Book Review.* "Timothy's malice arises from his chronic aloneness, so that it isn't possible, as the [character of] the vicar recognizes, to see the boy as evil."

Some critics see Timothy's rescue by the vicar at the novel's conclusion to be a weak solution to an otherwise excellent book. "To imply that sooner or later the shrinks and the socialists will put an end to evil is to drag out an old chestnut indeed," writes *Sewanee Review* contributor Walter Sullivan. Sullivan finds that this flaw negates "the fine performance which leads up to this foolishness." But Thomas R. Edwards asserts in the *New York Review of Books* that *The Children of Dynmouth* "succeeds in being funny, frightening, and morally poised and intelligent at once." Oates similarly concludes that it is "a skillfully written novel, a small masterpiece of understatement."

In another Whitbread Prize-winning novel, *Fools of Fortune,* Trevor chronicles the years of lonely isolation of two lovers separated by a tragic turn of fate. A "benchmark novel against which other contemporary novels will have to be measured," in *Washington Post Book World* critic Charles Champlin's assessment, *Fools of Fortune* also reflects the "last seven decades of English-Irish history." The novel relates how British soldiers misguidedly destroy Willie Quinton's family and home in the year 1918, and how Willie's revenge on a British officer leads to his exile from Ireland. Forced to leave his beloved English cousin, Marianne, he is denied the chance to see her or their daughter, Imelda, for years to come. The Quintons, remarks Jonathan Yardley in the *Washington Post Book World,* "are all good, honorable people, but they—like poor Ireland—are victims of mere chance, arbitrary and random."

With other tales, such as the central story of *The News from Ireland, and Other Stories* and the novel, *The Silence in the Garden,* Trevor relates the struggles in Ireland to the misfortunes of his characters and, as Richard Eder of the *Los Angeles Times* puts it, "the passing of a kind of civility that Yeats celebrated." In the case of *The Silence in the Garden,* the story of how war and terrorism ruin a once happy and prosperous Anglo-Irish family, *Washington Post Book World* critic Gregory A. Schirmer notes that Trevor "has much to say about the attitudes and patterns that lie behind the [British-Irish] violence, and about the ways in which the present is inevitably—and, in Ireland, often tragically—shaped by the past."

Although Trevor's stories and novels often involve dramatic events, he is mainly concerned with how these events preoccupy and obsess his characters. This inner tension is subtly portrayed through the author's quiet, understated writing style. Michiko Kakutani of the *New York Times* describes Trevor's style in a review of *Fools of Fortune,* as "spare, lilting prose, . . . delineat[ing] these melodramatic events with economy and precision." For some critics, however, Trevor's use of understatement is a drawback in his writing. Anatole Broyard, for one, writes in a *New York Times* review of *Beyond the Pale*: "Though everyone regards [Trevor] as a master of understatement, I wonder whether it isn't conceited in a way to insist on writing such carefully removed stories, so breathlessly poised on the edge of nonexistence."

In 1992, sixty of Trevor's short stories were published in *William Trevor: Collected Stories.* Reviewers have been generally enthusiastic about the quality of the collection. Joseph Coates writes in the *Tribune Books,* "The stories of this modern master often hinge on a slightness and subtlety that are the last thing we think of hefting a volume of this size." Coates goes on to say that "despite this massive output, the salient characteristic of his work is the careful craftsmanship that produces its deceptively transparent surfaces. . . . What gives Trevor's stories their paradoxical sparkle . . . is his fascination with the endless variety and sheer unaccountability of human life, the infinite inventiveness with which people make their odd, pathetic but always somehow dignified arrangements for getting through their days and nights, with or without satisfaction, with or without the slimmest of memories to sustain them."

Trevor's sympathy for outcasts is at the core of his 1994 novel, *Felicia's Journey.* The plot concerns a young Irish girl, Felicia, who travels to the gloomy industrial districts of England in search of the young man who seduced and then abandoned her. She is preyed upon by Mr. Hilditch, a huge, lonely man with hidden sociopathic tendencies. Cunningly he weaves his web around her, engineering "chance" meetings and making innocent-sounding offers of help to her. Felicia stays with him for a time, and then, sensing evil, turns to Mrs. Calligary, a door-to-door evangelist. But when the missionary-like retreat Mrs. Calligary offers becomes unbearable, Felicia returns to her doom at Mr. Hilditch's residence. Reviewers differed sharply in their assessment of *Felicia's Journey.* Some, such as *Spectator* contributor Peregrine Hodson, find the book's many references to brand names and other details to be pointless and tedious. "Having finished *Felicia's Journey,* I felt I had read an extremely long short story," remarks Hodson. "Some may find, in the author's descriptions of minutiae, evidence of the artist's eye, which misses nothing.

Others may feel the accumulation of trivia—'Marlboro, it said on the packet on the table'—clogs the narrative."

Richard Eder expresses a more serious objection to the book in the *Los Angeles Times Book Review.* He praises the author's rendering of Felicia, stating that "William Trevor, who is good at a great deal, is particularly good with the meek; and most particularly with the rural Irish meek. He finds the passion in them and he finds the ruses they devise to preserve . . . their lives." But Eder dismisses Mr. Hilditch as an unconvincing authorial device, one which unfortunately dominated the book: "True, he can do splendid bullies, tricksters and arrogant bastards; but in each case he builds on their humanity and warps it just enough. . . . A monster, on the other hand, is a kind of void. . . . A writer can portray a man with a hole—an absence—in him, but a writer needs to be a special kind of metaphysician . . . to make the hole the character. . . . Hilditch is not enough of a character to generate a moral or significant action; he is a device through which the author acts."

Jennifer Chen of the *Book Report* calls Trevor's collection of stories, *After Rain,* "a must for both long time Trevor fans and newcomers to the Irish master." In the familiar setting of Irish villages, more stories of failed relationships are displayed as Trevor runs "the whole, huge, messy gamut of human foibles and emotions," Chen states. Michiko Kakutani of the *New York Times* remarks that Trevor writes "with such assurance that he's able to collapse entire lives into a few brief pages, showing us how a character's past connects to his future, how his fate, in short, has been constructed." Some critics think the collection lacks humor, and Kakutani believes there is a decided "mood of resignation" that permeates the stories.

During his career, Trevor has been compared to such luminaries as Muriel Spark, Anton Chekov, and Andre Malraux, but most often to his Irish predecessor, James Joyce. *New York Times Book Review* critic Ted Solotaroff compares Joyce and Trevor this way: "Both Trevor and the early Joyce are geniuses at presenting a seemingly ordinary life as it is, socially, psychologically, morally, and then revealing the force of these conditions in the threatened individual's moment of resistance to them. This is the deeper realism: accurate observation turning into moral vision." "Yet like Joyce before him," concludes *Washington Post Book World* contributor Howard Frank Mosher, "Trevor is entirely his own writer, with his own uncompromised vision of human limitations made accessible by a rare generosity toward his characters and their blighted lives."

BIOGRAPHICAL/CRITICAL SOURCES:

BOOKS

Contemporary Dramatists, St. James Press (Detroit), 1993.
Contemporary Literary Criticism, Gale (Detroit), Volume 7, 1977; Volume 9, 1978; Volume 14, 1980; Volume 25, 1983; Volume 71, 1992.
Contemporary Novelists, St. James Press, 1991.
Dictionary of Literary Biography, Gale, Volume 14: *British Novelists since 1960,* 1983; Volume 139: *British Short-Fiction Writers, 1945-1980,* 1994.
Morrison, Kristin, *William Trevor,* Twayne, 1993.
Paulson, Suzanne Morrow, *William Trevor: A Study of the Short Fiction,* Twayne, 1993.
Schirmer, Gregory A., *William Trevor: A Study of His Fiction,* Routledge, 1990.

PERIODICALS

Atlantic Monthly, August, 1986.
Book Report (online journal), 1997.
Boston Book Review, 1998.
Boston Globe, November 15, 1992, p. 91; February 6, 1994, p. 89; February 13, 1994, p. A15; January 8, 1995, p. 47.
Chicago Tribune, November 13, 1987; September 30, 1988; November 22, 1992, section 14, p. 1; April 6, 1994, section 5, p. 3; January 15, 1995, section 14, p. 3.
Chicago Tribune Book World, July 29, 1979; March 15, 1981; February 14, 1982; October 30, 1983.
Christian Science Monitor, February 26, 1970; March 10, 1994, p. 14; January 10, 1995, p. 13.
Encounter, January, 1979.
Globe and Mail (Toronto), December 31, 1983; October 24, 1987; September 17, 1988.
Harper's, October, 1983, pp. 74-5.
Hudson Review, winter, 1991, pp. 686-90.
Irish Literary Supplement, spring, 1991, p. 20.
Irish Times, May 22, 1988.
Listener, July 21, 1988, pp. 25-6.
London Magazine, August, 1968.
London Review of Books, June 23, 1988, p. 22; December 16, 1993, pp. 22-3.
Los Angeles Times, October 2, 1983; September 29, 1988; February 10, 1994, p. E10; January 8, 1995, p. 3.
Los Angeles Times Book Review, January 11, 1981; March 11, 1984, p. 4; May 4, 1986, p. 3; August 6, 1989; May 20, 1990, p. 3; September 5, 1993, p. 6; February 13, 1994, p. 6; January 8, 1995.
Nation, December 3, 1983, pp. 574-77.
New Republic, February 4, 1967; November 28, 1983, pp. 37-9; June 9, 1986, pp. 28-30; February 6, 1989, pp. 37-40; October 1, 1990, pp. 40-1.
New Statesman, October 15, 1971; July 9, 1976; September 22, 1978.
New Statesman & Society, August 27, 1993, pp. 40-1.
Newsweek, June 14, 1976; February 22, 1982; October 10, 1983.
New Yorker, July 12, 1976.
New York Review of Books, April 19, 1979; March 19, 1981; December 22, 1983, pp. 53-4; June 26, 1986, pp. 32-3, 35; May 17, 1990; September 26, 1991, pp. 29-30.
New York Times, September 31, 1972; March 31, 1979; January 17, 1981; February 3, 1982; September 26, 1983; May 14, 1986; August 27, 1988; May 11, 1990, p. C33; January 3, 1995, p. B27; November 12, 1996.
New York Times Book Review, February 11, 1968; July 11, 1976; April 8, 1979; February 1, 1981; February 21, 1982; October 2, 1983, pp. 1, 22, 24; June 8, 1986, p. 14; January 17, 1988, p. 24; October 9, 1988, p. 12; June 3, 1990, p. 9; September 8, 1991, p. 3; February 3, 1993, p.1; February 28, 1993, pp. 1, 25-7; February 13, 1994, p. 7; January 8, 1995, pp. 1, 22.
Observer, June 11, 1980; April 6, 1986, p. 27; June 5, 1988; November 1, 1987; February 4, 1990; May 26, 1991.
Plays and Players, September, 1971.
Publishers Weekly, October 28, 1983.
San Francisco Review of Books, Volume 16, number 3, 1991, pp. 47-8.
Saturday Review, May 12, 1970, pp. 44-5.
Sewanee Review, spring, 1978, pp. 320-25.
Spectator, October 11, 1969; May 13, 1972; November 29, 1986, p. 25; June 1, 1991, p. 28; October 17, 1992, pp. 25-6; August 28, 1993, p. 32; August 20, 1994, p. 34.
Sunday Times, May 29, 1988, pp. 68-9; May 26, 1991, pp. 6-7.

Time, January 26, 1970; October 10, 1983.
Times (London), June 18, 1980; October 15, 1981; April 28, 1983; March 20, 1986; May 30, 1991, p. 12.
Times Literary Supplement, October 26, 1973; June 20, 1980; October 16, 1981; April 29, 1983; August 31, 1984; April 11, 1986; November 5, 1987; June 10, 1988; January 26, 1990, p. 87; May 31, 1991, p. 21; September 17, 1993, p. 24; August 19, 1994, p. 20.
Tribune Books (Chicago), September 10, 1989; November 22, 1992, p. 1.
Vogue, February 1, 1968.
Wall Street Journal, March 2, 1994, p. A9; January 26, 1995, p. A12.
Washington Post, March 11, 1995, p. A17.
Washington Post Book World, April 8, 1979; February 1, 1981; February 21, 1982; September 25, 1983, p. 3; March 4, 1984; May 25, 1986, p. 6; August 28, 1988; May 27, 1990; August 18, 1991; January 22, 1995, pp. 1, 10.
Writer, October, 1990.

* * *

COZZENS, James Gould 1903-1978

PERSONAL: Born August 19, 1903, in Chicago, IL; died August 9, 1978, of pneumonia following treatment for cancer of the spine, in Stuart, FL; cremated; son of Henry William and Bertha (Wood) Cozzens; married Sylvia Bernice Baumgarten (a literary agent), December 31, 1927 (died January 30, 1978). *Education:* Graduate of Kent (CT) School, 1922; attended Harvard University, 1922-24.

ADDRESSES: Office—c/o Harcourt Brace Jovanovich, 750 Third Ave., New York, NY 10017.

CAREER: Writer. Taught children of American engineers in Tuinucu, Cuba, 1925-26; spent one year in Europe as a traveling tutor, 1926-27; librarian at the New York Athletic Club, 1927; worked in advertising, 1928; associate editor of *Fortune* magazine, 1938; farmer. *Military service:* U.S. Army Air Forces, 1942-45; became major.

MEMBER: National Institute of Arts and Letters.

AWARDS, HONORS: O. Henry Award, Doubleday & Co., 1931, for short story "A Farewell to Cuba," and 1936, for short story "Total Stranger"; Pulitzer prize, 1949, for *Guard of Honor;* Litt.D., Harvard University, 1952; William Dean Howells Medal, American Academy of Arts and Letters, 1960, for *By Love Possessed.*

WRITINGS:

NOVELS

Confusion, B. J. Brimmer, 1924.
Michael Scarlett, A & C Boni, 1925.
Cock Pit, Morrow, 1928.
The Son of Perdition, Morrow, 1929.
S.S. San Pedro (Book-of-the-Month Club selection; also see below), Harcourt, 1931.
The Last Adam (Book-of-the-Month Club selection), Harcourt, 1933, original edition published in England as *A Cure of Flesh,* Longmans, Green, 1934.
Castaway (also see below), Random House, 1934, Elephant Paperbacks (Chicago), 1989.
Men and Brethren, Harcourt, 1936.

Ask Me Tomorrow, Harcourt, 1940, published as *Ask Me Tomorrow; or, The Pleasant Comedy of Young Fortunas,* Harcourt, 1969.

The Just and the Unjust (Book-of-the-Month Club selection), Harcourt, 1942.

Guard of Honor, Harcourt, 1948.

S.S. San Pedro [and] *Castaway,* Modern Library, 1956.

By Love Possessed (Book-of-the-Month Club selection; *Reader's Digest* condensed book selection), Harcourt, 1957.

Morning Noon and Night, Harcourt, 1968.

OTHER

(Contributor) Burton Rascoe, editor, *Morrow's Almanack for the Year of Our Lord 1929,* Morrow, 1928.

(Contributor) Thayer Hobson, editor, *Morrow's Almanack Every-Day Book for 1930,* Morrow, 1929.

Children and Others (stories), Harcourt, 1964.

(Author of introduction) James B. Meriwether, *James Gould Cozzens: A Checklist,* Gale, 1972.

A Flower in Her Hair, Bruccoli Clark, 1974.

A Rope for Dr. Webster (essay), Bruccoli Clark, 1976.

Bruccoli, Matthew J., editor, *Just Representations: A James Gould Cozzens Reader,* Southern Illinois University Press, 1978.

Bruccoli, editor, *A Time of War: Air Force Diaries and Pentagon Memos, 1943-1945,* Bruccoli Clark, 1984.

Bruccoli, editor, *Selected Notebooks, 1960-1967,* Bruccoli Clark, 1984.

Contributor of short stories, poems, and essays to periodicals, including the *Atlantic, Pictorial Review, Saturday Evening Post, Collier's, Redbook, Kent Quarterly, Bookman, Town & Country, Harvard Advocate,* and *Woman's Home Companion.* Some of Cozzens's novels have been translated into foreign languages, including Burmese, Italian, German, Portuguese, and Japanese. Cozzens's manuscripts and papers are located at the Princeton University Library.

MEDIA ADAPTATIONS: The Last Adam was made into a motion picture entitled *Doctor Bull,* 1933, starring Will Rogers; *By Love Possessed* was made into a motion picture by United Artists, 1961, starring Efrem Zimbalist, Jr., and Lana Turner.

SIDELIGHTS: After publishing four novels for which he received little money or critical recognition, James Gould Cozzens gained his first writing success with *S. S. San Pedro,* a novel based on the real-life sinking of the *Vestris* in a November gale with heavy loss of life. Only 133 pages long, *S.S. San Pedro,* the first novel in which Cozzens consistently maintained an objective tone and a detached point of view, was selected as a September 1931 choice by the Book-of-the-Month Club. As Matthew Bruccoli notes in *James Gould Cozzens: A Life Apart:* "The process of rewriting the novel through successive versions had brought control over his material and style. Having published four self-indulgent novels, he moved at twenty-eight into his unembellished middle style." Increasingly concerned with structure, Cozzens regarded *S.S. San Pedro* as his first mature work, though it is flawed by the obviously symbolic use of Dr. Percival, a grotesque figure, to prefigure death. After he experimented with allegory again in *Castaway* Cozzens then permanently abandoned it.

While working on *S.S. San Pedro* in 1929 and 1930, Cozzens resumed writing commercial short stories to improve his plotting and earn money. Cozzens soon began a novel situated in a small Connecticut town. "This setting," he wrote in an inscribed copy of *The Last Adam,* "is imagined to be Kent, Connecticut, with a

green like New Milford's along US 7 as it passes through Kent." Published in 1933, *The Last Adam* was Cozzens's most successful work to date, containing the qualities that distinguish his best novels. Not only does it scrutinize a profession through its central character, Dr. Bull, but it weaves cause and effect together in a dispassionate, objective style. The protagonist, moreover, acknowledges human limitations and acts within them. Harry John Mooney, in his critical work *James Gould Cozzens: Novelist of Intellect,* declares: "What *The Last Adam* revealed, above all else, was the rapidly developing direction of James Gould Cozzens himself."

The principal subject of the novel is the community of New Winton—its tight structure and the interrelations of its people. Cozzens, however, had not yet invested his central character with those traits generally belonging to his professional men. Barely competent and decidedly unconcerned about his patients, Dr. Bull's neglect is partly responsible for a typhoid epidemic; yet he nevertheless possesses an elemental force: "Something unkillable. Something here when the first men walked erect; here now. The last man would twitch with it when the earth expired. A good greedy vitality, surely the very vitality of the world and the flesh; it survived all blunders and injuries." Unlike Dr. Bull, however, the professionals in Cozzens's later novels believe firmly in responsibility and adherence to duty. Near the end of *The Last Adam,* Cozzens quotes from Milton's *Samson Agonistes:* "His servants he, with new acquist / Of true experience from this great event / With peace and consolation both dismissed, / And calm of mind." As Bruccoli notes in *James Gould Cozzens: A Life Apart,* "'New acquist of true experience' would become his test of literature: the presentation of convincing characters in convincing action, unimpaired by sentimental theories about human nature, to provide the reader with an undistorted recognition of behavior."

Early in 1933 the Cozzenses moved to Carrs Farm, three miles outside Lambertville, New Jersey. The move gave Cozzens a feeling of "extraordinary repose" and permitted him to garden extensively. The sixth revision of *Castaway* was completed in May.

Castaway opens with the protagonist, Mr. Lecky, emerging into the vast material abundance of a department store. Inexplicably, his watch has stopped, and though the store is unpopulated, he becomes almost incapacitated by unnamed fears and begins stalking his Doppelganger, or ghostly counterpart. Cozzens provides no reason for the situation or any account of the outside world, and the principle action in the novel may occur within Mr. Lecky's consciousness, though the work does not employ stream-of-consciousness techniques.

Cozzens's antidemocratic inclinations—particularly his suggestion that those endowed with breeding, superior education, and inherent disposition ought to order their communities—begin to manifest themselves in *Castaway.* Indeed, the novel reads as a study in the impoverishment of those less endowed individuals. Mr. Lecky has no survival skills, despite the store's abundance, and he becomes the victim of his own inadequacies. Intelligent enough only to recognize that he is not enjoying complete gratification from the material wealth about him, he does not know how to make any of it his own. Paralyzed by indecision and lacking self-reliance, Mr. Lecky embodies a mediocrity of intelligence and sensibility that renders him incapable of realistically viewing his world. Beginning with his next novel, *Men and Brethren,* Cozzens depicted an American aristocracy in which ability and a sense of duty were primarily discerned in those who possessed the advantages of family and position.

Men and Brethren constitutes the first novel in which Cozzens fully portrayed the concept of duty that characterizes his major fiction. Ernest Cudlipp, an Episcopalian minister, struggles with himself and the truth of appearances. As Louis Coxe observes in his 1955 *American Literature* essay, Cudlipp and such men as Colonel Ross in *Guard of Honor* "have worked out for themselves a mode of action and a standard of conduct by which they judge others and by which we as readers may judge them." Recognizing the burden placed upon him, the duty that makes him an early model of the Cozzens hero, Cudlipp explains to an adulterous woman whose abortion he has arranged, "This is the answer. A great obligation has been laid upon me to do or be whatever good thing I have learned I ought to be, or know I can do. I can't excuse myself from it. I dare not bury it or throw it away." The Cozzens hero is a man aware of requirements, a man of intelligence, determination, education, and analytical skills, who, because of his position and his ability to fulfill the duties of that position, helps hold society together.

Men and Brethren achieves a tight structure that enforces both the simultaneity of action and the complexity of causes. In *The Last Adam* Cozzens had depicted tangential events, but the time scheme was loose and the novel lacked a central intelligence. Limited to parts of only two days, *Men and Brethren* achieves unity because events in the novel are seen from Cudlipp's point of view. As Bruccoli notes in his critical biography, "The third-person narrative provides the impression of standing with the author behind Cudlipp and observing everything from Cudlipp's perspective, thereby providing the effect of detachment combined with close participation." The novel ends with Cudlipp's recitation of St. Matthew's parable of the talents: "For the kingdom of heaven is as a man traveling into a far country, who called his own servants and delivered unto them his goods." Depicting the faithful, good servant, Cozzens achieved a convincing portrait of a priest, despite his personal antipathy to religious people. Writing to his mother on July 23, 1935, he complained that the book was "a little thin probably because if I got right down to it I find it hard to conceive of a professional Christian who isn't a fool, or a knave."

Cozzens devoted himself primarily to short stories in 1936 as he studied possible subjects for another novel. Between 1934 and 1938 he published twelve stories, writing them now only for money because he regarded the form as too confining. "Total Stranger," published in the *Saturday Evening Post,* was awarded the O. Henry Prize for the best story of 1936. Only partly playful, Cozzens wrote his mother on December 4 that he considered it "a piece of damned impertinence for anyone to try to give me a prize. . . . I don't doubt that fundamentally the reason I prefer to live as nearly like a recluse as possible is that subconsciously I know that people, the world, never would and never will greet my entrances into it with the reverent applause required for my pleasure and if cannot have that I will not, in effect, play." Feeling it degrading to sell himself, Cozzens withdrew from literary life—though not from writing—while still in his early thirties.

Cozzens's most autobiographical novel, *Ask Me Tomorrow* attempts to explain the prideful behavior of Francis Ellery, a writer in reduced circumstances working in Europe as a traveling tutor. Early in the book, Ellery thinks: "The hard fact was, circumstances rarely misled, and appearances were always full of truth. . . . People who are poor, while they may be estimable and

virtuous, confess in the fact of poverty an incapacity for mastering their environment; and what excuse or justification their incapacity may have interests only themselves." At the end of the novel, Ellery realizes the insignificance of his place in the world. He reflects: "To or about the course of events you could say what you liked; but events never stopped to argue with you."

In an *American Scholar* essay, John William Ward declares: "To act in the full awareness of the conditions within which he must act is, for Cozzens, the dignity of man." Critics note that Ellery finally achieves a certain worthiness because he glimpses the interlocking simultaneity of events, but *Ask Me Tomorrow* lacks the narrative scope to permit adequate development of an epiphany. Despite the fact that the novel is the one on which he labored the longest and which he felt came nearest to fulfilling his intentions, its critical reception disappointed Cozzens. Even the favorable reviews were unenthusiastic.

Completed in March 1942, *The Just and the Unjust* covers three days of a murder trial. Judge Coates's concluding instruction to his son Abner, the assistant district attorney, echoes Ernest Cudlipp's position in *Men and Brethren* and states the familiar Cozzens directive. One should employ his talents, do his job, fulfill his responsibilities: "The world gets up in the morning and is fed and goes to work, and in the evening it comes home and is fed again and perhaps has a little amusement and goes to sleep. To make that possible, so much has to be done by so many people that, on the face of it, it is impossible. Well, every day we have to do it; and every day, come hell, come high water, we're going to have to go on doing it as well as we can."

Like *Men and Brethren, The Just and the Unjust* is structured around a multiplicity of events that affect the protagonist during a short time period. Cozzens weaves expository flashbacks to support the present time sequence and to suggest the complexity of concurrent actions; the method is one he would employ again in *Guard of Honor.* As Bruccoli observes in *James Gould Cozzens: A Life Apart*: "His major novels—more than those of any other American writer—simulate the chain of cause and effect (but in Cozzens it is frequently perceived as effect and cause) that determine behavior." Cozzens also depicts the mental processes of his characters while maintaining the objectivity of the third.person perspective, a method that reinforces what Coxe refers to as "the double vision of modern man, the central paradox of action and contemplation, of understanding and conduct, of the ironic view and the heroic efficacy."

On October 6, 1942, while stationed in Washington, D.C., Cozzens began keeping a detailed, typed diary that not only chronicled his daily service activities but also described the hundreds of people he met. Eventually, his assignment provided him access to almost all reports from every theater of the war, and though he had not yet begun planning an air force novel, Cozzens recognized the value of his experiences. When discharged, he had compiled 380 single-spaced pages of diaries that—supplemented by his Pentagon memos—formed a useful historical record. While preparing of his notes, Cozzens found the idea for *Guard of Honor.*

Tightly plotted, *Guard of Honor* covers seventy-two hours at Ocanara Air Base, Florida, in September 1943. The third-person omniscient narrator—recognizably Cozzens himself—is not so much seeking solutions as he is identifying the limitations inhibiting human conduct. The novel's actual subject is not General Beal's crisis—the challenge to segregated clubs by black pilots—but the overwhelming complexity of the U.S. Army Air

Forces. Both Colonel Ross, who provides the perspective of the professional officer, and Captain Hicks, who represents the viewpoint of the civilian drafted to be a soldier, come to realize the intricate chain of cause and effect that, together with the operation of good and bad luck, restricts human action. In his *New York Herald Tribune* review, Mark Shorer identified the theme as "power, the hierarchy of power, and the responsibility of power," for, as Colonel Ross thinks: "Downheartedness was no man's part. A man must stand up and do the best he can with what there is. If the thing he labored to uncover now seemed in danger of stultifying him, could a rational being find nothing to do? If mind failed you, seeing no pattern; and heart failed you, seeing no point, the stout, stubborn will must be up and doing. A pattern should be found; a point should be imposed. Was that too much? It was not." Despite Cozzens's ability to treat a profession with convincing familiarity, however, critics continued to complain that his characters lacked emotion. Brendan Gill in the *New Yorker* claimed that *Guard of Honor* failed to achieve great novel status because of "an absence of deep feeling, of a fastidious shying-off on the part of the novelist, of an inconspicuous but nagging failure to commit himself beyond irony."

In January 1949, Cozzens began *By Love Possessed,* a novel, he wrote his mother on April 3, that meant "to say something about the cardinal human need to do what you want to, at any cost to yourself or other people; and however indirectly or circuitously, however unreasonably or unwisely, which is what I think is meant by love or being possessed by it." Although he predicted that the novel would appear in 1952, Cozzens found that the complexity of his artistic method and the standards he set for himself had made writing more difficult, and the book was not published until 1957. On February 1, 1951, he described his method as "taking things that appear simple and reducing them to their essential complexity." *By Love Possessed* centers on forty-nine hours in the life of Arthur Winner, a lawyer involved in a complex of problems resulting from the many varieties of love altruism; marital, parental, and filial affection; lust; religion; and friendship.

Cozzens's style was becoming a concern of the critics, for he refused to make concessions to inattentive or ignorant readers. *By Love Possessed* contains long, complex sentences, with inverted syntax and heavy subordination, as well as parenthetical constructions and elaborate quotations; reviewers called it "baroque." However, Cozzens aimed at a precision of statement, and his unfamiliar words, inverted word order, and double negatives (for example, "not unlikely" instead of "likely") sought to present the truth of experience. The "complications" in certain paragraphs, he wrote Charles Phillips on May 22, 1958, "were indeed a studied attempt to so reproduce or simulate the process of thought that the reader would go through it instead of just hearing about it." Abandoning the inflated, romantic wordiness of his early novels and the unadorned style of the 1930s and 1940s, Cozzens adopted a qualifying and meditative style that critics consistently attacked.

Against Bernice's advice, Cozzens consented to an interview with *Time.* Entitled "The Hermit of Lambertville," the cover story of September 2, 1957, sold thousands of copies of *By Love Possessed*; but because Cozzens did not exercise his option of checking the piece for accuracy, factual errors and misrepresentations in the article resulted in readers viewing Cozzens as an arrogant crank.

After a series of false starts, Cozzens shifted the new work, *Morning Noon and Night,* to the first person, which, he wrote in his notebook on November 20, 1964, "seemed to release me at once." The novel opens with Henry Dodd Worthington making a statement of fact: "I have been young and now am old." The remainder of the book constitutes the narrator's attempt to depict what exactly his life has been and what, if anything, he has learned from it: "What is this life? Who am I; what is this 'I' in me." Worthington's narrative—a meditative memoir—is carried along principally by a process of association of ideas, for the simultaneity of events precludes any final unified understanding. The seemingly unstructured account provides the means not only by which Worthington examines himself and the roles he has played but also the way through which he relates the truths he has learned. The process of narration corresponds with what Worthington believes is the nature of memory—"Give it liberty, and order be damned"—and the inconsistencies inherent in memory's operation. Cozzens in *Morning Noon and Night* thus produced a narrative style that supported the matter of the novel.

Morning Noon and Night offers a perspective different from Cozzens's other novels. Previously, his characters—from Ernest Cudlipp through Arthur Winner—had insisted that the rational individual work within the limitations of the system or society of which he was a part. Colonel Ross in *Guard of Honor* maintains that "a pattern should be found; a point should be imposed" on the disorder characteristic of life. Worthington, however, the epitome of management acumen, sees only the pervasiveness of good or bad luck, though he believes the struggle for achievement is valuable in itself. The novel ends: "A calling or twittering of skylarks or other birds has ceased; the immense silence settles, and the child must soon be taken away to bed. Yes; good night, good night. Good night, any surviving dear old Carian guests. Good night, ladies. Good night, all." Such a closing motif can be viewed as Cozzens's valedictory. As Bruccoli observes in *James Gould Cozzens: A Life Apart*: "Although he expected to continue writing for publication the novel is virtually an inventory of things Cozzens valued (the Puritan ethic, ability, intelligence, reason, the lessons of experience) and depreciated (self-indulgent emotion, youth, the liberal establishment, the literary life)."

BIOGRAPHICAL/CRITICAL SOURCES:

BOOKS

Bruccoli, Matthew J., editor, *Just Representations: A James Gould Cozzens Reader,* Southern Illinois University, 1978.

Bruccoli, Matthew J., editor, *James Gould Cozzens: New Acquist of True Experience,* Southern Illinois University Press, 1979.

Bruccoli, Matthew, J., *James Gould Cozzens: A Descriptive Bibliography,* University of Pittsburgh Press, 1981.

Bruccoli, Matthew J., *James Gould Cozzens: A Life Apart,* Harcourt, 1983.

Contemporary Literary Criticism, Gale (Detroit), Volume 1, 1973; Volume 4, 1975; Volume 11, 1979.

Cramer, Ann Bryant, *Patterns of Imitation and Innovation: O'Hara, Marquand, and Cozzens and the Victorian Novel of Manners* (microfilm), University of Chicago, 1988.

Dictionary of Literary Biography, Volume 9: *American Novelists, 1910-1945,* Gale, 1981.

Dictionary of Literary Biography Documentary Series, Volume 2, Gale, 1982.

Dictionary of Literary Biography Yearbook: 1984, Gale, 1985.

French, Warren, *The Forties: Fiction, Poetry, Drama,* Everett/ Edwards, 1969.

Hicks, Granville, *James Gould Cozzens,* University of Minnesota Press, 1966.

Kunitz, Stanley J., and Howard Haycraft, editors, *Twentieth Century Authors,* Wilson, 1942.

Michel, Pierre, *James Gould Cozzens: An Annotated Checklist,* Kent State University Press, 1971.
Millgate, Michael, *American Social Fiction: James to Cozzens,* Barnes & Noble, 1964.
Mooney, Harry John, Jr., *James Gould Cozzens: Novelist of Intellect,* University of Pittsburgh Press, 1963.
Noble, David W., *The Eternal Adam and the New World Garden: The Central Myth in the American Novel since 1830,* Braziller, 1968.
Prescott, Orville, *In My Opinion,* Bobbs-Merrill, 1952.
Stuckey, W. J., *The Pulitzer Prize Novels: A Critical Backward Look,* University of Oklahoma Press, 1966.
Walcutt, Charles Child, *Man's Changing Mask: Modes and Methods of Characterization in Fiction,* University of Minnesota Press, 1966.
Whitbread, Thomas, *Seven Contemporary Authors,* University of Texas Press, 1966.

PERIODICALS

America, October 5, 1957.
American Literature, May, 1955.
American Scholar, winter, 1957-58; spring, 1958.
Antioch Review, summer, 1958.
Arizona Quarterly, summer, 1960; winter, 1962.
Atlantic, March, 1920; August, 1964; September, 1968.
Best Sellers, April 1, 1969; September 1, 1969.
Book-of-the-Month Club News, December, 1932.
Book Week, August 2, 1964.
Book World, September 8, 1968.
Christian Science Monitor, September 19, 1968.
College English, January, 1950; January, 1956; April, 1958.
Commentary, January, 1958; September, 1968; September, 1983.
Commonweal, January, 1958; April 4, 1958.
Critical Quarterly, spring, 1962.
Critique: Studies in Modern Fiction, winter, 1958.
Harper's, February, 1949; September, 1957; October, 1968.
Hudson Review, winter, 1957-58.
Kenyon Review, November, 1966.
Life, August 30, 1968.
Los Angeles Times Book Review, August 26, 1984.
Nation, January 15, 1936; November 2, 1957; September 9, 1968.
National Review, November 1, 1968.
New Leader, October 3, 1983.
New Mexico Quarterly Review, winter, 1949; winter, 1951.
New Republic, January 20, 1957; September 16, 1957; June 9, 1958.
Newsweek, April 28, 1958; August 26, 1968.
New Yorker, October 9, 1948; August 24, 1957; February 8, 1958; November 2, 1968.
New York Evening Post, September 29, 1928.
New York Herald Tribune, January 8, 1933; October 10, 1948; August 25, 1957.
New York Times, April 27, 1924; November 15, 1925; July 22, 1942; August 25, 1957; August 9, 1959; August 20, 1968; July 30, 1978.
New York Times Book Review, June 23, 1940; August 25, 1957; August 9, 1959; August 2, 1964; August 25, 1968; July 3, 1983.
Observer Review, January 29, 1969.
Pacific Spectator, winter, 1951; summer, 1955.
Princeton University Library Chronicle, autumn, 1957.
Saturday Review, August 24, 1957; August 8, 1959.
Shenandoah, winter, 1959.
Spectator, December 26, 1958; May 21, 1965; February 21, 1969.

Texas Studies in Literature and Language, spring, 1959.
Time, September 2, 1957; August 8, 1968.
Tomorrow, May, 1947.
Twentieth-Century Literature, July, 1960.
Virginia Quarterly Review, winter, 1969.
Vogue, November 15, 1957.
Washington Post Book World, July 25, 1982.
Western Humanities Review, autumn, 1965.

*   *   *

CRAIG, A. A.
See ANDERSON, Poul (William)

*   *   *

CRANE, (Harold) Hart 1899-1932

PERSONAL: Born July 21, 1899, in Garrettsville, OH; committed suicide, April 27 (some sources say April 26), 1932, in the Gulf of Mexico; son of Clarance A. (a store owner and manufacturer) and Grace Edna (Hart) Crane. *Education:* Attended public schools in Cleveland, OH.

CAREER: Writer. Worked as mechanic bench hand and shipyard laborer in Ohio in mid-1910s; newspaper reporter for *Cleveland Plain Dealer* in Cleveland, OH, 1919; advertising manager for *Little Review* in New York City, 1919; shipping clerk for Rheinthal and Newman in New York City, 1919; advertising copywriter for various firms in Cleveland and New York City in 1920s; in sales in New York City in mid-1920s.

AWARDS, HONORS: Helen Waire Levinson Prize, 1930; Guggenheim fellow, 1931-32.

WRITINGS:

White Buildings (poetry), foreword by Allen Tate, Boni & Liveright, 1926.
The Bridge (poetry), Black Sun Press, 1930, Liveright, 1930.
The Collected Poems of Hart Crane, edited by Waldo Frank, Liveright, 1933.
Voyages: Six Poems From White Buildings, illustrations by Leonard Baskin, Museum of Modern Art, 1957.
The Complete Poems and Selected Letters and Prose of Hart Crane, edited by Brom Weber, Doubleday/Anchor, 1966.
Twenty-one Letters From Hart Crane to George Bryan, edited by Joseph Katz, Hugh C. Atkinson, and Richard A. Ploch, Ohio State University Press, 1968.
Robber Rocks: Letters and Memories of Hart Crane, 1923-1932, edited by Susan Jenkins Brown, Wesleyan University Press, 1969.
Ten Unpublished Poems, Gotham Book Mart, 1972.
(With others) *The Letters of Hart Crane and His Family,* edited by Thomas S. W. Lewis, Columbia University Press, 1974.
(With Yvor Winters) *Hart Crane and Yvor Winters: Their Literary Correspondence,* edited by Thomas Parkinson, University of California Press, 1978.
The Poems of Hart Crane, edited by Marc Simon, Liveright, 1986.
O My Land, My Friends: The Selected Letters of Hart Crane, edited by Langdon Hammer and Brom Weber, Four Walls Eight Windows (New York City), 1997.

Work represented in numerous anthologies, including *The New Pocket Anthology of American Verse* and *The Norton Anthology of Modern Poetry.*

Contributor to periodicals, including *Bruno's Weekly, Modern School, Modernist, Pagan,* and *S4N.*

SIDELIGHTS: Hart Crane is a legendary figure among American poets. In his personal life he showed little self-esteem, indulging in great and frequent bouts of alcohol abuse and homosexual promiscuity. In his art, however, he showed surprising optimism. Critics have contended that for Crane, misery and despair were redeemed through the apprehension of beauty, and in some of his greatest verses he articulated his own quest for redemption. He also believed strongly in the peculiarly naive American Romanticism extending back through Walt Whitman to Ralph Waldo Emerson, and in his most ambitious work, *The Bridge,* Crane sought nothing less than an expression of the American experience in its entirety. His failure in this attempt, as many critics noted, was rather to be expected. His effort, however, not only impressed many of those same critics but prompted a few of them to see Crane as a pivotal figure in American literature, and he has since come to be regarded as both the quintessential Romantic artist and the embodiment of those extreme characteristics—hope and despair, redemption and damnation—that seemed to preoccupy many writers in his time. As Allen Tate wrote in *Essays of Four Decades,* "Crane was one of those men whom every age seems to select as the spokesman of its spiritual life; they give the age away."

Crane was born in Garrettsville, Ohio, in 1899 of bourgeois parents—his father was a businessman who produced chocolates, and his mother was an emotionally unstable woman known for her beauty. Crane's relationship with his mother was stifling in its intensity. His parents fought regularly, and his mother succeeded in engaging his sympathies against his father. In addition, his mother used him as an often inappropriate confidant in complaining about the sex act and her real and imagined health problems. During his mother's bouts of hypochondria, Crane often spent an inordinate amount of time in her company, comforting and consoling her. This unusual intimacy proved overwhelmingly distressful to Crane, but even in adulthood he often remained incapable of freeing himself from his mother's considerable control.

As a result of real and imagined problems, Crane's mother suffered a nervous collapse in 1908, and while she recuperated, he moved to his grandmother's home in Cleveland. There he spent most of his formative years and showed his first enthusiasm for poetry. Crane's formal education, however, was continually undermined by family problems necessitating prolonged absences from school. Finally, in 1916, he left Cleveland without graduating and moved to New York City to attend Columbia University, which he hoped to enter upon passing an entrance examination.

Once in New York City, however, Crane abandoned any pretence of acquiring a college education and began vigorously pursuing a literary career. Instead of seeking regular employment, he relied on his parents to provide financial support. Their continual squabbling, however, sometimes resulted in unfortunate delays of his funds, and so Crane occasionally sold advertising for the publication *Little Review,* which promoted the work of modernists such as Joyce and T. S. Eliot.

Initially, Crane found New York City invigorating and even inspiring. Although he abused alcohol and consistently indulged his sexual proclivity for sailors, he still managed to work diligently on his poetry. But his parents divorced in 1917, and afterwards his mother arrived—with her mother—to stay in his one-bedroom apartment. Bedridden from emotional exhaustion, Crane's mother demanded his near constant attention. His problems mounted when his father, increasingly prosperous in the chocolate business, nonetheless threatened to withhold further funds until Crane found a job. To escape the pressures of family life, Crane attempted to enlist in the Army, only to be rejected as a minor. He then left New York City for Cleveland and found work in a munitions plant for the duration of World War I.

After the war, Crane stayed in Cleveland and found work as a reporter for the *Cleveland Plain Dealer.* He held that job only briefly, however, before returning to New York City to work once again for the *Little Review.* In mid-1919 his father used his influence in obtaining a position for his son as a shipping clerk. But Crane stayed at that job for only a few months before moving back to Ohio to work for his father's own company.

By 1922 Crane had already written many of the poems that would comprise his first collection, *White Buildings.* Among the most important of these verses is "Chaplinesque," which he produced after viewing the great comic Charlie Chaplin's film *The Kid.* In this poem Chaplin's chief character—a fun-loving, mischievous tramp—represents the poet, whose own pursuit may be perceived as trivial but nonetheless profound. For Crane, the film character's optimism and sensitivity bears similarities to poets' own outlooks toward adversity, and the tramp's apparent disregard for his own persecution is indication of his innocence: "We will sidestep, and to the final smirk / Dally the doom of that inevitable thumb / That slowly chafes its puckered index toward us, / Facing the dull squint with what innocence / And what surprise!"

In "Lachrymae Christi," another major poem from this period, Crane expresses a more profound sympathy for the poet, whose suffering inevitably leads to redemption. Here, through mysterious imagery and symbolism, Crane portrays nature, specifically as it is renewed in springtime, as a reflection of the poet's own rejuvenation.

Aside from "Chaplinesque" and "Lachrymae Christi," the most impressive poem Crane produced before 1924 was probably "For the Marriage of Faustus and Helen," a relatively expansive work reveling in the optimism that Crane believed prevalent throughout America at the time—the early 1920s. With this poem, he reinforces his own optimism by setting the marriage in contemporary times: Faustus rides a streetcar, and Helen appears at a jazz club. Here Faustus represents the poet seeking ideal beauty, and Helen embodies that beauty. In the poem's concluding section, Helen's beauty encompasses the triumph of the times too, and Crane calls for recognition of the age as one in which the poetic imagination surpasses the despair of recent events, notably World War I.

Unfortunately, the optimism expressed in such poems as "For the Marriage of Faustus and Helen" was hardly indicative of Crane's emotional state at the time. Soon after completing the aforementioned poem in the spring of 1923, Crane moved back to New York City and found work at another advertising agency. Not surprisingly, he once again found the job tedious and unrewarding. By autumn Crane feared that his anxiety would soon lead to a nervous breakdown and so fled the city for nearby Woodstock. There he reveled in the relative tranquility of the rural environment and enjoyed the company of a few close friends.

Once revived, Crane traveled back to New York City. Soon afterwards he fell in love with a sailor, Emil Opffer, and their relationship—one of intense sexual passion and occasional turbulence—inspired "Voyages," a poetic sequence in praise of love. In *Hart Crane,* Vincent Quinn described this poem as "a celebration of the transforming power of love" and added that the work's "metaphor is the sea, and its movement is from the lover's dedication to a human and therefore changeable lover to a beloved beyond time and change." With its dazzling poeticism and mysteriously inspiring perspective, this poem is often hailed as Crane's greatest achievement. R. W. B. Lewis, for instance, wrote in *The Poetry of Hart Crane* that the poem was Crane's "lyrical masterpiece."

By the time he finished "Voyages" in 1924, Crane had already commenced the first drafts of his ambitious poem *The Bridge,* which he intended, at least in part, as an uplifting alternative to T. S. Eliot's bleak masterwork, *The Waste Land.* With this long poem, which eventually comprised fifteen sections and sixty pages, Crane sought to provide a panorama of what he called "the American experience." Adopting the Brooklyn Bridge as the poem's sustaining symbol, Crane celebrates, in often hopelessly obscure imagery, various peoples and places—from explorer Christopher Columbus and the legendary Rip Van Winkle to the contemporary New England landscape and the East River tunnel. The bridge, in turn, serves as the structure uniting, and representing, all that is America. In addition, it functions as the embodiment of uniquely American optimism and serves as a source of inspiration and patriotic devotion.

In 1926, while Crane worked on *The Bridge,* his verse collection *White Buildings* was published. This work earned him substantial respect as an imposing stylist, one whose lyricism and imagery recalled the French Romantics Baudelaire and Rimbaud. But it prompted speculation that Crane was an imprecise and confused artist, one who sometimes settled for sound instead of sense. Edmund Wilson, for instance, wrote in *New Republic* that "though [Crane] can sometimes move us, the emotion is oddly vague." For Wilson, whose essay was later reprinted in *The Shores of Light,* Crane possessed "a style that is strikingly original—almost something like a great style, if there could be such a thing as a great style which was . . . not . . . applied to any subject at all."

His self-confidence was shaken by the disappointing reception accorded *The Bridge* by critics, many of whom expressed respect for his effort but dissatisfaction with his achievement. But even critics that deemed Crane's work a failure readily expressed respect for his creative undertaking. William Rose Benet, for instance, declared in the *Saturday Review of Literature* that Crane had "failed in creating what might have been a truly great poem." But Benet nonetheless deemed *The Bridge* "fascinating" and declared that it "reveals potencies in the author that may make his next work even more remarkable."

Crane, however, had entered a creative slump from which he would not recover. Perhaps sensing a decline in his literary skills, he applied for a Guggenheim fellowship with intentions of studying European culture and the American poetic sensibility. After obtaining the fellowship, though, Crane traveled to Mexico and continued his self-destructive behavior. At this time he also experienced a heterosexual romance—presumably his only one—with Peggy Baird, who was then married to prominent literary figure Malcolm Cowley. During this time Crane wrote only infrequently, producing largely inferior work that only confirmed his own fear that his talent had declined significantly. Finally, in 1932, his despair turned all-consuming, and on April 27, while traveling by ship with Baird, Crane killed himself by leaping into the Gulf of Mexico.

In the years since his death, Crane has earned recognition as an ambitious and accomplished—if not entirely successful—poet, one whose goals vastly exceeded his capabilities (and, probably, anyone else's) but whose talent nonetheless enabled him to explore the limits of self-expression both provocatively and profoundly. Allen Tate, writing in his *Essays of Four Decades,* assessed Crane's artistic achievement as an admirable, but unavoidable, failure. Tate noted that Crane, like the earlier Romantics, attempted the overwhelming imposition of his own will in his poetry, and in so doing reached the point at which his will, and thus his art, became self-reflexive, and thus self-destructive. "By attempting an extreme solution to the romantic problem," Tate contended, "Crane proved that it cannot be solved."

BIOGRAPHICAL/CRITICAL SOURCES:

BOOKS

Adamson, Robert, *Waving to Hart Crane,* Angus & Robertson, 1994.

Clark, David R., editor, *Critical Essays on Hart Crane,* G. K. Hall, 1982.

Combs, Robert, *Vision of the Voyage: Hart Crane and the Psychology of Romanticism,* Memphis State University Press, 1978.

Cowley, Malcolm, *Exile's Return: A Literary Odyssey of the 1920's,* Viking, 1951.

Dembo, L. S., *Hart Crane's Sanskrit Charge: A Study of The Bridge,* Cornell University Press, 1960.

Dictionary of Literary Biography, Gale (Detroit), Volume 4: *American Writers in Paris, 1920-1939,* 1980; Volume 48: *American Poets, 1880-1945, Second Series,* 1986.

Hanley, Alfred, *Hart Crane's Holy Vision: "White Buildings,"* Duquesne University Press, 1981.

Lewis, R. W. B., *The Poetry of Hart Crane: A Critical Study,* Princeton University Press, 1967.

Nilsen, Helge Normann, *Hart Crane's Divided Vision: An Analysis of The Bridge,* Universitetssforlaget (Oslo, Norway), 1980.

Norton-Smith, John, *A Reader's Guide to Hart Crane's White Buildings,* Edwin Mellen Press, 1993.

Paul, Sherman, *Hart's "Bridge,"* University of Illinois Press, 1972.

Quinn, Vincent G., *Hart Crane,* Twayne, 1963.

Schwartz, Joseph, *Hart Crane: A Reference Guide,* G. K. Hall, 1983.

Smith, Ernest J., *The Imaged Word: The Infrastructure of Hart Crane's White Buildings (American University Study Series XXIV American Literature, Vol. 19),* Peter Lang Publishing, 1990.

Sugg, Richard P., *Hart Crane's "The Bridge": A Description of Its Life,* University of Alabama Press, 1976.

Tate, Allen, *Essays of Four Decades,* Swallow Press, 1968.

Trachtenbert, Alan, editor, *Hart Crane: A Collection of Critical Essays,* Prentice-Hall, 1982.

Twentieth-Century Literary Criticism, Gale, Volume 2, 1979; Volume 5, 1981.

Yingling, Thomas E., *Hart Crane and the Homosexual Text: New Thresholds, New Anatomies,* University of Chicago Press, 1990.

PERIODICALS

American Literature, March, 1967; March, 1968.
Arizona Quarterly, spring, 1964.
Commonweal, October 26, 1962.
Critical Inquiry, autumn, 1975.
New Republic, March 16, 1927; May 11, 1927; August 31, 1953; June 22, 1987.
Papers on Language and Literature, summer, 1980.
PMLA, March, 1951; January, 1981.
Poetry, October, 1926.
Prairie Schooner, summer, 1974.
Saturday Review of Literature, July 5, 1930.
Sewanee Review, January-March, 1950; July-September, 1965.
Southern Review, July, 1975.
Twentieth-Century Literature, October, 1967.
University of Kansas Review, winter, 1949.
Wisconsin Studies in Contemporary Literature, spring-summer, 1962.
Yale Review, winter, 1987.

*   *   *

CREELEY, Robert (White) 1926-

PERSONAL: Born May 21, 1926, in Arlington, MA; son of Oscar Slade (a physician) and Genevieve (Jules) Creeley; married Ann MacKinnon, 1946 (divorced, c. 1955); married Bobbie Louise Hall, January 27, 1957 (divorced, 1976); married Penelope Highton, 1977; children: (first marriage) David, Thomas, Charlotte; (second marriage) Kirsten (stepdaughter), Leslie (stepdaughter; deceased), Sarah, Katherine; (third marriage) William, Hannah. *Education:* Attended Harvard University, 1943-44 and 1945-46; Black Mountain College, B.A., c. 1955; University of New Mexico, M.A., 1960.

ADDRESSES: Home—64 Amherst St., Buffalo, NY 14207. *Office*—Department of English, State University of New York at Buffalo, Buffalo, NY 14260.

CAREER: Poet, novelist, short story writer, essayist, and editor. Divers Press, Palma, Mallorca, Spain, founder and publisher, 1950-54; Black Mountain College, Black Mountain, NC, instructor in English, 1954-55; instructor at school for young boys, Albuquerque, NM, beginning 1956; University of New Mexico, Albuquerque, instructor in English, 1961-62, lecturer, 1963-66, visiting professor, 1968-69 and 1978-80; University of British Columbia, Vancouver, instructor in English, 1962-63; University of New Mexico, lecturer in English, 1963-65; State University of New York at Buffalo, visiting professor, 1965-66, professor of English, 1967–, David Gray Professor of Poetry and Letters, 1978-89, Capen Professor of Poetry and Humanities, 1990–, director of poetics program, 1991-92; San Francisco State College, lecturer in creative writing, 1970-71; State University of New York at Binghampton, visiting professor, 1985 and 1986. Bicentennial chair of American studies at University of Helsinki, Finland, 1988. Participated in numerous poetry readings and writers' conferences. *Wartime service:* American Field Service, India and Burma, 1945-46.

MEMBER: American Academy of Arts and Letters.

AWARDS, HONORS: Levinson Prize, 1960, for group of ten poems published in *Poetry* magazine; D. H. Lawrence fellowship (for summer writing), University of New Mexico, 1960; National Book Award nomination, 1962, for *For Love;* Leviton-Blumenthal Prize, 1964, for group of thirteen poems published in *Poetry;* Guggenheim fellowship in poetry, 1964-65 and 1971; Rockefeller Foundation grant, 1966; Union League Civic and Arts Foundation Prize, 1967; Shelley Award, 1981, and Frost Medal, 1987, both from Poetry Society of America; National Endowment for the Arts grant, 1982; Deutsche Auftauschdienst Programme (DADD) providing residency in Berlin, 1983 and 1987; Leone d'Oro Premio Speziale, Venice, 1985; Frost Medal, Poetry Society of America, 1987; Fulbright Award, 1988, 1995; Walt Whitman citation of merit, 1989; named New York State Poet, 1989-91; distinguished award from State University of New York at Buffalo, 1989; D.Litt, University of New Mexico, 1993; Horst Bienek Preis fur Lyrick, Munich, 1993; The America Award for Poetry, Washington, 1995.

WRITINGS:

POETRY

Le Fou, Golden Goose Press, 1952.
The Kind of Act Of, Divers Press (Palma, Mallorca, Spain), 1953.
The Immoral Proposition, Jonathan Williams, 1953.
A Snarling Garland of Xmas Verse (published anonymously), Divers Press, 1954.
All That Is Lovely in Men, Jonathan Williams, 1955.
(With others) *Ferrin and Others,* Gerhardt (Germany), 1955.
If You, Porpoise Bookshop, 1956.
The Whip, Migrant Books, 1957.
A Form of Women, Jargon Books, 1959.
For Love: Poems, 1950-1960, Scribner, 1962.
Distance, Terrence Williams, 1964.
Mister Blue, Insel-Verlag, 1964.
Two Poems, Oyez, 1964.
Hi There! Finial Press, 1965.
Words (eight poems), Perishable Press, 1965.
Poems, 1950-1965, Calder & Boyars, 1966.
About Women, Gemini, 1966.
For Joel, Perishable Press, 1966.
A Sight, Cape Coliard Press, 1967.
Words (eighty-four poems), Scribner, 1967.
Robert Creeley Reads (with recording), Turret Books, 1967.
The Finger, Black Sparrow Press, 1968, enlarged edition published as *The Finger Poems, 1966-1969,* Calder & Boyars, 1970.
5 Numbers (five poems), Poets Press, 1968, published as *Numbers* (text in English and German), translation by Klaus Reichert, Galerie Schmela (Dusseldorf, Germany), 1968.
The Charm: Early and Collected Poems, Perishable Press, 1968, expanded edition published as *The Charm,* Four Seasons Foundation, 1969.
Divisions and Other Early Poems, Perishable Press, 1968.
Pieces (fourteen poems), Black Sparrow Press, 1968.
The Boy (poem poster), Gallery Upstairs Press, 1968.
Mazatlan: Sea, Poets Press, 1969.
Pieces (seventy-two poems), Scribner, 1969.
Hero, Indianakatz, 1969.
A Wall, Bouwerie Editions, 1969.
For Betsy and Tom, Alternative Press, 1970.
For Benny and Sabrina, Samuel Charters, 1970.
America, Press of the Black Flag, 1970.
In London, Angel Hair Books, 1970.
Christmas: May 10, 1970, Lockwood Memorial Library, State University of New York at Buffalo, 1970.
St. Martin's, Black Sparrow Press, 1971.
1-2-3-4-5-6-7-8-9-0, drawings by Arthur Okamura, Shambala, 1971.

Sea, Cranium Press, 1971.
For the Graduation, Cranium Press, 1971.
Change, Hermes Free Press, 1972.
One Day after Another, Alternative Press, 1972.
For My Mother: Genevieve Jules Creeley, 8 April 1887-7 October 1972 (limited edition), Sceptre Press, 1973.
His Idea, Coach House Press, 1973.
The Class of '47, Bouwerie Editions, 1973.
Kitchen, Wine Press, 1973.
Sitting Here, University of Connecticut Library, 1974.
Thirty Things, Black Sparrow Press, 1974.
Backwards, Sceptre Press, 1975.
Hello, Hawk Press, 1976, expanded edition published as *Hello: A Journal, February 29-May 3, 1976*, New Directions, 1978.
Away, Black Sparrow Press, 1976.
Presences (also see below), Scribner, 1976.
Selected Poems, Scribner, 1976.
Myself, Sceptre Press, 1977.
Later, Toothpaste, 1978, expanded edition, New Directions, 1979.
Desultory Days, Sceptre Press, 1979.
Corn Close, Sceptre Press, 1980.
Mother as Voice, Am Here Books/Immediate Editions, 1981.
The Collected Poems of Robert Creeley, 1945-1975, University of California Press, 1982.
Echoes, Toothpaste, 1982.
Going On: Selected Poems, 1958-1980, Dutton, 1983.
Mirrors, New Directions, 1983.
A Calendar: Twelve Poems, Coffee House Press, 1984.
The Collected Prose of Robert Creeley, Scribner, 1984.
Memories, Pig Press, 1984.
Memory Gardens, New Directions, 1986.
The Company, Burning Deck, 1988.
Window, edited by Richard Blevins, State University of New York at Buffalo, 1988.
(With Libby Larsen) *A Creeley Collection: For Mixed Voices, Solo Tenor, Flute, Percussion, and Piano*, E. C. Schirmer, 1989.
(With Francesco Clemente) *64 Pastels*, Bruno Bischofberger, 1989.
Places, Shuffaloff Press, 1990.
Windows, New Directions Publishing Corporation, 1990.
Places, Shuffaloff Books, 1990.
Have a Heart, Limberlost Press, 1990.
Selected Poems, University of California Press, 1991.
A Poetry Anthology, Edmundson Art Foundation, 1992.
Echoes, New Directions Publishing Corporation, 1994.

Also author of *The Old Days* and *Gnomic Verses*, both 1991.
Life and Death, Grenfell Press, 1993.

EDITOR

Charles Olson, *Mayan Letters*, Divers Press, 1953.
(With Donald M. Allen, and contributor) *New American Story*, Grove, 1965.
(And author of introduction) Olson, *Selected Writings*, New Directions, 1966.
(With Allen, and contributor) *The New Writing in the U.S.A.*, Penguin, 1967.
Whitman: Selected Poems, Penguin, 1973.
(And contributor) *The Essential Burns*, Ecco Press, 1989.
Tim Prythero, Peters Corporation, 1990.
Olson, *Selected Poems*, University of California Press, 1993.

PROSE

The Gold Diggers (short stories), Divers Press, 1954, expanded edition published as *The Gold Diggers and Other Stories*, J. Calder, 1965.
The Island (novel), Scribner, 1963.
A Day Book (poems and prose), Scribner, 1972.
Mabel: A Story, and Other Prose (includes *A Day Book* and *Presences*), Calder & Boyars, 1976.
Collected Prose, Marion Boyars, 1984, corrected edition, University of California Press, 1988.

NONFICTION

An American Sense (essay), Sigma Press, 1965.
A Quick Graph: Collected Notes and Essays, edited by Donald M. Allen, Four Seasons Foundation, 1970.
Notebook, Bouwerie Editions, 1972.
A Sense of Measure (essays), Calder & Boyars, 1972.
Inside Out (lecture), Black Sparrow Press, 1973.
The Creative (lecture), Black Sparrow Press, 1973.
Was That a Real Poem and Other Essays, Four Seasons Foundation, 1979.
Collected Essays, University of California Press, 1989.
Autobiography, Hanuman Books, 1990.

OTHER

Listen (play; produced in London, 1972), Black Sparrow Press, 1972.
Contexts of Poetry: Interviews, 1961-1971, Four Seasons Foundation, 1973.
Charles Olson and Robert Creeley: The Complete Correspondence, nine volumes, edited by George F. Butterick, Black Sparrow Press, 1980-90.
Jane Hammond, Exit Art, 1989.
Irving Layton and Robert Creeley: The Complete Correspondence, edited by Ekbert Faas and Sabrina Reed, University of Toronto Press, 1990.
Tales Out of School: Selected Interviews, University of Michigan Press, 1993.

Work represented in anthologies, including *The New American Poetry: 1945-1960*, edited by Allen, Grove, 1960; *A Controversy of Poets*, edited by Paris Leary and Robert Kelly, Doubleday, 1965; *Norton Anthology of Modern Poetry*, edited by Richard Ellmann and Robert O'Clair, Norton, 1973; *The New Oxford Book of American Verse*, edited by Ellmann, Oxford University Press, 1976; and *Poets' Encyclopedia*, edited by John Cage, Unmuzzled Ox Press, 1980. Contributor to literary periodicals, including *Paris Review, Nation, Black Mountain Review, Origin, Yugen*, and *Big Table*. Founder and editor, *Black Mountain Review*, c. 1954-57.

SIDELIGHTS: Once known primarily for his association with the group called the "Black Mountain Poets," Robert Creeley has become an important and influential literary figure in his own right. His poetry is noted as much for its concision as its emotional power. Albert Mobilio, writing in the *Voice Literary Supplement*, observes: "Creeley has shaped his own audience. The much imitated, often diluted minimalism, the compression of emotion into verse in which scarcely a syllable is wasted, has decisively marked a generation of poets."

Creeley first began to develop his writing talents while attending Holderness School in Plymouth, New Hampshire, on a scholarship. His articles and stories appeared regularly in the school's literary magazine, and in his senior year he became its editor in chief. Creeley was admitted to Harvard in 1943, but his academic life was disrupted when he served as an ambulance driver for the American Field Service in 1944 and 1945.

Creeley returned to Harvard after the war and became associated with such writers as John Hawkes, Mitchell Goodman, and Kenneth Koch. He began corresponding with Cid Corman and Charles Olson, two poets who were to have a substantial influence on the direction of his future work. Excited especially by Olson's ideas about literature, Creeley began to develop a distinctive and unique poetic style.

Throughout the 1950s, Creeley was associated with the "Black Mountain Poets," a group of writers including Denise Levertov, Ed Dorn, Fielding Dawson, and others who had some connection with Black Mountain College, an experimental, communal college in North Carolina that was a haven for many innovative writers and artists of the period. Creeley edited the *Black Mountain Review* and developed a close and lasting relationship with Olson, who was the rector of the college. The two engaged in a lengthy, intensive correspondence about literary matters that has been collected and published as *Charles Olson and Robert Creeley: The Complete Correspondence.* Olson and Creeley together developed the concept of "projective verse," a kind of poetry that abandoned traditional forms in favor of a freely constructed verse that took shape as the process of composing it was underway. Olson called this process "composition by field," and his famous essay on the subject, "Projective Verse," was as important for the poets of the emerging generation as T. S. Eliot's "Tradition and the Individual Talent" was to the poets of the previous generation. Olson credited Creeley with formulating one of the basic principles of this new poetry: the idea that "form is never more than an extension of content."

Creeley was a leader in the generational shift that veered away from history and tradition as primary poetic sources and gave new prominence to the ongoing experiences of an individual's life. Because of this emphasis, the major events of his life loom large in his literary work. Creeley's marriage to Ann McKinnon ended in divorce in 1955. The breakup of that relationship is chronicled in fictional form in his only novel, *The Island,* which drew upon his experiences on the island of Mallorca, off the coast of Spain, where he lived with Ann and their three children in 1953 and 1954. After the divorce Creeley returned to Black Mountain College for a brief time before moving west to make a new life. He was in San Francisco during the flowering of the "San Francisco Poetry Renaissance" and became associated for a time with the writers of the Beat Generation: Allen Ginsberg, Jack Kerouac, Michael McClure, and others. His work appeared in the influential "beat" anthology *The New American Poetry: 1945-1960,* edited by Donald Allen.

In 1956 Creeley accepted a teaching position at a boys' school in Albuquerque, New Mexico, where he met his second wife, Bobbie Louise Hawkins. Though Creeley published poetry and fiction throughout the 1950s and 1960s and had even established his own imprint, the Divers Press, in 1952, his work did not receive important national recognition until Scribner published his first major collection, *For Love: Poems 1950-1960,* in 1962. This book collected work that he had been issuing in small editions and little magazines during the previous decade. When *For Love* debuted, Mibilio writes, "it was recognized at once as a pivotal contribution to the alternative poetics reshaping the American tradition. . . . The muted, delicately contrived lyrics . . . were personal and self-contained; while they drew their life from the everyday, their

techniques of dislocation sprang from the mind's naturally stumbled syntax."

The very first poem in *For Love,* "Hart Crane," with its unorthodox, Williams-like line breaks, its nearly hidden internal rhymes, and its subtle assonance and sibilance, announces the Creeley style—a style defined by an intense concentration on the sounds and rhythms of language as well as the placement of the words on the page. This intensity produces a kind of minimal poetry, which seeks to extract the bare linguistic bones from ongoing life experiences. In his introduction to *The New Writing in the U.S.A.,* Creeley cites approvingly Herman Melville's definition of "visible truth"—"the apprehension of the absolute condition of present things"—and supplements it with William Burroughs's famous statement from *Naked Lunch* about the writer's task: "There is only one thing a writer can write about: what is in front of his senses at the moment of writing. . . . I am a recording instrument . . . I do not presume to impose 'story' 'plot' 'continuity'."

In *Pieces, A Day Book, Thirty Things,* and *Hello: A Journal, February 29-May 3, 1976,* all published between 1968 and 1978, Creeley attempted to break down the concept of a "single poem" by offering his readers sequential, associated fragments of poems with indeterminate beginnings and endings. All of these works are energized by the same heightened attention to the present that characterizes Creeley's earlier work, but in *Hello,* a book written as journal entries over a five-week period while Creeley traveled in the Orient and South Pacific, he speculates on the possibility of using memory rather than the present as a poetic source. The poetry remains stubbornly rooted in the present despite the insistent intrusion of memories, both recent and long past.

Many of the poems in *Hello* refer to the last days of Creeley's relationship with his second wife, Bobbie. That marriage ended in divorce in 1976, the same year he met Penelope Highton, his third wife, while traveling in New Zealand. In this sense, the book may be described in much the same terms as Sherman Paul, in his book *The Lost America of Love,* describes *For Love,* "Poems of two marriages, the breakup of one, the beginning of another." For all of Creeley's experimentation, he has always been in some ways an exceedingly domestic poet; his mother, children, wives, and close friends are the subjects of his best work. Because Creeley's second marriage lasted nearly twenty years, the sense of a major chunk of his life drifting away from him is very strong in *Hello.* Creeley here conveys the traumatic emotional state that almost always accompanies the breakup of long-term relationships. En route to Perth, he writes: "Sitting here in limbo, there are / people walking through my head." In Singapore he remarks on his tenuous hold on things: "Getting fainter, in the world, / fearing something's fading. . . ." Although *Hello* is superficially a record of Creeley's travels, the poems are not really about the countries he has visited, but rather about the landscape of mind he has brought with him.

It is not until Creeley's next major collection, 1979's *Later,* that the poetry seems to shift into a new phase characterized by a greater emphasis on memory, a new sense of life's discrete phases, and an intense preoccupation with aging. In "Myself," the first poem in *Later,* he writes: "I want, if older, / still to know / why, human, men / and women are / so torn, so lost / why hopes / cannot / find a better world / than this." This futile but deeply human quest captures the spirit of Creeley's later work. It embodies a commonly shared realization: one becomes older but still knows very little about essential aspects of life, particularly the mysteries of human relationships. And as Alan Williamson observes in his *New York Times Book Review* assessment of *Later,* "In general, the stronger the note of elegiac bafflement and rage (the past utterly gone, the compensating wisdom not forthcoming), the better the writing."

The ten-part title poem, "Later," was written over a period of ten days in September of 1977. The poem presents a kaleidoscopic view of various times and events important to Creeley's life, beginning with an evocation of lost youth. Youth, in later life, can only become a palpable part of the present through the evocative power of memory. Another section of the poem comments on how certain empirical sensations are repositories of memory. A taste, a smell, a touch, can evoke a lost world. "Later" continues to present a flood of childhood memories: a lost childhood dog that Creeley fantasizes running into again after all these years; memories of his mother and friends and neighbors; sights and sounds of his early days all evoked and made a part of the poetry he is composing in an attic room in Buffalo, September, 1977.

In the work produced after the material included in his *Collected Poems, 1945-1975* there is an increasing tendency to derive poetry from what the English Romantic poet William Wordsworth called "emotion recollected in tranquility." It is a poetry that remembers and reflects and seems much less tied to the exigencies of the present than the earlier work.

Mirrors reveals how much a part of our characters memories become with each passing year, so that as we age we accumulate the mannerisms of our parents and reexperience past situations. This theme of the present incorporating the past is most literal in "Prospect," one of the most memorable poems in *Mirrors*. It is an atypical Creeley poem because it utilizes conventional elements of poetry—symbolism, metaphor, and imagery—in a surprisingly traditional manner. In fact, the poem has a remarkably unique resonance because Creeley's physical description of nature conveys both present and past psychological states. It takes no deep looking into the poem to see the landscape as emblematic of the state of Creeley's later life, invigorated by a new marriage and the birth of a new child, his son William. The poem concludes with the reflections awakened by a contemplation of the landscape, which is described as peaceful and beautiful, yet in the end "faintly painful." The final phrase surprises, coming at the end of an otherwise tranquil and nearly celebratory poem. It reminds the reader that although embarking on a new life can create the illusion that it is possible to exist in an Edenic landscape apart from time, in reality the past remains an integral part of the present. "Faintly painful," with its echoing first syllable rhyme, is exactly right to convey the contrary feelings of both relief and regret that the poem ultimately leaves the reader with—relief that the thoughtfulness the landscape provokes is not more painful, regret that there is any pain at all.

But pain has been one of the most constant elements in Creeley's work, and this later poetry continues to search for words to express it with sensitivity and exactness and without the sometimes maudlin excesses of "confessional" verse. Though these poems are more rooted in memory than the earlier work, Creeley remains committed to the poetic task of getting things exactly right. This has been the task of his writing throughout his career, and as readers look into the "mirror" of Creeley's work, they can see not only his aging, but their own.

BIOGRAPHICAL/CRITICAL SOURCES:

BOOKS

Allen, Donald M., editor, *Robert Creeley, Contexts of Poetry: Interviews, 1961-1971,* Four Seasons Foundation, 1973.

Allen and Warren Tallman, editors, *The Poetics of the New American Poetry,* Grove, 1973.

Butterick, George F., editor, *Charles Olson and Robert Creeley: The Complete Correspondence,* Black Sparrow Press, 1980.

Clark, Tom, *Robert Creeley and the Genius of the American Common Place: Together with the Poet's Own Autobiography,* New Directions, 1993.

Contemporary Authors Autobiography Series, Volume 10, Gale (Detroit), 1989.

Contemporary Literary Criticism, Gale, Volume 1, 1973; Volume 2, 1974; Volume 4, 1975; Volume 8, 1978; Volume 11, 1979; Volume 15, 1980; Volume 36, 1986.

Corman, Cid, editor, *The Gist of Origin,* Viking, 1975.

Edelberg, Cynthia Dubin, *Robert Creeley's Poetry: A Critical Introduction,* University of New Mexico Press, 1978.

Faas, Ekbert, and Sabrina Reed, editors, *Irving Layton & Robert Creeley: The Complete Correspondence, 1953-1978,* McGill-Queen's University Press, 1990.

Foster, Edward Halsey, *Understanding the Black Mountain Poets,* University of South Carolina Press (Columbia, SC), 1995.

Novik, Mary, *Robert Creeley: An Inventory, 1945-1970,* Kent State University Press, 1973.

Paul, Sherman, *The Lost America of Love: Rereading Robert Creeley, Edward Dorn, and Robert Duncan,* Louisiana State University Press, 1981.

Sheffler, Ronald Anthony, *The Development of Robert Creeley's Poetry,* University of Massachusetts, 1971.

Wilson, John, editor, *Robert Creeley's Life and Work: A Sense of Increment,* University of Michigan Press, 1987.

PERIODICALS

American Book Review, May/June, 1984.

American Poetry Review, November/December, 1976; May, 1997, p. 9.

Atlantic, November, 1962; February, 1968; October, 1977.

Books Abroad, autumn, 1967.

Boundary 2, spring, 1975; spring and fall (special two-volume issue on Creeley), 1978.

Christian Science Monitor, October 9, 1969.

Contemporary Literature, spring, 1972.

Critique, spring, 1964.

Encounter, February, 1969.

Gentleman's Quarterly, June, 1996, p. 74.

Harper's, August, 1967; September, 1983.

Hudson Review, summer, 1963; summer, 1967; spring, 1970; summer, 1977.

Iowa Review, spring, 1982.

Kenyon Review, spring, 1970.

Library Journal, September 1, 1979; April 15, 1994, p. 81; April 1, 1997, p. 94.

Listener, March 23, 1967.

London Magazine, June/July, 1973.

Los Angeles Times Book Review, April 17, 1983; October 30, 1983; March 4, 1984; June 24, 1984; June 23, 1991, p. 8.

Modern Poetry Studies, winter, 1977.

Nation, August 25, 1962.

National Observer, October 30, 1967.

National Review, November 19, 1960.

New Leader, October 27, 1969.

New Republic, October 11, 1969; December 18, 1976.
New Statesman, August 6, 1965; March 10, 1987.
New York Review of Books, January 20, 1966; August 1, 1968.
New York Times, June 27, 1967.
New York Times Book Review, November 4, 1962; September 22, 1963; November 19, 1967; October 27, 1968; January 7, 1973; May 1, 1977; March 9, 1980; August 7, 1983; June 24, 1984; September 23, 1984.
Observer (London), September 6, 1970.
Paris Review, fall, 1968.
Parnassus, fall/winter, 1984.
Partisan Review, summer, 1968.
Poetry, March, 1954; May, 1958; September, 1958; March, 1963; April, 1964; August, 1966; January, 1968; March, 1968; August, 1968; May, 1970; December, 1970; September, 1984.
Publishers Weekly, March 18, 1968; March 28, 1994.
Review of Contemporary Fiction, fall, 1995, p. 82.
Saturday Review, August 4, 1962; December 11, 1965; June 3, 1967.
Sewanee Review, winter, 1961.
Southwest Review, winter, 1964.
Time, July 12, 1971.
Times Literary Supplement, March 16, 1967; August 7, 1970; November 12, 1970; December 11, 1970; May 20, 1977; May 30, 1980; February 20, 1981; November 4, 1983; May 10, 1991, p. 22.
Village Voice, October 22, 1958; December 10, 1979; November 25, 1981.
Virginia Quarterly Review, summer, 1968; winter, 1972; spring, 1973.
Voice Literary Supplement, September, 1991, p. 14.
Washington Post Book World, August 11, 1991, p. 13.
Western Humanities Review, spring, 1970.
World Literature Today, autumn, 1984; summer, 1992; spring, 1995.
Yale Review, October, 1962; December, 1969; spring, 1970.

*   *   *

CREWS, Harry (Eugene) 1935-

PERSONAL: Born June 6, 1935, in Alma, GA; son of Rey (a farmer) and Myrtice (Haselden) Crews; married Sally Thornton Ellis, January 24, 1960 (divorced); children: Patrick Scott (deceased), Byron Jason. *Education:* University of Florida, B.A., 1960, M.S.Ed., 1962.

CAREER: Writer. Broward Junior College, Ft. Lauderdale, FL, teacher of English, 1962-68; University of Florida, Gainesville, associate professor, 1968-74, professor of English, 1974-88. *Military service:* U.S. Marine Corps, 1953-56; became sergeant.

AWARDS, HONORS: Award from American Academy of Arts and Sciences, 1972.

WRITINGS:

NOVELS

The Gospel Singer, Morrow (New York City), 1968.
Naked in Garden Hills, Morrow, 1969.
This Thing Don't Lead to Heaven, Morrow, 1970.
Karate Is a Thing of the Spirit, Morrow, 1971.
Car, Morrow, 1972.
The Hawk Is Dying, Knopf (New York City), 1973.

The Gypsy's Curse, Knopf, 1974.
A Feast of Snakes, Atheneum (New York City), 1976.
All We Need of Hell, Harper (New York City), 1987.
The Knockout Artist, Harper, 1988.
Body, Poseidon Press (New York City), 1990.
Scar Lover, Poseidon Press, 1992.
The Mulching of America, Simon & Schuster (New York City), 1995.
Celebration, Simon & Schuster, 1998.

SHORT STORIES

The Enthusiast, Palaemon Press, 1981.
Two, Lord John (Northridge, CA), 1984.

Contributor of stories to *Florida Quarterly* and *Craft and Vision.*

OTHER

A Childhood: The Biography of a Place (autobiography), Harper, 1978.
Blood and Grits (nonfiction), Harper, 1979.
Florida Frenzy (essays and stories), University Presses of Florida (Gainesville), 1982.
Blood Issue (play), produced in Louisville, KY, 1989.
Madonna at Ringside, Lord John, 1991.
Classic Crews: A Harry Crews Reader, Poseidon Press, 1993.

Author of column "Grits" for *Esquire.* Contributor to *Sewanee Review, Georgia Review,* and *Playboy.*

SIDELIGHTS: Reading novelist Harry Crews, Allen Shepherd maintains in the *Dictionary of Literary Biography,* "is not something one wants to do too much of at a single sitting; the intensity of his vision is unsettling." This vision is both comic and tragic, nostalgic and grotesque, and is focused on the American South, where Crews was raised and still lives. His characters, often physically deformed or strangely obsessed, are grotesques in the southern gothic tradition, and his stories are violent and extreme. Michael Mewshaw, writing in the *Nation,* explains that Crews "has taken a cast of the misfit and malformed—freaks, side-show performers, psychopaths, cripples, midgets and catatonics—and yoked it to plots which are even more improbable than his characters." Frank W. Shelton of the *Southern Literary Journal* defines the world of Crews's fiction as "mysterious, violent and dangerous" and calls his vision "a lonely and extremely sad one." But Mewshaw does not find Crews's vision essentially sad. He finds that Crews is "beset by existential nausea but, like any normal American, is not blind to the humor of it all. Bleak, mordant, appalling, Harry Crews can also be hilarious." Vivian Mercier of the *World* echoes this idea, remarking that "reading Crews is a bit like undergoing major surgery with laughing gas."

Crews first began to create stories as a boy in rural Georgia during the Depression. Living in an area where, he claims in *A Childhood: The Biography of a Place,* "there wasn't enough cash money . . . to close up a dead man's eyes," Crews and his friends found a wonderland in the Sears, Roebuck mail order catalog. The boys called the catalog their dream book because the models seemed unnaturally perfect to them, and the merchandise was far beyond their reach. While poring over the catalog pictures, Crews entertained his friends by spinning stories about the models and products. "I had decided that all the people in the catalog were related," he explains in *A Childhood,* "not necessarily blood kin but knew one another. . . . And it was out of this knowledge that I first began to make up stories."

After serving four years in the U.S. Marines, which he joined at the age of seventeen, Crews went to the University of Florida, where he was inspired by writer in residence Andrew Lyle to begin writing seriously.

Crews writes of his native Georgia in *The Gospel Singer,* his first published novel. A popular traveling evangelist, the Gospel Singer appears in his hometown of Enigma during a concert tour. His local sweetheart has recently been murdered and, it is suspected, raped by a black man. The Singer is trailed into town by the Freak Fair, a sideshow of human oddities—including the show's owner, a man with an oversized foot—working the crowds attracted by the Singer's revival meetings. When the accused murderer is threatened with lynching, the Gospel Singer tries to save him by revealing that the murdered woman was not in fact a violated virgin but "the biggest whore who ever walked in Enigma," as Shepherd writes. In the resulting chaos the townspeople lynch both men.

Response to *The Gospel Singer* was generally favorable. Though Walter Sullivan of *Sewanee Review* finds the book has "all the hallmarks of a first novel: it is energetic but uneven, competent but clumsy, not finally satisfactory but memorable nonetheless," he believes that "Crews has a good eye, an excellent ear for voices, and a fine dramatic sense." Martin Levin of the *New York Times Book Review* thinks *The Gospel Singer* "has a nice wild flavor and a dash of Grand Guignol strong enough to meet the severe standards of Southern decadence." And Guy Davenport of *National Review* calls the novel "a frenetic sideshow of Georgia poor white trash and their *Hochkultur.*"

Crews followed *The Gospel Singer* with *Naked in Garden Hills,* a book Jean Stafford of the *New York Times Book Review* believes "lives up to and beyond the shining promise of . . . 'The Gospel Singer.' It is southern Gothic at its best, a Hieronymus Bosch landscape in Dixie inhabited by monstrous, darling pets." The novel revolves around the almost helpless Mayhugh Aaron, known as the Fat Man because of his six-hundred-pound frame, and his valet John Henry Williams, a tiny black man who takes care of him. Fat Man owns most of Garden Hills, a town where the local phosphate mine is the only source of employment. When the mine is exhausted and closed, the town faces financial collapse. To avoid ruin, Dolly Ferguson opens a nightclub with go-go dancers and a sideshow to attract the tourist trade. She wants Fat Man as her star sideshow exhibit, but he refuses. As his employees, including Williams the valet, are one by one hired away by Dolly, and as his financial situation deteriorates, the Fat Man is reduced to a humiliated and helpless figure. He is finally forced to join the sideshow. "Bleeding, beaten by the mob of tourists, naked, and drooling, he crawls to his waiting cage and is lifted high in the light," Shepherd recounts.

Writing in the *New York Times Book Review,* Jonathan Yardley finds *Naked in Garden Hills* "a convincing grotesque of a rotting American landscape and its decadent inhabitants." Shelton believes the novel "treats religion in an almost allegorical way." He cites the novel's title as a reference to the Garden of Eden, sees Jack O'Boylan, the out-of-state mine owner, as a God figure, and pictures Dolly Ferguson as a kind of savior meant to restore the town. But the novel's ending, in which "everyone is consumed by Dolly's voracious appetite for success," shows that "man's desire to find meaning in his life leads to degradation, exploitation and the denial of love," Shelton writes.

A religious dimension can be found in *Karate Is a Thing of the Spirit.* In this novel Crews writes of an outlaw karate class that meets on a Florida beach and is barred from tournament competition because of its deadly reputation. John Kaimon wanders into this circle and becomes a member, undergoing the rigorous training under the hot sun. The star member of the class, brown belt Gaye Nell Odell, becomes pregnant, possibly by Kaimon, and at novel's end the couple drive out of town together. Shelton finds both Kaimon and Odell searching for something— something they both find in the discipline of karate. The training, Shelton argues, "is an almost religious ritual through which people attempt to link and fulfill body and spirit." John Deck of the *New York Times Book Review* observes that, after a slow start, "the novel takes off, in the manner of a fire storm, rushing at amazing speed, eating up the oxygen, scorching everything it touches."

In *Car,* Crews examines another physical discipline, this one far less common than karate. Herman Mack, whose family is in the automobile junkyard business, decides it is his destiny to eat an automobile, four ounces at a time each day. His daily ingestion of the cut-up auto is broadcast on national television as a sports event. At first pleased with his instant notoriety, Herman falls in love with a prostitute and ends by abandoning his spectacle before it is finished. Yardley calls the ending "mere sentimentality" and a "flabby resolution," but also believes the novel "a marvelous idea" and "exceedingly funny, indeed painfully so." The reviewer for the *Times Literary Supplement* finds the novel "a satire on two alleged vices of the American people: an extravagant fondness for motor-cars, and a taste for ghoulish spectacle." Christopher Lehmann-Haupt of the *New York Times* also sees larger implications in the story, concluding that *Car* "may very well be the best metaphor yet made up about America's passionate love affair with the automobile."

Another obsession dominates Crews's novel *The Hawk Is Dying.* George Gattling becomes obsessed with training a wild hawk, an obsession that estranges him from his family and friends. But his efforts eventually reach fruition when "the hawk has finally been 'manned,' and flies free to kill and return again to Gattling's hand," resulting in "one moment of absolute value—and hence absolute beauty," as the critic for the *Times Literary Supplement* explains. The story is told in "comic-horrific scenes," the critic remarks. Mercier also finds this odd mix in the novel, writing that "beauty and pity and terror coexist with satire and grotesque humor." Similarly, Phoebe Adams of *Atlantic* calls *The Hawk Is Dying* "a bizarre mixture of tragedy and farce." But she goes on to say that, though "the events of this novel are hardly realistic, . . . the book becomes immensely convincing because the underlying pattern of desperation over wasted time and neglected abilities is real and recognizable."

Crews examines a town's obsession with rattlesnakes in *A Feast of Snakes.* He fictionalizes a unique yearly custom in Mystic, Georgia, where the townspeople hold a Rattlesnake Roundup at which they crown a rattlesnake queen, hold a snake fight, and even dine on rattlesnake. The novel follows local resident Joe Lon Mackey, who is unhappily married, illiterate, and bitter about his life. Crews shows the pressures which drive Mackey to go on a murderous rampage at the snake roundup.

The gruesome events leading up to this final outburst of violence are seen by many critics to be expertly handled by Crews. "Crews," Paul D. Zimmerman writes in *Newsweek,* "has an ugly knack for making the most sordid sequences amusing, for evoking an absolutely venomous atmosphere, unredeemed by charity or hope. Few writers could pull off the sort of finale that has mad-eyed red-necks rushing in sudden bursts across a snake-scattered, bonfire-bright field, their loins enflamed by the local beauty contestants, their blood racing with whisky, their hearts ready for violence. Crews does." The critic for the *New Yorker* judges Crews to be "a writer of extraordinary power. Joe Lon is a monster, but we are forced to accept him as human, and even as sympathetic. Mr. Crews' story makes us gag, but he holds us, in awe and admiration, to the sickening end."

Crews's nonfiction book *A Childhood* gives some insight into the sources of his fiction. In this book Crews recounts the first six years of his life. It was a period, he claims, when "what has been most significant in my life had all taken place." Crews's father died when he was two years old. His mother remarried his uncle, a man she later left because of his violent rages. Crews had a bout with polio, which paralyzed his legs for a time and forced him to hobble on the floor. A fall into a tub of scalding water, used for removing the skin off slaughtered hogs, removed the first layer of skin on most of Crews's body. "The skin on the top of the wrist and the back of my hand, along with the fingernails," he remembers in the book, "all just turned loose and slid on down to the ground."

Despite the hardships of his childhood, Crews presents the people of his home county in a warm, honest, and unapologetic manner. As Crews recounts, "It was a world in which survival depended on raw courage, a courage born out of desperation and sustained by a lack of alternatives." Robert Sherrill of the *New York Times Book Review* admits: "It's easy to despise poor folks. *A Childhood* makes it more difficult. It raises almost to a level of heroism these people who seem of a different century."

Critical reaction to *A Childhood* was generally positive, with several critics citing Crews's restraint in recounting his life. Mewshaw, for example, finds that throughout the book Crews "maintains a precarious balance between sentiment and sensation, memory and madness, and manages to convince the reader of two mutually exclusive imperatives which have shaped his life—the desire to escape Bacon County and the constant ineluctable need to go back, if only in memory." The *New Yorker* critic writes that Crews remembers his childhood with "a sense of grateful escape and shattering loss which have the confusing certainty of truth."

The author resumed writing longer works of fiction in late 1980s, producing the novels *All We Need of Hell* and *The Knockout Artist*. Like his books from previous decades, the works have been acclaimed for their gritty Southern flavor and offbeat characters. *All We Need of Hell* concerns Duffy Deeter, a driven attorney who constantly seeks to prove his manliness. When his wife throws him out of the house, Duffy commences a spree of exercise and drinking, a session that ends when a former enemy teaches Duffy the virtues of love, friendship, and forgiveness.

"If *All We Need of Hell* ran according to Harry Crews's earlier fictional form," remarks Christopher Lehmann-Haupt in the *New York Times,* "Duffy's misadventures would lead him to some bizarre or even ghoulish fate." Noting, though, that "something new has been added" to Crews's fiction, the reviewer laments that "there is something decidedly forced and even sentimental about [the story's positive] turn of events. . . . We come away from the novel regarding it as a distinctly lesser effort." Beaufort Cranford writing in the *Detroit News* was similarly disappointed, commenting that "we readers of Crews suddenly find ourselves on alarmingly cheerful ground. . . . [The ending to] *All We Need of Hell* is a . . . shock, much like a sudden infusion of sugar." Despite complaints that Crews has softened his fiction, Lehmann-

Haupt concludes that "we can't help forgiving him for it. There's still such a vividness to his characters. There's still such ease to his prose. . . . [And] he still has the power to make us smile and even laugh out loud."

Crews followed *All We Need of Hell* with *The Knockout Artist* in 1988. The story focuses on Eugene Biggs, a promising young boxer whose career ends after he develops a glass jaw and is rendered incapable of further fighting. To survive, Eugene earns money by staging shows wherein he knocks himself out. Humiliated by his own exploits and burdened by an assortment of unusual friends, Eugene finally decides to break the destructive pattern of his life and becomes a boxing trainer.

Crews's next novel, *Body,* centers around a backwoods Georgia girl, Dorothy Turnipseed, who takes to working out in a gym and eventually goes on to compete, under the name Shereel Dupont, in the Ms. Cosmos competition. "In the world of the Ms. Cosmos competition, sex is for losing weight, food is for fuel, other people for rivalry, love for exploitation, family for leaving," novelist Fay Weldon notes in her *New York Times Book Review* assessment of *Body*. Nevertheless, Dorothy/Shereel's family accompanies her all the way to the contest, where they are conspicuous among the bodybuilders because of their immense bulk. Merle Rubin is unforgiving in her criticism of the book in the *Wall Street Journal*, labeling it a "violent comic-strip of a novel" that "mixes clenched, muscle-bound humor with lashings of fairly standard-style pornography."

Weldon, however, is extremely enthusiastic about *Body,* describing it as "electric" and as "a hard, fast and brilliant book." She has special praise for Crews's ability to create convincing women: "Not for a moment, such is this male writer's skill, the throttled-back energy of his writing, do I doubt Mr. Crews's right to be as intimate as he is with his female characters. . . . Shereel's struggle between love and honor provides the book's tender, perfect fleshing out; the will-she-win, won't-she-win tension, mounting page by page, gives muscle, nerve and fervor to the whole." She adds, however, that "it's Harry Crews's ability to describe physical existence, bodily sensation, that most impresses."

Scar Lover, Crews's next novel, featured a typical cast of outcasts and misfits, including a pair of scarred Rastafarian lovers and a woman who sings lullabies to her husband's skull. The protagonist is Peter Butcher, a man tormented by guilt because of an accident in which he left his younger brother permanently brain-damaged. Filled with self-loathing and reviled by the rest of his family, Peter eventually drifts into true love, fighting it all the way. "It may surprise the followers of Harry Crews to hear that his twelfth novel is a love story that is both life-affirming and tender," advises Robert Phillips in the *Hudson Review*. It is "a comic morality play which is less fierce and more tender than any of his previous works." In the reviewer's estimation, however, the positive messages in *Scar Lover* in no way blunt the power of the author's work. *Chicago Tribune* writer Gary Dretzka concurs that *Scar Lover* "is successful in promoting the healing powers of love and forgiveness," and he notes that "Crews' familiar tenderness toward his outcast characters is here in spades, driven by typically muscular writing and energetic pacing."

A darker tone permeated Crews's next effort, *The Mulching of America,* a book described by a *Washington Post Book World* reviewer as "a satire of corporate America and the credo of success at any cost." The reviewer goes on to say that "Crews's wicked satire sends up corporate culture's celebration of conformity and boundless personal sacrifice." The central characters are Hickum Looney, a door-to-door salesman for a soap company; Gaye Nell Odell, a homeless prostitute (seen previously in *Karate Is a Thing of the Spirit*); and the Boss—the harelipped, hard-driving chief of the Soap for Life Company. Valerie Sayers, a contributor to the *New York Times Book Review,* finds the characters predictable enough "for reader discomfort to set in." Still, she adds that especially in the case of Hickum and Gaye Nell, "that their love story is sweetly compelling is the measure of Mr. Crews's ability to have his cartoon characters remind us, vaguely and laughably, of our own most compelling fears and humiliations." She further credits the author with creating a successful portrayal of "Americans terrified of taking a step or making a moral choice," and concludes that "Harry Crews is a storyteller who bears down on American enterprise with fierce eyes and a cackle. By the end of the story, he's not laughing and we are all ready to look away."

Some observers judge Crews's stories to be excessive. "His harshest critics claim that Crews always pushes things too far—to the point where his characters turn into caricatures and his plots become cartoons," Mewshaw explains. One such critic is Sarah Blackburn of the *New York Times Book Review,* who describes *The Hawk Is Dying* as "a festival of mangled animals, tortured sexuality and innocence betrayed." James Atlas in *Time* calls Crews "a Southern gothic novelist who often makes William Faulkner look pastoral by comparison." Crews's novel *A Feast of Snakes* was even banned in South Africa.

Crews's 1997 novel *Celebration* is set in a Florida retirement community where various outcasts have come to die in obscurity. Into this depressing world strides a voluptuous trailer park honey named Too Much, who seduces Stump, the deformed leader of the village. The romance awakens the long-dormant passions of the community's other members. Crews intended the novel to be a broad comic allegory about age and mortality, an approach that delighted some critics and alienated others. Christopher Lemann-Haupt of the *New York Times* stated that "The plot's often obscure grotesqueness gradually wears the reader down," but a *Publishers Weekly* critic felt that "No one escapes Crews' critical pen as his caricatures comically portray the elderly coming to grips with the brutal and messy reality of mortality."

Admirers of Crews cite his ability to transform unusual or extreme subjects into credible, moving stories. Doris Grumbach, writing in *Saturday Review,* admits that Crews's novels possess a "bizarre, mad, violent, and tragic quality," but believes that Crews "has a sympathy for maimed and deformed characters, a love of strange situations, and the talent to make it all, somehow, entirely believable." Shepherd, speaking of *Car, The Hawk Is Dying,* and *A Feast of Snakes* in an article for *Critique: Studies in Modern Fiction,* argues that Crews displays "in these strangely powerful, outlandish, excessive, grotesquely alive novels a gift at once formidable and frightening."

BIOGRAPHICAL/CRITICAL SOURCES:

BOOKS

Contemporary Literary Criticism, Gale (Detroit), Volume 6, 1976; Volume 23, 1983; Volume 49, 1988.
Dictionary of Literary Biography, Gale, Volume 6: *American Novelists since World War II, Second Series,* 1980; Volume 143: *American Novelists Since World War II, Third Series,* 1994.

Jeffrey, David K., editor, *A Grit's Triumph: Essays on the Works of Harry Crews,* Associated Faculty Press (Port Washington, NY), 1983.

PERIODICALS

Arkansas Review, spring, 1995, pp. 1, 82-94.
Atlanta Journal-Constitution, January 18, 1987, p. J8; June 26, 1988, p. J8; April 9, 1989, pp. N1, N2; September 2, 1990, p. N14; January 26, 1992, p. N8; March 8, 1992, p. N1; November 28, 1993, p. K8.
Atlantic, April, 1973.
Booklist, February 15, 1992, p. 1086; October 1, 1993, p. 244; January 1, 1998.
Boston Globe, January 13, 1987, p. 59; May 3, 1988, p. 73; October 1, 1990, p. 32; February 21, 1992, p. 40; November 23, 1995, p. A26.
Chicago Tribune, February 1, 1987, section 14, p. 3; April 10, 1988, section 14, p. 6; August 27, 1990, section 5, p. 3; February 23, 1992, p. 6.
Chicago Tribune Book World, October 29, 1978; March 11, 1979; July 18, 1982; July 31, 1983; February 23, 1992, section 14, p. 6.
Critique: Studies in Modern Fiction, September, 1978; fall, 1986, pp. 45-53.
Detroit News, February 1, 1987, p. H2.
Entertainment Weekly, February 28, 1992, p. 50; March 27, 1992, p. 69; November 17, 1995, p. 75.
Georgia Review, fall, 1987, pp. 627-31; fall, 1994, pp. 3, 537-53.
Harper's, August, 1986, p. 35.
Hudson Review, autumn, 1993, pp. 492-93.
Journal of American Culture, fall, 1988, pp. 2, 47-54.
Kirkus Reviews, December 1, 1997.
Library Journal, August, 1990, p. 139; February 1, 1992, p. 121; November 15, 1995, p. 98; December, 1997.
Los Angeles Times, May 3, 1987, p. B8; May 22, 1988, p. B6; January 31, 1992, p. E2.
Los Angeles Times Book Review, May 3, 1987; May 22, 1988, p. 6; September 23, 1990, p. 3; October 21, 1990, p. 3; January 14, 1996, p. 2.
Maclean's, March 26, 1979.
Mississippi Quarterly: The Journal of Southern Culture, winter, 1987-88, pp. 1, 69-88.
Nation, February 3, 1979.
National Review, April 21, 1970.
New Boston Review, February-March, 1979.
New Republic, March 31, 1973; May 8, 1989, p. 28.
Newsweek, August 2, 1976.
New Yorker, July 15, 1974; July 26, 1976; November 6, 1978.
New York Times, March 2, 1972; March 21, 1973; April 30, 1974; July 12, 1976; December 11, 1978; February 6, 1979; January 12, 1987, p. C19; February 1, 1987, section 7, p. 9; February 19, 1987; April 18, 1988, p. C21; May 1, 1988, section 7, p. 21; April 5, 1989, p. C19; November 20, 1995, p. C16; January 8, 1998.
New York Times Book Review, February 18, 1968; April 13, 1969; April 26, 1970; April 25, 1971; February 27, 1972; March 25, 1973; March 10, 1974; June 2, 1974; June 23, 1974; September 12, 1976; December 24, 1978; March 25, 1979; February 1, 1987, pp. 9, 11; May 1, 1988, p. 21; September 9, 1990, p. 14; March 15, 1992, p. 13; November 5, 1995, p. 18.
Observer (London), October 30, 1994, p. 4.
People, June 8, 1987, p. 75; October 1, 1990, p. 41.
Playboy, August, 1990, p. 64.

Prairie Schooner, spring, 1974.
Publishers Weekly, April 15, 1988; June 29, 1990, p. 86; December 13, 1991, p. 44; September 11, 1995; November 17, 1997.
Saturday Review, November 11, 1978.
Sewanee Review, winter, 1969.
Shenandoah, summer, 1974.
Southern Literary Journal, spring, 1980; spring, 1984, pp. 132-35; spring, 1992, pp. 2, 3-10.
Spectator, January 22, 1977.
Studies in the Literary Imagination, fall, 1994, pp. 2, 75-86.
Texas Review, spring-summer, 1988, pp. 1-2, 96-109.
Time, September 13, 1976; October 23, 1978; March 5, 1979; April 17, 1989, p. 70; March 2, 1992, p. 66.
Times Literary Supplement, February 2, 1973; January 11, 1974; January 24, 1975; January 21, 1977; December 7, 1979; December 30, 1994, p. 19.
Variety, April 19, 1989, p. 215.
Village Voice, October 30, 1978.
Virginia Quarterly Review, autumn, 1980, pp. 612-26.
Wall Street Journal, August 31, 1990, p. A9.
Washington Post, March 29, 1979.
Washington Post Book World, April 15, 1973; July 24, 1983; May 1, 1988; August 19, 1990, p. 3; February 16, 1992, p. 4; October 17, 1993, p. 3; February 4, 1996, p. 8.
World, April 24, 1973.
Writers Digest, June, 1982, p. 30.

*   *   *

CRICHTON, (John) Michael 1942-
(Michael Douglas, Jeffrey Hudson, John Lange)

PERSONAL: Surname is pronounced "*cry*-ton"; born October 23, 1942, in Chicago, IL; son of John Henderson (a corporate president) and Zula (Miller) Crichton; married Joan Radam, January 1, 1965 (divorced, 1970); married Kathleen St. Johns, 1978 (divorced, 1980); married Suzanne Childs (marriage ended); married Anne-Marie Martin, 1987; children: (fourth marriage) Taylor (a daughter). *Education:* Harvard University, A.B. (summa cum laude), 1964, M.D., 1969.

ADDRESSES: Office—Jenkins Fin Services, 433 N. Camden Dr., Suite 500, Beverly Hills, CA 90210-4443; Alfred A. Knopf, 201, E. 50th St., New York, NY 10022.

CAREER: Salk Institute for Biological Studies, La Jolla, CA, post-doctoral fellow, 1969-70; full-time writer of books and films; director of films and teleplays, including *Pursuit* (based on his novel *Binary*), American Broadcasting Companies, Inc. (ABC-TV), 1972, *Westworld,* Metro-Goldwyn-Mayer (MGM), 1973, *Coma,* United Artists (UA), 1978, *The Great Train Robbery,* UA, 1979, *Looker,* Warner Bros., 1981, and *Runaway,* Tri-Star Pictures, 1984. Creator of National Broadcasting Company (NBC-TV) series *ER.*

MEMBER: Mystery Writers Guild of America (West), Authors Guild, Authors League of America, Academy of Motion Picture Arts and Sciences, Directors Guild of America, PEN, Aesculaepian Society, Phi Beta Kappa.

AWARDS, HONORS: Edgar Award, Mystery Writers of America, 1968, for *A Case of Need,* and 1979, for *The Great Train Robbery;* writer of the year award, Association of American Medical Writers, 1970, for *Five Patients: The Hospital Explained.*

WRITINGS:

NOVELS

The Andromeda Strain, Knopf (New York City), 1969.
(With brother Douglas Crichton, under joint pseudonym Michael Douglas) *Dealing: Or, The Berkeley-to-Boston Forty-Brick Lost-Bag Blues,* Knopf, 1971.
The Terminal Man, Knopf, 1972.
Westworld (also see below), Bantam (New York City), 1974.
The Great Train Robbery (also see below), Knopf, 1975.
Eaters of the Dead: The Manuscript of Ibn Fadlan, Relating His Experiences with the Northmen in A.D. 922, Knopf, 1976.
Congo, Knopf, 1980.
Sphere, Knopf, 1987.
Jurassic Park, Knopf, 1990.
Rising Sun, Knopf, 1992.
Disclosure, Knopf, 1994.
The Lost World, Knopf, 1995.
Airframe, Knopf, 1996.
The Lost World, Jurassic Park: The Movie Storybook, based on the motion picture by David Koepp and the novel *The Lost World* by Michael Crichton, Grosset and Dunlap (New York City), 1997.

NONFICTION

Five Patients: The Hospital Explained, Knopf, 1970.
Jasper Johns, Abrams (New York City), 1977; revised and expanded, 1994.
Electronic Life: How to Think about Computers, Knopf, 1983.
Travels (autobiography), Knopf, 1988.

SCREENPLAYS

Extreme Close-up, National General, 1973.
Westworld (based on novel of same title), Metro-Goldwyn-Mayer, 1973.
Coma (based on novel of same title by Robin Cook), United Artists, 1977.
The Great Train Robbery (based on novel of same title), United Artists, 1978.
Looker, Warner Bros., 1981.
Runaway, Tri-Star Pictures, 1984.
Twister, Warner Bros., 1996, screenplay published by Ballantine (New York City), 1996.

UNDER PSEUDONYM JOHN LANGE

Odds On, New American Library (New York City), 1966.
Scratch One, New American Library, 1967.
Easy Go, New American Library, 1968, published as *The Last Tomb,* Bantam, 1974.
Zero Cool, New American Library, 1969.
The Venom Business, New American Library, 1969.
Drug of Choice, New American Library, 1970.
Grave Descend, New American Library, 1970.
Binary, Knopf, 1971.

UNDER PSEUDONYM JEFFREY HUDSON

A Case of Need, New American Library, 1968.

MEDIA ADAPTATIONS: The Andromeda Strain was filmed by Universal, 1971; *A Case of Need* was filmed by Metro-Goldwyn-Mayer, 1972; *Binary* was filmed as *Pursuit,* ABC-TV, 1972; *The Terminal Man* was filmed by Warner Bros., 1974; *Jurassic Park* was filmed by Steven Spielberg and released in 1994; *Congo* was filmed by Frank Marshall and released by Paramount, 1995; *Disclosure* was filmed and released in 1995.

SIDELIGHTS: Michael Crichton has had a number of successful careers—physician, teacher, film director, screenwriter—but he is perhaps best known for pioneering the "techno-thriller" with novels such as *The Andromeda Strain, Sphere,* and *Jurassic Park.* Whether writing about a deadly microorganism, brain surgery gone awry, or adventures in the Congo, Crichton's ability to blend the tight plot and suspense of the thriller with the technical emphasis of science fiction has made him a favorite with readers of all ages. Crichton's fame is not limited to literary endeavors; he has also directed a number of popular films with subjects ranging from body organ piracy (*Coma*) to advertising manipulation and murder (*Looker*) and he is the creator of the award-winning television drama *ER.* Summing up Crichton's appeal in the *Dictionary of Literary Biography Yearbook,* Robert L. Sims wrote: "His importance lies in his capacity to tell stories related to that frontier where science and fiction meet. . . . Crichton's best novels demonstrate that, for the immediate future at least, technological innovations offer the same possibilities and limitations as their human creators."

Crichton's first brush with literary success occurred after he entered medical school. To help pay for tuition and living expenses, he began writing paperback thrillers on the weekends and during vacations. One of these books, *A Case of Need,* became an unexpected hit. Written under a pseudonym, the novel revolves around a Chinese-American obstetrician who is unjustly accused of performing an illegal abortion on the daughter of a prominent Boston surgeon. Critical reaction to the book was very positive. "Read *A Case of Need* now," urged Fred Rotondaro in *Best Sellers,* "it will entertain you; get you angry—it will make you think." Allen J. Hubin, writing in the *New York Times Book Review,* similarly noted that the "breezy, fast-paced, up-to-date first novel . . . demonstrates again the ability of detective fiction to treat contemporary social problems in a meaningful fashion."

Also published while the author was still in medical school, *The Andromeda Strain* made Crichton a minor celebrity on campus (especially when the film rights were sold to Universal Studios). Part historical journal, the novel uses data such as computer printouts, bibliographic references, and fictional government documents to lend credence to the story of a deadly microorganism that arrives on Earth aboard a NASA space probe. The virus quickly kills most of the residents of Piedmont, Arizona. Two survivors—an old man and a baby—are taken to a secret government compound for study by Project Wildfire. The Wildfire team—Stone, a bacteriologist, Leavitt, a clinical microbiologist, Burton, a pathologist, and Hall, a practicing surgeon—must race against the clock to isolate the organism and find a cure before it can spread into the general population.

The mix of science and suspense in *The Andromeda Strain* brought varied reactions from reviewers. While admitting that he stayed up all night to finish the book, Christopher Lehmann-Haupt of the *New York Times* observed that he felt cheated by the conclusion. Richard Schickel, writing in *Harper's,* was more concerned with a shortage of character development. "The lack of interest in this matter is . . . amazing. Perhaps so much creative energy went into his basic situation that none was left for people," he wrote. Not all critics were as harsh in their evaluation of the novel, however. "The pace is fast and absorbing," claimed Alexander Cook in *Commonweal,* "the writing is spare and its quality is generally high; and the characters, if not memorable, are at any rate sufficiently sketched in and have been given little personal touches of their own."

Crichton also used the world of science and medicine as a backdrop for *The Terminal Man.* The title refers to computer scientist Harry Benson who, as the result of an automobile accident, suffers severe epileptic seizures. As the seizures grow in intensity, Benson has blackouts during which he commits violent acts. At the urging of his doctors, Benson decides to undergo a radical procedure in which an electrode is inserted into his brain. Hooked up to a packet in the patient's shoulder, the electrode is wired to locate the source of the seizures and deliver a shock to the brain every time an episode is about to occur. Unfortunately, something goes wrong, and Benson's brain is overloaded; as the shocks increase, Benson becomes more irrational, dangerous, and eventually, murderous.

John R. Coyne in the *National Review* found *The Terminal Man* "one of the season's best." He added: "Crichton proves himself capable of making the most esoteric material completely comprehensible to the layman. . . . Even more important, he can create and sustain that sort of suspense that forces us to suspend disbelief." And, in an *Atlantic Monthly* review of the novel, Edward Weeks opined that Crichton has "now written a novel quite terrifying in its suspense and implication."

In *The Great Train Robbery,* Crichton moved out of the realm of science and into the world of Victorian England. Loosely based on an actual event, the book explores master criminal Edward Pierce's attempt to steal a trainload of army payroll on its way to the Crimea. "*The Great Train Robbery* combines the pleasures, guilt, and delight of a novel of gripping entertainment with healthy slices of instruction and information interlarded," declared Doris Grumbach in the *New Republic.* Lehmann-Haupt enthused that he found himself "not only captivated because it is Mr. Crichton's best thriller to date . . . but also charmed most of all by the story's Victorian style and content." And Weeks, writing in the *Atlantic Monthly,* called the novel "an exciting and very clever piece of fiction."

Congo marked Crichton's return to the field of science and technology. In the novel, three adventurers travel through the dense rain forests of the Congo in search of a cache of diamonds with the power to revolutionize computer technology. The trio is accompanied by an intelligent, linguistically-trained gorilla named Amy, the designated intermediary between the scientists and a band of killer apes who guard the gems. The small band's search is hampered by cannibals, volcanos, and mutant primates; it is also marked by a sense of desperation, as the team fights to beat a Euro-Japanese rival company to the prize. In a review of *Congo* for *Best Sellers,* Justin Blewitt termed the novel "an exciting, fast-paced adventure. It rang very true and at the same time was a terrific page-turner. That's a rare combination. . . . [*Congo* is] really a lot of fun."

A scientific—and monetary—search is also the emphasis in *Sphere.* An American ship laying cable in the Pacific hits a snag; the snag turns out to be a huge spaceship, estimated to be at least three centuries old. An undersea research team is ordered to investigate the strange craft from the relative safety of an underwater habitat. Among the civilian and military crew is psychologist Norman Johnson, whose apprehension about the entire project is validated by a number of increasingly bizarre and deadly events: a bad storm cuts the habitat off from the surface, strange messages begin appearing on computer screens, and an unseen—but apparently huge—squid attacks the crew's quarters.

"Michael Crichton's new novel . . . kept me happy for two hours sitting in a grounded plane," wrote Robin McKinley in the *New*

York Times Book Review, adding that "no one can ask for more of a thriller. . . . Take this one along with you on your next plane ride." While noting that he had some problems with *Sphere*—including stilted dialogue and broad characterizations—James M. Kahn mused that Crichton "keeps us guessing at every turn. . . . [He is] a storyteller and a damned good one." And Michael Collins of the *Washington Post Book World* noted that "the pages turn quickly." He urged readers to "suspend your disbelief and put yourself 1,000 feet down."

Huge creatures—in this case, dinosaurs—are also integral to the plot of Crichton's thriller *Jurassic Park. Jurassic Park* chronicles the attempts of self-made billionaire John Hammond to build an amusement park on a remote island off the coast of Costa Rica. Instead of roller coasters and sideshows, the park features actual life-sized dinosaurs bred through the wonders of biotechnology and recombinant DNA. There are some problems before the park opens, however: workmen begin to die in mysterious accidents and local children are attacked by strange lizards. Fearful that the project's opening is in jeopardy, Hammond calls together a team of scientists and technicians to look things over. Led by a paleontologist named Grant, the group is initially amazed by Hammond's creation. Their amazement quickly turns to horror when the park's electronic security system is put out of commission and the dinosaurs are freed to roam at will. What ensues is a deadly battle between the vastly under-armed human contingent and a group of smarter-than-anticipated tyrannosaurs, pterodactyls, stegosaurs, and velociraptors.

Time correspondent John Skow considered *Jurassic Park* the author's "best [techno-thriller] by far since *The Andromeda Strain.*" Skow added that Crichton's "sci-fi is convincingly detailed." In a piece for the *Los Angeles Times Book Review,* Andrew Ferguson remarked that, "having read Crichton's fat new novel . . . I have a word of advice for anyone owning real estate within 10 miles of the La Brea tar pits: Sell." Ferguson ultimately stated that *Jurassic Park*'s "only real virtue" lies in "its genuinely interesting discussion of dinosaurs, DNA research, paleontology, and chaos theory." Gary Jennings of the *New York Times Book Review* was more appreciative, arguing that the book has "some good bits. . . . All in all, *Jurassic Park* is a great place to visit."

Crichton left the world of science in *Rising Sun,* a political thriller revolving around the murder of a young American woman during a party for a huge Japanese corporation. The case is given to detective Peter J. Smith, who finds himself up against an Oriental syndicate with great political and economic power. As Smith gets closer to the truth, the Japanese corporation uses all its influence to thwart his investigation—influence that includes corruption and violence. John Schwartz in *Newsweek* recognized that Crichton had "done his homework," but the critic still felt that *Rising Sun* is too full of "randy propaganda instead of a more balanced view" to be effective.

If *Rising Sun* was criticized as having a xenophobic view of the Far East, *Disclosure,* Crichton's 1994 best-seller, opened a whole new vista for debate and discussion. A techno-thriller with a twist, *Disclosure* opens as a computer company executive named Tom Sanders discovers that he has been passed over for a promotion in favor of a woman executive with whom he had once been romantically involved. When he arrives at his new boss's office, she makes a pass at him. Now happily married, Sanders dodges the boss's advances, only to find within days that he has been named as the aggressor in a sexual harassment suit. How Sanders digs his way from beneath the spurious charges—while simulta-

neously unearthing wider corruption in the computer company—forms the core of the novel.

While critics duly observed the theme of sexual harassment in *Disclosure,* they tended to dwell more upon the thriller aspect of the novel. In *New Statesman and Society,* Douglas Kennedy commended *Disclosure* as an "acidic glimpse into the nasty gamesmanship of U.S. corporate life," adding: "Sexual harassment becomes a minor consideration in a narrative more preoccupied by the wonders of virtual reality and the vicious corporate battlefield." *People* magazine reviewer Susan Toepfer found that by casting the woman as the wrongdoer, "Crichton offers a fresh and provocative story," but contended he did not sufficiently explore the situation's possibilities. *National Review* contributor Michael Coren likewise noted of the novel: "This is provocative stuff, for to question the racial or gender exclusivity of self-awarded victim status is to kick at the very foundations of modern liberalism."

Both *Disclosure* and *Jurassic Park* were produced as feature films, the latter proving to be one of the top-grossing movies of all time. Perhaps the vast success of *Jurassic Park* as a book and a film inspired Crichton to re-visit his scheming raptors and vicious tyrannosaurs in *The Lost World.* Also set on an island off the coast of Costa Rica, *The Lost World* follows the adventures of another team of scientists—with a return appearance by mathematical theorist Ian Malcolm—as they try to escape the clutches of the dinosaurs *and* thwart the ambitions of some egg-stealing opportunists. Noted Susan Toepfer in *People,* "Characteristically clever, fast-paced and engaging, Michael Crichton's . . . work accomplishes what he set out to do: offer the still-harrowing thrills of a by-now-familiar ride."

Although Crichton is best known for his works of fiction, he has also written a number of nonfiction books that reflect his varied interests. *Five Patients: The Hospital Explained* uses five case studies to explore how a modern hospital functions. The topics Crichton discusses in *Five Patients* include the rising cost of health care, advancing technology, and the relationships between doctors and their patients. According to Sims, "*Five Patients* is written by a doctor who prefers writing about medicine to practicing it." Some of the issues raised in *Five Patients* are also touched on in Crichton's autobiographical *Travels.* In *Travels,* the author talks with candor about both his personal and professional life, a life that includes journeys to mysterious lands. "I was ultimately swept away, not just by [Crichton's] richly informed mind, but his driving curiosity," remarked Patricia Bosworth in the *New York Times Book Review.*

Crichton's ability to mesh science, technology, and suspense is not limited to novels. Many of the films that the author has directed, such as *Westworld* and *Runaway,* feature a struggle between humans and technology. Despite the often grim outlook of both his films and novels, Crichton revealed in an interview with Ned Smith of *American Way* that his primary intention in making movies and writing books is to "entertain people." He noted that one of the rewards he gets from filmmaking and writing comes from telling stories. "It's fun to manipulate people's feelings and to be manipulated. To take a movie, or get a book and get very involved in it—don't look at my watch, forget about other things," he said. As for critical reaction to his work, Crichton told Smith: "Every critic assumes he's a code-breaker; the writer makes a code and the critic breaks it. And it doesn't work that way at all. As a mode of working, you need to become very uncritical."

BIOGRAPHICAL/CRITICAL SOURCES:

BOOKS

Authors and Artists for Young Adults, Volume 10, Gale (Detroit), 1993, pp. 63-70.
Contemporary Literary Criticism, Gale, Volume 2, 1974; Volume 6, 1976; Volume 54, 1989, pp. 62-77.
Dictionary of Literary Biography Yearbook: 1981, Gale, 1982.
Trembley, Elizabeth A., *Michael Crichton: A Critical Companion,* Greenwood Press (Westport, CT), 1996.

PERIODICALS

American Spectator, May, 1992, p. 71.
Atlantic Monthly, May, 1972, pp. 108-10.
Best Sellers, August 15, 1968, pp. 207-08; February, 1981, p. 388.
Booklist, November 15, 1996, p. 548; January 15, 1997, p. 763.
Commonweal, August 9, 1969, pp. 493-94.
Entertainment Weekly, December 3, 1990, p. 80; December 16, 1994, p. 16; December 30, 1994, p. 30; January 13, 1995, pp. 52-3; September 22, 1995, pp. 72-3.
Forbes, June 21, 1993, p. 24; September 13, 1993, p. 26; February 14, 1994, p. 26; February 21, 1994, p. 108.
Harper's, August, 1969, p. 97.
JAMA: Journal of the American Medical Association, September 8, 1993, p. 1252.
Library Journal, January, 1997, p. 172.
Los Angeles Times Book Review, July 12, 1987, pp. 1, 13; November 11, 1990, p. 4; October 29, 1995, p. 2; December 15, 1996, p. 3.
Nation, May 11, 1992, p. 637.
National Review, June 23, 1972, pp. 700-01; August 17, 1992, p. 40; February 21, 1994, p. 63.
New Republic, June 7, 1975, pp. 30-1.
New Statesman and Society, March 1, 1991, p. 34; February 4, 1994, p. 49; December 20, 1997, p. 121.
Newsweek, November 19, 1990, p. 69; February 17, 1992, p. 64; January 17, 1994, p. 52; December 9, 1996, p. 80.
New Yorker, February 7, 1994, p. 99; June 27, 1994, p. 81; December 16, 1996, p. 103.
New York Review of Books, April 23, 1992, p. 3; August 12, 1993, p. 51; February 29, 1996, pp. 20-2; January 9, 1997, p. 16.
New York Times, May 30, 1969, p. 25; June 10, 1975; December 5, 1996, p. 35.
New York Times Book Review, August 18, 1968, p. 20; July 12, 1987, p. 18; June 26, 1988, p. 30; November 1, 1990, pp. 14-15; November 11, 1990, p. 14; February 9, 1992, p. 1; January 23, 1994, p. 7; October 1, 1995, pp. 9-10; December 15, 1996, p. 12.
People, January 17, 1994, p. 24; September 18, 1995, p. 37.
Publishers Weekly, September 28, 1990, p. 84; January 27, 1992, p. 91; July 22, 1996, p. 142; November 11, 1996, p. 58; December 2, 1996, p. 30; December 16, 1996, p. 20.
Time, November 12, 1990, p. 97; February 24, 1992, p. 63; January 10, 1994, p. 52; September 25, 1995, pp. 60-7; December 9, 1996, p. 90.
U.S. News and World Report, March 9, 1992, p. 50.
Vanity Fair, January, 1994, p. 32.
Wall Street Journal, December 9, 1996, p. A12; December 11, 1996, p. B12.
Washington Monthly, April, 1994, p. 54.
Washington Post Book World, June 14, 1987, pp. 1, 14.

CRUZ, Victor Hernandez 1949-

PERSONAL: Born February 6, 1949, in Aguas Buenas, Puerto Rico; immigrated to the U.S., 1954; son of Severo and Rosa (Hernandez) Cruz; divorced; children: Vitin Ajani, Rosa Luz. *Education:* Attended high school in New York, NY.

ADDRESSES: Office—P.O. Box 40148, San Francisco, CA 94140; P.O. Box 1047, Aguas Buenas, PR 00607.

CAREER: Poet. East Harlen Gut Theatre, New York City, co-founder, 1968; University of California, Berkeley, guest lecturer, 1970; San Francisco State University, San Francisco, CA, instructor, beginning 1973. Also associated with the San Francisco Art Commission; co-founder, Before Columbus Foundation.

AWARDS, HONORS: Creative Artists public service award, 1974, for *Tropicalization;* National Endowment for the Arts fellow, 1980.

WRITINGS:

Papo Got His Gun! and Other Poems, Calle Once Publications, 1966.
Doing Poetry, Other Ways, 1968.
Snaps (poems), Random House, 1969.
(Editor with Herbert Kohl) *Stuff: A Collection of Poems, Visions, and Imaginative Happenings from Young Writers in Schools—Open and Closed,* Collins & World, 1970.
Mainland (poems), Random House, 1973.
Tropicalization (poems and prose), Reed, Canon, 1976.
The Low Writings, Lee/Lucas Press, 1980.
By Lingual Wholes, Momo's Press, 1982.
Rhythm, Content and Flavor: New and Selected Poems, Arte Publico Press, 1989.
Red Beans, Coffee House Press, 1991.
(Editor with Leroy V. Quintana and Virgil Suarez) *Paper Dance: Fifty-four Latino Poets,* Persea Books, 1994.
Panaramas, Coffee House Press (Minneapolis, MN), 1997.

Cruz's work has been included in anthologies, including *An Anthology of Afro-American Writing,* Morrow, 1968, and *Giant Talk: An Anthology of Third World Writings,* Random House, 1975. Contributor to *Evergreen Review, New York Review of Books, Ramparts, Down Here,* and *Revista del Instituto de Estudios Puertorriquenos.* Editor, *Umbra* magazine, 1967-69.

SIDELIGHTS: Victor Hernandez Cruz wrote: "My family life was full of music, guitars and conga drums, maracas and songs. My mother sang songs. Even when it was five below zero in New York she sang warm tropical ballads." He continued: "My work is on the border of a new language, because I create out of a consciousness steeped in two of the important world languages, Spanish and English. A piece written totally in English could have a Spanish spirit. Another strong concern in my work is the difference between a tropical village, such as Aguas Buenas, Puerto Rico, where I was born, and an immensity such as New York City, where I was raised. I compare smells and sounds, I explore the differences, I write from the center of a culture which is not on its native soil, a culture in flight, living half the time on memories, becoming something totally new and unique, while at the same time it helps to shape and inform the new environment. I write about the city with an agonizing memory of a lush tropical silence. This contrast between landscape and language creates an intensity in my work."

In a *New York Times Book Review* of *By Lingual Wholes,* Richard Elman remarks: "Cruz writes poems about his native Puerto Rico and elsewhere which often speak to us with a forked tongue, sometimes in a highly literate Spanglish. . . . He's a funny, hard-edged poet, declining always into mother wit and pathos: 'So you see, all life is a holy hole. Bet hard on that.'" And Nancy Sullivan reflects in *Poetry* magazine: "Cruz allows the staccato crackle of English half-learned, so characteristic of his people, to enrich the poems through its touching dictional inadequacy. If poetry is arching toward the condition of silence as John Cage and Susan Sontag suggest, perhaps this mode of inarticulateness is a bend on the curve. . . . I think that Cruz is writing necessary poems in a period when many poems seem unnecessary."

Cruz's 1991 work *Red Beans,* the title of which is a play on the words "red beings," referring to Puerto Ricans, has also received critical attention. Reviewers have characterized the volume as a highly imaginative exploration of Puerto Rican history as well as the Puerto Rican's history in America. In a review for the *San Francisco Review of Books,* Jose Amaya assessed, "Cruz experiments with the vast linguistic and cultural possibilities of 'indo-afro-hispano' poetry and comes up with a strong vision of American unity." Commenting on the development of Cruz's style, Amaya noted that "Cruz is at his best in *Red Beans* when he portrays . . . the distinct sounds and voices of Caribbean life which crash into his poetic consciousness like a wild ocean surf." Calling Cruz a "vigorous bilingual Latino troubadour," Frank Allen in *Library Journal* declared the book is "a dance on the edges."

BIOGRAPHICAL/CRITICAL SOURCES:

PERIODICALS

Bilingual Review, Volume 1, 1974, pp. 312-19.
Library Journal, October 1, 1997.
MELUS, spring, 1989-90, pp. 43-58.
New York Times Book Review, September 18, 1983.
Poetry, May, 1970.
Publishers Weekly, September 22, 1997.

                                    *   *   *

CULLEN, Countee 1903-1946

PERSONAL: Birth name Countee LeRoy Porter; first name pronounced "Coun-tay"; born May 30, 1903, in Louisville, KY (some sources say New York, NY or Baltimore, MD); died of uremic poisoning, January 9, 1946, in New York, NY; buried in Woodlawn Cemetery, New York City; married Nina Yolande DuBois, April 9, 1928 (divorced, 1930); married Ida Mae Roberson, September 27, 1940. *Education:* New York University, B.A., 1925; Harvard University, M.A., 1926.

CAREER: Poet, columnist, editor, novelist, playwright, children's writer, and educator. Assistant editor and author of monthly column "The Dark Tower" for *Opportunity: Journal of Negro Life,* 1926-28; traveled back and forth between France and the United States, 1928-34; Frederick Douglass Junior High School, New York City, teacher of English, French, and creative writing, 1934-45.

MEMBER: New York Civic Club, Phi Beta Kappa, Alpha Delta Phi.

AWARDS, HONORS: Witter Bynner Prize for poetry for "Poems," John Reed Memorial Prize from *Poetry* magazine for "Threnody for a Brown Girl," Amy Spingarn Award from *Crisis* magazine for "Two Moods of Love," and second prize winner in Palm Poetry Contest for "Wisdom Cometh With the Years," all 1925; second prize winner in *Crisis* Poetry Contest, 1926, for "Thoughts in a Zoo"; Harmon Foundation Literary Award from National Association for the Advancement of Colored People (NAACP), 1927, for "distinguished achievement in literature by a Negro"; Guggenheim Foundation fellowship, France, 1928-30.

WRITINGS:

POETRY

Color (includes "Heritage," "Atlantic City Waiter," "Near White," "To a Brown Boy," "For a Lady I Know," "Yet Do I Marvel," "Incident," "The Shroud of Color," "Oh, for a Little While Be Kind," "Brown Boy to Brown Girl," and "Pagan Prayer"), Harper, 1925.
Copper Sun (includes "If Love Be Staunch," "The Love Tree," "Nocturne," "Threnody for a Brown Girl," and "To Lovers of Earth: Fair Warning"), decorations by Charles Cullen, Harper, 1927.
(Editor) *Caroling Dusk: An Anthology of Verse by Negro Poets,* decorations by Aaron Douglas, Harper, 1927.
The Black Christ, and Other Poems (includes "The Black Christ," "Song of Praise," "Works to My Love," "In the Midst of Life," "Self Criticism," "To Certain Critics," and "The Wish"), decorations by Charles Cullen, Harper, 1929.
The Medea, and Some Poems (includes translation of Euripides' play *Medea,* "Scottsboro, Too, Is Worth Its Song," "Medusa," "The Cat," "Only the Polished Skeleton," "Sleep," "After a Visit," and "To France"), Harper, 1935.
On These I Stand: An Anthology of the Best Poems of Countee Cullen (includes "Dear Friends and Gentle Hearts," "Christus natus est," and some previously unpublished poems), Harper, 1947.

OTHER

The Ballad of the Brown Girl: An Old Ballad Retold, illustrations and decorations by Charles Cullen, Harper, 1927.
One Way to Heaven (novel), Harper, 1932 (also see below).
The Lost Zoo (a Rhyme for the Young, but Not Too Young), illustrations by Charles Sebree, Harper, 1940, new edition, with illustrations by Joseph Low, Follett, 1969.
My Lives and How I Lost Them (juvenile; autobiography of fictional character Christopher Cat), drawings by Robert Reid Macguire, Harper, 1942, new edition, with illustrations by Rainey Bennett, Follett, 1971.
(With Owen Dodson) *The Third Fourth of July* (one-act play), published in *Theatre Arts,* 1946.
(With Arna Bontemps) *St. Louis Woman* (musical adaptation of Bontemps's novel *God Sends Sunday*; first produced at Martin Beck Theater in New York City, March 30, 1946), published in *Black Theatre,* edited by Lindsay Patterson, Dodd, 1971.

Also author of unpublished plays, including *Let the Day Perish* (with Waters Turpin), *The Spirit of Peace,* and *Heaven's My Home* (an adaptation, with Harry Hamilton, of Cullen's novel, *One Way to Heaven*), and of book reviews. Author of introduction to *The House of Vanity* by Frank Ankenbrand and Isaac Benjamin, Leibman Press, 1928. Contributor to *America as Americans See It,* edited by Fred J. Ringel, Harcourt, 1932.

Contributor to *Crisis, Phylon, Bookman, Harper's, American Mercury, Century, Nation, Poetry,* and other periodicals.

SIDELIGHTS: Countee Cullen was perhaps the most representative voice of the Harlem Renaissance. His life story is essentially a tale of youthful exuberance and talent of a star that flashed across the Afro-American firmament and then sank toward the horizon. When his paternal grandmother and guardian died in 1918, the fifteen-year-old Countee LeRoy Porter was taken into the home of the Reverend Frederick A. Cullen, the pastor of Salem Methodist Episcopal Church, Harlem's largest congregation. There the young Countee entered the approximate center of black politics and culture in the United States and acquired both the name and awareness of the influential clergyman who was later elected president of the Harlem chapter of the National Association for the Advancement of Colored People (NAACP).

While Cullen's informal education was shaped by his exposure to black ideas and yearnings, his formal education derived from almost totally white influences. This dichotomy heavily influenced his creative work and his criticism, particularly because he did extremely well at the white-dominated institutions he attended and won the approbation of white academia. In high school Cullen earned academic honors that in turn garnered him the posts of vice-president of his class and editor of the school newspaper, as well as prizes for poetry and oratory. His glory continued at New York University, where he obtained first or second prizes in a number of poetry contests, including the national Witter Bynner Contests for undergraduate poetry and contests sponsored by *Poetry* magazine. Harvard University's Irving Babbitt publicly lauded Cullen's *The Ballad of the Brown Girl,* and in 1925, which proved a bumper year for the young man's harvest of literary prizes, Cullen graduated from New York University, was accepted into Harvard's masters program, and published his first volume of poetry, *Color.*

During the next four years Cullen reached his zenith. A celebrated young man about Harlem, he had in print by 1929 several books of his own poems and a collection of poetry he edited, *Caroling Dusk,* written by other Afro-Americans. His letters from Harvard to his Harlem friend Harold Jackman exuded self-satisfaction and sometimes the snide intolerance of the *enfant terrible.* The climax of those heady years may have come in 1928. That year Cullen was awarded a Guggenheim fellowship to write poetry in France, and he married Nina Yolande DuBois, the daughter of W. E. B. DuBois, a man who for decades was the acknowledged leader of the Afro-American intellectual community. Few social events in Harlem rivaled the magnitude of the latter event, and much of Harlem joined in the festivities that marked the joining of the Cullen and DuBois lineages, two of its most notable families.

Because of Cullen's success in both black and white cultures, and because of his romantic temperament, he formulated an aesthetic that embraced both cultures. He came to believe that art transcended race and that it could be used as a vehicle to minimize the distance between black and white peoples.

In poems such as "Heritage" and "Atlantic City Waiter," Cullen reflects the urge to reclaim African arts—a phenomenon called "Negritude" that was one of the motifs of the Harlem Renaissance. The cornerstone of his aesthetic, however, was the call for black-American poets to work conservatively, as he did, within English conventions. In his 1927 foreword to *Caroling Dusk,* Cullen observed that "since theirs is . . . the heritage of the English language, their work will not present any serious aberration from poetic tendencies of their times."

His dedication to oneness led Cullen to be cautious of any black writer's work that threatened to erect rather than pull down barricades between the races. Thus, in a February, 1926, "Dark Tower" column in which Cullen reviewed Langston Hughes's *The*

Weary Blues, Cullen pressed Hughes not to be a "racial artist" and to omit jazz rhythms from his poems. In a later column he prodded black writers to censor themselves by avoiding "some things, some truths of Negro life and thought . . . that all Negroes know, but take no pride in." For Cullen, showcasing unpleasant realities would "but strengthen the bitterness of our enemies" and thereby weaken the bridge of art between blacks and whites.

A paradox exists, however, between Cullen's philosophy and writing. While he argued that racial poetry was a detriment to the color-blindness he craved, he was at the same time so affronted by the racial injustice in America that his own best verse—indeed most of his verse—gave voice to racial protest. In fact, the title of Cullen's 1925 collection, *Color,* was not chosen unintentionally, nor did Cullen include sections with that same title in later volumes by accident. Both early and late in his career he was, in spite of himself, largely a racial poet. This is evident throughout Cullen's works from the *Color* pieces and the introduction of racial violence into his 1927 work *The Ballad of the Brown Girl* to the poems that he selected for the posthumously published *On These I Stand,* of which substantially more than half are racial poems.

Of the six identifiable racial themes in Cullen's poetry, the first is Negritude, or Pan-African impulse, a pervasive element of the 1920s international black literary movement that scholar Arthur P. Davis in a 1953 *Phylon* essay called "the alien-and-exile theme." Specific examples of this motif in Cullen's poetry include his attribution of descent from African kings to the girl featured in *The Ballad of the Brown Girl* as well as the submerged pride exhibited by the waiter in the poem "Atlantic City Waiter" whose graceful movement resulted from "Ten thousand years on jungle clues." Probably the best-known illustration of the Pan-African impulse in Cullen's poetry is found in "Heritage," where the narrator realizes that although he must suppress his African heritage, he cannot ultimately surrender his black heart and mind to white civilization. "Heritage," like most of the Negritude poems of the Harlem Renaissance and like political expression such as Marcus Garvey's popular back-to-Africa movement, powerfully suggests the duality of the black psyche—the simultaneous allegiance to America and rage at her racial inequities

Four similar themes recur in Cullen's poems, expressing other forms of racial bias. These include a kind of black chauvinism that prevailed at the time and that Cullen portrayed in both *The Ballad of the Brown Girl* and *The Black Christ,* when in those works he judged that the passion of blacks was better than that of whites. Likewise, the poem "Near White" exemplifies the author's admonition against miscegenation, and in "To a Brown Boy" Cullen propounds a racially motivated affinity toward death as a preferred escape from racial frustration and outrage. Another poem, "For a Lady I Know," presents a satirical view of whites obliviously mistreating their black counterparts as it depicts blacks in heaven doing their "celestial chores" so that upper-class whites can remain in their heavenly beds.

Using a sixth motif, Cullen exhibits a direct expression of irrepressible anger at racial unfairness. His outcry is more muted than that of some other Harlem Renaissance poets—Hughes, for example, and Claude McKay—but that is a matter of Cullen's innate and learned gentility. Those who overlook Cullen's strong indictment of racism in American society miss the main thrust of his work. His poetry throbs with anger as in "Incident" when he recalls his personal response to being called "nigger" on a Baltimore bus, or in the selection "Yet Do I Marvel," in which

Cullen identifies what he regards as God's most astonishing miscue that he could "make a poet black, and bid him sing!" In addition to his own personal experiences, Cullen also focuses on public events. For instance, in "Scottsboro, Too, Is Worth Its Song," he upbraids American poets, who had championed the cause of white anarchists in the controversial Sacco-Vanzetti trials, for not defending the nine black youths indicted on charges of raping two white girls in a freight car passing through Scottsboro, Alabama, in 1931.

On the subject of religion, Cullen waywardly progressed from uncertainty to Christian acceptance. Early on he was given to irony and even defiance in moments of youthful skepticism. In "Heritage," for example, he observes that a black Christ could command his faith better than the white one. When he was twenty-four, he provided a third-person description of himself in which he commented that his "chief problem has been that of reconciling a Christian upbringing with a pagan inclination. His life so far has not convinced him that the problem is insoluble." But before very long, his grandmother Porter's influence and that of the Cullen rectory won out. Outrage over racial injustice notwithstanding, he had fairly well controlled the "pagan inclination" in favor of Christian orthodoxy by 1929, when he published *The Black Christ, and Other Poems.* In the opening of the book's narrative title poem, the protagonist sings of embracing God in spite of certain earthly obstacles that he summarizes as "my country's shame." The speaker's brother has been beaten to death by a white lynch mob for an innocent relationship with a white woman; the narrator's resentment toward a savior who allows such evil to occur is overcome by his mother's proclamation of her unshakable faith, and any residue of doubt disappears when the murdered brother is resurrected.

To understand Cullen's treatment of love it is necessary first to examine the effete—weak or effeminate—quality of many of his love poems. David Levering Lewis, in *When Harlem Was in Vogue,* asserted that "impotence and death run through [Cullen's] poetry like dark threads, entangling his most affirmative lines." In general, Cullen's love poetry is clearly characterized not only by misgivings about women but also by a distrust of the emotion of heterosexual love. His "Medusa" and "The Cat," both contained in *The Medea, and Some Poems,* illustrate this vision of male-female relationships. In Cullen's version of the ancient myth, it is not the hideousness of Medusa that blinds the men who gaze upon her, but rather her beauty. So great is the destructive power of the attractive female that the narrator in "The Cat" imagines in the animal "A woman with thine eyes, satanic beast / Profound and cold as scythes to mow me down." Male lovers, on the other hand are often portrayed as sickly with apprehension that a relationship is about to be ended either by a fickle partner or by death. In "If Love Be Staunch," for example, the speaker warns that love lasts no longer than "water stays in a sieve" and in "The Love Tree" Cullen portrays love as a crucifixion whereby future lovers may realize that "'Twas break of heart that made the love tree grow." What Lewis identified in Cullen's love poems as a "corroding suspicion of life cursed from birth" may have resulted from Cullen's alleged homosexuality.

Cullen's treatment of death in his writing was shaped by his early encounters with the deaths of his parents, brother, and grandmother, as well as by a premonition of his own premature demise. Running through his poems are a sense of the brevity of life and a romantic craving for the surcease of death. In "Nocturne" and "Works to My Love," death is readily accepted as a natural element of life. "Threnody for a Brown Girl" and "In the Midst of Life" portray even warmer feelings towards death as a welcome escape. And in poems such as "Only the Polished Skeleton" death is gratefully anticipated to bring relief from racial oppression: A stripped skeleton has no race; it can but "measure the worth of all it so despised." Looking forward to death, Cullen meanwhile accepted sleep as an effective surrogate. In the poem "Sleep" he portrays slumber as "lovelier" and "kinder" than any alternative. It is both a feline killer and gentle nourisher that suckles the sleeper: "though the suck be short 'tis good." In April, 1943, less than three years before he died of uremic poisoning, Cullen related in "Dear Friends and Gentle Hearts" that "blessedly this breath departs."

After 1929 Cullen's production of verse dropped off dramatically. It was limited to his translation of Euripides' play *Medea,* which appeared along with some new poems in his 1935 collection *The Medea, and Some Poems* and later with half a dozen previously unpublished pieces that were included in his posthumously published collection, *On These I Stand.* A complexity of reasons contributed to the dimming of his poetic star. The Harlem Renaissance required a white audience to sustain it, and as whites became preoccupied with their own tenuous situation during the Great Depression, they lost interest in the Afro-American arts. Also, Cullen's idealism about building a bridge of poetry between the races had been sorely tested by the time the 1920s ended. Moreover, he seemed affected by legitimate doubts concerning his growth as a poet. In "Self Criticism" he reflected whether he would go on singing a "failing note still vainly clinging / To the throat of the stricken swan."

For a combination of causes, then, beginning in the early 1930s Cullen largely curtailed his poetic output and channeled his creative energy into other genres. He wrote a novel, *One Way to Heaven,* published in 1932, but its poor critical reception made it his only novel. The book reveals a flair for satire in its secondary plot, which centers around the Harlem salon of the irrepressible hostess Constancia Brandon; one particularly effective episode features a white intellectual bigot who is invited to read his tract, "The Menace of the Negro to Our American Civilization," to an audience of mainly black intellectuals. The novel itself, however, suffers from a fatal structural flaw. Cullen never successfully integrated the secondary plot—a takeoff on his own experience in Harlem intellectual circles—with the major story line, a melodrama in which itinerant con man Sam Lucas undergoes a fake religious conversion to edge his way into a Harlem congregation; marries and then cheats on his sweet young wife; and finally, on his death bed undergoes a change of heart. The characters in the main plot are generally based on stereotypes common in black-American folklore—the fast-talking trickster and the sagacious saintly old aunt, for example. Although Cullen displays some compassion toward them and a good deal of good-natured wit in dealing with the satirical figures, the two plots never adequately come together. As Rudolph Fisher said in a *New York Herald Tribune* review of *One Way to Heaven,* it was as if Cullen were "exhibiting a lovely pastel and cartoon on the same frame."

When thirty-one-year-old Cullen turned to teaching in 1934, he was determined to find some way other than literature to contribute to social change, but he did not abandon writing entirely. In 1935 he published his version of *Medea* (with the speeches and choral passages curiously attenuated) and collaborated with Harry Hamilton on "Heaven's My Home," a dramatic adaptation of *One Way to Heaven.* The play, which was never published, is actually more contrived than Cullen's novel, but unlike the original work, "Heaven's My Home" manages to integrate the two plots by introducing a sexual relationship between the protagonists Lucas and Brandon.

Toward the end of his life, in the 1940s, Cullen was relatively successful as a dramatist. With another collaborator, Owen Dodson, he worked on several projects, including "The Third Fourth of July," a one-act play printed in *Theatre Arts* in August, 1946. During this period Cullen rejected a professorship at Fisk University and instead remained in New York to work with Arna Bontemps on a dramatic version of her novel *God Sends Sunday*. Cullen, who suggested the adaptation, made this endeavor the center of his life, but the enterprise caused him much grief. By 1945 the play had become the musical "St. Louis Woman," and celebrated performer Lena Horne was expected to star in its Broadway and Hollywood productions. Then disaster struck. Walter White of the National Association for the Advancement of Colored People (NAACP) argued that the play, set in the black ghetto of St. Louis and featuring lower-class and seedy characters, was demeaning to blacks. Cullen was blamed for revealing the seamy side of black life, the very thing he had warned other black writers not to do. Many of Cullen's friends refused to defend him; some joined the attack, which was patently unjust. Admittedly, greed and criminality figure in the play, which focuses on the struggle between overbearing salon keeper-gambler Bigelow Brown and diminutive jockey Lil Augie for the affections of Della Greene, a hard-nosed and soft-hearted beauty.

Probably more than any other writer of the Harlem Renaissance, Cullen carried out the intentions of black American intellectual leaders such as W. E. B. DuBois and James Weldon Johnson. These men had nothing but the highest praise for Cullen, for he was brilliantly practicing what they advocated, and he came close to embodying Alain Locke's "New Negro." "In a time," DuBois wrote in a 1928 *Crisis* essay, "when it is vogue to make much of the Negro's aptitude for clownishness or to depict him objectively as a serio-comic figure, it is a fine and praiseworthy act for Mr. Cullen to show through the interpretation of his own subjectivity the inner workings of the Negro soul and mind." Johnson was pleased with Cullen's decision not to recognize "any limitation to 'racial' themes and forms." In Cullen's wish not to be "a negro poet," Johnson insisted, the writer was "not only within his right: he is right." As these authorities attest, to read Countee Cullen's work is to hear a voice as representative of the Harlem Renaissance as it is possible to find.

BIOGRAPHICAL/CRITICAL SOURCES:

BOOKS

Baker, Houston A., Jr., *A Many-Colored Coat of Dreams: The Poetry of Countee Cullen,* Broadside Press, 1974.

Bontemps, Arna, editor, *The Harlem Renaissance Remembered,* Dodd, Mead, & Co., 1972.

Davis, Arthur P., *From the Dark Tower: Afro-American Writers, 1900-1960,* Howard University Press, 1974.

Dictionary of Literary Biography, Gale (Detroit), Volume 4: *American Writers in Paris: 1920-1939,* 1980; Volume 48: *American Poets: 1880-1945, Second Series,* 1986; Volume 51: *Afro-American Writers from the Harlem Renaissance to 1940,* 1987.

Huggins, Nathan Irvin, *Harlem Renaissance,* Oxford, 1971.

Johnson, James Weldon, *The Book of American Negro Poetry,* Harcourt, 1922, revised edition, 1931, Harbrace, 1959.

Kramer, Victor A., *The Harlem Renaissance Re-examined,* AMS Press, 1987.

Lewis, David Levering, *When Harlem Was in Vogue,* Knopf, 1981.

Margolies, Edward, *Native Sons: A Critical Study of Twentieth-Century Negro American Authors,* Lippincott, 1968.

Perry, Margaret, *A Bio-Bibliography of Countee P. Cullen, 1903-1946,* Greenwood, 1971.

Rosenblatt, Roger, *Black Fiction,* Harvard University Press, 1974.

Shucard, Alan, *Countee Cullen,* Twayne, 1984.

Singh, Amritjit, *The Novels of the Harlem Renaissance: Twelve Black Authors, 1923-1933,* Pennsylvania State University Press, 1976.

Twentieth-Century Literary Criticism, Volume 4, Gale, 1981.

Wagner, Jean, *Black Poets of the United States: From Paul Laurence Dunbar to Langston Hughes,* University of Illinois Press, 1973.

PERIODICALS

Atlantic Monthly, No. 79, March, 1947.

CLA Journal, September, 1967; September, 1969; December, 1974.

College Language Association Journal, No. 13, 1970.

Crisis, No. 35, June, 1928.

Critique, No. 11, 1969.

Nation, March 12, 1930.

New Republic, No. 52, 1927.

New York Herald Tribune of Books, February 28, 1932.

Phylon, No. 14, 1953.

*   *   *

CUMMINGS, E(dward) E(stlin) 1894-1962

PERSONAL: Born October 14, 1894, in Cambridge, MA; died September 3, 1962, in North Conway, NH; buried in Forest Hills Cemetery, Boston, MA; son of Edward (a professor of sociology and political science and a Unitarian minister) and Rebecca Haswell (Clarke) Cummings; married Elaine Orr Thayer, March 19, 1924 (divorced, 1925); married Anne Minnerly Barton, May 1, 1929 (divorced, 1932); married (common law) Marion Morehouse, 1934; children: (first marriage) Nancy. *Education:* Harvard University, A.B. (magna cum laude), 1915, M.A., 1916.

CAREER: Poet, painter, novelist, and playwright. Charles Eliot Norton Professor of Poetry, Harvard University, 1952-53. One-man exhibitions at American British Art Centre, 1949, and Rochester Memorial Gallery, 1959. *Military service:* Served as an ambulance driver with the Norton-Harjes Ambulance Service in France, 1917; detained on suspicion of treason and held in a French internment camp, 1917; U.S. Army, private, 1918-1919.

MEMBER: National Academy of Arts and Letters.

AWARDS, HONORS: *Dial* (magazine) Award, 1925, for distinguished service to American letters; Guggenheim fellowship, 1933 and 1951; Levinson Prize, *Poetry* (magazine), 1939; Shelley Memorial Award, Poetry Society of America, 1944; Academy of American Poets fellowship, 1950; Harriet Monroe Poetry Award, 1950; Eunice Teitjens Memorial Prize, *Poetry,* 1952; National Book Award special citation, 1955, for *Poems, 1923-1954*; Festival Poet, Boston Arts Festival, 1957; Bollingen Prize in Poetry, Yale University, 1958; Oscar Blumenthal Prize, *Poetry,* 1962.

WRITINGS:

POEMS

(Contributor) *Eight Harvard Poets,* L. J. Gomme, 1917.
Tulips and Chimneys (also see below), T. Seltzer, 1923, enlarged edition, Golden Eagle Press, 1937.
Puella Mia, Golden Eagle Press, 1923.
XLI Poems, Dial, 1925.
& (also see below), privately printed, 1925.
is 5, Boni & Liveright, 1926.
Christmas Tree, American Book Bindery, 1928.
W(ViVa), Liveright, 1931.
(Contributor) Peter Neagoe, editor, *Americans Abroad: An Anthology,* Servire, 1932.
No Thanks, Golden Eagle Press, 1935.
1/20, Roger Roughton, 1936.
Collected Poems, Harcourt, 1938.
50 Poems, Duell, Sloan & Pearce, 1940.
1 x 1, Holt, 1944.
XAIPE: Seventy-One Poems, Oxford University Press, 1950.
Poems, 1923-1954, Harcourt, 1954.
95 Poems, Harcourt, 1958.
100 Selected Poems, Grove, 1958.
Selected Poems, 1923-1958, Faber, 1960.
73 Poems, Harcourt, 1963.
A Selection of Poems, Harcourt, 1965.
Complete Poems, 1923-1962, two volumes, MacGibbon & Kee, 1968; revised edition published in one volume as *Complete Poems, 1913-1962,* Harcourt, 1972.
Poems, 1905-1962, edited by Firmage, Marchim Press, 1973.
Tulips & Chimneys: The Original 1922 Manuscript with the 35 Additional Poems from &, edited by Firmage, Liveright, 1976.
(Contributor) Nancy Cummings De Forzet, *Charon's Daughter: A Passion of Identity,* Liveright, 1977.
Love Is Most Mad and Moonly, Addison-Wesley, 1978.
(Chaire), Liveright, 1979.
Complete Poems, 1910-1962, Granada, 1982.
Hist Whist and Other Poems for Children, edited by Firmage, Liveright, 1983.
Etcetera: The Unpublished Poems of E. E. Cummings, edited by Firmage and Richard S. Kennedy, Liveright, 1984.
In Just-Spring, Little, Brown, 1988.
Selected Poems, Liveright (New York City), 1994.
E. E. Cummings: Complete Poems 1904-1962, Liveright, 1994.
May I Feel Said He: Poem, Welcome Enterprises (New York City), 1995.

OTHER

The Enormous Room, Boni & Liveright, 1922, revised edition, Liveright, 1978.
Him (three-act play; first produced in New York at the Provincetown Playhouse, April 18, 1928), Boni & Liveright, 1927, new edition, Liveright, 1970.
[No title] (collection of stories), Covici Friede, 1930.
CIOPW (artwork), Covici Friede, 1931.
Eimi (travel diary), Covici Friede, 1933, 4th edition, Grove, 1958.
(Translator) Louis Aragon, *The Red Front,* Contempo, 1933.
Tom (ballet based on *Uncle Tom's Cabin* by Harriet Beecher Stowe), Arrow Editions, 1935.
Anthropos: The Future of Art, Golden Eagle Press, 1944.
Santa Claus: A Morality (play), Holt, 1946.
i: six nonlectures, Harvard University Press, 1953.

E. E. Cummings: A Miscellany, Argophile Press, 1958, revised edition edited by George Firmage, October Press, 1965.
(With wife Marion Morehouse) *Adventures in Value,* Harcourt, 1962.
Fairy Tales, Harcourt, 1965.
Three Plays and a Ballet, edited by Firmage, October House, 1967.
Selected Letters of E. E. Cummings, edited by F. W. Dupee and George Stade, Harcourt, 1969.
E. E. Cummings Reads His Collected Poetry, 1943-1958 (recording), Caedmon, 1977.
Little Tree (juvenile), Crown, 1987.
Pound/Cummings: The Correspondence of Ezra Pound and E. E. Cummings, edited by Barry Ahearn, University of Michigan Press (Ann Arbor), 1996.

SIDELIGHTS: "Among the most innovative of twentieth-century poets," according to Jenny Penberthy in the *Dictionary of Literary Biography,* E. E. Cummings experimented with poetic form and language to create a distinct personal style. A Cummings poem is spare and precise, employing a few key words eccentrically placed on the page. Some of these words were invented by Cummings, often by combining two common words into a new synthesis. He also revised grammatical and linguistic rules to suit his own purposes, using such words as "if," "am," and "because" as nouns, for example, or assigning his own private meanings to words. Despite their nontraditional form, Cummings' poems came to be popular with many readers. "No one else," Randall Jarrell claimed in his *The Third Book of Criticism,* "has ever made avant-garde, experimental poems so attractive to the general and the special reader." By the time of his death in 1962 Cummings held a prominent position in twentieth-century poetry. John Logan in *Modern American Poetry: Essays in Criticism* called him "one of the greatest lyric poets in our language." Stanley Edgar Hyman wrote in *Standards: A Chronicle of Books for Our Time*: "Cummings has written at least a dozen poems that seem to me matchless. Three are among the great love poems of our time or any time." Malcolm Cowley admitted in the *Yale Review* that Cummings "suffers from comparison with those [poets] who built on a larger scale—Eliot, Aiken, Crane, Auden among others—but still he is unsurpassed in his special field, one of the masters."

Cummings decided to become a poet when he was still a child. Between the ages of eight and twenty-two, he wrote a poem a day, exploring many traditional poetic forms. By the time he was in Harvard in 1916, modern poetry had caught his interest. He began to write avant-garde poems in which conventional punctuation and syntax were ignored in favor of a dynamic use of language. Cummings also experimented with poems as visual objects on the page. These early efforts were included in *Eight Harvard Poets,* a collection of poems by members of the Harvard Poetry Society.

After graduating from Harvard, Cummings spent a month working for a mail order book dealer. He left the job because of the tedium. In April of 1917, with the First World War raging in Europe and the United States not yet involved, he volunteered for the Norton-Harjes Ambulance Service in France. Ambulance work was a popular choice with those who, like Cummings, considered themselves to be pacifists. He was soon stationed on the French-German border with fellow American William Slater Brown, and the two young men became fast friends. To relieve the boredom of their assignment, they inserted veiled and provocative comments into their letters back home, trying to outwit and baffle the French censors. They also befriended soldiers in nearby units. Such activities led in September of 1917 to their being held on suspicion of treason and sent to an internment camp in Normandy for questioning. Cummings and Brown were housed in a large, one-room holding area along with other suspicious foreigners. Only outraged protests from his father finally secured Cummings' release in December of 1917; Brown was not released until April of the following year. In July of 1918, with the United States entering the war, Cummings was drafted into the U.S. Army and spent some six months at a training camp in Massachusetts.

The early twenties were an extremely productive time for Cummings. In 1922 he published his first book, *The Enormous Room,* a fictionalized account of his French captivity. Critical reaction was overwhelmingly positive, although Cummings' account of his imprisonment was oddly cheerful in tone and freewheeling in style. He depicted his internment camp stay as a period of inner growth. As David E. Smith wrote in *Twentieth Century Literature, The Enormous Room*'s emphasis "is upon what the initiate has learned from his journey. In this instance, the maimed hero can never again regard the outer world (i.e., 'civilization') without irony. But the spiritual lesson he learned from his sojourn with a community of brothers will be repeated in his subsequent writings both as an ironical dismissal of the values of his contemporary world, and as a sensitive, almost mystical celebration of the quality of Christian love." John Dos Passos, in a review of the book for *Dial,* claimed that "in a style infinitely swift and crisply flexible, an individual not ashamed of his loves and hates, great or trivial, has expressed a bit of the underside of History with indelible vividness." Writing of the book in 1938, John Peale Bishop claimed in the *Southern Review:* "*The Enormous Room* has the effect of making all but a very few comparable books that came out of the War look shoddy and worn."

Cummings' first collection of poems, *Tulips and Chimneys,* appeared in 1923. His eccentric use of grammar and punctuation are evident in the volume, though many of the poems are written in conventional language. "The language of *Tulips and Chimneys,* . . . like the imagery, the verse forms, the subject matter, and the thought, is sometimes good, sometimes bad," wrote Robert E. Maurer in the *Bucknell Review.* "But the book is so obviously the work of a talented young man who is striking off in new directions, groping for original and yet precise expression, experimenting in public, that it seems uncharitable to dwell too long on its shortcomings."

It was with these collections of the 1920s that Cummings established his reputation as an avant-garde poet conducting daring experiments with language. Speaking of these language experiments, M. L. Rosenthal wrote in *The Modern Poets: A Critical Introduction*: "The chief effect of Cummings' jugglery with syntax, grammar, and diction was to blow open otherwise trite and bathetic motifs through a dynamic rediscovery of the energies sealed up in conventional usage. . . . He succeeded masterfully in splitting the atom of the cute commonplace." "Cummings," Richard P. Blackmur wrote in *The Double Agent: Essays in Craft and Elucidation,* "has a fine talent for using familiar, even almost dead words, in such a context as to make them suddenly impervious to every ordinary sense; they become unable to speak, but with a great air of being bursting with something very important and precise to say." Bethany K. Dumas wrote in her *E. E. Cummings: A Remembrance of Miracles* that "more important than the specific devices used by Cummings is the use to which he puts the devices. That is a complex matter; irregular spacing . . . allows both amplification and retardation. Further, spacing of key words allows puns which would otherwise

be impossible. Some devices, such as the use of lowercase letters at the beginnings of lines . . . allow a kind of distortion that often re-enforces that of the syntax. . . . All these devices have the effect of jarring the reader, of forcing him to examine experience with fresh eyes."

This satirical aspect to Cummings' work drew both praise and criticism. His attacks on the mass mind, conventional patterns of thought, and society's restrictions on free expression, were born of his strong commitment to the individual. In the "nonlectures" he delivered at Harvard University Cummings explained his position: "So far as I am concerned, poetry and every other art was, is, and forever will be strictly and distinctly a question of individuality." As Penberthy noted, Cummings' consistent attitude in all of his work was "condemning mankind while idealizing the individual." "Cummings' lifelong belief," Bernard Dekle stated in *Profiles of Modern American Authors,* "was a simple faith in the miracle of man's individuality. Much of his literary effort was directed against what he considered the principal enemies of this individuality—mass thought, group conformity, and commercialism." For this reason, Cummings satirized what he called "mostpeople," that is, the herd mentality found in modern society. "At heart," Logan explained, "the quarrels of Cummings are a resistance to the small minds of every kind, political, scientific, philosophical, and literary, who insist on limiting the real and the true to what they think they know or can respond to. As a preventive to this kind of limitation, Cummings is directly opposed to letting us rest in what we believe we know; and this is the key to the rhetorical function of his famous language."

Cummings was also ranked among the best love poets of his time. "Love always was . . . Cummings' chief subject of interest," Friedman wrote in his *E. E. Cummings: The Art of His Poetry.* "The traditional lyric situation, representing the lover speaking of love to his lady, has been given in our time a special flavor and emphasis by Cummings. Not only the lover and his lady, but love itself—its quality, its value, its feel, its meaning—is a subject of continuing concern to our speaker." Love was, in Cummings' poems, equated to such other concepts as joy and growth, a relationship which "had its source," wrote Robert E. Wegner in *The Poetry and Prose of E. E. Cummings,* "in Cummings' experience as a child; he grew up in an aura of love. . . . Love is the propelling force behind a great body of his poetry." Friedman noted that Cummings was "in the habit of associating love, as a subject, with the landscape, the seasons, the times of day, and with time and death—as poets have always done in the past."

In addition to his poetry, Cummings was also known for his play, *Him,* and for the travel diary, *Eimi. Him* consisted of a sequence of skits drawing from burlesque, the circus, and the avant-garde, and jumping quickly from tragedy to grotesque comedy. The male character is named Him; the female character is Me. "The play begins," Harold Clurman wrote in *Nation,* "as a series of feverish images of a girl undergoing anaesthesia during an abortion. She is 'me,' who thinks of her lover as 'him.'" In the program to the play, staged at the Provincetown Playhouse, Cummings provided a warning to the audience: "Relax and give the play a chance to strut its stuff—relax, stop wondering what it's all 'about'—like many strange and familiar things, Life included, this Play isn't 'about,' it simply is. Don't try to enjoy it, let it try to enjoy you. DON'T TRY TO UNDERSTAND IT, LET IT TRY TO UNDERSTAND YOU."

In 1931 Cummings traveled to the Soviet Union. Like many other writers and artists of the time, he was hopeful that the communist revolution had created a better society. After a short time in the country, however, it became clear to Cummings that the Soviet Union was a dictatorship in which the individual was severely regimented by the state. His diary of the visit, in which he bitterly attacked the Soviet regime for its dehumanizing policies, was published in 1933 as *Eimi,* the Greek word for "I am." In it, he described the Soviet Union as an "uncircus of noncreatures." Lenin's tomb, in which the late dictator's preserved body is on display, especially revolted Cummings and inspired him to create the most impassioned writing in the book. "The style which Cummings began in poetry," Bishop wrote, "reaches its most complete development in the prose of *Eimi.* Indeed, one might almost say that, without knowing it, Cummings had been acquiring a certain skill over the years, in order that, when occasion arose, he might set down in words the full horror of Lenin's tomb." In tracing the course of his thirty-five day trip through the Soviet Union, Cummings made frequent allusion to Dante's *Inferno* and its story of a descent into Hell, equating the two journeys. It is only after crossing back into Europe at book's end that "it is once more possible for [Cummings] to assume the full responsibility of being a man. . . ," Bishop wrote. "Now he knows there is but one freedom. . . , the freedom of the will, responsive and responsible, and that from it all other freedoms take their course."

In 1952, Cummings was invited to give the Charles Eliot Norton lectures in poetry at Harvard University. His lectures, later published as *i: six nonlectures,* were highly personal accounts of his life and work, "autobiographical rambles," as Penberthy described them.

Critics of Cummings' work were divided into two camps as to the importance of his career. His detractors called his failure to develop as a writer a major weakness; Cummings' work changed little from the 1920s to the 1950s. Others saw him as merely clever but with little lasting value beyond a few technical innovations. Still others questioned the ideas in his poetry, or seeming lack of them. George Stade in the *New York Times Book Review* claimed that "intellectually speaking, Cummings was a case of arrested development. He was a brilliant 20-year-old, but he remained merely precocious to the end of his life. That may be one source of his appeal." James G. Southworth, writing in *Some Modern American Poets,* argued that Cummings "is too much out of the stream of life for his work to have significance." Southworth went on to say that "the reader must not mistake Mr. Cummings for an intellectual poet."

But Cummings' supporters acclaimed his achievement. In a 1959 essay reprinted in his collection *Babel to Byzantium,* James Dickey proclaimed: "I think that Cummings is a daringly original poet, with more vitality and more sheer, uncompromising talent than any other living American writer." Although admitting that Cummings' work was not faultless, Dickey stated that he felt "ashamed and even a little guilty in picking out flaws" in the poems, a process he likened to calling attention to "the aesthetic defects in a rose. It is better to say what must finally be said about Cummings: that he has helped to give life to the language."

BIOGRAPHICAL/CRITICAL SOURCES:

BOOKS

Berry, S. L., *E. E. Cummings* (juvenile biography), Creative Education (Mankato, MN), 1994.
Blackmur, Richard P., *The Double Agent: Essays in Craft and Elucidation,* Arrow Editions, 1935.

Contemporary Literary Criticism, Gale (Detroit), Volume 1, 1973; Volume 3, 1975; Volume 8, 1978; Volume 12, 1980; Volume 15, 1980.
Dekle, Bernard, *Profiles of Modern American Authors,* Tuttle, 1969.
Dickey, James, *Babel to Byzantium,* Farrar, 1968.
Dictionary of Literary Biography, Gale, Volume 4: *American Writers in Paris, 1920-1939,* 1980; Volume 48: *American Poets, 1880-1945,* second series, 1986.
Dumas, Bethany K., *E. E. Cummings: A Remembrance of Miracles,* Barnes & Noble, 1974.
Fairley, Irene, *E. E. Cummings & Ungrammar: A Study of Syntactic Deviance in His Poems,* Windmill Press, 1975.
Firmage, George J., *E. E. Cummings: A Bibliography,* Wesleyan University Press, 1960.
Friedman, Norman, *E. E. Cummings: The Art of His Poetry,* Johns Hopkins University Press, 1960.
Friedman, Norman, *Re Valuing Cummings: Further Essays on the Poet, 1962-1993,* University Press of Florida (Gainesville), 1996.
Hyman, Stanley Edgar, *Standards: A Chronicle of Books for Our Time,* Horizon, 1966.
Jarrell, Randall, *The Third Book of Criticism,* Farrar, 1969.
Kennedy, Richard S., *Dreams in the Mirror: A Biography of E. E. Cummings,* Liveright, 1980.
Kennedy, Richard S., *E. E. Cummings Revisited,* Twayne (New York City), 1994.
Kidder, Rushworth M., *E. E. Cummings: An Introduction to the Poetry,* Columbia University Press, 1979.
Kostelanetz, Richard, and John Rocco, editors, *Another E. E. Cummings,* Liveright (New York City), 1998.
Rosenthal, M. L., *The Modern Poets: A Critical Introduction,* Oxford University Press, 1960.
Rotella, Guy L., *E. E. Cummings: A Reference Guide,* G. K. Hall, 1979.
Southworth, James G., *Some Modern American Poets,* Basil Blackwell, 1950.
Webster, Michael, *Reading Visual Poetry after Futurism: Marinetti, Apollinaire, Schwitters, Cummings,* P. Lang (New York City), 1995.
Wegner, Robert E., *The Poetry and Prose of E. E. Cummings,* Harcourt, 1965.

PERIODICALS

Bucknell Review, May, 1955.
Contemporary Literature, autumn, 1976.
Dial, July, 1922.
Georgia Review, summer, 1978.
Journal of Modern Literature (special Cummings issue), April, 1979.
Nation, July 8, 1925; May 11, 1974.
New York Times Book Review, July 22, 1973.
Poetry, August, 1933; August, 1938.
Southern Review, summer, 1938; summer, 1941.
Twentieth Century Literature, July, 1965.
Wake, spring, 1976 (special Cummings issue).
Yale Review, spring, 1973.

*   *   *

CUNNINGHAM, E. V.
See FAST, Howard (Melvin)

CURTIS, Price
　　See ELLISON, Harlan (Jay)

*   *   *

CUTRATE, Joe
　　See SPIEGELMAN, Art

CZACZKES, Shmuel Yosef
　　See AGNON, S(hmuel) Y(osef Halevi)

D

DAHL, Roald 1916-1990

PERSONAL: Given name is pronounced "Roo-aal"; born September 13, 1916, in Llandaff, South Wales; died November 23, 1990, in Oxford, England; son of Harald (a shipbroker, painter, and horticulturist) and Sofie (Hesselberg) Dahl; married Patricia Neal (an actress), July 2, 1953 (divorced, 1983); married Felicity Ann Crosland, 1983; children: (first marriage) Olivia (deceased), Tessa, Theo, Ophelia, Lucy. *Education:* Graduate of British public schools, 1932.

CAREER: Shell Oil Co., London, England, member of eastern staff, 1933-37, member of staff in Dar-es-Salaam, Tanzania, 1937-39; writer. Host of a series of half-hour television dramas, *Way Out,* during early 1960s. *Military service:* Royal Air Force, fighter pilot, 1939-45; became wing commander.

AWARDS, HONORS: Edgar Award, Mystery Writers of America, 1954, 1959, and 1980; New England Round Table of Children's Librarians award, 1972, and Surrey School award, 1973, both for *Charlie and the Chocolate Factory*; Surrey School award, 1975, and Nene award, 1978, both for *Charlie and the Great Glass Elevator*; Surrey School award, 1978, and California Young Reader Medal, 1979, both for *Danny: The Champion of the World*; Federation of Children's Book Groups award, 1982, for *The BFG*; Massachusetts Children's award, 1982, for *James and the Giant Peach; New York Times* Outstanding Books award, 1983, Whitbread Award, 1983, and West Australian award, 1986, all for *The Witches*; World Fantasy Convention Lifetime Achievement Award, and Federation of Children's Book Groups award, both 1983; Maschler award runner-up, 1985, for *The Giraffe and the Pelly and Me; Boston Globe/Horn Book* nonfiction honor citation, 1985, for *Boy: Tales of Childhood*; International Board on Books for Young People awards for Norwegian and German translations of *The BFG,* both 1986; Smarties Award, 1990, for *Esio Trot.*

WRITINGS:

FOR ADULTS

Sometime Never: A Fable for Supermen (novel), Scribner, 1948.
My Uncle Oswald (novel), M. Joseph, 1979, Knopf, 1980.
Going Solo (autobiography), Farrar, Straus, 1986.

FOR CHILDREN

The Gremlins, illustrations by Walt Disney Productions, Random House, 1943.

James and the Giant Peach: A Children's Story (also see below), illustrations by Nancy Ekholm Burkert, Knopf, 1961, illustrations by Michel Simeon, Allen & Unwin, 1967.
Charlie and the Chocolate Factory (also see below), illustrations by Joseph Schindelman, Knopf, 1964, revised edition, 1973, illustrations by Faith Jaques, Allen & Unwin, 1967.
The Magic Finger (also see below), illustrations by William Pene du Bois, Harper, 1966, illustrations by Pat Marriott, Puffin, 1974.
Fantastic Mr. Fox (also see below), illustrations by Donald Chaffin, Knopf, 1970.
Charlie and the Great Glass Elevator: The Further Adventures of Charlie Bucket and Willy Wonka, Chocolate-Maker Extraordinary (also see below), illustrations by J. Schindelman, Knopf, 1972, illustrations by F. Jaques, Allen & Unwin, 1973.
Danny: The Champion of the World, illustrations by Jill Bennett, Knopf, 1975 (collected with *James and the Giant Peach* and *Fantastic Mr. Fox,* Bantam, 1983).
The Enormous Crocodile (also see below), illustrations by Quentin Blake, Knopf, 1978.
The Complete Adventures of Charlie and Mr. Willy Wonka (contains *Charlie and the Chocolate Factory* and *Charlie and the Great Glass Elevator*), illustrations by F. Jaques, Allen & Unwin, 1978.
The Twits, illustrations by Q. Blake, J. Cape, 1980, Knopf, 1981.
George's Marvelous Medicine, illustrations by Q. Blake, J. Cape, 1981, Knopf, 1982.
Roald Dahl's Revolting Rhymes, illustrations by Q. Blake, J. Cape, 1982, Knopf, 1983.
The BFG (also see below), illustrations by Q. Blake, Farrar, Straus, 1982.
Dirty Beasts (verse), illustrations by Rosemary Fawcett, Farrar, Straus, 1983.
The Witches (also see below), illustrations by Q. Blake, Farrar, Straus, 1983.
Boy: Tales of Childhood, Farrar, Straus, 1984.
The Giraffe and Pelly and Me, illustrations by Q. Blake, Farrar, Straus, 1985.
Matilda, illustrations by Q. Blake, Viking Kestrel, 1988.
Roald Dahl: Charlie and the Chocolate Factory, Charlie and the Great Glass Elevator, The BFG (boxed set), Viking, 1989.
Rhyme Stew (comic verse), illustrations by Q. Blake, J. Cape, 1989, Viking, 1990.
Esio Trot, illustrations by Q. Blake, Viking, 1990.

The Dahl Diary, 1992, illustrations by Q. Blake, Puffin Books, 1991.

The Minpins, Viking, 1991.

Three More from Roald Dahl (includes *The Witches, James and the Giant Peach,* and *Danny: The Champion of the World*), Puffin, 1991.

The Vicar of Nibbleswicke, illustrations by Q. Blake, Viking, 1992.

My Year, illustrations by Q. Blake, Viking Children's, 1994.

Roald Dahl's Revolting Recipes, illustrations by Quentin Blake, Viking (New York City), 1994.

SHORT FICTION

Over to You: Ten Stories of Flyers and Flying (also see below), Reynal, 1946.

Someone Like You (also see below), Knopf, 1953.

Kiss, Kiss (also see below), Knopf, 1959.

Selected Stories of Roald Dahl, Modern Library, 1968.

Twenty-nine Kisses from Roald Dahl (contains *Someone Like You* and *Kiss, Kiss*), M. Joseph, 1969.

Switch Bitch (also see below), Knopf, 1974.

The Wonderful World of Henry Sugar and Six More, Knopf, 1977 (published in England as *The Wonderful Story of Henry Sugar and Six More,* Cape, 1977).

The Best of Roald Dahl (selections from *Over to You, Someone Like You, Kiss Kiss,* and *Switch Bitch*), introduction by James Cameron, Vintage, 1978.

Roald Dahl's Tales of the Unexpected, Vintage, 1979.

Taste and Other Tales, Longman, 1979.

A Roald Dahl Selection: Nine Short Stories, edited and introduced by Roy Blatchford, photographs by Catherine Shakespeare Lane, Longman, 1980.

More Tales of the Unexpected, Penguin, 1980 (published in England as *More Roald Dahl's Tales of the Unexpected,* Joseph, 1980, and as *Further Tales of the Unexpected,* Chivers, 1981).

(Editor) *Roald Dahl's Book of Ghost Stories,* Farrar, Straus, 1983.

Two Fables (contains "Princess and the Poacher" and "Princess Mammalia"), illustrations by Graham Dean, Viking, 1986.

The Roald Dahl Omnibus, Hippocrene Books, 1987.

A Second Roald Dahl Selection: Eight Short Stories, edited by Helene Fawcett, Longman, 1987.

Ah, Sweet Mystery of Life, illustrations by John Lawrence, J. Cape, 1988, Knopf, 1989.

The Collected Short Stories, Michael Joseph, 1991.

SCREENPLAYS

Lamb to the Slaughter (teleplay), *Alfred Hitchcock Presents,* Columbia Broadcasting System (CBS-TV), 1958.

(With Jack Bloom) *You Only Live Twice,* United Artists, 1967.

(With Ken Hughes) *Chitty Chitty Bang Bang,* United Artists, 1968.

The Night-Digger (based on *Nest in a Falling Tree,* by Joy Crowley), Metro-Goldwyn-Mayer, 1970.

Willie Wonka and the Chocolate Factory (motion picture; adaptation of *Charlie and the Chocolate Factory*), Paramount, 1971.

Also author of screenplays *Oh Death, Where Is Thy Sting-a-Ling-a-Ling?,* United Artists, *The Lightning Bug,* 1971, and *The Road Builder.*

OTHER

The Honeys (play), produced in New York City, 1955.

(With wife Felicity Dahl) *Memories with Food at Gipsy House,* Viking, 1991.

Dahl recorded *Charlie and the Chocolate Factory,* Caedmon, 1975, *James and the Giant Peach,* Caedmon, 1977, *Fantastic Mr. Fox,* Caedmon, 1978, and *Roald Dahl Reads His "The Enormous Crocodile" and "The Magic Finger,"* Caedmon, 1980, as well as an interview, *Bedtime Stories to Children's Books,* Center for Cassette Studies, 1973. Contributor to anthologies and periodicals, including *Harper's, New Yorker, Playboy, Collier's, Town and Country, Atlantic, Esquire,* and *Saturday Evening Post.*

MEDIA ADAPTATIONS: 36 Hours (motion picture; adaptation of Dahl's short story "Beware of the Dog"), Metro-Goldwyn-Mayer, 1964. *Delicious Inventions* (motion picture; excerpted from film *Willie Wonka and the Chocolate Factory,* Paramount, 1971), Films, Inc., 1976. *The Witches,* screenplay by Allan Scott, Lorimar, 1990. *James and the Giant Peach* (animated motion picture; adapted from Dahl's novel of the same name), screenplay by Karey Kirkpatrick, Jonathan Roberts, and Steve Bloom, Walt Disney, 1996. *Matilda,* 1996, starring Mara Wilson and Danny DeVito. *Tales of the Unexpected,* WNEW-TV, 1979. *Roald Dahl's Charlie and the Chocolate Factory: A Play,* adapted by Richard George, introduction by Dahl, Knopf, 1976. *Roald Dahl's James and the Giant Peach: A Play,* adapted by Richard George, introduction by Dahl, Penguin, 1982.

SIDELIGHTS: Roald Dahl, best known as the author of children's books *Charlie and the Chocolate Factory* and *James and the Giant Peach,* was also noted for his short stories for adults, and his enchanting autobiographical descriptions of growing up in England and flying in World War II. His children's fiction is known for its sudden turns into the fantastic, its wheeling, fast-moving prose, and its decidedly harsh treatment of any adults foolish enough to cause trouble for the young heroes and heroines. Similarly, his adult fiction often relies on a sudden twist that throws light on what has been happening in the story, a trait most evident in *Tales of the Unexpected,* which was made into a television series.

Dahl was born on September 13, 1916, the son of an adventurous shipbroker. He was an energetic and mischievous child and from an early age proved adept at finding trouble. His very earliest memory was of pedaling to school at breakneck speed on his tricycle, his two sisters struggling to keep up as he whizzed around curves on two wheels. In *Boy: Tales of Childhood,* Dahl recounted many of these happy memories from his childhood, remembering most fondly the trips that the entire family took to Norway, which he always considered home.

In 1939, Dahl's adventures took on a more dangerous cast as he joined the Royal Air Force training squadron in Nairobi, Kenya. World War II was just beginning, and Dahl would soon make his mark as a fighter pilot combating the Germans all around the Mediterranean Sea. While strafing a convoy of trucks near Alexandria, Egypt, his plane was hit by machine-gun fire. The plane crashed to the ground and Dahl crawled from the wreckage as the gas tanks exploded. The crash left his skull fractured, his nose crumpled, and his eyes temporarily stuck shut. After six months of recovery he returned to his squadron in Greece and shot down four enemy planes, but frequent blackouts as a result of his earlier injuries eventually rendered him unable to fly.

Dahl was soon transferred to Washington, DC, to serve as an assistant air attache. One day C. S. Forester interviewed Dahl over lunch for an article he was writing for the *Saturday Evening Post,* but was too engrossed in eating to take notes himself. The notes that Dahl took for him turned out to be a story, which Forester sent to the magazine under Dahl's name. The magazine paid Dahl one thousand dollars for the story, which was titled *"Piece of Cake"* and later published in *Over to You: Ten Stories of Fliers and Flying.* Soon his stories appeared in *Collier's, Harper's, Ladies' Home Journal, Tomorrow* and *Town and Country.* Dahl indicated in a *New York Times Book Review* profile by Willa Petschek that "as I went on, the stories became less and less realistic and more fantastic. But becoming a writer was pure fluke. Without being asked to, I doubt if I'd ever have thought of it."

Dahl went on to publish numerous short story collections during the next several decades, some of which—notably 1953's *Someone Like You* and 1959's *Kiss, Kiss*—sold widely in the United States and earned Dahl a measure of fame. After 1960 Dahl's primary focus became children's fiction, although he did produce a short story collection, *Switch Bitch,* in 1974 as well as a novel, *My Uncle Oswald,* in 1979. Both of the latter works are marked by themes of sexual sadism and obsession; both were controversial and received criticism from reviewers for the sexual violence they portrayed. *Dictionary of Literary Biography* contributor John L. Grigsby summarized Dahl's achievements as a short fiction writer: "In his best stories Dahl presents skillfully composed plots that convey powerful insights into the frequently negative depths of the human psyche. . . . In his less effective works, however, Dahl's outsider status results in a kind of cynical condescension toward and manipulation of the reader in surprise-of-plot stories that stereotype characters outside his self-focused realm of psychological experience."

In 1943, Dahl wrote his first children's story, and coined a term, with *The Gremlins.* Gremlins were tiny saboteurs who lived on fighter planes and bombers and were responsible for all crashes. Mrs. Roosevelt, the president's wife, read the book to her children and liked it so much that she invited Dahl to dinner, and he and the president soon became friends. Through the 1940s and into the 1950s Dahl continued as a short story writer for adults, establishing his reputation as a writer of macabre tales with an unexpected twist. A *Books and Bookmen* reviewer called Dahl "a master of horror—an intellectual Hitchcock of the writing world." J. D. O'Hara, writing in *New Republic,* labeled him "our Supreme Master of Wickedness," and his stories earned him three Edgar Allan Poe Awards from the Mystery Writers of America.

In 1953 he married Hollywood actress Patricia Neal, star of such movies as *The Fountainhead* and, later, *Hud,* for which she won an Academy Award. Dahl recalled in *Pat and Roald* that "she wasn't at all movie-starish; no great closets filled with clothes or anything like that. She had a drive to be a great actress, but it was never as strong as it is with some of these nuts. You could turn it aside." Although the marriage did not survive, it produced five children. As soon as the children were old enough, he began making up stories for them each night before they went to bed. These stories became the basis for his career as a children's writer, which began in earnest with the publication of *James and the Giant Peach* in 1961. Dahl insisted that having to invent stories night after night was perfect practice for his trade, telling the *New York Times Book Review:* "Children are a great discipline because they are highly critical. And they lose interest so quickly. You have to keep things ticking along. And if you think a child is getting bored, you must think up something that jolts it back. Something that tickles. You have to know what children like." Sales of Dahl's books certainly attest to his skill: *Charlie and the Chocolate Factory* and *Charlie and the Great Glass Elevator* have

sold over one million hardcover copies in America, and *James and the Giant Peach* more than 350,000 copies.

James and the Giant Peach recounts the fantastic tale of a young boy who travels thousands of miles in a house-sized peach with as bizarre an assemblage of companions as can be found in a children's book. After the giant peach crushes his aunts, James crawls into the peach through a worm hole, making friends with a centipede, a silkworm, a spider, a ladybug, and a flock of seagulls that lifts the peach into the air and carries it across the ocean to Central Park. Gerald Haigh, writing in *Times Literary Supplement,* said that Dahl had the ability to "home unerringly in on the very nub of childish delight, with brazen and glorious disregard for what is likely to furrow the adult brow."

One way that Dahl delighted his readers was to exact often vicious revenge on cruel adults who harmed children. In *Matilda,* the Amazonian headmistress Miss Turnbull, who deals with unruly children by grabbing them by the hair and tossing them out windows, is finally banished by the brilliant, triumphant Matilda. *The Witches,* released as a movie in 1990, finds the heroic young character, who has been turned into a mouse, thwarting the hideous and diabolical witches who are planning to kill all the children of England. But even innocent adults receive rough treatment: parents are killed in car crashes in *The Witches,* and eaten by a rhinoceros in *James and the Giant Peach*; aunts are flattened by a giant peach in *James and the Giant Peach*; and pleasant fathers are murdered in *Matilda.* Many critics have objected to the rough treatment of adults. Eleanor Cameron, for example, in *Children's Literature in Education,* found that "Dahl caters to the streak of sadism in children which they don't even realize is there because they are not fully self-aware and are not experienced enough to understand what sadism is." And in *Now Upon a Time: A Contemporary View of Children's Literature,* Myra Pollack Sadker and David Miller Sadker criticized *Charlie and the Chocolate Factory* for its "ageism": "The message with which we close the book is that the needs and desires and opinions of old people are totally irrelevant and inconsequential."

In *Trust Your Children: Voices Against Censorship in Children's Literature,* Dahl contended that adults may be disturbed by his books "because they are not quite as aware as I am that children are different from adults. Children are much more vulgar than grownups. They have a coarser sense of humor. They are basically more cruel." Dahl often commented that the key to his success with children was that he conspired with them against adults. Vicki Weissman, in her review of *Matilda* in the *New York Times Book Review,* agreed that Dahl's books are aimed to please children rather than adults in a number of ways. She thought that "the truths of death and torture are as distant as when the magician saws the lady in half," and delighted that "anarchic and patently impossible plots romp along with no regard at all for the even faintly likely."

BIOGRAPHICAL/CRITICAL SOURCES:

BOOKS

Children's Literature Review, Gale (Detroit), Volume 1, 1976; Volume 7, 1984.
Contemporary Literary Criticism, Gale, Volume 1, 1973; Volume 6, 1976; Volume 18, 1981; Volume 79, 1993.
Dictionary of Literary Biography, Volume 139: *British Short-Fiction Writers, 1945-1980,* Gale, 1994.
Farrell, Barry, *Pat and Roald,* Random House, 1969.

McCann, Donnarae, and Gloria Woodard, editors, *The Black American in Books for Children: Readings in Racism,* Scarecrow, 1972.

Powling, Chris, *Roald Dahl,* Hamish Hamilton, 1983.

Sadker, Myra Pollack, and David Miller Sadker, *Now Upon a Time: A Contemporary View of Children's Literature,* Harper, 1977.

Treglown, Jeremy, *Roald Dahl: A Biography,* Farrar, Straus (New York City), 1994.

Twentieth-Century Children's Writers, 3rd edition, St. James Press, 1989, pp. 255-56.

Warren, Alan with Dale Salwak and Daryl F. Mallett, *Roald Dahl: From the Gremlins to the Chocolate Factory,* second edition, Borgo Press (San Bernadino, CA), 1994.

West, Mark I., interview with Roald Dahl in *Trust Your Children: Voices Against Censorship in Children's Literature,* Neal-Schuman, 1988, pp. 71-76.

Wintle, Justin, and Emma Fisher, *Pied Pipers: Interviews with the Influential Creators of Children's Literature,* Paddington Press, 1975.

PERIODICALS

Chicago Sunday Tribune, February 15, 1960; November 12, 1961.
Chicago Tribune, October 21, 1986.
Chicago Tribune Book World, August 10, 1980; May 17, 1981.
Christian Science Monitor, November 16, 1961.
Commonweal, November 15, 1961.
Entertainment Weekly, January 24, 1994, p. 57.
Horn Book, October, 1972; December, 1972; February, 1973; April, 1973; June, 1973; January/February 1989, p. 68; January/February 1992, p. 64.
Kenyon Review, Volume 31, number 2, 1969.
Library Journal, November 15, 1961.
Life, August 18, 1972.
New Republic, October 19, 1974, p. 23; April 19, 1980.
New Statesman, October 29, 1960; March 5, 1971; November 4, 1977.
New Statesman & Society, November 24, 1989, p. 34.
New York, December 12, 1988.
New Yorker, December 12, 1988, p. 157; November 25, 1991, p. 146.
New York Herald Tribune Book Review, November 8, 1953; February 7, 1960.
New York Review of Books, December 17, 1970; December 14, 1972.
New York Times, November 8, 1953; April 29, 1980.
New York Times Book Review, February 7, 1960; November 12, 1961; October 25, 1964; November 8, 1970; September 17, 1972; October 27, 1974; October 26, 1975; December 25, 1977, pp. 6, 15; September 30, 1979; April 20, 1980; March 29, 1981; January 9, 1983; January 20, 1985; October 12, 1986; January 15, 1989, p. 31; October 27, 1991, p. 27; May 1, 1994, p. 28.
Observer, September 8, 1991.
People, November 3, 1986; May 9, 1988.
Publishers Weekly, June 6, 1980; December 20, 1991, p. 82; January 24, 1994, p. 57; October 10, 1994, p. 69.
Punch, November 29, 1967; December 6, 1978.
Quill & Quire, November, 1991, p. 25.
School Library Journal, November, 1991, p. 92; May, 1992, p. 112; March, 1993, p. 155; April, 1994, p. 136; March, 1995, p. 210.
Sewanee Review, winter, 1975.
Spectator, December, 1977; December 11, 1993, p. 45.

Times (London), December 22, 1983; April 21, 1990.
Times Educational Supplement, November 19, 1982, p. 35.
Times Literary Supplement, October 28, 1960; December 14, 1967; June 15, 1973; November 15, 1974; November 23, 1979; November 21, 1980; July 24, 1981; July 23, 1982; November 30, 1984; September 12, 1986; May 6, 1988; July 12, 1991, p. 21; October 4, 1991, p. 28; November 22, 1991, p. 23.
Vanity Fair, January, 1994, p. 26.
Washington Post, October 8, 1986.
Washington Post Book World, November 13, 1977; April 20, 1980; May 8, 1983; January 13, 1985.
Wilson Library Bulletin, February, 1962; February, 1989; June, 1995, p. 125.

*　　*　　*

DALE, George E.
See ASIMOV, Isaac

*　　*　　*

DANOIS, N. le
See GOURMONT, Remy(-Marie-Charles) de

*　　*　　*

D'ANTIBES, Germain
See SIMENON, Georges (Jacques Christian)

*　　*　　*

DANTICAT, Edwidge 1969-

PERSONAL: Name pronounced "Ed-*weedj* Dan-ti-*cah*"; born January 19, 1969, in Port-au-Prince, Haiti; immigrated to the United States, 1981; daughter of Andre (a cab driver) and Rose (a textile worker; maiden name, Napoleon) Danticat. *Education:* Barnard College, 1990; Brown University, M.F.A., 1993.

ADDRESSES: Office—c/o Soho Press, 853 Broadway, No. 1903, New York, NY 10003.

CAREER: Writer, 1994–.

MEMBER: Alpha Kappa Alpha Sorority.

AWARDS, HONORS: Krik? Krak! was a finalist for the 1995 National Book Award; Danticat was also named one of *Granta's* "Best of American Novelists" in 1996.

WRITINGS:

FICTION

Breath, Eyes, Memory (novel), Soho Press (New York, NY), 1994.
Krik? Krak! (short stories), Soho Press, 1995.
The Farming of Bones (novel), Soho Press, 1998.

SIDELIGHTS: Fiction writer Edwidge Danticat was born in Haiti and lived there the first twelve years of her life. Then, in 1981, she came to the United States, joining her parents who had already begun to build a life for themselves in New York City. When she started attending junior high classes in Brooklyn, she had difficulty fitting in with her classmates because of her Haitian accent, clothing, and hairstyle. Danticat recalled for Garry Pierre-Pierre in the *New York Times* that she took refuge from the isolation she felt in writing about her native land. As an adolescent she began work on what would evolve into her first novel, 1994's highly acclaimed *Breath, Eyes, Memory*. Danticat followed her debut with a 1995 collection of short stories, *Krik? Krak!*—a volume which became a finalist for that year's National Book Award. According to Pierre-Pierre, the young author has been heralded as "'the voice' of Haitian-Americans," but Danticat told him: "I think I have been assigned that role, but I don't really see myself as the voice for the Haitian-American experience. There are many. I'm just one."

Danticat's parents wished for her to pursue a career in medicine, and with the goal of becoming a nurse, she attended a specialized high school in New York City. But she abandoned this aim to devote herself to her writing. An earlier version of *Breath, Eyes, Memory* served as her master of fine arts thesis at Brown University, and the finished version was published shortly thereafter. Like Danticat herself, Sophie Caco—the novel's protagonist—spent her first twelve years in Haiti, several of them in the care of an aunt, before coming wide-eyed to the United States. But there the similarities end. Sophie is the child of a single mother, conceived by rape. Though she rejoins her mother in the United States, it is too late to save the still-traumatized older woman from self-destruction. Yet women's ties to women are celebrated in the novel, and Sophie draws strength from her mother, her aunt, and herself in order to escape her mother's fate.

Breath, Eyes, Memory has caused some controversy in the Haitian-American community. Some of Danticat's fellow Haitians did not approve of her writing of the practice of "testing" in the novel. Female virginity is highly prized in Haitian culture, and Sophie's aunt "tests" to see whether Sophie's hymen is intact by inserting her fingers into the girl's vagina. Haitian-American women have for the most part abandoned this practice and many felt that Danticat's inclusion of it portrayed them as primitive and abusive. Critics, however, have widely lauded *Breath, Eyes, Memory*. Joan Philpott in *Ms.* hailed the book as "intensely lyrical." Danticat's writing has been favorably compared with that of African-American author Alice Walker, whose works include *The Color Purple,* and Pierre-Pierre reported that reviewers "have praised Ms. Danticat's vivid sense of place and her images of fear and pain." Jim Gladstone concluded in the *New York Times Book Review* that the novel "achieves an emotional complexity that lifts it out of the realm of the potboiler and into that of poetry."

Krik? Krak! takes its title from the practice of Haitian storytellers. Danticat told Deborah Gregory for *Essence* magazine that storytelling is a favorite entertainment in Haiti, and a storyteller inquires of his or her audience, "Krik?" to ask if they are ready to listen; the group then replies with an enthusiastic, "Krak!" The tales in this collection include one about a man attempting to flee Haiti in a leaky boat; another about a prostitute who tells her son that the reason she dresses up every night is that she is expecting an angel to descend upon their house; yet another explores the feelings of a childless housekeeper in a loveless marriage who finds an abandoned baby in the streets. Robert Houston, citing the fact that some of the stories in *Krik? Krak!* were written while Danticat was still an undergraduate at Barnard College, felt that these pieces were "out of place in a collection presumed to represent polished, mature work." Jordana Hart, opining in *Ms.,* declared that "the nine tales" of *Krik? Krak!* "are textured and deeply personal, as if the 26-year-old Haitian American author

had spilled her own tears over each." Even Houston conceded that readers "weary of stories that deal only with the minutiae of 'relationships' will rejoice that they have found work that is about something, and something that matters."

BIOGRAPHICAL/CRITICAL SOURCES:

BOOKS

Contemporary Literary Criticism, Volume 94, Gale, 1996.
Short Stories for Students, Volume 1, Gale, 1997.

PERIODICALS

Emerge, April, 1995, p. 58.
Essence, April, 1995, p. 56.
Ms., March/April, 1994, pp. 77-78; March/April, 1995, p. 75.
New York Times, January 26, 1995, pp. C1, C8; October 23, 1995, p. B3.
New York Times Book Review, July 10, 1994, p. 24; April 23, 1995, p. 22.
Progressive, January, 1997, p. 39.
Publishers Weekly, January 24, 1994, pp. 39-40.
School Library Journal, May, 1995, p. 135.

*   *   *

DARIO, Ruben 1867-1916

PERSONAL: Name originally Felix Ruben Garcia y Sarmiento; born January 18, 1867, in Metapa, Nicaragua; died February 6, 1916, in Leon, Nicaragua; married Rafaela Contrera, 1890 (died, 1892); married Francisca Sanchez; children: two sons (one from each marriage). *Education:* Attended a Jesuit school.

CAREER: Writer and poet. Began work as a journalist for newspapers in Santiago and Valparaiso, Chile, and Buenos Aires, Argentina, c. 1881. Became correspondent for *La Nacion,* Buenos Aires, and other Latin American papers in Latin America; Paris, France; and Madrid, Spain. Founder, with Gilberto Freyre, of *Revista de America,* 1896. Also served in various diplomatic and representative posts for Colombia and Nicaragua.

WRITINGS:

Primeras notas (title means "First Notes"), Tipografia Nacional, 1888.
Azul (poetry and short prose; title means "Blue"), [Chile], 1888, reprinted, Espasa-Calpe (Madrid), 1984 (also see below).
Los raros (literary biography and critical essays; title means "The Rare Ones"), 1893, reprinted, Universidad Autonoma Metropolitana (Mexico), 1985 (also see below).
Prosas profanas (title means "Profane Prose"), 1896, reprinted, introduction and notes by Ignacio M. Zuleta, Castalia (Madrid), 1983 (also see below).
Castelar, B. R. Serra (Madrid), 1899.
Espana contemporanea (title means "Contemporary Spain"), Garnier (Paris), 1901, reprinted, Lumen, 1987 (also see below).
Cantos de vida y esperanza, Los cisnes, y otros poemas (title means "Songs of Life and Hope, The Swans, and Other Poems"), [Madrid], 1905, reprinted, Nacional (Mexico), 1957 (also see below).
El canto errante (poetry; title means "The Wandering Song"), M. Perez Villavicencio (Madrid), 1907, reprinted, Espasa-Calpe, 1965 (also see below).

El viaje a Nicaragua; e, Intermezzo tropical (travel writings), Biblioteca Ateneo (Madrid), 1909, reprinted, Ministerio de Cultura, 1982 (also see below).

Poema del otono y otros poemas (title means "Poem of Autumn and Other Poems"), Biblioteca Ateneo, 1910, Espasa-Calpe, 1973 (also see below).

Muy antiguo y muy moderno (poetry; title means "Very Old and Very Modern"), Biblioteca Corona (Madrid), 1915.

El mundo de los suenos: Prosas postumas (title means "The World of Dreams: Posthumous Prose"), Libreria de la Viuda de Pueyo (Madrid), 1917.

Sol del domingo (title means "Sunday Sun"), Sucesores de Hernando (Madrid), 1917.

Alfonso XIII y sus primeras notas (addresses, essays, lectures and biographical text; title means "Alfonso the Thirteenth and His Principal Notes"), R. Dario Sanchez (Madrid), 1921.

Baladas y canciones (title means "Ballads and Songs"), prologue by Andres Gonzalez-Blanco, Biblioteca Ruben Dario Hijo (Madrid), 1923.

Sonetos (title means "Sonnets"), Biblioteca Ruben Dario (Madrid), 1929.

En busca del alba (poetry; title means "In Search of Dawn"), Aristides Quillet (Buenos Aires), 1941.

Brumas y luces (poetry; title means "Fogs and Lights"), Ediciones Argentinas S.I.A., 1943.

Wakonda: Poemas, Guillermo Kraft (Buenos Aires), 1944.

El ruisenor azul: Poemas ineditos y poemas olvidados (title means "The Blue Nightingale: Unpublished and Forgotten Poems"), prologue by Alberto Ghiraldo, Talleres Graficos Casa Nacional del Nino, c. 1945.

Quince poesias (title means "Fifteen Poems"), illustrated by Mallol Suazo, Argos (Barcelona), 1946.

Cerebros y corazones (biographical sketches; title means "Minds and Hearts"), Nova (Buenos Aires), 1948.

La amargura de la Patagonia (novella; title means "The Grief of Patagonia"), Nova (Buenos Aires), 1950.

El manto de nangasasu (novella; title means "The Cloak of Nangasasu"), S.A.C.D.I.C., 1958.

El sapo de oro (novella; title means "The Golden Toad"), G. Kraft (Buenos Aires), 1962.

Also author of *Epistolas y poemas* (title means "Epistles and Poems"), 1885; *Abrojos* (poetry; title means "Thorns"), 1887; *Canto epico a las glorias de Chile* (poetry; title means "Epic Song to the Glories of Chile"), 1887; *Emelina* (novel), with Eduardo Poirier, 1887; *Las rosas andinas: Rimas y contra-rimas* (title means "Andean Roses: Rhymes and Counter-Rhymes"), with Ruben Rubi, 1888; *Rimas* (title means "Poems"), 1888; *Peregrinaciones* (travel writings; title means "Journeys"), 1901 (also see below); *Oda a Mitre* (poetry; title means "Ode to Mitre"), 1906 (also see below); *Canto a la Argentina y otros poemas* (title means "Song to Argentina and Other Poems"), c. 1910 (also see below); *Historia de mis libros* (title means "The Story of My Books"), 1912; *Caras y caretas* (title means "Faces and Masks"), 1912; *Vida de Ruben Dario, escrita por el mismo* (title means "The Life of Ruben Dario, Written By Himself"), 1916; *Edelmira* (fiction), edited by Francisco Contreras, c. 1926; and *El hombre de oro* (title means "The Golden Man"), Zig-Zag.

IN ENGLISH

Eleven Poems, introduction by Pedro Henriquez Urena, translation by Thomas Walsh and Salomon de la Selva, Putnam, 1916, revised edition published as *Eleven Poems of Ruben Dario: Bilingual Edition,* Gordon, 1977.

Selected Poems of Ruben Dario, introduction by Octavio Paz, translated by Lysander Kemp, University of Texas Press, 1965, reprinted, 1988.

COLLECTIONS

Obras completas (title means "Complete Works"), twenty-two volumes, edited by author's son, Ruben Dario Sanchez, illustrations by Enrique Ochoa, Mundo Latino (Madrid), Volume 1: *La caravana pasa* (poetry; title means "The Caravan Passes"), prologue by Ghiraldo, 1917; Volume 2: *Prosas profanas,* 1917; Volume 3: *Tierras solares* (travel writings; title means "Lands of the Sun"), 1917; Volume 4: *Azul,* 1917; Volume 5: *Parisiana,* 1917; Volume 6: *Los raros,* 1918; Volume 7: *Cantos de vida y esperanza, Los cisnes, y otros poemas,* 1920; Volume 8: *Letras* (addresses, essays, lectures), 1918; Volume 9: *Canto a la Argentina, Oda a Mitre, y otros poemas,* 1918; Volume 10: *Opiniones,* 1918; Volume 11: *Poema del otono y otros poemas,* 1918; Volume 12: *Peregrinaciones,* 1918; Volume 13: *Prosas politicas: Las republicas americanas* (title means "Political Prose: The American Republics"), 1918; Volume 14: *Cuentos y cronicas* (title means "Stories and Chronicles"), 1918; Volume 15: *Autobiografia,* 1918; Volume 16: *El canto errante,* 1918; Volume 17: *El viaje a Nicaragua, e historia de mis libros* (title means "The Trip to Nicaragua and the Story of My Books"), 1919; Volume 18: *Todo al vuelo* (title means "All On the Fly"), 1919; Volume 19: *Espana contemporanea,* 1919; Volume 20: *Prosa dispersa* (title means "Random Prose"), 1919; Volume 21: *Lira postuma* (title means "Posthumous Verse"), 1919; Volume 22: *Cabezas: Pensadores y artistas, politicos* (biographical essays; title means "Heads: Thinkers, Artists, Politicians"), 1919.

Obras poeticas completas (title means "Complete Poetic Works"), twenty-one volumes, edited by Ghiraldo and Gonzalez-Blanco, [Madrid], 1923-29, new edition edited by A. Mendez Plancarte, [Madrid], 1952.

Cuentos completos (title means "Complete Stories"), edited with notes by Ernesto Mejia Sanchez, preliminary study by Raimundo Lida, Fondo de Cultura Economica (Mexico), 1950.

Poesias completas (title means "Complete Poems"), two volumes, edited by Alfonso Mendez Plancarte, 1952, revised edition edited by Antonio Oliver Belmas, 1967.

Several volumes of Dario's *Obras completas* were reissued separately during the 1980s. Works collected in other volumes, including *Obra poetica* (title means "Poetic Works"), four volumes, 1914-1916; *Textos socio-politicos,* [Managua], 1980; *Poesias escogidas,* 1982; and *Cuentos fantasticos,* Alianza (Madrid), 1982.

SIDELIGHTS: Nicaraguan writer Ruben Dario ranks among the most esteemed and enduring figures in South American literature. A journalist, critic, poet and author of short stories, he is credited with both founding and leading the *modernista* literary movement, which ended a period of creative latency among Spanish-language writers. Dario is probably best remembered for his innovative poetry, noted for its blending of experimental rhymes and meters with elements of French and Italian culture, classical literature, and mythology.

A bright and inquisitive child, Dario displayed a propensity for poetry while he was still quite young. His aunt, who raised him after the separation of his parents, nurtured his literary aspirations, and his early interest in journalism led to his association with members of the European and South American intelligentsia. By the turn of the twentieth century, Dario had taken his place among the literary and cultural elite and, as a foreign correspondent and diplomat, had become a symbol of a new bohemianism in Latin America. Stephen Kinzer, writing in the *New York Times,* summarized the author's career as that of a "vagabond poet who . . . influence[d] Latin American and Spanish literature forever and dazzle[d] Europe as no provincial ever had."

Though generally dismissed by critics as an uninspired and predictable contribution to the romance genre, *Emelina*—one of Dario's earliest writings and his only novel—offers a glimpse at the artistry that the poet would perfect in his 1888 volume *Azul* ("Blue"), a work that revolutionized Spanish letters. The poetry and short prose in *Azul* marks a deliberate break with the conventions of Romanticism, a bold experimentation with line and metre construction, and an introduction to Dario's celebration of literature as an *alcazar interior* ("tower of ivory"), a dreamlike shelter dedicated to pure art. Another collection, *Prosas profanas* (*Profane Prose*), first published in 1896, is a masterful, melodic display of the poet's fascination with Symbolism. The 1905 volume *Cantos de vida y esperanza* (*Songs of Life and Hope*), however, reveals a change in Dario's orientation as an artist—a move away from the idealistic "ivory tower" toward the global concerns of political and humanistic unity and nationalism among Hispanics. In *Studies in Spanish-American Literature,* Isaac Goldberg asserted: "*Cantos de vida y esperanza* is the keystone of Dario's poetical arch. It most exemplifies the man that wrote it; it most reveals his dual nature, his inner sincerity, his complete psychology; it is the artist at maturity."

Dario remains largely unknown among English-speaking readers, mainly because of the difficulty in translating his poetry while preserving the unique rhythms and linguistic nuances that the works possess in their original form. However, two volumes of the author's poems are available in English, and several critics have noted that the universality of Dario's themes precludes the problem of accessibility. Commenting on Dario's widespread appeal, Goldberg rated the poet among "the consecrated few who belong to no nation because they belong to all." And S. Griswold Morley, writing in *Dial,* concluded: "What cannot be denied is that Dario, single-handed, initiated a movement in Spain that affects today nearly every branch of literary art; that he renovated the technique of both poetry and prose; that he made his own many diverse styles; and that his verse is often so inevitable as to touch the finality of art."

BIOGRAPHICAL/CRITICAL SOURCES:

BOOKS

Ellis, Keith, *Critical Approaches to Ruben Dario,* University of Toronto Press, 1974.
Fiore, Dolores Ackel, *Ruben Dario in Search of Inspiration: Greco-Roman Mythology in His Stories and Poetry,* Las Americas Publishing Co., 1963.
Fitzmaurice-Kelly, James, *Some Masters of Spanish Verse,* Oxford University Press, 1924.
Goldberg, Isaac, *Studies in Spanish-American Literature,* Brentano's, 1920.
Peers, E. Allison, *A Critical Anthology of Spanish Verse,* University of California Press, 1949.
Twentieth-Century Literary Criticism, Volume 4, Gale, 1981.
Watland, Charles D., *Poet-Errant: A Biography of Ruben Dario,* Philosophical Library, 1965.

PERIODICALS

Dial, June 14, 1917.
Hispania, March, 1919; May, 1966.
Latin American Literary Review, spring, 1973.
New York Times, January 18, 1987.
Poetry, July, 1916.

*   *   *

DARWISH, Mahmud 1942-

PERSONAL: Born 1942, in al-Birwa, Israel; the son of a farmer and landowner; married Rana Qabanni (marriage ended). *Education:* Attended primary and secondary schools in Israel, attended one year of college in Moscow, 1970.

ADDRESSES: Office: c/o Riad el-Rayyes Books, 56 Knightsbridge, London SW1X 7NJ, England.

CAREER: Edited the magazines *Shuun Filastiniyya* and *Al Jadid;* currently edits the magazine *Al-Karmal.*

AWARDS: Lotus prize, 1969; Mediterranean prize, 1980; Lenin Peace prize, 1983.

WRITINGS:

Asafir bila ajnihah (poetry; title means "Sparrows without Wings"), 1960.
Awraq al-zaytun (poetry; title means "Olive Branches"), 1965.
Ashiq min Filastin (poetry; title means "A Lover of Palestine"), 1966.
Akhir al-layl (poetry; title means "The End of Night"), Aka matba at al-Jalil (Akka), 1967.
Habibati tanhadu min nawmiha (poetry; title means "My Beloved Awakens"), Dar al-Awdah (Beirut), 1969.
Yawmiyat jurh Filastini, Dar al-Awdah (Beirut), 1969.
(With Abd al-Rahman Yaghi) *Maa Mahmud Darwish fi diwanih asafir bila ajnihah,* Amman Maktabat (Ammon), 1969
Al-asafir tamut fi al-Jalil (poetry; title means "Sparrows Die in Galilee"), Dar al-Adab (Beirut), 1970.
Kitabah ala daw bunduqiyah, Dar al-Awdah (Beirut), 1970.
A Letter from Exile, League of Arab States Mission (New Delhi), 1970(?).
Shay an al-watan (prose; title means "Something About Home"), Dar al-Awdah (Beirut), 1971.
Matar naim fi kharif baid, Matbaat wa-Awfasit al-Hakim (al-Nasirah), 1971.
Youmiat muwaten bala watan, 1971; published in English as *Poems from Palestine,* Committee for a Free Palestine (Eugene, OR), 198(?).
Uhibbuki aw la uhibuk (poetry; title means "Love You, Love You Not"), Manshurat Dar al-Awdah (Beirut), 1972.
The Palestinian Chalk Circle, Arab Women's Information Committee (Beirut), 1972(?).
Selected Poems, translated by Ian Wedde and Fawwaz Tuqan, Carcanet (Manchester), 1973.
Birun az usturah ha, Amir Kabir (Teheran), 1973.
Yawmiyyat al-huzn al-adi (diary; title means "Diaries of Ordinary Grief"), 1973.
Wada an ayyatuha al-harb, wadaan ayyuha al-salam (poetry; title means "Farewell War, Farewell Peace"), Munazzamat al-Tahrir al-Filastiniya (Beirut), 1974.
Muhawalah raqm sab ah (poetry; title means "The Seventh Attempt"), Dar al-Awdah (Beirut), 1974.

Splinters of Bone, edited and translated by B. M. Bennani, Greenfield Review Press (New York), 1974; bilingual edition published as *Ahmad al-Zatar,* translated by Rana Kabbani, al-ittihad al-Amm lil-Kuttab al-Suhufiyin al-Filastiniyin (Beirut), 1977(?).

Tilk suratoha wa-hadha intihar al-ashiq (poetry; title means "That Is Her Picture and This Is Her Lover's Suicide"), Markaz al-Abhath, Munazzamat al-Tahrir al-Filastiniyah (Beirut), 1975.

Aras (poetry; title means "Weddings"), Dar al-Awdah (Beirut), 1977.

Diwan Mahmud Darwish (poetry; title means "Collected Poems of Mahmud Darwish"), Dar al-Awdah (Beirut), 1977.

The Music of Human Flesh, edited and translated by Denys Johnson-Davis, Heinemann (London) and Three Continents (Washington), 1980.

(With al-Hadi Taymumi) *al-Nashat al-Sihyuni bi-Tunis bayna 1897 & 1948,* al-Taududiyah al-Ummaliyah (Safaqis), 1982.

Madih al-dhil al-ali, Dar al-Awdah (Beirut), 1983.

(With Adunis and Samih al-Qasim) *Victims of a Map: A Bilingual Anthology of Arabic Poetry,* translated by Abdullah al-Udhari, Al-Saqi (London), 1984.

Hisar li-mada ih al-bahr (poetry; title means "Ban on Panegyrics to the Sea"), Arabask (Akka, al-Aswar), 1984.

Ward aqal (poetry; title means "Lesser Roses"), 1986.

Sand and Other Poems, edited and translated by Rana Kabbani, KPI (London), 1986.

Hiya ughniyah, jhiya ughniyah (poetry; title means "It is a Song, It Is a Song"), Dar al-Kalimah lil-Nashr (Beirut), 1986.

Zakirah lil-nisyan (memoir; title means "A Memory of Oblivion"), al-Muassasah al-Arabiyyah lil-Dirasat wa-al-Nashr (Beirut), 1987.

Fi wasf halatine: Maqalat mukhtarah, 1975-1985, Dar al-kalimah lil-Nashr (Beirut), 1987

Masat al-Nirjis wa-malhat al-fiddah (poetry; title means "The Tragedy of Narcissus and the Comedy of Silver"), Riad el-Rayyes (London), 1989.

Ara ma urid (poetry; title means "I See What I Want"), 1990.

(With Samih al-Qasim) *al-Rasail,* Dar al-Awdah (Beirut), 1990.

Ihda ashar kawkaba (poetry; title means "Eleven Planets"), Dar al-Jadid (Beirut), 1992.

Ara ma urid, Dar al-Jadid (Beirut), 1993.

From Beirut, translated by Stephen Kessler, Pygmy Forest Press (Albion), 1993.

(In French) *Une memoire pour l'oubli: Le temps, Beyrouth, Le Lieu, Un jour d'aout 1982* (memoir), Acts Sud (Arles), 1994; published in English as *Memory for Forgetfulness: August, Beirut, 1982,* translated by Ibrahim Muhawi, University of California Press (Berkeley and Los Angeles), 1995.

Psalms for Palestine, translated by Ben Bennani, Lynne Rienner (Boulder), 1995.

SIDELIGHTS: Mahmud Darwish is widely considered preeminent among contemporary Arab poets, having achieved great popularity in the Arab world while impressing scholars with his formal experimentations and innovations in language usage. His work is politically charged; he has devoted his talent to the Palestinian cause from the beginning of his career, having grown up in Israeli-controlled Galilee and seen, at age six, the village of his birth destroyed by the Israelis and his once-wealthy father compelled to work in a quarry to support his large family.

A controversial poem written in school at age 14 marked the beginning of Darwish's vocation. This poem, read at the school's annual party, has been described by Sabry Hafez as "a heartfelt cry from an Arab child to his Jewish peer at school about the simple things denied to an Arab boy and allowed to his Jewish counterpart." For reading this poem, young Darwish was warned by the district military ruler that any further poems of this nature might lead to his father's losing his job at the quarry. Inspired by the power of the written word, Darwish continued writing poems, publishing his first collection, *Asafir bila ajnihah* in 1960, at age 19. By the end of the decade, he had published a half-dozen poetry collections; and after the appearance of each, Darwish was either jailed or placed under house arrest for long periods. In 1970 he published a final collection while living in Israel, *Al-asafir tamut fi al-Jalil,* and then quickly left Galilee to continue his education in Moscow, an education denied him in Israel. The following year, having finished a one-year course in Russia, he moved to Egypt and then to Beirut. He lived, wrote, and published in Beirut until the Israelis invaded Lebanon in 1982 in response to Palestinian morter attacks on northern Israeli settlements. Leaving Beirut, Darwish moved to Paris, where he edits *Al-Karmal* magazine and continues to write poetry.

Since leaving Israel in 1970, Darwish has published many volumes of poetry and several prose works. His poetic canon can be divided into two distinct sections: what might be called the formative poetry (1960-70) and the poetry of exile (1971-present). Darwish's poems written while living in Israel comprise the first phase. These contain spare poems, written in unornamented language, evoking pride in Palestinian culture and resistance to Israeli designs on that culture. It is didactic, political, and deals in tactile objects, combining traditional forms and subject matter with innovations, building organically upon older forms to recast old truths in new ways. The second phase reflects to a great extent a maturing and synthesizing of the realpolitik of Arab culture with the need to stir the imagination of people grown apathetic, weary, and cynical of bloodletting and betrayal within their own ranks. During the period between the early 1970s and the Israeli incursion into Lebanon, the Palestinians had seen the rise and fall of the Black September movement, internecine fighting within Palestinian political and military groups, and the seeming futility of the Middle-East peace process. Darwish's poetry of this period displays a recurrent sense of hoping against hope, and of his people undergoing a purgatorial process. His poetry of exile in Paris continues and accentuates this sense of angry lament and exhortation.

BIOGRAPHICAL/CRITICAL SOURCES:

BOOKS

Chevalier, Tracy, ed. *Contemporary World Writers,* second edition, St. James Press (Detroit), 1993.

Jayyusi, Salma Khadra, ed. *Anthology of Modern Palestinian Literature,* Columbia University Press (New York), 1995.

Who's Who in the Arab World, 1981-1982, sixth edition, Publitec Publications (Beirut), 1981.

*   *   *

DAVIES, (William) Robertson 1913-1995 (Samuel Marchbanks)

PERSONAL: Born August 28, 1913, in Thamesville, Ontario, Canada; died of a stroke December 2, 1995; son of William Rupert (a publisher) and Florence Sheppard (McKay) Davies; married Brenda Matthews, February 2, 1940; children: Miranda, Jennifer (Mrs. C. T. Surridge), Rosamund (Mrs. John Cunnington). *Education:* Attended Upper Canada College, Toronto, and

Queen's University at Kingston; Balliol College, Oxford, B.Litt., 1938.

CAREER: Old Vic Company, London, England, teacher and actor, 1938-40; *Saturday Night,* Toronto, Ontario, literary editor, 1940-42; *Examiner,* Peterborough, Ontario, editor and publisher, 1942-62; University of Toronto, Toronto, professor of English, 1960-81, master of Massey College, 1962-81, emeritus professor and master, 1981-95. Also worked as a newspaperman for the Kingston Whig Standard (Ontario). Senator, Stratford Shakespeare Festival, Stratford, Ontario.

MEMBER: Royal Society of Canada (fellow), Playwrights Union of Canada, Royal Society of Literature (fellow), American Academy and Institute of Arts and Letters (honorary member), Authors Guild, Authors League of America, Dramatists Guild, Writers' Union (Canada), PEN International.

AWARDS, HONORS: Louis Jouvet Prize for directing, Dominion Drama Festival, 1949; Stephen Leacock Medal for Humour, 1954, for *Leaven of Malice;* Lorne Pierce Medal, Royal Society of Canada, 1961; Companion of the Order of Canada, 1972; Governor General's Award for fiction, 1973, for *The Manticore;* LL.D., University of Alberta, 1957, Queen's University, 1962, University of Manitoba, 1972, University of Calgary, 1975, and University of Toronto, 1981; D.Litt., McMaster University, 1959, University of Windsor, 1971, York University, 1973, Mount Allison University, 1973, Memorial University of Newfoundland, 1974, University of Western Ontario, 1974, McGill University, 1974, Trent University, 1974, University of Lethbridge, 1981, University of Waterloo, 1981, University of British Columbia, 1983, University of Santa Clara, 1985, Trinity College, Dublin, 1990, University of Oxford, 1991, and University of Wales, 1995; LH.D., University of Rochester, 1983, Dowling College, NY, 1992, and Loyola University, Chicago, 1994; D.C.L., Bishop's University, 1967; D.Hum. Litt., University of Rochester, 1983; honorary fellow of Balliol College, Oxford, 1986, and Trinity College, University of Toronto, 1987; World Fantasy Convention Award for *High Spirits;* City of Toronto Book Award, 1986; Canadian Authors Association Literary Award for Fiction, 1986, for *What's Bred in the Bone; What's Bred in the Bone* was shortlisted for Booker Prize, 1986; Banff Centre School of Fine Arts National Award, 1986; Lifetime Achievement Award from Toronto Arts Awards, 1986; Gold Medal of Honor for Literature from National Arts Club (New York), 1987; Order of Ontario, 1988; Diplome d'honneur, Canada Confederation of the Arts, 1988, Molson Prize in Arts, Canadian Council, 1988, Neil Gunn international fellow, Scottish Arts Council, 1988, Honorary fellowship, Royal Conservatory of Music, Toronto.

WRITINGS:

THE "SALTERTON TRILOGY"; NOVELS

Tempest-Tost, Clarke, Irwin, 1951; Rinehart, 1952.
Leaven of Malice, Clarke, Irwin, 1954; Scribners, 1955.
A Mixture of Frailties, Scribners, 1958.
The Salterton Trilogy (contains *Tempest-Tost, Leaven of Malice,* and *A Mixture of Frailties*), Penguin, 1986.

THE "DEPTFORD TRILOGY"; NOVELS

Fifth Business, Viking, 1970.
The Manticore, Viking, 1972.
World of Wonders, Macmillan (Toronto), 1975; Viking, 1976.
The Deptford Trilogy (contains *Fifth Business, The Manticore,* and *World of Wonders*), Penguin, 1985.

THE "CORNISH TRILOGY"; NOVELS

The Rebel Angels, Viking, 1982.
What's Bred in the Bone, Viking, 1985.
The Lyre of Orpheus, Viking, 1988.

OTHER FICTION

High Spirits (stories), Viking, 1983.
Murther & Walking Spirits (novel), Viking, 1991.
The Cunning Man (novel), McClelland & Stewart, 1994.

NONFICTION

Shakespeare's Boy Actors, Dent, 1939, Russell, 1964.
Shakespeare for Young Players: A Junior Course, Clarke, Irwin, 1942.
The Diary of Samuel Marchbanks (collection of newspaper pieces originally published under pseudonym Samuel Marchbanks), Clarke, Irwin, 1947.
The Table Talk of Samuel Marchbanks (collection of newspaper pieces originally published under pseudonym Samuel Marchbanks), Clarke, Irwin, 1949.
(With Tyrone Guthrie and Grant Macdonald) *Renown at Stratford: A Record of the Shakespearean Festival in Canada,* Clarke, Irwin, 1953, new edition, 1971.
(With Guthrie and Macdonald) *Twice Have the Trumpets Sounded: A Record of the Stratford Shakespearean Festival in Canada,* Clarke, Irwin, 1954.
(With Guthrie, Boyd Neal, and Tanya Moiseiwitsch) *Thrice the Brinded Cat Hath Mew'd: A Record of the Stratford Shakespearean Festival in Canada,* Clarke, Irwin, 1955.
A Voice from the Attic, Knopf, 1960, published in England as *The Personal Art: Reading to Good Purpose,* Secker & Warburg, 1961.
Le Jeu de centenaire, Comission du Centenaire, c. 1967.
Samuel Marchbanks' Almanack (collection of newspaper pieces originally published under pseudonym Samuel Marchbanks), McClelland & Stewart, 1967.
The Heart of a Merry Christmas, Macmillan (Toronto), 1970.
Stephen Leacock, McClelland & Stewart, 1970.
(Editor and author of introduction) *Feast of Stephen: An Anthology of Some of the Less Familiar Writings of Stephen Leacock,* McClelland & Stewart, 1970.
(With Michael R. Booth, Richard Southern, Frederick Marker, and Lise-Lone Marker) *The Revels History of Drama in English, Volume VI: 1750-1880,* Methuen, 1975.
One Half of Robertson Davies: Provocative Pronouncements on a Wide Range of Topics, Macmillan (Toronto), 1977, published as *One Half of Robertson Davies,* Viking, 1978.
The Enthusiasms of Robertson Davies, edited by Judith Skelton Grant, McClelland & Stewart, 1979.
(Contributor) Robert G. Lawrence and Samuel L. Macey, editors, *Studies in Robertson Davies' Deptford Trilogy,* English Literary Studies, University of Victoria, 1980.
The Well-Tempered Critic: One Man's View of Theatre and Letters in Canada, edited by Grant, McClelland & Stewart, 1981.
The Mirror of Nature (lectures), University of Toronto Press, 1983.
The Papers of Samuel Marchbanks (contains portions of *The Diary of Samuel Marchbanks, The Table Talk of Samuel Marchbanks,* and *Samuel Marchbanks' Almanack*), Irwin Publishing, 1985, Viking, 1986.
The Merry Heart: Reflections on Reading, Writing, and the World of Books, Viking, 1997.

Happy Alchemy: On the Pleasures of Music and the Theatre, Viking, 1998.

PLAYS

Fortune, My Foe (first produced in Kingston, Ontario, by the International Players, 1948), Clarke, Irwin, 1949.

Eros at Breakfast and Other Plays (contains "Eros at Breakfast" [first produced in Montreal, Quebec, at the Montreal Repertory Theatre, 1948], "Overlaid" [first produced in Peterborough, Ontario, at Peterborough Little Theatre, 1947], "The Voice of the People" [first produced in Montreal at the Montreal Repertory Theatre, 1948], "At the Gates of the Righteous" [first produced in Peterborough at the Peterborough Little Theatre, 1948], and "Hope Deferred" [first produced in Montreal at the Montreal Repertory Theatre, 1948]), with introduction by Tyrone Guthrie, Clarke, Irwin, 1949, revised edition published as *Four Favorite Plays,* 1968.

At My Heart's Core (first produced in Peterborough at the Peterborough Little Theatre, 1950), Clarke, Irwin, 1952.

A Masque of Aesop (first produced in Toronto, Ontario, at Upper Canada College, May, 1952), Clarke, Irwin, 1952.

A Jig for the Gypsy (first produced in Toronto at the Crest Theatre, 1954), Clarke, Irwin, 1955.

Love and Libel (based on *Leaven of Malice;* first produced in Toronto at the Royal Alexandra Theatre, November, 1960; first produced on Broadway at the Martin Beck Theatre, December, 1960), Studio Duplicating Service, 1960.

A Masque of Mr. Punch (first produced in Toronto at Upper Canada College, 1962), Oxford University Press, 1963.

The Voice of the People, Book Society of Canada, 1968.

Hunting Stuart and Other Plays (contains "Hunting Stuart" [first produced in Toronto at the Crest Theatre, 1955], "King Phoenix" [first produced in Peterborough, 1950], and "General Confession"), New Press, 1972.

"Brothers in the Black Art," first produced on Canadian Broadcasting Corporation, 1974.

Question Time (first produced in Toronto at the St. Lawrence Center, 1975), Macmillan, 1975.

"Pontiac and the Green Man," first produced in Toronto at the Macmillan Theatre, 1977.

"Hunting Stuart" & "The Voice of the People": Two Plays, Simon & Pierre (Niagara Falls, NY), 1994.

OTHER

Columnist under pseudonym Samuel Marchbank.

SIDELIGHTS: The *Deptford Trilogy*—consisting of the novels *Fifth Business, The Manticore,* and *World of Wonders*—brought Robertson Davies to international attention as one of Canada's leading men of letters. "These novels," Claude Bissell writes in *Canadian Literature,* "comprise the major piece of prose fiction in Canadian literature—in scope, in the constant interplay of wit and intelligence, in the persistent attempt to find a pattern in this, [as Davies states in the trilogy,] 'life of marvels, cruel circumstances, obscenities, and commonplaces.'"

The trilogy traces the lives of three Canadian men from the small town of Deptford, Ontario, who are bound together by a single tragic event from their childhood. At the age of ten, Dunstan Ramsay and Percy "Boy" Staunton are throwing snowballs at one another. Staunton throws a snowball at Ramsay which contains a rock. Ramsay ducks. The snowball strikes Mrs. Mary Dempster in the head, causing her to give birth prematurely to a son, Paul Dempster, and to have a mental breakdown that ends in her permanent hospitalization. Each novel of the trilogy revolves around this tragedy and deals primarily with one of the three men involved: *Fifth Business* with Dunstan Ramsay, who becomes a teacher; *The Manticore* with Boy Staunton, a politician; and *World of Wonders* with Paul Dempster, a stage magician. "*Fifth Business* provides the brickwork," John Alwyne writes in the *New Statesman,* "the two later volumes, the lath and plaster. But what a magnificent building is the result. [The trilogy] bears comparison with any fiction of the last decade."

The trilogy garnered extensive critical praise and each volume has been an international bestseller. The first volume, *Fifth Business,* is, Sam Solecki maintains in *Canadian Forum,* "Davies' masterpiece and . . . among the handful of Canadian novels that count." In the form of an autobiographical letter written by Dunstan Ramsay upon his retirement, the novel delineates the course of Ramsay's life and how it was shaped by the pivotal snowball incident. Because he avoided being hit, and thereby caused Mrs. Dempster's injury, Ramsay has lived his life suffering under a tremendous guilt. This guilt inspired an interest in hagiology, the study of saints, and Ramsay becomes in later years the foremost Protestant authority on the lives of the saints. "All the lore on saints and myth," Judith Skelton Grant states in *Book Forum,* "is firmly connected to the central character, reflecting his interests, showing how he thinks, influencing his life, and playing a part in his interpretation of events." It is in terms of hagiology that Ramsay eventually comes to a realization about himself. His autobiographical letter finally "leads Ramsay to comprehension of his own nature—which is not saintly," John Skow reports in *Time.*

Much of this same story is reexamined in *The Manticore,* the second novel of the trilogy, which takes place after the mysterious death of prominent Canadian politician Boy Staunton. Staunton has been found drowned in his car at the bottom of Lake Ontario, a rock in his mouth. Investigation proves the rock to be the same one that Staunton threw at Mrs. Dempster some sixty years before. Ramsay, obsessed with the incident, had saved it. But how Staunton died, and why he had the rock in his mouth, is unknown. During a performance by the magician Magnus Eisengrim (Paul Dempster's stage name), a floating brass head is featured that answers questions from the audience. Staunton's son David asks the head an explosive question, "Who killed Boy Staunton?" In the tumult caused by his outburst, David runs from the theater. His breakdown and subsequent Jungian psychoanalysis in Switzerland make up the rest of the novel. During his analysis, David comes to terms with his late father's career. "The blend of masterly characterization, cunning plot, shifting point of view, and uncommon detail, all fixed in the clearest, most literate prose, is superbly achieved," writes Pat Barclay in *Canadian Literature.*

The life story of Paul Dempster is told in *World of Wonders,* the final volume of the trilogy. As a young boy, Dempster is kidnaped by a homosexual stage magician while visiting a traveling carnival. Dempster stays with the carnival as it makes its way across Canada, intent on becoming a magician himself by learning the secrets of the man who abducted him. While learning the trade, Dempster works inside a mechanical fortune-telling gypsy, operating the gears that make it seem lifelike. When the carnival breaks up, Dempster heads for Europe where he finds work as a double for a popular stage actor. With his knowledge of magic and the stage manner he has acquired from the theater people he knows, Dempster strikes out on his own as a magician, becoming one of the most successful acts on the continent. *World of Wonders,* Michael Mewshaw states in the *New York Times Book Review,* is "a novel of stunning verbal energy and intelligence." L.

J. Davis of *New Republic* believes the novel's "situation is shamelessly contrived, and the language fairly reeks of the footlights (to say nothing of, yes, brimstone)." Furthermore, Davis contends that *World of Wonders* "isn't so much a novel as it is a brilliant act whose strength lies in the complexity of its symbolism and the perfection of its artifice." It is, Davis judges, "a splendid conclusion" to the trilogy.

Davies's 1994 novel *The Cunning Man* "is as substantial and as entertaining as any he has written," claims Isabel Colegate in the *New York Times Book Review*. According to Paul Gray in *Time*, "Canada's foremost living author . . . entertains with an old-fashioned fictional mixture that he seems to have invented anew: keen social observations delivered with wit, intelligence and free-floating philosophical curiosity." John Bemrose contends in *Maclean's* that "*The Cunning Man* takes the form of a memoir, but it reads more like an extended monologue by its narrator, Dr. Jonathan Hullah, a Toronto doctor nearing the end of his career." An aging physician who has assented to a series of interviews with a reporter writing a number of articles about "old Toronto," Hullah employs a notebook to separate his public reminiscences from his private reflections—those snippets of information and fact he agrees to reveal in print and those, some of which pertain to incidents in his own background, he prefers to reserve exclusively to himself. As the notebook containing his personal thoughts and musings grows, he realizes he is actually recording and defining his own character analysis, a true lifetime retrospective. Although as a physician Hullah relies on scientific observation and qualitative inquiry, he combines his diagnostic approach with consideration of other factors, including psychological and spiritual elements. In an interview with Mel Gussow in the *New York Times Book Review*, the reviewer notes, "Mr. Davies has said he is 'a moralist possessed by humor,' a description that would serve equally for Dr. Hullah, who, he says, 'is a moralist not because he dictates morals but because he observes what's wrong with his patients.' For both the author and the character, physical and emotional causes of disease are inseparable." As Stephen Smith describes in *Quill and Quire*: "Hullah makes his narration a guide through a landscape full of recognizable Davies landmarks. There is a suspicious death on a church altar, a miracle, a murder, a disappointment in love, and sundry asides into theatre, music, art and into the past of that most 'flat-footed, hard-breathing' of Canadian cities, Toronto, as seen from its upper crust."

The recurring theme of self-discovery follows the pattern established by psychologist Carl Jung, although Davies did not adhere strictly to Jungian psychology. He explored a number of models for "complete human identity," Patricia Monk writes in her *The Smaller Infinity: The Jungian Self in the Novels of Robertson Davies,* and though he has a "deep and long-lasting affinity with Jung, . . . Davies eventually moves beyond his affinity . . . to a more impartial assessment of Jungianism as simply one way of looking at the universe, one myth among a number of others." Still, in common with the Jungian belief in archetypal influence on the human mind, Davies presents in his fiction characters who "discover the meaning of their lives," Roger Sale writes in the *New York Review of Books,* "by discovering the ways those lives conform to ancient patterns." Peter Baltensperger, writing in *Canadian Literature,* sees this as a consistent theme in all of Davies's fiction, not only in the *Deptford Trilogy.* This theme Baltensperger defines as "the conquest of one's Self in the inner struggle and the knowledge of oneself as fully human."

Davies clarified the primary concern in all of his work. "The theme which lies at the root of all my novels is the isolation of the human spirit," he explained. "I have not attempted to deal with it in a gloomy fashion but rather to demonstrate that what my characters do that might be called really significant is done on their own volition and usually contrary to what is expected of them. This theme is worked out in terms of characters who are trying to escape from early influences and find their own place in the world but who are reluctant to do so in a way that will bring pain and disappointment to others."

Since he wrote a number of plays, had been a teacher and actor with the Old Vic Company, and served on the board of the Stratford Shakespeare Festival for many years, it is not surprising to find that Davies employed theatrical elements in his novels. He used theatricality to move his story along at a quicker pace. In *World of Wonders,* a *Time* critic states, the characters "are brilliant talkers, but when they natter on too long, the highly theatrical author causes a grotesque face to appear at a window, drops someone through a trap door or stages a preposterous recognition scene." These melodramatic touches came naturally to Davies who, Davis remarks, "is a player in love with the play, and the kind of play he loves is melodrama." In his collection of lectures entitled *The Mirror of Nature,* Davies made his case on behalf of melodrama and attempts, as Alberto Manguel writes in the Toronto *Globe & Mail,* "to save melodrama's lost honor." Davies argued in this book that "theatre is a coarse art. . . . It appeals immediately to primary, not secondary elements in human nature." Melodrama's emphasis on creating an emotional response in its audience, Davies continued, is true to theatre's fundamental purpose. Manguel concludes that Davies "succeeds" in justifying his own use of melodrama.

Davies' experience as an actor also gave him a certain mystique. Michael Peterman in *Books in Canada* writes of Davies: "He had in public and private the air of a performer about him; he dressed for the daily performance, he modulated his speech and his phrases for each occasion . . . and he had the bearings of someone who knew the script." In a 1994 interview with Michael Coren of *Saturday Night,* Davies acknowledged this. "'There is something funny about me,' he whispers, 'I create myths.' And then he turns in semi-profile and as his head sweeps round I swear that there is a twinkle in his eye. And he knows I can see it. . . . Robertson Davies has conjured up a magic, puckish effect and instantly reversed the balance between interviewer and interviewee." A biography of Davies by Judy Skelton Grant attempted to dispel this myth but Davies was "gently dismissive" of it: "'She hasn't got me. Or so I've heard. Haven't read it, you know; my secretary has though.'"

Calling Davies "a compellingly inventive storyteller" who garnered an "affectionate following," James Idema of the *Chicago Tribune Book World* explains the appeal of his fiction. It lies in "his way of placing ordinary humans in the midst of extraordinary events, of bringing innocent, resolutely straight characters into contact with bonafide exotics," Idema believes. "The 'real world' interests [Davies] only as a starting point. Enigma, myth, illusion and magic are the stuff of his elegant stories." Similarly, William Kennedy observes in the *New York Times Book Review* that Davies "conveys a sense of real life lived in a fully imagined if sometimes mythical and magical world." Comparing the role of the novelist with that of the magician, because both "mean us to believe in what never happened and to this end use many conjuror's tricks," Prescott defines Davies as one writer "who takes seriously his magician's role." In doing so, Davies became "one of the most gifted and accomplished literary entertainers now writing in English," as a writer for *Time* remarks. In a speech given at the University of Windsor and quoted by *Time* (Canada), Davies observed that "though it is always an unwise thing to say too loudly—because you never know who may be listening—I am a happy man."

BIOGRAPHICAL/CRITICAL SOURCES:

BOOKS

Buitenhuis, Elspeth, *Robertson Davies*, Forum House Publishing, 1972.
Contemporary Dramatists, 4th edition, St. James, 1988.
Contemporary Literary Criticism, Gale, Volume 2, 1974; Volume 7, 1977; Volume 13, 1980; Volume 25, 1983; Volume 42, 1987; Volume 75, 1993.
Contemporary Novelists, 5th edition, St. James, 1991.
Davis, J. Madison, editor, *Conversations with Robertson Davies*, University Press of Mississippi, 1989.
Dictionary of Literary Biography, Volume 68: *Canadian Writers, 1920-1959, First Series*, Gale, 1988.
Grant, Judith Skelton, *Robertson Davies*, McClelland & Stewart, 1978.
Grant, *Robertson Davies: Man of Myth*, Penguin, 1994.
Heath, Jeffrey M., editor, *Profiles in Canadian Literature #2*, Dundurn Press, 1980.
King, Bruce, *The New English Literatures: Cultural Nationalism in a Changing World*, St. Martin's Press, 1980.
Kirkwood, Hilda, *Between the Lines*, Oberon Press (Ottawa), 1994.
Klinck, Carl F., editor, *Literary History of Canada*, University of Toronto Press, 2nd edition, 1976.
Lawrence, Robert G. and Samuel L. Macey, editors, *Studies in Robertson Davies' Deptford Trilogy*, English Literary Studies, University of Victoria, 1980.
Lecker, Robert, and Jack David, editors, *The Annotated Bibliography of Canada's Major Authors*, Vol. 3, ECW Press, 1982.
Lecker, David, and Ellen Luigley, editors, *Canadian Writers and Their Works*, Vol. 6, ECW Press, 1985.
Little, Dave, *Catching the Wind in a Net: The Religious Vision of Robertson Davies*, ECW, 1996.
Monk, Patricia, *The Smaller Infinity: The Jungian Self in the Novels of Robertson Davies*, University of Toronto Press, 1982.
Morley, Patricia, *Robertson Davies*, Gage Educational Publishing, 1977.
Peterman, Michael, *Robertson Davies*, Twayne, 1986.
Stone-Blackburn, Susan, *Robertson Davies: Playwright*, University of British Columbia Press, 1985.
Stouck, David, *Major Canadian Authors: A Critical Introduction*, University of Nebraska Press, 1984.
Twigg, Alan, *For Openers: Conversations with 24 Canadian Writers*, Harbour Publishing, 1981.
Wyatt, David, *Prodigal Sons: A Study in Authorship and Authority*, Johns Hopkins University Press, 1980.

PERIODICALS

American Spectator, May, 1989.
Ariel, July, 1979.
Atlantic, June, 1993.
Bloomsbury Review, May/June, 1996.
Books in Canada, November, 1985; August, 1988; February, 1996, p. 2.
Book World, December 13, 1970.
Canadian Drama, 7, No. 2, 1981 (special Davies issue).

Canadian Forum, June, 1950; December, 1975; October, 1977; December-January, 1981-82; February-March, 1989; November, 1991.
Canadian Literature, spring, 1960; winter, 1961; winter, 1967; spring, 1973; winter, 1974; winter, 1976; spring, 1982; winter, 1986.
Canadian Review, fall, 1976.
Chicago Tribune, July 26, 1986.
Chicago Tribune Book World, January 31, 1982.
Christian Century, February 1, 1989; January 29, 1992.
Christian Science Monitor, July 14, 1986.
Commonweal, December 20, 1985.
Dalhousie Review, autumn, 1981; fall, 1986.
Design for Arts in Education, May-June, 1989
Detroit Free Press, January 22, 1989; February 6, 1989.
Economist, June 30, 1990.
English Studies in Canada, March, 1986; March, 1990.
Essays on Canadian Writing, spring, 1977; winter 1977-1978; winter, 1984-1985; spring, 1987; fall, 1989.
Globe & Mail (Toronto), March 5, 1977; January 7, 1984; September 10, 1988; September 17, 1988.
Insight on the News, September 17, 1990.
Interview, March, 1989.
Journal of Canadian Fiction, winter, 1972; no. 3, 1974; winter, 1982.
Journal of Canadian Studies, November, 1974; February, 1977 (special Davies issue).
Journal of Commonwealth Literature, 22, Number 1, 1987.
Library Journal, January, 1989; January, 1990; October 1, 1991; April 1, 1992.
Library Quarterly, April, 1969.
Listener, April 15, 1971.
London Review of Books, November 10, 1988.
Los Angeles Times, January 29, 1982.
Los Angeles Times Book Review, December 1, 1985; January 29, 1989; January 30, 1989.
Maclean's, March 15, 1952; September, 1972; November 18, 1985; October 19, 1987; September 12, 1988; December 26, 1988; September 23, 1991; October 24, 1994, p. 54.
Nation, April 24, 1982; October 24, 1994, p. 54.
New Republic, March 13, 1976; April 15, 1978; March 10, 1982; December 30, 1985; April, 24, 1989.
New Statesman, April 20, 1973; April 4, 1980; October 14, 1988; November 22, 1991.
Newsweek, January 18, 1971; March 22, 1976; February 8, 1982.
New Yorker, January 27, 1986; February 10, 1992.
New York Review of Books, February 8, 1973; February 27, 1986; April 13, 1989.
New York Times, February 8, 1982; November 6, 1985; December 28, 1988; December 29, 1988.
New York Times Book Review, December 20, 1970; November 19, 1972; April 25, 1976; February 14, 1982; December 15, 1985; October 30, 1988; January 8, 1989; November 17, 1991; December 1, 1991; February 5, 1995, pp. 1, 23, 24.
Observer (London) May 31, 1987; October 2, 1988.
Performing Arts & Entertainment, summer, 1992.
Publishers Weekly, October 14, 1988; February 2, 1990; September 6, 1991; January 25, 1993.
Queen's Quarterly, spring, 1986.
Quill & Quire, August, 1988; September, 1994, pp. 1, 59, 62, 64.
Rolling Stone, December 1, 1977.
San Francisco Review of Books, spring, 1987.
Saturday Night, April 26, 1947; December 13, 1947; February 14, 1953; November, 1967; October, 1985; December, 1987;

August, 1988; October, 1988; November, 1990; October, 1991; October, 1994, p. 58.
Saturday Review, December 26, 1970; April 3, 1976.
Spectator, August 21, 1982; October 8, 1988.
Studies in Canadian Literature, winter, 1978; 7, No. 2, 1982; 12, No. 1, 1987.
Sunday Times, September 1991.
Time, January 11, 1971; May 17, 1976; December 26, 1988; March 13, 1995, pp. 100-01.
Time (Canada), November 3, 1975.
Times Literary Supplement, March 26, 1982; February 28, 1986; October 16, 1987; September 23, 1988.
Tribune Books, December 25, 1988.
U.S. News & World Report, January 16, 1989.
Wall Street Journal, July 15, 1986.
Washington Post, January 11, 1989.
Washington Post Book World, May 30, 1976; February 7, 1982; October 30, 1983; November 17, 1985; July 20, 1986; June 5, 1988; December 18, 1988.
World Literature Today, autumn, 1995, p. 793.
World Press Review, November, 1988.

* * *

DAVIS, B. Lynch
See BIOY CASARES, Adolfo
See BORGES, Jorge Luis

* * *

DAVIS, Ossie 1917-

PERSONAL: Born December 18, 1917, in Cogdell, GA; son of Kince Charles (a railway construction engineer) and Laura (Cooper) Davis; married Ruby Ann Wallace (an actress and writer under name Ruby Dee), December 9, 1948; children: Nora, Guy, La Verne. *Education:* Attended Howard University, 1935-39, and Columbia University, 1948; trained for the stage with Paul Mann and Lloyd Richards.

ADDRESSES: Office—Emmalyn II Productions, P.O. Box 1318, New Rochelle, NY 10802. *Agent*—Artists Agency, 10000 Santa Monica Blvd., Suite 305, Los Angeles, CA 90067.

CAREER: Actor, playwright, screenwriter, novelist, director and producer of stage productions and motion pictures, civil rights activist. Worked as janitor, shipping clerk, and stock clerk in New York City, 1938-41. Actor in numerous stage productions, 1941–, including *Joy Exceeding Glory,* 1941, *Jeb,* 1946, *Anna Lucasta,* 1948, *Stevedore,* 1949, *The Green Pastures,* 1951, *No Time for Sergeants,* 1957, *A Raisin in the Sun,* 1959, *Purlie Victorious,* 1961, *Take It from the Top,* 1979, and *I'm Not Rappaport,* 1986. Actor in motion pictures and teleplays, including *The Joe Louis Story,* 1953, *The Emperor Jones,* 1955, *The Cardinal,* 1963, *Gone Are the Days,* 1963, *Man Called Adam,* 1966, *Teacher, Teacher* for Hallmark Hall of Fame, 1969, *Let's Do It Again,* 1976, *For Us the Living* for American Playhouse, 1983, *School Daze,* 1988, *Do the Right Thing,* 1989, *Jungle Fever,* 1991, *No Way Out, Harry and Son, Gladiator, Malcolm X, Grumpy Old Men, The Client,* 1994, and *Get on the Bus,* 1996; actor in television series *Evening Shade,* 1990-93, miniseries Alex Haley's *Queen,* 1993, and Stephen King's *The Stand,* 1994, television specials *The Ernest Green Story,* 1993 and *The Ray Alexander Mystery,* 1994; other

television appearances include *Name of the Game, Night Gallery, Bonanza,* and *B. L. Stryker.*

Director of motion pictures, including *Cotton Comes to Harlem,* 1970, *Kongi's Harvest,* 1971, *Black Girl,* 1972, *Gordon's War,* 1973, and *Countdown at Kusini,* 1976. Co-host of radio program *Ossie Davis and Ruby Dee Story Hour,* 1974-78, and of television series *With Ossie and Ruby,* Public Broadcasting System (PBS-TV), 1981. Co-producer of stage production *Ballad for Bimshire,* 1963. Narrator of motion picture *From Dreams to Reality: A Tribute to Minority Inventors,* 1986, and of television movie *The American Experience: Goin' Back to T'Town,* 1993. Chairperson of the board, Institute for New Cinema Artists; founder with wife Ruby Dee of Emmalyn II Productions. Performer on recordings for Caedmon and Folkways Records. *Military service:* U.S. Army, 1942-45; served as surgical technician in Liberia, West Africa, and with Special Services Department.

MEMBER: Actor's Equity Association, Screen Actors Guild, American Federation of Radio and Television Artists, Director's Guild of America, National Association for the Advancement of Colored People (advisory board), Southern Christian Leadership Conference (advisory board), Congress of Racial Equality, Masons.

AWARDS, HONORS: First Mississippi Freedom Democratic Party Citation, 1965; Emmy Award nomination from Academy of Television Arts and Sciences, best actor in a special, 1969, for *Teacher, Teacher,* and nomination, c. 1978, for *King*; Antoinette Perry Award nomination, best musical, 1970, for *Purlie*; recipient with Dee of Frederick Douglass Award from New York Urban League, for "distinguished leadership toward equal opportunity," 1970; Paul Robeson Citation from Actor's Equity Association, 1975, for "outstanding creative contributions in the performing arts and in society at large"; Coretta Scott King Book Award from American Library Association, and Jane Addams Children's Book Award from Jane Addams Peace Association, both 1979, for *Escape to Freedom: A Play about Young Frederick Douglass*; Jury Award from Neil Simon Awards, 1983, for *For Us the Living*; Father of the Year Award, 1987; Image Award from National Association for the Advancement of Colored People, for best performance by a supporting actor, and Hall of Fame Award for outstanding artistic achievement, both 1989, both for *Do The Right Thing*; Monarch Award, 1990; inducted into Theater Hall of Fame, 1994.

WRITINGS:

PLAYS

(And director) *Goldbrickers of 1944,* first produced in Liberia, West Africa, 1944.
Alice in Wonder (one-act), first produced in New York City at Elks Community Theatre, September 15, 1952; revised and expanded version produced as *The Big Deal in New York* at New Playwrights Theatre, March 7, 1953.
Purlie Victorious (first produced on Broadway at Cort Theatre, 1961; also see below), Samuel French (New York City), 1961.
Curtain Call, Mr. Aldridge, Sir (first produced in Santa Barbara at the University of California, summer, 1968), published in *The Black Teacher and the Dramatic Arts: A Dialogue, Bibliography, and Anthology,* edited by William R. Reardon and Thomas D. Pawley, Negro Universities Press, 1970.
(With Philip Rose, Peter Udell, and Gary Geld) *Purlie* (adaptation of *Purlie Victorious*; first produced on Broadway at Broadway Theatre, March 15, 1970), Samuel French, 1971.

Escape to Freedom: A Play about Young Frederick Douglass (first produced in New York City at the Town Hall, March 8, 1976), Viking (New York City), 1978.

Langston: A Play (first produced in New York City in 1982), Delacorte (New York City), 1982.

(With Hy Gilbert, and director) *Bingo* (baseball musical based on novel *The Bingo Long Traveling All-Stars and Motor Kings* by William Brashler), first produced in New York City at AMAS Repertory Theater, November, 1985.

Also author of *Last Dance for Sybil.*

SCREENPLAYS AND TELEPLAYS

Gone Are the Days (adaptation of *Purlie Victorious*; also released as *Purlie Victorious* and *The Man from C.O.T.T.O.N.*), Trans Lux, 1963.

(With Arnold Perl, and director) *Cotton Comes to Harlem* (based on a novel by Chester Himes), United Artists, 1970.

(And director) *Kongi's Harvest* (adapted from work by Wole Soyinka), Calpenny Films Nigeria Ltd., 1970.

Today Is Ours, Columbia Broadcasting System (CBS-TV), 1974.

(With Ladi Ladebo and Al Freeman, Jr.) *Countdown at Kusini* (based on a story by John Storm Roberts), CBS-TV, 1976.

Also writer of television episodes of *East Side/West Side,* 1963, *The Negro People,* 1965, *Just Say the Word,* 1969, *The Eleventh Hour, Bonanza,* and *N.Y.P.D.*; and for special *Alice in Wonder,* 1987.

OTHER

(With others) *The Black Cinema: Foremost Representatives of the Black Film World Air Their Views* (sound recording), Center for Cassette Studies 30983, 1975.

(With wife Ruby Dee) *Hands upon the Heart* (two-volume videotape), Emmalyn Enterprises, 1994.

(Author of foreword) Langston Hughes, *Black Magic: A Pictorial History of the African-American in the Performing Arts,* Da Capo (New York City), 1990.

(Author of foreword) G. William Jones, *Black Cinema Treasures: Lost and Found,* University of North Texas (Denton), 1991.

(Author of afterword) Malcolm X, *The Autobiography of Malcom X* (with the assistance of Alex Haley; introduction by M. S. Handler; epilogue by Alex Haley), Ballantine (New York City), 1992.

Just Like Martin (young adult novel), Simon & Schuster (New York City), 1992.

(Author of foreword with Dee) Barbara Brandon, *Where I'm Coming From,* Andrews and McMeel (Kansas City), 1993.

Purlie Victorious: A Commemorative (with commentary by Dee), Emmalyn Enterprises (New Rochelle, NY), 1993.

Also author of "Ain't Now But It's Going to Be" (song), for *Cotton Comes to Harlem,* 1970. Contributor to journals and periodicals, including *Negro History Bulletin, Negro Digest,* and *Freedomways.*

SIDELIGHTS: "Ossie Davis is best known as an actor, but his accomplishments extend well beyond the stage," writes Michael E. Greene in the *Dictionary of Literary Biography.* "In the theater, in motion pictures, and in television he has won praise both for his individual performances and those he has given with his wife, Ruby Dee. He has, however, also been a writer, director, producer, social activist, and community leader." The bond uniting all of Davis's work, according to Jayne F. Mulvaney in the *Dictionary of Literary Biography,* is Davis's commitment to "creating works that would truthfully portray the black man's experience."

Long active in the cause of racial justice, Davis was a prominent figure in the civil rights movement of the 1960s. He gave the eulogies at the funerals of black leaders Malcolm X and Dr. Martin Luther King Jr., and he acted as master of ceremonies at the famous "March on Washington" in 1963—the site of Dr. King's "I Have a Dream" speech. Throughout his life, Davis has used his many talents and experiences to expose wide audiences to his views. As the actor explains to Calvin Reid in *Publishers Weekly*: "I am essentially a storyteller, and the story I want to tell is about black people. Sometimes I sing the story, sometimes I dance it, sometimes I tell tall tales about it, but I always want to share my great satisfaction at being a black man at this time in history."

A native of Cogdell, Georgia, Davis began his career after enrolling at Howard University, where Alain Locke, a drama critic and professor of philosophy, spurred his budding interest in the theater. On Locke's counseling, Davis became involved in several facets of stage life, including maintenance and set construction, while biding time as an actor. He first appeared on the stage as a member of Harlem's Ross McClendon Players in a 1941 production of *Joy Exceeding Glory.* Few offers followed, however, and Davis was reduced to sleeping in parks and scrounging for food.

In 1942 in the midst of World War II, Davis was inducted into the U.S. Army, where he served as a medical technician in Liberia, West Africa. After his transfer to Special Services, he began writing and producing stage works to entertain military personnel. Upon discharge, though, Davis returned to his native Georgia. There he was reached by McClendon director Richard Campbell, who encouraged Davis to return to New York City and audition for Robert Ardrey's *Jeb.* Davis accepted Campbell's encouragement and eventually secured the title role in Ardrey's work. The play, which concerns a physically debilitated veteran's attempt to succeed as an adding machine operator in racist Louisiana, was poorly received, but Davis was exempted for his compelling performance.

Davis married fellow *Jeb* performer Ruby Dee in 1948 after they completed a stint with the touring company of *Anna Lucasta.* The pace of his acting career then accelerated as Davis received critical praise for his work in *Stevedore,* in which he played a servant who assumes a misplaced worldliness following a visit to Paris, and *The Green Pastures,* in which he portrayed one of several angels in a black-populated Heaven.

While acting, Davis also continued to devote attention to his writing. "As a playwright Davis was committed to creating works that would truthfully portray the black man's experience," says Mulvaney. In 1953, his play *Alice in Wonder,* which focused on McCarthy-era issues of integrity and blacklisting, was dimly received in Harlem; however, his 1961 opus *Purlie Victorious* generated a more favorable response. Mulvaney describes the play as a comedy about the schemes of an eloquent itinerant preacher who returns to his Georgia home with hopes of buying the old barn that once served as a black church, and establishing an integrated one. To realize his plan, he must secure the inheritance of his deceased aunt, a former slave, whose daughter has also died. Because Captain Cotchipee, the play's antagonist and holder of the inheritance, is unaware of the death of Purlie's cousin, Purlie plans to have a pretty young black girl impersonate his cousin so that he can claim the inheritance to finance the church of his dreams. "The action of the play involves the hilarious efforts of Purlie, his family, and the captain's liberal son, Charlie, to outwit the captain," says Mulvaney. Many critics were especially pleased with Davis's humorous portrayal of the black preacher's efforts to swipe the $500 inheritance from the white plantation owner.

Greene calls *Purlie Victorious* a "Southern fable of right against wrong with Purlie's faith in the cause of equality triumphing over the bigotry of Ol' Cap'n Cotchipee, the local redneck aristocrat." Considering the comedy's brilliance to derive "chiefly from how cliches and stereotypes are blown out of proportion," Mulvaney suggests that *Purlie Victorious* is "satire which proceeds toward reconciliation rather than bitterness. Its invective is not venomous." "Unfortunately, despite the reviews, the endorsement of the National Association for the Advancement of Colored People, and the play's seven-and-a-half month run, neither playwright nor producer made money," notes Mulvaney. "The financial support of the black community was not enough; the white audiences did not come." Greene suggests that the play would have been considerably more successful had it been written either ten years before or after it was. "Davis himself recognized that his handling of stereotypes, black and white, would have been offensive had a white writer created them," Greene observes. He adds that Davis "argues that one of his purposes in the play was to present justice as an ideal, as something that is not always the same as traditional law-and-order, which allows the Ol' Cap'ns of American society to win too often."

Purlie Victorious was adapted by Davis as the motion picture *Gone Are the Days*. A. H. Weiler, writing in the *New York Times,* complains that the film rarely availed itself of cinematic techniques, but adds that the work "is still speaking out against injustice in low, broad, comic fashion." Weiler praises the performances of Davis, who played the preacher Purlie Victorious, and Ruby Dee, the title character's lover.

Race relations are at the core of Davis's novel for young adults, *Just Like Martin.* A *Kirkus Reviews* contributor describes the story as "dramatic and simply told, with a cast of strong personalities." Set in 1963, the tale finds Isaac "Stone" and his father, Ike, struggling with their involvement in the civil rights movement. Ike will not let Stone, an all-A student, leave their Alabama home to go with a church youth group to a civil rights march in Washington, DC. Ike's fear that Stone would be harmed is compounded by his wife's recent death. Ike is also opposed to his son's devotion to nonviolence and belittles the boy's admiration of Martin Luther King. Stone, who hopes to become a preacher "just like Martin," eventually organizes a children's march after two friends are killed and another is maimed when a church youth meeting room is bombed.

In *Just Like Martin,* the church's Reverend Cable asks Stone and other members in the Creative Nonviolence Workshop for Children if they have the strength to let people strike them and not strike back. Stone believes he can endure a beating without resorting to violence, yet finds himself "fist fighting in the house of the Lord," according to Reverend Cable. Anne Scott in *Washington Post Book World* praises Davis's characters, despite their flaws, as they fight off "injustice . . . not always knowing how to respond to the history in which they find themselves."

Other reviewers of Davis's novel comment on Ike's coming to terms with the values of his son. Watching the youth's efforts, along with the shock of hearing of President John F. Kennedy's assassination, prompt Ike to resolve his inner conflict and lend his support to Stone. Lauding Davis's development of father and son, Lyn Miller-Lachmann notes in *Junior High Up* that the author

"realistically portrays the boy's struggle to apply King's values in his personal life, and the ending is hopeful but not happy." *Booklist* contributor Hazel Rochman points out some minor flaws in the story, but deemed that "what is riveting here is the sense of history being made—of struggle and commitment in one community."

Davis was also prominently featured in films such as Spike Lee's *School Daze, Do the Right Thing, Jungle Fever,* and *Malcolm X,* and the careers of Dee and Davis have remained intertwined as well. They have performed together in stage productions, films, and recordings; shared duties as hosts/performers on the brief PBS-TV series *With Ossie and Ruby;* and co-founded Emmalyn II Productions. When not on location, they live in New Rochelle, New York.

In addition to his career and his status as a role model, Davis has also been a direct source of encouragement and support for other African American artists. He founded the Institute of Cinema Artists in 1973, providing black students with training for careers in television and film. In recognition of his achievements in this area, Mulvaney calls Davis "a force in the development of black culture." Davis explains his commitment to nurturing other artists in the *Dictionary of Literary Biography:* "For if we can, in fact, create for our own people; work for our own people; belong to our own people; we will no longer be forced into artistic prostitution and self-betrayal in the mad scramble, imposed upon us far too long, to belong to some other people. . . . Only then can we begin to take a truly independent position within the confines of American culture, a black position."

BIOGRAPHICAL/CRITICAL SOURCES:

BOOKS

Abramson, Doris E., *Negro Playwrights in the American Theatre, 1925-1959,* Columbia University Press (New York City), 1969.
Dictionary of Literary Biography, Gale (Detroit), Volume 7: *Twentieth-Century American Dramatists,* 1981; Volume 38: *Afro-American Writers after 1955: Dramatists and Prose Writers,* 1985.
Funke, Lewis, *The Curtain Rises—The Story of Ossie Davis,* Grosset & Dunlap (New York City), 1971.
Patterson, Lindsay, editor, *Anthology of the American Negro in the Theatre,* Association for the Study of Life and History/ Publishers Company, 1967.

PERIODICALS

Booklist, September 1, 1992.
Detroit Free Press, November 11, 1983.
Ebony, February, 1961; December, 1979.
Essence, December, 1994, p. 76.
Freedomways, spring, 1962; summer, 1965; summer, 1968.
Junior High Up, October, 1992.
Kirkus Reviews, September 15, 1992, p. 1185.
Modern Maturity, July-August, 1994, p. 64.
Nation, April 6, 1970; July 24-31, 1989, pp. 144-48.
National Observer, March 22, 1970.
Negro Digest, February, 1966; April, 1966.
Negro History Bulletin, April, 1967.
Newsweek, March 30, 1970; December 17, 1990, p. 64.
New York, April, 1970; February 13, 1989, p. 71.
New Yorker, October 7, 1961; July 24, 1989, p. 78; March 26, 1990, p. 79.
New York Times, September 24, 1963; May 5, 1968; October 12, 1969; March 10, 1970; November 11, 1985.

People, February 13, 1989, p. 13; September 24, 1990, p. 7; August 1, 1994, p. 16.

Publishers Weekly, December 28, 1992, p. 27.

Variety, March 5, 1969; January 28, 1970; March 28, 1970.

Voice of Youth Advocates, April, 1993, p. 24.

Washington Post Book World, December 6, 1992, p. 20.

*　　*　　*

DAVISON, Lawrence H.
See LAWRENCE, D(avid) H(erbert Richards)

*　　*　　*

DAY LEWIS, C(ecil) 1904-1972
(Nicholas Blake)

PERSONAL: Born April 27, 1904, in Ballintubber, Ireland; died May 22, 1972; son of F. C. (a minister) and Kathleen Blake (Squires; a collateral descendant of Oliver Goldsmith) Day Lewis; married Constance Mary King, 1928 (divorced, 1951); married Jill Angela Henriette Balcon, April 27, 1951; children: (first marriage) Sean Francis, Nicholas Charles; (second marriage) Lydia Tamasin, Daniel Michael. *Education:* Attended Wadham College, Oxford.

CAREER: Assistant master at Summerfields, Oxford, England, 1927-28, at Larchfield, Helensburgh, Scotland, 1928-30, and at Cheltenham College, England, 1930-35; editor with Ministry of Information, 1941-46; Trinity College, Cambridge, England, Clark Lecturer, 1946; Oxford University, Oxford, professor of poetry, 1951-56; Harvard University, Cambridge, MA, Charles Eliot Norton Professor of Poetry, 1964-65. Appointed Poet Laureate of Britain by Queen Elizabeth II, 1968. Member of Arts Council, 1962-72; member of board of directors, Chatto & Windus Ltd. (publishers).

MEMBER: Royal Society of Literature (fellow; vice president, 1958-72), Royal Society of Arts (fellow), American Academy of Arts and Letters (honorary member), Athenaeum.

AWARDS, HONORS: Companion, Order of British Empire, 1950; D.Litt., University of Exeter, 1965, University of Hull, 1970; Litt.D., Trinity College, Dublin, 1968.

WRITINGS:

Beechen Vigil, and Other Poems, Fortune Press, 1925.

Country Comets (poetry), 1928.

Transitional Poem, Hogarth, 1929.

From Feathers to Iron (poetry), Hogarth, 1932.

Dick Willoughby (juvenile fiction), Basil Blackwell, 1933, Random House, 1938.

The Magnetic Mountain (poetry), Hogarth, 1933.

A Hope for Poetry (criticism), Basil Blackwell, 1934, reprinted with a postscript, Folcroft, 1969.

Collected Poems, 1929-1933, Hogarth, 1935, 2nd edition, 1945.

Collected Poems, 1929-1933 [and] *A Hope For Poetry,* Random House, 1935.

Revolution in Writing (commentary), Hogarth, 1935.

A Time to Dance, and Other Poems, Hogarth, 1935.

We're Not Going to Do Nothing (commentary), Left Review, 1936.

The Friendly Tree (novel), J. Cape, 1936, Harper, 1937.

Noah and the Waters (modern morality play), Hogarth, 1936.

A Time to Dance; Noah and the Waters, [and] *Revolution in Writing,* Random House, 1936.

(With L. S. Stebbing) *Imagination and Thinking,* Life and Leisure, 1936.

Starting Point (novel), J. Cape, 1937, Harper, 1938.

Overtures to Death, and Other Poems, J. Cape, 1938.

Child of Misfortune (novel), J. Cape, 1939.

Poems in Wartime, J. Cape, 1940.

Selected Poems, Hogarth, 1940, revised edition, Penguin, 1969.

Word Over All (poetry), J. Cape, 1943, Transatlantic, 1944.

Poetry for You: A Book for Boys and Girls on the Enjoyment of Poetry (juvenile), Basil Blackwell, 1944, Oxford University Press (New York), 1947.

Short is the Time: Poems, 1936-1943 (previously published as *Overtures to Death, and Other Poems* and *Word Over All*), Oxford University Press (New York), 1945.

The Poetic Image (criticism), Oxford University Press, 1947.

Enjoying Poetry, Cambridge University Press for National Book League, 1947.

The Colloquial Element in English Poetry (criticism), Literary and Philosophical Society of Newcastle-upon-Tyne, 1947.

Collected Poems, 1929-1936, Hogarth, 1948.

Poems, 1943-1947, Oxford University Press, 1948.

The Otterbury Incident (juvenile; adaptation of the French film *Nous le gosses,* released in England as *Us Kids*), Putnam, 1948, reissued, 1963.

The Poet's Task (criticism), Clarendon Press, 1951.

The Grand Manner (criticism), University of Nottingham, 1952.

An Italian Visit (narrative poem), Harper, 1953.

The Lyrical Poetry of Thomas Hardy (criticism), Oxford University Press, 1953, Folcroft, 1970.

Collected Poems, J. Cape, 1954, published as *Collected Poems, 1954,* 1970.

Christmas Eve, Faber, 1954.

Notable Images of Virtue: Emily Bronte, George Meredith, W. B. Yeats, Ryerson, 1954.

Pegasus, and Other Poems, J. Cape, 1957, Harper, 1958.

The Poet's Way of Knowledge, Cambridge University Press, 1957.

The Newborn: D. M. B., 29th April, 1957 (poetry), Favil Press of Kensington, 1957.

The Buried Day (autobiography), Harper, 1960.

English Lyric Poems, 1500-1900, Appleton, 1961 (published in England as *A Book of English Lyrics,* Chatto & Windus, 1961).

The Gate, and Other Poems, J. Cape, 1962.

Requiem for the Living (poetry), Harper, 1964.

On Not Saying Anything (poetry), privately printed, 1964.

The Lyric Impulse (Charles Eliot Norton lectures), Harvard University Press, 1965.

(With R. A. Scott-James) *Thomas Hardy* (criticism), Longman, 1965.

The Room, and Other Poems, J. Cape, 1965.

A Marriage Song for Albert and Barbara (poetry), privately printed, 1965.

Selected Poems, Harper, 1967, revised edition, Penguin, 1969.

Selections from His Poetry (also published as *C. Day Lewis: Selections from His Poetry*), edited by Patric Dickinson, Chatto & Windus, 1967.

The Abbey That Refused to Die: A Poem, Ballintubber Abbey, 1967.

A Need for Poetry?, University of Hull, 1968.

The Whispering Roots, and Other Poems, Harper, 1970 (published in England as *The Whispering Roots,* J. Cape, 1970).

Going My Way, [London], 1970.

The Poems of C. Day Lewis, edited by Ian Parson, J. Cape, 1970.
On Translating Poetry: A Lecture, Abbey Press, 1970.

DETECTIVE NOVELS; UNDER PSEUDONYM NICHOLAS BLAKE

A Question of Proof, Harper, 1935.
Shell of Death, Harper, 1936 (published in England as *Thou Shell of Death,* Collins, 1936).
There's Trouble Brewing, Harper, 1937.
The Beast Must Die, Harper, 1938.
The Smiler With the Knife, Harper, 1939.
The Summer Camp Mystery, Harper, 1940 (published in England as *Malice in Wonderland,* Collins, 1940; American paperback edition published as *Malice with Murder*).
The Corpse in the Snowman, Harper, 1941 (published in England as *The Case of the Abominable Snowman,* Collins, 1941).
Minute for Murder, Harper, 1947.
Head of a Traveler, Harper, 1949.
The Dreadful Hollow, Harper, 1953.
The Whisper in the Gloom, Harper, 1954.
A Tangled Web, Harper, 1956.
End of Chapter, Harper, 1957.
A Penknife in My Heart, Collins, 1958, Harper, 1959.
The Widow's Cruise, Harper, 1959.
The Worm of Death, Harper, 1961.
The Deadly Joker, Collins, 1963.
The Sad Variety, Harper, 1964.
The Morning after Death, Collins, 1966.
The Nicholas Blake Omnibus, Collins, 1966.
The Private Wound, Harper, 1968.

EDITOR

(With W. H. Auden) *Oxford Poetry,* Basil Blackwell, 1927-32.
The Mind in Chains: Socialism and the Cultural Revolution, Muller Ltd., 1937.
(With John Lehmann, T. A. Jackson Fox, and Ralph Winston) *Ralph Fox: Writer in Arms,* International Publishers, 1937.
(With Charles Fenby) *Anatomy of Oxford: An Anthology,* J. Cape, 1938.
(With L. A. G. Strong) *An Anthology of Modern Verse, 1920-1940* (also published as *A New Anthology of Modern Verse, 1920-1940*), Methuen, 1941.
The Echoing Green: An Anthology of Verse, three volumes, Basil Blackwell, 1941-43.
(With others) *Orion,* Nicholson & Watson, Volume II, 1945, Volume III, 1946.
(And author of introduction) Francis T. Palgrave, *The Golden Treasury of the Best Songs and Lyrical Poems in the English Language,* Collins, 1954.
(And author of introduction and notes) Wilfred Owen, *Collected Poems,* amended edition, New Directions, 1954.
(With John Lehmann) *The Chatto Book of Modern Poetry, 1915-1955,* Chatto & Windus, 1956.
Charles Dickens, *The Mystery of Edwin Drood,* Collins, 1956.
(With Kathleen Nott and Thomas Blackburn) *New Poems 1957,* M. Joseph, 1957.
(And author of introduction) Edmund Charles Blunden, *The Midnight Skaters: Poems for Young Readers,* Bodley Head, 1968.
The Poems of Robert Browning, Limited Editions Club (Cambridge), 1969, Heritage Press, 1971.
A Choice of Keats's Verse, Faber, 1971.
George Crabbe, *Crabbe,* Penguin, 1973.

TRANSLATOR

Virgil, *Georgics,* J. Cape, 1940.

Paul Valery, *Le Cimetiere marin,* Secker & Warburg, 1947.
Virgil, *Aeneid,* Oxford University Press, 1952, Doubleday Anchor, 1953.
Virgil, *Eclogues,* J. Cape, 1963.
The Eclogues and Georgics of Virgil, Doubleday Anchor, 1964 (published in England as *The Eclogues: Georgics and Aeneid,* Oxford University Press, 1966).
(With Matyas Sarkozi) Erzsi Gazdas, *The Tomtit in the Rain: Traditional Hungarian Rhymes,* Chatto & Windus, 1971.

SIDELIGHTS: When C. Day Lewis was appointed Poet Laureate of Great Britain, a reviewer in the *Beloit Poetry Journal* commented: "If one may judge by his past performance, it is an honor that he will till with a good deal more distinction than most of his predecessors. As this volume [*Selected Poems*] quickly demonstrates, he is a poet of superb range. Three themes seem to recur over the years: an admiration for all that is truly heroic, a feeling for the ephemeral quality of life, and a quest for pure and true identity. But there are other themes, too—lighter, less cerebral. But everything he writes is touched with a sense of the truly poetic. He is a major figure."

This regard has not always been shared by critics, nor have his poems been considered of uniformly high quality. Philip Booth offered an explanation: "To look to these poems for the verbal energy of Ted Hughes or the imagistic precision of Philip Larkin is to miss the personal perspective which characterizes this collection [*Selected Poems*]. . . . Day Lewis is not everyone's cup of tea, especially in an America where stronger, colder, and more bitter drinks are now more fashionable. But to ask these poems to be other than they are would be to deny the very civilization to which they are native; the collection is a wholly honorable brew."

Day Lewis's own history provides other clues to his diversity. The late Poet Laureate was once a poet of revolution, inextricably linked with the avant-garde Oxford poets of the 1930s, W. H. Auden, Stephen Spender, and Louis MacNeice. His poems of that period were mostly parodies, and considered highly imitative. Brian Jones wrote that it was not until 1943 that Day Lewis published verse "which gives the authentic shock of originality. . . . Since then, Day Lewis has continued in this much more personal vein . . . which seems to arise genuinely from his own personality. And it is clear from his 'Thirties verse that he could not at that time find a satisfactory voice because he knew only too well what it naturally was—a late Romantic's, words which it was a disgrace to utter at that time. And so he hid it, became a mimic, or at best used his true voice when he was pretending it was somebody elses's, as in his parodies."

His prose, on the other hand, was always highly regarded, from his early political essays, to his quite successful "Nicholas Blake" novels, which he began as pot-boilers. "From most of the news stories about the appointment of Cecil Day Lewis as Poet Laureate of Great Britain," noted Anthony Boucher, "you would gather that he is one of those lyric dons who dash off an occasional detective story in their lighter moments. In fact the poet is . . . a hardworking professional in crime, who . . . is also one of England's two or three leading reviewers of crime fiction. Blake's stature among mystery novelists is at least as high as that of Day Lewis among poets; he has excelled both in the straight detective puzzle and in the broader study of crime and character, as well as in happy blends of the two methods."

Often classified as a Georgian, Day Lewis was a skilled craftsman, excelling at highly disciplined traditional verse forms, at his best in meditative poems. "I always wished to be lucid," he once commented, and his best poems are noted for lucidity, simplicity, and quiet lyricism. "He is a quiet writer," observed John Wain, "with a preference for ordered syntax and regular form, who likes to brood rather than to exclaim." He called himself a member of the "derriere garde," and, according to Peter Gellatly, "derided his 'too meticulous words,' and disclaimed for his works that 'divine incontinence' which he considers an essential element in good poetry. He obviously admires the roistering, Dylan-like figure but cannot emulate him. Wild singing is not for Day Lewis. On the other hand, his temperateness and steadiness of outlook sometimes invest his poems with a glossy perfection that is rarely seen elsewhere."

As Poet Laureate he turned out official verse not noted for literary distinction. Yet he could still write in another vein; his last collection elicited this reassurance from Derek Stattford: "it is good to see Mr. Day Lewis in such a fine and charming fettle. . . . Those . . . who may have feared this poet would be throttled by his chain of office can breathe a deep sigh of relief and get down to enjoying *The Whispering Roots.*"

BIOGRAPHICAL/CRITICAL SOURCES:

BOOKS

Contemporary Literary Criticism, Gale, Volume 1, 1973; Volume 6, 1976; Volume 10, 1979.
Dictionary of Literary Biography, Gale, Volume 15: *British Novelists, 1930-1959,* 1983; Volume 20: *British Poets, 1914-1945,* 1983; Volume 77: *British Mystery Writers, 1920-1939,* 1988.
Dyment, Clifford, *C. Day Lewis,* Longmans, Green, for the British Council, 1955.
Gelpi, Albert, *Living in Time: The Poetry of C. Day Lewis,* Oxford University Press, 1997.
Handley-Taylor, Geoffrey and Timothy d'Arch Smith, *C. Day Lewis, The Poet Laureate: A Bibliography,* St. James Press, 1968.

PERIODICALS

New Republic, March 28, 1964.
New Statesman, June 14, 1958.
New York Review of Books, June 25, 1964.
New York Times Book Review, June 22, 1958.
Poetry, August, 1958.
Times Literary Supplement, March 6, 1959.
Washington Post Book World, June 21, 1981.

* * *

DE BEAUVOIR, Simone (Lucie Ernestine Marie Bertrand)
See BEAUVOIR, Simone de

* * *

DE GOURMONT, Remy(-Marie-Charles)
See GOURMONT, Remy(-Marie-Charles) de

* * *

DEIGHTON, Len
See DEIGHTON, Leonard Cyril

DEIGHTON, Leonard Cyril 1929-
(Len Deighton)

PERSONAL: Born February 18, 1929, in Marylebone, London, England; married Shirley Thompson (an illustrator), 1960. *Education:* Attended St. Martin's School of Art, London, three years; Royal College of Art, graduate.

ADDRESSES: Office—25 Newman St., London W.1, England. *Agent*—c/o Jonathan Clowes Ltd., 10 Iron bridge House, Bridge Approach, London, NW1 8BD, England.

CAREER: Author. Worked as a railway lengthman, an assistant pastry cook at the Royal Festival Hall, 1951, a manager of a gown factory in Aldgate, England, a waiter in Piccadilly, an advertising man in London and New York City, a teacher in Brittany, a co-proprietor of a glossy magazine, and as a magazine artist and news photographer; steward, British Overseas Airways Corporation (BOAC), 1956-57; producer of films, including "Only When I Larf," based on his novel of the same title, 1969.

WRITINGS:

UNDER NAME LEN DEIGHTON

Only When I Larf (novel), M. Joseph, 1968, published as *Only When I Laugh,* Mysterious Press, 1987.
Oh, What a Lovely War! (screenplay), Paramount, 1969.
Bomber: Events Relating to the Last Flight of an R.A.F. Bomber Over Germany on the Night of June 31, 1943 (novel), Harper, 1970.
Declarations of War (story collection), J. Cape, 1971, published as *Eleven Declarations of War,* Harcourt, 1975.
Close-Up (novel), Atheneum, 1972.
SS-GB: Nazi-Occupied Britain, 1941 (novel), J. Cape, 1978, Knopf, 1979.
Goodbye, Mickey Mouse (novel; Book-of-the-Month Club selection), Knopf, 1982.
Winter: A Novel of a Berlin Family (Book-of-the-Month Club alternate selection), Knopf, 1988.
Pests: A Play in Three Acts (limited edition), Mansfield Woodhouse, 1994.

Also author of television scripts "Long Past Glory," 1963, and "It Must Have Been Two Other Fellows," 1977. Also author of weekly comic strip on cooking, *Observer,* 1962–.

ESPIONAGE NOVELS; UNDER NAME LEN DEIGHTON

The Ipcress File, Fawcett, 1962.
Horse Under Water (Literary Guild selection), J. Cape, 1963, Putnam, 1967.
Funeral in Berlin, J. Cape, 1964, Putnam, 1965.
The Billion Dollar Brain, Putnam, 1966.
An Expensive Place to Die, Putnam, 1967.
Spy Story, Harcourt, 1974.
Yesterday's Spy, Harcourt, 1975.
Twinkle, Twinkle, Little Spy, J. Cape, 1976, published as *Catch a Falling Spy,* Harcourt, 1976.
XPD, Knopf, 1981.
Berlin Game, Knopf, 1983.
Mexico Set (Literary Guild selection), Knopf, 1985.
London Match, Knopf, 1985.
Spy Hook (Book-of-the-Month Club selection), Knopf, 1988.
Spy Line, Knopf, 1989.
Spy Sinker, HarperCollins, 1990.
MAMista, HarperCollins, 1991.
City of Gold, HarperCollins, 1992.

Violent Ward, HarperCollins, 1993.
Faith, HarperCollins, 1995.
Hope, HarperCollins (New York City), 1995.
Charity, HarperCollins, 1996.

NONFICTION; UNDER NAME LEN DEIGHTON

(Editor) *Drinks-man-ship: Town's Album of Fine Wines and High Spirits,* Haymarket Press, 1964.
Ou est le garlic; or, Len Deighton's French Cookbook, Penguin, 1965, revised edition published as *Basic French Cooking,* J. Cape, 1979.
Action Cookbook: Len Deighton's Guide to Eating, J. Cape, 1965.
Len Deighton's Cookstrip Cook Book, Bernard Geis Associates, 1966.
(Editor with Michael Rand and Howard Loxton) *The Assassination of President Kennedy,* J. Cape, 1967.
(Editor and contributor) *Len Deighton's London Dossier,* J. Cape, 1967.
Len Deighton's Continental Dossier: A Collection of Cultural, Culinary, Historical, Spooky, Grim and Preposterous Fact, compiled by Victor and Margaret Pettitt, M. Joseph, 1968.
Fighter: The True Story of the Battle of Britain, J. Cape, 1977, Knopf, 1978.
(With Peter Mayle) *How to Be a Pregnant Father,* Lyle Stuart, 1977.
(With Arnold Schwartzman) *Airshipwreck,* J. Cape, 1978, Holt, 1979.
(With Simon Goodenough) *Tactical Genius in Battle,* Phaidon Press, 1979.
Blitzkrieg: From the Rise of Hitler to the Fall of Dunkirk, Coward, 1980.
Battle of Britain, Coward, 1980.
ABC of French Food, Bantam (New York City), 1990.
Blood, Tears, and Folly: An Objective Look at World War II, HarperCollins, 1993.

MEDIA ADAPTATIONS: The Ipcress File was filmed by Universal in 1965, *Funeral in Berlin* by Paramount in 1966, *The Billion Dollar Brain* by United Artists in 1967, and *Only When I Larf* by Paramount in 1969; *Spy Story* was filmed in 1976; film rights to *An Expensive Place to Die* have been sold. Deighton's nameless British spy hero was given the name Harry Palmer in the film adaptations of his adventures.

SIDELIGHTS: With his early novels, especially *The Ipcress File* and *Funeral in Berlin,* Len Deighton established himself as one of the mainstays of modern espionage fiction. He is often ranked—along with Graham Greene, John le Carre, and Ian Fleming—among the foremost writers in the field. Deighton shows a painstaking attention to accuracy in depicting espionage activities, and in his early novels this realism was combined with a light ironic touch that set his work apart. Deighton, David Quammen remarks in the *New York Times Book Review,* is "a talented, droll and original spy novelist."

Deighton was an immediate success with his first novel, *The Ipcress File,* a book that the late Anthony Boucher of the *New York Times Book Review* admits "caused quite a stir among both critics and customers in England." Introducing Deighton's nameless protagonist in an adventure that takes him to a nuclear testing site on a Pacific atoll, to the Middle East, and behind the Iron Curtain, the book continues to be popular for its combination of a serious espionage plot with a parody of the genre. As Richard Locke observes in the *New York Times Book Review, The Ipcress*

File possesses "a Kennedy-cool amorality. . . , a cross of Hammett and cold war lingo."

Critics praise the book's gritty evocation of intelligence work, ironic narrative, and comic touches. Boucher calls it "a sharply written, ironic and realistic tale of modern spy activities." Deighton's humor attracts the most attention from John B. Cullen of *Best Sellers,* who claims that in *The Ipcress File* "Deighton writes with a tongue-in-cheek attitude. . . . No one is spared the needle of subtle ridicule, but the author still tells a plausible story which holds your attention throughout." However, for Robert Donald Spectar of the *New York Herald Tribune Book Review* Deighton's humor ruins the espionage story. "Deighton," Spectar writes, "has combined picaresque satire, parody, and suspense and produced a hybrid more humorous than thrilling." But this opinion is disputed by G. W. Stonier in the *New Statesman.* Comparing Deighton with James Bond creator Ian Fleming, Stonier finds Deighton to be "a good deal more expert and twice the writer" and believes "there has been no brighter arrival on the shady scene since Graham Greene." Even in 1979, some seventeen years after the book's initial publication, Julian Symons of the *New York Times Book Review* was moved to call *The Ipcress File* "a dazzling performance. The verve and energy, the rattle of wit in the dialogue, the side-of-the-mouth comments, the evident pleasure taken in cocking a snook at the British spy story's upper-middle-class tradition—all these, together with the teasing convolutions of the plot, made it clear that a writer of remarkable talent in this field had appeared."

Deighton's reputation as an espionage writer was enhanced by *Funeral in Berlin,* a story revolving around an attempt to smuggle a defecting East German biologist out of Berlin. With the assistance of a high-ranking Russian agent, former Nazi intelligence officers, and a freelance operator of doubtful allegiance, Deighton's unnamed hero arranges the details of the defection. The many plot twists, and Deighton's enigmatic presentation of his story, prompt Stephen Hugh-Jones of *New Statesman* to admit, "I spent most of the book wondering what the devil was going on." Boucher finds the mysterious goings-on to be handled well. "The double and triple crosses involved," Boucher writes, "are beautifully worked out." Published at the same time as John le Carre's classic espionage tale *The Spy Who Came in From the Cold,* a novel also set in Germany's divided city, *Funeral in Berlin* compares favorably with its competitor. Boucher calls its plot "very nearly as complex and nicely calculated," while Charles Poore of the *New York Times* maintains it is "even better" than le Carre's book. It is, Poore concludes, "a ferociously cool fable of the current struggle between East and West." Andy East of *Armchair Detective* claims that *Funeral in Berlin* "has endured as Deighton's most celebrated novel."

Of his later espionage novels, perhaps his most important work has been the trilogy comprised of *Berlin Game, Mexico Set,* and *London Match.* Here, Deighton spins a long story of moles (agents working within an enemy intelligence organization), defection, and betrayal that also comments on his own writing career, the espionage genre, and the cold war between East and West that has inspired such fiction. Derrick Murdoch of the Toronto *Globe and Mail* calls the trilogy "Deighton's most ambitious project; the conventional spy-story turned inside-out."

The first novel of the trilogy, *Berlin Game,* opens with two agents waiting near the Berlin Wall for a defector to cross over from East Berlin. "How long have we been sitting here?" asks Bernie Samson, British agent and the protagonist of the trilogy. "Nearly a quarter of a century," his companion replies. With that exchange Deighton underlines the familiarity of this scene in espionage fiction, in his own early work and in the work of others, while commenting on the continuing relevance of the Berlin Wall as a symbol of East-West conflict, notes Anthony Olcott in the *Washington Post Book World.* Deighton, Olcott argues, "is not only aware of this familiarity, it is his subject. . . . Berlin and the Wall remain as much the embodiment of East-West rivalry as ever. . . . To read *Berlin Game* is to shrug off 25 years of acclimatization to the Cold War, and to recall what espionage fiction is about in the first place."

Mexico Set continues the story begun in *Berlin Game.* In the first book, Samson uncovers the spy in British intelligence—his own wife—and she defects to East Germany. To redeem himself in the eyes of his superiors, who now harbor understandable doubts about his own loyalty, Samson works in *Mexico Set* to convince a Russian KGB agent to defect. But the agent may only be a plant meant to further discredit Samson and destroy his credibility. If Samson cannot convince him to defect, his superiors may assume that he is secretly working for the Russians himself. But the Russian may defect only to provide British intelligence with "proof" of Samson's treason. As in *Berlin Game,* Deighton relates this novel back to the origins of the cold war and, "just when you've forgotten what the Cold War was all about, Len Deighton takes you right back to the [Berlin] Wall and rubs your nose on it," as Chuck Moss writes in the *Detroit News.*

Samson's efforts to persuade the Russian agent to defect take him from London to Mexico, Paris, and Berlin. "Every mile along the way," Noel Behn writes in the *Chicago Tribune,* "objectives seem to alter, friends and enemies become indistinguishable, perils increase, people disappear, people die." Behn finds it is Deighton's characters that make the story believable: "They strut forward one after the other—amusing, beguiling, arousing, deceiving, threatening—making us look in the wrong direction when it most behooves the prestidigitator's purpose." Ross Thomas also sees Deighton's characters as an essential ingredient in the novel's success. Writing in the *Washington Post Book World,* Thomas reports that Deighton "serves up fascinating glimpses of such types as the nearly senile head of British intelligence; a KGB major with a passion for Sherlock Holmes; and Samson's boyhood friend and Jewish orphan, Werner Volkmann," all of whom Thomas finds to be "convincing characters." Thomas concludes that *Mexico Set* is "one of [Deighton's] better efforts," while Behn calls the novel "a pure tale, told by an author at the height of his power."

In the final novel of the trilogy, *London Match,* the Russian agent has defected to the British. But Samson must now decide whether the defector is telling the truth when he insists that a high-ranking member of British intelligence is a Russian mole. The situation grows more complicated when the suspected mole, one of Samson's superiors, comes to Samson for help in clearing his name. *London Match* "is the most complex novel of the trilogy," Julius Lester writes in the *New York Times Book Review.*

Deighton continues Samson's adventures in the 1988 *Spy Hook,* the first story in a second trilogy about the British intelligence agent. In this thriller, Samson is charged with accounting for the disappearance of millions in Secret Service funds. At first, he suspects his ex-wife—who defected in the earlier *Berlin Game*—as the thief, but later Samson learns that his superiors have begun to suspect him for the crime. *Spy Hook* was chosen as a Book-of-the-Month Club selection and became a best-seller. Critical

reception of the work was generally favorable, with reviewers praising the book's carefully developed and intricate plot, detailed settings, and suspenseful atmosphere. A number of reviewers, however, reacted negatively to the book's ending, which they feel is too ambiguous. "Deighton's craftsmanship—his taut action and his insightful study of complex characters under pressure—is very much in place here, but many. . . unanswered questions raised in *Spy Hook* remain just that at the novel's conclusion," states Don G. Campbell, for example, in the *Los Angeles Times Book Review.* Several critics, though, share Margaret Cannon's Toronto *Globe and Mail* assessment of *Spy Hook* as matching Deighton's previous achievements in the espionage genre. The novel, she writes, "promises to be even better than its terrific predecessors and proves that Deighton, the old spymaster, is still in top form."

Deighton followed *Spy Hook* with the trilogy's second installment, *Spy Line,* in 1989 and the concluding book, *Spy Sinker,* in 1990. *Spy Sinker* focuses on the clandestine efforts of Samson's wife to effect the fall of the Berlin Wall from inside East Germany. As it turns out, Samson's wife was working as a double-agent all along. Her earlier defection and callous abandonment of her husband was ordered by British Intelligence as part of a long-term strategic plan to subvert East German internal order. "Here *Spy Sinker* shows Deighton at the top of his form, in his concentration upon the one player in this series whose story is not yet told," writes Anthony Olcott in *Washington Post Book World.* Olcott adds, "Deighton is able now to close in *Spy Sinker* by exploring what betrayal costs the betrayer, a woman who for higher loyalties leaves husband, home, and country, to incur even more betrayals in a cycle which may, in the end, destroy her."

According to Albert Hunt in *New Statesmen & Society,* "Everything slots together beautifully—Len Deighton has done as professional a job as Bernard Samson ever did." A *Time* reviewer similarly praises *Spy Sinker,* noting that Deighton accomplishes the near impossible—"winding up a closely plotted six-volume thriller . . . and still writing a credible novel. He makes a good job of it with a clever change of focus." However, *New York Times Book Review* contributor Morton Kondracke strongly disagrees: "As a stand-alone spy novel, this book is implausible, often incomprehensible and, altogether, downright dull." Though acknowledging the rather convenient resolution achieved by Deighton as the omnipotent narrator, Hunt remarks, "Manipulation, rather than the Berlin Wall, is what these books are about—that, and the way what Bernard calls 'marital, professional and political' betrayals are enmeshed."

Deighton initiated another Samson trilogy with *Faith* and *Hope* in 1995. Set in Berlin in 1987, *Faith* involves Samson's participation in the defection of a Communist spy and relates complicated domestic circumstances surrounding the return of his wife after their long separation. "What raises Deighton's genre to art," according to Andy Solomon in *Washington Post Book World,* "is not only his absorbing characters but his metaphoric grace . . . droll wit . . . command of technical detail . . . and sure sense of place." Despite such praise, *New York Times Book Review* contributor Newgate Callendar describes *Faith* as "dull and turgid." Likewise *Kirkus Reviews* criticizes Deighton's "vapid characters, murky plot, and infelicitous descriptions." While noting slow passages concerning Samson's marital difficulties and Intelligence agency politics, *Times Literary Supplement* reviewer John-Paul Flintoff writes, "Deighton throws in plenty of plausible details—tricks of the trade, gun specifications, a picture of Berlin as a local would see it."

Deighton followed with *Hope,* in which Samson pursues his Polish brother-in-law despite official evidence of his death at the hands of Russian army deserters. Commenting on the strained relationship depicted between Samson and his wife, a *Times Literary Supplement* reviewer describes *Hope* as "an unexpectedly ambiguous novel, complicated by repressed emotions and jealousies as well as by double crosses and false identities." Scott Veale complains in the *New York Times Book Review,* "there's more secrecy than action in this novel, and too often it's easy to get lost in the plot's numerous byways." However, Chris Petrakos praises *Hope* in Chicago *Tribune Books,* noting that "as usual" Deighton puts forth "a taut, enigmatic effort." *Publishers Weekly* also commends *Hope* and hails Deighton as "the only author other than le Carre who deserves to be known as 'spymaster.'"

Although Deighton is best known for his espionage fiction, he has also written best-selling novels outside the espionage field, as well as books of military history. These other novels and books of history are usually concerned with the events and figures of the World War II. Among the most successful of his novels have been *SS-GB: Nazi-Occupied Britain, 1941* and *Goodbye, Mickey Mouse: The True Story of the Battle of Britain* has earned Deighton praise as a writer of military history. Deighton's writing in other fields has shown him, Symons writes, to be "determined not to stay within the conventional pattern of the spy story or thriller."

SS-GB takes place in an alternative history of World War II, a history in which England lost the crucial Battle of Britain and Nazi Germany conquered the country. The story takes place after the conquest when Scotland Yard superintendent Douglas Archer investigates a murder and finds that the trail leads to the upper echelons of the Nazi party. An underground plot to rescue the king of England, who is being held prisoner in the Tower of London, and the ongoing efforts of the Nazis to develop the atom bomb also complicate Archer's problems. "As is usual with Mr. Deighton," John Leonard writes in *Books of the Times,* "there are as many twists as there are betrayals."

Goodbye, Mickey Mouse, another Deighton novel about World War II, concerns a group of American pilots in England who run fighter protection for the bombers making daylight runs over Germany. It is described by Thomas Gifford of the *Washington Post Book World* as "satisfying on every imaginable level, but truly astonishing in its recreation of a time and place through minute detail." Equally high praise comes from Peter Andrews, who writes in his review for the *New York Times Book Review*: "Deighton's latest World War II adventure novel is such a plain, old-fashioned, good book about combat pilots who make war and fall in love that it defies a complicated examination. . . . 'Goodbye, Mickey Mouse' is high adventure of the best sort but always solidly true to life."

The crucial Battle of Britain, which figures prominently in *SS-GB,* and the air battles of that period, which appear in *Goodbye, Mickey Mouse,* are further explored in the nonfiction *Fighter,* a history of the Royal Air Force defense of England during the Battle of Britain. *Fighter* is a highly acclaimed popular account of what Noble Frankland of the *Times Literary Supplement* calls "among the handful of decisive battles in British history." In the *New York Times Book Review,* Drew Middleton lauds *Fighter* as "the best, most dispassionate story of the battle I have read . . . and I say that even though the book destroyed many of my illusions and, indeed, attacks the validity of some of what I wrote as an eyewitness of the air battle 38 years ago."

In all of his writing, whether fiction or nonfiction, Deighton shows a concern for an accurate and detailed presentation of the facts. He has included appendices in several novels to explain to his readers such espionage esoterica as the structure of foreign intelligence organizations and the effects of various poisons. Howard claims that Deighton "takes enormous, almost obsessional care to get the background to his books exactly right."

Part of Deighton's research involves extensive travel throughout the world; he is reported to have contacts in cities as far-flung as Anchorage and Casablanca. These research trips have sometimes proven dangerous. Hugh Moffett notes that Deighton was once "hauled into police barracks in Czechoslovakia when he neglected to renew his visa." And Russian soldiers once took him into custody in East Berlin. For *Bomber: Events Relating to the Last Flight of an R.A.F. Bomber Over Germany on the Night of June 31, 1943,* Deighton made three trips to Germany and spent several years in research, gathering some half million words in notes. Research for the books *Fighter* and *Blitzkrieg: From the Rise of Hitler to the Fall of Dunkirk* took nearly nine years.

Deighton turns to historical fiction in his 1987 book *Winter: A Novel of a Berlin Family.* The story of a well-to-do German family led by a banker and war financier, *Winter* depicts how cultural and historical factors influence the attitudes of his two sons, one of whom joins the murderous Nazi party, while the other moves to the United States and marries a Jewish woman. The mixed criticism for *Winter* revolves around Deighton's sympathetic portrayals of his Nazi characters and around the novel's wide historical scope, which some reviewers feel is inadequately represented, mainly through dialogue rather than plot.

"Unlike much of Deighton's work," writes Gary Dretzka in Chicago *Tribune Books,* "'Winter' isn't much concerned with military strategy, suspense and spies as with people and relationships." According to Elizabeth Ward in *Washington Post Book World,* "*Winter* is neither fiction nor history but docudrama, running like a film script in a series of dutifully dated vignettes from New Year's Eve 1899 . . . to 1945." Favorably describing *Winter* as a fictional counterpart to William L. Shirer's acclaimed historical work *The Rise and Fall of the Third Reich,* Ward maintains that "*Winter* is an altogether silkier, less demanding and more entertaining read," adding, "Len Deighton certainly knows how to move a narrative along, build suspense and weave mysteries, even if history did write the larger plot for him."

Deighton also produced *City of Gold* in 1992, another volume of historical fiction based on events during the Second World War. This novel is set in Cairo at the height of Nazi domination of North Africa under the command of General Erwin Rommel. The protagonist is Corporal Jim Ross, a British soldier who escapes court-martial by assuming the identity of Major Bert Cutler, a British Intelligence agent who dies of a heart attack on a train. With his new identity and security clearance, Ross (as Cutler) is assigned to uncover the source of Rommel's detailed information about Allied forces and their movements. Though critical of Deighton's unusually large cast of stereotyped characters, Michael Kernan writes in *Washington Post Book World,* "The action scenes in the desert are as good as anything he has written." *Kirkus Reviews* praises Deighton's "terrific return" to the Second World War and the "rich drama of heroes and villains" in *City of Gold.* "In the finest Deighton form," writes Dick Roraback in the *Los Angeles Times Book Review,* "the master sets up his row of people then surrounds them with the authentic sights, sounds, smells, the moods and mores of their locale."

Continuing the trilogy begun with *Faith* and *Hope,* the novel *Charity* begins with Bernard's wife, Fiona, returning home after a dangerous flirtation with spy life that has led to the death of her sister, Tessa. The action takes place more than a year before the fall of the Berlin Wall, and Bernard, assigned to Berlin, is nervous about leaving Fiona behind; he is convinced that something is fishy about Tessa's death. *Booklist* notes: "Bernard is at his stubborn, cynical best, exhibiting his trademark biting wit and subtle disregard for the rules as he pushes the envelope in his quest for the truth," and calls the book "brilliant."

Deighton's position as one of the most prominent of contemporary espionage writers is secure. Cannon describes him as "one of the finest living writers of espionage novels." Schorr relates that it was Rudyard Kipling who "first called espionage the 'Great Game,' and no one is more adept at providing a fictional play-by-play than Len Deighton."

BIOGRAPHICAL/CRITICAL SOURCES:

BOOKS

Contemporary Literary Criticism, Gale, Volume 4, 1975; Volume 7, 1977; Volume 22, 1982; Volume 46, 1988.
Keating, H. R. F., editor, *Whodunit?: A Guide to Crime, Suspense and Spy Fiction,* Van Nostrand, 1982.
Symons, Julian, *Mortal Consequences: A History—From the Detective Story to the Crime Novel,* Harper, 1972.

PERIODICALS

Armchair Detective, winter, 1986.
Booklist, June 1-15, 1993; November 15, 1995, p. 514; June 1, 1996, p. 1749.
Books and Bookmen, September, 1967; December, 1971.
Books of the Times, February, 1979; August, 1981.
Chicago Tribune Book World, March 18, 1979; January 19, 1986.
Detroit News, February 3, 1985; February 9, 1986.
Globe and Mail (Toronto), December 1, 1984; December 14, 1985.
Harper's, November, 1982.
Kirkus Reviews, May 1, 1992, p. 555; October 15, 1994, p. 1364; October 1, 1996, p. 1418.
Library Journal, December, 1995, p. 514.
Life, March 25, 1966.
London Review of Books, March 19-April 1, 1981.
Los Angeles Times, November 26, 1982; March 23, 1987.
Los Angeles Times Book Review, March 17, 1985; February 16, 1986; November 22, 1987; August 19, 1990, p. 8; July 26, 1992, p. 9.
National Review, December 23, 1996, p. 56.
New Leader, January 19, 1976.
New Republic, December 13, 1975.
New Statesman, December 7, 1962; September 8, 1964; May 12, 1967; June 18, 1976; August 25, 1978.
New Statesman and Society, September 14, 1990; September 6, 1991.
Newsweek, January 18, 1965; January 31, 1966; June 26, 1972; October 14, 1974; February 19, 1979; December 27, 1982; December 19, 1983; February 11, 1985; January 13, 1986.
New Yorker, February 3, 1968; May 7, 1979; February 6, 1984.
New York Herald Tribune Book Review, November 17, 1963.
New York Times, January 12, 1965; October 17, 1970; October 16, 1976; September 20, 1977; May 13, 1981; June 21, 1981; December 7, 1982; December 12, 1983; December 21, 1987.
New York Times Book Review, November 10, 1963; January 17, 1965; May 21, 1967; January 14, 1968; October 4, 1970; April 13, 1975; July 9, 1978; February 25, 1979; May 3, 1981; November 14, 1982; January 8, 1984; March 10, 1985; December 1, 1985; January 10, 1988; December 25, 1988; September 2, 1990, p. 6; June 28, 1992; August 15, 1993; January 29, 1995, p. 21; February 25, 1996, p. 21; February 25, 1996, p. 21; January 12, 1997, p. 21.
Playboy, May, 1966.
Publishers Weekly, November 27, 1995, p. 53; November 4, 1996, p. 64.
Saturday Review, January 30, 1965; June 10, 1978.
Spectator, September 24, 1977; September 2, 1978; April 18, 1981.
Time, March 12, 1979; April 27, 1981; January 13, 1986; December 28, 1987; December 5, 1988; September 17, 1990, p. 79.
Times Literary Supplement, February 8, 1963; June 1, 1967; June 22, 1967; September 25, 1970; June 16, 1972; May 3, 1974; October 28, 1977; September 15, 1978; March 13, 1981; October 21, 1983; October 21, 1994; October 6, 1995, p. 28; September 20, 1996, p. 23.
Tribune Books (Chicago), February 24, 1985; December 27, 1987; January 1, 1989; January 8, 1989; January 21, 1996, p. 6; January 19, 1997, p. 6.
Village Voice, February 19, 1979.
Wall Street Journal, May 21, 1980.
Washington Post, October 9, 1970; December 20, 1987; December 13, 1988; December 12, 1989; July 12, 1992.
Washington Post Book World, September 29, 1974; June 4, 1978; March 20, 1979; April 14, 1981; November 7, 1982; January 8, 1984; January 27, 1985; December 15, 1985; December 20, 1987; September 23, 1990; February 12, 1995.

*   *   *

de la MARE, Walter (John) 1873-1956 (Walter Ramal)

PERSONAL: Born April 25, 1873, in Charlton, Kent, England; died June 22, 1956, in Twickenham, Middlesex, England; buried at St. Paul's Cathedral, London, England; son of James Edward (a church warden) and Lucy Sophia (Browning) de la Mare; married Constance Elfrida Ingpen, 1899 (died, 1943); children: Dick, Florence, Jenny, Colin. *Education:* Attended St. Paul's Cathedral Choir School, London.

CAREER: Anglo-American (Standard) Oil Company, London, England, clerk in statistics department, 1890-1908; writer.

MEMBER: Athenaeum Club.

AWARDS, HONORS: Polignac prize, Royal Society of Literature, 1911; James Tait Black Memorial Prize for fiction, 1922, for *Memoirs of a Midget;* Carnegie Medal, Library Association, 1947, for *Collected Stories for Children;* Companion of Honour, 1948; Order of Merit, 1953; Foyle Poetry prize, 1954; honorary degrees from several universities, including Oxford, Cambridge, St. Andrews, Bristol, and London.

WRITINGS:

FOR CHILDREN

(Under name Walter Ramal) *Songs of Childhood* (poetry), Longman, 1902, Garland, 1976, revised edition (published under name Walter de la Mare), Longman, 1916, new edition published as *Songs of Childhood,* illustrated by Estella

Canziani, 1923, illustrated by Marion Rivers-Moore, Faber, 1956.

The Three Mulla-Mulgars (fiction), illustrated by J. R. Monsell, Duckworth, 1910, illustrated by Dorothy P. Lathrop, Knopf, 1919, illustrated by J. A. Shepherd, Selwyn & Blount, 1924, published as *The Three Royal Monkeys,* illustrated by Mildred E. Eldridge, Faber, 1969.

A Child's Day (poetry), illustrated by Carine Cadby and Will Cadby, Constable, 1912, illustrated by Winifred Bromhall, Holt, 1923.

Peacock Pie (poetry), Constable, 1913, illustrated by W. Heath Robinson, 1916, illustrated by Jocelyn Crow, Holt, 1936, illustrated by Edward Ardizzone, Faber, 1946, illustrated by Barbara Cooney, Knopf, 1961, revised edition, Faber, 1969.

Story and Rhyme (fiction), Dutton, 1921.

Crossings: A Fairy Play, music by Cecil Armstrong Gibbs, illustrated by Randolph Schwabe (produced by Hove, Sussex, 1919, London, 1925), Beaumont Press, 1921, illustrated by Lathrop, Knopf, 1923, illustrated by Gwendolen Raverat, Faber, 1942.

Down-Adown-Derry (poetry), illustrated by Lathrop, Holt, 1922.

(Editor with Alec Buckels) *Come Hither* (poetry), illustrated by Buckels, Knopf, 1923, revised edition, 1928.

(Editor with Thomas Quayle) *Readings: Traditional Tales Told by the Author,* illustrated by A. H. Watson and C. T. Nightingale, six volumes, Blackwell, 1925-28, one volume, Knopf, 1927.

Broomsticks and Other Tales (fiction; contains "Pigtails, Ltd.", "The Dutch Cheese," "Miss Jemima," "The Thief," "Broomsticks," "Lucy," "A Nose," "The Three Sleeping Boys of Warwickshire," "The Lovely Myfanwy," "Alice's Godmother," "Maria-Fly," and "Visitors"), illustrated by Bold, Knopf, 1925.

Miss Jemima (fiction), illustrated by Buckels, Basil Blackwell, 1925, Artists and Writers Guild, 1935, published as *The Story of Miss Jemima,* illustrated by Nellie H. Farnam, Grosset & Dunlap, 1940.

(With others) *Number Three Joy Street,* Appleton, 1925.

(With others) *Number Four Joy Street,* Appleton, 1926.

(With others) *Number Five Joy Street,* Appleton, 1927.

Lucy, illustrated by Hilda T. Miller, Basil Blackwell, 1927.

Old Joe (fiction), illustrated by C. T. Nightingale, Basil Blackwell, 1927.

Stuff and Nonsense and So On (poetry), woodcuts by Bold, Holt, 1927, revised edition, Faber, 1946, illustrated by Margaret Wolpe, Faber, 1957.

Told Again: Traditional Tales, illustrated by A. H. Watson, Blackwell, 1927, published as *Told Again: Old Tales Told Again,* Knopf, 1927, published as *Tales Told Again,* illustrated by Alan Howard, Faber/Knopf, 1959.

(With others) *Number Six Joy Street,* Appleton, 1928.

Stories from the Bible, illustrated by Theodore Nadejen, Cosmopolitan, 1929; illustrated by Ardizzone, 1977.

Poems for Children, Holt, 1930.

The Dutch Cheese and the Lovely Myfanwy (fiction), illustrated by Lathrop, Knopf, 1931, illustrated by Hawkins, Faber, 1946.

(Editor) *Tom Tiddler's Ground: A Book of Poetry for the Junior and Middle Schools,* illustrations from Thomas Bewick, three volumes, Collins, 1931, illustrated by Margery Gill, one volume, Knopf, 1962.

(Editor) *Old Rhymes and New, Chosen for Use in Schools,* two volumes, Constable, 1932.

The Lord Fish and Other Tales (fiction; contains "The Lord Fish," "A Penny a Day," "The Jacket," "Dick and the Beanstalk,"

"Hodmadod," "The Old Lion," and "Sambo and the Snow Mountains"), illustrated by Rex Whistler, Faber, 1933.

Letters from Mr. Walter de la Mare to Form Three, privately printed, 1936.

(With Harold Jones) *This Year: Next Year* (poetry), illustrated by Jones, Holt, 1937.

Animal Stories, Chosen, Arranged, and in Some Part Re-Written, Faber, 1939, Scribner, 1940.

Bells and Grass: A Book of Rhymes, illustrated by F. Rowland Emett, Faber, 1941, illustrated by Lathrop, Viking, 1942.

The Old Lion and Other Stories (fiction), illustrated by Irene Hawkins, Faber, 1942.

Mr. Bumps and His Monkey (fiction), illustrated by Lathrop, J. C. Winston, 1942.

The Magic Jacket, and Other Stories (contains "The Magic Jacket," "Miss Jemima," "Dick and the Beanstalk," and "The Riddle"), illustrated by Hawkins, Faber, 1943, illustrated by Paul Kennedy, Knopf, 1962.

The Scarecrow and Other Stories (contains "The Scarecrow or Hodmadod," "The Lovely Myfanwy," "Broomsticks," and "Visitors"), illustrated by Hawkins, Faber, 1945.

The Dutch Cheese and Other Stories (contains "The Dutch Cheese," "Lucy," "Alice's Godmother," "A Penny a Day," and "The Three Sleeping Boys of Warwickshire"), illustrated by Hawkins, Faber, 1946.

Dick Whittington (adapted from a story appearing in *Told Again*), illustrated by Ionicus, Hulton, 1951.

Jack and the Beanstalk (adapted from a story appearing in *Told Again*), illustrated by William and Brenda Stobbs, Hulton, 1951.

Selected Stories and Verses, edited by Eleanor Graham, Penguin, 1952.

The Story of Joseph, illustrated by Ardizzone, Faber, 1958.

The Story of Moses, illustrated by Ardizzone, Knopf, 1960.

The Story of Samuel and Saul, illustrated by Ardizzone, Faber, 1960.

A Penny a Day (fiction; contains "A Penny a Day," "The Three Sleeping Boys of Warwickshire," "The Lovely Myfanwy," "The Dutch Cheese," "Dick and the Beanstalk," and "The Lord Fish"), illustrated by Paul Kennedy, Knopf, 1960.

Molly Whuppie, illustrated by Errol Le Cain, Straus, 1983.

The Voice: A Sequence of Poems, edited and illustrated by Catherine Brighton, Faber, 1986, Delacorte, 1987.

Visitors, Creative Education, 1986.

The Lord Fish, Candlewick Press (Cambridge, MA), 1997.

FOR ADULTS

Henry Brocken: His Travels and Adventures in the Rich, Strange, Scarce-Imaginable Regions of Romance (novel), J. Murray, 1904, Knopf, 1924.

Poems, Murray, 1906.

M. E. Coleridge: An Appreciation, The Guardian, 1907.

The Return (novel), Arnold, 1910, Putnam, 1911, revised edition, Knopf, 1922.

The Listeners and Other Poems, Constable, 1912, Holt, 1916.

The Old Men (poetry), Flying Fame, 1913.

The Sunken Garden and Other Poems, Beaumont Press, 1917.

Motley and Other Poems, Holt, 1918.

Rupert Brooke and the Intellectual Imagination: A Lecture, Sidgwick & Jackson, 1919, Harcourt, 1920.

Flora (poetry), illustrated by Pamela Bianco, Lippincott, 1919.

The Veil and Other Poems, Constable, 1921, Holt, 1922.

Memoirs of a Midget (novel), Collins, 1921, Knopf, 1922.

Lispet, Lispett, and Vaine (short stories), Bookman's Journal, 1923.

The Riddle (contains "The Almond Tree," "The Count's Courtship," "The Looking-Glass," "Miss Duveen," "Sellna's Parable," "Seaton's Aunt," "The Bird of Travel," "The Bowl," "The Three Friends," "Lispet, Lispett, and Vaine," "The Tree," "Out of the Deep," "The Creatures," "The Riddle," and "The Vats"), Selwyn and Blount, 1923, published as *The Riddle and Other Tales,* Knopf, 1923.

Thus Her Tale: A Poem, illustrated by William Ogilvie, Porpoise Press, 1923.

Some Thoughts on Reading (lecture), Yellowsands Press, 1923.

A Ballad of Christmas (poetry), Selwyn and Blount, 1924.

Ding Dong Bell (contains the short stories "Lichen," "Benighted," and "Winter"), Knopf, 1924.

Two Tales: The Green-Room, The Connoisseur, Bookman's Journal, 1925.

The Hostage (poetry), Selwyn and Blount, 1925.

(With Rudyard Kipling) *St. Andrews: Two Poems* (includes "A Memory"), A. and C. Black, 1926.

The Connoisseur and Other Stories (contains "Mr. Kempe," "Missing," "The Connoisseur," "Disillusioned," "The Nap," "Pretty Poll," "All Hallows," "The Wharf," and "The Lost Track"), Knopf, 1926.

Alone (poetry), wood engravings by Blair Hughes-Stanton, Faber & Gwyer, 1927.

The Captive and Other Poems (contains "To Katherine Mansfield," "On the Esplanade," "The Strange Spirit," "The Captive," "Reconciliation," and "The Snail"), Bowling Green Press, 1928.

Self to Self (poetry), Faber, 1928.

At First Sight (short stories), Crosby Gaige, 1928.

A Snowdrop (poetry), illustrated by Claudia Guercio, Faber, 1929.

Some Women Novelists of the 'Seventies, Cambridge University Press, 1929.

News (poetry), illustrated by Barnett Freedman, Faber, 1930.

(Editor) *Desert Islands and Robinson Crusoe* (literary quotations and discussion), illustrated by Rex Whistler, Fountain Press, 1930, revised edition, Faber, 1932.

(Editor) Christina Rossetti, *Poems,* Gregynog Press, 1930.

(Editor) *The Eighteen-Eighties: Essays by Fellows of the Royal Society of Literature,* Macmillan, 1930.

On the Edge: Short Stories (contains "A Recluse," "Willows," "Crewe," "At First Sight," "The Green Room," "The Orgy: An Idyll," "The Picnic," and "An Ideal Craftsman"), wood engravings by Elizabeth Rivera, Faber, 1930, Knopf, 1931.

To Lucy (poetry), illustrated by Albert Rutherston, Faber, 1931.

The Sunken Garden and Other Verses, Birmingham School of Printing, 1931.

Two Poems, privately printed, 1931.

The Printing of Poetry (lecture), Cambridge University Press, 1931.

The Early Novels of Wilkie Collins, Cambridge University Press, 1932.

Lewis Carroll, Faber, 1932.

The Fleeting and Other Poems, Knopf, 1933.

A Froward Child (short stories), Faber, 1934.

Early One Morning in the Spring: Chapters on Children and on Childhood as It Is Revealed in Particular in Early Memories and in Early Writings, Macmillan, 1935.

Poetry in Prose (lecture), H. Milford, 1935, Oxford University Press, 1937.

The Nap and Other Stories, Nelson, 1936.

The Wind Blows Over (contains the short stories "What Dreams May Come," "Cape Race," "In the Forest," "Physic," "The Talisman," "A Froward Child," "Miss Miller," "The House," "A Revenant," "A Nest of Singing Birds," "The Trumpet," and "Strangers and Pilgrims") Macmillan, 1936.

Ghost Stories, illustrated by Freedman, Folio Society, 1936.

Poems, Corvinus Press, 1937.

Memory and Other Poems, Holt, 1938.

(With Arthur Rogers) *Two Poems,* privately printed, 1938.

Arthur Thompson: A Memoir, privately printed, 1938.

An Introduction to Everyman, Dent, 1938.

Haunted: A Poem, Linden Press, 1939.

(Editor) *Behold, This Dreamer!* Knopf, 1939.

Pleasures and Speculations (essays on literature; contains "The Great Adventurers," "Hans Christian Andersen," "Tennyson," "Naturalists," "The Thousand and One," "Poetry in Prose," "Rupert Brooke and the Intellectual Imagination," "Flowers and Poetry," "Some Women Novelists," "The Dream,'" "A Book of Words," and "Maps Actual and Imaginary"), Faber, 1940, Books for Libraries Press, 1969.

The Picnic and Other Stories, Faber, 1941.

Collected Poems, Holt, 1941.

Time Passes and Other Poems, edited by Anne Ridler, Faber, 1942.

(Editor) *Love,* Faber, 1943, Morrow, 1946.

The Burning-Glass (includes "The Traveller"), Viking Press, 1945, illustrated by John Piper, Faber, 1946.

The Traveller (poetry), Faber, 1946.

Two Poems: Pride, The Truth of Things, Dropmore Press, 1946.

Inward Companion (poetry), Faber, 1950.

Winged Chariot (poetry), Faber, 1951.

Winged Chariot and Other Poems, Viking Press, 1951.

O Lovely England, and Other Poems, Faber, 1953, Viking, 1956.

Private View (essays on literature), Faber, 1953, Hyperion, 1979.

The Winnowing Dream (poetry), illustrated by Robin Jacques, Faber, 1954.

The Morrow (poetry), privately printed, 1955.

A Beginning and Other Stories, Faber, 1955.

Some Stories, Faber, 1962.

Walter de la Mare (poetry), edited by John Hadfield, Vista Books, 1962.

Envoi (poetry), privately printed, 1965.

The Return, Dover Publications (Mineola, NY), 1997.

OTHER COLLECTIONS AND SELECTIONS

Poems 1901 to 1918, two volumes, Constable, 1920, published as *Collected Poems 1901 to 1918,* two volumes, Holt, 1920.

Walter de la Mare, edited by Edward Thompson, Benn, 1926.

Selected Poems, Holt, 1927.

Seven Short Stories (contains "Miss Duveen," "The Bird of Travel," "The Tree," "The Nap," "Missing," "The Wharf," and "Maria-Fly"), illustrated by John Nash, Faber, 1931.

Poems 1919 to 1934, Constable, 1935, Holt, 1936.

Stories, Essays, and Poems, edited by M. M. Bozman, Dent, 1938.

Best Stories of Walter de la Mare (contains "The Almond Tree," "Miss Duveen," "An Ideal Craftsman," "Seaton's Aunt," "Crewe," "Missing," "Miss Miller," "The Orgy," "The Nap," "Physic," "The Picnic," "All Hallows," "The Trumpet," "The House," "What Dreams May Come," and "The Vats"), Faber, 1942.

Collected Rhymes and Verse, illustrated by Berthold Wolpe, 1944, illustrated by Errol Le Cain, 1970, both Faber.

Collected Stories for Children (contains "Dick and the Beanstalk," "The Dutch Cheese," "A Penny a Day," "The Scarecrow,"

"The Three Sleeping Boys of Warwickshire," "The Lovely Myfanwy," "Lucy," "Miss Jemima," "The Magic Jacket," "The Lord Fish," "The Old Lion," "Broomsticks," "Alice's Godmother," "Maria-Fly," "Visitors," "Sambo and the Snow Mountains," and "The Riddle"), illustrated by Hawkins, Faber, 1947, illustrated by Jacques, 1967.

Rhymes and Verses: Collected Poems for Children, illustrated by Elinore Blaisdell, Holt, 1947.

The Collected Tales of Walter de la Mare, edited by Edward Wagenknecht, Knopf, 1950.

Selected Poems, edited by R. N. Green-Armytage, Faber, 1954.

Walter de la Mare: A Selection from His Writings, edited by Kenneth Hopkins, Faber, 1956.

Best Stories, Faber, 1957.

Collected Poems (contains "Poems," "The Listeners," "Motley," "The Veil," "The Fleeting," and "Memory"), illustrated by B. Wolpe, Faber, 1961.

Poems (edited by Eleanor Graham), illustrated by Margery Gill, Penguin, 1962.

A Choice of de la Mare's Verse, edited, and with an introduction by W. H. Auden, Faber, 1963.

Secret Laughter, illustrated by Gill, Penguin, 1969.

The Complete Poems of Walter de la Mare, edited by Leonard Clark and others, Faber, 1969, Knopf, 1970.

Eight Tales, Arkham House, 1971.

The Collected Poems of Walter de la Mare, Faber, 1979.

De la Mare's manuscripts are present in the collections of Syracuse University, Temple University, the University of Chicago, and King's College of Cambridge University.

SIDELIGHTS: Commenting on Walter de la Mare's literary diversity, *Dictionary of Literary Biography* contributor Michael Kirkham stated that the author "will be remembered chiefly as a poet and writer of children's verse, the two genres not always clearly distinguishable in his work. But until 1928 he was also a novelist and until the mid-1930s a short-story writer; he was an anthologist of great individuality, an essayist, and a reviewer." Born in 1873, de la Mare attended St. Paul's Cathedral school, where he became founder and editor of the *Choristers' Journal.* At age seventeen, he began working as a clerk for the Anglo-American Oil Company and he also edited and wrote for the company's internal publication. De la Mare retained his position with the Anglo-American Oil Company for eighteen years, until he received a government pension that enabled him to become a full-time writer.

In 1902, de la Mare published his first book, *Songs of Childhood.* Like his other early books and magazine stories, it was printed under the pseudonym Walter Ramal ("Ramal" being an anagram of "de la Mare"). In the introduction to *Bells and Grass,* de la Mare commented on the public's reception of *Songs of Childhood,* stating that "charming though the little volume was in outward appearance, its welcome hardly resembled that bestowed on hot cakes. But there it actually was, in print."

In order to entertain his own children, de la Mare wrote his best-known novel, *The Three Mulla-Mulgars* (later reprinted as *The Three Royal Monkeys*). The world of *The Three Mulla-Mulgars* "is inhabited primarily by the various races of monkeys ('Mulgars'), among whom man is only another sub-species (or 'Oomgar-Mulgar')," noted *Twentieth-Century Children's Writers* contributor Julia Briggs, who also observed that "the highest in rank are the 'Mulla-Mulgars' or royal monkeys such as the book's heroes, the brothers Thumb, Thimble, and Nod. Their quest for the

paradisal land of Tishnar, their destined home, provides the main narrative thread." Some critics who enjoyed reading *The Three Mulla-Mulgars* questioned whether the writing style is sufficiently accessible to young readers. For example, *Junior Bookshelf* reviewer M. S. Crouch asserted that *The Three Mulla-Mulgars* is "difficult for children to read themselves, for its strange names and its complex symbolism." However, Crouch also declared that "it is, for all that, a very great children's book, a great adventure-story, superbly told." De la Mare's novel is regarded by some critics as a precursor to such modern British fantasies as J. R. R. Tolkien's *The Lord of the Rings* and Richard Adams's *Watership Down.* "Today de la Mare's works are frequently overlooked in favor of more recent authors'," noted *Writers for Children* contributor Ellin Greene, who added that "the loss is ours. His fantasies are every bit as good as those by Tolkien, C. S. Lewis, and Lloyd Alexander. His poems and stories are part of the canon of children's literature."

In general, critics have especially praised de la Mare's appreciation for the imaginative life of childhood. "Looking back over the years since *Songs of Childhood* and *Peacock Pie* first became widely known," wrote *Horn Book* contributor Margery Bianco in a 1942 issue devoted to consideration of de la Mare, "one can only now begin to realize how great has been Walter de la Mare's influence upon the whole field of imaginative literature for children, and the full significance of his contribution. . . . When he speaks of a tree, a bird, a flower, it is as though one were seeing it—really seeing it—for the first time, through the eyes of one who is sensitive to beauty in whatever form, even under the guise of what is called ugliness."

Writing in the *London Mercury,* J. B. Priestley asserted that de la Mare's popularity resulted from his remembrance of childhood. The critic commented that de la Mare "remains one of that most lovable order of artists who never lose sight of their childhood, but re-live it continually in their work and contrive to find expression for their maturity in it, memories and impressions, its romantic vision of the world; the artists whose limitations and weaknesses are plain for any passing fool to see, but whose genius, and they are never without it, never mere men of talent, delights both philosophers and children; the artists who remember Eden." De la Mare, himself, declared in his introduction to *Bells and Grass* that *Peacock Pie* and *Songs of Childhood* "had been written by and through that self within which, in however small a degree, there still lurked *some*thing that might merit so precious a tribute as that of being described as young." Similarly, an anthology co-edited by de la Mare, *Come Hither,* was subtitled *A Collection of Rhymes and Poems for the Young of All Ages.*

De la Mare retained his interest in imagination throughout his life. In a second "Walter de la Mare" issue of *Horn Book* in 1957, Eleanor Farjeon reported that de la Mare was "increasingly possessed" by the theme of "the reality of his dreams compared with the reality of his waking life." She quotes him as asking, "'Don't you find as you grow older—I do—that life is much more *actual* in your dreams?'" In 1954, de la Mare had fallen and suffered a brain injury that hindered his writing. He died two years later, and was buried in St. Paul's Cathedral.

BIOGRAPHICAL/CRITICAL SOURCES:

BOOKS

Atkins, John, *Walter de la Mare: An Exploration,* Temple, 1947.

Brain, Russell, *Tea with Walter de la Mare,* Faber, 1957.

Children's Literature Review, Volume 23, Gale (Detroit), 1991, pp. 40-81.

Clark, Leonard, *Walter de la Mare,* Bodley Head, 1960, Walck, 1961.

Dictionary of Literary Biography, Volume 19: *British Poets, 1880-1914,* Gale, 1983, pp. 109-31.

Hopkins, Kenneth, *Walter de la Mare,* Longman, 1953.

McCrosson, Doris Ross, *Walter de la Mare,* Twayne, 1966.

Reid, Forrest, *Walter de la Mare: A Critical Study,* Holt, 1929.

Twentieth-Century Children's Writers, 3rd edition, St. James Press, 1989, pp. 276-79.

Twentieth-Century Literary Criticism, Volume 4, Gale, 1981, pp. 70-82.

Whistler, Theresa, *Imagination of the Heart: The Life of Walter de la Mare,* Duckworth (London), 1993.

Writers for Children, Scribner, 1988, pp. 173-80.

PERIODICALS

Horn Book, May/June 1942; June, 1957.
Junior Bookshelf, October, 1956, pp. 187-91.
London Mercury, May, 1924, pp. 33-43.

*   *   *

DELANEY, Franey
   See O'HARA, John (Henry)

*   *   *

DELANY, Samuel R(ay Jr.) 1942-
   (K. Leslie Steiner)

PERSONAL: Born April 1, 1942, in New York, NY; son of Samuel R. (a funeral director) and Margaret Carey (a library clerk; maiden name, Boyd) Delany; married Marilyn Hacker (a poet), August 24, 1961 (divorced, 1980); children: Iva Alyxander. *Education:* Attended City College (now of the City University of New York), 1960 and 1962-63.

ADDRESSES: Agent—Henry Morrison, Inc., Box 235, Bedford Hills, NY 10507.

CAREER: Writer. State University of New York at Buffalo, Butler Professor of English, 1975; University of Wisconsin—Milwaukee, senior fellow at the Center for Twentieth Century Studies, 1977; Cornell University, Ithaca, NY, senior fellow at the Society for the Humanities, 1987; University of Massachusetts—Amherst, professor of comparative literature, 1988–.

AWARDS, HONORS: Nebula Awards, Science Fiction Writers of America, 1966, for best novel *Babel-17,* 1967, for best novel *The Einstein Intersection,* 1967, for best short story "Aye and Gomorrah," and 1969, for best novelette "Time Considered as a Helix of Semi-Precious Stones"; Hugo Award for best short story, World Science Fiction Convention, 1970, for "Time Considered as a Helix of Semi-Precious Stones"; American Book Award nomination, 1980, for *Tales of Neveryon*; Pilgrim Award, Science Fiction Research Association, 1985; Bill Whitehead Award for Lifetime Achievement in Gay Literature, 1993.

WRITINGS:

SCIENCE FICTION

The Jewels of Aptor (abridged edition bound with *Second Ending* by James White), Ace Books, 1962, hardcover edition, Gollancz, 1968, complete edition published with an introduction by Don Hausdorff, Gregg Press, 1976.

Captives of the Flame (first novel in trilogy; bound with *The Psionic Menace* by Keith Woodcott), Ace Books, 1963, revised edition published under author's original title *Out of the Dead City* (also see below), Sphere Books, 1968.

The Towers of Toron (second novel in trilogy; also see below; bound with *The Lunar Eye* by Robert Moore Williams), Ace Books, 1964.

City of a Thousand Suns (third novel in trilogy; also see below), Ace Books, 1965.

The Ballad of Beta-2 (also see below; bound with *Alpha Yes, Terra No!* by Emil Petaja), Ace Books, 1965, hardcover edition published with an introduction by David G. Hartwell, Gregg Press, 1977.

Empire Star (also see below; bound with *The Three Lords of Imeten* by Tom Purdom), Ace Books, 1966, hardcover edition published with an introduction by Hartwell, Gregg Press, 1977.

Babel-17, Ace Books, 1966, hardcover edition, Gollancz, 1967, published with an introduction by Robert Scholes, 1976.

The Einstein Intersection, slightly abridged edition, Ace Books, 1967, hardcover edition, Gollancz, 1968, complete edition, Ace Books, 1972.

Nova, Doubleday, 1968.

The Fall of the Towers (trilogy; contains *Out of the Dead City, The Towers of Toron,* and *City of a Thousand Suns*), Ace Books, 1970, hardcover edition published with introduction by Joseph Milicia, Gregg Press, 1977.

Driftglass: Ten Tales of Speculative Fiction, Doubleday, 1971.

The Tides of Lust, Lancer Books, 1973.

Dhalgren, Bantam, 1975, hardcover edition published with introduction by Jean Mark Gawron, Gregg Press, 1978.

The Ballad of Beta-2 [and] *Empire Star,* Ace Books, 1975.

Triton, Bantam, 1976; published as *Trouble on Triton: An Ambiguous Heterotopia,* University Press of New England (Hanover, NH), 1996.

Empire: A Visual Novel, illustrations by Howard V. Chaykin, Berkley Books, 1978.

Distant Stars, Bantam, 1981.

Stars in My Pocket Like Grains of Sand, Bantam, 1984.

The Complete Nebula Award-Winning Fiction, Bantam, 1986.

The Star Pits (bound with *Tango Charlie and Foxtrot Romeo* by John Varley), Tor Books, 1989.

They Fly at Ciron, Incunabula, 1992.

Equinox, Masquerade, 1994.

The Mad Man, Masquerade, 1994.

Atlantis: Three Tales, Wesleyan University (Middletown, CT), 1995.

"RETURN TO NEVERYON" SERIES; SWORD AND SORCERY NOVELS

Tales of Neveryon, Bantam, 1979.
Neveryona; or, The Tale of Signs and Cities, Bantam, 1983.
Flight from Neveryon, Bantam, 1985.
The Bridge of Lost Desire, Arbor House, 1987.

OTHER

The Jewel-Hinged Jaw: Notes on the Language of Science Fiction, Dragon Press, 1977, revised edition, Berkley Publishing, 1978.

The American Shore: Meditations on a Tale of Science Fiction by Thomas M. Disch—"Angouleme" (criticism), Dragon Press, 1978.

Heavenly Breakfast: An Essay on the Winter of Love (memoir), Bantam, 1979.

Starboard Wine: More Notes on the Language of Science Fiction,
Dragon Press, 1984.

*The Motion of Light in Water: Sex and Science Fiction Writing in
the East Village, 1957-1965,* Arbor House, 1988.

*Wagner/Artaud: A Play of Nineteenth and Twentieth Century
Critical Fictions,* Ansatz Press, 1988.

Straits of Messina (essays; originally published in magazines
under pseudonym K. Leslie Steiner), Serconia Press, 1989.

*Silent Interviews; On Language, Race, Sex, Science Fiction, and
Some Comics: A Collection of Written Interviews,* Wesleyan
University Press, 1994.

Longer Views: Extended Essays, University Press of New England
(Hanover, NH), 1996.

Bread and Wine: An Erotic Tale of New York City, Juno, 1998.

Also author of scripts, director, and editor for two short films,
Tiresias, 1970, and *The Orchid,* 1971; author of two scripts for the
Wonder Woman Comic Series, 1972, and of the radio play *The
Star Pit,* based on his short story of the same title. Editor, *Quark,*
1970-71. Contributor to periodicals, including *The New York
Review of Science Fiction.*

SIDELIGHTS: "Samuel R. Delany is one of today's most
innovative and imaginative writers of science-fiction," comments
Jane Branham Weedman in her study of the author, *Samuel R.
Delany.* In his science fiction, which includes over fifteen novels
and several collections of short stories, the author "has explored
what happens when alien world views intersect, collide, or mesh,"
writes Greg Tate in the *Voice Literary Supplement.* Delany first
appeared on the science fiction horizon in the early 1960s, and in
the decade that followed he established himself as one of the stars
of the genre. Like many of his contemporaries who entered
science fiction in the 1960s, he is less concerned with the
conventions of the genre, more interested in science fiction as
literature, literature which offers a wide range of artistic opportunities. As a result, maintains Weedman, "Delany's works are
excellent examples of modern science-fiction as it has developed
from the earlier and more limited science-fiction tradition,
especially because of his manipulation of cultural theories, his
detailed futuristic or alternate settings, and his stylistic innovations."

Delany entered the world of science fiction in 1962 with the
publication of his novel *The Jewels of Aptor.* Over the next six
years, he published eight more, including *Babel-17, The Einstein
Intersection,* and *Nova,* his first printed originally in hardcover.
Douglas Barbour, writing in *Science Fiction Writers,* describes
these early novels as "colorful, exciting, entertaining, and
intellectually provocative to a degree not found in most genre
science fiction." Barbour adds that although they do adhere to
science fiction conventions, they "begin the exploration of those
literary obsessions that define [Delany's] oeuvre: problems of
communication and community; new kinds of sexual/love/family
relationships; the artist as social outsider. . . ; cultural interactions and the exploration of human social possibilities these allow;
archetypal and mythic structures in the imagination."

With the publication of *Babel-17* in 1966, Delany began to gain
recognition in the science fiction world. The novel, which earned
its author his first Nebula Award, is a story of galactic warfare
between the forces of the Alliance, which includes the Earth, and
the forces of the Invaders. The poet Rydra Wong is enlisted by
Alliance intelligence to decipher communications intercepted
from its enemy. When she discovers that these dispatches contain
not a code but rather an unknown language, her quest becomes

one of learning this mysterious tongue labeled *Babel-17.* While
leading an interstellar mission in search of clues, Rydra gains
insights into the nature of language and, in the process, discovers
the unique character of the enigmatic new language of the
Invaders.

Babel-17 itself becomes an exploration of language and its ability
to structure experience. A central image in the novel, as George
Edgar Slusser points out in his study *The Delany Intersection:
Samuel R. Delany Considered as a Writer of Semi-Precious
Words,* is that of "the web and its weaver or breaker." The web,
continues Slusser, "stands, simultaneously, for unity and isolation,
interconnectedness and entanglement." And, as Alterman points
out in *Science-Fiction Studies,* "the web is an image of the effect
of language on the mind and of the mind as shaper of reality."
Weedman elaborates in her essay on the novel: "The language one
learns necessarily constrains and structures what it is that one
says." In its ability to connect and constrain is the power of the
language/web. "Language . . . has a direct effect on how one
thinks," explains Weedman, "since the structure of the language
influences the processes by which one formulates ideas." At the
center of the language as web "is one who joins and cuts—the
artist-hero," comments Slusser. And, in *Babel-17,* the poet Rydra
Wong demonstrates that only she is able to master this new
language weapon and turn it against its creators.

Delany followed *Babel-17* with another Nebula winner, *The
Einstein Intersection.* This novel represents a "move from a
consideration of the relationship among language, thought, action
and time to an analytic and imaginative investigation of the
patterns of myths and archetypes and their interaction with the
conscious mind," writes Alterman. Slusser sees this development
in themes as part of a logical progression: "[Myths] too are seen
essentially as language constructs: verbal scenarios for human
action sanctioned by tradition or authority." Comparing this novel
to *Babel-17,* he adds that "Delany's sense of the language act, in
this novel, has a broader social valence."

The Einstein Intersection relates the story of a strange race of
beings that occupies a post-apocalyptic Earth. This race assumes
the traditions—economic, political, and religious—of the extinct
humans in an attempt to make sense of the remnant world in
which they find themselves. "While they try to live by the myths
of man," writes Barbour in *Foundation,* "they cannot create a
viable culture of their own. . . . Their more profound hope is to
recognize that they do not have to live out the old myths at all,
that the 'difference' they seek to hide or dissemble is the key to
their cultural and racial salvation."

Delany's next novel, *Nova,* "stands as the summation of [his]
career up to that time," writes Barbour in *Science Fiction Writers:
Critical Studies of the Major Authors from the Early Nineteenth
Century to the Present Day.* "Packing his story full of color and
incident, violent action and tender introspective moments, he has
created one of the grandest space operas ever written." In this
novel, Delany presents a galaxy divided into three camps, all
embroiled in a bitter conflict caused by a shortage of the fuel
illyrion on which they all depend. In chronicling one group's
quest for a new source of the fuel, the author examines, according
to Weedman, "how technology changes the world and philosophies for world survival. Delany also explores conflicts between
and within societies, as well as the problems created by people's
different perceptions and different reality models."

After the publication of *Nova,* Delany turned his creative urges to
forms other than the novel, writing a number of short stories,

editing four quarterlies of speculative fiction, and dabbling in such diverse media as film and comic books. Also at this time, he engaged himself in conceiving, writing, and polishing what would become his longest, most complex, and most controversial novel, *Dhalgren*—a work that would earn him national recognition. On its shifting surface, this novel represents the experience of a nameless amnesiac, an artist/criminal, during the period of time he spends in a temporally and spatially isolated city scarred by destruction and decay. As Alterman relates in the *Dictionary of Literary Biography,* "it begins with the genesis of a protagonist, one so unformed that he has no name, no identity, the quest for which is the novel's central theme." The critic goes on to explain that "at the end Kid has a name and a life, both of which are the novel itself; he is a persona whose experience in *Dhalgren* defines him."

Dhalgren's length and complexity provide a significant challenge to readers, but as Gerald Jonas observes in the *New York Times Book Review,* "the most important fact about Delany's novel . . . is that nothing in it is clear. Nothing is meant to be clear." He adds: "An event may be described two or three times, and each recounting is slightly disconcertingly different from the one before." What is more, continues the reviewer, "the nameless narrator experiences time discontinuously; whole days seem to be excised from his memory." According to Weedman, "Delany creates disorientation in *Dhalgren* to explore the problems which occur when reality models differ from reality." And in Jonas's estimation, "If the book can be said to be *about* anything, it is about nothing less than the nature of reality."

Following the exhaustive involvement with Kid necessary to complete *Dhalgren,* Delany chose to do a novel in which he distanced himself from his protagonist, giving him a chance to look at the relationship between an individual and his society in a new light. "I wanted to do a psychological analysis of someone with whom you're just not in sympathy, someone whom you watch making all the wrong choices, even though his plight itself is sympathetic," Delany explained in an interview with Larry McCaffery and Sinda Gregory published in their book *Alive and Writing: Interviews with American Authors of the 1980s.* The novel is *Triton*; its main character is Bron.

"*Triton* is set in a sort of sexual utopia, where every form of sexual behavior is accepted, and sex-change operations (not to mention 'refixations,' to alter sexual preference) are common," observes Michael Goodwin in *Mother Jones.* In this world of freedom lives Bron, whom Govan describes in *Black American Literature Forum* as "a narrow-minded, isolated man, so self-serving that he is incapable of reaching outside himself to love another or even understand another despite his best intentions." In an attempt to solve his problems, he undergoes a sex-change operation, but finds no happiness. "Bron is finally trapped in total social and psychological stasis, lost in isolation beyond any help her society can offer its citizens," comments Barbour in *Science Fiction Writers.*

In the 1980s, Delany continued to experiment in his fiction writing. In his *Neveryon* series, which includes *Tales of Neveryon, Neveryona; or, The Tale of Signs and Cities, Flight from Neveryon,* and *The Bridge of Lost Desire,* he chooses a different setting. "Instead of being set in some imagined future, [they] are set in some magical, distant past, just as civilization is being created," observes McCaffery in a *Science-Fiction Studies* interview with Delany. Their focus, suggests Gregory in the same

interview, is "power—all kinds of power: sexual, economic, even racial power via the issue of slavery."

Throughout these tales of a world of dragons, treasures, and fabulous cities Delany weaves the story of Gorgik, a slave who rises to power and abolishes slavery. In one story, the novel-length "Tale of Plagues and Carnivals," he shifts in time from his primitive world to present-day New York and back to examine the devastating effects of a disease such as acquired immune deficiency syndrome (AIDS). And, in the appendices that accompany each of these books, he reflects on the creative process itself. Of the four, it is *Neveryona,* the story of Pryn—a girl who flees her mountain home on a journey of discovery—that has received the most attention from reviewers. *Science Fiction and Fantasy Book Review* contributor Michael R. Collings calls it "a stirring fable of adventure and education, of heroic action and even more heroic normality in a world where survival itself is constantly threatened." Faren C. Miller finds the book groundbreaking; she writes in *Locus*: "Combining differing perspectives with extraordinary talent for the *details* of a world—its smells, its shadows, workaday furnishings, and playful frills—Delany has produced a sourcebook for a new generation of fantasy writers." The book also "presents a new manifestation of Delany's continuing concern for language and the magic of fiction, whereby words become symbols for other, larger things," Collings observes.

In *Stars in My Pocket Like Grains of Sand,* Delany returns to distant worlds of the future. The book is "a densely textured, intricately worked out novelistic structure which delights and astonishes even as it forces a confrontation with a wide range of thought-provoking issues," writes McCaffery in *Fantasy Review.* Included are "an examination of interstellar politics among thousands of far flung worlds, a love story, a meandering essay on the variety of human relationships and the inexplicability of sexual attractiveness, and a hypnotic crash-course on a fascinating body of literature which does not yet exist," notes H. J. Kirchhoff in the Toronto *Globe and Mail.*

"This is an astonishing new Delany," according to Somtow Sucharitkul in the *Washington Post Book World,* "more richly textured, smoother, more colorful than ever before." Jonas commends the novel because of the interaction it encourages with the reader. "Sentence by sentence, phrase by phrase, it invites the reader to collaborate in the process of creation, in a way that few novels do," writes the reviewer. "The reader who accepts this invitation has an extraordinarily satisfying experience in store for him/her." "*Stars in My Pocket Like Grains of Sand . . .* confirms that [Delany] is American SF's most consistently brilliant and inventive writer," McCaffery claims.

Delany's 1992 novel *They Fly at Ciron* grew out of a short story Delany wrote in 1962. Although a version of the story, produced in collaboration with James Sallis, was published in 1971, Delany was not satisfied with it and subsequently reworked it into a novel. The action takes place in a nameless world that consists of small, independent village-states living in isolated harmony. However, this harmony is shattered when a fierce, technologically advanced people known as the Myetrans begin pillaging the land, overpowering and slaughtering the inhabitants of every village they encounter. It is left to a pair of men—Kire, a former member of the Myetrans, and Rahm—to thwart the warring Myetrans. The two men eventually overcome their nemesis by joining forces with the Winged Ones, a species of intelligent, flying beings. *New York Times Book Review* critic Gerald Jones calls the novel "a biting parable about the bloody roots of civilization" and praises the "spare beauty" of Delany's prose. Likewise, an *Analog Science Fiction and Fact* contributor notes that "Delany is a fine, expressive, thoughtful writer."

With the publication of *The Motion of Light in Water*, Delany turned to writing about himself. This memoir of his early days as a writer in New York's East Village is "an extraordinary account of life experienced by a precocious black artist of the 1960s," as E. Guereschi writes in *Choice*. The book reveals much of Delany's sexual adventures, with partners of both sexes at the time, his nervous breakdown, and the general sense of living on the edge in an exciting and innovative period. Moreover, the book tells of Delany's realization and eventual acceptance of his homosexuality. Thomas M. Disch, writing in the *American Book Review*, finds that Delany "can't help creating legends and elaborating myths. Indeed, it is his forte, the open secret of his success as an SF writer. [Delany's] SF heroes are variations of an archetype he calls The Kid. . . . In his memoir, the author himself [is] finally assuming the role in which his fictive alter-egos have enjoyed their success. That is the book's strength even more than its weakness." Guereschi believes that the memoir "defines an arduous search for identity," while Disch concludes that *The Motion of Light in Water* "has the potential of being as popular, as representative of its era, as *On the Road*."

Silent Interviews contains ten written interviews with Delany as well as one interview by him (of composer Anthony Davis) and features Delany discussing topics such as the state of science fiction, race, sexuality, language, and literary criticism. Paul Miller, reviewing the work in the *Village Voice*, remarks that "the most interesting parts of *Silent Interviews* are not when [Delany] talks about the obvious aspects of sexuality and race, but when he discusses the ways they are encoded into our lives."

Delany followed *Silent Interviews* with *Longer Views: Extended Essays*, which explore issues of language, literature, sexuality, and identity. Gerald Jonas summarized the collection in the *New York Times Book Review*: "Few people are at home in both science fiction and post-structural literary criticism. Samuel R. Delany is one." Essays explore Hart Crane's classic poem, "The Bridge," and compare and contrast the German composer Richard Wagner with surrealist writer Antoin Artaud. Charles Nash wrote in *Library Journal* that "Delany brings a rare personal frankness and stunning erudition" to his work. *Booklist* reviewer Carl Hays also applauded "Delany's elegant command of language and deep insights into other authors' works."

BIOGRAPHICAL/CRITICAL SOURCES:

BOOKS

Bleiler, E. F., editor, *Science Fiction Writers: Critical Studies of the Major Authors from the Early Nineteenth Century to the Present Day*, Scribner, 1982.
Contemporary Literary Criticism, Gale, Volume 8, 1978; Volume 14, 1980; Volume 38, 1986.
Dictionary of Literary Biography, Gale, Volume 8: *Twentieth-Century American Science Fiction Writers*, 1981; Volume 33: *Afro-American Fiction Writers after 1955*, 1984.
Kostelanetz, Richard, editor, *American Writing Today*, Whitston, 1991.
McCaffery, Larry, and Sinda Gregory, editors, *Alive and Writing: Interviews with American Authors of the 1980s*, University of Illinois Press, 1987.
McEvoy, Seth, *Samuel R. Delany*, Ungar, 1984.

Peplow, Michael W., and Robert S. Bravard, *Samuel R. Delany: A Primary and Secondary Bibliography, 1962-1979*, G. K. Hall, 1980.
Platt, Charles, editor, *Dream Makers: The Uncommon People Who Write Science Fiction*, Berkley Books, 1980.
Sallis, James, *Ash of Stars: On the Writing of Samuel R. Delany*, University Press of Mississippi (Jackson), 1996.
Slusser, George Edgar, *The Delany Intersection: Samuel R. Delany Considered as a Writer of Semi-Precious Words*, Borgo Press, 1977.
Smith, Nicholas D., editor, *Philosophers Look at Science Fiction*, Nelson-Hall, 1982.
Weedman, Jane Branham, *Samuel R. Delany*, Starmont House, 1982.

PERIODICALS

American Book Review, January, 1989.
Analog Science Fiction/Science Fact, April, 1985; June, 1995, p. 168.
Black American Literature Forum, summer, 1984.
Booklist, May 1, 1996.
Choice, February, 1989.
Commonweal, December 5, 1975.
Extrapolation, fall, 1982; winter, 1989; fall, 1989.
Fantasy Review, December, 1984.
Foundation, March, 1975.
Globe and Mail (Toronto), February 9, 1985.
Library Journal, June 15, 1996.
Locus, summer, 1983; October, 1989; January, 1995, p. 54.
Los Angeles Times Book Review, March 13, 1988.
Magazine of Fantasy and Science Fiction, November, 1975; June, 1980; May, 1989.
Mother Jones, August, 1976.
Nation, October 28, 1996.
New York Review of Books, January 29, 1991.
New York Times Book Review, February 16, 1975; March 28, 1976; October 28, 1979; February 10, 1985; January 1, 1995, p. 22; October 29, 1995, p. 42; December 29, 1996, p. 15; December 29, 1996.
Publishers Weekly, January 29, 1988; October 19, 1992.
Science Fiction and Fantasy Book Review, July/August, 1983.
Science Fiction Chronicle, November, 1987; February, 1990.
Science-Fiction Studies, November, 1981; July, 1987; November, 1990.
Village Voice, January 24, 1995, p. 78.
Voice Literary Supplement, February, 1985.
Washington Post Book World, January 27, 1985; August 25, 1991; November 29, 1992, p. 11.

*   *   *

**DELAPORTE, Theophile
See GREEN, Julien (Hartridge)**

*   *   *

**DeLILLO, Don 1936-
(Cleo Birdwell)**

PERSONAL: Born November 20, 1936, in New York, NY; married; wife's name, Barbara (a bank worker). *Education:* Fordham University, graduated, 1958.

ADDRESSES: Agent—Wallace & Sheil, 177 East 70th St., New York, NY 10021.

CAREER: Writer. Worked as an advertising copywriter in early 1960s.

MEMBER: American Academy and Institute of Arts and Letters.

AWARDS, HONORS: Guggenheim fellowship, 1979; American Academy and Institute of Arts and Letters Award in Literature, 1984; American Book Award in fiction, and National Book Critics Circle Award nomination, both 1985, both for *White Noise*; *Irish Times*—Aer Lingus International Fiction Prize, American Book Award nomination and National Book Critics Circle Award nomination, all 1989, all for *Libra*; PEN/Faulkner Award, 1992, for *Mao II*.

WRITINGS:

NOVELS

Americana, Houghton, 1971.
End Zone, Houghton, 1972.
Great Jones Street, Houghton, 1973.
Ratner's Star, Knopf, 1976.
Players, Knopf, distributed by Random House, 1977.
Running Dog, Knopf, 1978.
The Names, Knopf, distributed by Random House, 1982.
White Noise, Viking, 1985.
Libra, Viking, 1988.
Mao II, Viking, 1991.
Underworld, Scribner, 1997.

Also author of *Amazons,* 1980, under the pseudonym Cleo Birdwell.

OTHER

The Day Room (play), Knopf (New York City), 1987.

Also author of plays *The Engineer of Moonlight,* 1979, and *The Rapture of the Athlete Assumed into Heaven,* 1990. Contributor to anthologies, including *Stories from Epoch,* edited by Baxter Hathaway, Cornell University Press, 1966; *The Secret Life of Our Times,* edited by Gordon Lish, Doubleday, 1973; *Cutting Edges,* edited by Jack Hicks, Holt, 1973; *On the Job,* edited by William O'Rourke, Random House, 1977; and *Great Esquire Fiction,* edited by L. Rust Hills, Viking, 1983. Contributor of short stories to periodicals, including *New Yorker, Esquire, Sports Illustrated,* and *Atlantic.*

SIDELIGHTS: With each of his novels Don DeLillo has enhanced his literary reputation and gained a wider audience for his carefully crafted prose. He first attracted critical attention in the early seventies when he published two ambitious and elusive novels about games: *End Zone,* an existential comedy which parlays football into a metaphor for thermonuclear war, and *Ratner's Star,* a surrealistic science fiction that is structurally akin to the mathematical formulas it employs. The verbal precision, dazzling intelligence, and sharp wit of these books made DeLillo a critical favorite, "but without bestseller sales figures or a dependable cult following, he has become something of a reviewer's writer," according to R. Z. Sheppard in *Time.*

DeLillo has yet to achieve bestsellerdom, but his early books have been reissued and, thanks largely to the impact of *White Noise,* his name has become more widely known. A major literary event, this 1985 novel received front page *New York Times Book Review* coverage and garnered the American Book Award in fiction that year. "In fact," writes *Chicago Tribune Book World* contributor

John W. Aldridge, "with this, his eighth novel, DeLillo has won the right not only to be ranked with [Thomas] Pynchon and [William] Gaddis but recognized as having surpassed them in brilliance, versatility, and breadth of imagination. DeLillo shares with them, but in a degree greater than theirs, that rarest of creative gifts, the ability to identify and describe, as if from the perspective of another galaxy, the exact look and feel of contemporary reality." DeLillo's next novel, *Libra,* is an account of the life of Lee Harvey Oswald, John F. Kennedy's assassin. A stunning success—*Libra* was nominated for the National Book Award and won the newly inaugurated International Fiction Prize from the *Irish Times*—Walter Clemons in *Newsweek* calls it "an overwhelming novel."

DeLillo's obsession with language links him to other members of literature's experimental school. "Like his contemporaries, William Gass, Robert Coover, and John Barth, he may be termed a 'metafictionist'," writes Michael Oriard in *Critique: Studies in Modern Fiction.* "Like these writers, he is strongly aware of the nature of language and makes language itself, and the process of using language, his themes." In his *Contemporary Literature* interview with Thomas LeClair, DeLillo suggests that after writing *End Zone,* he realized "that language was a subject as well as an instrument in my work." Later, he elaborated: "What writing means to me is trying to make interesting, clear, beautiful language. Working at sentences and rhythms is probably the most satisfying thing I do as a writer. I think after a while a writer can begin to know himself through his language. He sees someone or something reflected back at him from these constructions. Over the years it's possible for a writer to shape himself as a human being through the language he uses. I think written language, fiction, goes that deep."

DeLillo's anti-social sentiments may have frightened off readers, but they have not fazed critics. Rising to his challenge of commitment, they have lavished attention on his publications, offering thoughtful interpretations of his complex work. Those who have studied the body of his writing recognize recurring themes, which darken and turn more ominous as the work evolves. "From *Americana* to *End Zone* to *Great Jones Street* to *Ratner's Star* DeLillo traces a single search for the source of life's meaning," explains Oriard. "By the end of *Ratner's Star,* the quest has been literally turned inside out, the path from chaos to knowledge becomes a Moebius strip that brings the seeker back to chaos."

The quest in DeLillo's first novel, *Americana,* involves a disillusioned television executive's search for a national identity. Abandoning his job, producer David Bell embarks on a cross-country odyssey to "nail down the gas-driven, motel-housed American soul," *Village Voice* contributor Albert Mobilio explains. Even in this early work, DeLillo's obsession with language dominates the narrative: his first-person narrator describes his quest as a "literary venture," using images that compare the western landscape to linguistic patterns on a page. "For years I had been held fast by the great unwinding mystery of this deep sink of land, the thick paragraphs and imposing photos, the gallop of panting adjectives, prairie truth and the clean kills of eagles," says Bell. *Americana,* like most first novels, was not widely reviewed, but it did attract favorable notice from some established New York critics, who expressed enthusiasm for DeLillo's remarkable verbal gifts. "It is a familiar story by now, flawed in the telling," notes *New York Times* contributor Christopher Lehmann-Haupt in a representative review. "But the language soars and dips, and it imparts a great deal." *New York Times Book*

Review contributor Thomas R. Edwards deems it "a savagely funny portrait of middle-class anomie in a bad time," but also notes that the book was "too long and visibly ambitious, and too much like too many other recent novels, to seem as good as it should have."

Edwards finds DeLillo's second novel—in which the quest for meaning is transferred from the American roadside to the sports arena—a more successful venture. "In *'End Zone'*," writes Edwards, "DeLillo finds in college football a more original and efficient vehicle for his sense of things now." This episodic, largely plotless novel focuses on the final attempt college athlete Gary Harkness makes to prove himself as a football player in a small west Texas school. Gary, who spends his free time playing war games, is attracted to carefully structured systems of ordered violence that afford opportunities for complete control. Edwards speculates that "Gary's involvement with [football] is a version of his horrified fascination with the vocabulary, theory and technology of modern war." Out on the playing field, Gary wins all but one of his football games, but "it's a season of losses all the same," Edwards concludes, for not only do minor characters suffer setbacks and tragedies but Gary "ends up in the infirmary with a mysterious brain-fever being fed through plastic tubes."

Gary's hunger strike has been interpreted as a final existential attempt to exert control. "He's paring things down. He is struggling, trying to face something he felt had to be faced," DeLillo told LeClair. Thus the "end zone" of this novel becomes a symbolic setting that represents "not only the goal of the running back in a football game, but the human condition at the outer extremity of existence, a place where the world is on the verge of disintegration, and the characters teeter between genius and madness," Oriard believes. "In this region of end zones that DeLillo describes, characters struggle for order and meaning as their world moves inexorably towards chaos. DeLillo's men and women fight the natural law of entropy, while human violence hastens its inevitable consequences."

The next American milieu DeLillo tackled was the world of rock stars and the drug culture in the novel *Great Jones Street*. Walter Clemons's assessment of the novel as an "in-between book" is representative of critical opinion, and while critics realized that DeLillo was extending himself as a writer, they weren't completely satisfied with the result. "The rock stars, drug dealers and hangers-on that populate *'Great Jones Street'* are so totally freaked out, so slickly devoted to destruction and evil, so obsessed with manipulating and acquiring that they're beyond redemption," writes *New York Times Book Review* contributor Sara Blackburn, who deems the work "more of a sour, admirably written lecture than a novel, a book that is always puffing to keep up with the power and intensity of its subject."

DeLillo turned to the genre of science fiction for his fourth book, *Ratner's Star*, a pivotal work about a fourteen-year-old mathematical genius and Noble laureate, Billy Twilling. "There is no easy way to describe *Ratner's Star*, a cheerfully apocalyptic novel," writes Amanda Heller in the *Atlantic*. "Imagine *Alice in Wonderland* set at the Princeton Institute for Advanced Studies." A reviewer for the *New Yorker* finds it "a whimsical, surrealistic excursion into the modern scientific mind." *New York Times Book Review* contributor George Stade describes it as "not only interesting, but funny (in a nervous kind of way). From it comes an unambiguous signal that DeLillo has arrived, bearing many gifts. He is smart, observant, fluent, a brilliant mimic and an ingenious architect."

Modeled after Lewis Carroll's *Alice in Wonderland,* DeLillo's novel is comprised of two sections, "Adventures" and "Reflections," that mimic the structural divisions of Carroll's book. "The comic, episodic discontinuous style of the book's first half is reflected in reverse in its symmetrically opposite second part," writes G. M. Knoll in *America*. He continues, "All that has been asserted or hypothesized about the signals from Ratner's Star is here denied. Billy's assignment is now to assist in the development of a language to answer the star's message rather than decipher the meaning of the signals." DeLillo's goal in this venture, according to *Time*'s Paul Gray, "is to show how the codification of phenomena as practiced by scientists leads to absurdity and madness." In his interview with LeClair, however, DeLillo says that his primary intention was "to produce a book that would be naked structure. The structure would be the book."

Ratner's Star marks a turning point in DeLillo's fiction, say critics who note a shift in the pacing and tone of subsequent books. "Since *Ratner's Star*, the apogee or nadir of his mirrorgame experiments, DeLillo has opened his fiction to the possibilities of more extroverted action," observes *New Republic* contributor Robert Towers. "The speeded-up pace in both *Players* and *Running Dog* seems to me all to the good." Accompanying this accelerated narrative, however, is a noticeable change in the kinds of people DeLillo is writing about. Hardened by exposure to modern society, cynical in their views of life, these characters "are not sustained by the illusion that answers to cosmic questions can be found," Oriard believes. Nor are their self-serving quests particularly admirable, according to *Dictionary of Literary Biography* contributor Frank Day, who maintains that readers may have a hard time sympathizing with protagonists whose lives are "parables of betrayal and degeneration. The frail, confused youths of the early novels are here displaced by characters influenced by popular espionage fiction."

In *Players* DeLillo employs a prologue—a sophisticated bit of pure fiction in which the characters are temporarily suspended outside the apparatus of the story—to introduce his themes. Before the narrative starts, DeLillo collects his as-yet-unnamed protagonists on an empty airplane, seating them in the lounge to watch a grisly film. "The Movie," as this prelude is called, depicts an unsuspecting band of Sunday golfers being attacked and murdered by marauding hippies, who splatter the scenic green landscape with blood. Without earphones the passengers can't hear the dialogue, so the pianist improvises silent-movie music to accompany the scene. "The passengers laugh, cheer, clap," notes *New York Times Book Review* contributor Diane Johnson. "It is the terrorists whom they applaud." When the movie ends, the lights come up and the passengers, now identified as protagonists Lyle and Pammy Wynant and friends, step off the plane and into the story—a tale of terrorists, murder, and wasted lives.

A hip New York couple, Pammy and Lyle are bored to distraction by each other and their jobs. She's a promotional writer at the Grief Management Council, an organization that "served the community in its efforts to understand and assimilate grief." He's a stockbroker on Wall Street, who spends his free time parked in front of the TV set, flipping channels, not in hopes of finding a good program, but because "he simply enjoyed jerking the dial into fresh image burns."

Pammy moves out, heading off to Maine with a pair of homosexual lovers, one of whom will become her lover and commit suicide. She will return home. Lyle takes up with a mindless secretary who is linked to a terrorist group responsible for murdering a man on the Stock Exchange floor. Intrigued by the glamour of revolutionary violence, Lyle joins forces with the terrorists, but also covers himself by informing on their activities to law enforcement agencies. "The end," notes John Updike in the *New Yorker,* "finds him in a motel in Canada, having double-crossed everybody but on excellent terms, it seems, with himself." Both he and Pammy have become players in the game.

Noting that DeLillo is that rare kind of novelist who looks "grandly at the whole state of things," Johnson postulates that "since Freud, we've been used to the way novelists normally present a character: looks normal, is secretly strange and individual. In the first of many inversions of appearance and reality that structure the book, Pammy and Lyle look interesting and seem to do interesting things, but do not interest themselves. The richness is only superficial. . . . Pammy and Lyle have no history; they are without pasts, were never children, come from nowhere. They worry that they have become too complex to experience things directly and acutely, but the opposite is true. They are being reduced by contemporary reality to numb simplicity, lassitude."

DeLillo followed *Players* with two psychological thrillers, *Running Dog* and *The Names,* the latter of which was praised for its improved characterization. But it was with *White Noise* that DeLillo most impressed critics with his rendition of fully realized characters in a minimalist prose style. Noting that with each book DeLillo becomes increasingly elliptical, *Village Voice* contributor Albert Mobilio observes that "the distillation is matched by a more subtle and convincing treatment of his characters' inner lives. This broadened emotional vocabulary charges *White Noise* with a resonance and credibility that makes it difficult to ignore. Critics who have argued that his work is too clever and overly intellectual should take notice: DeLillo's dark vision is now hard-earned. It strikes at both heart and head."

A novel about technology and death, *White Noise* unfolds as the first-person narrative of Jack Gladney, chairman of the department of Hitler studies at a small liberal arts school, College-on-the-Hill. Gladney lives with his fourth wife Babette—an ample, disheveled woman who teaches an adult education class in posture and reads to the blind—and their four children from previous marriages, Wilder, Steffie, Denise, and Heinrich. Life seems full for the Gladneys, but early on, Jack confesses that he and Babette are obsessed with a troubling question: "Who will die first?" Even as they debate it, small signs of trouble begin to surface: the children are evacuated from grade school because of an unidentified toxin in the atmosphere, and Babette can't remember facts or incidents because she's secretly taking medication that impairs her memory. One clear winter day, a major chemical spill jeopardizes the whole city. Everyone is forced to evacuate and, on his way to the shelter Jack stops to get gas, inadvertently exposing himself to the "airborne toxic event." Informed that "anything that puts you in contact with actual emissions means we have a situation," Jack becomes convinced that he is dying. (As proof, his computerized health profile spews out "bracketed numbers with pulsing stars.") When Jack discovers that Babette's medication (which she has committed adultery to obtain) is an experimental substance said to combat fear of death, he vows to find more of the substance for himself. His quest to obtain the illicit drug at any cost forms the closing chapters of the novel.

Newsweek's Walter Clemons writes that *White Noise* should win DeLillo "wide recognition, till now only flickeringly granted as one of the best American novelists. Comic and touching,

ingenious and weird, *'White Noise'* looks, at first, reassuringly like an example of a familiar genre, the campus novel." But, he goes on to say, the novel "tunes us in on frequencies we haven't heard in other accounts of how we live now. Occult supermarket tabloids are joined with TV disaster footage as household staples providing nourishment and febrile attractions. Fleeting appearances or phone calls from the Gladneys' previous spouses give us the start of surprise we experience when we learn that couples we know have a previous family we haven't heard about." Also commenting on DeLillo's depiction of domestic scenes is Jay McInerney, who writes in the *New Republic* that "DeLillo's portrait of this postnuclear family is one of the simpler pleasures of this novel. Gladney's oldest, Heinrich, is a sullen and precocious fourteen-year-old who plays chess by mail with a convicted murderer and keeps his father off balance with sophistic deconstructions of conventional wisdom, and bulletins from the frontiers of high school chemistry. Denise, eleven, is engaged in a constant campaign to root out her mother's faults, particularly short-term memory loss, and to instruct her stepsister Steffie, in the cruel ways of the world. Wilder, the baby, is the holy innocent, the pre-verbal totem figure who gives the family a precious and fragile sense of identity." Bert Testa hypothesizes in the Toronto *Globe and Mail* that "*White Noise* plays off the familiar and the disturbing without ever tipping into the merely grotesque. When DeLillo constantly returns to Jack's quotidian family life, he means his readers to enter a firmly drawn circle that not even a little toxic apocalypse can break."

"The world of *Libra* is not the modern or technological brilliant world that characters in my other novels try to confront," DeLillo explained his 1988 fiction offering to the *New York Times*'s Herbert Mitgang. "This is a different kind of novel, a terminus of human feelings. It takes place at the far end of the map." In *Libra* DeLillo mixes fact with fiction in a discussion of the events that led to the assassination of President John F. Kennedy on November 22, 1963, in Dallas, Texas. He dispels the accepted truth that Kennedy was shot by a lone gunman, Lee Harvey Oswald, by uncovering information supporting a conspiracy theory, acknowledged by some historians. DeLillo spent three years researching and writing about Oswald's life, tracing his career as a Marxist in the American military and his consequent defection to the Soviet Union and return to the United States. DeLillo surmises that in America a coterie of underworld and government figures—enemies of Kennedy—recruited Oswald as a scapegoat for an assassination attempt that should have been botched.

"At what point exactly does fact drift over into fiction?" Anne Tyler asked in her *New York Times Book Review* critique of *Libra.* "The book is so seamlessly written that perhaps not even those people who own . . . copies of the Warren report could say for certain." Richard Eder in the *Los Angeles Times Book Review* agreed, noting that in the novel "DeLillo disassembles his plots with the finest of jigsaw cuts, scrambles their order and has us reassemble them. As the assorted characters go about their missions, we discern them more by intuition than by perception. The chronology goes back and forth, disorienting us. We do not so much follow what is going on as infiltrate it." Robert Dunn observed in *Mother Jones* that in his study of the president's assassin DeLillo "has found a story beyond imagination, one whose significance is indisputable and ongoing . . . and he carefully hews to known facts and approaches all events with respect, even awe. By giving Oswald and the forces he represents full body, DeLillo has written his best novel."

DeLillo's 1991 novel, *Mao II,* further solidified the author's place in the leading ranks of contemporary American novelists. The winner of the 1992 PEN/Faulkner Award for fiction, the novel revolves around a reclusive novelist, Bill Gray, whose first two works made him famous but who has since labored for more than twenty years to produce his third novel. Completely hidden from public view on his rural New York estate, Gray has human contact only with his secretary and helper, Scott, and a young woman, Karen, coping with the dissolution of her marriage. In typical DeLillo fashion, Karen's wasn't a standard marriage: the novel's opening scene shows her wedding her husband along with 6,000 other couples in a ceremony staged by the Reverend Sun Myung Moon at Yankee Stadium. Convinced that Gray's long-awaited novel is a failure, Scott urges him not to publish it, arguing that his already cult-like celebrity will increase if the novel never appears in print. Gray, however, tiring of his isolation, does something more momentous than publishing his novel: he allows himself to be photographed by Brita, a Swedish photographer.

In *Underworld,* DeLillo paints an encyclopedic portrait of late twentieth-century American life told through the story of Nick Shay, accused of murder, as his path collides with great moments of history, including the 1951 ball game in which the Giants won the pennant. Michiko Kakutani of the *New York Times* admired the novel, calling it a "remarkable" tale of "the effluvia of modern life, all the detritus of our daily and political lives" that has been "turned into a dazzling, phosphorescent work of art." Like most of DeLillo's novels, time is not a straight trajectory in *Underworld,* and a current of conspiracy, paranoia, and terrorism weaves through the story that brings the alienated protagonist in close contact with events that define the century, including the political suspense of the Cold War. In a review for the *New York Times,* writer Martin Amis, while claiming that *Underworld* "may or may not be a great novel," also states that "there is no doubt that . . . DeLillo is a great novelist." Hypothesizing that nuclear war is the central theme of the book, he praised the novel, which "surges with magisterial confidence through time . . . and through space . . . . And its main actors are psychological 'downwinders,' victims of the fallout from all the blasts—blasts actual and imagined."

BIOGRAPHICAL/CRITICAL SOURCES:

BOOKS

Civello, Paul, *American Literary Naturalism and Its Twentieth-Century Transformations: Frank Norris, Ernest Hemingway, Don DeLillo,* University of Georgia Press (Athens), 1994.
Contemporary Literary Criticism, Gale (Detroit), Volume 8, 1978; Volume 10, 1979; Volume 13, 1980; Volume 27, 1984; Volume 39, 1986; Volume 54, 1989; Volume 76, 1993.
Dictionary of Literary Biography, Volume 6: *American Novelists Since World War II, Second Series,* Gale, 1980.
Hantke, Steffen, *Conspiracy and Paranoia in Contemporary American Fiction: The Works of Don DeLillo and Joseph McElroy,* P. Lang (New York City), 1994.
LeClair, Tom, *In the Loop: Don DeLillo and the Systems Novel,* University of Illinois Press, 1988.
Lentricchia, Frank, editor, *New Essays on White Noise,* Cambridge University Press, 1991.
Lentricchia, Frank, *Introducing Don DeLillo,* Duke University Press, 1991.

PERIODICALS

America, August 7, 1976; July 6-13, 1985.
Antioch Review, spring, 1972; winter, 1983.
Atlantic, August, 1976; February, 1985.
Booklist, November 1, 1993, p. 499.
Chicago Tribune Book World, November 7, 1982; January 13, 1985; July 31, 1988.
Choice, April, 1988, p. 1242.
Commonweal, August 9, 1991, pp. 490-91.
Contemporary Literature, winter, 1982.
Critique: Studies in Modern Fiction, Volume XX, number 1, 1978.
Detroit News, February 24, 1985.
Globe and Mail (Toronto), March 9, 1985; August 27, 1988.
Harper's, September, 1977; December, 1982.
Journal of Modern Literature, spring, 1996, p. 453.
Library Journal, January, 1988, p. 96.
Los Angeles Times, July 29, 1984; August 12, 1988.
Los Angeles Times Book Review, November 7, 1982; January 13, 1985; July 31, 1988; June 9, 1991, p. 3.
Maclean's, November 13, 1978, pp. 62, 64; August 29, 1988.
Modern Fiction Studies, summer, 1994, p. 229.
Mother Jones, September, 1988.
Nation, September 17, 1977; October 18, 1980; December 11, 1982; February 2, 1985; September 19, 1988.
National Review, October 28, 1977.
New Republic, October 7, 1978; November 22, 1982; February 4, 1985.
New Statesman, February 2, 1979, p. 158.
Newsweek, June 7, 1976; August 29, 1977; October 25, 1982; January 21, 1985; August 15, 1988.
New Yorker, July 12, 1976; March 27, 1978; September 18, 1978; April 4, 1983; September 15, 1997, p. 42.
New York Review of Books, June 29, 1972; December 16, 1982; March 14, 1985; June 9, 1991, pp. 7, 49; June 27, 1991, pp. 17-18.
New York Times, May 6, 1971; March 22, 1972; April 16, 1973; May 27, 1976; August 11, 1977; September 16, 1980; October 12, 1982; January 7, 1985; December 20, 1987; December 21, 1987; July 19, 1988; May 18, 1989; September 24, 1989; September 16, 1997, p. E1; October 5, 1997, p. E2.
New York Times Book Review, May 30, 1971; April 9, 1972; April 22, 1973; June 20, 1976; September 4, 1977; November 12, 1978; October 10, 1982; January 13, 1985; May 28, 1991, p. C15; October 5, 1997, p. 12.
Partisan Review, Number 3, 1979.
Publishers Weekly, August 19, 1988.
Saturday Review, September 3, 1977; September 16, 1978.
Spectator, September 7, 1991, pp. 34-35.
Time, June 7, 1976; November 8, 1982; January 21, 1985; August 1, 1988; June 10, 1991, p. 68.
Times (London), January 23, 1986.
Times Literary Supplement, September 14, 1973; December 9, 1983; January 17, 1986.
Tribune Books (Chicago), June 23, 1991, pp. 1, 4.
USA Today, January 11, 1985.
Village Voice, April 30, 1985; June 18, 1991, p. 65.
Voice Literary Supplement, December, 1981; November, 1982; October, 1988.
Wall Street Journal, June 13, 1991, p. A14.
Washington Post, August 24, 1988; May 11, 1989.
Washington Post Book World, April 16, 1972; April 15, 1973; June 13, 1976; August 21, 1977; October 15, 1978; October 10, 1982; January 13, 1985; July 31, 1988; May 26, 1991, pp. 1-2.

World Literature Today, winter, 1992.
Yale Review, April, 1995, p. 107.

* * *

de MAN, Paul (Adolph Michel) 1919-1983

PERSONAL: Born December 6, 1919, in Antwerp, Belgium; immigrated to United States, 1947; died of cancer, December 21, 1983, in New Haven, CT; son of Robert (a manufacturer of X-ray equipment) and Magdalena (de Brey) de Man; married Anaide Baraghian, 1943 (marriage ended); married Patricia Kelley, 1950; children: (first marriage) Hendrik, Robert, Marc; (second marriage) Patricia, Michael. *Education:* University of Brussels, Candidature, 1942; Harvard University, M.A., 1958, Ph.D., 1960.

CAREER: Le Soir (daily newspaper), Brussels, Belgium, writer, 1940-42; worked as a translator and in publishing business in Brussels and Antwerp, Belgium, 1942-47; affiliated with faculty of University of Zurich, Zurich, Switzerland; Bard College, Annandale-on-Hudson, NY, teacher of French literature, 1949-51; Berlitz School, Boston, MA, French teacher, beginning in 1951; Harvard University, Cambridge, MA, lecturer, c. 1955-60; Cornell University, Ithaca, NY, teacher, 1960-67; Johns Hopkins University, Baltimore, MD, professor of humanistic studies, 1967-1970; Yale University, New Haven, CT, 1970-83, became Sterling Professor of Humanities and chairman of department of comparative literature.

WRITINGS:

(Translator) Paul Alverdes, *Le Double Visage,* Editions de la Toison d'Or (Brussels), 1942.
(Translator) Filip de Pillecyn, *Le Soldat Johan,* Editions de la Toison d'Or, 1942.
(Translator) Albert Erich Brinckmann, *Esprit des nations,* Editions de la Toison d'Or, 1943.
(Translator) Herman Melville, *Moby Dick,* Helicon, Kipdorp (Antwerp), 1945.
(Editor and translator) Gustave Flaubert, *Madame Bovary: Backgrounds and Sources; Essays in Criticism,* Norton, 1965.
Field of Comparative Literature: Analysis of Needs, [Ithaca, NY], 1967.
Blindness and Insight: Essays in the Rhetoric of Contemporary Criticism, Oxford University Press, 1971, 2nd edition, revised, with introduction by Wlad Godzich, University of Minnesota Press, 1983.
(Editor) Ranier Maria Rilke, *Oeuvres,* Editions du Seuil, 1972.
Allegories of Reading: Figural Language in Rousseau, Nietzsche, Rilke, and Proust, Yale University Press, 1979.
(With Harold Bloom, Jacques Derrida, Geoffrey H. Hartman, and J. Hillis Miller) *Deconstruction and Criticism,* Seabury Press, 1979.
The Rhetoric of Romanticism, Columbia University Press, 1984.
The Resistance to Theory, foreword by Wlad Godzich, University of Minnesota Press, 1986.
Aesthetic Ideology, edited by Andrzej Warminski, University of Minnesota Press, 1988.
Fugitive Writings, edited by Lindsay Waters, University of Minnesota Press, 1988.
Wartime Journalism, 1939-1943, University of Nebraska Press, 1988.
Lindsay Waters, editor, *Critical Writings, 1953-1978,* University of Minnesota Press (Minneapolis), 1989.

(With E. S. Burt and others) *Romanticism and Contemporary Criticism: The Gauss Seminar and Other Papers,* Johns Hopkins University Press (Baltimore), 1993.

Also author of foreword to Carol Jacobs's *The Dissimulating Harmony,* 1978. Contributor to American, Flemish, and French periodicals, including *Critical Inquiry, Critique, Het Vlaamsche Land, Les Cahiers du libre examen, Monde nouveau, Preuves,* and *Revue internationale de philosophie.*

SIDELIGHTS: "Venerated as a teacher and scholar, [Paul de Man] was the originator of a controversial theory of language that some say may place him among the greatest thinkers of his age," a *New York Times* reporter professed. De Man and French philosopher Jacques Derrida revolutionized literary criticism in America by devising deconstructionism, a theory that emphasizes the uncertainty of meaning caused by the imprecision of language. But after de Man's death in 1983 his work was clouded in controversy when a student compiling a bibliography of his works uncovered numerous articles that he had written for a pro-Nazi and anti-Semitic newspaper, *Le Soir,* in his native Belgium between 1940 and 1942.

Born in Antwerp and graduated from the University of Brussels, de Man immigrated to the United States following World War II and took his master's degree and doctorate at Harvard University. He subsequently taught at Cornell and Johns Hopkins universities before settling at Yale University in 1970, where he stayed until his death in 1983. His presence at Yale, as well as the presence of other outstanding deconstructive critics including J. Hillis Miller and Geoffrey Hartman, brought great prestige to the school, which subsequently became known as the seat of deconstructive theory in the United States.

During his second year at Yale, de Man published *Blindness and Insight: Essays in the Rhetoric of Contemporary Criticism,* a collection of articles that previously appeared in journals during de Man's tenure at Harvard and Cornell. Revised in 1983 with five additional essays, *Blindness and Insight* is considered by scholars to be the best introduction to de Man's early academic work. The volume includes such essays as "Criticism and Crisis," "Literary History and Literary Modernity," and an English translation of de Man's 1956 article "Impasse de la critique formaliste," which introduced French readers to New Criticism, an Anglo-American literary theory that was considered radical at the time. The New Critics maintained that a text's meaning could be discovered by reconciling its ambiguities and contradictions, disregarding the influences of an author's psychology, biography, culture, and politics on the text's meaning.

"To write critically about critics," de Man wrote in *Blindness and Insight,* "becomes a way to reflect on the paradoxical effectiveness of a blinded vision that has to be rectified by means of insights that it unwittingly provides," Jonathan Culler quoted the author in the *Dictionary of Literary Biography.* In *Blindness and Insight* de Man explains the principle behind a deconstructive reading: a scholar, when closely reading a text, can uncover many of the author's unstated philosophical, cultural, and linguistic assumptions by exposing contradictions that appear in the language of a text. In turn, a subsequent critic can discover the hidden assumptions in that scholar's analysis. Thus deconstruction posits the radical notion that the meaning of the text resides as much in the act of interpretation as in the words of the text itself.

Blindness and Insight contains deconstructive readings of texts such as "Heidegger's Exegesis of Holderlin," in which de Man critiques German philosopher Martin Heidegger's study of works by German poet Friedrich Holderlin. Also included is an essay on Hungarian Marxist philosopher and critic Gyorgy Lukacs's reading of French novelist Gustave Flaubert's *Education sentimentale,* as well as what many consider de Man's most influential work, an analysis of Derrida's criticism of writings by French author Jean-Jacques Rousseau. Articles such as these by de Man and other deconstructive scholars often brought scorn upon the new school of criticism; its detractors, such as *New York Review of Books* contributor Denis Donoghue, discounted the system as "mainly a commentary written in the margin of other philosophical and literary texts." Nonetheless, Culler attests, with *Blindness and Insight* scholars began reading literary criticism with the kind of attention that was only given previously to literary and philosophical works.

Allegories of Reading: Figural Language in Rousseau, Nietzsche, Rilke, and Proust, de Man's second collection of essays, consists of works published in journals during the 1970s. A volume of dense and difficult close readings of works by French and German writers, it contains analyses of Rousseau's novel *La Nouvelle Heloise* and *Discourse on the Origin of Language,* Friedrich Nietzsche's philosophical treatise *The Birth of Tragedy,* many of Ranier Maria Rilke's poems, and Marcel Proust's epic novel *Remembrance of Things Past.* In *Allegories of Reading* de Man pays extremely close attention to the use of language in these works, dissecting allegories and metaphors to answer the questions "precisely whether a literary text is *about* that which it describes, represents, or states," Anthony Thorlby cited de Man in the *Times Literary Supplement,* or "whether *all* language is about language."

The main assertion of *Allegories of Reading* (and of deconstructive theory) is that language cannot be taken literally. Because all language is metaphorical, where one set of signs are only substitutions for another, there is no reconcilability or oneness between a word and the idea of the specific object. Robert Alter in *New Republic* explained that deconstruction professes "the relation between word and referent, signifier and signified, is inevitably an arbitrary and conventional one. . . . [W]hat appears to be literal is necessarily metaphorical; what is proffered as reality is in fact fiction." Thus when language uses metaphors to be most authoritative it undermines its own intent by clearly revealing its fictive nature. Furthermore, when studying a literary text the reader cannot reconcile the difference between the opposing literal and the figurative meanings of the work, thus the text is considered "unreadable."

The first volume of de Man's essays collected after the author's death in 1983 was published the following year. *The Rhetoric of Romanticism,* compiled from articles written after 1956 and two never before issued, is considered an indispensable tool by scholars of romanticism. In this strictly linguistic approach to romantic and postromantic themes de Man studies the course toward greater concreteness in poetic diction (especially when writing of nature), the shift from the use of allegorical to symbolic language, and the development of the study of the union of imagination and nature. He writes on individual romantics, including Rousseau, William Wordsworth, Shelley, William Butler Yeats, and Holderlin, and examines the general relationship among German, French, and English trends in romanticism. Culler reflected that *The Rhetoric of Romanticism* was extremely influential; it forced literary critics to reassess the place of European romantic writings in the canon of world literature.

Three other collections of de Man's academic essays have been published posthumously. Both *The Resistance to Theory,* consisting of six recent essays focusing on contemporary literary criticism, and *Aesthetic Ideology,* featuring essays on German philosophers Immanuel Kant and Georg Hegel and German writer Friedrich von Schiller, explore the incompatibility of a linguistically oriented and an aesthetic approach to literature. *Fugitive Writings,* also published in 1988, is a group of essays on literary criticism de Man wrote during the 1950s for the French periodicals *Critique* and *Monde nouveau.*

In December, 1987, the *New York Times* revealed that from 1940 until 1942 de Man, under his own name, wrote more than one hundred articles for *Le Soir,* a pro-Nazi and strongly anti-Semitic daily newspaper in his native Belgium, then occupied by the German army. A Belgian graduate student, Ortwin de Graef, came across these essays and book and music reviews when compiling a list of de Man's works. The uncovering of de Man's writings for *Le Soir*—which have been collected in *Wartime Journalism, 1939-1943*—shocked many who knew de Man, for his colleagues considered him an unbiased and affable man. These articles "seem so at odds with the sense of the person I knew later on," reflected Neil Hertz, one of de Man's friends, quoted in the *New York Times.* Shochana Felman, a student of de Man's at Yale, added that she thought he was "almost entirely without prejudice," claiming de Man "took an ethical stance in all his daily life." Peter Brooks, with whom de Man worked at Yale, in a letter to the editor of the *New York Times,* claimed that he and many of de Man's friends and colleagues "wish to testify that [de Man's] life and character, as we knew them, suggested a complete repudiation of the hateful things he wrote in a sordid time."

Many scholars agree that in only one of the articles, "Jews in Contemporary Literature," does de Man take an overtly anti-Semitic stance. In the piece he states that Jews "pollute" modern fiction and that their influence in modern letters is negligible. However, some of de Man's detractors detect anti-Semitic sentiments in his other articles, including reviews of works by Austrian writer Franz Kafka and French historian Daniel Halevy. The revelation increased the existing controversy surrounding deconstruction theory, which the *New York Times* reporter alleged "always reflects the biases of its users." But Hartman, writing in the *New Republic,* rebutted the *New York Times* article, stating that de Man's "position is the very opposite of an idealism that confuses intellect and action, ideology and political praxis." De Man, Hartman asserted, stressed "the non-identity of these realms."

BIOGRAPHICAL/CRITICAL SOURCES:

BOOKS

Derrida, Jacques, *Memoires: Lectures for Paul de Man,* translated by Cecile Lindsay, Jonathan Culler, and Eduardo Cadava, Columbia University Press, 1986.

Dictionary of Literary Biography, Volume 67: *Modern American Critics Since 1955,* Gale (Detroit), 1988.

Eagleton, Terry, *Literary Theory: An Introduction,* University of Minnesota Press, 1983.

Gaschae, Rodolphe, *The Wild Card of Reading: on Paul de Man,* Harvard University Press, 1998.

Graef, Ortwin de, *Serenity in Crisis: A Preface to Paul de Man, 1939-1960,* University of Nebraska (Lincoln), 1993.

Graef, Ortwin de, *Titanic Light: Paul de Man's Post-Romanticism, 1960-1969,* University of Nebraska Press (Lincoln), 1995.

Herman, Luc, Kris Humbeeck, and Geert Lernout, editors, *(Dis)continuities: Essays on Paul de Man,* Rodopi (Atlanta), 1989.

Lehman, David, *Signs of the Times: Deconstruction and the Fall of Paul de Man,* Poseidon Press (New York City), 1991.

Loesberg, Jonathan, *Aestheticism and Deconstruction: Pater, Derrida, and de Man,* Princeton University Press (Princeton, NJ), 1991.

Morrison, Paul, *The Poetics of Fascism: Ezra Pound, T. S. Eliot, Paul de Man,* Oxford University Press (New York City), 1996.

Rosiek, Jan, *Figures of Failure: Paul de Man's Criticism 1953-1970,* Aarhaus University Press (Denmark), 1992.

Waters, Lindsay and Wlad Godzich, editors, *Reading de Man Reading,* University of Minnesota Press (Minneapolis), 1989.

PERIODICALS

Critical Inquiry, spring, 1982; summer, 1986.
Harper's, July, 1988.
Insight on the News, January 23, 1989, p. 61.
Nation, January 9, 1988; April 9, 1988.
New Republic, April 25, 1983; July 7, 1986; March 7, 1988; March 6, 1989, p. 30.
Newsweek, February 15, 1988.
New York Review of Books, June 12, 1980; June 29, 1989, p. 32; October 12, 1989, p. 69.
New York Times, December 1, 1987; August 28, 1988; October 2, 1988; January 25, 1989.
New York Times Book Review, May 24, 1992, p. 1.
Times Literary Supplement, February 29, 1980; January 17, 1986; November 6, 1987.
Village Voice Literary Supplement, April, 1988.
Washington Post Book World, February 24, 1980.

*   *   *

DEMIJOHN, Thom
See DISCH, Thomas M(ichael)

*   *   *

DENIS, Julio
See CORTAZAR, Julio

*   *   *

DENMARK, Harrison
See ZELAZNY, Roger (Joseph)

*   *   *

DE ROUTISIE, Albert
See ARAGON, Louis

*   *   *

DERRIDA, Jacques 1930-

PERSONAL: Born July 15, 1930, in El Biar, Algeria; son of Aime and Georgette (Safar) Derrida. *Education:* Attended Ecole Normale Superieure, 1952-56; University of Paris, Sorbonne, Licence es Lettres, 1953, Licence de Philosophie, 1953, Diplome d'Etudes Superieures, 1954; received Certificat d'Ethnologie, 1954, Agregation de Philosophie, 1956, Doctorat en Philosophie, 1967, Doctorat d'Etat es Lettres, 1980; graduate study at Harvard University, 1956-57.

ADDRESSES: Home—Paris, France. *Office*—Ecole des Hautes Etudes en Sciences Sociales, 54 bis Raspail, 75006 Paris, France; or, c/o University of Chicago Press, 5801 South Ellis Ave., Chicago, IL.

CAREER: Professeur de lettres superieures at Lycee du Mans, 1959-60; University of Paris, Sorbonne, Paris, France, professor of philosophy, 1960-64; Ecole Normale Superieure, Paris, professor of philosophy, 1964-84; Ecole des Hautes Etudes en Sciences Sociales, Paris, director, 1984–. College International de Philosophie, member of planning board, 1982-83, director, 1983-84, member of administrative council, 1986. Visiting professor and lecturer at numerous universities in Europe and the United States, including Johns Hopkins University, Yale University, University of California at Irvine, Cornell University, and City University of New York.

MEMBER: Institut des Textes et Manuscrits Modernes (member of steering committee, 1983-86), Groupe de Recherches sur l'Enseignement Philosophique (president), Association Jan Hus (vice-president), Fondation Culturelle Contre l'Apartheid, American Academy of Arts and Sciences (foreign honorary member), Modern Language Association of America (honorary member), Academy for the Humanities and Sciences (honorary member).

AWARDS, HONORS: Prix Cavailles from Societe des Amis de Jean Cavailles, 1964, for translation into French and introduction of Edmund Husserl's *Origin of Geometry*; named to Liste d'Aptitude a l'Enseignement Superieur, 1968; Chevalier, 1968, Officier, 1980, des Palmes Academiques; Commandeur des Arts et des Lettres, 1983; Prix Nietzsche from Association Internationale de Philosophie, 1988. Honorary doctorates from Columbia University, 1980, University of Louvain, 1983, University of Essex, 1987.

WRITINGS:

(Translator and author of introduction) Edmund Husserl, *L'Origine de la geometrie,* Presses Universitaires de France, 1962, translation by John P. Leavy, published as *Edmund Husserl's "Origin of Geometry": An Introduction,* Nicolas-Hays, 1977.

La Voix et le phenomene: Introduction au probleme du signe dans la phenomenologie de Husserl, Presses Universitaires de France, 1967, translation by David B. Allison, published as *Speech and Phenomena and Other Essays on Husserl's Theory of Signs,* Northwestern University Press, 1973.

L'Ecriture et la difference, Le Seuil, 1967, translation by Alan Bass, published as *Writing and Difference,* University of Chicago Press, 1978.

De la grammatologie, Minuit, 1967, translation by Gayatri Chakravorty Spivak, published as *Of Grammatology,* Johns Hopkins University Press, 1976.

La Dissemination, Le Seuil, 1972, translation by Barbara Johnson, published as *Dissemination,* University of Chicago Press, 1981.

Marges de la philosophie, Minuit, 1972, translation by Alan Bass, published as *Margins of Philosophy,* University of Chicago Press, 1982.

Positions: Entretiens avec Henri Ronse, Julia Kristeva, Jean-Louis Houdebine, Guy Scarpetta (interviews), Minuit, 1972, translation by Alan Bass, published as *Positions,* University of Chicago Press, 1981.

Glas, Galilee, 1974, translation by John P. Leavey, Jr., and Richard Rand, published as *Glas,* University of Nebraska Press, 1986.

L'Archeologie du frivole (first published as introduction to Etienne de Condillac, *L'Essai sur l'origine des connaissances humaines,* Galilee, 1973) Editions Denoel, 1976, translation by John P. Leavey, Jr., published as *The Archeology of the Frivolous: Reading Condillac,* Duquesne University Press, 1980.

Eperons: Les Styles de Nietzsche, Flammarion, 1976, translation by Barbara Harlow, published as *Spurs: Nietzsche's Styles,* University of Chicago Press, 1979.

Limited Inc: abc, Johns Hopkins University Press, 1977.

La Verite en peinture (title means "Truth in Painting"), Flammarion, 1978.

La Carte postale: De Socrate a Freud et au-dela, Flammarion, 1980, translation by Alan Bass, published as *The Post Card: From Socrates to Freud and Beyond,* University of Chicago Press, 1987.

L'Oreille de l'autre: Otobiographies, transferts, traductions; textes et debats avec Jacques Derrida, VLB (Montreal), 1982, translation by Peggy Kamuf, published as *The Ear of the Other: Otobiography, Transference, Translation,* Schocken, 1985.

D'un ton apocalyptique adopte naguere en philosophie, Galilee, 1983.

Feu la cendre/Cio'che resta del fuoco, Sansoni (Florence), 1984, published as *Feu la cendre,* Editions des Femmes, 1987.

Signeponge/Signsponge (French and English text; English translation by Richard Rand), Columbia University Press, 1984, revised, Le Seuil, 1988.

Otobiographies: L'Enseignement de Nietzsche et la politique du nom propre, Galilee, 1984.

Droit de regards, Editions de Minuit, 1985.

La Facultae de juger, Editions de Minuit, 1985.

Parages, Galilee, 1986.

De l'esprit: Heidegger et la question, Galilee, 1987, translation by Geoffrey Bennington and Rachel Bowlby, published as *Of Spirit: Heidegger and the Question,* University of Chicago Press, 1989.

Psyche: Inventions de l'autre, Galilee, 1987.

Memoires: Pour Paul de Man, Galilee, 1988, translation by Cecile Lindsay, Jonathan Culler, and Eduardo Cadava, published as *Memoires: Lectures for Paul de Man,* Columbia University Press, 1986.

Le problaeme de la genaese dans la philosophie de Husserl, Presses Universitaires de France, 1990.

De droit a la philosophie, Galilee, 1990.

Maemoires de'aveugle, L'autoportrait et autres ruins, Reunion des musees nationaux, 1990, translation by Pascale Ann Brault and Michael Nass, published as *Memoirs of the Blind, the Self-Portrait and Other Ruins,* University of Chicago Press, 1993.

Donner le temps, 1, Fausse monnai, Galilee, 1991, translation by Peggy Kamuf, published as *Given Time, 1: Counterfeit Money,* University of Chicago Press, 1992.

L'autre cap; suivre de La daemocratie ajournae, Editions de Minuit, 1991, translation by Pascale-Anne Brault and Michael Naas, published as *The Other Heading: Reflections of Today's Europe,* Indiana University Press, 1992.

A Derrida Reader: Between the Blinds, edited by Peggy Kamuf, Columbia University Press, 1991.

Cinders, translation by Ned Lukacher, University of Nebraska Press, 1991.

(With Geoffrey Derrida) *Jacques Derrida,* Seuil, 1991.

Prejuges, Edition Passagen, 1992.

Acts of Literature, edited by Derek Attridge, Routledge, 1992.

Donner la mort, Seuil, 1992, translation by David Wells, published as *The Gift of Death,* University of Chicago Press, 1995.

Passions, Galilee, 1993.

Khaora, Galilee, 1993.

Apories: mourir—s'attendre aux "limites de la verite," Galilee, 1993, translation by Thomas Dutoit, published as *Aporias: Dying-Awaiting (One Another at) the "Limits of Truth,"* Stanford University Press, 1993.

Spectres de Marx: l'etat de la dette, le travail du deuil et la nouvelle internationale, Galilee, 1993, translation by Peggy Kamuf, published as *Spectres of Marx, State of the Debt, the Work of Mourning, and the New International,* Routledge, 1994.

Force de loi; le "fondement mystique de l'autorite," Galilee, 1994.

On the Name, edited by Thomas Dutoit, translated by David Wood and others, Stanford University Press, 1995.

Politiques de l'amitie, Galilee, 1994, translation by George Collins, published as *The Politics of Friendship,* Verso, 1997.

Mal d'archive, une impression freudienne, Galilee, 1995, translation by Eric Predowitz, published as *Archive Fever: A Freudian Impression,* University of Chicago Press, 1996.

Deconstruction and Philosophy: The Texts of Jacques Derrida, translation by David Wells, University of Chicago Press, 1995.

Deconstruction and Pragmatism, 1996.

Resistances, de la psychanalyse, Galilee, 1996, published as *Resistances of Psychoanalysis,* Stanford University Press, 1998.

La monolinguisme de l'autre, ou La prothaese d'origine, Galilee, 1996, translation by Patrick Mensa, published as *Monolingualism of the Other; or, The Prosthesis of Origin,* Stanford University Press, 1998.

Passions de la littaerature: avec Jacques Derrida, Galilee, 1996.

(With Bernard Stiegler) *Echographies de la television,* Galilee, 1996.

(With Peter Eisenman) *Chora L Works,* Monacelli Press, 1997.

Deconstruction in a Nutshell: A Conversation with Jacques Derrida, edited by John D. Caputo, Fordham University Press, 1997.

(With Paule Thevenin) *Secret Art of Antonin Artaud,* translation by Mary AnnCaws, MIT Press, 1997.

Cosmopolites de tous les pays, encore un effort, Galilee, 1997.

Adieu a Emmanuel Levines, Galilee, 1997.

De L'hospitalite/Anne Duformantelle invite Jacques Derrida a repondre, Calmann Levy, 1997.

CONTRIBUTOR

Tableau de la litterature francaise, Gallimard, 1974.

Mimesis, Aubier-Flammarion, 1976.

Politiques de la philosophie, Grasset, 1976.

Qui a peur de la philosophie?, Flammarion, 1977.

Les Etats Generaux de la philosophie, Flammarion, 1979.

Deconstruction and Criticism, Seabury Press, 1979.

Philosophy in France Today, Cambridge University Press, 1983.

Joseph H. Smith and William Kerrigan, editors, *Taking Chances: Derrida, Psychoanalysis, and Literature,* Johns Hopkins University Press, 1984.

Text und Interpretation, Fink, 1984.

Post-Structuralist Joyce, Cambridge University Press, 1984.

La Faculte de juger, Minuit, 1985.

Qu'est-ce que Dieu?, [Brussels], 1985.

Difference in Translation, Cornell University Press, 1985.

Genese de Babel, Joyce et la creation, Editions du CNRS, 1985.

Paul Celan, Galilee, 1986.

La Graeve des philosophies: aecole et philosophie, Editions Osiris, 1986, published as *Raising the Tone of Philosophy,* edited by Peter Fenves, Johns Hopkins University Press, 1993.

La Case vide, Achitectural Association (London), 1986.

Pour Nelson Mandela, Gallimard, 1986.

Romeo et Juliette, Papiers, 1986.

OTHER

Co-director of the collection *La Philosophie en effet.* Member of editorial boards of *Critique, Structuralist Review, Contemporary Studies in Philosophy and the Human Sciences,* and *Revue senegalaise de philosophie.* Associated with *Tel Quel* during 1960s and 1970s.

SIDELIGHTS: French philosopher Jacques Derrida is the leading light of the post-structuralist intellectual movement that has significantly influenced philosophy, the social sciences, and literary criticism in recent years. By means of a "strategy of deconstruction" Derrida and other post-structuralists seek to reveal the play of multiple meanings in our cultural products and expose the tacit metaphysical assumptions that they believe underlie much of contemporary social thought. The deconstructionist project has ignited intense controversy among intellectuals in Europe and the United States, with detractors dismissing it as a particularly insidious form of nihilism, while its advocates argue that deconstructive practice allows the possibility of creating new values amid what they see as cynicism and spiritual emptiness of postmodern society.

Derrida first outlined his seminal ideas in a lengthy introduction to his 1962 French translation of German philosopher Edmund Husserl's *Origin of Geometry.* The strategy of deconstruction is rigorously delineated in Derrida's difficult masterwork, *Of Grammatology,* but the philosopher explains some of his basic concepts in more accessible terms in a 1972 collection of interviews called *Positions.* Derrida's thought builds on a variety of so-called subversive literature, including the writings of German philosophers Friedrich Nietzsche and Martin Heidegger, who both sought to overturn established values and depart from the traditional approach to the study of metaphysics; the political, social, and cultural insights of political economist Karl Marx and psychologist Sigmund Freud, who postulated underlying contradictory phenomena beneath the surface of everyday social life; and the linguistic analysis of the Swiss linguist Ferdinand de Saussure, who posited that language functions in a self-referential manner and has no "natural" relation to external reality. Many of Derrida's texts are subtle analyses of the writings of these thinkers and the literature of the modern structuralist movement, another strong influence on the philosopher. While accepting the structuralist notion, derived from Saussure, that cultural phenomena are best understood as self-referential systems of signs, Derrida denies the existence of a common intellectual structure capable of unifying the diverse cultural structures.

Derrida's insistence on the inadequacy of language to render a complete and unambiguous representation of reality forms the basis for his deconstructivist strategy of reading texts. In reading, Derrida studies texts for the multiple meanings that underlie and subvert the surface meaning of every piece of writing. To do this, he scrutinizes seemingly marginal textual elements such as idiosyncrasies of vocabulary and style and subverts what appear to be simple words and phrases with a battery of puns, allusions, and neologisms. He illuminates the continual play of differences in language—a movement he calls *differance.* As he wrote in *Positions, differance* prevents any simple element of language from being "*present* in and of itself, referring only to itself." Rather, every element contains differences and spaces within itself and *traces* of other elements that interweave to transform one text into another. There is, in Derrida's famous phrase, "nothing outside the text," that is, no clear and simple meaning represented by words, but only the play of *differance* and the multiplication of meanings in the deconstructive project. Although a deconstructive reading is never definitive, it is also not arbitrary, and the textual transformations can be followed systematically and even subjected to a structural analysis. Derrida's own deconstructive analyses of philosophical and literary texts include *Margins of Philosophy, Dissemination,* and *Spurs: Nietzsche's Styles.*

Given his devotion to textual analysis, Derrida has strongly influenced literary criticism, particularly in France and the United States. J. Hillis Miller and the late Paul de Man of Yale University are the best-known deconstructivists, but a wide spectrum of younger critics have also adopted the method in recent years. Derrida himself, meanwhile, has attempted to deconstruct the distinction between criticism and creative writing in his books such as *Glas* and *The Post Card.* The first work is considered one of the most unusual books ever printed. The pages of *Glas* are divided into two columns, one being a philosophical, psychological, and biographical portrait of the German philosopher G. W. F. Hegel, and the other a critical analysis of the writings of French playwright Jean Genet. The columns are in turn fractured within themselves into sub-columns and boxes. Both texts begin and end in mid-sentence and appear at first to be completely independent from each other—indeed, they can be read that way. But the reader can also create his or her own text by uncovering the textual traces that link the two columns and illuminate their differences. In fact, there is a virtually infinite number of ways to read and interpret *Glas,* which stoutly resists any totalized understanding. "The disorderly philosophical conduct of this work is so magnificent that it defies linear exposition," Geoffrey H. Hartman remarked in his critical study *Saving the Text: Literature/Derrida/Philosophy.* "Not since *Finnegans Wake* has there been such a deliberate and curious work: less original . . . and mosaic than the *Wake,* even flushed and overreaching, but as intriguingly, wearyingly allusive."

Derrida's strategy of deconstruction has implications far beyond literary criticism in the postmodern age, in the opinion of some moral philosophers. At a time when both religion and secular humanist ideologies have failed for many people, the post-structuralist celebration of difference offers an escape from alienated individualism. The metaphysical search is nostalgic and totalizing—seeking origin and end—while the deconstructive project recognizes no permanence and subverts all hierarchies. Dismissed by some readers and critics as nihilistic, this radical insistence on difference, incompleteness, and ephemerality impresses others as a positive grounding for social tolerance, mutual respect, and open discourse in the tumultuous world of the late twentieth century.

BIOGRAPHICAL/CRITICAL SOURCES:

BOOKS

Behler, Ernst, *Confrontations: Derrida/Heidegger/Nietzsche,* Standord University Press, 1991.

Caputo, John D., *The Prayers and Tears of Jacques Derrida: Religion without Religion,* Indiana University Press, 1997.

Collins, Jeff, *Introducing Derrida,* Totem Books, 1997.

Contemporary Literary Criticism, Volume 24, Gale, 1983.

Garver, Newton, *Derrida and Wittgenstein,* Temple University Press, 1994.

Gasche, Rodolphe, *The Train of the Mirror: Derrida and the Philosophy of Difference,* Harvard University Press, 1986.

Hartman, Geoffrey H., *Saving the Text: Literature/Derrida/Philosophy,* Johns Hopkins University Press, 1981.

Harvey, Irene E., *Derrida and the Economy of Difference,* Indiana University Press, 1986.

Llewelyn, John, *Derrida on the Threshold of Sense,* Macmillan, 1986.

Magliola, Robert R., *Derrida on the Mend,* Purdue University Press, 1984.

Megill, Allan, *Prophets of Extremity,* University of California Press, 1985.

Niall, Lucy, *Debating Derrida,* Melbourne University Press, 1995.

Norris, Christopher, *Derrida,* Harvard University Press, 1987.

Staten, Henry, *Wittgenstein and Derrida,* University of Nebraska Press, 1984.

Sturrock, John, editor, *Structuralism and Since: From Levi-Strauss to Derrida,* Oxford University Press, 1979.

PERIODICALS

Contemporary Literature, spring, 1979.

Critical Inquiry, summer, 1978.

Criticism, summer, 1979; winter, 1993.

New Literary History, autumn, 1978.

New Republic, April 16, 1977.

New York Review of Books, March 3, 1977; January 14, 1993.

New York Times Book Review, February 1, 1987.

Partisan Review, number 2, 1976; number 2, 1981.

Times Literary Supplement, February 15, 1968; September 30, 1983; December 5, 1986.

Virginia Quarterly Review, winter, 1992.

* * *

DERSONNES, Jacques
  See SIMENON, Georges (Jacques Christian)

* * *

DESAI, Anita 1937-

PERSONAL: Born June 24, 1937, in Mussoorie, India; daughter of D. N. (a businessperson) and Toni (Nime) Mazumdar; married Ashvin Desai (an executive), December 13, 1958; came to U.S., 1987; children: Rahul, Tani, Arjun, Kiran. *Education:* Delhi University, B.A. (with honors), 1957.

ADDRESSES: Office—c/o Deborah Rogers Ltd., 20 Powis Mews, London W11 1JN, England; Massachusetts Institute of Technology, Cambridge, MA 02139.

CAREER: Writer. Member of Advisory Board for English, Sahitya Akademi, New Delhi, India, 1972–. Smith College, Elizabeth Drew Professor, 1987-88; Mount Holyoke College, Purington Professor of English, 1988-93; Massachusetts Institute of Technology, Professor of writing, 1993–.

MEMBER: Royal Society of Literature (fellow).

AWARDS, HONORS: Winifred Holtby Prize, Royal Society of Literature, 1978, for *Fire on the Mountain*; Sahitya Academy award, 1979; *Guardian* Prize for Children's Fiction, 1983, for *The Village by the Sea*; Girton College, University of Cambridge, Helen Cam Visiting fellow, 1986-87, honorary fellow, 1988; Clare Hall, University of Cambridge, Ashby fellow, 1989, honorary fellow, 1991; *Hadassah* Prize, *Hadassah* (magazine), 1989, for *Baumgartner's Bombay*; Padma Sri, 1990; Literary Lion Award, New York Public Library, 1993; Neil Gunn fellowship, Scottish Arts Council, 1994.

WRITINGS:

NOVELS

Cry, the Peacock, P. Owen (London), 1963.
Voices in the City, P. Owen, 1965.
Bye-Bye, Blackbird, Hind Pocket Books, 1968.
Where Shall We Go This Summer?, Vikas Publishing House (India), 1975.
Fire on the Mountain, Harper (New York City), 1977.
Clear Light of Day, Harper, 1980.
In Custody, Heinemann (London), 1984, Harper, 1985.
Baumgartner's Bombay, Knopf (New York City), 1989.
Journey to Ithaca, Knopf, 1995.

JUVENILE

The Peacock Garden, India Book House, 1974.
Cat on a Houseboat, Orient Longmans (India), 1976.
Games at Twilight and Other Stories, Heinemann, 1978, Harper, 1980.
The Village by the Sea, Heinemann, 1982.
(Author of introduction) Lady Mary Wortley Montagu, *Turkish Embassy Letters,* edited by Malcolm Jack, University of Georgia Press (Athens), 1993.

Contributor of short stories to periodicals, including *Thought, Envoy, Writers Workshop, Quest, Indian Literature, Illustrated Weekly of India, Fesmina,* and *Harper's Bazaar.*

MEDIA ADAPTATIONS: The Village by the Sea was filmed in 1992, and *In Custody* was filmed in 1993.

SIDELIGHTS: Anita Desai focuses her novels upon the personal struggles of her Indian characters to cope with the problems of contemporary life. In this way, she manages to portray the cultural and social changes that her native country has undergone since the departure of the British. One of Desai's major themes is the relationships between family members, and especially the emotional tribulations of women whose independence is suppressed by Indian society. Her first novel, *Cry, the Peacock,* concerns a woman who finds it impossible to assert her individuality; the theme of the despairing woman is also explored in Desai's *Where Shall We Go This Summer?* Other novels explore life in urban India (*Voices in the City*), the clash between eastern and western cultures (*Bye-Bye, Blackbird*), and the differences between the generations (*Fire on the Mountain*).

Exile—physical as well as psychological—is also a prominent theme. In *Baumgartner's Bombay,* Desai (who is half-Indian and half-German) details the life of Hugo Baumgartner, a German Jew who flees Nazi Germany for India, where he "gradually drifts down through Indian society to settle, like sediment, somewhere near the bottom," writes Rosemary Dinnage in the *New York Review of Books.* She adds: "Baumgartner is a more thoroughly displaced person than Anglicized Indians, and more solitary, for Desai's Indian characters are still tied to family and community, however irksomely. She has drawn on her dual nationality to write on a subject new, I think, to English fiction—the experience of Jewish refugees in India." Pearl K. Bell makes a similar statement. "Baumgartner is the loneliest, saddest, most severely dislocated of Desai's fictional creatures," she notes in the *New Republic.* "But [he] is also a representative man, the German Jew to whom things happen, powerless to resist the evil wind that swept him like a vagrant weed from Berlin to India." Jean Sudrann of the *Yale Review* praises Desai's narrative skill "in making us feel the cumulative force of Hugo's alienation."

The author's descriptive powers are acclaimed by several critics. In the *New Leader* Betty Falkenberg calls *Baumgartner's Bombay* "a mathematical problem set and solved in exquisite prose." Bell observes that "there is a Dickensian rush and tumble to her portrayals of the bazaars, the crowded streets, the packed houses of an Indian metropolis." In general, Desai's "novels are quite short, but they convey a sharply detailed sense of the tangled complexities of Indian society, and an intimate view of the tug and pull of Indian family life."

While noting Desai's mixed German-Indian ancestry, *Spectator* contributor Caroline Moore nonetheless commends the author for the authentic Indian flavor of her works. "Westerners visiting India find themselves reeling under the outsider's sense of 'culture shock,' which is compounded more of shock than culture," the critic writes. "To Anita Desai, of course, the culture is second nature. Yet that intimacy never becomes mere familiarity: her achievement is to keep the shock of genuine freshness, the eyes of the perpetual outsider." This particular engagement with India is evident in many of Desai's novels, as A. G. Mojtabai notes in the *New York Times Book Review.* "Anita Desai is a writer of Bengali-German descent, who stands in a complicated but advantageous relation to India," says the reviewer. "Insiders rarely notice this much; outsiders cannot have this ease of reference." Mojtabai finds that Desai is able to delineate characters, settings, and feelings intricately yet economically, without extraneous detail or excessively populated scenes: "This author has no need of crowds. Properly observed, a roomful of people is crowd enough, and in the right hands—as Anita Desai so amply illustrates—*world* enough."

The complexities of outsiders facing Indian culture form the basis of Desai's 1995 novel, *Journey to Ithaca.* The story revolves around a hippie-era European couple who travel to India for quite different reasons—the husband to find enlightenment, the wife to enjoy a foreign experience. As the husband, Matteo, becomes involved with a spiritual guru known as the Mother, his wife, Sophie, goes on a quest of her own—to find the guru's roots in an effort either to debunk or to understand her. Calling the work "a kind of love triangle set against the madness of extreme spiritual searching," *New York Times* reviewer Richard Bernstein adds of *Journey to Ithaca*: "Ms. Desai writes with intelligence and power. She has a remarkable eye for substance, the things that give life its texture. Nothing escapes her power of observation, not the thickness of the drapes that blot out the light in a bourgeois Parisian home, or the enamel bowl in the office of an Indian doctor." Caroline Moore, in the *Spectator,* commends the book as

"superbly powerful . . . emotionally and intellectually haunting, teasing and tugging our minds even through its imperfections." Among these imperfections, Moore says, is the fact that the main characters are drawn rather sketchily.

Gabriele Annan, reviewing for the *Times Literary Supplement,* finds other flaws in *Journey to Ithaca.* "This is a curiously inept book for a novelist of Desai's experience," Annan writes. "The narrative is full of gaps and improbabilities, as well as cliches . . . the dialogue is stagey and unconvincing." The *Wall Street Journal*'s Brooke Allen, while admiring Desai's writing style, also finds much of the story unbelievable. Spiritually inclined readers may find the action plausible, but "others will remain incredulous," Allen asserts.

Desai is frequently praised by critics for her ability to capture the local color of her country and the ways in which eastern and western cultures have blended together there and for developing this skill further with each successive novel. A large part of this skill is due to her use of imagery, one of the most important devices in Desai's novels. Because of this emphasis on imagery, Desai is referred to by such reviewers as *World Literature Today* contributor Madhusudan Prasad as an "imagist-novelist. . . . [Her use of imagery is] a remarkable quality of her craft that she has carefully maintained in all her later fiction" since *Cry, the Peacock.* Employing this imagery to suggest rather than overtly explain her themes, Desai's stories sometimes appear deceptively simple; but, as Anthony Thwaite points out in the *New Republic,* "she is such a consummate artist that she [is able to suggest], beyond the confines of the plot and the machinations of her characters, the immensities that lie beyond them—the immensities of India." In the *Observer,* Salman Rushdie describes Desai's books as being "illuminated by the author's perceptiveness, delicacy of language and sharp wit."

BIOGRAPHICAL/CRITICAL SOURCES:

BOOKS

Afzal-Khan, Fawzia, *Cultural Imperialism and the Indo-English Novel: Genre and Ideology in R. K. Narayan, Anita Desai, Kamala Markandaya, and Salman Rushdie,* Pennsylvania State University Press (University Park), 1993.

Bellioppa, Meena, *The Fiction of Anita Desai,* Writers Workshop, 1971.

Choudhury, Bidulata, *Women and Society in the Novels of Anita Desai,* Creative Books (New Delhi), 1995.

Contemporary Literary Criticism, Gale (Detroit), Volume 19, 1981; Volume 37, 1986.

Khanna, Shashi, *Human Relationships in Anita Desai's Novels,* Sarup & Sons (New Delhi), 1995.

Parker, Michael and Roger Starkey, editors, *Postcolonial Literature: Achebe, Ngugi, Desai, Walcott,* St. Martin's (New York City), 1995.

Pathania, Usha, *Human Bonds and Bondages: The Fiction of Anita Desai and Kamala Markandaya,* Kanishka Publishers (New Delhi), 1992.

Sharma, Kajali, *Symbolism in Anita Desai's Novels,* Abhinav Publications (New Delhi), 1991.

Singh, Sunaina, *The Novels of Margaret Atwood and Anita Desai: A Comparative study in Feminist Perspectives,* Creative Books, 1994.

Sivanna, Indira, *Anita Desai as an Artist: A Study in Image and Symbol,* Creative Books, 1994.

Solanki, Mrinalini, *Anita Desai's Fiction: Patterns of Survival Strategies,* Kanishka Publishers, 1992.

PERIODICALS

Belles Lettres, summer, 1989, p. 4.
Boston Globe, August 15, 1995, p. 26.
Chicago Tribune, September 1, 1985.
Chicago Tribune Book World, August 23, 1981.
Globe and Mail (Toronto), August 20, 1988.
Kirkus Reviews, June 15, 1995, p. 799.
Los Angeles Times, July 31, 1980.
Los Angeles Times Book Review, March 3, 1985; April 9, 1989.
New Leader, May 1, 1989.
New Republic, March 18, 1985; April 3, 1989; April 6, 1992, p. 36; August 15, 1994, p. 43.
New York Review of Books, June 1, 1989; December 6, 1990, p. 53; January 16, 1992, p. 42; March 3, 1994, p. 41; May 23, 1996, p. 6.
New York Times, November 24, 1980; February 22, 1985; March 14, 1989; August 30, 1995, p. B2.
New York Times Book Review, November 20, 1977; June 22, 1980; November 23, 1980; March 3, 1985, p. 7; April 9, 1989, p. 3; January 27, 1991, p. 23; September 17, 1995, p. 12.
Observer (London), October 7, 1984, p. 22.
Spectator, June 3, 1995, pp. 41-42.
Time, July 1, 1985; August 21, 1995, p. 67.
Times (London), September 4, 1980.
Times Higher Education Supplement, April 7, 1995, pp. 16-17.
Times Literary Supplement, September 5, 1980; September 7, 1984; October 19, 1984; July 15-21, 1988, p. 787; June 2, 1995, p. 501.
Tribune Books (Chicago), March 5, 1989.
Wall Street Journal, August 24, 1995, p. A14.
Washington Post Book World, January 11, 1981, p. 3; October 7, 1984; March 31, 1985; February 26, 1989.
World Literature Today, summer, 1984, pp. 363-69; winter, 1997, p. 221.
Yale Review, Volume 79, spring, 1990, p. 414.

*   *   *

DE SAINT ROMAN, Arnaud
See ARAGON, Louis

*   *   *

De VRIES, Peter 1910-1993

PERSONAL: Born February 27, 1910, in Chicago, IL; died of pneumonia, September 28, 1993 in Norwalk, CT; son of Joost (a furniture warehouse owner) and Henrietta (Eldersveld) De Vries; married Katinka Loeser (a writer), October 16, 1943; children: Jan, Peter Jon, Emily (deceased), Derek. *Education:* Calvin College, A.B., 1931; attended Northwestern University, summer, 1931. *Politics:* Democrat.

ADDRESSES: Home—170 Cross Hwy., Westport, CT 06880.

CAREER: Writer and editor. Editor of community newspapers, Chicago, IL, 1931; candy vending machine operator, taffy apple peddler, lecturer, and radio actor, Chicago, 1931-38; freelance writer, 1931-93; *Poetry* magazine, Chicago, associate editor, 1938-42, co-editor, 1942-44; *The New Yorker,* staff member, 1944-87. Balch Lecturer, University of Virginia, Charlottesville, 1962; lecturer, 1968 Sophomore National Literary Festival,

University of Notre Dame; lecturer during 1960s at several universities in Germany as part of a U.S. State Department-sponsored program.

MEMBER: National Institute of Arts and Letters, American Academy of Arts and Letters.

AWARDS, HONORS: American Academy of Arts and Letters grant, 1946; D.H.L., University of Bridgeport, CT, 1968, University of Michigan, and Susquehanna University, PA; Arts Award, Connecticut Commission on the Arts, 1991.

WRITINGS:

NOVELS

But Who Wakes the Bugler?, Houghton, 1940.
The Handsome Heart, Coward, 1943.
Angels Can't Do Better, Coward, 1944.
The Tunnel of Love (also see below), Little, Brown, 1954.
Comfort Me with Apples (also see below), Little, Brown, 1956.
The Mackerel Plaza, Little, Brown, 1958.
The Tents of Wickedness (sequel to *Comfort Me with Apples*), Little, Brown, 1959.
Through the Fields of Clover, Little, Brown, 1961.
The Blood of the Lamb, Little, Brown, 1962.
Reuben, Reuben, Little, Brown, 1964.
Let Me Count the Ways, Little, Brown, 1965.
The Vale of Laughter, Little, Brown, 1967.
The Cat's Pajamas and Witch's Milk (contains the novellas "The Cat's Pajamas" and "Witch's Milk"), Little, Brown, 1968.
Mrs. Wallop, Little, Brown, 1970.
Into Your Tent I'll Creep, Little, Brown, 1971.
Forever Panting, Little, Brown, 1973.
The Glory of the Hummingbird, Little, Brown, 1974.
I Hear America Swinging, Little, Brown, 1976.
Madder Music, Little, Brown, 1977.
Consenting Adults; or, The Duchess Will Be Furious, Little, Brown, 1980.
Sauce for the Goose, Little, Brown, 1981.
Slouching towards Kalamazoo, Little, Brown, 1983.
The Prick of Noon, Little, Brown, 1985.
Peckham's Marbles, Putnam, 1986.

SHORT STORIES

No, But I Saw the Movie, Little, Brown, 1952.
Without a Stitch in Time: A Selection of the Best Humorous Short Pieces, Little, Brown, 1972.

OTHER

(With Joseph Fields) *The Tunnel of Love* (dramatization of the novel; produced on Broadway by Theatre Guild and in London, 1957), Little, Brown, 1957.

De Vries's manuscript collection is housed at the Boston University Library.

MEDIA ADAPTATIONS: The Tunnel of Love was filmed by Metro-Goldwyn-Mayer, 1958; *Reuben, Reuben* was adapted by Herman Shumlin and produced on Broadway at ANTA Theatre as *Spofford,* 1967, and filmed by Twentieth Century-Fox, 1983; *Let Me Count the Ways* was filmed by American Broadcasting Co. as *How Do I Love Thee?,* 1970; *Witch's Milk* was adapted by Julius J. Epstein and filmed by Universal as *Pete 'n' Tillie,* 1972.

SIDELIGHTS: Author Peter De Vries, described by Sybil S. Steinberg in *Publishers Weekly* as "something of a national humorist laureate," has made a career of satirizing society's shortcomings with wit, irony, and plenty of puns. "He is a serious man whose comic cast of mind developed as a defense against the severe Dutch Calvinist indoctrination of his formative years," Steinberg noted. Indeed, De Vries's background is reflected in his recurring themes of love, lust, marriage and its alternatives, and the unholy battles aroused by the topic of religion.

De Vries began his lucrative and long-lasting partnership with *The New Yorker* magazine in 1944, while working as editor of *Poetry* magazine in Chicago. De Vries invited humorist James Thurber to speak at a lecture to benefit his financially strapped publication, and Thurber in turn persuaded De Vries to contribute to *The New Yorker*. De Vries was soon offered the position of poetry editor. His affiliation with *Poetry* brought him another rewarding partnership—he met his wife, Katinka Loeser, also an author, when she won the magazine's Young Poet's Prize in 1942. Over the years, beyond his editorial duties, De Vries has contributed numerous short stories to *The New Yorker* which were later published in collected volumes. The magazine has served as a forum for his wife's work as well. "Often the coterie of loyal De Vries fans are the same ones who savor Katinka Loeser's memorable stories in *The New Yorker* and other magazines . . . , unaware that in private life Loeser is Mrs. De Vries," Steinberg reflected.

De Vries chose to disown his first three novels. "For a while I tried to buy up extant copies and burn them, but now it costs too much," he told Steinberg. The irony of a rare book catalog's listing of *But Who Wakes the Bugler?* at an exorbitant price was not lost on the author. *The Tunnel of Love,* the first novel De Vries acknowledges, sets his pattern of including at least one pun-addicted character in each work and introduces a favorite topic: marriage and its accompanying problems and delights. The book achieved best-seller status and was adapted for the stage; after a successful run on Broadway, it later became a film. *Comfort Me with Apples* and *Tents of Wickedness* both follow Chick Swallow through his marital discomforts and infidelities. "Typically, the overall movement of De Vries' novels is first a reaction against and then a comic acceptance of the adult community of marriage, and Swallow ends the second book by refusing the tempting offer of a tryst with an old girlfriend, 'Thanks just the same . . . but I don't want any pleasures interfering with my happiness,'" T. Jeff Evans observed in *American Humor: An Interdisciplinary Newsletter.*

The Mackerel Plaza, published between *Comfort Me with Apples* and *The Tents of Wickedness,* introduces the now-familiar discord wrought by religion in De Vries's novels. The story follows the plight of the Reverend Andrew (Holy) Mackerel, who faces opposition from his congregation when he expresses his wish to remarry after his saintly wife dies. Again his characters provide abundant De Vriesian commentary. "Some of De Vries's aphorisms are worthy of Oscar Wilde, and his characters are never short of repartee," Stuart Sutherland observed in *Times Literary Supplement.* "The ultramodern young clergyman of *Mackerel Plaza* is caught staring at a girl's legs; 'Stop looking at my legs,' she says, to which he replies, 'Don't worry, ma'am, my thoughts were on higher things.' Of twentieth-century novelists, only P. G. Wodehouse and Evelyn Waugh have De Vries's capacity to make the reader laugh out loud."

The Blood of the Lamb, which many critics consider his most important work, marked a turning point in De Vries's writing. His youngest daughter's death from leukemia in 1960 brought a deepening cynicism and somberness to De Vries's novels during the following decade, most noticeably to *The Blood of the Lamb,* in which a father wrestles with questions of religion and comes to terms with the tragic death of his child. The seemingly incongruous combination of comedy, always present in De Vries's work, and tragedy is successful; De Vries proves that "comedy is not the opposite of tragedy but its Siamese twin," *Time*'s R. Z. Sheppard noted. The author returned to farcical religious figures in *Let Me Count the Ways,* featuring agnostic Tom Waltz, the product of an evangelical mother and atheistic father who agreed to compromise on his spiritual upbringing. A pilgrimage to the healing shrine at Lourdes provides Tom with the disease that reunites him with his estranged wife.

De Vries's novels of the 1970s begin his exploration of the sociological phenomena of feminism, gender identity, and the sexual revolution. Here De Vries defends marriage in earnest, pointing up the shortcomings of excessive sexual freedom but also illuminating the difficulties of maintaining the necessary degree of wedded bliss. Critics remarked on the black humor and cynicism still evident in De Vries's work of this period, but generally agreed that *Consenting Adults; Or, The Duchess Will Be Furious* marked the author's return to a lighter, more humourous style. While still exploring the seamier sides of human existence, De Vries seemed once again able to embrace life and its myriad unknowns. "Question: Is it possible to cram into a novel every joke the theme and plot will allow, then add a couple of hundred more for good measure, and still maintain, from first page to last, a graceful, elegant and, above all, seemingly effortless prose style?," Christopher Cerf queried in the *New York Times Book Review.* "Answer: Absolutely—but probably only if you're Peter De Vries."

Washington Post Book World's Joseph McLellan summarizes *Consenting Adults* as a chronicle of the "social and sexual aspirations and misadventures of Ted Peachum of Pocock, Illinois, who is 16 years old when we first meet him and grows up (but not too much) in the course of the next 200 pages." McLellan finds the book's subject "of some interest but not really crucial, because in a De Vries novel the important point is not what he writes about but the way he writes about it." "*Consenting Adults* is rarely serious and only occasionally does it evoke pathos," Sutherland wrote in *Times Literary Supplement.* "It is more of a fun novel than a funny one—a literary romp." A young man's sexual awakening and subsequent troubles is again the subject in *Slouching towards Kalamazoo.* Anthony Thrasher, an under-achieving fifteen-year-old, finds himself a father-to-be after an indiscretion with his teacher during a tutoring session. The teacher, who shocked the small burg of Ulalume, North Dakota, by assigning *The Scarlet Letter* to her eighth-grade English class of 1961, leaves town to have the baby. Anthony follows, planning to make an honest woman of her, but falls for the baby's sitter, the nubile Bubbles Breedlove. *Slouching towards Kalamazoo* is "vintage De Vries, a perfect example of the sort of hilarious and expertly crafted comic novel that he amazingly seems to be able to turn out annually," Thomas Meehan declared in the *New York Times Book Review.*

De Vries employed a particularly thought-provoking double entendre as the title of *The Prick of Noon,* in which pornographer Eddie Teeters, known as Monty Carlo to his clientele, attempts to fit in with the society crowd while concealing his identity. "*The Prick of Noon* is in every respect a thoroughly characteristic De Vries novel," Jonathan Yardley commented in the *Washington Post.* "Its people have odd names and do odd things, but where it counts they are as human as any to be found in contemporary

American literature; its commentary is in equal measures perceptive and irreverent; its prose is facile and its puns outrageous. Not merely is De Vries the funniest of living American novelists, he is also one of the best." Among the book's memorable passages is "one of the most imaginative accounts of delirium in contemporary fiction," Elaine Kendall observed in the *Los Angeles Times Book Review,* "in which Teeters imagines himself going naked through a car wash, lathered by the rotary brushes, slapped by the hanging strips, blasted with suds like mad dog saliva, dried with powerful jets of hot air and finally waxed and finished off by avaricious attendants who expect a lavish tip for their attentions." Kendall concluded, "Like the preceding 21, this novel is well supplied with redeeming social value masquerading as risque frivolity." Sheppard remarked in *Time* that *The Prick of Noon* "may not be his strongest performance. But . . . De Vries still projects a vision that is fresh and sensuous. His is a comedy that does not reduce character with sociology and psychology but sees instincts and folly through the eyes of a naturalist."

In *Peckham's Marbles,* Earl Peckham, fresh out of a sanitarium after recovering from a case of hepatitis that forced him to "look on the world with a jaundiced eye," sets out to revive his literary career. Three copies of his book were sold to bookstores; he hopes to find and autograph them so they can't be returned to the publisher. Unfortunately for him, though, "Peckham tries to make things happen, but he is ultimately the sort of person to whom things happen," Christopher Buckley observed in *Washington Post Book World.* Remarking on Peckham's constant recitation of lines from the works of Mark Twain, F. Scott Fitzgerald, T. S. Eliot, Willa Cather, and a host of other literary icons, Buckley noted, "At times it seems as if the book has been crossbred with one of the tonier Writers on Writers quotebooks. But this is a book about writers and the lit'ry life, after all, and anyway, the sheer felicity of watching Peter De Vries handle the language vaporizes that objection like a blue neon Bug Zapper."

A popular writer both in the United States and Britain, De Vries was described by British author Kingsley Amis in the *London Times* as "the funniest serious writer to be found either side of the Atlantic." To those who have yet to read a De Vries novel, the *Observer's* Julian Barnes offers this suggestion: "Samuel Butler advised us to eat a bunch of grapes downwards, so that each grape gets bigger and sweeter. Perhaps you should read Mr De Vries backwards, so that each book will seem funnier and truer." The *New York Times Book Review's* Meehan advised, "If you've somehow never read Mr. De Vries, you should, starting . . . with *Slouching towards Kalamazoo* and working your way back to *The Tunnel of Love* and *Comfort Me with Apples,* for such highly intelligent literary pleasures as he has to offer are rare indeed to come upon these days."

BIOGRAPHICAL/CRITICAL SOURCES:

BOOKS

Bowden, Edwin T., *Peter De Vries: A Bibliography 1934-1977,* University of Texas Humanities Research Center, 1978.
Bowden, J. H., *Peter De Vries,* Twayne, 1983.
Campion, Dan, *Peter De Vries and Surrealism,* Bucknell University Press (Lewisburg), 1995.

PERIODICALS

American Humor: An Interdisciplinary Newsletter, fall, 1980, pp. 13-16.
Chicago Tribune, February 21, 1984; April 14, 1985.

Chicago Tribune Book World, August 10, 1980, sec. 7, p. 1; September 6, 1981, sec. 7, p. 1; June 6, 1982, p. 2; November 7, 1982, p. 7; July 17, 1983, p. 29.
Christian Century, November 26, 1975.
Detroit News, May 19, 1985.
Encounter, January, 1973.
Globe and Mail (Toronto), October 18, 1986.
Los Angeles Times, September 25, 1986.
Los Angeles Times Book Review, September 21, 1980, p. 1; September 13, 1981, p. 4; August 28, 1983, p. 7; May 8, 1985.
New Republic, October 23, 1976.
Newsweek, October 5, 1981, p. 82; August 1, 1983, p. 68.
New Yorker, March 11, 1974; March 26, 1979.
New York Times, July 31, 1980, p. C18; September 18, 1981; July 22, 1983; April 5, 1985; October 3, 1986; October 6, 1986.
New York Times Book Review, August 17, 1980, pp. 1, 22; September 20, 1981, p. 14; August 14, 1983, pp. 7, 20; May 19, 1985, p. 16; April 20, 1986, p. 38; November 2, 1986, p. 26.
Observer, January 26, 1986, p. 51.
Publishers Weekly, October 16, 1981, pp. 6-8.
Studies in American Humor, April, 1974.
Theology Today, April, 1975.
Time, September 21, 1981, p. 81; April 22, 1985, p. 69; October 13, 1986, p. 102.
Times (London), February 26, 1981.
Times Literary Supplement, January 30, 1981, p. 107; January 22, 1982, p. 76; August 26, 1983, p. 898; January 24, 1986, p. 82.
Tribune Books (Chicago), October 19, 1986, p. 6.
Washington Post, May 18, 1984; April 17, 1985.
Washington Post Book World, August 7, 1980; September 6, 1981, p. 3; March 14, 1982, p. 16; June 6, 1982, p. 12; July 17, 1983, p. 3; October 5, 1986, p. 5.

*   *   *

DEXTER, (Norman) Colin 1930-
(N. C. Dexter)

PERSONAL: Born September 29, 1930, in Stamford, Lincolnshire, England; son of Alfred (a taxi driver) and Dorothy (Towns) Dexter; married Dorothy Cooper (a physiotherapist), March 31, 1956; children: Sally, Jeremy. *Education:* Christ's College, Cambridge, B.A., 1953, M.A., 1958. *Politics:* Socialist ("lapsed"). *Religion:* Methodist ("lapsed").

ADDRESSES: Home—456 Banbury Rd., Oxford OX2 7RG, England.

CAREER: Wyggeston School, Leicester, England, assistant classics master, 1954-57; Loughborough Grammar School, Loughborough, England, sixth form classics master, 1957-59; Corby Grammar School, Corby, England, senior classics master, 1959-66; Oxford Local Examination Board, Oxford, England, assistant secretary, 1966-76, senior assistant secretary, 1976-87. *Military service:* Royal Corps of Signals, 1949-50.

MEMBER: Crime Writers Association, Detection Club.

AWARDS, HONORS: M.A., Oxford University, 1966; Silver Dagger Award, Crime Writers Association, 1979, for *Service of All the Dead,* and 1981, for *The Dead of Jericho;* Gold Dagger Award, Crime Writers Association, 1989, for *The Wench Is Dead,* and 1992, for *The Way through the Woods*; M.A., Leicester University, 1996; Medal of Merit, Lotus Club, 1996.

WRITINGS:

AS N. C. DEXTER

(With E. G. Rayner) *Liberal Studies: An Outline Course,* 2 volumes, Macmillan (New York City), 1964, revised edition, 1966.

(With Rayner) *Guide to Contemporary Politics,* Pergamon (London), 1966.

"INSPECTOR MORSE" MYSTERIES

Last Bus to Woodstock, St. Martin's (New York City), 1975.
Last Seen Wearing (also see below), St. Martin's, 1976.
The Silent World of Nicholas Quinn, St. Martin's, 1977.
Service of All the Dead, Macmillan (London), 1979, St. Martin's, 1980.
The Dead of Jericho, St. Martin's, 1981.
The Riddle of the Third Mile (also see below), Macmillan, 1983.
The Secret of Annexe 3 (also see below), Macmillan, 1986, St. Martin's, 1987.
The Wench Is Dead, Macmillan, 1989, St. Martin's, 1990.
The Jewel That Was Ours, Macmillan, 1991.
The Second Inspector Morse Omnibus (contains *The Secret of Annexe 3, The Riddle of the Third Mile,* and *Last Seen Wearing*) Macmillan (London), 1991.
The Way through the Woods, Macmillan, 1992.
Morse's Greatest Mystery (contains "As Good As Gold," "Morse's Greatest Mystery," "Evans Tries An O-Level," "Dead as a Dodo," "At the Lulu-Bar Motel," "Neighbourhood Watch," "A Case of Mis-Identity," "The Inside Story," "Monty's Revolver," "The Carpet-Bagger," and "Last Call"), Macmillan, 1993.
The Daughters of Cain, Macmillan, 1994.
Death Is Now My Neighbour, Macmillan, 1996.

OTHER

(With Martin Edwards) *Perfectly Criminal,* Severn House, 1997.

Work represented in several anthologies, including *Murder Ink,* edited by Dilys Winn, Workman, 1977; *Winter's Crimes 9,* edited by George Hardinge, St. Martin's, 1978; *Winter's Crimes 13,* edited by Hardinge, St. Martin's, 1982; *Winter's Crimes 21,* edited by Hilary Hale, Macmillan, 1989.

MEDIA ADAPTATIONS: Stories based on Dexter's Inspector Morse character have been adapted for television and shown in the United States on the PBS program *Mystery! Inspector Morse: Driven to Distraction* by Anthony Minghella is a screenplay based on characters created by Dexter and was published by University of Cambridge (NY), 1994. Several of his novels have also been recorded and released as audio books.

SIDELIGHTS: "To most readers of Colin Dexter's books," writes *Dictionary of Literary Biography* contributor Bernard Benstock, "his major accomplishment is the creation of his particular detective hero, Detective Chief Inspector Morse of the Thames Valley Constabulary of Kidlington, Oxon." Inspector Morse is an irascible figure, fond of beer and tobacco, but nonetheless held in awe by his associate Detective Sergeant Lewis. "At times," Benstock reveals, "his seediness is similar to the seediness of a Graham Greene character, his bluster and swagger similar to John Mortimer's Rumpole of the Bailey, but always there is an element of the pathetic to counterbalance the braggadocio. Morse's vulnerable and remarkable character unfolds serially from book to book, so that eventually there are no mysteries about him—except for his given name."

Dexter introduced Inspector Morse in 1975 in *Last Bus to Woodstock,* which established many of the central characteristics of Dexter's work. "*Last Bus to Woodstock* concerns the brutal murder (and possible sex-murder) of a scantily clad female hitchhiker, whose companion at the bus stop fails to identify herself," writes Benstock. "Several young women are likely possibilities for the companion, but Morse is frustrated by their refusal to be honest with him." Morse finds himself sidetracked after having identified the wrong person as the murderer. "The grisly deaths of a husband and wife, each of whom had confessed to the murder," Benstock continues, "bring matters to a head, and Morse apprehends the woman murderer—an attractive young woman he had admired, who confesses that she has fallen in love with him—as she is taken away to stand trial." Dexter treats each of the Morse mysteries as a puzzle, complete with misleading clues, red herrings, and false trails. "Once you chose the wrong word," explains a *Virginia Quarterly Review* contributor, "the whole puzzle can be filled incorrectly."

Morse's irritability is complimented by his companion in mystery-solving, Detective Sergeant Lewis. Cushing Strout, writing in *Armchair Detective,* compares the relationship between Lewis and Morse to that of Arthur Conan Doyle's Sherlock Holmes and John Watson, calling Dexter's work "the best contemporary English example of adapting and updating Doyle's technique." Like Holmes, Strout continues, "Morse is a bachelor," but, "in spite of his generally cynical expectations about human nature and the world, unlike Holmes he is always romantically vulnerable (in spite of disappointing experience) to being smitten by love at first sight for some attractive and intelligent, but quite inappropriate woman." In contrast to Morse, Strout continues, Sergeant Lewis "is working class, a family man, and a competent policeman in a routine way. He has a refreshing common sense that Morse often sorely lacks, and the two men (like Holmes and Watson in this respect) know how to tease each other."

Dexter, Strout explains, "has collated his novels under the heading of 'what may be termed (though it sounds a bit posh) the exploitation of reader-mystification.'" This is a traditional attribute of English detective fiction: the ability to mislead the reader in identifying the culprit. The classic mystery novel, as set forth by one of the earliest practitioners of the genre, G. K. Chesterton, should present the reader with all the clues available to the detective, but in such a way that the reader fails to make the connection with the criminal until after the detective uncovers the guilty party. "Inferior writers," Strout continues, "tend to cast suspicion on so many characters that it is . . . like hiding one card amid the rest of the deck, rather than performing the much more difficult classic trick, wherein the 'money card' is one of only three cards." "Dexter," the critic concludes, "keeps shifting the pieces, like a conjuror misdirecting the audience by giving a specious explanation of his trick, until they finally make a coherent and credible picture with the lagniappe of a last surprise." In a review of *The Daughters of Cain* for the *New York Times Book Review,* Marilyn Stasio advises readers "to get out their pencils, timetables and aspirin."

As the series progresses, Dexter also begins to play highly literate games with his readers, ranging from apparently gratis references to literature, such as James Joyce's *Ulysses* in *The Riddle of the Third Mile* and Sophocles' Oedipus trilogy of plays in *The Dead of Jericho.* He also uses inscriptions and epigraphs at the beginning of each chapter like a chorus in a Greek play to comment on the story's action and the state of Morse's mind. "The basic norm in the Dexter novels," Benstock declares, "is best characterized by the epigraph to chapter 14 of *The Riddle of the Third Mile*: 'Preliminary investigations are now in full swing, and Morse appears unconcerned about the contradictory evidence that emerges.'"

Morse demonstrates his best points in the Gold Dagger award-winning novel *The Wench Is Dead*. Critics have compared the book to Josephine Tey's classic detective novel *The Daughter of Time,* in which her detective Alan Grant, immobilized in hospital with a fractured spine, tries to solve an historical mystery—the disappearance of young Edward V and his brother Richard of York in the Tower of London during the reign of Richard III. Like Grant, Morse is hospitalized, with a bleeding ulcer, and to ease his boredom he reopens a Victorian murder case that took place in Oxford: the death by drowning of a female passenger on a canal boat in the mid-nineteenth century. Morse's wits and temper, writes Stasio in the *New York Times Book Review,* "tug the reader into the detective's hospital bed to share his single-minded pursuit of the truth."

Dexter's "Inspector Morse" novels have established him as a pivotal figure in modern English detective fiction. Throughout the series, Benstock states, "the comic vies with the grotesque, pathos with the tragic, within an effective evocation of the mundane. The surface realities of ordinary life consistently color the criminal situations without impinging on the careful artifice of the usual murders and the bumbling but brilliant methods of investigation undertaken almost in spite of himself by Chief Inspector E. Morse." Strout declares that "fans of the [detective story] will be grateful to Dexter, for some of its greatest luminaries are showing signs of restlessness with the genre." Ruth Rendell, famous as an author of police-procedural novels, mixes social issues such as unemployment and racism in her detective fiction. P. D. James's poet-detective hero Adam Dalgliesh "seems to be headed for retirement," Strout explains, "not by his own or Scotland Yard's decision but by his creator's restlessness with the genre." Strout concludes that "it is much to our benefit that Dexter is still fond of the form."

BIOGRAPHICAL/CRITICAL SOURCES:

BOOKS

Dictionary of Literary Biography, Volume 87: *British Mystery and Thriller Writers since 1940, First Series,* Gale (Detroit), 1989.

PERIODICALS

Armchair Detective, winter, 1989, pp. 76-77; fall, 1990, p. 497; summer, 1994, p. 272; fall, 1995, pp. 434-37.
Listener, July 8, 1976; June 30, 1977.
New Republic, March 4, 1978.
New York Times Book Review, May 20, 1990, p. 53; April 4, 1993; April 16, 1995, p. 29.
Time, April 26, 1993, p. 65.
Times Literary Supplement, September 26, 1975; April 23, 1976; August 26, 1977; June 5, 1981; October 25, 1991, p. 21; October 23, 1992, p. 22.
Virginia Quarterly Review, autumn, 1992, p. 131.
Washington Post Book World, December 20, 1987, p. 8.

DEXTER, John
See BRADLEY, Marion Zimmer

* * *

DEXTER, N. C.
See DEXTER, (Norman) Colin

* * *

DIAMANO, Silmang
See SENGHOR, Leopold Sedar

* * *

DI BASSETTO, Corno
See SHAW, George Bernard

* * *

DICK, Philip K(indred) 1928-1982
(Richard Phillips)

PERSONAL: Born December 16, 1928, in Chicago, IL; died of heart failure following a stroke, March 2, 1982, in Santa Ana, CA; son of Joseph Edgar (a government employee) and Dorothy (Kindred) Dick; married, 1949; wife's name Jeannette (divorced); married, 1951; wife's name Kleo (divorced); married, 1958; wife's name Ann (divorced); married April 18, 1967; wife's name Nancy (divorced); married Tessa Busby, April 18, 1973 (divorced); children: (third marriage) Laura; (fourth marriage) Isolde; (fifth marriage) Christopher. *Education:* Attended University of California, Berkeley, 1950. *Politics:* "Anti-war, pro-life." *Religion:* Episcopalian.

CAREER: Writer. Hosted classical music program on KSMO Radio, 1947; worked in a record store, 1948-52; occasional lecturer at California State University, Fullerton; active in drug rehabilitation and anti-abortion work.

MEMBER: Science Fiction Writers of America, Animal Protection Institute.

AWARDS, HONORS: Hugo Award, World Science Fiction Convention, 1962, for *The Man in the High Castle*; John W. Campbell Memorial Award, 1974, for *Flow My Tears, the Policeman Said*; guest of honor, Science Fiction Festival, Metz, France, 1978; the Philip K. Dick Memorial Award has been created by Norwescon, an annual science fiction convention in Seattle.

WRITINGS:

SCIENCE FICTION NOVELS

Solar Lottery (bound with *The Big Jump* by Leigh Brackett), Ace Books, 1955, reprinted separately, Gregg, 1976 (published separately in England as *World of Chance,* Rich & Cowan, 1956).
The World Jones Made (bound with *Agent of the Unknown* by Margaret St. Clair), Ace Books, 1956.
The Man Who Japed (bound with *The Space-Born* by E. C. Tubb), Ace Books, 1956.
Eye in the Sky, Ace Books, 1957.

The Cosmic Puppets (bound with *Sargasso of Space* by Andrew North), Ace Books, 1957, reprinted separately, Berkley Publishing, 1983.

Time Out of Joint, Lippincott, 1959.

Dr. Futurity (also see below; bound with *Slavers of Space* by John Brunner), Ace Books, 1960, reprinted (bound with *The Unteleported Man* by Dick), 1972, reprinted separately, Berkley Publishing, 1984.

Vulcan's Hammer (bound with *The Skynappers* by Brunner), Ace Books, 1960.

The Man in the High Castle, Putnam, 1962.

The Game-Players of Titan, Ace Books, 1963.

Martian Time-Slip, Ballantine, 1964.

The Penultimate Truth, Belmont-Tower, 1964.

The Simulacra, Ace Books, 1964.

Clans of the Alphane Moon, Ace Books, 1964.

Dr. Bloodmoney; or, How We Got Along after the Bomb, Ace Books, 1965.

The Three Stigmata of Palmer Eldritch, Doubleday, 1965.

Now Wait for Last Year, Doubleday, 1966.

The Crack in Space (also see below), Ace Books, 1966.

The Unteleported Man (also see below; bound with *The Mind Monsters* by Howard L. Cory), Ace Books, 1966, reprinted (bound with *Dr. Futurity* by Dick), 1972, reprinted separately, Berkley Publishing, 1983.

(With Ray Nelson) *The Ganymede Takeover,* Ace Books, 1967.

Counter-Clock World, Berkley Publishing, 1967.

The Zap Gun, Pyramid Publications, 1967.

Do Androids Dream of Electric Sheep?, Doubleday, 1968, published as *Blade Runner,* Ballantine, 1982.

Ubik (also see below), Doubleday, 1969.

Galactic Pot-Healer, Doubleday, 1969.

A Philip K. Dick Omnibus (contains *The Crack in Space, The Unteleported Man,* and *Dr. Futurity*), Sidgwick & Jackson, 1970.

A Maze of Death, Doubleday, 1970.

Our Friends from Frolix 8, Ace Books, 1970.

We Can Build You, DAW Books, 1972.

Flow My Tears, the Policeman Said, Doubleday, 1974.

(With Roger Zelazny) *Deus Irae,* Doubleday, 1976.

A Scanner Darkly, Doubleday, 1977.

VALIS, Bantam, 1981.

The Divine Invasion, Pocket Books, 1981.

The Transmigration of Timothy Archer, Pocket Books, 1982.

The Man Whose Teeth Were All Exactly Alike, Zeising, 1984.

Radio Free Albemuth, Arbor House, 1987.

Nick and the Glimmung, Gollancz, 1988.

The Little Black Box, Gollancz, 1990.

STORY COLLECTIONS

A Handful of Darkness, Rich & Cowan, 1955.

The Variable Man and Other Stories, Ace Books, 1957.

The Preserving Machine and Other Stories, Ace Books, 1969.

The Book of Philip K. Dick, DAW Books, 1973 (published in England as *The Turning Wheel and Other Stories,* Coronet, 1977).

The Best of Philip K. Dick, Ballantine, 1977.

The Golden Man, Berkley Publishing, 1980.

Robots, Androids, and Mechanical Oddities: The Science Fiction of Philip K. Dick, edited by Patricia Warrick and Martin H. Greenberg, Southern Illinois University Press, 1984.

Lies, Inc., Gollancz, 1984.

I Hope I Shall Arrive Soon, Doubleday, 1985.

The Collected Stories, 5 vols., Underwood Miller, 1987.

The Philip K. Dick Reader, Citadel Press, 1997.

CONTRIBUTOR

August Derleth, editor, *Time to Come,* Farrar, Straus, 1954.

Frederik Pohl, editor, *Star Science Fiction Stories #3,* Ballantine, 1955.

Anthony Boucher, editor, *A Treasury of Great Science Fiction,* Volume I, Doubleday, 1959.

Harlan Ellison, editor, *Dangerous Visions: 33 Original Stories,* Doubleday, 1967.

Edward L. Ferman and Barry N. Malzberg, editors, *Final Stage,* Charterhouse, 1974.

Willis E. McNelly, editor, *Science Fiction: The Academic Awakening,* College English Association, 1974.

Bruce Gillespie, editor, *Philip K. Dick: Electric Shepherd,* Norstrilia Press (Melbourne), 1975.

Peter Nicholls, editor, *Science Fiction at Large,* Gollancz, 1976, Harper, 1977.

OTHER

Confessions of a Crap Artist, Jack Isidore (of Seville, Calif.): A Chronicle of Verified Scientific Fact, 1945-1959 (novel), Entwhistle Books, 1975.

A Letter from Philip K. Dick (pamphlet), Philip K. Dick Society, 1983.

In Milton Lumky Territory (novel), Ultramarine, 1984.

Ubik: The Screenplay (based on novel of same title), Corroboree, 1985.

Puttering about in a Small Land (novel), Academy, 1985.

Mary and the Giant (novel), Arbor House, 1987.

The Broken Bubble(novel), Arbor House, 1988.

Williams, Paul, editor, *The Selected Letters of Philip K. Dick 1974,* Underwood-Miller (Novato, CA), 1991.

Gather Yourselves Together (novel), WCS Books (Herndon, VA), 1994.

Sutin, Lawrence, editor, *The Shifting Realities of Philip K. Dick: Selected Literary and Philosophical Writings,* Pantheon (New York City), 1995.

Also author of unpublished novels *A Time for George Stavros, Nicholas and the Higs,* and *Voices from the Street.* Author of radio scripts for the Mutual Broadcasting System. Contributor of over 100 stories, some under pseudonym Richard Phillips, to *Magazine of Fantasy and Science Fiction, Galaxy, Amazing Science Fiction Stories,* and other magazines.

MEDIA ADAPTATIONS: Do Androids Dream of Electric Sheep? was filmed as *Blade Runner* by Warner Bros. in 1982. The short story "We Can Remember It for You Wholesale" was filmed as *Total Recall* in 1990. Film rights for the story "Second Variety" have also been sold. *Ubik* has been optioned for a film adaptation.

SIDELIGHTS: The central problem in much of the late Philip K. Dick's science fiction is how to distinguish the real from the unreal. He once told *Contemporary Authors:* "My major preoccupation is the question, 'What is reality?'" In novel after novel, Dick's characters find that their familiar world is in fact an illusion, either self-created or imposed on them by others. Dick "liked to begin a novel," Patricia Warrick wrote in *Science-Fiction Studies,* "with a commonplace world and then have his characters fall through the floor of this normal world into a strange new reality." Drug-induced hallucinations, robots and androids, mystical visions, paranoic delusions, and alternate or artificial worlds are the stuff of which Dick's flexible universe is made. "All of his work," Charles Platt wrote in *Dream Makers: The Uncommon People Who Write Science Fiction,* "starts with the basic assumption that there cannot be one, single, objective reality. Everything is a matter of perception. The ground is liable to shift under your feet. A protagonist may find himself living out another person's dream, or he may enter a drug-induced state that actually makes better sense than the real world, or he may cross into a different universe completely."

Despite the mutable and often dangerous nature of Dick's fictional worlds, his characters retain at least a faint hope for the future, and manage to survive and comfort one another. Dick's characters are usually ordinary people—repairmen, housewives, students, salesmen—caught up in overwhelming situations that call into question their basic beliefs about themselves and their world. In *The Three Stigmata of Palmer Eldritch,* powerful drugs create such believable hallucinations that users find it difficult to know when the hallucination has ended and the real world has returned. A character in *Time Out of Joint* discovers that he does not really live in a mid-twentieth-century American town as he had believed. He lives in an artificial replica of an American town built by a government of the future for its own purposes. In *Eye in the Sky,* eight people at a research facility are pushed by a freak accident into a state of consciousness where each one's subjective reality becomes real for the entire group for a time. They experience worlds where the ideas of a religious cult member, a communist, a puritan, and a paranoid are literally true. The ability of Dick's characters to survive these situations, preserving their sanity and humanity in the process, is what Dick celebrated. His novels presented a "world where ordinary people do the best they can against death-driven, malevolent forces," Tom Whalen wrote in the *American Book Review.*

The Man in the High Castle, winner of the 1962 Hugo Award and generally considered Dick's best novel, is set in a world in which America lost the Second World War. The nation has been divided in two and occupied by the Germans and Japanese. Most of the novel takes place on the Japanese-occupied West Coast and revolves around a group of Americans who are trying to cope with their status as subject people. Concerned primarily with creating a believable alternate society, the novel reveals in the process "how easily this nation would have surrendered its own culture under a Japanese occupation and how compatible American fears, prejudices, and desires were with Nazism," as Hogan remarked. The novel's "man in the high castle" is the author of an underground bestseller about an alternate world where America won the war. "I did seven years of research for *The Man in the High Castle,*" Dick said in an interview for the *Missouri Review.* "I had prime-source material at the Berkeley-Cal library right from the gestapo's mouth—stuff that had been seized after World War II. . . . That's . . . why I've never written a sequel to it: it's too horrible, too awful. I started several times to write a sequel, but I [would have] had to go back and read about Nazis again, so I couldn't do it." Dick used the I Ching, an ancient Chinese divining system, to plot *The Man in the High Castle.* At each critical juncture in the narrative, Dick consulted the I Ching to determine the proper course of the plot.

The alternate universes in *The Three Stigmata of Palmer Eldritch* are created by powerful hallucinogenic drugs. The novel is set in the near-future when the increasing heat of the sun is making life on Earth impossible. The United Nations is forcing people to immigrate to Mars, an inhospitable desert waste where colonists must live in underground hovels. Because of the boredom of colony life, a drug-induced fantasy world has been devised which uses small dolls and miniature settings. When a colonist takes the drug Can-D, he becomes one of the dolls and lives for a brief time in an Earth-like setting. The manufacturer of the dolls and settings—a company named Perky Pat Layouts, after the female doll—also sells Can-D. When Palmer Eldritch returns from a deep-space exploration, he brings with him a supply of the new and more powerful drug Chew-Z. Eldritch has also acquired three "stigmata"—an artificial metallic arm, enormous steel teeth, and artificial eyes. His Chew-Z is cheaper and longer-lasting than Can-D and he soon is selling it to the Martian colonists. But Chew-Z doesn't seem to wear off. The user is moved into a world that seems like his own but with the important difference that Palmer Eldritch has god-like powers. Bruce Gillespie, writing in *Philip K. Dick: Electric Shepherd,* called *Palmer Eldritch* "one of the few masterpieces of recent science fiction."

In 1974 Dick received the John W. Campbell Memorial Award for *Flow My Tears, the Policeman Said,* a near-future novel in which popular television talk show host Jason Taverner wakes up one morning in a world where he is unknown. No record even exists of his having been born, an awkward situation in the records-conscious police state that Taverner's California has become. The explanation for this impossibility is that Taverner is living within the drug hallucination of Alys Buckner, and in that hallucination there is no place for him. The powerful drug, able to impose Alys's hallucination on reality itself, eventually kills her, and Taverner is set free. "Dick skillfully explores the psychological ramifications of this nightmare," Gerald Jonas commented in the *New York Times Book Review,* "but he is even more interested in the reaction of a ruthlessly efficient computerized police state to the existence of a man, who, according to the computers, should not exist."

Do Androids Dream of Electric Sheep? is Dick's most celebrated novel about simulacra, mechanical objects which simulate life. In this novel Dick posits a world in which androids are so highly developed that it is only by the most rigid testing that one can distinguish them from human beings. The key difference is the quality of empathy which humans have for other living things. When some androids escape from a work colony and make their way to Earth, bounty hunter Rick Deckard must find them. But Deckard gradually comes to feel compassion for the androids, realizing that the tests he gives measure only a subtle difference between androids and humans. In contrast to this officially-sanctioned tracking and killing of androids, this near-future society accepts artificial animals of all kinds—everything from sheep to spiders. With most real animals extinct, replicas are fashionable to own. One of the rarest animals is the toad, and when Deckard discovers one in the desert he believes he has made an important find. But even in the desert there are no real animals. Deckard notices a small control panel in the toad's abdomen. Nonetheless, he takes the toad home and cares for him. His wife, touched by his concern for the "creature," buys some electric flies for the toad to eat. "Against this bizarre background of pervasive fakery," Philip Strick wrote in *Sight and Sound,* "the erosion of authentic humanity by undetectable android imitations has all the plausibility of a new and lethal plague whereby evolution would become substitution and nobody would notice the difference." Writing in *Philip K. Dick,* Patricia S. Warrick called *Do Androids Dream of Electric Sheep?* "one of Dick's finest novels," citing its "complexity of structure and idea." *Androids* was loosely adapted as the film *Blade Runner* in 1982.

In writing several novels, Dick drew upon his own life experiences. *A Scanner Darkly,* for example, is dedicated to a list of Dick's friends who died or suffered permanent health damage because of drugs. The novel concerns undercover narcotics agent

Bob Arctor, who is assigned to investigate himself. His superiors are unaware of his undercover identity and Arctor cannot afford to reveal it. He investigates himself to avoid suspicion. While conducting the investigation, however, Arctor is taking the drug Substance D. The drug splits his personality until he no longer recognizes himself in surveillance videotapes. Arctor's condition worsens until he is finally put into a drug rehabilitation program. "The novel," Patrick Parrinder wrote in the *Times Literary Supplement,* "is a frightening allegory of the process of drug abuse, in which some of the alternative realities experienced are revealed as the hallucinations of terminal addicts." "Drug misuse is not a disease," Dick wrote in an author's note to the novel, "it is a decision, like the decision to step out in front of a moving car." Dick himself suffered pancreatic damage from his involvement with drugs. His use of amphetamines resulted in the high blood pressure which eventually ended in his fatal stroke. Dick told Platt that he had "regarded drugs as dangerous and potentially lethal, but I had a cat's curiosity. It was my interest in the human mind that made me curious. . . . These were essentially religious strivings that were appearing in me."

Prior to his success as a science-fiction writer, Dick attempted to find a niche as a mainstream author in the 1950s and 1960s. Two of the books Dick produced during this period were posthumously published as *Mary and the Giant* and *The Broken Bubble,* and both revolve around 1950s suburban California. The protagonist of *Mary and the Giant* is an undereducated twenty-year-old woman who whirls in the vacuum of her life options. These include marriage or love with several different lovers including an elderly record-store owner, an African-American lounge singer, and an underachieving pianist. A *Publishers Weekly* critic called Dick "one of the most compelling chroniclers of life and love in 1950s California that we have had." Colin Greenland of the *Times Literary Supplement* stated that "this neglected early novel reveals Philip K. Dick's remarkable insight into a society on the eve of change and a young woman on the edge of panic." "The narrative voice is ever clear and sensitive, forcing sympathies in unlikely places," noted Nancy Forbes in the *New York Times Book Review.* Forbes added, "In this *film noir* world, people may be good, but they are never nice." Greenland concluded that Dick's "bald, assertive style prefigures the work of contemporary writers like Frederick Barthelme, Tobias Wolff, and Ellen Gilchrist, who attempt to articulate, in their own terms, the dramas of individuals whose moral perceptions are smothered by a culture of compliance and consumption."

The Broken Bubble centers on narrator Jim Briskin, a radio announcer who is still in love with his ex-wife, Pat. The story unfolds as Jim introduces Pat to two of his fans, the teenage couple Art and Rachel, setting into motion a complex relationship between the four. George Blooston in the *New York Times Book Review* said of the characters: "Their willfulness is riveting. But by the time the dust clears and the morally strong have saved the weak, the rewards of the novel seem meager. Without the humor or wisdom of Dick's science fiction, this portrait of 1950's anomie is dominated by its bleak naturalism and soap-operate earnestness." John Clute of the *Times Literary Supplement* commented, "It is a slippery plot to hold, but although Dick sometimes loses control . . . the mature, deft, probing tenderness with which he presents his four protagonists exhibits a rather more than scattershot talent."

At his best, Dick is generally regarded as one of the finest science fiction writers of his time. Nicholls believed him to be "one of the greatest science fiction writers in history, and one of this century's

most important writers in any field." He was, Whalen maintained, "one of America's best writers. . . . He was a great science fiction writer, so much so, that one is reluctant to apply the SF label, with its undeserved stigma, to his writing." Similarly, Clute held that Dick was the "greatest of science fiction writers—though he's by no means the best writer of science fiction" to clarify that what Dick wrote was concerned with the human condition, not with the technological progress of the future. Kosek believed Dick had a "very intense and morally significant vision of life" which he made evident in "a long string of compelling, idiosyncratic novels. . . , most of which embodied a single urgent message: Things are not what they seem to be." In her evaluation of Dick's work, LeGuin stressed that it was easy to misinterpret him. A reader "may put the book down believing that he's read a clever sci-fi thriller and nothing more," LeGuin wrote. "The fact that what Dick is entertaining us about is reality and madness, time and death, sin and salvation—this has escaped most readers and critics. Nobody notices; nobody notices that we have our own homegrown [Jorge Luis] Borges, and have had him for 30 years."

BIOGRAPHICAL/CRITICAL SOURCES:

BOOKS

Contemporary Authors New Revision Series, Volume 16, Gale (Detroit), 1986.
Contemporary Literary Criticism, Gale, Volume 10, 1979; Volume 30, 1984; Volume 72, 1992.
Dick, Anne R., *Search for Philip K. Dick, 1928-1982: A Memoir and Biography of the Science Fiction Writer,* Edwin Mellen Press (Lewiston, NY), 1996.
Dictionary of Literary Biography, Volume 8: *Twentieth-Century American Science-Fiction Writers,* two volumes, Gale, 1981.
Gillespie, Bruce, editor, *Philip K. Dick: Electric Shepherd,* Norstrilia Press (Melbourne), 1975.
Greenberg, Martin Harry and Joseph D. Olander, editors, *Philip K. Dick,* Taplinger, 1983.
Ketterer, David, *New Worlds for Old: The Apocalyptic Imagination, Science Fiction, and American Literature,* Indiana University Press, 1974.
Levack, Daniel J. H. and Steven Owen Godersky, *PKD: A Philip K. Dick Bibliography,* Underwood/Miller, 1981.
Platt, Charles, *Dream Makers: The Uncommon People Who Write Science Fiction,* Berkley Publishing, 1980.
Rickman, Gregg, *Philip K. Dick: In His Own Words,* Fragments, 1984.
Scholes, Robert and Eric S. Rabkin, *Science Fiction: History, Science, Vision,* Oxford University Press, 1977.
Spinrad, Norman, *Modern Science Fiction,* Doubleday, 1974.
Taylor, Angus, *Philip K. Dick and the Umbrella of Light,* T-K Graphics, 1975.
Umland, Samuel J., *Philip K. Dick: Contemporary Critical Interpretations,* Greenwood Press (Westport, CT), 1995.
Wolfe, Gary K., editor, *Science Fiction Dialogues,* Academy Chicago, 1982.

PERIODICALS

American Book Review, January, 1984.
Best Sellers, November, 1976; May, 1977.
Chicago Tribune, March 4, 1982.
Chicago Tribune Book World, July 4, 1982.
Extrapolation, summer, 1979; summer, 1980; summer, 1983.
Fantasy Newsletter, April/May, 1982.
Fantasy Review, October, 1984.
Listener, May 29, 1975.
Los Angeles Times, March 8, 1982.

Los Angeles Times Book Review, September 6, 1981; February 9, 1986, p. 4.

Magazine of Fantasy and Science Fiction, June, 1963; August, 1968; January, 1975; August, 1978; July, 1980.

Missouri Review, Volume VII, number 2, 1984.

New Republic, October 30, 1976; November 26, 1977; December 6, 1993, p. 34.

New Statesman, December 17, 1976; December 16, 1977; October 9, 1987, p. 29.

Newsweek, March 15, 1982.

New Worlds, March, 1966; May, 1969.

New York Times, March 3, 1982.

New York Times Book Review, July 20, 1975; December 1, 1985, p. 24; January 12, 1986, p. 22; April 26, 1987, p. 24; October 16, 1988, p. 36; January 26, 1992, p. 24.

Observer, December 8, 1974.

Philip K. Dick Society Newsletter, 1983–.

Publishers Weekly, March 19, 1982; March 20, 1987, p. 68; May 27, 1988, p. 50.

San Francisco Review of Books, Volume 6, number 13, 1991.

Science Fiction Review, Volume V, number 2, 1976; Volume V, number 4, 1976; February, 1977; summer, 1983; November, 1983.

Science-Fiction Studies, March, 1975; July, 1980; July, 1982; July, 1983; March, 1984; March, 1992, p. 105.

s.f. chronicle, October, 1985, p. 42; May, 1986, p. 37; May, 1988, p. 42.

Sight and Sound, summer, 1982.

Spectator, November 19, 1977.

Time, March 15, 1982.

Times (London), March 15, 1982.

Times Literary Supplement, June 12, 1969; July 8, 1977; January 27, 1978; February 7, 1986, p. 150; February 19, 1988, p. 186; December 8, 1989, p. 1368.

Voice Literary Supplement, August, 1982.

Washington Post, March 4, 1982.

Washington Post Book World, February 22, 1981; May 23, 1982; June 30, 1985; May 25, 1986; August 2, 1987.

*   *   *

DICKEY, James (Lafayette) 1923-1997

PERSONAL: Born February 2, 1923, in Buckhead, GA; died January 19, 1997, in Columbia, SC, of complications from lung disease; son of Eugene (a lawyer) and Maibelle (Swift) Dickey; married Maxine Syerson, November 4, 1948 (died October 28, 1976); married Deborah Dodson, December 30, 1976; children: (first marriage) Christopher Swift, Kevin Webster; (second marriage) Bronwen Elaine. *Education:* Attended Clemson College (now University), 1942; Vanderbilt University, B.A. (magna cum laude), 1949, M.A., 1950.

CAREER: Poet, novelist, and essayist. Instructor in English at Rice Institute (now Rice University), Houston, TX, 1950 and 1952-54, and University of Florida, Gainesville, 1955-56; worked in advertising, 1956-60, first as copywriter for McCann-Erickson, New York City, then as official for Liller, Neal, Battle & Lindsey and Burke Dowling Adams, both in Atlanta, GA; poet in residence at Reed College, Portland, OR, 1963-64, San Fernando Valley State College (now California State University, Northridge), Northridge, CA, 1964-65, University of Wisconsin—Madison, 1966, University of Wisconsin—Milwaukee, 1967, and Washington University, St. Louis, MO, 1968; Georgia Institute of Technology, Atlanta, Franklin Distinguished Professor of English, 1968; University of South Carolina, Columbia, professor of English and poet in residence, 1969-97. Library of Congress, consultant in poetry, 1966-68, honorary consultant in American Letters, 1968-71; Yale Younger Poets contest, judge, 1989-1994.

Military service: U.S. Army Air Forces, served in World War II, flew 100 combat missions in 418th Night Fighter Squadron. U.S. Air Force, served in Korean War; awarded Air Medal.

MEMBER: American Academy of Arts and Sciences, American Academy of Arts and Letters, National Advisory Council on the Arts, National Institute of Arts and Letters, Fellowship of Southern Writers, South Carolina Academy of Authors, Writer's Guild of America, Phi Beta Kappa.

AWARDS, HONORS: Sewanee Review poetry fellowship, 1954-55; *Poetry* magazine, Union League Civic and Arts Foundation Prize, 1958, Vachel Lindsay Prize, 1959, and Levinson Prize, 1982; Guggenheim fellowship, 1961-62; National Book Award for poetry and Melville Cane Award of Poetry Society of America, both 1966, for *Buckdancer's Choice*; National Institute of Arts and Letters grant, 1966; Medicis prize for best foreign book of the year (Paris), 1971, for *Deliverance*; invited to read poem "The Strength of Fields" at Inauguration of U.S. President Jimmy Carter, 1977; *New York Quarterly* Poetry Day Award, 1977; invited to read poem "For a Time and Place" at second inauguration of Richard Riley, governor of South Carolina, 1983.

WRITINGS:

POETRY

Into the Stone, and Other Poems, Scribner (New York City), 1960.

Drowning with Others (also see below), Wesleyan University Press (Middletown, CT), 1962.

Helmets (also see below), Wesleyan University Press, 1964.

Two Poems of the Air, Centicore Press (Portland, OR), 1964.

Buckdancer's Choice, Wesleyan University Press, 1965.

Poems, 1957-1967 (selections issued as miniature edition prior to publication), Wesleyan University Press, 1968.

The Eye-Beaters, Blood, Victory, Madness, Buckhead, and Mercy, Doubleday (Garden City, NY), 1970.

Exchanges, Bruccoli Clark (Columbia, SC), 1971.

The Zodiac (long poem; based on Hendrik Marsman's poem of the same title), Doubleday and Bruccoli Clark, 1976.

The Strength of Fields (poem; also see below), Bruccoli Clark, 1977.

Tucky the Hunter (for children), Crown (New York City), 1978.

The Strength of Fields (collection; title poem previously published separately), Doubleday, 1979.

Head Deep in Strange Sounds: Improvisations from the UnEnglish, Palaemon Press (Winston-Salem, NC), 1979.

Scion, Deerfield Press (Deerfield, MA), 1980.

The Early Motion: "Drowning with Others" and "Helmets," Wesleyan University Press, 1981.

Falling, May Day Sermon, and Other Poems, Wesleyan University Press, 1981.

The Eagle's Mile (also see below), Bruccoli Clark, 1981.

Puella, Doubleday, 1982.

Vaermland: Poems Based on Poems, Palaemon Press, 1982.

False Youth: Four Seasons, Pressworks (Dallas, TX), 1983.

The Central Motion, Wesleyan University Press, 1983.

(With Sharon Anglin Kuhne) *Intervisions: Poems and Photographs,* Visualternatives, 1983.

Veteran Birth: The Gadfly Poems, 1947-1949, Palaemon Press, 1983.

Bronwen, the Traw, and the Shape Shifter: A Poem in Four Parts (for children), illustrations by Richard Jesse Watson, Harcourt, 1986.

Of Prisons and Ideas, Harcourt, 1987.

Summons, Bruccoli Clark, 1988.

The Eagle's Mile (collection), Wesleyan University Press, 1990.

The Whole Motion: Collected Poems, 1945-1992, Wesleyan University Press, 1992.

Poems represented in many anthologies, including: *Contemporary American Poetry,* edited by Donald Hall, Penguin, 1962; *Where Is Viet Nam? American Poets Respond,* edited by Walter Lowenfels, Doubleday, 1967; *The Norton Anthology of Poetry,* revised shorter edition, edited by Alexander W. Allison, Herbert Barrows, Caesar R. Blake, Arthur J. Carr, Arthur M. Eastman, and Hubert M. English, Jr., Norton, 1975; *The Norton Anthology of American Literature,* Volume 2, edited by Ronald Gottesman, Laurence B. Holland, William H. Pritchard, and David Kalstone, Norton, 1979.

PROSE

The Suspect in Poetry (criticism), Sixties Press (Madison, MN), 1964.

A Private Brinksmanship (lecture given at Pitzer College, June 6, 1965), Castle Press (Pasadena), 1965.

Spinning the Crystal Ball: Some Guesses at the Future of American Poetry (lecture given at Library of Congress, April 24, 1967), Library of Congress (Washington, DC), 1967.

Metaphor as Pure Adventure (lecture given at Library of Congress, December 4, 1967), Library of Congress, 1968.

Babel to Byzantium: Poets and Poetry Now (criticism), Farrar, Straus (New York City), 1968.

Deliverance (novel; Literary Guild selection; excerpt entitled "Two Days in September" published in *Atlantic Monthly,* February, 1970; also see below), Houghton (Boston), 1970.

Self-Interviews (informal monologues; excerpt entitled "The Poet Tries to Make a Kind of Order" published in *Mademoiselle,* September, 1970), recorded and edited by Barbara Reiss and James Reiss, Doubleday, 1970.

Sorties: Journals and New Essays, Doubleday, 1971.

(With Hubert Shuptrine) *Jericho: The South Beheld* (Book-of-the-Month Club alternate selection), Oxmoor (Birmingham, AL), 1974.

(With Marvin Hayes) *God's Images: The Bible, a New Vision,* Oxmoor, 1977.

The Enemy from Eden, Lord John Press (Northridge, CA), 1978.

In Pursuit of the Grey Soul, Bruccoli Clark, 1978.

The Water Bug's Mittens (Ezra Pound Lecture at University of Idaho), Bruccoli Clark, 1980.

The Starry Place between the Antlers: Why I Live in South Carolina, Bruccoli Clark, 1981.

Night Hurdling: Poems, Essays, Conversations, Commencements, and Afterwords, Bruccoli Clark, 1983.

Alnilam (novel), Doubleday, 1987.

Wayfarer: A Voice from the Southern Mountains, Oxmoor House, 1988.

Southern Light, with photography by James Valentine, Oxmoor House, 1991.

To the White Sea (novel), Houghton, 1993.

Contributor to books, including *Modern Southern Literature in Its Cultural Setting,* edited by Louis D. Rubin, Jr., and Robert D. Jacobs, Doubleday, 1961; *Poets on Poetry,* edited by Howard Nemerov, Basic Books, 1966; *Pages: The World of Books,*

Writers, and Writing, Volume 1, Gale, 1976; *Conversations with Writers,* Volume 1, Gale, 1977; *Dictionary of Literary Biography,* Volume 5: *American Poets since World War II,* Gale, 1980; and *From the Green Horseshoe: Poems by James Dickey's Students,* University of South Carolina Press, 1987.

OTHER

(Adapter with others of English version) Evgenii Evtushenko, *Stolen Apples: Poetry,* Doubleday, 1971.

Deliverance (screenplay; based on Dickey's novel of the same title; produced by Warner Bros., 1972), Southern Illinois University Press (Carbondale), 1982.

(With Charles Fries) *Call of the Wild* (screenplay; based on the novel by Jack London), produced by National Broadcasting Co. (NBC-TV), 1976.

Striking In: The Early Notebooks of James Dickey, edited by Gordon Van Ness, University of Missouri Press (Columbia), 1996.

Also author of screenplays *To Gene Bullard* and *The Sentence.* Contributor of poems, essays, articles, and reviews to more than thirty periodicals, including *Atlantic Monthly, Harper's, Hudson Review, Nation, New Yorker, Paris Review, Poetry, Sewanee Review, Times Literary Supplement,* and *Virginia Quarterly Review.*

SIDELIGHTS: James Dickey was widely regarded as a major American poet because of his unique vision and style. "It is clear," said Joyce Carol Oates in her *New Heaven, New Earth: The Visionary Experience in Literature,* "that Dickey desires to take on 'his' own personal history as an analogue to or a microscopic exploration of twentieth-century American history, which is one of the reasons he is so important a poet." Winner of both the 1966 National Book Award and the Melville Cane Award for *Buckdancer's Choice,* Dickey was called an expansional poet, not only because the voices in his work loomed large enough to address or represent facets of the American experience, but also because his violent imagery and eccentric style exceeded the bounds of more traditional norms, often producing a quality he described as "country surrealism."

Although he started writing poetry in 1947 at the age of twenty-four, Dickey did not become a full-time poet until thirteen years later. After earning a master's degree in 1950, he taught and lectured at several colleges for six years, but when some of his poems were construed to be obscene, he decided to forsake academic life for the advertising business. "I thought if my chosen profession, teaching, was going to fall out to be that sort of situation," he said in *Conversations with Writers,* "I'd rather go for the buck and make some damn dough in the market place. I had the confidence of Lucifer in myself by that time, and I was beginning to appear all over the place in the *Hudson Review, Partisan* [*Review*], *Sewanee* [*Review*], *Kenyon* [*Review*], and so on. I figured that the kind of thing that an advertising writer would be able to write, I could do with the little finger of the left hand, and they were getting paid good dough for it. I happened to have been right."

Dickey got a job with McCann-Erickson, the biggest ad agency in New York at the time, and wrote jingles for its Coca-Cola account. Later, he went to Liller, Neal, Battle & Lindsey in Atlanta, GA, for twice the salary, working on potato chips and fertilizer accounts, and then jumped agencies again for still another increase, becoming an executive with Burke Dowling Adams, where his primary concern was the Delta Airlines account. Robert W. Hill reported in *Dictionary of Literary*

Biography that by the late 1950s, Dickey was earning enough to have a secure future in the business. But after his first book, *Into the Stone, and Other Poems,* was published in 1960, Dickey left advertising to devote all his time to poetry. "There could have been no more unpromising enterprise or means of earning a livelihood than that of being an American poet," he admitted in *Conversations with Writers.* "It's different now. They're still having a relatively rocky road, but it ain't like it was when I used to give readings sometimes for maybe ten or fifteen dollars, where there would be five people in the audiences, three of them relatives."

In seeking the means to liberate his poetic spirit, Dickey concentrated at first on rhythms, on anapests and iambs. "Although I didn't care for rhyme and the 'packaged' quality which it gives even the best poems," he said in *Poets on Poetry,* "I did care very much for meter, or at least rhythm." With his prize-winning collection, *Buckdancer's Choice,* he began using the split line and free verse forms that came to be associated with his work. But perhaps the most recognizable feature of his stylistic development was his ambitious experimentation with language and form—inverted or odd syntax, horizontal spaces within lines, spread-eagled and ode-like shaped poems. Dickey's poems, wrote Paul Zweig in the *New York Times Book Review,* "are like richly modulated hollers; a sort of rough, American-style bel canto advertising its freedom from the constraints of ordinary language. Dickey's style is so personal, his rhythms so willfully eccentric, that the poems seem to swell up and overflow like that oldest of American art forms, the boast."

According to David Kalstone in another *New York Times Book Review* article, Dickey's "achievement has been to press the limit of language and, in his criticism, to point up the strengths of other writers who do: Hart Crane, [D. H.] Lawrence, [Theodore] Roethke." L. M. Rosenberg expressed a similar sentiment in the *Chicago Tribune Book World.* Claiming that for "sheer beauty and passion we have no greater spokesman, nor do we have any poet more powerfully, naturally musical [than Dickey]," Rosenberg maintained that Dickey's "experiments with language and form are the experiments of a man who understands that one of the strangest things about poetry is the way it looks on the page: It just isn't normal. The question of how to move the reader's eye along the page, particularly as it makes an unnatural jump from line to line . . . how to slow the reader down or speed him up, how to give words back their original, almost totemic power—that's something any poet thinks a lot about, and it's something Dickey works with almost obsessively."

A primary thematic concern of Dickey's, one well served by his vigorous style, was the need "to get back wholeness of being, to respond full-heartedly and full-bodiedly to experience," observed Anatole Broyard of the *New York Times.* In *Poets on Poetry,* Dickey recalled that the subject matter of his early poems came from the principal incidents of his life, "those times when I felt most strongly and was most aware of the intense reality of the objects and people I moved among. If I were to arrange my own poems in some such scheme, chronologizing them, they would form a sort of story of this kind."

Many of Dickey's poems explored moments of being as known by horses, dogs, deer, bees, boars, and other inhabitants of non-human worlds. In "The Sheep Child," for example, a creature half child and half sheep (the result of boys coupling with sheep) speaks out from a jar of formaldehyde. The poem "attains very nearly the power of mythic utterance," maintained Hill, for the

sheep child "shows its magnified view of the truth of two worlds," the fusion of man and nature, with an "eternal, unyielding vision." In Hill's opinion, "The Sheep Child" is "the most radical expression of Dickey's sense of transcendence in fusing man and nature to achieve 'imperishable vision,'" but it is not the only such expression.

Dickey was widely praised for having what Herbert Leibowitz in the *New York Times Book Review* called "a shrewd and troubled knowledge of the 'primal powers'" of nature, as well as "a dramatic skill in presenting the endless beauty of instinct, the feel of icy undertows and warm shallows, the bloodlettings which are a regular part of nature's law."

Although Dickey's images were often primitive, many reviewers considered it a mistake to see him as a spokesman for a return to savagery. Oates wrote that Dickey, "so disturbing to many of us, must be seen in a larger context, as a kind of 'shaman,' a man necessarily at war with his civilization because that civilization will not, cannot, understand what he is saying." A writer in the *Virginia Quarterly Review* observed that at the heart of Dickey's work lay a "desperate insistence that every human experience, however painful or ugly, be viewed as a possible occasion for the renewal of life, [and] with Dickey any renewal inevitably requires struggle."

According to Hill and Aronson, a typical case of misinterpretation involved "The Firebombing," the first poem in *Buckdancer's Choice.* In part a result of Dickey's own experiences in the air force as a fighter-pilot, the poem presents a speaker who, in a momentary flashback, recalls that twenty years ago he was dropping 300-gallon tanks filled with napalm and gasoline on neighborhoods much like his own. Aronson reported that some readers believe the poem portrays the "joy of destroying" experienced by men at war, or even suggests that destruction itself is natural, when actually the poem expresses the complex emotion of "guilt at the inability to feel guilt." Hill concurred: "The moral indignation that might flood so readily for artists and thinkers flows less surely and less fleetingly for one whose life has depended upon a certain screening out of moral subtleties in times of actual combat. The 'luxury' of moral pangs seems to come upon the fighter-pilot in 'The Firebombing' only after his war is over, his safety and his family's restored to allow the contemplation of distant and not-to-be-altered acts of horrible proportion."

In Dickey's internationally bestselling novel *Deliverance,* critics generally saw a thematic continuity with his poetry. A novel about how decent men kill, it is also about the bringing forth, through confrontation, of those qualities in a man that usually lie buried. Simply put, *Deliverance* is the story of four Atlanta suburbanites on a back-to-nature canoe trip that turns into a terrifying test of survival. Dickey, who made a number of canoe and bow-hunting trips in the wilds of northern Georgia, told Walter Clemons in the *New York Times Book Review* that much of the story was suggested by incidents that had happened to him or that he had heard about through friends. All those experiences, according to Dickey, shared the feeling of excitement and fear that "comes from being in an unprotected situation where the safeties of law and what we call civilization don't apply, they just don't. A snake can bite you and you can die before you could get treatment. There are men in those remote parts that'd just as soon kill you as look at you. And you could turn into a counter-monster yourself, doing whatever you felt compelled to do to survive."

"In writing *Deliverance,*" said the *New York Times*'s Christopher Lehmann-Haupt, "Dickey obviously made up his mind to tell a story, and on the theory that a story is an entertaining lie, he has produced a double-clutching whopper." Three ill-prepared businessmen join Lewis Medlock, an avid sportsman who constantly lectures about the purity of nature and the corruption of civilization, on a weekend escape from the banality of suburban living. Canoeing down a wild and difficult stretch of the Cahulawassee River, the men experience only the natural hazards of the river on the first day. Their idyllic sense of community with nature and of masculine camaraderie is shattered on the second, however, when two members of the party, resting from the unaccustomed strain, are surprised by two malicious strangers coming out of the woods. Ed Gentry, the novel's narrator, is tied to a tree while Bobby Trippe is held at gunpoint and sexually assaulted by one of the mountain men. Before the attack can go much further, Lewis catches up, kills one of the assailants by shooting an arrow into his back—thereby partially avenging the homosexual rape—and scares off the other. Fearing a trial conducted by city-hating hicks, the canoeists decide to bury the body and continue down the river. But after Drew, the sole member of the party to advocate informing the authorities, accidentally drowns, and Lewis suffers a broken leg, Ed must kill the other assailant who is gunning them from the cliffs above the Cahulawassee.

Critical reactions to *Deliverance* helped explain its popular success. "The story is absorbing," wrote Evan S. Connell, Jr., in the *New York Times Book Review,* "even when you are not quite persuaded Dickey has told the truth. He is effective and he is deft, with the fine hand of an archer." Lehmann-Haupt gave the book similar praise, stating that Dickey "has succeeded in hammering out a comparatively lean prose style (for a man in the habit of loading words with meaning) and built the elements of his yarn into its structure. And except for one blind lead and an irritating logical discrepancy, he has built well. Best of all, he has made a monument to tall stories."

Though Christopher Ricks, critiquing the novel in the *New York Review of Books,* believed *Deliverance* was "too patently the concoction of a situation in which it will be morally permissible—nay, essential—to kill men with a bow and arrow," Charles Thomas Samuels pointed out in the *New Republic* that Dickey "himself seems aware of the harshness of his substructure and the absurdity of some of his details" and overcomes these deficiencies through his stylistic maneuvers: "Such is Dickey's linguistic virtuosity that he totally realizes an improbable plot. How a man acts when shot by an arrow, what it feels like to scale a cliff or to capsize, the ironic psychology of fear: these things are conveyed with remarkable descriptive writing. His publishers are right to call *Deliverance* a *tour de force.*"

Deliverance represented only one of Dickey's ventures outside the realm of poetry. He not only adapted the novel for the screen but also appeared in the box-office smash as the redneck Sheriff Bullard, whom the canoeists face at the end of their journey. In addition to criticism, Dickey published a retelling of several biblical stories, *God's Images: The Bible, a New Vision,* as well as *Jericho: The South Beheld,* an exploration of "the rich prose language and sensual impressions of the American South, which Dickey has publicly championed," wrote Hill. "Like Whitman or [Mark] Twain," said Michael Dirda in the *Washington Post Book World,* "Dickey seems in a characteristic American tradition, ever ready to light out for new territories."

Dickey told *Publishers Weekly* that he spent thirty-six years working on his lengthy World War II novel *Alnilam,* which was published in 1987. Named for the central star in the belt of the constellation Orion, *Alnilam* concerns the recently blinded Frank Cahill's search for his son, Joel, whom he has never met. Cahill slowly discovers that his son, an extraordinary pilot thought to have been killed in an aircraft-training accident, had been the leader of a mysterious, dictatorial military training cult known as Alnilam. By interviewing anyone who knew Joel, Cahill forms an impressionistic and sometimes contradictory portrait of this unusual young man. Describing the novel to R. Z. Sheppard of *Time* magazine, Dickey said, "I've tried to do for the air what [Herman] Melville did for water." Sheppard elaborated: "Flying in the mechanical as well as transcendental sense, is basic to the action, which is surprisingly abundant for a book that is shaped by poetic impulses rather than plot."

The novel received mixed reviews, with most critics comparing it unfavorably to the powerful *Deliverance.* As Erling Friis-Baastad put it in the Toronto *Globe and Mail, Alnilam* "is an awkward and overworked book, but the touch of a master poet can still be experienced periodically throughout . . . at least by those who can endure the uphill read." Robert Towers, writing in the *New York Times Book Review,* said that *Alnilam* "is, for better and worse, very much a poet's novel, Mr. Dickey's extended hymn to air, light, wind and the ecstasies of flight." Although he found Cahill an engaging character, Towers faulted Dickey for the "inordinately slow pacing" of the novel. He noted that one of Dickey's innovative devices interrupts the flow of the already slow-moving narrative. Wrote Towers, "On many of its pages, the symbolic contrasts between blindness and sight, between darkness and light, are typographically rendered. The page is split down the middle into two columns. The left, which represents Cahill's internal sensations and thoughts, is printed in dark type; the right, which contains the objective narration of speech and events, is printed in ordinary type. Such a device has, of course, the effect not only of dividing one's attention, but also of modifying the degree of one's involvement in what is taking place."

In his final novel, *To the White Sea,* published in 1993, Dickey returned to the themes of his earlier novels. The book's one character, Muldrow, is an Air Force tail gunner whose plane is shot down over Tokyo during World War II. During the early stages of the novel, Muldrow endures supremely difficult circumstances as he struggles for survival. Fleeing Tokyo and heading north to the island of Hokkaido—whose cold and wintry climate appeals to his own childhood experiences growing up in Alaska—Muldrow kills several people in search of food and clothing. "Initially one identifies with . . . [Muldrow's] unbelievable courage and control in the face of almost hopeless odds," noted Steve Brzezinski in *The Antioch Review.* However, as the novel progresses, Muldrow's actions grow increasingly violent and shocking, as he enjoys his murderous actions. "His 'heart of ice' proves to be another heart of darkness," commented John Melmoth in the *Times Literary Supplement.* "Things take an apocalyptic turn and end in a welter of blood and feathers." During his journey, Muldrow comes to identify with the animals he encounters in the wilderness and seeks to transform himself into a facet of the harsh landscape around him.

As with *Alnilam,* critical reaction to *To the White Sea* was mixed, with critics praising Dickey's prose style but recoiling at the novel's disturbing plot. "Dickey takes language as far as it will go and sometimes overdoes it," remarked Melmoth, who added that "some of the writing has an eerie brilliance." While commending Dickey's "haunting" imagery and stylistic achievement, Brzezinski averred that *To the White Sea* "is a bleak and unsettling book."

In the end, concluded Ronald Curran in a *World Literature Today* review, "however the reader conceives of Muldrow's musings about his adaptive identifications with animals or his eventual transcendence into weather itself, the success of *To the White Sea* depends upon whether or not empathetic identification can be fostered" among readers.

Dickey once told *Contemporary Authors:* "I'm the same way about novels as I am about anything I write. I build them very slowly. I work on the principle that the first fifty ways I try to write a novel or a critical piece or a poem or a movie are going to be wrong. But you get a direction in some way or other. Keep drafting and redrafting and something emerges eventually. If the subject is intense, if you are intense about it, something will come. In my case, at least, the final work is nothing like what I started out with; generally I don't have a very good idea at first. But something begins to form in some unforeseen, perhaps unforeseeable, shape. It's like creating something out of nothing—creation ex nihilo, which is said to be impossible. God must have done it, I guess, but nobody else can—except poets."

BIOGRAPHICAL/CRITICAL SOURCES:

BOOKS

Baughman, Ronald, editor, *The Voiced Connections of James Dickey: Interviews and Conversations,* University of South Carolina Press (Columbia), 1989.
Bruccoli, Matthew J., and Judith S. Baughman, *James Dickey: A Descriptive Bibliography,* University of Pittsburgh Press (Pittsburgh), 1990.
Contemporary Authors New Revision Series, Volume 48, Gale (Detroit), 1995.
Contemporary Authors Bibliographical Series, Volume 2, *American Poets,* Gale, 1986.
Contemporary Literary Criticism, Gale, Volume 1, 1973; Volume 2, 1974; Volume 4, 1975; Volume 7, 1977; Volume 10, 1979; Volume 15, 1980; Volume 47, 1988.
Conversations with Writers, Volume 1, Gale, 1977.
De La Fuente, Patricia, editor, *James Dickey: Splintered Sunlight,* School of Humanities, Pan American University, 1979.
Dictionary of Literary Biography, Volume 5: *American Poets since World War II,* Gale, 1980.
Dictionary of Literary Biography Documentary Series, Volume 7, Gale, 1989.
Dictionary of Literary Biography Yearbook: 1982, Gale, 1983.
Dictionary of Literary Biography Yearbook: 1993, Gale, 1994.
Elledge, J., *James Dickey: A Bibliography, 1947-1974,* Scarecrow (Metuchen, NJ), 1979.
Finholt, Richard, *American Visionary Fiction: Mad Metaphysics as Salvation Psychology,* Kennikat (Port Washington, NY), 1978.
Kirschten, Robert, *Critical Essays on James Dickey,* G.K. Hall (New York City), 1994.
Kirschten, Robert, *'Struggling for Wings': The Art of James Dickey,* University of South Carolina Press, 1997.
Lieberman, Lawrence, *Unassigned Frequencies: American Poetry in Review, 1964-77,* University of Illinois Press (Champaign), 1978.
Oates, Joyce Carol, *New Heaven, New Earth: The Visionary Experience in Literature,* Vanguard, 1974.
Suarez, Ernest, *James Dickey and the Politics of Canon: Assessing the Savage Ideal,* University of Missouri Press, 1993.
Van Ness, Gordon, *Striking in: the early notebooks of James Dickey,* University of Missouri Press, 1996.

Weigl, Bruce, and Terry Hummer, editors, *James Dickey: The Imagination of Glory,* University of Illinois Press, 1984.
Writer's Yearbook, Writer's Digest (Cincinnati), 1981.

PERIODICALS

Alaska, February, 1994, p. 75.
American Literature, June, 1990, p. 370.
Antioch Review, fall-winter, 1970-71; spring, 1994, p. 358.
Atlantic Monthly, October, 1967; November, 1968; December, 1974; February, 1980.
Book World, June 30, 1968; March 15, 1970; December 6, 1970; April 25, 1971.
Bulletin of Bibliography, April-June, 1981, pp. 92-100; July-September, 1981, pp. 150-55.
Chicago Tribune, May 10, 1987.
Chicago Tribune Book World, January 27, 1980.
Christian Science Monitor, December 3, 1964; November 12, 1970; February 20, 1980.
Commonweal, December 1, 1967; February 19, 1971; September 29, 1972; December 3, 1976.
Contemporary Literature, summer, 1975.
Critic, May, 1970.
Critique, Volume 15, number 2, 1973.
English Journal, November, 1990, p. 84; January, 1992, p. 27.
Esquire, December, 1970.
Georgia Review, spring, 1968; summer, 1969; spring, 1974; summer, 1978; fall, 1993, p. 603.
Globe and Mail (Toronto), August 15, 1987.
Hudson Review, spring, 1966; autumn, 1967; autumn, 1968; spring, 1993, p. 223; spring, 1994, p. 133.
James Dickey Newsletter, 1984–.
Life, July 22, 1966; July, 1987, p. 35.
Literary News, May-June, 1967.
Los Angeles Times, May 19, 1968; February 26, 1980; July 9, 1987; December 8, 1987.
Los Angeles Times Book Review, June 27, 1982; January 18, 1987, p. 8; June 7, 1987, p. 1.
Mademoiselle, September, 1970; August, 1972.
Modern Fiction Studies, summer, 1975.
Mother Earth News, March-April, 1990.
Nation, June 20, 1966; April 24, 1967; March 23, 1970; April 6, 1970; February 5, 1983.
National Review, November 15, 1993, p. 64.
New Leader, May 22, 1967; May 20, 1968.
New Republic, September 9, 1967; June 29, 1968; April 18, 1970; December 5, 1970; August 5, 1972; November 30, 1974; November 20, 1976; January 5, 1980; January 12, 1980.
New Statesman, September 11, 1970.
Newsweek, March 30, 1970; August 7, 1972; December 6, 1976; January 31, 1977; August 30, 1993, p. 54.
New Yorker, May 2, 1970; August 5, 1972; September 27, 1993, p. 101.
New York Review of Books, April 23, 1970.
New York Times, March 16, 1966; September 10, 1966; March 27, 1970; December 17, 1971; July 31, 1972; August 20, 1972; January 22, 1977; June 1, 1987; May 19, 1988; October 27, 1990, p. 16; March 23, 1997.
New York Times Book Review, January 3, 1965; February 6, 1966; April 23, 1967; March 22, 1970; June 7, 1970; November 8, 1970; December 6, 1970; January 23, 1972; February 9, 1975; November 14, 1976; December 18, 1977; July 15, 1979; January 6, 1980; June 3, 1984, p. 23; February 15, 1987; March 8, 1987, p. 31; June 21, 1987, p. 7; September 19, 1993.

Paris Review, spring, 1976.

Partisan Review, summer, 1966.

People Weekly, July 6, 1987, p. 16; October 11, 1993, p. 29; January 31, 1994, p. 80.

Playboy, May, 1971; September, 1993, p. 78.

Poetry, October, 1966; March, 1968; July, 1971.

Publishers Weekly, May 29, 1987, p. 62; October 19, 1990, p. 52; June 7, 1993, p. 65; June 21, 1993, p. 82.

Rapport, Volume 17, number 5, 1993, p. 31.

Salmagundi, spring-summer, 1973.

Saturday Review, May 6, 1967; March 11, 1970; March 28, 1970; March 11, 1972.

Saturday Review of Science, August 5, 1972.

Sewanee Review, winter, 1963; summer, 1966; spring, 1969; summer, 1971.

Southern Review, winter, 1971; summer, 1971; winter, 1973; spring, 1973; spring, 1981; autumn, 1992, p. 971.

Southwest Review, spring, 1979.

Time, December 13, 1968; April 20, 1970; August 7, 1972; June 29, 1987; October 11, 1993, p. 88.

Times (London), February 3, 1990.

Times Literary Supplement, October 29, 1964; May 18, 1967; September 11, 1970; May 21, 1971; December 2, 1983, p. 1342; January 24, 1986, p. 95; May 10, 1991, p. 22; February 11, 1994, p. 21.

Tribune Books (Chicago), November 16, 1986, p. 4; May 24, 1987, p. 3.

Triquarterly, winter, 1968.

Village Voice, February 4, 1980.

Virginia Quarterly Review, autumn, 1967; autumn, 1968; winter, 1971; spring, 1990, p. 66; summer, 1991, p. 100; winter, 1994, p. 23.

Washington Post, March 31, 1987; May 24, 1987; December 8, 1987.

Washington Post Book World, November 21, 1976; December 30, 1979; May 24, 1987, p. 1; November 22, 1992, p. 8.

World Literature Today, summer, 1991, p. 489; spring, 1993, p. 384; autumn, 1994, p. 809.

Yale Review, October, 1962; December, 1967; winter, 1968; October, 1970.

OTHER

Lord Let Me Die but Not Die Out: James Dickey, Poet (film), Encyclopaedia Britannica, 1970.

*   *   *

DICKSON, Carr
See CARR, John Dickson

*   *   *

DICKSON, Carter
See CARR, John Dickson

*   *   *

DIDION, Joan 1934-

PERSONAL: Born December 5, 1934, in Sacramento, CA; daughter of Frank Reese and Eduene (Jerrett) Didion; married John Gregory Dunne (a writer), January 30, 1964; children: Quintana Roo (daughter). *Education:* University of California, Berkeley, B.A., 1956.

ADDRESSES: *Agent*—Lynn Nesbit, Janklow, and Nesbit, 598 Madison Ave., New York, NY 10022.

CAREER: Writer. *Vogue,* New York City, 1956-63, began as promotional copywriter, became associate feature editor. Visiting regents lecturer in English, University of California, Berkeley, 1976.

AWARDS, HONORS: First prize, *Vogue*'s Prix de Paris, 1956; Bread Loaf fellowship in fiction, 1963; National Book Award nomination in fiction, 1971, for *Play It as It Lays*; Morton Dauwen Zabel Award, National Institute of Arts and Letters, 1978; National Book Critics Circle Prize nomination in nonfiction, 1980, and American Book Award nomination in nonfiction, 1981, both for *The White Album*; *Los Angeles Times* Book Prize nomination in fiction, 1984, for *Democracy*; Edward MacDowell Medal, 1996.

WRITINGS:

NOVELS

Run River, Obolensky (New York City), 1963.

Play It as It Lays (also see below), Farrar, Straus (New York City), 1970.

A Book of Common Prayer, Simon & Schuster (New York City), 1977.

Democracy, Simon & Schuster, 1984.

The Last Thing He Wanted, Knopf (New York City), 1996.

SCREENPLAYS; WITH HUSBAND, JOHN GREGORY DUNNE

Panic in Needle Park (based on a James Mills book of the same title), Twentieth Century-Fox, 1971.

Play It as It Lays (based on Didion's book of the same title), Universal, 1972.

(With others) *A Star Is Born,* Warner Bros., 1976.

True Confessions (based on Dunne's novel of the same title), United Artists, 1981.

Hills Like White Elephants (based on Ernest Hemingway's short story), HBO, 1990.

Broken Trust (based on the novel *Court of Honor* by William Wood), TNT, 1995.

Up Close and Personal, Disney, 1996.

NONFICTION

Slouching towards Bethlehem, Farrar, Straus, 1968.

The White Album, Simon & Schuster, 1979.

Salvador, Simon & Schuster, 1983.

Miami, Simon & Schuster, 1987.

Robert Graham: The Duke Ellington Memorial in Progress, Los Angeles County Museum of Art (Los Angeles), 1988.

After Henry, Simon & Schuster, 1992, published in England as *Sentimental Journeys,* HarperCollins (London), 1993.

(Author of introduction) Robert Mapplethorpe, *Some Women,* Bulfinch Press (Boston), 1992.

Author of column, with Dunne, "Points West," *Saturday Evening Post,* 1967-69, and "The Coast," *Esquire,* 1976-77; former columnist, *Life.* Contributor of short stories, articles, and reviews to periodicals, including *Vogue, Saturday Evening Post, Holiday, Harper's Bazaar,* and *New York Times Book Review, The New Yorker,* and *The New York Review of Books.* Former contributing editor, *National Review.*

SIDELIGHTS: An elegant prose stylist and celebrated journalist, Joan Didion possesses a distinct literary voice, widely praised for its precision and control. She began, by her own admission, as a nonintellectual writer, more concerned with images than ideas and renowned for her use of telling detail. In addition to being "a gifted reporter," according to *New York Times Magazine* contributor Michiko Kakutani, Didion "is also a prescient witness, finding in her own experiences parallels of the times. The voice is always precise, the tone unsentimental, the view unabashedly subjective. She takes things personally." For years, Didion's favorite subject was her native California, a state that seemed to supply ample evidence of the disorder in society. Though her theme has not changed, she has broadened her perspective in more recent years and turned to the troubled countries of Central America and Southeast Asia for new material.

After graduating from the University of California at Berkeley in 1956, Didion took a job at *Vogue* magazine's New York office, where she remained for eight years, rising from promotional copywriter to associate feature editor. During this period, she met John Gregory Dunne and, after several years of friendship, they married, becoming not just matrimonial partners but collaborators as well. While still at *Vogue,* Didion began writing her first novel, *Run River,* which was published in 1963. The following year she moved back to the West Coast with Dunne, determined to earn a living as a freelance reporter. Working on a series of magazine columns about California for the *Saturday Evening Post,* the couple earned a meager $7,000 in their first year. But their writing did attract widespread attention, and when Didion's columns were collected and published in 1968 as *Slouching towards Bethlehem,* her reputation as an essayist soared.

Slouching towards Bethlehem takes its theme from Yeats's poem "The Second Coming," which reads: "Things fall apart; the center cannot hold; / Mere anarchy is loosed upon the world." For Didion those words sum up the chaos of the sixties, a chaos so far-reaching that it affected her ability to perform. Convinced "that writing was an irrelevant act, that the world as I had understood it no longer existed," Didion, as she states in the book's preface, realized, "If I was to work again at all, it would be necessary for me to come to terms with disorder." She went to Haight-Ashbury to explore the hippie movement and out of that experience came the title essay.

Most critics praise the book highly. Writing in the *Christian Science Monitor,* Melvin Maddocks suggests of Didion that "her melancholy voice is that of a last survivor dictating a superbly written wreckage report onto a tape she doubts will ever be played." And while *Best Sellers* reviewer T. O'Hara argues that "the devotion she gives to America-the-uprooted-the-lunatic-and-the-alienated is sullied by an inability to modulate, to achieve a respectable distance," most critics applaud her subjectivity. "Nobody captured the slack-jawed Haight-Ashbury hippies any better," states *Saturday Review* contributor Martin Kasindorf.

In 1970, Didion published *Play It as It Lays,* a best-selling novel that received a National Book Award nomination and, at the same time, created enormous controversy with its apparently nihilistic theme. The portrait of a woman on what *New York Times Book Review* contributor Lore Segal calls a "downward path to wisdom," *Play It as It Lays* tells the story of Maria Wyeth's struggle to find meaning in a meaningless world. "The setting is the desert; the cast, the careless hedonists of Hollywood; the emotional climate, bleak as the surroundings," Kakutani reports in the *New York Times Magazine.* Composed of eighty-four brief chapters, some less than a page in length, the book possesses a cinematic quality and such technical precision that Richard Shickel remarks in *Harper's* that it is "a rather cold and calculated fiction—more a problem in human geometry . . . than a novel that truly lives."

A Book of Common Prayer continues the author's theme of social disintegration with the story of Charlotte Douglas, a Californian "immaculate of history, innocent of politics." Until her daughter Marin abandoned home and family to join a group of terrorists, Charlotte was one who "understood that something was always going on in the world but believed that it would turn out all right." When things fall apart, Charlotte takes refuge in Boca Grande, a fictitious Central American country embroiled in its own domestic conflicts. There she idles away her days at the airport coffee shop, futilely waiting for her daughter to surface and eventually losing her life in a military coup.

Because Charlotte's story is narrated by Grace, an American expatriate and long-time Boca Grande resident, the book presented several technical problems. "The narrator was not present during most of the events she's telling you about. And her only source is a woman incapable of seeing the truth," Didion explained to Diehl. In her *New York Times Book Review* article, Joyce Carol Oates speculates that Didion employs this technique because Grace permits Didion "a free play of her own speculative intelligence that would have been impossible had the story been told by Charlotte. The device of an uninvolved narrator is a tricky one, since a number of private details must be presented as if they were within the range of the narrator's experience. But it is a measure of Didion's skill as a novelist that one never questions [Grace's] near omniscience in recalling Charlotte's story." Christopher Lehmann-Haupt, on the other hand, maintains in the *New York Times* that Didion "simply asks too much of Charlotte, and overburdened as she is by the pitiless cruelty of the narrator's vision, she collapses under the strain."

After *A Book of Common Prayer,* Didion published *The White Album,* a second collection of magazine essays similar in tone to *Slouching towards Bethlehem.* "I don't have as many answers as I did when I wrote *Slouching,*" Didion explained to Kakutani. She called the book *The White Album* in consideration of a famous Beatles album that captured for her the disturbing ambiance of the sixties. "I am talking here about a time when I began to doubt the premises of all the stories I had ever told myself," Didion writes in the title essay. "This period began around 1966 and continued until 1971." During this time, says Didion, "all I knew was what I saw: flash pictures in variable sequence, images with no 'meaning' beyond their temporary arrangement, not a movie but a cuttingroom experience."

While highly acclaimed for its literary merits, *Salvador* has been criticized on other grounds. *Newsweek* reviewer Gene Lyon, for example, allows that "Didion gets exactly right both the ghastliness and the pointlessness of the current killing frenzy in El Salvador" but then suggests that "ghastliness and pointlessness are Didion's invariable themes wherever she goes. Most readers will not get very far in this very short book without wondering whether she visited that sad and tortured place less to report than to validate the Didion world view." Others question Didion's credentials as a historian. Leonel Gomez Videz, former deputy director of the Agrarian Reform Institute in El Salvador, faults the book for mystifying a subject that desperately needs to be understood. "What she provides is a horrific description of atrocity: 'The dead and pieces of the dead turn up in El Salvador everywhere, every day, as taken for granted as in a nightmare, or a horror movie,'" he writes, quoting *Salvador* in the *New Republic.* "What point is Didion making? Such lurid details make for compelling prose, but in the absence of any analysis of why such murders occur, they seem at best to bolster her thesis of mindless terror and at worst to suggest a penchant for gratuitous special effects."

In 1984, one year after *Salvador* was published, Didion produced *Democracy.* The book was to have been the story of a family of American colonialists whose interests were firmly entrenched in the Pacific at a time when Hawaii was still a territory, but Didion abandoned this idea. The resulting novel features Inez Christian and her family. In the spring of 1975—at the time the United States completed its evacuation of Vietnam and Cambodia— Inez's father is arrested for a double murder with political and racial overtones. "The Christians and their in-laws are the emblems of a misplaced confidence," according to John Lownsbrough in Toronto's *Globe & Mail,* "the flotsam and jetsam of a Manifest Destiny no longer so manifest. Their disintegration as a family in the spring of 1975 . . . is paralleled by the fall of Saigon a bit later that year and the effective disintegration of the American expansionist dream in all its ethnocentric optimism." Somehow, her family's tragedy enables Inez to break free of her marriage to a self-serving politician and escape to Malaysia with Jack Lovett, a freelance CIA agent and the man she has always loved. Though he dies abruptly, Inez holds on to her freedom, choosing to remain in Kuala Lumpur where she works among the Vietnamese refugees.

New York Review of Books critic Thomas R. Edwards believes *Democracy* "finally earns its complexity of form. It is indeed 'a hard story to tell' and the presence in it of 'Joan Didion' trying to tell it is an essential part of its subject. Throughout one senses the author struggling with the moral difficulty that makes the story hard to tell—how to stop claiming what Inez finally relinquishes, 'the American exemption' from having to recognize that history records not the victory of personal wills over reality . . . but the 'undertow of having and not having, the convulsions of a world largely unaffected by the individual efforts of anyone in it.'"

Miami once again finds Didion on the literary high wire, in a work of nonfiction that focuses on the cultural, social, and political impact the influx of Cuban exiles has had upon Miami and, indeed, upon the entire United States. Culminating in an indictment of American foreign policy from the presidential administrations of John F. Kennedy through Ronald Reagan, *Miami* "is a thoroughly researched and brilliantly written meditation on the consequences of power, especially on power's self-addictive delusions," according to *Voice Literary Supplement* reviewer Stacey D'Erasmo. The book explores the thirty-year history of the community of Cuban immigrants which now comprises over half the population of that city.

Didion paints these emigres as existing within a country that threatens their political agenda, and a city full of enemies. "The shadowy missions, the secret fundings, the conspiracies beneath conspiracies, the deniable support by parts of the U.S. government and active discouragement by other parts," Richard Eder writes in the *Los Angeles Times Book Review,* paraphrasing Didion's argument, "all these things have fostered a tensely paranoid style in parts of our own political life. . . . Miami is us." While noting that Didion's intricate—if journalistic—style almost overwhelms her argument, Eder compares *Miami* to a luxury hunting expedition: "You may look out the window and see some casually

outfitted huntsman trudging along. You may wonder whether his experience is more authentic than yours. Didion's tour is overarranged, but that is a genuine lion's carcass strapped to our fender."

After Henry, published in the United Kingdom as *Sentimental Journeys,* is a collection of twelve essays organized loosely around three geographical areas that Didion has focused on throughout her writing career: Washington, DC, California, and New York City. "For her they are our Chapels Perilous," declares Robert Dana in the *Georgia Review,* "where power and dreams fuse or collide." The title essay is a tribute to Didion's friend and mentor Henry Robbins, who served as her editor prior to his death in 1979.

Politics are discussed in the section titled "Washington." The essay "In the Realm of the Fisher King" is an analysis of the years of the Reagan presidency. Didion's analytic style received mixed reactions. "Her difficulty with politics is that she really doesn't know it as well as she imagines," states Jonathan Yardley in the *Washington Post Book World,* "and brings to it no especially useful insights." However, reviewer Hendrik Hertzberg lauds "Inside Baseball," Didion's essay on the 1988 presidential campaign, in the *New York Times Book Review*: "Her cool eye sees sharply when it surveys the rich texture of American public folly. . . . What she has to say about the manipulation of images and the creation of pseudo-events makes familiar territory new again." But, Hertzberg adds, Didion's "focus on the swirl of 'narratives' is useful as a way of exploring political image-mongering, but surprisingly limited as a way of describing the brute political and social realities against which candidates and ideas must in the end be measured."

Included among the remaining works in *After Henry* is "Sentimental Journey," a three-part "attack on New York City and the sentimentality that distorts and obscures much of what is said and done there, and which has brought the city to the edge of bankruptcy and collapse," according to Dana. One section explores the way in which the highly publicized 1990 rape of a white investment banker jogging in New York City's Central Park—and the trial that followed—was transformed by the media into what Didion terms a "false narrative." Combined with her illuminating discussion of the many rapes occurring in the city that are not given such intensive press coverage and the decreasing competitive edge possessed by the city when viewed in real terms, "Didion's portrait is one of a city drugged nearly to death on the crack of its own myths," according to Dana, "its own 'sentimental stories told in defense of its own lazy criminality.'"

After a twelve-year hiatus, Joan Didion returned to fiction with *The Last Thing He Wanted.* Set in 1984, the year *Democracy* was published, it contains some of the same elements but this time in a different outpost of American foreign-policy gamesmanship, Central America. Told from the viewpoint of a "not quite omniscient" narrator, it is the story of Elena McMahon, a writer who walks away from a job covering the presidential campaign and returns to Florida and her widowed father. A shady wheeler-dealer fading into senility, her father sees a chance to turn a huge profit by supplying arms to Nicaragua's anti-communist *contras,* and Elena flies to Costa Rica to close the deal. Before long, she is caught in a web of gunrunners, CIA operatives, and a conspiracy that stretches from the JFK assassination to the Iran-Contra scandal. Some reviewers criticize the narrator, and by extension the novel, as too vague and unreal. "The problem of *The Last Thing He Wanted,*" according to *New Republic* critic James

Wood, "is not that our author is 'not quite omniscient.' It is that our narrator is not quite a person." Michiko Kakutani, writing in the daily *New York Times,* finds the novel equally unconvincing: "Despite Ms. Didion's nimble orchestration of emotional and physical details, despite her insider's ear for lingo, her conspiratorial view of history never feels terribly persuasive. . . . In the end, what's meant to be existential angst feels more like self-delusion; what's meant to be disturbing feels more like paranoia." Other critics, however, find this "unreality" oddly appropriate, with John Weir, in the *New Yorker,* writing, "A dream is disorienting but it adheres to its own particular logic. By contrast, the real life events on which novels are traditionally based have lately taken on a quality that almost defies their being retold. 'This is something different,' Didion's narrator writes about the story she's driven to tell. The result is entrancing—a dream without the logic of a dream, the way we live now."

Didion's continuing emphasis on self-reflection, image, and detail mirrors her personal orientation. In a lecture she delivered at her alma mater, she explained the way her mind works: "During the years I was an undergraduate at Berkeley, I . . . kept trying to find that part of my mind that could deal in abstracts. But my mind kept veering inexorably back like some kind of boomerang I was stuck with—to the specific, to the tangible, to what was generally considered by everyone I knew, the peripheral. I would try to think about the Great Dialectic and I would find myself thinking instead about how the light was falling through the window in an apartment I had on the North Side. How it was hitting the floor."

Didion knows her concerns are not the standard ones and in one of her better-known essays, "In the Islands," she describes herself as "a woman who for some time now has felt radically separated from most of the ideas that seem to interest other people." However, many critics and readers would hasten to disagree. "Her prose is a literary seismograph," describes Dana, "on which are clearly registered the tremors and temblors that increasingly shake the bedrock of the American social dream."

BIOGRAPHICAL/CRITICAL SOURCES:

BOOKS

Contemporary Literary Criticism, Gale (Detroit), Volume 1, 1973; Volume 3, 1975; Volume 8, 1978; Volume 14, 1980.
Dictionary of Literary Biography, Volume 2: *American Novelists since World War II,* Gale, 1978.
Dictionary of Literary Biography Yearbook, Gale, 1981, 1986.
Felton, Sharon, editor, *The Critical Response to Joan Didion,* Greenwood Press (Westport, CT), 1994.
Friedman, Ellen G., editor, *Joan Didion: Essays and Conversations,* Ontario Review Press, 1984.
Henderson, Katherine, *Joan Didion,* Ungar, 1981.
Loris, Michelle, *Innocence, Loss, and Recovery in the Art of Joan Didion,* Peter Lang, 1989.
Winchell, Mark, *Joan Didion,* Twayne, 1980.

PERIODICALS

American Scholar, winter, 1970-71.
American Spectator, September, 1992.
Atlantic, April, 1977.
Belles Lettres, fall, 1992, p. 14.
Booklist, March 1, 1992.
Boston Globe, May 17, 1992, p. 105.
Chicago Tribune, June 12, 1979.
Chicago Tribune Book World, July 1, 1979; April 3, 1983; April 15, 1984.

Chicago Tribune Magazine, May 2, 1982.
Christian Science Monitor, May 16, 1968; September 24, 1970; July 9, 1979; June 1, 1992, p. 13.
Commentary, June, 1984, pp. 62-67.
Commonweal, November 29, 1968; October 23, 1992.
Critique, spring, 1984, pp. 160-70.
Detroit News, August 12, 1979.
Dissent, summer, 1983.
Economist, August 22, 1992.
Esquire, March, 1996, p. 36.
Georgia Review, winter, 1992, pp. 799-802.
Globe and Mail (Toronto), April 28, 1984.
Harper's, August, 1970; December, 1971.
Harvard Advocate, winter, 1973.
London Review of Books, December 10, 1987, pp. 3, 5-6; October 21, 1993, p. 12-13.
Los Angeles Times, May 9, 1971; July 4, 1976.
Los Angeles Times Book Review, March 20, 1983; September 27, 1987, pp. 3, 6.
Miami Herald, December 2, 1973.
Ms., February, 1977.
Nation, September 26, 1979.
National Review, June 4, 1968; August 25, 1970; October 12, 1979; November 23, 1987; June 22, 1992, pp. 53-54.
New Republic, June 6, 1983; April 9, 1984; November 23, 1987; October 14, 1996.
Newsweek, August 3, 1970; December 21, 1970; March 21, 1977; June 25, 1979; March 28, 1983; April 16, 1984.
New Yorker, June 20, 1977; April 18, 1983; January 25, 1988, p. 112; September 16, 1996.
New York, February 15, 1971; June 13, 1979.
New York Review of Books, October 22, 1970; May 10, 1984.
New York Times, July 21, 1970; October 30, 1972; March 21, 1977; June 5, 1979; March 11, 1983; April 6, 1984; September 14, 1984; September 3, 1996.
New York Times Book Review, July 21, 1968; August 9, 1970; April 3, 1977; June 17, 1979; March 13, 1983; April 22, 1984; October 25, 1987, p. 3; May 17, 1992, pp. 3, 39.
New York Times Magazine, June 10, 1979; February 8, 1987.
Observer (London), March 27, 1988, p. 43; January 24, 1993, p. 53.
Quill and Quire, December, 1987, p. 30.
San Francisco Review of Books, May, 1977.
Saturday Review, August 15, 1970; March 5, 1977; September 15, 1979; April 1982.
Sewanee Review, fall, 1977.
Time, August 10, 1970; March 28, 1977; August 20, 1979; April 4, 1983; May 7, 1984; June 29, 1992.
Times Literary Supplement, February 12, 1970; March 12, 1971; July 8, 1977; November 30, 1979; June 24, 1983; January 29, 1993, p. 10; November 5, 1993, p. 28.
Tribune Books (Chicago), May 10, 1992, pp. 3, 7.
Village Voice, February 28, 1977; June 25, 1979; May 26, 1992, pp. 74-76.
Voice Literary Supplement, October 1987, pp. 21-22.
Washington Post, April 8, 1983.
Washington Post Book World, June 17, 1979; March 13, 1983; April 15, 1984; May 10, 1992, p. 3.

DILLARD, Annie 1945-

PERSONAL: Born April 30, 1945, in Pittsburgh, PA; daughter of Frank and Pam (Lambert) Doak; married Richard Dillard (a professor and writer), June 5, 1964 (divorced); married Gary Clevidence (a writer), April 12, 1980 (divorced); married Robert D. Richardson, Jr. (a professor and writer), 1988; children: (with Clevidence) Cody Rose; Carin, Shelly (stepchildren). *Education:* Hollins College, B.A., 1967, M.A., 1968.

ADDRESSES: Agent—Timothy Seldes, Russell & Volkening, 50 West 29th St., New York, NY 10001.

CAREER: Writer. The Wilderness Society, columnist in *The Living Wilderness,* 1973-75; *Harper's Magazine,* editor, 1973-85; Western Washington University, Bellingham, scholar in residence, 1975-79; Wesleyan University, Middletown, CT, distinguished visiting professor, beginning in 1979, full adjunct professor, beginning in 1983, writer in residence, beginning in 1987. Member of U.S. cultural delegation to China, 1982. Board member, Western States Arts Foundation, Milton Center, and Key West Literary Seminar; board member and chair (1991–), Wesleyan Writers' Conference. Member, New York Public Library National Literacy Committee, National Committee for U.S.-China relations, and Catholic Commission on Intellectual and Cultural Affairs. Member of usage panel, *American Heritage Dictionary.*

MEMBER: International PEN, Poetry Society of America, Society of American Historians, NAACP, Phi Beta Kappa.

AWARDS, HONORS: Pulitzer Prize (general nonfiction), 1975, for *Pilgrim at Tinker Creek;* New York Press Club Award for Excellence, 1975; Washington State Governor's Award for Literature, 1978; grants from National Endowment for the Arts, 1980-81, and Guggenheim Foundation, 1985-86; *Los Angeles Times* Book Prize nomination, 1982, for *Living by Fiction;* honorary degrees from Boston College, 1986, Connecticut College, and University of Hartford, both 1993; National Book Critics Circle award nomination, 1987, for *An American Childhood;* Appalachian Gold Medallion, University of Charleston, 1989; St. Botolph's Club Foundation Award, Boston, 1989; English-speaking Union Ambassador Book Award, 1990, for *The Writing Life;* Best Foreign Book Award (France), 1990, for *Pilgrim at Tinker Creek;* History Maker Award, Historical Society of Western Pennsylvania, 1993; Connecticut Governor's Arts Award, 1993; Campion Medal, 1994; Milton Prize, 1994.

WRITINGS:

Tickets for a Prayer Wheel (poems), University of Missouri Press (Columbia), 1974.
Pilgrim at Tinker Creek (also see below), Harper's Magazine Press, 1974.
Holy the Firm (also see below), Harper (New York City), 1978.
Living by Fiction (also see below), Harper, 1982.
Teaching a Stone to Talk: Expeditions and Encounters (also see below), Harper, 1982.
Encounters with Chinese Writers, Wesleyan University Press (Middletown, CT), 1984.
(Contributor) *Inventing the Truth: The Art and Craft of Memoir,* edited by William Zinsser, Houghton (Boston), 1987.
An American Childhood (also see below), Harper, 1987.
(Editor with Robert Atwan) *The Best American Essays, 1988,* Ticknor & Fields (New York City), 1988.

The Annie Dillard Library (contains *Living by Fiction, An American Childhood, Holy the Firm, Pilgrim at Tinker Creek,* and *Teaching a Stone to Talk*), Harper, 1989.
The Writing Life, Harper, 1989.
Three by Annie Dillard (contains *Pilgrim at Tinker Creek, An American Childhood,* and *The Writing Life*), Harper, 1990.
The Living (novel), HarperCollins (New York City), 1992.
The Annie Dillard Reader, HarperCollins, 1994.
(Editor with Cort Conley) *Modern American Memoirs,* HarperCollins, 1995.
Mornings Like This: Found Poems, HarperCollins, 1995.

Columnist, *Living Wilderness,* 1973-75. Contributing editor, *Harper's,* 1974-81, and 1983-85. Contributor of fiction, essays, and poetry to numerous periodicals, including *Atlantic Monthly, American Scholar, Poetry, New York Times Magazine, New York Times Book Review,* and *Chicago Review.*

SIDELIGHTS: Annie Dillard has carved a unique niche for herself in the world of American letters. Over the course of her career, Dillard has written essays, a memoir, poetry, literary criticism—even a western novel. In whatever genre she works, Dillard distinguishes herself with her carefully wrought language, keen observations, and original metaphysical insights. Her first significant publication, *Pilgrim at Tinker Creek,* drew numerous comparisons to Thoreau's *Walden;* in the years since *Pilgrim* appeared, Dillard's name has come to stand for excellence in writing.

Tickets for a Prayer Wheel was Dillard's first publication. This slim volume of poetry—which expressed the author's yearning for a hidden God—was praised by reviewers. Within months of *Tickets*'s appearance, however, the book was completely overshadowed by the release of *Pilgrim at Tinker Creek.* Dillard lived quietly on Tinker Creek in Virginia's Roanoke Valley, observing the natural world, taking notes, and reading voluminously in a wide variety of disciplines, including theology, philosophy, natural science, and physics. Following the progression of seasons, *Pilgrim* probes the cosmic significance of the beauty and violence coexisting in the natural world.

The author's next book delved into the metaphysical aspects of pain. *Holy the Firm* was inspired by the plight of one of Dillard's neighbors, a seven-year-old child badly burned in a plane crash. As Dillard reflects on the maimed child and on a moth consumed by flame, she struggles with the problem of reconciling faith in a loving god with the reality of a violent world. Only seventy-six pages long, the book overflows with "great richness, beauty and power," according to Frederick Buechner in the *New York Times Book Review. Atlantic* reviewer C. Michael Curtis concurred, adding that "Dillard writes about the ferocity and beauty of natural order with . . . grace."

Elegant writing also distinguishes *Living by Fiction,* Dillard's fourth book, in which the author analyzes the differences between modernist and traditional fiction. "Everyone who timidly, bombastically, reverently, scholastically—even fraudulently—essays to live 'the life of the mind' should read this book," advised Carolyn See in the *Los Angeles Times.* See went on to describe *Living by Fiction* as "somewhere between scholarship, metaphysics, an acid trip and a wonderful conversation with a most smart person." "Whether the field of investigation is nature or fiction, Annie Dillard digs for ultimate meanings as instinctively and as determinedly as hogs for truffles," remarked *Washington Post Book World* contributor John Breslin. "The resulting upheaval can be disconcerting . . . still, uncovered morsels are rich and tasty."

Dillard returned to reflections on nature and religion in a book of essays entitled *Teaching a Stone to Talk: Expeditions and Encounters.* In minutely detailed descriptions of a solar eclipse, visits to South America and the Galapagos Islands, and other, more commonplace events and locations, Dillard continues "the pilgrimage begun at Tinker Creek with an acuity of eye and ear that is matched by an ability to communicate a sense of wonder," stated Beaufort Cranford in the *Detroit News. Washington Post Book World* contributor Douglas Bauer was similarly pleased with the collection, judging the essays to be "almost uniformly splendid." In his estimation, Dillard's "art as an essayist is to move with the scrutinous eye through events and receptions that are random on their surfaces and to find, with grace and always-redeeming wit, the connections."

Dillard later chronicled her experiences as a member of a Chinese-American cultural exchange in a short, straightforward volume entitled *Encounters with Chinese Writers*; she then looked deeply into her past to produce another best-seller, *An American Childhood.* On one level, *An American Childhood* details Dillard's upbringing in an idiosyncratic, wealthy family; in another sense, the memoir tells the story of a young person's awakening to consciousness. In the words of *Washington Post* writer Charles Trueheart, Dillard's "memories of childhood are like her observations of nature: they feed her acrobatic thinking, and drive the free verse of her prose." Critics also applauded Dillard's keen insight into the unique perceptions of youth, as well as her exuberant spirit. "Loving and lyrical, nostalgic without being wistful, this is a book about the capacity for joy," said *Los Angeles Times Book Review* contributor Cyra McFadden, while Noel Perrin of the *New York Times Book Review* observed that "Ms. Dillard has written an autobiography in semimystical prose about the growth of her own mind, and it's an exceptionally interesting account."

The activity that had occupied most of Dillard's adulthood was the subject of her next book, *The Writing Life.* With regard to content, *The Writing Life* is not a manual on craft nor a guide to getting published; rather, it is a study of a writer at work and the processes involved in that work. Among critics, the book drew mixed reaction. "Annie Dillard is one of my favorite contemporary authors," Sara Maitland acknowledged in the *New York Times Book Review.* "Dillard is a wonderful writer and *The Writing Life* is full of joys. These are clearest to me when she comes at her subject tangentially, talking not of herself at her desk but of other parallel cases—the last chapter, a story about a stunt pilot who was an artist of air, is, quite simply, breathtaking. There are so many bits like this. . . . Unfortunately, the bits do not add up to a book." *Washington Post Book World* contributor Wendy Law-Yone voiced similar sentiments, finding the book "intriguing but not entirely satisfying" and "a sketch rather than a finished portrait." Nevertheless, she wondered, "Can anyone who has ever read Annie Dillard resist hearing what she has to say about writing? Her authority has been clear since *Pilgrim at Tinker Creek*—a mystic's wonder at the physical world expressed in beautiful, near-biblical prose."

Dillard ventured into new territory with her 1992 publication, *The Living,* a sprawling historical novel set in the Pacific Northwest. Reviewers hailed the author's first novel as masterful. "Her triumph is that this panoramic evocation of a very specific landscape and people might as well have been settled upon any other time and place—for this is, above all, a novel about the reiterant, precarious, wondrous, solitary, terrifying, utterly common condition of human life," wrote Molly Gloss in *Washington Post Book World.* Dillard's celebrated skill with words was also much in evidence here, according to Gloss, who noted that Dillard "uses language gracefully, releasing at times a vivid, startling imagery." Carol Anshaw concurred in the *Los Angeles Times Book Review*: "The many readers who have been drawn in the past to Dillard's work for its elegant and muscular language won't be disappointed in these pages."

Following the 1994 publication of *The Annie Dillard Reader,* a collection of poems, stories, and essays that prompted a *Publishers Weekly* reviewer to term Dillard "a writer of acute and singular observation," Dillard produced two works that were published in 1995. *Modern American Memoirs,* which Dillard edited with Cort Conley, is a collection of thirty-five pieces excerpted from various writers' memoirs. Authors whose work appears here include Ralph Ellison, Margaret Mead, Reynolds Price, Kate Simon, and Russell Baker. "Many of these memoirs are striking and memorable despite their brevity," commented Madeline Marget in a *Commonweal* review of the collection.

Mornings Like This: Found Poems, Dillard's other 1995 publication, is an experimental volume of poetry. To create these poems, Dillard culled lines from other writers' prose works—Vincent Van Gogh's letters and a Boy Scout Handbook, for example—and "arranged [the lines]in such a way as to simulate a poem originating with a single author," noted John Haines in *The Hudson Review.* While commenting that Dillard's technique in this book works better with humorous and joyful pieces than with serious ones, a *Publishers Weekly* critic remarked that "these co-op verses are never less than intriguing." Haines expressed serious concern with the implications of Dillard's experiment: "What does work like this say about the legitimacy of authorship?" He concluded, however, that "on the whole the collection has in places considerable interest."

BIOGRAPHICAL/CRITICAL SOURCES:

BOOKS

Authors and Artists for Young Adults, Volume 6, Gale (Detroit), 1991.
Contemporary Literary Criticism, Gale, Volume 9, 1978; Volume 60, 1990.
Dictionary of Literary Biography Yearbook: 1980, Gale, 1981.
Hassan, Ihab, *Selves at Risk: Patterns of Quest in Contemporary American Letters,* University of Wisconsin Press, 1991.
Johnson, Sandra Humble, *The Space Between: Literary Epiphany in the Works of Annie Dillard,* Kent State University Press, 1992.
Smith, Linda, *Annie Dillard,* Twayne, 1991.
Something about the Author, Volume 10, Gale, 1976.

PERIODICALS

America, April 20, 1974; February 11, 1978, pp. 363-64; May 6, 1978, pp. 363-64; November 25, 1989, p. 1; November 19, 1994, p. 2.
American Literature, March, 1987.
American Scholar, summer, 1990, p. 445.
Atlantic, December, 1977.
Best Sellers, December, 1977.
Chicago Tribune, October 1, 1987.
Chicago Tribune Book World, September 12, 1982, p. 7; November 21, 1982, p. 5.
Christian Century, November 15, 1989, p. 1063.
Christianity Today, May 5, 1978, pp. 14-19, 30-31; September 14, 1992, p. 46.
Commentary, October, 1974.

Commonweal, October 24, 1975, pp. 495-96; February 3, 1978; March 9, 1990, p. 151; April 5, 1996, p. 32.

Detroit News, October 31, 1982, p. 2H.

English Journal, April, 1989, p. 90; May 1, 1989, p. 69.

Globe and Mail (Toronto), November 28, 1987.

Hudson Review, winter, 1996, p. 666.

Los Angeles Times, April 27, 1982; November 19, 1982.

Los Angeles Times Book Review, November 18, 1984, p. 11; September 20, 1987, pp. 1, 14; October 31, 1982, p. 2; November 18, 1984, p. 11; July 6, 1986, p. 10; September 20, 1987, pp. 1, 14; May 31, 1992, pp. 1, 7.

Ms., August, 1974.

Nation, November 20, 1982, pp. 535-36; October 16, 1989, pp. 435-36; May 25, 1992, p. 692.

New Leader, June 24, 1974; August 10, 1992, p. 17.

New Republic, April 6, 1974.

New Statesmen and Society, December 23, 1988, p. 30; November 9, 1990, p. 34.

Newsweek, June 8, 1992, p. 57.

New Yorker, December 25, 1989, p. 106; July 6, 1992, p. 80.

New York Times, September 21, 1977; March 12 1982, p. C18; November 25, 1982.

New York Times Book Review, March 24, 1974 pp. 4-5; September 25, 1977, pp. 12, 40; May 9, 1982, pp. 10, 22-23; July 1, 1979, p. 21; November 28, 1982, pp. 13, 19; January 1, 1984, p. 32; September 23, 1984, p. 29; September 27, 1987, p. 7; September 17, 1989, p. 15; May 3, 1992, p. 9.

New York Times Magazine, April 26, 1992, p. 34.

People, October 19, 1987, p. 99.

Publishers Weekly, September 1, 1989, pp. 67-68; October 31, 1994, p. 45; April 24, 1995, p. 65.

Reason, April, 1990, p. 56.

South Atlantic Quarterly, spring, 1986, pp. 111-22.

Threepenny Review, summer, 1988.

Time, March 18, 1974; October 10, 1977.

Tribune Books (Chicago), September 13, 1987, pp. 1, 12; December 18, 1988, p. 3; August 27, 1989, p. 6.

Village Voice, July 13, 1982, pp. 40-41.

Virginia Quarterly Review, autumn, 1974, pp. 637-40; spring, 1996, p. 57.

Washington Post, October 28, 1987.

Washington Post Book World, October 16, 1977, p. E6; April 4, 1982, p. 4; January 2, 1983, p. 6; September 9, 1984, p. 6; July 6, 1986, p. 13; September 6, 1987, p. 11; August 14, 1988, p. 12; August 27, 1989, p. 6; September 24, 1989, p. 4; May 3, 1992, pp. 1-2.

Yale Review, October, 1992, p. 102.

*   *   *

DINESEN, Isak
See BLIXEN, Karen (Christentze Dinesen)

*   *   *

DISCH, Thomas M(ichael) 1940-
(Thom Demijohn, Tom Disch, Leonie Hargrave, Cassandra Knye)

PERSONAL: Born February 2, 1940, in Des Moines, IA; son of Felix Henry and Helen (Gilbertson) Disch. *Education:* Attended Cooper Union and New York University, 1959-62.

ADDRESSES: Agent—Karpfinger Agency, 500 Fifth Ave., Suite 2800, New York, NY 10110.

CAREER: Writer, 1964–. Majestic Theatre, New York City, part-time checkroom attendant, 1957-62; Doyle Dane Bernbach, New York City, copywriter, 1963-64; theater critic for *Nation,* 1987-91; theater critic for the *New York Daily News,* 1993–. Artist-in-residence, College of William and Mary, 1996–. Lecturer at universities.

MEMBER: PEN, National Book Critics Circle (board member, 1988-91), Writers Guild East.

AWARDS, HONORS: O. Henry Prize, 1975, for story "Getting into Death," and 1979, for story "Xmas"; John W. Campbell Memorial Award, and American Book Award nomination, both 1980, both for *On Wings of Song;* Hugo Award and Nebula Award nominations, 1980, and British Science Fiction Award, 1981, all for novella *The Brave Little Toaster.*

WRITINGS:

NOVELS

The Genocides, Berkley Publishing (New York City), 1965.

Mankind under the Leash (expanded version of his short story, "White Fang Goes Dingo" [also see below]), Ace Books (New York City), 1966, published in England as *The Puppies of Terra,* Panther Books, 1978.

(With John Sladek under joint pseudonym Cassandra Knye) *The House That Fear Built,* Paperback Library, 1966.

Echo Round His Bones, Berkley Publishing, 1967.

(With Sladek under joint pseudonym Thom Demijohn) *Black Alice,* Doubleday (New York City), 1968.

Camp Concentration, Hart-Davis, 1968, Doubleday, 1969.

The Prisoner, Ace Books, 1969.

334, MacGibbon & Kee, Avon (New York City), 1974.

(Under pseudonym Leonie Hargrave) *Clara Reeve,* Knopf (New York City), 1975.

On Wings of Song, St. Martin's (New York City), 1979.

Triplicity (omnibus volume), Doubleday, 1980.

(With Charles Naylor) *Neighboring Lives,* Scribner, 1981.

The Businessman: A Tale of Terror, Harper, 1984.

Amnesia (computer-interactive novel), Electronic Arts, 1985.

The Silver Pillow: A Tale of Witchcraft, M. V. Ziesing (Willimantic, CT), 1987.

The M.D.: A Horror Story, Knopf, 1991.

The Priest: A Gothic Romance, Knopf, 1995.

STORY COLLECTIONS

One Hundred and Two H-Bombs and Other Science Fiction Stories (also see below), Compact Books (Hollywood, FL), 1966, revised edition published as *One Hundred and Two H-Bombs,* Berkeley Publishing, 1969, published in England as *White Fang Goes Dingo and Other Funny S.F. Stories,* Arrow Books, 1971.

Under Compulsion, Hart-Davis, 1968, also published as *Fun with Your New Head,* Doubleday, 1969.

Getting into Death: The Best Short Stories of Thomas M. Disch, Hart-Davis, 1973, revised edition, Knopf, 1976.

The Early Science Fiction Stories of Thomas M. Disch (includes *Mankind under the Leash* and *One Hundred and Two H-bombs),* Gregg (Boston, MA), 1977.

Fundamental Disch, Bantam, 1980.

The Man Who Had No Idea, Bantam, 1982.

POETRY

(With Marilyn Hacker and Charles Platt) *Highway Sandwiches,* privately printed, 1970.

The Right Way to Figure Plumbing, Basilisk Press, 1972.

ABCDEFG HIJKLM NPOQRST UVWXYZ, Anvil Press Poetry (Millville, MN), 1981.

Orders of the Retina, Toothpaste Press (West Branch, IA), 1982.

Burn This, Hutchinson, 1982.

Here I Am, There You Are, Where Were We?, Hutchinson, 1984.

Yes, Let's: New and Selected Poetry, Johns Hopkins University Press (Baltimore, MD), 1989.

Dark Verses and Light, Johns Hopkins University Press, 1991.

(Under the pseudonym Tom Disch) *A Child's Garden of Grammar,* University Press of New England (Hanover, NH), 1997.

JUVENILE

The Tale of Dan de Lion: A Fable, Coffee House Press, 1986.

The Brave Little Toaster: A Bedtime Story for Small Appliances, Doubleday, 1986.

The Brave Little Toaster Goes to Mars, Doubleday, 1988.

EDITOR

The Ruins of the Earth: An Anthology of Stories of the Immediate Future, Putnam, 1971.

Bad Moon Rising: An Anthology of Political Foreboding, Harper, 1975.

The New Improved Sun: An Anthology of Utopian Science Fiction, 1975.

(With Naylor) *New Constellations: An Anthology of Tomorrow's Mythologies,* Harper, 1976.

(With Naylor) *Strangeness: A Collection of Curious Tales,* Scribner, 1977.

(Ghost editor with Robert Arthur) *Alfred Hitchcock Presents: Stories that Scared Even Me,* Random House, 1967.

(Librettist) *The Fall of the House of Usher* (opera), produced in New York City, 1979.

(Librettist) *Frankenstein* (opera), produced in Greenvale, NY, 1982.

Ringtime (short story), Toothpaste Press, 1983.

(Author of introduction) Michael Bishop, *One Winter in Eden,* Arkham House (Sauk City, WI), 1984.

Torturing Mr. Amberwell (short story), Cheap Street (New Castle, VA), 1985.

(Author of preface) Pamela Zoline, *The Heat Death of the Universe and Other Stories,* McPherson & Company (New Paltz, NY), 1988.

(Author of introduction) Philip K. Dick, *The Penultimate Truth,* Carroll & Graf, 1989.

Ben Hur (play), first produced in New York City, 1989.

The Cardinal Detoxes (verse play), first produced in New York City by RAPP Theater Company, 1990.

The Castle of Indolence: On Poetry, Poets, and Poetasters, Picador (New York City), 1995.

OTHER

The Dreams Our Stuff Is Made of: How Science Fiction Conquered the World, Simon & Schuster, 1998.

Contributor to *Science Fiction at Large,* edited by Peter Nicholls, Harper, 1976.

Contributor to numerous anthologies. Also contributor to periodicals, including *Playboy, Poetry,* and *Harper's.* Regular reviewer for *Times Literary Supplement* and *Washington Post Book World.*

MEDIA ADAPTATIONS: The Brave Little Toaster was produced as an animated film by Hyperion-Kushner-Lockec, 1987.

SIDELIGHTS: An author of science fiction, poetry, historical novels, opera librettos, and computer-interactive fiction, Thomas Disch has been cited as "one of the most remarkably talented writers around" by a reviewer for the *Washington Post Book World.* Disch began his career writing science fiction stories that featured dark themes and disturbing plots. Many of Disch's early themes reappear in his short stories and poetry; the result, according to Blake Morrison in the *Times Literary Supplement,* is "never less than enjoyable and accomplished." While many of his best-known works are aimed at an adult audience, Disch is also the author of well-received children's fiction, including two fantasies, *The Brave Little Toaster* and *The Brave Little Toaster Goes to Mars.* Describing the diversity of Disch's work in *Dream Makers: The Uncommon People Who Write Science Fiction,* Charles Platt notes that the author "has traveled widely, through almost every genre and technique. . . . And in each field [Disch] has made himself at home, never ill-at-ease or out-of-place, writing with the same implacable control and elegant manners."

Disch grew up in Minnesota and graduated from high school in St. Paul. As a youngster he devoured horror comic books and science fiction magazines, including the influential *Astounding Science Fiction.* He learned his craft by reading and re-reading the work of authors such as Robert A. Heinlein and Isaac Asimov—found in the pages of *Astounding Science Fiction.* After a series of low-paying jobs in Minnesota (which included employment as night watchman in a funeral parlor), Disch moved to New York City. While living in New York, he worked as a checkroom attendant and advertising copywriter. His first fiction appeared in a magazine called *Fantastic Stories* in 1962. Between that periodical and another one called *Amazing Stories* he would publish nine more stories that year and the next. Although Disch has admitted to not thinking that highly of his first publishing success, he found his second effort at writing a full-length story more satisfactory. This story, entitled "White Fang Goes Dingo," was first published in its short form, then in an expanded version as the author's second novel, *Mankind under the Leash* (later published under the title Disch prefers, *The Puppies of Terra*).

In 1964, having secured an advance from Berkley Books, Disch left advertising to become a full-time writer. He published his first novel the following year, a science fiction tale entitled *The Genocides.* In large part the story of an alien invasion of Earth, *The Genocides* describes the last grim days of human existence, an existence where people are reduced to little more than insects in the aliens' global garden. Critics found the book frightening. "The novel . . . is powerful in the way that it forces the reader to alter his perspective, to reexamine what it means to be human," writes Erich S. Rupprecht in the *Dictionary of Literary Biography.* Disch followed *The Genocides* with a series of thought-provoking science fiction tales, such as *Camp Concentration* and *334,* as well as horror novels such as *The Businessman* and *The M.D.*

Camp Concentration, 334, and *On Wings of Song* are widely considered Disch's best works. All three appeared in a mid-1980s survey by David Pringle entitled *Science Fiction: The 100 Best Novels.* In *Science Fiction: History, Science, Vision,* Robert Scholes and Eric S. Rabkin describe *Camp Concentration* as Disch's "first major breakthrough" under the influence of the New Wave. It is set at a secret prison camp run by the U.S. Army where selected prisoners are being treated with a new drug that increases their intelligence. Unfortunately, this drug also causes the prisoners' early deaths. The novel is in the form of a diary kept by one of the prisoners. The diary's style grows more complex as the narrative develops, reflecting the prisoner's increasing intelligence. According to Scholes and Rabkin, the novel "combines considerable technical resources in the management of the narrative . . . with a probing inquiry into human values." Rupprecht draws a parallel between *Camp Concentration* and *The Genocides*. In both novels, he argues, the characters must survive inescapable situations. Disch's continuing theme, Rupprecht summarizes, is "charting his characters' attempts to keep themselves intact in a world which grows increasingly hostile, irrational, inhuman."

This theme is also found in *334,* a novel set in a New York City housing project of the future. Divided into six loosely-related sections, the novel presents the daily lives of residents of the building, which is located at 334 East Eleventh Street. The characters live in boredom and poverty; their city is rundown and dirty. The world of the novel, Scholes and Rabkin believe, "is not radically different from ours in many respects but is deeply troubling for reasons that apply to the present New York as well. Above all, the aimlessness and purposelessness of the lives chronicled is affecting." In his analysis of the book Rupprecht also notes the similarity between the novel's setting and the world of the present. He finds *334* to be "a slightly distorted mirror image of contemporary life." Although the *Washington Post Book World* reviewer judges the setting to be "an interesting, plausible and unpleasant near-future world where urban life is even more constricted than now," he nonetheless believes that "survival and aspiration remain possible." Rupprecht praises *334* as Disch's "most brilliant and disturbing work. . . . One can think of few writers—of science fiction or other genres—who could convey a similar sense of emptiness, of yearning, of ruin with this power and grace. . . . Like all great writers, Disch forces his readers to see the reality of their lives in a way that is fresh, startling, disturbing, and moving."

Like *334, On Wings of Song* deals with a future time that resembles our own. Describing the general atmosphere of the novel in the *New York Times Book Review,* Gerald Jonas notes: "Politically and economically, things seem to be going downhill, but in between crises, people can still assure themselves that they are living in 'normal' times." In the *Village Voice,* John Calvin Batchelor calls *On Wings of Song* Disch's "grandest work." The critic maintains that the novel links Disch with other great social critics of the past, including H. G. Wells and George Orwell. "Disch," he writes, "is an unapologetic political writer, a high-minded liberal democrat, who sees doom in Western Civilization and says so, often with bizarre, bleak scenarios."

Continuing to explore many literary avenues, in the 1980s and 1990s Disch published novels, stories, poetry, a libretto and an interactive computer novel. Three novels published during this period further the social criticism seen in earlier works. In *The Businessman: A Tale of Terror, The M.D.: A Horror Story,* and *The Priest: A Gothic Romance,* Disch combines classic thriller techniques with a critical look at the corruption he sees in the three professions mentioned in the titles. The plots are replete with the type of strange occurrences Disch's readers have grown to expect, and the works show Disch's usual blend of styles. Writing about *The M.D.* in *Kliatt,* Larry W. Prater notes: "The novel combines elements of the macabre, of fantasy and of SF." Evidently, in life as well as literature, categories aren't important to Disch. In a *Publishers Weekly* interview with David Finkle, Disch refuses to see *The M.D.* as just a horror novel and with

equal fervor defends his right to remain unburdened by a convenient label. "Every book has its own slightly different ground rules from the others," he maintains. ". . . As long as the book plays by its own rules and those are clear, I don't think genre borderlines are especially helpful. I don't spend my life trying to determine what category I'm in." Disch tells Platt: "Part of my notion of a proper ambition is that one should excel at a wide range of tasks."

The variety found in Disch's novels and stories also extends to his poetry and work for children. Lehman praises Disch's poetry by noting that "the distinctive qualities of Disch's prose fiction—wit, invention, and the gift of gab—are the virtues of his verse as well. . . . Disch has . . . an excellent ear and clever tongue." Disch has also had success as a children's author with titles such as *The Brave Little Toaster* and *The Tale of Dan de Lion.* In these works, Disch fully embraces the fantastic. *The Brave Little Toaster* tells the story of a group of small appliances (including the toaster, a clock radio, and an electric blanket) who come to life in order to search for their missing master. *The Tale of Dan de Lion,* presented in a series of couplets, concerns the adventures of a dandelion, his weedy family, and the rose breeder who wants to destroy them. Critics praised Disch's children's works both for the author's use of language and sense of whimsy. *The Brave Little Toaster* gained further recognition when it was produced as a popular animated film in 1987.

BIOGRAPHICAL/CRITICAL SOURCES:

BOOKS

Aldiss, Brian W., *Trillion Year Spree: The History of Science Fiction,* Atheneum, 1986.
Bleiler, E. F., editor, *Science Fiction Writers: Critical Studies of the Major Authors from the Early Nineteenth Century to the Present Day,* Scribner, 1982, pp. 351-56.
Children's Literature Review, Volume 18, Gale (Detroit), 1989.
Contemporary Literary Criticism, Gale, Volume 7, 1977, pp. 86-87; Volume 36, 1986, pp. 123-28.
Contemporary Poets, St. James Press (Chicago), 5th edition, 1991.
Delany, Samuel R., *The American Shore: Meditations on a Tale of Science Fiction by Thomas M. Disch,* Dragon (Elizabethtown, NY), 1978.
Dictionary of Literary Biography, Volume 8: *Twentieth-Century Science Fiction Writers,* Gale, 1981, pp. 148-54.
Scholes, Robert, and Eric S. Rabkin, *Science Fiction: History, Science, Vision,* Oxford University Press, 1977.
Something about the Author Autobiography Series, Volume 15, Gale, 1993, pp. 107-23.
Stephens, Christopher P., *A Checklist of Thomas M. Disch,* Ultramarine (Hastings-on-Hudson, NY), 1991.

PERIODICALS

Chicago Tribune Book World, March 22, 1982.
Kliatt, September, 1992, p. 20.
Los Angeles Times, February 3, 1981; November 21, 1982, p. 13; August 13, 1989, p. 3.
New Statesman, July 13, 1984, p. 28.
Newsweek, March 9, 1981; July 2, 1984; July 11, 1988, pp. 66-67.
New York Times Book Review, March 21, 1976, p. 6; October 28, 1979, p. 15, 18; August 26, 1984, p. 31; April 20, 1986, p. 29.
Publishers Weekly, January 7, 1974, p. 56; January 5, 1976, p. 59; August 29, 1980, p. 363; April 19, 1991, pp. 48-49.
Science Fiction Chronicle, February, 1993, p. 35.

Spectator, May 1, 1982, p. 23.
Time, July 28, 1975; February 9, 1976, pp. 83-84; July 9, 1984, pp. 85-86.
Times Literary Supplement, February 15, 1974, p. 163; June 12, 1981, p. 659; August 27, 1982, p. 919; May 25, 1984, p. 573; November 28, 1986, p. 343; September 15-21, 1989, p. 1000; November 11, 1994, p. 19.
Village Voice, August 27-September 2, 1980, pp. 35-36.
Voice of Youth Advocates, April, 1981, p. 39.
Washington Post, September 23, 1979, p. 7.
Washington Post Book World, July 26, 1981, pp. 6-7; August 6, 1989, p. 5.

*   *   *

DISCH, Tom
See DISCH, Thomas M(ichael)

*   *   *

D'ISLY, Georges
See SIMENON, Georges (Jacques Christian)

*   *   *

DOCTOROW, E(dgar) L(aurence) 1931-

PERSONAL: Born January 6, 1931, in New York, NY; son of David R. (a music store proprietor) and Rose (a pianist; maiden name, Levine) Doctorow; married Helen Esther Setzer (a writer), August 20, 1954; children: Jenny, Caroline, Richard. *Education:* Kenyon College, A.B. (with honors), 1952; Columbia University, graduate study, 1952-53.

ADDRESSES: Home—New Rochelle, NY. *Office*—c/o Random House Publishers, 201 East 50th St., New York, NY 10022; c/o New York University, Department of English, New York, NY 10003.

CAREER: Script reader, Columbia Pictures Industries, Inc., New York City; New American Library, New York City, senior editor, 1959-64; Dial Press, New York City, editor-in-chief, 1964-69, vice president, 1968-69; University of California, Irvine, writer in residence, 1969-70; Sarah Lawrence College, Bronxville, NY, member of faculty, 1971-78; New York University, New York City, professor of English, 1982—. Creative writing fellow, Yale School of Drama, 1974-75; visiting professor, University of Utah, 1975; visiting senior fellow, Princeton University, 1980-81. *Military service:* U.S. Army, Signal Corps, 1953-55.

MEMBER: American Academy and Institute of Arts and Letters, Authors Guild (director), PEN (director), Writers Guild of America, East, Century Association.

AWARDS, HONORS: National Book Award nomination, 1972, for *The Book of Daniel;* Guggenheim fellowship, 1973; Creative Artists Service fellow, 1973-74; National Book Critics Circle Award and Arts and Letters award, 1976, both for *Ragtime;* L.H.D., Kenyon College, 1976; Litt.D., Hobart and William Smith Colleges, 1979; American Book Award, 1986, for *World's Fair;* L.H.D., Brandeis University, 1989; Edith Wharton Citation of Merit for Fiction and New York State Author, 1989-1991.

WRITINGS:

NOVELS

Welcome to Hard Times, Simon & Schuster, 1960, published in England as *Bad Man from Bodie,* Deutsch, 1961.
Big as Life, Simon & Schuster, 1966.
The Book of Daniel (also see below), Random House, 1971.
Ragtime (Book-of-the-Month Club selection), Random House, 1975.
Loon Lake, Random House, 1980.
World's Fair, Random House, 1985.
Billy Bathgate (Book-of-the-Month Club main selection), Random House, 1989.
Three Complete Novels, Wings (New York City), 1994.
The Waterworks Random House, 1994.

OTHER

(Contributor) Theodore Solotaroff, editor, *New American Review 2,* New American Library, 1968.
Drinks before Dinner (play; first produced off-Broadway at Public Theater, November 22, 1978), Random House, 1979.
American Anthem, photographs by Jean-Claude Suares, Stewart, Tabori, 1982.
Daniel (screenplay; based on author's *The Book of Daniel),* Paramount Pictures, 1983.
Lives of the Poets: Six Stories and a Novella, Random House, 1984.
Reading and Interview (sound recording), American Audio Prose Library, 1991.
Jack London, Hemingway, and the Constitution: Selected Writings, 1977-1992, Random House, 1993.

MEDIA ADAPTATIONS: In 1967, Metro-Goldwyn-Mayer produced *Billy Bathgate,* a movie version of *Welcome to Hard Times,* which starred Henry Fonda. Doctorow, who had nothing to do with the film adaptation, has referred to it as the second worst movie ever made. Unlike with *Welcome to Hard Times,* he was involved, at least for a time, with the film version of *Ragtime,* which was released in 1981. Dino De Laurentiis hired Robert Altman to direct the film, and after scrapping someone else's screenplay, Altman convinced Doctorow to write one. De Laurentiis eventually fired Altman, and then Doctorow's script was rejected for being too long. Milos Forman eventually took over the directing, and playwright Michael Weller wrote the screenplay; it starred James Cagney in his last screen performance. However, Doctorow did write the screenplay for *Daniel,* the film adaptation of *The Book of Daniel,* which was produced by Paramount Pictures in 1983 and starred Timothy Hutton. Another version of *Billy Bathgate* was filmed in 1991; it was written by Tom Stoppard, directed by Robert Benton, and starred Dustin Hoffman, Nicole Kidman, and Bruce Willis.

SIDELIGHTS: E. L. Doctorow is a highly regarded novelist and playwright known for his serious philosophical probings, the subtlety and variety of his prose style, and his unusual use of historical figures in fictional works. Doctorow's first novel, *Welcome to Hard Times,* was inspired, he told Jonathan Yardley of the *Miami Herald,* by his job as a reader for Columbia Pictures, where he "was accursed to read things that were submitted to this company and write synopses of them." "I had to suffer one lousy Western after another," continued Doctorow, "and it occurred to me that I could lie about the West in a much more interesting way than any of these people were lying. I wrote a short story, and it subsequently became the first chapter of that novel." The resulting book, unlike many Westerns, is concerned with grave issues. As

Wirt Williams notes in the *New York Times Book Review,* the novel addresses "one of the favorite problems of philosophers: the relationship of man and evil. . . . Perhaps the primary theme of the novel is that evil can only be resisted psychically: when the rational controls that order man's existence slacken, destruction comes. [Joseph] Conrad said it best in *Heart of Darkness,* but Mr. Doctorow has said it impressively. His book is taut and dramatic, exciting and successfully symbolic." Similarly, Kevin Stan, writing in the *New Republic,* remarks: "*Welcome to Hard Times* . . . is a superb piece of fiction: lean and mean, and thematically significant. . . . He takes the thin, somewhat sordid and incipiently depressing materials of the Great Plains experience and fashions them into a myth of good and evil. . . . He does it marvelously, with economy and with great narrative power."

After writing a Western of sorts, Doctorow turned to another form not usually heralded by critics: science fiction. In *Big as Life,* two naked human giants materialize in New York harbor. The novel examines the ways in which its characters deal with a seemingly impending catastrophe. Like *Hard Times, Big as Life* enjoyed much critical approval. A *Choice* reviewer, for example, comments that "Doctorow's dead pan manner . . . turns from satire to tenderness and human concern. A performance closer to James Purdy than to [George] Orwell or [Aldous] Huxley, but in a minor key." In spite of reviewers' praise, however, *Big as Life,* like *Welcome to Hard Times,* was not a large commercial success.

The Book of Daniel, Doctorow's third book, involves yet another traditional form, the historical novel. It is a fictional account based on the relationship between Julius and Ethel Rosenberg and their children. The Rosenbergs were Communists who were convicted of and executed for conspiracy to commit treason. Many feel that they were victims of the sometimes hysterical anti-communist fever of the 1950s. As with *Welcome to Hard Times* and *Big as Life,* Doctorow has modified the traditional form to suit his purposes. The work is not an examination of the guilt or innocence of the Rosenbergs, but as David Emblidge observes in *Southwest Review,* a look at the central character Daniel's psychology, his attempts to deal with the trauma he suffered from his parents' death. Thus many critics argue that the book, unlike typical historical novels, is largely independent of historical fact. Jane Richmond, writing in *Partisan Review,* believes that "if Julius and Ethel Rosenberg had never existed, the book would be just as good as it is." In like manner, Stanley Kauffmann, in the *New Republic,* remarks: "I haven't looked up the facts of the Rosenberg case; it would be offensive to the quality of this novel to check it against those facts."

Many critics were very impressed with the achievement of *The Book of Daniel.* Kauffmann terms it "the political novel of our age, the best American work of its kind that I know since Lionel Trilling's *The Middle of the Journey.*" P. S. Prescott of *Newsweek* adds that *The Book of Daniel* "is a purgative book, angry and more deeply felt than all but a few contemporary American novels, a novel about defeat, impotent rage, the passing of the burden of suffering through generations. . . . There is no question here of our suspending disbelief, but rather how when we have finished, we may regain stability." And Richmond calls it "a brilliant achievement and the best contemporary novel I've read since reading Frederick Exley's *A Fan's Notes.* . . . It is a book of infinite detail and tender attention to the edges of life as well as to its dead center."

In *Ragtime,* Doctorow forays deeper into historical territory. The novel interweaves the lives of an upper-middle-class WASP family, a poor immigrant family, and the family of a black ragtime musician with historical figures such as I. P. Morgan, Harry Houdini, Henry Ford, and Emma Goldman. Particularly intriguing to readers is that Doctorow shows famous people involved in unusual, sometimes ludicrous, situations. In the *Washington Post Book World,* Raymond Sokolov notes that "Doctorow turns history into myth and myth into history. . . . [He] continually teases our suspicion of literary artifice with apparently true historical description. . . . On the one hand, the 'fact' tugs one toward taking the episode as history. On the other, the doubt that lingers makes one want to take the narrative as an invention." Sokolov argues that Doctorow "teases" the reader in order to make him try "to sort out what the author is doing. That is, we find ourselves paying Doctorow the most important tribute. We watch to see what he is doing."

Newsweek's Walter Clemons also finds himself teased by *Ragtime*'s historical episodes: "The very fact that the book stirs one to parlor-game research is amusing evidence that Doctorow has already won the game: I found myself looking up details because I wanted them to be true." In addition, George Stade, in the *New York Times Book Review,* expresses a belief similar to Sokolov's. "In this excellent novel," Stade writes, "silhouettes and rags not only make fiction out of history but also reveal the fictions out of which history is made. It incorporates the fictions and realities of the era of ragtime while it rags our fictions about it. It is an anti-nostalgic novel that incorporates our nostalgia about its subject."

Ragtime's political content also generates debate. Several reviewers believe that *Ragtime* presents a simplistic leftist viewpoint. Hilton Kramer of *Commentary,* for instance, contends that "the villains in *Ragtime,* drawn with all the subtlety of a William Gropper cartoon, are all representatives of money, the middle class, and white ethnic prejudice. . . . *Ragtime* is a political romance. . . . The major fictional characters . . . are all ideological inventions, designed to serve the purposes of a political fable." Similarly, Jeffrey Hart, writing in the *National Review,* objects that Doctorow judges his revolutionary and minority characters much less harshly than the middle and upper-class WASP figures, which results in "what can be called left-wing pastoral," a form of sentimentality.

In *Loon Lake,* Doctorow continues to experiment with prose style and to evoke yet another period in American history, the Depression. The novel's plot revolves around the various relationships between an industrial tycoon, his famous aviatrix-wife, gangsters and their entourage, an alcoholic poet, and Joe, a young drifter who stumbles onto the tycoon's opulent residence in the Adirondacks. The novel works on several levels with "concentrically expanding ripples of implication," according to Robert Towers in the *New York Times Book Review.* For the most part, however, it is Doctorow's portrait of the American dream versus the American reality which forms the novel's core. As Christopher Lehmann-Haupt of the *New York Times* explains, "[*Loon Lake*] is a complex and haunting meditation on modern American history."

Time's Paul Gray believes that "Doctorow is . . . playing a variation on an old theme: The American dream, set to the music of an American nightmare, the Depression." Lehmann-Haupt infers a similar correlation and elaborates: "This novel could easily have been subtitled *An American Tragedy Revisited.* . . . *Loon Lake* contains [several] parallels to, as well as ironic comments on, the themes of [Theodore] Dreiser's story. . . . Had

Dreiser lived to witness the disruptions of post-World War II American society—and had he possessed Mr. Doctorow's narrative dexterity—he might have written something like *Loon Lake*."

Doctorow's extraordinary narrative style has generated much critical comment. "The written surface of *Loon Lake* is ruffled and choppy," Gray remarks. "Swatches of poetry are jumbled together with passages of computerese and snippets of mysteriously disembodied conversation. Narration switches suddenly from first to third person, or vice versa, and it is not always clear just who is telling what." A reviewer for the *Chicago Tribune* finds such "stylistic tricks" annoyingly distractive. "We balk at the frequent overwriting, and the clumsy run-on sentences," he reports. "We can see that Doctorow is trying to convey rootlessness and social unrest through an insouciant free play of language and syntax. . . ; the problem is that these eccentricities draw disproportionate attention to themselves, away from the characters and their concerns."

Doctorow's play, *Drinks before Dinner,* seems to have been created through an analogous act of exploration. In *Nation,* he states that the play "originated not in an idea or a character or a story but in a sense of heightened language, a way of talking. It was not until I had the sound of it in my ear that I thought about saying something. The language preceded the intention. . . . The process of making something up is best experienced as fortuitous, unplanned, exploratory. You write to find out what it is you're writing." In composing *Drinks before Dinner,* Doctorow worked from sound to words to characters. Does this "flawed" method of composition show a "defective understanding of what theater is supposed to do?" wonders Doctorow. His answer: "I suspect so. Especially if we are talking of the American theater, in which the presentation of the psychologized ego is so central as to be an article of faith. And that is the point. The idea of character as we normally celebrate it on the American stage is what this play seems to question."

Doctorow's experiment garners a mixed response from drama critics. In the *Village Voice,* Michael Feingold observes that in *Drinks before Dinner* Doctorow "has tried to do something incomparably more ambitious than any new American play has done in years—he has tried to put the whole case against civilization in a nutshell." According to Feingold, the intent is defeated by a "schizoid" plot and "flat, prosy, and empty" writing. "I salute his desire to say something gigantic," Feingold concludes; "how I wish he had found a way to say it fully, genuinely, and dramatically." Richard Eder of the *New York Times* responds more positively: "Mr. Doctorow's turns of thought can be odd, witty and occasionally quite remarkable. His theme—that the world is blindly destroying itself and not worrying about it—is hardly original, but certainly worth saying. And he finds thoughtful and striking ways of saying it, even though eventually the play becomes an endless epigram, a butterfly that turns into a centipede." "Still, a play of ideas is rare enough nowadays," Eder observes, "and Mr. Doctorow's are sharp enough to supplement intellectual suspense when the dramatic suspense bogs down."

Among Doctorow's more recent books, *World's Fair* and *Billy Bathgate* are both set in 1930s-era New York and have received wide critical acclaim. *World's Fair,* considered by many reviewers to be autobiographical in nature, relates a boy's experiences in New York City during the depression and ends with his visit to the 1939 World's Fair. Although *World's Fair* received an American Book Award, many critics view the author's next novel, *Billy Bathgate,* to be an even greater achievement. The story of 15-year-old Billy Behan's initiation into the world of organized crime is a "grand entertainment that is also a triumphant work of art," according to *Washington Post Book World* contributor Pete Hamill. A number of reviewers especially appreciated Doctorow's ability to avoid cliched characters: "Even the various gangsters [in *Billy Bathgate*] are multidimensional," Anne Tyler remarked with pleasure in the *New York Times Book Review.* The completion of *Billy Bathgate* was also a milestone for its author. Discussing *Billy Bathgate* in the *Washington Post,* Doctorow revealed that he felt he had been "liberated by it to a certain extent. . . . Certain themes and preoccupations, that leitmotif that I've been working with for several years. I think now I can write anything. The possibilities are limitless. I've somehow been set free by this book."

In *The Waterworks* (1994), Doctorow imaginatively revisits old New York of the 1870s, an era of widespread corruption in a city which enjoyed great prosperity because of profiteering during the Civil War. In this novel, Doctorow's protagonist is a journalist named McIlvaine, who investigates reports that a wealthy man, believed deceased, has been spotted in public on at least two occasions in the city. To his horror, McIlvaine discovers several such specimens of the living dead as well as their reanimator: a rogue scientist named Wrede Sartarius who is either a madman or a genius ahead of his time, capable of bringing to life the recently deceased using "fluids" obtained from anonymous street urchins held captive in his lair. Major scenes are set at the municipal waterworks, the holding reservoir into which flows Manhattan's water supply from upstate. In this novel, explains Luc Sante in the *New York Review of Books,* the waterworks facility "is identified with the machinery of civilization, a matter of considerable ambiguity. It is both the locus of possibly nefarious deeds and a marvel of engineering no less impressive today than it was then. Within its precincts Sartorius carries out his experiments, which are futuristic and quaint, morally questionable and straightforwardly inquisitive." Paul Gray, in *Time,* finds *The Waterworks* "an entertaining and sometimes truly haunting story." In the *Spectator,* John Whitworth calls *The Waterworks* "a marvelous book," a novel "of the prelapsarian state, a late 19th-century novel, something out of Conrad and James, out of Stevenson and Wells and Conan Doyle."

BIOGRAPHICAL/CRITICAL SOURCES:

BOOKS

Concise Dictionary of American Literary Biography: Broadening Views, 1968-1988, Gale (Detroit), 1989.
Contemporary Literary Criticism, Gale, Volume 6, 1976; Volume 11, 1979; Volume 15, 1980; Volume 18, 1981; Volume 37, 1986; Volume 44, 1987; Volume 65, 1991.
Dictionary of Literary Biography, Volume 2: *American Novelists since World War II,* 1978; Volume 28: *Twentieth-Century American-Jewish Fiction Writers,* 1984.
Dictionary of Literary Biography Yearbook: 1980, Gale, 1981.
Johnson, Diane, *Terrorists and Novelists,* Knopf, 1982.
Levine, Paul, *E. L. Doctorow,* Methuen, 1985.
Morris, Christopher, *Models of Misrepresentation: On the Fiction of E. L. Doctorow,* University Press of Mississippi, 1991.
Parks, John, *E. L. Doctorow,* Continuum, 1991.
Tokarczyk, Michelle, and E. L. Doctorow, *E. L. Doctorow: An Annotated Bibliography,* Garland, 1988.
Trenner, Richard, editor, *E. L. Doctorow: Essays and Conversations,* Ontario Review Press, 1983.

Williams, John, *Fiction as False Document: The Reception of E.L. Doctorow in the Postmodern Age,* Camden House (Columbia), 1996.

PERIODICALS

American Literary History, summer, 1992.
American Studies, spring, 1992.
Atlanta Journal and Constitution, February 8, 1998.
Atlantic Monthly, September, 1980.
Booklist, October 1, 1994, p. 238.
Chicago Tribune, September 28, 1980.
Commentary, October, 1975; March, 1986.
Detroit Free Press, February 19, 1989.
Detroit News, November 10, 1985.
Drama, January, 1980.
Entertainment Weekly, June 17, 1994, p. 46.
Globe and Mail (Toronto), March 11, 1989.
Hudson Review, summer, 1986.
London Magazine, February, 1986.
Los Angeles Times Book Review, November 24, 1985; March 5, 1989.
Maclean's, July 25, 1994, p. 54.
Manchester Guardian, February 23, 1986.
Midwest Quarterly, autumn, 1983.
The Nation, June 2, 1979; September 27, 1980; November 17, 1984; November 30, 1985; April 3, 1989; June 6, 1994.
National Review, August 15, 1975; March 14, 1986.
New Leader, December 16-30, 1985.
New Republic, June 5, 1971; July 5, 1975; September 6, 1975; September 20, 1980; December 3, 1984; July 18, 1994, p. 44.
New Statesman, June 17, 1994, p. 40.
Newsweek, June 7, 1971; July 14, 1975; November 4, 1985.
New York, September 29, 1980; November 25, 1985.
New Yorker, December 9, 1985; June 27, 1994, p. 41.
New York Herald Tribune, January 22, 1961.
New York Review of Books, August 7, 1975; December 19, 1985; June 23, 1994, p. 12.
New York Times, August 4, 1978; November 24, 1978; September 12, 1980; November 6, 1984; October 31, 1985; February 9, 1989; July 8, 1994.
New York Times Book Review, September 25, 1960; July 4, 1971; July 6, 1975; September 28, 1980; December 6, 1984; November 10, 1985; February 26, 1989; June 19, 1994, p. 1.
Partisan Review, fall, 1972.
People, March 20, 1989; July 4, 1994, p. 28.
Progressive, March, 1986.
Publishers Weekly, June 30, 1975; June 27, 1994, p. 51.
Saturday Review, July 17, 1971; July 26, 1975; September, 1980.
South Atlantic Quarterly, winter, 1982.
Southwest Review, autumn, 1977.
Spectator, May 28, 1994, p. 33.
Time, July 14, 1975; September 22, 1980; December 18, 1985; June 20, 1994, p. 66.
Times Literary Supplement, February 14, 1986.
Village Voice, July 7, 1975; August 4, 1975; December 4, 1978; November 26, 1985.
Wall Street Journal, February 7, 1986.
Washington Post, March 9, 1998.
Washington Post Book World, July 13, 1975; September 28, 1980; November 11, 1984; November 17, 1985; February 19, 1989.

DOMECQ, H(onorio) Bustos
See BIOY CASARES, Adolfo
See BORGES, Jorge Luis

*   *   *

DOMINI, Rey
See LORDE, Audre (Geraldine)

*   *   *

DOMINIQUE
See PROUST, (Valentin-Louis-George-Eugene-) Marcel

*   *   *

DONLEAVY, J(ames) P(atrick) 1926-

PERSONAL: Born April 23, 1926, in Brooklyn, NY; became Irish citizen, 1967; married Valerie Heron (divorced); married Mary Wilson Price, 1970 (divorced); children: (first marriage) Philip, Karen; (second marriage) Rebecca Wallis, Rory. *Education:* Attended Trinity College, Dublin.

ADDRESSES: Home and office— Levington Park, Mullingar, County Westmeath, Ireland.

CAREER: Writer and playwright. Founder with son Philip Donleavy and producer Robert Mitchell of De Alfonce Tennis Association for the Promotion of the Superlative Game of Eccentric Champions. *Military service:* U.S. Navy, served in World War II.

AWARDS, HONORS: Most Promising Playwright Award, *Evening Standard,* 1960, for *Fairy Tales of New York;* Brandeis University Creative Arts Award, 1961-62, for two plays, *The Ginger Man* and *Fairy Tales of New York;* citation from National Institute and American Academy of Arts and Letters, 1975; American Academy of Arts and Letters grantee, 1975; Worldfest Houston Gold Award, 1992; Cine Golden Eagle Award for writer and narrator, 1993.

WRITINGS:

FICTION

The Ginger Man (novel; also see below), Olympia Press (Paris), 1955, published with introduction by Arland Ussher, Spearman (London), 1956, Obolensky (New York City), 1958, complete and unexpurgated edition, Delacorte (New York City), 1965.
A Singular Man (novel), Little, Brown (Boston), 1963.
Meet My Maker the Mad Molecule (short stories; also see below), Little, Brown, 1964.
The Saddest Summer of Samuel S (novel; also see below), Delacorte/Seymour Lawrence (New York City), 1966.
The Beastly Beatitudes of Balthazar B (novel), Delacorte/Seymour Lawrence, 1968.
The Onion Eaters (novel), Delacorte, 1971, Penguin/Eyre & Spottiswoode (Andover, England), 1986.
A Fairy Tale of New York (novel; also see below), Delacorte/Seymour Lawrence, 1973.

The Destinies of Darcy Dancer, Gentleman (novel), illustrations by Jim Campbell, Delacorte/Seymour Lawrence, 1977.

Schultz (novel), Delacorte/Seymour Lawrence, 1979.

"Meet My Maker the Mad Molecule" and "The Saddest Summer of Samuel S," Dell (New York City), 1979.

Leila: Further in the Destinies of Darcy Dancer, Gentleman (novel; sequel to *The Destinies of Darcy Dancer, Gentleman*), Delacorte/Seymour Lawrence, 1983, published as limited edition with *A Special Message for the First Edition from J. P. Donleavy,* Franklin Library, 1983, published in England as *Leila: Further in the Life and Destinies of Darcy Dancer, Gentleman,* Allen Lane (London), 1983.

Are You Listening Rabbi Loew (novel; sequel to *Schultz*), Viking (New York City), 1987.

That Darcy, That Dancer, That Gentleman (novel; sequel to *Leila*), Viking, 1990.

The Lady Who Liked Clean Rest Rooms: The Chronicle of One of the Strangest Stories Ever to Be Rumored about around New York (novella), St. Martin's (New York City), 1997.

PLAYS

The Ginger Man (adaptation of his novel of same title; first produced at Fortune Theatre, London, September 15, 1959; produced at Gaiety Theatre, Dublin, October 26, 1959; produced on Broadway at Orpheum Theatre, November 21, 1963; contains introduction "What They Did in Dublin"; also see below), Random House (New York City), 1961, published in England as *What They Did in Dublin with The Ginger Man,* MacGibbon and Kee (London), 1961 (also see below).

Fairy Tales of New York (adaptation of his novel *A Fairy Tale of New York*; first produced at Comedy Theatre, London, January 24, 1961; also see below), Random House, 1961.

A Singular Man (first produced at Comedy Theatre, October 21, 1964; produced at Westport County [CT] Playhouse, September 4, 1967; also see below), Bodley Head (London), 1964.

The Plays of J. P. Donleavy (with a preface by the author; contains *What They Did in Dublin with The Ginger Man, The Ginger Man, Fairy Tales of New York, A Singular Man,* and *The Saddest Summer of Samuel S*), photographs of productions by Lewis Morley, Delacorte/Seymour Lawrence, 1973.

The Beastly Beatitudes of Balthazar B (adaptation of his novel of same title), first produced in London, 1981.

Also author of radio play, *Helen,* 1956.

OTHER

The Unexpurgated Code: A Complete Manual of Survival and Manners, illustrations by the author, Delacorte/Seymour Lawrence, 1975.

De Alfonce Tennis: The Superlative Game of Eccentric Champions, Its History, Accoutrements, Rules, Conduct, and Regimen, Dutton (New York City)/Seymour Lawrence, 1984.

J. P. Donleavy's Ireland: In All Her Sins and in Some of Her Graces, Viking, 1986, published in England as *Ireland: In All Her Sins and in Some of Her Graces,* M. Joseph (London), 1986.

A Singular Country, Ryan (Peterborough, England), 1989, Norton (New York City), 1990.

The History of the Ginger Man, Houghton (Boston), 1994.

Contributor of short fiction and essays to *Atlantic Monthly, Playboy, Queen, Saturday Evening Post,* and *Saturday Review.*

SIDELIGHTS: "If there is an archetypal post-World War II American writer-in-exile it may well be James Patrick Donleavy," writes William E. Grant in a *Dictionary of Literary Biography* essay. The son of Irish immigrant parents, J. P. Donleavy renounced the America of their dreams for an Ireland of his own, and became a citizen when Ireland granted tax-free status to its authors. Although literary success came several years after the publication of his stylistically innovative first novel, *The Ginger Man,* Donleavy is now internationally recognized for having written what many consider to be a modern classic.

Donleavy was resolved to achieve recognition and relates in a *Paris Review* interview with Molly McKaughan: "I realized that the only way you could ever tackle the world was to write something that no one could hold off, a book that would go everywhere, into everyone's hands. And I decided then to write a novel which would shake the world. I shook my fist and said I would do it." That novel, *The Ginger Man,* is set in post-World War II Dublin and details the hedonistic existence of Sebastian Dangerfield who, according to Alfred Rushton in the Toronto *Globe and Mail,* gave "moral turpitude a new lease on life." While still a student, Donleavy began crafting the novel, but he returned to New York to complete and publish it. He indicates in the *Paris Review* that Scribners, to whom he first took the manuscript, thought it was one of the best ever brought to them; its content, however, prevented them from publishing it. Forty-five publishers rejected the novel because they "thought it was a dirty book—scatological, unreadable, obscene," Donleavy tells David Remnick in the *Washington Post.* "My life literally depended on getting this book into print, and when I couldn't, it just drove me out of America." Despite "the potential for literary damage, publication by Olympia Press had the generally salutary effect of establishing the unexpurgated edition of *The Ginger Man* as an underground classic before complete editions became available," notes Grant.

In 1994 Donleavy's *The History of the Ginger Man* was published. In the book Donleavy chronicles his efforts to publish *The Ginger Man* and recounts his struggles to become a writer while supporting his family. The author also reprints his entire correspondence with Olympia Press publisher Maurice Girodias, with whom Donleavy waged a protracted battle for the rights to the novel. Even before the publication of *The History of the Ginger Man,* critics recognized the autobiographical aspects of Donleavy's best-known novel. Sally Eckhoff, writing in the *Voice Literary Supplement,* observes: "In Dangerfield, Donleavy created his prototypical diver into Irish society. Like his hero, the author has a history of Olympic pub-crawling—right down there under the rug with Flann O'Brien." Eckhoff also notes that Donleavy's writing exhibits a strong sense of setting. "Most of *The Ginger Man,*" writes Eckhoff, "takes place in Dublin—the world of dreams, populated by gullible shopkeepers, screaming kids, crooked priests, affectionate laundrywomen with time on their hands, and a pub on every corner with a weird name like 'The Bleeding Horse.'"

Despite the commercial success of Donleavy's subsequent work, the critics generally consider his reputation to rest solely on *The Ginger Man.* "So far as most critics and reviewers are concerned, the later works have been but pale shadows of the first brilliant success, and the publication of each succeeding novel has seen a decline in critical attention," writes Grant. Some critics believe that Donleavy has run out of ideas, that he is refurbishing old material, reworking or resurrecting earlier work. For instance, in a *Harper's* review of *The Destinies of Darcy Dancer, Gentleman,* Michael Malone compares a Donleavy book to Guinness stout:

"It's distinctive, it's carbonated, it's brimmed with what Hazlitt called 'gusto,' and those who like it can drink it forever. The ingredients never change."

According to Grant, the themes of love and loss are also important in much of Donleavy's work. *The Saddest Summer of Samuel S* is about an eminent literary figure in the United States who undergoes psychoanalysis in Vienna in order to live a more conventional life. Of this novel, Grant writes: "Longing for a love he has never had and cannot find because in spite of his need he cannot give, Samuel S is the victim of a life that cannot be lived over and a destiny that cannot be changed." The character, observes Grant, is withdrawn and "trapped in a life-in-death state of mind with neither belief nor passion to motivate him." Similarly, in *The Beastly Beatitudes of Balthazar B,* a novel that details the lonely life of a wealthy young man whose marriage collapses, the hero is "separated from those he loves . . . and seeks completion by loving others, a simple but impossible quest," says Shaun O'Connell in the *Nation.* Robert Scholes observes in the *Saturday Review* that although this "shy and gentle" character seeks love, "it proves elusive, even harder to keep than to find." And O'Connell sees in Donleavy "the joy of the artist who can embody his vision, however bleak, the self-certainty of the writer who can so eloquently move his hero to name his pain."

However, writing in the *Washington Post Book World* about Donleavy's *The Destinies of Darcy Dancer, Gentleman,* a novel in which a young aristocrat is thwarted in several of his attempts at love, Curt Suplee suggests that "Donleavy does not write novels so much as Oedipal fairy tales: semi-realistic fables in which the same patterns are obsessively reenacted. Invariably, a young man finds himself trapped in a society dominated by hostile father-figures and devoid of the uncritical comfort afforded by mothers. . . . Every time the young man attempts to assert his ego in this world, he fails or is beaten, and flees to succour—either to the manic medium of alcohol or the overt mother-surrogates who provide sex and self-esteem, for a while."

Focusing on the bawdy humor in Donleavy's work, critics sometimes fault it for what they consider to be gratuitously lewd language and a reliance upon sexual slapstick. A *Times Literary Supplement* reviewer of *The Onion Eaters,* for instance, states that "the scenes of violence and the sexual encounters suggest an attitude to the human body and its functions, weaknesses and pleasures, which is anything but tender, compassionate, or celebratory." The novel is about a young and handsome character named Clayton Claw Clever Clementine, who in addition to being somewhat freakishly over-endowed sexually, has inherited an Irish manor and must confront what a *New Statesman* contributor refers to as a "bizarre collection of servants and . . . an ever-growing crew of sex-obsessed weirdies." Guy Davenport finds in the *National Review* that "Donleavy is uninterruptedly bawdy, yet his obscenity is so grand and so open, that it rises above giving offense into a realm of its own, unchallenged and wild."

Writing in *Newsweek* about Donleavy's nonfiction book *The Unexpurgated Code: A Complete Manual of Survival and Manners,* Arthur Cooper describes Donleavy's humor: "Like Mel Brooks, he knows that bad taste is merely a joke that doesn't get a laugh. And like Brooks, Donleavy's demonic humor is utterly democratic, thrusting the needle into everyone regardless of race, creed, color, or ability to control one's bowels." Referring to the book as "a collection of bilious and often funny rules for living," Melvin Maddocks observes in *Time* that "between the lines, Donleavy's diatribes manage to say more." Maddocks believes

that Donleavy's "visions of grace, chivalry and order" reveal the author as "an inverted romantic, profoundly sad beneath his disguise because he and the world are no better than they happen to be."

Similarly, in a *Midwest Quarterly* assessment of *The Unexpurgated Code,* Charles G. Masinton suggests that "Donleavy normally proceeds by means of instinct, inspiration, and intuition—the tools of a romantic artist. He aims to produce belly laughs and . . . a sympathetic response to his chief characters; he does not set out to impose order and rationality on experience. And instead of elevated language (which he often parodies quite effectively), he records with great skill an earthy vernacular full of both comic and lyric possibilities." While Grant believes that Donleavy's "characteristic tone of pessimism, melancholia, alienation, and human failure . . . suggest Jonathan Swift's misanthropic humor," he also finds it reminiscent of Mark Twain's later work, "which combines pessimism and humor in an elegiac, melancholic, and misanthropic voice."

Another point of interest for critics of Donleavy's writing is the effect that leaving the United States for Ireland has had on the author. Grant believes that "Donleavy remains essentially the exile who once wrote of America, 'there it goes, a runaway horse, with no one in control.' " Donleavy recalls in his *Atlantic Monthly* essay, that "each time you arrive anew in America, you find how small you are and how dismally you impress against the giantness and power of this country where you are so obviously, and with millions like yourself, so totally fatally expendable." Grant notes that this vision is often expressed in Donleavy's portrayal of the United States as a nightmare. In *A Fairy Tale of New York,* for instance, the wife of the Brooklyn-born, Bronx-raised, and European-educated Cornelius Christian dies on their way to New York; and without money or friends, Christian is taken advantage of by everyone. "Affection, loathing, nostalgia and fear are the main components of the attitude he brings to bear upon his native place," writes Julian Moynahan in the *Washington Post Book World,* adding that "hidden away in the book for those who can find it is a good deal of personal revelation, a good deal of alembicated and metamorphosed autobiography." As D. Keith Mano states in the *New York Times Book Review,* the book is "about social impotence and despair. Valleys of humiliation, sloughs of despond." The story focuses on the brutality of New York City; and Christian, who lacks the funds to move, sees emigration as the only answer to his liberation. "Yet Donleavy's thunderous, superb humor has the efficacy of grace," says Mano. "It heals and conquers and ratifies." And a *Times Literary Supplement* contributor, who remarks that "few writers know how to enjoy verbal promiscuity like . . . Donleavy," considers that "it is largely because of the confidence of the style, too, that you come out of the welter of failure and misery feeling good— nastiness is inevitably laced with hilarity and sentiment in his telling it."

John Kelly writes in the *Times Literary Supplement* that "during a disconsolate return to his native America," Donleavy discovered that "Ireland is a state of mind" and his recent *J. P. Donleavy's Ireland: In All Her Sins and Some of Her Graces* "attempts a description of that state of mind." Donleavy recreates his own first exposure to the postwar Dublin that, says Kelly, provided the "raw material" for "Donleavy's myth-making imagination." In a Toronto *Globe and Mail* review of the book, Rushton thinks that "Donleavy belongs to the people he describes, and acknowledges their kinship by giving them their full due." As Kevin E. Gallagher comments in the *Los Angeles Times Book Review,* it is "a love story that, I think never ends for anyone who cares, like this, about a place."

Although Donleavy's *The Ginger Man* remains the standard by which the entirety of his work is measured, his writing has generated the full spectrum of critical response. Ken Lawless in an *Antioch Review* of *The Destinies of Darcy Dancer, Gentleman,* for example, writes that "no literary artist working in English today is better than J. P. Donleavy, and few merit comparison with him." On the other hand, in the *New York Times Book Review,* Geoffrey Wolff reacts to similar critical assessments of Donleavy's work with: "Nonsense. He is an Irish tenor who sets his blarney to short songs that are sometimes as soft as velvet or good stout, sometimes plangent, elliptical and coarse." However, Grant suggests that "at the very least, he represents the example of a writer who goes very much his own way, eschewing both the popular success of the best-sellers and the literary acclaim of the academic establishment. At best, a case can be made for a few of his novels as primary expressions within the black humorist tradition of modern literature. Certainly he is a foremost American exponent of the Kafkaesque vision of the modern world, and his better works strongly express that sense of universal absurdity at which we can only laugh."

BIOGRAPHICAL/CRITICAL SOURCES:

BOOKS

Contemporary Literary Criticism, Gale (Detroit), Volume 1, 1973; Volume 4, 1975; Volume 6, 1976; Volume 10, 1979; Volume 45, 1987.
Dictionary of Literary Biography, Volume 6: *American Novelists since World War II,* Gale, 1980.
Hassan, Ihab, *Radical Innocence: Studies in the Contemporary American Novel,* Princeton University Press (Princeton, NJ), 1961.
Masinton, Charles G., *J. P. Donleavy: The Style of His Sadness and Humor,* Popular Press, 1975.
Podhoretz, Norman, *Doings and Undoings,* Farrar, Straus (New York City), 1964.
Sharma, R. K., *Isolation and Protest: A Case Study of J. P. Donleavy's Fiction,* Ajanta (New Delhi), 1983.

PERIODICALS

America, May 3, 1969; May 10, 1980.
Antioch Review, winter, 1978; winter, 1980, p. 122.
Atlantic Monthly, December, 1968; December, 1976; December, 1977; June, 1979.
Books, November, 1987, p. 29.
Chicago Tribune, May 25, 1958; May 19, 1985.
Chicago Tribune Book World, October 28, 1979.
Commonweal, August 15, 1958; December 2, 1966; March 7, 1969; September 14, 1990, p. 518.
Contemporary Literature, Volume 12, number 3, 1971.
Critique: Studies in Modern Fiction, Volume 9, number 2, 1966; Volume 12, number 3, 1971; Volume 17, number 1, 1975.
Detroit News, October 2, 1983; June 9, 1985.
Economist, November 10, 1973.
Gentleman's Quarterly, April, 1994, p. 88.
Globe and Mail (Toronto), October 13, 1984; January 17, 1987; April 18, 1987.
Harper's, December, 1977.
Listener, May 11, 1978; December 13, 1984, p. 30; October 29, 1987, p. 32; November 2, 1989, p. 35; November 1, 1990, p. 34.
Los Angeles Times, October 28, 1983.

Los Angeles Times Book Review, October 7, 1979; May 5, 1985, p. 11; November 16, 1986, p. 11; November 13, 1988, p. 7; May 1, 1994, p. 8.
Midwest Quarterly, winter, 1977.
Nation, May 24, 1958; December 14, 1963; January 20, 1969.
National Review, October 18, 1971.
New Leader, December 19, 1977.
New Republic, December 14, 1963; March 1, 1969; July 24, 1971; December 15, 1979.
New Statesman, April 17, 1964; February 7, 1969; July 16, 1971; May 12, 1978; March 28, 1980, p. 483; October 14, 1983.
Newsweek, November 11, 1963; March 21, 1966; November 18, 1968; September 15, 1975.
New Yorker, October 25, 1958; May 16, 1964; October 15, 1966; October 8, 1973; December 19, 1977; July 16, 1990.
New York Herald Tribune Book Review, May 11, 1958.
New York Review of Books, January 2, 1969.
New York Times, May 11, 1958; November 16, 1979; April 17, 1987; October 12, 1988.
New York Times Book Review, November 24, 1963; November 7, 1965; December 5, 1965; March 20, 1966; December 29, 1968; September 5, 1971; September 23, 1973; November 6, 1977; October 7, 1979, p. 14; October 26, 1980; October 11, 1983; October 30, 1983; April 28, 1985, p. 24; November 27, 1988, p. 22; March 4, 1990, p. 38; December 2, 1990, p. 72.
Observer (London), October 28, 1984, p. 25; July 6, 1986, p. 24; November 8, 1987, p.28; November 4, 1990, p. 61.
Paris Review, fall, 1975.
Playboy, May, 1994, p. 34.
Publishers Weekly, October 31, 1986.
Punch, October 21, 1987, p. 64.
Saturday Review, May 10, 1958; November 23, 1963; November 23, 1968; November 12, 1977; January 20, 1979.
Spectator, September 22, 1973; May 13, 1978; April 12, 1980; December 8, 1984, p. 33; July 19, 1986, p. 29; November 28, 1987, p. 36.
Time, March 18, 1966; December 6, 1968; July 5, 1971; October 29, 1973; September 22, 1975; November 14, 1977; October 15, 1979.
Times (London), October 13, 1983; July 17, 1986, p. 15; October 29, 1987.
Times Literary Supplement, April 30, 1964; May 6, 1965; May 5, 1967; March 20, 1969; July 23, 1971; September 7, 1973; May 12, 1978; April 4, 1980, p. 382; October 28, 1983, p. 1185; November 16, 1984, p. 1302; December 19, 1986, p. 1433; February 1, 1991, p. 10; June 24, 1994, p. 36.
Tribune Books (Chicago), January 25, 1987, p. 6; October 2, 1988, p. 7; June 5, 1994, p. 5.
Twentieth Century Literature, January, 1968; July, 1972.
Village Voice, September 17, 1979.
Virginia Quarterly Review, spring, 1987, p. 56.
Voice Literary Supplement, October, 1988, p. 28.
Washington Post, October 30, 1979; February 24, 1985.
Washington Post Book World, September 30, 1973; November 13, 1977.
World Literature Today, summer, 1978; summer, 1980, p. 431; spring, 1984.
Yale Review, October, 1966.

DONOSO, Jose 1924-1996
(Jose Donoso Yanez)

PERSONAL: Born October 5, 1924, in Santiago, Chile; son of
Jose Donoso (a physician) and Alicia Yanez; died December 7,
1996; married Maria del Pilar Serrano (a translator), 1961.
Education: Attended University of Chile, beginning in 1947;
Princeton University, A.B., 1951.

ADDRESSES: Home—Galvarino Gallardo 1747, Santiago, 9
Chile.

CAREER: Writer, journalist, and translator. Shepherd in southern
Chile, 1945-46; dockhand in Buenos Aires, Argentina, c. 1946;
Kent School, Santiago, Chile, English teacher, c. 1953; Catholic
University of Chile, Santiago, professor of conversational English,
beginning in 1954; worked in Buenos Aires, 1958-60; *Ercilla*
(weekly newsmagazine), Santiago, journalist with assignments in
Europe, beginning in 1960, editor and literary critic, beginning in
1962; University of Chile, Santiago, lecturer at school of
journalism, beginning in 1962; *Siempre* (periodical), Mexico City,
Mexico, literary critic, 1965; University of Iowa, Dubuque,
teacher of writing and modern Spanish American literature at
Writers' Workshop, 1965-67; Colorado State University, Fort
Collins, teacher, 1969.

AWARDS, HONORS: Santiago Municipal Short Story Prize, 1955,
for *Veraneo y otros cuentos*; Chile-Italia Prize for journalism,
1960; William Faulkner Foundation Prize, 1962, for *Coronacion*;
Guggenheim awards, 1968 and 1973; Critics Award for best novel
in Spanish, 1979, for *Casa de campo*; National Literature Prize,
Chile, 1990; Woodrow Wilson Fellow, 1992.

WRITINGS:

Veraneo y otros cuentos (title means "Summertime and Other
Stories,") privately printed (Santiago, Chile), 1955.
Dos cuentos (title means "Two Stories"), Guardia Vieja, 1956.
Coronacion (novel), Nascimento, 1957, Seix Barral, 1981, trans-
lation by Jocasta Goodwin, published as *Coronation,* Knopf,
1965.
El charleston (short stories; title means "The Charleston"),
Nascimento, 1960.
Los mejores cuentos de Jose Donoso (short stories; title means
"The Best Stories of Jose Donoso"), Zig-Zag, 1965.
Este domingo (novel), Zig-Zag, 1965, translation by Lorraine
O'Grady Freeman, published as *This Sunday,* Knopf, 1967.
El lugar sin limites (novella; title means "The Place Without
Limits"), J. Moritz (Mexico), 1966; translation by Suzanne
Jill Levine and Hallie D. Taylor, published as *Hell Has No
Limits* in *Triple Cross,* Dutton, 1972.
(Editor with William A. Henkin and others) *The Tri-Quarterly
Anthology of Contemporary Latin American Literature,*
Dutton, 1969.
El obsceno pajaro de la noche (novel), Seix Barral, 1970,
translation by Hardie St. Martin and Leonard Mades,
published as *The Obscene Bird of Night,* Knopf, 1973.
Cuentos (title means "Stories"), Seix Barral, 1971, translation by
Andree Conrad, published as *Charleston and Other Stories,*
David Godine, 1977.
Historia personal del "boom" (memoir), Anagrama (Barcelona),
1972, translation by Gregory Kolovakos, published as *The
Boom in Spanish American Literature: A Personal History,*
Columbia University Press, 1977.

Tres novelitas burguesas (title means "Three Bourgeois Novellas"), Seix Barral, 1973, translation by Andree Conrad,
published as *Sacred Families: Three Novellas,* Knopf, 1977.
Casa de campo (novel), Seix Barral, 1978, translation by David
Pritchard and Suzanne Jill Levine, published as *A House in
the Country,* Knopf, 1984.
El jardin de al lado (novel; title means "The Garden Next Door"),
Seix Barral, 1981.
La misteriosa desparicion de la Marquesita de Loria (novel; title
means "The Mysterious Disappearance of the Young Mar-
chioness of Loria"), Seix Barral, 1981.
Poemas de un novelista (poems), Ganymedes (Santiago), 1981.
Cuatro para Delfina (novellas; title means "Four for Delfina"),
Seix Barral, 1982.
La desesperanza (novel; title means "Despair"), Seix Barral,
1986, translation by Alfred MacAdam, published as *Curfew,*
Weidenfeld & Nicolson, 1988.
(Contributor) Doris Meyer, editor, *Lives on the Line: The
Testimony of Contemporary Latin American Authors,* Uni-
versity of California Press, 1988.
Taratuta; Naturaleza muerta con cachimba (novellas), Mondadori
(Madrid), 1990; translation by Gregory Rabassa, published as
Taratuta; and, Still Life with Pipe: Two Novellas, W. W.
Norton (New York City), 1993.

Translator into Spanish of numerous works, including *The Life of
Sir Arthur Conan Doyle* by John Dickson Carr and *Last Tales* by
Isak Dinesen, and, with wife, Maria del Pilar Serrano, of *The
Scarlet Letter* by Nathaniel Hawthorne and *Les Personnages* by
Francoise Malet-Joris. Contributor of articles and short stories to
periodicals, including *Americas, mss.* (Princeton University), and
Review.

SIDELIGHTS: "I fear simplification more than anything," said
Chilean novelist Jose Donoso in *Partisan Review.* Donoso's
novels, noted for their complexity and insistent pessimism, seem
to embody his observation that life, society, and writing are each
an "adventure into [a] mad, dark thing." Donoso has often been
ranked among the finest Latin American authors of the twentieth
century; he has been hailed as a master by Mexican novelist
Carlos Fuentes and Spanish filmmaker Luis Bunuel, two of his
most renowned contemporaries. "He is an extraordinarily sophisticated writer," wrote *Newsweek*'s Walter Clemons, "in perfect
control of time dissolves, contradictory voices, gritty realism and
hallucinatory fugues."

Donoso was born into a family that kept a tenuous foothold in
Chile's respectable upper middle class. His father "was a young
physician more addicted to horse racing and to playing cards than
to his profession," the author recalled in *Review.* His mother, who
"somehow coped," came from "the ne'er-do-well branch of a
nouveau riche family." The father used family connections to get
a newspaper job, but he was fired; thereafter he became house
physician to three decrepit great-aunts whose fortunes he hoped to
inherit. When the aunts died, the Donosos inherited nothing. But
soon they were sheltering other relatives, including an irresponsible uncle and Donoso's grandmother, who lived with the family
for ten years while slowly succumbing to insanity. "The gradual
process of [my grandmother's] deterioration, intertwined with
lightning flashes of memory and family lore . . . is one of the
episodes that has most marked my life," Donoso declared, "not
because I loved this old woman but because her madness brought
the ironies of family life and the horrors of aging and dying so
cruelly into focus." He became a high-school truant and then a
dropout, associating with bums and spending a year as a shepherd

in the remote grasslands of southern Chile. In his early twenties he returned home and resumed his education, rejecting the traditional careers open to "an upper middle-class boy" by becoming an undergraduate English major.

Donoso describes his literary development in the memoir *Historia personal del "boom"* (*The Boom in Spanish American Literature: A Personal History*). The book introduces readers to one of the most renowned periods in Spanish American Literature—the "Boom," a flowering of literary activity during the 1960s—by showing its relationship to Donoso's own life. As an aspiring author in the 1950s, Donoso relates in his memoir, he shared with other young writers throughout Latin America the sense of being "asphyxiated" by the provincial cultural environment of his native land. Great authors of the past such as Mexico's Manuel Azuela, who saw the novel as a practical way to discuss contemporary social problems, seemed to members of Donoso's generation like "statues in a park." The earnest, simple style that such "grandfathers" had made popular seemed to rob the novel of creativity and expressiveness. The region's publishers, too poor to take risks on new talent, preferred to reprint literary classics and popular foreign works; accordingly, Donoso and his peers had difficulty getting published, often had to sell copies of their books on their own, and found it difficult to obtain each others' work in print.

In his first novel, *Coronacion* (*Coronation*), Donoso combined traditional realism with the more complex personal vision that would emerge in his later works. The book's main character is an affluent old woman who lives with her servants in a mansion; her vivid delusions and curses frighten her grandson, a repressed middle-aged bachelor. The old woman, Donoso admitted, is a portrait of his insane grandmother, and some relatives were indignant at the resemblance. Reviewers in Chile praised *Coronation* as a realistic depiction of that country's society, especially, recalled Donoso in *The Boom,* "the decadence of the upper class." Wishing to transcend realism, Donoso found such praise frustrating. The resolution of the novel, he suggested, was designed to challenge traditional literary style. The book's climax largely abandons the restraints of realism by dwelling on madness and the grotesque. The old woman, costumed and crowned by her maids during a drunken prank, dies convinced she has already gone to heaven. The grandson, confronting his mortality and his unfulfilling life, concludes that God himself must have been mad to create such a world and then follows his grandmother into insanity. *Coronation* brought Donoso an international reputation and won the 1962 William Faulkner Foundation Prize, established in Faulkner's will to encourage the translation of outstanding Latin American fiction into English.

Donoso's second novel, *Este domingo* (*This Sunday*), with its themes of upper-class decay and incipient chaos, has often been likened to *Coronation*. Many reviewers considered the later work a significant advance for Donoso, showing greater subtlety, impact, and stylistic sophistication. "As Donoso sees it," wrote Alexander Coleman in the *New York Times Book Review,* "the rich are different because they cannot live without the underworld of the poor to exploit and command." Don Alvaro is an affluent, middle-aged professional who has grown up weak and ineffective, but has kept a sense of virility by making a chambermaid his mistress. His wife Chepa, who has an obsessive need to minister to others, becomes the domineering patroness to a paroled murderer still drawn toward a life of crime. The novel's climax occurs when Chepa, unhappy with the parolee's conduct, seeks him out in the slum where he lives; she is hounded by poor neighborhood children and collapses on a trash heap. Throughout

the book Donoso experiments with differing points of view, showing parts of the story through the eyes of its obsessive participants, and part through the eyes of a young relative of Alvaro, too naive to understand the underlying brutality of the world around him. Noting Donoso's "cool and biting intelligence," Coleman praised the author's "perfect balance between compulsion and control as he exorcises his infernally driven characters."

Donoso delved much further into obsession and fantasy with his novella *El lugar sin limites* (*Hell Has No Limits*), written at about the same time as *This Sunday*. The work is set in an isolated small town owned by Don Alejo, a powerful, all-knowing, selfish aristocrat whom many reviewers saw as the satirical embodiment of an unfeeling God. The main character is Manuela, whose delusions about being a lithe, young female dancer are lavishly echoed by the story's narration; in fact, however, Manuela is an aging male transvestite who works as a dancer in his daughter's bordello and uses fantasy to transcend his absurd existence. The story culminates in violence when Pancho, a virile male truck driver attracted to Manuela, lashes out against his own underlying homosexuality by savagely assaulting the transvestite. Biographer George McMurray considered *Hell Has No Limits* a powerful comment on the futility of human aspirations, so pessimistic as to approach nihilism. The author's intentions, McMurray explained, "are to undermine traditional values, reveal the bankruptcy of reason, and jar the reader onto new levels of awareness by exposing the other side of reality."

When *El obsceno pajaro de la noche* (*The Obscene Bird of Night*) finally emerged in 1970, reviewers found it both masterful and indescribable—"How do you review a dream?" asked Wolfgang Luchtig in *Books Abroad*. The novel is narrated by Humberto, an unsuccessful writer who becomes the retainer to a decaying aristocratic family and the tutor of their only son and heir. The child, monstrously deformed, is seen by his father as an emblem of chaos and is surrounded by freaks so that he will seem "normal." Eventually Humberto apparently flees to one of the family's charitable ventures—a decrepit convent that houses some of society's castoff women, ranging from the elderly to young orphans. Throughout the novel past and present are confusingly intermingled, and characters undergo bizarre transformations, sometimes melting into one another. Humberto appears as a deaf-mute servant in the convent; is apparently transformed into a baby by the old women, who often seem to be witches; and is finally sealed in a bundle of rags and thrown onto a fire, where he turns to ashes as the book ends.

Until the 1980s Donoso continued to reside primarily in Spain. After he finished *The Obscene Bird of Night,* his writing began to change: his style became less hallucinatory and his narratives were less concerned with the Chilean aristocracy. Some of his work was set in Spain, including *Tres novelitas burguesas* (*Sacred Families*), novellas that portray that country's upper middle class with a blend of fantasy and social satire, and *El jardin de al lado* (*The Garden Next Door*), which features a novelist-in-exile who is haunted by his past. Throughout his years in Spain, Donoso reported in *Lives on the Line,* he found it impossible to cut his emotional ties to Chile. He did not feel nostalgia, he continued, but rather "the *guilt of absence*" or the "guilt of not being connected with action." His dilemma was heightened because he remained abroad by choice while Pinochet established his dictatorship. "All of us who lived abroad during that period who didn't have to," he explained in *Vogue,* "have a terrible feeling of guilt" because "we didn't share in the history of Chile during a very important time."

In the mid-1970s Donoso resolved to discuss Chile's turmoil in a novel, which became *Casa de campo* (*A House in the Country*). Aware that he was cut off from the daily life of Chileans—including the way they spoke—he wrote about them indirectly, creating what reviewers called a political allegory. Once more Donoso set his book in an aristocratic household. When the estate's owners leave on an excursion, their children (perhaps representing the middle class) and exploited Indians from the surrounding area (perhaps the working class) take over and wreak havoc. They are led by an aristocratic uncle (Salvador Allende?) who may be insane or may be the victim of injustice at the hands of his relatives. When the owners return, they use servants to ruthlessly re-establish order and then proclaim—despite all the bitterness they have engendered—that nothing has changed since they first left. Though some reviewers faulted the novel for being too intellectual and emotionally detached, others found it highly relevant and involving. "The combination of literary grace, political urgency and a fierce and untethered imagination," wrote Charles Champlin in the *Los Angeles Times Book Review*, "give Donoso and *A House in the Country* the power of an aimed projectile."

By the mid-1980s Donoso had resettled in Chile, and in 1986 he produced a more direct study of life under Pinochet in the novel *La desesperanza* (*Curfew*). Though the book describes both Pinochet's torturers and the dispossessed poor, its principal focus is the country's well-educated, dispirited political left. The two main characters—a onetime revolutionary and a political folksinger who fled to Paris—share deep feelings of guilt because they were not punished as much by the regime as were other leftists. Their old comrades, meanwhile, seem paralyzed by infighting, didacticism, and bitterness. The book was highly praised by prominent American critics and, notably, by Jacobo Timerman, an Argentine journalist respected worldwide as an eloquent victim of political oppression. "Donoso is a moderate who has written a revolutionary novel," Timerman observed in *Vogue*; in *New Yorker* he wrote that "it is a relief, finally, to read a work of Chilean literature in which none of the characters are above history or appear to dominate it." *Curfew*, reviewers suggested, displays the deep personal flaws of leftists and rightists alike: by avoiding simple conclusions, the novel makes plain that Chile abounds in uncertainty and despair.

The two novellas in Donoso's *Taratuta; and, Still Life with Pipe* "immerse readers in the intriguing interplay between art and reality," noted Larsen Olszewski in *Library Journal*. In "Taratuta" the narrator, a novelist, seeks to learn more about Lenin by tracing an obscure Russian revolutionary named "Taratuta." But the quest remains uncompleted when Taratuta's descendent, whom the narrator hopes will shed light on the revolutionary, mysteriously disappears. In "Still Life with Pipe" a young man becomes obsessed with a forgotten Chilean artist and wrecks his own life in the process.

BIOGRAPHICAL/CRITICAL SOURCES:

BOOKS

Contemporary Literary Criticism, Gale (Detroit), Volume 4, 1975; Volume 8, 1978; Volume 11, 1979; Volume 32, 1985.

Forster, Merlin H., editor, *Tradition and Renewal: Essays on Twentieth-Century Latin American Literature and Culture,* University of Illinois Press, 1975.

Hispanic Literature Criticism, Gale, Volume 1, 1994.

MacAdam, Alfred J., *Modern Latin American Narratives: The Dreams of Reason,* University of Chicago Press, 1977.

McMurray, George R., *Jose Donoso,* Twayne, 1979.

Meyer, Doris, editor, *Lives on the Line: The Testimony of Contemporary Latin American Authors,* University of California Press, 1988.

Schwartz, Ronald, *Nomads, Exiles, and Emigres: The Rebirth of the Latin American Narrative, 1960-80,* Scarecrow Press, 1980.

PERIODICALS

Americas, June 9, 1984; November/December, 1987, p. 8.

Atlanta Constitution, December 10, 1996

Book Forum, summer, 1977.

Booklist, December 15, 1992, p. 714.

Books Abroad, winter, 1968; winter, 1972; spring, 1972; spring, 1975.

Christian Science Monitor, June 27, 1973; June 2, 1988.

Commonweal, September 21, 1973; May 18, 1984.

Contemporary Literature, Volume 28, number 4, 1987.

Essays in Literature, spring, 1975.

Hispania, May, 1972.

Hudson Review, winter, 1978; winter, 1989.

Independent, December 14, 1996

Journal of Spanish Studies: Twentieth Century, winter, 1973.

Kirkus Reviews, November 15, 1992, p. 1393.

Library Journal, January, 1993, p. 168.

Los Angeles Times Book Review, February 5, 1984; May 15, 1988.

Modern Fiction Studies, winter, 1978.

Nation, March 11, 1968; June 11, 1973; February 11, 1978.

New Leader, October 1, 1973.

New Statesman, June 18, 1965; March 1, 1974.

Newsweek, June 4, 1973.

New Yorker, June 16, 1973; April 30, 1984; November 2, 1987; June 13, 1988; August 16, 1993, p. 86; December 23, 1996.

New York Review of Books, April 19, 1973; December 13, 1973; August 4, 1977; July 18, 1985.

New York Times Book Review, March 14, 1965; November 26, 1967; December 24, 1972; June 17, 1973; June 26, 1977; February 26, 1984; May 29, 1988.

Partisan Review, fall, 1974; number 1, 1982; number 2, 1986.

PMLA, January, 1978.

Pregonero, July 10, 1997.

Publishers Weekly, November 30, 1992, p. 30.

Punch, 1977.

Review, fall, 1973, January-May, 1984.

Revista de Estudios Hispanicos, January, 1975.

Saturday Review, March 13, 1965; December 9, 1967; January 23, 1971; July 2, 1971; February 10, 1978; April 6, 1984.

Studies in Short Fiction, winter, 1971.

Time, April 23, 1965; July 30, 1973; June 27, 1977; February 20, 1984.

Time International, December 23, 1996.

Times Literary Supplement, July 1, 1965; October 12, 1967; February 22, 1968; April 18, 1984.

UNESCO Courier, July-August, 1994, p. 4.

Village Voice, March 27, 1984.

Vogue, May, 1988.

Washington Post Book World, May 27, 1973; August 14, 1977; February 26, 1984; May 22, 1988.

World Literature Today, autumn, 1977; spring, 1981; summer, 1982; winter, 1983.

DOOLITTLE, Hilda 1886-1961
(H. D., John Helforth)

PERSONAL: Born September 19, 1886, in Bethlehem, PA; died of a heart attack, September 27, 1961, in Zurich, Switzerland; daughter of Charles Leander (a professor of mathematics and astronomy) and Helen Eugeneia (Woole) Doolittle; married Richard Aldington (a writer), October, 1913 (separated, 1919; divorced, 1938); children: Perdita (Mrs. John Schaffner). *Education:* Attended Bryn Mawr College, 1900-06.

CAREER: Poet, playwright, novelist, and translator. Literary editor of the *Egoist,* 1916-17; contributing editor of *Close-Up* (cinema journal), 1927-31. Actress with Paul Robeson in film "Borderline," c. 1930.

AWARDS, HONORS: Guarantors Prize from *Poetry,* 1915; Levinson Prize, 1938, and Harriet Monroe Memorial Prize, 1958, both for poetry published in *Poetry;* Brandeis University Creative Arts Medal, 1959, for lifetime of distinguished achievement; Award of Merit Medal for poetry from National Institute and American Academy of Arts and Letters, 1960.

WRITINGS:

UNDER NAME H. D.

Sea Garden (poems), Constable, 1916.

(Translator) *Choruses From the Iphigenia in Aulis by Euripides,* Clerk's Private Press, 1916.

The Tribute and Circe: Two Poems, Clerk's Private Press, 1917.

Hymen (poems), Holt, 1921.

Heliodora and Other Poems, Houghton, 1924.

Collected Poems of H. D., Boni & Liveright, 1925.

H. D. (poems), edited by Hugh Mearns, Simon & Schuster, 1926.

Palimpsest (novel), Houghton, 1926, revised edition, Southern Illinois University Press, 1968.

Hippolytus Temporizes: A Play in Three Acts, Houghton, 1927, revised, 1985.

Hedylus (novel), Houghton, 1928, revised edition, 1980.

Red Roses for Bronze (poems), Random House, 1929.

Borderline—A Pool Film with Paul Robeson, Mercury, 1930.

Kora and Ka (novel), Darantiere (Dijon, France), 1934, Bios, 1978.

The Usual Star (poems), Darantiere, 1934.

The Hedgehog (children's fiction), Brendin, 1936.

(Translator) Euripides, *Ion* (play), Houghton, 1937, revised, 1985.

What Do I Love? (poems), Brendin, 1944.

The Walls Do Not Fall (poems; also see below), Oxford University Press, 1944.

Tribute to the Angels (poems; also see below), Oxford University Press, 1945.

The Flowering of the Rod (poems; also see below), Oxford University Press, 1946.

By Avon River (poetry and prose), Macmillan, 1949, revised edition, 1986.

Tribute to Freud, with Unpublished Letters to Freud by the Author, Pantheon, 1956, enlarged edition, McGraw, 1975, 2nd edition published as *Tribute to Freud: Writing on the Wall,* New Directions, 1984.

Selected Poems, Grove, 1957.

Bid Me to Live: A Madrigal (novel), Grove, 1960, revised edition, 1983.

Helen in Egypt (poem), Grove, 1961.

Two Poems (originally published in *Life and Letters Today,* 1937), Arif, 1971.

Temple of the Sun, Arif, 1972.

Hermetic Definition, New Directions, 1972.

Trilogy: The Walls Do Not Fall, Tribute to the Angels, The Flowering of the Rod, New Directions, 1973.

The Poet and the Dancer (originally published in *Life and Letters Today,* December, 1935), Five Trees Press, 1975.

(Contributor) Eric Walter White, *Images of H. D.,* Enitharmon, 1976.

End to Torment: A Memoir of Ezra Pound, edited by Norman Holmes Pearson and Michael King, New Directions, 1979.

HERmione, New Directions, 1981, published as *Her,* Virago, 1984.

The Gift (memoir), New Directions, 1982.

Collected Poems 1912-1944, edited by Louis L. Martz, New Directions, 1983.

Notes on Thought and Vision and The Wise Sappho, City Lights Books, 1983.

Priest and A Dead Priestess Speaks (two poems), Copper Canyon Press, 1983.

Selected Poems, edited by Louis L. Martz, Carcanet Press, 1989.

Richard Aldington & H. D.: The Later Years in Letters, Manchester University Press (Manchester), 1995.

Between History and Poetry: The Letters of H. D. and Norman Holmes Pearson, edited by Donna Krolik Hollenberg, University of Iowa Press, 1997.

OTHER

(Under pseudonym John Helforth) *Nights,* Darantiere, 1935.

Work represented in anthologies, including *Des Imagistes: An Anthology,* edited by Ezra Pound, A. & C. Boni, 1914; *Some Imagist Poets: An Anthology,* edited by Amy Lowell, Houghton, 1915-17; *Contact Collection of Contemporary Writers,* edited by Robert McAlmon, Contact Editions, 1925. Contributor to *Poetry* and other periodicals. Translator of Euripides's *Hippolytus,* 1919. Collections of H. D.'s papers are housed at the Beinecke Library, Yale University.

SIDELIGHTS: As one of the founders of Imagism, Hilda Doolittle (known as H. D.) became known as much for her poetry as for her association with the group's distinguished writers. Yet her own stark and concrete poetry typified the demands of Imagism as set forth by Ezra Pound and a core of other avant-garde poets. By the mid-1920's, however, after a series of personal crises and the passing of the Imagist years, H. D. sought a more secluded life in Switzerland. But the events of her time—her psychoanalysis with Sigmund Freud, World War II, her advancing age and growing Christian faith—continued to be reflected in her writing. Although in many ways she wrote more productively and diversely than ever before, the influence she held early in her career has not been forgotten: H. D. remains known to many as "the perfect Imagist."

Clearly the most influential figure in H. D.'s early years was Ezra Pound. The two met when H. D. was fifteen, he sixteen, reported Melody Zajdel, and for a while were engaged—until H. D.'s father broke up the relationship. But they continued to share their love of literature, classical as well as modern, with Pound encouraging H. D. by bringing her "armfuls of books to read." Pound also introduced her to a close friend, William Carlos Williams. Pound, Williams, H. D., and her Bryn Mawr classmate, Marianne Moore, as undergraduates, were sharing the literary theories that would lead each of them to play a distinct role in changing the course of American poetry.

In 1906 H. D. left Bryn Mawr because of poor health. She continued to study on her own, though, and began to write seriously for the first time. When Pound left the United States for

Europe in 1908, publishing his first book in Venice and joining the literary circles in London, H. D. stayed behind, contributing poems, stories, and articles to a variety of newspapers and small journals.

H. D. fell under Pound's influence again in 1911. She had left on a summer vacation to Europe, where she eventually settled permanently, and met Pound in London. There she was introduced to many of his literary friends, among them Ford Maddox Ford, William Butler Yeats, F. S. Flint, and Richard Aldington. But Pound, at first, remained most influential: "I had never heard of *verse libre,*" H. D. recalled, "till I was 'discovered' by Ezra Pound. . . . I did a few poems that I don't think Ezra liked . . . , but later he was beautiful about my first authentic verses, . . . and sent my poems in for me to Miss Monroe [Harriet Monroe, editor of *Poetry* in Chicago]. He signed them for me 'H. D., Imagiste.'"

H. D., Pound, Flint, and Aldington formed the core of what became known as the Imagist movement. Living in Europe and publishing in the United States through *Poetry,* the group shaped the course of modern poetry. They abandoned the formalities of the poetry of the time as they set forth their Imagist tenets, calling for an economical verse in the language of common speech, composed "in sequence of the musical phrase, not in sequence of a metronome."

Though H. D. wrote in the Imagist mode throughout much of her career, the movement itself was short-lived. Pound, who by some accounts invented the school solely to bring attention to H. D.'s work, drifted away from the movement's center and was replaced by Amy Lowell. (Disgusted with Lowell's influence in the group, Pound then dubbed the school "Amygism.")

The highlight of H. D.'s personal life during these years was her relationship with fellow Imagist Richard Aldington. The two married in 1913, bonded by what Zajdel called a "mutual interest in classical literature, a mutual contempt of middle-class hypocrisy, and a mutual dedication to careers in poetry." They appeared to those around them as happy—Lowell thought them "a perfectly charming young couple"—but that joy was interrupted by World War I. Aldington went into service in 1916 while H. D. assumed his post as literary editor of the *Egoist.* Upon his return, however, their relationship began to deteriorate, leaving H. D. alone to endure a most difficult period of her life.

In addition to her marital problems, H. D. faced other serious personal crises at this time. In 1918 her brother was killed in action in France. Later that year, in poor health and pregnant for the second time (her first pregnancy had ended in miscarriage), H. D. separated from Aldington. Her daughter Perdita was born in 1919; but also in that year H. D.'s father died. H. D.'s despondency was broken only with the help of a new friend, Winnifred Ellerman, known pseudonymously as Bryher.

H. D.'s relationship with Bryher was the "single bright spot" of the time, reported Zajdel. Bryher stabilized her friend during her emotional crises, and offered H. D. encouragement as a writer as well. The two had met after Bryher had sent H. D. a letter praising *Sea Garden,* and Bryher continued to compliment H. D.'s work: she called *Hymen* "a beacon to those who, in a destructive age, believe in life." H. D., in turn, provided Bryher the encouragement she needed to pursue her own writing; she eventually became a successful novelist. Between 1919 and 1923 the two also traveled extensively, to Greece, Egypt, and America, spending most of their time in London between travels. H. D. finally settled in Switzerland in 1924.

By that time, the publication of *Hymen* and *Heliodora* had given H. D.'s poetry a significant platform from which to be judged. Readers praised her work for its economy of language and its precision, but also detected hints of emotion uncharacteristic of much Imagist work. "H. D. is that unique thing, an imagist poet with passion as well as pattern," wrote Mark Van Doren. "She goes on carving her Greek world out of pure, white rock, inlaying it all the while with Mediterranean purple and the hues of windflowers infinitely alive." Whether she chose as her subjects symbols from the Hellenic world or objects taken from nature, she fused her abilities to create and to control. As Willard Thorp wrote of the second part of the poem "Garden," H. D. displayed "perfectly in thirteen lines the oppressiveness of fructifying summer heat." Thorp also admired H. D.'s poetry for capturing its subjects "much as Cezanne's painting of still life does."

The publication of *Collected Poems* in 1925 is considered a watershed in H. D.'s career. The book helped establish H. D.'s reputation by bringing into one volume all of her poems and translations. To William Carlos Williams, *Collected Poems* presented H. D.'s work together "as a clear story. There is an extraordinary vista of a strong rise, beginning with youth and extending over a long period of a woman's growth and blossoming and further rise from that flower into a world beyond it, that should be to every American a source of strengthening pride." But at the same time, as Vincent Quinn suggested, the book has done H. D. one particular disservice: "the title suggests the end rather than the beginning of her career."

During the 1930's H. D. published little while living privately in Switzerland. A major influence on her in this time was the psychoanalysis she submitted to under the guidance of Sigmund Freud. Feeling the need "to dig down and dig out, root out my personal weeds, strengthen my purpose, reaffirm my beliefs, canalize my energies," H. D. first sought Freud's help in 1933 and visited him again a year later. She published her recollections of the experience in her 1956 book, *Tribute to Freud.* "Essentially," said Quinn, "the work is a self-portrait brought into focus by her confrontation with Freud." Freud helped H. D. to understand her dreams, Quinn reported, but the two differed in their beliefs in immortality. As H. D. herself wrote, Freud's argument was that a "belief in the soul's survival, in a life after death . . . was the last and greatest phantasy." H. D., in comparison, longed "for the Absolute," said Quinn. "She clung to the faith that the shortcomings of time would be overcome in eternity."

H. D. regained some attention as a poet with the release of the separate volumes of the "war trilogy" in the mid-1940's. Her most recent major publication before that, *Red Roses for Bronze* (1929), had been noted for some stylistic innovations but had also, according to Zajdel, "marked the end of H. D.'s popularity with the public." And while the trilogy did not bring her immediate fame, it was evidence of a renewed creative vigor. "The genesis of *Trilogy* lies in the catalytic effects on H. D. of living in war-time London," said Peter Scupham. "Her sense of living at a turning point in time led her to these meditations on the nature of the poet's role, the correspondences between Christian belief and the Egyptian pantheon, the presences of the spiritual world and the healing and unifying visions of reconciliation."

In *The Walls Do Not Fall,* the first volume of the trilogy, H. D. asserted her idealism—her belief in man's union with God—in the face of war, reported Quinn. *Tribute to the Angels* follows that same theme, focusing on the conflict between faith and war. With her faith firmly established, H. D. then seeks in *Flowering of the*

Rod, a mystical vision, "a transcendental union with God." This section of the trilogy has been criticized for being too mystical; but, as Quinn noted, "although the reader may be dismayed by H. D.'s theology, his sympathy is almost certain to be aroused by the candor and intensity of her quest for a religious experience."

After the war, H. D. returned to Switzerland, where she wrote her third major work of fiction, *Bid Me to Live.* The novel is her roman a clef about life in London in the 1920's. "I am Julia," H. D. told *Newsweek*'s Lionel Durand upon the novel's release in 1960, "and all the others are real people." Specifically, those others include D. H. Lawrence, his wife, and Aldington. In the novel Julia's marriage dissolves and she becomes involved in a Platonic relationship with another man. When that man withdraws from her, her solution, said Zajdel, "is a dedication to her life as an artist and an affirmation of her identity as a creator and poet."

H. D. offered a different sort of optimism in her last major poetic work, *Helen in Egypt.* A book-length mixture of poetry and prose in three parts, Helen is the author's recreation of the Helen-Achilles myth. Her theme, said Quinn, "is stark and transcendental: the perfect love that she and Achilles seek is to be found in death: 'the dart of Love/is the dart of Death.'" Horace Gregory reinforced this notion when he said "her overlying theme . . . is one of rebirth and resurrection." *Helen in Egypt* is also important as a representative display of the themes and techniques H. D. employed throughout her career. Emily Stipes Watts as well as other critics agreed that "Helen in Egypt is the climax of H. D.'s career both intellectually and poetically."

Though few would argue about H. D.'s importance as an influence on modern poetry, many are still unconvinced of the lasting merits of her work. Readers have been deterred from much of her writing because of the preciousness of her language, the abundance of mythology, the limited world of her focus. And though she did broaden her subject range after World War II, as Quinn noted, she did so at the expense of the clarity and conciseness that had been her trademark. Still, her technical achievements, her poignant portrayals of her personal struggles, and the beauty of her work have all earned a significant amount of praise. As Sisson pointed out, the prospective reader of H. D. might be a little surprised to find that "H. D. offers more than the formal virtues which are usually allowed to her work, and that . . . work abundantly repays the not very strenuous labor of reading it."

BIOGRAPHICAL/CRITICAL SOURCES:

BOOKS

Aldington, Richard, *Life for Life's Sake: A Book of Reminiscences,* Viking, 1941.

Bryher, *The Heart to Artemis: A Writer's Memoirs,* Harcourt, 1962.

Coffman, Stanley K., *Imagism: A Chapter for the History of Modern Poetry,* University of Oklahoma Press, 1950.

Contemporary Literary Criticism, Gale, Volume 3, 1975; Volume 8, 1978; Volume 14, 1980; Volume 31, 1985; Volume 34, 1985.

Dictionary of Literary Biography, Gale, Volume 4: *American Writers in Paris, 1920-39,* 1980; Volume 45: *American Poets, 1880-1945,* 1986.

Edmunds, Susan, *Out of Line: History, Psychoanalysis, and Montage in H. D.'s Long Poems,* Stanford University Press (Stanford), 1994.

Gregory, Eileen, *H. D. and Hellenism: Classic Lines,* Cambridge University Press, 1997.

Guest, Barbara, *Herself Defined: The Poet H. D. and Her World,* Doubleday, 1984.

Hughes, Glenn, *Imagism and the Imagists,* Humanities Press, 1931.

Laity, Cassandra, *H. D. and the Victorian Fin de Siecle: Gender, Modernism, Decadence,* Cambridge University Press (New York City), 1996.

Perkins, David, *A History of Modern Poetry: From the 1890's to the High Modernist Mode,* Harvard University Press, 1976.

Robinson, Janice S., *H. D.: The Life and Work of an American Poet,* Houghton, 1982.

Swann, Thomas Burnett, *The Classical World of H. D.,* University of Nebraska Press, 1962.

Sword, Helen, *Engendering Inspiration: Visionary Strategies in Rilke, Lawrence, and H. D.,* University of Michigan Press (Ann Arbor), 1995.

PERIODICALS

Best Sellers, February 15, 1974; June, 1975.

Books, February 14, 1932.

Christian Science Monitor, October 26, 1961.

College English, March, 1975.

Commonweal, April 18, 1958.

Contemporary Literature, autumn, 1969; spring, 1978.

Essays in Criticism, July, 1977.

Literary Review, May 23, 1925; November 27, 1926.

Mississippi Quarterly, fall, 1962.

Nation, April 26, 1922; November 12, 1924; August 19, 1925; October 8, 1973.

New Republic, January 2, 1929; February 16, 1974.

Newsweek, May 2, 1960.

New York Herald Tribune Book Review, November 28, 1926; June 12, 1960.

New York Times, August 31, 1924; November 21, 1926; November 18, 1928; January 31, 1932; July 31, 1949; September 22, 1957.

New York Times Book Review, May 1, 1960; December 24, 1961.

Poetry, March, 1922; November, 1932; April, 1947; January, 1958; June, 1962; June, 1974.

Poetry Nation, number 4, 1975.

Saturday Review, May 28, 1960.

Saturday Review of Literature, January 1, 1927; December 22, 1928; December 29, 1945; February 22, 1947; August 20, 1949.

Sewanee Review, spring, 1948.

Spectator, February 25, 1922; December 31, 1931.

Times Literary Supplement, July 3, 1924; July 27, 1946; March 23, 1973; March 15, 1974.

Triquarterly, spring, 1968.

Weekly Book Review, October 1, 1944.

*   *   *

DORRIS, Michael (Anthony) 1945-1997
(Milou North)

PERSONAL: Born January 30, 1945, in Louisville, KY (some sources say Dayton, WA); committed suicide, April 11, 1997, in Concord, NH; son of Jim and Mary Besy (Burkhardt) Dorris; married Louise Erdrich (a writer), in 1981; children: Reynold Abel (died in 1991), Jeffrey Sava, Madeline Hannah, Persia Andromeda, Pallas Antigone, Aza Marion. *Education:* Georgetown University, B.A. (cum laude), 1967; Yale University, M.Phil., 1970.

CAREER: University of Redlands, Johnston College, Redlands, CA, assistant professor, 1970; Franconia College, Franconia, NH, assistant professor, 1971-72; Dartmouth College, Hanover, NH, instructor, 1972-76, assistant professor, 1976-79, associate professor, 1979, professor of anthropology, 1979-88, adjunct professor, 1989-97, chair of Native American studies department, 1979-85, chair of Master of Arts in Liberal Studies program, 1982-85. University of New Hampshire, visiting senior lecturer, 1980. Director of urban bus program, Summers, 1967, 1968, and 1969. Society for Applied Anthropology, fellow, 1977-97; Save the Children Foundation, board member, 1991-92, advisory board member, 1992-97; U.S. Advisory Committee on Infant Mortality, member, 1992-97. Consultant to National Endowment for the Humanities, 1976-97, and to television stations, including Los Angeles Educational Television, 1976, and Toledo Public Broadcast Center, 1978. Appeared on numerous radio and television programs.

MEMBER: PEN, Author's Guild, Writer's Guild, Modern Language Association of America (delegate assembly and member of minority commission, 1974-77), American Anthropological Association, American Association for the Advancement of Science (opportunities in science commission, 1974-77), National Indian Education Association, National Congress of American Indians, National Support Committee (Native American Rights Fund), Save the Children (board of directors, 1993-94), Research Society on Alcoholism, National Organization for Fetal Alcohol Syndrome, Phi Beta Kappa, Alpha Sigma Nu.

AWARDS, HONORS: Woodrow Wilson fellow, 1967 and 1980; fellowships from National Institute of Mental Health, 1970 and 1971, John Simon Guggenheim Memorial Foundation, 1978, Rockefeller Foundation, 1985, National Endowment for the Arts, 1989, and Dartmouth College, 1992; Indian Achievement Award, 1985; best book citation, American Library Association, 1988, for *A Yellow Raft in Blue Water*; PEN Syndicated Fiction Award, 1988, for "Name Games"; honorary degree, Georgetown University, 1989; National Book Critics Circle Award for general nonfiction, 1989, and Christopher Award, Heartland Prize, and Outstanding Academic Book, *Choice,* all 1990, all for *The Broken Cord: A Family's Ongoing Struggle with Fetal Alcohol Syndrome*; Medal of Outstanding Leadership and Achievement, Dartmouth College, 1991; Sarah Josepha Hale Literary Award, 1991; Scott Newman Award, 1992, and Gabriel Award for National Entertainment Program, ARC Media Award, Christopher Award, Writers Guild of America award, and Media Award, American Psychology Association, all for the television film of *The Broken Cord: A Family's Ongoing Struggle with Fetal Alcohol Syndrome*; Montgomery Fellow, Dartmouth College, 1992; International Pathfinder Award, World Conference on the Family, 1992; Award for Excellence, Center for Anthropology and Journalism, 1992, for essays on Zimbabwe; Scott O'Dell Award for Historical Fiction, American Library Association, 1992, for *Morning Girl.*

WRITINGS:

Native Americans: Five Hundred Years After (nonfiction), with photographs by Joseph C. Farber, Crowell, 1977.
(As Michael A. Dorris, with Arlene B. Hirschfelder and Mary Gloyne Byler) *A Guide to Research on North American Indians* (nonfiction), American Library Association, 1983.
A Yellow Raft in Blue Water (novel), Holt, 1987.
The Broken Cord: A Family's Ongoing Struggle with Fetal Alcohol Syndrome (nonfiction), foreword by Louise Erdrich, Harper, 1989; published as *The Broken Cord: A Father's Story,* Collins, 1990.

(With Erdrich) *The Crown of Columbus* (novel), HarperCollins, 1991.
(With Erdrich) *Route Two and Back,* Lord John, 1991.
Morning Girl (young adult novel), Hyperion, 1992.
Rooms in the House of Stone (nonfiction), Milkweed Editions, 1993.
Working Men (stories), Holt, 1993.
Paper Trail (essays), HarperCollins, 1994.
Guests (young adult), Hyperion, 1995.
Sees Behind Trees, Hyperion (New York City), 1996.
Cloud Chamber (novel), Scribners, 1997.
The Window (juvenile), Hyperion, 1997.
(Editor) *The Most Wonderful Books: Writers on Discovering the Pleasures of Reading,* Milkweed Editions (Minneapolis, MN), 1997.

Also author of article "House of Stone" and the short story "Name Games." Contributor to books, including *Racism in the Textbook,* Council on Interracial Books for Children, 1976; *Separatist Movements,* edited by Ray Hall, Pergamon, 1979; and *Heaven Is under Our Feet,* edited by Don Henley and Dave Marsh, Longmeadow Press, 1991. Contributor of articles, poems, short stories, and reviews to periodicals, including *Chicago Tribune, Life, Los Angeles Times, Mother Jones, New York Times Book Review, Parents Magazine, Vogue,* and *Woman* (with Erdrich, under the joint pseudonym Milou North). *Viewpoint,* editor, 1967; *American Indian Culture and Research Journal,* member of editorial board, 1974-97; *MELUS: The Journal of the Society for the Study of the Multi-Ethnic Literature of the United States,* member of the editorial board, 1977-79. Author of the screen treatment *Sleeping Lady,* Mirage Films/Sydney Pollack, 1991; author of songs with Judy Rodman, Warner-Chappell Music, 1993.

MEDIA ADAPTATIONS: The Broken Cord: A Family's Ongoing Struggle with Fetal Alcohol Syndrome was produced for television by Universal Television and ABC-TV, 1992. *A Yellow Raft in Blue Water* and *The Broken Cord: A Family's Ongoing Struggle with Fetal Alcohol Syndrome* were released on audiocassette by HarperAudio in 1990; *The Crown of Columbus* was released on audiocassette by HarperAudio in 1991. Film rights to *The Crown of Columbus* were sold to Cinecom.

SIDELIGHTS: Deemed by many reviewers as one of the most renowned Native American writers, Michael Dorris helped to promote the study of Native American culture through his works of nonfiction and fiction. Part Modoc on his father's side, Dorris coauthored a North American Indian research guide, founded the Native American Studies Department at Dartmouth College, created juvenile stories about Native American life, and researched Fetal Alcohol Syndrome (FAS)—the abnormalities occurring in a child when alcohol consumption during pregnancy destroys the brain cells of the fetus. FAS is a particular concern of some Native Americans since the rate of alcohol abuse is higher than the national average on reservations.

Dorris first became aware of FAS when, as a single parent, he adopted a three-year-old Sioux boy who had been taken from his neglectful, alcoholic mother. Dorris, unaware of the physical and mental impact of FAS, initially believed that with love and security his adopted son would outgrow many of his health and behavior problems. Over time, however, developmental impairments in the child became more obvious and limitations more pronounced. In addition to seizures and physical dysfunctions, his son experienced poor vision, near deafness, and slow growth, and was unable to relate cause and effect. After consulting with numerous professionals, Dorris had to face the fact that his son was not getting better. In 1982 Dorris learned that his son's problems stemmed from FAS; the boy's biological mother, who died of alcohol poisoning, drank heavily during her pregnancy. The discovery inspired Dorris to confront the topic of alcoholism among Native Americans. His extensive research and personal story led to the publication of *The Broken Cord: A Family's Ongoing Struggle with Fetal Alcohol Syndrome* (also published as *The Broken Cord: A Father's Story*), a semi-autobiographical account of the events leading up to and succeeding the adoption of his son (called Adam in the book) along with the information he unearthed on FAS.

Granted the National Book Critics Circle Award for general nonfiction, *The Broken Cord* received widespread praise for Dorris's sharing of his personal story as well as the statistical information he gathered. "*The Broken Cord,* beautifully written, angry, dispassionate, painfully honest is the deeply moving and fierce story of Michael Dorris's search for answers. Part memoir, part mystery, part love story, polemic, and social and public-health study, this is that rare book that focuses attention like a magnifying glass on a hot, sunny day. It burns," noted the *Detroit News*' Stephen Salisbury. Contributor Carl A. Hammerschlag wrote in the *Los Angeles Times Book Review* that "it is not enough to say that *The Broken Cord . . .* is good. Written like a prayer from the heart of someone strong enough to share his pain, it tells a tale of crimes against Native American children that approach the dimensions of genocide. . . . Whatever the theories of causation, alcohol is threatening to destroy 1.5 million contemporary Indian people. The annihilation is almost unimaginable. Dorris gives all this a name, a face and a personal history that make it impossible for the reader to remain detached." According to Phyllis Theroux of the *Washington Post,* "Dorris gradually uncovers the ghastly dimensions of [FAS], clearly intending *The Broken Cord* to be an [alarm] that neither lay nor professional readers can ignore. He succeeds brilliantly."

In addition to nonfiction topics, Dorris wrote fictional accounts about such notable events as the arrival of Columbus in America. In 1992, the five-hundredth anniversary of Christopher Columbus's discovery of the Americas, Dorris published his first book for young adults, *Morning Girl,* a story of Bahamian youths living in 1492. Morning Girl, who loves the day, and Star Boy, who prefers the night, are siblings who are like two sides of the same coin and often display their conflicting feelings about one another. As their identities develop and emerge, however, the children discover similarities in their caring for their family. The daily adventures of the young narrators are the focus of the novel, and Dorris interweaves the backdrop of nature and the prominent role of the natural world in the children's native culture. The book comes to a close when Columbus's crew from the *Nina* lands on the island. "This sad, lovely and timely tale gives us an alternative view of America's 'discovery,'" related Suzanne Curley in the *Los Angeles Times Book Review.*

Dorris's second book for young adults, *Guests,* was published in 1995. It tells the story of Moss, a young Native American boy growing up several centuries ago. The guests are most likely Europeans invited by his father to a celebratory dinner in honor of the harvest. "As in *Morning Girl,* his first work of fiction for children, Mr. Dorris writes lyrically of nature. The descriptions fill the senses," wrote Linda Perkins in the *New York Times Book Review.* Nancy Vasilakis, writing in the *Horn Book Magazine,* stated, "The narrative voice in this book is natural and believable,

though this book, like [*Morning Girl,*] is very much an introspective novel." A reviewer for the Chicago *Tribune Books* concluded, "Dorris brings readers close to his characters at the same time he evokes how far away they were."

Dorris also wrote with his wife, author Louise Erdrich, an adult novel about Christopher Columbus, *The Crown of Columbus.* The book is a love story about two Dartmouth professors, Vivian Twostar and Roger Williams, with little in common but a physical attraction. Both are involved in the research of Christopher Columbus. Vivian, a Native American single parent, has been assigned the task of writing an academic piece on Columbus from the Native American viewpoint. Roger, an English professor and poet, is writing an epic poem about Columbus for *People* magazine. The research leads them on an adventure and eventually forces them to question the impact of Columbus's journey for the contemporary world, especially Native Americans.

The Crown of Columbus received mixed reactions. Some reviewers believed that the work was below the standards of Dorris's and Erdrich's previous books and claimed it was manufactured to become a best-seller rather than a literary effort, while other reviewers found Vivian and Roger's adventures amusing, vibrant, and charming. "Erdrich and Dorris, who write so convincingly elsewhere from their own experience, seem here to have been a little hasty in trying to exploit Columbus's," claimed contributor Kirkpatrick Sale in the *Nation.* Sale also found *The Crown of Columbus* "difficult to read without remembering that the Dorris-Erdrich team got some $1.5 million to turn out a book from their Indian perspective for the Quincentenary." But *Library Journal's* Ann Fisher declared the book "a sure-fire winner on all levels" and praised Dorris and Erdrich's depiction of the relationship of the two main characters as "funny, vivid, and life-affirming." *New York Times Book Review's* Robert Houston complimented the "moments of genuine humor and compassion, of real insight and sound satire," but also commented, "in the end, *The Crown of Columbus* never really finds itself."

Cloud Chamber, published just prior to Dorris's death in 1997, refers readers back to his 1987 novel *A Yellow Raft in Blue Water* which introduces the character of 15-year-old Rayona Taylor, part African American, part Native American. While *Yellow Raft* describes Rayona's adventures as a feisty tomboy including entering a bronco-riding contest, *Cloud Chamber* traces Rayona's lineage back to her great-great-grandmother from Ireland. In doing so, it relates the complex love relationships that have patterned the family over the years. John Skow of *Time* called the novel "intricate and brooding."

Dorris also published a book of short stories titled *Working Men.* A number of the stories included were previously published in other publications such as *Mother Jones, Ploughshares,* and *Northwest Review.* Despite its title, the collection examines the lives of men and women, straight and gay, young and old in a variety of settings. Noted Phillip Graham in the Chicago *Tribune Books,* "No two of these stories are the same, though each rests on the solid authority of a distinctive human voice and a slyly elastic definition of work."

The volume received praise from a number of reviewers. "All [of the stories] are strikingly different and are told with flair and efficiency and honed craftsmanship. *Working Men* is admirable not just for its mastery and variety, but for Michael Dorris's faith in the heroism and importance of ordinary American life," praised Ron Hansen in the *Los Angeles Times Book Review.* Mentioning the stories "The Vase" and "Jeopardy" specifically, Charles R.

Larson of *Washington Post Book World* wrote, "*Working Men* contains two stories as good as we are likely to find by anyone writing today, and that is all the measure needed for any artist worthy of serious attention."

While *The Crown of Columbus* was the first novel that Dorris and Erdrich did in complete collaboration, they worked closely together on all of their books. As Dorris explained to Dulcy Brainard in a *Publishers Weekly* interview: "The person whose name is on the book is the one who's done most of the primary writing. The other helps plan, reads it as it goes along, suggests changes in direction, in character and then acts as editor." Considering their popular following, the system seemed to work well for Dorris and Erdrich. *New York Times Magazine*'s Vince Passaro pointed out that "one senses the act of collaboration serves a vital, extra-literary function, perhaps as a fortification against an insinuating and inevitable competition. If every work that leaves their hands is in some sense a joint work, they can escape the awful consequences of one talent overshadowing another."

Despite seemingly successful careers intertwined with a solid marriage, Erdrich and Dorris quietly separated in 1996 and were undergoing divorce proceedings when Dorris ended his life in April of 1997. Following his death, it became public that Dorris was under investigation for child abuse and that he had previously attempted suicide two weeks prior to his death. However, in an interview with the *New York Times,* Erdrich said that Dorris's depression had existed throughout their marriage: "Suicide. It's a very tangled road, a tangle of paths and dead ends and clear places and it's gone. He descended inch by inch, fighting all the way."

BIOGRAPHICAL/CRITICAL SOURCES:

BOOKS

Erdrich, Louise, *Conversations with Louise Erdrich and Michael Dorris,* University Press of Mississippi (Jackson), 1994.
Native North American Literature, Gale, 1994.
Weil, Ann, *Michael Dorris,* Raintree Steck-Vaughn (Austin, TX), 1997.

PERIODICALS

Bloomsbury Review, May/June, 1995, p. 19.
Christian Science Monitor, March 2, 1989, pp. 16-17.
Georgia Review, summer, 1995, p. 523.
Horn Book Magazine, January/February, 1995, p.58.
Library Journal, March 15, 1991, p. 114.
Los Angeles Times, September 18, 1988, Section VI, pp. 8-9.
Los Angeles Times Book Review, June 21, 1987, p. 2; September 27, 1992, p. 12; August 3, 1993, p. 11; November 7, 1993, p. 2; October 30, 1994, p. 8.
Missouri Review, 1988, pp. 79-99.
New Statesman and Society, September 7, 1990, p. Y44.
New York Times, April 19, 1991, p. C5; February 2, 1992, Section L, pp. 29, 38.
New York Times Book Review, June 7, 1987, p. 7; July 30, 1989, pp. 1, 20; April 28, 1991, p. 10; August 1, 1993, p. 18; May 18, 1994, p. 18; January 1, 1995, p. 20; January 29, 1995, p. 20.
New York Times Magazine, April 21, 1991, pp. 35-40, 76.
North Dakota Quarterly, winter, 1987, pp. 196-218.
Publishers Weekly, August 4, 1989, pp. 73-74; August 10, 1992, p. 71.
Time, February 17, 1997.
Times Literary Supplement, August 24, 1990, p. 893; July 19, 1991, p. 21; December 2, 1994.

Tribune Books (Chicago), May 10, 1987, pp. 6-7; July 23, 1989, pp. 1, 11; April 28, 1991, p. 5; October 24, 1993, pp. 6-7; August 14, 1994, p. 7.
Washington Post Book World, October 17, 1993, p. 6.
Western American Literature, February, 1992, pp. 369-71.
Women's Review of Books, October, 1991, pp. 17-18.

*   *   *

DORRIS, Michael A.
See DORRIS, Michael (Anthony)

*   *   *

DORSAN, Luc
See SIMENON, Georges (Jacques Christian)

*   *   *

DORSANGE, Jean
See SIMENON, Georges (Jacques Christian)

*   *   *

DOS PASSOS, John (Roderigo) 1896-1970

PERSONAL: Born January 14, 1896, in Chicago, IL; died, apparently of a heart attack, September 28, 1970, in Baltimore, MD; buried in Westmoreland Co., VA; son of John Randolph Dos Passos (an attorney) and Lucy Addison Sprigg Madison; married Katherine F. Smith, August 21, 1929 (died, 1947); married Elizabeth Hamlin Holdridge, August 6, 1949; children: (second marriage) Lucy Hamlin. *Education:* Harvard University, B.A. (cum laude), 1916. *Politics:* Began left-wing, shifting to conservative in his later years. *Avocation:* Travel, sailing, canoeing, gardening, painting watercolors.

CAREER: Volunteered for ambulance duty in France with Norton-Harjes Ambulance Unit, 1917, in Italy with Red Cross, 1918, and with U.S. Army Medical Corps, 1918-19; traveled to Near East with Near East Relief, 1921; *New Masses,* founder, 1926, executive board member, beginning 1926; correspondent in Central America, 1932; correspondent for *Life* magazine in the Pacific, 1945, and in South America, 1948. Treasurer, National Committee for Defense of Political Prisoners, 1932.

MEMBER: American Academy of Arts and Letters, American Academy of Arts and Sciences, Authors League, Virginia Committee on Constitutional Government.

AWARDS, HONORS: Guggenheim fellowships, 1939, 1940, 1942; National Institute of Arts and Letters Gold Medal Award for fiction, 1957; Antonio Feltrinelli Prize from Italian Academia Nazionale dei Lincei, 1967, for innovation in narrative.

WRITINGS:

(Contributor) *Eight Harvard Poets,* Laurence J. Gomme, 1917.
One Man's Initiation—1917, Allen & Unwin, 1919, Doran, 1920, published as *First Encounter,* Philosophical Library, 1945, unexpurgated edition published with new introduction, Cornell University Press, 1969.
Three Soldiers, Doran, 1921.

Rosinante to the Road Again, Doran, 1922.

A Pushcart at the Curb, Doran, 1922.

Streets of Night, Doran, 1923.

Manhattan Transfer, Harper, 1925.

Orient Express, Harper, 1927.

Facing the Chair: Story of the Americanization of Two Foreign-born Workmen, Sacco-Vanzetti Defense Committee (Boston), 1927.

The 42nd Parallel (first book in "U.S.A." trilogy; also see below), Harcourt, 1930.

1919 (second book in "U.S.A." trilogy; also see below), Harcourt, 1932.

Culture and the Crisis: An Open Letter to the Writers, Artists, Teachers, Physicians, Engineers, Scientists, and Other Professional Workers of America, League of Professional Groups for Foster & Ford (New York), 1932.

In All Countries, Harcourt, 1934.

(Contributor) Henry Hart, editor, *American Writers Conference,* International Publishers, 1935.

The Big Money (third book in "U.S.A." trilogy; also see below), Harcourt, 1936.

The Villages Are the Heart of Spain, Esquire-Coronet, 1937.

Journeys between Wars, Harcourt, 1938.

U.S.A. (trilogy; contains *The 42nd Parallel, 1919,* and *The Big Money*), Harcourt, 1938.

Adventures of a Young Man (first book in "District of Columbia" trilogy; also see below), Houghton, 1939.

The Living Thoughts of Tom Paine, Presented by John Dos Passos, Longmans, Green, 1940.

The Ground We Stand On, Harcourt, 1941.

(Contributor) Herman Ould, editor, *Writers in Freedom,* Hutchinson, 1942.

Number One (second book in "District of Columbia" trilogy; also see below), Houghton, 1943.

State of the Nation, Houghton, 1944.

Tour of Duty, Houghton, 1946.

The Grand Design (third book in "District of Columbia" trilogy; also see below), Houghton, 1949.

The Prospect Before Us, Houghton, 1950.

Life's Picture History of World War II, Time Inc., 1950.

Chosen Country, Houghton, 1951.

District of Columbia (trilogy; contains *Adventures of a Young Man, Number One,* and *The Grand Design*), Houghton, 1952.

The Head and Heart of Thomas Jefferson, Doubleday, 1954.

Most Likely to Succeed, Prentice-Hall, 1954.

The Theme Is Freedom, Dodd, 1956.

The Men Who Made the Nation, Doubleday, 1957.

(Contributor) *Essays on Individuality,* University of Pennsylvania Press, 1958.

The Great Days, Sagamore, 1958.

Prospects of a Golden Age, Prentice-Hall, 1959.

Midcentury: A Contemporary Chronicle, Houghton, 1961.

Mr. Wilson's War, Doubleday, 1962.

Brazil on the Move (travel), Doubleday, 1963.

Occasions and Protests (essays, 1936-1964), Regnery, 1964.

Thomas Jefferson: The Making of a President, Houghton, 1964.

(Contributor) Allan Nevins, editor, *Lincoln and the Gettysberg Address,* University of Illinois Press, 1964.

The Shackles of Power: Three Jeffersonian Decades, 1801-1826, Doubleday, 1966.

The World in a Glass: A View of Our Century Selected from the Novels of John Dos Passos, Houghton, 1966.

The Best Times: An Informal Memoir, New American Library, 1966.

The Portugal Story: Three Centuries of Exploration and Discovery, Doubleday, 1969.

Easter Island: Island of Enigmas, Doubleday, 1971.

The Fourteenth Chronicle: Letters and Diaries of John Dos Passos, edited by Townsend Ludington, Gambit, 1973.

Century's Ebb: The Thirteenth Chronicle, Gambit, 1975.

Promise of U.S.A.: John Dos Passos' Thumbnail Biographies, edited by Edgar Stanton, Hwong Publishing, 1975.

PLAYS

The Garbage Man (produced, 1926; also see below), Harper, 1926.

Airways, Inc. (also see below), Macaulay, 1928.

Three Plays: The Garbage Man, Airways, Inc., Fortune Heights (produced in U.S.S.R., 1933), Harcourt, 1934.

(With Paul Shyre) *U.S.A.: A Dramatic Revue,* Samuel French, 1963.

OTHER

Translator from the French, and illustrator, of B. Cendrar's *Panama.* Contributor to *Nation, New Republic, New Masses, Common Sense, Esquire, Partisan Review, National Review,* and other periodicals.

An extensive collection of manuscripts and other working materials is housed at the Alderman Library of the University of Virginia.

SIDELIGHTS: Jean-Paul Sartre once called John Dos Passos "the best novelist of our time." Nevertheless, Gore Vidal noted that although he was "admired extravagantly in the '20's and '30's, Dos Passos was largely ignored in the '40's and '50's, his new works passed over either in silence or else noted with that ritual sadness we reserve for those whose promise to art has not been kept."

Reviews of his earlier works reflect the expectations that Dos Passos raised in the literary world. Sinclair Lewis heralded *Manhattan Transfer* as "a novel of the very first importance; a book which the idle reader can devour yet which the literary analyst must take as possibly inaugurating, at long last, the vast and blazing dawn we have awaited. It may be the foundation of a whole new school of novel-writing. Dos Passos may be, more than Dreiser, Cather, Hergesheimer, Cabell, or Anderson the father of humanized and living fiction . . . not merely for America but for the world!. . . I regard *Manhattan Transfer* as more important in every way than anything by Gertrude Stein or Marcel Proust or even the great white boar, Mr. Joyce's Ulysses." Mary Ross wrote of *1919:* "Mr. Dos Passos's writing is always distinguished by a remarkable sensuous perception, but more than that, he has a directness, independence and poignancy of thought and emotion that seems to me unexcelled in current fiction. . . . *1919* will disturb or offend some of its readers. Their recoil will be in itself a mark of its force. No novel with which I am familiar seems to me to have surpassed it in power, range, and beauty."

After the completion of the *U.S.A.* trilogy, Theodore Spencer declared: "No one concerned with the health of the novel as a living form can fail to . . . regard his achievement with respect. He writes from a wise and comprehending point of view; his construction is firm; his narrative is swift, realistic, and interesting. There are few novelists in this country today whose craftsmanship is as secure, and whose sense of American life as understanding and awake." However, Alfred Kazin noted that while *U.S.A.* became an epic, "it is a history of defeat. There are no flags for the spirit in it, and no victory save the mind's silent victory that integrity can acknowledge to itself. It is one of the saddest books ever written by an American." Even so, Kazin added, "what Waldo Frank said of Mencken is particularly relevant to Dos Passos: he brings energy to despair."

Viewed from the perspective of thirty years later, Peter Meinke's review of *The Fourteenth Chronicle* found Dos Passos "to be in that main American tradition beginning with Whitman that seeks to grasp the American experience by accumulation of detail, by great width and scope, by swallowing America whole, as it were, rather than carving out deep chunks from certain sections as his friends Hemingway, Fitzgerald, Faulkner and Cummings did. . . . While the book is ultimately sad, with the elderly out-of-step writer exclaiming that 'the rank idiocy of the younger generation is more than I can swallow' the main impression one gets from reading it is that of a decent and generous man of boundless enthusiasm and energy." D. J. Stewart's review of *Occasions and Protests* noted the "startling emphasis on vision, on seeing clear, rounded, individual shapes of things provides a kind of touchstone wherewith to reread and better understand what these pieces are about. For they are essentially the reactions to life of a man who uses his eyes intensely and voraciously, one who lives with and through his vision." Dos Passos sees things with the coolness and the clarity of the camera's eye, which accounts for one of his most frequently-mentioned faults: his two-dimensional vision tends to create types, defeating the creation of characters with any true individuality.

According to Don Gifford, Dos Passos explained his philosophy in *Occasions and Protests*—that "personal freedom and individual liberty constitute the highest good, and that this good is under attack by evil in the form of institutional authority in mass society (big government, big labor, big business, etc.) and in the form of 'the prescriptions of doctrine' (Communism, liberalism, conformism, etc.)." However, this philosophy does not produce an optimistic view of his characters. Edmund Wilson asserted many years ago that Dos Passos's "disapproval of capitalistic society becomes distaste for all the human beings who compose it." This same view was expressed in 1939 by Alfred Kazin, who wrote: "For Dos Passos irony itself has become the supreme style; the cold, methodical ferocity of his prose, with its light, bitter thrust, its extraordinary pliability and ease, becomes a cackling solemnity. [*Adventures of a Young Man*] really trembles with an internal disgust. Dos Passos has always disliked most of his characters, but here his characteristic repugnance and exasperation yield to pure hatred."

The effects of these emotions were examined by Sartre. "Dos Passos' hate, despair, and lofty contempt are real," he commented. "But that is precisely why his world is not real; it is a created object. I know of none—not even Faulkner's or Kafka's—in which the art is greater or better hidden. I know of none that is more precious, more touching or closer to us. This is because he takes his material from our world."

R. A. Fraser lamented that, in *Occasions and Protests,* "nothing is left of the Dos Passos style but his habit of omitting the hyphen. His prose could once—perhaps will again—slap life into the cheeks of the most commonplace landscape, the most banal event; here . . . it's rouge that's being applied, slowly, laboriously and inaccurately. Even his ear has betrayed him." John Gross wrote in his review of *Midcentury,* "All one can do for the sake of the man who once wrote *Manhattan Transfer* and *The Big Money* is look the other way." H. M. Robinson seems similarly inclined. He recalled: "Time was, when the publication of a novel by John Dos

Passos called for the lighting of bonfires on promontories. But no triumphant flare will greet the appearance of his latest work. . . . Kindly reviewers may regard the book as a temporary lapse of energy. . . . But Mr. Dos Passos deserves something more constructive than mercy. . . . The weakness of *The Grand Design* proceeds not so much from the waning of Mr. Dos Passos's creative powers—though there is a marked decline here—as from the exhaustion of the genre in which he is working." "Yet," Vidal noted, "there is something about Dos Passos which makes a fellow writer unexpectedly protective, partly out of compassion for the man himself, and partly because the fate of Dos Passos is a chilling reminder of those condemned to write for life that this is the way it almost always is in a society which, to put it tactfully, has no great interest in the development of writers, a process too slow for the American temperament. As a result our literature is rich with sprinters but significantly short of milers."

Examination of the decline in Dos Passos's popularity yields several conjectures as to what went wrong. Vance Bourjaily claimed: "Dos Passos, through the years, has become a better and better writer; but the appeal of his point of view has grown narrower and narrower. For a work of literature at its best, is a creation; and *The Grand Design,* with its caricatures and its atmosphere of intangible bias, is merely an interpretation." Early in Dos Passos's career Henry Hazlitt foresaw such difficulties. "Mr. Dos Passos is a writer of extraordinary talent," he wrote in his review of *The 42nd Parallel.* "He knows American cities, he knows a great deal about life, he has a shrewd insight into men and women. . . . But it leaves one wondering whether [his] present method is not more a handicap than a help to him. This kaleidoscopic shaking of the fragments of several novels into one no longer has the attraction of novelty, and its other advantages are not always clear." In 1961, John Wrenn demonstrated the validity of Hazlitt's misgivings. He explained: "Dos Passos has been admired for characteristics which today, with a perspective of twenty years, appear to be superficial: for his success in the novel of protest; for his brilliant technical innovations in such a work as *U.S.A.*; for his contemporaneity—his grasp of the problems and events of the time as they related to individual characters in his fiction. When the novel of protest became all too familiar, the innovations of *U.S.A.* no longer new, and the events of his major novels no longer current ones, even his best work seemed to become no longer relevant."

One of Dos Passos' loyal admirers, James T. Farrell, wrote in 1958: "John Dos Passos writes with great ease and he is technically inventive. . . . From *Three Soldiers* to *The Great Days,* we can see in Dos Passos the effort of one man of talent and sensibility to take hold of this changing play of forces in our life." But Wrenn observed that contemporary Americans were no longer his audience, principally because he had been stereotyped as "rebel of the twenties, ex-communist, political novelist, disillusioned social critic," and writers so labeled were out of fashion. Robie Macaulay felt that much of Dos Passos' work was "bound to taste rather stale to this generation, a spectacle not current enough to be news and not quite old enough to be history. . . . But, given enough distance, Dos Passos will have his day again. How he will be read in another time is hard to say. . . . I should say that it will be less as a social interpreter than as a primitive portraitist of American lives during a certain time." To this Thomas Lask added: "Dos Passos may become known as the author of one book, but in its range and reach, in its willingness to meet head on the possibilities of American life, it is large enough to be considered a life's work."

Arthur Mizener noted that, in spite of his faults, "Dos Passos is the only major American novelist of the twentieth century who has had the desire and the power to surround the lives of his characters with what Lionel Trilling once called 'the buzz of history'—the actual, homely, everyday sounds of current events and politics, of social ambitions and the struggle for money, of small pleasures and trivial corruptions, amidst which we all live. He has given us a major aspect of our experience that has hardly been touched by any other novelist of our time." Kazin echoed these sentiments when he wrote: "It is often assumed that Dos Passos was a 'left-wing' novelist in the Thirties who, like other novelists of the period, turned conservative and thus changed and lost his creative identity. . . . But [*U.S.A.*] is not simply a 'left-wing' novel, and its technical inventiveness and freshness of style are typical of the Twenties rather than the Thirties. In any event, Dos Passos has always been so detached from all group thinking that it is impossible to understand his development as a novelist by identifying him with the radical novelists of the Thirties. He began earlier. . . . In all periods he has followed his own perky, obstinately independent course. . . . It is not his values but the loss by many educated people of a belief in 'history' that has caused Dos Passos's relative isolation in recent years. Alone among his literary cronies, Dos Passos managed to add this idea of history as the great operative force to their enthusiasm for radical technique, the language of Joyce, and 'the religion of the world.'"

BIOGRAPHICAL/CRITICAL SOURCES:

BOOKS

Belkind, Allen, editor, *Dos Passos, the Critics, and the Writer's Intention,* Southern Illinois University Press, 1972.

Brantley, John, *The Fiction of John Dos Passos,* San Antonio College, 1964.

Brown, Frieda S., et al., editors, *Rewriting the Good Fight: Critical Essays on the Literature of the Spanish Civil War,* Michigan State University Press, 1989, pp. 215-28.

Carr, Virginia Spencer, *Dos Passos: A Life,* Doubleday & Co., 1984.

Casey, Janet Galligani, *Dos Passos and the Ideology of the Feminine,* Cambridge University Press, 1998.

Colley, Iain, *Dos Passos and the Fiction of Despair,* Rowman and Littlefield, 1978.

Concise Dictionary of American Literary Biography: The Age of Maturity, 1921-1941, Gale, 1989.

Contemporary Literary Criticism, Gale, Volume 1, 1973; Volume 4, 1975; Volume 7, 1978; Volume 11, 1979; Volume 15, 1980; Volume 25, 1983; Volume 34, 1985; Volume 82, 1994.

Cowley, Malcolm, *Exile's Return,* revised edition, Viking, 1951.

Dictionary of Literary Biography, Gale, Volume 4: *American Writers in Paris, 1920-1939,* 1980; Volume 9: *American Novelists, 1910-1945,* 1981.

Dictionary of Literary Biography Documentary Series, Volume 1, Gale, 1982.

Eastman, Mark, and others, *John Dos Passos: An Appreciation,* Prentice-Hall, 1954.

Filler, Louis, editor, *A Question of Quality: Popularity and Value in Modern Creative Writing,* Bowling Green University Popular Press, 1976, pp. 115-23.

Hook, Andrew, editor, *Dos Passos: A Collection of Critical Essays,* Prentice-Hall, 1974.

Kazin, Alfred, *Native Grounds,* Reynal, 1942.

Klein, Holger, editor, *The First World War in Fiction: A Collection of Critical Essays,* Macmillan Press, 1976.

Knox, G. A., and H. M. Stahl, *Dos Passos and the Revolting Playwrights,* Folcroft, 1976.

Landsberg, Melvin, *Dos Passos' Path to U.S.A.: A Political Biography, 1912-1936,* Colorado Associated University Press, 1972.

Longstreet, Stephen, *We All Went to Paris,* Macmillan, 1972.

Ludington, Townsend, *John Dos Passos: A Twentieth Century Odyssey,* Dutton, 1980.

Potter, Jack, *A Bibliography of John Dos Passos,* Normandie House, 1950.

Rogers, Francis M., *The Portuguese Heritage of John Dos Passos,* Portuguese Continental Union of the U.S.A., 1976.

Rohrkemper, John, *John Dos Passos: A Reference Guide,* G. K. Hall & Co., 1980.

Sanders, David, editor, *The Merrill Studies in U.S.A.,* Charles E. Merrill Publishing Co., 1972.

Sartre, Jean-Paul, *Literary and Philosophical Essays,* Rider, 1955.

Waldmeir, John Christian, *The American Trilogy, 1900-1937: Morris, Dreiser, Dos Passos, and the History of Mammon,* Locust Hill Press (West Cornwall), 1995.

Wilson, Edmund, *The Triple Thinkers,* revised edition, Oxford University Press, 1948.

Wrenn, John H., *John Dos Passos,* Twayne, 1961.

PERIODICALS

American Literature, November, 1976, pp. 340-64; March, 1978, pp. 85-105.

Booklist, October 15, 1994, p. 444.

Bookmen, December, 1922.

Books, March 13, 1932; April 29, 1934; July 1, 1934; June 4, 1939.

Catholic World, February, 1949.

Christian Century, November 28, 1962; November 4, 1964.

Christian Science Monitor, March 2, 1961.

Commonweal, June 2, 1939; March 5, 1943; January 28, 1949; October 8, 1954.

Esquire, May, 1961.

Forum, September, 1936.

Journal of Narrative Technique, fall, 1984, pp. 182-92.

Modern Fiction Studies (special Dos Passos issue), autumn, 1980.

Nation, November 15, 1922; March 12, 1930; June 3, 1939; April 14, 1956.

National Review, December 1, 1964; October 20, 1970.

New Leader, March 15, 1965.

New Literary History, spring, 1970, pp. 471-83.

New Republic, June 14, 1939; September 1, 1941; July 24, 1944; September 2, 1946; September 27, 1954; April 28, 1958.

New Statesman, October 27, 1961.

New Statesman and Nation, June 11, 1932.

Newsweek, October 12, 1970.

New Yorker, June 3, 1939; August 24, 1946; March 18, 1961.

New York Herald Tribune Books, December 2, 1962.

New York Herald Tribune Lively Arts, February 26, 1961.

New York Herald Tribune Weekly Book Review, January 2, 1949.

New York Times, May 6, 1934; May 20, 1934; August 31, 1941; July 23, 1944; September 29, 1970.

New York Times Book Review, December 20, 1959; December 25, 1960; April 7, 1963; January 10, 1965.

Paris Review, spring, 1969, pp. 147-72.

Review of Reviews, September, 1936.

San Francisco Chronicle, January 9, 1949; February 26, 1961.

Saturday Review, December 12, 1959; February 25, 1961; March 15, 1969.

Saturday Review of Literature, December 5, 1925; May 5, 1934; September 2, 1944; January 8, 1949.
Saturday Review/World, September 11, 1973.
Spectator, September 27, 1930.
Springfield Republican, March 13, 1932.
Texas Studies in Literature and Language, spring, 1964, pp. 22-38.
Time, September 27, 1954; March 3, 1961; October 12, 1970.
Times Literary Supplement, June 17, 1939; October 27, 1950; January 28, 1965.
Twentieth Century Literature, October, 1967, pp. 167-78; May, 1977, pp. 195-228.
Washington Post Book World, October 28, 1973.
Yale Review, summer, 1943.

*   *   *

DOSSAGE, Jean
See SIMENON, Georges (Jacques Christian)

*   *   *

DOUGLAS, Leonard
See BRADBURY, Ray (Douglas)

*   *   *

DOUGLAS, Michael
See CRICHTON, (John) Michael

*   *   *

DOVE, Rita (Frances) 1952-

PERSONAL: Born August 28, 1952, in Akron, OH; daughter of Ray A. (a chemist) and Elvira E. (Hord) Dove; married Fred Viebahn (a writer) March 23, 1979; children: Aviva Chantal Tamu Dove-Viebahn. *Education:* Miami University, B.A. (summa cum laude), 1973; attended Universitaet Tuebingen, West Germany, 1974-75; University of Iowa, M.F.A., 1977.

ADDRESSES: Office—Department of English, University of Virginia, Charlottesville, VA 22903.

CAREER: Arizona State University, Tempe, assistant professor, 1981-84, associate professor, 1984-87, professor of English, 1987-89; University of Virginia, Charlottesville, professor of English 1989-93, Commonwealth Professor of English, 1993–; United States Poet Laureate, 1993-95. Writer-in-residence at Tuskegee Institute, 1982. National Endowment for the Arts, member of literature panel, 1984-86, chair of poetry grants panel, 1985. Commissioner, Schomburg Center for the Preservation of Black Culture, New York Public Library, 1987–; judge, Walt Whitman Award, Academy of American Poets, 1990, Pulitzer Prize in poetry, 1991, Ruth Lilly Prize, 1991, National Book Award (poetry), 1991, Anisfield-Wolf Book Awards, 1992–.

MEMBER: PEN, Associated Writing Programs (member of board of directors, 1985-88; president, 1986-87), Academy of American Poets, Poetry Society of America, ASCAP, American Philosophical Society, Poets and Writers, Phi Beta Kappa, Phi Kappa Phi.

AWARDS, HONORS: Fulbright fellow, 1974-75; grants from National Endowment for the Arts, 1978, and Ohio Arts Council, 1979; International Working Period for Authors fellow for West Germany, 1980; Portia Pittman fellow at Tuskegee Institute from National Endowment for the Humanities, 1982; John Simon Guggenheim fellow, 1983; Peter I. B. Lavan Younger Poets Award, Academy of American Poets, 1986; Pulitzer Prize in poetry, 1987, for *Thomas and Beulah*; General Electric Foundation Award for Younger Writers, 1987; Bellagio (Italy) residency, Rockefeller Foundation, 1988; Ohio Governor's Award, 1988; Mellon fellow, National Humanities Center, North Carolina, 1988-89; Ohioana Award, 1991, for *Grace Notes*; Literary Lion citation, New York Public Libraries, 1991; inducted Ohio Hall of Fame, 1991; Women of the Year Award, Glamour Magazine, 1993; NAACP Great American Artist Award, 1993; Harvard University Phi Beta Kappa poetry award, 1993; Distinguished Achievement medal, Miami University Alumni Association, 1994; Renaissance Forum Award for leadership in the literary arts, Folger Shakespeare Library, 1994; Carl Sandburg Award, International Platform Association, 1994; U.S. Poet Laureate, 1994-1995; Heniz award in arts and humanities, 1996; Amy Lowell Fellowship, 1997; Shelley Memorial Award, 1997; honorary literary doctorates: Miami University, 1988, Knox College, 1989, Tuskegee University, 1994, University of Miami, 1994, Washington University, St. Louis, 1994, Case Western Reserve University, 1994, University of Akron, 1994, Arizona State University, 1995, Boston College, 1995, Dartmouth College, 1995, Spellman College, 1996, University of Pennsylvania, 1996, Notre Dame, 1997, Northeastern University, 1997, University of North Carolina, 1997.

WRITINGS:

Ten Poems (chapbook), Penumbra Press, 1977.
The Only Dark Spot in the Sky (poetry chapbook), Porch Publications, 1980.
The Yellow House on the Corner (poems), Carnegie-Mellon University Press, 1980.
Mandolin (poetry chapbook), Ohio Review, 1982.
Museum (poems), Carnegie-Mellon University Press, 1983.
Fifth Sunday (short stories), Callaloo Fiction Series, 1985.
Thomas and Beulah (poems), Carnegie-Mellon University Press, 1986.
The Other Side of the House (poems), photographs by Tamarra Kaida, Pyracantha Press, 1988.
Grace Notes (poems), W. W. Norton & Company, Inc., 1989.
Through the Ivory Gate (novel), Pantheon Books, 1992.
Selected Poems, Pantheon, 1993.
Lady Freedom among Us, Janus Press, 1993.
The Darker Face of the Earth: A Verse Play in Fourteen Scenes, Story Line Press, 1994.
Mother Love: Poems, W.W. Norton (New York City), 1995.
Multicultural Voices: Literature from the United States, Scott-Foresman (Glenview), 1995.
The Poet's World, Library of Congress (Washington, D.C.), 1995.

Work represented in anthologies. Contributor of poems, stories, and essays to magazines, including *Agni Review, Antaeus, Georgia Review, Nation,* and *Poetry.* Member of editorial board, *National Forum,* 1984–; poetry editor, *Callaloo,* 1986–; advisory editor, *Gettysburg Review,* 1987–, and *TriQuarterly,* 1988–.

SIDELIGHTS: Award-winning writer Rita Dove, former U.S. Poet Laureate, has been described as a quiet leader, a poet who does not avoid race issues, but does not make them her central focus. As Dove herself explains in the *Washington Post:*

"Obviously, as a black woman, I am concerned with race. . . . But certainly not every poem of mine mentions the fact of being black. They are poems about humanity, and sometimes humanity happens to be black. I cannot run from, I won't run from any kind of truth." As the first black poet laureate, Dove notes that, though it has less personal significance for her, "it is significant in terms of the message it sends about the diversity of our culture and our literature."

Born in Akron, Ohio, in 1952, Dove was a National Merit Scholar at Miami University in Ohio, after which she received a Fulbright Fellowship to attend the University of Tubingen and then completed an M.F.A. at the Iowa Writers' Workshop. Although Dove published two chapbooks of poetry in 1977 and 1980, she made her formal literary debut in 1980 with the poetry collection *The Yellow House on the Corner,* which received praise for its sense of history combined with individual detail. Dove's next volume, *Museum,* also received praise for its lyricism, its finely crafted use of language, and its detailed depiction of images drawn from Dove's travels in Europe. Alvin Aubert of *American Book Review,* however, faults the volume for an avoidance of personal issues and experiences, such as that of ethnicity. "I would like to know more about Rita Dove as a woman, including her ethnicity, and on her home ground," he asserts. Calvin Hernton of *Parnassus,* in contrast, praises the "universal" sensibility of the poems in *Museum,* which, he notes, "lack anything suggesting that they were written by a person of African, or African-American, artistic or cultural heritage."

Dove turned to prose fiction with the publication of *Fifth Sunday,* a short story collection. Reviewers emphasized Dove's minimalist style and her interest in what a critic for *Southern Humanities Review* called "the fable-like aspects of middle class life." While considered promising, the volume generally received mixed reviews, with many critics finding the quality and detail of the writing uneven.

Dove is best known for her book of poems *Thomas and Beulah,* which garnered her the 1987 Pulitzer Prize in poetry. The poems in *Thomas and Beulah* are loosely based on the lives of Dove's maternal grandparents, and are arranged in two sequences: one devoted to Thomas, born in 1900 in Wartrace, Tennessee, and the other to Beulah, born in 1904 in Rockmart, Georgia. *Thomas and Beulah* is viewed as a departure from Dove's earlier works in both its accessibility and its chronological sequence that has, to use Dove's words, "the kind of sweep of a novel." On the book's cover is a snapshot of the author's grandparents, and *New York Review of Books* contributor Helen Vendler observes that "though the photograph, and the chronology of the lives of Thomas and Beulah appended to the sequence, might lead one to suspect that Dove is a poet of simple realism, this is far from the case. Dove has learned . . . how to make a biographical fact the buried base of an imagined edifice."

The poems in *Grace Notes,* Dove's fourth book, are largely autobiographical. Alfred Corn remarks in *Poetry* that "glimpses offered in this collection of middle-class Black life have spark and freshness to them inasmuch as this social category hasn't had poetic coverage up to now." In *Parnassus,* Helen Vendler describes Dove's poems as "rarely without drama," adding, "I admire Dove's persistent probes into ordinary language of the black proletariat." Jan Clausen notes in *The Women's Review of Books* that Dove's "images are elegant mechanisms for capturing moods and moments which defy analysis or translation." In the *Washington Post Book World,* A. L. Nielsen finds that the poems

"abound in the unforgettable details of family character" and adds that Dove "is one of those rare poets who approach common experience with the same sincerity with which the objectivist poets of an earlier generation approached the things of our world."

A later work, the novel *Through the Ivory Gate,* tells the story of Virginia King, a gifted young black woman who takes a position as artist-in-residence at an elementary school in her hometown of Akron, Ohio. The story alternates between past and present as Virginia's return stirs up strong, sometimes painful memories of her childhood. Barbara Hoffert observes in the *Library Journal* that the "images are indelible, the emotions always heartfelt and fresh," and in the *New York Times Book Review,* Geoff Ryman notes: "Through the Ivory Gate is mature in its telling of little stories—Virginia's recollections of life with a troupe of puppeteers, of visiting the rubber factory where her father worked, of neighborhood boys daubing a house so that it looked as if it had measles." He concludes: "The book aims to present the richness of a life and its connections to family and friends, culture, place, seasons, and self. In this it succeeds."

In 1993 Dove published *Selected Poems,* which contains three of Dove's previously published volumes: *The Yellow House on the Corner, Museum,* and *Thomas and Beulah.* Reviewing the collection for *The Women's Review of Books,* Akasha (Gloria) Hull remarks, "In the guise of poet, [Dove] becomes many types of women and men, and takes us readers into their consciousness, helping us to feel whatever it is we all share that makes those journeys possible." In recognition of her achievements as a poet, Dove was appointed to the prestigious post of United States Poet Laureate, a position she held from 1994 to 1995.

Dove explores yet another genre with her first full-length play, *The Darker Face of the Earth.* "[T]here's no reason to subscribe authors to particular genres," comments Dove in *Black American Literature*; "I'm a writer, and I write in the form that most suits what I want to say." Depicting the events that ensue when a wealthy white woman named Amalia gives birth to a slave's child, *The Darker Face of the Earth* imbues the theme of slavery with the high drama as well as the murderous elements reminiscent of classical Greek drama. Hull, again writing for *The Women's Review of Books,* comments: "[The Darker Face of the Earth] transfers the oedipal myth of patricide and maternal incest to antebellum South Carolina, and though we can guess the end from the very beginning, we read with continuing interest, sustained by Dove's poetic dialogue."

While Dove's forays into fiction and drama have been well-received, some critics, such as Helen Vendler in *The New Yorker,* comment that Dove is "primarily a poet" because her greatest concern is language itself. Dove returned to writing poetry with her most recent volume, *Mother Love.* Dedicated to Dove's daughter Aviva, the volume takes its unifying structure from the Greek mother-daughter myth of Demeter and Persephone. Vendler praises Dove's unsentimental portrayal of motherhood, emphasizing her often wry and sometimes startling tone. "Dove brings into close focus the pained relation between mothers and daughters," notes Vendler. "Dove's handling of the variety of voices and styles woven through the book shows a wonderful control of register and music," affirms Sarah Maguire in *Times Literary Supplement.*

BIOGRAPHICAL/CRITICAL SOURCES:

BOOKS

Vendler, Helen Hennessy, *The Given and the Made: Strategies of Poetic Redefinition,* Harvard University Press (Cambridge), 1995.

PERIODICALS

American Book Review, July, 1985.
American Poetry Review, January, 1982, 36.
American Visions, April-May, 1994, p. 33.
Belles Lettres, Winter 1993-94, pp. 38-41.
Black American Literature Forum, Fall, 1986, pp. 227-40.
Booklist, February 1, 1981, p. 743; August, 1983; March 15, 1986, p. 1057; February 15, 1997.
Callaloo, winter, 1986; spring, 1991; winter, 1996.
Current Biography, May, 1994, p. 10.
Detroit Free Press, July 24, 1993, pp. 5A, 7A.
Georgia Review, summer, 1984; winter, 1986.
Kliatt, March, 1994, p. 25.
Library Journal, August, 1992; November 15, 1993, p. 81; March 1, 1994, p. 88; April 1, 1997.
Michigan Quarterly Review, spring, 1987, pp. 428-38.
New Yorker, May 15, 1995.
New York Review of Books, October 23, 1986.
New York Times Book Review, October 11, 1992.
North American Review, March, 1986.
Parnassus: Poetry in Review, spring/summer/fall/winter, 1985; Volume 16, number 2, 1991.
Poetry, October, 1984; October, 1990, pp. 37-39; March, 1996.
Publishers Weekly, August 3, 1992; January 31, 1994, p. 83.
Southern Humanities Review, winter, 1988, p. 87.
Times Literary Supplement, February 18, 1994; November 17, 1995, p. 29.
USA Weekend, March 25-27, 1994, p. 22.
Virginia Quarterly Review, spring, 1988, pp. 262-76.
Washington Post, April 17, 1987; May 19, 1993; November 7, 1997.
Washington Post Book World, April 8, 1990, p. 4; July 30, 1995, p. 8.
Women's Review of Books, July, 1990, pp. 12-13; May, 1994, p. 6; May, 1996.

*   *   *

DOYLE, A. Conan
   See DOYLE, Arthur Conan

*   *   *

DOYLE, Arthur Conan 1859-1930
   (A. Conan Doyle, Conan Doyle, Sir A. Conan Doyle, Sir Arthur Conan Doyle)

PERSONAL: Born May 22, 1859, in Edinburgh, Scotland; died of a heart attack, July 7, 1930, in Crowborough, Sussex, England; buried at Windlesham, Crowborough, Sussex, England; son of Charles Altamont (a civil servant and artist) and Mary (Foley) Doyle; married Louise Hawkins, August 6, 1885 (died, 1906); married Jean Leckie, September 18, 1907; children: (first marriage) Mary Louise, Kingsley; (second marriage) Denis, Adrian Malcolm, Lena Jean. *Education:* Edinburgh University, B.M., 1881, M.D., 1885.

CAREER: Assistant to physician in Birmingham, England, 1879; ship's surgeon on whaling voyage to Arctic, 1880; ship's surgeon on voyage to west coast of Africa, 1881-82; physician in Southsea, Portsmouth, England, 1882-90; ophthalmologist in London, England, 1891; writer. Lectured on spiritualism in Europe, Australia, the United States, and Canada, 1917-25, South Africa, 1928, and Sweden, 1929. *Wartime service:* Served during the Boer War as chief surgeon of a field hospital in Bloemfontein, South Africa, 1900.

AWARDS, HONORS: Knighted, 1902.

WRITINGS:

SHERLOCK HOLMES DETECTIVE FICTION

A Study in Scarlet (novel; first published in *Beeton's Christmas Annual,* November, 1887), illustrations by father, Charles Doyle, Ward, Lock, 1888, Lippincott, 1890, introduction by Hugh Greene, Doubleday, 1977.
The Sign of Four (novel; first published in *Lippincott's Monthly* magazine, February, 1890), Blackett, 1890, Collier, 1891, introduction by Graham Greene, Doubleday, 1977, published as *The Sign of the Four,* Conkey, 1900, illustrations by Frank Bolle, Lion Books, c. 1973, published as *The Sign of the Four; or, The Problem of the Sholtos,* introduction by P. G. Wodehouse, Ballantine, c. 1975.
The Adventures of Sherlock Holmes (short stories), illustrations by Paget, Newnes, 1892, Harper, 1892.
The Memoirs of Sherlock Holmes (short stories), illustrations by Sidney Paget, Newnes, 1893, illustrations by W. H. Hyde and Paget, Harper, 1894.
The Hound of the Baskervilles (novel; serialized in *Strand* magazine, 1901-02), illustrations by Paget, Newnes, 1902, McClure, Phillips, 1902, foreword and afterword by John Fowles, Doubleday, 1977.
The Return of Sherlock Holmes (short stories), illustrations by Paget, Newnes, 1905, McClure, Phillips, 1905.
The Valley of Fear (novel; serialized in *Strand* magazine, 1914-1915), Smith, Elder, 1915, published as *The Valley of Fear: A Sherlock Holmes Novel,* illustrations by Arthur I. Keller, Doran, 1915.
His Last Bow: Some Reminiscences of Sherlock Holmes (short stories), J. Murray, 1917, published as *His Last Bow: A Reminiscence of Sherlock Holmes,* Doran, 1917.
The Case-Book of Sherlock Holmes (short stories), J. Murray, 1927, Doran, 1927.
The Annotated Sherlock Holmes: The Four Novels and the Fifty-six Short Stories Complete, edited with introduction, notes, and bibliography by William S. Baring-Gould, illustrations by Charles Doyle and others, C. N. Potter, 1967.
The Uncollected Sherlock Holmes (short stories), compiled by Richard Lancelyn Green, Penguin, 1983.
Sherlock Holmes Reader (includes "The Red-Headed League" and "The Adventure of the Speckled Band"), Courage Books (Philadelphia), 1994.
The Mysteries of Sherlock Holmes, illustrations by Paul Bachem, Grosset & Dunlap (New York City), 1996.
Sir Arthur Conan Doyle: Three Adventure Novels (contains *The Lost World, The Poison Belt,* and *The White Company*), Gramercy (Avenel), 1996.

NOVELS

The Mystery of Cloomber, Ward & Downey, 1889, Munro, 1895.
The Firm of Girdlestone (semiautobiographical), Chatto & Windus, 1890, Lovell, 1890.

The Doings of Raffles Haw (serialized in *Answers*, 1891-92), Lovell, Coryell, 1891, Cassell, 1892.

Beyond the City, George Newnes, 1892.

The Parasite, Constable, 1894, published as *The Parasite: A Story*, illustrations by Howard Pyle, Harper, 1895.

The Stark Munro Letters: Being a Series of Sixteen Letters Written by J. Stark Munro, M.B., to his Friend and Former Fellow-Student, Herbert Swanborough, of Lowell, Massachusetts, During the Years 1881-1884 (autobiographical), Longmans, Green, 1895, Appleton, 1895.

Rodney Stone, illustrations by Paget, Smith, Elder, 1896, Appleton, 1896.

The Tragedy of the Korosko, illustrations by Paget, Smith, Elder, 1898, published as *A Desert Drama: Being the Tragedy of the Korosko*, Lippincott, 1898.

A Duet with an Occasional Chorus, Richards, 1899, Appleton, 1899.

The Lost World, Hodder & Stoughton, 1912, Doran, 1912.

The Poison Belt, illustrations by Harry Rountree, Hodder & Stoughton, 1913, Doran, 1913, introduction by John Dickson Carr, epilogue by Harlow Shapley, Berkley Publishing, 1966.

The Land of Mist, Hutchinson, 1925, Doran, 1926.

HISTORICAL NOVELS

Micah Clarke: His Statement as Made to His Three Grandchildren, Joseph, Gervas, and Reuben, During the Hard Winter of 1734, Longmans, Green, 1889, Harper, 1889.

The White Company (serialized in *Cornhill* magazine, 1891), Smith, Elder, 1891, Lovell, 1891, Burt, c. 1982.

The Refugees: A Tale of Two Continents (serialized in *Harper's Monthly* magazine, 1893), Longmans, Green, 1893, illustrations by T. De Thulstrup, Harper, 1893.

The Great Shadow (first published in *Arrowsmith's Christmas Annual*, 1892), Arrowsmith, 1893, Harper, 1893.

Uncle Bernac: A Memory of the Empire, illustrations by Robert Sauber, Smith, Elder, 1897, Appleton, 1897.

Sir Nigel (sequel to *The White Company*; serialized in *Strand* magazine, 1905-06), illustrations by Arthur Twidle, Smith, Elder, 1906, illustrations by the Kinneys, McClure, Phillips, 1906.

Sir Arthur Conan Doyle: The Historical Romances, 2 volumes, New Orchard England, 1986.

SHORT STORIES

Mysteries and Adventures, Scott, 1890, published as *The Gully of Bluemansdyke and Other Stories*, Scott, 1892, published as *My Friend the Murderer and Other Mysteries and Adventures*, Lovell, Coryell, 1893.

The Captain of the Polestar and Other Tales, Longmans, Green, 1890, Munro, 1894.

(With Campbell Rae Brown) *An Actor's Duel* [and] *The Winning Shot* (the former by Brown, the latter by Doyle), Dicks, 1894.

Round the Red Lamp: Being Facts and Fancies of Medical Life (horror), Methuen, 1894, Appleton, 1894.

The Surgeon of Gaster Fell (also see below), Ivers, 1895.

The Exploits of Brigadier Gerard (adventure), illustrations by W. B. Wollen, Newnes, 1896, Appleton, 1896.

The Green Flag and Other Stories of War and Sport, Smith, Elder, 1900, McClure, Phillips, 1900.

Adventures of Gerard, illustrations by W. B. Wollen, Newnes, 1903, McClure, Phillips, 1903.

Round the Fire Stories, Smith, Elder, 1908, McClure, 1908.

One Crowded Hour (also see below), Paget, 1911.

The Last Galley: Impressions and Tales, illustrations by N. C. Wyeth and Rountree, Smith, Elder, 1911, Doubleday, Page, 1911.

Danger! And Other Stories, J. Murray, 1918, Doran, 1919 (see above).

Tales of the Ring and Camp, J. Murray, 1922, published as *The Croxley Master and Other Tales of the Ring and Camp*, Doran, 1925.

Tales of Terror and Mystery, Murray, 1922; published as *The Black Doctor and Other Tales of Terror and Mystery*, Doran, 1925.

Tales of Twilight and the Unseen, J. Murray, 1922, published as *The Great Keinplatz Experiment and Other Tales of Twilight and the Unseen*, Doran, 1925.

Tales of Adventure and Medical Life, J. Murray, 1922, published as *The Man from Archangel and Other Tales of Adventure*, Doran, 1925.

Tales of Long Ago, J. Murray, 1922, published as *The Last of the Legions and Other Tales of Long Ago*, Doran, 1925.

The Three of Them: A Reminiscence, J. Murray, 1923.

The Macarot Deep and Other Stories, J. Murray, 1929, Doubleday, Doran, 1929.

Complete Professor Challenger Stories, Transatlantic, 1952.

Uncollected Stories: The Unknown Conan Doyle, compiled with an introduction by John Michael Gibson and Richard Lancelyn Green, Secker & Warburg, 1982.

Conan Doyle Stories, Hippocrene Books, 1985.

PLAYS

(With J. M. Barrie) *Jane Annie; or, The Good Conduct Prize* (comic opera; first produced in London at Savoy Theatre, May 13, 1893), Chappell, 1893.

Foreign Policy (one-act play; based on own short story "A Question of Diplomacy"), first produced in London at Terry's Theatre, June 3, 1893.

Waterloo (one-act play; based on own short story "A Straggler of '15"; first produced as *A Story of Waterloo* in Bristol, England, at Prince's Theatre, September 21, 1894), Samuel French, 1907.

Halves (prologue and three acts; based on story of same title by James Payn), first produced in Aberdeen, Scotland, at Her Majesty's Theatre, April 10, 1899.

(With William Gillette) *Sherlock Holmes* (four-act play; based on Doyle's short story "The Strange Case of Miss Faulkner"; first produced in London at Duke of York's Theatre, June 12, 1899; produced in Buffalo, NY, at Star Theatre, October 23, 1899; produced Off-Broadway at Garrick Theatre, November 6, 1899), Samuel French, 1922.

A Duet (A Duologue) (one-act comedy; based on own novel *A Duet with an Occasional Chorus*; first produced in London at Steinway Hall, October 27, 1902), Samuel French, 1903.

Brigadier Gerard (four-act comedy), first produced in London at Imperial Theatre, March 3, 1906; produced in New York City at Savoy Theatre, November 5, 1906.

The Fires of Fate (four-act; based on own novel *The Tragedy of the Korosko*), first produced in Liverpool, England, at Shakespeare Theatre, June 11, 1909; produced in New York City at Liberty Theatre, December 28, 1909.

The House of Temperley, first produced in London at Adelphi Theatre, February 11, 1910.

A Pot of Caviare (one-act play; based on own short story of same title), first produced in London at Adelphi Theatre, April 19, 1910.

The Speckled Band: An Adventure of Sherlock Holmes (three-act play; based on own short story "The Adventure of the Speckled Band"; first produced in London at Adelphi Theatre, June 4, 1910; produced Off-Broadway at Garrick Theatre, November 21, 1910; produced on the West End at Strand Theatre, February 6, 1911), Samuel French 1912.

The Crown Diamond (one-act play; first produced in Bristol, England, at the Hippodrome, May 2, 1921), privately printed, 1958.

It's Time Something Happened (one-act play), Appleton, 1925.

Exile: A Drama of Christmas Eve (one-act play), Appleton, 1925.

Also author of *Angels of Darkness* (three-acts), *Sir Charles Tregellis, Admiral Denver, The Stonor Case, The Lift,* and *Mrs. Thompson* (based on the novel of the same title by W. B. Maxwell).

WORKS ON SPIRITUALISM

The New Revelation, Hodder & Stoughton, 1918, Doran, 1918.

The Vital Message, Hodder & Stoughton, 1919, Doran, 1919.

Spiritualism and Rationalism, Hodder & Stoughton, 1920.

The Wanderings of a Spiritualist, Hodder & Stoughton, 1921, Doran, 1921.

The Evidence for Fairies, Doran, 1921.

Fairies Photographed, Doran, 1921.

The Coming of the Fairies, Hodder & Stoughton, 1922, Doran, 1922.

(With others) *The Case for Spirit Photography,* preface by Fred Barlow, Hutchinson, 1922, Doran, 1923.

Our American Adventure, Hodder & Stoughton, 1923, Doran, 1923.

(Compiler) *The Spiritualists' Reader,* Two Worlds, 1924.

Our Second American Adventure, Hodder & Stoughton, 1924, Little, Brown, 1924.

(Contributor) James Marchant, editor, *Survival,* Putnam, 1924, Doyle's contribution published separately as *Psychic Experiences,* Putnam, 1925.

The History of Spiritualism, 2 volumes, Cassell, 1926, Doran, 1926.

Pheneas Speaks: Direct Spirit Communications in the Family Circle, Psychic Press, 1927, Doran, 1927.

Our African Winter, J. Murray, 1929.

The Roman Catholic Church: A Rejoinder, Psychic Press, 1929.

The Edge of the Unknown (essays), J. Murray, 1930, Putnam, 1930.

OTHER

Songs of Action (poetry; also see below), Smith, Elder, 1898, Doubleday & McClure, 1898.

The Great Boer War, Smith, Elder, 1900, McClure, Phillips, 1900.

The War in South Africa: Its Cause and Conduct, Smith, Elder, 1902, McClure, Phillips, 1902.

The Story of Mr. George Edalji, privately printed, 1907, published as *The Case of Mr. George Edalji,* Blake, 1907.

Through the Magic Door (criticism), illustrations by W. Russell Flint, Smith, Elder, 1907, McClure, 1908, Doubleday, Page, 1925.

The Crime of the Congo, Hutchinson, 1909, Doubleday, Page, 1909.

Songs of the Road (poetry; also see below), Smith, Elder, 1911, Doubleday, Page, 1911.

The Case of Oscar Slater, Hodder & Stoughton, 1912.

Great Britain and the Next War, Small, Maynard, 1914.

To Arms!, preface by F. E. Smith, Hodder & Stoughton, 1914.

The German War (essays), Hodder & Stoughton, 1914.

Western Wanderings, Doran, 1915.

A Visit to Three Fronts: June, 1916, Hodder & Stoughton, 1916, published as *A Visit to Three Fronts: Glimpses of the British, Italian, and French Lines,* Doran, 1916.

The Origin and Outbreak of the War, Doran, 1916.

The British Campaign in France and Flanders, 6 volumes, Hodder & Stoughton, 1916-20, Doran, 1916-20, enlarged edition published as *The British Campaigns in Europe, 1914-1919,* Bles, 1928.

The Guards Came Through and Other Poems (also see below), J. Murray, 1919, Doran, 1920.

The Poems of Arthur Conan Doyle: Collected Edition (contains *Songs of Action, Songs of the Road,* and *The Guards Came Through and Other Poems,*), J. Murray, 1922.

Memories and Adventures (autobiography), Hodder & Stoughton, 1924, Little, Brown, 1924.

Strange Studies From Life: Containing Three Hitherto Uncollected Tales Based on the Annals of True Crime, additional material by Philip Trevor, edited with an introduction by Peter Ruber, Candlelight Press, 1963.

Essays on Photography: The Unknown Conan Doyle, compiled with an introduction by John Michael Gibson and Richard Lancelyn Green, Secker & Warburg, 1982.

Letters to the Press, edited with an introduction by John Michael Gibson and Richard Lancelyn Green, University of Iowa Press, 1986.

Contributor of works such as "The Truth About Sherlock Holmes" in a variety of genres to many magazines and newspapers, including *Strand, Chambers's Journal, Harper's, Blackwood's, Saturday Evening Post, McClure's, London Society, Cornhill, Lippincott's, Boston Herald, Philadelphia Inquirer, St. Louis Post-Dispatch,* and the *New York Times.* Translator from the French of *The Mystery of Joan of Arc* by Leon Denis, J. Murray, 1924, Dutton, 1925.

MEDIA ADAPTATIONS: Many of Doyle's works have been adapted for film, including *A Study in Scarlet, The Adventures of Sherlock Holmes, The Hound of the Baskervilles, His Last Bow, The Firm of Girdlestone,* and *The Exploits of Brigadier Gerard.* Doyle's writings have also been adapted for plays and television.

SIDELIGHTS: Sir Arthur Conan Doyle created one of the most famous characters in the history of fiction. Indeed, the name of Sherlock Holmes is synonymous with detective; and the deerstalker cap and calabash pipe suggest Holmes to people all over the world, even to those who have never read any of the four novels and fifty-six short stories Doyle wrote about him. Yet those kinds of cap and pipe are not mentioned and the phrase "Elementary, my dear Watson" is never uttered in any of the sixty tales. But Doyle was so afraid that Holmes would distract his own and his readers' attention from what he considered his more important work that he killed the detective in one story, only to be forced by public demand to resurrect him later. Doyle was a master storyteller. Even his weaker fictional efforts hold the reader's interest. Doyle prided himself on his ability to devise ingenious plots—the reader is carried along by the sheer power of the storyteller's art. In fact, his historical novels, which he intended as authentic recreations of life in earlier periods and which were supposed to educate Englishmen in the history of their country, were treated by reviewers only as exciting adventure yarns.

After Doyle gave up the practice of medicine in 1891, he lived and supported a large family on the income from his writing alone. By the 1920's he was the most highly paid writer in the world, commanding ten shillings a word. Market considerations occasionally entered into his decisions about what to write—especially in regard to the Sherlock Holmes stories. Most of his works appeared first in magazines and then in book form so that he was paid twice for each.

Doyle wrote in virtually every form and genre: detective stories, historical novels, science fiction, horror stories, domestic comedy, sports stories, poetry, and plays; he even collaborated on an operetta—one of his few failures. A significant portion of his writing was nonfiction, to which he brought the same stylistic and storytelling skills that made his fiction so popular. He was knighted not, as many people suppose, for writing the Sherlock Holmes stories, but for his pamphlet defending British actions in South Africa during the Boer War of 1899 to 1902. He also wrote histories of that war and of World War I, articles on military preparedness, literary criticism, histories and defenses of spiritualism, and vindications of men unjustly convicted of crimes.

Doyle was a true man of his time. Until his obsession with spiritualism began to make him look somewhat foolish, he was regarded on both sides of the Atlantic as the very symbol of British probity, stolidity, and common sense. He shared the prejudices of his time and place in his unswerving support of the British Empire, his steadfast opposition to women's suffrage, his unquestioning acceptance of the class system, and his hostility to labor unions.

Doyle started out as a doctor rather than a writer. While attending Edinburgh University in the late 1870s, he met Dr. Joseph Bell, a surgeon who was able to deduce his patients' occupations and other information from observing their appearance; Bell became the model for Sherlock Holmes, as professor of physiology William Rutherford did for another Doyle character, Professor Challenger. To help pay for his education, Doyle worked during vacations as an assistant to various doctors. The nephew of one of these physicians told Doyle that his letters were so vivid he ought to try to write something to sell. This encouragement launched Doyle's professional writing career. His first story was rejected, but the second, "The Mystery of Sasassa Valley," appeared anonymously in *Chambers's Journal* in 1879. It is the tale of three young adventurers in South Africa who investigate a native superstition about a demon with a glowing red eye and discover a huge diamond. Another story, "The American's Tale," written in imitation of Bret Harte, was published in the Christmas, 1880, issue of *London Society.*

Doyle indulged his taste for real-life adventure by signing on as a ship's surgeon on a seven-month Arctic whaling and sealing expedition in 1880; as Pearsall comments, "his whaler types crop up time and time again in his stories, sometimes dressed up in army uniform." After receiving his bachelor of medicine degree in 1881, he sailed to Africa as a surgeon on a freighter. On his return, he wrote an account of the voyage for the *British Journal of Photography* and submitted short stories for publication in *London Society* and *Blackwood's.*

In 1886 Doyle decided to try his hand at a detective novel. He said later that all the detective fiction he had read was unsatisfactory because the solution of the mystery was made to depend on chance or on some flash of intuition by the detective; Doyle, as he declared in "The Truth about Sherlock Holmes," wanted to try to "reduce this fascinating but unorganized business to something nearer to an exact science." Influenced by Poe's Dupin stories, the Lecoq novels of Emile Gaboriau, and Sergeant Cuff in Wilkie Collins's *The Moonstone* (1868), Doyle began work on a novel he

called "A Tangled Skein." His notes reveal that his detective protagonist was originally to be called "Sherrinford Holmes" and the narrator "Ormond Sacker"; but these names were quickly replaced by "Sherlock Holmes" and "John H. Watson, M.D.," and the title of the novel became *A Study in Scarlet.*

Doyle wrote the novel in three weeks during March and April, 1886, and sent it to the *Cornhill*; the editor, James Payn, liked but rejected it because it was too long to publish in one issue and too short to serialize. The novel was accepted by Ward, Lock for publication in their *Beeton's Christmas Annual* for 1887, more than a year away. They paid Doyle twenty-five pounds for the complete rights to the story—the only money he ever received for it. When *A Study in Scarlet* appeared, it caused no great stir; but the 1887 edition of *Beeton's Christmas Annual* sold out—it is now one of the rarest and most valuable publications in the world—and the novel received complimentary reviews in minor journals and newspapers. Ward, Lock republished it in book form in 1888 with six illustrations by Doyle's father, who had been in an asylum suffering from alcoholism since 1879.

In July 1887, Doyle started work on the first of his historical novels, *Micah Clarke,* dealing with the Duke of Monmouth's rebellion against his father, Charles II, in the seventeenth century. According to John Dickson Carr in *The Life of Sir Arthur Conan Doyle,* "The power of Micah Clarke, aside from its best action scenes—the bloodhounds on Salisbury Plain, the brush with the King's Dragoons, the fight in Wells Cathedral, the blinding battlepiece at Sedgemoor—still lies in its characterization: that other imagination, the use of homely detail, by which each character grows into life before ever a shot is fired in war." Charles Higham points out in *The Adventures of Conan Doyle: The Life of the Creator of Sherlock Holmes,* that "the descriptions of war have a remarkable intensity, being alive with the author's love of battle"—at this time Doyle had never experienced a real war—but says that "the book suffers from deliberately antiquated 'period' diction in the dialogue and some of the descriptive material." Like many of Doyle's fictional works, the novel is narrated in the first person—in this case by Micah, a supporter of Monmouth. Doyle later claimed to have spent two years in research and five months in writing the book.

Micah Clarke received enthusiastic reviews when it was published in February, 1889, and Doyle immediately began work on another historical novel, *The White Company,* set in the fourteenth century. Between researching and writing *The White Company,* Doyle received an offer from the American editor of *Lippincott's* magazine, which was published in both Philadelphia and London, for another Sherlock Holmes story. The proposal was made at a dinner in London that was also attended by Oscar Wilde; out of this meeting came both Doyle's *The Sign of Four* and Wilde's *The Picture of Dorian Gray* (1891). *The Sign of Four*—published in the United States as *The Sign of the Four*—is set in 1888 and involves an Indian treasure, a one-legged man, a vicious Pygmy with a deadly blowgun, a character closely modeled on Oscar Wilde, and a chase down the Thames River in a motor launch. *The Sign of Four* appeared complete in one issue of *Lippincott's* and also in book form in 1890. It was well received, particularly in America, but the sensational popularity of Sherlock Holmes was yet to come.

After writing *The Sign of Four,* Doyle went back to *The White Company.* The novel follows the adventures in England, France, and Spain of the knight Sir Nigel Loring, his squire Alleyne Edricson, Edricson's friend John of Hordle, and the bowman

Samkin Aylward. As Higham says, it is "somewhat dated today" but is "vigorously told and scrupulously accurate." Doyle felt that the novel illuminated the national traditions of England and revealed for the first time the significance of the rise of the longbowman. He was disturbed that critics regarded it simply as a rousing adventure story. *The White Company* was serialized in the *Cornhill* before appearing in book form in 1891, and went through numerous editions.

In 1891, Doyle set himself up as an eye specialist in London, though he never attracted a single patient. Instead, he contributed a humorous story about a phonograph, "The Voice of Science," to the March, 1891, issue of a new illustrated monthly, the *Strand*. Doyle soon realized that a series of stories with a continuing central character could build reader loyalty for the magazine; since he had already created Sherlock Holmes, he quickly wrote six short stories featuring Holmes. When the first of these, "A Scandal in Bohemia," appeared in the July, 1891, issue of the *Strand,* the phenomenal popularity of Sherlock Holmes began. Doyle received thirty-five pounds for each story.

The first twelve Holmes stories were collected as *The Adventures of Sherlock Holmes,* and the *Strand* asked for more. Hoping to quiet the editors' requests, Doyle demanded what he considered an outrageous amount, [1,000 pounds sterling] for another dozen stories. Again, the editors accepted. While working on these stories, the incredibly productive Doyle wrote a novel about suburban life, *Beyond the City,* and another historical novel, *The Great Shadow.* Higham calls the latter work "tedious," though Carr says that the description of the Battle of Waterloo at the end "rings in the ears and stifles the nostrils with gun smoke." Doyle also helped his friend James Barrie, who had fallen ill, complete an operetta, *Jane Annie; or, The Good Conduct Prize,* which was a resounding failure when it was performed at the Savoy Theatre in May, 1893.

In the fall of 1893, Doyle's wife, Louise, was diagnosed as having tuberculosis and given only months to live; in fact, she survived for thirteen years. Burdened with concern for his wife, tired of inventing new plots for the Holmes stories, and convinced that his detective was consuming the time and attention due his "better" work, Doyle killed Holmes in "The Final Problem," the last of the twelve stories he had promised the *Strand.* In this story, set in April, 1891 Holmes and Watson are pursued to Switzerland by the arch-criminal Professor James Moriarty, whose gang has been destroyed through Holmes's efforts. Watson returns to the brink of the Reichenbach Falls, after having been called away on a ruse, to find a note from Holmes and evidence that he and Moriarty have struggled and then fallen over the precipice to their deaths. When the story appeared in the *Strand* in December, 1893, twenty thousand readers canceled their subscriptions, businessmen dressed in mourning, and Doyle received letters addressing him as "You Brute." Unremorseful, Doyle collected the second twelve Holmes stories as *The Memoirs of Sherlock Holmes* and wrote *The Stark Munro Letters,* an autobiographical novel, based on Doyle's experiences with Dr. Budd, that contains some of his best comedy but ends when the protagonist and his wife are killed in a railroad accident.

Doyle then wrote the first series of Brigadier Gerard stories for the *Strand.* Gerard was based on the real-life French General Baron de Marbot, whose memoirs Doyle had read in 1892. The two series of stories, collected as *The Exploits of Brigadier Gerard* and *Adventures of Gerard,* form in Carr's judgment "the finest picture he ever did of the Napoleonic campaigns. And the reason

is this: that he saw it through the eyes of a Frenchman." Gerard's "naive boasting, his complacence, his firm conviction that every woman is in love with him, all blind the reader with mirth. Above everything, his serene good nature never fails. He curls his sidewhiskers, gives his mustache the Marengo twist, and rides living out of the page." The stories are exciting and frequently hilarious—sometimes with a grim humor, as characters are run through with swords or decapitated—and Gerard is one of Doyle's most memorable creations.

In the spring of 1898 Doyle began a new series of stories for the *Strand* which were collected as *Round the Fire Stories.* One of these, "The Lost Special," in which a train vanishes without a trace between stations, is, according to Carr, "by far his finest mystery (as distinguished from detective) story." In the fall, he wrote *A Duet with an Occasional Chorus,* a warm, gentle, humorous look at the ordinary life of a middle-class suburban couple. The book was always one of his favorites; he refused to allow it to be serialized, because he thought serialization would ruin it. Though H. G. Wells and Algernon Charles Swinburne admired it, the novel was too great a departure from what the public and critics expected from Doyle, and it was not successful.

When fighting broke out in South Africa between the governing British colonists and the Dutch-descended settlers known as the Boers, Doyle was too old at forty-one to enlist as a soldier. He instead served for three months in 1900 as a doctor in a private military hospital in Bloemfontein, South Africa. On his return to England he wrote *The Great Boer War,* an accurate and impartial history of the conflict up to that time. The book was and is highly respected; but its final chapter advocating the modernization of the British army—an argument he had earlier presented in the *Cornhill*—predictably earned him the scorn of the military establishment. However, all of the reforms he proposed were subsequently adopted. Later, angered by charges that the British committed atrocities during the Boer War, Doyle wrote in one week a sixty-thousand-word pamphlet in rebuttal. Published in January, 1902, *The War in South Africa: Its Cause and Conduct* was sold for sixpence per copy in Britain; thousands of translations were given away in France, Russia, Germany, and other countries. All profits from the sale of the book were donated to charity. For producing this propaganda triumph, Doyle was knighted on August 9, 1902.

In March, 1901, Doyle went on a golfing holiday with Fletcher Robinson, who told him the legend of a ghostly hound from Robinson's native Dartmoor, in Devonshire. After a trip to Dartmoor with Robinson, Doyle began writing what he called "a real creeper" of a novel based on the legend. Almost as an afterthought, he decided to use Sherlock Holmes in the novel, titled *The Hound of the Baskervilles*; but he was careful to set the story in 1899, before Holmes's death in the Reichenbach Falls. According to Carr, *The Hound of the Baskervilles* "is the only tale, long or short, in which the story dominates Holmes rather than Holmes dominating the story; what captures the reader is less the Victorian detective than the Gothic romance."

While *The Hound of the Baskervilles* was being serialized in the *Strand,* Gillette's play, *Sherlock Holmes,* which had already been a hit in the United States, opened in London with equal success. Gillette went on to make a career of portraying Holmes, which he did until he was an elderly man. It was he who was responsible for the popular conception of the detective puffing on a curved-stem pipe, which he adopted because it was easy for him to use on stage; over the years, cartoonists exaggerated the pipe into the monstrous calabash. In fact, the only pipes mentioned in the Doyle stories are a brier, a long-stemmed cherrywood, and an oily black clay.

In 1903 *McClure's* magazine in New York offered Doyle $5,000 per story if he would bring Sherlock Holmes back to life, and the *Strand* offered more than half that amount for the British rights. Persuaded by these astronomical sums, Doyle agreed. In "The Empty House," Holmes reappears in London and tells the shocked Watson that his knowledge of the Japanese martial art of baritsu enabled him to slip through Moriarty's grasp and that the evil professor had plunged into the Reichenbach Falls alone. For reasons that, upon close examination, do not make a great deal of sense, Holmes decided to fake his own death and disappear. He has returned in "The Empty House" to apprehend Moriarty's last remaining henchman, Colonel Sebastian Moran, "the most dangerous man in London." The story is set in April, 1894, meaning that Holmes had been away for three years; in actual time, it had been ten years since he had last shown himself in "The Final Problem."

The appearance of "The Empty House" in the *Strand* in October, 1903, created a sensation. Along with twelve more stories, which ran in the magazine until December 1904, it was collected in *The Return of Sherlock Holmes.* Holmes was as popular as ever, though some critics have contended that the stories written after what is known as "the Great Hiatus" are generally not up to the standard of the earlier ones. Doyle was aware of this opinion, and although he disagreed with it, he enjoyed reporting as he did in "The Truth About Sherlock Holmes"—the words of the Cornish boatman who said to him: "I think, sir, when Holmes fell over that cliff, he may not have killed himself, but all the same he was never quite the same man afterwards." Stephen Knight notes, in *Form and Ideology in Crime Fiction,* that some of the changes in the later Holmes stories correspond to changes in Doyle's own situation: "The older Doyle was a much more prosperous and prestigious man, and the later Sherlock Holmes becomes more respectable. . . . Holmes gives up cocaine, goes for healthy walks, gets on better with the police and is much less barbed towards Watson." Some of the stories Doyle wrote after reintroducing Holmes are set in the period after Holmes's return; others are purportedly records of cases that occurred before his disappearance.

Inspired by learning of the discovery near his home in Sussex of fossilized dinosaur footprints, Doyle in the fall and winter of 1911 wrote *The Lost World,* the story of four adventurers who find living prehistoric animals and people on an isolated mesa in Brazil. The young, naive journalist-narrator Edward Malone; the thin, sardonic, pipe-puffing Professor Summerlee; the dashing hunter Lord John Roxton; and above all, the squat, powerful, bellowing sarcastic genius Professor George Edward Challenger are all vividly and memorably drawn characters. The story presents scenes of high comedy, as when Malone tries to pass himself off as a scientist on his first meeting with Challenger but is trapped by the professor's pseudo-scientific doubletalk, and scenes of high adventure on the mesa. Furthermore, Doyle's descriptions of the pterodactyls and dinosaurs are scientifically accurate. At the end of 1912, Doyle produced another novel about Professor Challenger and his three friends. In *The Poison Belt,* the earth passes through a poisonous zone in the "ether," and everyone in the world except the four heroes—who are supplied with oxygen in an airtight room—appears to have died. In the end, what seemed to be death turns out to have been suspended animation.

Doyle's response to the outbreak of World War I was characteristic: he both took direct action forming a volunteer rifle company in his area and visiting the front and wrote about it in articles, lectures, and several books, including the six-volume *The British Campaign in France and Flanders.* He brought Holmes into the war in "His Last Bow," in which the sixty-year-old detective comes out of retirement—he has been keeping bees on the Sussex Downs since 1903—to capture a German spy. (While working undercover, Holmes uses the alias "Altamont," Doyle's father's middle name.) The story was written in 1917 but is set just before the outbreak of the war in August, 1914. It was made the title piece in a collection of stories that had been appearing in the *Strand* at long intervals since 1908.

Sherlock Holmes' stories continued to appear at irregular intervals over the years, and in 1927 the last twelve of them were collected as *The Case-Book of Sherlock Holmes.* In the book's preface Doyle announced his intention to write no more of the stories: "I fear that Mr. Sherlock Holmes may become like one of those popular tenors who, having outlived their time, are still tempted to make repeated farewell bows to their indulgent audiences. This must cease and he must go the way of all flesh, material or imaginary." To stop writing the Holmes narratives had also been Doyle's intention when he wrote "The Final Problem" in 1893, but thirty-four years later he held to his resolution.

Beginning with the 1933 founding in New York of the Baker Street Irregulars (named for the street urchins who assist Holmes in three of the stories), Sherlockians have been organized in clubs in at least thirteen countries, including Australia, Burma, Denmark, Germany, Holland, New Zealand, Venezuela, Sweden, and Japan. In the United States, the clubs are known as "scion societies" and take their names from titles of the stories, from cases alluded to by Watson but never recorded, or from something somehow connected with the stories: for example, the Greek Interpreters of East Lansing, Michigan; the Hounds of the Baskervilles of Chicago; the Naval Treaty of St. Louis; and the Red-Headed League of Westtown, Pennsylvania. These societies tend to come into and disappear from existence, but as of 1980 about two hundred of them were organized in the United States. In addition, two periodicals are devoted entirely to Sherlockian scholarship: the *Baker Street Journal,* published by the Baker Street Irregulars, and the *Sherlock Holmes Journal,* published by the Sherlock Holmes Society of London.

Yet although his "serious" fiction has not attracted the attention he desired, Doyle's creation of Sherlock Holmes has insured his immortality as a writer. No other character in the history of fiction has ever inspired such devotion and enthusiasm, and this fact must stand as a tribute to Doyle's talent. The Holmes stories were written carelessly, hastily, and almost always purely for money; but the unstudied and spontaneous nature of the narratives allowed Doyle's creative abilities to be exemplified more fully than did the historical novels for which he prepared so carefully and on which he labored so arduously.

BIOGRAPHICAL/CRITICAL SOURCES:

BOOKS

Adams, Cynthia, *Mysterious Case of Sir Arthur Conan Doyle,* Morgan Reynolds, 1998.
Atkinson, Michael, *The Secret Marriage of Sherlock Holmes, and Other Eccentric Readings,* University of Michigan Press (Ann Arbor), 1996.
Bell, H.W., *Baker Street Studies,* O. Penzler Books (New York City), 1995.

Blackbeard, Bill, *Sherlock Holmes in America,* Abrams, 1981.

Brown, Ivor, *Conan Doyle: A Biography of the Creator of Sherlock Holmes,* Hamilton, 1972.

Bullimore, Tom, *Baker Street Puzzles,* Sterling (New York City), 1994.

Bunson, Matthew, *Encyclopedia Sherlockiana: An A-to-Z Guide to the World of the Great Detective,* Macmillan (New York City), 1994.

Butters, Roger, *First Person Singular: A Review of the Life and Work of Sherlock Holmes, the World's First Consulting Detective,* Vantage, 1984.

Canton, Rolf J., *The Moriarty Principle: Ruminations on Sherlock Holmes,* Galde Press, 1997.

Carr, John Dickson, *The Life of Sir Arthur Conan Doyle,* Harper, 1949.

De Waal, Ronald B., *The Universal Sherlock Holmes,* G. A. Vanderburgh (Shelburne, Ontario), 1994.

Dictionary of Literary Biography, Gale, Volume 18: *Victorian Novelists,* 1983; Volume 70: *British Mystery Writers, 1860-1919,* 1988.

Doyle, Adrian Conan, *The True Conan Doyle,* J. Murray, 1945.

Dudley-Edwards, Owen, *The Quest for Sherlock Holmes: A Biographical Study of Arthur Conan Doyle,* B & N Imports, 1983.

Eyles, Allen, *Sherlock Holmes: A Centenary Celebration,* Harper, 1987.

Frost, Mark, *The Six Messiahs,* Morrow (New York City), 1995.

Goldfarb, Clifford S., *The Great Shadow: Arthur Conan Doyle, Brigadier Gerard and Napoleon,* Calabash Press, 1997.

Gut, Patricia, *Bacchus at Baker Street: Observations on the Bibulous References of Mr. Sherlock Holmes and His Associates,* Players Press (Studio City), 1995.

Holroyd, *Baker Street By-ways,* O. Penzler Books (New York City), 1994.

Hyder, William, *From Baltimore to Baker Street: Thirteen Sherlockian Studies,* [Toronto], 1995.

Jann, Rosemary, *The Adventures of Sherlock Holmes: Detecting Social Order,* Twayne (New York City), 1995.

Jenkins, William D., *The Adventure of the Detected Detective: Sherlock Holmes in James Joyce's "Finnegan's Wake",* Greenwood Press (Westport), 1994.

Kaye, Marvin, *The Game is Afoot: Parodies, Pastiches, and Ponderings of Sherlock Holmes,* St. Martin's Press (New York), 1995.

Kestner, Joseph A., *Sherlock's Men: Masculinity, Conan Doyle, and Cultural History,* Scolar Press, 1997.

King, Joseph A. Cutshall, Charles R. Putney, and Sally Sugarman, *Sherlock Holmes: From Victorian Sleuth to Modern Hero,* Scarecrow Press (Lanham, MD), 1996.

Park, Orlando, *The Sherlock Holmes Encyclopedia,* Carol Publishing Group (Secaucus, NJ), 1994.

Pearsall, Ronald, *Conan Doyle: A Biographical Solution,* St. Martin's, 1977.

Pearson, Hesketh, *Conan Doyle: His Life and Art,* Methuen, 1943.

Pointer, Michael, *The Public Life of Sherlock Holmes,* David & Charles, 1975.

Roberts, S. C., *Holmes & Watson: A Miscellany,* O. Penzler (New York City), 1994.

Rodin, A. E. and Jack D. Key, *Medical Casebook of Doctor Arthur Conan Doyle: From Practitioner to Sherlock Holmes and Beyond,* Krieger, 1984.

Ross, Thomas Wynne, *Good Old Index: The Sherlock Holmes Handbook,* Camden House (Columbia), 1996.

Satterthwait, Walter, *Escapade,* St. Martin's Press, 1995.

Shreffler, Philip A., editor, *The Baker Street Reader: Cornerstone Writings About Sherlock Holmes,* Greenwood Press, 1984.

PERIODICALS

American Scholar, autumn, 1968.

Atlantic Monthly, January, 1994, p. 103.

Bookman, December, 1892; February, 1901; July, 1901; May, 1902; August, 1903; November, 1912; July, 1914; July, 1922; October, 1927; August, 1929.

Collier's, August 15, 1908; December 29, 1923.

Harper's, May, 1948.

Hudson Review, winter, 1949.

Los Angeles Times, January 14, 1987; January 18, 1987.

Medical Times, July, 1971.

Modern Fiction Studies, spring, 1969.

New England Journal of Medicine, October 1, 1953.

Newsweek, August 24, 1959; November 18, 1974.

New Yorker, February 17, 1945.

New York Review of Books, August 17, 1978.

New York Times, March 9, 1952; January 17, 1987.

New York Times Book Review, April 2, 1944; January 21, 1968.

Pacific Quarterly, January, 1978.

Paris Match, August 8, 1959.

Playboy, December, 1966; January, 1975.

Punch, June 20, 1951.

Quarterly Review, July, 1904.

Reader, August, 1905.

San Francisco Review of Books, December, 1976; February, 1977; March, 1977.

Saturday Review, April 27, 1968.

Saturday Review of Literature, July 19, 1930; August 2, 1930; April 29, 1939; February 17, 1940.

Science 83, September, 1983.

Sports Illustrated, March 19, 1973.

Texas Quarterly, summer, 1968.

Twentieth Century (London), May, 1901.

West Coast Review of Books, April, 1975.

*   *   *

DOYLE, Conan
See DOYLE, Arthur Conan

*   *   *

DOYLE, John
See GRAVES, Robert (von Ranke)

*   *   *

DOYLE, Roddy 1958-

PERSONAL: Born in 1958 in Dublin, Ireland; married; wife's name, Belinda; children: two sons.

ADDRESSES: Home—Dublin, Ireland. *Agent*—Patti Kelly, Viking Books, 375 Hudson St., New York, NY 10014; Secker & Warburg, 54 Poland St., London W1V 3DF, England.

CAREER: Playwright, screenwriter, and novelist. Greendale Community School, Kilbarrack, Dublin, English and geography teacher, 1980–.

AWARDS, HONORS: The Van was shortlisted for Britain's Booker Prize, Book Trust (England), 1991; Booker Prize, 1993, for *Paddy Clarke Ha Ha Ha.*

WRITINGS:

NOVELS

The Commitments, Heinemann, 1988, Random House, 1989.
The Snapper, Secker & Warburg, 1990, Penguin, 1992.
The Van, Viking, 1991.
The Barrytown Trilogy, Secker & Warburg, 1992.
Paddy Clarke Ha Ha Ha, Secker & Warburg, 1993.
Brownbread; And, War, Minerva (London), 1993.
The Woman Who Walked into Doors, Viking (New York City), 1996.

SCREENPLAYS

(With Dick Clement and Ian La Frenais) *The Commitments* (based on the novel by Doyle), Twentieth Century-Fox, 1991.
The Snapper (based on the novel by Doyle), Miramax Films, 1993.

SIDELIGHTS: Roddy Doyle's trilogy of novels about the Irish Rabbitte family, known informally as the "Barrytown trilogy," has been internationally acclaimed for wit, originality, and powerful dialogue. Each of the three books—*The Commitments, The Snapper,* and *The Van*—focuses on a single character of the large Rabbitte family who live in Barrytown, Dublin. They are "a likeable, rough, sharp-witted clan," declared Lawrence Dugan in *Chicago Tribune.* Typical working-class citizens, the Rabbittes are a vivacious and resilient household, lustily displaying an often ribald sense of humor. "These books are funny all the way down to their syntax," claimed Guy Mannes-Abbott in *New Statesman & Society,* "enabling Doyle to sustain my laughter over two or three pages."

The Commitments is, perhaps, Doyle's most well-recognized work. The successful novel was adapted in 1991 into a very popular screenplay by Doyle, Dick Clement, and Ian La Frenais, and directed by award-winning filmmaker Alan Parker. In both the novel and the film, Doyle's wit and originality are evident. The main character, Jimmy Rabbitte, inspired by the rhythm and blues music of James Brown, B. B. King, and Marvin Gaye, resolves to form an Irish soul band in Dublin. He places a musicians-wanted ad in the paper: "Have you got Soul? If yes, . . . contact J. Rabbitte." And so is born the "Commitments," with Jimmy as the manager of a group which includes Imelda, a singer, and Joey "The Lips" Fagan, a musician who claims to have "jammed with the man" James Brown. "The rehearsals, as Mr. Doyle chronicles them," wrote Kinky Friedman in *New York Times,* "are authentic, joyous, excruciating and funny as hell." Dugan, in the *Chicago Tribune,* described *The Commitments* as "a beautifully told story about the culture that absorbed the Vikings, Normans, Scots and British now trying its luck with black America." Doyle "possesses a rare gift for capturing the metaphysical lift of live music," enthused David Fricke in *Rolling Stone.* "In Doyle's hands, the band . . . take[s] on an uncommon vibrancy." The film version stars an all-Irish cast, including Robert Arkins, Andrew Strong, and singer Maria Doyle performing such 1960s hits as "Mustang Sally" and "In the Midnight Hour." A *People* critic reviewed the film and concluded, "the cathartic power of music has never been more graphically demonstrated."

Doyle's second novel, *The Snapper,* focuses on Sharon Rabbitte, Jimmy's older sister, who is young, unmarried, and pregnant.

Refusing to reveal the identity of the father of her "snapper," Sharon's predicament has the Rabbitte household in a tizzy, and she becomes the target of humorous speculations by the Barrytown citizens. As a result of Sharon's pregnancy, relationships within the family undergo various transformations ranging from the compassionate (dad Jimmy Sr.) to the murderous (mom Veronica), while Sharon herself tries to understand the changes within her own body: "me uterus is pressin' into me bladder," she explains on one of her numerous trips to the "loo." A *Los Angeles Times Book Review* critic noted that "few novels depict parent-child relationships—healthy relationships, no less—better than this one, and few men could write more sensitively about pregnancy."

Like *The Commitments, The Snapper* is written in the Irish vernacular, with little descriptive intrusion, and with an enormous sense of humor. John Nicholson in the London *Times* pointed to Doyle's "astonishing talent for turning the humdrum into high comedy" in the novel. He also singled out the characters' vernacular banter for critical praise—"the dialogue of *The Snapper* crackles with wit and authenticity." This is a "very funny" novel, admitted Tania Glyde in the London *Times,* yet she further pointed out that "it is also sad . . . Sharon's life . . . would be tragic without the support of her large and singular family." *Times Literary Supplement* critic Stephen Leslie asserted that "*The Snapper* is a worthy successor to *The Commitments.*"

Shortlisted for Britain's prestigious Booker Prize, Roddy Doyle's third Rabbitte novel, *The Van,* changes the focus to Jimmy Sr., the ribald, fun-loving father of the Rabbitte family, who has been recently laid off work. Jimmy and his best friend, Bimbo, open a portable fast-food restaurant—Bimbo's Burgers—housed in a greasy van that is a health inspector's nightmare. The antics of the two friends running the business provide much of the hilarity of the book; for example, they mistakenly deep-fry a diaper, serve it up to a customer like cod, and then flee—restaurant and all—from his wrath, hurling frozen fish at their victim from the back of the van. Jimmy and his friends are Irish laborers "whose idea of wit and repartee is putting on fake Mexican accents and 'burstin' their shite' at jokes about farting," wrote Anne-Marie Conway in *Times Literary Supplement.* "*The Van* is not just a very funny book," insisted Mannes-Abbott, "it is also faultless comic writing."

Critical response towards *The Van* was enthusiastic, with many reviewers finding a special appeal in what a *Publishers Weekly* commentator called Doyle's "brash originality and humor that are both uniquely Irish and shrewdly universal." Reviewer Tim Appelo in the *Los Angeles Times Book Review* maintained that "Roddy Doyle has perfect pitch from the get-go. He can write pages of lifelike, impeccably profane dialogue without a false note or a dull fill, economically evoking every lark and emotional plunge in the life of an entire Irish family." Ann-Marie Conway sums up her comments by saying "*The Van* could have been depressing; that it is warm and funny . . . is a tribute to an interesting new writer on the Irish scene."

Doyle's next book, *Paddy Clarke Ha Ha Ha,* was awarded the prestigious Booker Prize in 1993. The novel is written from the point of view of Paddy Clarke, a ten-year-old Irish boy, whose often humorous escapades become gradually more violent and disturbing as the story progresses. John Gallagher in the *Detroit News and Free Press* commented on Doyle's effective use of a stream of consciousness narrative, and noted a "theme of undeserved suffering. . . . *Paddy Clarke Ha Ha Ha* matures into an unforgettable portrait of troubled youth."

In the *New York Times,* Mary Gordon established her admiration for Doyle by stating that "perhaps no one has done so much to create a new set of images for the Ireland of the late 20th century as Roddy Doyle." Doyle's book, *The Woman Who Walked into Doors,* is about an abused, beaten wife who continually goes to the hospital emergency room and is never questioned by the staff, who merely "chalk [her repeat visits] up to her drinking or clumsiness or bad luck." Paula came from a family with loving, affectionate parents and three sisters, and her marriage started out with a "blissful honeymoon at the seaside." Gordon ruminates about Doyle's description of "what it's like to be beaten by your lover, the father of your children," and feels that it "is a masterpiece of virtuoso moves. Nothing is blinked; nothing is simplified." Paula finally comes to her senses when she sees her husband "looking at their daughter, not with desire . . . but with hate and a wish to annihilate. She stops being a battered wife when she becomes a protective mother."

BIOGRAPHICAL/CRITICAL SOURCES:

PERIODICALS

Chicago Tribune, August 9, 1992, p. 5.
Detroit News and Free Press, December 12, 1993,
Los Angeles Times Book Review, July 19, 1992, p. 6; September 20, 1992, p. 3.
New Republic, September 16, 1991, p. 30.
New Statesman & Society, August 23, 1991, pp. 35-36; June 18, 1993, p. 39.
New Yorker, January 24, 1994, p. 91; February 5, 1996, p. 56.
New York Review of Books, February 3, 1994, p. 3.
New York Times, July 23, 1989, p. 11; May 16, 1997, p. B12.
New York Times Book Review, October 11, 1992, p. 15; October 8, 1993; January 2, 1994, pp. 1, 21; April 28, 1996, p. 7.
Newsweek, December 27, 1993, p. 48.
People, August 26, 1991, pp. 13-14.
Publishers Weekly, May 25, 1992, p. 36.
Rolling Stone, September 21, 1989, p. 27.
Time, December 6, 1993, p. 82
Times (London), August 16, 1990; October 5, 1991, p. 51.
Times Literary Supplement, December 21-27, 1990, p. 1381; August 16, 1991, p. 22; November 5, 1993, p. 14.
Washington Post Book World, August 10, 1992, p. B2.

* * *

DOYLE, Sir A. Conan
  See DOYLE, Arthur Conan

* * *

DOYLE, Sir Arthur Conan
  See DOYLE, Arthur Conan

* * *

DR. A
  See ASIMOV, Isaac

DRABBLE, Margaret 1939-

PERSONAL: Born June 5, 1939, in Sheffield, England; daughter of John Frederick (a judge) and Kathleen Marie (Bloor) Drabble; married Clive Walter Swift (an actor with the Royal Shakespeare Company), June, 1960 (divorced, 1975); married Michael Holroyd (an author), 1982; children: (first marriage) Adam Richard George, Rebecca Margaret, Joseph. *Education:* Newnham College, Cambridge, B.A. (first class honors), 1960.

ADDRESSES: Agent—Peters, Fraser, and Dunlop, 5th Floor, The Chambers, Chelsea Harbour, Lots Road, London SW10 0XF, England.

CAREER: Novelist, biographer, critic, editor, and short story writer. Member of Royal Shakespeare Company, one year.

MEMBER: National Book League (deputy chairperson, 1978-80; chairperson, 1980-82).

AWARDS, HONORS: John Llewelyn Rhys Memorial Award, 1966, for *The Millstone;* James Tait Black Memorial Book Prize, 1968, for *Jerusalem the Golden;* Book of the Year Award from *Yorkshire Post,* 1972, for *The Needle's Eye;* E. M. Forster Award from National Institute and American Academy of Arts and Letters, 1973; *The Middle Ground* was named a notable book of 1980 by the American Library Association, 1981; honorary fellow of Sheffield City Polytechnic, 1989; D.Litt. from University of Sheffield, 1976, University of Manchester, 1987, University of Keele, 1988, University of Bradford, 1988, University of Hull, 1992, University of East Anglia, 1994, and University of York, 1995.

WRITINGS:

NOVELS

A Summer Bird-Cage, Weidenfeld & Nicolson, 1963, Morrow, 1964.
The Garrick Year, Weidenfeld & Nicolson, 1964, Morrow, 1965.
The Millstone, Weidenfeld & Nicolson, 1965, Morrow, 1966; published with new introduction by Drabble and editorial material compiled by Michael Marland, Longman, 1970; published as *Thank You All Very Much* (also see below), New American Library, 1973.
Jerusalem the Golden, Morrow, 1967.
The Waterfall, Knopf, 1969.
The Needle's Eye, Knopf, 1972.
The Realms of Gold, Knopf, 1975.
The Ice Age, Knopf, 1977.
The Middle Ground, Knopf, 1980.
The Radiant Way (first novel in a trilogy), Knopf, 1987.
A Natural Curiosity (second novel in a trilogy), Viking, 1989.
The Gates of Ivory (third novel in a trilogy), Viking, 1991.
The Witch of Exmoor, Viking, 1996.

OTHER

Laura (television play), Granada Television, 1964.
Wordsworth (criticism), Evans Brothers, 1966, Arco, 1969.
(Author of dialogue) *Isadora* (screenplay), Universal, 1968.
Thank You All Very Much (screenplay; based on Drabble's novel, *The Millstone*), Columbia, 1969; released in England as *A Touch of Love,* Palomar Pictures, 1969.
Bird of Paradise (play), first produced in London, 1969.
(Editor with B. S. Johnson) *London Consequences* (group novel), Greater London Arts Association, 1972.
Virginia Woolf: A Personal Debt, Aloe Editions, 1973.
Arnold Bennett (biography), Knopf, 1974.

(Editor) Jane Austen, *Lady Susan, the Watsons and Sanditon,* Penguin, 1975.
(Editor with Charles Osborne) *New Stories 1,* Arts Council of Great Britain, 1976.
(Editor) *The Genius of Thomas Hardy,* Knopf, 1976.
For Queen and Country: Britain in the Victorian Age, Deutsch, 1978; published as *For Queen and Country: Victorian England,* Houghton, 1979.
A Writer's Britain: Landscape and Literature, photographs by Jorge Lewinski, Knopf, 1979.
(General editor) *The Oxford Companion to English Literature,* 5th edition, Oxford University Press, 1985.
(Editor with Jenny Stringer) *The Concise Oxford Companion to English Literature,* Oxford University Press, 1987, revised edition, 1995, abridged sixth edition, 1996.
Stratford Revisited, Celandine Press, 1989.
Safe as Houses, Chatto & Windus, 1990.
(Editor) Emily Bronte, *Wuthering Heights, and Poems,* Charles E. Tuttle Co., 1993.
Angus Wilson: A Biography, St. Martin's Press (New York City), 1996.

Also author of story for "A Roman Marriage," Winkast Productions. Contributor to numerous anthologies.

SIDELIGHTS: On the strength of her first three novels, *A Summer Bird-Cage, The Garrick Year,* and *The Millstone,* Margaret Drabble made her reputation in the early 1960s as the preeminent novelist of the modern woman. Her first three protagonists share the attributes of what Drabble calls "the high-powered girls": they are all young, attractive, talented, and smart.

Two of Drabble's characters, Sarah Bennett of *A Summer Bird-Cage* and Rosamund Stacey of *The Millstone,* are, like the author herself, Oxbridge graduates. Sarah has given up the notion of going on to get a higher degree because "you can't be a sexy don," and she has spent a year rather aimlessly looking for something to do that is worthy of her talents and education. In the course of the novel, she considers her options, partly represented by her beautiful sister Louise, who has sacrificed any ambition she had to marry a rich, fussy, rather sexless man, and partly by her Oxford friends, most of whom are working at dull jobs in London and falling short of their ambitions almost as badly as Louise is. In the end, Sarah is preparing to marry her long-time Oxford boyfriend, though she insists that she will "marry a don" as opposed to becoming "a don's wife." Rosamund, a Cambridge graduate, is more determined and less conventional. Not only does she earn her doctorate in English literature during the course of the novel, but she also becomes pregnant, has the baby on her own, and discovers the profound experience of mother-love at the same time.

At twenty-six, somewhat older than the other two characters and the mother of two small children, Emma Evans of *The Garrick Year* experiences more "adult" problems. Having just been offered a chance to escape from the domestic routine for part of the day by reading the news on television, she finds that she must move her family from London to Hereford, where her actor husband has a year's engagement with a provincial theatre company. There she tries to escape the even more intense boredom by having an affair with her husband's director. Like Rosamund, Emma finds that motherhood is the dominant factor in her life and that both she and her husband are bound to their marriage by that most important factor, the children.

Charles Burkhardt has remarked, "I do not believe anyone has written as intensely and movingly of pregnancy, childbirth, and young motherhood as Drabble, in her early novels, has." What makes her treatment of motherhood so important is the intense examination she gives it, the recognition that it is worthy of attention because it is the most significant event at that moment in the lives of the women she writes about, and by extension at some point in most of the lives of the women who in large part make up her readership. As Pamela Bromberg has noted, "Maternal love is, throughout Drabble, an agent of salvation both because she sees it as 'an image of unselfish love' and because it represents the fulfillment of biological destiny. Drabble understands and enjoys, as perhaps few other late twentieth century women writers do, the profound experience of rightness that many women find in their generativity."

The two novels that followed these early treatments of women, *Jerusalem the Golden* and *The Waterfall,* represent a considerable development for Drabble as a novelist. Rose contends that *Jerusalem the Golden* is Drabble's "first wholly realized novel, economical in its construction, finely precise in its characterization of the heroine. In later novels she will be more profound; never will she be more completely in control of her material than in this relatively early work."

Burkhardt has observed that Drabble's "efforts to liberate herself from the solipsistic constitute . . . the direction she's taken," and this drive is nowhere more evident than in *Jerusalem the Golden*'s determined expansion of subject beyond the individual to the social, familial, and physical environment. Clara Maugham is not an upper-middle-class Oxbridge type, but a working class girl from the north of England who has won for herself a scholarship to the University of London. Drabble's study of this "high-powered girl" and her eager pursuit of "the social joys" in her version of "Jerusalem the Golden," upper-class London, is also a study of Clara's working-class origins and values in confrontation with the world of the Denhams, the artistic and aristocratic family that provides her with her role-model Clelia and her lover Gabriel.

The Waterfall returns to the solipsistic protagonist, but treats her in a much more self-conscious way. The most "experimental" of Drabble's novels, *The Waterfall* has as its primary stylistic characteristic a divided narrative point of view. The first half of the book is in the third person, narrated from the point of view of the protagonist Jane Grey, a young woman on the verge of agoraphobia. She is the mother of a small child, and her husband has left her during the sixth month of her second pregnancy. The novel opens with the birth of her second child and her falling in love with her cousin's husband and continues with Jane's experience of the ensuing affair, which is presented as the highest and most consuming of passions. In the middle of the novel, however, Jane breaks out in the first person, exclaiming, "Lies, lies, it's all lies. A pack of lies. . . . What have I tried to describe? A passion, a love, an unreal life, a life in limbo, without anxiety, guilt, corpses." The two voices then alternate, the third-person narrator creating an intense and unreal story of passionate love and the first-person narrator training an objective, almost cynical eye on the novel's events and characters. In one sense, this split expresses a division that runs throughout Drabble's fiction, between a romantic yearning for coherence through love and a realistic skepticism prompted by the awareness of conflict and incoherence.

Critics have been divided both on the nature of the split in point of view and on its success. Writing in *Journal of Narrative*

Technique, Caryn Fuoroli maintains that it results from Drabble's "inability to control narration" and that the novel fails because the technique keeps her from realizing "the full potential of her material." Myer, on the other hand, has written that *The Waterfall* is Drabble's "neatest exposition of her central concern, and paradoxically the most conclusive in its dramatized recognition that there is no true solution to the conflict between instinct and morality." Rose believes that the novel works because its point of view is a dramatization of the conflict of the woman artist: "She has divided herself into Jane, the woman (whose experience is liquid), and Jane Grey, the artist (who gives form, order, and shapeliness to that experience)." Rose contends in *Contemporary Literature* that this is the fundamental truth the novel succeeds in expressing: "In order to be whole (and wholly a woman), Drabble suggests, a woman must reconcile these divisions. And if a woman writer is to articulate this experience of what it is to be a woman, she must devise a form, as Drabble has done in *The Waterfall,* which amalgamates feminine fluidity and masculine shapeliness."

The Needle's Eye reflects both Drabble's deep interest in ethics and morality and her lack of orthodoxy. Like her, the novel's heroine, Rose Vassiliou, is unsure of her theology but possessed of a conviction that she must do right. As a young heiress she achieved a certain amount of notoriety by giving up her inheritance to marry Christopher Vassiliou, an unsavory and radical young immigrant. After their marriage, she infuriated Christopher by giving away a thirty-thousand-pound legacy to a rather dubious African charity and refusing to move out of their working class house into a more fashionable middle-class neighborhood when he began to make his own fortune. At the time of the novel, Rose is living in her house with her children and has divorced the violent Christopher, who is trying to get her back or to get custody of the children. After flirting with the idea of leaving the children to Christopher and going off to do missionary work in the Third World, Rose finally decides that Christopher is her fate, that the way to her salvation is to take him back and maintain the family. Drabble has commented that "Rose has several possibilities. She can stay with the children and continue to live as she does in a selfish state of grace that excludes the pains of the world. She can go off and become really martyred, an act which she is aware would produce a state of grace of another kind of selfishness, though one can be absolutely certain that if one does do something dramatic like go to help the starving, one will be redeemed in some way. A person like Rose might have found a deep spiritual experience in quitting and going off, but Rose had to reject that, too, and what she accepts finally is no less painful."

Marion Vlastos Libby has written in *Contemporary Literature* that *The Needle's Eye* is a "complex and passionate evocation of a fatalism deriving from the human condition and the nature of the world" and that its greatness "lies in portraying the tension, real and agonizing, between the hounds of circumstance and the force of the individual will." This is certainly the book that shows the human will at its weakest and circumstance at its strongest. The best that Drabble can say for Rose is that she has been "weathered into identity" by the hostile forces that she confronts. In other words, she has developed a soul and found a way to grace, and in that sense she has won her battle. But she has "ruined her own nature against her own judgment, for Christopher's sake, for the children's sake. She had sold them for her own soul . . . the price she had to pay was the price of her own living death, her own conscious lying, her own lapsing, slowly, from grace." As Myer suggests, Drabble's fatalism constitutes a religious vision if

looked at as a means to salvation: "For Margaret Drabble the true end of life is to reconcile flesh and spirit by accepting one's own nature and living with it, in a context of love and responsibility for others. While this is far from easy, and any accommodation achieved is costly, the reconciliation of instinct and morality remains as a possibility worth striving for. This reconciliation, the author hopes, can come about by involvement in society."

If *The Needle's Eye* represents the human will at its weakest and circumstance at its strongest, Drabble moved to the opposite extreme in *The Realms of Gold.* Its protagonist, Frances Wingate, is the apotheosis of the high-powered heroine. A celebrated archaeologist in her mid-thirties, she has divorced the wealthy man she married at an early age and is raising their four children on her own. She has a satisfying love affair with Karel Schmidt, a historian and survivor of the holocaust, whom she eventually marries. She is rich, accomplished, and a little smug. She recognizes in herself "amazing powers of survival and adaptation," and she admits to herself that she is a "vain, self-satisfied woman."

Frances has her frailties, particularly of the body. She suffers quite a bit from two toothaches in the course of the novel, and she worries that her body is deteriorating. She knows she drinks too much and fears that she may share the fate of her alcoholic brother. And she suffers from bouts of hereditary depression, what Drabble calls the "midlands sickness." The important fact about Frances, however, is that she is not affected by these limitations in any fundamental way, because she does not allow them to affect her. She is Drabble's quintessential personification of will: "I must be mad, she thought to herself. I imagine a city, and it exists. If I hadn't imagined it, it wouldn't have existed. All her life things had been like that. She had imagined herself doing well, and had done well. Marrying, and had married. Bearing children, and had borne them. Being rich, and had become rich. Being free and was free. Finding true love, and had found it. Losing it, and had lost it."

Not everyone finds Frances attractive. Fox-Genovese calls her a "fatuous, self-satisfied bitch; too good at everything by half, not to mention too rich and unencumbered." She is an obvious extreme, and Drabble sets her in opposition to the other extremes in the novel. While she makes her mark on her family, her profession, her society, even—in discovering a lost city in the desert—upon nature, she is surrounded by people who are destroyed by circumstances: environment, heredity, psychology, and fate. Her Aunt Constance has starved to death, left alone by an indifferent society. Her nephew has committed suicide, killing his baby daughter as well, because he cannot face the state of the world and does not want her to grow up in it. His anorexic wife is slowly starving herself toward the same escape. Less drastically, Frances's cousin is caught in a miserable marriage in a miserable midlands town and dreams that the gas main will blow up and deliver her from her fate. The list goes on. As Mary Moran notes in *Margaret Drabble: Existing within Structures,* "Margaret Drabble's fiction portrays a bleak, often menacing universe, ruled over by a harsh deity who allows human beings very little free will." Drabble's emphatic statement in *The Realms of Gold,* however, is that the will does count for something, that what hope there is for survival lies precisely in the individual's exercise of will in the face of what may seem overwhelming external forces.

The two novels that followed *The Realms of Gold, The Ice Age* and *The Middle Ground,* present what has become the typical struggle of the individual in Drabble's work to survive and to maintain an identity in the face of a disintegrating social order. Drabble has remarked that *The Ice Age* is in one sense a novel about money. Its protagonist, Anthony Keating, is a thoughtful man who made a fortune in real estate development during the boom times of the 1960s and lost it during the recession of the early 1970s. At the beginning of the novel he is recuperating from a heart attack and trying to come to terms with his new position in life. Meanwhile, the spoiled teenaged daughter of his fiancee, Alison Murray, has gotten herself into trouble in an eastern European country, and his former partner, Len, has landed himself in prison through his shady dealings. The novel is about money in many senses: about the failing British economy, about the effects that making a lot of money has on people, about the interaction of old money and new money, and about the class structures that underlie everyone's thinking about money. However, it is also about the forces that individuals in contemporary Britain are up against, from the natural fact of Alison's retarded younger daughter to the threat that an alien totalitarian government poses to her older one.

The interesting artistic fact about *The Ice Age* is that its narrative is not centered in one character, but is divided among Anthony, Alison, Len, and Len's girlfriend, Maureen. This is in part a reflection of the general disintegration going on in the world Drabble is presenting, in part a somewhat ironic move toward community. Not one of these characters has the force of will that makes Frances Wingate the central presence she is. Each of them is severely handicapped in some way, but they do manage to function in concert. There is some power in community.

The Middle Ground returns to a central character, a character who is very much like Frances Wingate. Kate Armstrong is a successful writer with teenaged children who lives a very comfortable expense-account life. Because she resides in the world of *The Ice Age,* however, Kate is less confident than Frances of her future. In one sense *The Middle Ground* is about middle age. After the ending of a ten-year love affair and the abortion of a fetus with spina bifida, Kate at forty-one is asking what is left for her to do with the rest of her life: "Work? Living for others? Just carrying on, from day to day, enjoying as much of it as one could? Responding to demands as they came, for come they would?" Faced with the decay of urban London, the realities of the Third World visited upon her in the shape of a house-guest called Mujid, the apparent failure of the women's movement, and the turning off of the youth in her world, Kate is not sure what course she should take. In the end she decides to steer a middle ground between her friend Evelyn, a self-sacrificing social worker, and Evelyn's husband and Kate's former lover Ted, a biologist who uses Darwin to justify his self-interest. Kate decides somewhat ambiguously to settle for being "a nice woman," and Drabble leaves her looking toward the future with anticipation and excitement, a woman in the middle of her life.

More recently, Drabble has completed a trilogy that follows the lives of three women who began a friendship while they were students at Cambridge in the 1950s. In the first book, *The Radiant Way,* Drabble introduces Liz, a successful psychotherapist, Alix, an idealist whose socialistic principles have led her to work at low-paying, altruistic jobs, and Esther, a scholar whose main interest lies with minor artists of the Italian Renaissance. By following these three characters through the years in *The Radiant Way* and into their middle age in *A Natural Curiosity,* the author "also attempts to show us how a generation managed (or mismanaged) its hopes and dreams," comments Michiko Kakutani in the *New York Times.* Kakutani finds this approach similar to that of Mary McCarthy's *The Group,* a novel about former Vassar students, and criticizes the tendency in both books "to substitute exposition for storytelling, sociological observation for the development of character and drama." But in a *Newsweek* review by Laura Shapiro, the critic approves of Drabble's willingness to explore all the facets of her characters' lives "at a time when skimpy prose, skeletal characterizations, frail plots and a sense of human history that stops sometime around last summer have become the new standards for fiction." Shapiro concludes: "Drabble reminds us here as in all her books exactly why we still love to read."

The Gates of Ivory completes the trilogy, but it differs from *The Radiant Way* and *A Natural Curiosity* in several significant ways. For example, "in *The Gates of Ivory,*" declares *Concise Dictionary of British Literary Biography* contributor Barbara C. Millard, "Drabble eschews a conventional plot in favor of a compelling scrutiny of her ongoing characters." Also, while the first two books centered on crime—the murder of one of Alix's students in *The Radiant Way,* and Alix's attempts to understand the murderer's motivation in *A Natural Curiosity*—*The Gates of Ivory* follows Liz's actions on behalf of her friend, journalist Stephen Cox, in his attempt to interview Khmer Rouge leader Pol Pot. Cox disappears while travelling through rural Cambodia, and Liz becomes involved in the situation first in London, when she tries to trace his route, and then in Cambodia itself, when she travels there to look for him. In the process, Drabble combines elements of the traditional domestic novel, for which she is celebrated, with journalism and literary criticism, and examines such diverse topics as the Vietnam War, the novels of Joseph Conrad, and the restoration of the ancient temple complex at Angkor Wat.

In addition to her novels, Drabble has also written well-regarded works of criticism and biography and has edited several influential volumes, including the fifth edition of the esteemed *Oxford Companion to English Literature.* Her biographies include 1974's *Arnold Bennett* and 1996's *Angus Wilson.* In the latter work, Drabble chronicles the life of Angus Wilson, a well-known British writer who became a friend of Drabble's during the 1960s. While some reviewers felt that Drabble failed to offer a fully realized portrait of Wilson's inner life, others remarked that her own training as a novelist assisted her in analyzing Wilson's character and his writing. Commenting in the *London Review of Books,* Frank Kermode avers, "Altogether, with the assistance and consent of [Wilson's longtime companion] Tony Garrett, . . . she has given a minute, intimate and candid account . . . of Wilson's hectic life."

BIOGRAPHICAL/CRITICAL SOURCES:

BOOKS

Allan, Tuzyline Jita, *Womanist and Feminist Aesthetics: A Comparative Review,* Ohio University Press (Athens), 1995.
Concise Dictionary of British Literary Biography: Contemporary Writers, 1960 to the Present, Gale, 1992.
Contemporary Literary Criticism, Gale (Detroit), Volume 2, 1974; Volume 3, 1975; Volume 5, 1976; Volume 8, 1978; Volume 10, 1979; Volume 22, 1982; Volume 53, 1989.
Creighton, Joanne V., *Margaret Drabble,* Methuen, 1985.
Dictionary of Literary Biography, Gale, Volume 14: *British Novelists since 1960,* 1983; Volume 155: *Twentieth-Century British Literary Biographers,* 1995.
Moran, Mary Hurley, *Margaret Drabble: Existing within Structures,* Southern Illinois University Press, 1983.

Quiello, Rose, *Breakdowns and Breakthoughts: The Figure of the Hysteric in Contemporary Novels by Women,* P. Lang (New York City), 1996.

Rose, Ellen Cronan, *The Novels of Margaret Drabble: Equivocal Figures,* Barnes & Noble, 1980.

Schmidt, Dory, and Jan Seale, editors, *Margaret Drabble: Golden Realms,* Pan American University, 1982.

Showalter, Elaine, *A Literature of Their Own,* Princeton University Press, 1977.

Staley, Thomas F., editor, *Twentieth Century Women Novelists,* Barnes & Noble, 1982.

Todd, Janet, *Gender and Literary Voice,* Holmes & Meier, 1980.

Wojcik-Andrews, Ian, *Maragret Drabble's Female Bildungsromane: Theory, Genre, and Gender,* P. Lang (New York City), 1995.

PERIODICALS

Canadian Forum, November, 1977.

Chicago Tribune Book World, August 31, 1980.

CLA Journal, September, 1984.

College Literature, fall, 1982.

Contemporary Literature, Volume 14, 1973; Volume 16, 1975; Volume 21, 1980; Volume 23, 1982.

Detroit News, October 19, 1980.

English Studies, number 59, 1978.

Globe and Mail (Toronto), April 11, 1987; October 7, 1989.

Guardian Weekly, May 29, 1969; January 15, 1972; April 8, 1972; May 13, 1972; July 20, 1974; October 4, 1975; November 11, 1979; July 13, 1980.

Hudson Review, winter, 1970; winter, 1973; winter, 1975; summer, 1975; spring, 1978; spring, 1981.

Journal of Narrative Technique, spring, 1981.

London Review of Books, June 8, 1995, p. 3.

Los Angeles Times, December 28, 1980; November 25, 1982; June 21, 1987; October 23, 1989.

Los Angeles Times Book Review, October 18, 1987; September 24, 1989; June 9, 1996, p. 3.

Maclean's, September 29, 1980.

Midwest Quarterly, Volume 16, 1975.

Modern Fiction Studies, Volume 25, 1979-80.

Modern Language Review, April, 1971.

Ms., August, 1974; July, 1978; November, 1980.

Nation, October 23, 1972; April 5, 1975.

National Review, December 23, 1977; March 20, 1981.

New Leader, July 24, 1972; April 26, 1976; January 30, 1978; September 22, 1980.

New Republic, July 8, 1972; September 21, 1974; October 22, 1977.

New Statesman, May 23, 1969; March 31, 1972; July 12, 1974; September 26, 1975; March 19, 1976; September 9, 1977; December 7, 1979; July 11, 1980.

New Statesman & Society, May 26, 1995, p. 24.

Newsweek, September 9, 1974; October 17, 1977; October 6, 1980; November 2, 1987.

New Yorker, October 4, 1969; December 16, 1972; December 23, 1974; January 12, 1976; December 26, 1977; July 11, 1980.

New York Review of Books, October 5, 1972; October 31, 1974; November 27, 1975; November 10, 1977; July 19, 1979; November 20, 1980.

New York Times, October 31, 1975; October 4, 1977; July 4, 1985; October 21, 1987; August 22, 1989.

New York Times Book Review, November 23, 1969; June 11, 1972; December 3, 1972; September 1, 1974; December 1, 1974; December 7, 1975; April 18, 1976; June 26, 1977;

August 21, 1977; October 9, 1977; November 20, 1977; December 23, 1977; September 7, 1980; February 14, 1982; November 7, 1982; July 14, 1985; November 1, 1987; September 3, 1989; May 30, 1993.

New York Times Magazine, September 11, 1988.

Observer, April 2, 1972; September 23, 1973; July 14, 1974; September 28, 1975; December 14, 1975; March 21, 1976; April 17, 1977; September 4, 1977; December 18, 1977; June 29, 1980; July 13, 1980.

Prairie Schooner, spring-summer, 1981.

Progressive, January, 1981.

Publishers Weekly, May 31, 1985.

Saturday Review, November 15, 1975; January 10, 1976; February 21, 1976; August 20, 1977; January 7, 1978.

Sewanee Review, January, 1977; April, 1978; January, 1982.

Spectator, April 1, 1972; July 20, 1974; September 27, 1975; February 7, 1976; February 14, 1976; July 5, 1980; May 27, 1995, p. 38.

Time, September 9, 1974; November 3, 1975; June 26, 1976; October 17, 1977; September 15, 1980; November 16, 1987.

Times (London), June 30, 1980; April 25, 1985; April 27, 1987; April 30, 1987; July 8, 1987.

Times Literary Supplement, July 12, 1974; September 26, 1975; September 2, 1977; July 11, 1980; April 26, 1985; July 12, 1985; May 1, 1987; September 29, 1989; June 9, 1995, p. 24.

Tribune Books (Chicago), November 8, 1987; August 20, 1989.

Victorian Studies, spring, 1978.

Village Voice, November 24, 1975; October 24, 1977.

Virginia Quarterly Review, spring, 1976; summer, 1976; summer, 1978.

Voice Literary Supplement, May, 1982.

Washington Post, January 1, 1980.

Washington Post Book World, September 14, 1980; June 2, 1985; September 21, 1986; October 25, 1987; August 27, 1989.

Women's Studies, Volume 6, 1979.

World Literature Today, spring, 1993.

Yale Review, March, 1970; June, 1978.

*   *   *

DRAYHAM, James
See MENCKEN, H(enry) L(ouis)

*   *   *

DREISER, Theodore (Herman Albert) 1871-1945
(The Prophet)

PERSONAL: Born August 27, 1871, in Terre Haute, IN; died of a heart attack, December 28, 1945, in Los Angeles, CA (some sources say Hollywood, CA); son of John Paul and Sarah Schaenaeb Dreiser; married Sara Osborne White, December 28, 1898 (divorced, 1910); married Helen Patges Richardson, June 13, 1944. *Education:* Attended Indiana University, 1889-1890.

CAREER: Writer. *Globe,* Chicago, IL, reporter, 1892; worked as a reporter for *Globe-Democrat* and *Republic,* both St. Louis, MO, 1892-93; *Dispatch,* Pittsburgh, PA, reporter, 1894; *Ev'ry Month,* New York City, editor, 1895-97; freelance writer, 1897-1905; *Smith's Magazine,* New York City, editor, 1905-06; *Broadway Magazine,* New York City, editor, 1906-07; *Delineator,* New York City, editor, 1907-10; *American Spectator,* New York City, co-editor, 1932-34.

AWARDS, HONORS: Finalist, Nobel Prize in literature, 1930; Award of Merit, American Academy of Arts and Letters, 1945.

WRITINGS:

NOVELS

Sister Carrie (also see below), Doubleday, Page, 1900, abridged edition edited by Dreiser and Arthur Henry, Heinemann, 1901, Pennsylvania edition, edited by John C. Berkey and Alice M. Winters, University of Pennsylvania, 1981, reprinted without textual and historical notes, introduction by Alfred Kazin, Penguin Books, 1981.

Jennie Gerhardt (also see below), Harper, 1911.

The Financier (first novel in a trilogy; also see below), Harper, 1912, revised edition, Boni & Liveright (New York), 1927.

The Titan (second novel in a trilogy; also see below), John Lane (New York), 1914.

The "Genius," John Lane, 1915.

An American Tragedy, Boni & Liveright, 1925, abridged edition edited and with introduction by George Mayberry, New American Library, 1949.

The Bulwark, Doubleday, 1946.

The Stoic (third novel in a trilogy; also see below), Doubleday, 1947.

Trilogy of Desire (contains *The Financier, The Titan,* and *The Stoic*), Crowell, 1974.

OTHER

(Author of first verse and chorus) Paul Dresser, *On the Banks of the Wabash Far Away,* Howley, Haviland (New York), 1897.

A Traveler at Forty, Century (New York), 1913.

(Author of introduction) Oswald Fritz Bilse, *Life in a Garrison Town,* John Lane, 1914.

Plays of the Natural and the Supernatural, John Lane, 1916.

A Hoosier Holiday, John Lane, 1916.

The Girl in the Coffin (play), first produced in New York at Comedy Theatre, December 3, 1917.

The Hand of the Potter (play; first produced in New York at the Provincetown Playhouse, December 3, 1917), Boni & Liveright, 1919, revised edition, 1927.

Free and Other Stories, Boni & Liveright, 1918.

Twelve Men (short stories; also see below), Boni & Liveright, 1919.

Hey Rub-a-Dub-Dub: A Book of the Mystery and Wonder and Terror of Life, Boni & Liveright, 1920.

A Book about Myself, Boni & Liveright, 1922, published as *Newspaper Days,* Liveright, 1931.

The Color of a Great City, Boni & Liveright, 1923.

Moods, Cadenced and Declaimed (poems; also see below), Boni & Liveright, 1926, revised edition published as *Moods Philosophic and Emotional, Cadenced and Declaimed,* Simon & Schuster, 1935.

Chains: Lesser Novels and Stories by Theodore Dreiser, Boni & Liveright, 1927.

(Author of introduction) Dresser, *The Songs of Paul Dresser,* Boni & Liveright, 1927.

(Author of introduction) Frank Norris, *McTeague,* Doubleday, Doran, 1928.

Dreiser Looks at Russia, Liveright, 1928.

A Gallery of Women, Liveright, 1929.

Epitaph: A Poem, Heron Press (New York), 1929.

Dawn (autobiography), Liveright, 1931.

Tragic America, Liveright, 1931.

(Author of introduction) *Harlan Miners Speak: Report on Terrorism in the Kentucky Coal Fields,* Harcourt, 1932.

(Editor and author of introduction) Henry David Thoreau, *The Living Thoughts of Thoreau,* Longmans, Green, 1938.

America Is Worth Saving, Modern Age, 1941.

The Best Short Stories of Theodore Dreiser (also see below), edited and with introduction by Howard Fast, World Publishing, 1947.

Letters of Theodore Dreiser: A Selection, three volumes, edited and with preface and notes by Robert H. Elias, University of Pennsylvania Press, 1959.

Letters to Louise: Theodore Dreiser's Letters to Louise Campbell, edited and with commentary by Louise Campbell, University of Pennsylvania Press, 1959.

(Author of notes with Hy Craft) Borden Deal, *The Tobacco Men: A Novel Based on Notes By Theodore Dreiser and Hy Craft,* foreword by Craft, Bantam, 1965.

The Lost Phoebe and Other Stories (selections from *The Best Short Stories of Theodore Dreiser*; English language textbook with Japanese annotations), edited and with notes by Fujio Aoyama, Shimizu Shoin (Tokyo), 1967.

Selected Poems (from Moods), introduction and notes by Robert Palmer Saalbach, Exposition, 1969.

Notes on Life, edited by Marguerite Tjader and John J. McAleer, University of Alabama Press, 1974.

Theodore Dreiser: A Selection of Uncollected Prose, edited by Donald Pizer, Wayne State University Press, 1977.

Theodore Dreiser: American Diaries, 1902-1926, edited by Thomas P. Riggio and others, University of Pennsylvania Press, 1983.

An Amateur Laborer (autobiography), edited and introduced by Richard W. Dowell, with James L. W. West and Neda M. Westlake, University of Pennsylvania Press, 1983.

Selected Magazine Articles of Theodore Dreiser: Life and Art in the American 1890s, edited by Yoshinobu Hakutani, Fairleigh Dickinson University Press, 1985.

Dreiser-Mencken Letters: The Correspondence of Theodore Dreiser and H. L. Mencken, 1907-1945, edited by Riggio, University of Pennsylvania Press, 1986.

Sister Carrie; Jennie Gerhardt; Twelve Men (omnibus edition), Literary Classics of the United States, 1987.

Theodore Dreiser's "Heard in the Corridors" Articles and Related Writings, Iowa State University Press, 1988.

Journalism, University of Pennsylvania Press, 1988.

The Best Short Stories of Theodore Dreiser, Dee, Ivan R., Incorporated, 1989.

A Hoosier Holiday, Reprint Services Corporation, 1991.

Newspaper Days, University of Pennsylvania Press, 1991.

Fulfillment & Other Tales of Women & Men, Black Sparrow, 1992.

Contributor of articles and the column, "Reflections," under pseudonym The Prophet, to *Ev'ry Month.* Contributor to periodicals, including *Success.* Most of Dreiser's manuscripts are kept at the Theodore Dreiser Collection of the University of Pennsylvania Library; other collections are maintained in the Cornell University Library, the Lilly Library of Indiana University, the New York Public Library, the University of Texas Library, and the University of Virginia Library.

MEDIA ADAPTATIONS: In 1951 a movie adaptation of *An American Tragedy* was produced by Paramount Pictures.

SIDELIGHTS: One of the most prominent naturalistic authors in the United States during the early twentieth century, Theodore Dreiser was an instrumental figure in promoting a realistic portrayal of life in America. In such novels as *Sister Carrie* and

An American Tragedy, he described people who were motivated not by a higher sense of ethics, but rather by their own selfish impulses and the social class pressures that surrounded them. Many conservative critics like *Nation* contributor Stuart P. Sherman, who favored the gentility and Puritan moralism that was characteristic of most writing at the time, felt that such "a representation of the life of a man in contemporary society . . . is an artistic blunder"; criticism was often also aimed at Dreiser's poor command of language and style. The novelist's career was thus marked by his struggle to be accepted by the critical community. More recently, however, the author's significance in American literary history has been generally acknowledged. Joseph Warren Beach, author of *The Twentieth Century Novel: Studies in Technique,* asserted that what makes Dreiser a major American author is "his fearlessness, his honesty, his determination to have done with conventional posturings and evasions. It was extremely important that we should have some one bold enough to set down in the English language just as he saw it the unvarnished truth about American business life, American social life in its major reaches, and the sex-psychology of American men and women."

As recorded in his autobiography *Dawn,* Dreiser came from a poor Indiana farm family of German and Bohemian origin. Unlike many authors of his time, he never graduated from college—although he spent an unproductive year at Indiana University under the sponsorship of his high school English teacher—nor did he have easy access to books as a child. He did, however, gather a wealth of experience from his own family, which *Dictionary of Literary Biography* contributor Donald Pizer described as "poor, large, Catholic, ignorant, and superstitious. . . . The character and experiences of the Dreiser family in the years during which Theodore was growing up were later to supply the mature author with many of his themes. The underlying configuration of the family—the warm, forgiving, and loving mother; the narrow-minded, disciplinarian father; and the fun-loving, wayward, and seeking children—became that of Dreiser's fictional families."

Sister Carrie, Dreiser's first novel, was based on the experiences of his sister Emma, who had an affair with a married man and then fled with him to Canada after he had stolen thousands of dollars from his company's safe. Changing the names to Caroline Meeber and George Hurstwood, the young author soon composed a fictionalized account of his sister's adventures. He completed the book in 1900, with the help of his friend Arthur Henry and his wife Sara ("Jug"); but his efforts to publish the manuscript with Doubleday, Page, and Company resulted in "one of the most famous incidents in American literary history," according to Pizer. In its first edition, *Sister Carrie* sold only five hundred copies, and Dreiser blamed the poor sales on his publisher's refusal to promote the book.

The failure of *Sister Carrie* caused Dreiser to sink into a deep depression and even to consider committing suicide. Much of this low point in his life is recorded in *An Amateur Laborer,* a journal that Dreiser kept during the early 1900s, but that was not published until 1983. Here, Dreiser writes about his years of desperate poverty when he gave up writing—believing his creative powers had abandoned him—and instead sought work as a laborer. Reduced to living in a Brooklyn slum, Dreiser by chance met his brother Paul Dresser, the successful composer of "My Gal Sal" and "On the Banks of the Wabash Far Away," who had changed his name for professional reasons. Paul sent his destitute brother to Muldoon's Sanatorium, a spa and retreat for the upper classes.

In 1907 Dreiser had *Sister Carrie* reprinted by B. W. Dodge with much better results. This, in turn, encouraged him to complete his second novel, *Jennie Gerhardt.* Although not as well-known today as its predecessor, *Jennie Gerhardt,* commented Jonathan Yardley in the *Washington Post Book World,* was "a considerable commercial success and firmly established Dreiser's standing as a novelist—though it did not still the furor over his treatment of sexual and moral questions that had been stirred by *Sister Carrie.*" Once again using one of his sisters as a model for his novel's protagonist, Dreiser writes about another "fallen woman" in *Jennie Gerhardt.* Jennie sins by having a child out of wedlock, but she is a very different character compared to Carrie. Philip L. Gerber explained in another *Dictionary of Literary Biography* entry: "Unlike Carrie, who is all calculation and no genuine human feeling, Jennie Gerhardt is wholly without self-interest. Her actions are governed by her emotional responses, and she is known for her fidelity to those she loves." But despite these admirable qualities, Dreiser ends her story on a tragic note. By the novel's conclusion, Jennie has lost her child and the man she loves, but she overcomes her feelings of loss by adopting and caring for two children. Thus, wrote Gerber, she "never succumbs to self-pity, never *feels* victimized either by other human beings or by Life. In drawing such a portrait, Dreiser appears to suggest, as he does nowhere else, that one's perception of his fate can itself become a type of 'protective coloration' which will assist one to survive in a harsh world."

In revising his first two novels, however, Dreiser's faith that the strength of his characters would eventually bring them success is obscured. Initially in *Jennie Gerhardt,* the author planned to have Jennie marry her rich lover, Lester Kane, and have the couple live happily ever after despite Jennie's first affair with a senator that resulted in her pregnancy. But Dreiser had learned that such a conclusion would not have pleased moralistic readers, so, according to Kenneth S. Lynn in his *The Dream of Success: A Study of the Modern American Imagination,* the author rewrote the ending to "generate reader-sympathy for Jennie." The first conclusion for *Sister Carrie,* which was restored and published in the 1981 Pennsylvania edition of the novel, is even more revealing of Dreiser's Spencerian beliefs. In this version, the materialistic, unscrupulous Carrie meets a respectable Midwesterner, Bob Ames, after she and Hurstwood have gone their separate ways. She and Ames become attracted to one another with the "implication . . . that Carrie will ascend to the next rung of growth and perhaps marry Ames," reported Richard Lingman in the *Nation.* "In fact," the reviewer later added, "Dreiser created the possibility of a young woman who is immoral by all standards of polite society achieving the virtuous woman's ultimate reward: marrying the handsome, clean-cut young man rather than being punished." However, Dreiser's wife Jug, who played a large role in editing *Sister Carrie,* would not tolerate such an ending and persuaded her husband to change the book so that Carrie is condemned to living a lonely, chaste life of "dreamy solipsism." Even with these changes, though, many readers objected to the author's novels.

Having separated from his wife in 1910, Dreiser's later books were less influenced by others and therefore reflect his philosophy more clearly. Regarding his philosophical works, many critics found the author's expositions to be severely flawed, yet revealing. *Theodore Dreiser* author James Lindquist, for example, remarked that in books like *Hey, Rub-A-Dub-Dub!: A Book of the Mystery and Wonder and Terror of Life* "there are, along with many inconsistencies and much triteness, dozens of striking sentences, moods that are frequently charming, and reflections that occasionally make aspects of Dreiser's novels more understandable." Ronald E. Martin, author of *American Literature and the Universe of Force,* also opined that Dreiser's dogma was "shallow and inconsiderable stuff," although Dreiser himself felt his philosophizing brought him near "the brink of some great discovery." Martin and others have blamed Dreiser's intellectual sloppiness on his tendency to season his thought with his emotions and sense of wonder for life—"he arrived at an attitudinal sense of things rather than a consistent rational paradigm of the universe."

The "Genius," whose main character, Eugene Witla, strongly represents "Dreiser's self-image," according to Lindquist, is a good example of the author's tendency to mix rational with fanciful thinking. The novel mirrors its author's own life very closely, with the exception that Witla is a painter rather than a writer; it also reflects Dreiser's love of science and metaphysics. Both of these aspects flaw *The "Genius"* significantly in a number of critics' views. Pizer asserted, "Literalness mars Dreiser's extremely long reprise of his life in *The 'Genius'* from the beginning to the end of the novel." And Martin pondered, "What are we to make of the novel's strange mixture of mechanistic materialism and mystical idealism? Simply that Dreiser's own incomparable philosophical enthusiasms, which are always close to expression in this nearly autobiographical work, come through in the novel as an incoherent narrative approach."

If the character of Eugene Witla was considered amoral, Dreiser's Frank Cowperwood, whose life is portrayed in the trilogy consisting of *The Financier, The Titan,* and *The Stoic* (later published together as *The Trilogy of Desire*), is even more so. "The idea that civilization is a sham," said Sherman, takes on its most Social Darwinistic note in these novels. "Mr. Dreiser drives home the great truth that man is essentially an animal, impelled by temperament, instinct, physics, chemistry—anything you please that is irrational and uncontrollable." Cowperwood is based upon the real-life nineteenth-century traction magnate, Charles T. Yerkes. In writing this trilogy, the author hoped to present "both an expose and a celebration of the world of finance capitalism," explained Michael Spindler, author of *American Literature and Social Change: William Dean Howells to Arthur Miller.* Dreiser chose Yerkes over other prominent industrialists like John D. Rockefeller because he saw in him the possibility "to endow the entrepreneur with epic dimensions—to make him, in fact, a colossus of the age. Dreiser's irony is directed . . . at the hypocrisy, as he saw it, of the public and private moral codes. It was Yerkes' lack of such hypocrisy, his unabashed practice of dishonesty, which appealed so strongly to Dreiser, providing him with a foil against which to set the hollow sentiments which were supposed to govern American business life."

The Financier, which relates Cowperwood's early years in Philadelphia, "remains the most impressive" book in the trilogy in *New York Times Book Review* critic Malcolm Cowley's opinion. Cowley described the book as "an interweaving of finance and politics with a love story that, besides being effective in itself, is also essential to the climax of the novel." In this volume, Cowperwood rises from a middle-class childhood to a man of immense wealth and influence through his ruthless deals in the stock market. His fall from power comes when he has an affair with Aileen Butler, the daughter of one of Philadelphia's political bosses who, although easily as immoral a businessman as Cowperwood, is extremely conservative when it comes to his family values. His "moral outrage against Cowperwood on family grounds," revealed Spindler, "is the real motivation for his

determination to ruin the financier and bring him to trial for the embezzlement of Philadelphian City Council funds." Cowperwood is imprisoned for his crimes but receives a pardon from the governor, and, unrepentant, regains his fortune during the economic crisis of 1873. Once again a wealthy man, Cowperwood leaves Philadelphia with Aileen, thus proving his superiority over hypocrites such as Butler. "The moral of this story," summarized Walter Benn Michaels, a contributor to *American Realism: New Essays,* ". . . is the irrelevance of anything but strength in a world 'organized' so that the strong feed on the weak. Such a moral is, of course, congruent with the Spencerian's Social Darwinist tendency to find in natural law a justification for the robber-baron practices of the most predatory American businessmen."

Despite the flaws in these two novels, Granville Hicks commented in his *The Great Tradition: An Interpretation of American Literature since the Civil War* that in Frank Cowperwood Dreiser had "succeeded in creating such a figure as had not previously appeared in our literature." The author, however, did not return to the story of the financier's life until over thirty years later when he completed *The Stoic.* This tremendous interim between books in the trilogy resulted in the completely different nature of *The Stoic* compared to the other books. The Great Depression, related Lynn, "absolutely convinced Dreiser that capitalism was through, that the American atmosphere of 'zest and go' which he so loved was now only a memory." This, and Dreiser's own financial problems which he suffered in the time between *The Titan* and *The Stoic,* had an "effect on Dreiser's art [that] was catastrophic," and the last two major novels that he wrote, *The Stoic* and *The Bulwark,* became "curious, hollow shells of books, utterly lacking in conviction."

Dreiser's most powerful outcry against overwhelming social forces came before his disillusionment with the American dream. In *An American Tragedy,* the author resolved to write about "a certain kind of crime which he believed was significantly expressive of American life," according to Pizer. Basing his story on the true murder of Grace Brown by Chester Gilette in 1906, Dreiser set out to explain how an ordinary, middle-class American could be driven to commit homicide because of a deluded faith in the American dream. The novel follows the life story of Clyde Griffiths, a man who has been indoctrinated since his childhood to believe that the ultimate aim in life is to achieve financial success and that anyone who tries hard enough can reach this end. Only Clyde, for some reason he cannot comprehend, has found this goal to be unattainable. Working in his rich uncle's factory, he becomes envious of his relatives (who are condescending toward him) and disliked by his neighbors (who associate him with his snobbish relatives). Clyde's chance comes when Sondra Finchley, a wealthy, beautiful woman who embodies all of Clyde's hopes for success, takes an interest in him. But by this time he has already become involved with Roberta Alden, a poor woman who bears Clyde's child. Caught between the pressure to marry Roberta and his desire to wed Sondra, he resolves to kill Roberta. He intends to drown her on a boating trip, but Dreiser instead has her die accidentally, creating an ambiguous situation that allows the author to focus on the methods by which society will determine Clyde's guilt or innocence. Without any firm proof, Dreiser shows how the jury finds Clyde guilty and condemns him to death solely because of their class and sex prejudices, for as Elizabeth Langland explained in her *Society and the Novel,* the author saw "morality [as] a function of social class."

Reaction to *An American Tragedy* was generally optimistic. In a *New Republic* article, Irving Howe called the novel "a masterpiece, nothing less," observing that in this work the author "mines his talent to its very depth." Beach asserted that *An American Tragedy* "is doubtless the most neatly constructed of all Dreiser's novels, as well as the best written." Still, a number of reviewers found flaws in the book, most of which concerned problems that a number of critics found in all of Dreiser's books. For example, Arnold Bennett, author of *The Savour of Life: Essays in Gusto,* withheld his recommendation of *An American Tragedy* because it "is written abominably, by a man who evidently despises style, elegance, clarity, even grammar. Dreiser simply does not know how to write, never did know, never wanted to know." *The Shape of Books to Come* author, J. Donald Adams, added that "Dreiser's thinking was never more confused and never more sentimental than it was in the writing of *An American Tragedy.*"

Despite such criticism, the book was a popular success and brought Dreiser financial security until the Great Depression. But at least part of this popularity, attested Gerber, was because by the time of *An American Tragedy*'s publication—after World War I and the appearance of T. S. Eliot's *The Waste Land* and Sinclair Lewis's *Babbitt*—"the public was at last prepared for a book which would hold society itself accountable for the behavior of its individual members. Dreiser had not changed, but the times had caught up with him, and *An American Tragedy,* with its gloomy picture of the havoc worked on American youth by the nation's unquestioning embrace of the Success Myth, suddenly was *au courant.*"

BIOGRAPHICAL/CRITICAL SOURCES:

BOOKS

Algeo, Ann M., *The Courtroom as Forum: Homicide Trials by Dreiser, Wright Capote, and Mailer,* P. Lang (New York City), 1996.
Asselineau, Roger, *The Transcendentalist Constant in American Literature,* New York University Press, 1980.
Barrineau, Nancy, editor, *Theodore Dreiser's Ev'Ry Month,* University of Georgia Press, 1996.
Dictionary of Literary Biography Documentary Series, Gale, Volume 1, 1982.
Fleischmann, Fritz, editor, *American Novelists Revisited: Essays in Feminist Criticism,* G. K. Hall, 1982.
Gammel, Irene, *Sexualizing Power in Naturalism: Theodore Dreiser and Frederick Philip Grove,* University of Calgary Press (Calgary), 1994.
Gogol, Miriam, *Theodore Dreiser: Beyond Naturalism,* New York University Press (New York City), 1995.
Hakutani, Yoshinobu, *Young Dreiser: A Critical Study,* Fairleigh Dickinson University Press, 1980.
Hicks, Granville, *The Great Tradition: An Interpretation of American Literature since the Civil War,* Macmillan, 1935.
Langland, Elizabeth, *Society in the Novel,* University of North Carolina Press, 1984.
Lingeman, Richard, *Theodore Dreiser: An American Journey,* John Wiley & Sons, 1993.
Martin, Ronald E., *American Literature and the Universe of Force,* Duke University Press, 1981.
Spindler, Michael, *American Literature and Social Change: William Dean Howells to Arthur Miller,* Indiana University Press, 1983.
Sundquist, Eric J., editor, *American Realism: New Essays,* Johns Hopkins University Press, 1982.
Szekely, Yvette, *Dearest Wilding: A Memoir: With Love Letters from Theodore Dreiser,* University of Pennsylvania (Philadelphia), 1995.

Tjader, Marguerite, and Lawrence E. Hussman, editors, *Love That Will Not Let Me Go: My Time With Theodore Dreiser,* Peter Lang Publishing, 1998.
Twentieth Century Literary Criticism, Gale, Volume 10, 1983; Volume 18, 1985.
Waldmeir, John Christian, *The American Trilogy, 1900-1937: Norris, Dreiser, Dos Passos, and the History of Mammon,* Locust Hill Press (West Cornwall), 1995.
West, James L.W., *Dreiser's Jennie Gerhardt: New Essays on the Restored Text,* University of Pennsylvania (Philadelphia), 1995.

PERIODICALS

American Literature, March, 1981.
Arizona Quarterly, autumn, 1981.
Athenaeum, September 7, 1901.
Atlantic, August, 1993.
Bookman, December, 1912.
Forum, February, 1929.
Library Journal, March 1, 1987; July, 1988; August, 1991; November 1, 1992.
Nation, July 11, 1981.
New Yorker, March 23, 1946.
New York Review of Books, February 26, 1987; November 23, 1989.
New York Times Book Review, October 26, 1919; November 23, 1947; November 20, 1977; May 31, 1981; August 22, 1982; December 4, 1983; November 7, 1993.
Scribner's Magazine, April, 1926.
Times Literary Supplement, September 24, 1982; February 21, 1986; July 17, 1987.
Village Voice, January 24, 1984.
Washington Post Book World, July 21, 1974; July 4, 1982; January 25, 1987.

*   *   *

DR. SEUSS
See GEISEL, Theodor Seuss

*   *   *

DRUMMOND, Walter
See SILVERBERG, Robert

*   *   *

D'SOUZA, Dinesh 1961-

PERSONAL: Born April 25, 1961, in Bombay, India; immigrated to United States, 1978; son of Allan L. (an executive) and Margaret (a homemaker; maiden name, Fernandes) D'Souza. *Education:* Dartmouth College, A.B., 1983.

CAREER: Dartmouth Review, Hanover, NH, editor, 1982-83; *Prospect,* Princeton, NJ, editor, 1983-85; *Policy Review,* Washington, DC, managing editor, beginning in 1985; worked as an assistant domestic policy adviser in the Ronald Reagan administration, Washington, DC, 1987-88.

MEMBER: Phi Beta Kappa.

AWARDS, HONORS: Award from Society for Professional Journalists, 1982, for outstanding reporting.

WRITINGS:

Falwell: Before the Millennium, Regnery Gateway (Washington, DC), 1985.

The Catholic Classics, introduction by John J. O'Connor and William F. Buckley Jr., Our Sunday Visitor (Huntington, IN), 1986.

My Dear Alex: Letters from the KGB, Regnery Gateway, 1987.

Illiberal Education: The Politics of Race and Sex on Campus, Free Press (New York City), 1991.

The End of Racism: Principles for a Multi-Cultural Society, Free Press, 1995.

(With Alvin J. Schmidt) *The Menace of Multiculturalism: Trojan Horse in America,* Praeger, 1997.

Ronald Reagan: How an Ordinary Man Became an Extraordinary Leader, Free Press, 1997.

An abridged version of *Illiberal Education: The Politics of Race and Sex on Campus* was recorded on audio cassette and released by Dove, Audio, 1991.

Contributor to periodicals, including *New York Times, Washington Post, Boston Globe, Los Angeles Times,* and *Wall Street Journal.*

SIDELIGHTS: Dinesh D'Souza is a conservative who during the 1980s and 1990s pushed to continue the Reagan Revolution by challenging the nation's social, economic, and political thought. D'Souza's experience in the public policy arena has given him strongly conservative credentials.

D'Souza is an immigrant from India. His family was Catholic, so his father, a pharmaceutical company executive, sent him to Jesuit schools. In his final year of high school, D'Souza came to the United States as an exchange student. After graduation, he went to Dartmouth, where he began to pursue his interest in public policy. In addition to his studies and other campus activities, D'Souza went to work at the *Dartmouth Review,* a conservative magazine not affiliated with the college. He later became editor. After graduating from Dartmouth, he took the position of editor with *Prospect,* a magazine published by Princeton alumni. He also began contributing to conservative magazines like the *National Review* and *Policy Review.* In 1987, he joined the Reagan administration as an assistant in the domestic policy office.

While pursuing his interests and his career as a journalist, D'Souza began writing longer works on conservative issues. His biography of Jerry Falwell, *Falwell: Before the Millennium,* examines the life and career of the American fundamentalist preacher and leader of a conservative political lobby. Investigating numerous charges leveled against the minister by the liberal Left, the author argues that many are exaggerations or propaganda; he contends, for example, that accusations of segregations and anti-Semitism belie Falwell's vigorous support of civil rights issues and the perpetuation of Israel. D'Souza also sees the preacher's secular activities as twentieth-century methods to disseminate traditional fundamentalist teachings, disavowing the perceived threat of Falwell's political activism to the Bill of Rights' separation of Church and State. "Falwell did what Martin Luther King, William Sloane Coffin, Jesse Jackson, the Berrigans, and thousands of other leftist clergymen had been doing for generations, with liberal benedictions," asserted Joseph Sobran in a *National Review* summary of D'Souza's position. Falwell, Sobran concluded, "is a 'menace' only to liberalism."

Reproaching the publisher of *Falwell* for presenting it as a "critical biography," *New York Times Book Review* contributor Marty Zupan found D'Souza's treatment far from "an objective assessment" of Falwell. "Mr. D'Souza might object that he is careful to note Mr. Falwell's failings," wrote the reviewer. "Indeed, he does, and then he generally excuses them. . . . Meanwhile, Falwell's controversial positions are not discussed." Zupan dismissed the biography as a book "written for the faithful." Sobran, too, noted the volume's "friendly" approach but emphasized instead its factual and informative nature, commenting that the book "is written with unfailing color and energy. . . . Its main virtue is simply that it brings new information in every paragraph. The details add up to a warm but accurate portrait of the man." In the *American Spectator,* Malcolm T. Gladwell viewed *Falwell* as "a case of the right dealing with its own." Yet the critic discounted the publisher's mislabeling, remarking that the book "never pretends to be anything but a defense of Falwell." He added: "To his credit D'Souza treats his subject with grace and thoroughness, and turns what could easily be shrill justification into a genuinely good read. But in the process he steers clear of the implications of Falwell's move into the political arena. . . . D'Souza doesn't want to believe that Falwell's secular activities have tainted him and pushed him in any way from the traditional fundamentalist pattern."

In *Illiberal Education: The Politics of Race and Sex on Campus,* D'Souza examines the contemporary American university. The cultural revolution of the 1960s, he observes, has not disappeared from campuses, but rather has become institutionalized as the revolutionary students have become the faculty and administrators of today's academia. Ideas such as affirmative action, a multicultural curriculum, preferential treatment for some groups, and restrictions of speech to protect these groups have come to shape the university. These changes, D'Souza believes, have caused a decline in American higher education. He maintains that the study of classic literature is out, as is Western culture itself. Merit is out, with respect to disciplines, texts, faculty, and students. Instead, all choices are made with an eye to welcoming groups traditionally left out, groups defined by race, gender, and sexual orientation.

D'Souza's conclusions sparked debate among reviewers over the state of the American university. Charles J. Sykes, writing in *National Review,* found that "*Illiberal Education* is both a primer on the breadth of the crisis and a penetrating critique of the fundamental issues that underlie the assault on academic values, free speech, and intellectual integrity in American higher education." Sykes added, "The triumph of *Illiberal Education* is D'Souza's success in exposing the dishonesty and hypocrisy of what James Coleman has called policies of 'conspicuous benevolence.'" Catherine R. Stimpson, on the other hand, labeled the book "a document in a political campaign. Like most campaigns, it polarizes reality. The target is higher education." She concluded in her review in the *Nation,* "*Illiberal Education* saturates educational debate with slippery rhetoric, inconsistency and falsehood. *Illiberal Education* debases thought for a heap of bony power."

The End of Racism: Principles for a Multi-Cultural Society gives an outsider's view of racism in America. "Not since Gunnar Myrdal's classic, *An American Dilemma,* just over half a century ago," wrote Hoover Institution economist Thomas Sowell in *Forbes,* "has any book looked so searchingly at the role of race in American society as Dinesh D'Souza's new book, *The End of Racism.*" As Peter Brimelow explained in *National Review,* "By skillfully marshalling facts that are publicly available but rarely brought together in a systematic way, D'Souza argues that the plight of black Americans must be largely attributed to their own dysfunctional culture." To reach this conclusion, D'Souza reexamines the long history of blacks in America, through slavery, segregation, and discrimination. He reevaluates recent events, including the civil rights movement and policy and social trends since. What he finds is both a failure of liberal policies and the dependence on the part of some blacks on these failed policies. Overall, in the opinion of Sean Wilentz in the *New Yorker,* "D'Souza tells only half the story of our racial travails, and that obliquely. The part that he does describe is the tragedy of modern liberalism, especially that of the Democratic Party. . . . The other half of the story, the half that D'Souza does not tell, is the tragedy of modern conservatism—especially that of the Republican Party."

As with his previous books, *The End of Racism* stirred a great deal of discussion. Harvard historian Stephan Thernstrom disputed D'Souza's reassessment of the historical record. He contended in the *Times Literary Supplement,* "D'Souza has had no professional training in history, but that does not stop him from writing a good many pages on the history of slavery and the intellectual origins of racism. He is simply beyond his depth here and never should have made the attempt." Specifically, Thernstrom found that "D'Souza . . . is naively generous in his assessment of the motivation of the 'southern ruling elite,' which he believes favoured segregation because of its commitment to the benevolent 'code of the Christian and the gentleman.'" He offered stronger words to describe D'Souza's view of recent events. "His analysis is so muddled that it is difficult to criticize," maintained Thernstrom. "He tells us that the notion that 'the civil rights movement represented a triumph of justice and enlightenment over the forces of Southern racism and hate' is a mere 'myth.'"

In the eyes of some reviewers, *The End of Racism* provides justification for racism. A reviewer for the *Economist* commented, "This book is a defence of bigotry and prejudice. Its message, crudely put, is that discrimination against blacks in America is not racial but rational—meaning wise in circumstances—and that the disadvantages they suffer are largely their fault." It also overgeneralizes, according to this reviewer: "His whole book is written in the language of blame and in the language of stereotypes. It treats black America as 'the Other,' as an undifferentiated statistical mass, as a social 'dysfunction,' as a problem." Yet, for Thomas Sowell in *Forbes, The End of Racism* does not justify racism; rather, it deflates it. As he puts it, the book "argues that the explanatory power of racism is very weak when put to the test, and it now serves largely as a distraction from the hard work of dealing with other factors behind very real problems." In the estimation of Peter Brimelow, "In *The End of Racism,* D'Souza takes many courageous stands; his book has a powerful major argument and endlessly fascinating detail." He concluded, however, that "it remains ultimately incomplete, in terms both of fact and of theory." Sowell summed up the book in the following terms: "*The End of Racism* is . . . a thorough reappraisal of race and racism in American today."

BIOGRAPHICAL/CRITICAL SOURCES:

PERIODICALS

American Spectator, January, 1985; November, 1987, p. 46.
Chicago Tribune, February 4, 1985, sec. 1, p. 11.
Christian Science Monitor, November 30, 1987, p. 20.
Economist, October 14, 1995, p. 101.
Forbes, October 9, 1995, p. 74.

Los Angeles Times Book Review, June 28, 1987, p. 3.
Modern Language Journal, spring, 1993, p. 113.
Mother Jones, January, 1991, p. 74.
Nation, September 30, 1991, p. 378.
National Review, February 22, 1985; November 21, 1986, p. 67; April 15, 1991, p. 49; September 30, 1991, p. 378; November 27, 1995, p. 60.
Nature, September 30, 1991, p. 384.
New Republic, April 15, 1991, p. 30.
New Yorker, May 20, 1991, p. 101; October 2, 1995, p. 91.
New York Review of Books, July 18, 1991, p. 32.
New York Times Book Review, December 30, 1984; March 31, 1991, p. 12.
Time, May 6, 1991, p. 71.
Times Literary Supplement, May 31, 1991, p. 7; December 8, 1995, p. 4.
Village Voice, May 21, 1991, p. 71.
Wall Street Journal, March 28, 1991.
Washington Monthly, April, 1991, p. 56.
Washington Post, April 16, 1991, p. B1.

* * *

Du BOIS, W(illiam) E(dward) B(urghardt) 1868-1963

PERSONAL: Born February 23, 1868, in Great Barrington, MA; immigrated to Ghana, 1960, naturalized Ghanaian citizen, 1963; died August 27, 1963, in Accra, Ghana; buried in Accra; son of Alfred and Mary (Burghardt) Du Bois; married Nina Gomer, 1896 (died, 1950); married Shirley Graham (an author), 1951 (died, 1977); children: Burghardt (deceased), Yolande Du Bois Williams (deceased). *Education:* Fisk University, B.A., 1888; Harvard University, B.A. (cum laude) 1890, M.A., 1891, Ph.D., 1896; graduate study at University of Berlin, 1892-1894. *Politics:* Joined Communist Party, 1961.

CAREER: Wilberforce University, Wilberforce, OH, professor of Greek and Latin, 1894-96; University of Pennsylvania, PA, assistant instructor in sociology, 1896-97; Atlanta University, Atlanta, GA, professor of history and economics, 1897-1910; National Association for the Advancement of Colored People (NAACP), New York City, director of publicity and research and editor of *Crisis,* 1910-1934; Atlanta University, professor and chairman of department of sociology, 1934-1944; NAACP, director of special research, 1944-1948; Peace Information Center, New York City, director, 1950. Co-founder and general secretary of Niagra Movement, 1905-09. Organizer of the Pan-African Congress, 1919. Vice-chairman of the Council of African Affairs, 1949. American Labor Party candidate for U.S. Senator from New York, 1950.

AWARDS, HONORS: Spingarn Medal from NAACP, 1932; elected to the National Institute of Arts and Letters, 1943; Lenin International Peace Prize, 1958; Knight Commander of the Liberian Humane Order of African Redemption conferred by the Liberian Government; Minister Plenipotentiary and Envoy Extraordinary conferred by President Calvin Coolidge; LL.D. from Howard University, 1930, and Atlanta University, 1938; Litt.D. from Fisk University, 1938; L.H.D. from Wilberforce University, 1940; honorary degrees from Morgan State College, University of Berlin, and Charles University (Prague).

WRITINGS:

NOVELS

The Quest of the Silver Fleece, A. C. McClurg, 1911.
Dark Princess: A Romance, Harcourt, 1928.
The Ordeal of Mansart (first novel in trilogy; also see below), Mainstream Publishers, 1957.
Mansart Builds a School (second novel in trilogy; also see below), Mainstream Publishers, 1959.
Worlds of Color (third novel in trilogy; also see below), Mainstream Publishers, 1961.
The Black Flame (trilogy; includes *The Ordeal of Mansart, Mansart Builds a School,* and *Worlds of Color*), Kraus Reprint, 1976.

POETRY

Selected Poems, Ghana University Press, c. 1964.

PLAYS

Haiti, included in *Federal Theatre Plays,* edited by Pierre De Rohan, Works Progress Administration, 1938.

Also author of pageants, "The Christ of the Andes," "George Washington and Black Folk: A Pageant for the Centenary, 1732-1932," and "The Star of Ethiopia."

WORKS EDITED IN CONJUNCTION WITH THE ANNUAL CONFERENCE FOR THE STUDY OF NEGRO PROBLEMS; PUBLISHED BY ATLANTA UNIVERSITY PRESS

Mortality Among Negroes in Cities, 1896.
Social and Physical Condition of Negroes in Cities, 1897.
Some Efforts of American Negroes for Their Own Social Benefit, 1898.
The Negro in Business, 1899.
A Select Bibliography of the American Negro: For General Readers, 1901.
The Negro Common School, 1901.
The Negro Artisan, 1902.
The Negro Church, 1903.
Some Notes on Negro Crime, Particularly in Georgia, 1904.
A Select Bibliography of the Negro American, 1905.
The Health and Physique of the Negro American, 1906.
Economic Co-operation among Negro Americans, 1907.
The Negro American Family, 1908.
Efforts for Social Betterment Among Negro Americans, 1909.
(With Augustus Granville Dill) *The College-Bred Negro American,* 1910.
(With Dill) *The Common School and the Negro American,* 1911.
(With Dill) *The Negro American Artisan,* 1912.
(With Dill) *Morals and Manners among Negro Americans,* 1914.
Atlanta University Publications, two volumes, Hippocrene, 1968.

NONFICTION

The Suppression of the African Slave-Trade to the United States of America, 1638-1870, Longmans, Green, 1896.
The Conservation of Races, American Negro Academy, 1897.
The Philadelphia Negro: A Special Study (bound with *A Special Report on Domestic Service,* by Isobel Eaton), University of Pennsylvania, 1899.
The Souls of Black Folk: Essays and Sketches (young adult), A. C. McClurg, 1903.
(With Booker Taliaferro Washington) *The Negro in the South: His Economic Progress in Relation to His Moral and Religious Development* (lectures), G. W. Jacobs, 1907.
John Brown (biography), G. W. Jacobs, 1909, 2nd revised edition, International Publishing, 1974.

The Negro, Holt, 1915.
Darkwater: Voices from Within the Veil (semiautobiographical), Harcourt, 1920.
The Gift of Black Folk: The Negroes in the Making of America, Stratford Co., 1924.
Africa: Its Geography, People and Products (also see below), Haldeman-Julius Publications, 1930.
Africa: Its Place in Modern History, Haldeman-Julius Publications, 1930, reprinted in a single volume with *Africa: Its Geography, People and Products,* Unipub-Kraus International, 1977.
Black Reconstruction: An Essay Toward a History of the Part Which Black Folk Played in the Attempt to Reconstruct Democracy in America, 1860-1880, Harcourt, 1935, published as *Black Reconstruction in America, 1860-1880,* Atheneum, 1969.
Black Folk, Then and Now: An Essay in the History and Sociology of the Negro Race, Holt, 1939.
Dusk of Dawn: An Essay Toward an Autobiography of a Race Concept, Harcourt, 1940.
Color and Democracy: Colonies and Peace, Harcourt, 1945.
The World and Africa: An Inquiry Into the Part Which Africa Has Played in World History, Viking, 1947, revised edition, 1965.
(Editor) *An Appeal to the World: A Statement on the Denial of Human Rights to Minorities in the Case of Citizens of Negro Descent in the United States of America and an Appeal to the United Nations for Redress* [New York], 1947.
In Battle for Peace: The Story of My 83rd Birthday (autobiography), Masses and Mainstream, 1952.
The Autobiography of W. E. Burghardt Du Bois: A Soliloquy on Viewing My Life From the Last Decade of Its First Century, edited by Herbert Aptheker, International Publishers, 1968.
Black North in 1901: A Social Study, Ayer, 1970.

COLLECTIONS AND CORRESPONDENCE

An ABC of Color: Selections From Over Half a Century of the Writings of W. E. B. Du Bois, Seven Seas Publishers (Berlin), 1963.
Three Negro Classics, edited by John H. Franklin, Avon, 1965.
W. E. B. Du Bois Speaks: Speeches and Addresses, edited by Philip S. Foner, Pathfinder Press, 1970.
The Selected Writings of W. E. B. Du Bois, edited by Walter Wilson, New American Library, 1970.
W. E. B. Du Bois: A Reader, edited by Meyer Weinberg, Harper, 1970.
The Seventh Son: The Thought and Writings of W. E. B. Du Bois, edited by Julius Lester, Random House, 1971.
A W. E. B. Du Bois Reader, edited by Andrew G. Paschal, Macmillan, 1971.
W. E. B. Du Bois: The Crisis Writings, edited by Daniel Walden, Fawcett Publications, 1972.
The Emerging Thought of W. E. B. Du Bois: Essays and Editorials from "The Crisis," edited by Harvey Lee Moon, Simon & Schuster, 1972.
The Correspondence of W. E. B. Du Bois, edited by Aptheker, University of Massachusetts Press, Volume I: *1877-1934,* 1973; Volume II: *1934-1944,* 1976; Volume III: *1944-1963,* 1978.
The Education of Black People: Ten Critiques, 1906-1960, edited by Aptheker, University of Massachusetts Press, 1973.
The Writings of W. E. B. Du Bois, edited by Virginia Hamilton, Crowell, 1975.
Book Reviews, edited by Aptheker, KTO Press, 1977.

Prayers for Dark People, edited by Aptheker, University of Massachusetts Press, 1980.

(And editor) *Writings in Periodicals,* UNIPUB-Kraus International, 1985.

Creative Writings by W. E. B. Du Bois: A Pageant, Poems, Short Stories and Playlets, UNIPUB-Kraus International, 1985.

Pamphlets and Leaflets by W. E. B. Du Bois, UNIPUB-Kraus International, 1985.

Against Racism: Unpublished Essays, Papers, Addresses, 1887-1961, edited by Aptheker, University of Massachusetts Press, 1985.

W. E. B. Du Bois on Sociology and the Black Community, edited by Dan S. Greene and Edwin D. Driver, University of Chicago Press, 1987.

W. E. B. Writings, Library of America, 1987.

W. E. B. DuBois: A Reader, H. Holt and Company (New York City), 1995.

The Oxford W. E. B. DuBois Reader, Oxford University Press (New York City), 1996.

The Selected Speeches of W. E. B. DuBois, Modern Library (New York City), 1996.

OTHER

Columnist for newspapers, including *Chicago Defender, Pittsburgh Courier, New York Amsterdam News,* and *San Francisco Chronicle.* Contributor to numerous periodicals, including *Atlantic Monthly* and *World's Work.* Founder and editor of numerous periodicals, including *Moon,* 1905-06, *Horizon,* 1908-10, *Brownies' Book,* 1920-21, and *Phylon Quarterly,* 1940. Editor in chief of *Encyclopedia of the Negro,* 1933-46. Director of *Encyclopaedia Africana.*

Some of Du Bois's books have been published in French and Russian.

SIDELIGHTS: W. E. B. Du Bois was at the vanguard of the civil rights movement in America. Of French and African descent, Du Bois grew up in Massachusetts and did not begin to comprehend the problems of racial prejudice until he attended Fisk University in Tennessee. Later he was accepted at Harvard, but while he was at that institution he voluntarily segregated himself from white students. Trained as a sociologist, Du Bois began to document the oppression of black people and their strivings for equality in the 1890s. By 1903 he had learned enough to state in *The Souls of Black Folk* that "the problem of the twentieth century is the problem of the color line," and he spent the remainder of his long life trying to break down racial barriers.

The Souls of Black Folk was not well received when it first came out. Houston A. Baker, Jr. explained in his *Black Literature in America* that white Americans were not "ready to respond favorably to Du Bois's scrupulously accurate portrayal of the hypocrisy, hostility, and brutality of white America toward black America." Many blacks were also shocked by the book, for in it Du Bois announced his opposition to the conciliatory policy of Booker T. Washington and his followers, who argued for the gradual development of the Negro race through vocational training. Du Bois declared: "So far as Mr. Washington apologizes for injustice, North or South, does not rightly value the privilege and duty of voting, belittles the emasculating effects of caste distinctions, and opposes the higher training and ambition of our brighter minds—so far as he, the South, or the Nation, does this— we must unceasingly and firmly oppose him. By every civilized and peaceful method we must strive for the rights which the world accords to men." In retrospect, many scholars have pointed to *The*

Souls of Black Folk as a prophetic work. Harold W. Cruse and Carolyn Gipson noted in the *New York Review of Books* that "nowhere else was DuBois's description of the Negro's experience in American Society to be given more succinct expression. . . . *Souls* is probably his greatest achievement as a writer. Indeed, his reputation may largely rest on this remarkable document, which had a profound effect on the minds of black people."

A few years after *The Souls of Black Folk* was published, Du Bois banded with other black leaders and began the Niagra Movement, which sought to abolish all distinctions based on race. Although this movement disintegrated, it served as the forerunner of the National Association for the Advancement of Colored People (NAACP). Du Bois helped to establish the NAACP and worked as its director of publicity and research for many years. As the editor of *Crisis,* a journal put out by the NAACP, he became a well-known spokesman for the black cause. In 1973 Henry Lee Moon gathered a number of essays and articles written by Du Bois for *Crisis* and published them in a book, *The Emerging Thought of W. E. B. Du Bois.*

In addition to the articles and editorials he wrote for *Crisis,* Du Bois produced a number of books on the history of the Negro race and on the problems of racial prejudice. In *Black Reconstruction,* Du Bois wrote about the role that blacks played in the Reconstruction, a role that had been hitherto ignored by white historians. The history of the black race in Africa and America was outlined in *Black Folk: Then and Now.* H. J. Seligmann found the book impressive in the *Saturday Review of Literature:* "No one can leave it without a deepened sense of the part the Negro peoples have played and must play in world history." An even higher compliment was paid by Barrett Williams reviewing for the *Boston Transcript:* "Professor Du Bois has overlooked one of the strongest arguments against racial inferiority, namely, this book itself. In it, a man of color has proved himself, in the complex and exacting field of scholarship, the full equal of his white colleagues."

Although Du Bois's novels did not attract as much notice as his scholarly works, they also were concerned with the plight of the black race. His first novel, *The Quest of The Silver Fleece,* dramatizes the difficulties created by the low economic status of the Southern Negro. *Dark Princess* dealt with miscegenation. After reading *Dark Princess,* a reviewer for the *Springfield Republican* observed: "The truth is, of course, that DuBois is not a novelist at all, and that the book judged as a novel has only the slightest merit. As a document, as a program, as an exhortation, it has its interest and value."

Du Bois gradually grew disillusioned with the moderate policies of the NAACP and with the capitalistic system in the United States. When he advocated black autonomy and "non-discriminatory segregation" in 1934, he was forced to resign from his job at the NAACP. Later he returned to the NAACP and worked there until another rift developed between him and that organization's leaders in 1944. More serious conflicts arose between Du Bois and the U.S. government. Du Bois had become disenchanted with capitalism relatively early. In *Darkwater: Voices From Within the Veil,* he had depicted the majority of mankind as being subjugated by an imperialistic white race. In the 1940s he returned to this subject and examined it in more detail. *Color and Democracy: Colonies and Peace* presented a case against imperialism. "This book by Dr. Du Bois is a small volume of 143 pages," critic H. A. Overstreet observed in the *Saturday Review of Literature,* "but it contains enough dynamite to blow up the whole vicious system whereby we have comforted our white souls and lined the pockets of generations of free-booting capitalists." *The World and Africa* contained a further indictment of the treatment of colonials. Du Bois "does not seek exaggeration of Africa's role, but he insists the role must not be forgotten," Saul Carson remarked in the *New York Times.* "And his insistence is firm. It is persuasive, eloquent, moving. Considering the magnitude of the provocation, it is well-tempered, even gentle."

Du Bois not only wrote about his political beliefs; he acted upon them. He belonged to the Socialist party for a brief time in the early 1900s. Later he conceived a program of Pan-Africanism, a movement that he called "an organized protection of the Negro world led by American Negroes." In 1948 he campaigned for the Progressive Party in national elections, and in 1950 he ran for senator from New York on the American Labor Party ticket. Du Bois's radical political stance provoked some run-ins with the U.S. government, the first of which occurred in 1949, when he accepted an honorary position as vice-chairman of the Council on African affairs. This organization was labeled "subversive" by the attorney general. His work with the Peace Information Center, a society devoted to banning nuclear weapons, also embroiled him in controversy. Along with four other officers from the Peace Information Center, Du Bois was indicted for "failure to register as an agent of a foreign principal." The case was brought to trial in 1951 and the defendants were acquitted.

After the trial was over, Du Bois wanted to travel outside the United States, but he was denied a passport on the grounds that it was not in "the best interests of the United States" for him to journey abroad. Later the State Department refused to issue a passport to him unless he stated in writing that he was not a member of the Communist Party, a condition that Du Bois rejected. In 1958 the Supreme Court handed down a decision which declared that "Congress had never given the Department of State any authority to demand a political affidavit as prerequisite to issuing a passport." This decision enabled Du Bois and his wife to leave the country the same year. For several months they traveled in Europe, the U.S.S.R., and China.

Du Bois's travels abroad had a profound influence on his thinking. In 1961 he joined the Communist Party. He explained in his autobiography how he reached this decision: "I have studied socialism and communism long and carefully in lands where they are practiced and in conversation with their adherents, and with wide reading. I now state my conclusion frankly and clearly: I believe in communism. . . . I believe that all men should be employed according to their ability and that wealth and services should be distributed according to need. Once I thought that these ends could be attained under capitalism, means of production privately owned, and used in accord with free individual initiative. After earnest observation I now believe that private ownership of capital and free enterprise are leading the world to disaster."

After joining the Communist party, Du Bois moved to Ghana at the invitation of President Nkrumah. While there he served as the director of the *Encyclopaedia Africana* project. In August, 1963, the ninety-five-year-old leader inspired a protest march on the U.S. embassy in Accra to show support for the historic "March for Jobs and Freedom" taking place in Washington, D.C. that same month. Shortly afterward, Du Bois died. Although Du Bois was a controversial figure in his lifetime, his reputation has grown in the past decade. A large number of books and scholarly studies about him have recently appeared. In a discussion of the revival of

interest in Du Bois, Cruse and Gipson wrote: "It is important to remember that he continued to plead for a truly pluralistic culture in a world where the superiority of whites is still an *a priori* assumption. In so far as he grasped the basic dilemma of Western blacks as being a people with 'two souls, two thoughts, two unreconciled strivings,' Du Bois's attitudes have been vindicated. He was, as we can now see, one of those unique men whose ideas are destined to be reviled and then revived, and then, no doubt, reviled again, haunting the popular mind long after his death."

BIOGRAPHICAL/CRITICAL SOURCES:

BOOKS

Baker, Houston A., Jr., *Black Literature in America,* McGraw, 1971.

Bell, Bernard W.; Emily Grosholz; and James B. Stewart; *The Critique of Custom: W. E. B. DuBois and Philosophical Questions,* Routledge (New York), 1996.

Bell, Bernard W.; Emily Grosholz; and James B. Stewart, *W. E. B. Dubois on Race and Culture: Philosophy, Politics, and Poetics,* Routledge (New York), 1996.

Byerman, Keith Eldon, *Seizing the Word: History, Art, and Self in the Work of W. E. B. DuBois,* Univeristy of Georgia Press (Athens), 1994.

Concise Dictionary of American Literary Biography: Realism, Naturalism, and Local Color, 1865-1917, Gale, 1988.

Contemporary Literary Criticism, Gale, Volume 1, 1973; Volume 2, 1974.

Dictionary of Literary Biography, Gale, Volume 47: *American Historians, 1866-1912,* 1986; Volume 50: *Afro-American Writers Before the Harlem Renaissance,* 1986.

Du Bois, Shirley Graham, *His Day Is Marching On: A Memoir of W. E. B. Du Bois,* Lippincott, 1971.

Moss, Nathaniel, *W. E. B. DuBois: Civil Rights Leader,* Chelsea Juniors (New York), 1996.

Pobi-Asamani, Kwadwo, *W. E. B. DuBois: His Contribution to Pan-Africanism,* Borgo Press (San Bernardino), 1994.

Rampersad, Arnold, *Art and Imagination of W. E. B. Du Bois,* Harvard University Press, 1976.

Reed, Adolph L., *Fabianism and the Color Line: W. E. B. DuBois and American Political Thought in Black and White,* Oxford University Press (New York City), 1997.

Wintz, Cary D., *African-American Political Thought,* M.E. Sharpe (Armonk, NY), 1996.

Zamir, Shamoon, *Dark Voices: W. E. B. DuBois and American Thought, 1888-1903,* University of Chicago Press (Chicago), 1995.

PERIODICALS

American Visions, February-March, 1994, p. 24.
Boston Transcript, June 24, 1939.
Ebony, August, 1972; August, 1975; November, 1994, p. 102.
Forbes, December 5, 1994, p. 84.
Jet, November 14, 1994, p. 20.
Los Angeles Times Book Review, January 25, 1987.
New Republic, February 26, 1972; August 4, 1994, p. 28.
Newsweek, August 23, 1971.
New York Review of Books, November 30, 1972.
New York Times, March 9, 1947; October 24, 1979.
New York Times Book Review, September 29, 1985.
Saturday Review of Literature, July 29, 1939; June 23, 1945.
Springfield Republican, May 28, 1928.

DUERRENMATT, Friedrich 1921-1990
(Friedrich Durrenmatt)

PERSONAL: Born January 5, 1921, in Konolfingen, Bern, Switzerland; died December 14, 1990, in Neuchatel, Switzerland; son of Reinhold (a Protestant minister) and Hulda (Zimmermann) Duerrenmatt; married Lotti Geissler (an actress), 1946 (died, 1983); married Charlotte Kerr (a journalist), 1984; children: (first marriage) Peter, Barbara, Ruth. *Education:* Attended University of Zurich, 1941-42, and University of Bern, 1942. *Avocation:* Painting, astronomy.

CAREER: Playwright, novelist, short story writer, essayist, and critic.

MEMBER: Modern Language Association of America (honorary fellow).

AWARDS, HONORS: Welti-stiftung fuer das Drama, City of Bern, 1948, for *Es steht geschrieben*; Literaturpreis, City of Bern, 1954, for *Ein Engel kommt nach Babylon*; Hoerspielpreis der Kriegsblinden (Berlin), 1957, for *Die Panne*; Prix Italia, RAI (Venice), 1958, for *Abendstunde im Spaetherbst*; Preis zur Foerderung des Bernischen Schrifttums, 1959, for *Das Versprechen*; Schiller-Preis, City of Mannheim, 1959, for *Grieche sucht Griechin*; New York Drama Critics Circle Awards for best foreign play, 1959, for *The Visit*; Grillparzer-Preis, Oesterreich Akademie der Wissenschaften, 1968, for *Der Besuch der alten Dame*; Grosser Schiller-Preis, Schweizer Stiftung, 1969, for *Die Physiker*; Grosser Literaturpreis, Canton of Bern, 1969; doctor honoris causa, Temple University, 1969, Hebrew University, 1977, University of Nice, 1977, and University of Neuchatel, 1981; International Writers Prize, Welsh Arts Council, University of Wales, 1976; Buber-Rosenzweig-Medaille (Frankfort), 1977; Grosser Literaturpreis, City of Bern, 1979.

WRITINGS:

STAGE PLAYS

Es steht geschrieben: Ein Drama; mit zwei Zeichnungen vom Autor (title means "It Is Written"; first produced in Zurich, Switzerland, 1947), Schwabe (Basel), 1947, new version published as *Der Wiedertaeufer: Ein Komoedie in zwei Teilen* (title means "The Anabaptists"; first produced in Zurich, 1967), Arche (Zurich), 1967.

Der Blinde: Ein Drama (title means "The Blind Man"; first produced in Basel, Switzerland, 1948), Buehnenverlag Block Erben (Berlin), 1947, revised edition, Arche, 1965.

Romulus der Grosse: Eine ungeschichtliche historische Komoedie in vier Akten (first produced in Basel, 1949, new version produced in Zurich, 1957), Arche, 1958, revised version, 1964, 2nd edition, 1968, translation by Gerhard Nellhaus published as *Romulus the Great* with *An Angel Comes to Babylon*, Grove, 1964.

Die Ehe des Herrn Mississippi: Eine Komoedie (first produced in Munich, West Germany, 1952, translation by E. Peters and R. Schnorr, produced in London, England, 1959, as *The Marriage of Mr. Mississippi*), Oprecht (Zurich), 1952, revised edition published as *Die Ehe des Herrn Mississippi: Buehnenfassung und Drehbuch*, Arche, 1966.

Ein Engel kommt nach Babylon: Eine Komoedie in drei Akten (first produced in Munich, 1953, new version produced in Zurich, 1957), Arche, 1954, revised edition published as *Ein Engel kommt nach Babylon: Eine fragmentarishe Komoedie in drei Akten*, 1958, translation by George White (produced

at University of California, 1962) published as *An Angel Comes to Babylon*, K. Hellmer, c. 1962.

Der Besuch der alten Dame: Ein tragische Komoedie; mit einem Nachwort (first produced in Zurich, 1956, produced in New York City, 1958), Arche, 1956, translation published as *The Visit: A Play in Three Acts*, Random House, 1958, translation by Patrick Bowles published as *The Visit: A Tragi-Comedy*, Grove, 1962.

(With Paul Burkhard) *Frank der Fuenfte: Oper einer Privatbank* (satirical opera; title means "Frank the Fifth: Opera of a Private Bank"; first produced in Zurich, 1959), music by Burkhard, Arche, 1960, published as *Frank der Fuenfte: Eine Komoedie*, Bochumer Fassung (Zurich), 1960, revised edition, Arche, 1964.

Die Physiker: Eine Komoedie in zwei Akten (first produced in Zurich, 1962, produced in New York City, 1964), Arche, 1962, translation by James Kirkup published as *The Physicists: A Play in Two Acts*, Samuel French, 1963, published as *The Physicists*, Grove, 1964.

Herkules und der Stall des Augias: Eine Komoedie (expanded version of radio play; first produced in Zurich, 1963), Arche, 1963, translation by Agnes Hamilton published as *Hercules and the Augean Stables*, Dramatic Publishing, 1963.

An Angel Comes to Babylon [and] *Romulus the Great: Two Plays* (latter a translation of *Romulus der Grosse*), translated by William McElwee and Gerhard Nellhaus, respectively, Grove, 1964.

Four Plays, 1957-62 (contains *Romulus the Great, The Marriage of Mr. Mississippi, An Angel Comes to Babylon*, and *The Physicists*; bound with essay, Problems of the Theatre), translated by Gerhard Nellhaus and others, J. Cape, 1964, published as *Four Plays*, Grove, 1965.

Der Meteor: Eine Komoedie in zwei Akten (first produced in Zurich, 1966), Arche, 1966, translation by James Kirkup published as *The Meteor*, Dramatic Publishing, 1966, published as *The Meteor: A Comedy in Two Acts*, J. Cape, 1973, Grove, 1974.

(Adaptor) *Koenig Johann: Nach Shakespeare* (first produced in Basel, 1968), Arche, 1968.

Play Strindberg: Totentanz nach August Strindberg (first produced in Basel, 1969), Arche, 1969, translation by James Kirkup (produced in New York City at Lincoln Center, 1971), published as *Play Strindberg: Choreographed by Friedrich Duerrenmatt*, Dramatic Publishing, 1970, published as *Play Strindberg: The Dance of Death Choreographed*, Grove, 1973.

(Adaptor) *Goethes Urfaust: Ergaenzt durch das Buch von Doktor Faustus aus dem Jahre 1589* (first produced in Zurich, 1970), Diogenes, 1980.

Portraet eines Planeten (first produced in Dusseldorf, West Germany, 1970), Arche, 1971.

(Adaptor) *Titus Andronicus: Eine Komoedie nach Shakespeare* (first produced in Dusseldorf, 1970), Arche, 1970.

Der Mitmacher, ein Komplex: Text der Komoedie, Dramaturgie, Erfahrungen, Berichte, Erzaehlungen (includes play and commentary by Duerrenmatt), Arche, 1976, play published singularly as *Der Mitmacher: Eine Komoedie*, 1978.

Die Frist: Eine Komoedie (first produced in Zurich, 1977), Arche, 1977.

Die Panne: Komoedie (adaptation of novel), Diogenes, 1979.

(Adaptor) *Koenig Johann* [and] *Titus Andronicus: Shakespeare-Umarbeitungen*, Diogenes, 1980.

Der Meteor [and] *Dichterdaemmerung: Nobelpreistraegerstuecke*, Diogenes, 1980.

Achterloo: Eine Komoedie in zwei Akten (first produced in Zurich, 1983), Diogenes, 1983.

RADIO PLAYS

Herkules und der Stall des Augias: Mit Randnotizen eines Kugelschreibers, Arche, 1954.

Das Unternehmen der Wega: Ein Hoerspiel (title means "The Vega Enterprise"; broadcast in 1954), Arche, 1958.

Naechtliches gespraech mit einem verachteten Menschen: Ein Kurs fuer Zeitgenossen, Arche, 1957, translation by Robert David Macdonald published as *Conversation at Night with a Despised Character: A Curriculum for Our Times,* Dramatic Publishing, 1957.

Der Prozess um des Esels Schatten: Ein Hoerspiel (nach Wieland—aber nicht sehr) (title means "The Trial of the Ass's Shadow"), Arche, 1958.

Stranitzky und der Nationalheld: Ein Hoerspiel (title means "Stranitzky and the National Hero"), Arche, 1959.

Abendstunde im Spaetherbst: Ein Hoerspiel (produced by British Broadcasting Corp., 1959), Arche, 1959, translation by Gabriel Karminski published as *Episode on an Autumn Evening,* Dramatic Publishing, 1959, different translation published as *Incident at Twilight* in *Postwar German Theatre,* edited by M. Benedikt and G. E. Wellworth, Macmillan, 1968.

Der Doppelgaenger: Ein Spiel, Arche, 1960.

Die Panne: Ein Hoerspiel (first published as novel), Arche, 1961, published as *Die Panne: Ein Hoerspiel und eine Komoedie,* Diogenes, 1980.

Drei Hoerspiele, Harrap, 1966.

Vier Hoerspiele, Volk & Welt (Berlin), 1967.

Naechtliches Gespraech mit einem verachteten Menschen [and] *Stranitzky und der Nationalheld* [and] *Das Unternehmen der Wega: Hoerspiele und Kabarett,* Diogenes, 1980.

Also author of "Sammelband," 1960.

FICTION

Pilatus (story), Vereinigung Oltner Buecherfreunde (Olten), 1949.

Der Nihilist (story), Holunderpresse (Horgen), 1950, reprinted as *Die Falle,* Arche, 1952.

Der Tunnel (story), Arche, 1952.

Das Bild des Sisyphos (story), Arche, 1952.

Die Stadt: Prosa I-IV (title means "The City"; story collection), Arche, 1952.

Der Richter und sein Henker (novel; originally serialized in *Der Beobachter,* 1950), Benziger (Einsiedeln), 1952; translation by Cyrus Brooks published as *The Judge and His Hangman,* Jenkins, 1954; translation by Theresa Pol under same title, Harper, 1955.

Der Verdacht (novel; originally serialized in *Der Beobachter*), Benziger, 1953; translation by Eva H. Morreale published as *The Quarry,* Grove, 1961.

Grieche sucht Griechin: Eine Prosakomoedie (novel), Arche, 1955; new edition, 1957; translation by Richard Winston and Clara Winston published as *Once a Greek. . . ,* Knopf, 1965.

Die Panne: Ein noch moegliche Geschichte (title means "The Breakdown"; novel), Arche, 1956; new edition, 1960; translation by R. Winston and C. Winston published as *Traps,* Knopf, 1960 (published in England as *A Dangerous Game,* J. Cape, 1960).

Das Versprechen: Requiem auf den Kriminalroman (novel; originally written as screenplay), Arche, 1958; translation by R. Winston and C. Winston published as *The Pledge,* Knopf, 1959.

Die Panne [and] *Der Tunnel,* edited by F. J. Alexander, Oxford University Press, 1967.

Der Richter und sein Henker [and] *Die Panne,* Volk & Welt, 1969.

Der Sturz (story), Arche, 1971.

Der Hund [and] *Der Tunnel* [and] *Die Panne: Erzaehlungen* (stories), Diogenes, 1980.

Grieche sucht Griechin [and] *Mister X macht Ferien* [and] *Nachrichten ueber den Stand des Zeitungswesens in der Steinzeit: Grotesken,* Diogenes, 1980.

The Judge and His Hangman [and] *The Quarry: Two Hans Barlach Mysteries,* afterword by George Stade, David Godine, 1983.

Justiz: Roman (novel), Diogenes, 1985.

Minotaurus: Eine Ballade (story), drawings by Duerrenmatt, Diogenes, 1985.

Der Auftrag; oder, Vom Beobachten des Beobachters der Beobachter: Novelle in vierundzwanzig Saetzen (novel), Diogenes, 1986; translation by Joel Agee published as *The Assignment: or, On the Observing of the Observer of the Observers,* Random House, 1988.

The Execution of Justice (novel), translated by John E. Wood, Random House, 1989.

NONFICTION

Theaterprobleme (essay), Arche, 1955, translation by Gerhard Nellhaus published as *Problems of the Theatre* [with] *The Marriage of Mr. Mississippi: A Play Translated from the German by Michael Bullock,* Grove, 1964.

Friedrich Schiller: Eine Rede (speech), Arche, 1960.

(With Werner Weber) *Der Rest ist Dank* (speeches), Arche, 1961.

Theater-Schriften und Reden (essays and speeches), edited by Elisabeth Brock Sulzer, Arche, Volume 1: *Theater-Schriften und Reden,* 1966, Volume 2: *Dramaturgisches und Kritisches,* 1972; translation by H. M. Waidson published as *Writings on Theatre and Drama,* J. Cape, 1976.

Monstervortrag ueber Gerechtigkeit und Recht nebst einem helvetischen Zwischenspiel: Eine kleine Dramaturgie der Politik (lecture), Arche, 1969.

Saetze aus Amerika (travel book), Arche, 1970.

Zusammenhaenge: Essay ueber Israel; eine Konzeption, Arche, 1976.

Albert Einstein: Ein Vortrag (lecture), Diogenes, 1979.

Literature und Kunst: Essays, Gedichte und Reden, Diogenes, 1980.

Philosophie und Naturwissenschaft: Essays, Gedichte und Reden, Diogenes, 1980.

Politik: Essays, Gedichte und Reden, Diogenes, 1980.

Kritik: Kritiken und Zeichnungen, Diogenes, 1980.

Also author of *Israel: Eine Rede,* 1975.

OTHER

Friedrich Duerrenmatt liest: "Herkules und der Stall des Augias" [and] *"Eine Kurzfassung der Komoedie"* (recording), Deutsche Grammophon Gesselschaft, 1957.

It Happened in Broad Daylight (screenplay version of *The Pledge*), Continental, 1960.

Die Ehe des Herrn Mississippi: Ein Drehbuch mit Szenenbildern (filmscript adaptation of stage play), Sanssouci (Zurich), 1961.

Naechtliches Gespraech (recording), Platern Club, 1963.

Die Heimat im Plakat: Ein Buch fuer Schweizer Kinder (satirical drawings), Diogenes, 1963.

Problems of the Theatre: An Essay Translated from the German by Gerhard Nellhaus (translation of *Theaterprobleme*) [and] *The Marriage of Mr. Mississippi: A Play Translated from the German by Michael Bullock,* Grove, 1964.

(With Gore Vidal) *Romulus: The Broadway Adaptation, by Gore Vidal* [and] *The Original Romulus the Great, by Friedrich Duerrenmatt,* translated by G. Nellhaus, preface by Vidal, Grove, 1966.

Zeichnungen gerachtfertigt durch Friedrich Duerrenmatt, Diogenes, 1972.

(Author of introduction) Hans Falk, *Hans Falk,* ABC (Zurich), 1975.

Duerrenmatt: Bilder und Zeichnungen (paintings and drawings), edited by Christian Strich, Diogenes, 1978.

Lesebuch: Friedrich Duerrenmatt, Arche, 1978.

(Author of foreword) Tomi Ungerer, *Babylon,* Diogenes, 1979.

Herkules und der Stall des Augias [and] *Der Prozess um des Esels Schatten* [and] *Griechische Stuecke,* Diogenes, 1980.

Play Strindberg [and] *Portrait eines Planeten: Uebungsstucke fuer Schauspieler* (exercises for actors), Diogenes, 1980.

Stoffe I-III, Diogenes, 1981.

(With Dorothea Christ) *Hildi Hess: Mit Texten von Dorothea Christ und Friedrich Duerrenmatt,* edited by Daniel Keel, Diogenes, 1981.

Denken mit Duerrenmatt: Denkanstosse; ausgewahlt und zusammengestellt von Daniel Keel; mit sieben Zeichnungen des Dichters, drawings by Duerrenmatt, Diogenes, 1982.

Die Erde ist zu schoen. . .: Die Physiker [and] *Der Tunnel* [and] *Das Unternehmen der Wega,* Arche, 1983.

(With wife, Charlotte Kerr) *Rollenspiele: Protokoll einer fiktiven Inszenierung und Achterloo III* (includes play, *Achterloo III*), Diogenes, 1986.

Also author of television adaptation of *The Judge and His Hangman,* 1957. Work appears in numerous anthologies, including *The Modern Theatre,* edited by R. W. Corrigan, Macmillan, 1946; *The Best Plays of 1964-65,* edited by O. L. Guernsey, Jr., Dodd, 1965; *Postwar German Theatre,* edited by M. Benedikt and G. E. Wellwarth, Macmillan, 1968; and *Die Besten klassischen und modernene Hundegeschichten,* Diogenes, 1973. Drama critic for *Die Weltwoche,* 1951-52.

MEDIA ADAPTATIONS: The Visit: A Drama in Three Acts was adapted by Maurice Valency from *Der Besuch der Alten Dame* and published by Samuel French, 1956; Valency's adaptation was later published as *The Visit: A Play in Three Acts,* Random House, 1958, and produced in New York City in 1958. *Fools Are Passing Through* was adapted by Maximilian Slater from *Die Ehe des Herrn Mississippi* and produced in New York City at Jan Hus Auditorium, April 2, 1958. *The Deadly Game* was adapted by James Yaffe from *Traps* and produced in New York City at Longacre Theatre, February 2, 1960; Yaffe's *The Deadly Game: A Play in Two Acts; Adapted from the Novel "Traps" by Friedrich Duerrenmatt* was published by Dramatists Play Service, 1966. *The Jackass* was adapted by George White from *Der Prozess um des Esels Schatten* and produced in New York City at Barbizon Plaza Theatre, March 23, 1960. *Romulus: A New Comedy* was adapted by Gore Vidal from *Romulus the Great* and produced in New York City, 1962; Vidal's *Romulus: A New Comedy; Adapted from a Play of Friedrich Duerrenmatt* was published by Dramatists Play Service, 1962. *The Visit of the Old Lady: Opera in Three Acts by Gottfried von Einem* was adapted from *Der Besuch der Alten Dame* (English version by Norman Tucker) and published by Boosey & Hawkes, 1972. *Chicago Radio Theatre Production of Friedrich Duerrenmatt's Play "Strindberg"* was released as a cassette recording, Allmedia Dramatic Workshop, 1977.

A dramatization of *The Judge and His Hangman* was televised in the United States in 1956, and an adaptation of *The Deadly Game* in 1957. Duerrenmatt's works have also been adapted as motion pictures, including an adaptation of *The Visit* by Twentieth Century-Fox Film Corp., 1964, *Fools Are Passing Through* (an adaptation of *The Marriage of Mr. Mississippi*), 1961, and an adaptation of one of Duerrenmatt's short stories by Sergeo Amidei for an Italian film, 1972.

SIDELIGHTS: Acclaimed Swiss playwright and critic Friedrich Duerrenmatt is considered to be one of the most important German-language dramatists of the twentieth century. His most famous works include *Der Besuch der alten Dame* (*The Visit*), regarded by many to be his finest play, and *Der Physiker* (*The Physicists*), one of the most frequently performed plays of the German stage. *The Visit,* a huge success on Broadway in addition to Germany, is the story of a wealthy old woman who returns to her impoverished hometown with the intent of financially rewarding the townspeople if they enact revenge on an old suitor of the woman's. According to Frederick Lumley in *New Trends in Twentieth Century Drama, The Visit* "raises Duerrenmatt to the level of the leading playwright of our times. Not only is it a good play in itself, it is one of the most forceful statements ever made on the corruption of the power of money, a radical indictment of the values of our society and the hypocrisy on which it is built." The grotesque comedy *The Physicists* depicts three insane nuclear physicists in an asylum who believe they are Albert Einstein, Sir Isaac Newton, and August Ferdinand Moebius. Possessing the knowledge of how to destroy the world, each physicist goes as far as murdering others to prevent others from discovering what they know; the play raises questions regarding definitions of madness, in addition to the limits of scientific responsibility. A reviewer for the *Times Literary Supplement* comments that in both plays "drama is generated by the pursuit of a ruthless, absolute logic in the teeth of anarchy," while "success rests in part on the way in which a tragi-comic ambivalence of plot is carried through into the language and the stage-realization."

For Duerrenmatt, the playwright's task is to present a new, fantastic, even grotesque and bizarre world upon a stage by using everything at his command: language, irony, ideas, and what Adolf D. Klarmann calls "theatrical pyro-technics." Klarmann cites a few of these from Duerrenmatt's work: "Figures appear out of trap doors, enter through windows and clocks, scenery flies up and down in full view, torture wheels are outlines against the sky, moon dances are performed on roofs, angels alight on chandeliers, chickens run across the stage, in short, every conceivable trick of the trade of the theatre, of the cabaret, the burlesque, and the movies is applied with a lusty abandon."

Believing that true tragedy is impossible to create in a world, he calls his dramatic pieces comedies, though the comedy to be found therein is no more merry than gallows humor. Duerrenmatt writes: "The task of art, insofar as art can have a task at all, and hence also the task of drama today, is to create something concrete, something that has form. This can be accomplished best by comedy. . . . [But] we can achieve the tragic out of comedy. We can bring it forth as a frightening moment, as an abyss that opens suddenly. . . . [The conceit employed by comedy] easily transforms the crowd of theatregoers into a mass which can be attacked, deceived, outsmarted into listening to things it would otherwise not so readily listen to. Comedy is a mousetrap in which the public is easily caught and in which it will get caught over and over again. Tragedy on the other hand, predicates a true community, a kind of community whose existence in our day is but an embarrassing fiction."

Although he is primarily known as a dramatist, Duerrenmatt has also written acclaimed fiction and is best known for his mystery and detective novels, including *Der Richter und sein Henker* (*The Judge and His Hangman*) *Der Verdacht* (*The Quarry*), and *Das Versprechen* (*The Pledge*). *The Judge and His Hangman* was a German best-seller when it appeared in 1950 and, according to Saad Elkhadem in *International Fiction Review*, "is undoubtedly one of the most exciting and entertaining novels in German literature." Elkhadem contends that the novel's popularity is due mainly to "its gripping incidents and breath-taking plot," while "from a narrative point of view, [the] pure event-novel testifies to the remarkable talent of Duerrenmatt as an imaginative fabulist and beguiling storyteller." *Dictionary of Literary Biography* contributor Roger A. Crockett notes "there is a distinctly dramatic quality to Duerrenmatt's prose," adding that "the same pessimistic view of history, the same distrust of absolutes, and the same dominance of coincidence over rational planning which characterize his dramas also pervade his prose."

"Duerrenmatt is a disillusioned analyst of the human character," writes George Wellwarth in *The Theater of Protest and Paradox.* "Even the plays with political themes are ultimately about the human beings rather than issues. Like Ionesco, like Beckett, like all the writers of the dramatic avant-garde in fact, Duerrenmatt feels deep down in himself that the problems of humanity are insoluble. And so he takes refuge from this knowledge in a mordantly sardonic portrayal of life." Duerrenmatt's recurring themes, according to Wellwarth, are "the effect of the possession of power on the human souls," and the senselessness of death, which "renders human acts trivial." But, Wellwarth contends, "Duerrenmatt always implies that events must be resisted. Nothing is inevitable and determined in Duerrenmatt. The fact that things are insignificant from a cosmic viewpoint does not alter the fact that they are significant in the immediate present: it merely argues that they are finally insoluble and will always repeat themselves." Duerrenmatt once commented: "The universal escapes my grasp. I refuse to find the universal in a doctrine. The universal for me is chaos. The world (hence the stage which represents this world) is for me something monstrous, a riddle of misfortunes which must be accepted but before which one must not capitulate."

BIOGRAPHICAL/CRITICAL SOURCES:

BOOKS

Arnold, Heinz, Ludwig, editor, *Friedrich Duerrenmatt II*, Beck, 1977.

Block, H. M., and H. Salinger, editors, *Creative Vision*, Evergreen, 1960.

Chick, Edson M., *Dances of Death: Wedekind, Brecht, Duerrenmatt and the Satiric Tradition*, Camden House, 1984.

Contemporary Literary Criticism, Gale (Detroit), Volume 1, 1973; Volume 4, 1975; Volume 8, 1978; Volume 11, 1979; Volume 15, 1980; Volume 43, 1987.

Crockett, Roger A., *Understanding Friedrich Durrenmatt*, University of South Carolina Press, 1997.

Dictionary of Literary Biography, Volume 69: *Contemporary German Fiction Writers, First Series*, Gale, 1988.

Esslin, Martin, *Reflections: Essays on Modern Theatre*, Doubleday, 1969.

Knapp, Gerhard, *Friedrich Duerrenmatt*, Metzler, 1980.

Knopf, Jan, *Friedrich Duerrenmatt*, Beck, 1980.

Lazar, Moshe, Editor, *Play Duerrenmatt*, Undena, 1983.

Lumley, Frederick, *New Trends in Twentieth Century Drama*, Oxford University Press, 1967.

Wager, Walter, Editor, *The Playwrights Speak*, Delacorte Press, 1967.

Wellwarth, George, *The Theater of Protest and Paradox: Developments in the Avant-garde Drama*, New York University Press, 1964.

Whitton, Kenneth S., *Duerrenmatt: Reinterpretation in Retrospect*, Berg, 1990.

Whitton, Kenneth S., *The Theatre of Friedrich Duerrenmatt: A Study in the Possibility of Freedom*, Oswald Wolff, 1980.

Wilbert-Collins, E., *Bibliography of Four Contemporary Swiss-German Authors: Friedrich Duerrenmatt, Max Frisch, Robert Walser, Albin Zollinger*, Francke, 1967.

PERIODICALS

Christian Century, October 28, 1964.

Christian Science Monitor, July 22, 1965; August 7, 1965.

Comparative Drama, pring, 1982.

Contemporary Literature, autumn, 1966; summer, 1970; summer, 1981.

Esquire, May, 1961.

Forum for Modern Language Studies, January, 1976.

Genre, December, 1975.

Germanic Review, November, 1972.

German Life and Letters, January, 1974.

German Quarterly, January, 1962; May, 1967.

International Fiction Review, July, 1977.

Journal of Modern Literature, Volume 1, Number 1, 1971.

Kentucky Foreign Language Quarterly, 9, No. 4, 1962.

Library Journal, April 15, 1988; April 1, 1989.

Modern Drama, May, 1967; May, 1969; June, 1977.

Modern Fiction Studies, winter, 1971-72.

Mosaic, spring, 1972.

Nation, January 9, 1960; May 4, 1963; March 2, 1992.

New Leader, February 10, 1992.

New Republic, June 5, 1989.

New Statesman and Society, February 22, 1991.

New Yorker, February 3, 1992.

New York Times, October 18, 1964; July 10, 1965; June 4, 1971; February 5, 1989.

New York Times Book Review, June 13, 1965; June 12, 1988; August 6, 1989.

Publishers Weekly, March 11, 1988; February 17, 1989.

Renascence, winter, 1985.

Saturday Review, July 17, 1965.

Stage, January 20, 1972.

Time, December 10, 1973; December 24, 1990 (obituary); February 3, 1992.

Times (London), June 29, 1989.

Times Literary Supplement, January 11, 1964; July 14, 1966; October 27, 1972; October 16, 1981; October 29, 1982; May 16, 1986.

Tribune Books (Chicago), March 6, 1988.

Voice Literary Supplement, February, 1984.

Wisconsin Studies Contemporary Literature, autumn, 1966.

World Literature Today, winter, 1978; autumn, 1981; summer, 1982; summer, 1984; spring, 1986; summer, 1986; autumn, 1987.

du MAURIER, Daphne 1907-1989

PERSONAL: Born May 13, 1907, in London, England; died April 19, 1989, in Par, Cornwall, England; daughter of Gerald (an actor and manager) and Muriel (an actress; maiden name, Beaumont) du Maurier; married Frederick Arthur Montague Browning (a lieutenant-general and former treasurer to the Duke of Edinburgh), July 19, 1932 (died, 1965); children: Tessa (Mrs. David Montgomery), Flavia Browning Tower, Christian. *Education:* Attended schools in London, Paris, and Meudon, France. *Politics:* "Center." *Avocation:* Walking, sailing, gardening, country life.

CAREER: Writer, 1931-89.

MEMBER: Bronte Society, Royal Society of Literature (fellow).

AWARDS, HONORS: National Book Award, 1938, for *Rebecca*; Dame Commander, Order of the British Empire, 1969.

WRITINGS:

NOVELS

The Loving Spirit, Doubleday (Garden City, NY), 1931.
I'll Never Be Young Again, Doubleday, 1932.
The Progress of Julius, Doubleday, 1933.
Jamaica Inn (also see below), Doubleday, 1936, abridged edition, edited by Jay E. Greene, bound with *The Thirty-Nine Steps* by John Buchan, Globe Publications, 1951.
Rebecca (also see below), Doubleday, 1938.
Frenchman's Creek (also see below), Gollancz (London), 1941, Doubleday, 1942.
Hungry Hill (also see below), Doubleday, 1943.
The King's General, Doubleday, 1946, abridged edition, edited by Lee Wyndham, Garden City Books, 1954.
The Parasites, Gollancz, 1949, Doubleday, 1950.
My Cousin Rachel (also see below), Gollancz, 1951, Doubleday, 1952.
Mary Anne (fictionalized biography of author's great-great grandmother), Doubleday, 1954.
The Scapegoat, Doubleday, 1957.
Three Romantic Novels: Rebecca, Frenchman's Creek, Jamaica Inn, Doubleday, 1961.
(With Arthur Quiller-Couch) *Castle d'Or,* Doubleday, 1962.
The Glass-Blowers, Doubleday, 1963.
The Flight of the Falcon, Doubleday, 1965.
The House on the Strand (Literary Guild selection), Doubleday, 1969.
Rule Britannia, Gollancz, 1972, Doubleday, 1973.
Four Great Cornish Novels (contains *Jamaica Inn, Rebecca, Frenchman's Creek,* and *My Cousin Rachel*), Gollancz, 1978.

SHORT STORY COLLECTIONS

Come Wind, Come Weather, Heinemann (London), 1940, Doubleday, 1941.
The Apple Tree: A Short Novel and Some Stories, Gollancz, 1952, published as *Kiss Me Again, Stranger: A Collection of Eight Stories, Long and Short,* Doubleday, 1953, published as *The Birds, and Other Stories,* Pan Books (London), 1977.
The Breaking Point, Doubleday, 1959, published as *The Blue Lenses, and Other Stories,* Penguin (London), 1970.
Early Stories, Todd, 1959.
The Treasury of du Maurier Short Stories, Gollancz, 1960.
Don't Look Now, Doubleday, 1971, published as *Not after Midnight,* Gollancz, 1971.

Echoes from the Macabre: Selected Stories, Gollancz, 1976, Doubleday, 1977.
The Rendezvous, and Other Stories, Gollancz, 1980.

Also author of the short story "The Birds."

PLAYS

Rebecca (three-act; based on author's novel of same title; produced on the West End at Queen's Theatre, 1940, produced on Broadway at Ethel Barrymore Theatre, 1945), Gollancz, 1940, Dramatists Play Service (New York City), 1943.
The Years Between (two-act; produced in Manchester, England, 1944, produced on the West End at Wyndham's Theatre, 1945), Gollancz, 1945, Doubleday, 1946.
September Tide (three-act; produced on the West End at Aldwych Theatre, 1948), Gollancz, 1949, Doubleday, 1950, revised edition with Mark Rayment, Samuel French (New York City), 1994.
Gerald: A Portrait (biography of author's father), Gollancz, 1934, Doubleday, 1935.
The du Mauriers (family history and biography), Doubleday, 1937.
Happy Christmas, Doubleday, 1940.
Spring Picture, Todd, 1944.
(Coauthor) *Hungry Hill* (screenplay; based on author's novel of same title), Universal Pictures, 1947.
(Editor) *The Young George du Maurier: A Selection of His Letters, 1860-1867,* P. Davies, 1951, Doubleday, 1952.
The Infernal World of Branwell Bronte (biography), Gollancz, 1960, Doubleday, 1961.
(Editor) Phyllis Bottome, *Best Stories,* Faber, 1963.
Vanishing Cornwall (history and travel), Doubleday, 1967.
Golden Lads: Sir Francis Bacon, Anthony Bacon and Their Friends, Doubleday, 1975.
The Winding Stair: Francis Bacon, His Rise and Fall, Gollancz, 1976, Doubleday, 1977.
Myself When Young: The Shaping of a Writer (autobiography), Doubleday, 1977, published as *Growing Pains: The Shaping of a Writer,* Gollancz, 1977.
The "Rebecca" Notebook, and Other Memories, Doubleday, 1980.
Daphne du Maurier Classics, Doubleday, 1987.
Enchanted Cornwall: Her Pictorial Memoir, M. Joseph (London), 1990.
My Cousin Rachel (adapted from author's novel of same title), edited by Diana Morgan, Dramatists Play Service, 1990.
Letters from Menabilly: Portrait of a Friendship, edited by Oriel Malet, M. Evans (New York City), 1994.

MEDIA ADAPTATIONS: Alfred Hitchcock directed *Jamaica Inn* for Paramount Pictures in 1939, *Rebecca* for United Artists in 1940 (it won an Academy Award for best motion picture as well as a citation by the Film Daily Poll as one of the ten best pictures of the year), and *The Birds* for Universal Pictures in 1963. *Frenchman's Creek* was filmed by Paramount in 1944, *Hungry Hill* by I. Arthur Rank in 1947, *My Cousin Rachel* by Metro-Goldwyn-Mayer (MGM) in 1953, *The Scapegoat* by MGM in 1959, *Don't Look Now* by Paramount in 1973, and the novella "The Breakthrough" as *The Lifeforce Experiment* by Astral Film Enterprises, 1994. *Rebecca* was adapted as a television mini-series in 1979 by the British Broadcasting Corp. and adapted for the stage by Clifford Williams in 1994. *Jamaica Inn* was adapted for television in 1985 by Harlech Television. The television film *The Birds II: Land's End,* 1994, is a sequel to *The Birds.*

SIDELIGHTS: "Last night I dreamt I went to Manderley again." With these words, among the most recognizable in twentieth-century Gothic fiction, Daphne du Maurier began her classic novel *Rebecca.* Described by the *Spectator*'s Kate O'Brien as "a Charlotte Bronte story minus Charlotte Bronte," *Rebecca* takes a familiar situation (the arrival of a second wife in her new husband's home) and turns it into an occasion for mystery, suspense, and violence. Its primary features—an enigmatic heroine in a cold and hostile environment, a brooding hero tormented by a guilty secret, and a rugged seacoast setting—are now virtual staples of modern romantic novels. Though reviewers have long pointed out (and du Maurier agreed) that she could not take credit for inventing this formula, many critics believe that du Maurier's personal gift for storytelling places her novels a cut above other Gothic fiction.

Daughter of renowned actor Gerald du Maurier and granddaughter of artist and author George du Maurier (*Trilby*), young Daphne first turned to writing as a means of escape. Despite a happy and financially secure childhood, she often felt "inadequate" and desperately in need of solitude. She delighted in the imaginary world of books and play-acting and stubbornly resisted "growing up" until her late teens. After shunning the debutante scene and a chance at an acting career, du Maurier determined to succeed on her own terms—as a writer. During one ten-week stay at her parents' country home on the Cornish coast, the twenty-four-year-old Englishwoman wrote her first novel, *The Loving Spirit,* a romantic family chronicle. A best-seller that achieved a fair share of critical acclaim as well, *The Loving Spirit* so impressed a thirty-five-year-old major in the Grenadier Guards that he piloted his motor launch past the du Maurier home in the hope of meeting the author. Major Frederick "Boy" Browning and du Maurier married a few months later, setting off by boat on a honeymoon "just like the couple in *The Loving Spirit,*" according to Nicholas Wade in the *Times Literary Supplement.*

Perhaps because of the fairy-tale quality of her own life, du Maurier displayed a fondness for romance and intrigue throughout her entire writing career. While some critics feel her short stories, which include "The Birds" and "Don't Look Now," represent her best work in a literary sense, few dispute the fact that her novels form the basis of her immense popular success. As V. S. Pritchett remarked in a review of *Rebecca*: "Many a better novelist would give his eyes to be able to tell a story as Miss Du Maurier does, to make it move at such a pace and to go with such mastery from surprise to surprise. . . . From the first sinister rumors to the final conflagration the melodrama is excellent."

Despite the almost overwhelming critical praise for *Rebecca,* some critics believed du Maurier's other work exhibits too much melodrama, too many plot similarities, and too little character development and analysis. With the exception of *My Cousin Rachel,* a book several critics have hailed as another *Rebecca,* many of her later novels suffer in comparison. The *Spectator*'s Paul Ableman, for instance, declared that her "plots creak and depend on either outrageous coincidence or shamelessly contrived mood," that her prose is "both sloppy and chaotic," and that her dialogue consists of "rent-a-line, prefabricated units for the nobs or weird demotic for the yokels." And L. A. G. Strong, another *Spectator* critic, pointed out the "facile, out-of-character lines that disfigure the often excellent dialogue," as well as a certain "laziness over detail" and a "mixture of careful with perfunctory work." In addition, insisted Beatus T. Lucey of *Best Sellers,* "nowhere does the reader become engaged and involved in the action."

Du Maurier herself admitted that she was "not so much interested in people as in types—types who represent great forces of good or evil. I don't care very much whether John Smith likes Mary Robinson, goes to bed with Jane Brown and then refuses to pay the hotel bill. But I *am* passionately interested in human cruelty, human lust and human avarice—and, of course, their counterparts in the scale of virtue."

Despite the views of critics who complain about plot similarities and stereotyped characters, Jean Stubbs of *Books and Bookmen* remained convinced of the writer's success. "Daphne Du Maurier has the deserved reputation of being an outstanding storyteller," Stubbs wrote. "She has the gift of conveying mystery and holding suspense, above all of suggesting the grip of the unknown on ordinary lives. . . . She is passionately devoted to Cornwall, and insists on our participation. Her sense of theatre creates some characters a little larger than life, and her commonsense surrounds them with people we have met and known, so that the eccentric and dramatic is enhanced."

Furthermore, as a critic for the *Times Literary Supplement* pointed out in a review of *Rebecca,* it may not be to anyone's benefit to approach du Maurier's work as one would approach great literature. "If one chooses to read the book in a critical fashion—but only a tiresome reviewer is likely to do that—it becomes an obligation to take off one's hat to Miss du Maurier for the skill and assurance with which she sustains a highly improbable fiction," the critic stated. "Whatever else she may lack, it is not the story-teller's flow of fancy. All things considered, [hers] is an ingenious, exciting and engagingly romantic tale."

Critical wrangling aside, the number of notable film adaptations of du Maurier's work will insure her a place among notable novelists of the twentieth century. "There is no doubt that Du Maurier, right at the start of her career, hit on a brilliant combination of ingredients that will continue to hold readers spellbound for a long time," concluded Anstiss Drake in the *Chicago Tribune Book World.* Capturing the essence of her work, he noted that her characters "are as real to us as any of Dickens' creations. . . . She sweeps dust away and brings her stories alive. It is a rare talent. . . . In this century few English-speaking authors seem to keep that particular magic. Somerset Maugham was one, and Du Maurier is most definitely another."

BIOGRAPHICAL/CRITICAL SOURCES:

BOOKS

Cook, Judith, *Daphne: A Portrait of Daphne Du Maurier,* Ulverscroft Large Print Books, 1992.

Horner, Avril, and Sue Zlosnik, *Daphne Du Maurier: Writing, Identity and the Gothic Imagination,* St. Martin's Press, 1998.

Leng, Flavia, *Daphne Du Maurier: A Daughter's Memoir,* Mainstream Publication Company Ltd., 1995.

Shallcross, Martyn, *The Private World of Daphne Du Maurier,* Isis Large Print Books, 1992.

PERIODICALS

Atlantic, April 1942.
Best Sellers, May 1, 1963; October 15, 1969.
Books and Bookmen, January 1973.
Canadian Forum, October 1938.
Chicago Tribune Book World, September 21, 1980.
Christian Science Monitor, September 14, 1938; October 2, 1969; September 21, 1977.
Commonweal, April 10, 1942.

Critic, September 1978.
Detroit News, November 13, 1977.
Ladies' Home Journal, November 1956.
Life, September 11, 1944; February 6, 1970.
Listener, June 9, 1977.
Los Angeles Times, October 3, 1980.
Manchester Guardian, January 10, 1936; August 5, 1938; September 19, 1941; August 3, 1951.
Nation, November 11, 1931.
New Statesman and Nation, March 14, 1931; August 11, 1951.
Newsweek, September 26, 1938; January 9, 1950; June 24, 1954.
New Yorker, February 7, 1942; February 9, 1952; September 23, 1967.
New York Herald Tribune Book Review, February 10, 1952.
New York Times, August 2, 1931; April 26, 1936; September 25, 1938; February 1, 1942; February 10, 1952.
New York Times Book Review, October 26, 1969; November 6, 1977; September 21, 1980.
Observer (London), July 16, 1967.
Publishers Weekly, February 18, 1939; January 31, 1948.
Saturday Review, February 28, 1931; April 24, 1937; September 24, 1938; June 19, 1943; January 12, 1946; February 7, 1948; January 7, 1950; February 9, 1952; July 19, 1952; March 14, 1953; February 23, 1957; October 11, 1969.
Saturday Review of Literature, December 12, 1931; April 25, 1936; September 24, 1938; February 14, 1942.
Spectator, February 28, 1931; January 24, 1936; August 12, 1938; September 19, 1941; August 10, 1951; May 14, 1977; November 15, 1980.
Theatre Arts, March 1945.
Time, November 3, 1947; January 16, 1950; February 11, 1952; June 21, 1954; February 25, 1957; February 23, 1962.
Times Literary Supplement, March 5, 1931; January 11, 1936; August 6, 1938; September 13, 1941; June 3, 1977; December 26, 1980.

*   *   *

DUNCAN, Robert (Edward) 1919-1988
(Robert Symmes)

PERSONAL: Born January 7, 1919, in Oakland, CA; died February 3, 1988, of a heart attack in San Francisco, CA; name at birth, Edward Howard Duncan; son of Edward Howard (a day laborer) and Marguerite (Wesley) Duncan (who died at the time of his birth); adopted, March 10, 1920, by Edwin Joseph (an architect) and Minnehaha (Harris) Symmes; adopted name, Robert Edward Symmes; in 1941 he took the name Robert Duncan; companion of Jess Collins (a painter). *Education:* Attended University of California, Berkeley, 1936-38, 1948-50, studying the civilization of the Middle Ages under Ernst Kantorowicz.

CAREER: Poet. Worked at various times as a dishwasher and typist. Organizer of poetry readings and workshops in San Francisco Bay area, California. *Experimental Review,* co-editor with Sanders Russell, publishing works of Henry Miller, Anais Nin, Lawrence Durrell, Kenneth Patchen, William Everson, Aurora Bligh (Mary Fabilli), Thomas Merton, Robert Horan, and Jack Johnson, 1940-41; *Berkeley Miscellany,* editor, 1948-49; lived in Banyalbufar, Majorca, 1955-56; taught at Black Mountain College, Black Mountain, NC, spring and summer, 1956; assistant director of Poetry Center, San Francisco State College, under a Ford grant, 1956-57; associated with the Creative Writing Workshop, University of British Columbia, 1963; lecturer in

Advanced Poetry Workshop, San Francisco State College, spring, 1965. *Military service:* U.S. Army, 1941; discharged on psychological grounds.

AWARDS, HONORS: Ford Foundation grant, 1956-57; Union League Civic and Arts Foundation Prize, *Poetry* magazine, 1957; Harriet Monroe Prize, *Poetry,* 1961; Guggenheim fellowship, 1963-64; Levinson Prize, *Poetry,* 1964; Miles Poetry Prize, 1964; National Endowment for the Arts grants, 1965, 1966-67; Eunice Tietjens Memorial Prize, *Poetry,* 1967; nomination for National Book Critics Circle Award, 1984, for *Ground Work: Before the War;* first recipient of National Poetry Award, 1985, in recognition of lifetime contribution to the art of poetry; Before Columbus Foundation American Book Award, 1986, for *Ground Work: Before the War;* Fred Cody Award for Lifetime Literary Excellence from Bay Area Book Reviewers Association, 1986.

WRITINGS:

Heavenly City, Earthly City (poems, 1945-46), drawings by Mary Fabilli, Bern Porter, 1947.
Medieval Scenes (poems, 1947), Centaur Press (San Francisco), 1950, reprinted with preface by Duncan and afterword by Robert Bertholf, Kent State University Libraries, 1978.
Poems, 1948-49 (actually written between November, 1947, and October, 1948), Berkeley Miscellany, 1950.
The Song of the Border-Guard (poem), Black Mountain Graphics Workshop, 1951.
The Artist's View (San Francisco), 1952.
Fragments of a Disordered Devotion, privately printed, 1952.
Caesar's Gate: Poems, 1949-55, Divers Press (Majorca), 1956, 2nd edition, Sand Dollar, 1972.
Letters (poems, 1953-56), drawings by Duncan, J. Williams (Highlands, NC), 1958.
Faust Foutu: Act One of Four Acts, A Comic Mask, 1952-1954 (an entertainment in four parts; first produced in San Francisco, CA, 1955; produced in New York, 1959-60), decorations by Duncan, Part I, White Rabbit Press (San Francisco), 1958, entire play published as *Faust Foutu,* Enkidu sur Rogate (Stinson Beach, CA), 1959.
Selected Poems (1942-50), City Lights Books, 1959.
The Opening of the Field (poems, 1956-59), Grove, 1960, revised edition, New Directions, 1973.
(Author of preface) Jess [Collins], *O!* (poems and collages), Hawk's Well Press (New York), 1960.
(Author of preface) Jonathan Williams, *Elegies and Celebrations,* Jargon, 1962.
On Poetry (radio interview, broadcast on WTIC, Hartford, CT, May 31, 1964), Yale University, 1964.
Roots and Branches (poems, 1959-63), Scribner, 1964.
Writing Writing: A Composition Book of Madison 1953, Stein Imitations (poems and essays, 1953), Sumbooks, 1964.
As Testimony: The Poem and the Scene (essay, 1958), White Rabbit Press, 1964.
Wine, Auerhahn Press for Oyez Broadsheet Series (Berkeley), 1964.
Uprising (poems), Oyez, 1965.
The Sweetness and Greatness of Dante's "Divine Comedy," 1263-1965 (lecture presented at Dominican College of San Raphael, October 27, 1965), Open Space (San Francisco), 1965.
Medea at Kolchis; [or] *The Maiden Head* (play; first produced at Black Mountain College, 1956), Oyez, 1965.
Adam's Way: A Play on Theosophical Themes, [San Francisco], 1966.

(Contributor) Howard Nemerov, editor, *Poets on Poetry,* Basic Books, 1966.

Of the War: Passages 22-27, Oyez, 1966.

A Book of Resemblances: Poems, 1950-53, drawings by Jess, Henry Wenning, 1966.

Six Prose Pieces, Perishable Press (Rochester, MI), 1966.

The Years as Catches: First Poems, 1939-46, Oyez, 1966.

Boob (poem), privately printed, 1966.

Audit/Robert Duncan (also published as special issue of *Audit/Poetry,* Volume 4, number 3), Audit/Poetry, 1967.

Christmas Present, Christmas Presence! (poem), Black Sparrow Press, 1967.

The Cat and the Blackbird (children's storybook), illustrations by Jess, White Rabbit Press, 1967.

Epilogos, Black Sparrow Press, 1967.

My Mother Would Be a Falconress (poem), Oyez, 1968.

Names of People (poems, 1952-53), illustrations by Jess, Black Sparrow Press, 1968.

The Truth and Life of Myth: An Essay in Essential Autobiography, House of Books (New York), 1968.

Bending the Bow (poems), New Directions, 1968.

The First Decade: Selected Poems, 1940-50, Fulcrum Press (London), 1968.

Derivations: Selected Poems, 1950-1956, Fulcrum Press, 1968.

Achilles Song, Phoenix, 1969.

Playtime, Pseudo Stein; 1942, A Story [and] *A Fairy Play: From the Laboratory Records Notebook of 1953, A Tribute to Mother Carey's Chickens,* Poet's Press, c.1969.

Notes on Grossinger's "Solar Journal: Oecological Sections," Black Sparrow Press, 1970.

A Selection of Sixty-Five Drawings from One Drawing Book, 1952-1956, Black Sparrow Press, 1970.

Tribunals: Passages 31-35, Black Sparrow Press, 1970.

Poetic Disturbances, Maya (San Francisco), 1970.

Bring It up from the Dark, Cody's Books, 1970.

(Contributor) Edwin Haviland Miller, editor, *The Artistic Legacy of Walt Whitman: A Tribute to Gay Wilson Allen,* New York University Press, 1970.

A Prospectus for the Prepublication of Ground Work to Certain Friends of the Poet, privately printed, 1971.

An Interview with George Bowering and Robert Hogg, April 19, 1969, Coach House Press, 1971.

Structure of Rime XXVIII; In Memoriam Wallace Stevens, University of Connecticut, 1972.

Poems from the Margins of Thom Gunn's Moly, privately printed, 1972.

A Seventeenth-Century Suite, privately printed, 1973.

(Contributor) Ian Young, editor, *The Male Muse: Gay Poetry Anthology,* Crossing Press, 1973.

Dante, Institute of Further Studies (New York), 1974.

(With Jack Spicer) *An Ode and Arcadia,* Ark Press, 1974.

The Venice Poem, Poet's Mimeo (Burlington, VT), 1978.

Veil, Turbine, Cord & Bird: Sets of Syllables, Sets of Words, Sets of Lines, Sets of Poems, Addressing . . . , J. Davies, c. 1979.

Fictive Certainties: Five Essays in Essential Autobiography, New Directions, 1979.

The Five Songs, Friends of the University of California, San Diego Library, 1981.

Towards an Open Universe, Aquila Publishing, 1982.

Ground Work: Before the War, New Directions, 1984.

A Paris Visit, Grenfell Press, 1985.

The Regulators, Station Hill Press, 1985.

Ground Work II: In the Dark, New Directions, 1987.

Selected Poems, edited by Robert J. Bertholf, New Directions, 1993.

A Selected Prose, edited by Robert J. Bertholf, New Directions, 1995.

Copy Book Entries, Small Press Distribution, 1996.

Also author of *The H.D. Book,* a long work in several parts, published in literary journals. Represented in anthologies, including *Faber Book of Modern American Verse,* edited by W. H. Auden, 1956, *The New American Poetry: 1945-1960,* edited by Donald M. Allen, 1960, and many others. Contributor of poems, under the name Robert Symmes, to *Phoenix* and *Ritual.* Contributor to *Atlantic, Poetry, Nation, Quarterly Review of Literature,* and other periodicals.

SIDELIGHTS: Though the name Robert Duncan is not well known outside the literary world, within that world it has become associated with a number of superlatives. Kenneth Rexroth, writing in *Assays,* named Duncan "one of the most accomplished, one of the most influential" of the postwar American poets. The diverse range of his work links him with various literary movements, particularly the romantics, the Beats, and the "Black Mountain School" of poetry led by Charles Olson. Duncan became "probably the figure with the richest natural genius" from among the Black Mountain group, suggests M. L. Rosenthal in *The New Poets: American and British Poetry since World War II.* Duncan was also, in Rosenthal's opinion, perhaps "the most intellectual of our poets from the point of view of the effect upon him of a wide, critically intelligent reading." In addition, "few poets have written more articulately and self-consciously about their own intentions and understanding of poetry," reports *Dictionary of Literary Biography* contributor George F. Butterick. The homosexual companion of San Francisco painter Jess Collins, Duncan was also one of the first poets to call for a new social consciousness that would accept homosexuality. Largely responsible for the establishment of San Francisco as the spiritual hub of contemporary American poetry, Duncan has left a significant contribution to American literature through the body of his writings and through the many poets who have felt the influence of the theory behind his poetics.

Duncan's poetics were formed by the events of his early life. His mother died while giving him birth, leaving his father, a day-laborer, to care for him. Six months later, he was adopted by a couple who selected him on the basis of his astrological configuration. Their reverence for the occult in general, and especially their belief in reincarnation, and other concepts from Hinduism, was a lasting and important influence on his poetic vision.

Minnesota Review contributor Victor Contoski suggests that Duncan's essays in *The Truth and Life of Myth* may be "the best single introduction to his poetry," which, for Duncan, was closely related to mysticism. Duncan, says a London *Times* reporter, was primarily "concerned with poetry as what he called 'manipulative magic' and a 'magic ritual', and with the nature of what he thought of (in a markedly Freudian manner) as 'human bisexuality.'" Reports James Dickey in *Babel to Byzantium,* "Duncan has the old or pagan sense of the poem as a divine form of speech which works intimately with the animism of nature, of the renewals that believed-in ceremonials can be, and of the sacramental in experience; for these reasons and others that neither he nor I could give, there is at least part of a very good poet in him." While this emphasis on myth was an obstacle to some reviewers, critic Laurence Liebermann, writing in a *Poetry* review, said of

The Opening of the Field, Duncan's first mature collection, that it "announced the birth of a surpassingly individual talent: a poet of mysticism, visionary terror, and high romance."

Duncan wrote some of the poems in *The Opening of the Field* in 1956 when he taught at Olson's Black Mountain College. Olson promoted projective verse, a poetry shaped by the rhythms of the poet's breath, which he defined as an extension of nature. These poems would find their own "open" forms unlike the prescribed measures and line lengths that ruled traditional poetry. "Following Olson's death Duncan became the leading spokesman for the poetry of open form in America," notes Butterick. Furthermore, say some critics, Duncan fulfilled Olson's dictum more fully than Olson had done; whereas Olson projected the poem into a space bounded by the poet's natural breath, Duncan carried this process farther, defining the poem as an open field without boundaries of any kind.

Each Duncan poem builds itself by a series of organic digressions, in the manner of outward-reaching roots or branches. The order in his poems is not an imposed order, but a reflection of correspondences already present in nature or language. At times, the correspondences inherent in language become insistent so that the poet following an organic method of writing is in danger of merely recording what the language itself dictates as possible. Duncan was highly susceptible to impressions from other literature—perhaps too susceptible, he said in a *Boundary 2* interview. In several interviews, for example, Duncan referred to specific early poems as "received" from outside agents, "poems in which angels were present." After reading Rainer Marie Rilke's *Duino Elegies,* he came to dread what he called "any angelic invasion"—or insistent voice other than his own. One poem that expresses this preference is "Often I Am Permitted to Return to a Meadow," the first poem in *The Opening of the Field.* He told Jack R. Cohn and Thomas J. O'Donnell in an interview for *Contemporary Literature:* "When I wrote that opening line, . . . I recognized that this was my permission, and that this meadow, which I had not yet identified, would be the thematic center of the book. In other words, what's back of that opening proposition I understood immediately: twice *you* wanted to compel me to have a book that would have angels at the center, but *now* I am permitted, often you have permitted me, to return to a mere meadow." His originality consisted of his demand that the inner life of the poem be his own, not received from another spiritual or literary source. "Whether he is working from Dante's prose Renaissance meditative poems, or Thom Gunn's *Moly* sequence, he works *from* them and *to* what they leave open or unexamined," explains Thomas Parkinson in *Poets, Poems, Movements.*

Duncan's works express social and political ideals conversant with his poetics. The ideal environment for the poet, Duncan believed, would be a society without boundaries. In poetry, Duncan found a vocation where there was no prohibition against homosexuality, James F. Mersmann observes in *Out of the Viet Nam Vortex: A Study of Poets and Poetry against the War.* Duncan's theory, he goes on, "not only claims that the poem unfolds according to its own law, but envisions a compatible cosmology in which it may do so. It is not the poem alone that must grow as freely as the plant: the life of the person, the state, the species, and indeed the cosmos itself follows a parallel law. All must follow their own imperatives and volition; all activity must be free of external coercion."

Political commitment is the subject of *Bending the Bow.* Duncan was "one of the most astute observers of the malpractices of Western governments, power blocs, etc., who [was] always on the human side, the *right* side of such issues as war, poverty, civil rights, etc., and who therefore [did] not take an easy way out," though his general avoidance of closure sometimes weakened his case, Harriet Zinnes remarks in a *Prairie Schooner* review. Highly critical of the Viet Nam war, pollution, nuclear armament, and the exploitation of native peoples and natural resources, the poems in *Bending the Bow* include "Up-Rising," "one of the major political poems of our time," according to Michael Davidson in the *Dictionary of Literary Biography.* For Duncan, the essayist continues, "the American attempt to secure *one* meaning of democracy by eliminating all others represents a massive violation of that vision of polis desired by John Adams and Thomas Jefferson and projected through Walt Whitman." Though such poems voice an "essentially negative vision," says Robert C. Weber in *Concerning Poetry,* "it is a critical part of Duncan's search for the nature of man since he cannot ignore what man has become. . . . These themes emerge from within the body of the tradition of the poetry he seeks to find; politics are a part of the broad field of the poet's life, and social considerations emerge from his concern with the nature of man."

The difference between organic and imposed order, for Duncan, says Mersmann, "is the difference between life and death. The dead matter of the universe science dissects into tidy stacktables; the living significance of creation, the angel with which the poet wrestles, is a volatile whirlwind of sharp knees and elbows thrashing with a grace beyond our knowledge of grace." The only law in a dancing universe, he goes on, is its inherent "love of the dance itself." Anything opposed to this dance of freedom is seen as evil. Both Duncan's poetics and his lifestyle stem from "a truly different kind of consciousness, either a very old or a very new spirituality," Mersmann concludes.

Duncan's method of composition presents some difficulties for the critic, as well. The eclectic nature of *Bending the Bow,* for example, remarks Hayden Carruth in the *Hudson Review,* excludes it from "questions of quality. I cannot imagine my friends, the poets who gather to dismember each other in this review, asking of this book, as they would of the others in this review, those narrower in scope, smaller in style, 'Is it good or is it bad?' The question doesn't arise; not because Duncan is a good poet, though he is superb, but because the comprehensiveness of his imagination is too great for us."

After the publication of *Bending the Bow* in 1968, Duncan announced he would not publish a major collection for another fifteen years. During this hiatus he hoped to produce process-oriented poems instead of the "overcomposed" poems he wrote when he thought in terms of writing a book. In effect, this silence kept him from receiving the widespread critical attention or recognition he might otherwise have enjoyed. However, Duncan had a small but highly appreciative audience among writers who shared his concerns. Distraught when *Ground Work: Before the War,* the evidence of nearly twenty years of significant work, did not win the attention they thought it deserved from the publishing establishment, these poets founded the National Poetry Award and honored Duncan by making him the first recipient of the award in 1985. The award, described in a *Sagetrieb* article, was "a positive action affirming the admiration of the poetic community for the dedication and accomplishment of a grand poet." A major collection of his manuscripts is archived in the Bancroft Library at the University of California, Berkeley.

BIOGRAPHICAL/CRITICAL SOURCES:

BOOKS

Bertholf, Robert J. and Ian W. Reid, editors, *Robert Duncan: Scales of the Marvelous,* New Directions, 1979.

Contemporary Literary Criticism, Gale (Detroit), Volume 1, 1973; Volume 2, 1974; Volume 4, 1975; Volume 7, 1977; Volume 15, 1980; Volume 41, 1987.

Dickey, James, *Babel to Byzantium,* Farrar, Straus, 1968.

Dictionary of Literary Biography, Gale, Volume 5: *American Poets since World War II,* 1980; Volume 16: *The Beats: Literary Bohemians in Postwar America,* 1983.

Fass, Ekbert, *Young Robert Duncan: Portrait of the Homosexual in Society,* Black Sparrow Press, 1983.

Foster, Edward Halsey, *Understanding the Black Mountain Poets,* University of South Carolina Press (Columbia), 1995.

Mersmann, James F., *Out of the Viet Nam Vortex: A Study of Poets and Poetry Against the War,* University Press of Kansas, 1974.

Parkinson, Thomas, *Poets, Poems, Movements,* University of Michigan Research Press, 1987.

Rexroth, Kenneth, *Assays,* New Directions, 1961.

Rexroth, Kenneth, *American Poetry in the Twentieth Century,* Herder and Herder, 1971.

Rosenthal, M. L., *The New Poets: American and British Poetry since World War II,* Oxford University Press, 1967.

Rumaker, Michael, *Robert Duncan in San Franciso,,* Grey Fox Press, 1996.

PERIODICALS

Agenda, autumn/winter, 1970.
Audit/Poetry (special Duncan issue), Number 3, 1967.
Boundary 2, winter, 1980.
Centennial Review, fall, 1975; fall, 1985.
Concerning Poetry, spring, 1978.
Contemporary Literature, spring, 1975.
History Today, January, 1994, p. 56.
Hudson Review, summer, 1968.
Library Journal, March 1, 1993, p. 81; August, 1994, p. 132.
Maps (special Duncan issue), 1974.
Minnesota Review, fall, 1972.
New York Review of Books, June 3, 1965; May 7, 1970.
New York Times Book Review, December 20, 1964; September 29, 1968; August 4, 1985.
Poetry, March, 1968; April, 1969; May, 1970.
Publishers Weekly, February 15, 1993, p. 232; May 16, 1994, p. 63.
Sagetrieb, winter, 1983; (special Duncan issue) fall/winter, 1985.
Saturday Review, February 13, 1965; August 24, 1968.
School Library Journal, August, 1994, p. 132.
Southern Review, spring, 1969; winter, 1985.
Sulfur 12, Volume 4, number 2, 1985.
Times Literary Supplement, May 1, 1969; July 23, 1971.
Voice Literary Supplement, November, 1984.

*   *   *

DUNN, Katherine (Karen) 1945-

PERSONAL: Born October 24, 1945, in Garden City, KS; daughter of Jack (a linotype operator) and Velma (Golly) Dunn; children: Eli Malachy Dunn Dapolonia. *Education:* Attended Portland State College (now University) and Reed College. *Religion:* None.

ADDRESSES: 1603 Northwest 23rd, Portland, OR, 97210.

AWARDS, HONORS: Music Corporation of America writing grant; Rockefeller writing grant; National Book Award nomination for *Geek Love.*

WRITINGS:

Attic (novel), Harper, 1970.
Truck (novel), Harper, 1971.
Geek Love (novel), Knopf, 1989.
Why Do Men Have Nipples? and Other Low-life Answers to Real-life Questions, Warner, 1992.
Death Scenes: A Homicide Detective's Scrapbook, Feral House, 1996.
Guyana, Twin Palms, 1996.

Also author of film script of *Truck.*

SIDELIGHTS: Katherine Dunn told *Contemporary Authors*: "I have been a believer in the magic of language since, at a very early age, I discovered that some words got me into trouble and others got me out. The revelations since then have been practically continuous.

"There are other inclinations that have shaped the form and direction of my work: rampant curiosity, a cynical inability to accept face-values balanced by lunatic optimism, and the preoccupation with the effervescing qualities of truth that is probably common to those afflicted by absent-mindedness, prevarication, and general unease in the presence of facts. But the miraculous nature of words themselves contains the discipline."

Reviewing Dunn's novel *Geek Love,* the editor of *Horror Magazine* found the book a "wild, often horrifying novel about freaks, geeks and other aberrancies of the human condition" in which the *normal* and the *abnormal* experience a role reversal. Dunn's novel makes for a powerful emotional statement about our concepts of acceptable appearance and behavior. Her incessant curiosity about out-of-the-ordinary situations and people, pulls the unwary reader into a bizarre world. Reviewers find the book one which readers will either love or hate, with little middle ground for ambivalence. A 1997 issue of *Oregon Live* refers to Dunn as "hit[ting] her literary stride" with *Geek Love,* describing the novel as "the dark story of misfits and misfortune, centered around the albino dwarf named Olympia Binewski." In another review of this work, Margot Dougherty of *People Weekly* complimented Dunn's writing as "crisp, clear and light as her characters are twisted, dark and brooding."

As her alter-ego, "The Slicer," a question-and-answer columnist for a Portland, Oregon weekly newspaper, Dunn collected a series of questions unrelated except for their oddity. She expands upon these items in her short book, *Why Do Men Have Nipples? and Other Low-life Answers to Real-life Questions.* In its review of the volume, *Publishers Weekly* describes Dunn as "more irreverent than many advice columnist, taking on such issues as why orgasms clear the sinuses . . . [and] the psychology of women who leave droplets of urine on public toilet seats." *Publishers Weekly* goes on to note that some of the queries she answers are entertaining (such as her investigation of certain word origins) while others are more mundane (regarding laundered money and decaffeinated coffee, for example), while still others reveal dubious taste on Dunn's part (such as instructions on how to perform bar tricks with flies*). Why Do Men Have Nipples?* treats many local issues pertinent to the Portland area and was published in a limited edition under the name "The Slicer."

Dunn's passionate interest in the out-of-the-ordinary took her into the world of true crime with the publication of *Death Scenes: A Homicide Detective's Scrapbook.* The book does not make for light reading, containing stark, black-and-white photographs and text related to homicides investigated by the Los Angeles Police Department dating back to the 1930s and 1940s. Dunn's following increased with the publication of *Death Scenes,* with her readers giving high marks to this well-researched account of crime and how the American criminal justice system has changed throughout the twentieth century.

"Writing is, increasingly, a moral issue for me," Dunn told *Contemporary Authors.* "The evasion of inexpensive facility, the rejection of the flying bridges built so seductively into the language, require a constant effort of will. The determination required for honest exploration and analysis of the human terrain is often greater than I command. But the fruits of that determination seem worthy of all my efforts."

BIOGRAPHICAL/CRITICAL SOURCES:

BOOKS

Contemporary Authors, Volume 33-36R, Gale (Detroit), 1978.

PERIODICALS

Horror Magazine, 1996.
Life, October 24, 1969.
Nation, August 3, 1970.
New York Times, July 1, 1970.
New York Times Book Review, June 21, 1970.
Oregon Live, October 23, 1997.
People Weekly, April 17, 1989, p. 127.
Publishers Weekly, September 28, 1992.

* * *

DUNSANY, Edward John Moreton Drax Plunkett 1878-1957
(Lord Dunsany)

PERSONAL: Born July 24 (one source says August 25), 1878, in London, England; died October 25, 1957, in Dublin, Ireland; married Beatrice Villiers, 1904; children: one son. *Religion:* Atheist.

CAREER: Novelist, poet, playwright, and translator; also lectured in literature at the University of Athens in Greece during World War II. *Military service:* Served with the Coldstream Guards in Gibraltar and South Africa during the Boer War; later fought in World War I and in Ireland's Easter Rebellion.

WRITINGS:

AS LORD DUNSANY

The Gods of Pegana, Elkin Mathews (London), 1905, Luce (Boston), 1916.
Time and the Gods, Heinemann (London), 1906, Luce, 1917.
The Sword of Welleran, and Other Stories, Allen (London), 1908, Luce, 1916.
The Glittering Gate (play; produced at the Abbey Theatre, Dublin, Ireland, 1909, then Court Theatre, London, England, 1910), later published with an introduction by William-Alan Landes, Players Press (Studio City, CA), 1994.
A Dreamer's Tales, Allen, 1910, Luce, 1916.

King Argimenes and the Unknown Warrior (play; produced at the Abbey Theatre, 1911), later published with an introduction by Landes, Players Press, 1994.
The Gods of the Mountain (play; produced at the Haymarket Theatre, London, 1911), later published with an introduction by Landes, Players Press, 1994.
The Golden Doom (play; produced at the Haymarket Theatre, 1912), later published with an introduction by Landes, Players Press, 1994.
The Book of Wonder, Heinemann, 1912, Luce, 1913.
The Lost Silk Hat (play; produced at the Gaiety Theatre, Manchester, England, 1913), later published with an introduction by Landes, Players Press, 1994.
Five Plays, Richards (London), 1914, Kennerley, 1914.
Fifty-One Tales, Kennerley (New York City), 1915, later published as *The Food of Death: Fifty-One Tales,* Newcastle (Hollywood, CA), 1974.
A Night at an Inn (one-act play; produced at the Neighborhood Playhouse, New York City, 1916), Sunwise Turn (New York City), 1916.
The Queen's Enemies (play; produced at the Neighborhood Playhouse, 1916), French (New York City), 1916.
Tales of Wonder, Elkin Mathews, 1916, published in the United States as *The Last Book of Wonder,* Luce, 1916.
Plays of Gods and Men (contains *The Tents of the Arabs, The Laughter of the Gods, The Queen's Enemies,* and *A Night at an Inn*), Putnam's (New York City), 1917.
Tales of War, Unwin (London), 1918, Putnam's, 1922.
Tales of Three Hemispheres, Luce, 1919, later published with an introduction by H. P. Lovecraft and illustrated by Tim Kirk, Owlswick Press (Philadelphia), 1976.
The Murderers (play), produced at Shubert Murat Theatre, Indianapolis, IN, 1919.
Unhappy Far-Off Things, Little, Brown (Boston), 1919.
The Laughter of the Gods (play; produced at the Punch and Judy Theatre, New York City, 1919), Putnam's (London), 1922.
If (play; produced at the Ambassadors' Theatre, London, 1921), Putnam's (London), 1921, Putnam's (New York City), 1922.
Cheezo (play), produced at Everyman Theatre, London, 1921.
The Chronicles of Rodriguez, Putnam's, 1922, also published as *Don Rodriguez: Chronicles of Shadow Valley,* Putnam's, 1922.
Plays of Near and Far, Putnam's (New York City), 1922.
Lord Adrian (play), produced at Prince of Wales Theatre, Birmingham, England, 1923.
Fame and the Poet (play), produced at Albert Hall, Leeds, England, 1924.
The King of Elfland's Daughter, Putnam's, 1924.
The Compromise of the King of the Golden Isles (play), Grolier Club, 1924.
Alexander, Putnam's, 1925.
Alexander, & Three Small Plays, Putnam's, 1925.
His Sainted Grandmother (play), produced at Fortune Theatre, London, 1926.
The Charwoman's Shadow, Putnam's, 1926.
The Jest of Hahalaba (play), produced at Playroom 6, 1927.
My Faithful (play), produced at Q Theatre, London, 1927.
The Blessing of Pan, Putnam's, 1927.
Seven Modern Comedies, Putnam's, 1928.
Fifty Poems, Putnam's, 1929.
The Travel Tales of Mr. Joseph Jorkens, Putnam's, 1931.
The Curse of the Wise Woman, Longmans, Green (New York City), 1933.

If I Were Dictator: The Pronouncements of the Grand Macaroni, Methuen (London), 1934.

Mr. Jorkens Remembers Africa, Heinemann, 1934, published in the U.S. as *Jorkens Remembers Africa,* Longmans, Green, 1934.

Mr. Faithful: A Comedy in Three Acts, French, 1935.

Up in the Hills, Heinemann, 1935, Putnam's, 1936.

My Talks with Dean Spanley, Putnam's, 1936.

Rory and Bran, Heinemann, 1936, Putnam's, 1937.

Plays for Earth and Air, Heinemann, 1937.

My Ireland, Funk & Wagnalls (New York City), 1937.

Mirage Water, Putnam's (London), 1938, Dorrance (Philadelphia), 1939.

Patches of Sunlight, Reynal & Hitchcock (New York City), 1938.

The Story of Mona Sheehy, Heinemann, 1939, Harper (New York City), 1940.

Jorkens Has a Large Whiskey, Putnam's, 1940.

War Poems, Hutchinson (London), 1941.

Wandering Songs, Hutchinson, 1943.

A Journey, Macdonald (London), 1943.

While the Sirens Slept, Jarrolds (New York City), 1944.

The Sirens Wake, Jarrolds, 1945.

The Donnellan Lectures, 1943, Heinemann, 1945.

A Glimpse from a Watchtower, Jarrolds, 1946.

The Year, Jarrolds, 1946.

The Man Who Ate the Phoenix, Jarrolds, 1947.

The Fourth Book of Jorkens, Arkham (Sauk City, WI), 1948.

To Awaken Pegasus, Ronald (Oxford), 1949.

The Strange Journeys of Colonel Polders, Jarrolds, 1950.

The Last Revolution, Jarrolds (London), 1951.

His Fellow Men, Jarrolds, 1952.

The Little Tales of Smethers and Other Stories, Jarrolds (New York City), 1952.

Jorkens Borrows Another Whiskey, M. Joseph (London), 1954.

At the Edge of the World, edited by Lin Carter, Ballantine (New York City), 1970.

Beyond the Fields We Know, edited by Carter, Pan/Ballantine (London), 1972.

Gods, Men and Ghosts: The Best Supernatural Fiction of Lord Dunsany, selected and with an introduction by E. F. Bleiler, Dover Publications (New York City), 1972.

Over the Hills and Far Away, Ballantine (New York City), 1974.

The Ghosts of the Heaviside Layer, and Other Fantasms, illustrated by Tim Kirk, Owlswick Press, 1980.

The Ghosts, Creative Education (Mankato, MN), 1993.

Contributor of introduction to volumes by Francis Ledwidge, including *Songs of the Field,* Jenkins (London), 1916, *Songs of Peace,* Jenkins, 1917, *Last Songs,* Jenkins, 1918, and *The Complete Poems of Francis Ledwidge,* Jenkins, 1919; author of introduction to *The Golden Book of Modern English Poetry, 1870-1920,* edited by Thomas Caldwell, Dent (London and Toronto), 1922, *Tales from Bective Bridge* by Mary Lavin, M. Joseph (London), 1945, *The Egoist* by George Meredith, Oxford University Press (London), 1947, *Green and Gold* by Mary Hamilton, Wingate (London), 1948, *Bridie Stern* by Annie Crone, Heinemann (London), 1949, *Drift of the Storm* by Baroness Judith Anne Dorothea Wentworth Blunt-Lytton, Ronald (Oxford, England), 1951, *Time's Travellers* by Stanton A. Coblentz, Wings (Mill Valley, CA), 1952, and *A Hill of Dreams* by Arthur Machen, Richards (London), 1954. Author of foreword to *Gods in Motley* by Seumas MacCall, Constable (London), 1935. Contributor to periodicals, including *Punch.* Translator of *The Odes of Horace,* Heinemann, 1947, and, with Michael Oakley, of *The Collected*

Works of Horace, Dutton (New York City), 1961; provided vocals and text for *Poets I Have Known: A Lecture and Poetry Reading,* Library of Congress, 1955.

SIDELIGHTS: Lord Dunsany was the name under which Edward John Moreton Drax Plunkett (Baron Dunsany) wrote during an authorial career that spanned nearly five decades. An Irish aristocrat whose peerage stretched back to medieval times, Lord Dunsany is considered by scholars one of the earliest masters of the fantasy literary genre. He penned several dozen plays as well as poetry and short stories, but also enjoyed accolades as a chessmaster, big-game hunter, and elite soldier in several of the twentieth century's more notorious conflicts. Dunsany's sixty-plus volumes of drama, verse, and short stories were almost always written in longhand with an old-fashioned quill pen: he once told someone that the wild geese from which the quill feathers came carried on them the spirit and romance of far-off lands—lands similar to the fictitious countries he created on paper.

Born in 1878, Dunsany was reared in his family's ancestral Dunsany Castle in County Meath, Ireland. During his formative years he was schooled in Greek mythology and other classics, and at home was encouraged to read the Bible as one of the most noteworthy of English-language texts. He also became skilled in the game of chess. After Dunsany's father passed away in 1899, an uncle took over the family affairs and Dunsany assumed the baronetcy. This uncle introduced him to the writer William Butler Yeats, who would later become a literary collaborator of Dunsany's. He never attended college, but instead joined the Coldstream Guards and served in the Boer War in South Africa. Returning to civilian life, he married and by 1905 had produced his first book, *The Gods of Pegana,* inspired in part by a play called *The Darling of the Gods.*

The vignettes in *The Gods of Pegana* present a mythological kingdom and theogony created entirely by Dunsany. The land of Pegana is populated by deities with invented names and the legends that accompany the place's creation and existence. "For all their fantasy, however, the gods of Pegana succeed in impressing one with a sense of their identity," wrote Ernest A. Boyd in *Appreciations and Depreciations: Irish Literary Studies.* "They are conceived after a plan, the logic of imagination has gone towards their creation, so that the reader carries away an impression of coherence. . . . What greater praise can be awarded it than to say that it possesses precisely those elements which make all legendary and mythological stories convincing?"

Dunsany followed his debut with a similar tome called *Time and the Gods,* published in 1906. It chronicles the fate of the mythological city of Sardathrion, a city destroyed by time. Dunsany recreated this cataclysm through a series of vignettes that portrayed various deities, ordinary people, and events of the kingdom's history that led up to it. Boyd observed in *Appreciations and Depreciations* that "the various legends of *Time and the Gods* are all equally informed with the spirit of fantasy and many are of great poetic power. 'Night and Morning,' 'The South Wind,' and 'A Legend of the Dawn,' are typical of the charm with which Lord Dunsany's imagination can invest the commonest phenomena." Later books by Dunsany followed the trail of this and other mythological lands, such as 1910's *A Dreamer's Tales,* and *The Book of Wonder,* published in 1912.

In April of 1909 Dunsany saw the production of his first work for the stage, a play called *The Glittering Gate* that was staged at Dublin's Abbey Theatre. It was written at the invitation of Yeats and produced by him as well. Set on a cliff, the play uses actors as

English thieves (in a way, reversing the standard characterization of the Irish as ne'er-do-wells by some English playwrights of the day). They break into heaven only to find it empty—a setting perhaps reflective of Dunsany's professed atheism. His next play, 1911's *King Argimenes and the Unknown Warrior,* was also produced at the Abbey. The plot concerns a king held captive by another, King Darniack. One day Argimenes finds a long-buried sword belonging to a forgotten warrior of another era. With the weapon he gains the strength to overthrow his captor.

In Dunsany's *A Night at an Inn,* a work staged in 1916, the fantastic is evidenced when an Indian idol, whose ruby eye has been stolen by thieves, appears at the hostel where they are staying, hoping to retrieve it—the idol then eliminates them offstage. "A more perfect one-act play it would be difficult to conceive," stated Boyd in *Appreciations and Depreciations,* "so wonderfully is the atmosphere created, so tense the suspense, so devastatingly unexpected the denouement."

The onset of World War I interrupted Dunsany's literary pursuits, and he also fought and was wounded in Ireland's Easter Rebellion of 1916, which left part of his face paralyzed. His wartime experiences brought a sobriety to subsequent work, evident in 1918's *Tales of War* as well as *Tales of Three Hemispheres,* published the following year.

During the next few years Dunsany continued to write for the stage, and at one point in 1921 witnessed five of his dramas running simultaneously on Broadway. Yet he also experimented with other literary forms, including poetry and novels. *The Chronicles of Rodriguez,* published in 1922, was his first novel, but some critics term his 1924 volume *The King of Elfland's Daughter* his most successful foray into the genre. AE, the pseudonym under which George Russell wrote, said in the *Living Age* that the work is "the most purely beautiful thing Lord Dunsany has written." AE praised the lyrical descriptions of the fantasy kingdom and the characters, declaring that "his people loom before us like a dance of animated and lovely shadows and grotesques, but we follow their adventures with excitement, and that means in some way they are symbolic of our own spiritual adventures."

Another of Dunsany's novels, the 1926 work *The Charwoman's Shadow,* is the tale of an adventurer named Ramon who trades his shadow for gold. A wizened magician gives him a replacement shadow in return, but it really belongs to a charwoman; the novel follows Ramon's attempts to regain his own shadow back. During the 1920s Dunsany continued to write plays, poems, and short stories, and carried on with his own real-life adventures. He was Ireland's standing chess champion at one time, and traveled the world in search of adventure, including hunting big game in Africa. Many of these experiences were reflected in the "Jorkens" tales, short stories in which the garrulous adventurer Mr. Jorkens regales mates at the club. The first of these was 1931's *The Travel Tales of Mr. Joseph Jorkens,* followed intermittently through the years by *Mr. Jorkens Remembers Africa* (1934), *Jorkens Has a Large Whiskey* (1940), and *The Fourth Book of Jorkens* (1948). Patrick Mahony wrote of the tales in the journal *Eire-Ireland*: "We are served with adventures in putative hunting, talking dogs, enchanted swans, magic apples, and pookas that can entice human beings. The scenery Dunsany describes is often as fantastic as his themes, and he makes frequent use of obscurity and suspense. Action sometimes takes place within deep mysterious woods, or in a stormy piece of jagged coastline with Irish mountains sloping nearby."

In 1937 Dunsany wrote down his impressions of his native land in *My Ireland.* He describes the country, its character, and his perspective on it, in particular from a perspective gained through his hunting exploits. "Nostalgic and measured prose, that is at the same time vigorous, hangs over all this an iridescent veil," wrote Emma Garrett Boyd of the book in the *Forum.* "Considering Dunsany's intangible subject-matter, his imagination has an incredible vividness—the very wind that blows up over the edge of the world has a strange, metallic taste from the wandering stars. It is a highly romantic imagination, too: nature not only takes its coloring from the beholder's mood . . . but it anticipates and forebodes."

After a long and prolific career, Dunsany died in Dublin at the age of seventy-nine. Although Dunsany is considered by some to have been one of the greatest writers Ireland ever produced, his reputation among literary critics suffered somewhat after his death. Still, many credit him as an important early practitioner of the fantasy genre. A good deal of his works combine elements of the fantastic, the poetic, and the dramatic. Cornelius Weygandt felt the last category was perhaps Dunsany's best arena. "The plays of Dunsany belong to literature," he asserted in *Tuesdays at Ten: A Garnering from the Tales of Thirty Years on Poets, Dramatists and Essayists.* "He writes in prose, but his writing has about it the lift of poetry, so we accept him as what he claims to be, a poet. . . . We are thankful to Dunsany, too, for the aloofness of his plays from the moil and toil of today. We are thankful that they are so seldom concerned with such poor sinners as most of us are, that he deals with abstractions, with decorations, with symbols of romance."

BIOGRAPHICAL/CRITICAL SOURCES:

BOOKS

Boyd, Ernest A., *Appreciations and Depreciations: Irish Literary Studies,* Talbot Press, 1917.

Daniels, Keith Allen, *Arthur C. Clarke and Lord Dunsany: A Correspondence,* Anamnesis Press, 1998.

Dictionary of Literary Biography, Volume 77, *British Mystery Writers, 1920-1939,* Gale (Detroit), 1989.

Joshi, S. T., *The Weird Tale: Arthur Macken, Lord Dunsany, Algernon Blackwood, M. R. James, Ambrose Bierce, H. P. Lovecraft,* University of Texas Press, 1990.

Joshi, S. T., and Darrell Schweitzer, *Lord Dunsany: A Bibliography,* Scarecrow Books, 1993.

Joshi, S. T., *Lord Dunsany: Master of the Anglo-Irish Imagination,* Greenwood Publishing Group, 1995.

Twentieth Century Literary Criticism, Gale, Volume 2, 1979; Volume 59, 1995.

Weygandt, Cornelius, *Tuesdays at Ten: A Garnering from the Tales of Thirty Years on Poets, Dramatists, and Esayists,* 1928.

PERIODICALS

Atlantic Monthly, March, 1955, pp. 67-68, 70, 72.

Bookman, November, 1923.

Eire-Ireland, spring, 1979.

Forum, April, 1917.

Living Age, May 29, 1926, pp. 464-66.

Personalist, January, 1922, pp. 5-30.

Poetry Review, Vol. 49, number 2, 1958.

DUNSANY, Lord
See DUNSANY, Edward John Moreton Drax Plunkett

*   *   *

DU PERRY, Jean
See SIMENON, Georges (Jacques Christian)

*   *   *

DURANG, Christopher (Ferdinand) 1949-

PERSONAL: Born January 2, 1949, in Montclair, NJ; son of Francis Ferdinand and Patricia Elizabeth Durang. *Education:* Harvard University, B.A., 1971; Yale University, M.F.A., 1974. *Religion:* "Raised Roman Catholic."

ADDRESSES: Agent—Helen Merrill, 361 West 17th St., New York, NY 10011.

CAREER: Yale Repertory Theatre, New Haven, CT, actor, 1974; Southern Connecticut College, New Haven, teacher of drama, 1975; Yale University, New Haven, teacher of playwriting, 1975-76; playwright, 1976–. Actor in plays, including *The Idiots Karamazov* and *Das Lusitania Songspiel.*

MEMBER: Dramatists Guild, Actors Equity Association.

AWARDS, HONORS: Fellow of Columbia Broadcasting System (CBS), 1975-76; Rockefeller Foundation grant, 1976-77; Guggenheim fellow, 1978-79; Antoinette Perry Award (Tony) nomination for best book of a musical from League of New York Theatres and Producers, 1978, for *A History of the American Film*; grant from Lecomte du Nouy Foundation, 1980-81; off-Broadway Award (Obie) from *Village Voice*, 1980, for *Sister Mary Ignatius Explains It All for You*; Hull-Warriner Award, Dramatists Guild, 1985; Lila Wallace-*Reader's Digest* Fund Writer's Award, 1994.

WRITINGS:

PLAYS

The Nature and Purpose of the Universe (first produced in Northampton, MA, 1971; produced in New York City, 1975), Dramatists Play Service, 1979.
Robert, first produced in Cambridge, MA, 1971; produced as *'dentity Crisis* in New Haven, CT, 1975.
Better Dead Than Sorry, first produced in New Haven, CT, 1972; produced in New York City, 1973.
(With Albert Innaurato) *I Don't Generally Like Poetry, But Have You Read "Trees'?* first produced in New Haven, CT, 1972; produced in New York City, 1973.
(With Innaurato) *The Life Story of Mitzi Gaynor; or, Gyp,* first produced in New Haven, CT, 1973.
The Marriage of Betty and Boo (first produced in New Haven, CT, 1973; revised version produced in New York City, 1979), Dramatists Play Service, 1985.
(With Innaurato) *The Idiots Karamazov* (first produced in New Haven at Yale Repertory Theatre, October 10, 1974), Dramatists Play Service, 1980.
Titanic (also see below; first produced in New Haven, CT, 1974; produced off-Broadway at Van Dam Theatre, May 10, 1976), Dramatists Play Service, 1983.
Death Comes to Us All, Mary Agnes, first produced in New Haven, CT, 1975.

When Dinah Shore Ruled the Earth, first produced in New Haven, CT, 1975.
(With Sigourney Weaver) *Das Lusitania Songspiel,* first produced off-Broadway at Van Dam Theatre, May 10, 1976.
A History of the American Film (first produced in Hartford, CT, at Eugene O'Neill Playwrights Conference, summer, 1976; produced on Broadway at American National Theatre, March 30, 1978), Avon, 1978.
The Vietnamization of New Jersey (first produced in New Haven, CT, at Yale Repertory Theatre, October 1, 1976), Dramatists Play Service, 1978.
Sister Mary Ignatius Explains It All for You (first produced in New York at Ensemble Studio Theatre, December, 1979), Dramatists Play Service, 1980.
The Nature and Purpose of the Universe, Death Comes to Us All, Mary Agnes, 'dentity Crisis: Three Short Plays, Dramatists Play Service, 1979.
Beyond Therapy (first produced off-Broadway at Phoenix Theatre, January 5, 1981), Samuel French, 1983.
The Actor's Nightmare (first produced in New York at Playwrights Horizons, October 21, 1981), Dramatists Play Service, 1982.
Christopher Durang Explains It All for You (contains *The Nature and Purpose of the Universe, 'dentity Crisis, Titanic, The Actor's Nightmare, Sister Mary Ignatius Explains It All for You* and *Beyond Therapy*), Avon, 1982.
Baby with the Bathwater (first produced in Cambridge, MA, 1983; produced in New York City, 1983), Dramatists Play Service, 1984.
Sloth, first produced in Princeton, NJ, 1985.
Laughing Wild, first produced in New York City, 1987.
Cardinal O'Connor [and] *Woman Stand-up,* first produced as part of musical revue *Urban Blight,* New York City, 1988.
Chris Durang & Dawne (cabaret), first produced in New York City, 1990.
Naomi in the Living Room, first produced in New York City, 1991.
Media Amok, first produced in Boston, 1992.
Putting It Together, first produced in New York City, 1993.
For Whom the Southern Belle Tolls, first produced in New York City, 1994.
Durang Durang (six short plays, including *For Whom the Southern Belle Tolls* and *A Stye in the Eye*), first produced in New York City, 1994.
Twenty-Seven Short Plays, Smith and Kraus (Lyme, NH), 1995.
Complete Full-Length Plays, Smith and Kraus, 1996.
Sex and Longing, first produced at Cort Theater, 1996.

Also author, with Robert Altman, of screenplay *Beyond Therapy,* 1987. Writer for television series *Comedy Zone* and for *Carol Burnett Special.* Lyricist of songs for plays.

SIDELIGHTS: Early in Christopher Durang's career, a *New York Times* reviewer included him in the constellation of "new American playwrights," dramatists such as Michael Cristofer, Albert Innaurato, David Mamet, and Sam Shepard who follow in the footsteps of Tennessee Williams, Arthur Miller, and Edward Albee. Writers like Durang, the reviewer claimed, "are not one-play writers—a home run and back to the dugout—but artists with staying power and growing bodies of work."

Stylistically, Durang specializes in collegiate humor. He deals in cartoons and stereotypes, employing mechanical dialogue and brand names to exploit cliches. In one play, for instance, a character feels compelled to make small talk with a pharmacist, so he asks, "What's in Tylenol?" "The characteristic of [Durang's] humor," Richard Eder explains, "is that it does not step back for comic perspective. It does not really see its target. It leaps onto it, instead, engages it totally, and burrows its head into it as if it were a mock target; much in the same way that a mother is a mock target for a not terribly naughty child."

Thus far, Durang has parodied drama, literature, movies, families, the Catholic church, show business, and society. But his lampoons are not vicious or hostile; they are controlled comedies. He "is a parodist without venom," Antonio Chemasi writes in *Horizon* magazine. "At the moment he fixes his pen on a target, he also falls in love with it. His work brims with an unlikely mix of acerbity and affection and at its best spills into a compassionate criticism of life."

Durang's first target as a professional playwright was literature. In 1974 the Yale Repertory Theatre produced *The Idiots Karamazov*, a satire of Dostoyevsky's *The Brothers Karamazov*. The play, featuring Durang in a leading role, was applauded by critics for its "moments of comic inspiration." "I was . . . impressed—with their [Durang's and his co-author Albert Innaurato's] wit as well as their scholarship," Mel Gussow states in the *New York Times*. The playwright followed *The Idiots Karamazov* with *Das Lusitania Songspiel*, a musical travesty that met with critical and popular success. "From the evidence presented [in *Das Lusitania Songspiel*]," writes Oliver, "Mr. Durang is a spirited, original fellow . . . , who brings back to the theatre a welcome impudence and irreverence."

Durang's major success of the seventies was *A History of the American Film*, for which he was nominated for a Tony Award in 1978. A tribute to movie mania, the play illustrates America's perceptions of Hollywood from 1930 to the present. *A History of the American Film* parodies some two hundred motion pictures and chronicles the evolution of movie stereotypes in American culture. There are five characters: a tough gangster typified by James Cagney, an innocent Loretta Young type, a sincere guy, a temptress, and a girl who never gets the man of her dreams. The production parodies movies such as *The Grapes of Wrath*, *Citizen Kane*, and *Casablanca*. Show girls dressed up like vegetables satirize the razzmatazz of big Hollywood productions by singing "We're in a Salad." And the character portraying Paul Henreid's role in *Now, Voyager* is forced to smoke two cigarettes when Bette Davis's character refuses one because she does not smoke. "In Durang's hands," writes *Time*'s Gerald Clarke, "the familiar images always take an unexpected turn, however, and he proves that there is nothing so funny as a cliche of a different color."

After the success of *A History of the American Film*, Durang wrote two satires of suburban families, *The Vietnamization of New Jersey* and *The Nature and Purpose of the Universe*, as well as a parody of the Catholic church. Called a "savage cartoon" by Mel Gussow and a "clever and deeply felt work" by Frank Rich, *Sister Mary Ignatius Explains It All for You* uses the character of an elderly nun to expose the hypocrisies of Catholicism. The nun, Gussow writes, is "a self-mocking sister [who] flips pictures of hell, purgatory and heaven as if they are stops on a religious package tour." Her list of the damned includes David Bowie, Betty Comden, and Adolph Green, and she lists hijacking planes alongside murder as a mortal sin. "Anyone can write an angry play—all it takes is an active spleen," observes Rich. "But only a writer of real talent can write an angry play that remains funny and controlled even in its most savage moments. *Sister Mary*

Ignatius Explains It All for You confirms that Christopher Durang is just such a writer."

In October, 1981, the Obie-winning *Sister Mary Ignatius* was presented on the same playbill as *The Actor's Nightmare*, a satire of show business and the theater. Using the play-within-a-play technique for *The Actor's Nightmare*, Durang illustrates the comedy which ensues when an actor is forced to appear in a production he has never rehearsed. Earlier in 1981, the Phoenix Theatre produced Durang's *Beyond Therapy*, a parody in which a traditional woman, Prudence, and a bisexual man, Bruce, meet through a personal ad, only to have their relationship confounded by their psychiatrists. Hers is a lecherous, he-man Freudian; his is an absent-minded comforter. "Some of Durang's satire . . . is sidesplitting," comments a *New York* reviewer, "and there are many magisterial digs at our general mores, amores, and immores."

A writer heaped with honors early in his career may begin to feel the weight of the mantle later on. Recent criticism of Durang's work has been mixed. In a review in the *Daily News*, Douglas Watt turns a cold eye on Durang's 1983 drama, *Baby with the Bathwater*: "[Durang] continues to write like a fiendishly clever undergrad with some fresh slants but an inability to make them coalesce into a fully sustained evening of theater." Rich, writing in the *New York Times*, admits a note of irritation: "We can't ignore that Act I of *Baby with the Bathwater* is a strained variation on past Durang riffs. We're so inured by now to this writer's angry view of parental authority figures that at intermission we feel like shaking him and shouting: 'Enough already! Move on!'" Rich concludes: "The author's compulsive gag-making might also be in tighter control. . . . Some of the punchlines are indeed priceless, but not all of them are germane." John Simon sounds a similar theme in his review in *New York Magazine*: "Christopher Durang is such a funny fellow that his plays cannot help being funny; now, if they could only help being so undisciplined." Simon sums up: "Free-floating satire and rampant absurdism are all very well, but even the wildest play must let its characters grow in wildness and match up mouth with jokes." In a review in the *Nation*, Eliot Sirkin finds that Durang "is, at heart, a writer who divides humanity into the humiliators and the humiliated." Sirkin compares Durang's methods to those of Tennessee Williams: "When Williams created an overwhelming woman, he didn't create a psychopathic fiend—at least not always. . . . Durang's witches are *just* witches."

Durang's next play *The Marriage of Bette and Boo* draws from the playwright's own childhood. In his review for the *New York Post*, Clive Barnes summarizes the characters: "The father was a drunk, the mother rendered an emotional cripple largely by her tragic succession of stillborn children, the grandparents were certifiably nutty, the family background stained with the oppression of the Roman Catholic Church, and the son himself is primarily absorbed in a scholarly enquiry into the novels of Thomas Hardy. Just plain folks!" Rich, writing in the *New York Times*, finds that "*Bette and Boo* is sporadically funny and has been conceived with a structural inventiveness new to the writer's work. . . . But at the same time, Mr. Durang's jokemaking is becoming more mannered and repetitive. . . . *Bette and Boo* has a strangely airless atmosphere." Simon writes in *New York Magazine*: "Christopher Durang's latest, *The Marriage of Bette and Boo*, is more recycling than writing. Here again, the quasi-autobiographical boy-hero growing up absurd."

In a 1990 *Chicago Tribune* interview with Richard Christiansen, Durang revealed that he felt "burned out on New York, and that includes its theater." For a time Durang left the theater to tour with a one-hour cabaret act, *Chris Durang & Dawne.* Durang explained his "premise" to Christiansen: "I was fed up with being a playwright and had decided to form my own lounge act with two back-up singers and go on a tour of Ramada Inns across the country."

In 1992 Durang returned to the theater with *Media Amok,* a lampoon of the characters and obsessions of television talk-shows. Noting its content, Durang told Kevin Kelly of the *Boston Globe* that he had become "more political." The play features an elderly couple watching television talk shows which assault them constantly with the same three topics: abortion, gay rights, and racial tension. All of the topics are handled in a flippant and inflammatory fashion.

In 1994 *Durang Durang,* a series of six sketches taking swipes at fellow playwrights Tennessee Williams, Sam Shepard and David Mamet, debuted in New York City. One section, the one-act play entitled *For Whom the Southern Belle Tolls,* is a parody of *The Glass Menagerie,* while *A Stye in the Eye* focuses on Shepard's typical cowboy characters. In a *New Yorker* review, Nancy Franklin calls the play "Beckett with a joy buzzer." She concludes: "Sitting through *Durang Durang* is a little like going on the bumper cars at an amusement park: you're so caught up in the exhilarating hysteria that it doesn't matter to you that you're not actually going anywhere except—momentarily, blissfully—outside yourself." In a *New York Times* review, Ben Brantley finds *Durang Durang* "endearing and exasperating . . . juvenile and predictable."

Lulu, a nymphomaniac, and Justin, a nearly as insatiable homosexual, share an apartment in the play *Sex and Longing.* A philandering and drunkard senator and his puritanical wife, as well as a reverend from the political right, also figure into the plot. *Newsweek* critic Marc Peyser remarks: "This intersection of sex, religion, hypocrisy and spiritual emptiness was bracing two decades ago, . . . now it's trite and labored and, worst of all, almost devoid of humor." John Simon, who thinks the play's humorlessness stems from its silliness bordering on the ridiculous, comments in *New York* that the play "is strictly anti-realistic absurdist farce, but even as such it ought to know where it is going." He concludes: "It is all rather like automatic writing with a glitch in the automation." Greg Evans marvels in *Variety* that Durang "can mine any laughs at all from such perversity," and he notes that the "characters [are] so broadly drawn that to call them stereotypes would be an understatement." Still, Evans concedes, "Despite his misstep here, the playwright retains a distinctive voice—one that finds its way even through the indulgences of this play."

BIOGRAPHICAL/CRITICAL SOURCES:

BOOKS

American Theatre Annual, 1979-1980, Gale (Detroit), 1981.
Contemporary Literary Criticism, Gale, Volume 27, 1984; Volume 38, 1986.

PERIODICALS

Atlanta Constitution, March 18, 1994, p. P17.
Boston Globe, March 22, 1992, p. B25.
Chicago Tribune, January 21, 1990.
Daily News (New York), March 31, 1978; November 9, 1983.
Entertainment Weekly, April 16, 1993, p. 31.

Horizon, March, 1978.
Los Angeles Times, August 11, 1989, p. 8; November 25, 1994, p. 1.
Nation, April 15, 1978; February 18, 1984, pp. 202-204.
New Republic, April 22, 1978.
Newsweek, April 10, 1978; October 21, 1996, p. 89.
New York, April 17, 1978; January 19, 1981; October 23, 1989, p. 166; November 28, 1994, p. 76; October 21, 1996, pp. 76-77.
New Yorker, May 24, 1976; April 10, 1978; January 19, 1981; November 28, 1994, pp. 153-55.
New York Magazine, November 21, 1983, pp. 65-68; June 3, 1985, pp. 83-84.
New York Post, March 31, 1978; November 9, 1983; December 12, 1983, p. 80; May 17, 1985, pp. 268-69.
New York Times, November 11, 1974; February 13, 1977; March 17, 1977; May 11, 1977; August 21, 1977; June 23, 1978; December 27, 1978; February 24, 1979; December 21, 1979; February 8, 1980; August 6, 1980; January 6, 1981; October 22, 1981; November 9, 1983, p. C21; May 17, 1985, p. 3; June 27, 1994, p. C13; November 14, 1994, p. 11.
Saturday Review, May 27, 1978.
Time, May 23, 1977.
USA Today, May 17, 1985.
Variety, November 14, 1994, p. 54; October 14-20, 1996, p. 72.
Washington Post, December 11, 1994, p. 4.
Women's Wear Daily, May 20, 1985.
World Literature Today, summer, 1991, p. 487.

*   *   *

DURANT, Will(iam James) 1885-1981

PERSONAL: Born November 5, 1885, in North Adams, MA; died November 7, 1981, in Los Angeles, CA, of heart failure; son of Joseph (a superintendent of a Du Pont branch) and Marie (Allors) Durant; married Ariel Kaufman (a writer and researcher), October 31, 1913; children: Ethel Benvenuta (Mrs. Stanislas Kwasniewski), Louis R. (adopted). *Education:* St. Peter's College (Jersey City, NJ), B.A., 1907, M.A., 1908; Columbia University, Ph.D., 1917. *Religion:* "Agnostic, formerly Catholic."

ADDRESSES: Home—5608 Briarcliff Rd., Los Angeles, CA 90028.

CAREER: Seton Hall College (now University), South Orange, NJ, instructor in Latin and French, 1907-11; Ferrer Modern School, New York City, teacher, 1911-13; Labor Temple School, New York City, director and lecturer, 1914-27; Columbia University, New York City, instructor in philosophy, 1917; University of California, Los Angeles, professor of philosophy, 1935; full-time writer. Reporter, *New York Evening Journal,* 1908. Lecturer.

MEMBER: National Institute of Arts and Letters.

AWARDS, HONORS: L.H.D., Syracuse University, 1930; with wife, Ariel K. Durant, Huntington Hartford Foundation award for literature, 1963, for *The Age of Louis XIV*; with A. K. Durant, Pulitzer Prize, 1968, for *Rousseau and Revolution*; with A. K. Durant, California Literature Medal Award, 1971, for *Interpretations of Life*; with A. K. Durant, Medal of Freedom, 1977.

WRITINGS:

Philosophy and the Social Problem, Macmillan, 1917.

The Story of Philosophy, Simon & Schuster, 1926, revised edition, 1933.

Transition: A Sentimental Story of One Mind and One Era (autobiographical novel), Simon & Schuster, 1927.

(Editor) Arthur Schopenhauer, *Works,* Simon & Schuster, 1928, revised edition, Ungar, 1962.

Mansions of Philosophy: A Survey of Human Life and Destiny, Simon & Schuster, 1929, published as *The Pleasures of Philosophy: A Survey of Human Life and Destiny,* 1953.

The Case for India, Simon & Schuster, 1930.

Adventures in Genius (also see below; essays and articles; also see below), Simon & Schuster, 1931.

A Program for America, Simon & Schuster, 1931.

On the Meaning of Life (correspondence), R. R. Smith, 1932.

Tragedy of Russia: Impressions from a Brief Visit, Simon & Schuster, 1933.

100 Best Books for an Education (excerpt from *Adventures in Genius*), Simon & Schuster, 1933.

Great Men of Literature (excerpt from *Adventures in Genius*), Simon & Schuster, 1936.

The Story of Civilization, Simon & Schuster, Volume 1: *Our Oriental Heritage* (also see below), 1935, Volume 2: *The Life of Greece,* 1939, Volume 3: *Caesar and Christ: A History of Roman Civilization from Its Beginnings to A.D.337,* 1944, Volume 4: *The Age of Faith,* 1950, Volume 5: *The Renaissance,* 1953, Volume 6: *The Reformation,* 1957, Volume 7: (with wife, Ariel K. Durant) *The Age of Reason Begins,* 1961, Volume 8: (with A. K. Durant) *The Age of Louis XIV,* 1963, Volume 9: (with A. K. Durant) *The Age of Voltaire,* 1965, Volume 10: (with A. K. Durant) *Rousseau and Revolution,* 1967, Volume 11: (with A. K. Durant) *The Age of Napoleon,* 1975.

The Foundations of Civilization (introduction to Volume 1 of *The Story of Civilization*), Simon & Schuster, 1936.

(With A. K. Durant) *The Lessons of History,* Simon & Schuster, 1968.

(With A. K. Durant) *Interpretations of Life,* Simon & Schuster, 1970.

(With A. K. Durant) *A Dual Autobiography,* Simon & Schuster, 1977.

SIDELIGHTS: Will Durant was a prize-winning historian and philosopher whose chronicles of world history and civilization reached a mass audience. Perhaps his most enduring work is the eleven-volume *The Story of Civilization,* on which he collaborated with his wife, Ariel. In this collection, the pair endeavored to synthesize the developments in art, science, religion, politics, literature, and economics. It was an unusual approach, according to Bernard A. Weisberger in the *Washington Post Book World,* as these subjects and their progress are "usually treated separately." The Durants' purpose was to popularize history, to make a large and varied amount of information accessible and comprehensible to the average reader. Though their efforts were popular bestsellers, professional historians often insisted, as Weisberger reports, "that the attempt to handle sixty centuries of human history resulted fatally and inevitably in shallowness and error."

However, Weisberger contends that, notwithstanding the scholars' criticism, "the Durants fill a spiritual vacuum." He believes that "the key" to the popularity and success of *The Story of Civilization* was "[Will] Durant's late 19th-century faith in the simple concepts of history and civilization," his belief in "patterns and structures, tides and movements in history." The reviewer explains: "Somehow, out of chaos, civilizations emerged, and if one unravelled and went under in a civil war or a barbarian incursion, another painfully emerged. . . . People appear to need this assurance that there is a purposeful flow in the life of the whole human race; that their instant of existence matters in an overall scheme."

A *Time* critic argues that "the charge that [the Durants] are popularizers is meaningless. Of course they are popularizers—and great ones." Durant himself responded to his detractors in a *Publishers Weekly* interview with John F. Baker: "We're amateurs. . . . We want to make history meaningful for ordinary readers. . . . We need specialists who devote their time to research, and who work from first-hand materials, sure, but I reject the notion that only university professors can write history. There's room for an integral view, which looks at every aspect of an age—its art, its manners and morals, its philosophy, even its architecture—and shows how they all interrelate. That's how history works—it's not all in separate compartments."

The Durants wrote *The Lessons of History* as a follow-up to *The Story of Civilization.* In short thematic essays, they reflect on the changes humankind has undergone through history and draw conclusions about its achievements, conduct, and prospects.

Interpretations of Life contains some two dozen sketches by the Durants on notable twentieth-century American, British, and European writers. In the book's introduction Durant admits he is not a critic and finds authors more interesting than their works. Nonetheless, several critics note that the essays are interesting but provide few insights about the writers.

In *A Dual Autobiography,* the Durants share letters to each other and from well-known contemporaries, press clippings, book reviews, and alternate accounts of their life together. The pair met while Ariel was a student at the New York school where Will taught. They married when she was fourteen and he seventeen. Besides collaborating with his wife on books, Durant was a lecturer on topical subjects and philosophers and debated such eminent persons as Clarence Darrow on stage. Alden Whitman says in the *New York Times Book Review* that the Durants mention the numerous well-known people they met during their lives in their accounts, which are written in ordinary language, but reveal nothing of their own character and personality. He states, "The puzzle of *A Dual Autobiography* is that it recites the trivial and scants the substantial. It is all surface, and even that does not glitter very brightly."

The Durants garnered several important awards for their writings, including a Pulitzer Prize in 1968 for *Rousseau and Revolution.* Will Durant died in 1981 in Los Angeles, California.

BIOGRAPHICAL/CRITICAL SOURCES:

BOOKS

Frey, Raymond, *William James Durant: An Intellectual Autobiography,* E. Mellen Press (Lewiston, NY), 1991.

PERIODICALS

Book Week, September 15, 1963; October 10, 1965.

Christian Science Monitor, October 28, 1965; November 30, 1967.

Forbes, March 27, 1995, p. 26.

Life, October 18, 1963.

National Review, January 16, 1968.

New Republic, October 2, 1965.

Newsweek, September 16, 1957; September 11, 1961; September 16, 1963.

New York Herald Tribune Book Review, October 25, 1953.

New York Times Book Review, September 15, 1963; September 19, 1965; October 15, 1967; February 5, 1978.
Publishers Weekly, November 24, 1975.
Reader's Digest, October, 1969.
Saturday Review, September 9, 1961; September 21, 1963; October 23, 1965; September 23, 1967.
Time, September 28, 1953; September 27, 1963; August 13, 1965; October 8, 1965; October 6, 1967.
Washington Post Book World, November 27, 1977.
Yale Review, December, 1963.

*   *   *

DURAS, Marguerite 1914-1996

PERSONAL: Original name Marguerite Donnadieu; born April 4, 1914, in Giadinh, Indochina (now Vietnam); died March 3, 1996, in Paris, France; daughter of Henri (a mathematics teacher) and Marie (Legrand) Donnadieu; divorced; children: one son. *Education:* Graduated from Lycee de Saigon; University of Paris, Sorbonne, licences in law and political science; also studied mathematics.

ADDRESSES: Home—5 rue Saint-Benoit, Paris 75006, France.

CAREER: Novelist, screenwriter, and playwright. Emigrated from Indochina to Paris at age seventeen; secretary at French Ministry of Colonies, Paris, 1935-41.

AWARDS, HONORS: Prix Jean Cocteau, 1955; Prix Ibsen, 1970, for her play, *L'Amante anglaise;* Grand Prix Academie du Cinema, 1983; Goncourt Prize, 1984, for novel *L'Amant;* Ritz Paris Hemingway Prize, 1985, for *L'Amant.*

WRITINGS:

FICTION

Les Impudents, Plon (Paris), 1943.
La Vie tranquille, Gallimard (Paris), 1944.
Un Barrage contre le Pacifique, Gallimard, 1950, translation by Herma Briffault published as *The Sea Wall,* Pellegrini & Cudahy (London), 1952, same translation published with a preface by Germaine Bree, Farrar, Strauss (New York City), 1967, translation by Antonia White published as *A Sea of Troubles,* Methuen (New York City), 1953.
Le Marin de Gibraltar, Gallimard, 1952, translation by Barbara Bray published as *The Sailor from Gibraltar,* Grove (New York City), 1966.
Les Petits Chevaux de Tarquinia, Gallimard, 1953, translation by Peter DuBerg published as *The Little Horses of Tarquinia,* J. Calder (London), 1960.
Des Journees entieres dans les arbres (short stories; title means "Whole Days in the Trees"), Gallimard, 1954.
Le Square, Gallimard, 1955, translation by Sonia Pitt-Rivers and Irina Morduch published as *The Square,* Grove, 1959, French language edition, published under original French title, edited by Claude Morhange Begue, Macmillan (New York City), 1965.
Moderato cantabile, Editions de Minuit (Paris), 1958, translation by Richard Seaver published as *Moderato cantabile,* Grove, 1960, French language edition, edited by Thomas Bishop, Prentice-Hall (Englewood Cliffs, NJ), 1968, another French language edition, edited by W. S. Strachan, Methuen, 1968, also published with supplemental material as *Moderato cantabile* [suivi de] *L'Univers romanesque de Marguerite Duras,* Plon, 1962.

Dix heures et demie du soir en ete, Gallimard, 1960, translation by Anne Borchardt published as *Ten-thirty on a Summer Night,* J. Calder, 1962, Grove, 1963.
L'Apres Midi de Monsieur Andesmas, Gallimard, 1962, translation by Borchardt, published together with Bray's translation of *Les Eaux et forets* (play; also see below) as *The Afternoon of Monsieur Andesmas* [and] *The Rivers and Forests,* J. Calder, 1965.
Le Ravissement de Lol V. Stein, Gallimard, 1964, translation by Seaver published as *The Ravishing of Lol Stein,* Grove, 1966, translation by Eileen Ellenbogen published as *The Rapture of Lol V. Stein,* Hamish Hamilton (London), 1967.
Four Novels (contains *The Square, Moderato cantabile, Ten-thirty on a Summer Night,* and *The Afternoon of Monsieur Andesmas*), translations by Pitt-Rivers and others, introduction by Bree, Grove, 1965.
Le Vice-consul, Gallimard, 1966, translation by Ellenbogen published as *The Vice-consul,* Hamish Hamilton, 1968.
L'Amante anglaise, Gallimard, 1967, translation by Bray published as *L'Amante Anglaise,* Grove, 1968.
Detruire, ditelle, Editions de Minuit, 1969, translation by Bray published as *Destroy, She Said,* Grove, 1970.
Abahn, Sabana, David, Gallimard, 1970.
L'Amour, Gallimard, 1971.
India Song: Texte-theatre-film, Gallimard, 1973, translation by Bray published as *India Song,* Grove, 1976.
(With Xaviere Gauthier) *Les Parleuses,* Editions de Minuit, 1974.
Suzanna Andler; La Musica & L'Amante anglaise, translation by Bray, J. Calder, 1975.
(With Jacques Lacan and Maurice Blanchot) *Etude sur l'oeuvre litteraire, theatrale, et cinematographique de Marguerite Duras* (nonfiction), Albatros (Paris), 1976.
Le Camion, suivi de Entretien avec Michelle Porte, Editions de Minuit, 1977.
Le Navire Night; Cesaree; Les Mains negatives; Aurelia Steiner, Mercure de France (Paris), 1979.
Vera Baxter ou Les Plages de l'Atlantique, Albatros, 1980.
L'Homme assis dans le couloir, Editions de Minuit, 1980, translation by Bray published as *The Man Sitting in the Corridor,* North Star Line, 1992.
L'Ete '80, Editions de Minuit, 1981.
Outside, Albin Michel (Paris), 1981, translation by Arthur Goldhammer, published under title *Outside: Selected Writings,* Beacon Press (Boston), 1986.
L'Homme atlantique, Editions de Minuit, 1982.
La Maladie de la mort, Editions de Minuit, 1982, translation by Bray published as *The Malady of Death,* Grove, 1986.
Savannah Bay, Editions de Minuit, 1983.
L'Amant, Editions de Minuit, 1984, translation by Bray published as *The Lover,* Pantheon (New York City), 1985.
La Douleur, POL (Paris), 1985, translation by Bray published as *The War: A Memoir,* Pantheon, 1986.
La Mouette de Tchekhov, Gallimard, 1985.
Les Yeux bleus cheveux noirs, Editions de Minuit, 1986, translation by Bray published as *Blues Eyes, Black Hair,* Pantheon, 1988.
La Pute de la cote normande, Editions de Minuit, 1986.
Emily L., Editions de Minuit, 1987, translation by Bray, published under same title, Pantheon, 1989.
Green Eyes, translation of the French novel *Yeux verts* by Carol Barko, Columbia University Press (New York City), 1990.
L'Amante de la Chine du Nord, Gallimard, 1991, translation by Leigh Hafrey published as *The North China Lover,* New Press (New York City), 1992.

Summer Rain, Scribner (New York City), 1992.
Yann Andrea Steiner, translation by Bray, Hodder & Stoughton (London), 1994.

PLAYS

Les Viaducs de la Seine-et-Oise (translation by Bray, produced as *The Viaduct* in Guildford, England, at Yvonne Arnaud Theatre, February, 1967), Gallimard, 1960.
(With James Lord) *La Bete dans la jungle* (adaptation of *The Beast in the Jungle* by Henry James), produced, 1962.
Theatre I (contains *Les Eaux et forets, Le Square*, and *La Musica*; *La Musica* produced as *The Music* off-off-Broadway at West Side Actors Workshop and Repertory, March, 1967), Gallimard, 1965.
Three Plays, translation by Bray and Sonia Orwell (contains *The Square, Days in the Trees*, and *The Viaducts of Seine-et-Oise; Days in the Trees* produced in Paris at Theatre de France, and on BBC-Television *Wednesday Play*, 1967), Calder & Boyars, 1967.
Theatre II (contains *Suzanna Andler, Des Journees entieres dan les arbres, Yes, peut-etre, Le Shaga*, and *Un Homme est venue me voir*; *Suzanna Andler* first produced in Paris at Theatre Mathurins, December, 1969; translation by Bray produced on the West End at Aldwych Theatre, March 7, 1973), Gallimard, 1968.
L'Amante anglaise (based on the novel), produced in Paris at Theatre National Populaire, December, 1969, produced in French as *L'Amante Anglaise* on the West End at Royal Court Theatre, 1969, produced in French off-Broadway at Barbizon-Plaza Theatre, April 14, 1971, translation by Bray first produced as *A Place without Doors* in New Haven, CT, at Long Wharf Theatre, November 21, 1970, produced off-Broadway at Stairway Theatre, December 22, 1970, same translation produced as *Lovers of Viorne* on the West End at Royal Court Theatre, July 6, 1971.
La Danse de mort, produced in Paris, 1970.
Ah! Ernesto, F. Ruy-Vidal (Paris), 1971.
India Song (also see below), Gallimard, 1973, translation by Bray published under same title, Grove, 1976.
L'Eden cinema (produced in Paris, 1977), Mercure de France, 1977.
Agatha, Editions de Minuit, 1981, translation by Howard Limoli published as *Agatha* [and] *Savannah Bay: 2 Plays*, Post-Apollo Press (Sausalito, CA), 1992.
La Musica deuxieme (produced in Paris, 1985), Gallimard, 1985.

SCREENPLAYS

Hiroshima, mon amour: Scenario et dialogues (based on the novel by Alain Resnais; film produced in 1959), Gallimard, 1960, translation by Seaver published as *Hiroshima, mon amour: Text by Marguerite Duras for the Film by Alain Resnais*, Grove, 1961.
(With Gerard Jarlot) *Une Aussi longue absence* (based on the novel by Henri Colpi), Gallimard, 1961, translation by Wright published under original French title together with above translation as *Hiroshima, mon amour* [and] *Une Aussi longue absence* (movie scripts), Calder & Boyars, 1966.
Moderato cantabile (based on the novel), Royal Films International, 1964.
(With Jules Dassin) *Ten-thirty p.m. Summer* (film version of her novel, *Ten-thirty on a Summer Night*), Lopert, 1966.
Detruire, dit-elle (based on the novel), Ancinex/Madeleine Films, 1970.
La Musica (based on the play), United Artists, 1970.

Nathalie Granger (film produced by Monelet & Co., 1972), published in *Nathalie Granger* [suive de] *La Femme du Gange*, Gallimard, 1973.

Also author of screenplays *Jaune le soleil*, 1971, *India Song*, 1975, *Baxter, Vera Baxter*, 1975, *Son Nom de Venise dans Calcutta desert*, 1976, *Des Journees entieres dans les arbres*, 1976, *Le Camion*, 1977, *Le Navire Night*, 1978, *Cesaree*, 1979, *Les Mains negatives*, 1979, *Aurelia Steiner, dite Aurelia Melbourne*, 1979, *Aurelia Steiner, dite Aurelia Vancouver*, 1979, *Agatha et les lectures illimitees*, 1981, *L'Homme atlantique*, 1981, *Dialogue de Rome*, 1981, and *Les Enfants*, 1985.

OTHER

(With Michelle Porte) *Les Lieux de Marguerite Duras* (interview), Editions de Minuit, 1977.
La vie materielle, POL, 1987, translation by Barbara Bray published as *Practicalities: Marguerite Duras Speaks to Jerome Beaujour*, Grove, 1990.
La pluie d'ete, POL, 1990.
Le Monde Exterieur, POL, 1993.
Ecrire, Gallimard, 1994.
C'est tout, POL, 1995, translation by Richard Howard, published by Seven Stories Press, 1998.
La mer ecrite, Diffusion Harmonia Mundi, 1996.

MEDIA ADAPTATIONS: Un Barrage contre le Pacifique was filmed as *The Sea Wall* by Columbia Pictures, 1958, and was also translated and adapted by Sofka Skipworth as *A Dam against an Ocean*, for British Broadcasting Corp. (BBC), 1962; *The Sailor from Gibraltar* was filmed by Lopert, 1967; *L'Amant* was filmed as *The Lover* and released by Metro-Goldwyn-Mayer, 1992.

SIDELIGHTS: Marguerite Duras has written novels, films and plays for over four decades, often drawing upon the details of her own life to fashion her fictional narratives. "Her main raw material," writes Alan Riding in the *New York Times,* "is of course herself, an extraordinary life cut like cord into sections and variously displayed in her books as elegant bows or tight knots." Carol J. Murphy, in her article for the *Dictionary of Literary Biography,* explains that Duras "has evolved what might be called a core story of passionate love and desire undercut with death. Successive texts echo or decant the story in an increasingly fragmented, lyrical style which has come to characterize Duras's poetic prose."

Duras was born in the French colony of Indochina (now the nation of Vietnam) where her parents had moved to teach school. Following the death of her father when Duras was four years old, her mother spent the family's savings on a rice plantation, hoping the venture would prove viable enough to support her and her three young children. Unfortunately, the colonial officials who sold her the plantation were dishonest, the land was virtually worthless because of recurring flooding from the sea, and Duras's mother found herself broke and trying to raise her family far from home. The family's many troubles in Indochina form the backdrop for many of Duras's novels.

In 1932 Duras left Indochina to attend school in France. During World War II she was a member of the French Resistance movement working against the Nazi occupiers. She later joined the Communist Party, only to be dismissed in 1950 along with a number of other French intellectuals for ideological differences. Her continuing involvement with leftist political causes led to trouble with American officials over a travel visa in 1969. Duras, wishing to attend a New York Film Festival showing of her

Detruire, dit-elle, had to prove to officials her adherence to anti-communist principles. Duras was also an apologist for the student uprisings in Paris in 1968 and a supporter of French president Mitterand during the 1980s.

Although Duras first began writing during World War II, her first book to earn critical attention was 1950's *Un Barrage contre le Pacifique,* translated as *The Sea Wall.* Largely autobiographical, the novel revolves around her mother's failed efforts to save her rice plantation from destruction by building a sea wall to protect the crops from flooding. Within this framework are told the stories of Duras's unwelcome courtship by the son of a local Chinese planter and her brother's succumbing to a life of indolence. "Straightforward, chronologically ordered, and easy to read, *The Sea Wall* fits within the conventions of the nineteenth-century novel," writes Judith Graves Miller in *Theatre Journal.* "Indeed, of Duras's . . . novels, it is the most traditional." The story first told in *The Sea Wall* was to be retold in several later Duras's works.

In *Le Marin de Gibraltar,* translated as *The Sailor from Gibraltar,* Duras first turned from realistic fiction to a more symbolic representation of experience. The sailor of the novel, searched for by the character Anna and the male narrator, undergoes a series of transformations and becomes a criminal, a lover, and a folk hero in turn. Every clue followed by Anna and the narrator results in fresh stories about the sailor's possible identity until it is clear that there is no sailor at all, only Anna in search of him and the narrator chronicling the search. In *Le Marin,* Marilyn R. Schuster writes in the *French Review,* "Duras dismantles conventional character and demonstrates that it is through its absence that the female subject's story can begin to be articulated."

In 1959 Duras was invited by film director Alain Resnais to write the screenplay *Hiroshima, mon amour.* The story of a French actress working in Tokyo whose affair with a Japanese architect calls to mind her disastrous wartime affair with a Nazi officer, *Hiroshima, mon amour* was a worldwide success. Leslie Hill, writing in *Paragraph: The Journal of the Modern Critical Theory Group,* finds that in the film "private disaster is echoed, outstripped, overwhelmed, effaced by public catastrophe. . . . Like the comparison of the bombing of Hiroshima with a casual affair. . . , the association is scandalous. But the scandal, by transgressing the limit of what is properly imaginable, bears witness: to the unimaginable catastrophe of war and of representation." As Joanne Schmidt notes in *Belles Lettres,* however, "even after [Duras] wrote the screenplay for a film that became a landmark in world cinema, her reputation remained marginal."

In the Goncourt Prize-winning novel *L'Amant,* translated as *The Lover,* Duras returned to the autobiographical terrain first covered in *The Sea Wall,* this time focusing her attention on the love affair between the young woman character and the wealthy Chinese planter. Because of the thirty-year difference between publication of the two books, many of the family members Duras had fictionalized in *The Sea Wall* were dead by the time she wrote *The Lover,* allowing her to deal with some aspects of the story she had not attempted earlier. As Duras explains in the second novel: "I've written a good deal about the members of my family, but then they were still alive, my mother and my brothers. And I skirted around them, skirted around all these things without really touching them."

In *The Lover* Duras writes from the perspective of a sixty-year-old woman recalling her first sexual experience. Because of its focus on the memory of past events rather than on the events themselves, the novel sets the past into an emotional context apart from a strict chronological recounting. This technique gives the story what several critics see as a powerful intensity. Eva Hoffman, writing in the *New York Times,* finds *The Lover* to display a "compressed intensity" which combines "the seemingly irreconcilable perspectives of confession and objectivity, of lyrical poetry and nouveau roman." Similarly, Miranda Seymour in her review of the novel for *Spectator* remarks that "in a little more than a hundred pages, [Duras] creates a world more charged with passion, despair and hatred than most of us are likely to encounter in a lifetime" and further compliments the book's "hypnotically beautiful images and unswerving emotional frankness." Writing in the *New York Times Book Review,* Diane Johnson finds that *The Lover* contains "an unremitting intensity, an effect on some subliminal reserve of emotion in the reader that one might suspect or resist if the passion and sincerity of the author were for a moment in doubt."

Duras returned again to the autobiographical material covered in *The Sea Wall* and *The Lover* in the 1991 novel *L'Amant de la Chine du Nord,* translated as *The North China Lover.* This novel began as a series of notes Duras wrote while working on a screenplay version of *The Lover.* These notes, exploring ideas left untouched in the earlier novel, retell the story of a young woman and her older Chinese lover in a manner that combines cinematic techniques with the *nouveau roman.* As Elaine Romaine writes in *Belles Lettres,* the novel "contains wide spaces between short paragraphs, directions for a camera, and even chapters devoted to single line images." Although *The North China Lover* retells the story found in earlier Duras novels, its emphasis on "the sexual attraction all the characters share for one another" is its own, as David Plante writes in the *New York Times Book Review.* Ultimately, the novel "sends a strange thrill through you," Plante believes. "How Marguerite Duras manages to make that happen is amazing."

In *The War: A Memoir* Duras collects six narratives of her World War II experiences with the French Resistance. Two of these narratives are fiction; the other four are autobiography. Writing in the *New York Times Book Review,* Francine du Plessix Gray finds the book's title chapter, an account of Duras's husband being rescued from a concentration camp and nursed back to health, to be "the most powerful text I have read about that period. . . . It is equally sublime as a literary work and as an act of witness." Speaking of the same text, Maria Margaronis in the *Nation* praises how the story is "splintered into tiny, sharp sentences, pointing every which way, fixed painfully in the claustrophobic space of waiting." According to Frederick J. Harris in *America,* the story is a "very powerful and often beautiful and touching memoir."

Duras draws inspiration from a more recent period in her life in the novel *Yann Andrea Steiner,* transforming her real-life partner Yann Andrea into a fictional character. Centering on the couple's initial meeting twelve years earlier, the primary narrative is contrasted with the story of a young boy and girl whose family histories share the tragedy of French deportation of Jews during World War II. While James Woodall, writing in the *Guardian Weekly,* judges the novel to be "touching, certainly, but oblique almost to the point of opacity," Janet Barron in *New Statesman* finds more to praise. Calling *Yann Andrea Steiner* "a bleakly passionate novella and, at times, a poem in prose," she describes it as an "evocation of history that looks with horror on stories too painful to be told."

Speaking of the relationship between her fiction and her life, Duras is quoted by Riding as explaining: "Even when my books are completely invented, even when I think they have come from elsewhere, they are always personal." "The trajectory of Duras's fictional enterprise," Murphy concludes, "remains firmly entrenched in desire—the desire to know how to understand and express that which continually slips away from human understanding." Schmidt finds that "Duras is one of the most powerful and gifted French women writers of our time, with one of the richest and most fertile intellects."

BIOGRAPHICAL/CRITICAL SOURCES:

BOOKS

Ames, Sanford S., editor, *Remains to Be Seen: Essays on Marguerite Duras,* Peter Lang (New York City), 1988.

Bajomee, Danielle, and Ralph Heyndels, editors, *Ecrire dit-elle: Imaginaires de Marguerite Duras,* Editions de l'Universite de Bruxelles (Brussels, Belgium), 1988.

Beauclair, Michelle, *In Death's Wake: Mourning in the Works of Albert Camus and Marguerite Duras,* P. Lang (New York City), 1996.

Cohen, Susan D., *Women and Discourse in the Fiction of Marguerite Duras: Love, Legends, Language,* University of Massachusetts Press (Amherst), 1993.

Contemporary Literary Criticism, Gale (Detroit), Volume 3, 1975; Volume 6, 1976; Volume 20, 1982; Volume 34, 1985; Volume 40, 1986; Volume 68, 1991.

Corbin, Laurie, *The Mother Mirror: Self-Representation and the Mother-Daughter Relation in Colette, Simone de Beauvoir, and Marguerite Duras,* P. Lang (New York City), 1996.

Cranston, Mechthild, editor, *In Language and in Love, Marguerite Duras: The Unspeakable: Essays for Marguerite Duras,* Scripta Humanistica (Potomac, MD), 1992.

Dictionary of Literary Biography, Volume 83: *French Novelists since 1960,* Gale, 1989, pp. 71-83.

Gauthier, Xaviere, *Les Parleuses,* Editions de Minuit, 1974, translation by Katharine A. Jensen published as *Woman to Woman,* University of Nebraska Press (Lincoln), 1987.

Glassman, Deborah N., *Marguerite Duras: Fascinating Vision and Narrative Cure,* Fairleigh Dickinson University Press (Rutherford, NJ), 1991.

Hill, Leslie, *Marguerite Duras: Apocalyptic Desires,* Routledge & Kegan Paul (London), 1994.

Hofmann, Carol, *Forgetting and Marguerite Duras,* University Press of Colorado (Niwot, CO), 1991.

Kaivola, Karen, *All Contraries Confounded: The Lyrical Fiction of Virginia Woolf, Djuna Barnes, and Marguerite Duras,* University of Iowa Press (Ames), 1991.

Knapp, Bettina L., editor, *Critical Essays on Marguerite Duras,* G. K. Hall, 1998.

Lamy, Suzanne and Andre Roy, *Marguerite Duras a Montreal,* Editions Spirale (Montreal), 1981.

McNeece, Lucy Stone, *Art and Politics in Duras' India Cycle,* University Press of Florida (Gainesville), 1997.

Murphy, Carol J., *Alienation and Absence in the Novels of Marguerite Duras,* French Forum Monographs (Lexington, KY), 1982.

Ramsay, Raylene L., *The French New Autobiographies,* University Press of Florida (Gainesville), 1996.

Schneider, Ursula, W., *Ars Amandi: The Erotic of Extremes in Thomas Mann and Marguerite Duras,* P. Lang (New York City), 1995.

Schuster, Marilyn R., *Marguerite Duras Revisited,* Twayne, 1993.

Selous, Trista, *The Other Woman: Feminism and Femininity in the Work of Marguerite Duras,* Yale University Press (New Haven, CT), 1988.

Skoller, Eleanor Honig, *The In-Between of Writing: Experience and Experiment in Drabble, Duras, and Arendt,* University of Michigan Press (Ann Arbor), 1993.

Willis, Sharon, *Marguerite Duras: Writing on the Body,* University of Illinois Press (Urbana), 1987.

Williams, James S., *The Erotics of Passage: Pleasure, Politics, and Form in the Later Work of Marguerite Duras,* St. Martin's, 1997.

PERIODICALS

Belles Lettres, winter, 1989, pp. 12-13; spring, 1993, p. 9.

Books Abroad, winter, 1967; spring, 1968; summer, 1969; spring, 1970.

Christian Science Monitor, November 29, 1968; July 30, 1970.

College Literature, June, 1993, pp. 98-118; February, 1994, pp. 46-62.

Film Quarterly, summer, 1992, pp. 45-46.

French Review, October, 1984, pp. 48-57; October, 1992, pp. 77-88; December, 1993, p. 385.

Guardian Weekly, April 3, 1994, p. 29.

Harper's Bazaar, September, 1992, p. 374.

Hudson Review, autumn, 1967.

Illustrated London News, January 14, 1967; February 4, 1967.

Le Monde, January 12, 1990, p. 24; June 28, 1991, p. 18.

London Magazine, May, 1967; October, 1968.

Los Angeles Times Book Review, October 16, 1987, p. 20; April 30, 1989, p. 9; January 12, 1992, p. 10; June 14, 1992, p. 6.

Nation, March 16, 1963; January 11, 1971; November 8, 1986, pp. 493-96.

National Review, September 26, 1994.

New Leader, August 14, 1967; February 8, 1971.

New Republic, December 28, 1992, pp. 24-25.

New Statesman, January 20, 1967; April 7, 1967; September 29, 1967; May 3, 1968; July 14, 1970; July 16, 1971; January 12, 1990, p. 36; June 12, 1992, p. 40; January 28, 1994, pp. 70-71.

Newsweek, January 16, 1967; January 11, 1971.

New York, January 11, 1971; May 3, 1971; November 9, 1992.

New Yorker, November 8, 1968; July 14, 1986, p. 83.

New York Herald Tribune Book Review, February 7, 1960.

New York Times, March 15, 1953; September 14, 1969; August 23, 1970; January 3, 1971; September 7, 1972; June 10, 1985, p. C17; March 26, 1990, p. C11.

New York Times Book Review, November 8, 1959; February 19, 1967; July 2, 1967; November 17, 1968; June 23, 1985, pp. 1, 25; May 4, 1986, pp. 1, 48-49; July 13, 1986, p. 18; May 28, 1989, p. 18; May 20, 1990, p. 30; February 23, 1992, p. 12; December 27, 1992, p. 7; June 14, 1992.

New York Times Magazine, October 20, 1991, pp. 44-53.

Observer (London), February 26, 1967; September 24, 1967; May 5, 1968; October 13, 1968; September 6, 1970.

Paragraph: The Journal of the Modern Critical Theory Group, March, 1989, pp. 1-22.

Plays and Players, August, 1970; September, 1971; October, 1972.

PMLA, March, 1987, pp. 138-52.

Punch, January 11, 1967; November 6, 1968.

Saturday Review, November 23, 1968.

Signs: Journal of Women and Culture in Society, winter, 1975, pp. 423-34.

Spectator, January 4, 1986, p. 29.

Stage, June 17, 1971; July 15, 1971; October 21, 1971; January 27, 1972.

Theatre Arts, November, 1963.

Theatre Journal, December, 1981, pp. 431-52.

Time, July 7, 1967; November 1, 1968; December 14, 1970.

Times Literary Supplement, January 19, 1967; June 22, 1967; October 5, 1967; May 30, 1968; September 25, 1970; October 30, 1970; March 9, 1990, p. 248; June 26, 1992, p. 22; February 25, 1994, p. 24.

Variety, October 1, 1969; October 8, 1969; December 9, 1970; December 16, 1970; January 13, 1971; April 12, 1971; April 14, 1971; July 21, 1971; August 25, 1971; September 6, 1972; March 28, 1973.

Village Voice, March 16, 1967; July 15, 1986, pp. 47, 50.

Women's Review of Books, October, 1990, pp. 19-20.

World Literature Today, summer, 1988, pp. 436-37.

Yale French Studies, summer, 1959.

* * *

DURRELL, Lawrence (George) 1912-1990
(Charles Norden, Gaffer Peeslake)

PERSONAL: Name pronounced *Dur*-el; born February 27, 1912, in Jullundur, India; died of emphysema, November 7, 1990, in Sommieres, France; son of Lawrence Samuel (a British civil engineer) and Louise Florence (Dixie) Durrell; married Nancy Isobel Myers (an artist), 1935 (divorced, 1947); married Yvette Cohen, February 26, 1947 (divorced); married Claude-Marie Vincendon (a novelist), March 27, 1961 (died, 1967); married Ghyslaine de Boissons, 1973 (divorced, 1979) children: (first marriage) Penelope Berengaria; (second marriage) Sappho-Jane. *Education:* Attended College of St. Joseph, Darjiling, India, and St. Edmund's School, Canterbury, England. *Religion:* "Of course I believe in God; but every kind of God. But I rather dread the word 'religion' because I have a notion that the reality of it dissolves the minute it is uttered."

CAREER: Worked variously as an automobile racer, jazz pianist and composer, and real estate agent; ran a photographic studio with first wife. *The Booster,* Paris, France, editor with Henry Miller and Alfred Perles, 1937-39; British Institute, Kalamata, Greece, teacher, 1940; *Egyptian Gazette,* Cairo, columnist, 1941; British Information Office, Cairo, foreign press service officer, 1941-44; *Personal Landscape,* Cairo, co-editor, 1942-45; Alexandria, Egypt, press attache, 1944-45; Dodecanese Island, Greece, public relations director, 1946-47; British Institute, Cordoba, Argentina, director, 1947-48; British legation, Belgrade, Yugoslavia, press attache, 1949-52; teacher, 1951; British government, Cyprus, director of public relations, c. 1953; *The Economist,* special correspondent in Cyprus, 1953-55; *Cyprus Review,* Nicosia, editor, 1954-55; full-time writer, 1957-90. Andrew Mellon visiting professor of Humanities, California Institute of Technology, 1974.

MEMBER: Royal Society of Literature (fellow, 1954).

AWARDS, HONORS: Duff Cooper Memorial Prize, 1957, for *Bitter Lemons;* Prix du Meilleur Livre Etranger, 1959, for *Justine* and *Balthazar;* James Tait Black Memorial Prize, 1975, for *Monsieur; or, The Prince of Darkness;* first prize in international competition, Union of Hellenic Authors and Journalists of Tourism, 1979, for *The Greek Islands; Constance; or, Solitary Practices* was shortlisted for the Booker McConnell Prize, 1981;

Cholmondeley Award for Poetry, British Society of Authors, 1986.

WRITINGS:

NOVELS

Pied Piper of Lovers, Cassell, 1935.

(Under pseudonym Charles Norden) *Panic Spring* (thriller), Covici-Friede, 1937.

The Black Book; An Agon, Obelisk Press, 1938, Dutton, 1960.

Cefalu: A Novel (social satire), Editions Poetry, 1947, published as *The Dark Labyrinth,* Ace Books, 1958, Dutton, 1962.

White Eagles over Serbia (adventure), Criterion, 1957.

Justine: A Novel (also see below), Dutton, 1957, published with illustrations by David Palladini, Franklin Library, 1980.

Balthazar: A Novel (also see below), Dutton, 1958.

Mountolive: A Novel (also see below), Dutton, 1958.

Clea: A Novel (also see below), Dutton, 1960.

The Alexandria Quartet: Justine, Balthazar, Mountolive, Clea, Dutton, 1961.

Tunc: A Novel (also see below), Dutton, 1968.

Nunquam: A Novel (also see below), Dutton, 1970.

The Revolt of Aphrodite (includes *Tunc* and *Nunquam*), Faber, 1974.

Monsieur; or, The Prince of Darkness (first part of Avignon Quincux), Faber, 1974, Viking, 1975.

Livia; or, Buried Alive (second part of Avignon Quincux), Faber, 1978, Viking, 1979.

Constance, or, Solitary Practices (third part of Avignon Quincux), Viking, 1982.

Sebastian, or, Ruling Passions (fourth part of Avignon Quincux), Viking, 1983.

Quinx, or The Ripper's Tale (final part of Avignon Quincux), Viking, 1985.

POETRY

Quaint Fragment: Poems Written between the Ages of Sixteen and Nineteen, Cecil Press, 1931.

A Ballade of Slow Decay, [Bournemouth], 1931.

Ten Poems, Caduceus Press, 1932.

(Under pseudonym Gaffer Peeslake) *Bromo Bombastes: A Fragment from a Laconic Drama by Gaffer Peeslake, When Same Being a Brief Extract from His Compendium of Lisson Devices,* Caduceus Press, 1933.

Transitions: Poems, Caduceus Press, 1934.

Mass for the Old Year, [Bournemouth], 1935.

(With others) *Proems: An Anthology of Poems,* Fortune Press, 1938.

A Private Country, Faber, 1943.

The Parthenon: For T. S. Eliot, [London], c. 1945.

Cities, Plains, and People, Faber, 1946.

On Seeming to Presume, Faber, 1948.

A Landmark Gone, Reuben Pearson, 1949.

Deus Loci: A Poem, Di Mato Vito, 1950.

Nemea, [London], 1950.

Private Drafts, Proodos Press, 1955.

The Tree of Idleness and Other Poems, Faber, 1955.

Selected Poems, Grove, 1956.

Collected Poems, Faber, 1960, Dutton, 1968.

Poetry, Dutton, 1962.

Beccafico Le Becfigue, with French translation by F. J. Temple, La Licorne, 1963.

A Persian Lady, Tragara Press, 1963.

La Descente du Styx, with French translation by Temple, La Murene, 1964, published as *Down the Styx,* Capricorn Press, 1971.

Selected Poems 1935-63, Faber, 1964.

The Ikons and Other Poems, Faber, 1966, Dutton, 1967.

In Arcadia (also see below), Turret Books, 1968.

Faustus: A Poem, [London], 1970.

The Red Limbo Lingo: A Poetry Notebook for 1968-1970, Dutton, 1971.

On the Suchness of the Old Boy, illustrated by daughter, Sappho Durrell, Turret Books, 1972.

Vega and Other Poems, Overlook Press, 1973.

The Plant-Magic Man, Capra Press, 1973.

Lifelines: Four Poems, Tragara Press, 1974.

Selected Poems, edited and with an introduction by Alan Ross, Faber, 1977.

Collected Poems, 1931-1974, edited by James A. Brigham, Viking, 1980.

SHORT STORIES

Esprit de Corps: Sketches from Diplomatic Life (humor), illustrated by V. H. Drummond, Faber, 1957, published with illustrations by Vasiliu, Dutton, 1968.

Stiff Upper Lip: Life among the Diplomats (humor), Faber, 1958, Dutton, 1961.

Sauve qui peut, illustrated by Nicholas Bentley, Faber, 1966, Dutton, 1967.

The Best of Antrobus, illustrated by Bentley, Faber, 1974.

Antrobus Complete, Faber, 1985.

PLAYS

Sappho; A Play in Verse (broadcast on BBC-Radio, 1957, produced in Hamburg, Germany, 1959), Faber, 1950, Dutton, 1958.

An Irish Faustus: A Morality in Nine Scenes (produced in Sommerhausen, Germany, 1966), Faber, 1963, Dutton, 1964.

Acte: A Play (produced in Hamburg, Germany, 1961), Faber, 1964, Dutton, 1965.

Ulysses Come Back: Outline/Sketch of a Musical Based upon the Last Three Love Affairs of Ulysses the Greek Adventurer of Mythology, Adapted Rather Light-Heartedly from Homer (with recording), Turret Books, 1970.

OTHER

(Editor, with others) *Personal Landscape: An Anthology of Exile,* Editions Poetry, 1945.

Prospero's Cell: A Guide to the Landscape and Manners of the Island of Corcyra (travelogue), Faber, 1945, published with *Reflections on a Marine Venus* (also see below), Dutton, 1960, revised edition published with *Lear's Corfu* (also see below), Faber, 1975, Penguin, 1978.

(Translator) *Six Poems from the Greek of Sekilianos and Seferis,* [Rhodes], 1946.

Zero and Asylum in the Snow: Two Excursions into Reality, [Rhodes], published as *Two Excursions into Reality,* Circle Editions, 1947.

(Translator with Bernard Spenser and Nanos Valaoritis) Georges Seferis, *The King of Asine, and Other Poems,* John Lehmann, 1948.

(Translator) Emmanuel Royidis, *The Curious History of Pope Joan,* Rodney, Phillips, & Green, 1948, published as *Pope Joan: A Personal Biography,* Deutsch, 1960, Dutton, 1961.

A Key to Modern Poetry, Peter Nevill, 1952, published as *A Key to Modern British Poetry,* University of Oklahoma Press, 1952.

Reflections on a Marine Venus: A Companion to the Landscape of Rhodes, Faber, 1953, revised edition, Dutton, 1960.

Bitter Lemons (on Cyprus), Faber, 1957, Dutton, 1958, Marlowe (New York City), 1996.

Art and Outrage: A Correspondence about Henry Miller between Alfred Perles and Lawrence Durrell, with an Intermission by Henry Miller, Putnam, 1959, Dutton, 1961.

(Editor) *A Henry Miller Reader,* New Directions, 1959, published as *The Best of Henry Miller,* Heinemann, 1960.

Groddeck (biography), translated by Grete Weill, Limes-Verlag, 1961.

(Editor, with Elizabeth Jennings and R. S. Thomas) *Penguin Modern Poets I,* Penguin, 1962.

(Coauthor) *Cleopatra* (screenplay), Twentieth Century-Fox, 1963.

Lawrence Durrell and Henry Miller: A Private Correspondence, edited by George Wickes, Dutton, 1963.

(Editor) *New Poems 1963: A PEN Anthology of Contemporary Poetry,* Hutchinson, 1963.

(Editor) *Lear's Corfu: An Anthology Drawn from the Painter's Letters,* Corfu Travel, 1965.

Spirit of Place: Letters and Essays on Travel, edited by Alan G. Thomas, Dutton, 1969.

Le Grand suppositoire: Ententiens avec Marc Alyn, illustrated with paintings by Durrell, Editions Pierre Belfond, 1972, translation by Francine Barker published as *The Big Supposer: A Dialogue with Marc Alyn,* Abelard Schuman, 1973, Grove, 1974.

The Happy Rock (on Henry Miller), Village Press, 1973.

(Editor) *Wordsworth,* Penguin, 1973.

Blue Thirst, Capra Press, 1975.

Sicilian Carousel, Viking, 1977.

The Greek Islands, illustrated with maps, Viking, 1978.

A Smile in the Mind's Eye, Wildwood House, 1980, Universe, 1982.

(Translator) *Three Poems of Cavalry,* Tragara Press, 1980.

Literary Lifelines: The Richard Aldinton—Lawrence Durrell Correspondence, edited by Ian S. MacNiven and Harry T. Moore, Viking, 1981.

The Durrell—Miller Letters, 1935-1980, edited by MacNiven, New Directions, 1988.

Lawrence Durrell: Letters to Jean Fanchette, 1958-1963, Two Cities, 1988.

Caesar's Vast Ghost: A Portrait of Provence, Arcade, 1990.

Lawrence Durrell: Conversations, with Earl G. Ingersoll, Fairleigh Dickenson University Press, 1998.

Also author of numerous prefaces and other contributions to books and periodicals, including *Holiday*; author of television script, *The Lonely Road,* 1971. Author of story used as basis of screenplay by John Michael Hayes for *Judith,* Paramount, 1965. Author's manuscript included in collections at the University of California, Los Angeles and University of Illinois, Urbana. Author's work has been translated into other languages, including Danish, French, German, Italian, Spanish, Swedish, and Turkish.

MEDIA ADAPTATIONS: Nothing Is Lost, Sweet Self (poem), set to music by Wallace Southam, published by Turret Books, 1967; *In Arcadia* (poem), with music by Southam, Trigram Press, 1968.

SIDELIGHTS: The son of British citizens, Lawrence Durrell was born in Jullundur, India, where his father, a British civil engineer, had gone to assist in the construction of India's first railway. The author's early years were spent in that country, but after receiving some education at Darjiling's College of St. Joseph, Durrell moved to England to study at St. Edmund's School in Canterbury.

Refused admission to Cambridge University, Durrell left England when he was twenty-three, and spent his twenties and thirties predominantly in Greece or, during World War II, in Egypt. In 1957, he took up residence in France where he remained until his death in 1990 at the age of seventy-eight.

Regarding his earliest book, the novel *Pied Piper of Lovers* which was published in 1935, as the work of an apprentice, Durrell showed no interest in reissuing either it or *Panic Spring,* which followed two years later. *Pied Piper of Lovers* is linear in design and obviously a first novel, but *Panic Spring* is more interesting, for in his second novel Durrell was already experimenting with form and technique. "I've tried, just for an exercise in writing, to create characters on two continuous planes of life—the present—meaning the island [the Greek setting of the book] and their [the characters'] various pasts," he wrote, according to Alan G. Thomas in *Spirit of Place: Letters and Essays on Travel.* "It does not progress as an ordinary novel progresses. The tentacles push out sideways while the main body is almost static." The young author added: "I am beginning to feel that my pencil is almost sharpened. Soon I'll be ready to begin on a BOOK."

James A. Brigham viewed *Pied Pipers of Lovers* and *Panic Spring* as the first parts of an "unacknowledged trilogy" in his article in *Collected Essays on Lawrence Durrell.* Brigham contended that the culmination of the trilogy, the "BOOK" Durrell referred to, was *The Black Book.* Published in 1938, *The Black Book* proved to be Durrell's first foray into literary notoriety, and a giant step forward in his literary career. Brigham noted that Durrell himself always thought in terms of sets of novels. In a letter to Miller he had described a projected trilogy: "I have planned AN AGON, A PATHOS, AN ANAGNORISIS. If I write them they should be The Black Book, The Book of Miracles, The Book of the Dead." "The Book of the Dead" was his original title for *The Alexandria Quartet,* but its accomplishment lay twenty years in the future.

The Black Book is structured around the narrator, Lawrence Lucifer, who in composing his autobiography on a Greek island, recalls the "English Death" of a waste-land London and encloses within his life story parts of a fictional diary attributed to one "Death" Gregory. The book concerns itself with sickness, sex, prostitution, death, and decay—the stifling, destructive existence of the impoverished artist. In corrosive language the writer attacks England's smugness and sterility within his "scenario of despair," prompting G. S. Fraser to suggest in *Lawrence Durrell* that in *The Black Book* Durrell "explored Hell" and "just got out."

One of the most significant influences on Durrell during his search for his own voice as a writer was Henry Miller's *Tropic of Cancer.* Miller's 1934 novel, which opened whole new areas of frankness in subject matter and expression, was published in France, banned in England, and immediately joined James Joyce's *Ulysses* (1922) and D. H. Lawrence's *Lady Chatterley's Lover* (1928) as major books that were widely read "underground." Durrell was influenced by the innovations of all three writers: He admired Miller's openness, Joyce's formal experimentations, and Lawrence's erotic honesty and spirit of revolt. T. S. Eliot's *The Waste Land,* published in 1922, its surface of kaleidoscopic vignettes of modern London overlying layers of meaning below, also helped to inspire in Durrell a new fictional method. In *The Black Book* he had deliberately tried to create a plot that would move in memory but remain static in linear time, radiating instead out into space. He referred to this principle—which he would go on to refine in *The Alexandria Quartet*—as "heraldic."

In 1939 Durrell returned to Greece from his stay in Paris and London; when World War II began soon after, he fled ahead of the German troops into Egypt where he became a British foreign press officer, first in Cairo and then in Alexandria. After the war he filled diplomatic and teaching positions in such diverse locations as Rhodes, Argentina, Yugoslavia, and Cyprus, until he finally settled in Provence, France. Through the 1940s and 1950s Durrell continued to write, gaining serious recognition in two different genres—"island books" and poetry. It is for these two bodies of writing that his reputation is greatest among English readers.

Durrell's "island" or landscape books are drawn from the Greek world, but they are far more than travelogues, or catalogues of places to visit. Like the travel literature of Norman Douglas and D. H. Lawrence, they recreate the ambience of places loved, the characters of people known, and the history and mythology of each unique island world. The first three landscape books, *Prospero's Cell* (1945), *Reflections on a Marine Venus* (1953), and *Bitter Lemons* (1957), form a kind of trilogy mounting in intensity and power. *Prospero's Cell* is considered by critics to be the most beautiful of the three, evoking the Corfu of the young Durrell, his Greek friends, and the history of the island, and resonating with myths from Homer to Shakespeare and beyond. *Reflections on a Marine Venus* is, by comparison, a harsher, less romantic look at the life of the people of Rhodes immediately after the war. In *Reflections* Durrell classified his love of islands as "Islomania": "This book is by intention a sort of anatomy of islomania, with all its formal defects of inconsequence and shapelessness." *Bitter Lemons* is critically seen to be the finest of Durrell's island studies and among the most outstanding of his works. Published in 1957, the book was written immediately after he returned to England from Cyprus, where his romance with Greece had been tragically strained by the island's nationalistic uprisings. He felt helpless, caught between England's wavering paternalistic position and the intense desire for "Enosis"—union with Greece—developing among the island people he loved. The author's helplessness is expressed forcefully and vividly in *Bitter Lemons.* In the *New York Times Book Review,* Freya Stark praised its "integrity of purpose, . . . careful brilliant depth of language and . . . the feeling of destiny which pervades it," declaring that the book elevated Durrell to the first rank of writers.

Durrell drew upon his fascination with islands in *Cefalu,* a satiric novel written in 1947. Published under the title *The Dark Labyrinth* in the United States, the story follows a group of English tourists into a Cretan cave—perhaps the site of the ancient labyrinth—where a landslide prevents their exit. Forced into their inner selves in search of their destinies, one couple makes their way into a sort of mythic world beyond time. Describing it to Miller, Durrell referred to *Cefalu* "a queer cosmological tale." With mythic depths, philosophic quest, and breakthrough into the Heraldic Universe, it presages on a minor scale his work to come.

Durrell was critically considered a very good poet. In the 1930s and early 1940s, his was a beautifully modulated "new voice in a new time," as Fraser noted in *Lawrence Durrell.* Urbane, compassionate, often infused with loneliness yet filled with a sense of wry fun, his poems draw deeply on two traditions: the first of ancient Greece and its rebirth in the works of such modern Greek poets as Constantine Cavafy and George Seferis, and the second of the Renaissance, of Shakespeare and Donne as reinvented by the twentieth-century "metaphysicals" Eliot and W. H. Auden. Although Durrell journeyed with the moderns across a waste land, his poetry is suffused with Greek light. Hayden

Carruth wrote in *The World of Lawrence Durrell,* "the poet of the historic consciousness who is recording the end of a civilization is intimately aware of the beginning, and the figure of Homer, the blind brother in the mists of ancientness, overlooks these poems, overlooks the *Quartet* too, I think." Many of his lyrics, such as "Nemea," "Lesbos," and "Mneiae," recall the ancient Greek Anthology put together from many sources in the Byzantine period, while his character poems, with their interplay of art and idea, are closer to Cavafy. In this latter category can be placed "Petron, the Desert Father" and "A Portrait of Theodora," the second of which reflects not only the modern Greek woman but, through her, the Byzantine empress as a girl. The character poems, especially "Fangbrand: A Biography," display "a kind of golden fullness of expression," Derek Stanford declared in his essay collected in *The World of Lawrence Durrell.*

In his best poems, as in *The Alexandria Quartet,* a profound understanding both of the past and of mythology underlies Durrell's quick and lively awareness of the present, with its attendant humor and many sorrows. Among these poems is "Deus Loci," a kind of classical hymn to the "small sunburnt" god—a charming and elegant personification of the spirit of place. Friedman wrote in *Lawrence Durrell and The Alexandria Quartet* that "Deus Loci" "offers an archetypal treatment of place—that pervading, ever-recurring motif—that may serve as a paradigm not only for the bulk of Durrell's poetry but also for such works as *Sappho,* the island books, and the *Quartet.*" Another of his best-known poems, "Alexandria," evokes the atmosphere of the city and the poet's own loneliness, "the artist at his papers / Up there alone, upon the alps of night."

Durrell's poetry has been seen as moving from early lyrics to the classically-based and metaphysically strong poems of his middle years. His later poetry, more conversational in tone, becomes even stronger in its anguished concern with "the three big words of Durrell's poetic vocabulary . . . art, love, and death," according to Ian S. MacNiven in *Critical Essays.* One of the most moving of these poems is the elegy, "Seferis." Poems like "A Patch of Dust" and "Last Heard Of" evince a remarkable sureness and power. In reflecting a maturing style, Durrell's poetic works form a kind of *Ars poetica,* a portrait of the developing artist.

Sappho, the earliest and most lyrical of the plays, creates, as Fraser noted in *Critical Essays on Lawrence Durrell,* "an atmosphere of a lost civilization at once primitive and lucid." But, although its plot covers much time and ground, the play contains more talk than action. The writing in *Acte,* a Corneille-like tragedy set in Nero's Rome, is terser and more theatrically oriented than *Sappho,* but *Acte* also fails to achieve great power as drama. Here Durrell seems more interested in Petronius as the play's creative artist than in the play's central love story. *An Irish Faustus* is the most intriguing of the three dramas. Basing his philosopher-magician on the character portrayed in the works of both Christopher Marlowe and Johann Wolfgang von Goethe, Durrell portrays Faustus' need to understand both black and white magic before he can find peace. *An Irish Faustus* cleverly reverses Marlowe's *Dr. Faustus*; the concluding act finds Faustus high on a mountain top playing cards with Matthew the Hermit, Martin the Pardoner, and Mephisto, the primary devil in the Faust legend. Upon gaining the knowledge that "when nothing begins to happen . . . the dance of the pure forms begins," Faustus is allowed entrance to Durrell's Heraldic Universe. Both Jungian psychology and Eastern thought are woven into the play, expanding the medieval German legend through time and space. Although possibly his best play, Friedman perceived it as "nearly sterile." In

contrast, Fraser praised the work in *Collected Essays on Lawrence Durrell,* deeming *An Irish Faustus* "a small masterpiece."

With the publication of *Justine* in 1957, Durrell achieved worldwide fame. In the summer of 1956, he wrote Miller from Cyprus: "I have just finished a book about Alexandria called *Justine*—the first *serious* book since *The Black Book,* much clearer and better organized, I think. . . . It's a sort of prose poem to one of the great capitals of the heart, the Capital of Memory." In discussing the novel with Alyn he explained its genesis: "It took me years to evolve *Justine,* because I was having to work on so many levels at once; history, landscape (which had to be fairly *strange* to symbolize our civilization), the weft of occultism and finally the novel about the actual process of writing. What I was trying to achieve was a canvas that was both historic and ordinary; to get that I made use of every modern technique." Durrell wanted *Justine,* in its conception, "to turn, for example, to Einstein, or to go back to the origins: *The Book of the Dead,* Plato, to the occult traditions which are still alive in the East."

The Alexandria Quartet was an experiment in form. The outer plot, a story of love, mystery, and spies, is narrated by a young writer who takes an archetypal journey to find love, self-knowledge, and his artistic voice. He writes a first novel—*Justine*—about a love affair in Alexandria, follows with another—*Balthazar*—that, in quoting other people, contradicts the first. Finally, after the interjection of a third omniscient volume revealing the "facts"—*Mountolive*—the narrator adds a last novel—*Clea*—that moves forward in time toward his attainment of maturity and wisdom. George P. Elliott, discussing Durrell's fictional strategies in *Critical Essays,* found that the "shifting of the point of view from volume to volume is the most spectacular of these, its effect being the expansion, alteration, deepening of our knowledge of what has happened."

The form of the *Quartet* is intrinsic to the work; Durrell had been concerned for many years with how the new physics of space-time might apply to fiction. Deeply read in Sigmund Freud and Carl Jung and in Sir James Frazer's mythic theory, he saw modern thought returning full circle to Far Eastern and Indian philosophy, and he wanted to weave all these concepts into the tapestry of the novel. He explained in *Paris Review* that "Eastern and Western metaphysics are coming to a point of confluence in the most interesting way. It seems unlikely in a way, but nevertheless the two main architects of this breakthrough have been Einstein and Freud. . . . Well, this novel is a four-dimensional dance, a relativity poem." Durrell's concept of space-time has been greatly debated by critics of his work. Anthony Burgess contended in *The Novel Now,* that "To learn more and more as we go on is what we expect from any good novel, and we need no benefit of 'relativity.'" John Unterecker voiced the opposing point of view in *Lawrence Durrell:* "the relativity theory involves a reorientation for the modern writer not only toward the materials of his art but also toward himself, his audience, his world." In no sense a pretentious or superfluous theory imposed on the *Quartet,* space-time is, in many ways, the central structure of the work. Indeed, Durrell had presaged its use five years before *Justine.* In his *Key to Modern British Poetry* he discussed how modern writers were beginning to think in terms both of Einsteinian space-time and of Freudian and Jungian psychology.

The Revolt of Aphrodite is set in a futuristic world of big business and computers and deals with a company called "The Firm" that totally controls the lives of those under it. The "Aphrodite" of the title is a female robot created in the image of a dead movie star.

The theme of the work is the need for freedom in an increasingly mechanized world. At the end of *Nunquam* Durrell adds a note: "It's a sort of novel-libretto based on the preface to [Oswald Spengler's] *The Decline of the West*." He is again concerned with Freud, as he explained in an interview for *Ralits*, "In *Tunc* and *Nunquam* I play with the castration complex—much more terrifying than the Oedipus complex." In the *Paris Review* Durrell explained, "whatever I do will depend upon trying to crack forms." At least two critics have seen this experimentation with forms as a clue to the misunderstanding of *The Revolt of Aphrodite*. In *Lawrence Durrell* Fraser interpreted the work as a serious philosophic romance embodying both the popular and the intellectual, like William Godwin's *Caleb Williams* or Mary Shelley's *Frankenstein*. Reed Way Dasenbrock in *Twentieth Century Literature* maintained that whereas *The Alexandria Quartet* is modern, using the modes of modernism, *Tunc* and *Nunquam* are postmodern and "deliberately confront, mock, and subvert" these modes. They are ironic, unorthodox novels, "a fierce if funny, savage if entertaining attack on our complacencies," Dasenbrock declared. He saw *Revolt* as Durrell's "most powerful, and ultimately most satisfying work of art."

The Avignon Quintet, Durrell's next major work, was, perhaps, his most ambitious undertaking; a set of five novels designed partly after the medieval quincunx garden unit of five trees—one in the middle, the others four-square. The plot involves a search during and after World War II for the lost golden treasure of the Knights Templar, which becomes also a quest for understanding and wisdom. The work is informed by gnosticism, the philosophy that holds the things of this world evil but seeks, somewhere beyond, for a universal spirit of light. And the *Quintet* carries from the *Quartet*—while making other links to it—the belief in the disappearance of the discrete ego.

The first volume, *Monsieur*, published in 1974, is presented as a novel written by one of the characters of the *Quintet*. Exploring and illustrating methods of characterization, Durrell has the "created" novelist create characters who show up in other volumes alongside characters *not* created by the fictional novelist. Durrell makes clear, however, that even these characters are creations, adding an Old Testament Envoi to *Monsieur* beginning "So D./ begat. . ." that proclaims himself the god behind the machine. Through this device Durrell shows his continued self-consciousness about his art and his delight in the mirror play of illusion and reality.

Although critics have differed widely in their assessments of Durrell's canon, they have never questioned the quality of the "Island" books or the fine, restrained elegance of his poetry. But from the *Quartet* onward, contention swirled around his experiments with form, with characterization, with layering of ideas, and with language itself. Steiner insisted that Durrell's style was at the center of the controversy, that style being "the inward sanctuary of Durrell's meaning." Durrell himself said in a *Ralits* interview in 1969 that critics were "disconcerted by my changes of tone, by the mixture of poetry, meditation, humour, and *grand guignol* in my novels." Yet his work, viewed as a whole, finally takes on, as John Unterecker said in *On Contemporary Literature*, a "marble constancy" all its own; it "fuses together into something that begins to feel like an organic whole."

BIOGRAPHICAL/CRITICAL SOURCES:

BOOKS

Begnal, Michael, editor, *On Miracle Ground: Essays on the Fiction of Durrell*, 1990.

Bowker, Gordon, *Through the Dark Labyrinth: A Biography of Lawrence Durrell*, St. Martin's, 1997.

Burgess, Anthony, *Ninety-Nine Novels: The Best in English since 1939*, Allison & Bushy, 1984.

Closter, Susan Vander, *Joyce Cary and Lawrence Durrell: A Reference Guide*, G. K. Hall, 1985.

Concise Dictionary of British Literary Biography, Volume 7: *Writers after World War II, 1945-1960*, Gale (Detroit), 1991.

Contemporary Literary Criticism, Gale, Volume 1, 1973; Volume 4, 1975; Volume 6, 1976; Volume 8, 1978; Volume 13, 1980; Volume 27, 1984; Volume 41, 1987.

Contemporary Poets, St. James Press, 1980, pp. 407-10.

Dictionary of Literary Biography, Gale, Volume 15: *British Novelists, 1930-1959*, 1983; Volume 27: *Poets of Great Britain and Ireland, 1945-1960*, 1984.

Dictionary of Literary Biography Yearbook: 1990, Gale, 1991.

Durrell, Gerald, *My Family and Other Animals*, Rupert Hart-Davis, 1956.

Friedman, Alan Warren, *Lawrence Durrell and the Alexandria Quartet: Art for Love's Sake*, University of Oklahoma Press, 1970.

Kaczvinsky, Donald P., *Lawrence Durrell's Major Novels*, Associated University Presses, 1997.

Kersnowski, Frank L., *Into the Labyrinth: Essays on the Art of Lawrence Durrell*, UMI Research Press, 1989.

Kostelanetz, Richard, editor, *On Contemporary Literature*, Avon, 1964.

Lemon, Lee, *Portraits of the Artist in Contemporary Fiction*, University of Nebraska Press, 1985.

Moore, Harry T., editor, *The World of Lawrence Durrell*, Southern Illinois University Press, 1962.

Pine, Richard, *Lawrence Durrell: The Mindscape*, St. Martin's Press (New York City), 1994.

Raper, Julius Rowan; Melody L. Enscore; Paige Matthey Bynum; *Lawrence Durrell: Comprehending the Whole*, University of Missouri Press (Columbia), 1995.

Scholes, Robert, *Fabulation and Metafiction*, University of Illinois Press, 1979.

Thomas, Alan G., and James A. Brigham, *Lawrence Durrell: An Illustrated Checklist*, Southern Illinois University Press, 1983.

PERIODICALS

Architectural Digest, August, 1991, pp. 24-28.

Books and Bookmen, February, 1960.

Chicago Tribune, October 29, 1978; April 15, 1979.

Chicago Tribune Book World, February 22, 1981, p. 4; November 14, 1982, pp. 1, 2.

Detroit News, August 29, 1982, p. 1E; October 13, 1985.

Globe and Mail (Toronto), March 31, 1984.

Interview, March, 1988, pp. 119-20.

Los Angeles Times, October 20, 1980.

Los Angeles Times Book Review, September 9, 1979, p. 13; June 13, 1982, p. 6; June 18, 1982, p. 9; November 14, 1982, p. 3; July 15, 1984, p. 2; October 27, 1985, p. 3; February 2, 1986.

Modern Fiction Studies, summer, 1971.

New Statesman, November 13, 1987, p. 25.

New Statesman and Society, March 2, 1990, pp. 34.

New Republic, May 9, 1960, pp. 20-22.

New York Times Book Review, March 2, 1958, p. 6; April 3, 1960, pp. 1, 28; November 6, 1960, p. 7; April 14, 1969, pp. 4, 14; April 10, 1979, p. C13; April 22, 1979, p. 14; August 1, 1982, p. 27; December 2, 1982; April 1, 1984, p. 22; September 15, 1985, p. 16.

New York Review of Books, July 23, 1971, p. 8.
Saturday Review, April 2, 1960, p. 15; March 21, 1964.
Shenandoah, winter, 1971.
Sunday Times (London), November 6, 1983, p. 41; June 2, 1985, p. 44.
Times (London), July 5, 1980; October 14, 1982; October 27, 1983; May 30, 1985; October 24, 1985.
Times Literary Supplement, May 22, 1969; October 15, 1982, p. 1122; October 28, 1983, p. 1184; May 31, 1985, p. 597; December 20, 1985, p. 1453; November 27, 1987, p. 1397.
Virginia Quarterly Review, summer, 1967.
Washington Post, May 29, 1986, pp. B1, 4.
Washington Post Book World, June 19, 1979, p. B1; April 15, 1984, p. 4; October 14, 1984, p. 12; September 1, 1985, p. 9.

*   *   *

DURRENMATT, Friedrich
See DUERRENMATT, Friedrich

*   *   *

DWORKIN, Andrea 1946-

PERSONAL: Born September 26, 1946, in Camden, NJ; daughter of Harry (a guidance counselor) and Sylvia (a secretary; maiden name, Spiegel) Dworkin. *Education:* Bennington College, B.A., 1968. *Politics:* Radical feminist.

ADDRESSES: Agent—Elaine Markson, 44 Greenwich Ave., New York, NY 10011.

CAREER: Writer and lecturer. Has worked as a waitress, receptionist, secretary, typist, salesperson, factory worker, paid political organizer, and teacher.

MEMBER: PEN, Women's Institute for Freedom of the Press, Authors Guild, Authors League of America.

WRITINGS:

NONFICTION

Woman Hating, Dutton, 1974.
Last Days at Hot Slit: A Radical Look at Sexual Polarity, Dutton, 1974.
Our Blood: Prophecies and Discourses on Sexual Politics (essays), Harper, 1976.
Pornography: Men Possessing Women, Putnam, 1981.
Right-wing Women, Putnam, 1983.
Intercourse, Free Press, 1987.
(With Catharine A. MacKinnon) *Pornography and Civil Rights: A New Day for Women's Equality,* Organizing Against Pornography, 1988.
Letters from a War Zone: Writings, 1976-1989 (essays), Dutton, 1989.
Life and Death, Free Press, 1997.
(Editor, with Catherine A. MacKinnon) *In Harm's Way: The Pornography Civil Rights Hearings,* Harvard University Press, 1998.

Also contributor to *Take Back the Night: Women on Pornography,* Morrow, 1980, and contributor to periodicals, including *America Report, Christopher Street, Gay Community News, Ms., Social Policy,* and *Village Voice.*

FICTION

The New Woman's Broken Heart (short stories), Frog in the Well, 1980.
Ice and Fire, Secker & Warburg, 1986.
Mercy, Secker & Warburg, 1990.

Also author of the novel *Ruins.*

SIDELIGHTS: Called "one of the most compelling voices" in the women's movement by critic Carole Rosenthal in *Ms.,* Andrea Dworkin, self-proclaimed radical feminist, author, and lecturer, "is still out there fighting . . . against the way American culture treats women," observes Lore Dickstein in the *New York Times Book Review.* Author of fiction about victimized women, Dworkin is perhaps best known for the forceful expression of her politics in controversial nonfiction about sexual roles in contemporary society.

"The role polarity of sex in our culture, which stresses the differences of man and woman, creates problems of power and violence that a culture which stresses the similarities between the sexes can peacefully avoid," explains Jeanne Kinney in a *Best Sellers* review of Dworkin's 1974 book, *Woman Hating.* And although Dworkin's graphic examples of sexual abuses of women repelled her, Kinney states that "it also awakened me to Woman as Victim in ways I never knew existed." In *Our Blood: Prophecies and Discourses on Sexual Politics,* according to Rosenthal, Dworkin "scrutinizes historical and psychological issues, including female masochism, rape, the slavery of women in 'Amerika,' and the burning of nine million witches during the Middle Ages. Then she calls for—insists upon, really—a complete cultural transformation, the rooting out of sex roles from our society."

In *Right-wing Women,* almost ten years after the publication of her first book, Dworkin theorizes that fear of male violence has forced many women to seek protection by accepting the rigid, predetermined social order of conservatism, which promises "form, shelter, safety, rules, and love" in exchange for female subservience. She cautions that the price for this protection is high, suggesting that with the possibility of laboratory reproduction comes the only role sanctioned by men for women—the prostitute. Consequently, she envisions a "gynocide," or female holocaust, with survivors reduced to the status of worker ants in a brothel-ghetto. The problem with the book, suggests Anne Tyler in *New Republic,* however, is that Dworkin "avoids the particular and makes generalizations so sweeping that the reader blinks and draws back."

Intercourse, Dworkin's 1987 book, "consists of accounts of the attitudes and behavior of men in sexual relations with women," writes Naomi Black in the Toronto *Globe and Mail.* "Some of them documentary, most of them literary, these accounts are harrowing." Although she believes that "Dworkin uses texts selectively to support her argument," Black concludes that "it is surely crucial to accept women's own accounts of their experience, which distinguish by implication between more and less harmful versions of male sexuality." In Dworkin's opinion, writes Black, "heterosexuality is necessarily exploitative" because of the typically dominant role of the male, and such exploitation extends throughout heterosexual society. Some reviewers take exception to Dworkin's portrayal of men as uniformly given to violence and power, though. Accused of being a man-hater, Dworkin's response, reports Catherine Bennett in a London *Times* review of *Intercourse,* is: "Women are supposed to be loyal and devoted to men. And if you don't have loyalty and devotion you are called a man hater. I am not loyal and devoted but I am deeply responsive to men of integrity, who care about women's rights."

Although critics sometimes fault Dworkin on stylistic grounds, especially her use of language, Dworkin's strong convictions and passionate language usually impress even those reviewers who do not agree with her politics. Bennett, for example, points to "the unvarying, obstreperous crudity of her language," and the "relentless battering" of her prose style. However, in a *Punch* review of *Pornography: Men Possessing Women*, Stanley Reynolds proclaims that "Dworkin writes like a Leon Trotsky of the sex war. Short, sharp sentences, full of repetitions but never boring. She is full of power and energy. She writes—dare I say it?—with an aggressive manner, like a man. Except that no men write with such utter conviction these days." Similarly, Rosenthal states that although Dworkin's revolutionary demands are sometimes unrealistic, her "relentless courage" in calling for drastic social reform is admirable. "If she overstates her case, it is because she is a true revolutionary," notes Reynolds.

Dworkin believes that pornography is one of the primary weapons used by men to control women. It is not about sex, she says, but about male power. Her *Pornography: Men Possessing Women*, states Reynolds, analyzes numerous pornographic stories to illustrate that they "all—even those dealing with homosexuals— demonstrate the male lust for violence and power." By portraying women as masochistic, submissive playthings for men, "it creates hostility and aggression toward women, causing both bigotry and sexual abuse," she told *Contemporary Authors*. Dworkin discusses the subtle effects of pornography upon both the sexes and believes, as Sally O'Driscoll points out in the *Village Voice*, that "men make pornography to justify their treatment of women in real life, but at the same time men treat real women that way because pornography proves that's how they are. It's a vicious cycle."

Dworkin has not limited her crusade against pornography to her writings; she and lawyer Catharine A. MacKinnon, with whom she wrote *Pornography and Civil Rights: A New Day for Women's Equality* in 1988, are responsible for a controversial antipornography ordinance that has been passed in Indianapolis, was twice passed and twice vetoed in Minneapolis, and is being considered in many other cities. The ordinance defines pornography as a form of sex discrimination and allows any person who has been harried by pornography to sue its maker or seller.

Opponents of the legislation have said that it violates the First Amendment and restricts basic personal freedoms. Dworkin disagrees in *Ms.*: "The law really doesn't have anything to say about what people do in their private lives, unless they're forcing pornography on somebody or coercing somebody or assaulting somebody. If personal, private sexual practice involves the use of pornography that someone else has to produce, the question then is, do they have a right to that product no matter what it costs the people who have to produce it?'

In her fiction, which she has had difficulty publishing in the United States, Dworkin attempts to convey to the reader the emotional impact of her nonfictional topics. Her first novel, *Ice and Fire*, begins with recollections of childhood by a disillusioned young woman. Increasingly contemptuous of men and the violence she sees at their core, the narrator descends into a squalid life of drugs, prostitution, and pan-handling in New York City, and is eventually rescued by the act of writing. "Dworkin creates an atmosphere that evokes the suffocating intensity and impotent panic of a nightmare," writes Sherie Posesorski in the Toronto

Globe and Mail. "The scenes flash like strobe lights. Her short, punchy paragraphs and assertive syntax establish a rhythm of explosive anger." And although Jean Hanff Korelitz contends in the *Times Literary Supplement* that "Dworkin completely fails to flesh out any of the points made in her non-fiction works," Posesorski maintains that the novel "invades the consciousness like a migraine headache; its provocative aura and disturbing vision vibrate with unforgettable urgency."

Her more recent novel, *Mercy*, is about "a young woman whose journey through the misogynist world . . . constitutes an almost encyclopaedic survey of male sexual violence," writes Zoe Heller in a *Times Literary Supplement* review. Unable to verbalize her anger, she expresses it by beating up male tramps at night. The novel "offers a strangely moving account of the girl's recognition of the major and minor, deliberate and casual denigration of women," observes a *Time Out* contributor. Although Heller finds that "Dworkin has written a mad, bad novel; and one doesn't have to be a man, a rapist, or a self-hating woman to admit as much," Brian Morton calls Dworkin a "considerably underrated novelist," adding in his *Bookseller* review that "for all the skeltering violence and fury of her fiction, there is a unity of voice and a dim hope of transcendence in the telling that keeps one (this one; personally) to the page." And in the *Glasgow Herald*, Morton suggests, "There is hope, too, in Dworkin's writing. The fact that she *is* writing is a gesture of hope in itself."

BIOGRAPHICAL/CRITICAL SOURCES:

BOOKS

Contemporary Authors New Revision Series, Gale (Detroit), Volume 16, 1986; Volume 39, 1992.
Contemporary Literary Criticism, Volume 43, Gale, 1987.
Jenefsky, Cindy, and Ann Russo, *Without Apology: Andrea Dworkin's Art and Politics*, Westview Press, 1997.

PERIODICALS

Best Sellers, July 1, 1974.
Bookseller, September 21, 1990, p. 837.
Choice, October, 1974.
Current Biography, October, 1994, p. 11.
Glasgow Herald, October 4, 1990.
Globe and Mail (Toronto), August 2, 1986; July 11, 1987.
Library Journal, June 1, 1974.
Listener, December 3, 1981.
Los Angeles Times, August 10, 1983.
Los Angeles Times Book Review, May 3, 1987.
Ms., February, 1977; June, 1980; March, 1981; June, 1983; April, 1985; January-February, 1994, p. 32.
New Pages, spring, 1982.
New Republic, February 21, 1983; June 25, 1984; August 11-18, 1997, p. 36.
New Statesman, November 6, 1981; July 29, 1983.
Newsweek, March 18, 1985.
New Yorker, March 28, 1977.
New York Times Book Review, July 12, 1981; May 3, 1987; October 29, 1989.
Observer, May 16, 1982.
Playboy, October, 1992, p. 36.
Progressive, November, 1993, p. 38.
Publishers Weekly, February 25, 1974; December 30, 1996, p. 46.
Punch, February 10, 1982.
Time Out, September 26, 1990, p. 1049.
Times (London), June 4, 1987; May 18, 1988.

Times Literary Supplement, January 1, 1982; June 6, 1986, p. 622;
　　October 16, 1987; June 3-9, 1988; October 5-11, 1988;
　　October 5, 1990, p. 1072.

Village Voice, July 15-21, 1981.
Washington Post Book World, June 21, 1981.
West Coast Review of Books, March/April, 1983.

E

EAGLETON, Terence (Francis) 1943-
(Terry Eagleton)

PERSONAL: Born February 22, 1943, in Salford, England. *Education:* Trinity College, Cambridge, B.A., 1964; Jesus College, Cambridge, Ph.D., 1968. *Avocation:* Poetry, theater, Irish music.

ADDRESSES: Home and office—St. Catherine's College, Oxford University, Oxford, 0X1 3UJ England.

CAREER: Cambridge University, Jesus College, Cambridge, England, fellow, 1964-69; Oxford University, Wadham College, Oxford, England, fellow and tutor in poetry, 1969-89, lecturer in critical theory, 1989-92; Oxford University, St. Catherine's College, Thomas Warton professor of English and Literature, 1992–. Selector for Poetry Book Society, 1969-71; judge, Sinclair Fiction Prize, 1985.

MEMBER: Society for the Study of Narrative Literature (president).

AWARDS, HONORS: D. Litt., Salford, 1993.

WRITINGS:

The New Left Church (essays), Helicon, 1966.
Shakespeare and Society: Critical Studies in Shakespearean Drama, Schocken, 1967.

UNDER NAME TERRY EAGLETON

(Editor) *Directions: Pointers for the Post-Conciliar Church* (essays), Sheed, 1968.
(Editor with Brian Wicker) *From Culture to Revolution: The Slant Symposium, 1967* (essays), Sheed, 1968.
The Body as Language: Outline of a "New Left" Theology, Sheed, 1970.
Exiles and Emigres: Studies in Modern Literature, Schocken, 1970.
Myths of Power: A Marxist Study of the Brontes, Barnes & Noble, 1975.
Marxism and Literary Criticism, University of California Press, 1976.
Criticism and Ideology: A Study in Marxist Literary Theory, Verso (London), 1976, Schocken, 1978.
Walter Benjamin; or, Towards a Revolutionary Criticism, Schocken, 1981.

The Rape of Clarissa: Writing, Sexuality and Class Struggle in Samuel Richardson, University of Minnesota Press, 1982.
Literary Theory: An Introduction, University of Minnesota Press, 1983, second edition, Blackwell (Cambridge, MA), 1996.
The Function of Criticism: From the Spectator to Post-Structuralism, Verso, 1984.
(Editor) Laura Brown, *Alexander Pope,* Basil Blackwell, 1985.
(Editor) James Kavanaugh, *Emily Bronte,* Basil Blackwell, 1985.
(Editor) Stan Smith, *W. H. Auden,* Basil Blackwell, 1985.
William Shakespeare, Basil Blackwell, 1986.
Against the Grain: Selected Essays, 1975-1985, Verso, 1986.
Saints and Scholars (novel), Verso, 1987.
Myths of Power: A Marxist Study of the Brontes, second edition, Macmillan, 1988.
(Editor) *Raymond Williams: A Critical Reader,* Northeastern University Press, 1989.
The Ideology of the Aesthetics, Blackwell (Oxford, UK), 1990.
(With Fredric Jameson and Edward W. Said) *Nationalism, Colonialism, and Literature,* University of Minnesota Press (Minneapolis), 1990.
Saint Oscar (play), first produced in London, 1990.
Ideology: An Introduction, Verso (London), 1991.
Wittgenstein: The Terry Eagleton Script, the Derek Jarman Film, BFI (London), 1993.
Heathcliff and the Great Hunger: Studies in Irish Culture, Verso (London), 1995.
The Illusions of Postmodernism, Blackwell (Cambridge, MA), 1996.
(Editor) *Marxist Literary Theory: A Reader,* Blackwell (Cambridge, MA), 1996.

OTHER

Contributor to *Slant, Times Literary Supplement, Stand, Commonweal,* and other periodicals. Poetry reviewer, *Stand,* 1968–. Delivered lecture *The Crisis of Contemporary Culture* before the University of Oxford, 1992, published by Clarendon Press (Oxford), 1993.

SIDELIGHTS: Terry Eagleton is "widely regarded as the foremost young Marxist literary thinker in England," writes a *Washington Post Book World* contributor. Concerned with the ideologies found in literature, Eagleton examines the role of Marxism in discerning these ideologies. "Always alert to the underside or reversible lining of any intellectual model, Eagleton tracks the cross-currents and strategies of literary criticism with a uniquely agile understanding," states Chris Baldick in the *Times Literary Supplement.* Eagleton's books have not only clarified arcane critical theories of literature for the novice but have also posed provocative questions to the specialists. His polemical expositions in literary theory have generated a spirited critical response, and even those opposed to his stance speak readily about his "accessible" and persuasive prose. "Unlike too many other theorists, Marxist or otherwise," says Steven G. Kellman in *Modern Fiction Studies,* "Eagleton writes with grace, clarity, and force." In *Thought,* Walter Kendrick points also to Eagleton's "sprightly style and . . . lively sense of humor, rare commodities in his field."

Eagleton's brief but concise *Marxism and Literary Criticism* discusses the author of a work as producer, as well as the relationships between literature and history, form and content, and the writer and commitment. As George Woodcock observes in the *Sewanee Review,* Eagleton perceives Marxist criticism to be "part of a larger body of theoretical analysis that aims to understand *ideologies*—the ideas, values and feelings by which men experience their societies at various times. And certain of those ideas, values and feelings are available to us only in literature." Woodcock praises Eagleton's clear and vigorous writing, adding that he is "brisk and specific, and tells us a great deal . . . about the more important continental European Marxist critics, their books, and their theories." Peter Conrad, however, sees a need for more textual examples in *Marxism and Literary Criticism,* and he refers to it in the *Spectator* as "a case of theory talking about itself." Michael Wilding similarly finds the book "academic and self-referential," suggesting in *Modern Language Review* that Eagleton approaches Marxist literary criticism "as a subject, rather than as an instrument for revealing other subjects."

According to Jonathan Culler in *Poetics Today,* Eagleton's academic best-seller, *Literary Theory: An Introduction,* is a "vigorous articulation of what has become a common theme today in the realm of critical theory: the call for criticism and for literary theory to assume a relationship to history, both by confronting the question of their insertion in social and political history and by taking account of their own history." As John Lucas notes in a *Times Literary Supplement* review of *Against the Grain: Selected Essays, 1975-1985,* Eagleton is "one of a number of critics and theorists on the left who have necessarily drawn attention to improper or at least ideologically-based privileging of certain authors and texts." In *Literary Theory,* Eagleton begins with the observation that "literary criticism is by nature a political act, even (or especially) when it eschews direct political engagement," writes Kendrick, and in this volume, Eagleton connects each school of literary study with the ideology of its particular time and place.

Literary Theory is a "remarkable and important book," writes Charles Sugnet in *American Book Review,* adding that it "does what a good introduction should do—it synthesizes tendencies already in the air and makes them widely accessible in clear prose." Culler believes it to be Eagleton's "best work: provocative, efficient, and for the most part well-informed." Praising the stylistic grace and precision with which Eagleton distills complex theories of literature, critics especially address the book's provocative premise. "A Marxist with wit, Terry Eagleton is magisterial in his deployment of a wide range of ideas, but rarely dispassionate, . . ." says Kellman. "After patient scrutiny of the writings of numerous contemporary critics, Eagleton confesses that he has not come to praise theory but to bury it."

David Forgacs questions Eagleton's proposal of subsuming literature into a wider study and wonders in *Poetics Today,* "[w]ho is going to supply the methodologies and the courses, and with what claims to expertise in the field." Among other criticisms, Denis Donoghue in the *New York Review of Books* faults Eagleton for failing to adequately define "history" or how it "proves invulnerable to the irony he so relentlessly directs against other ultimate categories." But in *South Atlantic Quarterly,* Wallace Jackson thinks that Eagleton "de-mythologizes the high-cultural pretensions of literary study in the university, recognizes that in fact such study underwrites the practices of state capitalism, and effectively nullifies whatever radical power literature may have as an instrument of social criticism and social change." Kendrick notes in the *New York Times Book Review* that while *Literary Theory* is intended for a nonacademic audience, "academics will be unable to ignore it. . . . Eagleton's expositions render even the most jargon-ridden of contemporary theories accessible to the ordinary educated person, and the questions posed by *Literary Theory* will have to be answered, either by the theoreticians themselves or by those who validate them by accepting their authority." Kellman, who believes that Eagleton successfully assimilates "a motley crowd of structuralists, feminists, hermeneuticians, psychoanalysts, and deconstructionists to his argument that there are no innocent readings, that every literary experience is shaped by ideology," recommends that it "ought to be read with the same blend of enthusiasm and wariness with which it was written, but it ought to be read by anyone concerned with contemporary theory."

Eagleton's *The Function of Criticism: From the Spectator to Post-Structuralism* augments *Literary Theory* in that it traces the history of English literary criticism "from its earliest recognizable appearance around the turn of the eighteenth century to its present institutionalized form," writes Kendrick in the *Voice Literary Supplement.* It is a "polemical history, not of criticism as such," observes Patrick Parrinder in the *London Review of Books,* "but of the 'critical institution' within which it acquired what Eagleton recognises as social significance." And David Montrose points out in the *New Statesman* that Eagleton "seeks to 'recall criticism to its traditional role'—engagement in cultural politics—from what he considers a position of crisis, where it is narrowly preoccupied with literary texts and estranged from social life through confinement to Academe and 'the literary industry.'" "But the heart of this book," says Christopher Norris in *British Book News,* "is clearly to be found in Eagleton's use of the 'public sphere' as a concept to articulate and clarify the relation between criticism and ideology."

Eagleton further articulates his theoretical positions in *Saints and Scholars,* a novel of ideas whose characters are philosopher Ludwig Wittgenstein, Irish revolutionary James Connolly, Leopold Bloom from James Joyce's *Ulysses,* and Nikolai Bakhtin, brother of famed Marxist literary critic Mikhail. Their fictitious conversations while gathered together in an Irish cottage during 1916 serve as a forum for Eagleton to debate the practical and theoretical limitations of thought and social action. Though noting that "facts blended with fiction make a difficult genre, and the connections between realism and surrealism are not always easily made," Roy Foster praises the novel in the *Times Literary Supplement* as "ingenious, erudite and entertaining." *Observer* contributor Maureen Freely commends Eagleton's courage to write such a book, described by Freely as "an experimental, non-bourgeois anti-novel" whose "*raison d'etre* is discourse, and the subject of the discourse is revolution."

Eagleton followed with *The Ideology of Aesthetics,* which, according to *Times Literary Supplement* reviewer Sebastian Gardner, "is Terry Eagleton's most substantial work to date,. . . a comprehensive engagement with the history of modern philosophical aesthetics." Eagleton's analysis considers the work of Immanuel Kant, G. W. F. Hegel, Friedrich Nietzsche, Walter Benjamin, Martin Heidegger, and Theodor Adorno, among other major philosophers and social theorists, in an attempt to further penetrate and reveal the interplay of social and political forces in the formation of aesthetic thought. While challenging conventional Marxist principles and the "libertarian pessimism" of post-structuralism, as Frank Kermode writes in the *London Review of Books,* "Eagleton states his own faith in a community purged of the imperialism of the bourgeois aesthetic—a community in which all will recognise that 'our shared material conditions bind us ineluctably together, and in doing so open up the possibilities of friendship and love.'"

With *Heathcliff and the Great Hunger: Studies in Irish Culture,* Eagleton launched an assault on the perceived revisionism of Irish history that, in his view, denies the impact of the great potato famine and nineteenth-century colonial politics on Victorian English literature and subsequent writers such as Oscar Wilde and W. B. Yeats. The book consists of a series of eight essays on Irish culture and society from the period of the famine, referred to by Eagleton as "the Irish Auschwitz," through the early decades of the twentieth century. Commenting on Eagleton's interpretation of Heathcliff, a character from Emily Bronte's *Wuthering Heights,* as an Irish famine victim, Andrew Hadfield writes in the *Times Literary Supplement,* "This is Eagleton at his best: lucid, original and witty, goading the reader to challenge his unmasking of the complacent assumptions we all, probably, share." Hadfield continues, "Elsewhere in the work, he explores a fundamental paradox: why was Ireland, the most backward nation in nineteenth-century Europe, able to produce some of the most avant-garde writing? Answer: mainland Britain was too wedded to an ideology of organic progress which allowed realism to flourish as a genre, whereas in Ireland, traumatized by the famine, nature and culture were out of sympathy and no one dominant tradition emerged, rather, a whole range of genres flourished."

Norris concludes in *Southern Humanities Review* that "Eagleton is a stylist of great resource whose arguments derive much of their power from the presently embattled situation of literary theory." And Parrinder suggests that while "one does not go to Eagleton's works for true judgment, by and large, and it is hard to know what contribution he has made to the emancipation of the masses," he nonetheless maintains that "Eagleton remains one of the most spectacular orators in the park, and English criticism would be a good deal less entertaining without his pamphlets."

BIOGRAPHICAL/CRITICAL SOURCES:

BOOKS

Contemporary Literary Criticism, Volume 63, Gale (Detroit), 1991.

PERIODICALS

American Book Review, May-June, 1985.
British Book News, February, 1985.
Canadian Literature, autumn, 1992, p. 108.
Commentary, March, 1984.
London Review of Books, February 7, 1985; September 3, 1987, p. 19; April 5, 1990, p. 14.
Modern Fiction Studies, summer, 1984.
Modern Language Review, January, 1979; April, 1985.

Nation, December 24, 1983; January 21, 1984.
New Republic, November 10, 1986; June 20, 1994, p. 34; August 21, 1995, p. 42.
New Statesman, June 3, 1983; October 5, 1984; October 6, 1989, p. 42; June 21, 1991, p. 44; June 16, 1995, p. 37.
New York Review of Books, July 21, 1983; December 8, 1983; November 6, 1986.
New York Times, April 18, 1986.
New York Times Book Review, September 4, 1983; October 18, 1987; August 18, 1991, p. 14.
Observer, September 13, 1987; March 4, 1990, p. 64.
Poetics Today, Volume 5, number 1, 1984; Volume 5, number 2, 1985; Volume 7, number 1, 1986.
Sewanee Review, fall, 1978.
South Atlantic Quarterly, summer, 1985; spring, 1986.
Southern Humanities Review, summer, 1985.
Spectator, August 21, 1976.
Thought, December, 1984.
Times Literary Supplement, July 13, 1967; January 23, 1969; August 14, 1970; October 23, 1970; May 20, 1977; November 12, 1982; February 4, 1983; June 10, 1983; November 23, 1984; July 4, 1986; September 4, 1987, p. 947; March 30-April 5, 1990, p. 337; July 7, 1995, p. 24.
Voice Literary Supplement, June, 1983; March, 1985.
Washington Post Book World, October 2, 1983.
World Literature Today, winter, 1977.

*   *   *

EAGLETON, Terry
    See EAGLETON, Terence (Francis)

*   *   *

EAST, Michael
    See WEST, Morris L(anglo)

*   *   *

ECHO
    See PROUST, (Valentin-Louis-George-Eugene) Marcel

*   *   *

ECO, Umberto 1932-

PERSONAL: Born January 5, 1932, in Alessandria, Italy; son of Giulio and Giovanna (Bisio) Eco; married Renate Ramge (a teacher) September 24, 1962; children: Stefano, Carlotta. *Education:* University of Turin, Ph.D., 1954.

ADDRESSES: Office—Universita di Bologna, Via Toffano 2, Bologna, Italy.

CAREER: RAI (Italian Radio-Television), Milan, Italy, editor for cultural programs, 1954-59; University of Turin, Turin, Italy, assistant lecturer, 1956-63, lecturer in aesthetics, 1963-64; University of Milan, Milan, lecturer in architecture, 1964-65; University of Florence, Florence, Italy, professor of visual communications, 1966-69; Milan Polytechnic, Milan, professor of semiotics, 1969-71; University of Bologna, Bologna, Italy, associate professor, 1971-75, professor of semiotics, 1975–, director of doctorate program in semiotics, 1986–, chair of Corso di Laurea in Scienze della comunicazione, 1993–. Visiting professor, New York University, 1969, 1976, Northwestern University, 1972, University of California, San Diego, 1975, Yale University, 1977, 1980, 1981, and Columbia University, 1978; visiting fellow of The Italian Academy,and Columbia University. Lecturer on semiotics at various institutions throughout the world, including Tanner Lecturer, Cambridge University, 1990, Norton Lecturer, Harvard University, 1992-93, University of Antwerp, Ecole Pratique des Hautes Etudes, University of London, Nobel Foundation, University of Warsaw, University of Budapest, University of Toronto, Murdoch University—Perth, and Amherst College. Member of the Council for the United States and Italy. *Military service:* Italian Army, 1958-59.

MEMBER: International Association for Semiotic Studies (secretary-general, 1972-79, vice president, 1979–), James Joyce Foundation (honorary trustee).

AWARDS, HONORS: Premio Strega and Premio Anghiari, both 1981, both for *Il nome della rosa*; named honorary citizen of Monte Cerignone, Italy, 1982; Prix Medicis for best foreign novel, 1982, for French version of *Il nome della rosa*; *Los Angeles Times* fiction prize nomination, 1983, and best fiction book award from Association of Logos Bookstores, both for *The Name of the Rose*; Marshall McLuhan Teleglobe Canada Award from UNESCO's Canadian Commission, 1985, for achievement in communications; Commandeor de l'Ordre des Arts et des Lettre (France), 1985; Chevalier de la Legion d'Honneur (France), 1993; Golden Cross of the Dodecannese, Patmos (Greece), 1995; Cavaliere di Gran Croce al Merito dell a Repubblica Italiana, 1996; honorary degrees from Catholic University, Leuven, 1985, Odense University, 1986, Loyola University, Chicago, 1987, State University of New York at Stony Brook, 1987, Royal College of Arts, London, 1987, Brown University, 1988, University of Paris, Sorbonne Nouvelle, 1989, University of Glasgow, 1990, University of Tel Aviv and University of Buenos Aires, both 1994, University of Athens, Laurentian University at Sudbury, Ontario, and Academy of Fine Arts, Warsaw, all 1996.

WRITINGS:

IN ITALIAN

Filosofi in liberta, Taylor (Turin), 1958, 2nd edition, 1959.
(Contributor) *Momenti e problema di storia dell'estetica,* Marzorati, 1959.
Apocalittici e integrati: Comunicazioni di massa e teoria della cultura di massa, Bompiani, 1964, revised edition, 1977.
Le poetiche di Joyce, Bompiani, 1965, 2nd edition published as *Le poetiche di Joyce dalla "Summa" al "Finnegans Wake,"* 1966.
(Editor with Eugenio Carmi) *La Bomba e il generale,* Bompiani, 1966, revised edition, 1988.
(Editor with Carmi) *I tre cosmonauti,* Bompiani, 1966, revised edition, 1988.
Appunti per una semiologia delle comunicazioni visive (also see below), Bompiani, 1967.
(Author of introduction) Mimmo Castellano, *Noi vivi,* Dedalo Libri, 1967.
La struttura assente (includes *Appunti per una semiologia delle comunicazioni visive*), Bompiani, 1968, revised edition, 1983.
La definizione dell'arte (title means *The Definition of Art*), U. Mursia, 1968.

(Editor) *L'uomo e l'arte,* Volume 1: *L'arte come mestiere,* Bompiani, 1969.
(Editor with Remo Faccani) *I sistemi di segni e lo strutturalismo sovietico,* Bompiani, 1969, 2nd edition published as *Semiotica della letteratura in URSS,* 1974.
(Editor) *L'Industria della cultura,* Bompiani, 1969.
(Editor) *Dove e quando? Indagine sperimentale su due diverse edizioni di un servizio di 'Almanacco,'* Rai, 1969.
(Editor) *Socialismo y consolacion: Reflexiones en torno a "Los misterios de Paris" de Eugene Sue,* Tusquets, 1970, 2nd edition, 1974.
Le forme del contenuto, Bompiani, 1971.
(Editor with Cesare Sughi) *Cent'anni dopo: Il ritorno dell'intreccio,* Bompiani, 1971.
Il segno, Isedi, 1971, 2nd edition, Mondadori.
(Editor with M. Bonazzi) *I pampini bugiardi,* Guaraldi, 1972.
(Editor) *Estetica e teoria dell'informazione,* Bompiani, 1972.
(Contributor) *Documenti su il nuovo medioevo,* Bompiani, 1973.
(Editor) *Eugenio Carmi: Una pittura de paesaggio?,* G. Prearo, 1973.
Il costume di casa: Evidenze e misteri dell'ideologia italiano, Bompiani, 1973.
Beato di Liebana: Miniature del Beato de Fernando I y Sancha, F. M. Ricci, 1973.
Il superuomo di massa: Studi sul romanzo popolare, Cooperativa Scrittori, 1976, revised edition, Bompiani, 1978.
(Coeditor) *Storia di una rivoluzione mai esistita l'esperimento Vaduz,* Servizio Opinioni, RAI, 1976.
Dalla periferia dell'Impero, Bompiani, 1976.
Come si fa una tesi di laurea, Bompiani, 1977.
(Contributor) *Convegno su realta e ideologie dell'informazione,* [Milan], 1978, Il Saggiatore, 1979.
Lector in fabula: La cooperazione interpretative nei testi narrativa, Bompiani, 1979; also published as *The Role of the Reader: Explorations in the Semiotics of Texts,* Indiana University Press (Bloomington), 1979.
(Contributor) *Carolina Invernizio, Matilde Serao, Liala,* La Nuova Italia, 1979.
(With others) *Perche continuiamo a fare e a insegnare arte?,* Cappelli, 1979.
Sette anni di desiderio, Bompiani, 1983.
Conceito de texto, Queiroz, 1984.
Sugli specchi e altri saggi, Bompiani, 1985.
Lo strano caso della Hanau 1609, Bompiani, 1989.
I Limiti dell'interpretazione, Bompiani, 1990.
Stelle e stellette, Melangolo, 1991.
Vocali, Guida, 1991.
(With Eugenio Carmi) *Gli gnomi di gnu,* Bompiani, 1992.
L'Isola del giorno prima (also see below), Bompiani, 1994.
(Editor) *Povero Pinocchio,* Comix, 1995.
Incontro, Guernica Editions, 1997.

IN ENGLISH TRANSLATION

Il problema estetico in San Tommaso, Edizioni di Filosofia, 1956, 2nd edition published as *Il problema estetico in Tommaso d'Aquino,* Bompiani, 1970, translation by Hugh Bredin published as *The Aesthetics of Thomas Aquinas,* Harvard University Press, 1988.
(Editor with G. Zorzoli) *Storia figurata delle invenzioni: Dalla selce scheggiata al volo spaziali,* Bompiani, 1961, translation by Anthony Lawrence published as *The Picture History of Inventions from Plough to Polaris,* Macmillan (New York City), 1963, 2nd Italian edition, Bompiani, 1968.

Opera aperta: Forma e indeterminazione nelle poetiche contemporanee (includes *Le poetiche di Joyce*; also see below), Bompiani (Milan), 1962, revised edition, 1972, translation by Anna Cancogni published as *The Open Work,* Harvard University Press (Cambridge, MA), 1989.

Diario minimo, Mondadori, 1963, 2nd revised edition, 1976, translation by William Weaver published as *Misreadings,* Harcourt (San Diego, CA), 1993.

(Editor with Oreste del Buono) *Il caso Bond,* Bompiani, 1965, translation by R. Downie published as *The Bond Affair,* Macdonald, 1966.

(Editor with Jean Chesneaux and Gino Nebiolo) *I fumetti di Mao,* Laterza, 1971, translation by Frances Frenaye published as *The People's Comic Book: Red Women's Detachment, Hot on the Trail, and Other Chinese Comics,* Anchor Press (New York City), 1973.

Il nome della rosa (novel), Bompiani, 1980, translation by William Weaver published as *The Name of the Rose,* Harcourt, 1983.

Postscript to "The Name of the Rose" (originally published in Italian), translation by William Weaver, Harcourt, 1984.

Art and Beauty in the Middle Ages (originally published in Italian), translation by Hugh Bredin, Yale University Press (New Haven, CT), 1986.

Travels in Hyper Reality (originally published in Italian), edited by Helen Wolff and Kurt Wolff, translation by William Weaver, Harcourt, 1986.

Il pendolo di Foucault (novel), Bompiani, 1988, translation by William Weaver published as *Foucault's Pendulum,* Harcourt, 1989.

The Aesthetics of Chaosmos: The Middle Ages of James Joyce (originally published in Italian), translation by Ellen Esrock, Harvard University Press, 1989.

The Bomb and the General (juvenile; originally published in Italian), translation by William Weaver, illustrations by Eugenio Carmi, Harcourt, 1989.

La ricerca della lingua perfetta nella cultura europea, Laterza (Bari), 1993, translation by James Fentress published as *The Search for the Perfect Language,* Blackwell (Oxford), 1994.

How to Travel with a Salmon and Other Essays (originally published in Italian as *Il Secondo diario minimo*), translation by William Weaver, Harcourt, 1994.

L'Isola del giorno prima (novel), Bompiani, 1994, translation by William Weaver published as *The Island of the Day Before,* Harcourt, 1995.

IN ENGLISH

A Theory of Semiotics, Indiana University Press, 1976, translation from original English manuscript published as *Trattato di semiotica generale,* Bompiani, 1975.

Semiotics and the Philosophy of Language, Indiana University Press, 1984.

(Editor with Thomas A. Sebeok) *Sign of the Three: Dupin, Holmes, Peirce,* Indiana University Press, 1984.

Leonardo Cremonini: Paintings and Watercolors 1976-1986, Bernard, Claude, Gallery, Ltd., 1987.

(Editor with others) *Meaning and Mental Representations,* Indiana University Press, 1988.

The Three Astronauts (for children), Harcourt, 1989.

(Editor with Costantino Marmo) *On the Medieval Theory of Signs,* John Benjamins, 1989.

The Limits of Interpretation, Indiana University Press, 1990.

(With Richard Torty, Jonathan Culler, and Christine Brooke-Rose) *Interpretation and Overinterpretation,* Cambridge University Press (Cambridge), 1992.

Misreadings, Harcourt, 1993.

Apocalypse Postponed: Essays, Indiana University Press, 1994.

Six Walks in the Fictional Woods, Harvard University Press, 1994.

The Cult of Vespa, Gingko Press, 1997.

Contributor to numerous encyclopedias, including *Enciclopedia Filosofica* and *Encyclopedic Dictionary of Semiotics.* Also contributor to proceedings of the First Congress of the International Association for Semiotic Studies. Columnist for *Il giorno, La stampa, Corriere della Sera,* and other newspapers and magazines. Contributor of essays and reviews to numerous periodicals, including *Espresso, Corriere della Sera, Times Literary Supplement, Revue Internationale de Sciences Sociales,* and *Nouvelle Revue Francaise.*

Member of editorial board, *Semiotica, Poetics Today, Degres, Structuralist Review, Text, Communication, Problemi dell'informazione,* and *Alfabeta*; nonfiction senior editor, Casa Editrice Bompiani, Milan, 1959-75; editor, *VS-Semiotic Studies.*

MEDIA ADAPTATIONS: Jean-Jacques Annaud directed a 1986 film adaptation of Eco's novel, *The Name of the Rose*; the movie starred Sean Connery as William of Baskerville.

SIDELIGHTS: No one expected *The Name of the Rose* to become an internationally acclaimed best-seller, least of all Umberto Eco, the man who wrote the book. A respected Italian scholar, Eco had built his literary reputation on specialized academic writing about semiotics—the study of how cultures communicate through signs. Not only was *The Name of the Rose* his first novel, it was also a complex creation, long on philosophy and short on sex—definitely not blockbuster material, especially not in Italy where the market for books is small.

Some experts attribute its success to the current interest in fantasy literature. "For all its historical accuracy, *The Name of the Rose* has the charm of an invented world," Drenka Willen, Eco's editor at Harcourt, told *Newsweek.* Others chalk it up to snob appeal. "Every year there is one great *unread* best-seller. A lot of people who will buy the book will never read it," Howard Kaminsky, president of Warner Books, suggests in that same *Newsweek* article.

But perhaps the most plausible explanation is the one offered by Franco Ferrucci in *New York Times Book Review*: "The answer may lie in the fact that Mr. Eco is the unacknowledged leader of contemporary Italian culture, a man whose academic and ideological prestige has grown steadily through years of dazzling and solid work." On one level *The Name of the Rose* is a murder mystery in which a number of Catholic monks are inexplicably killed. The setting is an ancient monastery in northern Italy, the year is 1327, and the air is rife with evil. Dissension among rival factions of the Franciscan order threatens to tear the church apart, and each side is preparing for a showdown. On one side stand the Spiritualists and the emperor Louis IV who endorse evangelical poverty; on the other, the corrupt Pope John XXII and the monks who believe that the vow of poverty will rob the church of earthly wealth and power. In an effort to avoid a confrontation, both sides agree to meet at the monastery—a Benedictine abbey that is considered neutral ground. To this meeting come William of Baskerville, an English Franciscan empowered to represent the emperor, and Adso, William's disciple and scribe. Before the council can convene, however, the body of a young monk is discovered at the bottom of a cliff, and William, a master logician in the tradition of Sherlock Holmes, is recruited to solve the crime, assisted by Adso, in Watson's role.

Nowhere is the importance of decoding symbols more apparent than in the library—an intricate labyrinth that houses all types of books, including volumes on pagan rituals and black magic. The secret of the maze is known to only a few, among them the master librarian whose job it is to safeguard the collection and supervise the circulation of appropriate volumes. William suspects that the murders relate to a forbidden book—a rare work with "the power of a thousand scorpions"—that some of the more curious monks have been trying to obtain. "What the temptation of adultery is for laymen and the yearning for riches is for secular ecclesiastics, the seduction of knowledge is for monks," William explains to Adso. "Why should they not have risked death to satisfy a curiosity of their minds, or have killed to prevent someone from appropriating a jealously guarded secret of their own?"

If William speaks for reason, Adso—the young novice who, in his old age, will relate the story—represents the voice of faith. Ferrucci believes that Adso reflects the author's second side: "The Eco who writes *The Name of the Rose* is Adso: a voice young and old at the same time, speaking from nostalgia for love and passion. William shapes the story with his insight; Adso gives it his own pathos. He will never think, as William does, that 'books are not made to be believed but to be subjected to inquiry'; Adso writes to be believed."

Another way Eco's novel can be interpreted is as a parable of modern life. The vehement struggle between church and state mirrors much of recent Italian history with its "debates over the role of the left and the accompanying explosion of terrorist violence," writes Sari Gilbert in the *Washington Post*. Eco acknowledges the influence that former Italian premier Aldo Moro's 1978 kidnapping and death had on his story, telling Gilbert that it "gave us all a sense of impotence," but he also warned that the book was not simply a *roman a clef*. "Instead," he told Herbert Mitgang in a *New York Times Book Review* article, "I hope readers see the roots, that everything that existed then—from banks and the inflationary spiral to the burning of libraries—exists today. We are always approaching the time of the anti-Christ. In the nuclear age, we are never far from the Dark Ages."

As with his first novel, Eco's second novel was an international best-seller. Published in 1989 in English as *Foucault's Pendulum*, the book is similar to *The Name of the Rose* in that it is a semiotic murder mystery wrapped in several layers of meaning. The plot revolves around Casaubon, the narrator, and two Milan editors who break up the monotony of reviewing manuscripts on the occult by combining information from all of them into one computer program called the Plan. Initially conceived as a joke, the Plan connects the Knights Templar—a medieval papal order who fought in the Crusades—with other occult groups throughout history. The program produces a map indicating the geographical point at which the powers of the earth can be controlled. That point is in Paris, France, at Foucault's Pendulum. When occult groups, including Satanists, get wind of the Plan, they go so far as to kill one of the editors in their quest to gain control of the earth. Beyond the basic plot, readers will also encounter William Shakespeare, Rene Descartes, Tom and Jerry, Karl Marx, Rhett Butler and Scarlett O'Hara, Sam Spade, Frederick the Great of Prussia, Nazis, Rosicrucians, and Jesuits. Eco orchestrates all of these and other diverse characters and groups into his multilayered semiotic story.

Some of the interpretations of the book critics have suggested include reading it as nothing more than an elaborate joke, as an exploration of the ambiguity between text as reality and reality as text, and as a warning that harm comes to those who seek knowledge through bad logic and faulty reasoning. Given this range of interpretation and Eco's interest in semiotics, *Foucault's Pendulum* is probably best described as a book about many things, including the act of interpretation itself.

Foucault's Pendulum generated a broad range of commentary. Some critics faulted the book for digressing too often into scholarly minutia, and others felt Eco had only mixed success in relating the different levels of his tale. Several reviewers, however, praised *Foucault's Pendulum*. Comparing the work to his first novel, Herbert Mitgang, for example, said in the *New York Times* that the book "is a quest novel that is deeper and richer than 'The Name of the Rose.' It's a brilliant piece of research and writing—experimental and funny, literary and philosophical—that bravely ignores the conventional expectations of the reader." Eco offered his own opinion of his novel in *Time*: "This was a book conceived to irritate the reader. I knew it would provoke ambiguous, nonhomogeneous responses because it was a book conceived to point up some contradictions."

The Search for the Perfect Language is a history of the attempts to reconstruct a "natural" original language. *London Review of Books* contributor John Sturrock calls it "a brisk, chronological account of the many thinkers about language, from antiquity onwards, who have conceived programmes for undoing the effects of time and either recovering the ur-language that they believed must once have existed only later to be lost, or else inventing a replacement for it." Eco pursues this search as a semiotician, because he believes language is the most common human symbol. However, as *The Search for the Perfect Language* reveals, more often than not the thinkers only reveal their own linguistic prejudices in their conclusions. This search for the primal tongue is, Sturrock continues, a "history of a doomed but often laudably ingenious movement to go against the linguistic grain and rediscover a truly natural language: a language of Nature or of God as it were, the appropriateness of whose signs there could be no denying."

With the publication of *The Island of the Day Before*, Eco returned to writing fiction. His third novel, like *The Search for the Perfect Language*, explains Toronto *Globe and Mail* contributor Patrick Rengger, "is also, and in more ways than one, attempting to excavate truths by sifting language and meaning." The book takes place during the early seventeenth century and tells the story of an Italian castaway, Roberto della Griva, who is marooned on an otherwise deserted ship in the South Pacific. "While exploring the ship," states Mel Gussow in the *New York Times,* "the protagonist drifts back into his past and recalls old battles as well as old figments of his imagination." "Eco's 'The Island of the Day Before' is dazzling in its range," *Los Angeles Times Book Review* contributor Marina Warner declares, "its linguistic fireworks ('Babelizing' as Eco calls it) and sheer learning."

Eco's *Apocalypse Postponed* is a collection of essays on culture that were written from the 1960s through the 1980s. The book discusses a variety of topics, including cartoons, literacy, Federico Fellini, and the counterculture movement. A reviewer for *Kirkus Reviews* opines that "Eco offers refreshing commentary on cultural life, primarily in Italy, from the mid-1960s to the late '80s, when intellectuals were especially alarmed by the emergence of a mass or pop culture." Divided into four parts, which reflect the topics of mass culture, mass media, countercultures, and

Italian intellectualism, the book is summarized by *Kirkus Reviews* as "substantial, lucid, humane, and a great deal of fun."

BIOGRAPHICAL/CRITICAL SOURCES:

BOOKS

Bondanella, Peter E., *Umberto Eco and the Open Text: Semiotics, Fiction, Popular Culture,* Cambridge University Press, 1997.

Capozzi, Rocco, editor, *Reading Eco: An Anthology,* Indiana University Press, 1997.

Contemporary Literary Criticism, Gale, Volume 28, 1984; Volume 60, 1991.

Inge, Thomas M., editor, *Naming the Rose: Essays on Eco's "The Name of the Rose,"* University Press of Mississippi (Jackson), 1988.

Tanner, William E., Anne Gervasi and Kay Mizell, editors, *Out of Chaos: Semiotics; A Festschrift in Honor of Umberto Eco,* Liberal Arts Press (Arlington, TX), 1991.

PERIODICALS

America, August 3, 1983.
American Scholar, autumn, 1987.
Antioch Review, winter, 1993, p. 149.
Atlantic, November, 1989.
Bloomsbury Review, September, 1992.
Boston Globe, March 30, 1994, p. 75.
Corriere della Sera, June 1, 1981.
Drama Review, summer, 1993.
Economist, October 28, 1989.
Esquire, August, 1994, p. 99.
Globe and Mail (Toronto), January 6, 1996, p. C7.
Harper's, August, 1983; May, 1993, p. 24; January, 1995, p. 33.
International Philosophical Quarterly, June, 1980.
Interview, November, 1989.
Kirkus Reviews, March 15, 1994.
Journal of Communication, autumn, 1976.
Language, Volume 53, number 3, 1977.
Language in Society, April, 1977.
London Review of Books, October 5, 1995, p. 8; November 16, 1995.
Los Angeles Times, November 9, 1989; June 1, 1993, p. E4.
Los Angeles Times Book Review, June 4, 1989; April 13, 1994; November 13, 1994, p. 6; December 17, 1995.
Maclean's, July 18, 1983.
Nation, January 6, 1997, p. 35.
National Review, January 22, 1990.
New Republic, September 5, 1983; November 27, 1989.
New Statesman and Society, December 15, 1989; April 22, 1994.
Newsweek, July 4, 1983; September 26, 1983; September 29, 1986; November 13, 1989.
New Yorker, May 24, 1993, p. 30; August 21-28, 1995, p. 122.
New York Review of Books, July 21, 1983; February 2, 1995; June 9, 1994, p. 24; June 22, 1995, p. 12; April 10, 1997, p. 4.
New York Times, June 4, 1983; December 13, 1988; October 11, 1989; January 9, 1991, p. C15; November 28, 1995, pp. B1-B2.
New York Times Book Review, June 5, 1983; July 17, 1983; October 15, 1989; July 25, 1993, p. 17; October 22, 1995; March 14, 1993, p. 31.
People Weekly, August 29, 1983.
Publishers Weekly, February 24, 1989, p. 232.
San Francisco Review of Books, spring, 1991, pp. 18-19.
Sight and Sound, November, 1994, p. 37.
Spectator, June 12, 1993, pp. 49-50; November 19, 1994, p. 48.
Time, June 13, 1983; March 6, 1989; November 6, 1989.

Times (London), September 29, 1983; November 3, 1983.
Times Literary Supplement, July 8, 1977; March 3, 1989; April 7-13, 1989, p. 380; February 1, 1991, p. 9; December 6, 1991, p. 12; July 30, 1993, p. 8.
UNESCO Courier, June, 1993.
U.S. News and World Report, November 20, 1989.
Village Voice Literary Supplement, October, 1983; November, 1989.
Wall Street Journal, June 20, 1983; November 14, 1989.
Washington Post, October 9, 1983; November 26, 1989.
Washington Post Book World, June 19, 1983; October 29, 1989.

* * *

EDMONDSON, Wallace
    See ELLISON, Harlan (Jay)

* * *

EDWARDS, Eli
    See McKAY, Festus Claudius

* * *

EFRON, Marina Ivanovna Tsvetaeva
    See TSVETAEVA (EFRON), Marina (Ivanovna)

* * *

EHRENREICH, Barbara 1941-

PERSONAL: Born August 26, 1941, in Butte, MT; daughter of Ben Howes and Isabelle Oxley (Isely) Alexander; married John Ehrenreich, August 6, 1966 (marriage ended); married Gary Stevenson, December 10, 1983; children: (first marriage) Rosa, Benjamin. *Education:* Reed College, B.A., 1963; Rockefeller University, Ph.D., 1968. *Politics:* "Socialist and feminist." *Religion:* None.

CAREER: Health Policy Advisory Center, New York City, staff member, 1969-71; State University of New York College at Old Westbury, assistant professor of health sciences, 1971-74; writer, 1974–; *Seven Days* magazine, editor, 1974–; *Mother Jones* magazine, columnist, 1986-89; Time magazine, essayist, 1990; *The Guardian,* London, columnist, 1992–. New York Institute for the Humanities, associate fellow, 1980–; Institute for Policy Studies, fellow, 1982–. Co-chair, Democratic Socialists of America, 1983–.

AWARDS, HONORS: National Magazine award, 1980; Ford Foundation award for Humanistic Perspectives on Contemporary Issues, 1981; Guggenheim fellowship, 1987.

WRITINGS:

(With husband, John Ehrenreich) *Long March, Short Spring: The Student Uprising at Home and Abroad,* Monthly Review Press (New York City), 1969.

(With J. Ehrenreich) *The American Health Empire: Power, Profits, and Politics, a Report from the Health Policy Advisory Center,* Random House (New York City), 1970.

(With Deirdre English) *Witches, Midwives, and Nurses: A History of Women Healers,* Feminist Press (Old Westbury, NY), 1972.

(With English) *Complaints and Disorders: The Sexual Politics of Sickness,* Feminist Press, 1973.

(With English) *For Her Own Good: One Hundred Fifty Years of the Experts' Advice to Women,* Doubleday (New York City), 1978.

The Hearts of Men: American Dreams and the Flight from Commitment, Doubleday, 1983.

(With Annette Fuentes) *Women in the Global Factory* (pamphlet), South End Press (Boston), 1983.

(With Elizabeth Hess and Gloria Jacobs) *Re-making Love: The Feminization of Sex,* Anchor Press/Doubleday, 1986.

(With Fred Block, Richard Cloward, and Frances Fox Piven) *The Mean Season: An Attack on the Welfare State,* Pantheon (New York City), 1987.

Fear of Falling: The Inner Life of the Middle Class, Pantheon, 1989.

The Worst Years of Our Lives: Irreverent Notes from a Decade of Greed, Pantheon, 1990.

Kipper's Game, Farrar, Straus (New York City), 1993.

The Snarling Citizen: Essays, Farrar, Straus, 1995.

Contributor to magazines, including *Radical America, Nation, Esquire, Vogue, New Republic,* and *New York Times Magazine.* Contributing editor, *Ms.,* 1981–, and *Mother Jones,* 1988–.

SIDELIGHTS: An outspoken feminist and socialist party leader, Barbara Ehrenreich crusades for social justice in her books. Although many of her early works were shaped by her formal scientific training—she earned a Ph.D. in biology—her later works have moved beyond health care concerns to the plight of women and the poor. In addition to her numerous nonfiction books, Ehrenreich is widely known for her weekly columns in *Time* and *The Guardian.*

Early in her career, while working for the Health Policy Advisory Center, Ehrenreich published a scathing critique of the American health "empire," exposing its inefficiency, inhumanity, and self-serving policies. Then, turning from the population in general to women in particular, Ehrenreich and her co-author Deirdre English unveiled the male domination of the female health care system in *Complaints and Disorders: The Sexual Politics of Sickness* and *For Her Own Good: One Hundred Fifty Years of the Experts' Advice to Women.* In her most controversial book to date, *The Hearts of Men: American Dreams and the Flight from Commitment,* Ehrenreich takes on the whole male establishment, challenging the assumption that feminism is at the root of America's domestic upheaval.

Describing *The Hearts of Men* as a study of "the ideology that shaped the breadwinner ethic," Ehrenreich surveys the three decades between the 1950s and the 1980s, showing how male commitment to home and family collapsed during this time. "The result," according to *New York Times* contributor Eva Hoffman, "is an original work of cultural iconography that supplements—and often stands on its head—much of the analysis of the relations between the sexes that has become the accepted wisdom of recent years." Ehrenreich's interpretation of the evidence led her to the surprising conclusion that anti-feminism evolved not in response to feminism—but to men's abdication of their breadwinner role.

The seeds of male revolt were planted as far back as the 1950s, according to Ehrenreich, when what she calls "the gray flannel dissidents" began to balk at their myriad responsibilities. "The

gray flannel nightmare of the commuter train and the constant pressure to support a houseful of consumers caused many men to want to run away from it all," Carol Cleaver writes in the *New Leader.* What held these men in check, says Ehrenreich, was the fear that, as bachelors, they would be associated with homosexuality. Hugh Hefner banished that stigma with the publication of *Playboy,* a magazine whose name alone "defied the convention of hard-won maturity," Ehrenreich says in her book. "The magazine's real message was not eroticism, but escape . . . from the bondage of breadwinning."

In the decades that followed, men's increasing "flight from commitment" was sanctioned by pop psychologists and other affiliates of the Human Potential Movement, who banished guilt and encouraged people to "do their own thing." Unfortunately for women, Ehrenreich concludes that men abandoned the breadwinner role "without overcoming the sexist attitudes that role has perpetuated: on the one hand, the expectation of female nurturance and submissive service as a matter of right; on the other hand a misogynist contempt for women as 'parasites' and entrappers of men." In response to male abdication, women increasingly adopted one of two philosophies: they became feminists, committed to achieving economic and social parity with men, or they became anti-feminists, who tried to keep men at home by binding themselves ever more tightly to them. Despite such efforts, Ehrenreich concludes that women have not fared well, but instead have found themselves increasingly on their own "in a society that never intended to admit us as independent persons, much less as breadwinners for others."

Widely reviewed in both magazines and newspapers, *The Hearts of Men* was hailed for its provocative insights—even as individual sections of the study were soundly criticized. In her *Village Voice* review, for instance, Judith Levine is both appreciative of the work and skeptical of its conclusions: "Barbara Ehrenreich—one of the finest feminist-socialist writers around—has written a witty, intelligent book based on intriguing source material. *The Hearts of Men* says something that needs saying: men have not simply reacted to feminism—skulking away from women and children, hurt, humiliated, feeling cheated of their legal and emotional rights. Men, as Ehrenreich observes, have, as always, done what they want to do. . . . I applaud her on-the-mark readings of *Playboy,* medical dogma, and men's liberation; her insistence that the wage system punishes women and children when families disintegrate; her mordant yet uncynical voice. . . . But I believe *The Hearts of Men* is wrong. When she claims that the glue of families is male volition and the breadwinner ideology—and that a change in that ideology caused the breakup of the family—I am doubtful. The ideology supporting men's abdication of family commitment is not new. It has coexisted belligerently with the breadwinner ethic throughout American history."

In the 1986 *Re-making Love: The Feminization of Sex,* co-authored with Elizabeth Hess and Gloria Jacobs, Ehrenreich reports and applauds the freer attitudes towards sex that women adopted in the 1970s and 1980s. The authors assert that women have gained the ability to enjoy sex just for the sake of pleasure, separating it from idealistic notions of love and romance. In her review of *Re-making Love* for the *Chicago Tribune,* Joan Beck noted that the book "is an important summing up of what has happened to women and sex in the last two decades and [that it] shows why the sex revolution requires re-evaluation." Beck, however, argued that the authors ignore the "millions of walking wounded"—those affected by sexually transmitted diseases, unwanted pregnancy, or lack of lasting relationships. *Washington*

Post Book World contributor Anthony Astrachan also expresses a wish for a deeper analysis, but nevertheless finds *Re-making Love* "full of sharp and sometimes surprising insights that come from looking mass culture full in the face."

Ehrenreich's next work to attract critical notice, *Fear of Falling: The Inner Life of the Middle Class,* examines the American middle class and its attitudes towards people of the working and poorer classes. Jonathan Yardley writes in the *Washington Post* that what Ehrenreich actually focuses on is a class "composed of articulate, influential people. . . . in fact what most of us think of as the upper-middle class." According to Ehrenreich this group perceives itself as threatened, is most concerned with self-preservation, and has isolated itself—feeling little obligation to work for the betterment of society. This attitude, Ehrenreich maintains, is occurring at a time when the disparity in income between classes has reached the greatest point since World War II and has become "almost as perilously skewed as that of India," Joseph Coates quotes from *Fear of Falling* in *Tribune Books.*

Globe and Mail contributor Maggie Helwig, though praising the book as "witty, clever, [and] perceptive," describes as unrealistic Ehrenreich's hope for a future when everyone could belong to the professional middle class and hold fulfilling jobs. Similarly, David Rieff remarks in the *Los Angeles Times Book Review* that Ehrenreich's proposed solutions to class polarization are overly optimistic and tend to romanticize the nature of work. "Nonetheless," Rieff concludes, "'Fear of Falling' is a major accomplishment, a breath of fresh thinking about a subject that very few writers have known how to think about at all." The book elicited even higher praise from Coates, who deems it "a brilliant social analysis and intellectual history, quite possibly the best on this subject since Tocqueville's."

In *The Worst Years of Our Lives: Irreverent Notes from a Decade of Greed,* Ehrenreich discusses in a series of reprinted articles what some consider to be one of the most self-involved and consumeristic decades in American history: the 1980s. Most of these articles first appeared in *Mother Jones,* but some come from such periodicals as *Nation, Atlantic, New York Times,* and *New Republic.* Together, they summarize "what Ms. Ehrenreich sees as the decade's salient features: blathering ignorance, smug hypocrisy, institutionalized fraud and vengeful polarization—all too dangerous to be merely absurd," says H. Jack Geiger in the *New York Times Book Review.* "One of Mrs. Ehrenreich's main themes," observes *New York Times* reviewer Herbert Mitgang, ". . . is that the Reagan Administration, which dominated the last decade, cosmeticized the country and painted over its true condition. The author writes that the poor and middle class are now suffering the results of deliberate neglect."

The Snarling Citizen: Essays collects fifty-seven previously published essays, most of which Ehrenreich contributed to *Time* and *The Guardian.* The essays once again reveal the author's passion for social justice and feminism. Although some reviewers take exception with Ehrenreich's opinions in these pieces, nearly all lavish praise on her well-honed writing style. Writing in the Chicago *Tribune Books,* for example, Penelope Mesic remarks that the pieces in *The Snarling Citizen* "startle and invigorate because those who espouse liberal causes—feminism, day care and a strong labor movement—all too often write a granola: a mild, beige substance that is, in a dull way, good for us. Ehrenreich is peppery and salacious, bitter with scorn, hotly lucid." *Women's Review of Books* contributor Nan Levinson commends the author for her "writing, a hymn to pithiness and

wit, and her ear, attuned to the ways in which language redefined becomes thought reconstructed and politics realigned." Andrew Ferguson, however, commenting in the *American Spectator,* takes issue with what he calls the author's habit of building entire essays around "casual misstatements" of fact. In addition, while conceding that Ehrenreich "knows that caricature can be a verbal art," Ferguson maintains that "too often her fondness for exaggeration and hyperbole drags her into mere buffoonery." While noting that the collection's pieces are all so similar in "size, . . . voice and essentially . . . subject" that they "resemble a box of Fig Newtons," Levinson declares: "Ehrenreich is a rare thing in American public life today—a freelance thinker."

Although she has long been known as a journalist and social critic, Ehrenreich in 1993 published her first novel, *Kipper's Game.* Part science fiction novel and part thriller, the work is "set in a futuristic world that bears a decided resemblance to the present-day United States," explains *New York Times* critic Michiko Kakutani. This world features decaying cities plagued by foliage-eating caterpillars, hazardous waste, and unscrupulous computer companies. The complex plot involves Della Markson's search for her missing son, Kipper, a young computer hacker who mysteriously disappears after he creates a revolutionary computer game.

The novel elicited mixed reviews from critics. Kakutani, for instance, remarks that "Unfortunately, little of the irreverent wit that animates Ms. Ehrenreich's essays is in evidence in these pages." He does, however, commend those instances where the author describes scenes of "ordinary life." Reviewing the novel for *New Statesman & Society,* however, Vicky Hutchings avers that "*Kipper's Game* is . . . sharp and funny, in a dry sort of way. Sometimes the observations make your hair stand on end." In an interview with Wendy Smith for *Publishers Weekly,* Ehrenreich commented on her reasons for writing about a wide variety of subjects and moving between nonfiction and fiction: "People have sometimes thought I was a sociologist or a historian, but since I have no formal education in any of these things, I'm not tied to a discipline, so I can rampage through any kind of material I want."

BIOGRAPHICAL/CRITICAL SOURCES:

PERIODICALS

American Spectator, August, 1995, p. 66.
Chicago Tribune, September 25, 1986.
Globe and Mail (Toronto), August 26, 1986.
Humanist, January-February, 1992, p. 11.
Los Angeles Times, July 24, 1983.
Los Angeles Times Book Review, August 20, 1989.
Ms., May-June, 1995, p. 75.
Nation, December 24, 1983.
New Leader, July 11, 1983.
New Republic, July 11, 1983.
New Statesman & Society, May 17, 1991, p. 37, May 20, 1994, p. 37.
New York Review of Books, July 1, 1971.
New York Times, January 20, 1971; August 16, 1983; May 16, 1990; July 13, 1993, p. C18.
New York Times Book Review, March 7, 1971; June 5, 1983; August 6, 1989; May 20, 1990, August 8, 1993, p. 18; May 28, 1996, p. 12.
New York Times Magazine, June 26, 1996, p. 28.
Progressive, January, 1995, p. 47; February, 1995, p. 34.
Publishers Weekly, July 26, 1993, p. 46.
Time, May 7, 1990.
Times Literary Supplement, July 22, 1977.

Tribune Books (Chicago), November 8, 1987; September 24, 1989; May 13, 1990; May 28, 1995, p. 3.
Utne Reader, May-June, 1995, p. 70.
Village Voice, February 5, 1979; August 23, 1983.
Washington Post, August 23, 1989.
Washington Post Book World, August 19, 1979; July 24, 1983; November 9, 1986.
Whole Earth Review, winter, 1995, p. 86.
Women's Review of Books, October, 1995, p. 25.

*   *   *

EINSTEIN, Albert 1879-1955

PERSONAL: Born March 14, 1879, in Ulm, Germany; naturalized Swiss citizen, 1901; immigrated to United States, 1933, naturalized citizen, 1940; died of a ruptured aorta, April 18, 1955, in Princeton, NJ; son of Hermann and Pauline (Koch) Einstein; married Mileva Maric, 1903 (divorced, 1919); married cousin, Elsa Einstein Lowenthal, 1919 (died, 1936); children: (first marriage) Hans Albert, Edward. *Education:* Graduated from Swiss Federal Institute of Technology, 1901; University of Zurich, Ph.D., 1905. *Avocation:* Playing the violin, sailing.

CAREER: Theoretical physicist, peace activist, and writer. Teacher at Winterthur Technical School, 1901; Swiss Patent Office, Bern, Switzerland, technical assistant, 1902-09; University of Bern, Bern, lecturer, 1908-09; University of Zurich, Zurich, Switzerland, associate professor of physics, 1909-11; German University, Prague, Czechoslovakia, professor of physics, 1911-12; Swiss Federal Institute of Technology, Zurich, professor of physics, 1912-14; University of Berlin, Berlin, Germany, professor of physics, 1914-c. 1932; Kaiser Wilhelm Institute for Physics, Berlin, director, 1914-c. 1932; Institute for Advanced Study, Princeton University, Princeton, NJ, professor of theoretical physics, 1933-45, life member, 1933-55. Herbert Spencer Lecturer at Oxford University, 1933. Participated in World Government Movement.

MEMBER: Prussian Academy of Sciences, Royal Society (fellow), French Academy of Sciences (fellow).

AWARDS, HONORS: Nobel Prize in physics, 1921; named first honorary citizen of Tel Aviv, 1923; Copley Medal, Royal Society of London, 1925; Gold Medal, Royal Astronomical Society, London, 1926; Franklin Institute Medal, 1935; offered presidency of Israel, 1952 (declined); received honorary degrees from Universities of Geneva, Zurich, Rostock, Madrid, Brussels, Buenos Aires, Paris, London, Glasgow, Leeds, and Manchester, and Cambridge, Oxford, Harvard, Princeton, New York State, and Yeshiva Universities.

WRITINGS:

PHYSICS

Eine neue Bestimmung der Molekueldimensionen, K. J. Wyss (Bern), 1905.
(With Marcel Grossman) *Entwurf einer verallgemeinerten Relativitaetstheorie und eine Theorie der Gravitation,* Teubner (Leipzig), 1913.
Die Grundlage der allgemeinen Relativitaetstheorie, J. A. Barth (Leipzig), 1916 (also see below).
Ueber die spezielle und allgemeine Relativitaetstheorie, gemeinverstaendlich, F. Vieweg (Braunschweig), 1917, translation by Robert W. Lawson published as *Relativity: The Special and General Theory,* Holt, 1920, 17th edition, Crown, 1961.

(With H. Minkowski) *The Principle of Relativity* (includes *Die Grundlage der allgemeinen Relativitaetstheorie*), translated by M. N. Saha and S. N. Bose, introduction by P. C. Mahalanobis, University of Calcutta, 1920.
Aether und Relativitaetstheorie, J. Springer (Berlin), 1920 (also see below).
Geometrie und Erfahrung, J. Springer, 1921 (also see below).
Sidelights on Relativity (contains translations by G. B. Jeffery and W. Perrett of *Aether und Relativitaetstheorie* and *Geometrie und Erfahrung*), Methuen, 1922, Dutton, 1923.
The Meaning of Relativity: Four Lectures Delivered at Princeton University, translated by Edwin Plimpton Adams, Methuen, 1922, Princeton University Press, 1923, 5th edition, 1955, revised edition, Methuen, 1956.
Untersuchjungen ueber die Theorie der Brownschen Bewegung, Akademische Verlagsgesellschaft (Leipzig), 1922, translation by A. D. Cowper published as *Investigations on the Theory of the Brownian Movement,* edited with notes by R. Furth, Methuen, 1926, Dover, 1956.
On the Method of Theoretical Physics, Oxford University Press, 1933 (also see below).
The Origins of the General Theory of Relativity, Jackson, Wylie (Glasgow), 1933 (also see below).
(With Leopold Infeld) *The Evolution of Physics: The Growth of Ideas From Early Concepts to Relativity and Quanta,* Simon & Schuster, 1938, new edition, 1967.
The Theory of Relativity, and Other Essays, Carol Publishing (Secaucus, NJ), 1950; also published as *Essays in Physics,* Citadel Press.
Grundzuge der Relativitaetstheorie, F. Vieweg, 1956.
(With Erwin Schroedinger, Max Planck, and H. A. Lorentz) *Letters on Wave Mechanics: Schroedinger, Planck, Einstein, Lorentz,* edited by K. Przibram, translated by Martin J. Klein, Philosophical Library, 1967.
Einstein's 1912 Manuscript on the Special Theory of Relativity: A Facsimile, George Braziller (New York City), 1996.

Also author of *The Unitary Field Theory,* 1929, and *Builders of the Universe,* 1932.

OTHER

About Zionism (speeches and letters), translated and edited with an introduction by Leon Simon, Soncino Press, 1930, Macmillan, 1931.
Cosmic Religion, Covici-Friede (New York), 1931.
(With others) *Living Philosophies,* Simon & Schuster, 1931.
The Fight Against War, edited by Alfred Lief, John Day Company (New York), 1933.
(With Sigmund Freud) *Why War?,* International Institute of Intellectual Cooperation, League of Nations, 1933.
Mein Weltbild (essays; also see below), Querido Verlag (Amsterdam), 1934, translation by Alan Harris published as *The World As I See It* (includes *On the Method of Theoretical Physics* and *The Origins of the General Theory of Relativity*), Covici-Friede, 1934, abridged edition, Philosophical Library, 1949.
Test Case for Humanity, Jewish Agency for Palestine (London), 1944.
(With Eric Kahler) *The Arabs and Palestine,* Christian Council on Palestine and American Palestine Committee (New York), 1944.
(With others) *Albert Einstein: Philosopher-Scientist,* edited by Paul Arthur Schilpp, Library of Living Philosophers (Evanston, IL), 1949 (also see below).
Essays in Humanism, Philosophical Library, 1950.

Out of My Later Years (essays), Philosophical Library, 1950, revised edition, Greenwood Press, 1970.

Ideas and Opinions (based on *Mein Weltbild*), edited by Carl Seelig, Crown, 1954, third edition, Crown (New York City), 1995.

Essays in Science (selected essays from *Mein Weltbild*), Philosophical Library, 1955.

Lettres a Maurice Solovine, Gauthier-Villars (Paris), 1956, translation published as *Letters to Solovine,* introduction by Maurice Solovine, Philosophical Library, 1987.

Einstein on Peace, edited by Otto Nathan and Heinz Norden, preface by Bertrand Russell, Simon & Schuster, 1960.

(With Arnold Sommerfeld) *Briefwechsel: 60 Briefe aus dem goldenen Zeitalter der modernen Physik,* Schwabe (Stuttgart), 1968.

(With Max and Hedwig Born) *Briefwechsel, 1916-1955,* Nymphenburger Verlagshandlung (Munich), 1969, translation by Irene Born published as *The Born-Einstein Letters: Correspondence Between Albert Einstein and Max and Hedwig Born From 1916 to 1955,* Walker, 1971.

Albert Einstein, the Human Side: New Glimpses From His Archives, selected and edited by Helen Dukas and Banesh Hoffmann, Princeton University Press, 1979.

Autobiographical Notes (first published in *Albert Einstein: Philosopher-Scientist*), translated and edited by Paul Arthur Schilpp, Open Court, 1979.

Einstein: A Centenary Volume, edited by A. P. French, Harvard University Press, 1979.

(With Elie Cartan) *Elie Cartan-Albert Einstein: Letters on Absolute Parallelism, 1929-1932,* translated by Jules Leroy and Jim Ritter, edited by Robert Debever, Princeton University Press, 1979.

Some Strangeness in the Proportion: A Centennial Symposium to Celebrate the Achievements of Albert Einstein, edited by Harry Woolf, Addison-Wesley, Advanced Book Program, 1980.

The Collected Papers of Albert Einstein, Princeton University Press, 1987-1995, Volume 1: *The Early Years: 1879-1901,* edited by John Stachel, Volume 2: *The Swiss Years: Writings, 1900-1909,* Volume 3: *The Swiss Years: Writings, 1909-1911,* Volume 4: *The Swiss Years: Writings, 1912-1914,* Volume 5: *The Swiss Years: Correspondence, 1902-1914,* edited by Martin J. Klein, A. J. Kox, and Robert Schulmann.

Albert Einstein/Mileva Maric: The Love Letters, Princeton University Press (Princeton, NJ), 1992.

Essential Einstein, Pomegranate Artbooks (San Francisco), 1995.

The Quotable Einstein, edited by Alice Calaprice, Princeton University Press (Princeton, NJ), 1996.

SIDELIGHTS: Albert Einstein is generally considered the greatest scientist of the twentieth century. Creator of the theory of relativity and recipient of a Nobel Prize, the theoretical physicist is acclaimed for revolutionizing the world's understanding of space, time, and matter. Einstein is also revered for his longtime commitment to pacifism, but it is for his pioneering research on laws governing the physical universe that he will be most remembered. According to historians, Einstein's achievements in physics place him among the ranks of scientists Archimedes, Galileo Galilei, and Isaac Newton.

Born to Jewish parents in Ulm, Germany, Einstein grew up in Munich, where his father operated a small electrochemical plant. A rebellious student, he resisted the stringent discipline of German schools and instead indulged in independent readings of philosophy, math, and science. When his father's business failed in 1895, the family moved to Milan, leaving Einstein behind to finish his education. The student, though, soon quit school to join his family in Italy. Enjoying there a short period of unstructured learning, Einstein taught himself calculus and higher scientific principles. Despite his advanced intelligence, he failed an entrance examination to the Swiss Federal Institute of Technology in Zurich. Dedicating the following year to preparation, Einstein retook the examination and earned acceptance in 1896. At the Institute he studied physics and mathematics, graduating in 1901 and becoming a Swiss citizen.

Einstein significantly nurtured his profound understanding of science while working at the Swiss Patent Office in Bern as a technical assistant. Relishing the job's relatively undemanding work, he was able to concentrate on his own theoretical scientific investigations. Einstein described such subjects as capillarity, intermolecular forces, and applications of statistical thermodynamics in a number of papers, one of which was accepted in 1905 as a doctoral dissertation at the University of Zurich. Other papers produced that same year would distinguish him as a preeminent thinker among scientists of his day.

One significant document of this time illustrates Einstein's theory concerning Brownian motion, the random movement of particles suspended in liquid. By observing liquid under a microscope, Einstein determined that the particle motion was caused by collisions with unseen molecules, thus verifying for the first time the existence of molecules. Another major paper published in 1905 described Einstein's revolutionary research into light, which he determined was dualistic in its ability to exist as either a wave or a particle. Theorizing that light energy travels in discrete packets of photons, or quanta, Einstein helped shape the modern quantum theory of light and furthered research on the nature of matter and the molecular process.

While these discoveries significantly advanced the science of physics, they are considered minor when compared to Einstein's major proposal of 1905, his theory of special relativity. Discarding the existing concept that time and space are absolute, the theory proposes that time and space vary with circumstances and can only be measured relative to two systems or frames of reference. Mind-bending postulates of this discovery theorize that time slows down for a moving body, nothing can travel faster than light, and all objects become more massive as they seem to travel faster.

Following the publication of his findings, Einstein received substantial academic attention. He worked as a professor of physics at universities in Zurich and Czechoslovakia before returning to Germany in 1914 to become a professor at the University of Berlin and director of the Kaiser Wilhelm Institute for Physics. Despite his opposition to the German cause during World War I at this time—adopting instead a stance of pacifism—Einstein restored his German citizenship and was elected a member of the prestigious Prussian Academy of Sciences. This secure professional stature allowed the physicist to devote time and money toward scientific research.

In 1915 Einstein produced significant discoveries that expanded his 1905 theory of special relativity. In what he termed the general theory of relativity, Einstein, upon observing the behavior of light as it reacts to gravitational forces in the universe, was able to postulate that energy and mass interact in a four-dimensional continuum called space-time. Summed up in the now well-known equation "energy equals mass times the speed of light squared," this theory, according to John Maddox writing in the *Washington*

Post Book World, "provided for the first time a way of calculating how the universe behaves." Additional related discoveries by Einstein include his theory of an expanding universe, in which the physicist reconciled seemingly conflicting notions of finite mass and infinite space. His findings were published in such books as *The Principle of Relativity, Sidelights on Relativity,* and *The Meaning of Relativity.*

Einstein's brilliant scientific findings earned him the 1921 Nobel Prize for physics, among other prestigious prizes. Although he had attained worldwide admiration, he came under increasing attack in Germany for his continued commitment to pacifism and for his scientific theories that conflicted with those of other prominent German scientists. Einstein nevertheless persisted in his independent studies of physics and continued to espouse pacifist causes, including supporting the peace efforts of the League of Nations and becoming a spokesperson for Zionist issues. Eventually, though, he was unable to reconcile his humanitarianism with the rising fascist ideals and militant nationalism permeating German culture; Einstein left his country, and, in so doing, avoided the 1933 rise to power of Nazi leader Adolf Hitler.

Einstein settled permanently in Princeton, New Jersey, where he became a professor of theoretical physics at the Institute for Advanced Study. While he continued intense scientific investigations, he remained active in propagating pacifist ideals, producing such books as *The Fight Against War* and, with Austrian psychoanalyst Sigmund Freud, *Why War?* At the onset of World War II, however, Einstein realized the importance of thwarting German expansion and, reluctantly concluding that U.S. military superiority was essential, appealed to President Franklin D. Roosevelt to step up nuclear fission research. The scientist, though, played no role in subsequent developments of the atomic bomb and was ultimately horrified by the United States's atomic bombing of Japan during the closing months of World War II. He consequently renewed his pacifist position, arduously campaigning for the abolition of war and controlled development of nuclear arms in order to ensure the survival of humanity.

Following World War II, Einstein produced a number of books reflecting his firm commitment to world peace, including *Essays in Humanism* and *Ideas and Opinions.* While his later years seem to have been dominated by political activism, Einstein remained dedicated to furthering his understanding of the universe through science. "Equations are more important to me," the scientist was quoted by Stephen W. Hawking in *A Brief History of Time.* "Politics is for the present, but an equation is something for eternity." Einstein spent the final thirty years of his life in pursuit of what he called a grand unified theory of physics. Striving to develop a model of nature that would express the properties of matter and energy in a single formula, Einstein was ultimately unsuccessful. He died in 1955 at the age of seventy-six.

Since his death, many of Einstein's writings, both personal and professional, have been published. Many of these are found in the five-volume *Collected Papers of Albert Einstein,* published between 1987 and 1995. Among the collections of private letters published are *Letters to Solovine, Elie Cartan-Albert Einstein: Letters on Absolute Parallelism, 1929-1932,* and *Albert Einstein/ Mileva Maric—The Love Letters.* The latter volume, published in 1992, contains fifty-four letters exchanged by Einstein and his first wife, Mileva Maric, between 1897 and 1903. All but eleven of the letters were written by Einstein. As Carol Anshaw explained in *Voice Literary Supplement,* the letters "stop just two years before Einstein's annus mirabilis, the year (1905) in which,

at 26, he would introduce three startling concepts-light quanta; Brownian motion; . . . and the special theory of relativity, his revolution of the notions of space and time." Critics noted that these letters provide little insight into the genius behind Einstein's achievements; rather, the letters reveal a young man grappling with love, courtship, marriage, and quotidian concerns such as finding a job. Although *Times Literary Supplement* reviewer Michael Neve commented that "eleven short letters cannot allow for any quick unlocking of the secrets of Mileva Maric's personality," Robert Kanigel of the *New York Times Book Review* remarked that "it's plain from this correspondence that theirs was an intellectual bond as well as a physical and emotional one."

When once asked what motivated his relentless quest for scientific truth, Einstein, as quoted by Ronald W. Clark in *Einstein: The Life and Times,* replied: "The important thing is not to stop questioning. . . . Curiosity has its own reason for existence. One cannot help but be in awe when [one] contemplates the mysteries of eternity, of life, of the marvelous structure of reality. It is enough if one tries merely to comprehend a little of this mystery each day. Never lose a holy curiosity."

BIOGRAPHICAL/CRITICAL SOURCES:

BOOKS

Bernstein, *Albert Einstein,* Oxford University Press (New York City), 1996.
Bernstein, Jeremy, *Albert Einstein and the Frontiers of Physics,* Oxford University Press (New York City), 1996.
Bharucha, Filita P., *Buddhist Theory of Causation and Einstein's Theory of Relativity,* Sri Satguru (Delhi, India), 1992.
Born, Max, *Einstein's Theory of Relativity,* Dover, 1962.
Brian, Denis, *Einstein: A Life,* J. Wiley (New York City), 1995.
Bucky, Peter A., *The Private Albert Einstein,* Andrews and McMeel (Kansas City), 1992.
Calaprice, Alice, editor, *The Quotable Einstein,* Princeton University Press, 1996.
Cassidy, David C., *Einstein and Our World,* Humanities Press (Atlantic Highlands, NJ), 1995.
Charpa, Ulrich, *Albert Einstein,* Campus Verlag (New York City), 1993.
Clark, Ronald W., *Einstein: The Life and Times,* World Publishing Company, 1971, Wings Books (New York City), 1995.
Davies, P.C.W., *About Time: Einstein's Unfinished Revolution,* Simon & Schuster (New York City), 1995.
Elkana, Yehuda, *Albert Einstein: Historical and Cultural Perspectives: The Centennial Symposium in Jerusalem,* edited by Gerald Holton, Dover Publications, 1997.
Fine, Arthur, *The Shaky Game: Einstein, Realism, and the Quantum Theory,* University of Chicago Press, 1986, second edition, 1997.
Finkelstein, David, *Quantum Relativity: A Synthesis of the Ideas of Einstein and Heisenberg,* Springer-Verlag (New York City), 1996.
Folsing, Albrecht, *Albert Einstein: A Biography,* translated from the German by Ewald Osers, Viking (New York City), 1997.
Friedman, Alan J. and Carol C. Donley, *Einstein as Myth and Muse,* Cambridge University Press, 1985.
Goldenstern, Joyce, *Albert Einstein, Physicist and Genius,* Enslow (Springfield, NJ), 1995.
Goldman, Robert N., *Einstein's God: Albert Einstein's Quest As a Scientist and As a Jew to Replace a Forsaken God,* Jason Aronson (Northvale, NJ), 1997.
Goldsmith, Maurice and other editors, *Einstein: The First Hundred Years,* Pergamon Press, 1980.

Hawking, Stephen W., *A Brief History of Time: From the Big Bang to Black Holes,* Bantam, 1988.

Hentschel, Klaus, *The Einstein Tower: An Intertexture of Dynamic Construction, Relativity Theory, and Astronomy,* translated by Ann M. Hentschel, Stanford University Press (Stanford, CA), 1997.

Hermanns, William, *Einstein and the Poet: In Search of the Cosmic Man,* Branden Press, 1983.

Hey, Tony and Patrick Walters, *Einstein's Mirror,* Cambridge University Press (New York City), 1996.

Highfield, Roger, *The Private Lives of Albert Einstein,* St. Martin's Griffin (New York City), 1995.

Holton, Gerald James, *Einstein, History, and Other Passions,* AIP (Woodbury, NY), 1995, Addison-Wesley (Reading, MA), 1996.

Kaufmann, Ronald, *Albert Einstein's Magic: Envisioning, Interpreting, Entertaining,* Heridonius Enlightened Light (Las Vegas), 1995.

Lightman, Alan P., *Einstein's Dreams,* Pantheon (New York City), 1993.

MacDonald, Fiona, *The World in the Time of Albert Einstein,* Dillon Press, 1998.

McPherson, Stephanie Sammartino, *Ordinary Genius: The Story of Albert Einstein,* Carolrhoda Books (Minneapolis), 1995.

Miller, Arthur I., *Albert Einstein's Special Theory of Relativity: Emergence (1905) and Early Interpretation, 1905-1911,* Springer (New York City), 1997.

Morrison, Roy Dennis, *Science, Theology, and the Transcendental Horizon: Einstein, Kant, and Tillich,* Scholars Press (Atlanta), 1994.

Pais, Abraham, *Subtle Is the Lord: The Science and Life of Albert Einstein,* Oxford University Press, 1982.

Pais, *Einstein Lived Here: Essays for the Layman,* Oxford University Press (New York City), 1994.

Parker, Steve, *Albert Einstein and Relativity,* Chelsea House (New York City), 1995.

Swisher, Clarice, *Relativity: Opposing Viewpoints,* Greenhaven Press (San Diego), 1990.

Swisher, *Albert Einstein,* Lucent (San Diego), 1994.

Whitaker, Andrew, *Einstein, Bohr, and the Quantum Dilemma,* Cambridge University Press (Cambridge, NY), 1996.

White, Michael, *Einstein: A Life in Science,* Dutton (New York City), 1994.

PERIODICALS

New York Times, April 19, 1955.

New York Times Book Review, September 27, 1987; July 19, 1992, p. 15.

Science, May 18, 1990, p. 878; November 9, 1990, p. 770.

Science Digest, February, 1979.

Scientific American, January, 1994, p. 26.

Time, February 19, 1979; April 30, 1990, p. 108.

Times Literary Supplement, January 15, 1970; July 17, 1992, p. 11.

Voice Literary Supplement, April, 1993, p. 22.

Washington Post, March 8, 1990.

Washington Post Book World, March 25, 1979.

*   *   *

EKWENSI, C. O. D.
See EKWENSI, Cyprian (Odiatu Duaka)

EKWENSI, Cyprian (Odiatu Duaka) 1921-
(C. O. D. Ekwensi)

PERSONAL: Born September 26, 1921, in Minna, Nigeria; son of Ogbuefi David Duaka and Uso Agnes Ekwensi; married Eunice Anyiwo; children: five. *Education:* Attended Achimota College, Ghana, and Ibadan University; received B.A.; further study at Chelsea School of Pharmacy, London, and University of Iowa. *Avocation:* Hunting game, swimming, photography, motoring, weightlifting.

ADDRESSES: Home—12 Hillview, Independence Layout, P.O. Box 317, Enugu, Anambra, Nigeria.

CAREER: Novelist and writer of short stories and stories for children. Igbodi College, Lagos, Nigeria, lecturer in biology, chemistry, and English, 1947-49; School of Pharmacy, Lagos, lecturer in pharmacognosy and pharmaceutics, 1949-56; pharmacist superintendent for Nigerian Medical Services, 1956-57; head of features, Nigerian Broadcasting Corporation, 1957-61; Federal Ministry of Information, Lagos, director of information, 1961-66; chairman of Bureau for External Publicity during Biafran secession, 1967-69, and director of an independent Biafran radio station; chemist for plastics firm in Enugu, Nigeria; managing director of Star Printing & Publishing Co. (publishers of *Daily Star*), 1975-79; managing director of Niger Eagle Publishing Company, 1980-81; managing director of Ivory Trumpet Publishing Co. Ltd., 1981-83. Owner of East Niger Chemists and East Niger Trading Company. Chairman of East Central State Library Board, 1972-75. Newspaper consultant to *Weekly Trumpet* and *Daily News* of Anambra State and to *Weekly Eagle* of Imo State, 1980-83; consultant on information to the executive office of the president; consultant to Federal Ministry of Information; public relations consultant.

MEMBER: PEN, Society of Nigerian Authors, Pharmaceutical Society of Great Britain, Institute of Public Relations (London), Institute of Public Relations (Nigeria; fellow).

AWARDS, HONORS: Dag Hammarskjold International Prize for Literary Merit, 1969.

WRITINGS:

NOVELS

People of the City, Andrew Dakers, 1954, Northwestern University Press, 1967, revised edition, Fawcett, 1969.

Jagua Nana, Hutchinson, 1961.

Burning Grass, Heinemann, 1962.

Beautiful Feathers, Hutchinson, 1963.

Divided We Stand, Fourth Dimension Publishers, 1980.

JUVENILE

(Under name C. O. D. Ekwensi) *Ikolo the Wrestler and Other Ibo Tales,* Thomas Nelson, 1947.

(Under name C. O. D. Ekwensi) *The Leopard's Claw,* Thomas Nelson, 1950.

The Drummer Boy, Cambridge University Press, 1960.

The Passport of Mallam Ilia, Cambridge University Press, 1960.

An African Night's Entertainment (folklore), African Universities Press, 1962.

Yaba Roundabout Murder (short novel), Tortoise Series Books (Lagos, Nigeria), 1962.

The Great Elephant-Bird, Thomas Nelson, 1965.

Juju Rock, African Universities Press, 1966.

The Boa Suitor, Thomas Nelson, 1966.

Trouble in Form Six, Cambridge University Press, 1966.

Coal Camp Boy, Longman, 1971.

Samankwe in the Strange Forest, Longman, 1973.

The Rainbow Tinted Scarf and Other Stories (collection), Evans Africa Library, 1975.

Samankwe and the Highway Robbers, Evans Africa Library, 1975.

Masquerade Time, Heinemann Educational Books, 1992.

King Forever!, Heinemann Educational Books, 1992.

OTHER

(Under name C. O. D. Ekwensi) *When Love Whispers* (novella), Tabansi Bookshop (Onitsha, Nigeria), 1947.

The Rainmaker and Other Short Stories (short story collection), African Universities Press, 1965.

Lokotown and Other Stories (short story collection), Heinemann, 1966.

Iska, Hutchinson, 1966.

The Restless City and Christmas Gold, Heinemann, 1975.

Survive the Peace, Heinemann, 1976.

(Editor) *Festac Anthology of Nigerian Writing,* Festac, 1977.

Motherless Baby (novella), Fourth Dimension Publishers, 1980.

For a Roll of Parchment, Heinemann, 1987.

Jagua Nana's Daughter, Spectrum, 1987.

Gone to Mecca, Heinemann, 1991.

Also author of *Behind the Convent Wall,* 1987. Writer of plays and scripts for BBC radio and television, Radio Nigeria, and other communication outlets. Contributor of stories, articles, and reviews to magazines and newspapers in Nigeria and England, including *West African Review, London Times, Black Orpheus, Flamingo,* and *Sunday Post.* Several of Ekwensi's novels have been translated into other languages, including Russian, Italian, German, Serbo-Croatian, Danish, and French. His novellas have been used primarily in schools as supplementary readers.

SIDELIGHTS: "Cyprian Ekwensi is the earliest and most prolific of the socially realistic Nigerian novelists," according to Martin Tucker in his *Africa in Modern Literature: A Survey of Contemporary Writing in English.* "His first writings were mythological fragments and folk tales. From these African materials he turned to the city and its urban problems, which he now feels are the major issues confronting his people." Reviewing Cyprian Ekwensi's *Beautiful Feathers* in *Critique: Studies in Modern Fiction,* John F. Povey writes: "The very practice of writing, the developing professionalism of his work, makes us find in Ekwensi a new and perhaps important phenomenon in African writing. . . . Other Nigerian novelists have sought their material from the past, the history of missionaries and British administration as in Chinua Achebe's books and the schoolboy memoirs of Onuora Nzekwu. Ekwensi faces the difficult task of catching the present tone of Africa, changing at a speed that frighteningly destroys the old certainties. In describing this world, Ekwensi has gradually become a significant writer."

Born in Northern Nigeria in 1921, Ekwensi grew up in various cities and had ample opportunity to observe what one critic called the "urban politics" of Nigeria. He went to schools in Ibadan, Lagos, and the Gold Coast, excelling in English, mathematics, and science; a high school record indicates that only his temper and occasional sullen moods kept him from being the ideal student. In the early 1940s he enrolled at the School of Forestry in Western Nigeria; successfully completing his degree requirements in 1944, he began his work as a forestry officer. According to biographer Ernest Emenyonu, "it was . . . while wandering in the domains of animals and trees that ekwensi decided to become a writer. Taking advantage of his wild and lonely environment he began to create

adventure stories with forest backgrounds." Among his early works are the short stories "Banana Peel," "The Tinted Scarf," and "Land of Sani," which he published together with a collection of Igbo folk tales under the title *Ikolo the Wrestler and Other Ibo Tales* in 1947. Other early works include *When Love Whispers* and *The Leopard's Claw;* he also published several adventure stories for children. In addition to being a professional writer, Ekwensi has worked as a pharmacist and a teacher. Most recently he has been involved with the Nigerian Broadcasting Corporation and various newspaper and publishing organizations.

Despite his popularity as folklorist and writer of children's literature, Ekwensi's fans frequently cite his urban novels as their favorites. *People of the City, Jagua Nana, Beautiful Feathers,* and *Iska* are all set in the city of Lagos, and according to Juliet Okonkwo, Ekwensi "revels in the excitement of city life and loves to expose its many faces of modernity. He writes about . . . its criminals, prostitutes, band-leaders, ministers of state, businessmen, civil servants, professionals, policemen on duty, thugs, thieves, and many other types that are found in the city. . . . Employing a naturalistic narrative technique reminiscent of Emile Zola, Ekwensi has been able to capture both the restless excitement and the frustrations of life in the city." *Burning Grass: A Story of the Fulani of Northern Nigeria* and *Survive the Peace* are exceptions to his "city novels." The former centers on Mai Sunsaye, a Fulani cattleman living on the grassy plains of Nigeria, and the latter on James Oduga, a radio journalist who tries to rebuild his life after a war.

Of Ekwensi's city novels, *Jagua Nana* is considered his best work. It focuses on Jagua Nana, an aging prostitute who thrives on Lagos nightlife—"They called her Jagua because of her good looks and stunning fashions. They said she was Ja-gwa, after the famous British prestige car." When the novel opens she is in love with Freddie Namme, an ambitious young teacher. She continues to sleep with other men for money, to Freddie's dismay, because she wants to "wear fine cloth": "She loved Freddie well, but his whole salary would not buy that dress. He must understand that taking money from the Syrian did not mean that she loved him less." Freddie claims to despise Jagua's lifestyle but doesn't refuse the luxuries that her income provides. Seeking consolation, Freddie has an affair with a younger woman, but before Jagua can unleash her jealous rage, he leaves for England. When Jagua and Freddie meet again, Freddie is running for office against Uncle Taiwo, a large, crass, power-hungry politician "who has chosen to absorb and use all that is worst in European ways," according to critic John Povey. The novel ends with Freddie and Uncle Taiwo both murdered and Jagua fleeing Lagos for her life. "Through Jagua, her career, her pursuits and her fluctuating fortune," Okonkwo observed, "Ekwensi reveals the common wickedness, squalor, materialism and immorality of the city, together with its crimes and violence." Since its publication in 1961, *Jagua Nana* has attracted bitter controversy. Church organizations and women's groups vehemently attacked it, prompting some schools to ban it from their libraries. The Nigerian Parliament refused an Italian studio's request to film the book. Some readers called it "obscene" and "pornographic," while others praised it as a masterpiece. Similarly, literary critics were equally divided in their opinions: some were impressed with *Jagua Nana,* particularly by Ekwensi's use of language and depth of characterization, but others dismissed it as another "whore-with-a-heart-of-gold" story commonly found in bad American movies and books.

Controversy appears to follow all of Ekwensi's fiction; while *Jagua Nana* has received the most attention, his other books have also been scrutinized. Assessing Ekwensi as a writer, critic Bernth Lindfors declared: "not one [of his works] is entirely free of amateurish blots and blunders, not one could be called the handiwork of a careful, skilled craftsman." Ekwensi's supporters, most notably Povey, have argued otherwise. Acknowledging Ekwensi's weaknesses as a writer, Povey explained: "He often dangerously approaches the senstimental, the vulgar and melodramatic. Behind his work stands a reading of American popular fiction and paperback crime stories. Yet Ekwensi's writing cannot be dismissed wtih such assertions. . . . Ekwensi is interesting because he is concerned with the present, with the violence of the new Lagos slums, the dishonesty of the new native politicians. . . . Only Ekwensi has dared to approach the contemporary scene with critical satire." A contributor to *African Authors: A Companion to Black African Writing 1800-1973* likewise noted: "Ekwensi is not an accomplished stylist, but he writes with vivacity and can paint a scene quickly and convincingly. His work expresses a very warm sensuality and there is little preciosity or primness in all his work."

Ekwensi states that his life in government and quasi-government organizations like the Nigerian Broadcasting Corporation has prevented him from expressing any strong political opinions, but adds, "I am as much a nationalist as the heckler standing on the soap-box, with the added advantage of objectivity." During the late 1960s Biafran war, in which the eastern region of Biafra seceded temporarily from the rest of Nigeria, Ekwensi visited the United States more than once to help raise money for Biafra and to purchase radio equipment for the independent Biafran radio station of which he was director. He has also traveled in western Europe.

J. O. J. Nwachukwu-Agbada, in *World Literature Today,* describes Ekwensi as the "Nigerian Defoe": "Ekwensi has been writing fiction since the 1940s. He is prolific and versatile, especially in the subject matter of his works, which can range from sex to science. . . . The 'new' work [*For a Roll of Parchment*] also reveals considerable artistic development, particularly in language and descriptive power."

In a later edition of *World Literature Today,* Nwachukwu-Agbada talks of "Cyprian Ekwensi's Rabelaisian jeu d'esprit whose obscene flavor sparked considerable outrage among Nigerian readers of the sixties [upon the release of *Jagua Nana* in 1961]. The new novel's [*Jagua Nana's Daughter*] bawdiness twenty-five years later has not attracted similar attention, probably due to the increased permissiveness and decreased influence of tradition in modern-day Nigeria."

Ekwensi's stature as a novelist is still debated. Emenyonu believes that Ekwensi's commitment "to portray the naked truth about the life of modern man" is the reason for the existing controversy over *Jagua Nana* and all of Ekwensi's fiction. "When one looks at his works over the past three decades," he observed, "one sees the deep imprints of a literature of social awareness and commitment, and this is Ekwensi's greatest achievement in the field of modern African writing."

BIOGRAPHICAL/CRITICAL SOURCES:

BOOKS

Contemporary Literary Criticism, Volume 4, Gale (Detroit), 1975.
Emenyonu, Ernest N., *The Essential Ekwensi: A Literary Celebration of Cyprian Ekwensi's Sixty-Fifth Birthday,* Heinemann, 1987.

Tucker, Martin, *Africa in Modern Literature: A Survey of Contemporary Writing in English,* Ungar, 1967.

PERIODICALS

Books Abroad, autumn, 1967.
Critique: Studies in Modern Fiction, October, 1965.
Times Literary Supplement, June 4, 1964.
World Literature Today, autumn, 1988; winter, 1989.

*   *   *

ELIOT, Dan
See SILVERBERG, Robert

*   *   *

ELIOT, T(homas) S(tearns) 1888-1965
(Charles Augustus Conybeare, Reverend Charles James Grimble, Gus Krutzch, Muriel A. Schwartz, J. A. D. Spence, Helen B. Trundlett)

PERSONAL: Born September 26, 1888, in St. Louis, MO; moved to England, 1914, naturalized British subject, 1927; died January 4, 1965, in London, England; buried in Westminster Abbey; son of Henry Ware (president of Hydraulic Press Brick Co.) and Charlotte Chauncey (a teacher, social worker and writer; maiden name Stearns) Eliot; married Vivienne Haigh Haigh-Wood (a dancer), January, 1915 (divorced c. 1930; died, 1947); married (Esme) Valerie Fletcher (his private secretary before their marriage), 1957; children: none. *Education:* Attended Smith Academy (of Washington University), St. Louis, 1898-1905; Milton Academy, Milton, MA, graduated, 1906; Harvard University, B.A. (philosophy), 1909, M.A. (philosophy), 1910, graduate study, 1911-14 (his doctoral dissertation "Experience and the Objects of Knowledge in the Philosophy of F. H. Bradley," was accepted in 1916 but never presented for the degree; the dissertation was published in 1964 as *Knowledge and Experience in Philosophy of F. H. Bradley*); attended University of Paris (Sorbonne), 1910-11; studied in Munich, 1914; read philosophy at Merton, Oxford, 1914-15; also studied under Edward Kennard Rand, Irving Babbitt, and Alain Fournier, and attended courses given by Henri Bergson. *Politics:* Conservative ("royalist"). *Religion:* Church of England, Anglo-Catholic wing; confirmed, 1927.

CAREER: Harvard University, Cambridge, MA, assistant in philosophy department, 1913-14; teacher of French, Latin, mathematics, drawing, geography, and history at High Wycombe Grammar School, London, then at Highgate School, London, 1915-17; Lloyds Bank Ltd., London, clerk in the Colonial and Foreign Department, 1917-25; *The Egoist,* London, assistant editor, 1917-19; founder of the *Criterion* (literary quarterly), London, 1922, and editor, 1922-39 (ceased publication, at Eliot's decision, in 1939 because of the war and paper shortage); Faber and Gwyer Ltd. (publishers), later Faber & Faber Ltd., London, literary editor and member of the advisory board, 1925-65. Clark Lecturer at Trinity College, Cambridge, 1926; Charles Eliot Norton Professor of Poetry at Harvard University, six months, 1932-33; Page-Barbour Lecturer at University of Virginia, 1933; resident at Institute for Advanced Study at Princeton University, 1948; Theodore Spencer Memorial Lecturer at Harvard University, 1950; lecturer at University of Chicago during the fifties; lecturer at Library of Congress, at University of Texas, at

University of Minnesota, and before many other groups. President of London Library, 1952-65.

MEMBER: Classical Association (president, 1941), Virgil Society (president, 1943), Books Across the Sea (president, 1943-46), American Academy of Arts and Sciences (honorary member), Accademia dei Lincei (Rome; foreign member), Bayerische Akademie der Schoenen Kuenste (Munich; foreign member), Athenaeum, Garrick Club, Oxford and Cambridge Club.

AWARDS, HONORS: Sheldon Travelling Fellowship for study in Munich, 1914; Dial award, 1922, for *The Waste Land*; Nobel Prize for literature, 1948; Order of Merit, 1948; Commander, Ordre des Arts et des Lettres; Officier de la Legion d'Honneur; New York Drama Critics Circle Award, 1950, for *The Cocktail Party* as best foreign play; Hanseatic Goethe Prize of Hamburg University, 1954; Dante Gold Medal (Florence), 1956; Ordre pour le Merite (West Germany), 1959; Emerson-Thoreau Medal of the American Academy of Arts and Sciences, 1959; honorary fellow of Merton College, Oxford, and of Magdalene College, Cambridge; honorary citizen of Dallas, TX; honorary deputy sheriff of Dallas County, TX; Campion Medal of the Catholic Book Club, 1963, for "long and distinguished service to Christian letters"; received President Johnson's award for distinguished contribution to American literature and public life. Honorary degrees: Litt.D., Columbia University, 1933, Cambridge University, 1938, University of Bristol, 1938, University of Leeds, 1939, Harvard University 1947, Yale University, 1947, Princeton University, 1947, Washington University, 1953, University of Rome, 1958, University of Sheffield, 1959; LL.D., University of Edinburgh, 1937, St. Andrews' University, 1953; D.Litt., Oxford University, 1948, University of London, 1950; D.Philos., University of Munich, 1959; D. es L., University of Paris, 1959, Universite d'Aix-Marseille, 1959, University of Rennet, 1959.

WRITINGS:

POETRY

Prufrock, and Other Observations (contains 11 poems and a prose piece, "Hysteria"; the title poem, "The Love Song of J. Alfred Prufrock," was first published in *Poetry,* June, 1915; five other poems were originally published in *Catholic Anthology,* edited by Ezra Pound, 1915), *The Egoist* (London), 1917.
Poems by T. S. Eliot, Hogarth, 1919.
Ara Vos Prec (includes *Poems by T. S. Eliot,* above), Ovid Press (London), 1920, published in America as *Poems,* Knopf, 1920.
The Waste Land (first published in *Criterion,* first issue, October, 1922), Boni & Liveright, 1922.
Poems, 1909-1925 (contains all works cited above and "The Hollow Men"; earlier drafts and sections of "The Hollow Men" appeared in *Chapbook, Commerce, Criterion,* and *Dial,* 1924-25), Faber, 1925.
Journey of the Magi (one of the "Ariel Poems"), Faber, 1927.
Animula (one of the "Ariel Poems"), Faber, 1929.
Ash-Wednesday (first 3 parts originally published in French, American, and English magazines, respectively; Part 2, first published as *Salutation* in *Saturday Review of Literature,* was intended as another of the "Ariel Poems" and as a complement to *Journey of the Magi;* the publisher also intended to issue this part separately as a Christmas card), Putnam, 1930.
Marina (one of the "Ariel Poems"), Faber, 1930.
Triumphal March, Faber, 1931.

The Waste Land and Other Poems, Harcourt, 1934.
Words for Music, [Bryn Mawr], 1935.
Collected Poems, 1909-1935, Harcourt, 1936.
A Song for Simeon (written in the 1920s; one of the "Ariel Poems"), Faber, 1938.
(With Geoffrey Faber, Frank Morley, and John Hayward) *Noctes Binanianae* (limited edition of 25 copies for the authors and friends; never reprinted), privately printed (London), 1939.
Old Possum's Book of Practical Cats, Harcourt, 1939.
East Coker, Faber, 1940.
Burnt Norton, Faber, 1941.
The Dry Salvages, Faber, 1941.
Later Poems, 1925-1935, Faber 1941.
Little Gidding, Faber, 1942.
Four Quartets (consists of *Burnt Norton, East Coker, The Dry Salvages,* and *Little Gidding*), Harcourt, 1943.
A Practical Possum, Harvard Printing Office, 1947.
Selected Poems, Penguin, 1948, Harcourt, 1967.
The Undergraduate Poems, Harvard *Advocate* (unauthorized reprint of poems originally published in the *Advocate*), 1949.
Poems Written in Early Youth, privately printed by Bonniers (Stockholm), 1950, new edition prepared by Valerie Eliot and John Hayward, Farrar, Straus, 1967.
The Cultivation of Christmas Trees (one of the "Ariel Poems"), Faber, 1954, Farrar, Straus, 1956.
Collected Poems, 1909-1962, Harcourt, 1963.
The Waste Land: A Facsimile of the Original Drafts, Including the Annotations of Ezra Pound, edited and with introduction by Valerie Eliot, Harcourt, 1971.
Inventions of the March Hare: Poems, 1909-1917, edited by Christopher Ricks, Harcourt, 1997.

PLAYS

Fragment of a Prologue, [London], 1926.
Fragment of the Agon, [London], 1927.
Sweeney Agonistes: Fragments of an Aristophanic Melodrama (provisionally titled *Wanna Go Home, Baby?* during composition; consists of two fragments cited above; first produced in New York at Cherry Lane Theater, March 2, 1952), Faber, 1932.
The Rock: A Pageant Play (a revue with scenario by E. Martin Browne and music by Martin Shaw; first produced in London at Sadler Wells Theatre, May 9, 1934), Faber, 1934.
Murder in the Cathedral (provisionally titled *Fear in the Way* during composition; first produced in an abbreviated form for the Canterbury Festival in the Chapter House of Canterbury Cathedral, June, 1935; produced in London at Mercury Theatre, November 1, 1935; first produced in America at Yale University, January, 1936; first produced in New York at Manhattan Theater, March 20, 1936), Harcourt, 1935.
The Family Reunion (often cited as a rewriting of the unfinished *Sweeney Agonistes*; first produced in London at Westminster Theatre, March 21, 1939; produced in New York at Phoenix Theater, October 20, 1958), Harcourt, 1939.
The Cocktail Party (provisionally titled *One-Eyed Riley* during composition; first produced for the Edinburgh Festival, Scotland, August, 1949; produced in New York at Henry Miller's Theater, January 21, 1950), Harcourt, 1950.
The Confidential Clerk (first produced for the Edinburgh Festival, August, 1953; produced in London at Lyric Theatre, September 16, 1953; produced in New York at Morosco Theater, February 11, 1954), Harcourt, 1954.

The Elder Statesman (first produced for the Edinburgh Festival, August, 1958; produced in London at Cambridge Theatre, September 25, 1958), Farrar, Straus, 1959.
Collected Plays, Faber, 1962.

PROSE

Ezra Pound: His Metric and Poetry (published anonymously) Knopf, 1917.
The Sacred Wood (essays on poetry and criticism), Methuen, 1920, 7th edition, 1950, Barnes & Noble, 1960.
Homage to John Dryden (three essays on 17th-century poetry), L. and V. Woolf at Hogarth Press, 1924, Doubleday, 1928.
Shakespeare and the Stoicism of Seneca (an address), Oxford University Press, for the Shakespeare Association, 1927.
For Lancelot Andrewes: Essays on Style and Order, Faber, 1928, Doubleday, 1929.
Thoughts After Lambeth (a criticism of the *Report* of the Lambeth Conference, 1930), Faber, 1931.
Charles Whibley: A Memoir, Oxford University Press, for the English Association, 1931.
Selected Essays, 1917-1932, Harcourt, 1932, 2nd edition published as *Selected Essays,* Harcourt, 1950, 3rd edition, Faber, 1951.
John Dryden, the Poet, the Dramatist, the Critic (three essays), T. & Elsa Holiday (New York), 1932.
The Use of Poetry and the Use of Criticism: Studies in the Relation of Criticism to Poetry in England (the Charles Eliot Norton lectures), Harvard University Press, 1933, 2nd edition, Faber, 1964.
Elizabethan Essays (includes *Shakespeare and the Stoicism of Seneca*), Faber, 1934, Haskell House, 1964.
After Strange Gods: A Primer of Modern Heresy (the Page-Barbour lectures), Harcourt, 1934.
Essays, Ancient and Modern (first published in part as *For Lancelot Andrewes*), Harcourt, 1936.
The Idea of a Christian Society (three lectures), Faber, 1939, Harcourt, 1940.
Christianity and Culture (contains *The Idea of a Christian Society* and *Notes Towards the Definition of Culture*), Harcourt, 1940.
Points of View (selected criticism), edited by John Hayward, Faber, 1941.
The Classics and the Man of Letters (an address), Oxford University Press, 1942.
The Music of Poetry (lecture), Jackson (Glasgow), 1942.
Reunion by Destruction: Reflections on a Scheme for Church Union in South India (an address), Pax House (London), 1943.
What Is a Classic? (an address), Faber, 1945.
Die Einheit der europaischen Kultur, Carl Havel, 1946.
On Poetry, [Concord], 1947.
A Sermon, [Cambridge], 1948.
From Poe to Valery (first published in *Hudson Review,* 1948), privately printed for friends by Harcourt, 1948.
Milton (lecture), Cumberlege (London), 1948.
Notes Towards the Definition of Culture (seven essays; a few copies erroneously stamped *Notes Towards a Definition of Culture*), Harcourt, 1949.
The Aims of Poetic Drama, Galleon, 1949.
Poetry by T. S. Eliot: An NBC Radio Discussion, [Chicago], 1950.
Poetry and Drama (the Theodore Spencer lecture), Harvard University Press, 1951.
The Value and Use of Cathedrals in England Today, [Chichester], 1951.

American Literature and the American Language (an address and an appendix entitled "The Eliot Family and St. Louis," the latter prepared by the English Department at Washington University), Washington University Press, 1953.
The Three Voices of Poetry (lecture), Cambridge University Press, for the National Book League, 1953, Cambridge University Press (New York), 1954.
Selected Prose, edited by John Hayward, Penguin, 1953.
Religious Drama, House of Books (New York), 1954.
The Literature of Politics (lecture), foreword by Sir Anthony Eden, Conservative Political Centre, 1955.
The Frontiers of Criticism (lecture), University of Minnesota, 1956.
Essays on Elizabethan Drama (contains nine of the eleven essays originally published as *Elizabethan Essays*), Harcourt, 1956.
On Poetry and Poets (essays), Farrar, Straus, 1957.
Essays on Poetry and Criticism, introduction and notes in Japanese by Kazumi Yano, Shohakusha (Tokyo), 1959.
William Collin Brooks (an address), The Statist (London), 1959.
Geoffrey Faber, 1889-1961, Faber, 1961.
George Herbert, Longmans, Green, for the British Council and the National Book League, 1962.
Elizabethan Dramatists, Faber, 1963.
Knowledge and Experience in the Philosophy of F. H. Bradley (doctoral dissertation), Farrar, Straus, 1964.
To Criticize the Critic, and Other Writings (contains *From Poe to Valery*; *American Literature and the American Language*; *The Literature of Politics*; *The Classics and the Man of Letters*; *Ezra Pound: His Metric and Poetry*; and new essays), Farrar, Straus, 1965.

OTHER

(Translator) St. John Perse (pseudonym of Alexis Saint-Leger Leger) *Anabasis* (poem; published in a bilingual edition with the original French), Faber, 1930, revised edition, Harcourt, 1949.
(With George Hoellering) *Murder in the Cathedral* (screenplay based on Eliot's play), Harcourt, 1952.
The Letters of T. S. Eliot, Volume 1: 1898-1922, Harcourt, 1988.
Mr. Mistoffelees; with Mungojerrie and Rumpelteazer, Faber, 1990, Harcourt, 1991.
The Varieties of Metaphysical Poetry: The Clark Lectures at Trinity College, Cambridge, 1926, and the Turnbull Lectures at the Johns Hopkins University, 1933, Harcourt Brace (New York City), 1994.

Also lyricist for songs "For An Old Man," [New York], 1951, and "The Greater Light," [London], released in 1956, with music by David Diamond and Martine Shaw. A complete run of Eliot's periodical, *Criterion* (1922-1939), was published by Barnes & Noble, 1967. Also author under pseudonyms Charles Augustus Conybeare, Reverend Charles James Grimble, Gus Krutzch, Muriel A. Schwartz, J. A. D. Spence, and Helen B. Trundlett. Editor of the *Harvard Advocate,* 1909-1910. Member of the editorial boards of *New English Weekly, Inventario, Christian News-Letter,* and other periodicals.

MEDIA ADAPTATIONS: "The Hollow Men" was set for baritone solo, male voice chorus, and orchestra, published by Oxford University Press, 1951; Stravinsky set sections of "Little Gidding" to music; *Murder in the Cathedral* was filmed in 1952, and Eliot wrote some new lines for the script and himself read the part of The Fourth Tempter, who is never seen on the screen; The Old Vic issued a recording of *Murder in the Cathedral* in 1953; "Sweeney Agonistes" was adapted into a jazz musical by John

Dankworth for "Homage to T. S. Eliot"; *Old Possum's Book of Practical Cats* was adapted as the stage musical *Cats,* 1981.

SIDELIGHTS: When T. S. Eliot died, wrote Robert Giroux, "the world became a lesser place." Certainly the most imposing poet of his time, Eliot was revered by Igor Stravinsky "not only as a great sorcerer of words but as the very key keeper of the language." For Alfred Kazin he was "the *mana* known as 'T. S. Eliot,' the model poet of our time, the most cited poet and incarnation of literary correctness in the English-speaking world." Northrop Frye, in *T.S. Eliot,* simply states: "A thorough knowledge of Eliot is compulsory for anyone interested in contemporary literature. Whether he is liked or disliked is of no importance, but he must be read."

In *After Strange Gods,* Eliot wrote: "I should say that in one's prose reflections one may be legitimately occupied with ideals, whereas in the writing of verse one can deal only with actuality."

Like Emerson, Eliot recognized the duality of man's soul "struggling," as Kazin writes, "for its own salvation"—and the world, "meaning everything outside the soul's anxious efforts," so that this duality is more "real" than society. Just as Eliot never accepted the statement that *The Waste Land* represented "the disillusionment of a generation," Neville Braybrooke submits in *T. S. Eliot,* he would never admit that his use of broken images "meant a separation from belief, since for him doubts and certainties represented varieties of belief." As G. Wilson Knight astutely points out, the "wonderful lyric in *East Coker* [beginning] 'The wounded surgeon plies the steel' [is] surely the grimmest statement on the Christian world-view ever penned by a devotee [and] offers a universe so riddled with negations and agonies that we must go to the anti-Christian polemics of Nietzsche—which its cutting phraseology recalls—for an analogy." But as always, Eliot is applying to the city and to the institutions of men his own peculiar vision in order to make a poetry which he in turn uses to test the validity of poetry. There is no deceit; from the outset he tells us that he will take us through half-deserted streets "that follow like a tedious argument / Of insidious intent / To lead you to an overwhelming question." Eliot presents us with a pattern which, as Frank Kermode writes in his discussion of *The Waste Land,* "suggests a commitment, a religion; and the poet retreats to it. But the poem is a great poem because it will not force us to follow him. It makes us wiser without committing us. . . . It joins the mix of our own minds but it does not tell us what to believe. . . . The poem resists an imposed order; it is a part of its greatness that it can do so."

Eliot told Donald Hall in 1959 that he considered *The Four Quartets* to be his best work; "and," he added, "I'd like to feel that they get better as they go on. The second is better than the first, the third is better than the second, and the fourth is the best of all. At any rate, that's the way I flatter myself." Neville Braybrooke writes: "It is . . . generally agreed . . . that in his *Four Quartets* [Eliot] attempted . . . to achieve a poetry so transparent that in concentrating on it attention would not fall so much on the words, but on the words pointed to. And in his rigorous stripping away of the poetic, such a pure poetry is sustained." Further, Eliot shaped the *Quartets* into a gyre, and, by imposing such a form, directed us to see the work as a totality in which each part contributes to and is enhanced by the process of synthesis.

Although many critics have commented on the cyclical nature of the *Four Quartets,* Frye has actually diagrammed these poems. "Draw a horizontal line on a page," he says, "then a vertical line of the same length cutting it in two and forming a cross, then a circle of which these lines are diameters, then a smaller circle

inside with the same centre. The horizontal line is clock time, the Heraclitean flux, the river into which no one steps twice. The vertical line is the presence of God descending into time, and crossing it at the Incarnation, forming the 'still point of the turning world.' The top and bottom of the vertical line represent the goals of the way up and the way down, though we cannot show that they are the same point in two dimensions. The top and bottom halves of the larger circle are the visions of plenitude and of vacancy respectively; the top and bottom halves of the smaller circle are the world of the rose-garden and (not unnaturally for an inner circle) of the subway, innocence and experience. . . . What lies below experience is ascesis or dark night. There is thus no hell in *Four Quartets,* which belong entirely to the purgatorial vision." "The archetype of this cycle is the Bible," he continues, "which begins with the story of man in a garden." So in Eliot we begin and end at the same point, "with the Word as the circumference of reality, containing within itself time, space, and poetry viewed in the light of the conception of poetry as a living whole of all the poetry that has ever been written." All this to say, as A. Alvarez writes in *Stewards of Excellence,* that "the triumphant achievement of the *Four Quartets* is in the peculiar wholeness and isolation of their poetic world. . . . Eliot has always worked obliquely, by suggestion and by his penetrating personal rhythms. His power is in his sureness and mastery of subject and expression. And this sense of inviolable purpose seems to remove his verse from the ordinary realm of human interchange. He has created a world of formal perfection. It lacks the dimension of human error."

Eliots strong sense of purpose extended to other literary efforts, particularly his playwriting. "Eliot's desire," writes Carol H. Smith, "was for a dramatic form which would make drama conform to the criterion of all art: the harmonious relationship of the parts to the whole." And, she continues, "Eliot's ideal of dramatic form was a work which would re-create in its theme, its form and its language the harmony which explained the untidy surface of life. The dramatist's mission was thus both artistic and religious, and it was envisioned as a process of transformation." In 1949, Eliot wrote in a letter to Lawrence Durrell: "We have got to make plays in which the mental movements cannot find physical equivalents. But when one comes to the big moment (and if we can't get it we can't do drama) there must be some simple fundamental emotion (expressed, of course, in deathless verse) which *everybody* can understand."

Eliot himself believed that *The Family Reunion,* at least poetically, was the best of all his plays. Helen Gardner, among several others, believes that *The Cocktail Party* and *The Confidential Clerk* are his finest. Gardner, in *The Art of T. S. Eliot,* says of these plays: "No other plays of our generation present with equal force, sympathy, wisdom, and wit the classic subject of comedy: our almost, but mercifully not wholly, unlimited powers of self-deception, and the shocks and surprises that life gives to our poses and pretenses." But history will almost certainly endow *Murder in the Cathedral* with the longest life and the greatest fame. John Gross notes: "Whether or not *Murder in the Cathedral* augments our ability to live, it is certainly a remarkable piece of work. It is Eliot's one indubitable theatrical triumph, and the one English addition to the classic repertoire since Shaw."

Eliot's concern for the lasting value of his (or any) criticism is paralleled by his own awareness of those who preceded him. As John Paul Pritchard explains, "Eliot required that for the understanding of any living artist he be set for contrast and comparison among those dead artists" before him; and "the poet's contribution is not that in which he differs from tradition, but that part of his work most in harmony with the dead poets who preceded him. From these premises Eliot concluded that the poet's work must be judged by standards from the past." And since, as Richard Poirier suggests, he "chooses to devalue literature in the interests of the pre-eminent values of language," Eliot is again led to a poetry which primarily serves the language as it has been invested with life by tradition. But, Mario Praz points out, "the critic's task should be to see literature *not* as consecrated by time, but to see it beyond time; to see the best work of our time and the best work of twenty-five hundred years ago with the same eyes.'" In other words, the poetry itself "does not matter" for Eliot in this sense; as he told Lawrence Durrell, the "prose sense comes first, and . . . poetry is merely prose developed by a knowledge of aeronautics."

Eliot's type of criticism, writes Praz, "in his own words, is meant to be an integration of scholarly criticism. In *The Music of Poetry* he said that his method was that of a poet 'always trying to defend the kind of poetry he is writing.'" Since Eliot wanted to write poetry "with the greatest economy of words, and with the greatest austerity in the use of metaphor, simile, verbal beauty, and elegance," he turned to Dante, whose language, says Praz, "is the perfection of a common language." Also, Praz continues, "what Eliot [saw] in Dante—who is almost the sole poet for whom he [had] kept up a constant cult—is more the fruit of a poet's sensibility than of a critical evaluation. He [saw] in Dante clear visual images [and] a concise and luminous language." Thus, in establishing criteria for his own poetry, Eliot formalized critical "theories" useful to his own thinking. The resultant eclecticism is, according to Austin Warren, a theory of poetry which "falls neither into didacticism nor into its opposite heresies, imagism and echolalia. The real 'purity' of poetry—to speak in terms at once paradoxical and generic—is to be constantly and richly impure: neither philosophy, nor psychology, nor imagery, nor music alone, but a significant tension between all of them."

Regardless of his imposing stature as a literary critic, Eliot, in his later years, seemed to re-examine his earlier statements with mistrust. Eliot told Donald Hall in 1959 that, "as one gets older, one is not quite confident in one's ability to distinguish new genius among younger men." Perhaps the same diminishing confidence in his critical ability led to the various recantations (most notable in his Milton criticism) which characterized much of his later work. I. A. Richards writes: "Gentleness and justness, these are the marks of his later criticism, with its elaborate measures taken to repair any injustices—to Milton, to Shelley, to Coleridge, or to *meaning* or to *interpretation* or even to *education*—that his earlier pronouncements seemed to him to have committed. I doubt if another critic can be found so ready to amend what he had come to consider his own former aberrations." (Conrad Aiken recently quoted from a very early letter in which Eliot called Ezra Pound's poetry "touchingly incompetent." When Hall asked him about this evaluation Eliot replied, "Hah! That was a bit brash, wasn't it?")

A review of Eliot's lectures, only recently published in *The Varieties of Metaphysical Poetry: The Clark Lectures at Trinity College, Cambridge, 1926, and the Turnbull Lectures at the Johns Hopkins University, 1933,* reveals that Eliot "repeatedly cannibalized" them for "subsequent essays," as Helen Vendler notes in *The New Republic.* "And many of their seminal ideas—from the decline of culture since the thirteenth century to a consequent 'dissociation of sensibility' (as intellect detached itself from emotion)—made their way rapidly into critical discourse." Vendler remarks on the profound influence Eliot's ideas had on other

critics. "Eliot's writings were always so fertile in suggestion, that cultural critics, religious writers, poets and professors all mined them as sources of provocative obiter dicta."

The lectures themselves are somewhat scattered, written "hurriedly" and during a time of great personal distress for Eliot—his marriage to his wife Vivienne was ending (the relationship later became the subject of a film, *Tom and Viv*) and he was about to convert to the Anglican Church. "And so it isn't surprising," finds Alexander Theroux in the Chicago *Tribune Books,* "to note Eliot's compulsion in the Clark Lectures to put something in order, to seek some sort of wholeness, cultural if not personal." Theroux continues, "The lectures were fulsome scholarship and far from easy to grasp." Robert Craft, writing for *Washington Post Book World,* states, "In general, Eliot's lectures are less finely concentrated than his essays." To assist readers, the editor, Ronald Schuchard, clarified and corrected Eliot's notes and pointed out themes reused by Eliot elsewhere. However, Eric Griffith pronounces in the *Times Literary Supplement,* "They make uncomfortable reading, and may be supposed to have made uncomfortable listening in the black and gold splendour of the hall at Trinity, overlooked as it is by the dominating, narrowed gaze of Henry VIII, who had a shorter way with marital dissatisfactions." Theroux notes the lectures received mixed reviews in their day and concedes, "Even upon reading, there is a pithiness wanting, much needless erudition and unintentional obfuscation." However, he concludes, "there is nothing false or weakly undeliberated in *The Varieties of Metaphysical Poetry*. These are the observations of a man who loved poetry . . . and for that they are eminently important."

One can read the reminiscences of his friends and guess at personal things about "Tom" Eliot (although he would be highly pleased, one is sure, to be able to invalidate our conclusions). Stephen Spender, for instance, writes: "[Eliot's] first wife, who had been a dancer, . . . was gay, talkative, a chatter-box. She wanted to enjoy life, found Eliot inhibiting and inhibited, yet worshipped him. . . . There was a time when the Eliots separated, and Eliot lived by himself, wore a monocle, was known to the neighbours as Captain Eliot." Aldous Huxley once told Robert Craft that "the marriage in *The Cocktail Party* was inspired—if that is the word—by Tom's own [first] marriage. His wife, Vivienne, was an ether addict, you know, and the house smelled like a hospital. All that dust and despair in Eliot's poetry is to be traced to this fact." Derek Stanford, too, has done some conjecturing about the subjectivity of Eliot's work. Citing the well-known lines, "Go, said the bird, for the leaves were full of children, / Hidden excitedly, containing laughter. / Go, go, go, said the bird: human kind / Cannot bear very much reality," Stanford writes: "This is as near to confession as Eliot need ever come. *The Four Quartets* are deeply concerned with first and last things, with archetypal experience and states: birth, pro-creation, death, judgment, salvation, damnation; and if I read this passage aright it originates in Eliot's loss and need of domestic life before his second marriage." But, as Stanford later points out, the origin doesn't really matter.

Eliot has said that his poetry "has obviously more in common with my distinguished contemporaries in America than with anything written in my generation in England. That I'm sure of." He admits that, in his own youth, he had very little sense of the literary times, that he felt no dominating presence of an older poet as one now feels the immediate influence of Eliot, Pound, and Stevens. "I think it was rather an advantage not having any living poets in England or America in whom one took any particular interest," he told Hall. "I don't know what it would be like, but I think it would be a rather troublesome distraction to have such a lot of dominating presences . . . about. Fortunately we weren't bothered by each other. . . . There was Yeats, but it was the early Yeats. It was too much Celtic twilight for me. There was really nothing except the people of the 90s who had all died of drink or suicide or one thing or another."

Publication of Eliot's *Inventions of the March Hare: Poems, 1909-1917* in 1997 sheds new light on the young poet. As Sarah Lyall notes in the *New York Times,* these poems were not meant by Eliot for publication. Sold to his friend and patron, John Quinn in 1922, "The poet's instructions could not have been more clear. 'I beg you fervently to keep them to yourself and see that they are never printed.'" While Eliot found them inferior, much was made over the poems' content. As Paul Levy notes in *The Wall Street Journal:* "These 'poems' are not helpful to those who wish to defend Eliot from charges of racism and anti-Semitism." They include "bawdy, scatalogical limericks with racist imagery that describe, among other things, the encounter of a highly sexed Christopher Columbus with King Bolo, a well-endowed black monarch," states Lyall. The editor, Christopher Ricks, notes these were previously published in other collections and were commented on by Conrad Aiken almost fifty years ago. The collection as a whole provides additional insight into Eliot's evolution as a poet. Concludes Levy, "These formerly lost early works are meaning-laden exceptions to . . . Eliot's magpie poetic method, the making of patchwork patterns of phrases and strings of words, very often borrowed from other poets' verses, without the use of quotation marks. We can now more easily trace the development of the (relatively) meaning-free mature works and see, in his concern for formal configuration, the evolution of a genuine modernist."

Today, as always, critical evaluations include sincere dislike of Eliot's work. In 1963, John Frederick Nims observed that Eliot "woos the lugubrious," that his poems "are a bore, obtruding and exhorting, buttonholing us with 'Redeem the time' and so forth." Though Nims concedes that Eliot "outranks . . . just about all [contemporary poets]," he is concerned because Eliot does not readily enchant the reader, and because his poetry tends to translate easily. The sterility, inaction, detachment, and despair which dominate Eliot's poetry are, in the opinion of several critics, epitomized in V.S. Pritchett's description of Eliot as "a trim anti-Bohemian with black bowler and umbrella . . . ushering us to our seats in hell." But for most, Eliot was, at the time of his death, the most imposing literary figure in the world. As early as 1917 Eliot declared: "The existing order is complete before the new work arrives; for order to persist after the supervention of novelty, the *whole* existing order must be, if ever so slightly, altered." Stephen Spender writes: "I think it can now be said that the novelties he introduced—none more striking than the reappearance of *ideas* in poetry—have been assimilated and become part of that marvelous order, now slightly altered, of imperishable works in English." Frank Kermode adds: "Eliot certainly has the marks of a modern kind of greatness, those beneficial intuitions of irregularity and chaos, the truth of the foul rag-and-bone shop. Yet we remember him as celebrating order. Over the years he explored the implications of his attitudes to order, and it is doubtful whether many people capable of understanding him now have much sympathy with his views. His greatness will rest on the fruitful recognition of disorder, though the theories will have their interest as theories held by a great man." And R. A. Scott-James has said that Eliot "brought into poetry something which in this generation was needed: a language spare, sinewy, modern; a fresh and

springy metrical form; thought that was adult; and an imagination aware of what is bewildering and terrifying in modern life and in all life. He has done more than any other [contemporary] English poet to make this age conscious of itself, and, in being conscious, apprehensive."

BIOGRAPHICAL/CRITICAL SOURCES:

BOOKS

Ackroyd, Peter, *T. S. Eliot: A Life,* Simon & Schuster, 1984.
Aiken, Conrad, *A Reviewer's ABC,* World Publishing, 1958.
Albright, Daniel, *Quantum Poetics: Yeats, Pound, Eliot, and the Science of Modernism,* Cambridge University Press (New York), 1997.
Alvarez, A., *Stewards of Excellence,* Scribner, 1958.
Asher, Kenneth George, *T.S. Eliot and Ideology,* Cambridge University Press (New York City), 1995.
Austin, William James, *A Deconstruction of T.S. Eliot: The Fire and the Rose,* Edwin Mellen Press (Lewiston, NY), 1997.
Braybrooke, Neville, *T. S. Eliot,* Eerdmans, 1967.
Blalock, Susan E., *Guide to the Secular Poetry of T.S. Eliot,* G.K. Hall (New York City), 1996.
Brooker, Jewel Spears, *Mastery and Escape: T.S. Eliot and the Dialectic of Modernism,* University of Massachusetts Press (Amherst), 1994.
Childs, Donald J., *T.S. Eliot: Mystic, Son, and Lover,* St. Martin's (New York City), 1997.
Concise Dictionary of American Literary Biography: The New Maturity, 1929-1941, Gale, 1989.
Contemporary Literary Criticism, Gale, Volume 1, 1973; Volume 2, 1974; Volume 3, 1975; Volume 6, 1976; Volume 9, 1978; Volume 10, 1979; Volume 13, 1980; Volume 15, 1980; Volume 24, 1983; Volume 34, 1985; Volume 41, 1987; Volume 55, 1989.
Cooper, John Xiros, *T.S. Eliot and the Ideology of Four Quarters,* Cambridge University Press (New York City), 1995.
Dawson, J.L., *A Concordance to the Complete Poems and Plays of T.S. Eliot,* Cornell University Press (Ithaca), 1995.
Dictionary of Literary Biography, Gale, Volume 7: *Twentieth-Century American Dramatists,* 1981; Volume 10: *Modern British Dramatists, 1940-1945,* 1982; Volume 45: *American Poets, 1880-1945, First Series,* 1986; Volume 63: *Modern American Criticism, 1920-1955,* 1988.
Enig, Rainer, *Modernism in Poetry: Motivation, Structures, and Limits,* Longman (New York City), 1996.
Frye, Northrup, *T. S. Eliot,* Oliver & Boyd, 1963.
Gardner, Helen, *The Art of T. S. Eliot,* Dutton, 1959.
Gordon, Lyndall, *Eliot's Early Years,* Oxford University Press, 1977.
Gordon, Lyndall, *Eliot's New Life,* Farrar, Straus, 1988.
Gregory, Elizabeth, *Quotation and Modern American Poetry: Imaginary Gardens with Real Toads,* Rice University Press (Houston), 1995.
Harwood, John, *Eliot to Derrida: The Poverty of Interpretation,* St. Martin's Press (New York City), 1995.
Julius, Anthony, *T.S. Eliot, Anti-Semitism, and Literary Form,* Cambridge University Press (New York City), 1995.
Kim, Dal-Yong, *Puritan Sensibility in T.S. Eliot's Poetry,* P. Lang (New York City), 1994.
Lentricchia, Frank, *Modernist Quartet,* Cambridge University Press (New York City), 1994.
Malamud, Randy, *Where the Words are Valid: T.S. Eliot's Communities of Drama,* Greenwood Press (Westport, CT), 1994.

Moody, Anthony David, editor, *The Cambridge Companion to T.S. Eliot,* Cambridge University Press (New York City), 1994.

Moody, *Thomas Stearns Eliot, Poet,* Cambridge University Press (Cambridge), 1994.

Moody, *Mapping T.S. Eliot's Peregrinations,* Cambridge University Press (New York City), 1996.

Morrison, Paul A., *The Poetics of Fascism: Ezra Pound, T.S. Eliot, Paul de Man,* Oxford University Press (New York City), 1996.

Phillips, Caroline, *The Religious Quest in the Poetry of T.S. Eliot,* Edwin Mellen Press (Lewiston, NY), 1995.

Pritchard, John Paul, *Criticism in America,* University of Oklahoma Press, 1956.

Rexroth, Kenneth, *Assays,* New Directions, 1961.

Scott-James, R. A., *Fifty Years of English Literature,* 1900-1950, Longmans, Green, 1951.

Sharma, R. S., *Indian Response to T.S. Eliot,* Atlantic Publishers (New Delhi), 1994.

Smith, Grover Cleveland, *T.S. Eliot and the Use of Memory,* Bucknell University Press (Lewisburg, PA), 1996.

Southam, B.C., *A Guide to the Selected Poems of T.S. Eliot,* Harcourt Brace (San Diego), 1996.

Timmerman, John H., *T.S. Eliot's Ariel Poems: The Poetics of Recovery,* Bucknell University Press (Lewisburg, PA), 1994.

Tratner, Michael, *Modernism and Mass Politics: Joyce, Woolf, Eliot, Yeats,* Stanford University Press (Stanford), 1995.

Wolosky, Shira, *Language Mysticism: The Negative Way of Language in Eliot, Beckett, and Celan,* Stanford University Press (Stanford), 1995.

PERIODICALS

America, September 17, 1994, p. 26.
Atlantic Monthly, May, 1965.
Book Week, February 13, 1966.
Canadian Forum, February, 1965.
Contemporary Literature, winter, 1968.
Criticism, fall, 1966; winter, 1967.
Drama, summer, 1967.
Encounter, March, 1965; April, 1965; November, 1965.
Esquire, August, 1965.
Listener, June 25, 1967.
Nation, October 3, 1966.
New Leader, November 6, 1967.
New Republic, May 20, 1967; December 19, 1994, p. 34.
New Statesman, October 11, 1963; March 13 1964.
New York Review of Books, March 3, 1966.
New York Times, January 5, 1965; June 14, 1965; August 22, 1989; September 23, 1996, p. B1.
New York Times Book Review, November 19, 1967; July 14, 1996, p. 30.
New York Times Magazine, September 21, 1958.
Observer, June 11, 1967.
Paris Review, spring-summer, 1959.
Partisan Review, spring, 1966.
Publishers Weekly, December 10, 1962.
Quarterly Review of Literature, numbers 1-2 (double issue), 1967.
Saturday Review, September 13, 1958; October 19, 1963; February 8, 1964.
Sewanee Review, winter, 1962, spring, 1967.
Southwest Review, summer, 1965.
Times (London), September 29, 1958.
Times Educational Supplement, September 26, 1958.
Times Literary Supplement, June 1, 1967; October 2, 1992, p. 10; July 8, 1994, p. 3.
Tribune Books (Chicago), July 24, 1994, p. 5.
Virginia Quarterly Review, autumn, 1967.
Wall Street Journal, September 12, 1996, p. A12.
Washington Post Book World, May 22, 1994, p. 4.

*   *   *

ELKIN, Stanley L(awrence) 1930-1995

PERSONAL: Born May 11, 1930, in New York, NY; died May 31, 1995, of heart failure in St. Louis, MO; son of Phil (a salesman) and Zelda (Feldman) Elkin; married Joan Marion Jacobson, February 1, 1953; children: Philip Aaron, Bernard Edward, Molly Ann. *Education:* University of Illinois, A.B., 1952, M.A., 1953, Ph.D., 1961. *Religion:* Jewish.

CAREER: Washington University, St. Louis, MO, instructor, 1960-62, assistant professor, 1962-66, associate professor, 1966-69, professor of English, 1969-95. Visiting professor at Smith College, 1964-65, University of California, Santa Barbara, 1967, University of Wisconsin—Milwaukee, 1969, University of Iowa, 1974, Yale University, 1975, and Boston University, 1976. *Military service:* U.S. Army, 1955-57.

MEMBER: Modern Language Association of America, American Academy and Institute of Arts and Letters.

AWARDS, HONORS: Longview Foundation award, 1962; *Paris Review* humor prize, 1965; Guggenheim fellow, 1966-67; Rockefeller Foundation grant, 1968-69; National Endowment for the Arts and Humanities grant, 1972; American Academy of Arts and Letters award, 1974; Richard and Linda Rosenthal Award, 1980; *Sewanee Review* prize, 1981, for *Stanley Elkin's Greatest Hits*; National Book Critics Circle Award, 1982, for *George Mills*; Brandeis University, creative arts award, 1986; New York University, Elmer Holmes Bobst award, 1991; National Book Critics Circle Award for Fiction, 1995, for *Mrs. Ted Bliss*; honorary degrees: L.H.D., University of Illinois, 1986, D.Litt., Bowling Green State University, 1992.

WRITINGS:

Boswell: A Modern Comedy (novel), Random House, 1964.
Criers and Kibitzers, Kibitzers and Criers (stories), Random House, 1966.
A Bad Man (novel), Random House, 1967.
The Dick Gibson Show (novel), Random House, 1971.
The Making of Ashenden (novella; also see below), Covent Garden Press, 1972.
Searches and Seizures (contains *The Bailbondsman, The Making of Ashenden,* and *The Condominium*), Random House, 1973 (published in England as *Eligible Men: Three Short Novels,* Gollancz, 1974), published as *Alex and the Gypsy: Three Short Novels,* Penguin, 1977.
The Franchiser (novel), Farrar, Straus, 1976.
The Living End (contains three contiguous novellas, *The Conventional Wisdom, The Bottom Line,* and *The State of the Art,* which first appeared, in slightly different form, respectively in *American Review, Antaeus,* and *TriQuarterly*), Dutton, 1979.
Stanley Elkin's Greatest Hits, foreword by Robert Coover, Dutton, 1980.
(Editor with Shannon Ravenel and author of introduction) *The Best American Short Stories, 1980,* Houghton, 1980.

The First George Mills (novel), Pressworks, 1981.
George Mills, Dutton, 1982.
The Magic Kingdom, Thunder's Mouth Press, 1985.
Early Elkin, Bamberger Books, 1985.
The Rabbi of Lud, 1987.
The Six-Year Old Man, Bamberger Books, 1987.
The Coffee Room, 1988.
The MacGuffin: A Novel, Viking Penguin, 1991.
Pieces of Soap, Simon and Schuster, 1992.
Van Gogh's Room at Arles: Three Novellas, Viking Penguin, 1992.
Mrs. Ted Bliss, Hyperion, 1995.

Also author of film scenario "The Six-Year-Old Man," published in *Esquire,* December, 1968. Stories appear in *The Best American Short Stories,* Houghton, 1962, 1963, 1965, and 1978. Contributor to *Epoch, Views, Accent, Esquire, American Review, Antaeus, TriQuarterly, Perspective, Chicago Review, Journal of English and Germanic Philology, Southwest Review, Paris Review, Harper's, Oui,* and *Saturday Evening Post.*

MEDIA ADAPTATIONS: Of his novellas, "The Bailbondsman" was filmed as "Alex and the Gypsy." The film rights to *Boswell* and *A Bad Man* have been purchased.

SIDELIGHTS: "'What happens next?' is a question one doesn't usually ask in Stanley Elkin's [works]," writes Christopher Lehmann-Haupt of the *New York Times.* "Plot is not really Mr. Elkin's game. His fiction runs on language, on parody, on comic fantasies and routines. Give him conventional wisdom and he will twist it into tomfoolery. . . . Give [him] cliche and jargon and he will fashion of it a kind of poetry." Long recognized and praised for his extraordinary linguistic vitality and comic inventiveness, Elkin, though he dislikes these terms, has been described as a "stand-up literary comedian" and a "black humorist" who invites us to laugh at the painful absurdities, frustrations, and disappointments of life. His books "aren't precisely satires," according to Bruce Allen in the *Chicago Tribune Book World,* but rather are "unillusioned yet affectionate commemorations of rascally energy and ingenuity."

Searches and Seizures, a collection of three novellas, "should provide the uninitiated with an ideal introduction to [Elkin's] art even as it confirms addicts like me in our belief that no American novelist tells us more about where we are and what we're doing to ourselves," claims Thomas R. Edwards in the *New York Times Book Review.* "This is an art that takes time—his scenes are comic turns that build cunningly toward climax in deflative bathos, and in the novels there's an inclination toward the episodic, the compulsive storyteller's looseness about connections and logic. [The first novella,] *The Bailbondsman,* . . . is just about perfectly scaled to Elkin's imagination; we have a tight focus, one day in the life of an aging Cincinnati bondsman of Phoenician descent, which nevertheless accommodates an astonishing thickness of texture, a weaving of events and psychic motifs that is as disturbing as it is funny."

The other two stories in *Searches and Seizures* are "The Making of Ashenden" and "The Condominium." The former is, in the words of Clancy Sigal in the *New Republic,* "a fantasy satirizing Brewster Ashenden, an idle wastrel in love with Jane Loes Lipton, a kind of Baby Jane Holzer with a Schweitzerian yen to do good. The 'shocking' climax, within the dream landscape of a rich Englishman's private zoo, has Brewster interminably screwing a bear." The man-bear sex scene "is vigorous, raunchy, painful, smelly—and downright *touching*," exclaims Bruce Allen in the

Hudson Review, and it forces Brewster, humbly and hilariously, to admit his animal nature.

According to Michael Wood in the *New York Review of Books,* "the real subject of the three short novels contained in *Searches and Seizures* is a complicated invention of character by means of snowballing language. The writer invents characters who invent themselves as they talk and thereby invent him, the writer." The protagonist of "The Bailbondsman," for example, introduces himself as "Alexander Main the Bailbondsman. I go surety. . . . My conditions classic and my terms terminal. Listen, I haven't much law—though what I have is on my side, binding as clay, advantage to the house—but am as at home in replevin, debenture, and gage as someone on his own toilet seat with the door closed and the house empty." "The motive force of Elkin's writing," says William Plummer in the *New Republic,* "is 'the conventional wisdom' itself. His aggressive, high energy rhetoric comes into being under the pressure of cliche, which is not to suggest that his *metier* is either satire or camp. Rather, he seems to share with Emerson the vaguely platonic idea that the hackneyed is 'fossile poetry'—the Truth in tatters, in its fallen condition."

The Dick Gibson Show, Elkin's third novel, "contains enough comic material for a dozen nightclub acts," notes R. Z. Sheppard in *Time,* "yet it is considerably more than an entertainment." Joseph McElroy claims in the *New York Times Book Review* that this "absolutely American compendium . . . may turn out to be our classic about radio." The hero of the book is a disc jockey who has worked for dozens of small-town radio stations across the country. "As the perpetual apprentice, whetting his skills and adopting names and accents to suit geography," says Sheppard, "he evolves into part of American folklore. As Dick Gibson, the paradox of his truest identity is that he is from Nowhere, U.S.A."

A radio talk-show host, Gibson is the principal listener for a bizarre cast of callers: Norman, the "caveman from Africa," whose linguistic equivalent for "chief" is "Aluminum Siding Salesman"; a rich orphaned boy—his skydiving parents accidentally parachuted into a zoo's tiger den—who has fears of being adopted for his money; a woman who wants to trade a bow and arrow, and in exchange will accept nothing but used puppets. Sheppard surmises that Gibson is "a McLuhan obfuscation made flesh—a benevolent witch doctor in an electronic village of the lonely, the sick, and the screwed up." McElroy concurs, arguing that Elkin "unites manic narrative and satiric wit to ensure that we know Dick Gibson [as] . . . receiver of an America whose invisibility speaks live into the great gap of doubt inside him, itinerant listener in this big-hearted country where it's so hard to get anyone to listen."

Christopher Lehmann-Haupt, however, believes that while it could be argued that Dick Gibson is "the sound of American silence, . . . this is forcing things somewhat. . . . The bittersweet and seriocomic truth is that Stanley Elkin is [merely] stringing routines together. . . . Which is not to say that I didn't love . . . passages like 'the wide laps beneath her nurse's white uniform with its bas-relief of girdle and garter like landmarks under a light snow.' Or that I didn't sink to my knees from laughing time and again. It's just that after a while one gets tired, can predict the patterns, begins to look for more than gags, and can't really find much."

John Leonard, writing in *Saturday Review,* considers *The Franchiser* to be the closest of Elkin's novels to *The Dick Gibson Show;* he also deems it Elkin's best. "It is a brilliant conceit—the franchising of America on the prime interest rate; manifest destiny on credit," states Leonard. "It is also considerably more than a conceit. It is a frenzied parable, rather as though the Wandering Jew and Willy Loman had gotten together on a vaudeville act. Who, after all, is displaced by the franchise? Ben Flesh [the protagonist] knows: 'Kiss off the neighborhood grocers and corner druggists and little shoemakers.' Kiss off, in other words, ethnicity, roots. Assimilate. Homogenize. What's in the melting pot? Campbell's soup, Kraft cheese, Kool-Aid. . . . The immigrants who shortened their names, the Jews who changed them, the slaves who borrowed new ones from their masters, were consequently diminished. They tailored who they were to the specifications of a culture that wanted someone else, insofar as the culture knew anything at all about what it wanted."

Despite Leonard's explication and the fact that his assessment is shared by other reviewers, some critics fault the book for its digressiveness—a common flaw in Elkin's novels according to Lehmann-Haupt, Robert Towers, and John Irving. Towers says in the *New York Times Book Review*: "While he can invent wonderful scenes full of madness and power, Elkin seems unable to create a sustaining comic action or plot that could energize the book as a whole and carry the reader past those sections where invention flags or becomes strained. Without the onward momentum of plot—no matter how zany—we are left with bits, pieces and even large chunks that tend to cancel each other out and turn the book into a kind of morass. . . . The need is especially felt in a book as long as *The Franchiser*, where the potentials of situation, character, and theme—very rich potentials—are never fully mobilized into a truly memorable novel." Novelist John Irving, also writing in the *New York Times Book Review*, declares that the "rap against Elkin is that he's too funny, and too fancy with his prose, for his own good. . . . It is brilliant comedy, but occasionally stagnant: the narrative flow is interrupted by Elkin's forays into some of the best prose-writing in English today; it is extraordinary writing, but it smacks at times of showing off—and it is digressive. Despite the shimmering language, the effect is one of density; I know too many readers who say they admire Stanley Elkin as a writer, but they haven't finished a single Elkin novel."

The Living End is, in the opinion of many critics, Elkin's best work. John Irving, for example, calls it a "narrative marvel [with] a plot and such a fast pace that a veteran Elkin reader may wonder about the places where he lost interest, or lost his way, in reading Elkin before." The book consists of three contiguous novellas, "The Conventional Wisdom," "The Bottom Line," and "The State of the Art," which provide the kind of conventional, "beginning-middle-end," structure often lacking in Elkin's other novels. The titles of the novellas also reflect Elkin's characteristic attention to cliche, according to Harold Robbins in the *Washington Post Book World*. Echoing William Plummer's comment on *Searches and Seizures*, Robbins points out that Elkin "knows that cliches are the substance of our lives, the coinage of human intercourse, the ways and means that hold our messy selves and sprawling nation intact. To exploit their vigor and set them forth with unexpected force has been the basis of his success as a novelist; no writer has maneuvered life's shoddy stock-in-trade into more brilliantly funny forms."

In addition to the strenuous language and the book's structural balance, "in *The Living End* Elkin has finally found a subject worthy of him," writes Geoffrey Stokes in the *Village Voice*. "No more does he diddle with the surrogates, no more leave us wiping the laughter from our eyes and wondering if we really care quite all that much about One-Hour Martinizing. This time, Elkin goes directly for the big one: God, He Who, etc." *Time*'s R. Z.

Sheppard believes that with *The Living End*, "Elkin must finally be recognized as the grownup's Kurt Vonnegut, the Woody Allen for those who prefer their love, death, and cosmic quarrels with true bite and sting."

With a vision that is sometimes blasphemous, the book begins with Ellerbee, a Minneapolis liquor-store owner and "the nicest of guys," notes Sheppard, who goes to Heaven after being gunned down behind the counter during a robbery. His surprise at Heaven's unsurprising sights, sounds, and smells—pearly gates, angels with harps, ambrosia, manna, and a choir that sings "Oh dem golden slippers"—however, turns to shock when St. Peter tells him, "beatifically," to go to Hell. The "ultimate ghetto," Hell also gives Ellerbee a sense of *deja vu*, with the devils' horns and pitchforks, and the sinners raping and mugging each other endlessly and pointlessly; moreover, there is cancer, angina, indigestion, headache, toothache, earache, and a painful, third-degree burning itch everywhere. "What Ellerbee discovers," declares Irving, "is that everything [about the afterlife] is true. . . . It's like life itself, of course, but so keenly exaggerated that Elkin manages to make the pain more painful, and the comedy more comic."

After several years God visits Hell, and Ellerbee asks why he, a good man, has been condemned. A mean-spirited and petty God charges him with selling the demon rum, keeping his store open on the Sabbath, uttering an occasional oath, having impure thoughts, and failing to honor his parents, even though he was orphaned as an infant. Sheppard infers that Ellerbee "ignored what Elkin labels 'the conventional wisdom.' The corollary: in a cosmos ruled by an unforgiving stickler, 'one can never have too much virtue.'"

Jeffrey Burke points out in *Harper's* that Elkin "founds his irreverence on the truths of contemporary religion, that is, on the myriad inconsistencies, cliches, superstitions, and insanities derived from centuries of creative theology," but claims that Elkin's purpose lies beyond satire. Harold Robbins explains: "Unlike others of his generation, . . . Elkin does not identify with the laughter of the gods, he does not dissociate himself from the human spectacle by taking out a franchise on the cosmic joke. Hard and unyielding as his comic vision becomes, Elkin's laughter is remission and reprieve, a gesture of willingness to join the human mess, to side with the damned, to laugh in momentary grace at whatever makes life Hell."

In his seventeenth (and presumably final) novel, *Mrs. Ted Bliss*, Elkin details the autumn years of 70-year-old Dorothy Bliss, a Russian-Jewish immigrant, whose comfortable life becomes unexpectedly complicated. Living alone in her Miami Beach condominium and nearly deaf, Dorothy, a "candidate for death by heartbreak" after her husband's death, learns to come to terms with her life and the loss of her illusions after being subpoenaed to testify at the trial of a drug king to whom she sells the family car and commences a friendship with her late husband's business partner. "Family, friends, love fall away," she reflects at the novel's bittersweet end. "Even madness stilled at last. until all that's left is obligation." Walter Goodman, writing in the *New York Times Book Review*, says, "Elkin's own language—rich, musical and playful, like that of a Joyce who grew up on Yiddish—serves as a kind of momentary stay, a protest, against these implacable facts of mortality." "A great critic of society, Elkin created a host of vivid and compelling characters," writes Donna Seaman in *Booklist*, "and his final heroine, the unflappable Mrs. Ted Bliss, may well be one of his most enduring. Elkin was always fascinated by the conflict between brain and heart, between what we think and what we feel, yet in Dorothy Bliss, he forged a consciousness notable for its steadfastness of spirit."

BIOGRAPHICAL/CRITICAL SOURCES:

BOOKS

Bailey, Peter Joseph, *Reading Stanley Elkin,* University of Illinois Press, 1985.

Bargen, Doris G., *The Fiction of Stanley Elkin,* P. Lang, 1980.

Charney, Maurice, *Jewish Wry: Essays on Jewish Humor,* Indiana University Press, 1987.

Cohen, Sarah Blacher, editor, *Jewish Wry,* Wayne State University Press, 1987.

Contemporary Literary Criticism, Gale (Detroit), Volume 4, 1975; Volume 6, 1976; Volume 9, 1978; Volume 14, 1980; Volume 27, 1984; Volume 51, 1989.

Dougherty, David C., *Stanley Elkin,* Twayne, 1991.

Dictionary of Literary Biography, Gale, Volume II: *American Novelists since World War II,* 1978; *Yearbook: 1980,* 1981.

Guttman, Allan, *The Jewish Writer in America: Assimilation and the Crisis of Identity,* Oxford University Press, 1971, pp. 79-86.

Lebowitz, Naomi, *Humanism and the Absurd in the Modern Novel,* Northwestern University Press, 1971, pp. 126-29.

Olderman, Raymond M., *Beyond the Waste Land: A Study of the American Novel in the 1960s,* Yale University Press, 1972, pp. 53-73, 175-81.

Pughe, Thomas, *Comic Sense: Reading Robert Coover, Stanley Elkin, and Philip Roth,* Birkhauser Verlag (Boston), 1994.

Short Story Criticism, Gale, Volume 12, 1993.

Tanner, Tony, *City of Words,* J. Cape, 1971.

PERIODICALS

America, December 12, 1992.

Booklist, December 15, 1992; February 1, 1992; August, 1995, p. 1909.

Chicago, June, 1987; January, 1988; March, 1991; February, 1992.

Chicago Tribune Book World, July 8, 1979.

Christian Science Monitor, May 12, 1966.

Contemporary Literature, Spring, 1975, pp. 131-62.

Critique, Volume XXI, Number 2, 1979.

Encounter, February, 1975.

Esquire, November, 1980.

Fiction International Spring/Fall, 1974, pp. 140-44.

Harper's, July, 1979; November, 1982; May, 1988; January, 1993.

Hollins Critic, June, 1982.

Hudson Review, Spring, 1974.

Iowa Review, Winter, 1976, pp. 127-39.

Library Journal, January 15, 1966; October 15, 1987; February 1, 1991; January, 1993.

Life, October 27, 1967.

Listener, March 28, 1968.

Los Angeles Times Book Review, July 15, 1979.

Massachusetts Review, Summer, 1966, pp. 597-600.

Nation, November 27, 1967; August 28, 1976; June 1, 1985.

New Leader, December 4, 1967.

New Republic, November 24, 1973; March 23, 1974; June 12, 1976; June 23, 1979; June, 1980; May 20, 1991.

Newsweek, April 19, 1971; June 18, 1979.

New York, June 18, 1979; October 12, 1987; February 25, 1991; March 8, 1993.

New Yorker, February 24, 1968; April 19, 1993.

New York Review of Books, February 3, 1966; January 18, 1967; March 21, 1974; August 5, 1976; August 16, 1979.

New York Times, February 17, 1971; October 9, 1973; May 21, 1976; May 25, 1979.

New York Times Book Review, July 12, 1964; January 23, 1966; October 15, 1967, p. 40; February 21, 1971; October 21, 1973; June 13, 1976; June 10, 1979; March 24, 1985; November 8, 1987; March 10, 1991; March 21, 1993; September 17, 1995, p. 7.

New York Times Magazine, March 3, 1991.

Publishers Weekly, October 22, 1973; September 11, 1987; January 18, 1991; December 13, 1991; December 14, 1992.

Saturday Review, August 15, 1964; January 15, 1966; November 18, 1967; May 29, 1976.

Studies in American Jewish Literature, Volume 2, 1982, pp. 132-43.

Studies in Short Fiction, Fall, 1974.

Time, October 27, 1967; March 1, 1971; October 29, 1973; May 24, 1976; June 4, 1979; November 10, 1980; March 25, 1991.

Times Literary Supplement, October 22, 1964; August 27, 1971; January 18, 1980.

Village Voice, August 20, 1979.

Washington Post Book World, October 22, 1967; October 29, 1967; March 7, 1971; October 28, 1973; June 13, 1976; January 7, 1979; July 1, 1979.

Yale Review, July, 1993.

*   *   *

ELLERMAN, Annie Winifred 1894-1983 (Bryher)

PERSONAL: Name legally changed to Bryher; born September 2, 1894, in Margate, Kent, England; died January 28, 1983, in Vevey, Switzerland; daughter of Sir John Reeves (an industrialist and financier) and Hannah (Glover) Ellerman; married Robert McAlmon (a writer and publisher), 1921 (divorced, 1927); married Kenneth Macpherson (a writer and editor), 1927 (divorced, 1947). *Education:* Educated in Eastbourne, Sussex, England, and by private tutor.

ADDRESSES: Home—Kenwin, Burier, Vaud, Switzerland.

CAREER: Writer, critic, and poet. *Close-Up* (film magazine), Territet, Switzerland, and London, England, co-founder and co-editor, 1927-33.

MEMBER: Interplanetary Association.

WRITINGS:

NOVELS UNDER NAME BRYHER, EXCEPT AS NOTED

(Under name Annie Winifred Ellerman) *Region of Lutany and Other Poems* (poems), Chapman & Hall, 1914.

Development, preface by Amy Lowell, Macmillan, 1920.

(With others) *Arrow Music* (poems), J. & E. Bumpus, 1922.

Two Selves, Contact Press, 1923, Chaucer Head, c. 1927.

Civilians, Pool (Territet, Switzerland), 1927.

(With Trude Weiss) *The Lighthearted Student,* Pool (London), 1930.

The Fourteenth of October, Pantheon, 1952.

The Player's Boy, Pantheon, 1953.

The Roman Wall, Pantheon, 1954.

Beowulf: Roman d'une maison de dans Londres bombarde, Mercure de France, 1948, translation from the French published as *Beowulf,* Pantheon, 1956.

Gate to the Sea, Pantheon, 1958.

Ruan, Pantheon, 1960.

The Coin of Carthage, Harcourt, 1963.

Visa for Avalon, Harcourt, 1965.

This January Tale, Harcourt, 1966.

The Colors of Vaud, Harcourt, 1969.

OTHER

Amy Lowell: A Critical Appreciation, Eyre & Spottiswoode, 1918.

(Translator) Bion of Smyrna, *The Lament for Adonis,* A. L. Humphreys, 1918.

A Picture Geography for Little Children, Part One: Asia, J. Cape, 1925.

West (travel), J. Cape, 1925.

Film Problems of Soviet Russia, Pool (London), 1929.

(With Robert Herring and Dallas Bower) *Cinema Survey,* Brendin, 1937.

Paris 1900, translated by Sylvia Beach and Adrienne Monnier, La Maison des Amis Livres, 1938.

The Heart to Artemis: A Writer's Memoirs, Harcourt, 1962.

(Editor with husband, Kenneth Macpherson) *Close-Up: A Magazine Devoted to the Art of Films,* ten volumes, Arno, 1970.

The Days of Mars: A Memoir, 1940-46, Harcourt, 1972.

Regular contributor of reviews and articles to *Saturday Review* and *Sphere,* 1917-18. Contributor of poetry, articles, and reviews to numerous periodicals, including *Bookman, North American Review, Poetry, Contact, Transatlantic Review, Transition, Seed, Life and Letters Today, Fortnightly Review, Little Review,* and *This Quarter.*

SIDELIGHTS: The daughter of wealthy parents, Bryher traveled extensively in her youth. The Ellermans' journeys often prevented Bryher from going to regular schools, so she was privately tutored. The author feels she was fortunate not to have been sent to school. "Fate was kind and I did few formal lessons in my childhood, with the result that my mind developed freely and was ravenous for knowledge." During the family's meanderings through Egypt, Europe, the Middle East, and the Mediterranean, Bryher acquired a lifelong fascination with history and archaeology, and participated in archaeological expeditions until the onset of World War I. She used her knowledge of these subjects to fuel her historical novels.

Bryher began contributing articles and reviews to the *Saturday Review* and *Sphere* in 1917. She attributes much of her maturation as a writer to the influence of the editors of these magazines, A. A. Baumann and Clement Shorter, respectively. Also influential were her friend Havelock Ellis and Sigmund Freud's work in psychoanalysis. When she began to write, the author legally changed her name to Bryher so as not to take advantage of her father's powerful influence in British publishing firms. Bryher, the name of one of the Scilly Isles off the coast of England, was an island she often visited as a child.

Eventually, Bryher met Hilda Doolittle (H.D.), who became a close friend. Sylvia Beach noted in her book *Shakespeare and Company* that H. D. introduced Bryher into her literary circle. "H.D. was one of the most admired of the so-called Imagists," asserted Beach, "a group that included Ezra Pound, John Gould Fletcher, and others." Bryher gradually numbered among her acquaintances such luminaries as James Joyce, Andre Gide, Ernest Hemingway, and Gertrude Stein. With H.D., the author

visited the United States in 1920 and 1921. On this trip Bryher met her first husband. A writer from Minnesota, Robert McAlmon also published avant-garde literature at the Contact Press. The two married the day after they met.

In 1927 Bryher and McAlmon divorced, and later that year she married Kenneth Macpherson, an authority on the cinema. Together they founded and edited the magazine *Close-Up.* This publication is often praised as the finest periodical on the art of silent films. Bryher and Macpherson divorced in 1947.

Although she has also written poetry and nonfiction, Bryher's historical novels have received the greatest recognition. Many critics are impressed with her mastery of history and her ability to write as if she were an actual spectator of events she describes. Shelby Martin observed in the *Bulletin of the New York Public Library*: "Bryher's novels deal with a wide variety of periods—from Switzerland of the Roman outposts to England of the Norman Conquest—and yet the documentation for each period is accurate and unobtrusive. All of the novels focus upon periods of chaos when the old foundations of cultures are destroyed and new foundations must be developed. Her characters are ordinary people forced by circumstances to deal with the collapse of the world as they have known it. The problem of loyalty to culture, religion, and/or friendship under the new conditions is developed both realistically for that moment in time and metaphorically for twentieth-century crises. Her prose is spare and yet her images convey haunting beauty." Writing in the *Observer Review,* Susanna Eliot described Bryher's novel *This January Tale* as a picture of "the past without the comforts of romance, and for all its starkness gives you the uneasy feeling that the author was somehow there when it happened."

Eleventh-century England is the setting of Bryher's first historical novel, and the event described is the Battle of Hastings. "Her attention to detail, ability to recreate the terrain of Cornwall and the countryside around Hastings, her . . . knowledge of the age and history of the period—all are superbly realized" in *The Fourteenth of October,* complimented P. J. Driscoll of *Commonweal.* "One stands in admiration of her achievement, and particularly of the verbal beauty with which she colors her descriptive writing." J. H. Jackson agreed in the *San Francisco Chronicle.* "Bryher tells the story with all the warmth and spirit of one long soaked in the atmosphere of the period," he remarked. "Her narrative is convincing, pulsing with life."

The author's next effort, *The Player's Boy,* takes place in England after the death of Elizabeth I. Horace Gregory of the *New York Times* asserted that it "is written with the intensity and sharpness of a dramatic poem." *The Roman Wall* tells the story of an outpost of the Roman Empire about to be invaded by Germanic tribes. In the *New York Herald Tribune Book Review,* Geoffrey Bruun disclosed: "She can banish time and make the past as real and credible as the present. This is her special secret and her special charm."

Returning to her own time in *Beowulf,* Bryher depicts London during World War II and the Battle of Britain. Again she received favorable reviews. *Commonweal*'s R. T. Horchler appraised the novel as "intelligent, ingenious, beautifully and subtly written, and completely without pretension," while David Daiches took note of its realism. "This is no romantic story of heroism, no flamboyant demonstration that 'Britain can take it,' " he contended, "but a quiet, perceptive, authentic account of the worries, the discomforts and the almost casual endurance of a small number of representative characters."

In *Poetry,* Marianne Moore named *Gate to the Sea* the best of Bryher's novels. "Of them all," she reflected, *Gate to the Sea* "is the most compactly vivid and expertly absorbing—a masterpiece." Other reviewers were similarly taken with this story of fourth-century Poseidonia's defeat at the hands of an Italic tribe. Geoffrey Bruun declared that Bryher's "mastery of mood owes something to her zest for archaeology, but her art is concentrated in her flawless prose." Horace Gregory elaborated: "No one living today writes prose with more quiet, unstressed authority than Bryher's."

Ruan evokes a view of sixth-century Britain, which, as the *Chicago Sunday Tribune's* W. J. Igoe mused, "has something of the formal perfection of the Grecian friezes one sees perpetuated in Wedgewood china and yet . . . [it has] a remote ghostly vitality that is strangely moving." *The Coin of Carthage* takes place in Italy and Carthaginian North Africa after the second Punic War. "This is the most accomplished of Bryher's . . . books," heralded W. G. Rogers in the *New York Times Book Review.* "Her novel serves Rome and Carthage as handsomely as Edith Hamilton's essays serve Greece."

This January Tale introduces a different view of the Norman conquest of the Saxons in 1066. Bryher claims in this historical novel that contrary to the popular theory, the invasion did not bring a greater civilization to the Anglo-Saxons. She maintained: "Art and learning virtually disappeared. A magnificent language was destroyed." *Book Week's* Richard Winston applauded the work: "Like all of Bryher's fiction, it vibrates with a kind of frozen music: it is both swiftly moving and perfectly static, full of action and yet fixed in time and space, slight yet comprehensive. It is a mysterious effect, and I do not pretend to understand how it is achieved; but it is there all the same."

In addition to her writing, Bryher was involved in a number of philanthropic activities. Beach revealed in her book that the author maneuvered the rescue of dozens of Nazi victims during World War II and helped them establish new lives in the United States. She also has "done more than anyone knows to maintain international contacts throughout wars, and to keep together her large family of intellectuals, who are dispersed in many countries. She looked after them in war and peace, and her correspondence is vast." In her memoir, *The Days of Mars,* Bryher upheld that "it is friendship that counts in the long dreary days that are full of hardships rather than valor."

BIOGRAPHICAL/CRITICAL SOURCES:

BOOKS

Beach, Sylvia, *Shakespeare and Company,* Harcourt, 1959.

PERIODICALS

Book Week, November 6, 1966.
Boston Transcript, November 20, 1920.
Bulletin of the New York Public Library, summer, 1976.
Chicago Sunday Tribune, December 18, 1960.
Christian Science Monitor, February 18, 1970.
Commonweal, May 30, 1952; August 20, 1954; October 12, 1956; October 10, 1958; December 2, 1960.
Listener, February 1, 1968.
New Republic, January 14, 1967.
New York Herald Tribune Book Review, May 24, 1953; May 16, 1954; September 14, 1958; November 13, 1960.
New York Herald Tribune Books, June 2, 1963.
New York Times, May 17, 1953; August 26, 1956; September 14, 1958; November 6, 1960.

New York Times Book Review, June 2, 1963; April 25, 1965; November 27, 1966; February 8, 1970.
Observer Review, January 7, 1968.
Poetry, February, 1959.
Publishers Weekly, January 28, 1983.
San Francisco Chronicle, June 10, 1952.
Saturday Review, September 1, 1956; November 12, 1960.
Springfield Republican, December 18, 1960.
Time, June 21, 1963.

*　　*　　*

ELLIOTT, Don
See SILVERBERG, Robert

*　　*　　*

ELLIOTT, William
See BRADBURY, Ray (Douglas)

*　　*　　*

ELLIS, Alice Thomas
See HAYCRAFT, Anna

*　　*　　*

ELLIS, Bret Easton 1964-

PERSONAL: Born March 7, 1964, in Los Angeles, CA; son of Robert Martin (a real estate investment analyst) and Dale (a housewife; maiden name, Dennis) Ellis. *Education:* Bennington College, B.A., 1986. *Avocation:* Piano, playing keyboards in bands, reading, sculling.

ADDRESSES: Home—Sherman Oaks, CA. *Agent*—Amanda Urban, International Creative Management, 40 West 57th St., New York, NY 10019.

CAREER: Writer.

MEMBER: Authors Guild.

WRITINGS:

Less Than Zero (novel), Simon & Schuster, 1985.
The Rules of Attraction (novel), Simon & Schuster, 1987.
American Psycho (novel), Simon & Schuster, 1991.
Informers (novel), Knopf, 1994.

Contributor of articles to periodicals, including *Rolling Stone, Vanity Fair, Wall Street Journal,* and *Interview.*

MEDIA ADAPTATIONS: Less Than Zero was adapted as a film, produced by Twentieth-Century Fox, 1988.

SIDELIGHTS: In 1985 twenty-one-year-old Bret Easton Ellis jolted the literary world with his first novel, *Less Than Zero.* Many reviewers' reactions to the book echoed that of *Interview* magazine's David Masello, who called it "startling and hypnotic." Eliot Fremont-Smith of the *Voice Literary Supplement* pronounced the book "a killer"—and, like other critics, was impressed not only with the novel itself but also with its author's youth. "As a first novel, [*Less Than Zero*] is exceptional," John

Rechy declared in the *Los Angeles Times Book Review*; it is "extraordinarily accomplished," a *New Yorker* critic concurred. *Less Than Zero,* wrote Larry McCarthy in *Saturday Review,* "is a book you simply don't forget." A college undergraduate at the time of novel's publication, Ellis has been hailed by more than one critic as the voice of the new generation. Upon the publication of his third novel, *American Psycho,* Ellis again attracted attention, this time for writing a story so disturbing and violent that Matthew Tyrnauer of *Vanity Fair* called Ellis "the most reviled writer in America, the Salman Rushdie of too much, too fast."

The somewhat-autobiographical *Less Than Zero* grew out of a writing project Ellis began at Bennington College under his professor, writer Joe McGinniss. Comprised of vignettes about his high school experiences in a wealthy section of Los Angeles, the book centers on Clay, an eighteen-year-old freshman at an eastern college who returns to Los Angeles for Christmas vacation. Drugs, sex, expensive possessions, and an obsession with videotapes, video games, and music videos fill the lives of Clay and his jaded peers. Events others might find horrifying—hard-core pornography, a corpse in an alley, and a girl who is kidnapped, drugged, and raped—become passive forms of entertainment.

The novel's grim subject matter is related in a detached, documentary-style prose, leading *New York Times* reviewer Michiko Kakutani to state that *Less Than Zero* was "one of the most disturbing novels [she had] read in a long time." *Time* magazine's Paul Gray, asserted that "Ellis conveys the hellishness of aimless lives with economy and skill," while Alan Jenkins of the *Times Literary Supplement* found that "at times [the novel] reproduces with numbing accuracy the intermittent catatonic lows of a psycho-physical system artificially stimulated beyond normal human endurance."

Some critics drew comparisons between *Less Than Zero* and J. D. Salinger's *Catcher in the Rye,* the 1950s classic of disaffected youth. But Anne Janette Johnson, writing in the *Detroit Free Press,* explained that such comparisons could not extend "beyond the fact that both [novels] concern teenagers coming of age in America. Salinger's [Holden Caulfield] had feelings—anger, self-pity, desire. The youths in [*Less Than Zero*] are merely consuming automatons, never energetic enough to be angry or despairing." For some critics, the novel brought to mind Jack Kerouac and similar "beat generation" writers of the 1950s. And Kakutani found echoes of Raymond Chandler, Joan Didion, and Nathanael West in Ellis's evocation of Los Angeles.

Ellis's second novel, *The Rules of Attraction,* continued in the vein of *Less Than Zero*; as R. Z. Sheppard of *Time* magazine noted, "the village of the damned goes East." *Rules* is set at Camden College, a fictional East Coast school which bears a striking similarity to Bennington College in Vermont, where Ellis earned his degree. Despite the academic setting, many reviewers noted the absence of the usual rigors of higher education. Richard Eder announced in the *Los Angeles Times Book Review* that "we actually catch a glimpse of one professor . . . and he is asleep on his office couch and reeks of pot." What is present, however, are "drunken parties, drugs, sex, shoplifting, [and] pop music," according to Campbell Geeslin in *People.* The three main characters, Paul, Sean, and Lauren, are involved in a frustrating love triangle: Paul, a homosexual, desires the bisexual Sean; Sean meanwhile longs to deepen his involvement with Lauren, who is pining after someone else. *New York Times Book Review* contributor Scott Spencer stated that these characters "live in a world of conspicuous and compulsive consumption—consuming first one another, and then drugs, and then anything else they can lay their hands on."

Spencer praised Ellis for "portraying the shallowness of [his characters'] desires," but objected to what he deemed the author's gratuitous use of brand names which served no function in the narrative. Spencer also surmised that Ellis is a potentially adept satirist, but that in *The Rules of Attraction* "his method of aping the attitudes of the burnt-out works against him. . . . One closes the book feeling that this time out the author has stumbled over the line separating cool from cold. Where we ought to be saying, 'Oh my God, no,' we are, instead, saying, 'Who cares?'" *Newsweek* reviewer David Lehman also found Ellis's authorial skill to be somewhat deficient, and he concluded that "like *Less Than Zero, The Rules of Attraction* is more effective as a sociological exhibit than as a work of literary art."

A minor character from *The Rules of Attraction*—Sean's older brother Patrick—became the central figure in Ellis's third novel, *American Psycho.* Like Ellis's other protagonists, Patrick Bateman is young, greedy, wealthy, and devoid of morals. A Wall Street executive who shops at the most expensive stores and dines at the trendiest restaurants, Patrick also enjoys torturing, mutilating, and murdering people at random, mostly from New York City's underclass. His crimes are described in the same emotionless detail that he devotes to his observations on food, clothing, and stereo equipment. Though he drops many hints of his covert activities to friends and authorities, he is never caught, and none of the victims seems to be missed.

Ellis has stated that he intended *American Psycho* to be a satirical black comedy about the lack of morality in modern America, and some critics agree that he achieved this aim. Other commentators, however, accused him of pandering to readers' most base desires by producing a novel with all the artistic worth of a low-budget horror movie. Man, woman, child, and animal all meet grisly ends at the hands of Bateman, and the book's violence towards women in particular prompted one chapter of the National Organization for Women to organize a boycott not only of the book itself, but of all books by its publisher, Vintage, and its parent company, Random House.

Some critics saw little literary merit in the book. In a *Washington Post* review, Jonathan Yardley called *American Psycho* "a contemptible piece of pornography, the literary equivalent of a snuff flick" and urged readers to forego the experience. Andrew Motion echoed Yardley's sentiments in the London *Observer,* calling the book "deeply and extremely disgusting. . . . [S]ensationalist, pointless except as a way of earning its author some money and notoriety." Similarly, Albert Manguel of *Saturday Night* also reported that his reaction to the book was not as the author intended: "not intellectual terror, which compels you to question the universe, but physical horror—a revulsion not of the senses but of the gut, like that produced by shoving a finger down one's throat." John Leonard of the *Nation,* however, argued that "There is no reason this couldn't have been funny: if not Swiftian, at least a sort of *Bonfire of the Vanities* meets *The Texas Chainsaw Massacre.* . . . Ellis has an ear for the homophobic and misogynistic fatuities of his social set. . . . When Patrick tells people that he's 'into murders and executions,' what they hear him say is 'mergers and acquisitions.'"

Unlikely proponents of the book include Gore Vidal, who Tyrnauer quotes as remarking, "I thought it was really rather inspired. . . . These nutty characters, each on his own track—and the tracks keep crossing. It was a wonderfully comic novel." Director David Cronenberg considered making a film version, and author Michael Tolkin argued, as Tyrnauer reports, that "There was a massive denial about the strengths of the book. . . . People scapegoated the violence, but that wasn't his sin. He made a connection between the language of fashion writing and serial murder."

The debate over Ellis's style continued with his 1994 publication, *The Informers.* A novel constructed from loosely related short pieces which take place once again in Los Angeles and concern rich and beautiful college students, the book displays the deadpan prose and scenes of horror on which Ellis's reputation has been built. The book contains graphic depictions of vampirism and murder on a par with those in *American Psycho,* but violence is not the novel's focus. A multitude of friends and acquaintances, mostly tan, blonde, and sleeping with each other, find their lives uprooted by several random murders and mutilations of their relatives and peers. As it turns out, two of these young trendy types, Dirk and Jamie, are vampires. But once again Ellis focuses on the emptiness of the 1980s and on characters consumed with style and materialism who have contempt for any real analysis of their lives. "The *Informers* is full of scintillating chitchat," wrote Leonard in the *Nation.* "What Ellis has digitized, instead of a novel, is a video. He channel-surfs—from bloody bathroom to bloodier bedroom; from herpes to anorexia," he continued.

For Neal Karlen, reviewer for the *Los Angeles Times Book Review, The Informers* represented "a further slide down for an author who long ago had it." Karlen dismissed the book as full of "a rancid phoniness" and characterized all of Ellis's later work as being "opaque and bitter, devoid of both humanity and meaning" because "Ellis apparently has not learned the lesson of empathy, either on the page or in life." Conversely, for *New York Times Book Review* contributor George Stade, *The Informers* was "spare, austere, elegantly designed, telling in detail, coolly ferocious, sardonic in its humor." Stade concluded that Ellis himself was "a covert moralist and closet sentimentalist, the best kind, the kind who leaves you space in which to respond as your predispositions nudge you, whether as a commissar or hand-wringer or, like me, as an admirer of his intelligence and craft."

In Tyrnauer's interview with Ellis, he noted that "a certain slangy level of ironic detachment informs even his most serious statements—and not everybody gets it. 'I am an incredibly moralistic person. . . . A lot of people totally mistake the books in some cases as advocating a certain behavior or as glorifying a certain form of behavior.'" Commenting on his role as a spokesperson for his generation, Ellis told *Contemporary Authors* that "I . . . don't believe that there's one or two spokespeople for a generation, one collective voice who's going to speak for the whole lot. . . . What you have to do . . . is just feel safe enough about your own opinion and go ahead and state it."

BIOGRAPHICAL/CRITICAL SOURCES:

BOOKS

Contemporary Authors New Revision Series, Volume 51, Gale (Detroit), 1996.
Contemporary Literary Criticism, Gale, Volume 39, 1986; Volume 71, 1992.

PERIODICALS

Chicago Tribune, September 13, 1987.
Current Biography, November, 1994, p. 23.
Detroit Free Press, August 18, 1985.

Detroit News, August 11, 1985.
Entertainment Weekly, August 19, 1994.
Esquire, October, 1994, p. 158.
Film Comment, December, 1985.
Interview, June, 1985; January, 1991, p. 54.
Library Journal, January, 1991; July, 1994.
Los Angeles Times Book Review, May 26, 1985; September 13, 1987.
Mademoiselle, June, 1986.
Nation, April 1, 1991, p. 426; September 5, 1994, p. 238.
National Review, February 14, 1986; June 24, 1991; September 12, 1994, p. 86; June 17, 1996, p. 56.
New Republic, June 10, 1985; September 5, 1994, p. 46.
New Statesman, November 11, 1994, p. 40.
Newsweek, July 8, 1985; September 7, 1987; March 4, 1991, p. 58.
New Yorker, July 29, 1985; October 26, 1987, p. 142.
New York Review of Books, May 29, 1986.
New York Times, June 8, 1985.
New York Times Book Review, June 16, 1985; June 22, 1986; September 13, 1987, p. 14; December 16, 1990, p. 3; September 18, 1994, p. 14.
Observer, April 21, 1991, p. 61.
People Weekly, July 29 1985; September 28, 1987.
Playboy, July, 1991, p. 26.
Publishers Weekly, June 13, 1994.
Rolling Stone, September 26, 1985.
Saturday Night, July-August, 1991, pp. 46-47, 49.
Saturday Review, July/August, 1985.
Time, June 10, 1985; October 19, 1987; March 18, 1991, p. 14.
Times Literary Supplement, February 28, 1986.
Vanity Fair, April, 1994, p. 108; August, 1994, p. 94.
Voice Literary Supplement, May, 1985.
Washington Post, February 27, 1991, pp. B1, B3; April 28, 1991, pp. C1, C4.
Writer's Digest, December, 1986.

*　　*　　*

**ELLIS, Landon
  See ELLISON, Harlan (Jay)**

*　　*　　*

ELLISON, Harlan (Jay) 1934-
(Cordwainer Bird, Jay Charby, Ellis Hart, Paul Merchant, Jay Solo; Clyde Mitchell, Ellis Robertson, joint pseudonyms; Lee Archer, Phil "Cheech" Beldone, Robertce Curtis, Wallace Edmondson, Landon Ellis, Sley Harson, E. K. Jarvis, Ivar Jorgensen, Alan Maddern, Nalrah Nosille, Bert Parker, Derry Tiger, house pseudonyms)

PERSONAL: Born May 27, 1934, in Cleveland, OH; son of Louis Laverne (a dentist and jeweler) and Serita (Rosenthal) Ellison; married Charlotte B. Stein, February 19, 1956 (divorced, 1960); married Billie Joyce Sanders, November 13, 1960 (divorced, 1963); married Lory Patrick, January 30, 1966 (divorced, 1966); married Lori Horwitz, June 5, 1976 (divorced, 1977); married Susan Toth, 1986. *Education:* Attended Ohio State University, 1953-54.

ADDRESSES: Home—P.O. Box 55548, Sherman Oaks, CA, 91413. *Office*—The Kilimanjaro Corporation, 3484 Coy Dr., Sherman Oaks, CA 91423. *Agent*—Richard Curtis Associates, Inc., 171 East 74th St., New York, NY 10021.

CAREER: Writer, 1954–. Editor, *Rogue* (magazine), 1959-60; founder and editor, Regency Books, 1961-62. Editorial commentator, Canadian Broadcasting Co. (CBC), 1972-78; president of The Kilimanjaro Corp., Sherman Oaks, CA, 1979–. Creator of weekly television series (sometimes under pseudonym Cordwainer Bird), including *The Starlost,* syndicated, 1973, *Brillo* (with Ben Bova), American Broadcasting Companies, Inc. (ABC), 1974, and *The Dark Forces* (with Larry Brody), National Broadcasting Corporation, Inc. (NBC), 1986; creative consultant and director of television series (sometimes under pseudonym Cordwainer Bird), including *The Twilight Zone,* Columbia Broadcasting Systems, Inc. (CBS), 1984-85, and *Cutter's World,* 1987-88; conceptual consultant, *Babylon 5,* syndicated, 1993–; host of cable magazine show, *Sci-Fi Buzz,* the Sci-Fi Channel, 1993; actor and voice-over talent. Has lectured at various universities, including Yale Political Union, Harvard University, Massachusetts Institute of Technology, London School of Economics, Michigan State University, University of California—Los Angeles, Duke University, Ohio State University, and New York University. West Coast spokesman, Chevrolet GEO Imports, 1988-89. Member of board of advisors, Great Expectations (video dating service). *Military service:* U.S. Army, 1957-59.

MEMBER: PEN, Science Fiction Writers of America (co-founder; vice-president, 1965-66), Writers Guild of America, West (former member of board of directors), Lewis Carroll Society, Cleveland Science Fiction Society (co-founder), Screen Actors Guild.

AWARDS, HONORS: Writers Guild of America Awards, 1965, for *Outer Limits* television series episode "Demon with a Glass Hand," 1967, for original teleplay of *Star Trek* television series episode "The City on the Edge of Forever," 1973, for original teleplay of *Starlost* television pilot episode "Phoenix without Ashes," and 1986, for *Twilight Zone* television series episode "Paladin of the Lost Hour"; Nebula Awards, Science Fiction Writers of America, best short story, 1965, for "'Repent, Harlequin!' Said the Ticktockman," and 1977, for "Jeffty Is Five," best novella, 1969, for "A Boy and His Dog."

Hugo Awards, World Science Fiction Convention, best short fiction, 1965, for "'Repent, Harlequin!' Said the Ticktockman," best short story, 1967, for "I Have No Mouth, and I Must Scream," 1968, for "The Beast That Shouted Love at the Heart of the World," 1977, for "Jeffty Is Five," and 1986, for "Paladin of the Lost Hour," best dramatic presentation, 1967, for *Star Trek* television series episode "The City on the Edge of Forever," and 1976, for film "A Boy and His Dog," best novelette, 1973, for "The Deathbird," 1974, for "Adrift, Just Off the Islets of Langerhans. . . ," George Melie Awards for Cinematic Achievement, 1972, 1973; special plaques from the World Science Fiction Convention, 1968, for *Dangerous Visions: 33 Original Stories,* and 1972, for *Again, Dangerous Visions: 46 Original Stories*; Nova Award, 1968, for most outstanding contribution to the field of science fiction.

Locus Awards, *Locus* (magazine), best short fiction, 1970, for "The Region Between," 1972, for "Basilisk," 1973, for "The Deathbird," 1975, for "Croatoan," 1977, for "Jeffty Is Five," 1978, for "Count the Clock That Tells the Time," 1985, for "With Virgil Oddum at the East Pole," and 1988, for "Eiddons," best original anthology, 1972, for *Again, Dangerous Visions,* and

1986, for *Medea: Harlan's World,* best novelette, 1974, for "Adrift, Just Off the Islets of Langerhans, . . ." 1982, for "Djinn, No Chaser," 1985, for "Paladin of the Lost Hour," and 1988, for "The Function of Dream Sleep," best nonfiction, 1984, for *Sleepless Nights in the Procrustean Bed,* best short story collection, 1988, for *Angry Candy.*

Edgar Allan Poe Awards, Mystery Writers of America, 1974, for "The Whimper of Whipped Dogs," and 1988, for "Soft Monkey"; Jupiter Awards, Instructors of Science Fiction in Higher Education, best novelette, 1973, for "The Deathbird," and best short story, 1977, for "Jeffty Is Five"; Bram Stoker Awards, Horror Writers of America, 1988, for *The Essential Ellison: A Thirty-five Year Retrospective,* and 1990, for *Harlan Ellison's Watching*; Certificate of Merit, Trieste Film Festival, 1970; British Fantasy Award, 1978; PEN International Award for Journalism, 1982; PEN International Silver Pen award for journalism, 1988, for column, "An Edge in My Voice"; World Fantasy Awards, best short story collection, 1989, for *Angry Candy,* and 1993, for lifetime achievement; *Angry Candy* was named one of the major works of American literature by *Encyclopedia Americana Annual,* 1988; honored by PEN for continuing commitment to artistic freedom and battle against censorship, 1990; inducted into Swedish National Encyclopedia, 1992; selection of short story "The Man Who Rowed Christopher Columbus to Freedom" for inclusion in *The Best American Short Stories,* 1993; nominated for Nebula Award, 1993, for "The Man Who Rowed Christopher Columbus to Freedom," and 1994 for novella *Mefisto in Onyx*; World Fantasy Convention Life Achievement Award, 1993; recipient of Milford Award for lifetime achievement in editing.

WRITINGS:

SHORT STORY COLLECTIONS

The Deadly Streets, Ace Books, 1958.
(Under pseudonym Paul Merchant) *Sex Gang,* Nightstand, 1959.
A Touch of Infinity, Ace Books, 1960.
Children of the Streets (also published as *The Juvies*), Ace Books, 1961.
Gentleman Junkie, and Other Stories of the Hung-Up Generation, Regency Books, 1961.
Ellison Wonderland, Paperback Library, 1962.
Paingod, and Other Delusions (includes "'Repent, Harlequin!' Said the Ticktockman"), Pyramid Books, 1965.
I Have No Mouth and I Must Scream (also see below), Pyramid Books, 1967.
From the Land of Fear, Belmont, 1967.
Love Ain't Nothing But Sex Misspelled, Trident, 1968.
The Beast That Shouted Love at the Heart of the World, Avon, 1969.
Over the Edge: Stories from Somewhere Else, Belmont, 1970.
Alone against Tomorrow: Stories of Alienation in Speculative Fiction, Macmillan, 1971, abridged editions published in England as *All the Sounds of Fear,* Panther, 1973, and *The Time of the Eye,* Panther, 1974.
(With others) *Partners in Wonder: SF Collaborations with Fourteen Other Wild Talents,* Walker & Co., 1971.
Approaching Oblivion: Road Signs on the Treadmill toward Tomorrow, Walker & Co., 1974.
Deathbird Stories: A Pantheon of Modern Gods (includes "The Whimper of Whipped Dogs"; also see below), Harper, 1975.
No Doors, No Windows, Pyramid Books, 1975.
Strange Wine: Fifteen New Stories from the Nightside of the World, Harper, 1978.

The Illustrated Harlan Ellison, edited by Byron Preiss, Baronet, 1978.

Strange Wine: Fifteen New Stories from the Nightside of the World, Harper & Row, 1978.

The Fantasies of Harlan Ellison, Gregg, 1979.

Shatterday (also see below), Houghton, 1980.

Stalking the Nightmare, Phantasia Press, 1982.

The Essential Ellison: A Thirty-five Year Retrospective, edited by Terry Dowling, with Richard Delap and Gil Lamont, with an introduction by Dowling, Nemo Press, 1986.

Angry Candy, Houghton, 1988.

Dreams with Sharp Teeth (includes revised editions of *I Have No Mouth and I Must Scream, Deathbird Stories,* and *Shatterday*), Book-of-the-Month-Club, 1991.

Mind Fields: The Art of Jacek Yerka, the Fiction of Harlan Ellison, Morpheus International (Beverly Hills), 1994.

Slippage, Houghton, 1994.

Contributor of short story to Mel Odom's *I Have No Mouth, and I Must Scream: The Official Strategy Guide,* Prima (Rocklin, CA), 1995. Also contributor of over eleven hundred short stories, some under pseudonyms, to numerous publications, including *Magazine of Fantasy and Science Fiction, Ariel, Twilight Zone, Cosmopolitan, Datamation, Omni, Ellery Queen's Mystery Magazine, Analog, Heavy Metal,* and *Galaxy.*

NOVELS

Rumble, Pyramid Books, 1958, published as *Web of the City,* 1975.

The Man with Nine Lives (novel; also see below) [and] *A Touch of Infinity* (stories), Ace Books, 1960.

The Sound of a Scythe (originally published as *The Man with Nine Lives*), Ace Books, 1960.

Spider Kiss (also published as *Rockabilly*), Fawcett, 1961.

Doomsman (bound with *Telepower* by Lee Hoffman), Belmont, 1967, reprinted (bound with *The Thief of Thoth* by Lin Carter), 1972.

(With Edward Bryant) *The Starlost #1: Phoenix without Ashes,* Fawcett, 1975.

All the Lies That Are My Life, Underwood-Miller, 1980.

Footsteps, illustrated by Ken Snyder, Footsteps Press, 1989.

Run for the Stars (bound with *Echoes of Thunder* by Jack Dann and Jack C. Haldeman II), Tor Books, 1991.

Mefisto in Onyx, Zeising Books, 1993.

ESSAYS

Memos from Purgatory: Two Journeys of Our Times, Regency Books, 1961.

The Glass Teat: Essays of Opinion on the Subject of Television, Ace Books, 1970.

The Other Glass Teat: Further Essays of Opinion on Television, Pyramid Books, 1975.

The Book of Ellison, edited by Andrew Porter, Algol Press, 1978.

Sleepless Nights in the Procrustean Bed, edited by Marty Clark, Borgo, 1984.

An Edge in My Voice, Donning, 1985.

Harlan Ellison's Watching, Underwood-Miller, 1989.

The Harlan Ellison Hornbook (autobiographical), Penzler, 1990.

EDITOR

Dangerous Visions: 33 Original Stories, Doubleday, 1967.

Nightshade and Damnations: The Finest Stories of Gerald Kersh, Fawcett, 1968.

Again, Dangerous Visions: 46 Original Stories, Doubleday, 1972.

With others, and contributor, *Medea: Harlan's World* (includes "With Virgil Oddum at the East Pole"), Bantam, 1985.

EDITOR; "DISCOVERY" SERIES OF FIRST NOVELS

James Sutherland, *Stormtrack,* Pyramid Books, 1974.

Marta Randall, *Islands,* Pyramid Books, 1976.

Terry Carr, *The Light at the End of the Universe,* Pyramid Books, 1976.

Arthur Byron Cones, *Autumn Angels,* Pyramid Books, 1976.

Bruce Sterling, *Involution Ocean,* Pyramid Books, 1977.

SCREENPLAYS

(With Russell Rouse and Clarence Greene) *The Oscar* (based on the novel by Richard Sale), Embassy, 1966.

Harlan Ellison's Movie: An Original Screenplay, Twentieth Century-Fox, Mirage Press, 1990.

(With Isaac Asimov) *I, Robot: The Illustrated Screenplay* (see also below), Warner, 1994.

Also author of screenplays *Would You Do It for a Penny?,* Playboy Productions, *Stranglehold,* Twentieth Century-Fox, *Seven Worlds, Seven Warriors,* De Laurentis, *I, Robot,* Warner Bros., *Swing Low, Sweet Harriet,* Metro-Goldwyn-Mayer, *The Dream Merchants,* Paramount, *Rumble,* American International, *Khadim,* Paramount, *Bug Jack Barron,* Universal, *None of the Above, Blind Voices, The Whimper of Whipped Dogs, Nick the Greek,* and *Best by Far.*

TELEPLAYS

The Starlost (series), syndicated, 1973.

Brillo (series), ABC, 1974.

The Tigers Are Loose (special), NBC, 1974.

The Dark Forces (series), NBC, 1986.

The Twilight Zone (series), CBS, 1986.

Also author of *The City on the Edge of Forever* (episode of *Star Trek* television series), 1967. Author of telefilms and pilots *A Boy and His Dog, The Spirit, Dark Destroyer, Man without Time, The Other Place, The Tigers Are Loose, Cutter's World, Our Man Flint, Heavy Metal, Tired Old Man, Mystery Show, Astral Man, Astra/Ella, Project 120, Bring 'Em Back Alive, Postmark: Jim Adam, The Contender,* and *The Sniper.*

Author of teleplays for series, including *Star Trek, Outer Limits, Voyage to the Bottom of the Sea, Dark Room, Circle of Fear, Rat Patrol, Amos Burke—Secret Agent, The Great Adventure, Empire, Batman, Ripcord, The Man from UNCLE, Cimarron Strip, Burke's Law, The Young Lawyers, The Name of the Game, Manhunter, The Flying Nun, Route 66, The Alfred Hitchcock Hour, Logan's Run, Twilight Zone,* and *Babylon 5.*

OTHER

(Contributor) Jack Dann and George Zebrowski, editors, *Faster than Light,* Harper, 1976.

The City on the Edge of Forever (play; based on the teleplay by Ellison), published in *Six Science Fiction Plays,* edited by Roger Elwood, Pocket Books, 1976.

Demon With a Glass Hand (graphic novel; illustrated by Marshall Rogers), D.C. Comics, 1986.

Night and the Enemy (graphic novel; illustrated by Ken Steacy), Comico, 1987.

Vic and Blood: The Chronicles of a Boy and His Dog (graphic novel; based on the novella by Ellison), edited by Jan Strand, illustrated by Richard Corben, St. Martin's, 1989.

Mind Fields: Thirty Short Stories Inspired by the Art of Jacek Yerka, art by Yerka, Morpheus, 1994.

(Contributor) Clifford Lawrence Meth and Ricia Mainhardt, *Strange Kaddish: Tales You Won't Hear from Bubbie,* Aardwolf Publishing, 1996.

Also author of "A Boy and His Dog" (novella), 1968. Author of four books on juvenile delinquency. Former author of columns "The Glass Teat" and "Harlan Ellison Hornbook," *Los Angeles Free Press,* and of "An Edge in My Voice," *L.A. Weekly*; author of syndicated film review column "Watching"; publisher of *Dimensions* magazine (originally *Science Fantasy Bulletin*).

MEDIA ADAPTATIONS: A Boy and His Dog was filmed in 1975; much of Ellison's work has been cited as the inspiration for the motion picture *The Terminator,* Orion, 1984; several of Ellison's short stories have been adapted for television. The film rights to *Mefisto in Onyx* have been optioned by Metro-Goldwyn-Mayer.

SIDELIGHTS: Described by fellow author J. G. Ballard as "an aggressive and restless extrovert who conducts his life at a shout and his fiction at a scream," Harlan Ellison is a writer who actively resists being labeled. Though he has written or edited sixty books and has authored more than eleven hundred short stories, he dislikes being called prolific; though his works of fiction and nonfiction are often considered iconoclastic, opinionated, and confrontational, he bristles at the label "irrepressible"; and, though he has garnered numerous major awards from science fiction organizations, he adamantly refuses to be categorized as a science fiction writer, preferring the term "magic realism" to define his writing.

Ellison began his writing career in the mid-1950s after being dismissed from college over a disagreement with a writing teacher who told Ellison that he had no talent. Ellison moved to New York City to become a freelance writer and in his first two years there sold some 150 short stories to magazines in every genre from crime fact to science fiction. It was the science fiction genre, however, that most appreciated Ellison's talent—both to Ellison's benefit and chagrin. Reviewers quickly associated him with the New Wave of science fiction writers—a group that included such authors as Brian W. Aldiss, J. G. Ballard, and Robert Silverberg. James Blish, writing under the pseudonym William Atheling, Jr., proclaimed in *More Issues at Hand,* "Harlan Ellison is not only the most audible but possibly the most gifted of the American members of the New Wave." Donald A. Wolheim concurred in *The Universe Makers*: "Harlan Ellison is one of those one-man phenomena who pop up in a field, follow their own rules, and have such a terrific charisma and personal drive that they get away with it. They break all the rules and make the rest like it."

Some critics, such as Joseph McLellan of the *Washington Post,* have suggested that to call Ellison a science fiction writer is too limiting. McLellan maintained that "the categories are too small to describe Harlan Ellison. Lyric poet, satirist, explorer of odd psychological corners, moralist, one-line comedian, purveyor of pure horror and of black comedy; he is all these and more."

Ellison employs the term "magic realism" to describe his writing, a term which he says can be applied to the work of many other writers, including Kurt Vonnegut, John Barth, Jorge Luis Borges, and Luisa Valenzuela. In 1967, after reading a short story by Thomas Pynchon, Ellison was inspired to edit a collection of "magic realism" stories as a means of better defining the term and distinguishing it from science fiction. The result was *Dangerous Visions: 33 Original Stories.* Specifically designed to include those stories too controversial, too experimental, or too well written to appear in the popular magazines, *Dangerous Visions*

broke new ground in both theme and style. "[*Dangerous Visions*] was intended to shake things up," Ellison wrote in his introduction to the book. "It was conceived out of a need for new horizons, new forms, new styles, new challenges in the literature of our times."

Critical reaction to the book was largely favorable. "You should buy this book immediately," Algis Budrys urged his readers. "There has never been a collection like this before," James Blish, again as Atheling, wrote in *Amazing Stories.* "It will entertain, infuriate, and reward you for years." Damon Knight, writing in the *Saturday Review,* called it "a gigantic, shapeless, exuberant, and startling collection [of] vital, meaningful stories." Of the thirty-three stories in *Dangerous Visions,* seven became winners of either the Hugo or Nebula Award while another thirteen stories were nominees. The collection received a special plaque from the World Science Fiction Convention. *Again, Dangerous Visions: 46 Original Stories,* Ellison's sequel to *Dangerous Visions,* met with the same success as its predecessor: J. B. Post of *Library Journal* predicted that *Again, Dangerous Visions* "will become a historically important book," and W. E. McNelly of *America* claimed that the collection was "so experimental in design, concept, and execution that this one volume may well place science fiction in the very heart of mainstream literature."

However provocative it may be, Ellison's fiction has been ranked among America's best. Blish noted in *More Issues at Hand* that Ellison is "a born writer, almost entirely without taste or control but with so much fire, originality and drive, as well as compassion, that he makes the conventional virtues of the artist seem almost irrelevant." In his book-length study, *Harlan Ellison: Unrepentant Harlequin,* George Edgar Slusser called Ellison "a tireless experimenter with forms and techniques" and concludes that he "has produced some of the finest, most provocative fantasy in America today." George R. R. Martin wrote in the *Washington Post Book World* that Ellison "is one of the great living American short story writers."

Of all his short stories, the one most often singled out by critics and fans alike as Ellison's best is "'Repent, Harlequin!' Said the Ticktockman." It describes a future civilization in which citizens are held responsible for every second of their day; value is determined by productivity, and tardiness is loathed above all things. Promptness is enforced by the tyrannical Master Time-keeper, known colloquially as the Ticktockman. The protagonist is the Harlequin, who dresses in a motley style, is always late, and who plays pranks on his coworkers simply to make them laugh. Though in the end the Harlequin is brainwashed and subsumed by the system, his actions create ripples in the pond, planting within his coworkers the seeds of civil disobedience. The moral of "'Repent, Harlequin!'" is, according to Slusser, that "the 'real' men in society are not those who abdicate all freedom of judgment to serve the machine, but those who resist dehumanization through acts of conscience, no matter how small. . . . If such a sacrifice brings even the slightest change, it is worth it." "'Repent, Harlequin!' Said the Ticktockman" is one of the ten most reprinted stories in the English language.

Another popular work of Ellison's is the 1968 novella *A Boy and His Dog,* which was made into a movie in 1975. In the year 2024, shortly after the devastating climax of World War IV, Vic and his dog Blood wander the wastes of the American southwest. The relationship between boy and dog is unusual for two reasons: first, Blood is telepathic, allowing him to communicate with Vic; second, the roles of human and animal have been reversed—Vic is little more than a scavenger, while Blood is literate and cultured. Blood teaches his "master" reading, speech, arithmetic, and history; however, he has forgotten his animal instincts, and must rely upon Vic to hunt game and find shelter. John Crow and Richard Erlich, reviewing *A Boy and His Dog* for *Extrapolation,* described the novella as "a cautionary fable" which "demands consideration of just how consciously our own society is proceeding into its technological future."

Ellison continued to produce successful fiction during the 1990s. The novella *Mefisto in Onyx* features Rudy Pairis, a gifted black man whose ability to read minds is employed by Deputy District Attorney Allison Roche to exonerate a convicted serial killer who awaits an impending death sentence. Though Roche prosecuted the convicted murderer herself, days before his execution she doubts his guilt and persuades Pairis to probe his mind for evidence of his innocence. David Gianatasio praised the Pairis character in an *Armchair Detective* review. "Like most Ellison anti-heroes, Pairis's inability to fully accept his heightened mental powers—and in a larger sense, to accept himself—makes him an outcast in his own world." Gianatasio added, "Pairis's ability to accept who and what he is. . . is the key to his final transcendence." Tom Auer concluded in *Bloomsbury Review,* "This story is a page-turner, quick, lively, and entertaining, and very funny in parts, but colored throughout with a deep sense of humankind's insufferable inhumanity."

Ellison also published *I, Robot: The Illustrated Screenplay,* co-authored with Isaac Asimov, after a protracted and ultimately failed attempt to produce a film version of the story. As Michael Rogers noted in *Library Journal,* this unproduced script achieved near legendary status as "the greatest science fiction movie *never* made." Based on Asimov's *I, Robot* series and elements of Orson Welles's *Citizen Kane,* Ellison grafts various Asimov subplots and his own material into a story about a journalist's persistent effort to interview Susan Calvin, a reclusive octogenarian, upon the death of her reputed lover Stephen Byerly. Though commending Ellison's achievement, *Locus* reviewer Gary K. Wolfe wrote, "*I, Robot* was probably never a very good idea for a movie" because "most of the stories were intellectual puzzles based on permutations of the laws of robotics." However, Wolfe added, "As a potential moviegoer, there's nothing here to convince me that this relatively simple story about a lonely woman in a lost future is impossible to film." An *Analog* reviewer similarly concluded, "Ellison did indeed make a compelling story of Asimov's material, and the script would indeed make a grand movie."

Commenting on Ellison's style and central themes, Auer wrote, "Ellison's prose is powerful and ingenious, but often angry, sometimes sinister, occasionally gloomy, and often with an edge that can cut quickly to and through the heart of his subject, or that of his reader for that matter." As Auer observed, "The bloody truth of our violent times, a subject he writes about with regularity and ease, practically drips from some of his finely crafted pages. He also has a sense of humor, but we don't see it often, and it is frequently black as midnight when we do."

"I write because I cannot *not* write," Ellison once explained in *Bloomsbury Review.* "That's what I *do.* . . . It amazes me when I get an interview with someone who says, 'You're so prolific, you've done forty-two books and thousands of short stories.' And I say, 'If I were a plumber, and I had fixed a thousand toilets, you wouldn't say that, you wouldn't say what a prolific plumber I am.' That's what I *do.*"

BIOGRAPHICAL/CRITICAL SOURCES:

BOOKS

Atheling, Jr., William, *More Issues at Hand,* Advent, 1970.
Contemporary Literary Criticism, Gale (Detroit), Volume 1, 1973; Volume 13, 1980; Volume 42, 1987.
Dictionary of Literary Biography, Volume 8: *Twentieth-Century American Science Fiction Writers,* Gale, 1981.
Platt, Charles, *The Dream Makers: The Uncommon People Who Write Science Fiction,* Berkley, 1980.
Porter, Andrew, editor, *The Book of Ellison,* Algol Press, 1978.
Slusser, George Edgar, *Harlan Ellison: Unrepentant Harlequin,* Borgo, 1977.
Swigart, Leslie Kay, *Harlan Ellison: A Bibliographical Checklist,* Williams Publishing (Dallas), 1973.
Walker, Paul, *Speaking of Science Fiction: The Paul Walker Interviews,* Luna, 1978.
Wolheim, Donald A., *The Universe Makers,* Harper, 1971.

PERIODICALS

America, June 10, 1972.
Analog, September, 1960; December, 1962; May, 1968; June, 1968; August, 1970; April, 1973; September, 1995, p. 185.
Armchair Detective, spring, 1994, p. 245.
Bloomsbury Review, January, 1985; February, 1985; May/June, 1994, p. 1.
Chicago Tribune, September 24, 1961; June 2, 1985; January 17, 1989.
Esquire, January, 1962.
Extrapolation, May, 1977; winter, 1979.
Fantasy Newsletter, April, 1981.
Galaxy, April, 1968; May, 1972.
Library Journal, April 15, 1972; February 1, 1995, p. 75.
Locus, November, 1994, p. 61.
Los Angeles Times, September 20, 1988; October 26, 1997.
Los Angeles Times Book Review, October 24, 1982, p. 14; June 30, 1985, p. 7; January 1, 1989, p. 9.
Magazine of Fantasy and Science Fiction, January, 1968; November, 1971; September, 1972; October, 1975; July, 1977; June, 1994.
Manchester Guardian, July 4, 1963.
National Review, July 12, 1966; May 7, 1968.
New Statesman, March 25, 1977.
New York Times Book Review, October 26, 1958; June 30, 1960; August 20, 1961; June 30, 1968; September 3, 1972; March 23, 1975; April 1, 1979; January 8, 1989, p. 31; September 17, 1989, p. 12; March 18, 1990, p. 32.
Publishers Weekly, February 10, 1975.
Renaissance, summer, 1972.
Review of Contemporary Literature, fall, 1994, p. 229.
Saturday Review, December 30, 1967.
Science Fiction Review, January, 1971; September/October, 1978.
Spectator, January, 1971.
Times Literary Supplement, April 16, 1971; January 14, 1977; July 9, 1982, p. 739.
Tribune Books (Chicago), June 2, 1985, p. 35.
Variety, July 8, 1970; March 17, 1971.
Washington Post, August 3, 1978; July 30, 1985.
Washington Post Book World, January 25, 1981; December 26, 1982; June 30, 1985; September 25, 1988, p. 8; October 28, 1990, p. 10; February 2, 1992, p. 12.

ELLISON, Ralph (Waldo) 1914-1994

PERSONAL: Born March 1, 1914, in Oklahoma City, OK; died of cancer, April 16, 1994, in New York, NY; son of Lewis Alfred (a construction worker and tradesman) and Ida (Millsap) Ellison; married Fanny McConnell, July, 1946. *Education:* Attended Tuskegee Institute, 1933-36. *Avocation:* Jazz and classical music, photography, electronics, furniture-making, bird-watching, gardening.

CAREER: Writer, 1937-94. Worked as a researcher and writer on Federal Writers' Project in New York City, 1938-42; edited *Negro Quarterly,* 1942; lecture tour in Germany, 1954; lecturer at Salzburg Seminar, Austria, fall, 1954; U.S. Information Agency, tour of Italian cities, 1956; Bard College, Annandale-on-Hudson, NY, instructor in Russian and American literature, 1958-61; New York University, New York City, Albert Schweitzer Professor in Humanities, 1970-79, professor emeritus, 1979-94. Alexander White Visiting Professor, University of Chicago, 1961; visiting professor of writing, Rutgers University, 1962-64; visiting fellow in American studies, Yale University, 1966. Gertrude Whittall Lecturer, Library of Congress, January, 1964; delivered Ewing Lectures at University of California, Los Angeles, April, 1964. Lecturer in African-American culture, folklore, and creative writing at other colleges and universities throughout the United States, including Columbia University, Fisk University, Princeton University, Antioch University, and Bennington College.

Member of Carnegie Commission on Educational Television, 1966-67; honorary consultant in American letters, Library of Congress, 1966-72. Trustee, Colonial Williamsburg Foundation, John F. Kennedy Center for the Performing Arts, 1967-77, Educational Broadcasting Corp., 1968-69, New School for Social Research, 1969-83, Bennington College, 1970-75, and Museum of the City of New York, 1970-86. Charter member of National Council of the Arts, 1965-67, and of National Advisory Council, Hampshire College. *Military service:* U.S. Merchant Marine, World War II.

MEMBER: PEN (vice president, 1964), Authors Guild, Authors League of America, American Academy and Institute of Arts and Letters, Institute of Jazz Studies (member of board of advisors), Century Association (resident member).

AWARDS, HONORS: Rosenwald grant, 1945; National Book Award and National Newspaper Publishers' Russwurm Award, both 1953, both for *Invisible Man*; Certificate of Award, *Chicago Defender,* 1953; Rockefeller Foundation award, 1954; Prix de Rome fellowships, American Academy of Arts and Letters, 1955 and 1956; *Invisible Man* selected as the most distinguished postwar American novel and Ellison as the sixth most influential novelist by *New York Herald Tribune Book Week* poll of two hundred authors, editors, and critics, 1965; recipient of award honoring well-known Oklahomans in the arts from governor of Oklahoma, 1966; Medal of Freedom, 1969; Chevalier de l'Ordre des Arts et Lettres (France), 1970; Ralph Ellison Public Library, Oklahoma City, named in his honor, 1975; National Medal of Arts, 1985, for *Invisible Man* and for his teaching at numerous universities; honorary doctorates from Tuskegee Institute, 1963, Rutgers University, 1966, Grinnell College, 1967, University of Michigan, 1967, Williams College, 1970, Long Island University, 1971, Adelphi University, 1971, College of William and Mary, 1972, Harvard University, 1974, Wake Forest College, 1974, University of Maryland, 1974, Bard College, 1978, Wesleyan University, 1980, and Brown University, 1980.

WRITINGS:

Invisible Man (novel), Random House (New York City), 1952, published in a limited edition with illustrations by Steven H. Stroud, Franklin Library, 1980, thirtieth-anniversary edition with new introduction by author, Random House, 1982, edited and with an introduction by Harold Bloom, Chelsea House (New York City), 1996.

(Author of introduction) Stephen Crane, *The Red Badge of Courage and Four Great Stories,* Dell (New York City), 1960.

Shadow and Act (essays), Random House, 1964.

(With Karl Shapiro) *The Writer's Experience* (lectures; includes "Hidden Names and Complex Fate: A Writer's Experience in the U.S.," by Ellison, and "American Poet?," by Shapiro), Gertrude Clarke Whittall Poetry and Literature Fund for Library of Congress, 1964.

(With Whitney M. Young and Herbert Gans) *The City in Crisis,* introduction by Bayard Rustin, A. Philip Randolph Education Fund, 1968.

(Author of introduction) Romare Bearden, *Paintings and Projections* (catalogue of exhibition, November 25-December 22, 1968), State University of New York at Albany, 1968.

(Author of foreword) Leon Forrest, *There Is a Tree More Ancient than Eden,* Random House, 1973.

Going to the Territory (essays), Random House, 1986.

The Collected Essays of Ralph Ellison, Modern Library, 1995.

Flying Home and Other Stories, edited by John F. Callahan, preface by Saul Bellow, Random House (New York City), 1996.

OTHER

Ralph Ellison: An Interview with the Author of Invisible Man (sound recording), Center for Cassette Studies, 1974.

(With William Styron and James Baldwin) *Is the Novel Dead?: Ellison, Styron and Baldwin on Contemporary Fiction* (sound recording), Center for Cassette Studies, 1974.

Conversations with Ralph Ellison, edited by Maryemma Graham and Amritjit Singh, University Press of Mississippi (Jackson), 1995.

Contributor to books, including *The Living Novel: A Symposium,* edited by Granville Hicks, Macmillan (New York City), 1957; *Education of the Deprived and Segregated* (report of seminar on education for culturally-different youth, Dedham, MA, September 3-15, 1963), Bank Street College of Education, 1965; *Who Speaks for the Negro?,* by Robert Penn Warren, Random House, 1965; *To Heal and to Build: The Programs of Lyndon B. Johnson,* edited by James MacGregor Burns, prologue by Howard K. Smith, epilogue by Eric Hoffer, McGraw (New York City), 1968; and *American Law: The Third Century, the Law Bicentennial Volume,* edited by Bernard Schwartz, F. B. Rothman for New York University School of Law, 1976. Work represented in numerous anthologies, including *American Writing,* edited by Hans Otto Storm and others, J. A. Decker, 1940; *Best Short Stories of World War II,* edited by Charles A. Fenton, Viking (New York City), 1957; *The Angry Black,* edited by John Alfred Williams, Lancer Books, 1962, 2nd edition published as *Beyond the Angry Black,* Cooper Square (Totowa, NJ), 1966; *Soon, One Morning: New Writing by American Negroes, 1940-1962* (includes previously unpublished section from original manuscript of *Invisible Man*), edited by Herbert Hill, Knopf (New York City), 1963, published in England as *Black Voices,* Elek Books (London), 1964; *Experience and Expression: Reading and Responding to Short Fiction,* edited by John L. Kimmey, Scott, Foresman (Glenview, IL), 1976; *and The*

Treasury of American Short Stories, compiled by Nancy Sullivan, Doubleday (New York City), 1981.

SIDELIGHTS: Growing up in Oklahoma, a "frontier" state that "had no tradition of slavery" and where "relationships between the races were more fluid and thus more human than in the old slave states," Ralph Ellison became conscious of his obligation "to explore the full range of American Negro humanity and to affirm those qualities which are of value beyond any question of segregation, economics or previous condition of servitude." This sense of obligation, articulated in his 1964 collection of critical and biographical essays, *Shadow and Act,* led to his staunch refusal to limit his artistic vision to the "uneasy sanctuary of race" and commit instead to a literature that explores and affirms the complex, often contradictory frontier of an identity at once black and American and universally human. For Ellison, whom John F. Callahan in a *Chant of Saints: A Gathering of Afro-American Literature, Art, and Scholarship* essay called a "moral historian," the act of writing was fraught with both great possibility and grave responsibility. As Ellison asserted, writing "offers me the possibility of contributing not only to the growth of the literature but to the shaping of the culture as I should like it to be. The American novel is in this sense a conquest of the frontier; as it describes our experience, it creates it."

For Ellison, then, the task of the novelist was a moral and political one. In his preface to the thirtieth anniversary edition of *Invisible Man,* Ellison argued that the serious novel, like the best politics, "is a thrust toward a human ideal." Even when the ideal is not realized in the actual, he declared, "there is still available that fictional *vision* of an ideal democracy in which the actual combines with the ideal and gives us representations of a state of things in which the highly placed and the lowly, the black and the white, the Northerner and the Southerner, the native-born and the immigrant are combined to tell us of transcendent truths and possibilities such as those discovered when Mark Twain set Huck and Jim afloat on the raft." Ellison saw the novel as a "raft of hope" that may help readers stay above water as they try "to negotiate the snags and whirlpools that mark our nation's vacillating course toward and away from the democratic ideal."

Early in his career, Ellison conceived of his vocation as a musician, as a composer of symphonies. When he entered Alabama's Tuskegee Institute in 1933 he enrolled as a music major; he wonders in *Shadow and Act* if he did so because, given his background, it was the only art "that seemed to offer some possibility for self-definition." The act of writing soon presented itself as an art through which he could link the disparate worlds he cherished, could verbally record and create the "affirmation of Negro life" he knew was so intrinsic a part of the universally human. To move beyond the old definitions that separated jazz from classical music, vernacular from literary language, the folk from the mythic, he would have to discover a prose style that could equal the integrative imagination of the "Renaissance Man."

Because Ellison did not get a job that paid him enough to save money for tuition, he stayed in New York, working and studying composition until his mother died in Dayton, Ohio. After his return to Dayton, he and his brother supported themselves by hunting. Though Ellison had hunted for years, he did not know how to wing-shoot; it was from Hemingway's fiction that he learned this process. Ellison studied Hemingway to learn writing techniques; from the older writer he also learned a lesson in descriptive accuracy and power, in the close relationship between fiction and reality. Like his narrator in *Invisible Man,* Ellison did not return to college; instead he began his long apprenticeship as a writer, his long and often difficult journey toward self-definition.

Ellison's early days in New York, before his return to Dayton, provided him with experiences that would later translate themselves into his theory of fiction. Two days after his arrival in "deceptively 'free' Harlem," he met black poet Langston Hughes who introduced him to the works of Andre Malraux, a French writer defined as Marxist. Though attracted to Marxism, Ellison sensed in Malraux something beyond a simplistic political sense of the human condition. Said Ellison: Malraux "was the artist-revolutionary rather than a politician when he wrote *Man's Fate,* and the book lives not because of a political position embraced at the time, but because of its larger concern with the tragic struggle of humanity." Ellison began to form his definition of the artist as a revolutionary concerned less with local injustice than with the timelessly tragic.

Ellison's view of art was furthered after he met black novelist Richard Wright. Wright urged him to read Joseph Conrad, Henry James, James Joyce, and Feodor Dostoevsky and invited Ellison to contribute a review essay and then a short story to the magazine he was editing. Wright was then in the process of writing *Native Son,* much of which Ellison read, he declared in *Shadow and Act,* "as it came out of the typewriter." Though awed by the process of writing and aware of the achievement of the novel, Ellison, who had just read Malraux, began to form his objections to the "sociological," deterministic ideology which informed the portrait of the work's protagonist, Bigger Thomas. In *Shadow and Act,* which Arthur P. Davis in *From the Dark Tower: Afro-American Writers, 1900 to 1960* described as partly an *apologia pro vita sua* (a defense of his life), Ellison articulated the basis of his objection: "I, for instance, found it disturbing that Bigger Thomas had none of the finer qualities of Richard Wright, none of the imagination, none of the sense of poetry, none of the gaiety." Ellison thus refuted the depiction of the black individual as an inarticulate victim whose life is one only of despair, anger, and pain. He insisted that art must capture instead the complex reality, the pain and the pleasure of black existence, thereby challenging the definition of the black person as something less than fully human. Such a vision of art, which is at the heart of *Invisible Man,* became the focal point of an extended debate between Ellison and Irving Howe, who in a 1963 *Dissent* article accused Ellison of disloyalty to Wright in particular and to "protest fiction" in general.

From 1938 to 1944, Ellison published a number of short stories and contributed essays to journals such as *New Masses.* As with other examples of Ellison's work, these stories have provoked disparate readings. In an essay in *Black World,* Ernest Kaiser called the earliest stories and the essays in *New Masses* "the healthiest" of Ellison's career. The critic praised the economic theories that inform the early fiction, and he found Ellison's language pure, emotional, and effective. Lamenting a change he attributed to Ellison's concern with literary technique, Kaiser charged the later stories, essays, and novels with being no longer concerned with people's problems and with being "unemotional." Other critics, like Marcus Klein in *After Alienation: American Novels in Mid-Century,* saw the early work as a progressive preparation for Ellison's mature fiction and theory. In the earliest of these stories, "Slick Gonna Learn," Ellison drew a character shaped largely by an ideological, naturalistic conception of existence, the very type of character he later repudiated. From this imitation of proletarian fiction, Ellison's work moved towards psychological and finally metaphysical explorations of the human condition. His characters thus were freed from restrictive definitions as Ellison developed a voice that was his own, Klein maintains.

In the two latest stories of the 1938-1944 period, "Flying Home" and "King of the Bingo Game," Ellison created characters congruent with his sense of pluralism and possibility and does so in a narrative style that begins to approach the complexity of *Invisible Man.* As Arthur P. Davis noted, in "Flying Home" Ellison combined realism, folk story, symbolism, and a touch of surrealism to present his protagonist, Todd. In a fictional world composed of myriad levels of the mythic and the folk, the classical and the modern, Todd fights to free himself of imposed definitions. In "King of the Bingo Game," Ellison experimented with integrating sources and techniques. As in all of Ellison's early stories, the protagonist is a young black man fighting for his freedom against forces and people that attempt to deny it. In "King of the Bingo Game," Robert G. O'Meally argued in *The Craft of Ralph Ellison,* "the struggle is seen in its most abstracted form." This abstraction results from the "dreamlike shifts of time and levels of consciousness" that dominate the surrealistic story and also from the fact that "the King is Ellison's first character to sense the frightening absurdity of everyday American life." In an epiphany which frees him from illusion and which places him, even if for only a moment, in control, the King realizes "that his battle for freedom and identity must be waged not against individuals or even groups, but against no less than history and fate," O'Meally declared. The parameters of the fight for freedom and identity have been broadened. Ellison saw his black hero as one who wages the oldest battle in human history: the fight for freedom to be timelessly human, to engage in the "tragic struggle of humanity," as the writer asserted in *Shadow and Act.*

Whereas The King achieves awareness for a moment, the Invisible Man not only becomes aware but is able to articulate fully the struggle. As Ellison noted in his preface to the anniversary edition of the novel, too often characters have been "figures caught up in the most intense forms of social struggle, subject to the most extreme forms of the human predicament but yet seldom able to articulate the issues which tortured them." The Invisible Man is endowed with eloquence; he is Ellison's radical experiment with a fiction that insists upon the full range and humanity of the black character.

Ellison began *Invisible Man* in 1945. Although he was at work on a never-completed war novel at the time, Ellison recalled in his 1982 preface that he could not ignore the "taunting, disembodied voice" he heard beckoning him to write *Invisible Man.* Published in 1952 after a seven-year creative struggle, and awarded the National Book Award in 1953, *Invisible Man* received critical acclaim. Although some early reviewers were puzzled or disappointed by the experimental narrative techniques, many now agree that these techniques give the work its lasting force and account for Ellison's influence on later fiction. The novel is a fugue of cultural fragments—echoes of Homer, Joyce, Eliot, and Hemingway join forces with the sounds of spirituals, blues, jazz, and nursery rhymes. The Invisible Man is as haunted by Louis Armstrong's "What did I do / To be so black / And blue?" as he is by Hemingway's bullfight scenes and his matadors' grace under pressure. The linking together of these disparate cultural elements allows the Invisible Man to draw the portrait of his inner face that is the way out of his wasteland.

In the novel, Ellison clearly employed the traditional motif of the *Bildungsroman,* or novel of education: the Invisible Man moves from innocence to experience, darkness to light, from blindness to sight. Complicating this linear journey, however, is the narrative frame provided by the Prologue and Epilogue which the narrator composes after the completion of his above-ground educational journey. Yet readers begin with the Prologue, written in his underground chamber on the "border area" of Harlem where he is waging a guerrilla war against the Monopolated Light & Power Company by invisibly draining their power. At first denied the story of his discovery, readers must be initiated through the act of re-experiencing the events that led them and the narrator to this hole. Armed with some suggestive hints and symbols, readers then start the journey toward a revisioning of the Invisible Man, America, and themselves.

The act of writing, of ordering and defining the self, is what gives the Invisible Man freedom and what allows him to manage the absurdity and chaos of everyday life. Writing frees the self from imposed definitions, from the straitjacket of all that would limit the productive possibilities of the self. Echoing the pluralism of the novel's form, the Invisible Man insists on the freedom to be ambivalent, to love and to hate, to denounce and to defend the America he inherits. Ellison himself was well-acquainted with the ambivalence of his American heritage; nowhere is it more evident than in his name. Named after the nineteenth-century essayist and poet Ralph Waldo Emerson, whom Ellison's father admired, the name created for Ellison embarrassment, confusion, and a desire to be the American writer his namesake called for. And Ellison placed such emphasis on his unnamed yet self-named narrator's breaking the shackles of restrictive definitions, of what others call reality or right, he also freed himself, as Robert B. Stepto in *From Behind the Veil: A Study of Afro-American Narrative* argued, from the strictures of the traditional slave narratives of Frederick Douglas and W. E. B. DuBois. By consciously invoking this form but then not bringing the motif of "ascent and immersion" to its traditional completion, Ellison revoiced the form, made it his own, and stepped outside it.

In her 1979 *PMLA* essay, Susan Blake argued that Ellison's insistence that black experience be ritualized as part of the larger human experience results in a denial of the unique social reality of black life. Because Ellison so thoroughly adapted black folklore into the Western tradition, Blake found that the definition of black life becomes "not black but white"; it "exchanges the self-definition of the folk for the definition of the masters." Thorpe Butler, in a 1984 *College Language Association Journal* essay, defended Ellison against Blake's criticism. He declared that Ellison's depiction of specific black experience as part of the universal does not "diminish the unique richness and anguish" of that experience and does not "diminish the force of Ellison's protest against the blind, cruel dehumanization of black Americans by white society." This debate extends arguments that have appeared since the publication of the novel. Underlying these controversies is the old, uneasy argument about the relationship of art and politics, of literary practice and social commitment.

Although the search for identity is the major theme of *Invisible Man,* other aspects of the novel have also received critical attention. Among them, as Joanne Giza noted in her essay in *Black American Writers: Bibliographical Essays,* are literary debts and analogies, comic elements, the metaphor of vision, use of the blues, and folkloric elements. Although all of these concerns are part of the larger issue of identity, Ellison's use of blues and folklore has been singled out as a major contribution to contemporary literature and culture. Since the publication of *Invisible Man,* scores of articles have appeared on these two topics, a fact which in turn has led to a rediscovery and revisioning of the importance of blues and folklore to American literature and culture in general.

Much of Ellison's groundbreaking work is presented in *Shadow and Act*. Published in 1964, this collection of essays, said Ellison, is "concerned with three general themes: with literature and folklore, with Negro musical expression—especially jazz and the blues—and with the complex relationship between the Negro American subculture and North American culture as a whole." This volume has been hailed as one of the more prominent examples of cultural criticism of the century. Writing in *Commentary,* Robert Penn Warren praised the astuteness of Ellison's perceptions; in *New Leader,* Stanley Edgar Hyman proclaimed Ellison "the profoundest cultural critic we have." In the *New York Review of Books,* R. W. B. Lewis explored Ellison's study of black music as a form of power and found that "Ellison is not only a self-identifier but the source of self-definition in others." Published in 1986, *Going to the Territory* is a second collection of essays reprising many of the subjects and concerns treated in *Shadow and Act*—literature, art, music, the relationships of black and white cultures, fragments of autobiography, tributes to such noted black Americans as Richard Wright, Duke Ellington, and painter Romare Beardon. With the exception of "An Extravagance of Laughter," a lengthy examination of Ellison's response to Jack Kirkland's dramatization of Erskine Caldwell's novel *Tobacco Road,* the essays in *Going to the Territory* are reprints of previously published articles or speeches, most of them dating from the 1960s.

Ellison's influence as both novelist and critic, as artist and cultural historian, has been enormous. In special issues of *Black World* and *College Language Association Journal* devoted to Ellison, strident attacks appear alongside equally spirited accolades. Perhaps another measure of Ellison's stature and achievement was his readers' vigil for his long-awaited second novel. Although Ellison often refused to answer questions about the work-in-progress, there is enough evidence to suggest that the manuscript was very large, that all or part of it was destroyed in a fire and was being rewritten, and that its creation was a long and painful task. Most readers waited expectantly, believing that Ellison, who said in *Shadow and Act* that he "failed of eloquence" in *Invisible Man,* intended to wait until his second novel equaled his imaginative vision of the American novel as conqueror of the frontier, equaled the Emersonian call for a literature to release all people from the bonds of oppression.

Eight excerpts from this novel-in-progress have been published in journals such as *Quarterly Review of Literature, Massachusetts Review,* and *Noble Savage.* Set in the South in the years spanning the Jazz Age to the Civil Rights movement, these fragments seem an attempt to recreate modern American history and identity. The major characters are the Reverend Hickman, a one-time jazz musician, and Bliss, the light-skinned boy whom he adopts and who later passes into white society and becomes Senator Sunraider, an advocate of white supremacy. As O'Meally noted in *The Craft of Ralph Ellison,* the major difference between Bliss and Ellison's earlier young protagonists is that despite some harsh collisions with reality, Bliss refuses to divest himself of his illusions and accept his personal history. Said O'Meally: "Moreover, it is a renunciation of the blackness of American experience and culture, a refusal to accept the American past in all its complexity."

After Ellison's death on April 16, 1994, speculation about the existence of the second novel reignited. In an article in the *New York Times,* William Grimes assembled the information available on the subject. "Joe Fox, Mr. Ellison's editor at Random House, and close friends of the novelist say that Mr. Ellison has left a manuscript of somewhere between 1,000 and 2,000 pages," Grimes reported. "At the time of his death, he had been working on it every day and was close to completing the work, whose fate now rests with his widow, Fanny." A close friend of Ellison's, John F. Callahan, a college dean from Portland, Oregon, told Grimes that he had seen parts of the manuscript not already published in other sources. "From what I've read, if 'Invisible Man' is akin to Joyce's 'Portrait of the Artist,' then the novel in progress may be his 'Ulysses.'" Callahan added that "it's a weaving together of all kinds of voices, and not simply voices in the black tradition, but white voices, too: all kinds of American voices." As Grimes suggested, "If Mr. Ellison, as his final creative act, were to top 'Invisible Man,' it would be a stunning bequest," given that the first novel is considered a literary classic. *Invisible Man* "has never been out of print," Grimes pointed out. "It has sold millions of copies worldwide. On college campuses it is required reading in 20th-century American literature courses, and it has been the subject of hundreds of scholarly articles."

BIOGRAPHICAL/CRITICAL SOURCES:

BOOKS

Benstion, Kimberly W., editor, *Speaking for You: The Vision of Ralph Ellison,* Howard University Press (Washington, DC), 1987.
Bishop, Jack, *Ralph Ellison,* Chelsea House (New York City), 1988.
Bloom, Harold, editor, *Ralph Ellison: Modern Critical Views,* Chelsea Publishing, 1986.
Busby, Mark, *Ralph Ellison,* Twayne (Boston), 1991.
Callahan, John F., *In the African-American Grain: The Pursuit of Voice in Twentieth-Century Black Fiction,* University of Illinois Press (Urbana, IL), 1988.
Concise Dictionary of American Literary Biography: The New Consciousness, 1941-1948, Gale (Detroit), 1987.
Contemporary Literary Criticism, Gale, Volume 1, 1973; Volume 3, 1975; Volume 11, 1979; Volume 54, 1989.
Cooke, Michael, *Afro-American Literature in the Twentieth Century: The Achievement of Intimacy,* Yale University Press, 1984.
Davis, Arthur P., *From the Dark Tower: Afro-American Writers, 1900 to 1960,* Howard University Press, 1974.
Davis, Charles T., *Black Is the Color of the Cosmos: Essays on Afro-American Literature and Culture, 1942-1981,* edited by Henry Louis Gates, Jr., Garland Publishing (New York City), 1982.
Dictionary of Literary Biography, Gale, Volume 2: *American Novelists since World War II,* 1978; Volume 76: *Afro-American Writers, 1940-1955,* 1988.
Graham, Maryemma, and Amritjit Singh, editors, *Conversations with Ralph Ellison,* University Press of Mississippi (Jackson, MS), 1995.
Inge, M. Thomas, editor, *Black American Writers: Bibliographic Essays, Volume 2: Richard Wright, Ralph Ellison, James Baldwin, and Amiri Baraka,* St. Martin's, 1978.
Jothiprakash, R., *Commitment as a Theme in African American Literature: A Study of James Baldwin and Ralph Ellison,* Wyndham Hall Press (Bristol, IN), 1994.
Klein, Marcus, *After Alienation: American Novels in Mid-Century,* World Publishing, 1964.

Kostelanetz, Richard, *Politics in the African-American Novel: James Weldon Johnson, W. E. B. DuBois, Richard Wright, and Ralph Ellison,* Greenwood Press (New York City), 1991.

Lynch, Michael F., *Creative Revolt: A Study of Wright, Ellison, and Dostevsky,* P. Lang (New York City), 1990.

McSweeney, Kerry, *Invisible Man: Race and Identity,* Twayne (Boston), 1988.

Nadel, Alan, *Invisible Criticism: Ralph Ellison and the American Canon,* University of Iowa Press (Iowa City, IA), 1988.

O'Meally, Robert G., *New Essays on Invisible Man,* Cambridge University Press (Cambridge, England), 1988.

O'Meally, Robert G., *The Craft of Ralph Ellison,* Harvard University Press, 1980.

Parr, Susan Resneck, and Pancho Savery, editors, *Approaches to Teaching Ellison's "Invisible Man,"* Modern Language Associates of America, 1989.

Schor, Edith, *Visible Ellison: A Study of Ralph Ellison's Fiction,* Greenwood Press, 1993.

Stepto, Robert B., *From Behind the Veil: A Study of Afro-American Narrative,* University of Illinois Press, 1979.

Sundquist, Eric J., editor, *Cultural Contexts for Ralph Ellison's Invisible Man,* Bedford Books (Boston), 1995.

Watts, Jerry Gafio, *Heroism and the Black Intellectual: Ralph Ellison, Politics, and Afro-American Intellectual Life,* University of North Carolina Press (Chapel Hill, NC), 1994.

PERIODICALS

America, August 27, 1994, p. 26.
Atlantic, July, 1952; December, 1970; August, 1986.
Black American Literature Forum, summer, 1978.
Black World, December, 1970 (special Ellison issue).
Carleton Miscellany, winter, 1980 (special Ellison issue).
Chicago Review, Volume 19, number 2, 1967.
Chicago Tribune, June 18, 1992, p. 1.
Chicago Tribune Book World, August 10, 1986.
College Language Association Journal, December, 1963; June, 1967; March, 1970 (special Ellison issue); September, 1971; December, 1971; December, 1972; June, 1973; March, 1974; September, 1976; September, 1977; Number 25, 1982; Number 27, 1984.
Commentary, November, 1953; Number 39, 1965.
English Journal, September, 1969; May, 1973; November, 1984.
Harper's, October, 1959; March, 1967; July, 1967.
Los Angeles Times, August 8, 1986.
Massachusetts Review, autumn, 1967; autumn, 1977.
Modern Fiction Studies, winter, 1969-70.
Nation, May 10, 1952; September 9, 1964; November 9, 1964; September 20, 1965.
Negro American Literature Forum, July, 1970; summer, 1973; Number 9, 1975; spring, 1977.
Negro Digest, May, 1964; August, 1967.
Negro History Bulletin, May, 1953; October, 1953.
New Criterion, September, 1983.
New Leader, October 26, 1964.
New Republic, November 14, 1964; August 4, 1986.
Newsweek, August 12, 1963; October 26, 1964; May 2, 1994, p. 58.
New Yorker, May 31, 1952; November 22, 1976; March 14, 1994, p. 34.
New York Herald Tribune Book Review, April 13, 1952.
New York Review of Books, January 28, 1964; January 28, 1965.
New York Times, April 13, 1952; April 24, 1985; April 17, 1994, p. A38; April 20, 1994, p. C13; April 18, 1996, pp. B1, B2.

New York Times Book Review, April 13, 1952; May 4, 1952; October 25, 1964; January 24, 1982; August 3, 1986.
New York Times Magazine, November 20, 1966; January 1, 1995, p. 22.
PMLA, January, 1979.
Renascence, spring, 1974; winter, 1978.
Saturday Review, April 12, 1952; March 14, 1953; December 11, 1954; January 1, 1955; April 26, 1958; May 17, 1958; July 12, 1958; September 27, 1958; July 28, 1962; October 24, 1964.
Southern Humanities Review, winter, 1970.
Southern Literary Journal, spring, 1969.
Southern Review, fall, 1974; summer, 1985.
Studies in American Fiction, spring, 1973.
Studies in Black Literature, autumn, 1971; autumn, 1972; spring, 1973; spring, 1975; spring, 1976; winter, 1976.
Time, April 14, 1952; February 9, 1959; February 1, 1963; April 6, 1970.
Times Literary Supplement, January 18, 1968.
Tribune Books (Chicago), April 24, 1994, p. 3.
Village Voice, November 19, 1964.
Washington Post, August 19-21, 1973; April 21, 1982; February 9, 1983; March 30, 1983; July 23, 1986; April 18, 1994, p. C1; April 25, 1994, p. C2.
Washington Post Book World, May 17, 1987.

*   *   *

ELLMANN, Richard (David) 1918-1987

PERSONAL: Born March 15, 1918, in Highland Park, MI; died May 13, 1987, of pneumonia brought on by amyotrophic lateral sclerosis (Lou Gehrig's disease) in Oxford, England; son of James I. (a lawyer) and Jeanette (Barsook) Ellmann; married Mary Donahue (a writer), August 12, 1949; children: Stephen, Maud, Lucy. *Education:* Yale University, B.A., 1939, M.A., 1941, Ph.D., 1947; Trinity College, Dublin, B.Litt., 1947; Oxford University, England, M.A., 1970.

CAREER: Harvard University, Cambridge, MA, instructor, 1942-43, 1947-48, Briggs-Copeland Assistant Professor of English Composition, 1948-51; Northwestern University, Evanston, IL, professor of English, 1951-63, Franklin Bliss Snyder Professor, 1963-68; Yale University, New Haven, CT, professor of English, 1968-70; Oxford University, Oxford, England, Goldsmiths' Professor of English Literature, 1970-1984, New College, fellow, 1970-84, honorary fellow, 1984-87; Wolfson College, extraordinary fellow, 1984-87. Frederick Ives Carpenter Visiting Professor, University of Chicago, 1959, 1967, and 1975-77; Emory University, visiting professor, 1978-81, Woodruff Professor of English, 1982-87. Member of United States/United Kingdom Educational Commission, 1970-85. Consultant to "The World of James Joyce," Public Broadcasting Service, 1983. *Military service:* U.S. Navy and Office of Strategic Services, 1943-46.

MEMBER: British Academy (fellow), Modern Language Association of America (chairman of English Institute, 1961-62; member of executive council, 1961-65), English Institute (chairman, 1961-62), Royal Society of Literature (fellow), American Academy and Institute of Arts and Letters (fellow), American Academy and Institute of Arts and Letters (fellow), Phi Beta Kappa, Chi Delta Theta, Athenaeum, Elizabethan Club, Signet.

AWARDS, HONORS: Rockefeller Foundation fellow in humanities, 1946-47; Guggenheim fellow, 1950, 1957-58, and 1970;

grants from American Philosophical Society and Modern Language Association of America, 1953; *Kenyon Review* fellowship in criticism, 1955-56; School of Letters fellow, Indiana University, 1956 and 1960, senior fellow, 1966-72; National Book Award for nonfiction, Friends of Literature Award in biography, Thormond Monson Award from Society of Midland Authors, and Carey-Thomas Award for creative book publishing to Oxford University Press, all for *James Joyce*, 1960, and Duff Cooper Prize and James Tair Black Prize for new and revised edition, 1982; George Polk Memorial Award, 1970, for *The Artist As Critic: Critical Writings of Oscar Wilde;* New College fellow, Oxford University, 1970-84, honorary fellow, 1984-87; Extraordinary fellow, Wolfson College, 1984-87; National Book Critics Circle Award for best biography/autobiography, 1989, for *Oscar Wilde*. D.Litt. from National University of Ireland, 1975, Emory University, 1979, Northwestern University, 1980, and McGill University, 1986; National Endowment for the Humanities research grant, 1977; Ph.D., University of Gothenburg (Sweden), 1978; D.H.L. from Boston College and University of Rochester, both 1979.

WRITINGS:

Yeats: The Man and the Masks, Macmillan, 1948, corrected edition with new preface, Oxford University Press, 1979.
The Identity of Yeats, Oxford University Press, 1954, 2nd edition, 1964.
James Joyce, Oxford University Press, 1959, new and revised edition with corrections, 1982.
Edwardians and Late Victorians, Columbia University Press, 1960.
(With E. D. H. Johnson and Alfred L. Bush) *Wilde and the Nineties: An Essay and an Exhibition,* edited by Charles Ryskamp, Princeton University Library, 1966.
Eminent Domain: Yeats among Wilde, Joyce, Pound, Eliot, and Auden, Oxford University Press, 1967.
Ulysses on the Liffey, Oxford University Press, 1972, corrected edition, Faber and Faber, 1984.
Golden Codgers: Biographical Speculations, Oxford University Press, 1973.
(With John Espey) *Oscar Wilde: Two Approaches* (Papers Read at a Clark Library Seminar, April 17, 1976), Williams Andrews Clark Memorial Library, 1977.
The Consciousness of Joyce, Oxford University Press, 1977.
Four Dubliners: Wilde, Yeats, Joyce, and Beckett, U.S. Government Printing Office, 1986.
Oscar Wilde, Hamish Hamilton, 1987, Knopf, 1988.
a long the riverrun: Selected Essays, Knopf (New York City), 1989.

EDITOR

(And translator, and author of introduction) Henri Michaux, *Selected Writings,* Routledge & Kegan Paul, 1952.
Stanislaus Joyce, *My Brother's Keeper: James Joyce's Early Years,* Viking, 1958.
(With others) *English Masterpieces,* 2nd edition, two volumes, Prentice-Hall, 1958.
Arthur Symons, *The Symbolist Movement in Literature,* Dutton, 1958.
(With Ellsworth Mason) *The Critical Writings of James Joyce,* Faber and Faber, 1959.
(With Charles Feidelson, Jr.) *The Modern Tradition: Backgrounds of Modern Literature,* Oxford University Press, 1965.
James Joyce, *Letters of James Joyce,* Volumes 2-3, Viking, 1966.

(Of corrected holograph) James Joyce, *A Portrait of the Artist As a Young Man,* drawings by Robin Jacques, Cape, 1968.
Oscar Wilde, *The Artist As Critic: Critical Writings of Oscar Wilde,* Random House, 1969.
Oscar Wilde: A Collection of Critical Essays, Prentice-Hall, 1969.
(With Robert O'Clair) *The Norton Anthology of Modern Poetry,* Norton, 1973, second edition published as *Modern Poems: A Norton Introduction,* Norton (New York City), 1989.
James Joyce, *Selected Letters of James Joyce,* Viking, 1975.
(With O'Clair) *Modern Poems: An Introduction to Poetry,* Norton, 1976.
The New Oxford Book of American Verse, Oxford University Press, 1976.
(And author of introduction) Oscar Wilde, *The Picture of Dorian Gray and Other Writings,* Bantam, 1982.

OTHER

(Contributor of "A Chronology on the Life of James Joyce") James Joyce, *Letters,* Volume 1, edited by Stuart Gilbert, Viking, 1957.
Ulysses the Divine Nobody (monograph), Yale University Press, 1957.
Joyce in Love (monograph), Cornell University Library, 1959.
(Contributor of "Overtures to Wilde's Salome") *Twentieth Anniversary, 1968,* Indiana University School of Letters, 1968.
(Author of introduction and notes) James Joyce, *Giacomo Joyce,* Faber, 1968.
(Contributor of "Ulysses: A Short History") James Joyce, *Ulysses,* Penguin, 1969.
James Joyce's Tower (monograph), Eastern Regional Tourism Organisation (Dublin), 1969.
Literary Biography (monograph; inaugural lecture, University of Oxford, May 4, 1971), Clarendon Press, 1971.
The Poetry of Yeats (phono tape), BFA Educational Media, 1974.
James Joyce's Hundredth Birthday, Side and Front Views (monograph), Library of Congress, 1982.
Oscar Wilde at Oxford (monograph), Library of Congress, 1984.
(Author of introduction) Michael Moscato and Leslie LeBlanc, *The United States of America vs. One Book Entitled Ulysses by James Joyce; Documents and Commentary: 50-Year Retrospective,* University Publications of America, 1984.
Henry James among the Aesthetes (lectures), Longwood Publishing Group, 1985.
W. B. Yeats' Second Puberty (monograph), Library of Congress, 1985.
Samuel Beckett, Nayman of Noland (monograph), Library of Congress, 1986.
Also author of monographs *Wallace Stevens' Ice-Cream,* 1957, and *The Background of Joyce's The Dead,* 1958.

SIDELIGHTS: A renowned biographer, literary critic, and educator, Richard Ellmann held professorial posts at such universities as Harvard, Northwestern, and Yale before becoming the first American to teach English literature at Oxford University, a position he held for many years. Ellmann devoted most of his distinguished academic career to the study of the Irish literary renaissance. "It is difficult to think of the great writers of Irish literature—W. B. Yeats, James Joyce, or Oscar Wilde—without thinking of Ellmann," remarked Steven Serafin in a *Dictionary of Literary Biography Yearbook, 1987* essay. Ellmann's scholarship on Yeats remains a standard reference, and he is widely acknowledged as having been the foremost authority on Joyce. His much heralded, National Book Award-winning biography *James Joyce,* not only represents the definitive work on the artist but, in the opinion of many, casts its shadow as the best literary biography ever written. Referring to him as "an extraordinary individual of rare and exceptional talent," Serafin believed that "Ellmann essentially redefined the art of biography." And in a *Times Literary Supplement* review of Ellmann's National Book Critics Circle Award-winning final work, the biography *Oscar Wilde,* Gore Vidal deemed him "our time's best academic biographer."

Ellmann's scholarship sought the literary influences upon and connections among writers and their work. Calling Ellmann "particularly sensitive to the impingement of one talent upon another," Denis Donoghue added in a *New York Times Book Review* essay about *Eminent Domain: Yeats among Wilde, Joyce, Pound, Eliot, and Auden*: "As critics we look for corresponding moments in the work, moments of representative force and definition. Mr. Ellmann is a keen student of these epiphanies in life and art. He finds them more often than not in the pressure of one mind upon another, and he delights in these occasions." In Ellmann's *Eminent Domain,* "Yeats's greatness as a poet is seen as illustrated by his gift for expropriating or confiscating, from youth to age, ideas or tactics from other writers," stated a *Times Literary Supplement* contributor.

Ellmann, whose work on Yeats "set the tone of much subsequent criticism," stated Kevin Sullivan in a *Nation* review of *Eminent Domain,* believed that as "a young poet in search of an aesthetic," Yeats was significantly indebted to Wilde, whose "professional reputation rested . . . on his skill as a talker before all else." Yeats "pillaged freely" of this talk during their London meetings and believed that "Wilde's dazzling conversation was an aristocratic counterpart to the oral culture that had persisted among the Irish peasantry at home," explained Sullivan. "But what really attracted him was Wilde's easy assumption of the superiority of imagination to reason and intellect, and the corollary that followed almost at once upon that assumption—the primacy and autonomy of art." And about the relationship between Yeats and Joyce, the *Times Literary Supplement* contributor noted that while "Joyce's attitude to Yeats was that of a rebel in the Irish literary movement," according to Sullivan, Ellmann believed that "Joyce turned from verse to prose out of an awareness of Yeats's unchallengeable mastery as a poet." Praised by Sullivan for describing "a wide and graceful arc that encompasses many of the major developments in English poetry during a full half-century," *Eminent Domain* was labeled "lucid, perceptive, urbane, in itself a graceful occasion" by Donoghue.

James Joyce, Ellmann's masterwork, was hailed with critical superlatives. "This immensely detailed, massive, completely detached and objective, yet loving biography, translates James Joyce's books back into his life," wrote Stephen Spender in the *New York Times.* "Here is the definitive work," assessed Dwight Macdonald in *New Yorker,* "and I hope it will become a model for future scholarly biographies." And according to Mark Schorer in the *San Francisco Chronicle,* "This is not only the most important book that we have had on James Joyce until now (and the only reliable biography), it is also, almost certainly, one of the great literary biographies of this century, a book that will last for years, probably for generations." A few critics, however, faulted the biography for the enormity of its detail. A *Times Literary Supplement* contributor, for example, contended that "much of the difficulty with Mr. Ellmann's book is in seeing the wood for the trees." But in the *Saturday Review,* Stuart Gilbert echoed the widely shared critical recognition that Ellmann performed commendably, calling *James Joyce* "a masterpiece of scholarly objectivity and exact research, in which the facts are marshaled

and set forth with fine lucidity, and the imposing mass of detail never clogs the analysis."

In 1982, more than twenty years after the publication of *James Joyce,* Ellmann marked the centennial year of Joyce's birth with a new and revised edition of his biography. Having had access to Joyce's private library and other previously unavailable material, Ellmann was able to define the influences upon Joyce's art, especially *Ulysses.* "Ellmann's task was a dual one," wrote Thomas Flanagan in the *Washington Post Book World.* "He re-created for the reader what had become one of the exemplary lives of modern literature, conveying its color and its textures, its characterizing movements and stances, by the adroit but unobtrusive deployment of many thousands of details." The *New York Time*'s Christopher Lehmann-Haupt, who felt that this minutely detailed new material was "entirely appropriate and desirable, considering the obsessive sort of attachment that Joyce's art inspires," remarked: "And the effect of this experience is fairly stunning, not alone because of the remarkable wealth of details that the author has gathered up and artfully pieced together. What also strikes the reader is the number of those details that wound up in Joyce's fiction, or, to put it the other way around, the degree to which Joyce's art was grounded in actuality."

Although *Newsweek*'s Peter S. Prescott regarded it "a pleasure to salute this masterly book as it marches past again," critics such as Hugh Kenner in the *Times Literary Supplement* acknowledged the book's achievement while pondering its veracity. Kenner suggested that because much of Ellmann's data was based upon interviews with those who claimed a link to Joyce, it was essentially unreliable, citing in particular Ellmann's use of "Irish Fact, definable as anything you get told in Ireland, where you get told a great deal." Kenner further maintained: "'Definitive' in 1959, was a word that got thrown around rather thoughtlessly by reviewers stunned beneath an avalanche of new information. But there can be no 'definitive' biography. Biography is a narrative form: that means, a mode of fiction. Many narratives can be woven from the same threads. Biography incorporates 'facts', having judged their credibility. Its criteria for judgment include assessment of sources . . . and, pervasively, assessment of one's man." Moreover, Kenner also questioned whether Ellmann's detachment from his subject was sufficient: "Tone is a delicate matter; we don't want a hagiography. We'd like, though, to feel the presence of the mind that made the life worth writing and makes it worth reading." Conversely, Flanagan concluded that it was "because of the unsparing scrupulousness of his own methods," that Ellmann wrote "the kind of book which has become unhappily rare—a work of exacting scholarship which is also a humane and liberating document. Joyce found the proper biographer, and there can be no higher praise." John Stallworthy concurred in the *Times Literary Supplement,* "Speaking with his master's voice, his master's elegance, and his master's wit, Ellmann has produced a biography worth its place on the shelf beside *Dubliners, Ulysses,* and *Finnegans Wake.* "

James Joyce marked a turning point for Ellmann, even though he was encouraged by its critical reception, said Serafin: "Shortly after its publication he ruminated about the future of his career: 'There really aren't any other modern writers that measure up to Yeats or Joyce. I can't think of anyone else I'd want to work on the way I've worked on them.'" Gore Vidal suggested that "since Ellmann had already written magisterial works on two of the four [subjects of his essays, *Four Dubliners: Wilde, Yeats, Joyce, and Beckett*], symmetry and sympathy plainly drew him to a third." Ellmann spent the last twenty years of his life working on *Oscar

Wilde. Suffering from Lou Gherig's disease, "during the last weeks of his life, with the help of small machines on which he typed out messages that were then printed on a screen or on paper, he made final revisions on his long-awaited biography," reported Walter Goodman in the *New York Times.*

"While the literary world will continue to mourn his passing, we must all be grateful that he lived long enough to complete his magnificent life of Oscar Wilde . . . ," wrote Robert E. Kuehn in *Tribune Books.* "Like his earlier life of James Joyce, this book is biography on the grand scale: learned, expansive, judicious, magnanimous, and written with care and panache." Ellmann perceived Wilde, said Michael Dirda of the *Washington Post Book World,* "chiefly as a fearless artist and social critic who, like a kamikaze pilot, used himself as the bomb to explode the bourgeois values, pretentions and hypocrisies of late Victorian society." Likening Wilde's fate to that of "a hero of classic tragedy [who] plummeted from the heights of fame to utter ruin," Dirda pointed out that although Wilde has been the subject of several biographies, "they cannot compete with this capacious, deeply sympathetic and vastly entertaining new life of Richard Ellmann."

"There's no question that *Oscar Wilde* is brilliant," declared Walter Kendrick in the *Voice Literary Supplement*; "its posthumous publication splendidly caps Ellmann's career and, like his *James Joyce,* it belongs on the short shelf of biographies correctly labeled definitive." Although praising Ellmann as "a masterful biographer," Eslpeth Cameron continued in the Toronto *Globe and Mail* that "no biography is definitive, and this one is not without its flaws. Ellmann's intellectual grasp of Wilde is firmer than his comprehension of Wilde's emotional life." However, Kuehn found that "when it comes to interpretation, the psychological patterns he traces tend to be all the more persuasive for his refusal to overstate the case." Declaring that "Oscar Wilde is not easily led," Richard Eder acknowledged in the *Los Angeles Times Book Review* that "Ellmann does everything a biographer could do, and some things that few biographers have the courage and talent to do. He refuses to net the butterfly Wilde; he flies with him instead."

At the time of his death, Ellmann was planning to collect many of his own essays for publication. While he was unable to complete this task, his family gathered a number of Ellmann's essays and published them as *a long the riverrun: Selected Essays* in 1989. The title phrase refers to the words that link the beginning and ending sections of Joyce's *Finnegans Wake.* Consisting of twenty essays, all but one of which were previously published, the volume finds Ellmann ruminating on a wide range of literary subjects, from the authors—Joyce, Wilde, Yeats—whose lives he chronicled to the discipline of literary biography. "These twenty essays testify to Ellmann's versatility and interests," commented Kark Beckson in the *Times Literary Supplement,* adding that the work inspires many re-readings: "when one turns the last page of this volume, one is impelled to begin again." According to *World Literature Today* reviewer John L. Brown, despite the numerous writers that Ellmann discusses in the collection, "the leading man in the cast . . . remains Yeats." *New York Times Book Review* contributor Angeline Goreau termed the volume "witty, ironic, [and] unfailingly astute" and remarked that it "offers one final glimpse of a matchless literary mind at work, unearthing the 'mysterious armature' (as Mallarme called it) that binds the life of writing to its creation fiction."

BIOGRAPHICAL/CRITICAL SOURCES:

BOOKS

Contemporary Literary Criticism, Volume 50, Gale (Detroit), 1988.
Dictionary of Literary Biography, Volume 103: *American Literary Biographers, First Series,* Gale, 1991.
Dictionary of Literary Biography Yearbook, 1987, Gale, 1988.
Heaney, Seamus, *The Place of Writing,* Scholars Press (Atlanta), 1989.
Schroeder, Horst, *Additions and Corrections to Richard Ellmann's Oscar Wilde,* H. Schroeder (Braunschweig), 1989.

PERIODICALS

Chicago Sun Times, May 15, 1987.
Detroit Free Press, May 14, 1987.
English Journal, January, 1995, p. 116.
Globe and Mail (Toronto), December 26, 1987.
Guardian, October 30, 1959.
Hudson Review, spring, 1968.
Los Angeles Times, May 16, 1987.
Los Angeles Times Book Review, November 14, 1982; February 14, 1988.
Maclean's, December 21, 1987.
Nation, October 17, 1959; November 13, 1967; June 23, 1969; June 19, 1972; November 20, 1981; February 13, 1988.
New Republic, June 3, 1972; February 15, 1988.
Newsweek, September 27, 1982.
New Yorker, December 12, 1959; March 21, 1988.
New York Review of Books, August 26, 1965; October 18, 1973; September 19, 1974; October 13, 1977; February 18, 1988.
New York Times, October 25, 1959; January 1, 1968; October 25, 1969; November 25, 1969; May 17, 1972; December 15, 1975; June 1, 1977; September 21, 1982; May 14, 1987.
New York Times Book Review, December 10, 1967; January 21, 1968; May 14, 1972; June 19, 1977; April 19, 1981; February 21, 1988; March 19, 1989, p. 21.
Publishers Weekly, January 27, 1989, p. 461.
San Francisco Chronicle, November 1, 1959.
Saturday Review, October 24, 1959; May 24, 1969; March 28, 1970; May 13, 1972.
Spectator, November 13, 1959; February 12, 1977; October 23, 1982.
Time, January 4, 1988.
Times (London), November 20, 1959; January 5, 1967; July 25, 1968; March 17, 1972; February 18, 1977; October 8, 1987.
Times Literary Supplement, December 30, 1965; July 25, 1968; April 2, 1970; March 17, 1972; October 26, 1973; January 24, 1975; December 17, 1982; March 23, 1984; November 14, 1986; October 2-8, 1987; November 4, 1988, p. 1234.
Tribune Books (Chicago), February 7, 1988.
Virginia Quarterly Review, spring, 1968.
Washington Post Book World, May 21, 1972; March 29, 1981; October 31, 1982; October 30, 1983; January 24, 1988.
World Literature Today, winter, 1979; summer, 1983; winter, 1990, p. 114.

*   *   *

ELLROY, James 1948-

PERSONAL: Born March 4, 1948, in Los Angeles, CA; son of Geneva (a nurse; maiden name, Hillaker) Ellroy; married Mary

Doherty, 1988 (marriage ended); married Helen Knode (journalist and author).

ADDRESSES: Home—New Canaan, CT. *Agent*—Nat Sobel, Sobel Weber Associates, Inc., 146 East 19th St., New York, NY 10003.

CAREER: Writer. Worked at a variety of jobs, including as a golf caddy in California and New York, 1977-84. *Military service:* U.S. Army, 1965.

AWARDS, HONORS: Edgar Award nomination, Mystery Writers of America, 1982, for *Clandestine*; Prix Mystere Award, 1990, for *The Big Nowhere.*

WRITINGS:

"L.A. QUARTET" CRIME NOVELS

The Black Dahlia, Mysterious Press, 1987.
The Big Nowhere, Mysterious Press, 1988.
L.A. Confidential, Mysterious Press, 1990.
White Jazz, Knopf, 1992.

OTHER CRIME NOVELS

Brown's Requiem, Avon, 1981.
Clandestine, Avon, 1982.
Blood on the Moon, Mysterious Press, 1984.
Because the Night, Mysterious Press, 1984.
Killer on the Road, Avon, 1986.
Suicide Hill, Mysterious Press, 1986.
Silent Terror, introduction by Jonathan Kellerman, Avon, 1986.
Hollywood Nocturnes, O. Penzler Books (New York City), 1994.
American Tabloid: A Novel, Knopf (New York City), 1995.
L.A. Noir, Mysterious Press, 1998.

OTHER

(Author of introduction) *Heed the Thunder,* by Jim Thompson, Armchair Detective Library, 1991.
My Dark Places: An L.A. Crime Memoir, Knopf, 1996.

MEDIA ADAPTATIONS: Blood on the Moon was filmed as *Cop,* Atlantic, 1988. *L.A. Confidential* was filmed in 1997 by New Regency, directed by Curtis Hanson and starring Kevin Spacey, Danny DeVito, and Kim Basinger. The film won Academy Awards for best adapted screenplay (Hanson and Brian Helgeland) and best supporting actress (Basinger).

SIDELIGHTS: James Ellroy is a prominent crime novelist who has won acclaim for his vivid portraits of Los Angeles's seamier aspects. Ellroy himself spent many years on the Los Angeles streets. After an arduous childhood—his parents divorced when he was four, his mother was murdered six years later, and his father died seven years after that—Ellroy took to the streets. Having already been expelled from both high school (for excessive truancy) and the military (for faking a nervous breakdown), he turned to crime, committing petty burglaries to fund his increasing alcohol dependency. From 1965 to 1977 Ellroy was arrested—for such crimes as drunkenness, shoplifting, and trespassing—on approximately thirty occasions. Twelve times he was actually convicted, and for eight months he was imprisoned.

In 1977 Ellroy's life changed radically after he was hospitalized for double pneumonia. Profoundly shaken by his brush with death, he entered an Alcoholics Anonymous program and then managed—through a friend, another recovering alcoholic—to obtain employment as a caddy at posh Hollywood golf courses. By this time Ellroy was already determined to pursue a literary career. Earlier, before he had been hospitalized, Ellroy had spent many hours in public libraries, where he would drink discreetly while poring through twentieth-century American literature. He also read more than two hundred crime novels that he had stolen from various markets and bookstores. It was the crime genre that eventually enticed him into commencing his own literary career, and in 1979, while he continued with his job as a caddy, he also began writing his first book. The result, after more than ten months of steady writing in longhand, was *Brown's Requiem,* the story of a private investigator who uncovers a deadly band of extortionists roaming the streets of Los Angeles.

Brown's Requiem won Ellroy immediate acceptance from an agent who, in turn, quickly managed to place the manuscript with Avon publishers. Ellroy's actual earnings from the novel, though, were not enough to support him, and so he remained a golf caddy while he produced a second novel, *Clandestine.* This novel, in which a former police officer tracks down his ex-lover's killer, received a nomination for the crime genre's prestigious Edgar Award from the Mystery Writers of America.

Ellroy followed *Clandestine* with *Blood on the Moon,* the story of two brilliant men—a somewhat unstable police detective, Lloyd Hopkins, and a psychopathic murderer—who clash in Los Angeles. In 1984, the year that this novel appeared in print, Ellroy finally managed to leave his caddying job and devote himself fully to writing. Among the next few novels he published were *Because the Night, Killer on the Road,* and *Suicide Hill,* in which Lloyd Hopkins, the temperamental protagonist of the earlier *Blood on the Moon,* opposes a vicious bank robber.

In 1987, Ellroy produced *The Black Dahlia,* the first volume in what would become known as the "L.A. Quartet." *The Black Dahlia* is based on an actual incident, the 1947 unsolved murder of prostitute Elizabeth Short (also known as the Black Dahlia), whose completely severed body was found on a Los Angeles street. The murder bears similarities to that of Ellroy's own mother, who was found naked and strangled to death after reportedly accompanying a man and a woman from a bar. Like the Black Dahlia case, the murder of Ellroy's mother was never solved. In Ellroy's novel, however, he proposes a possible solution to the Black Dahlia mystery. "Ellroy's novel is true to the facts as they are known," wrote David Haldane in the *Los Angeles Times.* "But it provides a fictional solution to the crime consistent with those facts." Haldane added that in tracing the Black Dahlia case Ellroy "conducts an uncompromising tour of the obscene, violent, gritty, obsessive, darkly sexual world of [Los Angeles's] underbelly in the 1940s, complete with names and places."

Ellroy continued to chart the Los Angeles underworld in *The Big Nowhere,* in which two criminal investigations converge with shocking results during the McCarthy era of the 1950s, when fear of communism in the United States was widespread. In one investigation, a deputy sheriff probes a rash of killings in the homosexual community. The other case involves a city investigator's efforts to further his career by exposing a band of alleged communists circulating within the film industry. The two cases become one when the ambitious investigator employs the deputy as a decoy to lure an influential leftist known as the Red Queen. This collaborative operation leads to unexpected discoveries.

The Big Nowhere won Ellroy substantial recognition as a proficient writer. According to London *Times* writer Peter Guttridge, it established Ellroy "among that handful of crime writers whose work is regarded as literature." Among the novel's enthusiasts was Bruce Cook, who proclaimed in the *Washington Post Book World* that Ellroy had produced "a first-rate crime novel, a violent picture in blood-red and grays, set against a fascinating period background."

Ellroy realized further acclaim with *L.A. Confidential,* in which three police officers cross paths while conducting affairs in 1950s Los Angeles. The protagonists here are wildly different: Bud White is a brutish, excessively violent law enforcer; Trashcan Vincennes is a corrupt narcotics investigator; and Ed Exley is a rigid, politically ambitious sergeant. The three men come together in probing a bizarre incident in which several coffee shop patrons were gunned down. The ensuing plot, reported Kevin Moore in Chicago *Tribune Books,* "plays itself out with all the impact—and excess—of a shotgun blast." *People* reviewer Lorenzo Carcaterra judged that *L.A. Confidential* is "violently unsettling" and "ugly yet engrossing."

White Jazz, the concluding volume in the "L.A. Quartet," appeared in 1992. Forthcoming works by Ellroy include what Guttridge described, in his London *Times* piece, as "a sprawling police thriller set in 1942." This novel, though set in Los Angeles, is not part of the "L.A. Quartet." Ellroy also plans to produce a series of possibly ten novels in which he will trace twentieth-century America through crime. "I think," Ellroy told Guttridge in the London *Times,* "it's time I moved beyond Los Angeles." Ellroy added, however, that he will continue to pursue what he called his "one goal—to be the greatest crime writer of all time."

Move beyond Los Angeles he did in his next novel, *American Tabloid,* an ambitious, tightly plotted narrative of national and international conspiracy and crime in the 1960s, culminating with the great "unsolved" American crime of the Kennedy assassination. Two FBI agents and a CIA operative make up the three central characters through which Ellroy spins this complex, disturbing, and visceral tale of American history "from the bottom up," in the words of a *Booklist* critic. *American Tabloid,* rife with Ellroy's signature staccato language and over-the-top violence, sold well and invited positive reviews and colorful critical descriptions. *Booklist* characterized the novel as being about the "most potent drug of all"—power. "It's as if Ellroy injects us with a mainline pop of the undiluted power that surges through the veins of his obsessed characters," the critic said. Paul Gray of *Time* magazine called *American Tabloid* "American history as well as Hellzapoppin, a long slapstick routine careening around a manic premise: What if the fabled American innocence is all shuck and jive?" Gray went on to praise the novel as "a big, boisterous, rude and shameless reminder of why reading can be so engrossing and so much fun."

With his next project, 1996's "crime memoir," *My Dark Places,* Ellroy returns not only to L.A., but also to his own unresolved past. With his early novel *The Black Dahlia,* Ellroy may have attempted to kill his demons by offering a fictional solution to an unsolved murder similar to that of his mother, but here he sets out to solve that true-crime murder itself. He enlists the help of a retired Los Angeles cop and starts retracing the evidence of the almost 30-year-old crime. Ellroy reports the facts of the investigation in great detail, using a style similar to that of his crime novels, a decision critics found only partially successful. A writer for *Kirkus Reviews* described the language as "a punchy but monotonous rhythm that's as relentless as a jackhammer" and Bruce Jay Friedman of the *New York Times Review* compared it to something that "might've been fired out of a riveting gun." Ellroy never finds the murderer but he does speculate on the impact of his mother's death on his character and career and learns more about her life. A *Kirkus Review* writer warned, "Those expecting

an autobiographical expose of the writer's psychological clockwork will feel stonewalled by macho reserve," but Friedman found the psychological dimension satisfying. "All in all, a rough and strenuously involving book," he assessed. "Early on, Mr. Ellroy makes a promise to his dead mother that seems maudlin at first: 'I want to give you breath.' But he's done just that and—on occasion—taken ours away."

BIOGRAPHICAL/CRITICAL SOURCES:

BOOKS

Twentieth-Century Crime and Mystery Writers, Third edition, St. James Press, 1991, pp. 347-48.

PERIODICALS

Armchair Detective, spring, 1987, p. 206; winter, 1991, p. 31.
Booklist, January 15, 1995.
Christian Science Monitor, October 2, 1987, p. B5.
Interview, December, 1996, p. 70.
Kirkus Reviews, September 15, 1996.
Los Angeles Times, October 4, 1987; May 27, 1990.
Los Angeles Times Book Review, June 3, 1984, p. 18; September 13, 1987, p. 16; October 9, 1988, p. 12; July 8, 1990, p. 8.
Nation, December 2, 1996, p. 25.
New Statesman, June 19, 1987, p. 31; January 22, 1988, p. 33.
New York Times Book Review, July 22, 1984, p. 32; July 6, 1986, p. 21; November 8, 1987, p. 62; October 9, 1988, p. 41; September 3, 1989, p. 20; July 15, 1990, p. 26; June 30, 1991, p. 32; November 24, 1996.
Observer, May 13, 1984, p. 23.
People, December 14, 1987; July 2, 1990; November 25, 1996, p. 93.
Publishers Weekly, June 15, 1990, pp. 53-54.
Spectator, July 21, 1984, p. 29.
Time, April 10, 1995, p. 74; November 25, 1996, p. 115.
Times (London), November 10, 1990.
Tribune Books (Chicago), September 3, 1989, p. 5; June 10, 1990, p. 1.
Washington Post Book World, October 23, 1988, p. 10.
West Coast Review of Books, January, 1983, p. 43; September, 1983, p. 20; September, 1986, p. 27.

*   *   *

ELRON
See HUBBARD, L(afayette) Ron(ald)

*   *   *

EL-SHABAZZ, El-Hajj Malik
See LITTLE, Malcolm

*   *   *

ELYTIS, Odysseus 1911-1996
(Odysseus Alepoudelis)

PERSONAL: Original name, Odysseus Alepoudelis; born November 2, 1911, in Heraklion, Crete, Greece; died March 18, 1996; son of Panayiotis and Maria Alepoudelis. *Education:* Attended University of Athens, 1930-35, and Sorbonne, University of Paris, 1948-52.

CAREER: Poet and writer. Hellenic National Broadcasting Institution, Athens, Greece, broadcasting and program director, 1945-47 and 1953-54; art and literary critic for *Kathimerini* (newspaper) in Greece, 1946-48. Adviser to Art Theatre, 1955-56, and to Greek National Theatre, 1965-68; member of administrative board, Greek National Theatre, 1974-76; president of administrative board, Greek Broadcasting and Television, 1974; represented Greece at Second International Gathering of Modern Painters, in Geneva, Switzerland, 1948, and at Congress of International Association of Art Critics, in Paris, France, 1949; president of governing board of Greek Ballet, 1956-58. *Military service:* First Army Corps, 1940-41; served in Albania; became second lieutenant.

MEMBER: International Union of Art Critics, Societe Europienne de Culture.

AWARDS, HONORS: National Poetry Prize and National Book Award, both 1960, both for *To axion esti*; Order of the Phoenix, 1965; honorary doctorate from the University of Thessaloniki, 1975; Nobel Prize for literature, 1979; honorary doctorate from the University of Paris, 1980; honorary doctorate from the University of London, 1981; Commander de la Legion d'Honneur, 1989.

WRITINGS:

POETRY IN ENGLISH TRANSLATION

To axion esti (title means "Worthy It Is"), Ikaros, 1959, translation by Edmund Keeley and George Savidis published as *The Axion Esti of Odysseus Elytis*, University of Pittsburgh Press, 1974.

O ilios o iliatoras, Ikaros, 1971, translation by Kimon Friar published as *The Sovereign Sun: Selected Poems*, Temple University Press, 1974.

What I Love: Selected Poems of Odysseus Elytis, translated by Olga Broumas, Copper Canyon, 1978.

Maria Nefeli: Skiniko piima (title means "Maria the Cloud: Dramatic Poem"), [Athens, Greece], 1978, 3rd edition published as *Maria Nefeli*, 1979, translation by Athan Anagnostopoulos published as *Maria Nephele*, Houghton, 1981.

O mikros naftilos (title means "The Little Navigator," Ikaros, 1985); translation by Olga Broumas published as *The Little Mariner*, Copper Canyon Press, 1988.

The Collected Poems of Odysseus Elytis, translated by Jeffrey Carson and Nikos Sarros, John Hopkins University Press, 1997.

Work represented in anthologies, including *Six Poets of Modern Greece*, edited and translated by Edmund Keeley and Philip Sherrard, Knopf, 1961; *Modern Greek Poetry: From Cavafis to Elytis*, edited by Kimon Friar, Simon & Schuster, 1973.

POETRY IN GREEK

Prosanatolizmi (title means "Orientations"), first published in *Makedhonikes Imeres*, 1936, published under same title, Pirsos, 1939.

Ilios o protos, mazi me tis parallayies pano se mian ahtidha (title means "Sun the First Together With Variations on a Sunbeam"), O Glaros, 1943.

Iroiko kai penthimo asma ghia ton hameno anthypolohagho tis Alvanias (title means "A Heroic and Elegiac Song of the Lost Second Lieutenant of the Albanian Campaign"), first published in *Tetradhio*, August-September, 1945, published under same title, Ikaros, 1962.

Hexe kai mia typheis gia ton ourano (title means "Six and One Regrets for the Sky"), Ikaros, 1960.

Ho helios ho protos, Ikaros, 1963.

To fotodhendro ke i dhekati tetarti omorfia (title means "The Light Tree and the Fourteenth Beauty"), Ikaros, 1971.

Thanatos ke anastasis tou Konstandinou Paleologhou (title means "Death and Resurrection of Constandinos Paleologhos"), Duo d'Art, 1971.

Ta ro tou erota (title means "The Ro of Eros"), Asterias, 1972.

To monograma (title means "The Monogram"), first published in *L'Oiseau*, 1971, published under same title, Ikaros, 1972.

O fillomandis (title means "The Leaf Diviner"), Asterias, 1973.

Ta eterothali (title means "The Stepchildren"), Ikaros, 1974.

Imeroloyio enos atheatou Apriliou (title means "Journal of an Unforeseen April" or "Diary of an Invisible April"), Ipsilon, 1984.

Krinagoras, Ypsilon, 1987.

Ta elegia tis Oxopetras (title means "The Elegies of Oxopetras"), Ikaros, 1991.

Author of "I kalosini stis likopories" (title means "Kindness in the Wolfpasses"), published in *Tetradhio,* December, 1946, and "Alvaniadha. Piima yia dhio phones. Meros proto." (title means "Albaniad. Poems for Two Voices. First Part."), published in *Panspoudhastiki,* December 25, 1962.

OTHER

Ho zographos Theophilos (art criticism; title means "The Painter Theophilos"), Asterias, 1973.

Anihta hartia (essays; title means "Open Book"), Asterias, 1974; translation published as *Open Papers,* Copper Canyon Press, 1994.

I mayia tou papadhiamandhi (essays; title means "The Magic of Papadiamantis"), Ermias, 1978.

Anafora ston Andrea Embiriko (title means "Report to Andreas Embirikos"), Ypsilon, 1980.

To Domatio me tis ikones (title means "The Room of Images"), Ikaros, 1986.

Ta Dimosia ke ta idiotika (title means "Public and Private Matters"), Ikaros, 1990.

I idiotiki odos (title means "Private Way"), Ypsilon, 1990.

En lefko (title means "In White"), Ikaros, 1992.

TRANSLATOR

Arthur Rimbaud and others, *Defteri Graphi* (title means "The Second Writing"), Ikaros, 1976.

(From ancient Greek) *Sappho—Anasinthesi ke apodosi*, Ikaros, 1985.

(From ancient Greek) *Ioannis, I apokalipsi* (title means "The Apocalypse of John"), Ypsilon, 1985.

SIDELIGHTS: Odysseus Elytis was relatively unknown outside his native Greece when he was awarded the Nobel Prize for literature in 1979. Although the Swedish Academy of Letters has in recent years bestowed the honor upon other previously little-known writers—notably Eugenio Montale, Vicente Aleixandre, and Harry Martison—their choice of Elytis came as a surprise nonetheless. The academy declared in its presentation that his poetry "depicts with sensual strength and intellectual clearsightedness modern man's struggle for freedom and creativeness. . . . [In] its combination of fresh, sensuous flexibility and strictly disciplined implacability in the face of all compulsion, Elytis' poetry gives shape to its distinctiveness, which is not only very personal but also represents the traditions of the Greek people."

To be a Greek and a part of its twenty-five-century-old literary tradition is to Elytis a matter of great pride. His words upon acceptance of the Nobel Prize give evidence of this deep regard for his people and country: "I would like to believe that with this year's decision, the Swedish Academy wants to honor in me Greek poetry in its entirety. I would like to think it also wants to draw the attention of the world to a tradition that has gone on since the time of Homer, in the embrace of Western civilization."

Elytis was born Odysseus Alepoudelis in the city of Heraklion on the island of Crete. To avoid any association to his wealthy family of soap manufacturers, he later changed his surname to reflect those things he most treasured. Frank J. Prial of the *New York Times* explained that the poet's pseudonymous name is actually "a composite made up of elements of Ellas, the Greek word for Greece; elpidha, the word for hope; eleftheria, the word for freedom, and Eleni, the name of a figure that, in Greek mythology, personifies beauty and sensuality."

Prosanatolizmi (*Orientations*), published in 1936, was Elytis's first volume of poetry. Filled with images of light and purity, the work earned for its author the title of the "sun-drinking poet." Keeley, a frequent translator of Elytis's work, observed that these "first poems offered a surrealism that had a distinctly personal tone and a specific local habitation. The tone was lyrical, humorous, fanciful, everything that is young." In a review of a later work, *The Sovereign Sun,* a writer for the *Virginia Quarterly Review* echoed Keeley's eloquent praise: "An intuitive poet, who rejects pessimism and engages in his surrealistic images the harsh realities of life, Elytis is a voice of hope and naked vigor. There is light and warmth, an awakening to self, body, and spirit, in Elytis."

The poet, however, bridles at such descriptions of his work. He has suggested that "my theory of analogies may account in part for my having been frequently called a poet of joy and optimism. This is fundamentally wrong. I believe that poetry on a certain level of accomplishment is neither optimistic nor pessimistic. It represents rather a third state of the spirit where opposites cease to exist. There are no more opposites beyond a certain level of elevation. Such poetry is like nature itself, which is neither good nor bad, beautiful nor ugly; it simply *is*. Such poetry is no longer subject to habitual everyday distinctions."

With the advent of World War II, Elytis interrupted his literary activities to fight with the First Army Corps in Albania against the fascists of Benito Mussolini. His impressions of this brutal period of his life were later recorded in the long poem *Iroiko kai penthimo asma ghia ton maneno anthypolohagho tis Alvanias* (*A Heroic and Elegiac Song of the Lost Second Lieutenant of the Albanian Campaign*). Regarded as one of the most touchingly human and poignant works inspired by the war, the poem has since become one of the writer's best-loved works.

Elytis's next work, *To axion esti* (*Worthy It Is*), came after a period of more than ten years of silence. Widely held to be his *chef d'oeuvre*, it is a poetic cycle of alternating prose and verse patterned after the ancient Byzantine liturgy. As in his other writings, Elytis depicts the Greek reality through an intensely personal tone. Keeley, the translator of the volume into English, suggested that *To axion esti* "can perhaps be taken best as a kind of spiritual autobiography that attempts to dramatize the national and philosophical extensions of the poet's personal sensibility. Elytis's strategy in this work . . . is to present an image of the contemporary Greek consciousness through the developing of a

persona that is at once the poet himself and the voice of his country."

After the overwhelming success of *To axion esti,* questions were raised regarding what new direction Elytis would pursue and whether it would be possible to surpass his masterpiece. When *Maria Nefeli* was first published in 1978, it met with a curious yet hesitant public. M. Byron Raizis related in *World Literature Today* that "some academicians and critics of the older generations still [wanted] to cling to the concept of the 'sun-drinking' Elytis of the Aegean spume and breeze and of the monumental *Axion Esti,* so they [approached] *Maria Nefeli* with cautious hesitation as an experimental and not-so-attractive creation of rather ephemeral value."

The reason behind the uncertainty many Elytis devotees felt toward this new work stemmed from its radically different presentation. Whereas his earlier poems dealt with the almost timeless expression of the Greek reality, "rooted in my own experience, yet . . . not directly [transcribing] actual events," he once stated, *Maria Nefeli* is based on a young woman he actually met. Different from the women who graced his early work, the woman in Elytis's poem has changed to reflect the troubled times in which she lives. "This Maria then is the newest manifestation of the eternal female," noted Raizis, "the most recent mutation of the female principle which, in the form of Maria, Helen and other more traditional figures, had haunted the quasi-idyllic and erotic poems of [Elytis's youth]." Raizis explained further that Maria is the "attractive, liberated, restless or even blase representative of today's young woman. . . . This urban Nefeli is the offspring, not the sibling, of the women of Elytis's youth. Her setting is the polluted city, not the open country and its islands of purity and fresh air."

The poem consists of the juxtaposed statements of Maria Nefeli, who represents the ideals of today's emerging woman, and Antifonitis, or the Responder, who stands for more traditional views. Through Maria, the Responder is confronted with issues which, though he would like to ignore them, he is forced to come to terms with. Rather than flat, lifeless characters who expound stale and stereotyped maxims, however, "both are sophisticated and complex urbanites who express themselves in a wide range of styles, moods, idioms and stanzaic forms," maintained Raizis.

Despite the initial reservations voiced by some critics, *Maria Nefeli* has come to be regarded as the summa of Elytis's later writings. Gini Politi, for example, announced: "I believe that *Maria Nefeli* is one of the most significant poems of our times, and the response to the agony it includes *is written*; this way it saves for the time being the language of poetry and of humaneness." Kostas Stamatiou, moreover, expressed a common reaction to the work: "After the surprise of a first reading, gradually the careful student discovers beneath the surface the *constants* of the great poet: faith in surrealism, fundamental humanism, passages of pure lyricism."

In an interview with Ivar Ivask for *Books Abroad,* Elytis summarized his life's work: "I consider poetry a source of innocence full of revolutionary forces. It is my mission to direct these forces against a world my conscience cannot accept, precisely so as to bring that world through continual metamorphoses more in harmony with my dreams. I am referring here to a contemporary kind of magic whose mechanism leads to the discovery of our true reality. It is for this reason that I believe, to the point of idealism, that I am moving in a direction which has never been attempted until now. In the hope of obtaining a freedom from all constraint and the justice which could be identified with absolute light, I am an idolator who, without wanting to do so, arrives at Christian sainthood."

BIOGRAPHICAL/CRITICAL SOURCES:

BOOKS

Contemporary Literary Criticism, Gale (Detroit), Volume 15, 1981; Volume 49, 1988.
Ivask, Ivar, editor, *Odysseus Elytis: Analogies of Light,* University of Oklahoma Press, 1981.

PERIODICALS

Books Abroad, spring, 1971; (Elytis issue) autumn, 1975.
Chicago Tribune, October 19, 1979.
Comparative Literature, No. 3, 1984.
Hudson Review, winter, 1975-76.
Journal of Modern Greek Studies, No. 2, 1983.
New Statesman, June 12, 1987, p. 26.
New York Times, October 19, 1979.
New York Times Book Review, February 7, 1982.
Publishers Weekly, October 29, 1979.
Times Literary Supplement, October 9, 1981.
Virginia Quarterly Review, spring, 1975.
Washington Post, October 19, 1979.
World Literature Today, spring, 1980; No. 1, 1988.

*   *   *

EMECHETA, (Florence Onye) Buchi 1944-

PERSONAL: Born July 21, 1944, in Yaba, Lagos, Nigeria; daughter of Jeremy Nwabudike (a railway worker and molder) and Alice Ogbanje (Okwuekwu) Emecheta; married Sylvester Onwordi, 1960 (separated, 1966); children: Florence, Sylvester, Jake, Christy, Alice. *Education:* University of London, B.Sc. (with honors), 1972. *Religion:* Anglican. *Avocation:* Gardening, attending the theatre, listening to music, reading.

ADDRESSES: Home—7 Briston Grove, Crouch End, London N8 9EX, England.

CAREER: British Museum, London, England, library officer, 1965-69; Inner London Education Authority, London, youth worker and sociologist, 1969-76; community worker, Camden, NJ, 1976-78. Writer and lecturer, 1972–. Visiting professor at several universities throughout the United States, including Pennsylvania State University, University of California, Los Angeles, and University of Illinois at Urbana-Champaign, 1979; senior resident fellow and visiting professor of English, University of Calabar, Nigeria, 1980-81; lecturer, Yale University, 1982, London University, 1982–; fellow, London University, 1986. Proprietor, Ogwugwu Afor Publishing Company, 1982-83. Member of Home Secretary's Advisory Council on Race, 1979–, and of Arts Council of Great Britain, 1982-83.

AWARDS, HONORS: Jock Campbell Award for literature by new or unregarded talent from Africa or the Caribbean, *New States-man,* 1978; selected as the Best Black British Writer, 1978, and one of the Best British Young Writers, 1983.

WRITINGS:

In the Ditch, Barrie & Jenkins, 1972.
Second-Class Citizen (novel), Allison & Busby, 1974, Braziller, 1975.

The Bride Price: A Novel (paperback published as *The Bride Price: Young Ibo Girl's Love; Conflict of Family and Tradition*), Braziller, 1976.
The Slave Girl: A Novel, Braziller, 1977.
The Joys of Motherhood: A Novel, Braziller, 1979.
Destination Biafra: A Novel, Schocken, 1982.
Naira Power (novelette directed principally to Nigerian readers), Macmillan (London), 1982.
Double Yoke (novel), Schocken, 1982.
The Rape of Shavi (novel), Ogwugwu Afor, 1983, Braziller, 1985.
Adah's Story: A Novel, Allison & Busby, 1983.
Head above Water (autobiography), Ogwugwu Afor, 1984, Collins, 1986.
A Kind of Marriage (novelette), Macmillan, 1987.
The Family (novel), Braziller, 1990.
Gwendolen (novel), Collins, 1990.
Kehinde, Heinemann (Portsmouth, NH), 1994.

JUVENILE

Titch the Cat (based on story by daughter, Alice Emecheta), Allison & Busby, 1979.
Nowhere to Play (based on story by daughter, Christy Emecheta), Schocken, 1980.
The Moonlight Bride, Oxford University Press in association with University Press, 1981.
The Wrestling Match, Oxford University Press in association with University Press, 1981, Braziller, 1983.
Family Bargain (publication for schools), British Broadcasting Corp., 1987.

OTHER

(Author of introduction and commentary) Maggie Murray, *Our Own Freedom* (book of photographs), Sheba Feminist (London), 1981.
A Kind of Marriage (teleplay; produced by BBC-TV), Macmillan (London), 1987.

Also author of teleplays "Tanya, a Black Woman," produced by BBC-TV, and "The Juju Landlord." Contributor to journals, including *New Statesman, Times Literary Supplement,* and *Guardian.*

SIDELIGHTS: Although Buchi Emecheta has resided in London since 1962, she is "Nigeria's best-known female writer," comments John Updike in the *New Yorker.* "Indeed, few writers of her sex . . . have arisen in any part of tropical Africa. "Emecheta enjoys much popularity in Great Britain, and she has gathered an appreciative audience on this side of the Atlantic as well. Although Emecheta has written children's books and teleplays, she is best known for her historical novels set in Nigeria, both before and after independence. Concerned with the clash of cultures and the impact of Western values upon agrarian traditions and customs, Emecheta's work is strongly autobiographical; and, as Updike observes, much of it is especially concerned with 'the situation of women in a society where their role, though crucial, was firmly subordinate and where the forces of potential liberation have arrived with bewildering speed.'

Born to Ibo parents in Yaba, a small village near Lagos, Nigeria, Emecheta indicates that the Ibos "don't want you to lose contact with your culture," writes Rosemary Bray in the *Voice Literary Supplement.* Bray explains that the oldest woman in the house plays an important role in that she is the "big mother" to the entire family. In Emecheta's family, her father's sister assumed this role, says Bray: "She was very old and almost blind," Buchi recalls, "And she would gather the young children around her after dinner and tell stories to us." The stories the children heard were about their origins and ancestors; and, according to Bray, Emecheta recalls: "I thought to myself, "No life could be more important than this." So when people asked me what I wanted to do when I grew up I told them I wanted to be a storyteller—which is what I'm doing now."

In the Ditch, her first book, originally appeared as a series of columns in the *New Statesman.* Written in the form of a diary, it "is based on her own failed marriage and her experiences on the dole in London trying to rear alone her many children," state Charlotte and David Bruner in *World Literature Today.* Called a "sad, sonorous, occasionally hilarious. . .extraordinary first novel," by Adrianne Blue of the *Washington Post Book World,* it details her impoverished existence in a foreign land, as well as her experience with racism, and "illuminates the similarities and differences between cultures and attitudes," remarks a *Times Literary Supplement* contributor, who thinks it merits "special attention."

Similarly autobiographical, Emecheta's second novel, *Second-Class Citizen,* "recounts her early marriage years, when she was trying to support her student-husband—a man indifferent to his own studies and later indifferent to his job searches, her childbearing, and her resistance to poverty," observe the Bruners. The novel is about a young, resolute and resourceful Nigerian girl who, despite traditional tribal domination of females, manages to continue her own education; she marries a student and follows him to London, where he becomes abusive toward her. "Emecheta said people find it hard to believe that she has not exaggerated the truth in this autobiographical novel," reports Nancy Topping Bazin in *Black Scholar.* "The grimness of what is described does indeed make it painful to read." Called a "brave and angry book" by Marigold Johnson in the *Times Literary Supplement,* Emecheta's story, however, "is not accompanied by a misanthropic whine," notes Martin Levin in the *New York Times Book Review.* Alice Walker, who thinks it is "one of the most informative books about contemporary African life" that she has read, observes in *Ms.* that "it raises fundamental questions about how creative and prosaic life is to be lived and to what purpose."

"Emecheta's women do not simply lie down and die," observes Bray. "Always there is resistance, a challenge to fate, a need to renegotiate the terms of the uneasy peace that exists between them and accepted traditions." Bray adds that "Emecheta's women know, too, that between the rock of African traditions and the hard place of encroaching Western values, it is the women who will be caught." Concerned with the clash of cultures, in *The Bride Price: A Novel,* Emecheta tells the story of a young Nigerian girl "whose life is complicated by traditional attitudes toward women," writes Richard Cima in *Library Journal.* The young girl's father dies when she is thirteen; and, with her brother and mother, she becomes the property of her father's ambitious brother. She is permitted to remain in school only because it will increase her value as a potential wife. However, she falls in love with her teacher, a descendant of slaves; and because of familial objections, they elope, thereby depriving her uncle of the "bride price." When she dies in childbirth, she fulfills the superstition that a woman would not survive the birth of her first child if her bride price had not been paid; and Susannah Clapp maintains in the *Times Literary Supplement,* that the quality of the novel "depends less on plot or characterization than on the information conveyed about a set of customs and the ideas which underlay them." Calling it "a captivating Nigerian novel lovingly but unsentimentally written, about the survival of ancient marriage customs in modern Nigeria," Valerie Cunningham adds in *New Statesman* that this book "proves Buchi Emecheta to be a considerable writer."

Emecheta's *Slave Girl: A Novel* is about "a poor, gently raised Ibo girl who is sold into slavery to a rich African marketwoman by a feckless brother at the turn of the century," writes a *New Yorker* contributor. Educated by missionaries, she joins the new church where she meets the man she eventually marries. In *Library Journal,* Cima thinks that the book provides an "interesting picture of Christianity's impact on traditional Ibo society." Perceiving parallels between marriage and slavery, Emecheta explores the issue of "freedom within marriage in a society where slavery is supposed to have been abolished," writes Cunningham in the *New Statesman,* adding that the book indicts both "pagan and Christian inhumanity to women." And although a contributor to *World Literature Today* suggests that the "historical and anthropological background" in the novel tends to destroy its "emotional complex," another contributor to the same journal believes that the sociological detail has been "unobtrusively woven into" it and that *The Slave Girl* represents Emecheta's "most accomplished work so far. It is coherent, compact and convincing."

The Joys of Motherhood is about a woman "who marries but is sent home in disgrace because she fails to bear a child quickly enough," writes Bazin. "She then is sent to the city by her father to marry a man she has never seen. She is horrified when she meets this second husband because she finds him ugly, but she sees no alternative to staying with him. Poverty and repeated pregnancies wear her down; the pressure to bear male children forces her to bear child after child since the girls she has do not count." Eustace Palmer in *African Literature Today* observes that "clearly, the man is the standard and the point of reference in this society. It is significant that the chorus of countrymen say, not that a woman without a child is a failed woman, but that a woman without a child *for her husband* is a failed woman." Bazin observes that in Emecheta's novels, "a woman must accept the double standard of sexual freedom: it permits polygamy and infidelity for both Christian and non-Christian men but only monogamy for women. These books reveal the extent to which the African woman's oppression is engrained in the African mores."

Acknowledging that "the issue of polygamy in Africa remains a controversial one," Palmer states that what Emecheta stresses in *The Joys of Motherhood* is "the resulting dominance, especially sexual, of the male, and the relegation of the female into subservience, domesticity and motherhood." Nonetheless, despite Emecheta's "angry glare," says Palmer, one can "glean from the novel the economic and social reasons that must have given rise to polygamy. . . . But the author concentrates on the misery and deprivation polygamy can bring." Palmer praises Emecheta's insightful psychological probing of her characters's thoughts: "Scarcely any other African novelist has succeeded in probing the female mind and displaying the female personality with such precision." Blue likewise suggests that Emecheta "tells this story in a plain style, denuding it of exoticism, displaying an impressive, embracing compassion." Calling it a "graceful, touching, ironically titled tale that bears a plain feminist message," Updike adds that "in this compassionate but slightly distanced and stylized story of a life that comes to seem wasted, [Emecheta] sings a dirge for more than African pieties. The lives within *The Joys of Motherhood* might be, transposed into a different cultural key, those of our own rural ancestors."

Emecheta's *Destination Biafra: A Novel* is a story of the "history of Nigeria from the eve of independence to the collapse of the Biafran secessionist movement," writes Robert L. Berner in *World Literature Today.* The novel has generated a mixed critical response, though. In the *Times Literary Supplement,* Chinweizu feels that it "does not convey the feel of the experience that was Biafra. All it does is leave one wondering why it falls so devastatingly below the quality of Buchi Emecheta's previous works." Noting, however, that Emecheta's publisher reduced the manuscript by half, Robert L. Berner in *World Literature Today* suggests that "this may account for what often seems a rather elliptical narrative and for the frequently clumsy prose which too often blunts the novel's satiric edge." Finding the novel "different from any of her others . . . larger and more substantive," the Bruners state: "Here she presents neither the life story of a single character nor the delineation of one facet of a culture but the whole perplexing canvas of people from diverse ethnic groups, belief systems, levels of society all caught in a disastrous civil war." Moreover, the Bruners feel that the "very objectivity of her reporting and her impartiality in recounting atrocities committed by all sides, military and civilian, have even greater impact because her motivation is not sadistic."

The Rape of Shavi represents somewhat of a departure in that "Emecheta attempts one of the most difficult of tasks: that of integrating the requirements of contemporary, realistic fiction with the narrative traditions of myth and folklore," writes Somtow Sucharitkul in the *Washington Post Book World.* Roy Kerridge describes the novel's plot in the *Times Literary Supplement:* "A plane crashes among strange tribespeople, white aviators are made welcome by the local king, they find precious stones, repair their plane and escape just as they are going to be forcibly married to native girls. The king's son and heir stows away and has adventures of his own in England." Called a "wise and haunting tale" by a *New Yorker* contributor, *The Rape of Shavi* "recounts the ruination of this small African society by voracious white interlopers," says Richard Eder in the *Los Angeles Times.* A few critics suggest that in *The Rape of Shavi,* Emecheta's masterful portrayal of her Shavian community is not matched by her depiction of the foreigners. Eder, for instance, calls it a "lopsided fable," and declares: "It is not that the Shavians are noble and the whites monstrous; that is what fables are for. It is that the Shavians are finely drawn and the Westerners very clumsily. It is a duet between a flute and a kitchen drain." However, Sucharitkul thinks that portraying the Shavians as "complex individuals" and the Westerners as "two dimensional, mythic types" presents a refreshing, seldom expressed, and "particularly welcome" point of view.

Although in the *New York Times* Michiko Kakutani calls *The Rape of Shavi* "an allegorical tale, filled with ponderous morals about the evils of imperialism and tired aphorisms about nature and civilization," Sucharitkul believes that "the central thesis of [the novel] is brilliantly, relentlessly argued, and Emecheta's characters and societies are depicted with a bittersweet, sometimes painful honesty." The critic also praises Emecheta's "persuasive" prose: "It is prose that appears unusually simple at first, for it is full of the kind of rhythms and sentence structures more often found in folk tales than in contemporary novels. Indeed, in electing to tell her multilayered and often very contemporary story within a highly mythic narrative framework, the author walks a fine line between the pitfalls of preciosity and pretentiousness. By and large, the tightrope act is a success."

BIOGRAPHICAL/CRITICAL SOURCES:

BOOKS

Allan, Tuzyline Jita, *Womanist and Feminist Aesthetics: A Comparative Review,* Ohio University Press (Athens), 1995.
Contemporary Literary Criticism, Gale (Detroit), Volume 14, 1980; Volume 28, 1984.
Fishburn, Katherine, *Reading Buchi Emecheta: Cross-Cultural Conversations,* Greenwood Press (Westport, CT), 1995.
Umeh, Marie, *Emerging Perspectives on Buchi Emecheta,* Africa World Press (Trenton, NJ), 1995.
Zell, Hans M., and others, *A New Reader's Guide to African Literature,* 2nd revised and expanded edition, Holmes & Meier, 1983.

PERIODICALS

African Literature Today, Number 3, 1983.
Atlantic, May, 1976.
Black Scholar, November/December, 1985; March/April, 1986.
Essence, August, 1990, p. 50.
Library Journal, September 1, 1975; April 1, 1976; January 15, 1978; May 1, 1979; May 15, 1994, p. 98.
Listener, July 19, 1979.
Los Angeles Times, October 16, 1983; March 6, 1985; January 16, 1990.
Ms., January, 1976; July, 1984; March, 1985; July/August, 1990, p. 68.
New Statesman, June 25, 1976; October 14, 1977; June 2, 1978; April 27, 1979.
New Yorker, May 17, 1976; January 9, 1978; July 2, 1979; April 23, 1984; April 22, 1985.
New York Times, February 23, 1985; June 2, 1990.
New York Times Book Review, September 14, 1975; November 11, 1979; January 27, 1980; February 27, 1983; May 5, 1985; April 29, 1990.
School Library Journal, September, 1994, p. 255.
Times Literary Supplement, August 11, 1972; January 31, 1975; June 11, 1976; February 26, 1982; February 3, 1984; February 27, 1987; April 20, 1990.
Voice Literary Supplement, June, 1982.
Washington Post Book World, May 13, 1979; April 12, 1981; September 5, 1982; September 25, 1983; March 30, 1985.
World Literature Today, spring, 1977; summer, 1977; spring, 1978; winter, 1979; spring, 1980; winter, 1983; autumn, 1984; winter, 1985.

*   *   *

EMPSON, William 1906-1984

PERSONAL: Born September 27, 1906, in Yokefleet, Howden, East Yorkshire, England; died April 15, 1984, in London, England; son of A. R. and Laura (Micklethwait) Empson; married Hester Henrietta Crouse, 1941; children: William Hendrick Mogador, Jacobus Arthur Calais. *Education:* Winchester College, 1920-25; Magdalen College, Cambridge, B.A., 1929, M.A., 1935.

CAREER: Bunrika Daigaku, Tokyo, Japan, chair of English literature, 1931-34; Peking National University (then part of South-Western Combined Universities), Peking, China, professor of English literature, 1937-39; British Broadcasting Co., London, England, editor in monitoring department, 1940-41, Chinese editor, 1941-46; Peking National University, Peking, China, professor of English, 1947-52; Sheffield University, Sheffield, England, professor of English literature, 1953-1971, became professor emeritus. Visiting fellow, Kenyon College, Gambier, Ohio, summers, 1948, 1950, and 1954; visiting professor, University of Toronto, 1973-74, and Pennsylvania State University, University Park, 1974-75.

AWARDS, HONORS: Ingram Merrill Foundation Award for Literature, 1968; D.Litt., from University of East Anglia, Norwich, 1968, University of Bristol, 1971, and University of Sheffield, 1974; knighted, 1979.

WRITINGS:

Letter IV (poems), privately printed, 1929.
Seven Types of Ambiguity: A Study of its Effects on English Verse (criticism), Chatto & Windus, 1930, revised edition, 1947, Meridan, 1957.
Poems, privately printed, 1934, Chatto & Windus, 1935.
Some Versions of Pastoral, Chatto & Windus, 1935, New Directions, 1950, published as *English Pastoral Poetry,* Norton, 1938.
(Editor and translator from technical into basic English) John Haldane, *Outlook of Science,* Routledge & Kegan Paul, 1935.
(Editor and translator from technical into basic English) Haldane, *Science and Well-Being,* Routledge & Kegan Paul, 1935.
(With George Garrett) *Shakespeare Survey,* Brendin Publishing Co., 1937.
The Gathering Storm (poems), Faber, 1940.
Collected Poems of William Empson, Harcourt, 1949, enlarged edition, 1961.
The Structure of Complex Words, New Directions, 1951, 3rd edition, Rowman, 1979.
(Contributor) Derek Hudson, *English Critical Essays: Twentieth Century, Second Series,* Oxford University Press, 1958.
Milton's God, Chatto & Windus, 1961, New Directions, 1962, enlarged edition, Cambridge University Press, 1981.
(Author of introduction) John R. Harrison, *The Reactionaries: Yeats, Lewis, Pound, Eliot, Lawrence,* Schocken, 1967.
(Editor) *Shakespeare's Poems,* New American Library, 1969.
(Editor with David Pirie) *Coleridge's Verse: A Selection,* Faber, 1972, Schocken, 1973.
Using Biography (criticism), Harvard University Press, 1984.
Essays on William Shakespeare, edited by Pirie, Cambridge University Press, 1986.
The Royal Beasts and Other Works, edited by John Haffenden, Chatto & Windus, 1986.
Faustus and the Censor: The English Faust-Book and Marlowe's Dr. Faustus, edited by John Henry Jones, Basil Blackwell, 1987.
Argufying: Essays on Literature and Culture, edited by Haffenden, Chatto & Windus, 1988.
Essays on Renaissance Literature, edited by John Haffenden, Cambridge University Press, Volume 1: *Donne and the New Philosophy,* 1993, *The Drama,* Volume 2, 1994.
The Strengths of Shakespeare's Shrew: Essays, Memoirs, Reviews, edited by John Haffenden, Sheffield Academic Press, 1996.

SIDELIGHTS: Sir William Empson, professor of English literature at Sheffield University for nearly twenty years, "revolutionized our ways of reading a poem," notes a London *Times* writer. The school of literary criticism known as New Criticism gained important support from Empson's *Seven Types of Ambiguity: A Study of Its Effects on English Verse.* This work, together with his other published essays, has become "part of the furniture of any good English or American critic's mind," G. S. Fraser remarks in *Great Writers of the English Language: Poets.* Empson will also

be remembered for "the peculiar, utterly original and startling tenor of his works," says the *Times* writer. Radically different from the romantic poetry produced by Dylan Thomas and Empson's other peers, Empson's poetry employed a more objective, nonsentimental language that reflected his competence as a mathematician and his reverence for science. The *Times* article relates that his first collection, *Poems,* "made an immediate, deserved, and explosive impact such as the literary scene in Britain knows only two or three times in a century."

Perhaps most helpful to erstwhile readers of poetry is Empson's first book-length work of criticism, *Seven Types of Ambiguity.* In general usage, a word or reference is deemed ambiguous if it has more than one possible meaning. In *Seven Types,* Empson wrote, "I propose to use the word in an extended sense, and shall think relevant to my subject any verbal nuance, however slight, which gives room for alternative reactions to the same piece of language." Empson's seven types are briefly defined in the table of contents: "First-type ambiguities arise when a detail is effective in several ways at once. . . . In second-type ambiguities two or more alternative meanings are fully resolved into one. . . . The condition for the third type ambiguity is that two apparently unconnected meanings are given simultaneously. . . . In the fourth type the alternative meanings combine to make clear a complicated state of mind in the author. . . . The fifth type is a fortunate confusion, as when the author is discovering his idea in the act of writing . . . or not holding it in mind all at once. . . . In the sixth type what is said is contradictory or irrelevant and the reader is forced to invent interpretations. . . . The seventh type is that of full contradiction, marking a division in the author's mind."

Ambiguity impedes communication when it results from the writer's indecision, Empson wrote in *Seven Types:* "It is not to be respected in so far as it is due to weakness or thinness of thought, obscures the matter at hand unnecessarily . . . or when the interest of the passage is not focussed upon it, so that it is merely an opportunism in the handling of the material, if the reader will not understand the ideas which are being shuffled, and will be given a general impression of incoherence." However, the protean properties of words—their ability to carry multiple meanings in a variety of ways—are a major component of poetic language, and being aware of how this facet of language operates is one of the pleasures of poetry, said Empson. "*Seven Types* is primarily an exercise intended to help the reader who has already felt the pleasure understand the nature of his response," a *Contemporary Literary Critics* contributor suggests.

Some Versions of Pastoral addresses the modern propensity to express nostalgia for idyllic world views that belong to the past. According to Empson, pastoral literature implied "a beautiful relation between rich and poor [and made] . . . simple people express strong feelings. . . in learned and fashionable language (so that you wrote about the best subject in the best way)." Empson maintains that contemporary expressions of the pastoral are for the most part pretenses: "in pastoral you take a limited life and pretend it is the full and normal one." Writing in *Modern Heroism: Essays on D. H. Lawrence, William Empson, and J. R. R. Tolkien,* Roger Sale contends that by examining a series of leader/heroes from the sixteenth century forward, Empson means to say that the moieties that used to bind leaders to their people no longer exist—in Sale's words, "the people have become a mob and the hero painfully alienated"—and that, therefore, the role of hero or Christ-figure is not attainable.

Sale believes that *Some Versions of Pastoral* is Empson's best book, although it too has been misjudged as a literary work and misused as a critical tool. Sale notes that "in [this book] he can move from the work at hand to his vision with almost no shoving of the evidence, so even though his prose and organization may seem difficult on first reading, he turns with almost indescribable grace from the smallest particular to the largest generalization and then back to various middle grounds. When one becomes used to the book and begins to hear the massive chords of its orchestrations supporting even the most irrelevant aside, the effect is one only the greatest books can produce—it envelopes and controls such large areas of the imagination that for a while one is willing to admit it is the only book ever written. As a modern work of persuasion it is unrivaled."

Milton's God is "a diatribe against Christianity which Empson feels has had a monopoly on torture-worship, sexual repression and hypocrisy," the *Contemporary Literary Critics* essayist relates. Milton's God, Empson maintains, seems to want to set aside the cruelty of his absolute rule, and "has cut out of Christianity both the torture-horror and the sex-horror, and after that the monster seems almost decent." Questioning Milton's orthodoxy on these grounds, Empson presents Milton as a humanist—a view that raised a "furor" among the "entrenched Miltonic establishment," says Robert M. Adams in the *New York Review of Books*. It was, he says, the eccentric professor's "last raid on the academic chicken coop" before his retirement from the University of Sheffield in 1971.

Empson's own humanism accounts in part for his open-minded approach to the topic of meaning in literature. In *Gnomon: Essays on Contemporary Literature*, Hugh Kenner notes: "'The object of life, after all,' [Empson] tells us late in *Ambiguity*, 'is not to understand things, but to maintain one's defenses and equilibrium and live as well as one can; it is not only maiden aunts who are placed like this.'" In *Milton's God*, he declared his agreement with philosopher Jeremy Bentham "that the satisfaction of any impulse is in itself an elementary good, and that the practical ethical question is how to satisfy the greatest number." Empson's poetry and criticism are the natural extensions of his views. Empson offers "not a theory of literature or a single method of analysis but a model of how to read with pleasure and knowledge," notes *New Statesman* reviewer Jon Cook. In *Using Biography*, for example, he demonstrates how familiarity with an author's life helps the critic to empathize with the author, allowing the critic to apply corresponding personal experiences to see into an author's intentions. The resulting insights on Andrew Marvell and W. B. Yeats, says James Fenton in the London *Times*, owe more to Empson's speculations and free associations than to systematic analysis of biographical detail. According to Cook, Empson makes it clear that it is far worse to succumb to "the critical habit of pressing literary works into the service of authoritarian and repressive ideologies, all this, of course, under the comforting guise that to receive authority in this way does us good."

Empson's two-volume *Essays on Renaissance Literature*, like *Argufying*, was edited by Empson's authorized biographer, John Haffenden. Volume 1, *Donne and the New Philosophy*, is a collection of essays about the man whose poetry greatly influenced Empson. Volume 2 includes miscellaneous essays focusing on Shakespeare's *A Midsummer Night's Dream* as well as a host of other Renaissance writers including Christopher Marlowe and Ben Jonson. "Empson was a true miracle-worker in his criticism; he made the dead live again and gave the silenced speech.

Fielding comes alive when Empson writes about him, as Donne's poems do under the critic's deftly charitable hands," notes Eric Griffiths in a *Times Literary Supplement* review of Volume 1. Stephen Greenblatt, however, reviewing Volume 2 in the *London Review of Books*, states that "None of this is close to the level of Empson's major work." While Charles Rosen, writing in the *New York Review of Books*, admits that Empson was "wrong . . . often enough" as a critic, he contends that "Empson's achievement here as elsewhere comes from the generosity of spirit which made him consistently a great critic."

Although Empson is best known for his criticism, *Preliminary Essays* author John Wain writes: "It may well be that criticism will be read and remembered while poetry is forgotten, for criticism breeds fresh criticism more easily than poetry breeds fresh poetry; but in Empson's case it would be a pity if he were known simply as the 'ambiguity' man, and not as a poet." A. Alvarez writes in *Stewards of Excellence*, "The poetry of William Empson has been more used [as a model] than that of any other English poet of our time." As the upheavals of World War II threatened to render romanticism and pastoralism obsolete, poets were challenged to find language and forms equal to the age. "Empson's verse was read with an overwhelming sense of relief after the brash and embarrassed incoherence of wartime and post-war poetry," notes Alvarez, who elaborates, "there is something in his work which encourages other writers to use it for their own ends. It has, I think, an *essential* objectivity. . . . In the later poems what goes in as strong personal feeling comes out as something more general; whilst in the earlier work all the personal energy goes into a particularly impersonal business."

In addition, Empson's best verses "have a quality of mystery and incantation which runs quite counter to his professed rationalism," notes Robert Nye in the London *Times*. The poems, says a writer for the London *Times*, were perceived by some critics to be like "exercises: ingenious, resembling staggeringly clever crossword puzzles, abstruse, riddling—in a word, over-intellectual. But as Edwin Muir and other shrewder readers noted, their real keynote was passion. They represent, as Empson put it in one of the most famous of them, a style learned from a despair. The subject matter of the great ones . . . is the nature of sexual passion and the nature of political passion." Writers found in Empson's verse the balance between intense emotion and detachment that seemed appropriate to describe life in the contemporary world.

While Empson focused on poetry when he was not writing criticism, he did attempt several fictional works during his lifetime. *The Royal Beasts and Other Works*, edited by Haffenden, collects several of Empson's unpublished fictional works, including poems, a satirical fable, and the outline for a ballet. The title of the collection comes from Empson's fable, *The Royal Beasts*, written while Empson was teaching in China in 1937. This work "explores the possibility of a race of apelike creatures, the Wurroos, who by a quirk of evolution evolved rational capacities of thought," notes Tyrus Miller in *Modern Language Notes*. The ballet sketch, also inspired by Empson's stint in the Far East, examines both Eastern and Western religious myths.

BIOGRAPHICAL/CRITICAL SOURCES:

BOOKS

Alvarez, A., *Stewards of Excellence*, Scribner, 1958.
Constable, John, *Critical Essays on William Empson*, Ashgate (Brookfield, VT), 1993.

Contemporary Literary Criticism, Gale (Detroit), Volume 3, 1975; Volume 8, 1981; Volume 19, 1981; Volume 33, 1985; Volume 34, 1985.

Contemporary Literary Critics, St. James, 1977.

Dictionary of Literary Biography, Volume 20: *British Poets, 1914-1945,* Gale, 1983.

Fry, Paul H., *William Empson: Prophet Against Sacrifice,* Routledge (New York), 1991.

Gill, Roma, editor, *William Empson: The Man and His Work,* Routledge & Kegan Paul, 1974.

Hamilton, Ian, editor, *The Modern Poet: Essays from "The Review",* MacDonald, 1968.

Hyman, Stanley Edgar, *The Armed Vision: A Study in the Methods of Modern Literary Criticism,* Knopf, 1948, revised edition, 1955.

Kenner, Hugh, *Gnomon: Essays on Contemporary Literature,* McDowell, 1958.

Makers of Modern Culture, Facts on File, 1981.

Norris, Christopher, *William Empson and the Philosophy of Literary Criticism,* Athlone Press, 1978.

Norris, Christopher and Nigel Mapp, *William Empson: The Critical Achievement,* Cambridge University Press (New York City), 1993.

Sale, Roger, *Modern Heroism: Essays on D. H. Lawrence, William Empson, and J. R. R. Tolkien,* University of California Press, 1973.

Vinson, James, editor, *Great Writers of the English Language: Poets,* St. Martins, 1979.

Wain, John, *Preliminary Essays,* Macmillan (London), 1957.

William Empson: The Man and His Work, Routledge & Kegan Paul, 1974.

PERIODICALS

Agenda, winter, 1994, p. 309.

Criticism, fall, 1966.

Hudson Review, spring, 1952; autumn, 1966.

London Review of Books, July 22, 1993, p. 15; October 20, 1994, p. 31.

Modern Language Notes, December, 1988, p. 1155.

Nation, June 16, 1962.

New Statesman, October 12, 1984; April 19, 1996, p. 39.

New York Review of Books, April 11, 1985; October 21, 1993, p. 72.

New York Times Book Review, May 20, 1984.

Observer, September 30, 1984.

Review of English Studies, November, 1989, p. 551.

Scrutiny, Volume 2, number 3, December, 1933.

Southern Review, autumn, 1938.

Time, April 18, 1949; August 10, 1962.

Times (London), October 25, 1984; February 8, 1985; November 13, 1986.

Times Literary Supplement, November 14, 1986; January 1, 1988; February 26, 1988; July 30, 1993, p. 6.

Washington Post Book World, May 19, 1985.

Yale Review, June, 1962.

*   *   *

ENDO, Shusaku 1923-1996

PERSONAL: Born March 27, 1923, in Tokyo, Japan; died September 29, 1996; son of Tsuneshia and Iku (Takei) Endo; married Junko Okado, September 3, 1955; children: Ryunosuke (son). *Education:* Keio University, Tokyo, B.A., 1949; Lyon University, Lyon, France, student in French literature, 1950-53. *Religion:* Roman Catholic.

MEMBER: International PEN (president of Japanese Center, 1969), Association of Japanese Writers (member of executive committee, 1966).

AWARDS, HONORS: Akutagawa prize (Japan), 1955, for *Shiroihito;* Tanizaki prize (Japan), 1967, and Gru de Oficial da Ordem do Infante dom Henrique (Portugal), 1968, both for *Chinmoku;* Sanct Silvestri, awarded by Pope Paul VI, 1970; Noma Prize, 1980.

WRITINGS:

IN ENGLISH TRANSLATION

Umi to Dokuyaku (novel), Bungeishunju, 1958, translation by M. Gallagher published as *The Sea and Poison,* P. Owen, 1971, Taplinger, 1980.

Kazan (novel), [Japan], 1959, translation by Richard A. Schuchert published as *Volcano,* P. Owen, 1978, Taplinger, 1980.

Obaka-san, [Japan], 1959, translation by Francis Mathy published as *Wonderful Fool,* Harper, 1983.

Chinmoku (novel), Shinkosha, 1966, translation by William Johnston published as *Silence,* P. Owen, 1969, Taplinger, 1979.

Ougon no Ku (play), Shinkosha, 1969, translation by Mathy published as *The Golden Country,* Tuttle (Tokyo), 1970.

Iseu no shogai, [Japan], 1973, translation by Schuchert published as *A Life of Jesus,* Paulist Press, 1978.

Kuchibue o fuku toki (novel), [Japan], 1974, translation by Wan C. Gessel published as *When I Whistle,* Taplinger, 1979.

Juichi no iro-garasu (short stories), [Japan], 1979, translation published as *Stained Glass Elegies,* Dodd, 1985.

Samurai (novel), [Japan], 1980, translation by Gessel published as *The Samurai,* Harper, 1982.

Scandal, translated by Gessel, Dodd, 1988.

Foreign Studies, translated by Mark Williams, P. Owen, 1989.

The Final Martyrs, translated by Gessel, New Directions, 1994.

Deep River, translated by Gessel, New Directions (New York City), 1994.

Watashi ga suteta onna (see also below), translation by Williams published as *The Girl I Left Behind,* New Directions (New York City), 1995.

IN JAPANESE

Shiroihito (novel), Kodansha, 1955.

Seisho no Naka no Joseitachi (essays; title means "Women in the Bible"), Shinchosha, 1968.

Bara no Yakat (play), Shinchosha, 1969.

Yumoa shosetsu shu (short stories), Kodansha, 1974.

France no daigakusei (essays on travel in France), Kadokawasho-ten, 1974.

Kitsunegata tanukigata (short stories), Kodansha, 1976.

Watashi ga suteta onna, Kodansha, 1976.

Yukiaru kotoba (essays), Shinchosha, 1976.

Nihonjin wa Kirisuto kyo o shinjirareru ka, Shogakukan, 1977.

Kare no ikikata, Shinchosha, 1978.

Kirisuto no tanjo, Shinchosha, 1978.

Ningen no naka no X (essays), Chuokoronsha, 1978.

Rakuten taisho, Kodansha, 1978.

Ju to jujika (biography of Pedro Cassini), Shuokoronsha, 1979.

Marie Antoinette (fiction), Asahi shinbunsha, 1979.

Chichioya, Shinchosha, 1980.

Kekkonron, Shufunotomosha, 1980.

Sakka no nikki (diary excerpts), Toju-sha, 1980.

Endo Shusaku ni yoru Endo Shusaku, Seidosha, 1980.
Meiga Iesu junrei, Bungei Shunju, 1981.
Onna no issho (fiction), Asahi Shinbunsha, 1982.
Endo Shusaku to Knagaeru, PHP Kekyujo, 1982.
Fuyu no yasashisa, Bunka Shuppakyoku, 1982.

Also author of *Watakusi no Iesu,* 1976, *Usaba kagero nikki,* 1978, *Shinran,* 1979, *Tenshi,* 1980, *Ai to jinsei o meguru danso,* 1981, and *Okuku e no michi,* 1981.

SIDELIGHTS: Of all leading modern Japanese novelists, Shusaku Endo is considered by many critics to be the one whose novels are easiest for Western readers to grasp. His Roman Catholic upbringing is often cited as the key to his accessibility, for it gave him a philosophical background shaped by Western traditions rather than those of the East. Christianity is a rarity in Japan, where two sects of Buddhism predominate. As Garry Wills explains in the *New York Review of Books,* "Christ is not only challenging but embarrassing [to the Japanese] because he has absolutely no 'face'. . . . He will let anyone spit on him. How can the Japanese ever honor such a disreputable figure?" While strongly committed to his adopted religion, Endo often described the sense of alienation felt by a Christian in Japan. Most of his novels translated into English address the clash of Eastern and Western morals and philosophy, as well as illustrate the difficulty and unlikelihood of Christianity's establishment in Japan.

John Updike writes in the *New Yorker* that Endo's first novel in English translation, *Silence,* is "a remarkable work, a somber, delicate, and startlingly empathetic study of a young Portuguese missionary during the relentless persecution of the Japanese Christians in the early seventeenth century." The young missionary, Rodrigues, travels to Japan to investigate rumors that his former teacher, Ferreira, has not only converted to Buddhism, but is even participating in the persecution of Christians. Updike notes, "One can only marvel at the unobtrusive, persuasive effort of imagination that enables a modern Japanese to take up a viewpoint from which Japan is at the outer limit of the world."

Rodrigues is captured soon after his clandestine entry into Japan, and is handed over to the same jailer who effected Ferreira's conversion. Rodrigues is never physically harmed but is forced to watch the sufferings of native converts while repeatedly being told that his public denouncement of Christ is the only thing that will save them. At first he resists, anticipating a glorious martyrdom for himself, but eventually a vision of Christ convinces him of the selfishness of this goal. He apostatizes, hoping to save at least a few of the Japanese converts by his example. This "beautifully simple plot," writes Updike, "harrowingly dramatizes immense theological issues."

Endo sought to illustrate Japan's hostility toward a Christ figure in another of his translated novels, *Wonderful Fool.* Set in modern times, this story centers on a Frenchman, Gaston Bonaparte. Gaston is a priest who longs to work with missionaries in Japan; after being defrocked, he travels there alone to act as a lay missionary. Completely trusting, pure-hearted, and incapable of harming anyone, Gaston is seen only as a bumbling fool by the Japanese. At their hands he is "scorned, deceived, threatened, beaten and finally drowned in a swamp," reports *Books Abroad* contributor Kinya Tsuruta. "In the end, however, his total faith transforms all the Japanese, not excluding even a hardened criminal. Thus, the simple Frenchman has successfully sowed a seed of good will in the corrupting mud swamp, Endo's favorite metaphor for non-Christian Japan."

Wonderful Fool is seen by some reviewers as Endo's condemnation of his country's values. "What shocks him. . .," notes a *Times Literary Supplement* contributor, "is the spiritual emptiness of what he calls 'mud-swamp Japan,' an emptiness heightened by the absence of any appropriate sense of sin. . . . [But] is it not, perhaps, too self-righteous to ask whether Japan needs the sense of sin which the author would have it assume?" Addressing this issue in a *New Republic* review, Mary Jo Salter believes that "ultimately it is the novelist's humor—slapstick, corny, irreverent—that permits him to moralize so openly."

Louis Allen concurs in the *Listener* that Endo "is one of Japan's major comic writers." Praising the author's versatility, he continues, "In *When I Whistle,* he explores yet another vein, a plain realism behind which lingers a discreet but clear symbolism." *When I Whistle* tells two parallel stories, that of Ozu and his son, Eiichi. Ozu is an unsuccessful businessman who thinks nostalgically of his childhood in pre-war Japan and his youthful romance with the lovely Aiko. Eiichi is a coldly ambitious surgeon who "despises his father—and his father's generation—as sentimentally humanist," explains Allen. The parallel stories merge when Eiichi, in the hopes of furthering his career, decides to use experimental drugs on a terminal cancer patient—Ozu's former sweetheart, Aiko.

Like *Wonderful Fool, When I Whistle* presents "an unflattering version of postwar Japan," notes Allen. But while *Wonderful Fool* is marked by its humor, "Sadness is the keynote [of *When I Whistle*], and its symbol the changed Aiko: a delicate beauty, unhoused and brought to penury by war, and ultimately devoured by a disease which is merely a pretext for experiment by the new, predatory generation of young Japan." *When I Whistle* differs from many of Endo's novels in its lack of an overtly Christian theme, but here as in all his fiction, believes *New York Times Book Review* contributor Anthony Thwaite, "what interests Mr. Endo—to the point of obsession—are the concerns of both the sacred and secular realms: moral choice, moral responsibility. . . . 'When I Whistle' is a seductively readable—and painful—account of these issues."

Endo returned to the historical setting of *Silence*—the seventeenth century—with *The Samurai.* This work has proved to be his most popular in Japan, and like *Silence,* it is based on historical fact. Whereas *Silence* gave readers a Portuguese missionary traveling to Japan, *The Samurai* tells of a Japanese warrior journeying to Mexico, Spain, and finally the Vatican. The samurai, Hasekura, is an unwitting pawn in his shogun's complex scheme to open trade routes to the West. Instructed to feign conversion to Christianity if it will help his cause, Hasekura does so out of loyalty to the shogun, although he actually finds Christ a repulsive figure. Unfortunately, by the time he returns to Japan five years later, political policy has been reversed, and he is treated as a state enemy for his "conversion." Finally, through his own suffering, Hasekura comes to identify with Jesus and becomes a true Christian.

Geoffry O'Brien judges *The Samurai* to be Endo's most successful novel, giving particular praise to its engrossing storyline and to Endo's "tremendously lyrical sensory imagination" in his *Village Voice* review. *Washington Post Book World* reviewer Noel Perrin agrees that *The Samurai* functions well as an adventure story but maintains that "Endo has done far more than write a historical novel about an early and odd encounter between East and West. Taking the history of Hasekuru's embassy as a mere base, he has written a really quite profound religious novel. . . . It is calm and understated and brilliantly told. Simple on the surface, complex underneath. Something like a fable from an old tapestry. . . . If you're interested in how East and West really met, forget Kipling. Read Endo."

In *Scandal,* Endo relates the self-referential story of Suguro, an aging Japanese Catholic novelist who, upon receiving crowning accolades in a public ceremony, is accused of leading a double life in the brothels of Tokyo. Haunted by his striking semblance in a portrait displayed in a sordid hotel and hounded by Kobari, a muckraking journalist, Suguro immerses himself in the Tokyo underworld to pursue his doppelganger. Here Suguro is introduced to Mrs. Naruse, a sadomasochist nurse who engages the author's lurid yearnings and arranges for him to view his double as he engages in sex with Mitsu, a young girl. The distinction between reality and illusion becomes ambiguous as Suguro discovers his shocking other self and struggles to reconcile the moral dichotomy. According to Charles Newman in the *New York Times Book Review,* "Suguro is left with a knowledge more complex than that of a moral hypocrite and more human than that of a writer who had commonly confused the esthetic dualism with the spiritual," reflecting instead "the irreducible evil at the core of his own character." In the end, as Louis Allen observes in the *Times Literary Supplement,* "The sure grip Suguro thought he had on his world is gradually pried loose. His relationship to his wife is falsified, and his art is seen to be built on self-deception. He realizes that 'sin' and the salvation which can arise from it are somehow shallow and superficial things." Nicci Gerrard praises *Scandal* in the *Observer,* writing that Endo "is fastidious and yet implacable in exposing the dark side of human nature and is painstakingly lucid about unresolvable mysteries."

Foreign Studies, originally published in Japan in 1965, is a collection of three tragic stories that portray the reception of Japanese students in Europe, reflecting Endo's own education in France. The first, *A Summer in Rouen,* describes a Japanese student's stay with a Catholic family in post-war France. Kudo, the student, is viewed as a reincarnation of the hostess's dead son and is even called by his name. Unable to express himself because of his poor French and taciturn nature, Kudo retreats into quiet misery among his European sponsors. The brief second piece, *Araki Thomas,* anticipates the themes of *Silence* and *The Samurai* in the story of a seventeenth century Japanese student who travels to Rome to study theology. Upon his return to Japan, however, a changed political climate and torture induce Araki Thomas to apostatize his new religion. As a result he suffers from his dual betrayal of self and his fellow Christians who continue to receive punishment. The third and longest story, *And You, Too,* is generally regarded as the most significant. Described by Endo as "a prelude to *Silence,*" *And You, Too* conveys the acute psychological pain caused by acculturation. Tanaka, a Japanese student, visits Paris in the mid-1960s to study literature, in particular the writings of the Marquis de Sade. His preference for European writers is the source of scorn among the other Japanese expatriates, except for a failed architecture student whom he befriends until tuberculosis forces the friend's premature departure. Isolated and disconsolate in Paris, Tanaka ventures to Sade's castle near Avignon where, in a highly symbolic denouement, he wanders about the ruins and coughs blood onto the snow as he leaves, signifying his final inability to reconcile the cultures of East and West and his imminent return to Japan. As John B. Breslin notes in a *Washington Post Book World* review, Endo's prefatory comments for the English translation indicate his belief that "East and West could never really understand one another on the deep level of 'culture,' only on the relatively superficial level

of 'civilization.'" Marleigh Grayer Ryan praises the collection in *World Literature Today,* writing that "the three pieces taken together constitute a strong statement of the abyss that separates the Japanese mind and the sensibility from the West."

The Final Martyr is a collection of eleven short stories produced by Endo between 1959 and 1985. However, as Karl Schoenberger qualifies in the *Los Angeles Times Book Review,* "these are not short stories at all, but rather character sketches and rambling essays in the confessional *zuihitsu* style," some with extensive footnotes that display Endo's incorporation of historical detail. As several reviewers observe, the collection reveals Endo's frequent use of the short story to develop themes and characters for later novels. Joseph R. Graber writes in the *San Francisco Review of Books* that "*The Final Martyrs* is a fascinating study of how the writer's mind works." The title story, originally published in 1959, describes the persecution of nineteenth century Catholic villagers in southern Japan and foreshadows the novel *Silence.* Here the central figure is a weak-minded villager who renounces Christianity under torture and experiences acute guilt as he betrays both state and God. Endo also offers unabashed autobiographic examination in *A Sixty-Year-Old Man,* written upon the author's sixtieth birthday, which describes an aging Catholic writer's lust for a young girl he encounters at the park. In the final story, *The Box,* Endo contemplates whether talking to plants encourages their growth as he recounts wartime events revealed in an old box of postcards and photographs. Paul Binding concludes in a *New Statesman and Society* review, "It is Endo's triumph that his sense of the totalitarian power of suffering does not diminish his insights into quotidian, late twentieth century urban life—and vice versa."

In *Deep River,* set in India along the Ganges, Endo describes the spiritual quest of Otsu, a rejected Catholic priest who carries corpses to the funeral pyres, and a Japanese tourist group, including a recently widowed businessman who pursues the reincarnation of his wife, a former soldier who survived the Burmese Highway of Death during the Second World War, a nature story writer, and Mitsuko, a cynical, divorced woman who once seduced and spurned Otsu. Through their experiences Endo explores the transcendent wisdom and salvation of Hinduism, Buddhism, and Catholicism, symbolically reflected in Mitsuko's characterization of God as an onion. Robert Coles comments in the *New York Times Book Review,* "Mr. Endo is a master of the interior monologue, and he builds 'case' by 'case,' chapter by chapter, a devastating critique of a world that has 'everything' but lacks moral substance and seems headed nowhere." Praising the novel as among Endo's most effective, Andrew Greeley writes in *Washington Post Book World,* "this moving story about a pilgrimage of grace, must be rated as one of the best of them all."

The Girl I Left Behind, written some thirty-five years earlier but not published until a year before the author's death in 1996, recounts lifelong encounters between Yoshioka Tsutomu, a Japanese salesman, and Mitsu, a simple country girl whom he seduced as a college student. Though Endo himself acknowledged the immaturity of this early work in an afterward, the sentimental story adumbrates the author's skill for characterization and powerful Christian allusions, here represented by Mitsu's Christ-like goodness and charity. Confined to a leprosarium managed by Catholic nuns until informed of her misdiagnosis, Mitsu learns to live among the lepers and devotes her life to their care. Despite its noted awkwardness and technical shortcomings, P.J. Kavanagh regards the novel as "remarkably convincing" in the *Spectator,* and a *Publishers Weekly* reviewer concludes that Endo's writing is redeemed by "moments of sparkling intelligence and clarity."

BIOGRAPHICAL/CRITICAL SOURCES:

BOOKS

Contemporary Literary Criticism, Gale (Detroit), Volume 7, 1977; Volume 14, 1980; Volume 19, 1981; Volume 54, 1989.

Rimer, J. Thomas, *Modern Japanese Fiction and Its Traditions: An Introduction,* Princeton University Press, 1978.

PERIODICALS

America, June 21, 1980; February 2, 1985; October 13, 1990; August 1, 1992; November 19, 1994, pp. 18, 28.

Antioch Review, winter, 1983.

Best Sellers, November, 1980.

Books Abroad, spring, 1975.

Chicago Tribune Book World, October 7, 1979.

Christianity Today, March 17, 1989.

Commonweal, November 4, 1966; September 22, 1989; May 19, 1995.

Kirkus Reviews, October 1, 1995.

Listener, May 20, 1976; April 12, 1979.

London Magazine, April/May, 1974.

London Review of Books, May 19, 1988.

Los Angeles Times, November 13, 1980; December 1, 1983.

Los Angeles Times Book Review, December 5, 1982; September 18, 1994.

New Republic, December 26, 1983.

New Statesman, May 7, 1976; April 13, 1979.

New Statesman and Society, April 30, 1993.

Newsweek, December 19, 1983.

New Yorker, January 14, 1980.

New York Review of Books, February 19, 1981; November 4, 1982.

New York Times Book Review, January 13, 1980; June 1, 1980; December 26, 1982; November 13, 1983; July 21, 1985; August 28, 1988; May 6, 1990; May 28, 1995.

Observer, April 24, 1988; August 29, 1993.

Publishers Weekly, July 4, 1994, p. 25; September 11, 1995, p. 72.

San Francisco Review of Books, October/November, 1994.

Saturday Review, July 21, 1979.

Spectator, May 1, 1976; April 14, 1979; May 15, 1982; November 19, 1994.

Times (London), April 18, 1985.

Times Literary Supplement, July 14, 1972; January 25, 1974; May 5, 1978; May 21, 1982; October 26, 1984; April 29, 1988; October 28, 1994.

Vanity Fair, February, 1991.

Village Voice, November 16, 1982.

Washington Post Book World, September 2, 1979; October 12, 1980; October 24, 1982; June 23, 1985; May 6, 1990; June 25, 1995.

World Literature Today, summer, 1979; winter, 1984; winter, 1990; winter, 1996.

*   *   *

ENGELHARDT, Frederick
 See HUBBARD, L(afayette) Ron(ald)

*   *   *

EPERNAY, Mark
 See GALBRAITH, John Kenneth

EPSILON
 See BETJEMAN, John

*   *   *

ERDRICH, Louise 1954-
 (Heidi Louise, Milou North)

PERSONAL: Born Karen Louise Erdrich June 7 (one source says July 6), 1954, in Little Falls, MN; daughter of Ralph Louis (a teacher with the Bureau of Indian Affairs) and Rita Joanne (affiliated with the Bureau of Indian Affairs; maiden name, Gourneau) Erdrich; married Michael Anthony Dorris (a writer and professor of Native American studies) October 10, 1981 (committed suicide April 11, 1997); children: Reynold Abel (died in 1991), Jeffrey Sava, Madeline Hannah, Persia Andromeda, Pallas Antigone, Aza Marion. *Education:* Dartmouth College, B.A., 1976; Johns Hopkins University, M.A., 1979. *Politics:* Democrat. *Religion:* "Anti-religion." *Avocational interests:* Quilling, running, drawing, "playing chess with daughters and losing, playing piano badly, speaking terrible French."

CAREER: Writer. North Dakota State Arts Council, visiting poet and teacher, 1977-78; Johns Hopkins University, Baltimore, MD, writing instructor, 1978-79; Boston Indian Council, Boston, MA, communications director and editor of *The Circle,* 1979-80; Charles-Merrill Co., textbook writer, 1980. Previously employed as a beet weeder in Wahpeton, ND; waitress in Wahpeton, Boston, and Syracuse, NY; psychiatric aide in a Vermont hospital; poetry teacher at prisons; lifeguard; and construction flag signaler. Has judged writing contests.

MEMBER: International Writers, PEN (member of executive board, 1985-88), Authors Guild, Authors League of America.

AWARDS, HONORS: Johns Hopkins University teaching fellow, 1978; MacDowell Colony fellow, 1980; Yaddo Colony fellow, 1981; Dartmouth College visiting fellow, 1981; First Prize, Nelson Algren fiction competition, 1982, for "The World's Greatest Fisherman"; National Endowment for the Arts fellowship, 1982; Pushcart Prize, 1983; National Magazine Fiction awards, 1983 and 1987; *Love Medicine* received the Virginia McCormack Scully Prize for best book of the year dealing with Indians or Chicanos in 1984, the National Book Critics Circle Award for best work of fiction in 1984, the *Los Angeles Times Award* for best novel, the Sue Kaufman Prize for the Best First Novel from the American Academy and Institute of Arts and Letters, the American Book Award from the Before Columbus Foundation, and was named one of the best eleven books of 1985 by the *New York Times Book Review;* Guggenheim fellow, 1985-86; *The Beet Queen* was named one of *Publishers Weekly's* best books, 1986; First Prize, O. Henry awards, 1987; National Book Critics Circle Award nomination.

WRITINGS:

NOVELS

Love Medicine, Holt (New York City), 1984, expanded edition, 1993.

The Beet Queen, Holt, 1986.

Tracks, Harper, 1988.

(With Michael Dorris) *The Crown of Columbus,* HarperCollins (New York City), 1991.

The Bingo Palace, HarperCollins, 1994.

Tales of Burning Love, HarperCollins, 1996.

The Antelope Wife, HarperCollins, 1998.

POETRY

Jacklight, Holt, 1984.
Baptism of Desire, Harper, 1989.

OTHER

Imagination (textbook), C. E. Merrill, 1980.
(Author of preface) Michael Dorris, *The Broken Cord: A Family's Ongoing Struggle with Fetal Alcohol Syndrome,* Harper, 1989.
(Author of preface) Desmond Hogan, *A Link with the River,* Farrar, Straus, 1989.
(With Allan Richard Chavkin and Nancy Feyl Chavkin) *Conversations with Louise Erdrich and Michael Dorris,* University Press of Mississippi (Jackson), 1994.
The Falcon: A Narrative of the Captivity and Adventures of John Tanner, Penguin (New York City), 1994.
The Blue Jay's Dance: A Birth Year (memoir), HarperCollins (New York City), 1995.
Grandmother's Pigeon (children's book), illustrated by Jim LaMarche, Hyperion (New York City), 1996.

Author of short story, "The World's Greatest Fisherman"; contributor to anthologies, including the *Norton Anthology of Poetry*; *Best American Short Stories* of 1981-83, 1983, and 1988; and *Prize Stories: The O. Henry Awards,* in 1985 and 1987. Contributor of stories, poems, essays, and book reviews to periodicals, including *New Yorker, New England Review, Chicago, American Indian Quarterly, Frontiers, Atlantic, Kenyon Review, North American Review, New York Times Book Review, Ms., Redbook* (with her sister Heidi, under the joint pseudonym Heidi Louise), and *Woman* (with Dorris, under the joint pseudonym Milou North).

MEDIA ADAPTATIONS: The Crown of Columbus has been optioned for film production.

SIDELIGHTS: Award-winning author Louise Erdrich published her first two books—*Jacklight,* a volume of poetry, and *Love Medicine,* a novel—at the age of thirty. The daughter of a Chippewa Indian mother and a German-American father, the author explores Native American themes in her works, with major characters representing both sides of her heritage. The first in a multi-part series, *Love Medicine* traces two Native American families from 1934 to 1984 in a unique seven-narrator format. The novel was extremely well-received, earning its author numerous awards, including the National Book Critics Circle Award in 1984. Since then, Erdrich has gone on to publish *The Beet Queen, Tracks, The Bingo Palace,* and *Tales of Burning Love,* all of which are related through recurring characters and themes.

Erdrich's first year at Dartmouth, 1972, was the year the college began admitting women, as well as the year the Native American studies department was established. The author's future husband and collaborator, anthropologist Michael Dorris, was hired to chair the department. In his class, Erdrich began the exploration of her own ancestry that would eventually inspire her novels.

After receiving her master's degree, Erdrich returned to Dartmouth as a writer-in-residence. Dorris—with whom she had remained in touch—attended a reading of Erdrich's poetry there, and was impressed. A writer himself—Dorris would later publish the best-selling novel *A Yellow Raft in Blue Water* and receive the 1989 National Book Critics Circle Award for his nonfiction work *The Broken Cord*—he decided then that he was interested in working with Erdrich and getting to know her better. When he left for New Zealand to do field research and Erdrich went to Boston to work on a textbook, the two began sending their poetry and fiction back and forth with their letters, laying a groundwork for a literary relationship. Dorris returned to New Hampshire in 1980, and Erdrich moved back there as well. The two began collaborating on short stories, including one titled "The World's Greatest Fisherman." When this story won five thousand dollars in the Nelson Algren fiction competition, Erdrich and Dorris decided to expand it into a novel—*Love Medicine.* At the same time, their literary relationship led to a romantic one. In 1981, they were married.

Erdrich's novels *Love Medicine, The Beet Queen, Tracks, The Bingo Palace,* and *Tales of Burning Love* encompass the stories of three interrelated families living in and around a reservation in the fictional town of Argus, North Dakota, from 1912 through the 1980s. The novels have been compared to those of William Faulkner, mainly due to the multi-voice narration and nonchronological storytelling which he employed in works such as *As I Lay Dying.* Erdrich's works, linked by recurring characters who are victims of fate and the patterns set by their elders, are structured like intricate puzzles in which bits of information about individuals and their relations to one another are slowly released in a seemingly random order, until three-dimensional characters—with a future and a past—are revealed. Through her characters' antics, Erdrich explores universal family life cycles while also communicating a sense of the changes and loss involved in the twentieth-century Native American experience.

Erdrich published her first novel, *Love Medicine,* in 1984. "With this impressive debut," stated *New York Times Book Review* contributor Marco Portales, "Louise Erdrich enters the company of America's better novelists." *Love Medicine* was named for the belief in love potions which is a part of Chippewa folklore. The novel explores the bonds of family and faith which preserve both the Chippewa tribal community and the individuals that comprise it.

The novel begins at a family gathering following the death of June Kashpaw, a prostitute. The characters introduce one another, sharing stories about June which reveal their family history and their cultural beliefs. Albertine Johnson, June's niece, introduces her grandmother, Marie, her grandfather, Nector, and Nector's twin brother, Eli. Eli represents the old way—the Native American who never integrated into the white culture. He also plays a major role in *Tracks,* in which he appears as a young man. The story of Marie and Nector brings together many of the important images in the novel, including the notion of "love medicine." As a teenager in a convent, Marie is nearly burned to death by a nun who, in an attempt to exorcize the devil from within her, pours boiling water on Marie. Immediately following this incident, Marie is sexually assaulted by Nector. Marie and Nector are later married, but in middle age, Nector begins an affair with Lulu Lamartine, a married woman. In an attempt to rekindle Nector and Marie's passion, their grandson Lipsha prepares "love medicine" for Nector. But Lipsha has difficulty obtaining a wild goose heart for the potion. He substitutes a frozen turkey heart, which causes Nector to choke to death.

Reviewers responded positively to Erdrich's debut novel, citing its lyrical qualities as well as the rich characters who inhabit it. *New York Times* contributor D. J. R. Bruckner was impressed with Erdrich's "mastery of words," as well as the "vividly drawn" characters who "will not leave the mind once they are let in."

Portales, who called *Love Medicine* "an engrossing book," applauded the unique narration technique which produces what he termed "a wondrous prose song."

Her 1986 novel, *The Beet Queen,* deals with whites and half-breeds, as well as American Indians, and explores the interactions between these worlds. The story begins in 1932, during the Depression. *The Beet Queen* begins when Mary and Karl Adare's recently-widowed mother flies off with a carnival pilot, abandoning the two children and their newborn brother. The baby is taken by a young couple who have just lost their child. Karl and eleven-year-old Mary ride a freight train to Argus, seeking refuge with their aunt and uncle. When they arrive in the town, however, Karl, frightened by a dog, runs back onto the train and winds up at an orphanage. Mary grows up with her aunt and uncle, and the novel follows her life—as well as those of her jealous, self-centered cousin Sita and their part-Chippewa friend Celestine James—for the next forty years, tracing the themes of separation and loss that began with Mary's father's death and her mother's grand departure.

The Beet Queen was well-received by critics, some of whom found it even more impressive than *Love Medicine.* Many noted the novel's poetic language and symbolism; Robert Bly in the *New York Times Book Review* noted that Erdrich's "genius is in metaphor," and that the characters "show a convincing ability to feel an image with their whole bodies." Josh Rubins, writing in *New York Review of Books,* called *The Beet Queen* "a rare second novel, one that makes it seem as if the first, impressive as it was, promised too little, not too much."

While more political than her previous novels, *Tracks,* Erdrich's 1989 work, also deals with spiritual themes, exploring the tension between the Native Americans' ancient beliefs and the Christian notions of the Europeans. *Tracks* takes place between 1912 and 1924, before the settings of Erdrich's other novels, and reveals the roots of *Love Medicine*'s characters and their hardships. One of the narrators, Nanapush, is the leader of a tribe that is suffering on account of the white government's exploitation. He feels pressured to give up their land in order to avoid starvation. While Nanapush represents the old way, Pauline, the other narrator, represents change. The future mother of *Love Medicine*'s Marie Lazarre, Pauline is a young half-breed from a mixed-blood tribe "for which the name was lost." She feels torn between her Indian faith and the white people's religion, and is considering leaving the reservation. But at the center of *Tracks* is Fleur, a character whom *Los Angeles Times Book Review* contributor Terry Tempest Williams called "one of the most haunting presences in contemporary American literature." Nanapush discovers this young woman—the last survivor of a family killed by consumption—in a cabin in the woods, starving and mad. Nanapush adopts Fleur and nurses her back to health.

Reviewers found *Tracks* distinctly different from Erdrich's earlier novels, and some felt that her third novel lacked the characteristics that made *Love Medicine* and *The Beet Queen* so outstanding. *Washington Post Book World* critic Jonathan Yardley felt that, on account of its more political focus, the work has a "labored quality." Robert Towers stated in *New York Review of Books* that he found the characters too melodramatic and the tone too intense. Katherine Dieckmann, writing in the *Voice Literary Supplement,* affirmed that she "missed [Erdrich's] skilled multiplications of voice," and called the relationship between Pauline and Nanapush "symptomatic of the overall lack of grand orchestration and

perspectival interplay that made Erdrich's first two novels polyphonic masterpieces."

Erdrich and Dorris's jointly-authored novel, *The Crown of Columbus,* explores Native American issues from the standpoint of the authors' current experience, rather than the world of their ancestors. Marking the quincentennial anniversary of Spanish explorer Christopher Columbus's voyage in a not-so-celebratory fashion, Erdrich and Dorris raise important questions about the meaning of that voyage for both Europeans and Native Americans today. The story is narrated by the two central characters, both Dartmouth professors involved in projects concerning Columbus. Vivian Twostar is a Native American single mother with eclectic tastes and a teenage son, Nash. Vivian is asked to write an academic article on Columbus from a Native American perspective and is researching Columbus's diaries. Roger Williams, a stuffy New England Protestant poet, is writing an epic work about the explorer's voyage. Vivian and Roger become lovers—parenting a girl named Violet—but have little in common. Ultimately acknowledging the destructive impact of Columbus's voyage on the Native American people, Vivian and Roger vow to redress the political wrongs symbolically by changing the power structure in their relationship. In the end, as Vivian and Roger rediscover themselves, they rediscover America.

Some reviewers found *The Crown of Columbus* unbelievable and inconsistent, and considered it less praiseworthy than the individual authors' earlier works. However, *New York Times Book Review* contributor Robert Houston appreciated the work's timely political relevance. He also stated, "There are moments of genuine humor and compassion, of real insight and sound satire." Other critics also considered Vivian and Roger's adventures amusing, vibrant, and charming.

Erdrich returned to the descendants of Nanapush with her 1994 novel, *The Bingo Palace.* The fourth novel in the series which began with *Love Medicine, The Bingo Palace* weaves together a story of spiritual pursuit with elements of modern reservation life. Erdrich also provided continuity to the series by having the novel primarily narrated by Lipsha Morrisey, the illegitimate son of June Kapshaw and Gerry Nanapush from *Love Medicine.* After working at a Fargo sugar beet factory, Lipsha has returned home to the reservation in search of his life's meaning. He finds work at his uncle Lyman Lamartine's bingo parlor and love with his uncle's girlfriend, Shawnee Ray Toose. Thanks to the magic bingo tickets provided to him by the spirit of his dead mother, June, he also finds modest wealth. The character of Fleur Pillager returns from *Tracks* as Lipsha's great-grandmother. After visiting her, Lipsha embarks on a spiritual quest in order to impress Shawnee and learn more about his own tribal religious rites. Family members past and present are brought together in his pursuit, which comprises the final pages of the novel.

Reviewers' comments on *The Bingo Palace.* were generally positive. While Lawrence Thornton in the *New York Times Book Review* found "some of the novel's later ventures into magic realism . . . contrived," his overall impression was more positive: "Ms. Erdrich's sympathy for her characters shines as luminously as Shawnee Ray's jingle dress." Pam Houston, writing for the *Los Angeles Times Book Review,* was especially taken by the character of Lipsha Morrissey, finding in him "what makes this her most exciting and satisfying book to date."

Erdrich turned to her own experience as mother of six for her next work, *The Blue Jay's Dance.* Her first book of nonfiction, *The Blue Jay's Dance* chronicles Erdrich's pregnancy and the birth year of her child. The title refers to a blue jay's habit of defiantly "dancing" towards an attacking hawk, Erdrich's metaphor for "the sort of controlled recklessness that having children always is," noted Jane Aspinall in *Quill & Quire*. Erdrich has been somewhat protective of her family's privacy and has stated the narrative actually describes a combination of her experience with several of her children. Sue Halpern in the *New York Times Book Review* remarked on this difficult balancing act between public and private lives but found "Ms. Erdrich's ambivalence inspires trust . . . and suggests that she is the kind of mother whose story should be told."

Some reviewers averred that Erdrich's description of the maternal relationship was a powerful one: "the bond between mother and infant has rarely been captured so well," commented a *Kirkus Reviews* contributor. While the subject of pregnancy and motherhood is not a new one, Halpern noted that the book provided new insight into the topic: "What makes *The Blue Jay's Dance* worth reading is that it quietly places a mother's love and nurturance amid her love for the natural world and suggests . . . how right that placement is." Although the *Kirkus Reviews* contributor found *The Blue Jay's Dance* to be "occasionally too self-conscious about the importance of Erdrich's role as Writer," others commented positively on the book's examination of the balance between the work of parenting and one's vocation. A *Los Angeles Times* reviewer remarked: "this book is really about working and having children, staying alert and . . . focused through the first year of a child's life."

Within the same year, Erdrich returned to the character of June Kasphaw of *Love Medicine* in her sixth novel, *Tales of Burning Love*. More accurately, it is the story of June's husband, Jack Mauser, and his five (including June) ex-wives. To begin the tale, Jack meets June while they are both inebriated and marries her that night. In reaction to his inability to consummate their marriage, she walks off into a blizzard and is found dead the next day. His four subsequent marriages share the same elements of tragedy and comedy, culminating in Jack's death in a fire in the house he built. The story of each marriage is told by the four ex-wives as they are stranded together in Jack's car during a blizzard after his funeral. Again, Erdrich references her previous work in the characters of Gerry and Dot Nanapush, Dot as one of Jack's ex-wives and Gerry as Dot's imprisoned husband.

Reviewers continued to note Erdrich's masterful descriptions and fine dialogue in this work. According to Penelope Mesic in the *Chicago Tribune*, "Erdrich's strength is that she gives emotional states—as shifting and intangible, as indefinable as wind—a visible form in metaphor." A *Times Literary Supplement* contributor compared her to both Tobias Wolff—"(like him), she is . . . particularly good at evoking American small-town life and the space that engulfs it"—as well as Raymond Carver, noting her dialogues to be "small exchanges that . . . map out the barely navigable distance between what's heard, what's meant, and what's said."

While Erdrich covers familiar territory in *Tales of Burning Love*, she seems to be expanding her focus slightly. Roxana Robinson in *Washington Post Book World* remarked, "The landscape, instead of being somber and overcast . . . is vividly illuminated by bolts of freewheeling lunacy: This is a mad Gothic comedy." Or as Verlyn Klinkenborg noted in the *Los Angeles Times Book Review*, "this book marks a shift in (Erdrich's) career, a shift that is suggested rather than fulfilled . . . there is new country coming

into (her) sight, and this novel is her first welcoming account of it."

BIOGRAPHICAL/CRITICAL SOURCES:

BOOKS

Authors and Artists for Young Adults, Volume 10, Gale (Detroit), 1993.
Contemporary Literary Criticism, Gale, Volume 39, 1986; Volume 54, 1989.
Dictionary of Literary Biography, Volume 152: *American Novelists since World War II, Fourth Series,* Gale, 1995.
Pearlman, Mickey, *American Women Writing Fiction: Memory, Identity, Family, Space,* University Press of Kentucky, 1989, pp. 95-112.

PERIODICALS

America, May 14, 1994, p. 7.
American Indian Culture and Research Journal, 1987, pp. 51-73.
American Literature, September, 1990, pp. 405-22.
Belles Lettres, Summer, 1990, pp. 30-31.
Booklist, January 15, 1995, p. 893.
Chicago Tribune, September 4, 1988, pp. 1, 6; January 1, 1994, pp. 1, 9; April 21, 1996, pp. 1, 9.
College Literature, October, 1991, pp. 80-95.
Commonweal, October 24, 1986, pp. 565, 567; November 4, 1988, p. 596.
Kirkus Reviews, February 15, 1996, p. 244; April 15, 1996, p. 600.
Los Angeles Times Book Review, October 5, 1986, pp. 3, 10; September 11, 1988, p. 2; May 12, 1991, pp. 3, 13; February 6, 1994, p. 1, 13; May 28, 1995, p. 8; June 16, 1996, p. 3.
Nation, October 21, 1991, pp. 465, 486-90.
New Republic, October 6, 1986, pp. 46-48; January 6-13, 1992, pp. 30-40.
Newsday, November 30, 1986.
New York Review of Books, January 15, 1987, pp. 14-15; November 19, 1988, pp. 40-41; May 12, 1996, p. 10.
New York Times, December 20, 1984, p. C21; August 20, 1986, p. C21; August 24, 1988, p. 41; April 19, 1991, p. C25.
New York Times Book Review, August 31, 1982, p. 2; December 23, 1984, p. 6; October 2, 1988, pp. 1, 41-2; April 28, 1991, p. 10; July 20, 1993, p. 20; January 16, 1994, p. 7; April 16, 1995, p.14; April 12, 1998, p. 6.
People, June 10, 1991, pp. 26-27.
Playboy, March, 1994, p. 30.
Publishers Weekly, August 15, 1986, pp. 58-59; April 22, 1996, p. 71.
Quill & Quire, August, 1995, p. 30.
Time, February 7, 1994, p. 71.
Times Literary Supplement, February 14, 1997, p. 21.
Voice Literary Supplement, October, 1988, p. 37.
Washington Post Book World, August 31, 1986, pp. 1, 6; September 18, 1988, p. 3; February 6, 1994, p. 5; April 21, 1996, p. 3.
Western American Literature, February, 1991, pp. 363-64.
Writer's Digest, June, 1991, pp. 28-31.

*   *   *

ERICSON, Walter
See FAST, Howard (Melvin)

ERIKSON, Erik H(omburger) 1902-1994
(Erik Homburger)

PERSONAL: Born June 15, 1902, in Frankfurt-am-Main, Germany; came to U.S., 1933, naturalized citizen, 1939; died May 12, 1994, Harwich, MA; son of Danish parents; after mother's second marriage used stepfather's surname Homburger until his naturalization; married Joan Mowat Serson, April 1, 1930; children: Kai T., Jon M., Sue (Mrs. Harland G. Bloland). *Education:* Graduated from the Vienna Psychoanalytic Institute in 1933; received certificate from the Maria Montessori School; studied under Anna Freud; also studied at Harvard University Psychological Clinic.

ADDRESSES: Home—1705 Centro West, Tiburon, CA 94920.

CAREER: Practicing psychoanalyst, 1933-94. Training psychoanalyst, 1942-94. Teacher and researcher at Harvard University, School of Medicine, Department of Neuropsychiatry, Cambridge, MA, 1934-35, Yale University, School of Medicine, New Haven, CT, 1936-39, University of California, Berkeley, and San Francisco, 1939-51, San Francisco Psychoanalytic Institute, San Francisco, CA, and Menninger Foundation, Topeka, KS, 1944-50; Austen Riggs Center, Stockbridge, MA, senior staff member, 1951-60; visiting professor, 1951-60, Western Psychiatric Institute, Pittsburgh, PA., Massachusetts Institute of Technology, Boston, MA, and University of Pittsburgh, School of Medicine, Pittsburgh; Harvard University, professor of human development and lecturer on psychiatry, 1969-70, distinguished visiting professor, Erikson Center, 1982-94, professor emeritus, 1970-94. Trustee of Radcliffe College, Cambridge.

MEMBER: American Psychological Association (fellow), American Psychoanalytic Association (life member), American Academy of Arts and Science (fellow), National Academy of Education (emeritus), Cambridge Scientific Club, Signet Society, Phi Beta Kappa (honorary).

AWARDS, HONORS: Harvard University, M.S., 1960, LL.D., 1978; University of California, LL.D., 1968; Loyola University, Sc.D., 1970; National Book Award for philosophy and religion, and Pulitzer Prize, both 1970, both for *Gandhi's Truth;* Yale University, Soc.Sc.D., 1971; Brown University, LL.D., 1972; National Association for Mental Health research award, and Aldrich Award from American Academy of Pediatrics, both 1974; Golden Bagel award from Mt. Zion Hospital, San Francisco, CA, 1976; Lund University, Fil.Dr.H.C., 1980; Copenhagen University, Soc.Sc.D., 1987.

WRITINGS:

Observations on the Yurok: Childhood and World Image, University of California Press, 1943.
Childhood and Society, Norton, 1950, revised edition, 1963.
Young Man Luther: A Study in Psychoanalysis and History, Norton, 1958.
Identity and the Life Cycle, International Universities Press, 1959.
   (Editor) *Youth: Change and Challenge,* Basic Books, 1963, published as *The Challenge of Youth,* Doubleday, 1963.
Insight and Responsibility: Lectures on the Ethical Implications of Psychoanalytic Insight, Norton, 1964.
Identity: Youth and Crisis, Norton, 1968.
Gandhi's Truth: On the Origins of Militant Nonviolence, Norton, 1969.
(With Huey P. Newton) *In Search of Common Ground,* edited by Kai T. Erikson, Norton, 1973.

Dimensions of a New Identity: The 1973 Jefferson Lectures, Norton, 1974. *Life History and the Historical Moment,* Norton, 1975.
Toys and Reasons: Stages in the Ritualizations of Experience, Norton, 1976.
Identity and the Life Cycle: A Reissue, Norton, 1980.
The Life Cycle Completed: A Review, Norton, 1982.
(With Joan M. Erikson and Helen Q. Kivnick) *Vital Involvement in Old Age: The Experience of Old Age in Our Time,* Norton, 1986.
A Way of Looking at Things: Selected Papers From 1930 to 1980, edited by Stephen Schlein, Norton, 1987.

CONTRIBUTOR

P. G. Davis, editor, *The Cyclopedia of Medicine,* Volume XII, Davis, 1940.
R. C. Barker and others, *Child Behavior and Development,* McGraw, 1943.
O. Fenichel and others, editors, *The Psychoanalytic Study of the Child,* Volume I, International Universities Press, 1945.
Phyllis Greenacre and others, editors, *The Psychoanalytic Study of the Child,* Volume II, International Universities Press, 1946.
M. J. E. Seen, editor, *Symposium on the Healthy Personality,* Josiah Macy, Jr. Foundation, 1950.
C. J. Friedrich, editor, *Totalitarianism,* Harvard University Press, 1954. Clara Thompson, *An Outline of Psychoanalysis,* Random House, 1955.
Helen Witmer and Ruth Kotinsky, editors, *New Perspectives for Research in Juvenile Delinquency,* U.S. Department of Health, Education, and Welfare, 1956.
B. Schaffner, editor, *Group Processes,* Josiah Macy, Jr. Foundation, 1956. J. M. Tanner and B. Inhelder, editors, *Discussions on Child Development,* International Universities Press, Volume III, 1958, Volume IV, 1960.
Daniel H. Funkenstein, editor, *The Student and Mental Health,* World Federation of Mental Health and International Association of Universities, 1959.
Psychological Issues, Volume I, International Universities Press, 1959. (Author of introduction) Blaine and McArthur, *Emotional Problems of the Student,* Crofts, 1961.
Sir Julian Huxley, editor, *The Humanist Frame,* Harper, 1961.
(And editor) *Adulthood: Essays,* Norton, 1978.

SIDELIGHTS: David Elkind calls Erik H. Erikson "the most widely known and read psychoanalyst in America today." He adds: "like the other giants of psychology, Freud and Piaget, Erikson is not an experimentalist but rather a gifted and sensitive observer and classifier of human behavior and experience. Like Freud, Erikson knows how to use his own psyche as a delicate register of what is universal in man and of what is particular to himself. And, like Piaget, Erikson has been concerned with epigenesis, with the emergent phenomena in human growth. In Erikson's case, this has amounted to a concern with how new feelings, attitudes, and orientations arise in the course of personality development, and how these new features fit within the continuous pattern that is the human life cycle."

Reviewing Erikson's Pulitzer Prize-winning biography, *Gandhi's Truth,* Christopher Lasch writes that this book "even more brilliantly than its predecessor, *Young Man Luther,* shows that psychoanalytic theory, in the hands of an interpreter both resourceful and wise, can immeasurably enrich the study of 'great lives' and of much else besides. With these books Erikson has single-handedly rescued psychoanalytic biography from neglect and disrepute." Elizabeth Hardwick states that "*Gandhi's Truth* opens up for our enlightenment so many thoughts about Gandhi that one almost loses sight of the peculiar, tranquil contribution of Erikson's own temperament upon that of his subject. There is a sort of hidden fullness and richness in this work—hidden in the discreet, rather genteel style, in the mood always courteous and forever wondering. Erikson's mind is free of the temptation to dramatize in a journalistic way and to schematize in the way of his profession, psychoanalysis." Geoffrey Gorer agrees: "In his earlier writings Erik Erikson showed himself to be one of the most insightful and innovative writers on psychoanalytical themes, above all in his work with young children and adolescents. More recently he has shown his awareness of the relevance of cultural differences in the interpretation of the behaviour of members of different societies and in *Young Man Luther,* of the importance of historical context." However, he then adds that "these critical and analytical faculties are almost entirely replaced by a pious uncritical acceptance of the whole myth about Gandhi as a modern saint who, with his unparalleled insight and skills, single-handedly mobilised the whole Indian population and enabled them to throw out the wicked British Empire."

BIOGRAPHICAL/CRITICAL SOURCES:

BOOKS

Maier, Henry W., *Three Theories of Child Development,* Harper, 1965.
Roazen, Paul, *Erik H. Erikson: The Power and Limits of a Vision,* Jason Aronson (Northvale, NJ), 1997.
Wallerstein, Robert S., and Leo Goldberger, *Ideas and Identities: The Life and Work of Erik Erikson,* International Universities Press (Madison, WI), 1997.

PERIODICALS

American Scholar, summer, 1965.
American Sociological Review, December, 1960.
Antioch Review, winter, 1969-70.
Canadian Forum, February, 1970.
Chicago Tribune, December 17, 1986; June 29, 1987.
Christian Century, April 17, 1968; April 8, 1970.
Commonweal, March 13, 1970.
Los Angeles Times Book Review, February 1, 1987.
Nation, June 3, 1968; November 22, 1969.
New Leader, April 8, 1968.
New Republic, October 18, 1969.
New Statesman, January 17, 1969.
Newsweek, August 10, 1964; August 18, 1969; December 21, 1970.
New York Herald Tribune Book Review, November 16, 1958.
New York Times, June 14, 1988.
New York Times Book Review, November 19, 1950; March 31, 1968; September 14, 1969; April 5, 1987.
Observer, January 4, 1970.
Saturday Review, January 16, 1971.
Time, November 30, 1970.
Times Literary Supplement, September 9, 1983; February 26, 1988.
Village Voice, November 20, 1969.
Vogue, December, 1969.
Washington Post, June 29, 1968.
Washington Post Book World, November 9, 1986; June 14, 1987.

ERIKSSON, Buntel
See BERGMAN, (Ernst) Ingmar

*   *   *

ESEKI, Bruno
See MPHAHLELE, Ezekiel

*   *   *

ESQUIVEL, Laura 1951(?)-

PERSONAL: Born c. 1951, in Mexico; daughter of Julio Caesar Esquivel (a telegraph operator) and Josephina Esquivel; married Alfonso Arau (a film director); children: Sandra. *Education:* Attended Escuela Normal de Maestros, Mexico. *Avocation:* Cooking.

ADDRESSES: Home—Mexico City, Mexico. *Office*—Doubleday, 666 5th Avenue, New York, NY 10103

CAREER: Novelist and screenwriter; writer and director for children's theater. Worked as a teacher for eight years.

AWARDS, HONORS: Ariel Award nomination for best screenplay, Mexican Academy of Motion Pictures, Arts and Sciences, for *Chido One.*

WRITINGS:

SCREENPLAYS

Like Water for Chocolate, based on her novel of the same title, Miramax, c. 1993.

Also author of *Chido One,* released in 1985, and *Little Ocean Star,* a children's feature, released in 1994.

NOVELS

Como agua para chocolate: novela de entregas mensuales con recetas, amores, y remedios caseros, Editorial Planeta Mexicana, 1989, translation by Carol Christensen and Thomas Christensen published as *Like Water for Chocolate: A Novel in Monthly Installments, with Recipes, Romances, and Home Remedies,* Doubleday, 1991.
Ley del amor, translation by Margaret Sayers Peden published as *The Law of Love,* Crown Publishers (New York City), 1996.

SIDELIGHTS: Mexican author Laura Esquivel, who gained international recognition with her first novel, *Como agua para chocolate* (*Like Water for Chocolate*), began her literary career as a screenwriter. Working in partnership with her husband, the Mexican director Alfonso Arau, Esquivel wrote the screenplay for a 1985 Mexican release *Chido One,* which Arau directed. The film's success prompted the couple to continue their collaboration, and Arau became the director when Esquivel adapted *Like Water for Chocolate* for the screen. Both the novel and movie have been enormously popular. A number one best-seller in Mexico in 1990, the book has been translated into numerous languages, including an English version, which enjoyed a longstanding run on the *New York Times Book Review* best-seller list in 1993. The movie, according to *Publishers Weekly,* has reported record-breaking attendance, to become one of the highest-grossing foreign films of the decade. Employing in this work the brand of magic realism that Gabriel Garcia Marquez popularized, Esquivel blends culinary knowledge, sensuality, and alchemy with fables and cultural lore to capture what *Washington Post* reviewer Mary Batts

Estrada calls "the secrets of love and life as revealed by the kitchen."

Like Water for Chocolate is the story of Tita, the youngest of three daughters born to Mama Elena, the tyrannical owner of the De La Garza ranch. Tita is a victim of tradition: as the youngest daughter in a Mexican family she is obliged to remain unmarried and to care for her mother. Experiencing pain and frustration as she watches Pedro, the man she loves, marry her older sister Rosaura, Tita faces the added burden of having to bake the wedding cake. But because she was born in the kitchen and knows a great deal about food and its powers, Tita is able to bake her profound sense of sorrow into the cake and make the wedding guests ill. "From this point," as James Polk remarks in the *Tribune Books,* "food, sex and magic are wondrously interwoven." For the remainder of the novel, Tita uses her special culinary talents to provoke strange reactions in Mama Elena, Rosaura, Tita's other sister, Gertrudis, and many others.

Food has played a significant role in Esquivel's life since she was a child. Remembering her early cooking experiences and the aromas of foods cooked in her grandmother's house, she told Molly O'Neill of the *New York Times* that "I watch cooking change the cook, just as it transforms the food. . . . Food can change anything." For Esquivel, cooking is a reminder of the alchemy between concrete and abstract forces. Esquivel's novel of cooking and magic has been well-received by critics. Writing in the *Los Angeles Times Book Review,* Karen Stabiner remarks that Esquivel's novel "is a wondrous, romantic tale, fueled by mystery and superstition, as well as by the recipes that introduce each chapter." James Polk, in the *Chicago Tribune,* writes that "*Like Water for Chocolate* (a Mexican colloquialism meaning, roughly, agitated or excited) is an inventive and mischievous romp—part cookbook, part novel."

Esquivel followed with *The Law of Love,* a highly imaginative novel that features reincarnation, cosmic retribution, and attests to the primacy of love. The story opens with the sixteenth century Spanish conquest of Tenochtitlan, the future site of Mexico City, and the rape of an Aztec princess atop a temple. Many centuries later the principal actors of this earlier drama reappear as astro-analyst Azucena, her missing soul mate Rodrigo, and planetary presidential candidate Isabel in a confrontation that finally breaks the cycle of vengeance and hatred with love and forgiveness. The text is accompanied by a compact disc with music and cartoon illustrations. This "multimedia event," as described by Lilian Pizzichini in the *Times Literary Supplement,* incorporates elements of magic realism, science fiction, and New Age philosophy. "The result," writes *Library Journal* reviewer Barbara Hoffert, "is at once wildly inventive and slightly silly, energetic and cliched." Pizzichini concludes, "Esquivel dresses her ancient story in a collision of literary styles that confirm her wit and ingenuity. She sets herself a mission to explore the redemptive powers of love and art and displays boundless enthusiasm for parody."

BIOGRAPHICAL/CRITICAL SOURCES:

PERIODICALS

Entertainment Weekly, April 23, 1993, p. 52; December 31, 1993, p. 203-204; January 7, 1994, p. 47.
Hispanic Times, December/January 1996, p. 42.
Kirkus Reviews, July 1, 1996, p. 917.
Library Journal, January, 1996, p. 81; July, 1996, p. 156.
Los Angeles Times Book Review, November 1, 1992, p. 6.
Ms., November/December, 1993, p. 75.
Nation, June 14, 1993, p. 846.
New Republic, March 1, 1993, pp. 24-25.
New Yorker, June 27, 1994, p. 80.
New York Times, March 31, 1993, pp. C1, C8.
New York Times Book Review, November 17, 1996, p. 11.
Publishers Weekly, May 17, 1993, p. 17; August 15, 1994, p. 13; October 3, 1994, p. 40; February 5, 1996, p. 24.
Time, April 5, 1993, pp. 62-63.
Times Literary Supplement, October 18, 1996, p. 23.
Tribune Books (Chicago), October 18, 1992, p. 8.
Washington Post, September 25, 1992, p. B2.
World Press Review, February, 1996, p. 43.

* * *

ESSLIN, Martin (Julius) 1918-

PERSONAL: Born June 8, 1918, in Budapest, Hungary; came to Great Britain, 1939; naturalized British citizen, 1947; son of Paul (a journalist) and Charlotte (Schiffer) Pereszlenyi; married Renate Gerstenberg, 1947; children: Monica. *Education:* Attended University of Vienna, 1936-38; received degree from Reinhardt Seminar of Dramatic Art, Vienna, 1938. *Avocation:* Reading, book-collecting.

ADDRESSES: Home—64 Loudoun Rd., London NW8, England; and Ballader's Plat, Winchelsea, Sussex, England. *Office*—Department of Drama, Stanford University, Stanford, Calif. 94305. *Agent*—Curtis Brown Ltd., 162-168 Regent St., London W1R 5TB, England.

CAREER: British Broadcasting Corp. (BBC), London, England, director and writer on theater, 1940-77, producer and scriptwriter for European services, 1941-55, became assistant head of European productions, 1955, became assistant head of drama (sound), 1961, head of drama (radio), 1963-77; Stanford University, Stanford, California, professor of drama, 1977–. Visiting professor of theater at Florida State University, 1969-76. Royal Shakespeare Company, London, literary advisor, 1963-72. Magic Theatre, San Francisco, dramaturg, 1977.

MEMBER: Arts Council of Great Britain (member of drama panel), Garrick Club.

AWARDS, HONORS: Title of Professor by president of Austria, 1967; member of the Order of the British Empire, 1972; D.Litt., Kenyon College, 1978.

WRITINGS:

Brecht: A Choice of Evils; A Critical Study of the Man, His Work, and His Opinions, Eyre & Spottiswoode, 1959, published as *Brecht: The Man and His Work,* Doubleday, 1960, 4th revised edition, Methuen, 1984.
The Theatre of the Absurd, Doubleday, 1961, third revised edition, Penguin, 1983.
(Editor with others) *Sinn oder Unsinn? Das Groteske im Modernen Drama,* Basilius, 1962.
(Editor) *Samuel Beckett: A Collection of Critical Essays,* Prentice-Hall, 1965.
(Editor) *Absurd Drama,* Penguin (London), 1965.
Harold Pinter, Friedrich Verlag, 1967.
(Editor and author of introduction) *The Genius of the German Theater,* New American Library, 1968.
Bertolt Brecht, Columbia University Press, 1969.

Reflections: Essays on Modern Theatre, Doubleday, 1969 (published in England as *Brief Chronicles: Essays on Modern Theatre,* Maurice Temple Smith, 1970).

(Editor) *The New Theatre of Europe,* Volume IV, Dell, 1970.

The Peopled Wound: The Work of Harold Pinter, Doubleday, 1970, revised edition published as *Pinter: A Study of His Plays,* Methuen, 1973, 4th revised edition, 1982, 5th revised edition published as *Pinter, the Playwright,* 1992.

An Anatomy of Drama, T. Smith, 1976, Hill & Wang, 1977.

Artaud, J. Calder, 1976, Penguin, 1977.

(Editor and author of introduction) *The Encyclopedia of World Theater,* Scribner, 1977 (published in England as *The Illustrated Encyclopaedia of World Theatre,* Thames & Hudson, 1977).

Mediations: Essays on Brecht, Beckett, and the Media, Louisiana University Press, 1980.

The Age of Television, Stanford, 1981.

(Author of introduction) Jan Kott, *The Theater of Essence and Other Essays,* Northwestern University Press, 1984.

The Field of Drama, Methuen, 1987.

Antonin Artaud, Riverrun Press, 1993.

Contributor of reviews and essays on theatre to numerous periodicals. Advisory editor of *Drama Review*; drama editor of *Kenyon Review.*

SIDELIGHTS: Martin Esslin has been a prominent, and sometimes controversial, critic of contemporary theater. Besides volumes on individual playwrights such as Bertolt Brecht, Antonin Artaud, and Harold Pinter, he has written and edited numerous other books on theatre, most notably *The Theatre of the Absurd.*

The Theatre of the Absurd is considered a major study of the school of avant-garde dramatists who emerged in the late 1950s and early 1960s. Such playwrights as Samuel Beckett, Jean Genet, and Eugene Ionesco had bewildered many critics and audiences who found no recognizable plot, theme, characterization, or any other "typical" elements of drama in their work. Instead, in Esslin's words, viewers saw an expression "of the senselessness of the human condition and the inadequacy of the rational approach by the open abandonment of rational devices and discursive thought." To better comprehend these works, then, a new set of judgments had to be used, those which Esslin sought to define and clarify in his book.

One of Esslin's major theses expressed in *The Theatre of the Absurd* held that these plays, often dismissed as "nonsense or mystification, *have* something to say and *can* be understood." Essentially, he said, the theatre of the absurd reflected the absurdity of human life not by argument or theory, but by actually presenting the experience; it strove for "an integration between the subject matter and the form." Esslin cited changing critical response to Beckett's *Waiting for Godot* as evidence that audiences have come to look past their preconceived notions of what a play should be: While the 1955 premier of *Godot* met with "a wide measure of incomprehension," its 1964 London revival was criticized for having "one great fault: its meaning and symbolism were a little too obvious."

Another playwright whose avant-garde style warrants Esslin's attention is Pinter. With such plays as *The Caretaker* and *The Birthday Party,* Pinter creates a stage where domination and self-doubt boil together into a hazy neo-reality. In Esslin's study *The Peopled Wound: The Work of Harold Pinter,* the author "has moved in on Pinter as remorselessly as one Pinter character moves in on another Pinter character," according to *New York Review of Books* critic Nigel Dennis. And while Dennis doesn't claim to agree with Esslin's assessments of Pinter's work, the reviewer notes that among Pinter scholars, Esslin is "the kindest and gentlest." *New York Times Book Review* writer Richard Gilman expresses similar mixed feelings, remarking that Esslin is a critic "whose usefulness lies less in original thinking or insightfulness than in lucid exposition, the kind of critic who possesses thoroughness in place of brilliance, breadth instead of depth." While citing Esslin's tendency to "encircle the [Pinter] plays with [descriptive] terminology and his narrow experience of them as sensuous, independent, unprogrammatic works," Gilman also finds that "at his best . . . Esslin is able to offer some helpful illustrations of how Pinter's dialogue achieves its effects and some minor illumination of the way he departs from traditional dramaturgy." And in a *Times Literary Supplement* critic's opinion, *The Peopled Wound* (published in a revised edition as *Pinter: A Study of His Plays*) "holds its place as the most straightforwardly useful account of Pinter's work to date."

With such works as *Brief Chronicles, Mediations: Essays on Brecht, Beckett, and the Media,* and *The Field of Drama,* Esslin draws the usual mixed critical reaction. All three books contain the author's thoughts on the direction of modern drama in its many manifestations. "In *Brief Chronicles* the best pieces are those in which [Esslin] focuses on a play, a playwright or a performance," says another *Times Literary Supplement* critic. "He provides, for example, a fine structural analysis of Ibsen's *Hedda Gabler.* Another excellent piece deals with three plays by Edward Bond: The remarks on *Early Morning* are a first-rate exposition of that mordant piece." And while London *Times* writer Peter Ackroyd acknowledges that some of Esslin's views are controversial, he says of *The Field of Drama*: "It is not necessary to agree with this book in order to be impressed by it. It is engagingly written, elegantly argued, and filled with those genuine perceptions which spring from what might be described as cross-cultural magnanimity."

BIOGRAPHICAL/CRITICAL SOURCES:

PERIODICALS

Books and Bookmen, January, 1977, March, 1978.
Drama Review, winter, 1970; spring, 1974.
Economist, October 23, 1976.
Journal of Modern Literature, spring, 1993, p. 281.
New Theatre Quarterly, November, 1994, p. 377; November, 1995, p. 381.
New York Review of Books, December 17, 1970; June 3, 1971.
New York Times, December 14, 1984.
New York Times Book Review, January 23, 1966; September 13, 1970; July 17, 1977.
Review of Contemporary Fiction, fall, 1997, pp. 79-101.
Times (London), July 2, 1987.
Times Literary Supplement, July 23, 1970; July 6, 1973; December 17, 1976; April 10, 1981.
World Literature Today, summer, 1978; winter, 1982.

*   *   *

ESTERBROOK, Tom
See HUBBARD, L(afayette) Ron(ald)

ESTLEMAN, Loren D. 1952-

PERSONAL: Born September 15, 1952, in Ann Arbor, MI; son of Leauvett Charles (a truck driver) and Louise (a postal clerk; maiden name, Milankovich) Estleman; married Carole Ann Ashley (a marketing and public relations specialist), September 5, 1987. *Education:* Eastern Michigan University, B.A., 1974.

ADDRESSES: Home—Whitmore Lake, MI. *Agent*—c/o Morgan and Associates, P.O. Box 2976, Ann Arbor, MI 48106.

CAREER: Writer. *Michigan Fed,* Ann Arbor, MI, cartoonist, 1967-70; *Ypsilanti Press,* Ypsilanti, MI, reporter, 1973; *Community Foto-News,* Pinckney, MI, editor in chief, 1975-76; *Ann Arbor News,* Ann Arbor, special writer, 1976-77; *Dexter Leader,* Dexter, MI, staff writer, 1977-80. Has been an instructor for Friends of the Dexter Library, and a guest lecturer at colleges.

MEMBER: Mystery Writers of America, Author's Guild, Western Writers of America (vice president and president-elect, 1998), Private Eye Writers of America, Napoleonic Association of America.

AWARDS, HONORS: American Book Award nomination, 1980, for *The High Rocks; New York Times Book Review* notable book citations, 1980, for *Motor City Blue,* and 1982, for *The Midnight Man;* Golden Spur Award for best western historical novel, Western Writers of America, 1982, for *Aces & Eights;* Shamus Award nomination for best private eye novel, Private Eye Writers of America, 1984, for *The Glass Highway;* Pulitzer Prize in letters nomination, 1984, for *This Old Bill;* Shamus Awards, 1985, for novel *Sugartown,* and for short story "Eight Mile and Dequindre"; Golden Spur Award for best western short story, 1986, for "The Bandit"; Michigan Arts Foundation Award for Literature, 1986; Michigan Library Association Author of the Year Award, 1997.

WRITINGS:

The Oklahoma Punk (crime novel), Major Books (Canoga Park, CA), 1976.

Sherlock Holmes vs. Dracula; or, The Adventure of the Sanguinary Count (mystery-horror novel), Doubleday, 1978.

Dr. Jekyll and Mr. Holmes (mystery-horror novel), Doubleday, 1979.

The Wister Trace: Classic Novels of the American Frontier (criticism), Jameson Books, 1987.

Red Highway (novel), PaperJacks, 1988.

Peeper (mystery novel), Bantam, 1989.

The Best Western Stories of Loren D. Estleman, edited by Bill Pronzini and Martin H. Greenberg, Ohio University Press, 1989.

Sweet Women Lie, Thorndike Press, 1990.

Whiskey River, Bantam Books, Inc., 1990.

Motown, Bantam Books, Inc., 1992.

Sudden Country, Bantam Books, Inc., 1992.

Crooked Way, Eclipse Books, 1993.

King of the Corner, Bantam Books, Inc., 1993.

City of Widows, Tor Books, 1994.

The Judge, Forge, 1994.

Edsel, Mysterious Press, 1995.

Stress, Mysterious Press, 1996.

"AMOS WALKER" MYSTERY SERIES

Motor City Blue, Houghton, 1980.

Angel Eyes, Houghton, 1981.

The Midnight Man, Houghton, 1982.

The Glass Highway, Houghton, 1983.

Sugartown, Houghton, 1984.

Every Brilliant Eye, Houghton, 1986.

Lady Yesterday, Houghton, 1987.

Downriver, Houghton, 1988.

General Murders (short story collection), Houghton, 1988.

Silent Thunder, Houghton, 1989.

Never Street, Mysterious Press, 1997.

The Witchfinder, Mysterious Press, 1998.

"PETER MACKLIN" MYSTERY SERIES

Kill Zone, Mysterious Press, 1984.

Roses Are Dead, Mysterious Press, 1985.

Any Man's Death, Mysterious Press, 1986.

WESTERN NOVELS

The Hider, Doubleday, 1978.

Aces & Eights (first book in historical western trilogy), Doubleday, 1981.

The Wolfer, Pocket Books, 1981.

Mister St. John, Doubleday, 1983.

This Old Bill (second book in historical western trilogy), Doubleday, 1984.

Gun Man, Doubleday, 1985.

Bloody Season, Bantam, 1988.

Western Story, Doubleday, 1989.

Billy Gashade, Forge (New York City), 1997.

Journey of the Dead, Forge, 1998.

"PAGE MURDOCK" WESTERN SERIES

The High Rocks, Doubleday, 1979.

Stamping Ground, Doubleday, 1980.

Murdock's Law, Doubleday, 1982.

The Stranglers, Doubleday, 1984.

OTHER

(Contributor) Robert J. Randisi, editor, *The Eyes Have It: The First Private Eye Writers of America Anthology,* Mysterious Press, 1984.

(Contributor) Edward D. Hoch, editor, *The Year's Best Mystery and Suspense Stories, 1986,* Walker & Co., 1986.

(Editor, with Martin H. Greenberg) *P. I. Files,* Ivy Books, 1990.

Contributor to periodicals, including *Alfred Hitchcock's Mystery Magazine, Baker Street Journal, Fiction Writers Magazine, A Matter of Crime, Mystery, New Black Mask, Pulpsmith, Roundup, Saint Magazine, TV Guide, Writer,* and *Writer's Digest.*

MEDIA ADAPTATIONS: The Amos Walker mysteries *Motor City Blue, Angel Eyes, The Midnight Man, Sugartown, The Glass Highway,* and *Every Brilliant Eye* were recorded on audio cassettes in unabridged readings by David Regal for Brilliance Corp. (Grand Haven, MI) in 1988. *Sherlock Holmes vs. Dracula* was broadcast by the British Broadcasting Corporation. One of Estleman's western novels has been optioned by a California film company.

SIDELIGHTS: Loren D. Estleman, the prolific author of what James Kindall describes in *Detroit* as "hard-bitten mysteries, a herd of reality-edged westerns and an occasional fantasy or two," is perhaps best known for his series of hard-boiled mysteries that unravel in an authentically evoked Detroit. "A country boy who has always lived outside of Detroit, he writes with convincing realism about inner city environments," states Kindall, adding that "probably no other area pensmith can lay as convincing a claim to the title of Detroit's private eye writer as Estleman." Had it not been for the success of fellow Detroiter and mystery writer

Elmore Leonard, pronounces William A. Henry in *Time,* "Estleman would doubtless be known as the poet of Motor City."

Estleman has crafted an increasingly popular series of mysteries around the character of Amos Walker, a witty and rugged Detroit private investigator who recalls Chandler's Philip Marlowe and Hammett's Sam Spade. Considered "one of the best the hard-boiled field has to offer" by Kathleen Maio in *Wilson Library Bulletin,* "Walker is the very model of a Hammett-Chandler descendant," observes the *New York Times Book Review*'s Newgate Callendar. "He is a big man, very macho, who talks tough and is tough. He hates hypocrisy, phonies and crooks. He pretends to cynicism but is a teddy bear underneath it all. He is lonely, though women swarm all over him." Conceding to Ross that the character represents his "alter ego," Estleman once refused a six-figure offer from a major film company for exclusive rights to Walker, explaining to Kindall: "Twenty years from now, the money would be spent and I'd be watching the umpteenth movie with Chevy Chase or Kurt Russell playing Amos with the setting in Vegas or L.A. and blow my brains out."

Amos Walker "deals with sleaze from top to bottom—Motor City dregs, cop killers and drug dealers," remarks Andrew Postman in *Publishers Weekly,* and reviewers admire the storytelling skills of his creator. Walker made his debut searching the pornographic underworld of Detroit for the female ward of an aging ex-gangster in *Motor City Blue,* a novel that Kristiana Gregory appraises in the *Los Angeles Times Book Review* as "a dark gem of a mystery." About *Angel Eyes,* in which a dancer who anticipates her own disappearance hires Walker to search for her, the *New Republic* 's Robin W. Winks believes that "Estleman handles the English language with real imagination . . . so that one keeps reading for the sheer joy of seeing the phrases fall into place." In *Midnight Man,* which Callendar describes as "tough, side-of-the-mouth stuff, well written, positively guaranteed to keep you awake," Walker encounters a contemporary bounty hunter in his pursuit of three cop killers; and writing about *The Glass Highway,* in which Walker is hired to locate the missing son of a television anchor and must contend with a rampaging professional killer, Callendar believes that Estleman "remains among the top echelon of American private-eye specialists."

Amos Walker disappeared for most of the 1990s as Estleman worked on other projects, then made a comeback in *Never Street* after a seven-year hiatus. *Never Street* spins an intriguing and self-reflexive tale by setting up a mystery based on one character's obsession with the classic film noir *Pitfall,* which leaves Walker "wandering the '90s in search of 1952," in the words of a writer for *Booklist.* Estleman refers to plot devices and conventions of the film noir genre and scenes from the actual movie as the mystery unwinds, "producing a novel that is part parody, part tribute," according to *Booklist. Mystery Editor* praised the novel as a "pure noir gem," and the *New York Times Book Review*'s Marilyn Stasio applauded Walker's return, saying that he had come back "just in time to slap some sense into a genre that's getting dumber and dumber by the minute."

General Murders contains a collection of ten previously published short stories and novelettes featuring Walker. "Dating from 1982 to 1987, these samplings are good indicators of the pleasures in Estleman's longer works," remarks a reviewer for *Publishers Weekly,* while a *Booklist* contributor says, "Like the best short story writers, Estleman creates characters with a phrase and sets scenes with a sentence." But *New York Times Book Review* contributor Edna Stumpf concludes, "In general, however, the

short story form reveals the intense stylization of Loren Estleman's fiction in an unkind way."

In another series of mysteries, Estleman slants the perspective to that of a criminal, Peter Macklin, who also free-lances out of Detroit. "Macklin is the result of my wanting to do an in-depth study of a professional killer," Estleman tells Bob McKelvey in the *Detroit Free Press.* "It presents a challenge to keep a character sympathetic who never has anything we would call morals." Kindall suggests that "although a killer, he always seems to end up facing opponents even lower on the evolutionary scale, which shades him into the quasi-hero side." However, in a review of *Kill Zone,* the first novel in the Macklin series, Callendar feels that "not even Mr. Estleman's considerable skill can hide the falsity of his thesis" that even hired killers can be admirable characters. The plot of the novel concerns the seizure of a Detroit riverboat by terrorists who hold hundreds of passengers hostage, attracting other professional killers from organized crime and a governmental agency as well—a plot that a *Publishers Weekly* contributor finds "confusing and glutted with a plethora of minor characters who detract from the story's credibility." And although Peter L. Robertson detects an implausibility of plot in the second of the series' novels, *Roses Are Dead,* in which Macklin tries to determine who and why someone has contracted to kill him, he says in *Booklist* that the novel is "a guaranteed page-turner that features an intoxicating rush of brutal events and a fascinating anti-hero in Macklin." Describing the action of *Any Man's Death,* in which Macklin is hired to guard the life of a television evangelist and is caught in the struggle between rival mob families for control of a proposed casino gambling industry in Detroit, Wes Lukowsky suggests in *Booklist* that Estleman "has created a surprisingly credible and evolving protagonist." And as a *Time* contributor remarks: "For urban edge and macho color . . . nobody tops Loren D. Estleman."

The Hider, a novel about the last buffalo hunt in America, was Estleman's first western novel and was purchased immediately—a rarity in the genre. He has since written several other successful western novels plus a critical analysis of western fiction itself, *The Wister Trace: Classic Novels of the American Frontier;* and several of his books about the American West have earned critical distinction. *The High Rocks,* for instance, which is set in the mountains of Montana and relates the story of a man's battle with the Indians who murdered his parents, was nominated for an American Book Award. And the first two books of his proposed historical western trilogy have also earned honors: *Aces & Eights,* about the murder of Wild Bill Hickok, was awarded the Golden Spur; and *This Old Bill,* a fable based on the life of William Frederick "Buffalo Bill" Cody, was nominated for a Pulitzer Prize.

In the *Los Angeles Times Book Review,* David Dary discusses Estleman's *Bloody Season,* an extensively researched historical novel about the gunfight at the O.K. Corral: "The author's search for objectivity and truth, combined with his skill as a fine writer, have created a new vision of what happened in Tombstone . . . ,and he avoids the hackneyed style that clutters the pages of too many Westerns." Dary concludes that although it is a fictional account, the novel "probably comes closer to the truth" than anything else published on the subject. In *Twentieth-Century Western Writers,* Bill Crider observes: "All of Estleman's books appear solidly researched, and each ends in a way which ties all the story threads together in an effective pseudo-historical manner, giving each an air of reality and credibility."

Estleman again displayed his ability to balance parody and tribute in the 1997 western *Billy Gashade.* The novel tells the story of a young man from a wealthy family who flees his New York home after the 1863 draft riots and lights out for the territories, encountering on his journey such figures as Jesse James, Calamity Jane, Billy the Kid, and Crazy Horse. The narrative, told from the vantage point of the 88-year-old protagonist living in depression-era Hollywood, tells of Billy's wanderings as an itinerant piano player. *Publishers Weekly* called the novel "a song, lyrical and alive with biting wit, drama, and grace," praising Estleman's ability to take "potshots at our conventional understanding of western heroes and their legends," while a critic for *Booklist* was impressed that the novel "somehow manages to avoid collapsing under the weight of its epic scope." A writer for *Kirkus Reviews* assessed *Billy Gashade* as "a fine, picaresque tale that brings to vivid, mock-heroic life many of American history's western icons."

Estleman followed the upbeat *Billy Gashade* with a western of a much darker tone. *Journey of the Dead* picks up the thread of another figure whose life was touched by the legendary Billy the Kid—his killer, Sheriff Pat Garrett. Garrett's life, described in *Kirkus Reviews* as "sunbaked torture," was irreparably shaken by his intervention in history. A writer for *Publishers Weekly* described Garrett as "a convincingly tragic western figure who never quite understands the praise and blame attached to him for an act he can never live down." The novel tells not only of the violent events themselves, but also of Garrett's lingering night-mares, taking place on a bleak strip of landscape called La Journada del Muerto, from which the novel takes its title. *Journey of the Dead* "deserves blue ribbons and rosettes," according to the *Kirkus Reviews* critic, "As he shows once more, [Estleman] has no rival—not even Louis L'Amour—in invoking the American Southwest."

The city of Detroit is the central character of Estleman's crime series originally projected to be a trilogy but now encompassing additional volumes. The first installment, *Whiskey River,* covers the wars between rival gangs during the Prohibition years and is narrated by newspaper columnist Connie Minor. "Estleman's novel is a wizard piece of historical reconstruction, exciting as a gangster film but with a texturing of the characters and the times that rises well above genre," hails Charles Champlin in the *Los Angeles Times Book Review.* "Occasionally the details fail," remarks Walter Walker in the *New York Times Book Review.* "But [Estleman] does a marvelous job of setting clues, bringing seemingly loose ends together and surprising his readers, leaving them nearly incapable of stopping at the end of any given chapter." *Motown* is set in the turbulent year of 1966, when big cars, mobs, labor unions, racial tension, and power politicians dominated Detroit. Intertwining real and fictional events, Estle-man weaves plots concerning race wars between the black and Italian mobs, racketeering, and the safety records of the cars produced by the Big Three automakers. Connie Minor appears again, this time as an investigative reporter who finds an incriminating photograph of a labor leader. Thomas Morawetz declares in *Washington Post Book World* that "this wonderful cornucopia of a novel [has] quicksilver dialogue, incisive charac-terizations and canny interweaving of observations and events." The series' third novel is *King of the Corner,* which continues the themes of racial tension, dirty politics, and organized crime. The central character is "Doc" Miller, an overweight ex-Tigers baseball pitcher just out of prison for the death of a girl in his hotel room. Though he intends to do honest work, Miller soon finds himself involved with Detroit's black drug dealers and

political corruption. "Neither as colorful nor as vigorous as the earlier volumes-but, still, a pleasing if rather rambling mystery-thriller," comments a *Kirkus Reviews* contributor.

The additional novels in the series focus on other decades in the Motor City. In *Edsel,* Connie Minor has become a copywriter for the Ford Motor Company touting its new dream car of the 1950s, the Edsel. But because of his questioning of guys on the line, Minor comes under suspicion of spying on the rank-and-file and gets caught up in intrigue by the unions. "The conspiracy he ultimately discovers and untangles may be fairly anticlimactic, but Minor's observation and irreverence combine to keep the reader comfortably-even avidly-in the passenger's seat," declares Jean Hanff Korelitz in *Washington Post Book World.* Notes Marilyn Stasio in the *New York Times Book Review,* "Mr. Estleman is a pithy, punchy writer who can also deliver the action by spitting images out of the side of his mouth." *Stress* takes place in the 1970s as Detroit is recovering from the sixties riots. Charlie Battle is a young black cop confronting a racist department and violent black militant groups. Wes Lukowsky of *Booklist* calls the novel "a fine installment in an innovative series," while a *Publishers Weekly* reviewer states: "It's difficult to believe that Detroit will ever find a more eloquent poet than Estleman, who here . . . celebrates the gristle and sinew of the city as well as its aching heart."

BIOGRAPHICAL/CRITICAL SOURCES:

BOOKS

Contemporary Literary Criticism, Volume 48, Gale (Detroit), 1988, pp. 102-107.
Twentieth-Century Crime and Mystery Writers, 2nd edition, St. Martin's, 1985.
Twentieth-Century Western Writers, Gale, 1982.

PERIODICALS

Ann Arbor News, September 24, 1978.
Ann Arbor Observer, July, 1978.
Armchair Detective, summer, 1987, p. 311; spring, 1988, p. 218; summer, 1989, p. 329; fall, 1989, p. 434; summer, 1990, p. 250; spring, 1991, p. 250; winter, 1991, pp. 5-11, p. 28; summer, 1995, p. 285.
Booklist, November 15, 1984; September 1, 1985; October 15, 1986; September 15, 1988, p. 123; April 1, 1990, p. 1530; June 15, 1991, pp. 1932, 1948; March 15, 1994, p. 1327; March 15, 1996, p. 1242.
Chicago Tribune Book World, January 18, 1981; August 10, 1986.
Detroit, March 8, 1987.
Detroit Free Press, September 26, 1984.
Detroit News, May 18, 1979; August 21, 1983.
Kirkus Reviews, August 1, 1988, p. 1100; August 1, 1989, p. 1116; June 15, 1991, p. 746; April 1, 1992, p. 412; February 15, 1994, p. 160; February 1, 1995, p. 90; December 1, 1997.
Library Journal, September 1, 1989, p. 219; March 15, 1994, p. 100; March 1, 1996, p. 109.
Los Angeles Times Book Review, August 21, 1983, p. 7; January 19, 1986, p. 9; January 24, 1988, p. 12; September 9, 1990, p. 10; April 11, 1991, p. 5; August 11, 1991, p. 5; May 10, 1992, p. 17.
New Republic, November 25, 1981.
New York Times Book Review, November 11, 1979, p. 24; October 26, 1980, p. 20; November 1, 1981, p. 41; August 22, 1982, p. 26; August 14, 1983, p. 27; October 23, 1983, p. 38; December 2, 1984; December 23, 1984, p. 24; March 24, 1985, p. 29; November 24, 1985, p. 43; April 20, 1986, p. 32;

October 26, 1986, p. 47; March 6, 1988, p. 22; January 29, 1989, p. 34; April 9, 1989, p. 42; April 16, 1989, p. 31; October 15, 1989, p. 45, p. 56; May 20, 1990, p. 53; July 8, 1990, p. 28; October 14, 1990, p. 50; September 15, 1991, p. 34; February 9, 1992, p. 28; July 5, 1992, p. 17; May 8, 1994, p. 18; March 19, 1995, p. 29; February 22, 1998.

Observer (London), September 16, 1990, p. 55

Publishers Weekly, August 23, 1985; August 12, 1988, p. 442; January 22, 1988; May 3, 1991, p. 64; March 14, 1994, p. 64; January 29, 1996, p. 84.

Time, July 31, 1978, p. 83; December 22, 1986, p. 75; August 17, 1987, p. 63; February 1, 1988, p. 66; March 16, 1998, p. 80.

Times (London), November 20, 1986; November 29, 1986; December 31, 1987.

Times Literary Supplement, March 14, 1986; April 10, 1987; August 12, 1988, p. 893; September 8, 1989, p. 969; August 10, 1990, p. 855; September 13, 1991, p. 22.

Tribune Books (Chicago), February 24, 1987, p. 41; March 1, 1987, p. 8; January 31, 1988, p. 6; March 26, 1989, p. 6; November 5, 1989, p. 6; July 21, 1991, p. 3; May 3, 1992, p. 6.

Village Voice, February 24, 1987.

Washington Post Book World, September 21, 1980, p. 14; October 18, 1981, p. 6; May 17, 1987, p. 6; October 21, 1990, p. 10; August 18, 1991, p. 10; July 26, 1992, p. 1; August 16, 1992, p. 6; March 26, 1995, p. 2.

Wilson Library Bulletin, March, 1985, p. 487.

*   *   *

EWING, Frederick R.
    See STURGEON, Theodore (Hamilton)

F

FAIR, A. A.
See GARDNER, Erle Stanley

* * *

FAIRBAIRN, Roger
See CARR, John Dickson

* * *

FALUDI, Susan 1959(?)-

PERSONAL: Born c. 1959; daughter of Steven (a photographer) and Marilyn Lanning (an editor) Faludi. *Education:* Received B.A. (summa cum laude) from Harvard University.

ADDRESSES: Home—San Francisco, CA. *Agent*—Sandra Dijkstra, Sandra Dijkstra Literary Agency, 1155 Camino del Mar, Suite 515, Del Mar, CA 92014.

CAREER: Worked as a copy clerk for the *New York Times*; previously a reporter at *Miami Herald, Atlanta Constitution,* and *Mercury News*; affiliated with *Wall Street Journal,* beginning in 1990. Writer.

AWARDS, HONORS: Pulitzer Prize, Columbia University Graduate School of Journalism, 1991, for *Wall Street Journal* article on the leveraged buyout of Safeway supermarkets; National Book Critics Circle Award nomination, for *Backlash: The Undeclared War against American Women.*

WRITINGS:

Backlash: The Undeclared War against American Women, Crown, 1991.

Contributor of articles to periodicals, including *Mother Jones* and *Ms.*

SIDELIGHTS: Pulitzer Prize-winning journalist Susan Faludi gained nationwide attention with her first book, *Backlash: The Undeclared War against American Women,* in which the author investigates the attacks she observed on feminism and women's social, economic, and political progress in the 1980s. From advertisements for plastic surgery that term small breasts a "disease" to blue-collar men who harass their few female coworkers, and from right-wing preachers who denounce feminists as "witches" and "whores" to Hollywood films that depict single career women as desperate and crazed, Faludi finds a "backlash" against women virtually everywhere. The culmination of four years of research, *Backlash* drew praise and stirred controversy, with some critics maintaining that Faludi essentially claims society conspires to keep women oppressed.

Faludi was inspired to write *Backlash* by a 1986 marriage study that made national headlines. The study, which was conducted by researchers at Harvard and Yale universities and was unfinished at the time, stated that college-educated thirty-year-old women had only a twenty percent chance of ever getting married, and by thirty-five the odds dropped to five percent. After one of the researchers talked to a reporter about the unpublished study's findings, newspapers, popular magazines, and talk shows began running stories about the "marriage crunch" and "man shortage" in America. Women who postponed marriage in favor of educations and careers, the researchers reasoned, would have difficulty finding a husband.

Skeptical of the researchers' statistics, Faludi contacted the U.S. Census Bureau and other sources and learned that the methodology used to generate the marriage study was flawed and that the report's conclusions were suspect. She and other journalists wrote articles about this discovery, but the story was virtually ignored by the national media. "What was remarkable to me," Faludi told Kim Hubbard in *People,* "was that there was so little interest in finding out whether the study was true or false. The story simply fit the notion of where women were at that point in history."

Faludi points out in *Backlash* that many accepted ideas about women's status in the 1980s were also myths. In addition to the nationally trumpeted marriage study, the author discredits other media trend stories in her book, including accounts of professional women who were leaving the work force in large numbers to care for their homes and children, and reports of single and career women who suffered from depression, nervous breakdowns, and burnout in epidemic proportions. Upon examining these claims, Faludi discovered that they had no empirical basis. A number of studies comparing working and nonworking women, for example, concluded that women who work are actually mentally and physically healthier than their nonworking counterparts.

In what some critics consider *Backlash*'s most effective section, Faludi profiles a number of notable antifeminists, including

George Gilder, a speechwriter for former President Ronald Reagan and author of *Wealth and Poverty*; Allen Bloom, author of *The Closing of the American Mind,* a book that decries feminism's influence in higher education; Robert Bly, a founder of the men's movement and author of *Iron John*; and Sylvia Ann Hewlett, author of *A Lesser Life: The Myth of Women's Liberation in America.* She also interviews philosophy professor Michael Levin, who wrote *Feminism and Freedom,* a book that denounces feminism as an "antidemocratic, if not totalitarian, ideology," Faludi notes. Levin also claims that men are naturally better at math and that women prefer to take on household duties such as cooking. During her interview with Levin, Faludi learned that his wife, Margarita, was a professor of the philosophy of mathematics, that the Levins split child care and household tasks equally, and that cooking was the favorite activity of one of their young sons. Gayle Greene remarked in a *Nation* review that "Faludi must be a crackerjack interviewer, letting subjects babble on until they blurt out marvelously self-incriminating revelations, offering up the real reasons they hate and fear feminists—motives that are self-serving, silly, often sinister—which Faludi simply, deadpan, recounts."

Published in 1991, *Backlash* quickly became a best-seller. And though the response from critics was generally favorable, some reviewers found the book to be overlong or disagreed that a backlash against women's progress existed. *Business Week* writer Walecia Konrad commented that "even for committed feminists, Faludi's analysis is an eye-opener. But her relentless presentation of facts, figures, anecdotes, polls, and interviews is so dense that at times the book is hard to read." In *Commentary,* Charlotte Allen opined that *Backlash* has "none of the sustained theorizing or distanced observation that we might expect from a work of cultural criticism." But *Newsweek* contributor Laura Shapiro, who compared Faludi's book to Simone de Beauvoir's *The Second Sex* and Betty Friedan's *The Feminine Mystique,* described *Backlash* as "less visionary than theirs but just as gripping. She's not a theorist, she's simply a reporter."

Backlash's success soon made Faludi a sought-after guest on talk shows and the subject of a *Time* magazine cover story with noted feminist Gloria Steinem. But despite the attention she has received, she is reluctant to promote herself as feminism's new spokeswoman. "It's strange, since in my book I'm fairly critical of instant experts," Faludi told Hubbard. "I don't want to set myself up as a sort of seer." The author remarked to Carol Pogash in *Working Woman,* "To the extent that *Backlash* arms women with information and a good dose of cynicism, I think it will have served its purpose." She added, "It's also very large, so it can be thrown at misogynists."

BIOGRAPHICAL/CRITICAL SOURCES:

PERIODICALS

Atlantic, December, 1991, pp. 123-26.
Business Week, November 4, 1991, pp. 12, 17.
Commentary, February, 1992, pp. 62-64.
Nation, February 10, 1992, pp. 166-70.
New Republic, March 16, 1992, pp. 30-34.
New Statesman and Society, April 3, 1992, pp. 44-45.
Newsweek, October 21, 1991, pp. 41-44.
New Yorker, December 23, 1991, p. 108.
New York Times Book Review, October 27, 1991, pp. 1, 36.
People, November 11, 1991, pp. 138-40.
Time, March 9, 1992, pp. 56-57.
Times (London), March 26, 1992.

Working Woman, April, 1992, pp. 64-67, 104.

*   *   *

FARRELL, James T(homas) 1904-1979
(Jonathan Titulescu Fogarty, Esq.)

PERSONAL: Born February 27, 1904, in Chicago, IL; died of a heart attack, August 22, 1979, in New York, NY; son of James Francis and Mary (Daly) Farrell; married Dorothy Patricia Butler, 1931 (divorced); married Hortense Alden (divorced September, 1955); remarried Dorothy Butler Farrell, September, 1955 (separated, 1958); children: (with second wife) Kevin. *Education:* Attended night classes at De Paul University, one semester, 1924-25; attended University of Chicago, eight quarters, until 1929; attended New York University, one semester. *Avocation:* Baseball.

CAREER: Writer. Worked wrapping shoes in a chain store in Chicago, IL; as a clerk for the American Railway Express Co. in Chicago; a filling-station attendant; a cigar store clerk in New York City; an advertising salesman for Donnelly's *Red Book* in Queens, NY; in an undertaking parlor in Chicago; as a campus reporter for the *Chicago Herald Examiner*; and, for two weeks, as a scenario writer in Hollywood, CA. Served as chairman of the national board, Workers Defense League, New York City, and as a member of the Spanish Refugee Aid Committee.

MEMBER: National Institute of Arts and Letters, Authors League of America, American Civil Liberties Union, Overseas Press Club.

AWARDS, HONORS: Guggenheim fellowship for creative writing, 1936; Book-of-the-Month Club prize, 1937, for *Studs Lonigan: A Trilogy*; Messing Award, St. Louis University Library Association; honorary degrees from Miami University, Oxford University, Ohio State University, Columbia University, University of Chicago, and Glassboro State College.

WRITINGS:

Young Lonigan: A Boyhood in Chicago Streets (also see below), Vanguard, 1932, reprinted with new introduction, World Publishing, 1943, published as *Young Lonigan: The Studs Lonigan Story,* Avon, 1972.
Gas-House McGinty, Vanguard, 1933.
Calico Shoes, and Other Stories (also see below), Vanguard, 1934 (published in England as *Seventeen, and Other Stories,* Panther, 1959).
The Young Manhood of Studs Lonigan (also see below), Vanguard, 1934, reprinted with new introduction, World Publishing, 1944.
Judgment Day, Vanguard, 1935, reprinted with new introduction, World Publishing, 1945.
Studs Lonigan: A Trilogy (contains *Young Lonigan, The Young Manhood of Studs Lonigan,* and *Judgment Day*), Vanguard, 1935, reprinted with new introduction, Modern Library, 1938, published with an introduction and a new epilogue by the author, Vanguard, 1978.
Guillotine Party, and Other Stories (also see below), Vanguard, 1935.
A World I Never Made, Vanguard, 1936, reprinted with new introduction, World Publishing, 1947.
A Note on Literary Criticism, Vanguard, 1937, Columbia University Press (New York City), 1992.
Fellow Countrymen: Collected Stories, Vanguard, 1937.

Can All This Grandeur Perish?, and Other Stories (also see below), Vanguard, 1937.

The Short Stories of James T. Farrell (contains *Calico Shoes, and Other Stories, Guillotine Party, and Other Stories,* and *Can All This Grandeur Perish?, and Other Stories*), Vanguard, 1937.

No Star Is Lost, Vanguard, 1938, reprinted with new introduction, World Publishing, 1947.

Father and Son, Vanguard, 1940, reprinted with new introduction, World Publishing, 1947 (published in England as *Father and His Son,* Routledge & Kegan Paul, 1943).

Ellen Rogers, Vanguard, 1941.

Short Stories, Blue Ribbon Books, 1941.

$1000 a Week, and Other Stories (also see below), Vanguard, 1942.

My Days of Anger, Vanguard, 1943, reprinted with new introduction, World Publishing, 1947.

Fifteen Selected Stories, Avon, 1943.

To Whom It May Concern, and Other Stories, Vanguard, 1944 (also see below), published as *More Stories,* Sun Dial Press, 1946.

Twelve Great Stories, Avon, 1945.

The League of Frightened Philistines, and Other Papers, Vanguard, 1945.

When Boyhood Dreams Come True, Vanguard, 1946, published as *Further Short Stories,* Sun Dial Press, 1948.

More Fellow Countrymen, Routledge & Kegan Paul, 1946.

Bernard Clare, Vanguard, 1946, published as *Bernard Carr,* New American Library, 1952.

The Fate of Writing in America, New Directions, 1946.

The Life Adventurous, and Other Stories (also see below), Vanguard, 1947.

Literature and Morality, Vanguard, 1947.

A Hell of a Good Time, and Other Stories, Avon, 1947.

Yesterday's Love, and Eleven Other Stories, Avon, 1948.

The Road Between, Vanguard, 1949.

A Misunderstanding, House of Books, 1949.

An American Dream Girl, and Other Stories, Vanguard, 1950.

(Under pseudonym Jonathan Titulescu Fogarty, Esq.) *The Name Is Fogarty: Private Papers on Public Matters,* Vanguard, 1950.

This Man and This Woman, Vanguard, 1951.

(Contributor of "The Frontier and James Whitcomb Riley") *Poet of the People,* Indiana University Press, 1951.

Yet Other Waters, Vanguard, 1952.

The Face of Time, Vanguard, 1953.

Reflections at Fifty, and Other Essays, Vanguard, 1954.

French Girls Are Vicious, and Other Stories, Vanguard, 1955.

(Author of introduction) Theodore Dreiser, *Best Short Stories,* World Publishing, 1956.

An Omnibus of Short Stories (contains *$1000 a Week, and Other Stories, To Whom It May Concern, and Other Stories,* and *The Life Adventurous, and Other Stories*), Vanguard, 1956.

My Baseball Diary, A. S. Barnes, 1957.

A Dangerous Woman, and Other Stories, Vanguard, 1957.

Saturday Night, and Other Stories, Hamish Hamilton, 1958.

It Has Come to Pass, T. Herzl Press, 1958.

(Editor) H. L. Mencken, *Prejudices,* Vintage, 1958.

The Girl at the Sphinx (collection of short stories previously published by Vanguard), Hamish Hamilton, 1959.

(With others) *Dialogue on John Dewey,* edited by Corliss Lamont and Mary Redmer, Horizon, 1959.

Boarding House Blues, Paperback Library, 1961.

Side Street, and Other Stories, Paperback Library, 1961.

Sound of a City (short stories), Paperback Library, 1962.

The Silence of History (first of a projected 29-volume series), Doubleday, 1963.

Selected Essays, edited by Luna Wolf, McGraw, 1964.

What Time Collects, Doubleday, 1964.

The Collected Poems of James T. Farrell, Fleet, 1965.

Lonely for the Future, Doubleday, 1966.

When Time Was Born (prose poem), The Smith, 1966.

The Letters to Theodore Dreiser, The Smith, 1966.

New Year's Eve, 1929, The Smith, 1967.

A Brand New Life (novel), Doubleday, 1968.

Childhood Is Not Forever, Doubleday, 1969.

Judith (also see below), Duane Schneider Press, 1969.

Invisible Swords, Doubleday, 1971.

(Contributor) Ray Boxer and Harry Smith, editors, *The Smith-Fourteen,* The Smith, 1972.

Judith, and Other Stories, Doubleday, 1973.

The Dunne Family, Doubleday, 1976.

Literary Essays, 1954-1974, edited by Jack Alan Robbins, Kennikat Press, 1976.

Olive and Maryanne, Stonehill Publishing, 1977.

The Death of Nora Ryan, Doubleday, 1978.

Eight Short Stories and Sketches, Arts End, 1981.

On Irish Themes, University of Pennsylvania Press (Philadelphia), 1982.

Sam Holman: A Novel, Prometheus Books (Buffalo), 1983.

Hearing Out James T. Farrell: Selected Lectures, edited by Donald Phelps, The Smith (New York City), 1985.

(With Alain Dugrand) *Trotsky in Mexico,* Carcanet (Manchester), 1992.

Chicago Stories, selected and edited by Charles Fanning, University of Illinois Press, 1998.

Also author of *Tommy Gallagher's Crusade,* 1939, and editor of *A Dreiser Reader,* 1962. Contributor to magazines and to the Asian press.

MEDIA ADAPTATIONS: Studs Lonigan was filmed by United Artists in 1960.

SIDELIGHTS: In 1941, in *American Fiction, 1920-1940,* Joseph Warren Beach described James T. Farrell's writing as "perhaps the plainest, soberest, most straightforward of any living novelist," thus citing the basis of both the criticism and praise of Farrell's work. Farrell is most often recognized as a naturalistic writer, a school to which he adhered even during the 1930s when symbolism was increasingly popular. In *Reflections at Fifty,* Farrell wrote, "I have been called a naturalist and I have never denied it. However, my own conception of naturalism is not that which is usually attributed to me. By naturalism I mean that whatever happens in this world must ultimately be explainable in terms of events in this world, in terms of natural origins rather than of extranatural or supernatural origins." In *The Modern Novel in Britain and the United States,* Walter Allen wrote: "James T. Farrell, for all his indebtedness to Joyce, began as a naturalist and has remained one, unrepentant and defiant. He is the true heir of Dreiser. If he lacks Dreiser's tragic sense, he has an icily relentless passion that transforms his best work into a formidable indictment of society."

Beach wrote: "Farrell's type of naturalism is not a kind to appeal to the common run of readers. It has little to offer those who go to fiction for light entertainment, the glamour of the stage, or the gratification of their bent for wishful thinking. There is no reason why the squeamish or tender-minded should put themselves through the ordeal of trying to like his work. But there will always be a sufficient number of those whom life and thought have ripened and disciplined, who have a taste for truth, however unvarnished, provided it be honestly viewed, deeply pondered, and imaginatively rendered. For many such it may well turn out that James T. Farrell is the most significant of American novelists writing in 1940."

Farrell's ambition and direction as a writer, as well as his thematic material, sprang directly from his own youth in Chicago's South Side. Blanche Housman Gelfant noted in *The American City Novel* that, although the South Side was a slum, without variety, beauty, or surprise, "it provided Farrell with the substance of his art and his purpose as a city novelist. . . . Few city writers are as much the insider as he; and of the writers who have the same kind of inmost knowledge of manners, none has exploited his material to such powerful effect." Beach added, "His literary performance is determined by his pity and loathing for all that was mean, ugly, and spiritually poverty stricken in the mores and culture to which he was born. All his work is a representation, patient, sober, feeling, tireless, pitiless, of a way of living and a state of mind which he abhors, and from which he has taken flight as one flees from the City of Destruction."

During the 1930s, Farrell decided that certain literary critics were "perpetrating error and should be exposed before they could do further damage," noted Walter B. Rideout in *The Radical Novel in the United States, 1900-1954*. In 1936 Farrell published *A Note on Literary Criticism,* which, according to Rideout, was the "only extended discussion of Marxist aesthetics written from a Marxist standpoint in the United States during the thirties." Rideout contended that "the book constitutes a simultaneous attack and defense. The attack is directed against both 'revolutionary sentimentalism,' as represented by [Michael] Gold, and 'mechanical Marxism,' as represented by [Granville] Hicks. Since each of these two 'Leftist' tendencies in literary criticism has, in its extreme emphasis on the functional ('use-value') aspect of literature, ignored the aesthetic aspect, they have together, Farrell argued, kept Marxist criticism weak, because they substitute measurement for judgment. Hence, the critic's task, which is ultimately one of judgment, of evaluation, has been avoided." Rideout added later: "If Farrell's own statement of the critic's function is not strikingly original, if his dissection of the deficiencies of proletarian literature and criticism is, stylistically speaking, performed as much with a meat ax as with a scalpel, still the dissection itself was a thorough one." Farrell, in fact, aroused so much critical feeling with this work that *The New Masses* summarized his comments, and those of his supporters, with the arguments of his opponents under the heading "The Farrell Controversy."

Many critics believed that Farrell's Studs Lonigan trilogy was extremely successful as a work of "social consequence." Rideout contended that Farrell was the only writer who succeeded in chronicling "with great zest and passion the slow downward spiral of what [was then] considered both a dull and ideologically unimportant class. [Farrell succeeded] because setting down the minutely detailed degradation of Studs Lonigan represented for [Farrell] an angry act of catharsis." Rideout believed that the Studs Lonigan trilogy is one of the "most durable achievements of the radical novel of the thirties."

Farrell's later work, however, received less critical acclaim. James R. Frakes wrote of *Lonely for the Future*: "At this late date Farrell's style reads like vicious self-parody. In this world of human wrecks and pointless waste, James T. Farrell continues to chronicle his bleak Chicago inferno like a bleeding Virgil." Although the *Time* reviewer called Farrell "the most heroic figure in modern American letters," he wrote in his review of *When Time Was Born*: "Farrell calls his latest literary enterprise a prose poem. It is neither prose nor poem, but it appears to be an attempt to rewrite the first chapters of the Book of Genesis. The first sentence blithers and blathers and blunders along for five pages and 1,390 words. Reading it can only be likened to the experience of a man who, having lost an election bet, has undertaken to eat a pad of Brillo and is wondering which is the more unpalatable—the steel-wool structure or the pink soapy filling." But Beach summarized: "The best single test for a writer of fiction is the creation of characters that live in the imagination. Farrell has brought to life an unusual number of such living characters. Studs Lonigan, Jim O'Neill, Al O'Flaherty, Aunt Margaret, and grandmother O'Flaherty are among the memorable people in English fiction."

Farrell's last novel was *Sam Holman,* which tells the story of a young and brilliant encyclopedia editor in New York City in the 1930s. The work has been disparaged for concentrating mainly on Sam's sexual exploits and his ponderous philosophical disquisitions with his fellow overly earnest Communist Party members. John W. Aldridge wrote in *The New York Times Book Review*—summing up his feelings about *Sam Holman* and Farrell's career—that the novel "contains all the faults for which Farrell has always been famous, but here they are unredeemed by the presence of his former virtues. From the beginning Farrell was a peculiarly graceless and tone-deaf writer whose prose often appeared to have been laid on the page with a dump truck and shovel. Yet in the best of his early work one sensed a current of evangelical rage that gained special authenticity from being expressed with bludgeoning artlessness."

BIOGRAPHICAL/CRITICAL SOURCES:

BOOKS

Allen, Walter, *The Modern Novel in Britain and the United States,* Dutton, 1964.

Beach, Joseph Warren, *American Fiction, 1920-1940,* Macmillan, 1941.

Branch, Edgar Marquess, *A Bibliography of James T. Farrell's Writings, 1921-1957,* University of Pennsylvania Press, 1959.

Branch, Edgar Marquess, *James T. Farrell,* University of Minnesota Press, 1963.

Branch, Edgar Marquess, *Studs Lonigan's Neighborhood and the Making of James T. Farrell,* Arts End Books (Newton, MA), 1996.

Contemporary Literary Criticism, Gale (Detroit), Volume 1, 1973; Volume 4, 1975; Volume 8, 1978; Volume 11, 1979.

Conversations With Writers, Volume 2, Gale, 1978.

Dictionary of Literary Biography, Gale, Volume 4: *American Writers in Paris, 1920-1939,* 1980; Volume 9: *American Novelists, 1910-1945,* 1981.

Dictionary of Literary Biography Documentary Series, Volume 2, Gale, 1982.

Fried, Lewis, *Makers of the City,* University of Massachusetts Press (Amherst), 1990.

Gelfant, Blanche Housman, *The American City Novel,* University of Oklahoma Press, 1954.

Kazin, Alfred, *On Native Grounds,* Harcourt, 1942.

Rideout, Walter B., *The Radical Novel in the United States, 1900-1954,* Harvard University Press, 1956.

Walcutt, Charles Child, editor, *Seven Novelists in the American Naturalist Tradition,* University of Minnesota Press, 1974.

Wald, A. M., *James T. Farrell,* New York University Press, 1978.

PERIODICALS

American Book Collector, May, 1967.
American Book Review, December, 1993-January, 1994.
American Heritage, April, 1995, pp. 135, 150.
American Quarterly, winter, 1977.
Best Sellers, May 15, 1971.
Esquire, December, 1962.
Harper's, October, 1954.
Humanist, November-December, 1983.
Literary Times, April, 1965.
Nation, June 3, 1968; October 16, 1976.
National Observer, June 29, 1964.
New Yorker, March 18, 1974.
New York Herald Tribune Book Week, February 27, 1966.
New York Times, December 3, 1967.
New York Times Book Review, August 12, 1962; January 7, 1968; July 14, 1968; January 19, 1969; November 25, 1973; September 16, 1979; October 9, 1983.
People, March 12, 1979.
Prairie Schooner, spring, 1967.
Saturday Review, June 20, 1964.
Time, May 27, 1966.
Twentieth Century Literature, February, 1976.
Washington Post, September 11, 1968.

* * *

FARREN, Richard J.
See BETJEMAN, John

* * *

FARREN, Richard M.
See BETJEMAN, John

* * *

FAST, Howard (Melvin) 1914-
(E. V. Cunningham, Walter Ericson)

PERSONAL: Born November 11, 1914, in New York, NY; son of Barney (an ironworker, cable car gripper, tin factory worker, and dress factory cutter) and Ida (a homemaker; maiden name, Miller) Fast; married Bette Cohen (a painter and sculptor), June 6, 1937; children: Rachel, Jonathan. *Education:* Attended National Academy of Design. *Religion:* Jewish. *Avocation:* "My home, my family, the theater, the film, and the proper study of ancient history. And the follies of mankind."

ADDRESSES: Home—Greenwich, CT. *Agent*—Sterling Lord Agency, 65 Bleeker St., New York, NY 10012.

CAREER: Worked at several odd jobs and as a page in the New York Public Library prior to 1932; writer, 1932–. Foreign correspondent for *Esquire* and *Coronet,* 1945. Taught at Indiana University, 1947; member of World Peace Council, 1950-55; American Labor Party candidate for U.S. Congress, 23rd New York District, 1952; owner, Blue Heron Press, New York, 1952-57; film writer, 1958-67; chief news writer, Voice of America,

1982-88. Has given numerous lectures and made numerous appearances on radio and television programs. *Military service:* Affiliated with U.S. Office of War Information, 1942-44; correspondent with special Signal Corps unit and war correspondent in China-India-Burma theater, 1945.

MEMBER: Century Club, Fellowship for Reconciliation.

AWARDS, HONORS: Bread Loaf Literary Award, 1937; Schomburg Award for Race Relations, 1944, for *Freedom Road*; Newspaper Guild award, 1947; National Jewish Book Award, Jewish Book Council, 1949, for *My Glorious Brothers*; International Peace Prize from the Soviet Union, 1954; Screenwriters annual award, 1960; Secondary Education Board annual book award, 1962; American Library Association "notable book" citation, 1972, for *The Hessian*; Emmy Award for outstanding writing in a drama series, American Academy of Television Arts and Sciences, 1975, for episode of *Benjamin Franklin*; Literary Lions Award, New York Public Library, 1985; Prix de la Policia Award (France), for books under name E. V. Cunningham.

WRITINGS:

Two Valleys, Dial (New York City), 1933, Lovat Dickson, 1933.
Strange Yesterday, Dodd (New York City), 1934.
Place in the City, Harcourt (New York City), 1937.
Conceived in Liberty: A Novel of Valley Forge (also see below), Simon & Schuster (New York City), 1939, Michael Joseph (London), 1939.
The Last Frontier, Duell, Sloan & Pearce (New York City), 1941, Bodley Head (London), 1948.
The Romance of a People, Hebrew Publishing (New York City), 1941.
Lord Baden-Powell of the Boy Scouts, Messner (New York City), 1941.
Haym Salomon, Son of Liberty, Messner, 1941.
The Unvanquished (also see below), Duell, Sloan & Pearce, 1942, John Lane (London), 1947.
The Tall Hunter, Harper (New York City), 1942, Harper (London), 1942.
(With wife, Bette Fast) *The Picture-Book History of the Jews,* Hebrew Publishing, 1942.
Goethals and the Panama Canal, Messner, 1942.
Citizen Tom Paine (also see below), Duell, Sloan & Pearce, 1943, John Lane, 1945.
The Incredible Tito, Magazine House (New York City), 1944.
Freedom Road, Duell, Sloan & Pearce, 1944, new edition with foreword by W. E. B. DuBois, introduction by Eric Foner, M. E. Sharpe (Armonk, NY), 1995.
Patrick Henry and the Frigate's Keel and Other Stories of a Young Nation, Duell, Sloan & Pearce, 1945.
The American: A Middle Western Legend, Duell, Sloan & Pearce, 1946.
(With William Gropper) *Never Forget: The Story of the Warsaw Ghetto,* Book League of the Jewish Fraternal Order, 1946.
(Editor) Thomas Paine, *The Selected Works of Tom Paine,* Modern Library (New York City), 1946.
The Children, Duell, Sloan & Pearce, 1947.
(Editor) Theodore Dreiser, *Best Short Stories of Theodore Dreiser,* World Publishing, 1947.
Clarkton, Duell, Sloan & Pearce, 1947.
Tito and His People, Contemporary Publishers (Winnipeg, Canada), 1948.
My Glorious Brothers, Little, Brown (Boston), 1948, new edition, Hebrew Publications, 1977, Bodley Head, 1950.
Departure and Other Stories, Little, Brown, 1949.

Intellectuals in the Fight for Peace, Masses & Mainstream (New York City), 1949.

The Proud and the Free (also see below), Little, Brown, 1950.

Literature and Reality, International Publishers (New York City), 1950.

Spartacus (also see below), Blue Heron (New York City), 1951, Citadel (Secaucus, NJ), 1952, Bodley Head, 1952, reprinted with new introduction, North Castle Books (Armonk, NY), 1996.

Peekskill, U.S.A.: A Personal Experience, Civil Rights Congress (New York City), 1951.

Tony and the Wonderful Door, Blue Heron, 1952.

Spain and Peace, Joint Anti-Fascist Refugee Committee, 1952.

The Passion of Sacco and Vanzetti: A New England Legend, Blue Heron, 1953, Bodley Head, 1954.

Silas Timberman, Blue Heron, 1954, Bodley Head, 1954.

The Last Supper, and Other Stories, Blue Heron, 1955, Bodley Head, 1956.

The Story of Lola Gregg, Blue Heron, 1956, Bodley Head, 1957.

The Naked God: The Writer and the Communist Party (memoir), Praeger (New York City), 1957, Bodley Head, 1958.

Moses, Prince of Egypt, Crown (New York City), 1958, Methuen (London), 1960.

The Winston Affair, Crown, 1959, Methuen, 1960.

The Howard Fast Reader, Crown, 1960.

April Morning, Crown, 1961, Methuen, 1961.

The Edge of Tomorrow (stories), Bantam (New York City), 1961.

Power, Doubleday (New York City), 1962, Methuen, 1963.

Agrippa's Daughter, Doubleday, 1964, Methuen, 1965.

The Hill, Doubleday, 1964.

Torquemada, Doubleday, 1966, Methuen, 1967.

The Hunter and the Trap, Dial, 1967.

The Jews: Story of a People, Dial, 1968, Cassell (London), 1960.

The General Zapped an Angel, Morrow (New York City), 1970.

The Crossing (based on his play of the same title; also see below), Morrow, 1971, Eyre Methuen (London), 1972, New Jersey Historical Society, 1985.

The Hessian (based on his screenplay of the same title; also see below), Morrow, 1972, Hodder & Stoughton, 1975, reprinted with new foreword, North Castle Books (Armonk, NY), 1996.

A Touch of Infinity: Thirteen Stories of Fantasy and Science Fiction, Morrow, 1973.

Time & the Riddle: Thirty-One Zen Stories, Ward Richie Press, 1975.

The Immigrants, Houghton (Boston), 1977, Hodder & Stoughton (London), 1978.

The Art of Zen Meditation, Peace Press (Culver City, CA), 1977.

The Second Generation, Houghton, 1978, Hodder & Stoughton, 1979.

The Establishment, Houghton, 1979, Hodder & Stoughton, 1979.

The Legacy, Houghton, 1980.

The Magic Door (juvenile), Avon (New York City), 1980.

Max, Houghton, 1982.

The Outsider, Houghton, 1984.

The Immigrant's Daughter, Houghton, 1985.

The Dinner Party, Houghton, 1987.

The Call of Fife and Drum: Three Novels of the Revolution (contains *The Unvanquished, Conceived in Liberty,* and *The Proud and the Free*), Citadel, 1987.

The Pledge, Houghton, 1988.

The Confession of Joe Cullen, Houghton, 1989.

Being Red: A Memoir (memoir), Houghton, 1990.

The Trial of Abigail Goodman: A Novel, Crown, 1993.

War and Peace: Observations on Our Times, M. E. Sharpe, 1993.

Seven Days in June: A Novel of the American Revolution, Carol (Secaucus, NJ), 1994.

The Bridge Builder's Story, M. E. Sharpe, 1995.

An Independent Woman, Harcourt Brace and Co. (New York City), 1997.

Author of weekly column, *New York Observer,* 1989-92; also columnist for *Greenwich Time* and *Stamford Advocate.*

PLAYS

The Hammer, produced in New York, 1950.

Thirty Pieces of Silver (produced in Melbourne, 1951), Blue Heron, 1954.

George Washington and the Water Witch, Bodley Head (London), 1956.

The Crossing, produced in Dallas, TX, 1962.

The Hill (screenplay), Doubleday, 1964.

David and Paula, produced in New York City at American Jewish Theater, November 20, 1982.

Citizen Tom Paine: A Play in Two Acts (produced in Washington, DC, at the John F. Kennedy Center for the Performing Arts, 1987), Houghton, 1986.

The Novelist (produced in Mamaroneck, NY, 1991), published as *The Novelist: A Romantic Portrait of Jane Austen,* Samuel French (New York City), 1992.

Also author of *The Hessian,* 1971, and teleplay, *What's a Nice Girl Like You. . .!,* based on his novel *Shirley.* Also wrote television episode for series *Benjamin Franklin,* 1975.

UNDER PSEUDONYM E. V. CUNNINGHAM; NOVELS

Sylvia, Doubleday, 1960, published under name Howard Fast, Carol, 1992.

Phyllis, Doubleday, 1962.

Alice, Doubleday, 1963.

Shirley, Doubleday, 1963.

Lydia, Doubleday, 1964.

Penelope, Doubleday, 1965.

Helen, Doubleday, 1966.

Margie, Morrow, 1966.

Sally, Morrow, 1967, published under name Howard Fast, Chivers, 1994.

Samantha, Morrow, 1967.

Cynthia, Morrow, 1968.

The Assassin Who Gave Up His Gun, Morrow, 1969.

Millie, Morrow, 1973.

The Case of the One-Penny Orange, Holt (New York City), 1977.

The Case of the Russian Diplomat, Holt, 1978.

The Case of the Poisoned Eclairs, Holt, 1979.

The Case of the Sliding Pool, Delacorte (New York City), 1981.

The Case of the Kidnapped Angel, Delacorte, 1982.

The Case of the Angry Actress, Delacorte, 1984.

The Case of the Murdered Mackenzie, Delacorte, 1984.

The Wabash Factor, Doubleday, 1986.

UNDER PSEUDONYM WALTER ERICSON

Fallen Angel, Little, Brown, 1951.

MEDIA ADAPTATIONS: *Spartacus* was filmed in 1960 by Universal Pictures, directed by Stanley Kubrick (uncredited) and Anthony Mann, starring Kirk Douglas, Laurence Olivier, Tony Curtis, Jean Simmons, Charles Laughton, and Peter Ustinov; many of Fast's other works have been adapted to the screen, including *Man in the Middle,* based on his novel *The Winston Affair,* 1964, *Mirage,* based on a story he wrote under the pseudonym Walter Ericson, 1965, *Penelope,* based on his novel of the same title, 1966, *Jigsaw,* based on his novel *Fallen Angel,* 1968, and *Freedom Road,* based on his novel of the same title, 1980; *The Immigrants* was broadcast as a television miniseries in 1979; *April Morning* was adapted as a television program, 1988; *The Crossing* was recorded on cassette, narrated by Norman Dietz, Recorded Books, 1988; *The Immigrant's Daughter* was recorded on cassette, narrated by Sandra Burr, Brilliance Corporation, 1991.

SIDELIGHTS: Howard Fast has published novels, plays, screenplays, stories, historical fiction, and biographies in a career that dates from the early days of the Great Depression. Fast's works have been translated into some eighty-two languages and have sold millions of copies worldwide; some observers feel that he may be the most widely read writer of the twentieth century. *Los Angeles Times* contributor Elaine Kendall writes: "For half a century, Fast's novels, histories and biographies have appeared at frequent intervals, a moveable feast with a distinct political flavor." *Washington Post* correspondent Joseph McLellan finds Fast's work "easy to read and relatively nourishing," adding that the author "demands little of the reader, beyond a willingness to keep turning the pages, and he supplies enough activity and suspense to make this exercise worthwhile."

The grandson of Ukrainian immigrants and son of a British mother, Fast grew up in New York City. His family struggled to make ends meet, so Fast went to work as a teen and found time to indulge his passion—writing—in his spare moments. His first novel, *Two Valleys,* was published in 1933 when he was only eighteen. Thereafter Fast began writing full time, and within a decade he had earned a considerable reputation as a historical novelist with his realistic tales of American frontier life.

Fast found himself drawn to the downtrodden peoples in America's history—the Cheyenne Indians and their tragic attempt to regain their homeland (*The Last Frontier*), the starving soldiers at Valley Forge (*Conceived in Liberty: A Novel of Valley Forge*), and black Americans trying to survive the Reconstruction era in the South (*Freedom Road*). In *Publishers Weekly,* John F. Baker calls these works "books on which a whole generation of radicals was brought up." A *Christian Science Monitor* contributor likewise notes: "Human nature rather than history is Howard Fast's field. In presenting these harassed human beings without any heroics he makes us all the more respectful of the price paid for American liberty." *Freedom Road* in particular was praised by the nation's black leaders for its depiction of one race's struggle for liberation; the book became a bestseller and won the Schomberg Award for Race Relations in 1944.

During the Second World War, Fast worked as a correspondent for several periodicals and for the Office of War Information. After the conflict ended he found himself at odds with the Cold War mentality developing in the United States. At the time Fast was a member of the Communist Party and a contributor of time and money to a number of anti-fascist causes. His writing during the period addressed such issues as the abuse of power, the suppression of labor unions, and communism as the basis for a utopian future. Works such as *Clarkton, My Glorious Brothers,* and *The Proud and the Free* were widely translated behind the Iron Curtain and earned Fast the International Peace Prize in 1954.

Baker notes that Fast's political views "made him for a time in the 1950s a pariah of the publishing world." The author was jailed for three months on a contempt of Congress charge for refusing to testify about his political activities. Worse, he found himself blacklisted to such an extent that no publishing house would accept his manuscripts. Fast's persecution seemed ironic to some observers, because in the historical and biographical novels he had already published—like *Conceived in Liberty: A Novel of Valley Forge* and *The Unvanquished*—as well as in his work for the Office of War Information, Fast emphasized the importance of freedom and illuminated the heroic acts that had built American society. He made the relatively unknown or forgotten history of the United States accessible to millions of Americans in books like *The Last Frontier,* and as a correspondent for the radio program that would become the Voice of America, he was entrusted with the job of assuring millions of foreigners of the country's greatness and benevolence during World War II. Yet even after Fast learned of Stalin's atrocities, which convinced him that he had been betrayed by the Communist Party and caused him to break his ties with it, he did not regret the decision he had made in 1944. His experience as the target of political persecution evoked some of his best and most popular works. It also led Fast to establish his own publishing house, the Blue Heron Press.

Fast published *Spartacus* under the Blue Heron imprint in 1951. A fictional account of a slave revolt in ancient Rome, *Spartacus* became a bestseller after it was made into a feature film in 1960, starring Kirk Douglas, Sir Laurence Olivier, and Tony Curtis. By that time Fast had grown disenchanted with the Communist Party and had formally renounced his ties to it. In a discussion of Fast's fiction from 1944 through 1959, *Nation* correspondent Stanley Meisler contends that the "older writings must not be ignored. They document a unique political record, a depressing American waste. They describe a man who distorted his vision of America to fit a vision of communism, and then lost both."

Fast published five books chronicling the fictional Lavette family, beginning with *The Immigrants* in 1977. The saga ends with 1985's *The Immigrant's Daughter,* the story of Barbara Lavette, Dan Lavette's daughter, and her political aspirations. Denise Gess in the *New York Times Book Review* calls *The Immigrant's Daughter* "satisfying, old-fashioned story-telling" despite finding the novel occasionally "soap-operatic and uneven." Barbara Conaty, reviewing the novel in *Library Journal,* calls Fast a "smooth and assured writer." A reviewer for *Publishers Weekly* concurs, commenting that "[s]moothly written, fast-paced, alive with plots and subplots, the story reads easily."

The prolific Fast published another politically charged novel in 1989, with *The Confession of Joe Cullen.* Focussing on U.S. military involvement in Central America, *The Confession of Joe Cullen* is the story of a C.I.A. pilot who confesses to New York City police that, among other things, he murdered a priest in Honduras, and has been smuggling cocaine into the United States. Arguing that the conspiracy theory that implicates the federal government in drug trafficking and gun running has never been proved, Morton Kondracke in the *New York Times Book Review* has reservations about the "political propaganda" involved in *The Confession of Joe Cullen.* Robert H. Donahugh, however, highly recommends the novel in *Library Journal,* calling it "unexpected and welcome," and lauding both the "fast-moving" storyline and the philosophical probing into Catholicism. Denise Perry Donavin, in *Booklist,* concurs, finding the politics suiting the characters "without lessening the pace of a powerful tale."

Fast focuses on another controversial subject, the issue of abortion, in his 1993 novel *The Trial of Abigail Goodman.* As a *Publishers Weekly* critic notes, Fast views America's attitude toward abortion as "parochial" and is sympathetic to his protagonist, a college professor who has an abortion during the third trimester in a southern state with a retroactive law forbidding such acts. Critical reaction to the novel was mixed. Ray Olson in *Booklist* argues that "every anti-abortion character" is stereotyped, and that Fast "undermines . . . any pretensions to evenhandedness," calling the novel "an execrable work." The *Publishers Weekly* critic, on the other hand, finds *The Trial of Abigail Goodman* "electrifying" and calls Fast "a master of courtroom pyrotechnics." Many critics, including Susan Dooley in the *Washington Post,* view the novel as too polemical, failing to flesh out the characters and the story. Dooley argues that Fast "has not really written a novel; his book is a tract for a cause, and like other similar endeavors, it concentrates more on making converts than creating characters." A reviewer for *Armchair Detective* concurs, concluding that the novel would have been much stronger if "there were some real sincerity and some well-expressed arguments from the antagonists." A *Rapport* reviewer agrees, and comments: "Fast is more than capable of compelling character studies. There's a kernel of a powerful trial novel here, but this prestigious writer chooses not to flesh it out."

Fast returned to the topic of the American Revolution in his 1994 novel *Seven Days in June: A Novel of the American Revolution.* A *Publishers Weekly* critic summarizes: "Fictionalizing the experiences of British commanders, loyalists to the crown and a motley collection of American revolutionaries, Fast . . . fashions this dramatic look at a week of profound tension that will erupt [into] the battle of Bunker Hill." Some critics see *Seven Days in June* as inferior to Fast's *April Morning,* considered by some to be a minor masterpiece. Charles Michaud in *Library Journal* finds that *Seven Days* "is very readable pop history, but as a novel it is not as involving as . . . April Morning." A *Kirkus Reviews* critic faults the novel for repetitiveness and a disproportionate amount of focus on the sexual exploits of the British commanders, concluding that *Seven Days* "has a slipshod, slapdash feel, cluttered with hurried, lazy characterizations." The critic for *Publishers Weekly,* however, argues that the novel "ekes genuine suspense" and lauds Fast's "accomplished storytelling."

The Bridge Builder's Story tells of Scott Waring and his young bride, Martha, who honeymoon in Europe during the Nazi era and find themselves persecuted by Hitler's thuggish minions. After Martha is killed by the Gestapo, Scott makes his way to New York, where his ensuing sessions with a psychiatrist provide much of the narrative. While Albert Wilheim, writing in *Library Journal,* finds this novel to perhaps "test the limits of credibility," he praises Fast's "skillful narration." And Alice Joyce, in *Booklist,* opines that in *The Bridge Builder's Story* "Fast's remarkable prowess for storytelling" results in a "riveting tale, sure to satisfy readers."

Fast's time as a Communist in Cold War America provided him with an extraordinary story to share in his autobiographical works, including *Being Red: A Memoir.* Charles C. Nash of *Library Journal* calls *Being Red* "indispensable to the . . . literature on America's terrifying postwar Red Scare." Fast explains to Jean W. Ross in a *Contemporary Authors* interview: "There is no way to imagine war or to imagine jail or to imagine being a father or a mother. These things can only be understood if you live through them. Maybe that's a price that a writer should pay." Fast tells Ken Gross in *People Weekly* that he wrote the book with the inspiration of his son, Jonathan, who wanted to show it to his own children. Rhoda Koenig of *New York* magazine remarks that Fast's story is "a lively and gripping one," and that he "brings

alive the days of parochial-school children carrying signs that read KILL A COMMIE FOR CHRIST."

With a critical eye, Ronald Radosh asserts in *Commentary* that *Being Red* contains information and perspectives that contradict portions of Fast's 1957 memoir, *The Naked God: The Writer and the Communist Party.* In Radosh's opinion, *Being Red* was the author's attempt to "rehabilitate" the Communist Party he had admonished in *The Naked God.* "Now, nearly thirty-five years later, it almost sounds as though Fast wants to end his days winning back the admiration of those unreconstructed Communists," Radosh claims, even calling them "some of the noblest human beings I have ever known."

Fast has also published a number of detective novels under the pseudonym E. V. Cunningham, for which he received a Prix de la Policia Award. Many of these feature a fictional Japanese-American detective named Masao Masuto who works with the Beverly Hills Police Department. Fast tells *Publishers Weekly,* "Critics can't stand my mainline books, maybe because they sell so well, [but] they love Cunningham. Even the *New Yorker* has reviewed him, and they've never reviewed me." In the *New York Times Book Review,* Newgate Callendar calls detective Masuto "a well-conceived character whose further exploits should gain him a wide audience." Toronto *Globe and Mail* contributor Derrick Murdoch also finds Masuto "a welcome addition to the lighter side of crime fiction." "Functional and efficient, Fast's prose is a machine in which plot and ideals mesh, turn and clash," Kendall concludes. "The reader is constantly being instructed, but the manner is so disarming and the hectic activity so absorbing that the didacticism seldom intrudes upon the entertainment."

Fast's voice has interpreted America's past and present and helped shape its reputation at home and abroad. One of his own favorites among his novels, *April Morning,* has been standard reading about the American Revolution in public schools for generations, the film *Spartacus* has become a popular classic, and *Being Red* offers an account of American history that Americans may never want to forget, whether or not they agree with Fast's perspectives. As Victor Howes comments in *Christian Science Monitor,* if Howard Fast "is a chronicler of some of mankind's most glorious moments, he is also a register of some of our more senseless deeds."

BIOGRAPHICAL/CRITICAL SOURCES:

BOOKS

Contemporary Authors New Revision Series, Volume 33, Gale (Detroit), 1991.
MacDonald, Andrew, *Howard Fast: A Critical Companion,* Greenwood, 1996.

PERIODICALS

Armchair Detective, spring, 1994, p. 218.
Atlantic, September, 1944; June, 1970.
Best Sellers, February 1, 1971; September 1, 1973; January, 1979; November, 1979.
Booklist, June 15, 1989, p. 1739; July, 1993, p. 1916; October 1, 1995, p. 252.
Book Week, May 9, 1943.
Chicago Tribune, February 8, 1987, pp. 6-7; April 21, 1987; January 20, 1991, section 14, p. 7.
Christian Science Monitor, July 8, 1939; August 23, 1972, p. 11; November 7, 1977, p. 18; November 1, 1991, p. 12.
Commentary, March, 1991, pp. 62-64.
Detroit News, October 31, 1982.

Globe and Mail (Toronto), September 15, 1984; March 1, 1986.
Kirkus Reviews, June 15, 1994, p. 793.
Library Journal, November 15, 1978; September 15, 1985, p. 92; May 15, 1989, p. 88; October 1, 1990, p. 96; August, 1991, p. 162; July, 1994, p. 126; September 1, 1995, p. 206.
Los Angeles Times, November 11, 1982; November 11, 1985; November 21, 1988.
Los Angeles Times Book Review, December 9, 1990.
Nation, April 5, 1952; May 30, 1959.
New Republic, August 17, 1942, p. 203; August 14, 1944; November 4, 1978; May 27, 1992.
New Statesman, August 8, 1959.
New York, November 5, 1990, pp. 124-25.
New Yorker, July 1, 1939; May 1, 1943.
New York Herald Tribune Book Review, July 21, 1963.
New York Herald Tribune Books, July 27, 1941, p. 3.
New York Times, October 15, 1933; June 25, 1939; April 25, 1943; February 3, 1952; September 24, 1984; February 9, 1987, p. C16; March 10, 1987; April 21, 1991, pp. 20-21; October 23, 1991, p. C19; November 19, 1993, p. A2.
New York Times Book Review, October 13, 1933; April 25, 1943; February 3, 1952; March 4, 1962; July 14, 1963; February 6, 1966; October 2, 1977, p. 24; October 30, 1977; May 14, 1978; June 10, 1979; September 15, 1985, p. 24; March 29, 1987, p. 22; August 20, 1989, p. 23.
People Weekly, January 28, 1991, pp. 75-79.
Publishers Weekly, August 6, 1979; April 1, 1983; July 19, 1985, p. 48; November 28, 1986, p. 66; July 22, 1988, p. 41; June 30, 1989, p. 84; June 21, 1993, p. 83; July 11, 1994, p. 66.
Rapport, Number 1, 1994, p.38.
Saturday Review, March 8, 1952; January 22, 1966; September 17, 1977.
Saturday Review of Literature, July 1, 1939; July 26, 1941, p. 5; May 1, 1943; December 24, 1949.
Time, November 6, 1977.
Times Literary Supplement, November 11, 1939.
Tribune Books (Chicago), February 8, 1987, p. 6.
Washington Post, October 4, 1979; September 26, 1981; September 25, 1982; September 3, 1985; February 9, 1987; March 3, 1987; September 6, 1993, p. C2.
Washington Post Book World, October 23, 1988; November 25, 1990.

*   *   *

FAULKNER, William (Cuthbert) 1897-1962

PERSONAL: Surname originally Falkner, later changed to Faulkner; born September 25, 1897, in New Albany, MS; died July 6, 1962, in Byhalia, MS; son of Murry Cuthbert (a railroad worker, owner of a cottonseed oil and ice plant, livery stable operator, hardware store employee, secretary and business manager at University of Mississippi) and Maud (Butler) Falkner; married Lida Estelle Oldham Franklin, June 20, 1929; children: Alabama (died, 1931), Jill (Mrs. Paul Dilwyn Summers, Jr.); (step-children) Victoria, Malcolm Argyle. *Education:* Attended University of Mississippi, 1919-20. *Avocation:* Aviation, raising and training horses, hunting, sailing.

CAREER: First National Bank, Oxford, MS, clerk, 1916; Winchester Repeating Arms Co., New Haven, CT, ledger clerk, 1918; Lord & Taylor, New York, NY, bookstore clerk, 1921; University of Mississippi, Oxford, postmaster, 1921-24; worked as roof painter, carpenter, and paper hanger, New Orleans, LA, 1925;

deckhand on Genoa-bound freighter, 1925; full-time writer, 1925-62. Coal shoveler at Oxford Power Plant, 1929. Screenwriter for Metro-Goldwyn-Mayer, 1932-33, and for Warner Bros., 1942-45, 1951, 1953, and 1954. Chairman of Writer's Group People-to-People Program, 1956-57. Writer in residence, University of Virginia, 1957-62. *Military service:* British Royal Air Force, cadet pilot, 1918; became honorary second lieutenant.

MEMBER: American Academy of Arts and Letters, Sigma Alpha Epsilon.

AWARDS, HONORS: Elected to National Institute of Arts and Letters, 1939; O. Henry Memorial Short Story Awards, 1939, 1940, and 1949; elected to American Academy of Arts and Letters, 1948; Nobel Prize in literature, 1949; William Dean Howells Medal, American Academy of Arts and Letters, 1950; National Book Award, 1951, for *Collected Stories*; Legion of Honor of Republic of France, 1951; National Book Award and Pulitzer Prize, both 1955, both for *A Fable*; Silver Medal of the Greek Academy, 1957; gold medal for fiction, National Institute of Arts and Letters, 1962.

WRITINGS:

POETRY

Vision in Spring, privately printed, [Mississippi], 1921.
The Marble Faun (also see below), Four Seas (Boston), 1924.
This Earth, a Poem, drawings by Albert Heckman, Equinox, 1932.
A Green Bough (includes *The Marble Faun*), H. Smith and R. Haas, 1933, published as *The Marble Faun* [and] *A Green Bough,* Random House, 1965.
Mississippi Poems (also see below), limited edition with introduction by Joseph Blotner and afterword by Luis Daniel Brodsky, Yoknapatawpha Press (Oxford, Mississippi), 1979.
Helen, a Courtship [and] *Mississippi Poems,* introductory essays by Carvel Collins and Joseph Blotner, Tulane University and Yoknapatawpha Press, 1981.

NOVELS

Soldiers' Pay, Boni & Liveright, 1926, published with author's speech of acceptance of Nobel Prize, New American Library of World Literature, 1959.
Mosquitoes, Boni and Liveright, 1927.
Sartoris (also see below), Harcourt, 1929.
The Sound and the Fury, J. Cape & H. Smith, 1929, 2nd edition published as *The Sound and the Fury: An Authoritative Text, Backgrounds and Contexts, Criticism,* Norton (New York City), 1994.
As I Lay Dying, J. Cape & H. Smith, 1930, new and corrected edition, Random House, 1964.
Sanctuary, J. Cape & H. Smith, 1931, published as *Sanctuary: The Original Text,* edited with afterword and notes by Noel Polk, Random House, 1981, published as *Sanctuary: The Corrected Text,* Random House, 1993.
Light in August, H. Smith and R. Haas, 1932.
Pylon, H. Smith and R. Haas, 1935.
Absalom, Absalom!, Random House, 1936, casebook edition edited by Elisabeth Muhlenfeld published as *William Faulkner's Absalom, Absalom!,* Garland Publishing, 1984.
The Unvanquished, drawings by Edward Shenton, Random House, 1938.
The Wild Palms, Random House, 1939, published as *If I Forgot Thee Jerusalem: The Wild Palms* by Vintage (New York City), 1995.

The Hamlet (first book in the "Snopes Trilogy"; also see below),
Random House, 1940.

Intruder in the Dust, Random House, 1948.

Requiem for a Nun, Random House, 1951.

A Fable, Random House, 1954.

The Town (second book of the "Snopes Trilogy"; also see below),
Random House, 1957.

*The Long Hot Summer: A Dramatic Book from the Four-Book
Novel; The Hamlet,* New American Library, 1958.

The Mansion (third book in the "Snopes Trilogy"; also see below),
Random House, 1959.

The Reivers, a Reminiscence, Random House, 1962 (condensation
published as *Hell Creek Crossing,* illustrations by Noel
Sickles, Reader's Digest Association, 1963), New American
Library, 1969.

Snopes: A Trilogy, Volume 1: *The Hamlet,* Volume 2: *The Town,*
Volume 3: *The Mansion,* Random House, 1965.

Flags in the Dust (unabridged version of *Sartoris*), edited with an
introduction by Douglas Day, Random House, 1973, published as *Three Novels of the Snopes Family: The Hamlet,
The Town, The Mansion,* Random House, 1994.

Mayday, University of Notre Dame Press, 1976.

Father Abraham, Random House, 1984, published as *Father
Abraham, 1926,* Garland Publishing, 1987.

Elmer, edited by Dianne L. Cox, foreword by James B.
Meriwether, Seajay Society, 1984.

*The Collected William Faulkner: The Sound and the Fury, Light
in August, As I Lay Dying,* Random House, 1992.

Novels, 1942-1944 (includes *Go Down, Moses, Intruder in the
Dust, Requiem for a Nun,* and *A Fable*), Library of America,
1994.

SHORT FICTION

These Thirteen (also see below; contains "Victory," "Ad Astra,"
"All the Dead Pilots," "Crevasse," "Red Leaves," "A Rose
for Emily," "A Justice," "Hair," "That Evening Sun," "Dry
September," "Mistral," "Divorce in Naples," and "Carcas-
sonne"), J. Cape & H. Smith, 1931.

Doctor Martino, and Other Stories (also see below), H. Smith and
R. Haas, 1934.

Go Down, Moses, and Other Stories (also see below), Random
House, 1942 (also published in a limited edition), published
as *Go Down, Moses,* Vintage, 1973.

Three Famous Short Novels (contains "Spotted Horses," "Old
Man," and "The Bear"), Random House, 1942, published as
*Three Famous Short Novels: Spotted Horses; Old Man; The
Bear,* Vintage, 1978.

Knight's Gambit, Random House, 1949 (published in England as
Knight's Gambit: Six Stories, Chatto & Windus, 1960).

Collected Stories, Random House, 1950, published as *Collected
Stories of William Faulkner,* Vintage, 1977, published in
England as *Collected Short Stories,* Volume 1: *Uncle Willy
and Other Stories,* Volume 2: *These Thirteen,* Volume 3: *Dr.
Martino and Other Stories,* Chatto & Windus, 1958.

Mirrors of Chartres Streets (includes sketches), introduction by
William Van O'Connor, illustrations by Mary Demopoulous,
Faulkner Studies (Minneapolis), 1953.

Big Woods (contains "The Bear," The Old People, A Bear Hunt,
and Race at Morning), drawings by Edward Shenton,
Random House, 1955, published as *Big Woods: The Hunting
Stories,* Random House, 1994.

Jealousy, and Episode (originally published in New Orleans
Times-Picayune, 1925), limited edition, Faulkner Studies
(Minneapolis), 1955.

Uncle Willy, and Other Stories, Chatto & Windus, 1958.

Selected Short Stories, Modern Library, 1961.

*Bear, Man, and God: Seven Approaches to William Faulkner's
"The Bear"* (contains "The Bear," "Delta Autumn," and
selections from other works), edited by Francis Lee Utley,
Lynn Z. Bloom, and Arthur F. Kinney, Random House,
1964.

The Wishing Tree (children's fiction), with illustrations by Don
Bolognese, Random House, 1964.

The Tall Men and Other Stories, edited with notes by K. Sakai,
Apollonsha (Kyoto), 1965.

A Rose for Emily, edited by M. Thomas Inge, Merrill, 1970.

Fairchild's Story, limited edition, Warren Editions (London),
1976.

Uncollected Stories of William Faulkner, edited by Joseph
Blotner, Random House, 1979.

Helen: A Courtship and Mississippi Poems, Yoknapatawpha
Press, 1981.

SCREENPLAYS

Today We Live, Metro-Goldwyn-Mayer, 1933.

(With Joel Sayre) *The Road to Glory* (Twentieth Century-Fox,
1936), with afterword by George Garrett, Southern Illinois
University Press, 1981.

(With Nunnally Johnson) *Banjo on My Knee,* Twentieth Century-
Fox, 1936.

(With Sam Hellman, Lamar Trotti, and Gladys Lehman) *Slave
Ship,* Twentieth Century-Fox, 1937.

(With Sayre, Fred Guiol, and Ben Hecht) *Gunga Din,* 1939.

(With Jean Renoir) *The Southerner,* Universal, 1945.

(With Jules Furthman) *To Have and Have Not* (Warner Bros.,
1945), based on novel by Ernest Hemingway, edited with
introduction by Bruce F. Kawin, University of Wisconsin
Press, 1980.

(With Leigh Brackett and Jules Furthman) *The Big Sleep,* Warner
Bros., 1946.

(With Harry Kurnitz and Harold Jack Bloom) *Land of the
Pharoahs,* Warner Bros., 1955.

Faulkner's MGM Screenplays, University of Tennessee Press,
1982.

Country Lawyer and Other Stories for the Screen, University
Press of Mississippi, 1987.

Stallion Road: A Screenplay by William Faulkner, University
Press of Mississippi, 1990.

OTHER

Marionettes (one-act play) first produced at University of Mississippi, March 4, 1921; published as *The Marionettes,* limited
edition, Bibliographical Society, University of Virginia,
1975, published as *The Marionettes: A Play in One Act,*
Yoknapatawpha Press (Oxford, MS), 1978.

*Sherwood Anderson and Other Famous Creoles: A Gallery of
Contemporary New Orleans,* drawings by William Spratling,
Pelican Bookshop Press, 1926.

Idyll in the Desert, limited edition, Random House, 1931.

Miss Zilphia Gant, limited edition, Book Club of Texas, 1932.

Salmagundi (contains poem by Ernest M. Hemingway), limited
edition, Casanova Press (Milwaukee), 1932.

The Portable Faulkner, edited by Malcolm Cowley, Viking, 1946,
revised and expanded edition, 1967 (published in England as
The Essential Faulkner, Chatto & Windus, 1967).

Notes on a Horsethief, illustrations by Elizabeth Calvert, Levee
Press (Greenville, MS), 1950.

William Faulkner's Speech of Acceptance upon the Award of the Nobel Prize for Literature, Delivered in Stockholm on the Tenth of December, 1950, [New York], 1951.

(And author of foreword) *The Faulkner Reader: Selections from the Works of William Faulkner,* Random House, 1954.

Faulkner's County: Tales of Yoknapatawpha County, Chatto & Windus, 1955.

Faulkner on Truth and Freedom: Excerpts from Tape Recordings of Remarks Made by William Faulkner during His Recent Manila Visit, Philippine Writer's Association (Manila), 1956.

Faulkner at Nagano, edited by Robert A. Jelliffe, Kenkyusha (Tokyo), 1956.

New Orleans Sketches, introduction by Carvel Collins, Rutgers University Press, 1958.

Faulkner in the University: Class Conferences at the University of Virginia, 1957-1958 (interviews and conversations), edited by Frederick L. Gwynn and Joseph Blotner, University Press of Virginia, 1959.

William Faulkner: Early Prose and Poetry, compiled and introduced by Carvel Collins, Little, Brown, 1962.

Faulkner's University of Mississippi Pieces, compiled and introduced by Carvel Collins, Kenkyusha (Tokyo), 1962.

William Faulkner's Library: A Catalogue, compiled with an introduction by Joseph Blotner, University Press of Virginia, 1964.

Faulkner at West Point (interviews), edited by Joseph L. Fant III and Robert Ashley, Random House, 1964.

The Faulkner-Cowley File: Letters and Memories, 1944-1962, edited by Cowley, Viking, 1966.

Essays, Speeches and Public Letters, edited by James B. Merriwether, Random House, 1966.

The Best of Faulkner, Chosen by the Author, special edition, World Books Society, 1967.

Man, introduction by Bernard H. Porter, limited edition, [Rockland, ME], 1969.

Faulkner's University Pieces, compiled with an introduction by Carvel Collins, Folcroft Press, 1970.

Selected Letters of William Faulkner, edited by Joseph Blotner, limited edition, Franklin Library, 1976, Random House, 1977.

The Faulkner Reader, Random House, 1989.

Faulkner and Psychology, University Press of Mississippi, 1994.

Also author of *Faulkner on Love: A Letter to Marjorie Lyons,* limited edition edited by Richard Lyons, Merrykit Press (Fargo, ND), 1974; and *Faulkner's Ode to the Louver, Speech at Teatro Municipal, Caracas, 1961,* edited by James B. Merriwether, State College of Mississippi, 1979. Featured on sound recordings: *William Faulkner Reads Selections from His Novel: The Sound and the Fury—Dilsey,* Listening Library, 1976; *William Faulkner Reads a Selection from His Novel: Light in August,* Listening Library, 1979. Also contributor of poems, short stories, and articles to magazines and newspapers, including *New Orleans Times-Picayune, New Republic, Saturday Evening Post, Scribner's,* and *Sports Illustrated.*

MEDIA ADAPTATIONS: Requiem for a Nun was adapted by Ruth Ford for the stage (first produced on Broadway, January 30, 1959, Hart Stenographic Bureau, 1959), *A Rose for Emily,* read by Tammy Grimes, Caedmon, 1980, *Tomorrow,* by Horton Foote, Dramatists Play Service, 1963, Maddow, Ben, *Intruder in the Dust,* 1978. The following novels by Faulkner have been adapted for movies: "Intruder in the Dust," Metro-Goldwyn-Mayer, 1949; "Tarnished Angels" (based on *Pylon*), Universal, 1957; "The Long Hot Summer" (based on *The Hamlet*), Twentieth Century-Fox, 1958; "The Sound and the Fury," Twentieth Century-Fox, 1959; "Sanctuary" (also includes parts of *Requiem for a Nun*), Twentieth Century-Fox, 1961; "The Reivers," Cinema Center Films, 1969. *The Sound and the Fury* was adapted for television in 1955, and several of Faulkner's short stories have been adapted for television, including "An Error in Chemistry" and "The Brooch."

SIDELIGHTS: William Faulkner is considered one of America's greatest twentieth-century novelists. He spent most of his literary career in the South, which both inspired and informed his fiction. Many critics have expressed amazement that Faulkner, in many ways such an isolated and provincial artist, was able to produce such impressive, universal work. Perhaps John W. Aldridge put it best in *The Devil in the Fire* when he wrote, "Working alone down there in that seemingly impenetrable cultural wilderness of the sovereignly backward state of Mississippi, he managed to make a clearing for his mind and a garden for his art, one which he cultivated so lovingly and well that it has come in our day to feed the imagination of literate men throughout the civilized world."

Most of the biographical facts about Faulkner have been thoroughly documented. He was born into a genteel Southern family that had played a significant part in the history of Mississippi. His great-grandfather, William Clark Falkner, was a colorful figure who had built railroads, served in the Confederate Army, and written a popular novel, *The White Rose of Memphis.* An indifferent student, Faulkner dropped out of Oxford High School in 1915 and then worked for a time as a clerk in his grandfather's bank. During this period he wrote bad imitative verse and contributed drawings to the University of Mississippi's yearbook, *Ole Miss.* When the United States declared war on Germany, Faulkner tried to enlist but was rejected because of his small stature.

Instead of going to war, Faulkner went to New Haven, Connecticut, to visit his friend Phil Stone, then a student at Yale. Stone had recognized Faulkner's talent early on and had encouraged his literary bent. The two men read and discussed Balzac and the French Symbolist poets. Although some critics have pointed to Stone as the determining factor in Faulkner's success, Michael Millgate theorized in *Faulkner's Place* that the "apparent passivity of the younger man [Faulkner], his willingness to accept the position of listener, learner, recipient, and protege, undoubtedly led Stone to exaggerate in his own mind, and in public and private statements, the real extent of his influence. . . . Inevitably, Faulkner grew beyond Stone." At this time, however, Stone and Faulkner were still close friends. With Stone's help, Faulkner hatched a scheme to get admitted into the Royal Canadian Air Force. By affecting a British accent and forging letters of recommendation from nonexistent Englishmen, Faulkner was accepted into the RAF.

The war ended before Faulkner saw combat duty. He returned to his hometown, where he intermittently attended Ole Miss as a special student. His dandified appearance and lack of a stable job led townspeople to dub him "Count No Count." On August 6, 1919, he surprised them when his first poem, "L'Apres-midi d'un faune," was published in *New Republic*; later in the same year the *Mississippian* published one of his short stories, "Landing in Luck." After Faulkner dropped out of Ole Miss, he went to New York City at the invitation of Stark Young, a Mississippi novelist and drama critic. While he was there, Faulkner worked for Elizabeth Prall as a bookstore clerk.

When he returned to Oxford, Faulkner was hired as university postmaster, but his mind was rarely on his duties. Before putting magazines into the proper subscriber's post office box, he read through the issues. He brought his writing to the post office with him and became so immersed in what he was doing that he ignored patrons. Eventually his laxness came to the attention of the postal inspector, and he resigned rather than be fired. Faulkner remarked that he quit the job because he "didn't want to be at the beck and call of every son-of-a-bitch with the price of a two-cent stamp."

His career in the postal service over, Faulkner called on Elizabeth Prall in New Orleans. She was now married to novelist Sherwood Anderson, and the two men struck up a friendship. The association with Anderson helped Faulkner realize that his true metier was not poetry but the novel. Faulkner's first book, *The Marble Faun,* a collection of verse, was published after he arrived in New Orleans in 1924. Sales were so poor that most of the five hundred copies were sold to a bookstore for a mere ten cents a volume. Acting upon Anderson's advice, Faulkner wrote a novel and set it in the South. Anderson told Faulkner he would recommend the novel, entitled *Soldiers' Pay,* to a publisher as long as he didn't have to read it. Although the two men were very close for several months, a rift developed between them. Millgate postulated that "Faulkner's early realization that Anderson's way was not to be his way must always have been a source of strain in their relationship." During this period in New Orleans, Faulkner also contributed short stories and sketches to the *Times-Picayune.*

In 1925, Faulkner joined the American literary expatriates and went to Europe. He did not remain there long, however, and after a brief stay in New Orleans, he returned to Oxford, where he finally settled down. While he had been in Europe, *Soldiers' Pay* had appeared on the bookstands. It attracted some favorable notices but was not a commercial success. It was *The Sound and the Fury* that helped Faulkner establish a solid reputation among critics. Stirred by Faulkner's novel, Lyle Saxon wrote, "I believe simply and sincerely this is a great book." A reviewer for the *Boston Evening Transcript* called *The Sound and the Fury* a novel "worthy of the attention of a Euripides."

When writing his next novel, *As I Lay Dying,* Faulkner did not experience the same rapture he had felt when he was working on *The Sound and the Fury. As I Lay Dying* was written in a six-week period while Faulkner was working the night shift at a powerhouse. The constant humming noise of a dynamo serenaded him while he wrote his famous tour de force on the nature of being. By the time *As I Lay Dying* came out in 1930, John Bassett observed that "Faulkner's name, if not a household word, was at least known to many critics and reviewers, who spoke of him no longer as a neophyte, or a new voice in fiction, but as one either continuing his development in fruitful ways or floundering after several attempts, in either case as a writer known to the literary world."

Faulkner was not recognized by the general public until *Sanctuary,* one of his most violent and shocking novels, appeared in 1931. When he wrote *Sanctuary,* Faulkner later admitted, he had one purpose in mind: to make money. By this time he had a family to support, and out of desperation he concocted a book he thought would sell to the masses. Faulkner was ashamed when he saw the printer's galleys of the book and extensively rewrote his potboiler so that it would have a more serious intent. The scandalous subject matter of *Sanctuary* appealed to the reading public, and it sold well. For a brief time Faulkner became a minor celebrity, but the

rest of the decade did not go as well. Many reviewers had favorable comments to make about *Sanctuary*—Andre Malraux declared it "marks the intrusion of Greek tragedy into the detective story"—but in the view of others, the novel proved that Faulkner was merely a purveyor of the monstrous, the gory, and the obscene, and they judged his subsequent books in the same light. Faulkner was also a victim of the times. The Depression caused book sales in general to plummet, but his novels were particularly unpopular because they were not in keeping with the nation's mood. Warren speculated that critics and the public became disenchanted with Faulkner because his books offered no practical solutions to the pressing problems of the day—feeding the hungry and providing jobs for the millions of unemployed. Some readers were offended by Faulkner's novels because they were not written in the optimistic spirit of the New Deal, while still others discerned fascist tendencies in his work.

During the 1930s and 1940s Faulkner wrote many of his finest books, including *Light in August, Absalom, Absalom!, The Wild Palms, The Hamlet,* and *Go Down, Moses.* They brought in very little revenue, however, and he was forced to work in Hollywood as a screenwriter. Faulkner worked on and off in Hollywood for a number of years, but he was never happy there. He fled from the movie capital as soon as he had amassed enough money to pay his bills.

Despite Faulkner's stature in literary circles at home and abroad, in the 1940s his books gradually began dropping out of print, partly because of lack of popular interest, partly because of the war effort. By 1945 all seventeen of his books were out of print. In 1946 the publication of *The Portable Faulkner,* edited by Malcolm Cowley, created a resurgence of interest in Faulkner. Cowley's introduction to the volume, with its emphasis on the Southern legend that Faulkner had created in his works, served as a springboard for future critics. "Faulkner performed a labor of imagination that has not been equaled in our time, and a double labor," Cowley asserted. "First, to invent a Mississippi county that was like a mythical kingdom, but was complete and living in all its details; second, to make his story of Yoknapatawpha County stand as a parable or legend of all the Deep South."

Fifteen of Faulkner's novels and many of his short stories are set in Yoknapatawpha County, which bears a close resemblance to the region in northern Mississippi where Faulkner spent most of his life. Faulkner defined Yoknapatawpha as an "Indian word meaning water runs slow through flat land." The county is bounded by the Tallahatchie River on the north and by the Yoknapatawpha River on the south. Jefferson, the county seat, is modeled after Oxford. Up the road a piece is Frenchman's Bend, a poverty-stricken village. Scattered throughout the countryside are ramshackle plantation houses, farmhouses, and the hovels of tenant farmers. Depicted in both the past and the present, Yoknapatawpha is populated with a vast spectrum of people—the Native Americans who originally inhabited the land, the aristocrats, those ambitious men who fought their way into the landed gentry, yeoman farmers, poor whites, blacks, carpetbaggers, and bushwhackers. Faulkner was proud of the kingdom he had erected in his imagination. On a map of Yoknapatawpha County he prepared for the first edition of *Absalom, Absalom!,* he wrote, "William Faulkner, Sole Owner & Proprietor."

Most often, Faulkner's style is keyed to his themes. One of Faulkner's chief thematic preoccupations is the past, and this theme is also reflected in his form. In a famous analogy, Jean-Paul Sartre compared the Faulknerian character's point of view to that "of a passenger looking backward from a speeding car, who sees, flowing away from him, the landscape he is traversing. For him the future is not in view, the present is too blurred to make out, and he can see clearly only the past as it streams away before his obsessed and backward-looking gaze." Faulkner's pages are filled with characters who are fettered to the past. Millgate pointed out that in *The Sound and the Fury* the suicidal Quentin Compson searches "for a means of arresting time at a moment of achieved perfection, a moment when he and Caddy could be eternally together in the simplicity of their childhood relationship." The Reverend Gail Hightower in *Light in August* is also locked in the past, endlessly reliving the glory of his grandfather's cavalry charge. Robert Hemenway believed that in *As I Lay Dying* Faulkner is showing "that the South, like the Bundrens, must bury the past; that it cannot remain true—without courting tragedy or absurdity—to the promises given to dead ancestors or to the illusions of former glory." In "A Rose for Emily," Emily Grierson's embracing of her dead lover becomes a gruesome symbol of what happens when one clings to the past.

The stylistic methods most closely associated with Faulkner's treatment of the past are his use of long sentences, flashbacks, and multiple viewpoints. Aiken suggested that Faulkner utilizes complicated sentence structures because he wants "a medium without stops or pauses, a medium which is always *of the moment,* and of which the passage from moment to moment is as fluid and undetectable as in the life itself which he is purporting to give." Helen Swink posited that the confusing sentences that withhold meaning from the reader "intensify the emotional experience," while Millgate claimed that these sentences enable Faulkner "to hold a single moment in suspension while its full complexity is explored." The flashbacks are even more clearly related to Faulkner's interest in the past. Edward Murray pointed out that in *Light in August* the minds of Joe Christmas, Gail Hightower, Joanna Burden, and Lena Grove frequently revert back to the past, but "the flashbacks are not there merely to supply expository material for the actions in the present that need further explanation. Since the past is Faulkner's subject—or a large part of it—the flashbacks are not simply 'functional': they are thematically necessary."

"Faulkner's true domain is that of the eternal myths, particularly those popularized by the Bible," Maurice Coindreau observed in *The Time of William Faulkner.* "The themes that he prefers, his favorite images and metaphors, are those which ornament the fabric of the Old Testament." Like the writers of the Old Testament, Faulkner believes that the sins of the fathers are visited upon their children. Many of his characters are plagued by guilt, precipitated by their own sins as well as by the actions of their forefathers, who had callously shoved aside the Indians, enslaved the blacks, and laid waste the land.

Perhaps the greatest moral burden borne by Southerners was slavery. Much of Faulkner's fiction shows the evil that results from the failure to recognize the humanity of black people. Certainly many of the slave owners he depicts are cruel to their human property. In *Go Down, Moses,* Carothers McCaslin seduces Eunice, one of his Negroes. Years later he seduces the daughter who resulted from that union, thus driving Eunice to suicide. One of the reasons that Thomas Sutpen's grand design fails in *Absalom, Absalom!* is his acceptance of racism. When Sutpen leaves Haiti to found a dynasty in Mississippi, he abandons his black wife and infant son because their color would not be acceptable to Southerners. That deed comes back to haunt Sutpen and the children from his second marriage, Judith and

Henry. Sutpen's mulatto son shows up and wants to marry Judith. As horrified by the thought of miscegenation as he is by the possibility of incest, Henry guns down his half brother. This is only one incident in *Absalom, Absalom!* that demonstrates, as John V. Hagopian pointed out, how "the novel as a whole clearly repudiates Southern racism."

Another important aspect of Faulkner's fiction is love between family members. Cowley observed that Faulkner's books "have what is rare in the novels of our time, a warmth of family affection, brother for brother and sister, the father for his children—a love so warm and proud that it tries to shut out the rest of the world." But family life has eroded in Faulkner's fiction, at least partially because society is debilitated. "Faulkner's recurrent dramatization of the decay of families," Philip Momberger reflected, "e.g., the deterioration of the Compson, Sutpen, and Sartoris lines—is an expression in the domestic sphere of a more general, public disintegration: the collapse of the ideal of 'human family' in the modern world and the resulting deracination of the individual." Momberger went on to say that the social ideal that underpins Faulkner's work is "a state of communal wholeness within which, as within a coherent and loving family, the individual's identity would be defined, recognized, and sustained."

Established religion also comes under close scrutiny in Faulkner's fiction, and his characters are often deeply disturbed by the rigid attitudes of the church-going populace. In *Sanctuary,* Horace Benbow is taken aback when the Christian community refuses to help a man who is falsely accused of murder. Calvinist righteousness is also attacked in *Light in August,* where Hightower comes to realize that rigid religious attitudes encourage people to crucify themselves and others. One of the people they feel compelled to crucify is Joe Christmas, who is clearly an outcast in the community. The major significance in Christmas's name, Flannery O'Connor noted, "is the irony of Joe Christmas' being pursued and harassed throughout his life by voices of Christian righteousness."

M. E. Bradford pointed out that the thematic corollary to Faulkner's consideration of a young man's coming into his majority is the question of pride, "or pride's proper role in the formation of good character and of its necessary limitation in contingency. The gentleman, the exemplar of ordinate pride and enactor of a providentially assigned place, sums up in his person the possibility of a civil and religiously grounded social order. In him either presumption or passivity is communal and spiritual disaster." Closely linked to pride is the Faulknerian concept of honor, the need for a man to prove himself. In Faulkner's novels, exaggerated notions of honor lead to trouble. Quentin Compson's fanatic defense of his sister's honor is narcissistic; his "insistence upon honor and dignity have become extreme, forms of self love," O'Connor noted. In *As I Lay Dying,* the Bundren family's attempt to honor Addie's dying wish is ludicrous, yet Cleanth Brooks in *William Faulkner: The Yoknapatawpha Country* pointed out that Cash and Jewel "exhibit true heroism—Cash in his suffering, Jewel in his brave actions." The scruple of honor is also of great significance in *The Hamlet.* After Eula Varner becomes pregnant, her honor is ironically preserved when her father pays Flem Snopes to marry her. Even Mink Snopes has a warped sense of honor that compels him to kill Zack Houston. But Mink discovers that his cousin Flem is so devoid of honor that he won't even help Mink when he is arrested. Mink evens this score in a later novel, *The Mansion.* When he is released from prison, Mink kills Flem for the sake of honor.

When Faulkner's characters are initiated into manhood, they lose their innocence and are forced to face reality. The world they discover is one in which good and evil are intermingled. The "Snopes Trilogy," Stanley Edgar Hyman claimed, that is "Faulkner's fullest exploration of natural evil." In *The Hamlet*, the heartless Flem Snopes is pitted against V. K. Ratliff, an itinerant sewing machine salesman. Flem is almost the perfect embodiment of evil, whereas Ratliff, John Lewis Longley demonstrated, is a man "who is willing to actively commit himself against evil, but more important, to form actions of positive good." Although Flem is depicted as the incarnation of evil in *The Hamlet*, commentators have noted that he is portrayed more sympathetically in the succeeding two books in the trilogy. This treatment is in keeping with Faulkner's view of the nature of man. "I think that you really can't say that any man is good or bad. I grant you there are some exceptions, but man is the victim of himself or his fellows, or his own nature, or his environment, but no man is good or bad either. He tries to do the best he can within his rights," the Faulkner once said.

Though Faulkner occasionally failed greatly, he usually succeeded mightily. Whatever the faults of his later books, few would dispute the general excellence of his canon. Even Faulkner seemed overwhelmed by his achievement. Toward the end of his life, he wrote to a friend: "And now I realize for the first time what an amazing gift I had: uneducated in every formal sense, without even very literate, let alone literary, companions, yet to have made the things I made. I don't know where it came from. I don't know why God or gods or whoever it was, elected me to be the vessel. Believe me, this is not humility, false modesty: it is simply amazement."

BIOGRAPHICAL/CRITICAL SOURCES:

BOOKS

Aldridge, John W., *The Devil in the Fire*, Harper's Magazine Press, 1972.

Arnold, Edwin T. and Dawn Trouard, *Reading Faulkner, Sanctuary: Glossary and Commentary*, University Press of Mississippi (Jackson), 1996.

Barbour, James, and Tom Quirk, editors, *Writing the American Classics*, University of North Carolina Press, 1990, pp. 156-76.

Bassett, John E., *William Faulkner: An Annotated Checklist of Criticism*, Lewis, 1972.

Bassett, John E., *William Faulkner: An Annotated Checklist of Recent Criticism*, Kent State University Press, 1983.

Blotner, Joseph L. and Frederick L. Gwynn, *Faulkner in the University*, University Press of Virginia (Charlottesville), 1995.

Blotner, Joseph L., editor, *Selected Letters of William Faulkner*, Random House, 1977.

Bockting, Ineke, *Character and Personality in the Novels of William Faulkner: A Study in Psychostylistics*, University Press of America (Lanham, MD), 1995.

Brooks, Cleanth, *William Faulkner: The Yoknapatawpha Country*, Yale University Press, 1963.

Brooks, Cleanth, *William Faulkner: Toward Yoknapatawpha and Beyond*, Yale University Press, 1978.

Carothers, James B., *William Faulkner's Short Stories*, UMI Research Press, 1985.

Clarke, Deborah, *Robbing the Mother: Women in Faulkner*, University Press of Mississippi (Jackson), 1994.

Coindreau, Maurice, *The Time of William Faulkner*, University of South Carolina Press, 1971.

Concise Dictionary of Literary Biography: The Age of Maturity, 1929-1941, Gale (Detroit), 1989.

Contemporary Literary Criticism, Gale, Volume 1, 1973; Volume 3, 1975; Volume 6, 1976; Volume 8, 1978; Volume 9, 1978; Volume 11, 1979; Volume 14, 1980; Volume 18, 1981; Volume 28, 1984; Volume 52, 1989; Volume 68, 1991.

Cowley, Malcolm, editor, *The Faulkner-Cowley File: Letters and Memories*, Viking, 1966.

Cowley, *A Second Flowering: Works and Days of the Lost Generation*, Viking, 1973, pp. 130-55.

Cowley, *And I Worked at the Writer's Trade*, Viking, 1978.

Dictionary of Literary Biography, Gale, Volume 9: *American Novelists, 1910-1945*, 1981; Volume 11: *American Humorists, 1800-1950*, 1982; Volume 44: *American Screenwriters, Second Series*, 1986.

Dictionary of Literary Biography Documentary Series, Volume 2, Gale, 1982.

Dictionary of Literary Biography Yearbook 1986, Gale, 1987.

Faulkner, Jim and others, *Talking About William Faulkner: Interviews with Jimmy Faulkner and Others*, Louisiana State University Press (Baton Rouge), 1996.

Fowler, Doreen, *Faulkner: The Return of the Repressed*, University Press of Virginia, 1997.

Godden, Richard, *Fictions of Labor: William Faulkner and the South's Long Revolution*, Cambridge University Press, 1997.

Gray, Richard J., *The Life of William Faulkner: A Critical Biography*, Blackwell (Cambridge, MA), 1994.

Hahn, Stephen and Arthur F. Kinney, *Approaches to Teaching Faulkner's The Sound and the Fury*, Modern Language Association (New York City), 1996.

Hines, Thomas S., *William Faulkner and the Tangible Past: The Architecture of Yoknapatawpha*, University of California Press (Berkeley), 1996.

Hinkle, James, *Reading Faulkner. The Unvanquished: Glossary and Commentary*, University Press of Mississippi (Jackson), 1995.

Holmes, Catherine D., *Annotations to William Faulkner's The Hamlet*, Garland (New York City), 1996.

Honnighausen, Lothar, *Faulkner: Masks and Metaphors*, University Press of Mississippi, 1997.

Hyman, Stanley Edgar, *Standards: A Chronicle of Books for Our Time*, Horizon Press, 1966.

Inge, M. Thomas, *William Faulkner—The Contemporary Reviews*, Cambridge University Press (New York City), 1995.

Irwin, John T., *Doubling and Incest/Repetition and Revenge: A Speculative Reading of Faulkner*, Johns Hopkins University Press, 1975, expanded edition, 1996.

Johnson, Carol Siri, and Laurie Kalmanson, *William Faulkner's Absalom, Absalom!* Research and Education Association, 1996.

Jones, Diane Brown, *A Reader's Guide to the Short Stories of William Faulkner*, Maxwell Macmillan International (New York City), 1994.

Karl, Frederick R., *William Faulkner: American Writer*, Weidenfeld & Nicolson, 1989.

Kartiganer, Donald M. and Ann J. Abadie, *Faulkner and Ideology*, University Press of Mississippi (Jackson), 1994.

Kartiganer, Donald M. and Ann J. Abadie, *Faulkner and Psychology*, University Press of Mississippi (Jackson), 1994.

Kartiganer, Donald M. and Ann J. Abadie, *Faulkner and the Artist*, University Press of Mississippi (Jackson), 1996.

Kartiganer, Donald M. and Ann J. Abadie, *Faulkner and Gender*, University Press of Mississippi, 1996.

Kartiganer, Donald M. and Ann J. Abadie, *Faulkner in Cultural Context,* University Press of Mississippi, 1997.

Kaufmann, Michael, *Textual Bodies: Modernism, Postmodernism, and Print,* Bucknell University Press (Lewisburg, PA), 1994.

Kinney, Arthur F., *Critical Essays on William Faulkner: The Sutpen Family,* G.K.Hall (New York), 1996.

Kinney, Arthur F., *Go Down, Moses: The Miscegenation of Time,* Twayne (New York City), 1996.

LaLonde, Christopher A., *William Faulkner and the Rites of Passage,* Mercer University Press (Macon, GA), 1996.

Millgate, Michael, *Faulkner's Place,* University of Georgia Press, 1997.

Roberts, Diane, *Faulkner and Southern Womanhood,* University of Georgia Press (Athens), 1994.

Ross, Stephen, *Fiction's Inexhaustible Voice: Speech and Writing in Faulkner,* University of Georgia Press, 1989.

Ross, Stephen and Noel Polk, *Reading Faulkner. The Sound and the Fury,* University Press of Mississippi (Jackson), 1996.

Ruppersburg, Hugh M., *Reading Faulkner. Light in August: Glossary and Commentary,* University Press of Mississippi (Jackson), 1994.

Short Story Criticism, Gale, Volume 1, 1988.

Singel, Daniel J., *William Faulkner: The Making of a Modernist,* University of North Carolina Press, 1997.

Vanderwerken, David L., *Faulkner's Literary Children: Patterns of Development,* Peter Lang (New York City), 1997.

Visser, Irene, *Compassion in Faulkner's Fiction,* Edwin Mellen Press (Lewiston, NY), 1996.

Wagner-Martin, Linda, *New Essays on Go Down, Moses,* Cambridge University Press (New York City), 1996.

Weinstein, Philip M., editor, *The Cambridge Companion to William Faulkner,* Cambridge University Press (New York City), 1995.

PERIODICALS

American Literature, May, 1973.
Georgia Review, summer, 1972.
Journal of Popular Culture, summer, 1973.
Modern Fiction Studies, summer, 1973; winter, 1973-74; summer, 1975.
New Republic, September 8, 1973.
Sewanee Review, winter, 1970; autumn, 1971.
Southern Review, summer, 1968; autumn, 1972.
Studies in Short Fiction, summer, 1974.
Twentieth Century Literature, July, 1973.

*   *   *

FENNO, Jack
See CALISHER, Hortense

*   *   *

FERBER, Edna 1887-1968

PERSONAL: Born August 15, 1887, in Kalamazoo, MI; died of cancer, April 16, 1968, in New York, NY; daughter of Jacob Charles (Hungarian-born small businessman) and Julia (Newmann) Ferber. *Education:* Graduated from Ryan High School, Appleton, WI.

CAREER: Novelist, short story writer, playwright. At seventeen, began working as a full-time reporter for *Appleton Daily Crescent,* Appleton, WI; later worked as a writer and reporter for *Milwaukee Journal. Wartime service:* During World War II, served in civilian capacity as war correspondent for U.S. Army Air Forces.

MEMBER: National Institute of Arts and Letters, Authors League of America, Authors Guild, Dramatists Guild.

AWARDS, HONORS: Pulitzer Prize in fiction, 1924, for *So Big;* Litt.D., Columbia University and Adelphi College.

WRITINGS:

NOVELS

Dawn O'Hara, the Girl Who Laughed, Stokes, 1911.
Fanny Herself, Stokes, 1917.
The Girls, Doubleday, 1921.
So Big, Doubleday, 1924, with introduction by Maria K. Mootry, University of Illinois Press (Urbana), 1995.
Show Boat, Doubleday, 1926.
Cimarron, Doubleday, 1930, revised edition, Grosset, 1942, new edition by Frederick H. Law, Globe, 1954.
American Beauty, Doubleday, 1931.
Come and Get It, Doubleday, 1935.
Nobody's In Town (two novellas, including "Trees Die at the Top"), Doubleday, 1938.
Saratoga Trunk, Doubleday, 1941.
Great Son, Doubleday, 1945.
Giant, Doubleday, 1952.
Ice Palace, Doubleday, 1958.

SHORT STORIES

Buttered Side Down, Stokes, 1912.
Roast Beef, Medium: The Business Adventures of Emma McChesney, Stokes, 1913.
Personality Plus: Some Experiences of Emma McChesney and Her Son, Jock, Stokes, 1914.
Emma McChesney & Co., Stokes, 1915.
Cheerful, by Request, Doubleday, 1918.
Half Portions, Doubleday, 1920.
Gigolo (includes "Old Man Minick"; also see below), Doubleday, 1922.
Mother Knows Best: A Fiction Book, Doubleday, 1927.
They Brought Their Women: A Book of Short Stories, Doubleday, 1933.
No Room at the Inn, Doubleday, 1941.
One Basket: Thirty-One Short Stories, Simon & Shuster, 1947.

PLAYS

(With George V. Hobart) *Our Mrs. McChesney,* first produced in New York at Lyceum Theater, October 19, 1915.
(With George S. Kaufman) *Minick* (dramatization of her short story, "Old Man Minick"; also see below), first produced in New York at Booth Theater, September 24, 1924.
The Eldest: A Drama of American Life, Appleton, 1925.
(With Kaufman) *The Royal Family* (first produced in New York at Selwyn Theater, December 28, 1927; produced as television play, 1954), Doubleday, 1928.
(With Kaufman) *Dinner at Eight* (first produced on Broadway at Music Box Theater, October 22, 1932), Doubleday, 1932.
(With Kaufman) *Stage Door* (first produced on Broadway at Music Box Theater, October 22, 1936), Doubleday, 1936.
(With Kaufman) *The Land Is Bright* (first produced on Broadway at Music Box Theater, October 28, 1941), Doubleday, 1941.

(With Kaufman) *Bravo!* (first produced in New York at Lyceum Theater, November 11, 1948), Dramatists Play Service, 1949.

OTHER

(Author of filmscript) "A Gay Old Dog," Pathe Exchange, 1919.

(With Newman Levy) *$1200 a Year,* Doubleday, 1920.

(Contributor) *My Story That I Like Best,* International Magazine Co., 1924.

Old Man Minick [and] *Minick* (the story and the play; the latter with Kaufman), Doubleday, 1924.

(With Kaufman, author of filmscript) "Welcome Home," Paramount, 1925.

A Peculiar Treasure (autobiography), Doubleday, 1939.

Your Town, World, 1948.

Show Boat, So Big, [and] *Cimarron: Three Living Novels of American Life,* Doubleday, 1962.

A Kind of Magic (autobiography; sequel to *A Peculiar Treasure*), Doubleday, 1963.

MEDIA ADAPTATIONS: The following films were based on Ferber's work: *Our Mrs. McChesney,* Metro, 1918; *No Woman Knows* (based on *Fanny Herself*), Universal, 1921; *Classified* (based on her short story of the same title), Corinne Griffith Productions, 1925; *Gigolo,* Cinema Corporation of America, 1926; *Mother Knows Best,* Fox, 1928; *The Home Girl* (based on a short story), Paramount, 1928; *Show Boat,* Universal, 1929, remade by Universal, 1936, and M-G-M, 1951; *The Royal Family of Broadway* (based on the play "The Royal Family," by Ferber and Kaufman), Paramount, 1930; *Cimarron,* RKO, 1931, remade by M-G-M, 1960; *The Expert* (based on her short story, "Old Man Minick"), Warner Bros., 1932; *So Big,* Warner Bros., 1932, remade by Warner Bros., 1953; *Dinner at Eight* (based on play written with Kaufman), M-G-M, 1933; *Come and Get It,* United Artists, 1936; *Stage Door,* RKO, 1937; *No Place to Go* (based on the play, *Minick,* by Ferber and Kaufman), Warner Bros., 1939; *Saratoga Trunk,* Warner Bros., 1945; *Giant,* Warner Bros., 1956; *Ice Palace,* Warner Bros., 1960. *Show Boat* was adapted for the stage with music by Jerome Kern, and was first produced in New York at Ziegfeld Theater, December 27, 1927. *Saratoga Trunk* was adapted for a musical, *Saratoga,* with a libretto by Harold Arlen; it was first produced on Broadway at Winter Garden Theater, December 7, 1959.

SIDELIGHTS: Edna Ferber loved America and all of her stories in many ways depict a vanishing American way of life. Along with her great love for America, Edna Ferber greatly admired the characters she portrayed. These characters, drawn from the Midwestern lower middle and middle classes, exemplify the American ideal for her. (She always found the conversation of a truck driver more vigorous and stimulating than the conversation of a Cadillac owner.) When Edna Ferber died at the age of 82, the *New York Times* stated: "Ferber was a dramatic writer with a keen eye for a story, a wholesome respect for the color and harmony of words and a precise ability at portraiture. She [owed] much of this to early journalistic training as a reporter. . . . Reporting, she maintained, developed in her a super-camera eye, a sense of the dramatic and a 'vast storehouse of practical and psychological knowledge' that proved invaluable in her creative writing. . . . Like all good reporters, Miss Ferber was indefatigably curious. The ideas for many of her novels came from snatches of conversation that piqued her interest." She attributed her success to her ability to project herself into any environment. Whatever captured her fancy she could easily write about. Although her books were not profound, they were vivid representations and as a result afford pleasurable reading. (Many of her books and stories are required reading in schools.)

Ms. Ferber continued writing about the United States for four decades. Even though her father, a Hungarian Jew, was an unsuccessful storekeeper and she was forced to work instead of attending college where she wanted to study drama, she learned to write "smoothly and brightly, with . . . so wide-awake a style and so clever a selection of detail," Louis Kronenberger perceived. Her enthusiasm made her books especially enjoyable reading for young people. Though a *Dial* reviewer was critical of Edna Ferber—her "talents go to polishing the bright pebbles of life, rather than to touching the bedrock of reality"—this comment may as well be taken as a compliment to her talent. Edna Ferber gave us a fragment of life important to her. Her "sentimentality" was typical of an era we may never see again. William Allen White believed that "the historian will find no better picture of America in the first three decades of this century than Edna Ferber has drawn."

Critics of the twenties and thirties did not hesitate to call her the greatest American woman novelist of her day. *So Big,* her Pulitzer Prize-winning novel of 1924, is the story of Selina Peake Dejong, who is left penniless when her gambler father dies of a bullet wound. "Selina's victory in the novel is Ferber's extended homily on the gospel of rugged individualism," W. T. Stuckey concluded. She continued writing with the "escapist" technique in *Show Boat,* living in James Adams' Floating Theater for two months to get the right atmosphere; in 1924, she dramatized her own personal doubts in *Cimarron* (she had been fired by a new city editor after working on the paper for a year and a half). Her eleventh novel, *Giant,* was, according to the author, "not only a story of Texas today but, I hope, Texas tomorrow." Her last novel, *Ice Palace,* which concerns Alaska, "was given much credit for the admission of the territory," noted William Rutledge III.

In later years, Ms. Ferber often helped young writers and used her leisure time for travel (in her youth, she wrote more than 1,000 words a day, 350 days a year). Her own philosophy continued to help the talented young writers in whom she was so interested: "Life," she said, "can't ever really defeat a writer who is in love with writing, for life itself is a writer's lover until death—fascinating, cruel, lavish, warm, cold, treacherous, constant; the more varied the moods the richer the experience."

BIOGRAPHICAL/CRITICAL SOURCES:

BOOKS

Contemporary Literary Criticism, Volume 18, Gale (Detroit), 1981.

Cournos, John, and Sybil Norton (pseudonym of H. S. N. K. Cournos), *Famous American Modern Novelists,* Dodd, 1952.

Dickinson, R., *Edna Ferber,* Doubleday, 1925.

Dictionary of Literary Biography, Gale, Volume 9: *American Novelists, 1910-1945,* 1981; Volume 28: *Twentieth-Century American-Jewish Fiction Writers,* 1984.

Dodd, Loring Holmes, *Celebrities at Our Hearthside,* Dresser, 1959.

Van Gelder, Robert, *Writers and Writing,* Scribner, 1946.

Witham, W. Tasker, *Panorama of American Literature,* Doubleday, 1947.

PERIODICALS

Atlantic, November, 1912; December 1941.

Atlantic Bookshelf, December, 1931.

Chicago Sunday Tribune Book Review, March 30, 1958.

Christian Science Monitor, March 27, 1958.
Dial, November 20, 1950.
Literary Journal, November 1, 1941.
Literary Review, October 28, 1922; August 21, 1926.
Nation, April 23, 1930.
New Republic, April 30, 1930.
New Yorker, February 4, 1939.
New York Times, April 17, 1968.
New York Times Book Review, August 22, 1926; April 17, 1927; March 23, 1930; May 14, 1933; April 17, 1968.
New York World, March 20, 1930.
Saturday Review, October 17, 1931; September 27, 1952; March 29, 1958.
Springfield Republican, March 2, 1924.
Times (London), April 17, 1968.
United States Quarterly Booklist, September, 1947.
Variety, April 24, 1968.

*　　　*　　　*

FERLING, Lawrence
See FERLINGHETTI, Lawrence (Monsanto)

*　　　*　　　*

FERLINGHETTI, Lawrence (Monsanto) 1919(?)- (Lawrence Ferling)

PERSONAL: Born Lawrence Ferling, March 24, c. 1919, in Yonkers, NY; original family name of Ferlinghetti restored, 1954; son of Charles S. (an auctioneer) and Clemence (Mendes Monsanto) Ferling; married Selden Kirby-Smith, April, 1951 (divorced); children: Julie, Lorenzo. *Education:* University of North Carolina, A.B., 1941; Columbia University, M.A., 1947; Sorbonne, University of Paris, Doctorat de l'Universite (with honors), 1949. *Politics:* "Now an enemy of the State." *Religion:* "Catholique manque."

ADDRESSES: Home—San Francisco, CA. *Office*—City Lights Books, 261 Columbus Ave., San Francisco, CA 94133.

CAREER: Poet, playwright, editor, and painter; worked for *Time,* New York City, post-World War II; taught French in a adult education program, San Francisco, CA, 1951-52; City Lights Pocket Bookshop (now City Lights Books), San Francisco, co-owner, 1953–, founder and editor of City Lights Books (publisher), 1955–. Participant in numerous national and international literary conferences, art exhibitions, and poetry readings. *Military service:* U.S. Naval Reserve, 1941-45; became lieutenant commander; was commanding officer during Normandy invasion.

AWARDS, HONORS: National Book Award nomination, 1970, for *The Secret Meaning of Things;* Notable Book of 1979 citation, *Library Journal,* 1980, for *Landscapes of Living & Dying;* Silver Medal for poetry, Commonwealth Club of California, 1986, for *Over All the Obscene Boundaries;* recipient of poetry prize, City of Rome, 1993; San Francisco street named in his honor, 1994.

WRITINGS:

(Translator) Jacques Prevert, *Selections From Paroles,* City Lights, 1958.
Her (novel), New Directions, 1960.
Howl of the Censor (trial proceedings), edited by J. W. Ehrlich, Nourse Publishing, 1961.

(With Jack Spicer) *Dear Ferlinghetti,* White Rabbit Press, 1962.
The Mexican Night: Travel Journal, New Directions, 1970.
A World Awash with Fascism and Fear, Cranium Press, 1971.
A Political Pamphlet, Anarchist Resistance Press, 1976.
Northwest Ecolog, City Lights, 1978.
(With Nancy J. Peters) *Literary San Francisco: A Pictorial History from the Beginning to the Present,* Harper, 1980.
(With Nancy J. Peters) *Literary San Francisco: A Pictorial History from its Beginnings to the Present Day,* Harper & Row, 1980.
The Populist Manifestos (includes "First Populist Manifesto"), Grey Fox Press, 1983.
Seven Days in Nicaragua Libre (journal), City Lights, 1985.
Leaves of Life: Fifty Drawings From the Model, City Lights, 1985.
(Translator with others) Nicanor Parra, *Antipoems: New & Selected,* New Directions, 1985.
(Translator with Francesca Valente) Pier Paolo Pasolini, *Roman Poems,* City Lights, 1986.
Love in the Days of Rage (novel), Dutton, 1988.
(With Alexis Lykiard) *The Cool Eye: Lawrence Ferlinghetti Talks to Alexis Lykiard,* Stride, 1993.

POETRY

Pictures of the Gone World, City Lights, 1955, enlarged edition, 1995.
Tentative Description of a Dinner Given to Promote the Impeachment of President Eisenhower, Golden Mountain Press, 1958.
A Coney Island of the Mind, New Directions, 1958.
Berlin, Golden Mountain Press, 1961.
One Thousand Fearful Words for Fidel Castro, City Lights, 1961.
Starting From San Francisco, with recording of poems, New Directions, 1961, revised edition without recording, 1967.
(With Gregory Corso and Allen Ginsberg) *Penguin Modern Poets 5,* Penguin, 1963.
Thoughts of a Concerto of Telemann, Four Seasons Foundation, 1963.
Where Is Vietnam?, City Lights, 1965.
To F—Is to Love Again, Kyrie Eleison Kerista; or, The Situation in the West, Followed by a Holy Proposal, F—You Press, 1965.
Christ Climbed Down, Syracuse University, 1965.
An Eye On the World: Selected Poems, MacGibbon & Kee, 1967.
Moscow in the Wilderness, Segovia in the Snow, Beach Books, 1967.
After the Cries of the Birds, Dave Haselwood Books, 1967.
Fuclock, Fire Publications, 1968.
Reverie Smoking Grass, East 128, 1968.
The Secret Meaning of Things, New Directions, 1969.
Tyrannus Nix?, New Directions, 1969.
Back Roads to Far Places, New Directions, 1971.
Love Is No Stone on the Moon, ARIF Press, 1971.
The Illustrated Wilfred Funk, City Lights, 1971.
Open Eye, Open Heart, New Directions, 1973.
Director of Alienation: A Poem, Main Street, 1976.
Who Are We Now? (also see below), City Lights, 1976.
Landscapes of Living and Dying (also see below), New Directions, 1979.
Mule Mountain Dreams, Bisbee Press Collective, 1980.
A Trip to Italy and France, New Directions, 1980.
Endless Life: Selected Poems (includes "Endless Life"), New Directions, 1984.

Over All the Obscene Boundaries: European Poems and Transitions, New Directions, 1985.

Inside the Trojan Horse, Lexikos, 1987.

Wild Dreams of a New Beginning: Including "Landscapes of Living & Dying" and "Who Are We Now?", New Directions, 1988.

When I Look at Pictures, Peregrine Smith Books, 1990.

These Are My Rivers: New & Selected Poems 1955-1993, New Directions (New York City), 1993.

A Far Rockaway of the Heart, New Directions, 1997.

PLAYS

Unfair Arguments with Existence: Seven Plays for a New Theatre (contains *The Soldiers of No Country* [produced in London, 1969], *Three Thousand Red Ants* [produced in New York City, 1970; also see below], *The Alligation* [produced in San Francisco, 1962; also see below], *The Victims of Amnesia* [produced in New York City, 1970; also see below], *Motherlode, The Customs Collector in Baggy Pants* [produced in New York City, 1964], and *The Nose of Sisyphus*), New Directions, 1963.

Routines (contains thirteen short plays, including *The Jig Is Up, His Head, Ha-Ha,* and *Non-Objection*), New Directions, 1964.

3 by Ferlinghetti: Three Thousand Red Ants, The Alligation, [and] *The Victims of Amnesia,* produced in New York City, 1970.

EDITOR

Beatitude Anthology, City Lights, 1960.

Pablo Picasso, *Hunk of Skin,* City Lights, 1969.

Charles Upton, *Panic Grass,* City Lights, 1969.

City Lights Anthology, City Lights, 1974, 1995.

City Lights Pocket Poets Anthology, City Lights, 1995.

(With Peters) *City Lights Review, No. 1,* City Lights, 1987.

(With Peters) *City Lights Review, No. 2,* City Lights, 1988.

RECORDINGS

(With Kenneth Rexroth) *Poetry Readings in "The Cellar,"* Fantasy, 1958.

Tentative Description of a Dinner To Impeach President Eisenhower, and Other Poems, Fantasy, 1959.

Tyrannus Nix? and Assassination Raga, Fantasy, 1971.

(With Corso and Ginsberg) *The World's Greatest Poets 1,* CMS, 1971.

OTHER

Author of narration, *Have You Sold Your Dozen Roses?* (film), California School of Fine Arts Film Workshop, 1957. Contributor to numerous periodicals, including *San Francisco Chronicle, Nation, Evergreen Review, Liberation, Chicago Review, Transatlantic Review,* and *New Statesman.* Editor, *Journal for the Protection of All Beings, Interim Pad,* and *City Lights Journal.*

Ferlinghetti's manuscripts are collected at Columbia University, New York City.

MEDIA ADAPTATIONS: Ferlinghetti's poem "Autobiography" was choreographed by Sophie Maslow, 1964. *A Coney Island of the Mind* was adapted for the stage by Steven Kyle Kent, Charles R. Blaker, and Carol Brown and produced at the Edinburgh Festival, Scotland, 1966; poem was adapted for television by Ted Post on *Second Experiment in Television,* 1967.

SIDELIGHTS: As poet, playwright, publisher, and spokesman, Lawrence Ferlinghetti helped to spark the San Francisco literary renaissance of the 1950s and the subsequent Beat movement in American poetry. Ferlinghetti was one of a group of writers—later labeled the "Beat Generation"—who felt strongly that art should be accessible to all people, not just a handful of highly educated intellectuals. Ferlinghetti's career has been marked by a constant challenge to the status quo in art. His poetry engages readers, defies popular political movements, and reflects the influence of American idiom and modern jazz. In *Lawrence Ferlinghetti: Poet-at-Large,* Larry Smith notes that the author "writes truly memorable poetry, poems that lodge themselves in the consciousness of the reader and generate awareness and change. And his writing sings, with the sad and comic music of the streets."

Ferlinghetti performed numerous functions essential to the establishment of the Beat movement while also creating his own substantial body of work. His City Lights bookstore provided a gathering place for the fertile talents of the San Francisco literary renaissance, and his City Lights press offered a forum for publication of Beat writings. He also became "America's best-selling poet of the twentieth century," according to Paul Varner in *Western American Literature.* As Smith puts it in the *Dictionary of Literary Biography,* "What emerges from the historical panorama of Ferlinghetti's involvement is a pattern of social engagement and literary experimentation as he sought to expand the goals of the Beat movement." Smith adds, however, that Ferlinghetti's contribution far surpasses his tasks as a publisher and organizer. "Besides molding an image of the poet in the world," the critic writes, "he created a poetic form that is at once rhetorically functional and socially vital." *Dictionary of Literary Biography* essayist Thomas McClanahan likewise contends that Ferlinghetti "became the most important force in developing and publicizing antiestablishment poetics."

Ferlinghetti was born Lawrence Monsanto Ferling, the youngest of five sons of Charles and Clemency Ferling. His father, an Italian immigrant, had shortened the family name upon arrival in America. Only years later, when he was a grown man, did Ferlinghetti discover the lengthier name and restore it as his own.

A series of disasters struck Ferlinghetti as a youngster. Before he was born, his father died suddenly. When he was only two, his mother suffered a nervous breakdown that required lengthy hospitalization. Separated from his brothers, Lawrence went to live with his maternal uncle, Ludovic Monsanto, a language instructor, and his French-speaking wife, Emily. The marriage disintegrated, and Emily Monsanto returned to France, taking Lawrence with her. During the following four years, the youngster lived in Strasbourg and spoke only French.

Ferlinghetti's return to America began with a stay in a state orphanage in New York. His aunt placed him there while she sought work in Manhattan. Eventually the pair were reunited when the aunt found a position as governess to the wealthy Bisland family in Bronxville. The youngster endeared himself to the Bislands to such an extent that when his aunt disappeared suddenly, he was allowed to stay. Surrounded by fine books and educated people, he was encouraged to read and learn fine passages of literature by heart. His formal education proceeded first in the elite Riverdale Country Day School and later in Bronxville public schools. As a teenager he was sent to Mount Hermon, a preparatory academy in Massachusetts.

Calling himself Lawrence Monsanto Ferling, Ferlinghetti enrolled at the University of North Carolina in 1937. There he majored in journalism and worked with the student staff of the *Daily Tarheel.* He earned his bachelor's degree in the spring of 1941 and joined the United States Navy that fall. His wartime service included patrolling the Atlantic coast on submarine watch and commanding a ship during the Normandy invasion. After his discharge he took advantage of the G.I. Bill to continue his education. He did graduate study at Columbia University, receiving his master's degree in 1948, and he completed his doctoral degree at the University of Paris in 1951.

Ferlinghetti returned from Paris in 1951 and moved to San Francisco. For a short time he supported himself by teaching languages at an adult education school and by doing freelance writing for art journals and the *San Francisco Chronicle*. In 1953 he joined with Peter D. Martin to publish a magazine, *City Lights*, named after a Charlie Chaplin silent film. In order to subsidize the magazine, Martin and Ferlinghetti opened the City Lights Pocket Book Shop in a neighborhood on the edge of Chinatown.

Before long the City Lights Book Shop was a popular gathering place for San Francisco's avant-garde writers, poets, and painters. "We were filling a big need," Ferlinghetti told the *New York Times Book Review*. "City Lights became about the only place around where you could go in, sit down, and read books without being pestered to buy something. That's one of the things it was supposed to be. Also, I had this idea that a bookstore should be a center of intellectual activity; and I knew it was a natural for a publishing company too."

Ferlinghetti was busy creating his own poetry, and in 1955 he launched the City Lights Pocket Poets publishing venture. First in the "Pocket Poets" series was a slim volume of his work, *Pictures of the Gone World*. In *Lawrence Ferlinghetti*, Smith observes that from his earliest poems onwards, the author became "the contemporary man of the streets speaking out the truths of common experience, often to the reflective beat of the jazz musician. As much as any poet today he . . . sought to make poetry an engaging oral art." McClanahan writes: "The underlying theme of Ferlinghetti's first book is the poet's desire to subvert and destroy the capitalist economic system. Yet this rather straightforward political aim is accompanied by a romantic vision of Eden, a mirror reflecting the Whitmanesque attempts to be free from social and political restraints."

These sentiments found an appreciative audience among young people agonizing over the nuclear arms race and Cold War politics. By 1955 Ferlinghetti counted among his friends such poets as Kenneth Rexroth, Allen Ginsberg, and Philip Whalen, as well as the novelist Jack Kerouac. Ferlinghetti was in the audience at the watershed 1955 poetry reading "Six Poets at the Six Gallery," at which Ginsberg unveiled his poem *Howl*. Ferlinghetti immediately recognized *Howl* as a classic work of art and offered to publish it in the "Pocket Poets" series. The first edition of *Howl and Other Poems* appeared in 1956 and sold out quickly. A second shipment was ordered from the British printer, but United States customs authorities seized it on the grounds of alleged obscenity. When federal authorities declined to pursue the case and released the books, the San Francisco Police Department arrested Ferlinghetti on charges of printing and selling lewd and indecent material.

Ferlinghetti engaged the American Civil Liberties Union for his defense and welcomed his court case as a test of the limits to freedom of speech. Not only did he win the suit on October 3, 1957, he also benefitted from the publicity generated by the case. In the *Dictionary of Literary Biography*, Smith writes: "The importance of this court case to the life and career of Ferlinghetti as well as to the whole blossoming of the San Francisco renaissance in poetry and the West Coast Beat movement is difficult to overestimate. Ferlinghetti and Ginsberg became national as well as international public figures leading a revolution in thinking as well as writing. The case solidified the writing into a movement with definite principles yet an openness of form."

For Ferlinghetti, the "principles" included redeeming poetry from the ivory towers of academia and offering it as a shared experience with ordinary people. He began reading his poems to the accompaniment of experimental jazz and reveled in an almost forgotten oral tradition in poetry. In 1958, New Directions press published Ferlinghetti's *A Coney Island of the Mind,* a work that has since sold well over one million copies in America and abroad. In his *Dictionary of Literary Biography* piece, Smith contends that *A Coney Island of the Mind* "is one of the key works of the Beat period and one of the most popular books of contemporary poetry. . . . It launched Ferlinghetti as a poet of humor and satire, who achieves an open-form expressionism and a personal lyricism." Walter Sutton offers a similar assessment in *American Free Verse: The Modern Revolution in Poetry*. Sutton feels that the general effect of the book "is of a kaleidoscopic view of the world and of life as an absurd carnival of discontinuous sensory impressions and conscious reflections, each with a ragged shape of its own but without any underlying thematic unity or interrelationship." Sutton adds, "To this extent the collection suggests a Surrealistic vision. But it differs in that meanings and easily definable themes can be found in most of the individual poems, even when the idea of meaninglessness is the central concern."

In *Lawrence Ferlinghetti,* Smith suggests that the poems in *A Coney Island of the Mind* demonstrate the direction Ferlinghetti intended to go with his art. Ferlinghetti "enlarged his stance and developed major themes of anarchy, mass corruption, engagement, and a belief in the sureality and wonder of life," to quote Smith. "It was a revolutionary art of dissent and contemporary application which jointly drew a lyric poetry into new realms of social-and self-expression. It sparkles, sings, goes flat, and generates anger or love out of that flatness as it follows a basic motive of getting down to reality and making of it what we can." Smith concludes: "Loosely, the book forms a type of 'Portrait of the Artist as a Young Poet of Dissent.' There are some classic contemporary statements in this Ferlinghetti's—and possibly America's—most popular book of modern poetry. The work is remarkable for its skill, depth, and daring."

If certain academics grumbled about Ferlinghetti's work, others found it refreshing for its engagement in current social and political issues and its indebtedness to a bardic tradition. "Ferlinghetti has cultivated a style of writing visibly his own," claims Linda Hamalian in the *American Book Review*. "He often writes his line so that it approximates the rhythm and meaning of the line. He also has William Carlos Williams' gift of turning unlikely subjects into witty poems. . . . He introduces the unexpected, catching his readers open for his frequently sarcastic yet humorous observations." *Poetry* magazine contributor Alan Dugan maintains that the poet "has the usual American obsession, asking, 'What is going on in America and how does one survive it?' His answer might be: By being half a committed outsider and half an innocent Fool. He makes jokes and chants seriously with equal gusto and surreal inventiveness, using spoken American in a romantic, flamboyant manner."

Two recent collections of Ferlinghetti's poetry provide insight into the development of his style and thematic approach: *Endless Life: Selected Poems* and *These Are My Rivers: New & Selected*

Poems 1955-1993. Ferlinghetti chose selections from his eight books of poetry and work in progress, written over twenty-six years, for inclusion in *Endless Life.* The poems reflect the influences of E. E. Cummings, Kenneth Rexroth, and Kenneth Patchen and are concerned with contemporary themes, such as the anti-war and anti-nuclear movements. Some critics dismiss Ferlinghetti "as either sentimental or the literary entrepreneur of the Beat generation," notes John Trimbur in *Western American Literature,* labels he feels are unjustified. Trimbur maintains Ferlinghetti writes a "public poetry to challenge the guardians of the political and social status quo for the souls of his fellow citizens," while "risking absurdity" in doing so. In *World Literature Today,* J. Martone acknowledges that Ferlinghetti has produced heralded poetry but finds the poet's work stagnant. Martone writes, "Ferlinghetti never moves beyond—or out-grows—the techniques of [his] early poems, and his repertoire of devices (deliberately casual literary allusion, self-mockery, hyper-bole) becomes a bit tedious with repetition." However, Joel Oppenheimer praises Ferlinghetti in the *New York Times Book Review,* saying Ferlinghetti had "learned to write poems, in ways that those who see poetry as the province of the few and the educated had never imagined."

Ferlinghetti focuses on current political and sexual matters in *These Are My Rivers.* As Rochelle Ratner notes in *Library Journal,* the poems are experimental in technique, often lacking common poetic devices such as stanza breaks, and they appear in unusual ways on the page, "with short lines at the left margin or moving across the page as hand follows eye." Yet despite its visual effect, Ashley Brown says in *World Literature Today,* "Ferlinghetti writes in a very accessible idiom; he draws on pop culture and sports as much as the modern poets whom he celebrates." Ratner avers that "Ferlinghetti is the foremost chronicler of our times." Indeed, the collection shows "Ferlinghetti still speaking out against academic poetry just as he did when the Beat Movement began," remarks Varner in *Western American Literature.* He adds, "Ferlinghetti, always the poet of the topical now, still sees clearly the 1990s."

Drama also proved a fertile ground for Ferlinghetti. He carried his political philosophies and social criticisms into experimental plays, many of them short and surrealistic. In *Lawrence Ferlinghetti,* Smith contends that the writer's stint as an experimental dramatist "reflects his stronger attention to irrational and intuitive analogy as a means of suggesting the 'secret meaning' behind life's surface. Though the works are provocative, public, and oral, they are also more cosmic in reference, revealing a stronger influence from Buddhist philosophy." In *Dialogue in American Drama,* Ruby Cohn comments that the plays "are brief sardonic comments on our contemporary life-style. . . . The themes may perhaps be resolved into a single theme—the unfairness of industrial, consumer-oriented, establishment-dominated exis-tence—and the plays are arguments against submission to such existence."

In 1960 Ferlinghetti's sole novel, *Her,* was published. An autobiographical, experimental work that focuses on the narrator's pursuit of a woman, the novel received very little critical comment when it was published. According to Smith in *Dictionary of Literary Biography:* "[*Her*] is an avant-garde work that pits character and author in a battle with the subjective relativity of experience in a quest for ideals; a surrealistic encounter with the subconscious—filled with phallic symbols and prophetic visions of desire. At once existential, absurd, symbolic, expressionistic, cinematic and surrealistic in vision and form, *Her* is controlled, as

all of Ferlinghetti's work is, by a drive toward expanded consciousness." Smith concludes, "The book is truly a spirited, though somewhat self-mocking, projection of the optimistic goals the Beat and San Francisco poetry movements placed on a grand imaginative scale."

Ferlinghetti continues to operate the City Lights bookstore, and he travels frequently to give poetry readings. His paintings and drawings have been exhibited in San Francisco galleries; his plays have been performed in experimental theaters. Smith observes in the *Dictionary of Literary Biography* that Ferlinghetti's life and writing "stand as models of the existentially authentic and engaged. . . . His work exists as a vital challenge and a living presence to the contemporary artist, as an embodiment of the strong, anticool, compassionate commitment to life in an absurd time." *New York Times Book Review* correspondent Joel Oppen-heimer cites Ferlinghetti's work for "a legitimate revisionism which is perhaps our best heritage from those raucous [Beat] days—the poet daring to see a different vision from that which the guardians of culture had allowed us." *New Pages* contributor John Gill concludes that reading the works of Lawrence Ferlinghetti "will make you feel good about poetry and about the world—no matter how mucked-up the world may be."

BIOGRAPHICAL/CRITICAL SOURCES:

BOOKS

Cherkovski, Neeli, *Ferlinghetti: A Biography,* Doubleday, 1979.
Cohn, Ruby, *Dialogue in American Drama,* Indiana University Press, 1971.
Contemporary Literary Criticism, Gale (Detroit), Volume 2, 1974; Volume 6, 1976; Volume 10, 1979; Volume 27, 1984.
Dictionary of Literary Biography, Volume 16: *The Beats: Literary Bohemians in Post-War America,* Gale, 1983.
Parkinson, Thomas, *Poets, Poems, Movements,* UMI Research Press, 1987.
Poetry Criticism, Volume 1, Gale, 1991.
Rexroth, Kenneth, *American Poetry in the Twentieth Century,* Herder & Herder, 1971.
Rexroth, *Assays,* New Directions, 1961.
Silesky, Barry, *Ferlinghetti: The Artist in His Time,* Warner Books, 1990.
Smith, Larry, *Lawrence Ferlinghetti: Poet-at-Large,* Southern Illinois University Press, 1983.
Sutton, Walter, *American Free Verse: The Modern Revolution in Poetry,* New Directions, 1973.

PERIODICALS

American Book Review, March/April, 1984.
American Poetry Review, September/October, 1977.
Arizona Quarterly, autumn, 1982.
Chicago Tribune, May 19, 1986; September 13, 1988.
Chicago Tribune Book World, February 28, 1982.
Critique: Studies in Modern Fiction, Volume 19, number 3, 1978.
Georgia Review, winter, 1989.
Library Journal, November 15, 1960; October 1, 1993, p. 98.
Life, September 9, 1957.
Listener, February 1, 1968.
Los Angeles Times, July 20, 1969; March 18, 1980; September 27, 1985.
Los Angeles Times Book Review, August 24, 1980; October 19, 1980; March 24, 1985; September 4, 1988.
Midwest Quarterly, autumn, 1974.
Minnesota Review, July, 1961.
Nation, October 11, 1958.

New Pages, spring/summer, 1985.

New York Times, April 14, 1960; April 15, 1960; April 16, 1960; April 17, 1960; February 6, 1967; February 27, 1967; September 13, 1970.

New York Times Book Review, September 2, 1956; September 7, 1958; April 29, 1962; July 21, 1968; September 8, 1968; September 21, 1980; November 1, 1981; November 6, 1988; November 6, 1994.

Observer, November 1, 1959; April 9, 1967.

Parnassus: Poetry in Review, spring/summer, 1974.

Poetry, November, 1958; July, 1964; May, 1966.

Prairie Schooner, fall, 1974; summer, 1978.

Publishers Weekly, September 26, 1994, p. 59; March 31, 1997.

Punch, April 19, 1967.

San Francisco Chronicle, March 5, 1961.

San Francisco Review of Books, September, 1977.

Saturday Review, October 5, 1957; September 4, 1965.

Sewanee Review, fall, 1974.

Sunday Times (London), June 20, 1965.

Times (London), October 27, 1968.

Times Literary Supplement, April 27, 1967; November 25, 1988.

Virginia Quarterly Review, autumn, 1969; spring, 1974.

Washington Post Book World, August 2, 1981.

West Coast Review, winter, 1981.

Western American Literature, spring, 1982, p. 79; winter, 1995, p. 372.

World Literature Today, summer, 1977; spring, 1982, p. 348; autumn, 1994, p. 815.

*   *   *

FERRE, Rosario 1942-

PERSONAL: Born July 28, 1942, in Ponce, Puerto Rico; daughter of Luis A. (an engineer and governor of Puerto Rico from 1968 to 1972) and Lorenza Ramirez Ferre; married Benigno Trigo (a merchant), 1960 (divorced); children: Rosario, Benigno, Luis. *Education:* University of Puerto Rico, M.A.; University of Maryland, Ph.D., 1986. *Religion:* Catholic.

ADDRESSES: Agent—Tomas Colchie, 5 rue de la Villette, Paris, France 75019.

CAREER: Writer. Founder and director of *Zona de carga y descarga,* a Latin American journal devoted to new Puerto Rican literature.

AWARDS, HONORS: National Book Award nomination, 1996, for *The House on the Lagoon.*

WRITINGS:

Papeles de Pandora (title means "Pandora's Roles"), Joaquin Mortiz (Mexico City), 1976, translation by the author published as *The Youngest Doll,* University of Nebraska Press (Lincoln, NE), 1991.

El medio pollito: Siete cuentos infantiles (title means "The Half Chicken"; children's stories), Ediciones Huracan (Rio Piedras, Puerto Rico), 1976.

La muneca menor/The Youngest Doll (bilingual edition), illustrations by Antonio Martorell, Ediciones Huracan, 1980.

Sitio a Eros: Trece ensayos literarios (title means "Eros Besieged"), Joaquin Mortiz, 1980, translation by Ferre and Diana L. Velez published as "The Writer's Kitchen" in *Lives on the Line: The Testimony of Contemporary Latin American*

Authors, edited by Doris Meyer, University of California Press (Berkeley, CA), 1988.

Los cuentos de Juan Bobo (title means "The Tales of Juan Bobo"; children's stories), Ediciones Huracan, 1980.

La mona que le pisaron la cola (title means "The Monkey Whose Tail Got Stepped On"; children's stories), Ediciones Huracan, 1981.

Fabulas de la garza desangrada (title means "Fables of a Bleeding Crane"), Joaquin Mortiz, 1982.

La caja de cristal, La Maquina de Escribir (Mexico), 1982.

Maldito amor (title means "Cursed Love"), Joaquin Mortiz, 1986, revised and translated by Ferre and published as *Sweet Diamond Dust* (see also below), Ballantine (New York City), 1988.

El acomodor: Una lectura fantastica de Felisberto Hernandez, Fondo de Cultura Economica, 1986.

Sonatinas, Ediciones Huracan, 1989.

El arbol y sus sombras, Fondo de Cultura (Mexico), 1989.

El coloquio de las perras, Cultural (San Juan, Puerto Rico), 1990, selections translated by the author and published as "On Destiny, Language, and Translation; or, Ophelia Adrift in the C & O Canal," in *The Youngest Doll,* 1991.

El cucarachita Martina, Ediciones Huracan, 1990.

Cortazar, Literal (Washington, DC), 1991.

Las dos Venecias (title means "The Two Venices"), Joaquin Mortiz, 1992.

Memorias de Ponce: Autobiografia de Luis A. Ferre, Editorial Norma (Barcelona, Spain), 1992.

La batalla de las virgenes, Editorial de la Universidad de Puerto Rico (San Juan, Puerto Rico), 1993.

The House on the Lagoon, Farrar, Straus (New York City), 1995.

Sweet Diamond Dust and Other Stories, Plume (New York City), 1996.

Eccentric Neighborhoods, Farrar Straus, 1998.

CONTRIBUTOR

Teresa Mindez-Faith, editor, *Contextos: Literarios hispanoamericanos,* Holt (New York City), 1985.

Anthology of Contemporary Latin American Literature, 1960-1984, Fairleigh Dickinson University Press, 1986.

Reclaiming Medusa: Short Stories by Contemporary Puerto Rican Women, Spinsters Aunt Lute (San Francisco, CA), 1988.

Marie-Lisa Gazarian Gautier, editor, *Interviews with Latin American Writers,* Dalkey Archive Press, 1989.

Some of Ferre's writings have also been anthologized in *Ritos de iniciacion: Tres novelas cortas de Hispanoamerica,* a textbook for intermediate and advanced students of college Spanish, by Grinor Rojo, and *Anthology of Women Poets.*

SIDELIGHTS: "Rosario Ferre," writes *Dictionary of Literary Biography* contributor Carmen S. Rivera, "has become the 'translator' of the reality of Puerto Rican women, opening the doors for the feminist movement on the island. By combining classical mythology with indigenous folktales that usurp the traditional actions of female characters, Ferre has interpreted, translated, and rewritten a more active and satisfying myth of Puerto Rican women." Ferre—the daughter of a former governor of Puerto Rico—writes about politics (she favors Puerto Rican independence), about literature, and about the status of women in modern Puerto Rican society. A former student of Angel Rama and Mario Vargas Llosa, she often utilizes magic realist techniques to communicate her points. "Many critics believe that with the publication of her first book," Rivera continues, ". . . Ferre began the feminist movement in Puerto Rico and became, if not its only voice, one of its most resonant and forceful spokespersons."

Chronologically, Ferre's first work was the short story collection *Papeles de Pandora.* Its original Spanish-language version was published in Mexico in 1976, but it was not until 1991 that an English-language translation by the author became available. "Defiant magic feminism challenges all our conventional notions of time, place, matter and identity in Rosario Ferre's spectacular new book, *The Youngest Doll,*" declares Patricia Hart in the *Nation. New York Times Book Review* contributor Cathy A. Colman states, "Ms. Ferre . . . writes with an irony that cloaks anger about the oppression and danger inherent in being either a protected upper-class woman or a marginalized working-class woman caught in Puerto Rico's patriarchal society." In "Sleeping Beauty," for example, a young woman's desire to become a dancer is railroaded by her family, who wants her to marry an aristocratic young man. The protagonist of "The Poisoned Story" starts out as a Cinderella figure (she marries a sugarcane planter) but ends up playing the role of a wicked stepmother to his daughter. "From beginning to end . . . whether she is conceiving stories, translating them or providing commentary," Hart concludes, "Rosario Ferre shines, and it is high time for English-speaking readers to bask in her light."

Ferre's first work to be translated into English was *Sweet Diamond Dust,* a short novel telling the stories of influential Puerto Rican women in different time periods. "Ferre parodies novels about the land, a popular genre during the first half of the century, as she sets out to rewrite Puerto Rican history from a woman's perspective," Rivera declares. "She describes how the island (*isla* is a female noun in Spanish) is oppressed by the government and American businesses—both of which are rendered as masculine in Spanish—while drawing parallels to the situation of women." Reviewer Alan Cheuse, writing in the *Chicago Tribune,* called Ferre "one of the most engaging young Latin American fiction writers at work today," and added, "Ferre shows off her linguistic talent as well as her inventiveness by giving us her own English version of the book."

The House on the Lagoon was Ferre's first work composed in English and was nominated for the National Book Award in 1996. "Most of this novel," declares a *Publishers Weekly* reviewer, "is comprised of . . . semi-fictionalized family history." The book tells of a Puerto Rican couple, Quintin Mendizabal and Isabel Monfort, who come into conflict over politics (she favors independence for the island, he favors close ties with the United States), their attitudes (he believes in traditional women's roles, she favors feminism) and the history she is writing, which includes stories about her husband's family. The family's black servant Petra Aviles also plays a role in the family dynamic. "The novel's conclusion affirms in the strongest terms the necessity of interracial alliances, both sexual and familial, to the future of a Puerto Rican community," writes Judith Grossman in the *Women's Review of Books.* "Ferre dramatizes the issue of who gets to write history," states the *Publishers Weekly* contributor, "gracefully incorporating it into a compelling panorama of Puerto Rican experience that is rich in history, drama and memorable characters." "*The House on the Lagoon,*" Grossman concludes, "gives us a performance of great accomplishment and wit, and the sense of a world held in measured but deeply affectionate memory."

Ferre followed the successful *House on the Lagoon* with 1998's *Eccentric Neighborhoods,* her second book in English. *Eccentric Neighborhoods* tells the story of modern Puerto Rican history

through the family heritage of its narrator, Elvira Vernet, following the two main branches of her maternal ancestors in order to illustrate the conflicts and contradictions of Puerto Rican society. *Time*'s Walter Kirn described Ferre's project as "a panoramic landscape dominated by two great family trees, both with deep roots and broad, overlapping branches." On one side, Elvira descends from the passive women of a privileged family made rich by its sugar plantations, on the other, from ambitious men who prosper as commercial careerists and are participants in the struggle for Puerto Rican independence. Through Elvira's family, Ferre draws broad outlines of the gender, class, and political strife that have defined modern Puerto Rico. Critics lauded this ambitious goal but tended to agree that Ferre's dense network of characters and events overwhelmed her purpose. A *Kirkus Reviews* writer opined that "it's difficult to absorb all the particulars of Ferre's crowded narrative and to distinguish among her many characters and their convoluted relationships." Mark Childress of the *New York Times* made a similar observation that "the more dramatic of her stories keep the narrative rolling along, but there are simply too many of them." The *Kirkus Reviews* writer nevertheless evaluated *Eccentric Neighborhoods* as the "most demanding of [Ferre's] novels so far and probably her best." Childress commented that though Ferre may fall short of her lofty goal, "we can still admire her lovely flow of language, the wit and intelligence she brings to the task."

BIOGRAPHICAL/CRITICAL SOURCES:

BOOKS

Dictionary of Literary Biography, Volume 145: *Modern Latin American Fiction Writers, Second Series,* Gale (Detroit), 1994.
Hintz, Suzanne S., *Rosario Ferre: A Search for Identity,* P. Lang (New York City), 1995.

PERIODICALS

Chicago Tribune, January 13, 1989.
Kirkus Reviews, December 1, 1997.
Library Journal, August, 1995, p. 115.
Nation, May 6, 1991, pp. 597-98.
New York Times Book Review, March 24, 1991, p. 24; February 22, 1998.
Publishers Weekly, July 3, 1995, p. 47.
Time, March 16, 1998, p. 80.
Women's Review of Books, February, 1996, p. 5.

*   *   *

FIEDLER, Leslie A(aron) 1917-

PERSONAL: Born March 8, 1917, in Newark, NJ; son of Jacob J. (a pharmacist) and Lillian (Rosenstrauch) Fiedler; married Margaret Ann Shipley, October 6, 1939 (divorced, 1973); married Sally Andersen, February, 1973; children: (first marriage) Kurt, Eric, Michael, Deborah, Jenny, Miriam; (second marriage; stepchildren) Soren Andersen, Eric Andersen. *Education:* New York University, B.A., 1938; University of Wisconsin, M.A., 1939, Ph.D., 1941; Harvard University, postdoctoral study, 1946-47. *Religion:* Jewish.

ADDRESSES: Home—154 Morris Ave., Buffalo, NY 14214. *Office*—Department of English, State University of New York at Buffalo, Buffalo, NY 14260.

CAREER: Montana State University, Missoula, assistant professor, 1941-48, associate professor, 1948-52, professor of English, 1954-64, department chair and director of humanities courses, 1954-56; State University of New York at Buffalo, professor of English, 1964-72, Samuel L. Clemens Professor of Literature, 1972–. Fulbright fellow and lecturer, universities of Rome and Bologna (Italy), 1951-53, and University of Athens (Greece), 1961-62; junior fellow, School of Letters, Indiana University, 1953; resident fellow in creative writing and Gauss Lecturer, Princeton University, 1956-57; associate fellow, Calhoun College, Yale University, 1969. Visiting professor, University of Sussex (England), 1967-68, and University of Vincennes (France), 1971. Summer professor at New York University, Columbia University, University of Vermont, and Indiana University. Lecturer. National Book Awards judge, 1956 and 1972. *Military service:* U.S. Naval Reserve, 1942-46; Japanese interpreter; became lieutenant junior grade.

MEMBER: American Association of University Professors, Modern Language Association of America, English Institute, Dante Society of America, PEN, Phi Beta Kappa.

AWARDS, HONORS: Rockefeller fellow, Harvard University, 1946-47; Furioso poetry prize, 1951; *Kenyon Review* fellow in literary criticism, 1956-57; National Institute of Arts and Letters prize for excellence in creative writing, 1957; American Academy grant, 1957; American Council of Learned Societies grants-in-aid, 1960 and 1961; Guggenheim fellow, 1970-71; Alumni Award, New York University (Heights), 1985; Chancellor Charles P. Norton Medal, State University of New York at Buffalo, 1989; Hubbell Medal, Modern Language Association, 1994, for lifetime contribution to the study of American literature.

WRITINGS:

LITERARY CRITICISM

An End to Innocence: Essays on Culture and Politics, Beacon Press, 1955.
The Jew in the American Novel, Herzl Press, 1959, second edition, 1966.
Love and Death in the American Novel, Criterion, 1960, revised edition, Stein & Day, 1966, with afterword by the author, Anchor Books (New York City), 1992.
No! In Thunder: Essays on Myth and Literature, Beacon Press, 1960.
The Riddle of Shakespeare's Sonnets, Basic Books, 1962.
Waiting for the End, Stein & Day, 1964 (published in England as *Waiting for the End: The American Literary Scene from Hemingway to Baldwin,* J. Cape, 1965).
The Return of the Vanishing American, Stein & Day, 1968.
Collected Essays (includes *An End to Innocence* [also see above], *The Jew in the American Novel* [also see above], *No! In Thunder* [also see above], *Unfinished Business* [also see below], *To the Gentiles* [also see below], and *Cross the Border, Close the Gap* [also see below]), two volumes, Stein & Day, 1971.
The Stranger in Shakespeare, Stein & Day, 1972.
Unfinished Business, Stein & Day, 1972.
To the Gentiles, Stein & Day, 1972.
Cross the Border, Close the Gap, Stein & Day, 1972.
A Fiedler Reader, Stein & Day, 1977.
Freaks: Myths and Images of the Secret Self, Simon & Schuster, 1978.
The Inadvertent Epic: From Uncle Tom's Cabin to Roots, Simon & Schuster, 1980.

Olaf Stapledon, Oxford University Press, 1982.
What Was Literature? Class Culture and Mass Society, Simon & Schuster, 1982.
Tyranny of the Normal: Essays on Bioethics, Theology, & Myth, D.R. Goodine (Boston), 1996.

NOVELS

The Second Stone: A Love Story, Stein & Day, 1963.
Back to China, Stein & Day, 1965.
The Messengers Will Come No More, Stein & Day, 1974.

SHORT STORIES

Pull Down Vanity and Other Stories, Lippincott, 1962.
The Last Jew in America, Stein & Day, 1966.
Nude Croquet and Other Stories, Stein & Day, 1969.

EDITOR

The Art of the Essay, Crowell, 1958, revised edition, 1969.
(And author of introduction) *Walt Whitman: Selections from "Leaves of Grass,"* Dell, 1959.
(With Jacob Vinocur) *The Continuing Debate: Essays on Education,* St. Martin's, 1965.
(With Arthur Zeiger) *A Critical Anthology of American Literature,* Volume 1: *O Brave New World: American Literature From 1600 to 1840,* Dell, 1968.
(With J. W. Field) *Bernard Malamud and the Critics,* New York University Press, 1970.
In Dreams Awake: A Historical-Critical Anthology of Science Fiction, Dell, 1976.
(With Houston A. Baker Jr.) *English Literature: Opening Up the Canon,* Johns Hopkins Press, 1981.

Advisory editor, *Ramparts* and *Studies in Black Literature*; advisory editor in English, St. Martin's Press.

OTHER

(With others) *Negro and Jew: Encounter in America,* [New York], 1956.
Being Busted, Stein & Day, 1969.
Fiedler on the Roof: Essays on Literature and Jewish Identity, Godine (Boston), 1991.

Regular columnist for *American Judaism.* Contributor to periodicals, including *Kenyon Review, Partisan Review, Poetry, Commentary, New Republic,* and *Encounter.*

SIDELIGHTS: In his major critical work *Love and Death in the American Novel,* Leslie A. Fiedler examines American and European novels and claims that the principal difference lies in the way the themes of death and adult sexuality are treated. He believes that American novelists are not only obsessed with death but also are incapable of portraying adult heterosexual relationships. He writes, "American authors have shied away from permitting in their fiction the presence of any full-fledged mature women, giving us instead monsters of virtue or bitchery, symbols of the rejection or fear of sexuality."

Statements such as this one have divided Fiedler's audience into those who find him provocative and those who find him provoking. This polarity is apparent in the critical evaluation of *Love and Death in the American Novel.* In the *Spectator* Kingsley Amis praises the book as "witty, exasperating, energetic, penetrating" while in the *Guardian* Donald Davie declares it "a sustained fouling of the American nest." Granville Hicks, writing in the *Saturday Review,* describes the book as "a serious and impressively well-informed attempt to look at American fiction in a new way." On the other hand, a *Times Literary Supplement* reviewer believes that the book offers "under the guise of criticism . . . a spiritual autobiography: a confession of the impact upon [Fiedler] of 'the American Experience.'"

No! In Thunder received similar critical response. "There is something here to offend almost everyone," contends *Catholic World*'s S. P. Ryan. "Much of [the book] seems close to angry raving; but there are passages of sheer brilliance." *New York Herald Tribune*'s Perry Miller calls the book "a set of lively, witty, stimulating pieces" which have been marred by Fiedler's feeling "obliged . . . to make himself offensive to somebody or other." A *Kirkus* reviewer sums up the general opinion of *No! In Thunder*: "Fiedler's critical theories have generated a great deal of partisanship and no doubt this collection will prove as continuingly provocative and/or provoking."

Later summations of Fiedler's work generally accept his eccentricities and acknowledge his contribution to the field of literary criticism. "By now the objections to Fiedler's procedures are virtually standardized," remarks Thomas R. Edwards in the *Partisan Review*. "He can be careless about little accuracies . . . and silly with his analogies . . . and his habit of melodramatizing history will not be to everyone's taste. . . . Fiedler is an incorrigible rascal, and to forbid him his tricks would deprive us of the often brilliant insights he has up his sleeve."

In an article for *Literary Review*, Charles R. Larson describes Fiedler's method as "a frontal attack based on shock, entertainment . . . and the destruction of shibboleths and prejudices. . . . [His] criticism remains for the most part highly readable and almost uniformly fresh." Larson also believes that many critics have misunderstood Fiedler simply because they have insisted on taking him at face value: "Fiedler's work so frequently approaches the superlative that one would think that by now the critics would be catching on."

New Republic critic Jonathan Yardley observes that Fiedler, then in middle age with a substantial body of publications, "can no longer lay claim to the title of *enfant terrible* of American letters." As the dust jacket of Fiedler's novel *The Messengers Will Come No More* notes, *Love and Death in the American Novel* "is now being taught by the same people who were originally outraged by it." Yardley comments, "Even if he has moved perilously close to membership in the literary establishment Fiedler has shown little evidence of losing his refreshing talent for slaying dragons and tilting at windmills, his instinct for the jugular and the provocative."

Fiedler produced an incendiary attack on contemporary elitist culture with *What Was Literature? Class Culture and Mass Society*. His retrospective analysis of American fiction, including Harriet Beecher Stowe's *Uncle Tom's Cabin*, Margaret Mitchell's *Gone With the Wind* and Alex Haley's *Roots*, aims to distinguish the validity of popular culture versus high art. John McGowan summarizes Fiedler's position in a *Dictionary of Literary Biography* essay: "Fiedler now argues that high art, by following the path of elitism, lost contact with both its audience and the mythic energies that sustain art. Such 'minority literature' appeals only to a small, highly educated audience, and its prestige is maintained by educational institutions that subject students to a forced diet of books they would never read otherwise." In Fiedler's view, as Lennard J. Davis observes in the *Nation*, "The best TV shows and schlock novels are the ones that tap universal emotions—except in repressed, university-conditioned critics and academics."

In *Fiedler on the Roof: Essays on Literature and Jewish Identity*, the septuagenarian author offers his idiosyncratic personal views on topics surrounding the Holocaust, the Book of Job, Norman Mailer, James Joyce's Leopold Bloom character in *Ulysses*, and the Grail legend. "As the show-biz title suggests," writes *New York Times Book Review* contributor Morris Dickstein, "the critic himself takes the spotlight. . . . Whatever the topic at hand, the subject of this book is Leslie Fiedler." As Sanford Pinsker observes in the *Virginia Quarterly Review*, Fiedler draws attention to the achievements of postwar Jewish-American writers and laments what he considers the declining quality of this literature in recent decades. "In Fiedler's self-styled mythology," Pinsker remarks, "he is the 'last Jew'—as Indian, as shaman, as maverick, as archetypal bad boy."

Dickstein notes, "Leslie Fiedler's desire to shock, his ambivalence about being a Jew, a critic and an intellectual, has always galvanized his writing but also finally limited it." Reflecting on the Fiedler's considerable notoriety and influence, McGowan concludes, "Fiedler's continued desire to be provocative has led him to the margins of received thought again and again, and his work provides one final proof that examination of the excluded is both dangerous and fruitful."

BIOGRAPHICAL/CRITICAL SOURCES:

BOOKS

Amis, Kingsley, *What Became of Jane Austen? and Other Questions*, J. Cape, 1970, Harcourt Brace, 1971.
Contemporary Literary Criticism, Gale (Detroit), Volume 4, 1975; Volume 13, 1980; Volume 24, 1983.
Dictionary of Literary Biography, Gale, Volume 28: *Twentieth-Century American Jewish Fiction Writers*, 1984; Volume 67: *Modern American Critics since 1955*, 1988.
Marudanayagam, P., *Quest for Myth: Leslie Fiedler's Critical Theory and Practice*, Reliance Publishing (New Delhi, India), 1994.
Winchell, Mark Royden, *Leslie Fiedler*, edited by Warren French, Twayne, 1985.

PERIODICALS

Catholic World, December, 1960.
Chicago Sun-Times, May 17, 1978.
Chicago Tribune, February 12, 1978.
Commentary, June, 1991, p. 58.
Commonweal, December 9, 1960; January 6, 1967.
Georgia Review, fall, 1980.
Guardian, January 13, 1961.
Harper's, January, 1970; February, 1978.
Kirkus Reviews, January 15, 1960; September 15, 1960; June 1, 1996.
Literary Review, fall, 1970.
Los Angeles Times Book Review, November 31, 1982, p. 3; June 16, 1991, p. 6; October 13, 1996.
Nation, August 15, 1959; September 22, 1969; December 11, 1982, p. 628.
New Republic, December 5, 1960; May 22, 1965; November 9, 1974; December 20, 1982, p. 30.
Newsweek, August 2, 1971; January 9, 1984.
New York Herald Tribune, January 1, 1961.
New York Herald Tribune Book Review, April 10, 1960.
New York Review of Books, April 10, 1969.
New York Times, April 9, 1988; September 30, 1996.
New York Times Book Review, August 4, 1991, p. 3.
Partisan Review, fall, 1968.

Publishers Weekly, March 22, 1991, p. 64; June 28, 1991, p. 84;
  June 3, 1996, p. 67.
Saturday Review, July 2, 1960.
Spectator, January 13, 1961.
Time, April 18, 1960; February 20, 1978.
Times Literary Supplement, March 17, 1961; October 15, 1982;
  October 23, 1983.
Village Voice, December 25, 1969; January 30, 1978.
Village Voice Literary Supplement, November, 1982; October,
  1993.
Virginia Quarterly Review, spring, 1978; autumn, 1993.
Washington Post Book World, November 14, 1982; September 1,
  1991, p. 13.

*   *   *

FINK, William
See MENCKEN, H(enry) L(ouis)

*   *   *

FISHER, M(ary) F(rances) K(ennedy) 1908-1992
(Mary Frances Parrish; Victoria Berne, a joint pseudonym)

PERSONAL: Born July 3, 1908, in Albion, MI; died of Parkinson's disease, June 22, 1992, in Glen Ellen, CA; daughter of Rex Brenton (a newspaper editor and publisher) and Edith Oliver (Holbrook) Kennedy; married Alfred Young Fisher, 1929 (divorced, 1938); married Dillwyn Parrish (a painter), 1940 (died, 1942); married Donald Friede (a literary agent), 1945 (divorced, 1951); children: (third marriage) Anna Kennedy Friede Maginnis, Kennedy Wright. *Education:* Attended Illinois College, Occidental College, University of California, Los Angeles, and University of Dijon, 1929-32.

CAREER: Writer, 1934-92.

MEMBER: American Academy of Arts and Letters.

AWARDS, HONORS: California Literature Silver Medal award, 1970, for *With Bold Knife and Fork*; Robert Kirsch Award, *Los Angeles Times,* 1984, for a body of work by an author from the West or featuring the West.

WRITINGS:

(With husband, Dillwyn Parrish, under joint pseudonym Victoria
  Berne) *Touch and Go* (novel), Harper, 1939.
Here Let Us Feast: A Book of Banquets, Viking, 1946, revised
  edition, North Point Press, 1986.
Not Now but Now (novel), Viking, 1947.
An Alphabet for Gourmets (also see below), Viking, 1949.
(Editor and translator) Jean Anthelme Brillat-Savarin, *The Physiology of Taste,* Limited Editions Club, 1949, published as *M. F. K. Fisher's Translation of The Physiology of Taste, or, Meditations on Transcendental Gastronomy,* North Point Press, 1986.
The Art of Eating: The Collected Gastronomical Works of M. F. K. Fisher (contains *Serve It Forth, Consider the Oyster, How to Cook a Wolf, The Gastronomical Me,* and *An Alphabet for Gourmets*), World Publishing, 1954, reprinted as *The Art of Eating, Five Gastronomical Works,* Vintage, 1976.
A Cordial Water: A Garland of Odd and Old Recipes to Assuage the Ills of Man or Beast, Little, Brown, 1961.

The Story of Wine in California, University of California Press,
  1962.
Maps of Another Town: A Memoir of Provence (also see below),
  Little, Brown, 1964.
The Cooking of Provincial France, Time-Life, 1968.
With Bold Knife and Fork, Putnam, 1969.
Among Friends, Knopf, 1971.
A Considerable Town (also see below), Knopf, 1978.
(With Lynn Newberry) *The Food Book* (juvenile), Goodheart-
  Willcox, 1981.
As They Were, Knopf, 1983.
Two Towns in Provence (contains *Maps of Another Town* and *A Considerable Town*) Vintage, 1983.
Sister Age, Knopf, 1983.
Spirits of the Valley, Grenfell Press, 1985.
Fine Preserving: M. F. K. Fisher's Annotated Edition of Catherine Plagemann's Cookbook, illustrated by Earl Thollander, Aris Books, 1986.
Dubious Honors, North Point Press, 1988.
The Boss Dog, North Point Press, 1991.
Long Ago in France: The Years in Dijon, Prentice-Hall, 1991.
Conversations with M. F. K. Fisher, edited by David Lazar, University Press of Mississippi, 1992.
To Begin Again: Stories and Memoirs, 1908-1929, Pantheon, 1992.
Stay Me, Oh Comfort Me: Journals and Stories, 1933-1945, Pantheon, 1993.
M. F. K. Fisher: A Life in Letters: Correspondence 1929-1991, compiled by Norah K. Barr, Patrick Moran, and Marsha Moran, Counterpoint, 1997.

UNDER NAME MARY FRANCES PARRISH

Serve It Forth, Harper, 1937.
Consider the Oyster, Duell, Sloan & Pearce, 1941.
How to Cook a Wolf, Duell, Sloan & Pearce, 1942, revised edition, 1951.
The Gastronomical Me, Duell, Sloan & Pearce, 1943.

SIDELIGHTS: "It seems to me that our three basic needs, for food, and security and love, are so mixed and mingled and entwined that we cannot straightly think of one without the others, so it happens that when I write of hunger, I am really writing about love and the hunger for it, and warmth and the love of it and the hunger for it." These words from M. F. K. Fisher's 1943 book, *The Gastronomical Me,* summarize the philosophy she presented in numerous works. Although Fisher was often called a "food writer," her books were only superficially concerned with food and were more about remembering and savoring the details of life and relationships.

Raised primarily in Whittier, California, a Quaker community that shunned her Protestant family, the young Fisher enjoyed cooking meals for her family. Encouraged in literary pursuits by academically inclined parents, Fisher combined her favorite pastimes and began writing about cooking as early as 1929 when she moved to Dijon, France, with her first husband, Alfred Fisher. By 1938 she had settled in Vevey, Switzerland, with her second husband, the artist Dillwyn Parrish. Guests to their country home frequently included artists and writers. After Parrish's death in 1942, Fisher lived for a time in Hollywood where she worked as a screenwriter and served as a model for Man Ray.

Beginning with *Serve It Forth,* a combination cookbook and storybook published in 1937, Fisher developed her world view as seen from the dining room table. Stories of the preparation and celebration of delicacies from ancient times to the present abound, along with Fisher's statement that the most unfortunate are those who "never taste because they are stupid, or, more often, because they have never been taught to search for differentiations of flavour."

The publication of *The Art of Eating* in 1954 was the culmination of Fisher's early career. A compendium of her first five food-related books, it chronicles her experience of being young and naive in Europe during the 1930s and 1940s; "at a time when only the very rich or the very bohemian knew the fleshpots of Europe in depth, she shared with American readers her pleasure in French gastronomic voluptuousness," wrote Victoria Glendinning in the *New York Times Book Review.* Fisher's wit and practicality are revealed in such passages as the one from *How to Cook a Wolf,* in which she suggests that "when the wolf is at the door one should invite him and have him for dinner," quoted Molly O'Neill in the *New York Times.* Written during World War II when food shortages were common, the book offers suggestions on how to survive on rations and basics in difficult times, beginning with the task of boiling water. Stacey D'Erasmo, writing in the *Voice Literary Supplement,* summarized Fisher's tone in these books as "flirtatious but strict—to be a gourmet, one must be extremely brave and resourceful, unafraid to look at the slimy guts and sexual ambiguities of the natural world."

Because her subject matter was considered frivolous, Fisher often maintained, she was dismissed by critics for years. This sentiment was reinforced by Raymond Sokolov of the *New York Times Book Review,* who claimed that "in a properly run culture, Mary Frances Kennedy Fisher would be recognized as one of the great writers this country has produced in this century." Fisher made no effort to conceal the autobiographical nature of her writings, revealing to readers details of her upbringing in California and the early marriage that took her to Dijon, where she first became a serious gourmand. Later books include stories of her second and third husbands, accounts of traveling through France with two young daughters, and reflections on living in the wine region of California—in all of these cases using food as a metaphor for the joys and tribulations of life. Passages about heating tangerines on a radiator at the dawn of World War II or the appropriateness of oysters in various social situations are often cited as examples of Fisher's recollections on how food provides more than nourishment.

Fisher reconsidered her early years in Europe in *Long Ago in France: The Years in Dijon.* It was a place, Fisher recalled, where "I started to grow up, to study, to make love, to eat and drink, to be me and not what I was expected to be." In Fisher's accounts of temperamental landladies, dingy apartments, and comforting cafes, "her exquisite perception seems also to co-exist comfortably with a Rabelaisian coarseness," wrote Joseph Coates in the Chicago *Tribune Books.* Caroline Moorehead of the *Times Literary Supplement* characterized the memoir as a reminiscence "in loving and nostalgic detail, [of] the life of a small French provincial town between the wars, when its inhabitants lived simply, ate well, and gossiped." One of Fisher's most enduring works from this period as well as one of her personal favorites is the translation of *The Physiology of Taste,* written in 1825 by French philosopher Jean Anthelme Brillat-Savarin. Enveloped in her own comments and observances of food, the work became "as much a contemporary American commentary as it is French and classic," wrote Jeannette Ferrary in the *New York Times Book Review.*

Although she co-wrote a romance novel with her second husband in 1939, Fisher's only other novel was *Not Now but Now,* originally published in 1947. The novel's time-traveling heroine, Jennie, who appears in four separate episodes, has brought comparisons to Virginia Woolf's *Orlando.* A tale of illicit affairs with the familiar culinary details, the novel begins with Jennie entertaining four friends, each of whom she goes back in time and meets under different circumstances. "Jennie is a difficult hero, self-contained, manipulative, afraid of feeling; she arranges relationships that force her into a corner and she runs away, to arrive in another era, on another train," summarized Jeff Weinstein in the *Village Voice.*

Critics did not receive the book as warmly as Fisher's more autobiographical writings. Noting that the author was prompted to write the book by two of the men in her life, *Nation* writer Blair T. Birmelin remarked that "one is reminded of Scheherazade spinning her tales on command." Iris Barry, writing in *New York Herald Tribune Weekly,* admitted that the premise was "bold . . . [but] it does not entirely convince." A more complete verdict was offered by Weinstein: "Fisher apparently does not possess the gift for writing extended fiction. . . . [but she] does, however, have the gift for storytelling." Sokolov wrote that with the novel Fisher "misfired—with elegance." Conversely, Andrew Sinclair of the London *Times,* upon reviewing a reprint of the novel thirty-seven years after its first appearance, called it "a delight of refined wit and grace under no pressure."

In *As They Were,* a collection of essays published in 1983, Fisher shares vivid memories of her childhood, like the luxurious Saturday afternoon at boarding school she spent cooped up in her room eating hoarded chocolate bars. The essay "Two Kitchens in Provence" describes the simple, fly-filled French kitchens that she called home in the 1950s. In one reminiscence Fisher describes a trip home from the market: "Sometimes I would want [the driver] to go faster, for I could almost feel the food in the baskets swelling with juice, growing soft, splitting open in an explosive rush toward ripeness and disintegration." Criticism of Fisher's writing is prompted by her redundancy on certain topics; according to Carolyn See of the *Los Angeles Times*: "We are lectured once again on good red wines and perfect little lettuces, and you want to shriek." In addition, See commented that the people in Fisher's life seem like undifferentiated "cutouts," and that one never knows which husband she is referring to. But other critics admire this trait of Fisher's—"she had learned everything Hemingway and Colette had to teach her about literary control and about the importance of what is left out," wrote Sokolov.

In *Sister Age,* a book "about aging and ending and living and whatever else the process of human being is about," Fisher confronts the effects of growing old. The collection of short stories covers familiar territory with such stories as "The Oldest Man," an account of a hundred-year-old man with whom Fisher stayed in the French countryside with her two young daughters, and a character sketch of her landlady in Aix-en-Provence. Other stories incorporate supernatural elements and thus become more fictitious than what Fisher normally wrote. Though confronting the effects of time may seem natural for a writer in her mid-70s, Ann Hulbert of the *New Republic* noted that Fisher first approached the topic in *Serve It Forth,* when she advised "sparse but appreciative eating; [to] 'ease our body's last years by lightening its burden.'" "Remarkably few tears are shed in *Sister Age,*" wrote Patricia Blake in *Time,* "but those that fall linger in the memory." Commenting on the interactions of the main characters, often a woman and her young daughters, with the people they meet while traveling, Caroline Thompson of *Los Angeles Times Book Review* stated that "what goes unspoken here is enough to break any reader's heart." However, these subtleties prompted Kay Dick of the London *Times* to pronounce the collection full of "self-consciousness [and] a prevailing patronizing generalization, which I feel to be American."

Most critics consider *The Gastronomical Me* to be the pinnacle of Fisher's career. An accumulation of culinary tales from 1912 through 1941, the book contains vignettes of meals and memories from Fisher's childhood through the rising tension in Europe between the wars. In one passage, for example, Fisher reveals "the confusing stirrings of sexuality [that] are remembered through the trauma of eating an oyster for the first time at a boarding school banquet," summarized Patricia Storace in the *New York Review of Books,* "while senior girls danced with junior girls in an eerie atmosphere of social rigidity and repressed lust."

Fisher lived for many years on a farm in northern California, enjoying the surrounding vineyards and the foods of the region and continuing to write even after she was bedridden. She died on June 22, 1992, from Parkinson's disease. "Her genius has been her absolute insistence that life's small moments are the important ones," wrote Ruth Reichl in the *Los Angeles Times Book Review.* "She alone seems to have the silence, exile, and cunning a writer would need to stalk people in their kitchens," added D'Erasmo.

BIOGRAPHICAL/CRITICAL SOURCES:

BOOKS

Contemporary Literary Criticism, Volume 76, Gale, 1993.
Ferrary, Jeannette, *Between Friends: M. F. K. Fisher and Me,* Atlantic Monthly Press, 1991.
Fussell, Betty, *Masters of American Cookery—M. F. K. Fisher, James Andrews Beard, Raymond Craig Claiborne, Julia McWilliams Child,* Times Books, 1983.
Lazar, David, editor, *Conversations with M. F. K. Fisher,* University Press of Mississippi, 1992.

PERIODICALS

Los Angeles Times, June 14, 1982.
Los Angeles Times Book Review, November 20, 1983, p. 3; June 6, 1991, pp. H1, H9; August 28, 1993, p. 11.
Nation, December 11, 1982, pp. 632, 634.
New Republic, June 6, 1983, pp. 36-37.
New Yorker, August 16, 1982, pp. 87-89.
New York Herald Tribune Weekly, August 17, 1947, p. 8.
New York Review of Books, December 7, 1989, pp. 42-45.
New York Times, June 24, 1992, p. A18.
New York Times Book Review, June 6, 1982, p. 19; May 31, 1987; June 9, 1991, p. 15.
New York Times Magazine, October 27, 1985.
Time, May 16, 1983.
Times (London), January 12, 1984; January 19, 1984.
Times Literary Supplement, June 28, 1991, p. 24.
Tribune Books (Chicago), March 10, 1991, p. 6.
Village Voice, January 11, 1983, p. 41.
Voice Literary Supplement, April, 1993, pp. 10-11.
Washington Post Book World, June 13, 1982; April 28, 1991, pp. 4-5.

*   *   *

FISKE, Tarleton
See BLOCH, Robert (Albert)

FITCH, Clarke
See SINCLAIR, Upton (Beall)

*   *   *

FITCH, John IV
See CORMIER, Robert (Edmund)

*   *   *

FITZGERALD, Captain Hugh
See BAUM, L(yman) Frank

*   *   *

FITZGERALD, F(rancis) Scott (Key) 1896-1940

PERSONAL: Born September 24, 1896, in St. Paul, MN; died of a heart attack, December 21, 1940, in Hollywood, CA; buried in Rockville Union Cemetery, Rockville, MD; reburied near his parents in St. Mary's Cemetery, Rockville, MD, in 1975; son of Edward (in business) and Mary (an heiress; maiden name, McQuillan) Fitzgerald; married Zelda Sayre (an artist, dancer, and writer), April 3, 1920 (died March 10, 1948); children: Frances Scott Fitzgerald Smith (formerly Mrs. Samuel J. Lanahan). *Education:* Attended Princeton University, 1913-17. *Religion:* Catholic.

CAREER: Novelist, poet, playwright, screenwriter, and author of short stories. Worked briefly as a copywriter at Barron Collier Advertising Agency in New York, 1919; worked sporadically as a screenwriter at motion picture studios in Los Angeles, CA, including Metro-Goldwyn-Mayer and United Artists, 1927-40, contributing to film scripts such as "Winter Carnival," "The Women," and "Gone With the Wind," all 1939. *Military service:* U.S. Army, 1917-19; became second lieutenant.

WRITINGS:

NOVELS

This Side of Paradise, Scribner, 1920.
The Beautiful and Damned (first published serially in *Metropolitan Magazine,* September, 1921-March, 1922), revised edition of original text, Scribner, 1922.
The Great Gatsby, Scribner, 1925, Chelsea House, 1986.
Tender Is the Night: A Romance, decorations by Edward Shenton, Scribner, 1934, new edition with Fitzgerald's final revisions, preface by Malcolm Cowley, 1951, revised from original text as *Tender Is the Night,* Scribner, 1960, revised edition published in England as *Tender Is the Night,* with Fitzgerald's final revisions, preface by Cowley, Grey Walls Press, 1953.
The Last Tycoon, first published as *The Last Tycoon: An Unfinished Novel, Together with "The Great Gatsby" and Selected Stories* (includes "Notes for *The Last Tycoon*"), with additional notes by Fitzgerald, foreword by Edmund Wilson, Scribner, 1941, published as *The Last Tycoon: An Unfinished Novel,* with notes by Fitzgerald, foreword by Wilson, Scribner, 1958, reprinted as *The Last Tycoon,* 1983, reprinted as *The Love of the Last Tycoon: A Western,* 1994; published in England as *The Last Tycoon: An Unfinished Novel,* Grey Walls Press, 1949, as *The Last Tycoon,* Penguin, 1960, 1977,

reprinted with notes by Fitzgerald, foreword by Wilson, 1965, 1974.

SHORT STORIES

Flappers and Philosophers (includes "The Offshore Pirate," "The Ice Palace", "Head and Shoulders", and "Bernice Bobs Her Hair"), Scribner, 1920, reprinted, with introduction by Arthur Mizener, 1959, 1972.

Tales of the Jazz Age (contains "The Camel's Back," "May Day," and "The Diamond as Big as the Ritz"), Scribner, 1922, revised as *Six Tales of the Jazz Age, and Other Stories,* introduction by Frances Fitzgerald Lanahan, Scribner, 1960.

All the Sad Young Men (includes "The Rich Boy," "Winter Dreams," and "Absolution"), Scribner, 1926.

Taps at Reveille (includes "Crazy Sunday" and "Babylon Revisited"), Scribner, 1935.

The Pat Hobby Stories, introduction by Arnold Gingrich, Scribner, 1962.

The Basil and Josephine Stories (includes "The Scandal Detectives"), edited with an introduction by Jackson R. Bryer and John Kuehl, Scribner, 1973.

(With wife, Zelda Fitzgerald) *Bits of Paradise: Twenty-one Uncollected Stories by F. Scott and Zelda Fitzgerald,* selected by Matthew J. Bruccoli, with the assistance of Scottie Fitzgerald Smith, Scribner, 1973.

The Price Was High: The Last Uncollected Stories of F. Scott Fitzgerald (contains "Myra Meets His Family" and "The Pusher-in-the-Face"), edited by Bruccoli, Harcourt, 1979.

The Fantasy and Mystery Stories of F. Scott Fitzgerald, edited by Peter Haining, Robert Hale, 1991.

PLAYS

(And lyricist) *Fie! Fie! Fi-Fi!* (two-act musical comedy; first produced in Princeton, NJ, at Princeton University, December 19, 1914), published in pamphlet form for distribution at performances (extent of Fitzgerald's authorship disputed in some sources [also see below]).

(And lyricist) *The Evil Eye* (two-act musical comedy; first produced at Princeton University, December 18, 1915), published in pamphlet form for performances (extent of Fitzgerald's authorship disputed in some sources [also see below]).

(And lyricist) *Safety First* (two-act musical comedy; first produced at Princeton University, December 15, 1916), published in pamphlet form for performances (extent of Fitzgerald's authorship disputed in some sources [also see below]).

The Vegetable; or, From President to Postman (first produced at Apollo Theatre, Atlantic City, November 19, 1923), Scribner, 1923, revised and enlarged edition, with previously unpublished scenes and corrections, introduction by Charles Scribner III, Scribner, 1976.

F. Scott Fitzgerald's St. Paul Plays, 1911-1914, edited with an introduction by Alan Margolies, Princeton University Library, 1978.

CORRESPONDENCE

The Letters of F. Scott Fitzgerald, edited by Andrew Turnbull, Scribner, 1963.

Scott Fitzgerald: Letters to His Daughter, edited by Turnbull, introduction by Frances Fitzgerald Lanahan, Scribner, 1965.

Dear Scott, Dear Max: The Fitzgerald-Perkins Correspondence, edited by Kuehl and Bryer, Scribner, 1971.

As Ever, Scott Fitz—: Letters Between F. Scott Fitzgerald and His Literary Agent, Harold Ober, 1919-1940, edited by Matthew J. Bruccoli, with Jennifer McCabe Atkinson, foreword by Scottie Fitzgerald Smith, Lippincott, 1972.

Correspondence of F. Scott Fitzgerald, edited by Bruccoli and Margaret M. Duggan, with Susan Walker, Random House, 1980.

Fitzgerald: A Life in Letters, edited by Bruccoli and Judith S. Baughman, Macmillan, 1994.

COLLECTIONS

The Crack-Up: With Other Uncollected Pieces, Note-Books, and Unpublished Letters (includes "The Crack-Up," "Handle With Care," and "Early Success"), edited by Edmund Wilson, J. Laughlin, 1945, published in England as *The Crack-Up, With Other Pieces and Stories,* Penguin, 1965.

The Portable F. Scott Fitzgerald (includes novels and short stories), selected by Dorothy Parker, introduction by John O'Hara, Viking, 1945, reprinted as *The Indispensable F. Scott Fitzgerald,* Book Society, 1949, 1951.

The Diamond as Big as the Ritz, and Other Stories, first published in limited edition, with an introduction by Louis Untermeyer, for the U.S. Armed Services, 1946, Penguin, 1962.

The Stories of F. Scott Fitzgerald: A Selection of Twenty-eight Stories (includes "Three Hours Between Planes"), introduction by Malcolm Cowley, Scribner, 1951.

Three Novels: The Great Gatsby, With an Introduction by Malcolm Cowley. Tender Is the Night, With the Author's Final Revisions; Edited by Malcolm Cowley. The Last Tycoon, an Unfinished Novel; Edited by Edmund Wilson, Scribner, 1953.

Afternoon of an Author: A Selection of Uncollected Stories and Essays (includes "How to Live on $36,000 a Year"), introduction and notes by Mizener, Princeton University Library, 1957, Scribner, 1958.

The Bodley Head Scott Fitzgerald, six volumes, introduction by J. B. Priestley, Bodley Head, 1958-63.

Babylon Revisited, and Other Stories, Scribner, 1960.

The Stories of F. Scott Fitzgerald, five volumes, Penguin, 1962-68.

The Fitzgerald Reader, edited by Mizener, Scribner, 1963.

The Apprentice Fiction of F. Scott Fitzgerald, edited with an introduction by Kuehl, Rutgers University Press, 1965.

F. Scott Fitzgerald in His Own Time: A Miscellany, edited by Bruccoli and Bryer, Kent State University Press, 1971.

Bernice Bobs Her Hair and Other Stories, Signet (New York City), 1996.

F. Scott Fitzgerald: Selected Works, Gramercy (New York City), 1996.

F. Scott Fitzgerald: The Princeton Years, Cypress House Press, 1996.

OTHER

Let's Go Out and Play (radio script), first broadcast in New York City on WABC-Radio (CBS), October 3, 1935.

(With Edward E. Paramore, Jr.) *Three Comrades* (screenplay; based on English translation of novel of the same title by Erich Maria Remarque), Metro-Goldwyn-Mayer, 1938 (also see below).

Thoughtbook of Francis Scott Fitzgerald, With an Introduction by John R. Kuehl, Princeton University Library, 1965.

F. Scott Fitzgerald's Ledger: A Facsimile, introduction by Bruccoli, NCR/Microcard Editions, 1972.

The Great Gatsby: A Facsimile, edited with an introduction by Bruccoli, Microcard Editions Books, 1973.

F. Scott Fitzgerald's Screenplay for "Three Comrades," by Erich Maria Remarque (includes original version by Fitzgerald alone), edited with afterword by Bruccoli, Southern Illinois University Press, 1978.

The Notebooks of F. Scott Fitzgerald, edited by Bruccoli, Harcourt/Bruccoli Clark, 1978.

F. Scott Fitzgerald: Triangle Club Songs (cassette recording; songs from three plays produced at Princeton University), performed by After-Dinner Opera Co. of New York, Bruccoli Clark, 1979.

Poems, 1911-1940, edited by Bruccoli, foreword by James Dickey, Bruccoli Clark, 1981.

F. Scott Fitzgerald on Writing, edited by Larry W. Phillips, Scribner, 1985.

F. Scott Fitzgerald on Authorship, University of South Carolina Press (Columbia), 1996.

Author of unproduced screenplays, such as "Red-Headed Woman" and "Lipstick." Contributor to film scripts, among them "A Yank at Oxford," 1937; "Infidelity" and "Madame Curie," both 1938; "Winter Carnival," "The Women," and "Gone With the Wind," all 1939; and "Cosmopolitan," 1940.

MEDIA ADAPTATIONS: Writings adapted for film include "Head and Shoulders," adapted as *The Chorus Girl's Romance,* Metro Pictures, 1920; "Myra Meets His Family," adapted as *The Husband Hunter,* Fox Film Corp., 1920; *The Offshore Pirate,* Metro Pictures, 1921; *The Beautiful and Damned,* Warner Bros., 1922; "The Camel's Back," adapted as *Conductor 1492,* Warner Bros., 1924; *The Great Gatsby,* Players-Lasky-Paramount, 1926, Paramount, 1949 and 1974; "The Pusher-in-the-Face," adapted as a movie short, Paramount, 1929; "Babylon Revisited," adapted as *The Last Time I Saw Paris,* Metro-Goldwyn-Mayer, 1954; *Tender Is the Night,* Twentieth-Century Fox, 1962; and *The Last Tycoon,* Paramount, 1976. The 1924 Film Guild movie *Grit* was based on an original story by Fitzgerald.

Works adapted for stage include *The Great Gatsby,* first produced in New York City at the Ambassador Theatre, February 2, 1926, and produced as a ballet by the Pittsburgh Ballet Theater at State University of New York, State University College at Purchase, N.Y., March 31, 1989; "Three Hours Between Planes," adapted as a one-act play, 1958; and *This Side of Paradise,* adapted as an off-Broadway play, 1962.

SIDELIGHTS: Beginning early in his life, F. Scott Fitzgerald strove to become a great writer. In a 1944 essay, "Thoughts on Being Bibliographed," Edmund Wilson wrote that Fitzgerald told him soon after college, "I want to be one of the greatest writers who have ever lived, don't you?" Although today most college-level American literature survey courses usually include at least one of his works, during Fitzgerald's lifetime he was regarded mainly as a portrayer of the 1920s Jazz Age and of flaming youth, but not as one of this country's most important writers. And while close to fifty thousand copies of his first novel, *This Side of Paradise,* were printed in 1920 and 1921, he was never a best-selling novelist. Fewer than twenty-nine thousand copies of *The Great Gatsby* and some fifteen thousand copies of *Tender Is the Night* were published in the United States during Fitzgerald's lifetime. By the time of his death in 1940, very few copies of his books were being sold, and he was earning his living as a freelance film writer. Since then, however, Fitzgerald's popularity has increased dramatically.

Even at an early age, F. Scott Fitzgerald exhibited talent. At St. Paul Academy, he wrote stories for the school magazine and participated in dramatics. According to Andrew Turnbull in his biography *Scott Fitzgerald,* C. N. B. Wheeler—one of Fitzgerald's teachers at St. Paul Academy—said years later: "I helped him by encouraging his urge to write adventures. It was also his best work, he did not shine in his other subjects. He was inventive in all playlets we had and marked his course by his pieces for delivery before the school. . . . I imagined he would become an actor of the variety type, but he didn't. . . . It was his pride in his literary work that put him in his real bent."

From 1911 to 1913, Fitzgerald attended the Newman School in Hackensack, New Jersey, where he continued to write for various school publications. There he fell under the influence of Father Sigourney Fay, who was to be fictionalized as Monsignor Darcy in Fitzgerald's first novel, *This Side of Paradise.* In *Some Sort of Epic Grandeur,* Matthew J. Bruccoli explained that "Fay soon became Scott's surrogate father." Fay introduced Fitzgerald to Anglo-Irish writer Shane Leslie who, Fitzgerald later wrote in a review-essay titled "Homage to the Victorians" (1922), "came into my life as the most romantic figure I had ever known."

At this time Fitzgerald had other interests as well. He played on the Newman School football team, and he was admitted to Princeton University in 1913. But there were better and heavier candidates for the team, and he soon devoted most of his time to writing short stories, poems, plays, book reviews, and even jokes for the *Nassau Literary Magazine* and the humor magazine *Princeton Tiger.* These extracurricular activities impinged on his classroom work, however, and in January, 1916, Fitzgerald withdrew from Princeton because of low grades. He returned the following school year but never graduated. World War I intervened; he applied for a U.S. Army commission, and in October, 1917, he was appointed second lieutenant.

Fitzgerald's army career was a disappointment to him. He never served overseas and, as he later declared in "Early Success" (1937), spent two of his fifteen months' service as "the army's worst aide-de-camp." And yet, during this period he completed a draft of a novel, "The Romantic Egotist." In a January 10, 1918, letter, reprinted in *The Letters of F. Scott Fitzgerald,* he told Edmund Wilson that the work was the story of a young man's boyhood "from the San Francisco fire thru school, Princeton, to the end, where at twenty-one he writes his autobiography at the Princeton aviation school." Although the publishing house Charles Scribner's Sons did not accept his manuscript, he was encouraged to rewrite and resubmit it. Further, while stationed at Camp Sheridan near Montgomery, Alabama, he met and soon fell in love with the eighteen-year-old Zelda Sayre, daughter of Minnie Machen Sayre and Judge Anthony Dickinson Sayre of the Alabama Supreme Court.

Fitzgerald was discharged from the army in 1919 and subsequently worked for a short while at a New York advertising agency. Eventually he returned to St. Paul where he rewrote his novel, retitling it *This Side of Paradise.* In the letter of acceptance, collected in *Dear Scott, Dear Max,* Scribner editor Maxwell Perkins wrote Fitzgerald, "We are all for publishing your book. . . . I think you have improved it enormously. . . . It abounds in energy and life."

On publication *This Side of Paradise* was greeted enthusiastically. Harry Hansen wrote in the *Chicago Daily News* for March 31, 1920: "It is one of the few American novels extant. . . . Fitzgerald has taken a real American type—the male flapper of our best colleges—and written him down with startling verisimilitude. He has taken a slice of American life, part of the pie-crust.

Only a man on the inside could have done it." And critic H. L. Mencken in the August, 1920, *Smart Set* found the work "a truly amazing first novel—original in structure, extremely sophisticated in manner, and adorned with a brilliancy that is as rare in American writing as honesty is in American statecraft." Today, while one can understand the reaction at the time, *This Side of Paradise* is not considered one of Fitzgerald's best works. Bruccoli noted in *Some Sort of Epic Grandeur*: "Although *This Side of Paradise* now seems naive after sixty years, it was received in 1920 as an iconoclastic social document—even as a testament of revolt." Bruccoli went on to point out that what "was regarded as an experimental or innovative narrative because of the mixture of styles and the inclusion of plays and verse" was actually the result of "the circumstance that Fitzgerald did not yet know how to structure a novel."

This Side of Paradise was published on March 26, 1920, and Fitzgerald married Zelda Sayre the following week, on April 3. Meanwhile, he was publishing short stories, and in September, 1920, his first collection, *Flappers and Philosophers,* appeared. While Fitzgerald admitted that most of his short stories were written much more quickly and carelessly than his novels, many hold up well today. Of this first collection, two stories are probably most memorable: "The Ice Palace," the story of a Southern girl who finds herself unable to adjust to the cold North of her fiance and, after being trapped in an ice palace, returns home; and "Bernice Bobs Her Hair," about another young girl who gives in to the dares of her cousin and others and bobs her hair. While some of the critics praised the collection, for the most part the reviews reflected a feeling that the book was not up to the level of *This Side of Paradise.* William Huse, for example, in the September 24, 1920, *Chicago Evening Post* lamented that the book was "scarcely as satisfying," and Mencken in the December, 1920, *Smart Set* deemed it "a collection that shows both the very good and the very bad."

In March, 1922, Fitzgerald's next major work, *The Beautiful and Damned,* was published. This second novel, Fitzgerald's story of the disintegration of the lives of the once young and glamorous Anthony and Gloria Patch, was a much more carefully constructed novel than *This Side of Paradise.* Many of the book's reviewers, however, were disappointed. Louise Maunsell Field in the March 5, 1922, *New York Times Book Review,* for example, began her assessment by stating, "It would not be easy to find a more thoroughly depressing book than this new novel by F. Scott Fitzgerald." On the other hand, Mencken asserted in the *Smart Set* for April, 1922: "There are a hundred signs in it of serious purpose and unquestionable skill." Further, he compared it with Fitzgerald's previous novel and stated that Fitzgerald had "tried something much more difficult, and if the result is not a complete success, it is nevertheless near enough to success to be worthy of respect."

Then in September, 1922, Fitzgerald's second collection of short stories, *Tales of the Jazz Age*—which included the well-known fantasy "The Diamond as Big as the Ritz" as well as "May Day," a powerful tale of post-World War I days in New York City—was published. Much of the remainder, however, was not at all representative of Fitzgerald at his best. Jackson R. Bryer related in *Scott Fitzgerald: The Critical Reception* that the reviewers of the time "were, for the most part, charmed by its table of contents—in which the author humorously described each story and its genesis—but they found the collection itself uneven, although many applauded Fitzgerald's apparent shift away from stories about flappers into what he himself called his 'second manner.'"

And Bruccoli in *Some Sort of Epic Grandeur* assessed: "Despite the inclusion of two major stories, 'May Day' and 'Diamond,' the collection was a grab bag; Fitzgerald did not have enough good material for a volume and padded it with pieces that had been left out of *Flappers and Philosophers.*"

The Great Gatsby was a great advance over Fitzgerald's two earlier novels. The intricate pattern he mentioned to Perkins reveals itself in the book's time span from spring to fall of one year with the climax, the reunion between Jay Gatsby and Daisy Buchanan, taking place exactly in the center of the novel. And yet, as it moves forward in time, it also moves backward, as Fitzgerald makes the reader aware of events in Jay Gatsby's past. In addition, *The Great Gatsby* also marked progress in Fitzgerald's method of narration. In the novel all information is filtered through the narrator, Nick Carraway. To assist Nick, Fitzgerald employed in the character of Jordan Baker a device that writer Henry James had popularized—that of a confidante, a person whose major purpose is to bring information to the narrator. Sometimes, information in the novel is filtered through several people, a device previously used by writer Joseph Conrad. As a result of this technique, the reader does not know what is true and what isn't in the novel's tale of love and murder.

Fitzgerald's plot was equal to his method of storytelling. His story of the vulgar and yet romantic Jay Gatsby who attempts, through illicit means, to rewin the hand of the now married Daisy Buchanan, however, was only part of his story. Rich versus poor, old rich versus new rich, East versus West, and America when it was still new versus more recent times were just some of the novel's issues. Of Tom and Daisy Buchanan, representatives of the old rich, Fitzgerald wrote: "They were careless people, Tom and Daisy—they smashed up things and creatures and then retreated back into their money or their vast carelessness, or whatever it was that kept them together, and let other people clean up the mess they had made." But contrasting with the Buchanans and the evil East is the still innocent West with what Nick Carraway identified as its "thrilling returning trains of my youth, and the street lamps and sleigh bells in the frosty dark and the shadows of holly wreaths thrown by lighted windows on the snow." And contrasting with both of these symbols is the virgin past of the United States when the "vanished trees, the trees that had made way for Gatsby's house, had once pandered in whispers to the last and greatest of all human dreams."

While a few reviewers criticized the work (the headline in the April 12, 1925, *New York World* was "F. Scott Fitzgerald's Latest a Dud"), most recognized the advance in Fitzgerald's art. Fanny Butcher in the April 18, 1925, *Chicago Daily Tribune,* for example, wrote, "*The Great Gatsby* proves that Scott Fitzgerald is going to be a writer, and not just a man of one book." And Gilbert Seldes went even further when he wrote in *Dial* for August, 1925: "Fitzgerald has more than matured; he has mastered his talents and gone soaring in a beautiful flight, leaving behind him everything dubious and tricky in his earlier work, and leaving even farther behind all the men of his own generation and most of his elders." Many of Fitzgerald's peers agreed. Writer T. S. Eliot, in a letter to Fitzgerald that was later published in *The Crack-Up,* called the novel "the first step that American fiction has taken since Henry James."

After the completion of *The Great Gatsby* in 1925, Fitzgerald began his fourth novel. Completion, however, took some nine years of noncontinuous work with at least three major plot changes and many other revisions. During this period Fitzgerald's alcohol abuse worsened, while Zelda Fitzgerald's increasingly apparent mental illness eventually necessitated, starting in 1930, periods of hospitalization. Further, Fitzgerald was falling more and more into debt. All of these factors negatively affected his writing.

Nonetheless, in February, 1926, Fitzgerald's third collection of short stories, *All the Sad Young Men,* appeared. This volume included three of Fitzgerald's best and most popular stories, "Winter Dreams," originally published in the December, 1922, *Metropolitan Magazine*; "Absolution," published in *American Mercury* for June, 1924; and "The Rich Boy," published in January and February, 1926, issues of *Redbook* magazine. Critical reaction to *All the Sad Young Men* was far more favorable than that attracted by Fitzgerald's earlier short story collections. A reviewer in the May, 1926, *Bookman,* for example, wrote: "As F. Scott Fitzgerald continues to publish books, it becomes apparent that he is head and shoulders better than any writer of his generation. *All the Sad Young Men* contains several stories of compelling fineness, along with more conventional pieces of story telling that are sufficiently amusing with the old Fitzgerald talent."

In December, 1926, the Fitzgeralds returned to the United States, eventually living for a year in "Ellerslie," near Wilmington, Delaware. In January, 1927, Fitzgerald worked for two months in Hollywood on "Lipstick," a treatment for a silent film with a college setting for actress Constance Talmadge; but the treatment was judged unsatisfactory and the movie was never made. While in Hollywood, however, Fitzgerald met Metro-Goldwyn-Mayer (MGM) producer Irving Thalberg, who later served as the primary model for the hero of *The Last Tycoon*—Fitzgerald's final but unfinished novel. Also during this period he wrote, among other short stories, a series of eight tales based on his childhood in St. Paul, the adventures of young Basil Duke Lee. These were published in the *Saturday Evening Post,* beginning with "The Scandal Detectives" on April 28, 1928.

In April, 1934, Scribner published Fitzgerald's fourth novel, *Tender Is the Night,* the story of the deterioration of psychiatrist Richard Diver, who falls in love with and marries his patient Nicole Warren. Utilizing an international setting, the novel also reflects destructive impulses implicit in the United States. The wealthy Nicole, Fitzgerald wrote, "was the product of much ingenuity and toil. For her sake trains began their run at Chicago and traversed the round belly of the continent to California; chicle factories fumed and link belts grew link by link in factories; men mixed toothpaste in vats and drew mouthwash out of copper hogsheads; girls canned tomatoes quickly in August or worked rudely at the Five-and-Tens on Christmas Eve; half-breed Indians toiled on Brazilian coffee plantations and dreamers were muscled out of patent rights in new tractors."

Milton R. Stern in *The Golden Moment: The Novels of F. Scott Fitzgerald* noted that in this fourth novel Fitzgerald was continuing themes that he had touched on in his first two novels and had expressed even more clearly in *The Great Gatsby.* In *Tender Is the Night,* according to Stern, "the corrupt new world of soulless wealth becomes identified with the new America as the new America spreads over the world, is internationalized, and loses its old unique identity." Here, "the destroyed, old world of our Gatsby-youth, Dick Diver's lost 'safe, beautiful world' of promise, hope, passion, charm, virtues, and graces, is identified with an older America that is forever buried, as with Dick, we say goodbye to all our fathers."

In 1938 Fitzgerald suggested a revised edition of *Tender Is the Night.* "Its great fault is that the *true* beginning—the young psychiatrist in Switzerland—is tucked away in the middle of the book," he wrote Perkins in a letter later published in *Dear Scott, Dear Max.* "If pages 151-212 were taken from their present place and put at the start," Fitzgerald argued, "the improvement in appeal would be enormous." He revised his own copy by tearing out these pages and placing them at the beginning as well as making other changes. In the front of this copy, as noted in Bruccoli's *Some Sort of Epic Grandeur,* Fitzgerald wrote: "This is the *final version* of the book as I would like it." In 1951 Scribner published this revised version edited by Malcolm Cowley, but today the 1934 version is considered the standard text. As Bruccoli noted: "Whatever its flaws, the 1934 version has been vindicated by reader preference."

Critical reaction to *Tender Is the Night* has also reversed itself, especially since Fitzgerald's death, thus vindicating a 1935 statement by Ernest Hemingway; as reported in *Dear Scott, Dear Max,* Hemingway had written Perkins, "A strange thing is that in retrospect his *Tender Is the Night* gets better and better." One recent explanation for the original disappointing reception has been suggested by Bryer in *F. Scott Fitzgerald: The Critical Reputation*: "The world that greeted *Tender Is the Night* on April 12, 1934, was far different from that of 1920 or 1925. Readers who had been charmed earlier by the excesses and harmless eccentricities of Fitzgerald's young people were now living through the deprivations caused by a depression. Their responses to a novel about wealthy expatriates cavorting on the Riviera were, predictably, varied, more so than to any other Fitzgerald book."

Very few publications reviewed Fitzgerald's last collection of short stories, *Taps at Reveille,* which appeared in 1935. Bryer viewed this lack of critical response as "a further indication that readers and critics were no longer interested in his Jazz Age subject matter." Bryer continued: "The silence of the reviewers implied that their minds were made up—they had either forgotten or dismissed Fitzgerald."

Between February, 1935, and July, 1937, Fitzgerald, when not living in Baltimore, divided his time between Tryon, Asheville, and Hendersonville, North Carolina. "One harassed and despairing night I packed a brief case," he wrote of his flight to Tryon in "Handle With Care" (1936), "and went off a thousand miles to think it over. I took a dollar room in a drab little town where I knew no one and sunk all the money I had with me in a stock of potted meat, crackers and apples." He treated this difficult period in three confessional essays published in *Esquire* in 1936. In the first, "The Crack-Up," he compared himself to an old plate that suddenly cracks. He wrote: "I began to realize that for two years my life had been a drawing on resources that I did not possess, that I had been mortgaging myself physically and spiritually up to the hilt."

By mid-1937 Fitzgerald's health had improved somewhat and he was able to curb his drinking. To help pay debts and defray new expenses he went to Hollywood in July, 1937, to work as a scriptwriter, spending the first eighteen months at Metro-Goldwyn-Mayer and then working at other studios as a freelancer. Shortly after his arrival in Hollywood, Fitzgerald met film columnist Sheilah Graham and soon began a relationship with her that was to last, though somewhat stormily at times because of his drinking, until the novelist's death.

During this final Hollywood period Fitzgerald worked on some fourteen films, including two weeks on "Gone With the Wind." However, his only screen credit, shared with Edward E. Paramore, Jr., was for MGM's "Three Comrades." In addition he was taking notes on this Hollywood experience for his final novel, *The Last Tycoon*. As work opportunities dwindled, he began writing a series of brief humorous stories for *Esquire* about a hack film writer named Pat Hobby. More importantly, he was able to devote more time to the novel despite tenuous health and discouragement at times. "I am a forgotten man," he wrote his wife in March, 1940, in a letter later printed in *The Letters of F. Scott Fitzgerald*; "*Gatsby* had to be taken out of the Modern Library because it didn't sell, which was a blow." And Fitzgerald's last royalty statement in August, 1940, reported that his publishers had sold only forty copies of all of his books for a total royalty of $13.13.

In this final novel Fitzgerald portrayed the Hollywood of the 1930s, with special emphasis on the studio system and its need for a strong leader, embodied in the character Monroe Stahr. Stahr is fashioned in the tradition of the great leaders who have contributed to the success of the United States despite flaws in their natures. Stahr displays great sensitivity in his relationship with Kathleen, the young woman with whom he falls in love, and with the many employees in his studio, especially (as suggested by Edmund Wilson in his synopsis of the unfinished ending based on Fitzgerald's notes, outlines, and other information) when he sides with them in a wage fight with stockholders. But eventually, as conceived but not carried out by Fitzgerald, Stahr was to have a falling out with his partner, Brady, and, fearing that the latter would murder him, was to arrange with a gangster to have Brady murdered. The novel, however, was never finished. On December 21, 1940, at the age of forty-four, Fitzgerald died suddenly of a heart attack.

Ten months later Scribner published Wilson's edition of what Fitzgerald had completed of *The Last Tycoon*: five chapters and a fraction of a sixth, some of the notes, and Fitzgerald's plan for the novel. Not only were the reviewers in full agreement as to the worth of the volume, but many also used the occasion to praise Fitzgerald's entire body of work. Clifton Fadiman in the November 15, 1941, *New Yorker* stated, for example, "that Fitzgerald was on the point of becoming a major novelist." And J. Donald Adams on the front page of the *New York Times Book Review* for November 9, 1941, said that *The Last Tycoon* "would have been Fitzgerald's best novel." Poet Stephen Vincent Benet concluded in the December 6, 1941, *Saturday Review of Literature*: "You can take off your hats, gentlemen, and I think perhaps you had better. This is not a legend, this is a reputation—and, seen in perspective, it may well be one of the most secure reputations of our time."

BIOGRAPHICAL/CRITICAL SOURCES:

BOOKS

Berman, Ronald, *The Great Gatsby and Modern Times,* University of Illinois Press (Urbana), 1994.

Berman, Ronald, *The Great Gatsby and Fitzgerald's World of Ideas,* University of Alabama Press, 1997.

Bloom, Harold, *F. Scott Fitzgerald's The Great Gatsby,* Chelsea House (New York City), 1995.

Bruccoli, Matthew J., *Fitzgerald and Hemingway: A Dangerous Friendship,* Carroll & Graf (New York City), 1994.

Bruccoli, Matthew J., *Reader's Companion to F. Scott Fitzgerald's Tender is the Night,* University of South Carolina Press (Columbia), 1996.

Bruccoli, Matthew J., *Some Sort of Epic Grandeur: The Life of F. Scott Fitzgerald,* Harcourt, 1981.

Bryer, Jackson R., *The Critical Reputation of F. Scott Fitzgerald: A Bibliographical Study,* supplement, Archon Books, 1984.

Bryer, Jackson R., *New Essays on F. Scott Fitzgerald's Neglected Stories,* University of Missouri Press (Columbia), 1996.

Bryer, Jackson R., editor, *Scott Fitzgerald: The Critical Reception,* Burt Franklin, 1978.

Concise Dictionary of American Literary Biography: The Twenties, 1917-1929, Gale, 1989.

Cowley, Malcolm and Robert Cowley, editors, *Fitzgerald and the Jazz Age,* Scribner, 1966.

de Koster, Katie, *Readings on F. Scott Fitzgerald,* Greenhaven Press, 1997.

Dictionary of Literary Biography, Gale, Volume 4: *American Writers in Paris, 1920-1939,* 1980; Volume 9: *American Novelists, 1910-1945,* 1981.

Dictionary of Literary Biography Documentary Series, Volume 1, Gale, 1982.

Dictionary of Literary Biography Yearbook: 1981, Gale, 1982.

Dillard, Mary, *F. Scott Fitzgerald's The Great Gatsby,* Research & Education Association (Piscataway, NJ), 1994.

Dolan, Marc, *Modern Lives: A Cultural Re-reading of the "Lost Generation,"* Purdue University Press (West Lafayette, IN), 1996.

Gale, Robert L., *An F. Scott Fitzgerald Encyclopedia,* Greenwood Press, 1998.

Gross, Dalton, *Understanding The Great Gatsby: A Student Casebook to Issues, Sources, and Historical Documents,* Greenwood Press, 1998.

Kennedy, J. Gerald and Jackson R. Bryer, editors, *French Connections: Hemingway and Fitzgerald Abroad,* St. Martin's Press, 1998.

Meyers, Jeffrey, *Scott Fitzgerald: A Biography,* HarperCollins (New York City), 1994.

Milford, Nancy, *Zelda: A Biography,* Harper, 1970.

Roulston, Robert, *The Winding Road to West Egg: The Artistic Development of F. Scott Fitzgerald,* Bucknell University Press (Lewisburg, PA), 1995.

Schlacks, Deborah Davis, *American Dream Visions: Chaucer's Surprising Influence on F. Scott Fitzgerald,* P. Lang (New York), 1994.

Short Story Criticism, Gale, Volume 6, 1990.

Stern, Milton R., *The Golden Moment: The Novels of F. Scott Fitzgerald,* University of Illinois Press, 1970.

Stern, Milton R., *Tender is the Night: The Broken Universe,* Maxwell Macmillan International (New York City), 1994.

Sufrin, Mark, *F. Scott Fitzgerald,* Maxwell Macmillan International (New York City), 1994.

Tate, Mary Jo, *Fitzgerald A to Z,* Facts on File, 1997.

Turnbull, Andrew, editor, *The Letters of F. Scott Fitzgerald,* Scribner, 1963.

Twentieth-Century Literary Criticism, Gale, Volume 1, 1978; Volume 6, 1982; Volume 14, 1984; Volume 28, 1988; Volume 55, 1995.

Washington, Bryan R., *The Politics of Exile: Ideology in Henry James, F. Scott Fitzgerald, and James Baldwin,* Northeastern University Press (Boston), 1995.

Westbrook, Robert, *Intimate Lies: F. Scott Fitzgerald and Sheilah Graham: Her Son's Story,* HarperCollins (New York City), 1995.

Weston, Elizabeth A., *The International Theme in F. Scott Fitzgerald's Literature,* P. Lang (New York City), 1995.

Wilson, Edmund, *Letters on Literature and Politics, 1912-1972,* edited by Elena Wilson, introduction by Daniel Aaron, foreword by Leon Edel, Farrar, Straus, 1977.

Zhang, Aiping, *Enchanted Places: The Use of Setting in F. Scott Fitzgerald's Fiction,* Greenwood Press, 1997.

PERIODICALS

Bookman, May, 1926.
Chicago Daily News, March 31, 1920.
Chicago Daily Tribune, April 18, 1925.
Chicago Evening Post, September 24, 1920.
Dial, August, 1925.
Esquire, February, 1936; April, 1936; August, 1936.
Nation, May 9, 1934.
New Yorker, November 15, 1941.
New York Evening Journal, April 12, 1934.
New York Times, April 4, 1989.
New York Times Book Review, March 5, 1922; November 9, 1941.
New York Tribune, May 7, 1922.
New York World, April 12, 1925.
Saturday Evening Post, April 5, 1924.
Saturday Review of Literature, December 6, 1941.
Smart Set, August, 1920; December, 1920; April, 1922.
Washington Post, September 25, 1989.

*   *   *

FITZGERALD, Penelope 1916-

PERSONAL: Born December 17, 1916, in Lincoln, England; daughter of Edmund Valpy (editor of *Punch*), and Christina (Hicks) Knox; married Desmond Fitzgerald, August 15, 1953 (died, 1976); children: Edmund Valpy, Maria. *Education:* Somerville College, Oxford, degree in English literature (first class honors), 1939. *Religion:* Christian.

ADDRESSES: Office—c/o HarperCollins, 78-85 Fulham Palace Rd., London W6 8JB, England.

CAREER: Writer. Broadcasting House (British Broadcasting Corporation), London, recorded program assistant, 1939-53; has also worked in a bookstore and as a teacher affiliated with Westminster Tutors, London.

AWARDS, HONORS: Booker Prize shortlist for fiction, 1978, for *The Bookshop*; Booker Prize for fiction, 1979, for *Offshore*; National Book Critics Circle Prize, 1998, for *Blue Flower.*

WRITINGS:

NOVELS

The Golden Child, Scribner (New York City), 1977.
The Bookshop, Duckworth (London), 1978.
Offshore, Collins (London), 1979, Holt (New York City), 1987.
Human Voices, Collins, 1980.
At Freddie's, Collins, 1982, Godine (Boston), 1985.
Innocence, Holt, 1986.
The Beginning of Spring, Collins, 1988, Holt, 1989.
The Gate of Angels, Collins, 1990, Doubleday (Garden City, NY), 1992.
The Blue Flower, Flamingo (London), 1995, Houghton (Boston), 1997.

BIOGRAPHIES

Edward Burne-Jones, M. Joseph (London), 1975.

The Knox Brothers, Macmillan (London), 1977, published as *The Knox Brothers: Edmund (Evoe), 1881-1971, Dillwyn, 1883-1943, Wilfred, 1886-1950, Ronald, 1888-1957,* Coward, McCann & Geoghegan (New York City), 1977.

Charlotte Mew and Her Friends, Collins, 1984, published as *Charlotte Mew and Her Friends: With a Selection of Her Poems,* Addison-Wesley (Reading, MA), 1988.

SIDELIGHTS: Penelope Fitzgerald published her first novel when she was fifty-nine years old. Some two decades and a Booker Prize later, she has established a reputation as an ironic, spare, and richly comic author. Even when the settings for her novels range as far afield as Florence, pre-revolutionary Moscow, and Germany in the 1790s, she is praised for her sense of detail and her clear observations of human nature. In *Spectator,* Anita Brookner characterizes Fitzgerald as "one of the mildest and most English of writers," adding: "Mild, yes, but there is authority behind those neat, discursive and unresolved stories of hers. . . . She is so unostentatious a writer that she needs to be read several times. What is impressive is the calm confidence behind the apparent simplicity of utterance." *Los Angeles Times Book Review* contributor Richard Eder notes that Fitzgerald's writing is "so precise and lilting that it can make you shiver . . . an elegy that nods at what passes without lamentation or indifference."

Some of Fitzgerald's early novels are loosely based upon her own work experiences. Born of a "writing family," she was educated at Oxford and was employed by the British Broadcasting Corporation during World War II. After her marriage in 1953, she worked as a clerk in a bookstore in rural East Suffolk; later she and her family lived on a barge on the Thames. These episodes in her life helped Fitzgerald to present, in her fiction, "a small, specialist world which she opens for the reader's inspection," to quote *Dictionary of Literary Biography* contributor Catherine Wells Cole. In *The Bookshop,* for instance, a courageous entrepreneur named Florence Green defies the stuffy prejudices of her town, Hardborough, by stocking Vladimir Nabokov's novel *Lolita* for sale. *The Bookshop* is described by Valentine Cunningham in the *Times Literary Supplement* as "on any reckoning a marvelously piercing fiction. . . . [There] are the small circumstances that give rise naturally to a Hardy-like gothic, complete with a rapping poltergeist, and to a fiction where character inevitably comes to 'characters.' And Penelope Fitzgerald's resources of odd people are impressively rich."

Offshore, published in 1979 in England, presents a community of eccentric characters living in barges on Battersea Reach on the Thames River. As the tide ebbs and flows, so do the lives in the unconventional community, in both comic and tragic ways. *Offshore* won the Booker Prize for Fitzgerald, who, at sixty-three, was still something of a novice writer. In *Books and Bookmen,* reviewer Mollie Hardwick describes the work as "a delicate water-colour of a novel . . . a small, charming, Whistler etching." Similar praises greeted *Human Voices,* Fitzgerald's novelistic take on wartime work at Broadcasting House in London. There, one character wishes for a quick peace because he might be called upon to provide more typewriters than he has available; another one muses about the challenge of recording the sounds of tanks rolling across a beach. In *Encounter,* correspondent Penelope Lively finds the novel "a clever fictional rendering of the way in which a random selection of people, flung together for impersonal reasons, will set up a pattern of relationships and reactions . . . told in a voice that is both idiosyncratic and memorable."

Beginning in 1986 with the publication of *Innocence*, Fitzgerald began to range farther afield for her stories. Set in Florence, Italy, during the post-war era, *Innocence* follows the fortunes of a patrician family in decline. In a *Times Literary Supplement* review of the work, Anne Duchene writes of Fitzgerald: "Her writing, as ever, has a natural authority, is very funny, warm, and gently ironic, and full of tenderness towards human beings and their bravery in living." *The Beginning of Spring* presents an off-beat comedy of manners set in the household of a British expatriate in 1913 Moscow. As the thoughtful and upright Frank Reid faces the sudden departure of his wife—leaving him with three young children—he receives dubious assistance from some of his friends, both English and Russian. To quote *New York Times Book Review* correspondent Robert Plunket, with *The Beginning of Spring* Fitzgerald has become "that refreshing rarity, a writer who is very modern but not the least bit hip. Ms. Fitzgerald looks into the past, both human and literary, and finds all sorts of things that are surprisingly up to date. Yet as *The Beginning of Spring* reaches its triumphant conclusion, you realize that its greatest virtue is perhaps the most old-fashioned of all. It is a lovely novel."

Fitzgerald continued her writing career into the 1990s, producing the well-received novels *The Gate of Angels* and *The Blue Flower*. *The Gate of Angels*, published in the United States in 1992, concerns a fictitious Cambridge college for physicists in Edwardian England, and describes how the cloistered academy changes after one of its junior fellows, Fred Fairly, suffers a bicycle accident. "This funny, touching, wise novel manages, despite its brevity, to seem leisurely," writes Nina King in the *New York Times Book Review*. "It is vibrant with wonderful minor characters, ablaze with ideas." *Listener* reviewer Kate Kellaway notes that, in *The Gate of Angels*, Fitzgerald "unostentatiously fills her story with quietly original observations so that you are constantly recognising and discovering through her eyes." Observes John Bayley in the *New York Review of Books*: "Penelope Fitzgerald is not only an artist of a high order but one of immense originality, wholly her own woman. She composes with an innocent certainty which avoids any suggestion that she might have a feminist moral in mind, or a dig against science, or a Christian apologetic. The translucent little tale keeps quite clear of such matters, and yet it is certainly about goodness, and . . . successful at giving us the experience and conviction of it."

In addition to her many novels, Fitzgerald has published several works of nonfiction, including a biography of Pre-Raphaelite painter Edward Coley Burne-Jones, and *The Knox Brothers*, which recounts the lives of her father and his brothers, each of whom contributed to British society in a special—and individual—way. In an essay for the *Contemporary Authors Autobiography Series*, Fitzgerald writes of herself: "Biographies and novels are the forms which I feel I can just about manage. They are the outcome of intense curiosity about other people and about oneself." That "intense curiosity" has produced a body of work that casts an eye on such intangibles as personal relationships, social institutions, history, and the interactions between them. "On a superficial reading Fitzgerald's novels may appear slight," concludes Catherine Wells Cole, "but their real strength lies in what they omit, in what has been pared away. Their skill and grace is not simply displayed technical achievement, but derives instead from Fitzgerald's absolute concern, often conveyed through humor and comedy, for the moral values of the tradition she follows so precisely."

Fitzgerald once told *Contemporary Authors*: "I've begun to write at rather a late stage in life because I love books and everything to do with them. I believe that people should write biographies only about people they love, or understand, or both. Novels, on the other hand, are often better if they're about people the writer doesn't like very much."

BIOGRAPHICAL/CRITICAL SOURCES:

BOOKS

Contemporary Authors, Gale (Detroit), Volume 85, 1974; Volume 86, 1974; Volume 87, 1974; Volume 88, 1974.
Contemporary Authors Autobiography Series, Volume 10, Gale (Detroit), 1989, pp. 101-9.
Contemporary Authors New Revision Series, Volume 56, Gale, 1997.
Contemporary Literary Criticism, Gale, Volume 19, 1981, pp. 172-75; Volume 51, 1989, pp. 123-27; Volume 61, 1989, pp. 114-24.
Dictionary of Literary Biography, Volume 14: *British Novelists since 1960*, Gale, 1983, pp. 302-8.

PERIODICALS

Booklist, September 1, 1997, p. 57.
Books and Bookmen, December 1979, pp. 16-17.
Encounter, January 1981, pp. 53-59.
Library Journal, September 1, 1997, p. 217.
Listener, August 23, 1990, p. 24.
London Review of Books, October 13, 1988, pp. 20-21.
Los Angeles Times Book Review, April 23, 1989, p. 3; January 12, 1992, pp. 3, 7.
New Statesman, October 3, 1980, p. 24.
New Statesman and Society, October 6, 1995, p. 38.
New York Review of Books, April 9, 1992, p. 13; October 5, 1995, p. 7.
New York Times, March 26, 1998, p. B11.
New York Times Book Review, May 2, 1989, p. 15; March 1, 1992, pp. 7, 9; September 7, 1997, p. 11; December 7, 1997, p. 12.
Publishers Weekly, July 21, 1997, p. 183.
Spectator, October 1, 1988, pp. 29-30.
Times Literary Supplement, November 17, 1978, p. 1333; September 12, 1986, p. 995.
Washington Post Book World, February 23, 1992, pp. 1, 8.

*   *   *

FLEMING, Ian (Lancaster) 1908-1964 (Atticus)

PERSONAL: Born May 28, 1908, in London, England; died August 12, 1964; son of Valentine (a major in the armed forces and a Conservative member of the British Parliament) and Evelyn Beatrice (Ste. Crois Rose) Fleming; married Anne Geraldine Charteris (formerly Lady Rothermere), March 24, 1952; children: Caspar. *Education:* Attended Eton, Royal Military Academy at Sandhurst, University of Munich, and University of Geneva. *Avocation:* Swimming, gambling, golf.

CAREER: Moscow correspondent for Reuters Ltd., London, England, 1929-33; associated with Cull & Co. (merchant bankers), London, England, 1933-35; stockbroker with Rowe & Pitman, London, England, 1935-39; returned to Moscow, 1939, officially as a reporter for *The Times*, London, unofficially as a representative of the Foreign Office; Kemsley (later Thomson) Newspapers, foreign manager, 1945-59; publisher of *The Book*

Collector, 1949-64. *Military service:* Royal Naval Volunteer Reserve, 1939-45; lieutenant; did secret service work as a personal assistant to the director of Naval Intelligence, 1939-45.

MEMBER: Turf Club, Broodle's Club, Portland Club.

AWARDS, HONORS: Order of the Dannebrog, 1945; Young Reader's Choice Award, 1967, for *Chitty-Chitty-Bang-Bang.*

WRITINGS:

"JAMES BOND" SERIES

Casino Royale (also see below), J. Cape (London), 1953, Macmillan (New York City), 1954, published in paperback as *You Asked for It,* Popular Library (New York City), 1955.

Live and Let Die (also see below), J. Cape, 1954, Macmillan (New York City), 1955.

Moonraker (also see below), Macmillan, 1955, published as *Too Hot to Handle,* Perma Books (New York City), 1957.

Diamonds Are Forever (also see below), Macmillan, 1956.

From Russia, with Love (also see below), Macmillan, 1957.

Doctor No (also see below), Macmillan, 1958.

Goldfinger (also see below), Macmillan, 1959.

For Your Eyes Only: Five Secret Exploits of James Bond, Viking (New York City), 1960, published in England as *For Your Eyes Only: Five Secret Occasions in the Life of James Bond,* J. Cape, 1960.

Gilt-Edged Bonds: Casino Royale, From Russia, with Love, Doctor No, introduction by Paul Gallico, Macmillan, 1961.

Thunderball (also see below), Viking (New York City), 1961.

The Spy Who Loved Me (also see below), Viking, 1962.

On Her Majesty's Secret Service (also see below), New American Library (New York City), 1963.

You Only Live Twice (also see below), New American Library, 1964.

Bonded Fleming: A James Bond Omnibus (contains *Thunderball, For Your Eyes Only,* and *The Spy Who Loved Me*), Viking, 1965.

The Man with the Golden Gun (also see below), New American Library, 1965.

More Gilt-Edged Bonds (contains *Live and Let Die, Moonraker,* and *Diamonds Are Forever*), Macmillan, 1965.

Octopussy (also see below; includes story "The Living Daylights"), New American Library, 1965, published in England as *Octopussy, and The Living Daylights,* J. Cape, 1966.

A James Bond Quartet (contains *Casino Royale, Live and Let Die, Moonraker,* and *From Russia, with Love*), J. Cape, 1992.

A James Bond Quintet (contains *Diamonds Are Forever, Doctor No, Goldfinger, For Your Eyes Only,* and *The Spy Who Loved Me*), J. Cape, 1993.

The Essential James Bond (includes *Thunderball, On Her Majesty's Secret Service, You Only Live Twice, The Man with the Golden Gun, Octopussy,* and *The Living Daylights*), J. Cape, 1994.

Ian Fleming's James Bond (includes *Moonraker, From Russia with Love, Dr No, Goldfinger, Thunderball,* and *On Her Majesty's Secret Service*), Chancellor Press (London), 1994.

OTHER

The Diamond Smugglers (novel), J. Cape, 1957, Macmillan, 1958.

Thrilling Cities (essays), J. Cape, 1963, New American Library, 1964.

Chitty-Chitty-Bang-Bang: The Magical Car (juvenile), illustrations by John Burningham, Random House (New York City), 1964.

Fleming Introduces Jamaica (nonfiction), edited by Morris Cargill, Deutsch (London), 1965, Hawthorn (New York City), 1966.

Also author, with Kevin McClory and Jack Whittington, of screenplay adaptation of his novel *Thunderball,* 1965. Columnist, under pseudonym Atticus, for the *Sunday Times,* London, during the 1950s. Contributor to *Horizon, Spectator,* and other magazines.

A collection of Fleming's letters, manuscripts, and other papers and memorabilia is housed at Lilly Library, Indiana University, and additional material is owned by Glidrose Productions.

MEDIA ADAPTATIONS: Films adapted from Fleming's works and/or based on his characters include *Dr. No,* 1962, *From Russia with Love,* 1963, *Goldfinger,* 1964, *Thunderball,* 1965, *The Poppy Is Also a Flower,* 1966, *Casino Royale,* 1967, *You Only Live Twice,* 1967, *Chitty-Chitty-Bang-Bang,* 1968, *On Her Majesty's Secret Service,* 1969, *Diamonds Are Forever,* 1971, *Live and Let Die,* 1973, *The Man with the Golden Gun,* 1974, *The Spy Who Loved Me,* 1977, *Moonraker,* 1979, *For Your Eyes Only,* 1981, *Never Say Never Again,* 1983, *Octopussy,* 1983, *A View to a Kill,* 1985, *The Living Daylights,* 1987, *License to Kill,* 1989, and *Goldeneye,* 1995.

SIDELIGHTS: The success of Ian Fleming's espionage adventure tales about the fictional secret agent James Bond has been astounding, both in the English versions and in translations, even though the author himself called his works "trivial piffle." Bond, a special agent for British intelligence, is a cynical, cold man with a suave exterior, physically tough, endowed with numerous gadgets and luxury accouterments, and irresistible to women. Malcolm Muggeridge proposed that the Bond books became so wildly popular because "Fleming's squalid aspirations and dream fantasies happened to coincide with a whole generation's. He touched a nerve. The inglorious appetites for speed at the touch of a foot on the accelerator and for sex at the touch of a hand on the flesh, found expression in his books. We live in the Century of the Common Bond, and Fleming created him." William Plomer put forth another, loftier view of the stories: "They are brilliant, romantic fairy-tales in which a dragon-slaying maiden-rescuing hero wins battle after battle against devilish forces of destruction, and yet is indestructible himself: an ancient kind of myth skilfully re-created in a modern idiom. They are, like life, sexy and violent, but I have never thought them corrupting. Compared with some of the nasty stuff that gets into print, they have a sort of boyish innocence." Sarel Eimerl noted one difference between Fleming's stories and most espionage novels, a difference which may account for part of this success. Fleming, who had worked with British Intelligence, had, or gave the impression of having, "the inside dope." He sounded authentic.

Fleming and Bond often became confused in the public mind. John Pearson, in *James Bond: The Authorised Biography of 007,* described Fleming as a modern-day Lord Byron, "tall, saturnine, hollow-cheeked, his face lopsided with its magnificently broken nose, his brow half-covered by that thoughtful comma of black hair which he was to pass on to his hero. . . ." Like Bond, Ian Fleming enjoyed travel and luxury. He was a "noted womanizer," related Joan DelFattore in *Dictionary of Literary Biography,* whose "attitude toward women is surely one of the reasons for the uneven quality of James Bond's relationships with the female characters in his novels." He had some training as a secret agent, but failed a key test designed to see whether or not he could kill in cold blood.

Bond's genesis occurred during World War II, when, as Plomer reported, Fleming came to him "with a diffidence that came surprisingly from so buoyant a man, [and] said he had a wish to write a thriller. . . . I at once made it . . . plain how strongly I believed in his ability to write such a book, and in its probable originality. 'But,' I said, 'it's no good writing just *one*. With that sort of book, you must become regular in your habits. You must hit the nail again and again with the same hammer until it's driven into the thick head of your potential public.' " Muggeridge, who recalls discussing Fleming's writing with him when he was at work on *Casino Royale* remembers that Fleming "was insistent that he had no 'literary' aspiration at all, and that his only purpose was to make money and provide entertainment." By the time he died, Fleming reportedly had made 2.8 million dollars from his books alone, to say nothing of what he earned from the many films made of them.

From *Casino Royale* to *The Man with the Golden Gun*, the Bond books evoked strong responses from critics, both positive and negative. Some reviewers described Bond's adventures as wonderful entertainment, others found them to be a significant reflection of modern culture and fantasies, while still others considered Fleming's books offensively bad, filled with racism, snobbery, misogynism, excessive violence, and poor writing. Discussing what he perceived to be a moral void in the Bond books, Bernard Bergonzi wrote in *Twentieth Century,* "Where the relations between the sexes are concerned, Mr Fleming's characteristic mode of fantasy seems to be that of a dirty-minded schoolboy." Bergonzi went on to decry the "strongly marked streak of voyeurism and sado-masochism" he found in Fleming's books, and remarked that the author "describes scenes of violence with uncommon relish. . . . It is these that really bring his books down to the horror-comic level. . . . In *Casino Royale,* for instance, Bond is captured by a Communist agent. . . . [He] is stripped naked and tied to a chair from which the seat has been removed; he is then systematically beaten on the genitals with a carpet-beater for about an hour."

Reviewing *Dr. No* for *New Statesman,* Paul Johnson called it "badly written to the point of incoherence" and "the nastiest book I have ever read." He found three basic ingredients in the story, "all unhealthy, all thoroughly English: the sadism of a schoolboy bully, the mechanical, two-dimensional sex-longings of a frustrated adolescent, and the crude, snob-cravings of a suburban adult. Mr. Fleming has no literary skill, the construction of the book is chaotic, and entire incidents and situations are inserted, and then forgotten, in a haphazard manner. But the three ingredients are manufactured and blended with deliberate, professional precision."

On the other end of the critical spectrum, Kingsley Amis held Bond up as the modern embodiment of the romantic heroes of Lord Byron. Like them, Amis suggested in his *The James Bond Dossier,* Bond is "lonely, melancholy, of fine natural physique, which has become in some way ravaged, of similarly fine but ravaged countenance, dark and brooding in expression, of a cold or cynical veneer, above all *enigmatic,* in possession of a sinister secret." He applauded Fleming's skill in bringing off "the unlikely feat of enclosing this wildly romantic, almost narcissistic, and (one would have thought) hopelessly out-of-date persona inside the shellac of a secret agent, so making it plausible, mentally actable, and, to all appearance, contemporary." Bond was also evaluated quite seriously by George Grella, who wrote in *The Critic as Artist: Essays on Books 1920-1970* that "James Bond is the Renaissance man in mid-century guise, lover, warrior,

connoisseur. He fights the forces of darkness, speaks for the sanitary achievements of the age, enjoys hugely the fruits of the free enterprise economy. He lives the dreams of countless drab people, his gun ready, his honor intact, his morals loose: the hero of our anxiety-ridden, mythless age: the savior of our culture."

"Don't try to read any of the Bond adventures seriously!" warned Ann S. Boyd in *The Devil with James Bond!* "Bond was meant for fun, for escape." Still, she contended that in rereading Fleming's books, one may "discover that there is more to his series of thriller adventures than one originally might suspect." In Boyd's estimation, the Bond canon is really "the saga of a modern knight of faith whose adventures involve a gallery of modern demons which have been attacking contemporary mankind just as diabolically as Medusa and all the other legendary demons and dragons attacked mankind in ages past. Rather than casting pearls before swine, Fleming's genius has cast swine as the personifications of the devil before a hero who is willing to sacrifice all for the great pearl of life and faith."

Writing in *Dictionary of Literary Biography,* Joan DelFattore summed up the good and bad points of the Bond novels: "Fleming's books are superficial, implausible, and erratically structured, and they have unquestionably been overshadowed in popularity by the Bond films, which are even more superficial, implausible, and erratically structured. On the other hand, Fleming's work is, for the most part, imaginative, readable, and, most important, outrageously entertaining."

"The phenomenon of James Bond [has] always troubled both his admirers and his detractors, who have great difficulty simply accounting for it," declared George Grella in *St. James Guide to Crime and Mystery Writers.* "The major sources of his appeal are not entirely obscure. For one thing, the James Bond novels are a perfect example of the right thing at the right time, as appropriate an expression and index of their age as, for example, the Sherlock Holmes stories or the novels of Dashiell Hammett." Evaluating Fleming's literary achievement, Grella found that the author "in his own way mastered one of the most enviable and admirable feats in all of literature—the mingling of the barely credible, the utterly incredible, and the specifically identifiable in an excitingly sustained narrative fiction."

BIOGRAPHICAL/CRITICAL SOURCES:

BOOKS

Amis, Kingsley, *The James Bond Dossier,* New American Library, 1965.

Benson, Raymond, *The James Bond Bedside Companion,* Dodd (New York City), 1984.

Boyd, Ann S., *The Devil with James Bond!* John Knox, 1966.

Bruce, Ivar, *You Only Live Once: Memories of Ian Fleming,* Weidenfeld and Nicolson (London), 1975, University Publications of America (Frederick, MA), 1985.

Concise Dictionary of British Literary Biography, Volume 7: *Writers after World War II, 1945-1960,* Gale (Detroit), 1991.

Contemporary Literary Criticism, Gale, Volume 3, 1975; Volume 30, 1984.

Contosta, David R., *The Private Life of James Bond,* Sutter House (Lititz, PA), 1993.

Dictionary of Literary Biography, Volume 87: *British Mystery and Thriller Writers since 1940, First Series,* Gale, 1989.

Gardner, John E., *Ian Fleming's James Bond,* Avenet (New York City), 1987.

Haining, Peter, *James Bond: A Celebration,* W. H. Allen (London), 1987.

Lycett, Andrew, *Ian Fleming: The Intimate Story of the Man Who Created James Bond,* Turner (Atlanta), 1996.

McCormick, Donald, *The Life of Ian Fleming,* P. Owen (London), 1993.

Panek, LeRoy L., *The Special Branch: The British Spy Novel, 1890-1980,* Bowling Green University Popular Press (Bowling Green, OH), 1981.

Pearson, John, *James Bond: The Authorised Biography of 007,* Granada (London), 1985, Grove (New York), 1986.

Pearson, John, *The Life of Ian Fleming,* McGraw (New York City), 1966.

Reference Guide to English Literature, second edition, St. James Press (Detroit), 1991.

Rosenberg, Bruce A., and Ann Steward, *Ian Fleming,* Twayne (Boston), 1989.

Rubin, Steven Jay, *The James Bond Films,* Arlington (London), 1982.

St. James Guide to Crime and Mystery Writers, St. James Press, 1996.

Sauerberg, Lars Ole, *Secret Agents in Fiction: Ian Fleming, John le Carre and Len Deighton,* St. Martin's (New York City), 1984.

Symons, Julian, *Mortal Consequences: From the Detective Story to the Crime Novel,* Harper, 1972.

Twentieth-Century Crime and Mystery Writers, third edition, St. James Press, 1991.

Twentieth-Century Young Adult Writers, St. James Press, 1994.

Van Dover, J. Kenneth, *Murder in the Millions: Erle Stanley Gardner, Mickey Spillane, Ian Fleming,* Ungar (New York City), 1984.

PERIODICALS

Commentary, July, 1968.
Critic, October-November, 1965.
Encounter, January, 1965.
Life, August 10, 1962.
Nation, June 21, 1958, pp. 566-67.
National Review, September 7, 1965, pp. 776-77.
New Republic, July 2, 1966, p. 29.
New Statesman, April 5, 1958, pp. 430, 432; April 2, 1965, pp. 540-41.
Newsweek, June 15, 1964, p. 103.
New Yorker, April 21, 1962.
New York Times, February 16, 1967; April 25, 1967.
New York Times Book Review, July 4, 1961; November 5, 1961; April 1, 1962; December 11, 1966.
Publishers Weekly, August 24, 1964.
Spectator, April 17, 1953, p. 494; April 12, 1957, p. 493; December 13, 1957, pp. 844-45; April 4, 1958, p. 438.
Sunday Herald Tribune Book World, August 29, 1965, pp. 1, 17.
Times Literary Supplement, April 17, 1953, p. 249; October 27, 1966.
Twentieth Century, March, 1958, pp. 220-28; May, 1958, pp. 478-779.

*　　*　　*

FLEUR, Paul
See POHL, Frederik

FLOOGLEBUCKLE, Al
See SPIEGELMAN, Art

*　　*　　*

FLYING OFFICER X
See BATES, H(erbert) E(rnest)

*　　*　　*

FO, Dario 1926-

PERSONAL: Born March 24, 1926, in San Giano, Lombardy, Italy; son of Felice (a railroad stationmaster) and Pina (Rota) Fo; married Franca Rame (a playwright and actress), June, 1954; children: three. *Education:* Attended Accademia di Belle Arti, Milan.

ADDRESSES: Home—Milan, Italy. *Agent*—Maria Nadotti, 349 East 51st St., New York, NY 10022.

CAREER: Playwright, director, actor, and theatrical company leader. Has written more than forty plays, many of which have been translated and performed in more than thirty countries, beginning in 1953; performs plays in Italy, Europe, and the United States, and runs classes and workshops for actors, 1970s-. Worked as a member of small theatrical group, headed by Franco Parenti, performing semi-improvised sketches for radio before local audiences, 1950; wrote and performed comic monologues for his own radio program, *Poer nana* ("Poor Dwarf"), broadcast by the Italian national radio network RAI, 1951; formed revue company, *I Dritti* ("The Stand-Ups"), with Giustino Durano and Parenti, 1953; screenwriter in Rome, 1956-58; formed improvisational troupe *Compagnia Fo-Rame,* with wife, Franca Rame, 1958; named artistic director of Italian state television network's weekly musical revue, *Chi l'ha visto?* ("Who's Seen It?"), and writer and performer of sketches for variety show *Canzonissima* ("Really Big Song"), 1959; formed theater cooperative *Nuova Scena,* with Rame, 1968, and *La Comune,* 1970.

AWARDS, HONORS: Recipient of Sonning Award, Denmark, 1981; Obie Award, 1987; Nobel Prize in literature, 1997.

WRITINGS:

PLAYS

Teatro comico, Garzanti, 1962.
Le commedie, Einaudi, 1966, enlarged edition published as *Le commedie di Dario Fo,* 6 volumes, Einaudi, 1974.
Vorrei morire anche stasera se dovessi pensare che no e servito a niente, E.D.B., 1970.
Morte e resurrezione di un pupazzo, Sapere Edizioni, 1971.
Ordine! Per Dio, Bertani, 1972.
Pum, pum! Chi e? La polizia! (title means "Knock, Knock! Who's There? Police!"), Bertani, 1972.
Tutti uniti! Tutti insieme! Ma scusa quello non e il padrone? (title means "United We Stand! All Together Now! Oops, Isn't That the Boss?"), Bertani, 1972.
Guerra di popolo in Cile (title means "The People's War in Chile"), Bertani, 1973.
Mistero buffo (title means "The Comic Mystery"; first produced in Milan, 1969; produced on Broadway at the Joyce Theater, May 27, 1986), Bertani, 1973, revised, 1974.

Ballate e canzoni (title means "Ballads and Songs"), introduction by Lanfranco Binni, Bertani, 1974.

Morte accidentale di un anarchico (first produced in Milan, December, 1970; produced on Broadway at Belasco Theater, November 15, 1984), Einaudi, 1974, translation by Gavin Richards published as *Accidental Death of an Anarchist,* Pluto Press, 1980.

Non si paga, non si paga (first produced in Milan, 1974), La comune, 1974, translation by Lino Pertite published as *We Can't Pay? We Won't Pay!,* adapted by Bill Colvill and Robert Walker, Pluto Press, 1978, translation by Pertite reprinted as *Can't Pay? Won't Pay!* Pluto Press, 1982, North American version by R. G. Davis published as *We Won't Pay! We Won't Pay!* Samuel French, 1984.

La guillarata, Bertani, 1975.

Il Fanfani rapito, Bertani, 1975.

La marjuana della mamma e la piu bella, Bertani, 1976.

La signora e da buttare (title means "The Old Girl's for the Scrapheap"), Einaudi, 1976.

Il teatro politico, G. Mazzotta, 1977.

(With wife, Franca Rame) *Tutta casa, letto e chiesa* (title means "All House, Bed, and Church"), Bertani, 1978, translation published as *Orgasmo Adulto Escapes From the Zoo,* adapted by Estelle Parsons, Broadway Play Publishing, 1985.

La storia di un soldato, photographs by Silvia Lelli Masotti, commentary by Ugo Volli, Electa, 1979.

Storia vera di Piero d'Angera: Che alla crociata non c'era, La comune, 1981.

OTHER PLAYS IN ENGLISH TRANSLATION

(With Rame) *Female Parts: One Woman Plays,* translated by Margaret Kunzle and Stuart Hood, adapted by Olwen Wymark, Pluto Press, 1981.

Car Horns, Trumpets and Raspberries (first produced in Milan, January, 1981; produced in the United States at the Yale Repertory Theater as *About Face,* 1981), translated by R. C. McAvoy and A. H. Giugni, Pluto Press, 1981.

(With Rame) *The Open Couple—Wide Open Even,* Theatretexts, 1984.

The Tale of a Tiger, Theatretexts, 1984.

One Was Nude and One Wore Tails, Theatretexts, 1985.

The Open Couple and an Ordinary Day, Heinemann, 1990.

The Pope and the Witch, Heinemann, 1993.

(With Rame) *Plays, Two* (contains *Can't Pay? Won't Pay!, The Open Couple,* and *An Ordinary Day*), Methuen (London), 1994.

Abducting Diana, Theater Communications Group, 1998.

OTHER PLAYS; PRODUCED ONLY

Il dito nell'occhio (title means "A Finger in the Eye"), first produced in Milan at Piccolo Teatro, June, 1953.

I sani da legare (title means "A Madhouse for the Sane"), first produced in Milan at Piccolo Teatro, 1954.

Ladri, manachini e donne nude (title means "Thieves, Dummies, and Naked Women"), first produced in Milan at Piccolo Teatro, 1958.

Gli arcangeli non giocano a flipper (title means "Archangels Don't Play Pinball"), first produced in Milan at Teatro Odeon, September, 1959.

Isabella, tre caravelle, e un cacciaballe (title means "Isabella, Three Ships, and a Con Man"), first produced in Milan at Teatro Odeon, 1963.

Also author of numerous other plays first produced in Italy, including "Aveva due pistole con gli occhi bianchi e neri" (title means "He Had Two Pistols With White and Black Eyes"), 1960; "Grande pantomima con bandiere e pupazzi piccoli e medi" (title means "Grand Pantomime With Flags and Small and Medium-Sized Puppets"), October, 1968; "Fedayn," 1971; "Il fabulazzo osceno" (title means "The Obscene Fable"), 1982; "Quasi per caso una donna: Elisabetta" (title means "A Woman Almost by Chance: Elizabeth"), 1984; "Hellequin, Arlekin, Arlechino," 1986. Other stage credits include an adaptation of Bertolt Brecht's *Threepenny Opera,* for Teatro Stabile di Torino and Teatro Il Fabbricone of Prato, and *Patapumfete,* for the clown duo I Colombaioni.

OTHER

Manuale minimo dell'attore (title means "Basic Handbook for the Actor"), Einaudi, 1987.

The Tricks of the Trade, translation by Joe Farrell, Routledge, 1991.

Tot o: Manuale dell'Attor Comico, Vallecchi (Florence), 1995.

SIDELIGHTS: Noted Italian playwright Dario Fo began refining his animated method of storytelling as a child, listening to the tales told by the locals in San Giano, the small fishing village in northern Italy where he was born. After leaving Milan's Academy of Fine Arts without earning a degree, Fo wrote and performed with several improvisational theatrical groups. He first earned acclaim as a playwright in 1953 with *Il dito nell'occhio* (*A Finger in the Eye*), a socially satiric production that presented Marxist ideas against a circus-like background. His 1954 attack on the Italian government in *I sani de legare* (*A Madhouse for the Sane*), in which Fo labeled several government officials fascist sympathizers, resulted in the cutting of some material from the original script and the mandated presence of state inspectors at each performance of the play to insure that the country's strict libel laws were not violated.

Following a brief stint as a screenwriter in Rome, Fo, together with his wife, actress Franca Rame, returned to the theater and produced a more generalized, less explicitly political brand of social satire. Widely regarded as his best work during this phase of his career, *Gli arcangeli non giocano a flipper* (*Archangels Don't Play Pinball*) was the first of Fo's plays to be staged outside of Italy. As quoted by Irving Wardle in the London *Times,* the heroic clown in *Archangels* voices the playwright's basic contention, stating, "My quarrel is with those who organize our dreams."

In 1968 Fo and Rame rejected the legitimate theater as an arm of the bourgeoisie and, backed by the Italian Communist party, they formed Nuova Scena, a noncommercial theater group designed to entertain and inform the working class. The plays produced by this company centered on political issues and grew increasingly radical in tone. The communist government withdrew its support from Nuova Scena after the staging of *Grande pantomima con bandiere e pupazzi piccoli e medi* (*Grand Pantomime With Flags and Small and Medium-Sized Puppets*), a satire of Italy's political history in the wake of World War II. The highly symbolic play depicts the birth of capitalism (portrayed by a beautiful woman) from fascism (a huge monster puppet) and the subsequent seduction of communism by capitalism. Through the play Fo demonstrated his disenchantment with the authoritative, antirevolutionary policies of the Italian Communist party, allowing communism to succumb to capitalism's enticement.

Steeped in an atmosphere of political and social unrest, the 1960s proved to be a decade of increased popularity for Fo, providing him with new material and a receptive audience. He first performed *Mistero buffo,* generally considered his greatest and most controversial play, in 1969. An improvised production based on a constantly changing script, the play is a decidedly irreverent retelling of the gospels that indicts landowners, government, and, in particular, the Catholic church as public oppressors. Fo based the show's format on that of the medieval mystery plays originally parodied by *giullari,* strolling minstrel street performers of the Middle Ages. *Mistero buffo* was written in Italian as a series of sketches for a single actor—Fo—to perform on an empty stage. The playwright introduces each segment of the work with an informal prologue to establish a rapport with his audience. He links together the satiric religious narratives, portraying up to a dozen characters at a time by himself. The sketches include a reenactment of Lazarus's resurrection, complete with opportunists who pick the pockets of the awestruck witnesses; the tale of a contented cripple's efforts to avoid being cured by Jesus; an account of the wedding feast at Cana as told by a drunkard; and an especially dark portrait of the corrupt Pope Boniface VIII.

Fo's penchant for justice prompted him to compose the absurdist play *Morte accidentale di un anarchico* (*Accidental Death of an Anarchist*) in response to the untimely death of anarchist railway man Giuseppi Pinelli in late 1969. Pinelli's death was apparently connected to efforts by right-wing extremists in Italy's military and secret service agencies to discredit the Italian Communist party by staging a series of seemingly leftist-engineered bombings. The railway worker was implicated in the worst of these bombings, the 1969 massacre at Milan's Agricultural Bank. While being held for interrogation, Pinelli fell—it was later shown that he was pushed—from the fourth-floor window of Milan's police headquarters.

In *Accidental Death,* Fo introduces a stock medieval character, the maniac, into the investigation of the bombing to illuminate the truth. Fo commented in *American Theatre,* "When I injected absurdity into the situation, the lies became apparent. The maniac plays the role of the judge, taking the logic of the authorities to their absurd extremes," thus demonstrating that Pinelli's death could not have occurred in the way the police had described. John Lahr reported in the *Los Angeles Times* that because of their part in the exposure of the police cover-up, Fo was assaulted and jailed and Rame kidnapped and beaten in the first few years that the play was staged.

Accidental Death of an Anarchist was a smash hit in Italy, playing to huge crowds for more than four years. When officials pressured a theater in Bologna to halt plans for production, the play was alternatively staged in a sports stadium for an audience of more than six thousand people. After receiving rave reviews throughout Europe—Lahr, writing in *New Society,* called the show "loud, vulgar, kinetic, scurrilous, smart, [and] sensational. . . . Everything theatre should be"—and enjoying a thirty-month run in London, *Accidental Death* opened in the United States in 1984, only to close a short time later.

Because Fo's plays are often either loosely translated or performed in Italian and center on historical, political, and social events that bear more significance for audiences in Italy than in the States, American versions of the playwright's works are frequently considered less dazzling than their Italian counterparts. In an article for the *New York Times,* Mel Gussow pointed out that "dealing with topical Italian materials in colloquial Italian language . . . presents problems for adapters and directors." For instance, a few critics found the presence of a translator on stage during *Mistero buffo* mildly distracting. And many reviewers agreed that the English translation of *Accidental Death* lacked the

power of the Italian production. Frank Rich insisted in the *New York Times* that adapter Richard Nelson's introduction of timely American puns into the *Accidental Death* script "wreck[ed] the play's farcical structure and jolt[ed] both audience and cast out of its intended grip."

Fo's 1978 collaboration with Rame, *Tutta casa, letto e chiesa,* produced in the United States as *Orgasmo Adulto Escapes From the Zoo,* also "may have lost some of its punch crossing the Atlantic," asserted David Richards in the *Washington Post.* A cycle of short sketches written for a single female player, *Orgasmo* focuses on women's status in a patriarchal society. Richards felt that, to an American audience in the mid-1980s (when the play was produced in the United States), "the women in *Orgasmo* seem to be fighting battles that have long been conceded on these shores." Still, if not timely, the performances were judged favorably for their zest and honesty in portraying Italian sexism.

The Tricks of the Trade, published in 1991, is a collection of notes, talks, and workshop transcripts by Fo that deal with numerous aspects of the theater and their historical origins and modern roles: mimes and clowns, masks, and puppets and marionettes. Fo also discusses his own plays and his distinctive approach to playwriting and performing. "*The Tricks of the Trade* offers inspiration for theatre practitioners of all sorts, while celebrating a revival of the power and predominance of the politically inspired clown," remarked James Fisher in *Drama Review.* Writing in *World Literature Today,* Giovanni d'Angelo commented that the book "is technically robust and exhaustive" and termed Fo's style "fluent and graceful."

Gussow noted, "For Mr. Fo, there are no sacred cows, least of all himself or his native country," and concluded that Fo's social commentary is more "relevant" than "subversive." Commenting on the underlying philosophy that shapes and informs his works, Fo asserted in *American Theatre,* "My plays are provocations, like catalysts in a chemical solution. . . . I just put some drops of absurdity in this calm and tranquil liquid, which is society, and the reactions reveal things that were hidden before the absurdity brought them out into the open."

BIOGRAPHICAL/CRITICAL SOURCES:

BOOKS

Contemporary Literary Criticism, Volume 32, Gale, 1985.
McAvoy, R. C., editor, *Fo Dario and Franca Rame: The Theatre Workshops at Riverside Studios,* Red Notes, 1983.
Mitchell, Tony, *Dario Fo: People's Court Jester,* Methuen, 1984.

PERIODICALS

American Theatre, June, 1986.
Atlantic Monthly, September, 1985.
Choice, March, 1992, p. 1090.
Drama, summer, 1979.
Drama Review, winter, 1992, p. 171.
Los Angeles Times, January 16, 1983; January 21, 1983.
Maclean's, October 20, 1997, p. 32.
Nation, November 3, 1997, p. 4, 5; November 10, 1997, p. 8.
National Catholic Reporter, November 13, 1992.
New Republic, December 17, 1984; November 24, 1997, p. 30.
New Society, March 13, 1980.
New Statesman, August 7, 1981.
New Yorker, February 23, 1981.
New York Times, December 18, 1980; April 17, 1983; August 5, 1983; August 14, 1983; August 27, 1983; February 15, 1984;

October 31, 1984; November 16, 1984; May 29, 1986; May 30, 1986; May 9, 1987; November 27, 1987.

New York Times Book Review, February 1, 1998, p. 31.

Opera News, October, 1993.

Times (London), November 17, 1984; September 22, 1986; September 25, 1986.

Times Literary Supplement, December 18, 1987.

Variety, August 4, 1982; May 11, 1992.

Washington Post, August 27, 1983; November 17, 1984; January 17, 1985; June 12, 1986.

World Literature Today, autumn, 1992, p. 707.

*   *   *

FOGARTY, Jonathan Titulescu Esq.
    See FARRELL, James T(homas)

*   *   *

FOLKE, Will
    See BLOCH, Robert (Albert)

*   *   *

FOOTE, Shelby 1916-

PERSONAL: Born November 17, 1916, in Greenville, MS; son of Shelby Dade (a business executive) and Lillian (Rosenstock) Foote; married Gwyn Rainer, September 6, 1956; children: Margaret Shelby, Huger Lee. *Education:* Attended University of North Carolina, 1935-37.

ADDRESSES: Home and office—542 East Parkway S., Memphis, TN 38104.

CAREER: Novelist, historian, and playwright. Novelist-in-residence, University of Virginia, Charlottesville, 1963; playwright-in-residence, Arena Stage, Washington, D.C., 1963-64; writer-in-residence, Hollins College, Roanoke, VA, 1968. Judge, National Book Award in history, 1979. *Military service:* U.S. Army, artillery, 1940-44; became captain. U.S. Marine Corps, 1944-45.

MEMBER: American Academy of Arts and Letters, Society of American Historians, Fellowship of Southern Writers.

AWARDS, HONORS: Guggenheim fellowships, 1955, 1956, 1957, 1958, 1959, and 1960; Ford Foundation grant, 1963; Fletcher Pratt Award, 1964, for *The Civil War: A Narrative;* named distinguished alumnus, University of North Carolina, 1974; Dos Passos Prize for Literature, 1988; Charles Frankel Award, 1992; St. Louis Literary Award, 1992; Nevins-Freeman Award, 1992; received honorary D.Litt degrees from University of the South, 1981, Southwestern University, 1982, University of South Carolina, 1991, University of North Carolina, 1992, Millsaps University, 1992, and Notre Dame University, 1994.

WRITINGS:

NOVELS, EXCEPT AS INDICATED; PUBLISHED BY DIAL, EXCEPT AS INDICATED

Tournament, 1949.

Follow Me Down (also see below), 1950.

Love in a Dry Season (also see below), 1951.

Shiloh, 1952.

Jordan County: A Landscape in Narrative (also see below), 1954.

The Civil War: A Narrative (history), Random House, Volume I: *Fort Sumter to Perryville,* 1958, Volume II: *Fredericksburg to Meridian,* 1963, Volume III: *Red River to Appomattox,* 1974.

Three Novels (contains *Follow Me Down, Love in a Dry Season,* and *Jordan County: A Landscape in Narrative*), 1964.

September September, Random House, 1979.

A Novelist's View of History (nonfiction), 1981.

(Editor) *Chickamunga, and Other Civil War Stories* (short stories), Dell, 1993.

Stars in Their Courses: The Gettysburg Campaign (history), Random House, 1994.

The Beleaguered City: The Vicksburg Campaign, December 1862-July 1863 (originally published in Volume 2 of *The Civil War: A Narrative*), Modern Library (New York City), 1995.

Child by Fever, Random House, 1995.

Ride Out, Modern Library, 1996.

The Correspondence of Shelby Foote and Walker Percy, edited by Jay Tolson, Center for Documentary Studies (New York City), 1997.

Also author of play, "Jordan County: A Landscape in the Round," produced in Washington, D.C., 1964.

SIDELIGHTS: Although his novels have been favorably received, Shelby Foote is best known for his three-volume narrative history of the Civil War. Originally envisioned as a one-volume work, Foote's effort grew into what critics call a "monumental" project that took some twenty years to complete. In the *New York Times Book Review,* Nash K. Burger explains: "After writing five novels, one of which, *Shiloh,* dealt with the Civil War, Mississippi-born Shelby Foote was asked by a New York publisher to write a short, one-volume history of that conflict. Foote agreed. It seemed a nice change of pace before his next novel. Now, 20 years later, the project is completed: Three volumes . . . , 2,934 pages, a million and a half words." Burger follows his account of the writing of *The Civil War: A Narrative* with this assessment, "It is a remarkable achievement, prodigiously researched, vigorous, detailed, absorbing."

Other reviewers have voiced similar praise. *Newsweek*'s Peter S. Prescott states that "the result [of Foote's labor] is not only monumental in size, but a truly impressive achievement." He reports that "Foote the novelist cares less for generalizations about dialectics, men and motives than for creating 'the illusion that the observer is not so much reading a book as sharing an experience.'" According to M. E. Bradford in *National Review,* in this endeavor the author has succeeded: "There is, of course, a majesty inherent in the subject [of the Civil War]. . . . [And] the credit for recovering such majesty to the attention of our skeptical and unheroic age will hereafter belong . . . to Mr. Foote."

Foote's account of the war is strictly a military one, detailing the battles, men, and leaders on both sides of the conflict. "The War itself . . . is indeed Foote's subject," Bradford remarks. "The *war,* the *fighting*—and not its economic, intellectual, or political causes." Lance Morrow echoes this summation in a *Time* review: "[Foote's] attention is focused on the fighting itself—fortification, tactics, the strange chemistries of leadership, the workings in the generals' minds. Foote moves armies and great quantities of military information with a lively efficiency."

Critics note that though such military histories concerning the Civil War are not uncommon, Foote's is one of the most comprehensive, covering as it does the Union and Confederate Armies in both the eastern and western theaters of the war. Moreover, they express admiration for the author's balanced and objective view of the conflict. C. Vann Woodward of the *New York Review of Books* contends that "in spite of his Mississippi origins, Foote . . . attempts to keep an even hand in giving North and South their due measure of praise and blame." Burger agrees and adds that although Foote's chronicle begins and ends with reports on the activities of Jefferson Davis, this "is not indicative of any bias in favor of the South or its leader. . . . The complete work," the critic continues, "is a monumental, even-handed account of this country's tragic, fratricidal conflict."

In discussing Foote's concentration on the war itself and "therefore the persons who made, died in, or survived that conflict," Bradford asserts that it is not "an exaggeration to speak of the total effect produced by this emphasis as epic." Prescott concludes: "To read Foote's chronicle is an awesome and moving experience. History and literature are rarely so thoroughly combined as here; one finishes [the last] volume convinced that no one need undertake this particular enterprise again."

Foote became something of a national celebrity during the early 1990s for his on-camera commentary in Ken Burns's PBS documentary *The Civil War,* originally aired in 1990. Since that time, interest in Foote's life and work has increased markedly.

BIOGRAPHICAL/CRITICAL SOURCES:

BOOKS

Carter, William C., editor, *Conversations with Shelby Foote,* University Press of Mississippi, 1995.
Phillips, Robert L., Jr., *Shelby Foote: Novelist and Historian,* University Press of Mississippi, 1992.
Tolson, Jay, *The Correspondence of Shelby Foote and Walker Percy,* Center for Documentary Studies, 1997.
White, Helen, and Redding S. Sugg Jr., *Shelby Foote,* Twayne Publishers, 1982.

PERIODICALS

American Heritage, July-August, 1991.
Atlantic, May, 1952; December, 1963.
Book Week, December 15, 1963.
Chicago Sunday Tribune, November 16, 1958.
Christian Science Monitor, December 4, 1963.
Commonweal, January 9, 1959.
National Review, February 14, 1975.
Newsweek, December 2, 1974; January 30, 1978.
New York Herald Tribune Book Review, July 16, 1950; October 21, 1951; April 6, 1952; May 2, 1954; November 23, 1958.
New York Review of Books, March 6, 1975.
New York Times, September 25, 1949; September 23, 1951; April 6, 1952; April 25, 1954; November 16, 1958; December 1, 1996.
New York Times Book Review, December 1, 1963; December 15, 1974; March 5, 1978.
San Francisco Chronicle, November 28, 1958.
Saturday Review, November 19, 1949; June 5, 1954; December 13, 1958.
Time, July 3, 1950; January 27, 1975.

FORCHE, Carolyn (Louise) 1950-

PERSONAL: Surname is pronounced "for-*shay*"; born April 28, 1950, in Detroit, MI; daughter of Michael Joseph (a tool and die maker) and Louise Nada (a journalist; maiden name, Blackford) Sidlosky; married Henry E. Mattison (a news photographer), December 27, 1984; children: one son. *Education:* Michigan State University, B.A., 1972; Bowling Green State University, M.F.A., 1975.

ADDRESSES: Home—430 Greenwich St., New York, NY 10013. *Agent*—Virginia Barber, 353 West 21st St., New York, NY 10011.

CAREER: Michigan State University, Justin Morrill College, East Lansing, visiting lecturer in poetry, 1974; San Diego State University, San Diego, CA, visiting lecturer, 1975, assistant professor, 1976-78; University of Virginia, Charlottesville, visiting lecturer, 1979, visiting associate professor, 1982-83; University of Arkansas, Fayetteville, assistant professor, 1980, associate professor, 1981; New York University, New York City, visiting writer, 1983 and 1985; Vassar College, Poughkeepsie, NY, visiting writer, 1984; Writer's Community, New York City, visiting poet, 1984; State University of New York at Albany, Writer's Institute, writer in residence, 1985; George Mason University, Fairfax, VA, associate professor, 1994–. Columbia University, adjunct associate professor, 1984-85; University of Minnesota, visiting associate professor, summer, 1985. Journalist and human rights activist in El Salvador, 1978-80; correspondent for National Public Radio's *All Things Considered* in Beirut, 1983; consultant on Central America and member of Commission on U.S.-Central American Relations. Lecturer on human rights; gives poetry readings.

MEMBER: Amnesty International, PEN American Center (member of Freedom to Write and Silenced Voices committees), Poetry Society of America, Academy of American Poets, Associated Writing Programs (president, 1994–), Institute for Global Education, Coalition for a New Foreign Policy, Theta Sigma Phi.

AWARDS, HONORS: Devine Memorial fellowship in poetry, 1975; First Award in Poetry, *Chicago Review,* 1975; Yale Series of Younger Poets Award, 1975, for *Gathering the Tribes;* Tennessee Williams fellowship in poetry, Bread Loaf Writers Conference, 1976; National Endowment for the Arts fellowships, 1977 and 1984; John Simon Guggenheim Memorial fellowship, 1978; Emily Clark Balch Prize, *Virginia Quarterly Review,* 1979; Alice Fay di Castagnola Award, Poetry Society of America, 1981; Lamont Poetry Selection Award, Academy of American Poets, 1981, for *The Country between Us; Los Angeles Times* Book Award nominee, 1982, for *The Country between Us;* H.D.L., Russell Sage College, 1985; *Los Angeles Times* Book Award for Poetry, 1994, for *The Angel of History.*

WRITINGS:

(With Martha Jane Soltow) *Women in the Labor Movement, 1835-1925: An Annotated Bibliography,* Michigan State University Press (East Lansing, MI), 1972.
Gathering the Tribes (poetry), Yale University Press (New Haven, CT), 1976.
The Colonel, Bieler Press, 1978.
(Editor) *Women and War in El Salvador,* Women's International Resource Exchange (New York City), 1980.
The Country between Us (poetry), Copper Canyon Press (Port Townsend, WA), 1981.

(Translator) Claribel Alegria, *Flowers from the Volcano,* University of Pittsburgh Press (Pittsburgh, PA), 1982.

(Author of text) *El Salvador: The Work of Thirty Photographers,* edited by Harry Mattison, Susan Meiselas, and Fae Rubenstein, Writers and Readers Publishing Cooperative (New York City), 1983.

(Editor and author of introduction) *Against Forgetting: Twentieth-Century Poetry of Witness,* Norton (New York City), 1993.

The Angel of History (poetry), HarperCollins (New York City), 1994.

Colors Come from God—Just Like Me! Abingdon Press, 1995.

(With others) *Lani Maestro/Cradle Cradle Ugoy* (catalog for an exhibition), Art in General (New York City), 1996.

Contributing editor of *The Pushcart Prize: Best of the Small Presses,* Volume III; poetry co-editor of *The Pushcart Prize: Best of the Small Presses,* Volume VIII. Work represented in anthologies, including *The Pushcart Prize: Best of the Small Presses,* Volume VI and Volume VIII; *The American Poetry Anthology*; and *Anthology of Magazine Verse: Yearbook of American Poetry.* Contributor of poetry, articles, and reviews to periodicals, including *Parnassus: Poetry in Review, New York Times Book Review, Washington Post Book World, Ms., Antaeus, Atlantic Monthly,* and *American Poetry Review.* Poetry editor of *New Virginia Review,* 1981; contributing editor of *Tendril.*

SIDELIGHTS: "Perhaps no one better exemplifies the power and excellence of contemporary poetry than Carolyn Forche, who is not only one of the most affecting younger poets in America, but also one of the best poets writing anywhere in the world today," Jonathan Cott wrote in the introduction to his interview with Forche for *Rolling Stone.* Such praise was not new to Forche. Her first book of poetry, *Gathering the Tribes,* recounts experiences of the author's adolescence and young adult life and won the 1975 Yale Series of Younger Poets Award, and her second, *The Country between Us,* was named the 1981 Lamont Poetry Selection and became a poetry best-seller. In a critique for the *Los Angeles Times Book Review,* Art Seidenbaum maintained that the poems of the second volume "chronicle the awakening of a political consciousness and are themselves acts of commitment: to concepts and persons, to responsibility, to action." According to Joyce Carol Oates in the *New York Times Book Review,* Forche's ability to wed the "political" with the "personal" places her in the company of such poets as Pablo Neruda, Philip Levine, and Denise Levertov.

By the time she was twenty-four, Forche had completed *Gathering the Tribes,* described by Stanley Kunitz in the book's foreword as a work centering on kinship. In these poems Forche "remembers her childhood in rural Michigan, evokes her Slovak ancestors, immerses herself in the American Indian culture of the Southwest, explores the mysteries of flesh, tries to understand the bonds of family, race, and sex," related Kunitz. "Burning the Tomato Worms," for example, deals with a young woman's sexual coming of age. But this poetic tale of "first sexual experience," Mark Harris stated in a *Dictionary of Literary Biography* essay, "is told against the larger backdrop of her grandmother's life and death and their meaning to a woman just grown."

If *Gathering the Tribes* "introduced a poet of uncommon vigor and assurance," Oates wrote, then *The Country between Us* "is a distinct step forward." A *Ms.* reviewer called that second book "a poetry of dissent from a poet outraged." Forche herself told Cott: "The voice in my first book doesn't know what it thinks, it doesn't make any judgments. All it can do is perceive and describe and use language to make some sort of re-creation of moments in time. But I noticed that the person in the second book makes an utterance."

Forche's first two volumes of poetry were separated by a period of five years, during the course of which she was involved with Amnesty International and with translating the work of Salvadoran poets. In those years she also had the opportunity to go to Central America as a journalist and human rights advocate and learned firsthand of violations against life and liberty. While there, she viewed inadequate health facilities that had never received the foreign aid designated for them and discovered that sixty-three out of every thousand children died from gastrointestinal infections before age one; she saw for herself the young girls who had been sexually mutilated; she learned of torture victims who had been beaten, starved, and otherwise abused; and she experienced something of what it was like to survive in a country where baby food jars are sometimes used as bombs.

Her experiences found expression in *The Country between Us.* As reviewer Katha Pollitt observed in the *Nation,* Forche "insists more than once on the transforming power of what she has seen, on the gulf it has created between herself and those who have seen less and dared less." The poet herself admitted to the compelling nature of her Central American experience. "I tried not to write about El Salvador in poetry, because I thought it might be better to do so in journalistic articles," she told Cott. "But I couldn't—the poems just came." El Salvador became the primary subject of *The Country between Us.* In these poems Forche "addresses herself unflinchingly to the exterior, historical world," Oates explained. She did so at a time when most of her contemporaries were writing poetry in which there is no room for politics—poetry, Pollitt stated, "of wistful longings, of failed connections, of inevitable personal loss, expressed in a set of poetic strategies that suit such themes."

Forche is considered particularly adept at depicting cruelty and helpless victims, and in so doing, Paul Gray wrote in *Time,* she "makes pain palpable." More than one critic singled out her poem "The Colonel," centering on her now-famous encounter with a Salvadoran colonel who, as he made light of human rights, emptied a bag of human ears before Forche. The poem concludes: "Something for your poetry, no? he said. Some of the ears on the floor caught this scrap of his voice. Some of the ears on the floor were pressed to the ground." Pollitt remarked that "at their best, Forche's poems have the immediacy of war correspondence, postcards from the volcano of twentieth-century barbarism."

A dozen years passed between the publication of *The Country between Us* and *Against Forgetting: Twentieth-Century Poetry of Witness,* her anthology of poets speaking of human rights violations on a global level. The poems in this anthology present what Matthew Rothschild in the *Progressive* called "some of the most dramatic antiwar and anti-torture poetry written in this benighted century." The poems provide, as Gail Wronsky pointed out in the *Antioch Review,* "irrefutable and copious evidence of the human ability to record, to write, to speak in the face of those atrocities." Building on the tradition of social protest and the antiwar poems of the late 1960s, Forche presents a range of approaches: "Many of the poems here are eyes-open, horrifyingly graphic portrayals of human brutality," observed Rothschild. "But others are of defiance, demonstrating resolve and extracting hope even in the most extreme circumstances."

Against Forgetting begins with poets who witnessed the Ottoman Turk genocide of 1.5 million Armenians between 1909 and 1918. In this section the executed Armenian poet Siamento seems to speak for all the other poets in the collection: "Don't be afraid. I must tell you what I say / so people will understand / the crimes men do to men." Another section includes poems by Americans, Germans, and Japanese about the effects of World War II upon those who witnessed and recorded the events. There are also sections on the Holocaust, the Spanish Civil War, the Soviet Union, Central and Eastern Europe, the Mediterranean, the Middle East, Latin America, South Africa, and China.

Critics are divided upon both the selections in and the importance of *Against Forgetting*. Wronsky, for example, questioned why "women of all races and ethnicities are underrepresented here (124 male poets to 20 female)." But Phoebe Pettingell in the *New Leader* argued that the work's flaws were "outweighed by the anthology's breadth and scope, and by the excellence of most of its entries. *Against Forgetting* preaches the hope that humanity, after a century of unparalleled brutality met largely by helplessness, can finally learn to mend its ways." John Bayley in the *New York Review of Books* called it "a remarkable book. Not only in itself and for the poems it contains, but for the ideas that lie behind their selection as an anthology."

The year following the publication of *Against Forgetting* saw Forche bring out her own book of witness, *The Angel of History*, which won the 1994 *Los Angeles Times* Book Award for Poetry. The book is divided into five sections, dealing with the atrocities of war in France, Japan, and Germany and with references to the poet's own experiences in Beirut and El Salvador. The title figure, the Angel of History—a figure imagined by German philosopher and critic Walter Benjamin—can record the miseries of humanity yet is unable either to prevent these miseries from happening or from suffering from the pain associated with them.

Kevin Walker in the *Detroit Free Press* called the book "a meditation on destruction, survival and memory." Don Bogen in the *Nation* saw this as a logical development, since Forche's work with *Against Forgetting* was "instrumental in moving her poetry beyond the politics of personal encounter. *The Angel of History* is rather an extended poetic mediation on the broader contexts—historical, aesthetic, philosophical—which include our century's atrocities."

Critical response to *The Angel of History* was generally supportive. Calvin Bedient of the *Threepenny Review* claimed that *The Angel of History* is "instantly recognizable as a great book, the most humanitarian and aesthetically 'inevitable' response to a half-century of atrocities that has yet been written in English." Steven Ratiner in *Christian Science Monitor* called the collection one which "addresses the terror and inhumanity that have become standard elements in the 20th-century political landscape—and yet affirms as well the even greater reservoir of the human spirit."

Forche is a poet of social and political conscience in an era when poetry is often criticized for being self-centered and self-absorbed. But Forche's verse does not always succeed, according to some critics. Pollitt identified an "incongruity between Forche's themes and her poetic strategies," also commenting on a certain lack of "verbal energy" in her work. William Logan, critiquing for the *Times Literary Supplement*, explained that "in her attempt to offer a personal response to the horrors she has witnessed, Forche too often emphasizes herself at their expense. . . . Forche's work relies on sensibility, but she has not found a language for deeper feeling." Nevertheless, recognizing Forche's achievement, Pollitt

commended the poet for "her brave and impassioned attempt to make a place in her poems for starving children and bullet factories, for torturers and victims." She might not be a reassuring poet but, in the words of Paul Gray, "she is something better, an arresting and often unforgettable voice."

BIOGRAPHICAL/CRITICAL SOURCES:

BOOKS

Contemporary Literary Criticism, Gale (Detroit), Volume 25, 1983; Volume 83, 1994; Volume 86, 1995.
Contemporary Poets, fifth edition, St. James Press (Detroit), 1991.
Dictionary of Literary Biography, Volume 5: *American Poets since World War II,* Gale, 1980.
Poetry Criticism, Volume 10, Gale, 1994.

PERIODICALS

American Poetry, spring, 1986, pp. 51-69.
American Poetry Review, November-December, 1976, p. 45; July-August, 1981, pp. 3-8; January-February, 1983, pp. 35-39; November-December, 1988, pp. 35-40.
Antioch Review, summer, 1994, p. 536.
Bloomsbury Review, September/October, 1994, p. 19.
Book Forum, 1976, pp. 369-99.
Boston Globe, July 24, 1994, p. 42.
Centennial Review, spring, 1986, pp. 160-80.
Chicago Tribune, December 13, 1982, pp. 1-3.
Christian Science Monitor, April 20, 1994, p. 20.
Commonweal, November 25, 1977.
Detroit Free Press, May 27, 1982; May 22, 1994, p. 8.
Detroit News, June 8, 1982.
Georgia Review, winter, 1982, pp. 911-22; summer, 1994, pp. 361-66.
Library Journal, May 1, 1993, p. 88.
Los Angeles Times, August 24, 1982; October 17, 1982; February 22, 1984.
Los Angeles Times Book Review, May 23, 1982; October 17, 1982.
Ms., January, 1980; September, 1982.
Nation, May 8, 1982; October 16, 1982; December 27, 1993, pp. 809, 814; October 24, 1994, p. 464.
New England Review, spring, 1994, p. 144-154.
New Leader, May 17, 1993, pp. 23-24.
New York Review of Books, June 24, 1993, pp. 20-22.
New York Times Book Review, August 8, 1976; April 4, 1982; April 19, 1982; December 4, 1983.
Parnassus, spring-summer, 1982, pp. 9-21.
Progressive, October, 1993, pp. 45-46.
Publishers Weekly, February 1, 1993, p. 78; January 31, 1994, p. 7.
Rolling Stone, April 14, 1983, pp. 81, 83-87, 110-11.
Text and Performance Quarterly, January, 1990, pp. 61-70.
Threepenny Review, summer, 1994, pp. 19-20.
Time, March 15, 1982.
Times Literary Supplement, June 10, 1983.
Triquarterly, winter, 1986, pp. 30, 32-38.
Village Voice, March 29, 1976.
Virginia Quarterly Review, autumn, 1994, p. 136.
Washington Post Book World, May 30, 1982.
Whole Earth Review, spring, 1996, p. 70.
Women's Review of Books, July, 1995, p. 3.

FORD, Elbur
See HIBBERT, Eleanor Alice Burford

*   *   *

FORD, Ford Madox 1873-1939
(Ford Madox Hueffer; pseudonyms: Daniel Chaucer, Fenil Haig, Baron Ignatz von Aschendrof)

PERSONAL: Birth name Ford Hermann Madox Hueffer; name legally changed, 1919; born December 17, 1873, in Merton, Surrey, England; died of heart failure June 26, 1939, in Deauville, France; son of Francis (formerly Franz; an author and music critic for the London *Times*) and Catherine Madox (an artist; maiden name, Brown) Hueffer; married Elsie Martindale, May 17, 1894 (separated, 1909); children: Christina, Katherine; (with Stella Bowen) Esther Julia. *Education:* Educated at schools in England. *Religion:* Roman Catholic.

CAREER: Novelist, poet, critic, and editor. Founder and editor, 1908-10, *English Review*; founder and editor, *transatlantic review*, Paris, France, 1924; writer and critic in residence, Olivet College, Olivet, MI, 1937. *Military service:* British Army, World War I, beginning 1915; transportation officer.

AWARDS, HONORS: Doctor of Literature, Olivet College, 1938.

WRITINGS:

FICTION; UNDER NAME FORD MADOX HUEFFER

The Brown Owl: A Fairy Story (for children), Stokes, 1891.
The Feather (for children), frontispiece by grandfather, Ford Madox Brown, Cassell, 1892.
The Shifting of the Fire, Putnam, 1892.
The Queen Who Flew: A Fairy Tale (for children), Bliss, Sands & Foster, 1894.
(With Joseph Conrad) *The Inheritors: An Extravagant Story,* McClure, Phillips, 1901.
(With Conrad) *Romance: A Novel,* Smith, Elder, 1903, McClure, Phillips, 1904.
The Benefactor: A Tale of a Small Circle, Brown, Langham, 1905.
Christina's Fairy Book (for children), Alston Rivers, 1906.
The Fifth Queen: And How She Came to Court (first novel in "Fifth Queen" trilogy; also see below), Alston Rivers, 1906.
Privy Seal: His Last Venture (second novel in "Fifth Queen" trilogy; also see below), Alston Rivers, 1907.
An English Girl: A Romance, Methuen, 1907.
The Fifth Queen Crowned: A Romance (third novel in "Fifth Queen" trilogy; also see below), E. Nash, 1908.
Mr. Apollo: A Just Possible Story, Methuen, 1908.
The "Half Moon": A Romance of the Old World and the New, Doubleday, Page, 1909.
A Call: The Tale of Two Passions, Chatto & Windus, 1910.
The Portrait, Methuen, 1910.
Ladies Whose Bright Eyes: A Romance, Constable, 1911, Doubleday, 1912, revised edition published under name Ford Madox Ford, Lippincott, 1935.
The Panel: A Sheer Comedy, Constable, 1912, revised and expanded version published as *Ring for Nancy: A Sheer Comedy,* Bobbs-Merrill, 1913.
Mr. Fleight, Latimer, 1913.
The Young Lovell: A Romance, Chatto & Windus, 1913.
The Good Soldier: A Tale of Passion (novel), John Lane, 1915, reprinted under name Ford Madox Ford, Vintage, 1989, reprinted as *The Good Soldier: Authoritative Text, Textual Appendices, Contemporary Reviews, Literary Impressionism, Biographical and Critical Commentary,* Norton (New York City), 1995.
(With Conrad) *The Nature of a Crime* (novel), Duckworth, 1923, Doubleday, Page, 1924.

FICTION; UNDER NAME FORD MADOX FORD

The Marsden Case: A Romance, Duckworth, 1923.
Some Do Not . . . (first novel in tetralogy; also see below), Seltzer, 1924.
No More Parades (second novel in tetralogy; also see below), A. & C. Boni, 1925.
A Man Could Stand Up (third novel in tetralogy; also see below), A. & C. Boni, 1926.
The Last Post (fourth novel in tetralogy; also see below), A. & C. Boni, 1928.
A Little Less Than Gods: A Romance, Viking, 1928.
No Enemy: A Tale of Reconstruction, Macaulay, 1929.
When the Wicked Man, Liveright, 1931.
The Rash Act, Long & Smith, 1933.
Henry for Hugh (sequel to *The Rash Act*), Lippincott, 1934.
Vive le Roy, Lippincott, 1936.
Parade's End (contains *Some Do Not . . .*, *No More Parades*, *A Man Could Stand Up*, and *The Last Post*), Knopf, 1950, revised edition, 1961.
The Fifth Queen (contains *The Fifth Queen*, *Privy Seal*, and *The Fifth Queen Crowned*), Ecco Press, 1980.

MEMOIRS

(Under name Ford Madox Hueffer) *Memories and Impressions: A Study in Atmospheres,* Harper, 1911 (published in England as *Ancient Lights and Certain New Reflections, Being the Memories of a Young Man,* Chapman & Hall, 1911).
(Under name Ford Madox Hueffer) *Thus to Revisit: Some Reminiscences of Ford Madox Hueffer,* Chapman & Hall, 1921.
Joseph Conrad: A Personal Remembrance, Little, Brown, 1924.
Return to Yesterday: Reminiscences 1894-1914, Gollancz, 1931, Liveright, 1932.
It Was the Nightingale, Lippincott, 1933.
Portraits from Life: Memories and Criticisms, Houghton, 1937 (published in England as *Mightier Than the Sword: Memories and Criticisms,* Allen & Unwin, 1938).

UNDER NAME FORD MADOX HUEFFER

Ford Madox Brown: A Record of His Life and Work (biography), Longmans, Green, 1896.
The Cinque Ports: A Historical and Descriptive Record, Blackwood, 1900.
Poems for Pictures and for Notes of Music, Macqueen, 1900.
Rossetti: A Critical Essay on His Art, Dutton, 1902.
The Face of the Night: A Second Series of Poems for Pictures, Macqueen, 1904.
The Soul of London: A Survey of a Modern City (also see below), Alston Rivers, 1905.
Hans Holbein, the Younger: A Critical Monograph, Dutton, 1905.
The Heart of the Country: A Survey of a Modern Land (also see below), Alston Rivers, 1906.
The Pre-Raphaelite Brotherhood: A Critical Monograph, Dutton, 1907.
The Spirit of the People: An Analysis of the English Mind (also see below), Alston Rivers, 1907.
From Inland and Other Poems, Alston Rivers, 1907.

England and the English: An Interpretation (contains *The Soul of London, The Heart of the Country,* and *The Spirit of the People*), McClure, Phillips, 1907.
Songs from London, Elkin Mathews, 1910.
The Critical Attitude (essays), Duckworth, 1911.
High Germany: Eleven Sets of Verse, Duckworth, 1911.
Henry James, a Critical Study, Secker, 1913, A. & C. Boni, 1915.
Collected Poems, Goschen, 1913.
Antwerp (poem), Poetry Bookshop, 1914.
Between St. Dennis and St. George: A Sketch of Three Civilizations, Hodder & Stoughton, 1915.
When Blood Is Their Argument: An Analysis of Prussian Culture, Hodder & Stoughton, 1915.
(With Violet Hunt) *Zeppelin Nights: A London Entertainment,* John Lane, 1916.
(Translator) Pierre Loti, *The Trail of the Barbarians,* Longmans, 1917.
On Heaven, and Poems Written on Active Service, John Lane, 1918.
A House: Modern Morality Play, Monthly Chapbook, Number 21, 1921.

OTHER

(Under pseudonym Fenil Haig) *The Questions at the Well: With Sundry Other Verses for Notes of Music,* Digby, Long, 1893.
(Under pseudonym Daniel Chaucer) *The Simple Life Limited* (novel), John Lane, 1911.
(Under pseudonym Daniel Chaucer) *The New Humpty-Dumpty* (novel), John Lane, 1912.
Women and Men, Three Mountains Press (Paris), 1923.
Mister Bosphorus and the Muses; or, A Short History of Poetry in Britain: Variety Entertainment in Four Acts, Duckworth, 1923.
A Mirror to France, A. & C. Boni, 1926.
New Poems, W. E. Rudge, 1927.
New York Essays, W. E. Rudge, 1927.
New York Is Not America: Being a Mirror to the States, A. &. C. Boni, 1927.
The English Novel, from the Earliest Days to the Death of Joseph Conrad (criticism), Lippincott, 1929.
Provence: From Minstrels to the Machine (travel), drawings by Janice Biala, Lippincott, 1935.
Collected Poems, Oxford University Press, 1936.
Great Trade Route (travel), drawings by Biala, Oxford University Press, 1937.
The March of Literature, from Confucius' Day to Our Own, Dial, 1938 (published in England as *The March of Literature from Confucius to Modern Times,* Allen & Unwin, 1939).
The Bodley Head Ford Madox Ford (collected works), Bodley Head, Volumes 1-4, edited by Graham Greene, 1962, Volume 5, edited by Michael Killigrew, 1971.
Critical Writings of Ford Madox Ford, edited by Frank McShane, University of Nebraska Press, 1964.
Letters of Ford Madox Ford, edited by Richard M. Ludwig, Princeton University Press, 1965.
Buckshee (poems), Pym-Randall Press, 1966.
(With Ezra Pound) *Pound-Ford: The Story of a Literary Friendship* (letters), edited by Brita L. Seyersted, New Directions, 1982.
The Ford Madox Ford Reader (collected works), edited by Sondra Stang, foreword by Greene, Ecco Press, 1986.
A History of Our Own Times, edited by Stang and Solon Beinfeld, Indiana University Press, 1988.

SIDELIGHTS: "Though a controversial writer and often an easy target for critics because of his literary and personal excesses, Ford Madox Ford played a key role in the development of modern literature," Richard F. Peterson maintained in a *Dictionary of Literary Biography* essay. A prolific writer of novels, memoirs, nonfiction, and criticism, Ford also introduced and supported the efforts of such writers as D. H. Lawrence, Ezra Pound, and James Joyce through his editing of two progressive periodicals, the *English Review* and *Transatlantic Review.* He "firmly believed that he had played a major role in shaping the most important literary movement of the modern age, a movement he termed impressionism," Peterson continued. In works such as *The Good Soldier* and the *Parade's End* tetralogy, Ford developed his impressionistic techniques of time shift and point of view into complex narratives that arrived at subtle human truths through seemingly simple incidents and details. "He succeed[ed], more often than not, in his ingenious system of getting at the inside of things by looking intensely at the surface alone," V. S. Pritchett commented in *The Working Novelist.*

Ford's memoirs in particular exhibited the dual nature that aggravated his critics and delighted his supporters. *Joseph Conrad: A Personal Remembrance,* Ford's account of his relationship with the famous novelist, was faulted for its inaccuracies, and Conrad's widow publicly denounced it as pandering to Ford's vanity at her husband's expense. But "in its peculiar way, [*Joseph Conrad*] is quite a clever production," noted *Nation and Athenaeum* reviewer E. Garnett, "and does, with all its exaggerations and distortions of facts, contain many interesting picturesque impressions of Conrad as he 'revealed himself' to his collaborator." American critic H. L. Mencken similarly observed that while Ford was prone to exaggeration, "what he says, even when he is most impudent, always has a well-greased reasonableness," he wrote in the *American Mercury.*

His efforts as chronicler and editor of a literary age notwithstanding, Ford wrote several renowned fictions that are acknowledged as his greatest contributions. One of his earlier works, *The Fifth Queen* trilogy (consisting of *The Fifth Queen, Privy Seal,* and *The Fifth Queen Crowned*), exhibits qualities that distinguish his later masterpieces. Set in the court of Henry VIII, the trilogy follows the efforts of Katherine Howard—the fifth of Henry's wives—to neutralize the immoral and corrupt influences of her husband's advisors. As with his literary memoirs, the strong point of Ford's historical trilogy is his construction of atmosphere and detail; London *Times* reviewer Anne Barnes, for instance, noted that "the story is built up through a mass of impressions" and likened the book's descriptions to "a film [Ford] sees in his own mind." As Arthur Mizener recounted in *The Saddest Story: A Biography of Ford Madox Ford,* "the remarkable moments of Ford's *Fifth Queen* trilogy are its dazzling historical scenes. . . . These scenes are dazzling reconstructions, paintings in the tradition of [Ford's grandfather, painter] Ford Madox Brown," the biographer added, and the work's "pageantry" reveals "the complex political purposes that cause these events, and the scenes of plotting and planning that bring them about."

While *The Fifth Queen* treated the traditional subjects of historical fiction, it was also a precursor to Ford's later, more impressionistic work. "No doubt *The Fifth Queen* is too close to the eye in a cinematic way to have the spacious historical sense of a great historical novel," Pritchett commented, ". . . but it makes most of our historical fiction up to 1914 look like the work of interior decorators." In *Bookman,* Granville Hicks elaborated on the nature of the trilogy: "The author's interest [in the series] is centered in the presentation of states of mind and the rendering of sequences that are largely psychological."

While Ford wrote over thirty novels, it is *The Good Soldier* that "stands out as a masterpiece of modern fiction," Peterson claimed, calling it "a masterstroke of impressionistic fiction that ranks with [other modern classics] in its perfect balance of point of view, character, and theme." "*The Good Soldier* is 'A Tale of Passion,'" Samuel Hynes related in the *Sewanee Review,* "a story of seduction, adultery, and suicide told by a deceived husband." For several years, American John Dowell and his wife Florence have sustained a friendly relationship with Edward and Leonora Ashburnham, a British couple they met at a European spa. Dowell, who narrates the story, makes clear his admiration for Edward Ashburnham's gentlemanly virtues, even though, as the reader learns, the former soldier indulged in several affairs, including one with Dowell's wife that led to her suicide. "These are melodramatic materials," maintained Hynes; "yet the novel is not a melodrama, because the action of which it is an imitation is not the sequence of passionate gestures which in another novel we would call the plot, but rather the action of the narrator's mind as it gropes for the meaning, the reality of what has occurred."

Complementing Ford's use of time shift in *The Good Soldier* is Dowell's narrative point of view, which adds another dimension of irony to the novel. As Dowell continues to reconsider the events of his narrative, he creates an ironic contrast between his present and past interpretations. As Mizener stated: "The ironic wit of *The Good Soldier*'s style depends . . . on a discrepancy between Dowell's attitude as a participant in the events and Dowell's attitude as a narrator of them. All the perception, the tolerance, the humility that recognizes the limitations of its own understanding; all the poetic wit of the book's figures of speech; all the powerful ironies of the narration; all these things are Dowell's." "In choosing for the narrator a dull and unemotional man who fumbles his way through a tale of passion which leads to death and madness," Pritchett asserted, "Ford has found someone who will perfectly put together the case of the [passionate] heart versus conventional society, for he is a mild American Quaker perpetually astonished by Catholic puritanism. Meanwhile," the critic added, "his own do-gooding wife is, unknown to him, a destroyer and nymphomaniac." Further, wrote Mizener, Edward Ashburnham's gentlemanly behavior contains its own contradictions, for the novel "includes a judgment of the world in which Edward Ashburnham has to exist and an ironic awareness of the impossibility of Edward's conduct in that world."

This conflict in *The Good Soldier* between the ideal of being a gentleman in the rural tradition and the reality of modern industrial life was one of Ford's most common themes. As John A. Meixner related in *Ford Madox Ford's Novels: A Critical Study*: "In *The Good Soldier,* a book which dramatizes the emotional meaning of this change in the life of modern man, Ford's great theme . . . finds its quintessential rendering." "Ford has taken the most common materials and used them artistically," Robie Macauley maintained in the *Kenyon Review:* "he has employed the wandering style of narration and used it for a series of brilliant *progressions d'effet*; he has used a commonplace vocabulary sensitively and precisely, making it sound fresh; he has taken the threadbare plot of unhappy marriage—even the 'triangle'—and given it such new life and meaning that it becomes a passionate and universal story." As a result, Meixner concluded, *The Good Soldier* is "one of the literary triumphs of the twentieth century—a creation of the very highest art which must also be ranked among the more powerful novels that have been written."

Many critics have observed that *Parade's End* contains Ford's most convincing rendition of his theme of the virtuous gentleman ruined by modern society. Frank MacShane, for example, reported in the *New Republic* that this theme is "more clearly defined and more satisfactorily projected in *Parade's End*" than in his other works. Tietjens's "chivalric behavior, his complete honesty, his willingness always to turn the other cheek—all these qualities so enrage his fellows that he meets disaster . . . in a world run on the principles of dog-eat-dog," the critic added. In the Tietjens tetralogy, Marlene Griffith proposed in a *Modern Fiction Studies* article, Ford "had . . . to show an individual coming to grips with the new dichotomy of private man and social man, and at the same time to show how the social and private worlds relate. It is a remarkable accomplishment that Ford was able to resolve this complex task."

Parade's End is Ford's "most wide-ranging and serious judgment of the failure of the modern world to sustain the essential truths and traditions that most define culture and civilization," Peterson stated, and the optimum setting for this theme is "the critical years surrounding World War I when the values of Western civilization changed so dramatically." A *Saturday Review* critic, among others, found the tetralogy's war sequences most convincing, commenting that they "easily surpass everything else that has yet been written in English about the physical circumstances and moral atmosphere of the [First World] War." Ford's descriptions of war, however, are not graphic but rather ironic; "there is not a great deal of mud, blood, tears, and death, but what there is is awful—and it is not merely awful, but hideously silly," Kenneth Rexroth claimed in the *Saturday Review.* "No book has ever revealed more starkly the senselessness of the disasters of war, nor shown up with sharper X-ray vision, under the torn flesh of war, the hidden, all-corrupting sickness of the vindictive world of peace-behind-the-lines." "We catch the true Fordian note from the start," Ambrose Gordon, Jr., noted in *Sewanee Review,* for "the prose is the quietest and suavest imaginable." In the tetralogy's second volume, *No More Parades,* the critic concluded, "we are given a glimpse of [war's] violence in a matrix of quietness, of intimacy being violated by more than sound."

"There is no other living writer whose work is more generally effective than Mr. Ford Madox Ford's," Charles Williams wrote in a 1938 *Time & Tide* article. In *Parade's End,* for example, "the quietness and the accuracy [of his narrative] were so extreme that the voice seemed to come from under one's own skin; if the experiences of those books were not one's own, yet the nightmare of them was." "As a story-teller Ford recognised life when he saw complication and chance," Pritchett summarized, explaining the author's fondness for exploring incongruities. As C. H. Sisson elaborated in *The Presence of Ford Madox Ford*: "The surface of Ford's writing is wavering, offering sometimes sharp, definite sketches and assertions which are inconsistent with one another; yet one carries away from his work the impression of a truthfulness hidden somewhere in this unstable mass. At the center, wherever it is, there is a passionate and painful care for good writing." "If [Ford] neither was nor thought himself the greatest writer of his time, he was nonetheless a superbly talented man," Mizener declared. "It is almost literally true that he could . . . write anything and write it well. He wrote poetry that anticipates—in style if not feeling—some of the essential qualities of twentieth-century poetry. He was, at moments, a fine novelist and . . . even more frequently he was a very good novelist who wrote half-a-dozen period books that will stand comparison with the work of contemporaries . . . and several clever experimental novels." "Ford is now generally perceived as a legitimate member of an exclusive company of artists who shaped modern literature because of their belief in the autonomy of the artist and the primacy of literature in defining the values of civilization," Peterson remarked. Ford's achievements both as an author and in discovering and supporting the writing of others, concluded the critic, entitle him "to be regarded as one of the main architects of modern literature."

BIOGRAPHICAL/CRITICAL SOURCES:

BOOKS

Bender, Todd K. *Literary Impressionism in Jean Rhys, Ford Madox Ford, Joseph Conrad, and Charlotte Bronte,* Garland, 1997.
Cassell, Richard A., *Ford Madox Ford: A Study of His Novels,* Johns Hopkins Press, 1961.
Dictionary of Literary Biography, Volume 34: *British Novelists, 1890-1929: Traditionalists,* Gale, 1985.
Greene, Graham, *Collected Essays,* Viking, 1969.
Harvey, David Dow, *Ford Madox Ford, 1873-1939: A Bibliography of Works and Criticism,* Princeton University Press, 1962.
MacShane, Frank, editor, *Ford Madox Ford: The Critical Heritage,* Routledge & Kegan Paul, 1972.
Meixner, John A., *Ford Madox Ford's Novels: A Critical Study,* University of Minnesota Press, 1962.
Mizener, Arthur, *The Saddest Story: A Biography of Ford Madox Ford,* World Publishing, 1971.
Pound, Ezra, *Pavannes and Divisions,* Knopf, 1918.
Pritchett, V. S., *The Working Novelist,* Chatto & Windus, 1965.
Saunders, Max, *Ford Madox Ford: A Dual Life,* Oxford University Press (New York City), 1996.
Snitow, Ann Barr, *Ford Madox Ford and the Voice of Uncertainty,* Louisiana State University Press, 1984.
Stang, Sondra J., editor, *The Presence of Ford Madox Ford: A Memorial Volume of Essays, Poems, and Memoirs,* University of Pennsylvania Press, 1981.
Twentieth-Century Literary Criticism, Gale, Volume 1, 1978; Volume 15, 1985.

PERIODICALS

American Mercury, April, 1925.
Bookman, December, 1930.
Books, January 17, 1932.
Hudson Review, autumn, 1971.
Kenyon Review, spring, 1949.
Modern Fiction Studies (special Ford issue), spring, 1963.
Nation, July 30, 1949.
Nation and Athenaeum, December 6, 1924.
New Republic, April 4, 1955.
New Yorker, February 12, 1972.
New York Herald Tribune Book Review, October 1, 1950.
New York Herald Tribune Books, October 17, 1926.
New York Times, September 17, 1950.
San Francisco Chronicle, September 24, 1950.
Saturday Review, February 18, 1928; May 16, 1964; September 4, 1965; March 16, 1968.
Sewanee Review, spring, 1961; summer, 1962.
Spectator, November 21, 1931.
Time & Tide, March 12, 1938.
Times (London), September 8, 1984.
Times Literary Supplement, June 14, 1985.
Vogue, July, 1971.

FORD, Richard 1944-

PERSONAL: Born February 16, 1944, in Jackson, MS; son of Parker Carrol (in sales) and Edna (Akin) Ford; married Kristina Hensley (a research professor), 1968. *Education:* Michigan State University, B.A., 1966; University of California, Irvine, M.F.A., 1970.

ADDRESSES: Agent—Amanda Urban, International Creative Management, 40 W. 57th St., New York, NY 10019.

CAREER: Writer. Lecturer at University of Michigan, Ann Arbor, 1974-76, and at Princeton University, Princeton, NJ, 1979-80; assistant professor of English, Williams College, Williamstown, MA, 1978-79.

MEMBER: Writers Guild (East), PEN.

AWARDS, HONORS: University of Michigan Society of Fellows, 1971-74; Guggenheim fellow, 1977-78; National Endowment for the Arts fellow, 1979-80, 1985-86; *The Sportswriter* was chosen one of the five best books of 1986, *Time* magazine; PEN/Faulkner citation for fiction, 1987, for *The Sportswriter;* literature award, Mississippi Academy of Arts and Letters, 1987; literature award, American Academy and Institute of Arts and Letters, 1989; Literary Lion Award, New York Public Library, 1989; Echoing Green Foundation award, 1991; Pulitzer Prize, 1995, for *Independence Day;* PEN/Faulkner Award for Fiction, 1995, for *Independence Day;* Rea Short Story Award, 1995.

WRITINGS:

FICTION

A Piece of My Heart (novel), Harper, 1976.
The Ultimate Good Luck (novel), Houghton, 1981.
The Sportswriter (novel), Vintage, 1986.
Rock Springs: Stories (includes "Children" and "Great Falls"), Atlantic Monthly Press, 1987.
Wildlife (novel), Atlantic Monthly Press, 1990.
Independence Day (novel), Knopf (New York City), 1995.
Women with Men: Three Stories, Knopf, 1997.

OTHER

(Contributor) L. Rust Hills, editor, *Fifty Great Years of Esquire Fiction,* Viking, 1983.
American Tropical (play), produced at Louisville's Actors Theater, Louisville, KY, 1983.
My Mother, in Memory, Raven Editions, 1988.
(Editor with Shannon Ravenel) *The Best American Short Stories 1990,* Houghton, 1990.
(Author of introduction) *Juke Joint: Photographs by Birney Imes,* University Press of Mississippi, 1990.
Bright Angel (screenplay; based on Ford's short stories "Children" and "Great Falls,"), Hemdale, 1991.
(Editor) *The Granta Book of the American Short Story,* Viking Penguin, 1992.
(Editor and author of introduction) A. J. Liebling, *The Fights,* Chronicle Books (San Francisco), 1996.

Ford's stories have appeared in *Esquire* and *The New Yorker.*

SIDELIGHTS: "Writing is the only thing I've done with persistence, except for being married," claimed Richard Ford in an interview with *Publishers Weekly,* "and yet it's such an inessential thing. Nobody cares if you do it, and nobody cares if you don't." The author undoubtedly believed that statement, yet numerous reviewers have demonstrated how much they do care about Ford's work by lavishing it with praise. He is "a formidably talented novelist" and "one of the best writers of his generation," according to Walter Clemons of *Newsweek*; he is also "the leading short story writer in the United States today," in the opinion of Toronto *Globe & Mail* contributor Alberto Manguel.

Writing in the *New York Times Book Review,* novelist Larry McMurtry raised comparisons between Ford and William Faulkner, but they were unfavorable. "If the vices this novel shares with its many little Southern cousins could be squeezed into one word, the word would be neo-Faulknerism. It reads like the worst, rather than the best, of Faulkner. . . . Portentousness, overwriting, pronouns drifting toward a shore only dimly seen, a constant backward tilt toward a past that hasn't the remotest causal influence on what is actually happening, plus a more or less constant tendency to equate eloquence with significance: these are the familiar qualities in which Mr. Ford's narrative abounds." Still, McMurtry acknowledged that he saw a great deal of promise in Ford's first work, and concluded: "One would hope that . . . these vices won't prove incurable. [Ford's] minor characters are vividly drawn, and his ear is first-rate. If he can weed his garden of some of the weeds and cockleburrs of his tradition, it might prove very fertile."

Ford himself was very impatient with the whole subject of "Faulknerism," and, in fact, with any attempt to categorize his writing as being part of the Southern tradition—or any other school of writing, for that matter. "Personally, I think there is no such thing as Southern writing or Southern literature or Southern ethos, and I'm frankly sick of the whole subject," he declared in *Harper's.* "Categorization (women's writing, gay writing, Illinois writing) inflicts upon art exactly what art strives at its best never to inflict on itself: arbitrary and irrelevant limits, shelter from the widest consideration and judgment, exclusion from general excellence. When writing achieves the level of great literature, of great art (even good art), categories go out the window. William Faulkner, after all, was not a great Southern writer: he was a great writer who wrote about the South."

Ford went even farther south—to Mexico—for the setting of his second novel, *The Ultimate Good Luck.* It was the tale of a Vietnam veteran who, in an attempt to reclaim the affections of his ex-girlfriend, journeys to Mexico to rescue her brother from prison, where he is being held for his part in a drug deal. Gilberto Perez panned the book in the *Hudson Review,* writing that it "calls to mind a cheap action picture in which hastily collaborating hacks didn't quite manage to put a story together"; but *Newsweek* reviewer Walter Clemons differed sharply in his assessment, calling *The Ultimate Good Luck* "a tighter, more efficient book [than *A Piece of My Heart*], and a good one." Clemons did feel that Ford had "jimmied himself into the confines of the existentialist thriller with a conspicuous sacrifice of his robust gift for comedy," and noted his belief that the author had "larger capabilities" than those manifested in *The Ultimate Good Luck,* but he nonetheless declared that "sentence by sentence, *The Ultimate Good Luck* is the work of a formidably talented novelist." Toronto *Globe & Mail* reviewer Douglas Hill was even more enthusiastic, crediting Ford with creating "a thriller that is also a love story, and at its core a meditation upon the precariousness and impotence of post-Vietnam U.S. values."

The total sales of *A Piece of My Heart* and *The Ultimate Good Luck* combined were under 12,000 copies, but Ford's reputation and popularity soared with the publication of his third book, *The Sportswriter,* which sold more than 60,000 copies. Described by James Wood in the London *Times* as "a desperately moving and

important book, at once tremulous and tough," *The Sportswriter* is narrated by its protagonist, Frank Bascombe. Bascombe is "deceptively amiable, easygoing and sweet natured," reports Clemons. "As he tells his story in a chipper, uncomplaining tone, we gradually learn that he's a damaged man who's retreated into cushioned, dreamy detachment to evade grief and disappointment." Once a promising novelist and short-story writer, Bascombe abandoned the difficulties of creating fiction for the simpler, more immediate gratifications of sports reporting and suburban life in New Jersey. The death of his son brings on a spiritual crisis he tries to avoid, distracting himself with extramarital affairs that eventually lead his wife to divorce him.

Although he continually asserts his happiness, Bascombe "asserts so hard that we are made to feel the hollowness," explained *Los Angeles Times* book critic Richard Eder. "Negation by assertion is the narrative's central device, in fact, giving it a flatness and a dead tone." Eder explained that "the point of 'The Sportswriter' is not the plot, but the quality of thought and feeling with which the narrator assays his life." The reviewer found it to be "a dull point" because, in his opinion, "Bascombe is not very nice and not very interesting." Clemons concurred that Bascombe's behavior was often "less than admirable," but in his view this increased Ford's literary achievement, for "only a scrupulously honest novelist could make us sympathetic to such an unheroic nature. Ford makes us feel we're more like Bascombe than we often care to admit." *New York Times* reviewer Michiko Kakutani called the novel "powerful," and noted that while Bascombe's monologue was occasionally "long winded and overly meditative . . . his voice, as rendered by Mr. Ford, is so pliant and persuasive that we are insistently drawn into his story. . . . We come to see Frank not only as he sees himself (hurt, alienated, resigned to a future of diminishing returns) but also as he must appear to others— essentially kind and decent, but also wary, passive and unwilling to embrace the real possibilities for happiness that exist around him."

"*The Sportswriter* . . . established a glittering reputation. The stories in *Rock Springs* confirm it," asserted a *Time* reviewer in his evaluation of Ford's first collection of short stories. Set mostly in Montana, the stories in *Rock Springs* tell of characters in transit, moving from one town or one way of life to another. The book elicited raves from most reviewers. "If the term 'perfect' still means 'thoroughly accomplished,' then *Rock Springs* is a perfect book," said Manguel. The *New York Times*'s Michiko Kakutani, too, found the collection to be an impressive work. "Mr. Ford has managed to find a wholly distinctive narrative voice . . . a voice that can move effortlessly between neat, staccato descriptions and rich, lyrical passages. . . . [His] stories stand as superb examples of the storyteller's craft, providing us with both the pleasures of narrative and the sad wisdom of art." Kakutani pronounced enthusiastically: "This volume should confirm his emergence as one of the most compelling and eloquent storytellers of his generation."

Ford returned to the novel with 1990's *Wildlife.* Describing the inner workings of the Brinson family, the novel uses the central metaphor of a raging forest fire to symbolize the uncontrolled forces sweeping through the family. Reviewers were divided in their assessment of this work. Jonathan Yardley, reviewing *Wildlife* for the *Washington Post,* was not pleased with the way the characters smoothed "each other's passage through life with pearls of pop-psychological wisdom" or with the abundance of metaphors in the narrative. "Like a puppy with a slipper, Ford sinks his teeth into those metaphors, shakes them all over the place and refuses to let them go," noted Yardley. Victoria Glendinning commented in the London *Times* that "there is something obsessional and over-tidy in the jigsaw neatness of his writing, his interlocking themes and images, his modest conclusions," but she allowed that the story is "beautifully made" and noted that Ford "has far more to teach Europeans about ordinary American life and the American psyche than have the flashier East Coast novelists."

The controversy and varied responses to Ford's work are the proof of its worth, according to Toronto *Globe & Mail* contributor Trevor Ferguson, who rated *Wildlife* "a superb novel." Ferguson concluded: "[The novel] is also, like its characters and like its vision of America, strangely contradictory—at once affirmative and self-limiting. Applaud or berate him as he assumes a position in the front rank of American letters, Ford and his stylistic decisions deserve heated debate."

Ford's *Independence Day* reunites the reader with Frank Bascombe from *The Sportswriter*. The book takes place seven years later and Bascombe has experienced the death of one son, the breakup of a marriage and the crisis of watching another son fail in his own life. Over a long holiday weekend, Bascombe attempts to repair family relationships and deal with his own mid-life crisis. A murder and other failed relationships add to his sense of detachment.

In a *New York Times* review of *Independence Day,* Michiko Kakutani described Ford as "Not only . . . [doing] a finely nuanced job of delineating Frank's state of mind . . . but he also moves beyond Frank, to provide a portrait of a time and a place, of a middle-class community caught on the the margins of change and reeling . . . from the wages of loss and disappointment and fear." She further lauded Ford's "consummate ear for dialogue" and his narrative, which is "as gripping as it is affecting." The novel won Ford a Pulitzer Prize in 1995.

Women with Men: Three Stories deals with the attempts of men to come to terms with the sensitivities of the women in their lives. Two of the three stories are set in France, unlikely ground for Ford, and the third story takes place in the American West and is narrated by a teenage boy who is visiting his mother. A *Publishers Weekly* reviewer credited Ford as "a writer whose directness of utterance and keen eye is combined with a remarkably subtle sense of the human comedy." Kevin Nance of the *Lexington Herald-Leader* expressed disappointment in the book, however, writing that the collection "centering on broken male-female relationships, is dispirited and aimless." Conversely, Michael Gorra of the *New York Times* referred to it as a "superb volume," stating that Ford's "ear for cliche has perfect pitch." Comparing Ford's writing with Ernest Hemingway's stories, Gorra summarized his feelings about *Women with Men* by saying that "In a way that would have seemed utterly alien to Hemingway, Richard Ford has throughout his work acknowledged the central importance that women and marriage have in the lives of men. He has had the originality—the strength—to bend the Hemingway tradition."

BIOGRAPHICAL/CRITICAL SOURCES:

BOOKS

Contemporary Literary Criticism, Volume 46, Gale (Detroit), 1988.

PERIODICALS

Antioch Review, winter, 1977, p. 124.
Boston Globe, October 19, 1987.
Canadian Literature, autumn, 1995, p. 51.

Chicago Tribune Book World, April 19, 1981.
Christian Century, March 1, 1989, p. 227.
Entertainment Weekly, July 28, 1995, p. 55.
Globe & Mail (Toronto), July 18, 1987; October 3, 1987; July 7, 1990.
Harper's, August, 1986, pp. 35, 42-43.
Hudson Review, winter, 1981-82, pp. 606-20.
Lexington Herald-Leader, July 20, 1997.
Library Journal, July, 1995, p. 40.
Los Angeles Times, March 12, 1986.
Los Angeles Times Book Review, October 30, 1988, p. 10; June 30, 1991, p. 14.
National Review, November 12, 1976, pp. 1240-41.
Newsweek, May 11, 1981, pp. 89-90; April 7, 1986, p. 82; June 12, 1995, p. 64.
New York Review of Books, April 24, 1986, pp. 38-39.
New York Times, February 26, 1986, p. C21; September 20, 1987; April 10, 1988; June 1, 1990; April 18, 1996, p. C17; August 22, 1995, p. C13; October 17, 1996, p. A27.
New York Times Book Review, October 24, 1976, p. 16; May 31, 1981, p. 13, 51; March 23, 1986, p. 14; June 13, 1995; July 13, 1997.
Publishers Weekly, May 18, 1990, pp. 66-67; April 24, 1995, p. 16.
Time, November 16, 1987, p. 89.
Times (London), August 28, 1986; June 11, 1987; June 20, 1987; July 11, 1987; May 5, 1988; August 9, 1990.
TriQuarterly, spring, 1990, p. 125.
Washington Post, June 20, 1990.
Washington Post Book World, February 20, 1977, p. N3; March 30, 1986, p. 3.

*   *   *

FORD, Webster
See MASTERS, Edgar Lee

*   *   *

FOREZ
See MAURIAC, Francois (Charles)

*   *   *

FORSTER, E(dward) M(organ) 1879-1970

PERSONAL: Born January 1, 1879, in London, England; died June 7, 1970, in Coventry, England; son of Edward Morgan Llewellyn and Alice Clara (Whichelo) Forster. *Education:* King's College, Cambridge, B.A. (second-class honors in classics), 1900, B.A. (second-class honors in history), 1901, M.A., 1910.

CAREER: Lived in Greece and Italy after leaving Cambridge in 1901, remaining abroad until 1907, except for a brief visit to England in 1902; lectured at Working Men's College, London, for a period beginning in 1907; made first trip to India in 1912; Red Cross volunteer in Alexandria, 1915-19; returned to England after the war where he was literary editor of the Labor Party's *Daily Herald* for a time, and contributed reviews to journals including *Nation* and *New Statesman;* served as private secretary to the Maharajah of Dewas State Senior, 1921; lived in England, writing and lecturing, 1921-70. Gave annual Clark Lectures at Cambridge

University, 1927, Rede Lecturer, 1941, W. P. Ker Lecturer, 1944; made lecture tour of United States in 1947. Member of general advisory council, British Broadcasting Corp., and writer of numerous broadcasts; was a vice-president of the London Library.

MEMBER: American Academy of Arts and Letters (honorary corresponding member), Bavarian Academy of Fine Arts (honorary corresponding member), Cambridge Humanists (president), Reform Club.

AWARDS, HONORS: James Tait Black Memorial Prize, and Prix Femina Vie Heureuse, both 1925, both for *A Passage to India*; LL.D., University of Aberdeen, 1931; Benson Medal, Royal Society of Literature, 1937; honorary fellow, King's College, Cambridge, 1946; Litt.D., University of Liverpool, 1947, Hamilton College, 1949, Cambridge University, 1950, University of Nottingham, 1951, University of Manchester, 1954, Leiden University, 1954, and University of Leicester, 1958; Tukojimo III Gold Medal; Companion of Honour, 1953; Companion of Royal Society of Literature; Order of Merit, 1969.

WRITINGS:

Where Angels Fear to Tread (novel), Blackwood, 1905, Knopf, 1920, recent edition, Holmes & Meier, 1978.

The Longest Journey (novel), Blackwood, 1907, Knopf, 1922, recent edition, Holmes & Meier, 1985.

A Room With a View (novel), Edward Arnold, 1908, Putnam, 1911, recent edition, Random House, 1989.

Howards End (novel), Putnam, 1910, Random House, 1989; published with appendices and criticism, edited by Paul B. Armstrong, Norton, 1997; also with history and criticism, edited by Alistair M. Duckworth, Bedford Books, 1997.

The Celestial Omnibus, and Other Stories, Sidgwick & Jackson, 1911, Knopf, 1923, recent edition, Random House, 1976.

The Story of the Siren (short story), Hogarth Press, 1920.

The Government of Egypt (history), Labour Research Department, 1921.

Alexandria: A History and a Guide, W. Morris, 1922, 3rd edition, Doubleday-Anchor, 1961, recent edition, Oxford University Press, 1986.

Pharos and Pharillon (history), Knopf, 1923, 3rd edition, Hogarth Press, 1943.

A Passage to India (novel), Harcourt, 1924, recent edition, Holmes & Meier, 1979.

Anonymity: An Enquiry, V. Woolf, 1925.

Aspects of the Novel (Clark Lecture, 1927), Harcourt, 1927, recent edition, Holmes & Meier, 1978.

The Eternal Moment, and Other Stories, Harcourt, 1928.

A Letter to Madan Blanchard (belles lettres), Hogarth Press, 1931, Harcourt, 1932.

Goldsworthy Lowes Dickinson (biography), Harcourt, 1934, new edition, Edward Arnold, 1945, recent edition, Holmes & Meier, 1978.

Abinger Harvest (essays), Harcourt, 1936.

What I Believe (political), Hogarth Press, 1939.

Nordic Twilight (political), Macmillan, 1940.

England's Pleasant Land (pageant play), Hogarth Press, 1940.

Virginia Woolf (criticism; Rede Lecture, 1941) Harcourt, 1942.

The Development of English Prose Between 1918 and 1939 (criticism; W. P. Ker Lecture, 1944), Jackson & Co. (Glasgow), 1945.

The Collected Tales of E. M. Forster (previously published as *The Celestial Omnibus* and *The Eternal Moment*), Knopf, 1947 (published in England as *Collected Short Stories of E. M. Forster,* Sidgwick & Jackson, 1948).

(Author of libretto with Eric Crozier) *Billy Budd* (based on the novel by Herman Melville; music by Benjamin Britten), Boosey & Hawkes, 1951, revised edition, 1961.

Two Cheers for Democracy (essays), Edward Arnold, 1951.

Desmond MacCarthy, Mill House Press, 1952.

The Hill of Devi, Harcourt, 1953 (published in England as *The Hill of Devi: Being Letters from Dewas State Senior,* Edward Arnold, 1953; also see below).

Battersea Rise (first chapter of *Marianne Thornton* see below), Harcourt, 1955.

Marianne Thornton: A Domestic Biography, 1797-1887, Harcourt, 1956.

E. M. Forster: Selected Writings, edited by G. B. Parker, Heinemann Educational, 1968.

Albergo Empedocle and Other Writings (previously unpublished material, written 1900-15), edited by George H. Thomson, Liveright, 1971.

Maurice (novel), Norton, 1971.

The Life to Come and Other Stories, Norton, 1973.

The Hill of Devi and Other Indian Writings (includes *The Hill of Devi*), edited by Oliver Stallybrass, Holmes & Meier, 1983.

Selected Letters of E. M. Forster, edited by Mary Lago and P. N. Furbank, Harvard University Press, Volume 1: *1879-1920,* 1983, Volume 2: *1921-1970,* 1984.

Commonplace Book, edited by Philip Gardner, Stanford University Press, 1985.

Original Letters from India, Hogarth Press, 1986.

The New Collected Short Stories by E. M. Forster, Sidgwick & Jackson, 1987.

Also author of *Reading as Usual* (criticism), 1939. Author of unfinished novel, "Arctic Summer," published in *Tribute to Benjamin Britten on His Fiftieth Birthday,* edited by Anthony Gishford, Faber, 1963. Author of plays, "The Heart of Bosnia," 1911, and "The Abinger Pageant," 1934, and script for film, "Diary for Timothy."

CONTRIBUTOR

Arnold W. Lawrence, editor, *T. E. Lawrence by His Friends,* J. Cape, 1937.

Hermon Ould, editor, *Writers in Freedom,* Hutchinson, 1942.

George Orwell, editor, *Talking to India,* Allen & Unwin, 1943.

Peter Grimes: Essays, John Lane, for the governors of Sadler's Wells Foundation, 1945.

Hermon Ould, editor, *Freedom of Expression: A Symposium,* Hutchinson, 1945.

S. Radhakrishnan, *Mahatma Gandhi: Essays and Reflections on His Life and Work,* 2nd edition, Allen & Unwin, 1949.

Hermon Ould: A Tribute, [London], 1952.

The Fearful Choice: A Debate on Nuclear Policy, conducted by Philip Toynbee, Wayne State University Press, 1959.

Also contributor to *Aspects of England,* 1935, and *Britain and the Beast,* 1937.

OTHER

Author of notes for various books, including William Golding's *Lord of the Flies,* Coward, 1955. Work is represented in collections, including *The Challenge of Our Time,* Percival Marshall, 1948, and *Fairy Tales for Computers,* Eakins Press, 1969.

Contributor to journals and periodicals, including *Listener, Independent Review, Observer, New Statesman, Nation, Albany Review, Open Window, Athenaeum, Egyptian Mail,* and *Horizon.*

MEDIA ADAPTATIONS: A Passage to E. M. Forster, a play based on his works, was compiled by William Roerick and Thomas Coley, and produced in New York, NY at Theatre de Lys in October, 1970. *A Room With a View* was adapted as a play by Stephen Tait and Kenneth Allcott, produced in Cambridge, February, 1950, and published by Edward Arnold, 1951; it was adapted for film by Merchant-Ivory Productions and released by Cinecom in 1986. *A Passage to India* was adapted for the stage by Santha Rama Rau, and published by Edward Arnold, 1960; it was produced in London in 1960 and on Broadway in 1962; the television adaptation by John Maynard was produced by the BBC, and broadcast by NET in 1968; it was adapted into a film, directed by David Lean, and released by Columbia Pictures in 1984. *Where Angels Fear to Tread* was adapted as a play by Elizabeth Hart, S. French, 1963, and produced as a film in 1991 by Charles Sturridge, starring Rupert Graves, Judy Davis, and Helena Bonham Carter. *Howards End* was adapted for stage by Lance Sieveking and Richard Cottrell and produced in London in 1967; the BBC production, adapted by Pauline Macaulay, was broadcast in 1970; a film version by Merchant-Ivory Productions, starring Anthony Hopkins and Emma Thompson, was produced in 1992. *Maurice* was adapted into a film by Merchant-Ivory Productions and released by Cinecom in 1987, starring Hugh Grant and Rupert Graves.

SIDELIGHTS: E. M. Forster's talent is now labeled "genius" as a matter of course—Graham Greene called it "the gentle genius"; another critic once wrote: "So erratically and spasmodically has he worked that one cannot think of his genius as in course of development; it comes and goes, apparently as it wills."

His production of novels was sparse—he had published five by 1924, and the sixth, *Maurice,* was issued posthumously after a hiatus of almost fifty years. Yet what Rose Macaulay concluded of Forster's position before his death in 1970 was undoubtedly true: "If you asked a selection of educated English readers of fiction to pick out our most distinguished living novelist, nine out of ten, I should say, would answer E. M. Forster."

It was once said that "his reputation goes up with every book he doesn't write." Morton Dauwen Zabel wrote, in *Craft and Character,* that Forster had "no stylistic followers and perhaps few disciples in thought, yet if one were fixing the provenance of Auden's generation, Forster's name—whatever the claim of James, Lawrence, or Eliot—would suggest the most accurate combination of critical and temperamental forces, the only one stamped by the peculiarly English skeptical sensibility that survived the war with sanity. . . ."

Though his novels were early established as classics, Forster never enjoyed tremendous popular success. Zabel commented that during his lifetime Forster "practiced the difficult strategy of writing little but making it count for much. . . ." His writings are concerned with the complexity of human nature. What he called the "Primal Curse" is not the knowledge of good and evil, but the knowledge of good-and-evil in its inextricable and unknowable complexity. Such a complex relationship cannot be explained by dogma. In 1939, Forster wrote: "I do not believe in Belief. Faith, to my mind, is a stiffening process, a sort of mental starch, which ought to be applied as sparingly as possible. I dislike the stuff. . . . My law givers are Erasmus and Montaigne, not Moses and St. Paul. My temple stands not upon Mount Moriah, but in that Elysian Field where even the immoral are admitted. My motto is: 'Lord, I disbelieve—help thou my unbelief.'"

Another time Forster wrote: "Truth, being alive, is not halfway between anything." Seeking the wholeness of truth he searched for a "synthesis of matter and essence, of civilization with its inhibitions and nature with its crude energy," wrote Zabel. "And like Andre Gide, whom he respected, he is one of the 'free minds'. . . . He too makes it his task to transmit not 'life's greatness,' which he has called 'a Nineteenth Century perquisite, a Goethean job,' but 'life's complexity, and the delight, the difficulty, the duty of registering that complexity and conveying it.'"

In 1941, at a time when such tenets were losing influence, he proclaimed his support of art for art's sake. He wrote: "The work of art stands by itself, and nothing else does. It achieves something which has often been promised by society but always delusively. Ancient Athens made a mess—but the Antigone stands up. Renaissance Rome made a mess—but the ceiling of the Sistine got painted; Louis XIV made a mess—but there was Phedre; Louis XV continued it, but Voltaire got his letters written."

Forster's style is meticulous. Macaulay writes that "his present-ment of people . . . is most delicately exact. Tones of speech, for instance. He is perhaps the only novelist, apart from Jane Austen, none of whose characters could, when speaking, be confused with any others in the book. And this without any of the obvious tricks and slogans which those whom he calls 'flat' characters in fiction fly like identifying flags."

Austin Warren, however, in *Rage for Order,* observed certain shortcomings: "Neither at wholeness nor at steadiness do his novels completely succeed. There are wide and deep *lacunae:* except for the Basts [in *Howards End*], there are no poor. From poverty, hunger, lust, and hate, his people are exempt. Love between the sexes, though recognized with sympathy, is never explored and is central to none of his novels. Except in *A Passage to India,* the individual is not portrayed in relation to society. . . ."

Forster told his *Paris Review* interviewers that he wrote only under inspiration, but that the act of writing inspired him. His childhood was very literary—"I was the author of a number of works between the ages of six and ten," he recalled. He thought highly of his own works and read them often. ("I go gently over the bits I think are bad.") He also said: "I have always found writing pleasant, and don't understand what people mean by 'throes of creation.' I've enjoyed it, but believe that in some ways it is good. Whether it will last, I have no idea."

BIOGRAPHICAL/CRITICAL SOURCES:

BOOKS

Armstrong, Paul B., editor, *Howards End: Authoritative Text, Textual Appendix, Backgrounds and Contexts, Criticism,* Norton, 1997.

Bakshi, Parminder Kaur, *Distant Desire: Homoerotic Codes and the Subversion of the English Novel in E. M. Forster's Fiction,* P. Lang (New York City), 1995.

Bandyopaadhyaacya, Surabhi, *E. M. Forster: A Critical Linguistic Approach,* Allied (New Delhi), 1995.

Beauman, Nicola, *E. M. Forster: A Biography,* Knopf (New York City), 1994.

Beer, J. B., editor, *"A Passage to India": Essays in Interpretation,* Barnes & Noble, 1985.

Bradbury, Malcolm, editor, *Forster,* Prentice-Hall, 1966.

Contemporary Literary Criticism, Gale (Detroit), Volume 1, 1973; Volume 2, 1974; Volume 3, 1975; Volume 4, 1975;

Volume 9, 1978; Volume 10, 1979; Volume 13, 1980; Volume 15, 1980; Volume 22, 1982; Volume 45, 1987; Volume 77, 1993.

Cowley, Malcolm, editor, *Writers at Work: The Paris Review Interviews,* First Series, 1958.

Dictionary of Literary Biography, Volume 34: *British Novelists, 1890-1929: Traditionalists,* Gale, 1985.

Duckworth, Alistair M. (editor), *Howards End: Complete, Authoritative Text with Biographical and Historical Contexts, Critical History, and Essays from Five Contemporary Critical Perspectives,* Bedford Books, 1997.

Eldridge, C. C., *The Imperial Experience: From Carlyle to Forster,* St. Martin's Press (New York City), 1996.

Furbank, P. N., *E. M. Forster: A Life,* Harcourt Brace Jovanovich, 1978.

Gardner, Philip, *E. M. Forster,* Longman, 1977.

Herz, Judith Scherer, *The Short Narratives of E. M. Forster,* St. Martin's Press, 1988.

Herz, Judith Scherer and Robert K. Martin, editors, *E. M. Forster: Centenary Revaluations,* Macmillan, 1982.

Lago, Mary, *E. M. Forster: A Literary Life,* St. Martin's Press (New York City), 1995.

Land, Stephen K., *Challenge and Conventionality in the Fiction of Forster,* 1990.

Lavin, Audrey A. P., *Aspects of the Novelist: E. M. Forster's Pattern and Rhythm,* P. Lang (New York City), 1995.

Macaulay, Rose, *Writings of E. M. Forster,* Harcourt, 1938, new edition, Barnes & Noble, 1970.

Martin, Robert K., and George Piggford, editors, *Queer Forster,* University of Chicago Press, 1997.

May, Brian, *The Modernist as Pragmatist: E. M. Forster and the Fate of Liberalism,* University of Missouri Press, 1997.

Rapport, Nigel, *The Prose and the Passion: Anthropology, Literature, and the Writing of E. M. Forster,* St. Martin's Press (New York City), 1994.

Sahni, Chaman L., *Forster's " A Passage to India": The Religious Dimension,* Arnold Heinemann, 1981.

Summers, Claude J., *E. M. Forster,* Ungar, 1983.

Tambling, Jeremy, *E. M. Forster,* St. Martin's Press (New York City), 1995.

Warren, Austin, *Rage for Order,* University of Michigan Press, 1948.

Zabel, Morton Dauwen, *Craft and Character,* Viking, 1957.

PERIODICALS

Books and Bookmen, August, 1970.

Chicago Tribune, April 9, 1986; April 1, 1987.

Christian Century, July 22, 1970.

Criterion, October, 1934.

Critical Inquiry, autumn, 1985, pp. 59-87.

Criticism, winter, 1980, pp. 40-56.

Globe and Mail (Toronto), January 14, 1984; March 8, 1986.

Journal of Modern Literature, March, 1983, pp. 109-24; summer, 1988, pp. 121-40.

Listener, July 9, 1970.

Literary Half-Yearly, July, 1992, pp. 23-30.

Los Angeles Times, March 31, 1987; October 1, 1987; November 22, 1987.

Los Angeles Times Book Review, August 3, 1986.

Mademoiselle, June, 1964.

Modern Fiction Studies, autumn, 1961, pp. 258-70; summer, 1967, pp. 195-210.

Modern Philology, August, 1981, pp. 45-60.

Nation, June 29, 1970; November 29, 1971.

New Republic, October 5, 1949; January 1, 1964.

Newsweek, June 22, 1970; September 21, 1987.

New Yorker, September, 1959.

New York Times, December 18, 1985; March 7, 1986; May 30, 1986; September 13, 1987; September 18, 1987; October 4, 1987.

New York Times Book Review, December 29, 1968; January 8, 1984.

Novel, fall, 1988, pp. 86-105.

PMLA, December, 1955, pp. 934-54; January, 1984, pp. 72-88.

Textual Practice, summer, 1991, pp. 195-218.

Theology, April, 1940.

Times (London), February 4, 1982; December 29, 1983; March 14, 1987.

Times Literary Supplement, June 22, 1962; April 16, 1982; April 5, 1985; May 24, 1985.

Twentieth Century Literature, July, 1961, pp. 51-63; (E. M. Forster issue) summer-fall, 1985; winter, 1992, pp. 365-85.

Vogue, January 1, 1965.

Washington Post, October 2, 1987.

Washington Post Book World, January 1, 1984.

Wide Angle, October, 1989, pp. 42-51.

Yale Review, June, 1944.

*   *   *

FORSYTH, Frederick 1938-

PERSONAL: Born in 1938 in Ashford, Kent, England; son of a furrier, shopkeeper, and rubber tree planter; married, September, 1973; wife's name, Carole ("Carrie"; a model); children: Frederick Stuart, Shane Richard. *Education:* Attended University of Granada. *Avocational interests:* Sea fishing, snooker.

ADDRESSES: Home—St. John's Wood, London, England. *Office*—c/o Hutchinson Publishing Group, 62-65 Chandos Pl., London WC2N 4NW, England.

CAREER: Novelist. *Eastern Daily Press,* Norwich, England, and King's Lynn, Norfolk, reporter, 1958-61; Reuters News Agency, reporter in London, England, and Paris, France, and bureau chief in East Berlin, East Germany, 1961-65; British Broadcasting Corporation (BBC), London, England, reporter, 1965-67, assistant diplomatic correspondent, 1967-68; freelance journalist in Nigeria, 1968-70. *Military service:* Royal Air Force, pilot, 1956-58.

AWARDS, HONORS: Edgar Allan Poe Award, Mystery Writers of America, 1971, for *The Day of the Jackal.*

WRITINGS:

NOVELS

The Day of the Jackal, Viking (New York City), 1971.

The Odessa File, Viking, 1972.

The Dogs of War, Viking, 1974.

The Shepherd, Hutchinson (London), 1975, Viking, 1976.

The Novels of Frederick Forsyth (contains *The Day of the Jackal, The Odessa File,* and *The Dogs of War*), Hutchinson, 1978, published as *Forsyth's Three,* Viking, 1980, published as *Three Complete Novels,* Avenel Books (New York City), 1980.

The Devil's Alternative, Hutchinson, 1979, Viking, 1980.

The Four Novels (contains *The Day of the Jackal, The Odessa File, The Dogs of War,* and *The Devil's Alternative*), Hutchinson, 1982.

The Fourth Protocol, Viking, 1984.

The Negotiator, Bantam (New York City), 1989.
The Deceiver, Bantam, 1991.
The Fist of God, Bantam, 1994.
Icon, Bantam, 1996.

OTHER

The Biafra Story (nonfiction), Penguin (London), 1969, revised edition published as *The Making of an African Legend: The Biafra Story,* 1977.
(Contributor) *Visitor's Book: Short Stories of Their New Homeland by Famous Authors Now Living in Ireland,* Arrow Books, 1982.
Emeka (biography of Chukwuemeka Odumegwu-Ojukwu), Spectrum Books (Ibadan), 1982.
No Comebacks: Collected Short Stories, Viking, 1982.
(And executive producer) *The Fourth Protocol* (screenplay; based on his novel), Lorimar, 1987.
Chacal, French and European Publications, 1990.
(Editor) *Great Flying Stories,* Norton (New York City), 1991.
I Remember: Reflections on Fishing in Childhood, Summersdale (London), 1995.

Also author of *The Soldiers,* a documentary for BBC. Contributor of articles to newspapers and magazines, including *Playboy.*

MEDIA ADAPTATIONS: *The Day of the Jackal* was filmed by Universal in 1973; *The Odessa File* was filmed by Columbia in 1974; *The Dogs of War* was filmed by United Artists in 1981. The Mobil Showcase Network filmed two of Forsyth's short stories ("A Careful Man" and "Privilege") under the title *Two by Forsyth* in 1984; "A Careful Man" was also videotaped and broadcast on Irish television.

SIDELIGHTS: Realism is the key word behind the novels of Frederick Forsyth. Often credited as the originator of a new genre, the "documentary thriller," Forsyth found sudden fame with the publication of his smash best-seller, *The Day of the Jackal,* a book that combines the suspense of an espionage novel with the detailed realism of the documentary novel, first made popular by Truman Capote's *In Cold Blood.* The detail in Forsyth's novels depends not only on the months of research he spends on each book, but also on his own varied personal experiences which lend even greater authenticity to his writing. As *Dictionary of Literary Biography* contributor Andrew F. Macdonald explains, "the sense of immediacy, of an insider's view of world affairs, of all-too-human world figures," as well as quick-paced plots, are the keys to the author's popularity.

Impatient to experience life for himself, Forsyth left school at the age of seventeen and went to Spain, where he briefly attended the University of Granada while toying with the idea of becoming a matador. However, having previously trained as a Tiger Moth biplane pilot, Forsyth decided to join the Royal Air Force in 1956. He learned to fly a Vampire jet airplane, and—at the age of nineteen—he was the youngest man in England at the time to earn his wings.

But Forsyth still dreamed of becoming a foreign corespondent, and towards that end he left the service to join the staff of the *Eastern Daily Press.* His talent for languages (Forsyth is fluent in French, German, Spanish, and Russian) later landed him his dream job as a correspondent for Reuters News Agency and then for the British Broadcasting Corporation (BBC). It was during an assignment for the BBC that Forsyth's career took a sudden turn. Assigned to cover an uprising in the Nigerian region of Biafra, Forsyth began his mission believing he was going to meet an upstart rebellious colonel who was misleading his followers. He soon realized, though, that this leader, Colonel Ojukwu, was actually an intelligent man committed to saving his people from an English-supported government whose corrupt leaders were allowing millions to die of starvation in order to obtain their oil-rich lands. When Forsyth reported his findings, he was accused of being unprofessional and his superiors reassigned him to covering politics at home. Outraged, Forsyth resigned, and he tells Henry Allen in a *Washington Post* article that this experience destroyed his belief "that the people who ran the world were men of good will." This disillusionment is reflected in his writing.

Going back to Africa, Forsyth did freelance reporting in Biafra and wrote an account of the war, *The Biafra Story,* which *Spectator* critic Auberon Waugh asserts "is by far the most complete account, from the Biafran side [of the conflict], that I have yet read." In 1970, when the rebels were finally defeated and Ojukwu went into exile, Forsyth returned to England to find that his position on the war had effectively eliminated any chances he had of resuming a reporting career. He decided, however, that he could still put his journalism experience to use by writing fiction. Recalling his days in Paris during the early 1960s when rumors were spreading that the Secret Organization Army had hired an assassin to shoot President Charles de Gaulle, Forsyth sat down and in just over a month wrote *The Day of the Jackal* based on this premise.

The fascinating part of *The Day of the Jackal* lies in Forsyth's portrayal of the amoral, ultra-professional killer known only by his code name, "Jackal," and detective Claude Lebel's efforts to stop him. Despite what *New York Times Book Review* critic Stanley Elkin calls Forsyth's "graceless prose style," and characterization that, according to J. R. Frakes in a *Book World* review, uses "every stereotype in the filing system," the author's portrayal of his nemesis weaving through a non-stop narrative has garnered acclaim from many critics and millions of readers. By boldly switching his emphasis from the side of the law to the side of the assassin, Forsyth adds a unique twist that gives his novel its appeal. "So plausible has Mr. Forsyth made his implausible villain . . . and so exciting does he lead him on his murderous mission against impossible odds," says Elkin, "that even saintly readers will be hard put not to cheer this particular villain along his devious way." The author, however, notes that he considered the positive response to his villain a distinctly American response. "There is this American trait of admiring efficiency," he explains to a *Washington Post* interviewer, "and the Jackal is efficient in his job."

"*The Day of the Jackal* established a highly successful formula," writes Macdonald, "one repeated by Forsyth and a host of other writers." Using a tight, journalistic style, Forsyth creates an illusion of reality in his writing by intermixing real-life people and historical events with his fictional characters and plots; "the ultimate effect is less that of fiction than of a fictional projection into the lives of the real makers of history," Macdonald attests. The author also fills his pages with factual information about anything from how to assemble a small nuclear device to shipping schedules and restaurant menus. But the main theme behind the author's novels is the power of the individual to make a difference in the world, and even change the course of history. Macdonald describes the Forsyth protagonist as "a maverick who succeeds by cutting through standard procedure and who as a result often has difficulty in fitting in, [yet he] lives up to his own high professional standards. Forsyth suggests that it is the lone professionals, whether opposed to the organization or part of it, who truly create history, but a history represented only palely on the front pages of newspapers."

Since Forsyth had a three-book contract with Viking, he quickly researched and wrote his next two novels, *The Odessa File,* about a German reporter's hunt for a Nazi war criminal, and *The Dogs of War,* which concerns a mercenary who orchestrates a military coup in West Africa. Forsyth drew on his experience as a reporter in East Berlin for *The Odessa File,* as well as interviewing experts like Nazi hunter Simon Weisenthal, to give the novel authenticity. Background for *The Dogs of War* also came from the author's personal experiences—in this case, his time spent in Biafra. When it comes to details about criminal doings, however, Forsyth goes right to the source. In a Toronto *Globe and Mail* interview with Rick Groen, Forsyth says, "There are only two kinds of people who really know the ins and outs of illegal activities: those who practice them and those who seek to prevent them from being practiced. So you talk to cops or criminals. Not academics or criminologists or any of those sorts." This tactic has gotten Forsyth into some dangerous situations. In a *Chicago Tribune* interview the author regales Michael Kilian with one instance when he was researching *The Dogs of War.* Trying to learn more about gun trafficking in the black market, Forsyth posed as a South African interested in buying arms. The ploy worked until one day when the men he was dealing with noticed a copy of *The Day of the Jackal* in a bookstore window. It was "probably the nearest I got to being put in a box," says the author.

The Dogs of War became a highly controversial book when a London *Times* writer accused Forsyth of paying two-hundred-thousand dollars to mercenaries attempting a coup against the President of Equatorial Guinea, Francisco Marcias Nguema. At first, the novelist denied any involvement. Later, however, David Butler and Anthony Collins reported in *Newsweek* that Forsyth admitted to having "organized a coup attempt for research purposes, but that he had never intended to go through with it." The controversy did not hurt book sales, though, and *The Dogs of War* became Forsyth's third best-seller in a row.

Forsyth continued with *The Devil's Alternative,* an intricately plotted, ambitious novel about an American president who must choose between giving in to the demands of a group of terrorists and possibly causing a nuclear war in the process, or refusing their demands and allowing them to release the biggest oil spill in history from the tanker they have hijacked. "The vision is somewhat darker than in Forsyth's earlier works, in which a moral choice was possible," notes Macdonald. "Here . . . somebody must get hurt, no matter which alternative is chosen." The usual complaints against Forsyth's writing have been trained against *The Devil's Alternative.* Peter Gorner, for one, argues in the *Chicago Tribune Book World* that "his characters are paper-thin, the pages are studded with cliches, and the plot is greased by coincidence." But Gorner adds that ". . .things move along so briskly you haven't much time to notice." *Los Angeles Times* critic Robert Kirsch similarly notes that "Forsyth's banal writing, his endless thesaurus of cliches, his Hollywood characters do not interfere with page turning." Nevertheless, *New York Times Book Review* contributor Irma Pascal Heldman expresses admiration for Forsyth's abilities to accurately predict some of the political crises that came to pass not long after the book was published. She also praises the "double-whammy ending that will take even the most wary reader by surprise. *The Devil's Alternative* is a many-layered thriller."

As with *The Devil's Alternative,* Forsyth's *The Fourth Protocol* and *The Negotiator* offer intrigue on a superpower scale. *The Fourth Protocol* is the story of a Soviet plot to detonate a small atomic device in a U.S. airbase in England. The explosion is meant to be seen as an American error which helps put the leftist, antinuclear Labour Party into power. Reviews on the novel have been mixed. *Time* magazine reviewer John Skow faults the author for being too didactic: "[Forsyth's] first intention is not to write an entertainment but to preach a political sermon. Its burden is that leftists and peaceniks really are fools whose habitual prating endangers civilization." Michiko Kakutani of the *New York Times* also feels that, compared to Forsyth's other novels, *The Fourth Protocol* "becomes predictable, and so lacking in suspense." But other critics, like *Washington Post Book World* reviewer Roderick MacLeish, maintain a contrary view. MacLeish asserts that it is Forsyth's "best book so far" because the author's characters are so much better developed. "Four books and a few million pounds after *Jackal* Frederick Forsyth has become a well-rounded novelist."

Of *The Negotiator,* Forsyth's tale of the kidnapping of an American president's son, *Globe and Mail* critic Margaret Cannon declares that "while nowhere nearly as good as *The Day of the Jackal* or *The Odessa File,* it's [Forsyth's] best work in recent years." Harry Anderson, writing in *Newsweek,* also calls the novel "a comparative rarity; a completely satisfying thriller." Some critics like *Washington Post* reviewer John Katzenbach have resurrected the old complaints that Forsyth "relies on shallow characters and stilted dialogue," and that while "the dimensions of his knowledge are impressive, rarely does the information imparted serve any greater purpose." Acknowledging that *The Negotiator* has "too many characters and a plot with enough twists to fill a pretzel factory," Cannon nevertheless adds that ". . . the endless and irrelevant descriptive passages are gone and someone has averted Forsyth's tendency to go off on tiresome tangents."

The author revisits the changing world order in *The Fist of God,* which tells of a secret mission to Iraq in an attempt to prevent the use of a catastrophic doomsday weapon. The intelligence situation in Iraq's closed society has become critical, and the western allies recruit a young version of Sam McCready—Major Mike Martin—to obtain the information they need. Martin's mission is to contact an Israeli "mole," a secret agent planted in Iraq by the Mossad, Israel's secret service, years before. In the process he also encounters rumors of Saddam Hussein's ultimate weapon—a weapon he must destroy in order to ensure a western victory. "As with his best works," writes Macdonald in the *St. James Guide to Crime and Mystery Writers,* "Forsyth gives a sense of peering behind the curtains created by governments and media, allowing a vision of how the real battles, mostly invisible, were carried out."

In *Icon,* Forsyth turns to contemporary Russian politics for a thriller about a presidential candidate with ties to the Russian mafia and plans for wholesale ethnic cleansing at home and renewed Russian aggression abroad. Jason Monk, ex-CIA agent, is hired by an unlikely group of Russian and American global players to get rid of candidate Igor Komarov before the election. "As usual," writes the reviewer for *Publishers Weekly,* "Forsyth interweaves speculation with historical fact, stitching his plot pieces with a cogent analysis of both Russian politics and the world of espionage." Although Anthony Lejeune in *National Review* believes that "the scale is too large, the mood too chilly, for much personal involvement" with the novel's characters, J. D. Reed in *People* claims that "*Icon* finds the master in world-class form."

BIOGRAPHICAL/CRITICAL SOURCES:

BOOKS

Contemporary Literary Criticism, Gale (Detroit), Volume 2, 1974; Volume 5, 1976; Volume 36, 1986.
Dictionary of Literary Biography, Volume 87: *British Mystery and Thriller Writers since 1940, First Series,* Gale, 1989.
St. James Guide to Crime and Mystery Writers, 4th edition, St. James Press (Detroit), 1996.

PERIODICALS

Armchair Detective, May, 1974; winter, 1985.
Atlantic, December, 1972; August, 1974.
Book and Magazine Collector, June, 1989.
Booklist, March 1, 1994, p. 1139.
Book World, September 5, 1971.
Chicago Tribune, October 16, 1984; April 16, 1989; June 14, 1989.
Chicago Tribune Book World, March 2, 1980.
Christian Science Monitor, September 7, 1984.
Daily News (New York), September 30, 1984.
Detroit News, February 10, 1980; August 15, 1982; April 30, 1989.
Economist, December 7, 1996, p. S3.
Entertainment Weekly, May 20, 1994, p. 55.
Globe and Mail (Toronto), September 8, 1984; August 29, 1987; April 29, 1989.
Guardian, August 16, 1994, p. 3.
Insight on the News, July 11, 1994, p. 28.
Life, October 22, 1971.
Listener, June 17, 1971; September 28, 1972; January 10, 1980.
Los Angeles Times, March 19, 1980; March 28, 1980; May 7, 1982; August 28, 1987.
Los Angeles Times Book Review, April 16, 1989.
National Observer, October 30, 1971.
National Review, August 2, 1974; December 23, 1996, p. 56.
New Leader, April 7, 1980.
New Statesman, September 20, 1974; January 15, 1988.
New Statesman & Society, September 6, 1991, pp. 35-36.
Newsweek, July 22, 1974; May 1, 1978; April 24, 1989.
New York Post, September 21, 1974.
New York Times, October 24, 1972; April 18, 1978; January 17, 1980; August 30, 1984; August 28, 1987.
New York Times Book Review, August 15, 1971; December 5, 1971; November 5, 1972; July 14, 1974; October 16, 1977; February 24, 1980; March 2, 1980; May 9, 1982; September 2, 1984; April 16, 1989; May 22 *Observer,* June 13, 1971; September 24, 1972; September 22, 1974.
People Weekly, October 22, 1984; July 18, 1994, p. 24; October 21, 1996, p. 40.
Playboy, July, 1989, p. 26; November, 1991, p. 34.
Publishers Weekly, August 9, 1971; September 30, 1974; March 17, 1989; August 9, 1991, p. 43; March 7, 1994, p. 51; August 12, 1996, p. 61.
Saturday Review, September 4, 1971; September 9, 1972.
Spectator, August 2, 1969.
Time, September 3, 1984.
Times (London), August 22, 1982; March 17, 1987; May 13, 1989.
Times Literary Supplement, July 2, 1971; October 25, 1974; December 19, 1975.
Wall Street Journal, April 12, 1989; April 18, 1989.

Washington Post, August 19, 1971; September 26, 1971; December 12, 1978; February 13, 1981; March 28, 1984; August 29, 1987; April 21, 1989.
Washington Post Book World, February 3, 1980; August 26, 1984.
World Press Review, March, 1980; May, 1987.

*   *   *

FOUCAULT, Michel 1926-1984

PERSONAL: Born October 15, 1926, in Poitiers, France; died of a neurological disorder, June 25, 1984, in Paris, France; son of Paul (a doctor) and Anne (Malapert) Foucault. *Education:* Attended Ecole Normale Superieure; Sorbonne, University of Paris, license, 1948 and 1950, diploma, 1952.

CAREER: Writer. Worked as teacher of philosophy and French literature at University of Lill, University of Uppsala, University of Warsaw, University of Hamburg, University of Clermont-Ferrand, University of Sao Paulo, and University of Tunis, 1960-68; University of Paris, Vincennes, France, professor, 1968-70; chairman of history of systems of thought at College de France, 1970-84.

AWARDS, HONORS: Medal from Center of Scientific Research (France), 1961, for *Madness and Civilization.*

WRITINGS:

Folie et deraison: Histoire de la folie a l'age classique, Plon, 1961, abridged edition, Union Generale, 1964, translation by Richard Howard published as *Madness and Civilization: A History of Insanity in the Age of Reason,* Pantheon, 1965.
Maladie mentale et psychologie, Presses Universitaires de France, 1962, translation by Alan Sheridan published as *Mental Illness and Psychology,* Harper, 1976.
Naissance de la clinique: Une Archeologie du regard medical, Presses Universitaires de France, 1963, translation by A. M. Sheridan Smith published as *The Birth of the Clinic: An Archaeology of Medical Perception,* Pantheon, 1973.
Raymond Roussel, Gallimard, 1963, translation published as *Death and the Labyrinth: The World of Raymond Roussel,* Doubleday, 1986.
Les Mots el les choses: Une Archeologie des sciences humanes, Gallimard, 1966, translation published as *The Order of Things: An Archaeology of the Human Sciences,* Pantheon, 1971.
L'Archeologie du savoir, Gallimard, 1969, translation by Smith published as *The Archaeology of Knowledge* (includes "The Discourse on Language"; also see below), Pantheon, 1972.
L'Ordre du discours, Gallimard, 1971 (translation by Smith published in *The Archaeology of Knowledge* as "The Discourse on Language"; also see above).
(Editor) *Moi, Pierre Riviere, ayant egorge ma mere, ma soeur et mon frere* [France], 1973, translation by Frank Jellinek published as *I, Pierre Riviere, Having Slaughtered My Mother, My Sister, and My Brother . . . : A Case of Parricide in the 19th Century,* Pantheon, 1975.
Ceci n'est pas une pipe: Deux Lettres et quatre dessins de Rene Magritte, Fata Morgana, 1973, translation by James Harkness published as *This Is Not a Pipe: Illustrations and Letters by Rene Magritte,* University of California Press, 1983.

Surveiller et punir: Naissance de la prison, Gallimard, 1975, translation by Sheridan published as *Discipline and Punish: The Birth of the Prison,* Pantheon, 1977.

Histoire de la sexualite, Gallimard, Volume 1: *La Volonte de savoir* (title means "The Will to Know"; translation by Robert Hurley published as *The History of Sexuality,* Pantheon, 1978), 1976; Volume 2: *L'Usage of des Plaisirs* (translation by Hurley published as *The Use of Pleasure,* Pantheon, 1985), 1984; Volume 3: *Souci de Soi* (translation by Hurley published as *The Care of the Self,* Pantheon, 1987), 1984.

Language, Counter-Memory, Practice: Selected Essays and Interviews, edited by Donald F. Bouchard, translated by Bouchard and Sherry Simon, Cornell University Press, 1977.

(Author of introduction) *Herculine Barbin: Being the Recently Discovered Memoirs of a Nineteenth-Century French Hermaphrodite,* translation by Richard McDougall, Pantheon, 1980.

Power/Knowledge: Selected Interviews and Other Writings, 1972-1977, Pantheon, 1981.

The Foucault Reader, edited by Paul Rabinow, Pantheon, 1984.

(With Ludwig Binswanger) *Dream and Existence,* edited by Keith Hoeller, translation from the French and German by Forrest Williams and Jacob Needleman, Rev. Exist. Psych., 1986.

(With Maurice Blanchot) *Foucault-Blanchot,* translation by Jeffrey Mehlman and Brian Massumi, Zone Books, 1987.

Politics, Philosophy, Culture: Interviews and Other Writings, 1977-1984, edited by Lawrence D. Kritzman, introduction by Alan Sheridan, Routledge, 1988.

(With Graham Burchell, Colin Gordon, and Peter Miller) *The Foucault Effect: Studies in Governmentality: With Two Lectures by and and Interview with Michel Foucault,* University of Chicago Press (Chicago), 1991.

Ethics: Subjectivity and Truth, edited by Paul Rabinow, New Press, 1997.

Director of *Zone des tempetes,* 1973-84. Contributor to periodicals, including *Critique.*

SIDELIGHTS: In the *New York Times Book Review,* Peter Cawes wrote, "Michel Foucault is one of a handful of French thinkers who have . . . given an entirely new direction to theoretical work in the so-called 'human sciences,' the study of language, literature, psychiatry, intellectual history and the like." But according to Frank Kermode, Foucault is not "writing history of ideas, or indeed history of anything. Unlike historians, he seeks not origin, continuities, and explanations which will fill in documentary breaches of continuity, but rather 'an epistemological space specific to a particular period.' He attempts to uncover the *unconscious* of knowledge."

D. W. Harding explained Foucault's disdain for the history of knowledge: "Foucault believes that our own current intellectual life and systems of scientific thought are built on assumptions profoundly taken for granted and normally not exposed to conscious inspection, and yet likely in time . . . to be discarded." *Nation's* Bruce Jackson agreed. "Foucault is one of the few social analysts whose work regularly unfits readers to continue looking at things or ideas or institutions in the same way," he wrote. "His archaeologies uncover architectures that make sensible order of what previously seemed sloppiness or incompetence or foolishness or malevolence."

Sherry Turkle characterized Foucault's method as "constructive," though a more apt definition might be "reconstructive." As Jackson noted, "Foucault works to uncover, to unearth." Similar-ly, Peter Cawes wrote in *New Republic,* "The archaeologist, finding a coin here, a pot there, reconstructs cities and civilizations. Foucault, turning over words with immense scholarship and erudition, reconstructs a group of intellectual activities collectively called in French the *sciences humaines.*"

Foucault introduced his archaeological method in *The Order of Things,* in which he presents the idea that "in any given culture and at any given moment there is only one *episteme* [a system of instinctual knowledge] that defines the conditions of possibility of all knowledge." Foucault then attempts "to dig up and display the 'archaeological' form or forms which would be common to all mental activity," and he traces these forms throughout historic cultures.

In *The Order of Things,* Foucault also presented his concept of "the disappearance of man." He explains that "there was no epistemological consciousness of man" before the eighteenth century. According to Foucault, only upon the advent of biology, economics, and philology did man appear "as an object of knowledge and as a subject that knows." He then describes the twentieth century as the "death of man." Foucault attributes man's decline to objectivity, which eliminates the necessity of making man the focus of history.

Foucault addressed his archaeological methods in *The Archaeology of Knowledge.* Cawes described the book as "an attempt to decide just what it is about certain utterances or inscriptions—real objects in a real world which leave traces behind to be discovered, classified and related to one another—that qualifies them as 'statements' . . . belonging to various bodies of knowledge." The English-language edition of *The Archaeology of Knowledge* included "The Discourse on Language," an investigation into the ways in which society manipulates language for purposes of politics and power. Cawes described Foucault's perception of language as "a net *thrown over* the world: it criticized, classified, analyzed."

During the 1970s, Foucault shifted his emphasis from the archaeological method to a genealogical method. Whereas the former consisted of unearthing scholarly minutia from the past to understand the types of knowledge possible during a given time period, the genealogical method sought to understand how power structures shaped and changed the boundaries of "truth." Donald F. Bouchard discusses Foucault's conception of genealogy and truth in *Thinkers of the Twentieth Century:* "The classic philosophical question, 'What is the surest path to the Truth?' has been refashioned . . . into a new basis for historical interrogation: 'what is the hazardous career that Truth has followed?'—the question of genealogy for which the will to truth, in Western culture, is the most deeply enmeshed historical phenomenon. In Foucault's works, truth is no longer an unchanging, universal essence, but the perpetual object of appropriation, domination."

Foucault employed his genealogical approach in *Discipline and Punish,* published in French in 1975 and English in 1977. The work provides a history of how society has approached crime and punishment over the years. In *New Republic,* Frank McConnell noted that *Discipline and Punish,* rather than merely tracing the evolution of penal institutions, presents the argument "that the invention of the prison is the crucial, inclusive image for all those modes of brutalization, in industry, in education, in the very fabric of citizenship, which defines the modern era of humanistic tyranny, the totalitarianism of the norm."

Foucault also followed the genealogical approach in the first volume of his last work, *The History of Sexuality,* a proposed series of six volumes of which Foucault completed three and most of the fourth before his death in 1984. But, as Michael Ignatieff observed in the *Times Literary Supplement,* volumes two and three "will surprise readers expecting Foucault to continue his genealogy of modern reason. Indeed, in the interval between the publication of the first volume . . . in 1976 and the appearance of these two further volumes eight years later, the axis of his work shifted so radically that the continuity of the whole project must be put in doubt." Ignatieff remarked that Foucault's new scope expanded to include the history of "Western reason itself since the dawn of Greek philosophy."

The focus of *The History of Sexuality* is on how the self has variously perceived itself through its views on human sexuality. The first volume introduces the series and, in Turkle's words, "challenges standard interpretations of modern sexual history as a history of repression." Volume two, translated into English as *The Use of Pleasure,* examines the sexual questions and moral problems that the ancient Greeks pondered, and volume three, translated as *The Care of the Self,* centers on the Christian influence on the Romans regarding issues of marriage and procreation. In Foucault's estimation the Romans represent a transitional group between the ancient Greeks—who regularly practiced homosexuality and who did not equate sexual practice with sin—and the Christian Europeans, whose concept of sin caused them to approach sexuality with considerable anxiety. Ignatieff concluded, "Because the *History of Sexuality* will remain unfinished, the history [of] modern asceticism we are offered is only a sketchy outline. . . . [Foucault's history] begins, now, not with the confinement of the insane, the criminal and the sick in the seventeenth century, but with that sense of sin and that sense of desire which date back to the meeting between the pagan and Christian languages of the self."

Foucault's work has met with resistance, much of which stems from his manner of presentation. He has been accused of writing "obliquely" and "rhetorically," and Paul Robinson called him "one of those authors who write with their ears, not with their heads." Christopher Lasch declared, "His writing is difficult, the argument hard to follow, the arrangement of chapters seemingly arbitrary and the whole very difficult to summarize." Cawes described Foucault as "never a man to use one word where five will do, or to say straightforwardly what can be said obliquely." Similarly, Robinson contended, "What he tries to create, above all else, is a certain tone—highfalutin, patronizing . . . and, whenever the argument threatens to run thin, opaque."

Turkle defended Foucault's style as the French method of putting "poetry into science." She declared, "In order to put into question assumptions deeply embedded in our ordinary language, one has to use language in extraordinary ways." Harding summarized: "Foucault has the dreadful gift . . . of diffusing his meaning very thinly throughout an immense verbal spate, no part of which is quite empty of meaning, redundant, or merely repetitive. But behind all the abstract jargon and intimidating erudition there is undoubtedly an alert and sensitive mind which can ignore the familiar surfaces of established intellectual codes and ask new questions."

BIOGRAPHICAL/CRITICAL SOURCES:

BOOKS

Armstrong, Timothy J., *Michel Foucault, Philosopher: Essays Translated from the French and German,* Routledge (New York City), 1992.

Barker, Philip, *Michel Foucault: Subversions of the Subject,* St. Martin's Press (New York City), 1993.

Barry, Andrew, Thomas Osborne, and Nikolas Rose, editors, *Foucault and Political Reason: Liberalism, Neo-Liberalism, and Rationalities of Government,* University of Chicago Press, 1996.

Bell, Vikki, *Interrogating Incest: Feminism, Foucault, and the Law,* Routledge (New York City), 1993.

Burke, Sean, *The Death and Return of the Author: Criticism and Subjectivity in Barthes, Foucault, and Derrida,* Edinburgh University Press (Edinburgh), 1992.

Caputo, John D. and Mark Yount, *Foucault and the Critique of Institutions,* Pennsylvania University Press (University Park), 1993.

Coles, Romand, *Self/Power/Other: Political Theory and Dialogical Ethics,* Cornell University Press (Ithaca), 1992.

Cook, Deborah, *The Subject Finds a Voice: Foucault's Turn Toward Subjectivity,* P. Lang (New York City), 1993.

Dean, Mitchell, *Critical and Effective Histories: Foucault's Methods and Historical Sociology,* Routledge (New York City), 1994.

During, Simon, *Foucault and Literature: Towards a Genealogy of Writing,* Routledge (New York City), 1992.

Fillingham, Lydia Alix, *Foucault for Beginners,* Writers and Readers (New York City), 1993.

Gane, Mike and Terry Johnson, *Foucault's New Domains,* Routledge (New York City), 1993.

Goldstein, Jan Ellen, *Foucault and the Writing of History,* Blackwell (Cambridge, MA), 1994.

Gutting, Gary, editor, *The Cambridge Companion to Foucault,* Cambridge University Press (New York City), 1994.

Hekman, Susan J. *Feminist Interpretations of Michel Foucault,* Pennsylvania State University (University Park), 1996.

Lanigan, Richard L., *The Human Science of Communicology: A Phenomenology of Discourse of Discourse in Foucault and Merleau-Ponty,* Duquesne University Press (Pittsburgh), 1992.

Lloyd, Moya and Andrew Thacker, editors, *The Impact of Michel Foucault on the Social Sciences and Humanities,* St. Martin's Press (New York City), 1996.

MacEy, David, *The Lives of Michel Foucault: A Biography,* Pantheon (New York City), 1993.

Mahon, Michael, *Foucault's Nietzschean Geneaology: Truth, Power, and the Subject,* State University of New York Press (Albany), 1992.

May, Todd, *Between Genealogy and Epistemology: Psychology, Politics, and Knowledge in the Thought of Michel Foucault,* Pennsylvania State University Press (University Park), 1993.

May, *The Moral Theory of Poststructuralism,* Pennsylvania State University Press (University Park), 1995.

McNay, Lois, *Foucault and Feminism: Power, Gender, and the Self,* Northeastern University Press (Boston), 1993.

McNay, *Foucault: A Critical Introduction,* Continuum (New York City), 1994.

Miller, Jim, *The Passion of Michel Foucault,* Simon & Schuster (New York City), 1993.

Nilson, Herman, *Michel Foucault and the Games of Truth,* St. Martin's Press, 1998.

O'Hara, Daniel T., *Radical Parody: American Culture and Critical Agency after Foucault,* Columbia University Press (New York City), 1992.

Privitera, Walter, *Problems of Style: Michel Foucault's Epistemology,* State University of New York Press (Albany), 1995.

Quinby, Lee, *Freedom, Foucault, and the Subject of America,* Northeastern University Press (Boston), 1991.

Rajchman, John, *Truth and Eros: Foucault, Lacan, and the Question of Ethics,* Routledge (New York City), 1991.

Ramazanoglu, Caroline, *Up Against Foucault: Explorations of Some Tensions Between Foucault and Feminism,* Routledge (New York City), 1993.

Sawicki, Jana, *Gender/Power/Knowledge: Feminism and Foucault,* Routledge (New York City), 1991.

Shumway, David R., *Michel Foucault,* University Press of Virginia (Charlottesville), 1992.

Simons, Jon, *Foucault & the Political,* Routledge (New York City), 1995.

Smart, Barry, *Michel Foucault: Critical Assessments,* Routledge (New York City), 1994.

Stoler, Ann Laura, *Race and the Education of Desire: Foucault's History of Sexuality and the Colonial Order of Things,* Duke University Press (Durham), 1995.

Thinkers of the Twentieth Century, Gale, 1987.

PERIODICALS

American Historical Review, April, 1993, pp. 338, 354, 364, 376.
Commonweal, May 12, 1978.
Esquire, July, 1975.
Globe and Mail (Toronto), June 7, 1986.
Horizon, autumn, 1969.
Library Quarterly, October, 1992, p. 408.
Los Angeles Times Book Review, November 24, 1985.
Nation, July 5, 1971; January 26, 1974; March 4, 1978; January 27, 1979.
New Republic, March 27, 1971; November 10, 1973; April 1, 1978; October 28, 1978; February 15, 1993, p. 27; June 27, 1994, p. 39.
New Yorker, January 29, 1979; July 16, 1979.
New York Review of Books, August 12, 1971; May 17, 1973; January 22, 1976.
New York Times Book Review, October 22, 1972; February 24, 1974; December 7, 1975; February 19, 1978; January 14, 1979; February 25, 1979; November 25, 1979; January 27, 1980; June 12, 1980; January 18, 1987; January 10, 1993, p. 1.
Spectator, October 9, 1971.
Times Literary Supplement, June 9, 1972; February 1, 1974; June 16, 1978; April 27, 1984; September 28, 1984.
Washington Post Book World, January 7, 1979; March 15, 1981; January 5, 1986.
Whole Earth Review, winter, 1995, p. 72.

*　　*　　*

FOWLES, John (Robert) 1926-

PERSONAL: Born March 31, 1926, in Essex, England; son of Robert John and Gladys May (Richards) Fowles; married Elizabeth Whitton, April 2, 1954 (died, 1990); children: Anna (stepdaughter). *Education:* Edinburgh University, 1944; New College, Oxford, B.A. (with honours in French), 1950.

ADDRESSES: Home—Lyme Regis, Dorset, England. *Office*—Jonathan Cape Ltd., 20 Vauxshall Bridge Rd., London, SW1V 2SA England. *Agent*—Anthony Sheil Associates, 43 Doughty St., London WC1N 2LF, England.

CAREER: Writer. University of Poitiers, France, lecturer in English, 1950-51; Anargyrios College, Spetsai, Greece, teacher, 1951-52; taught at various schools in London, England, including Ashridge College and St. Godric's College, 1953-63. *Military service:* Royal Marines, 1945-46; became lieutenant.

AWARDS, HONORS: Silver Pen Award from English Centre of International PEN, 1970; W. H. Smith and Son Literary Award, 1970, for *The French Lieutenant's Woman;* Christopher Award, 1982, for *The Tree.* D.Litt., Exeter University, 1983.

WRITINGS:

The Aristos: A Self-Portrait in Ideas, Little, Brown (Boston), 1964, 2nd revised edition published as *The Aristos,* J. Cape (London), 1980.
(Author of introduction, glossary, and appendix) Sabine Baring-Gould, *Mehalah: A Story of the Salt Marshes,* Chatto & Windus (London), 1969.
Poems, Ecco Press (New York City), 1973.
The Ebony Tower (collection of short fiction), Little, Brown, 1974.
Shipwreck, illustrated with photographs by the Gibsons of Scilly, J. Cape, 1974, Little, Brown, 1975.
(Adaptor and translator) Charles Perrault, *Cinderella,* J. Cape, 1974, Little, Brown, 1976.
(Translator) Clairie du Fort, *Ourika,* W. Thomas Taylor (Austin, TX), 1977.
Islands, illustrated with photographs by Fay Godwin, Little, Brown, 1978.
The Tree, illustrated with photographs by Frank Horvat, Little, Brown, 1980.
The Enigma of Stonehenge, illustrated with photographs by Barry Brukoff, Summit Books (New York City), 1980.
(Editor) John Aubrey, *Monumenta Brittanica,* Little, Brown, Parts 1 and 2, 1980, Part 3 and Index, 1982.
A Short History of Lyme Regis, Little, Brown, 1983.
(Editor and author of introduction) *Thomas Hardy's England,* Little, Brown, 1985.
(Editor) *Land,* illustrated with photographs by Fay Godwin, Little, Brown, 1985.
Lyme Regis Camera, Little, Brown, 1990.
(Translator with Robert D. MacDonald and Christopher Hampton) Corneille, *Landmarks of French Classical Drama,* Heinemann (London), 1991.
(Author of afterword) David H. Lawrence, *The Man Who Died: A Story,* Ecco Press, 1994.
Wormholes: Essays and Occasional Writings, edited by Jan Relf, Holt, 1998.

NOVELS

The Collector (also see below), Little, Brown, 1963.
The Magus (also see below), Little, Brown, 1966, revised edition, 1977.
The French Lieutenant's Woman (also see below), Little, Brown, 1969.
Daniel Martin, Little, Brown, 1977.
Mantissa, Little, Brown, 1982.
A Maggot, Little, Brown, 1985.

SCREENPLAYS

(With Stanley Mann and John Kohn) *The Collector* (based on Fowles's novel of the same title), Columbia, 1965.

The Magus (based on Fowles's novel of the same title), Twentieth Century-Fox, 1969.

(Author of foreword) Harold Pinter, *The French Lieutenant's Woman: A Screenplay* (based on Fowles' novel of the same title), Little, Brown, 1981.

OTHER

Contributor to books and anthologies, including *Afterwords: Novelists on Their Novels,* 1969, *New Visions of Franz Kafka,* 1974, *The Novel Today,* 1977, *Thomas Hardy after Fifty Years,* 1977, *Steep Holm: A Case History in the Study of Evolution,* 1978, *Britain: A World by Itself: Reflections on the Landscape by Eminent British Writers,* 1984. Author of forewords, introductions, and afterwords to several books.

MEDIA ADAPTATIONS: The Collector was adapted for the stage and produced in London at the King's Head Theatre in 1971; a version of Fowles's novella *The Ebony Tower* was broadcast on television in 1984; *The Collector, The Magus,* and *The French Lieutenant's Woman,* have all been adapted for film.

SIDELIGHTS: The concept of freedom has played a significant role throughout much of John Fowles's writing career. It has lead him to investigate and question both its thematic importance and its stylistic value. Not only does Fowles refuse to be put into a "cage labelled 'novelist,'" as he says in *The Aristos: A Self-Portrait in Ideas,* he also rejects any label limiting him to a particular kind of writing. Known primarily as a novelist, Fowles seems to write every possible kind of novel, as well as works of poetry and short fiction.

A review of Fowles's diverse writings helps to explain why some readers find his works to be perplexing. Many who enjoyed *The Collector,* a thriller and Fowles's first novel, were subsequently puzzled when *The Magus* departed from its pattern. Unlike the tight and compact form of the thriller, *The Magus* spreads to the length of an "apprentice novel," a form which, like Charles Dickens' *Great Expectations,* usually follows the chronology of a youth's development. *The French Lieutenant's Woman,* a historical novel set in the 1860s, overtly guides readers into Fowles's method of transforming and recreating established forms for a new era. *The Ebony Tower* is unique, for it contains short works that are connected thematically to each other and to several of Fowles's earlier books.

The driving force for Fowles's constant variation can be found in his central theme: freedom. That is, the question of whether a human being can act independently from the psychological and social pressures of his/her environment. While this is not his only theme, he says in his nonfiction manifesto, *The Aristos,* that the very "terms of existence encourage us to change, to evolve" if we are to be free; and thus the theme provides a unifying thread throughout much of his work.

Fowles's first published work, *The Collector,* deals with freedom on a variety of levels. Fred Clegg, a lower-class clerk who has won a fortune in a football pool, buys an isolated house and rigs up a basement room as a secret cell for Miranda, a twenty-year-old, upper-middle-class scholarship art student, whom he has kidnapped. The action of the novel consists of the working out of two lines of freedom, both based on Miranda's response to Clegg's imposition of his illegitimate authority over her. One line of freedom is Miranda's tentative, temporary, or pretended acceptance of the imposed authority that wins her small degrees of freedom within the limited boundaries that Clegg will permit. The second line consists of Miranda's successive attempts to escape Clegg's control altogether, a struggle that takes on societal and universal human dimensions as the novel progresses.

While the imprisonment of a young woman in a locked room dramatizes lost freedom in *The Collector,* Fowles deals with the issue more subtly and ironically in *The Magus.* Nicholas, the novel's main character, must learn that freedom in a world of psychological and societal influences requires self-knowledge. Although Nicholas has embraced the concepts of existentialism precisely because of their emphasis on the possibility of knowing one's self and acting authentically upon such knowledge, Fowles demonstrates how the character, in fact, uses them as an almost ironclad defense against self-knowledge.

The French Lieutenant's Woman again addresses the issues of freedom starkly dramatized in *The Collector* and more developed in *The Magus.* While Fowles again depicts characters struggling for physical and psychic liberation, he places them in the restrictive atmosphere of Victorian England. He also desires to see his characters freed, not only from society but also from his own control of them as author; thus the composing process becomes part of the novel's subject. And finally, Fowles liberates even himself from the limitations of the novel form; he devises three separate endings for the novel, making the reader his implied consultant on the creation of the book.

By giving characters their freedom, Fowles also liberates himself from the tyranny of the rigid plan; but there remains a more basic limitation of fiction, and from this Fowles frees himself by means of his multiple endings: "The novelist is still a god," Fowles says in *The French Lieutenant's Woman,* "since he creates (and not even the most aleatory avant-garde modern novel has managed to extirpate its author completely); what has changed is that we are no longer the gods of the Victorian image, omniscient and decreeing; but in the new theological image, with freedom our first principle, not authority."

Fowles says in his personal note set in the middle of *The Ebony Tower* that he "meant to suggest variations on both certain themes in previous books of mine and in methods of narrative presentation." Themes and narrative methods combine to weave an intricate pattern of connection, not only with earlier works but among the novella, the translation of a Celtic medieval romance, and the three short stories that make up this collection. Such an approach allows Fowles to display his freedom as a writer, even within the boundaries of his own works.

A Maggot, which Fowles explains in his prologue is not a historical novel but rather a whim, a quirk, a perverse fancy-all obsolete senses of the word *maggot*—is set in southwestern England in the early eighteenth century; the plot unveils the evolution of a new era. Pat Rogers, in the *Times Literary Supplement,* calls *A Maggot* "Fowles' most political work of fiction to date" and says "as the novel progresses, the mystical and socio-religious aspects take over." The book opens with four men and a woman traveling across the countryside, their identities and relationships enigmatic. When one member is found hanged from a tree and another, a nobleman, disappears, the other three face trial. The story unfolds as London barrister Henry Ayscough investigates the mysterious events surrounding the party. One such event is a vision by the woman, who is a prostitute and the future mother of the founder and leader of the American Shaker movement. In *Time* Christopher Porterfield writes that *A Maggot* "makes gripping reading indeed, part detective story, part crackling courtroom drama. A vivid gallery of the English underclasses passes under the lawyer's scrutiny. Testimony is offered on London brothel life, moonlit rituals at Stonehenge, witchcraft and an odd prefiguring of science fiction in a cavern beneath the Devon moors." Yet the novel leaves loose ends. Fallon Evans writes in the *Los Angeles Times Book Review*, "John Fowles' *A Maggot* is a wonderful book, unless you are the kind of reader who wants to know what really happened."

Fowles's refusal to limit himself opens his work to much of life. He sifts elements of culture, art, and historical experience into such familiar structures as the thriller, the adolescent-learning novel, the historical novel, the book of short fiction, and the mainstream modernist novel. He always re-creates and makes these forms his own, mixing his insight about human beings and life into the transformed structures. Literature and myth enter through the many allusions that he makes central to the movement of the novels. History emerges most noticeably in *The French Lieutenant's Woman,* and Fowles works to open his own creative processes to the reader, especially in *The French Lieutenant's Woman* and *Mantissa.*

Finally, while many of Fowles's novels make significant social comments and provide insights into human character, his variety of forms opens continual opportunities for new possibilities. Such diversity, though presenting the reader with difficulties of adjustment from novel to novel, surely supplies evidence that Fowles pushes ahead, activated by his own major theme: the drive for freedom.

BIOGRAPHICAL/CRITICAL SOURCES:

BOOKS

Acheson, James, *John Fowles,* St. Martin's, 1998.

Arlett, Robert, *Epic Voices: Inner and Global Impulse in the Contemporary American and British Novel,* Susquehanna University Press (Selinsgrove, PA), 1996.

Aubrey, James R., *John Fowles: A Reference Companion,* Greenwood Press, 1991.

Barnum, Carol M., *The Fiction of John Fowles: A Myth for Our Time,* Penkevill Pub. (Greenwood, FL), 1988.

Begiebing, Robert J., *Toward a New Synthesis: John Fowles, John Gardner, Norman Mailer,* UMI Research Press (Ann Arbor, MI), 1989.

Conradi, Peter, *John Fowles,* Methuen (London), 1982.

Contemporary Literary Criticism, Gale (Detroit), Volume 1, 1973; Volume 2, 1974; Volume 3, 1975; Volume 4, 1975; Volume 6, 1976; Volume 9, 1978; Volume 10, 1979; Volume 15, 1980; Volume 33, 1985; Volume 87, 1995.

Cooper, Pamela, *The Fiction of John Fowles: Power, Creativity, Femininity,* University of Ottawa Press, 1991.

Dictionary of Literary Biography, Gale, Volume 14: *British Novelists since 1960,* 1983; Volume 139: *British Short-Fiction Writers, 1945-1980,* 1994.

Eriksson, Bo H. T., *The "Structuring Forces" of Detection: the Cases of C. P. Snow and John Fowles,* University of Uppsala, 1995.

Fawkner, H. W., *The Timescapes of John Fowles,* Fairleigh Dickinson University Press (East Brunswick, NJ), 1984.

Foster, Thomas C., *Understanding John Fowles,* University of South Carolina Press (Columbia, SC), 1994.

Garard, Charles, *Point of View in Fiction and Film: Focus on John Fowles,* Peter Lang, 1991.

Loveday, Simon, *The Romances of John Fowles,* St. Martin's, 1985.

Neary, John, *Something and Nothingness: The Fiction of John Updike and John Fowles,* Southern Illinois University Press, 1992.

Olshen, Barry, and Toni Olshen, *John Fowles: A Reference Guide,* G. K. Hall (Boston), 1980.

Onega Jaen, Susana, *Form and Meaning in the Novels of John Fowles,* UMI Research Press, 1989.

Tarbox, Katherine, *The Art of John Fowles,* University of Georgia Press (Athens), 1988.

Wolfe, Peter, *John Fowles: Magus and Moralist,* Bucknell University Press (Cranbury, NJ), 1976, revised edition, 1979.

Woodcock, Bruce, *Male Mythologies: John Fowles and Masculinity,* Barnes & Noble (New York City), 1984.

PERIODICALS

Ariel, July, 1989, pp. 39-52.

Boston Review, February, 1983.

Chicago Tribune, October 29, 1986.

Chicago Tribune Book World, November 2, 1969; August 29, 1982; July 7, 1985.

Contemporary Literature, winter, 1974; summer, 1975, pp. 328-39; spring, 1976, pp. 204-22; autumn, 1976, pp. 455-69; summer, 1986, pp. 160-81.

Contemporary Literature Studies, Volume 17, 1980; winter, 1986, pp. 324-34.

Critical Quarterly, winter, 1973, pp. 317-34; spring, 1982.

Critique: Studies in Modern Fiction, Volume 20, summer, 1968; Volume 23, number 3, 1972; Volume 31, number 2, 1979.

Encounter, August, 1970; January, 1978.

Film Literature Quarterly, July, 1988, pp. 144-54.

Globe & Mail (Toronto), September 14, 1985; September 21, 1985.

Harper's, July, 1968.

Hollins Critic, December, 1969, pp. 1-12.

Hudson Review, summer, 1966.

Journal of Modern Literature, No. 2, 1980-1981, pp. 235-46 and 275-86; spring, 1988, pp. 579-84.

Journal of Narrative Technique, September, 1973, pp. 193-207.

Life, May 29, 1970, pp. 55-58, 60.

Listener, October 31, 1974; October 7, 1982.

Literature Film Quarterly, January, 1987, pp. 8-14.

London Magazine, March, 1971, pp. 34-46; March, 1975.

Los Angeles Times, March 16, 1980; November 30, 1980; September 29, 1982.

Los Angeles Times Book Review, July 21, 1985; September 15, 1985, p. 10; November 6, 1985; September 21, 1986.

Modern Fiction Studies (issue devoted to John Fowles), spring, 1985, pp. 3-210; summer, 1991, pp. 217-33.

Mosaic, fall, 1989, pp. 31-44.

Nation, December 15, 1969; September 13, 1975.

New Republic, October 18, 1982; October 7, 1985.

New Statesman, June 21, 1963; July 2, 1965; October 11, 1974; November 28, 1986.

Newsweek, November 25, 1974; October 7, 1985.

New York Herald Tribune Book Review, July 28, 1963.

New York Review of Books, December 8, 1977; December 5, 1985.

New York Times, November 10, 1969; September 13, 1977; August 31, 1982; October 5, 1982; September 2, 1985.

New York Times Book Review, January 28, 1963; July 28, 1963; January 9, 1966; November 9, 1969, pp. 1, 74-75; November 9, 1969, pp. 2, 52-53; November 10, 1974, pp. 2-3, 20;

September 25, 1977; November 13, 1977, pp. 3, 84-85;
March 19, 1978; March 30, 1980; August 29, 1982;
September 8, 1985; October 5, 1986; May 31, 1998, p. 37.

Philosophy and Literature, April, 1991, pp. 1-18.

Poetics Today, No. 3, 1986, pp. 397-420.

Spectator, June 14, 1970; November 16, 1974; September 21, 1985.

Time, November 20, 1964; January 14, 1966; December 2, 1974; September 27, 1982; September 9, 1985, p. 67.

Times (London), April 22, 1985; September 19, 1985.

Times Literary Supplement, May 17, 1963; June 12, 1969; December 6, 1974; April 17, 1981; October 8, 1982; September 20, 1985, p. 1027.

Twentieth Century Literature, Volume 19, 1973; Volume 28, 1982.

Village Voice, September 12, 1977; February 20, 1978.

Village Voice Literary Supplement, September, 1982.

Washington Post, December 11, 1974.

Washington Post Book World, November 23, 1980; February 14, 1982; September 19, 1982; September 8, 1985; December 8, 1985; September 14, 1986, p. 12.

World Literature Today, summer, 1986.

*   *   *

FRAME, Janet
See CLUTHA, Janet Paterson Frame

*   *   *

FRANCE, Anatole
See THIBAULT, Jacques Anatole Francois

*   *   *

FRANCIS, Dick 1920-

PERSONAL: Full name, Richard Stanley Francis; born October 31, 1920, in Tenby, Pembrokeshire, Wales; son of George Vincent (a professional steeplechase rider and stable manager) and Molly (Thomas) Francis; married Mary Brenchley (a teacher and assistant stage manager), June 21, 1947; children: Merrick, Felix. *Education:* Attended Maidenhead County School. *Religion:* Church of England. *Avocation:* Boating, fox hunting, tennis.

ADDRESSES: Home—P. O. Box 30866 SMB Grand Cayman, West Indies. *Agent*—Andrew Hewson, John Johnson Authors' Agent, 45/47 Clerkenwell Green, London EC1R 0HT, England; Sterling Lord Literistic, Inc., 1 Madison Ave., New York, NY 10010.

CAREER: Novelist. Amateur steeplechase rider, 1946-48; professional steeplechase jockey, 1948-57; *Sunday Express,* London, England, racing correspondent, 1957-73. Exercises racehorses in winter; judges hunters at horse shows in summer. *Military service:* Royal Air Force, 1940-46; became flying officer (pilot).

MEMBER: Crime Writers Association (chair, 1973-74), Mystery Writers of America, Writers of Canada, Detection Club, Racecourse Association.

AWARDS, HONORS: Steeplechase jockey championship, 1954; Silver Dagger Award, Crime Writers Association, 1965, for *For Kicks;* Edgar Allan Poe Award, Mystery Writers of America, 1969, for *Forfeit,* and 1980, for *Whip Hand;* Gold Dagger Award, Crime Writers Association, 1980, for *Whip Hand;* Order of the British Empire, 1984; L.H.D., Tufts University, 1991; Grand Master Award and Best Novel award, both from the Mystery Writers of America, Shamus Award finalist, all 1996, all for *Come to Grief.*

WRITINGS:

MYSTERY NOVELS

Dead Cert, Holt, 1962.
Nerve, Harper, 1964.
For Kicks, Harper, 1965.
Odds Against, M. Joseph, 1965, Harper, 1966.
Flying Finish, M. Joseph, 1966, Harper, 1967.
Blood Sport, Harper, 1967.
Forfeit, Harper, 1968.
Enquiry, Harper, 1969.
Three to Show: A Trilogy, Harper, 1969.
Rat Race, Harper, 1970.
Bonecrack, Harper, 1971.
Smokescreen, Harper, 1972.
Slay-ride, Harper, 1973.
Knockdown, Harper, 1974.
High Stakes, Harper, 1975.
Across the Board: A Trilogy, Harper, 1975.
In the Frame, Harper, 1976.
Risk, Harper, 1977.
Trial Run, Harper, 1978.
Whip Hand, Harper, 1979.
Reflex, M. Joseph, 1980, Putnam, 1981.
Twice Shy, M. Joseph, 1981, Putnam, 1982.
Banker, M. Joseph, 1982, Putnam, 1983.
The Danger, M. Joseph, 1983, Putnam, 1984.
Proof, M. Joseph, 1984, Putnam, 1985.
Break In, M. Joseph, 1985, Putnam, 1986.
Bolt, M. Joseph, 1986, Putnam, 1987.
Hot Money, M. Joseph, 1987, Putnam, 1988.
The Edge, M. Joseph, 1988, Putnam, 1989.
Straight, Putnam, 1989.
Longshot, Putnam, 1990.
Comeback, Putnam, 1991.
Driving Force, Putnam, 1992.
Decider, Putnam, 1993.
Wild Horses, Putnam, 1994.
Come to Grief, Putnam, 1995.
To the Hilt, Thorndike Press (Thorndike, ME), 1996.
Three Complete Novels, Putnam, 1997.
10 lb. Penalty, Putnam, 1997.

OTHER

The Sport of Queens (racing autobiography), M. Joseph, 1957.
(Editor with John Welcome) *Best Racing and Chasing Stories,* Faber, 1966.
(Editor with Welcome) *Best Racing and Chasing Stories II,* Faber, 1969.
The Racing Man's Bedside Book, Faber, 1969.
A Jockey's Life: The Biography of Lester Piggott, Putnam, 1986, published in England as *Lester, the Official Biography,* M. Joseph, 1986.
(Editor with Welcome) *The New Treasury of Great Racing Stories,* Norton, 1991.
(Editor with Welcome) *The Dick Francis Treasury of Great Racing Stories,* G. K. Hall, 1991.

Contributor to anthologies, including *Winter's Crimes 5,* edited by Virginia Whitaker, Macmillan, 1973; *Stories of Crime and Detection,* edited by Joan D. Berbrich, McGraw, 1974; *Ellery Queen's Crime Wave,* Putnam, 1976; and *Ellery Queen's Searches and Seizures,* Davis, 1977. Contributor to periodicals, including *Horseman's Year, Sports Illustrated, In Praise of Hunting,* and *Stud and Stable.*

MEDIA ADAPTATIONS: Dead Cert was filmed by United Artists in 1973; *Odds Against* was adapted for Yorkshire Television as *The Racing Game,* 1979, and also broadcast by the PBS-TV series *Mystery!,* 1980-81; Francis's works adapted for television series *Dick Francis Mysteries* by Dick Francis Films Ltd., 1989; *Blood Sport* was adapted for television as *Dick Francis: Blood Sport* by Comedia Entertainment, 1989. Many of Francis's books have been recorded on audiocassette.

SIDELIGHTS: When steeple jockey Dick Francis retired from horseracing at age thirty-six, he speculated in his autobiography that he would be remembered as "the man who didn't win the National," England's prestigious Grand National steeplechase. If he hadn't turned to fiction, his prediction might have been correct, but with the publication of his first novel, *Dead Cert,* in 1962, Francis launched a second career that was even more successful than his first: he became a mystery writer.

Since that time, Francis has averaged a thriller a year, astounding critics with the fecundity of his imagination and garnering awards such as Britain's Silver Dagger (in 1965 for *For Kicks*) and two Edgars (for *Forfeit* in 1969 and *Whip Hand* in 1980). However, talking about his books and their success Francis says in *Sport of Queens,* his autobiography, that, "I still find the writing . . . grindingly hard, and I approach Chapter 1 each year with deeper foreboding." Gina MacDonald, writing in the *Dictionary of Literary Biography,* says that Francis's method of writing his books is very precise. He usually thinks of a plot by midsummer, and spends the rest of the year researching the book. He finally starts writing the following year and finishes the book by spring. Since most of his books concern horses, racing still figures in his life. His affinity for the racetrack actually enhances his prose, according to Julian Symons, who writes in the *New York Times Book Review* that "what comes most naturally to [Francis] is also what he does best—writing about the thrills, spills and chills of horse racing."

Before he began writing, Francis experienced one of racing's most publicized "spills" firsthand. In 1956, when he was already a veteran jockey, Francis had the privilege of riding Devon Loch—the Queen Mother's horse—in the annual Grand National. Fifty yards from the finish line, with the race virtually won, the horse inexplicably faltered. Later examination revealed no physical injury and no clue was ever found. "I still don't have the answer," Francis told Peter Axthelm of *Newsweek.* "Maybe he was shocked by the noise of 250,000 people screaming because the royal family's horse was winning. But the fact is that with nothing wrong with him, ten strides from the winning post he fell. The other fact is," he added, "if that mystery hadn't happened, I might never have written all these other ones."

While critics initially speculated that Francis's specialized knowledge would provide only limited fictional opportunities, most have since changed their minds. "It is fascinating to see how many completely fresh and unexpected plots he can concoct about horses," marvels Anthony Boucher in the *New York Times Book Review.* Philip Pelham takes this approbation one step further, writing in *London Magazine* that "Francis improves with every

book as both a writer of brisk, lucid prose and as a concocter of ingenious and intricately worked-out plots." His racetrack thrillers deal with such varied story lines as crooks transporting horses by air (*Flying Finish*), stolen stallions (*Blood Sport*), and a jockey who has vanished in Norway (*Slay-ride*). To further preserve the freshness of his fiction, Francis creates a new protagonist for each novel and often develops subplots around fields unrelated to racing. "His books," notes Axthelm, "take him and his readers on global explorations as well as into crash courses in ventures like aviation, gold mining and, in *Reflex,* amateur photography."

Barry Bauska, writing in the *Armchair Detective,* offers a more detailed version of the "typical" Francis thriller: "At the outset something has happened that looks wrong (a jockey is set down by a board of inquiry that seemed predetermined to find him guilty; a horse falls going over a final hurdle it had seemed to clear; horses perfectly ready to win consistently fail to do so). The narrator protagonist (usually not a detective, but always inherently curious) begins to poke around to try to discover what has occurred. In so doing he inevitably pokes too hard and strikes a hornets' nest. The rest of the novel then centers on a critical struggle between the searcher-after-truth and the mysterious agent of evil, whose villainy had upset things in the first place."

Despite the formulaic nature of his work, Francis deals with problems prevalent in modern society, says Marty Knepper in *Twelve Englishmen of Mystery.* He feels that Francis's works deal with social and moral issues "seriously and in some depth . . . including some topics generally considered unpleasant." For example, in *Blood Sport* the hero is struggling with his own suicidal urges. In Knepper's words, "To read *Blood Sport* . . . is to learn what it feels like to be lonely, paranoid and suicidal."

Character development also plays an important part in Francis's novels. Knepper says that biographical similarities between Francis's heroes may blind the reader to the important differences between them. For example, Francis's heroes have a wide variety of professions. This gives him a chance to examine professionalism, and the responsibilities that accompany it, in fields other than racing and detection. Each of Francis's heroes, according to Knepper, is "a unique person, but each hero . . . changes as a result of his adventures." In the end, characters learn from their experiences and have evolved.

While a number of Francis's books include a love story, a much more pressing theme, according to Axthelm, is that of pain. "Again and again," he writes in *Newsweek,* the author's "villains probe the most terrifying physical or psychic weakness in his heroes. A lifetime's most treasured mementos are destroyed by mindless hired thugs; an already crippled hand is brutally smashed until it must be amputated. The deaths in Francis novels usually occur 'off-camera.' The tortures are more intimate affairs, with the reader forced to watch at shudderingly close range."

While the violence of his early novels is largely external, his later novels emphasize more internal stress, according to critics who believe that this shift has added a new dimension to Francis's work. John Welcome, for instance, comments that in *Reflex* Francis's lessened emphasis on brutality has enabled him to "flesh out his characters. The portrait of Philip More, the mediocre jockey nearing the end of his career, is created with real insight; as is the interpretation of his relations with the horses he rides." MacDonald comments that Francis's later books "concentrate more specifically on psychological stress." In her opinion, his writing has gone beyond the "dramatic presentation of heroic action" to a deeper level, where the hero "is less a man who can endure torture than one who has the strength to face self-doubt, fear, and human inadequacy and still endure and thrive." And Bauska expresses a similar view when he says that Francis's later works, although not that different in the plot, focus on the protagonist. According to Bauska, Francis is increasingly "considering what goes into the making not so much of a 'hero' as of a good man." The focus of Francis's work is no longer the war outside, though the books are still action-packed, but on the struggle within the protagonist's mind and his attempts to conquer his own doubts and fears. Bauska attributes this shift in focus to Francis's own growing distance from his racing days. The result, he says, "is that Dick Francis is becoming less a writer of thrillers and more a creator of literature."

For example, in *To the Hilt*, Alexander Kinloch severs all ties to his family estate and brewing business in order to paint the bucolic vistas of the Scottish highlands. Upon learning that his stepfather, Sir Ivan, has been bilked out of millions by a trusted assistant, Kinloch returns and becomes the reluctant savior of his family fortune and honor. *Booklist*'s Emily Melton writes that "remarkably, after more than 35 novels, Dick Francis is still getting better," evidencing "more emotion and humanity than his last few efforts." The *Atlantic Monthly*'s Phoebe-Lou Adams and Marilyn Stasio in the *New York Times Book Review* call *To the Hilt* an exhilarating tale; the latter states, "*To the Hilt* delivers the pleasures people pay for: an exciting story told with great narrative drive," while the former declares, "The tale starts with a bang and ends with a crash, both highly satisfactory."

In *10 lb. Penalty* (an expression referring to the handicap the favored horse must carry on race day) young apprentice jockey Ben Juliard is abruptly forbidden to race on suspicion of drug abuse and then pushed into political campaigning when his father, George, runs for a seat in the House of Commons. Years pass, and then a scandal borne by enemies' rumors about a past crime threatens to halt George's rise to national eminence. Former jockey Ben, now an insurance investigator, pitches in to solve the mystery of his father's tormentors and the truth of their accusations, this time imperiling his life in the process. David Murray, in the *New York Times Book Review*, states that *10 lb. Penalty* has all of the basic ingredients of a Dick Francis novel: "unusual characters, an intricate story, fast-moving prose and no end of surprises." *Publishers Weekly* says of the author and his novel, "He may be turning 77 this year, but Francis narrates his new thriller through the eyes of a 17 year old without missing a step."

Francis's consistent ability to continually engage both new readers and old fans alike in his stories is perhaps his greatest strength. Christopher Wordsworth, reviewing *Wild Horses* for the *Observer*, calls Francis "an institution." Indeed, as Elizabeth Tallent notes in the *New York Times Book Review*, while Francis's former position as jockey for the Queen Mother is often mentioned in reviews of the writer, "At this point in his illustrious writing career, the Queen Mother might wish to note in her *vita* that the writer Dick Francis once rode for her."

BIOGRAPHICAL/CRITICAL SOURCES:

BOOKS

Bargainnier, Earl F., editor, *Twelve Englishmen of Mystery*, Bowling Green University Popular Press, 1984, pp. 222-48.
Barnes, Melvyn, *Dick Francis*, New York: Ungar, 1986.
Contemporary Literary Criticism, Gale (Detroit), Volume 2, 1974; Volume 22, 1982; Volume 42, 1987.
Davis, J. Madison, *Dick Francis*, Boston: Twayne, 1989.
Dictionary of Literary Biography, Volume 87: *British Mystery and Thriller Writers since 1940, First Series*, 1989.

PERIODICALS

Architectural Digest, Vol. 42, June, 1985.
Armchair Detective, July, 1978; Vol. 15, spring, 1982; Vol. 19, No. 1, winter, 1986; Vol. 26, No. 3, summer, 1993; Vol. 29, No. 1, winter, 1996, p. 102.
Atlantic Monthly, March, 1969; November, 1996, p. 122.
Booklist, January 15, 1986; September 1, 1996, p. 29.
British Book News, October, 1984.
Chicago Tribune, October 2, 1994, p. 9; September 3, 1995, p. 4.
Christian Science Monitor, July 17, 1969; July 17, 1969.
Family Circle, July, 1970.
Forbes, November 21, 1994, p. 26.
Globe and Mail (Toronto), November 16, 1985; August 12, 1989.
Kirkus Reviews, July 15, 1995, p. 986.
Life, Vol. 66, June 6, 1969.
London Magazine, February-March, 1975; March, 1980; February-March, 1981.
Los Angeles Times, March 27, 1981; April 9, 1982; September 12, 1984.
National Review, Vol. 44, January 20, 1992.
Newsweek, April 6, 1981.
New Yorker, March 15, 1969; Vol. LX, No. 9, April 16, 1984; Vol. LXI, No. 9, April 22, 1985.
New York Times, March 6, 1969; April 7, 1971; March 20, 1981; December 18, 1989.
New York Times Book Review, March 21, 1965; March 10, 1968; March 16, 1969; June 8, 1969; July 26, 1970; May 21, 1972; July 27, 1975; September 28, 1975; June 13, 1976; July 10, 1977; May 20, 1979; June 1, 1980; March 29, 1981; April 25, 1982; February 12, 1989; March 27, 1983; March 18, 1984; March 24, 1985; March 16, 1986; October 18, 1992, p. 32; October 2, 1994, p. 26; October 13, 1996, p. 29; October 19, 1997.
New York Times Magazine, March 25, 1984.
Observer, October 2, 1994, p. 18.
People Weekly, June 7, 1976; November 23, 1982; January 24, 1994, p. 32.
Publishers Weekly, Vol. 229, No. 4, January 24, 1986; August 25, 1997, p. 47.
School Library Journal, January, 1995, p. 145.
Sports Illustrated, Vol. 79, November 15, 1993.
Time, March 11, 1974; July 14, 1975; May 31, 1976; July 7, 1978; May 11, 1981.
Times (London), December 18, 1986.
Times Literary Supplement, October 28, 1977; October 10, 1980; December 10, 1982; October 30, 1992, p. 21; October 7, 1994, p. 30; November 17, 1995, p. 28.
U.S. News and World Report, March 28, 1988.
Washington Post, October 3, 1986.
Washington Post Book World, April 30, 1972; February 18, 1973; April 19, 1980; April 18, 1982; March 27, 1983; March 17, 1985; February 21, 1988; February 5, 1989.

*   *   *

FRANK, Anne(lies Marie) 1929-1945

PERSONAL: Born June 12, 1929, in Frankfurt on the Main, Germany; died of typhoid fever and malnutrition in March, 1945, in the Bergen-Belsen concentration camp near Belgen, Germany; daughter of Otto (banker and business owner) and Edith Frank.

WRITINGS:

Het achterhuis (diary; foreword by Annie Romein-Verschoor), Contact (Amsterdam), 1947, translation from Dutch by B. M. Mooyaart-Doubleday published as *Diary of a Young Girl,* introduction by Eleanor Roosevelt, Doubleday, 1952; with new preface by George Stevens, Pocket Books, 1958; published as *Anne Frank: The Diary of a Young Girl,* Washington Square Press, 1963; published as *The Diary of Anne Frank,* foreword by Storm Jameson, illustrations by Elisabeth Trimby, Heron Books, 1973; published as *The Diary of Anne Frank: The Critical Edition,* edited by David Barnouw and Gerrold van der Stroom, translated by Arnold J. Pomerans and B. M. Mooyaart-Doubleday, introduction by Harry Paape, Gerrold van der Stroom, and David Barnouw, Doubleday, 1989; published as *The Diary of Anne Frank: The Definitive Edition,* edited by Otto Frank and Mirjam Pressler, Doubleday, 1995.

The Works of Anne Frank, introduction by Ann Birstein and Alfred Kazin, Doubleday, 1959 (also see below).

Tales From the House Behind: Fables, Personal Reminiscences, and Short Stories, translation from original Dutch manuscript, *Verhalen rondom het achterhuis,* by H. H. B. Mosberg and Michel Mok, World's Work, 1962; with drawings by Peter Spier, Pan Books, 1965 (also see below).

Anne Frank's Tales From the Secret Annex, with translations from original manuscript, *Verhaaltjes en gebeurtenissen uit het Achterhuis,* by Ralph Manheim and Michel Mok, Doubleday, 1983 (portions previously published in *The Works of Anne Frank* and *Tales From the House Behind*).

MEDIA ADAPTATIONS: Frances Goodrich and Albert Hackett adapted *Anne Frank: Diary of a Young Girl* for a two-act stage play titled *Diary of Anne Frank,* first produced in New York, 1955, and published with a foreword by Brooks Atkinson, Random House, 1956. The diary was also adapted for the film *The Diary of Anne Frank,* released by Twentieth Century-Fox, 1959, and a television movie of the same name, starring Melissa Gilbert, 1980. A new adaptation of the play by Wendy Kesselman, starring Natalie Portman, was published on Broadway in 1998.

SIDELIGHTS: Anne Frank, a victim of the Holocaust during World War II, became known throughout the world through her eloquent diary, describing the two years she and seven others hid from Nazis in an attic above her father's business office in Amsterdam. In the diary Anne relates the fear of being discovered and the aggravations of life in hiding as well as the feelings and experiences of adolescence that are recognized by people everywhere. Anne received the first notebook as a present from her parents on her thirteenth birthday in 1942, about a month before the family went into hiding. She wrote in the diary until the discovery of the hiding place in August, 1944. Anne's father, Otto Frank, the only one of them to survive the concentration camps to which they were sent, agreed to publish the diary in 1946.

Since then, Anne has been for many people a source of inspiration, a model of courage, and a symbol of the persecution, tragic suffering, and loss of life inflicted by the Nazis. Meyer Levin declared in the *New York Times Book Review,* "Because the diary was not written in retrospect, it contains the trembling life of every moment—Anne Frank's voice becomes the voice of six million vanished Jewish souls." This is not because there were no other journals found from that time. Upon reading a copy of Anne's diary in 1946, Jan Romein declared in the Dutch newspaper *Het Parool*: "The Government Institute for War Documentation is in possession of about two hundred similar diaries, but it would amaze me if there was *one* among them as pure, as intelligent, and yet as human as [Anne's]."

The Franks moved from Frankfurt, Germany—where Anne was born—to Amsterdam in 1933 after Germany ruled that Jewish and German children had to attend segregated schools. In July, 1942, after Anne's sister Margot received notice to report to the Dutch Nazi organization, the Franks immediately went into hiding in the "Secret Annex," as Anne dubbed the attic of the Amsterdam warehouse. Soon after, Mr. and Mrs. Frank and their two girls welcomed Mr. and Mrs. Van Daan (pseudonymous names used by Anne) and their son Peter into their rooms, and lastly Mr. Dussel, an elderly dentist. In an entry about her family's flight into hiding, Anne wrote that the diary was the first thing she packed. It meant a great deal to her; she viewed the diary as a personal friend and confidant, as she remarked June 20, 1942, in a reflection about the diary itself: "I haven't written for a few days, because I wanted first of all to think about my diary. It's an odd idea for someone like me to keep a diary; not only because I have never done so before, but because it seems to me that neither I—nor for that matter anyone else—will be interested in the unbosomings of a thirteen-year-old schoolgirl. Still, what does that matter? I want to write, but more than that, I want to bring out all kinds of things that lie buried deep in my heart. . . . [T]here is no doubt that paper is patient and as I don't intend to show this . . . 'diary' to anyone, unless I find a real friend, boy or girl, probably nobody cares. And now I come to the root of the matter, the reason for my starting a diary; it is that I have no such real friend. . . . [I]t's the same with all my friends, just fun and joking, nothing more. I can never bring myself to talk of anything outside the common round. . . . Hence, this diary. . . . I don't want to set down a series of bald facts in a diary as most people do, but I want this diary itself to be my friend, and I shall call my friend Kitty."

"What child of 13 hasn't had these feelings, and resolved to confide in a diary?" wrote Levin. Apart from interest in the diary for its historical value and for the extreme circumstances under which it was written, some have admired the diary for its accurate, revealing portrait of adolescence. "She described life in the 'Annex' with all its inevitable tensions and quarrels," wrote L. De Jong in *A Tribute to Anne Frank*. "But she created first and foremost a wonderfully delicate record of adolescence, sketching with complete honesty a young girl's feelings, her longings and loneliness."

At the age of thirteen, when Anne began the diary, she was struggling with the problems of growing up. Lively and vivacious, she was chastised at school—and later in the annex—for her incessant chattering. In the annex she was forced to whisper throughout the day. It was a great trial for Anne, who wrote on October 1, 1942, "We are as quiet as mice. Who, three months ago, would ever have guessed that quicksilver Anne would have to sit still for hours—and, what's more—could?" After a year of this silence, combined with confinement indoors, she expressed her feelings of depression, writing on October 29, 1943, "The atmosphere is so oppressive, and sleepy and as heavy as lead. You don't hear a single bird singing outside, and a deadly close silence hangs everywhere, catching hold of me as if it will drag me down deep into an underworld. . . . I wander from one room to another, downstairs and up again, feeling like a songbird whose wings have been clipped and who is hurling himself in utter darkness against the bars of his cage."

During the course of writing the diary, Anne became certain she wanted to be a writer. She envisioned a novel based on her diary.

Additionally she wrote stories, later collected in *The Works of Anne Frank* and *Tales From the House Behind*. According to *New York Times Book Review* critic Frederick Morton, the stories "show that Anne followed instinctively the best of all platitudes: Write whereof you know. Not even her little fairy tales are easy escapes into make-believe, but rather pointed allegories of reality—the two elves who are imprisoned together to learn tolerance; or Blurry the Baby who runs away from home to find the great, free, open world, and never does. . . . Still none of these . . . , not even a charming little morality tale like "The Wise Old Dwarf," has the power of any single entry in the diary."

The diary ends August 1, 1944, three days before the group was arrested and sent to the concentration camp at Auschwitz, Poland. They were separated, and Margot and Anne were later transferred to Bergen-Belsen. According to a survivor who knew her at the concentration camp, Anne never lost her courage, deep sensitivity, or ability to feel. An excerpt of Ernst Schnabel's *Anne Frank: A Portrait in Courage*, reprinted in *A Tribute to Anne Frank*, states that "Anne was the youngest in her group, but nevertheless she was the leader of it. She also distributed the bread in the barracks, and she did it so well and fairly that there was none of the usual grumbling. . . . Here is another example. We were always thirsty. . . . And once, when I was so far gone that I almost died because there was nothing to drink, Anne suddenly came to me with a cup of coffee. To this day I don't know where she got it." The woman continued: "She, too, was the one who saw to the last what was going on all around us. . . . we were beyond feelings. . . . Something protected us, kept us from seeing. But Anne had no such protection, to the last. I can still see her standing at the door and looking down the camp street as a herd of naked gypsy girls was driven by, to the crematory, and Anne watched them going and cried. And she cried also when she marched past the Hungarian children who had already been waiting half a day in the rain in front of the gas chambers, because it was not yet their turn. And Anne nudged me and said: 'Look, look. Their eyes. . . .'"

Both Anne and Margot died of typhoid fever at Bergen-Belsen in March, 1945. Their mother had died earlier at Auschwitz. Otto Frank, liberated from Auschwitz by Russian troops in 1945, returned to Amsterdam. He already knew of his wife's death, but he had hope that Margot and Anne were alive. He soon received a letter informing him of their deaths. It was then that Miep Gies, who had worked for Mr. Frank as a secretary and helped hide the family, gave Anne's writings to him. Gies had discovered the diaries strewn on the floor after the Franks' arrest, and she kept the writings at her home but did not read them. It took Anne's father several weeks to read the diary as he could only bear to read a little at a time. Urged by friends, he published an edited version of the diary, deleting a number of passages he thought too personal.

Fifty years after the diary was first published, a new edition was published that included the passages Otto had originally deleted. Titled *The Diary of Anne Frank: The Definitive Edition* and edited by German author Mirjam Pressler, the new version includes thirty percent more material than the original publication. Writing in the *New York Times Book Review*, Patricia Hampl remarked, "There are more searching passages about her erotic feelings and her urgent curiosity about sexuality, more emphatic distancing from her dignified but apparently critical mother."

Mr. Frank, who received numerous letters in response to the diary, cautioned in the preface to *A Tribute to Anne Frank*, "However touching and sincere the expressions of sympathy I receive may be, I always reply that it is not enough to think of Anne with pity or admiration. Her diary should be a source of inspiration toward the realization of the ideals and hopes she expressed in it."

The Anne Frank Foundation has preserved the Franks' hiding place in Amsterdam, and schools in several countries, as well as a village at Wuppertal, Germany, have been named for Anne.

BIOGRAPHICAL/CRITICAL SOURCES:

BOOKS

Bettelheim, Bruno, *Surviving and Other Essays*, Knopf, 1979.
Brenner, Rachel Feldhay, *Writing As Resistance: Four Women Confronting the Holocaust: Edith Stein, Simone Weil, Anne Frank, Etty Hillesum*, Pennsylvania State University Press (University Park, PA), 1997.
Epstein, Rachel, *Anne Frank*, F. Watts (New York City), 1997.
Fradin, Dennis B., *Remarkable Children: Twenty Who Made History*, Little, Brown, 1987.
Gies, Miep, and Alison Leslie Gold, *Anne Frank Remembered: The Story of the Woman Who Helped to Hide the Franks*, Simon & Schuster, 1987.
Gold, Alison Leslie, *Memories of Anne Frank: Reflections of a Childhood Friend*, Scholastic (New York City), 1997.
Goodrich, Frances, and Albert Hackett, *Diary of Anne Frank*, Random House, 1956.
Graver, Lawrence, *An Obsession with Anne Frank: Meyer Levin and The Diary*, University of California Press (Berkeley, CA), 1995.
Katz, Sandor, *Anne Frank*, Chelsea House (New York), 1996.
Kopf, Hedda Rosner, *Understanding Anne Frank's The Diary of a Young Girl: A Student Casebook to Issues, Sources, and Historical Documents*, Greenwood Press (Westport, CT), 1997.
Melnick, Ralph, *The Stolen Legacy of Anne Frank: Meyer Levin, Lillian Hellman, and the Staging of the Diary*, Yale University Press (New Haven, CT), 1997.
Schnabel, Ernst, *Anne Frank: A Portrait in Courage*, translated from German by Richard and Clara Winston, Harcourt, 1958 (published in England as *Footsteps of Anne Frank*, Longmans, 1959).
Steenmeijer, Anna G., editor, in collaboration with Otto Frank and Henri van Praag, *A Tribute to Anne Frank*, Doubleday, 1970.
Twentieth-Century Writing: A Reader's Guide to Contemporary Literature, Transatlantic, 1969.
Tridenti, Lina, *Anne Frank*, translated by Stephen Thorne, Silver Burdett, 1985.

PERIODICALS

Christian Century, May 6, 1959.
Commonweal, October 31, 1958.
Horn Book, November-December, 1994, p. 706.
Ladies' Home Journal, September, 1967.
Life, August 18, 1958.
Los Angeles Times, April 13, 1984.
McCall's, July, 1958.
New Statesman and Nation, May 17, 1952.
Newsweek, June 25, 1979.
New York Times Book Review, June 15, 1952; September 20, 1959; May 10, 1987; July 2, 1989; March 5, 1995.
New York Times Magazine, April 21, 1957.
People Weekly, September 16, 1984.
Saturday Review, July 19, 1952.
Time, June 16, 1952; February 17, 1958; January 30, 1984.

Women's Review of Books, January, 1996, p. 12.

* * *

FRANKLIN, Benjamin
See HASEK, Jaroslav (Matej Frantisek)

* * *

FRANKLIN, (Stella Maria Sarah) Miles (Lampe) 1879-1954
(Brent of Bin Bin)

PERSONAL: Born October 14, 1879, in Talbingo, Australia; died, September 19, 1954, in Sydney, Australia; daughter of John (a rancher and landowner) and Margaret Susannah Eleanor (Lampe) Franklin. *Education:* Attended public school, 1880s-1890s.

ADDRESSES: Sydney, Australia.

CAREER: Served with the Scottish Women's Hospital Unit in the Balkans, 1916-17; delivered Commonwealth Literary Fund lectures at the University of Western Australia, 1950; contributor of essays short fiction to the Sydney *Bulletin* and other periodicals.

AWARDS: Winner of Prior Memorial Prize, 1936 and 1939.

WRITINGS:

My Brilliant Career, Blackwood (Edinburgh), 1901.
Some Everyday Folk and Dawn, Blackwood (Edinburgh), 1909.
The Net of Circumstance, Mills and Boon (London), 1915.
(As Brent of Bin Bin) *Up the Country: A Tale of the Early Australian Squattocracy,* Blackwood (Edinburgh), 1928.
(As Brent of Bin Bin) *Ten Creeks Run: A Tale of the Horse and Cattle Stations of the Upper Murrumbidgee,* Blackwood (Edinburgh), 1930.
(As Brent of Bin Bin) *Back to Bool Bool: A Ramiparous Novel with Several Prominent Characters and a Hantle of Others Disposed as the Atolls of Oceania's Archipelagoes,* Blackwood (Edinburgh), 1931.
Old Blastus of Bandicoot: Opuscule on a Pioneer Tufted with Ragged Rhymes, Palmer (London), 1931.
Bring the Monkey, Endeavour Press (Sydney), 1933.
All That Swagger, Angus & Robertson (Sydney), 1936.
(With Dymphna Cusack) *Pioneers on Parade,* Angus & Robertson (Sydney), 1939.
(With Kate Baker) *Joseph Furphy: The Legend of a Man and His Book,* Angus & Robertson (Sydney), 1944.
My Career Goes Bung: Purporting to Be the Autobiography of Sybylla Penelope Melvyn, Georgian House (Melbourne), 1946.
Sydney Royal: Divertisement, Shakespeare Head (Sydney), 1947.
(As Brent of Bin Bin) *Prelude to Waking,* Angus & Robertson (Sydney), 1950.
(As Brent of Bin Bin) *Cockatoos: A Story of Youth and Exodists,* Angus & Robertson (Sydney), 1954.
(As Brent of Bin Bin) *Gentlemen at Gyang Gyang: A Tale of the Jambuck Pads on the Summer Runs,* Angus & Robertson (Sydney), 1956.
Laughter, Not for a Cage: Notes on Australian Writing, Angus & Robertson (Sydney), 1956.
Childhood at Brindabella, Angus & Robertson (Sydney), 1963.
The End of My Career, St. Martin's (New York), 1981.

On Dearborn Street, University of Queensland Press (St. Lucia), 1981.
My Congenials: Miles Franklin and Friends in Letters, edited by Jill Roe, Angus & Robertson (Pymble), 1993.

SIDELIGHTS: Franklin appeared suddenly on the literary scene with her first novel, *My Brilliant Career,* written when she was sixteen. Although the work contains the flaws of structure and composition that might be expected from such a young author, it also displays vigor, budding talent, a pervasive feminism, and the strong nationalism that was developing in Australia. A. G. Stephens, editor of the Sydney *Bulletin,* praised *My Brilliant Career* as "the very first Australian novel to be published . . . that might not have been written by a stranger or a sojourner."

Franklin was born on her grandmother's cattle station in southern New South Wales and grew up in the Australian outback. She later recounted her youth in *Childhood at Brindabella,* an idealized autobiography. *My Brilliant Career,* when it first appeared, proved an embarrassment to Franklin's family and friends, who, along with most contemporary critics, assumed the poverty, drunkenness and melodramatic episodes portrayed in the novel were more autobiographical than fictional. In fact, while her heroine's attitudes were Franklin's, the details of her heroine's life were not. Upset by the misinterpretation, Franklin wrote a satiric sequel, *My Career Goes Bung,* which was not published for forty-five years. Franklin eventually suppressed her first book, making provisions for its publication ten years after her death. She referred to the novel in her volume of literary criticism, *Laughter, Not for a Cage,* as a "girl's story . . . conceived and tossed off on impulse in a matter of weeks." She withdrew the work from print because of "the stupid literalness with which it was taken to be her own autobiography," which "startled and disillusioned then constrained her." After *My Brilliant Career* was published, Franklin worked briefly in Sydney as a freelance journalist before traveling to the United States. She worked in Chicago for the National Women's Trade Union League, and wrote the novel *Some Everyday Folk and Dawn,* in which she attempted unsuccessfully to write about the United States with the same informal intimacy that had characterized her Australian stories. At the start of World War I Franklin moved to London, becoming active in social work, and did not return to Australia until 1933. Later in life, she established the Miles Franklin Award, a prize of five hundred pounds awarded annually to the best novel illuminating a phase of Australian life.

In 1930, *Up the Country* appeared under the pseudonym "Brent of Bin Bin." Since at that time Franklin had published only her first two books, she was not thought of as the possible author. But as more of her works appeared, along with five more novels by "Brent of Bin Bin," critics began to note the similarities of style, vocabulary, characterization, theme, and setting in both Franklin's and "Brent's" works. Events in the Bin Bin books, which corresponded to events in Franklin's own life, seemed to support the argument of her authorship. Franklin never publicly claimed authorship of the Bin Bin books, but friends have said that in her last years she privately admitted having written them. Most critics today believe that she did so, though some cite her steadfast public denial as proof of alternate authorship. Some critics have conjectured that she possibly wrote them in collaboration with another author, or that she worked almost directly from existing records. The novels signed by "Brent of Bin Bin" share with those signed by Miles Franklin pride and joy in Australian nationalism, dissatisfaction with the status of women, and great admiration for the pioneer, the squatter, the farmer, and the swagman, who explored, homesteaded, and opened up the new continent.

Aside from *My Brilliant Career,* Franklin's most significant work is *All That Swagger,* a saga spanning well over a hundred years in the lives of a family of European immigrants in Australia. The chief figure in the chronicle is Danny Delacey, called Franklin's most skillful male characterization. Delacey was based, as was the hero of the earlier *Old Blastus of Bandicoot,* on Franklin's grandfather; in fact, most of Franklin's plots and characters were drawn from her life and family history. It is when she attempted to write about non-Australian places and people that her writing was weakest. *All That Swagger,* and the "Brent of Bin Bin" novel series, helped to popularize the saga form in English writing.

Franklin is not recognized for style and technique; she never fully mastered either. Rather, it is for her vivid portrayal of a unique period in the history of Australia that she is remembered. She recreated Australia's pastoral age from the point of view of those who, as Franklin's biographer Marjorie Barnard phrased it, brought about "the peaceful conquest of a continent."

BIOGRAPHICAL/CRITICAL SOURCES:

BOOKS

Barnard, Marjorie, *Miles Franklin,* Twayne (Boston), 1967.
Coleman, Verna, *Miles Franklin in America: Her Unknown (Brilliant) Career,* Angus & Robertson (London), 1981.
Dutton, Geoffrey, editor, *The Literature of Australia,* Penguin (Sydney), 1976.
Ewers, John K., *Creative Writing in Australia: A Selective Survey,* Georgian House (Melbourne), 1959.
Ferrier, Carole, editor, *Gender, Politics and Fiction: Twentieth Century Australian Women's Novels,* University of Queensland Press (St. Lucia), 1985.
Goodwin, Ken, *A History of Australian Literature,* St. Martin's (New York City), 1986.
Hadgraft, Cecil, *Australian Literature: A Critical Account to 1955,* Heinemann (London), 1960.
Henry, Alice, *Memoirs of Alice Henry,* edited by Nettie Palmer, Melbourne, 1944.
Mathew, Ray, *Miles Franklin,* Lansdowne Press (Melbourne), 1963.
Roderick, Colin Arthur, *Miles Franklin: Her Brilliant Career,* Rigby (New York City), 1982.

PERIODICALS

Australian Literary Studies, May, 1980, pp. 275-85.
Best Sellers, February, 1981, p. 389.
Southerly, 1951, pp. 196-202; 1955, pp. 83-85.

*   *   *

FRASER, (Lady) Antonia (Pakenham) 1932-
(Antonia Pakenham)

PERSONAL: Born August 27, 1932, in London, England; daughter of Francis Aungier Pakenham, seventh Earl of Longford (a politician and writer) and Elizabeth Pakenham, Countess of Longford (a writer; maiden name, Harman); married Sir Hugh Charles Patrick Joseph Fraser (member of Parliament), September 25, 1956 (marriage ended, 1977); married Harold Pinter (a playwright), November 27, 1980; children: (first marriage) Rebecca, Flora, Benjamin, Natasha, Damian, Orlando. *Education:* Oxford University, B.A., 1953; received M.A. *Religion:* Roman

Catholic. *Avocational interests:* Swimming, "life in the garden," and spending time with her grandchildren.

ADDRESSES: Home—Haymarket House 28/29 Haymarket, SWIY 4SP London, England. *Agent*—Curtis Brown Ltd., 162-168 Regent St., London W1R 5TA, England.

CAREER: Writer, 1963–. Also worked as broadcaster and lecturer; panelist on British Broadcasting Corporation's *My Word!* radio program. Member of Arts Council, 1970-71.

MEMBER: English PEN (vice president, 1990–), Society of Authors (chairperson, 1974-75), Crimewriters Association (vice chairperson, 1984; chairperson, 1985-86), Detection, Vanderbilt, Writers in Prison Committee (chairman, 1985-88, 1990–).

AWARDS, HONORS: James Tait Black Memorial Prize for biography, 1969, for *Mary, Queen of Scots;* Woltsor Prize for history, 1984, and Prix Caumont-La Force, 1985, both for *The Weaker Vessel;* D. Litt., Hull, 1986, Sussex, 1990, Nottingham, 1993, St. Andrew's College, 1994.

WRITINGS:

HISTORICAL NONFICTION

Dolls, Putnam (New York City), 1963.
A History of Toys, Delacorte (New York City), 1966, revised edition, Springer Books, 1972.
Mary, Queen of Scots (biography), Delacorte, 1969.
Cromwell, the Lord Protector (biography), Knopf (New York City), 1973, published in England as *Cromwell, Our Chief of Men,* Weidenfeld & Nicolson (London), 1973.
Mary, Queen of the Scots, and the Historians, Royal Stuart Society (Ilford, Essex), 1974.
King James VI of Scotland, I of England (biography), Weidenfeld & Nicolson, 1974, Knopf, 1975.
Royal Charles: Charles II and the Restoration (biography), Knopf, 1979, published in England as *King Charles II,* Weidenfeld and Nicolson, 1979, revised edition published as *Charles II: His Life and Times,* London, Weidenfeld and Nicolson, 1993.
The Weaker Vessel: Woman's Lot in Seventeenth-Century England, Knopf, 1984.
The Warrior Queens, Knopf, 1988, published in England as *Boadicea's Chariot: The Warrior Queens,* Weidenfeld & Nicolson, 1988.
The Wives of Henry VIII, Knopf, 1992, published in England as *The Six Wives of Henry VIII,* Weidenfeld & Nicolson, 1992.
Faith and Treason: The Story of the Gunpowder Plot, Doubleday (New York City), 1996.

"JEMIMA SHORE" MYSTERY SERIES

Quiet as a Nun, Viking (New York City), 1977.
The Wild Island: A Mystery, Norton (New York City), 1978.
A Splash of Red, Norton, 1981.
Cool Repentance, Norton, 1982.
Oxford Blood, Norton, 1985.
Jemima Shore's First Case and Other Stories, Methuen (New York City), 1986.
Your Royal Hostage, Atheneum (New York City), 1988.
The Cavalier Case, Bantam (New York City), 1990.
Jemima Shore at the Sunny Grave and Other Stories, Bloomsbury (London), 1991, Bantam, 1993.
Political Death, Bantam, 1996.

EDITOR

The Lives of the Kings and Queens of England, Knopf, 1975.

Scottish Love Poems: A Personal Anthology, Canongate (Edinburgh), 1975, Viking (New York City), 1976.

Love Letters: An Anthology, Weidenfeld & Nicolson, 1976, Knopf, 1977, reprinted as *Love Letters: An Illustrated Anthology,* Contemporary Books (Chicago), 1989.

Heroes and Heroines, Weidenfeld & Nicolson, 1980.

Mary, Queen of Scots: An Anthology of Poetry, Eyre Methuen (London), 1981.

Oxford and Oxfordshire in Verse, illustrated by Rebecca Fraser, Secker & Warburg (London), 1982.

Love Letters: An Illustrated Anthology, Contemporary Books, 1989.

The Pleasure of Reading, Random House (New York City), 1992.

OTHER

(Under name Antonia Pakenham) *King Arthur and the Knights of the Round Table* (juvenile), Weidenfeld & Nicolson, 1954, Knopf, 1970.

(Translator under name Antonia Pakenham) Jean Monsterleet, *Martyrs in China,* Longman (London), 1956.

(Under name Antonia Pakenham) *Robin Hood* (juvenile), Weidenfeld & Nicolson, 1957, Knopf, 1971.

(Translator under name Antonia Pakenham) *Dior by Dior: The Autobiography of Christian Dior,* Weidenfeld & Nicolson, 1957.

Mary, Queen of Scots (phonodisc), National Portrait Gallery, 1971.

(With Gordon Donaldson) *Sixteenth-Century Scotland* (phonotape), Holt Information Systems, 1972.

(Contributor) Rosemary Herbert, *The Fatal Art of Entertainment: Interviews with Mystery Writers,* G. K. Hall, 1996.

Contributor to *Winter's Crimes 10,* edited by Hilary Watson, Macmillan, 1978; *The Fourth Bedside Book of Great Detective Stories,* edited by Herbert Van Thal, Barker, 1979; *Winter's Crimes 15,* edited by George Hardinge, St. Martin's Press (New York City), 1983; and *John Creasey's Crime Collection 1983,* edited by Herbert Harris, Gollancz, 1983. Also author of scripts for television series *Jemima Shore Investigates,* 1983. Also author of radio plays *On the Battlements,* 1975, *The Heroine,* 1976, and *Penelope,* 1976; author of television play *Charades,* 1977, "Mister Clay, Mister Clay" for the *Time for Murder* series, 1985, *Have a Nice Death,* 1985. General editor, "Kings and Queens of England" series, Weidenfeld & Nicolson, 1953-55.

MEDIA ADAPTATIONS: The novel *A Splash of Red* was adapted for television as *Jemima Shore Investigates.*

SIDELIGHTS: Antonia Fraser "has won many accolades for her meticulous research and attention to detail," writes Edie Gibson in the *Chicago Tribune,* "[and for] bringing a lively narrative style to historical writing, capturing readers who typically shun such scholarly endeavors." Fraser secured her position as a noteworthy biographer with *Mary, Queen of Scots,* and has subsequently chronicled the lives of other British figures such as Oliver Cromwell, James I, and Charles I. In *The Weaker Vessel,* Fraser examines the place of women in seventeenth century England, and *The Warrior Queens* illuminates the leadership roles women often assume in times of war. Her works of fiction detail the adventures of Jemima Shore, a liberated investigative television reporter who has a knack for solving mysteries.

Mary, Queen of Scots, Fraser's first biography, established the standard for her historical writing: thorough research, vivid character portraits, and sound scholarship presented in a manner that appealed to a wide audience. Jean Stafford of *Book World*

notes that Fraser conveys "a vivid sense of the mores of the sixteenth century" in *Mary, Queen of Scots.* In addition, "she succeeds in almost completely clarifying the muddied maelstrom in which Europe and the British Isles were thrashing and trumpeting," Stafford continues, with "a narrative dexterity that makes her sad tale seem told for the first time." "Mary emerges neither as a Jezebel nor as a saint," declares a reviewer for *Time,* "but as a high-spirited woman who was brave, rather romantic, and not very bright." "Satisfying to scholars," comments a *Times Literary Supplement* critic, "the book is eminently one for the general reader, its style both spirited and graceful." The book won the prestigious James Tait Black Memorial Prize for historical writing in 1969.

Fraser's early works, critics have noted, are strict biography in the sense that they examine the life of a single person, but they do not attempt to discuss the individual's actions in terms of the age in which he or she lived. In *Cromwell, the Lord Protector, King James VI of Scotland, I of England,* and *Royal Charles,* Fraser's portrayals of eminent historical figures are brought "so vividly to life that the history of the age in which they play so arresting a part tends to lose itself in the background," according to Peter Stansky of the *New York Times Book Review.* In reviewing *Royal Charles,* Stansky comments on the difference between pure biography and historical biography: "Unlike, for example, Barbara Tuchman, who sees biography as a 'Prism of History,' and admits to using it 'less for the sake of the individual subject than as a vehicle for exhibiting an age,' Lady Antonia is wholeheartedly committed to the life of the individual subject."

Fraser altered her strict biographical approach with her 1984 award-winning study *The Weaker Vessel: Woman's Lot in Seventeenth-Century England.* Rather than focusing on a single character as her earlier biographies had done, *The Weaker Vessel* looks at many roles of women in the 1600s, with special emphasis on "marriage, birth, widowhood, divorce, prostitution, the stage, business, and so forth," summarizes Brigitte Weeks in the *Washington Post.* "Each chapter is a maze of interconnected life stories of women, almost always pregnant, ending all too often in sudden death, mostly in childbirth," Weeks continues. Fraser investigated women's varied responsibilities during the English Civil War: holding custody of castles, leading troops into battle, writing treatises, and presenting petitions to parliament. After the war, however, these newly-won liberties were rescinded, leaving women in much the same position as they were before the conflict. "One of the lies about historical progress," declares Peter S. Prescott in a *Newsweek* review of *The Weaker Vessel* "is that it hunches inexorably along its way. In fact, progress is cyclical; it jumps sporadically, only to be set back again." Fraser's analysis of the gamut of class roles, from dairymaid to actress to heiress, prompts Maureen Quilligan of the *Nation* to acknowledge that "it will be hard for anyone to paint a fuller, more vivid or more abundantly detailed portrait of women in seventeenth-century England."

The Warrior Queens, another survey of women's history, grew out of the research Fraser did for *The Weaker Vessel.* The work focuses on women who have led their countries into war, women such as the Egyptian queen Cleopatra, the British tribal leader Boadicea, and Zenobia, the third-century Queen of the desert city of Palmyra, all of whom led forces against the Roman Empire. Also included are modern-day leaders such as Israel's Golda Meir and Great Britain's Margaret Thatcher. "Seeking explanations for these women's rise to power and their enormous personal magnetism," writes Barbara Benton in *MHQ: The Quarterly*

Journal of Military History, "she attempts to isolate common themes in their stories."

In *The Warrior Queens,* Fraser categorizes the patterns of behavior that these women leaders have utilized in wielding their power. Victoria Glendenning enumerates these in the London *Times*: "The Appendance Syndrome, according to which the Warrior Queen justifies herself by stressing her connection with a famous father or husband, or fights allegedly on behalf of her son; the Shame Syndrome, otherwise the Better-man Syndrome, which means she shows up the chaps by being braver than they are; the Tomboy Syndrome, which implies that she never played with dolls when she was a little girl; and the Only-a-Weak-Woman Syndrome, when she puts on a sudden show of weakness or modesty for strategic purposes." In addition to these is the "voracity syndrome" in which powerful women are separated into models of virtue or monsters of lust. Fraser's conclusions, summarizes Margaret Atwood in the *Los Angeles Times Book Review,* show that "public women are put through different tests of nerve, attract different kinds of criticism, and are subject to different sorts of mythologizing than are men, and *The Warrior Queens* indicates what kinds."

Continuing her interest in the lives of prominent women in history, Fraser wrote *The Wives of Henry VIII,* which provided new interpretations of the six women who, according to Fraser, are often "defined in a popular sense not so much by their lives as by the way these lives ended," quotes Angeline Goreau in the *New York Times Book Review.* During his reign from 1509-1547, Henry VIII's unsuccessful quest to produce a male heir to succeed him left four wives dead and two in the unceremonious state of being divorced. From Catherine of Aragon to Catherine Parr, Fraser explores the lives of those she proclaims were "intelligent and fascinating people who were variously misused, abandoned, and executed" by the king, according to Bonnie Angelo in *Time.* Fraser analyzes the effect of divorce on Catherine of Aragon and Anne of Cleves and illustrates its impact on the rest of their lives; an aspect that prompted Goreau to deem the book "a deeply engaging portrait of a marriage—in serial." About this notorious episode of history, Angelo concludes that "Fraser brings to it insights—and a keen feminist edge—based on meticulous research."

In *Faith and Treason: The Story of the Gunpowder Plot,* Fraser shed new light on the events that are now commemorated every year on Guy Fawkes' Day—a November 5 holiday that is celebrated with huge bonfires and the burning in effigy of the Pope. In 1605, Roman Catholics were subject to terrible persecution in England, despite the fact that King James I was the son of one Catholic, and the husband of another. Dissidents hatched a plan to blow up the unsympathetic king and most of his nobles at the opening of Parliament that year. The plan failed miserably, and the unsuccessful rebels have been reviled throughout most of English history. "Antonia Fraser, with her usual combination of careful scholarship and a nose for a good subject, has now told the plotters' story," advises Michael Elliott in the *New York Times.* "It is such a good yarn that one wonders why nobody has tried to popularize it before."

"Fraser's searching look at the failed conspiracy of Robert Catesby (the actual planner) and Guy Fawkes could not be more timely," reports a *Publishers Weekly* writer. The author draws parallels between the Gunpowder Plot and modern terrorism, asking "the old but difficult questions: When does persecution excuse violence? How far should a cause of conscience be

defended?" said Elliott. Another reviewer, *New Statesman* contributor Diarmaid MacCulloch, notes that there are many books on the Gunpowder Plot, but names Fraser's as "a good place to start for a serious, balanced treatment of the still-mysterious affair. She manages to combine scholarly breadth and historical sympathy with readability and wit. Writing with fellow-feeling for the Roman Catholic plotters and those they dragged down to disaster, she nevertheless avoids . . . partisanship."

"Despite the fact that she was able to bring a personal style to the writing of history," declares Rosemary Herbert in a *Publishers Weekly* interview with the author, "in the mid-'70s Fraser 'felt that there was something in myself that history didn't express.' She gave in to the impulse to write fiction and created the TV commentator/sleuth Jemima Shore, a stylish, liberated woman who shares some of the author's characteristics." Fraser further tells Herbert that mystery writing fulfilled her need to "preserve a sort of order. I'm very interested in good and evil and the moral nature of my [characters]. People in my books tend to get their just desserts." P. D. James, herself a well-known mystery writer, greeted the investigator's debut in *Quiet as a Nun* with pleasure, noting that the story "is written with humour and sympathy and has a heroine of whom, happily, it is promised that we shall know more."

Though not as "lovably eccentric as Peter Wimsey, Jane Marple, Hercule Poirot, or the great Sherlock Holmes," writes Anne Tolstoi Wallach in the *New York Times Book Review,* Jemima Shore is nevertheless "prettier, sexier, and far more in tune with today's London." Margaret Cannon, writing in the Toronto *Globe and Mail,* was fascinated by the details that Fraser provides about the upper class settings through which Shore moves—circles in which Fraser herself travels. In the seventh Jemima Shore mystery, *The Cavalier Case,* Shore ventures to a haunted estate to produce a television segment about the ghost of a seventeenth century poet who has apparently caused several deaths. During her investigation, Shore becomes involved with the new viscount of the manor. Though crime is not in short supply in Fraser's Jemima Shore novels, the incidents tend to be relatively mild because, as Fraser states in the *St. James Guide to Crime and Mystery Writers,* she has "a horror of blood dripping from the page," adding, "my books are therefore aimed at readers who feel likewise."

Jemima Shore at the Sunny Grave and Other Stories is a collection of nine mystery stories, most of which involve Fraser's well-known heroine and are set on remote islands. The title story involves the murder of an elderly heiress at her plantation mansion in the Caribbean, where Jemima Shore is preparing a television documentary. In another story, "The Moon Was To Blame," Fraser recounts an Englishman's Greek-island vacation with his wife punctuated by murder and eroticism. Brad Hooper notes in a *Booklist* review that Fraser displays "precision" and "characteristic elan." The collection is described by *Kirkus Reviews* as "highly civilized, suavely written—and immensely readable."

In *Political Death,* Jemima Shore resolves a longstanding British political scandal from the 1960s. During a heated political campaign, Lady Imogen Swain, the aged former mistress of a contemporary political candidate, reveals her intimate knowledge of the "Faber Mystery," involving the disappearance of a man accused of selling government secrets. After offering her story and incriminating diaries to Shore, Lady Imogen dies from a suspicious fall, prompting Shore to pursue a trail of evidence through the British theater and political scenes to solve the case.

Many critics agree that Fraser's detective stories are worthy additions to the illustrious heritage of British detective writing. Beverly Lyon Clark writes in the *New York Times Book Review* that *Oxford Blood* is "in the tradition of the British whodunit, especially that of the Tea Cake and Country House mystery—or, in this case, the Champagne and Maserati sort. . . . Antonia Fraser is not quite Dorothy Sayers, not quite P. D. James. But she does have a seductive style." Shore believes, according to Cannon, that "there's nothing in the detective code of ethics that says you have to dress badly, get married or pass up an interesting one-night stand. It's a long way from St. Mary Mead, but I somehow think that [Agatha Christie's detective] Miss Marple, shrewd student of human nature that she was, would approve."

BIOGRAPHICAL/CRITICAL SOURCES:

BOOKS

St. James Guide to Crime and Mystery Writers, 4th edition, St. James Press (Detroit), 1996.

PERIODICALS

Booklist, November 15, 1992, p. 563; March 15, 1996, p. 1242.
Book World, November 16, 1969.
Chicago Tribune, March 16, 1988.
Chicago Tribune Book World, September 30, 1984.
Christian Science Monitor, December 7, 1979; December 18, 1996.
Globe and Mail (Toronto), August 25, 1984.
Kirkus Reviews, November 1, 1992, p. 1336; January 15, 1996, p. 104.
Los Angeles Times, September 25, 1980; January 31, 1997.
Los Angeles Times Book Review, September 23, 1984; April 2, 1989.
MHQ: The Quarterly Journal of Military History, autumn, 1989.
Nation, September 22, 1984, pp. 244-46.
New Statesman, August 30, 1996, p. 48.
Newsweek, September 10, 1984.
New Yorker, November 11, 1996, p. 119.
New York Review of Books, April 11, 1985; May 15, 1997, pp. 35-37.
New York Times, November 13, 1979; November 14, 1984; October 13, 1985, p. 24; May 17, 1989, p. 15; April 9, 1989, page 47; January 6, 1991; October 27, 1996; December 4, 1996.
New York Times Book Review, November 18, 1984; April 2, 1989; January 6, 1991; December 20, 1992, p. 11; July 31, 1994, p. 28; October 27, 1996, p. 7.
People Weekly, February 3, 1997, p. 35.
Publishers Weekly, June 19, 1987, pp. 104-5; February 5, 1996, p. 79; August 26, 1996, p. 86.
Spectator, September 26, 1987, pp. 34-35.
Time, October 17, 1969; September 17, 1984; December 21, 1992.
Times (London), May 3, 1984; October 7, 1988; October 15, 1988; March 3, 1990.
Times Literary Supplement, July 3, 1969; May 27, 1977; June 8, 1984; November 11-17, 1988; August 30, 1996, p. 25.
Tribune Books (Chicago), April 2, 1989.
Vogue, January, 1993, p. 71.
Washington Post, October 7, 1984.
Washington Post Book World, March 12, 1989; April 21, 1996.

FRASER, George MacDonald 1925-
(Dand MacNeill)

PERSONAL: Born April 2, 1925, in Carlisle, England; son of William (a doctor) and Anne Struth (Donaldson) Fraser; married Kathleen Margarette Hetherington, April 16, 1949; children: Simon, Caroline, Nicholas. *Education:* Educated in England and Scotland. *Politics:* "Totally independent and firmly opposed to all party politics." *Religion:* "Sentimental Presbyterian."

ADDRESSES: Home and office—Bungalow, Baldrine, Isle of Man 1M4 6DS, Britain. *Agent*—Curtis Brown, Haymarket House, 28/29 Haymarket, London, England.

CAREER: Carlisle Journal, Carlisle, England, reporter, 1947-49; *Leader-Post,* Regina, Saskatchewan, Canada, reporter, 1949-50; *Cumberland News,* Carlisle, reporter and subeditor, 1950-53; *Glasgow Herald,* Glasgow, Scotland, features editor, leader writer, and deputy editor, 1953-69; writer. *Military service:* British Army, 1943-45. Indian Army, Gordon Highlanders, 1945-47; became lieutenant.

MEMBER: Society of Authors, Authors Guild.

AWARDS, HONORS: British Arts Council Prize, 1972, for *The Steel Bonnets; Playboy* editorial awards, 1973 and 1975; Writers Guild of Great Britain award for best comedy screenplay, 1974.

WRITINGS:

Flashman: From the Flashman Papers, 1839-1842, World Publishing (New York City), 1969.
(Editor and arranger) *Royal Flash: From the Flashman Papers, 1842-3 and 1847-8,* Knopf (New York City), 1970.
The General Danced at Dawn (short stories), Knopf, 1970.
The Steel Bonnets, Knopf, 1971.
Flash for Freedom!, Knopf, 1971.
Flashman at the Charge, Knopf, 1973.
McAuslan in the Rough, Knopf, 1974.
Flashman in the Great Game: From the Flashman Papers, 1856-1858, Knopf, 1975.
(With others) *The World of the Public School,* St. Martin's (New York City), 1977.
Flashman's Lady, Knopf, 1977.
Mr. American, Simon & Schuster (New York City), 1980.
Flashman and the Redskins, Knopf, 1982.
The Pyrates, Knopf, 1984.
Flashman and the Dragon, Knopf, 1986.
The Hollywood History of the World: From One Million Years B.C. to Apocalypse Now (film stills), Beech Tree Books (New York City), 1988.
(Editor and arranger) *Flashman and the Mountain of Light: From the Flashman Papers, 1845-46,* Knopf, 1991.
The Candlemass Road, HarperCollins (New York City), 1993.
Quartered Safe Out Here, HarperCollins, 1994.
Flashman and the Angel of the Lord, HarperCollins, 1994.
Black Ajax, Carroll & Graf, 1998.

Contributor to numerous journals and newspapers, sometimes under the pseudonym Dand MacNeill.

SCREENPLAYS

The Three Musketeers, Twentieth Century-Fox, 1973.
The Four Musketeers, Twentieth Century-Fox, 1975.
Royal Flash (based on his novel of the same title), Twentieth Century-Fox, 1975.

Prince and the Pauper, Warner Bros., 1977, released in America as *Crossed Swords,* 1978.
Octopussy, MGM/United Artists, 1983.
Red Sonja, MGM/United Artists, 1985.

Also author of *Casanova,* 1987, and *The Return of the Musketeers,* 1989.

SIDELIGHTS: George MacDonald Fraser's novels, notes W. Keith Kraus of *Best Sellers,* are "the continuing story of Harry Flashman, a nineteenth-century rogue who zoomed to stardom in a first volume over the bodies of a few thousand Afghans . . . and a handful of reviewers. Masquerading as a true account, *Flashman: From the Flashman Papers, 1839-1842* chronicled the misadventures of a young British captain in India who always managed to end up the hero while running from danger. The book was as funny as it was spurious and reviewers from Texas to, alas, Shippensburg, Pennsylvania, assumed the account was on the level. When the publisher, 'motivated solely by a desire to set the record aright,' broke the story in the *New York Times* the book became a best seller."

Other Flashman books feature the hero in various historical settings. In *Flashman and the Redskins,* for instance, Flashman travels to the United States and tries to persuade President Grant to give General Custer his job back. Jonathan Yardley, in *Washington Post Book World,* finds this adventure, though not "quite as hilarious as promised in the promotional material," still "consistently entertaining" and "eminently satisfying." Jack Kapica, of the Toronto *Globe and Mail,* considering the hero's exploits in *Flashman and the Dragon* less predictable than the previous Flashman books, declares that "there is a more mature hand at work here, and one that is oddly even more satisfying."

In addition to publishing volumes of his "discovery" (the memoirs of Harry Flashman, soldier), Fraser has presented stories of other rascals. Many reviewers have welcomed Fraser's work. W. F. Graham of *Best Sellers,* for example, finds *The General Danced at Dawn* a "good, humorous [collection] that keeps one pleasantly engaged during its reading. While it is not at all so gripping that you can't put it down once you start it, it is a delightful book to have around." And in the *New York Times Book Review,* Martin Levin remarks that *McAuslan in the Rough* "is loaded with good humor and Scottish charm, and if you have charm, as J. M. Barrie observed, you don't need anything else." *The Pyrates* is a high-seas lark that Flashman and McAuslan admirer John Nicolson, writing in the London *Times,* deems "not really vintage stuff." In the Toronto *Globe and Mail,* however, H. J. Kirchhoff describes the swashbuckling romp as "a rollicking good read."

Fraser's second Flashman book, *Royal Flash,* was made into a 1975 Twentieth Century-Fox movie, for which Fraser wrote the screenplay. Among his other screenplays are *The Three Musketeers,* a tongue-in-cheek version of the classic by Alexandre Dumas, and *The Four Musketeers*; the 1983 James Bond movie *Octopussy,* which Gene Siskel found weakly scripted but entertaining nonetheless and *New York Times* reviewer Vincent Canby called "actually better" than most of the previous twelve James Bond fantasies; and the less successful *Red Sonja.* Fraser's interest in movies is apparent as well in *The Hollywood History of the World: From One Million Years B.C. to Apocalypse Now,* a 1988 collection of film stills that document the movies' treatment of history through what he calls in his accompanying narrative the "Seven Ages of Hollywood."

Flahsman and the Angel of the Lord relates the story of John Brown and Harper's Ferry. A reviewer from the *IBIC Editor's Journal* says the story "although well told, simply is not interesting enough to sustain an entire novel." The reviewer goes on to say that "ignorant, extremist, symbolic political violence . . . is ultimately uninteresting."

James Teacher, in a *Spectator* review of Fraser's *Black Ajax,* refers to the "witty and raffish pen of MacDonald Fraser," as he grapples with the synopsis of the book. At the basis of the story is Tom Molineaux, the *Black Ajax* of the title, an American ex-slave who challenges the heroic, English bare-knuckle boxer champion, Tom Cribb, for his title in 1810. The story is told through a series of flashbacks which enable Fraser to "parade a motley selection of dubious characters for the prurient delectation of the reader."

Fraser is best known for his Flashman series, where he mixes fact with fiction to draw the reader into his intricately plotted historical epics. Teacher warns the reader that "this is not a book that panders to the sensibilities of the politically correct and will doubtless fall foul of the furies from the Ministry for Women and the men from the race relations board." He concludes that "*Black Ajax* is another splendid feather in the already bristling bonnet of MacDonald Fraser."

BIOGRAPHICAL/CRITICAL SOURCES:

BOOKS

Contemporary Literary Criticism, Volume 7, Gale (Detroit), 1977.

PERIODICALS

Atlantic, May, 1991; October, 1988.
Best Sellers, June 15, 1969; October 15, 1970; April 1, 1973.
Books and Bookmen, July, 1976.
Chicago Tribune, June 10, 1983; July 5, 1985.
Globe and Mail (Toronto), May 26, 1984; March 8, 1986; September 3, 1988.
IBIC (online journal), 1997.
Los Angeles Times, June 10, 1983; July 3, 1985.
Los Angeles Times Book Review, September 25, 1988.
National Review, November 8, 1974; April 7, 1989; November 29, 1993, p. 62; May 15, 1995, p. 66; October 9, 1995, p. 58; January 26, 1998, p. 47.
New Republic, November 26, 1977; August 11, 1986.
Newsweek, May 5, 1986.
New York Times, June 10, 1983; July 3, 1985.
New York Times Book Review, October 26, 1969; October 18, 1970; May 20, 1973; November 24, 1974; October 21, 1984; May 4, 1985; June 11, 1995.
Observer (London), December 18, 1977.
Saturday Review, July, 1981.
Spectator, July 19, 1997.
Time, August 3, 1981; June 2, 1986.
Times (London), December 1, 1983; April 1, 1989.
Times Literary Supplement, June 12, 1969; May 31, 1974; July 16, 1982; December 2, 1983; October 11, 1985; June 12, 1992; August 26, 1994; December 23, 1994; September 5, 1997, p. 23.
Washington Post, October 6, 1974; June 10, 1983.
Washington Post Book World, July 12, 1981; August 25, 1982; August 26, 1984; May 4, 1986.

FRAYN, Michael 1933-

PERSONAL: Born September 8, 1933, in London, England; son of Thomas Allen (a manufacturer's representative) and Violet Alice (Lawson) Frayn; married Gillian Palmer (a psychotherapist), February 18, 1960 (divorced, 1989); married Claire Tomalin (an author), June 5, 1996; children: three daughters. *Education:* Emmanuel College, Cambridge University, B.A., 1957.

ADDRESSES: Agent—Greene & Heaton Ltd., 37a Goldhawk Road, London W12 8QQ, England.

CAREER: Novelist and playwright. *Guardian,* Manchester, England, general-assignment reporter, 1957-59, "Miscellany" columnist, 1959-62; *Observer,* London, England, columnist, 1962-68. Contributor to weekly comedy series, "Beyond a Joke," British Broadcasting Corp., 1972; has made regular appearances on Granada Television's "What the Papers Say." *Military service:* British Army, 1952-54.

MEMBER: Royal Society of Literature.

AWARDS, HONORS: Somerset Maugham Award, 1966, for *The Tin Men*; Hawthornden Prize, 1967, for *The Russian Interpreter*; National Press Club Award for distinguished reporting, International Publishing Corporation, 1970, for series of *Observer* articles on Cuba; Best Comedy of the Year award, *Evening Standard,* 1975, for *Alphabetical Order,* and 1982, for *Noises Off*; Society of West End Theatre Award for best comedy of the year, 1976, for *Donkeys' Years,* and 1982, for *Noises Off*; Best Play of the Year award, *Evening Standard,* 1984, for *Benefactors*; Society of West End Theatre Award for best play of the year, 1984, for *Benefactors*; American Theatre Wing's Antoinette Perry Award nomination for best play, 1984, Laurence Olivier Award for best play, 1984, *Plays and Players* award for best new play, 1986, and New York Drama Critics Circle award for best new foreign play, 1986, all for *Benefactors*; International Emmy Award, 1989, for *First and Last*; Emmy Award, 1990; *Sunday Express* Book of the Year Award, 1991, for *A Landing on the Sun.*

WRITINGS:

The Day of the Dog (selections from his *Guardian* column), illustrations by Timothy Birdsall, Collins (London), 1962, Doubleday (New York City), 1963.

The Book of Fub (selections from his *Guardian* column), Collins, 1963, published as *Never Put off to Gomorrah,* Pantheon (New York City), 1964.

On the Outskirts, Collins, 1964.

At Bay in Gear Street (selections from his *Observer* column), Fontana (Huntington, NY), 1967.

Constructions (philosophy), Wildwood House, 1974.

The Original Michael Frayn: Satirical Essays, Salamander Press (Edinburgh), 1983.

Speak after the Beep (collection of *Guardian* and other columns), Methuen (London), 1995.

NOVELS

The Tin Men, Collins, 1965, Little, Brown (Boston), 1966.

The Russian Interpreter, Viking (New York City), 1966.

Towards the End of the Morning, Collins, 1967, published as *Against Entropy,* Viking, 1967.

A Very Private Life, Viking, 1968.

Sweet Dreams, Collins, 1973, Viking, 1974.

The Trick of It, Viking, 1989.

A Landing on the Sun, Viking, 1991.

Now You Know, Viking, 1992.

PLAYS

(With John Edwards) *Zounds!* (musical comedy), first produced in Cambridge, England, May, 1957.

The Two of Us: Four One-Act Plays for Two Players (contains *Black and Silver, The New Quixote, Mr. Foot,* and *Chinamen*; first produced on West End at Garrick Theatre, July 30, 1970), Fontana, 1970.

The Sandboy (first produced in London at Greenwich Theatre, September 16, 1971), Fontana, 1971.

Alphabetical Order (also see below), first produced in London at Hampstead Theatre Club, March 11, 1975; transferred to May Fair Theatre on West End, April 8, 1975; produced in New Haven, CT, at Long Wharf Theatre, October 14, 1976.

Donkeys' Years (first produced on West End at Globe Theatre, July 15, 1976; produced off-off Broadway at New Theatre of Brooklyn, March, 1987; also see below), French (New York City), 1977.

Clouds (also see below; first produced in London at Hampstead Theatre Club, August 16, 1976; produced on West End at Duke of York's Theatre, November 1, 1978), French, 1977.

Alphabetical Order [and] *Donkeys' Years,* Methuen, 1977.

Liberty Hall (first produced in London at Greenwich Theatre, January 24, 1980), Methuen, 1977.

Make and Break (also see below; first produced in Hammersmith, England, at Lyric Theatre, March 18, 1980; transferred to Haymarket Theatre Royal on West End, April 24, 1980; produced in Washington, D.C., at John F. Kennedy Center for the Performing Arts, 1982), Methuen, 1980.

Noises Off: A Play in Three Acts (also see below; first produced in Hammersmith at Lyric Theatre, February 11, 1982; transferred to Savoy Theatre on West End, March 31, 1982; produced in Washington, D.C., at Eisenhower Theater, November, 1983; produced on Broadway at Brooks Atkinson Theatre, December, 1983), Methuen, 1982, acting edition, French, 1982.

Benefactors: A Play in Two Acts (first produced on West End at Vaudeville Theatre, April, 1984; produced on Broadway at Brooks Atkinson Theatre, December, 1985), Methuen, 1984.

Plays: One (contains *Alphabetical Order, Donkeys' Years, Clouds, Make and Break,* and *Noises Off*), Methuen, 1985.

(Translator from French) Jean Anouilh, *Number One* (play; first produced at Queens Theatre, 1984), French, 1985.

Balmoral: Methuen Modern Play, Routledge, Chapman & Hall (London), 1988.

Look Look (also see below; first produced as *Spettattori* at Teatro Santa Vittoria, Rome, 1989), Aldwych, 1990.

Listen to This (various short plays, including the four from *The Two of Us*), Methuen, 1990.

Audience (first act of *Look Look*), French, 1991.

Plays: Two (contains *Benefactors, Balmoral,* and *Wild Honey*), Methuen, 1992.

Here (first produced at Donmar Warehouse, 1993), Methuen, 1993.

(Translator from French) Jacques Offenbach, *La Belle Vivette* (opera), first produced at the Coliseum, 1995.

Now You Know (first produced at Hampstead Theatre, London, 1995), Methuen, 1995.

TRANSLATOR FROM THE RUSSIAN, AND ADAPTER

(And author of introduction) Anton Chekhov, *The Cherry Orchard: A Comedy in Four Acts* (first produced on West End at National Theatre, 1978), Methuen, 1978.

(And author of introduction) Leo Tolstoy, *The Fruits of Enlight-enment: A Comedy in Four Acts* (first produced on West End at National Theatre, 1979), Methuen, 1979.

(And author of introduction) *Three Sisters: A Drama in Four Acts* (first produced in Manchester, England, at Royal Exchange Theatre, 1985), Methuen, 1983.

Chekhov, *Wild Honey: The Untitled Play* (unofficially known as Platonov; first produced on West End at National Theatre, 1984; produced in New York at Virginia Theatre, December 18, 1986), Methuen, 1984.

(And author of introduction) Chekhov, *The Seagull* (first produced on West End at the Palace Theatre, 1986), Methuen, 1986.

Chekhov, *Uncle Vanya* (first produced at Vaudeville Theatre, 1988), Methuen, 1987.

Chekhov, *The Sneeze* (short stories and sketches, first produced on West End at Aldych Theatre, November, 1988), Methuen, 1989.

Exchange (first produced at Guildhall School of Drama, 1986), Methuen, 1990.

OTHER

(Editor) John Bingham Morton, *The Best of Beachcomber*, Heinemann (London), 1963.

(Contributor) Michael Sissons and Philip French, *Age of Austerity*, Hodder & Stoughton (London), 1963.

(Editor with Bamber Gascoigne) *Timothy: The Drawings and Cartoons of Timothy Birdsall*, M. Joseph (London), 1964.

Jamie, On a Flying Visit (teleplay), British Broadcasting Corp. (BBC-TV), January, 1968.

One Pair of Eyes (documentary film), BBC-TV, 1968.

Birthday (teleplay), BBC-TV, 1969.

Laurence Stern Lived Here (documentary film), BBC-TV, 1973.

Making Faces (comedy broadcast in six parts), BBC-TV, September 25-October 30, 1975.

Imagine a City Called Berlin (documentary film), BBC-TV, 1975.

Vienna: The Mask of Gold (documentary film), BBC-TV, 1977.

Alphabetical Order (adapted from the stage play), Granada, 1978.

Three Streets in the Country (documentary film), BBC-TV, 1979.

Donkeys' Years (adapted from the stage play), ATV, 1980.

The Long Straight, BBC-TV, 1980.

(With others) *Great Railway Journeys of the World* (based on film broadcast by BBC-TV; contains Frayn's segment on Australia), BBC, 1981, Dutton (New York City), 1982.

Jerusalem (documentary film), BBC-TV, 1984.

Clockwise: A Screenplay (produced and released by Universal, 1986), Methuen, 1986.

Make and Break (adapted from the stage play), BBC-TV, 1987.

Benefactors (adapted from the stage play), BBC-TV, 1989.

First and Last (film for television), BBC-TV, 1989.

Magic Lantern: Prague (documentary film), BBC-TV, 1993.

A Landing on the Sun (film made for television; adapted from the novel), BBC-TV, 1994.

Budapest: Written in Water (documentary film), BBC-TV, 1996.

SIDELIGHTS: Though best known in the United States as the author of the hit stage farce *Noises Off,* British playwright Michael Frayn has actually produced a wide variety of writing. His beginnings as a columnist and critic for two newspapers, the Manchester *Guardian* and the London *Observer,* led to a number of published collections. Frayn's novels, including *The Tin Men* and *The Russian Interpreter,* have garnered praise for both their humor and their insights into complicated modern times. Among his other plays, Frayn's translations of Anton Chekhov's classics draw particular attention. In 1986 the writer ventured into cinema, with a produced screenplay, *Clockwise.*

Comparing Frayn's "wit, sophistication, and imagination" to "that of American humorist S. J. Perelman," Mark Fritz of the *Dictionary of Literary Biography* declares that Frayn's "satire is sharper." That sense of satire, along with an emerging seriousness, carried the author to his first novel, *The Tin Men.* The story, about the suitability of computers to take over the burden of human dullness, won the Somerset Maugham Award for fiction in 1963. A year later, Frayn produced *The Russian Interpreter,* "a spy story which deals more with the deceit between individuals than between nations," according to Fritz. That novel took the Hawthornden Prize.

Frayn's novel *A Very Private Life,* written in the future tense, "explains how life has grown more private, first through physical privacy, then through the development of drugs to cope with anger and uncertainty," writes Malcolm Page in *File on Frayn.* To *Spectator* reviewer Maurice Capitanchik, "Frayn, in his parable of the horrific future, does not escape the impress which [George] Orwell and [Aldous] Huxley have made upon the genre, nor does he really go beyond the area of authoritarian oppression so brilliantly illumined by [Franz] Kafka, but he does something else both valuable and unique: he shows that his 'Brave New World' is really our cowardly old world, if we did but, shudderingly, know it, in a prose which is often beautiful and, almost, poetry." And in *Sweet Dreams* a young architect dies and goes to a distinctly familiar sort of English heaven, "a terribly decent place, really, where one's pleasantest dreams come true and one's most honest longings are fulfilled," as *Washington Post Book World* critic L. J. Davis describes.

In *The Trick of It,* a young lecturer in literature becomes involved with a slightly older, celebrated author on whom he is an expert. Through his involvement with her, which includes marriage, the man hopes to unravel the secret to her creative success. George Craig of the *Times Literary Supplement* calls the novel "an intensely discomfiting novel, precisely because the elements of farce, social comedy and adventure remain present throughout as potential directions, even as darker and more destructive elements proliferate."

Civil servants are leading characters in Frayn's novels *A Landing on the Sun* and *Now You Know.* In the former, civil servant Brian Jessel is assigned to investigate the supposedly accidental death of another civil servant, Stephen Summerchild, fifteen years earlier. Jessel uncovers that Summerchild was overseeing government research into happiness by Elizabeth Serafin, an Oxford philosophy don, and that the two had set up a hidden garret for meetings. "*A Landing on the Sun* tells the wacky and exhilarating story of how Summerchild and Serafin got up into the garret, what they did there and what became of them," explains Richard Eder in the *Los Angeles Times Book Review.* "On that level, it is loony comedy with a mournful ending. Intermittently, it is a lovely satirical speculation on the ways of bureaucracies and academics, on the uses of order and disorder, and the deepest opposite twists in men and women." In *Now You Know* Hilary Wood quits her job at the Home Office after meeting Terry Little, who heads OPEN, an organization demanding truth from the government. When she leaves, she illegally takes a file about a police fatality case, the details of which OPEN wants made known. Yet, despite all the talk of openness, secrecy abounds. *Now You Know* is "ingenious, witty, thoughtful and smart. . . . [I]t is also a provocative meditation on the pitfalls of letting it all-most particularly, the truth-hang out," Jonathan Yardley notes in *Washington Post Book World.*

Frayn's dramatic work began with a number of television plays. His prior theatrical background included a sojourn with the Cambridge Footlights revue, and a walk-on in a production of Nikolai Gogol's *The Inspector General*—a disaster that prefigured the backstage slapstick of *Noises Off*. "I pulled instead of pushed at the door, it jammed in the frame, and there was no other way off," the writer tells Benedict Nightingale for a *New York Times Magazine* profile. "So I waited for what seemed like many, many hours while stagehands fought with crowbars on the other side and the audience started to slow-handclap. I've never been on the stage since."

Frayn has, however, brought to the stage many critically acclaimed productions. Among his stage plays, *Alphabetical Order* and *Donkeys' Years* earned plaudits, profits, and some measure of reputation for their author. In *Alphabetical Order,* the happy disarray of a newspaper's research department—the "morgue"—is changed forever when a hyperefficient young woman joins the staff. "By the second act she has transformed [the morgue] into a model of order and efficiency. But somehow the humanness is gone," notes Fritz. "The young woman then proceeds to reorganize the personal lives of the other characters as well. She is not a total villain, however. In a way, the newspaper staff needs her: without a strong-willed person to manipulate them, weak-willed people often stagnate. At the heart of the play is the question: which is better, order or chaos?" The successful *Donkeys' Years* focuses upon a group of university graduates reunited twenty years later, only to revert to their adolescent roles and conflicts. Voted the best comedy of 1982 by London's West End Theatre Society, the play was dubbed by Stephen Holden in the *New York Times,* a "well-made farce that roundly twits English propriety."

Frayn's 1980 production *Make and Break,* a comedy-drama about a salesman whose aggressive talent for business overshadows his humanity, played to capacity audiences in London, but premiered in the United States to mixed reviews. Finding the play "wretchedly constructed," *Drama* critic Harold Hobson, for instance, was also disappointed in its "old-fashioned . . . views of women." But more favorable notices came from other reviewers, including *Observer* contributor Michael Ratcliffe, who considered the production Frayn's "best play to date." Describing it as "an excessively neat, neoclassical sort of piece which draws on only a fraction of his imaginative range," the critic pointed out that the only "real problem with the play is simply that the men remain shadows and only the women come to life."

Although many renowned comedies and dramas have used the play-within-a-play format in the past—it is a device that predates Shakespeare—perhaps no self-referential play has been so widely received in this generation as *Noises Off,* a no-holds-barred slapstick farce. Using the kind of manic entrances and mistaken identities reminiscent of the French master Georges Feydeau, *Noises Off* invites the audience to witness the turmoil behind a touring company of has-beens and never-weres as they attempt to perform a typically English sex farce called 'Nothing On.' Referring to the production as "a show that gave ineptitude a good name," *Insight* writer Sheryl Flatow indicates that *Noises Off* was criticized by some as nothing more than a relentless, if effective, laugh-getting machine. The charge of being too funny, however, is not the sort of criticism that repels audiences, and *Noises Off* enjoyed a long run on the West End and Broadway.

Noises Off established Frayn in America as a farceur, on the order of Feydeau and Ben Travers. To that end, the author tells *Los Angeles Times* reporter Barbara Isenberg that farce is serious business. Its most important element, he says, is "the losing of power for coherent thought under the pressure of events. What characters in farce do traditionally is try to recover some disaster that occurred, by a course of behavior that is so ill-judged that it makes it worse. In traditional farce, people are caught in a compromising situation, try to explain it with a lie and, when they get caught, have then to explain both the original situation *and* the lie. And, when they're caught in that lie, they have to have another one."

Frayn's first produced screenplay, *Clockwise,* closely resembles *Noises Off* in its wild construction. Like the play, the film takes a simple premise and lets circumstances run amok. In *Clockwise,* protagonist Brian Stimpson, a small-town headmaster and a man obsessed with punctuality, wins Headmaster of the Year honors and must travel by train to a distant city to deliver his acceptance speech. Inevitably, Brian catches the wrong train, and the thought that he may arrive late drives him to desperate means. By the film's end, he has stolen a car, invaded a monastery, robbed a man of his suit, and set two squadrons of police on his trail. "It isn't the film's idea of taking a prim, controlled character and letting him become increasingly unhinged that makes *Clockwise* so enjoyable; it's the expertise with which Mr. Frayn's screenplay sets the wheels in motion and keeps them going," according to Janet Maslin's *New York Times* critique. Noting that *Clockwise* is "far from perfect—it has long sleepy stretches and some pretty obvious farce situations," *Washington Post* critic Paul Attanasio nonetheless adds, "but at its best, here is a comedy unusual in its layered complexity, in the way Frayn has worked everything out. 'Gonna take a bit o' sortin' out, this one,' says one of the pursuing bobbies. The joke, of course, is in the understatement. And rarely has the 'sortin' out' been so much fun."

Departing from farce, Frayn has written the stage work *Benefactors* as an acerbic look at a 1960s couple wrestling with their ideals as they try to cope with their troubled neighbors, a couple caught in a failing marriage. Frank Rich, who so enjoyed *Noises Off,* saw a production of *Benefactors* and writes in the *New York Times,* "It's hard to fathom that these two works were written by the same man. Like *Noises Off, Benefactors* is ingeniously constructed and has been directed with split-second precision . . . but there all similarities end. Mr. Frayn's new play is a bleak, icy, microcosmic exploration of such serious matters as the nature of good and evil, the price of political and psychological change and the relationship of individuals to the social state. Though *Benefactors* evokes Chekhov, *Othello* and *The Master Builder* along its way, it is an original, not to mention demanding, achievement that is well beyond the ambitions of most contemporary dramatists." Likewise, Mel Gussow of the same newspaper finds strong ties between Chekhov and Frayn: "Thematically, . . . the work remains [close] to Chekhov; through a closely observed, often comic family situation we see the self-defeating aspects of misguided social action."

Fluent in Russian, Frayn served with the British Army in 1952 and was sent to Cambridge, where he trained as an interpreter and used the opportunity to hone his "passion that started in late adolescence for things Soviet," as *New York Times Magazine* writer Benedict Nightingale puts it. From his early days, Frayn has emulated the Russian writer Anton Chekhov; and references to Chekhov are more than apt to describe Frayn also. After working on English versions of Chekhov's classics *The Cherry Orchard, Three Sisters,* and *The Seagull,* Frayn embarked on a more unusual project—reworking for the stage "an unwieldy, six-hour play discovered in 1920 with its title page missing," writes

Flatow. "The work is usually called Platonov,' after its leading character, a roguish teacher who is the object of affection of every woman in town." Flatow finds Frayn's version, *Wild Honey,* to be "very much a collaboration," and offers the author's own remarks about the difficulty separating his own work from Chekhov's: "It's hard to say how much is mine and how much is his. As I wrote in the introduction to the play, I thought the only thing to do was treat it as if it were a rough draft of one of my own plays and proceed from there. If that meant giving one character's speech to another or rewriting dialogue or adding my own speeches, fine—anything to make a better second draft."

Scholars have noted that the original manuscript was left largely to the archives because when he was thought to have written the work—in his late teens or early twenties—Chekhov had hardly made his reputation as a creative artist. According to Rich in his *New York Times* column, "*Wild Honey* isn't the only distillation of ['Platonov'], but it may be the most economical and witty. Even Mr. Frayn, a master of theatrical construction . . . and Chekhovian nuance, . . . cannot turn a journeyman's work into the masterpiece it sometimes prefigures (*The Cherry Orchard*). Yet the adapter has achieved his goal, as stated in his published introduction, of making 'a text for production' rather than 'an academic contribution or a pious tribute.'" As Rich goes on, "Let academics have fun detailing, applauding or deploring the transpositions, telescopings, elisions and outright alterations Mr. Frayn has made in the original work. What's fascinating about *Wild Honey* is how elegantly the embryonic Chekhovian cartography pops into relief."

"Although one cannot say that Michael Frayn's plays revolutionized the British stage during [our era], they certainly helped to enliven it," concludes Fritz. "Frayn contributed a string of lively, witty comedies with some serious philosophical questions lurking beneath the surfaces. Like many other playwrights of [the 1970s and 1980s,] Frayn experimented with dramatic structures borrowed from film and television—perhaps an attempt to find new methods of expression." And in Malcolm Page's opinion, the playwright "has such gifts for humor that his reputation is for comedy; however, he may be disappointed that the more solemn implications have yet to be perceived. His future may be in less comic theatre, as he continues to focus mainly on people of his age, class, and education."

BIOGRAPHICAL/CRITICAL SOURCES:

BOOKS

Contemporary Literary Criticism, Gale (Detroit), Volume 3, 1975; Volume 7, 1977; Volume 31, 1985; Volume 47, 1988.
Dictionary of Literary Biography, Gale, Volume 13: *British Dramatists since World War II,* 1982; Volume 14: *British Novelists since 1960,* 1983.
Page, Malcolm, *File on Frayn,* Methuen Drama (London), 1994.

PERIODICALS

Chicago Tribune, November, 1988.
Drama, summer, 1975; July, 1980.
Horizon, January/February, 1986.
Insight, February 3, 1986.
Kirkus Reviews, November 15, 1991, p. 1421.
Listener, January 21, 1965; January 15, 1966; March 20, 1975.
London Review of Books, October 8, 1992, p. 13.
Los Angeles Times, October 30, 1984; February 3, 1985; February 12, 1985; October 10, 1986; July 20, 1987.
Los Angeles Times Book Review, February 16, 1992, p. 3.
New Statesman, October 4, 1968; November 1, 1974.

Newsweek, February 18, 1974; January 20, 1986.
New York Review of Books, May 14, 1992, p.41.
New York Times, September 11, 1970; June 13, 1971; June 3, 1979; December 12, 1983; July 23, 1984; January 28, 1985; December 23, 1985; January 5, 1986; March 19, 1986; September 4, 1986; October 10, 1986; December 14, 1986; December 19, 1986; March 12, 1987.
New York Times Book Review, September 15, 1968; March 18, 1990; February 16, 1992; January 17, 1993, p. 1.
New York Times Magazine, December 8, 1985.
Observer (London), June 11, 1967; July 18, 1976; April 27, 1980; April 4, 1984.
Opera News, August, 1996, p. 49.
Plays and Players, September, 1970; March, 1982; December, 1984.
Publishers Weekly, December 6, 1991; November 23, 1992.
Spectator, November 23, 1962; October 4, 1968; December 10, 1983; August 29, 1992, p. 28.
Sunday Times (London), January 27, 1980.
Time, September 27, 1968; July 12, 1982; January 5, 1987.
Times (London), February 25, 1982; February 15, 1983; April 6, 1984; March 14, 1986; November 10, 1986.
Times Literary Supplement, February 1, 1980; March 5, 1982; September 22-28, 1989.
Variety, July 27, 1997, p. 39.
Washington Post, October 16, 1983; October 27, 1983; December 24, 1985; October 25, 1986.
Washington Post Book World, January 10, 1974; January 31, 1993, p. 3.

*   *   *

FRENCH, Marilyn 1929-
(Mara Solwoska)

PERSONAL: Born November 21, 1929, in New York, NY; daughter of E. Charles and Isabel (Hazz) Edwards; married Robert M. French, Jr. (a lawyer), June 4, 1950 (divorced, 1967); children: Jamie, Robert M. III. *Education:* Hofstra College (now University), B.A., 1951, M.A., 1964; Harvard University, Ph.D., 1972. *Avocation:* Amateur musician; parties, cooking, travel.

ADDRESSES: Home—New York, NY. *Agent*—Charlotte Sheedy Literary Agency, 145 West 86th St., New York, NY 10024.

CAREER: Writer and lecturer. Hofstra University, Hempstead, NY, instructor in English, 1964-68; College of the Holy Cross, Worcester, MA, assistant professor of English, 1972-76; Harvard University, Cambridge, MA, Mellon fellow in English, 1976-77. Artist-in-residence at Aspen Institute for Humanistic Study, 1972.

MEMBER: Modern Language Association of America, Society for Values in Higher Education, Virginia Woolf Society, James Joyce Society, Phi Beta Kappa.

WRITINGS:

The Book As World: James Joyce's "Ulysses", Harvard University Press, 1976.
The Women's Room (novel), Summit Books, 1977.
The Bleeding Heart (novel; Book-of-the-Month Club alternate selection), Summit Books, 1980.
Shakespeare's Division of Experience, Summit Books, 1981.
(Author of introduction) Edith Wharton, *House of Mirth,* Jove Books, 1981.
(Author of introduction) Wharton, *Summer,* Jove Books, 1981.

Beyond Power: On Women, Men, and Morals (essays), Summit Books, 1985.

Her Mother's Daughter (novel), Summit Books, 1987.

The War against Women (nonfiction), Summit, 1992.

Our Father (novel), Little, Brown, 1994.

My Summer with George, Knopf (New York), 1996.

(With George Sand and Sian Mills) *Marianne,* Carroll & Graf, 1998.

Women's History of the World, Ballantine, 1998.

Contributor of articles and stories, sometimes under pseudonym Mara Solwoska, to journals, including *Soundings* and *Ohio Review.*

MEDIA ADAPTATIONS: *The Women's Room* was produced as a television movie in 1980.

SIDELIGHTS: Novelist, educator, and literary scholar Marilyn French is perhaps best known for the cogent, feminist aspect of her work. "My goal in life," she asserts in an *Inside Books* interview with Ray Bennett, "is to change the entire social and economic structure of western civilization, to make it a feminist world." Divorced in 1967, French earned a doctorate from Harvard through fellowships, and then launched an impressive academic career marked by the publication of her thesis, *The Book As World: James Joyce's "Ulysses."* In 1977, her explosive and provocative first novel, *The Women's Room,* not only granted her the financial freedom to pursue writing full-time but has, itself, become a major novel of the women's movement. And although the critical response to her work frequently focuses upon its polemics—praising in the nonfiction what the fiction challenges—her many readers identify with and admire what French has to say.

"I wanted to tell the story of what it is like to be a woman in our country in the middle of the twentieth century," French explained to a *New York Times* interviewer about *The Women's Room.* Calling it "a collective biography of a large group of American citizens," Anne Tyler describes the novel's characters in the *New York Times Book Review*: "Expectant in the '40s, submissive in the '50s, enraged in the '60s, they have arrived in the '70s independent but somehow unstrung, not yet fully composed after all they've been through." The novel is about Mira, a submissive and repressed young woman whose conventional childhood prepares her for a traditional marriage, which ends suddenly in divorce and leaves her liberated but alone. "The tone of the book is rather turgid, but exalted, almost religious," says Anne Duchene in the *Times Literary Supplement,* "a huge jeremiad for a new kind of Fall, a whole new experience of pain and loss."

Writing about *The Women's Room* in the *Washington Post Book World,* Brigitte Weeks contends that "the novel's basic thesis— that there is little or no foreseeable future for coexistence between men and women—is powerfully stated, but still invokes a lonely chaos repellent to most readers." Uncomfortable with what she perceives as the woman-as-victim perspective in *The Women's Room,* Sara Sanborn elaborates in *Ms.,* "My main objection is not that French writes about the sufferings of women; so have other women writers. But the women of, say, George Eliot or Virginia Woolf, hampered as they are, live in the world of choice and consequence. They are implicated in their own fates, which gives them both interest and stature. The characters in this book glory in the condition which some men have ascribed to women: they are not responsible."

"French wonders not only if male-female love is *possible,* but whether it's *ethical* in the contemporary context," writes Lindsy

Van Gelder in a *Ms.* review of French's second novel, *The Bleeding Heart.* "How, in other words, does one reconcile one's hard-won feminist insights about the way the System works with one's longing to open one's heart completely to a man who, at the very least, benefits from an oppressive System buttressed, in part, by women's emotional vulnerability?" *The Bleeding Heart* centers on Dolores, a liberated professor of Renaissance literature on leave researching a new book at Oxford, when she meets Victor, an unhappily married father of four in England on business. Compromising her feminist principles by engaging in an impassioned but frustratingly combative affair with him, Dolores ultimately realizes that she cannot live with him without descending into predictably prescribed roles. Commenting in *Newsweek* that "French makes her point and touches lots of raw contemporary nerves," Jean Strouse queries, "What happens when nobody wants to be the wife?" According to Rosellen Brown in the *New York Times Book Review, The Bleeding Heart* represents "an admirably honest admission of the human complications that arise after a few years of lonely integrity: What now? Must one wait for love until the world of power changes hands? Is there a difference between accommodation and compromise among lovers? Accommodation and surrender? How to spell out the terms of a partial affirmation?"

A criticism frequently leveled at French is that "her novels suffer from a knee-jerk feminist stereotype in which all men are at worst, brutal and, at best, insensitive," notes Susan Wood in the *Washington Post Book World.* Astonished at the bitterness and anger that French expresses in *The Women's Room* and *The Bleeding Heart,* critics often object to the anti-male stance in her fiction. For example, Libby Purves writes in the London *Times* that *The Women's Room* is "a prolonged—largely autobiographical—yell of fury at the perversity of the male sex. . . . The men in the novel are drawn as malevolent stick figures, at best appallingly dull and at worst monsters." And referring in the *Chicago Tribune Book World* to a "persistently belligerent anti-male bias" in *The Bleeding Heart,* Alice Adams feels this one-sided characterization only serves to disenfranchise many readers who might otherwise read and learn from French's literature.

Praising French's skill in eliciting response from her readers, Weeks declares that "as a polemic [*The Women's Room*] is brilliant, forcing the reader to accept the reactions of the women as the only possible ones." Noting that "the reader, a willing victim, becomes enmeshed in mixed feelings," Weeks observes that the novel "forces confrontations on the reader mercilessly." Although Weeks acknowledges the novel's flaws, she concludes, "*The Women's Room* is a wonderful novel, full of life and passions that ring true as crystal. Its fierceness, its relentless refusal to compromise are as stirring as a marching song." Yet, as Van Gelder points out in *Ms.,* despite the fact that it "is a book whose message is 'the lesson all women learn: men are the ultimate enemy,'" men do not seem to be "especially threatened by the book"; those who choose to read it probably have some degree of commitment to feminism in the first place. "The best compliment I can pay it is that I kept forgetting that it was fiction," remarks the *New York Times's* Christopher Lehmann-Haupt. "It seized me by my preconceptions and I kept struggling and arguing with its premises. Men can't be that bad, I kept wanting to shout at the narrator. There must be room for accommodation between the sexes that you've somehow overlooked. And the damnable thing is, she's right."

In *Her Mother's Daughter,* a forgiving look at motherhood, French writes about the maternal legacy bequeathed to daughters by examining four generations of an immigrant family through the experiences of its women. Anastasia, the narrator, attempts to overcome several generations of wrongs by living like a man, sexually free and artistically and commercially successful. Her success, however, is juxtaposed with the hardships and sufferings endured by the women before her, and her emancipation, according to Anne Summers in the *Times Literary Supplement,* "is shown to be more illusory than real; despite every conceivable change in outward forms, it is the older women's experience which imprints itself on her inner life." Reviewing the novel in *Tribune Books,* Beverly Fields indicates that the novel "elaborates a theme that runs more or less quietly through her first two books: the ways in which female submission to male society, with its accompanying suppression of rage, is passed like contagion from mother to daughter." Marie Olesen Urbanski observes in the *Los Angeles Times Book Review* that "the more educated or liberated the mother is, the more pervasive is her sense of a guilt from which there is no absolution. . . . 'Her Mother's Daughter' celebrates mothers. It depicts the high price mothers pay for children who say they do not want, but who must have their sacrifices."

French's nonfiction seeks the origins of male dominance in society. In *Shakespeare's Division of Experience,* for example, she posits that the female's capacity to bear children has historically aligned her with nature and, consequently, under man's compulsion to exercise power over it. In the *New York Times Book Review,* Geoffrey H. Hartman describes the subject of the book as "the relationship between political power and the 'division' of experience according to gender principles. It is a division that has proved disastrous for both sexes, she writes: To the male is attributed the ability to kill; to the female the ability to give birth; and around these extremes there cluster 'masculine' and 'feminine' qualities, embodied in types or roles that reinforce a schizoid culture and produce all sorts of fatal contradictions." Calling it "the finest piece of feminist criticism we have yet had," Laurence Lerner notes in the *Times Literary Supplement* that "her concern is not merely with Shakespeare." Recognizing that "she believes the identification of moral qualities with genders impoverishes and endangers our society," Lerner adds that French thinks "every human experience should be reintegrated."

Remarking that "French is intelligent, nothing if not ingenious, and obviously sincere," Anne Barton suggests in the *New York Review of Books* about *Shakespeare's Division of Experience* that "there is something very limiting, however, about the assumption upon which all her arguments are based." For example, Barton continues, "Although she does grudgingly admit from time to time that rationality, self-control, individualism, and 'permanencies' may have some little value, she is distrustful of 'civilization,' and of the life of the mind."

Beyond Power: On Women, Men, and Morals, writes Lawrence Stone in the *New York Times Book Review,* "is a passionate polemic about the way men have treated women over the past several millenniums." And according to Paul Robinson in the *Washington Post Book World,* "Nothing in her previous books, however, prepares one for the intellectual range and scholarly energy of *Beyond Power,* which is nothing less than a history of the world (from the cavewomen to the Sandinistas) seen through the critical prism of contemporary feminism." Mary Warnock explains in the *Times Literary Supplement* that French's "general thesis is that men, who have hitherto governed the world, have always sought power above all else, and, in the interests of power, have invented the system of patriarchy which dominates all

Western art, philosophy, religion and education. Above all it now dominates industry and politics."

French's *The War against Women* surveys the oppression of women on a global scale. Considering such activities as ritualized female genital mutilation in Africa and bride burning in India, along with economic disparities between women and men, French argues that women have become "increasingly disempowered, degraded and subjugated" by patriarchal societies. Comparing the book with Susan Faludi's more popular feminist tract, *Backlash: The Undeclared War against Women,* Julie Wheelwright of *New Statesman and Society* finds *The War Against Women* simplistic in light of recent developments in contemporary feminist thought. In particular, Wheelwright objects to French's insistence on the universal victimization and "moral superiority" of women. Isabelle de Courtivron of *New York Times Book Review,* however, praises "French's chilling and well-documented research," noting the disturbing validity of many of her observations.

French's novel *Our Father* depicts the troubled "family reunion" that occurs after a wealthy man, Stephen Upton, suffers a stroke, sparking a visit from his four estranged daughters (all of whom have different mothers). Each hoping to gain either money or acknowledgment from their father, the women initially compete and bicker. The daughters' discovery that they have all been the victims of incest during their childhood, however, becomes a source of bonding and mutual support. Reviews of the work have been mixed. Citing an element of flatness in French's characters and scenes, Georgia Jones-Davis in *Los Angeles Times Book Review* comments: "Marilyn French has written a polemic, not a novel. . . . [The work] is too preachy and badly written to count as literature and too static to be good mind candy." Maude McDaniel of Chicago *Tribune Books* also finds the author's prose style "pedestrian," but nevertheless argues that "*Our Father* should strike a chord with every woman who is willing to think honestly about the place of femaleness in the world."

My Summer with George concerns an unlikely romance between Hermione Beldame, a romance novelist, and a dark-spirited, low-class journalist named George. Were her head ruling her heart instead of the reverse, George's tenure in the relationship would have been brief. Instead, Hermione, conditioned by old-fashioned ideas of romance, is carried away by her imagination and tries to make someone special out of George. A *Publishers Weekly* reviewer expressed disappointment with the novel: "The passionate indignation and insight into women's lives that made French a household name in the 1970s . . . has dwindled to a few dim sparks here." Concurring, Barbara Kemp in *Library Journal* says that George is a "flat uninteresting character" and that French fails to provide any reason why such an "intelligent woman would be obsessed with such a cretin." Carolyn See, writing in the *Washington Post,* notes that "there's one kind of person who never makes an appearance in these pages. . . . That's a regular, decent, okay guy," and suggests that such portrayals of men ultimately cause both women and men to become irritated with feminists.

BIOGRAPHICAL/CRITICAL SOURCES:

BOOKS

Contemporary Literary Criticism, Gale (Detroit), Volume 10, 1979; Volume 18, 1981; Volume 60, 1990.

PERIODICALS

Booklist, March 15, 1992; October 15, 1993.
Chicago Tribune, May 4, 1980; February 7, 1988.

Chicago Tribune Book World, March 9, 1980; June 23, 1985.
Detroit News, April 20, 1980.
Economist, March 21, 1992.
Entertainment Weekly, April 24, 1992.
Library Journal, November 15, 1977; October 15, 1987; May 1, 1992; November 15, 1993; August, 1996, p. 111.
Los Angeles Times Book Review, May 4, 1980; April 19, 1981, August 25, 1985; October 18, 1987; February 27, 1994, p. 12.
Modern Language Review, January, 1979.
Ms., January, 1978; April, 1979; May, 1980; April, 1987; April, 1989; July-August, 1990; March-April, 1991.
Nation, January 30, 1988.
New Statesman & Society, February 21, 1986; April 3, 1992, p. 44.
Newsweek, March 17, 1980; January 24, 1994, p. 66.
New York, October 12, 1987.
New York Review of Books, June 11, 1981.
New York Times, October 27, 1977; March 10, 1980; March 16, 1981; July 9, 1995.
New York Times Book Review, October 16, 1977; November 11, 1977; March 16, 1980; March 22, 1981; June 12, 1983; June 23, 1985; October 25, 1987; July 17, 1988; September 24, 1989; July 5, 1992, p. 8; January 16, 1994, p. 12; August 25, 1996.
Observer, January 26, 1986.
People, February 20, 1978; January 24, 1994.
Psychology Today, August, 1985.
Publishers Weekly, August 29, 1977; August 21, 1978; March 7, 1980; September 11, 1987; September 2, 1988; March 2, 1992; October 18, 1993.
Spectator, April 4, 1992, p. 39.
Time, March 17, 1980; July 29, 1985.
Times (London), March 18, 1982; January 22, 1986; October 15, 1987; October 19, 1987.
Times Literary Supplement, February 18, 1977; April 21, 1978; May 9, 1980; June 4, 1982; January 24, 1986; October 23, 1987; June 19, 1992, p. 3.
Tribune Books (Chicago), October 11, 1987; January 2, 1994.
Village Voice, March 24, 1980.
Virginia Quarterly Review, Volume 54, Number 2, 1978.
Washington Post, May 7, 1980; September 20, 1996.
Washington Post Book World, October 9, 1977; March 9, 1980; March 8, 1981; June 2, 1985; October 18, 1987.
Weekly Tribune Plus, September 16, 1996, p. 8.
Women's Review of Books, October, 1986; April, 1988.

*   *   *

FRENCH, Paul
See ASIMOV, Isaac

*   *   *

FREUD, Sigmund 1856-1939

PERSONAL: Name originally Sigismund Solomon Freud; born May 6, 1856, in Freiberg, Moravia (now Pribor, Czechoslovakia); died of cancer, September 23, 1939, in London, England; cremated; son of Jacob (a merchant) and Amalia Freud; married Martha Bernays, 1886; children: Martin, Anna, four others. *Education:* University of Vienna, M.D., 1881.

CAREER: Worked at the Physiological Institute of Vienna, 1876-1882; Vienna Central Hospital, Vienna, assistant physician, 1882-85; private psychiatric practice in Vienna, 1886-1938; University of Vienna, Vienna, 1886-1938, began as lecturer in neuropathology, became professor of neurology. Co-founder of the Vienna Psycho-Analytic Society and the International Psychoanalytical Association; visiting lecturer at universities in the United States and Europe, including Clark University and the University of London.

AWARDS, HONORS: Honorary member of the American Psychiatric Association, the American Psychoanalytic Association, the New York Neurological Society, the French Psychoanalytic Society, and the Royal Medico-Psychological Association; honorary doctoral degree from Clark University; Goethe Prize, 1930; fellow of the Royal Society of Medicine (London).

WRITINGS:

Zur Auffassung der Aphasien: Eine kritische Studie, Deuticke, 1891, translation with introduction by E. Stengel published as *On Aphasia: A Critical Study,* International Universities Press, 1953.
(With Josef Breuer) *Studien uber Hysterie,* Deuticke, 1895, translation by A. A. Brill published as *Selected Papers on Hysteria and Other Psychoneuroses,* Journal of Nervous and Mental Disease Publishing Co., 1909, enlarged edition translated by James Strachey published as *Studies on Hysteria,* Basic Books, 1957.
Die infantile Cerebrallaehmung, Hoelder, 1897, translation by Lester A. Russin published as *Infantile Cerebral Paralysis,* University of Miami Press, 1968.
Die Traumdeutung, Deuticke, 1900, translation by Brill published as *The Interpretation of Dreams,* Macmillan, 1913, translation by J. Strachey published under the same title, Basic Books, 1955.
Zur Psychopathologie des Alltagslebens (Ueber Vergessen, Versprechen, Vergreifen, Aberglaube und Irrtum), Karger, 1904, translation by Brill published as *Psychopathology of Everyday Life,* Macmillan, 1914, translation by Alan Tyson published as *The Psychopathology of Everyday Life,* Norton, 1965.
Drei Abhandlungen zur Sexualtheorie, Deuticke, 1905, translation by Brill published as *Three Contributions to the Sexual Theory,* Journal of Nervous and Mental Disease Publishing Co., 1910, 2nd enlarged edition published as *Three Contributions to the Theory of Sex,* 1916, translation by James Strachey published as *Three Essays on the Theory of Sexuality,* Imago Publishing Co., 1949, Basic Books, 1962.
Der Witz und seine Beziehung zum Unbewussten, Deuticke, 1905, translation by Brill published as *Wit and Its Relation to the Unconscious,* Moffat, 1916, translation by J. Strachey published as *Jokes and Their Relation to the Unconscious,* Norton, 1960, published under original title with a new foreword by A. A. Brill, Dover (New York), 1993.
Ueber Psychoanalyse: Fuenf Vorlesungen gehalten zur zwanzigjaehrigen Gruendungsfeier der Clark University in Worcester, Massachusetts, September, 1909, Deuticke, 1910, translation published as *The Origin and Development of Psychoanalysis,* Clark University Press, 1910, translation by James Strachey published as *Five Lectures on Psycho-Analysis,* Norton, 1977.
Eine Kindheitserinnerung des Leonardo da Vinci, Deuticke, 1910, translation by Brill published as *Leonardo da Vinci: A Psychosexual Study of Infantile Reminiscence,* Moffat, 1916,

translation by Tyson published as *Leonardo da Vinci and A Memory of His Childhood,* Norton, 1966.

Ueber den Traum, Bergmann, 1911, translation by M. D. Eder published as *On Dreams,* Rebman, 1914, translation by J. Strachey published under the same title, Norton, 1952.

Totem und Tabu: Ueber einige Ueberinstimmungen im Seelenleben der Wilden und der Neurotiker, Heller, 1913, translation by Brill published as *Totem and Taboo: Resemblances Between the Psychic Lives of Savages and Neurotics,* Moffat, 1917, translation by James Strachey published as *Totem and Taboo: Some Points of Agreement Between the Mental Lives of Savages and Neurotics,* Routledge & Paul, 1950, Norton, 1952.

"Zeitgemaesses ueber Krieg und Tod," originally published in German periodical *Imago,* 1915, translation by Brill and Alfred B. Kuttner published as *Reflections on War and Death,* Moffat, 1918.

Vorlesungen zur Einfuehrung in die Psychoanalyse, three volumes, Heller, 1916, translation by Joan Riviere published as *A General Introduction to Psychoanalysis,* Boni & Liveright, 1920.

The History of the Psychoanalytic Movement, translated by A. A. Brill, Journal of Nervous and Mental Disease Publishing Co., 1917.

Dream Psychology: Psychoanalysis for Beginners, translated by Eder, McCann, 1920.

Jenseits des Lustprinzips, Internationaler Psychoanalytischer Verlag, 1920, translation by C. J. M. Hubback published as *Beyond the Pleasure Principle,* International Psychoanalytic Press, 1922, translation by James Strachey published under the same title, Liveright, 1961.

Massenpsychologie und Ich-Analyse, Internationaler Psychoanalytischer Verlag, 1921, translation by James Strachey published as *Group Psychology and the Analysis of the Ego,* International Psychoanalytic Press, 1922, Norton, 1975.

Das Ich und das Es, Internationaler Psychoanalytischer Verlag, 1923, translation by Riviere published as *The Ego and the Id,* Hogarth Press, 1927, Norton, 1962.

Selbstdarstellungen, Meiner, 1925, translation by James Strachey published as *An Autobiographical Study,* Hogarth Press, 1935, Norton, 1952.

Hemmung, Symptom und Angst, Internationaler Psychoanalytischer Verlag, 1926, translation supervised by L. Pierce Clark published as *Inhibition, Symptom and Anxiety,* Psychoanalytic Institute, 1927, translation by Alix Strachey published as *Inhibitions, Symptoms and Anxiety,* Hogarth Press, 1936, revised edition, Norton, 1959.

Die Frage der Laienanalyse: Underredung mit einem Unparteiischen, Internationaler Psychoanalytischer Verlag, 1926, translation by A. Paul Maerker-Branden published as *The Problem of Lay-Analysis,* Brentano, 1927, translation by James Strachey published as *The Question of Lay-Analysis: An Introduction to Psycho-Analysis,* Imago Publishing Co., 1947.

Zie Zukunft einer Illusion, Internationaler Psychoanalytischer Verlag, 1927, translation by W. D. Robson-Scott published as *The Future of an Illusion,* Liveright, 1928, translation by James Strachey published under the same title, Norton, 1975.

Das Unbehagen in der Kultur, Internationaler Psychoanalytischer Verlag, 1930, translation by Riviere published as *Civilization and Its Discontents,* J. Cape and H. Smith, 1930, translation by James Strachey published under the same title, Norton, 1961.

Neue Folge der Vorlesungen zur Einfuehrung in die Psychoanalyse, Internationaler Psychoanalytischer Verlag, 1933, translation by W. J. H. Sprott published as *New Introductory Lectures on Psycho-Analysis,* Norton, 1933, translation by James Strachey published under the same title, Hogarth, 1974.

(With Albert Einstein) *Why War?,* International Institute of Intellectual Cooperation, 1933.

The Problem of Anxiety, translated by Henry Alden Bunker, Norton, 1936.

Der Mann Moses und die monotheistiche Religion: Drei Abhandlungen, Allert de Lange, 1939, translation by Katherine Jones published as *Moses and Monotheism,* Knopf, 1939.

An Outline of Psycho-Analysis, translated by James Strachey, Norton, 1949.

The Origins of Psycho-Analysis: Letters to Wilhelm Fliess, Drafts and Notes, 1889-1902, translated by Erich Mosbacher and J. Strachey, Basic Books, 1954.

(With D. E. Oppenheim) *Dreams in Folklore,* translated by A. M. O. Richards, International Universities Press, 1958.

On Creativity and the Unconscious: Papers on the Psychology of Art, Literature, Love, Religion, selected by Benjamin Nelson, Harper, 1958.

Briefe 1873-1939, edited by E. L. Freud, Fischer, 1960, translation by Tania and James Stern published as *The Letters of Sigmund Freud,* Basic Books, 1960.

The Cocaine Papers, Dunquin Press, 1963, Stonehill, 1975.

Sigmund Freud/Oskar Pfister: Briefe 1909 bis 1939, edited by E. L. Freud and H. Meng, Fischer, 1963, translation by Erich Mosbacher published as *Psychoanalysis and Faith: The Letters of Sigmund Freud and Oskar Pfister,* Basic Books, 1963.

Character and Culture, Collier Books, 1963.

Freud: A Dictionary of Psychoanalysis, edited by Nandor Fodor and Frank Gaynor, Fawcett, 1963.

Sigmund Freud/Karl Abraham: Briefe 1907 bis 1926, edited by H. C. Abraham and E. L. Freud, Fischer, 1965, translation by Bernard Marsh and Hilda C. Abraham published as *A Psychoanalytic Dialogue: The Letters of Sigmund Freud and Karl Abraham, 1907-1926,* Basic Books, 1965.

General Psychological Theory: Papers on Metapsychology, Collier Books, 1966. *Sigmund Freud/Lou Andreas-Salome, Briefwechsel* (letters), edited by E. Pfeiffer, Fischer, 1966, translation by William and Elaine Robson-Scott published as *Sigmund Freud and Lou Andrea-Salome,* Harcourt, 1972.

(With William C. Bullitt) *Thomas Woodrow Wilson, Twenty-Eighth President of the United States: A Psychological Study,* Houghton, 1967.

The Complete Introductory Lectures on Psychoanalysis, translated by James Strachey, Norton, 1967.

Briefwechsel von Sigmund Freud und Arnold Zweig, 1927-1939, edited by E. L. Freud, Fischer, 1968, translation published as *The Letters of Sigmund Freud and Arnold Zweig, 1927-1939,* Harcourt, 1970.

Briefwechsel, edited by William McGuire and Wolfgang Sauerlaender, Fischer, 1974, translation by Ralph Manheim and R. F. C. Hull published as *The Freud/Jung Letters: The Correspondence Between Sigmund Freud and C. G. Jung,* Princeton University Press, 1974.

The Complete Letters of Sigmund Freud to Wilhelm Fliess, 1887-1904, edited by Jeffrey Moussaieff Masson, Harvard University Press, 1985.

A Phylogenetic Fantasy: Overview of the Transference Neuroses, edited by Ilse Grubrich-Simitis, translation by Axel Hoffer and Peter T. Hoffer, Belknap Press of Harvard University Press, 1987.

Freud on Women: A Reader, edited by Elisabeth Young-Bruehl, Norton (New York), 1990.

The Letters of Sigmund Freud and Eduard Silberstein, 1871-1881, edited by Walter Boehlich, Belknap Press of Harvard University Press, 1990.

The Major Works of Sigmund Freud, 2nd edition, Encyclopedia Britannica (Chicago), 1990.

The Diary of Sigmund Freud, 1929-1939: A Record of the Final Decade, edited by Michael Molnar, Scribner's (New York), Macmillan Canada (Toronto), 1992.

The Letters of Sigmund Freud, edited by Ernst L. Freud, Dover (New York), 1992.

The Complete Correspondence of Sigmund Freud and Ernest Jones, 1908-1939, edited by Andrew R. Paskauskas, Belknap Press of Harvard University Press, 1993.

The Correspondence of Sigmund Freud and Saandor Ferenczi: Volume 1: 1908-1914, edited by Eva Brabant, Ernst Falzeder, and Patrizia Giampieri-Deutsch, Belknap Press of Harvard University Press, 1993.

The Case of the Wolfman (From the History of an Infantile Neurosis), edited by Richard Wollheim, Jim Dine, and James Strachey, Arion Press (San Francisco), 1993.

Psychological Writings and Letters, edited by Sander L. Gilman, Continuum (New York), 1995.

Also author of *Three Case Histories, Lettres de Jeunesse, Notes Upon a Case of Obsessional Neurosis, Dora: An Analysis of a Case of Hysteria,* and *Sexuality and the Psychology of Love.*

COLLECTIONS

Sammlung kleiner Schriften zur Neurosenlehre, five volumes, Volumes 1-3, Deuticke, Volume 4, Heller, Volume 5, Internationaler Psychoanalytischer Verlag, 1906-22.

Gesammelte Schriften, twelve volumes, Internationaler Psychoanalytischer Verlag, 1924-34.

Collected Papers, five volumes, translation supervised by Riviere, International Psychoanalytic Press, 1924-50, Basic Books, 1959.

The Basic Writings of Sigmund Freud, edited by Brill, Random House, 1938.

Gesammelte Werke, seventeen volumes, Imago Publishing Co., 1940-52.

The Standard Edition of the Complete Psychological Works of Sigmund Freud, twenty-four volumes, edited by James Strachey, Macmillan, 1953-74, *Abstracts* published by National Institute of Mental Health, 1971, *A Concordance to the Standard Edition,* edited by Samuel A. Cuttman, et. al. published by G. K. Hall, 1980.

Civilization, War and Death: Selections From Three Works by Sigmund Freud, edited by John Rickman, Hogarth Press, 1968.

The Essentials of Psychoanalysis, Hogarth Press, 1986.

OTHER

Contributor to psychology journals; editor of psychoanalytic journals, including the *International Journal of Psychoanalysis;* translator into the German of works by J. M. Charcot, H. M. Bernheim, and Marie Bonaparte.

SIDELIGHTS: Sigmund Freud, the Viennese father of psychoanalysis, began his career as a medical neurologist studying the nervous system. He became an internationally recognized expert on the causes of children's paralysis and collaborated with the noted neurologist J. M. Charcot and the physician Josef Breuer on research to determine the origin and nature of hysteria. Breuer broke new ground by recognizing this nervous disorder as a psychological rather than a physical disturbance, and he and Freud had some success treating patients with hypnosis. Freud's work with hysterics led him to the strikingly original insight that would form the core of psychoanalysis: the idea that neurotic behavior is motivated by unconscious desires that can be revealed through the discursive method of free association.

Early on, Freud hypothesized that the sexual drive (or "libido") lay behind many of these unconscious desires, a view that was deeply shocking to nineteenth-century European society. The radical theorist found himself isolated from the main currents in academic psychology, and he labored alone in the 1890s to refine his theories by analyzing himself and a succession of patients. The psychoanalytic method Freud pioneered sought to reveal the unconscious conflicts and frustrations, often stemming from childhood, that he believed to be responsible for much irrational behavior. By talking spontaneously about his or her feelings under the analyst's guidance, the psychoanalytic patient undertook the slow and painful process of discovering and resolving these unconscious conflicts.

Freud published the results of his work in a series of groundbreaking books, beginning with *Die Traumdeutung (The Interpretation of Dreams)* in 1900. In this book, which remains one of his most widely read works, the psychiatrist postulated that dreams often express unconscious desires in symbolic form. Freud theorized that the mechanism of repression, whereby the mind keeps unconscious material from surfacing into consciousness, relaxed during sleep: dream interpretation thus offered an important way of making contact with the deep recesses of the psyche. Freud explored other possible paths to the unconscious in *Zur Psychopathologie des Alltagslebens* and *Der Witz und seine Beziehung zum Unbewussten* (respectively translated as *The Psychopathology of Everyday Life* and *Wit and Its Relation to the Unconscious*). These innovative works suggested that such seemingly innocuous behavior as slips of the tongue, superstitious quirks, and joke telling could yield psychoanalytic clues to unconscious desires. Freud concluded that psychoanalysis could render useful insights about normal as well as neurotic behavior.

Drei Abhandlungen zur Sexualtheorie, published in 1905 and translated five years later as *Three Contributions to the Sexual Theory,* secured Freud's international reputation and notoriety. The Viennese psychiatrist outlined here the childhood stages of sexual development whose successful passage he thought vital to adult happiness and psychic equilibrium. Dismissing the Victorian image of the sexually innocent child, Freud saw childhood as consisting of stages charged with sexual feelings, focused successively on the mouth, the anus, and the genitals. These bodily organ stages are associated with a developing psychosexual orientation from love of the self to love of the image of the self in another person and, finally, sexual attraction to another person recognized as such. Freud postulated that a development watershed is generally reached between the ages of three and five, when the child feels a strong attraction to the parent of opposite sex and intense rivalry toward the same-sex parent (the so-called Oedipal and Electra stages). Freud theorized that unresolved conflicts in negotiating these developmental stages were major contributors to adult neurosis.

This bold and original sexual theory provoked controversy that continues even today. Freud's insistence on the libido as the dominant human drive led to breaks with some of his illustrious followers, notably Alfred Adler and Carl Jung, who respectively emphasized a "will to power" and a mythic/spiritual questing as important sources of unconscious energy. But the Freud-led international psychoanalytic movement gained considerable influence in professional circles in the period before World War I, and Freudian theory had been popularized in Europe and the United States by the 1920s. Freud's *Vorlesungen zur Einfuehrung in die Psychoanalyse (General Introduction to Psychoanalysis)*, published in 1916 and translated into English four years later, introduced his basic ideas about dreams, errors, sexual development, and neurosis to a general readership.

While continuing to give prime importance to sexual energy and individual childhood development, Freud refined and extended psychoanalytic theory significantly during the early 1920s. Responding in part to the carnage of World War I, he wrote of a powerful human aggressive drive and death instinct in *Jenseits des Lustprinzips (Beyond the Pleasure Principle)*. The deepest instinct of life, he theorized, is to return to an original state of relative equilibrium or stable diffusion in the broader world—that is, death. In *Das Ich und das Es,* translated as *The Ego and the Id,* Freud introduced a conceptual framework for the basic structure of the psyche. According to this theory, the individual experiences a basic conflict between the instinctual, gratification-driven *id* and the inhibitory controls derived from parents and society and internalized in the *superego.* The task of the third psychic structure, the *ego,* is to reconcile—as much as possible—these conflicting demands according to the opportunities and constraints presented by the outside world. "A neurosis," Freud wrote, "is the result of a conflict between the ego and the id; the person is at war with himself. A psychosis is the outcome of similar disturbance between the ego and the outside world."

In his other writings Freud devoted attention to cultural and historical influences in psychic development. In *Totem und Tabu (Totem and Taboo)*, published in 1913, the psychologist analyzed, as indicated by the book's subtitle, the "resemblances between the psychic lives of savages and neurotics," as shown especially in their approaches to totemic or proscribed objects. "The book is extraordinarily provocative," wrote a *New Republic* reviewer in 1918. "There is a thrilling sense of having had contact with a mind at work on the root-problems of human behavior." *Das Unbehagen in der Kultur,* translated as *Civilization and Its Discontents* and one of Freud's best-known works, discusses the basic, irreconcilable conflict between the claims of society and the individual. The very essence of civilization is frustration and denial, Freud argues, and all the products of art, science, and culture in general owe their existence to rechannelled (or "sublimated") sexual energy. Yet Freud did not deny the value of civilization or the fact that culture and its products could become independently desirable. "If Mr. Freud's is not a thoroughly trustworthy mind, it is none the less, one need hardly add, an immensely interesting one, and surely one of the most seminal of our era," wrote Henry Hazlitt in a 1930 *Nation* review. "*Civilization and Its Discontents,* in spite of its few vagaries, must be set down as an impressive and absorbing contribution to the great problem of happiness under our civilization."

In the early 1990s several volumes of Freud's personal writing and correspondence appeared in collected translations. *The Letters of Sigmund Freud and Eduard Silberstein, 1871-1881* consists of Freud's correspondence with his closest childhood friend, in whom he confided his early interests and experiences. D. A. Harris noted in a *Choice* review that the 73 letters and postcards

produced by Freud between age 15 and 24 "can be breathtaking" as "his youthful brilliance" and "extraordinary self-consciousness are apparent throughout." *The Diary of Sigmund Freud, 1929-1939* contains laconic entries from the last decade of the psychiatrist's life. Supplemented by extensive annotations, an index of entries referring to Freud's various illnesses, and previously unpublished photographs of the Freud family, Freud's brief notations document family affairs and his own physical suffering with somber resignation, though they provide little comment on his scientific work or the momentous events surrounding the outbreak of the Second World War.

The Complete Correspondence of Sigmund Freud and Ernest Jones sheds light on the relationship between Freud and his most devoted follower and administrator over a period of three decades. In addition to personally rescuing Freud from the Nazis, Jones is credited with popularizing Freud's ideas in the English-speaking world, particularly through translations which he meticulously supervised, the founding of both the London and British Psycho-Analytical societies, and an influential three-volume biography of his idol. The extensive correspondence between the two men, consisting of some 700 letters, provides many interesting insights into the formative years of the psychoanalytic movement and tensions among its leading personalities. Liam Hudson commented in the *Times Literary Supplement,* "While the present volume adds to our knowledge of psychoanalysis's strange history, its real value lies elsewhere. It documents the steps whereby two starkly dissimilar but equally driven men joined forces and changed the world."

The Correspondence of Sigmund Freud and Saandor Ferenczi reveals the intimate relationship between Freud and his favorite disciple, containing more than a third of the 1200 letters produced between the two men over twenty-five years. Freud met the younger Ferenczi in 1908 and immediately recognized him as a brilliant scientific collaborator and close companion. Robert Stewart noted in the *New York Times Book Review* that the Freud-Ferenczi letters "prove to be as riveting as they are revealing, and I know of no other correspondence of Freud's that is this conversational in tone, this un-self-conscious and full of feeling." Their exchanges discuss important psychoanalytic discoveries and intellectual revelations, their personal relationship, and ventures into the study of the occult and psychic phenomena.

While Freudian concepts and language now suffuse Western culture, psychoanalytic theory remains highly controversial more than half a century after the psychologist's death. Freud continues to be criticized for exaggerating unconscious sexual motivations, and many of his theories about female sexuality are now widely dismissed. Freud's ideas have also come under fire for what critics see as their narrow positivism and antispiritualism; cited in particular are his characterizations of art as essentially neurotic and religion as "the collective neurosis." More fundamentally, psychoanalysis itself has been questioned as a less than scientific approach with results that are difficult to measure, and therefore to assess.

BIOGRAPHICAL/CRITICAL SOURCES:

BOOKS

Bakan, David, *Sigmund Freud and the Jewish Mystical Tradition,* Free Association Books (London), 1990.

Berliner, Arthur K., *Psychoanalysis and Society: The Social Thought of Sigmund Freud,* University Press of America, 1983.

Bernheimer, Charles and Claire Kahane, editors, *In Dora's Case: Freud, Hysteria, Feminism,* Columbia University Press, 1985.

Bloom, Harold, editor, *Sigmund Freud,* Chelsea House, 1985.

Chasseguet-Smirgel, Janine and Bela Grunberger, *Freud or Reich? Psychoanalysis and Illusion,* Yale University Press, 1986.

Clark, Ronald W., *Freud: The Man and the Cause,* Random House, 1980.

Cohen, Ira H., *Ideology and Consciousness: Reich, Freud, and Marx,* New York University Press, 1982.

Dilman, Ilham, *Freud and the Mind,* Blackwell, 1984.

Draenos, S., *Freud's Odyssey,* Yale University Press, 1982.

Erdelyi, Matthew Hugh, *Freud's Cognitive Psychology,* W. H. Freeman, 1985.

Farrell, John, *Freud's Paranoid Quest: Psychoanalysis and Modern Suspicion,* New York University Press, 1996.

Fast, Irene, *Event Theory: A Piaget-Freud Interpretation,* L. Erlbaum, 1985.

Feffer, Melvin, *The Structure of Freudian Thought: The Problem of Immutability and Discontinuity in Development Theory,* International Universities Press, 1982.

Ferguson, Harvie, *The Lure of Dreams: Sigmund Freud and the Construction of Modernity,* Routledge (New York City), 1996.

Ferris, Paul, *Dr. Freud, A Life,* Counterpoint, 1998.

Fischer, Seymour and Roger P. Greenberg, *The Scientific Credibility of Freud's Theories and Therapy,* Columbia University Press, 1985.

Fisher, Seymour and Roger P. Greenberg, *Freud Scientifically Reappraised: Testing the Theories and Therapy,* Wiley & Sons (New York City), 1996.

Forrester, John, *Dispatches from the Freud Wars: Psychoanalysis and Its Passions,* Harvard University Press, 1997.

Freud, Martin, *Sigmund Freud: Man and Father,* Vanguard, 1958.

Fromm, Erich, *The Greatness and Limitations of Freud's Thought,* Harper, 1980.

Gabriel, Yiannis, *Freud and Society,* Routledge, 1983.

Garcia, Emanuel E., editor, *Understanding Freud: The Man and His Ideas,* New York University Press, 1997.

Gay, Peter, *A Godless Jew: Freud, Atheism, and the Making of Psychoanalysis,* Yale University Press, 1987.

Gay, *Freud: A Life for Our Time,* Norton, 1988.

Grinstein, Alexander, *Freud's Rules of Dream Interpretation,* International Universities Press, 1983.

Grubrich-Simitis, Ilse, *Early Freud and Late Freud: Reading Anew Studies on Hysteria and Moses and Monotheism,* translated by Philip Slotkin, Routledge, 1997.

Hogenson, George B., *Jung's Struggle with Freud,* University of Notre Dame Press, 1983.

Jones, Ernest, *The Life and Work of Sigmund Freud,* three volumes, Basic Books, 1953-57.

Lewis, Helen Block, *Freud and Modern Psychology,* Plenum, 1983.

Macmillan, Malcolm, *Freud Evaluated: The Completed Arc,* MIT Press (Cambridge), 1996.

Malcolm, Janet, *In the Freud Archives,* Knopf, 1984.

Mann, Thomas, *Freud, Goethe, Wagner,* Knopf, 1937.

Masson, Jeffrey Moussaieff, *The Assault on Truth: Freud's Suppression of the Seduction Theory,* Farrar, 1984.

Muckenhoupt, Margaret, *Sigmund Freud,* Oxford University Press (New York City), 1996.

Nye, Robert D., *Three Psychologies: Perspectives from Freud, Skinner, and Rogers,* Brooks/Cole (Pacific Grove, CA), 1996.

O'Neill, John, editor, *Freud and the Passions,* Pennsylvania State University Press (University Park), 1996.

Stafford-Clark, David, *What Freud Really Said,* Schocken, 1997.

Steele, Robert S., *Freud and Jung: Conflicts of Interpretation,* Routledge, 1982.

Stepansky, Paul E., editor, *Freud: Appraisals and Reappraisals: Contributions to Freud Studies,* Analytic Press, 1986.

PERIODICALS

American Imago, winter, 1992, pp. 371, 411; fall, 1994, p. 247; spring, 1995, p. 9; fall, 1995, p. 243; winter, 1995, p. 439.

American Scholar, winter, 1993, p. 150; spring, 1994, p. 315.

Choice, October, 1991, p. 355; July/August, 1994, p. 1797.

Commentary, January, 1992, p. 48.

Lancet, March 9, 1996, p. 669.

London Review of Books, August 5, 1993, p. 9; October 6, 1994, p. 3.

Nation, September 17, 1930.

New Republic, July 20, 1918.

Newsweek, October 29, 1990, p. 84.

New York Review of Books, August 18, 1988; October 24, 1991, p. 25; December 5, 1991, p. 27.

New York Times Book Review, March 12, 1967; January 29, 1989; January 17, 1991, p. 34; April 22, 1993, p. 49; October 31, 1993, p. 41; March 6, 1994, p. 1.

New York Times Magazine, May 6, 1956; October 4, 1970.

Observer, May 3, 1992, p. 55; May 23, 1993, p. 70.

Spectator, May 16, 1992, p. 27.

Time, November 29, 1993, p. 46.

Times Literary Supplement, May 10, 1974; October 29, 1993, p. 4.

Yale Review, July, 1994, p. 1.

*   *   *

FRIEDAN, Betty (Naomi) 1921-

PERSONAL: Born February 4, 1921, in Peoria, IL; daughter of Harry (a jeweler) and Miriam (Horowitz) Goldstein; married Carl Friedan (a theater producer), June, 1947 (divorced May, 1969); children: Daniel, Jonathan, Emily. *Education:* Smith College, A.B. (summa cum laude), 1942; further study at University of California, Berkeley, University of Iowa, and Esalen Institute. *Politics:* Democrat.

ADDRESSES: Home—31 West 93rd St., New York, NY 10023. *Office*—One Lincoln Plaza, No. 40K, New York, NY 10023.

CAREER: Feminist organizer, writer, and lecturer at universities, institutes, and professional associations worldwide, including Harvard Law School, University of Chicago, Vassar College, Smithsonian Institution, New York Bar Association, U.S. Embassy in Bogota, Colombia, and in Sweden, the Netherlands, Brazil, Israel, and Italy, beginning in the 1960s; organizer and director, First Women's Bank & Trust Co., New York City, 1974–. Organizer, Women's Strike for Equality, 1970, International Feminist Congress, 1973, and Economic Think Tank for Women, 1974; consultant for President's Commission on the Status of Women, 1964-65, and Rockefeller Foundation project on education of women, 1965. Delegate, White House Conference on Family, 1980, United Nations Decade for Women Conferences in Mexico City, Copenhagen, and Nairobi. Instructor in creative writing and women's studies, New York University, 1965-73;

visiting professor, Yale University, 1974, and Queens College of the City University of New York, 1975; visiting scholar, University of Southern Florida, Sarasota, 1985; distinguished visiting professor, School of Journalism and Social Work, University of Southern California.

MEMBER: National Organization for Women (NOW; founding president, 1966-70; member of board of directors of legal defense and education fund), National Women's Political Caucus (founder; member of national policy council, 1971-73), National Association to Repeal Abortion Laws (vice-president, 1972-74), National Conference of Public Service Employment (member of board of directors), Girl Scouts of the U.S.A. (member of national board), Women's Forum, American Sociological Association, Association for Humanistic Psychology, Gerontological Society of America, PEN, American Federation of Television and Radio Artists (AFTRA), American Society of Journalists and Authors, Authors Guild, Authors League of America, Women's Ink, Women's Forum, Society of Magazine Writers, Phi Beta Kappa, Coffee House.

AWARDS, HONORS: New World Foundation-New York State Education Department grant, 1958-62; Wilhelmina Drucker Prize for contribution to emancipation of men and women, 1971; Humanist of the Year award, 1975; American Public Health Association citation, 1975; Mort Weisinger Award for outstanding magazine article, American Society of Journalists and Authors, 1979; Author of the Year, American Society of Journalists and Authors; L.H.D., Smith College, 1975, State University of New York at Stony Brook, 1985, and Cooper Union, 1987; Chubb fellow, Yale University, 1985; Andrus Center for Gerontology fellow, University of Southern California, 1986; Eleanor Roosevelt Leadership Award, 1989; Doctorate (honorary), Columbia University, 1994.

WRITINGS:

The Feminine Mystique, Norton, 1963, revised edition, 1974, twentieth-anniversary edition, 1983.
It Changed My Life: Writings on the Women's Movement, Random House, 1976, published with a new introduction by the author, Norton, 1985.
The Second Stage, Summit Books, 1981, revised edition, 1986.
The Fountain of Age, Simon & Schuster (New York), 1993.
The Feminine Mystique, W.W. Norton (New York City), 1997.
Beyond Gender: The New Politics of Work and Family, Woodrow Wilson Center Press (Washington, D.C.), 1997.

Contributor to books, including *Voices of the New Feminism,* edited by Mary Lou Thompson, Beacon Press, 1970, and to anthologies, including *Anatomy of Reading,* edited by L. L. Hackett and R. Williamson, McGraw, 1966; *Gentlemen, Scholars, and Scoundrels: Best of "Harper's" 1850 to the Present*; and *A College Treasury.* Contributor of articles to periodicals, including *Saturday Review, New York Times Magazine, Harper's, Redbook, Mademoiselle, Ladies' Home Journal, Newsday,* and *Working Woman*; contributing editor and columnist for *McCall's,* 1971-74; member of editorial board for *Present Tense.*

The Schlesinger Library of Radcliffe College maintains a collection of Friedan's personal papers.

SIDELIGHTS: When Betty Friedan's first book, *The Feminine Mystique,* was published in 1963 it helped launch the modern women's movement by debunking the myth of the post-war woman—a content homemaker who deferred her own ambitions and interests to take care of her family. Friedan was the first writer

to analyze how the perpetration of this stereotype belied the complexity of most women's lives; she called this phenomenon "the feminine mystique." With the publication of the book, she immediately became one of the women's movement's most visible proponents, participating in the founding of the National Organization for Women (NOW) in 1966 and lobbying incessantly for such causes as the passage of the Equal Rights Amendment and legalization of abortion. By the 1990s her concerns had shifted to issues pertaining to aging. Her book *The Fountain of Age* was prompted by "feelings of *deja vu* [that washed] over me as I hear[d] geriatric experts talk about the aged with the same patronizing 'compassionate' denial of their personhood that I heard when experts talked about women 20 years ago," Friedan wrote in the *New York Times Magazine.*

Friedan's journey to political activism began in the early 1960s when she lost her job as a newspaper reporter after requesting her second maternity leave. Although she graduated from college with honors in psychology, she turned down a fellowship at University of California at Berkeley in order to devote herself to her growing family. In her spare time she began to write articles for women's magazines and soon discovered a pattern of bias on the part of the magazines' editors. "They claimed a woman painting a crib was interesting to their readers, but a woman painting a picture was not," summarized Marilyn French in *Esquire.* "The reality of women's lives . . . was censored; what appeared was a fantasy, a picture-book image of happy female domesticity," French continued. *The Feminine Mystique* addressed this generation of women whose lives were supposed to be made more convenient by the proliferation of time-saving appliances and the trappings of suburbia. Instead, many of these women turned to tranquilizers or lived with vague feelings of uneasiness and unfulfillment. A *Times Literary Supplement* reviewer defined the mystique as a "victorian homelife made roseate by the women's magazines and the ad-men, and made intellectually respectable by pseudo-Freud."

Criticism of the book was diverse. Sylvia Fleis Fava, writing in the *American Sociological Review,* noted that "Friedan tends to set up a counter-mystique; that all women must have creative interests outside the home to realize themselves. This can be just as confining and tension-producing as any other mold." Fava also explained that Friedan was not warmly received by all feminists in those early years—especially the movement's more radical elements who saw her views as somewhat reactionary and bourgeois. This discord resulted in the fracturing of the women's movement in the early 1970s in which other prominent feminists, most notably Gloria Steinem and Bella Abzug, gained control of the National Women's Political Caucus and NOW, two of the most powerful feminist organizations at the time.

Friedan's next two books, *It Changed My Life: Writings on the Women's Movement* and *The Second Stage,* document the women's movement as it pertains to her own experiences. *It Changed My Life* is a compilation of Friedan's writings from the 1960s and 1970s in which she sorts out the healthy, productive elements of the movement from the petty, divisive ones in an attempt to gain a new focus—"She wants us to *get together* in a cause that is right and good for all of us, women, men, children, grandparents, single people, everybody," wrote Eliot Fremont-Smith in the *Village Voice.* Accounts of the activities of the National Women's Political Caucus detail the maneuvering that typified the movement at that point, as alliances shifted and allegations were made that resulted in a less-than-unified front. However, Stephanie Harrington of the *New York Times Book*

Review questioned Friedan's "half-light between innuendo and substantiated accusation, juxtaposing names and her version of events and letting the implications fall where they may" approach. Friedan also received criticism for her assertion that lesbianism is a private matter and therefore should not be an issue for the women's movement—an opinion that infuriated many lesbians who considered themselves integral to the movement. Such fringe groups, Friedan argued, threatened basic gains for all women, especially passage of the Equal Rights Amendment. Many critics further faulted Friedan for her maternal attitude towards her accomplishments; Sara Sanborn in the *Saturday Review* described it as "a self-justifying, even self-regarding tone . . . as though Friedan were afraid that we might forget our debt to her."

The Second Stage explains how the backlash from the first wave of feminism caused a "feminist mystique" to emerge in the form of the "superwoman" stereotype—she who effortlessly combines family, career, and satisfying social life. This new prevailing wisdom enabled "the Moral Majority, Ronald Reagan, and various Neanderthal forces [to] bear down with a wrecker" and threaten the gains women have made, wrote Webster Schott of the *Washington Post Book World.* Friedan defines the "second stage" as "the restructuring of our institutions on the basis of real equality for women and men, so we can live a new 'yes' to life and love, and *choose* to have children." She urges those in the women's movement to make the family its central focus. Furthermore, she proposes revised standards of performance for women's roles, because expecting women to perform at their highest levels in both the workplace and the home is unrealistic; they no longer have the luxury of concentrating on a single role as previous generations of women did. The "feminist mystique," Friedan said in an interview with Paula Gribetz Gottlieb in *Working Woman*, refers to "an agenda so concentrated on that which had been denied . . . that it denies that there are other aspects to her life. . . . What is needed now is an integration of the two."

With the publication of *The Fountain of Age* in 1993, Friedan moved to the forefront of another emerging movement—one that seeks to improve the quality of life and amount of respect for older people. The goal of this movement, Friedan states, is for society to see aging not as a process whereby individuals become useless, but as a new phase of life that is none the less vital or interesting than youth. Enumerating statistics illustrating that people are living longer than ever, that women live longer than men, and that people over sixty-five are the fastest growing demographic in the country, Friedan sets out to overturn stereotypes that cast the elderly as nonparticipants in society. According to Friedan, the "age mystique" is the unacceptable view "that aging is acceptable only if it passes for youth," wrote Carol Kleiman in Chicago *Tribune Books.*

After three decades of promoting her own strain of feminism, Friedan finally admits in *The Fountain of Age* "with relief and excitement, my liberation from the power politics of the women's movement. I recognized my own compelling need now to transcend the war between the sexes, the no-win battles of women as a whole sex, oppressed victims, against men as a whole sex, the oppressors. . . . The unexpectedness of this new quest has been my adventure into age." However, Friedan does credit feminism for providing women with a greater ability to adapt to the challenges of aging. Though Friedan's ideas are not necessarily ground-breaking or revolutionary—"word has been out for years that old age need not be synonymous with deterioration," stated David Gates in *Newsweek*—they bring the issue into the main-stream with discussions and anecdotes about life after menopause, mountain-climbing expeditions, and maintaining healthy relationships.

Criticism of *The Fountain of Age* came from Nancy Mairs in the *New York Times Book Review,* who warned that the author "generalizes from the conditions and experiences of a predominately white middle-class population . . . for people from diverse ethnic and economic backgrounds aging may present altogether different challenges." Others have faulted Friedan's writing for what they see as a lack of organization and excessive length due to repetition; "a prose style that resembles nothing so much as a community bulletin board, full of flabby words," according to Christopher Lehman-Haupt in the *New York Times.* Kleiman was puzzled by Friedan's support for the lifestyle *Playboy* magnate Hugh Hefner has adopted in his later years while simultaneously dismissing Steinem, now in her fifties, who is still a high-profile feminist activist. Diane Middlebrook, writing in the *Los Angeles Times Book Review,* also commented on Friedan's interpretation of cultural attitudes toward aging by determining that "Friedan is better as a muckraker challenging the disease model by which the conditions of aging are approached by medical and social institutions." When it comes to research priorities and allocation of funds, for example, Friedan thinks the medical establishment focuses too heavily on sickness and disability while ignoring the healthy, active populace over sixty-five. Despite this, Kleiman wrote, "She shows no desire to evade issues, no matter how delicate and difficult." Middlebrook concluded that "readers not turned off by her occasional nervous preening will find much to enlighten and provoke as they join her in the contemplation of possibilities."

BIOGRAPHICAL/CRITICAL SOURCES:

BOOKS

Contemporary Issues Criticism, Volume 2, Gale (Detroit), 1984.
Mitchell, Juliet, *Psychoanalysis and Feminism,* Random House, 1974.

PERIODICALS

American Sociological Review, December, 1963, pp. 1053-54.
Business Week, November 1, 1993, p. 18.
Chicago Tribune Book World, November 8, 1981.
Encounter, February, 1983.
Esquire, December, 1983.
Humanist, January/February, 1991, pp. 26-27.
Insight on the News, October 25, 1993, p. 12; June 27, 1994, p. 40.
Life, fall, 1990, p. 107.
Los Angeles Times, December 27, 1981.
Los Angeles Times Book Review, September 19, 1993.
Nation, November 14, 1981; November 28, 1981.
National Review, February 5, 1982.
New Republic, April 27, 1974; January 20, 1982; July 1, 1983; October 11, 1993, p. 49.
Newsweek, October 4, 1993, p. 78.
New York Times, August 3, 1976; April 25, 1983; June 2, 1986; October 11, 1993.
New York Times Book Review, July 4, 1976, pp. 7-8; November 22, 1981; October 3, 1993, p. 1.
New York Times Magazine, July 5, 1981; February 27, 1983; November 3, 1985.
People Weekly, October 4, 1993, p. 26.
Psychology Today, November-December, 1993, p. 20.
Publishers Weekly, June 28, 1993, p. 61.

Saturday Review, July 24, 1976; October, 1981.
Tikkun, March-April, 1994, p. 79.
Times Literary Supplement, May 31, 1963; July 30, 1982.
Tribune Books (Chicago), September 12, 1993.
Village Voice, June 28, 1976, pp. 43-44.
Washington Post Book World, August 8, 1976, p. F7; November 1, 1981; October 19, 1983.
Working Woman, February, 1982.

*   *   *

FRIEDMAN, Milton 1912-

PERSONAL: Born July 31, 1912, in New York, NY; son of Jeno Saul and Sarah Ethel (Landau) Friedman; married Rose Director, June 25, 1938; children: Janet, David. *Education:* Rutgers University, A.B., 1932; University of Chicago, A.M., 1933; Columbia University, Ph.D., 1946. *Avocation:* Tennis, carpentry.

ADDRESSES: Office—Hoover Institution, Stanford, CA 94305-6010.

CAREER: University of Chicago, Social Science Research Committee, Chicago, IL, research assistant, 1934-35; National Resources Committee, Washington, DC, associate economist, 1935-37; National Bureau of Economic Research, New York City, member of research staff, 1937-45, 1948-81; U.S. Treasury Department, Division of Tax Research, Washington, DC, principal economist, 1941-43; Columbia University, Division of War Research, New York City, associate director of statistical research group, 1943-45; University of Minnesota, Minneapolis, associate professor of economics and business administration, 1945-46; University of Chicago, Chicago, associate professor, 1946-48, professor, 1948-62, Committee on White House Fellows (president), 1971-74, Hoover Institution, Stanford, CA, senior research fellow, 1977, Paul Snowden Russell Distinguished Service Professor of Economics, 1962-82, President's Economic Advisory Board, 1981-88, Paul Snowden Russell Distinguished Service Professor Emeritus, 1982.

Columbia University, part-time lecturer, 1937-40, and Wesley Clair Mitchell Research Professor of Economics, 1964-65. Visiting Fulbright lecturer, Cambridge University, 1953-54; visiting professor, University of California, Los Angeles, 1967, and University of Hawaii, 1972; visiting scholar, Federal Reserve Bank of San Francisco, 1977. Member of President's Commission on White House Fellows, 1971-73, and Federal Reserve System advisory committee on monetary statistics, 1974. Host of ten-part television series "Free to Choose," Public Broadcasting Service, 1980, and discussion leader of three-part series "Tyranny of the Status Quo," Public Broadcasting Service, 1984. Chief economic advisor to Senator Barry Goldwater, 1964. Consultant to Economic Cooperation Administration, Paris, 1950, and International Cooperation Administration, India, 1955.

MEMBER: National Academy of Sciences, American Statistical Association (fellow), American Economic Association (member of executive committee, 1955-57; president, 1967), Econometric Society (fellow), Institute of Mathematical Statistics (fellow), American Philosophical Society, Mont Pelerin Society (American secretary, 1957-62; member of council, 1962-65; vice-president, 1967-70, 1972–; president, 1970-72), American Enterprise Institute for Public Policy Research (member of council of academic advisors, 1956-78), Royal Economic Society, Western Economic Association (president, 1984-85), Philadelphia Society (member

of board of trustees, 1965-67, 1970-72, 1976–), Quadrangle Club (Chicago).

AWARDS, HONORS: John Bates Clark Medal, American Economic Association, 1951; Center for Advanced Study in the Behavioral Sciences fellow, 1957-58; Ford faculty research fellow, 1962-63; LL.D. from St. Paul's University, Tokyo, 1963, Kalamazoo College, 1968, Rutgers University, 1968, Lehigh University, 1969, Loyola University, 1971, University of New Hampshire, 1975, Harvard University, 1979, Brigham Young University, 1980, Dartmouth College, 1980, and Gonzaga University, 1981; L.H.D. from Rockford College, 1969, Roosevelt University, 1975, Hebrew Union College, Los Angeles, 1981, and Jacksonville University, 1993; D.Sc. from University of Rochester, 1971; named Chicagoan of the Year, Chicago Press Club, 1972; named Educator of the Year, Chicago United Jewish Fund, 1973; Nobel Prize for economic science, 1976; Scopus Award from American Friends of the Hebrew University, 1977; Ph.D. from Hebrew University of Jerusalem, 1977; D.C.S. from Francisco Marroquin University, 1978; Freedoms Foundation, Private Enterprise Exemplar Medal, 1978, Valley Forge Honor Certificate, 1978, for speech "The Future of Capitalism," and George Washington Honor Medal, 1978, for television series "Open Mind," WPIX, New York City; gold medal from National Institute of Social Sciences, 1978; Statesman of the Year Award, Sales and Marketing Executives International, 1981; Ohio State Award, New Perspectives Award, and Tuck Media Award, all 1981, all for television series "Free to Choose"; Grand Cordon Sacred Treasure, Japan, 1986; National Medal of Science, 1988; Presidential Medal of Freedom, 1988; Prize in Moral-Cultural Affairs, Institution of World Capitalism, 1993.

WRITINGS:

(With Carl Shoup and Ruth P. Mack) *Taxing to Prevent Inflation,* Columbia University Press, 1943.
(With Simon Kuznets) *Income from Independent Professional Practice,* National Bureau of Economic Research, 1945.
(With H. A. Freeman, F. Mosteller, and W. Allen Wallis) *Sampling Inspection,* McGraw, 1948.
Essays in Positive Economics, University of Chicago Press, 1953.
(Editor and contributor) *Studies in the Quantity Theory of Money,* University of Chicago Press, 1956.
A Theory of the Consumption Function, Princeton University Press, 1957.
A Program for Monetary Stability, Fordham University Press, 1960.
Price Theory: A Provisional Text, Aldine, 1962, revised edition, 1976.
(With wife, Rose D. Friedman) *Capitalism and Freedom,* University of Chicago Press, 1962, reprinted with new preface, 1981.
Inflation: Causes and Consequences, Asia Publishing House (Bombay), 1963.
(With Anna I. Schwartz) *A Monetary History of the United States, 1867-1960* (also see below), Princeton University Press, 1963.
The Great Contraction, 1929-1933: Chapter Seven of "Monetary History of the United States, 1867-1960", National Bureau of Economic Research, 1965.
(With Robert V. Roosta) *The Balance of Payments: Free Versus Fixed Exchange Rates,* American Enterprise Institute for Public Policy Research, 1967.
Dollars and Deficits: Inflation, Monetary Policy, and the Balance of Payments, Prentice-Hall, 1968.

The Optimum Quantity of Money and Other Essays, Aldine, 1969.

(With Walter W. Heller) *Monetary Versus Fiscal Policy,* Norton, 1969.

Preparation of Leases, Practising Law Institute, 1969.

(With Schwartz) *Monetary Statistics of the United States: Estimates, Sources, Methods,* Columbia University Press, 1970.

The Counter-Revolution in Monetary Theory, Institute of Economic Affairs, 1970, Transatlantic, 1972.

(With Wilbur I. Cohen) *Social Security: Universal or Selective?,* American Enterprise Institute for Public Policy Research, 1972.

An Economist's Protest: Columns on Political Economics (collection of magazine columns), Thomas Horton, 1972, 2nd edition, 1975, 2nd edition also published as *There's No Such Thing as a Free Lunch,* Open Court, 1975, 3rd edition published as *Bright Promises, Dismal Performance: An Economist's Protest,* edited by William R. Allen, Harcourt, 1983.

(Contributor) *The Futures Market in Foreign Currencies* (Chicago), 1972.

Money and Economic Development, Praeger, 1973.

Milton Friedman's Monetary Framework: A Debate with His Critics, edited by Robert I. Gordon, University of Chicago Press, 1974.

Essays on Inflation and Indexation, American Enterprise Institute for Public Policy Research, 1974.

Indexing and Inflation, American Enterprise Institute for Public Policy Research, 1974.

Contracts and Conveyances of Real Property, Practising Law Institute, 1975.

Monetary Correction, Transatlantic Arts, 1975.

Unemployment Versus Inflation, Institute of Economic Affairs, 1975.

The Nobel Prize in Economics, Hoover Institute Press, 1976.

From Galbraith to Economic Freedom, Institute of Economic Affairs, 1977.

(Contributor) Frederick E. Webster, editor, *The Business System: A Bicentennial View,* University Press of New England, 1977.

Has the Economic Tide Turned? Strathclyde Business School, 1978.

Tax Limitation, Inflation, and the Role of Government, Fisher Institute, 1979.

(With R. D. Friedman) *Free to Choose: A Personal Statement* (Book-of-the-Month Club alternate selection), Harcourt, 1980.

(With Paul A. Samuelson) *Milton Friedman and Paul A. Samuelson Discuss the Economic Responsibility of Government,* Center for Education and Research in Free Enterprise, 1980.

Milton Friedman Speaks, Harcourt, 1980.

The Invisible Hand in Economics and Politics, Institute of Southeast Asian Studies [Singapore], 1981.

Market Mechanisms and Central Economic Planning, American Enterprise Institute for Public Policy Research, 1981.

(With Schwartz) *Monetary Trends in the United States and the United Kingdom: Their Relation to Income, Prices, and Interest Rates, 1867-1975,* University of Chicago Press, 1982.

On Milton Friedman, Fraser Institute, 1982.

(Contributor) *Money Talks: Five Views of Britain's Economy,* edited by Alan Horrox and Gillian McCredie, Thames Methuen, 1983.

(With R. D. Friedman) *Tyranny of the Status Quo,* Harcourt, 1984.

Politics and Tyranny: Lessons in Pursuit of Freedom, Pacific Institute for Public Policy Research, 1985.

The Essence of Friedman, edited by Kurt R. Leube, foreword by W. Glenn Campbell, introduction by Anna J. Schwartz, Hoover Institution Press, 1987.

Monetarist Economics (part of "IEA Masters of Modern Economics" series), Blackwell (Oxford, England), 1991.

Money Mischief: Episodes in Monetary History, Harcourt, 1992.

(With Thomas Stephen Szasz) *Friedman and Szasz on Liberty and Drugs: Essays on the Free Market and Prohibition,* edited with a preface by Arnold S. Trebach and Kevin B. Zeese, Drug Policy Foundation Press (Washington, DC), 1992.

Input and Output in Medical Care (public policy essays), Hoover Institute on War, Revolution, and Peace, Stanford University (Stanford, CA), 1992.

Why Government Is the Problem, Hoover Institute on War, Revolution, and Peace, 1993.

Foreign Economic Aid: Means and Objectives, foreword by Peter Duigan, Hoover Institute on War, Revolution, and Peace, 1995.

(With Rose D. Friedman) *Two Lucky People: Memoirs,* University of Chicago Press, 1998.

Also author of *Theoretical Framework for Monetary Analysis, Inflation and Unemployment: The New Dimension of Politics,* and other monographs, published speeches, and booklets. Columnist, *Newsweek,* 1966-84. Contributor of articles and reviews to economic and statistics journals. Member of board of directors, Aldine Publishing Co., 1961-76. Member of board of editors, *American Economic Review,* 1951-53, and *Econometrica,* 1957-69. Member of advisory board, *Journal of Money, Credit,* and Banking, 1968.

MEDIA ADAPTATIONS: Free to Choose: A Personal Statement was written in conjunction with the television series *Free to Choose,* Public Broadcasting Service, 1980; *Tyranny of the Status Quo* was written in conjunction with the television series *Tyranny of the Status Quo,* Public Broadcasting Service, 1984. The texts of the books and series are different.

SIDELIGHTS: "Economic freedom," Nobel laureate Milton Friedman declares in *Free to Choose: A Personal Statement,* "is an essential requisite for political freedom. By enabling people to cooperate with one another without coercion or central direction, it reduces the area over which political power is exercised. In addition, by dispersing power, the free market provides an offset to whatever concentration of political power may arise. The combination of economic and political power in the same hands is a sure recipe for tyranny." Friedman's defense of freedom is the foundation of his economic thought. It has led him in his many books, his years of teaching at the University of Chicago, and in two widely-seen educational television series, to promote the ideas of a free market economic system.

As the leader of the Chicago School of Economics, a school of economic thought that calls for an end to government intervention in all aspects of the economy, Friedman has seen his position gain the ascendancy in recent years. "Events in Eastern Europe, the experience of prolonged inflation, disillusion with the welfare state in particular, resentment at the spread of bureaucratic intrusion and alarm at the unchecked growth of government expenditures along with a concomitant growth in the popularity of tax evasion—all have undoubtedly contributed to the change in political climate," E. I. Mishan explains in the *Times Literary*

Supplement. Friedman was awarded the Nobel Prize for economic science in 1976. And with the election of President Ronald Reagan in the United States and Prime Minister Margaret Thatcher in England, both of whom are followers of Friedman, some of Friedman's economic proposals have become government policy.

Friedman's belief in the free market system is argued in his book *Capitalism and Freedom,* cowritten with his wife, Rose D. Friedman. The book's major theme, the authors state, "is the role of competitive capitalism—the organization of the bulk of economic activity through private enterprise operating in a free market as a system of economic freedom and a necessary condition for political freedom." The book also delineates the proper role of government in a free market system. Two broad principles define this ideal government, the Friedmans write: "First, the scope of government must be limited. Its major function must be to protect our freedom both from the enemies outside and from our fellow-citizens. . . . The second broad principle is that government power must be dispersed. If government is to exercise power, better in the county than in the state, better in the state than in Washington."

Because Friedman holds these beliefs, he criticizes much of the social legislation enacted by the United States Government since the New Deal of the 1930s. Friedman fears that those who promote current social legislation are all too ready "to rely on the state for the furtherance of welfare and equality," Abba P. Lerner writes in the *American Economic Review.* This reliance on the state results in an encroachment on individual liberty, as it gives power over individual decisions to the government.

In *A Monetary History of the United States, 1867-1960,* cowritten with Anna J. Schwartz, Friedman traces the history of the nation's money supply. In doing so, he also writes extensively about the Federal Reserve System, the government agency regulating the nation's money supply. Organized in 1914 in response to alleged banking abuses, the Federal Reserve has caused, Friedman believes, even more serious abuses. The Great Depression of the 1930s would not have been so catastrophic, Friedman argues, had not the Federal Reserve stepped in and worsened the situation. Friedman's *A Monetary History of the United States* is considered to be "the definitive history and is as useful to his critics as to his cohorts," according to Eliot Janeway of the *Los Angeles Times Book Review.*

In *Free to Choose* and *Tyranny of the Status Quo,* both written with his wife, Friedman presents his economic views for a popular audience. Both books were companions to nationally broadcast television programs and are meant not for the academic audience of Friedman's previous books but for the general reader. Mishan describes *Free to Choose* as "a popular version of the more fastidious but no less cogently argued statement of his views elaborated in Friedman's *Capitalism and Freedom.*" As such, the book is meant to "persuade readers to embrace a certain set of principles," Donald J. Yankovic explains in the *Journal of Economic History.*

Sidney Weintraub of the *New York Times Book Review* describes *Free to Choose* as "clear, cogent, sure and humorless," and believes that it is "sweeping and surgical in cutting up economic absurdities perpetrated by government agencies since the New Deal." Although he is "skeptical of its message," Weintraub nonetheless concludes that *Free to Choose* is "noteworthy for its clarity, logic, candor and unequivocal stand on political implications." Yankovic sees the Friedmans' strong defense of the free market system as a prime aspect of the book's importance. "The Friedmans offer," Yankovic writes, "a sound prescription for improving the economic well-being of the bulk of the population by widening the range of individual choices. . . . [*Free to Choose*] reminds us that there are many protections for us, in our various economic roles, in the market itself. It also reminds us that when we turn to government for protection, good intentions can lead to perverse results."

Many of the same arguments found in *Free to Choose* are restated in *Tyranny of the Status Quo,* but the focus of the book is on the economic policies of President Reagan's first term in office. Though Reagan came to the presidency with the idea "that Big Government is the sworn enemy of economic progress and individual freedom. . . the bureaucrats survived the first years of his regime unscarred," writes Ron Grossman in the *Chicago Tribune Book World.* The Friedmans try to determine why Reagan, who was elected in part because he sought to limit the size of government, was able to reform relatively little of it. They find that "a new administration has six to nine months to achieve major changes." Any changes attempted beyond this initial period will probably fail, although Reagan was able to institute a sweeping tax reform in his second term. "In the end," Susan Lee states in the *New York Times Book Review,* "the Friedmans blame Mr. Reagan for not being bold enough during his honeymoon period." To insure a limited federal government, since even a president is limited in what he can accomplish in this area, the Friedmans propose several constitutional amendments, including one requiring a balanced budget.

"Whatever your political persuasion," Marjorie Lewellyn Marks writes of the book in the *Los Angeles Times,* "many Friedman arguments, backed by statistical and historical documentation are quite convincing." But Wayne Godley of the *Times Literary Supplement* disagrees. *Tyranny of the Status Quo,* Godley states, "is full of simple, plausible and dogmatic statements. . . . I disagree totally with the Friedmans' economics and passionately with their political beliefs." Grossman, too, has some reservations about the book. He sees it as calling for institutional change yet failing to present a workable strategy for this change. But he does believe that "Rose and Milton Friedman offer a compelling description of what ails American society."

In *Money Mischief: Episodes in Monetary History,* Friedman examines the unintended and wide-ranging consequences of various monetary reforms in the United States and abroad. Focusing primarily on events from the late nineteenth and early twentieth centuries, Friedman recounts circumstances and implications surrounding the Coinage Act of 1873, William Jennings Bryan's "Cross of Gold" campaign in 1896, Franklin D. Roosevelt's silver purchase program and its connection to Chinese politics, as well as contemporary issues related to the creation of the European Monetary System and attempts to peg the currency of Third World nations to the U.S. dollar. "The unchanging theme underlying all of these reforms," according to Alan Reynolds in *National Review,* "is the importance of preventing the value of money from being determined by the whim of politicians and bankers." Kenneth Silber writes in *Commentary,* "Drawing on a range of examples, [Friedman] defends his well-known thesis that excessive monetary growth is the crucial factor underlying inflation." Summarizing Friedman's lesson, Reynolds adds, "Starting with stone money on the island of Yak, we are quickly led to understand what affects people's willingness to hold money for short or long periods, how real and nominal quantities of money differ, and how the perception of individuals about the delights of having more money clashes with what is actually possible for the entire economy and thus leads to monetary mischief."

Evaluations of Friedman's career point to his many contributions to economic science. James Tobin of the *Economist* explains that "Friedman was a pioneer in developing and applying the fruitful idea of 'human capital.' In 1957, Friedman showed how the distinction between permanent and transient income resolved puzzles in consumption and saving statistics for whole economies and for samples of households. His monumental monetary history. . . is an indispensable treatise packed with theoretic insights and policy analysis as well as historical and statistical narrative." Writing in the *New Statesman,* Wilfred Beckerman maintains: "If Nobel Prizes are awarded according to the intellectual power of the recipients and the extent to which they have stimulated research and analysis in their fields. . . Milton Friedman certainly deserves one. If they are awarded according to the extent to which the recipients have correctly analysed some aspects of the phenomena they have studied, he may still deserve one, but it is not yet possible to be sure about this."

BIOGRAPHICAL/CRITICAL SOURCES:

BOOKS

Contemporary Issues Criticism, Volume 1, Gale (Detroit), 1982.
Cunningham, John, editor, *Milton Friedman: Critical Assessments,* Routledge (London), 1990.
Frazer, William Johnson, *Power and Ideas: Milton Friedman and the Big U-turn,* Gulf/Atlantic (Gainesville, FL), 1988.
Frazer, William [Johnson], *The Friedman System: Economic Analysis of Time Series,* Praeger (Westport, CN), 1997.
Hammond, Daniel J., *Theory and Measurement: Casuality Issues in Milton Friedman's Monetary Economics,* Cambridge University Press (New York), 1996.
Hirsch, Abraham, and Neil de Marchi, *Milton Friedman: Economics in Theory and Practice,* University of Michigan Press (Ann Arbor, MI), 1990.
Selden, Richard T., editor, *Capitalism and Freedom: Problems and Prospects; Proceedings of a Conference in Honor of Milton Friedman,* University Press of Virginia, 1975.

PERIODICALS

American Economic Review, June, 1963; September, 1965.
American Political Science Review, March, 1977.
Annals of the American Academy of Political and Social Science, November, 1963.
Business History Review, fall, 1971.
Business Week, July 19, 1969; November 1, 1976.
Canadian Journal of Political Science, March, 1968.
Chicago Tribune Book World, March 11, 1984.
Christian Century, November 25, 1970.
Christian Science Monitor, February 11, 1980.
Commentary, July, 1969; May, 1992, p. 61.
Commonweal, February 23, 1973.
Economist, July 1, 1972; October 9, 1976; October 23, 1976.
Esquire, September, 1970.
Forbes, May 27, 1991, p. 294; August 17, 1992, p. 42.
Fortune, June 1, 1967; July 3, 1989, p. 66.
Journal of American History, June, 1964.
Journal of Economic History, March, 1975; June, 1981.
Journal of Political Economy, December, 1963.
Kirkus Reviews, December 1, 1993, p. 1512.
Listener, September 26, 1974.
Los Angeles Times, May 6, 1984; September 14, 1988.
Los Angeles Times Book Review, May 29, 1983.
Money, September, 1976.
Monthly Review, November, 1990, p. 35.
Nation, November 20, 1976; January 22, 1977.
National Review, September 10, 1971; November 9, 1973; September 16, 1977; August 3, 1992, p. 38.
New Republic, November 6, 1976; March 22, 1980.
New Statesman, October 22, 1976.
Newsweek, January 31, 1972; October 25, 1976.
New York Review of Books, April 17, 1980.
New York Times, July 12, 1970; January 14, 1980; July 14, 1981.
New York Times Book Review, February 24, 1980; February 26, 1984.
New York Times Magazine, January 25, 1970.
Publishers Weekly, December 13, 1991, p. 43.
Reason, April, 1993, p. 64; June, 1995, p. 32.
Saturday Evening Post, May, 1977.
Science, November 5, 1976.
Scientific American, December, 1976.
Social Service Review, March, 1963.
Time, January 10, 1969; December 19, 1969; February 1, 1971.
Times Literary Supplement, April 16, 1970; September 5, 1980; September 14, 1984.
U.S. News & World Report, April 4, 1966; March 7, 1977.
Wall Street Journal, May 23, 1968; January 10, 1969.
Washington Post, November 24, 1963; February 1, 1980.

*　　*　　*

FRISCH, Max (Rudolf) 1911-1991

PERSONAL: Born May 15, 1911, in Zurich-Hottingen, Switzerland; died of cancer, April 4, 1991, in Zurich, Switzerland; son of Franz Bruno (an architect) and Lina (Wildermuth) Frisch; married Gertrud Anna Constance von Meyenburg (an architecture student), July 30, 1942 (divorced, 1959); married Marianne Oellers, December, 1968 (divorced); children: (first marriage) Ursula, Hans Peter, Charlotte. *Education:* Attended University of Zurich, 1931-33; Federal Institute of Technology, Zurich, diploma in architecture, 1940.

CAREER: Freelance journalist for various Swiss and German newspapers, including *Neue Zuercher Zeitung* and *Frankfurter Zeitung,* beginning 1933; architect in Zurich, Switzerland, 1945-55; full-time writer, 1955-1991, *Military service:* Swiss Army, 1939-45, served as cannoneer and later as border guard on the Austrian and Italian frontiers.

MEMBER: Deutsche Akademie fuer Sprache und Dichtung, Akademie der Kuenste, PEN, American Academy and Institute of Arts and Letters (honorary member), American Academy of Arts and Sciences (honorary member), Comunita degli Scrittori.

AWARDS, HONORS: Conrad Ferdinand Meyer Prize, 1938; Rockefeller Foundation grant for drama, 1951; Georg Buechner Prize, German Academy of Language and Poetry, 1958; Literature Prize of the City of Zurich, 1958; Literature Prize of Northrhine-Westphalia, 1963; Prize of the City of Jerusalem, 1965; Grand Prize, Swiss Schiller Foundation, 1974; Peace Prize, German Book Trade, 1976; Commandeur de l'Ordre des Arts et des Lettres, 1985; Common Wealth Award, Modern Language Association of America, 1986; International Neustadt Prize for Literature, University of Oklahoma, 1987. Has received honorary doctorates from the City University of New York, 1982, Bard

College, Philipps University, Marburg, West Germany, and Technische Universitaet, Berlin.

WRITINGS:

NOVELS

Juerg Reinhart: Eine sommerliche Schicksalsfahrt, Deutsche Verlags-Anstalt, 1934, revised edition published as *J'adore ce qui me brule; oder, Die Schwierigen: Roman,* Atlantis (Zurich), 1943, 2nd revised edition published as *Die Schwierigen; oder, J'adore ce qui me brule,* Atlantis, 1957.

Antwort aus der Stille: Eine Erzaehlung aus den Bergen (title means "Answer Out of the Silence: A Tale from the Mountains"), Deutsche Verlags-Anstalt, 1937.

Bin; oder, Die Reise nach Peking (title means "Am; or, the Trip to Peking"), Atlantis, 1945.

Stiller: Roman, Suhrkamp (Frankfurt on the Main), 1954, translation by Michael Bullock published as *I'm Not Stiller,* Abelard, 1958, with a new foreword by Michael Bullock, Harcourt Brace, 1994.

Homo Faber: Ein Bericht, Suhrkamp, 1957, translation by Bullock published as *Homo Faber: A Report,* Abelard, 1959.

Meine Name sei Gantenbein, Suhrkamp, 1964, translation by Bullock published as *A Wilderness of Mirrors,* Methuen, 1965, Random House, 1966.

Montauk: Eine Erzaehlung, Suhrkamp, 1975, translation by Geoffrey Skelton published as *Montauk,* Harcourt, 1976.

Der Mensch erscheint im Holozaen: Eine Erzaehlung, Suhrkamp, 1979, translation by Skelton published as *Man in the Holocene: A Story,* Harcourt, 1980.

Blaubart: Eine Erzaehlung, Suhrkamp, 1982, translation by Skelton published as *Bluebeard,* Harcourt, 1984.

PLAYS

Nun singen sie wieder: Versuch eines Requiems (two-act; title means "Now They Sing Again: An Attempt at a Requiem"; first produced in Zurich at the Schauspielhaus, March 29, 1945), Schwabe (Switzerland), 1946, translation by David Lommen published as *Now They Sing Again* in *Contemporary German Theatre,* edited by Michael Roloff, Avon, 1972.

Santa Cruz: Eine Romanz (five-act; first produced at the Schauspielhaus, March 7, 1946), Suhrkamp, 1946.

Die chinesische Mauer: Eine Farce (also see below; first produced at the Schauspielhaus, October 10, 1946), Schwabe, 1947, 2nd revised edition, 1972, translation by James L. Rosenberg published as *The Chinese Wall,* Hill & Wang, 1961.

Als der Kriege zu Ende war: Schauspiel (also see below; title means "When the War Was Over"; first produced at the Schauspielhaus, January 8, 1948), Schwabe, 1949, edited by Stuart Friebert, Dodd, 1967.

Graf Oederland: Ein Spiel in Zehn Bildern (also see below; title means "Count Oederland: A Play in Ten Scenes"; first produced at the Schauspielhaus, February 10, 1951; produced in Washington, D.C., at Arena Stage as *A Public Prosecutor Is Sick of It All,* 1973), Suhrkamp, 1951, revised edition published as *Graf Oederland: Eine Moritat in zwoelf Bildern,* Suhrkamp, 1963, edited by George Salamon, Harcourt, 1966.

Don Juan; oder, die Liebe zur Geometrie: Eine Komoedie in fuenf Akten (also see below; title means "Don Juan; or, The Love of Geometry: A Comedy in Five Acts"; first produced at the Schauspielhaus, May 5, 1953), Suhrkamp, 1953.

Rip van Winkle: Hoerspiel (radio play; first produced in Germany, 1953), Reclam (Stuttgart), 1969.

Herr Biedermann und die Brandstifter: Hoerspiel (also see below; radio play; first produced in Germany, 1953; first stage adaptation produced as *Biedermann und die Brandstifter: Eine Lehrstueck ohne Lehre, mit einem Nachspiel* at the Schauspielhaus, March 29, 1958; produced in London as *The Fire Raisers,* 1961; produced at the Maidman Playhouse as *The Firebugs,* February, 1963), Suhrkamp, 1958, translation by Bullock published as *The Fire Raisers: A Morality without Moral, with an Afterpiece,* Methuen, 1962, translation by Mordecai Gorelick published as *The Firebugs: A Learning Play without a Lesson,* Hill & Wang, 1963.

Die grosse Wut des Philipp Hotz (also see below; one-act; first produced at the Schauspielhaus, March 29, 1958; produced at the Barbizon-Plaza Theatre as *The Great Fury of Philipp Hotz,* November, 1969), translation published as *Philipp Hotz's Fury* in *Esquire,* October, 1962.

Andorra: Stueck in zwoelf Bildern (also see below; one-act radio play; first broadcast in West Germany, 1959; stage adaptation first produced at the Schauspielhaus, November 2, 1961; produced on Broadway at the Biltmore Theatre, February 9, 1963), Suhrkamp, 1962, translation by Bullock published as *Andorra: A Play in Twelve Scenes,* Hill & Wang, 1964.

Three Plays (contains "The Fire Raisers," "Count Oederland," and "Andorra"), translation by Bullock, Methuen, 1962.

Zurich-Transit: Skizze eines Films (television play; first produced on German television, January, 1966), Suhrkamp, 1966.

Biografie: Ein Spiel (also see below; two-act; first produced at the Schauspielhaus, February 1, 1968), Suhrkamp, 1967, revised edition, 1968, translation by Bullock published as *Biography: A Game,* Hill & Wang, 1969.

Three Plays (contains *Don Juan; or, the Love of Geometry: A Comedy in Five Acts, The Great Rage of Philipp Hotz,* and *When the War Was Over*), translation by J. L. Rosenberg, Hill & Wang, 1967.

Four Plays: The Great Wall of China, Don Juan; or, the Love of Geometry, Philipp Hotz's Fury, Biography: a Game, translation by Bullock, Methuen (London), 1969.

Triptychon: Drei szenische Bilder, Suhrkamp, 1978, translation by Skelton published as *Triptych: Three Scenic Panels,* Harcourt, 1981.

Also author of plays *Stahl* (title means "Steel"), 1927, and *Judith,* 1948, and *Herr Quixote,* a radio play, 1955.

OTHER

Geschrieben im Grenzdienst 1939, [Germany], 1940.

Blaetter aus dem Brotsack (diary; title means "Pages from the Knapsack"), Atlantis (Zurich), 1940.

Marion und die Marionetten: Ein Fragment, Gryff-Presse (Basel, Switzerland), 1946.

Das Tagebuch mit Marion (title means "Diary with Marion"), Atlantis, 1947, revised and expanded version published as *Tagebuch, 1946-1949,* Droemer Knaur (Munich), 1950, translation by Skelton published as *Sketchbook, 1946-49,* Harcourt, 1977.

(Author of annotations) Robert S. Gessner, *Sieben Lithographien,* Huerlimann (Zurich), 1952.

(With Lucius Burckhardt and Markus Kutter) *Achtung, die Schweiz: Ein Gespraech ueber unsere Lage und ein Vorschlag zur Tat,* Handschin (Basel), 1956.

(Author of foreword) Markus Kutter and Lucius Burckhardt, *Wir selber bauen unsere Stadt: Ein Hinweis auf die Moeglichkeiten staatlicher Baupolitik,* Handschin (Basel), 1956.

(With Burckhardt and Kutter) *Die Neue Stadt: Beitraege zur Diskussion,* Handschin, 1956.

(Author of afterword) Bertold Brecht, *Drei Gedichten,* [Zurich], 1959.

(Contributor) Albin Zollinger, *Gesammelte Werke,* Volume 1, Atlantis (Zurich), 1961.

Ausgewaehlte Prosa, edited by Stanley Corngold, Suhrkamp, 1961, Harcourt, 1968.

Stuecke, two volumes, Suhrkamp, 1962.

(Author of texts with Kurt Hirschfeld and Oskar Waelterlin) Teo Otto, *Skizzen eines Buehnenbildners: 33 Zeichnungen,* Tschudy (St. Gallen, Switzerland), 1964.

(Contributor) Alexander J. Seiler, *Siamo italiani/Die Italiener: Gespraeche mit italienischen Arbeitern in der Schweiz,* EVZ Verlag (Zurich), 1965.

(Author of preface) Gody Suter, *Die grossen Staedte: Was sie zerstoert und was sie retten kann,* Luebbe (Bergisch Gladbach, West Germany), 1966.

Oeffentlichkeit als Partner (essays), Suhrkamp, 1967.

Erinnerungen an Brecht, Friedenauer (West Berlin), 1968.

Dramaturgisches: Ein Briefwechsel mit Walter Hoellerer, Literarisches Colloquium (West Berlin), 1969.

(Author of postscript) Andrei Sakharov, *Wie ich mir die Zukunft vorstelle: Gedanken ueber Fortschritt, friedliche Koexistenz und geistige Freiheit,* Diogenes (Zurich), 1969.

(With Rudolf Immig) *Der Mensch zwischen Selbstentfremdung und Selbstverwirklichung,* Calwer (Stuttgart), 1970.

Glueck: Eine Erzaehlung, Brunnenturm-Presse, 1971.

Wilhelm Tell fuer die Schule, Suhrkamp, 1971.

Tagebuch, 1966-71, Suhrkamp, 1972, translation by Skelton published as *Sketchbook, 1966-71,* Harcourt, 1974.

Dienstbuchlein, Suhrkamp, 1974.

Stich-Worte, Suhrkamp, 1975.

(With Hartmut von Hentig) *Zwei Reden zum Friedenspreis des Deutschen Buchhandels 1976,* Suhrkamp, 1976.

Gesammelte Werke in zeitlicher Folge, six volumes, Suhrkamp, 1976.

Frisch: Kritik, Thesen, Analysen, Francke (Bern, Switzerland), 1977.

Erzaehlende Prosa, 1939-1979, Volk und Welt (West Berlin), 1981.

Forderungen des Tages, Suhrkamp, 1983.

Also author of *Schweize ohne Armee? Ein Palavar* (title means "Switzerland without an Army? A Palaver"), 1989. Contributor to periodicals in West Germany and Switzerland, including *Neue Schweizer Rundschau, Der Spiegel,* and *Atlantis;* contributor to newspapers, including *Neue Zuercher Zeitung* and *Sueddeutsche Zeitung.*

SIDELIGHTS: Along with fellow Swiss dramatist Friedrich Duerrenmatt, Max Frisch "has been a major force in German drama for the generation since 1945," declares Arrigo Subiotto in *The German Theatre: A Symposium.* Best known for such works as *I'm Not Stiller* and *The Firebugs,* Frisch is esteemed as both a novelist and playwright. Winning numerous literary awards, including the Georg Buechner Prize and Neustadt International Prize, he was also a perennial candidate for the Pulitzer Prize for several years. His writing, characterized by its surrealistic style, "is a sort of poetry," remarks Joseph McLellan in the *Washington Post Book World,* "but a poetry of the mind rather than the senses—sparse and austere, with every detail chosen for its resonances." Several critics have commented on not only the remarkable consistency of this style, which *Dictionary of Literary Biography* contributor Wulf Koepke avers to be "discernable since the early 1940s," but also on Frisch's inventiveness in

expressing "a single theme: the near impossibility of living truthfully," concludes Sven Birkerts in his *New Republic* article.

As a student of German literature at the University of Zurich, Frisch admired such writers as Albin Zollinger and Gottfried Keller. His father's death, however, made it necessary for him to leave school to support himself and his mother. Becoming a freelance journalist for various German and Swiss newspapers, he traveled widely in Europe throughout the 1930s. During this time, Frisch also wrote fiction; but, as Koepke notes, he "grew increasingly disenchanted with his writing, and in 1937 he burned all his manuscripts." Opting for a more utilitarian career, he temporarily abandoned his writing goals to attend architecture classes at the Federal Institute of Technology in Zurich, where he received his diploma in 1940. However, he was not able to refrain totally from writing, and, while serving as a border guard in the Swiss army, he wrote *Juerg Reinhart: Eine sommerliche Schicksalsfahrt, Antwort aus der Stille: Eine Erzaehlung aus den Bergen, Blaetter aus dem Brotsack,* and *Bin; oder, die Reise nach Peking.*

These lesser-known works, considering they were written during the time of Hitler's Third Reich, "astound the reader by their absolutely apolitical character," observe Mona and Gerhard Knapp in *World Literature Today.* Frisch was by no means unconcerned with the war's effects, however. Characterized by *New York Times Book Review* contributor Richard Gilman as "politically liberal, a pacifist," the author "was very much aware of his own unique position regarding the war; as a Swiss, apparently unaffected by the conflict surrounding his own country, Frisch could only attempt to present the lessons of the war from a bipartisan point of view," observes Manfred Jurgensen in *Perspectives on Max Frisch.* This is precisely what the dramatist attempts to do in his first plays written after the war.

Invited in 1945 by the director of the Zurich Schauspielhaus, Kurt Hirschfield, to write plays for his theater, the author's *Nun singen sie wieder: Versuch eines Requiems* ("Now They Sing Again: An Attempt at a Requiem") explores prejudice by placing characters from both the Axis and Ally countries into the world of the afterlife, where they become equals. In his next play about the war, *Als der Krieg zu Ende war* ("When the War Was Over"), Frisch writes of a German woman who falls in love with a Russian soldier, demonstrating, as Carol Petersen says in his book, *Max Frisch,* "that by true human feelings all kinds of prejudices can and must be overcome."

However, "Frisch has no real hope that [such social] evils can be remedied," remarks Koepke, and his plays and novels are therefore largely pessimistic. For example, in *The Theater of Protest and Paradox: Developments in the Avant-Garde Drama,* George Wellwarth asserts that "Frisch's two best plays, [*The Chinese Wall*] and [*The Firebugs: A Learning Play without a Lesson*], are consciously foredoomed pleas for a better world. The irony implicit in them no longer sounds like the scornful laughter of the gods we hear in Duerrenmatt; it sounds like the self-reproaching wailing of the damned." Underlying this pessimism is, as Jurgensen remarks, Frisch's frustration with "man's incorrigible selfishness and his inability or unwillingness to learn, to change, to think dynamically." According to Petersen, the lesson of *The Chinese Wall* is therefore that "freedom is only in the realm of the spirit; for, in the real world, the possessors of power end up by doing the same things over and over again."

Approaching this theme from another angle in what *World Literature Today* contributor Adolf Muschg calls Frisch's "most successful play internationally," *The Firebugs* creates a character who, instead of trying to prevent disaster, actually fosters it. In this play, a weak-willed hair lotion manufacturer named Gottlieb Biedermann is unable to admit to himself the true intentions of two arsonists, and knowingly allows them to enter and destroy his home. Several interpretations of the political implications of this play have been proposed, as Subiotto explains: "[*The Firebugs*] can be seen as a metaphor of Hitler's legitimate 'seizure of power' or of the way in which the nations of the world are playing with nuclear bombs as deterrents. . . . It also offers a 'model' of liberal societies allowing freedom of action, in the name of liberty, to extremist elements in their midst (whether of right or left) whose avowed aim is to destroy those societies." According to Koepke, the author endorses the interpretation that *The Firebugs* is about "the weakness of capitalist society." What is also significant about *The Firebugs* is how it further develops Frisch's "theme of the true identity behind an artificial mask, the destruction of false conventions, and the feeling of the self from deeply ingrained prejudices," writes Alex Natan in his introduction to *German Men of Letters: Twelve Literary Essays*.

According to the Knapps, *Andorra: A Play in Twelve Scenes*, along with *The Firebugs*, "catapulted [Frisch] to international theatrical prominence." *Andorra* revolves around the theme of anti-semitism to illustrate the imposition of images. The story concerns the deception of a schoolteacher, living in fictional Andorra, who hides the identity of his illegitimate son Andri by telling his neighbors that Andri is a Jewish boy whom he has saved from the oppressive "Blacks." With the increasing strength of the Blacks, the Andorrans begin to impose more and more stereotypes on Andri until he eventually accepts himself as Jewish. Even when he learns the truth about who he really is, however, Andri is unable to shed this false identity; and, when the Blacks invade Andorra, he chooses to die under their persecution.

The struggle for self-truth in a world which prefers the stereotypes and simplicity of the image to an authentic existence is also evident in *Don Juan; or, the Love of Geometry*. Here, in what Petersen calls "an uncommonly clever, wittily pointed play, which offers a broad view of the relativity of all human sentiment," Frisch twists the legend of Don Juan by describing Juan as a lover of geometry who is forced into the role of philanderer by the demands and expectations of society. He actually prefers the logic and precision of geometry to the capricious ways of the women who surround him. Compared to the traditional version of Don Juan, critics like Petersen believe that "the twentieth-century man, inclined to rationalism, can more readily recognize himself in Frisch's Don Juan."

The three novels that deal with the theme of identity on its most introspective, individual level are *I'm Not Stiller*, *Homo Faber: A Report*, and *A Wilderness of Mirrors*. Along with a number of other critics, Charles Hoffman, a contributor to *The Contemporary Novel in German: A Symposium*, feels that with these books, Frisch "has created three of the most important novels of [the mid-nineteenth century]. Taken together, these books are perhaps the most meaningful [in] recent German writing." The years in which they were written, from 1954 to 1964, were also "of singular importance in establishing Frisch's international reputation," add the Knapps.

Like *Don Juan*, *Homo Faber* appeals to the modern man, but on a much more serious note. Submerging himself in a love of technology over actual human emotions, Frisch's protagonist, engineer Walter Faber, unwittingly enters into a relationship with a woman whom he later discovers to be his illegitimate daughter. Because he cannot face the emotions that result from this discovery, Faber "is punished for his 'blindness' by her loss" when she dies of a snake bite, explain the Knapps. In this description of a man who becomes alienated from his own identity through his reverence for modern technology, "Frisch has captured that essential anguish of modern man which we find in the best of Camus," asserts Richard Plant in *Spectator*. But *Homo Faber* is also one of Frisch's more optimistic works because, notes Koepke, in the "last period of his life, characterized by a growing awareness of human existence, [Faber] not only comes into contact with his own past failures and their long-term consequences but also begins to see the truth of nontechnological realities."

I'm Not Stiller, which Michael Butler in his *The Novels of Max Frisch* says "established [for Frisch] a claim to major status in the history of the novel in post-war Germany and Switzerland," is his most critically acclaimed novel concerning the theme of escape from the self. Told mostly through the point-of-view of the sculptor Anatol Stiller, *I'm Not Stiller* is the story of a man who assumes the identity of an American named White in an effort to flee his feelings of failure as an artist, husband, and lover. Confronted with his true identity by the Swiss government, which has accused him of having worked with the Communists, Stiller is forced to face his true identity, and the resulting personal struggle that Frisch chronicles in Stiller's journal, "consumes not only all his own moral and artistic energy," say the Knapps, "but also that of his frail wife Julika, who soon dies." The last section of *I'm Not Stiller* is told by Stiller's prosecutor, who moralizes: "As long as a person does not accept himself, he will always have the fear of being misunderstood and misconstrued by his environment." Although some critics like Plant feel that the novel's "provocative idea [has] been spoiled . . . by excessive detail and overdecoration," a number of others think that *I'm Not Stiller* is one of Frisch's best works. Butler opines, for example, that in *I'm Not Stiller* "Frisch suddenly produced a narrative work of unsuspected depth and fascination."

After *Montauk* the author's books betray his awareness of his advancing years. Koepke explains: "While in *Montauk* numerous quotes from Frisch's earlier works indicate self-acceptance, the past has become threatening in the last works. Old age and death are dominant themes, but even more prevalent may be regret of the past—one's own and that of the human race." For example, Jurgensen states that in *Triptychon* "Frisch shows . . . how all acts, thoughts, and misunderstandings are repeated in death; death becomes the stage for re-enacting our lives. The finality does not lie in death but in our unthinking life, in our inability to do anything other than repeat ourselves." "*Triptychon*'s real subject is a social death," Jurgensen concludes, "in fact: the death of society."

Jurgensen also notes that this pessimistic theme is similar to that in *The Firebugs*; and his next book, *Man in the Holocene*, also resembles *The Firebugs* in its "unsettling notion that some rational, well-meaning force is actually *willing* catastrophe," according to *Nation* reviewer Arthur Sainer. In what McLellan asserts to be "a small book but a major achievement," *Man in the Holocene* relates the last few days in the life of a ageing man named Geiser who becomes trapped in his alpine valley home by a landslide. Battling against his own encroaching senility and a dwindling food supply, Geiser ironically passes up the chance to escape his isolation, eventually suffering from a stroke before he finally dies. *Man in the Holocene*, like *Triptychon*, reiterates

Frisch's suspicion of the transience of the human race. McLellan phrases it this way: In *Man in the Holocene* "the old man's life itself is being eroded, as are all men's lives—as is, perhaps, the life of the entire species."

Frisch returns to his more familiar theme of identity in *Bluebeard*. But, avers Sven Birkerts in a *New Republic* review, the author "is not so much returning to earlier themes as he is bringing the preoccupations of a lifetime under a more calculated and intense pressure." As in *I'm Not Stiller*, the story's events are related by the protagonist, Dr. Schaad, through his memories about his trial. This time, the main character is accused of being a wife murderer, like the infamous Bluebeard; and this role is forced upon him to the point where he eventually assimilates it. Marga I. Weigel notes the similarity between Dr. Schaad's identity crisis and that of another Frisch character. Writing in *World Literature Today*, Weigel observes: "[Dr. Schaad] works himself more and more into the role of the murderer. He is now convinced he is the person others consider him to be—an attitude identical to the reaction of Andri in *Andorra*."

BIOGRAPHICAL/CRITICAL SOURCES:

BOOKS

Butler, Michael, *The Novels of Max Frisch*, Oswald Wolff, 1976.
Contemporary Literary Criticism, Gale (Detroit), Volume 3, 1975; Volume 9, 1978; Volume 14, 1980; Volume 18, 1981; Volume 32, 1985; Volume 44, 1987.
Daemmrich, Horst S., and Diether H. Haenicke, *The Challenge of German Literature*, Wayne State University Press, 1971.
Dictionary of Literary Biography, Volume 69: *Contemporary German Fiction Writers*, Gale, 1988.
Esslin, Martin, *Reflections: Essays on Modern Theatre*, Doubleday, 1969.
Garten, Hugh Frederic, *Modern German Drama*, Methuen, 1959.
Hayman, Ronald, *The German Theatre: A Symposium*, Barnes & Noble, 1975.
Heitner, Robert R., editor, *The Contemporary Novel in German: A Symposium*, University of Texas Press, 1967.
Lumley, Frederick, *New Trends in 20th Century Drama*, Oxford University Press, 1967.
Natan, Alex, editor, *German Men of Letters: Twelve Literary Essays*, Volume 3, Oswald Wolff, 1968.
Petersen, Carol, *Max Frisch*, translated by Charlotte La Rue, Ungar, 1972.
Probst, Gerhard F., and Jay F. Bodine, editors, *Perspectives on Max Frisch*, University Press of Kentucky, 1982.
Weber, Brom, editor, *Sense and Sensibility in Twentieth-Century Writing*, Southern Illinois University Press, 1970.
Weisstein, Ulrich, *Max Frisch*, Twayne, 1967.
Wellwarth, George, *The Theater of Protest and Paradox: Developments in the Avant-Garde Drama*, New York University Press, 1964.
White, Alfred D., *Max Frisch, the Reluctant Modernist*, E. Mellen Press, 1995.

PERIODICALS

Biography News, June, 1974.
Books Abroad, winter, 1968.
Chicago Sun-Times, May 5, 1974.
Chicago Tribune Book World, September 28, 1980.
Christian Science Monitor, February 12, 1968.
Forum for Modern Language Studies, July, 1982.
German Life and Letters, October, 1974.
Los Angeles Times Book Review, August 10, 1980.

Modern Drama, December, 1975.
Nation, July 3, 1976; September 20, 1980.
New Republic, July 11, 1983.
New Statesman, August 6, 1982.
New Yorker, May 24, 1976; July 11, 1977.
New York Review of Books, September 24, 1981.
New York Times, July 2, 1968; November 27, 1969; May 17, 1970; May 22, 1980.
New York Times Book Review, February 20, 1966; April 28, 1974; May 16, 1976; May 27, 1976; April 3, 1977; March 19, 1978; May 11, 1980; June 22, 1980; July 10, 1983; September 29, 1983.
Observer, July 25, 1982; March 13, 1983.
Saturday Review, April 12, 1958; May 7, 1960; February 26, 1966.
Spectator, April 11, 1958; May 7, 1960.
Times (London), February 24, 1983.
Times Literary Supplement, November 11, 1965; January 25, 1968; September 29, 1972; September 12, 1980; June 4, 1982; July 30, 1982.
Tulane Drama Review, March, 1962.
Village Voice, July 11, 1968.
Washington Post Book World, July 18, 1976; July 27, 1980; July 17, 1983.
World Literature Today, spring, 1977; spring, 1979; spring 1983; autumn, 1984; autumn, 1986.

*   *   *

FROST, Robert (Lee) 1874-1963

PERSONAL: Born March 26, 1874, in San Francisco, CA; died January 29, 1963, in Boston, MA; son of William Prescott (a newspaper reporter and editor) and Isabel (a teacher; maiden name, Moodie) Frost; married Elinor Miriam White, December 19, 1895 (died, 1938); children: Elliott (deceased), Lesley (daughter), Carol (son; deceased), Irma, Marjorie (deceased), Elinor Bettina (deceased). *Education:* Attended Dartmouth College, 1892, and Harvard University, 1897-99.

CAREER: Poet. Held various jobs between college studies, including bobbin boy in a Massachusetts mill, cobbler, editor of a country newspaper, schoolteacher, and farmer. Lived in England, 1912-15. Tufts College, Medford, MA, Phi Beta Kappa poet, 1915 and 1940; Amherst College, Amherst, MA, professor of English and poet-in-residence, 1916-20, 1923-25, and 1926-28; Harvard University, Cambridge, MA, Phi Beta Kappa poet, 1916 and 1941; Middlebury College, Middlebury, VT, co-founder of the Bread-Loaf School and Conference of English, 1920, annual lecturer, beginning 1920; University of Michigan, Ann Arbor, professor and poet-in-residence, 1921-23, fellow in letters, 1925-26; Columbia University, New York City, Phi Beta Kappa poet, 1932; Yale University, New Haven, CT, associate fellow, beginning 1933; Harvard University, Charles Eliot Norton Professor of Poetry, 1936, board overseer, 1938-39, Ralph Waldo Emerson Fellow, 1939-41, honorary fellow, 1942-43; associate of Adams House; fellow in American civilization, 1941-42; Dartmouth College, Hanover, NH, George Ticknor Fellow in Humanities, 1943-49, visiting lecturer.

MEMBER: International PEN, National Institute of Arts and Letters, American Academy of Arts and Letters, American Philosophical Society.

AWARDS, HONORS: Levinson Prize, *Poetry* magazine, 1922; Pulitzer Prize for poetry, 1924, for *New Hampshire,* 1931, for *Collected Poems,* 1937, for *A Further Range,* and 1943, for *A Witness Tree;* Golden Rose Trophy, New England Poetry Club, 1928; Russell Loines Prize for poetry, National Institute of Arts and Letters, 1931; Mark Twain medal, 1937; Gold Medal of the National Institute of Arts and Letters, 1939; Gold Medal of the Poetry Society of America, 1941 and 1958; Gold Medal, Limited Editions Club, 1949; unanimous resolution in his honor and gold medal from the U.S. Senate, March 24, 1950; American Academy of Poets Award, 1953; Medal of Honor, New York University, 1956; Huntington Hartford Foundation Award, 1958; Emerson-Thoreau Medal, American Academy of Arts and Sciences, 1958; participated in President John F. Kennedy's inauguration ceremonies, 1961, by reading his poems "Dedication" and "The Gift Outright"; Congressional Gold Medal, 1962; Edward MacDowell Medal, 1962; Bollingen Prize in Poetry, 1963; inducted into American Poet's Corner at Cathedral of St. John the Divine, 1986. Chosen poet laureate of Vermont by the State League of Women's Clubs; more than forty honorary degrees from colleges and universities, including Oxford and Cambridge Universities, Amherst College, and the University of Michigan.

WRITINGS:

POETRY

Twilight, [Lawrence, MA], 1894.
A Boy's Will, D. Nutt, 1913, Holt, 1915.
North of Boston, D. Nutt, 1914, Holt, 1915.
Mountain Interval, Holt, 1916.
New Hampshire, Holt, 1923.
Selected Poems, Holt, 1923.
Several Short Poems, Holt, 1924.
West-Running Brook, Holt, 1928.
Selected Poems, Holt, 1928.
The Lovely Shall Be Choosers, Random House, 1929.
The Lone Striker, Knopf, 1933.
Two Tramps in Mud-Time, Holt, 1934.
The Gold Hesperidee, Bibliophile Press, 1935.
Three Poems, Baker Library Press, 1935.
A Further Range, Holt, 1936.
From Snow to Snow, Holt, 1936.
A Witness Tree, Holt, 1942.
A Masque of Reason (verse drama), Holt, 1942.
Steeple Bush, Holt, 1947.
A Masque of Mercy (verse drama), Holt, 1947.
Greece, Black Rose Press, 1948.
Hard Not to Be King, House of Books, 1951.
Aforesaid, Holt, 1954.
The Gift Outright, Holt, 1961.
"Dedication" and "The Gift Outright" (poems read at the presidential inaugural, 1961; published with the inaugural address of J. F. Kennedy), Spiral Press, 1961.
In the Clearing, Holt, 1962.
Stopping by Woods on a Snowy Evening, Dutton, 1978.
Early Poems, Crown, 1981.
A Swinger of Birches: Poems of Robert Frost for Young People (with audiocassette), Stemmer House, 1982.
Spring Pools, Lime Rock Press, 1983.
Birches, illustrated by Ed Young, Holt, 1988.
The Runaway (juvenile poetry), illustrated by Glenna Lang, Godine (Boston), 1996.

Also author of *And All We Call American,* 1958.

POEMS ISSUED AS CHRISTMAS GREETINGS

Christmas Trees, Spiral Press, 1929.
Neither Out Far Nor In Deep, Holt, 1935.
Everybody's Sanity, [Los Angeles], 1936.
To a Young Wretch, Spiral Press, 1937.
Triple Plate, Spiral Press, 1939.
Our Hold on the Planet, Holt, 1940.
An Unstamped Letter in Our Rural Letter Box, Spiral Press, 1944.
On Making Certain Anything Has Happened, Spiral Press, 1945.
One Step Backward Taken, Spiral Press, 1947.
Closed for Good, Spiral Press, 1948.
On a Tree Fallen Across the Road to Hear Us Talk, Spiral Press, 1949.
Doom to Bloom, Holt, 1950.
A Cabin in the Clearing, Spiral Press, 1951.
Does No One but Me at All Ever Feel This Way in the Least, Spiral Press, 1952.
One More Brevity, Holt, 1953.
From a Milkweed Pod, Holt, 1954.
Some Science Fiction, Spiral Press, 1955.
Kitty Hawk, 1894, Holt, 1956.
My Objection to Being Stepped On, Holt, 1957.
Away, Spiral Press, 1958.
A-Wishing Well, Spiral Press, 1959.
Accidentally on Purpose, Holt, 1960.
The Woodpile, Spiral Press, 1961.
The Prophets Really Prophesy as Mystics, the Commentators Merely by Statistics, Spiral Press, 1962.
The Constant Symbol, [New York], 1962.

COLLECTIONS

Collected Poems of Robert Frost, Holt, 1930, new edition, 1939.
Selected Poems, Holt, 1934.
Come In, and Other Poems, edited by Louis Untermeyer, Holt, 1943, enlarged edition published as *The Road Not Taken: An Introduction to Robert Frost,* reprinted as *The Pocket Book of Robert Frost's Poems,* Pocket Books, 1956.
The Poems of Robert Frost, Modern Library, 1946.
You Come Too: Favorite Poems for Young Readers, Holt, 1959.
A Remembrance Collection of New Poems by Robert Frost, Holt, 1959.
Poems, Washington Square Press, 1961.
Longer Poems: The Death of the Hired Man, Holt, 1966.
Selected Prose, edited by Hyde Cox and Edward Connery Lathem, Holt, 1966.
Complete Poems of Robert Frost, Holt, 1968.
The Poetry of Robert Frost, edited by Lathem, Holt, 1969.
Robert Frost: Poetry and Prose, edited by Lawrence Thompson and Lathem, Holt, 1972.
Selected Poems, edited by Ian Hamilton, Penguin, 1973.
Collected Poems, Plays, and Prose, Library of America (New York), 1995.
Early Frost: The First Three Books, Ecco (Hopewell, NJ), 1996.
Edward Connery Lathem, editor, *Versed in Country Things,* Little, Brown, 1996.

LETTERS

The Letters of Robert Frost to Louis Untermeyer, Holt, 1963.
Selected Letters, edited by Thompson, Holt, 1964.

OTHER

A Way Out: A One-Act Play, Harbor Press, 1929.
The Cow's in the Corn: A One-Act Irish Play in Rhyme, Slide Mountain Press, 1929.

(Contributor) John Holmes, editor, *Writing Poetry,* Writer, Inc., 1960.

(Contributor) Milton R. Konvitz and Stephen E. Whicher, editors, *Emerson,* Prentice-Hall, 1962.

Robert Frost on "Extravagance" (the text of Frost's last college lecture, Dartmouth College, November 27, 1962), [Hanover, N.H.], 1963.

Robert Frost: A Living Voice (contains speeches by Frost), edited by Reginald Cook, University of Massachusetts Press, 1974.

(With Caroline Ford) *The Less Travelled Road,* Bern Porter, 1982.

Stories for Lesley, edited by Roger D. Sell, University Press of Virginia, 1984.

Frost's papers are collected at the libraries of the University of Virginia, Amherst College, and Dartmouth College, and the Huntington Library in San Marino, California.

SIDELIGHTS: Robert Frost holds a unique position in American letters. "Though his career fully spans the modern period and though it is impossible to speak of him as anything other than a modern poet," writes James M. Cox in *Robert Frost: A Collection of Critical Essays,* "it is difficult to place him in the main tradition of modern poetry." In a sense, Frost stands at the crossroads of nineteenth-century American poetry and modernism, for in his verse may be found the culmination of many nineteenth-century tendencies and traditions as well as parallels to the works of his twentieth-century contemporaries. Taking his symbols from the public domain, Frost developed, as many critics note, an original, modern idiom and a sense of directness and economy that reflect the imagism of Ezra Pound and Amy Lowell. On the other hand, as Leonard Unger and William Van O'Connor point out in *Poems for Study,* "Frost's poetry, unlike that of such contemporaries as Eliot, Stevens, and the later Yeats, shows no marked departure from the poetic practices of the nineteenth century." Although he avoids traditional verse forms and only uses rhyme erratically, Frost is not an innovator and his technique is never experimental.

Critics frequently point out that Frost complicated his problem and enriched his style by setting traditional meters against the natural rhythms of speech. Drawing his language primarily from the vernacular, he avoided artificial poetic diction by employing the accent of a soft-spoken New Englander. In *The Function of Criticism,* Yvor Winters faulted Frost for his "endeavor to make his style approximate as closely as possible the style of conversation." But what Frost achieved in his poetry was much more complex than a mere imitation of the New England farmer idiom. He wanted to restore to literature the "sentence sounds that underlie the words," the "vocal gesture" that enhances meaning. That is, he felt the poet's ear must be sensitive to the voice in order to capture with the written word the significance of sound in the spoken word. "The Death of the Hired Man," for instance, consists almost entirely of dialogue between Mary and Warren, her farmer-husband, but critics have observed that in this poem Frost takes the prosaic patterns of their speech and makes them lyrical. To Ezra Pound "The Death of the Hired Man" represented Frost at his best—when he "dared to write . . . in the natural speech of New England; in natural spoken speech, which is very different from the 'natural' speech of the newspapers, and of many professors."

Frost's use of New England dialect is only one aspect of his often discussed regionalism. Within New England, his particular focus was on New Hampshire, which he called "one of the two best states in the Union," the other being Vermont. In an essay entitled "Robert Frost and New England: A Revaluation," W. G.

O'Donnell noted how from the start, in *A Boy's Will,* "Frost had already decided to give his writing a local habitation and a New England name, to root his art in the soil that he had worked with his own hands." Reviewing *North of Boston* in the *New Republic,* Amy Lowell wrote, "Not only is his work New England in subject, it is so in technique. . . Mr. Frost has reproduced both people and scenery with a vividness which is extraordinary." Many other critics have lauded Frost's ability to realistically evoke the New England landscape; they point out that one can visualize an orchard in "After Apple-Picking" or imagine spring in a farmyard in "Two Tramps in Mud Time." In this "ability to portray the local truth in nature," O'Donnell claims, Frost has no peer. The same ability prompted Pound to declare, "I know more of farm life than I did before I had read his poems. That means I know more of 'Life.' "

The austere and tragic view of life that emerges in so many of Frost's poems is modulated by his metaphysical use of detail. As Frost portrays him, man might be alone in an ultimately indifferent universe, but he may nevertheless look to the natural world for metaphors of his own condition. Thus, in his search for meaning in the modern world, Frost focuses on those moments when the seen and the unseen, the tangible and the spiritual intersect. John T. Napier calls this Frost's ability "to find the ordinary a matrix for the extraordinary." In this respect, he is often compared with Emily Dickinson and Ralph Waldo Emerson, in whose poetry, too, a simple fact, object, person, or event will be transfigured and take on greater mystery or significance. The poem "Birches" is an example: it contains the image of slender trees bent to the ground—temporarily by a boy's swinging on them or permanently by an ice-storm. But as the poem unfolds, it becomes clear that the speaker is concerned not only with child's play and natural phenomena, but also with the point at which physical and spiritual reality merge.

Such symbolic import of mundane facts informs many of Frost's poems, and in "Education by Poetry" he explained: "Poetry begins in trivial metaphors, pretty metaphors, 'grace' metaphors, and goes on to the profoundest thinking that we have. Poetry provides the one permissible way of saying one thing and meaning another. . . . Unless you are at home in the metaphor, unless you have had your proper poetical education in the metaphor, you are not safe anywhere."

Frost's own poetical education began in San Francisco where he was born in 1874, but he found his place of safety in New England when his family moved to Lawrence, Massachusetts, in 1884 following his father's death. The move was actually a return, for Frost's ancestors were originally New Englanders. The region must have been particularly conducive to the writing of poetry because within the next five years Frost had made up his mind to be a poet. In fact, he graduated from Lawrence High School, in 1892, as class poet (he also shared the honor of co-valedictorian with his wife-to-be Elinor White); and two years later, the *New York Independent* accepted his poem entitled "My Butterfly," launching his status as a professional poet with a check for $15.00.

Since 1915 Frost's position in American letters has been firmly rooted; in the years before his death he came to be considered the unofficial poet laureate of the United States. On his seventy-fifth birthday, the U.S. Senate passed a resolution in his honor which said, "His poems have helped to guide American thought and humor and wisdom, setting forth to our minds a reliable representation of ourselves and of all men." In 1955, the State of

Vermont named a mountain after him in Ripton, the town of his legal residence; and at the presidential inauguration of John F. Kennedy in 1961, Frost was given the unprecedented honor of being asked to read a poem, "The Gift Outright," which he wrote for the occasion.

Though Frost allied himself with no literary school or movement, the imagists helped at the start to promote his American reputation. *Poetry: A Magazine of Verse* published his work before others began to clamor for it. It also published a review by Ezra Pound of the British edition of *A Boy's Will,* which Pound said "has the tang of the New Hampshire woods, and it has just this utter sincerity. It is not post-Miltonic or post-Swinburnian or post Kiplonian. This man has the good sense to speak naturally and to paint the thing, the thing as he sees it." Amy Lowell reviewed *North of Boston* in the *New Republic,* and she, too, sang Frost's praises: "He writes in classic metres in a way to set the teeth of all the poets of the older schools on edge; and he writes in classic metres, and uses inversions and cliches whenever he pleases, those devices so abhorred by the newest generation. He goes his own way, regardless of anyone else's rules, and the result is a book of unusual power and sincerity." In these first two volumes, Frost introduced not only his affection for New England themes and his unique blend of traditional meters and colloquialism, but also his use of dramatic monologues and dialogues. "Mending Wall," the leading poem in *North of Boston,* describes the friendly argument between the speaker and his neighbor as they walk along their common wall replacing fallen stones; their differing attitudes toward "boundaries" offer symbolic significance typical of the poems in these early collections.

Mountain Interval marked Frost's turn to another kind of poem, a brief meditation sparked by an object, person or event. Like the monologues and dialogues, these short pieces have a dramatic quality. "Birches," discussed above, is an example, as is "The Road Not Taken," in which a fork in a woodland path transcends the specific. The distinction of this volume, the *Boston Transcript* said, "is that Mr. Frost takes the lyricism of *A Boy's Will* and plays a deeper music and gives a more intricate variety of experience."

Several new qualities emerged in Frost's work with the appearance of *New Hampshire,* particularly a new self-consciousness and willingness to speak of himself and his art. The volume, for which Frost won his first Pulitzer Prize, "pretends to be nothing but a long poem with notes and grace notes," as Louis Untermeyer described it. The title poem, approximately fourteen pages long, is a "rambling tribute" to Frost's favorite state and "is starred and dotted with scientific numerals in the manner of the most profound treatise." Thus, a footnote at the end of a line of poetry will refer the reader to another poem seemingly inserted to merely reinforce the text of "New Hampshire." Some of these poems are in the form of epigrams, which appear for the first time in Frost's work. "Fire and Ice," for example, one of the better known epigrams, speculates on the means by which the world will end. Frost's most famous and, according to J. McBride Dabbs, most perfect lyric, "Stopping by Woods on a Snowy Evening," is also included in this collection; conveying "the insistent whisper of death at the heart of life," the poem portrays a speaker who stops his sleigh in the midst of a snowy woods only to be called from the inviting gloom by the recollection of practical duties. Frost himself said of this poem that it is the kind he'd like to print on one page followed with "forty pages of footnotes."

West-Running Brook, Frost's fifth book of poems, is divided into six sections, one of which is taken up entirely by the title poem. This poem refers to a brook which perversely flows west instead of east to the Atlantic like all other brooks. A comparison is set up between the brook and the poem's speaker who trusts himself to go by "contraries"; further rebellious elements exemplified by the brook give expression to an eccentric individualism, Frost's stoic theme of resistance and self-realization. Reviewing the collection in the *New York Herald Tribune Books,* Babette Deutsch wrote: "The courage that is bred by a dark sense of Fate, the tenderness that broods over mankind in all its blindness and absurdity, the vision that comes to rest as fully on kitchen smoke and lapsing snow as on mountains and stars—these are his, and in his seemingly casual poetry, he quietly makes them ours."

A Further Range, which earned Frost another Pulitzer Prize and was a Book-of-the-Month Club selection, contains two groups of poems subtitled "Taken Doubly" and "Taken Singly." In the first, and more interesting, of these groups, the poems are somewhat didactic, though there are humorous and satiric pieces as well. Included here is "Two Tramps in Mud Time," which opens with the story of two itinerant lumbermen who offer to cut the speaker's wood for pay; the poem then develops into a sermon on the relationship between work and play, vocation and avocation, preaching the necessity to unite them. Of the entire volume, William Rose Benet wrote, "It is better worth reading than nine-tenths of the books that will come your way this year. In a time when all kinds of insanity are assailing the nations it is good to listen to this quiet humor, even about a hen, a hornet, or Square Matthew. . . . And if anybody should ask me why I still believe in my land, I have only to put this book in his hand and answer, 'Well—here is a man of my country.'"

Most critics acknowledge that Frost's poetry in the forties and fifties grew more and more abstract, cryptic, and even sententious, so it is generally on the basis of his earlier work that he is judged. His political conservatism and religious faith, hitherto informed by skepticism and local color, became more and more the guiding principles of his work. He had been, as Randall Jarrell points out, "a very odd and very radical radical when young" yet became "sometimes callously and unimaginatively conservative" in his old age. He had become a public figure, and in the years before his death, much of his poetry was written from this stance.

Reviewing *A Witness Tree* in *Books,* Wilbert Snow noted a few poems "which have a right to stand with the best things he has written": "Come In," "The Silken Tent," and "Carpe Diem" especially. Yet Snow went on: "Some of the poems here are little more than rhymed fancies; others lack the bullet-like unity of structure to be found in *North of Boston.*" On the other hand, Stephen Vincent Benet felt that Frost had "never written any better poems than some of those in this book." Similarly, critics were let down by *In the Clearing.* One wrote, "Although this reviewer considers Robert Frost to be the foremost contemporary U.S. poet, he regretfully must state that most of the poems in this new volume are disappointing. . . . [They] often are closer to jingles than to the memorable poetry we associate with his name." Another maintained that "the bulk of the book consists of poems of 'philosophic talk.' Whether you like them or not depends mostly on whether you share the 'philosophy.'"

Indeed, many readers do share Frost's philosophy, and still others who do not nevertheless continue to find delight and significance in his large body of poetry. In October, 1963, President John F. Kennedy delivered a speech at the dedication of the Robert Frost

Library in Amherst, Massachusetts. "In honoring Robert Frost," the President said, "we therefore can pay honor to the deepest source of our national strength. That strength takes many forms and the most obvious forms are not always the most significant. . . . Our national strength matters; but the spirit which informs and controls our strength matters just as much. This was the special significance of Robert Frost." The poet would probably have been pleased by such recognition, for he had said once, in an interview with Harvey Breit: "One thing I care about, and wish young people could care about, is taking poetry as the first form of understanding. If poetry isn't understanding all, the whole world, then it isn't worth anything."

BIOGRAPHICAL/CRITICAL SOURCES:

BOOKS

Breit, Harvey, *The Writer Observed,* World Publishing, 1956.
Concise Dictionary of American Literary Biography: The Twenties, 1917-1929, Gale (Detroit), 1989.
Contemporary Literary Criticism, Gale, Volume 1, 1973; Volume 3, 1975; Volume 4, 1975; Volume 9, 1978; Volume 10, 1979; Volume 13, 1980; Volume 15, 1980; Volume 26, 1983; Volume 34, 1985; Volume 44, 1987.
Cox, James M., *Robert Frost: A Collection of Critical Essays,* Prentice-Hall, 1962.
Cramer, Jefferey S., *Robert Frost among His Poems: A Literary Companion to the Poet's Own Biographical Contexts and Associations,* McFarland (Jefferson, NC), 1996.
Dictionary of Literary Biography, Volume 54: *American Poets, 1880-1945, Third Series,* Gale, 1987.
Dodd, Loring Holmes, *Celebrities at Our Hearthside,* Dresser, 1959.
Doyle, John R., Jr., *Poetry of Robert Frost: An Analysis,* Hallier, 1965.
Evans, William R., editor, *Robert Frost and Sidney Cox: Forty Years of Friendship,* University Press of New England, 1981.
Faggen, Robert, *Robert Frost and the Challenge of Darwin,* University of Michigan Press, 1997.
Fleissner, Robert F., *Frost's Road Taken,* Peter Lang (New York), 1996.
Francis, Lesley Lee, *The Frost Family's Adventure in Poetry: Sheer Morning Gladness at the Brim,* University of Missouri Press (Columbia), 1994.
Frost, Lesley, *New Hampshire's Child: Derry Journals of Lesley Frost,* State University of New York Press, 1969.
Hall, Donald, *Remembering Poets,* Hater, 1977.
Ingebretsen, Ed, *Robert Frost: Star and a Stone Boat: Aspects of a Grammar of Belief,* International Scholars Publications (San Francisco), 1994.
Isaacs, Emily Elizabeth, *Introduction to Robert Frost,* A. Swallow, 1962.
Jarrell, Randall, *Poetry and the Age,* Vintage, 1955.
Kearns, Katherine, *Robert Frost and a Poetics of Appetite,* Cambridge University Press (Cambridge, England), 1994.
Lentriccia, Frank, *Robert Frost: Modern Poetics and the Landscapes of Self,* Duke University Press, 1975.
Maxson, H.A., *On the Sonnets of Robert Frost,* McFarland and Co., 1997.
Mertins, Marshall Louis and Esther Mertins, *Intervals of Robert Frost: A Critical Bibliography,* University of California Press, 1947.
Meyers, Jeffrey, *Robert Frost: A Biography,* Houghton Mifflin (Boston), 1996.
Muir, Helen, *Frost in Florida: A Memoir,* Valiant Press (Miami), 1995.

Newdick, Robert Spangler, *Newdick's Season of Frost: An Interrupted Biography of Robert Frost,* edited by William A. Sutton, State University of New York Press, 1976.
Reeve, Franklin D., *Robert Frost in Russia,* Little, Brown, 1964.
Richardson, Mark, *The Ordeal of Robert Frost: The Poet and His Poetics,* University of Illinois Press, 1997.
Rosenthal, M. L., *The Modern Poets,* Oxford University Press, 1965.
Shepley, Elizabeth, *Robert Frost: The Trial by Existence,* Holt, 1960.
Sohn, David A. and Richard Tyre, *Frost: The Poet and His Poetry,* Holt, 1967.
Thompson, Lawrence, *Fire and Ice: The Art and Thought of Robert Frost,* Holt, 1942.
Thompson, Lawrence, *Robert Frost,* University of Minnesota Press, 1959.
Thompson, Lawrence, editor, *Selected Letters of Robert Frost,* Holt, 1964.
Thompson, Lawrence, *Robert Frost: The Early Years, 1874-1915,* Holt, 1966.
Thompson, Lawrence, *Robert Frost: The Years of Triumph, 1915-1938,* Holt, 1970.
Thompson, Lawrence and R. H. Winnick, *Robert Frost: The Later Years, 1938-1963,* Holt, 1976.
Tutein, David W., *Robert Frost's Reading: An Annotated Bibliography,* Edwin Mellen, 1997.
Unger, Leonard and William Van O'Connor, *Poems for Study,* Holt, 1953.
Untermeyer, Louis, *Lives of the Poets,* Simon & Schuster, 1959.
Untermeyer, Louis, *Robert Frost: A Backward Look,* U.S. Government Printing Office, 1964.
Van Egmond, Peter, *The Critical Reception of Robert Frost,* G. K. Hall, 1974.
Waggoner, Hyatt H., *American Poetry from the Puritans to the Present,* Houghton, 1968.
Wagner, Linda Welshimer, editor, *Robert Frost: The Critical Reception,* B. Franklin, 1977.
West, Herbert Faulkner, *Mind on the Wing,* Coward, 1947.
Wilcox, Earl J., *His "Incalculable" Influence on Others: Essays on Robert Frost in Our Time,* English Literary Studies, University of Victoria (Victoria, British Columbia), 1994.
Winters, Yvor, *The Function of Criticism,* A. Swallow, 1957.

PERIODICALS

America, December 24, 1977.
American Literature, January, 1948.
Atlantic, February, 1964; November, 1966.
Bookman, January, 1924.
Books, May 10, 1942.
Boston Transcript, December 2, 1916.
Commonweal, May 4, 1962; April 1, 1977.
New Republic, February 20, 1915.
New York Herald Tribune Books, November 18, 1928.
New York Times, October 19, 1986.
New York Times Book Review, July 17, 1988.
New York Times Magazine, June 11, 1972; August 18, 1974.
Poetry, May, 1913.
Saturday Review of Literature, May 30, 1936; April 25, 1942.
South Atlantic Quarterly, summer, 1958.
Times Literary Supplement, December 14, 1967.
Virginia Quarterly Review, summer, 1957.
Wisconsin Library Bulletin, July, 1962.
Yale Review, spring, 1934; summer, 1948.

FRY, Christopher 1907-

PERSONAL: Name originally Christopher Fry Harris; born December 18, 1907, in Bristol, England; son of Charles John (an architect) and Emma Marguerite Fry (Hammond) Harris; married Phyllis Marjorie Hart, December 3, 1936 (died 1987); children: one son. *Education:* Attended Bedford Modern School, Bedford, England, 1918-26. *Religion:* Church of England.

ADDRESSES: Home—The Toft, East Dean, near Chichester, West Sussex PO18 0JA, England. *Agent*—ACTAC Ltd., 16 Cadogan Ln., London S.W.1., England.

CAREER: Bedford Froebel Kindergarten, teacher, 1926-27; Citizen House, Bath, England, actor and office worker, 1927; Hazelwood Preparatory School, Limpsfield, Surrey, England, schoolmaster, 1928-31; secretary to H. Rodney Bennett, 1931-32; Tunbridge Wells Repertory Players, founding director, 1932-35, 1940, 1944-46; Dr. Barnardo's Homes, lecturer and editor of school magazine, 1934-39; Oxford Playhouse, director, 1940; Arts Theatre Club, London, England, director, 1945, staff dramatist, 1947. Visiting director, Oxford Playhouse, 1945-46, Arts Theatre Club, 1947. Composer. *Military service:* Pioneer Corps, 1940-44.

MEMBER: Dramatists Guild, Garrick Club.

AWARDS, HONORS: Shaw Prize Fund award, 1948, for *The Lady's Not for Burning;* William Foyle Poetry Prize, 1951, for *Venus Observed;* New York Drama Critics Circle Award, 1951, for *The Lady's Not for Burning,* 1952, for *Venus Observed,* and 1956, for *Tiger at the Gates;* Queen's Gold Medal for Poetry, 1962; Heinemann Award, Royal Society of Literature, 1962, for *Curtmantle;* D.A., 1966, and Honorary Fellow, 1988, Manchester Polytechnic, 1966; Writers Guild Best British Television Dramatization award nomination, 1971, for "The Tenant of Wildfell Hall"; Doctor of Letters, Lambeth and Oxford University, 1988, De Monfort University and University of Sussex, both in 1994; Royal Society of Literature Fellow.

WRITINGS:

PLAYS

(With Monte Crick and F. Eyton) *She Shall Have Music,* first produced in London, England, 1934.

Open Door, first produced in London, England, 1936.

The Boy with a Cart: Cuthman, Saint of Sussex, first produced in Coleman's Hatch, Sussex, England, 1938; produced in the West End at Lyric Theatre, January 16, 1950), Oxford University Press, 1939, 2nd edition, Muller, 1956.

(Author of libretto) *Robert of Sicily: Opera for Children,* first produced in 1938.

The Tower (pageant), first produced at Tewkesbury Festival, Tewkesbury, England, July 18, 1939.

Thursday's Child: A Pageant (first produced in London, 1939), Girl's Friendly Press (London), 1939.

(Author of libretto) *Seven at a Stroke: A Play for Children,* first produced in 1939.

A Phoenix Too Frequent (first produced in London at Mercury Theatre, April 25, 1946; produced on Broadway, 1950), Hollis & Carter, 1946, Oxford University Press, 1949.

The Firstborn (broadcast on radio, 1947; first produced at Gateway Theatre, Edinburgh, Scotland, September 6, 1948), Cambridge University Press, 1946, 3rd edition, Oxford University Press, 1958.

The Lady's Not for Burning (first produced in London at Arts Theatre, March 10, 1948; produced in the West End, May 11, 1949, produced on Broadway at Royale Theatre, November

8, 1950), Oxford University Press, 1949, revised edition, 1973.

Thor, with Angels (first produced at Chapter House, Canterbury, England, June, 1948; produced in the West End at Lyric Theatre, September 27, 1951), H. J. Goulden, 1948, Oxford University Press, 1949.

Venus Observed (first produced in London at St. James Theatre, January 18, 1950; produced on Broadway at Century Theatre, February 13, 1952), Oxford University Press, 1950.

A Sleep of Prisoners (first produced in Oxford, England, at University Church, April 23, 1951; produced in London at St. Thomas's Church, May 15, 1951), Oxford University Press, 1951, 2nd edition, 1965.

The Dark Is Light Enough: A Winter Comedy (first produced in the West End at Aldwych Theatre, April, 30, 1954; produced on Broadway at ANTA Theatre, February 23, 1955) Oxford University Press, 1954.

Curtmantle (first produced in Dutch in Tilburg, Netherlands, at Stadsschouwburg, March 1, 1961, produced on the West End at Aldwych Theatre, October 6, 1962), Oxford University Press, 1961.

A Yard of Sun: A Summer Comedy (first produced at Nottingham Playhouse, Nottingham, England, July 11, 1970; produced on the West End at Old Vic Theatre, August 10, 1970), Oxford University Press, 1970.

One Thing More, or Caedmon Construed (first produced at Chelmsford Cathedral, England, 1986; broadcast on radio, 1986), Oxford University Press, 1985, Dramatists Play Service, 1987.

Also author of "Youth of the Peregrines," produced at Tunbridge Wells with premiere production of George Bernard Shaw's "Village Wooing." Author of radio plays for "Children's Hour" series, 1939-40, and of "Rhineland Journey," 1948.

SCREENPLAYS AND TELEPLAYS

The Canary, British Broadcasting Corp. (BBC-TV), 1950.

The Queen Is Crowned (documentary), Universal, 1953.

(With Denis Cannan) *The Beggar's Opera,* British Lion, 1953.

Ben Hur, Metro-Goldwyn-Mayer, 1959.

Barabbas, Columbia, 1961.

(With Jonathan Griffin, Ivo Perilli, and Vittorio Bonicelli) *The Bible: In the Beginning,* Twentieth Century-Fox, 1966.

The Tenant of Wildfell Hall, BBC-TV, 1968.

The Brontes of Haworth (four teleplays), BBC-TV, 1973.

The Best of Enemies, BBC-TV, 1976.

Sister Dora, BBC-TV, 1977.

Star Over Bethlehem, BBC-TV, 1981.

TRANSLATOR

(And adaptor from *L'Invitation au Chateau* by Jean Anouilh), *Ring Round the Moon: A Charade with Music* (first produced in the West End at Globe Theatre, January 26, 1950), Oxford University Press, 1950.

(And adaptor) Jean Giraudoux, *Tiger at the Gates* (first produced in the West End at Apollo Theatre, October 3, 1955), Methuen, 1955, 2nd edition, 1961, Oxford University Press, 1956, produced as *The Trojan War Will Not Take Place* (London, 1983), Methuen, 1983.

(And adaptor) Anouilh, *The Lark* (first produced in the West End at Lyric Theatre, May 11, 1955; produced on Broadway at Longacre Theatre, November 17, 1955), Methuen, 1955, Oxford University Press, 1956.

(And adaptor from *Pour Lucrece* by Giraudoux), *Duel of Angels* (first produced in the West End at Apollo Theatre, April 22,

1958; produced on Broadway at Helen Hayes Theatre, April 19, 1960), Methuen, 1958, Oxford University Press, 1959.

(And adaptor) Giraudoux, *Judith* (first produced in the West End at Her Majesty's Theatre, June 20, 1962), Methuen, 1962.

Sidonie Gabrielle Colette, *The Boy and the Magic,* Dobson, 1964, Putnam, 1965.

(And adaptor) Henrik Ibsen, *Peer Gynt* (first produced at Chichester Festival Theatre, Chichester, England, May 13, 1970), Oxford University Press, 1970, revised edition, 1989.

(And adaptor) Edmond Rostand, *Cyrano de Bergerac* (first produced at Chichester Festival Theatre, May 14, 1975), Oxford University Press, 1975.

OMNIBUS VOLUMES

Three Plays: The Firstborn; Thor, with Angels; A Sleep of Prisoners, Oxford University Press, 1960.

(Translator) Giraudoux, *Plays* (contains *Judith, Tiger at the Gates,* and *Duel of Angels*), Methuen, 1963.

Plays (contains *Thor, with Angels* and *The Lady's Not for Burning*), Oxford University Press, 1969.

Plays (contains *The Boy with a Cart: Cuthman, Saint of Sussex, The Firstborn,* and *Venus Observed*), Oxford University Press, 1970.

Plays (contains *A Sleep of Prisoners, The Dark Is Light Enough,* and *Curtmantle*), Oxford University Press, 1971.

Selected Plays (contains *The Boy with a Cart: Cuthman, Saint of Sussex, A Phoenix Too Frequent, The Lady's Not for Burning, A Sleep of Prisoners, Curtmantle*), Oxford University Press, 1985.

OTHER

(Contributor) Kaye Webb, editor, *An Experience of Critics and the Approach to Dramatic Criticism,* Perpetua, 1952, Oxford University Press, 1953.

(Author of libretto) Crown of the Year (cantata), first produced in 1958.

(Contributor) Robert W. Corrigan, editor, *The Modern Theatre,* Macmillan, 1964.

The Boat That Mooed (juvenile fiction), Macmillan, 1965.

(Contributor) H. F. Rubinstein, editor, *The Drama Bedside Book,* Atheneum, 1966.

(With Jonathan Griffin) *The Bible: Original Screenplay,* Pocket Books, 1966.

The Brontes of Haworth, published in two volumes, Davis-Poynter, 1975.

Root and Sky: Poetry from the Plays of Christopher Fry, edited by Charles E. Wadsworth and Jean G. Wadsworth, Godine, 1975.

Can You Find Me: A Family History, Oxford University Press, 1978.

(Adaptor) *Paradise Lost* (first produced in Chicago, 1978), Schott, 1978.

Death Is a Kind of Love (lecture; drawings by Charles E. Wadsworth), Tidal Press, 1979.

(Author of introduction) *Charlie Hammond's Sketch Book,* Oxford University Press, 1980.

Genius, Talent, and Failure (lecture), King's College, 1987.

(Author of foreword) Fry, Phyl, *A Sprinkle of Nutmeg: Letters to Christopher Fry, 1943-45,* Enitharmon Press, 1992.

(Author of introduction) *Cyrano de Bergerac: A Heroic Comedy in Five Acts,* Oxford University Press (New York City), 1996.

The Early Days (lecture), Society for Theatre Research (London), 1997.

SIDELIGHTS: British playwright, screenwriter, translator, and critic Christopher Fry is best known for his elegant verse plays, which emerged in the 1940s and 1950s as a sharp contrast to the naturalism and realism popular since the late nineteenth century. When Fry's blank-verse comedy *The Lady's Not for Burning* first appeared on stage in London during the 1950s, it became an immediate sensation. According to Harold Hobson in *Drama:* "It is difficult to exaggerate the sense of freshness and excitement that swept through the theatrical world when *The Lady's Not for Burning,* with the extraordinary brilliance of the fancies, the conceits, and the imagination of its dialogue, the originality of its verse-form, and the joyous medieval paradox of its story seemed to shatter the by then somnolent reign of naturalism on the British stage." Derek Stanford recalls in *Christopher Fry:* "Without the creaking machinery of any cranked-up manifesto, the plays of Fry appeared on the stage, receiving a progressive succession of applause. For the first time for several centuries, we were made to realise that here was a poet addressing the audience from the boards with that immediacy of effect which had seemed to have deserted the muse as far as its dramatic office was concerned. . . . Like a man who is conscious of no impediment, and does not anticipate embarrassing rebuffs, Fry spoke out with a power natural to him. He was heard—with surprise, with pleasure, and relief."

Fry's style attracted as many detractors as devotees; some complained that his rapidly moving, glittering language masked weak plots and shallow characterizations. In a *Times Literary Supplement* review of *The Lady's Not for Burning,* a critic finds the play "without the comparatively pedestrian power of developing character and situation," and adds: "It is surprising how rich a play may be in fine speeches and yet be a bad play because the speeches alter nothing." But Stanford determines that "so readily magniloquent and rich, in fact, is Fry that in an age of verbal paucity his own Elizabethan munificence of diction appears to our 'austerity' reviewers as suspect. None of these critics, it is true, has been able to deny the impact of his language, but have rather tended to minimise its import by treating it as the playwright's sole talent."

The Lady's Not for Burning, directed by and starring John Gielgud, was the first installment of a series of four comedies, each corresponding to a different season. The series continued with *Venus Observed* (autumn), *The Dark Is Light Enough* (winter), and concluded, twenty-two years after its commencement, with *A Yard of Sun* (summer). While the other plays, especially *Venus Observed,* received critical acclaim, none surpassed *The Lady's Not for Burning* in popularity. *The Lady's Not for Burning* is set in a somewhat fantastic medieval world, and primarily concerns two characters: Thomas, an embittered ex-soldier who wishes to die, and Jennet, a wealthy young orphan who loves life, but has been sentenced to burn on a trumped-up witchcraft charge so that the town may inherit her property. The play intertwines irony and comedy, with a dense mayor, his practical wife, and their two quarrelling sons all playing clownish roles. In *Dictionary of Literary Biography,* Audrey Williamson describes the play as "a lyric of spring: it has an April shimmer, like the dust of pollination shot by sunlight." Williamson continues: "There is a kind of golden haze about it that is penetrated by the occasional bawdiness of the humor: for Fry has combined the robustness of the Elizabethans with touches of the cheerful blasphemy that mingled with piety in the medieval morality play. But the sense of the abundance, mystery, and poetry of life is unimpaired."

Venus Observed involves an emotionally remote and aging duke who intends to choose a wife from his many ex-lovers. But in the process he becomes infatuated with the young woman his son also loves. The role of the elderly man was played by Laurence Olivier in London and Rex Harrison in New York; *Theatre Arts* contributor L. N. Roditte writes of the character: "The Duke is a hero of considerable magnitude; his story, though mild and witty, has an element of tragedy. . . . [Fry] has created an extraordinary part that other great actors will want to play." Although *Venus Observed* was well received by the public and critics, Fry's style again received criticism. According to *Saturday Review* contributor John Mason Brown: "Mr. Fry is blessed with one of the most delightful talents now contributing to the theatre. He has a wit, nimble and original; an agile and unpredictable mind, as playful as it is probing; and a love of language which can only be described as a lust." But Brown continues that Fry "is an anachronism, if you will; a fellow who has wandered from one Elizabethan age into another," and concludes: "Mr. Fry concentrates on all the sensuous splendors of the flesh, ignoring the skeleton of sustained ideas or dramatic structure." Harold Clurman in the *New Republic*, however, strongly objects to this view: "Let no one say that Fry's work consists of playful, euphonious words and no more. The meaning is clear to anyone who will pay attention. . . . And the meaning . . . is historically or (socially) revealing. Fry's plays are poems of resignation in which tragic substance is flattened into lovely ornament."

The Dark Is Light Enough delves into the past, this time using the background of revolutions on the Hungarian border in 1848. The heroine, Countess Rosmarin, is an elderly lady who attempts to rescue her ex-son-in-law, an army deserter, from execution. While the play ends with the Countess's death, "the viewer senses a summer radiance on which winter has set its feathered touch, light and cold as the snowflakes descending outside the window," explains Williamson. In *Ariel*, Stanley Wiersma also sees the conclusion as a positive one: "The Countess . . . finds warmth enough in the winter of our discontent, goodness enough in a wicked world, life enough in death." *Chicago Sunday Tribune* contributor F. E. Faverty sees a conflict between the plot and dialogue, however. "In spite of the heavy themes, the dialogue is light and sparkling," he writes. "There is a quotable epigram on every page. Nonetheless, one's final impression is that there is too much talk and too little action." But Williamson admires the interplay: "Fry adapts his verse to his theme, conveying wisdom and a new verbal austerity," she continues. "It makes for a play of dramatic tension and fascination."

Fry's abhorrence of violence is an important part of *The Dark Is Light Enough*. Wiersma identifies the play's themes as "violence as self-assertion, violence as loyalty to the state, violence as loyalty to God, and, finally, violence to be endured but not to be inflicted," and explains that the playwright sees such violence as "an infection with its own irrational necessities. The violence in the situation and within the people is moving toward a duel; who fights it or against whom is beside the point." Fry's answer to violence is love: love that endures pain but refuses to inflict it. Emil Roy, in his monograph on Fry, finds this treatment unique: "Unlike most of his contemporaries, Fry has not given man's meanness, animality, and evil a central position in his work. If men are selfish, egoistic, and blind to love, it belongs to his more enlightened, self-controlled, and discerning characters to bring their understanding and tolerance to bear upon the pain and anguish that results."

A Yard of Sun ends the quartet; it deals with the return of two absent members of an Italian family: the black sheep and a betrayed friend. A *Times Literary Supplement* reviewer calls the characters and situation "stereotyped" and claims they "receive a thick coating of Fry's Christmas-tree versification which serves to convert cliches into fanciful imagery and camouflage the fact that no issue is being squarely faced." But according to Williamson, the play contains "a concentrated glow of language, pared to a new, more austere structure. The Italianate characterization is vivid and varied, and the story line taut and gripping." And a *Newsweek* reviewer finds that *A Yard of Sun* "shimmers with poetry and affirms Fry's belief in a basically mystical Christian benevolence."

Overall, Stanford sees Fry as a joyous free-thinker in a narrow world: "In a universe often viewed as mechanic, he has posited the principle of mystery; in an age of necessitarian ethics, he has stood unequivocally for ideas of free-will. In theatre technique, he has gaily ignored the sacrosanct conventions of naturalistic drama; and in terms of speech he has brought back poetry onto the stage with undoctored abandon." Roy states: "Fry has occasionally seemed wordy, sentimental, and lacking in conventional kinds of conflict, but he has more than compensated with vital and compassionate characters, the courage to deal with contemporary human conflicts and issues, and some of the most vital language in the theater today." And Williamson concludes: "In Fry's hands the English theater turned, for an elegantly creative period, away from prosaic reality and explored both the poetry and the mystery of life."

BIOGRAPHICAL/CRITICAL SOURCES:

BOOKS

Dictionary of Literary Biography, Volume 13: *British Dramatists Since World War II,* Gale (Detroit), 1982.
Leeming, Glenda, *Poetic Drama,* Macmillan, 1989.
Leeming, Glenda, *Christopher Fry,* Twayne, 1990.
Roy, Emil, *Christopher Fry,* Southern Illinois University Press, 1968.
Sangal, Mahendra Pratap, *Christopher Fry and T. S. Eliot,* Brij Prakashan, 1968.
Stanford, Derek, *Christopher Fry: An Appreciation,* Peter Nevill, 1951.
Wiersma, Stanley, *More Than the Ear Discovers: God in the Plays of Christopher Fry,* Loyola University Press, 1983.
Wiersma, Stanley, *Christopher Fry: A Critical Essay,* Eerdmans, 1970.

PERIODICALS

Ariel, October, 1975.
Drama, spring, 1979.
Literary Half-Yearly, July, 1971.
New Republic, August 20, 1951; March 3, 1952; December 2, 1978.
Newsweeek, July 27, 1970.
New York Times Book Review, January 21, 1979.
New York Times Magazine, March 12, 1950.
Plays and Players, December, 1987.
Saturday Review, March 1, 1952; March 21, 1953.
Theatre Arts, September, 1950.
Times Literary Supplement, April 2, 1949; August 21, 1970; October 20, 1978.

FRYE, (Herman) Northrop 1912-1991

PERSONAL: Born July 14, 1912, in Sherbrooke, Quebec, Canada; died of a heart attack, January 22, 1991, in Toronto, Ontario, Canada; son of Herman Edward (a hardware merchant) and Catherine Maud (Howard) Frye; married Helen Kemp, August 24, 1937 (died, 1986); married Elizabeth Brown, 1988. *Education:* University of Toronto, B.A. (philosophy and English; with honors), 1933; Emmanuel College, ordained, 1936; Merton College, Oxford, M.A., 1940. *Religion:* United Church of Canada.

CAREER: Worked as a pastor of a congregation near Shaunavon, Saskatchewan, 1934; University of Toronto, Victoria College, Toronto, Ontario, lecturer in English, 1939-41, assistant professor, 1942-46, associate professor, 1947, professor of English, 1948-91, chair of department, 1952-59, principal, 1959-67, University Professor, 1967-91. Chancellor, Victoria University, Toronto, 1978-91. Visiting professor at Harvard University, Princeton University, Columbia University, Indiana University, University of Washington, University of British Columbia, Cornell University, University of California, Berkeley, and Oxford University. Andrew D. White Professor-at-Large, Cornell University, 1970-75; Charles Eliot Norton Poetry Professor, Harvard University, 1974-75. Member of board of governors, Ontario Curriculum Institute, 1960-63; chair of Governor-General's Literary Awards Committee, 1962. Canadian Radio Television and Telecommunications Commission, advisory member, 1968-77.

MEMBER: Modern Language Association of America (executive council member, 1958-62; president, 1976), English Institute (former chair), Royal Society of Canada (fellow), American Academy of Arts and Sciences (foreign honorary member), British Academy (corresponding fellow), American Philosophical Society (foreign member), American Academy and Institute of Arts and Letters (honorary member).

AWARDS, HONORS: Guggenheim fellow, 1950-51; Lorne Pierce Medal of the Royal Society of Canada, 1958; Canada Council Medal, 1967; Pierre Chauveau Medal of the Royal Society of Canada, 1970; Canada Council Molson Prize, 1971; Companion of the Order of Canada, 1972; honorary fellow, Merton College, Oxford, 1974; Civic Honour, City of Toronto, 1974; Royal Bank Award, 1978; Governor General's Award, 1987. Thirty-six honorary degrees from colleges and universities in Canada and the United States, including Dartmouth College, Harvard University, Princeton University, and University of Manitoba.

WRITINGS:

Fearful Symmetry: A Study of William Blake, Princeton University Press, 1947.

Anatomy of Criticism: Four Essays, Princeton University Press, 1957.

(With others) *The English and Romantic Poets and Essayists: A Review of Research and Criticism,* Modern Language Association of America, 1957.

Culture and the National Will, Carleton University, for Institute of Canadian Studies, 1957.

(With Kluckhohn and Wigglesworth) *Three Lectures,* University of Toronto, 1958.

By Liberal Things, Clarke, Irwin, 1959.

(Editor) William Shakespeare, *The Tempest,* Penguin, 1959.

(Editor) *Design for Learning,* University of Toronto Press, 1962.

(With L. C. Knights and others) *Myth and Symbol: Critical Approaches and Applications,* edited by Bernice Slote, University of Nebraska Press, 1963.

The Developing Imagination (published together with an essay by A. R. MacKinnon), Harvard University Press, 1963.

The Changing Pace of Canadian Education, Sir George Williams University (Montreal), 1963.

The Well-Tempered Critic, Indiana University Press, 1963.

T. S. Eliot: An Introduction, Grove, 1963.

Fables of Identity: Studies in Poetic Mythology, Harcourt, 1963.

(Editor) *Romanticism Reconsidered: Selected Papers from the English Institute,* Columbia University Press, 1963.

The Educated Imagination, Indiana University Press, 1964.

A Natural Perspective: The Development of Shakespearean Comedy and Romance, Columbia University Press, 1965.

The Return of Eden: Five Essays on Milton's Epics, University of Toronto Press, 1965.

(Editor) *Selected Poetry and Prose,* McGraw, 1966.

(Editor) *Blake: A Collection of Critical Essays,* Prentice-Hall, 1966.

Fools of Time: Studies in Shakespearean Tragedy, University of Toronto Press, 1967.

The Modern Century (Whidden Lectures), Oxford University Press, 1967.

A Study of English Romanticism, Random House, 1968.

Silence in the Sea, Memorial University of Newfoundland, 1969.

The Stubborn Structure: Essays on Criticism and Society, Methuen, 1970.

The Bush Garden: Essays on the Canadian Imagination, House of Anansi Press, 1971.

The Critical Path: An Essay on the Social Context of Literary Criticism, Indiana University Press, 1971.

On Teaching Literature, Harcourt, 1972.

The Secular Scripture: A Study of the Structure of Romance, Harvard University Press, 1976.

Spiritus Mundi: Essays on Literature, Myth and Society, Indiana University Press, 1976.

Northrop Frye on Culture and Literature: A Collection of Review Essays, edited by Robert Denham, Chicago University Press, 1978.

Creation and Recreation, University of Toronto Press, 1980.

Criticism As Education, School of Library Service, Columbia University, 1980.

The Great Code: The Bible and Literature, Harcourt, 1982.

Divisions on a Ground: Essays on Canadian Culture, House of Anansi Press, 1982.

The Myth of Deliverance: Reflections on Shakespeare's Problem Comedies, University of Toronto Press, 1982.

(Editor with Sheridan Baker and George W. Perkins) *The Harper Handbook to Literature,* Harper, 1985, 1997.

Northrop Frye on Shakespeare, edited by Robert Sandler, Yale University Press, 1986.

(With others) *The Practical Imagination,* Harper, 1987.

On Education, University of Michigan Press, 1988.

Northrop Frye—Myth and Metaphor: Selected Essays, University Press of Virginia, 1990.

Reading the World: Selected Writings, Peter Lang, 1990.

Words with Power: Being a Second Study of "The Bible and Literature," Harcourt, 1990.

The Double Vision: Language and Meaning in Religion, University of Toronto Press, 1991.

A World in a Grain of Sand: Twenty-Two Interviews with Northrop Frye, edited by Robert D. Denham, Peter Lang, 1992.

Northrop Frye in Conversation (interviews by David Cayley), Anansi, 1992.

The Eternal Act of Creation: Essays, 1979-1990, Indiana University Press, 1994.

Genre, Trope, Gender: Critical Essays by Northrop Frye, Linda Hutcheon, and Shirley Neuman, Carleton University Press, 1994.

The Correspondence of Northrop Frye and Helen Kemp, 1932-1939, University of Toronto Press, 1996.

Northrop Frye's Student Essays 1932-1938, with Robert D. Denham, University of Toronto Press, 1997.

Has written educational radio and television programs for the Canadian Broadcasting Co. Work represented in anthologies. Contributor to professional journals. *Canadian Forum,* literary editor, 1947-49, editor, 1949-52.

SIDELIGHTS: Because of the influential theories on literary criticism that he presented in *Anatomy of Criticism: Four Essays* and other books, Northrop Frye was regarded as one of the most important literary critics of his generation. Although Frye made no effort during his life to form a school of criticism based on his ideas, his ability to categorize the different approaches used to analyze literature put the field of criticism as a whole into new perspective. The critic and educator was also once a pastor for the United Church of Canada, and even though he abandoned this career for that of a university professor his religious background led to an interest in the relationship between the Bible and Western literature. Influenced by the poet William Blake, Frye saw the Bible not as something holy in itself, but rather as a text that could lead one to higher spirituality through contact with the Holy Spirit dwelling within each human being. According to Harold Bloom in the *New York Times,* Frye's "true greatness" was his advocacy "of a Protestant and Romantic tradition that has dominated much of British and American literature, the tradition of the Inner Light, by which each person reads Scripture for himself or herself without yielding to a premature authority imposed by Church or State or School." But for others familiar with Frye's work, like *New York Times Book Review* contributor Robert M. Adams, the critic will be remembered primarily as "one of the bold, inventive—and unhappily rare—schematizers of our literature."

Many of Frye's ideas about literature came from Blake, the eighteenth-century English poet, artist, and critic about whom Frye wrote *Fearful Symmetry: A Study of William Blake.* Before the publication of this book, critics approached Blake's poetry as being "private, mystical, or deranged," according to *Dictionary of Literary Biography* contributor Robert D. Denham. But Frye showed ". . .that Blake's poetry is typical, that he belongs squarely in the tradition of English literature, and that he should be read in imaginative, rather than simply historical, terms." Although Blake's use of symbolism was unique, Frye argued that the basis of this symbolism was universal and could be compared to writings by "Edmund Spenser and John Milton, and especially the Bible." By studying the unity of imagination in Blake's work, Frye extrapolated in *Fearful Symmetry* "that all symbolism in all art and religion is mutually intelligible among all men, and that there is such a thing as the iconography of the imagination."

Frye elaborated upon this theory in *Anatomy of Criticism,* a book that "forced itself" on him when he was trying to write about another subject. After writing *Fearful Symmetry,* Frye was determined at first to apply Blake's principles of literary symbolism and Biblical analysis to the poet Edmund Spenser. But "the introduction to Spenser became an introduction to the theory of allegory, and that theory obstinately adhered to a much larger

theoretical structure," Frye explained in *Anatomy*'s preface. "The basis of argument became more and more discursive, and less and less historical and Spenserian. I soon found myself entangled in those parts of criticism that have to do with such words as 'myth,' 'symbol,' 'ritual,' and 'archetype'. . . . Eventually, the theoretical and the practical aspects of the task I had begun completely separated." But rather than abandon the project, Frye simply shifted his focus, writing not about Spenser in particular, but about literature in general. When he finished, he had produced four essays of what he calls "pure critical theory." Published together in 1957, these essays comprise *Anatomy of Criticism,* a schematic, non-judgmental theory of literature and the first, according to David Schiller in *Commentary,* "which enables a student to tell where, in the totality of his literary experiences, an individual experience belongs."

One of the most controversial features of Frye's schema is the role it assigns critics. The historical function of criticism, from the time of Samuel Johnson to T. S. Eliot, has been to provide a means of discriminating good writing from bad. But Frye's interest was in what makes works of literature similar to one another, not what makes them different, and he adamantly rejected the notion of critic as judge. It is not, he asserted, the critic's responsibility to evaluate poetry or to say that one poem is better than another because his judgment, while informed, is really nothing more than a reflection of taste. And, "the history of taste is no more a part of the structure of criticism than the Huxley-Wilberforce debate is part of the structure of biological science," Frye wrote. Matters of judgment are best left to book reviewers, not critics, in Frye's point of view.

But W. K. Wimsatt, in an essay in *Northrop Frye in Modern Criticism,* charged Frye with inconsistency: "He can and is willing to distinguish 'ephemeral rubbish,' mediocre works, random and peripheral experience, from the greatest classics, the profound masterpieces in which may be discerned the converging patterns of the primitive formulas. At other moments, however, he says that criticism has nothing whatever to do with either the experience or the judging of literature. The direct experience of literature is central to criticism, yet somehow this center is excluded from it." The effect, Wimsatt concluded, is that the reader remains unsure whether Frye "wishes to discredit all critical valuing whatever, or only the wrong kinds of valuing."

With *The Great Code: The Bible and Literature* and its companion study, *Words with Power: Being a Second Study of "The Bible and Literature,"* Frye attempted "his most ambitious literary ascent: a two-volume assault on the central and highest massif in Western civilization," according to John B. Breslin in *Washington Post Book World.* The Bible was for Frye the single most important book upon which the overall structure and mythology behind literature could be based. Indeed, he asserted in *The Great Code* that a "student of English literature who does not know the Bible does not understand a good deal of what is going on in what he reads." Viewing the New and Old Testaments with the eye of a critic rather than a theologian or historian, Frye professed that the Bible could only be fully understood when subjected to systematic literary study.

The Great Code, as the title implies, analyzes the words of the Bible. Frye examined the text typologically, that is, as words representing things, people, and events in the Old Testament that foreshadow those in the New Testament. According to *New York Review of Books* contributor J. M. Cameron, this approach was necessary in Frye's view, "not because this is an interesting pattern after we have given the kaleidoscope a shake, but because this is how the Biblical authors, in the main, wrote." Viewing the Bible this way, the reader can see the relationship between the Old and New Testaments, such as how the twelve tribes of Israel are reflected in the twelve apostles, how Moses receiving the Ten Commandments is reflected by Jesus's "Sermon on the Mount," and how Israel's defeat of its enemies in Canaan is reflected by the victory of the Resurrection, to give only a few examples.

The Great Code thus illustrates the imaginative unity of the Bible, and how its use of myths and symbols combine to convey a message (or "theme") of salvation. In Frye's terms, according to W. J. Keith in the *Globe and Mail*, *The Great Code* is therefore a study of the "'centripetal' coherence" of the Bible. The companion book to *The Great Code*, on the other hand, "moves outward in a 'centrifugal' manner to demonstrate 'the extent to which the canonical unity of the Bible indicates or symbolizes a much wider imaginative unity in secular European literature.'" *New York Times* critic Michiko Kakutani summarized that *Words with Power* "helps the reader recognize some of the recurring myths that connect religious and secular literature, and [Frye] shows how ideological and social changes can cause changes in the interpretation and emphasis of those myths."

Frye published *Words with Power* just before his death early in 1991, thus completing the last part of "the big book about the Bible" that he had "set out to write as long ago as 1957," but which was set aside for what was to become *Anatomy of Criticism*, according to *New York Times Book Review* contributor Hugh Kenner. As with his other books, Frye set out to study his subject as systematically and scientifically as possible. But a few critics felt that some of Frye's personal beliefs still linger behind his attempted objective analysis. "Frye's career has been devoted unswervingly to the delicate task of placing the Christian religion on a scientific footing," declared Paul H. Fry in the *Yale Review*. "This he has attempted by claiming, first, that his method is indeed scientific,. . . and second, somewhat less candidly, I think, that the object of his discipline is not the Christian revelation, but mythopoetic thinking wherever it appears. It seems to me that Frye is caught in a bind that he cannot acknowledge, one that is perforce more apparent in *The Great Code* than hitherto: he cannot admit the religious basis of his undertaking without admitting that his analytic point of departure. . . is not quite dispassionately chosen."

Two significant volumes of Frye's lectures appeared shortly after his death. *The Double Vision: Language and Meaning in Religion* represents a brief and accessible overview of Frye's ambitious study of the Bible as put forth in *The Great Code* and *Words with Power*. Based on three lectures delivered at the University of Toronto within a year of his death, Frye considers the paradox, or "double vision," of language, nature, time, and God. "The purpose of these brilliantly readable—almost inhabitable—essays," wrote Gary Michael Dault in *Books in Canada*, "is to persuade us that a 'simple sense perception' is not enough to guide us through the unfolding meaning of our progressions within time, space (nature), and consciousness (language). Humanity's primary duty, Frye points out, is not to be natural but to be human." A second posthumous publication, *The Eternal Act of Creation: Essays, 1979-1990*, also reveals the acumen and impressive range of Frye's critical analysis. This collection consists of a dozen addresses delivered by Frye in the last decade of his life on diverse topics such as computers, medical metaphors, and therapeutic uses for literature. As David Rampton concluded in

Canadian Literature, "No critic of our time has gained such a hold on our imaginations or been the object of so many accolades."

While Frye's ideas on structuralism have given way to other schools of criticism since the publication of *Anatomy of Criticism*, the critic and his work are still widely admired. "[Frye's] was a hard mind with an intricate and completely assured gift for the patterning of concepts and attitudes," wrote Adams. "[His] wit was concise and dry, his erudition compendious. The first two books [he wrote] expressed exactly the nature of his interests: one was an anatomy, the other laid bare a symmetry. He was always getting down to the bare bones of things while demonstrating the way they could be articulated into larger and larger structures."

BIOGRAPHICAL/CRITICAL SOURCES:

BOOKS

Ayre, John, *Northrop Frye: A Critical Biography*, General Publishing (Don Mills, Canada), 1988.
Contemporary Literary Criticism, Volume 24, Gale (Detroit), 1983.
Denham, Robert, *Northrop Frye and Critical Method*, Pennsylvania State University Press, 1978.
Denham, Robert, *Northrop Frye: An Annotated Bibliography of Primary and Secondary Sources*, University of Toronto Press, 1988.
Dictionary of Literary Biography, Gale, Volume 67: *Modern American Critics since 1955*, 1988; Volume 68: *Canadian Writers, 1920-1959, First Series*, 1988.
Hoffman, Daniel, editor, *Harvard Guide to Contemporary American Writing*, Belknap Press, 1979.
Krieger, Murray, editor, *Northrop Frye in Modern Criticism: Selected Papers from the English Institute*, Columbia University Press, 1966.
Lee, Alvin A., and Robert D. Denham, *The Legacy of Northrop Frye*, University of Toronto Press (Toronto), 1994.
Sauerberg, Lars Ole, *Versions of the Past-Visions of the Future: The Canonical in the Criticism of T.S. Eliot, F.R. Leavis, Northrop Frye, and Harold Bloom*, St. Martin's, 1997.
Russell, Ford, *Northrop Frye on Myth: An Introduction*, Garland, 1998.

PERIODICALS

Books in Canada, September, 1991, p. 42.
Cambridge Review, May 7, 1971.
Canadian Literature, summer, 1994, p. 141.
Chicago Tribune Book World, May 16, 1982.
Commentary, September, 1968.
Comparative Literature, spring, 1995, p. 160.
Globe and Mail (Toronto), October 4, 1986; December 1, 1990.
Nation, February 19, 1968.
New York Review of Books, April 14, 1977; April 15, 1982; April 9, 1992, p. 25.
New York Times, April 18, 1976; December 4, 1990.
New York Times Book Review, April 18, 1976; April 11, 1982; November 30, 1986; March 31, 1991.
Partisan Review, winter, 1969.
Sewanee Review, January, 1980.
South Atlantic Quarterly, spring, 1967.
Times Literary Supplement, August 12, 1965; July 2, 1982; February 17, 1984; April 26, 1985.
Washington Post Book World, May 16, 1982.
Yale Review, autumn, 1957; spring, 1964; spring, 1967; March, 1971; summer, 1983.

FUENTES, Carlos 1928-

PERSONAL: Born November 11, 1928, in Panama City, Panama; Mexican citizen; son of Rafael Fuentes Boettiger (a career diplomat) and Berta Macias Rivas; married Rita Macedo (a movie actress), 1959 (divorced, 1969); married Sylvia Lemus (a television journalist), 1973; children: (first marriage) Cecilia; (second marriage) Carlos Rafael, Natasha. *Education:* National University of Mexico, LL.B., 1948; graduate study, Institute des Hautes Etudes, Geneva, Switzerland. *Politics:* Independent leftist. *Avocation:* Reading, travel, swimming, visiting art galleries, listening to classical and rock music, motion pictures, the theater.

ADDRESSES: Home—716 Watchung Rd., Bound Brook, NJ 08805. *Office*—401 Boylston Hall, Harvard University, Cambridge, MA 02138. *Agent*—c/o Brandt & Brandt, 1501 Broadway, New York, NY 10036.

CAREER: Writer. International Labor Organization, Geneva, Switzerland, began as member, became secretary of the Mexican delegation, 1950-52; Ministry of Foreign Affairs, Mexico City, Mexico, assistant chief of press section, 1954; National University of Mexico, Mexico City, secretary and assistant director of cultural dissemination, 1955-56, head of department of cultural relations, 1957-59; Mexico's ambassador to France, 1975-77; Cambridge University, Norman Maccoll Lecturer, 1977, Simon Bolivar professor, 1986-87; Barnard College, New York City, Virginia Gildersleeve Professor, 1977; Columbia University, New York City, Henry L. Tinker Lecturer, 1978; Harvard University, Cambridge, MA, Robert F. Kennedy Professor of Latin American studies, 1987–. Fellow at Woodrow Wilson International Center for Scholars, 1974; Lecturer or visiting professor at University of Mexico, University of California at San Diego, University of Oklahoma, University of Concepcion in Chile, University of Paris, University of Pennsylvania, and George Mason University; Modern Humanities Research Association, president, 1989–; member of Mexican National Commission on Human Rights.

MEMBER: American Academy and Institute of Arts and Letters (honorary).

AWARDS, HONORS: Centro Mexicano de Escritores fellowship, 1956-57; Biblioteca Breve Prize from Seix Barral (publishing house; Barcelona), 1967, for *Cambio de piel*; Xavier Villaurrutia Prize (Mexico), 1975; Romulo Gallegos Prize (Venezuela), 1977, for *Terra Nostra*; Alfonso Reyes Prize (Mexico), 1979, for body of work; National Award for Literature (Mexico), 1984, for "Orchids in the Moonlight"; nominated for *Los Angeles Times* Book Award in fiction, 1986, for *The Old Gringo*; Miguel de Cervantes Prize from Spanish Ministry of Culture, 1987; Ruben Dario Order of Cultural Independence (Nicaragua) and literary prize of Italo-Latino Americano Institute, both 1988, for *The Old Gringo*; Medal of Honor for Literature, National Arts Club, New York City, 1988; Rector's Medal, University of Chile, 1991; Casita Maria Medal, 1991; Order of Merit (Chile), 1992; French Legion of Honor, 1992; Menedez Pelayo International Award, University of Santander, 1992; named honorary citizen of Santiago de Chile, Buenos Aires, and Veracruz, 1993; Principe de Asturias Prize, 1994; Premiio Grinzane-Cavour, 1994; candidate for Neustadt International Prize for Literature, 1996; honorary degrees from Bard College, Cambridge University, Columbia College, Chicago State University, Dartmouth College, Essex University, Georgetown University, Harvard University, and Washington University.

WRITINGS:

NOVELS

La region mas transparente, Fondo de Cultura Economica, 1958, translation by Sam Hileman published as *Where the Air Is Clear,* Ivan Obolensky, 1960, Hileman's translation published as *Where the Air Is Clear: A Novel,* Farrar, Straus, 1982.

Las buenas consciencias, Fondo de Cultura Economica, 1959, translation published as *The Good Conscience,* Ivan Oblensky, 1961.

La muerte de Artemio Cruz, Fondo de Cultura Economica, 1962, translation by Hileman published as *The Death of Artemio Cruz,* Farrar, Straus, 1964.

Aura (also see below), Era, 1962, translation by Lysander Kemp, Farrar, Straus, 1965.

Zona sagrada, Siglo XXI, 1967, translation by Suzanne Jill Levine published as *Holy Place* (also see below), Dutton, 1972.

Cambio de piel, Mortiz, 1967, translation by Hileman published as *A Change of Skin,* Farrar, Straus, 1968.

Cumpleanos, Mortiz, 1969, translation published as Birthday (also see below).

Terra Nostra (also see below), Seix Barral, 1975, translation by Levine, afterword by Milan Kundera, Farrar, Straus, 1976.

La cabeza de hidra, Mortiz, 1978, translation by Margaret Sayers Peden published as *Hydra Head,* Farrar, Straus, 1978.

Una familia lejana, Era, 1980, translation by Peden published as *Distant Relations,* Farrar, Straus, 1982.

El gringo viejo, Fondo de Cultura Economica, 1985, translation by Peden and Fuentes published as *The Old Gringo,* Farrar, Straus, 1985.

Christopher Unborn (translation of *Cristobal Nonato*), Farrar, Straus, 1989.

The Orange Tree, introduction by Mac Adam, Farrar, Straus, & Giroux, 1994.

Diana, the Goddess Who Hunts Alone, introduction by Alfred J. Mac Adam, Farrar, Straus, & Giroux (New York), 1995.

Voluptuario, St. Martin's Press (New York City), 1996.

Also author of *Holy Place & Birthday: Two Novellas,* Farrar, Straus.

SHORT STORIES

Los dias enmascarados (also see below), Los Presentes, 1954.

Cantar de ciegos (also see below), Mortiz, 1964.

Dos cuentos mexicanos (title means "Two Mexican Stories"; two short stories previously published in *Cantar de ciegos*), Instituto de Cultura Hispanica de Sao Paulo, Universidade de Sao Paulo, 1969.

Poemas de amor: Cuentos del alma, Imp. E. Cruces (Madrid), 1971.

Chac Mool y otros cuentos, Salvat, 1973.

Agua quemada (anthology), Fondo de Cultura Economica, 1981, translation by Peden published as *Burnt Water,* Farrar, Straus, 1980.

Constancia and Other Stories for Virgins, Farrar, Straus, 1989.

The Crystal Frontier: A Novel in Nine Stories, Farrar, Straus, 1997.

PLAYS

Todos los gatos son pardos (also see below), Siglo XXI, 1970.

El tuerto es rey (also see below; first produced [in French], 1970), Mortiz, 1970.

Los reinos originarios (contains *Todos los gatos son pardos* and *El tuerto es rey*), Seix Barral, 1971.

Orquideas a la luz de la luna (first produced in English as *Orchids in the Moonlight* at American Repertory Theater in Cambridge, MA, June 9, 1982), Seix Barral, 1982.

NONFICTION

The Argument of Latin America: Words for North Americans, Radical Education Project, 1963.

(Contributor) *Whither Latin America?* (political articles), Monthly Review Press, 1963.

Paris: La revolucion de mayo, Era, 1968.

La nueva novela hispanoamericana, Mortiz, 1969.

(Contributor) *El mundo de Jose Luis Cuevas,* Tudor (Mexico City), 1969.

Casa con dos puertas (title means "House With Two Doors"), Mortiz, 1970.

Tiempo mexicano (title means "Mexican Time"), Mortiz, 1971.

Cervantes; o, La critica de la lectura, Mortiz, 1976, translation published as *Don Quixote; or, The Critique of Reading,* Institute of Latin American Studies, University of Texas at Austin, 1976.

On Human Rights: A Speech, Somesuch Press (Dallas), 1984.

Latin America: At War With the Past, CBC Enterprises, 1985.

Myself With Others: Selected Essays, Farrar, Straus, 1988.

A New Time for Mexico, Farrar, Straus, & Giroux, 1996.

OTHER

(Editor and author of prologue) Octavio Paz, *Los signos en rotacion, y otros ensayos,* Alianza, 1971.

Cuerpos y ofrendas (anthology; includes selections from *Los dias enmascarados, Cantar de ciegos, Aura,* and *Terra Nostra,*) introduction by Octavio Paz, Alianza, 1972.

(Author of introduction to Spanish translation) Milan Kundera, *La vida esta en otra parte,* Seix Barral, 1977.

(Author of introduction) Omar Cabezas, *Fire From the Mountain,* Crown, 1988.

Valiente Mundo Nuevo, Fondo de Cultura Economica (Mexico City), 1990.

The Campaign, Farrar, Straus, 1991.

Buried Mirror: Reflections on Spain in the New World, Houghton, 1992.

Geografia de la novela, Fondo de Cultura Economica (Mexico City), 1993.

El naranjo, o los circulos del Tempe, Alfaguara, Mexico, 1993.

La frontera de cristal, Alfaguara, Mexico, 1995.

(Author of introduction) *The Diary of Frida Kahlo; An Intimate Self-Portrait,* published by Harry N. Abrams, 1995.

Collaborator on several film scripts, including *Pedro Paramo,* 1966, *Tiempo de morir,* 1966, and *Los caifanes,* 1967. Work represented in numerous anthologies, including *Antologia de cuentos hispanoamericanos,* Nueva Decada (Costa Rica), 1985. Contributor to periodicals in the United States, Mexico, and France, including *New York Times, Washington Post,* and *Los Angeles Times.* Founding editor, *Revista Mexicana de Literatura,* 1954-58; coeditor, *El Espectador,* 1959-61, *Siempre,* 1960, and *Politica,* 1960.

MEDIA ADAPTATIONS: Two short stories from *Cantar de ciegos* were made into films in the mid-1960s; *The Old Gringo* was adapted into a film of the same title by Fonda Films, 1989.

SIDELIGHTS: "Carlos Fuentes," states Robert Maurer in *Saturday Review,* is "without doubt one of Mexico's two or three greatest novelists." He is part of a group of Latin American writers whose writings, according to Alistair Reid's *New Yorker* essay, "formed the background of the Boom," a literary phenomenon Reid describes as a period in the 1960s when "a sudden surge of hitherto unheard-of writers from Latin America began to be felt among [U.S.] readers." Fuentes, however, is singled out from among the other writers of the Boom in Jose Donoso's autobiographical account, *The Boom in Spanish American Literature: A Personal History,* in which the Chilean novelist calls Fuentes "the first active and conscious agent of the internationalization of the Spanish American novel." And since the 1960s, Fuentes has continued his international influence in the literary world: his 1985 novel, *The Old Gringo,* for example, was the first written by a Mexican to ever appear on the *New York Times* best-seller list.

Fuentes's novels *The Death of Artemio Cruz* and *Terra Nostra* are especially good examples of his experimental techniques. The first narrative deals with a corrupt Mexican millionaire who on his deathbed relives his life in a series of flashbacks. In the novel Fuentes uses three separate narrations to tell the story, and for each of these narrations he uses a different narrative person. *New York Review of Books* contributor A. Alvarez explains the three-part narration of the novel: "Cruz's story is told in three persons. 'I' is the old man dying on his bed; 'you' is a slightly vatic, 'experimental' projection of his potentialities into an unspecified future. . . ; 'he' is the real hero, the man whose history emerges bit by bit from incidents shuffled around from his seventy-one years." In John S. Brushwood's *Mexico in Its Novel: A Nation's Search for Identity,* the critic praises Fuentes's technique, commenting: "The changing narrative viewpoint is extremely effective, providing a clarity that could not have been accomplished any other way. I doubt that there is anywhere in fiction a character whose wholeness is more apparent than in the case of Artemio Cruz."

Robert Coover observes in the *New York Times Book Review* that in *Terra Nostra* Fuentes once again uses a variety of narrators to tell his story. Commenting favorably on Fuentes's use of the "you" narrative voice in the novel, Coover writes: "Fuentes's second person [narration] is not one overheard on a stage: the book itself, rather than the author or a character, becomes the speaker, the reader or listener a character, or several characters in succession." Spanish novelist Juan Goytisolo similarly states in *Review:* "One of the most striking and most successful devices [in *Terra Nostra*] is the abrupt shift in narrative point of view (at times without the unwary reader's even noticing), passing from first-person narration to second,. . . and simultaneously rendering objective and subjective reality in one and the same passage with patent scorn for the rules of discourse that ordinarily govern expository prose." In the *Paris Review* Fuentes comments on his use of the second person narrative, calling it "the voice poets have always used and that novelists also have a right to use."

Fuentes's use of the second person narrative and other experimental techniques makes his novels extremely complex. The author's remarks in a *New York Times Book Review* interview with Frank MacShane concerning the structure of *Terra Nostra* describe the intricacy of the work: "My chief stylistic device in *Terra Nostra* is to follow every statement by a counter statement and every image by its opposite." This deliberate duplicity by the author, along with the extensive scope of the novel, causes some reviewers to criticize *Terra Nostra* for being inaccessible to the average reader. Maurer, for instance, calls the novel "a huge, sprawling, exuberant, mysterious, almost unimaginably dense work of 800 pages, covering events on three continents from the creation of man in Genesis to the dawn of the twenty-first century," and adds that

"Terra Nostra presents a common reader with enormous problems simply of understanding what is going on." *Newsweek*'s Peter S. Prescott notes: "To talk about [*Terra Nostra*] at all we must return constantly to five words: excess, surreal, baroque, masterpiece, [and] unreadable."

In 1992 Fuentes produced *The Buried Mirror: Reflections on Spain in the New World,* a historical work that discusses the formation and development of the Latin American world. The title refers to polished rocks found in the tombs of ancient Mediterranean and Amerindian peoples, presaging, in Fuentes's view, the convergence of these distant cultures. Fuentes writes that his book is "dedicated to a search for the cultural continuity that can inform and transcend the economic and political destiny and fragmentation of the Hispanic world." Attempting to disentangle the complex legacy of Spanish settlement in the New World, Fuentes first addresses the mixed ethnicity of the Spanish conquerors, whose progeny include Celts, Phoenicians, Greeks, Romans, Arabs, and Jews, and the consequent diversity produced in Latin America through war, colonization, and miscegenation.

Praising Fuentes's intriguing though broad subject, Nicolas Shumway writes in the *New York Times Book Review,* "The range of the book is both its principal defect and its chief virtue. Beginning with the prehistoric cave paintings at Altamira in Spain and ending with contemporary street art in East Los Angeles, Mr. Fuentes seeks to cover all of Spanish and Spanish-American history, with frequent digressions on a particular artist, political figure, novel or painting." *The Buried Mirror,* according to David Ewing Duncan in a *Washington Post Book World* review, is "invigorated by the novelist's sense of irony, paradox and sensuality. Here is a civilization, he says, that defies whatever stereotypes we may hold, a society at once erotic and puritanical, cruel and humane, legalistic and corrupt, energetic and sad." Guy Garcia notes in *Time* that the book "represents an intellectual homecoming for Fuentes, who conceived of the project as 'a fantastic opportunity to write my own cultural biography.'"

Four years later Fuentes followed with *A New Time for Mexico,* a collection of essays on the internal injustice and international indignity suffered by Mexico. Viewed as a sequel to his 1971 publication *Tiempo mexicano,* translated as "Mexican Time," Fuentes addresses current events in his native country, including political reform, the Chiapas rebellion, social inequities, and the significance of the North American Free Trade Agreement (NAFTA) for Mexico and its perception in the United States. Though noting the bias of Fuentes's strong nationalism, Roderic A. Camp maintains in *Library Journal* that his "brief cultural vignettes" are "appealing and insightful." A *Publishers Weekly* reviewer commends Fuentes's "lapidary, lyrical meditations on Mexico as a land of continual metamorphosis."

In *The Orange Tree* Fuentes offers five novellas whose subjects span several centuries, each connected by the image of the orange and its perennial source. For Fuentes the orange tree signifies the possibilities of beauty, sustenance, transplantation, and rejuvenation, as its seeds were introduced to Spain through Roman and Moorish invaders, reached the New World with the conquistadors, and have flourished since. Fuentes illustrates various manifestations of violence, deception, and suffering by recounting episodes from the conquest of Roman Iberia and Mexico, a contemporary corporate takeover, and the death wish of an American actor.

"In all this intercourse between Old World and New, Rome and Africa and Spain, past and present," Alan Cheuse writes in Chicago *Tribune Books,* "Fuentes makes the older material resonate with all of the exotic and yet familiar attraction of compelling human behavior." Michael Kerrigan praises the work in a *Times Literary Supplement* review noting that "The challenge and opportunity *The Orange Tree* presents its reader are those of escaping from 'a more or less protected individuality' into a wider existence of multiple possibility and a cyclical history which holds past and present in simultaneity and in ceaseless renewal." Kerrigan concludes, "What strikes the reader first in Fuentes' work may be his erudition and intellectual rigour, but what remains in the mind is his sympathy, his concern to commemorate the countless lives sacrificed in pain and obscurity so that we might live."

In 1995 Fuentes published *Diana, the Goddess Who Hunts Alone,* a semi-autobiographical novel that follows a love affair between an unnamed, married Mexican novelist and an American film actress, Diana Soren. The fictional romance, however, contains obvious parallels to the author's real-life affair with film actress Jean Seberg. Mirroring actual events surrounding the liaison between Fuentes and Seberg, the writer meets Soren at a New Year's Eve party in 1969 and follows her to a Santiago film location where they enjoy a passionate, albeit brief, relationship. After several months of literary conversation and tenuous intimacy, the self-absorbed writer is abandoned by the unstable actress who maintains a second relationship via telephone with a Black Panther and keeps a photograph of her last lover, Clint Eastwood, by her bed.

Though the book received mixed reviews, Rosanne Daryl Thomas observes in Chicago *Tribune Books* that the novel reveals "the tensions between imagination, language and reality, between generosity born of love and the profound selfishness often found in artists." Thomas concludes, "Carlos Fuentes takes off the mask of literary creation and reveals a man nakedly possessed by a desperate passion. Then he raises the mask to his face and tells a fascinating, frightening tale of heartbreak."

Fuentes's 1997 work *The Crystal Frontier,* subtitled "a novel in nine stories," looks at relations between the U.S. and Mexico through the prism of Leonardo Barroso, a political wheeler-dealer around whom the various tales revolve. The title refers to the U.S.-Mexico border, lying only a few miles from Barroso's villa. The metaphoric distance between the two countries is reflected in the relationships between Mexicans and Americans in the fiction. "Girlfriends," for example, depicts the relationship between an affluent white woman and her Mexican maid, while the title story recasts the characters as a window washer and a businessman.

The story cycle earned decidedly mixed critical reviews. Writing in the *New York Times Book Review,* Jay Parini bewailed its "woefully unimagined central character." Other reviewers found the material didactic and lacking in feel for its American characters. "[F]or a book that seeks to depict the ways in which Americans misunderstand Mexicans and Mexico," observed a reviewer in *Publishers Weekly,* "there are a surprising number of stereotypes and cliches of life in the States." However, Jack Shreve of *Library Journal* excused these excesses, calling *The Crystal Frontier* "a brilliant update on relations between an extremely poor country and the richest in the world."

BIOGRAPHICAL/CRITICAL SOURCES:

BOOKS

Authors and Artists for Young Adults, Volume 4, Gale (Detroit), 1990.

Brushwood, John S., *Mexico in Its Novel: A Nation's Search for Identity,* University of Texas Press, 1966.

Contemporary Literary Criticism, Gale, Volume 3, 1975; Volume 8, 1978; Volume 10, 1979; Volume 13, 1980; Volume 22, 1982; Volume 41, 1987; Volume 60, 1991.

Dictionary of Literary Biography, Volume 113: *Modern Latin American Fiction Writers, First Series,* Gale, 1992.

Donoso, Jose, *The Boom in Spanish American Literature: A Personal History,* Columbia University Press, 1977.

Helmuth, Chalene, *The Postmodern Fuentes,* Bucknell University Press (Cranbury, NJ), 1997.

Hispanic Literature Criticism, Gale, 1994.

Plimpton, George, editor, *Writers at Work: The Paris Review Interviews, Sixth Series,* Penguin Books, 1984.

Williams, R. L., *The Writings of Carlos Fuentes,* University of Texas Press (Austin), 1996.

World Literature Criticism, Gale, 1992.

Van Delden, Marteen, *Carlos Fuentes, Mexico and Modernity,* Vanderbilt University Press (Nashville, TN), 1997.

PERIODICALS

Booklist, September 15, 1996; July 19, 1997.
Boston Globe Magazine, September 9, 1984.
Forbes, April 21, 1997.
Hispania, May, 1978.
Independent on Sunday, October 19, 1997.
Kirkus Reviews, April 15, 1996, p. 575; September 1, 1997.
Library Journal, January, 1994, p. 96; January, 1995, p. 77; January, 1996, p. 81; May 1, 1996, p. 112; August, 1997.
London Review of Books, May 10, 1990, p. 26.
Los Angeles Times, October 24, 1997.
Nation, February 17, 1992, p. 205.
New Perspectives, spring, 1994, p. 54.
New Statesman and Society, August 26, 1994, p. 37; September 29, 1995, p. 57.
Newsweek, November 1, 1976.
New Republic, August 25, 1997.
New Yorker, March 4, 1961; January 26, 1981; February 24, 1986.
New York Review of Books, June 11, 1964.
New York Times Book Review, November 7, 1976; October 19, 1980; October 6, 1991, p. 3; April 26, 1992, p. 9; October 22, 1995, p. 12; August 11, 1996; October 26, 1997.
Observer, April 1, 1990, p. 67.
Paris Review, winter, 1981.
Publishers Weekly, April 15, 1996, p. 55; August 11, 1997.
Review, winter, 1976.
Saturday Review, October 30, 1976.
Time, June 29, 1992, p. 78.
Times Literary Supplement, June 10, 1994, p. 23; September 29, 1995, p. 27.
Tribune Books (Chicago), April 19, 1992; April 11, 1994, p. 6; December 17, 1995, p. 3.
Village Voice, January 28, 1981; April 1, 1986.
Washington Post, May 5, 1988.
Washington Post Book World, October 26, 1976; January 14, 1979; March 29, 1992.
World Literature Today, autumn, 1994, p. 794.

*   *   *

FULLER, Buckminster
See FULLER, R(ichard) Buckminster (Jr.)

FULLER, R(ichard) Buckminster (Jr.) 1895-1983
(Buckminster Fuller)

PERSONAL: Born July 12, 1895, in Milton, MA; died of a heart attack, July 1, 1983, in Los Angeles, CA; son of Richard Buckminster (a merchant) and Caroline Wolcott (Andrews) Fuller; married Anne Hewlett, July 12, 1917 (died July, 1983); children: Alexandra Willets (deceased), Allegra (Mrs. Robert Snyder). *Education:* Attended Harvard University, 1913-15, and U.S. Naval Academy, 1917.

CAREER: Writer and lecturer. Richards, Atkinson & Kaserick, Boston, MA, apprentice machine fitter, 1914; Armour & Co., New York, NY, apprentice, 1915-17, assistant export manager, 1919-21; national account sales manager, Kelly Springfield Truck Co., 1922; president, Stockade Building System, 1922-27; 4-D Co., Chicago, IL, founder, 1927, president, 1927-32; assistant director of research, Pierce Foundation-American Radiator-Standard Sanitary Manufacturing Co., 1930; Dymaxion Corp., Bridgeport, Conn., founder, 1932, director and chief engineer, 1932-36, vice-president and chief engineer, 1941-42; assistant to director of research and development, Phelps Dodge Corp., 1936-38; technical consultant, *Fortune* magazine, 1938-40; chief of mechanical engineering section, Board of Economic Warfare, 1942-44; special assistant to director, Foreign Economic Administration, 1944; chairman of board and administrative engineer, Dymaxion Dwelling Machines, 1944-46; Fuller Research Foundation, Wichita, KS, chairman of board of trustees, 1946-54; president, Geodesics, Inc., 1954-56; Synergetics, Inc., Raleigh, NC, president, 1954-59; Southern Illinois University, Carbondale, 1956-83, began as research professor, became professor emeritus; Plydomes, Inc., Des Moines, IA, president, beginning 1957; Tetrahelix Corp., Hamilton, OH, chairman of board, beginning 1959. Chairman of board, Buckminster Fuller Institute, beginning 1959; U.S. representative to American-Russian Protocol Exchange, U.S.S.R., 1959; trustee, Research and Design Institute, 1966; director, Temcor Corporation, 1967; University of Detroit, Detroit, MI, R. Buckminster Fuller Professor of Architecture, beginning 1970. *Military service:* U.S. Navy, 1917-19; became lieutenant.

MEMBER: World Academy of Art and Science (fellow), World Society for Ekistics (vice-president; international president, 1975-77), International Society for Stereology, Royal Society of Arts (Benjamin Franklin life fellow), Royal Institute of British Architects, Society of Venezuelan Architects, Mexican College and Institute of Architects, Institute for Advanced Philosophic Research, Mensa (international president, 1975-83), Institute of General Semantics (fellow and honorary trustee), Institute of Human Ecology, American Association for the Advancement of Science (life fellow), American Institute of Architects (honorary life member), National Academy of Sciences (member of Building Research Institute), National Institute of Arts and Letters (life member), American Society of Professional Geographers, American Association of University Professors, American Academy of Arts and Letters (academician, 1980), American Society for Metals, Society of Architectural Historians, Harvard Engineering Society, Lincoln Academy of Illinois, Architectural League of New York, Phi Beta Kappa, Sigma Xi, Alpha Rho Chi, Tau Sigma Delta, Century Club (New York), New York Yacht Club, Northeast Harbor Fleet, Camden Yacht Club, Somerset Club (Boston), Authors Club (London).

AWARDS, HONORS: Award of merit from New York chapter of American Institute of Architects, 1952; award of merit from U.S.

Marine Corps, 1954; Gran Premio, Trienniale de Milano, 1954 and 1957; Centennial Award, Michigan State University, 1955; gold medal scarab, National Architectural Society, 1958; gold medal, Philadelphia chapter of American Institute of Architects, 1960; Frank P. Brown Medal, Franklin Institute, 1960; Allied Professions gold medal, American Institute of Architects, 1963; Plomade de Oro Award, Society of Mexican Architects, 1963; Brandeis University Special Notable Creative Achievement Award of the Year, 1964; Delta Phi Delta Gold Key Laureate, 1964; Industrial Designers Society of America Award of Excellence, 1966; Graham Foundation fellow, 1966-67; Lincoln Academy of Illinois, fellow and Order of Lincoln Medal, 1967; gold medal, National Institute of Arts and Letters, 1968; named Humanist of the Year, American Association of Humanists, 1969; Dean's Award, State University of New York, 1980; named to Housing Hall of Fame, 1981; Presidential Medal of Freedom, 1983. Recipient of about forty honorary degrees from numerous colleges and universities, including University of North Carolina, 1954, University of Michigan, 1955, Washington University, 1957, Southern Illinois University, 1959, Rollins College, 1960, University of Colorado, 1964, University of New Mexico, 1964, Clemson University, 1964, Monmouth College, 1965, Long Island University, 1966, Clarkson College, 1967. "Buckminster Fuller Recognition Day" declared by University of Colorado, 1963, state of Massachusetts, 1977, cities of Boston and Cambridge, 1977, state of Minnesota, 1978, state of Illinois, 1980, city of Buffalo, 1980, city of Austin, 1981.

WRITINGS:

4D Time-Lock, privately printed, 1927, reprinted, N. M. Lama Foundation, 1972.
Nine Chains to the Moon, Lippincott, 1938.
(With others) *New Worlds in Engineering,* Chrysler Co., 1940.
Industrialization of Brazil, Board of Economic Warfare, 1943.
Survey of the Industrialization of Housing, U.S. Foreign Economics Administration, 1944.
(With Robert W. Marks; under name Buckminster Fuller) *The Dymaxion World of Buckminster Fuller,* Reinhold, 1960.
Geoscope 1960, edited by James Robert Hillier, Princeton University, 1960.
New Approaches to Structure, [Washington, DC], 1961.
Untitled Epic Poem of the History of Industrialization, J. Williams, 1962.
No More Second Hand God, and Other Writings, Southern Illinois University Press, 1963.
Ideas and Integrities: A Spontaneous Autobiographical Disclosure, edited by Robert W. Marks, Prentice-Hall, 1963.
Education Automation: Freeing the Scholar to Return to His Studies, Southern Illinois University Press, 1963.
Charles Eliot Norton 1961-1962 Lectures at Harvard University, Harvard University Press, 1963.
Governor's Conference with Buckminster Fuller, Governor's Office (Raleigh), 1963.
(With John McHale) *World Design Science Decade, 1965-1975: Inventory of World Resources, Human Trends, and Needs—Phase 1 of 5 Two-Year Increments of World Retooling Design Decade Proposed to the International Union of Architects,* Southern Illinois University, 1963.
(With McHale) *World Resources Inventory, Human Trends and Needs,* Southern Illinois University, 1963.
World Design Science Decade, 1965-1975: The Design Initiative (includes phase 1, [1964], document 2, also brief outlines of phases 2, 3, 4, and 5), Southern Illinois University, 1964.

Comprehensive Thinking, edited by McHale, Southern Illinois University, 1965.
What I Am Trying to Do, Cape Goliard, 1968.
(Author of foreword) Isamu Noguchi, *A Sculptor's World,* Harper, 1968.
(Contributor) Richard Kostelanetz, editor, *Beyond Left and Right: Radical Thought for Our Times,* Morrow, 1968.
Operating Manual for Spaceship Earth, Southern Illinois University Press, 1969.
(With others) *The Arts and Man,* Prentice-Hall, 1969.
Utopia or Oblivion: The Prospects for Humanity, Bantam, 1969.
Reprints and Selected Articles, Bern Porter, 1969.
Planetary Planning, Jawaharlal Nehru Memorial Fund, 1969.
Fifty Years of the Design Science Revolution and the World Game: A Collection of Articles and Papers on Design, Southern Illinois University, 1969.
(With others) *Approaching the Benign Environment: The Franklin Lectures in the Sciences and Humanities,* University of Alabama Press, 1970.
I Seem to Be a Verb, Bantam, 1970.
(Author of introduction) Samuel Rosenberg, *The Come As You Are Masquerade Party,* Prentice-Hall, 1970.
The Buckminster Fuller Reader, edited by James Miller, J. Cape, 1970.
The World Game: Integrative Resource Utilization Planning Tool, Southern Illinois University, 1971.
Old Man River: An Environmental Domed City, Parsimonious Press, 1972.
(Editor with Henry Dreyfuss) *Symbol Sourcebook: An Authoritative Guide to International Graphic Symbols,* McGraw, 1972.
Intuition, Doubleday, 1972, second revised edition, Impact, 1983.
Buckminster Fuller to Children of Earth, Doubleday, 1972.
Earth, Inc., Doubleday-Anchor, 1973.
Synergetics: Explorations in the Geometry of Thinking, Macmillan, 1975.
And It Came to Pass—Not to Stay, Macmillan, 1976.
(With Edgar J. Applewhite) *Synergetics Two: Explorations in the Geometry of Thinking,* Macmillan, 1979.
R. Buckminster Fuller on Education, edited by Robert D. Kahn and Peter H. Wagschal, University of Massachusetts Press, 1979.
(With Kiyoshi Kuromiya) *Critical Path,* St. Martin's, 1981.
Tetrascroll: A Cosmic Fairy Tale, St. Martin's, 1982.
Grunch of Giants, St. Martin's, 1983.
Cosmography: A Posthumous Scenario for the Future of Humanity, Macmillan (New York), 1992.

Also produced recordings "Designing Environments," Big Sur Recordings, 1976, "Anticipating Tomorrow's Schools," [Philadelphia], 1975, and "R. Buckminster Fuller Thinks Aloud," Credo 2. Contributor to journals. Editor, *Convoy* (magazine), 1918-19; publisher, *Shelter* (magazine), 1931-32; editor and author, "Notes on the Future" column, *Saturday Review,* beginning 1964.

SIDELIGHTS: In 1927, when he was thirty-two years old, Richard Buckminster ("Bucky") Fuller, Jr., stood at the shores of Lake Michigan and contemplated whether to take his own life. Despondent over the death of his four-year-old daughter, in disgrace with his family because he was the first Fuller in five generations to have been expelled (twice) from Harvard University, the young man had also just lost his job and was a debt-ridden alcohol abuser. As he would later recall, Fuller paused for a while at the lake's edge on "a jump-or-think basis." The answer came to him, as a *New York Times* article reported, when Fuller realized that "you do not have the right to eliminate yourself. You do not belong to you. You belong to the universe." With that, Fuller turned from the shore and embarked on what would become an illustrious career as one of America's most innovative engineers and inventors, as well as a noted philosopher, poet, educator, and environmentalist.

Best known for his invention of the geodesic dome, the self-described "citizen of the twenty-first century" was a major proponent of using science to improve life on what he coined Spaceship Earth. Acclaim, even acceptance, did not come easily at first; early in his career Fuller was regarded by some as a crackpot because of such utopian inventions as the Dymaxion House, a fully self-sufficient prefabricated dwelling, and the Dymaxion Bathroom, the whole of which could be produced en masse, like an auto body. Perhaps the most controversial of these early innovations was the Dymaxion Car. Built in the 1930s, the car was a fuel efficient egg-shaped three-wheeler (efficiency estimated at 40 miles per gallon) that could reach speeds of up to 120 miles per hour. The promising prototype succumbed to poor publicity after a 1935 accident in which, as the *New York Times* stated, "one of the cars collided with a sedan in Chicago and both vehicles overturned. By the time reporters arrived, the other car had been towed away. The driver of the Dymaxion car was killed, and under such headlines as 'Three Wheeled Car Kills Driver,' newspaper accounts did not mention that another car had been involved."

Despite such setbacks, Fuller's enthusiasm for Dymaxion products (the word is an amalgam of "dynamic, maximum" [efficiency], and "ion" [of power]) and other futuristic concepts continued unabated. And while the tide of public approval began to turn his way with the production of the Dymaxion Ariocean World Map—the first flat chart that displayed the entire surface of the earth without distortion—Fuller's reputation as an engineer of vision was cemented with the 1947 unveiling of the geodesic dome.

Defining geodesic as "the most economical momentary relationship among a plurality of points and events," the self-taught architect had designed that rare thing—a "structure [that] occurs in nature and can be built by man," according to the *New York Times*. The dome is "as self-sufficient as a butterfly's wing and as strong as an egg shell," the *Times* continued. "It depends on no heavy vaults or flying buttresses to support it. Its strength is derived instead from a complex of alternating squares and triangles which produce a phenomenal strength-to-weight ratio when pressure is applied to any point on the structure. It crops up all over in nature—in viruses, in the cornea of the eye. Fuller patented it in 1953—almost like getting a patent on gravity." Within a short time of its introduction, the geodesic dome was being used as everything from a cover for an automobile plant to a hangar for a Marine Corps helicopter station. "Radomes" housed radar equipment along miles of the Distant Early Warning Lines in the Arctic. Russian premier Nikita Khrushchev was impressed by the structure and invited its inventor to lecture to Soviet engineers.

As an author, Fuller often described a technological utopia waiting for those willing to shed the old ideas about science and society. A passage from his study *Synergetics: Explanations in the Geometry of Thinking,* for instance, predicts a future "moving intuitively toward an utterly classless, raceless, omnicooperative, omniworld humanity." Naturally, some critics took exception to this kind of speculation; Robert Wood and O. B. Hardison, Jr., found *Synergetics* an engrossing if somewhat difficult read. Wood, writing in *Saturday Review,* was "exasperated" by the

book's "approach to evidence and validation. [The author] interweaves strangely disparate elements: fact and value, commentary on life and the universe, quantity and quality, evidence and inference. And he does this majestically, carelessly, in a manner calculated to infuriate the conscientious scholar in whatever field he happens to be writing about."

New York Times Book Review critic Hardison called *Synergetics* "a kind of *summa theologica* of Fuller's mathematics, philosophy and design theories." Citing the numerous graphs, charts, and equations the author included in the work, Hardison remarked that as a reader "you grope for analogies. The Notebooks of Leonardo. The Opera of Paracelsus. Pascal's *Pensees.* Or Alexander Pope's remark about Creation: 'A mighty maze, but not without a plan.' [The book] is alternately brilliant and obscure, opaque and shot through with moments of poetry. What becomes clear with patience is that the virtues and the liabilities are one. *Synergetics* could not have been written in any other way because its language and mathematics are vehicles for a vision. They embody the vision and if they were different the vision itself would be different—perhaps impossible to express, but certainly impossible to express convincingly."

One of the last major books published before his death, Fuller's *Critical Path,* was called by its author "by far the most important thing" he had ever done, according to Guy Murchie in the *Chicago Tribune Book World.* Essentially a long-range plan for the revitalization of Spaceship Earth, Critical Path employs some of the author's most startling scientific views, as well as an admonishment for its readers to stop being wary of technology and to start appreciating the potential gifts that science offers. For instance, Fuller wrote that the "most effective educational system for human beings is to be derived from the home video cassette system and supporting books, the pages of which are also to be called forth on world-satellite-interlinked video 'library' screens as published in any language." "Some will consider *Critical Path* too far up in the clouds for practical use because they are biased against technology," stated Murchie, "but if they could only let themselves consider his message with a fully open mind, I think they just might discover something profoundly spiritual there."

Fuller's last book, *Grunch of Giants,* summarizes some of Fuller's most significant theories with an emphasis on his warning against the pervasive fear and greed generated by life in a society largely controlled by corporations. (Fuller's word "Grunch" is actually an acronym for "Gross universal Cash Heist.") Reviewers found the book fascinating, although some faulted Fuller's tendency toward political diatribe and an occasional lack of clarity in his explanations. Responding to criticisms of Fuller's views as impractical and excessively idealistic, Art Seidenbaum of *Los Angeles Times Book Review* commented: "[Fuller's] example is a life lived in constant search of fresh perception, of ways to translate formulations of philosophical good news through physical invention." Several critics noted that while Fuller's writings are flawed, his life suggests greatness. Nearly completed at the time of his death in 1983, *Cosmography: A Posthumous Scenario for the Future of Humanity* articulates Fuller's response to the question of humankind's purpose in the universe. In the volume he advocates the realization of human potential through principles of science and technology. "Fuller saw the human race as still living in the Dark Ages, locked into a futile circle of misinformation, perverted by big business, militarism and organized religion. He sought the rebirth of humanity in a better future, a world in which individual genius would be nurtured rather than suppressed," commented Ian Stewart in *Nature.*

BIOGRAPHICAL/CRITICAL SOURCES:

BOOKS

Baldwin, J., *Bucky Works: Buckminster Fuller's Ideas Today,* John Wiley, 1996.

Casper, Dale E., *Richard Buckminster Fuller, Architect: Twenty Years of Journal Reviews,* Vance Bibliographies (Monticello, IL), 1988.

Close, G. W., *R. Buckminster Fuller,* Council of Planning Libraries, 1977.

Hatch, Alden, *Buckminster Fuller: At Home in the Universe,* Crown, 1974.

Kenner, Hugh, *Bucky: A Guided Tour of Buckminster Fuller,* Morrow, 1973.

Lord, Athena V., *Pilot for Spaceship Earth: R. Buckminster Fuller, Architect, Inventor and Poet* (for juveniles), Macmillan, 1978.

McHale, John, R., *Buckminster Fuller,* Braziller, 1962.

Moore, Joe S., *Basic Bucky,* J. S. Moore (Salinas, CA), 1992.

Pawley, Martin, *Buckminster Fuller,* Trefoil Publications (London), 1990.

Potter, Robert R., *Buckminster Fuller,* Silver Burdett Press (Englewood Cliffs, NJ), 1990.

Rosen, Sidney, *Wizard of the Dome: R. Buckminster Fuller, Designer for the Future,* Little, Brown, 1969.

Sieden, Lloyd Steven, *Buckminster Fuller's Universe: An Appreciation,* foreword by Norman Cousins, Plenum Press (New York), 1989.

Snyder, R., editor, *R. Buckminster Fuller,* St. Martin's, 1980.

PERIODICALS

Architectural Forum, October, 1963.
Business Week, May 10, 1958.
Chicago Tribune Book World, March 22, 1981.
Futurist, November-December, 1989, p. 14.
Horizon, summer, 1968.
Los Angeles Times Book Review, April 26, 1981; September 19, 1982.
Life, February 26, 1971.
Nation, June 15, 1970.
National Review, July 22, 1983.
Nature, April 16, 1992, p. 633.
Newsweek, July 13, 1959; August 5, 1963.
New Yorker, October 10, 1959.
New York Times, August 28, 1978.
New York Times Book Review, July 28, 1963; May 5, 1968; April 20, 1969; June 29, 1975; April 19, 1981; July 17, 1983.
New York Times Magazine, August 23, 1959; April 23, 1967; July 6, 1975.
People Weekly, July 21, 1980.
Saturday Review, May 2, 1970; May 31, 1975; September-October, 1983.
Science Digest, October, 1964.
Time, October 20, 1958; January 10, 1964; March 10, 1967; March 1, 1968; May 11, 1970.
Times (London), April 14, 1983.
Times Literary Supplement, September 6, 1963; August 6, 1964; September 11, 1969; October 28, 1983.
Washington Post, June 10, 1970.
Whole Earth Review, fall, 1991, p. 50; spring, 1996, p. 6.

FUSSELL, Paul 1924-

PERSONAL: Surname rhymes with "Russell"; born March 22, 1924, in Pasadena, CA; son of Paul (an attorney) and Wilhma (Sill) Fussell; married Betty Ellen Harper (a journalist), June 17, 1949 (divorced 1987); married Harriette Behringer, April 11, 1987; children: Rosalind, Sam. *Education:* Pomona College, B.A., 1947; Harvard University, M.A., 1949, Ph.D., 1952.

ADDRESSES: Home—2020 Walnut St., Apt. 4-H, Philadelphia, PA 19103. *Office*—Department of English, University of Pennsylvania, Philadelphia, PA 19104-6273.

CAREER: Connecticut College, New London, instructor in English, 1951-54; Rutgers University, New Brunswick, NJ, assistant professor, 1955-59, associate professor, 1959-64, professor of English, 1964-76, John DeWitt Professor of English Literature, 1976-83; University of Pennsylvania, Philadelphia, Donald T. Regan Professor of English Literature, 1983-94. Fulbright lecturer, University of Heidelberg, 1957-58. Regional chairman, Woodrow Wilson National Fellowship Foundation, 1962-64. Consulting editor, Random House, Inc., 1964-65. Lecturer, American University, 1965–. Visiting professor, King's College, London, 1990-92. *Military service:* U.S. Army, Infantry, 1943-47; became first lieutenant; received Bronze Star and two Purple Hearts.

MEMBER: Modern Language Association of America, Academy of Literary Studies, Society of American historians; English Institute (secretary, 1964-70), Royal Society of Literature (fellow).

AWARDS, HONORS: James D. Phelan Award, 1965, for nonfiction; Lindback Foundation Award, 1971; National Endowment for the Humanities senior fellowship, 1973-74; National Book Critics Circle Award and National Book Award, both 1976, both for *The Great War and Modern Memory*; Ralph Waldo Emerson Award, Phi Beta Kappa, 1976; Guggenheim fellow, 1977-78; American Academy and Institute of Arts and Letters award, 1980, for excellence in literature; *Abroad: British Literary Traveling between the Wars* was nominated for a National Book Critics Circle Award, 1980; Litt.D., Pomona College, 1981; M.A., University of Pennsylvania, 1983; Litt.D., Monmouth College, 1985; Rockefeller fellow, 1983-84.

WRITINGS:

Theory of Prosody in Eighteenth-Century England, Connecticut College, 1954.

(Co-author) *The Presence of Walt Whitman,* Columbia University Press, 1962.

The Rhetorical World of Augustan Humanism: Ethics and Imagery from Swift to Burke, Oxford University Press, 1965.

Poetic Meter and Poetic Form, Random House, 1965, revised edition, 1979.

Samuel Johnson and the Life of Writing, Harcourt, 1971.

The Great War and Modern Memory, Oxford University Press, 1975.

(Editor) *The Ordeal of Alfred M. Hale,* Leo Cooper, 1975.

Abroad: British Literary Traveling between the Wars, Oxford University Press, 1980.

The Boy Scout Handbook and Other Observations, Oxford University Press, 1982.

(Editor) *Siegfried Sassoon's Long Journey: Selections from the Sherston Memoirs,* Oxford University Press, 1983.

Class: A Guide through the American Status System, Summit Books, 1983, published as *Class,* Ballantine, 1984 (published in England as *Caste Marks: Style and Status in the USA,* Heinemann, 1984).

(Editor) *The Norton Book of Travel,* Norton, 1987.

Thank God for the Atom Bomb and Other Essays, Summit Books (New York), 1988.

Wartime: Understanding and Behavior in the Second World War, Oxford University Press, 1989.

(Editor) *The Norton Book of Modern War,* Norton, 1991.

BAD, or, The Dumbing of America, Summit Books, 1991.

(Editor) *The Bloody Game: An Anthology of Modern War,* Scribners, 1992.

The Anti-Egotist: Kingsley Amis, Man of Letters, Oxford University Press (New York), 1994.

Doing Battle: The Making of a Skeptic, Little, Brown (Boston), 1996.

Contributor of reviews and essays to *Saturday Review, Encounter, Virginia Quarterly Review, Partisan Review,* and other publications. Contributing editor to *Harper's,* 1979-83, and *New Republic,* 1979-85.

SIDELIGHTS: It was not until Paul Fussell "got tired of writing" what he was "supposed to write," as he told Robert Dahlin of *Publishers Weekly,* that he became a successful author. For twenty years, Fussell wrote critical works on poetic theory and eighteenth-century English literature, none of which sold more than 8,000 copies. But with *The Great War and Modern Memory,* a study of the cultural impact of the First World War, came the realization that he could reach a general audience. *The Great War and Modern Memory* has sold over 50,000 copies and won Fussell a National Book Award and the National Book Critics Circle Award. "It was the perfect moment in a writer's life," he told Dahlin, "the right subject, the right time. It was an accidental masterpiece." Since his successful break with academic writing, Fussell has continued to write nonfiction for a general audience.

As Fussell explains in the preface, *The Great War and Modern Memory* is about "the British experience of the Western Front from 1914 to 1918 and some of the literary means by which it has been remembered, conventionalized and mythologized." Fussell argues that the modernist sensibility—what Robert Hughes of *Time* defines as "the sense of absurdity, disjuncture and polarization, the loathing of duly constituted authorities, the despair and the irony"—derives from the horrors of the First World War.

By comparing the art and literature dealing with earlier wars to that about the First World War, Fussell traces the differences between prewar and postwar culture. The war is likened by Hughes to "a fault line [that] had opened in history, and all that had been taken as normal vanished into its rumbling cleft." Writing in the *New York Times Book Review,* Frank Kermode states that "the national imagination, even the texture of our culture, have been permanently qualified by those years, and by men's understanding of what happened in them."

The winner of the National Book Award and the National Book Critics Circle Award, *The Great War and Modern Memory* also received praise from the critics. Hughes calls the book "a scrupulously argued and profoundly affecting account of what the Great War changed," while a *New Yorker* critic finds it "a learned and well-balanced book that is also bright and sensitive." Although having doubts about some of Fussell's conclusions, Kermode thinks that "one's sense of the whole book is that on the major issues it is right, skillful and compassionate. . . . This book is an important contribution to our understanding of how we came to make [the First World War] part of our minds."

In *Abroad: British Literary Traveling between the Wars,* Fussell examines the literary record left by the postwar generation of travelers, drawing a clear distinction between the traditional traveler of that time and the modern tourist. Richard Rodriguez of the *Los Angeles Times Book Review* finds that Fussell is "concerned with British travelers and travel writing in the years between the wars. The '20's and '30's were, argues Fussell, the great years of modern travel. After wartime gray, cold, deprivation and confinement, 'imaginative and sensitive' Englishmen sought release in travel 'to the glittering regions of the sun: the Mediterranean, the Middle East, Africa, and Latin America." Writing in the Washington Post Book World, Peter Stansky observes that the "heyday of travel began in the aftermath of the First World War, about which [Fussell] wrote with so much originality and force in *The Great War and Modern Memory.* The present book, which might serve as a coda to its distinguished predecessor, looks back again and again to the first war to explain the peculiarities and excitements of the postwar reaction, not least among them the phenomena of travel and travel writing." Dahlin believes that in both books Fussell "peels away layers of history and experience to uncover English literary observations underlying them."

Fussell maintains that the period between the world wars was the last great age of travel, now replaced by mere tourism. When travelers wrote books about their experiences, they created what Fussell believes is a distinct literary form. Stansky notes that "it is hard to imagine the case for travel writing, a genre worthy of a place alongside poetry and the novel, being made more impressively." Fussell devotes chapters to the travel writing of D. H. Lawrence, Graham Greene, Evelyn Waugh, and other British literary figures. He also resurrects Robert Byron's *The Road to Oxiana* as a masterpiece of the genre. Jonathan Raban of the *New York Times Book Review* calls *Abroad: British Literary Traveling between the Wars* "an exemplary piece of criticism. It is immensely readable. It bristles with ideas. It disinters a real lost masterpiece from the library stacks. It admits a whole area of writing—at last!—to its proper place in literary history."

Fussell's contention that travel has been replaced by tourism—and that travel books are therefore no longer written—is rebuked by Raban, who points out that "two of the best books ever written in the genre, Mark Twain's *Innocents Abroad* and Evelyn Waugh's own *Labels,* happen to be about tourists on a package holiday." Raban makes clear that the essential condition on travel writing remains with us: "the experience of living among strangers, away from home." Stansky, too, disagrees that travel is dead. "The spirit of travel," he writes, "will prove inextinguishable: the space ship is waiting, the hotel is on Mars."

In *The Boy Scout Handbook and Other Observations* Fussell returns to some of the concerns with war found in *The Great War and Modern Memory.* A collection of reviews and essays on a variety of literary topics, the book is "actually the elaborate, multifaceted working out of traumas suffered during World War II, when Fussell was plunged from boyhood into manhood by his experiences as a line officer in Europe," as Joseph McLellan maintains in the *Washington Post.* Peter Ackroyd of the London *Times* believes that "some of the most powerful writing in the book comes from [Fussell's] account of his own experiences as an infantryman in France during the Second World War."

Fussell argues that his own war experiences altered his later life. The war, Ackroyd explains, "left him with a profound irony, a certain detachment, and a scepticism about human motives which runs through this book as its unacknowledged theme." D. Keith Mano agrees with this assessment in a *People* article, noting that "when you read Fussell, you can hear a disgruntled giant talking underneath his elegant and explosive prose style." Mano quotes Fussell as explaining: "I'm proud of that. I've created a character out of myself." Ronald B. Shwartz of the *American Spectator* describes Fussell's character as "a kind of thinking man's John Wayne, wielding prose with a certain fetching swagger and acid humor, and blaming it all on nothing less than his stint as a combat platoon leader in WW II."

With the publication of *Class: A Guide through the American Status System,* Fussell turned his attention to a topic touched upon briefly in *The Boy Scout Handbook and Other Observations*: the nature of class distinctions in the United States. He finds these distinctions to be primarily in matters of taste. Fussell claims that our choice of clothes, houses, cars, books, and other items, as well as our language, reveal our class origins. "Of the many guides to social travel that have appeared recently, Mr. Fussell's is surely the most comprehensive, as well as one of the wittiest," Alison Lurie writes in the *New York Times Book Review.*

In his examination of class differences Fussell explains why owning a Mercedes-Benz automobile is hopelessly upper middle class; why red geraniums are gauche; and how a threadbare Oriental rug on your floor can move you into a higher class. Fussell finds American class distinctions so pervasive that he includes a do-it-yourself living room rating test for determining which social class you occupy. Points are awarded for items of furniture, number of books displayed, artwork on the walls, and for other contents. "Most of the author's judgments," Cleveland Amory comments in the *Chicago Tribune Book World,* "are extremely accurate and most of his examples unfailingly interesting."

For those who wish to live outside the class system, Fussell offers an "X" group who are unhindered by class limitations and are able to enjoy true liberty. These X's avoid the pretensions of the upper classes and the insecurities of the proles while commenting ironically on the rest of society. "X's always dress down a peg. . . . They drink cheap but 'excellent' wine; they seldom eat out, . . . ; they favor ironic lawn furniture, if any. In short, they are academics, manfully keeping up with last year's unconventions," as Wilfrid Sheed writes in the *Atlantic.* "'X people' are just wonderful," Yardley states, "and all the rules for living the X life can be found in [the book]; there seem to be at least as many of them as there are for living middle-class life, and they are every bit as rigid."

Returning to a more disturbing subject, Fussell has gained more critical attention with *Wartime: Understanding and Behavior in the Second World War.* Though spoken of as a "good" war because it put an end to the Jewish holocaust, the war, like any war, was abominable, Fussell maintains. This controversial opinion, supported by numerous examples of needless slaughter, has been hailed by some readers as a long-overdue account of the actual horrors of the war as they experienced it. Others have denounced the book, claiming that Fussell's criticisms stem from sympathy with Nazi Germany. "The reaction to this book. . . shows how precious the second [world] war was to the self-esteem of Americans," Fussell told Richard Bernstein of the *New York Times.* Not claiming, as some have said, that the war should not have been fought, Fussell explained, "the war was both necessary and awful. The war was necessary and just and it caused a mess of intellectual and moral ruin." The ground warfare, he claims,

demoralized soldiers who then had a hard time reconciling the brutality of combat experience with their reception as heroes when they came home. *Washington Post Book World* editor Nina King explains, "the war as it was known by the men in the infantry combat units [was] a war of bodies hideously dismembered or blown into a thousand pieces, of grinding, humiliating fear that caused many men to lose control of their bowels and some to go mad. . . . But if the myth of the 'good war' persists 50 years later, it is because many of the survivors who knew the reality accept the myth, either because it is easier to live with, or because the idealistic, 'highminded' side of the war was also part of their understanding."

Thank God for the Atom Bomb and Other Essays declares that the use of nuclear weapons such as the bomb that destroyed Hiroshima is preferable to the carnage Fussell witnessed in Europe and the Pacific. Critics of the decision to use the bomb can easily forget that the minimization of casualties was a factor in reaching that decision, Fussell points out. He addresses this issue—and other war-related topics—to answer the facile comments of critics whose opinions are not informed by experience. Fussell told John Blades of the *Chicago Tribune* that future books will look at other topics. "I finished what I like to think is my last book on the subject [of war], 'The Norton Book of Modern War,' an anthology of war writings from the First War through Vietnam, with my commentary and interpretation. I found it so depressing, really, that I'd like to write a cheerful book, about the circus or the theater or something a little elevating. I'm tired of writing about mass murder and its meaning. After a while, you're persuaded that it doesn't have any meaning."

In *BAD, or, The Dumbing of America,* Fussell finds a source of humor in the banal idiosyncrasies of American culture and habit. In this alphabetically arranged compendium of scorn, he defines BAD, in all capital letters, as "something phony, clumsy, witless, untalented, vacant, or boring that many Americans can be persuaded is genuine, graceful, bright or fascinating." Joseph Epstein observes in the *Times Literary Supplement,* "In Fussell's view, boring is BAD, pretentious is BAD, euphemistic is BAD, not appreciating irony is BAD, unearned informality is BAD, and BAD, too, is much else in America, from public signs to television to U.S. Naval missile firing." Though commended for instances of incisive satire, Fussell received criticism for evincing pretentious and mean-spirited derision toward his fellow citizens, particularly the middle and lower classes. "As a checklist of Socially Correct opinion," Gertrude Himmelfarb writes in *The New Republic,* "and as a cross-reference of the Socially Correct and the Politically Correct, this book is invaluable." Christopher Buckley concludes in the *New York Times Book Review,* "[Fussell] has seen the future and it is broken. 'The new Goddess of Dullness is in the saddle, attended by her outriders Greed, Ignorance, and Publicity.'"

Fussel produced *Doing Battle: The Making of a Skeptic* in 1996, recounting his early experiences in Pasadena, student life at Pomona College and Harvard, his horrific and disillusioning service in World War II, and long career as a professor, historian, literary critic, and relentless commentator on the mediocrity and pernicious distortions of American society. According to Michael Coleman in a *Library Journal* review, Fussell's description of combat experience "is one of the most sordid and compelling war memoirs in recent years." *Kirkus Reviews* similarly notes Fussell's "forthright portrayal of war's horrors and lasting ill effects." Richard Bernstein writes in the *New York Times* that Fussell's memoir "is elegant, witty, caustic, and moving, a frank and at the same time discreet summing up of a well-lived life." Bernstein adds that after exposing the realities of war, *Doing Battle* becomes "a memoir of embattled intellectual life."

BIOGRAPHICAL/CRITICAL SOURCES:

PERIODICALS

American Historical Review, June, 1991, p. 843.
American Scholar, spring, 1992, p. 303.
American Spectator, July, 1983; April, 1984.
Atlantic, October, 1983.
Chicago Tribune, October 1, 1980; November 23, 1989.
Chicago Tribune Book World, November 13, 1983.
Christian Science Monitor, September 10, 1982.
Globe and Mail (Toronto), June 24, 1985; September 23, 1989; March 2, 1991.
Harper's, September, 1995, p. 66.
Kirkus Reviews, July 15, 1996, p. 1023.
Library Journal, August, 1996, p. 82.
Los Angeles Times, November 23, 1980; December 26, 1983; June 23, 1988; December 25, 1989.
Los Angeles Times Book Review, November 6, 1983.
Magazine of Fantasy and Science Fiction, May, 1992, p. 55.
National Review, February 24, 1997.
New Republic, October 28, 1991, p. 27.
New Yorker, October 20, 1975.
New York Review of Books, October 16, 1975.
New York Times, September 1, 1980; November 2, 1980; December 16, 1980; October 8, 1982; November 18, 1983; August 17, 1989; October 11, 1989; October 9, 1996.
New York Times Book Review, August 31, 1975; August 31, 1980; August 29, 1982; November 13, 1983; August 7, 1988; September 3, 1989; October 13, 1991, p. 9; September 11, 1994, p. 12; September 29, 1996.
People Weekly, February 7, 1983.
Philadelphia, December, 1991, p. 63.
Publishers Weekly, October 3, 1980; June 23, 1989; September 13, 1991, p. 69; July 18, 1994, p. 231.
Saturday Review, February 21, 1976.
Time, October 20, 1975; October 31, 1983.
Times (London), March 19, 1981; January 27, 1983.
Times Literary Supplement, March 20, 1981; February 11, 1983; July 6, 1984; September 22, 1989; December 20, 1991, p. 9.
Tribune Books (Chicago), July 27, 1988; August 13, 1989.
Voice Literary Supplement, November, 1983.
Washington Monthly, December 1996.
Washington Post, September 6, 1982; September 28, 1982; July 4, 1988.
Washington Post Book World, September 21, 1980; June 27, 1982; November 6, 1983; August 13, 1989.
Yale Review, July 1997.

G

GADDIS, William 1922-

PERSONAL: Born in 1922, in New York, NY; children: one son, one daughter. *Education:* Attended Harvard College, 1941-45.

ADDRESSES: Agent—Candida Donadio & Associates, 121 West 27th St., New York, NY 10001-6207.

CAREER: New Yorker, New York, NY, fact checker, 1946-47; lived in Latin America, Europe, and North Africa, 1947-52; freelance writer of filmscripts, speeches, and corporate communications, 1956-70; novelist. Has also taught at universities. Distinguished visiting professor at Bard College, 1977.

MEMBER: American Academy of Arts and Letters, American Academy of Arts and Sciences.

AWARDS, HONORS: National Institute of Arts and Letters grant, 1963; National Endowment for the Arts grants, 1967 and 1974; Rockefeller grant and National Book Award for fiction, both 1976, both for *J R;* Guggenheim Fellowship, 1981; MacArthur Foundation Fellowship, 1982; nomination for PEN/Faulkner Award, 1985, for *Carpenter's Gothic;* National Book Award, 1994, and National Book Critics' Circle Award, 1995, for *A Frolic of His Own.*

WRITINGS:

NOVELS

The Recognitions, Harcourt (New York City), 1955, corrected edition, Penguin Books (New York City), 1993.
J R, Knopf (New York City), 1975, corrected edition, Penguin Books, 1993.
Carpenter's Gothic, Viking (New York City), 1985.
A Frolic of His Own, Simon & Schuster (New York City), 1994.

OTHER

Contributor to periodicals, including *Atlantic, Antaeus, New Yorker, New York Times,* and *Harper's.*

SIDELIGHTS: William Gaddis is one of the most highly regarded yet least read novelists in America. In 1976, *New York Times Book Review* contributor George Stade described Gaddis as "a presiding genius . . . of post-war American fiction." Although many readers remain unfamiliar with his work, certain critics have made extravagant claims for it. Richard Toney, in the *San Francisco Review of Books,* describes Gaddis's first book, *The Recognitions,* as "a novel of stunning power, 956 pages of linguistic pyrotechnics and multi-lingual erudition unmatched by any American writer in this century—perhaps in any century." L. J. Davis, in the *National Observer,* writes that Gaddis's second novel, *J R,* "is the equal of—if not superior to—its predecessor"; but the work remains, as Frederick Karl asserts in *Conjunctions,* "perhaps the great unread novel of the postwar era." With the publication in 1994 of *A Frolic of His Own,* which won a National Book Award, Gaddis's work has received wider recognition.

Gaddis has drawn heavily on his own background for the settings of his novels. Born in Manhattan in 1922, he was raised in Massapequa, Long Island, in the house that was the model for the Bast home in *J R.* Like the Basts, Gaddis's maternal relatives were Quakers, though he himself was raised in a Calvinist tradition, as is Wyatt Gwyon in *The Recognitions.* Like Otto in the same novel and Jack Gibbs in *J R,* Gaddis grew up without a father. Haunting all four novels, in fact, is the spirit of a dead or absent father who leaves a ruinous state of affairs for his children, a situation that may be extrapolated to include Gaddis's literary vision of a world abandoned by God and plunged into disorder. The writer's fifth through thirteenth years were spent at a boarding school in Berlin, Connecticut, which not only furnished the fictional Jack Gibbs with the bleak memories recalled in *J R* but also provided the unnamed New England setting for the first chapter of *The Recognitions.* Returning to Long Island to attend Farmingdale High School, Gaddis contracted the illness that debilitates Wyatt in the first novel and that kept Gaddis out of World War II. Instead he attended Harvard and edited the *Harvard Lampoon* until circumstances required him to leave in 1945 without a degree.

Back in New York, Gaddis worked as a fact checker at the *New Yorker,* a job that he later recalled as "terribly good training, a kind of post-graduate school for a writer, checking everything, whether they were stories or profiles or articles. . . A lot of the complications of high finance and so forth in *J R*—I tried very hard to get them all right. And it was very much that for two years at the *New Yorker,*" he told Miriam Berkley in a *Publishers Weekly* interview. At this time he also mingled in the Greenwich Village milieu recreated in the middle section of *The Recognitions.* Here he became acquainted with future Beat writers William Burroughs, Allen Ginsberg, Alan Ansen, Chandler Brossard and Jack Kerouac. (In fact, Kerouac converted Gaddis into a character named Harold Sand in his 1958 novel *The Subterraneans.*) In 1947 Gaddis set off on five years of wandering through Mexico, Central America, Spain, France, and North Africa until, in 1952, he returned to America to complete his first novel.

Published in 1955, *The Recognitions* is an account of personal integration amid collective disintegration, of an individual finding himself in a society losing itself. Protagonist Wyatt Gwyon, a failed seminarian, turns to forging Old Masters in an earnest but misguided attempt to return to an era when art was authentic and sanctioned by God. Gaddis sets Wyatt in stark contrast to most of the other artist figures in the novel: Otto, the playwright; Esme, the poet; Max, the painter; Sinisterra, the counterfeiter—all of whom plagiarize, falsify, or discredit the artistic process. These personages, along with the rest of the novel's large cast of characters, are representative of a society crumbling in a shoddy world so encrusted with counterfeit that "recognitions" of authenticity are nearly impossible.

The action in *The Recognitions* runs on two narrative planes that occasionally intersect. On one plane lives Wyatt, whom Karl in *Conjunctions* calls "an avenging Messiah . . . because he perceives himself as bringing a purifying and cleansing quality, a 'recognition,' to a society that has doomed itself with corruptive sophistication." But Wyatt is hobbled in his pursuit of a "vision of order" (as it is later defined in *Carpenter's Gothic*) by a psychologically crippling boyhood that has instilled in him a mixture of guilt, secrecy, and alienation. The author exposes the compromised worlds of religion and art in the first two chapters, and Wyatt's brief fling with conventionality (complete with wife and nine-to-five job) fails by chapter three, leaving him open to the temptations of the novel's Mephistopheles, Recktall Brown, a corrupt art dealer. Selling his soul to the devil, Wyatt retreats offstage for the entrance of his parodic counterpart, Otto Pivner, whose comic misadventures in Central America and Greenwich Village constitute the second narrative plane of the novel.

Here the "corruptive sophistication" mentioned by *Conjunctions*'s Karl appear as endless discussions of art and religion are carried on through endless parties and bar conversations by those whom Gaddis lampoons as "the educated classes, an ill-dressed, underfed, overdrunken group of squatters with minds so highly developed that they were excused from good manners, tastes so refined in one direction that they were excused for having none in any other, emotions so cultivated that the only aberration was normality, all afloat here on sodden pools of depravity calculated only to manifest the pricelessness of what they were throwing away, the three sexes in two colors, a group of people all mentally and physically the wrong size."

The Recognitions had little immediate critical impact upon publication. Unfortunately, 1955 was "one of American criticism's weakest hours," as Maurice Dolbier noted in a *New York Herald Tribune* article seven years later, and most reviewers were put off by this gargantuan novel by an unknown writer. A few readers recognized its greatness immediately, but only in later years did a historical perspective allow critics to gauge its importance. In his 1975 *Saturday Review* assessment of Gaddis's second novel, John W. Aldridge, an early champion, writes from such a perspective: "As is usually the case with abrasively original work, there had to be a certain passage of time before an audience could begin to be educated to accept *The Recognitions*. The problem was not simply that the novel was too long and intricate or its vision of experience too outrageous, but that even the sophisticated reading public of the mid-Fifties was not yet accustomed to the kind of fiction it represented. . . The most

authoritative mode in the serious fiction of the Fifties was primarily realistic, and the novel of fabulation and Black Humor—of which *The Recognitions* was later to be identified as a distinguished pioneering example—had not yet come into vogue."

Little was heard of Gaddis in the decade and a half after 1955. Denied the life of a "successful" novelist, he began a long line of jobs in industry, working first in publicity for a pharmaceutical firm, then writing films for the army, and later writing speeches for corporate executives (as does Thomas Eigen in *J R*, who has also published an important but neglected novel). With the 1970 appearance in the *Dutton Review* of what would later become the opening pages of his second novel, Gaddis broke his fifteen-year silence. Two more fragments from *J R* appeared, in *Antaeus* and *Harper's*, before the novel was published in the fall of 1975 to much stronger reviews than those received by *The Recognitions*. *J R* won the National Book Award for the best fiction of the year and has since earned the praise of such writers as Saul Bellow, Mary McCarthy, William H. Gass, Stanley Elkin, Joseph McElroy, and Don DeLillo.

Although this intricate, 726-page novel resists easy summary, it is essentially a satire of corporate America, a "country" so obsessed with money that failure is all but inevitable for anyone who doesn't sell his soul to Mammon. The first word of the novel is "money," a word that reappears throughout the novel as its debasing touch besmirches everything from education to science, from politics to marriage, from the arts to warfare. At the center of the novel is eleven-year-old J. R. Vansant, a slovenly but clever boy who transforms a small "portfolio" of mail order acquisitions and penny stocks into an unwieldy paper empire in an improbably short time. The most radical feature of the novel is its narrative mode: except for an occasional transitional passage, the novel is composed entirely of dialogue. While novels composed totally of dialogue had been written before, none followed Gaddis's extreme format. For his dialogue is not the literary dialogue of most novels, tidied up and helpfully sprinkled with conversational conventions and explanatory asides by the author helping to clarify what the characters actually mean. Instead, *J R* reads like a tape-recorded transcription of real voices: ungrammatical, often truncated, with constant interruptions by other characters (and by telephones, radios, and televisions), with rarely an identifying or interpretive remark by the author.

Such a literary mode makes unusual demands upon the reader; it requires that he read actively with involvement and concentration, rather than passively, awaiting entertainment. Jack Gibbs, a major character, pinpoints this problem during a drunken conversation with Edward Bast, a young composer: " . . . problem most God damned readers rather be at the movies. Pay attention here bring something to it take something away problem most God damned writing's written for readers perfectly happy who they are rather be at the movies, come in empty-handed go out the same God damned way I told him Bast. Ask them to bring one God damned bit of effort want everything done for them they get up and go to the movies." In his interview with *Publishers Weekly,* Gaddis reiterated the point: "For me it is very much a proposition between the reader and the page. That's what books are about. And he must bring something to it or he won't take anything away. . . Television is hot, it provides everything. In the so-called situation comedies, you go with a completely blank mind, which is preoccupied for a half hour, and then you turn it off. You have brought nothing to it and you take nothing home. Much bad fiction is like this. Everything is provided for you, and you forget it a week later." What the attentive reader takes home from *J R* is a ringing in the ears from what Sarah E. Lauzen, in *Postmodern Fiction,* labels "the constant cacophony of America selling America."

Like its predecessor, *J R* is primarily a comic novel. As Alicia Metcalf Miller writes in the Cleveland *Plain Dealer,* "If Gaddis is a moralist, he is also a master of satire and humor. *J R* is a devastatingly funny book. Reading it, I laughed loudly and unashamedly in public places, and at home, more than once, I saw my small children gather in consternation as tears of laughter ran down my face." Such is the reader response for which *J R* aims.

For this novel—originally titled *That Time of Year: A Romance* but published in the summer of 1985 as *Carpenter's Gothic*—Gaddis turned away from the "mega-novel" and set out to write a shorter (262 pages), different sort of book. As he explained in a *Washington Post* interview with Lloyd Grove: "I wanted it to move very fast. Everything that happens on one page is preparing for the next page and the next chapter and the end of the book. When I started I thought, 'I want 240 pages'—that was what set I out for. It preserved the unity: one place, one very small amount of time, very small group of characters, and then, in effect, there's a nicer word than 'cliche,' what is it? Staples. That is, the staples of the marriage, which is on the rocks, the obligatory adultery, the locked room, the mysterious stranger, the older man and the younger woman, to try to take these and make them work."

Gaddis restores to worn-out literary cliches some of their original drama and intensity, particularly in *Carpenter's Gothic*. Like *The Recognitions,* his third novel is concerned with the ambiguous nature of reality; "there's a very fine line between the truth and what really happens" is an oft-repeated line in *Carpenter's Gothic.* It also attacks the perversions done in the name of religion. From *J R* it takes its narrative technique—an almost total dependence on dialogue—and its contempt for the motivating factor of capitalism. Sometimes seen by critics as a smaller, less important reflection of the author's two preceding novels, this novel presents Gaddis's most characteristic themes and techniques with economy and flair.

Carpenter's Gothic is rooted in a specific time and place: the action takes place over a month's time (internal references date it October-November 1983) in a "carpenter gothic" style Victorian house in a small Hudson River Valley town. (Gaddis owned just such a house on Ritie Street in Piermont, New York.) Almost continuously on stage is Elizabeth Booth: "Bibbs" to her brother Billy, "Liz" to her husband Paul, and "Mrs. Booth" to McCandless, the house's owner and a failed novelist. These men subject Liz to the bullying, self-serving dialogue that makes up the bulk of the novel and that brings the outside world onto Gaddis's one-set stage. With newspapers and telephone calls filling the roles of messengers, a complicated plot quickly unfolds concerning Christian fundamentalism, political chicanery, African mineral rights, and a half-dozen family disputes. Long-suffering Liz endures it all, helpless to prevent her men from rushing headlong into—and even creating—the Armageddon that looms on the final pages of the novel.

In *Carpenter's Gothic,* as in all of Gaddis's novels, the males do most of the talking and create most of the problems. Like Esme in *The Recognitions* and Amy in *J R,* Liz is the still point in a frantic male world, "the only thing that holds things together," as her brother Billy admits. Though flawed, she is perhaps the most sympathetic figure in all three of Gaddis's novels. For that reason, her sudden death at the end gives *Carpenter's Gothic* its bleaker, more despairing tone.

Throughout Gaddis's novels there is a sense of bitter disappointment at America for not fulfilling its potential, for events not working out as planned. In this regard Gaddis resembles his beloved Russian novelists of the nineteenth century; in the *New York Times Book Review* William H. Gass reports a talk of Gaddis's in Lithuania where he insisted "the comic and satiric side of his work was attempting to save his version of his country as the earlier Russian writers had endeavored to redeem theirs." In the third novel, however, America seems to have reached the bottom of the psychosocial abyss. *Carpenter's Gothic* implies that it is too late to reverse the tide, to restore the promise of the American dream, too late for anything more than "one last ridiculous effort at something worth doing."

Emphasizing litigiousness and greed as characteristics of contemporary American society, Gaddis's award-winning novel *A Frolic of His Own* focuses on Oscar Crease, his family, his friends, and the various lawsuits in which they are all enmeshed. Employing elements of humor and farce, Gaddis exhaustively details the absurdities of his characters' suits and subsequent countersuits. For example, Oscar is plaintiff in a plagiarism case he has brought against Constantine Kiester, a top Hollywood producer whose real name is Jonathan Livingston Siegal. Oscar is also, paradoxically, plaintiff and defendant in a suit concerning a hit-and-run accident in which he was hit by his own car—a Sosumi ("so sue me"). Taking its title from a British legal phrase used to describe an employee's actions which, though they resulted in on-the-job injuries, do not entitle the employee to compensation, *A Frolic of His Own* is largely noted for its satire of justice and law in contemporary American society and for its unusual narrative structure.

Except for the inclusion of excerpts from Oscar's writings, legal documents, and court opinions, the novel is told primarily through dialogue that is unattributed and only lightly punctuated. Critics have praised Gaddis's realistic depiction of everyday speech—complete with pauses, interruptions, and unfinished thoughts—and stressed the difficulty such a narrative technique, reminiscent of stream-of-consciousness writing, places on readers. Steven Moore observes in the *Nation*: "*A Frolic of His Own* is both cutting-edge, state-of-the-art fiction and a throwback to the great moral novels of Tolstoy and Dickens. That it can be both is just one of the many balancing acts it performs: It is bleak and pessimistic while howlingly funny; it is a deeply serious exploration of such lofty themes as justice and morality but is paced like a screwball comedy; it is avant-garde in its fictional techniques but traditional in conception and in the reading pleasures it offers; it is a damning indictment of the United States, Christianity and the legal system, but also a playful frolic of Gaddis's own." Zachary Leader in the *Times Literary Supplement* calls *A Frolic of His Own* a "bleak, brilliant, exhausting novel."

BIOGRAPHICAL/CRITICAL SOURCES:

BOOKS

Aldridge, John W., *In Search of Heresy,* McGraw, 1956.

Comnes, Gregory, *The Ethics of Indeterminacy in the Novels of William Gaddis,* University Press of Florida, 1994.

Contemporary Literary Criticism, Gale (Detroit), Volume 1, 1973; Volume 3, 1975; Volume 6, 1976; Volume 8, 1978; Volume 10, 1979; Volume 19, 1981; Volume 43, 1987; Volume 86, 1995.

Dictionary of Literary Biography, Volume 2: *American Novelists since World War II,* Gale, 1978.

Gardner, John, *On Moral Fiction,* Basic Books, 1978.

Knight, Christopher J., *Hints and Guesses: William Gaddis and the Longing for an Enlarged Culture,* University of Wisconsin Press, 1998.

Kuehl, John, and Steven Moore, editors, *In Recognition of William Gaddis,* Syracuse University Press, 1984.

Madden, David, *Rediscoveries,* Crown, 1971.

Magill, Frank N., editor, *Survey of Contemporary Literature,* supplement, Salem Press, 1972.

Magill, Frank N., editor, *Literary Annual,* Salem Press, 1976.

McCaffery, Larry, editor, *Postmodern Fiction,* Greenwood Press, 1986.

Moore, Steven, *A Reader's Guide to William Gaddis's "The Recognitions,"* University of Nebraska Press, 1982.

Tanner, Tony, *City of Words,* Harper, 1971.

Wiener, Norbert, *The Human Use of Human Beings,* Houghton, 1954.

Wolfe, Peter, *A Vision of His Own: The Mind and Art of William Gaddis,* Fairleigh Dickinson University Press (Madison, NJ), 1996.

PERIODICALS

Atlantic, April, 1985.
Chicago Tribune Book World, July 14, 1985.
Christian Science Monitor, September 17, 1985, pp. 25-26.
Commentary, December, 1985, pp. 62-65.
Commonweal, April 15, 1955.
Conjunctions, number 7, 1985; number 8, 1985.
Contemporary Literature, winter, 1975.
Critique, winter, 1962-63; Volume 19, number 3, 1978; Volume 22, number 1, 1980.
Hollins Critic, April, 1977.
Hungry Mind Review, spring, 1994, pp. 34, 42-43.
International Fiction Review, Volume 10, number 2, 1983.
Listener, March 13, 1986, pp. 28-29.
London Review of Books, May 12, 1994, pp. 20-21.
Los Angeles Times Book Review, July 14, 1985.
Modern Fiction Studies, number 27, 1981-82.
Nation, April 30, 1955; November 16, 1985, p. 496; April 25, 1994, pp. 569-71.
National Observer, October 11, 1975.
New Leader, January 17-31, 1994, pp. 18-19.
New Republic, September 2, 1985, pp. 30-32; February 7, 1994, pp. 27-30.
Newsweek, March 14, 1955; November 10, 1975; July 15, 1985; January 17, 1994, p. 52.
New York, January 3, 1994, p. 34.
New Yorker, April 9, 1955.
New York Herald Tribune, April 14, 1962.
New York Review of Books, February 17, 1994, pp. 3-4, 6.
New York Times, July 3, 1985, p. C22; November 15, 1987; January 4, 1994, p. C20.
New York Times Book Review, March 13, 1955; July 14, 1974; November 9, 1975; June 20, 1976; June 6, 1982; July 7, 1985; February 2, 1986; January 9, 1994, pp. 1, 22.
New York Times Magazine, November 15, 1987.
People Weekly, May 9, 1994, p. 29.
Plain Dealer (Cleveland), October, 1975.
Publishers Weekly, July 12, 1985; November 21, 1994, p. 26; January 6, 1997.
Pynchon Notes, Number 11, 1983.
Review of Contemporary Fiction, Volume 2, number 2, 1982.
San Francisco Review of Books, February, 1976.
Saturday Review, March 12, 1955; October 4, 1975.
Studies in American Humor, Number 1, 1982.
Time, March 14, 1955; July 22, 1985; January 24, 1994, p. 67.
Times Literary Supplement, February 28, 1986; June 3, 1994, p. 22.
United States Quarterly Book Review, June, 1955.
Village Voice, November 1, 1962.
Village Voice Literary Supplement, April, 1991, p. 26.
Virginia Quarterly Review, summer, 1976.
Wall Street Journal, August 26, 1985, p. 14.
Washington Post, August 23, 1985.
Washington Post Book World, July 7, 1985, p. 1; January 23, 1994, pp. 1, 10.

*   *   *

GAGE, Walter
See INGE, William Motter

*   *   *

GAINES, Ernest J(ames) 1933-

PERSONAL: Born January 15, 1933, in Oscar (some sources cite River Lake Plantation, near New Roads, Pointe Coupee Parish), LA; son of Manuel (a laborer) and Adrienne J. (Colar) Gaines. *Education:* Attended Vallejo Junior College; San Francisco State College (now University), B.A., 1957; graduate study at Stanford University, 1958-59.

ADDRESSES: Office—Department of English, University of Southwestern Louisiana, P.O. Box 44691, Lafayette, LA 70504. *Agent*—JCA Literary Agency, Inc., 242 West 27th St., New York, NY 10001.

CAREER: "Writing, five hours a day, five days a week." Denison University, Granville, OH, writer in residence, 1971; Stanford University, Stanford, CA, writer in residence, 1981; University of Southwestern Louisiana, Lafayette, professor of English and writer in residence, 1983–. Whittier College, visiting professor, 1983, and writer in residence, 1986. Subject of the film, *Louisiana Stories: Ernest Gaines,* which aired on WHMM-TV in 1993. *Military service:* U.S. Army, 1953-55.

AWARDS, HONORS: Wallace Stegner fellow, Stanford University, 1957; Joseph Henry Jackson Award from San Francisco Foundation, 1959, for "Comeback" (short story); award from National Endowment for the Arts, 1967; Rockefeller grant, 1970; Guggenheim fellow, 1971; award from Black Academy of Arts and Letters, 1972; fiction gold medal from Commonwealth Club of California, 1972, for *The Autobiography of Miss Jane Pittman,* and 1984, for *A Gathering of Old Men;* award from Louisiana Library Association, 1972; honorary doctorate of letters from Denison University, 1980, Brown University, 1985, Bard College, 1985, and Louisiana State University, 1987; award for excellence of achievement in literature from San Francisco Arts Commission, 1983; D.H.L. from Whittier College, 1986; literary award from American Academy and Institute of Arts and Letters, 1987; John D. and Catherine T. MacArthur Foundation fellowship, 1993.

WRITINGS:

FICTION

Catherine Carmier (novel), Atheneum, 1964.
Of Love and Dust (novel), Dial, 1967.
Bloodline (short stories; also see below), Dial, 1968, Vintage Contemporaries (New York City), 1997.

A Long Day in November (story originally published in *Bloodline*), Dial, 1971.
The Autobiography of Miss Jane Pittman (novel), Dial, 1971.
In My Father's House (novel), Knopf, 1978.
A Gathering of Old Men (novel), Knopf, 1983.
A Lesson Before Dying (novel), Knopf, 1993.

MEDIA ADAPTATIONS: The Autobiography of Miss Jane Pittman, adapted from Gaines's novel, aired on the Columbia Broadcasting System (CBS-TV), January 31, 1974, starring Cicely Tyson in the title role; the special won nine Emmy Awards. "The Sky Is Gray," a short story originally published in *Bloodline*, was adapted for public television in 1980. *A Gathering of Old Men*, adapted from Gaines's novel, aired on CBS-TV, May 10, 1987, starring Lou Gossett, Jr., and Richard Widmark.

SIDELIGHTS: The fiction of Ernest J. Gaines, including his 1971 novel *The Autobiography of Miss Jane Pittman*, is deeply rooted in the black culture and storytelling traditions of rural Louisiana where the author was born and raised. His stories have been noted for their convincing characters and powerful themes presented within authentic—often folk-like—narratives that tap into the complex world of Southern rural life. Gaines depicts the strength and dignity of his black characters in the face of numerous struggles: the dehumanizing and destructive effects of racism; the breakdown in personal relationships as a result of social pressures; and the choice between secured traditions and the sometimes radical measures necessary to bring about social change. Although the issues presented in Gaines's fiction are serious and often disturbing, "this is not hot-and-breathless, burn-baby-burn writing," Melvin Maddocks points out in *Time*; rather, it is the work of "a patient artist, a patient man." Expounding on Gaines's rural heritage, Maddocks continues: "[Gaines] sets down a story as if he were planting, spreading the roots deep, wide and firm. His stories grow organically, at their own rhythm. When they ripen at last, they do so inevitably, arriving at a climax with the absolute rightness of a folk tale."

Gaines's boyhood experiences growing up on a Louisiana plantation provide many of the impressions upon which his stories are based. Particularly important, he told Paul Desruisseaux in the *New York Times Book Review*, were "working in the fields, going fishing in the swamps with the older people, and, especially, listening to the people who came to my aunt's house, the aunt who raised me." Although Gaines moved to California at the age of fifteen and subsequently went to college there, his fiction has been based in an imaginary Louisiana plantation region named Bayonne, which a number of critics have compared to William Faulkner's Yoknapatawpha County. Gaines has acknowledged looking to Faulkner, in addition to Ernest Hemingway, for language, and to French writers such as Gustave Flaubert and Guy de Maupassant for style. A perhaps greater influence, however, has been the writings of nineteenth-century Russian authors.

Gaines's first novel, *Catherine Carmier*, is "an apprentice work more interesting for what it anticipates than for its accomplishments," notes William E. Grant in the *Dictionary of Literary Biography*. The novel chronicles the story of a young black man, Jackson Bradley, who returns to Bayonne after completing his education in California. Jackson falls in love with Catherine, the daughter of a Creole sharecropper who refuses to let members of his family associate with anyone darker than themselves, believing Creoles racially and socially superior. The novel portrays numerous clashes of loyalty: Catherine torn between her love for Jackson and love for her father; Jackson caught between a bond to

the community he grew up in and the experience and knowledge he has gained in the outside world. "Both Catherine and Jackson are immobilized by the pressures of [the] rural community," writes Keith E. Byerman in the *Dictionary of Literary Biography*, which produces "twin themes of isolation and paralysis [that] give the novel an existential quality. Characters must face an unfriendly world without guidance and must make crucial choices about their lives." The characters in *Catherine Carmier*—as in much of Gaines's fiction—are faced with struggles that test the conviction of personal beliefs. Winifred L. Stoelting in *CLA Journal* explains that Gaines is concerned more "with how they [his characters] handle their decisions than with the rightness of their decisions— more often than not predetermined by social changes over which the single individual has little control."

Gaines sets *Catherine Carmier* in the time of the Civil Rights movement, yet avoids making it a primary force in the novel. Grant comments on this aspect: "In divorcing his tale from contemporary events, Gaines declares his independence from the political and social purposes of much contemporary black writing. Instead, he elects to concentrate upon those fundamental human passions and conflicts which transcend the merely social level of human existence." Grant finds Gaines "admirable" for doing this, yet also believes Jackson's credibility marred because he remains aloof from contemporary events. For Grant, the novel "seems to float outside time and place rather than being solidly anchored in the real world of the modern South." Byerman concurs, stating that the novel "is not entirely successful in presenting its major characters and their motivations." Nonetheless, he points out that in *Catherine Carmier*, "Gaines does begin to create a sense of the black community and its perceptions of the world around it. Shared ways of speaking, thinking, and relating to the dominant white society are shown through a number of minor characters."

Gaines's next novel, *Of Love and Dust*, is also a story of forbidden romance, and, as in *Catherine Carmier*, a "new world of expanding human relationships erodes the old world of love for the land and the acceptance of social and economic stratification," writes Stoelting. *Of Love and Dust* is the story of Marcus Payne, a young black man bonded out of prison by a white landowner and placed under the supervision of a Cajun overseer, Sidney Bonbon. Possessed of a rebellious and hostile nature, Marcus is a threat to Bonbon, who in turn does all that he can to break the young man's spirit. In an effort to strike back, Marcus pays special attention to the overseer's wife; the two fall in love and plot to run away. The novel ends with a violent confrontation between the two men, in which Marcus is killed. After the killing, Bonbon claims that to spare Marcus would have meant his own death at the hands of other Cajuns. Grant notes a similarity between *Of Love and Dust* and *Catherine Carmier* in that the characters are "caught up in a decadent social and economic system that determines their every action and limits their possibilities." Similarly, the two novels are marked by a "social determinism [which] shapes the lives of all the characters, making them pawns in a mechanistic world order rather than free agents."

Of Love and Dust demonstrates Gaines's development as a novelist, offering a clearer view of the themes and characters that dominate his later work. Stoelting writes that "in a more contemporary setting, the novel . . . continues Gaines's search for human dignity, and when that is lacking, acknowledges the salvation of pride," adding that "the characters themselves grow into a deeper awareness than those of [his] first novel. More sharply drawn . . . [they] are more decisive in their actions." Byerman writes that the novel "more clearly condemns the economic, social, and racial system of the South for the problems faced by its characters." Likewise, the first-person narrator in the novel—a co-worker of Marcus—"both speaks in the idiom of the place and time and instinctively asserts the values of the black community."

Gaines turns to a first-person narrator again in his next novel, *The Autobiography of Miss Jane Pittman,* which many consider to be his masterwork. Miss Jane Pittman—well over one hundred years old—relates a personal history that spans the time from the Civil War and slavery up through the Civil Rights movement of the 1960s. "To travel with Miss Pittman from adolescence to old age is to embark upon a historic journey, one staked out in the format of the novel," writes Addison Gayle, Jr., in *The Way of the World: The Black Novel in America.* "Never mind that Miss Jane Pittman is fictitious, and that her 'autobiography,' offered up in the form of taped reminiscences, is artifice," adds Josh Greenfield in *Life,* "the effect is stunning." Gaines's gift for drawing convincing characters reaches a peak in *The Autobiography of Miss Jane Pittman.* "His is not . . . an 'art' narrative, but an authentic narrative by an authentic ex-slave, authentic even though both are Gaines's inventions," Bryant comments. "So successful is he in *becoming* Miss Jane Pittman, that when we talk about her story, we do not think of Gaines as her creator, but as her recording editor."

The character of Jane Pittman could be called an embodiment of the black experience in America. "Though Jane is the dominant personality of the narrative—observer and commentator upon history, as well as participant—in her odyssey is symbolized the odyssey of a race of people; through her eyes is revealed the grandeur of a people's journey through history," writes Gayle. "The central metaphor of the novel concerns this journey: Jane and her people, as they come together in the historic march toward dignity and freedom in Sampson, symbolize a people's march through history, breaking old patterns, though sometimes slowly, as they do." The important historical backdrop to Jane's narrative—slavery, Reconstruction, the Civil Rights movement, segregation—does not compromise, however, the detailed account of an individual. "Jane captures the experiences of those millions of illiterate blacks who never had a chance to tell their own stories," Byerman explains. "By focusing on the particular yet typical events of a small part of Louisiana, those lives are given a concreteness and specificity not possible in more general histories."

In his fourth novel, *In My Father's House,* Gaines focuses on a theme which appears in varying degrees throughout his fiction: the alienation between fathers and sons. As the author told Desruisseaux: "In my books there always seems to be fathers and sons searching for each other. That's a theme I've worked with since I started writing. Even when the father was not in the story, I've dealt with his absence and its effects on his children. And that is the theme of this book." *In My Father's House* tells of a prominent civil rights leader and reverend (Phillip Martin) who, at the peak of his career, is confronted with a troubled young man named Robert X. Although Robert's identity is initially a mystery, eventually he is revealed to be one of three offspring from a love affair the reverend had in an earlier, wilder life. Martin hasn't seen or attempted to locate his family for more than twenty years. Robert arrives to confront and kill the father whose neglect he sees as responsible for the family's disintegration: his sister has been raped, his brother imprisoned for the murder of her attacker, and his mother reduced to poverty, living alone. Although the son's intent to kill his father is never carried out, the reverend is forced "to undergo a long and painful odyssey through his own past and the labyrinthine streets of Baton Rouge to learn what really happened to his first family," writes William Burke in the *Dictionary of Literary Biography Yearbook.* Larry McMurtry, in the *New York Times Book Review,* notes that as the book traces the lost family, "we have revealed to us an individual, a marriage, a community and a region, but with such an unobtrusive marshaling of detail that we never lose sight of the book's central thematic concern: the profoundly destructive consequences of the breakdown of parentage, of a father's abandonment of his children and the terrible and irrevocable consequences of such an abandonment."

A Gathering of Old Men, Gaines's fifth novel, presents a cast of aging Southern black men who, after a life of subordination and intimidation, make a defiant stand against injustice. Seventeen of them, together with the 30-year-old white heiress of a deteriorating Louisiana plantation, plead guilty to murdering a hostile member (Beau Boutan) of a violent Cajun clan. While a confounded sheriff and vengeful family wait to lynch the black they've decided is guilty, the group members—toting recently fired shotguns—surround the dead man and "confess" their motives. "Each man tells of the accumulated frustrations of his life—raped daughters, jailed sons, public insults, economic exploitation—that serve as sufficient motive for murder," writes Byerman. "Though Beau Boutan is seldom the immediate cause of their anger, he clearly represents the entire white world that has deprived them of their dignity and manhood. The confessions serve as ritual purgings of all the hostility and self-hatred built up over the years." Fifteen or so characters—white, black, and Cajun—advance the story through individual narrations, creating "thereby a range of social values as well as different perspectives on the action," notes Byerman. Reynolds Price writes in the *New York Times Book Review* that the black narrators "are nicely distinguished from one another in rhythm and idiom, in the nature of what they see and report, especially in their specific laments for past passivity in the face of suffering," observes Elaine Kendall in the *Los Angeles Times Book Review,* is that the "individual stories coalesce into a single powerful tale of subjugation, exploitation and humiliation at the hands of landowners."

Another theme of *A Gathering of Old Men,* according to Ben Forkner in *America,* is "the simple, natural dispossession of old age, of the traditional and well-loved values of the past, the old trades and the old manners, forced to give way to modern times." Sam Cornish writes in the *Christian Science Monitor* that the novel's "characters—both black and white—understand that, before the close of the novel, the new South must confront the old, and all will be irrevocably changed. Gaines portrays a society that will be altered by the deaths of its 'old men,' and so presents an allegory about the passing of the old and birth of the new."

A Lesson Before Dying, issued ten years after *A Gathering of Old Men,* continues the author's historical reflections on the Southern world captured in all of his novels to date. The setting remains relatively the same—a plantation and jail in Bayonne during a six-month span in 1948. The unlikely hero is Jefferson, a scarcely literate, twenty-one-year-old man-child who works the cane fields of the Pichot Plantation. Trouble finds the protagonist when he innocently hooks up with two men, who rob a liquor store and are killed in the process along with the shop's proprietor, leaving Jefferson as an accomplice. The young man's naivete in the crime is never recognized as he is brought to trial before a jury of twelve white men and sentenced to death. Jefferson's defense attorney ineffectively attempts to save his client by presenting him as a dumb animal, as "a thing that acts on command. A thing to hold the handle of a plow, a thing to load your bales of cotton." When Jefferson's godmother learns of this analogy, she determines that her nephew will face his execution as a man, not as an animal. Thus, she enlists the help of a young teacher named Grant Wiggins, who is initially resistant but works to help Jefferson achieve manhood in his final days.

According to Sandra D. Davis in the *Detroit Free Press,* "*A Lesson Before Dying* begins much like many other stories where racial tension brews in the background." Yet, as in Gaines's other works, the racial tension in this novel is more of a catalyst for his tribute to the perseverance of the victims of injustice. Unexpectantly, pride, honor, and manhood in a dehumanizing environment emerge as the themes of this novel. Through Wiggins, the young narrator and unwilling carrier of the "burden" of the community, and his interaction with the black community, as represented by Jefferson's godmother and the town's Reverend Ambrose, Gaines "creates a compelling, intense story about heroes and the human spirit," contends Davis. Ironically, Jefferson and Reverend Ambrose ultimately emerge as the real teachers, showing Wiggins that, as Davis asserts, "education encompasses more than the lessons taught in school." Wiggins is also forced to admit, according to Jonathan Yardley in *Washington Post Book World,* "his own complicity in the system of which Jefferson is a victim."

Of that community which yields the lessons of Gaines' fiction and his relation to it, Alice Walker writes in the *New York Times Book Review* that Gaines "claims and revels in the rich heritage of Southern Black people and their customs; the community he feels with them is unmistakable and goes deeper even than pride. . . Gaines is mellow with historical reflection, supple with wit, relaxed and expansive because he does not equate his people with failure." Gaines has been criticized by some, however, who feel his writing does not more directly focus on problems facing blacks. Gaines responds to Desruisseaux that he feels "too many blacks have been writing to tell whites all about 'the problems,' instead of writing something that all people, including their own, could find interesting, could enjoy." Gaines has also remarked that more can be achieved than strictly writing novels of protest. In an interview for *San Francisco,* the author states: "So many of our writers have not read any farther back than [Richard Wright's] *Native Son.* So many of our novels deal only with the great city ghettos; that's all we write about, as if there's nothing else." Gaines continues: "We've only been living in these ghettos for 75 years or so, but the other 300 years—I think this is worth writing about."

BIOGRAPHICAL/CRITICAL SOURCES:

BOOKS

Babb, Valerie-Melissa, *Ernest Gaines,* Twayne, 1991.

Beavers, Herman, *Wrestling Angels into Song: The Fictions of Ernest J. Gaines and James Alan McPherson,* University of Pennsylvania Press (Philadelphia), 1995.

Bruck, Peter, editor, *The Black American Short Story in the Twentieth Century: A Collection of Critical Essays,* B. R. Gruner (Amsterdam), 1977.

Carmean, Karen, *Ernest J. Gaines: A Critical Companion,* Greenwood Press, 1998.

Concise Dictionary of American Literary Biography: Broadening Views, 1968-1988, Gale (Detroit), 1989.

Contemporary Literary Criticism, Gale, Volume 3, 1975; Volume 11, 1979; Volume 18, 1981.

Conversations with Ernest Gaines, University Press of Mississippi (Jackson), 1995.

Dictionary of Literary Biography, Gale, Volume 2: *American Novelists since World War II,* 1978; Volume 33: *Afro-American Fiction Writers after 1955,* 1984.

Dictionary of Literary Biography Yearbook: 1980, Gale, 1981.

Estes, David C., *Critical Reflections on the Fiction of Ernest J. Gaines,* University of Geogia Press (Athens), 1994.

Gaudet, Marcia, and Carl Wooton, *Porch Talk with Ernest Gaines: Conversations on the Writer's Craft,* Louisiana State University Press, 1990.

Gayle, Addison, Jr., *The Way of the New World: The Black Novel in America,* Doubleday, 1975.

Hicks, Jack, *In the Singer's Temple: Prose Fictions of Barthelme, Gaines, Brautigan, Piercy, Kesey, and Kosinski,* University of North Carolina Press, 1981.

Hudson, Theodore R., *The History of Southern Literature,* Louisiana State University Press, 1985.

O'Brien, John, editor, *Interview with Black Writers,* Liveright, 1973.

PERIODICALS

African American Review, fall, 1994, p. 489.

America, June 2, 1984.

Atlanta Journal and Constitution, October 26, 1997.

Black American Literature Forum, Volume 11, 1977; Volume 24, 1990.

Callaloo, Volume 7, 1984; Volume 11, 1988.

Chicago Tribune Book World, October 30, 1983.

Christian Science Monitor, December 2, 1983.

Chronicle of Higher Education, May 11, 1994, p. 23A.

CLA Journal, March, 1971; December, 1975.

Detroit Free Press, June 6, 1993, p. 7J.

Essence, August, 1993, p. 52.

Iowa Review, winter, 1972.

Life, April 30, 1971.

Los Angeles Times, March 2, 1983.

Los Angeles Times Book Review, January 1, 1984.

Meleus, Volume 11, 1984.

Nation, February 5, 1968; April 5, 1971; January 14, 1984.

Negro Digest, November, 1967; January, 1968; January, 1969.

New Orleans Review, Volume 1, 1969; Volume 3, 1972; Volume 14, 1987.

New Republic, December 26, 1983.

New Statesman, September 2, 1973; February 10, 1984.

Newsweek, June 16, 1969; May 3, 1971.

New Yorker, October 24, 1983.

New York Times, July 20, 1978.

New York Times Book Review, November 19, 1967; May 23, 1971; June 11, 1978; October 30, 1983.

Observer, February 5, 1984.

Publishers Weekly, March 21, 1994, p. 8.

San Francisco, July, 1974.

Southern Review, Volume 10, 1974; Volume 21, 1985.

Studies in Short Fiction, summer, 1975.

Time, May 10, 1971, December 27, 1971.

Times Literary Supplement, February 10, 1966; March 16, 1973; April 6, 1984.

Village Voice Literary Supplement, October, 1983.

Washington Post, January 13, 1976.

Washington Post Book World, June 18, 1978; September 21, 1983; March 28, 1993, p. 3; May 23, 1993.

GALBRAITH, John Kenneth 1908-
(Mark Epernay, Herschel McLandress)

PERSONAL: Born October 15, 1908, in Iona Station, Ontario, Canada; naturalized United States citizen, 1937; son of William Archibald (a politician and farmer) and Catherine (Kendall) Galbraith; married Catherine Atwater, September 17, 1937; children: John Alan, Peter, James, Douglas (deceased). *Education:* University of Toronto, B.S. (agriculture), 1931; University of California, Berkeley, M.S., 1933, Ph.D. (economics), 1934; attended Cambridge University, 1937-38. *Politics:* Democrat.

ADDRESSES: Home—30 Francis Ave., Cambridge, MA 02138; Newfane, VT (summer); Gstaad, Switzerland (winter). *Office*—206 Littauer Center, Harvard University, Cambridge, MA 02138.

CAREER: Harvard University, Cambridge, MA, instructor and tutor, 1934-39; Princeton University, Princeton, NJ, assistant professor of economics, 1939-42; U.S. Office of Price Administration, Washington, DC, administrator in charge of price division, 1941-42, department administrator, 1942-43; *Fortune* magazine, member of board of editors, 1943-48; Harvard University, lecturer, 1948-49, professor, 1949-59, Paul M. Warburg Professor of Economics, 1959-75; Paul M. Warburg Professor emeritus, 1975–; U.S. Ambassador to India, 1961-63. Reith Lecturer, 1966; Trinity College, visiting fellow, Cambridge, 1970-71. Director of U.S. Strategic Bombing Survey, 1945, and Office of Economic Security Policy, U.S. Department of State, 1946. Presidential adviser to John F. Kennedy and Lyndon B. Johnson. Affiliated with television series *The Age of Uncertainty,* on the British Broadcasting Corporation (BBC), 1977.

MEMBER: American Academy and Institute of Arts and Letters (president, 1984-87), American Academy of Arts and Sciences (fellow), American Economic Association (president, 1972), Americans for Democratic Action (chairman, 1967-69), American Agricultural Economics Association, Twentieth Century Fund (trustee), Century Club (New York), Federal City Club (Washington DC), Harvard Club (New York), Saturday Club (Boston).

AWARDS, HONORS: Research fellowship, University of California, 1931-34; Social Science Research Council fellowship, 1937-38; Medal of Freedom, 1946; Sarah Josepha Hale Award, Friends of the Richards Free Library, 1967; President's Certificate of Merit. LL.D., Bard College, 1958, Miami University (Ohio), 1959, University of Toronto, 1961, Brandeis University, 1963, University of Massachusetts, 1963, University of Guelph, 1965, University of Saskatchewan, 1965, Rhode Island College, 1966, Boston College, 1967, Hobart and William Smith Colleges, 1967, University of Paris, 1975, Harvard University, 1988, Moscow State University, 1988, Smith College, 1989, Oxford University, 1990, and many others; Lifetime Achievement Award, Robert F. Kennedy Book Awards, 1996-1997.

WRITINGS:

(With Henry Sturgis Dennison) *Modern Competition and Business Policy,* Oxford University Press, 1938.

A Theory of Price Control, Harvard University Press, 1952, reprinted with new introduction by Galbraith, 1980.

American Capitalism: The Concept of Countervailing Power, Houghton, 1952, reprinted with new introduction by Galbraith, M. E. Sharpe, 1980, revised edition, Transaction Publishers, 1993.

Economics and the Art of Controversy, Rutgers University Press, 1955.

The Great Crash, 1929, Houghton, 1955, reprinted with new introduction by Galbraith, 1988.

(With Richard H. Holton and others) *Marketing Efficiency in Puerto Rico,* Harvard University Press, 1955.

Journey to Poland and Yugoslavia, Harvard University Press, 1958.

The Affluent Society, Houghton, 1958, 4th edition, 1984.

The Liberal Hour, Houghton, 1960.

Economic Development in Perspective, Harvard University Press, 1962, revised edition published as *Economic Development,* 1964.

(Under pseudonym Mark Epernay) *The McLandress Dimension* (satire), Houghton, 1963, revised edition, New American Library, 1968.

The Scotch (memoir), Houghton, 1964, 2nd edition, 1985 (published in England as *Made to Last,* Hamish Hamilton, 1964, and as *The Non-potable Scotch: A Memoir on the Clansmen in Canada,* Penguin, 1964).

The Underdeveloped Country (text of five radio broadcasts), Canadian Broadcasting Corp., 1965.

The New Industrial State, Houghton, 1967, 4th edition, 1985.

How to Get Out of Vietnam: A Workable Solution to the Worst Problem of Our Time, New American Library, 1967.

The Triumph: A Novel of Modern Diplomacy, Houghton, 1968.

(With Mohinder Singh Randhawa) *Indian Painting: The Scene, Themes and Legends,* Houghton, 1968.

How to Control the Military, Doubleday, 1969.

Ambassador's Journal: A Personal Account of the Kennedy Years, Houghton, 1969.

(Author of introduction) David Levine, *No Known Survivors: David Levine's Political Prank,* Gambit, 1970.

Who Needs the Democrats, and What It Takes to Be Needed, Doubleday, 1970.

A Contemporary Guide to Economics, Peace, and Laughter (essays), edited by Andrea D. Williams, Houghton, 1971.

Economics and the Public Purpose, Houghton, 1973.

A China Passage, Houghton, 1973.

(Author of introduction) Frank Moraes and Edward Howe, editors, *India,* McGraw-Hill, 1974.

Money: Whence It Came, Where It Went, 1975, revised edition, Houghton, 1995.

The Age of Uncertainty (based on the 1977 BBC television series), Houghton, 1977.

The Galbraith Reader: From the Works of John Kenneth Galbraith, selected and with commentary by the editors of *Gambit,* Gambit, 1977.

(With Nicole Salinger) *Almost Everyone's Guide to Economics,* Houghton, 1978.

Annals of an Abiding Liberal, edited by Williams, Houghton, 1979.

The Nature of Mass Poverty, Harvard University Press, 1979.

A Life in Our Times: Memoirs, Houghton, 1981.

The Anatomy of Power, Houghton, 1983.

The Voice of the Poor: Essays in Economic and Political Persuasion, Harvard University Press, 1983.

A View from the Stands: Of People, Politics, Military Power, and the Arts, edited by Williams, Houghton, 1986.

Economics in Perspective: A Critical History, Houghton, 1987, published as *A History of Economics,* 1987.

(With Stanislav Menshikov) *Capitalism, Communism and Coexistence: From the Bitter Past to a Better Present,* Houghton, 1988.

A Tenured Professor (novel), Houghton, 1990.

The Culture of Contentment, Houghton, 1992.

(Editor and author of introduction) Thomas H. Eliot, *Recollections of the New Deal: When the People Mattered,* Northeastern University Press, 1992.

A Short History of Financial Euphoria: A Hymn of Caution, Whittle Books/Viking, 1993.

The Triumph: A Novel of Modern Diplomacy, Houghton, 1993.

A Journey through Economic Time: A Firsthand View, Houghton, 1994.

The World Economy since the Wars: An Eyewitness Account, Houghton, 1994.

The Good Society: The Humane Dimension, Houghton, 1996.

Contributor to books, including *Can Europe Unite?* Foreign Policy Association (New York City), 1950, and *The Past Speaks to the Present,* by Yigael Yadin, Granada TV Network Limited, 1962. Author of drafts of speeches for political leaders, including Franklin D. Roosevelt, Adlai Stevenson, John F. Kennedy, Lyndon B. Johnson, and Robert Kennedy. Editor of "Harvard Economic Studies" series, Harvard University Press. Contributor to scholarly journals. Reviewer, under pseudonym Herschel McLandress, of *Report from Iron Mountain.*

SIDELIGHTS: John Kenneth Galbraith is considered one of the twentieth century's foremost writers on economics and among its most influential economists. A prolific and diverse writer, whose more than thirty books range over a variety of topics, Galbraith is the author of such classic texts as *The Affluent Society* and *The New Industrial State.* In addition to his writings, he has also held positions as a government economist, presidential adviser, foreign ambassador, and for over twenty years was the Paul M. Warburg Professor of Economics at Harvard University. Galbraith's blend of skills make him a rarity among economists. "As a raconteur and a literary stylist, he stands with the best," states James Fallows in the *New York Times Book Review,* while "as a thinker," notes Lowell Ponte in the *Los Angeles Times Book Review,* "Galbraith has made major contributions to the economic arguments of our time." In addition to originating several terms that are part of the vernacular of economists and laymen alike—such as "affluent society," "conventional wisdom," and "countervailing power"—Galbraith is famous as a witty guide to twentieth-century economics. A *New Yorker* reviewer calls him "a wizard at packing immense amounts of information into a style so entertaining that the reader does not realize he is being taught." Eugene D. Genovese writes in the *New York Times Book Review* that Galbraith "has admirably demonstrated that respect for the English language provides everything necessary to demystify economics and render its complexities intelligible."

The son of a Canadian politician and farmer, Galbraith became interested in the study of economics during the Depression. In the 1930s and early 1940s, he taught at both Harvard University and Princeton University, and became influenced by economist John Maynard Keynes. In 1941, at the age of 33, he was appointed administrator of the price operations of the U.S. Office of Price Administration, and was responsible for setting prices in the United States. His 1952 book, *A Theory of Price Control,* outlines many of Galbraith's fundamental economic principles, as does another early book, *American Capitalism: The Concept of Countervailing Power,* which explores postwar American economy and the role of labor as a countervailing force in a market economy. Samuel Lubell in the *New York Herald Tribune Book Review* called *American Capitalism* "one of the most provocative economic essays since the writings of the late John Maynard Keynes," adding that "even where one disagrees, [Galbraith's] ideas stimulate a spring cleaning of old beliefs and outworn, if

cherished, notions—which is perhaps all that can be asked of any new theory." Galbraith commented to Victor Navasky in the *New York Times Book Review* on his decision to write about economics: "I made up my mind I would never again place myself at the mercy of the technical economists who had the enormous power to ignore what I had written. I set out to involve a large community. I would involve economists by having the larger public say to them 'Where do you stand on Galbraith's idea of price control?' They would *have* to confront what I said."

Galbraith broadened his readership with his 1955 book, *The Great Crash, 1929,* which recounts the harried days leading up to the stock market crash and Great Depression. Written at the suggestion of historian Arthur Schlesinger, Jr., who queried Galbraith as to why no one had ever written an economic account of the depression, *The Great Crash, 1929* was praised for being both illuminating and readable. "Economic writings are seldom notable for their entertainment value, but this book is," C. J. Rolo commented in *Atlantic,* adding, "Mr. Galbraith's prose has grace and wit, and he distills a good deal of sardonic fun from the whopping errors of the nation's oracles and the wondrous antics of the financial community." R. L. Heilbroner wrote in the *New York Herald Tribune Book Review*: "Mr. Galbraith has told the tale of the great bust with all the verve, pace, and suspense, of a detective story. . . For any one who is interested in understanding the recent past or attempting to achieve a perspective on the future of American economic history,. . . this book will be of great interest."

Following these books, Galbraith wrote the bestselling *The Affluent Society.* A major assessment of the U.S. economy, *The Affluent Society* questions priorities of production and how wealth is to be divided. As Galbraith states in the book: "The final problem of the productive society is what it produces. This manifests itself in an implacable tendency to provide an opulent supply of some things and a niggardly yield of others. This disparity carries to the point where it is a cause of social discomfort and social unhealth." According to Heilbroner, Galbraith raises three important issues: "One of these is the moral problem of how an Affluent Society may be prevented from becoming merely a Rich one. A second is the efficacy of Mr. Galbraith's reforms to offset the inertia and the vested interests of a powerful social structure. A third is what form of social cohesion can replace our troublesome but useful absorption in Production." Heilbroner called *The Affluent Society* "as disturbing as it is brilliant. . . with which it is easy to cavil or to disagree, but which it is impossible to dismiss."

Galbraith's 1967 bestseller *The New Industrial State,* a sequel to *The Affluent Society,* examines the diminishing role of individual choice in the market enterprise. "I reached the conclusion that in 'The Affluent Society' I had only written half the book I should have," Galbraith commented to the *New York Times Book Review.* "'The Affluent Society' says the more you have the more you want. And for obvious reasons, as people become richer it is easier to persuade them as to their wants. But I hadn't really examined the role of the great corporations, the industrial system, in the persuasion process." Arthur Selwyn Miller commented in the *New Republic*: "If Galbraith is correct—and I am inclined to agree in large part with him—then we. . . are ruled by nameless and faceless managers in the technostructures of the private governments of the supercorporations and their counterparts in the public bureaucracy. That's an event of considerable significance." Raymond J. Saulnier in the *New York Times Book Review* called *The New Industrial State* "a tightly organized, closely reasoned book, notable for what it says about the dynamics of institutional change and for certain qualities of its author: a sardonic wit, exercised liberally at the expense of conservatives, and unusual perception."

In his 1973 book, *Economics and the Public Purpose,* Galbraith, according to Leonard Silk in the *New York Times,* goes "beyond his earlier books to describe the whole modern capitalist economy, which he sees as split roughly in twain between 'the planning system' and what he calls 'the market system'—a collection of imperfect competitors and partial monopolists that includes such producers as farmers, television repairmen, retailers, small manufacturers, medical practitioners, photographers and pornographers. He regards the market system as the exploited and relatively feeble half of the economy—although it obviously includes some not particularly exploited people. . . Yet, although some members of the market system make out quite nicely, it is the planning system of the great corporations, he says, that dominates the state, unbalances social and economic development, exacerbates inequality, corrupts foreign policy and befouls the atmosphere."

In addition to over twenty-five other books on economics, the prolific Galbraith is also the author of three novels and of acclaimed volumes of memoirs. As in his other books, these writings display Galbraith's characteristic wit and insight. His 1968 novel *The Triumph,* set amidst a revolution in a fictional Latin American nation, depicts the bungled efforts of U.S. foreign policy officials to put an acceptable leader in power. Robert Brown in the *New Republic,* while expressing reservations about the novel's tone which he described as "loftily condescending and relentlessly witty," called the book "quite devastating" and acknowledged Galbraith's "detailed knowledge of the scene." Galbraith's 1990 novel, *A Tenured Professor,* is the tale of a professor who, with his wife, develops a successful stock forecasting mechanism that makes them very wealthy. With their new money, the couple begins supporting various liberal causes, such as identifying companies that do not employ women in top executive positions. "Lurking in the background of his story is enough economics to satisfy Wall Street game players and enough of a cheerful fairy tale for grown-ups to please the most liberal dreamers. . .," notes Herbert Mitgang in the *New York Times.* "A whimsical fellow is John Kenneth Galbraith, who knows that money makes people and institutions jump through hoops and over their own cherished principles." He added: "Readers who know and admire the author as an acerbic political voice are not shortchanged in his biting new novel. . . Satirical one-liners and paragraphs fall lightly from the pen of the author and from the lips of his characters all through the story."

In *The Culture of Contentment,* Galbraith "scathingly denounces a society in which the affluent have come to dominate the political arena, guaranteeing their continued comfort while refusing to address the needs of the less fortunate," claims Victor Dwyer in *Maclean's.* Galbraith asserts that satisfied citizens—the top twenty percent regarding annual earnings who live a moneyed lifestyle—tend to, by their very prosperity, guarantee their eventual downfall by ignoring the fundamental requirements of the underclasses. Their blindness to social reform has historically led to inflation and the need for greater government intervention, thereby causing a resulting eventual decline in economic security even for the elite, maintains the author. Galbraith warns that the upper-class ignores economic, political, and social necessities of the lower classes at their own peril. Galbraith told Dwyer that *The Culture of Contentment* exceeds the scope of his other books: "'What I am attempting is to formulate the political consequences

of self-satisfied well-being,' said Galbraith. 'In the wake of Mr. Reagan and Mr. Bush,' he added, 'it seemed that the time was right.'" Robert N. Bellah observes in the *New York Times Book Review,* "'The Culture of Contentment' is certainly no savage jeremiad. It is a very amusing volume, but by the end one's laughter has turned hollow and one wants to weep. For all its gentle appearances, it is a bombshell of a book, and the story it tells is one of devastation."

About *A Short History of Financial Euphoria,* Robert Krulwich explains in the *New York Times Book Review* that it "is John Kenneth Galbraith's quick tour through four centuries of financial bubbles, panics and crashes, with an eye toward instructing today's investors on how to see cautionary signs before it is too late." Galbraith describes, through myriad examples, a historic pattern of financial ebb and flow creating highs and lows in the economic climate. He denounces the oblivious attitude engendered by successful investments, blinding individuals to warning signs and potential disasters. As Krulwich simplifies, "How people become blockheads is the real subject of his treatise," concluding that Galbraith reminds readers that "rich people aren't smart. They're just lucky."

A Journey through Economic Time traces economic development from the time of World War I (or the "Great War") through the highlights of the twentieth century, including other wars and military conflicts, the philosophies of influential pundits, and the practices and ideologies of various presidential administrations. "Somehow, with an astonishing and no doubt deceptive ease, Mr. Galbraith is able to compress eras, reducing their unwieldy bulk to graspable essence and extracting coherence from their thematic tangle," remarks Alan Abelson in the *New York Times Book Review.* Abelson admired the readability of the book, asserting, "He's opinionated, incorrigibly sardonic and murder on fools. . . In a profession in which statistical surfeit, abused syntax and impenetrable prose are prerequisites to standing, Mr. Galbraith's lucidity and grace of articulation are excommunicable offenses." Donald McCloskey hails Galbraith's tome in the Chicago *Tribune Books,* summarizing, "What makes it good is the Old Economist showing you page after page how to think like one," ultimately urging readers to "buy it or borrow it. You'll be a better citizen and will not believe so easily the latest economic idiocy from Washington or the Sierra Club or the other fonts of conventional wisdom."

William Keegan notes in *New Statesman and Society* that *The World Economy since the Wars* "can be thoroughly recommended to those interested in the economic debate, but [who are] not quite sure where to start." Galbraith's efforts involve "sifting and reducing a lifetime's observations to an essential core," describes Keegan. While the reviewer suggests that much of this volume has already appeared in other forms in earlier books, he nevertheless maintains, "This is a highly engaging memoir, which holds the attention even of people, such as myself, who are thoroughly familiar with most of Galbraith's work."

Two years after the Republicans won control of Congress in the 1994 elections, Galbraith produced *The Good Society,* reiterating his economic and political vision for the creation of a just and equitable society. While suggesting that big government and the welfare state are the products of historical forces rather than liberal policies, Galbraith advocates reform on behalf of the poor and disenfranchised, including health care, unemployment compensation, government regulation of working conditions, education, environmental protection, and progressive taxation. Paul

Craig Roberts summarizes in *National Review,* Galbraith "defines 'the good society' as one that is politically organized to coerce 'the favored' for the poor. The instrument for this coercion 'must be the Democratic Party.'" According to Todd Gitlin in *The Nation,* "Galbraith has written perhaps the most chastened manifesto in American history. Deliberately so. His goal in this brief handbook is to sketch 'the achievable, not the perfect.'" *The Good Society,* as Matthew Miller observes in the *New York Times Book Review,* contains "Mr. Galbraith's vintage cultural complaints. He denounces the equation of wealth with intelligence, the role of advertising in ginning up consumer desire, the injustice of private affluence alongside public squalor. . . and, of course, the perils of bureaucracy."

BIOGRAPHICAL/CRITICAL SOURCES:

BOOKS

Contemporary Issues Criticism, Volume 1, Gale (Detroit), 1982.
Reisman, D. A., *Galbraith and Market Capitalism,* New York University Press, 1980.
Reisman, D. A., *Tawney, Galbraith, and Adam Smith,* St. Martin's, 1982.
Stanfield, J. Ron, *John Kenneth Galbraith,* St. Martin's, 1996.

PERIODICALS

American Economic Review, December, 1952.
Atlantic Monthly, June, 1955; January, 1987.
Chicago Tribune, June 1, 1958.
Chicago Tribune Book World, April 19, 1981.
Fortune, June 13, 1994, p. 149.
Kirkus Reviews, February 15, 1996, p. 273.
Library Journal, May 15, 1993, pp. 78-79.
Look, March 27, 1970.
Los Angeles Times, December 3, 1986.
Los Angeles Times Book Review, May 24, 1981; November 11, 1987; March 4, 1990; June 19, 1994, pp. 4, 11.
Maclean's, May 25, 1992, pp. 61-62.
Nation, July 30, 1955; May 6, 1996, p. 28.
National Review, October 10, 1994, p. 75; June 17, 1996, p. 52.
New Republic, June 9, 1958; July 8, 1967; May 4, 1968.
New Statesman and Society, January 28, 1994, p. 14; February 18, 1994, p. 24; July 22, 1994, p. 47.
Newsweek, June 26, 1967; July 3, 1967.
New Yorker, January 6, 1968; December 31, 1973; May 2, 1977.
New York Herald Tribune Book Review, June 29, 1952; April 24, 1955; June 9, 1958.
New York Review of Books, May 26, 1994, p. 40.
New York Times, June 1, 1958; September 18, 1973; February 24, 1990.
New York Times Book Review, June 25, 1967; September 7, 1975; May 3, 1981; February 11, 1990; April 5, 1992, p. 10; July 18, 1993, p. 8; June 19, 1994, p. 9; May 19, 1996.
Playboy (interview), June, 1968.
Publishers Weekly, May 17, 1993, p. 58.
Spectator, November 10, 1967.
Time, February 16, 1968.
Times Literary Supplement, March 13, 1987; May 29, 1992, p. 26.
Tribune Books (Chicago), February 18, 1990; September 25, 1994, p. 4.
Washington Monthly, July-August, 1994, p. 20; September, 1996.
Washington Post Book World, October 21, 1979; February 11, 1990.

GALINDO, P.
See HINOJOSA(-SMITH), Rolando (R.)

*   *   *

GALLANT, Mavis 1922-

PERSONAL: Born Mavis Young, August 11, 1922, in Montreal, Quebec, Canada. *Education:* Educated at schools in Montreal and New York City.

ADDRESSES: Home—14 rue Jean Ferrandi, Paris 6, France. *Agent*—Georges Borchardt, 136 East 57th St., New York, NY 10022.

CAREER: Worked at National Film Board of Canada, Montreal, early 1940s; *The Standard,* Montreal, Quebec, feature writer and critic, 1944-50; freelance writer, 1950–. Writer in residence at University of Toronto, 1983-84.

MEMBER: PEN, Authors Guild, Authors League of America, American Academy and Institute of Arts and Letters (foreign honorary member), Royal Society of Literature (fellow).

AWARDS, HONORS: Canadian Fiction Prize, 1978; named Officer of the Order of Canada, 1981; Governor General's Award, 1981, for *Home Truths: Selected Canadian Stories;* honorary doctorates from University of St. Anne, Nova Scotia, and York University, Ontario, both 1984, University of Western Ontario, 1990, Queen's University, 1992, and University of Montreal and Birnap's University, both 1995; Canada-Australia Literary Prize, 1985. Received Canada Council Molson Prize for the Arts, 1997.

WRITINGS:

FICTION

The Other Paris (short stories), Houghton, 1956.
Green Water, Green Sky (novel), Houghton, 1959.
My Heart Is Broken: Eight Stories and a Short Novel, Random House, 1964, published in England as *An Unmarried Man's Summer,* Heinemann, 1965).
A Fairly Good Time (novel), Random House, 1970.
The Pegnitz Junction: A Novella and Five Short Stories, Random House, 1973.
The End of the World and Other Stories, McClelland & Stewart, 1974.
From the Fifteenth District: A Novella and Eight Short Stories, Random House, 1979.
Home Truths: Selected Canadian Stories, Macmillan, 1981.
Overhead in a Balloon: Stories of Paris, Macmillan, 1985.
In Transit: Twenty Stories, Random House, 1989.
Across the Bridge: Nine Short Stories, Random House, 1993.
The Moslem Wife and Other Stories, McClelland & Stewart, 1993.
The Collected Stories of Mavis Gallant, Random House, 1996.

OTHER

(Author of introduction) Gabrielle Russier, *The Affair of Gabrielle Russier,* Knopf, 1971.
(Author of introduction) J. Hibbert, *The War Brides,* PMA (Toronto), 1978.
What Is To Be Done? (play; first produced in Toronto at Tarragon Theatre, November 11, 1982), Quadrant, 1983.
Paris Notebooks: Essays and Reviews, Macmillan (Toronto), 1986.

Contributor of essays, short stories, and reviews to numerous periodicals, including *New Yorker, New York Times Book Review, New Republic, New York Review of Books,* and *Times Literary Supplement.*

SIDELIGHTS: Canadian-born Mavis Gallant is widely considered one of the finest crafters of short stories in the English language. Her works, most of which appear initially in the *New Yorker* magazine, are praised for sensitive evocation of setting and penetrating delineation of character. In the words of *Maclean's* magazine contributor Mark Abley, Gallant "is virtually unrivalled at the art of short fiction," an exacting artist whose pieces reveal "an ability to press a lifetime into a few resonant pages as well as a desire to show the dark side of comedy and the humor that lurks behind despair." *Time* magazine correspondent Timothy Foote calls Gallant "one of the prose masters of the age," and adds that no modern writer "casts a colder eye on life, on death and all the angst and eccentricity in between." Since 1950 Gallant has lived primarily in Paris, but she has also spent extended periods of time in the United States, Canada, and other parts of Europe. Not surprisingly, her stories and novellas show a wide range of place and period; many feature refugees and expatriates forced into self-discernment by rootlessness. As Anne Tyler notes in the *New York Times Book Review,* each Gallant fiction "is densely-woven, . . . rich in people and plots—a miniature world, more satisfying than many full-scale novels. . . There is a sense of limitlessness: each story is like a peephole opening out into a very wide landscape."

At the age of twenty-one Gallant became a reporter with the Montreal *Standard,* a position that honed her writing talents while it widened her variety of experiences. Journalism, she told the *New York Times,* "turned out to be so valuable, because I saw the interiors of houses I wouldn't have seen otherwise. And a great many of the things, particularly in. . . [fiction] about Montreal, that I was able to describe later, it was because I had seen them, I had gone into them as a journalist." She added: "If I got on with the people, I had no hesitation about seeing them again. . . I went right back and took them to lunch. I could see some of those rooms, and see the wallpaper, and what they ate, and what they wore, and how they spoke,. . . and the way they treated their children. I drew it all in like blotting paper." From these encounters Gallant began to write stories. In 1950 she decided to leave Montreal and begin a new life as a serious fiction writer in Paris. At the same time she began to send stories to the *New Yorker* for publication. Her second submission, a piece called "Madeline's Birthday," was accepted, beginning a four-decade relationship with the prestigious periodical. Gallant used the six-hundred-dollar check for her story to finance her move abroad. Paris has been her permanent home ever since.

Expatriation provided Gallant with new challenges and insights that have formed central themes in her fiction. In *The Other Paris* and subsequent story collections, her characters are "the refugee, the rootless, the emotionally disinherited," to quote a *Times Literary Supplement* reviewer, who adds: "It is a world of displacement where journeys are allegorical and love is inadequate." Gallant portrays postwar people locked into archaic cultural presuppositions; often dispossessed of their homes by haphazard circumstances, they are bewildered and insecure, seeking refuge in etiquette and other shallow symbols of tradition. *Time* correspondent Patricia Blake maintains that Gallant's "natural subject is the varieties of spiritual exile. . . All [her characters] are bearers of a metaphorical 'true passport' that transcends nationality and signifies internal freedom. For some this serves as a safe-conduct to independence. For others it is a

guarantee of loneliness and despair." Gallant also presents the corollary theme of the past's inexorable grip on its survivors. In her stories, *New York Review of Books* essayist V. S. Pritchett contends, "we are among the victims of the wars in Europe which have left behind pockets of feckless exiles. . . History has got its teeth into them and has regurgitated them and left them bizarre and perplexed."

Gallant is best known for her short stories and novellas, but she has also written two novels, *Green Water, Green Sky* and *A Fairly Good Time.* Ronald B. Hatch in the *Dictionary of Literary Biography* contends that these works continue the author's "exploration of the interaction between an individual's thoughts and his external world." In *Green Water, Green Sky,* according to Constance Pendergast in the *Saturday Review,* Gallant "writes of the disaster that results from a relationship founded on the mutual need and antagonism of a woman and her daughter, where love turns inward and festers, bringing about inevitably the disintegration of both characters." Lighter in tone, *A Fairly Good Time* follows the blundering adventures of a Canadian, Shirley Perrigny, who lives in France. Hatch notes that the novel "may well be the funniest of all her works. . . As a satire on the self-satisfied habits of the French, *A Fairly Good Time* proves enormously high-spirited. Yet the novel offers more than satire. As the reader becomes intimately acquainted with Shirley, her attempts to defeat the rigidity of French logic by living in the moment come to seem zany but commendable."

Home Truths: Selected Canadian Stories, first published in 1981, has proven to be one of Gallant's most popular collections. In Abley's view, the volume "bears repeated witness to the efforts made by this solitary, distant writer to come to terms with her own past and her own country." The stories focus on footloose Canadians who are alienated from their families or cultures; the characters try "to puzzle out the ground rules of their situations, which are often senseless, joyless and contradictory," to quote *Nation* reviewer Barbara Fisher Williamson. *New York Times Book Review* contributor Maureen Howard observes that in *Home Truths,* Canada "is not a setting, a backdrop; it is an adversary, a constraint, a comfort, the home that is almost understandable, if not understanding. It is at once deadly real and haunting, phantasmagoric." Phyllis Grosskurth elaborates in *Saturday Night:* "Clearly [Gallant] is still fighting a battle with the Canada she left many years ago. Whether or not that country has long since vanished is irrelevant, for it has continued to furnish the world of her imagination. . . She knows that whatever she writes will be in the language that shaped her sensibility, though the Canada of her youth imposed restraints from which she could free herself only by geographic separation. Wherever she is, she writes out of her roots. . . Her Montreal is a state of mind, an emotion recalled, an apprenticeship for life." *Home Truths* won the 1981 Governor General's Award, Canada's highest literary honor. *Books in Canada* correspondent Wayne Grady concludes that it is not a vision of Gallant's native country that emerges in the book, but rather "a vision of the world, of life: it is in that nameless country of the mind inhabited by all real writers, regardless of nativity, that Mavis Gallant lives. We are here privileged intruders."

In Transit, published in 1989, consists of twenty stories that appeared in the *New Yorker* during the 1950s and 1960s. Most of the stories in this well-praised collection are set in Europe and portray the sense of dislocation experienced by various expatriates, refugees, tourists, and natives. In the title story, French newlyweds overhear the dispute of an older American couple while waiting in a Helsinki airport lounge, inducing private reflection on their own nuptial misgivings. Gerald Mangan writes in the *Times Literary Supplement,* "Elegant wit and a pin-sharp intelligence give her prose a dazzling surface; but her characters live entirely by their own lights, by virtue of a compassionate imagination, and she is generous enough to leave all the judgments to the reader." According to Ronald Bryden in the *New York Times Book Review,* "Transit, noise, and the symbiosis between them, one might argue, are Mavis Gallant's major themes—noise, that is, in the philosopher's definition of data that carry no meaning to the senses they fall on." He adds that Gallant "spends much of her work demonstrating quietly how much of language, culture, and their ideological designs on us is simply noise to most people, in this shifting world where fewer and fewer of us are at home, linguistically or otherwise."

Across the Bridge, a collection of eleven short stories, appeared in 1993. In each of these pieces, most set in either Montreal or Paris, Gallant explores the familiar themes of dislocation and alienation as reflected in arranged marriage, language, national identity, and modern consumer society. John McGahern writes in the *New York Times Book Review,* "French is the natural language of many of her characters, and it is a palpable presence in her lucid, elegant sentences." McGahern adds, "The general climate of the bourgeois or petit-bourgeois world she describes is philistine, never more so than when airbrushed with culture: Proust or Chateaubriand is interchangeable with Gucci or Armani." Barbara Gabriel writes in a *Canadian Forum* review, "As always in Gallant, the main protagonist in these stories is history itself. Readers who have followed her as one of the great chroniclers of the human fallout of World War II and its redrawn borders, will see the special ironies in the new twists and turns of fate inaugurated by the fall of the Berlin Wall." McGahern similarly notes "Gallant's remarkable gift for introducing whole lives and future histories in a few swift, brief strokes." Rita Donovan observes in a *Books in Canada* review, "Gallant writes of her origins from 'away'; this is interesting, first, because her grasp of Montreal, and the Montreal of the past, is undiluted and, second, because it ties in nicely with many of her other stories that deal with the emigre experience."

The critical reception for Gallant's work has been very positive. *Washington Post Book World* reviewer Elizabeth Spencer suggests that there is "no writer in English anywhere able to set Mavis Gallant in second place. Her style alone places her in the first rank. Gallant's firmly drafted prose neglects nothing, leaves no dangling ends for the reader to tack up. . . She is hospitable to the metaphysics of experience as well as to the homeliest social detail." Grosskurth writes: "Gallant's particular power as a writer is the sureness with which she catches the ephemeral; it is a wry vision, a blend of the sad and the tragi-comic. She is a born writer who happens to have been born in Canada, and her gift has been able to develop as it has only because she could look back in anger, love, and nostalgia." *New York Times Book Review* contributor Phyllis Rose praises Gallant for her "wicked humor that misses nothing, combined with sophistication so great it amounts to forgiveness." The critic concludes: "To take up residence in the mind of Mavis Gallant, as one does in reading her stories, is a privilege and delight."

BIOGRAPHICAL/CRITICAL SOURCES:

BOOKS

Contemporary Literary Criticism, Gale (Detroit), Volume 7, 1977; Volume 18, 1981; Volume 38, 1986.
Dictionary of Literary Biography, Volume 53: *Canadian Writers since 1960, First Series,* Gale, 1986.
Lecker, Robert, and Jack David, editors, *The Annotated Bibliography of Canada's Major Authors,* Volume 5, ECW (Ontario), 1984.
Merler, Grazia, *Mavis Gallant: Narrative Patterns and Devices,* Tecumseh, 1978.
Moss, John, editor, *Present Tense,* NC Press (Toronto), 1985.
Reference Guide to Short Fiction, St. James Press, 1993.
Short Story Criticism, Volume 5, Gale, 1990.

PERIODICALS

America, March 5, 1994, p. 28.
Atlantis, autumn, 1978.
Books and Bookmen, July, 1974.
Books in Canada, October, 1979; October, 1981; April, 1984; October, 1985; October 1993, p. 38.
Canadian Fiction, number 28, 1978; number 43, 1982.
Canadian Forum, February, 1982; November, 1985; March, 1994, p. 38; April, 1997.
Canadian Literature, spring, 1973; spring, 1985; winter, 1991, p. 235.
Chicago Tribune Book World, November 11, 1979.
Christian Science Monitor, June 4, 1970.
Globe and Mail (Toronto), October 11, 1986; October 15, 1988.
Los Angeles Times, April 15, 1985.
Los Angeles Times Book Review, November 4, 1979; May 24, 1987.
Maclean's, September 5, 1964; November 9, 1981; November 22, 1982; February 3, 1997.
Nation, June 15, 1985; October 18, 1993, p. 66.
New Republic, August 25, 1979; May 13, 1985; March 28, 1994, p. 43; November 25, 1996.
New York Review of Books, June 25, 1964; January 24, 1980.
New York Times, June 5, 1970; October 2, 1979; April 20, 1985; July 9, 1985; March 4, 1987.
New York Times Book Review, February 26, 1956; September 16, 1979; May 5, 1985; March 15, 1987; May 28, 1989, p. 3; September 12, 1993, p. 7; December 8, 1996.
Observer, February 4, 1990, p. 60.
People Weekly, January 13, 1997.
Publishers Weekly, August 5, 1996, p. 431.
Quill and Quire, October, 1981; June, 1984.
Rubicon, winter, 1984-85.
Saturday Night, September, 1973; November, 1981.
Saturday Review, October 17, 1959; August 25, 1979; October 13, 1979.
Spectator, August 29, 1987; February 20, 1988.
Time, November 26, 1979; May 27, 1985.
Times (London), February 28, 1980.
Times Literary Supplement, March 14, 1980; February 28, 1986; January 22-28, 1988; September 25-October 1, 1987; April 13, 1990, p. 403.
Virginia Quarterly Review, spring, 1980.
Washington Post Book World, April 14, 1985; March 29, 1987.

*   *   *

GALSWORTHY, John 1867-1933
(John Sinjohn, A. R. P-M)

PERSONAL: Born August 14, 1867, in Kingston Hill, Surrey, England; died of a brain tumor, January 31, 1933, in London, England; son of John (a solicitor and in business) and Blanche (Bartleet) Galsworthy; married Ada Cooper Galsworthy (his first cousin Arthur Galsworthy's ex-wife), September 23, 1905. *Education:* New College, Oxford, second-class degree, 1889.

CAREER: English novelist, playwright, and short story writer. Called to Bar in 1890. Practiced law at Lincoln's Inn, beginning in 1890; established private practice, c. 1893; began literary career, c. 1895. Founder of PEN Club. *Military service:* Volunteered at a military hospital in France, 1916-17.

AWARDS, HONORS: Received honorary Litt.D. degrees from Manchester, Dublin, Sheffield, Cambridge, Oxford, and Princeton universities, between 1920 and 1931; offered knighthood for literary achievement (refused by author); Order of Merit, 1929; Nobel Prize for literature, 1932.

WRITINGS:

UNDER PSEUDONYM JOHN SINJOHN

From the Four Winds (short stories), Unwin (London), 1897.
Jocelyn (novel), Duckworth (London), 1898, reissued under Galsworthy's real name, Scholarly Press (St. Clair Shores, MI), 1972.
Villa Rubein: A Novel, Duckworth, 1900, Putnam's (New York City), 1908.
A Man of Devon (short stories), Blackwood (London), 1901.
Corduroys, privately printed (Kansas City), 1937.
The Rocks, privately printed (Kansas City), 1937.

UNDER NAME JOHN GALSWORTHY

The Island Pharisees (novel), Putnam's, 1904, revised edition, Heinemann (London), 1908.
The Man of Property (novel), Putnam's, 1906.
The Silver Box (play; three-act; produced at Royal Court Theatre, London, 1906; also see below), Duckworth, 1910.
The Country House, Putnam's, 1907.
A Commentary, Putnam's, 1908.
Fraternity, Putnam's, 1909.
Plays: The Silver Box, Joy, Strife (three-acts; also see below), Putnam's, 1909, *Joy* published separately as *Joy: A Play on the Letter "I",* Duckworth, 1910, *Strife,* published separately, Scribner, 1920.
Justice: A Tragedy in Four Acts (play; also see below), Scribner (New York City), 1910.
A Motley, Scribner, 1910.
The Patrician, Scribner, 1911.
A Little Dream: An Allegory in Six Scenes (play; also see below), Scribner, 1911.
The Pigeon: A Fantasy in Three Acts (play; also see below), Scribner, 1912.
Moods, Songs, and Doggerels, Scribner, 1912.
The Inn of Tranquility: Studies and Essays, Scribner, 1912.
The Eldest Son: A Domestic Drama in Three Acts (play; also see below), Scribner, 1912.
The Fugitive: A Play in Four Acts (also see below), Scribner, 1913.
Plays: Second Series (contains *The Eldest Son, The Little Dream,* and *Justice*), Scribner, 1913.
The Dark Flower (novel; also see below), Scribner, 1913.
The Mob: A Play in Four Acts (also see below), Scribner, 1914.
Memories, illustrated by Maud Earl, Scribner, 1914.
Some Slings and Arrows, selected by Elsie E. Morton, E. Mathews, 1914.
Plays: Third Series (contains *The Fugitive, The Pigeon,* and *The Mob*), Scribner, 1914.
The Little Man, and Other Satires, Scribner, 1915.

A Bit o' Love: A Play in Three Acts (also see below), Scribner, 1915, also published as *The Full Moon: A Play in Three Acts,* Duckworth, 1915.
The Freelands, Scribner, 1915.
A Sheaf, Scribner, 1916.
Beyond (novel; also see below), Scribner, 1917.
Five Tales (includes Indian Summer of a Forsyte), Scribner, 1918.
The Land: A Plea, Allen & Unwin (London), 1918.
Another Sheaf, Scribner, 1919.
Addresses in America, Scribner, 1919.
Saint's Progress (novel; also see below), Scribner, 1919.
Tatterdemalion, Scribner, 1920.
The Foundations: An Extravagant Play in Three Acts (also see below), Scribner, 1920.
The Skin Game: A Tragi-comedy in Three Acts (play; also see below), Scribner, 1920.
Plays: Fourth Series (contains *A Bit o' Love, The Foundations,* and *The Skin Game*), Scribner, 1920.
In Chancery (play; also see below), Scribner, 1920.
Awakening (play; also see below), Scribner, 1920.
The First and the Last, Heinemann, 1920, enlarged edition, Scribner, 1925.
To Let (play; also see below), Scribner, 1921.
Six Short Plays, Scribner, 1921.
The Works of John Galsworthy, eighteen volumes, Heinemann, 1921-25.
The Forsyte Saga (novels and short stories; contains *Awakening, In Chancery, To Let,* and Indian Summer of a Forsyte [1918]), Scribner, 1922.
A Family Man, in Three Acts (play; also see below), Scribner, 1922.
The Works of John Galsworthy, Manaton Edition, twenty-five volumes, Scribner, 1922-29.
Windows: A Comedy in Three Acts for Idealists and Others (play; also see below), Duckworth, 1922, Scribner, 1923.
Loyalties: A Drama in Three Acts (play; also see below), Scribner, 1923.
Captures, Scribner, 1923.
International Thought, W. Heffer & Sons (Cambridge), 1923.
Plays: Fifth Series (contains *A Family Man, Loyalties,* and *Windows*), Scribner, 1923.
The Forest: A Drama in Four Acts (play; also see below), Scribner, 1924.
The White Monkey (novel; also see below), Scribner, 1924.
Abracadabra & Other Satires, Heinemann, 1924.
On Expression, Oxford University Press, 1924.
Representative Plays, introduction by George P. Baker, Scribner, 1924.
Old English: A Play in Three Acts (play; also see below), Duckworth, 1924, Scribner, 1925.
Caravan: The Assembled Tales of John Galsworthy (short stories), Scribner, 1925.
The Show: A Drama in Three Acts (play; also see below), Scribner, 1925.
The Silver Spoon (novel; also see below), Scribner, 1926.
Verses New and Old, Scribner, 1926.
Plays: Sixth Series (contains *The Forest, Old English,* and *The Show*), Scribner, 1926.
The Novels, Tales and Plays of John Galsworthy, Devon Edition, twenty-two volumes, Scribner, 1926-29.
Escape: An Episodic Play in a Prologue and Two Parts (also see below), Duckworth, 1926, Scribner, 1927.
Castles in Spain, and Other Screeds, Scribner, 1927.
. . . Satires, Scribner, 1927.

Two Forsyte Interludes: A Silent Wooing [and] *Passers By* (short stories; also see below), Heinemann, 1927, Scribner, 1928.

Swan Song (novel; also see below), Scribner, 1928.

Plays, Scribner, 1928.

Exiled: An Evolutionary Comedy in Three Acts (play; also see below), Duckworth, 1929, Scribner, 1930.

Four Forsyte Stories, Fountain (New York), 1929.

A Modern Comedy (novels and short stories; contains *The White Monkey, The Silver Spoon, Two Forsyte Interludes: A Silent Wooing [and] Passers By,* and *Swan Song*), Scribner, 1929.

The Roof: A Play in Seven Scenes (also see below), Duckworth, 1929, Scribner, 1931.

The Plays of John Galsworthy, Duckworth, 1929.

A Rambling Discourse, Mathews & Marrot (London), 1929.

On Forsyte 'Change (short stories), Scribner, 1930.

Soames and The Flag, Scribner, 1930.

Plays: Seventh Series (contains *Escape, Exiled,* and *The Roof*), Duckworth, 1930.

Two Essays on Conrad, privately printed (Cincinnati, OH), 1930.

The Creation of Character in Literature, Clarendon Press (Oxford, England), 1931.

Maid in Waiting (novel; also see below), Scribner, 1931.

Flowering Wilderness (novel; also see below), Scribner, 1932.

Worshipful Society, Scribner, 1932.

Candelabra: Selected Essays and Addresses, Heinemann, 1932, Scribner, 1933.

Three Novels of Love (contains *The Dark Flower, Beyond,* and *Saint's Progress*), Scribner, 1933.

Author and Critic, House of Books (New York), 1933.

Autobiographical Letters of John Galsworthy: A Correspondence with Frank Harris, Hitherto Unpublished, English Book Shop (New York City), 1933.

Over the River (novel; also see below), Heinemann, 1933, published as *One More River*, Scribner, 1933.

Ex Libris John Galsworthy (quotations from his writings), compiled by John and Ada Galsworthy, Heinemann, 1933.

End of the Chapter (novels; contains *Maid in Waiting, Flowering Wilderness,* and *Over the River*), Scribner, 1934.

The Collected Poems of John Galsworthy, Scribner, 1934.

Letters from John Galsworthy, 1900-1932, edited by Edward Garnett, Scribner, 1934.

The Apple Tree, Scribner, 1934.

Forsytes, Pendyces, and Others, Scribner, 1935.

The Winter Garden: Four Dramatic Pieces, Duckworth, 1935.

Galsworthy in His Humour, Duckworth, 1935.

Glimpses and Reflections, Heinemann, 1937.

Ten Famous Plays, Duckworth, 1941.

John Galsworthy's Letters to Leon Lion, edited by Asher Boldon Wilson, Mouton (The Hague), 1968.

Five Plays, introduction by Benedict Nightingale, Methuen (New York City), 1984.

OTHER

(Under pseudonym A. R. P-M) *The Burning Spear, Being the Experiences of Mr. John Lavender in Time of War*, Chatto & Windus, 1919, issued under Galsworthy name, Scribner, 1923.

Portions of Galsworthy's manuscript and letters are housed at Oxford University's Bodleian Library, Harvard University's Houghton Library, and Princeton University's Firestone Library.

SIDELIGHTS: Known primarily as the author of plays examining contemporary social problems during the early twentieth century, British author John Galsworthy is best remembered for his collection of novels and short stories known as the "Forsyte Chronicles," which contain a meticulous depiction of upper-middle-class English life. Loosely modeled on Galsworthy's relatives, the Forsytes are members of a family of wealthy industrialists who value material success above all else. While the "Chronicles" would fall out of favor in the years after World War II, in later years, Galsworthy's magnum opus has been revisited by critics in a less harsh light. A revival of interest in Galsworthy's work during the mid-1960s stemmed from the British Broadcasting Company's massive production of *The Forsyte Saga* that aired throughout the United Kingdom and the United States.

Born on a family estate in Kingston Hill, Surrey, near London, Galsworthy was the second child of an upper-middle-class family. His father was a successful solicitor who had a financial interest in mining companies in Canada and Russia; he later served as the model for Old Jolyon Forsyte in the "Forsyte Chronicles." At the age of nine Galsworthy was sent to the Saugeen Preparatory School, a boarding school in Bournemouth. Five years later he entered the prestigious Harrow School in London, where he excelled in athletics. In 1886 he went to Oxford University to study law, graduating with second degree honors in 1889. The following year he was called to the bar and began writing legal briefs for his father's firm. Galsworthy, however, had little interest in a legal career. In 1891 his father sent him on an extended inspection tour of the family's mining interests in Canada, and during the next few years he traveled widely. During a two-month voyage aboard the *Torrens* in 1893, he formed a close friendship with the first mate of the ship, Joseph Conrad, who was then at work on his first novel. Conrad later encouraged and guided Galsworthy in his literary efforts. Between 1897 and 1901 Galsworthy published two novels and two volumes of short stories under the pseudonym John Sinjohn. The last of these works, *A Man of Devon* (1901), contains his first short story dealing with the Forsytes.

After his father's death in 1904, Galsworthy began publishing under his own name. In 1906 the first "Forsyte" novel, *The Man of Property*, appeared, and a production of his play *The Silver Box* was favorably reviewed by critics. Galsworthy wrote prolifically until his death, gaining international recognition for his works. During World War I he donated the income from his writings to the war effort and volunteered as a masseur in a Red Cross hospital in France. In 1917 Galsworthy was offered a knighthood, which he declined; he later accepted the Order of Merit for his literary achievements. For twelve years he served as the first president of PEN, the international writers' organization. In 1932, shortly before his death, Galsworthy was awarded a Nobel Prize in literature.

Galsworthy first achieved prominence as a dramatist. His most esteemed plays are noted for their realistic technique and insightful social criticism. While working for his father, Galsworthy collected rents from the tenants of London slum properties, and several of his plays examine the contrast between the rights of the privileged upper classes and the poor. In *The Silver Box*, for example, the son of a wealthy member of Parliament steals a purse from a prostitute. Later, the husband of one of the family's servants steals a cigarette box from the purse. While the wealthy young man is released, the servant's husband is convicted and sent to prison. *Justice* (1910) examines the practice of solitary confinement in prisons and has been credited with prompting Winston Churchill to introduce legislation for prison reforms. Although a few critics consider Galsworthy's social plays his most important works, his accomplishments as a dramatist have been largely overshadowed by the renown of the "Forsyte Chronicles."

Publication of *The Forsyte Saga* in 1922 established Galsworthy's reputation as a novelist. In fact, he became somewhat of a publishing phenomenon: Over two million copies of the *Forsyte Saga* were sold in a space of only a few months after its initial 1922 publication. The works known as the "Forsyte Chronicles" include the novels and short fiction collected both *The Forsyte Saga* and *A Modern Comedy* (1929), as well as in the short stories collected as *On Forsyte 'Change* (1930) and others published elsewhere. Galsworthy modeled many of the characters in these works upon his ancestors and immediate family members; for example, Soames Forsyte, the central figure of the "Chronicles," is based on Galsworthy's cousin Arthur. Tracing the rise and decline of the Forsyte clan, the narrative of the "Chronicles" begins in the 1820s with a short story eventually published in *On Forsyte 'Change* and ends with the death of Soames in 1926 in *Swan Song* (1928). The "Chronicles" consists of a series of trilogies, the first encompassing the three novels eventually published in a single volume as *The Forsyte Saga: The Man of Property, In Chancery,* and *To Let,* their narratives interlinked with short stories. A follow-up trilogy, 1929's *Modern Comedy,* contains *The White Monkey, The Silver Spoon,* and *Swan Song,* which were each published separately between 1924 and 1928 and mortared together, as was characteristic of Galsworthy, with shorter fictional works. Galsworthy wrote a third trilogy, aptly titled *End of the Chapter* and released in 1934, which, related to the "Forsyte" books, encompassed the novels *Maid in Waiting, Flowering Wilderness,* and *One More River,* completed in 1933.

In *The Man of Property,* Soames Forsyte's wife, Irene, has an affair with an architect commissioned to build the Forsyte mansion. Soames takes revenge by ruining the architect and raping Irene. The architect later dies in a mysterious accident. *To Let* finds Irene befriended and financially provided for by the elder Forsyte, Old Jolyon; she is able to live in France, out of the reach of her vengeful husband after Jolyon's death. Soames and Irene divorce in *In Chancery* and Soames remarries, this time taking a wife who bears him a daughter named Fleur. Irene, meanwhile, marries Soames' brother, Jolyon Jr., and bears him a son and heir to the Forsyte family fortunes.

Somewhat predictably, Irene's son, Jon, falls in love with his cousin, Fleur, and that love is quickly returned. However, their marriage is not to be, not because of objections on the part of Soames (who has grudgingly agreed to the match to please the daughter he adores) but due to the hurt it would cause Irene, as, Jolyon Jr. counsels his son, the couple's "children . . . would be the grandchildren of Soames, as much as of your mother, of a man who once owned your mother as a man might own a slave." Fleur reacts by marrying the first eligible man she can—Michael Mont, the son of a large landowner destined to gain the title of baronet. By the group of novels published as *A Modern Comedy,* Galsworthy's attitude towards the Forsyte clan has mellowed, his perspective more sympathetic. In *The White Monkey* Soames' business decisions are ruled by ethical considerations as much as a lust for money. *The Silver Spoon* finds Fleur's father rebuking a woman who insults his daughter, only to find himself sued as a result. Ultimately, Soames is acquitted of any wrongdoing, leaving him to serve as her protector until, ultimately, he dies while rescuing Fleur from a fire in 1928's *Swan Song,* the final volume of *A Modern Comedy.* "Quite literally," noted *Dictionary of Literary Biography* essayist Brian Murray, "[Galsworthy's]

villain becomes a hero." When the book's publication was announced in July of 1928, along with the news that Soames Forsyte had been killed, the story made the headlines of more than one newspaper around London.

Maid in Waiting, the first volume in Galsworthy's final trilogy, *End of the Chapter,* depicts the lives of Fleur and Michael Mont and their family. Reflecting Galsworthy's own interest in addressing social injustice, the characters of Mr. and Mrs. Hilary Cherrell (who are related to the Michael Mont who married Fleur Forsyte in a previous novel), formulate a scheme that would put the unemployed to work cleaning up the city's slum areas. The Cherrells stand in stark contrast to the Forsytes in their acceptance of responsibility for those less fortunate as a result of their wealth and social stature. In *Flowering Wilderness,* daughter Dinny Cherrell supports her poet-lover Wilfred Desert for his religious beliefs, even though, during a trip to the Middle East, he been forced to pretended to accept Islam upon threats of death. According to Murray, *Flowering Wilderness* is one of Galsworthy's better efforts, lacking in "long stretches of ornate prose" and without "meandering subplots."

Indeed, the ornate prose and convoluted plots were central to a great deal of critical reaction levelled at Galsworthy's magnum opus in the year's after the author's death. They reflect the shifts in society occurring with rapidity during the early part of the twentieth century. "Critics [originally]praised the trilogy for its sweep and control," noted Murray, "and proclaimed Galsworthy a modern Thackeray." But then there appeared other reviews, most notably those by more outre writers Virginia Woolf and D. H. Lawrence. "The Forsytes are all parasites," fumed Lawrence in an article critical of the "Chronicles" in a 1928 edition of the magazine *Scrutinies,* "and Mr. Galsworthy set out, in a really magnificent attempt, to let us see it. They are parasites upon the thought, the feelings, the whole body of life of really living individuals who have gone before them and who exist alongside with them. . . As far as I can see, there is nothing but Forsyte in Galsworthy's books." Lawrence's harsh appraisal of the "Chronicles" was not unusual for his day; Galsworthy's literary star was beginning to set as early as 1924 when Woolf argued in her monograph *Mr. Bennett and Mrs. Brown* that his characters were superficial, his plots predictable and rife with stereotypes. He began to be viewed as an anachronism: a sentimentalist writing in an archaic literary style in the age of James Joyce, Woolf, Proust, and others.

In addition to his plays and his massive "Forsyte Chronicle," Galsworthy produced fourteen volumes of short stories and sketches and several collections of essays and poetry. Although his dramas and novels were highly regarded during his lifetime, critical and popular interest in his works declined shortly after his death, and continued in the decades following. Indeed, in 1953 critic Arnold Kettle, in his introduction to *An Introduction to the English Novel,* cited Galsworthy's work as "outstanding examples of 'middlebrow' literature. . . inferior literature adapted to the special tastes and needs of the middle class. . . . it must maintain, whatever its particular brand of inferiority, certain proprieties sacred to the bulk of readers of the more superior lending libraries. Though permitted to titillate with the mention and even the occasional vision of the unmentionable, it must never fundamentally shake, never stretch beyond breaking-point, certain secure complacencies." Fortunately, Galsworthy's literary reputation would be somewhat redeemed a decade later, following the British Broadcasting Corporation's twenty-six-hour serial adaptation of *The Forsyte Saga* on television. Broadcast in 1967 and again the following year, and syndicated in more than forty countries around the world, this adaptation has been credited with renewing interest in Galsworthy's novels. Today Galsworthy is recognized as an important chronicler of English life, with Sanford Sternlicht praising his works as "the finest written portrait of the passing from power of England's upper middle class."

BIOGRAPHICAL/CRITICAL SOURCES:

BOOKS

Batchelor, John, *The Edwardian Novelists,* Duckworth, 1982.
Dictionary of Literary Biography, Volume 34: *British Novelists, 1890-1929: Traditionalists,* Gale, 1985.
Dictionary of Literary Biography, Volume 98: *Modern British Essayists, First Series,* Gale, 1990.
Dictionary of Literary Biography, Volume 162: *British Short-Fiction Writers, 1915-1945,* Gale, 1996.
Dupre, Catherine, *John Galsworthy: A Biography,* Coward, 1976.
Fisher, John, *The World of the Forsytes,* Secker & Warburg, 1976.
Frechet, Alec, *John Galsworthy: A Reassessment,* Barnes & Noble, 1982.
Gindin, James, *The English Climate: An Excursion into a Biography of John Galsworthy,* University of Michigan Press, 1979.
Gindin, James, *John Galsworthy's Life and Art: An Alien's Fortress,* University of Michigan Press, 1987.
Leavis, J. D., *Fiction and the Reading Public,* Chatto & Windus, 1932.
Mooti, Farouk Abdel, *The Language and Style of John Galsworthy's Novels,* Mansoura University (Mansurah, Egypt), 1982.
Morris, Margaret, *My Galsworthy Story, Including Sixty-seven Hitherto Unpublished Letters,* Owen, 1967.
Mottram, R. H., *For Some We Loved: An Intimate Portrait of John and Ada Galsworthy,* Hutchinson, 1956.
Reynolds, M. E., *Memories of John Galsworthy by his Sister,* Stokes (New York), 1937.
Ronning, Anne Holden, *Hidden and Visible Suffrage: Emancipation and the Edwardian Women in Galsworthy, Wells, and Forster,* P. Lang (Bern, NY), 1995.
Sauter, Rudolf, *Galsworthy the Man: An Intimate Portrait,* Owen, 1967.
Short Story Criticism, Volume 22, Gale, 1997.
Sternlict, Sanford, *John Galsworthy,* Twayne, 1987.
Stevens, Earl E., and H. Ray Stevens, *John Galsworthy: An Annotated Bibliography of Writings about Him,* Northern Illinois University Press, 1980.
Twentieth-Century Literary Criticism, Gale (Detroit), Volume 1, 1978, Volume 25, 1988.
Woolf, Virginia, *Mr. Bennett and Mrs. Brown,* Hogarth, 1924.

PERIODICALS

American Mercury, April, 1936, pp. 448-59.
Bookman, January-February, 1932, pp. 483-93.
English Literature in Transition, Volume 19, 1976, pp. 283-98; Volume 21, 1978, pp. 149-57; Volume 23, 1980, pp. 99-114.
Illinois Quarterly, summer, 1981, pp. 41-50.
Madison Quarterly, Volume 4, 1944, pp. 84-94.
Saturday Review of Literature, March 18, 1933, pp. 485-87.
Texas Studies in Language and Literature, Volume 17, 1975, pp. 653-72.

GANDHI, M. K.
See GANDHI, Mohandas Karamchand

*   *   *

GANDHI, Mahatma
See GANDHI, Mohandas Karamchand

*   *   *

GANDHI, Mohandas Karamchand 1869-1948
(M. K. Gandhi, Mahatma Gandhi)

PERSONAL: Born October 2, 1869, in Probandar, Kathiawar, India; assassinated, January 30, 1948, in New Delhi, India; son of Karamchand (a provincial political official) and Putlibai Gandhi; married wife Kasturbai, 1883 (died, 1944); children: four sons; one daughter (adopted). *Education:* Attended University of Bombay; attended Samaldas College, Bhavnagar, India, 1887-88; received law degree from Inner Temple, London, 1891.

CAREER: Called to the bar, London, England, 1891; private law practice in Bombay and Rajkot, India, 1891-93; moved to Natal, South Africa, and worked for an Indian business firm, 1893-94; private law practice in Durban and Johannesburg, South Africa, 1894-1914; founded the Natal Indian Congress, 1894, to advance the political and civil rights of Indians in South Africa and served as the organization's secretary; organized the Indian Ambulance Corps to assist British forces during the Boer War, 1899-1902; launched *satyagraha* non-cooperation campaign for Indian rights, 1906, and led movement until 1914; returned to India and engaged in social work and community organizing in the Indian countryside, c. 1915-18; became president of the Indian National Congress and founded Satyagraha League, 1919; led *satyagraha* non-cooperation campaign for home rule against the British colonial government, 1919-22; imprisoned for seditious conspiracy, 1922-24; led new *satyagraha* campaigns and was repeatedly imprisoned in the 1930s; imprisoned for demanding Indian independence and opposing the British war effort, 1942-44; helped negotiate Indian independence, 1945-47; engaged in social work, 1947; fatally shot in 1948 by a Hindu extremist opposed to Gandhi's policies toward Muslims.

AWARDS, HONORS: Boer War Medal, c. 1902, and Kaisar-i-Hind Medal, 1906, from the British government in South Africa (Gandhi returned both in 1928).

WRITINGS:

WORKS ON POLITICS, SOCIETY, RELIGION, AND MORALITY

Hind Swaraj or Indian Home Rule, [South Africa], 1909, Navajivan, 1939.
Speeches and Writings, Natesan, 1918.
Swaraj and Non-Cooperation, Chakravartty, 1920.
Swaraj in One Year, Ganesh, 1921.
Mahatma Gandhi on Spinning, compiled by Manoranjan Bhattacharya, Bhattacharya, 1921.
Freedom's Battle: Being a Comprehensive Collection of Writings and Speeches on the Present Situation, Ganesh, 1922.
The Wheel of Fortune, Ganesh, 1922.
Non-Cooperation: Recent Speeches and Writings, Ganesh, 1922.
India on Trial, Ahimsa Ashram, 1922.
Mahatma Gandhi's Jail Experiences, Tagore, 1922.
The Tug of War, Book Club (Calcutta), 1922.

Young India (collection of articles published in journal *Young India*), Ganesan, Volume I: *1919-1922,* 1923, Volume II: *1924-1926,* 1927, Volume III: *1927-1928,* 1935.

Mahatma Gandhi: His Life, Writings, and Speeches, Ganesh, 1923.

A Guide to Health, Ganesan, 1923.

Sermon on the Sea, Universal Publishing Co., 1924.

Hindu-Muslim Tension: Its Cause and Cure, Young India Office, 1924.

Is India Different? The Class Struggle in India, Communist Party (London), 1927.

Satyagraha in South Africa, Navajivan, 1928, Academic Reprints, 1954.

Ethical Religion, Ganesan, 1930.

How to Compete With Foreign Cloth, Calcutta Book Co., 1931.

India's Case for Swaraj: Being Selected Speeches, Writings, Interviews, etc., of Mahatma Gandhi in England and India, September 1931-January 1932, Yeshanand, 1932.

My Soul's Agony: Being Statements Issued From Yeravda Prison about the Removal of Untouchability, Servants of Untouchables Society (Bombay), 1932.

The Bleeding Wound! Being a Most Up-to-Date Collection of Gandhiji's Writings and Statements on Untouchability, Shyam Lal, 1932.

Views on Untouchability: Being Extracts From Speeches and Writings, edited by Mukut Beharilal, privately printed (Kashi), 1932.

Self-Restraint Versus Self Indulgence, two volumes, Navajivan, 1933-39.

To the Students, edited by Anand T. Hingorani, Hingorani, 1935, new version edited by Bharatan Kumarappa, Navajivan, 1952.

Cent Percent Swadeshi or the Economics of Village Industries, Navajivan, 1938.

Swadeshi: True or False, Chandrashankar Shukla, 1940.

Birth Control Versus Self Control, edited by Dewan Ram Parkash, Dewan, 1941.

Christian Missions: Their Place in India, Navajivan, 1941, revised edition, 1957.

Economics of Khadi, Navajivan, 1941.

The Indian States' Problems, Navajivan, 1941.

To the Women, edited by Hingorani, Hingorani, 1941.

Non-Violence in Peace and War, two volumes, Navajivan, 1942-49, Garland Publishing, 1972.

To the Hindus and Muslims, edited by Hingorani, Hingorani, 1942.

To the Princes and Their People, edited by Hingorani, Hingorani, 1942.

Women and Social Injustice, Navajivan, 1942.

Our Language Problem, Hingorani, 1942; edited by Hingorani, Bharatiya Vidya, 1965.

Conquest of Self: Being Gleanings From His Writings and Speeches, compiled by R. K. Prabhu and U. R. Rao, Thacker, 1943.

Gandhi Against Fascism, edited by Jag Parvesh Chander, Free India Publications, 1943.

Ethics of Fasting, edited by Chander, Indian Printing Works, 1944.

The Mind of Mahatma Gandhi, compiled by Prabhu and U. R. Rao, Oxford University Press, 1945.

Swaraj Through Charkha, compiled by Kanu Gandhi, All India Spinners' Association, 1945.

Teachings of Mahatma Gandhi, edited by Chander, Indian Printing Works, 1945.

Daridra-Narayana, edited by Hingorani, Hingorani, 1946.

Communal Unity, Navajivan, 1947.

Gita the Mother, edited by Chander, 4th edition, Indian Printing Works, 1947.

India of My Dreams, compiled by Prabhu, Hind Kitabs, 1947.

Ramanama: The Infallible Remedy, edited by Hingorani, Hingorani, 1947.

To the Protagonists of Pakistan, edited by Hingorani, Hingorani, 1947.

Delhi Diary: Prayer Speeches From 10-9-1947 to 30-1-1948, Navajivan, 1948.

Precious Pearls, compiled by R. S. Kaushala, Glifton, 1948.

Selections from Gandhi, compiled by N. K. Bose, Navajivan, 1948.

Why the Constructive Programme, All India Congress Committee, 1948.

Diet and Diet Reform, Navajivan, 1949.

Food Shortage and Agriculture, Navajivan, 1949.

For Pacifists, Navajivan, 1949.

The Mahatma and the Missionary: Selected Writings, edited by Clifford Manshardt, Regnery, 1949.

Conversations of Gandhiji, edited by Chandrashankar Shukla, Vora, 1949.

The Gandhi Sutras: The Basic Teachings of Mahatma Gandhi, edited by D. S. Sarma, Devin-Adair, 1949.

Mohanmala: A Gandhian Rosary: Being a Thought for Each Day of the Year Gleaned From the Writings and Speeches of Mahatma Gandhi, compiled by Prabhu, Hind Kitabs, 1949.

Hindu Dharma, edited by Kumarappa, Navajivan, 1950.

The Good Life, edited by Chander, third enlarged edition, Indian Printing Works, 1950.

Health, Wealth and Happiness, Bharatiya Karmayogi Samaj, 1950.

Thus Spake Mahatma, Vichar Sahitya, 1950.

A Day Book of Thoughts From Mahatma Gandhi, edited by K. T. Narasimha Char, Macmillan, 1951.

Selected Writings of Mahatma Gandhi, edited by Ronald Duncan, Beacon, 1951.

Ruskin's Unto This Last: A Paraphrase, Navajivan, 1951.

Basic Education, Navajivan, 1951.

The Ideology of the Charkha: A Collection of Some of Gandhiji's Speeches and Writings About Khadi, edited by Shrikrishnadas Jaju, All India Spinners' Association, 1951.

Satyagraha: Non-Violent Resistance, edited by Kumarappa, Navajivan, 1951, Schocken, 1961.

Towards Non-Violent Socialism, edited by Kumarappa, Navajivan, 1951.

The Wit and Wisdom of Gandhi, edited by Homer A. Jack, Beacon, 1951.

Rebuilding Our Villages, edited by Kumarappa, Navajivan, 1953.

How to Serve the Cow, edited by Kumarappa, Navajivan, 1954.

Medium of Instruction, edited by Kumarappa, Navajivan, 1954.

Sarvodaya: The Welfare of All, edited by Kumarappa, Navajivan, 1954.

Untouchability, edited by Kumarappa, Navajivan, 1954.

Ashram Observances in Action, Navajivan, 1955.

Gokhale: My Political Guru, Navajivan, 1955.

Khadi: Why and How, edited by Kumarappa, Navajivan, 1955.

My Religion, edited by Kumarappa, Navajivan, 1955.

On Removal of Untouchability, Director of Publicity (Bombay), 1956.

Truth of God: Gleanings From the Writings of Mahatma Gandhi Bearing on God, God-Realization and the Godly Way, compiled by Prabhu, Navajivan, 1956.

Thoughts on National Language, Navajivan, 1956.

The Gandhi Reader: A Source Book of His Life and Writings, edited by Homer A. Jack, Indiana University Press, 1956.

Towards Lasting Peace, edited by Hingorani, Bharatiya Vidya, 1956.

Economic and Industrial Life and Relations, three volumes, edited by V. B. Kher, Navajivan, 1957.

Food for the Soul, edited by Hingorani, Bharatiya Vidya, 1957.

The Science of Satyagraha, edited by Hingorani, Bharatiya Vidya, 1957.

The Socialism of My Conception, edited by Hingorani, Bharatiya Vidya, 1957.

All Men Are Brothers: Life and Thoughts of Mahatma Gandhi as Told in His Own Words, Columbia University Press, 1958.

A Gandhi Anthology, compiled by Valji Govindji Desai, Navajivan, 1958.

Homage to the Departed, edited by V. B. Kher, Navajivan, 1958.

Women, Navajivan, 1958.

Jawaharlal Nehru: The Jewel of India, edited by Hingorani, Pearl, 1960.

My Non-Violence, edited by Sailesh Kumar Bandyopadhaya, Navajivan, 1960.

Writings and Speeches of Gandhi Relating to Bihar, 1917-1947, edited by K. K. Datta, Government of Bihar, 1960.

The Art of Living, edited by Hingorani, Pearl, 1961.

My Philosophy of Life, edited by Hingorani, Pearl, 1961.

Search of the Supreme, three volumes, edited by V. B. Kher, Navajivan, 1961-62.

Economic Thought, edited by J. S. Mathur and A. S. Mathur, Chaitanya Publishing House, 1962.

Bapu and Children, edited by Prabhu and Shewak Bhojraj, Navajivan, 1962.

All Religions Are True, edited by Hingorani, Pearl, 1962.

Birth Control, edited by Hingorani, Bharatiya Vidya, 1962.

The Law and the Lawyers, edited by S. B. Kher, Navajivan, 1962.

The Problem of Education, Navajivan, 1962.

The Teachings of the Gita, edited by Hingorani, Bharatiya Vidya, 1962.

True Education, Navajivan, 1962.

Varnashramadharma, compiled by Prabhu, Navajivan, 1962.

The Essential Gandhi: An Anthology, edited by Louis Fischer, Random House, 1962.

The Message of Jesus Christ, edited by Hingorani, Bharatiya Vidya, 1963.

The Supreme Power, edited by Hingorani, Bharatiya Vidya, 1963.

The Way to Communal Harmony, edited by U. R. Rao, Navajivan, 1963.

Caste Must Go and the Sin of Untouchability, compiled by Prabhu, Navajivan, 1964.

The Law of Continence: Brahmacharya, edited by Hingorani, Bharatiya Vidya, 1964.

The Role of Women, edited by Hingorani, Bharatiya Vidya, 1964.

Stone Walls Do Not a Prison Make, compiled and edited by V. B. Kher, Navajivan, 1964.

Through Self-Control, edited by Hingorani, Bharatiya Vidya, 1964.

Gandhi Expects: What the Father of the Nation Expected of People's Representatives, compiled by H. M. Vyas, Navajivan, 1965.

Gita My Mother, edited by Hingorani, Bharatiya Vidya, 1965.

Glorious Thoughts of Gandhi, edited by N. B. Sen, New Book Society (New Delhi), 1965.

The Hindu-Muslim Unity, edited by Hingorani, Bharatiya Vidya, 1965.

My Picture of Free India, edited by Hingorani, Bharatiya Vidya, 1965.

The Health Guide, edited by Hingorani, Bharatiya Vidya, 1965.

My Varnashrama Dharma, edited by Hingorani, Bharatiya Vidya, 1965.

Industrialize—and Perish! compiled by Prabhu, Navajivan, 1966.

The Nature Cure, edited by Hingorani, Bharatiya Vidya, 1966.

Man Versus Machine, edited by Hingorani, Bharatiya Vidya, 1966.

To Be Perplexed, edited by Hingorani, Bharatiya Vidya, 1966.

The Village Reconstruction, edited by Hingorani, Bharatiya Vidya, 1966.

The Gospel of Swadeshi, edited by Hingorani, Bharatiya Vidya, 1967.

The Wisdom of Gandhi, Philosophical Library, 1967.

The Selected Works of Mahatma Gandhi, edited by Shriman Narayan, Navajivan, 1968.

The Message of Mahatma Gandhi, compiled and edited by U. S. Mohan Rao, Publications Division of the Government of India, 1968.

Pen-Portraits and Tributes by Gandhiji: Sketches of Eminent Men and Women by Mahatma Gandhi, compiled and edited by U. S. Mohan Rao, National Book Trust (New Delhi), 1969.

Essential Writings, selected and edited by V. V. Remana Murti, Gandhi Peace Foundation (New Delhi), 1970.

Modern Versus Ancient Civilization, edited by Hingorani, Bharatiya Vidya, 1970.

My Views on Education, edited by Hingorani, Bharatiya Vidya, 1970.

Political and National Life and Affairs, three volumes, compiled and edited by V. B. Kher, Navajivan, 1967-68.

Service Before Self, edited by Hingorani, Bharatiya Vidya, 1971.

Epigrams From Gandhiji, compiled by S. R. Tikekar, Publications Division of the Government of India, 1971.

Pathway to God, compiled by M. S. Deshpande, Navajivan, 1971.

Why Fear or Mourn Death? edited by Hingorani, Bharatiya Vidya, 1971.

Gandhi and Haryana: A Collection of His Speeches and Writings Pertaining to Haryana, edited by J. Chandra, Usha, 1977.

The Words of Gandhi, selected by Richard Attenborough, Newmarket, 1982.

The Quintessence of Gandhi in His Own Words, compiled by Madhu Muskan, 1984.

The Moral and Political Writings of Mahatma Gandhi, edited by Raghavan Iyer, Oxford University Press, 1986.

Gandhi in India: In His Own Words, University Press of New England, 1987.

Gandhi on Nonviolence: Selected Texts from Mohandas K. Gandhi's Nonviolence in Peace and War, edited with an introduction by Thomas Merton, Shambhala (Boston), 1996.

Mahatma Gandhi: Selected Political Writings, edited with a foreword by Dennis Dalton, Hackett (Indianapolis, IN), 1996.

Gandhi (book of quotations for juveniles), illustrated by Beatrice Tanaka, Four Walls Eight Windows (New York), 1997.

Hind Swaraj and Other Writings, Cambridge University Press (New York), 1997.

Works published under name variation M. K. Gandhi and under Mahatma Gandhi. Also author of numerous pamphlets on political, social, religious, and moral issues.

CORRESPONDENCE AND OTHER

The Story of My Experiments With Truth, translated by Mahadev Desai, Navajivan, 1927-29; 2nd edition published as *An*

Autobiography, or the Story of My Experiments With Truth, 1940; abridged edition, Hind Kitabs, 1950.

My Early Life (1869-1914) (autobiography), arranged and edited by Mahadev Desai, Oxford University Press, 1932.

Songs From Prison (translation of Hindu lyrics made in prison by Gandhi), edited by John S. Hoyland, George Allen, 1934.

Gandhi-Jinnah Talks: Text of Correspondence and Other Relevant Matter, July-October 1944, Hindustan Times, 1944.

Correspondence Between Gandhiji and P. C. Joshi, People's Publishing House, 1945.

Gandhi's Correspondence With the Government, 1942-1944, Navajivan, 1945.

Famous Letters of Mahatma Gandhi, compiled and edited by R. L. Khipple, Indian Printing Works, 1947.

Selected Letters, two volumes, translated by Valji Govindji Desai, Navajivan, 1949-62.

Bapu's Letters to Mira, 1924-1948, Navajivan, 1949, published by Harper as *Gandhi's Letters to a Disciple,* 1950.

(Letters) to a Gandhian Capitalist: Correspondence Between Gandhi and Jamnalal Bajaj and Members of His Family, edited by Kaka Kalelkar, Jamnalal Seva Trust, 1951; second revised and enlarged edition, Sevak Prakashan, 1979.

(Letters) to Ashram Sisters (6-12-1926 to 30-12-1929), edited by Kaka Kalelkar, Navajivan, 1952.

My Dear Child: Letters to Esther Faering, edited by Alice M. Barnes, Navajivan, 1956.

Gandhi-Rajabhoj Correspondence, 1932-1946, edited by M. P. Mangudkar and G. B. Nirantar, Bharat Sevak Sangh, 1956.

Letters to Rajkumari Amrit Kaur, Navajivan, 1961.

Letters to Manibahen Patel, translated and edited by Valji Govindji Desai and Sudarshan V. Desai, Navajivan, 1963.

Works published under name variation M. K. Gandhi and under Mahatma Gandhi. Contributor of articles to newspapers and magazines, including *Young India.* Founder of and contributor to journal *Indian Opinion,* 1904.

COLLECTED WORKS

Collected Works, ninety volumes (expected), Publications Division of the Government of India, 1958–.

Thomas Merton, editor, *Gandhi on Non-Violence,* Random House, 1996.

Fatima Meer, editor, *The South African Gandhi,* University of Natal, 1996.

Beatrice Tanaka, editor, *Gandhi: Lifelines,* Four Walls Eight Windows (New York City), 1997.

SIDELIGHTS: The Indian independence leader Mohandas Karamchand Gandhi, called the Mahatma ("Great Soul") by many of his countrymen, changed the world far beyond his successful struggle to end British imperial rule in India. Gandhi's philosophy of nonviolent resistance to illegitimate authority and his mass civil disobedience campaigns introduced a new form of popular political struggle that has since been adopted around the globe, notably by the civil rights movement in the United States. The Indian leader's religious and social convictions, centered on the ideals of tolerance, community, equality, simplicity, and self-sacrifice and elaborated in his voluminous writings, have also entered the currency of modern thought. Above all, Gandhi's personal example of self-abnegation, his courage and perseverance, and his tolerance and humanity remain a source of inspiration to millions worldwide.

The son of a provincial official from the *Vaisya* Hindu caste, Gandhi studied law in England and struggled to overcome a painful shyness that threatened to abort his career. His political initiation occurred in Natal, South Africa, where he went to work for an Indian company and found himself victimized by the country's policies of racial discrimination. Gandhi refused to endure this treatment passively and formed the Natal Indian Congress in 1894 to further the large Indian minority's political and civil rights and press reform on the British colonial government. Supported by his now-thriving legal practice in Johannesburg, Gandhi founded the journal *Indian Opinion* in 1904 to rouse support for Indian rights, and he also began exploring spiritually-based paths to social change. Gandhi's innovative melding of political, social, and religious thinking led him to the key concept of *satyagraha,* or nonviolent but often extra-legal resistance to illegitimate authority. He launched a mass civil disobedience campaign in Johannesburg in 1906 to protest the Transvaal government's plan to register and better police the Indian population and continued to promote *satyagraha* until he left the country to return to India eight years later. Gandhi's efforts to improve the lot of South African Indians produced few concrete gains but helped bolster Indian confidence and self-esteem and also encouraged the country's oppressed black majority in its struggle for political and civil rights. The Indian leader described his South African campaign in *Satyagraha in South Africa,* published in 1928.

Gandhi's political work in South Africa had been well-publicized in India, and he returned a recognized leader to his native country. He joined the Indian National Congress, a moderate reformist organization composed largely of the Western-educated Indian elite that sought greater local self-government under British rule. As in South Africa, however, Gandhi found his political *metier* in direct, mass organizing rather than party building and political deal making. He spent two years traveling to remote Indian villages, where he inspired the rural poor with his moral and spiritual teachings as well as by his political vision of a self-reliant, emancipated nation.

Gandhi's developing spiritual politics overturned the traditional political opposition of means and ends and advanced the proposition that individual morality, social justice, and political self-determination are mutually interdependent and must all advance or fall together. He came to regard *satya* (truth) and *ahimsa* (nonviolence) as absolute moral values that transcend any particular creed or philosophy but that can only become real through active individual engagement in social life. Gandhi saw modern industrial society and power politics as often inimical to these values, and he counterposed an Indian vision of decentralized, egalitarian village communities engaged in agriculture and traditional handicrafts. He launched his famous *khadi* (homespun) movement as a symbol of self-reliance and native industry that would also help emancipate India from its dependence on imported cloth. Gandhi's emphasis on spirituality and rejection of Western-styled industrialism struck many progressive Indian independence leaders as reactionary, but he won a wide following among the Indian masses. Humble yet charismatic, a self-deprecating but inspiring leader, Gandhi took up residence in voluntary poverty and celibacy in a remote *ashram* (spiritual commune) near Ahmadabad and was soon known throughout India as the Mahatma, or "great soul."

In 1919, Gandhi became president of the Indian National Congress and formed the Satyagraha League to launch a mass civil disobedience campaign against repressive colonial laws. The non-cooperation movement's broader goal was the achievement of *Swaraj,* or home rule, to be won through such tactics as boycotting British goods and institutions and courting mass arrests and jailings. The generally peaceful movement provoked a savage British response, most notoriously when British troops massacred four hundred Indians attending a nonviolent demonstration in Armitsar, Punjab state. Along with thousands of others, Gandhi himself was arrested in 1922 and sentenced to six years in prison for seditious conspiracy.

Released because of illness after two years, Gandhi confronted a weakened and divided Congress movement in the mid-1920s. Rising religious tensions prompted Muslims to leave the predominantly Hindu organization and form their own Moslem League, while radicals demanded a commitment to complete political independence and a thoroughgoing social reform program. Gandhi and other *satyagraha* leaders were accused of eviscerating the movement and martyring the Congress rank-and-file in their anxiety to avoid violence.

Gandhi suspended much of his activist work in the mid-1920s in response to these criticisms, although he remained very much in the public eye through his widely-circulated writings. Two collections of articles on non-cooperation and the nationalist movement that originally appeared in the journal *Young India* were published during this period, and his *Story of My Experiments With Truth,* written during his years in prison, appeared in 1927. This last work "is extraordinary for candor and quality of self-criticism," remarked *Los Angeles Times Book Review* critic Malcolm Boyd. Writing in the *Yale Review,* Merle Curti commented, "The book is without literary distinction, but it is, nevertheless, great . . . because of the supreme sincerity and humility with which Gandhi reveals his limitations and strength in his never-ending struggle to approach Absolute Truth or God."

Gandhi's political semiretirement was short-lived, however, and he returned to active leadership of the Congress as British intransigence helped the nationalist movement recover strength and unity in the late 1920s. Gandhi joined more radical Congress leaders in raising a new demand for full political independence instead of British dominion status and then launched his famous *satyagraha* campaign against the colonial salt tax in March, 1930. The movement received worldwide press attention when Gandhi led thousands of followers on a dramatic march across India to the seaport of Dandi, where he was arrested for illegally making salt out of sea water. Successive non-cooperation campaigns punctuated by arrest, imprisonment, protest fasts, and inconclusive negotiations with the British authorities defined Gandhi's political activity in the 1930s and early 1940s and brought him and the Congress movement much international attention and respect. Gandhi's nonviolent tactics and moral rectitude sowed self doubt among the British colonists themselves and undermined their willingness to crush the independence movement by force.

The end of the World War II raised the issue of decolonization to the forefront of the international political agenda, and the new British Labour government bowed to political reality by beginning serious negotiations with Indian independence leaders to end British rule in India. The talks culminated in a 1947 tripartite agreement between the British, the Indian National Congress, and the Moslem League to partition the Indian subcontinent into the states of India and Pakistan, with respective Hindu and Muslim majority populations. Gandhi was dismayed by partition and counseled against acceptance of the agreement, but he could not moderate the deep religious hatreds dividing his countrymen. With independence at hand, he turned from politics to the immense task of promoting his program of social justice, which he

believed would be achieved through the voluntary actions of morally enlightened individuals. When rising communal violence threatened to make the newly free subcontinent ungovernable, Gandhi spoke out passionately for religious tolerance and began a "fast unto death" to protest the bloodshed. A Hindu fanatic enraged by this plea for brotherhood assassinated the Indian leader in the midst of his fast on January 30, 1948.

Scores of books attributed to Gandhi have appeared since the Mahatma's death, and his collected writings are expected to fill ninety volumes when they are published in their entirety by the Indian government. Some of these books are compilations of overlapping articles on topical political issues, but much of Gandhi's writing is devoted to political, social, and spiritual themes of enduring interest. His better known works include *The Mind of Mahatma Gandhi,* a selection of basic writings from 1909 to 1948, and *All Men Are Brothers: Life and Thoughts of Mahatma Gandhi, as Told in His Own Words,* which was published under the auspices of the United Nations Educational, Scientific, and Cultural Organization (UNESCO). "To read this book is an education in itself," *Saturday Review* critic Ranjee Shahani observed of the latter work. "Gandhi stands out in our murky era as a lighthouse of uncommon commonsense."

BIOGRAPHICAL/CRITICAL SOURCES:

BOOKS

Addressing Gandhi, Sahmat (New Delhi, India), 1995.

Bakshi, S. R., *Gandhi and the Status of Women,* Criterion, 1987.

Barraclough, John, *Gandhi,* Heinemann Interactive Library, 1997.

Bharathi, K. S., *Thoughts of Gandhi and Vinoba,* Concept (New Delhi), 1995.

Brown, and Martin Prozesky, editors, *Gandhi in South Africa: Principles and Politics,* St. Martin's Press (New York City), 1996.

Carter, April, *Mahatma Gandhi: A Selected Bibliography,* Greenwood Press (Westport, CT), 1995.

Chatterjee, Margaret, *Gandhi's Religious Thought,* Macmillan, 1983.

Dasgupta, Ajit Kumar, *Gandhi's Economic Thought,* Routledge (New York City), 1996.

Easwaran, Eknath, *Gandhi, the Man: The Story of His Transformation,* Nilgiri Press, 1997.

Emilsen, William W., *Violence and Atonement: The Missionary Experiences of Mohandas Gandhi, Samuel Stokes, and Verrier Elwin in India before 1935,* Peter Lang (New York), 1994.

Erikson, Erik H., *Gandhi's Truth: On the Origins of Militant Nonviolence,* Norton, 1969.

Gandhi, Prabhudas, *My Childhood with Gandhiji,* Navajivan, 1957.

Gandhi, Rajmohan, *The Good Boatman: A Portrait of Gandhi,* Viking (New York), 1995.

Gardner, Howard, *Extraordinary Minds,* Basic Books, 1997.

Green, Martin, *Tolstoy and Gandhi, Men of Peace: A Biography,* Basic Books, 1983.

Jain, Vidya, *M. K. Gandhi, Leader of the Masses,* Deep & Deep Publications (New Delhi), 1995.

Jesudasan, Ignatius, *A Gandhian Theology of Liberation,* Orbis, 1984.

Jordens, G.T.F., *Gandhi's Religion,* St. Martin's Press, 1997.

Murthy, B. Srinivasa, *Mahatma Gandhi and Christianity,* Long Beach Publications, 1998.

Nair, Keshavan, *A Higher Standard of Leadership: Lessons from the Life of Gandhi,* Publishers Group West (San Francisco), 1994.

Nanda, B. R., *Gandhi and His Critics,* Oxford University Press, 1985.

Nanda, *Mahatma Gandhi 125 Years: Remembering Gandhi, Understanding Gandhi, Relevance of Gandhi,* Indian Council for Cultural Relations and New Age International Publishers (New Delhi), 1995.

Pandiri, Ananda M., *A Comprehensive, Annotated Bibliography on Mahatma Gandhi,* Greenwood Press (Westport, CT), 1995.

Parekh, Bhikhu, *Gandhi,* Oxford University Press, 1997.

Ramakrishnan, Padma, *Gandhi and Indian Independence,* Blaze (New Delhi), 1994.

Richards, Glyn, *The Philosophy of Gandhi: A Study of His Basic Ideas,* Barnes & Noble, 1982.

Severance, John B., *Gandhi, Great Soul,* Clarion Books (New York), 1997.

Shirer, William L., *Gandhi: A Memoir,* Simon & Schuster, 1979.

Tendulkar, D. G., *Mahatma,* eight volumes, Pradesh, 1951-54.

PERIODICALS

Daedalus, Fall, 1989.
History Today, October, 1990.
Los Angeles Times Book Review, January 16, 1983.
Nation, January 23, 1924.
National Catholic Reporter, October 14, 1994.
New York Herald Tribune Weekly Book Review, November 7, 1948.
New York Times Magazine, May 25, 1969.
Saturday Review, September 26, 1959.
Scholastic Update, March 10, 1989.
Times Literary Supplement, July 26, 1934; March 31, 1972.
UN Chronicle, June, 1988.
UNESCO Courier, February, 1989; June, 1992.
Yale Review, Spring, 1949.

*   *   *

GARCIA LORCA, Federico 1898-1936

PERSONAL: Commonly known by mother's surname, Lorca; born June 5, 1898, in Fuentevaqueros, Granada, Spain; executed August 19, 1936, in Viznar, Granada, Spain; son of Federico Garcia Rodriguez (a landowner) and Vicenta Lorca (a teacher). *Education:* Attended University of Granada, 1914-19; received law degree from University of Madrid, 1923; attended Columbia University, 1929.

CAREER: Writer. Artistic director, serving as director and producer of plays, for University Theater (state-sponsored traveling theater group, known as *La Barraca* ['The Hut']), 1932-35. Director of additional plays, including *Blood Wedding,* 1933. Lecturer; illustrator, with work represented in exhibitions; musician, serving as arranger and pianist for recordings of Spanish folk songs, 1931. Helped to organize Festival of *Cante Jondo* (Granada, Spain), 1922.

WRITINGS:

POETRY

Libro de poemas (title means "Book of Poems"), Maroto (Madrid), 1921 (also see below).

Canciones (1921-1924), [Malaga, Spain], 1927, translation by Phillip Cummings published as *Songs,* Duquesne University Press, 1976 (also see below).

Primer romancero gitano (1924-1927) (contains poem "Romance de la guardia civil espanola"), Revista de Occidente (Madrid), 1928, 2nd edition (and most later editions) published as *Romancero gitano,* 1929, translation by Langston Hughes published as *Gypsy Ballads,* Beloit College, 1951, translation by Rolfe Humphries published as *The Gypsy Ballads, With Three Historical Ballads,* Indiana University Press, 1953, translation by Michael Hartnett published as *Gipsy Ballads,* Goldsmith Press (Dublin), 1973, translation and commentary by Carl W. Cobb published as *Lorca's "Romancero gitano": A Ballad Translation and Critical Study,* University Press of Mississippi, 1983 (also see below).

Poema del cante jondo, Ulises (Madrid), 1931, translation by Carlos Bauer published as *Poem of the Deep Song/Poema del cante jondo* (bilingual edition), City Lights Books, 1987 (also see below).

Oda a Walt Whitman (title means "Ode to Walt Whitman"), Alcancia, 1933, translation by Bauer published in *"Ode to Walt Whitman" and Other Poems,* City Lights, 1988.

Llanto por Ignacio Sanchez Mejias (title means "Lament for Ignacio Sanchez Mejias"; commonly known as "Lament for the Death of a Bullfighter"), Arbol, 1935 (also see below).

Seis poemas galegos (title means "Six Galician Poems"; written in Galician with assistance from others), Nos (Santiago de Compostela), 1935 (also see below).

Primeras canciones (title means "First Songs"), Heroe (Madrid), 1936.

Lament for the Death of a Bullfighter, and Other Poems (bilingual edition), translation by A. L. Loyd, Oxford University Press, 1937.

Poems, translation by Stephen Spender and J. L. Gili, Oxford University Press, 1939.

Poeta en Nueva York, Seneca (Mexico), 1940, translations published as *Poet in New York* (bilingual edition), by Ben Belitt, introduction by Angel del Rio, Grove Press, 1955, by Stephen Fredman, Fog Horn Press, 1975, by Greg Simon and Steven F. White, Farrar, Straus, 1988 (also see below).

The Poet in New York, and Other Poems (includes "Gypsy Ballads"), translation by Rolfe Humphries, introduction by J. Bergamin, Norton, 1940.

Selected Poems of Federico Garcia Lorca, translation by Stephen Spender and J. L. Gili, Hogarth Press (London), 1943, Transatlantic Arts (New York), 1947.

Poemas postumos, Canciones musicales, Divan del Tamarit, Mexicanas (Mexico), 1945.

Siete poemas y dos dibujos ineditos, edited by Luis Rosales, Cultura Hispanica, 1949.

The Selected Poems of Federico Garcia Lorca (bilingual edition), edited by Francisco Garcia Lorca and Donald M. Allen, introduction by Francisco Garcia Lorca, New Directions, 1955.

Lorca, translation and introduction by J. L. Gili, Penguin, 1960-65.

(With Juan Ramon Jimenez) *Lorca and Jimenez: Selected Poems,* translation by Robert Bly, Sixties Press, 1967.

Divan and Other Writings (includes *Divan del Tamarit*; title means "Divan of the Tamarit"), translation by Edwin Honig, Bonewhistle Press, 1974.

Lorca/Blackburn: Poems, translation by Paul Blackburn, Momo's Press, 1979.

The Cricket Sings: Poems and Songs for Children (bilingual edition), translation by Will Kirkland, New Directions, 1980.

Suites (reconstruction of a collection planned by Lorca), edited by Andre Belamich, Ariel (Barcelona), 1983.

Ineditos de Federico Garcia Lorca: Sonetos del amor oscuro, 1935-1936 (title means "Unpublished Works of Federico Garcia Lorca: Sonnets of the Dark Love, 1935-1936"), compiled by Marta Teresa Casteros, Instituto de Estudios de Literatura Latinoamericana (Buenos Aires), c. 1984.

Sonnets of Love Forbidden, translation by David K. Loughran, Windson, 1989.

The Poetical Works of Federico Garcia Lorca, two volumes, edited by Maurer, Farrar, Straus, 1988-91.

At Five in the Afternoon, translated by Francisco Aragon, Vintage Books, 1997.

Robert Bly, editor and translator, *Lorca and Jimenez: Selected Poems,* Beacon Press, 1997.

PLAYS

El maleficio de la mariposa (two-act; title means "The Butterfly's Evil Spell"), first produced in Madrid at Teatro Eslava, 1920.

Mariana Pineda: Romance popular en tres estampas (three-act; first produced in Barcelona at Teatro Goya, 1927; first published as *Romance de la muerte de Torrijos* in *El Dia Grafico,* June 25, 1927), Rivadeneyra (Madrid), 1928, translation by James Graham-Lujan published as *Mariana Pineda: A Popular Ballad in Three Prints* in *Tulane Drama Review,* winter, 1962, translation by Robert G. Havard published as *Mariana Pineda: A Popular Ballad in Three Engravings,* Aris & Phillips, 1987 (also see below).

La zapatera prodigiosa: Farsa violenta (two-act; title means "The Shoemaker's Prodigious Wife"), first produced in Madrid at Teatro Espanol, 1930.

El publico (title means "The Public"; one scene apparently missing; produced in San Juan, Puerto Rico, 1978), excerpts published in *Los Cuatro Vientos,* 1933; enlarged version published in *El publico: Amor, teatro, y caballos en la obra de Federico Garcia Lorca,* edited by R. Martinez Nadal, Dolphin (Oxford), 1970, revised edition published as *El publico: Amor y muerte en la obra de Federico Garcia Lorca,* J. Moritz (Mexico), 1974, translation published as *Lorca's "The Public": A Study of an Unfinished Play and of Love and Death in Lorca's Work,* Schocken, 1974; Lorca's manuscript published by Dolphin, 1976 (also see below).

Bodas de sangre: Tragedia (three-act; first produced in Madrid at Teatro Beatriz, 1933), Arbol, 1935, translation by Jose A. Weissberger produced as *Bitter Oleander* in New York City, 1935, translation by Gilbert Neiman published as *Blood Wedding,* New Directions, 1939 (also see below).

Amor de Don Perlimplin con Belisa en su jardin (title means "The Love of Don Perlimplin with Belisa, in His Garden"), first produced in Madrid on April 5, 1933.

Yerma: Poema tragico (three-act; first produced in Madrid on December 29, 1934), Anaconda (Buenos Aires), 1937, translation by Ian Macpherson and Jaqueline Minett published as *Yerma: A Tragic Poem* (bilingual edition), general introduction by John Lyon, Aris & Phillips, 1987 (also see below).

Retablillo de Don Cristobal (puppet play; title means "Don Cristobal's Puppet Show"; first produced in Buenos Aires, Argentina, at Teatro Avenida, March, 1934; revised version produced in Madrid at Feria del Libro, May 12, 1935), Subcomisariado de Propaganda del Comisariado General de Guerra (Valencia), 1938 (also see below).

Dona Rosita la soltera; o, El lenguaje de las flores: Poema granadino del novecientos (three-act; title means "Dona Rosita the Spinster; or, The Language of Flowers: Poem of Granada in the Nineteenth Century"), first produced in Barcelona, at the Principal Palace, December, 1935.

Los titeres de Cachiporra: Tragecomedia de Don Cristobal y la sena Rosita: Farsa (puppet play; title means "The Billy-Club Puppets: Tragicomedy of Don Cristobal and Mam'selle Rosita: Farce"; first produced in Madrid at Zarzuela Theater, December, 1937), Losange, 1953.

From Lorca's Theater: Five Plays (contains *The Shoemaker's Prodigious Wife, The Love of Don Perlimplin with Belisa, in His Garden, Dona Rosita the Spinster, Yerma,* and *When Five Years Pass* [produced as *Asi que pasen cinco anos* in Madrid, 1978]), translation by Richard L. O'Connell and James Graham-Lujan, introduction by Stark Young, Scribner, 1941.

La casa de Bernarda Alba: Drama de mujeres en los pueblos de Espana (three-act; title means "The House of Bernarda Alba: Drama of Women in the Villages of Spain"; first produced in Buenos Aires at Teatro Avenida, March 8, 1945), Losada, 1944 (also see below).

Three Tragedies (contains *Blood Wedding, Yerma,* and *The House of Bernarda Alba*), translation by Richard L. O'Connell and James Graham-Lujan, introduction by Francisco Garcia Lorca, New Directions, 1947, Greenwood Press, 1977, translation by Sue Bradbury, Folio Society (London), 1977.

Cinco forsas breves; seguidas de "Asi que pasen cinco anos," Losange, 1953.

Comedies (contains *The Butterfly's Evil Spell, The Shoemaker's Prodigious Wife, The Love of Don Perlimplin with Belisa, in His Garden, Dona Rosita the Spinster*), translation by Richard L. O'Connell and James Graham-Lujan, introduction by Francisco Garcia Lorca, New Directions, 1954, enlarged edition published as *Five Plays: Comedies and Tragicomedies* (includes *The Billy-Club Puppets*), 1963, Penguin, 1987.

Comedia sin titulo (one act of an incomplete play; title means *Play without a Title*; also known as *El sueno de la vida* ["The Dream of Life"]), first produced in Madrid, 1989.

El publico [and] Comedia sin titulo: Dos obras postumas, edited by R. Martinez Nadal and M. Laffranque, Seix Barral, 1978, translation by Carlos Bauer published as *The Public [and] Play Without a Title: Two Posthumous Plays,* New Directions, 1983.

Teatro inconcluso, edited by Laffranque, Universidad de Granada, 1986.

The Rural Trilogy: Blood Wedding [and] Yerma [and] The House of Bernarda Alba, translation by Michael Dewell and Carmen Zapata, introduction by Douglas Day, Bantam, 1987.

Three Plays (contains *Blood Wedding, Dona Rosita the Spinster,* and *Yerma*), translation by Gwynne Edwards and Peter Luke, introduction by Edwards, Methuen, 1987.

Once Five Years Pass, and Other Dramatic Works, translation by William B. Logan and Angel G. Orrios, Station Hill Press, 1989.

Two Plays of Misalliance: The Love of Don Perlimplin [and] The Prodigious Cobbler's Wife, Aris & Phillips, 1989.

Barbarous Nights: Legends and Plays from the Little Theater, translation by Christopher Sawyer-Laucanno, City Lights, 1991.

Blood Wedding; and Yerma, introduction by W. S. Merwin, Theatre Communications Group, 1994.

Four Major Plays (includes "Blood Wedding," "Yerma," "The House of Bernarda Alba," and "Dona Rosita the Spinster"), translated by John Edmunds, Oxford University Press, 1997.

Also author of short dramatic sketches, including "La donacella, el marinero, y el estudiante" (title means "The Maiden, the Sailor, and the Student") and "El paseo de Buster Keaton" (title means "Buster Keaton's Stroll"), both 1928, and "Quimera" (title means "Chimera"). Adapter of numerous plays, including *La dama boba* and *Fuente Ovejuna,* both by Lope de Vega. Plays represented in collections and anthologies.

OMNIBUS VOLUMES

Obras completas (title means "Complete Works"; includes *Asi que pasen cinco anos* and "Divan of the Tamarit"), edited by Guillermo de Torre, Losada (Buenos Aires), 1938-46.

Obras completas (title means "Complete Works"; includes "The Butterfly's Evil Spell"), edited with commentary by Arturo de Hoyo, introductions by Jorge Guillen and Vicente Aleixandre, Aguilar, 1954.

Obras (title means "Works"), edited with commentary by Mario Hernandez, several volumes, Alianza, 1981–, 2nd edition, revised, 1983–.

OTHER

Impresiones y paisajes (travelogue), P. V. Traveset (Granada), 1918, translation by Lawrence H. Klibbe published as *Impressions and Landscapes,* University Press of America, 1987.

Federico Garcia Lorca: Cartas a sus amigos (letters), edited by Sebastian Gasch, Cobalto (Barcelona), 1950.

Conferencias y charlas, Consejo Nacional de Cultura, 1961.

Garcia Lorca: Cartas, postales, poemas, y dibujos (includes letters and poems), edited by Antonio Gallego Morell, Monedo y Credito (Madrid), 1968.

Casidas, Arte y Bibliofilia, 1969.

Prosa, Alianza, 1969.

Granada, paraiso cerrado y otras paginas granadinas, Sanchez, 1971.

Autografos, edited by Rafael Martinez Nadal, Dolphin, Volume 1, 1975, Volume 2, 1976, Volume 3, 1979.

Deep Song, and Other Prose, translation by Christopher Maurer, New Directions, 1980.

Viaje a la luna (filmscript; translation by Richard Diers published as *Trip to the Moon* in *Windmill,* spring, 1963), edited by Laffranque, Braad, 1980.

From the Havana Lectures, 1928: "Theory and Play of the Duende" and "Imagination, Inspiration, Evasion" (lectures; bilingual edition), translation by Stella Rodriguez, preface by Randolph Severson, introduction by Rafael Lopez Pedraza, Kanathos (Dallas, TX), 1981.

Lola, la comedianta, edited by Piero Menarini, Alianza, 1981.

Epistolario, two volumes, edited by Maurer, Alianza, 1983, parts translated by David Gershator as *Selected Letters,* New Directions, 1983.

Conferencias, two volumes, edited by Maurer, Alianza, 1984.

How a City Sings from November to November (lecture; bilingual edition), translation by Maurer, Cadmus Editions, 1984.

Alocuciones argentinas, edited by Mario Hernandez, Fundacion Federico Garcia Lorca/Crotalon, 1985.

Tres dialogos, Universidad de Granada/Junta de Andalucia, 1985.

Alocucion al pueblo de Fuentevaqueros, Comision del Cincuecentenario, 1986.

Treinta entrevistas a Federico Garcia Lorca, edited by Andres Soria Olmedo, Aguilar, 1989.

Line of Light and Shadow: The Drawings of Federico Garcia Lorca (previously published as *Dibujos,* 1987), edited by Mario Hernandez, translation by Maurer, Duke University Press/Duke University Museum of Art, 1991.

Selected Verse, introductions by Christopher Maurer and Francisco Aragon, Farrar, Straus, & Giroux (New York), 1995.

Illustrator of several books, including *El fin del viaje* by Pablo Neruda; drawings represented in collections, including *Federico Garcia Lorca: Dibujos,* Ministerio de Cultura (Granada), 1986, and Helen Oppenheimer, *Lorca—The Drawings: Their Relation to the Poet's Life and Work,* F. Watts, 1987. Co-editor of *gallo* (Granada literary magazine; title means "rooster"), 1928.

Garcia Lorca's manuscripts are housed at Fundacion Garcia Lorca, Consejo Superior de Investigaciones Cientificas, Madrid.

MEDIA ADAPTATIONS: Several of Lorca's plays have been adapted for opera and ballet, including *Blood Wedding, Yerma,* and *The Love of Don Perlimplin with Belisa, in His Garden. Blood Wedding* was adapted by Antonio Gades for a ballet, which was in turn adapted by Carlos Saura for a film of the same title, 1981.

SIDELIGHTS: Federico Garcia Lorca was "a child of genius beyond question," declared Jorge Guillen in *Language and Poetry.* A Spanish poet and dramatist, Lorca was at the height of his fame in 1936 when he was executed by Fascist rebels at the age of thirty-eight; in the years thereafter, Guillen suggested, the writer's prominence in European culture matched that of his countryman Pablo Picasso. Lorca's work has been treasured by a broad spectrum of the reading public throughout the world. His complete works have been reprinted in Spain almost every year since the 1950s, and observers believe he is more widely recognized in the English-speaking world than any Spanish writer except Miguel de Cervantes, author of *Don Quixote.* Lorca was familiar with the artistic innovators of his time, and his work shares with theirs a sense of sophistication, awareness of human psychology, and overall pessimism. But while his contemporaries often preferred to appeal to the intellect, Lorca gained wide popularity by addressing basic human emotions. He possessed an engaging personality and a dynamic speaking style, and he imbued his writing with a wide range of human feeling, including awe, lust, nostalgia, and despair. "Those who knew him," wrote his brother Francisco in a foreword to *Three Tragedies,* "will not forget his gift . . . of enlivening things by his presence, of making them more intense."

During his youth Lorca experienced both Spain's traditional rural life and its entry into the modern world. Born in 1898, he grew up in a village in Andalusia—the southernmost region of Spain, then largely untouched by the modern world. Such areas were generally dominated by the traditional powers of Spanish society, including political conservatism, the Catholic church, and affluent landowners. Lorca's father, a landowning liberal, confounded his wealthy peers by marrying a village schoolteacher and by paying his workers generously. Though Lorca was a privileged child he knew his home village well, attending school with its children, observing its poverty, and absorbing the vivid speech and folktales of its peasants. "I have a huge storehouse of childhood recollections in which I can hear the people speaking," Lorca observed, according to biographer Ian Gibson. "This is poetic memory, and I trust it implicitly." The sense of lost innocence that recurs in Lorca's writings, Gibson averred, focuses on his early rural years, probably the happiest of his life.

But once Lorca moved with his parents to the Andalusian city of Granada in 1909, many forces propelled him into the modern world. Spain was undergoing a lengthy crisis of confidence, spurred by the country's defeat by the United States in the War of 1898. Some Spaniards wished to strengthen traditional values and revive past glory, but others hoped their country would moderate its conservatism, foster intellectual inquiry, and learn from more modernized countries. With his parents' encouragement Lorca encountered Spain's progressives through his schooling, first at an innovative, nonreligious secondary school, and then at the University of Granada, where he became a protege of such intellectual reformers as Fernando de los Rios and Martin Dominguez Berrueta. By his late teens Lorca was already known as a multi-talented artist—his first book, the travelogue *Impresiones y paisajes* (*Impressions and Landscapes*), appeared before he was twenty—but he was also a poor student. Skilled as a pianist and singer, he would probably have become a musician if his parents had not compelled him to stay in school and study law. "I am a great Romantic," he wrote to a friend at the time, according to Gibson. "In a century of Zeppelins and idiotic deaths, I weep at my piano dreaming of the Handelian mist."

In 1919 Lorca's parents let him transfer to the University of Madrid, where he ignored classes in favor of socializing and cultural life. The move helped Lorca's development as a writer, however, for some of the major trends of modern European culture were just beginning to reach Spain through Madrid's intellectual community. As Western writers began to experiment with language, Madrid became a center of ultraism, which sought to change the nature of poetry by abandoning sentiment and moral rhetoric in favor of "pure poetry"—new and startling images and metaphors. Surrealism, aided by Sigmund Freud's studies of psychology, tried to dispense with social convention and express the hidden desires and fears of the subconscious mind. New ideas surrounded Lorca even in his dormitory—an idealistic private foundation, the Residencia de Estudiantes, which tried to re-create in Spain the lively intellectual atmosphere found in the residence halls of England's elite universities. At the Residencia Lorca met such talented students as Luis Bunuel and Salvador Dali, who soon became prominent in the surrealist movement. The friendship between Lorca and Dali became particularly close, and at times painful to both. Dali, somewhat withdrawn in his youth, resisted becoming Lorca's lover but was clearly drawn to Lorca's ebullient personality. Lorca, who came to view Dali with feelings of unrequited love, was impressed by his friend's audacity as a social critic and as a painter. "You are a Christian tempest," Dali told Lorca, according to Gibson, "and you need my paganism."

Lorca's early poems, Carl Cobb suggested in *Lorca's "Romancero gitano": A Ballad Translation and Critical Study,* show his "search . . . for a permanent manner of expression"; the results are promising but sometimes awkward. Lorca quickly showed a gift for imagery and dramatic imagination, adeptly describing, for instance, the experience of a bird being shot down by a hunter. But he had to struggle to shed the vague, overemotional style of romanticism—a difficult task because he often seemed to be making veiled comments about his unhappiness as a homosexual. For example, Lorca's poem about the doomed love of a cockroach for a butterfly became an artistic disaster when it was presented in 1920 as the play *El maleficio de la mariposa* (*The Butterfly's Evil Spell*). Lorca's Madrid audience derided the play, and even when he became a successful dramatist he avoided discussing the experience. A more successful poem, which Gibson called "one of Lorca's most moving," is "Encuentro" ("Meeting"), in which the poet speaks with the loving wife he might have known as a

heterosexual. (At his death Lorca left behind many unpublished works—generally dominated by frustration or sadness—on homosexual themes, apparently presuming that the general public would not accept the subject matter.) Lorca tried many poetic forms, particularly in *Canciones* (*Songs*), which contains poems written between 1921 and 1924. He wrote several extended odes, including the "Ode to Salvador Dali," which was widely praised as a defense of modern art although it can also be read as a love poem. The form and rhythm of music inspired a group of poems titled *Suites,* which were not published as a unified collection until 1983.

Gypsy Ballads shows Lorca at the height of his skill as a poet, in full control of language, imagery, and emotional suggestion. The characters inhabit a world of intense, sometimes mysterious, emotional experience. In the opening ballad a gypsy boy taunts the moon, which appears before him as a sexually attractive woman; suddenly the moon returns to the sky and takes the child with her, while other gypsies wail. Observers have tried to explain the ballad as everything from a comment on Lorca's sense of being sexually "different" to a metaphor for death. Some of the ballads appear to celebrate sexual vitality. In an unusually delicate poem, Lorca describes a gypsy nun who is fleetingly aroused by the sound of men on horseback outside her convent; in another a gypsy man describes his nighttime tryst with a woman by a riverbank. Much of the book conveys menace and violence: a girl runs through the night, her fear of being attacked embodied by the wind, which clutches at her dress; a gypsy is murdered by others who envy his good looks; in the final ballad, derived from the Bible, a prince rapes his sister. In his lecture "On the Gypsy Ballads," reprinted in *Deep Song, and Other Prose,* Lorca suggests that the ballads are not really about gypsies but about pain—"the struggle of the loving intelligence with the incomprehensible mystery that surrounds it." "Lorca is not deliberately inflicting pain on the reader in order to shock or annoy him," wrote Roy Campbell in *Lorca,* but the poet "feels so poignantly that he has to share this feeling with others." Observers suggest that the collection describes the force of human life itself—a source of both energy and destructiveness.

The intensity of *Gypsy Ballads* is heightened by Lorca's mastery of the language of poetry. "Over the years," observed Cobb in his translation of the work, "it has become possible to speak of the 'Lorquian' metaphor or image, which [the poet] brought to fruition" in this volume. When Lorca says a gypsy woman bathes "with water of skylarks," Cobb explained, the poet has created a stunning new image out of two different words that describe something "soothing." Sometimes Lorca's metaphors boldly draw upon two different senses: he refers to a "horizon of barking dogs," for instance, when dogs are barking in the distance at night and the horizon is invisible. Such metaphors seem to surpass those of typical avant-garde poets, who often combined words arbitrarily, without concern for actual human experience. Lorca said his poetic language was inspired by Spanish peasants, for whom a seemingly poetic phrase such as "oxen of the waters" was an ordinary term for the strong, slow current of a river. Campbell stressed that Lorca was unusually sensitive to "the *sound* of words," both their musical beauty and their ability to reinforce the meaning of a poem. Such skills, practiced by Spain's folksingers, made Lorca "musician" among poets, Campbell averred; interestingly, Lorca greatly enjoyed reading his work aloud before audiences and also presented Spanish folk songs at the piano. Reviewers often lament that Lorca's ear for language is impossible to reproduce in translation.

The first product of Lorca's emotional turmoil was the poetry collection *Poeta en Nueva York* (*Poet in New York*). In the book, Cobb observed, New York's social problems mirror Lorca's personal despair. The work opens as the poet reaches town, already deeply unhappy; he surveys both New York's troubles and his own; finally, after verging on hopelessness, he regathers his strength and tries to resolve the problems he has described. *Poet in New York* is far more grim and difficult than *Gypsy Ballads,* as Lorca apparently tries to heighten the reader's sense of alienation. The liveliness of the earlier volume gives way to pessimism; the verse is unrhymed; and, instead of using vivid metaphors about the natural world, Lorca imitates the surrealists by using symbols that are strange and difficult to understand. In poems about American society Lorca shows a horror of urban crowds, which he compares to animals, but he also shows sympathy for the poor. Unlike many white writers of his time, he is notably eloquent in describing the oppression of black Americans, particularly in his image of an uncrowned "King of Harlem"—a strong-willed black man humiliated by his menial job. Near the end of the collection he predicts a general uprising in favor of economic equality and challenges Christianity to ease the pain of the modern world. In more personal poems Lorca contrasts the innocent world of his childhood with his later unhappiness, alludes to his disappointments in love, and rails at the decadence he sees among urban homosexuals. He seems to portray a positive role model in his "Ode to Walt Whitman," dedicated to a nineteenth-century American poet—also a homosexual—who attempted to celebrate common people and the realities of everyday life. Lorca's final poem is a song about his departure from New York for Cuba, which he found much more hospitable than the United States. Commentators disagreed greatly about the merits of *Poet in New York,* which was not published in its entirety until after Lorca's death. Many reviewers, disappointed by the book's obscure language and grim tone, dismissed it as a failed experiment or an aberration. By contrast, Cobb declared that "with the impetus given by modern critical studies and translations, *Poet in New York* has become the other book which sustains Lorca's reputation as a poet."

Before Lorca returned to Spain in 1930, he had largely completed what many observers would call his first mature play, *El publico* (*The Public*). Written in a disconcerting, surrealist style comparable to *Poet in New York,* the play confronts such controversial themes as the need for truth in the theater and for truth about homosexuality, in addition to showing the destruction of human love by selfishness and death. After his disastrous experience with "The Butterfly's Evil Spell," Lorca had spent the 1920s gradually mastering the techniques of drama, beginning with the light, formulaic Spanish genres of farce and puppet plays. From puppet theater, observers have suggested, Lorca learned to draw characters rapidly and decisively; in farces for human actors, he developed the skills required to sustain a full-length play. For instance, the farce *La zapatera prodigiosa* (*The Shoemaker's Prodigious Wife*), begun in the mid-1920s, shows Lorca's growing ease with extended dialogue and complex action. In *Amor de Don Perlimplin con Belisa en su jardin* (*The Love of Don Perlimplin with Belisa, in His Garden*), begun shortly thereafter, Lorca toys with the conventions of farce, as the play's object of ridicule—an old man with a lively young wife—unexpectedly becomes a figure of pity. By 1927 Lorca gained modest commercial success with his second professional production, *Mariana Pineda.* The heroine of this historical melodrama meets death rather than forsake her lover, a rebel on behalf of

democracy. By the time the play was staged, however, Lorca said he had outgrown its "romantic" style.

Accordingly, in *The Public* Lorca proposed a new theater that would confront its audience with uncomfortable truths. As the play opens, a nameless Director of popular plays receives three visitors, who challenge him to present the "theater beneath the sand"—drama that goes beneath life's pleasing surface. The three men and the Director rapidly change costumes, apparently revealing themselves as unhappy homosexuals, locked in relationships of betrayal and mistrust. The Director then shows his audience a play about "the truth of the tombs," dramatizing Lorca's pessimistic belief that the finality of death overwhelms the power of love. Apparently the Director reshapes William Shakespeare's "Romeo and Juliet," in which young lovers die rather than live apart from each other. In *The Public* Juliet appears on stage after her love-inspired suicide, realizing that her death is meaningless and that she will now remain alone for eternity. The Director's audience riots when faced with such ideas, but some theater students, perhaps representing the future of drama, are intrigued. Back in Spain Lorca read *The Public* to friends, who were deeply shocked and advised him that the play was too controversial and surrealistic for an audience to accept. Lorca apparently agreed: he did not release the work and, according to biographer Reed Anderson, dismissed it in interviews as "a poem to be booed at." Nonetheless, Lorca observed, it reflected his "true intention."

Lorca's four best-known plays from the 1930s—*Dona Rosita la soltera* (*Dona Rosita the Spinster*), *Bodas de sangre* (*Blood Wedding*), *Yerma,* and *La casa de Bernarda Alba* (*The House of Bernarda Alba*)—show notable similarities. All are set in Spain during Lorca's lifetime; all spotlight ordinary women struggling with the impositions of Spanish society. *Dona Rosita* is set in the Granada middle class that Lorca knew as a teenager. In three acts set from 1885 to 1911, Lorca first revels in nostalgia for turn-of-the-century Spain, then shows Rosita's growing despair as she waits helplessly for a man to marry her. By the play's end, as Rosita faces old age as an unwanted, unmarried woman, her passivity seems as outdated as the characters' costumes. The three remaining plays, called the "Rural Trilogy," are set in isolated villages of Lorca's Spain. *Yerma*'s title character is a woman whose name means "barren land." She dutifully allows relatives to arrange her marriage, then gradually realizes, to her dismay, that her husband does not want children. Torn between her desire for a baby and her belief in the sanctity of marriage, Yerma resorts to prayer and sorcery in a futile effort to become a mother. Finally she strangles her husband in a burst of uncontrollable frustration. In *The House of Bernarda Alba,* the repressive forces of society are personified by the play's title character, a conservative matriarch who tries to confine her unmarried daughters to the family homestead for eight years of mourning after the death of her husband. The daughters grow increasingly frustrated and hostile until the youngest and most rebellious commits suicide rather than be separated from her illicit lover. *Blood Wedding* is probably Lorca's most successful play with both critics and the public. A man and woman who are passionately attracted to each other enter loveless marriages out of duty to their relatives, but at the woman's wedding feast the lovers elope. In one of the most evocative and unconventional scenes of all Lorca's plays, two characters representing the Moon and Death follow the lovers to a dark and menacing forest, declaring that the couple will meet a disastrous fate. The woman's vengeful husband appears and the two men kill each other. The play ends back at the village where the woman, who has lost both her husband and her lover, joins other villagers in grieving but is isolated from them by mutual hatred. In each of the four plays, an individual's desires are overborne by the demands of society, with disastrous results.

After *Blood Wedding* premiered in 1933, Lorca's fame as a dramatist quickly matched his fame as a poet, both in his homeland and in the rest of the Hispanic world. A short lecture tour of Argentina and Uruguay stretched into six months, as Lorca was greeted as a celebrity and his plays were performed for enthusiastic crowds. He was warmly received by such major Latin American writers as Chile's Pablo Neruda and Mexico's Alfonso Reyes. Neruda, who later won the Nobel Prize for his poetry, called Lorca's visit "the greatest triumph ever achieved by a writer of our race." Notably, while Lorca's most popular plays have achieved great commercial success with Spanish-speaking audiences, they have been respected, but not adulated, by the English-speaking public. Some observers suggested that the strength of the plays is limited to their language, which is lost in translation. But others, including Spaniard Angel del Rio and American Reed Anderson, have surveyed Lorca's stagecraft with admiration. In the opening scenes of *Blood Wedding,* for instance, Lorca skillfully contrasts the festive mood of the villagers with the fierce passions of the unwilling bride; in *Yerma* he confronts his heroine with a shepherd whose love for children subtly embodies her dreams of an ideal husband. In an article that appeared in *Lorca: A Collection of Critical Essays,* del Rio wondered if the plays were too steeped in Hispanic culture for other audiences to easily appreciate.

Lorca's triumphs as a playwright were marred by growing troubles in Spain, which became divided between hostile factions on the political left and right. Though Lorca steadily resisted efforts to recruit him for the Communist party, his social conscience led him to strongly criticize Spanish conservatives, some of whom may have yearned for revenge. Meanwhile Lorca seemed plagued by a sense of foreboding and imminent death. He was shocked when an old friend, retired bullfighter Ignacio Sanchez Mejias, was killed by a bull while attempting to revive his career in the ring. Lorca's elegy—*Llanto por Ignacio Sanchez Mejias* (*Lament for the Death of a Bullfighter*)—has often been called his best poem, endowing the matador with heroic stature as he confronts his fate. Later, friends recalled Lorca's melodramatic remark that the bullfighter's death was a rehearsal for his own. In 1936 civil war broke out in Spain as conservative army officers under General Francisco Franco revolted against the liberal government. Lorca, who was living in Madrid, made the worst possible decision by electing to wait out the impending conflict at his parents' home in Granada, a city filled with rebel sympathizers. Granada quickly fell to rebel forces, who executed many liberal politicians and intellectuals. One was Lorca, who was arrested, shot outside town, and buried in an unmarked grave.

BIOGRAPHICAL/CRITICAL SOURCES:

BOOKS

Anderson, Andrew A., *Lorca's Late Poetry: A Critical Study,* Francis Cairns, 1990.

Anderson, Reed, *Federico Garcia Lorca,* Grove, 1984.

Campbell, Roy, *Lorca: An Appreciation of His Poetry,* Yale University Press, 1952.

Cavanaugh, Cecelia J., *Lorca's Drawings and Poems: Forming the Eye of the Reader,* Bucknell University Press (Lewisburg, PA), 1995.

Dictionary of Literary Biography, Volume 108: *Twentieth-Century Spanish Poets,* Gale (Detroit), 1991, pp. 136-60.

Drama Criticism, Volume 2, Gale, 1992.

Duran, Manuel, editor, *Lorca: A Collection of Critical Essays,* Prentice-Hall, 1962.

Edwards, Gwynne, *Lorca: The Theatre Beneath the Sand,* Boyars, 1980.

Gibson, Ian, *The Assassination of Federico Garcia Lorca,* W. H. Allen, 1979.

Gibson, *Federico Garcia Lorca: A Life,* Pantheon, 1989.

Guillen, Jorge, *Language and Poetry: Some Poets of Spain,* Harvard University Press, 1961.

Hispanic Literature Criticism, Gale, 1994.

Londre, Felicia Hardison, *Federico Garcia Lorca,* Ungar, 1984.

Loughran, David K., *Federico Garcia Lorca: The Poetry of Limits,* Tamesis, 1978.

Morris, C. Brian, *Son of Andalusia: The Lyrical Landscapes of Federico Garcia Lorca,* Vanderbilt University Press, 1997.

Newton, Candelas, *Understanding Federico Garcia Lorca,* University of South Carolina Press (Columbia), 1995.

Poetry Criticism, Volume 3, Gale, 1991.

Pollin, Alice M. and Philip H. Smith, editors, *A Concordance to the Plays and Poems of Federico Garcia Lorca,* Cornell University Press, 1975.

Smith, Paul Julian, *The Theatre of Garcia Lorca: Text, Performance, Psychoanalysis,* Cambridge University Press, 1998.

Soufas, C. Christopher, *Audience and Authority in the Modernist Theater of Federico Garcia Lorca,* University of Alabama (Tuscaloosa), 1996.

Twentieth-Century Literary Criticism, Gale, Volume 1, 1978; Volume 7, 1982; Volume 49, 1994.

World Literature Criticism, Gale, 1992.

Young, Howard T., *The Victorious Expression: A Study of Four Contemporary Spanish Poets,* University of Wisconsin Press, 1966.

PERIODICALS

Commonweal, November 3, 1939; April 20, 1945; August 12, 1955; September 2, 1955; October 21, 1955.

Kenyon Review, summer, 1955.

Nation, September 18, 1937; November 1, 1941; December 27, 1947.

New Republic, February 27, 1935; November 10, 1937; October 11, 1939; September 2, 1940; October 13, 1941.

New York Times, October 19, 1980; July 5, 1989.

New York Times Book Review, September 3, 1939; June 14, 1953; October 9, 1955; November 20, 1988; October 8, 1989.

Parnassus, spring, 1981.

Poetry, December, 1937; September, 1940.

Saturday Review, October 2, 1937; August 26, 1939; January 13, 1940; November 26, 1960.

Time, December 22, 1947; April 17, 1964.

Times Literary Supplement, October 16, 1937; May 27, 1939; September 2, 1965; September 2, 1977; November 21, 1980; August 2, 1984.

*   *   *

GARCIA MARQUEZ, Gabriel (Jose) 1928-

PERSONAL: Born March 6, 1928, in Aracataca, Colombia; son of Gabriel Eligio Garcia (a telegraph operator) and Luisa Santiaga Marquez Iguaran; married Mercedes Barcha, March, 1958; children: Rodrigo, Gonzalo. *Education:* Attended Universidad Nacional de Colombia, 1947-48, and Universidad de Cartagena, 1948-49.

ADDRESSES: Home—P.O. Box 20736, Mexico City D.F., Mexico. *Agent*—Agencia Literaria Carmen Balcells, Diagonal 580, Barcelona 08021, Spain.

CAREER: Began career as a journalist, 1947; reporter for *Universal,* Cartegena, Colombia, late 1940s, *El heraldo,* Baranquilla, Colombia, 1950-52, and *El espectador,* Bogota, Colombia, until 1955; freelance journalist in Paris, London, and Caracas, Venezuela, 1956-58; worked for *Momento* magazine, Caracas, 1958-59; helped form Prensa Latina news agency, Bogota, 1959, and worked as its correspondent in Havana, Cuba, and New York City, 1961; writer, 1965–. Fundacion Habeas, founder, 1979, president, 1979–.

MEMBER: American Academy of Arts and Letters (honorary fellow).

AWARDS, HONORS: Colombian Association of Writers and Artists Award, 1954, for story "Un dia despues del sabado"; Premio Literario Esso (Colombia), 1961, for *La mala hora*; Chianciano Award (Italy), 1969, Prix de Meilleur Livre Etranger (France), 1969, and Romulo Gallegos prize (Venezuela), 1971, all for *Cien anos de soledad*; LL.D., Columbia University, 1971; Books Abroad/Neustadt International Prize for Literature, 1972; Nobel Prize for literature, 1982; *Los Angeles Times* Book Prize nomination for fiction, 1983, for *Chronicle of a Death Foretold*; *Los Angeles Times* Book Prize for fiction, 1988, for *Love in the Time of Cholera*; Serfin Prize, 1989.

WRITINGS:

FICTION

La hojarasca (novella; title means "Leaf Storm"; also see below), Ediciones Sipa (Bogota), 1955, reprinted, Bruguera (Barcelona), 1983.

El coronel no tiene quien le escriba (novella; title means "No One Writes to the Colonel"; also see below), Aguirre Editor (Medellin, Colombia), 1961, reprinted, Bruguera, 1983.

La mala hora (novel; also see below), Talleres de Graficas "Luis Perez" (Madrid), 1961, reprinted, Bruguera, 1982, English translation by Gregory Rabassa published as *In Evil Hour,* Harper, 1979.

Los funerales de la Mama Grande (short stories; title means "Big Mama's Funeral"; also see below), Editorial Universidad Veracruzana (Mexico), 1962, reprinted, Bruguera, 1983.

Cien anos de soledad (novel), Editorial Sudamericana (Buenos Aires), 1967, reprinted, Catedra, 1984, English translation by Rabassa published as *One Hundred Years of Solitude,* Harper, 1970, with a new foreword by Rabassa, Knopf, 1995.

Isabel viendo llover en Macondo (novella; title means "Isabel Watching It Rain in Macondo"; also see below), Editorial Estuario (Buenos Aires), 1967.

No One Writes to the Colonel and Other Stories (includes "No One Writes to the Colonel," and stories from *Los Funerales de la Mama Grande*), translated by J. S. Bernstein, Harper, 1968.

La increible y triste historia de la candida Erendira y su abuela desalmada (short stories; also see below), Barral Editores, 1972.

El negro que hizo esperar a los angeles (short stories), Ediciones Alfil (Montevideo), 1972.

Ojos de perro azul (short stories; also see below), Equisditorial (Argentina), 1972.

Leaf Storm and Other Stories (includes "Leaf Storm," and "Isabel Watching It Rain in Macondo"), translated by Rabassa, Harper, 1972.

El otono del patriarca (novel), Plaza & Janes Editores (Barcelona), 1975, translation by Rabassa published as *The Autumn of the Patriarch,* Harper, 1976.

Todos los cuentos de Gabriel Garcia Marquez: 1947-1972 (title means "All the Stories of Gabriel Garcia Marquez: 1947-1972"), Plaza & Janes Editores, 1975.

Innocent Erendira and Other Stories (includes "Innocent Erendira and Her Heartless Grandmother" and stories from *Ojos de perro azul*), translated by Rabassa, Harper, 1978.

Dos novelas de Macondo (contains *La hojarasca* and *La mala hora*), Casa de las Americas (Havana), 1980.

Cronica de una muerte anunciada (novel), La Oveja Negra (Bogota), 1981, translation by Rabassa published as *Chronicle of a Death Foretold,* J. Cape (London), 1982, Knopf (New York City), 1983.

Viva Sandino (play), Editorial Nueva Nicaragua, 1982, 2nd edition published as *El asalto: el operativo con que el FSLN se lanzo al mundo,* 1983.

El rastro de tu sangre en la nieve: El verano feliz de la senora Forbes, W. Dampier Editores (Bogota), 1982.

El secuestro: Guion cinematografico (unfilmed screenplay), Oveja Negra (Bogota), 1982.

Erendira (filmscript; adapted from his novella *La increible y triste historia de la candida Erendira y su abuela desalmada*), Les Films du Triangle, 1983.

Collected Stories, translated by Rabassa and Bernstein, Harper, 1984.

El amor en los tiempos del colera, Oveja Negra, 1985, English translation by Edith Grossman published as *Love in the Time of Cholera,* Knopf, 1988.

A Time to Die (filmscript), ICA Cinema, 1988.

Diatribe of Love against a Seated Man (play; first produced at Cervantes Theater, Buenos Aires, 1988), Arango Editores (Santafe de Bogota), 1994.

El general en su labertino, Mondadori (Madrid), 1989, English translation by Grossman published as *The General in His Labyrinth,* Knopf, 1990.

Collected Novellas, HarperCollins (New York City), 1990.

Doce cuentos peregrinos, Mondadori (Madrid), 1992, English translation by Grossman published as *Strange Pilgrims: Twelve Stories,* Knopf, 1993.

The Handsomest Drowned Man in the World: A Tale for Children, translated by Rabazza, Creative Education (Mankato, MN), 1993.

Del amor y otros demonios, Mondadori (Barcelona), 1994, English translation by Grossman published as *Of Love and Other Demons,* Knopf, 1995.

NONFICTION

(With Mario Vargas Llosa) *La novela en America Latina: Dialogo,* Carlos Milla Batres (Lima), 1968.

Relato de un naufrago (journalistic pieces), Tusquets Editor (Barcelona), 1970, English translation by Randolph Hogan published as *The Story of a Shipwrecked Sailor,* Knopf, 1986.

Cuando era feliz e indocumentado (journalistic pieces), Ediciones El Ojo de Camello (Caracas), 1973.

Cronicas y reportajes (journalistic pieces), Oveja Negra, 1978.

Periodismo militante (journalistic pieces), Son de Maquina (Bogota), 1978.

De viaje por los paises socialistas: 90 dias en la "Cortina de hierro" (journalistic pieces), Ediciones Macondo (Colombia), 1978.

(Contributor) *Los sandanistas,* Oveja Negra, 1979.

(Contributor) Soledad Mendoza, editor, *Asi es Caracas,* Editorial Ateneo de Caracas, 1980.

Obra periodistica (journalistic pieces), edited by Jacques Gilard, Bruguera, Volume 1: *Textos constenos,* 1981, Volumes 2-3: *Entre cachacos,* 1982, Volume 4: *De Europa y America (1955-1960),* 1983.

El olor de la guayaba: Conversaciones con Plinio Apuleyo Mendoza (interviews), Oveja Negra, 1982, English translation by Ann Wright published as *The Fragrance of Guava,* Verso, 1983.

(With Guillermo Nolasco-Juarez) *Persecucion y muerte de minorias: dos perspectivas,* Juarez Editor (Buenos Aires), 1984.

(Contributor) *La Democracia y la paz en America Latina,* Editorial El Buho (Bogota), 1986.

La aventura de Miguel Littin, clandestino en Chile: Un reportaje, Editorial Sudamericana, 1986, English translation by Asa Zatz published as *Clandestine in Chile: The Adventures of Miguel Littin,* Holt, 1987.

Primeros reportajes, Consorcio de Ediciones Capriles (Caracas), 1990.

(Author of introduction) Mina, Gianni, *An Encounter with Fidel: An Interview,* translated by Mary Todd, Ocean Press (Melbourne), 1991.

Notas de prensa, 1980-1984, Mondadori (Madrid), 1991.

Elogio de la utopia: Una entrevista de Nahuel Maciel, Cronista Ediciones (Buenos Aires), 1992.

News of a Kidnapping, translated from the Spanish by Edith Grossman, Knopf (New York City), 1997.

MEDIA ADAPTATIONS: A play, *Blood and Champagne,* has been based on Garcia Marquez's *One Hundred Years of Solitude.*

SIDELIGHTS: Winner of the 1982 Nobel Prize for literature, Gabriel Garcia Marquez "is one of the small number of contemporary writers from Latin America who have given to its literature a maturity and dignity it never had before," asserted John Sturrock in the *New York Times Book Review.* "More than any other writer in the world," declared David Streitfeld in the *Washington Post,* "Gabriel Garcia Marquez combines both respect (bordering on adulation) and mass popularity (also bordering on adulation)." *One Hundred Years of Solitude* is perhaps Garcia Marquez's best-known contribution to the awakening of interest in Latin American literature. It has sold more than twenty million copies and has been translated into over thirty languages. According to an *Antioch Review* critic, the popularity and acclaim for *One Hundred Years of Solitude* signaled that "Latin American literature will change from being the exotic interest of a few to essential reading and that Latin America itself will be looked on less as a crazy subculture and more as a fruitful, alternative way of life." So great was the novel's initial popularity, notes Mario Vargas Llosa in *Garcia Marquez: Historia de un deicido,* that not only was the first Spanish printing of the book sold out within one week, but for months afterwards Latin American readers alone exhausted each successive printing. Translations of the novel similarly elicited enthusiastic responses from critics and readers around the world.

In this outpouring of critical opinion, which *Books Abroad* contributor Klaus Muller-Bergh called "an earthquake, a maelstrom," various reviewers termed *One Hundred Years of Solitude* a masterpiece of modern fiction. For example, Chilean poet Pablo Neruda, himself a Nobel laureate, was quoted in *Time* as calling the book "the greatest revelation in the Spanish language since the *Don Quixote* of Cervantes." Similarly enthusiastic was William Kennedy, who wrote in the *National Observer* that "*One Hundred Years of Solitude* is the first piece of literature since the Book of Genesis that should be required reading for the entire human race." And Regina Janes, in her study *Gabriel Garcia Marquez: Revolutions in Wonderland,* described the book as "a 'total novel' that [treats] Latin America socially, historically, politically, mythically, and epically," adding that *One Hundred Years of Solitude* is also "at once accessible and intricate, lifelike and self-consciously, self-referentially fictive."

The novel is set in the imaginary community of Macondo, a village on the Colombian coast, and follows the lives of several generations of the Buendia family. Chief among these characters are Colonel Aureliano Buendia, perpetrator of thirty-two rebellions and father of seventeen illegitimate sons, and Ursula Buendia, the clan's matriarch and witness to its eventual decline. Besides following the complicated relationships of the Buendia family, *One Hundred Years of Solitude* also reflects the political, social, and economic troubles of South America. Many critics have found the novel, with its complex family relationships and extraordinary events, to be a microcosm of Latin America itself.

The mixture of historical and fictitious elements that appears in *One Hundred Years of Solitude* places the novel within that genre of Latin American fiction that critics have termed magical realism. Janes attributed the birth of this style of writing to Alejo Carpentier, a Cuban novelist and short story writer, and concluded that Garcia Marquez's fiction follows ideas originally formulated by the Cuban author. The critic noted that Carpentier "discovered the duplicities of history and elaborated the critical concept of 'lo maravilloso americano' the 'marvelous real,' arguing that geographically, historically, and essentially, Latin America was a space marvelous and fantastic . . . and to render that reality was to render marvels." Garcia Marquez presented a similar view of Latin America in his *Paris Review* interview with Peter H. Stone: "It always amuses me that the biggest praise for my work comes for the imagination while the truth is that there's not a single line in all my work that does not have a basis in reality." The author further explained in his *Playboy* interview with Claudia Dreifus: "Clearly, the Latin American environment is marvelous. Particularly the Caribbean. . . . The coastal people were descendants of pirates and smugglers, with a mixture of black slaves. To grow up in such an environment is to have fantastic resources for poetry. Also, in the Caribbean, we are capable of believing anything, because we have the influences of all those different cultures, mixed in with Catholicism and our own local beliefs. I think that gives us an open-mindedness to look beyond apparent reality."

In *The Autumn of the Patriarch* Garcia Marquez uses a more openly political tone in relating the story of a dictator who has reigned for so long that no one can remember any other ruler. Elaborating on the kind of solitude experienced by Colonel Aureliano Buendia in *One Hundred Years,* Garcia Marquez explores the isolation of a political tyrant. "In this fabulous, dream-like account of the reign of a nameless dictator of a fantastic Caribbean realm, solitude is linked with the possession of absolute power," described Ronald De Feo in *National Review.* Rather than relating a straightforward account of the general's life, *The Autumn of the Patriarch* skips from one episode to another using detailed descriptions. *Times Literary Supplement* contributor John Sturrock found this approach appropriate to the author's subject, calling the work "the desperate, richly sustained hallucination of a man rightly bitter about the present state of so much of Latin America." Sturrock noted that "Garcia Marquez's novel is sophisticated and its language is luxuriant to a degree. Style and subject are at odds because Garcia Marquez is committed to showing that our first freedom—and one which all too many Latin American countries have lost—is of the full resources of our language." *Time* writer R. Z. Sheppard similarly commented on Garcia Marquez's elaborate style, observing that "the theme is artfully insinuated, an atmosphere instantly evoked like a puff of stage smoke, and all conveyed in language that generates a charge of expectancy." The critic concluded: "Garcia Marquez writes with what could be called a stream-of-consciousness technique, but the result is much more like a whirlpool."

Some critics, however, found both the theme and technique of *The Autumn of the Patriarch* lacking. J. D. O'Hara, for example, wrote in the *Washington Post Book World* that for all his "magical realism," Garcia Marquez "can only remind us of real-life parallels; he cannot exaggerate them." "For the same reason," the critic added, "although he can turn into grisly cartoons the squalor and paranoia of actual dictatorships, he can scarcely parody them; reality has anticipated him again." *Newsweek*'s Walter Clemons found the novel somewhat disappointing: "After the narrative vivacity and intricate characterization of the earlier book [*The Autumn of the Patriarch*] seems both oversumptuous and under-populated. It is—deadliest of compliments—an extended piece of magnificent writing."

"With its run-on, seemingly free-associative sentences, its constant flow of images and color, Gabriel Garcia Marquez's last novel, *The Autumn of the Patriarch,* was such a dazzling technical achievement that it left the pleasurably exhausted reader wondering what the author would do next," commented De Feo in the *Nation.* This next work, *Chronicle of a Death Foretold* "is, in miniature, a virtuoso performance," stated Jonathan Yardley of the *Washington Post Book World.* In contrast with the author's "two masterworks, *One Hundred Years of Solitude* and *The Autumn of the Patriarch,*" continued the critic, "it is slight . . . its action is tightly concentrated on a single event. But in this small space Garcia Marquez works small miracles; *Chronicle of a Death Foretold* is ingeniously, impeccably constructed, and it provides a sobering, devastating perspective on the system of male 'honor.'" In the novella, described Douglas Hill in the Toronto *Globe and Mail,* Garcia Marquez "has cut out an apparently uncomplicated, larger-than-life jigsaw puzzle of passion and crime, then demonstrated, with laconic diligence and a sort of concerned amusement, how extraordinarily difficult the task of assembling the pieces can be." The story is based on a historical incident in which a young woman is returned after her wedding night for not being a virgin and her brothers set out to avenge the stain on the family honor by murdering the man she names as her "perpetrator." The death is "foretold" in that the brothers announce their intentions to the entire town, but circumstances conspire to keep Santiago Nasar, the condemned man, from this knowledge, and he is brutally murdered.

"In telling this story, which is as much about the townspeople and their reactions as it is about the key players, Garcia Marquez might simply have remained omniscient," observed De Feo. But instead "he places himself in the action, assuming the role of a former citizen who returns home to reconstruct the events of the tragic day—a day he himself lived through." This narrative maneuvering, claimed the critic, "adds another layer to the book, for the narrator, who is visible one moment, invisible the next, could very well ask himself the same question he is intent on asking others, and his own role, his own failure to act in the affair contributes to the book's odd, haunting ambiguity."

In approaching the story from this re-creative standpoint, Garcia Marquez once again utilizes journalistic techniques. As *Chicago Tribune Book World* editor John Blades maintained, "Garcia Marquez tells this grisly little fable in what often appears to be a straight-faced parody of conventional journalism, with its dependence on 'he-she-they told me' narrative techniques, its reliance on the distorted, contradictory and dreamlike memories of 'eyewitnesses.'" Blades added, however, that "at the same time, this is precision-tooled fiction; the author subtly but skillfully manipulates his chronology for dramatic impact." The *New York Times*'s Christopher Lehmann-Haupt similarly noted a departure from the author's previous style: "I cannot be absolutely certain whether in *Chronicle* Gabriel Garcia Marquez has come closer to conventional storytelling than in his previous work, or whether I have simply grown accustomed to his imagination." The critic added that "whatever the case, I found *Chronicle of a Death Foretold* by far the author's most absorbing work to date. I read it through in a flash, and it made the back of my neck prickle." "It is interesting," remarked *Times Literary Supplement* contributor Bill Buford, that Garcia Marquez chose to handle "a fictional episode with the methods of a journalist. In doing so he has written an unusual and original work: a simple narrative so charged with irony that it has the authority of political fable." Buford concluded: "If it is not an example of the socialist realism [Garcia] Marquez may claim it to be elsewhere, *Chronicle of a Death Foretold* is in any case a mesmerizing work that clearly establishes [Garcia] Marquez as one of the most accomplished, and the most 'magical' of political novelists writing today."

Despite this journalistic approach to the story, *Chronicle of a Death Foretold* does contain some of the "magical" elements that characterize Garcia Marquez's fiction. As Robert M. Adams observed in the *New York Review of Books,* there is a "combination of detailed factual particularity, usually on irrelevant points, with vagueness, confusion, or indifference on matters of more importance." The result, Adams suggested, is that "the investigation of an ancient murder takes on the quality of a hallucinatory exploration, a deep groping search into the gathering darkness for a truth that continually slithers away."

Another blending of fable and fact, based in part on Garcia Marquez's recollections of his parents' marriage, *Love in the Time of Cholera* "is an amazing celebration of the many kinds of love between men and women," according to Elaine Feinstein of the London *Times.* "In part it is a brilliantly witty account of the tussles in a long marriage, whose details are curiously moving; elsewhere it is a fantastic tale of love finding erotic fulfilment in ageing bodies." The novel begins with the death of Dr. Juvenal Urbino, whose attempt to rescue a parrot from a tree leaves his wife of fifty years, Fermina Daza, a widow. Soon after Urbino's death, however, Florentino Ariza appears on Fermina Daza's doorstep. The rest of the novel recounts Florentino's determination to resume the passionate courtship of a woman who had given him up over half a century ago. In relating both the story of Fermina Daza's marriage and her later courtship, *Love in the Time of Cholera* "is a novel about commitment and fidelity under circumstances which seem to render such virtues absurd," recounted *Times Literary Supplement* contributor S. M. J. Minta. "[It is] about a refusal to grow old gracefully and respectably, about the triumph sentiment can still win over reason, and above all, perhaps, about Latin America, about keeping faith with where, for better or worse, you started out from."

Although the basic plot of *Love in the Time of Cholera* is fairly simple, some critics have accused Garcia Marquez of over-embellishing his story. Calling the plot a " boy-meets-girl" story, Chicago *Tribune Books* contributor Michael Dorris remarked that "it takes a while to realize this core [plot], for every aspect of the book is attenuated, exaggerated, overstated." The critic also argued that "while a Harlequin Romance might balk at stretching this plot for more than a year or two of fictional time, Garcia Marquez nurses it over five decades," adding that the "prose [is] laden with hyperbolic excess." Some critics have claimed that instead of revealing the romantic side of love, *Love in the Time of Cholera* "seems to deal more with libido and self-deceit than with desire and mortality," as Angela Carter termed it in the *Washington Post Book World*. Dorris expressed a similar opinion, writing that while the novel's "first 50 pages are brilliant, provocative, . . . they are [an] overture to a discordant symphony" which portrays an "anachronistic" world of machismo and misogyny. In contrast, Toronto *Globe and Mail* contributor Ronald Wright believed that the novel works as a satire of this same kind of "hypocrisy, provincialism and irresponsibility of the main characters' social milieu." Wright concluded: "*Love in the Time of Cholera* is a complex and subtle book; its greatest achievement is not to tell a love story, but to meditate on the equivocal nature of romanticism and romantic love."

For his next novel, *The General in His Labyrinth,* Garcia Marquez chose another type of story. His protagonist, the General, is Simon Bolivar. Known as "the Liberator," Bolivar is remembered as a controversial and influential historical figure. His revolutionary activities during the early-nineteenth century helped free South America from Spanish control. The labyrinth evoked in the title consists of what John Butt described in the *Times Literary Supplement* as "the web of slanders and intrigues that surrounded [Bolivar's] decline." The book focuses on Bolivar's last months, once the leader had renounced the Colombian presidency and embarked on a long journey that ended when he died near the Caribbean coast on December 17, 1830. Even as he neared death, Bolivar staged one final, failed attempt to reassert leadership in the face of anarchy. In the *New York Times Book Review* author Margaret Atwood declared: "Had Bolivar not existed, Mr. Garcia Marquez would have had to invent him." Atwood called the novel "a fascinating literary tour de force and a moving tribute to an extraordinary man," as well as "a sad commentary on the ruthlessness of the political process."

The political process is, indeed, an integral aspect of *The General in His Labyrinth.* "Latin American politicians and intellectuals have long relied on a more saintly image of Bolivar to make up for the region's often sordid history," Tim Padgett wrote in *Newsweek*. Although Garcia Marquez presents a pro-Bolivar viewpoint in his novel, the book was greeted with controversy. Butt observed that Garcia Marquez had "managed to offend all sides. . . . From the point of view of some pious Latin Americans he blasphemes a local deity by having him utter the occasional obscenity and by showing him as a relentless womanizer, which he was. Others have detected the author's alleged 'Caribbean' tropical and lowland dislike of *cachacos* or upland and *bogotano* Colombians." The harshest criticism, Butt asserted, emanated from some Colombian historians "who claim that the novel impugns the basis of their country's independence by siding too openly with the Liberator" to the detriment of some of Bolivar's political contemporaries. Garcia Marquez earned wide praise for the quality of documentary research that contributed to the novel, although Butt, for one, lamented that the book "leaves much unexplained about the mental processes of the Liberator." He elaborated: "We learn far more about Bolivar's appearance, sex-life, surroundings and public actions than about his thoughts and motives."

In the works, off and on, for nearly two decades, *Strange Pilgrims: Twelve Stories* marked Garcia Marquez's return to the short story collection. Garcia Marquez's pilgrims are Latin American characters placed in various European settings, many of them in southern Italy. "Thematically, these dozen stories explore familiar Marquesan territory: human solitude and quiet desperation, unexpected love (among older people, between generations), the bizarre turns of fate, the intertwining of passion and death," Michael Dirda asserted in the *Washington Post Book World*. At each story's core, however, "lies a variant of that great transatlantic theme—the failure of people of different cultures, ages or political convictions to communicate with each other." In *Strange Pilgrims,* Margaret Sayers Peden asserted in the *Chicago Tribune,* "Latins do not fare well in their separation from native soil." In "The Saint," for example, an old Colombian man has brought the intact corpse of his young daughter to Rome. For decades he journeys through the Vatican bureaucracy, trying to get his child canonized. "Absurd and oddly serene," Richard Eder wrote in the *Los Angeles Times Book Review,* "['The Saint'] says a great deal about Latin American boundlessness in a bounded Europe." In another story, "I Only Came to Use the Phone," a Mexican woman is mistakenly identified as a mental patient and is trapped in a Spanish insane asylum—no one heeds her cry that she only entered the building to place a telephone call.

Garcia Marquez returned to his Maconderos in his next novel, *Of Love and Other Demons.* The story stems from an event the author witnessed early in his journalistic career. As a reporter in Cartagena in 1949, he was assigned to watch while a convent's tomb was opened to transfer burial remains—the convent was being destroyed to clear space for a hotel. There soon emerged twenty-two meters of vibrant human hair, attached to the skull of a young girl who had been buried for two centuries. Remembering his grandparents' stories about a twelve-year-old aristocrat who had died of rabies, Garcia Marquez began to reconstruct the life and death of a character named Sierva Maria. Jonathan Yardley remarked in the *Washington Post Book World* that the author's mood in this novel "is almost entirely melancholy and his manner is, by contrast with his characteristic ebullience, decidedly restrained." In the *Los Angeles Times Book Review,* Eder judged the novel to be "a good one though not quite among [Garcia Marquez's] best."

As the daughter of wealthy but uninterested parents, Sierva Maria grows up with the African slaves on her family's plantation. When she is bitten by a rabid dog, a local bishop determines that she requires exorcism. The girl is taken to the Convent of Santa Clara, where the bishop's pious delegate, Father Cayetano Delaura, is charged with her case. But Delaura himself is soon possessed, by the demon of love, a forbidden love for the young woman. Yardley wrote: "Here most certainly we are in the world of Gabriel Garcia Marquez, where religious faith and human love collide in agony and passion." In *Time* magazine R. Z. Sheppard asserted that in telling "a story of forbidden love," Garcia Marquez "demonstrates once again the vigor of his own passion: the daring and irresistible coupling of history and imagination." Yardley warned, however, that "readers hoping to re-experience 'magical realism' at the level attained in the author's masterpieces will be disappointed." In the *Nation,* John Leonard stated: "My only complaint about this marvelous novella is its rush toward the end. Suddenly, [the author is] in a hurry . . . when we want to spend more time" with his characters.

Garcia Marquez again drew upon his experience as a journalist to write a nonfiction account of a bizarre episode in the history of twentieth-century Colombia in *News of a Kidnapping,* published in 1997. Set in 1992, this work recounts the abduction of ten prominent Colombians, mostly journalists, by thugs attached to the powerful Medellin drug cartel. The kidnapping and holding of hostages was ordered by Pablo Escobar, the drug cartel's kingpin, who sought to arrange some sort of deal with Colombian authorities which would lessen the chances of his being arrested and extradited to the U.S., where he would face a trial and near-certain life imprisonment. As days passed, hostages were gradually released, and Garcia Marquez seized upon one hostage's story to buttress his own investigative findings and write of what he calls "the biblical holocaust that has been consuming Colombia for more than twenty years." In *Booklist,* Bonnie Smothers writes, "Garcia Marquez is dealing with reality, and at times his tone is that of the journalist reporting a newsworthy event; but his material involves intrigue, victims in hideaways, captors in hoods, incandescent meetings between negotiators from all sides, and the tyranny of fate. A complex situation but just the sort of human snakepit that Garcia Marquez finds a home in." *Kirkus Reviews* hailed *News of a Kidnapping* as "a tale featuring real-life heroes, almost comically absurd events, endless terror, and a satisfyingly dramatic ending," while Robert Stone, writing in the *New York Times Book Review,* praised the author's "quick eye for the illuminating detail and a capacity for assembling fact."

Because of this history of political involvement, Garcia Marquez has often been accused of allowing his politics to overshadow his work, and has also encountered problems entering the United States. When asked by the *New York Times Book Review*'s Marlise Simons why he is so insistent on becoming involved in political issues, the author replied that "If I were not a Latin American, maybe I wouldn't [become involved]. But underdevelopment is total, integral, it affects every part of our lives. The problems of our societies are mainly political." The Colombian further explained that "the commitment of a writer is with the reality of all of society, not just with a small part of it. If not, he is as bad as the politicians who disregard a large part of our reality. That is why authors, painters, writers in Latin America get politically involved."

BIOGRAPHICAL/CRITICAL SOURCES:

BOOKS

Bell, Michael, *Gabriel Garcia Marquez: Solitude and Solidarity,* St. Martin's Press (New York City), 1993.

Bell-Villada, Gene H., *Garcia Marquez: The Man and His Work,* University of North Carolina Press (Chapel Hill, NC), 1990.

Brotherson, Gordon, *The Emergence of the Latin American Novel,* Cambridge University Press, 1979.

Contemporary Literary Criticism, Gale (Detroit), Volume 2, 1974; Volume 3, 1975; Volume 8, 1978; Volume 10, 1979; Volume 15, 1980; Volume 27, 1984; Volume 47, 1988; Volume 55, 1989.

Dictionary of Literary Biography Yearbook: 1982, Gale, 1983.

Dictionary of Literary Biography, Volume 113: *Modern Latin-American Fiction Writers,* Gale, 1992.

Dolan, Sean, *Gabriel Garcia Marquez,* Chelsea House (New York City), 1994.

Fiddian, Robin W., *Garcia Marquez,* Longman (New York), 1995.

Gabriel Garcia Marquez, nuestro premio Nobel, La Secretaria de Informacion y Prensa de la Presidencia de la Nacion (Bogota), 1983.

Gonzalez, Nelly S., *Bibliographic Guide to Gabriel Garcia Marquez, 1986-1992,* Greenwood Press (Westport, CT), 1994.

Janes, Regina, *Gabriel Garcia Marquez: Revolutions in Wonderland,* University of Missouri Press (Columbia, MO), 1981.

McGuirk, Bernard, and Richard Cardwell, editors, *Gabriel Garcia Marquez: New Readings,* Cambridge University Press, 1988.

Pritchett, V. S., *The Myth Makers,* Random House (New York City), 1979.

Vargas Llosa, Mario, *Garcia Marquez: Historia de un deicido,* Barral Editores, 1971.

Wood, Michael, *Gabriel Garcia Marquez: One Hundred Years of Solitude,* Cambridge University Press (Cambridge, England), 1990.

PERIODICALS

Antioch Review, winter, 1991, p. 154.

Booklist, May 1, 1997, p. 1458.

Books Abroad, winter, 1973; summer, 1973; spring, 1976.

Book World, June 29, 1997.

Chicago Tribune, March 6, 1983; October 31, 1993.

Chicago Tribune Book World, November 11, 1979; November 7, 1982; April 3, 1983; November 18, 1984; April 27, 1986.

Detroit News, October 27, 1982; December 16, 1984.

Globe and Mail (Toronto), April 7, 1984; September 19, 1987; May 21, 1988.

Hispania, September, 1976; September, 1993, pp. 439-45; March, 1994, pp. 80-81.

Kirkus Reviews, May 1, 1997, p. 693.

London Magazine, April/May, 1973; November, 1979.

Los Angeles Times, October 22, 1982; January 25, 1987; August 24, 1988; June 1, 1997.

Los Angeles Times Book Review, April 10, 1983; November 13, 1983; December 16, 1984; April 27, 1986; June 7, 1987; April 17, 1988; October 24, 1993, pp. 3, 10; May 14, 1995, pp. 3, 5.

Maclean's, July 24, 1995, p. 50.

Nation, December 2, 1968; May 15, 1972; May 14, 1983; June 12, 1995, pp. 836-40; June 16, 1997.

National Observer, April 20, 1970.

National Review, May 27, 1977; June 10, 1983.

New Republic, April 9, 1977; October 27, 1979; May 2, 1983.

New Statesman, June 26, 1970; May 18, 1979; February 15, 1980; September 3, 1982.

Newsweek, March 2, 1970; November 8, 1976; July 3, 1978; December 3, 1979; November 1, 1982; October 8, 1990, p. 70.

New York Review of Books, March 26, 1970; January 24, 1980; April 14, 1983; January 11, 1996, p. 37.

New York Times, July 11, 1978; November 6, 1979; October 22, 1982; March 25, 1983; December 7, 1985; April 26, 1986; June 4, 1986; April 6, 1988.

New York Times Book Review, September 29, 1968; March 8, 1970; February 20, 1972; October 31, 1976; July 16, 1978; September 16, 1978; November 11, 1979; November 16, 1980; December 5, 1982; March 27, 1983; April 7, 1985; April 27, 1986; August 9, 1987; April 10, 1988; September 16, 1990, pp. 1, 30; May 28, 1995, p. 8; June 15, 1997, p. 16.

Paris Review, winter, 1981.

People Weekly, July 24, 1995, p. 26.

Playboy, February, 1983.

Publishers Weekly, May 13, 1974; December 16, 1983; March 27, 1995, pp. 72-73; June 10, 1996, p. 45.

Review, number 24, 1979; September/December, 1981.

Spectator, October 16, 1993, pp. 40-41.
Time, March 16, 1970; November 1, 1976; July 10, 1978; November 1, 1982; March 7, 1983; December 31, 1984; April 14, 1986; May 22, 1995; June 2, 1997.
Times (London), November 13, 1986; June 30, 1988.
Times Literary Supplement, April 15, 1977; February 1, 1980; September 10, 1982; July 1, 1988; July 14-20, 1989, p. 781; July 7, 1995; July 11, 1997.
Tribune Books (Chicago), June 28, 1987; April 17, 1988.
UNESCO Courier, February, 1996, p. 4.
Variety, March 25, 1996, p. 55.
Washington Post, October 22, 1982; April 10, 1994, p. F1.
Washington Post Book World, November 14, 1976; November 25, 1979; November 7, 1982; March 27, 1983; November 18, 1984; July 19, 1987; April 24, 1988; October 31, 1993, p. 7; May 14, 1995, p. 3.
World Literature Today, winter, 1982; winter, 1991, p. 85; autumn, 1993, pp. 782-83.
World Press Review, April, 1982.
World Research INK, September, 1977.

*   *   *

GARDNER, Erle Stanley 1889-1970
(A. A. Fair, Carleton Kendrake, Charles J. Kenny)

PERSONAL: Born July 27, 1889, in Malden, MA; died March 11, 1970, in Temecula, CA; son of Charles Walter (a mining engineer) and Grace Adelma (Waugh) Gardner; married Natalie Talbert, April 9, 1912 (separated, 1935; died, February, 1968); married Agnes Jean Bethell, August 7, 1968; children: (first marriage) Natalie Grace (Mrs. Toby Naso). *Education:* Attended high school.

CAREER: Writer. Admitted to California Bar, 1911; attorney, Oxnard, CA, 1911-16; Consolidated Sales Co., president, 1918-21; Sheridan, Orr, Drapeau, and Gardner, Ventura, CA, attorney, 1921-33; founder and member, Court of Last Resort, 1948-60; founder, Paisano Productions, 1957; consultant and editor, *Perry Mason* television show, 1957-66.

MEMBER: American Bar Association, American Judicature Society, Academy of Scientific Interrogation, American Academy of Forensic Sciences, Law Science Academy of America, American Society of Criminology, California Bar Association, American Polygraph Association (honorary life member), Harvard Association of Political Science, New Hampshire Medico Society, Kansas Peace Officers Association, Elks, Adventurers (Chicago and New York).

AWARDS, HONORS: Mystery Writers of America, Edgar Allan Poe Award, 1953, for *The Court of Last Resort,* Grand Master Award, 1961; honorary alumnus, Kansas City University; Doctor of Law, McGeorge College of Law, 1956, and New Mexico University.

WRITINGS:

ALL PUBLISHED BY MORROW, EXCEPT AS INDICATED

(Under pseudonym Carleton Kendrake) *The Clue of the Forgotten Murder,* 1935.
(Under pseudonym Charles J. Kenny) *This Is Murder,* 1935.
Two Clues (novelettes), 1947.
The Case of the Musical Cow, 1950.

"PERRY MASON" SERIES, PUBLISHED BY MORROW EXCEPT AS INDICATED

The Case of the Velvet Claws, 1933.
The Case of the Sulky Girl, 1933.
The Case of the Lucky Legs, 1934.
The Case of the Howling Dog, 1934.
The Case of the Curious Bride, 1934.
The Case of the Counterfeit Eye, 1935.
The Case of the Caretaker's Cat, 1935.
The Case of the Sleepwalker's Niece, 1936.
The Case of the Stuttering Bishop, 1936.
The Case of the Dangerous Dowager, 1937.
The Case of the Lame Canary, 1937.
The Case of the Substitute Face, 1938.
The Case of the Shoplifter's Shoe, 1938.
The Case of the Perjured Parrot, 1939.
The Case of the Rolling Bones, 1939.
The Case of the Baited Hook, 1940.
The Case of the Silent Partner, 1940.
The Case of the Haunted Husband, 1941.
The Case of the Empty Tin, 1941.
The Case of the Drowning Duck, 1942.
The Case of the Careless Kitten, 1942.
The Case of the Buried Clock, 1943.
The Case of the Drowsy Mosquito, 1943.
The Case of the Crooked Candle, 1944.
The Case of the Black-Eyed Blonde, 1944.
The Case of the Golddigger's Purse, 1945.
The Case of the Half-Wakened Wife, 1945.
The Case of the Borrowed Brunette, 1946.
The Case of the Fan Dancer's Horse, 1947.
The Case of the Lazy Lover, 1947.
The Case of the Lonely Heiress, 1948.
The Case of the Vagabond Virgin, 1948.
The Case of the Dubious Bridegroom, 1949.
The Case of the Cautious Coquette, 1949.
The Case of the Negligent Nymph, 1950.
The Case of the One-Eyed Witness, 1950.
The Case of the Fiery Fingers, 1951.
The Case of the Angry Mourners, 1951.
The Case of the Moth-Eaten Mink, 1952.
The Case of the Grinning Gorilla, 1952.
The Case of the Hesitant Hostess, 1953.
The Case of the Green-Eyed Sister, 1953.
The Case of the Fugitive Nurse, 1954.
The Case of the Runaway Corpse, 1954.
The Case of the Restless Redhead, 1954.
The Case of the Glamorous Ghost (also see below), 1955.
The Case of the Sun Bather's Diary, 1955.
The Case of the Nervous Accomplice, 1955.
The Case of the Terrified Typist (also see below), 1956.
The Case of the Demure Defendant, 1956.
The Case of the Gilded Lily, 1956.
The Case of the Lucky Loser (also see below), 1957.
The Case of the Screaming Woman (also see below), 1957.
The Case of the Daring Decoy, 1957.
The Case of the Long-Legged Models (also see below), 1958.
The Case of the Foot-Loose Doll (also see below), 1958.
The Case of the Calendar Girl, 1958.
The Case of the Deadly Toy, 1959.
The Case of the Mythical Monkeys, 1959.
The Case of the Singing Skirt, 1959.
The Case of the Waylaid Wolf (also see below), 1960.
The Case of the Duplicate Daughter, 1960.

The Case of the Shapely Shadow, 1960.
The Case of the Spurious Spinster, 1961.
The Case of the Bigamous Spouse, 1961.
The Case of the Reluctant Model, 1962.
The Case of the Blonde Bonanza, 1962.
The Case of the Ice-Cold Hands, 1962.
The Case of the Mischievous Doll, 1963.
The Case of the Step-daughter's Secret, 1963.
The Case of the Amorous Aunt, 1963.
The Case of the Daring Divorcee, 1964.
The Case of the Phantom Fortune, 1964.
The Case of the Horrified Heirs, 1964.
The Case of the Troubled Trustee, 1965.
The Case of the Beautiful Beggar, 1965.
The Case of the Worried Waitress, 1966.
The Case of the Queenly Contestant, 1967.
The Case of the Careless Cupid, 1968.
The Case of the Fabulous Fake, 1969.
The Case of the Fenced-in Woman, 1972.
The Case of the Postponed Murder, 1973.

"DOUG SELBY" SERIES

The D.A. Calls It Murder, 1937.
The D.A. Holds a Candle, 1938.
The D.A. Draws a Circle, 1939.
The D.A. Goes to Trial, 1940.
The D.A. Cooks a Goose, 1942.
The D.A. Calls a Turn, 1944.
The D.A. Breaks a Seal, 1946.
The D.A. Takes a Chance, 1948.
The D.A. Breaks an Egg, 1949.

"TERRY CLANE" SERIES

Murder Up My Sleeve, 1938.
The Case of the Backward Mule, 1946.

"GRAMPA WIGGINS" SERIES:

The Case of the Turning Tide, 1941.
The Case of the Smoking Chimney, 1943.

SHORT STORIES

The Case of the Murderer's Bride, and Other Stories, edited by Ellery Queen, Davis Publications, 1969.
The Case of the Crimson Kiss, 1971.
The Case of the Crying Swallow, and Other Stories, 1971.
The Case of the Irate Witness, 1972.
The Amazing Adventures of Lester Leith, Dial, 1981.

CONTRIBUTOR

Howard Haycroft, editor, *The Art of the Mystery Story,* Simon & Schuster, 1946.
The President's Mystery Plot, Prentice-Hall, 1967.
The Fear Merchant, New English Library, 1974.

OMNIBUS VOLUMES

Erle Stanley Gardner: Seven Complete Novels (contains *The Case of the Glamorous Ghost, The Case of the Terrified Typist, The Case of the Lucky Loser, The Case of the Screaming Woman, The Case of the Long-Legged Models, The Case of the Foot-Loose Doll,* and *The Case of the Waylaid Wolf*), Crown, 1979.

NONFICTION

The Land of Shorter Shadows, 1948.
The Court of Last Resort, 1952.
Neighborhood Frontiers, 1954.

The Case of the Boy Who Wrote "The Case of the Missing Clue" with Perry Mason, 1959.
Hunting the Desert Whale, 1960.
Hovering over Baja, 1961.
The Hidden Heart of Baja, 1962.
The Desert Is Yours, 1963.
The World of Water: Exploring the Sacramento Delta, 1964.
Hunting Lost Mines by Helicopter, 1965.
Off the Beaten Track in Baja, 1967.
Gypsy Days on the Delta, 1967.
Mexico's Magic Square, 1968.
Drifting Down the Delta, 1969.
Host with the Big Hat, 1970.
Cops on Campus and Crime in the Streets, 1970.
Whispering Sands: Stories of Gold Fever and the Western Desert, edited by Charles G. Waugh and Martin H. Greenberg, 1981.

UNDER PSEUDONYM A. A. FAIR

The Bigger They Come, 1939, published in England as *Lam to the Slaughter,* Hamish Hamilton, 1939.
Turn on the Heat, 1940.
Gold Comes in Bricks, 1940.
Spill the Jackpot, 1941.
Double or Quits, 1941.
Owls Don't Blink, 1942.
Bats Fly at Dusk, 1942.
Cats Prowl at Night, 1943.
Give 'em the Ax, 1944, published in England as *An Axe to Grind,* Heinemann, 1951.
Crows Can't Count, 1946.
Fools Die on Friday, 1947.
Bedrooms Have Windows, 1949.
Top of the Heap, 1952.
Some Women Won't Wait, 1953.
Beware the Curves, 1956.
You Can Die Laughing, 1957.
Some Slips Don't Show, 1957.
The Count of Nine, 1958.
Pass the Gravy, 1959.
Kept Women Can't Wait, 1960.
Bachelors Get Lonely, 1961.
Shills Can't Cash Chips, 1961, published in England as *Stop at the Red Light,* Heinemann, 1962.
Try Anything Once, 1962.
Fish or Cut Bait, 1963.
Up for Grabs, 1964.
Cut Thin to Win, 1965.
Widows Wear Weeds, 1966.
Traps Need Fresh Bait, 1967.
All Grass Isn't Green, 1970.

MEDIA ADAPTATIONS: Warner Bros. filmed *The Case of the Howling Dog* in 1934, *The Case of the Curious Bride* in 1935, *The Case of the Lucky Legs* in 1935, *The Case of the Velvet Claws* in 1936, *The Case of the Black Cat* in 1936, and *The Case of the Stuttering Bishop* in 1937. Columbia Broadcasting System ran a Perry Mason radio series, 1943-55, the television series *Perry Mason,* 1957-66, and *The New Adventures of Perry Mason,* 1973-74.

SIDELIGHTS: The late mystery writer Erle Stanley Gardner "often insisted," Albin Krebs stated in the *New York Times,* "that he was 'not really a writer at all,' and to be sure, there were many critics who enthusiastically agreed with him. But millions of readers . . . looked upon Mr. Gardner . . . as a master storyteller." Gardner enjoyed being called a "fiction factory" or "the Henry Ford of detective novelists," references to the assembly-line nature of his prolific literary output. With over 200 million copies of his books sold, and sales at one time peaking at 26,000 copies a day, Gardner ranked as the best-selling American author of all time. "In terms of total readership," Hank Burchard of the *Washington Post* reported, "he ranks right up there with Homer, Matthew, Mark, Luke, and John."

The hard-hitting defense lawyer Perry Mason was easily Gardner's most popular character, appearing in some eighty of his novels. Mason, Otto Penzler stated in *The Private Lives of Private Eyes, Spies, Crimefighters, and Other Good Guys,* "is the most famous lawyer in fiction." "Perry Mason," Isaac Anderson of the *New York Times* believed, "is not only a shrewd lawyer and a brilliant detective, he is a master of stage-craft, who knows how to stage dramatic climaxes in the courtroom when they will do the most good for his client." The Mason books are based on Gardner's own years as a lawyer in rural California, with each novel being a composite of several actual cases. Many of the techniques employed by Mason were first used by Gardner himself who was, Burchard stated, "noted for his deft use of little-known statutes, penetrating cross-examination and colorful court-room demeanor." On one occasion Gardner defended a group of Chinese accused of illegal gambling by filling the courtroom with Chinese and daring the prosecuting attorney to match the indictments with the accused men. The charges were dropped. On another occasion Gardner's client was accused of causing a woman's nervous breakdown with his loose talk about her. A small earthquake shook the California courthouse during the proceedings and Gardner quickly used the unexpected event to his advantage, pointing out to the jury that the plaintiff had been the only person in the courthouse to stay calm during the quake. His client was acquitted. Gardner's clients were usually poor, members of minority groups, or those whom Gardner considered unjustly accused. *Time* quoted him as saying that he defended "vagrants, peeping Toms and chicken thieves as if they were statesmen." In 1948, Gardner founded the Court of Last Resort, an organization of lawyers who took on seemingly hopeless cases from across the country. In the twelve years of its existence, the Court of Last Resort was responsible for saving a number of defendants from prison terms.

In the 1920s, Gardner began to write fiction at night while working by day as a lawyer. His hectic schedule at the time included a full day of court appearances, several hours of researching points of law at the library, and then writing a self-imposed quota of 4,000 words of fiction when he returned home in the evening. His determination soon paid off. In 1921, the pulp magazine *Breezy Stories* published "Nellie's Naughty Nightie," Gardner's first published work. He was soon selling his stories to a wide variety of pulp magazines at such a steady rate that he cut back his legal practice to two days a week to devote more time to writing. At its peak, Gardner's output reached some one million words of published fiction per year, with his stories appearing in the pulp magazines at a rate of better than one per week.

In these early days Gardner experimented with a variety of story genres, including westerns, confession stories, and mysteries. Out of these writing experiments came the publication in 1933 of *The Case of the Velvet Claws,* the first Perry Mason novel. With the publication of this book Gardner's writing career took a new turn. Thayer Hobson, the president of Gardner's publishing house, suggested that Gardner concentrate his efforts on his new character, turning Perry Mason into a series character. Gardner

took the advice. Although he would later write mysteries featuring other characters, and some nonfiction books, the bulk of Gardner's later writing concerned Perry Mason. "It is a matter of loyalty to the characters one has created," *Newsweek* quoted Gardner as explaining, "and loyalty to one's associates."

The Perry Mason books, Burchard explained, "are formula books." In each one Mason defended a client charged with murder. The client is always entangled in a set of suspicious circumstances which makes him look guilty. When it seems as if all is lost and his client will be convicted, Mason risks everything—his life, disbarment, and/or a jail sentence—on a desperate last bid, confident that he can win acquittal. In a surprise ending, Mason's desperate bid pays off and he saves his client in a climatic courtroom scene, producing evidence at the last moment which not only clears the defendant but reveals the real murderer as well. "Defying all odds," Penzler observed, "Mason never loses a case." This despite Mason's own admission in *The Case of the Counterfeit Eye*: "I don't ask a client if he's guilty or innocent. Either way he's entitled to a day in court." Cyril Ray of *Spectator* described the Mason books as coming "off a conveyor-belt, of course, but with all the neatness and finish of the machine-made article."

The typical Perry Mason book, Burchard believed, "isn't great, but it isn't bad, either. The prose is mostly workmanlike, with a clinker here and there, the plot turns are less outrageous than many that can be found on any bookstand. . . . Gardner always put in interesting and often informative factual detail . . . , and the legal details are always scrupulously accurate." This attention to detail was noted by several critics, including James Sandoe of the *New York Herald Tribune Book Review.* Sandoe wrote that Gardner's "real assurance lies in the tricks of plotting and the accurate language of trial law." O. L. Bailey of the *Saturday Review of the Arts* stated that Gardner "never pretended to be anything but a commercial writer. His stock in trade was the great care he took to make sure that all the details of his complex plots were right." Gardner went so far as to purchase a new gun for each murder mystery he wrote. During a court trial, he said, the murder weapon's serial number must be entered into the court record. "If I give a phony one [in a Perry Mason book]," Gardner told *Newsweek,* "people write in and say there isn't any such serial number. If I give a real serial number, I face a lawsuit. So every time I commit a murder, I have to buy the gun." At the time of his death, Gardner was reported to have had a large gun collection.

In the 1940s, a Perry Mason radio show was broadcast five days a week in soap opera fashion. This show was superceded in 1957 by "Perry Mason," a television series starring Raymond Burr. Gardner served as consultant and editor to the series, which used many of his original Perry Mason novels as sources for its episodes. The show was a tremendous success, running nine seasons in prime time and becoming the most popular lawyer series in television history. Because Gardner was the majority owner of Paisano Productions, the packagers of "Perry Mason" for the Columbia Broadcasting System, he was said to have earned some fifteen million dollars from the show. "Perry Mason" is still broadcast in reruns in nearly every major American city, and broadcast overseas in 16 different languages. In 1973, CBS revived the series as "The New Adventures of Perry Mason" with Monte Markham as Mason. The show lasted one season.

"I write to make money," Krebs quoted Gardner as once saying, "and I write to give the reader sheer fun." Burchard quoted Gardner explaining his popularity this way: "Ordinary readers see in me somebody they can identify with. I'm for the underdog. Justice is done in my books. The average man is always in a state of supreme suspense because his life is all complications with no conclusions. In my books, he sees people in trouble get out of trouble."

BIOGRAPHICAL/CRITICAL SOURCES:

BOOKS

Bounds, J. Dennis, *Perry Mason: The Authorship and Reproduction of a Popular Hero,* Greenwood Press (Westport, CT), 1996.
Fugate, Francis L. and Roberta B. Fugate, *Secrets of the World's Best-Selling Writer: The Story-telling Techniques of Erle Stanley Gardner,* Morrow, 1980.
Hughes, Dorothy B., *Erle Stanley Gardner: The Case of the Real Perry Mason,* Morrow, 1978.
Johnson, Alva, *The Case of Erle Stanley Gardner,* Morrow, 1947.
Mott, Frank Luther, *Golden Multitudes,* Macmillan, 1947.
Mundell, E. H., *Erle Stanley Gardner: A Checklist,* Kent State University Press, 1969.
Penzler, Otto, *The Private Lives of Private Eyes, Spies, Crime-fighters, and Other Good Guys,* Grosset, 1977.
Senate, Richard L., *Erle Stanley Gardner's Ventura: The Birth-place of Perry Mason,* Charon Press, 1996.

PERIODICALS

Atlantic, January, 1967.
Books and Bookmen, March, 1971.
Christian Science Monitor, January 17, 1973.
Coronet, February, 1956.
Newsweek, October 25, 1943; October 7, 1957; January 18, 1960.
New Yorker, November 11, 1950.
New York Herald Tribune Book Review, November 16, 1952; May 25, 1958.
New York Times, June 24, 1934; November 18, 1934; January 6, 1957; May 11, 1958.
New York Times Book Review, September 13, 1959; February 4, 1973.
New York Times Magazine, March 21, 1965.
Publishers Weekly, January 27, 1958; August 11, 1958.
Reader's Digest, August, 1963.
Saturday Evening Post, May 30, 1942; September 1, 1956; January 30, 1960.
Saturday Review of Literature, July 16, 1938.
Saturday Review of the Arts, February, 1973.
Spectator, March 28, 1970.
Time, May 9, 1949.
Variety, April 1, 1970.
Washington Post, March 12, 1970.

*   *   *

GARDNER, John (Champlin), Jr. 1933-1982

PERSONAL: Born July 21, 1933, in Batavia, NY; died in a motorcycle accident, September 14, 1982, in Susquehanna, PA; son of John Champlin (a dairy farmer) and Priscilla (a high school literature teacher; maiden name, Jones) Gardner; married Joan Louise Patterson, June 6, 1953 (divorced, 1976); married Liz Rosenberg, 1980 (divorced); children: Joel, Lucy. *Education:* De Paul University, student, 1951-53; Washington University, St. Louis, A.B., 1955; State University of Iowa, M.A., 1956, Ph.D., 1958.

CAREER: Oberlin College, Oberlin, OH, instructor, 1958-59; Chico State College (now California State University), Chico, CA, instructor, 1959-62; San Francisco State College (now San Francisco State University), San Francisco, CA, assistant professor of English, 1962-65; Southern Illinois University, Carbondale, professor of English, 1965-74; Bennington College, VT, instructor, 1974-76; Williams College, Williamstown, MA, and Skidmore College, Saratoga Springs, NY, instructor, 1976-77; George Mason University, Fairfax, VA, instructor, 1977-78; founder and director of writing program, State University of New York at Binghamton, 1978-82; author, 1976-82. Distinguished visiting professor, University of Detroit, 1970-71; visiting professor, Northwestern University, Evanston, IL, 1973.

MEMBER: Modern Language Association of America, American Association of University Professors.

AWARDS, HONORS: Woodrow Wilson fellowship, 1955-56; Danforth fellowship, 1972-73; Guggenheim fellowship, 1973-74; National Education Association award, 1972; *Grendel* named one of 1971's best fiction books by *Time* and *Newsweek; October Light* named one of the ten best books of 1976 by *Time* and *New York Times*; National Book Critics Circle award for fiction, 1976, for *October Light*; Armstrong Prize, 1980, for *The Temptation Game.*

WRITINGS:

NOVELS

The Resurrection, New American Library, 1966.
The Wreckage of Agathon, Harper, 1970.
Grendel, Knopf, 1971.
The Sunlight Dialogues, Knopf, 1972.
Jason and Medeia (novel in verse), Knopf, 1973.
Nickel Mountain: A Pastoral Novel, Knopf, 1973.
October Light, Knopf, 1976.
Freddy's Book, Knopf, 1980.
Mickelsson's Ghosts, Knopf, 1982.

JUVENILES

Dragon, Dragon and Other Timeless Tales, Knopf, 1975.
Gudgekin the Thistle Girl and Other Tales (Junior Literary Guild selection), Knopf, 1976.
In the Suicide Mountains, Knopf, 1977.
A Child's Bestiary (light verse), Knopf, 1977.
King of the Hummingbirds, and Other Tales, Knopf, 1977.
Vlemk, the Box Painter, Lord John Press, 1979.

CRITICISM

(Editor with Lennis Dunlap) *The Forms of Fiction,* Random House, 1961.
(Editor and author of introduction) *The Complete Works of the Gawain-Poet in a Modern English Version with a Critical Introduction,* University of Chicago Press, 1965.
(Editor with Nicholas Joost) *Papers on the Art and Age of Geoffrey Chaucer,* Southern Illinois University Press, 1967.
(Editor and author of notes) *The Gawain-Poet: Notes on Pearl and Sir Gawain and the Green Knight, with Brief Commentary on Purity and Patience,* Cliffs Notes, 1967.
Morte D'Arthur Notes, Cliffs Notes, 1967.
Sir Gawain and the Green Knight Notes, Cliffs Notes, 1967.
(Editor and author of notes) *The Alliterative Morte Arthure, The Owl and the Nightingale and Five Other Middle English Poems* (modern English version), Southern Illinois University Press, 1971.

The Construction of the Wakefield Cycle, Southern Illinois University Press, 1974.
The Construction of Christian Poetry in Old English, Southern Illinois University Press, 1975.
The Life and Times of Chaucer, Knopf, 1977.
The Poetry of Chaucer, Southern Illinois University Press, 1978.
On Moral Fiction, Basic Books, 1978.
On Becoming a Novelist, Harper, 1983.
The Art of Fiction: Notes on Craft for Young Writers, Knopf, 1984.
On Writers and Writing, foreword by Stewart O'Nan, Addison-Wesley (Reading, MA), 1994.

OTHER

The King's Indian and Other Fireside Tales (novellas), Knopf, 1974, published in England as *The King's Servant,* J. Cape, 1975.
(Contributor) Matthew Bruccoli and C. E. Frazer Clark, Jr., editors, *Pages,* Volume 1, Gale (Detroit), 1976.
William Wilson (libretto; also see below), New London Press, 1978.
Poems, Lord John Press, 1978.
Three Libretti (includes *William Wilson, Frankenstein,* and *Rumpelstiltskin*), New London Press, 1979.
MSS: A Retrospective, New London Press, 1980.
The Art of Living and Other Stories, Knopf, 1981.
(Editor with Shannon Ravenel) *The Best American Short Stories of 1982,* Houghton, 1982.
(Translator with Nobuko Tsukui) Kikuo Itaya, *Tengu Child,* Southern Illinois University Press, 1983.
(Translator with John R. Maier) *Gilgamesh: A Translation,* Knopf, 1984.
Stillness and Shadows, edited by Nicholas Delbanco, Knopf, 1986.

Also author of *The Temptation Game* (radio play), 1980. Contributor of short stories to *Southern Review, Quarterly Review of Literature,* and *Perspective*; of poetry to *Kenyon Review, Hudson Review,* and other literary quarterlies; and of articles to *Esquire, Saturday Evening Post,* and other magazines. Founder and editor, *MSS* (a literary magazine).

MEDIA ADAPTATIONS: An animated film version of *Grendel* called *Grendel, Grendel, Grendel* was produced by Victorian Film Corporation in Australia in 1981.

SIDELIGHTS: John Champlin Gardner—not to be confused with the John Edmund Gardner who writes satiric mystery novels or John L. Gardner who was once the head of the Department of Health, Education and Welfare—was a philosophical novelist, a medievalist well versed in the classics, an educator, and an opinionated critic. Described by *Village Voice* contributor Elizabeth Stone as "Evel Knievel at the typewriter," Gardner stood for conservation of values from the past yet maintained a lifelong love-hate relationship with "the rules." Though he championed the moral function of literature, his long hair, leather jacket, and motorcycle classed him with nonconformists. The typical conflict in his work pits individual freedom against institutions that dominate by means of cultural "myths." In novels and stories, Paul Gray of *Time* summarizes, "Gardner sets conflicting metaphysics whirling, then records the patterns thrown out by their lines of force. One situation consistently recurs,. . . an inherited past must defend itself against a plotless future."

Gardner's novels provoked a wide range of critical responses, and, unlike many "academic" fictions, were appreciated by a large audience. Three of his novels were bestsellers. "Very few writers, of any age, are alchemist enough to capture the respect of the intellectual community *and* the imagination of others who lately prefer [Jacqueline] Susann and [Judith] Krantz. Based on critical acclaim, and sales volume, it would seem that this man accomplished both," Craig Riley wrote in *Best Sellers.* Carol A. MacCurdy reported in *Dictionary of Literary Biography Yearbook, 1982,* "Many critics consider *Grendel* (1971) a modern classic, *The Sunlight Dialogues* an epic of the 1970s, and *October Light* [which won the National Book Critics Circle Award for fiction in 1976] a dazzling piece of Americana."

Gardner's notes on *Morte D'Arthur, Sir Gawain and the Green Knight,* and the Gawain poet have helped younger readers to appreciate these classics. His books for children also draw from his knowledge of medieval literature. They are fairy tales retold with original twists, "hip" tales in which familiar characters speak in today's cliches, or where unlikely contemporary characters are revived by the magic of the past. For example, in *Dragon, Dragon and Other Tales,* losers win and heroes lose. "Kings prove powerless, young girls mighty. The miller wins the princess, but she proves to be a witch. Tables are turned this way and that, with consequences that are hilarious and wonderful," Jonathan Yardley related in the *New York Times Book Review.* Like most of Gardner's fairy tales, *In the Suicide Mountains*—the story of three outcasts who find happiness after hearing some old folktales—is for adults as well.

Gardner always worked on several book projects at a time and did not publish his novels in the order that they were finished. Gardner's first published novel, *The Resurrection,* traces a philosophy professor's thoughts after he learns his life will be shortened by leukemia. David Cowart observed in *Dictionary of Literary Biography,* "The book asks the question Gardner would ask in every succeeding novel: how can existential man—under sentence of death—live in such a way as to foster life-affirming values, regardless of how ultimately provisional they may prove?" *The Resurrection* introduces features that recur in later books: an embedded second narrative, usually a "borrowed" text; a facility with fictional techniques; and an emotional impact Cowart describes as "harrowing."

Gardner's second published novel, *The Wreckage of Agathon,* proved his skill as an antiquarian, as a writer who could bring forward materials from ancient history and weave them into "a novel transcending history and effectively embracing all of it, a philosophical drama that accurately describes the wreckage of the 20th century as well as of Agathon, and a highly original work of imagination," wrote Christopher Lehmann-Haupt of the *New York Times.* Built of mostly dialogue, it exposed Gardner's "manic glee in disputation," or "delight in forensic and rhetorical flashiness for its own sake," Cowart observed. Its themes include the relation between individuals and the social orders they encounter. *The Wreckage of Agathon* "delineates the mental motion of the individual as sacred, whether he's a seer or not. . . and it exuberantly calls into question society's categorical insistances—the things brought into being at our own expense to protect us against ourselves, other people, and, putatively, other societies," Paul West wrote in the *New York Times Book Review.*

The Sunlight Dialogues also grapples with this theme. In a *Washington Post Book World* review, Geoffrey Wolff called *The Sunlight Dialogues* "an extended meditation on the trench warfare between freedom and order." The Sunlight Man—a policeman-turned-outlaw embittered by the loss of his family—and Police

Chief Fred Clumly, obsessed with law and order, duel to the death in this novel. Emerging in the conflict between them is Gardner's examination of how these two forces impinge on art. Wolff commented, "While all men wish for both—freedom and order—the conflict between them is dramatized by every decision that an artist makes. The artist will do what he will. . . . No: the artist does what he must, recognizes the limits, agrees to our rules so that we can play too. No;. . . it's *his* cosmos. And so it goes."

Grendel retells the *Beowulf* tale from the monster's point of view. This new tack on the sea of the familiar hero myth allowed Gardner to fathom new insights into the conflict between order and chaos. In the *New York Times,* Richard Locke explained how the uncivil behavior of "civilized" man contributed to Grendel's murderous career: "Though twice he attempts to shed his monsterhood, become human, join these other verbal creatures,. . . he's misunderstood on both occasions, and the rat-like humans attack him in fear. So, racked with resentment, pride and vengeful nihilism, outraged by mankind's perversity (for the noble values of the poet's songs are betrayed in a trice by the beery warlords), Grendel commences his cynical war." Though confirmed in cynicism, the monster remains haunted by the words of The Shaper, the poet who revives inspiration and hope in the hearts of his listeners. In this way, Gardner demonstrated the power of art and its role in Western culture.

Nickel Mountain: A Pastoral Novel explored again the complex relationship between order and chaos, particularly as they relate to human responsibility for events in a world that seems to give random accident free play. Narrator Henry Soames, proprietor of an all-night diner, has a ringside seat to the "horror of the random," to cite Cowart, in the lives of his patrons. Slow-moving and dominated by routine, the pastoral life around the diner is interrupted by a series of fatal accidents, including auto wrecks and house fires. Touching Henry more closely is the man who fell to his death on the stairs while recoiling from Henry's shout. Debates ensue about limits to the assignment of blame. Some of Gardner's characters feel that the assignment of guilt, though painful, is preferable to seeing themselves as victims of mere chance. As *London Magazine* contributor Herbert Lomas put it, recognitions of personal failure or weakness are "what lead you to love, brotherhood and God. It's through weakness and failure that you find warmth,. . . see your need for mercy and forgiveness, and thus everyone's, and feel the beginnings of sacramental consciousness." "Here, as in his other fiction," wrote Michael Wood in the *New York Review of Books,* "Gardner shows a marvelous gift for making *stories* ask balanced, intricate questions, for getting his complex questions into tight stories."

Henry's bout with guilt in *Nickel Mountain* stemmed from a personal tragedy Gardner suffered early in his life. The eleven-year-old Gardner was at the wheel of a tractor that ran over and killed his seven-year-old brother David. Though it was an accident, he believed he could have prevented it. Daily flashbacks to the accident troubled him until he had written the story "Redemption" in 1979, a story based on his memory of the accident. Because writing the story demanded concentration on the scene in order to take narrative control of it, his terror was diffused. But the question of human responsibility versus chance continued to surface in many of Gardner's novels and stories, suggesting that this question had become, for him, a habit of mind.

What was an internal conflict in *Nickel Mountain* became open debate in Gardner's next bestseller. *October Light* pits American conservativism against liberalism embodied in a seventy-year-old Vermont farmer and his eighty-year-old feminist sister. In a characteristic rage about declining morals, James shoots Sally's television set and locks her into an upstairs room. They shout their arguments through the closed door. Sally finds a store of apples in the attic and parts of a "trashy" book about marijuana smugglers, *The Smugglers of Lost Soul's Rock,* and refuses to come out, even after her niece unlocks the door. She sees correspondences between the book's plot and her conflict with James. More vulnerable to his intimidating anger is James's son Richard, who commits suicide. Gardner exposed the regrettable stubbornness of both sides of their conflict and at the same time implied the paucity of absurdist literature in the "trashy" parody of postmodern literature Sally reads.

By the novel's end, James revises his opinions to accommodate a wider range of sensibility. "In *October Light,* then," reasoned Cowart, "we have a rustic world where the same horrors obtain as in the black-comic, nihilistic, 'smart-mouth satirical' novels typified by *Smugglers,* but Gardner convinces us that James Page can, at the age of seventy-two, come to self-knowledge—and that the thawing of this man's frozen heart holds much promise for all people who, bound in spiritual winter, have ever despaired of the spring."

While writing *Mickelsson's Ghosts,* Gardner deliberately tried to make the novel radically different from his prior works. The result, by comparison, said Curt Suplee of the *Washington Post,* "is a highbrow potboiler. . . . And it takes a wide-bodied and fast-moving narrative to carry all Gardner's themes, aiming them at the totalitarian threats in modern culture (metaphorically embedded in the Mormons and tax men) and a grand theological synthesis." Gardner explained to Suplee, "The two sort of big ghosts in the thing are Nietzsche and Luther: Luther's saying none of your works mean anything; and Nietzsche's saying works are everything. And if you get those two things together, you have courtly love. The lover does the most that he can possibly do, and then the grace of the lady saves him."

The title character, a philosophy professor, is troubled with a proliferation of "ghosts." The farm on which he has taken refuge from the world is haunted by apparitions of its previous owners, including the founder of Mormonism, Joseph Smith, and the still-living Hell's Angel who sold him the farm. Harassed by the Internal Revenue Service and the Sons of Dan (a fictional group of fanatic assassins), Mickelsson is haunted by his own crimes. After a teen he sleeps with gets pregnant, he robs an elderly man, hoping to pay the girl not to have an abortion. During the robbery, the man dies of a heart attack. Should Mickelsson, or should he not, think of himself as the murderer of the elderly miser? This and other questions of ethics—including how to assess the worth of individual human lives, Jack Miles noted in the *Los Angeles Times Book Review*—are the center of "this huge and ambitious book." Woiwode suggests that "its grappling hook at your heart . . . is its questioning of our premises of what is real, or what 'reality' is; and in its brave examination of this, and of borderline states of supposed health, it becomes the kind of book that can alter one's way of looking at life."

In addition to these novels, Gardner wrote a number of thought-provoking works on the purpose and craft of fiction. His criticism was hailed, as were his novels, as "disturbing." *On Moral Fiction,* written in part before his novels were published, contained many blunt statements that negatively assessed the works of other major novelists. Some of his statements contradicted others, such that his position was at times overstated, understated, or unclear. Some took these judgments as insults; and some critics, picking up the gauntlet, evaluated Gardner's subsequent works from a fighting stance. Yet others forgave the book's faults because they agreed with Gardner about the essentially humane quality of great literature.

On Becoming a Novelist expressed Gardner's many thoughts about his vocation and outlined what it takes to be a professional novelist. Most important, he claimed, are "drive"—an unyielding persistence to write and publish; and faith—confidence in one's own abilities, belief in one's eventual success. The book restated his moral aesthetic. *Los Angeles Times Book Review* contributor Richard Rodriguez was struck by Gardner's passionate rejection of fictions that substitute "inconclusiveness," "pointlessly subtle games," or obsessive "puzzle-making" for essential storytelling. *The Art of Fiction: Notes on Craft for Young Writers* "originated as the so-called 'Black Book,' an underground text passed from hand to hand in university creative-writing departments," Stuart Schoffman noted in the *Los Angeles Times Book Review,* citing Gardner's comment from its preface that "it is the most helpful book of its kind." John L'Heureux remarked in the *New York Times Book Review* that "Gardner was famous for his generosity to young writers, and *The Art of Fiction* is his posthumous gift to them."

Twelve years after his tragic death in a motorcycle accident, a volume of Gardner's literary reviews and essays appeared as *On Writers and Writing.* The collection includes Gardner's critical response to the fiction of John Steinbeck, William Styron, John Cheever, Walker Percy, and Bernard Malamud, among others, as well as an autobiographical essay and a posthumously discovered plan for *The Sunlight Dialogues.* According to William Hutchings in *World Literature Today,* "Gardner's essays are remarkable for his astringent intelligence, his pugnaciousness, his lucid style, and his relentless pontifications about The True Nature of Art and the 'great persons' who create it." Commenting on Gardner's extreme "seriousness" and daunting standards, *New York Times Book Review* contributor Brooke Allen wrote, "what Gardner always sought was great art, something to place alongside Melville and Tolstoy, the literary yardsticks against which he continually measured lesser writers. Needless to say, he was usually disappointed, therefore unnecessarily harsh in his judgements."

BIOGRAPHICAL/CRITICAL SOURCES:

BOOKS

Bellamy, Joe David, editor, *The New Fiction: Interviews with Innovative American Writers,* University of Illinois Press, 1974, pp. 169-93.

Burns, Alan and Charles Sugnet, *The Imagination on Trial: British and American Writers Discuss Their Working Methods,* Allison & Busby, 1981.

Contemporary Literary Criticism, Gale (Detroit), Volume 2, 1974; Volume 3, 1975; Volume 5, 1976; Volume 7, 1977; Volume 8, 1978; Volume 10, 1979; Volume 18, 1981; Volume 28, 1984; Volume 34, 1985.

Cowart, David, *Arches and Light: The Fiction of John Gardner,* Southern Illinois University Press, 1983.

Dictionary of Literary Biography, Volume 2: *American Novelists since World War II,* Gale, 1978.

Dictionary of Literary Biography Yearbook, 1982, Gale, 1983.

Ekelund, Bo G., *In the Pathless Forest: John Gardner's Literary Project,* Coronet Books, 1994.

Henderson, Jeff, editor, *Thor's Hammer: Essays on John Gardner,* University of Central Arkansas Press, 1985.

Howell, John M., *John Gardner: A Bibliographical Profile,* Southern Illinois University Press, 1980.

Howell, John M., *Understanding John Gardner,* University of South Carolina Press, 1993.

Morace, Robert A., *John Gardner: An Annotated Secondary Bibliography,* Garland Publishing, 1984.

Morace, Robert A. and Kathryn Van Spanckeren, editors, *John Gardner: Critical Perspectives,* Southern Illinois University Press, 1982.

Nutter, Ronald Grant, *A Dream of Peace: Art and Death in the Fiction of John Gardner,* Peter Lang, 1997.

Plimpton, George, editor, *Writers at Work: The Paris Review Interviews,* Viking, 1981.

Short Story Criticism, Gale, Volume 7, 1991.

Winther, Per, *The Art of John Gardner: Instruction and Exploration,* State University of New York Press, 1992.

PERIODICALS

Atlantic, May, 1977, pp. 43-47; January, 1984.

Best Sellers, April, 1984.

Chicago Review, spring, 1978, pp. 73-87.

Chicago Tribune, March 16, 1980; April 13, 1980.

Chicago Tribune Book World, May 24, 1981; April 13, 1980; June 13, 1982; April 1, 1984.

Choice, October, 1994, p. 280.

Contemporary Literature, autumn, 1979, pp. 509-12.

Critique, No. 2, 1977, pp. 86-108.

Esquire, January, 1971; June, 1982.

Los Angeles Times Book Review, May 30, 1982; December 5, 1982; June 12, 1983; May 30, 1982; February 12, 1984.

Midwest Quarterly, summer, 1979, pp. 405-15.

Mosaic, fall, 1975, pp. 19-31.

National Review, November 23, 1973.

New Republic, February 5, 1977; March 10, 1979, pp. 25, 28-33.

Newsweek, December 24, 1973; April 11, 1977.

New York Review of Books, March 21, 1974; June 24, 1982.

New York Times, September 4, 1970; November 14, 1976; December 26, 1976; January 2, 1977.

New York Times Book Review, November 16, 1975; March 23, 1980; May 17, 1981; May 31, 1981; June 20, 1982; February 26, 1984; July 20, 1986; March 27, 1994, p. 26.

New York Times Magazine, July 8, 1979, pp. 13-15, 34, 36-39.

Paris Review, spring, 1979, pp. 36-74.

Prairie Schooner, winter, 1980-81, pp. 70-93.

Sewanee Review, summer, 1977, pp. 520-31.

Time, January 1, 1973; December 30, 1974; December 20, 1976.

Times Literary Supplement, October 23, 1981; October 22, 1982; July 29, 1983.

Village Voice, December 27, 1976.

Washington Post, July 25, 1982; March 1, 1983.

Washington Post Book World, December 24, 1972; March 23, 1980; May 3, 1981; May 14, 1982.

World Literature Today, autumn, 1994, p. 819.

*　　*　　*

GARDNER, Miriam
See BRADLEY, Marion Zimmer

GARDONS, S. S.
See SNODGRASS, W(illiam) D(e Witt)

*   *   *

GARNER, Alan 1934-

PERSONAL: Born October 17, 1934, in Cheshire, England; son of Colin and Marjorie Garner; married first wife, Ann Cook, in 1956; married Griselda Greaves, 1972; children: (first marriage) Adam, Ellen, Katharine; (second marriage) Joseph, Elizabeth. *Education:* Attended Magdalen College, Oxford.

ADDRESSES: Home—Blackden, Holmes Chapel, Cheshire CW4 8BY, England.

CAREER: Author; writer and director of documentary films. *Military service:* British Army; became second lieutenant.

MEMBER: Portico Library Club (Manchester).

AWARDS, HONORS: Carnegie Medal, 1967, and Guardian Award, 1968, both for *The Owl Service;* Lewis Carroll Shelf Award, 1970, for *The Weirdstone of Brisingamen;* first prize, Chicago International Film Festival, for *Images,* 1981; Mother Goose Award for *A Bag of Moonshine,* 1987; Phoenix Award, Children's Book Association, 1996, for *The Stone Book.*

WRITINGS:

The Weirdstone of Brisingamen: A Tale of Alderley, Collins, 1960, published as *The Weirdstone: A Tale of Alderley,* F. Watts (New York City), 1961, revised edition, Walck, 1969.
The Moon of Gomrath, Walck, 1963.
Elidor, Walck, 1965.
Holly from the Bongs, Collins (London), 1966.
The Owl Service, Walck, 1967.
The Old Man of Mow, illustrated by Roger Hill, Doubleday (New York City), 1967.
(Editor) *A Cavalcade of Goblins,* illustrated by Krystyna Turska, Walck, 1969 (published in England as *The Hamish Hamilton Book of Goblins,* Hamish Hamilton, 1969).
Red Shift (also see below), Macmillan, 1973.
The Breadhorse, Collins, 1975.
The Guizer, Greenwillow Books (New York City), 1976.
The Stone Book, Collins, 1976, Collins & World, 1978.
Tom Fobble's Day, Collins, 1977, Collins & World, 1979.
Granny Reardun, Collins, 1977, Collins & World, 1979.
The Aimer Gate, Collins, 1978, Collins & World, 1979.
The Golden Brothers, Collins, 1979.
The Girl of the Golden Gate, Collins, 1979.
The Golden Heads of the Well, Collins, 1979.
The Princess and the Golden Mane, Collins, 1979.
Alan Garner's Fairytales of Gold, Philomel Books, 1980.
The Lad of the Gad, Collins, 1980, Philomel Books, 1981.
Alan Garner's Book of British Fairytales, Collins, 1984.
A Bag of Moonshine (folk stories), Delacorte (New York City), 1986.
The Stone Book Quartet, Dell (New York City), 1988.
(Reteller) *Jack and the Beanstalk,* illustrated by Julek Heller, Doubleday, 1992.
Once upon a Time, Though It Wasn't in Your Time, and It Wasn't in My Time, and It Wasn't in Anybody Else's Time. . . . , Dorling Kindersley, 1993.
The Alan Garner Omnibus (contains "Elidor," "The Weirdstone of Brisingamen," and "The Moon of Gomrath"), Lions, 1994.

(Reteller) *Little Red Hen,* illustrated by Norman Messenger, D.K. Publishers, 1996.
Strandloper, Harvill Press (London), 1996.
Lord Flame (play), Harvill Press, 1996.
Pentecost (play), Harvill Press, 1997.
The Voice that Thunders, Harvill Press, 1997.
The Well of the Wind (fairy tale), illustrated by Hervae Blondon, DK Publishing, 1998.

Also author of play *Holly from the Bongs,* 1965, and of dance drama *The Green Mist,* 1970; author of libretti for *The Bellybag* (music by Richard Morris), 1971, and *Potter Thompson* (music by Gordon Crosse), 1972; author of plays *Lamaload,* 1978, *Lurga Lom,* 1980, *To Kill a King,* 1980, *Sally Water,* 1982, and *The Keeper,* 1983; author of screenplays for documentary films *Places and Things,* 1978, and *Images,* 1981, and for feature film *Strandloper,* 1992; author of film adaptation of *Red Shift,* 1978. Member of International Editorial Board, Detskaya Literatura Publishers (Moscow), 1991–.

SIDELIGHTS: Considered among the most important children's authors since 1960, Alan Garner is noted for his use of folk traditions and the multiple layers of meaning contained in his stories. His early books, including *The Weirdstone of Brisingamen: A Tale of Alderley, The Moon of Gomrath,* and *Elidor* are reminiscent of the fantasy popularized by J. R. R. Tolkien. With such later works as *The Owl Service* and *The Stone Book Quartet,* however, Garner's interest in fantasy has become more closely enmeshed with the realistic English landscape of his childhood.

Born into a family of craftsmen who have lived for several generations near Alderley Edge in Cheshire, England, Garner proved unsuited for pursuing the way of life that had been in his family for many years. Following an education at Manchester Grammar School, Garner attended Magdalen College, Oxford, where he read classics. Returning to Cheshire without completing his degree, Garner began working on his first work of fiction, *The Weirdstone of Brisingamen.* His development as a writer was closely related to his embrace of his Cheshire homeland and dialect, reflecting what Roderick McGillis of *Dictionary of Literary Biography* calls his "Romantic quest to rediscover the mother tongue."

Though Garner was once considered a "children's" author, the increasing complexity of his stories has led many reviewers to reevaluate their original assessment of his work. For many, the turning point in his status was the publication of *The Owl Service,* an eerie tale of supernatural forces that interweaves ancient symbolism from Welsh folklore with a modern plot and original details. A story "remarkable not only for its sustained and evocative atmosphere, but for its implications," *The Owl Service* is "a drama of young people confronted with the challenge of a moral choice; at the same time it reveals, like diminishing reflections in a mirror, the eternal recurrence of the dilemma with each generation," according to the *Children's Book World.* A critic from the *Christian Science Monitor* describes it as "a daring juxtaposition of legend from the *Mabinogion,* and the complex relationship of two lads and a girl [in which] old loves and hates are . . . reenacted. Mr. Garner sets his tale in a Welsh valley and touches with pity and terror the minds of the reader who will let himself feel its atmosphere. This is not a book 'for children'; its subtle truth is for anyone who will reach for it." A writer for the *Times Literary Supplement* echoes this sentiment, noting that with *The Owl Service* "Alan Garner has moved away from the world of children's books and has emerged as a writer unconfined by reference to age-groups; a writer whose imaginative vein is rich enough to reward his readers on several different levels."

One book so complex that some critics find it almost impenetrable is *Red Shift*, a novel comprised of three different stories with separate sets of characters who are linked only by a Bronze Age axe-head, which functions as a talisman, and a rural setting in Cheshire. Composed almost wholly of dialogue, *Red Shift* jump-cuts from the days of the Roman conquest to the seventeenth century to the present time. Writing in *Horn Book*, Aidan Chambers compares the book to "a decorated prism which turns to show—incident by incident—first one face, then another. In the last section, the prism spins so fast that the three faces merge into one color, one time, one place, one set of people, one meaning." Michael Benton believes that "*Red Shift* expresses the significance of place and the insignificance of time. . . . Certainly in style and structure the book is uncompromising: the familiar literary surface of the conventional novel is stripped away and one is constantly picking up hints, catching at clues, making associations and allowing the chiselled quality of the writing to suggest new mental landscapes."

Derived from the folklore of the British Isles, Garner's *A Bag of Moonshine* presents twenty-two short stories that some have described as fables of human cunning and folly. Critics have praised Garner's use of the folk tradition, including what E. F. Bleiler of *Washington Post Book World* terms "fascinating rustic and archaic turns of phrase." Neil Philip of *Times Educational Supplement* concurs, observing that "Garner has taken a number of lesser-known English and Welsh stories and, as it were, set them to music, establishing in each text a tune or cadence based on local speech patterns." Also a unique retelling of folk tales for children, Garner's *Once upon a Time* presents "The Fox, the Hare, and the Cock," "The Girl and the Geese"—both Russian tales—and "Battibeth," which Joanne Schott of *Quill & Quire* describes as "a surrealistic and dreamlike story of a girl's search for her mother's missing knife." *Alan Garner's Fairytales of Gold* employs the author's successful technique of drawing upon the plots and themes of traditional stories and then embellishing this material with a highly original use of language and detail. The collection presents four English tales: "The Golden Brothers," "The Girl of the Golden Gate," "The Three Golden Heads of the Well," and "The Princess and the Golden Mane." Reviewers have observed that Garner's retellings maintain the general moral perspective, along with many of the thematic tenets of the original stories: the magic power of words, the use of incantations, the motif of fantastic quests, and the morality of kindness rewarded and evil punished. "Garner's interest is in reanimating a tradition of British stories; he laments the passing of traditional fairy tales that were meant for the whole family, not just the children," comments Roderick McGillis in *Dictionary of Literary Biography*. "The fairy tales he re-creates are a link to the British past, and, as he writes, 'a healthy future grows from its past'."

With *The Stone Book*, Garner presents a "quartet" of interrelated stories depicting four generations of a working-class family in Cheshire, England, spanning the mid-nineteenth-century through the World War II era. Set in Victorian England, the first volume of the series, *The Stone Book*, tells the story of a young girl who begins to learn the significance of history, cultural meaning, and time when her father takes her to a remote cave and tells her to "read" the ancient paintings on the wall. "[T]he ultimate idea [of the book] shines through with an elemental wisdom," asserts Paul Heins of *Horn Book*, "the continuity of life, the perception of a collective past." *Granny Reardun*, the second volume of the

series, treats the theme of family and history through another angle, depicting a boy who decides to abandon his grandfather's stone masonry trade in favor of apprenticeship to a blacksmith. The saga continues with the final stories of the quartet, *The Aimer Gate*, in which the destructive impact of World War I is addressed, followed by *Tom Fobble's Day*, a coming-of-age story in which a young boy acquires the courage and confidence to sled down one of the highest hills he can find. Although reviewers occasionally question the accessibility of Garner's historical setting and English idiom to contemporary American children, *The Stone Book* has consistently received high praise for the multi-layered quality of its treatment of the theme of family history. Offering a laudatory assessment of the series in *Times Literary Supplement*, Margaret Meek comments: "In the Stone Book Quartet we have moved away from a kind of nineteenth-century writing which is still found in books for twentieth-century children. This is a book of our day, for all its Victorian and Edwardian settings."

Garner continued to display his interest in folktales with 1993's *Once Upon a Time, though It Wasn't in Your Time, and It Wasn't in My Time, and It Wasn't in Anybody Else's Time*, in which he retells three uncommon but traditional-sounding stories. The whimsical title prepares the reader for the dreamlike, symbolic stories and the rich, surreal illustrations. Included in the volume, which a critic for *Kirkus Reviews* called "compact and intriguingly mysterious," are "The Fox, the Hare, and the Cock," "The Girl and the Geese," and "Battibeth." The simple stories are based on traditional nursery stories and are "distinguished by a folkloric lilt and [Garner's] own fresh imagery," according to *Kirkus Reviews*. A *Booklist* reviewer also praised *Once Upon a Time*, saying "Garner's elegant text doesn't waste a word."

With *Strandloper*—published in 1996, but in the works for twelve years—Garner returned to adult fiction. *Strandloper* combines elements of realist fiction with the spiritual folkways of Garner's native land, rendering a dense, original, and enigmatic novel. Set in the late eighteenth century, *Strandloper* tells the story of an English villager who is arrested for participating in an ancient pagan fertility ritual and sent to the prison colony of "New Holland," or Australia. There he spends the next thirty years becoming involved with the Aborigines and eventually serving as their spiritual leader. The novel closes with the protagonist's ambivalent return to his much-changed homeland. Paul Binding of *New Statesman & Society* described the novel's central concern as being "with humankind's need for a home and with the traumas of severance." Binding characterized the project as "a venture of great imaginative and intellectual boldness," matched by Garner's "astounding mastery of technique." While a writer for *Kirkus Reviews* found Garner's "crabbed, terse prose . . . often very beautiful," this critic was less convinced of the novel's overall success, citing its extreme obscurity.

The Voice that Thunders, Garner's 1997 collection of lectures and essays, sheds a great deal of light on the strange, dark, and mysterious writings of his long career. The pieces are collected from the course of many years, and includes speculation on Garner's attachment to his home village of Aldedey, Cheshire, and that locale's influence on his work, as well as the influence of Arthurian, Celtic, and Indian myths. He discusses the distinction between children's literature and his, which he says is for everyone, and he includes letters from his child fans. Perhaps most illuminating is Garner's revelation that he lived most of his life as an undiagnosed manic depressive, which may explain the hallucinatory darkness of his novels and his obsession with a narrow range of subjects. After reading *The Voice that Thunders*, particularly its account of Garner's psychological qualities, Nicci Gerard of *New Statesman* reported, "I am struck by how the cold terror of his novels imitates the terror he has lived through."

BIOGRAPHICAL/CRITICAL SOURCES:

BOOKS

British Children's Books in the Twentieth Century, Dutton, 1971.
Contemporary Literary Criticism, Volume 17, Gale (Detroit), 1981.
Dictionary of Literary Biography, Volume 161: *British Children's Writers since 1960, First Series*, Gale, 1996.

PERIODICALS

Booklist, March 1, 1981, p. 963; December 1, 1993.
Books for Keeps, May, 1987, p. 15.
Chicago Tribune Book World, November 10, 1985.
Children's Book World, November 3, 1968.
Children's Literature in Education, March, 1974.
Christian Science Monitor, November 2, 1967.
Globe and Mail (Toronto), April 4, 1987.
Horn Book, October, 1969, p. 531; February, 1970, p. 45; October, 1973; December, 1976, p. 636; April, 1979, p. 192; October, 1979, p. 533.
Kirkus Reviews, December 1, 1993, p. 1523; April 15, 1997.
Library Journal, December 15, 1970, p. 4349.
New Statesman & Society, May 24, 1996, p. 38; August 1, 1997, p. 45.
New York Times Book Review, October 22, 1967, p. 62; October 28, 1973; July 22, 1979.
Observer, October 7, 1979, p. 39.
Quill & Quire, January, 1994, p. 39.
School Library Journal, October, 1976, p. 116; March, 1981, p. 132; March, 1982, p. 157; April, 1987, p. 94; March, 1994, p. 215.
Spectator, April 12, 1975, p. 493.
Times Educational Supplement, December 5, 1986, p. 25.
Times Literary Supplement, May 25, 1967; November 30, 1967; September 28, 1973; March 25, 1977; December 2, 1977; September 29, 1978; November 30, 1984; November 28, 1986, p. 1346, December 5, 1995; May 24, 1996, p. 24.
Village Voice, December 25, 1978.
Washington Post Book World, July 8, 1979; November 10, 1985; November 9, 1986, p. 19; November 8, 1992, p. 11.

*   *   *

GARNETT, David 1892-1981
(Leda Burke)

PERSONAL: Born March 9, 1892, in Brighton, England; died February 17, 1981, in Montocq, France; son of Edward (a literary critic and editor) and Constance (a translator; maiden name, Black) Garnett; married Rachel Alice Marshall, 1921 (died, 1940); married Angelica Vanessa Bell, 1942; children: (first marriage) Richard Duncan, William Tomlin Kasper; (second marriage) Amaryllis Virginia, Henrietta Catherine Vanessa, Frances Olivia, Nerissa Stephen. *Education:* Imperial College of Science and Technology, A.R.C.S., 1913, D.I.C., 1915.

ADDRESSES: Agent—A. P. Watt & Son, 26/28 Bedford Row, London WC1R 4HL, England.

CAREER: Writer, bookseller, and publisher. Operated bookstore in Soho district of London, England, 1920; cofounder of Nonesuch Press, London, 1923-32; literary editor, *New Statesman,* 1932-34; Rupert Hart-Davis Ltd. (publishers), London, director. *Wartime service:* Conscientious objector during World War I; served with a Quaker relief organization in Europe and as a farm laborer; Royal Air Force, 1940; worked in intelligence section and as planning officer and historian.

AWARDS, HONORS: Commander, Order of the British Empire; James Tait Black Memorial Prize and Hawthornden Prize, both 1923, both for *Lady into Fox*; fellow, Imperial College of Science and Technology, 1956.

WRITINGS:

(Translator) Vincent Alfred Gressent, *The Kitchen Garden and Its Management,* Selwyn, Blount, 1919.
(Under pseudonym Leda Burke) *Dope-Darling: A Story of Cocaine,* T. Warner Laurie, 1919.
Lady into Fox (also see below), Chatto & Windus, 1922, Knopf, 1923.
A Man in the Zoo (also see below), Knopf, 1924.
The Sailor's Return, Knopf, 1925.
Go She Must!, Knopf, 1927.
The Old Dovecote and Other Stories, Mathews & Marrot, 1928.
(Translator) Andre Maurois, *A Voyage to the Island of the Articoles,* J. Cape, 1928, Appleton, 1929.
Never Be a Bookseller, Knopf, 1929.
Lady into Fox [and] *A Man in the Zoo*, Chatto & Windus, 1929.
No Love, Knopf, 1929.
The Grasshoppers Come, Brewer, Warren & Putnam, 1931.
A Rabbit in the Air: Notes from a Diary Kept While Learning to Handle an Aeroplane, Brewer, Warren & Putnam, 1932.
A Terrible Day, William Jackson, 1932.
Pocahontas: or, The Nonpareil of Virginia, Harcourt, 1933.
Beany-Eye, Harcourt, 1935.
(Editor) T. E. Lawrence, *The Letters of T. E. Lawrence,* J. Cape, 1938, Doubleday, Doran, 1939, published as *Selected Letters of T. E. Lawrence,* Hyperion Press, 1979.
War in the Air: September, 1939-May, 1941, Doubleday, 1941.
(Editor) Henry James, *Fourteen Stories,* Hart-Davis, 1946.
(Editor) *The Novels of Thomas Love Peacock,* Hart-Davis, 1948.
(Editor) *The Essential T. E. Lawrence,* Dutton, 1951.
The Golden Echo (memoirs), Volume I: *The Golden Echo,* Chatto & Windus, 1953, Harcourt, 1954, Volume II: *Flowers of the Forest,* Chatto & Windus, 1955, Harcourt, 1956, Volume III: *The Familiar Faces,* Chatto & Windus, 1962, Harcourt, 1963.
Aspects of Love, Harcourt, 1955.
A Shot in the Dark, Little, Brown, 1958.
A Net for Venus, Longmans, Green, 1959.
(Translator) Lawrence, *338171 T. E. (Lawrence of Arabia),* Dutton, 1963.
Two by Two: A Story of a Survival, Longmans, Green, 1963, Atheneum, 1964.
Ulterior Motives, Longmans, Green, 1966, Harcourt, 1967.
An Old Master and Other Stories, Yamaguchi Shoten (Tokyo), 1967.
(Editor) *The White/Garnett Letters,* Viking, 1968.
(Editor and author of introduction) Dora de Houghton Carrington, *Carrington: Letters and Extracts from Her Diaries,* J. Cape, 1970, Holt, 1971.
First "Hippy" Revolution, San Marcos Press, 1970.
A Clean Slate, Hamish Hamilton, 1971.

The Sons of the Falcon, Macmillan, 1972.

Plough over the Bones, Macmillan, 1973.

Purl and Plain and Other Stories, Macmillan, 1973.

The Master Cat: The True and Unexpurgated Story of Puss in Boots, Macmillan, 1974.

Up She Rises, St. Martin's, 1977.

Great Friends: Portraits of Seventeen Writers, Macmillan (London), 1979, Atheneum, 1980.

(Editor with Michael Moorcock) *New Worlds One,* VGSF (London), 1991.

(Editor with Michael Moorcock) *New Worlds Two,* VGSF, 1992.

(Selector) *The Essential T.E. Lawrence,* Oxford University Press (New York City), 1992.

Sylvia and David: The Townsend Warner and Garnett Letters, edited by Richard Garnett, Sinclair-Stevenson (London), 1994.

SIDELIGHTS: David Garnett came by his literary career naturally. His grandfather was an author and head of the British Museum reading room. His father, Edward Garnett, was a publisher's reader who discovered and encouraged such authors as Joseph Conrad and D. H. Lawrence. His mother, Constance Garnett, was the first translator into English of Leo Tolstoy, Anton Chekhov, Fedor Mikhailovich Dostoevski, and other Russian authors of the nineteenth century. Advised by his father, according to the London *Times,* to "never try to write, but above all never have anything to do with publishing or the book trade," Garnett nevertheless became a novelist, bookstore owner, and a partner in the publishing firm of Rupert Hart-Davis. His association with the Bloomsbury Group, a circle of British writers that included E. M. Forster, John Maynard Keynes, and Virginia Woolf, and his award-winning novel *Lady into Fox,* brought Garnett to literary prominence.

After taking his degree in botany in 1915, Garnett published his first book, a translation of a gardening manual. Garnett later claimed that his second book, a novel entitled *Dope-Darling: A Story of Cocaine,* was written "deliberately badly," as Roland Dille recounted in the *Dictionary of Literary Biography.* It was published under a pseudonym in 1919. Garnett first attracted critical notice with his third book, *Lady into Fox,* the first written under his own name. The novel about Mrs. Tebrick—a woman who becomes a fox, leaves her husband, and goes to live in the woods—won both the James Tait Black Memorial Prize and the Hawthornden Prize. It brought Garnett "popular acclaim and serious critical attention," Ann S. Johnson wrote in *Contemporary Literature.*

It is Garnett's style in *Lady into Fox* that attracted the most critical praise. Writing in *The Modern Novel in Britain and the United States,* Walter Allen remarked on the book's casual quality. Although the plot is fantastic, Garnett "merely narrates it as a true story," Allen stated, "telling it in a style a little archaic, a little mannered, suggestive of [Daniel] Defoe. . . . A triumph, if you like, of artificiality, it is also a triumph of story-telling." Frank Swinnerton, in his *The Georgian Literary Scene, 1910-1935,* argued that "the demureness of such a book as 'Lady into Fox' . . . is proper to the theme." But Swinnerton also allowed that Garnett "was telling [the] story with a false gravity which amused himself and his friends."

In his next novel, *A Man in the Zoo,* Garnett explored another whimsical situation. The novel concerns two lovers who quarrel during a visit to the city zoo. Enraged by John Cromartie's suggestion that they live together, Josephine Lackett tells John that he is nothing but an animal who deserves to be a zoo exhibit himself. He acts upon her suggestion, having himself displayed in the ape-house as an example of *homo sapiens.* At first ashamed of the scandalous attention this generates, Josephine eventually realizes her love for John and the novel ends with their reunion. By his flamboyant action, John "demonstrates that man in his natural place in the world is unencumbered by the artificialities with which society has surrounded him," Dille explained. The *Saturday Review* critic thought Garnett showed "more than a whimsical point of view and an austere style: he has a perception of the infinite sanity underlying the insane antics of mankind."

In *The Sailor's Return,* Garnett turned to a more realistic situation. William Targett, a sailor who has been to sea for many years, returns to his hometown with his black wife and child to find that the townspeople cannot accept him. An attempt is made to burn down Targett's inn. The couple is forced to remarry at the local church, having originally been married in Africa in a native ceremony the villagers refuse to recognize. Targett is eventually killed in a fight with some men who have insulted his wife. The novel, Johnson maintained, exposes "an intolerable system of racial and sexual caste." Calling it a "tragical rolling ballad," Laura Benet of *Nation* pointed out that in this novel, Garnett displayed his "poetic sense of irony and pity." Noting the brevity of these first three novels, Benet wrote: "Some day, perhaps, instead of these small, compressed prints [Garnett] will give us a powerful and heroic canvas."

No Love, the novel Garnett considered his best work, is judged by Allen to be "fully realized. The prose is as pure and formal as ever, but much more contemporary; one no longer has the impression that the characters are figures in a tapestry; one feels they have their own independent life." The novel is the story of two boys from two very different English families. Benedict's family is tolerant and open-minded, while Simon's family holds Victorian values. Simon grows up and marries a woman he does not love. When she falls in love with Benedict, Benedict gives her up, convinced that it would not be right to take his friend's wife. "The style of this book," the *Boston Transcript* critic noted, "is clear, succinct, direct. It is like a perfectly played fugue heard on a crisp morning."

These early novels show Garnett to reject many of the "conventional values that restrict human feeling," as Dille argued. But, Dille continued, "the judgment he makes of society is balanced by a melancholy that owes less to the losses imposed by the unthinking and the unfeeling than to a regret for death, separation, and the failure of love." After writing *The Grasshoppers Come,* a novel about an attempted long-distance flying record, and *Pocahontas; or, The Nonpareil of Virginia,* an historical novel, Garnett gave up the novel for some twenty years, turning his attention to editing books and writing nonfiction works. Among these items, perhaps the most important is the collection of T. E. Lawrence's letters that Garnett edited. Lawrence, better known as Lawrence of Arabia, was Garnett's close friend.

The three-volume memoirs, *The Golden Echo, Flowers of the Forest,* and *The Familiar Faces,* and the autobiographical *Great Friends: Portraits of Seventeen Writers,* trace the course of Garnett's long life. Because his parents knew many prominent literary figures, and because Garnett himself was a member of the influential Bloomsbury Group, these memoirs furnish many anecdotes and insights concerning the British literary scene over several decades. Nora Sayre wrote in the *New York Times Book Review* that in Garnett's memoirs his contemporaries "are portrayed with such natural ease that these men and women seem as accessible as one's own contemporaries." The memoirs are, Dille wrote, "a portrait of Bloomsbury and one of the best records of literary London between the wars." They are also, Dille concluded, "the self-portrait of a man who writes without malice and is revealed as tolerant, wise, and full of sympathy and affection." The three volumes begin with Garnett's childhood and end with his first wife's death in 1940.

The first volume of the memoirs, *The Golden Echo,* covers the years of Garnett's childhood and recounts some of his early memories of his parents' literary friends. Garnett's mother knew Russian authors and political leaders through her work as a translator. She served as Nikolai Lenin's translator when he visited London at the turn of the century. Garnett's father knew British authors because of his work as a publisher's reader. Their house in the English countryside was a literary gathering place. Such figures as Ford Madox Ford, D. H. Lawrence, and Joseph Conrad were frequent visitors. Garnett remembers that Ford had a propensity for embellishing his stories. Lawrence was judged by the young Garnett as not being "a gentleman." As David Stone stated in the *Spectator,* these memories are "re-created, rather than remembered . . .; we grow up with the book—an exceptional and delightful effect."

Flowers of the Forest, the second volume of memoirs, concerns the period of the First World War, when Garnett joined the Bloomsbury Group. The Bloomsbury Group began about 1906 as a casual meeting of literary friends. The association continued until the 1930s and came to include a number of prominent British writers and artists. The binding philosophy of the group was taken from a passage in George Edward Moore's *Principia Ethica* in which it is argued that the "most valuable things" are "the pleasures of human intercourse and the enjoyment of beautiful objects." The Bloomsbury writers were, Kathleen Nott stated in the *Observer,* "probably the last group . . . able to maintain the illusion of liberal and humane influence, particularly for the artist." Writing in the *Atlantic,* Edward Weeks found Garnett's character drawings of his literary friends to be "delightfully acute. What they wore and where they lived, their likes and dislikes, their impetuosities, political opinions, and love affairs are set down with a dry, scrupulous fidelity." As a volume of reminiscences, Aileen Pippett wrote in the *New York Times, Flowers of the Forest* is "incomparable. . . . Seldom has so much been written about so many with such precision."

The Familiar Faces covers the 1920s and 1930s, a period when Garnett became a bookseller and a partner in the publishing firm of Rupert Hart-Davis. It was through his role as publisher, K. T. Willis wrote in *Library Journal,* that Garnett "knew everyone in England and America who had genius for writing." His portraits of these people are successful, the critic for the *Times Literary Supplement* believed, because "Garnett's main virtues as a writer and surely as a person, derive from his love for his fellows, men and women, whom he is able to describe with the light and shade of real life." The book is "singularly free," J. D. Scott wrote in *Saturday Review,* "from the writer's occupational diseases of malice and self-pity." It also possesses, Scott continued, "a very pleasant, likable quality, like good, friendly conversation." Scott recommended the book "if you want to read a shrewd, urbane, yet feeling account of English literary life seen from its center."

Much of the same period covered in his memoirs is also covered in *Great Friends,* a book containing extended remembrances of seventeen writers Garnett knew during his career. It is, Michael

Dirda wrote in the *Washington Post Book World,* "an anecdotal, sentimental collection, and one sure to please anyone who enjoys literary gossip." One of these remembrances concerns a visit by Joseph Conrad to the Garnett residence when Garnett was five years old. To amuse the boy, Conrad fashioned a make-believe sailboat from a large laundry basket and a bedsheet, and he and Garnett "sailed" about the lawn. Garnett also remembers how Virginia Woolf entertained his own children by getting on her hands and knees and chasing them about the house. "*Great Friends,*" wrote Jonathan Raban in the *New Statesman,* "is a triumph of informal, unvarnished portraiture."

BIOGRAPHICAL/CRITICAL SOURCES:

BOOKS

Allen, Walter, *The Modern Novel in Britain and the United States,* Dutton, 1964.
Contemporary Literary Criticism, Volume 3, Gale (Detroit), 1975.
Dictionary of Literary Biography, Volume 34: *British Novelists, 1890-1929: Traditionalists,* Gale, 1985.
Edel, Leon, *Bloomsbury: A House of Lions,* Lippincott, 1979.
Garnett, Richard, editor, *Sylvia and David: The Townsend Warner and Garnett Letters,* Sinclair-Stevenson, 1994.
Heilburn, Carolyn, *The Garnett Family,* Macmillan, 1961.
Moore, George Edward, *Principia Ethica,* Cambridge University Press, 1903.
Swinnerton, Frank, *The Georgian Literary Scene, 1910-1935,* Hutchinson, revised edition, 1969.

PERIODICALS

Atlantic, October, 1956.
Books and Bookmen, June, 1973.
Book Week, March 1, 1964; July 2, 1967.
Boston Transcript, July 13, 1929.
Commonweal, October 26, 1956; June 19, 1959.
Contemporary Literature, spring, 1973.
International Book Review, September, 1923.
Library Journal, March 1, 1963.
Times (London), February 19, 1981.
Los Angeles Times, May 25, 1980.
Nation, May 23, 1923; November 4, 1925; March 3, 1956.
New Republic, December 30, 1925; May 8, 1971.
New Statesman, April 26, 1924; February 26, 1927; July 21, 1968; March 22, 1977; June 15, 1979.
New Yorker, February 4, 1956.
New York Herald Tribune Book Review, June 2, 1929; May 30, 1954; January 29, 1956.
New York Times, April 15, 1923; June 15, 1924; September 2, 1956; April 10, 1980.
New York Times Book Review, April 27, 1980.
New York World, May 6, 1923; October 4, 1925.
Observer, June 24, 1979.
Saturday Review, July 17, 1954; March 2, 1963; February 8, 1964.
Saturday Review of Literature, May 10, 1924; September 19, 1925; October 17, 1925; January 29, 1927; November 19, 1935.
Spectator, November 25, 1922; September 26, 1925; January 29, 1927; October 11, 1935; December 25, 1953; June 21, 1968.
Time, May 23, 1954; September 3, 1956.
Times Literary Supplement, September 17, 1925; January 20, 1927; May 8, 1931; November 21, 1958; October 26, 1962; December 8, 1966; June 27, 1968.
Washington Post Book World, May 4, 1980.

GARRISON, Frederick
See SINCLAIR, Upton (Beall)

*   *   *

GASS, William H(oward) 1924-

PERSONAL: Born July 30, 1924, in Fargo, ND; son of William Bernard and Claire (Sorensen) Gass; married Mary Patricia O'Kelly, June 17, 1952; married Mary Alice Henderson, September 13, 1969; children: (first marriage) Richard G., Robert W., Susan H.; (second marriage) Elizabeth, Catherine. *Education:* Kenyon College, A.B., 1947; Cornell University, Ph.D., 1954.

ADDRESSES: Home—6304 Westminster Pl., St. Louis, MO. 63130. *Office*—Washington University Campus, Box 1071, 1 Brookings Dr., St. Louis, MO. 63130. *Agent*—Lynn Nesbit, International Creative Management, 40 West 57th St., New York, NY 10019.

CAREER: College of Wooster, Wooster, OH, instructor in philosophy, 1950-54; Purdue University, Lafayette, IN, assistant professor, 1954-60, associate professor, 1960-66, professor of philosophy, 1966-69; Washington University, St. Louis, MO, professor of philosophy, 1969-79, David May Distinguished University Professor in the Humanities, 1979–. Visiting lecturer in English and philosophy, University of Illinois, 1958-59. Member of Rockefeller Commission on the Humanities, 1978-80; member of literature panel, National Endowment for the Arts, 1979-82; director of International Writers Center, 1990–. *Military service:* U.S. Navy, 1943-46; served in China and Japan; became ensign.

MEMBER: PEN, American Philosophical Association, American Academy and Institute of Arts and Letters, National Academy of Arts and Sciences.

AWARDS, HONORS: Longview Foundation Award in fiction, 1959, for "The Triumph of Israbestis Tott"; Rockefeller Foundation grant for fiction, 1965-66; Standard Oil Teaching Award, Purdue University, 1967; Sigma Delta Chi Best Teacher Award, Purdue University, 1967 and 1968; *Chicago Tribune* award for Big-Ten teachers, 1967; Guggenheim fellowship, 1969-70; Alumni Teaching Award, Washington University, 1974; National Institute for Arts and Letters prize for literature, 1975; National Medal of Merit for fiction, 1979; National Book Critics Circle award for criticism, 1986, for *The Habitations of the Word*; PEN/ Faulkner Award for Fiction and American Book Award, both 1996, for *The Tunnel*; National Book Critics Circle criticism award, 1997, for *Finding a Form*; Lifetime Achievement Award, The Lannan Foundation Literary Awards, 1997; Honorary degrees include D.Litt., Kenyon College, 1974 and 1985; D.Litt., George Washington University, 1982; D.Litt., Purdue University, 1985.

WRITINGS:

FICTION

Omensetter's Luck (novel), New American Library, 1966.
First Winter of My Married Life, Lord John Press, 1979.
In the Heart of the Heart of the Country (short stories), Harper, 1968, revised edition, David R. Godine, 1981.
Willie Masters' Lonesome Wife (novella; first published in *TriQuarterly* magazine, 1968), Knopf, 1971.
Culp, Grenfell Press, 1985.
The Tunnel (novel), Ticknor & Fields, 1994.
Cartesian Sonata and Other Novellas, Knopf, 1998.

NONFICTION

Fiction and the Figures of Life, Knopf, 1970.
(Author of introduction) *The Geographical History of America,* Random House, 1973.
On Being Blue, David R. Godine, 1975.
The World within the Word, Knopf, 1978.
The Habitations of the Word: Essays, Simon & Schuster, 1984.
Fifty Literary Pillars: A Temple of Texts: An Exhibition to Inaugurate the International Writers Center, Special Collections, Olin Library, Washington University, 1991.
Finding a Form: Essays, Knopf, 1996.
(Editor with Lorin Cuoco) *The Writer in Politics,* Southern Illinois University Press, 1996.
Art and Science: Investigating Matter, Nazraeli Press, 1996.
Writing in Politics, Southern Illinois University Press, 1996.
(With Johanna Drucker) *The Dual Muse: The Writer as Artist, the Artist as Writer* (essays), John Benjamins, 1997.

OTHER

Gerald Early and William H. Gass Reading from Their Work (sound recording), 1993.

Contributor to numerous periodicals, including *New York Review of Books, New York Times Book Review, New Republic, Nation, TriQuarterly, Salmagundi,* and to philosophical journals. William Gass's manuscripts have been collected in the Washington University Library.

SIDELIGHTS: "Both as an essayist and as a writer of fiction, William Gass has earned the reputation of being one of the most accomplished stylists of his generation," writes Arthur M. Saltzman in *Contemporary Literature.* Gass, who is the David May Distinguished Professor in the Humanities at Washington University, is a principal advocate of the primacy of language in literature and of the self-referential integrity of literary texts. *Times Literary Supplement* reviewer Robert Boyers contends that Gass's fictions—represented by novels, novellas, and short stories—"give heart to the structuralist enterprise," while his essays "may be said to promote the attack on realist aesthetics." Viewed as a whole, Boyers concludes, Gass's work constitutes "the most vigorous anti-realist literary 'programme' we have had in our time." A philosopher by training, Gass "maintains an art-for-art's-sake 'ethic' of infinite aesthetic value, in a structure of the sublime grotesque, as his principle of creativity," to quote *Criticism* contributor Reed B. Merrill.

Although born in Fargo, North Dakota, Gass grew up primarily in Warren, Ohio, as the son of an alcoholic mother and a father who was crippled by arthritis. His schooling at Kenyon College was briefly interrupted by his service as an ensign in the Navy in World War II. He returned to Kenyon to receive a bachelor's degree in philosophy in 1947. According to Larry McGaffery in the *Dictionary of Literary Biography,* "Gass was a voracious reader, his tastes focusing on such literary formalists as James, Faulkner, Joyce and—somewhat later—the three writers who would probably most directly influence his own writing career: Rilke, Gertrude Stein, and Valery." He also attended Cornell as a graduate student, later working with Max Black studying the philosophy of language and the theory of metaphor. He taught philosophy at the College of Wooster and eventually received his Ph.D. from Cornell in 1954. At that point, he began teaching at Purdue University, remaining there for fifteen years. Since then, he has taught a variety of subjects in the philosophy and English departments at Washington University in St. Louis.

His training in the philosophy of language under Black manifests itself in his later work principally in a sense of the musical and intellectual nature of words, sentences, and paragraphs. *Los Angeles Times Book Review* correspondent Jonathan Kirsch observes that Gass "does not merely celebrate language; quite the contrary, he is gifted with the nagging intellectual curiosity that prompts a precocious child to take apart a pocket watch to see what makes it tick." In the *Saturday Review,* Brom Weber comments on the fusion of fiction and philosophy in Gass's view. "Gass holds that philosophy and fiction are alike in that both are fictional constructions, systems based on concepts expressed linguistically, worlds created by minds whose choice of language specifies the entities and conditions comprising those worlds," Weber explains.

Omensetter's Luck, Gass's first novel, was "immediately recognized as a stunning achievement," according to Larry McCaffery in the *Dictionary of Literary Biography.* Published in 1966 after numerous rejections, the book established the unique verbal qualities that would come to be associated with all of Gass's work. The novel resists summarization; set in an Ohio river town, it explores the relationship between Brackett Omensetter, a happily unselfconscious "prelapsarian Adam," to quote McCaffery, and two conscious and thoughtful men, Henry Pimber and Jethro Furber. A *Newsweek* correspondent calls the book "a masterpiece of definition, a complex and intricate creation of level within level, where the theme of Omensetter's luck becomes an intense debate on the nature of life, love, good and evil, and finally, of death. . . . [It] is a story of life and death in the little countries of men's hearts." Richard Gilman offers a different interpretation in *The Confusion of Realms.* The novel, writes Gilman, "is Gass's prose, his style, which is not committed to something beyond itself, not an instrument of an idea. In language of amazing range and resiliency, full of the most exact wit, learning and contemporary emblems, yet also full of lyric urgency and sensuous body, making the most extraordinary juxtapositions, inventing, coining, relaxing at the right moments and charging again when they are over, never settling for the rounded achievement or the finished product, he fashions his tale of the mind, which is the tale of his writing a novel."

Given the difficulty Gass endured trying to find a publisher for *Omensetter's Luck,* he must have been immensely gratified by the critical reception the work received once it found its way into print. Gilman has called it "the most important work of fiction by an American in this literary generation . . . marvelously original, a whole Olympic broad jump beyond what almost any other American has been writing, the first full replenishment of language we have had for a very long time, the first convincing fusion of speculative thought and hard, accurate sensuality that we have had, it is tempting to say, since [Herman] Melville." *Nation* reviewer Shaun O'Connell describes *Omensetter's Luck* as "a difficult, dazzling first novel, important in its stylistic achievement and haunting in its dramatic evocation of the most essential human questions." Not every assessment has been entirely favorable, however. In his *Bright Book of Life: American Novelists & Storytellers from Hemingway to Mailer,* Alfred Kazin writes: "Everything was there in *Omensetter's Luck* to persuade the knowing reader of fiction that here was a great step forward: the verve, the bursting sense of possibility, the gravely significant atmosphere of contradiction, complexity of issue at every step. But it was all in the head, another hypothesis to dazzle the laity with. Gass had a way of dazzling himself under the storm of his style."

Gass followed *Omensetter's Luck* with *In the Heart of the Heart of the Country,* a short story collection "whose highly original form exactly suits its metafictional impulses," to quote McCaffery. McCaffery describes the book as a development of the related themes of isolation and the difficulties of love through the use of experimental literary forms. The characters "control their lives only to the extent that they can organize their thoughts and descriptions into meaningful patterns. Not surprisingly, then, we come to know them mainly as linguistic rather than psychological selves, with their actions usually less significant to our understanding of them than the way they project their inner selves through language." Again critics have praised the volume as a significant contribution to American letters. *Hudson Review* correspondent Robert Martin Adams notes that Gass's techniques, "which are various and imaginative, are always in the service of vision and feeling. Mr. Gass's stories are strict and beautiful pieces of writing without waste or falsity or indulgence." In the *New Republic,* Richard Howard writes: "This is a volume of fictions which tell the truth, and speak even beyond the truth they tell; it is in that outspokenness, the risk of leaving something standing in his mind, that the authority of William Gass persists." *Nation* contributor Philip Stevick concludes that *In the Heart of the Heart of the Country* "finally amounts to an eccentric and ingratiating book, like no other before it, full of grace and wit, displaying a mind in love with language, the human body, and the look of the world."

No Gass work reveals "a mind in love with language" more clearly than *Willie Masters' Lonesome Wife,* the author's 1971 novella. Merrill feels that the piece "stands, along with his fascinating, impressionistic literary criticism, as perhaps [Gass's] best work to date. . . . Structurally, it is clear from the beginning that the subject of this book is the act of creation, and that [the narrator] Babs is William Gass's 'experimental structure' composed of language and imagination. The book *is* literally Babs. The book is a woman from beginning to end. The covers are the extrinsic flesh, the pages are the intrinsic contents of Bab's consciousness—her interior world. It would be difficult to find a better example of the use of structural principles than in Gass's stylistic combination of form and content in his book." In a *Critique* essay, McCaffery calls the novella "a remarkably pure example of metafiction" and adds: "As we watch 'imagination imagining itself imagine,' . . . we are witnessing a work self-consciously create itself out of the materials at hand—words. As the best metafiction does, *Willie Masters' Lonesome Wife* forces us to examine the nature of fiction-making from new perspectives. If Babs (and Gass) have succeeded, our attention has been focused on the act of reading words in a way we probably have not experienced before. The steady concern with the *stuff* of fiction, words, makes Gass's work unique among metafictions which have appeared thus far."

Gass's magnum opus, *The Tunnel,* took him nearly 30 years to write. He began the novel in 1966, publishing portions of it in a number of small, literary journals such as the *Review of Contemporary Fiction* and as "fine press books," according to Steven Moore in the *Review of Contemporary Fiction.* It is the story of William Frederick Kohler, "fat and fifty-something . . . a bitter man, but a literate one," as Moore points out, who has almost completed *his* magnum opus, *Guilt and Innocence in Hitler's Germany.* All that remains is the introduction but he is unable to write it. Instead, he begins to write his own life story which is what the reader of *The Tunnel* ends up reading. In an interview with Tobin Harshaw of the *New York Times Book Review,* Gass said of his protagonist, "Better to have him on the page than inside of you." According to Harshaw, Gass "describes *The Tunnel* as an exploration of 'the inside of history'—the ambiguity and confusion hidden beneath any intellectual attempt at understanding the past."

Not surprisingly, the novel received a great deal of critical acclaim. In 1996, *The Tunnel* received both the PEN/Faulkner Award for Fiction and the American Book Award. Critics continue to laud Gass's amazing gift for language. Notes Moore, "The sheer beauty and bravura of Gass's sentences are overwhelming, breathtaking; the novel is a pharaoh's tomb of linguistic treasures." He continues, warning that readers who "prefer their prose straight are advised to look elsewhere." Michael Dirda in *Washington Post Book World* has a similar comment, calling *The Tunnel* "an extraordinary achievement, a literary treat." He continues, "For 650 pages one of the consummate magicians of English prose pulls rabbits out of sentences and creates shimmering metaphors before your very eyes. He dazzles and amazes. But be warned: He does so on his own terms and some readers may be confused, bored or repulsed."

Reviewers have compared his work to that from a weighty group of writers, among them Dreiser, Dostoevsky, Pynchon, Joyce, and Beckett. James McCourt in *The Yale Review* gushes, "Reading Gass is like reading Thomas Mann: *The Tunnel's* moral seriousness matches *The Magic Mountain's* and *Doctor Faustus's,* but I find Gass the better writer." Critics also placed *The Tunnel* in literary history, noting that students would be reaping additional treasures from its pages for years to come. Concludes Moore, "It will take years of study to excavate fully the artistry of *The Tunnel.*"

Whatever the subject at hand, Gass's essays are invariably artistic creations in and of themselves. *Village Voice* reviewer Sam Tanenhaus notes that each piece "is a performance or foray: [Gass] announces a topic, then descants with impressive erudition and unbuttoned ardor for the surprising phrase. The results often dazzle, and they're unfailingly original, in the root sense of the word—they work back toward some point of origin, generally a point where literature departs from the external world to invent a world of its own." Gass may serve as a spokesman for technical experimentation in fiction and for the value of innovative form, but his nonfiction also "asks us to yield ourselves in loving attentiveness to the being of language, poetic word, and concept, as it unfolds and speaks through us," according to Jeffrey Maitland in *Modern Fiction Studies.* V. S. Pritchett offers a similar view in the *New Yorker.* Writes Pritchett, "Gass is a true essayist, who certainly prefers traveling to arriving, who treats wisdom as a game in which no one wins. . . . His personality, his wit and affectations are part of the game."

Gass's 1996 collection of essays, *Finding a Form,* is loosely grouped around the subject of writing. Essays on the Pulitzer Prize (entitled "Pulitzer: The People's Prize"), the present tense, Ezra Pound, and the state of nature emphasize Gass's "belief in the autonomy of language in fiction," according to Christopher Lehmann-Haupt in the *New York Times.* Lehmann-Haupt finds this particular grouping a mixed bag, noting "Many in this volume are incisively to the point" while in a few "the author labors the obvious . . . and wanders aimlessly straining at gnats." Nevertheless, the collection received the National Book Critics Circle criticism award in 1997.

As Candyce Dostert notes in the *Wilson Library Bulletin,* to read William Gass "is to accompany an extraordinary mind on a quest for perfection, an invigorating voyage for the strong of heart."

Gass is acclaimed equally for his ground-breaking fiction and for the essays that defend the fiction's aesthetics. In the *Dictionary of Literary Biography,* McCaffery states: "Certainly no other writer in America has been able to combine his critical intelligence with a background as a student of both the literary and philosophical aspects of language and to make this synthesis vital." Edmund White arrives at a similar conclusion in the *Washington Post Book World.* Gass's "discursive prose always reminds us that he is an imaginative writer of the highest order," White contends. "Indeed, among contemporary American writers of fiction, he is matched as a stylist only by a very select group." Another *Washington Post Book World* contributor, Paul West, observes that Gass's world "*is* words, *his* way of being. . . . Gass sings the flux, under this or that commercial pretext, and in the end renders what he calls 'the interplay of genres . . . skids of tone and decorum' into cantatas of appreciative excess. A rare gift that yields startling art."

BIOGRAPHICAL/CRITICAL SOURCES:

BOOKS

Bellamy, Joe David, editor, *The New Fiction: Interviews with Innovative American Writers,* University of Illinois Press, 1974.
Contemporary Fiction in America and England, 1950-1970, Gale (Detroit), 1976.
Contemporary Literary Criticism, Gale, Volume 1, 1973; Volume 2, 1974; Volume 8, 1978; Volume 11, 1979; Volume 15, 1980; Volume 39, 1986.
Dictionary of Literary Biography, Volume 2: *American Novelists since World War II,* Gale, 1978.
Gilman, Richard, *The Confusion of Realms,* Random House, 1969.
Holloway, Watson L., *William Gass,* Twayne (Boston), 1990.
Kazin, Alfred, *Bright Book of Life: American Novelists & Storytellers from Hemingway to Mailer,* Little, Brown, 1973.
McCaffery, Lawrence, *Metafictional Muse,* Pittsburgh University Press, 1982.
Vidal, Gore, *Matters of Fact and of Fiction: Essays 1973-1976,* Random House, 1977.

PERIODICALS

Atlantic Monthly, June, 1995, p. 122.
Chicago Review, autumn, 1978.
Contemporary Literature, summer, 1984.
Criticism, fall, 1976.
Critique: Studies in Modern Fiction, December, 1972; summer, 1976.
Delaware Literary Review, Volume 1, 1972.
Esquire, March, 1995, p. 164.
Harper's, May, 1972; October, 1978; February, 1990, p. 38.
Harvard Advocate, winter, 1973.
Hudson Review, spring, 1968.
Iowa Review, winter, 1976.
Kirkus Reviews, June 15, 1996, p. 873.
Los Angeles Times Book Review, March 24, 1985; January 26, 1986.
Modern Fiction Studies, autumn, 1973; winter, 1977-78; winter, 1983.
Nation, May 9, 1966; April 29, 1968; March 22, 1971; January 29, 1977; March 27, 1995, p. 388.
National Review, May 1, 1995, p. 82.
New Republic, May 7, 1966; May 18, 1968; March 20, 1971; October 9, 1976; May 20, 1978; March 11, 1985; March 27, 1995, p. 29.
Newsweek, April 18, 1966; February 15, 1971; March 25, 1985.
New Yorker, January 10, 1977.

New York Review of Books, June 23, 1966; April 11, 1968; December 14, 1972; July 15, 1974; April 17, 1975; May 1, 1975; May 15, 1975; August 5, 1976; October 14, 1976; July 13, 1995, p. 8.
New York Times, October 4, 1976; February 14, 1985; February 23, 1995, p. C17; December 19, 1996, p. B2.
New York Times Book Review, April 17, 1966; April 21, 1968; February 21, 1971; November 14, 1971; November 7, 1976, July 9, 1978; June 3, 1979; March 10, 1985; February 26, 1995, p. 1, 18.
Partisan Review, summer, 1966.
Publishers Weekly, October 3, 1994, p. 13; January 2, 1995, p. 59; June 3, 1996, p. 66.
Review of Contemporary Fiction, spring, 1989.
Salmagundi, fall, 1973.
Saturday Review, March 2, 1968; September 21, 1968; May 29, 1971.
Shenandoah, winter, 1976.
Southern Review, spring, 1967.
Southwest Review, spring, 1979; autumn, 1985.
Time, November 15, 1976.
Times Literary Supplement, May 18, 1967; August 14, 1969; April 22, 1977; November 3, 1978.
Twentieth Century Literature, May, 1976.
Village Voice, June 4, 1985.
Washington Post Book World, July 9, 1978; March 3, 1985; February 2, 1992, p. 12; March 12, 1995, p. 1.
Western Humanities Review, winter, 1978.
Wilson Library Bulletin, May, 1985.
World Literature Today, spring, 1979; winter, 1987.
Yale Review, July, 1995, p. 159.

* * *

GASSET, Jose Ortega y
See ORTEGA y GASSET, Jose

* * *

GATES, Henry Louis, Jr. 1950-

PERSONAL: Born September 16, 1950, in Keyser, WV; son of Henry Louis and Pauline Augusta (Coleman) Gates; married Sharon Lynn Adams (a potter), September 1, 1979; children: Maude Augusta Adams, Elizabeth Helen-Claire. *Education:* Yale University, B.A. (summa cum laude), 1973; Clare College, Cambridge, M.A., 1974, Ph.D., 1979. *Religion:* Episcopalian. *Avocation:* Jazz, pocket billiards.

ADDRESSES: Office—Dept. of English, 302 Allen Bldg., Duke University, Durham, NC, 27706. *Agent*—Carl Brandt, Brandt & Brandt Literary Agents, Inc., 1501 Broadway, New York, NY 10036.

CAREER: Anglican Mission Hospital, Kilimatinde, Tanzania, general anesthetist, 1970-71; John D. Rockefeller gubernatorial campaign, Charleston, WV, director of student affairs, 1971, director of research, 1972; *Time,* London Bureau, London, England, staff correspondent, 1973-75; Yale University, New Haven, CT, lecturer, 1976-79, assistant professor, 1979-84, associate professor of English and Afro-American Studies, 1984-85, director of undergraduate Afro-American studies, 1976-79; Cornell University, Ithaca, NY, professor of English, comparative

literature, and African studies, 1985-88, W. E. B. DuBois Professor of Literature, 1988-90; Duke University, Durham, NC, John Spencer Bassett Professor of English and Literature, 1990–; Harvard University, Cambridge, MA, W. E. B. DuBois Professor of the Humanities, professor of English, chair of Afro-American studies, and director of W. E. B. DuBois Institute for Afro-American Research, 1991–. Virginia Commonwealth, visiting professor, 1987. Created the television series *The Image of the Black in the Western Imagination,* Public Broadcasting Service (PBS), 1982.

MEMBER: Council on Foreign Relations; American Antiquarian Society; Union of Writers of the African Peoples; Association for Documentary Editing; African Roundtable; African Literature Association; Afro-American Academy; American Studies Association; Trans Africa Forum Scholars Council; Association for the Study of Afro-American Life and History (life); Caribbean Studies Association; College Language Association (life); Modern Language Association; Stone Trust; Zora Neale Hurston Society; Cambridge Scientific Club; American Civil Liberties Union National Advisory Council; German American Studies Association; National Coalition Against Censorship; American Philosophical Society; Saturday Club; New England Historic Genealogical Society; Phi Beta Kappa.

AWARDS, HONORS: Carnegie Foundation Fellowship for Africa, 1970-71; Phelps Fellowship, Yale University, 1970-71; Mellon fellowships, Cambridge University, 1973-75, and National Humanities Center, 1989-90; grants from Ford Foundation, 1976-77 and 1984-85, and National Endowment for the Humanities, 1980-86; A. Whitney Griswold Fellowship, 1980; Rockefeller Foundation fellowships, 1981 and 1990; MacArthur Prize Fellowship, MacArthur Foundation, 1981-86; Yale Afro-American teaching prize, 1983; award from Whitney Humanities Center, 1983-85; Princeton University Council of the Humanities lectureship, 1985; Award for Creative Scholarship, Zora Neale Hurston Society, 1986; associate fellowship from W. E. B. DuBois Institute, Harvard University, 1987-88 and 1988-89; John Hope Franklin Prize honorable mention, American Studies Association, 1988; Woodrow Wilson National Fellow, 1988-89 and 1989-90; Candle Award, Morehouse College, 1989; American Book Award and Anisfield-Wolf Book Award for Race Relations, both 1989, both for *The Signifying Monkey: Towards a Theory of Afro-American Literary Criticism*; recipient of honorary degrees from Dartmouth College, 1989, University of West Virginia, 1990, University of Rochester, 1990, Pratt Institute, 1990, University of Bridgeport, 1991 (declined), University of New Hampshire, 1991, Bryant College, 1992, Manhattan Community College, 1992, George Washington University, 1993, University of Massachusetts at Amherst, 1993, Williams College, 1993, Emory University, 1995, Colby College, 1995, Bard College, 1995, and Bates College, 1995; Richard Wright Lecturer, Center for the Study of Black Literature and Culture, University of Pennsylvania, 1990; Potomac State College Alumni Award, 1991; Bellagio Conference Center Fellowship, 1992; Clarendon Lecturer, Oxford University, 1992; Best New Journal of the Year award (in the humanities and the social sciences), Association of American Publishers, 1992; elected to the American Academy of Arts and Sciences, 1993; Golden Plate Achievement Award, 1993; African American Students Faculty Award, 1993; George Polk Award for Social Commentary, 1993; Heartland Prize for Nonfiction, 1994, for *Colored People: A Memoir*; Lillian Smith Book Award, 1994; West Virginian of the Year, 1995; Humanities Award, West Virginia Humanities Council, 1995; Ethics Award, Tikun (magazine), 1996; Distinguished Editorial Achievement, *Critical Inquiry,* 1996; W. D. Weatherford Award.

WRITINGS:

Figures in Black: Words, Signs, and the Racial Self, Oxford University Press (New York City), 1987.
The Signifying Monkey: Towards a Theory of Afro-American Literary Criticism, Oxford University Press, 1988.
Loose Canons: Notes on the Culture Wars (essays), Oxford University Press, 1992.
Colored People: A Memoir, Knopf (New York City), 1994.
Speaking of Race: Hate Speech, Civil Rights, and Civil Liberties, New York University Press, 1995.
(With Cornel West) *The Future of the Race,* Knopf, 1996.
Thirteen Ways of Looking at a Black Man, Random House (New York City), 1997.
(Author of introduction) Douglass, Frederick, *Narrative of the Life of Frederick Douglass, an American Slave,* Laurel Leaf, 1997.

EDITOR

(And author of introduction) *Black Is the Color of the Cosmos: Charles T. Davis's Essays on Afro-American Literature and Culture, 1942-1981,* Garland Publishing (New York City), 1982.
(And author of introduction) Harriet E. Wilson, *Our Nig; or, Sketches from the Life of a Free Black,* Random House (New York City), 1983.
(And author of introduction) *Black Literature and Literary Theory,* Methuen (New York City), 1984.
(And author of introduction with Charles T. Davis) *The Slave's Narrative: Texts and Contexts,* Oxford University Press, 1986.
(And author of introduction) *"Race," Writing, and Difference,* University of Chicago Press (Chicago), 1986.
(And author of introduction) *The Classic Slave Narratives,* New American Library (New York City), 1987.
(And author of introduction) *In the House of Oshugbo: A Collection of Essays on Wole Soyinka,* Oxford University Press, 1988.
(Series editor) *The Oxford-Schomburg Library of Nineteenth-Century Black Women Writers,* 30 volumes, Oxford University Press, 1988–.
W. E. B. Du Bois, *The Souls of Black Folk,* Bantam Books (New York City), 1989.
James Weldon Johnson, *The Autobiography of an Ex-Coloured Man,* Vintage, 1989.
Three Classic African American Novels, Vintage, 1990.
Zora Neale Hurston, *Their Eyes Were Watching God* (introduction by Mary Helen Washington), Harper (New York City), 1990.
Hurston, *Jonah's Gourd Vine* (introduction by Rita Dove), Harper, 1990.
Hurston, *Tell My Horse* (introduction by Ishmael Reed), Harper, 1990.
Hurston, *Mules and Men* (introduction by Arnold Rampersad), Harper, 1990.
Reading Black, Reading Feminist: A Critical Anthology, Meridian Book, 1990.
Voodoo Gods of Haiti (introduction by Ishmael Reed), Harper, 1991.
The Schomburg Library of Nineteenth-Century Black Women Writers, 10 volume supplement, Oxford University Press, 1991.

(With Randall K. Burkett and Nancy Hall Burkett) *Black Biography, 1790-1950: A Cumulative Index,* Chadwyck-Healey (Teaneck, NJ), 1991.
(With George Bass) Langston Hughes and Zora Neale Hurston, *Mulebone: A Comedy of Negro Life,* HarperPerennial (New York City), 1991.
Bearing Witness: Selections from African American Autobiography in the Twentieth Century, Pantheon Books (New York City), 1991.
(With Anthony Appiah) *Gloria Naylor: Critical Perspectives Past and Present,* Amistad (New York City), 1993.
(With Appiah) *Alice Walker: Critical Perspectives Past and Present,* Amistad, 1993.
(With Appiah) *Langston Hughes: Critical Perspectives Past and Present,* Amistad, 1993.
(With Appiah) *Richard Wright: Critical Perspectives Past and Present,* Amistad, 1993.
(With Appiah) *Toni Morrison: Critical Perspectives Past and Present,* Amistad, 1993.
(With Appiah) *Zora Neale Hurston: Critical Perspectives Past and Present,* Amistad, 1993.
The Amistad Chronology of African American History from 1445-1990, Amistad, 1993.
(And annotations) *Frederick Douglass: Autobiographies,* Library of America, 1994.
(With Appiah) *The Dictionary of Global Culture,* Knopf, 1995.
The Complete Stories of Zora Neale Hurston, HarperCollins, 1995.
(With Appiah) *Identities,* University of Chicago, 1996.
Ann Petry: Critical Perspectives Past and Present, Amistad, 1997.
Chinua Achebe: Critical Perspectives Past and Present, Amistad, 1997.
Harriet A. Jacobs: Critical Perspectives Past and Present, Amistad, 1997.
Ralph Ellison: Critical Perspectives Past and Present, Amistad, 1997.
Wole Soyinka: Critical Perspectives Past and Present, Amistad, 1997.
Frederick Douglass: Critical Perspectives Past and Present, Amistad, 1997.
The Essential Soyinka: A Reader, Pantheon, 1998.

Also editor, with Appiah, of "Amistad Critical Studies in African American Literature" series, 1993, and editor of the Black Periodical Literature Project. Advisory editor of "Contributions to African and Afro-American Studies" series for Greenwood Press (Westport, CT), "Critical Studies in Black Life and Culture" series for Garland Press, and "Perspectives on the Black World" series for G. K. Hall (Boston). General editor of *A Dictionary of Cultural and Critical Theory; Middle-Atlantic Writers Association Review.* Coeditor of *Transition.* Associate editor of *Journal of American Folklore.* Member of editorial boards including, *Critical Inquiry, Studies in American Fiction, Black American Literature Forum, PMLA, Stanford Humanities Review,* and *Yale Journal of Law and Liberation.*

OTHER

(Compiler with James Gibb and Ketu H. Katrak) *Wole Soyinka: A Bibliography of Primary and Secondary Sources,* Greenwood Press, 1986.
(With N. Y. McKay) *The Norton Anthology of African American Literature,* Norton (New York City), 1996.

SIDELIGHTS: Henry Louis Gates, Jr. is one of the most controversial and respected scholars in the field of African-American studies. Gates was recognized early on by an English instructor at Potomac State Community College, who encouraged his student to transfer to Yale University. Gates graduated from that institution with highest honors in 1973. While in Africa on a Carnegie Foundation Fellowship and a Phelps Fellowship during 1970-1971, he visited fifteen countries and became familiar with various aspects of African culture. His knowledge of Africa deepened when the celebrated African writer Wole Soyinka became his tutor at Cambridge University, where Gates worked on his master's and doctoral degrees. In 1981 he was awarded one of the so-called "genius grants" from the MacArthur Foundation. He moved quickly from a teaching post at Yale to a full professorship at Cornell to an endowed chair at Duke, and in 1991, he became the W. E. B. DuBois Professor of the Humanities at Harvard and head of its Afro-American Studies program. Gates breathed new life and enthusiasm into the program and hired lecturers, such as film director Spike Lee and authors Jamaica Kincaid and Wole Soyinka. Under Gates's leadership, the number of students in the program tripled within a few years.

Gates has his detractors as well as his admirers, however. Some of his colleagues have faulted him for being insufficiently Afro-centric, while others have criticized his high-profile activities—such as publicly testifying at the obscenity trial of rap group 2 Live Crew—as inappropriate self-promotion. Yet even those who take exception to Gates's showmanship cannot argue with his credentials or deny his prolific contributions to Afro-American scholarship, as he has written and edited numerous books of literary and social criticism. According to James Olney in the *Dictionary of Literary Biography,* Gates's mission is to reorder and reinterpret "the literary and critical history of Afro-Americans in the context of a tradition that is fully modern but also continuous with Yoruba modes of interpretation that are firmly settled and at home in the world of black Americans."

In his approach to literary criticism, Gates is avowedly eclectic and defines himself as a centrist who rejects extreme positions, whether they be on the right (guardians of a Western tradition) or on the left (Afrocentricists). Gates insists that we need to transcend "ethnic absolutism" of all kinds. Like the American novelist Ralph Ellison, Gates sees the fluid, indeed porous, relationship between black and white culture in the United States. Gates argues that our conception of the literary canon needs to be enlarged accordingly.

Gates's *Black Literature and Literary Theory,* which he edited, is considered by many reviewers to be an important contribution to the study of black literature. Calling it "an exciting, important volume," Reed Way Dasenbrock wrote in *World Literature Today*: "It is a collection of essays . . . that attempts to explore the relevance of contemporary literary theory, especially structuralism and poststructuralism, to African and Afro-American literature. . . . Anyone seriously interested in contemporary critical theory, in Afro-American and African literature, and in black and African studies generally will need to read and absorb this book." R. G. O'Meally wrote in *Choice* that in *Black Literature and Literary Theory* Gates "brings together thirteen superb essays in which the most modern literary theory is applied to black literature of Africa and the U.S. . . . For those interested in [the] crucial issues—and for those interested in fresh and challenging readings of key texts in black literature—this book is indispensable." Finally, Terry Eagleton remarked in the *New York Times Book Review* that "the most thought-provoking contribu-

tions to [this] collection are those that not only enrich our understanding of black literary works but in doing so implicitly question the authoritarianism of a literary 'canon.'"

One of Gates's best-known works is *Loose Canons: Notes on the Culture Wars,* in which he discusses gender, literature, and multiculturalism and argues for greater diversity in American arts and letters. Writing in the *Virginia Quarterly Review,* Sanford Pinsker noted that according to Gates "the cultural right . . . is guilty of 'intellectual protectionism,' of defending the best that has been thought and said within the Western Tradition because they are threatened by America's rapidly changing demographic profile; while the cultural left 'demands changes to accord with population shifts in gender and ethnicity.' *Loose Canons* makes it clear that Gates has problems with both positions." "The society we have made," Gates argues in *Loose Canons,* "simply won't survive without the values of tolerance. And cultural tolerance comes to nothing without cultural understanding. . . . If we relinquish the ideal of America as a plural nation, we've abandoned the very experiment that America represents." Writing in the *Los Angeles Times,* Jonathan Kirsch praised the humor and wit that infused Gates's arguments. *Loose Canons,* Kirsch concluded, is "the work of a man who has mastered the arcane politics and encoded language of the canon makers; it's an arsenal of ideas in the cultural wars. But it is also the outpouring of a humane, witty and truly civilized mind."

Colored People: A Memoir played to a wider audience than did *Loose Canons.* In it, Gates recalls his youth in Piedmont, West Virginia, at a time when the town was becoming integrated. It "explores the tension between the racially segregated past and the integrated modernity that the author himself represents," commented David Lionel Smith in *America.* While affirming the progress brought by desegregation, Gates also laments the loss of the strong, united community feeling that segregation created among blacks—a feeling epitomized in the annual all-black picnic sponsored by the paper mill that provided jobs to most of Piedmont's citizens. Numerous reviewers pointed out the gentle, reminiscent tone of Gates's narrative, but some considered this a weakness in light of the momentous changes Gates lived through. Smith remarked: "From an author of Gates's sophistication, we expect more than unreflective nostalgia." Comparing it to other recent African-American memoirs and autobiographies, he concluded, "Some of them address social issues more cogently and others are more self-analytical, but none is more vivid and pleasant to read than *Colored People.*" *Los Angeles Times Book Review* contributor Richard Eder affirmed that *Colored People* was an "affecting, beautifully written and morally complex memoir," and Joyce Carol Oates, in her *London Review of Books* assessment, described it as an "eloquent document to set beside the grittier contemporary testimonies of black male urban memoirists; in essence a work of filial gratitude, paying homage to such virtues as courage, loyalty, integrity, kindness; a pleasure to read and, in the best sense, inspiring."

Gates wrote *The Future of the Race* with Cornel West, a professor of Afro-American studies at Harvard University. This work contains an essay by Gates, an essay by West, and two essays by black intellectual W. E. B. DuBois, the latter of which are preceded by a foreword by Gates. Writing in the *New York Times Book Review,* Gerald Early noted: "The question . . . that the authors wish to answer—what is their duty to the lower or less fortunate class of blacks?—indicates the black bourgeoisie's inability to understand precisely what their success means to themselves or blacks generally." Early also observed that while "the pieces seem hastily written," Gates's essay is "engagingly witty and journalistic" as well as "charming and coherent."

Gates offers insight into the position of the black male in American society in *Thirteen Ways of Looking at a Black Man*. Through a series of discussions recorded over several years and documented in various magazine articles, Gates brings a broad cross-section of African-American hopes and ideals to the reader's attention. Interviewees include such major black American figures as James Baldwin, Harry Belafonte, Colin Powell, and Bill T. Jones. Writing in *Library Journal*, Michael A. Lutes refers to *Thirteen Ways of Looking at a Black Man* as a "riveting commentary on race in America."

BIOGRAPHICAL/CRITICAL SOURCES:

BOOKS

Dictionary of Literary Biography, Volume 67: *Modern American Critics since 1955*, Gale (Detroit), 1988.

PERIODICALS

America, December 31, 1994, p. 24.
American Spectator, April-May, 1994, p. 69.
Boston Globe, October 20, 1990, p. 3; May 12, 1991, p. 12; April 23, 1992, p. 70; November 7, 1992, p. 15; December 1, 1992, p. 23; April 29, 1993, p. 53; May 29, 1994, p. A13.
Callaloo, spring, 1991.
Chicago Tribune, February 18, 1993, section 5, p. 3; November 18, 1993, section 1, p. 32; July 17, 1994, section 14, p. 3; August 24, 1994, section 5, p. 1.
Choice, May, 1985; March, 1995, p. 1059.
Christian Century, January 19, 1994, p. 53-54.
Christian Science Monitor, April 10, 1992, p. 11; June 7, 1994, p. 13.
Commonweal, December 18, 1992, pp. 22-23.
Criticism, winter, 1994, pp. 155-61.
Emerge, November, 1990, p. 76.
Humanities Magazine, July/August, 1991, pp. 4-10.
Library Journal, February, 1997.
London Review of Books, July 21, 1994, p. 22-23; January 12, 1995, p. 14.
Los Angeles Times, October 29, 1990, p. A20; March 25, 1992, p. E2; June 3, 1994, p. E1.
Los Angeles Times Book Review, May 8, 1994, pp. 3, 12.
New Leader, September 12, 1994, pp. 12-13.
New Literary History, autumn, 1991.
New Republic, July 4, 1994, p. 33; June 16, 1997.
New Statesman & Society, February 10, 1995, p. 43.
New York Times, December 6, 1989, p. B14; April 1, 1990, section 6, p. 25; June 3, 1992, p. B7; May 16, 1994, p. C16.
New York Times Book Review, December 9, 1984; August 9, 1992, p. 21; June 19, 1994, p. 10; April 21, 1996, p. 7; February 9, 1997.
New York Times Magazine, April 1, 1990.
Spectator, February 18, 1995, pp. 31-32.
Time, April 22, 1991, pp. 16, 18; May 23, 1994, p. 73.
Times Literary Supplement, May 17, 1985; February 24, 1995, p. 26.
Tribune Books (Chicago), July 17, 1994, pp. 3, 5; October 9, 1994, p. 11.
U.S. News and World Report, March, 1992.
Village Voice, July 5, 1994, p. 82.
Virginia Quarterly Review, summer, 1993, pp. 562-68.
Voice Literary Supplement, June, 1985.
U. S. News and World Report, March, 1992.

Washington Post, October 20, 1990, p. D1; August 11, 1992, p. A17.
Washington Post Book World, July 3, 1983; June 7, 1992, p. 6; May 15, 1994, p. 3.
World Literature Today, summer, 1985.

*   *   *

GAWSWORTH, John
    See BATES, H(erbert) E(rnest)

*   *   *

GEISEL, Theodor Seuss 1904-1991
    (Theo. LeSieg, Dr. Seuss; Rosetta Stone, a joint pseudonym)

PERSONAL: Surname is pronounced *Guy*-zel; born March 2, 1904, in Springfield, MA; died of cancer, September 24, 1991, in La Jolla, CA; son of Theodor Robert (superintendent of Springfield public park system) and Henrietta (Seuss) Geisel; married Helen Palmer (an author and vice-president of Beginner Books), November 29, 1927 (died, October 23, 1967); married Audrey Stone Diamond, August 6, 1968. *Education:* Dartmouth College, A.B., 1925; graduate study at Lincoln College, Oxford, 1925-26, and Sorbonne, University of Paris.

ADDRESSES: Home—La Jolla, CA. *Office*—Random House, Inc., 201 E. 50th St., New York, NY 10022. *Agent*—International Creative Management, 40 W. 57th St., New York, NY 10019.

CAREER: Author and illustrator. Freelance cartoonist, beginning 1927; advertising artist, Standard Oil Company of New Jersey, 1928-41; *PM* (magazine), New York, NY, editorial cartoonist, 1940-42; publicist, War Production Board of U.S. Treasury Department, 1940-42; Beginner Books, Random House, Inc., New York, NY, founder and president, 1957-1991. Correspondent in Japan, *Life* (magazine), 1954. Trustee, La Jolla (CA) Town Council, beginning 1956. One-man art exhibitions at San Diego Arts Museum, 1950, Dartmouth College, 1975, Toledo Museum of Art, 1975, La Jolla Museum of Contemporary Art, 1976, and Baltimore Museum of Art, 1987. *Military service:* U.S. Army Signal Corps, Information and Education Division, 1942-46; became lieutenant colonel; received Legion of Merit.

MEMBER: Authors League of America, American Society of Composers, Authors and Publishers (ASCAP), Sigma Phi Epsilon.

AWARDS, HONORS: Academy Award, 1946, for "Hitler Lives," 1947, for "Design for Death," and 1951, for "Gerald McBoing-Boing"; Randolph Caldecott Honor Award, Association for Library Services for Children, American Library Association, 1948, for *McElligot's Pool*, 1950, for *Bartholomew and the Oobleck*, and 1951, for *If I Ran the Zoo*; Young Reader's Choice Award, Pacific Northwest Library Association, 1950, for *McElligot's Pool*; L.H.D., Dartmouth College, 1956, American International College, 1968, Lake Forest College, 1977, and Brown University, 1987; Lewis Carroll Shelf Award, 1958, for *Horton Hatches the Egg*, and 1961, for *And to Think That I Saw It on Mulberry Street*; Boys' Club Junior Book Award, Boys' Club of America, 1966, for *I Had Trouble in Getting to Solla Sollew*.

Peabody Award, 1971, for animated cartoons "How the Grinch Stole Christmas" and "Horton Hears a Who"; Critics' Award from

International Animated Cartoon Festival and Silver Medal from International Film and Television Festival of New York, both 1972, both for "The Lorax"; Los Angeles County Library Association Award, 1974; Southern California Council on Literature for Children and Young People Award, 1974, for special contribution to children's literature; named "Outstanding California Author," California Association of Teachers of English, 1976; Emmy Award, 1977, for "Halloween Is Grinch Night"; Roger Revelle Award, University of California, San Diego, 1978; winner of Children's Choice Election, 1978; grand marshall of Detroit's Thanksgiving Day Parade, 1979.

D.Litt., Whittier College, 1980; Laura Ingalls Wilder Award, Association for Library Services for Children, American Library Association, 1980; "Dr. Seuss Week" proclaimed by State Governors, March 2-7, 1981; Regina Medal, Catholic Library Association, 1982; National Association of Elementary School Principals special award, 1982, for distinguished service to children; Pulitzer Prize, 1984, for his "special contribution over nearly half a century to the education and enjoyment of America's children and their parents"; PEN Los Angeles Center Award for children's literature, 1985, for *The Butter Battle Book*; D.F.A., Princeton University, 1985; D.H.L., University of Hartford, 1986.

WRITINGS:

UNDER PSEUDONYM DR. SEUSS; SELF-ILLUSTRATED, EXCEPT WHERE NOTED

And to Think That I Saw It on Mulberry Street, Vanguard, 1937.
The 500 Hats of Bartholomew Cubbins, Vanguard, 1938.
The Seven Lady Godivas, Random House, 1939.
The King's Stilts, Random House, 1939.
Horton Hatches the Egg, Random House, 1940.
McElligot's Pool, Random House, 1947.
Thidwick, the Big-Hearted Moose, Random House, 1948.
Bartholomew and the Oobleck, Random House, 1949.
If I Ran the Zoo, Random House, 1950.
Scrambled Eggs Super! (also see below), Random House, 1953.
The Sneetches and Other Stories, Random House, 1953.
Horton Hears a Who! (also see below), Random House, 1954.
On Beyond Zebra, Random House, 1955.
If I Ran the Circus, Random House, 1956.
Signs of Civilization! (booklet), La Jolla Town Council, 1956.
The Cat in the Hat (also see below), Random House, 1957, French/English edition published as *La Chat au chapeau,* Random House, 1967, Spanish/English edition published as *El Gato ensombrerado,* Random House, 1967.
How the Grinch Stole Christmas (also see below), Random House, 1957.
The Cat in the Hat Comes Back!, Beginner Books, 1958.
Yertle the Turtle and Other Stories, Random House, 1958.
Happy Birthday to You!, Random House, 1959.
One Fish, Two Fish, Red Fish, Blue Fish, Random House, 1960.
Green Eggs and Ham, Beginner Books, 1960.
Dr. Seuss' Sleep Book, Random House, 1962.
Hop on Pop, Beginner Books, 1963.
Dr. Seuss' ABC, Beginner Books, 1963.
(With Philip D. Eastman) *The Cat in the Hat Dictionary, by the Cat Himself,* Beginner Books, 1964.
Fox in Socks, Beginner Books, 1965.
I Had Trouble in Getting to Solla Sollew, Random House, 1965.
Dr. Seuss' Lost World Revisited: A Forward-Looking Backward Glance (nonfiction), Award Books, 1967.
The Cat in the Hat Songbook, Random House, 1967.
The Foot Book, Random House, 1968.

I Can Lick 30 Tigers Today! and Other Stories, Random House, 1969.
My Book About Me, By Me Myself, I Wrote It! I Drew It! With a Little Help from My Friends Dr. Seuss and Roy McKie, illustrated by Roy McKie, Beginner Books, 1969.
Mr. Brown Can Moo! Can You?, Random House, 1970.
I Can Draw It Myself, Random House, 1970.
The Lorax, Random House, 1971.
Marvin K. Mooney, Will You Please Go Now?, Random House, 1972.
Did I Ever Tell You How Lucky You Are?, Random House, 1973.
The Shape of Me and Other Stuff, Random House, 1973.
Great Day for Up!, illustrated by Quentin Blake, Beginner Books, 1974.
There's a Wocket in My Pocket!, Random House, 1974.
Dr. Seuss Storytime (includes *Horton Hears a Who*), Random House, 1974.
Oh, the Thinks You Can Think!, Random House, 1975.
The Cat's Quizzer, Random House, 1976.
I Can Read with My Eyes Shut, Random House, 1978.
Oh Say Can You Say?, Beginner Books, 1979.
The Dr. Seuss Storybook (includes *Scrambled Eggs Super!*), Collins, 1979.
Hunches in Bunches, Random House, 1982.
The Butter Battle Book (also see below), Random House, 1984.
You're Only Old Once, Random House, 1986.
The Tough Coughs as He Ploughs the Dough: Early Writings and Cartoons by Dr. Seuss, edited by Richard Marschall, Morrow, 1986.
I Am Not Going to Get Up Today!, illustrated by James Stevenson, Beginner Books, 1987.
Oh, the Places You'll Go!, Random House, 1990.
Six by Seuss (includes *And To Think I Saw It On Mulberry Street*), Random House, 1991.
Daisy-head Mayzie, Random House, 1994.
My Many Colored Days, illustrated by Steve Johnson and Lou Fancher, Knopf (New York), 1996.
What Was I Scared Of?, Random House, 1997.
A Hatful of Seuss (includes *The Sneetches and Other Stories*), Random House, 1997.
Hooper Humperdink—? Not Him!, illustrated by James Stevenson, Beginner Books, 1997.

UNDER PSEUDONYM THEO. LeSIEG

Ten Apples up on Top!, illustrated by McKie, Beginner Books, 1961.
I Wish That I Had Duck Feet, illustrated by B. Tokey, Beginner Books, 1965.
Come Over to My House, illustrated by Richard Erdoes, Beginner Books, 1966.
The Eye Book, illustrated by McKie, Random House, 1968.
(Self-illustrated) *I Can Write—By Me, Myself,* Random House, 1971.
In a People House, illustrated by McKie, Random House, 1972.
The Many Mice of Mr. Brice, illustrated by McKie, Random House, 1973.
Wacky Wednesday, illustrated by George Booth, Beginner Books, 1974.
Would You Rather Be a Bullfrog?, illustrated by McKie, Random House, 1975.
Hooper Humperdink . . .? Not Him!, Random House, 1976.
Please Try to Remember the First of Octember!, illustrated by Arthur Cummings, Beginner Books, 1977.

Maybe You Should Fly a Jet! Maybe You Should Be a Vet, illustrated by Michael J. Smullin, Beginner Books, 1980.

The Tooth Book, Random House, 1981.

SCREENPLAYS

"Your Job in Germany" (documentary short subject), U.S. Army, 1946, released under title "Hitler Lives," Warner Bros., 1946.

(With wife, Helen Palmer Geisel) "Design for Death" (documentary feature), RKO Pictures, 1947.

"Gerald McBoing-Boing" (animated cartoon), United Productions of America (UPA)/Columbia, 1951.

(With Allen Scott) "The 5,000 Fingers of Dr. T" (musical), Columbia, 1953.

Also author of screenplays for "Private Snafu" film series, for Warner Bros.

TELEVISION SCRIPTS

"How the Grinch Stole Christmas," Columbia Broadcasting System, Inc. (CBS-TV), first aired December 18, 1966.

"Horton Hears a Who," CBS-TV, first aired March 19, 1970.

"The Cat in the Hat," CBS-TV, first aired March 10, 1971.

"Dr. Seuss on the Loose," CBS-TV, first aired October 15, 1973.

"Hoober-Bloob Highway," CBS-TV, first aired February 19, 1975.

"Halloween Is Grinch Night," American Broadcasting Companies, Inc. (ABC-TV), first aired October 28, 1977.

"Pontoffel Pock, Where Are You?," ABC-TV, first aired March 2, 1980.

"The Grinch Grinches the Cat in the Hat," ABC-TV, first aired May 20, 1982.

"The Butter Battle Book," Turner Network Television (TNT-TV), first aired November 13, 1989.

OTHER

(Illustrator) *Boners,* Viking, 1931.

(Illustrator) *More Boners,* Viking, 1931.

(Under pseudonym, Dr. Seuss) *Great Day for Up!,* illustrated by Quentin Blake, Random House, 1974.

(With Michael Frith, under joint pseudonym Rosetta Stone) *Because a Little Bug Went Ka-Choo!,* illustrated by Frith, Beginner Books, 1975.

Dr. Seuss from Then to Now (museum catalog), Random House, 1987.

The Secret Art of Dr. Seuss, Random House (New York), 1995.

(Illustrator) Alexander Abingdon, *Herrings Go About the Sea in Shawls: And Other Classic Howlers from Classrooms and Examination Papers,* Viking, 1997.

Contributor of cartoons and prose to magazines, including *Judge, College Humor, Liberty, Vanity Fair,* and *Life.* Editor, *Jack-o'-Lantern* (Dartmouth College humor magazine), until 1925. The manuscript of *The 500 Hats of Bartholomew Cubbins* is in the collection of Dartmouth College in Hanover, New Hampshire. Other manuscripts are in the Special Collections Department of the University of California Library in Los Angeles.

MEDIA ADAPTATIONS: Dr. Seuss' animated cartoon character Gerald McBoing-Boing appeared in several other UPA pictures, including "Gerald McBoing-Boing's Symphony," 1953, "How Now McBoing-Boing," 1954, and "Gerald McBoing-Boing on the Planet Moo," 1956. In December of 1956, Gerald McBoing-Boing appeared in his own animated variety show, "The Gerald McBoing-Boing Show," which aired on CBS-TV on Sunday evenings. The program ran through October of 1958.

SIDELIGHTS: Theodor Seuss Geisel, better known under his pseudonym "Dr. Seuss," was "probably the best-loved and certainly the best-selling children's book writer of all time," wrote Robert Wilson of the *New York Times Book Review.* Seuss entertained several generations of young readers with his zany nonsense books. Speaking to Herbert Kupferberg of *Parade,* Seuss claimed: "Old men on crutches tell me, 'I've been brought up on your books.'" His "rhythmic verse rivals Lewis Carroll's," stated Stefan Kanfer of *Time,* "and his freestyle drawing recalls the loony sketches of Edward Lear." Because of his work in publishing books for young readers and for the many innovative children's classics he wrote himself, Seuss "has had a tremendous impact," Miles Corwin of the *Los Angeles Times* declared, "on children's reading habits and the way reading is taught and approached in the school system."

Seuss had originally intended to become a professor of English, but soon "became frustrated when he was shunted into a particularly insignificant field of research," reported Myra Kibler in the *Dictionary of Literary Biography.* After leaving graduate school in 1926, Seuss worked for a number of years as a freelance magazine cartoonist, selling cartoons and humorous prose pieces to the major humor magazines of the 1920s and 1930s. Many of these works are collected in *The Tough Coughs as He Ploughs the Dough.* One of Seuss' cartoons—about "Flit," a spray-can pesticide—attracted the attention of the Standard Oil Company, manufacturers of the product. In 1928 they hired Seuss to draw their magazine advertising art and, for the next fifteen years, Seuss created grotesque, enormous insects to illustrate the famous slogan "Quick, Henry! The Flit!" He also created monsters for the motor oil division of Standard Oil, including the Moto-Raspus, the Moto-Munchus, and the Karbo-Nockus, that, said Kibler, are ancestral to his later fantastic creatures.

It was quite by chance that Seuss began writing for children. Returning from Europe by boat in 1936, Seuss amused himself during the long voyage by putting together a nonsense poem to the rhythm of the ship's engine. Later he drew pictures to illustrate the rhyme and in 1937 published the result as *And to Think That I Saw It on Mulberry Street,* his first children's book. Set in Seuss' home town of Springfield, Massachusetts, *Mulberry Street* is the story of a boy whose imagination transforms a simple horse-drawn wagon into a marvelous and exotic parade of strange creatures and vehicles. Many critics regard it as Seuss' best work.

Mulberry Street, along with *The 500 Hats of Bartholomew Cubbins, Horton Hatches the Egg* and *McElligot's Pool,* introduces many of the elements for which Seuss has become famous. *Mulberry Street* features rollicking anapestic tetrameter verse that compliments Seuss's boisterous illustrations. Jonathan Cott, writing in *Pipers at the Gates of Dawn: The Wisdom of Children's Literature,* declared that "the unflagging momentum, feeling of breathlessness, and swiftness of pace, all together [act] as the motor for Dr. Seuss's pullulating image machine." Whimsical fantasy characterizes *The 500 Hats of Bartholomew Cubbins,* while *Horton Hatches the Egg* introduces an element of morality and *McElligot's Pool* marks the first appearance of the fantasy animal characters for which Seuss became famous.

The outbreak of World War II forced Seuss to give up writing for children temporarily and to devote his talents to the war effort. Working with the Information and Education Division of the U.S. Army, he made documentary films for American soldiers. One of these Army films—"Hitler Lives"—won an Academy Award, a feat Seuss repeated with his documentary about the Japanese war effort "Design for Death," and the UPA cartoon "Gerald McBoing-Boing," about a little boy who can only speak in sound effects. "The 5,000 Fingers of Dr. T," which Seuss wrote with Allen Scott, achieved cult status during the 1960s among music students on college campuses. Later, Seuss adapted several of his books into animated television specials, the most famous of which—"How the Grinch Stole Christmas"—has become a holiday favorite.

The success of his early books confirmed Seuss as an important new children's writer. However, it was *The Cat in the Hat* that really established his reputation and revolutionized the world of children's book publishing. By using a limited number of different words, all simple enough for very young children to read, and through its wildly iconoclastic plot—when two children are alone at home on a rainy day, the Cat in the Hat arrives to entertain them, wrecking their house in the process—*The Cat* provided an attractive alternative to the simplistic "Dick and Jane" primers then in use in American schools, and critics applauded its appearance. For instance, Helen Adams Masten of *Saturday Review* marveled at the way Seuss, using "only 223 different words, . . . has created a story in rhyme which presents an impelling incentive to read." The enthusiastic reception of *The Cat in the Hat* led Seuss to found Beginner Books, a publishing company specializing in easy-to-read books for children. In 1960, Random House acquired the company and made Seuss president of the Beginner Books division.

Seuss and Beginner Books created many modern classics for children, from *Green Eggs and Ham,* about the need to try new experiences, and *Fox in Socks,* a series of increasingly boisterous tongue-twisters, to *The Lorax,* about environmental preservation, and *The Butter Battle Book,* a fable based on the nuclear arms race. In 1986, at the age of 82, however, Seuss produced *You're Only Old Once,* a book for the "obsolete children" of the world. The story follows an elderly gentleman's examination at "The Golden Age Clinic on Century Square," where he's gone for "Spleen Readjustment and Muffler Repair." The gentleman, who is never named, is subjected to a number of seemingly pointless tests by merciless physicians and grim nurses, ranging from a diet machine that rejects any appealing foods to an enormous eye chart that asks, "Have you any idea how much these tests are costing you?" Finally, however, he is dismissed, the doctors telling him that "You're in pretty good shape/For the shape that you're in!"

In its cheerful conclusion *You're Only Old Once* is typically Seuss; "The other ending is unacceptable," Seuss confided to *New York Times Book Review* contributor David W. Dunlap. In other ways, however, the book is very different. Seuss told Dunlap that *You're Only Old Once* is much more autobiographical than any of his other stories. Robin Marantz Henig, writing in the *Washington Post Book World,* said *You're Only Old Once* "is lighthearted, silly, but with an undertone of complaint. Being old is sometimes tough, isn't it . . . Seuss seems to be saying." *Los Angeles Times Book Review* contributor Jack Smith declared that in it Seuss "reveals himself as human and old, and full of aches and pains and alarming symptoms, and frightened of the world of geriatric medicine, with its endless tests, overzealous doctors, intimidating nurses, Rube Goldberg machines and demoralizing paperwork." Nonetheless, Henig concluded, "We should all be lucky enough to get old the way this man, and Dr. Seuss himself, has gotten old."

BIOGRAPHICAL/CRITICAL SOURCES:

BOOKS

Children's Literature Review, Gale (Detroit), Volume 1, 1976; Volume 9, 1985.
Cott, Jonathan, *Pipers at the Gates of Dawn: The Wisdom of Children's Literature,* Random House, 1983.
Dictionary of Literary Biography, Volume 61: *American Writers for Children since 1960: Poets, Illustrators, and Nonfiction Authors,* Gale, 1987.
Fensch, Thomas, *Of Sneetches and Whos and the Good Dr. Seuss: Essays on the Writings and Life of Theodor Geisel,* McFarland and Co., 1997.
Greene, Carol, *Dr. Seuss: Writer and Artist for Children,* Children's Press (Chicago), 1993.
Lanes, Selma G., *Down the Rabbit Hole: Adventures and Misadventures in the Realm of Children's Literature,* Atheneum, 1972.
Lathem, Edward Connery (editor), *Theodor Seuss Geisel, Reminiscences and Tributes,* Dartmouth College, 1996.
Morgan, Judith, and Neil Morgan, *Dr. Seuss & Mr. Geisel: A Biography,* Random House, 1995.
Weidt, Maryann N., *Oh, the Places He Went: A Story about Dr. Seuss—Theodor Seuss Geisel,* illustrated by Kerry Maguire, Carolrhoda Books (Minneapolis, MN), 1994.

PERIODICALS

Chicago Tribune, May 12, 1957; April 15, 1982; April 17, 1984; June 29, 1986; January 14, 1987.
Education Digest, December, 1992.
English Journal, December, 1992.
Horn Book, September-October, 1992.
Interview, April, 1995.
Los Angeles Times, November 27, 1983; October 7, 1989.
Los Angeles Times Book Review, March 9, 1986.
New York Review of Books, December 20, 1990.
New York Times, May 21, 1986; December 26, 1987.
New York Times Book Review, November 11, 1952; May 11, 1958; March 20, 1960; November 11, 1962; November 16, 1975; April 29, 1979; February 26, 1984; March 23, 1986; February 26, 1995.
Parade, February 26, 1984.
Publishers Weekly, February 10, 1984; August 9, 1993; January 23, 1995.
Reader's Digest, April, 1992.
Saturday Review, May 11, 1957; November 16, 1957.
Time, May 7, 1979.
Washington Post, December 30, 1987.
Washington Post Book World, March 9, 1986.
Yankee, December, 1995.

*　　　*　　　*

GENET, Jean 1910-1986

PERSONAL: Born December 19, 1910, in Paris, France; died of throat cancer, April 15, 1986 in Paris, France; never knew his parents; was abandoned by his mother, Gabrielle Genet, to the *Assistance publique,* and was raised by a family of peasants.

CAREER: Joined the French Foreign Legion, under a false name, and subsequently deserted; was a beggar, thief, and homosexual prostitute; was thrown out of five countries and spent time in thirteen jails before he was thirty-five; novelist, dramatist, and poet.

AWARDS, HONORS: Village Voice Off-Broadway (Obie) Awards, 1960, for *The Balcony,* and 1961, for *The Blacks.* Literary Grand Prix (France), 1983.

WRITINGS:

Notre-Dame-des-Fleurs (novel), dated from Fresnes prison, 1942, limited edition, L'Arbalete, 1943, revised edition published by Gallimard (Paris), 1951, French & European Publications (New York), 1966, translation by Bernard Frechtman published as *Our Lady of the Flowers,* Morihien (Paris), 1949, published with introduction by Jean-Paul Sartre, Grove, 1963.

Miracle de la rose (prose-poem), dated from La Sante and Tourelles prisons, 1943, L'Arbalete, 1946, 2nd edition, L'Arbalete, 1956, translation by Frechtman published as *Miracle of the Rose,* Blond, 1965, Grove, 1966.

Chants secrets (poems), privately printed (Lyons), 1944.

Querelle de Brest, privately printed, 1947, translation by Gregory Streatham published as *Querelle of Brest,* Blond, 1966, translation by Anselm Hollo published as *Querelle,* Grove, 1974.

Pompes funebres, privately printed, c. 1947, revised edition, 1948, translation by Frechtman published as *Funeral Rites,* Grove, 1969.

Poemes, L'Arbalete, 1948, 2nd edition, 1962.

Journal du voleur, Gallimard, 1949, French & European Publications, 1966, translation by Frechtman published as *The Thief's Journal,* foreword by Sartre, Olympia Press, 1954, Grove, 1964.

Haute surveillance (play; first performed at Theatre des Mathurins, February, 1949), Gallimard, 1949, French & European Publications, 1965, translation by Frechtman published as *Deathwatch: A Play* (also see below; produced as *Deathwatch,* off-Broadway at Theatre East, October 9, 1958), Faber, 1961.

L'Enfant criminel et 'Adame Miroir, Morihien, 1949.

Les beaux gars, [Paris], 1951.

Les Bonnes (play; first performed in Paris, April 17, 1947), Pauvert, 1954, French & European Publications, 1963, translation by Frechtman published as *The Maids* (also see below; produced in New York at Tempo Playhouse, May 6, 1955), introduction by Sartre, Grove, 1954, augmented French edition published as *Les Bonnes et comment jouer Les Bonnes,* M. Barbezat, 1963.

The Maids [and] *Deathwatch,* introduction by Sartre, Grove, 1954, revised edition, 1962.

Le Balcon (play; produced in Paris at Theatre du Gymnase, May 18, 1960), illustrated with lithographs by Alberto Giacometti, L'Arbalete, 1956, French & European Publications, 1962, translation by Frechtman published as *The Balcony* (produced in London at London Arts Theatre Club, April 22, 1957; produced on Broadway at Circle in the Square, March 3, 1960), Faber, 1957, Grove, 1958, revised edition, Grove, 1960, reprint of French edition edited by David Walker, published under original title, Century Texts, 1982.

Les Negres: Clownerie (play; first produced at Theatre de Lutece, October 28, 1959), M. Barbezat, 1958, 3rd edition, published with photographs, M. Barbezat, 1963, translation by Frechtman published as *The Blacks: A Clown Show* (produced as *The Blacks* off-Broadway at St. Mark's Playhouse, May 4, 1961), Grove, 1960.

Les Paravents (play; produced in Stockholm, Sweden at Alleteatern Theatre, 1964), M. Barbezat, 1961, French & European Publications, 1976, translation by Frechtman published as *The Screens* (produced in Brooklyn, NY, at Brooklyn Academy of Music, November, 1971), Grove, 1962.

Lettres a Roger Blin, Gallimard, 1966, translation by Richard Seaver published as *Letters to Roger Blin: Reflections on the Theater,* Grove, 1969 (same translation published in England as *Reflections on the Theatre, and Other Writings,* Faber, 1972).

May Day Speech (delivered in 1970 at Yale University), with description by Allen Ginsberg, City Lights, 1970.

The Complete Poems of Jean Genet, Man-Root, 1980.

Treasures of the Night: Collected Poems of Jean Genet, Gay Sunshine, 1981.

The Selected Writings of Jean Genet, edited by Edmund White, Ecco Press, 1995.

OMNIBUS VOLUMES

Oeuvres completes, Volume I (contains *Saint Genet: Co-medien et martyr,* by Jean-Paul Sartre), Volume II (contains *Notre-Dame-des-Fleurs, Le Condamne a mort, Miracle de la rose,* and *Un Chant d'amour*), Volume III (contains *Pompes funebres, Le Pecheur du suquet,* and *Querelle de Brest*), Volume IV (contains *Les Bonnes, Le Balcon,* and *Haute Surveillance*), Volume V (contains *Le Funambule, Le Secret de Rembrandt, L'Atelier d'Alberto Giacometti, Les Negres, Les Paravents,* and *L'Enfant criminel*), Gallimard, 1951-79, Volumes I-IV (with Volume IV containing additional works, *L'Etrange Mot d'. . . . , Ce qui est reste d'un Rembrant dechire en petits carres, Comment jouer Les Bonnes,* and *Comment jouer Le Balcon*), French & European Publications, 1951-53.

L'Atelier d'Alberto Giacometti; Les Bonnes, suivi d'une lettre; L'Enfant criminel [and] *Le Funambule,* L'Arbalete, 1958.

OTHER

Work is represented in anthologies, including *Seven Plays of the Modern Theatre,* edited by Harold Clurman, Grove, 1962. Creator of the film, "A Song of Love," based on Genet's poem "Un Chant d'amour." Author of scenario, "Mademoiselle," Woodfall Films, 1966. Contributor to *Esquire.*

MEDIA ADAPTATIONS: Le Balcon was filmed and released as *The Balcony* by Continental in 1963; *Querelle de Brest* was filmed as *Querelle of Brest* and *Haute surveillance* was filmed as *Deathwatch*; a filmed stage performance of *The Maids* was released in 1975. Selections from Genet's works have been recorded on Caedmon Records, including a reading by Genet, in French, from *Journal du voleur.*

SIDELIGHTS: Jean Genet's works rarely inspire indifference. For some readers, he was a creative genius; for others, he was a mere pornographer. Indeed, his works, his attitudes, his theories, and the criticism written about him seem founded on irreconcilable oppositions.

Although the facts of Genet's life are mixed with fiction, it is certain that he was born in 1910 in Paris. His father was unknown, and his mother, Gabrielle Genet, abandoned him at birth. As a ward of the *Assistance publique,* he spent his early childhood in an orphanage. As a young boy he was assigned to a peasant family in the Morvan region of France. The foster parents, who were paid by the state to raise him, accused him of theft, and some time between the age of ten and fifteen he was sent to the Mettray Reformatory, a penal colony for adolescents. After escaping from Mettray and joining and deserting the Foreign Legion, Genet spent the next twenty years wandering throughout Europe where he made his living as a thief and male prostitute.

According to the legend, he began writing his first novels in jail and quickly rose to literary prominence. Having been sentenced to life in prison for a crime he did not commit, he received a presidential pardon from Vincent Auriol in 1948, primarily because of a petition circulated by an elite group of Parisian writers and intellectuals. After 1948 Genet devoted himself to literature, the theatre, the arts, and various social causes—particularly those espoused by the Black Panthers.

Francois Mauriac, a fervent opponent of Genet's work, rebuked him in a 1949 article "The Case of Jean Genet" ("Le Cas Jean Genet") for what Mauriac considered "worse than vice and crime, namely the *literary* utilization of vice and crime, their methodical exploitation." Mauriac, in conceding Genet's talent but deploring its use, ironically helped confirm Genet's stature as a writer. At the opposite end of the critical pole were the Parisian intellectuals, led by Jean-Paul Sartre and Jean Cocteau, who quickly became ardent defenders of Genet and his work. Sartre's 1952 portrayal of the writer as existential hero in *Saint Genet: Actor and Martyr (Saint Genet, comedien et martyr)* elevated him to the status of cult hero and his work to a legitimate object of scholarly research.

Recent analyses of Genet's works have become less occupied with their morality than with their complexities of style, thematic structures, aesthetic theories, and transformations of the life into the legend. In addition, scholarship has revised many of the early opinions of his works. It is now clear, for example, that Genet purposely created myths about his life and art. The once widely accepted story of the uneducated convict creating works of genius in a jail cell was undoubtedly created to enhance his opportunities for financial and literary success. It is now certain that Genet had read Proust and that he was aware of his literary ancestors, such as de Sade, Rimbaud, Lautreamont, Celine, Jouhandeau, Pirandello, and the surrealists.

One useful aspect of the Genet myth is the idea that his development as a writer was from poetry to novels to plays. According to the legend, his initial creative effort was a poem written in prison, and, in fact, his first published work was his poem "The Condemned Man" ("Le condamne a mort"), of 1942. The period from 1942 to 1948 was dominated by four major novels and one fictionalized autobiography. He also wrote two plays, of which one, *The Maids (Les Bonnes)*, was produced by Louis Jouvet in 1947. Although Genet made two films between 1949 and 1956 (*Imagenetions* and *Song of Love*), he commented in a 1965 *Playboy* interview that "Sartre's book created a void which made for a kind of psychological deterioration . . . [and I] remained in that awful state for six years." His most successful theatrical period was from 1956 to 1962. During that time, he wrote and presented three plays—all successful major productions. Various ballets, mimes, films, aesthetic criticism and sociopolitical statements were interspersed throughout his years of productivity, from about 1937 to 1979. Weakened by ill health, Genet published little after 1979.

From his first poem *The Condemned Man,* to his last work, the play *The Screens (Les Paravents)*, Genet dealt with constant subjects: homosexuality, criminality (murder, theft, corruption), saintliness, reality and illusion, history, politics, racism, revolution, aesthetics, solitude. Many people have been shocked not only by his themes but also by his attitude toward himself, his life, and his material—and most of all by his stated intention to corrupt. He openly professed his homosexuality, his admiration for crime and criminals, his joy in theft, and his contempt for the society that rejected him. His vitriolic and scatological attacks on accepted social values made him the target of innumerable moralists.

Genet's early success as a novelist may certainly be attributed to various factors—to the support of Cocteau and Sartre, to the scandal arising from his subject matter, and to the notoriety of the thief as novelist. The critics long continued to accept the simplistic legend of the unlettered convict genius despite the classical references and other literary allusions, the sophisticated structures, and the sheer volume of work purportedly created between 1942 and 1948. The legend persisted until 1970 when Richard N. Coe published, in *The Theatre of Jean Genet: A Casebook,* an essay by Lily Pringsheim in which she reported that the Genet she had known in Germany in 1937 was of "a truly astonishing intelligence. . . . I could scarcely believe the extent of his knowledge of literature." She also revealed that Genet begged her "to store away a number of manuscripts . . . and that he shared [with her friend Leuschner] an uncontrollable thirst for knowledge, for Leuschner, like Genet, carried books about with him everywhere he went: Shakespeare, language textbooks, scientific treatises."

A simple count of the major works supposedly created by Genet between 1942 and 1948, when he was in and out of prison, should have led some critics to question the legend. The staggering production of this period allegedly included four novels, an autobiography, two plays, three poems, and a ballet. Pringsheim's testimony supports the idea that a major portion of the work was done at an earlier date and in libraries with reference sources. In his very first novel, *Our Lady of the Flowers (Notre-Dame-des-Fleurs)*, supposedly written in Fresnes prison, Genet accurately quoted from *The Constitutional and Administrative History of France* by the nineteenth-century historian Jean-Baptiste-Honore-Raymond Capefigue. Furthermore, in a letter to the author of this essay, Genet confirmed that he had read *The Memoires on the Private Life of Marie Antoinette* by Madame Genet-Campan. The fact that Genet had read these rather unusual works, had quoted accurately from one of them (supposedly while in prison), and had used the other as a source for material in his play *The Maids,* leads one to several conclusions: major portions of *Our Lady* were written outside prison, Genet was extremely well read and undoubtedly an habitue of libraries, and he probably received the basics of a traditional French education while incarcerated as a boy at the Mettray reformatory.

Of the five novels, counting the fictionalized autobiography, *The Thief's Journal (Journal du voleur)*, critics consider *Our Lady of the Flowers* and *Miracle of the Rose (Miracle de la rose)* to be the best. Genet's first novel was brought to Jean Cocteau's attention by three young men who had become acquainted with Genet who was then selling books (some stolen) from a bookstall along the Seine. Cocteau recognized the literary merit of *Our Lady,* which is a tour de force. This novel is unique for several reasons: its basic philosophy, its sophisticated literary technique, and its composite central character Genet-Divine-Culafroy. Some critics think that Genet, the uneducated convict, should be considered a precursor of the "new novel"—that literary movement which came into being as a protest against the traditional novel. Genet's works, like those of the well-known "new novelists" Alain Robbe-Grillet and Michel Butor, may be considered untraditional in their disregard of conventional psychology, their lack of careful transitions, their confused chronologies, and their disdain for coherent plot structures.

To understand *Our Lady,* or any of Genet's works, one must turn to Sartre's *Saint Genet* for an explanation of the "sophistry of the Nay." Sartre explained Genet's view of the world by relating it to the concept of the saint. According to Sartre, saintliness results from refusing something—honors, power, or money, for example—and the seekers after saintliness soon "convince themselves and others that they have refused everything": "With these men appeared the sophistry of the Nay . . . [and] in a destructive society which places the blossoming of being at the moment of its annihilation, the Saint, making use of divine meditation, claims that a Nay carried to the extreme is necessarily transformed into a Yea. Extreme poverty is wealth, refusal is acceptance, the absence of God is the dazzling manifestation of his presence, to live is to die, to die is to live, etc. One step further and we are back at the sophisms of Genet: sin is the yawning chasm of God. In going to the limit of nothingness, one finds being, to love is to betray, etc." From this concept, Sartre postulated the concept of the "eternal couple of the criminal and the saint": hence, the legitimacy of the pursuit of saintliness by the homosexual thief Genet-Divine-Culafroy, the hero/heroine of *Our Lady.* The plot of this "epic of masturbation," as Sartre first labeled it, is difficult to follow because Genet wanders from past to present without transition in an episodic celebration of perversity. Louis Culafroy, a twenty-year-old peasant, arrives in Paris from the provinces. He assumes the name Divine and makes his living as a thief and male prostitute. Through the story of Our Lady's conviction for the murder of a helpless old pederast, it is the development of the Genet-Divine-Culafroy character which focuses the novel and provides its true literary merit.

In his next two "novels," Genet followed the successful formula used in *Our Lady. Miracle of the Rose* relates the story of Harcamone, "graduate" of the Mettray reformatory, who, betrayed by a fellow convict, murders a prison guard in order to die "gloriously" rather than serve a life sentence. The novel concludes with the mystical experience that Genet, the work's narrator, supposedly underwent the night prior to Harcamone's execution. Although this novel provides certain insights into Genet's life, the reader must be cautious about regarding the work as strictly autobiographical. The writer stipulated that his life must "be a legend, in other words, legible, and the reading of it must give birth to a certain new emotion that I call poetry." *Miracle,* which is easier to follow than *Our Lady,* may be marred by the excessive self-consciousness of its technique. Yet, as in *Our Lady,* Genet set forth in *Miracle* his inversion of good and evil, his longing for deification through degradation, and his homo-eroticism.

In *The Thief's Journal* Genet revealed much about his incredible odyssey through the criminal underworld and the sordid prisons of Europe in the 1930s and 1940s. Even if only partially factual, the book remains a fascinating social document. But whether Genet's works are primarily social documents or private mythologies is a question that frequently occupies critics. For example, Lucian Goldmann, in *La Creation culturelle dans la societe moderne (Cultural Creation in Modern Society),* labels Genet the "greatest advocate of social revolt in contemporary French literature." Yet, in *Narcissus Absconditus, the Problematic Art of Autobiography in Contemporary France,* Germaine Bree stresses the mythological aspect of his work saying that *Journal* "gyrates upon itself, proclaiming its symbol-laden ceremonies to be fiction."

Funeral Rites (Pompes funebres) and *Querelle of Brest (Querelle de Brest)* are Genet's least successful works. *Funeral* is Genet's lament for a lover killed during the liberation of Paris, and *Querelle* relates the depressing story of a sailor who is a murderer, thief, and opium smuggler. Both works concentrate on homosexuality, and *Querelle* is the only Genet novel that is not fictionalized autobiography. The critical judgments about his novels reflect the antitheses so often associated with the author and his works: the novels are considered poetic eroticism or pornographic trash, lyrical incantations or demented exhibitionism, sociological documents or masturbatory fantasies. They have been described—and this is only a partial catalogue of labels employed—as existentialist, solipsistic, ambiguous, mythological, homosexual, popular, Freudian, semi-mystical, humorous, basically romantic, adolescent, obscene, blasphemous, ahistorical, archetypal.

Genet's works for the theater may be divided into two periods—1947 to 1949 and 1956 to 1962. It is generally accepted that although *The Maids* was the first play produced, *Deathwatch (Haute Surveillance)* was written earlier. The several revisions that Genet made of *Deathwatch* suggest that he was little satisfied with the original version of the play so often compared to Sartre's *No Exit.* This first play by the "convict-genius" is tightly constructed, almost classical in conception and presentation. The unities of time, place, and action are strictly observed. However, the concept of decorum is violated by the on-stage murder of Maurice by Lefranc, and the language and premise of the author are definitely not classical. Once again, the spectators and the critic are confronted with the concept of the "criminal and the saint."

Genet established a criminal-religious hierarchy—that is, the more serious the crime the more "saintly" the criminal. Within this hierarchy Genet developed those subjects consistently found throughout his work: betrayal, murder, homosexuality, theft, and solitude. Although there is some dispute over who the "hero" really is, it seems obvious that Lefranc, not Green Eyes, is the preferred Genetian hero because he chooses his murder and opts for prison, whereas Green Eyes repudiates his murder. Furthermore, Lefranc admits that he is provoked to murder Maurice by an imaginary spray of lilacs, symbol of fate and death. Lefranc seeks to become the "Lilac Murderer" in imitation of other thugs who have acquired exotic nicknames appropriate to their crimes—the Avenger, the Panther, the Tornado, for example. *Deathwatch* thus serves as an excellent example of Genet's creative process. As the author of this essay has commented in the *French Review,* "he began with a basic symbol, that is, it is unlucky to take lilacs into a house for they will cause a death, and then expanded this symbol to include the basic themes of the play—murder, betrayal, fate, sex, and the criminal-religious hierarchy. By bedecking his criminals with lilacs, Genet has created a gigantic and a new flower-symbol."

The Maids, based on an actual murder committed by the Papin sisters, is a one-act play that serves as a brilliant example of Genet's ability to create complex structures for what Sartre called his "whirligig of reality and illusion." Genet wanted very much to have the female roles performed by young men. He also wanted a sign posted to inform the audience of the deception. This would have added two more levels of illusion to the already complicated role-playing wherein one of the maids assumes the guise of their mistress and her sister plays the role of the sister playing the mistress. As the author of this essay discusses in *Kentucky Romance Quarterly,* a remarkably complicated work results: "The complexity of Genet's genius is such that he can create a play such as *The Maids* based on 'historical materials' which is at the same time an illustration of the philosophical concept of the eternal couple of the criminal and the saint, a 'Fable' based on the history of Marie Antoinette and the French Revolution, and an example of a black mass."

The Balcony, unlike the first two plays in which there is a certain classical simplicity of form, is a long and complex series of scenes that take place primarily in Madame Irma's "House of Illusions," a brothel where various rooms are reserved for the ritualized performance of erotic fantasies based on such equations as sex/power, sex/religion, and sex/revolution. In the preface to the definitive edition of the play, Genet stressed that his play was not a satire but the "glorification of the Image and the Reflection. . . ." Richard N. Coe, in *The Vision of Jean Genet,* considers *The Balcony* an example of Genet's essential conception of drama: "The highest, most compelling form of experience—the experience which Genet describes as sacred and which forms the basis of all his mysticism—occurs when the human consciousness becomes simultaneously aware of the two co-existent dimensions of existence: the real and the transcendental. This, as Genet sees it, is the underlying miracle of the Christian Eucharist; and it is also the principle of all true theatre." Given Genet's obsession with religion and saintliness, it becomes more understandable why he objected so strenuously to Zadek's realistic London production of *The Balcony.* For, as Martin Esslin points out in *The Theatre of the Absurd,* Genet desired that "his fantasies of sex and power . . . be staged with the solemnity and the outward splendor of the liturgy in one of the world's great cathedrals."

Genet's last two major artistic creations, *The Blacks (Les Negres)* and *The Screens* may well have provided him with his most satisfying moments in his war on society. Both plays, in which racism or colonialism are presented within the context of Genetian ritual and ceremony, are vitriolic attacks on bourgeois values. *The Blacks,* written in 1957 and performed in 1959, is a play within a play. The audience, which must always include a white person or an effigy of one, is entertained with a ritual re-enactment of the murder of a white woman by a black man. The murderer is convicted by a white court—blacks wearing white masks. However, the trial of the murderer is a diversion from the real crime—a black traitor's execution—that is supposedly taking place off-stage. Presenting blacks acting out their hatred of whites and of white society, the play had its greatest success and most profound impact at the time of the race riots in America in the late 1960s. Although Bettina Knapp declares in *Jean Genet* that nothing real occurs on stage, that "The whole ritual on stage, then, is a big joke, a game, a 'clownerie' (the subtitle of the play)," it is more often believed that Genet's play was one of the first theatrical productions in which black actors confronted a primarily white audience with an expression of their suppressed hatreds and prejudices. It was certainly instrumental in the creation of a true black theater movement.

Criticism of *The Blacks* attests that, even in the black community, there was, as usual, a wide divergence of opinion. E. Bullins, the editor of *Black Theatre,* attacked the play and its author: "Jean Genet is a white, self-confessed homosexual with dead, white Western ideas—faggoty ideas about Black Art, Revolution, and people. His empty masochistic activities and platitudes on behalf of the Black Panthers should not con Black people. . . . Beware of whites who plead the Black cause." However, most critics, black or white, saw the play as an expression of black liberation, of black psychology, and of the bitterness in race relations. Very few critics accepted what director Roger Blin insisted was Genet's intention: to present a play that was an exercise in aesthetics, not in politics or psychology.

Genet's last work, *The Screens,* must also have provided him with endless hours of amused satisfaction at critical reactions. The play, an obvious attack on French colonialism and a virulent condemnation of the war in Algeria, naturally provoked hostile reactions from the right-wing element in France. Published in 1961, the play was not performed in its entirety until 1964 in Stockholm. Due to its explosive content, *The Screens* was banned in France until 1966, when it was presented for a total of forty performances at the behest of Andre Malraux, Minister of Culture. It must have delighted Genet's sense of irony to see his play produced at the Odeon, the theater of France, for the play is an attack on the nation. Even more ironic was the need for police protection because of the violence directed at the actors and the author by "honest patriots." The outcast, the rejected orphan, the despised homosexual and thief, had had the last word.

The word "complexity" is constantly present in critics' discussions of Genet's works. Whether the complexity was intentional or the result of literary, educational, or philosophic insufficiency depends on what education Genet received while at the Mettray reformatory and on when exactly he began writing. If we accept Pringsheim's statements, Genet was not only experimenting with verse and prose in 1937, he had already written several manuscripts and was in possession of and reading Shakespeare, language textbooks, and other material—all of this many years before he supposedly wrote *Our Lady of the Flowers* in Fresnes prison and long before he had met either Cocteau or Sartre. His first published novel does clearly reveal sophisticated techniques and classical allusions indicating that the legend of the uneducated convict genius was greatly exaggerated by Sartre, Cocteau, and Genet himself. He may have been primarily self-taught, and it is certain that he spent long hours reading and doing research in libraries. But the story that he was miraculously endowed in prison with literary talent and a vast store of classical and literary knowledge is clearly apocryphal.

BIOGRAPHICAL/CRITICAL SOURCES:

BOOKS

Bree, Germaine, *Narcissus Absconditus, the Problematic Art of Autobiography in Contemporary France,* Clarendon Press, 1978.

Brooks, Peter, and Joseph Halpern, editors, *Genet: A Collection of Critical Essays,* Prentice-Hall, 1979.

Brophy, Brigid, *Don't Never Forget: Collected Views and Reviews,* Holt, 1966.

Brustein, Robert, *The Theatre of Revolt: An Approach to Modern Drama,* Little, Brown, 1964, pp. 361-411.

Burgess, Anthony, *The Novel Now: A Guide to Contemporary Fiction,* Norton, 1967.

Cetta, Lewis T., *Profane Play, Ritual and Jean Genet: A Study of His Drama,* University of Alabama Press, 1974.

Choukri, Mohamed, *Jean Genet in Tangier,* Ecco Press, 1974.

Coe, Richard N., *The Theatre of Jean Genet: A Casebook,* Grove, 1970.

Coe, Richard N., *The Vision of Jean Genet,* Grove, 1968.

Contemporary Literary Criticism, Gale (Detroit), Volume 1, 1973; Volume 2, 1974; Volume 5, 1976; Volume 10, 1979; Volume 14, 1980; Volume 44, 1987; Volume 46, 1988.

Driver, Tom F., *Jean Genet,* Columbia University Press, 1966.

Esslin, Martin, *The Theatre of the Absurd,* Anchor Books, 1961, pp. 140-67.

Goldmann, Lucian, *La Creation culturelle dans la societe moderne (Cultural Creation in Modern Society),* Denoel, 1971.

Grossvogel, D. I., *Four Playwrights and a Postscript,* Cornell University Press, 1962, pp. 133-74.

Guicharnaud, Jacques, *Modern French Theatre: From Giraudoux to Genet,* revised edition, Yale University Press, 1967, pp. 259-77.

Hauptman, Robert, *The Pathological Vision,* Peter Lang, 1983, pp. 1-50.

Hayman, Ronald, *Theatre and Anti-theatre: New Movements since Beckett,* Oxford University Press, 1979.

Jacobsen, Josephine, and William R. Mueller, *Ionesco and Genet,* Hill & Wang, 1968.

Kennelly, Brian Gordon, *Unfinished Business: Tracing Incompletion in Jean Genet's Posthumously Published Plays,* Editions Rodopi, 1997.

Knapp, Bettina, *Jean Genet,* Twayne, 1968.

Kostelanetz, Richard, editor, *On Contemporary Literature,* Avon, 1964.

McMahon, J. H., *The Imagination of Jean Genet,* Yale University Press, 1964.

Naish, Camille, *A Genetic Approach to Structures in the Work of Jean Genet,* Harvard University Press, 1978.

Sartre, Jean-Paul, *Saint Genet, comedien et martyr,* Gallimard, 1952, translation by Bernard Frenchtman published as *Saint Genet: Actor and Martyr,* Braziller, 1963.

Savona, Jeanette L., *Jean Genet,* Macmillan, 1983.

Thody, Phillip, *Jean Genet: A Study of His Novels and Plays,* Stein & Day, 1969.

Webb, Richard C., and Suzanne A. Webb, *Jean Genet: An Annotated Bibliography, 1943-1980,* Scarecrow, 1982.

Winkler, Josef, *Flowers for Jean Genet,* translated by Michael Roloff, Ariadne (Riverside, CA), 1996.

PERIODICALS

American Cinematographer, May, 1963.
Atlantic, January, 1965.
Black Theatre, number 5, 1971.
Book Week, October 6, 1963.
Commentary, July, 1994.
Contemporary Literature, autumn, 1975.
Dance, December, 1969.
Dance News, September, 1957.
Drama, summer, 1972.
Drama Review, fall, 1969.
Drama Survey, spring-summer, 1967.
French Review, December, 1971; October, 1974; December, 1974; April, 1980; December, 1981; May, 1984.
Harper, January, 1965; September, 1974.
Horizon, November 29, 1964.
Kentucky Romance Quarterly, number 3, 1985.
Kenyon Review, March, 1967.
Modern Drama, September, 1967; September, 1969; March, 1974; September, 1976.
Nation, March 20, 1954; November 2, 1963; January 14, 1964; December 27, 1971.
New Leader, October 28, 1974.
New Republic, November 23, 1963.
New Statesman, January 10, 1964.
Newsweek, December 20, 1971; May 9, 1983.
New Yorker, January 16, 1965; October 21, 1974.
New York Times, January 19, 1986.
New York Times Book Review, September 29, 1963; February 19, 1967; June 15, 1969; September 8, 1974.
Partisan Review, April, 1949.
Playboy, April, 1964, pp. 45-55.
Saturday Review, June 18, 1960; November 14, 1964; July 12, 1969; November 15, 1969.
Southern Review, March, 1975; March, 1978.
Times Literary Supplement, October 31, 1958; April 8, 1965.
Village Voice, March 18, 1965.
Vogue, December, 1988.
Washington Post Book World, November 3, 1974.

*   *   *

GEORGES, Georges Martin
See SIMENON, Georges (Jacques Christian)

*   *   *

GEROME
See THIBAULT, Jacques Anatole Francois

*   *   *

GIBB, Lee
See WATERHOUSE, Keith (Spencer)

*   *   *

GIBBONS, Kaye 1960-

PERSONAL: Born in 1960, in Nash County, NC; married once (divorced); partner of Frank Ward (an attorney); children: three daughters. *Education:* Attended North Carolina State University and the University of North Carolina at Chapel Hill.

ADDRESSES: Home—Raleigh, NC.

CAREER: Novelist.

AWARDS, HONORS: Sue Kaufman Prize for First Fiction, American Academy and Institute of Arts and Letters, and citation from Ernest Hemingway Foundation, both for *Ellen Foster;* National Endowment for the Arts fellowship, for *A Virtuous Woman;* Nelson Algren Heartland Award for Fiction, *Chicago Tribune,* 1991, and PEN/Revson Foundation Fellowship, both for *A Cure for Dreams.*

WRITINGS:

NOVELS

Ellen Foster, Algonquin Books (Chapel Hill, NC), 1987.
A Virtuous Woman, Algonquin Books, 1989.
A Cure for Dreams, Algonquin Books, 1991.
Charms for the Easy Life, Putnam (New York), 1993, large print edition, Wheeler, 1993.
Sights Unseen, Putnam, 1995, large print edition, G. K. Hall, 1995.
On the Occasion of My Last Afternoon, Putnam, 1998.

Contributor to the *New York Times Book Review.*

SIDELIGHTS: Kaye Gibbons has won a number of literary awards and much praise for her body of fiction, a group of novels predominantly set in rural Southern communities not unlike Nash County, North Carolina, where their author grew up. From the matriarchal folk healer to the uncompromising eleven-year-old, Gibbons's strong central characters—almost always female—

possess a grounding and wisdom that transcends the often-difficult circumstances of lives. Writing in *Publishers Weekly,* critic Bob Summer termed them "Southern women who shoulder the burdens of their ordinary lives with extraordinary courage."

Ellen Foster began life as a poem Gibbons started writing while a student at the University of North Carolina at Chapel Hill, initially in the voice of the protagonist's young African-American friend, Starletta. The author admitted to being influenced by the work of early twentieth-century African-American poet James Weldon Johnson, and his use of common speech patterns and idioms in his prose. "I wanted to see if I could have a child use her voice to talk about life, death, art, eternity—big things from a little person," Gibbons told Summer. Ellen Foster's title character is a mere eleven years of age, and the story follows her travails in the rural southern states as she bounces from relative to relative. Told in the first person, Gibbons's heroine refers to herself as "old Ellen," and recounts her difficulties in flashback form. Deanna D'Errico described her in *Belles Lettres* as "the embodiment of tenacity, surviving with the tools of intelligence, sensitivity, a strong will, and a remarkable sense of humor." In the novel, Ellen's mother was the frail scion of a well-to-do family whom she alienated by marrying beneath her, and their offspring has it rough from the start. When her mother commits suicide, Ellen is left with a parent whom she describes as "a monster." His attempt at sexual abuse one drunken night leads Ellen to the jurisdiction of the court system, and a judge sends her to live with her wealthy, but extremely resentful, maternal grandmother.

Ellen's grandmother vents her grief at her daughter's suicide on her granddaughter, forcing her to work the family cotton fields and inflicting verbal and emotional abuse upon her. Over the course of Gibbons's novel, Ellen faces her problems with a good nature and determination: she learns to hoard money in a small box that contains all of her other vital belongings. She also befriends the aforementioned Starletta, who is mute. "Gibbons, unlike so many writers of the New South, doesn't evade the racism of Southern life," wrote Pearl K. Bell in a review of *Ellen Foster* for the *New Republic.* Growing up hearing the racial prejudices of her family, Ellen also feels such biases, and reminds herself that no matter how bad her own situation is, it would be worse to be "colored."

When Ellen's grandmother dies, she is sent to live with an aunt, and the aunt and Ellen's cousin also heap abuse upon her—at one point, ridiculing the picture she has drawn for them for a Christmas present as "cheap-looking." When the aunt sends her away, Ellen spends a night at Starletta's home, which eventually leads to the protagonist's realization that "now I know it is not the germs you cannot see . . . that will hurt you or turn you colored. What you had better worry about though is the people you knew and trusted they would be like you because you were all made in the same batch." In the end, Ellen discovers that her small town contains a "foster" family—a single woman who takes in children. She shows up on their doorstep and offers the one hundred-sixty-dollar contents of her box in exchange for a home.

In the *New Republic* review, Bell praised Gibbons's evocation of Ellen's unique personality through her narrative, as did many other reviewers. "The voice of this resourceful child is mesmerizing because we are right inside her head," she noted. Alice Hoffman reviewed *Ellen Foster* for the *New York Times Book Review* and asserted that the first-time author "is so adept at drawing her characters that we know Ellen, and, yes, trust her from the start." Hoffman further noted that "in many ways this is

an old-fashioned novel about traditional values and inherited prejudices. . . . What might have been grim, melodramatic material in the hands of a less talented author is instead filled with lively humor. . ., compassion and intimacy." *Sunday Times* critic Linda Taylor termed Gibbons's debut "fresh, instant and enchanting . . . a first novel that does not put a foot wrong in its sureness of style, tone and characterisation."

In her second novel, *A Virtuous Woman,* Gibbons again sets her characters in the rural South and allows them to speak in the idiomatic, direct language of her own upbringing. The 1989 work opens as Jack Stokes laments the loss of Ruby, his wife of many years, from lung cancer. "She hasn't been dead four months and I've already eaten to the bottom of the deep freeze," the farmer thinks to himself; despite her illness, Ruby had prepared months worth of meals ahead of time for Jack. Such details pointing to the ordinary, yet loving familiarities of the institution of marriage are what Gibbons attempts to call forth in the story. *A Virtuous Woman* is told in alternating first-person flashbacks for most of its course—Jack looking back after she is gone, alternating with Ruby's ruminations on their life together in the months before her death. The reader learns how Ruby's disastrous first marriage ultimately resulted in her inoperable tumors, and why her marriage to Jack was less vivid than her first, but over time, ultimately more satisfying.

As both characters in *A Virtuous Woman* come to grips with their impending tragedy, the interior monologues that Gibbons has Jack and Ruby voice in the novel propel it forward. Toward the end, Gibbons switches to a third-person perspective as the motivations and actions of other characters involved in Jack and Ruby's life come into play. "Too often, lacking a conflict of its own, the story wanders off to peek in at the neighbors," remarked *Los Angeles Times Book Review* critic Susan Heeger of this literary construction. "Pages are spent on the meanness of peripheral folk, whose main raison d'etre is to show up Jack's and Ruby's saintliness and to raise the question of why bad things happen to good people." The critic D'Errico, writing again for *Belles Lettres,* also found this switch disconcerting. "Technique suddenly looms over the tale," she lamented, "and it is difficult to view the scene without fretting over the strings that are showing."

Gibbons's third novel, 1991's *A Cure for Dreams,* won the *Chicago Tribune*'s Nelson Algren Heartland award for fiction that same year. In it, Gibbons recounts the multigenerational family saga of a trio of three women: Lottie, her daughter Betty, and granddaughter Marjorie. The novel begins as Marjorie introduces her recently-deceased mother Betty to the reader, and relates how much her mother loved to talk. "Talking was my mother's life," she says, and the story is soon overtaken by Betty's own narrative voice. Betty describes her indomitable Irish immigrant grandmother—Lottie's mother—and the harsh life Lottie suffered in rural Kentucky during the early years of the twentieth century. Lottie escapes by marriage, but her workaholic husband isolates her emotionally until Betty arrives as a newborn in 1920.

As some reviewers noted, most of the male characters in *A Cure for Dreams* seem unsympathetic figures, absorbed in their own world of nonverbal communication, while the women ultimately triumph over adversity by virtue of their need to communicate with one another, resulting in strong bonds. In coming together, they manage to overcome both petty and grievous abuses inflicted upon them by the men of their families. Throughout the course of *A Cure for Dreams,* Gibbons lets Betty continue the decades-long tale of her family, recalling how her mother Lottie became the de facto community leader of the women around North Carolina's Milk Farm Road in the 1920s. She organized card parties, passed along useful gossip and wisdom, and at one point even protected a friend who may or may not have shot her abusive husband. Betty's own saga of coming of age in the South of the 1930s is also recounted, and the novel ends with the birth of her daughter Marjorie during World War II.

The overwhelming successes of Gibbons's literary career were also accompanied by some periods of behind-the-scenes strife during the early 1990s. She went through a divorce, relocated to New York City—but returned to North Carolina—and changed publishers. In 1993, her fourth novel, *Charms for the Easy Life,* was published. Like *A Cure for Dreams,* the story follows the exploits of a family of strong women, and develops through the recollections of its youngest member. Set over a forty-year span that ends during World War II, narrator Margaret begins the novel by recounting the courtship of her grandparents in Pasquotank County, North Carolina. Her grandmother, Charlie (Clarissa) Kate, becomes the central figure in the novel through her work as a local midwife and faith healer. Gibbons had originally modeled the character on an African-American midwife who served as the best friend of Lottie in her previous novel, but reconsidered doing a sequel after she began, and instead made Charlie into a completely separate entity.

Like Lottie in *A Cure for Dreams,* Charlie becomes a vital and important force in her rural community. When she saves an African-American man from a lynching, he gives her a rabbit's foot, her "easy-life charm." A folk healer who reads the *New England Journal of Medicine,* Charlie promotes sex education and manages to put a halt to the damaging medical treatment meted out by the charlatan local "trained" doctor. She is also the first person in the community to own a toilet. "She's an implacable force of nature, a pillar of intellect, with insight and powers of intuition so acute as to seem nearly supernatural," remarked Stephen McCauley of Gibbons's creation in the *New York Times Book Review.* As in previous works, the author allowed few compassionate male characters into the story of the three women. "The men in their lives are largely ineffectual," observed McCauley. "They can be relied upon only to disappoint, disappear and die." Charlie's husband simply does not return home one evening, an act which has little impact upon her young daughter Sophie. Like her mother, Sophie later enter into a marriage with the wrong man, who passes away in the middle of the night; the two then move in with Charlie. Now all three women are free to pursue their ambitions and lend support to one another. They debate literature, Sophie and Margaret act as assistants to Charlie's unofficial doctor/dentist/midwife practice, and Charlie meddles in the affairs of her granddaughter, who in turn finds inspiration from the older woman.

Gibbons's fifth novel, *Sights Unseen,* was published in 1995. The novel tells the story, from the perspective of twelve-year-old daughter Hattie, of a mother's struggle with mental illness and its pervasive influence on her family's life. Comparing *Sights Unseen* to Gibbons' first novel, *Ellen Foster, New Yorker* critic James Wolcott notes that the narrator in each novel portrays "an avid need for normality and acceptance in a world of precarious well-being." A *Publishers Weekly* reviewer cites Gibbons' "restrained prose of unflinching clarity" and praises the novel, declaring it "a haunting story that begs to be read in one sitting."

Despite the praise bestowed by critics—and the numerous awards she has received—Gibbons admits that the writer's life is a strenuous one. "Nobody ever told me it was going to be easy," she noted in the interview with Summer for *Publishers Weekly.* "If I weren't a writer, I'd probably be a lawyer or an architect. I wouldn't want to do anything easy, and I chose to be a writer." The author reflected that, "as a writer, it's my job to come up with three hundred pages or so every two years. Each time I begin, I know it's going to happen, but I'm scared it won't. It's working with that element of fear that keeps a book going," a process she also likened to "looking over an abyss and knowing I have to jump."

BIOGRAPHICAL/CRITICAL SOURCES:

BOOKS

Watkins, James, editor, *Southern Selves, from Mark Twain and Eudora Welty to Maya Angelou and Kaye Gibbons: A Collection of Autobiographical Writing,* Vintage, 1998.

PERIODICALS

Belles Lettres, summer, 1989, p. 7; winter 1993-94, pp. 16-18.
Chicago Tribune Books, September 15, 1991, p. 7.
Los Angeles Times Book Review, June 11, 1989, p. 15; May 19, 1991, p. 13.
New York Times Book Review, April 12, 1989, pp. 12-13; May 12, 1991, pp. 13-14; April 11, 1993, pp. 9-10; September 24, 1995, p. 30.
New Yorker, June 21, 1993, p. 101; August 21 and 28, 1995, pp. 115-16.
Publishers Weekly, February 8, 1993, pp. 60-61; June 5, 1995, p. 48.
San Francisco Review of Books, spring, 1991, pp. 31-32.
Times Literary Supplement, September 15, 1989, p. 998.
Women's Review of Books, July, 1989, p. 21; October, 1993, p. 24.

*   *   *

GIBRAN, Kahlil 1883-1931
(Khalil Gibran, Kahlil Jibran, Kahlil Jabran, Khalil Jibran, Khalil Jabran)

PERSONAL: Born in 1883, in Bechari, Lebanon; immigrated to the United States, 1904; died of liver disease, April 10, 1931, in New York, NY. *Education:* Studied art at the Ecole des Beaux Arts. *Religion:* Maronite Christian.

CAREER: Poet, prose writer, painter, and sculptor.

WRITINGS:

'Ar' is al-muruj (short stories), 1910, translation by H. M. Nahmad published as *Nymphs of the Valley,* Knopf (New York), 1948.
Dam 'ah wabtisamah (poetry and prose), 1914, translation by Anthony Rizcallah Ferris published as *Tears and Laughter,* edited by Martin L. Wolf, Philosophical Library (New York), 1949; also published as *A Tear and a Smile,* translation by Nahmad, introduction by Robert Hillyer, Knopf, 1950.
The Madman: His Parables and Poems (poetry and prose), Knopf, 1918.
The Forerunner: His Parables and Poems (poetry and prose), Knopf, 1920.
Al-arwah al-mutamarridah (short stories), 1922, translation by Ferris published as *Spirits Rebellious,* Philosophical Library, 1946.
The Prophet (poetry), Knopf, 1923.

Sand and Foam: A Book of Aphorisms, Knopf, 1926.

Jesus the Son of Man: His Words and His Deeds as Told and Recorded by Those Who Knew Him (prose), Knopf, 1928.

The Earth Gods (poetry and prose), Knopf, 1931.

The Wanderer: His Parables and His Sayings (aphorisms and prose), Knopf, 1932.

The Garden of the Prophet, Knopf, 1933.

Manzumat (poetry), 1934, translation by Andrew Ghareeb published as *Prose Poems,* foreword by Barbara Young, Knopf, 1934.

The Secrets of the Heart (poetry and prose), Philosophical Library, 1947; later edition published as *The Secrets of the Heart: A Special Selection,* translated from the Arabic by Ferris and edited by Wolf, Wisdom Library (New York), 1971.

A Treasury of Kahlil Gibran, translated from the Arabic by Ferris and edited by Wolf, Citadel Press (New York), 1951.

The Broken Wings (poetry; original title, *Ajnihah al-mutakassirah;* translated by Ferris), Citadel Press, 1957.

The Procession, edited, translated and with a biographical sketch by George Kheirallah, Philosophical Library, 1958.

Voice of the Master, translated from the Arabic by Ferris, Citadel Press, 1958.

Kahlil Gibran: A Self-Portrait, translated from the Arabic and edited by Ferris, Citadel Press, 1959.

Thoughts and Meditations, translated from the Arabic and edited by Ferris, Citadel Press, 1960.

Spiritual Sayings, translated from the Arabic and edited by Ferris, Citadel Press, 1962.

A Second Treasury of Kahlil Gibran, translated from the Arabic by Ferris, Citadel Press, 1962.

Mirrors of the Soul, translated and with biographical notes by Joseph Sheban, Philosophical Library, 1965.

The Wisdom of Gibran: Aphorisms and Maxims, edited by Sheban, Philosophical Library, 1966.

(With Mary Haskell) *Beloved Prophet: The Love Letters of Kahlil Gibran and Mary Haskell, and Her Private Journal,* edited and arranged by Virginia Hilu, Barrie & Jenkins (London), 1972.

Between Night and Morn: A Special Selection, translated from the Arabic by Ferris and edited by Wolf, Wisdom Library, 1972.

Lazarus and His Beloved: A One-Act Play, introduction by the author's cousin and namesake Kahlil Gibran and wife, Jean Gibran, New York Graphic Society (Greenwich, CT), 1973.

Twenty Drawings, with an introductory essay by Alice Raphael, Vintage Books (New York), 1974.

I Care about Your Happiness: Quotations from the Love Letters of Kahlil Gibran and Mary Haskell, selected by Susan Polis Schutz and Nancy Hoffman, designed and illustrated by Stephen Schutz, Blue Mountain Arts (Boulder, CO), 1976.

Dramas of Life, with introduction by the author's cousin and namesake Kahlil Gibran and wife, Jean Gibran, Westminster Press (Philadelphia), 1981.

Blue Flame: The Love Letters of Kahlil Gibran to May Ziadah, edited and translated by Suheil Bushrui and Salma Kuzbari, Longman (Harlow, England), 1983.

Kahlil Gibran: Paintings and Drawings, 1905-1930, with essay by Aram Saroyan, Vrej Baghoomian Gallery (New York), 1989.

(With Jean Gibran), *Kahlil Gibran, His Life and World,* Interlink Books, 1991, republished 1998.

Spirit Brides, translated by Juan R. I. Cole, White Cloud Press (Santa Cruz, CA), 1993.

The Storm, translation by John Walbridge, White Cloud Press, 1993.

The Beloved: Reflections on the Path of the Heart, translated by Walbridge, White Cloud Press, 1994.

The Vision: Reflections on the Way of the Soul, translated by Cole, White Cloud Press, 1994.

The Kahlil Gibran Reader: Inspirational Writings, Carol Publishing (Secaucus, NJ), 1995.

Visions of the Prophet, translated by Margaret Crosland, Frog, Ltd. (Berkely, CA), 1997.

Also author of *The Death of the Prophet.*

SIDELIGHTS: Since World War II, Kahlil Gibran has emerged as one of the most popular authors in the bookselling world. His best known work, *The Prophet,* has been translated into at least twenty different languages, and lyrical passages from Gibran's body of work are commonly read at weddings, baptisms, and funerals throughout the Western world. He has been called the most successful writer that the Arabic region has ever produced, and critics often cite the influence of biblical literature upon Gibran's style. Much of his work was infused with mysticism and dramatize a quest for self-fulfillment. Scholars have suggested comparisons between the Lebanese-American writer and nineteenth-century predecessors such as the American poet Walt Whitman, or German philosopher Friedrich Nietzsche, but overall Gibran's work has received little academic examination. As an introductory essay in *Twentieth Century Literary Criticism* pointed out, "Generally, most critics agree that Gibran had the refined sensibility of a true poet and a gift for language, but that he often marred his work by relying on shallow epigrams and trite parables."

Gibran was born in Bechari, Lebanon, in 1883. From an early age he displayed a range of artistic skills, especially in the visual arts; he continued to draw and paint throughout his life, even illustrating many of his books. Gibran's family immigrated to the United States when he was twelve and settled in the Boston area, but he returned to the Middle East for schooling two years later. Pursuing his artistic talents further, he entered the famed Ecole des Beaux Arts in Paris, where he studied under the French sculptor Auguste Rodin. Gibran's first efforts at writing were poems and short plays originally penned in Arabic that attracted a modest success. In 1904 Gibran returned to the United States, where he befriended Mary Haskell, headmistress of a Boston school. She became his advisor, and the two wrote lengthy romantic missives to one another for a number of years. These were later reproduced in the 1972 book *Beloved Prophet: The Love Letters of Kahlil Gibran and Mary Haskell, and Her Private Journal.*

During these early adult years, Gibran lived in Boston's Chinatown, and scholars note that the works from this period show a preoccupation with his homeland and a sadness stemming from his status as an exile. One of his first published books, 1910's *'Ar' is al-muruj* (later published in English as *Nymphs of the Valley*), was a collection of three stories set in Lebanon; two subsequent works written during this era, later published as *Spirits Rebellious* and *The Broken Wings,* are, respectively, a collection of four stories and one novella. In each, a young man is the hero figure, rebelling against those inside Lebanon who are corrupting it; common literary targets include the Lebanese aristocracy and the Christian church.

Gibran's first collection of poetry appeared in Arabic in 1914 and was translated into English several years later and published as *A*

Tear and a Smile. "The tears, which are much more abundant here than the smiles," observed N. Naimy in *Journal of Arabic Literature,* "are those of Gibran the misfit rather than of the rebel in Boston, singing in an exceedingly touching way of his frustrated love and estrangement, his loneliness, homesickness and melancholy." Naimy called this book a bridge between a first and second stage of Gibran's career: the writer's longing for Lebanon gradually evolved into a dissatisfaction with the destructive attitude of humankind in general. By now Gibran's body of work was received enthusiastically in the extensive Arabic-speaking world, winning a readership that stretched from Asia to the Middle East to Europe, as well as across the Atlantic. Soon his writings were being deemed "Gibranism," a concept that "Gibran's English readers will have no difficulty in divining," wrote Claude Bragdon in his book *Merely Players.* "Mystical vision, metrical beauty, a simple and fresh approach to the so-called problems of life."

In 1912 Gibran left Boston and moved to New York City. During World War I his growing success as an emigre writer was tempered by Lebanon's abysmal wartime situation, when many of its citizens starved to death. Scholars of the poet's body of work hypothesize that Gibran's sorrow manifested itself in a more pronounced quest for self-fulfillment in his works, and a spirituality that sought wisdom and truth without the aid of an organized religion. At one point in his career the writer was excommunicated from the Christian Maronite church. His first work both written and published in English was 1918's *The Madman: His Parables and Poems.* Its title comes from a previously published prose work in which the hero sees existence as "a tower whose bottom is the earth and whose top is the world of the infinite . . . to clamour for the infinite in one's life is to be considered an outcast and a fool by the rest of men clinging to the bottom of the tower," explained Naimy in the *Journal of Arabic Literature.*

Gibran's most critically acclaimed work is *The Prophet,* first published in 1923. The author planned it to be first in a trilogy, followed by *The Garden of the Prophet* and *The Death of the Prophet.* The initial book *The Prophet* chronicles, through the title character Almustafa's own sermons, his life and teachings. Much of it is given in orations to the Orphalese, the people among whom Almustafa has been placed. Gibran's biographer, Mikhail Naimy, found similarities in *The Prophet* with Nietzsche's *Thus Spake Zarathrustra.* In each the author speaks through a created diviner, Naimy asserts, and both prophets walk among humankind as outsiders. Some elements are autobiographical: the critic saw a parallel in Gibran's dozen-year stay in New York City with the twelve-year wait Almustafa endured before returning home from the land of the Orphalese. "In this book, more than in any other of his books, Gibran's style reaches its very zenith," declared Naimy. "Many metaphors are so deftly formed that they stand out like statues chiselled in the rock."

Another critic compared *The Prophet* to Walt Whitman's *Song of Myself.* Mysticism, asserted Suhail ibn-Salim Hanna in *Literature East and West,* is a theme common to both, with Gibran having rejected the attitudes termed Nietzschean in favor of the more benign European ideology that unfolded during the Enlightenment of the eighteenth century. "Like Whitman, Gibran came to see, even accept, the reality of a benevolent and harmonious universe," wrote Hanna. Critiquing *The Prophet* from a more practical standpoint, Gibran's biographer, Khalil S. Hawi, faulted its structure. Writing in *Kahlil Gibran: His Background, Character and Works,* Hawi noted that "behind the attempts to perfect the

sermons and each epigrammatical sentence in them lies an artistic carelessness which allowed him to leave the Prophet standing on his feet from morning to evening delivering sermon after sermon, without pausing to consider that the old man might get tired, or that his audience might not be able to concentrate on his sermons for so long."

Despite any shortcomings, *The Prophet* went on to become the best-selling title in Alfred A. Knopf's history. It was followed by two more works in the trilogy Gibran had planned, *The Garden of the Prophet* and *The Death of the Prophet,* both published after their author's death. Another of Gibran's books considered noteworthy by scholars is *Jesus the Son of Man: His Words and His Deeds as Told and Recorded by Those Who Knew Him,* published in 1928. Personalities from the Bible—as well as ordinary characters created by Gibran—who came into contact with Christ recall their encounters with and impressions of the religious leader, although not all are adherents to what would become the Christian faith. In a review of the work for *New York Herald Tribune Books,* John Haynes Holmes termed Gibran well-suited to undertake such an ambitious work. "First of all he is a countryman of Jesus. . . . He therefore knows Palestine, its people, the cadences of their speech and the insights of their spirit," Holmes declared. "It is as though a contemporary sat down, at a belated hour, to write another and different gospel."

Gibran died of a liver ailment in 1931, and he had specified in his will that all future royalties due his estate should be donated to Bechari, his birthplace in Lebanon. Ironically, the writer's generous impulse provoked a legal battle. When copyright renewal came up for some of the works two decades later, Gibran's will was challenged, and the issue was kept in litigation for several years. At the same time, the increasing wealth entering the village from the growing international popularity of Gibran's works caused another legal conflict over the administration of the funds.

BIOGRAPHICAL/CRITICAL SOURCES:

BOOKS

Bragdon, Claude, *Merely Players,* Knopf (New York), 1929.
Gibbon, Monk, editor, *The Living Torch,* Macmillan (New York), 1938.
Hawi, Khalil S., *Kahlil Gibran: His Background, Character and Works,* Arab Institute for Research and Publishing, 1972.
Hillyer, Robert, introduction to *A Tear and a Smile* by Kahlil Gibran, Knopf (New York), 1950.
Naimy, Mikhail, *Kahlil Gibran: A Biography,* Philosophical Library (New York), 1934.
Twentieth Century Literary Criticism, Gale (Detroit), Volume 1, 1978; Volume 9, 1983.

PERIODICALS

Booklist, October 15, 1993, p. 417.
Canadian Forum, March, 1948.
Christian Century, February 4, 1948.
Dial, November 30, 1918; September, 1927.
Inc., January, 1991, p. 105.
Journal of Arabic Literature, volume 5, 1974, pp. 55-71.
Library Journal, October 15, 1993, p. 65.
Literary Review, December 8, 1923, p. 334.
Literature East and West, volume 12, numbers 2, 3, and 4, 1968, pp. 174-98.
MELUS, summer, 1980, pp. 21-36.
Nation, December 28, 1918, p. 812.
New York Herald Tribune Books, December 2, 1928, p. 6.

New York Times Book Review, May 17, 1931; April 18, 1948, p. 27; July 25, 1948, p. 19; February 19, 1950, p. 5; November 24, 1991, p. 20.

New York Times Magazine, June 25, 1972, pp. 8-9, 24, 26, 28, 30.

Saturday Review, May 20, 1950, p. 21; March 13, 1971, pp. 54-55, 70.

Times Literary Supplement, April 7, 1927.

* * *

GIBRAN, Khalil
See GIBRAN, Kahlil

* * *

GIBSON, William 1914-
(William Mass)

PERSONAL: Born November 13, 1914, in New York, NY; son of George Irving (a bank clerk) and Florence (Dore) Gibson; married Margaret Brenman (a psychoanalyst), September 6, 1940; children: Thomas, Daniel. *Education:* Attended College of City of New York (now City College of the City University of New York), 1930-32. *Politics:* Democrat.

ADDRESSES: Home—Stockbridge, MA. *Agent*——Flora Roberts, 157 West 57th St., New York, NY 10022.

CAREER: Author and playwright. Piano teacher at intervals in early writing days to supplement income. President and cofounder of Berkshire Theatre Festival, Stockbridge, 1966–.

MEMBER: PEN, Authors League of America, Dramatists Guild.

AWARDS, HONORS: Harriet Monroe Memorial Prize, 1945, for group of poems published in *Poetry;* Topeka Civic Theatre Award, 1947, for *A Cry of Players;* Sylvania Award, 1957, for television play *The Miracle Worker.*

WRITINGS:

PLAYS

I Lay in Zion (one-act; produced in at Topeka Civic Theatre, 1943), Samuel French (acting edition), 1947.

(Under pseudonym William Mass) *The Ruby* (one-act lyrical drama), with libretto (based on Lord Dunsany's *A Night at an Inn*) by Norman Dello Joio, Ricordi, 1955.

The Miracle Worker (three-act; originally written as a television drama; produced by Columbia Broadcasting System for *Playhouse 90* in 1957 and by National Broadcasting Company in 1979; rewritten for stage and produced on Broadway at Playhouse Theatre, October 19, 1959; rewritten for screen and produced by United Artists in 1962; also see below), Knopf, 1957.

Dinny and the Witches [and] *The Miracle Worker* (the former produced off-Broadway at Cherry Lane Theatre, December 9, 1959; also see below), Atheneum, 1960.

Two for the Seesaw (three-act comedy; copyrighted in 1956 as *After the Verb to Love;* produced on Broadway at Booth Theatre, January 16, 1958; also see below), Samuel French, 1960.

Dinny and the Witches: A Frolic on Grave Matters, Dramatists Play Service, 1961.

(With Clifford Odets) *Golden Boy* (musical adaptation of Odet's original drama, with lyrics by Lee Adams, and music by Charles Strouse; first produced on Broadway at Majestic Theatre, October 20, l964), Atheneum, 1965.

A Cry of Players (three-act; produced at Topeka Civic Theatre, February, 1948; produced on Broadway at the Vivian Beaumont Theatre, November 14, 1968), Atheneum, 1969.

John and Abigail (three-act drama; produced at Berkshire Theatre Festival, 1969, later in Washington, DC, at Ford's Theatre, January 9, 1970), published as *American Primitive: The Words of John and Abigail Adams Put into a Sequence for the Theater, with Addenda in Rhyme,* Atheneum, 1972.

The Body and the Wheel (produced in Lenox, MA, at Pierce Chapel, April 5, 1974), Dramatists Play Service, 1975.

The Butterfingers Angel, Mary and Joseph, Herod the Nut, and the Slaughter of 12 Hit Carols in a Pear Tree (produced at Pierce Chapel, December, 1974), Dramatists Play Service, 1975.

Golda (produced on Broadway at the Morosco Theatre, November 14, 1977), Samuel French, 1977.

Goodly Creatures (produced in Washington, DC, at the Round House Theatre, January, 1980), Dramatists Play Service, 1990.

Monday after the Miracle (produced in Charleston, SC, at the Dock Street Theatre, May, 1982, later produced on Broadway at the Eugene O'Neill Theatre, December 14, 1982), Dramatists Play Service, 1990.

Handy Dandy (produced in New York, 1984), Dramatists Play Service, 1986.

Raggedy Ann and Andy (musical; music and lyrics by Joe Raposo), first produced in Albany, New York, 1984, produced in New York City, 1986, as *Raggedy Ann.*

OTHER

Winter Crook (poems), Oxford University Press, 1948.

(Under pseudonym William Mass) *The Cobweb* (novel), Knopf, 1954.

The Seesaw Log (a chronicle of the stage production, including the text of *Two for the Seesaw*), Knopf, 1959.

A Mass for the Dead (chronicle and poems), Atheneum, 1968.

A Season in Heaven (chronicle), Atheneum, 1974.

Shakespeare's Game (criticism), Atheneum, 1978.

MEDIA ADAPTATIONS: The Cobweb was filmed by Metro-Goldwyn-Mayer, 1957; *Two for the Seesaw* was filmed by United Artists, 1962.

SIDELIGHTS: While William Gibson has published poetry, plays, fiction, and criticism, he is best known for his 1957 play *The Miracle Worker.* Originally written and performed as a television drama, and adapted in later years for both stage and screen, *The Miracle Worker* remains Gibson's most widely revived piece. It was refilmed for television in 1979 and also formed the basis for Gibson's 1982 play, *Monday after the Miracle,* which picks up the characters almost twenty years later. Writing in the *Dictionary of Literary Biography,* Stephen C. Coy calls the drama "a classic American play—and television play, and film—the full stature of which has yet to be realized."

The story, which is based on real people and actual events, concerns the relationship between Helen Keller, a handicapped child who has been deaf and blind since infancy, and Annie Sullivan, the formerly blind teacher who has been called in to instruct her. When Annie arrives, she finds that Helen has been utterly spoiled by well-intentioned parents who, in their sympathy, allow her to terrorize the household. Annie's efforts to civilize Helen and Helen's resistance result in a fierce, and frequently physical, struggle that forms the central conflict of the play. The "miracle" occurs when, after months of frustration, Annie is finally able to reach the child. Coy explains: "Just as the struggle appears to be lost, Helen starts to work the pump in the Keller yard and the miracle—her mind learning to name things—happens before the audience as she feels the water and the wet ground. Annie and others realize what is happening as Helen, possessed, runs about touching things and learning names, finally, to their great joy, 'Mother' and 'Papa.' The frenzy slows as Helen realizes there is something she needs to know, gets Annie to spell it for her, spells it back, and goes to spell it for her mother. It is the one word which more than any other describes the subject of *The Miracle Worker*: 'Teacher.'"

Praising the play's "youthfulness and vigor," the *New York Times* reviewer Bosley Crowther described the tremendous concentration of energy apparent in the battle scenes between Helen and Annie: "The physical vitality and passion are absolutely intense as the nurse, played superbly by Anne Bancroft moves in and takes on the job of 'reaching the soul' of the youngster, played by Patty Duke. . . . When the child, who is supposed to be Helen Keller in her absolutely primitive childhood state, kicks and claws with the frenzy of a wild beast at the nurse who is supposed to be Annie Sullivan, the famous instructor of Miss Keller, it is a staggering attack. And when Annie hauls off and swats her or manhandles her into a chair and pushes food into her mouth to teach her habits, it is enough to make the viewer gasp and grunt."

The Broadway production of the play was so well-received that a film version with the same stars was made in 1962 and enjoyed similar success. Later revivals have not fared so well. When *The Miracle Worker* was filmed for television in 1979 (with Patty Duke playing Annie Sullivan), Tom Shales commented in the *Washington Post* that the only point in doing *The Miracle Worker* again "was to give Patty Duke Astin a chance on the other side of the food." His objections range from what he calls "careless casting" to the inappropriateness (almost an insult, he calls it) of making a television movie from a screenplay written for live television. For the writing itself, however, Shales has nothing but praise. "William Gibson's play . . . remains, even when not perfectly done, a nearly perfect joy, one of the most assuredly affirmative dramatic works to come out of the optimistic '50s."

BIOGRAPHICAL/CRITICAL SOURCES:

BOOKS

Contemporary Literary Criticism, Volume 23, Gale (Detroit), 1983.
Dictionary of Literary Biography, Volume 7: *Twentieth Century American Dramatists,* Gale, 1981.

PERIODICALS

America, November 10, 1990, p. 350.
Cosmopolitan, August; 1958.
Los Angeles Times, October 19, 1982.
Nation, December 2, 1968.
New England Theatre, spring, 1970.
New Leader, December 16, 1968.
Newsweek, March 16, 1959; July 27, 1970.
New York, November 5, 1990, p. 127.
New Yorker, November 23, 1968; November 5, 1990, p. 120.
New York Times, May 24, 1962; May 27, 1962; June 3, 1962; November 16, 1977; December 9, 1980; May 26, 1982; December 15, 1982.
New York Times Book Review, April 14, 1968.
Saturday Review, March 23, 1968.

Tulane Drama Review, May, 1960.
Variety, February 21, 1971.
Washington Post, October 13, 1979; January 20, 1980; January 26, 1980; November 27, 1981; December 3, 1981; October 3, 1982; October 14, 1982.

*   *   *

GIBSON, William (Ford) 1948-

PERSONAL: Born March 17, 1948, in Conway, SC; immigrated to Canada; son of William Ford (a contractor) and Otey (a homemaker; maiden name, Williams) Gibson; married Deborah Thompson (a language instructor), June, 1972; children: Graeme Ford Gibson, Claire Thompson Gibson. *Education:* University of British Columbia, B.A., 1977.

ADDRESSES: Home—Vancouver, British Columbia, Canada. *Agent*—Martha Millard Literary Agency, 204 Park Ave., Madison, NJ 07940; (for film and television) Martin S. Shapiro, Shapiro-Lichtman Talent, 8827 Beverly Blvd., Los Angeles, CA 90048.

CAREER: Writer.

AWARDS, HONORS: Nebula Award nomination from Science Fiction Writers of America, c. 1983, for short story "Burning Chrome"; Hugo Award for best novel of 1984 from World Science Fiction Society, Philip K. Dick Award for best U.S. original paperback of 1984 from Philadelphia Science Fiction Society, Nebula Award for best novel of 1984 from Science Fiction Writers of America, and Porgie Award for best paperback original novel in science fiction from *West Coast Review of Books,* all 1985, and Ditmar Award from Australian National Science Fiction Convention, all for *Neuromancer.*

WRITINGS:

Neuromancer (novel; first in "Cyberspace" trilogy), Ace, 1984.
Count Zero (novel; second in "Cyberspace" trilogy), Arbor House, 1986.
(With John Shirley, Bruce Sterling, and Michael Swanwick) *Burning Chrome* (short stories; includes "Burning Chrome," "Johnny Mnemonic," "New Rose Hotel," and one story with each coauthor), introduction by Sterling, Arbor House, 1986.
Mona Lisa Overdrive (novel; third in "Cyberspace" trilogy), Bantam, 1988.
Dream Jumbo (text to accompany performance art by Robert Longo), produced in Los Angeles, California, at UCLA Center for the Performing Arts, 1989.
(With Sterling) *The Difference Engine* (novel), Gollancz, 1990, Bantam, 1991.
Virtual Light, Viking, 1993.
Johnny Mnemonic (screenplay; based on Gibson's short story of the same name), TriStar, 1995.
Idoru, Putnam (New York City), 1996.

Work represented in anthologies, including *Shadows 4,* Doubleday, 1981; *Nebula Award Stories 17,* Holt, 1983; and *Mirrorshades: The Cyberpunk Anthology,* edited with an introduction by Sterling, Arbor House, 1986. Contributor of short stories, articles, and book reviews to periodicals, including *Omni, Rolling Stone,* and *Science Fiction Review.*

SIDELIGHTS: Science fiction author William Gibson had published only a handful of short stories when he stunned readers with his debut novel, *Neuromancer.* Published in 1984, *Neuromancer* became the first work ever to sweep the major honors of science fiction—the Hugo, Nebula, and Philip K. Dick awards. Combining the hip cynicism of the rock music underground and the dizzying powers of high technology, the novel was hailed as the prototype of a new style of writing, promptly dubbed "cyberpunk." Gibson, who was also earning praise as a skillful prose stylist, disliked the trendy label but admitted that he was challenging science fiction traditions. "I'm not even sure what cyberpunk means," he told the *Philadelphia Inquirer,* "but I suppose it's useful as a tip-off to people that what they're going to read is a little wilder."

The surface features of Gibson's allegedly cyberpunk style— tough characters facing a tough world, frantic pacing, bizarre high-tech slang—alienated some reviewers. "Like punk rock . . . Cyberpunk caters to the wish-fulfillment requirements of male teenagers," complained science fiction novelist Thomas M. Disch in the *New York Times Book Review,* "and there is currently no more accomplished caterer than William Gibson." In *Science Fiction Review,* Andrew Andrews blasted the "style and execu- tion" of *Count Zero,* a novel typical of Gibson's work during the 1980s. "It is hodgepodge; spastic; incomprehensible in spots, somehow just *too much,*" the reviewer declared. "I prefer a novel that is concise, with fleshy, human characters." Beneath the flash, however, admirers detected a serious purpose. Writers like Gibson, suggested J. R. Wytenbroeck in *Canadian Literature,* are really describing the world "in which we live today, with all its problems taken to their logical extreme." In particular, the advance of technology is shown to cause as many problems as it solves.

Gibson grew up in a small town in southwest Virginia, on the edge of the Appalachian Mountains. "It was a boring, culturally deprived environment," he recalled in the *Sacramento Union.* "The library burned down in 1910, and nobody bothered to rebuild it." In such a place, he told *Interview,* "science fiction books were the only source I had for subversive information." By his late teens Gibson had left behind the conventional authors who filled the genre with shining cities and benevolent scientists. Instead he began to prefer iconoclasts, such as J. G. Ballard and Philip K. Dick, who described a grim and frightening future. Some of his favorites might not qualify with purists as science fiction writers at all: both William S. Burroughs and Thomas Pynchon were intricate stylists whose core following was among literary intellectuals. Such writers used the fantastic element of science fiction as a device to explore the ugly potentials of the human heart. Science fiction, Gibson realized, was a way to comment on the reality of the present day.

The 1960s youth culture also drew Gibson's attention. (A long- term rock fan, he counts the hard-edged music of Lou Reed as a major influence.) In 1967 he dropped out of high school and journeyed to Canada, ending up in Toronto, which had a thriving hippie scene. "I was clueless," he recalled in the *Chicago Tribune.* "A lot of my friends were becoming lawyers and librarians, things that filled me with horror." So he became a science fiction writer, even though at the time "it seemed like such a goofy, unhip thing to do," as he told *Rolling Stone.*

His writing blossomed with amazing speed. By the early 1980s he was a favorite of fiction editor Ellen Datlow, who helped make *Omni* magazine a showcase of rising science fiction talent. In *Omni* stories such as "Johnny Mnemonic" (1981) and "Burning Chrome" (1982) Gibson began to sketch his own grim version of the future, peopled with what *Rolling Stone* called "high-tech lowlifes." The title character of "Johnny Mnemonic," for instance,

stashes stolen computer data on a microchip in his brain. He is marked for murder by the Yakuza, a Japanese syndicate that has moved into high-tech crime, but he is saved by Molly Millions, a bionic hitwoman with razors implanted under her fingernails. "I thought I was on this literary kamikaze mission," Gibson informed *Rolling Stone.*

Neuromancer, together with its sequels *Count Zero* and *Mona Lisa Overdrive,* fleshes out the future society of Gibson's short stories. Here technology is the main source of power over others, and the multinational corporations that develop and control technology are more important than governments. The world is a bewildering splatter of cultures and subcultures; Gibson skirts the issue of whether the United States or Canada are still viable countries, but his multinationals are generally based in Europe or Japan. While shadowy figures run the world for their own benefit, a large underclass—the focus of Gibson's interest—endures amid pollution, overcrowding, and pointlessness. People commonly drug themselves with chemicals or with "simstims," a form of electronic drug that allows users to experience vicariously the life of another, more glamorous, human being.

Though such a future seems hopeless, Gibson remains in some sense a romantic, observers note, for he chronicles the efforts of individuals to carve out a life for themselves in spite of hostile surroundings. His misfit heroes often exist on the crime-infested fringes of society, thus lending his works some of the atmosphere of a traditional crime thriller. Along with the expected cast of smugglers, prostitutes, murderers, and thieves, Gibson celebrates a distinctly modern freebooter, the computer hacker. Computers of the future, Gibson posits, will be linked worldwide through "cyberspace"—an electronically generated alternate reality in which all data, and the security programs that protect it, will appear as a palpable three-dimensional universe. Computer operators will access cyberspace by plugging into it with their brains, and hackers—known as "cowboys"—will sneak in to steal data, fill their bank accounts with electronic money, or suffer death when a security program uses feedback to destroy their minds. "The Street," wrote Gibson in *Rolling Stone,* "finds its own uses for things—uses the manufacturers never imagined."

The plots of Gibson's works, some reviewers suggest, are less important than the way of life he describes: even admirers find the narratives rather complicated and difficult to summarize. As Gibson told *Interview,* he "do[es]n't really start with stories" but prefers to assemble images, "like making a ball out of rubber bands." *Neuromancer* centers on Henry Case, a skilled computer "cowboy" who has been punished for his exploits by being given a powerful nerve poison that leaves him unable to plug into cyberspace. As the book opens he is scrounging a living on the seamy side of Japan's Chiba City when a mysterious patron offers him restorative surgery in exchange for more computer hacking. Case assents, and in the company of Molly Millions (one of Gibson's many recurring characters) he travels from one bizarre setting to the next in pursuit of a goal he cannot even understand.

"*Neuromancer* was a bit hypermanic—simply from my terror at losing the reader's attention," Gibson recalled in *Rolling Stone.* For the sequel, *Count Zero,* "I aimed for a more deliberate pace. I also tried to draw the characters in considerable detail. People have children and dead parents in *Count Zero,* and that makes for different emotional territory." Thus instead of taking one main character on a manic ride throughout human society, *Count Zero* tells the stories of three more fleshed-out individuals whose lives gradually intertwine. The "Count Zero" of the title is really Bobby

Newmark, a poor teenage computer "cowboy" with dreams of greatness. On his first illicit run into cyberspace, he finds it much more colorful than Case did a few years earlier: the Artificial Intelligences of *Neuromancer* seem to have broken apart into many cyberspace entities, some of whom manifest themselves as voodoo gods. The "gods" have human worshippers who take custody of Bobby after he apparently has a religious experience while he is hacking. Meanwhile, art dealer Marly Krushkova tries to find an artist with mysterious powers, only to encounter an old "cowboy" who also believes that God lives in cyberspace. And Turner, a mercenary who rounds up scientists for multinationals, finds himself the protector of a strange young woman named Angie Mitchell. Angie has a unique gift: her scientist father placed microchips in her brain that give her direct access to cyberspace and sometimes make her the mouthpiece for its ghostly inhabitants. "The resolution [of the plot] is figuratively left in the hands of the Haitian Computer Gods," wrote Dorothy Allison of the *Village Voice.* "They are particularly marvelous, considering that the traditional science fiction model of an intelligent computer has been an emotionless logician."

Gibson's third novel, *Mona Lisa Overdrive,* "brilliantly pyramids the successes of its predecessors," wrote Edward Bryant in *Bloomsbury Review.* The book is set several years after *Count Zero,* using a similar structure of plot-lines that slowly interconnect. When *Mona Lisa* opens, Bobby Newmark has grown up into an accomplished cowboy. Now he leaves his body in a coma so that he can explore the electronically generated universe inside a unique and costly microchip that he stole from the Tessier-Ashpool clan. Angie Mitchell, Bobby's sometime girlfriend, has become a simstim star, struggling against drug abuse and unsure of her future. In *Mona Lisa Overdrive,* wrote Richard Mathews of the *St. Petersburg Times,* "Gibson employs the metaphor of addiction as the central fact of existence. Addictions to drugs, information, and sensuality permeate society and form the basis of all economic transactions." The drug-abusing Angie, for example, is herself a "mere fix . . . piped to millions of simstim addicts to enrich [her producers]." Bobby is also a junkie—"a metaphor for society, increasingly techno-dependent, and hopelessly addicted to the excitement of high-tech power trips and head games."

As *Mona Lisa* unfolds amid complex intrigues, the power of technology looms so large as to challenge the meaning of human identity itself. Characters seek friendship and advice from the personalities recorded on microchips; Angie comes face-to-face with "Mona Lisa," a confused teenage junkie who has been surgically altered to resemble Angie herself as part of a bizarre abduction plot. In the violent climax of the novel, during which Angie dies of a brain hemorrhage, the simstim producers stumble upon Mona and gladly recruit her as a new star. Then, in an astonishing burst of fantasy, Gibson shows Angie reunited with Bobby in his microchip universe—a computer-generated heaven. By then, Mathews observed, "Gibson has us re-evaluating our concepts of 'life,' 'death' and 'reality,' all of which have been redefined by the impact of the information matrix. What makes Gibson so exceptional a writer is that you haven't just seen or thought about this future; you've been there."

By the time *Mona Lisa Overdrive* was published in 1988, Gibson and many reviewers were glad to say farewell to the cyberpunk era. "It's becoming fashionable now to write 'cyberpunk is dead' articles," he noted in the *Bloomsbury Review.* The author teamed with fellow novelist Bruce Sterling to write *The Difference Engine,* a sort of retroactive science fiction novel set in Victorian England. The book is named for one of several mechanical

computers that were designed during the nineteenth century by mathematician Charles Babbage. Babbage failed to build his most sophisticated machines, for their manufacture was beyond his budget and he was unable to secure public funding. Gibson and Sterling, however, imagine the consequences if he had succeeded. With the help of mechanical computers, the Victorians develop airplanes, cybernauts, and a huge steam-powered television. *The Difference Engine,* Gibson warned, "sounds cuter than it is. It's really a very, very chilly semi-dystopia." In this novel, as in most of Gibson's work, technology proves corrupting, and society is painfully divided between the haves and have-nots. Gibson knows that a Victorian fantasy may baffle his old fans; at last, however, he might free himself of labels. "One of the reasons we cooked this up was so people wouldn't be able to say it was more cyberpunk writing," Gibson told the *Chicago Tribune.* "There won't be one guy with a silver Mohawk in the whole book."

After the short vacation from Cyberpunk that *The Difference Engine* afforded him, Gibson returned to a familiar dystopian future with his next novel, *Virtual Light.* Set in the geographic conglomerate known as the Sprawl (which is most likely a fusion of most of North America), the novel centers on the adventures of an unlikely pair of allies who are thrown together by circumstance. While Gibson's trademarks are still present: biotechnology, evil corporate empires, and ghosts in the machines, *Virtual Light* was perceived by critics as more character-driven than the author's previous Cyberpunk work. The technology serves the advancement of the plot rather than existing as the locus of the narrative.

In addition to his return to Cyberpunk writing, Gibson also revisited the arena of Hollywood scriptwriting. Although his efforts for *Alien 3* were fruitless, he returned with a produced screenplay in 1995. Adapting his short story "Johnny Mnemonic," Gibson worked closely with director and artist Robert Longo (who had previously collaborated with the author on a performance art piece titled *Dream Jumbo*) to bring his vision of the near future to the screen. With slight alterations to the original story—the remorselessly fierce Molly Millions character was turned into a softer, more accessible female mercenary—the film was released to mixed reviews.

BIOGRAPHICAL/CRITICAL SOURCES:

BOOKS

Contemporary Literary Criticism, Volume 39, Gale (Detroit), 1986.
McCaffery, Larry, editor, *Across the Wounded Galaxies: Interviews with Contemporary American Science Fiction Writers,* University of Illinois Press, 1990.
Sterling, Bruce, editor, *Mirrorshades: The Cyberpunk Anthology,* Arbor House, 1986.

PERIODICALS

Analog, November, 1984; December, 1986; January, 1987; April, 1989; October, 1989; March, 1997.
Best Sellers, July, 1986.
Bloomsbury Review, September, 1988.
Canadian Literature, summer, 1989.
Chicago Tribune, November 18, 1988; November 23, 1988.
Entertainment Weekly, August 13, 1993, p. 66.
Fantasy Review, July, 1984; April, 1986.
Film Comment, January, 1990.
Fortune, November 1, 1993.
Interview, January, 1989.
Isaac Asimov's Science Fiction Magazine, August, 1986.

Listener, October 11, 1990.

Locus, August, 1988.

Los Angeles Times Book Review, January 29, 1989.

Maclean's, April 29, 1991, p. 63; November 25, 1996.

Magazine of Fantasy and Science Fiction, August, 1985; August, 1986; fall, 1997.

Mississippi Review, Volume 16, numbers 2 and 3, 1988.

Nation, May 8, 1989.

New Statesman, June 20, 1986; September 26, 1986.

New York Times Book Review, November 24, 1985; December 11, 1988; March 10, 1991, p. 5; September 8, 1996.

People Weekly, October 25, 1993, p. 45.

Philadelphia Inquirer, April 15, 1986; October 30, 1988.

Pittsburgh Press, October 19, 1986.

Playboy, August, 1993, p. 32.

Publishers Weekly, July 12, 1993, p. 72.

Punch, February 6, 1985.

Rolling Stone, December 4, 1986; June 15, 1989.

Sacramento Union, October 26, 1988.

St. Petersburg Times, December 18, 1988.

San Francisco Chronicle, January 1, 1987.

Saturday Night, March, 1989.

Science Fiction Review, fall, 1985; summer, 1986; winter, 1986.

Spin, December, 1988.

Times Literary Supplement, December 7, 1984; June 20, 1986; August 12, 1988; September 27, 1996.

Utne Reader, July, 1989.

Village Voice, July 3, 1984; July 16, 1985; May 6, 1986; January 17, 1989; September 24, 1996.

Washington Post Book World, July 29, 1984; March 23, 1986; October 25, 1987; November 27, 1988.

West Coast Review of Books, September, 1985.

Whole Earth Review, summer, 1989.

*   *   *

GIDE, Andre (Paul Guillaume) 1869-1951

PERSONAL: Born November 22 (one source says November 21), 1869, in Paris, France; died of pneumonia, February 19, 1951, in Paris, France; buried in Cuverville-en-Caux, Normandy, France; son of Paul (a professor) and Juliette (Rondeaux) Gide; married cousin, Madeleine Rondeaux, in 1895; children: (with Elisabeth van Rysselberghe) Catherine. *Education:* Educated privately and in public schools in Paris, France.

CAREER: Novelist, playwright, essayist, diarist, and translator. Cofounder of *La Nouvelle Revue francaise* in 1909 and of *L'Arche,* a literary magazine in North Africa; literary critic for *La Revue blanche.* Mayor of La Roque, a commune in Normandy, France, 1896; juror in Rouen, France, 1912; special envoy of the Colonial Ministry in Africa, 1925-26. Worked with the Red Cross and, later, in a convalescent home for soldiers, and became director of the Foyer Franco-Belge during World War I. Traveled extensively in Europe and Africa.

MEMBER: Royal Society of London (elected honorary fellow, 1924), American Academy of Arts and Letters (elected honorary corresponding member, 1950).

AWARDS, HONORS: Goethe Medal, 1932; honorary doctorate in letters from University of Oxford, 1947; Nobel Prize in literature from Nobel Foundation, 1947; Goethe Plaque from the city of Frankfort on the Main, 1949.

WRITINGS:

NOVELS AND NOVELLAS

Le voyage d'Urien, Librairie de l'Art Independant, 1893, second edition, 1894, translation with introduction and notes by Wade Baskin published as *Urien's Voyage,* Philosophical Library, 1964.

Paludes (satire; also see below), Librairie de l'Art Independant, 1895, Gallimard, 1973.

Le Promethee mal enchaine (satire; also see below), Mercure, 1899, new edition, Gallimard, 1925, translation by Lilian Rothermere published as *Prometheus Illbound,* Chatto & Windus, 1919.

L'immoraliste, Mercure, 1902, translation by Dorothy Bussy published as *The Immoralist,* Knopf, 1930, translation by Richard Howard published as *The Immoralist,* Knopf, 1970, with a new foreword by Stanley Appelbaum, Dover (New York), 1996.

La porte etroite, Mercure, 1909, revised edition, 1959, translation by Dorothy Bussy published as *Strait Is the Gate,* Knopf, 1924.

Isabelle (also see below), Gallimard, 1911, translation by Dorothy Bussy published as *Isabelle,* Knopf, 1968.

Les caves du Vatican: Sotie (satire; also see below), Gallimard, 1914, Macmillan, 1956, translation by Dorothy Bussy published as *The Vatican Swindle,* Knopf, 1925, published as *Lafcadio's Adventures,* Knopf, 1928 (published in England as *The Vatican Cellars,* Cassell, 1952).

La symphonie pastorale (also see below), Editions de la Nouvelle Revue Francaise, 1919, translation by Dorothy Bussy published as *The Pastoral Symphony,* Knopf, 1968.

Les faux-monnayeurs, Gallimard, 1926, translation by Dorothy Bussy published as *The Counterfeiters* (also see below), Knopf, 1927 (published in England as *The Coiners,* Cassell, 1950).

L'ecole des femmes (also see below), Gallimard, 1929, translation by Dorothy Bussy published as *The School for Wives,* Knopf, 1929.

Robert: Supplement a "L'ecole des femmes" (also see below), Gallimard, 1929.

Genevieve; ou, La confidence inachevee (also see below), Gallimard, 1936.

L'ecole des femmes [suivi de] Robert [et de] Genevieve, Gallimard, 1944, translation by Dorothy Bussy published as *The School for Wives, Robert, [and] Genevieve; or, The Unfinished Confidence,* Knopf, 1950.

Thesee (also see below), Pantheon, 1946, translation by John Russell published as *Theseus,* New Directions Publishing, 1949.

Marshlands [and] Prometheus Misbound: Two Satires, translation by George D. Painter, New Directions Publishing, 1953, McGraw, 1965.

Two Symphonies: Isabelle [and] The Pastoral Symphony, translation by Dorothy Bussy, Knopf, 1931 (published in England as *La symphonie pastorale [and] Isabelle,* Penguin Books, 1963).

LYRICAL WORKS IN VERSE AND PROSE

Les cahiers d'Andre Walter (title means "The Notebooks of Andre Walter"; also see below), Librairie de l'Art Independant, 1891, translation of first half with introduction by Wade Baskin published as *The White Notebook,* Philosophical Library, 1964, translation with introduction and notes by

Baskin published as *The Notebooks of Andre Walter*, Philosophical Library, 1968.

Le traite du Narcisse: Theorie du symbole (title means "Treatise of the Narcissus: Theory of the Symbol"; also see below), Librairie de l'Art Independant, 1891.

Les poesies d'Andre Walter (title means "The Poems of Andre Walter"; also see below), Librairie de l'Art Independent, 1892.

La tentative amoureuse; ou, Le traite du vain desir (title means "The Attempt at Love; or, The Treatise of Vain Desire"; also see below), Librairie de l'Art Independant, 1893.

Les nourritures terrestres, Mercure, 1897.

Corydon, Gallimard, 1924, translation published by Farrar, Strauss, 1950.

Les nouvelles nourritures, Gallimard, 1935.

The Fruits of the Earth, translated by Dorothy Bussy, Knopf, 1949 (published in England as *Fruits of the Earth,* Secker & Warburg, 1962, published as *Fruits of the Earth* [and] *Later Fruits of the Earth,* Penguin Books/Secker & Warburg, 1970).

Les nourritures terrestres [et] *Les nouvelles nourritures,* Club des Libraires de France, 1956.

PLAYS

Philoctete (also see below), first performed privately, April 3, 1919.

Le roi Candaule (first produced in Paris, France, at Nouveau Theatre, May 9, 1901; also see below), Editions de la Revue Blanche, 1901.

Saul: Drame en cinq actes (first produced in Paris, France, at Theatre du Vieux-Colombier, June 16, 1922; also see below), Mercure, 1903, enlarged edition, 1904.

Le retour de l'enfant prodigue (first produced in Monte Carlo, Monaco, at Theatre de Monte-Carlo, December 4, 1928; text first published in *Vers et Prose,* 1907; also see below), Bibliotheque de l'Occident, 1909, translation by Aldyth Thain published as *The Return of the Prodigal Son,* Utah State University Press, 1960.

Bethsabe (first published in *L'Ermitage,* 1903; also see below), Bibliotheque de l'Occident, 1912.

Oedipe: Drame en trois actes (first produced in Antwerp, Belgium, at Cercle Artistique, December 10, 1931; also see below), Gallimard, 1931.

Persephone (first produced in Paris, France, at l'Opera, April, 1934; also see below), Gallimard, 1934, translation by Samuel Putnam published as *Persephone,* Gotham Book Mart, 1949.

Le treizieme arbre (title means "The Thirteenth Tree"; one-act farce), first produced in Marseilles, France, at Rideau Gris, May 8, 1935.

Le retour (title means "The Return"), Ides et Calendes, 1946.

(With Jean-Louis Barrault) *Le proces: Piece tiree du roman de Kafka* (dramatization of Franz Kafka's novel *Der Prozess;* first produced October 10, 1947), Gallimard, 1947, translation and adaptation by Jacqueline and Frank Sundstrom published as *The Trial,* Secker & Warburg, 1950, translation by Leon Katz and Joseph Katz published as *The Trial: A Dramatization Based on Franz Kafka's Novel,* Schocken, 1964.

Robert; ou, L'interet general (title means "Robert; or, The General Interest"; five-act play; first produced in Tunis, Tunisia, at Theatre Municipal, April 30, 1946), Ides et Calendes, 1949.

Les caves du Vatican: Farce en trois actes et dix-neuf tableaux (first produced in Montreux, Switzerland, at Societe des Belles-Lettres, December 9, 1933; revised script produced in Paris, France, at the Comedie-Francaise, December 13, 1950), Ides et Calendes, 1948, Gallimard, 1950.

Persephone: Melodrame en trois tableaux d'Andre Gide (opera libretto), music by Igor Fedorovich Stravinski, Boosey & Hawkes, 1950.

COLLECTED WORKS

Philoctete; *Le traite du narcisse*; *La tentative amoureuse*; *El Hadj,* Mercure, 1899.

Morceaux choisis (title means "Selections"; collection of previously published and unpublished works), Editions de la Nouvelle Revue Francaise, 1921.

Pages choisise (collection of previously published and unpublished works), Georges Cres, 1921.

Divers: Caracteres; Un Esprit non prevenu; Dictees; Lettres, Gallimard, 1931.

Oeuvres completes, fifteen volumes, edited by Louis Martin Chauffier, Gallimard and Editions de la Nouvelle Revue Francaise, 1932-39.

Le retour de l'enfant prodigue, precede de cinq autres traites: Le traite du narcisse, La tentative amoureuse, El Hadj, Philoctete, Bethsabe, Gallimard, 1932, translation by Dorothy Bussy published as *The Return of the Prodigal, Preceded by Five Other Treatises; With "Saul," a Drama in Five Acts,* Secker & Warburg, 1953.

Theatre (contains *Saul, Le roi Candaule, Oedipe, Persephone, Le treizieme arbre*), Gallimard, 1942.

Theatre complet, eight volumes, Ides et Calendes, 1947-49.

Recits, roman, soties (collection of prose and poetry), Gallimard, 1948.

My Theater: Five Plays and an Essay (contains Saul, Bathsheba, Philoctetes, King Candaules, Persephone, The Evolution of the Theater), translation by Jackson Mathews, Knopf, 1952.

Poesie; Journal; Souvenirs (collection of lyrical and autobiographical works), Gallimard, 1952.

Ne jugez pas; Souvenirs de la cour d'assises; L'affaire Redureau; La sequestree de Poitiers, Gallimard, 1957.

Romans, recits, et soties: Oeuvres lyriques (collection of works, including *Le voyage d'Urien, Paludes, La porte etroite, La symphonie pastorale, Les faux-monnayeurs, Le journal des faux-monnayeurs, Le traite du Narcisse, El Hadj*), edited with notes and bibliography by Yvonne Davet and Jean-Jacques Thierry, La Pleiade/Gallimard, 1958.

Oeuvres (collection of journals and lyrical works), Gallimard, 1960.

OTHER

Si le grain ne meurt (autobiography; first part printed privately, Imprimerie Ste. Catherine, 1920, second part printed privately, 1921), Gallimard, 1926, translation by Dorothy Bussy published as *If It Die: An Autobiography,* Random House, 1935 (published in England as *If It Die,* Secker & Warburg 1950).

Numquid et tu. . .?, Imprimerie Sainte-Catherine, 1922.

The Journals of Andre Gide, four volumes, selected, edited, and translated by Justin O'Brien, Knopf, 1947-51 (published in England as *Journals,* Secker & Warburg, 1948-55, and as *Journals, 1889-1949,* Penguin Books, 1967), published as *The Journals of Andre Gide, 1889-1949,* Vintage Trade, 1956, abridged edition published as *The Journals of Andre*

Gide, Volume 1: 1889-1924, Volume 2: 1924-1949, Northwestern University Press, 1987.

Ainsi soit-il; ou, Les jeux sonts faits, Gallimard, 1959, translation by Justin O'Brien published as *So Be It; or, The Chips Are Down,* Knopf, 1960.

Travels in the Congo, translation by Dorothy Bussy, Ecco (Hopewell, NJ), 1994.

Also author of volumes of essays, criticism, travel writings, and correspondence. Translator of numerous works into French.

MEDIA ADAPTATIONS: La symphonie pastorale was adapted into a motion picture script of the same title by Pierre Bost and Jean Aurenche and published by Nouvelle Edition, with a preface by J. Delannoy, in 1948; the book was adapted into a play in three acts and published by F. De Wolfe & Robert Stone in 1954. *L'immoraliste* was adapted into a play titled *Andre Gide's "The Immoralist"* by Ruth and Augustus Goetz and published by Dramatists Play Service in 1962.

SIDELIGHTS: As a master of prose narrative, occasional dramatist and translator, literary critic (particularly of Fyodor Dostoyevsky), letter writer, essayist, and diarist, Andre Gide provided twentieth-century French literature with one of its most intriguing examples of the man of letters. Gide continued the tradition of reflection on culture—its books and its institutions—established by the sixteenth-century essayist Michel de Montaigne, who had introduced the record of the self as a subject for serious literature in France. Inasmuch as it reflects the complex personality behind it, Gide's work enlarges this permission to take the self as subject. Inasmuch as that personality is ironic, however, the record of the self is deliberately subverted. While Gide lent the authorial pronoun "I" to any number of heroes and heroines in his narratives, he simultaneously cast aspersions on their credibility; while he recorded in his voluminous *Journal* the activities and thought of an eighty-year lifetime, he refused to recognize his authentic portrait in anything he had written if it were considered separately from the self-examinations in the rest of his works. "Hardly a day goes by that I don't put everything back into question," he wrote in his *Journal* in 1922. Each volume was intended to challenge itself, what had preceded it, and what could conceivably follow it. This characteristic, according to Daniel Moutote in his *Cahiers Andre Gide* essay, is what makes Gide's work "essentially modern": the "perpetual renewal of the values by which one lives."

In an article reprinted in *Gide: A Collection of Critical Essays,* Alain Girard pointed out that the published *Journal* is not the complete private diary of its author, who admittedly tore out or withheld parts of it. Nevertheless, the *Journal* faithfully records the importance Gide gave to sincerity and truthfulness to the self as moral values mediating between culturally defined notions of good and evil. It is also clear to what extent sincerity and obligation to the self required the author's discipline and effort of will: "Certainly I could have been more easily a naturalist, doctor or pianist . . . than a writer," Gide wrote in his *Journal* in 1910, "but I can bring more diverse qualities to this career; the others would have been more exclusive; but it's to this one that I must bring the most willpower."

Gide's pseudonymous *Cahiers d'Andre Walter,* a confessional work presented as a journal published posthumously, marked in 1891 Gide's entry into literary Paris. *Les Poesies d'Andre Walter* was published in 1892. In 1910, Gide remarked in his *Journal* that his present undertaking, *Corydon,* was his first work in twenty years to restore to him the "feeling of indispensability" that had

dictated *Andre Walter.* Again in his 1924 *Journal* Gide recalled his earliest prose experiment: "I began to write before knowing French very well—and especially: before knowing how to use it well. But I was bursting. . . At that time, I thought I could bend the language to my purposes." From the beginning, however, the French classical tradition of the word in obedience to the idea dominated Gide's concept of style; the tone and language of each work had to be perfectly suited to the subject being dealt with. He defined the beauty of a work in terms of the harmony of its composition and the exactitude and rigorousness of its style, writing, for example, in undated *Journal* notes this defense of the lack of imagery in *Andre Walter*: "Beginning with my *Notebooks of Andre Walter* I practiced a style that aimed toward a more secret and more essential beauty. . . I wanted this language 'poorer' still, more strict, more refined, judging that the only purpose of ornamentation is to hide one's faults and that only thoughts insufficiently beautiful in themselves should fear perfect nudity [of style]."

Gide's first major narrative work, *L'Immoraliste,* is flanked, on one side, by a short novel and a group of plays, and on the other, by a period of depression and difficulty during which Gide reworked much of his old material and wrote and rewrote *La Porte etroite,* which, in 1909, brought him his first real success. In 1899, the short novel *Le Promethee mal enchaine* introduced what would be Gide's major theme of the "gratuitous act"; the play *Philoctete* was published in the same year, followed by a second play, *Le Roi Candaule,* in 1901 and a third, *Saul,* in 1903. Although they met with little critical success and are not considered major works, Gide's plays from this period are, according to Germaine Bree in *Andre Gide: L'Insaissisable protee,* so unique as to bear little resemblance to classical, naturalist, or symbolist theater. Rather, with their "ambiguity unresolved by the denouement" and Gide's evocation of a "special world in which language and gesture approach an encoded language," Bree declared, they "opened the way" for French theater as Sartre and Camus would develop it after World War II. During this period between *L'Immoraliste* and *La Porte etroite,* there also appeared, to little critical fanfare, *Pretextes,* a collection of articles and short pieces; the evocative *Amyntas,* that Gide in his 1910 *Journal* called his "most perfect" work to date; and *Le Retour de l'enfant prodigue,* a parable that Gide completed, contrary to his usual practice, within just three weeks during the winter of 1907, partly because, he explained in his *Journal* at the time, "I was tired of not writing any more and all the other subjects I have within me presented too many difficulties to be dealt with right away." His most important contribution to literature during this interim, however, turned out to be not a written work but the literary journal and publishing house he cofounded in 1909. With its goal of publishing the best of contemporary writing (of course, including Gide's), the history of the *Nouvelle Revue francaise* became, in the words of Gide's biographer Pierre de Boisdeffre in his *Cahiers Andre Gide* essay, "the history of all of French literature from the 1910's to the 1950's."

In 1931, when his *Journal* and even his correspondence were being widely published, Gide reflected in the *Journal* that "the absence of echo"—or critical attention—for his earliest works had been the true guarantee of their value; writing for future readers, he said, he had written for timelessness. Pierre de Boisdeffre estimated in his *Vie d'Andre Gide, 1869-1951* that *L'Immoraliste* had had "only a handful" of reviewers, and Gide himself pessimistically predicted in his 1902 *Journal* that an edition of only three hundred copies would be sufficient to meet demand;

however, Claude Martin has documented in *La Maturite d'Andre Gide* the fairly extensive critical "echo" the book received in 1902 and 1903, pointing out that Gide was upset not that his book wasn't being read, but that it wasn't being read well. Among the flurry of articles about *L'Immoraliste,* Martin cites an essay by Marcel Drouin (Gide's brother-in-law writing under the pseudonym "Michel Arnauld") in *La Revue blanche* of November, 1902, an essay that constituted the authorized response to what Gide perceived as his readers' errors. Drouin wrote that the book would give rise to fewer misconceptions if "more people knew how to read, within the lines and between the lines, then reread, then reflect on their reading" of this book in which "the antithesis is next to the thesis, the objection with the argument,. . . united in the same soul and the single life [of the protagonist]."

Gide's sensitivity to the critical reaction aroused by his works is well documented. Charles Du Bos described in *Le Dialogue avec Andre Gide* the author's "fear of and passion for compromising himself"; according to an entry in Gide's 1922 *Journal,* Madeleine Gide wrote to her husband in January of that year: "What very much disturbs me is the nasty campaign begun against you. . . if you were invulnerable, I wouldn't worry. But you are vulnerable, and you know it, and I know it." It was precisely by his refusal to choose a definitive ethical position within his works that Gide rendered himself most vulnerable to critical attack by partisan thinkers and keepers of public morality. He, in fact, repeatedly provoked such attacks, as demonstrated by this comment about *La Porte etroite,* which Jean-Jacques Thierry quotes in his "Notice" to the Pleiade edition: "It's to the gratuitousness of the work of art that the Protestant remains refractory; he wants the work to have meaning, instruction, usefulness." By his term "gratuitousness," Gide suggested the function of his works as art, proposing with his heroes and heroines—"against whom [I] cannot side any more than [I] set them up as exemplary"—not solutions, but enigmas and stimuli to his readers' reflection. The Catholic critic Henri Massis, a principal adversary whose articles always appeared, Gide complained in his *Journal* for 1921, the very day the writer's books went on sale, refused in his *Jugements* to accept an argument from aesthetic grounds in defense of moral nonpartisanship; for Massis, Gide's "classicism" and the "gratuitousness of [his] art" were simply code words for hypocrisy, moral turpitude, and evasion of responsibility.

With the exception of *The Fruits of the Earth,* Gide eventually insisted, all of his works had to be read "ironically" or "critically," and even in this book, he wrote in his *Journal* for 1926, "there is, for whoever consents to read well and without prejudice, the critique of the book within the book itself, as it should be." In a 1950 letter to Pierre Lafille, a letter quoted by Lafille in his *Cahiers Andre Gide* essay, Gide wrote, "You have admirably noted that in each of my books there coexist and are juxtaposed, at one and the same time, the depiction of a psychological state and the critique of that very state." Jean Hytier, in *Andre Gide,* explained this irony as a play of sympathy and antipathy, identification and distance, skillfully balanced in the recits: "By sympathy, [Gide] makes these first persons singular speak with an accent of truth unequaled in French fiction;. . . by antipathy, he maintains all his reserve, marks the distances which separate him from his creatures. . . Readers let themselves be carried away, and react naively to the story they are being told,. . . but [Gide] also intends the reader to withdraw his identification, either by the story's end, or . . . as it is being told." The characters themselves are the first victims of Gide's irony, for as Germaine Bree observed in a 1951 *Yale French Studies* essay, they "are rather

like players who, in a football game, persist in playing basketball, with the conviction that that is the game being played."

A happier critical fate attended the memoirs, published in 1926 as *Si le grain ne meurt,* and recounting Gide's life up to his engagement to Madeleine in 1895. A number of Gide's friends, who were in a position to judge the completed work against his expressed desire for clarity and sincerity, expressed either their disappointment at his excessive discretion or their opinion that too great a concern for clarity had vastly oversimplified Gide's portrait of himself. For Du Bos in the *Dialogue, Si le grain ne meurt* was long on preparation and short on revelation, finally only "caricatural" of a "Gide larger, fuller, more moving, I was going to say than his entire work, in any case than this rasping and grating sketch." More perceptively, however, Gide's friend Jacques Raverat acknowledged—as Gide approvingly noted in his *Journal* for 1920—that the only way to have a full portrait of the author was to read all of Gide's works at the same time, since "all the states that, for artistic reasons, you depict as successive can be simultaneous with you." Gide's biographers, particularly Jean Delay, have drawn attention to the numerous inaccuracies and omissions in Gide's recollections of his past in this work; tantalizingly related to both autobiography and fiction (Gide's own and fiction as a genre), however, *Si le grain ne meurt* has been regarded as a masterpiece of the genre called "literary autobiography" by C. D. E. Tolton in his *Andre Gide and the Art of Autobiography.*

In 1919 Gide began his early sketches for *The Counterfeiters,* explaining to Elisabeth van Rysselberghe that what he had in mind was "a work, a novel that would make people say: 'Ah yes! we understand why he claimed not to have written any before this.'" *The Counterfeiters* was intended to leave behind the "monographs" of the recits in favor of multiplicity and counterpoint: "I conceive of the novel in the same manner as Dostoyevsky, [as] a struggle between points of view," he told van Rysselberghe in a 1919 interview. Still working on the book in 1923, he wrote at that time in his *Journal,* "What I want a novel to be? an intersection—a rendez-vous of problems." From its inception, the notion of "journal" was integral to this work. To help keep track of his uncharacteristically broad range of material ("there's enough here to feed half a dozen novels," he observed in the 1921 *Journal*), Gide kept a special journal detailing his plans for and progress on the novel; the resulting *Journal des Faux-Monnayeurs* is Gide's record of, in Thierry's description, "the architecture of the novel [that shows] not a plot as it develops but a novel as it is being written." In addition, a fictional journal kept within the novel by the character Edouard (in preparation for his novel, also entitled *The Counterfeiters*) is the means by which Gide intended to de-center his narrative focus and make of *The Counterfeiters* "the critique of the novel . . . in general," as he explained to van Rysselberghe: "There isn't one center to my novel, there are two, as in an ellipse: the events on the one hand and their reaction in 'Edouard.' Ordinarily, when one writes a novel, one either starts with the characters and makes up events to develop them, or starts with the events and creates characters as needed to explain them. But 'Edouard,' who holds the psychological strings of a series of beings who confide in him, rather than writing a novel, dreams of making them act in reality, and he doesn't succeed in substantiating the characters by the events. These characters give him events, that he can't do anything with! and that becomes part of the subject."

While *The Counterfeiters* was in press, Gide went on an extended tour of the Congo, the first of many voyages he would undertake and write about during the final third of his life. "All the long trips I haven't taken are like remorse within me," van Rysselberghe overheard him say before this departure, "traveling seems to me almost a duty, a kind of piety; I think the Good Lord must not be very happy with the way we honor Him, He must think, 'What! I gave them all that and look how little they make of it!'" Gide's *Voyage au Congo* and *Retour du Tchad* have been presented in support of a social conscience that had first surfaced in his *Souvenirs de la cour d'assises* before largely disappearing from the intervening works; Gide's descriptions in the *Voyage* of the economic exploitation of French equatorial Africa led to a public debate on colonialism upon his return to Paris. Similarly, his observations on his trip to Moscow as an honored guest at Maxim Gorki's funeral, the *Retour de l'U.R.S.S.,* and its supplement, *Retouches a mon "Retour de l'U.R.S.S.,"* sharply critiqued the Soviet system and announced Gide's estrangement from the Communist movement, which he had supported financially and ideologically during the early 1930s.

Gide's final works returned to what had always been for him a fertile source, equal to Christianity in imaginative possibility and moral instruction: Greek mythology. His version of *Oedipe,* which added, he said in his 1932 *Journal,* "jokes, trivialities and incongruities" to Sophocles' classic text, seemed to him a dramatization of the tragic "struggle between individualism and submission to religious authority"; his intention, he wrote in a *Journal* entry for 1933, was to evoke not terror and pity—the aims of the original Greek tragedy—but reflection. Evaluating his *Oedipe* in his 1931 *Journal,* he envisioned as a separate work a "decisive meeting" between the mythological king Theseus, whose life he had long wanted to write, and Oedipus, "each measuring himself against the other and illuminating, each under cover of the other, their two lives"; the meeting takes place near the end of Gide's final recit, his "testament" *Thesee,* which Claude Martin called, in *Andre Gide par lui-meme,* "at the evening of his life, . . . an intelligent extract of his wisdom."

BIOGRAPHICAL/CRITICAL SOURCES:

BOOKS

Babcock, Arthur E., *Portraits of Artists: Reflexivity in Gidean Fiction, 1902-1946,* French Literature Publications, 1982.

Boisdeffre, Pierre de, *Metamorphoses de la litterature,* Alsatia, 1950, excerpted in *Les Critiques de notre temps et Gide,* edited by Michel Raimond, Garnier, 1971.

Boisdeffre, Pierre de, *Cahiers Andre Gide,* Gallimard, 1969–.

Boisdeffre, Pierre de, *Vie d'Andre Gide, 1869-1951: Essai de biographie critique,* Hachette, 1970.

Bree, Germaine, *Andre Gide: L'Insaisissable protee,* Belles Lettres, 1953, English revision and translation published as *Andre Gide,* Rutgers University Press, 1963, excerpted in *Les Critiques de notre temps et Gide,* edited by Michel Raimond, Garnier, 1971.

Cordle, Thomas, *Andre Gide,* Twayne, 1969.

Delay, Jean, *La Jeunesse d'Andre Gide,* two volumes, Gallimard, 1956, translation by June Guicharnaud published as *The Youth of Andre Gide,* University of Chicago Press, 1963.

Driskill, Richard T., *Madonnas and Christs, Maidens and Knights: Sexual Confusion in the Bildungsromans of D.H. Lawrence and Andre Gide,* Peter Lang, 1998.

Du Bos, Charles, *Le Dialogue avec Andre Gide,* Correa, 1947.

Fryer, Jonathan, *Andre and Oscar: The Literary Friendship of Andre Gide and Oscar Wilde,* St. Martin's Press, 1998.

Guerard, Albert J., *Andre Gide,* Harvard University Press, 1969.

Hytier, Jean, *Andre Gide,* Charlot, 1945, excerpted in *Gide: A Collection of Critical Essays,* edited by David Littlejohn, Prentice-Hall, 1970.

Lucey, Andre, *Gide's Bent: Sexuality, Politics, Writing,* Oxford University Press (New York), 1995.

Martin, Claude, *La Maturite d'Andre Gide: De "Paludes" a "L'Immoraliste,"* Klincksieck, 1977.

Massis, Henri, *Jugements,* Plon, 1924.

O'Keefe, Charles, *Void and Voice: Questioning Narrative Conventions in Andre Gide's Major First-person Narratives,* Department of Romance Languages, University of North Carolina at Chapel Hill, 1996.

Painter, George D., *Andre Gide: A Critical Biography,* Atheneum, 1968.

Tolton, C. D. E., *Andre Gide and the Art of Autobiography: A Study of "Si legrain ne meurt,"* Macmillan (Toronto), 1975.

Walker, David H., editor, *Andre Gide,* Longman (New York City), 1996.

West, Russell, *Conrad and Gide: Translation, Transference and Intertextuality,* Rodopi, 1996.

PERIODICALS

New York Times, December 27, 1983; November 3, 1987.
New York Times Book Review, October 2, 1983.
Perspectives on Contemporary Literature, number 8, 1982.
Times Literary Supplement, June 26, 1981; March 7, 1986.
Yale French Studies, number 7, 1951.

*   *   *

GILCHRIST, Ellen 1935-

PERSONAL: Born February 20, 1935, in Vicksburg, MS; daughter of William Garth (an engineer) and Aurora (Alford) Gilchrist; children: Marshall Peteet Walker, Jr., Garth Gilchrist Walker, Pierre Gautier Walker. *Education:* Millsaps College, B.A., 1967; University of Arkansas, postgraduate study, 1976. *Avocation:* Love affairs (mine or anyone else's), all sports, children, inventions, music, rivers, forts and tents, trees.

ADDRESSES: Home and office—Fayetteville, AK.

CAREER: Author and journalist. *Vieux Carre Courier,* contributing editor, 1976-79. National Public Radio, Washington, DC, commentator on *Morning Edition* (news program), 1984-85.

MEMBER: Authors Guild, Authors League of America.

AWARDS, HONORS: Poetry award, Mississippi Arts Festival, 1968; poetry award, University of Arkansas, 1976; craft in poetry award, *New York Quarterly,* 1978; National Endowment for the Arts grant in fiction, 1979; Pushcart Prizes, Pushcart Press, 1979-80, for the story *Rich,* and 1983, for the story *Summer, An Elegy;* fiction award, *Prairie Schooner,* 1981; Louisiana Library Association Honor book, 1981, for *In the Land of Dreamy Dreams;* fiction awards, Mississippi Academy of Arts and Science, 1982 and 1985; Saxifrage Award, 1983; American Book Award for fiction, Association of American Publishers, 1984, for *Victory over Japan;* J. William Fulbright Award for literature, University of Arkansas, 1985; literature award, Mississippi Institute of Arts and Letters, 1985, 1990, 1991; national scriptwriting award, National Educational Television Network, for the play *A Season of Dreams;* D. Litt., Millsaps College, 1987; L. H. D., University of Southern Illinois, 1991; Pushcart Prize, 1995; O. Henry Award, 1995.

WRITINGS:

SHORT STORIES

In the Land of Dreamy Dreams, University of Arkansas Press, 1981, reissued, Little, Brown, 1985.
Victory over Japan: A Book of Stories, Little, Brown, 1984.
Drunk with Love, Little, Brown, 1986.
Two Stories: "Some Blue Hills at Sundown" and "The Man Who Kicked Cancer's Ass," Albondocani Press, 1988.
Light Can Be Both Wave and Particle: A Book of Stories, Little, Brown, 1989.
I Cannot Get You Close Enough, Little, Brown, 1990.
The Age of Miracles: Stories, Little, Brown (Boston), 1995.
Rhoda: A Life in Stories, Little, Brown (Boston), 1995.
The Courts of Love: A Novella and Stories, Little, Brown (Boston), 1996.

NOVELS

The Annunciation, Little, Brown, 1983.
The Anna Papers, Little, Brown, 1988.
Net of Jewels, Little, Brown, 1992.
Starcarbon: A Meditation of Love, Little, Brown, 1994.
Anabasis: A Journey to the Interior, University of Mississippi, 1994.
Sarah Conley, Little Brown, 1997.

OTHER

The Land Surveyor's Daughter (poetry), Lost Roads (Fayetteville, AK), 1979.
Riding out the Tropical Depression (poetry), Faust, 1986.
Falling through Space: The Journals of Ellen Gilchrist, Little, Brown, 1987.

Also author of *A Season of Dreams* (play; based on short stories by Eudora Welty), produced by the Mississippi Educational Network. Work represented in anthologies, including *The Pushcart Prize: Best of the Small Presses,* Pushcart, 1979-80, 1983. Contributor of poems, short stories, and articles to magazines and journals, including *Atlantic Monthly, California Quarterly, Cincinnati Poetry Review, Cosmopolitan, Iowa Review, Ironwood, Kayak, Mademoiselle, New Laurel Review, New Orleans Review, New York Quarterly, Poetry Northwest, Pontchartrain Review, Prairie Schooner,* and *Southern Living.*

SIDELIGHTS: With the publication of her first short story collection in 1981, Gilchrist gained the attention of literary critics, publishers, and, most importantly, the reading public. In its first few months in print, *In the Land of Dreamy Dreams* sold nearly ten thousand copies in the Southwest alone, a phenomenon particularly impressive since the book was published by a small university press, unaccompanied by major promotional campaigns. The book's popular appeal continued to spread, generating reviews in major newspapers, until it reached the attention of Little, Brown & Co. which offered Gilchrist a cash advance on both a novel and a second collection of short stories. In the meantime, the critical review of *In the Land of Dreamy Dreams* reflected that of the public. As Susan Wood remarked in a review for the *Washington Post Book World,* "Gilchrist may serve as prime evidence for the optimists among us who continue to believe that few truly gifted writers remain unknown forever. And Gilchrist is the real thing alright. In fact," added Wood, "it's difficult to review a first book as good as this without resorting to every known superlative cliche—there are, after all, just so many ways to say 'auspicious debut.'"

In the Land of Dreamy Dreams is a collection of fourteen short stories. Most are set in the city of New Orleans and many focus on the lives and concerns of young people. They are "traditional stories" according to Wood, "full of real people to whom things really happen—set, variously, over the last four decades among the rich of New Orleans, the surviving aristocracy of the Mississippi Delta, and Southerners transplanted . . . to southern Indiana." The main characters in the stories, many of them adolescents, exhibit such flaws of character as envy, lust, and avarice; however Wood noted that more positive motivations lay underneath the surface: "It is more accurate to say that *In the Land of Dreamy Dreams* is about the stratagems, both admirable and not so, by which we survive our lives." Jim Crace, in a *Times Literary Supplement* review of *In the Land of Dreamy Dreams,* indicated that Gilchrist's text "is obsessively signposted with street names and Louisiana landmarks. . . But *In the Land of Dreamy Dreams* cannot be dismissed as little more than an anecdotal street plan. . . The self-conscious parading of exact Southern locations is a protective screen beyond which an entirely different territory is explored and mapped. Gilchrist's 'Land of Dreamy Dreams' is Adolescence."

The adolescent struggle to come to terms with the way one's dreams and aspirations are limited by reality figures largely in these fourteen stories. Gilchrist introduces her readers to a variety of characters: an eight-year-old girl who delights in masquerading as an adult and commiserates with a newly widowed wartime bride; a girl who fantasizes about the disasters that could befall the brothers who have excluded her from their Olympic-training plans; a young woman who gains her father's help in obtaining an abortion; another girl who discovers the existence of her father's mistress; and an unruly teenager who disrupts the order of her adoptive father's world, challenges his self-esteem, and so aggravates him that he finally shoots her and then commits suicide.

Gilchrist completed her second collection of short stories, *Victory over Japan,* three years later. Winner of the 1984 American Book Award for fiction, *Victory over Japan* was hailed by reviewers as a return to the genre, style, and several of the characters of *In the Land of Dreamy Dreams.* Beverly Lowry, critiquing *Victory over Japan* in the *New York Times Book Review,* commented: "Those who loved *In the Land of Dreamy Dreams* will not be disappointed. Many of the same characters reappear . . . Often new characters show up with old names . . . These crossovers are neither distracting nor accidental . . . Ellen Gilchrist is only changing costumes, and she can 'do wonderful tricks with her voice.'" *Drunk with Love,* published in 1987, and *Light Can be Both Wave and Particle,* released two years later, expanded the author's exploration of her characters' many facets. While continuing to praise her voice, critics have found Gilchrist's later work to be of a more "uneven" quality than her early writing. Reviewing the volume in the *Chicago Tribune,* Greg Johnson noted that Gilchrist "seems to get carried away with her breezy style and verbal facility. The stories read quickly and are often enjoyable, but they lack the thought and craft that make for memorable fiction." However, Roy Hoffman praised the book in the *New York Times Book Review* as full of "new energy" and noted of the title story that "it brings together lovers from different cultures more spiritedly than any past Gilchrist story."

In 1983, Gilchrist's first novel, *The Annunciation,* was published. It recounts the life of Amanda McCarney, from her childhood on a Mississippi Delta plantation where she falls in love with and, at the age of fourteen, has a child by her cousin Guy, to her marriage to a wealthy New Orleans man and a life of high society and heavy drinking. Eventually rejecting this lifestyle, Amanda returns to school where she discovers a gift for languages that has lain dormant during the forty-some years of her life and is offered the chance to translate the rediscovered poetry of an eighteenth-century Frenchwoman. She divorces her husband and moves to a university town in Arkansas to pursue her translating where, in addition to her work, Amanda finds love and friendship among a commune of hippie-type poets and philosophers in the Ozarks. *The Annunciation* received mixed reviews from critics. Yardley, critiquing the book in the *Washington Post Book World,* asserted that for most of its length *"The Annunciation* is a complex, interesting, occasionally startling novel; but as soon as Gilchrist moves Amanda away from the conflicts and discontents of New Orleans, the book falls to pieces." Yardley agreed, noting that once Amanda moves to the Ozarks *The Annunciation* "loses its toughness and irony. Amid the potters and the professors and the philosopher-poets of the Ozarks, Amanda McCarney turns into mush." However Frances Taliaferro, reviewing *The Annunciation* in *Harper's,* deemed Gilchrist's novel "'women's fiction' par excellence" and described the book as "a cheerful hodgepodge of the social and psychological fashions of the past three decades." Taliaferro explained that "Amanda is in some ways a receptacle for current romantic cliches, but she is also a vivid character of dash and humor . . . Even a skeptical reader pays her the compliment of wondering what she will do next in this surprisingly likable novel." Taliaferro concluded that, despite some tragedy, the "presiding spirit of this novel is self-realization, and Amanda [in the end] has at last made her way to autonomy."

Gilchrist has gone on to write several more books in the novel or novella genre. *The Anna Papers* takes as its start the short story "Anna, Part I" that concluded *Drunk with Love.* Published in 1988, the novel begins with the suicide of 43-year-old Anna Hand, who decides to conclude her life after being diagnosed with cancer. The work deals with the aftermath of her death as family and friends are left to the influence of Anna's legacy; the recollection of her full and joyous, yet unconventional, life. Although the critical reception of the novel was mixed, *The Anna Papers* was praised for both the quality of its prose and the complexity of Gilchrist's fictional characters. Ann Vliet ascribed to its author "a stubborn dedication to the uncovering of human irony, a tendency, despite temptations toward glamour and comfort, to opt for the harder path, often using 'poorly disguised' autobiographical fiction, usually the short story, to dredge up the order in messy human relationships" in a review in the *Washington Post Book World. I Cannot Get You Close Enough,* published in 1991, is a continuation of *The Anna Papers* in the form of three novellas, each taking as its focus one of the characters of the previous book. Ilene Raymond of the *Washington Post Book World* praised the work. "Not since J. D. Salinger's Glass family has a writer lavished so much loving attention on the eccentricities and activities of an extended clan," Raymond commented, adding that the novellas were not "easy tales, but stories rich with acrimony, wisdom, courage and, finally, joy."

In 1987 Gilchrist published *Falling through Space,* a collection of brief journal excerpts. Originally intended as segments of her National Public Radio commentary, the book's segments reflect the life of a working writer. "I write to learn and to amuse myself and out of joy and because of mystery and in praise of everything that moves, breathes, gives, partakes, is," Gilchrist once told *Contemporary Authors.* "I like the feel of words in my mouth and the sound of them in my ears and the creation of them with my hands. If that sounds like a lot of talk, it is. What are we doing here anyway, all made out of stars and talking about everything and telling everything? The more one writes the clearer it all becomes and the simpler and more divine. A friend once wrote to me and ended the letter by saying: 'Dance in the fullness of time.' I write that in the books I sign. It may be all anyone needs to read."

Critics have repeatedly praised Gilchrist for her subtle perception, unique characters, and sure command of her writer's voice. Yardley remarked of *In the Land of Dreamy Dreams,* "Certainly it is easy to see why reviewers and readers have responded so strongly to Gilchrist; she tells home truths in these stories, and she tells them with style." Crace concluded that her "stories are perceptive, her manner is both stylish and idiomatic—a rare and potent combination." Miranda Seymour, reviewing her first short story collection for the London *Times,* noted that "Gilchrist's stories are elegant little tragedies, memorable and cruel" and compared her writing to that of fellow southerners Carson McCullers and Tennessee Williams in that all three writers share "the curious gift for presenting characters as objects for pity and affection." And Wood observed: "Even the least attractive characters become known to us, and therefore human, because Gilchrist's voice is so sure, her tone so right, her details so apt."

In her novel *Sarah Conley,* published in 1997, Gilchrist depicts another strong-minded woman, an editor at *Time* magazine and successful novelist who grew up poor in Kentucky and supported her mother. Sarah returns to Kentucky to be at her dying friend Eugenie's bedside—and to rekindle the torch she had long held for Eugenie's husband Jack. After Eugenie dies, Sarah must choose between Jack and an important career opportunity. *Booklist* found the novel one of Gilchrist's weaker efforts, and claimed that Sarah's dilemma over whether to "sell out" for love fails to make the reader care, concluding that, while Sarah might not sell out, "it sure feels as though Gilchrist has." On the other hand, *Kirkus Review* conceded that Gilchrist had accomplished much within the parameters of her story, writing, "The most familiar and best-loved potboiler quandaries take on new life under Gilchrist's direction, lending a good deal of shading (if not depth) to a fairly unoriginal plot."

BIOGRAPHICAL/CRITICAL SOURCES:

BOOKS

Contemporary Authors New Revision Series, Volume 41, Gale (Detroit), 1994.
Contemporary Literary Criticism, Gale, Volume 34, 1985; Volume 48, 1988, pp. 114-22.
McCay, Mary, *Ellen Gilchrist,* Twayne, 1997.

PERIODICALS

Booklist, January 15, 1994; September 1, 1994; August 19, 1997.
Chicago Tribune, October 14, 1986; October 9, 1987; October 2, 1988; October 1, 1989.
Harper's, June, 1985.
Kirkus Reviews, August 1, 1997.
Library Journal, March 1, 1994; August, 1994.
Listener, January 6, 1983.
Los Angeles Times Book World, September 14, 1986; November 27, 1988.
Ms., June, 1985.
New Statesman, March 16, 1984.
Newsweek, January 14, 1985; February 18, 1985.
New Yorker, November 19, 1984.
New York Times Book Review, September 23, 1984; October 5, 1986; January 3, 1988; January 15, 1989; October 22, 1989;

November 4, 1990; October 13, 1991; April 12, 1992; June 19, 1994; October 30, 1994, p. 48.

Observer, November 24, 1991.

Publishers Weekly, March 2, 1992; January 31, 1994; August 8, 1994.

Times (London), November 25, 1982; June 7, 1990; November 21, 1991.

Times Literary Supplement, October 15, 1982; April 6, 1984; May 24, 1985; March 6, 1987; October 27, 1989; November 29, 1991; September 7, 1990.

Vogue, May, 1994, p. 184.

Washington Post, September 12, 1984; September 28, 1986; December 31, 1987; October 20, 1988; December 15, 1989.

Washington Post Book World, January 24, 1982; March 21, 1982; May 29, 1983; December 31, 1987; December 16, 1990.

*   *   *

GILL, Brendan 1914-1997

PERSONAL: Born October 4, 1914, in Hartford, CT; son of Michael Henry Richard (a physician) and Elizabeth Pauline (Duffy) Gill; died December 27, 1997; married Anne Barnard, June 20, 1936; children: Brenda, Michael, Holly, Madelaine, Rosemary, Kate, Charles. *Education:* Yale University, A.B., 1936.

ADDRESSES: Home—1 Howe Place, Bronxville, NY 10708. *Office*—New Yorker, 20 West 43rd St., New York, NY 10036.

CAREER: New Yorker, New York, NY, regular contributor, 1936-1997, film critic, 1960-67, drama critic, 1968-87, author of architecture column, "The Sky Line," 1987-1997. Chairman of board of directors, October Fund. Member of New York City Commission on Cultural Affairs and Mayor's Committee in the Public Interest. Chairman of the Warhol Foundation for Visual Arts. Member of board of directors, Whitney Museum of American Art, Pratt Institute, Film Society of Lincoln Center, and MacDowell Colony. Chairman emeritus of the Institute for Art and Urban Resources, NY, and the Landmarks Conservancy of New York.

MEMBER: American Academy of Arts and Letters, Irish Georgian Society (board member), Victorian Society (vice-president), Municipal Art Society (board chairman), Film Society of Lincoln Center (vice-president), Coffee House (New York City), Century Association (New York City).

AWARDS, HONORS: National Institute and American Academy of Arts and Letters grant, 1951; National Book Award, 1951, for *The Trouble of One House.*

WRITINGS:

Death in April and Other Poems, Hawthorne House, 1935.

The Trouble of One House (novel), Doubleday, 1950.

The Day the Money Stopped (novel), Doubleday, 1957.

La Belle (play), first produced in Philadelphia, 1962.

(With Robert Kimball) *Cole: A Book of Cole Porter Lyrics and Memorabilia,* Holt, 1971 (published in England as *Cole: A Biographical Essay,* M. Joseph, 1972).

Tallulah, Holt, 1972.

(Author of introduction) *The Portable Dorothy Parker,* Viking, 1973.

The Malcontents, Harcourt, 1973.

(Editor) *Happy Times,* photography by Jerome Zerbe, Harcourt, 1973.

Ways of Loving: Two Novellas and Eighteen Short Stories, Harcourt, 1974.

(Editor) Philip Barry, *States of Grace: Eight Plays,* Harcourt, 1975.

Here at "The New Yorker" (Book-of-the-Month Club alternate selection), Random House, 1975, with a new introduction by the author, Da Capo Press (New York City), 1997.

The New York Custom House on Bowling Green, New York Landmarks Conservancy, 1976.

Lindbergh Alone, Harcourt, 1977.

Summer Places, photography by Dudley Witney, Stewart & McClelland, 1977.

(Author of introduction) *St. Patrick's Cathedral: A Centennial History,* Quick Fox, 1979.

The Dream Come True: Great Houses of Los Angeles, with photographs by Derry Moore, Lippincott, 1980.

Wooings: Five Poems, Plain Wrapper Press (Verona, Italy), 1980.

(Author of foreword) Gene Schermerhorn, *Letters to Phil: Memories of a New York Boyhood,* New York Bound, 1982.

John F. Kennedy Center for the Performing Arts, Abrams, 1982.

A Fair Land to Build In: The Architecture of the Empire State, Press League of New York State, 1984.

Many Masks: A Life of Frank Lloyd Wright, Putnam, 1987.

A New York Life: Of Friends and Others, Poseidon, 1990.

Late Bloomers, Artisan (New York City), 1996.

Contributor to anthologies, including *World's Great Tales of the Sea,* World Publishing, 1944, *The Best American Short Stories, 1945,* Houghton, 1945, *Fireside Book of Yuletide Tales,* Bobbs Merrill, 1948, and *Girls from Esquire,* Random House, 1952. Contributor of short stories to *Saturday Evening Post, New Yorker, Collier's,* and *Virginia Quarterly Review.*

MEDIA ADAPTATIONS: Gill's novel *The Day the Money Stopped* was adapted as a play by Maxwell Anderson.

SIDELIGHTS: In his book *Here at "The New Yorker,"* Brendan Gill writes fondly of his long career at the magazine: "I started out at the place where I wanted most to be and with much pleasure and very little labor have remained here since." Beginning at the *New Yorker* just after leaving college in 1936, Gill has written a wide range of articles, stories, and columns over the years, serving as both the theater and architecture critic in his time, and as a frequent writer for the "Talk of the Town" section. Gill has also published several biographies of prominent people and *A New York Life: Of Friends and Others,* a collection of character portraits.

Here at "The New Yorker," published to coincide with the magazine's fiftieth anniversary, is Gill's account of his many years at the popular magazine. His memories of his magazine work, and of those with whom he worked, are combined in *Here at "The New Yorker"* with such things as floor plans of the magazine's offices, humorous memos that made the rounds among staff members, photographs of such famous *New Yorker* writers as James Thurber and John O'Hara, and old cartoons from the magazine itself. As John Leonard remarks in the *New York Times Book Review,* Gill's "memoir is a splendid artichoke of anecdotes, in which not merely the heart and leaves but the thistles as well are edible."

In *A New York Life,* Gill expands his reminiscences to include the many interesting personalities he has met during his magazine career, including such figures as Eleanor Roosevelt, Dorothy Parker, and George Plimpton. Some 47 characters are covered in all. "Many of Mr. Gill's anecdotes," notes Caroline Seebohm in the *New York Times Book Review,* "shed new light on a character." Among Gill's more controversial pronouncements in the book are his charges regarding the late Joseph Campbell, a popular writer on mythology best known for his *The Power of Myth* television series on PBS. Gill characterizes Campbell as a racist and anti-Semite who "was uttering a vicious message," as Gill tells John Blades in the *Chicago Tribune.* Although Campbell's friends and associates have denied the charges, Gill insists that his characterization is accurate. For the most part, *A New York Life* is "a book of heroes," Gill explains to Blades. The character portraits "give the sense of what it was like to have lived in New York over the last half-century."

Gill has also written several biographies of famous personalities, including Tallulah Bankhead, Charles Lindbergh, Cole Porter, and Frank Lloyd Wright. In *Many Masks: A Life of Frank Lloyd Wright,* Gill portrayed the famous architect of modernism in sometimes unflattering terms. "The Frank Lloyd Wright who emerges . . . ," Michiko Kakutani writes in the *New York Times,* "is an architect of genius, but he's also an arrogant con man—a self-promoter and prevaricator, who uses his gift of gab to seduce women and clients, and enhance his own mythic stature as a visionary artist." More sympathetically, Witold Rybczynski, writing in the Toronto *Globe and Mail,* finds that Gill presents a version of Wright as "the owner of an extraordinary talent" who was "in many ways a very ordinary man—or rather a man with very ordinary impulses." *Late Bloomers,* published in 1996, contains 75 biographical portraits of famous people "who at whatever cost and whatever circumstances have succeeded in finding themselves," notes Gill in the book. Among the individuals profiled by Gill are Mother Theresa, Joseph Conrad, Ruth Gordon, and King Edward VII.

A diversified writer who has produced novels, short stories, biographies, essays, film and drama reviews, Gill told *Contemporary Authors:* "Fiction is my chief interest, followed by architectural history, followed by literary and dramatic criticism. If these fields were to be closed to me, I would write copy for a bird-seed catalogue. In any event, I would write."

When Gill died in late 1997, at age 83, he was remembered by the *Los Angeles Times* as "the perfect companion to experience, through his transparent prose, the pleasures to be had by a certain ideal of urban culture." The *New York Times* remembered him as a member of "that nearly extinct cultural species, the man of letters." *National Review* claimed that when Gill joined the *New Yorker,* he stood out among his fellow writers because "he knew more than most of his colleagues and had interests beyond his Talk of the Town feature. His style was a perfection of lightly held but formidable erudition; some of what he produced almost certainly will outlive the work of the Algonquin Roundtable wits." In an appreciation published in the *New Yorker,* John Updike described Gill's as "an Enlightenment personality, exhilarated by the possibilities of liberation; like Voltaire, he mocked in defense of life."

BIOGRAPHICAL/CRITICAL SOURCES:

BOOKS

Contemporary Authors New Revision Series, Volume 37, Gale (Detroit), 1992.

PERIODICALS

Chicago Tribune, October 9, 1990.
Chicago Tribune Book World, December 7, 1980.
Globe and Mail (Toronto), February 6, 1988.

Los Angeles Times, November 29, 1987; December 13, 1987; December 28, 1998.
Los Angeles Times Book Review, March 22, 1981; September 20, 1987; November 22, 1987; November 29, 1987.
National Review, January 26, 1998.
New Yorker, January 12, 1998.
New York Times, September 21, 1979; December 9, 1987; December 28, 1997.
New York Times Book Review, February 16, 1975; April 24, 1977; December 13, 1987; October 21, 1990, p. 11.
Publishers Weekly, February 26, 1996, p. 89.
Saturday Evening Post, August 9, 1941.
Saturday Review of Literature, February 17, 1951.
Time, February 24, 1975.
Times Literary Supplement, November 14, 1980; March 24, 1989.
Tribune Books (Chicago), November 8, 1987; October 7, 1990, p. 6.
Wall Street Journal, October 22, 1990.
Washington Post, February 24, 1987; April 13, 1987.
Washington Post Book World, November 22, 1987; November 18, 1990.

*   *   *

GILMAN, Charlotte (Anna) Perkins (Stetson) 1860-1935
(Charlotte Perkins Stetson)

PERSONAL: Born July 3, 1860, in Hartford, CT; committed suicide, August 17, 1935; daughter of Frederick Beecher (a librarian and magazine editor) and Mary (Fritch) Perkins; married Charles Walter Stetson (an artist), 1884 (divorced); married George Houghton Gilman, 1900; children: (first marriage) Katharine.

CAREER: Writer. Worked as teacher and commercial artist; periodicals editor in California, c. 1890s; lecturer and social activist. Cofounded Women's Peace Party.

WRITINGS:

FICTION

(Under name Charlotte Perkins Stetson) *The Yellow Wallpaper* (novella), Small Maynard (Boston, MA), 1899, published as *The Yellow Wall-Paper, and Other Stories,* edited with an introduction by Robert Shulman, Oxford University Press (New York City), 1995, published as *The Yellow Wall-Paper,* afterword by Elaine R. Hedges, Feminist Press at the City University of New York (New York City), 1996.
What Diantha Did (novel), Charlton (New York), 1910.
The Crux (novel), Charlton, 1911.
Moving the Mountain (novel), Charlton, 1911.
Benigna Machiavelli (originally published in *Forerunner,* 1914), Bandanna Books, 1994.
Herland (science fiction; originally published in *Forerunner,* 1915), Pantheon (New York), 1979.
The Later Poetry of Charlotte Perkins Gilman, edited by Denise D. Knight, University of Delaware Press (Newark), 1996.
Unpunished: A Mystery, edited and with an afterword by Catherine J. Golden and Denise D. Knight, Feminist Press (New York City), 1997.
With Her in Ourland: Sequel to Herland, edited by Mary Jo Deegan and Michael R. Hill, with an introduction by Mary Jo Deegan, Praeger (Westport, CT), 1997.

With Her in Ourland (science fiction) originally published in *Forerunner*, 1916. Fiction also represented in numerous anthologies and collections.

VERSE

(Under name Charlotte Perkins Stetson) *In This Our World,* McCombs and Vaughan (Oakland, CA), 1893.
Suffrage Songs and Verses, Charlton, 1911.

COLLECTIONS

The Charlotte Perkins Gilman Reader: The Yellow Wallpaper, and Other Fiction, edited by Ann J. Lane, Pantheon, 1980.
Charlotte Perkins Gilman: A Nonfiction Reader, edited by Larry Ceplair, Columbia University Press (New York), 1991.

OTHER

(Under name Charlotte Perkins Stetson) *A Clarion Call to Redeem the Race!,* Shaker Press (Mt. Lebanon, NY), 1890.
(Under name Charlotte Perkins Stetson) *Women and Economics,* Small Maynard, 1898, published as *Women and Economics: A Study of the Economic Relation Between Men and Women as a Factor in Social Evolution,* with a new introduction by Sheryl L. Meyering, Dover Publications (Mineola, NY), 1997.
Concerning Children, Small Maynard, 1900.
The Home: Its Work and Influence, McClure Phillips (New York), 1903.
Human Work, McClure Phillips, 1904.
The Punishment that Educates, Crist Scott (Cooperstown, NY), 1907.
The Man-Made World; or, Our Androcentric Culture, Charlton, 1911.
His Religion and Hers: A Study of the Faith of Our Fathers and the Work of Our Mothers, Century (New York), 1923.
The Living of Charlotte Perkins Gilman: An Autobiography, Appleton-Century (New York), 1935.
Forerunner (collection of material originally published in *Forerunner*), Greenwood Reprint, 1968.
The Diaries of Charlotte Perkins Gilman, edited by Denise D. Knight, University Press of Virginia, 1994.
A Journey from Within: The Love Letters of Charlotte Perkins Gilman, 1897-1935, edited by Mary A. Hill, Bucknell University Press, 1995.

Principal writer, editor, and publisher of periodical *Forerunner,* 1909-16. Contributor to periodicals, including *Nationalist.*

SIDELIGHTS: Charlotte Perkins Gilman is an important figure in feminist activism and literature. Her father, Frederick Perkins, was a librarian and editor who abandoned the family when Gilman was only an infant; in later years, relations between Gilman and her father revived only to the extent that he provided her with lists of books that he considered worthwhile. Gilman's relationship with her mother proved similarly peculiar, for her mother knowingly abstained from affection. (In behaving in this way, her mother reasoned, she would prevent Gilman from developing a need or desire for human affection.) In addition, Gilman was prevented by her mother from reading fiction or developing strong friendships. Her father's literary counsel constituted, perhaps, a halfhearted defiance of her mother's stern orders.

As a consequence of her father's desertion, Gilman, her mother and siblings were regularly in the company of relatives. Among these family relations were Harriet Beecher Stowe, the prominent abolitionist who wrote *Uncle Tom's Cabin*; and the feminist activists Isabella Beecher Hooker and Catherine Beecher. Under the tutelage of these women, Gilman also pursued independence and equality.

In her early adulthood, Gilman supported herself as a teacher and as a commercial artist. But in her mid-20s she married Charles Walter Stetson, who was himself an artist. Within a year of marrying, and after having given birth to a daughter, Gilman entered into a profound depression. Under the advice of a noted neurologist, S. Weir Mitchell, Gilman undertook a cure consisting largely of bedrest and minimal intellectual stimulation. Not surprisingly, the cure, far from enabling Gilman to recover her emotional equilibrium, further exacerbated her instability. Gilman eventually undertook responsibility for her own recovery and ended her rest cure. She also separated from her husband, for she had become convinced that the stifling domesticity of her marriage had contributed, if only somewhat, to her chronic despair.

Upon leaving her husband, Gilman settled in California, where she became active in a range of feminist concerns, including preparations for the state's Women's Congresses of the mid-1890s. She also toured extensively in both the United States and England and became a staunch advocate of reform in women's rights and labor.

During the 1890s Gilman, who had been producing verse and journal entries since childhood, became increasingly active as a writer, and in 1893 she published (as Charlotte Perkins Stetson) *In This Our World,* a collection of poems. Gilman's verses are marked, predictably, by a concern with feminist issues, but they are also accessible and, frequently, quite amusing. "Here is a woman with a sense of humor," Henry Austin proclaimed, perhaps rather patronizingly, in *Bookman.* Likewise, an *American Fabian* reviewer noted Gilman's flair for humor and added that the writer, whose ancestors—the Beechers—distinguished themselves in both literature and the clergy, "has shown evidences of possessing both strains of the Beecher talent, humor, pathos and graphic descriptive ability as a writer, combined with the power of the preacher."

In This Our World was well received, particularly for an initial effort. The *American Fabian* reviewer acknowledged Gilman as a compelling speaker and noted that in her poetry she likewise succeeds in articulating the folly of social injustice and inequality. The critic deemed *In This Our World* "a collection of singularly fresh and vigorous pieces." And Henry Austin, in his *Bookman* appraisal, lauded Gilman's literary debut as "one of the most quaint and startling verse-books of the year."

After publishing *In This Our World* Gilman, still writing under the Stetson surname, produced *Women and Economics,* in which she articulates the predicament of women as the equivalent of economic slaves in America's male-oriented, capitalist society. *Arena* reviewer Annie L. Muzzey, who described Gilman as a "bold, logical thinker who fearlessly strips the illusion of false sentiment from what passes in the world as love and wedlock." Another reviewer, Arthur B. Woodford, wrote in *Dial* that Gilman's *Women and Economics* states "a profound social philosophy" and added that Gilman accomplishes this "with enough wit and sarcasm to make the book very entertaining reading."

Gilman followed *Women and Economics* with *The Yellow Wallpaper,* a grim tale of madness and despair. *The Yellow Wallpaper,* her last major work as Charlotte Perkins Stetson, is a disturbing autobiographical novella in which a woman recounts the horrific circumstances of her treatment by her neurologist husband. In the course of the first-person narrative, the heroine degenerates from mere melancholia to sheer lunacy. She has been taken to the country by her well-meaning husband and prescribed utter rest. Despite craving intellectual stimulation, the heroine is kept alone in a room with dismal yellow wallpaper. As her mind falters further, the heroine comes to discern what appears to be the image of a woman behind the wallpaper. Soon she convinces herself that several women are concealed by the wallpaper. Desperately, she tears at the wallpaper to find the women behind; as she becomes engulfed in her madness, she rants to her husband that she has escaped from the tattered wallpaper and cannot return to it.

The Yellow Wallpaper is generally considered to be Gilman's greatest literary achievement and has been reprinted regularly since its 1899 publication. In an afterword to a 1973 edition of the tale, Elaine R. Hedges acknowledged it as "a small literary masterpiece" and declared that it "deserve(s) the widest possible audience." Hedges also noted that the tale "was wrenched out of Gilman's own life, and is unique in the canon of her works."

Incredibly, *The Yellow Wallpaper* was scarcely designed as an artistic achievement but merely as a Poe-like rebuke to the neurologist who had so mishandled Gilman's own illness several years earlier. Gilman conceded as much when she wrote in *The Living of Charlotte Perkins Gilman: An Autobiography* that "the real purpose of the story was to reach Dr. S. Weir Mitchell, and convince him of the error of his ways." Gilman added that she was later informed that Mitchell "had changed his treatment of nervous prostration" after reading the story. "If that is a fact," Gilman wrote, "I have not lived in vain."

In 1900, the year after *The Yellow Wallpaper* appeared, Gilman married a cousin, George Houghton Gilman, who encouraged her feminist endeavors. Throughout the next several years Gilman devoted herself, at least as a writer, to activism. In 1900 she published *Concerning Children,* in which she argued that children were being victimized by a prejudicial society that compelled some women to work, and at reduced wages, without affording them adequate alternative provisions for childcare. Alexander Black, writing about *Concerning Children* in a 1923 issue of the periodical *Century,* described it as "a disturbing and epoch-marking plea."

With ensuing volumes, notably *The Home: Its Work and Influence, Human Work,* and *The Punishment that Educates,* Gilman persevered in her efforts to prompt social change. In *The Home,* for example, she argued that conventional domesticity, with the wife-mother merely a fixture not unlike an appliance, was counter-productive to the happiness of all family members concerned. She argued instead for the notion of homes as family centers in which professionals might play increasing roles, particularly with regards to teaching and even childcaring. Carl N. Degler, writing about *The Home* in a 1956 issue of *American Quarterly,* called it "a full-scale, full battle-dress assault," and he prized the book particularly for "Gilman's insights into the position of women, and the consequences thereof for the two sexes and society."

In the ensuing decade, the 1910s, Gilman became increasingly active in fiction and poetry. In 1910 she published more novels, including *Moving the Mountain, Herland,* and *With Her in Ourland,* and she completed a second poetry collection, *Suffrage Songs and Verses.* Throughout the first half of the 1910s Gilman also published regularly in *Forerunner,* a periodical devoted to

feminist concerns. Much of her fiction, including *Herland* and *With Her in Ourland,* appeared initially in *Forerunner,* for which Gilman also served as editor and publisher.

Moving the Mountain, Herland, and *With Her in Ourland* are all essentially utopian tales. In *Moving the Mountain,* a traveler suffers from amnesia and recovers thirty years later to find himself in a socialist state free of prejudice and inequality. Similarly, the surprisingly comic *Herland* concerns a trio of male adventurers who come upon a society in which women are the equal of men. *With Her in Ourland* is a less accomplished sequel to *Herland,* set after World War I, in which Gilman's didacticism is generally conceded to have overwhelmed the actual narrative.

After leaving *Forerunner* in 1916, Gilman considerably slowed her writing. Her next book, *His Religion and Hers: A Study of the Faith of Our Fathers and the Work of Our Mothers,* was not published until 1923. Twelve more years passed before another of Gilman's books, her autobiography, appeared. That same year, 1935, Gilman ended her own life after learning that she suffered from cancer.

BIOGRAPHICAL/CRITICAL SOURCES:

BOOKS

Allen, Polly Wynn, *Building Domestic Liberty: Charlotte Perkins Gilman's Architectural Feminism,* University of Massachusetts Press, 1988.

Bauer, Dale, editor, *The Yellow Wallpaper: Charlotte Perkins Gilman,* St. Martin's Press, 1998.

Beer, Janet, *Kate Chopin, Edith Wharton, and Charolotte Perkins Gilman: Studies in Short Fiction,* St. Martin's Press (New York City), 1997.

Davidson, Cathy N., *Charlotte Perkins Gilman: The Woman and Her Work,* UMI Research Press, 1989.

Dock, Julie Bates, compiler and editor, *Charlotte Perkins Gilman's "The Yellow Wall-paper" and the History of Its Publication and Reception,* Pennsylvania State University Press (University Park, PA), 1998.

Hedges, Elaine R., afterword to *The Yellow Wallpaper* by Charlotte Perkins Gilman, Feminist Press, 1973, pp. 37-63.

Hill, Mary A., *Charlotte Perkins Gilman: The Making of a Radical Feminist, 1860-1896,* Temple University Press, 1980.

Kessler, Carol Farley, *Charlotte Perkins Gilman: Her Progress Toward Utopia with Selected Writings,* Syracuse University Press (New York City), 1995.

Knight, Denise D., *Charlotte Perkins Gilman: A Study of the Short Fiction,* Twayne Publishers (New York City), 1997.

Lane, Ann J., introduction to *Herland* by Charlotte Perkins Gilman, Pantheon, 1979.

Lane, *To Herland and Beyond: The Life and Work of Charlotte Perkins Gilman,* Pantheon, 1990.

Scharnhorst, Gary, *Charlotte Perkins Gilman,* Twayne, 1985.

Scharnhorst, *Charlotte Perkins Gilman: A Bibliography,* Scarecrow Press, 1985.

Short Story Criticism, Volume 13, Gale, 1993.

Twentieth-Century Literary Criticism, Gale, Volume 9, 1983; Volume 37, 1991.

PERIODICALS

American Fabian, January, 1987, pp. 1-3.

American Literature, December, 1985, pp. 588-99.

American Quarterly, spring, 1956, pp. 21-39.

Arena, August, 1899, pp. 263-72.

Bookman, September, 1898, pp. 50-53.

Century, November, 1923, pp. 33-42.
Dial, February 1, 1899, pp. 83-86.
Nation, June 8, 1899, p. 443.
Studies in American Fiction, spring, 1983, pp. 31-46.
Tulsa Studies in Women's Literature, spring-fall, 1984, pp. 61-77.
Women's Studies: An Interdisciplinary Journal, March, 1986, pp. 271-92.

*   *   *

GILRAY, J. D.
See MENCKEN, H(enry) L(ouis)

*   *   *

GINSBERG, Allen 1926-1997

PERSONAL: Born June 3, 1926, in Newark, NJ; died of cancer April 5, 1997, in New York, NY; son of Louis (a poet and teacher) and Naomi (Levy) Ginsberg. *Education:* Columbia University, A.B., 1948. *Politics:* "Space Age Anarchist." *Religion:* "Buddhist-Jewish."

CAREER: Poet. Spot welder, Brooklyn Naval Yard, Brooklyn, NY, 1945; dishwasher, Bickford's Cafeteria, New York City, 1945; worked on various cargo ships, 1945-56; literary agent, reporter for New Jersey union newspaper, and copy boy for *New York World Telegram,* 1946; night porter, May Co., Denver, CO, 1946; book reviewer, *Newsweek,* New York City, 1950; market research consultant in New York City and San Francisco, 1951-53; instructor, University of British Columbia, Vancouver, 1963; founder and treasurer, Committee on Poetry Foundation, 1966-97; organizer, Gathering of the Tribes for a Human Be-In, San Francisco, 1967; cofounder, codirector, and teacher, Jack Kerouac School of Disembodied Poetics, Naropa Institute, Boulder, CO, 1974-97. Has given numerous poetry readings at universities, coffee houses, and art galleries in the United States, England, Russia, India, Peru, Chile, Poland, and Czechoslovakia; has addressed numerous conferences, including Group Advancement Psychiatry Conference, 1961, Dialectics of Liberation Conference, 1967, LSD Decade Conference, 1977, and World Conference on Humanity, 1979. Has appeared in numerous films, including *Pull My Daisy,* 1960; *Guns of the Trees,* 1962; *Couch,* 1964; *Wholly Communion, Chappaqua,* and *Allen for Allen,* all 1965; *Joan of Arc* and *Galaxie,* both 1966; *Herostratus, The Mind Alchemists,* and *Don't Look Back,* all 1967; *Me and My Brother,* 1968; *Dynamite Chicken,* 1971; *Renaldo and Clara,* 1978; *It Doesn't Pay to Be Honest,* 1984; *It Was 20 Years Ago Today,* 1987; *Heavy Petting,* 1988; *John Bowles: The Complete Outsider,* and *Jonas in the Desert,* both 1994; narrator of *Kaddish* (TV film), 1977.

MEMBER: National Institute of Arts and Letters, PEN, New York Eternal Committee for Conservation of Freedom in the Arts.

AWARDS, HONORS: Woodbury Poetry Prize; Guggenheim fellow, 1963-64; National Endowment for the Arts grant, 1966, and fellowship, 1986; National Institute of Arts and Letters award, 1969; National Book Award for Poetry, 1974, for *The Fall of America*; National Arts Club Medal of Honor for Literature, 1979; Poetry Society of America gold medal, 1986; Golden Wreath, 1986; Before Columbus Foundation award, 1990, for lifetime achievement; Harriet Monroe Poetry Award, University of Chicago, 1991; American Academy of Arts and Sciences fellowship, 1992.

WRITINGS:

POETRY

Howl and Other Poems, introduction by William Carlos Williams, City Lights (San Francisco), 1956, revised edition, Grabhorn-Hoyem, 1971, 40th-anniversary edition, City Lights, 1996.
Siesta in Xbalba and Return to the States, privately printed, 1956.
Kaddish and Other Poems, 1958-1960, City Lights, 1961.
Empty Mirror: Early Poems, Corinth Books (Chevy Chase, MD), 1961, new edition, 1970.
A Strange New Cottage in Berkeley, Grabhorn Press, 1963.
Reality Sandwiches: 1953-1960, City Lights, 1963.
The Change, Writer's Forum, 1963.
Kral Majales (title means "King of May"), Oyez (Kensington, CA), 1965.
Wichita Vortex Sutra, Housmans (London), 1966, Coyote Books (Brunswick, ME), 1967.
TV Baby Poems, Cape Golliard Press, 1967, Grossman, 1968.
Airplane Dreams: Compositions from Journals, House of Anansi (Toronto), 1968, City Lights, 1969.
(With Alexandra Lawrence) *Ankor Wat,* Fulcrum Press, 1968.
Scrap Leaves, Tasty Scribbles, Poet's Press, 1968.
Wales—A Visitation, July 29, 1967, Cape Golliard Press, 1968.
The Heart Is a Clock, Gallery Upstairs Press, 1968.
Message II, Gallery Upstairs Press, 1968.
Planet News, City Lights, 1968.
For the Soul of the Planet Is Wakening . . . , Desert Review Press, 1970.
The Moments Return: A Poem, Grabhorn-Hoyem, 1970.
Ginsberg's Improvised Poetics, edited by Mark Robison, Anonym Books, 1971.
New Year Blues, Phoenix Book Shop (New York City), 1972.
Open Head, Sun Books (Melbourne), 1972.
Bixby Canyon Ocean Path Word Breeze, Gotham Book Mart (New York City), 1972.
Iron Horse, Coach House Press (Chicago), 1972.
The Fall of America: Poems of These States, 1965-1971, City Lights, 1973.
The Gates of Wrath: Rhymed Poems, 1948-1952, Grey Fox (San Francisco), 1973.
Sad Dust Glories: Poems during Work Summer in Woods, 1974, Workingman's Press (Seattle), 1975.
First Blues: Rags, Ballads, and Harmonium Songs, 1971-1974, Full Court Press (New York City), 1975.
Mind Breaths: Poems, 1972-1977, City Lights, 1978.
Poems All Over the Place: Mostly Seventies, Cherry Valley (Wheaton, MD), 1978.
Mostly Sitting Haiku, From Here Press (Fanwood, NJ), 1978, revised and expanded edition, 1979.
Careless Love: Two Rhymes, Red Ozier Press, 1978.
(With Peter Orlovsky) *Straight Hearts' Delight: Love Poems and Selected Letters,* Gay Sunshine Press (San Francisco), 1980.
Plutonian Ode: Poems, 1977-1980, City Lights, 1982.
Collected Poems, 1947-1980, Harper (New York City), 1984, expanded edition published as *Collected Poems: 1947-85,* Penguin (New York City), 1995.
Many Loves, Pequod Press, 1984.
Old Love Story, Lospecchio Press, 1986.
White Shroud, Harper, 1986.
Cosmopolitan Greetings: Poems, 1986-1992, HarperCollins (New York City), 1994.
Illuminated Poems, illustrated by Eric Drooker, Four Walls Eight Windows (New York City), 1996.
Selected Poems, 1947-1995, HarperCollins, 1996.

Also author, with Kenneth Koch, of *Making It Up: Poetry Composed at St. Mark's Church on May 9, 1979.*

OTHER

(Author of introduction) Gregory Corso, *Gasoline* (poems), City Lights, 1958.

(With William Burroughs) *The Yage Letters* (correspondence), City Lights, 1963.

(Contributor) David Solomon, editor, *The Marijuana Papers* (essays), Bobbs-Merrill (New York City), 1966.

Prose Contribution to Cuban Revolution, Artists Workshop Press, 1966.

(Translator with others) Nicanor Parra, *Poems and Antipoems,* New Directions (Newton, NJ), 1967.

(Contributor) Charles Hollander, editor, *Background Papers on Student Drug Abuse,* U.S. National Student Association, 1967.

(Author of introduction) John A. Wood, *Orbs: A Portfolio of Nine Poems,* Apollyon Press, 1968.

(Contributor) Bob Booker and George Foster, editors, *Pardon Me, Sir, but Is My Eye Hurting Your Elbow?* (plays), Geis, 1968.

(Author of introduction) Louis Ginsberg, *Morning in Spring* (poems), Morrow (New York City), 1970.

(Compiler) *Documents on Police Bureaucracy's Conspiracy against Human Rights of Opiate Addicts and Constitutional Rights of Medical Profession Causing Mass Breakdown of Urban Law and Order,* privately printed, 1970.

(Contributor of commentary) Jean Genet, *May Day Speech,* City Lights, 1970.

Indian Journals: March 1962-May 1963; Notebooks, Diary, Blank Pages, Writings, City Lights, 1970, Grove Press, 1996.

Notes after an Evening with William Carlos Williams, Portents Press, 1970.

Declaration of Independence for Dr. Timothy Leary, Hermes Free Press, 1971.

(Author of introduction) William Burroughs, Jr., *Speed* (novel), Sphere Books, 1971.

(Author of foreword) Ann Charters, *Kerouac* (biography), Straight Arrow Books, 1973.

(Contributor of interview) Donald M. Allen, editor, *Robert Creeley, Contexts of Poetry: Interviews 1961-1971,* Four Seasons Foundation (San Francisco), 1973.

The Fall of America Wins a Prize (text of speech), Gotham Book Mart, 1974.

Gay Sunshine Interview: Allen Ginsberg with Allen Young, Grey Fox, 1974.

The Visions of the Great Rememberer (correspondence), Mulch Press (San Francisco), 1974.

Allen Verbatim: Lectures on Poetry, Politics, and Consciousness, edited by Gordon Ball, McGraw (New York City), 1975.

Chicago Trial Testimony, City Lights, 1975.

The Dream of Tibet, City Moon, 1976.

To Eberhart from Ginsberg (correspondence), Penmaen Press (Great Barrington, MA), 1976.

Journals: Early Fifties, Early Sixties, edited by Gordon Ball, Grove (New York City), 1977.

(With others) *Madeira and Toasts for Basil Bunting's 75th Birthday,* edited by Jonathan Williams, Jargon Society (East Haven, CT), 1977.

(With Neal Cassady, and author of afterword) *As Ever: Collected Correspondence of Allen Ginsberg and Neal Cassady,* Creative Arts, 1977.

(Author of introduction) Anne Waldman and Marilyn Webb, editors, *Talking Poetics from Naropa Institute: Annals of the Jack Kerouac School of Disembodied Poetics,* Volume I, Shambhala (Boulder, CO), 1978.

Composed on the Tongue (interviews), edited by Donald Allen, Grey Fox, 1980.

(With others) *Nuke Chronicles,* Contact Two (Bowling Green, NY), 1980.

Your Reason and Blake's System, Hanuman Books, 1989.

Allen Ginsberg: Photographs, Twelvetrees Press (Pasadena, CA), 1991.

(Author of introduction) Ernesto Cardenal, *Ergo! The Bumbershoot Literary Magazine,* Bumbershoot, 1991.

(Author of foreword) Anne Waldman, editor, *Out of This World: The Poetry Project at the St. Mark's Church in the Bowery, an Anthology, 1966-1991,* Crown (New York City), 1991.

(Author of introduction) Andy Clausen, *Without Doubt,* Zeitgeist Press, 1991.

(Author of introduction) Jack Kerouac, *Poems All Sizes,* City Lights, 1992.

(Author of introduction) Sharkmeat Blue, *King Death: And Other Poems,* Underground Forest/Selva Editions, 1992.

(Author of afterword) Louis Ginsberg, *Collected Poems,* edited by Michael Fournier, Northern Lights, 1992.

Snapshot Poetics: Allen Ginsberg's Photographic Memoir of the Beat Era, introduction by Michael Kohler, Chronicle Books (San Francisco), 1993.

(Editor with Peter Orlovsky) *Francesco Clemente: Evening Raga 1992,* Rizzoli International (New York City), 1993.

Honorable Courtship: From the Author's Journals, January 1-15, 1955, edited and illustrated by Dean Bornstein, Coffee House Press (Minneapolis), 1994.

(Author of introduction) Edward Leffingwell, *Earthly Paradise,* Journey Editions, 1994.

Journals Mid-Fifties, 1954-1958, edited by Gordon Ball, Harper-Collins, 1995.

(Contributor and author of foreword) *The Beat Book: Poems and Fiction of the Beat Generation,* edited by Anne Waldman, Shambhala (Boston), 1996.

(Author of foreword) Ko Un, *Beyond Self: 108 Korean Zen Poems,* Parallax Press (Berkeley, CA), 1997.

Performer on numerous recordings, including *San Francisco Poets,* Evergreen Records, 1958; *Howl and Other Poems,* Fantasy, 1959; and *Holy Soul Jelly Roll: Poems and Songs, 1949-1993,* Rhino/Word Beat, 1995. Work appears in numerous anthologies, including *The Beat Generation and the Angry Young Men,* edited by Gene Feldman and Max Gartenberg, Citadel Press, 1958; and *The New Oxford Book of American Verse,* edited by Richard Ellmann, Oxford University Press, 1976. Contributor of poetry and articles to periodicals, including *Evergreen Review, Journal for the Protection of All Beings, Playboy, Nation, New Age, New Yorker, Atlantic Monthly, Partisan Review,* and *Times Literary Supplement.* Correspondent, *Evergreen Review,* 1965; former contributing editor, *Black Mountain Review;* former advisory guru, *Marijuana Review.*

Ginsberg's papers are housed at Stanford University.

MEDIA ADAPTATIONS: "Kaddish" was adapted as a film, with Ginsberg as narrator, and broadcast by National Educational Television in 1977.

SIDELIGHTS: Allen Ginsberg enjoyed a long career as a leading figure in contemporary poetry and culture because of his creative work, his social and political activities, and his interest in the visionary. Ginsberg first came to public attention in 1956 with the publication of *Howl and Other Poems.* "Howl," a long-line poem in the tradition of Walt Whitman, is an outcry of rage and despair against a destructive, abusive society. The poem's raw, honest language and its "Hebraic-Melvillian bardic breath," as Ginsberg called it, stunned many traditional critics. James Dickey, for instance, refers to "Howl" as "a whipped-up state of excitement" and concludes that "it takes more than this to make poetry. It just does." Critic Walter Sutton, in *American Free Verse: The Modern Revolution in Poetry,* dubs "Howl" "a tirade revealing an animus directed outward against those who do not share the poet's social and sexual orientation." Other critics responded more positively. Richard Eberhart, for example, calls "Howl" "a powerful work, cutting through to dynamic meaning. . . . It is a howl against everything in our mechanistic civilization which kills the spirit. . . . Its positive force and energy come from a redemptive quality of love." Paul Carroll, in *The Poem in Its Skin,* judges it "one of the milestones of the generation."

In addition to stunning many critics, *Howl* also stunned the San Francisco Police Department. Because of the graphic sexual language of the poem, they declared the book obscene and arrested the publisher, poet Lawrence Ferlinghetti. The ensuing trial attracted national attention, as prominent literary figures such as Mark Schorer, Kenneth Rexroth, and Walter Van Tilberg Clark spoke in defense of *Howl.* Schorer testified that "Ginsberg uses the rhythms of ordinary speech and also the diction of ordinary speech. I would say the poem uses necessarily the language of vulgarity." Clark called *Howl* "the work of a thoroughly honest poet, who is also a highly competent technician." The testimony eventually persuaded Judge Clayton W. Horn to rule that *Howl* was not obscene.

The qualities cited in its defense helped make *Howl* the manifesto of the Beat literary movement. The Beats, popularly known as Beatniks, included such novelists as Jack Kerouac and such poets as Gregory Corso, Michael McClure, Gary Snyder, and Ginsberg, all of whom wrote in the language of the street about previously forbidden and unliterary topics. The ideas and art of the Beats would greatly influence popular culture during the 1950s and 1960s.

Ginsberg followed *Howl* in 1961 with *Kaddish and Other Poems.* "Kaddish," a poem similar in style and form to "Howl," is based on the traditional Hebrew prayer for the dead and tells the life story of Ginsberg's mother, Naomi. The poet's complex feelings for his mother, colored by her struggle with mental illness, are at the heart of this long-line poem. It is considered to be one of Ginsberg's better poems. Thomas F. Merrill, in *Allen Ginsberg,* dubs it "Ginsberg at his purest and perhaps at his best"; Helen Vendler, commenting in the *New Republic,* considers "Kaddish" Ginsberg's "great elegy for his mother"; Louis Simpson, writing in *A Revolution in Taste,* simply refers to it as "a masterpiece."

Ginsberg's early poems were greatly influenced by fellow Paterson, New Jersey resident William Carlos Williams. Ginsberg recalled being taught at school that Williams "was some kind of awkward crude provincial from New Jersey," but upon talking to Williams about his poetry, Ginsberg "suddenly realized [that Williams] was hearing with raw ears. The sound, pure sound and rhythm—as it was spoken around him, and he was trying to adapt his poetry rhythms out of the actual talk-rhythms he heard rather than metronome or sing-song archaic literary rhythms." Ginsberg acted immediately on his sudden understanding. "I went over my prose writings," he told an interviewer, "and I took out little four-or-five line fragments that were absolutely accurate to some-

body's speak-talk-thinking and rearranged them in lines, according to the breath, according to how you'd break it up if you were actually to talk it out, and then I sent 'em over to Williams. He sent me back a note, almost immediately, and he said 'These are it! Do you have any more of these?'"

Another major influence was Ginsberg's friend Kerouac, who wrote novels in a "spontaneous prose" style that Ginsberg admired and adapted in his own work. Kerouac had written some of his books by putting a roll of white paper into a typewriter and typing continuously in a "stream of consciousness." Ginsberg began writing poems not, as he states, "by working on it in little pieces and fragments from different times, but remembering an idea in my head and writing it down on the spot and completing it there." Both Williams and Kerouac emphasized a writer's emotions and natural mode of expression over traditional literary structures. Ginsberg cited as historical precedents for this idea the works of poet Walt Whitman, novelist Herman Melville, and writers Henry David Thoreau and Ralph Waldo Emerson.

Ginsberg's political activities were called strongly libertarian in nature, echoing his poetic preference for individual expression over traditional structure. In the mid-1960s he was closely associated with the hippie and antiwar movements. He created and advocated "flower power," a strategy in which antiwar demonstrators would promote positive values like peace and love to dramatize their opposition to the death and destruction caused by the Vietnam War. The use of flowers, bells, smiles, and mantras (sacred chants) became common among demonstrators for some time. In 1967 Ginsberg was an organizer of the "Gathering of the Tribes for a Human Be-In," an event modeled after the Hindu *mela,* a religious festival. It was the first of the hippie festivals and served as an inspiration for hundreds of others. In 1969, when some antiwar activists staged an "exorcism of the Pentagon," Ginsberg composed the mantra they chanted. He testified for the defense in the Chicago 7 Conspiracy Trial in which antiwar activists were charged with "conspiracy to cross state lines to promote a riot."

Ginsberg's political activities caused him problems in other countries as well. In 1965 he visited Cuba as a correspondent for *Evergreen Review.* After he complained about the treatment of gays at the University of Havana, the government asked Ginsberg to leave the country. In the same year the poet traveled to Czechoslovakia where he was elected "King of May" by thousands of Czech citizens. The next day the Czech government requested that he leave, ostensibly because he was "sloppy and degenerate." Ginsberg attributes his expulsion to the Czech secret police who were embarrassed by the acclaim given to "a bearded American fairy dope poet."

A continuing concern reflected in Ginsberg's poetry is a focus on the spiritual and visionary. His interest in these matters was inspired by a series of visions he had while reading William Blake's poetry. Ginsberg recalled hearing "a very deep earthen grave voice in the room, which I immediately assumed, I didn't think twice, was Blake's voice . . . the peculiar quality of the voice was something unforgettable because it was like God had a human voice, with all the infinite tenderness and anciency and mortal gravity of a living Creator speaking to his son."

These visions prompted an interest in mysticism that led Ginsberg to experiment, for a time, with various drugs. He has claimed that some of his best poetry was written under the influence of drugs: the second part of "Howl" with peyote, "Kaddish" with amphetamines, and "Wales—A Visitation" with LSD. After a trip to

India in 1962, however, during which he was introduced to meditation and yoga, Ginsberg changed his mind about drugs. He has since maintained that meditation and yoga are far superior to drugs in raising one's consciousness, although he still believes that psychedelics could prove helpful in writing poetry. Psychedelics, he said, are "a variant of yoga and [the] exploration of consciousness."

Ginsberg's study of Eastern religions was spurred on by his discovery of mantras, rhythmic chants used for spiritual effects. Their use of rhythm, breath, and elemental sounds seemed to him a kind of poetry. In a number of poems he incorporated mantras into the body of the text, transforming the work into a kind of poetic prayer. During poetry readings he often began by chanting a mantra in order to set the proper mood.

Ginsberg's interest in Eastern religions eventually led him to the Venerable Chogyam Trungpa, Rinpoche, a Buddhist abbot from Tibet who had a strong influence on Ginsberg's writing. The early 1970s found the poet taking classes at Trungpa's Naropa Institute in Colorado as well as teaching poetry classes there. In 1972 Ginsberg took the Refuge and Boddhisattva vows, formally committing himself to the Buddhist faith.

In 1974 Ginsberg and fellow-poet Anne Waldman cofounded the Jack Kerouac School of Disembodied Poetics as a branch of Trungpa's Naropa Institute. "The ultimate idea is to found a permanent arts college," Ginsberg said of the school, "sort of like they have in Tibetan tradition where you have teachers and students living together in a permanent building which would go on for hundreds of years. Sort of a center where you'd have a poet old enough to really be a teacher or guru poet." Ginsberg attracted such prominent writers as Diane di Prima, Ron Padgett, and William Burroughs to speak and teach at the school. "Trungpa wants the presence of poets at Naropa," Ginsberg said, "to inspire the Buddhists towards becoming articulate, and he also sees the advantage of having the large scale Buddhist background to inspire the poets to silence; to the appreciation of silent space in meditation and breath."

Ginsberg lived a kind of literary "rags to riches"—from his early days as the feared, criticized, and "dirty" poet to his present position within what Richard Kostelanetz calls "the pantheon of American literature." He has been one of the most influential poets of his generation, and, in the words of James F. Mersmann in *Out of the Vietnam Vortex: A Study of Poets and Poetry against the War,* he is "a great figure in the history of poetry." According to *Times Literary Supplement* contributor James Campbell, "No one has made his poetry speak for the whole man, without inhibition of any kind, more than Ginsberg." Because of his rise to influence and his continued staying power as a figure in American art and culture, Ginsberg remains the object of much scholarly attention. A documentary directed by Jerry Aronson, *The Life and Times of Allen Ginsberg,* was released in 1994. The same year, Stanford University paid Ginsberg a reported one million dollars for his personal archives. New poems and collections of Ginsberg's previous works are published regularly. And his letters, journals, and even his photographs of fellow Beats have given critics and scholars new insights into the life and work of this poet.

Journals Mid-Fifties, 1954-1958, published in 1995, is an example of the new information available on Ginsberg. Jim Krusoe, writing in the *Los Angeles Times Book Review,* maintains that this book "provides plenty of food for thought about genius in general and about Ginsberg's development in particular." For some reviewers, however, these journals shed less light on the poet than previous works. Alexander Theroux comments in *Tribune Books,* "Sadly these pages are often remarkably dull and rarely original and insightful." According to Guy Mannes-Abbott in the *New Statesman and Society,* these journals "have interest but lack the vitality of earlier and later journals, or the generosity of his letters from this time." A reviewer for the *Economist* recognizes the shortcomings of these personal writings, but sees through to their merits. "Though maddeningly interested in his most banal reactions . . . [Ginsberg] is at least open about his self-fascination," writes the reviewer. "In a 'me-too', instant-playback world where every voice counts, why not write as it all is, here and now, for him?" This reviewer continues, "In most writers self-preoccupation is usually mortal. But Mr Ginsberg has the balancing gifts of promiscuous curiosity and an almost sappy, American optimism." For Krusoe, in the end, "the brilliance of these journals is exactly the brilliant persistence of a man who will not quit until his dream life, his love life and his poems are melded into a single whole."

BIOGRAPHICAL/CRITICAL SOURCES:

BOOKS

Carroll, Paul, *The Poem in Its Skin,* Follett, 1968.

Concise Dictionary of American Literary Biography: 1941-1968, Gale (Detroit), 1987.

Contemporary Literary Criticism, Gale, Volume 1, 1973; Volume 2, 1974; Volume 3, 1975; Volume 4, 1975; Volume 6, 1976; Volume 13, 1980; Volume 36, 1986; Volume 69, 1992.

Contemporary Poets, sixth edition, St. James Press (Detroit), 1996.

Cook, Bruce, *The Beat Generation,* Scribner (New York City), 1971.

Dictionary of Literary Biography, Gale, Volume 5: *American Poets since World War II,* 1980; Volume 16: *The Beats: Literary Bohemians in Postwar America,* 1983; Volume 169: *American Poets since World War II, Fifth Series,* 1996.

Erlich, J. W., editor, *Howl of the Censor,* Nourse Publishing, 1961.

Kramer, Jane, *Allen Ginsberg in America,* Random House (New York City), 1969, new edition, Fromm International Publishing, 1997.

Merrill, Thomas F., *Allen Ginsberg,* Twayne, 1969.

Mersmann, James F., *Out of the Vietnam Vortex: A Study of Poets and Poetry against the War,* University Pres of Kansas, 1974.

McNally, Dennis, *Desolate Angel: Jack Kerouac, the Beats, and America,* Random House, 1979.

Morgan, Bill, *The Response to Allen Ginsberg, 1926-1994: A Bibliography of Secondary Sources,* foreword by Ginsberg, Greenwood Press, 1996.

Poetry Criticism, Volume 4, Gale, 1992.

Roszak, Theodore, *The Making of a Counter Culture,* Doubleday (Garden City, NY), 1969.

Schumacher, Michael, *Dharma Lion,* St. Martin's (New York City), 1994.

Shaw, Robert B., editor, *American Poetry since 1960: Some Critical Perspectives,* Dufour (Chester Springs, PA), 1974.

Simpson, Louis, *A Revolution in Taste,* Macmillan, 1978.

Sutton, Walter, *American Free Verse: The Modern Revolution in Poetry,* New Directions, 1973.

Tyrell, John, *Naked Angels,* McGraw, 1976.

PERIODICALS

Advocate, February 22, 1994.

American Poetry Review, September, 1977.

Antioch Review, spring, 1994, p. 374.

Ariel, October, 1993, pp. 21-32.

Atlanta Journal and Constitution, November 19, 1994, p. WL23.

Best Sellers, December 15, 1974.

Bloomsbury Review, March, 1993, p. 5.

Booklist, April 15, 1994, p. 1503; April 15, 1995, p. 1468.

Chicago Review, summer, 1975.

Detroit News, April 18, 1997.

Dionysos, winter, 1993, pp. 30-42.

East West Journal, February, 1978.

Economist, November 11, 1995, p. 8.

Encounter, February, 1970.

Entertainment Weekly, October 11, 1996, p. 92.

Esquire, April, 1973.

Globe and Mail (Toronto), February 23, 1985.

Harper's, October, 1966.

Hudson Review, autumn, 1973.

Interview, June, 1994, p. 16.

Journal of American Culture, fall, 1993, pp. 81-88.

Journal of Popular Culture, winter, 1969.

Lambda Book Report, July, 1993, p. 42; July, 1994, p. 47; September, 1994, p. 34.

Library Journal, June 15, 1958; February 1, 1987; May 1, 1994; August, 1995, p. 79.

Life, May 27, 1966.

Los Angeles Times, April 18, 1985; February 16, 1994, p. F1; February 17, 1994, p. F3.

Los Angeles Times Book Review, January 2, 1994, p. 12; May 29, 1994, p. 8; September 3, 1995, p. 4.

Michigan Quarterly Review, spring, 1994, pp. 350-59.

Nation, February 25, 1957; November 11, 1961; November 12, 1977; May 20, 1991.

National Observer, December 9, 1968.

National Review, September 12, 1959; May 19, 1997, p. 54.

New Republic, July 25, 1970; October 12, 1974; October 22, 1977.

New Statesman and Society, May 12, 1995, p. 38; October 27, 1995, p. 47.

New Times, February 20, 1978.

New Yorker, August 17, 1968; August 24, 1968; May 28, 1979.

New York Times, February 6, 1972; May 21, 1994, p. A13; September 20, 1994, p. C15; September 25, 1994, sec. 2, p. 34; October 29, 1994, p. A19; September 29, 1995, p. C18.

New York Times Book Review, September 2, 1956; May 11, 1969; August 31, 1969; April 15, 1973; March 2, 1975; October 23, 1977; March 19, 1978; May 29, 1994, p. 14.

New York Times Magazine, July 11, 1965.

Observer (London), June 11, 1995, p. 16.

Parnassus: Poetry in Review, spring/summer, 1974.

Partisan Review, number 2, 1959; number 3, 1967; number 3, 1971; number 2, 1974.

People, July 3, 1978; November 25, 1996, p. 27.

Playboy, April, 1969; January, 1995, p. 24.

Poetry, September, 1957; July, 1969; September, 1969.

Progressive, May, 1994, p. 48; August, 1994, pp. 34-39.

Salmagundi, spring/summer, 1973.

Saturday Review, October 5, 1957.

Small Press Review, July/August, 1977.

Time, February 9, 1959; November 18, 1974; March 5, 1979.

Times Literary Supplement, July 7, 1978; September 1, 1995, p. 22.

Tribune Books (Chicago), June 11, 1995, p. 5.

USA Today, July, 1995, p. 96.

Vanity Fair, March, 1994, p. 186.

Village Voice, April 18, 1974.

Washington Post, March 17, 1985.

Washington Post Book World, March 20, 1994, p. 12.

Western American Literature, spring, 1995, pp. 3-28.

Whole Earth Review, fall, 1995, p. 90.

World Literature Today, winter, 1995, p. 146.

OTHER

The Life and Times of Allen Ginsberg (film), First Run Features, 1994.

*   *   *

GINZBURG, Natalia 1916-1991
(Alessandra Tournimparte)

PERSONAL: Born July 14 (one source says July 5), 1916, in Palermo, Italy; died October 7 (one source says October 8), 1991; daughter of Carlo (a novelist and professor of biology) and Lidia (Tanzi) Levi; married Leone Ginzburg (an editor and political activist), 1938 (died, 1944); married Gabriele Baldini, 1950.

ADDRESSES: Home—Piazza Camp Marzio 3, Rome, Italy.

CAREER: Novelist, short story writer, dramatist, and essayist. Worked for Einaudi (publisher), Turin, Italy. Member of Italian parliament. Elected representative of Independent Left Party Parliament of Italy, 1983.

AWARDS, HONORS: Strega Prize, 1964, for *Lessico famigliare;* Marzotto Prize for European Drama, 1968, for *The Advertisement;* Milan Club Degli Editori Award, 1969; Bagutto Award, 1984; Ernest Hemingway Prize, 1985.

WRITINGS:

(Under pseudonym Alessandra Tournimparte) *La strada che va in citta* (two short novels), Einaudi (Turin, Italy), 1942, reprinted under own name, 1975, translation by Frances Frenaye published under own name as *The Road to the City* (contains "The Road to the City" and "The Dry Heart"), Doubleday, 1949.

E stato cosi, Einaudi, 1947.

Valentino (novella; also see below), Einaudi, 1951.

Tutti i nostri ieri (novel), Einaudi, 1952, translation by Angus Davidson published as *A Light for Fools,* Dutton, 1956, translation published as *Dead Yesterdays,* Secker & Warburg, 1956.

(With Giansiro Ferrata) *Romanzi del 900,* Ediziono Radio Italiana (Turin), 1957.

Sagittario (novella; also see below), Einaudi, 1957, translation published as *Sagittarius,* 1975.

Le voci della sera, Einaudi, 1961, new edition edited by Sergio Pacilici, Random House, 1971, translation by D. M. Low published as *Voices in the Evening,* Dutton, 1963.

Le piccole virtu (essays), Einaudi, 1962, translation by Dick Davis published as *The Little Virtues,* Seaver Books, 1986.

Lessico famigliare (novel), Einaudi, 1963, translation by Low published as *Family Sayings,* Dutton, 1967.

Cinque romanzi brevi (short novels and short stories), Einaudi, 1964.

Ti ho sposato per allegria (plays), Einaudi, 1966.

The Advertisement (play; translation by Henry Reed first produced in London at Old Vic Theatre, September 24, 1968), Faber, 1969.

Teresa (play), [Paris], 1970.

Mai devi domandarmi (essays), Garzanti (Milan) 1970, translation by Isabel Quigly published as *Never Must You Ask Me,* M. Joseph, 1973.

Caro Michele (novel), Mondadori (Milan), 1973, translation by Sheila Cudahy published as *No Way,* Harcourt, 1974, published as *Dear Michael,* Owen, 1975.

Paese di mare e altre commedie, Garzanti, 1973.

Vita immaginaria (essays), Mondadori, 1974.

Famiglia (contains novellas "Borghesia" and "Famiglia"), 1977, translation by Beryl Stockman published as *Family,* Holt, 1988.

La citte e la casa, 1984, translation by Davis published as *The City and the House,* Seaver Books, 1987.

All Our Yesterdays, translation by Davidson, Carcanet, 1985.

The Manzoni Family, translation by Marie Evans, Seaver Books, 1987.

Valentino and Sagittarius, translation by Avril Bardoni, Holt, 1988.

Also author of *Fragola e panna,* 1966, *La segretaria,* 1967, and "I Married You for the Fun of It," 1972.

SIDELIGHTS: Natalia Ginzburg is one of the best-known postwar Italian writers. Her cool, controlled, simple style of writing has impressed critics, while her intimate explorations of domestic life have been praised for their authenticity and concern for traditional values. Annapaola Concogni of the *New York Times Book Review* explained that Ginzburg possessed an "ear tuned in to the subtlest frequencies of domestic life, its accents, its gestures, its ups and downs and constant contradictions." Isabel Quigly compared Ginzburg to Chekhov, finding that, when reading Ginzburg's fiction, "Inevitably, Chekhov comes to mind: not only because the long summer days, the endless agreeable but unrewarding chat, the whole provincial-intellectual set-up, recall him, but because the Italian charm, and volatility, and loquacity, and unselfconscious egocentricity, and inability to move out of grooves, and so on, that Miss Ginzburg so brilliantly captures, are all Chekhovian qualities."

"Natalia Ginzburg is at her best when dealing with detail," Marc Slonim wrote of *A Light for Fools,* "and her descriptions of children and adolescents have a definite poetic flavor. Most of the incidents and characters are seen through the eyes of an adolescent, and the book has much of the naivete and charm of a child's vision. This 'point of view' in the Jamesian sense gives a unity of diction to the whole narrative." Similarly, Quigly commented, "She has an extraordinary gift for what you might call cumulative characterization-a method that dispenses almost entirely with description and builds up solid and memorable people by the gradual mounting up of small actions, oblique glances, other people's opinions."

Other reviewers were critical of Ginzburg's method of characterization. Thomas G. Bergin wrote that the characters in *Voices in the Evening* "are, for the most part, like excellent line drawings, quite real but somehow not 'filled in.' Their bone structure is magnificent, but there is no flesh." And although Otis K. Burger found the same novel to be "crisp, brittle, entertaining, and informative," he also remarked that "the very coolness of the style tends to defeat the subtle theme of the death of a family (and a love) through sheer lack of gumption. The brevity of the book and its semicomic treatment of a muted tragedy come to seem, not a strength but part of the general, fatal weariness. The 'voices in the evening' tend to cancel each other out—succeeding only too well

in presenting people who, pallid to begin with, end as mere phantoms."

Although *Family Sayings* is on the surface a simple family tale, what is beneath and between the lines reveals the weight and worth of the novel. Raymond Rosenthal wrote that "what started as a simple family chronicle takes on the timeless, magnificent aspect of an ancient tale, a Homeric saga. It is magical, exhilarating. In the last pages, after all is accomplished and the deaths, the bereavements, the terrible losses of war and social struggle have been counted up, so to speak, the mere fact that Natalia's mother is still telling the same old stories, and that her father—the counter-muse, the rationalistic ogre—is still there to provide the antiphonic accompaniment of grumbles and complaints, becomes mythical in the truest sense. The surface of this book is also its depths."

Gavin Ewart also praised *Family Sayings.* The book exhibits, Ewart noted, "a simple, distilled style, a reliance on the virtues of repetition, an awareness of the ridiculousness of human beings; a great love (reading between the lines) for both her father and her mother; the shadow of Proust. All these are in it. Dealing with more 'tragic' material, it has the control and the only slightly edited reality that one finds in *My Life and Hard Times* (remember Thurber?). Though this is verbal comedy and not farce, it still seems, like that masterpiece, to imply that life can be terrible, but also terribly funny."

No Way concerns Michael, a young revolutionary living in a basement apartment. Ginzburg develops the relationships between Michael and his friends through letters (most of which are written to Michael, few of which he answers). "While Michael is expending what turn out to be his last days," Martin Levin comments, "his father dies, his girlfriend Mara runs through a half dozen patrons, and his mother is jilted by her lover Philip. All of these relationships are assembled by epistolary connections that have the intricacy and the fragility of an ant city. The wit is mordant and comes directly out of paradox." Lynne Sharon Schwartz noted, "The contours of [Ginzburg's] sentences linger in the ear like phrases from great music, familiar, basic truths. Her characters, sad, thwarted, often drab types, are memorable in the manner of people one knew very long ago."

"What makes this book so wonderful," L. E. Sissman declared, "magical even—is that we are never bored by the imprisoned pacings and abortive flights of its people. They all become real and individual and fascinating through the technical gifts of the author. . . *No Way* is a novel of the curdling of aspirations and the enfeebling of powers among those who heretofore held sway. Its quality lies in its reportorial accuracy, in its fine, warm, rueful equanimity, in its balance in the face of toppling worlds. It is a most remarkable book."

Writing in the *Los Angeles Times Book Review,* Peter Brunette called Ginzburg "the undisputed doyenne of contemporary Italian letters. Both a successful playwright and essayist, she has also become, through a steady outpouring of quietly memorable fiction over the last four decades, a world-class novelist."

BIOGRAPHICAL/CRITICAL SOURCES:

BOOKS

Bullock, Alan, *Natalia Ginzburg: Human Relationships in a Changing World,* St. Martin's Press (New York City), 1991.

Contemporary Literary Criticism, Gale, Volume 5, 1976; Volume 11, 1979; Volume 54, 1989.

PERIODICALS

Commonweal, December 4, 1992.
London Magazine, May, 1967.
Los Angeles Times Book Review, December 27, 1987.
New Leader, March 13, 1967.
New Republic, September 14, 1974.
New Yorker, October 21, 1974.
New York Review of Books, January 23, 1975.
New York Times, January 5, 1957; October 6, 1963.
New York Times Book Review, September 1, 1974; June 26, 1988.
Saturday Review, September 21, 1963.
Spectator, August 24, 1956.
Times Literary Supplement, February 5, 1971; April 13, 1973; June 15, 1973; February 21, 1975; March 28, 1975; June 2, 1978.
World Literature Today, August, 1991.

*   *   *

GIOVANNI, Nikki 1943-

PERSONAL: Birth name, Yolande Cornelia Giovanni, Jr.; born June 7, 1943, in Knoxville, TN; daughter of Jones (a probation officer) and Yolande Cornelia (a social worker; maiden name, Watson) Giovanni; children: Thomas Watson. *Education:* Fisk University, B.A. (with honors), 1967; postgraduate studies at University of Pennsylvania, Social Work School, and Columbia University, School of the Arts.

ADDRESSES: Office—English Department, Virginia Polytechnic Institute and State University, Blacksburg, Virginia, 24061; c/o William Morrow, Inc., 1350 Avenue of the Americas, New York, NY 10019.

CAREER: Poet, writer, lecturer, and educator. Queens College of the City University of New York, Flushing, NY, assistant professor of black studies, 1968; Rutgers University, Livingston College, New Brunswick, NJ, associate professor of English, 1968-72; Ohio State University, Columbus, visiting professor of English, 1984; College of Mount St. Joseph on the Ohio, Mount St. Joseph, Ohio, professor of creative writing, 1985-87; Virginia Polytechnic Institute and State University, Blacksburg, VA, professor, 1987–; Texas Christian University, visiting professor in humanities, 1991. Founder of publishing firm, Niktom Ltd., 1970.

MEMBER: National Council of Negro Women, Society of Magazine Writers, National Black Heroines for PUSH, Winnie Mandela Children's Fund Committee, Delta Sigma Theta.

AWARDS, HONORS: Grants from Ford Foundation, 1967, National Endowment for the Arts, 1968, and Harlem Cultural Council, 1969; named one of ten "Most Admired Black Women," *Amsterdam News,* 1969; outstanding achievement award, *Mademoiselle,* 1971; Omega Psi Phi Fraternity Award, 1971, for outstanding contribution to arts and letters; Meritorious Plaque for Service, Cook County Jail, 1971; Prince Matchabelli Sun Shower Award, 1971; life membership and scroll, National Council of Negro Women, 1972; National Association of Radio and Television Announcers Award, 1972, for *Truth Is on Its Way;* Woman of the Year Youth Leadership Award, *Ladies' Home Journal,* 1972; National Book Award nomination, 1973, for *Gemini;* "Best Books for Young Adults" citation, American Library Association, 1973, for *My House;* "Woman of the Year" citation, Cincinnati Chapter of YWCA, 1983; elected to Ohio Women's Hall of Fame, 1985; "Outstanding Woman of Tennessee" citation, 1985; Post-Corbett Award, 1986; Woman of the Year, NAACP (Lynchburg chapter), 1989.

Honorary Doctorate of Humanities, Wilberforce University, 1972, Fisk University, 1988; Honorary Doctorate of Literature, University of Maryland (Princess Anne Campus), 1974, Ripon University, 1974, and Smith College, 1975; Honorary Doctorate of Humane Letters, The College of Mount St. Joseph on the Ohio, 1985, Indiana Univesity, 1991, Otterbein College, 1992, Widener University, 1993, Albright College, 1995, Cabrini College, 1995, and Allegheny College, 1997. Jeanine Rae Award for the Advancement of Women's Culture, 1995; Langston Hughes Award, 1996.

WRITINGS:

POETRY

Black Feeling, Black Talk (also see below), Broadside Press (Highland Park, MI), 1968, third edition, 1970.
Black Judgement (also see below), Broadside Press, 1968.
Black Feeling, Black Talk/Black Judgement (contains *Black Feeling, Black Talk,* and *Black Judgement*), Morrow (New York City), 1970.
Re: Creation, Broadside Press, 1970.
Poem of Angela Yvonne Davis, Afro Arts, 1970.
Spin a Soft Black Song: Poems for Children, illustrations by Charles Bible, Hill & Wang (New York City), 1971, illustrations by George Martins, Lawrence Hill (Westport, CT), 1985, revised edition, Farrar, Straus (New York City), 1987.
My House, foreword by Ida Lewis, Morrow, 1972.
Ego Tripping and Other Poems for Young People, illustrations by George Ford, Lawrence Hill, 1973.
The Women and the Men, Morrow, 1975.
Cotton Candy on a Rainy Day, introduction by Paula Giddings, Morrow, 1978.
Vacation Time: Poems for Children, illustrations by Marisabina Russo, Morrow, 1980.
Those Who Ride the Night Winds, Morrow, 1983.
Knoxville, Tennessee, Scholastic (New York City), 1994.
Shimmy Shimmy Shimmy Like My Sister Kate: Looking at the Harlem Renaissance through Poems, Holt (New York City), 1995.
The Genie in the Jar, Holt, 1996.
The Selected Poems of Nikki Giovanni (1968-1995), Morrow, 1996.
The Sun Is So Quiet: Poems, Holt, 1996.
Love Poems, Morrow, 1997.

NONFICTION

Gemini: An Extended Autobiographical Statement on My First Twenty-five Years of Being a Black Poet, Bobbs-Merrill (New York City), 1971.
(With James Baldwin) *A Dialogue: James Baldwin and Nikki Giovanni,* Lippincott (Philadelphia), 1973.
(With Margaret Walker) *A Poetic Equation: Conversations between Nikki Giovanni and Margaret Walker,* Howard University Press (Washington, DC), 1974.
Sacred Cows . . . and Other Edibles (essays; includes "Reflections on My Profession," "Four Introductions," and "An Answer to Some Questions on How I Write"), Morrow, 1988.
Racism 101, Morrow, 1994.

SOUND RECORDINGS

Truth Is on Its Way, Right-On, 1971.

Like a Ripple on a Pond, Niktom, 1973.
The Way I Feel, Atlantic, 1974.
Legacies: The Poetry of Nikki Giovanni, Folkways, 1976.
The Reason I Like Chocolate, Folkways, 1976.

OTHER

(Editor) *Night Comes Softly: An Anthology of Black Female Voices,* Medic (Redmond, WA), 1970.
(Author of introduction) Adele Sebastian, *Intro to Fine* (poems), Woman in the Moon, 1985.
(Editor) *Appalachian Elders: A Warm Hearth Sampler,* Pocahontas Press, 1991.
(Author of foreword) *The Abandoned Baobob: The Autobiography of a Woman,* Chicago Review Press, 1991.
Grand Mothers: Poems, Reminiscences, and Short Stories about the Keepers of Our Traditions, Holt, 1994.
Knoxville, Tennessee, Scholastic, 1994.

Contributor to numerous anthologies. Also contributor of columns to newspapers and magazines, including *Black Creation, Black World, Ebony, Essence, Freedom Ways, Journal of Black Poetry, Negro Digest,* and *Umbra.* Editorial consultant, *Encore American and Worldwide News.*

A selection of Giovanni's public papers are at Mugar Memorial Library, Boston University.

MEDIA ADAPTATIONS: Spirit to Spirit: The Poetry of Nikki Giovanni (television film), 1986, produced by Public Broadcasting Corporation, Corporation for Public Broadcasting, and Ohio Council on the Arts.

SIDELIGHTS: One of the most prominent poets to emerge from the black literary movement of the late 1960s, Nikki Giovanni is famous for strongly voiced poems that testify to her own evolving awareness and experience: as a daughter and young girl, a black woman, a revolutionary in the Civil Rights movement, and a mother. A popular reader and lecturer in both the United States and Europe, Giovanni has been nicknamed "The Princess of Black Poetry," a title warranted by the crowds of fans which gather at her speaking engagements. Popular for her adult poetry and essays, as well as best-selling recorded albums of her poetry, Giovanni has also published three books of acclaimed verse for children: *Spin a Soft Black Song, Ego Tripping and Other Poems for Young People,* and *Vacation Time.* Like her adult works, "Nikki Giovanni's poems for children . . . exhibit a combination of casual energy and sudden wit," wrote Nancy Klein in the *New York Times Book Review.* Giovanni "explores the contours of childhood with honest affection, sidestepping both nostalgia and condescension. Her poems focus on the experiences of children—naps and baths and getting bigger, dreams and fears and growing up."

Giovanni was born in 1943 in Knoxville, Tennessee, a city nestled in the Smoky Mountains. "The mountains cause you to raise your eyes upward and ponder the heavens," she wrote in *Fifth Book of Junior Authors and Illustrators.* 'They help to create a larger vision. You are small but not alone." Her family life was a happy one, and Nikki, a strong-willed and independent child, was particularly close to her older sister Gary, who studied music, and her maternal grandmother, Louvenia Terrell Watson. Her grandmother—an outspoken women—instilled in the young Nikki an intense admiration and appreciation for her race. Other members of her family influenced her in the oral tradition of poetry. "I come from a long line of storytellers," she once commented. "My grandfather was a Latin scholar and he loved the myths, and my mother is a big romanticist, so we heard a lot of stories growing up. . . . I appreciated the quality and the rhythm of the telling of the stories, and I know when I started to write that I wanted to retain that—I didn't want to become the kind of writer that was stilted or that used language in ways that could not be spoken."

When Giovanni was still young, she moved with her family to a suburb of Cincinnati, Ohio, but remained close to her grandmother and spent several of her teen years in Knoxville. As a teenager, she was conservative in her outlook—a supporter of Republican presidential candidate Barry Goldwater and a follower of writer Ayn Rand, who was famous for her philosophy of objectivism. In 1960, at the age of seventeen, Giovanni enrolled in Nashville's all-black Fisk University, yet her independent nature caused her to abide by her own rules, and she was eventually asked by school officials to leave. After several years, however, she returned to Fisk in 1964 and became a dedicated student—one focused on both political and literary activities. She edited a campus literary magazine, *Elan,* and also participated in writing workshops. Politically awakened to the changes occurring on the American social scene in the 1960s, she helped restore Fisk's chapter of the SNCC (Student Non-Violent Coordinating Committee) at a time when SNCC was pressing the concept of "black power" to bring about social and economic reform. In 1967, Giovanni graduated from Fisk with an honors degree in history, as well as a commitment to become a poet herself and voice of the black movement.

Giovanni's first three books of poetry—*Black Feeling, Black Talk*; *Black Judgement*; and *Re: Creation*—display a strongly black perspective as she recounts her growing political awareness. According to Mozella G. Mitchell in the *Dictionary of Literary Biography,* these early poems, published between 1968 and 1970, are "a kind of ritualistic exorcism of former nonblack ways of thinking and an immersion in blackness. Not only are they directed at other black people whom [Giovanni] wanted to awaken to the beauty of blackness, but also at herself as a means of saturating her own consciousness." These early books quickly established Giovanni as a prominent new voice in black poetry; her books sold numerous copies and she became an increasingly popular figure on the reading and speaking circuit. In 1971, she recorded the first of several poetry albums, *Truth Is on Its Way,* featuring Giovanni reading her poetry to a background of gospel music. *Truth Is on Its Way* became the best-selling spoken-word album of the year, furthering her nationwide celebrity status as a poet.

Giovanni's personal life, meanwhile, underwent changes which would affect her future evolution as a writer. In 1969, she accepted a teaching position at Rutgers University, and during the summer of that year decided to bear a child out of wedlock. As a single mother, Giovanni reordered her priorities, lessening her commitment to the black movement. Her writing in the early 1970s began to reflect this change. In addition to a collection of autobiographical essays on her early life as a poet, *Gemini,* she published her first book of children's verse, *Spin a Soft Black Song.* These were then followed by two new books of adult verse (*My House* and *The Women and the Men*) which showed a change in Giovanni's work. Mitchell described it as "a more developed individualism and greater introspection, and a sharpening of [Giovanni's] creative and moral powers, as well as of her social and political focus and understanding."

Spin a Soft Black Song was followed by two other books of poetry for young readers, *Ego Tripping* and *Vacation Time. Spin a Soft*

Black Song focuses on the everyday experiences of black children; "some of the poems deal with universal childhood feelings and concerns while others are unique to the black experience," wrote a contributor to *Booklist,* "but all are honest and nonsentimental in concept and expression." *Ego Tripping* contains poems "directed at older readers able to handle heavier subjects and more ambitious poetry," wrote Nancy Rosenberg in the *New York Times Book Review.* "They are sly and seductive, freewheeling and winsome, tough, sure and proud."

Giovanni's later adult poetry shows a continuing evolution from her earlier work. Her 1978 book, *Cotton Candy on a Rainy Day,* according to Alex Batman in *Dictionary of Literary Biography,* stands out for its "poignancy. . . . One feels throughout that here is a child of the 1960s mourning the passing of a decade of conflict, of violence, but most of all, of hope." While such an outlook, Batman continues, might "lend itself too readily to sentimentality and chauvinism, . . . Giovanni is capable of countering the problems with a kind of hard matter-of-factness about the world that has passed away from her and the world she now faces."

In her 1983 book, *Those Who Ride the Night Winds,* Giovanni takes an altered political stance, offering sketches and tributes to various characters in Afro-American history, including Phillis Wheatley, Martin Luther King, Jr., and Rosa Parks. "In most cases," notes Mitchell, "the poems are meditation pieces that begin with some special quality in the life of the subject, and with thoughtful, clever, eloquent and delightful words amplify and reconstruct salient features of her or his character."

In addition to her books of poetry, Giovanni has coauthored acclaimed books of critical essays with two other noted black writers, James Baldwin and Margaret Walker. She is also a frequent teacher of poetry, which, as she told Ross, "enriches" the "lonely profession" of being a poet by "reminding . . . that there are other concerns out there." In the introduction to *Cotton Candy on a Rainy Day,* Paula Giddings praises Giovanni's commitment to her work: "Nikki Giovanni is a witness. Her intelligent eye has caught the experience of a generation and dutifully recorded it. . . . I have never known anyone who cares so much and so intensely about the things she sees around her as Nikki."

Giovanni returned to combining the personal and political in a collection of essays titled *Racism 101.* Published in 1994, it ruminates over lessons learned in the 1960s, in light of her more recent experience teaching at Virginia Polytechnic. Giovanni rails against icons such as Spike Lee, whom she finds "self-serving," while reflecting on her own career path. A contributor to *Kirkus Reviews* finds Giovanni, "mellower with age, but (her) ability to provoke with barbed comments remains much in evidence." A reviewer for *Publishers Weekly* comments that the essays are "often perceptive musings" but that they "beg for more substance." Giovanni also included advice to black students on academics and racism, "outlining . . . how the black collegian can become not merely certified as 'educated,' but *educated,*" notes Dale Edwyna Smith in *Belles Lettres.* Smith praises the work, confessing, "It seems to me that I have always loved the writing of Nikki Giovanni. I still do."

Grandmothers: Poems, Reminiscences and Short Stories About the Keepers of Our Traditions, edited by Giovanni and also published in 1994, is a collection of contributions on the figure of the grandmother, from a number of known and lesser-known writers. Established contributors include Maxine Hong Kingston, Gloria Naylor, and Gwendolyn Brooks; however, a *Publishers*

Weekly contributor comments that "the real treasures here are offered by relatively unknown authors," noting Susan Power and Anna Esaki-Smith in particular. The collection also includes works by Giovanni's writing students at a retirement home that provide "the feel of spontaneous personal reminiscences, the rough-edged, homespun manner of their telling contributing to their power, their charm," notes a *Voice of Youth Advocates* contributor.

Giovanni's work continued to focus on the image of strong women in 1996 with the publication of *The Genie in the Jar.* This children's poem, which Giovanni wrote for the singer Nina Simone, depicts a young black girl surrounded and supported by the love of her mother and a circle of women, creating a "loom of love" that "spins the notes of life's song," as a contributor to the *Children's Book Review Service* notes. But, comments a *Kirkus Reviews* contributor, "Readers don't need to know anything about Simone to hear this book sing." Kate McClelland, writing for *School Library Journal* finds the book to be "Symbolic on many levels . . . its message is undeniably universal. It is as cautionary and as reassuring as a creative life, lived with both risk and self-fulfillment."

Booklist notes that much of Giovanni's poetry is shaped by love, and her 1994 collection, *Love Poems,* is "as dreamy-eyed, passionate, and hopeful for better tomorrows as ever," according to Leslie Lockhart of the *Quarterly Black Review.* Dedicated to rap singer Tupac Shakur, the collection, which includes both old and new poems, glorifies sensuality, laments lost love, and revels in the joy of new love. As always, Lockhart comments, the poet's word is "playful on the page and committed to change." As the *Booklist* reviewer comments, Giovanni is one of America's most popular poets, because "she speaks her mind clearly and has a good time doing it." The *Midwest Review* describes the book as an excellent gathering of Giovanni classics centered on a powerful theme.

BIOGRAPHICAL/CRITICAL SOURCES:

BOOKS

Black Literature Criticism, Gale (Detroit), 1992.
Children's Literature Review, Volume 6, Gale, 1984.
Contemporary Authors Autobiography Series, Volume 6, Gale, 1988.
Contemporary Literary Criticism, Gale, Volume 2, 1974; Volume 4, 1975; Volume 19, 1981; Volume 64, 1991.
Dictionary of Literary Biography, Gale, Volume 5: *American Poets since World War II,* 1980; Volume 41: *Afro-American Poets since 1955,* 1985.
Evans, Mari, editor, *Black Women Writers, 1950-1980: A Critical Evaluation,* Doubleday (New York City), 1984.
Fowler, Virginia, *Nikki Giovanni,* Twayne (Boston), 1992.
Fowler, *Conversations with Nikki Giovanni,* University Press of Mississippi (Jackson), 1992.
Strickland, Michael R. *African-American Poets,* Enslow, 1996.
Tate, Claudia, editor, *Black Women Writers at Work,* Continuum, 1997.
Twentieth-Century Children's Writers, St. Martin's (New York City), 1978.

PERIODICALS

African American Review, summer, 1993, p. 318.
America, February 19, 1972.
Belles Lettres, spring, 1995, p. 68-70.
Booklist, May 1, 1972, p. 770; November 15, 1992, p. 572; December 15, 1995, p. 682; March 15, 1996, p. 1250; April

1, 1996, p. 1367; January, 1997, p. 809; February 15, 1997, p. 1014.

Children's Book Review Service, March, 1994, p. 87; September, 1994, p. 11; April, 1996, p. 102.

Ebony, February, 1972, pp. 48-50.

Harper's Bazaar, July, 1972, p. 50.

Horn Book, September-October, 1994, p. 575; fall, 1996, p. 367; spring, 1997, p. 150, 152.

Jet, April 4, 1994, p. 29.

Kirkus Reviews, December 1, 1993, p. 1503; March 15, 1996, p. 447; April 1, 1996, p. 529.

Library Journal, January, 1996, p. 103; November 1, 1996; February 1, 1997, p. 84.

Los Angeles Times Book Review, December 18, 1994, p. 9; June 9, 1996, p. 15.

New York Times Book Review, November 28, 1971, p. 8; February 13, 1972, pp. 6, 26; May 5, 1974, p. 38.

Publishers Weekly, December 13, 1993, p. 54; January 24, 1994, p. 54; August 8, 1994, p. 450; December 18, 1995, p. 51-52; February 19, 1996, p. 215; September 16, 1996; October 21, 1996; December 30, 1996, p. 62.

Quarterly Black Review (online), 1995.

School Library Journal, April, 1994, p. 119; October, 1994, p. 152; May, 1996, pp. 103-4, 139.

Voice of Youth Advocates, December, 1994, p. 298.

Washington Post Book World, February 13, 1994, pp. 4-5; July 3, 1994, p. 11.

Writer's Digest, February, 1989, pp. 30-34.

*   *   *

GLASGOW, Ellen (Anderson Gholson), 1873-1945

PERSONAL: Born April 22, 1873, in Richmond, VA; died November 21, 1945, in Richmond; daughter of Francis Thomas (an industrialist) and Anne Jane (Gholson) Glasgow. *Education:* privately educated at home.

CAREER: Writer.

AWARDS, HONORS: Honorary doctorates of literature from University of North Carolina, 1930; University of Richmond, 1938, Duke University, 1938, College of William and Mary, 1939; National Institute of Arts and Letters, 1932-45; American Academy of Arts and Letters, 1938-45; William Dean Howells Medal of the American Academy of Arts and Letters, 1940; *Saturday Review of Literature* Award, 1941; Southern Women's National Democratic Organization Prize for *In This Our Life,* 1942; Pulitzer Prize for *In This Our Life,* 1942.

WRITINGS:

The Descendant: A Novel, Harper & Brothers, 1897.
Phases of an Inferior Planet, Harper, 1898.
The Voice of the People, Doubleday, Page, 1900.
The Battle-Ground, Doubleday, 1902.
The Freeman, and Other Poems, Doubleday, 1902.
The Deliverance: A Romance of the Virginia Tobacco Fields, Doubleday, 1904.
The Wheel of Life, Doubleday, 1906.
The Ancient Law, Doubleday, 1908.
The Romance of a Plain Man, Macmillan, 1909.
The Miller of Old Church, Doubleday, 1911.
Virginia (novel), Doubleday, 1913.

Life and Gabriella: The Story of a Woman's Courage, Doubleday, 1916.
The Builders, Doubleday, 1919.
One Man in His Time, Doubleday, 1922.
The Shadowy Third, and Other Stories, Doubleday, 1923.
Barren Ground, Doubleday, 1925, reprinted with a preface by Glasgow, Sagamore Press, 1933.
The Romantic Comedians, Doubleday, 1926.
They Stooped to Folly: A Comedy of Morals, Doubleday, 1929.
The Old Dominion Edition of the Works of Ellen Glasgow (collection), 8 vols., Doubleday, 1929-33.
(Contributor of introduction) *A Memorial Volume of Virginia Historical Portraiture, 1585-1830,* edited by Alexander Wilbourne Weddell, William Byrd Press, 1930.
The Sheltered Life, Doubleday, 1932.
Vein of Iron, Harcourt, Brace, 1935.
(With James Branch Cabell) *Of Ellen Glasgow: An Inscribed Portrait,* Maverick Press, 1938.
The Virginia Edition of the Works of Ellen Glasgow (collection), 12 vols., Scribner, 1938.
In This Our Life, Harcourt, 1941.
A Certain Measure: An Interpretation of Prose Fiction (essays), Harcourt, 1943.
The Woman Within (autobiography), Harcourt, 1954.
Virginia (address), 1957.
Letters of Ellen Glasgow, edited by Blair Rouse, Harcourt, 1958.
Five Letters from Ellen Glasgow Concerning Censorship and Other Matters of Interest to a Library Board Member, introduction by Louis D. Rubin Jr., Friends of the Richmond Public Library, 1962.
The Collected Stories of Ellen Glasgow, edited by Richard K. Meeker, Louisiana State University Press, 1963.
Beyond Defeat: An Epilogue to an Era, edited by Luther Y. Gore, University Press of Virginia, 1966.
Ellen Glasgow's Reasonable Doubts: A Collection of Her Writings, edited by Julius Rowan Raper, Louisiana State University Press, 1988.

Contributor of poems and essays to the *New York Times Book Review, Harper's, New York Herald Tribune Books, Saturday Review of Literature,* and other periodicals.

SIDELIGHTS: Glasgow was one of America's foremost regional writers, and her work is often credited as being the first of the powerful new Southern literature which dominated the American literary scene during the early twentieth century. Glasgow began her career at a time when most southern fictions were romanticized portraits of the ideals and institutions lost after the Civil War. She rebelled against this unrealistic tradition, depicting the South's social and moral code as restrictive and false, and satirizing its idealization of the past.

Born in Richmond, Virginia, to a wealthy family, Glasgow was privately tutored and received much of her education from the classics in her father's large library. She grew up reading Plato, David Hume, Henry Fielding, Jane Austin, Leo Tolstoy, and Thomas Hardy, whose philosophy of fate and social determinism had a profound effect on much of her work. At eighteen she secretly wrote and destroyed her first novel, for in her family's eyes it would not hare been proper for a young woman to write fiction. Her first published novel, *The Descendant,* was written after her mother's death and appeared anonymously. She did not, however, successfully come to terms with her subject and style until she wrote *The Voice of the People* three years later. Here, in a somewhat romantic manner, Glasgow determined to write the truth about the South and its people. In 1913 she received recognition for *Virginia,* an historical novel laden with irony. But she did not gain wide critical acclaim until after World War I and the publication of *Barren Ground.* This work is considered by many critics as Glasgow's greatest achievement and the one novel in which she most poignantly expressed the feminist struggle for freedom and individuality in a hostile environment. Often compared to Glasgow herself, Dorinda Oakley is the author's concept of the model woman who refuses to feel guilt or repentance over an illegitimate child; instead she utilizes her talents and reaps success from the "barren" land.

Like no other writer of her time, Glasgow attempted to relate the American South to the rest of the world. Her fiction is an account of the old plantation civilization invaded by industrialization and a rising middle class; of a society dying under outmoded manners, opinions, and methods; and of a woman's place in such an environment. Her novels modulate in range and tone from the comic to the tragic, the two opposing realms bridged by her ironic sense of the disparities in human existence. In her best works, *Barren Ground* and *Vein of Iron,* Glasgow created fiction of epic and, occasionally, tragic depth and fullness. These novels are notable for their lifelike characters, controlled language, and the infusion of what Glasgow called "blood and irony," a phrase she coined for the realistic, critical focus of her narration. Glasgow's art can be divided into three stages. Her early novels, such as *The Descendant* and *The Battle-Ground,* belong to the very school she later satirized. Nevertheless, one may see in these "sword-and-cape" romances the young author's first attacks on the romanticized traditions of the South. Glasgow's work matured in the years following World War I. This was perhaps her greatest period, including such novels as *Barren Ground* and her "comedies of manners"—*The Romantic Comedians, They Stooped to Folly,* and *The Sheltered Life*—wherein Glasgow criticized the social manners of Virginian men and women with penetrating satire. Among her repertoire, these works are unsurpassed in their brilliant style and in their mostly sympathetic, though sometimes malicious, representation of character. In her third stage, which includes such works as *Vein of Iron* and *In This Our Life,* for which she won a Pulitzer Prize, Glasgow became more conservative. Whereas in her early work she empathized with the doubts of the aged and the protests of the young, her advice now was to simply endure the hardships that life offered. Glasgow was most efficient in presenting the struggle of human life through the development of her heroines, such as Dorinda Oakley in *Barren Ground* and Gabriella Carr in *The Sheltered Life.* These women were the survivors of a dying aristocracy, existing solely by their stoicism and self-reliance, though often at the expense of their own humanness.

Early in Glasgow's career, critical opinion of her work varied according to its origin: in the South she was severely criticized for her negative portrayals; in the North she was lauded as the South's first realist and as a master of satire. With the passage of time, Glasgow's realism was interpreted as something more akin to idealization; her plots were often felt to be unreal, and the uncommon success of her heroines led many critics to believe that she refused to accept the world as it was. Though many have praised her for her knowledge of Virginia social life and manners, her ability to interpret the complexities of southern history, and her insight into the intricacies of human nature, other critics have attacked Glasgow for her inability to use symbol, her failure to pay closer attention to the structure and form of her novels, and the lack of psychological depth of many of her characters. Her work has also been criticized for its lack of tragedy. Glasgow

rebuked this claim, saying that her major theme was the conflict of individuals with human nature, and that "tragedy lies not in defeat but in surrender."

Despite her lack of wide popularity, Glasgow remains an important figure in American literature. She was, as Henry Seidel Canby has said in *Literary History of the United States,* "a major historian of our times, who, almost singlehandedly, rescued southern fiction from the glamorous sentimentality of the Lost Cause."

BIOGRAPHICAL/CRITICAL SOURCES:

BOOKS

Auchincloss, Louis, *Pioneers & Caretakers: A Study of 9 American Novelists,* University of Minnesota Press, 1965.
Brooks, Van Wyck, *The Confident Years, 1885-1915,* Dutton, 1952.
Budd, Louis J., Edwin H. Cady, and Carl L. Anderson, editors, *Toward a New American Literary History: Essays in Honor of Arlin Turner,* Duke University Press, 1980.
Cabell, James Branch, *Let Me Lie: Being in the Main an Ethnological Account of the Remarkable Commonwealth of Virginia and the Making of Its History,* Farrar, Straus, 1947.
De Graffenried, Thomas P., editor, *The de Graffenried Family Scrap Book,* University Press of Virginia, 1945.
Ekman, Barbro, *The End of a Legend: Ellen Glasgow's History of Southern Women,* Almqvist & Wiksell, 1979.
Geismar, Maxwell, *Rebels and Ancestors: The American Novel, 1890-1915,* Houghton Mifflin, 1953.
Goodman, Susan, *Ellen Glasgow: A Biography,* Johns Hopkins University Press, 1998.
Kazin, Alfred, *On Native Grounds: An Interpretation of Modern American Prose Literature,* Reynal & Hitchcock, 1942.
McDowell, Frederick P. W., *Ellen Glasgow and the Ironic Art of Fiction,* University of Wisconsin Press, 1960.
Raper, J[ulius] R[owan], *Without Shelter: The Early Career of Ellen Glasgow,* Louisiana State University Press, 1971.
Raper, *From the Sunken Garden: The Fiction of Ellen Glasgow, 1916-1945,* Louisiana State University Press, 1980.
Rouse, Blair, *Ellen Glasgow,* Twayne, 1962.
Rubin, Louis D., Jr., *No Place on Earth,* University of Texas Press, 1959.
Santas, Joan Foster, *Ellen Glasgow's American Dream,* University Press of Virginia, 1965.
Spiller, Robert, E., Henry Seidel Canby, et al, editors, *Literary History of the United States,* vol. 2, Macmillan, 1948.
Thiebaux, Marcelle. *Ellen Glasgow,* Ungar, 1982.
Wagenknecht, Edward, *Cavalcade of the American Novel,* Holt, 1952.

PERIODICALS

American Mercury, October, 1929, pp. 251-52.
Bookman, August, 1909, pp. 613-18.
Dial, May 16, 1897, pp. 310-11.
Mississippi Quarterly, fall, 1979, pp. 565-76, 577-90.
Nation, November 16, 1943, pp. 442, 444.
Southern Review, October, 1935, pp. 397-401.

*   *   *

GLASSCOCK, Amnesia
See STEINBECK, John (Ernst)

GLUCK, Louise (Elisabeth) 1943-

PERSONAL: Surname is pronounced *Glick*; born April 22, 1943, in New York, NY; daughter of Daniel (an executive) and Beatrice (Grosby) Gluck; married Charles Hertz (divorced); married John Dranow (a writer and vice-president of the New England Culinary Institute), 1977 (divorced); children: Noah Benjamin. *Education:* Attended Sarah Lawrence College, 1962, and Columbia University, 1963-66, 1967-68.

ADDRESSES: Home—Creamery Rd., Plainfield, VT 05667. *Office*—Department of English, Williams College, Williamstown, MA 01267.

CAREER: Poet. Fine Arts Work Center, Provincetown, MA, visiting teacher, 1970; Goddard College, Plainfield, VT, artist-in-residence, 1971-72, member of faculty, 1973-74; poet in residence, University of North Carolina, Greensboro, spring, 1973, and Writer's Community, 1979; visiting professor, University of Iowa, 1976-77, Columbia University, 1979, and University of California, Davis, 1983; Goddard College, member of faculty and member of board of M.F.A. Writing Program, 1976-80; University of Cincinnati, Cincinnati, OH, Ellison Professor of Poetry, spring, 1978; Warren Wilson College, Swannanoa, NC, member of faculty and member of board of M.F.A. Program for Writers, 1980-84; University of California, Berkeley, Holloway Lecturer, 1982; Williams College, Williamstown, MA, Scott Professor of Poetry, 1983, senior lecturer in English, part time, 1984–. Phi Beta Kappa Poet, Harvard University, 1990. Poetry panelist or poetry reader at conferences and foundations, including Mrs. Giles Whiting Foundation and PEN Southwest Conference; judge of numerous poetry contests, including Discovery Contest.

MEMBER: PEN (member of board, 1988–).

AWARDS, HONORS: Academy of American Poets Prize, Columbia University, 1967; Rockefeller Foundation grant in poetry, 1968-69; National Endowment for the Arts creative writing fellowships, 1969-70, 1979-80, 1988-89; Eunice Tietjens Memorial Prize, *Poetry* magazine, 1971; John Simon Guggenheim Memorial Fellowship in Poetry, 1975-76, 1987-88; Vermont Council for the Arts individual artist grant, 1978-79; American Academy and Institute of Arts and Letters Award in Literature, 1981; National Book Critics Circle Award for Poetry, 1985, for *The Triumph of Achilles*; Melville Cane Award, Poetry Society of America, 1985; Sara Teasdale Memorial Prize, Wellesley College, 1986; corecipient of Bobbitt National Prize, 1992; William Carlos Williams Award, 1993; PEN/Martha Albrand Award for nonfiction, 1995; Poet Laureate of Vermont, 1996; Pulitzer Prize, 1996. Honorary degrees from Williams College, 1993, Skidmore College, 1995, Middlebury College, 1996.

WRITINGS:

POETRY

Firstborn, New American Library, 1968.
The House on Marshland, Ecco Press, 1975.
The Garden, Antaeus Editions, 1976.
Descending Figure, Ecco Press, 1980.
The Triumph of Achilles, Ecco Press, 1985.
Ararat, Ecco Press, 1990.
The Wild Iris, Ecco Press, 1992.
Proofs and Theories: Essays on Poetry, Ecco Press, 1994.
Meadowlands, Ecco Press, 1996.

Work represented in numerous anthologies, including *The New Yorker Book of Poems,* Viking, 1970; *New Voices in American Poetry,* Winthrop Publishing, 1973; and *The American Poetry Anthology,* Avon, 1975. Contributor to various periodicals, including *Antaeus, New Yorker, New Republic, Poetry, Salmagundi,* and *American Poetry Review.*

SIDELIGHTS: Considered by many critics to be one of America's more gifted and talented contemporary poets, Louise Gluck creates poetry that has been described as technically precise as well as sensitive, insightful, and gripping. In her work, Gluck freely shares her most intimate thoughts on such commonly shared human experiences as love, family, relationships, and death. "Gluck demands a reader's attention and commands his respect," states R. D. Spector in the *Saturday Review.*

From her first book of poetry, *Firstborn,* to her most recent work, Gluck has become internationally recognized as a very skilled, yet perceptive author who pulls the reader into her poetry and shares the poetic experience equally with her audience. Helen Vendler comments in her review of Gluck's second book, *The House on Marshland,* that "Gluck's cryptic narratives invite our participation: we must, according to the case, fill out the story, substitute ourselves for the fictive personages, invent a scenario from which the speaker can utter her lines, decode the import, 'solve' the allegory. Or such is our first impulse. Later, I think, . . . we read the poem, instead, as a truth complete within its own terms, reflecting some one of the innumerable configurations into which experience falls."

For admirers of Gluck's work, the poetry in books such as *Firstborn, The House on Marshland, The Garden, Descending Figure, The Triumph of Achilles, Ararat,* and *The Wild Iris* takes readers on a journey to explore their deepest and most intimate feelings. "Gluck has a gift for getting the reader to imagine with her, drawing on the power of her audience to be amazed," observes Anna Wooten in the *American Poetry Review.* "She engages a 'spectator' in a way that few other poets can do." Stephen Dobyns maintains in the *New York Times Book Review* that "no American poet writes better than Louis Gluck, perhaps none can lead us so deeply into our own nature."

One reason reviewers cite for Gluck's seemingly unfailing ability to capture her reader's attention is her expertise at creating poetry that many people can understand, relate to, and experience so intensely and completely. Gluck's poetic voice is uniquely distinctive and her language is deceptively straightforward. In her review of Gluck's *The Triumph of Achilles* Wendy Lesser notes in the *Washington Post Book World* that "'Direct' is the operative word here: Gluck's language is staunchly straightforward, remarkably close to the diction of ordinary speech. Yet her careful selection for rhythm and repetition, and the specificity of even her idiomatically vague phrases, give her poems a weight that is far from colloquial." Lesser goes on to remark that "the strength of that voice derives in large part from its self-centeredness—literally, for the words in Gluck's poems seem to come directly from the center of herself."

Because Gluck writes so effectively about disappointment, rejection, loss, and isolation, reviewers frequently refer to her poetry as "bleak" or "dark." For example, Deno Trakas observes in the *Dictionary of Literary Biography* that "Gluck's poetry has few themes and few moods. Whether she is writing autobiographically or assuming a persona, at the center of every poem is an 'I' who is isolated from family, or bitter from rejected love, or disappointed with what life has to offer. Her world is bleak; however, it is depicted with a lyrical grace, and her poems are attractive if disturbing. . . Gluck's poetry, despite flaws, is remarkable for its consistently high quality."

Writing on the somber nature of Gluck's recurring themes in *Nation*, Don Bogen admits that Gluck's "basic concerns—betrayal, mortality, love and the sense of loss that accompanies it—are serious. She is at heart the poet of a fallen world. . . Gluck's work to define that mortal part shows dignity and sober compassion." Bogen elaborates further: "Fierce yet coolly intelligent, Gluck's poem disturbs not because it is idiosyncratic but because it defines something we feel yet rarely acknowledge; it strips off a veil. Gluck has never been content to stop at the surfaces of things. Among the well-mannered forms, nostalgia and blurred resolutions of today's verse, the relentless clarity of her work stand out."

Readers and reviewers have also marvelled at Gluck's custom of creating poetry with a dreamlike quality that at the same time deals with the realities of passionate and emotional subjects. Holly Prado declares in a *Los Angeles Times Book Review* piece on Gluck's fifth book, *The Triumph of Achilles*, "Gluck's poems succeed because she has an unmistakable voice that resonates and brings into our contemporary world the old notion that poetry and the visionary are intertwined." Prado continues to reflect: "The tone of her work is eerie, philosophical, questioning. Her poems aren't simply mystical ramblings. Far from it. They're sternly well-crafted pieces. But they carry the voice of a poet who sees, within herself, beyond the ordinary and is able to offer powerful insights, insights not to be quickly interpreted."

"Gluck's ear never fails her; she manages to be conversational and lyrical at the same time, a considerable achievement when so much contemporary poetry is lamentably prosaic," asserts Wooten in the *American Poetry Review*. "Her range is personal and mythical, and the particular genius of the volume rests in its fusion of both approaches, rescuing the poems from either narrow self-glorification or pedantic myopia."

In *Proofs and Theories*, Gluck examines the styles and attitudes of Eliot, Williams, Dickinson, George Oppen, and other poets, describes her own feelings and attitudes about reading and her work, and discusses her education as a poet. *Booknews* calls the essay collection "well worth the wait. Passionate, penetrating, and thankfully unpostmodern." Allen Hoey, in the *American Poetry Review*, comments that "her essays chart the responses of a careful and incisive mind as it considers poetic problems," and that "her intent seems less an effort to originate or articulate a theory which helps us constellate literary works than to provide insight into the minds that generate those works."

Gluck begins the book by explaining what writing is not: "Writing is not decanting of personality." And as she notes elsewhere in the book, in order for experience to become authentic, it must be "changed—heightened, distilled, made memorable," and that these processes "have nothing to do with actuality. The truth, on the page, need not have been lived. It is, instead, all that can be envisioned." Although, as Patrick O'Malley comments in the *Boston Book Review*, Gluck seems to prefer to talk about what poetry is not rather than what it is. Most of the book concentrates on particular poets and critics. O'Malley notes that despite her insistence that poetry is not necessarily connected with actuality, "Gluck's understanding of the poetic drive remains deeply rooted in the personal, and especially in a notion of suffering." Gluck was anorexic as a child, and she describes the illness and its suffering as a kind of failed poetry, written with and on the body of the young woman. According to O'Malley, her understanding of suffering and loss serves her well in her studies of these poets.

Meadowlands, Gluck's first book of poems since she won a Pulitzer Prize for *The Wild Iris,* weaves the story of the dissolution of a marriage with the classical tale of the Odyssey. A *Publishers Weekly* reviewer notes that the stories are "grimly serious parables, amusing but disquieting spousal conversations and insightful commentaries written in the voice of Telemachus." Deborah Garrison of the *New York Times Book Review* comments that "Gluck lays out the dialogue of the doomed couple, as Front did, as if she were repeating it verbatim." Nevertheless, Garrison says that Gluck "captures the way that a marriage itself has a tone," and in the end she "skewers the division of labor that even in our age makes up a large part of marriage, and dramatizes the old but accurate cliche that in order to be truly together, a husband and wife must honor their separateness—or in this case, must simply separate."

Looking over Gluck's entire body of work, Dave Smith appraises her ability in a review of *Descending Figure* published in the *American Poetry Review*: "There are poets senior to Louise Gluck who have done some better work and there are poets of her generation who have done more work. But who is writing consistently better with each book? Who is writing consistently so well at her age? Perhaps it is only my own hunger that wants her to write more, that hopes for the breakthrough poems I do not think she has yet given us. She has the chance as few ever do to become a major poet and no one can talk about contemporary American poetry without speaking of Louise Gluck's accomplishment."

BIOGRAPHICAL/CRITICAL SOURCES:

BOOKS

Contemporary Literary Criticism, Gale (Detroit), Volume 7, 1977, pp. 118-20; Volume 22, 1982, pp. 173-78; Volume 44, 1987, pp. 214-24.
Directory of Literary Biography, Volume 5: *American Poets since World War II,* Gale, 1980, pp. 290-95.

PERIODICALS

American Poetry Review, July/August, 1975, pp. 5-6; January/February, 1982, pp. 36-46; September/October, 1982, pp. 37-46; November/December, 1986, pp. 33-36; January, 1997, p. 37.
Belles Lettres, November/December, 1986, pp. 6, 14; spring, 1991, p. 38.
Boston Book Review (online), 1997.
Georgia Review, winter, 1985, pp. 849-63.
Library Journal, September 15, 1985, p. 84; July, 1990, p. 17; March 15, 1996, p. 74; April 1, 1997, p. 94.
Los Angeles Times Book Review, February 23, 1986, p. 10.
Nation, January 18, 1986, pp. 53-54; April 15, 1991, p. 490; April 29, 1996, p. 28.
New Letters, spring, 1987, pp. 3-4.
New Republic, June 17, 1978, pp. 34-37.
New Yorker, May 13, 1996, p. 93.
New York Review of Books, October 23, 1986, p. 47.
New York Times Book Review, April 6, 1975, pp. 37-38; December 22, 1985, pp. 22-23; September 2, 1990, p. 5; August 4, 1996, p. 6.
Poetry, April, 1986, pp. 42-44; March, 1997, p. 339.
Publishers Weekly, May 11, 1992, p. 58; March 18, 1996, p. 66.
Saturday Review, March 15, 1969, p. 33.
Washington Post Book World, February 2, 1986, p. 11.

Women's Review of Books, November, 1996, p. 24.
World Literature Today, autumn, 1995, p. 805; winter, 1997, p. 156.

*   *   *

GODOY ALCAYAGA, Lucila 1889-1957
(Gabriela Mistral)

PERSONAL: Born April 7, 1889, in Vicuna, Chile; died in 1957 in Hempstead, NY; daughter of Jeronimo Godoy Villanueva (a schoolteacher and minstrel) and Petronila Alcayaga; children: Yin Yin (adopted; deceased). *Education:* Attended Pedagogical College, Santiago, Chile.

CAREER: Poet and author. Primary and secondary school teacher and administrator in Chile, including position as principal of Liceo de Senoritas, Santiago, 1910-22; adviser to Mexican minister of education Jose Vasconcelos, 1922; visiting professor at Barnard and Middlebury colleges and the University of Puerto Rico. League of Nations, Chilean delegate to Institute of Intellectual Cooperation, member of Committee of Arts and Letters; consul in Italy, Spain, Portugal, Brazil, and the United States.

AWARDS, HONORS: Juegos Florales laurel crown and gold medal from the city of Santiago, Chile, 1914, for *Sonetos de la muerte;* Nobel Prize for literature from the Swedish Academy, 1945; honorary degree from the University of Chile.

WRITINGS:

UNDER PSEUDONYM GABRIELA MISTRAL

Desolacion (poetry and prose; title means "Desolation"), preliminary notes by Instituto de las Espanas, Instituto de las Espanas en los Estados Unidos (New York), 1922, 2nd edition augmented by Mistral, additional prologue by Pedro Prado, Nascimento, 1923, 3rd edition, prologues by Prado and Hernan Diaz Arrieta (under pseudonym Alone), 1926, new edition with prologue by Roque Esteban Scarpa, Bello, 1979 (variations in content among these and other editions).

(Editor and contributor) *Lecturas para mujeres* (essays; also see below), introduction by Mistral, Secretaria de Educacion (Mexico), 1923, 4th edition, edited with an apology by Palma Guillen de Nicolau, Porrua (Mexico), 1967.

Ternura: Canciones de ninos (title means "Tenderness"), Saturnino Calleja (Madrid), 1924, enlarged edition, Espasa Calpe, 1945, 8th edition, 1965.

Nubes blancas (poesias), y la oracion de la maestra (poetry and prose; includes selections from *Desolacion* and *Ternura* and complete text of *Oracion de la maestra*), B. Bauza (Barcelona), 1925.

Poesias, Cervantes (Barcelona), c. 1936.

Tala (poetry; title means "Felling"; also see below), Sur (Buenos Aires), 1938, abridged edition, Losada, 1946, reprinted with introduction by Alfonso Calderon, Bello, 1979.

Antologia: Seleccion de la autora (includes selections from *Desolacion, Tala,* and *Ternura*), selected by Mistral, prologue by Ismael Edwards Matte, ZigZag, 1941, 3rd edition published as *Antologia,* prologue by Alone, 1953.

Pequena antologia (selected poetry and prose), Escuela Nacional de Artes Graficas, 1950.

Poemas de las madres, epilogue by Antonio R. Romero, illustrations by Andre Racz, Pacifico, 1950.

Lagar (poetry; title means "Wine Press"), Pacifico, 1954.

Obras selectas, Pacifico, 1954.

Los mejores versos, prologue by Simon Latino, Nuestra America (Buenos Aires), 1957.

Canto a San Francisco, El Eco Franciscano, 1957.

Epistolario, introduction by Raul Silva Castro, Anales de la Universidad de Chile, 1957.

Mexico maravilloso (essays and poetry originally published in *Lecturas para mujeres* and periodical *El Maestro*), selected with an introduction by Andres Henestrosa, Stylo (Mexico), 1957.

Produccion de Gabriela Mistral de 1912 a 1918 (poetry, prose, and letters, most previously unpublished), edited by Silva Castro, Anales de la Universidad de Chile, 1957.

Recados: Contando a Chile, selected with prologue by Alfonso M. Escudero, Pacifico, 1957.

Selected Poems of Gabriela Mistral, translated by Langston Hughes, Indiana University Press, 1957.

Croquis mexicanos: Gabriela Mistral en Mexico (contains prose selections from *Lecturas para mujeres,* poetry, and a pedagogical lecture titled Imagen y palabra en la educacion), B. Costa-Amic (Mexico), c. 1957.

Poesias completas, edited by Margaret Bates, prologues by Julio Saavedra Molina and Dulce Maria Loynaz, Aguilar (Madrid), 1958, 3rd edition, introduction by Esther de Caceres, 1966.

Poema de Chile, revisions by Doris Dana, Pomaire, 1967.

Antologia de Gabriela Mistral, selected with prologue by Emma Godoy, B. Costa-Amic, 1967.

Poesias, edited with a prologue by Eliseo Diego, Casa de las Americas, 1967.

Homenaje a Gabriela Mistral, Orfeo, 1967.

Selected Poems of Gabriela Mistral, translated by Dana, Johns Hopkins Press, 1971.

Todas ibamos a ser reinas, Quimantu, 1971.

Antologia general de Gabriela Mistral (poems, essays, and letters; portions originally published in periodical *Orfeo,* 1969), Comite de Homenaje a Gabriela Mistral, 1973.

Antologia poetica de Gabriela Mistral, selected with a prologue by Calderon, Universitaria, 1974.

Cartas de amor de Gabriela Mistral, Bello, 1978.

Prosa religiosa de Gabriela Mistral, notes and introduction by Luis Vargas Saavedra, Bello, 1978.

Gabriela presente, selected by Ines Moreno, Literatura Americana Reunida, 1987.

A Gabriela Mistral Reader, edited by Marjorie Agosin, White Pine Press, 1993.

Also author of *Sonetos de la muerte,* 1914, and "An Appeal to World Conscience: The Genocide Convention," 1956. Author of fables, including *Grillos y ranas,* translation by Dana published as *Crickets and Frogs,* Atheneum, 1972, and *Elefante y su secreto,* adaptation and translation by Dana published as *The Elephant and His Secret,* Atheneum, 1974. Poetry for children published as *El nino en la poesia de Gabriela Mistral,* 1978. Correspondence between Mistral and Matilde Ladron de Guevara published as *Gabriela Mistral, "rebelde magnifica,"* 1957.

Contributor to periodicals, including *Bulletin, Commonweal, Living Age,* and *Poetry.*

SIDELIGHTS: Nobel laureate Gabriela Mistral—whose actual name was Lucila Godoy Alcayaga—was a prominent Latin American poet, educator, and diplomat. A Chilean native of Spanish, Basque, and Indian descent, she was raised in a northern rural farming community. Following the example of her father, Mistral initially pursued a career in education, beginning as a primary school teacher at the age of fifteen. Over the next decade, she went on to become a secondary school professor, inspector general, and ultimately a school director. A leading authority on rural education, Mistral served as an adviser to Mexican minister of education Jose Vasconcelos in the early 1920s. Her background in teaching and value as an educational consultant led to her active service in the Chilean government. Mistral is probably best known, however, for her brand of rich but unpretentious lyrical poetry.

The tragic suicide of her fiance in the early 1900s prompted Mistral to compose her first lines of melancholy verse. Within several years she completed a small body of poetry that she would later publish under the Mistral pseudonym (which is said to be either a tribute to poets Gabriele D'Annunzio and Frederic Mistral or a combined reference to the archangel Gabriel and the brutal northerly wind, or "mistral," of southern France). Having entered her *Sonetos de la muerte* (*Sonnets on Death*) in a Santiago writing contest in 1914, she earned first prize and instant fame, developing in ensuing years a reputation as one of Latin America's most gifted poets.

Critics have noted the joint influences of biblical verse and the works of Hindu poet Rabindranath Tagore and Nicaraguan poet Ruben Dario on the literary development of Mistral. She frequently expressed through her verse an urgent concern for outcasts, underprivileged or otherwise impoverished people, and ancestors—the poet donated profits from her third book to Basque children orphaned in the Spanish Civil War. Her simple, unadorned writings evoke a sense of mystery and isolation, centering on themes of love, death, childhood, maternity, and religion. Mistral had turned to religion for solace in her despair over the loss of her intended husband. Her first volume of poetry, *Desolacion (Desolation)*, is imbued with the spirit of an individual's struggle to reconcile personal fulfillment with the will of God. In expressing her grief and anguish throughout the collection with characteristic passion and honesty, Mistral "talks to Christ as freely as to a child," commented Mildred Adams in *Nation*.

Several critics on Mistral, including Adams, have suggested that both her lover's death and her failure to bear his child inspired in the poet a fervent dedication to children. *Ternura (Tenderness)*, her 1924 volume of children's poetry, is a celebration of the joys of birth and motherhood. While *Desolacion* reflects the pain of a lost love and an obsession with death, *Ternura* is generally considered a work of renewed hope and understanding. Infused with a decidedly Christian temper, the poems in the latter collection are among the most sentimental written by Mistral, and they evoke the poet's overriding desire to attain harmony and peace in her life.

Correlating Mistral's treatment of the love theme with her frequent depiction of mother and child, Sidonia Carmen Rosenbaum theorized in *Modern Women Poets of Spanish America*: "Her conception of love is . . . profoundly religious and pure. Its purpose is not to appease desire, to satisfy carnal appetites, but soberly to give thought to the richest, the most precious, the most sacred heritage of woman: maternity." *Saturday Review* contributor Edwin Honig expressed a similar view, noting that for Mistral, "Childbearing . . . approximates a mystic condition: it is like finding union with God. . . . The experience of gestating another life inside oneself is the supreme act of creation."

Though consistently stark, simple, and direct, Mistral's later verse is marked by a growing maturity and sense of redemption and deliverance. The 1938 collection *Tala (Felling)*, according to

Rosenbaum, possesses "a serenity that reveals an emotion more contained (whose key note is hope) and . . . an expression less tortured" than the early works and therefore continues Mistral's path toward renewal. The poet achieved a greater objectivity in both this work and her final volume of poetry, *Lagar (Wine Press)*, which was published in 1954. Through pure and succinct language, *Lagar* conveys Mistral's acceptance of death and marks her growing freedom from bitterness. Several critics have implied that this collection—the culmination of her literary career—is both a refinement of her simple and skillful writing style and a testament to her strengthened faith and ultimate understanding of God. As Fernando Alegria explained in *Las fronteras del realismo,* "Here we have the secret dynamism [of the poet's verse]; it contains a salvation."

In *Gabriela Mistral: The Poet and Her Work,* Margot Arce de Vazquez concluded: "[Mistral's] poetry possesses the merit of consummate originality, of a voice of its own, authentic and consciously realized. The affirmation within this poetry of the intimate 'I,' removed from everything foreign to it, makes it profoundly human, and it is this human quality that gives it its universal value."

BIOGRAPHICAL/CRITICAL SOURCES:

BOOKS

Alegria, Fernando, *Las fronteras del realismo: Literatura chilena del siglo XX,* ZigZag, 1962.
de Vazquez, Margot Arce, *Gabriela Mistral: The Poet and Her Work,* translated by Helene Masslo Anderson, New York University Press, 1964.
Foster, David William and Virginia Ramos Foster, editors, *Modern Latin American Literature,* Volume 2, Ungar, 1975.
Horan, Elizabeth, *Gabriela Mistral: An Artist and Her People,* Organization of American States (Washington, DC), 1994.
Rosenbaum, Sidonia Carmen, *Modern Women Poets of Spanish America: The Precursors, Delmira Agustini, Gabriela Mistral, Alfonsina Storni, Juana de Ibarbourou,* Hispanic Institute in the United States, 1945.
Szmulewicz, Efraim, *Gabriela Mistral: Biografia emotiva,* Sol de Septiembre, 1967.
Taylor, Martin C., *Gabriela Mistral's Religious Sensibility,* University of California Press, 1968.
Twentieth-Century Literary Criticism, Volume 2, Gale, 1979.
Vargas Saavedra, Luis, editor, *El otro suicida de Gabriela Mistral,* Universidad Catolica de Chile, 1985.

PERIODICALS

Living Age, November 29, 1924.
Nation, December 29, 1945.
Saturday Review, March 22, 1958; July 17, 1971.

*   *   *

GODWIN, Gail (Kathleen) 1937-

PERSONAL: Born June 18, 1937, in Birmingham, AL; daughter of Mose Winston and Kathleen (a teacher and writer; maiden name, Krahenbuhl) Godwin; married Douglas Kennedy (a photographer), 1960 (divorced, 1961); married Ian Marshall (a psychiatrist), 1965 (divorced, 1966). *Education:* Attended Peace Junior College, 1955-57; University of North Carolina, B.A., 1959; University of Iowa, M.A., 1968, Ph.D. in English, 1971.

ADDRESSES: Home—P.O. Box 946, Woodstock, NY 12498-0946. *Agent*—John Hawkins, Paul R. Reynolds, Inc., 71 W. 23rd St., New York, NY 10010.

CAREER: Miami Herald, Miami, FL, reporter, 1959-60; U.S. Embassy, London, England, travel consultant in U.S. Travel Service, 1962-65; *Saturday Evening Post,* editorial assistant, 1966; University of Iowa, Iowa City, instructor in English literature, 1967-71, instructor in Writer's Workshop, 1972-73; University of Illinois, Center for Advanced Studies, Urbana-Champaign, fellow, 1971-72; writer. Special lecturer in Brazil for United States Information Service, State Department Cultural Program, spring, 1976; lecturer in English and creative writing at colleges and universities, including Vassar College, spring, 1977, and Columbia University, 1978-81.

MEMBER: PEN, Authors Guild, Authors League, American Society of Composers, Authors, and Publishers (ASCAP).

AWARDS, HONORS: National Endowment for the Arts grant in creative writing, 1974-75; nominated for a National Book Award, 1974, for *The Odd Woman*; Guggenheim fellowship in creative writing, 1975-76; National Endowment for the Arts grant for librettists, 1977-78; nominated for American Book Awards, 1980, for *Violet Clay,* and 1982, for *A Mother and Two Daughters*; Award in Literature, American Institute and Academy of Arts and Letters, 1981. Thomas Wolfe Memorial award, Lipinsky Endowment of Western North Carolina Historical Association, 1988; Janet Kafka award, University of Rochester, 1988.

WRITINGS:

NOVELS

The Perfectionists, Harper, 1970.
Glass People, Knopf, 1972.
The Odd Woman, Knopf, 1974.
Violet Clay, Knopf, 1978.
A Mother and Two Daughters, Viking, 1982.
The Finishing School, Viking, 1985.
A Southern Family, Morrow, 1987.
Father Melancholy's Daughter, Morrow, 1991.
The Good Husband, Ballantine, 1994.

OTHER

Dream Children (short stories), Knopf, 1976.
Mr. Bedford and the Muses (a novella and short stories), Viking, 1983.
(Author of introduction) *Pushcart Prize VIII: Best of the Small Presses, 1983-84 edition,* edited by Bill Henderson, Pushcart Press, 1983.
(Editor with Shannon Ravenel) *The Best American Short Stories, 1985,* Houghton, 1985.

Contributor to books, including *The Writer on Her Work* (essays), edited by Janet Sternburg, Norton, 1980; and *Real Life* (short stories), Doubleday, 1981. Also contributor of essays and short stories to periodicals, including *Atlantic, Antaeus, Ms., Harper's, Writer, McCall's, Cosmopolitan, North American Review, Paris Review,* and *Esquire.* Reviewer for *North American Review, New York Times Book Review, Chicago Tribune Book World,* and *New Republic.* Member of editorial board of *Writer.*

Librettist of musical works by Robert Starer, *The Last Lover,* produced in Katonah, NY, 1975; *Journals of a Songmaker,* produced in Pittsburgh, PA, with Pittsburgh Symphony Orchestra, 1976; *Apollonia,* produced in Minneapolis, MN, 1979; *Anna*

Margarita's Will, recorded by C.R.I., 1980; and *Remembering Felix,* 1987, recorded by Spectrum, 1989.

SIDELIGHTS: "More than any other contemporary writer, Gail Godwin reminds me of 19th century pleasures, civilized, passionate about ideas, ironic about passions," states Carol Sternhell in a *Village Voice* review of *The Finishing School.* "Her characters—sensible, intelligent women all—have houses, histories, ghosts; they comfortably inhabit worlds both real and literary, equally at home in North Carolina, Greenwich Village and the England of *Middlemarch.*" Godwin's protagonists are modern women, though, often creative and frequently Southern. And like many other writers of her era, she tends to focus "sharply on the relationships of men and women who find their roles no longer clearly delineated by tradition and their freedom yet strange and not entirely comfortable," as Carl Solana Weeks says in *Dictionary of Literary Biography.* "Godwin's great topic," notes Lee Smith, reviewing *Father Melancholy's Daughter* in the *Los Angeles Times Book Review,* "is woman's search for identity: A death in the family frequently precipitates this search. The tension between art and real life (many of her women are artists or would-be artists) is another thematic constant in her work. Her literate, smart women characters possess the free will to make choices, to take responsibility for their lives."

Literature has figured in Godwin's life from an early age. She grew up in Asheville, North Carolina, in the shadow of another writer, Thomas Wolfe. During the war her mother was a reporter, and Godwin recalls in an essay in *The Writer on Her Work* that "whenever Mrs. Wolfe called up the paper to announce, 'I have just remembered something else about Tom,'" her mother "was sent off immediately to the dead novelist's home on Spruce Street." Godwin's parents were divorced, and while Godwin was growing up, her mother taught writing and wrote love stories on the weekend to support her daughter while Godwin's grandmother ran the house.

Godwin didn't meet her father until he showed up many years later at her high school graduation when, she recalls in the essay, he introduced himself and she flung herself, "weeping," into his arms. He invited her to come and live with him, which she did, briefly, before he shot and killed himself like the lovable ne'er-do-well Uncle Ambrose in *Violet Clay.*

After graduating from the University of North Carolina, Godwin was hired as a reporter for the *Miami Herald* and was reluctantly fired a year later by a bureau chief who had failed to make a good reporter out of her. She married her first husband, newspaper photographer Douglas Kennedy, around that time. After her divorce, she completed her first novel, *Gull Key,* the story of "a young wife left alone all day on a Florida island while her husband slogs away at his job on the mainland," according to Godwin in *The Writer on Her Work.*

Not satisfied with her work at the time, Godwin found focusing on characters and themes outside of herself to be helpful. She got the idea for one of her most highly-regarded short stories, "An Intermediate Stop" (now included in her collection *Dream Children*), in a writing class at the London City Literary Institute after the teacher instructed the students to write a 450-word story beginning with the sentence, "'*Run away,' he muttered to himself, sitting up and biting his nails.*" Godwin writes in *The Writer on Her Work* that "when that must be your first sentence, it sort of excludes a story about a woman in her late twenties, adrift among the options of wifehood, career, vocation, a story that I had begun too many times already—both in fiction and reality—and could not resolve. My teacher wisely understood Gide's maxim for himself as writer: 'The best means of learning to know oneself is seeking to understand others.'"

Godwin describes "An Intermediate Stop" as a story "about an English vicar who has seen God, who writes a small book about his experience, and becomes famous. He gets caught up in the international lecture-tour circuit. My story shows him winding up his exhausting American tour at a small Episcopal college for women in the South. He is at his lowest point, having parroted back his own written words until he has lost touch with their meaning." *New York Times* critic Anatole Broyard indicates that, here, "another kind of epiphany—in the form of a [young woman]—restores his faith. The brilliance with which this girl is evoked reminds us that love and religion both partake of the luminous." A draft of the story also got the author accepted into the University of Iowa Writer's Workshop.

Godwin's novel, *The Perfectionists,* a draft of which was her Ph.D. thesis at Iowa, was published in 1970. It relates the story of the disintegrating "perfect" marriage of a psychiatrist and his wife while they are vacationing in Majorca with the man's son. Robert Scholes in *Saturday Review* writes that "the eerie tension that marks this complex relationship is the great achievement of the novel. It is an extraordinary accomplishment, which is bound to attract and hold many readers." Scholes describes the book as "too good, too clever, and too finished a product to be patronized as a 'first novel.'" Joyce Carol Oates in the *New York Times Book Review* calls it "a most intelligent and engrossing novel" and "the paranoid tragedy of our contemporary worship of self-consciousness, of constant analysis."

In Godwin's *Glass People,* Francesca Bolt, pampered and adored wife in a flawless but sterile marital environment, leaves her husband in a brief bid for freedom. This book, too, is praised as "a formally executed, precise, and altogether professional short novel" by Oates in *Book World.* Weeks indicates, however, that in *Glass People,* Godwin is exploring "a theme introduced in *The Perfectionists,* that of a resolution of woman's dilemma through complete self-abnegation; but the author, already suspicious of this alternative in her first novel, presents it here as neither fully convincing nor ironic." As the *New York Times Book Review* critic asks: "Are we really to root for blank-minded Francesca to break free, when her author has promised us throughout that she's totally incapable of doing so?" Genevieve Stuttaford, though, in *Saturday Review,* argues that "the characters in *Glass People* are meticulously drawn and effectively realized, the facets of their personalities subtly, yet precisely, laid bare. The author is coolly neutral, and she makes no judgements. This is the way it is, Godwin is saying, and you must decide who the villains are."

"Marking a major advance in Godwin's development as a novelist," reports Weeks in *Dictionary of Literary Biography,* "her third book, *The Odd Woman,* is twice as long as either of her previous novels, not from extension of plot but from a wealth of incidents told in flashback and in fantasy and a more thorough realization of present action." The odd woman of the book, "odd" in this case meaning not paired with another person, is Jane Clifford, a thirty-two-year-old teacher of Romantic and Victorian literature at a midwestern college, who is engaged in a sporadic love affair with an art historian who teaches at another school. For Jane, Susan E. Lorsch point out in *Critique,* "the worlds of fiction and the 'real' world are one." Not only does Jane experience "literary worlds as real," continues Lorsch, "she treats the actual world as if it were an aesthetic creation." Lorsch further notes that

"the entire book moves toward the climax and the completion of Jane's perception that the worlds of life and art are far from identical."

The Odd Woman's major theme, Anne Z. Mickelson suggests in *Reaching Out: Sensitivity and Order in Recent American Fiction by Women,* is "how to achieve freedom while in union with another person, and impose one's own order on life so as to find self-fulfillment." Because literature is explored in the novel as one means of giving shape to life, the book is generally regarded as cerebral and allusive. In *Times Literary Supplement* critic Victoria Glendinning's words, the book is "too closely or specifically tied to its culture" to be considered universal. Lore Dickstein, however, in the *New York Times Book Review,* calls the novel "a pleasure to read. Godwin's prose is elegant, full of nuance and feeling, and sparkling with ironic humor."

Violet Clay, Weeks comments, confirms Godwin's "mastery of the full, free narrative technique of *The Odd Woman*—the integration of fantasy and flashback into the narrative line—while also recalling the clean, classic structure of her two earlier novels." Weeks continues, "In *Violet Clay* Godwin raises a question that is central to understanding her work as a whole: what is the relationship between the artist and her art? The answer implied in Violet Clay's achievement as a painter reflects directly Godwin's ideals as a writer."

The title character of the novel, Violet Clay, leaves the South for New York at age twenty-four to become an artist, but "nine years later," John Leonard explains in the *New York Times,* "all that she paints are covers on Gothic romances for a paperback publishing house." Violet finally loses her job at Harrow House because the new art director wants to use photographs of terrorized women on the jackets of the romances rather than the idealized paintings Violet creates. When Violet finds out that her only living relative, Uncle Ambrose, a failed writer, has shot himself, she journeys to the Plommet Falls, New York, cabin in which he died to claim his body and bury him. And, in *Washington Post Book World* critic Susan Shreve's words, "she decides to stay on and face the demons with her paint and brush."

Violet Clay reflects "the old-fashioned assumption that character develops and is good for something besides the daily recital to one's analyst," points out a *Harper's* critic. In Leonard's opinion, however, *Violet Clay* is "too intelligent for its own good. It is overgrown with ideas. You can't see the feelings for the ideas." Katha Pollitt in the *New York Times Book Review* comments that *Violet Clay* "has the pep-talk quality of so many recent novels in which the heroine strides off the last page, her own woman at last." As Sternhell argues, though, Godwin's novels "are not about book-ness, not about the *idea* of literature, but about human beings who take ideas seriously. Clever abstracts are not her medium: her 'vital artistic subject,' like Violet Clay's is, will always be the 'living human figure.'"

Godwin's next novel, *A Mother and Two Daughters,* is a comedy of manners which portrays women who "are able to achieve a kind of balance, to find ways of fully becoming themselves that don't necessitate a rejection of everything in their heritage," Susan Wood relates in *Washington Post Book World.* Set against a current-events background of the Iranian revolution, Three Mile Island, and Skylab, the novel opens in the changing town of Mountain City, North Carolina (a fictional city), with the death of Leonard Strickland of a heart attack as he is driving home with his wife from a party. The book records "the reactions and relationships of his wife Nell and daughters Cate and Lydia, both in their late thirties, as the bereavement forces each of them to evaluate the achievement and purpose of their own lives," Jennifer Uglow writes in the *Times Literary Supplement.* Josephine Hendin writes in the *New York Times Book Review,* "As each woman exerts her claims on the others, as each confronts the envy and anger the others can inspire, Gail Godwin orchestrates their entanglements with great skill." And "for the first time," according to John F. Baker in *Publishers Weekly,* "Godwin enters several very different minds and personalities, those of her three protagonists."

A Mother and Two Daughters is "the richest, and most universal" of Godwin's books, "with a wholeness about its encompassing view of a large Southern family," according to Louise Sweeney in *Christian Science Monitor,* and is widely regarded as an unusually artful bestseller, appealing not only to the general public but also to Godwin's longtime followers. *Washington Post Book World* reviewer Jonathan Yardley finds *A Mother and Two Daughters* "a work of complete maturity and artistic control, one that I'm fully confident will find a permanent and substantial place in our national literature." He further comments that Godwin "turns out—this was not really evident in her four previous books—to be a stunningly gifted novelist of manners."

In *The Finishing School,* Godwin uses a first-person voice to create "a narrative of humanly impressive energies, as happy-sad in its texture as life itself may be said to be," according to William H. Pritchard in the *New Republic.* Shifting from one age perspective to another, Justin Stokes, a successful forty-year-old actress, tells the story of the summer she turns fourteen and her life is changed forever when she undergoes what *Time* reviewer Paul Gray calls "a brief but harrowing rite of passage toward maturity." After her father and grandparents die in quick succession, the young Justin, her mother, and her brother leave Fredericksburg, Virginia, to live with her aunt in an upstate New York industrial town. There she makes friends with the local bohemian, Ursula DeVane, a forty-four-year-old failed actress who lives with her brother Julian, a talented musician of little consequence, in an old rundown home.

Ursula takes Justin on as her protege, and they begin to meet in an old stone hut in the woods, the "Finishing School," in which Ursula "enthralls Justin with tales of her past and encourages her artistic aspirations," as Susan Wood puts it in the *Washington Post Book World.* The novel "charts the exhilaration, the enchantment, the transformation, then the inevitable disillusionment and loss inherent in such a friendship and self-discovery," according to Frances Taliaferro in the *New York Times Book Review.* And, as Sternhell relates, it is essentially "the tale of a daughter with two mothers." Where *A Mother and Two Daughters* "was symphonic—many movements, many instruments—*The Finishing School* plays a gentle, chilling theme with variations." Sternhell further comments that the book, despite its realistic form, "often reads like a fable, a contemporary myth; daughters love mothers, and—variations on a theme—daughters betray mothers, repeatedly, inevitably."

With her seventh novel, *A Southern Family,* published in 1987, Godwin returns to the setting of Mountain City first found in *A Mother and Two Daughters.* Another novel of manners in the Victorian tradition, this work revolves around the death of a member of the Quick family. Theo, a twenty-eight-year-old divorced father of a young son, is found dead after he apparently killed his girlfriend and committed suicide. The novel focuses on reactions from family members, including novelist Clare, her quirky mother Lily, and Clare's alcoholic half-brother Rafe. *A*

Southern Family, according to Susan Heeger in the *Los Angeles Times Book Review,* "takes off from Theo's death on a discursive exploration of family history and relationships as the Quicks struggle to measure their blame and—belatedly—to know the brother and son they failed in life." Several reviewers consider *A Southern Family* to be one of Godwin's most accomplished works. "Suffice it to say that *A Southern Family* is an ambitious book that entirely fulfills its ambitions," declares Yardley in *Washington Post Book World.* "Not merely is it psychologically acute, it is dense with closely observed social and physical detail that in every instance is exactly right." Likewise, Beverly Lowry, writing in the *New York Times Book Review,* proclaims that Godwin's *A Southern Family* "is the best she's written," concluding that Godwin's works "all give evidence of a supple intelligence working on the page."

Father Melancholy's Daughter, published in 1991, is the story of Margaret Gower, whose mother Ruth, when Margaret is six years old, leaves the family and is killed in a car crash a year later. Margaret and her father, Walter, an Episcopal priest, are thrust into an especially close father-daughter relationship in which much of their time is devoted to puzzling over Ruth's absence. The narrative switches time tracks from twenty-two-year-old Margaret, who is in love with a fortyish counselor named Adrian Bonner, to the younger Margaret of Ruth's disappearance. Calling the novel "a penetrating study of a child's coming to terms with her world," Nancy Wigston in the Toronto *Globe and Mail* writes in her conclusion that "The real achievement here is Margaret herself: Gail Godwin has created that rarity in fiction, a character who evolves, believably." *New York Times Book Review* contributor Richard Bausch, however, expresses dissatisfaction with Margaret's lack of self-awareness, but he attests that the novel has "a number of real satisfactions, namely the characters that surround Margaret and her father—the parishioners of St. Cuthbert's. . . . Gail Godwin is almost Chaucerian in her delivery of these people, with their small distinguishing characteristics and their vibrant physicality." Gray writes in *Time,* "Born in the South, Godwin appears to be one of those writers who inherited a subject for life; then she developed the wisdom and talent to make her birthright seem constantly fresh and enthralling."

In her ninth novel, *The Good Husband,* Godwin portrays four characters undergoing profound change. Magda is a middle-aged English professor who is dying of cancer, while her dutiful husband, Francis, copes gamely with her impending death. Meanwhile, their friends Alice and Hugo Henry are facing the collapse of their marriage. As Alice visits Magda to comfort her during her illness, Alice gradually falls in love with Francis. "It is [Alice's] chaste pursuit of [Francis,] which the dying woman encourages, that holds our attention through much of the novel," remarks Chicago *Tribune Books* reviewer Penelope Mesic. Although critical of the "small defects" in Godwin's prose—"Sentences too often trickle to a vague conclusion"—Mesic praises the author's handling of Magda's feverish, combative decline and "steady, lucid exposition of the action." Writing in the *New York Times Book Review,* Sara Maitland commends many of the novel's elements: "The four main characters are interesting and convincing; their difficulties are real and persuasive; the principal plot is well constructed and involving." However, Maitland faults Godwin for trying to infuse the plot with more symbolic significance than it can carry. She concludes, "Gail Godwin is a good writer, but 'The Good Husband' is not a good novel." While conceding that readers will find the novel "either extremely moving or extremely sentimental," Anita Brookner in

The Spectator commends Godwin's "calm and unassuming" style and contends that the book is "guileless, dignified, and ultimately persuasive."

BIOGRAPHICAL/CRITICAL SOURCES:

BOOKS

Contemporary Literary Criticism, Gale (Detroit), Volume 5, 1976; Volume 8, 1978; Volume 31, 1985; Volume 69, 1992.
Dictionary of Literary Biography, Volume 6: American Novelists since World War II, edited by James E. Kibler, Jr., Gale, 1981.
Kissel, Susan S., *Moving On: The Heroines of Shirley Ann Grau, Anne Tyler, and Gail Godwin,* Bowling Green State University Popular Press (Ohio), 1996.
Mickelson, Anne Z., *Reaching Out: Sensitivity and Order in Recent American Fiction by Women,* Scarecrow, 1979.
Sheldon, Barbara, *Daughters and Fathers in Feminist Novels,* P. Lang (New York City), 1997.
Sternburg, Janet, editor, *The Writer on Her Work,* Norton, 1980.
Xie, Lihong, *The Evolving Self in the Novels of Gail Godwin,* Louisiana State University Press (Baton Rouge), 1995.

PERIODICALS

America, December 21, 1974; April 17, 1982.
Atlantic, May, 1976; October, 1979.
Booklist, June 1, 1994, p. 1724.
Book World, October 1, 1972.
Boston Globe, February 21, 1982.
Chicago Tribune Book World, January 10, 1982; October 16, 1983; January 27, 1984; October 25, 1987.
Christian Century, November 6, 1991, p. 103; November 16, 1994, p. 1088.
Christian Science Monitor, November 20, 1974; April 1, 1976; June 23, 1978; July 21, 1983; September 2, 1983.
Commonweal, June 1, 1984; March 25, 1988, p. 187.
Critique, winter, 1978.
Critique: Studies in Modern Fiction, number 3, 1980.
Detroit Free Press, March 10, 1985.
Detroit News, April 11, 1982; October 16, 1983; February 10, 1985.
Entertainment Weekly September 16, 1994, p. 109.
Globe and Mail (Toronto), April 13, 1991, p. C6.
Harper's, July, 1978.
Library Journal, January, 1988, p. 41; February 1, 1991, p. 103; June 1, 1994, p. 158; December, 1995, p. 165.
Listener, June 9, 1977.
Los Angeles Times, November 13, 1981.
Los Angeles Times Book Review, September 11, 1983; February 24, 1985; February 9, 1986; October 4, 1987; March 3, 1991, pp. 2, 11; November, 1996, p. 856.
Miami Herald, February 29, 1976.
Ms., January, 1982.
National Review, September 15, 1978.
New Republic, January 25, 1975; July 8, 1978; February 17, 1982; December 19, 1983; February 25, 1985; February 29, 1988, p. 38.
New Statesman, August 15, 1975.
Newsweek, February 23, 1976; January 11, 1982; September 12, 1983; February 25, 1985.
New York, March 11, 1991, p. 86.
New Yorker, November 18, 1974; January 18, 1982.
New York Review of Books, February 20, 1975; April 1, 1976; July 20, 1978.
New York Times, September 21, 1972; September 30, 1974; February 16, 1976; May 18, 1978; December 22, 1981; September 6, 1983; October 4, 1983; January 24, 1985; December 15, 1985; September 21, 1987.
New York Times Book Review, June 7, 1970; October 15, 1972; October 20, 1974; February 22, 1976; May 21, 1978; January 10, 1982; September 18, 1983; January 27, 1985; August 10, 1986; October 11, 1987; March 3, 1991, p. 7; September 4, 1994, p. 5; December 3, 1995, p. 86.
New York Times Magazine, December 15, 1985.
Progressive, October, 1978.
Publishers Weekly, January 15, 1982; August 14, 1987, p. 93; August 1, 1994, p. 94.
Saturday Review, August 8, 1970; October 28, 1972; February 21, 1976; June 10, 1978; January, 1982.
Spectator, January 15, 1977; September 2, 1978; February 6, 1982; November 5, 1994, p. 51.
Time, January 25, 1982; February 11, 1985; October 5, 1987, p. 82; March 25, 1991, p. 70; September 26, 1994, p. 82.
Times (London), February 18, 1982; March 28, 1985.
Times Literary Supplement, July 23, 1971; July 4, 1975; September 15, 1978; March 5, 1982; February 17, 1984; November 20, 1987, p. 1274; May 24, 1991, p. 21; November 4, 1994, p. 22.
Tribune Books (Chicago), August 28, 1994, p. 3.
Village Voice, March 30, 1982; February 26, 1985.
Washington Post, February 7, 1983; March 7, 1991, p. D1.
Washington Post Book World, May 21, 1978; December 13, 1981; September 11, 1983; February 3, 1985; September 13, 1987; March 17, 1991, p. 4.
Writer, September, 1975; December, 1976.

*   *   *

GOLDING, William (Gerald) 1911-1993

PERSONAL: Born September 19, 1911, in St. Columb Minor, Cornwall, England; died of a heart attack, June 19, 1993, in Perranarworthal, near Falmouth, England; son of Alex A. (a schoolmaster) and Mildred A. Golding; married Ann Brookfield, 1939; children: David, Judith. *Education:* Brasenose College, Oxford, B.A., 1935, M.A., 1960. *Avocation:* Sailing, archaeology, and playing the piano, violin, viola, cello, and oboe.

CAREER: Writer. Was a settlement house worker after graduating from Oxford University; taught English and philosophy at Bishop Wordsworth's School, Salisbury, Wiltshire, England, 1939-40, 1945-61; wrote, produced, and acted for London equivalent of "very, very far-off-Broadway theatre," 1934-40, 1945-54. Writer in residence, Hollins College, 1961-62; honorary fellow, Brasenose College, Oxford University, 1966. *Military service:* Royal Navy, 1940-45; became rocket ship commander.

MEMBER: Royal Society of Literature (fellow), Savile Club.

AWARDS, HONORS: Commander, Order of the British Empire, 1965; D.Litt., University of Sussex, 1970, University of Kent, 1974, University of Warwick, 1981, Oxford University, 1983, and University of Sorbonne, 1983; James Tait Black Memorial Prize, 1980, for *Darkness Visible*; Booker McConnell Prize, 1981, for *Rites of Passage*; Nobel Prize for literature, 1983, for body of work; LL.D., University of Bristol, 1984; knighted, 1988.

WRITINGS:

FICTION

Lord of the Flies, Faber (London), 1954, published with an introduction by E. M. Forster, Coward, 1955, adapted for screen, 1963, casebook edition with notes and criticism, edited by James R. Baker and Arthur P. Ziegler Jr., Putnam, 1964.

The Inheritors, Faber, 1955, Harcourt (New York City), 1962.

Pincher Martin, Faber, 1955, new edition, 1972, published as *The Two Deaths of Christopher Martin,* Harcourt, 1957.

(With John Wyndham and Mervyn Peake) *Sometime, Never: Three Tales of Imagination,* Eyre & Spottiswoode (London), 1956, Ballantine (New York City), 1957.

Free Fall, Faber, 1959, Harcourt, 1960.

The Spire, Harcourt, 1964.

The Pyramid (novellas), Harcourt, 1967.

The Scorpion God: Three Short Novels (includes "Clonk Clonk," "Envoy Extraordinary" [also see below], and "The Scorpion God"), Harcourt, 1971.

Darkness Visible, Farrar, Straus (New York City), 1979.

Rites of Passage (first novel in trilogy), Farrar, Straus, 1980.

The Paper Men, Farrar, Straus, 1984.

Close Quarters (second novel in trilogy), Farrar, Straus, 1987.

Fire Down Below (third novel in trilogy), Farrar, Straus, 1989.

The Double Tongue: A Draft of a Novel, Farrar, Straus, 1995.

OTHER

Poems, Macmillan, 1934.

The Brass Butterfly: A Play in Three Acts (based on "Envoy Extraordinary"; first produced in Oxford, England, at New Theatre, 1958; produced in London, England, at Strand Theatre, April, 1958; produced in New York at Lincoln Square Theatre, 1965), Faber, 1958, new edition with introduction by Golding, 1963.

Break My Heart (play), produced for BBC Radio, 1962.

The Hot Gates, and Other Occasional Pieces (nonfiction), Harcourt, 1965.

A Moving Target (essays and lectures), Farrar, Straus, 1982.

Nobel Lecture, 7 December 1983, Sixth Chamber (Leamington Spa, UK), 1984.

An Egyptian Journal (travel), Faber, 1985.

Also author of radio plays and contributor to periodicals, including *Encounter, Holiday, Listener, New Left Review,* and *Spectator.*

MEDIA ADAPTATIONS: Pincher Martin was produced as a radio play for the British Broadcasting Corp. in 1958; *Lord of the Flies* was filmed by British Lion Films in 1963 (from Golding's screenplay) and by Castle Rock Entertainment in 1990.

SIDELIGHTS: William Golding has been described as pessimistic, mythical, spiritual—an allegorist who used his novels as a canvas to paint portraits of man's constant struggle between his civilized self and his hidden, darker nature. With the appearance of *Lord of the Flies,* Golding's first published novel, the author began his career as both a campus cult favorite and one of the late twentieth century's distinctive—and much debated—literary talents. Golding's appeal was summarized by the Nobel Prize committee, which issued this statement when awarding the author its literature prize in 1983: "[His] books are very entertaining and exciting. They can be read with pleasure and profit without the need to make much effort with learning or acumen. But they have also aroused an unusually great interest in professional literary critics [who find] deep strata of ambiguity and complication in Golding's work, . . . in which odd people are tempted to reach beyond their limits, thereby being bared to the very marrow."

The novel that established Golding's reputation, *Lord of the Flies,* was rejected by twenty-one publishers before Faber & Faber accepted the forty-three-year-old schoolmaster's book. While the story has been compared to such works as Daniel Defoe's *Robinson Crusoe* and Richard Hughes's *A High Wind in Jamaica,* Golding's novel is actually the author's "answer" to nineteenth-century writer R. M. Ballantyne's children's classic *The Coral Island: A Tale of the Pacific Ocean.* These two books share the same basic plot line and even some of the same character names (two of the lead characters are named Ralph and Jack in both books). The similarity, however, ends there. Ballantyne's story, about a trio of boys stranded on an otherwise uninhabited island shows how, by pluck and resourcefulness, the young castaways survive with their morals strengthened and their wits sharpened. *Lord of the Flies,* on the other hand, is "an allegory on human society today, the novel's primary implication being that what we have come to call civilization is, at best, not more than skin-deep," James Stern explained in the *New York Times Book Review.*

Initially, the tale of a group of schoolboys stranded on an island during their escape from atomic war received mixed reviews and sold only modestly in its hardcover edition. But when the paperback edition was published in 1959, thus making the book more accessible to students, the novel began to sell briskly. Teachers, aware of the student interest and impressed by the strong theme and stark symbolism of the work, assigned *Lord of the Flies* to their literature classes. As the novel's reputation grew, critics reacted by drawing scholarly theses out of what was previously dismissed as just another adventure story.

In his study *The Tragic Past,* David Anderson saw Biblical implications in Golding's novel. "*Lord of the Flies,*" wrote Anderson, "is a complex version of the story of Cain—the man whose smoke-signal failed and who murdered his brother. Above all, it is a refutation of optimistic theologies which believed that God had created a world in which man's moral development had advanced *pari passu* with his biological evolution and would continue so to advance until the all-justifying End was reached." *Lord of the Flies* presents moral regression rather than achievement, Anderson argued. "And there is no all-justifying End," the critic continued, "the rescue-party which takes the boys off their island comes from a world in which regression has occurred on a gigantic scale—the scale of atomic war. The human plight is presented in terms which are unqualified and unrelieved. Cain is not merely our remote ancestor: he is contemporary man, and his murderous impulses are equipped with unlimited destructive power."

The work has also been called Golding's response to the popular artistic notion of the 1950s that youth was a basically innocent collective, victims of adult society. In 1960, C. B. Cox deemed *Lord of the Flies* "probably the most important novel to be published . . . in the 1950s." Cox, writing in *Critical Quarterly,* continued: "[To] succeed, a good story needs more than sudden deaths, a terrifying chase and an unexpected conclusion. *Lord of the Flies* includes all these ingredients, but their exceptional force derives from Golding's faith that every detail of human life has a religious significance. This is one reason why he is unique among new writers in the '50s. . . . Golding's intense conviction [is] that every particular of human life has a profound importance. His children are not juvenile delinquents, but human beings realising for themselves the beauty and horror of life."

Golding took his theme of tracing the defects of society back to the defects of human nature a step further with his second novel, *The Inheritors.* This tale is set at the beginning of human existence itself, during the prehistoric age. A tribe of Neanderthals, as seen through the characters of Lok and Fa, live a peaceful, primitive life. Their happy world, however, is doomed: evolution brings in its wake the new race, *Homo sapiens,* who demonstrate their acquired skills with weapons by killing the Neanderthals. The book, which Golding has called his favorite, is also a favorite with several critics. And, inevitably, comparisons were made between *The Inheritors* and *Lord of the Flies.*

To Peter Green, in *A Review of English Literature,* for example, "it is clear that there is a close thematic connection between [the two novels]: Mr. Golding has simply set up a different working model to illustrate the eternal human verities from a new angle. Again it is humanity, and humanity alone, that generates evil; and when the new men triumph, Lok, the Neanderthaler, weeps as Ralph wept for the corruption and end of innocence [in *Lord of the Flies*]." Bernard Oldsey, quoted in the *Dictionary of Literary Biography,* saw the comparison in religious terms: "[The *Homo sapiens*] represent the Descent of Man, not simply in the Darwinian sense, but in the Biblical sense of the Fall. Peculiarly enough, the boys [in *Lord of the Flies*] slide backward, through their own bedevilment, toward perdition; and Lok's Neanderthal tribe hunches forward, given a push by their *Homo sapiens* antagonists, toward the same perdition. In Golding's view, there is precious little room for evolutionary slippage: progression in *The Inheritors* and retrogression in *Lord of the Flies* have the same results."

Just as *Lord of the Flies* is Golding's rewriting, in his own terms, of *The Coral Island,* Golding claimed that he wrote *The Inheritors* to refute H. G. Wells's controversial sociological study *Outline of History.* "[One] can see that between the two writers there is a certain filial relation, though strained," commented a *Times Literary Supplement* critic. "They share the same fascination with past and future, the extraordinary capacity to move imaginatively to remote points in time, the fabulizing impulse, the need to moralize. There are even similarities in style. And surely now, when Wells's reputation as a great writer is beginning to take form, it will be understood as high praise of Golding if one says that he is our Wells, as good in his own individual way as Wells was in his." Taken together, the author's first two novels are, according to Lawrence R. Ries in *Wolf Masks: Violence in Contemporary Fiction,* "studies in human nature, exposing the kinds of violence that man uses against his fellow man. It is understandable why these first novels have been said to comprise [Golding's] 'primitive period.'"

Golding's "primitive period" ended with the publication of his third novel, *Pincher Martin* (published in America as *The Two Deaths of Christopher Martin,* out of the publishers' concern for American readers who would not know that "pincher" is British slang for "petty thief"). Stylistically similar to Ambrose Bierce's famous short story "An Occurrence at Owl Creek Bridge," *Pincher Martin* is about a naval officer who, after his ship is torpedoed in the Atlantic, drifts aimlessly before latching on to a barren rock. Here he clings for days, eating sea anemones and trying his best to retain consciousness. Delirium overtakes him, though, and through his rambling thoughts he relives his past. The discovery of the sailor's corpse at the end of the story in part constitutes what has been called a "gimmick" ending, and gives the book a metaphysical turn—the reader learns that Pincher Martin has been dead from the beginning of the narrative.

The author's use of flashbacks throughout the narrative of *Pincher Martin* was discussed by Avril Henry in *Southern Review:* "On the merely narrative level [the device] is the natural result of Martin's isolation and illness, and is the process by which he is gradually brought to his ghastly self-knowledge." In fact, said Henry, the flashbacks "function in several ways. First the flashbacks relate to each other and to the varied forms in which they themselves are repeated throughout the book; second, they relate also to the details of Martin's 'survival' on [the rock]. . . . Third, they relate to the six-day structure of the whole experience: the structure which is superficially a temporal check for us and Martin in the otherwise timeless and distorted events on the rock and in the mind, and at a deeper level is a horrible parody of the six days of Creation. What we watch is an unmaking process, in which man attempts to create himself his own God, and the process accelerates daily."

While acknowledging the influences present in the themes of *Pincher Martin*—from Homer's *Odysseus* to *Robinson Crusoe* again—Stephen Medcalf in *William Golding* suggests that the novel is Golding's most autobiographical work to date. The author, said Medcalf, "gave [to] Martin more of the external conditions of his own life than to any other of his characters, from [his education at] Oxford . . . through a period of acting and theatre life to a commission in the wartime Navy." Golding, too, has added another dimension from his own past, noted Medcalf: "His childhood fear of the darkness of the cellar and the coffin ends crushed in the walls from the graveyard outside [his childhood home]. The darkness universalizes him. It becomes increasingly but always properly laden with symbolism: the darkness of the thing that cannot examine itself, the observing ego: the darkness of the unconscious, the darkness of sleep, of death and, beyond death, heaven."

To follow *Pincher Martin,* Golding "said that he next wanted to show the patternlessness of life before we impose our patterns on it," according to Green. However, the resulting book, *Free Fall,* Green noted, "avoids the amoebic paradox suggested by his own prophecy, and falls into a more normal pattern of development: normal, that is, for Golding." Not unlike *Pincher Martin, Free Fall* depicts through flashbacks the life of its protagonist, artist Sammy Mountjoy. Imprisoned in a darkened cell in a Nazi prisoner-of-war camp, Mountjoy, who has been told that his execution is imminent, has only time to reflect on his past.

Despite the similarity in circumstance to *Pincher Martin,* Oldsey found one important difference between that novel and *Free Fall.* In *Free Fall,* a scene showing Sammy Mountjoy's tortured reaction on (symbolically) reliving his own downfall indicates a move toward atonement. "It is at this point in Golding's tangled tale that the reader begins to understand the difference between Sammy Mountjoy and Pincher Martin," Oldsey said. "Sammy escapes the machinations of the camp psychiatrist, Dr. Halde, by making use of man's last resource, prayer. It is all concentrated in his cry of 'Help me! Help me!'—a cry which Pincher Martin refuses to utter. In this moment of desperate prayer, Sammy spiritually bursts open the door of his own selfishness."

Medcalf saw the story as Dantesque in nature (Mountjoy's romantic interest is even named Beatrice) and remarked: "Dante, like Sammy, came to himself in the middle of his life, in a dark wood [the cell, in Sammy's case], unable to remember how he came there. . . . His only way out is to see the whole world, and himself in its light. Hell, purgatory and heaven are revealed to him directly, himself and this world of sense in glimpses from the standpoint of divine justice and eternity." In *Free Fall* Golding's intent "is to show this world directly, in other hints and guesses. He is involved therefore in showing directly the moment of fall at which Dante only hints. He has a hero without reference points, who lives in the vertigo of free fall, therefore, reproachful of an age in which those who have a morality or a system softly refuse to insist on them: a hero for whom no system he has will do, but who is looking for his own unity in the world—and that, the real world, is 'like nothing, because it is everything.' Golding, however, has the advantage of being able to bring Dante's world in by allusion: and he does so with a Paradise hill on which Beatrice is met."

In Golding's fifth novel, *The Spire,* "the interest is all in the opacity of the man and in a further exploration of man's all-sacrificing will," wrote Medcalf. Fourteenth-century clergyman Dean Jocelin "is obsessed with the belief that it is his divine mission to raise a 400-foot tower and spire above his church," Oldsey related. "His colleagues protest vainly that the project is too expensive and the edifice unsuited for such a shaft. His master builder (obviously named Roger Mason) calculates that the foundation and pillars of the church are inadequate to support the added weight, and fruitlessly suggests compromises to limit the shaft to a lesser height. The townspeople—amoral, skeptical, and often literally pagan—are derisive about 'Jocelin's Folly.' " Dean Jocelin, nonetheless, strives on. The churchman, in fact, "neglects all his spiritual duties to be up in the tower overseeing the workmen himself, all the while choosing not to see within and without himself what might interrupt the spire's dizzying climb," Oldsey continued. The weight of the tower causes the church's foundations to shudder; the townspeople increasingly come to see Jocelin as a man dangerously driven.

The Spire "is a book about vision and its cost," observed *New York Review of Books* critic Frank Kermode. "It has to do with the motives of art and prayer, the phallus turned spire; with the deceit, as painful to man as to God, involved in structures which are human but have to be divine, such as churches and spires. But because the whole work is a dance of figurative language such an account of it can only be misleading." Characteristic of all Golding's work, *The Spire* can be read on two levels, that of an engrossing story and of a biting analysis of human nature. As Nigel Dennis found in the *New York Times Book Review,* Golding "has always written on these two levels. But *The Spire* will be of particular interest to his admirers because it can also be read as an exact description of his own artistic method. This consists basically of trying to rise to the heights while keeping himself glued to the ground. Mr. Golding's aspirations climb by clinging to solid objects and working up them like a vine. This is particularly pronounced in [*The Spire*], where every piece of building stone, every stage of scaffolding, every joint and ledge, are used by the author to draw himself up into the blue."

Thus, by 1965, Golding was evidently on his way to continuing acclaim and popular acceptance—but "then matters changed abruptly," as Oldsey related. The writer's output dropped dramatically: for the next fifteen years he produced no novels and only a handful of novellas, short stories, and occasional pieces. Of this period, *The Pyramid,* a collection of three related novellas (and considered a novel proper by some critics), is generally regarded as one of the writer's weaker efforts. The episodic story of a man's existence in the suspiciously named English town of Stilbourne, *The Pyramid* proved a shock to "even Golding's most faithful adherents [who] wondered if the book was indeed a novel or if it contributed anything to the author's reputation. To some it

seemed merely three weak stories jammed together to produce a salable book," said Oldsey. *The Pyramid,* however, did have its admirers, among them John Wakeman of the *New York Times Book Review,* who felt the work was Golding's "first sociological novel. It is certainly more humane, exploratory, and life-size than its predecessors, less Old Testament, more New Testament." And to a *Times Literary Supplement* critic the book "will astonish by what it is not. It is not a fable, it does not contain evident allegory, it is not set in a simplified or remote world. It belongs to another, more commonplace tradition of English fiction; it is a low-keyed, realistic novel of growing up in a small town—the sort of book H. G. Wells might have written if he had been more attentive to his style."

The Scorpion God: Three Short Novels, another collection of novellas, was somewhat better received. One *Times Literary Supplement* reviewer, while calling the work "not major Golding," nevertheless found the book "a pure example of Golding's gift. . . . The title story is from Golding's Egyptological side and is set in ancient Egypt. . . . By treating the unfamiliar with familiarity, explaining nothing, he teases the reader into the strange world of the story. It is as brilliant a *tour de force* as *The Inheritors,* if on a smaller scale."

Golding's reintroduction to the literary world was acknowledged in 1979 with the publication of *Darkness Visible.* Despite some fifteen years' absence from novel writing, the author "returns unchanged," Samuel Hynes observed in a *Washington Post Book World* article. "[He is] still a moralist, still a maker of parables. To be a moralist you must believe in good and evil, and Golding does; indeed, you might say that the nature of good and evil is his only theme. To be a parable-maker you must believe that moral meaning can be expressed in the very fabric of the story itself, and perhaps that some meanings can only be expressed in this way; and this, too, has always been Golding's way."

The title *Darkness Visible* derives from Milton's description of Hell in *Paradise Lost,* and from the first scenes of the book Golding confronts the reader with images of fire, mutilation, and pain—which he presents in Biblical terms. For instance, noted *Commonweal* reviewer Bernard McCabe, the novel's opening describes a small child, "horribly burned, horribly disfigured, [who walks] out of the flames at the height of the London blitz. . . . The shattered building he emerges from . . . is called 'a burning bush,' the firemen stare into 'two pillars of lighted smoke,' the child walks with a 'ritual gait,' and he appears to have been 'born from the sheer agony of a burning city.' " The rescued youth, dubbed Matty, the left side of whose face has been left permanently mutilated, grows up to be a religious visionary.

"If Matty is a force for light, he is opposed by a pair of beautiful twins, Toni and Sophy Stanhope," continued Susan Fromberg Schaeffer in her *Chicago Tribune Book World* review. "These girls, once symbols of innocence in their town, discover the seductive attractions of darkness. Once, say the spirits who visit Matty, the girls were called before them, but they refused to come. Instead, obsessed by the darkness loose in the world, they abandon morality, choosing instead a demonic hedonism that allows them to justify anything, even mass murder." "Inevitably, the two girls will . . . [embark on a] spectacular crime, and just as inevitably, Matty, driven by his spirit guides, must oppose them," summarized *Time*'s Peter S. Prescott. "The confrontation, as you may imagine, ends happily for no one."

Some of the ideas explored in this book trace back to *Lord of the Flies* "and to the view [the author] held then of man as a fallen being capable of a 'vileness beyond words,'" stated *New Statesman* reviewer Blake Morrison. Set in the early nineteenth century, *Rites of Passage* tells of a voyage from England to Australia as recounted through the shipboard diary of young aristocrat Edmund Talbot. "He sets down a vivid record of the ship and its characters," explained Morrison. They include "the irascible Captain Anderson . . . , the 'wind-machine Mr Brockle-band,' the whorish 'painted Magdalene' called Zenobia, and the meek and ridiculous 'parson,' Mr. Colley, who is satirised as mercilessly as the clerics in [Henry] Fielding's *Joseph Andrews*." This latter character is the one through which much of the dramatic action in *Rites of Passage* takes place. For Colley, this "country curate . . . this hedge priest," as Golding's Talbot describes him, "is the perfect victim—self-deluding, unworldly, sentimentally devout, priggish, and terrified. Above all he is ignorant of the powerful homosexual streak in his nature that impels him toward the crew and especially toward one stalwart sailor, Billy Rogers," said Robert Towers in the *New York Review of Books*. Driven by his passion yet torn by doubt, ridiculed and shunned by the other passengers on the ship, Colley literally dies of shame during the voyage.

The author faced his harshest criticism to date with the publication of his 1984 novel, *The Paper Men*. A farce-drama about an aging, successful novelist's conflicts with his pushy, overbearing biographer, *The Paper Men* "tells us that biography is the trade of the con man, a fatuous accomplishment, and the height of impertinence in both meanings of the word," according to London *Times* critic Michael Ratcliff. Unfortunately for Golding, many critics found *The Paper Men* to be sorely lacking in the qualities that distinguish the author's best work. Typical of their commentary is this observation from Michiko Kakutani of the *New York Times*: "Judging from the tired, petulant tone of [the novel], Mr. Golding would seem to have more in common with his creation than mere appearance—a 'scraggy yellow-white beard, yellow-white thatch and broken-toothed grin.' He, too, seems to have allowed his pessimistic vision of man to curdle his view of the world and to sour his enjoyment of craft."

Golding saw the publication of two more novels before his death in 1993. *Close Quarters,* published in 1987, and *Fire Down Below,* published in 1989, completed a trilogy begun with *Rites of Passage.* This first volume, according to Bernard F. Dick in *World Literature Today,* "portrayed a voyage to Australia on a ship that symbolized class-conscious Britain (circa 1810) facing the rise of the middle class. . . . *Close Quarters* continues the voyage, but this time the ship, which is again a symbol of Britain, is near collapse." The story is told through the journal entries of Edmund FitzHenry Talbot, "a well-meaning, somewhat uncertain, slightly pompous officer and gentleman enroute to Sydney and a career in His Majesty's service," a *Publishers Weekly* reviewer observed. When an inexperienced sailor's error destroys the ship's masts, the crew and passengers are left to ponder their mortality. "As with most of Golding's fiction," David Nokes asserted in the *Times Literary Supplement,* "it is impossible to escape a brooding, restless intensity which turns even the most trivial incident or observation into a metaphysical conceit." As the ship founders and its captives become increasingly agitated, it seems to become a living thing itself, with twigs sprouting from its timbers and discernable creeping movements in its deck planks underfoot. "As a story-teller [Golding's] touch never falters," Nokes concluded. "His attention to details of idiom and setting show a reverence for his craft that would do credit to a master-shipwright. It is in the dark undertow of his metaphors and in the literary ostentation of his allusions that a feeling of strain and contrivance appears. As he

steers us through the calms and storms, we are never quite sure whether we are in the safe hands of a master-mariner or under the dangerous spell of an Old Man of the Sea."

New York Times Book Review contributor Robert M. Adams had high hopes for the final book of the trilogy based on his reading of *Close Quarters.* He asserted that the second volume "will not stand up by itself as an independent fiction the way *Rites of Passage* did. . . . But this is the wrong time to pass final judgment on a project, the full dimensions of which can at this point only be guessed. In one sense, the very absence from this novel of strong scenes and sharply defined ironies confirms one's sense of a novelist who is still outward bound, firmly in control of his story, and preparing his strongest effects for the resolutions and revolutions to come." The *Los Angeles Times Book Review*'s Richard Hough also found *Close Quarters* unable to stand alone: "This reviewer confesses to being totally mystified by Golding's sequel to *Rites of Passage.* It is neither an allegory, nor a fantasy, nor an adventure, nor even a complete novel, as it has a beginning, a middle (of sorts) but an ending only at some unspecified future date when Golding chooses to complete it, if he does."

The final volume of the trilogy, *Fire Down Below,* appeared in 1989. The title refers to the plan for repairing the ship's masts which entails creating iron bands to pull together the split wood preventing the masts from bearing the weight of the sails, but which also carries the danger of fire in the hold. *Quill and Quire* reviewer Paul Stuewe described *Fire Down Below* as an "ambitious and satisfying novel" and "a rousing finale to an entertaining exercise in historical pastiche." While asserting that neither *Fire Down Below* nor *Close Quarters* "works as powerfully and coherently as *Rites of Passage* with its strongly structured story of a parson who literally died of shame," *New Statesman & Society*'s W. L. Webb observed that "what keeps one attending still, as to the other ancient mariner's tales of ice mast-high, are [Golding's] magic sea pictures: faces on the quarter-deck masked in moonlight, the eerie 'shadow' that falls behind solid bodies in mist and spray, storm-light and a droning wind, and the sailors swarming out like bees as the wounded ship yaws close to the ice cliffs. There's nothing quite like it in our literature."

"As a novelist, William Golding had the gift of terror," Joseph J. Feeney wrote in an obituary for *America*. "It is not the terror of a quick scare—a ghost, a scream, a slash that catches the breath—but a primal, fearsome sense of human evil and human mystery. . . . William Golding was, with Graham Greene, the finest British novelist of our half-century. His fellow novelist Malcolm Bradbury memorialized him as 'a writer who was both impishly difficult, and wonderfully monumental,' and a teller of 'primal stories—about the birth of speech, the dawn of evil, the strange sources of art.'"

BIOGRAPHICAL/CRITICAL SOURCES:

BOOKS

Anderson, David, *The Tragic Past,* John Knox Press, 1969.
Biles, J. I., and Robert O. Evans, editors, *William Golding: Some Critical Considerations,* University Press of Kentucky, 1979.
Bloom, Harold, *William Golding's Lord of the Flies,* Chelsea House (New York City), 1996.
Burgess, Anthony, *The Novel Now: A Guide to Contemporary Fiction,* Norton, 1967.
Contemporary Literary Criticism, Gale (Detroit), Volume 1, 1973; Volume 2, 1974; Volume 3, 1975; Volume 8, 1978; Volume 10, 1979; Volume 18, 1981; Volume 27, 1984; Volume 58, 1990; Volume 81, 1994.

Dictionary of Literary Biography, Volume 15: *British Novelists, 1930-1959,* Gale, 1983.

Dictionary of Literary Biography Yearbook: 1983, Gale, 1984.

Friedman, Lawrence S., *William Golding,* Continuum (New York City), 1993.

Johnson, Arnold, *Of Earth and Darkness: The Novels of William Golding,* University of Missouri Press, 1980.

McCarron, Kevin, *The Coincidence of Opposites: William Golding's Later Fiction,* Sheffield Academic Press, 1995.

Medcalf, Stephen, *William Golding,* Longman, 1975.

Reilly, Patrick, *Lord of the Flies: Fathers and Sons,* Twayne, 1992.

Ries, Lawrence R., *Wolf Masks: Violence in Contemporary Fiction,* Kennikat Press, 1975.

Siegl, Karin, *The Robinsonade Tradition in Robert Michael Ballantyne's The Coral Island and William Golding's Lord of the Flies,* Edwin Mellen Press, 1996.

PERIODICALS

America, July 31, 1993, pp. 6-7.
Atlantic, May, 1965; April, 1984.
Chicago Tribune, October 7, 1983.
Chicago Tribune Book World, December 30, 1979; October 26, 1980; April 8, 1984.
Commentary, January, 1968.
Commonweal, October 25, 1968; September 26, 1980.
Critical Quarterly, summer, 1960; autumn, 1962; spring, 1967.
Critique: Studies in Modern Fiction, Volume 14, number 2, 1972.
Detroit News, December 16, 1979; January 4, 1981; April 29, 1984.
Kenyon Review, autumn, 1957.
Life, November 17, 1967.
Listener, October 4, 1979; October 23, 1980; January 5, 1984.
London Magazine, February-March, 1981.
London Review of Books, June 17, 1982.
Los Angeles Times Book Review, November 9, 1980; June 20, 1982; June 3, 1984; June 7, 1987, pp. 3, 6.
New Republic, December 8, 1979; September 13, 1982.
New Statesman, August 2, 1958; April 10, 1964; November 5, 1965; October 12, 1979; October 17, 1980; June 11, 1982.
New Statesman & Society, April 14, 1989, p. 34.
Newsweek, November 5, 1979; October 27, 1980; April 30, 1984.
New Yorker, September 21, 1957.
New York Post, December 17, 1963.
New York Review of Books, April 30, 1964; December 7, 1967; February 24, 1972; December 6, 1979; December 18, 1980.
New York Times, September 1, 1957; November 9, 1979; October 15, 1980; October 7, 1983; March 26, 1984; June 22, 1987.
New York Times Book Review, October 23, 1955; April 19, 1964; November 18, 1979; November 2, 1980; July 11, 1982; May 31, 1987, p. 44.
Publishers Weekly, May 15, 1987, p. 267.
Quill and Quire, July, 1989, p. 47.
Saturday Review, March 19, 1960.
South Atlantic Quarterly, autumn, 1970.
Southern Review, March, 1976.
Spectator, October 13, 1979.
Time, September 9, 1957; October 13, 1967; October 17, 1983; April 9, 1984; June 8, 1987.
Times (London), February 9, 1984; June 11, 1987.
Times Literary Supplement, October 21, 1955; October 23, 1959; June 1, 1967; November 5, 1971; November 23, 1979; October 17, 1980; July 23, 1982; March 2, 1984; June 19, 1987, p. 653.

Twentieth Century Literature, summer, 1982.
Village Voice, November 5, 1979.
Washington Post, July 12, 1982; October 7, 1983; January 12, 1986.
Washington Post Book World, November 4, 1979; November 2, 1980; April 15, 1984.
World Literature Today, spring, 1988, p. 81; autumn, 1989, p. 681.
Yale Review, spring, 1960.

*   *   *

GOLDSMITH, Peter
See PRIESTLEY, J(ohn) B(oynton)

*   *   *

GORDIMER, Nadine 1923-

PERSONAL: Born November 20, 1923, in Springs, South Africa; daughter of Isidore (a jeweler) and Nan (Myers) Gordimer; married Gerald Gavronsky, March 6, 1949 (divorced, 1952); married Reinhold H. Cassirer (owner and director of art gallery), January 29, 1954; children: (first marriage) Oriane Taramasco; (second marriage) Hugo. *Education:* Attended private schools and the University of the Witwatersrand.

ADDRESSES: Agent—Russell & Volkening, Inc., 50 West 29th St., New York, NY 10001.

CAREER: Writer. Ford Foundation visiting professor, under auspices of Institute of Contemporary Arts, Washington, DC, 1961; lecturer, Hopwood Awards, University of Michigan, Ann Arbor, 1970; writer in residence, American Academy in Rome, 1984; has also lectured and taught writing at Harvard, Princeton, Northwestern, Columbia, and Tulane universities.

MEMBER: International PEN (vice-president), Congress of South African Writers, Royal Society of Literature, American Academy of Arts and Sciences (honorary member), American Academy of Literature and Arts (honorary member).

AWARDS, HONORS: W. H. Smith & Son Literary Award, 1961, for short story collection *Friday's Footprint and Other Stories;* Thomas Pringle Award, English Academy of South Africa, 1969; James Tait Black Memorial Prize, 1973, for *A Guest of Honour;* Booker Prize for Fiction, National Book League, 1974, for *The Conservationist;* Grand Aigle d'Or, 1975; CNA awards, 1974, 1979, 1981, and 1991; Neil Gunn fellowship, Scottish Arts Council, 1981; Commonwealth Award for Distinguished Service in Literature, 1981; Modern Language Association of America award, 1982; Nelly Sachs Prize, 1985; Premio Malaparte, 1986; Bennett Award, *Hudson Review,* 1986; Benson Medal, 1990; Commander de l'Ordre des Arts et des Lettres (France), 1991; Nobel Prize for literature, Nobel Foundation, 1991. D.Litt., University of Leuven, 1980, Smith College, City College of the City University of New York, and Mount Holyoke College, all 1985, and honorary degrees from Harvard University and Yale University, both 1987, and New School for Social Research, 1988.

WRITINGS:

NOVELS

The Lying Days, Simon & Schuster (New York City), 1953, published with new introduction by Paul Bailey, Virago (New York City), 1983.

A World of Strangers, Simon & Schuster, 1958.

Occasion for Loving, Viking, 1963, published with new introduction by Bailey, Virago, 1983.

The Late Bourgeois World, Viking, 1966.

A Guest of Honour, Viking, 1970.

The Conservationist, J. Cape (London), 1974, Viking, 1975.

Burger's Daughter, Viking, 1979.

July's People, Viking, 1981.

A Sport of Nature (Book-of-the-Month Club dual selection), Knopf (New York City), 1987.

My Son's Story, Farrar, Straus (New York City), 1990.

None to Accompany Me, Farrar, Straus, 1994.

Harald, Claudia, and Their Son Duncan, Bloomsbury, 1996.

The House Gun, Farrar, Straus, 1998.

SHORT STORIES

Face to Face (also see below), Silver Leaf Books (Johannesburg), 1949.

The Soft Voice of the Serpent and Other Stories (contains many stories previously published in *Face to Face*), Simon & Schuster, 1952.

Six Feet of the Country (also see below), Simon & Schuster, 1956.

Friday's Footprint and Other Stories, Viking, 1960.

Not for Publication and Other Stories, Viking, 1965.

Livingstone's Companions, Viking, 1971.

Selected Stories (contains stories from previously published collections), J. Cape, 1975, Viking, 1976, also published in England as *No Place Like: Selected Stories,* Penguin, 1978.

Some Monday for Sure, Heinemann Educational (London), 1976.

A Soldier's Embrace, Viking, 1980.

Town and Country Lovers, Sylvester and Orphanos (Los Angeles, CA), 1980.

Six Feet of the Country (contains stories from previously published collections selected for television series of same title), Penguin, 1982.

Something Out There, Viking, 1984.

Crimes of Conscience: Selected Short Stories, Heinemann, 1991.

Jump and Other Stories, Farrar, Straus, 1991.

Why Haven't You Written?: Selected Stories, 1950-1972, Viking, 1993.

Reflections of South Africa: Short Stories, Systime, 1986.

OTHER

(Editor with Lionel Abrahams) *South African Writing Today,* Penguin, 1967.

African Literature: The Lectures Given on This Theme at the University of Cape Town's Public Summer School, February, 1972, Board of Extra Mural Studies, University of Cape Town, 1972.

The Black Interpreters: Notes on African Writing, Spro-Cas/Ravan (Johannesburg), 1973.

On the Mines, photographs by David Goldblatt, C. Struik (Cape Town), 1973.

(Author of appreciation) *Kurt Jobst: Goldsmith and Silversmith; Art Metal Worker,* G. Bakker (Johannesburg), 1979.

(With others) *What Happened to Burger's Daughter; or, How South African Censorship Works,* Taurus (Johannesburg), 1980.

Lifetimes under Apartheid, photographs by Goldblatt, Knopf, 1986.

The Essential Gesture: Writing, Politics and Places, edited and introduced by Stephen Clingman, Knopf, 1988.

Three in a Bed: Fiction, Morals, and Politics, Bennington College, 1991.

(With Ruth Weiss) *Zimbabwe and the New Elite,* Tauris & Co., 1993.

Also author of *Writing and Being: The Charles Eliot Norton Lectures,* 1995.

Also author of television plays and documentaries, including *A Terrible Chemistry,* 1981, *Choosing for Justice: Allan Boesak,* with Hugo Cassirer, 1985, *Country Lovers, A Chip of Glass Ruby, Praise,* and *Oral History,* all part of *The Gordimer Stories* series adapted from stories of the same title, 1985. Contributor to periodicals, including *Atlantic, Encounter, Granta, Harper's, Holiday, Kenyon Review, Mother Jones, New Yorker, Paris Review,* and *Playboy.*

MEDIA ADAPTATIONS: City Lovers, based on Gordimer's short story of the same title, was filmed by TeleCulture Inc./TelePool in South Africa in 1982.

SIDELIGHTS: "Nadine Gordimer has become, in the whole solid body of her work, the literary voice and conscience of her society," declares Maxwell Geismar in *Saturday Review.* In numerous novels, short stories, and essays, she has written of her South African homeland and its apartheid government—under which its blacks, coloreds, and whites subsisted for nearly half a century. "This writer . . . has made palpable the pernicious, pervasive character of that country's race laws, which not only deny basic rights to most people but poison many relationships," maintains Miriam Berkley in *Publishers Weekly.* Her insight, integrity, and compassion inspire critical admiration. "She has mapped out the social, political and emotional geography of that troubled land with extraordinary passion and precision," says Michiko Kakutani of the *New York Times,* observing in a later essay that "taken chronologically, her work not only reflects her own evolving political consciousness and maturation as an artist—an early lyricism has given way to an increased preoccupation with ideas and social issues—but it also charts changes in South Africa's social climate." She was honored with the Nobel Prize in literature for her novels in 1991—a sign of the esteem in which the literary world holds her work.

Gordimer was originally only one of a series of novelists working in South Africa after World War II. "Some of the writers, like [Alan] Paton, turned to nonfiction or political work; even more, most notably [Peter] Abrahams and Dan Jacobson, expatriated," explains John Cooke in *The Novels of Nadine Gordimer: Private Lives/Public Landscapes.* "By the early sixties Gordimer was almost the only member of the postwar group to continue producing fiction from within the country. That she should be the survivor was not altogether surprising, for she was in essential ways more a product of South Africa than her contemporaries. She attended university at home, not in England as colonial writers so regularly have; she did not travel abroad until she was thirty."

"Gordimer seemed particularly unsuited to prosper as a writer in her arid land," Cooke continues, "because of the disjunction between her temperament and the situation she confronted. More than any of her contemporaries, Gordimer was initially drawn to private themes." Her novels and short stories are, at bottom, about complicated individuals caught in awkward or impossibly complex situations. "Her writing [is] so subtle that it forces readers to find their way back from her works into her mind," says Firdaus Kanga in the *Times Literary Supplement*; "her characters are powerful precisely because you cannot sum them up in a line or even a page."

Much of Gordimer's fiction focuses upon white middle-class lives. It frequently depicts what Geismar describes as "a terrified white consciousness in the midst of a mysterious and ominous sea of black humanity." But the "enduring subject" of her writing has been "the consequences of apartheid on the daily lives of men and women, the distortions it produces in relationships among both blacks and whites," says Kakutani. Her first novel, *The Lying Days,* is drawn from her own personal experience and tells about a young woman who comes into contact with the effects of apartheid when she has an affair with a social worker. *A World of Strangers* is about the efforts of a British writer to bring together his white intellectual friends with his black African intellectual friends. In *Burger's Daughter,* Gordimer examines white ambivalence about apartheid in the person of Rosa, who can no longer sustain the anti-apartheid cause of her imprisoned Afrikaner father after his death. The author "was increasingly frustrated as racial separation was more rigidly enforced during the fifties and sixties," Cooke explains. "Her response was to withdraw from her world, to examine it from an increasingly detached perspective."

Both *The Lying Days* and *A World of Strangers* end with a note of hope for a better future for South Africans. Gordimer's later novels, however, take a more pessimistic tone. *A Guest of Honour,* which won the James Tait Black Memorial Prize in 1973, tells of the return of Colonel James Bray to his African homeland. Bray had been exiled by the previous government for his espousal of black revolutionary ideology. Upon his return, however, Bray discovers that the new revolutionary government is just as corrupt and self-interested as the previous government was. When he speaks out publicly against the new government, it targets him for assassination. *The Conservationist,* awarded the Booker Prize (Great Britain's highest literary honor) the following year, tells about the uneasy relationship between a white landowner and the black squatters who have settled on his estate. "Beginning with *A Guest of Honour,*" Cooke concludes, "Gordimer's novels are informed by a tension between . . . two impulses: she at once observes her world from without and envisions it from within. Through this double process, the fruit of her long apprenticeship, Gordimer creates masterful forms and shapes despite the 'low cultural rainfall' of her world."

These forms and shapes also appear in Gordimer's short fiction. *Jump and Other Stories*—published shortly before the author received the Nobel Prize—contains stories that approach her favorite themes in a variety of ways. She tells about a white man out for a jog, who is caught up in a black gang-killing and is saved by a black woman who shelters him. "A single truth is witnessed," writes John Edgar Wideman in the *New York Times Book Review,* "a truth somehow missing in most fiction by white Americans that purports to examine our national life. No matter how removed one feels oneself from the fray, race and race relations lie at the heart of the intimate, perplexing questions we need to ask of ourselves: Where have I been? Where am I going? Who am I?" "Ms. Gordimer can be a merciless judge and jury," Wideman concludes. "Her portraits obtain a Vermeer-like precision, accurate and remorseless, with no room for hope, for self-delusion, no room even for the small vanities of ego and self-regard that allow

us to proceed sometimes as if at least our intentions are honorable."

The Swedish Academy had considered Gordimer as a Nobel Prize nominee for years before she finally received the award in 1991. Several commentators, while congratulating her on her accomplishment, noted that the struggle against apartheid remained unfinished. "On the day of the announcement that Nadine Gordimer would receive the 1991 Nobel Prize for literature, a tribute to the complex and intimate stories she has written about racism's toll on people's lives in her native South Africa," writes Esther B. Fein in the *New York Times,* "Nelson Mandela still did not have the right to vote." Mandela had been released from his political prison, but the basic tenets of apartheid prevented him from exercising the rights of citizenship. When President F. W. De Klerk announced that the policy of separation would end, reviewers wondered where the Nobel laureate would turn her attention. "With apartheid finally ended," Diana Jean Schemo declares in the *New York Times,* "the novelist waxes exultant over a sense of renewal in her homeland; the urgency is gone, but the turn of mind remains."

As in *None to Accompany Me, House Gun* explores the relationships between blacks and whites in post-apartheid South Africa. The Lindegards are an affluent white couple who learn that their only son Duncan has committed a murder. Duncan hires a black lawyer to represent him. This series of events sets up an exploration of the question, "Does a violent society provoke violence in nonviolent individuals?" Underlying this question is another, which asks if the level of violence in South Africa is higher than in Europe because of its large black population. "This is the racial question that haunts Gordimer's novel," according to Jack Miles in the *New York Times Book Review.* Miles goes on to describe *House Gun* as an "elegantly conceived, flawlessly executed novel." Conversely, Michiko Kakutani in the *New York Times* describes the novel as "little more than a courtroom thriller, dressed up with some clumsy allusions to apartheid's legacy of violence and the uses and misuses of freedom."

Gordimer's turn of mind reaches out in two directions: politically, she follows the fortunes of other first-class "third-world" writers such as Egyptian Naguib Mahfouz, Nigerian Chinua Achebe, and Israeli Amos Oz. "Her attention is turned on writers whose work seems most engaged in the questions that have absorbed her for much of her life," Schemo writes: "how justice, wealth, power and freedom are parceled out in a society, and the repercussions for its people." She also looks at the problems faced by racially polarized South Africa as it moves from apartheid into democracy. *None to Accompany Me* looks at the fortunes of two families—one black, one white—as they move into the new era. "For the past 40 years," Anne Whitehouse writes in *Tribune Books,* "Gordimer's fiction has reflected and illuminated her country's troubled history and the passions of individuals with integrity and detachment. *None to Accompany Me* is a sustaining achievement, proving Gordimer once again a lucid witness to her country's transformation and a formidable interpreter of the inner self."

"I began to write, I think, out of the real source of all art, and that is out of a sense of wonderment about life, and a sense of trying to make sense out of the mystery of life," Gordimer tells interviewer Beth Austin in the *Chicago Tribune.* "That hasn't changed in all the years that I've been writing. That is the starting point of everything that I write."

BIOGRAPHICAL/CRITICAL SOURCES:

BOOKS

Bazine, N. T., and M. D. Seymour, editors, *Conversations with Nadine Gordimer,* University Press of Mississippi, 1990.

Brodsky, Joseph, *New Censors: Nadine Gordimer and Others on Publishing Now,* Cassell Academic, 1996.

Clingman, Stephen, *The Novels of Nadine Gordimer: History from the Inside,* University of Massachusetts Press, 1992.

Cooke, John, *The Novels of Nadine Gordimer: Private Lives/ Public Landscapes,* Louisiana State University (Baton Rouge), 1985.

Ettin, Andrew Vogel, *Betrayals of the Body Politic: The Literary Commitments of Nadine Gordimer,* University Press of Virginia, 1993.

Head, Dominic, *Nadine Gordimer,* Cambridge University Press, 1995.

King, Bruce, editor, *The Later Fiction of Nadine Gordimer,* St. Martin's Press, 1993.

Newman, Judie, *Nadine Gordimer,* Routledge, 1990.

Smith, Rowland, *Critical Essays on Nadine Gordimer,* G. K. Hall, 1990.

Wagner, Kathrin, *Rereading Nadine Gordimer,* Indiana University Press, 1994.

PERIODICALS

Atlantic, January, 1960; February, 1998.

Booklist, October 1, 1958; January 10, 1960.

Chicago Sunday Tribune, September 21, 1958.

Chicago Tribune, May 18, 1980; December 7, 1986; November 12, 1987; October 4, 1991.

Chicago Tribune Book World, September 9, 1979; June 7, 1981; July 29, 1984; December 11, 1988, pp. 8-9; September 25, 1994, section 14, pp. 1, 9.

Christian Science Monitor, January 10, 1963; November 4, 1971; May 19, 1975; September 10, 1979.

Commonweal, October 23, 1953; July 9, 1965; November 4, 1966; November 30, 1984, pp. 667-68.

Detroit News, September 2, 1979; June 7, 1981; May 31, 1989.

Encounter, August, 1971; February, 1975.

Entertainment Weekly, January 24, 1992, p. 52.

Extrapolation, spring, 1992, pp. 73-87.

Globe and Mail (Toronto), July 28, 1984; June 6, 1987; January 5, 1991; October 5, 1991.

Harper's, February, 1963; April, 1976; November, 1990, p. 27.

Hudson Review, spring, 1980.

Library Journal, September 1, 1958.

London Magazine, April/May, 1975.

Los Angeles Times, July 31, 1984; December 7, 1986.

Los Angeles Times Book Review, August 10, 1980; April 19, 1987; April 3, 1988; April 2, 1989; October 28, 1990.

Modern Fiction Studies, summer, 1987.

Mother Jones, December, 1988.

Ms., July, 1975; September, 1987, p. 28.

Nation, June 18, 1971; August 18, 1976; May 2, 1987.

New Statesman and Nation, August 18, 1956.

Newsweek, May 10, 1965; July 4, 1966; March 10, 1975; April 19, 1976; September 22, 1980; June 22, 1981; July 9, 1984; May 4, 1987; October 14, 1991, p. 40.

New Yorker, June 7, 1952; November 21, 1953; November 29, 1958; May 12, 1975.

New York Herald Tribune Book Review, May 25, 1952; October 4, 1953; October 21, 1956; September 21, 1958; January 10, 1960; April 7, 1963.

New York Review of Books, June 26, 1975; July 15, 1976; March 30, 1989, p. 12; December 5, 1991, p. 16.

New York Times, June 15, 1952; October 4, 1953; October 7, 1956; September 21, 1958; May 23, 1965; October 30, 1970; September 19, 1979; August 20, 1980; May 27, 1981; December 28, 1981; July 9, 1984; January 14, 1986; April 22, 1987; December 28, 1987; October 5, 1990; January 1, 1991; October 4, 1991, pp. A1, C28; October 10, 1991, p. C25; December 8, 1991, p. 22; September 16, 1994, p. C31; November 28, 1994, pp. C11, C15.

New York Times Book Review, January 10, 1960; September 11, 1966; October 31, 1971; April 13, 1975; April 18, 1976; August 19, 1979; August 24, 1980; June 7, 1981; July 29, 1984; May 3, 1987; November 27, 1988, p. 8; October 21, 1990; June 2, 1991, p. 21; September 29, 1991, p. 7; September 24, 1994, p. 7; October 6, 1996, p. 102; January 16, 1998; February 1, 1998.

Paris Review, summer, 1983.

People, May 4, 1987; October 18, 1991, p. 14.

Progressive, January, 1992, p. 30.

Publishers Weekly, March 6, 1987; April 10, 1987; September 30, 1988; October 18, 1991, p. 14.

San Francisco Chronicle, May 26, 1952; November 9, 1953; January 24, 1960.

Saturday Review, May 24, 1952; October 3, 1953; September 13, 1958; January 16, 1960; May 8, 1965; August 20, 1966; December 4, 1971; March 8, 1975; September 29, 1979.

Sewanee Review, spring, 1977.

Spectator, February 12, 1960.

Time, October 15, 1956; September 22, 1958; January 11, 1960; November 16, 1970; July 7, 1975; June 8, 1981; July 23, 1984; April 6, 1987; October 14, 1991, p. 91.

Times (London), December 16, 1982; March 22, 1984; April 2, 1987; September 6, 1990.

Times Literary Supplement, October 30, 1953; July 13, 1956; June 27, 1958; February 12, 1960; March 1, 1963; July 22, 1965; July 7, 1966; May 14, 1971; May 26, 1972; January 9, 1976; July 9, 1976; April 25, 1980; September 4, 1981; March 30, 1984; April 17, 1987; September 23-29, 1988; October 4, 1990; October 11, 1991, p. 14; April 1, 1994, pp. 10-11.

Tribune Books (Chicago), April 26, 1987; December 11, 1988, pp. 8-9; October 14, 1990; September 25, 1994, pp. 1, 9.

U.S. News & World Report, May 25, 1987.

Village Voice, September 17, 1980.

Voice Literary Supplement, September, 1984.

Washington Post, December 4, 1979.

Washington Post Book World, November 28, 1971; April 6, 1975; August 26, 1979; September 7, 1980; May 31, 1981; July 15, 1984; May 3, 1987; November 20, 1988; October 2, 1994.

World Literature Today, autumn, 1984; spring, 1992, pp. 390-91.

Yale Review, winter, 1988.

*   *   *

GORDON, Caroline 1895-1981

PERSONAL: Born October 6, 1895, in Trenton, KY; died April 11, 1981, in San Cristobal de las Casas, Chiapas, Mexico, following surgery; daughter of James (director of a school for boys) and Nancy Minor (Meriwether) Morris; married Allen Tate (a poet and critic), November 2, 1924 (divorced, 1954); children: Nancy Meriwether (Mrs. Percy H. Wood, Jr.). *Education:* Bethany College, A.B., 1916. *Religion:* Roman Catholic.

CAREER: High school teacher, 1917-20; *Chattanooga News,* Chattanooga, TN, reporter, 1920-24; University of North Carolina, Woman's College, Greensboro, professor of English, 1938-39; Columbia University, School of General Studies, New York, NY, lecturer in creative writing, beginning 1946; University of Dallas, Dallas, TX, director of master's creative writing program. Visiting professor of English at University of Washington, Seattle, 1953, University of Kansas, 1956, and Purdue University; writer-in-residence at University of California, Davis, 1962-63; lecturer in creative writing at New School for Social Research, University of Utah, and University of Virginia.

MEMBER: Alpha Xi Delta.

AWARDS, HONORS: Guggenheim fellowship for creative writing, 1932; second prize, O. Henry Memorial Award, 1934; Litt.D., Bethany College, 1946; National Institute Grant in Literature, 1950; D.Litt., St. Mary's College, Notre Dame, IN, 1964; grants from National Arts Council, 1966, National Endowment for the Arts, 1967.

WRITINGS:

The Forest of the South (stories), Scribner, 1945.
(Editor with Allen Tate) *The House of Fiction: An Anthology of the Short Story, with Commentary,* Scribner, 1950, 2nd edition, 1960.
How to Read a Novel, Viking, 1957.
(Contributor) Thomas E. Connolly, editor, *Joyce's Portrait: Criticism and Critiques,* Appleton, 1962.
Old Red and Other Stories, Scribner, 1963.
A Good Soldier: A Key to the Novels of Ford Madox Ford, University of California Library (Davis), 1963.
The Collected Stories of Caroline Gordon, Farrar, Straus, 1981.
Southern Mandarins: Letters of Caroline Gordon to Sally Wood, 1924-1937, Louisiana State University Press, 1984.

NOVELS

Penhally, Scribner, 1931.
Aleck Maury, Sportsman, Scribner, 1934, published in England as *The Pastimes of Aleck Maury: The Life of a True Sportsman,* Dickson, 1935.
The Garden of Adonis, Scribner, 1937.
None Shall Look Back, Scribner, 1937 (published in England as *None Shall Look Back: A Story of the American Civil War,* Constable, 1937).
Green Centuries, Scribner, 1941.
The Women on the Porch, Scribner, 1944.
The Strange Children, Scribner, 1951.
The Malefactors, Harcourt, 1956.
The Glory of Hera, Doubleday, 1972.

Contributor to periodicals, including *Harper's, Sewanee Review,* and *Kenyon Review.*

SIDELIGHTS: In his introduction to *The Collected Stories of Caroline Gordon,* Robert Penn Warren grouped Caroline Gordon with such other Southern women writers as Eudora Welty, Flannery O'Connor and Katherine Anne Porter—writers "who have been enriching our literature uniquely in this century." A member of the Southern Renaissance of the 1920s and 1930s, Gordon wrote of the traditional values of the American South. In particular, according to Ashley Brown in the *Dictionary of Literary Biography Yearbook, 1981,* Gordon's work gives "an impressive image of Western man and the crisis which his restlessness has created." Also writing in the *Yearbook,* Andrew Lytle explained that Gordon's "view was historic and tragic. The

defeat of the Confederacy and the consequent destruction of Southern, that is the transplanted segment of European, society, its effects upon the succeeding generations, gave her the substance for her earlier fiction. Her later fiction concerns the damage into the third generation of what cracked and broken forms do to human beings." Among Gordon's most respected books is the novel *Aleck Maury, Sportsman,* which Brown called "an American classic" and a *Nation* reviewer described as "one of the most distinguished and beautiful novels to come out of the South." Writing in the *Dictionary of Literary Biography,* W. J. Stuckey claimed that at their best, Gordon's novels "are written with a lucidity that makes them timeless as well as moving accounts of human conduct."

An opponent of the more experimental fiction advocated by such writers as Gertrude Stein, whom she had met during the 1930s in Paris, Gordon asserted the primacy of personal experience as a source for fiction. Her stories and novels are often based on her own life. *Penhally* tells of the decline of a Southern aristocratic family and is inspired in part by Gordon's own family. *Aleck Maury* is based on Gordon's father, an avid sportsman and a teacher of classical literature, while *The Strange Children* and *The Malefactors* draw from Gordon's circle of friends in Paris during the 1930s. As Cynthia H. Rogers commented in the *Dictionary of Literary Biography,* Gordon believed that "the only proper subject for fiction is the realistic portrayal of experience."

This realism was meant to capture the unique qualities of a particular time and place. Margaret Dickie Uroff, writing in *National Review,* found that in Gordon's stories there was "not a lament for the dead, but rather an evocation of a world that is passing away, a celebration of things enjoyed in every particular precisely because they will not come again. It is not just the inevitability but the propriety of time's passage that Miss Gordon's narratives acknowledge. For her the changing world is cherished in its details, arrested for a moment in an image or a comment but then released to its flux."

Gordon also believed in rendering personal experience in an objective style. Stuckey, writing in his *Caroline Gordon,* credited her with trying "to efface herself as a person as completely as she can, to get herself out of her writing, and to allow her story to tell itself." This objectivity led critics like Lytle to ascribe a certain "coldness" to her writing: "Her tension at times seems too severe, as if her image as mask penetrates the passion and, instead of objectifying, freezes it. It causes her characters at times to appear immobile or cold." E. H. Walton believed that "Gordon fails to interest one crucially in any of her characters. She portrays them perfunctorily and without real warmth."

Critics like D. B. Collins, however, exemplify a more favorable critical judgment of Gordon's writing. Her work, Collins wrote, "is shapely, it has vitality, it illuminates a major aspect of American life, it is written in a style so perfectly suited to its matter that it goes straight to that heaven of all lovers of style: although . . . one feels a constant quiet reassurance running so deep that it rarely emerges into conscious appreciation; it is overlooked, and only seen in retrospect for the remarkable literary feat that it really is." Frederick P. W. McDowell, writing in his study *Caroline Gordon,* explained that she "made creative use of the tragic dimensions of human life, the aborted aspirations of most human beings, the sense of evil infecting the good and true, the glories and the burdens of a legendary past, the sense of cultures and individuals in conflict, and a feeling for place that becomes a muted passion." Writing in the *Dictionary of Literary*

Biography Yearbook, 1981, Howard Baker called Gordon "a stylist of the highest order."

BIOGRAPHICAL/CRITICAL SOURCES:

BOOKS

Contemporary Literary Criticism, Gale (Detroit), Volume 6, 1976; Volume 13, 1980; Volume 29, 1984.
Dictionary of Literary Biography, Gale, Volume 4: *American Writers in Paris, 1920-1939,* 1980; Volume 9: *American Novelists, 1910-1945,* 1981.
Dictionary of Literary Biography Yearbook, 1981, Gale, 1982.
Dunaway, John M. and Jacques Maritain, editors, *Exiles and Fugitives: The Letters of Jacques and Raeissa Maritain, Allen Tate, and Caroline Gordon,* Louisiana State University Press (Baton Rouge), 1992.
Jonza, Nancylee Novell, *The Underground Stream: The Life and Art of Caroline Gordon,* University of Georgia Press (Athens), 1995.
McDowell, Frederick P. W., *Caroline Gordon,* University of Minnesota Press, 1966.
O'Connor, William Van, *The Grotesque: An American Genre and Other Essays,* Southern Illinois University Press, 1962.
Rubin, Louis D., and Robert D. Jacobs, editors, *South: Modern Southern Literature in Its Cultural Setting,* Doubleday, 1961.
Stuckey, William J., *Caroline Gordon,* Twayne, 1972.
Tate, Allen, *Memoirs and Opinions, 1926-1974,* Swallow Press, 1975.
Walker, William Edward, and Robert L. Walker, editors, *Reality and Myth: Essays in American Literature,* Vanderbilt University Press, 1964.

PERIODICALS

Books, September 27, 1931; November 4, 1934; February 21, 1937; November 2, 1941.
Book Week, May 21, 1944; October 20, 1963.
Christian Science Monitor, March 8, 1937.
Commonweal, October 26, 1945.
Critique, winter, 1956.
Library Journal, September 15, 1957.
Nation, October 7, 1931; January 9, 1935; March 20, 1937.
National Review, December 31, 1963; July 10, 1981.
New Republic, November 4, 1931; January 2, 1935; March 31, 1937; January 5, 1942; April 20, 1956.
New Yorker, November 1, 1941; June 3, 1944; September 22, 1945; March 17, 1956.
New York Times, September 20, 1931; December 2, 1934; February 21, 1937; November 2, 1941; May 21, 1944; October 7, 1945; July 30, 1950; March 4, 1956; October 27, 1957.
New York Times Book Review, October 20, 1963; April 19, 1981.
Publishers Weekly, November 2, 1992, p. 60.
Saturday Review, November 21, 1931; February 20, 1937; May 27, 1944; October 27, 1945; June 17, 1950; November 16, 1957.
Sewanee Review, autumn, 1949.
Southern Literary Journal, spring, 1982.
Southern Review, summer, 1937; spring, 1971.
Times Literary Supplement, August 7, 1937; November 13, 1981.
Wilson Library Bulletin, September, 1937.

GORENKO, Anna Andreevna
  See AKHMATOVA, Anna

*   *   *

GORKY, Maxim
  See PESHKOV, Alexei Maximovich

*   *   *

GORYAN, Sirak
  See SAROYAN, William

*   *   *

GOTTESMAN, S. D.
  See POHL, Frederik

*   *   *

GOULD, Stephen Jay 1941-

PERSONAL: Born September 10, 1941, in New York, NY; son of Leonard (a court reporter) and Eleanor (an artist; maiden name, Rosenberg) Gould; married Deborah Lee (an artist and writer), October 3, 1965; children: Jesse, Ethan. *Education:* Antioch College, A.B., 1963; Columbia University, Ph.D., 1967.

ADDRESSES: Office—Museum of Comparative Zoology, Harvard University, Cambridge, MA 02138.

CAREER: Antioch College, Yellow Springs, OH, instructor in geology, 1966; Harvard University, Cambridge, MA, assistant professor and assistant curator, 1967-71, associate professor and associate curator, 1971-73, professor of geology and curator of invertebrate paleontology at Museum of Comparative Zoology, 1973–, Alexander Agassiz Professor of Zoology, 1982–. Member of advisory board, Children's Television Workshop, 1978-81, and *Nova,* 1980-92.

MEMBER: American Association for the Advancement of Science, American Academy of Arts and Sciences, American Society of Naturalists (president, 1979-80), National Academy of Sciences, Paleontological Society (president, 1985-86), Society for the Study of Evolution (vice-president, 1975, president, 1990), Society of Systematic Zoology, Society of Vertebrate Paleontology, History of Science Society, European Union of Geosciences (honorary foreign fellow), Society for the Study of Sports History, Royal Society of Edinburgh, Linnaean Society of London (foreign member), Sigma Xi.

AWARDS, HONORS: National Science Foundation, Woodrow Wilson, and Columbia University fellowships, 1963-67; Schuchert Award, Paleontological Society, 1975; National Magazine Award, 1980, for "This View of Life"; Notable Book citation, American Library Association, 1980, and National Book Award in science, 1981, both for *The Panda's Thumb: More Reflections in Natural History*; Scientist of the Year citation, *Discover,* 1981; National Book Critics Circle Award, 1982, American Book Award nomination in science, 1982, and outstanding book award, American Educational Research Association, 1983, all for *The Mismeasure of Man*; MacArthur Foundation Prize fellowship,

1981-86; medal of excellence, Columbia University, 1982; F. V. Haydn Medal, Philadelphia Academy of Natural Sciences, 1982; Joseph Priestley Award and Medal, Dickinson College, 1983; Neil Miner Award, National Association of Geology Teachers, 1983; silver medal, Zoological Society of London, 1984; Bradford Washburn Award and gold medal, Museum of Science (Boston), 1984; distinguished service award, American Humanists Association, 1984; Tanner Lectures, Cambridge University, 1984, and Stanford University, 1989; meritorious service award, American Association of Systematics Collections, 1984; Founders Council Award of Merit, Field Museum of Natural History, 1984; John and Samuel Bard Award, Bard College, 1984; Phi Beta Kappa Book Award in science, 1984, for *Hen's Teeth and Horse's Toes: Further Reflections in Natural History*; Sarah Josepha Hale Medal, 1986; creative arts award for nonfiction, Brandeis University, 1986; Terry Lectures, Yale University, 1986; distinguished service award, American Geological Institute, 1986; Glenn T. Seaborg Award, International Platform Association, 1986; In Praise of Reason Award, Committee for the Scientific Investigation of Claims of the Paranormal, 1986; H. D. Vursell Award, American Academy and Institute of Arts and Letters, 1987; National Book Critics Circle Award nomination, 1987, for *Time's Arrow, Time's Cycle: Myth and Metaphor in the Discovery of Geological Time*; Anthropology in Media Award, American Anthropological Association, 1987; History of Geology Award, Geological Society of America, 1988; T. N. George Medal, University of Glasgow, 1989; Sue T. Friedman Medal, Geological Society of London, 1989; Distinguished Service Award, American Institute of Professional Geologists, 1989; Associe du Museum National D'Historie Naturelle, Paris, 1989; fellow, Royal Society of Edinburgh, 1990; City of Edinburgh Medal, 1990; Britannica Award and Gold Medal, 1990, for dissemination of public knowledge; Forkosch Award, Council on Democratic Humanism, and Phi Beta Kappa Book Award in Science, both 1990, and Pulitzer Prize finalist and Rhone-Poulenc Prize, both 1991, all for *Wonderful Life: The Burgess Shale and the Nature of History*; Iglesias Prize, 1991, for Italian translation of *The Mismeasure of Man*; Distinguished Service Award, National Association of Biology Teachers, 1991; Golden Trilobite Award, Paleontological Society, 1992; Homer Smith Medal, New York University School of Medicine, 1992; UCLA medal, 1992; James T. Shea Award, National Association of Geology Teachers, 1992; Commonwealth Award in Interpretive Science, State of Massachusetts, 1993; J. P. McGovern Award and Medal in Science, Cosmos Club, 1993; St. Louis Libraries Literary Award, University of St. Louis, 1994; Gold Medal for Service to Zoology, Linnaean Society of London; Distinguished Service Medal, Teachers College, Columbia University. Recipient of numerous honorary degrees from colleges and universities.

WRITINGS:

NONFICTION

Ontogeny and Phylogeny, Belknap Press (Cambridge, MA), 1977.
Ever since Darwin: Reflections in Natural History (essays), Norton (New York City), 1977.
The Panda's Thumb: More Reflections in Natural History (essays), Norton, 1980.
(With Salvador Edward Juria and Sam Singer) *A View of Life*, Benjamin-Cummings (Menlo Park, CA), 1981.
The Mismeasure of Man, Norton, 1981, revised and expanded edition, 1996.
Hen's Teeth and Horse's Toes: Further Reflections in Natural History (essays), Norton, 1983.

The Flamingo's Smile: Reflections in Natural History (essays), Norton, 1985.
(With Rosamund Wolff Purcell) *Illuminations: A Bestiary*, Norton, 1986.
Time's Arrow, Time's Cycle: Myth and Metaphor in the Discovery of Geological Time, Harvard University Press (Cambridge, MA), 1987.
An Urchin in the Storm: Essays About Books and Ideas, Norton, 1987.
(With others) *Frederic Edwin Church*, National Gallery of Art, 1989.
Wonderful Life: The Burgess Shale and the Nature of History, Norton, 1989.
The Individual in Darwin's World: The Second Edinburgh Medal Address, Edinburgh University Press (Edinburgh), 1990.
Bully for Brontosaurus: Reflections in Natural History, Norton, 1991.
(With Purcell) *Finders, Keepers: Eight Collectors*, Norton, 1992.
(Editor) *The Book of Life*, W. W. Norton, 1993.
Eight Little Piggies: Reflections in Natural History, Norton, 1993.
Dinosaur in a Haystack: Reflections in Natural History, Harmony Books (New York City), 1995.
Full House: The Spread of Excellence from Plato to Darwin, Harmony Books, 1996.
Questioning the Millenium: A Rationalist's Guide to a Precisely Arbitrary Countdown, Random House, 1997.
Leonardo's Mountain of Clams and the Diet of Worms: Essays on Natural History, Harmony, 1998.

Author of *An Evolutionary Microcosm: Pleistocene and Recent History of the Land Snail P. (Poecilozonites) in Bermuda* (Cambridge, MA), 1969. Also author, with Eric Lewin Altschuler, of *Bachanalia: The Essential Listener's Guide to Bach's 'Well-Tempered Clavier.'*

OTHER

(Contributor, with Niles Eldredge) T. J. M. Schopf, editor, *Models in Paleobiology*, Freeman, Cooper (San Francisco), 1972.
(Contributor) Ernst Mayr, editor, *The Evolutionary Synthesis: Perspectives on the Unification of Biology*, Harvard University Press, 1980.
(Editor, with Eldredge) Mayr, *Systematics and the Origin of Species*, Columbia University Press (New York City), 1982.
(Editor, with Eldredge) Theodosius Dobzhansky, *Genetics and the Origin of Species*, Columbia University Press, 1982.
(Contributor) Charles L. Hamrum, editor, *Darwin's Legacy: Nobel Conference XVIII, Gustavus Adolphus College, St. Peter, Minnesota*, Harper (New York City), 1983.
(Author of foreword) Gary Larson, *The Far Side Gallery 3*, Andrews & McMeel (Fairway, KS), 1988.
(Contributor) *Between Home and Heaven: Contemporary American Landscape Photography*, National Museum of American Art (Washington, DC), 1992.
(Contributor) *Understanding Scientific Prose*, edited by Jack Selzer, University of Wisconsin Press (Madison), 1993.

Contributor to proceedings of International Congress of Systematic and Evolutionary Biology Symposium, 1973; contributor to *Bulletin of the Museum of Comparative Zoology*, Harvard University. Contributor of more than one hundred articles to scientific journals. Author of monthly column, "This View of Life," in *Natural History*.

General editor, *The History of Paleontology*, twenty volumes, Ayer, 1980; and *The Book of Life*, Norton, 1993. Associate editor,

Evolution, 1970-72; member of editorial board, *Systematic Zoology,* 1970-72, *Paleobiology,* 1974-76, and *American Naturalist,* 1977-80; member of board of editors, *Science,* 1986-91.

SIDELIGHTS: Stephen Jay Gould, a Harvard University professor and evolutionary biologist, is renowned for his ability to translate difficult scientific theories into prose understandable to the layman. In his books and essays on natural history, Gould, a paleontologist and geologist by training, popularizes his subjects without trivializing them, "simultaneously entertaining and teaching," according to James Gorman in the *New York Times Book Review.* With essay collections that include *Ever since Darwin: Reflections in Natural History* and *The Flamingo's Smile: Reflections in Natural History,* and book-length studies on specific topics, such as *The Mismeasure of Man* and *Time's Arrow, Time's Cycle: Myth and Metaphor in the Discovery of Geological Time,* Gould has won critical acclaim for bridging the gap between the advancing frontier of science and the literary world. "As witty as he is learned, Gould has a born essayist's ability to evoke the general out of fascinating particulars and to discuss important scientific questions for an audience of educated laymen without confusion or condescension," Gene Lyons comments in *Newsweek.* "He is a thinker and writer as central to our times as any whose name comes to mind." Lee Dembart offers similar praise in the *Los Angeles Times*: "Stephen Jay Gould is one of our foremost expositors of science, a man of extraordinary intellect and knowledge and an uncanny ability to blend the two. He sees familiar things in fresh ways, and his original thoughts are textured with meaning and powerfully honed. . . . The publication of a new book by Gould is a cause for celebration."

Gould's focus on the unexpected within nature reflects a view that permeates his work: that natural history is significantly altered by events out-of-the-ordinary and is largely revealed by examining its "imperfections." "Catastrophes contain continuities," explains Michael Neve in the *Times Literary Supplement.* "In fact Gould has made it his business to see the oddities and small-scale disasters of the natural record as the actual historical evidence for taking evolution seriously, as a real event." Through imperfections, "we can . . . see how things have altered by looking at the way organic life is, as it were, cobbled together out of bits and pieces some of which work, but often only just." The thumb of the panda, highlighted in Gould's 1981 American Book Award-winning essay collection *The Panda's Thumb: More Reflections in Natural History,* particularly demonstrates this. Not really a thumb at all, the offshoot on the panda's paw is actually an enlarged wristbone that enables the panda to strip leaves from bamboo shoots. "If one were to design a panda from scratch, one would not adapt a wrist bone to do the job of a thumb," observes *Times Literary Supplement* reviewer D. M. Knight. An imperfection, the appendage "may have been fashioned by a simple genetic change, perhaps a single mutation affecting the timing and rate of growth."

Gould's writings emphasize science as a "culturally embedded" discipline. "Science is not a heartless pursuit of objective information," he told the *New York Times Book Review,* "it is a creative human activity." Raymond A. Sokolov, in the same publication, remarks that Gould's "method is at bottom, a kind of textual criticism of the language of earlier biologists, a historical analysis of their 'metaphors,' their concepts of the world." Gould frequently examines science as the output of individuals working within the confines of specific time periods and cultures. In a *New Yorker* review of *The Flamingo's Smile,* John Updike writes of "Gould's evangelical sense of science as an advancing light,

[which] gives him a vivid sympathy with thinkers in the dark." Updike continues: "Gould chastens us ungrateful beneficiaries of science with his affectionate and tactile sense of its strenuous progress, its worming forward through fragmentary revelations and obsolete debates, from relative darkness into relative light. Even those who were wrong win his gratitude." Sue M. Halpern notes in *Nation*: "Gould is both a scientist and a humanist, not merely a scientist whose literary abilities enable him to build a narrow-bridge between the two cultures in order to export the intellectual commodities of science to the other side. [His writing] portrays universal strivings, it expresses creativity and it reveals Gould to be a student of human nature as well as one of human affairs."

Gould also demonstrates instances where science, by factually "verifying" certain cultural prejudices, has been misused. *The Flamingo's Smile* contains several accounts of individuals victimized as a result of cultural prejudices used as scientific knowledge, such as the "Hottentot Venus," a black southern African woman whose anatomy was put on public display in nineteenth-century Europe, and Carrie Buck, an American woman who was legally sterilized in the 1920s because of a family history of mentally "unfit" individuals. And in his award-winning *The Mismeasure of Man,* Gould focuses on the development of IQ testing and debunks the work of scientists purporting to measure human intelligence objectively. "This book," writes Gould, "is about the abstraction of intelligence as a single entity, its location within the brain, its quantification as one number for each individual, and the use of these numbers to rank people in a single series of worthiness, invariably to find that oppressed or disadvantaged groups—races, classes or sexes—are innately inferior and deserve their status." Halpern points out a theme that runs throughout Gould's work: "Implicit in Gould's writing is a binding premise: while the findings of science are themselves value-free, the uses to which they are put are not."

In a *London Review of Books* essay on *Hen's Teeth and Horse's Toes: Further Reflections in Natural History,* John Hedley Brooke summarizes some of the major themes that appear in Gould's writings: "The 'fact' of evolution is 'proved' from those imperfections in living organisms which betray a history of descent. The self-styled 'scientific creationists' have no leg to stand on and are simply playing politics. Natural selection must not be construed as a perfecting principle in any strong sense of perfection. Neo-Darwinists who look to adaptive utility as the key to every explanation are as myopic as the natural theologians of the early 19th century who saw in the utility of every organ the stamp of its divine origin." Citing yet another recurrent theme, Brooke notes Gould's focus on "the extent to which the course of evolution has been constrained by the simple fact that organisms inherit a body structure and style of embryonic development which impose limits on the scope of transformation." This last principle has been enhanced by Gould's field work with the Bahamian land snail genus *Cerion,* a group that displays a wide variety of shapes, in addition to a permanent growth record in its shell. "More orthodox evolutionists would assume that the many changes of form represent adaptations," notes James Gleick in the *New York Times Magazine.* "Gould denies it and finds explanations in the laws of growth. Snails grow the way they do because there are only so many ways a snail *can* grow."

Wonderful Life: The Burgess Shale and the Nature of History focuses on the fossil-rich remains discovered in a small area in the Canadian Rockies in 1909. The organisms preserved there display a much greater diversity than fossils sites from later eras, and their meaning has been hotly debated ever since their discovery. Gould chronicles the early studies of the Burgess Shale, then offers his own speculations on what the fossils reveal. In the process, he discredits the long-held notion that evolution is inevitably a progression toward higher and increasingly perfect life forms. Reviewing *Wonderful Life* in *New Statesman & Society*, Steven Rose relates: "Far from being the mechanism of ordered transformation along a great chain of being towards adaptive perfection, evolution is a lottery in which winners and losers are determined by forces over which they have little control. Nearly everything is possible; what survives, including ourselves, confirms the truth that nothing in biology makes sense except in the context of history." High praise for *Wonderful Life* also comes from Robin McKie, who writes in the *Observer* that Gould's "book is written with such clarity and breathtaking leaps of imagination that it successfully moulds a mass of detail and arcane taxonomy into a lucid and highly entertaining whole." McKie takes exception to Gould's contention that biologists have purposely presented evolution in anthropomorphic terms, yet he concludes that "*Wonderful Life* remains a masterly scientific explanation" of the Burgess Shale and evolution in general.

In essay collections that include *Eight Little Piggies: Reflections in Natural History, Bully for Brontosaurus: Reflections in Natural History,* and *Dinosaur in a Haystack: Reflections in Natural History,* Gould has upheld the standards of accessibility and scientific integrity he set in earlier books. "What makes Gould so good?" Robert Kanigel asks in the *Washington Post Book World*. The critic goes on to answer his own question: "Each of these 31 essays draws us into a cozy little world where we are left in intimate touch with Gould's heart and mind. Gould is one part Harvard intellectual, nine parts curious little boy; that's one element of his distinctive appeal. For another, he has a commanding knowledge of his discipline, evolutionary biology, and the fields, like geology and paleontology, that flank it. He doesn't have to parade it around; but he has so much to draw upon, and does." Kanigel further lists Gould's characteristic technique of beginning with some odd fact and proceeding from there to sweeping insights as another special charm, along with his delight in interesting digressions. "This is a feast," declares Bryan C. Clarke in his *Nature* commentary on *Eight Little Piggies,* citing the work as "a lovely mixture of bizarre facts, nice arguments, clever insights into the workings of evolution and a quality of writing that can make your skin prickle."

While some reviewers have commented that Gould's writings display a repetition of key principles and themes—in critiquing *Hen's Teeth and Horse's Toes,* Brooke remarks that "the big implications may begin to sound familiar"—Gould earns consistent praise for the range of subjects through which he illustrates evolutionary principles. "Gould entices us to follow him on a multifaceted Darwinian hunt for answers to age-old questions about ourselves and the rest of the living world," writes John C. McLoughlin in the *Washington Post Book World*. "Like evolution itself, Gould explores possibilities—any that come to hand—and his range of interest is stupendous. . . . Throughout, he displays with force and elegance the power of evolutionary theory to link the phenomena of the living world as no other theory seems able." Steven Rose writes in the *New York Times Book Review*: "Exploring the richness of living forms, Mr. Gould, and we, are constantly struck by the absurd ingenuity by which fundamentally inappropriate parts are pressed into new roles like toes that become hooves, or smell receptors that become the outer layer of the brain. Natural selection is not some grandiose planned event but a continual tinkering. . . . Mr. Gould's great strength is to recognize that, by demystifying nature in this way, he increases our wonder and our respect for the richness of life."

In the *New York Times Book Review* article on *Full House: The Spread of Excellence from Plato to Darwin,* David Papineau states that Gould's "central contention is that trends, in any area, should never be considered in isolation, but only as aspects of an overall range of variation (the 'full house' of the title)." In terms of evolution, this means that the mechanism of natural selection does not always progress toward greater complexity; in fact, according to Gould, it is just as likely to run toward simplicity. Gould bases this argument on "a very clear statistical insight. . . . The first is his own experience as a statistic, when he was a cancer patient. The second is an extended analysis of the disappearance of .400 batters in major league baseball," states Lucy Horwitz in the *Boston Book Review,* who concludes that Gould's argument is "convincing" and "elegantly presented."

Questioning the Millenium focuses on three questions: "What does the millennium mean? When does a millennium arrive Why are we interested in it and other divisions of time?" Gould uses "wit and style" to "launch an inquiry into the human 'fascination with numerical regularity'" and to seek this regularity "as one way of ordering a confusing world." Michiko Kakutani states in the *New York Times* that the book "is not one of Mr. Gould's more important books, but . . . it beguiles and entertains, even as it teaches us to reconsider our preconceptions about the natural world."

BIOGRAPHICAL/CRITICAL SOURCES:

PERIODICALS

America, May 24, 1986.
Antioch Review, spring, 1978.
Boston Book Review, March 1, 1997.
Chicago Tribune, December 2, 1981; January 20, 1988.
Chicago Tribune Book World, November 30, 1980; June 26, 1983.
Christian Science Monitor, July 15, 1987.
Detroit News, May 22, 1983.
Economist, May 16, 1987.
Listener, June 11, 1987.
London Review of Books, December 1, 1983.
Los Angeles Times, June 2, 1987.
Los Angeles Times Book Review, July 17, 1983; November 29, 1987.
Nation, June 18, 1983; November 16, 1985.
Natural History, January, 1988.
Nature, November 19, 1987.
New Republic, December 3, 1977; November 11, 1981.
Newsweek, November 9, 1981; August 1, 1983.
New Yorker, December 30, 1985.
New York Review of Books, June 1, 1978; February 19, 1981; October 22, 1981; May 28, 1987.
New York Times, October 17, 1987; November 11, 1997, p. E8.
New York Times Book Review, November 20, 1977; September 14, 1980; November 1, 1981; May 8, 1983; September 22, 1985; December 7, 1986; September 11, 1987; November 15, 1987; January 21, 1996, p. 9; September 22, 1996, p. 9; November 9, 1997, p. 9.
New York Times Magazine, November 20, 1983.
Observer, February 18, 1990, p. 57.
People, June 2, 1986.
Rolling Stone, January 15, 1987.
Science, May, 1983.
Time, May 30, 1983; September 30, 1985.

Times Literary Supplement, May 22, 1981; February 10, 1984;
　　October 25, 1985; June 6, 1986; September 11-17, 1987.
Voice Literary Supplement, June, 1987.
Washington Post Book World, November 8, 1981; May 8, 1983;
　　September 29, 1985; April 26, 1987.

*　　　*　　　*

GOURMONT, Remy(-Marie-Charles) de 1858-1915 (M. Coffe, N. le Danois, J. Drexelius; L'Ymagier, a joint pseudonym)

PERSONAL: Born April 4, 1858, in Bazouches-en-Houlme, Orne,
Normandy, France; died of a cerebral hemorrhage following a
stroke, September 27, 1915; son of Auguste-Marie (the Comte de
Gourmont), and Mathilde (de Montfort) de Gourmont. *Education:*
Attended Lycee Coutances, 1868-76, and graduated from University of Caen, Normandy, 1879. *Religion:* "Catholic turned
skeptic."

CAREER: Poet, critic, journalist and author, 1882-1915. Member
of staff, Bibliotheque Nationale, Paris, France, 1881-91.

WRITINGS:

En ballon, A. Degorce-Cadot (Paris), 1884, and Librairie generale
　　de vulgarisation (Paris), 1884.
Merlette (novel), [Paris], 1886.
Les Francais au Canada et en Arcadie, Firmin-Didot (Paris),
　　1888.
*Chez les lapons: moeurs, coutumes et legendes de la Laponie
　　norvegienne,* Firmin-Didot, 1890.
Sixtine: Roman de la vie cerebrale (novel), A. Savine (Paris),
　　1890, translation published as *A Very Woman,* translated by
　　J. L. Barrets, N. L. Brown (New York City), 1922.
Theodat (play), first produced at Theatre Moderne, Paris, 1891,
　　published in Paris, 1893, translation published as *Theodat,
　　the Old King,* 1916.
Lilith (play), [Paris], 1892, published in *Poet Lore,* 1945.
Fleurs de jadis (poems), [Paris], 1893.
Le fantome (novel), [Paris], 1893.
Histoires magiques, [Paris], 1894.
Proses moroses (short stories), published in 1894, Bibliotheque
　　artistique et litteraire (Montpellier), 1979.
*Le latin mystique: les poetes de l'antiphonaire et la symbolique au
　　moyen age* (criticism), Mercure de France (Paris), 1895,
　　AMS Press (New York City), 1981.
Le pelerin du silence (novel), [Paris], 1896.
Le livre des masques (criticism), Mercure de France, 1896,
　　translation by Jack Lewis published as *The Book of Masks,*
　　introduction by Ludwig Lewisohn, J.W. Luce (Paris), 1921.
Le vieux roi (play), [Paris], 1897.
Les chevaux de Diomede (novel), Mercure de France, 1897,
　　translation by C. Sartoris published as *The Horses of
　　Diomedes,* J.W. Luce, 1923.
Le songe d'une femme (novel), [Paris], 1899, translation by Lewis
　　Galantiere published as *The Dream of a Woman,* Boni and
　　Liveright (New York City), 1927.
*Esthetique de la langue francaise: la deformation, la metaphore,
　　le cliche, le vers libre, le vere populaire,* Societe du Mercure
　　de France (Paris), 1899.
La culture des idees, Societe du Mercure de France, 1900,
　　translation by William Aspenwall Bradley published as
　　Decadence and Other Essays on the Culture of Ideas,
　　Harcourt, Brace (New York City), 1921.

Oraisons mauvaises (poems), [Paris], 1900.
Simone: poeme champetre (poems), [Paris], 1901.
Le chemin de velours: nouvelles dissociations de'idees (criticism),
　　Mercure de France, 1902.
Le probleme du style (criticism), [Paris], 1902.
Physique de l'amour, [Paris], 1903, translation and postscript by
　　Ezra Pound published as *The Natural Philosophy of Love,*
　　Boni and Liveright, 1931, and G. Routledge (London), 1931,
　　and with an introduction by Burton Rascoe and decorations
　　by G. T. Hartmann, Liveright, 1932, published as *The
　　Physiology of Love,* Rarity Press (New York City), 1932.
Promenades litteraires (criticism), 7 volumes, Mercure de France,
　　1904-27.
Promenades philosophiques, 3 volumes, Mercure de France,
　　1905-09.
Un nuit au Luxembourg (novel), [Paris], 1906, translation
　　published as *A Night in the Luxembourg,* preface and
　　appendix by Arthur Ransome, S. Swift (London), 1912,
　　Modern Library (New York City), 1926.
Un coeur virginal (novel), [Paris], 1907, translation by Aldous
　　Huxley published as *A Virgin Heart,* N.L. Brown, 1921.
Couleurs (short stories), [Paris], 1908, translation and two
　　supplementary colours by Frederic Reeves Ashfield pub-
　　lished as *Colours,* Blue Faun (New York City), 1929,
　　published as *Colors,* Panurge Press (New York City), 1931.
*Nouveaux dialogues des amateurs sur les choses du temps 1907-
　　1910* (essays), Mercure de France, 1910.
Divertissements (poems), [Paris], 1912.
Lettres d'un satyre, [Paris], 1913, translation by John Howard,
　　published as *Mr. Antiphilos, Satyr,* introduction by Jack
　　Lewis, Lieber and Lewis (New York City), 1922.
La petite ville: paysages, [Paris], 1913.
Lettres a l'Amazone (letters), [Paris], 1914, translation and
　　introduction by Richard Aldington published as *Letters to the
　　Amazon,* Chatto and Windus (London), 1931.
Pendant l'orage (essays), E. Champion (Paris), 1915.
La Belgique litteraire, G. Cres (Paris), 1915.
Dans la tourmente, preface by Jean de Gourmont, [Paris], 1916.
Pendant la guerre: lettres pour l'Argentine (letters), preface by
　　Jean de Gourmont, Mercure de France, 1917.
Les idees du jour, [Paris], 1918.
Monsieur Croquant, illustrated by Raoul Dufy, [Paris], 1918.
Litanies de la rose, ouvrage illustre et decore par Andre Domin,
　　Editions R. Kiefer (Paris), 1919.
La patience de Griseledis, illustrations by P. A. Moras, Editions
　　du "Sagittaire" (Paris), 1920.
Les pas sur le sable, published in 1919, translation published as
　　Epigrams of Remy de Gourmont, selected by Isaac Goldberg,
　　Haldeman-Julius (Girard, KS), 1923.
Pensees inedites, Imprime par A. Jourde pour le compte de
　　Editions de la Sirene (Paris), 1920.
*Philosophic Nights in Paris, Being Selections from Promenades
　　philosophiques,* translation by Isaac Goldberg, J.W. Luce,
　　1920, Books for Libraries Press (Freeport, NY), 1969.
Remy de Gourmont: Dust for Sparrows (poems), translation by
　　Ezra Pound published in the *Dial,* 1920-21.
Lettres a Sixtine (letters), Mercure de France, 1921.
Petits crayons, [Paris], 1921.
*Dante, Beatrice et la poesie amoureuse: essai sur l'ideal feminin
　　en Italie a la fin du xiii siecle,* Mercure de France, 1922.
Le vase magique (essays), [Paris], 1923.
L'ombre d'une femme (play), [Paris], 1923.
Journal intime, [Paris], edited by Jean de Gourmont, 1923.
Dernieres pensees inedites, E. Champion (Paris), 1924.

Nouvelles dissociations, Editions du siecle (Paris), 1925.

Les femmes et le language, [Paris], 1925.

La fin de l'art, Les cahiers de Paris (Paris), 1925.

Deux poetes de la nature: Bryant et Emerson, La Centaine (Paris), 1925.

Le joujou et trois autres essais, [Paris], 1926.

Lettres intime a l'Amazone (letters), Mercure de France, 1927.

Le joujou patriotisme (essay), Les Editions de la Belle page, 1927.

Remy de Gourmont: Selections from All His Works, selected and translated by Richard Aldington, illustrated with photographs, drawings, and woodcuts by Andre Rouveyre, P. Covici (Chicago), 1928.

Selected Writings (essays and criticism), translated and edited by Glenn S. Burne, University of Michigan Press (Ann Arbor), 1966.

Rimes retrouvees (poems), Editions du Fourneau (Bannes, Marne), 1979.

Lettres a l'amazone; suivi de Lettres intimes a l'amazone, Mercure de France, 1988.

The Angels of Perversity, translation by Francis Amery, Dedalus/Hippocrene, 1992.

Also author of *Un volcan en eruption,* 1882, *Une ville ressuscitee,* 1882, *Bertrand du Guesclin,* 1883, *Tempetes et naufrages,* 1883, *Les derniers jours de Pompei,* 1884, *Les Canadiens de France,* 1893, *Le Chateau singulier,* 1894, *Histoire tragique de la princesse Phenissa,* 1894, *Phocas,* 1894, and *Almanach de l'Ymagier,* 1897; author of the six volume collection of essays *Epilogues: reflexions sur la vie,* 1903-13; author of the poetry volumes *Litanies de la rose,* 1892, *Hieroglyphes,* 1894, and *Les saints du paradis,* 1898; author of the short story volume *D'un pays lointain,* 1898; author of the criticism volume *Le deuxieme livre des masques,* 1898; author of the unpublished novel *Patrice*; author of *Chronique stendhalienne,* under pseudonym M. Coffe, and of *Le chat de mysere.* Author of *Stories in Green, Zinzinolin, Rose Purple, Mauve, Blue and Orange,* 1924, and *Stories in Yellow, Black, White, Blue, Violet, and Red.* Contributor to small magazines, often under pseudonyms M. Coffe, N. le Danois, J. Drexelius, and L'Ymagier. Founder (with Alfred Vallette and Henri de Regnier) and contributor, *Mercure de France,* 1889-1915.

SIDELIGHTS: Remy de Gourmont, wrote the Italian critic Giovanni Papini in his *Four and Twenty Minds,* "was the most intelligent man in France, and one of the keenest intellects in the whole world. His brain was an instrument of precision. His thought had the lucidity of distilled alcohol, as clear as water of a mountain spring, yet drawn from purple clusters, and carrying the inebriation, the vertigo, the wild fancy of a year's experience compressed into a single hour." Gourmont was a critic and journalist as well as a novelist, poet, and playwright whose works helped establish the Symbolist movement in French literature. Amy Lowell, Ezra Pound, and T. S. Eliot were among the poets and writers of a later generation that he influenced. "M. de Gourmont," observed a reviewer in a 1903 edition of the *Saturday Review,* "aims at evoking the atmosphere of the imaginary world of which, for the time, he has been an inhabitant, not only through his words, but before a page has been read, or before the book has been opened."

Gourmont was born into the minor French nobility in the mid-nineteenth century. His father was a Norman count who had his son educated at the University of Caen in Normandy. After graduating, Gourmont moved to Paris, where he found a position as a librarian in the Bibliotheque Nationale in 1881. Around this time he became intimate with the exotic Berthe de Courriere, a *parisienne* who introduced the young man to black magic, occultism, and oriental religions. She also introduced him to a number of literary friends, including the prominent Decadent novelist Joris-Karl Huysmans. The Decadent movement prefigured the work of the Symbolist movement and shared several characteristics with it, including a taste for the exotic and rampant individualism. In conjunction with two other Symbolists, Alfred Valette and Henri de Regnier, Gourmont founded the prominent Symbolist journal *Mercure de France* in 1889. Gourmont contributed to every issue of the periodical until his death in 1915.

The function of *Mercure de France,* as Gourmont and his co-founders conceived it, was to confront the contemporary French intellectual and artistic establishment. One of Gourmont's earliest contributions was the long essay "Le joujou patriotisme," published in the *Mercure* in April, 1891 (and as a book in 1927), in which he mocked the anti-German sentiment that passed for patriotism in contemporary France. He claimed that France and Germany could be allies and partners if it were not for the false patriotism and militarism of the French. The establishment took offense at Gourmont's remarks, and on April 28, 1891, he was fired from his position at the Bibliotheque Nationale. He was also blacklisted by many of the major French publishers. Retreating from public life, he became a recluse, living in seclusion and rarely seeing even his literary friends. Part of the reason for Gourmont's retreat may have been an attack of lupus, a disfiguring disease from which he suffered for the rest of his life.

Later Symbolists celebrated Gourmont's position and influence through his own writings. American poet Amy Lowell wrote in her *Six French Poets* in 1915 that Gourmont's second novel, "*Sixtine,* came out in 1890. Its second title was *Roman de la vie cerebrale,* and that might stand as subtitle for all his work. Oh, the delightful book that *Sixtine* is! I remember reading it in a sort of breathless interest. The hero is a writer, and everything that happens to him he translates almost bodily into his work. Two stories are carried on at the same time, the real one and the one he is writing. The chapters follow each other with no regular order, the reader only knows which story is which by the context." Richard Aldington, editor of the influential journal *The Egotist* and first husband of the poet Hilda Doolittle, stated in the periodical *The Drama,* "He is the synthesis of a great period of intellectual activity (1885-1914), inferior perhaps to some of his contemporaries in their own particular sphere, but superior to them all in the width of his interests and in the diversity of his accomplishments. If he was not supreme in any one branch of literary creation, there exists none in which he has not achieved fine, sometimes magnificent, work." "Gourmont arouses the senses of the imagination, preparing the mind for receptivities," stated poet Ezra Pound in his study *Make It New.* "His wisdom, if not of the senses, is at any rate via the senses. We base our 'science' on perceptions, but our ethics have not yet attained this palpable basis."

Gourmont expressed his adherence to the basic precepts of Symbolism in many works, including the critically acclaimed *Book of Masks.* "Remy de Gourmont, like all the very great critics—Goethe, Ste. Beuve, Hazlitt, Jules Lemaitre—knew the creative instinct and exercised the creative faculty," commented the critic Ludwig Lewisohn in his introduction to Gourmont's *The Book of Masks.* "All that we have to contribute to mankind, what is it but just—our selves? . . . This, in brief, is the critical theory of Gourmont," Lewisohn informed, "this is the background of that startling and yet, upon reflection, so clear and necessary saying of his: 'The only excuse a man has for writing is that he express himself, that he reveal to others the kind of world reflected in the mirror of his soul; his only excuse is that he be original.'"

BIOGRAPHICAL/CRITICAL SOURCES:

BOOKS

Aldington, Richard, *Remy de Gourmont, a Modern Man of Letters,* University of Washington Press (Seattle, WA), 1928.

Burne, Glenn S., *Remy de Gourmont: His Ideas and Influence in England and America,* Southern Illinois University Press, 1963.

Dantzig, Charles, *Remy de Gourmont: cher vieux Daim!* Editions du Rocher (Monaco), 1990.

Escoube, Paul, *Remy de Gourmont et son oeuvre,* Mercure de France (Paris), 1921.

Galletti, Marina, *La nascita della linguistica e Remy de Gourmont,* Bulzoni (Rome), 1985.

Goruppi, Tiziana, *Remy de Gourmont: L'idea dell'intelletuale e la crisi del romanzo,* Pacini Editori (Pisa), 1989.

Lewisohn, Ledwig, introduction to *The Book of Masks* by Remy de Gourmont, translated by Jack Lewis, J.W. Luce (Paris), 1921.

Lowell, Amy, *Six French Poets: Studies in Contemporary Literature,* 1915.

Papini, Giovanni, *Four and Twenty Minds,* edited and translated by Ernest Hatch Wilkins, Thomas Y. Crowell, 1922.

Pound, Ezra, *Make It New,* Scholarly Press, Inc., 1971, pp. 251-333.

Sieburth, Richard, *Instigations: Ezra Pound and Remy de Gourmont,* Harvard University Press (Cambridge, MA), 1978.

Twentieth-Century Literary Criticism, Volume 17, Gale, 1985.

Voivenel, Paul, *Remy de Gourmont vu par son medecin: essai de physiologie litteraire,* Cepadues editions (Toulouse), 1979.

PERIODICALS

Drama, May, 1916, pp. 167-83.

Saturday Review, November 28, 1903, pp. 675-76.

*   *   *

GOYTISOLO, Juan 1931-

PERSONAL: Born January 5, 1931, in Barcelona, Spain; immigrated to France, 1957. *Education:* Attended University of Barcelona and University of Madrid, 1948-52.

CAREER: Writer. Worked as reporter in Cuba, 1965; associated with Gallimard Publishing Co., France. Visiting professor at universities in the United States.

AWARDS, HONORS: Received numerous awards for *Juegos de Manos*; Premio Europalia, 1985.

WRITINGS:

NOVELS

Juegos de manos, Destino, 1954, recent edition, 1975, translation by John Rust published as *The Young Assassins,* Knopf, 1959.

Duelo en el paraiso, Planeta, 1955, Destino, 1981, translation by Christine Brooke-Rose published as *Children of Chaos,* Macgibbon & Kee, 1958.

El circo (title means "The Circus"), Destino, 1957, recent edition, 1982.

Fiestas, Emece, 1958, Destino, 1981, translation by Herbert Weinstock published as *Fiestas,* Knopf, 1960.

La resaca (title means "The Undertow"), Club del Libro Espanol, 1958, J. Mortiz, 1977.

La isla, Seix Barral, 1961, translation by Jose Yglesias published as *Island of Women,* Knopf, 1962 (published in England as *Sands of Torremolinos,* J. Cape, 1962).

Senas de identidad, J. Mortiz, 1966, translation by Gregory Rabassa published as *Marks of Identity,* Grove, 1969.

Reivindicacion del Conde don Julian, J. Mortiz, 1970, Catedra, 1985, translation by Helen R. Lane published as *Count Julian,* Viking, 1974.

Juan sin tierra, Seix Barral, 1975, translation by Lane published as *Juan the Landless,* Viking, 1977.

Makbara, Seix Barral, 1980, translation by Lane published as *Makbara,* Seaver Books, 1981.

Paisajes despues de la batalla, Montesinos, 1982, translation by Lane published as *Landscapes after the Battle,* Seaver Books, 1987. *Quarantine,* translated by Peter Bush, Dalkey Archive Press, 1994.

Also author of novels *Las virtudes del parajo solitario,* 1988, published as *The Virtues of the Solitary Bird,* 1993; and *La cuarentena,* 1991.

SHORT STORIES

Para vivir aqui (title means "To Live Here"), Sur, 1960, Bruguera, 1983.

Fin de fiesta: Tentativas de interpretacion de una historia amorosa, Seix Barral, 1962, translation by Yglesias published as *The Party's Over: Four Attempts to Define a Love Story,* Weidenfeld & Nicolson, 1966, Grove, 1967.

TRAVEL NARRATIVES

Campos de Nijar, Seix Barral, 1960, Grant & Cutler, 1984, translation by Luigi Luccarelli published as *The Countryside of Nijar* in *The Countryside of Nijar* [and] *La chanca,* Alembic Press, 1987.

La Chanca, Libreria Espanola, 1962, Seix Barral, 1983, translation by Luccarelli published in *The Countryside of Nijar* [and] *La chanca,* Alembic Press, 1987.

Pueblo en marcha: Instantaneas de un viaje a Cuba (title means "People on the March: Snapshots of a Trip to Cuba"), Libreria Espanola, 1963.

Cronicas sarracinas (title means "Saracen Chronicles"), Iberica, 1982.

OTHER

Problemas de la novela (literary criticism; title means "Problems of the Novel"), Seix Barral, 1959.

Las mismas palabras, Seix Barral, 1963.

Plume d'hier: Espagne d'aujourd'hui, compiled by Mariano Jose de Larra, Editeurs francais reunis, 1965.

El furgon de cola (critical essays; title means "The Caboose"), Ruedo Iberico, 1967, Seix Barral, 1982.

Spanien und die Spanien, M. Bucher, 1969.

(Author of prologue) Jose Maria Blanco White, *Obra inglesa,* Formentor, 1972.

Obras completas (title means "Complete Works"), Aguilar, 1977.

Libertad, libertad, libertad (essays and speeches), Anagrama, 1978.

(Author of introduction) Chukri, Mohamed, *El pan desnudo* (title means "For Bread Alone"), translation from Arabic by Abdellah Djibilou, Montesinos, 1982.

Coto vedado (autobiography), Seix Barral, 1985, translation by Peter Bush published as *Forbidden Territory: The Memoirs of Juan Goytisolo,* North Point Press, 1989.

(Author of commentary) Omar Khayyam, *Estances,* translation into Catalan by Ramon Vives Pastor, del Mall, 1985.

Contracorrientes, Montesinos, 1985.

En los reinos de taifa (autobiography; title means "Realms of Strife: The Memoirs of Juan Goytisolo, 1956-1982"), Seix Barral, 1986.

Space in Motion (essays), translation by Lane, Lumen Books, 1987.

Also author of *Disidencias* (essays), 1977. Work represented in collections and anthologies, including *Juan Goytisolo,* Ministerio de Cultura, Direccion General de Promocion del Libro y la Cinematografia, 1982. Contributor to periodicals.

SIDELIGHTS: "Juan Goytisolo is the best living Spanish novelist," wrote John Butt in the *Times Literary Supplement.* The author, as Butt observed, became renowned as a "pitiless satirist" of Spanish society during the dictatorship of Francisco Franco, who imposed his version of conservative religious values on the country from the late 1930s until his death in 1975. Goytisolo, whose youth coincided with the rise of Franco, had a variety of compelling reasons to feel alienated from his own country. He was a small child when his mother was killed in a bombing raid, a casualty of the civil war that Franco instigated to seize power from a democratically elected government. The author then grew up as a bisexual in a country dominated, in Butt's words, by "frantic machismo." Eventually, said Goytisolo in his memoir *Coto Vedado (Forbidden Territory),* he became "that strange species of writer claimed by none and alien and hostile to groups and categories." In the late 1950s, when his writing career began to flourish, he left Spain for Paris and remained in self-imposed exile until after Franco died.

The literary world was greatly impressed when Goytisolo's first novel, *Juegos de manos (The Young Assassins),* was published in 1954. David Dempsey found that it "begins where the novels of a writer like Jack Kerouac leave off." Goytisolo was identified as a member of the Spanish "restless generation" but his first novel seemed as much akin to Fedor Dostoevski as it did to Kerouac. The plot is similar to Dostoevski's *The Possessed:* a group of students plot the murder of a politician but end up murdering the fellow student chosen to kill the politician. Dempsey wrote, "Apparently, he is concerned with showing us how self-destructive and yet how inevitable this hedonism becomes in a society dominated by the smug and self-righteous."

Duelo en el paraiso (Children of Chaos) was seen as a violent extension of *The Young Assassins.* Like Anthony Burgess's *A Clockwork Orange* and William Golding's *Lord of the Flies, Children of Chaos* focuses on the terror wrought by adolescents. The children have taken over a small town after the end of the Spanish Civil War causes a breakdown of order.

Fiestas begins a trilogy referred to as "The Ephemeral Morrow" (after a famous poem by Antonio Machado). Considered the best volume of the trilogy, it follows four characters as they try to escape life in Spain by chasing their dreams. Each character meets with disappointment in the novel's end. Ramon Sender called *Fiestas* "a brilliant projection of the contrast between Spanish official and real life," and concluded that Goytisolo "is without doubt the best of the young Spanish writers."

El circo, the second book in "The Ephemeral Morrow," was too blatantly ironic to succeed as a follow-up to *Fiestas.* It is the story of a painter who manages a fraud before being punished for a murder he didn't commit. The third book, *La resaca,* was also a disappointment. The novel's style was considered too realistic to function as a fitting conclusion to "The Ephemeral Morrow."

After writing two politically oriented travelogues, *Campos de Nijar (The Countryside of Nijar)* and *La Chanca,* Goytisolo returned to fiction and the overt realism he'd begun in *La resaca.* Unfortunately, critics implied that both *La isla (Island of Women)* and *Fin de Fiesta (The Party's Over)* suffered because they ultimately resembled their subject matter. *The Party's Over* contains four stories about the problems of marriage. Although Alexander Coleman found that the "stories are more meditative than the full-length novels," he also observed, "But it is, in the end, a small world, limited by the overwhelming ennui of everything and everyone in it." Similarly, Honor Tracy noted, "Every gesture of theirs reveals the essence of the world, they're absolutely necessary, says another: we intellectuals operate in a vacuum. . . . Everything ends in their all being fed up."

Goytisolo abandoned his realist style after *The Party's Over.* In *Senas de identidad (Marks of Identity),* wrote Barbara Probst Solomon, "Goytisolo begins to do a variety of things. Obvious political statement, he feels, is not enough for a novel; he starts to break with form—using a variety of first, second and third persons, he is looking and listening to the breaks in language and . . . he begins to break with form—in the attempt to describe what he is really seeing and feeling, his work becomes less abstract." Robert J. Clements called *Marks of Identity* "probably his most personal novel," but also felt that the "most inevitable theme is of course the police state of Spain." Fusing experimentation with a firm political stance, Goytisolo reminded some critics of James Joyce while others saw him elaborating his realist style to further embellish his own sense of politics.

Reivindicacion del Conde don Julian (Count Julian), Goytisolo's next novel, is widely considered to be his masterpiece. In it, he uses techniques borrowed from Joyce, Celine, Jean Genet, filmmaker Luis Bunuel, and Pablo Picasso. Solomon remarked that, while some of these techniques proved less than effective in many of the French novels of the 1960s, "in the hands of this Spanish novelist, raging against Spain, the results are explosive." *Count Julian* is named for a legendary Spanish nobleman who betrayed his country to Arab invaders in the Middle Ages. In the shocking fantasies of the novel's narrator, a modern Spaniard living as an outcast in Africa, Julian returns to punish Spain for its cruelty and hypocrisy. Over the course of the narration, the Spanish language itself gradually transforms into Arabic. Writing in the *New York Times Book Review,* Carlos Fuentes called *Count Julian* "an adventure of language, a critical battle against the language appropriated by power in Spain. It is also a search for a new/old language that would offer an alternative for the future."

With the publication of *Juan sin tierra (Juan the Landless),* critics began to see Goytisolo's last three novels as a second trilogy. However, reviews were generally less favorable than those for either *Marks of Identity* or *Count Julian.* Anatole Broyard, calling attention to Goytisolo's obsession with sadistic sex and defecation, remarked, "Don Quixote no longer tilts at windmills, but toilets." A writer for *Atlantic* suggested that the uninformed reader begin elsewhere with Goytisolo.

Even after the oppressive Franco regime was dismantled in the late 1970s, Goytisolo continued to write novels that expressed deep alienation by displaying an unconventional, disorienting view of human society. *Makbara,* for example, is named for the cemeteries of North Africa where lovers meet for late-night trysts. "What a poignant central image it is," wrote Paul West in *Washington Post Book World,* "not only as an emblem of life in death . . . but also as a vantage point from which to review the human antic in general, which includes all those who go about their daily chores with their minds below their belts." "The people [Goytisolo] feels at home with," West declared, "are the drop-outs and the ne'er do wells, the outcasts and the misfits." In *Paisajes despues de la batalla (Landscapes After the Battle),* the author moved his vision of alienation to Paris, where he had long remained in exile. This short novel, made up of seventy-eight nonsequential chapters, displays the chaotic mix of people—from French nationalists to Arab immigrants—who uneasily coexist in the city. "The Paris metro map which the protagonist contemplates . . . for all its innumerable permutations of routes," wrote Abigail Lee in the *Times Literary Supplement,* "provides an apt image for the text itself." *Landscapes* "looked like another repudiation, this time of Paris," Butt wrote. "One wondered what Goytisolo would destroy next."

Accordingly, Butt was surprised to find that the author's memoir of his youth, published in 1985, had a markedly warmer tone than the novels that had preceded it. "Far from being a new repudiation," Butt observed, *Forbidden Territory* "is really an essay in acceptance and understanding. . . . Gone, almost, are the tortuous language, the lurid fantasies, the dreams of violation and abuse. Instead, we are given a moving, confessional account of a difficult childhood and adolescence." Goytisolo's recollections, the reviewer concluded, constitute "a moving and sympathetic story of how one courageous victim of the Franco regime fought his way out of a cultural and intellectual wasteland, educated himself, and went on to inflict a brilliant revenge on the social system which so isolated and insulted him."

BIOGRAPHICAL/CRITICAL SOURCES:

BOOKS

Amell, Samuel, editor, *Literature, the Arts, and Democracy: Spain in the Eighties,* Fairleigh Dickinson University Press, 1990.
Contemporary Literary Criticism, Gale (Detroit), Volume 5, 1976; Volume 10, 1979; Volume 23, 1983.
Epps, Bradley S., *Significant Violence: Oppression and Resistance in the Later Narrative of Juan Goytisolo,* Clarendon (New York City), 1996.
Gazarian Gautier, Marie-Lise, *Interviews with Spanish Writers,* Dalkey Archive Press, 1991.
Pope, Randolph D., *Understanding Juan Goytisolo,* University of South Carolina Press (Columbia), 1995.
Schwartz, Kessel, *Juan Goytisolo,* Twayne, 1970.
Schwartz, Ronald, *Spain's New Wave Novelists 1950-1974: Studies in Spanish Realism,* Scarecrow Press, 1976.
Six, Abigail Lee, *Juan Goytisolo: The Case for Chaos,* Yale University Press, 1990.

PERIODICALS

Atlantic, August, 1977.
Best Sellers, June 15, 1974.
Journal of Spanish Studies, winter, 1979, pp. 353-64.
Lettres Peninsulares, fall-winter, 1990, pp. 259-78.
Library Journal, October 1, 1990, p. 89; March 1, 1994, p.117.
Los Angeles Times Book Review, January 22, 1989.
Nation, March 1, 1975.

New Republic, January 31, 1967.
New Statesman & Society, December 17, 1993, p. 46.
New York Times Book Review, January 22, 1967; May 5, 1974; September 18, 1977; June 14, 1987; July 3, 1988; February 12, 1989.
Publishers Weekly, March 7, 1994, p. 55.
Saturday Review, February 14, 1959; June 11, 1960; June 28, 1969.
Texas Quarterly, spring, 1975.
Times Literary Supplement, May 31, 1985; September 9, 1988; May 19, 1989; November 17, 1989.
Washington Post Book World, January 17, 1982; June 14, 1987.
World Press Review, April, 1994. p. 51.

*   *   *

GRAHAM, Tom
See LEWIS, (Harry) Sinclair

*   *   *

GRAHAME, Kenneth 1859-1932

PERSONAL: Born March 8, 1859, in Edinburgh, Scotland; died of a cerebral hemorrhage, July 6, 1932, in Pangbourne, England; buried in Holywell Churchyard, Oxford; son of J. C. (a lawyer) and Bessie Grahame; married Elspeth Thomson, 1899; children: Alistair. *Education:* Educated in London, England.

CAREER: Bank of England, London, 1878-1907, began as clerk, became secretary of the bank, 1898; writer.

MEMBER: New Shakespeare Society.

AWARDS, HONORS: Lewis Carroll Shelf Award, 1958, for *The Wind in the Willows,* and 1963, for *The Reluctant Dragon.*

WRITINGS:

CHILDREN'S FICTION

The Golden Age (includes "A Holiday," "Alarums and Excursions," and "The Whitewashed Uncle"), Stone & Kimball, 1895, new edition illustrated by Maxfield Parrish, John Lane, 1900.
Dream Days (sequel to *The Golden Age*; includes "The Reluctant Dragon," "The Magic Ring," and "Saga of the Seas"), John Lane, 1898, new edition illustrated by Maxfield Parrish, 1902.
The Reluctant Dragon (excerpt from *Dream Days*; also see below), illustrated by Ernest H. Shepard, Holiday House, 1938.
The Wind in the Willows, Scribner, 1907, new edition illustrated by Paul Bransom, 1913.
The Kenneth Grahame Book (contains *The Golden Age, Dream Days,* and *The Wind in the Willows*), Methuen, 1932.
The First Whisper of "The Wind in the Willows" (includes correspondence and story "Bertie's Escapade"), edited by wife, Elspeth Grahame, Methuen, 1944, Lippincott, 1945.
Bertie's Escapade, illustrated by Ernest H. Shepard, Lippincott, 1949.
The River Bank and Other Stories From The Wind in the Willows, illustrated by Inga Moore, Candlewick Press (Cambridge, MA), 1996.

Works all published in new editions featuring various illustrators. Some excerpts published in various self-contained volumes. Work represented in anthologies.

OTHER CHILDREN'S BOOKS

(Editor) Eugene Field, *Lullaby-Land: Songs of Childhood,* illustrated by John Lawrence, Scribner, 1897.

(Editor) *The Cambridge Book of Poetry for Children* (two volumes), illustrated by Maude Fuller, Putnam, 1916, revised edition illustrated by Gwen Ravverat, Cambridge University Press, 1932, Putnam, 1933.

My Dearest Mouse: "The Wind in the Willows" Letters, Pavilion, 1988.

FOR ADULTS

Pagan Papers (essays; includes "The Lost Centaur," "Orion," "The Rural Pan," and "The Olympians"), Elkin Mathews and Lane, 1893, Stone & Kimball, 1894.

The Headswoman (stories), Bodley Head, 1898, new edition illustrated by Marcia Lane Foster, John Lane, 1921.

(Author of introduction) *Lord George Sanger, Seventy Years a Showman,* Dent, 1926, introduction published separately as *Fun o' the Fair,* Dent, 1929.

The Kenneth Grahame Day Book, edited by Margery Coleman, Methuen, 1937.

Paths to the River Bank: The Origins of "The Wind in the Willows," edited by Peter Haining, Souvenir Press, 1983.

Contributor to periodicals, including *National Observer, St. James Gazette,* and *Yellow Book.*

MEDIA ADAPTATIONS: Portions of *The Wind in the Willows* have been adapted for the stage by A. A. Milne as *Toad of Toad Hall* (adaptation published by Scribner, 1929), and for film by John Hench as *The Adventures of Mr. Toad* (adaptation published by Simon & Schuster, 1949); screenwriter Romeo Muller's adaptation of the entire work was filmed as a television musical (songs by Maury Laws and Jules Bass), American Broadcasting Company (ABC-TV), 1985. *The Reluctant Dragon* was filmed in 1938. Numerous other adaptations also exist in various audio and/ or visual forms.

SIDELIGHTS: Kenneth Grahame is author of the beloved children's book *The Wind in the Willows,* which recounts the adventures of such popular characters as Mr. Toad, Rat, and Mole. Grahame is known for the sensitivity with which he writes about childhood. He claimed to remember everything between the ages of four and seven and, consequently, that age group became his favorite audience. Margaret B. McDowell, writing in *Dictionary of Literary Biography,* restated the author's belief that "a child . . . should have a 'secret kingdom' within his mind in which to live when under stress or when bored by the rest of the world." McDowell added that Grahame insisted "only children between ages four and seven have the full ability to develop imaginatively, because they constantly view the detail of life with . . . 'wonderment.'"

Grahame himself had an unhappy childhood. He was born in 1859 in Scotland. His mother died of scarlet fever when he was only five years old. Grahame, too, contracted the disease, which left him with a lasting bronchial ailment. After his mother's death, Grahame and his siblings were surrendered by their father, an alcoholic, to Grahame's maternal grandmother. This woman, however, was hardly more devoted to the children, and Grahame often withdrew into fantasies and daydreams.

In his youth Grahame aspired to academic study, but an unsympathetic uncle—who controlled the family finances—refused to fund his continued schooling. Grahame was thus compelled to find work, and in 1876 he began working as a clerk for that same uncle. In 1878 Grahame left his uncle's office and assumed a clerk's position at the Bank of England. He held that post for the next ten years, then worked briefly in the chief cashier's office before settling in the secretary's office, where he remained until his retirement from the bank in 1907.

In 1887 Grahame's father died. Three years later Grahame began writing for various magazines and journals. In such essays as "The Lost Centaur" and "Orion" he extolled the need for people to regain their more animalistic aspects, which Grahame claimed were increasingly repressed as a result of the industrial revolution. In another essay, "The Rural Pan," Grahame writes of the mythical pagan god—half man, half goat—whom he perceived as the embodiment of human/animal unification. In "The Rural Pan," the pagan creature appears as a storyteller haunting countryside pubs and inns.

Grahame's tales and essays were collected in 1893 as *Pagan Papers,* to only a mixed critical reception. But one reader, *National Observer* editor William Ernest Henley, was impressed with the book, particularly the "The Olympians," a retrospective appraisal of childhood. Henley encouraged Grahame to further develop this perspective.

Grahame accepted Henley's advice and began producing a series of tales and vignettes about several orphans residing with uncaring relatives in a country house. In these accounts, adults (known as Olympians) and children, though residing together, live decidedly different lives. The adults are preoccupied with mundane matters, and the children thrive by indulging their imaginations. The perspective, however, is that of an adult recalling childhood, and the tone is often satiric, but it is never sentimental.

These new writings were collected in 1895 as *The Golden Age* and won Grahame his first widespread acclaim. Among the tales in this volume are "A Holiday," in which a child lets the wind dictate his own travels; "Alarums and Excursions," where a band of children pretends to be the Knights of the Round Table, then pursues an actual cavalry in hopes of seeing a bloody conflict; and "The Whitewashed Uncle," in which the children condemn an uncle for his apparent insincerity.

Popular with both children and adults, and with both British and American readers, *The Golden Age* established Grahame as a prominent new literary figure. "In *The Golden Age* [Grahame] has given us a book, a foursquare piece of literature, complete in itself," wrote a reviewer for *Academy.* "Many a literary man writes hard all his life, and never a book—in the best sense of the word—is forthcoming. Mr. Grahame made one the first time." Another reviewer, writing in *Bookman,* recommended *The Golden Age* to anyone interested in understanding how the world appears to children. The critic added: "Several of these stories are fine studies of the workings of a child's imagination, reproducing the very glamour in which the Golden Age is bathed."

Grahame continued his literary success with *Dream Days,* a sequel featuring the same characters—albeit slightly older—from the earlier *Golden Age.* Among the best-known tales in *Dream Days* is "The Reluctant Dragon," in which the monster of the St. George legend is characterized as a likeable creature. Roger Lancelyn Green later wrote in the *Junior Bookshelf* that "The Reluctant Dragon" constituted "perhaps the most perfect star in

Kenneth Grahame's crown: the jewel without any flaw." And Margaret Blount, in her book *Animal Land: The Creatures of Children's Fiction,* pronounced "The Reluctant Dragon" a "near-perfect story." Other notable tales in *Dream Days* are "The Magic Ring," about a first visit to the circus; and "Saga of the Seas," where the children play as pirates.

Critics lauded *Dream Days* as another successful and unique evocation of childhood. A critic for *Athenaeum* noted the various sketches are "well written" and added that "the book is full of quaint things." A *Bookman* reviewer welcomed the book as another opportunity to visit the characters of Grahame's earlier work. "Our old friends of the Golden Age are all here," the critic declared, "as full of life and fancy and rebellion as ever." And another *Bookman* reviewer, writing in 1922, affirmed, "There is no book about children like *The Golden Age,* unless it is [*Dream Days*]."

In the early 1900s Grahame was still reaping the benefits of *The Golden Age* and *Dream Days,* which sustained their popularity with reprints featuring works of accomplished illustrator Maxfield Parrish. By this time Grahame was a family man, having married Elspeth Thomson in 1899 and fathering a son, Alistair, the following year. Grahame was deeply fond of Alistair, who was born with substantially impaired vision (blindness in one eye; partial blindness in the other). Beginning on Alistair's fourth birthday, Grahame would regale his son at bedtime with a series of tales involving Mr. Toad, Mole, and Rat, and other characters who, though animals, nonetheless behave as humans. Young Alistair was quite fond of Grahame's tales, which continued as letters when the child was vacationing seaside.

Grahame eventually committed the entire series of stories to print and published them in 1907 as *The Wind in the Willows.* This highly episodic work recounts the various escapades of the aforementioned animal creatures. It begins with Mole conducting the spring cleaning of his hovel, after which he discovers a river. There he befriends the gregarious Rat, who acquaints Mole with the pleasures of water life. They also meet the asocial Badger, who nonetheless occasionally comes to their rescue. Perhaps most engaging of the book's character is Mr. Toad, a devil-may-care fellow who flees from home in a stolen car and is eventually captured by the authorities and imprisoned. He escapes, though, and slowly finds his way back to his ancestral home, Wild Wood, which he is forced to rid of squatters, including weasels and ferrets.

With its vivid characters and amusing episodes, *The Wind in the Willows* is considered a classic of children's literature. A critic prophesied as much in 1908 by writing in the *New York Times Saturday Review,* "This book is not easily classified—it is simply destined to be one of those dog-eared volumes which one laughs over and loves." Other critics at the time found *The Wind in the Willows* a wise and poignant, though continually engaging work. In the ensuing years, it has sustained that stature. Another children's writer, A. A. Milne, hailed it in his *Not That It Matters* as an endearing, beloved work, one "which is read aloud to every new guest, and is regarded as the touchstone of his worth." And Frank Swinnerton, writing in his volume *Tokefield Papers: Old and New,* remarked, "To read *The Wind in the Willows* is to be very profoundly amused, to have the mind set free for unlimited speculation, and to be brought . . . to dreamland itself."

Marriage to the moderately wealthy Elspeth Thompson, together with the success of *The Wind in the Willows,* had enabled Grahame to resign from the Bank of England, where he last served as secretary, in 1907. In the ensuing years, though, he wrote little, preferring to live quietly, and at his death in 1932 he was still best remembered as the author of *The Wind in the Willows* and, to a lesser extent, *The Golden Age* and *Dream Days.* But these works, particularly *The Wind in the Willows,* still hold considerable literary prominence, and it is likely that Grahame will remain an author beloved by young and old alike, for his achievement remains unique. "Most writers and most people find that when they have tossed off adult tasks and human curses they have, left over only a rather empty space," wrote Roger Sale in his *Fairy Tales and After: From Snow White to E. B. White.* "But Grahame could fill that space and invite us into the charmed circle he thereby created. He could make little sounds seem like bustle, make gestures of invitation seem like love, make food and fire seem like home."

BIOGRAPHICAL/CRITICAL SOURCES:

BOOKS

Blount, Margaret, *Animal Land: The Creatures of Children's Fiction,* Morrow, 1975, p. 119.
Children's Literature Review, Volume 5, Gale (Detroit), 1983, pp. 109-36.
Dictionary of Literary Biography, Volume 34: *British Novelists, 1890-1929: Traditionalists,* Gale, 1985, pp. 181-89.
Milne, A. A., *Not That It Matters,* Methuen, 1927.
Prince, Alison, *Kenneth Grahame: An Innocent in the Wild Wood,* Alison and Busby, 1995.
Sale, Roger, *Fairy Tales and After: From Snow White to E. B. White,* Harvard University Press, 1978, pp. 190-93.
Swinnerton, Frank, *Tokefield Papers: Old and New,* Hamish Hamilton, 1949, pp. 180-81.
Yesterday's Authors of Books for Children, Volume 1, Gale, 1977, pp. 144-53.

PERIODICALS

Academy, December 4, 1897, p. 493.
Athenaeum, February 4, 1899, p. 142.
Bookman, August-September, 1895, pp. 49-50; March, 1899, p. 187; December, 1922, p. 187; January, 1933, pp. 69-74.
Elementary English, December, 1968, pp. 1024-35.
Junior Bookshelf, March, 1959, pp. 54-55.
London Mercury, September, 1932, pp. 446-49.
New York Times Saturday Review, October 24, 1949, p. 593.

*   *   *

GRANT, Skeeter
See SPIEGELMAN, Art

*   *   *

GRASS, Guenter (Wilhelm) 1927-
(Artur Knoff)

PERSONAL: Born October 16, 1927, in the Free City of Danzig (now Gdansk, Poland); married Anna Schwarz in 1954; married Utte Grunert in 1979; children: (first marriage) Franz, Raoul, Laura, Bruno. *Education:* Attended Kunstakademie, Duesseldorf, Germany; attended Berlin Academy of Fine Arts, 1953-55. *Politics:* Social Democrat. *Religion:* Roman Catholic.

ADDRESSES: Home—Glockengiesserstrasse 21, 23552, Luebeck, Germany. *Office*—Niedstrasse 13, Berlin-Grunewald 41, Germany.

CAREER: Novelist, poet, playwright, graphic artist, and sculptor. Former farm laborer in the Rhineland; worked in potash mine near Hildesheim, Germany; black marketeer; apprentice stonecutter during the late 1940s, chiseling tombstones for firms in Duesseldorf, Germany; worked as a drummer and washboard accompanist with a jazz band. Speechwriter for Willy Brandt during his candidacy for the election of Bundeskanzler in West Germany. Visited the United States in 1964 and 1965, giving lectures and readings at Harvard University, Yale University, Smith College, Kenyon College, and at Goethe House and Poetry Center of YM and YWCA, New York, NY; writer in residence at Columbia University, 1966. Has exhibited his drawings, lithographs, and sculptures. *Wartime service:* Drafted into the German Army during World War II; aide with the Luftwaffe; prisoner of war in Marienbad, Czechoslovakia, 1945-46.

MEMBER: American Academy of Arts and Sciences, Berliner Akademie der Kuenste (president, 1983-86), Deutscher PEN, Zentrum der Bundesrepublik, Verband Deutscher Schriftsteller, Gruppe 47.

AWARDS, HONORS: Lyrikpreis, Sueddeutscher Rundfunk, 1955; prize from Gruppe 47, 1958; Bremen Literary Award, 1959; literary prize from the Association of German Critics, 1960; *Die Blechtrommel (The Tin Drum)* was selected by a French jury as the best foreign-language book of 1962; a plaster bust of Grass was placed in the Regensburger Ruhmestempel Walhalla, 1963; Georg Buechner Prize, 1965; Theodor Heuss Preis, 1969; Berliner Fontane Preis, 1969; *Local Anaesthetic* was selected as one of 1970's ten best books by *Time,* 1970; Carl von Ossiersky Medal, 1977; Premio Internazionale Mondello, Palermo, 1977; International Literatur Award, 1978; *The Flounder* was selected as one of 1978's best books of fiction by *Time,* 1979; Antonio Feltrinelli Award, 1982; awarded distinguished service medal from the Federal Republic of Germany (but Grass declined to accept award), 1980; honorary doctorates from Harvard University and Kenyon College.

WRITINGS:

Die Vorzuege der Windhuehner (poems, prose, and drawings; title means "The Advantages of Windfowl"; also see below), Luchterhand, 1956, 3rd edition, 1967.

(Author of text) *O Susanna: Ein Jazzbilderbuch: Blues, Balladen, Spirituals, Jazz,* Kiepenheuer & Witsch, 1959.

Die Blechtrommel (novel; also see below), Luchterhand, 1959, translation by Ralph Manheim published as *The Tin Drum,* Vintage Books, 1962.

Gleisdreieck (poems and drawings; title means "Rail Triangle"), Luchterhand, 1960.

Katz und Maus (novella; also see below), Luchterhand, 1961, translation by Manheim published as *Cat and Mouse,* Harcourt, 1963.

Hundejahre (novel; also see below), Luchterhand, 1963, translation by Manheim published as *Dog Years,* Harcourt, 1965.

Rede ueber das Selbstverstaendliche (speech), Luchterhand, 1965.

(Illustrator) Ingeborg Buchmann, *Ein Ortfuer Zufaelle,* Wagenbach, 1965.

Dich singe ich, Demokratie, Luchterhand, 1965.

Fuenf Wahlreden (speeches; contains Was ist des Deutschen Vaterland?, Loblied auf Willy, Es steht zur Wahl, Ich klage an, and Des Kaisers neue Kleider), Nuewied (Berlin), 1965.

Selected Poems (in German and English; includes poems from *Die Vorzuege der Windhuehner* and *Gleisdreieck;* also see below), translations by Michael Hamburger and Christopher Middleton, Harcourt, 1966, published as *Poems of Guenter Grass,* Penguin, 1969.

Ausgefragt (poems and drawings; title means "Questioned") Luchterhand, 1967.

Der Fall Axel C. Springer am Beispiel Arnold Zweig: Eine Rede, ihr Anlass, und die Folgen, Voltaire Verlag, 1967.

New Poems (includes poems from *Ausgefragt;* also see below), translation by Hamburger, Harcourt, 1968.

Ueber das Selbstverstaendliche: Reden, Aufsaetze, offene Briefe, Kommentare (title means "On the Self-Evident"; also see below), Luchterhand, 1968, revised and supplemented edition published as *Ueber das Selbstverstaendliche: Politische Schriften,* Deutscher Taschenbuch-Verlag 1969.

Briefe ueber die Grenze: Versuch eines Ost-West-Dialogs by Guenter Grass and Pavel Kohout (letters), C. Wegner, 1968.

Ueber meinen Lehrer Doeblin und andere Vortraege (title means "About My Teacher Doeblin and Other Lectures"), Literarisches Collequium Berlin, 1968.

Guenter Grass: Ausgewaehlte Texte, Abbildungen, Faksimiles, Bio-Bibliographie, edited by Theodor Wieser, Luchterhand, 1968, also published as *Portraet und Poesie,* 1968.

Kunst oder Pornographie? J. F. Lehmann, 1969.

Speak Out: Speeches, Open Letters, Commentaries (includes selections from *Ueber das Selbstverstaendliche: Reden, Aufsaetze, offene Briefe Kommentare*), translated by Manheim, Harcourt, 1969.

Oertlich betaeubt (novel), Luchterhand, 1969, translation by Manheim published as *Local Anaesthetic,* Harcourt, 1970.

Die Schweinekopfsuelze, Merlin Verlag, 1969.

Originalgraphik (poem with illustrations), limited edition, Argelander, 1970.

Gesammelte Gedichte ("Collected Poems"; also see below), introduction by H. Vormweg, Luchterhand, 1971.

Dokumente zur politischen Wirkung, edited by Heinz Ludwig Arnold and Franz Josef Goertz, Richard Boorherg, 1971.

Aus dem Tagebuch einer Schnecke, Luchterhand, 1972, translation by Manheim published as *From the Diary of a Snail,* Harcourt, 1973.

Mariazuehren Hommageamarie Inmarypraise, Bruckmann, 1973, bilingual edition with translation by Middleton published as *Inmarypraise,* Harcourt, 1974.

Liebe geprueft (poems), [Bremen], 1974.

Der Buerger und seine Stimme (title means "The Citizen and His Voice"), Luchterhand, 1974.

Guenter Grass Materialienbuch, edited by Rolf Geissler, Luchterhand, 1976.

Der Butt, Luchterhand, 1977, translation by Manheim published as *The Flounder,* Harcourt, 1978.

Denkzettel (title means "Note for Thought"), Luchterhand, 1978.

In the Egg and Other Poems (contains poems from *Selected Poems* and *New Poems*), translated by Hamburger and Middleton, Secker & Warburg, 1978.

Das Treffen in Telgte, Luchterhand, 1978, translation by Manheim published as *The Meeting at Telgte,* Harcourt, 1981.

Werkverzeichnis der Radierungen (catalogue), A. Dreher, 1979.

(With Volker Schlondorff) *Die Blechtrommel als Film,* Zweitausendeins, 1979.

(Contributor) *Danzig 1939: Treasures of a Destroyed Community,* Wayne State University Press, 1980.

Aufsaetze zur Literatur, 1957-1979 (title means "Essays on Literature, 1957-1979"), Luchterhand, 1980.

Danziger Trilogie (title means "Danzig Trilogy"; contains *Die Blechtrommel, Katz und Maus,* and *Hundejahre*), Luchterhand, 1980.

Kopfgeburten; oder Die Deutschen sterben aus, Luchterhand, 1980, translation by Manheim published as *Headbirths; or, The Germans Are Dying Out,* Secker & Warburg, 1982.

Zeichnen and Schreiben: Das bildnerische Werk des Schriftstellers Guenter Grass, Luchterhand, 1982, translation published as *Graphics and Writing,* Harcourt, 1983.

Kinderlied (poems and etchings; originally published in *Gesammelte Gedichte*), Lord John, 1982.

Zeichnungen und Texte, 1954-1977, Luchterhand, 1982, translation by Hamburger and Walter Arndt published as *Drawings and Words, 1954-1977,* Harcourt, 1983.

Ach, Butt!: Dein Maerchen geht boese aus, Luchterhand, 1983.

Radierungen und Texte, 1972-1982, Luchterhand, 1984, translation by Hamburger and others published as *Etchings and Words, 1972-1982,* Harcourt, 1985.

Widerstand lernen: Politische Gegenreden, 1980-1983 (title means "Learning Resistance: Political Countertalk"), Luchterhand, 1984.

On Writing and Politics: 1967-1983 (essays), translated by Manheim, Harcourt, 1985.

Geschenkt Freiheit, Akademie der Kuenste, 1985.

Die Raettin, Luchterhand, 1986, translation by Manheim published as *The Rat,* Harcourt, 1987.

Werkausgabe, ten volumes, edited by Volker Neuhaus, Luchterhand, 1987.

Die Gedichte 1955-1986, Luchterhand, 1988.

Zunge Zeigen, Luchterhand, 1988, translation by John E. Woods published as *Show Your Tongue,* Harcourt, 1989.

Deutscher Lastenausgleich: Wider das dumpfe Einheitsgebot; Reden und Gesprache, Texte zur Zeit, Aufbau, 1990.

Ein Schnappchen namens DDR: Letzte Reden vorm Glockengelaut, Luchterhand, 1990.

Skizzenbuch, Steidl, 1990.

Schreiben nach Auschwitz, Luchterhand, 1990.

Totes Holz, illustrated by Grass, Gottingen, 1990.

Two States—One Nation? Harcourt, 1990.

Ukenrufe: Eine Erzahlung, Gottingen, 1992.

The Call of the Toad, translation by Ralph Manheim, Harcourt, 1992.

Unkenrufe (title means "Toad Croaks," Gottingen, 1992.

In Kupfer, auf Stein: Das grafische Werk, edited by G. Fritze Margull, Steidl, 1994.

Cat and Mouse and Other Writings, Continuum (New York City), 1994.

Ein Weites Feld, Steidl, 1995.

(With Kenzaburo Oe) *Gestern, vor 50 Jahren: ein Deutsch-Japanischer Briefwechsel,* Steidl, 1995.

Die Deutschen und Ihre Dichter, Deutscher Taschenbuch Verlag, 1995.

Novemberland: Selected Poems, 1956-1993, Harcourt Brace (New York City), 1996.

Aesthetik Des Engagements, P. Lang, 1996.

Rede uber den Standort, Steidl, 1997.

PLAYS

Die boesen Koeche: Ein Drama in fuenf Akten (first produced in West Berlin in 1961; translation by A. Leslie Willson produced as *The Wicked Cooks* on Broadway at Orpheum Theatre, January 23, 1967), Luchterhand, 1982.

Hochwasser: Ein Stueck in zwei Akten (two acts; also see below), Suhrkamp, 1963, 4th edition, 1968.

Onkel, Onkel (four acts; title means "Mister, Mister"; also see below), Wagenbach 1965.

Die Plebejer proben den Aufstand: Ein deutsches Trauerspiel (also see below; first produced in West Berlin at Schiller Theatre, January 15, 1966), Luchterhand, 1966, translation by Manheim published as *The Plebeians Rehearse the Uprising: A German Tragedy* (produced in Cambridge, MA, at the Harvard Dramatic Club, 1967), Harcourt, 1966.

The World of Guenter Grass, adapted by Dennis Rosa, produced off-Broadway at Pocket Theatre, April 26, 1966.

Hochwasser [and] *Noch zehn Minuten bis Buffalo* (title of second play means "Only Ten Minutes to Buffalo"; also see below), edited by Wilson, Appleton, 1967.

Four Plays (includes *The Flood* [produced in New York at Project III Ensemble Theater, June, 1986], *Onkel, Onkel,* [cited in some sources as "Mister, Mister"], *Only Ten Minutes to Buffalo,* and *The Wicked Cooks*), Harcourt, 1967.

Davor: Ein Stuck in dreizehn Szenen (also see below), first produced in West Berlin at Schiller Theatre, February 16, 1969, translation by Wilson and Manheim produced as *Uptight* in Washington, DC, at Kreeger Theatre, March 22, 1972, published as *Davor: Ein Stuck in dreizehn Szenen,* Harcourt, 1973 translation published as *Max: A Play,* Harcourt, 1972.

Theaterspiele (includes *Hochwasser, Onkel, Onkel, Die Plebejer proben den Aufstand,* and *Davor*; first produced in West Berlin at the German Opera, 1970), Luchterhand, 1970.

Other plays include *Beritten hin und zurueck* (title means "Rocking Back and Forth"), *Goldmaeulchen,* 1964, and *Zweiunddreizig Zaehne.*

OTHER

Also collaborator with Jean-Claude Carriere, Volker Schlondorff and Franz Seitz on screenplay for film adaptation of *Katz und Maus,* released by Modern Art Film, 1967. Author of material for catalogues to accompany his art work. Work represented in anthologies, including *Deutsche Literatur seit 1945 in Einzeldarstellunger,* edited by Dietrich Weber, Kroener, 1968. A recording of selected readings by the author, *oertlich betaeubt,* has been produced by Deutsche Grammophon Gesellschaft, 1971. Editor with Heinrich Boell and Carola Stern, *L-80.* Author of foreward, *Seventeenth Century German Prose,* Hans J. von Grimmelshausen, Continuum, 1992.

MEDIA ADAPTATIONS: Die Blechtrommel (*The Tin Drum*) was filmed and released by New World Pictures, April, 1980 and won several awards, including the Golden Palm Award from the Cannes Film Festival and an Oscar for the best foreign picture from the Academy of Motion Picture Arts and Sciences, both 1980.

SIDELIGHTS: Guenter Grass, together with such other authors as Heinrich Boell, Uwe Johnson, and Martin Walser, represents a generation of post-World War II German writers, all of whom joined an informal workshop named Group 47. When, in 1955, Grass first attended a meeting of this group, at the invitation of its founder Hans Werner Richter, he had no other literary credentials than a third prize from a radio network poetry contest. But his verse was well received by the members of Group 47, and the following year Grass published his first volume, a slim book of drawings and poetry entitled *Die Vorzuege der Windhuehner* (*The Advantages of Windfowl*). While this collection of apparently surrealistic poems and fine-lined drawings of oversized insects was hardly noticed at the time (an English translation of certain of its poems was first published in *Selected Poems* in 1965), it contains the seed of much of his future work. To this day, Grass's specific kind of creative imagination can be identified as the graphic and plastic arts combined with lyric inspiration. As Kurt Lothar Tank writes in *Guenter Grass:* "One thinks of Paul Klee when one takes . . . lines in this volume of poetry and, instead of actually reading them, visualizes them. One feels with tender fervor the gaiety, light as a dream with which the poet nourishes the windfowl of his own invention that lend wings to his creative act."

In 1958 Grass won the coveted prize of Group 47 for a reading from his manuscript *Die Blechtrommel* (*The Tin Drum*), published the following year. This book transformed the author into a controversial international celebrity. Grass commented on the inspiration for and evolution of the book, which he wrote while living with his wife in a basement apartment in Paris, in a 1973 radio lecture, "Retrospective on 'The Tin Drum' or 'The Author as Questionable Witness'" (reprinted in *Guenter Grass Materialienbuch*). He said that while he was travelling in France in 1952 and constantly occupied with drawing and writing, he conceived a poem whose protagonist was a "Saint on a Column" and who, from this "elevated perspective," would describe life in the village. But, later, tiny Oskar Matzerath, the tin-drummer, became the exact reverse of a pillar-dweller. By staying closer to the earth than normal, the protagonist of *The Tin Drum* acquired a unique point of view. Presumably it took not merely an adventurer in imagination but also a student of sculpture and drawing (as Grass had been since 1948 at the academies of Duesseldorf and Berlin) to discover this unusual perspective.

The viewpoint of a precocious three-year-old allowed Grass an honest insider's approach to the problem that all the writers of Group 47 were struggling with: the task of coming to grips with the overwhelming experience of World War II, with what had led up to it, and with what had followed in its wake as "economic miracle." In January of 1963, shortly before *The Tin Drum* was published in the United States, a writer for *Time* pronounced Grass's work the "most spectacular example" of recent German literature "trying to probe beneath the surface prosperity to the uneasy past." The reviewer called Grass, whose *Tin Drum* was winning prizes and stirring anger all over Europe, "probably the most inventive talent to be heard from anywhere since the war" and described his central character, Oskar, as "the gaudiest gimmick in his literary bag of tricks. . . . For Oskar is that wildly distorted mirror which, held up to a wildly deformed reality, gives back a recognizable likeness." Two decades later, while reviewing Grass's latest volume, John Irving wrote in *Saturday Review:* "In the more than 20 years since its publication, *Die Blechtrommel*—as it is called in German—has not been surpassed; it is the greatest novel by a living author."

In Germany, reaction to Grass's bestselling novel ranged from critical endorsement to moral outrage. Characteristic of the honors and scandals surrounding the book was the literature prize of Bremen, voted by the jury but withheld by the city senate on moral grounds. Similar charges against Grass's writings took the form of law suits in 1962, were repeated with political overtones on the occasion of the Buechner Prize award in 1965, and continued as confrontations with the Springer Press and others.

The formidable task of coming to grips with his country's past, however, is not something Grass could accomplish in one novel no matter how incisive. By 1963 when *The Tin Drum* appeared in the United States, he had published a second volume of poetry and

drawings, *Gleisdreieck* (*Rail Triangle*); a novella, *Katz und Maus* (translated as *Cat and Mouse*); and another novel of epic dimensions, *Hundejahre* (translated as *Dog Years*). The drawings and poems of *Gleisdreieck* (which are translated in *Selected Poems* and in *In the Egg and Other Poems*) make up a volume of more imposing format than Grass's first poetry collection and clearly show his development from a playful style obsessed with detail to a bolder, more encompassing form of expression.

In the novella *Cat and Mouse,* set as is *The Tin Drum* in the region around the city of Danzig, the central focus and, with it, a sense of guilt are diverted from the first person narrator, Pilenz, to Mahlke, his high school friend. Mahlke's protruding adam's apple causes his relentless pursuit of the Iron Cross—never referred to by name—with which he intends to cover up his "mouse." But in the end the narrator, who has set up the cat-and-mouse game, can no longer fathom the depth of his friend's fatal complex nor his own role in it.

The years from the prewar to the postwar era are presented in *Dog Years* through the perspective of three different narrators, a team directed by Amsel, alias Brauxel, who makes scarecrows in man's image. The seemingly solid childhood friendship of Amsel and Matem evolves into the love-hate relationship between Jew and non-Jew under the impact of Nazi ideology. When the former friends from the region of the Vistula finally meet again in the west, the ominous Fuehrer dog, who followed Matem on his odyssey, is left behind in Brauxel's subterranean world of scarecrows. While *Dog Years,* like *The Tin Drum,* again accounts for the past through the eyes of an artist, the artist is no longer a demonic tin-drummer in the guise of a child but the ingenious maker of a world of objects reflecting the break between the creations of nature and those of men. Referring to Amsel's "keen sense of reality in all its innumerable forms," John Reddick writes in *The Danzig Trilogy of Guenter Grass:* "Any serious reader of Grass's work will need little prompting to recognize that Grass is in fact describing his own, as well as his persona's art."

In 1961, well into his *Tin Drum* fame, Grass revealed at a meeting of theater experts in Hamburg that, departing from his early poetry he had written four long plays and two one-act plays during "the relatively short time, from 1954 to 1957." Not all of the plays to which he referred had been staged or published at that time; some, like *Onkel, Onkel* (*Mister, Mister*), appeared later in revised editions. Grass's earliest plays, *Beritten hin und zurueck* (*Rocking Back and Forth*) and *Noch zehn Minuten bis Buffalo* (*Only Ten Minutes to Buffalo*), have clearly programmatic character. They stage diverse attitudes about approaches to drama or poetry. As presentations of Grass's "poetics" they belong in the same category as his important early essays, "Die Ballerina" ("The Ballet Dancer") of 1956 and "Der Inhalt als Widerstand" ("Content as Resistance") of 1957.

Die boesen Koeche (*The Wicked Cooks*), written in 1956 in Paris and initially performed in 1961 in Berlin, is Grass's first play to have been staged in the United States (New York, 1967). In 1961 Martin Esslin had included discussion of Grass's early dramatic works in *The Theatre of the Absurd.* But in 1966 Peter Spycher argued in a *Germanisch-Romanische Monatsschrift* article that, at least in the case of *The Wicked Cooks,* the criteria of absurdist theater do not apply. In the play a team of five restaurant cooks find their reputations threatened by the popular "Gray Soup" cooked on occasion by a guest referred to as "the Count." The play revolves around the intrigues of the cooks to obtain the Count's soup recipe. They even try to trade him a nurse, the girlfriend of one of them, in return for the secret. Unfortunately for the cooks, the Count and the nurse fall in love, and when the cooks invade their idyllic existence, the Count shoots both the woman and himself. Spycher justifiably sees the play as an "allegorical parable" or "anti-tale," for the Count assures the cooks that "it is not a recipe, it's an experience, a living knowledge, continuous change."

Grass's initial limited success as a playwright took on the dimensions of a scandal with the 1966 production in Berlin of *Die Plebejer proben den Aufstand: Ein deutsches Trauerspiel* (*The Plebeians Rehearse the Uprising*), subtitled *A German Tragedy*. Andrzej Wirth in his essay for *A Guenter Grass Symposium* explains why this "semi-documentary" drama, based on the 1953 workers' revolt in Berlin, provoked a negative reaction in that city: "In Berlin's Schiller Theater Grass's *Plebeians* tested Bertolt Brecht's credibility *vis a vis* the Uprising. The outcome of this test was a negative one. The Boss [of the play] was a Versager [failure], a Hamletic victim of his own theorems which confused his insights of reality. . . . And the Berlin audience interpreted the play as a challenge to Brecht's image, as a case of Guenter Grass versus Bertolt Brecht." However, as Wirth continues, "the American premiere of *The Plebeians Rehearse the Uprising* (1967) in the Harvard Dramatic Club presented an interesting alternative." Due to the English translation and certain changes in the staging, "the play succeeded in exposing a more universal theme—the dilemma of the artist: the aesthetic man versus the man of action, ideal versus reality." Although "the play was thus more impoverished than embellished," it could arrive at such an interpretation.

Grass's third volume of poetry and drawings, *Ausgefragt* ("Questioned," selections translated in *New Poems*), reflects the political controversies of the 1960s. One cycle of poems in this volume is entitled "Indignation, Annoyance, Rage" and is inspired by the protest songs of the early sixties. Intoning the "powerlessness" of the guitar protesters, Grass points to the futility of their ritualistic peace marches. But the student protests gained momentum after 1966 and became a force to be reckoned with. Thus Grass's hope of engaging the protesters in constructive election activity was crushed by the demands of the new, increasingly radical Left. Within the literary developments of the 1960s, Grass's *New Poems,* which ranged in subject matter from the private to the public sphere, and from aesthetics to politics, have been described by H. Vormweg—in the introduction to Grass's *Gesammelte Gedichte* (*Collected Poems*)—as reality training. The perception of individual and social reality has been exceptional in German literature, and as Vormweg points out, Grass, in his poems, ignores the most obvious change in the literature of the late 1950s and 1960s. The new objective of literature, as reflected for example in "concrete poetry," has been to expose language itself as an unreliable medium, inadequate for identifying things and situations as they are. Grass, however, evinces a fundamental trust in language and its ability to communicate reality. In his *New Poems* he attempts to make perfectly visible the inescapable contradictions and conflicts of everyday life, including his own.

Grass's political essays of this period are collected in the volume *Ueber das Selbstverstaendliche* (translated as *On the Self-Evident*). The title comes from his acceptance speech for the prestigious Buechner Prize in 1965; in that year the Social Democrats had lost the elections, and Grass was dubbed a bad loser by critics of his speech. Another collection of his speeches, open letters, and commentaries from the 1960s is translated in the volume, *Speak Out!,* which also contains Grass's 1966 address—

"On Writers as Court Jesters and on Non-Existent Courts"—at the meeting of Group 47 in Princeton. While Grass's references to some of his writing colleagues and himself were rigorously criticized in Germany, the last statement of his Princeton speech became renowned: "A poem knows no compromise, but men live by compromise. The individual who can stand up under this contradiction and act is a fool and will change the world." Three more volumes of political essays and commentaries—*Der Buerger und seine Stimme* (*The Citizen and His Voice*), *Denkzettel* (*Note for Thought*) and *Widerstand lernen: Politische Gegenreden* (*Learning Resistance: Political Countertalk*)—show that Grass remained politically outspoken through the 1970s and 1980s.

In 1969, six years after *Dog Years,* Grass published another novel, *Oertlich betaeubt* (translated as *Local Anaesthetic*). For the first time he left the Danzig origins of his earlier prose works, concentrating instead on his new home town, the Berlin of the 1960s, and on the student protests against the Vietnam War. Starusch, a high school teacher, while undergoing extensive dental treatment, is confronted with the plan of his favorite student Scherbaum to set fire to his dog on Kurfuerstendamm. By this act the seventeen-year-old hopes to awaken the populace to the realities of the war. Yet in the end the dog is not burned, and the student is about to undergo a dental treatment similar to his teacher's.

The reception of this novel in Germany was predictably negative. War protest reduced to the level of a dachshund was conceived as belittlement of the real problems at hand. In the United States, however, *Local Anaesthetic* earned Grass some enthusiastic reviews and a *Time* cover story. The caption read, "Novelist between the Generations: A Man Who Can Speak to the Young." Perhaps the only problem with this hopeful statement was that "the young" didn't listen, nor did they read the book; they preferred Hesse's "Siddhartha." However, the *Time* essay provided a lucid interpretation of *Local Anaesthetic* while other reviewers of the book found it difficult to make the switch from the generous epic panorama of the "Danzig Trilogy" to the contemporary outrages of the 1960s.

However, a play preceding the book, *Davor,* was performed successfully as *Uptight* in Washington, DC, in 1972. (The English translation was published as *Max: A Play.*) The play, based on the dialectics of the middle part of *Local Anaesthetic,* portrays the conflicts among the three major characters and two of their female partners: the middle-aged, liberal but skeptical, teacher and his dentist who believe in talk to prevent action and the student who wants to act to the point of sacrificing his dog. The teacher's female colleague and the student's Maoist girlfriend provide, as Henry Hewes declares in his *Saturday Review* essay, "the more emotionally radical attitudes of the World War II and present generations."

From the Diary of a Snail contains his most openly autobiographical statements to date. It is also a diary recording his experience during Willy Brandt's election campaign of 1969 for the Social Democrats. Most important, however, this book marks a change of emphasis from politics to the more private occupation with the visual arts. Grass writes in the *Diary*: "It's true: I am not a believer; but when I draw, I become devout. . . . But I draw less and less. It doesn't get quiet enough any more. I look out to see what the clamor is; actually it's me that's clamoring and somewhere else." In the context of this self-portrait in the *Diary,* we also find revealing remarks about Grass's inspiration and technique as graphic artist: "I draw what's left over. . . . A rich, that is, broken line, one that splits, stutters in places, here passes over in silence, there thickly proclaims. Many lines. Also bordered spots. But sometimes niggardly in disbursing outlines."

The image of the snail indicates Grass's withdrawal into an increasingly meditative phase. Although he adopted the snail as his political emblem ("the snail is progress"), his entire field of vision is affected by it. The snail replaces one of the eyeballs in two self-portraits, etchings in copper produced in 1972. Moreover, the English version of the *Diary* contains a reproduction of Duerer's engraving "Melancolia I." The "Variations on Albrecht Duerer's Engraving" are summarized in a speech celebrating the Duerer anniversary of 1971 and appended to the *Diary*. The personifications of both "Melancholy" and her twin sister, "Utopia," are supplemented by a narrative on "Doubt," whose story provides an excursion into the past—a report to the children about the fate of the Jewish community of Danzig during the war. With the exception of this narrative thread, the *Diary* dispenses almost entirely with plot; yet the importance of this book in defining Grass's concerns and motivations has gradually become clear to critics of his work.

Around 1974 Grass again began work on a major novel. At first he referred to it as a "Cookbook." Already in *The Diary of a Snail* he had toyed with plans of writing "a narrative cookbook: about ninety-nine dishes, about guests, about man as an animal who can cook." At a later stage, the working title for the new novel was modified: "The (female) cook in me." At a still later stage the book was said to be a variation on the Grimms' tale of "The Fisherman and His Wife." When after numerous public readings, including one in New York, the work was published in August 1977, it was entitled *Der Butt* (translated as *The Flounder*) and comprised 699 pages of prose laced with forty-six poems.

The Flounder is structured around the nine months of a pregnancy and "nine or eleven" female cooks, each representing a major phase in prehistory and history from the neolithic to the present. The talking flounder functions as an archetypal male element, the tempter, who gradually destroys the mythic golden age of the matriarch. He is duly sentenced and punished by a group of feminists but will resume his destructive influence as future advisor and assistant to womankind instead of mankind. Clearly, the novel is purporting to correct some misconceptions about the roles of women in history and in the present. But the strength of this epic account lies not in its feminist argument but rather, as is usual with Grass, in its historical panorama. The setting for the mythical and historical events, all told by an ever-present first person narrator, is once again the Baltic shore around the mouth of the Vistula. The representation of major cultural phases and personages, through individual female characters who provide life and nourishment, accounts for much of the fascination the work exerts. In the context of historical settings and figures, many of the images Grass had etched in copper—the fishheads, the mushrooms, and the portraits of women—became dynamic agents of the narrative.

A majority of reviewers, including *New Yorker* contributor John Updike, feel that the richness of the "stew" demands too much digestion. They object to its length, its preoccupation with food and cooking, with sex and scatology. For some readers, Grass's cooks do not come across as real characters. Nigel Dennis in the *New York Review of Books* labels *The Flounder* "a very bad novel." Morris Dickstein, on the other hand, concludes in the *New York Times*: "Mr. Grass's cooks save him for they give body to his politics. . . . The cooks bring together Grass the novelist and Grass the socialist." With regard to the issue of feminism, *The Flounder* is labeled by Richard Howard in his *New Leader* review as both "an antifeminist tract" and "a feminist tract." In a more thorough study of *The Flounder* within the context of Grass's overall work, Michael Hollington speculates "that critical reaction to the book in English-speaking countries was short-sighted" and "that as the novel is digested its distinction will gradually be recognized." *Time* magazine listed *The Flounder* under "Best Fiction of 1978" and under "Editor's Choice" through May 1979.

In 1978, the year following the completion of *The Flounder,* Grass exercised a long-standing option. Since 1959 he had received numerous offers to film *The Tin Drum*. However as he declared in a June 1978 interview—reprinted in *"Die Blechtrommel": Tagebuch einer Verfilmung*—Franz Seitz received the right to film *The Tin Drum* only after he presented Grass with a written plan followed by a prize-winning screenplay. But it was his acquaintance with the director, Volker Schlondorff, that really won Grass over for work on the movie. Schlondorff found the ideal actor for Oskar Matzerath in the twelve-year-old David Brennent, and Grass heartily approved this choice. He worked closely with Schlondorff on dialogue, accompanied the team during the filming in Gdansk, and produced two portrait etchings of young David as the tin drummer. The movie won a Cannes film festival prize and also an American Oscar as best foreign film for 1979-1980. Richard Schickel wrote in *Time*: "From the interplay of literary conceit and hard-edged, artfully compressed observations of a very real world, [Schlondorff] has created a film that has the dislocating immediacy of a nightmare that anyone anywhere might conjure up."

In 1979 Grass published *Das Treffen in Telgte* (translated as *The Meeting at Telgte*). This relatively short narrative is dedicated to Hans Werner Richter, founder of Group 47, in honor of his seventieth birthday. *The Meeting at Telgte,* like *The Flounder,* employs historical material, but because of its compact action, provides more suspenseful reading. Set in 1647, the novel portrays some twenty historical German writers who undertake a fictitious journey to Westphalia because they wish to contribute their share to the peace negotiations toward the end of the devastating Thirty Years' War. Clearly, the situation parallels that of the writers of Group 47 after World War II. But the story is not a *roman a clef,* although several of the seventeenth-century writers in Grass's "meeting" have twentieth-century counterparts in Group 47. For example, the mischievous Gelnhausen, who becomes the author of the *Simplicissimus* epic, reflects certain traits of Grass himself, and Simon Dach functions as a seventeenth-century image of Richter. The iconography on the dust jacket, a human hand with a quill rising above a sea of rubble, may represent as wishful a dream for the modern age as it was for the seventeenth century. But its execution in *The Meeting at Telgte* produces a masterpiece, as *German Quarterly* contributor Richard Schade has shown, by means of the thistle and writer's hand imagery.

Described alternately as science fiction and fable, Grass's novel *The Rat* opens with a Christmas scene in which the protagonist—Grass himself—asks for and receives a rat as his present. As the rat observes Grass at work, the author becomes increasingly distracted until, eventually, the rat begins to tell a dream-like, prophetic tale about the extinction of the human race as a result of atomic war, followed by the survival of a race of rats. "This is not a book about what *may* happen; it is a novel, built on our profound need for fable, about what *has* happened to western civilization," asserts Eugene Kennedy in Chicago *Tribune Books*. Also offering praise for the novel, Richard Locke of *Washington Post Book*

World comments: "*The Rat* asks to be read as a kind of modern Book of Revelation, with Grass the St. John of our time, the delirious prophet of Apocalypse, a nuclear Big Bang that will end human life and leave the earth populated with rats feasting on radioactive human garbage." Unlike *The Rat,* Grass's novel *The Call of the Toad* received mixed reviews. *The Call of the Toad* depicts a couple who sell cemetery plots located in the Polish city of Gdansk to Germans who wish to be buried in their Polish homeland. While the business is successful, the couple becomes plagued by escalating greed and tyranny: "[what they] had envisioned as a peace-promoting, free-will enterprise becomes a symbol of German greed and tyranny in the wake of reunification," asserts Donna Rifkind of *Washington Post Book World.* Reviewers faulted the novel for a stylistic flatness, often commenting that Grass's characters lack depth and interest, despite the interesting intellectual premise of the book. Grass's novel *Ein Weites Feld* also generated controversy and skeptical reviews. Objecting to the novel's approach to the satirizing contemporary politics in Germany "in the harsh light of history," *Spectator* reviewer Christian Caryl notes that "the construction [of *Ein Weites Feld*] takes absolute precedence over the life of the characters. . . . Never before has [Grass] allowed his self-image as the Great German Writer to weigh so heavily on his style." The novel in fact draws upon the historical figure Theodore Fontane, a nineteenth-century writer who, like Grass himself, was skeptical of Germany's earlier unification. Contradicting Caryl, a critic for *The Economist Review* finds *Ein Weites Feld* "a perfect vehicle for tracing echoes and parallels across German writing and history."

With *Two States—One Nation?* Grass presents a collection of essays and speeches voicing his opposition to the unification of East and West Germany. Throughout the volume, Grass points to the atrocities of the Holocaust as evidence of the potentially destructive force of a powerful Germany motivated by national self-interest and fear: "German unity has so often proved a threat to our neighbors that we cannot expect them to put up with it anymore," he comments. While a reviewer for *Los Angeles Times Book Review* finds the collection "a challenging and disturbing book," J. P. Stern of *Observer* rejects Grass's arguments as "gripes and sour grapes" without foundation in terms of the contemporary social reality in Germany. The subject of German unification is also a focus of the essays and speeches collected in *On Writing and Politics: 1967-1983.* "Grass, as these speeches show, remains stubbornly loyal to his own vision of Europe, to a 'third force' notion of a continent which must liberate itself from Soviet and American hegemony and from the burden of their armaments," observes Neal Ascherson in *London Review of Books.* Grass also addresses larger political questions concerning the nature of political power on a global scale and the implications for the future of a world characterized by what Jon Cook of *New Statesman* calls "a pretense of democracy," in which "everything is done in the name of the popular will, but in reality crucial areas of decision-making are withheld from the difficult, democratic process of negotiating consent."

Novemberland: Selected Poems 1956-1993, a bilingual volume of Grass's poems, was published in 1996. The fifty-four poems, in German and translated into English, cover the tumultuous period of German history from World War II to the beginning of German reunification. *America* notes that "Grass's style is allegorical, or perhaps fable-esque; readers familiar and comfortable with a direct access to the poet in a 'confessional' mode may not always know what to do with these poems." Grass's personal connection with the material is not always clear, according to the reviewer, as the style is surrealistic and works against such direct connections.

For example, some poems include a lamentation over the ruins of Berlin, two bitten apples that recall Paradise, and prophetic glove at the beach. *Library Journal* comments that the poems treat many of the same motifs as his novels do, and that all relate to his fascination with Poland, Danzig, and recent German history.

BIOGRAPHICAL/CRITICAL SOURCES:

BOOKS

Contemporary Literary Criticism, Gale (Detroit), Volume 1, 1973; Volume 2, 1974; Volume 4, 1975; Volume 6, 1976; Volume 11, 1979; Volume 15, 1980; Volume 22, 1982; Volume 32, 1985; Volume 49, 1988; Volume 88, 1995.

Dictionary of Literary Biography, Gale, Volume 75: *Contemporary German Fiction Writers,* second series, 1988; Volume 124: *Twentieth-Century German Dramatists, 1919-1992,* 1992.

Diller, Edward, *A Mythic Journey: Guenter Grass's "Tin Drum,"* University Press of Kentucky, 1974.

Enright, D. J., *Man Is an Onion: Reviews and Essays,* Open Court, 1972.

Esslin, Martin, *Reflections: Essays on Modern Theatre,* Doubleday, 1960.

Esslin, Martin, *The Theatre of the Absurd,* Doubleday, 1961.

Hollington, Michael, *Guenter Grass: The Writer in a Pluralistic Society,* Marion Boyars, 1980.

Leonard, Irene, *Guenter Grass,* Oliver & Boyd, 1974.

Mason, Ann L., *The Skeptical Muse: A Study of Guenter Grass' Conception of the Artist,* Herbert Lang, 1974.

Mayer, Hans, *Steppenwolf and Everyman,* translated by Jack D. Zipes, Crowell, 1971.

Mews, Siegfried, editor, *Guenter Grass's "The Flounder" in Critical Perspective,* AMS Press, 1983.

Miles, Keith, *Guenter Grass,* Barnes & Noble, 1975.

Neuhaus, Volker, *Guenter Grass,* Metzler, 1979.

O'Neill, Patrick, *Guenter Grass: A Bibliography, 1955-1975,* University of Toronto Press, 1976.

Panichas, George, editor, *The Politics of Twentieth Century Novelists,* Hawthorn, 1971.

Reddick, John, *The Danzig Trilogy of Guenter Grass,* Harcourt, 1974.

Steiner, George, *Language and Silence,* Atheneum, 1967.

Tank, Kurt Lothar, *Guenter Grass,* 5th edition, Colloquium, 1965, translation by John Conway published as *Guenter Grass,* Ungar, 1969.

Thomas, Noel, *The Narrative Works of Guenter Grass,* John Benjamins, 1982.

Willson, A. Leslie, editor, *A Guenter-Grass Symposium,* University of Texas Press, 1971.

PERIODICALS

America, October 26, 1996, p. 26.
Atlantic, June, 1981, June, 1989.
Books Abroad, spring, 1972.
Chicago Review, winter, 1978.
Chicago Tribune, October 29, 1978; June 27, 1980.
Chicago Tribune Book World, May 10, 1981; March 21, 1982.
Commonweal, May 8, 1970.
Contemporary Literature, summer, 1973; winter, 1976.
Critique: Studies in Modern Fiction, number 3, 1978.
Detroit News, May 9, 1982.
Diacritics, number 3, 1973.
Dimension, summer, 1970.
Encounter, April, 1964; November, 1970.
German Quarterly, number 54, 1981; number 55, 1982.

Germanisch-Romanische Monatsschrift, number 47, 1966.

Harper's, December, 1978.

Journal of European Studies, September, 1979.

Library Journal, May 15, 1996, p. 65.

Literary Review, summer, 1974.

London Magazine, October, 1978.

London Review of Books, February 5-18, 1981, May 6-19, 1982; October 17, 1985, p. 6; October 17, 1996, p. 3.

Los Angeles Times, May 22, 1981, April 18, 1982, May 20, 1983, July 21, 1985; August 13, 1989; November 29, 1992.

Los Angeles Times Book Review, November 17, 1991, p. 14.

Michigan Quarterly Review, winter, 1975.

Modern Fiction Studies, spring, 1971; summer, 1986, p. 334.

Nation, December 23, 1978; April 24, 1982; December 24, 1990; November 16, 1992.

New Leader, October 29, 1973; December 4, 1978.

New Republic, June 20, 1970; April 14, 1982; July 13, 1987.

New Review, May, 1974,

New Statesman, June 7, 1974; June 26, 1981; September 20, 1985, p. 27; June 26, 1987.

New Yorker, April 25, 1970; October 15, 1973; November 27, 1978; June 14, 1982.

New York Review of Books, November 23, 1978; June 11, 1981; July 5, 1987; May 21, 1989; September 30, 1990; November 1, 1992.

New York Times, April 15, 1977; November 9, 1978; November 25, 1978; May 31, 1979; January 26, 1980; April 30, 1981; March 6, 1983; June 2, 1986.

New York Times Book Review, August 14, 1966; March 29, 1970; September 30, 1973; November 12, 1978; November 23, 1978; May 17, 1981; March 14, 1982; May 16, 1982; February 27, 1983; March 27, 1983; February 19, 1984; June 23, 1985; May 21, 1989, p. 12; September 30, 1990, p. 9; October 22, 1995, p. 47.

Observer, July 16, 1989, p. 43; October 14, 1990, p. 64.

San Francisco Review of Books, July/August, 1981.

Saturday Review, May 20, 1972; November 11, 1978; May, 1981; March, 1982.

Scala, number 6, 1981; number 1, 1982.

Spectator, May 18, 1974; January 27, 1996, p. 28.

Time, January 4, 1963; April 13, 1978; April 28, 1980; May 18, 1981; January 27, 1986.

Times (London), June 22, 1981; April 22, 1982; September 19, 1985.

Times Literary Supplement, October 13, 1978; September 26, 1980; June 26, 1981; April 23, 1982; October 13, 1995, p. 26.

Tribune Books (Chicago), May 21, 1989; November 15, 1992.

Village Voice, October 25, 1973.

Virginia Quarterly Review, spring, 1975.

Washington Post, March 2, 1972; April 10, 1982.

Washington Post Book World, September 23, 1973; November 5, 1978; August 9, 1981; August 11, 1985; July 12, 1987, p. 5; November 8, 1992, p. 6.

World Literature Today, spring, 1981; autumn, 1981; winter, 1986, p. 194; summer, 1995, p. 578; spring, 1996, p. 387.

GRAVES, Robert (von Ranke) 1895-1985
(John Doyle; Barbara Rich, a joint pseudonym)

PERSONAL: Born July 24, 1895, in London, England; died after a long illness, December 7, 1985, in Deya, Majorca, Spain; buried in village cemetery in Deya, Majorca, Spain; son of Alfred Perceval (an Irish poet and ballad writer) and Amalia (von Ranke) Graves; married Nancy Nicholson, 1918 (divorced, 1929); married Beryl Pritchard, 1950; children: (first marriage) Jenny, David, Catherine, Samuel; (second marriage) William, Lucia, Juan, Tomas. *Education:* Attended King's College School and Rokeby School, Wimbledon, Copthorne School, Sussex, Charterhouse School, Godalming, Surrey, 1907-14; St. John's College, Oxford, B.Litt., 1926. *Religion:* None.

CAREER: Egyptian University, Cairo, Egypt, professor of English literature, 1926; cofounder with Laura Riding of Seizin Press, 1928, and *Epilogue* semiannual magazine, 1935, coeditor with Riding of *Epilogue,* 1935-37; Clarke Lecturer, Trinity College, Cambridge University, 1954-55; lecturer in United States, 1958; Oxford University, Oxford, England, professor of poetry, 1961-65; lecturer in United States, 1966-67. Arthur Dehon Little Memorial Lecturer at Massachusetts Institute of Technology, 1963. *Military service:* Royal Welch Fusiliers, 1914-18; served in France; became captain.

MEMBER: American Academy of Arts and Sciences (honorary member).

AWARDS, HONORS: Bronze Medal for poetry at Olympic Games in Paris, 1924; James Tait Black Memorial Prize, 1935, for *I, Claudius* and *Claudius, the God and His Wife Messalina;* Hawthornden Prize, 1935, for *I, Claudius;* Femina-Vie Heureuse Prize and the Stock Prize, both 1939, for *Count Belisarius;* Russell Loines Memorial Fund Award, 1958; Gold Medal of Poetry Society of America, 1959; Foyle Poetry Prize, 1960; honorary M.A., Oxford University, 1961; Arts Council award, 1962; Italia Prize for radio play, 1965; Gold Medal for poetry at Cultural Olympics in Mexico City, 1968; Queen's Gold Medal for Poetry, 1969; honorary fellow of St. John's College, 1971; Sol de Oro Medal, Madrid, 1973.

WRITINGS:

POETRY

Over the Brazier, Poetry Bookshop, 1916.

Goliath and David, Chiswick Press, 1916.

Fairies and Fusiliers, Heinemann, 1917, Knopf, 1918.

The Treasure Box, Chiswick Press, 1919.

Country Sentiment, Knopf, 1920.

The Pier-Glass, Knopf, 1921.

The Feather Bed, L. and V. Woolf, 1923.

Whipperginny, Knopf, 1923.

Mock Beggar Hall, Hogarth Press, 1924.

Welchman's Hose, The Fleuron, 1925.

Robert Graves, Benn, 1925.

(Under pseudonym John Doyle) *The Marmosite's Miscellany,* Hogarth Press, 1925.

Poems, 1914-1926, Heinemann, 1927, Doubleday, Doran & Co., 1929.

Poems, 1914-1927, Heinemann, 1927.

Poems, 1929, Seizin Press, 1929.

Ten Poems More, Hours Press (Paris), 1930.

Poems, 1926-1930, Heinemann, 1931.

To Whom Else? Seizin Press, 1931.

Poems, 1930-1933, Barker, 1933.

Collected Poems, Random House, 1938.
No More Ghosts: Selected Poems, Faber, 1940.
(With Alan Hodge and Norman Cameron) *Work in Hand,* Hogarth, 1942.
Poems, 1938-1945, Creative Age Press, 1946.
Collected Poems, 1914-1947, Cassell, 1948.
Poems and Satires, Cassell, 1951.
Poems, 1953, Cassell, 1953.
Collected Poems, 1955, Doubleday, 1955.
Robert Graves: Poems Selected by Himself, Penguin Books, 1957.
The Poems of Robert Graves Chosen by Himself, Doubleday, 1958.
Collected Poems, 1959, Cassell, 1959, Doubleday, 1961, 3rd edition, Cassell, 1962.
The Penny Fiddle: Poems for Children, Cassell, 1960, Doubleday, 1961.
More Poems, 1961, Cassell, 1961.
Selected Poetry and Prose, edited, introduced, and annotated by James Reeves, Hutchinson, 1961.
Poems, Collected by Himself, Doubleday, 1961.
The More Deserving Cases: Eighteen Old Poems for Reconsideration, Marlborough College Press, 1962.
New Poems 1962, Cassell, 1962, Doubleday, 1963.
Ann at Highwood Hall: Poems for Children, Cassell, 1964.
Man Does, Woman Is, Doubleday, 1964.
Love Respelt, Cassell, 1965, Doubleday, 1966.
Collected Poems, 1965, Cassell, 1965.
Collected Poems, 1966, Doubleday, 1966.
Seventeen Poems Missing From Love Respelt, Stellar Press, 1966.
Colophon to "Love Respelt," Bertram Rota, 1967.
(With D. H. Lawrence) *Poems,* edited by Leonard Clark, Longman, 1967.
Poems, 1965-1968, Cassell, 1968.
Beyond Giving, Bertram Rota, 1969.
Love Respelt Again, Doubleday, 1969.
Poems About Love, Cassell, 1969.
Poems, 1968-1970, Cassell, 1970, Doubleday, 1971.
Advice From a Mother, Poem-of-the-Month Club, 1970.
Green-Sailed Vessel, Bertram Rota, 1971.
Poems, 1970-1972, Cassell, 1972.
Timeless Meeting, Bertram Rota, 1973.
At the Gate, Bertram Rota, 1974.
Collected Poems 1975, Cassell, 1975, published as *New Collected Poems,* Doubleday, 1977.
Poems about War, Moyer Bell, 1992.
Across the Gulf, New Seizin Press, 1994.
Robert Graves: The Centenary Selected Poems, edited by Patrick Quinn, Carcanet, 1995.
Complete Poems, Volume I, edited by Beryl Graves and Dunstan Ward, Carcanet, 1995.

Also author of *Deya,* 1973, *Eleven Songs,* 1983, *Selected Poems,* edited by Paul O'Prey, 1986.

FICTION

My Head! My Head! Being the History of Elisha and the Shunamite Woman; With the History of Moses as Elisha Related It, and Her Questions Put to Him, Secker, 1925.
The Shout, Mathews and Marrot, 1929.
(With Laura Riding, under joint pseudonym Barbara Rich) *No Decency Left,* J. Cape, 1932.
The Real David Copperfield, Barker, 1933.
I, Claudius, Smith & Haas, 1934, revised edition, Random House, 1977.

Claudius, the God and His Wife Messalina, Barker, 1934, Smith & Haas, 1935.
"Antigua, Penny, Puce," Seizin Press and Constable, 1936, published as *The Antigua Stamp,* Random House, 1937.
Count Belisarius, Random House, 1938.
Sergeant Lamb of the Ninth, Methuen, 1940, published as *Sergeant Lamb's America,* Random House, 1940.
Proceed, Sergeant Lamb, Random House, 1941.
The Story of Marie Powell, Wife to Mr. Milton, Cassell, 1943, published as *Wife to Mr. Milton: The Story of Marie Powell,* Creative Age Press, 1944.
The Golden Fleece, Cassell, 1944, published as *Hercules, My Shipmate,* Creative Age Press, 1945.
King Jesus, Creative Age Press, 1946, 6th edition, Cassell, 1962.
The Islands of Unwisdom, Doubleday, 1949 (published in England as *The Isles of Unwisdom,* Cassell, 1950).
Watch the North Wind Rise, Creative Age Press, 1949 (published in England as *Seven Days in New Crete,* Cassell, 1949).
Homer's Daughter, Doubleday, 1955.
Catacrok! Mostly Stories, Mostly Funny, Cassell, 1956.
They Hanged My Saintly Billy: The Life and Death of Dr. William Palmer, Doubleday, 1957.
Collected Short Stories, Doubleday, 1964, published as *The Shout and Other Stories,* Penguin Books, 1978.
Complete Short Stories, edited by Lucia Graves, St. Martin's Press (New York City), 1996.

NONFICTION

On English Poetry; Being an Irregular Approach to the Psychology of This Art, From Evidence Mainly Subjective, Knopf, 1922.
The Meaning of Dreams, Palmer, 1924.
Poetic Unreason and Other Studies, Palmer, 1925.
Contemporary Techniques of Poetry: A Political Analogy, Hogarth Press, 1925.
Another Future of Poetry, Hogarth Press, 1926.
Impenetrability; or, The Proper Habit of English, L. and V. Woolf, 1926.
(With Riding) *A Survey of Modernist Poetry,* Heinemann, 1927, Doubleday, Doran, 1928.
Lawrence and the Arabs, J. Cape, 1927, published as *Lawrence and the Arabian Adventure,* Doubleday, Doran, 1928.
Lars Porsena; or, The Future of Swearing and Improper Language, Dutton, 1927, revised edition published as *The Future of Swearing and Improper Language,* K. Paul, Trench, Trubner, 1936.
Mrs. Fisher; or, The Future of Humour, K. Paul, Trench, Trubner, 1928.
(With Riding) *A Pamphlet Against Anthologies,* J. Cape, 1928.
Goodbye to All That: An Autobiography, J. Cape, 1929, J. Cape & H. Smith, 1930, revised edition, Doubleday, 1957.
T. E. Lawrence to His Biographer, Doubleday, 1938, published with Liddell Hart's work as *T. E. Lawrence to His Biographers,* Doubleday, 1963, 2nd edition, Cassell, 1963.
(With Alan Hodge) *The Long Week-End: A Social History of Great Britain, 1918-1939,* Faber, 1940, Macmillan, 1941.
(With Hodge) *The Reader Over Your Shoulder: A Handbook for Writers of English Prose,* Macmillan, 1943, revised edition published as *The Use and Abuse of the English Language,* Paragon, 1990.
The White Goddess: A Historical Grammar of Poetic Myth, Creative Age Press, 1948, amended and enlarged edition, Vintage Books, 1958.

The Common Asphodel: Collected Essays on Poetry, 1922-1949, H. Hamilton, 1949.

(With Joshua Podro) *The Nazarene Gospel Restored,* Cassell, 1953, Doubleday, 1954.

(With Podro) *Nazarene Gospel,* Cassell, 1955.

Adam's Rib, and Other Anomalous Elements in the Hebrew Creation Myth: A New View, Trianon Press, 1955, Yoseloff, 1958.

The Greek Myths, two volumes, Penguin Books, 1955, condensed edition, Viking, 1992, as *The Greek Myths: Complete Edition,* Viking, 1993.

The Crowning Privilege: The Clark Lectures, 1954-1955 (includes sixteen new poems), Cassell, 1955, Doubleday, 1956.

(With Podro) *Jesus in Rome: A Historical Conjecture,* Cassell, 1957.

5 Pens in Hand, Doubleday, 1958.

Steps: Stories, Talks, Essays, Poems, Studies in History, Cassell, 1958.

Food for Centaurs: Stories, Talks, Critical Studies, Poems, Doubleday, 1960.

Greek Gods and Heroes, Doubleday, 1960 (published in England as *Myths of Ancient Greece,* Cassell, 1961).

Oxford Addresses on Poetry, Doubleday, 1962.

Nine Hundred Iron Chariots, Massachusetts Institute of Technology, 1963.

(With Raphael Patal) *Hebrew Myths: The Book of Genesis,* Doubleday, 1964.

Mammon (lecture; also see below), London School of Economics, 1964.

Mammon and the Black Goddess (one section previously published as *Mammon*), Doubleday, 1965.

Majorca Observed, Doubleday, 1965.

Spiritual Quixote, Oxford University Press, 1967.

Poetic Craft and Principle (collection of Oxford lectures), Cassell, 1967.

(Author of introduction) *Greece, Gods, and Art,* Viking, 1968.

The Crane Bag, Cassell, 1969.

Difficult Questions, Easy Answers, Cassell, 1972, Doubleday, 1973.

Selected Letters of Robert Graves, edited by Paul O'Prey, Hutchinson, Volume I: *In Broken Images: 1914-1946,* 1982, Volume II: *Between Moon and Moon: 1946-1972,* 1984.

Conversations with Robert Graves, edited by Frank L. Kersnowski, University Press of Mississippi, 1989.

Dear Robert, Dear Spike: The Graves-Milligan Correspondence, edited by Pauline Scudamore, Sutton, 1991.

Robert Graves: Collected Writings on Poetry, edited by Paul O'Prey, Carcanet, 1995.

FOR CHILDREN

The Big Green Book, illustrated by Maurice Sendak, Crowell, 1962.

The Siege and Fall of Troy, Cassell, 1962, Doubleday, 1963.

Two Wise Children, Harlin Quist, 1966.

The Poor Boy Who Followed His Star, Cassell, 1968, Doubleday, 1969.

The Ancient Castle, P. Owen, 1980.

EDITOR

(And author of introduction and critical notes) *The English Ballad: A Short Critical Survey,* Benn, 1927, revised edition, Heinemann, 1957, published as *English and Scottish Ballads,* Macmillan, 1957.

John Skelton (Laureate), 1460(?)-1529, Benn, 1927.

(Compiler) *The Less Familiar Nursery Rhymes,* Benn, 1927.

(And author of foreword) Algernon Charles Swinburne, *An Old Saying,* J. S. Mayfield, 1947.

(And author of foreword) *The Comedies of Terence,* Doubleday, 1962, published as *Comedies,* Aldine, 1962.

Condensed Merrill P. Paine's edition of *David Copperfield,* by Charles Dickens, Harcourt, 1934.

TRANSLATOR

(With Laura Riding) Georg Schwarz, *Almost Forgotten Germany,* Random House, 1937.

Lucius Apuleius, *The Transformations of Lucius, Otherwise Known as "The Golden Ass,"* Farrar, Straus, 1951.

Manuel de Jesus Galvan, *The Cross and the Sword,* Indiana University Press, 1954.

Pedro Antonio de Alarcon, *The Infant With the Globe,* Faber, 1955.

Marcus Annaeus Lucanus, *Pharsalia: Dramatic Episodes of the Civil Wars,* Penguin Books, 1956.

George Sand, *Winter in Majorca,* illustrated by Maurice Sand, Cassell, 1956.

Suetonius, *The Twelve Caesars,* Cassell, 1957.

The Anger of Achilles: Homer's "Iliad" (produced at Lincoln Center, New York, 1967), Doubleday, 1959.

Hesiodu Stamperia del Santuccio, *Fable of the Hawk and the Nightingale,* 1959.

(With Omar Ali-Shah) *The Rubaiyyat of Omar Khayaam* (based on the twelfth-century manuscript), Cassell, 1967, published as *The Original Rubaiyyat of Omar Khayaam,* Doubleday, 1968.

Solomon's "Song of Songs," Cassell, 1968, Doubleday, 1969.

OTHER

John Kemp's Wager: A Ballad Opera, S. French, 1925.

But Still It Goes On: An Accumulation (includes the play "But It Still Goes On"), J. Cape, 1930, J. Cape & H. Smith, 1931.

(Rewriter) Frank Richards, *Old Soldiers Never Die,* Faber & Faber, 1933.

(Rewriter) Richards, *Old-Soldier Sahib,* Smith & Haas, 1936.

Occupation: Writer (includes the play "Horses"), Creative Age Press, 1950.

Nausicaa (opera libretto adapted from his novel *Homer's Daughter;* music by Peggy Glanville-Hicks), produced in Athens, Greece, 1961.

Also author of television documentary, *Greece: The Inner World,* 1964. Many of Graves' letters and worksheets, as well as an autograph diary, is in the Graves Manuscript Collection at the University of Victoria, British Columbia, Canada. Other papers are in the collections of Lockwood Memorial Library, State University of New York at Buffalo; Berg Collection, New York City Library; Humanities Research Center, University of Texas, Austin; and University of Southern Illinois, Carbondale.

Graves made several recordings of his work, including *Robert Graves Reading His Own Poems,* for Argo and Listen; *Robert Graves Reading His Own Poetry and The White Goddess,* for Caedmon; and *The Rubaiyyat of Omar Khayyam,* for Spoken Arts.

SIDELIGHTS: Robert Graves often stirred controversy in his endeavors as a poet, novelist, critic, mythographer, translator, and editor. Stephen Spender of the *New York Times Book Review* characterized Graves as a free thinker: "All of his life Graves has been indifferent to fashion, and the great and deserved reputation he has is based on his individuality as a poet who is both intensely idiosyncratic and unlike any other contemporary poet and at the same time classical." A rebel socially, as well as artistically, Graves left his wife and four children in 1929 to live in Majorca with Laura Riding, a Russian Jewish poet. Douglas Day commented on the importance of this move in *Swifter Than Reason: The Poetry and Criticism of Robert Graves*: "The influence of Laura Riding is quite possibly the most important single element in his poetic career: she persuaded him to curb his digressiveness and his rambling philosophizing and to concentrate instead on terse, ironic poems written on personal themes. She also imparted to him some of her own dry, cerebral quality, which has remained in much of his poetry. There can be little doubt that some of his best work was done during the years of his literary partnership with Laura Riding."

Critics often described the *White Goddess* in paradoxical terms. Patrick Callahan, writing in the *Prairie Schooner,* called her a blend of the "cruelty and kindness of woman." He contended: "Cerridwen, the White Goddess, is the apotheosis of woman at her most primitive. Graves finds the women he has loved an embodiment of her. If Cerridwen is to be adored, she is also to be feared, for her passing can rival the passing of very life, and the pendulum of ecstasy and anguish which marks human love reaches its full sweep in her." Martin Seymour-Smith also noted the complex personality of the Muse, describing her in *Robert Graves* as "the Mother who bears man, the Lover who awakens him to manhood, the Old Hag who puts pennies on his dead eyes. She is a threefold process of Birth, Copulation, and Death." Brian Jones, however, found the Goddess one-dimensional. He wrote in *London Magazine*: "It is interesting that it is often impossible to tell whether the feminine pronoun [in *Poems, 1965-1968*] refers to woman or Goddess or both; not that this is necessarily an adverse criticism, but in Graves both the woman and the Goddess [are] sentimental, belittled, simplified male creation[s]. The dignity and 'otherness' of the woman is missing."

Graves explored and reconstructed the White Goddess myth in his book *The White Goddess: A Historical Grammar of Poetic Myth.* J. M. Cohen noted in his *Robert Graves*: "The mythology of The White Goddess, though its elements are drawn from a vast field of ancient story and legends, is in its assemblage Graves's own creation, and conforms to the requirements of his own poetic mind." One of Graves's prerequisites is spontaneity. Muse poetry, wrote Graves in his *Oxford Addresses on Poetry,* "is composed at the back of the mind; an unaccountable product of a trance in which the emotions of love, fear, anger, or grief are profoundly engaged, though at the same time powerfully disciplined." Graves gave an example of such inspiration, explaining that while writing *The Golden Fleece* he experienced powerful feelings of "a sudden enlightenment." According to Cohen, this insight was into a subject Graves knew "almost nothing" about. Cohen wrote that "a night and day of furious cogitation was followed by three weeks of intense work, during which the whole 70,000 words of the original were written." Monroe K. Spears deplored this method of composition in the *Sewanee Review*: "Graves's theory of poetry— if it can be dignified by the name of theory—is essentially a perfectly conventional late Romantic notion of poetry as emotional and magical; it is remarkable only in its crude simplicity and vulnerability." Still, Randall Jarrell asserted that "Graves's richest, most moving, and most consistently beautiful poems— poems that almost deserve the literal *magical*—are his mythic/ archaic pieces, all those the reader thinks of as 'White Goddess' poems."

The story of Graves's translation of *The Rubaiyyat of Omar Khayaam* served to exemplify the stir he was capable of making when he brought his own theories about history to his writing. First, critics and scholars questioned the veracity of his text. Graves had worked from an annotated version of the poem given him by Ali-Shah, a Persian poet; although Ali-Shah alleged that the manuscript had been in his family for 800 years, L. P. Elwell-Sutton, an Orientalist at Edinburgh University, decried it as a "clumsy forgery." Next came the inevitable comparisons with Edward FitzGerald's standard translation, published in 1859. FitzGerald's depiction of romanticized Victorian bliss is epitomized by the much-quoted lines, "A Book of Verse underneath the Bough / A Jug of Wine, a Loaf of Bread, and Thou." Graves's translation, on the other hand, reads: "Should our day's portion be one mancel loaf, / a haunch of mutton and a gourd of wine." A *Time* critic defended FitzGerald's translation by quoting FitzGerald himself: "'A translation must live with a transfusion of one's own worse life if he can't retain the original's better. Better a live sparrow than a stuffed eagle.'" The critic added that "Graves's more dignified *Rubaiyyat* may be an eagle to FitzGerald's sparrow. But FitzGerald's work is still in living flight, while Graves's already sits there on the shelf—stuffed." Similarly, Martin Dodsworth commented in *Listener*: "Graves does not convince here. He has produced a prosy New English Bible sort of Khayaam, whose cloudy mysticism raises more questions than it answers."

Despite his detractors, Graves maintained his characteristically independent stance (he once told his students that "the poet's chief loyalty is to the Goddess Calliope, not to his publisher or to the booksellers on his publisher's mailing list") in defending his translation against the more commercially directed attempt he felt FitzGerald made. In Graves's opinion, the poet was writing about the ecstasy of Sufi mysticism, not—as he says FitzGerald implies—more earthly pleasures. In an extensive apologia for his translation, Graves wrote in *Observations*: "Any attempt at improving or altering Khayaam's poetic intentions would have seemed shocking to me when I was working on the *Rubaiyyat*. . . . My twin principles were: 'Stick as strictly to the script as you can' and 'Respect the tradition of English verse as first confirmed by the better Tudor poets: which is to be as explicit as possible on every occasion and never play down to ignorance.'"

The publication of *The Centenary Selected Poems* and *Collected Writings on Poetry* offers additional insight into Graves's creative preoccupations. *Collected Writings on Poetry* is based on a series of lectures Graves delivered at Cambridge in 1954 and 1955 and Oxford between 1961 and 1965, as well as several addresses made during visits to the United States. "[Graves] believed you had to *live* like a poet, and so he did," wrote Lorna Sage in *Observer,* adding, "He spoke with an Outsider's edgy authority, as you can see in *Collected Writings on Poetry*." Neil Powell noted in the *Times Literary Supplement*, "[Graves] was certainly not a reliable nor even a wholly competent critic, yet the essays and lectures are worth reading for quite other reasons. One consequence of his curiously innocent egocentricity is that his comments on other poets often reveal much more about himself than about their ostentatious subjects." While praising *Collected Writings on Poetry,* Powell questioned the omission of Graves's love poetry and humorous verse from *The Centenary Selected Poems* which, in his view, "present[s] Graves as a much duller writer than he is."

Together *Dear Robert, Dear Spike,* a volume of correspondence, and Miranda Seymour's biography *Robert Graves: Life on the Edge* expand public and critical understanding of the poet. *Dear*

Robert, Dear Spike, contains selected letters from the decade-long correspondence between Graves and Spike Mulligan, a veteran of war twenty years Graves's junior and the author of *Adolf Hitler, My Part in His Downfall.* Despite the age difference and their widely dissimilar social backgrounds, they apparently shared much in common, particularly the lasting physical and emotional scars of combat experience. "Both had compelling reasons to hate war," remarked Patrick Skene Catling in *Spectator.* "As a result, they both rejected authority and always maintained a defiant sort of artistic integrity." According to Mulligan, quoted by Catling, "The common bonding of our friendship was his mischievous, iconoclastic perorations on all stratas of stupidity and unreasonableness."

An *Observer* review praised the "great insight" provided by the Graves-Mulligan correspondence which began in 1964. Their letters, as Catling noted, appear "in the easy style of love letters, recounting the small colorful details of their work, opinions, domestic arrangements and moods." Sage similarly commended Seymour's *Robert Graves: Life on the Edge,* described by the critic as a "balanced, convincing, rounded" portrait. Commenting on the biographer's description of Graves's near death wounding on the Somme in 1916, Sage noted, "as Miranda Seymour says—it would have been hard [for Graves] not to feel a touch mythic, 'as if he had been borne again.'"

BIOGRAPHICAL/CRITICAL SOURCES:

BOOKS

Carter, D. N. G., *Robert Graves: The Lasting Poetic Achievement,* Barnes & Noble, 1989.
Cohen, J. M., *Robert Graves,* Oliver & Boyd, 1960.
Concise Dictionary of British Literary Biography, Volume 6: *Modern Writers, 1914-1945,* Gale (Detroit), 1991.
Contemporary Literary Criticism, Gale, Volume 1, 1973; Volume 2, 1974; Volume 6, 1976; Volume 11, 1979; Volume 39, 1986; Volume 44, 1987; Volume 45, 1987.
Day, Douglas, *Swifter Than Reason: The Poetry and Criticism of Robert Graves,* University of North Carolina Press, 1963.
Dictionary of Literary Biography, Gale, Volume 20, *British Poets, 1914-1945,* 1983; Volume 100: *Modern British Essayists, Second Series,* 1991.
Dictionary of Literary Biography Yearbook: 1985, Gale, 1986.
Graves, William, *Wild Olives: Life in Majorca with Robert Graves,* Pimlico, 1996.
Jarrell, Randall, *The Third Book of Criticism,* Farrar, Straus, 1969.
Poetry Criticism, Volume 6, Gale, 1993.
Quennell, Peter, *Casanova in London,* Stein & Day, 1971.
Seymour, Miranda, *Robert Graves: A Life on the Edge,* Henry Holt (New York City), 1995.
Seymour-Smith, Martin, *Robert Graves: His Life and Work* (originally published in 1982), revised edition, Bloomsbury, 1995.

PERIODICALS

Atlantic, January, 1966.
Chicago Tribune, December 9, 1985.
Commentary, February, 1967.
Harper's, August, 1967.
Horizon, January, 1962.
Hudson Review, spring, 1967.
Life, June 24, 1963; October 15, 1965.
Listener, May 4, 1967; November 9, 1967; December 24, 1970.
Literary Times, April, 1965.
London Magazine, February, 1969.

London Review of Books, September 7, 1995, p. 26.
Los Angeles Times, December 8, 1985.
Los Angeles Times Book Review, December 28, 1980; January 23, 1983.
Nation, March 18, 1978.
National Observer, March 17, 1969.
National Review, December 31, 1985.
New Leader, October 27, 1969.
New Statesman, December 3, 1965.
Newsweek, May 20, 1968; July 28, 1969; December 16, 1985.
New York Times, December 1, 1966; October 26, 1967; September 20, 1979; December 25, 1981; December 8, 1985.
New York Times Book Review, July 20, 1969; October 12, 1969; March 11, 1973; April 29, 1979; May 30, 1982; October 17, 1982; January 18, 1987, p. 34.
New York Times Magazine, October 30, 1966.
Observations, July, 1968.
Observer, July 2, 1995, p. 15; July 16, 1995, p. 13.
Playboy, December, 1970.
Poetry, January, 1969.
Prairie Schooner, summer, 1970.
Publishers Weekly, August 11, 1975; December 20, 1985.
School Library Journal, February, 1986.
Sewanee Review, fall, 1965.
Shenandoah, spring, 1966.
Spectator, March 16, 1991, p. 40.
Time, November 3, 1967; May 31, 1968; December 16, 1985.
Times (London), May 27, 1982; July 26, 1985; December 9, 1985.
Times Literary Supplement, October 7, 1965; December 7, 1967; June 26, 1969; November 21, 1980; September 27, 1985; November 3, 1995, p. 6.
Variety, July 26, 1972.
Washington Post, December 8, 1985; December 9, 1985.
Washington Post Book World, November 29, 1981.
Yale Review, autumn, 1968.

*   *   *

GRAVES, Valerie
See BRADLEY, Marion Zimmer

*   *   *

GRAY, Alasdair (James) 1934-

PERSONAL: Born December 28, 1934, in Glasgow, Scotland; son of Alex Gray (a machine operator) and Amy (Fleming) Gray (a homemaker); married Inge Sorensen (divorced); married Morag McAlpine, 1991; children: Andrew. *Education:* Glasgow Art School, diploma, 1957. *Politics:* "Devolutionary Scottish C.N.D. (Campaign for Nuclear Disarmament) Socialist." *Religion:* None.

ADDRESSES: Home—39 Kersland St., Glasgow G12 8BP, Scotland. *Agent*—Xandra Hardy, 9 Elsworth Terrace, London NW3, England.

CAREER: Part-time art teacher in area of Glasgow, Scotland, 1958-62; theatrical scene painter in Glasgow, 1962-63; freelance playwright and painter in Glasgow, 1963-75; People's Palace (local history museum), Glasgow, artist-recorder, 1976-77; University of Glasgow, writer in residence, 1977-79; freelance painter and maker of books in Glasgow, 1979–.

MEMBER: Society of Authors, Scottish Society of Playwrights, Glasgow Print Workshop, various organizations supporting coal miners and nuclear disarmament.

AWARDS, HONORS: Three grants from Scottish Arts Council, between 1968 and 1981; award from Saltire Society, 1982, for *Lanark: A Life in Four Books;* award from Cheltenham Literary Festival, 1983, for *Unlikely Stories, Mostly;* award from Scottish branch of P.E.N., 1986; Bellhouston Travelling Scholarship; Booker Prize nomination, Book Trust (England), for *Lanark: A Life in Four Books.*

WRITINGS:

Old Negatives: Four Verse Sequences, J. Cape (London), 1962.

Lanark: A Life in Four Books (novel), self-illustrated, Harper (New York City), 1981, revised edition, Braziller (New York City), 1985.

Unlikely Stories, Mostly (short stories; includes "The Star," "The Spread of Ian Nicol," and "Five Letters from an Eastern Empire"), self-illustrated, Canongate (Edinburgh), 1983, revised edition, Penguin (London), 1984.

1982 Janine (novel), Viking (London), 1984, revised edition, Penguin, 1985.

The Fall of Kelvin Walker: A Fable of the Sixties (novel; adapted from his television play of the same title; also see below), Canongate, 1985, Braziller, 1986.

(With James Kelman and Agnes Owens) *Lean Tales* (short story anthology), J. Cape, 1985.

Saltire Self-Portrait 4, Saltire Society Publications (Edinburgh), 1988.

(Editor) *The Anthology of Prefaces,* Canongate, 1989.

McGrotty and Ludmilla; or, The Harbinger Report: A Romance of the Eighties, White Leaf, 1989.

Something Leather (novel), Random House (New York City), 1990.

Poor Things: Episodes from the Early Life of Archibald McCandless, M.D., Scottish Public Health Officer (novel), Harcourt (New York City), 1992.

Why Scots Should Rule Scotland, Canongate, 1992.

Ten Tales Tall and True: Social Realism, Sexual Comedy, Science Fiction, and Satire, Harcourt Brace (New York City), 1993.

A History Maker, Harcourt Brace (San Diego), 1996.

Mavis Belfrage: A Romantic Tale, Bloomsbury (London), 1996.

PLAYS

Dialogue (one-act), first produced in Edinburgh at Gateway Theatre, 1971.

The Fall of Kelvin Walker (two-act; adapted from his television play of the same title; also see below), first produced in Stirling, Scotland, at McRoberts Centre, University of Stirling, 1972.

The Loss of the Golden Silence (one-act), first produced in Edinburgh at Pool Theatre, 1973.

Homeward Bound (one-act), first produced in Edinburgh at Pool Theatre, 1973.

(With Tom Leonard and Liz Lochhead) *Tickly Mince* (two-act), first produced in Glasgow at Tron Theatre, 1982.

(With Liz Lochhead, Tom Leonard, and James Kelman) *The Pie of Damocles* (two-act), first produced in Glasgow at Tron Theatre, 1983.

RADIO PLAYS

Quiet People, British Broadcasting Corporation (BBC), 1968.

The Night Off, BBC, 1969.

Thomas Muir of Huntershill, BBC, 1970.

The Loss of the Golden Silence, BBC, 1974.

McGrotty and Ludmilla, BBC, 1976.

The Vital Witness, BBC, 1979.

Near the Driver, translation into German by Berndt Rullkotter broadcast by Westdeutsche Rundfunk, 1983, original text broadcast by BBC, 1988.

TELEVISION PLAYS

The Fall of Kelvin Walker, BBC, 1968.

Dialogue, BBC, 1972.

Triangles, Granada, 1972.

The Man Who Knew about Electricity, BBC, 1973.

Honesty, BBC, 1974.

Today and Yesterday (series of three twenty-minute educational documentaries), BBC, 1975.

Beloved, Granada, 1976.

The Gadfly, Granada, 1977.

The Story of a Recluse, BBC, 1987.

SIDELIGHTS: After more than twenty years as a painter and a scriptwriter for radio and television, Alasdair Gray rose to literary prominence with the publication of several of his books in the 1980s. His works have been noted for their mixture of realistic social commentary and vivid fantasy, augmented by the author's own evocative illustrations. Jonathan Baumbach wrote in the *New York Times Book Review* that Gray's work "has a verbal energy, an intensity of vision, that has been mostly missing from the English novel since D. H. Lawrence." And David Lodge of the *New Republic* said that Gray "is that rather rare bird among contemporary British writers—a genuine experimentalist, transgressing the rules of formal English prose . . . boldly and imaginatively."

In his writing Gray often draws upon his Scottish background, and he is regarded as a major force in the literature of his homeland. Author Anthony Burgess, for instance, said in the London *Observer* that he considered Gray the best Scottish novelist since Sir Walter Scott became popular in the early nineteenth century. Unlike Scott, who made his country a setting for historical romance, Gray focuses on contemporary Scotland, where the industrial economy deteriorates and many citizens fear that their social and economic destiny has been surrendered to England. Critics praised Gray for putting such themes as Scotland's decline and powerlessness into a larger context that any reader could appreciate. "Using Glasgow as his undeniable starting point," Douglas Gifford wrote in *Studies in Scottish Literature,* "Gray . . . transforms local and hitherto restricting images, which limited [other] novelists of real ability, . . . into symbols of universal prophetic relevance."

Gray said that although his first novel took years to complete, the story-line of what would become his now acclaimed first novel, *Lanark: A Life in Four Books,* had essentially been worked out in his mind by the time he was eighteen. A long and complex work that some reviewers considered partly autobiographical, *Lanark* opens in Unthank, an ugly, declining city explained in reviews as a comment on Glasgow and other Western industrial centers. As in George Orwell's *Nineteen Eighty-four,* citizens of Unthank are ruled by a domineering and intrusive bureaucracy. Lanark is a lonely young man unable to remember his past. Along with many of his fellow-citizens, he is plagued with "dragonhide," an insidious, scaly skin infection seen as symbolic of his emotional isolation. Cured of his affliction by doctors at a scientific institute below the surface of the earth, Lanark realizes to his disgust that the staff is as arrogant and manipulative as the ruling elite on the surface. Before escaping from this underworld, Lanark has a vision in which he sees the life story of a young man who mysteriously resembles him—Duncan Thaw, an aspiring artist who lives in twentieth-century Glasgow.

Thaw's story, which comprises nearly half the book, is virtually a novel within a novel. It echoes the story of Lanark while displaying a markedly different literary technique. As William Boyd explained in the *Times Literary Supplement,* "The narration of Thaw's life turns out to be a brilliant and moving evocation of a talented and imaginative child growing up in working-class Glasgow. The style is limpid and classically elegant, the detail solidly documentary and in marked contrast to the fantastical and surrealistic accoutrements of the first 100 pages." Like Gray, Thaw attends art school in Glasgow, and, as with Lanark, Thaw's loneliness and isolation are expressed outwardly in a skin disease, eczema. With increasing desperation, Thaw seeks fulfillment in love and art, and his disappointment culminates in a violent outburst in which he kills—or at least thinks he kills—a young woman who had abandoned him. Bewildered and hopeless, he commits suicide.

Critics have generally lauded *Lanark,* although some expressed concern that it was hampered by its size and intricacy. Boyd, for instance, felt that the parallel narratives of Thaw and Lanark "do not happily cohere." *Washington Post Book World*'s Michael Dirda said that Lanark was "too baggy and bloated," but he stressed that "there are such good things in it that one hardly knows where it could be cut." Many critics echoed Boyd's overall assessment that "*Lanark* is a work of loving and vivid imagination, yielding copious riches." Moreover, Burgess featured *Lanark* in his book *Ninety-nine Novels: The Best in English Since 1939—A Personal Choice,* declaring, "It was time Scotland produced a shattering work of fiction in the modern idiom. This is it."

Although *Lanark* rapidly achieved critical recognition in Britain, it was Gray's second novel, *1982 Janine,* that was the first to be widely known in the United States. When asked why his work had now attained critical notice in the United States, Gray replied to *Contemporary Authors:* "*Lanark* was the first novel I had published in the U.S.A., by Harper & Row in 1981. It was speedily remaindered, because Harper & Row classified it as science fiction, only sent it to sci-fi magazines for review, and the sci-fi reviewers were not amused. . . . I suppose my books have been published in the United States because they sell well in Britain, and were praised by authors of *A Clockwork Orange* [Anthony Burgess] and *The History Man* [Malcolm Bradbury]."

1982 Janine records the thoughts of Jock McLeish, a disappointed, middle-aged Scottish businessman, during a long night of heavy drinking. In his mind Jock plays and replays fantasies in which he sexually tortures helpless women, and he gives names and identities to his victims, including the Janine of the title. Burgess spoke for several reviewers when he wrote in the *Observer* that such material was offensive and unneeded. But admirers of the novel, such as Richard Eder of the *Los Angeles Times,* felt that Jock's sexual fantasies were a valid metaphor for the character's own sense of helplessness. Jock, who rose to a managerial post from a working-class background, now hates himself because he is financially dependent on the ruling classes he once hoped to change.

As Eder observed, Jock's powerlessness is in its turn a metaphor for the subjugation of Scotland. Jock expounds on the sorry state of his homeland in the course of his drunken railings. Scotland's economy, he charges, has been starved in order to strengthen the country's political master, England; what is more, if war with the Soviet Union breaks out, Jock expects the English to use Scotland as a nuclear battlefield. As the novel ends, Jock resolves to quit his job and change his life for the better. Eder commended Gray for conveying a portrait of helplessness and the search for self-realization "in a flamboyantly comic narrator whose verbal blue streak is given depth by a winning impulse to self-discovery, and some alarming insight."

Gray's short-story collection *Unlikely Stories, Mostly* is "if anything more idiosyncratic" than *1982 Janine,* according to Jonathan Baumbach of the *New York Times Book Review.* Many reviewers praised the imaginativeness of the stories while acknowledging that the collection, which includes work dating back to Gray's teenage years, is uneven in quality. As Gary Marmorstein observed in the *Los Angeles Times Book Review,* some of the stories are "slight but fun," including "The Star," in which a boy catches a star and swallows it, and "The Spread of Ian Nicol," in which a man slowly splits in two like a microbe reproducing itself.

Gray's third novel, *The Fall of Kelvin Walker,* was inspired by personal experience. Still struggling to establish his career several years after his graduation from art school, Gray was tapped as the subject of a documentary by a successful friend at the British Broadcasting Corporation (BBC). Gray, who had been living on welfare, suddenly found himself treated to airline flights and limousine rides at the BBC's expense. In *Kelvin Walker* the title character, a young Scotsman with a burning desire for power, has a similar chance to use the communications media to fulfill his wildest fantasies. Though Kelvin arrives in London with few assets but self-confidence and a fast-talking manner, his persistence and good luck soon win him a national following as an interviewer on a television show. But in his pride and ambition Walker forgets that he exercises such influence only at the whims of his corporate bosses, and when he displeases them his fall from grace is as abrupt as his rise.

Kelvin Walker, which Gray adapted from his 1968 teleplay of the same title ("I sent it to a [BBC] director I know. He gave it to a producer who liked it"), is shorter and less surrealistic than his previous novels. The *Observer*'s Hermione Lee, though she stressed that Gray "is always worth attending to," felt that this novel "doesn't allow him the big scope he thrives on." By contrast, Larry McCaffery of the *New York Times Book Review* praised *Kelvin Walker* for its "economy of means and exquisite control of detail." Gray "is now fully in command of his virtuoso abilities as a stylist and storyteller," McCaffery said, asserting that Gray's first four books—"each of which impresses in very different ways—indicate that he is emerging as the most vibrant and original new voice in English fiction."

As Gray continued to write, critical reception of his work varied widely. Though most reviewers acknowledged his genius in such works as *Lanark,* books such as *Something Leather* and *McGrotty and Ludmilla; or, The Harbinger Report: A Romance of the Eighties* were criticized for lacking the intensity of his earlier work. Gray himself was remarkably candid about the quality and intent of some of these efforts. For example, he described *McGrotty and Ludmilla* as an Aladdin story set in modern Whitehall "with the hero a junior civil servant, wicked uncle Abanizir a senior one, and the magic lamp a secret government paper which gave whoever held it unlimited powers of blackmail." And works such as *Something Leather,* said Gerald Mangan in the *Times Literary Supplement,* placed Gray in "an unfortunate tradition in Scottish fiction, whereby novelists have tended to exhaust their inspiration in the effort of a single major achievement." That *Lanark* was a major achievement Mangan had no doubt. "*Lanark* is now so monumental a Scottish landmark," he wrote, "that few readers would have reproached him if a decade of silence had followed it." Instead, Gray brought out "a good deal of inferior material that had evidently subsidized or distracted him during the composition of his epic."

With the publication of *Poor Things: Episodes from the Early Life of Archibald McCandless, M.D., Scottish Public Health Officer,* purportedly edited by Gray, the author returns to form, suggested Philip Hensher in the *Spectator,* "after a rather sticky patch." The work drew comparisons to such authors as Daniel Defoe and Laurence Sterne, partly because of its eccentric humor and setting and partly because of Gray's skillful use of the traditions of the Victorian novel, which, according to Barbara Hardy in the *Times Literary Supplement,* "embodied their liberal notions of providence and progress in realistic narratives which often surge into optimistic or melioristic visions on the last page."

Set in Glasgow during the 1880s, the novel is narrated by Archie McCandless, a young medical student, who befriends the eccentric Godwin Baxter, another medical student. Baxter, who has been experimenting on the body of a beautiful and pregnant young suicide, has created "Bella" by transplanting the brain of the fetus into its mother's skull. Bella is sexually mature and wholly amoral, and McCandless wants to marry her. She, however, elopes with a wicked playboy whom she soon drives insane. After the death of her lover, Bella works for a time in a Parisian brothel before returning to Scotland. Here she runs into her ex-husband just as she is getting married to McCandless. A happy ending is combined with a clever final twist to produce a book that, said Hensher, becomes "a great deal more than entertaining only on finishing it. Then your strongest urge is to start reading it again."

Gray uses his visual and writing talents in *Ten Tall Tales and True: Social Realism, Sexual Comedy, Science Fiction, and Satire.* He illustrates the cover with ten animal tails; within the covers, he shows the entire animals. A critic for *Review of Contemporary Fiction* asked: "Is Gray suggesting perhaps the fragmented and nonhuman character of our life when we do not exist in a state of wholeness?" Set in present-day Scotland, the stories explore human relationships with humor and feeling. "[Gray's] stories most often dramatize those symbioses of oppression in which people find just the right partner, family or group to dominate or be dominated by," wrote Ron Loewinsohn in the *New York Times Book Review.* Observed Christopher Bray in the *Spectator,* "Stories and characters like these ought to make you downcast, and they would, were it not for the pithy intensity with which Gray sketches things in."

Gray expresses his concern for modern society in *A History Maker,* a political allegory. In a twenty-third-century Scotland that is reminiscent of ancient times, conflicts are mediated by war games governed by rules. When warrior Wat Dryhope becomes clan chieftain in the Ettrick Forest, he also becomes the leader of a mass militaristic movement. But he gives up war after meeting the evil Delilah Puddock, who destroys most of the world's food supply by infecting him with a virus. "Gray's touch is light and wry, and there is enough strangeness in his future to whet conventional SF appetites. But there is no mistaking the relevance of his allegory to the situation of nation-states in today's uneasy post-Cold War peace," maintained a *Village Voice Literary Supplement* reviewer.

BIOGRAPHICAL/CRITICAL SOURCES:

BOOKS

Burgess, Anthony, *Ninety-nine Novels: The Best in English since 1939—A Personal Choice,* Allison & Busby (London), 1984.
Contemporary Authors New Revision Series, Volume 47, Gale (Detroit), 1995.
Contemporary Literary Criticism, Volume 41, Gale, 1987.

PERIODICALS

Books, September, 1993, p. 9.
Christian Science Monitor, October 5, 1984.
Kirkus Reviews, February 1, 1994, p. 87; February 15, 1996, p. 247.
Los Angeles Times, November 21, 1984.
Los Angeles Times Book Review, December 9, 1984.
New Republic, November 12, 1984.
New Statesman, November 25, 1994, p. 48.
New York Review of Books, April 25, 1991.
New York Times Book Review, October 28, 1984; May 5, 1985; December 21, 1986; August 4, 1991; March 6, 1994, p. 11; August 18, 1996, p. 18; August 18, 1996, p. 18.
Observer (London), April 15, 1984; March 31, 1985; September 27, 1994, p. 21; December 10, 1995, p. 15.
Publishers Weekly, March 4, 1996, p. 61.
Review of Contemporary Fiction, fall, 1994, p. 204.
Spectator, February 28, 1981; September 5, 1992; October 30, 1993, p. 35.
Stage, November 30, 1972.
Studies in Scottish Literature, Volume 18, 1983.
Times (London), April 1, 1986.
Times Literary Supplement, February 27, 1981; March 18, 1983; April 13, 1984; March 29, 1985; May 10, 1985; July 6-12, 1990; April 3, 1992; August 28, 1992; December 9, 1994, p. 22.
Village Voice Literary Supplement, December, 1984; April, 1996, p. 8.
Washington Post Book World, December 16, 1984; August 31, 1986; June 16, 1991.
Whole Earth Review, winter, 1995, p. 62.

* * *

GRAY, Francine du Plessix 1930-

PERSONAL: Born September 25, 1930, in Warsaw, Poland (some sources say France); came to United States in 1941; naturalized citizen, 1952; daughter of Bertrand Jochaud (a diplomat and pilot for the Resistance) and Tatiana (Iacovleff) du Plessix; married Cleve Gray (a painter), April 23, 1957; children: Thaddeus Ives, Luke Alexander. *Education:* Attended Bryn Mawr College, 1948-50, and Black Mountain College, summers, 1951-52; Barnard College, B.A., 1952. *Politics:* Democrat. *Religion:* Roman Catholic. *Avocation:* Tennis, gardening, cooking Provencal food.

ADDRESSES: Home—Greystones, Cornwall Bridge, CT 06754. *Agent*—Georges Borchardt, Inc., 136 East 57th St., New York, NY 10022.

CAREER: United Press International, New York City, reporter at night desk, 1952-54; *Realities* (magazine), Paris, France, editorial assistant for French edition, 1954-55; freelance writer, 1955–; *Art in America,* New York City, book editor, 1964-66; *New Yorker,* New York City, staff writer, 1968–. Distinguished visiting professor at City College of the City University of New York, spring, 1975; visiting lecturer at Saybrook College, Yale University, 1981; adjunct professor, School of Fine Arts, Columbia University, 1983–; Ferris professor, Princeton University, 1986. Judge of 1974 National Book Award in philosophy and religion. Attended Soviet-American Writers' Workshop in Batumin, U.S.S.R., 1979.

MEMBER: International PEN, Authors Guild, Authors League of America, American Academy of Arts and Letters, National Book Critics Circle.

AWARDS, HONORS: Putnam Creative Writing Award from Barnard College, 1952; National Catholic Book Award from Catholic Press Association, 1971, for *Divine Disobedience: Profiles in Catholic Radicalism*; Front Page Award from Newswomen's Club of New York, 1972, for *Hawaii: The Sugar-Coated Fortress*; Annenberg fellow, Brown University, 1997. LL.D. from City University of New York, 1981, Oberlin College, 1985, University of Santa Clara, 1985, St. Mary's College, and University of Hartford; Guggenheim fellow, 1991-92.

WRITINGS:

Divine Disobedience: Profiles in Catholic Radicalism, Knopf, 1970.
Hawaii: The Sugar-Coated Fortress, Random House, 1972.
Lovers and Tyrants (novel), Simon & Schuster, 1976.
World Without End (novel), Simon & Schuster, 1981.
October Blood (novel), Simon & Schuster, 1985.
Adam and Eve and the City: Selected Nonfiction, Simon & Schuster, 1987.
Soviet Women: Walking the Tightrope, Doubleday, 1990.
Rage & Fire: A Life of Louise Colet—Pioneer Feminist, Literary Star, Flaubert's Muse, Simon & Schuster, 1994.

Contributor of articles, stories, and reviews to periodicals, including *Vogue, New Yorker, Saturday Review, New York Review of Books, New York Times Book Review,* and *New Republic.*

SIDELIGHTS: In 1976 *New Yorker* columnist Francine du Plessix Gray published *Lovers and Tyrants,* a book Caryl Rivers describes in *Ms.* as being "as rich in its texture as the lace tablecloths women of my grandmother's generation used to crochet." The novel, a startling and often touching autobiographical *bildungsroman,* gained the attention of many critics. "Every woman's first novel about her own break-through into adulthood is significant—liberation of any kind is significant—but Francine du Plessix Gray has created, in hers, something memorable," comments Kathleen Cushman in the *National Observer.* "To the cathartic throes of autobiography she has added a good dose each of humor, irony, and skill; *Lovers and Tyrants* transcends its limited possibilities as a book about *Woman Oppressed* and crosses into the realm of art."

The eight parts of this novel of "ascent and liberation," as Joan Peters calls it in the *Nation,* describe various periods in the life of Stephanie, the heroine. It begins with her childhood in Paris as the daughter of a Russian mother and an aristocratic French father who wanted her to be a boy. She is raised by a hypochondriac governess and her childhood, she writes in the opening lines of the book, was "muted, opaque, and drab, the color of gruel and of woolen gaiters, its noises muted and monotonous as a sleeper's pulse. . . . My temperature was taken twice a day, my head was perpetually wrapped in some woolen muffler or gauze veiling. I was scrubbed, spruced, buffed, combed, polished, year round, like a first communicant." After her father's death in the Resistance, Stephanie and her mother move to New York where Stephanie attends a fancy boarding school. Later, a young adult, she returns

to France to visit her relatives and has an affair with a French prince who describes himself as "style incarnate." Nearing thirty, she marries an architect, bears two sons, and continues her career as a journalist. She feels confined and dissatisfied in her marriage and leaves to tour the Southwest, writing about bizarre religious cults and taking up with a twenty-five-year-old homosexual who longs to be both a bisexual and a photographer and who continuously begs Stephanie to feed him. The theme of the novel, as Stephanie points out, is the tyranny of love: "Every woman's life is a series of exorcisms from the spells of different oppressors: nurses, lovers, husbands, gurus, parents, children, myths of the good life. The most tyrannical despots can be the ones who love us the most."

That theme, Gray acknowledges, came from experiences in her own life. In an essay for the *New York Times Book Review,* Gray writes that her late start in writing fiction was partially due to fear of disapproval from her father—even though he had died when she was eleven. *Lovers and Tyrants* grew out of her frustration as a young wife and mother. "I was married and had two children," Gray stated in the *New York Times Book Review* "The Making of an Author" column, "and since I live deep in the country and in relative solitude, encompassed by domestic duties, the journal [that I kept] became increasingly voluminous, angry, introspective. The nomad, denied flight and forced to turn inward, was beginning to explode. One day when I was 33, after I'd cooked and smiled for a bevy of weekend guests whom I never wished to see again, I felt an immense void, a great powerlessness, the deepest loneliness I'd ever known. I wept for some hours, took out a notebook, started rewriting one of the three stories that had won me my Barnard prize. It was the one about my governess. . . . It was to become, 12 years and two books of nonfiction later, the first chapter for *Lovers and Tyrants.* The process of finishing that book was as complex and lengthy as it was painful."

World Without End, Gray's second novel, is also noted for its sensitivity and intelligence. The story of three lifelong friends who reunite in middle age to tour Russia and, hopefully, to "learn how to live the last third of our lives," *World Without End* is "an ambitious novel about love and friendship, faith and doubt, liberty and license," comments Judith Gies in *Saturday Review.* D. M. Thomas, writing in the *Washington Post Book World,* considers *World Without End* to be "clearly the work of a richly talented writer. . . . The book is struggling with an important subject: the conflict within each of us between the psychological hungers symbolized by America and Russia—individualism and brotherhood, anarchy and order. It is no small achievement to have explored interestingly one of the most crucial dilemmas of our age."

Doris Grumbach in *Commonweal* calls *World Without End* "a prime entry in the novel of intelligence. It is just that: the lives [Gray] tells about ring with authenticity for their times and their place." It is the novel's "intelligence—"its lengthy discourses on a variety of subjects and the articulate growing self-awareness of its characters—that holds the attention of many of its reviewers. The *New York Times*'s John Leonard notes the "lyric excess" of the characters's musings, but believes that Gray "has chosen to satirize the art, the religion and the politics of the last 35 years" through characters Sophie, Claire, and Edmund. "[Gray] has also chosen to forgive the creatures of her satire," says Leonard. "They are more disappointed in themselves than readers will be in them as characters."

For other critics, the intellectual discussions in *World Without End* are a hindrance to an appreciation of the novel. "Anyone not conversant with the intellectual and esthetic upheavals in American art and politics over the last 30 years ought not attempt to read this novel," suggests Henrietta Epstein in the *Detroit News,* "for these concerns, along with those of friendship and love, are at the heart of Francine du Plessix Gray's work." *Newsweek* reviewer Annalyn Swan concurs with Leonard that "some of this is obviously satire" and says that "when Gray is not trying to be wry, or brilliant, she can be wonderful." Swan concludes that Gray, "like many social critics who cross the line into fiction, . . . has not yet mastered the difference between show and tell, between writing fiction that lives and using fiction as a forum for ideas. What she aspires to here is a highbrow critique of art and society in the last twenty years. What she has written is a novel that strives too hard to impress. The prose is full of bad breathiness, the characters suffer from terminal solipsism, and the social criticism is often as cliched as the attitudes it attacks."

Esquire columnist James Wolcott also comments on Gray's satiric designs: "Tripping through *World Without End,* I kept telling myself that the book might be a spoofy lark—a Harlequin romance for art majors—but I have a lurking suspicion that Gray is serious. After all, the novel's theme—the pull and persistence of friendship—is buttressed by quotations from Catullus and from Roland Barthes, and floating through the text are the sort of flowery phrases only a tremulously sincere epicurean would use." *Commentary*'s Pearl K. Bell is also highly critical of Gray's second novel. "Francine Gray's sententious dialogue about love and death and self-fulfillment does not blind us to the poverty of thought in what seems to have been conceived as a novel of ideas," the critic contends. "*World Without End* is not a novel of ideas, it is an adolescent daydream, an orgy of pseudo-intellectual posturing, a midnight bull session in a college dorm."

Gray's second father was artist Alexander Liberman, art director of *Vogue* magazine. Her mother once worked at Saks Fifth Avenue, New York City, in the fashion industry. Drawing from this heritage, *October Blood* satirizes "the peculiar world of high fashion" and "sets out to tell a serious, even painful, story about three generations of remarkable women," Judith Viorst remarks in the *New York Times Book Review.* Though *October Blood* received mixed reviews, Joanne Kaufman of *Book World* notes that "Gray is successful at showing that the concerns of the fashion world are as lightweight as a Chanel chemise."

Gray's next bestselling nonfiction book looks at another facet of her heritage, the Soviet ancestry of her mother and the other emigres who raised her in Paris. *Soviet Women: Walking the Tightrope* records Gray's observations of contemporary Soviet life and women's concerns she gathered on a visit to her mother's homeland. "The distinguished American journalist and novelist Francine du Plessix Gray has now brought us a rich and contradictory selection of Soviet women's opinions," Mary F. Zirin comments in the *Los Angeles Times Book Review.* Reading it, says Zirin, "is like turning a kaleidoscope—a new pattern emerges with every chapter. . . . Gray uses her novelistic skills to record talks with some women in which psychological pressure and suppressed rage can be sensed under a facade of stoic cheer." The government encourages women to hold jobs and to raise large families; abortion is the most well-known method of birth control, Gray reports. Each woman expects to have between seven and fourteen abortions before menopause; there are between five and eight abortions for every live birth, and one out of five babies is born with a defect. Women form deep commitments to each other but tend to see men as crude liabilities.

Carroll Bogert of *Newsweek* relates that *Soviet Women* offers some surprises: "Gray turns a predictable tale of oppression upside down. . . . Traditions have ensured a peculiar female dominance in a society where tremendous male chauvinism persists. . . . Ninety-two percent of Soviet women work, and they do nearly all domestic chores. One woman admits many women have 'a need to control that verges on the tyrannical, the sadistic.'" Furthermore, though the reforms of *glasnost* are viewed by outsiders as a move toward greater personal liberty for Soviet citizens, "the Bolshevik ideal of sexual equality is being trampled in the retreat from socialism," Bogert points out. Bogert concludes, "For Westerners who think Gorbachev's reforms will make Them more like Us, this fine writer has a valuable lesson to teach."

Gray's biography *Rage and Fire: A Life of Louise Colet, Pioneer Feminist, Literary Star, Flaubert's Muse,* portrays the life of Louise Colet, Flaubert's mistress from 1846 to 1855. Reviewers noted that the passionate nature of Colet's life, in addition to her affiliation with such major figures as Flaubert, constitutes fascinating material for biography. Born in Provence, Colet moved to Paris at a young age and employed what Gray calls "her great gift for self-promotion" to establish her own literary salon. Gray's biography recounts Colet's series of distinguished lovers including Flaubert, her ongoing struggle to assert herself as a successful writer, and her loneliness and decline during her later years. Throughout the biography, Gray refutes Colet's trivialized historical reputation (largely based on negative comments written by Flaubert's friends) as merely a beautiful and volatile woman with whom Flaubert had an affair, emphasizing the fact that some of Flaubert's most important insights concerning the writing process were articulated in letters to Colet, as well as the fact of Colet's literary fame during her lifetime. While critics acknowledged the often slanderous nature of earlier commentary on Colet, opinions diverged on the subject of Colet's status as a writer and feminist. Most noted that while her life and career were impressive, her writings evidence a modest and uneven level of skill. "The difficult truth is that a rereading of Colet's considerable creative legacy does not prove her testiest critics wrong," observes Barbara Meister in *Belles Lettres.* Gabriele Annan of the *Times Literary Supplement* also expresses skepticism concerning Gray's attempt to rehabilitate Colet as a writer: "Unfortunately, Colet doesn't emerge as a better feminist than she was a writer." *Rage and Fire* is nevertheless regarded as an important and successful biography in its depiction of an outstanding woman's life and for the historical insights Gray provides. "Ms. Gray gives rich background material on the mores of the times and has interesting things to say about the repression of female militancy in the wake of the Revolution," observes Victor Brombert in *New York Times Book Review.*

BIOGRAPHICAL/CRITICAL SOURCES:

BOOKS

Contemporary Authors Autobiography Series, Volume 2, Gale (Detroit), 1985.
Contemporary Literary Criticism, Volume 22, Gale, 1982.

PERIODICALS

American Spectator, January, 1982; July, 1990.
Belles Lettres, summer, 1994.
Books and Bookmen, March, 1971.
Book World, October 13, 1985.

Chicago Tribune Book World, May 31, 1981; August 15, 1982; March 25, 1990.

Commentary, August, 1981.

Commonweal, May 22, 1981.

Contemporary Review, January, 1996, p. 53.

Detroit News, December 16, 1981.

Esquire, June, 1981.

Harpers, November, 1976.

Listener, February 25, 1971; June 2, 1977.

Los Angeles Times Book Review, March 25, 1990.

Maclean's, April 9, 1990.

Ms., November, 1976; July, 1981.

Nation, February 1, 1971; November 20, 1976; June 4, 1990.

National Observer, December 18, 1976.

National Review, November 12, 1976.

New Republic, June 27, 1970; May 9, 1994.

Newsweek, October 11, 1976; June 22, 1981; March 26, 1990.

New York Review of Books, November 11, 1976; May 26, 1994, p. 12.

New York Times, October 8, 1976; September 15, 1979; May 19, 1981; August 20, 1981.

New York Times Book Review, May 31, 1970; October 17, 1976; May 24, 1981; September 12, 1982; October 6, 1985; March 11, 1990; March 20, 1994.

Progressive, November, 1981.

Quill & Quire, July, 1990.

Saturday Review, June 13, 1970; October 30, 1976; May, 1981.

Time, November 1, 1976.

Times Literary Supplement, May 20, 1977; July 22, 1994.

Village Voice, November 22, 1976.

Wall Street Journal, October 25, 1976; June 1, 1981.

Washington Post Book World, August 29, 1976; October 24, 1976; May 24, 1981; March 11, 1990.

Women's Review of Books, December, 1990.

*   *   *

GRAY, Spalding 1941-

PERSONAL: Born June 5, 1941, in Providence, RI; son of Rockwell (a factory employee) and Margeret Elizabeth (a homemaker; maiden name, Horton) Gray; married Renee Shafransky (a writer and stage director), August, 1991 (divorced); children: one son (not by marriage). *Education:* Emerson College, B.A., 1965. *Politics:* "None." *Religion:* "None."

ADDRESSES: Home and office—22 Wooster St., New York, NY 10013. *Agent*—Suzanne Gluck, International Creative Management, 40 West 57th St., New York, NY 10019.

CAREER: Actor in Cape Cod, MA, and Saratoga, NY, 1965-67; actor with Alley Theater, Houston, 1967; actor with Performance Group (experimental theater company), New York City, 1967-79; co-founder of Wooster Group (theater company), New York City, 1977; writer, 1979–. Actor in summer stock plays, including *The Curious Savage, Long Day's Journey into Night,* and *The Knack*; actor in films, including *The Killing Fields,* 1983, *Swimming to Cambodia,* 1985, *True Stories,* 1987, *Stars and Bars,* 1988, *Clara's Heart,*1988, *Beaches,* 1989, and *Bad Company.* Visiting instructor at University of California, Santa Cruz, summer, 1978, and at Columbia University, 1985; artist-in-residence at Mark Taper Forum, Los Angeles, 1986-87.

AWARDS, HONORS: Grants from National Endowment for the Arts, 1978, Rockefeller Foundation, 1979, and Edward Albee

Foundation, 1985; fellowships from National Endowment for the Arts, 1978, and Rockefeller Foundation, 1979; Guggenheim fellowship, 1985; Obie Award, *Village Voice,* 1985, for *Swimming to Cambodia.*

WRITINGS:

DRAMATIC MONOLOGUES

Sex and Death to the Age 14 (also see below), produced off-Broadway, 1979.

Booze, Cars, and College Girls (also see below) produced off-Broadway, 1979.

India (and After), produced off-Broadway, 1979.

A Personal History of the American Theatre, produced off-Broadway, 1980.

(With Randal Levenson) *In Search of the Monkey Girl* (produced off-Broadway, 1981), Aperture Press, 1982.

Swimming to Cambodia (produced off-Broadway, 1985; also see below), Theatre Communications Group, 1985.

Sex and Death to the Age 14 (collection; includes *Sex and Death to the Age 14* and *Booze, Cars, and College Girls*), Random House, 1986.

Travels through New England, produced off-Broadway, 1986.

Terrors of Pleasure, produced in New York at Lincoln Center, 1986.

Rivkala's Ring (based on Anton Chekhov's short story "A Witch"; produced in Chicago, 1986, as part of a production titled *Orchards*), in *Orchards* (anthology), Knopf, 1986.

Swimming to Cambodia: The Collected Works of Spalding Gray (includes *Swimming to Cambodia, Sex and Death to the Age 14, Booze, Cars, and College Girls, 47 Beds, Nobody Wanted to Sit behind a Desk, Travels through New England,* and *Terrors of Pleasure*), Picador, 1987.

Monster in a Box (produced in New York at Lincoln Center, 1990), Vintage (New York City), 1992.

Gray's Anatomy (produced in New York, 1993), Vintage, 1994.

It's a Slippery Slope, produced in New York at Lincoln Center, 1996, published by Noonday Press, 1997.

OTHER

(With Elizabeth LeCompte) *Sakonnet Point* (one-act play), produced off-Broadway, 1975.

(With LeCompte) *Rumstick Road* (one-act play), produced off-Broadway, 1977.

(With LeCompte) *Nyatt School* (one-act play), produced off-Broadway, 1978.

(With LeCompte) *Three Places in Rhode Island* (play trilogy; includes *Sakonnet Point, Rumstick Road,* and *Nyatt School*), produced off-Broadway, 1979.

Point Judith (one-act play; epilogue to *Three Places in Rhode Island*), produced off-Broadway, 1979.

Seven Scenes from a Family Album (short stories), Benzene Press, 1981.

Impossible Vacation (novel), Knopf, 1992.

Also producer of improvisations, including "Interviewing the Audience," 1981, and "Art in the Anchorage," 1985. Contributor of articles to drama journals and periodicals, including *Elle, Rolling Stone, Gentleman's Quarterly, Performing Arts Journal,* and *Drama Review.*

MEDIA ADAPTATIONS: Several of Gray's performances of *Swimming to Cambodia* were adapted by director Jonathan Demme for the 1987 film of the same title, with music by Laurie Anderson; *Terrors of Pleasure* was filed as an HBO Comedy Special; *Monster in a Box* was released as a film by Fine Line

Features in 1992, with music by Anderson; *Gray's Anatomy* was directed by Steven Soderberg and filmed in 1997.

SIDELIGHTS: Actor and performance artist Spalding Gray is known for his critically acclaimed autobiographical dramatic monologues in which he draws upon some of the most intimate areas of his personal history in order to produce observant, humorous, and insightful stories of contemporary life. "Recycling negative experience is one of the things the monologues are about," Gray explained to Don Shewey in the *New York Times.* "I go out and digest what could be disturbing situations and convert them into humor in front of an audience."

Born in Rhode Island to middle-class parents, Gray became interested in the theater as a teenager. He studied acting at Emerson College, and after his 1965 graduation he performed for two years in summer stock theater in New England and in New York state. In 1967 Gray traveled to Texas and Mexico, and upon his return several months later he learned his mother had committed suicide. The loss and subsequent family trauma caused him to suffer a prolonged depression that resulted in a nervous breakdown nine years later. Gray eventually used events from his childhood and college life as well as experiences as a struggling actor as material for his dramas and monologues.

In the late 1960s Gray moved to New York City, where he joined the Performance Group, an experimental off-Broadway theater company. There he composed his first autobiographical dramatic works, and in 1977 he founded the Wooster Group with Elizabeth LeCompte. Also with LeCompte, Gray wrote *Sakonnet Point* and *Rumstick Road,* two experimental dramas which explored his mother's mental illness and suicide and their effects on his youth and on his family, and *Nyatt School,* a satire of poet and dramatist T. S. Eliot's play *The Cocktail Party.* The three plays made up a trilogy titled *Three Places in Rhode Island,* which Gray produced collectively in 1979.

Gray became interested in the dramatic monologue's possibilities during his tenure as a summer workshop instructor at the University of California's Santa Cruz campus in 1978. As related by David Guy in the *New York Times Book Review,* Gray lamented what he foresaw as the demise of white middle-class life to a friend who replied, "During the collapse of Rome the last artists were the chroniclers." Gray consequently decided to "chronicle" his own life orally in dramatic monologue form; the performer felt that writing it down implied a faith in the future that he did not possess. In 1979 Gray performed *Sex and Death to the Age 14,* his first monologue, at SoHo's Performing Garage. This confessional account of Gray's boyhood experiences with family turmoil and sexuality was followed by an examination of his life at college titled *Booze, Cars, and College Girls* and then by *India (and After),* the story of his nervous collapse when he returned from a tour of India in 1976. "I'll never run out of material as long as I live," *Newsweek*'s Cathleen McGuigan quoted the actor describing his work's content. "The only disappointment is that I probably won't be able to come back after I die and tell that experience." After the success of these first monologues, Gray began giving performances across the country.

In the early 1980s Gray used the monologue form to produce *Interviewing the Audience* and *In Search of the Monkey Girl.* In the former Gray elicited stories from audience members, while the latter was the product of a trip that Gray, hoping to generate new material for his monologues, took to interview carnival members and sideshow freaks at the 1981 Tennessee State Fair. The resulting monologue was published as the text of a book of

photographs by the same name in 1982. During this time Gray also published his first fictional work, *Seven Scenes from a Family Album,* a book of short, interrelated autobiographical sketches depicting, with satire as well as humor, the sexual tensions and complex emotional relationships in a suburban family.

Publicity from Gray's one-man performances resulted in his being cast as an American ambassador's aide in the 1983 feature film *The Killing Fields,* the story of the friendship between an American correspondent and his Asian assistant during the 1970s war in Cambodia. The two months Gray spent filming on location in Thailand became the subject of his next effort, *Swimming to Cambodia,* considered by many critics to be his masterpiece. The monologue premiered in 1985 and evolved improvisationally at New York City's Performing Garage. Gray, who performed the monologue sitting at a desk with only a glass of water, a notebook, and two maps of Southeast Asia as props, narrated anecdotes and observations from several levels of his own experience—as an individual coping with personal problems, as a professional actor in a large-scale movie production, as an American facing the aftermath of U.S. policy in Cambodia since the Vietnam War, and as a human being learning of the atrocities committed by the Khmer Rouge, a guerrilla group that terrorized the country in 1975. The monologue takes its title, as quoted by Janet Maslin in the *New York Times,* from Gray's remark in the piece that "explaining the upheaval in that country 'would be a task equal to swimming there from New York.'"

Swimming to Cambodia met with an enthusiastic reception. Critics admired the pace and fluidity of Gray's narrative, the numerous descriptive details in his recollections, and the honesty with which he presented his stories. "What really makes [*Swimming to Cambodia*] work is its shifting frames of reference, as Gray contracts and expands his point of view to move from meticulously described immediate experience to a detached global-historical vision," assessed Dave Kehr in the *Chicago Tribune. New York Times* writer Mel Gussow was similarly impressed, asserting that Gray's "stream of experience has the zestful, first-hand quality of a letter home from the front." And David Richards, writing for the *Washington Post,* called the actor "an original and disciplined artistic temperament at work," concluding that when Gray is "talking about himself—with candor, humor, imagination and the unfailingly bizarre image—he ends up talking about all of us."

Gray's stage success with *Swimming to Cambodia* inspired him to collaborate with future wife Renee Shafransky on a movie version of the monologue. The film version of *Swimming to Cambodia* was produced by Shafransky, directed by Jonathan Demme, and released in 1987 to widespread critical acclaim. Deemed by Kehr a "documentary on the face and voice of Spalding Gray," the movie was filmed in the Performing Garage and later embellished only with music and a few clips from *The Killing Fields.*

Gray has published as well as performed his monologues. *Swimming to Cambodia,* issued in 1985, 1993's *Gray's Anatomy,* and a 1986 collection titled *Sex and Death to the Age 14* are among the transcriptions of Gray's many performances through which the printed form of each monologue evolved. "Almost all of my writing has grown out of speaking it in front of an audience," Gray once explained to *Contemporary Authors.* "Then, after a great number of performances, I take the best tape, get it transcribed, and rework it for print." Critical responses to Gray's monologues in book form, however, have been mixed: some readers, while admiring the author's storytelling ability, have questioned the literary merit of his material. Lisa Zeidner, for instance, wrote in the *New York Times Book Review* that *Swimming to Cambodia* "is surprisingly successful on the page—breezy and theatrical," while *New Statesman* reviewer Nick Kimberley complained that in the writing Gray "simply comes across as a cartoon version of the self-dramatising, all-American alternative culturist. . . . He lazily spews up the world in an endless burble of 'me-me-me.'"

Gray followed the popular *Swimming to Cambodia* with two more monologues: *Terrors of Pleasure,* which premiered at the Lincoln Center for the Performing Arts in New York City in 1986, and *Rivkala's Ring.* The story of Gray's purchase of a dilapidated house in New York's Catskill Mountains and his resultant frustration in learning that the structure's rotting foundations were causing it to sink, *Terrors of Pleasure* was praised by Gussow, who remarked that the "narrative has dramatic cohesiveness as well as comic insight." Gray was also commissioned in 1986 by the Juilliard Theater School's Acting Company to write a theatrical adaptation of a short story by Russian author and dramatist Anton Chekhov for a production called *Orchards.* For the project Gray wrote *Rivkala's Ring*—a monologue to be performed by an actor other than Gray in which an insomniac, upon receiving a copy of Chekhov's short story "The Witch" in the mail, begins a winding narrative having little overt connection to the story. Some reviewers found Gray's contribution to the program too far removed from Chekhovian themes, but John Beaufort in the *Christian Science Monitor* called the monologue "a windy word-scape, effectively recited." Again Gussow admired Gray's work, describing his contribution to *Orchards* as "a stream of fascinating experience," and concluded that "even more clearly than before, one realizes the extent of Mr. Gray's creativity as dramatist as well as performance artist."

In line with his autobiographical bent, Gray has also written an autobiographical novel. Titled *Impossible Vacation* and published in 1992, the novel had its genesis in the monologue *Monster in a Box,* which was first performed at New York's Lincoln Center in 1990. The monologue featured "a man who can't write a book about a man who can't take a vacation"; the "monster" of the title refers to the stack of handwritten manuscript pages that multiply—but to no conclusive "The End"—during the monologue's performance. In *Impossible Vacation* that man becomes Brewster North—a thinly disguised Gray—who can't hold down a job because of his belief that something better is just around the corner, whose emotionally troubled mother eventually commits suicide, and whose own emotional and financial instability occasionally topples him into lulls of depression as well. The continuous frustration of each of North's goals is the lifeblood of the work; while David Montrose commented in the *Times Literary Supplement* that later portions of the novel are "without Gray's usual humour and charm," *Spectator* reviewer Cressida Connolly noted of *Impossible Vacation*: "Its hero spends many years trying to relax, hang out and enjoy life: his failure to do so makes hilarious reading."

BIOGRAPHICAL/CRITICAL SOURCES:

BOOKS

Contemporary Authors, Volume 128, Gale (Detroit), 1990.

PERIODICALS

Chicago Tribune, July 9, 1986; April 7, 1987; May 20, 1987.
Christian Science Monitor, April 30, 1986.
Los Angeles Times, January 15, 1985; January 18, 1985; April 3, 1987; May 20, 1987; January 8, 1988.
Nation, April 18, 1987.

New Statesman, September 7, 1987.
Newsweek, July 28, 1986.
New York Times, November 16, 1984; March 28, 1986; April 23, 1986; May 11, 1986; May 15, 1986; March 7, 1987; March 13, 1987; March 22, 1987; April 24, 1987; November 11, 1996.
New York Times Book Review, January 12, 1986; May 4, 1986; May 22, 1992; July 12, 1992, pp. 9-10; October 12, 1997.
New York Times Magazine, March 8, 1987.
Observer, February 15, 1987.
Publishers Weekly, January 20, 1992, p. 59; November 22, 1993, p. 58.
Spectator, January 16, 1993, p. 30.
Time, April 27, 1987.
Times (London), February 7, 1987.
Times Literary Supplement, January 8, 1993, p. 17.
Village Voice, January 27, 1982.
Washington Post, June 2, 1979; April 1, 1985; May 1, 1987.

*   *   *

GREELEY, Andrew M(oran) 1928-

PERSONAL: Born February 5, 1928, in Oak Park, IL; son of Andrew T. (a corporation executive) and Grace (McNichols) Greeley. *Education:* St. Mary of the Lake Seminary, A.B., 1950, S.T.B., 1952, S.T.L., 1954; University of Chicago, M.A., 1961, Ph.D., 1962. *Politics:* Democrat. *Religion:* Roman Catholic.

ADDRESSES: Home—1012 East 47th St., Chicago, IL 60653. *Office*—National Opinion Research Center, University of Chicago, 1155 East 60th St., Chicago, IL 60637; and Department of Sociology, University of Arizona, Tucson, AZ 85721.

CAREER: Ordained Roman Catholic priest, 1954. Church of Christ the King, Chicago, IL, assistant pastor, 1954-64; University of Chicago, National Opinion Research Center, Chicago, IL, senior study director, 1961-68, program director for higher education, 1968-70, director of Center for the Study of American Pluralism, 1971-85, research associate, 1985–; University of Chicago, lecturer in sociology of religion, 1962-72, professor of social science, 1991–; University of Arizona, Tucson, professor of sociology, beginning 1978, currently adjunct professor. Professor of sociology of education, University of Illinois at Chicago. Member of planning committee, National Conference on Higher Education, 1969; member of board of advisers on student unrest, National Institute of Mental Health; consultant, Hazen Foundation Commission. Has made a number of appearances on radio and television programs.

MEMBER: American Sociological Association, American Catholic Sociological Society (former president), Society for the Scientific Study of Religion, Religious Research Association.

AWARDS, HONORS: Thomas Alva Edison Award, 1962, for *Catholic Hour* radio broadcasts; Catholic Press Association award for best book for young people, 1965; C. Albert Kobb award, National Catholic Education Association, 1977; Mark Twain Award, Society for the Study of Midwestern Literature, 1987; Popular Culture Award, Center for the Study of Popular Culture (Bowling Green State University), 1986; Freedom to Read Award, Friends of the Chicago Public Library, 1989; U.S. Catholic Award, 1993. LL.D., St. Joseph's College (Rensselaer, IN), 1967; Litt.D., St. Mary's College (Winona, MN), 1967; honorary Doctor of Humane Letters, Bowling Green State University (Bowling

Green, OH), 1986; honorary Doctorate of Humanities, St. Louis University (St. Louis, MO), 1991; honorary Doctorate, Northern Michigan University.

WRITINGS:

RELIGION

The Church and the Suburbs, Sheed, 1959.

Strangers in the House: Catholic Youth in America, Sheed, 1961, revised edition, Doubleday, 1967.

(Editor with Michael E. Schlitz) *Catholics in the Archdiocese of Chicago,* Chicago Archdiocesan Conservation Council, 1962.

Religion and Career: A Study of College Graduates, Sheed, 1963.

Letters to a Young Man, Sheed, 1964.

Letters to Nancy, from Andrew M. Greeley, Sheed, 1964.

Priests for Tomorrow, Ave Maria Press, 1964.

And Young Men Shall See Visions: Letters from Andrew M. Greeley, Sheed, 1964.

(With Peter H. Rossi) *The Education of Catholic Americans,* Aldine, 1966.

The Hesitant Pilgrim: American Catholicism after the Council, Sheed, 1966.

The Catholic Experience: An Interpretation of the History of American Catholicism, Doubleday, 1967.

(With William Van Cleve and Grace Ann Carroll) *The Changing Catholic College,* Aldine, 1967.

The Crucible of Change: The Social Dynamics of Pastoral Practice, Sheed, 1968.

Uncertain Trumpet: The Priest in Modern America, Sheed, 1968.

Youth Asks, "Does God Talk?," Nelson, 1968, published as *Youth Asks, "Does God Still Speak?",* 1970.

(With Martin E. Marty and Stuart E. Rosenberg) *What Do We Believe? The Stance of Religion in America,* Meredith, 1968.

From Backwater to Mainstream: A Profile of Catholic Higher Education, McGraw, 1969.

A Future to Hope In: Socio-Religious Speculations, Doubleday, 1969.

Life for a Wanderer: A New Look at Christian Spirituality, Doubleday, 1969.

Religion in the Year 2000, Sheed, 1969.

New Horizons for the Priesthood, Sheed, 1970.

The Life of the Spirit (also the Mind, the Heart, the Libido), National Catholic Reporter, 1970.

(With William E. Brown) *Can Catholic Schools Survive?,* Sheed, 1970.

The Jesus Myth, Doubleday, 1971.

The Touch of the Spirit, Herder & Herder, 1971.

What a Modern Catholic Believes about God, Thomas More Press, 1971.

Priests in the United States: Reflections on a Survey, Doubleday, 1972.

The Sinai Myth, Doubleday, 1972.

The Unsecular Man: The Persistence of Religion, Schocken, 1972.

What a Modern Catholic Believes about the Church, Thomas More Press, 1972.

The Catholic Priest in the United States: Sociological Investigations, United States Catholic Conference, 1972.

(Editor with Gregory Baum) *The Persistence of Religion,* Seabury, 1973.

The Devil, You Say! Man and His Personal Devils and Angels, Doubleday, 1974.

(With Baum) *The Church as Institution,* Herder & Herder, 1974.

May the Wind Be at Your Back: The Prayer of St. Patrick, Seabury, 1975.

(With William C. McCready and Kathleen McCourt) *Catholic Schools in a Declining Church,* Sheed, 1976.

The Communal Catholic: A Personal Manifesto, Seabury, 1976.

Death and Beyond, Thomas More Press, 1976.

The American Catholic: A Social Portrait, Basic Books, 1977.

The Mary Myth: On the Femininity of God, Seabury, 1977.

An Ugly Little Secret: Anti-Catholicism in North America, Sheed, 1977.

Everything You Wanted to Know about the Catholic Church but Were Too Pious to Ask, Thomas More Press, 1978.

(Editor with Baum) *Communication in the Church Concilium,* Seabury, 1978.

Crisis in the Church: A Study of Religion in America, Thomas More Press, 1979.

The Making of the Popes, 1978: The Politics of Intrigue in the Vatican, Sheed, 1979.

Catholic High Schools and Minority Students, Transaction Publications, 1982.

The Bottom Line Catechism for Contemporary Catholics, Thomas More Press, 1982.

Religion: A Secular Theory, Free Press, 1982.

The Catholic WHY? Book, Thomas More Press, 1983.

How to Save the Catholic Church, Penguin, 1984.

(With Mary G. Durka) *Angry Catholic Women,* Thomas More Press, 1984.

American Catholics since the Council: An Unauthorized Report, Thomas More Press, 1985.

Patience of a Saint, Warner Books, 1986.

Catholic Contributions: Sociology and Policy, Thomas More Press, 1987.

When Life Hurts: Healing Themes from the Gospels, Thomas More Press, 1988.

Religious Indicators, 1940-1985, Harvard University Press, 1989.

God in Popular Culture, Thomas More Press, 1989.

Myths of Religion, Warner Books, 1989.

Religious Change in America, Harvard University Press, 1989.

Complaints against God, Thomas More Press, 1989.

Year of Grace: A Spiritual Journal, Thomas More Press, 1990.

(With Jacob Neusner) *The Bible and Us: A Priest and a Rabbi Read Scripture Together,* Warner Books, 1990, revised edition published as *Common Ground: A Priest and a Rabbi Read Scripture Together,* Pilgrim Press (Cleveland), 1996.

The Book of Irish American Prayers and Blessings, Thomas More, 1991.

The Catholic Myth: The Behavior and Beliefs of American Catholics, Macmillan, 1991.

(Contributor) *The Seven Deadly Sins: Stories on Human Weakness and Virtue,* Liguori Publications, 1992.

Love Affair: A Prayer Journal, Crossroad, 1992.

Religion as Poetry, Thomas More Press, 1994.

Sociology and the Religion: A Collection of Readings, Harper, 1994.

Sacraments of Love: A Prayer Journal, Crossroad, 1994.

Windows: A Prayer Journal, Crossroad (New York City), 1995.

Forging a Common Future: Catholic, Judaic, and Protestant Relations for a New Millennium, Pilgrim Press (Cleveland, OH), 1997.

Also author of *Teenage World: Its Crises and Anxieties,* Divine Word Publications, and of a number of shorter works. Author of syndicated column "People and Values," appearing in approximately eighty newspapers. Contributor to Catholic magazines.

SOCIOLOGY

Why Can't They Be Like Us?: Facts and Fallacies about Ethnic Differences and Group Conflicts in America (also see below), Institute of Human Relations Press, 1969.

A Fresh Look at Vocations, Clarentian, 1969.

(With Joe L. Spaeth) *Recent Alumni and Higher Education,* McGraw, 1970.

Why Can't They Be Like Us?: America's White Ethnic Groups (includes portions of *Why Can't They Be Like Us?: Facts and Fallacies about Ethnic Differences and Group Conflicts in America*), Dutton, 1971.

The Denominational Society: A Sociological Approach to Religion in America, Scott, Foresman, 1972.

That Most Distressful Nation: The Taming of the American Irish, Quadrangle, 1972.

The New Agenda, Doubleday, 1973.

Building Coalitions: American Politics in the 1970s, New Viewpoints, 1974.

Ethnicity in the United States: A Preliminary Reconnaissance, Wiley, 1974.

MEDIA: Ethnic Media in the United States, Project IMPRESS (Hanover, NH), 1974.

The Sociology of the Paranormal: A Reconnaissance, Sage Publications, 1975.

Ethnicity, Denomination, and Inequality, Sage Publications, 1976.

The Great Mysteries: An Essential Catechism, Seabury, 1976.

(With McCready) *The Ultimate Values of the American Population,* Sage Publications, 1976.

Neighborhood, photographs by Greeley, Seabury, 1977.

No Bigger Than Necessary: An Alternative to Socialism, Capitalism, and Anarchism, New American Library, 1977.

(Editor) *The Family in Crisis or in Transition: A Sociological and Theological Perspective,* Seabury, 1979.

The Irish Americans: The Rise to Money and Power, Times Books, 1980.

(With McCready) *Ethnic Drinking Subcultures,* Praeger, 1980.

The Sociology of Andrew M. Greeley, Scholars Press, 1993.

Editor, *Ethnicity.* Contributor to sociology and education journals.

RELATIONSHIPS

The Friendship Game, Doubleday, 1970.

Sexual Intimacy, Thomas More Press, 1973.

Ecstasy: A Way of Knowing, Prentice-Hall, 1974.

Love and Play, Thomas More Press, 1975.

Faithful Attraction: Discovering Intimacy, Love and Fidelity in American Marriage, Tor, 1991.

The Sense of Love, Ashland Poetry Press, 1992.

NOVELS

Nora Maeve and Sebi, illustrated by Diane Dawson, Paulist/Newman, 1976.

The Magic Cup: An Irish Legend, McGraw, 1979.

Death in April, McGraw, 1980.

The Cardinal Sins, Warner Books, 1981.

Thy Brother's Wife (book 1 of the "Passover Trilogy"), Warner Books, 1982.

Ascent into Hell (book 2 of the "Passover Trilogy"), Warner Books, 1984.

Lord of the Dance (book 3 of the "Passover Trilogy"), Warner Books, 1987.

Love Song, Warner Books, 1988.

All about Women, Tor, 1989.

The Search for Maggie Ward, Warner Books, 1991.

The Cardinal Virtues, Warner Books, 1991.

An Occasion of Sin, Jove, 1992.

Wages of Sin, Putnam, 1992.

Fall from Grace, Putnam, 1993.

Irish Gold, Forge, 1994.

Angel Light: An Old-Fashioned Love Story, Forge (New York City), 1995.

Irish Lace, Forge, 1996.

White Smoke: A Novel about the Next Papal Conclave, Forge, 1996.

Summer at the Lake, Forge, 1997.

Star Bright!: A Christmas Story, Forge, 1997.

Irish Whiskey: A Nuala Anne McGrail Novel, Forge, 1998.

Contract with an Angel, Forge, 1998.

FATHER "BLACKIE" RYAN MYSTERY NOVELS

Virgin and Martyr, Warner Books, 1985.

Happy Are the Meek, Warner Books, 1985.

Happy Are Those Who Thirst for Justice, Mysterious Press, 1987.

Rite of Spring, Warner Books, 1987.

Happy Are the Clean of Heart, Warner Books, 1988.

St. Valentine's Night, Warner Books, 1989.

Happy Are the Merciful, Jove, 1992.

Happy Are the Peacemakers, Jove, 1993.

Happy Are the Poor in Spirit, Jove, 1994.

Happy Are Those Who Mourn, Jove, 1995.

Happy Are the Oppressed: A Blackie Ryan Novel, Beeler Large Print (Hampton Falls, NH), 1997.

The Bishop at Sea, Berkley, 1997.

SCIENCE FICTION NOVELS

Angels of September, G. K. Hall, 1986.

God Game, Warner Books, 1986.

The Final Planet, Warner Books, 1987.

Angel Fire, Random House, 1988.

OTHER

Come Blow Your Mind with Me (essays), Doubleday, 1971.

(With J. N. Kotre) *The Best of Times, the Worst of Times* (biography), Nelson Hall, 1978.

Women I've Met (poetry), Sheed, 1979.

A Piece of My Mind . . . on Just about Everything (selection of newspaper columns), Doubleday, 1983.

Confessions of a Parish Priest: An Autobiography, Simon & Schuster, 1986.

An Andrew Greeley Reader (essays), edited by John Sprague, Thomas More Press, 1987.

Andrew Greeley's Chicago, Contemporary Books, 1989.

(Author of introduction) John Appel, *Pat-Riots to Patriots: American Irish in Caricature and Comic Art,* Michigan State University Museum, 1990.

Andrew Greeley (autobiography), Tor, 1990.

(Editor with Michael Cassutt) *Sacred Visions* (science fiction anthology), Tor, 1991.

(Author of foreword) Mary E. Andereck, *Ethnic Awareness and the School: An Ethnographic Study,* Sage, 1992.

SIDELIGHTS: Andrew Greeley is, according to a *Time* writer, "a Roman Catholic priest, a sociologist, a theologian, a weekly columnist, the author of [numerous] books, and a celibate sex expert. He is an informational machine gun who can fire off an article on Jesus to the *New York Times Magazine,* on ethnic groups to the *Antioch Review,* and on war to *Dissent.*" *Time* reports that Greeley's friend, psychologist-priest Eugene Kennedy, calls him "obsessive, compulsive, a workaholic. . . . He's a natural resource. He should be protected under an ecological act."

While dividing his time between the National Opinion Research Center at the University of Chicago, where he has been involved in sociological research since 1961, and the University of Arizona, where he holds a professorship, Greeley has also published scores of books and hundreds of popular and scholarly articles, making him one of the nation's leading authorities on the sociology of religion.

Greeley has further fueled the fires of controversy by writing more than a dozen bestselling mystery, fantasy, and science fiction novels, often filled with corruption, murder, and lurid sex. Because many of these novels—such as *The Cardinal Sins* and *Thy Brother's Wife*—feature priests and other members of the clergy as principle characters, they are regarded by critics as a forum in which Greeley can air the church's dirty laundry. Other critics have simply dismissed him as a pulp writer. Greeley writes in *Contemporary Authors Autobiography Series (CAAS)*: "I became in the minds of many the renegade priest who wrote 'steamy' novels to make money." Furthermore, he has been ostracized from the Archdiocese of Chicago, refused a parish, and treated as a "non-person" by the Catholic church. (He relates in *CAAS*: "When I tried to pledge a million dollars from my book royalties for the inner-city Catholic schools, [Chicago's] Cardinal Bernardin bluntly turned down the pledge without giving a reason—arguably the first time in history the Catholic Church has turned down money from anyone.")

As a young man in Catholic school, Greeley was enthralled by the works of such Catholic poets and novelists as G. K. Chesterton and Evelyn Waugh. "It seemed to me that fiction was a brilliant way of passing on religion," he recalls in *CAAS*. "I thought that it must be challenging and rewarding to write 'Catholic fiction,' even if I never expected to do it myself." Still, within a few years Greeley was contributing articles and essays to Catholic magazines and conferences; the first of these were written pseudonymously, but later he grew bold enough to use his own name. In 1958 an editor at the Catholic publishers Sheed and Ward offered to expand two of Greeley's articles into a book entitled *The Church and the Suburbs*. He writes in *CAAS*: "This was a big step, much bigger, it would turn out, than I had expected. For a priest to set a word on paper in those days was a dangerous move (it still is). To write a book was to cut oneself off from most of the rest of the priesthood."

Greeley's writings have covered myriad topics, many of which deal with the role of religion in modern life. His subjects have included ethnicity, religious education, church politics, secular politics, the family, death and dying, vocations, history, and the future. His opinions in most of these areas have proven controversial to some extent, but when he tackles the subject of sex— particularly as it relates to religion today—he stirs up more than the usual amount of critical commentary. A good example is his book *Sexual Intimacy*, which the *Time* writer calls "a priest's enthusiastic endorsement of inventive marital sex play," and which J. W. Gartland of *Library Journal* recommends to Catholics who "seek a 'sexier' sexual relationship with their spouse and need supportive religious sanctions." In a much-quoted chapter entitled *"How to Be Sexy,"* Greeley portrays a wife greeting her husband "wearing only panties and a martini pitcher—or maybe only the martini pitcher." According to *Time*: "One right-wing Catholic columnist declared that even discussing the book would be an occasion of sin." But, Greeley explains to Pamela Porvaznik in an interview for the *Detroit News Sunday Magazine,* "a vigorous sexual life is one of the biggest problems confronting married couples. How can people grow in intimacy? How can

they consistently reassure themselves and each other of their own worth? These are real issues, and it's time the Church put them into perspective."

One of Greeley's best-known nonfiction works is *The Making of the Popes, 1978: The Politics of Intrigue in the Vatican.* In this book he details the series of startling events that took place in Rome beginning in the summer of 1978: the death of Pope Paul VI in July; the subsequent election of John Paul I, who died after only thirty-three days in office; and the election of John Paul II, the first non-Italian pope since 1522. The book is particularly noteworthy for its inclusion of little-known "inside information" on the process of electing a new pope, much of it supplied by an informant that Greeley calls "Deep Purple." The title of the book and the use of stylistic devices such as a diary format are intentionally reminiscent of Theodore H. White's *Making of the President* books, reinforcing Greeley's thesis that papal elections have all of the mystery, the jockeying for power, and the behind-the-scenes intrigue of an American presidential election. Several reviewers, including R. A. Schroth of the *New York Times Book Review,* note that Greeley's choice of the name "Deep Purple" for his unnamed source suggests that "he clearly identifies with Woodward and Bernstein." Thus, although the author sees himself as a journalist covering what is, essentially, a political event, he still leaves himself the option of injecting personal comments (as White is known to do) on the various candidates, the election process, and the diverse political powers that subtly influence the voting. "The White model works pretty well," writes Robert Blair Kaiser of the *New York Times,* "freeing the author to present an account of [the] doings in Rome, which, for all its ambiguous partisanship, tells us more about the election of two popes (and the future of the church) than less knowing reporters ever could."

The gap between Greeley and the rest of the Catholic Church was further widened in 1981 with the publication of *The Cardinal Sins.* Though not his first work of fiction, *The Cardinal Sins* was attacked by church officials for its unflattering portrayal of Cardinal Patrick Donahue, a fictional character who swiftly ascends to the top of Chicago's religious hierarchy despite his penchant for brutal sex. The church accused Greeley of using this character to slander the late John Cardinal Cody, then Archbishop of Chicago and a longtime rival of Greeley's. These accusations are not unsubstantiated: *The Cardinal Sins*'s Patrick Donahue funnels church funds to his mistress sister-in-law in South America; at the time of the novel's publication, coincidentally, Cardinal Cody was under investigation for allegedly channeling close to one million dollars to a female companion who also happened to be his step-cousin. Greeley denies any connection between the fictional cardinal and Chicago's Archbishop. "Patrick Donahue is a much better bishop than Cody and a much better human being [than Cardinal Cody]," he explains in the *New York Times.*

Greeley produced several additional novels in the 1990s. *Fall from Grace* centers on Irish Catholic clergy and laity in Chicago and their involvement in several scandals, mainly a priest's alleged pedophilia and an aspiring political candidate's secret homosexuality and spousal abuse. Though reflecting actual events in contemporary Chicago, Greeley notes in the introduction that the novel "was drafted before the explosion of the pedophile crisis in the Archdiocese." In *Irish Gold* an American commodities broker embarks for Dublin to investigate mysterious circumstances surrounding his grandparents' emigration to Chicago in 1922. There he falls for a beautiful Trinity College student who translates his grandmother's diaries, leading to the discovery that his grandparents knew who murdered a prominent Free Irish patriot during the period of the "Troubles" in Ireland. Mary Ellen Elsbernd praises Greeley's "piquant characters" and "delightful Irish mystery" in a *Library Journal* review.

In *White Smoke: A Novel about the Next Papal Conclave,* reminiscent of his expose *The Making of Popes,* Greeley reintroduces the character Father "Blackie" Ryan to address the contentious and often vicious politics behind the selection of a new pontiff. Upon the death of the incumbent pope, Father Blackie leaves Chicago for Rome with Cardinal Cronin to lobby for the election of a more liberal successor. Their cause is aided by a *New York Times* reporter and his ex-wife, a CNN correspondent, who implicate the Vatican in an investment scandal. A *Publishers Weekly* reviewer concludes, "Greeley knows his material *and* his opinions, and sets both into delicious spins here." In *The Bishop at Sea,* Bishop Ryan, who spends more time solving crimes than he does on spiritual matters, is sent to a nuclear-powered aircraft carrier, supposedly to perform a confirmation. Once on board, his talents as a detective are more in demand than his priestly ones, as he finds a mystery that seems as deep—and as dangerous—as the ocean. *Thriller* recommended the book as "sure to delight . . . Greeley's faithful fans."

In general, Greeley's novels have not received much critical praise. Christine B. Vogel of the *Washington Post Book World* describes them as "distinctly unscholarly and unpriestly," bearing "dubious literary merit." *America*'s Sean O'Faolain observes that the author is "all too visible" in his novels, "constantly manipulating both character and plot and infusing everybody, most notably the women, with his own often silly romantic notions." The novels' protagonists are, according to Elaine Kendall of the *Los Angeles Times Book Review,* "so tormented by temptations of the flesh that a questioning reader wonders whatever made them take the vow of celibacy in the first place." And the *New York Times Book Review*'s Sheila Paulos proclaims: "Andrew M. Greeley may be a great priest, a great sociologist, even a great fellow. But . . . a great novelist he is not."

If not a great novelist, Greeley is undeniably a popular one. His novels consistently reach the bestseller lists and linger there for weeks or months. Even his critics have admitted, at times, to his novels' appeal. "To give credit where it's due," *Washington Post Book World* reviewer Maude McDaniel writes, "anybody who reads Andrew Greeley's fiction gets involved." Webster Schott supports this claim in the *New York Times Book Review*: "He is never dull, he spins wondrous romances and he has an admirable ideal for what his church should become." Toronto *Globe and Mail* critic John Doyle attributes the author's popularity to the mystique of the clergy: "Greeley's novels have all been bestsellers because they help satisfy a natural need to know about the private lives of powerful, celibate men. Ecclesiastical power is as much an aphrodisiac as any other type." Abigail McCarthy of the *Chicago Tribune* agrees, noting Greeley's ability to combine "an apparently inside view of Catholic Church politics" with "a judicious mixture of money and clinically detailed sex."

In 1994 Greeley published *Sacraments of Love: A Prayer Journal,* containing the author's private meditations recorded between September 1991 and December 1992. Greeley reports daily activities and shares his own struggles with mortality, public personae, conflicting demands as priest and novelist, church reform and scandals, friendships, and most importantly his relationship with God, whom he addresses as "My Love." According to *Kirkus Reviews,* the book represents "the journal of

an exceptionally active man whose life, or so he prays, is 'possessed by love.'" A *Publishers Weekly* reviewer notes that Greeley's avowed "relationship with Spirit is indeed intimate and accessible."

As R. Stephen Warner noted in the *New York Times Book Review,* Greeley is a "well-trained, abundantly energetic and imaginatively gifted sociologist of religion," and in *The Catholic Myth: The Behavior and Beliefs of American Catholics,* Greeley presents "the fascinating, wonderful, and slightly daffy story of American Catholicism since the end of the Second Vatican Council." Drawing on three decades of Greeley's experience and research as a sociologist and as a priest, and based on scientific survey methods, the book attempts to battle myths and stereotypes about American Catholics. In particular, the book rejects the idea that Catholics are blue-collar reactionaries and that Catholics who become educated and middle-class eventually leave the church. Warner suggests that the book has a few loose ends, but calls it a success, claiming that it "dispels many myths, and gives new meaning to the word 'Catholic'."

Greeley once said: "I never courted controversy, but I also never walked away from it." That willingness to create and confront controversy, Jacob Neusner claims in *America,* makes Greeley exactly what the Catholic Church has needed: a catalyst. "He has defined the issues, set forth the propositions for analysis and argument and brought public discourse to the public at large. . . . He has taught us what it means to be religious in the United States in our time." Neusner concludes: "Had Greeley not lived and done his work, I may fairly claim that we religious people in the United States—Christians and Jews alike—should understand ourselves less perspicaciously than we do."

BIOGRAPHICAL/CRITICAL SOURCES:

BOOKS

Contemporary Authors Autobiography Series, Volume 7, Gale (Detroit), 1988.
Contemporary Literary Criticism, Volume 28, Gale, 1984.
Harrison, Elizabeth, *Andrew M. Greeley: An Annotated Bibliography,* Scarecrow Press (Metuchen, NJ), 1994.
Shafer, Ingrid, *The Womanliness of God: Andrew Greeley's Romances of Renewal,* Loyola University Press, 1986.
Shafer, Ingrid, editor, *Andrew Greeley's World: A Collection of Critical Essays, 1986-1988,* Warner Books, 1989.

PERIODICALS

America, February 10, 1968, p. 196; March 2, 1968, p. 297; May 4, 1968, p. 617; September 11, 1971, p. 153; November 20, 1971, p. 438; October 7, 1972, p. 270; December 8, 1973; November 30, 1974, p. 352; April 26, 1975, p. 326; May 15, 1976, p. 425; November 13, 1976, p. 326; April 9, 1977; May 26, 1979; September 15, 1979, p. 117; June 4, 1982, p. 342; October 22, 1983, p. 236; October 4, 1986, p. 170; May 13, 1989, p. 459; May 12, 1990, p. 481; June 16, 1990, p. 611; August 25, 1990, p. 113; June 1, 1991, p. 604; August 14, 1992, p. 18; December 16, 1995, p. 25.
Best Sellers, November 15, 1973.
Booklist, January 1, 1993, p. 771.
Chicago Tribune, March 3, 1985; August 22, 1989.
Chicago Tribune Book World, May 24, 1981; May 2, 1982; June 26, 1983; November 25, 1984; August 31, 1986.
Christian Century, February 20, 1985, p. 196; September 30, 1987, p. 836; April 18, 1990, p. 410; March 20, 1991, p. 345.
Commonweal, December 14, 1973; June 18, 1976; August 31, 1979; July 17, 1987, pp. 412-17; January 23, 1988, pp. 63-

66; May 18, 1990, p. 323; December 7, 1990, p. 727; August 14, 1992, pp. 18-21.

Detroit News, September 7, 1980; May 20, 1984; February 23, 1986.

Detroit News Sunday Magazine, February 2, 1975.

Economist, April 7, 1990, p. 102.

Globe and Mail (Toronto), March 2, 1985; August 20, 1988; July 13, 1991, p. C6.

Kirkus Reviews, December 15, 1992, p. 1524; December 1, 1993, p. 1504; September 15, 1994, p. 1230; April 1, 1996, p. 467.

Library Journal, November 15, 1973; January 1994, p. 126; November 1, 1994, p. 110; May 15, 1996, p. 84.

Los Angeles Times, May 6, 1982.

Los Angeles Times Book Review, March 28, 1982; September 4, 1983, p. 6; December 9, 1984, p. 16; April 7, 1985, p. 4; March 16, 1986, p. 4; September 14, 1986, p. 3; February 15, 1987, p. 4; April 30, 1989, p. 6; April 15, 1990, p. 8; September 16, 1990, p. 10; April 28, 1991, p. 14; March 14, 1993, p. 7.

National Catholic Reporter, January 15, 1988, p. 7; March 4, 1988, p. 9.

National Review, April 15, 1977; February 22, 1985, p. 42; December 5, 1986, p. 48; April 16, 1990, p. 51; December 5, 1994, p. 77.

New Republic, December 17, 1984, p. 35; September 24, 1990, p. 33.

Newsweek, July 30, 1990, p. 46.

New York Review of Books, March 4, 1976.

New York Times, March 13, 1972; March 6, 1977; September 21, 1979; March 22, 1981; October 31, 1985; March 24, 1993, p. B2.

New York Times Book Review, June 24, 1979; July 26, 1981; April 11, 1982; July 3, 1983, p. 8; January 6, 1985, p. 18; March 10, 1985, p. 13; September 29, 1985, p. 46; March 30, 1986, p. 10; September 14, 1986, p. 14; September 21, 1986, p. 31; February 8, 1987, p. 31; July 31, 1988, p. 32; August 14, 1988, p. 16; January 22, 1989, p. 23; September 17, 1989, p. 24; January 7, 1990, p. 18; April 22, 1990, p. 9; September 2, 1990, p. 9; December 30, 1990, p. 14; June 23, 1991, p. 28; June 30, 1991, p. 20; October 6, 1991, p. 32; December 24, 1995, p. 10; August 11, 1996, p. 16.

New York Times Magazine, May 6, 1984, p. 34.

People Weekly, July 9, 1979; May 3, 1993, p. 36.

Publishers Weekly, April 10, 1987, p. 78; December 14, 1992, p. 38; February 14, 1994, p. 65; October 17, 1994, p. 65; April 29, 1996, p. 50.

Thriller (online), 1998.

Time, January 7, 1974; July 16, 1978; August 10, 1981; July 1, 1991, p. 71.

Times Literary Supplement, August 31, 1984.

Tribune Books (Chicago), January 27, 1991, p. 6.

Village Voice, January 29, 1985, p. 47.

Virginia Quarterly Review, winter, 1990, p. 27.

Wall Street Journal, March 4, 1986, p. 28.

Washington Post, June 11, 1981; January 24, 1984; April 6, 1984, p. D8; June 27, 1986; July 21, 1986; August 19, 1986; June 13, 1987; November 16, 1987.

Washington Post Book World, July 10, 1983, pp. 3, 18; February 24, 1985, p. 1; March 24, 1985, p. 6; January 27, 1986; March 11, 1990, p. 13.

West Coast Review of Books, May, 1985, p. 32; Number 4, 1986, p. 33; Number 6, 1988, p. 44; Number 2, 1989, p. 26; Number 2, 1991, p. 35.

GREEN, Brian
See CARD, Orson Scott

*   *   *

GREEN, Julien (Hartridge) 1900-
(Theophile Delaporte)

PERSONAL: Born September 6, 1900, in Paris, France; christened Julian, but has used the French spelling, Julien, since the late 1920s; son of U.S. citizens, Edward Moon (a business agent) and Mary Adelaide (Hartridge) Green; children: Eric Jourdan (adopted). *Education:* Attended Lycee Janson-de-Sailly, Paris; attended University of Virginia, 1919-22; studied drawing at La Grande Chaumiere, Paris, 1922-23. *Religion:* Roman Catholic.

ADDRESSES: Agent—Editions Fayard, 75 rue des Saints-Peres, 75006, Paris, France.

CAREER: Writer, 1924–. Stayed several times in the United States, including a visit to Virginia, 1933-34; went to America in 1940 after France fell to Germany; lectured on French writers at Princeton University, Goucher College, Mills College, and a Jesuit college, 1940-1942; returned to Paris, 1945. *Wartime service:* World War I—Volunteered for the American Field Service, 1917; served on the French front at Verdun; later worked for six months with the Norton-Harjes Service (now the Red Cross) in Italy until May, 1918; joined the French Army as an American, training at the artillery school, Fontainebleau; served in the region of Metz, and, after the armistice, went with his regiment to the Saar on occupation duty; demobilized, 1919. World War II—Joined U.S. Army, 1942; later held post in the U.S. Office of War Information; made radio broadcasts to France, 1943.

MEMBER: Academie de Baviere, L'Academie Royale de Belgique, Academie Francaise, Academy of Arts and Letters, Academie of Mainz, Conseil litteraire de Monaco, Phi Beta Kappa, Raven Club, Jefferson Society.

AWARDS, HONORS: Prix Paul Flat, Academie Francaise, and Femina-Bookman Prize, both 1928, both for *Adrienne Mesurat*; Harper Prize, 1929-30, for *Leviathan*; Harper 125th Anniversary Award, 1942, for *Memory of Happy Days*; Officier de la Legion d'Honneur; Grand Prix Litteraire de Monaco, 1951, for the whole of his work; Grand Prix National des Lettres, 1966; Prix Ibico Reggino, 1968; Grand Prix, Academie Francaise, 1970; James Biddle Eustace Franco-American Award, 1972; Prix Marcel Proust, 1974; Grand Prix Litterature de Pologne, 1985; Prix des Universites Alemaniques; Grand Prix Arts, Sciences et Lettres de Paris.

WRITINGS:

FICTION

Mont-Cinere (novel), Plon, 1926, translation of complete version by Marshall A. Best published as *Avarice House,* Harper, 1927, complete French edition, Plon, 1928, new English edition published as *Monte-Cinere,* edited by C. T. Stewart, Harper, 1937.

Adrienne Mesurat (novel), Plon, 1927, translation by Henry Longan Stuart published as *The Closed Garden,* Harper, 1928, new French edition (containing some manuscript pages), Club des Libraires de France, 1957, revised edition, Holmes & Meier, 1989, revised English edition, 1991.

Le Voyageur sur la terre (story; illustrated with a portrait of the author by Jean Cocteau), Gallimard, 1927, translation by Courtney Bruerton published as *The Pilgrim on the Earth,* Harper, 1929.

Christine (story), F. Paillart, 1927.

La Traversee inutile (story), Plon, 1927, published as "Leviathan" in *Christine, suivi de Leviathan,* Editions des Cahiers Libres, 1928.

Les Clefs de la mort (story; title means "The Keys of Death"), J. Schiffrin (Paris), 1928.

Leviathan (novel; not the same work as the story, "Leviathan"), Plon, 1929, revised edition with a preface by J. C. Brisville, Editions Recontre (Lausanne), 1962, translation by Vyvyan Holland published as *The Dark Journey,* Harper, 1929.

Le Voyageur sur la terre (collection; contains "Leviathan," "Christine," "The Keys of Death," and "The Pilgrim on the Earth"), Plon, 1930, translation by Bruerton published as *Christine, and Other Stories,* Harper, 1930.

L'Autre Sommeil (novel), Gallimard, 1931.

Epaves (novel), Plon, 1932, translation by Holland published as *The Strange River,* Harper, 1932.

Le Visionnaire (novel), Plon, 1934, translation by Holland published as *The Dreamer,* Harper, 1934.

Minuit (novel), Plon, 1936, translation by Holland published as *Midnight,* Harper, 1936.

Varouna (novel), Plon, 1940, translation by James Whitall published as *Then Shall the Dust Return,* Harper, 1941.

Si j'etais vous (novel), Plon, 1947, revised edition, 1970, translation by J. H. F. McEwen published as *If I Were You,* Harper, 1949.

Moira (novel), Plon, 1950, translation by Denise Folliot published under same title, Macmillan, 1951.

Le Malfaiteur (novel), Plon, 1955, general edition, 1956, augmented edition, 1974, translation by sister, Anne Green, published as *The Transgressor,* Pantheon 1957.

Chaque homme dans sa nuit (novel), Plon, 1960, translation by A. Green published as *Each in His Darkness,* Pantheon, 1961.

L'Autre (novel), Plon, 1971, translation by Bernard Wall published as *The Other One,* Harcourt, 1973.

La Nuit des fantomes (children's book; title means "Halloween"), Plon, 1976.

Le Mauvais Lieu (novel), Plon, 1977.

L'apprenti psychiatre (story; first published in English as *The Apprentice Psychiatrist* in *Quarterly Review,* 1920), translation by son, Eric Jourdan, Le Livre de Poche, 1977.

Histoires de vertige (stories), Le Seuil, 1984.

Les Pays lointains (first novel in trilogy), Le Seuil, 1987, published in English as *The Distant Lands,* M. Boyars (New York City), 1991.

Les Etioles du Sud (second novel in trilogy), Seuil, 1989, published in English as *The Stars of the South.*

Ralph et la Quatrieme Dimension, Flammarion (Paris), 1991.

The Apprentice Writer, M. Boyars (New York City), 1993.

Dixie (third novel in trilogy), Fayard, 1995.

AUTOBIOGRAPHY

Journal, Volume 1: *Les Annees faciles, 1928-34,* Plon, 1938, revised edition published as *Les Annees faciles, 1926-34,* 1970; Volume 2: *Derniers beaux jours, 1935-39,* Plon, 1939; Volume 3: *Devant la porte sombre, 1940-43,* Plon, 1946; Volume 4: *L'Oeil de l'ouragan, 1943-46,* Plon, 1949; Volume 5: *Le Revenant, 1946-50,* Plon, 1951; Volume 6: *Le Miroir interieur, 1950-54,* Plon, 1955; Volume 7: *Le Bel aujourd'hui, 1955-58,* Plon, 1958; Volume 8: *Vers l'invisible, 1959-66,* Plon, 1967; Volume 9: *Ce qui reste de jour, 1966-72,* Plon, 1972; Volume 10: *La bouteille a la Mer, 1972-76,* Plon, 1976; Volume 11: *La terre est si belle, 1976-78,* Le Seuil, 1982; Volume 12: *La lumiere du monde, 1978-81,* Le Seuil, 1982, Volume 13: *L'arc-en-ciel, 1981-88,* 1988; Volume 14: *L'Expatrie, 1984-1990,* Seuil (Paris), 1990.

Personal Record, 1928-39 (contains *Journal,* Volumes 1 and 2), translation by Jocelyn Godefroi, Harper, 1939.

Memories of Happy Days (memoir), Harper, 1942.

(Contributor) *Les Oeuvres nouvelles* (includes "Quand nous habitions tous ensemble," reminiscences), Editions de la Maison Francaise (New York), 1943.

Journal: 1928-1958 (omnibus edition; contains Volumes 1-7), Plon, 1961, translation by A. Green published in abridged edition as *Diary, 1928-57,* edited by Kurt Wolff, Harcourt, 1964, new omnibus edition published as *Journal, 1928-66* (contains Volumes 1-8), two volumes, Plon, 1969.

Jeunes Annees (autobiography), Volume 1: *Partir avant le jour,* Grasset, 1963, translation by A. Green published as *To Leave before Dawn,* Harcourt, 1967, also published as *The Green Paradise,* M. Boyars (New York City), 1993; Volume 2: *Mille chemins ouverts,* Grasset, 1964, published in English as *The War at Sixteen: 1916-1920,* M. Boyars (New York City), 1993; Volume 3: *Terre Lointaine,* Grasset, 1966, published in English as *Love in America,* M. Boyars, 1994; Volume 4: *Restless Youth,* M. Boyars, 1996.

Jeunesse, Plon, 1974; published in two volumes, Le Seuil, 1984.

Memories of Evil Days, edited by Jean-Pierre J. Piriou, University Press of Virginia, 1976.

Dans la gueule de Tempo (journals), illustrated with 500 photographs, Plon, 1978.

Ce qu'il faut d'amour a l'homme, Plon, 1978.

Journal du Voyageur, Seuil (Paris), 1990.

L'homme et son ombre, Seuil (Paris), 1991.

PLAYS

Sud (three-act; produced in Paris, 1953), Plon, 1953, translation produced as "South," London, 1955, published in *Plays of the Year,* Volume 12, Elek, 1955, operatic version, with music by Kenton Coe, produced at Opera de Paris, 1973.

L'Ennemi (three-act; produced in Paris, 1954), Plon, 1954.

L'Ombre (three-act; produced at Theatre Antoine, 1956), Plon, 1956.

Demain n'exite pas; L'Automate (three and four-act), Le Seuil, 1985.

NONFICTION

(Under pseudonym Theophile Delaporte) *Pamphlet contre les Catholiques de France* (essay), Editions de la Revue des Pamphletaires (Paris), 1924, new edition, preface by Jacques Maritain, Plon, 1963.

Suite anglaise (essays), Cahiers de Paris, 1927.

Un Puritain homme de lettres: Nathaniel Hawthorne, Editions des Cahiers Libres, 1928.

Liberte (essay), Plon, 1974.

Paris (essay), Editions du Champ Vallon, 1983.

Frere Francois, Le Seuil, 1983, translation by Peter Heinegg published as *God's Fool: The Life and Times of Francis of Assisi,* Harper, 1985.

Le Langage et son double/The Language and Its Shadow (essays; bilingual edition with translations by the author), Editions de la Difference, 1985.

OTHER

(Translator with A. Green) Charles Peguy, *Basic Verities: Prose and Poetry,* Pantheon, 1943.

(Translator with Anne Green) Peguy, *Men and Saints,* Pantheon, 1944.

(Translator) Peguy, *God Speaks: Religious Poetry,* Pantheon, 1945.

(Translator) Peguy, *The Mystery of the Charity of Joan of Arc,* Pantheon, 1949.

Oeuvres Completes (collected works), ten volumes, Plon, 1954-65.

Bibliotheque de la Pleiade (collected works), five volumes, Gallimard, 1971-75.

Pamphlet contre les catholiques de France, suivi de Ce qu'il faut d'amour a l'homme; L'Appel du desert; La Folie de Dieu, Gallimard, 1982.

(With Jacques Maritain) *Un grande amitie: Correspondance, 1926-1972,* edited by Piriou, Plon, 1979, complete edition, Gallimard, 1982, English translation by Bernard Doering published as *The Story of Two Souls: The Correspondence of Jacques Maritain and Julien Green,* edited by Henry Bars and Jourdan, Fordham University Press, 1988.

Also author of filmscripts *Leviathan,* 1962, and, with Jourdan, *La Dame de pique,* 1965; author, with Jourdan, of television and radio scripts *Je est un autre,* 1954, and *La Mort de Ivan Ilytch,* 1955. Contributor to *Revue Hebdomadaire, Revue Europeenne, Nouvelle Revue Francaise, Revue Universelle, La Parisienne, Revue des Deux Mondes, University of Virginia Magazine, American Scholar,* and other periodicals.

SIDELIGHTS: In 1930 Courtney Bruerton wrote: "As Julien Green is the first American novelist to choose French as his medium of expression, so he is the first American to be ranked by competent critics as a great French writer." L. Clark Keating comments on the "irresistible appeal" which Green's work has held for critics, "many of whom have tried to find American sources and models for his characters and situations." Among his works which have American settings is *Avarice House*; this story, notes Keating, "is laid in a Virginia farmhouse, modeled on an uncle's manor house near Warrenton [where] Green spent several weeks during his first American sojourn." Discussing the similarities between Green and novelist Nathaniel Hawthorne, the critic suggests that "Green's sombre and fantastic imagination, and his preoccupation with violence and death, are often reminiscent of the nineteenth-century New Englander." He concludes that Hawthorne, "if not a model, has been an inspiration."

Green's interest in language and religion is evident in his early novel *Le Voyageur sur la terre,* which appeared in 1927. The story centers around Daniel O'Donovan, a conflicted man whose duality as the author and destroyer of his own personal writings underscores complex notions of self-identity and the autonomy of language as a vehicle of meaning. Robert Ziegler notes in *French Review,* "The antipathy that Green had voiced for his peers' indifference to the sacraments, their lukewarm spirituality, and ignorance of Scripture finds an echo in the absolutism that will characterize Daniel O'Donovan." Green also expresses his rejection of the literary endeavor itself and the apparent futility of written expression, with the exception of that found in the Bible. "The story of Daniel O'Donovan," according to Ziegler, "involves a process of verbal ascesis, the destruction of the documents that overlay the word of God, and an acquiescence to the silence that will enable him to hear the speech that he can understand and that will finally set him free. Indeed the value of the record of Daniel's

spiritual itinerary, like the purpose of Green's writing, is to affirm and testify to the supersession of their own texts by another which transcends them."

Adrienne Mesurat, also published in 1927, involves a young girl, Adrienne, and her suffocating residence in an isolated country villa with her controlling father and chronically ill sister. When Adrienne's sister finally escapes to a sanatorium, her father vents his wrath on Adrienne by imprisoning her in the house. Adrienne finally kills her father when she lunges at him and knocks him to the ground. However, she anguishes over her role in his death, which can only be partially justified as accidental, and finally lapses into a mental breakdown as a result. Praising Green's superior descriptive ability in *Review of Contemporary Literature,* Thomas Filbin writes, "His concentrated, mystical, detailed prose has been compared to both [Marcel] Proust and [Edgar Allan] Poe." Noting parallels between Green's characters and the author during the painful years of his spiritual abandonment, John L. Brown observes in *World Literature Today,* "Perhaps for Adrienne . . . madness might bring her the liberation which she had so desperately sought and had never found."

In addition to his many works of fiction, Green is well-known for his extensive journals and autobiographic writings. In *Jeunes Annees,* a four-volume autobiography, Green recounts the first three decades of his life. The first installment, *The Green Paradise,* spans his early years to age sixteen, including his first self-conscious experience at age five and mounting tension caused by his attraction to both sexes. Commenting on Green's difficult sexual awakening, Richard Eder writes in the *Los Angeles Times Book Review,* "[Green] tells of a childhood and adolescence marked by obsessive attachments both to purity and impurity, and to the mother from whom the mixed messages came." Eder also finds Green's reticence on the outcome of events "exasperating." He writes, "We learn of Julian's stunned bewilderment as his mother lies dying; we never learn what she died of. We learn about his gropings at the hands of fellow schoolboys in intense emotional detail, but we don't quite know what happened. Green does not so much visit his past as haunt it."

Michael Upchurch praises *The Green Paradise,* in the *New York Times Book Review*: "Mr. Green's supple prose—a mix of dreamy rapture and pointed precision—is matched by the fluid contradictions of his subject matter: himself. Ascetic in his aspirations but frankly alive to every sensual stimulus, luminously chaste in his spiritual impulses yet dryly urbane in his wit, Mr. Green is a fascinating paradox." David O'Connell similarly notes in *Commonweal,* "The limpid style, the sensitivity, the *delicatesse,* the discretion in talking of his sexual awakening are all in the French tradition of restraint, sobriety, and good taste." Donna Seaman adds in *Booklist,* "Parisian street life, and moments of inexplicable joy are all described with a sense of wonder and devoted self-study."

The second volume, *The War at Sixteen,* covers the next four years of Green's life in scrupulous detail, including his deeply affecting experiences in the First World War as an ambulance driver and thoughts about entering into a monastic life. Again, Green's sexual preoccupations temper his emotional sensibilities and, as *New York Times Book Review* contributor William H. Pritchard notes, "World War I is stripped of its particulars and turned into the abstract 'war.' The book's particulars emerge rather in the disturbingly powerful sensations other men cause in Mr. Green, who, he reminds us frequently, is notable for his 'astonishing innocence.'" While the war serves as a backdrop for his "inner exploration," according to *Kirkus Reviews,* Green's "journey to self-discovery, sexual identity, and religious belief" are the dominant themes.

The third volume, *Love in America,* spans only two years of Green's life while in the United States attending classes at the University of Virginia. This brief but important period of his development centers around his isolation as a student in an unfamiliar ancestral land, as a Roman Catholic in the predominantly Protestant South, and frustrations over unrequited and restrained homosexual love. However, visits with his maternal relatives and several new friendships softened his feelings toward the South and even inspired Confederate sympathies that later emerged in his writing. *Kirkus Reviews* praises the "excoriating candor that makes Green such a master and exemplar of the confessional voice."

Green concluded with *Restless Youth,* which recounts his return to Paris, association with the Jean Cocteau and Andre Gide literary scene, and successful publication of his first several novels. During this period between 1922 and 1929, Green abandoned painting to take up writing and continued to struggle with his conflicting spirituality and sexuality, a theme that became the hallmark of his fiction. "Whether writing of the progress of his literary career or of his love-affairs," writes Francis King in *Spectator,* "Green achieves an always arresting vividness." Upon the publication of the third volume of his autobiography, John Weightman concludes in the *New York Times Review of Books,* "I should expect the complete text to be his major achievement and to survive as a singular classic of confessional literature."

With *Paris,* a collection of essays and prose poems written during the 1940s and 1950s, Green reflects on the city in which he was born and lived most of his life. The text is accompanied by photographs taken by Green himself. "The tone is mainly elegiac," writes Weightman, "contrasting the charm of the old Paris of his childhood with the brashness of the new, and the style is exquisitely literary in a traditional French manner." Commenting on Green's nostalgic lamentations and professed dislike of the Eiffel Tower, *New York Times Book Review* contributor Richard Goodman writes, "Julian Green's Paris is mysterious and phantom-filled." Leighton Klein concludes in the *San Francisco Review of Books,* "the lifelong Parisian writes with astonishing fluidity and power, his images brooding and shimmering. . . . his *Paris* discards all the conventional terms of address and observation."

Green received renewed interest in the United States with the American publication of *The Distant Lands* in 1991. Set in the antebellum South, the novel centers around the experiences of Elizabeth Escridge, a young English woman who relocates to Georgia in 1850 with her widowed mother. There she witnesses the deceptive pleasures of plantation life, including duels, witchcraft, rural gentility, and compromising romantic affairs that proceed to complicate her life. Green began the novel in the 1930s but abandoned it when he thought it too similar to Margaret Mitchell's *Gone With the Wind.* While noting the novel's excessive length and almost non-existent plot, *New York Times Book Review* contributor Jeffrey Paine praises Green's ability to evoke the atmosphere of a bygone age: "A reader will be initiated almost bodily, inducted experientially, into the slower pulse of an earlier era. Yielding to the spell, you will discover no additional action in the narrative, but the very absence of action lets the luxurious ambiance—the exquisite interior decoration—reverberate with the force of an event."

A commercial success in France, *The Distant Land* was less-enthusiastically received by stateside readers. Despite Green's resort to trademark Southern stereotypes, as Clive Davis notes in *New Statesman,* "The subtle exposition of a young girl's moral and emotional development sits uneasily alongside a narrative full of stock devices and lovers with riding crops." Patrick Lindsay Bowles writes in the *Times Literary Supplement,* "It is not the translator but Green whose shameless repetitiveness, posh vulgarity and whose outrageous padding finally, here as in far too much of his work, obscure his true gifts as a master of chiaroscuro and a peerless story-teller." Green expanded his Southern epic into a trilogy with the addition of *The Stars of the South* in 1989 and *Dixie* in 1995, both of which received similar critical assessment. John L. Brown writes in a *World Literature Today* review of *Dixie,* "It certainly will not enhance the reputation of Julien Green, one of the most gifted and enigmatic writes of his generation. But, after all, at ninety-five, he possesses a reputation that needs no enhancement!"

BIOGRAPHICAL/CRITICAL SOURCES:

BOOKS

Burne, Glenn S., *Julian Green,* Twayne, 1972.
Contemporary Literary Criticism, Gale, Volume 3, 1975; Volume 11, 1979.
Cooke, M. G., *Hallucination and Death as Motifs of Escape in the Novels of Julien Green,* Catholic University of America Press, 1960.
Dictionary of Literary Biography, Gale, Volume 4: *American Writers in Paris, 1920-1939,* 1980; Volume 72: *French Novelists, 1930-1960,* 1988.
Dunaway, John M., *The Metamorphoses of the Self: The Mystic, the Sensualist, and the Artist in the Works of Julien Green,* University Press of Kentucky, 1978.
Gaddis, Marilyn, *The Critical Reaction to Julien Green (1926-56),* unpublished thesis, University of Missouri, 1958.
Green, Anne, *With Much Love,* Harper, 1948.
Stokes, Samuel, *Julian Green and the Thorn of Puritanism,* King's Crown Press, Columbia University, 1955.

PERIODICALS

Booklist, January 1, 1993, p. 785; September 1, 1996, p. 62.
Bookman, August, 1932.
Choice, February, 1992, p. 901.
Commonweal, September 24, 1993, p. 26.
French Review, March, 1950; May, 1955; April, 1990, p. 819.
Kirkus Reviews, June 1, 1991, p. 711; October 15, 1993, p. 1308; June 15, 1994, p. 820; January 1, 1996, p. 41.
Library Journal, July, 1994, p. 92; November 1, 1996, p. 106.
London Magazine, January, 1967.
Los Angeles Times Book Review, December 20, 1992; December 12, 1993.
New Statesman, September 28, 1990, p. 36.
New Yorker, September 1, 1951.
New York Review of Books, December 5, 1991, p. 53.
New York Times Book Review, May 11, 1941; October 1, 1967; August 11, 1991, p. 20; December 22, 1991, p. 10; July 11, 1993, p. 18; January 9, 1994, p. 25.
PMLA, June, 1939.
Publishers Weekly, June 7, 1991, p. 53; July 19, 1991, p. 46; September 7, 1992, p. 85; November 23, 1992, p. 49; November 1, 1993, p. 57; July 11, 1994, p. 71; February 5, 1996, p. 72; July 15, 1996, p. 54.
Review of Contemporary Literature, spring, 1992, p. 161.
San Francisco Review of Books, March, 1991, p. 24.

Saturday Review of Literature, November, 1939.
Sewanee Review, April, 1932.
Spectator, March 9, 1996, p. 33.
Times Literary Supplement, May 17, 1991, p. 6; February 14, 1992, p. 10.
Washington Post Book World, December 15, 1991, p. 13; January 30, 1994, p. 13.
World Literature Today, summer, 1995, p. 549; autumn, 1995, p. 764.

*   *   *

GREENE, Graham (Henry) 1904-1991

PERSONAL: Born October 2, 1904, in Berkhamsted, Hertfordshire, England; died of a blood disease, April 3, 1991, in Vevey, Switzerland; son of Charles Henry (headmaster of Berkhamsted School) and Marion Raymond Greene; married Vivien Dayrell Browning, 1927; children: one son, one daughter. *Education:* Attended Berkhamsted School; Balliol College, Oxford, B.A., 1925. *Religion:* Catholic convert, 1926.

CAREER: Writer. *Times,* London, England, sub-editor, 1926-30; film critic for *Night and Day* during the 1930s; *Spectator,* London, England, film critic, 1935-39, literary editor, 1940-41; with Foreign Office in Africa, 1941-44; Eyre & Spottiswoode Ltd. (publishers), London, England, director, 1944-48; Indo-China correspondent for *New Republic,* 1954; Bodley Head (publishers), London, England, director, 1958-68. Member of Panamanian delegation to Washington for signing of Canal Treaty, 1977.

AWARDS, HONORS: Hawthornden Prize, 1940, for *The Labyrinthine Ways* (published in England as *The Power and the Glory*); James Tait Black Memorial Prize, 1949, for *The Heart of the Matter;* Catholic Literary Award, 1952, for *The End of the Affair;* Boys' Clubs of America Junior Book Award, 1955, for *The Little Horse Bus;* Pietzak Award (Poland), 1960; D.Litt., Cambridge University, 1962; Balliol College, Oxford, honorary fellow, 1963; Companion of Honour, 1966; D.Litt., University of Edinburgh, 1967; Shakespeare Prize, 1968; Legion d'Honneur, chevalier, 1969; John Dos Passos Prize, 1980; medal of the city of Madrid, 1980; Jerusalem Prize, 1981; Grand Cross of the Order of Vasco Nunez de Balboa (Panama), 1983; named commander of the Order of Arts and Letters (France), 1984; named to British Order of Merit, 1986; named to the Order of Ruben Dario (Nicaragua), 1987; Royal Society of Literature Prize; honorary doctorate, Moscow State University, 1988.

WRITINGS:

FICTION, EXCEPT AS INDICATED

Babbling April (poems), Basil Blackwell, 1925.
The Man Within, Doubleday, 1929.
The Name of Action, Heinemann, 1930, Doubleday, 1931.
Rumour at Nightfall, Heinemann, 1931, Doubleday, 1932.
Orient Express, Doubleday, 1932 (published in England as *Stamboul Train,* Heinemann, 1932).
It's a Battlefield, Doubleday, 1934, reprinted with new introduction by author, Heinemann, 1970.
The Basement Room, and Other Stories, Cresset, 1935, title story revised as The Fallen Idol and published with *The Third Man* (also see below), Heinemann, 1950.
England Made Me, Doubleday, 1935, published as *The Shipwrecked,* Viking, 1953, reprinted under original title with new introduction by author, Heinemann, 1970.

The Bear Fell Free, Grayson & Grayson, 1935.
Journey Without Maps (travelogue; also see below), Doubleday, 1936, 2nd edition, Viking, 1961.
This Gun for Hire, Doubleday, 1936 (also see below; published in England as *A Gun for Sale,* Heinemann, 1936).
Brighton Rock, Viking, 1938, reprinted with new introduction by author, Heinemann, 1970.
The Confidential Agent (also see below), Viking, 1939, reprinted with new introduction by author, Heinemann, 1971.
Another Mexico, Viking, 1939, published in England as *The Lawless Roads,* Longmans, Green, 1939 (also see below).
The Labyrinthine Ways, Viking, 1940 (published in England as *The Power and the Glory,* Heinemann, 1940), reprinted under British title, Viking, 1946, reprinted under British title with new introduction by author, Heinemann, 1971.
British Dramatists (nonfiction), Collins, 1942.
The Ministry of Fear (also see below), Viking, 1943.
Nineteen Stories, Heinemann, 1947, Viking, 1949, later published with some substitutions and additions as *Twenty-one Stories,* Heinemann, 1955, Viking, 1962.
The Heart of the Matter, Viking, 1948, reprinted with new introduction by author, Heinemann, 1971.
The Third Man (also see below), Viking, 1950.
The Lost Childhood, and Other Essays, Eyre & Spottiswoode, 1951, Viking, 1952.
The End of the Affair, Viking, 1951.
The Living Room (two-act play; produced in London, 1953), Heinemann, 1953, Viking, 1957.
The Quiet American, Heinemann, 1955.
Loser Takes All, Heinemann, 1955, Viking, 1957.
The Potting Shed (three-act play; produced in New York, 1957, and in London, 1958), Viking, 1957.
Our Man in Havana (also see below), Viking, 1958, reprinted with new introduction by author, Heinemann, 1970.
The Complaisant Lover (play; produced in London, 1959), Heinemann, 1959, Viking, 1961.
A Burnt-Out Case, Viking, 1961.
In Search of a Character: Two African Journals, Bodley Head, 1961, Viking, 1962.
Introductions to Three Novels, Norstedt (Stockholm), 1962.
The Destructors, and Other Stories, Eihosha Ltd. (Japan), 1962.
A Sense of Reality, Viking, 1963.
Carving a Statue (two-act play; produced in London, 1964, and in New York, 1968), Bodley Head, 1964.
The Comedians, Viking, 1966.
(With Dorothy Craigie) *Victorian Detective Fiction: A Catalogue of the Collection,* Bodley Head, 1966.
May We Borrow Your Husband?, and Other Comedies of the Sexual Life, Viking, 1967.
(With Carol Reed) *The Third Man: A Film* (annotated filmscript), Simon & Schuster, 1968.
Collected Essays, Viking, 1969.
Travels With My Aunt, Viking, 1969.
(Author of introduction) Al Burt and Bernard Diederich, *Papa Doc,* McGraw, 1969.
A Sort of Life (autobiography), Simon & Schuster, 1971.
Graham Greene on Film: Collected Film Criticism, 1935-1940, Simon & Schuster, 1972 (published in England as *The Pleasure Dome,* Secker & Warburg, 1972).
The Portable Graham Greene (includes *The Heart of the Matter,* with a new chapter; *The Third Man;* and sections from eight other novels, six short stories, nine critical essays, and ten public statements), Viking, 1972, updated and revised, Penguin (New York City), 1994.

The Honorary Consul, Simon & Schuster, 1973.

Collected Stories, Viking, 1973.

Lord Rochester's Monkey, Being the Life of John Wilmot, Second Earl of Rochester, Viking, 1974.

The Return of A. J. Raffles (three-act comedy based on characters from E. W. Hornung's *Amateur Cracksman*; produced in London, 1975), Simon & Schuster, 1976.

The Human Factor, Simon & Schuster, 1978.

Dr. Fischer of Geneva; or, The Bomb Party, Simon & Schuster, 1980.

Ways of Escape, Simon & Schuster, 1981.

Monsignor Quixote, Simon & Schuster, 1982.

J'accuse: The Dark Side of Nice, Bodley Head, 1982.

Yes and No [and] *For Whom the Bell Chimes* (comedies; produced together in Leicester, England, at Haymarket Studio, March, 1980), Bodley Head, 1983.

Getting to Know the General: The Story of an Involvement, Simon & Schuster, 1984.

The Tenth Man, Bodley Head, 1985.

(Author of preface) *Night and Day* (selections from London periodical), edited by Christopher Hawtree, Chatto & Windus, 1985.

Granta 17, Penguin, 1986.

Collected Short Stories, Penguin, 1988.

The Captain and the Enemy, Viking, 1988.

Yours, etc.: Letters to the Press, 1945-1989, edited by Hawtree, Reinhardt, 1989.

Reflections (essays), Viking, 1990.

The Graham Greene Film Reader: Reviews, Essays, Interviews & Film Stories, Applause Theatre Book Publishers (New York City), 1994.

A World of My Own: A Dream Diary, Reinhardt (New York City), 1994.

OMNIBUS VOLUMES

3: This Gun for Hire; The Confidential Agent; The Ministry of Fear, Viking, 1952, reprinted as *Three by Graham Greene: This Gun for Hire; The Confidential Agent; The Ministry of Fear,* 1958.

Three Plays, Mercury Books, 1961.

The Travel Books: Journey Without Maps [and] *The Lawless Roads,* Heinemann, 1963.

Triple Pursuit: A Graham Greene Omnibus (includes *This Gun for Hire, The Third Man,* and *Our Man in Havana*), Viking, 1971.

JUVENILE

This Little Fire Engine, Parrish, 1950, published as *The Little Red Fire Engine,* Lothrop, Lee & Shepard, 1952.

The Little Horse Bus, Parrish, 1952, Lothrop, Lee & Shepard, 1954.

The Little Steamroller, Lothrop, Lee & Shepard, 1955.

The Little Train, Parrish, 1957, Lothrop, Lee & Shepard, 1958.

EDITOR

The Old School (essays), J. Cape, 1934.

H. H. Munro, *The Best of Saki,* 2nd edition, Lane, 1952.

(With brother, Hugh Greene) *The Spy's Bedside Book,* British Book Service, 1957.

(Author of introduction) Marjorie Bowen, *The Viper of Milan,* Bodley Head, 1960.

The Bodly Head Ford Madox Ford, Volumes 1 and 2, Bodley Head, 1962.

(And author of epilogue) *An Impossible Woman: The Memories of Dottoressa, Moor of Capri,* Viking, 1976.

(With brother, Hugh Greene) *Victorian Villainies,* Viking, 1984.

MEDIA ADAPTATIONS: Screenplays based on his books and stories: "Orient Express," 1934; "This Gun for Hire," 1942; "The Ministry of Fear," 1944; "The Confidential Agent," 1945; "Brighton Rock," screenplay by Greene and Terrence Rattigan, 1947; "The Smugglers," 1948; "The Fallen Idol" (based on Greene's 1935 short story "The Basement Room"), screenplay by Greene, 1949; "The Third Man," screenplay by Greene, 1950; "The Heart of the Matter," 1954; "The End of the Affair," 1955; "Loser Takes All," 1957; "The Quiet American," 1958; "Across the Bridge," 1958; "Our Man in Havana," screenplay by Greene, 1960; "The Power and the Glory," 1962; "The Comedians," screenplay by Greene, 1967; "The Living Room," 1969; "The Shipwrecked," 1970; "May We Borrow Your Husband?," 1970; "The End of the Affair," 1971; "Travels with My Aunt," 1973; "England Made Me," 1973; "A Burned-Out Case," 1973; "The Human Factor," screenplay by Tom Stoppard, directed by Otto Preminger, 1980; "Beyond the Limit," 1983; "Strike It Rich" (based on Greene's 1955 novella *Loser Takes All*), 1990.

SIDELIGHTS: Graham Greene is among the most widely read of all major English novelists of the twentieth century. Yet Greene's popular success—which David Lodge in *Graham Greene* holds partly responsible for a "certain academic hostility" towards Greene—came neither quickly nor easily. Of Greene's initial five novels, the first two were never published; and two others, *The Name of Action* and *Rumour at Nightfall* sold very poorly and have never been reprinted. In his first autobiographical volume, *A Sort of Life,* Greene lamented that, in his earliest novels, he did not know "how to convey physical excitement": the ability to write a "simple scene of action . . . was quite beyond my power to render exciting." Even as late as 1944, Greene confessed in his introduction to *The Tenth Man,* he had "no confidence" in sustaining his literary career.

Greene's string of literary failures drove him to write *Stamboul Train,* a thriller that Greene hoped would appeal to film producers. The novel, filmed two years later as *Orient Express,* is recognized by critics as Greene's coming-of-age work. Writing in a taut, realistic manner, Greene set *Stamboul Train* in contemporary Europe, gathered a train load of plausibly motivated characters, and sent them on their journey. Retaining such stock melodramatic devices as cloak-and-dagger intrigue, flight and pursuit, hair-breadth escapes, and a breakneck narrative pace, Greene shifted the focus away from the conventional hero—the hunter—and onto the villain and/or ostensible villain. What emerged was less a formula than a set of literary hardware that Greene would be able to use throughout the rest of his career, not just to produce further entertainments, but to help give outward excitement to his more morally centered, more philosophical novels.

Stamboul Train was the first of several thrillers Greene referred to as "entertainments"—so named to distinguish them from more serious novels. In his next two entertainments, *A Gun for Sale* (published in the United States as *This Gun for Hire*) and *The Confidential Agent,* Greene incorporated elements of detective and spy fiction, respectively. He also injected significant doses of melodrama, detection, and espionage into his more serious novels *Brighton Rock, The Power and the Glory* (published in the United States as *The Labyrinthine Ways*),*The Heart of the Matter, The End of the Affair, The Quiet American, A Burnt-Out Case, The Comedians, The Honorary Consul,* and *The Human Factor.* Indeed, so greatly did Greene's entertainments influence his other novels that, after 1958, he dropped the entertainment label.

Intrigue and contemporary politics are key elements of Greene's entertainments. In at least two of his thrillers Greene eulogized the tranquility of European life before the First World War. "It was all so peaceful," Dr. Hasselbacher muses about Germany in *Our Man in Havana,* "in those days. . . . Until the war came." And Arthur Rowe, dreaming in *The Ministry of Fear,* notes that his mother, who "had died before the first great war, . . . could [not] have imagined" the blitz on London of the second. He tells his mother that the sweet Georgian twilight—"Tea on the lawn, evensong, croquet, the old ladies calling, the gentle unmalicious gossip, the gardener trundling the wheelbarrow full of leaves and grass"—'isn't real life any more." He continues: "I'm hiding underground, and up above the Germans are methodically smashing London to bits all round me. . . . It sounds like a thriller, doesn't it, but the thrillers are like life . . . spies, and murders, and violence . . . that's real life."

Greene's characters inhabit a world in which lasting love, according to the narrator of the story "May We Borrow Your Husband?," means the acceptance of "every disappointment, every failure, every betrayal." By Greene's twenty-second novel, *Doctor Fischer of Geneva; or, The Bomb Party,* suffering had become a sufficient cause for having a soul. When the narrator of *Doctor Fischer* tells his wife, "If souls exist you certainly have one," and she asks "Why?," he replies, "You've suffered." This statement may well sound masochistic—"Pain is part of joy," the whiskey priest asserts in *The Power and the Glory,* "pain is a part of pleasure"; but as Greene wrote in the essay "Hans Anderson," it is really the "Catholic ideal of the acceptance of pain for a spiritual benefit." This ideal is behind the saintly Sarah's striking statement in *The End of the Affair:* "How good You [God] are. You might have killed us with happiness, but You let us be with You in pain."

Although Greene's Catholicism has generated the most intense critical debate, only five or six of his more than twenty novels actually focus on the religion: *Brighton Rock, The Power and the Glory, The Heart of the Matter* (the so-called "Catholic trilogy" analyzed by R. W. B. Lewis in *The Picaresque Saint* and by Marie-Beatrice Mesnet in *Graham Greene and the Heart of the Matter*), *The End of the Affair, Monsignor Quixote,* and, perhaps, *A Burnt-Out Case.* In exploring Catholicism in his fiction, Greene eschewed propaganda. He noted in *Ways of Escape,* his second volume of autobiography, that he was "not a Catholic writer but a writer who happens to be a Catholic." That is, Catholicism did not provide a dogma he wished to promulgate in his novels but instead supplied a framework within which he could measure the human situation. "I'm not a religious man," Greene told *Catholic World* interviewer Gene D. Phillips, "though it interests me. Religion is important, as atomic science is."

Despite the attention paid his Catholicism, Greene told Phillips that religion occupied only "one period" of his writing career: "My period of Catholic novels was preceded and followed by political novels." Greene's first successful novels were written in the 1930s, a decade G. S. Fraser in *The Modern Writer and His World* has said "forced the writer's attention back on the intractable public world around him." In *Ways of Escape* Greene defined the mid-1930s as "clouded by the Depression in England . . . and by the rise of Hitler. It was impossible in those days not to be committed, and it is hard to recall details of ones' private life as the enormous battlefield was prepared around us." Greene's earlier political novels are set in Europe, usually in England; but the later political novels move from one third-world trouble spot to another, even as they explore the themes found throughout

Greene's work: commitment, betrayal, corruption, sin, suffering, and the nature of human sexuality, often against a backdrop of Catholicism.

In both religion and politics Greene opposed the dogmatic and the doctrinaire, sided against those who sacrifice the corrupt but living human spirit for a grand but bloodless thesis. For example, in *Monsignor Quixote,* however much the good-natured priest and the equally good-natured communist politician quibble, both reject the intellectual rigidities of those whose commitment to their respective causes is ideologically absolute. Politics and religion, then, are closely related. *Monsignor Quixote* is at once political and religious in nature; and, while nobody denies that *The Power and the Glory* is one of Greene's Catholic works, it can also be studied as a political novel.

Not only a novelist, Greene wrote in more than a dozen other genres, including novellas, short stories, plays, radio plays, screenplays, essays, memoirs, biographies, autobiographies, travel books, poetry, and children's literature. Although Greene made his mark primarily in the novel, at least his stories, plays, and nonfiction prose, as well as his work in film, deserve consideration.

About the short story genre, Greene wrote in *Ways of Escape*: "I remain in this field a novelist who happens to have written short stories." Unfailingly modest in appraising his own literary efforts, Greene said in a note to his collection *Nineteen Stories,* "I am only too conscious of the defects of these stories. . . . The short story is an exacting form which I have not properly practised." His stories, he said, are "merely . . . the by-products of a novelist's career." However true this evaluation might be for *Nineteen Stories,* and however correct Lodge might be in calling the short story a "form in which [Greene] has never excelled," some of Greene's stories do merit reading. Even John Atkins, who in *Graham Greene* concurs with Lodge that the "short story is not one of Greene's successful forms," concedes that the four newer works in *Twenty-One Stories* "show an improvement" over those in the earlier volume. And in *Ways of Escape* Greene registered contentment with "The Destructors," "A Chance for Mr. Lever," "Under the Garden," and "Cheap in August": "I have never written anything better than" these works, he declared.

Less distinguished than his fiction, Greene's dramas provided him with, if nothing else, diversion. He recorded, almost bragged about, his life-long attempt to escape depression and boredom, starting with Russian roulette as a teenager and culminating in a career as a restless, wandering novelist who, when his mainstay got boring, tried to escape by shifting genres. Writing plays, he declared in *Ways of Escape,* "offered me novelty, an escape from the everyday"; "I needed a rest from novels."

As with his short stories, critics have not been enthusiastic about Greene's plays. *The Complaisant Lover,* however, has attracted applause. Philip Stratford in *Faith and Fiction* calls it an "outstanding and original achievement," and to Atkins it is as "vital as many of the Restoration comedies." A minority of critics have mentioned that the characters in his plays do not seem vivid enough. On the whole most critics would agree with Lodge's assessment: "it does not seem likely that Greene will add a significant chapter to the history of British drama."

Greene's nonfiction prose, though not widely analyzed, has been more appreciated. Metaphorical and speculative, the travel books are distinctly literary; Greene's narratives record spiritual no less than physical journeys. Greene's first travel book, *Journey*

Without Maps, is representative of his work in the genre. Believing Africa to be "not a particular place, but a shape, . . . that of the human heart," Greene imagined his actual trip as, simultaneously, a descent, with Freud as guide, into the collective soul of humanity in quest of "those ancestral threads which still exist in our unconscious minds." Greene found in Africa "associations with a personal and racial childhood"; and when in the end he returned to civilization, the conclusion he drew about his experience affirmed the "lost childhood" theme about which he so frequently wrote: "This journey, if had done nothing else, had reinforced a sense of disappointment with what man had made out of the primitive, what he had made out of childhood."

Other essay collections include *Reflections,* which brings together various nonfiction pieces such as film reviews, travel essays, and examinations of communism, Catholicism, and major literary figures; and *A World of My Own: A Dream Diary,* which presents dreams Greene recorded throughout his life. Malcolm Bradbury, writing in *The New York Times Book Review,* concludes of the latter volume: "It's not surprising that the strange tales told here—and they do emerge as tales, not as random notes on disconnected, chaotic events—are as powerful as his fiction, and interweave with it. Greene's *World of My Own*—a carefully organized and edited selection from his dream diaries, which he made and introduced himself, just before his death—is equally the world of his novels, his distinctive, adventurous life as an author, his enigmatic character as a man"

Although acclaimed for his work in various genres, it is as a novelist that he is most respected. Some critics even recognize him as the leading English novelist of his generation. In Lodge's words, among the British novelists who were Greene's contemporaries, "it is difficult to find his equal." Smith's evaluation that Greene's was "one of the more remarkable careers in twentieth-century fiction" is understated, especially alongside the judgment of the anonymous *Times Literary Supplement* reviewer who wrote that Greene is the "principal English novelist now writing in [the 'great'] tradition" of Henry James, Joseph Conrad, and Ford Madox Ford. But it was, perhaps, Francis Wyndham who came closest to explaining Greene's sustained popularity when he stated, simply, that "everything [Greene wrote] is readable."

BIOGRAPHICAL/CRITICAL SOURCES:

BOOKS

Allain, Marie-Francoise, *The Other Man: Conversations with Graham Greene,* Bodley Head, 1983.

Allott, Kenneth, and Miriam Farris Allott, *The Art of Graham Greene,* Hamish Hamilton, 1951, Russell & Russell, 1965.

Atkins, John, *Graham Greene,* Roy, 1958.

Cassis, A. F., editor, *Graham Greene: Man of Paradox,* Loyola Press, 1994.

Contemporary Literary Criticism, Gale (Detroit), Volume 1, 1973; Volume 3, 1975; Volume 6, 1976; Volume 9, 1978; Volume 14, 1980; Volume 18, 1981; Volume 27, 1984; Volume 37, 1986; Volume 70, 1992; Volume 72, 1992.

Crawford, Fred D., *Mixing Memory and Desire: The Waste Land and British Novels,* Pennsylvania State University Press, 1982, pp. 103-23.

Dictionary of Literary Biography, Gale, Volume 13: *British Dramatists Since World War II,* 1982; Volume 15: *British Novelists, 1930-1959,* 1983; Volume 77: *British Mystery Writers, 1920-1939,* 1989.

Dictionary of Literary Biography Yearbook: 1985, Gale, 1986.

Duraan, Leopoldo, *Graham Greene: An Intimate Portrait by His Closest Friend and Confidant,* Harper (San Francisco), 1994.

Duraan, *Graham Greene: Friend and Brother,* HarperCollins (London), 1994.

Evans, R. O., editor, *Graham Greene: Some Critical Considerations,* University of Kentucky Press, 1963.

Falk, Quentin, *Travels in Greeneland: The Cinema of Graham Greene,* Quartet, 1984.

Gordon, Haim, *Fighting Evil: Unsung Heroes in the Novels of Graham Greene,* Greenwood Publishing Group, 1997.

Lodge, David, *Graham Greene,* Columbia University Press, 1966.

Malamet, Elliott, *The World Remade: Graham Greene and the Art of Detection,* Peter Lang, 1997.

Pendleton, Robert, *Graham Greene's Conradian Masterplot: The Arabesques of Influence,* St. Martin's Press (New York City), 1996.

Shelden, Michael, *Graham Greene: The Enemy Within,* Random House (New York City), 1994.

Sherry, Norman, *The Life of Graham Greene, Volume 1: 1904-1939,* Viking, 1989.

Sherry, Norman, *The Life of Graham Greene: 1939-1955,* Viking, 1995.

Stratford, Philip, *Faith and Fiction,* University of Notre Dame Press, 1964.

West, W. J., *The Quest for Graham Greene,* St. Martin's Press, 1998.

Wyndham, Francis, *Graham Green,* Longmans, Green, 1955.

PERIODICALS

America, January 25, 1941.

Catholic World, December, 1954, pp. 172-75; August, 1969, pp. 218-21.

College English, October, 1950, pp. 1-9.

Globe and Mail (Toronto), September 29, 1984.

Life, February 4, 1966.

London Magazine, June-July, 1977, pp. 35-45.

Los Angeles Times, September 25, 1980; January 2, 1981; March 20, 1985.

Los Angeles Times Book Review, October 23, 1988; October 23, 1994.

Modern Fiction Studies, autumn, 1957, pp. 249-88.

New Republic, December 5, 1994, p. 30.

New Yorker, April 11, 1994, p. 46.

New York Review of Books, March 3, 1966; June 8, 1995; June 22, 1995.

New York Times, February 27, 1978; May 19, 1980; January 18, 1981; September 24, 1982; October 25, 1984; March 4, 1985; June 6, 1985; October 17, 1988; January 17, 1995.

New York Times Book Review, January 23, 1966; January 8, 1995.

Playboy, November, 1994, p. 32.

Southwest Review, summer, 1956, pp. 239-50.

Time, September 20, 1982.

Times (London), September 6, 1984; September 7, 1984; March 14, 1985; February 5, 1990.

Times Literary Supplement, January 27, 1966; March 28, 1980; March 15, 1985.

Washington Post, April 3, 1980; September 20, 1988.

Washington Post Book World, May 18, 1980; October 16, 1988; March 12, 1995.

World Press Review, December, 1981, pp. 31-2; April, 1983, p. 62.

GREER, Germaine 1939-
(Rose Blight)

PERSONAL: Born January 29, 1939, near Melbourne, Australia; daughter of Eric Reginal (a newspaper advertising manager) and Margaret May Mary (Lanfrancan) Greer; married Paul de Feu (a journalist), 1968 (divorced, 1973). *Education:* University of Melbourne, B.A., 1959; University of Sydney, M.A., 1961; Newnham College, Cambridge, Ph.D., 1967. *Politics:* Anarchist. *Religion:* Atheist.

ADDRESSES: Home—Tuscany, Italy. *Agent*—c/o Aitken and Stone, 29 Fernshaw Road, London SW10 0TG, England.

CAREER: Taught at a girls' school in Australia; University of Warwick, Coventry, England, lecturer in English, 1967-73; founder and director of Tulsa Centre for the Study of Women's Literature, 1979-82; director of Stump Cross Books, 1988–; special lecturer unofficial fellow, Newnham College, Cambridge, 1989–; writer. Has been an actress on a television comedy show in Manchester, England.

AWARDS, HONORS: J. R. Ackerly Prize, 1989, Internationazionale Mondello, for *Daddy, We Hardly Knew You.* Honorary degree from University of Griffith, 1996.

WRITINGS:

The Female Eunuch, MacGibbon & Kee, 1969, McGraw, 1971.
The Obstacle Race: The Fortunes of Women Painters and Their Work, Farrar, Straus, 1979.
Sex and Destiny: The Politics of Human Fertility, Harper, 1984.
Shakespeare (literary criticism), Oxford University Press, 1986.
The Madwoman's Underclothes: Essays and Occasional Writings, Picador, 1986, Atlantic Monthly Press, 1987.
(Editor with Jeslyn Medoff, Melinda Sansone, and Susan Hastings) *Kissing the Rod: An Anthology of Seventeenth-Century Women's Verse,* Farrar, Straus, 1989.
(Editor and author of introduction) *The Uncollected Verse of Aphra Behn,* Stump Cross Books, 1989.
Daddy, We Hardly Knew You, Viking Penguin, 1989.
The Change: Women, Aging, and the Menopause, Hamish Hamilton (London), 1991.
Slip-Shod Sibyls: Recognition, Rejection, and the Woman Poet, Viking, 1995.

Contributor to *River Journeys,* Hippocrene Books, c. 1985. Contributor to periodicals, including *Esquire, Listener, Oz, Spectator,* and, under pseudonym Rose Blight, *Private Eye.* Columnist, *London Sunday Times,* 1971-73. Co-founder of *Suck.*

SIDELIGHTS: Germaine Greer's writings, which include *The Female Eunuch, The Obstacle Race: The Fortunes of Women Painters and Their Work, Sex and Destiny: The Politics of Human Fertility,* a literary study titled *Shakespeare,* and the essay collection *The Madwoman's Underclothes,* have earned her both praise and disparagement from mainstream, academic, and feminist critics. The praise has typically been offered for her scholarly insight—which is perhaps most notable in *Shakespeare* and her study of great but unrecognized women artists, *The Obstacle Race*—and the criticism for her refusal to routinely espouse whatever literary or feminist ideas are most popular at a given time.

Greer had become a media success upon the American publication of *The Female Eunuch* in 1971. Such celebrity was consistent with her roles as a television performer and as a self-avowed London "groupie" (her enthusiasm for jazz and popular music had brought her into contact with musicians and other members of Britain's underground culture); but critics seized upon her slick and frankly sexual image as counterproductive to the feminist cause she espoused. While her book climbed the best-seller charts in both the United States and England and *Vogue* magazine hailed her as "a super heroine," many members of the women's liberation movement questioned her authority. While *Newsweek* described her as "a dazzling combination of erudition, eccentricity and eroticism," some feminist writers wondered whether an indisputably attractive Shakespearean scholar could speak with understanding about the plight of women in general.

Greer's basic argument, as explained in the book's introduction, is that women's "sexuality is both denied and misrepresented by being identified as passivity." She explains that women, urged from childhood to live up to an "Eternal Feminine" stereotype, are valued for characteristics associated with the castrate—"timidity, plumpness, languor, delicacy and preciosity"—hence the book's title. From the viewpoint of this primary assumption, Greer examines not only the problems of women's sexuality, but their psychological development, their relationships with men, their social position, and their cultural history. What most struck early critics of the book was that she considered "the castration of our true female personality. . . not the fault of men, but our own, and history's." Thus *Newsweek* considered Greer's work "women's liberation's most realistic and least anti-male manifesto"; and Christopher Lehmann-Haupt called it "a book that combines the best of masculinity *and* femininity."

In 1989 she published a more personal book than her previous volumes, *Daddy, We Hardly Knew You,* which records her painstaking investigations into the life and personality of her father, Reginald "Reg" Greer, after his death in 1983. Greer's "quest" to reconstruct her father's lineage leads to an international tour through the landscape and archives of Britain, Australia, South Africa, India, Tuscany, Malta, and finally Tasmania, where she discovers her father's humble upbringing as a foster child whose lifelong reticence was intended to bury his illegitimate origin. According to Jill Johnston in the *New York Times Book Review,* the story of Reg Greer "is a very sad story, which his daughter glosses with her rage and transcends with her vast knowledge of all sorts of things." The paucity of information produced by her frustrating research is supplemented by expansive digressions that portray the land and people encountered on her travels, including an entire chapter entitled "Sidetrack" that documents various physical and historical aspects of the Australian continent. Nancy Mairs describes the book in the *Los Angeles Times Book Review* as "part childhood reminiscence, part travelogue, part genealogy, part history, part social commentary." As the author can no longer view her father as a "hero" or "prince in disguise," Johnston concludes, "In the end Germaine Greer can't reconcile her father's lack of love with her understanding of the fear that made him lie to conceal his lowly origins."

Greer produced a forceful indictment of modern youth culture with *The Change: Women, Aging, and the Menopause,* renaming the later female life stage "climacteria" and invoking the term "anophobia" to describe the irrational fear and hostility directed toward older women. As Joan Frank observes in the *San Francisco Review of Books,* Greer identifies menopause as "a real and crucial transition in a woman's life for which no—repeat, *no*—reliable information, clear role models, rites of passage, historic or cultural sanctions exist as they do for comparable transitions: birth, the onset of menarche, marriage, childbirth, and death." Gleaning evidence from diverse and unlikely sources such as "historical accounts, memoirs, correspondence from the court of Louis XIV, old medical textbooks, anthropology tracts, novels, and poems both familiar and obscure," as Natalie Augier notes in the *New York Times Book Review*, Greer "talks with unvarnished candor about the invisibility of the middle-aged woman in our own culture, the unfairness of a system that lionizes the silver-haired male while scorning his female counterpart as beyond use, pathetic, desiccated, desexualized, a crone." Katha Pollitt remarks in a *New Yorker* review that Greer's version of post-menopausal life is "so charming, so seductively rendered—especially when it's contrasted with the situation of the wistful wives, desperate party girls, and breast-implanted exercise addicts which for her constitutes the only alternative—that the reader may find herself barely able to wait." Greer views menopause as "a liberation, an unwanted liberation," as quoted by Sarah Boxer in the *New York Times Book Review*.

In *Slip-Shod Sibyls: Recognition, Rejection, and the Woman Poet*, Greer challenges the validity of feminist revisionism and the status of celebrated female poets in the Western canon, including Sappho, Aphra Behn, Christina Rossetti, and Elizabeth Barrett Browning. Carol Rumens writes in a *Times Literary Supplement* review, "Though Greer admits we should carry on reclaiming women's work, she believes that 'to insist on equal representation or positive discrimination so that She-poetry appears on syllabuses in our schools and universities is to continue the system of false accounting that produced the double standard in the first place.'" Camille Paglia notes in the *Observer Review*, "the absence of pre-modern female poets from the curriculum," in Greer's view, "is not entirely due to sexism but rather to a lack of quality." Citing the life and work of Sylvia Plath and Anne Sexton, Greer similarly dismisses contemporary female poetry for its futile, and often fatal, narcissism. According to Greer, as Margaret Anne Doody summarizes in the *London Review of Books*: "The 20th century merely adds to the heap of sickly, self-regarding and self-destructive female poets. Lacking education, training in the Great Tradition, certainty about voice or subject-matter—and in the absence of any sense of how the culture of publicity and publication can work—woman writers of poetry over three centuries have exhibited themselves delving into their emotions. Poetry with them constantly becomes a morbid exercise." Furthermore, Greer contends that women poets were often responsible for their own artistic shortcomings. Fleur Adcock writes in a *New Statesman and Society* review that Greer suggests such female writers "took bad advice; they fell for flattery; they wrote fast and without revising sufficiently; and they failed to understand 'what was involved in making a poem.'" Praising *Slip-Shod Sibyls* and Greer's significant contribution to feminist criticism, Paglia concludes, "When the history of modern women is written, Germaine Greer will be seen as one who, like Jane Austen, permanently redefined female intellect."

BIOGRAPHICAL/CRITICAL SOURCES:

PERIODICALS

America, November 22, 1997, p. 18.
Chicago Tribune Books, January 11, 1990, p. 6.
Contemporary Review, November, 1996, p. 277.
Detroit News, May 9, 1971.
Globe and Mail (Toronto), February 25, 1984; October 17, 1987; April 29, 1989; August 5, 1989.
Life, May 7, 1971.
Listener, October 22, 1970.
London Review of Books, December 14, 1995, p. 14-5.

Los Angeles Times, March 7, 1984; November 26, 1987.
Los Angeles Times Book Review, September 6, 1987; April 8, 1990.
Meanjin, February, 1996, p. 208.
National Review, January 18, 1993, p. 49.
New Republic, January 31, 1994, p. 29.
New Statesman and Society, March 24, 1989, pp. 36-7; October 6, 1995, pp. 37-8.
Newsweek, March 22, 1971; November 16, 1992, p. 79.
New Yorker, April 16, 1990, p. 116; November 2, 1992, p. 106.
New York Times, April 20, 1971; November 1, 1979; March 5, 1984; April 23, 1984.
New York Times Book Review, October 11, 1987; January 28, 1990; October 11, 1992, pp. 1, 33.
Observer (London), October 11, 1970.
Observer Review, October 8, 1995, p. 14.
Publishers Weekly, May 25, 1984; December 1, 1989, p. 42; August 24, 1992, p. 66.
San Francisco Review of Books, January, 1992, p. 6.
Time, April 16, 1984; October 26, 1992, p. 80.
Times (London), March 20, 1986; October 23, 1986; March 20, 1989; March 25, 1989.
Times Literary Supplement, June 17, 1988; March 17, 1989; October 13, 1995, p. 29.
Washington Post, November 22, 1979; January 24, 1990.
Women's Review of Books, January, 1993.

* * *

GREER, Richard
See SILVERBERG, Robert

* * *

GREGOR, Lee
See POHL, Frederik

* * *

GRENVILLE, Pelham
See WODEHOUSE, P(elham) G(renville)

* * *

GREY, Zane 1872-1939

PERSONAL: Name originally Pearl Zane Gray; born January 31, 1872, in Zanesville, OH; died October 23, 1939, in Altadena, CA; son of Lewis M. (a travelling preacher and dentist) and Josephine (Zane) Gray; married Lina Elise Roth, November 21, 1905; children: Romer, Elizabeth, Loren. *Education:* University of Pennsylvania, D.D.S., 1896.

CAREER: Writer. Practiced dentistry in New York City, 1896-1904; traveled in the West, 1907-18.

WRITINGS:

WESTERN WRITINGS

Betty Zane, Charles Francis Press, 1903, abridged edition, Saalfield, 1940.

The Spirit of the Border: A Romance of the Early Settlers in the Ohio Valley, A. L. Burt, 1906, abridged edition, Saalfield, 1940.

The Last of the Plainsmen, Outing, 1908.

The Last Trail: A Story of Early Days in the Ohio Valley, A. L. Burt, 1909, abridged edition, Saalfield, 1940, authorized edition, University of Nebraska Press (Lincoln), 1996.

The Heritage of the Desert: A Novel, Harper, 1910.

Riders of the Purple Sage: A Novel, Harper, 1912, authorized edition, University of Nebraska Press (Lincoln), 1994.

Desert Gold: A Romance of the Border, Harper, 1913, abridged edition published as *Prairie Gold,* Sphere Books, 1967.

The Light of Western Stars: A Romance, Harper, 1914.

The Rustlers of Pecos County, Munsey, 1914.

The Lone Star Ranger: A Romance of the Border, Harper, 1915.

The Rainbow Trail: A Romance, Harper, 1915, authorized edition, University of Nebraska Press (Lincoln), 1995.

The Border Legion, Harper, 1916.

Wildfire, Harper, 1917.

The U.P. Trail: A Novel, Harper, 1918, published in England as *The Roaring U.P. Trail,* Hodder & Stoughton, 1918.

The Desert of Wheat: A Novel, Harper, 1919.

The Man of the Forest: A Novel, Harper, 1920.

The Mysterious Rider: A Novel, Harper, 1921.

To the Last Man: A Novel, Harper, 1922.

Wanderer of the Wasteland, Harper, 1923.

The Call of the Canyon, Harper, 1924.

Roping Lions in the Grand Canyon, Harper, 1924.

The Thundering Herd, Harper, 1925, with foreword by Loren Grey, University of Nebraska Press (Lincoln), 1996.

The Vanishing American, Harper, 1925, published in England as *The Vanishing Indian,* Hodder & Stoughton, 1926.

Under the Tonto Rim, Harper, 1926.

Forlorn River: A Romance, Harper, 1927, authorized edition (University of Nebraska Press (Lincoln), 1995.

Nevada: A Romance of the West, Harper, 1928, authorized edition, University of Nebraska Press (Lincoln), 1995.

Wild Horse Mesa, Harper, 1928.

Fighting Caravans, Harper, 1929.

The Shepherd of Guadaloupe, Harper, 1930.

Sunset Pass, Harper, 1931.

Arizona Ames, Harper, 1932.

Robber's Roost, Harper, 1932.

The Drift Fence, Harper, 1933.

The Hash Knife Outfit, Harper, 1933.

The Code of the West, Harper, 1934.

Thunder Mountain, Harper, 1935.

The Trail Driver, Harper, 1936.

The Lost Wagon Train, Harper, 1936.

West of the Pecos, Harper, 1937.

Majesty's Rancho, Harper, 1938.

Raiders of Spanish Peaks, Harper, 1938.

Knights of the Range, Harper, 1939.

Western Union, Harper, 1939.

30,000 on the Hoof, Harper, 1940.

Twin Sombreros, Harper, 1941.

Stairs of Sand, Harper, 1943.

Shadow on the Trail, Harper, 1946.

Valley of Wild Horses, Harper, 1947.

Rogue River Feud (originally serialized under title *Rustlers of Silver River*), Harper, 1948.

The Deer Stalker, Harper, 1949.

The Maverick Queen, Harper, 1950.

The Dude Ranger, Harper, 1951.

Captives of the Desert, Harper, 1952.

Wyoming, Harper, 1953.

Lost Pueblo, Harper, 1954.

Black Mesa, Harper, 1955.

Stranger from the Tonto, Harper, 1956.

The Fugitive Trail, Harper, 1957.

The Arizona Clan, Harper, 1958.

Horse Heaven Hill, Harper, 1959.

Boulder Dam, Harper, 1963.

Zane Grey's Greatest Western Stories, edited by Loren Grey, Belmont, 1975.

Zane Grey's Greatest Indian Stories, edited by Loren Grey, Belmont, 1975.

Zane Grey's Greatest Animal Stories, edited by Loren Grey, Belmont, 1975.

The Big Land, edited by Loren Grey, Belmont, 1976.

Yaqui and Other Great Indian Stories, edited by Loren Grey, Belmont, 1976.

The Buffalo Hunter, edited by Loren Grey, Belmont, 1977.

The Westerner, edited by Loren Grey, Belmont, 1977.

Tenderfoot and *The Secret of Quaking Asp Cabin,* Belmont, 1977.

Lost in the Never Never and Silvermane, Belmont, 1977.

Savage Kingdom, Henry, 1979.

Three Complete Novels, contains *Riders of the Purple Sage, The Rainbow Trail,* and *The Lone Star Ranger,* Gramercy Books (New York City), 1994.

The Last of the Duanes, Thorndike Press (Thorndike, ME), 1996.

JUVENILES

The Short-Stop, McClurg, 1909.

The Young Forester, Harper, 1910.

The Young Pitcher, Harper, 1911.

The Young Lion Hunter, Harper, 1911.

Ken Ward in the Jungle: Thrilling Adventures in Tropical Wilds, Harper, 1912.

The Red-Headed Outfield and Other Baseball Stories, Grosset & Dunlap, 1920.

Tappan's Burro and Other Stories, Harper, 1923.

Don: The Story of a Lion Dog, Harper, 1928.

The Wolf Tracker, Harper, 1930.

Zane Grey's Book of Camps and Trails, Harper, 1931.

The Ranger and Other Stories, Harper, 1960.

Blue Feather and Other Stories, Harper, 1961.

The Adventures of Finspot, D-J Books, 1974.

Rangers of the Lone Star: A Western Story, Five Star, 1997.

Also author of seven volumes of "King of the Royal Mounted" series of "Big-Little" books for Whitman, 1936-46.

OTHER

Nassau, Cuba, Yucatan, Mexico: A Personal Note of Appreciation of These Nearby Foreign Lands, New York and Cuba Mail, 1909.

Tales of Fishes, Harper, 1919.

Tales of Lonely Trails, Harper, 1922.

The Day of the Beast, Harper, 1922.

Tales of Southern Rivers, Harper, 1924.

Tales of Fishing Virgin Seas, Harper, 1925.

Tales of an Angler's Eldorado—New Zealand, Harper, 1926.

Tales of Swordfish and Tuna, Harper, 1927.

(With others) *Zane Grey: The Man and His Work,* Harper, 1928.

Tales of Fresh-Water Fishing, Harper, 1928.

Tales of Tahitian Waters, Harper, 1931.

An American Angler in Australia, Harper, 1937.

The Zane Grey Omnibus, edited by Ruth G. Gentles, Harper, 1943.

Wilderness Trek: A Novel of Australia, Harper, 1944.

Adventures in Fishing, edited and with notes by Ed Zern, Harper, 1952.

Zane Grey, Outdoorsman: Zane Grey's Best Hunting and Fishing Tales, Prentice-Hall, 1972.

Shark! Zane Grey's Tales of Man-Eating Sharks, edited by Loren Grey, Belmont, 1976.

The Reef Girl: A Novel of Tahiti, edited by Loren Grey, Harper, 1977.

Zane Grey's Tales from the Fisherman's Log, Hodder & Stoughton, 1979.

The Undiscovered Zane Grey Fishing Stories, edited by George Reiger, New Century, 1983.

Zane Grey: A Photographic Odyssey (photographs), text by Loren Grey, Taylor, 1985.

George Washington, Frontiersman, edited by Carlton Jackson, University Press of Kentucky (Lexington), 1994.

Also coauthor of screenplays *The Vanishing Pioneer,* 1928, and *Rangle River,* 1936.

SIDELIGHTS: "Perhaps more than any other modern American novelist," declares Ann Ronald in the *Dictionary of Literary Biography,* "Zane Grey caught the imaginations of several generations of readers." In books such as *The Heritage of the Desert* and *Riders of the Purple Sage,* Grey helped popularize the American West as a subject for fiction. Although writers such as James Fenimore Cooper (with *The Deerstalker* and *The Last of the Mohicans*) and Owen Wister (with *The Virginian*) also used the American frontier as the setting for their stories, Grey's vivid descriptions of Western landscapes and popular, formulaic plots established the "Western" genre. "From 1910 until 1925," Ronald continues, "his books appeared regularly on best-seller lists, and even today, in both hardcover and paperback, his fiction remains popular."

In his Western novels, Grey broke free from the nineteenth-century dime novel approach to adventure stories. He made three important innovations: he created the figure of the mysterious outlaw or gunfighter enlisted to fight for good; he wrote Western stories—particularly *The Light of Western Stars*—from a woman's point of view, and examined the love between an Indian chief and a white girl in *The Vanishing American*; and he established the Western environment as a test of character. Critics now believe that Grey should be read as a romantic rather than a realistic writer—that, although he gained his knowledge of the West through firsthand experience, making many trips there, and performed extensive research on historical background, especially in *The U.P. Trail* (his history of the transcontinental railroad), he was in fact more interested in portraying types rather than characters pitted against forces of evil or forces of nature, to triumph or perish.

Riders of the Purple Sage, the novel that brought Grey his greatest popular acclaim, demonstrates some of these elements. In Lassiter, the taciturn gunslinger, and Jane Withersteen, the proud Mormon heiress, the book "matched a superhuman hero with a virginal heroine and placed them against a backdrop of ruggedness and violence in a struggle against unmitigated evil," states Danney Goble in the *Journal of Arizona History.* Another pattern Grey frequently used, Ronald states, was "an adaptation of the 'easterner goes West to learn about life' embellished with his own richly pictorial imagination." Yet, although other authors had

used these formulas before, says Ronald in her *Zane Grey,* Grey's work is different because it is "an outgrowth of the author's personal experiences, a reiteration of his own journey to the frontier." "Within a few years the plots and characters would become standard," Goble concludes. "But Grey's combination of brutal violence and saccharine romance—a heady mixture all but unknown to his predecessors in the writing of frontier fiction—established his claim to a gold mine which he exploited time and again."

Grey's vivid depiction of the Western landscape was one of the strongest elements of his writing, critics agree. "He portrays it as an acid test of those elemental traits of character which he admires," writes T. K. Whipple in *Study Out the Land: Essays.* "It kills off the weaklings, and among the strong it makes the bad worse and the good better. Nature to him is somewhat as God is to a Calvinist—ruthlessly favoring the elect and damning the damned." "Grey may have fallen short of what Emerson had in mind in 'The American Scholar' in calling for a literature on indigenous American themes," declares Gary Topping in *Western American Literature,* "but for millions of readers he did provide an introduction, at least, to the literary potential of many common aspects of Western life."

"My long labors have been devoted to making stories resemble the times they depict," Grey wrote in the foreword to his novel *To the Last Man.* "I have loved the West for its vastness, its contrasts, its beauty and color and life, for its wildness and violence, and for the fact that I have seen how it developed great men and women who died unknown and unsung." "Romance," he continued, "is only another name for idealism; and I contend that life without ideals is not worth living. . . . Walter Scott wrote romance; so did Victor Hugo; and likewise Kipling, Hawthorne, Stevenson. It was Stevenson, particularly, who wielded a bludgeon against the realists. People live for the dream in their hearts." "We are all dreamers," he concluded, "if not in the heavy-lidded wasting of time, then in the meaning of life that makes us work on."

BIOGRAPHICAL/CRITICAL SOURCES:

BOOKS

Cawelti, John G., *Adventure, Mystery, and Romance,* University of Chicago Press, 1976.

Cawelti, John G., *The Six-Gun Mystique,* Bowling Green University Popular Press, 1971.

Dictionary of Literary Biography, Volume 9: *American Novelists, 1910-1945,* Gale, 1981.

Etulain, Richard W. and Marsden, Michael T., editors, *The Popular Western,* Bowling Green University Popular Press, 1974.

Farley, G. M., *Zane Grey, a Documented Portrait: The Man, the Bibliography, the Filmography,* Portals Press, 1985.

Farley, *The Many Faces of Zane Grey,* Silver Spruce, 1993.

Folsom, James K., *The American Western Novel,* College & University Press, 1966.

Garland, Hamlin, *Hamlin Garland's Diaries,* edited by Donald Pizer, Huntington Library, 1968.

Gay, Carol, *Zane Grey, Story-Teller,* State Library of Ohio, 1979.

Grey, Loren, *Zane Grey: A Photographic Odyssey,* Taylor Publications (Dallas), 1985.

Gruber, Frank, *Zane Grey: A Biography,* World Publishing, 1970.

Jackson, Carlton, *Zane Grey,* Twayne, 1973.

Kant, Candace C., *Zane Grey's Arizona,* Northland Press, 1984.

Karr, Jean, *Zane Grey: Man of the West,* Greenberg, 1949.

Kimball, Arthur G., *Ace of Hearts: The Westerns of Zane Grey,* Texas Christian University Press (Fort Worth), 1993.

May, Stephen J., *Zane Grey: Romancing the West,* Ohio University Press, 1997.

Mott, Frank Luther, *Golden Multitudes: The Story of Best Sellers in the United States,* Macmillan, 1947.

Nye, Russel B., *The Unembarrassed Muse: The Popular Arts in America,* Dial, 1970.

Powell, Lawrence Clark, *Southwest Classics: The Creative Literature of the Arid Lands—Essays on the Books and Their Writers,* Ward Ritchie Press, 1974.

Ronald, Ann, *Zane Grey,* Boise State University, 1975.

Scott, Kenneth W., *Zane Grey, Born to the West: A Reference Guide,* G. K. Hall, 1979.

Twentieth-Century Literary Criticism, Volume 6, Gale, 1982.

Warren, Don, *A Bibliographical Checklist of the Writings of Zane Grey,* Country Lane Books (Collinsville, CT), 1986.

Whipple, T. K., *Study Out the Land: Essays,* University of California Press, 1943.

PERIODICALS

American Review of Reviews, June, 1912.
Brigham Young University Studies, summer, 1978.
Journal of American Culture, winter, 1989.
Journal of Arizona History, spring, 1973.
Markham Review, February, 1970.
New York Times, September 12, 1908; October 8, 1910; February 18, 1912.
Playboy, January, 1994, p. 41.
Saturday Review of Literature, November 11, 1939.
South Dakota Review, autumn, 1985; spring, 1988.
Western American Literature, spring-summer, 1973, pp. 15-31.

*   *   *

GRIGSON, Geoffrey (Edward Harvey) 1905-1985

PERSONAL: Born March 2, 1905, in Pelynt, Cornwall, England; died November 28, 1985; son of William Shuckforth (a canon) and Mary (Boldero) Grigson; married Frances Galt, 1929 (died, 1937); married Burta Kunert, 1938 (marriage dissolved); married Jane McIntire (a writer); children: (first marriage) one daughter; (second marriage) one son, one daughter; (third marriage) one son. *Education:* St. Edmund Hall, Oxford, graduated. *Politics:* Labour. *Religion:* None.

ADDRESSES: Home—Broad Town Farm, Broad Town, Swinton, Wiltshire, England. *Agent*—David Higham Associates, 5-8 Lower John St., London W1R 4HA, England.

CAREER: Poet and professional writer. After college became member of London staff of *Yorkshire Post*; in 1929 began working on *Morning Post,* London, became literary editor; founded and edited *New Verse,* 1933-39, an avant-garde poetry magazine which published early poems of Auden, MacNeice, Dylan Thomas, and others; had worked in publishing formerly in Talks Department of British Broadcasting Corp. and member of BBC Literary Advisory Committee.

AWARDS, HONORS: Duff Cooper Memorial Prize, 1971; Oscar Blumenthal Prize, 1971.

WRITINGS:

POETRY

Several Observations: Thirty-Five Poems, Cresset Press (London), 1939.
Under the Cliff and Other Poems, Routledge, 1943.
The Isles of Scilly and Other Poems, Routledge, 1946.
Legenda Suecana, privately printed, 1953.
The Collected Poems of Geoffrey Grigson: 1924-1962, Phoenix House (London), 1963.
A Skull in Salop and Other Poems, Dufour, 1967.
Ingestion of Ice-Cream and Other Poems, Macmillan, 1969.
Discoveries of Bones and Stones, and Other Poems, Macmillan, 1971.
Sad Grave of an Imperial Mongoose, Macmillan, 1973.
Angles and Circles and Other Poems, Gollancz, 1974.
The Fiesta and Other Poems, Secker & Warburg, 1978.
History of Him, Secker & Warburg, 1980.
Collected Poems, 1963-1980, Allison & Busby, 1982.
The Cornish Dancer and Other Poems, Secker & Warburg, 1983.
Montaigne's Tower and Other Poems, Secker & Warburg, 1984.
Persephone's Flowers and Other Poems, Secker & Warburg, 1986.

NONFICTION

Henry Moore, Penguin, 1943.
Wild Flowers in Britain, Hastings House, 1944.
Samuel Palmer: The Visionary Years, Kegan Paul, 1947.
English Romantic Art (catalogue prepared for an Arts Council of Great Britain Exhibition), [London], 1947.
An English Farmhouse and Its Neighbourhood, Parrish, 1948.
The Scilly Isles, with drawings and watercolors by Fred Uhlman, Elek, 1948, revised edition, Duckworth, 1977.
The Harp of Aeolus, and Other Essays on Art, Literature, and Nature, Routledge, 1948.
Places of the Mind (essays, some originally appeared in periodicals), Routledge & Kegan Paul, 1949.
Flowers of the Meadow, with illustrations by Robin Tanner, Penguin, 1950.
The Crest on the Silver: An Autobiography, Cresset, 1950.
Wessex, Collins, 1951.
A Master of Our Time: A Study of Wyndham Lewis, Methuen, 1951.
Essays from the Air (radio talks), Routledge & Kegan Paul, 1951.
West Country, Collins, 1951.
Gardenage; or, The Plants of Ninhursaga, Routledge & Kegan Paul, 1952.
(With Jean Cassou) *The Female Form in Painting,* Harcourt, 1953.
Freedom of the Parish, Phoenix House, 1954.
Gerard Manley Hopkins, Longmans, for the British Council, 1955, revised edition, 1968.
The Englishman's Flora, Phoenix House, 1955, revised edition, 1975.
English Drawing from Samuel Cooper to Gwen John, Thames & Hudson, 1955.
The Shell Guide to Flowers of the Countryside (also see below), Phoenix House, 1955.
Jean Baptiste Camille Corot (Book-of-the-Month Club selection), Metropolitan Museum, 1956.
England, photographs by Edwin Smith, Thames & Hudson, 1957, Studio Publications, 1958.
(Author of commentary) Stevan Celebonovic, *Old Stone Age,* Philosophical Library, 1957.

(Author of commentary) Celebonovic, *The Living Rocks,* preface by Andre Maurois, translation by Joyce Emerson and Stanley Pococks, Philosophical Library, 1957.

Fossils, Insects, and Reptiles (also see below), Phoenix House, 1957.

The Painted Caves, Phoenix House, 1957.

Art Treasures of the British Museum, preface by Sir Thomas Kendrick, Abrams, 1957.

The Wiltshire Book, Thames & Hudson, 1957.

(Author of commentary) Henry Moore, *Heads, Figures and Ideas,* New York Graphic Society, 1958.

Looking and Finding and Reading and Investigating and Much Else (juvenile), drawings by Christopher Chamberlin, Phoenix House, 1958.

Shell Guide to Trees and Shrubs (also see below), Phoenix House, 1958.

English Villages in Colour, Batsford, 1958.

A Herbal of All Sorts, Macmillan, 1959.

Shell Guide to Wild Life (also see below), Phoenix House, 1959.

English Excursions, Macmillan, 1959.

Samuel Palmer's Valley of Vision, Phoenix House, 1960.

Christopher Smart, Longmans, for the British Council, 1961.

The Shell Country Book, Phoenix House, 1962, Dent, 1973.

Poets in Their Pride, Phoenix House, 1962, Basic Books, 1964.

(With others) *The Shell Nature Book* (contains *The Shell Guide to Flowers of the Countryside, Fossils, Insects, and Reptiles, Shell Guide to Trees and Shrubs,* and *Shell Guide to Wild Life*), Basic Books, 1964.

The Shell Book of Roads, illustrated by David Gentleman, Ebury Press, 1964.

(With wife, Jane Grigson) *Shapes and Stories: A Book about Pictures* (juvenile), J. Baker, 1964, Vanguard, 1965.

The Shell Country Alphabet, M. Joseph, in association with George Rainbird, 1966.

(With J. Grigson) *Shapes and Adventures,* Marshbank, 1967, published as *More Shapes and Stories: A Book about Pictures,* Vanguard, 1967.

Ben Nicholson: Twelve New Works (brochure for exhibition), Marlborough Fine Art Ltd. and Marlborough New London Gallery, 1967.

Poems and Poets, Dufour, 1969.

Shapes and People: A Book about Pictures (juvenile), Vanguard, 1969.

Notes from an Odd Country, Macmillan, 1970.

Shapes and Creatures: A Book about Pictures (juvenile), Black, 1973.

The Contrary View: Glimpses of Fudge and Gold, Rowman & Littlefield, 1974.

A Dictionary of English Plant Names (and Some Products of Plants), Allen Lane, 1974.

Britain Observed: The Landscape through Artists' Eyes, Phaidon, 1975.

The Englishman's Flora, Hart-Davis MacGibbon, 1975.

The Goddess of Love: The Birth, Triumph, Death, and Return of Aphrodite, Constable, 1976, Stein & Day, 1977.

Twists of the Way, Mandeville, 1981.

Blessings, Kicks and Curses, Allison & Busby, 1982.

The Private Art: A Poetry Notebook, Allison & Busby, 1982.

Recollections: Mainly of Artists and Writers (memoir), Chatto & Windus, 1984.

(With J. Grigson) *Shapes, Animals and Special Creatures,* Vanguard, in press.

EDITOR

(With Denys Kilham Roberts, Gerald Gould, and John Lehmann) *The Year's Poetry,* John Lane, 1934.

(And author of introduction) *The Arts Today,* John Lane, 1935.

(With Roberts) *The Year's Poetry, 1937-38,* John Lane, 1938.

New Verse: An Anthology (originally appeared in the first six years of the periodical *New Verse*), Faber, 1939.

(And author of introduction) *The Journals of George Sturt,* Cresset, 1941.

The Romantics: An Anthology, Routledge, 1942, Granger, 1978.

Visionary Poems and Passages; or, The Poet's Eye, with original lithographs by John Craxton, F. Muller (London), 1944.

The Mint: A Miscellany of Literature, two volumes, Routledge, 1946-48.

Before the Romantics: An Anthology of the Enlightenment, Routledge, 1946.

Poetry of the Present: An Anthology of the Thirties and After, Phoenix House, 1949.

Poems of John Clare's Madness, Routledge & Kegan Paul, 1949, Harvard University Press, 1951.

(And author of introduction) William Barnes, *Selected Poems,* Harvard University Press, 1950 (published in England as *Selected Poems of William Barnes,* Routledge & Kegan Paul, 1950).

(And author of introduction) *Selected Poems of John Dryden,* Grey Walls Press (London), 1950.

(And author of introduction) George Crabbe, *Poems,* Grey Walls Press, 1950.

(And author of introduction) John Clare, *Selected Poems,* Routledge & Kegan Paul, 1950.

The Victorians: An Anthology, Routledge & Kegan Paul, 1950.

(And author of commentary) Robert John Thomton, *Temple of Flora,* Collins, 1951.

About Britain, thirteen volumes, Collins, 1951.

(And author of introduction) Samuel Taylor Coleridge, *Poems,* Grey Walls Press, 1951.

(With Charles Harvard Gibbs-Smith) *People, Places, and Things,* four volumes, Grosvenor Press, 1954, published as *People, Places, and Things,* Hawthorn, Volume I: *People,* 1954, 2nd edition, 1957, Volume II: *Places,* 1954, 2nd edition, 1957, Volume III: *Things,* 1954, 2nd edition, 1957, Volume IV: *Ideas,* 1954, 2nd edition, 1957.

The Three Kings: A Christmas Book of Carols, Poems, and Pieces, G. Fraser (Bedford), 1958.

The Cherry Tree: A Collection of Poems (juvenile), Vanguard, 1959.

Country Poems, Hutton, 1959.

The Concise Encyclopedia of Modern World Literature, Hawthorn, 1963, revised 2nd edition, 1970.

O Rare Mankind!: A Short Collection of Great Prose, Phoenix House, 1963.

Watter Savage Landor, *Poems,* Centaur Press, 1964, Southern Illinois University Press, 1965.

The English Year from Diaries and Letters, Oxford University Press, 1967.

A Choice of William Morris's Verse, Faber, 1969.

A Choice of Thomas Hardy's Poems, Macmillan (London), 1969.

A Choice of Robert Southey's Verse, Faber, 1970.

Pennethorne Hughes, *Thirty-Eight Poems,* Baker, 1970.

(And author of introduction) *Faber Book of Popular Verse,* Faber, 1971, published as *Gambit Book of Popular Verse,* Gambit, 1971.

Rainbows, Fleas, and Flowers: A Nature Anthology Chosen by Geoffrey Grigson (juvenile), Baker, 1971, Vanguard, 1974.

Unrespectable Verse, Allen Lane, 1971.

The Faber Book of Love Poems: Love Expected, Love Begun, The Plagues of Loving, Love Continued, Absences, Doubts, Division, Love Renounced, and Love in Death, Faber, 1973.

Poet to Poet: Charles Cotton, Penguin, 1975.

The Penguin Book of Ballads, Penguin, 1975.

The Faber Book of Epigrams and Epitaphs, Faber, 1977.

The Faber Book of Nonsense Verse, Faber, 1979.

The Oxford Book of Satirical Verse: Chosen by Geoffrey Grigson, Oxford University Press, 1980, revised edition, 1995.

The Faber Book of Poems and Places, Faber, 1980.

The Faber Book of Reflective Verse, Faber, 1984.

SIDELIGHTS: The poet Geoffrey Grigson remained in Britain's literary forefront for half a century, though his poetry often received less recognition than his critical essays and numerous anthologies of others' works. As a critic Grigson established a considerable reputation in the 1930s, when he simultaneously edited his prestigious periodical *New Verse* and served as the literary editor of the conservative newspaper *Morning Post.* In both of these publications, and subsequently in the pages of the *Times Literary Supplement, New Statesman,* the *New York Review of Books* and other journals, Grigson reviewed with "a ferocity and personal animus foreign to the general, indulgent tone of modern criticism," according to a London *Times* reporter. In a *Times Literary Supplement* article, Samuel Hynes wrote of Grigson: "Every review is . . . a headlong charge with beaver down and lance at the ready, against the slackness, the wrongheadedness, the vulgarity, the un-Grigsonness of the rest of the world." In his later years, however, Grigson increased his output of published poetry, and Hynes noted: "If posterity, that shadowy reader, returns to Grigson, it will probably not be for his prose. The poetry has a better chance. . . . For Grigson belongs to the class of habitual poets, the kind who write poetry all the time, as other people write journals or diaries or letters, as a means of self-definition and self-sustenance, a way of arresting the daily losses that time exacts."

Grigson was born in Pelynt, Cornwall in 1905, when his father, a canon, was fifty-nine years old. Perceiving a distance between himself and his natural parents, the young Grigson adopted a surrogate mother named Bessie from amongst the Pelynt villagers, and she nurtured within him a delight for the Cornish landscape and for gardening. *Dictionary of Literary Biography* contributor Douglas Loney suggested that Grigson's love for the vicarage garden of his childhood became "the deepest foundation stone of his eclectic, observing, curious poetry. . . . The young Grigson had discovered that the nature which he so loved could be ordered by a careful and patient art and so could achieve a significance reaching beyond its own borders." At every opportunity throughout the years of schooling he called "long purgatory," Grigson escaped to favorite rural areas to observe wildlife and indulge in amateur archaeology. He then brought with him to Oxford University, Loney wrote, "an intense appreciation of the poetry of Herbert, Coleridge, and Hopkins, for the vigor of their poetic language and their stylistic discipline, for their romantic questing, for their insistence . . . on the immediate and the particular, on nature, and on nature's reflection of something rather more elusive, something of the spirit."

After graduating from Oxford, Grigson briefly held a position with the *Yorkshire Post,* writing short articles and book reviews. In 1929 he moved to the *Morning Post,* where he eventually became literary editor. Using the proceeds from the sales of review copies sent to the *Morning Post,* he founded *New Verse* in

1933. The avant-garde periodical, published for six years and never boasting a circulation greater than one thousand, achieved a prestige that far outstripped its modest dimensions. According to Loney, *New Verse* "made in its brief life an important contribution to letters, more perhaps in providing a forum for the works of some of England's finest young poets between the wars than for Grigson's attacks upon critics and authors who dared to disagree with him." Hynes conversely claimed: "In his early *New Verse* days, Grigson marred his achievement as an editor by abusing writers whose only offense was not to please him; *New Verse* was an extraordinarily good journal, and the editing of it was a heroic act, but what one remembers most clearly about it now is likely to be not the high quality of its verse, but the violence of its attacks."

Even after he discontinued *New Verse* in 1939 and began to publish his own poetry in books, Grigson maintained his reputation as an assessor of literary works. Other critics welcomed his forthright approach. In the *Spectator,* Peter Levi wrote: "Grigson fulfills perfectly the most important function of a critic even if he muffs some of the others. That is, he extends the reader's range and understanding, he shows one new things, he points to what is alive." P. J. Kavanagh stated in the *Spectator*: "Geoffrey Grigson has been a figure of such general cultural utility, . . . for so long . . . that it is odd to realize that anyone who praises him acquires a large number of unseen enemies. . . . This is because, in his detestation of the false, the merely fashionable, he has never been able to resist putting the boot in or, if that metaphor is too inelegant, planting a poisoned dart in the tenderest place, and then twisting." In 1974 a *Times Literary Supplement* reviewer claimed: "It would he hard to point to any critic who has so successfully combined an educated traditional taste with an acute awareness of what is going on around him. He has never succumbed either to the ineptitudes of academic criticism or to the standards of the flea-market by which most contemporary verse is judged."

Though a London *Times* writer suggests that the bitter tone of Grigson's criticism "may have sprung partly from the comparative non-recognition of his poetry," Grigson's verse was widely, and generally favorably, reviewed. Hynes described the work as springing from a tradition of "quotidian poetry . . . the poetry of the small, the homely, the contingent, the low-voiced, the ordinary. . . . It is a private record, a self alone in the world: there is rarely another person present, not many poems are direct address, almost none are third person narratives. The observations are exact but reticent, visual but not descriptive, and though they are full of natural details, they are painterly rather than nature poems." A *Times Literary Supplement* reviewer likewise noted Grigson's "interest in small, compact, isolated objects" in poems where "the density is pared down by his finely-wrought verse to a set of clean, separate perceptions, half-lights and ambiguities dispelled by a fastening on silhouetted shapes." "Quirky Mr. Grigson certainly is," wrote another *Times Literary Supplement* critic, who explained: "he enjoys oddments and oddities, and he seems to feel and think in short, sharp bursts, so that his poems are moments of delight and of irritation, little scraps and brief petulances. His touch is surer with objects and creatures than it is with people, even in the love poems." Loney concluded of Grigson's verse: "Although he may find it impossible to affirm any lasting reality beyond that which his senses reveal, he continues to celebrate the fleeting graces which he observes in the objects and events surrounding him." Roger Garfitt offered a similar assessment in *London Magazine:* "Grigson is particularly good at catching moments of subjective illumination and relating them to precise backgrounds, so that they form a kind of critique and history of present times. . . . The result is a poetry, of positive humanism, a redoubt of humane sensibility."

Unimpressed by the British academic community, Grigson never sought to align himself with a university. He worked instead at preparing anthologies, writing nature books, editing art books and museum catalogues, and even publishing an occasional book for children. The author of a *Times Literary Supplement* profile wrote of Grigson's eclectic oeuvre: "Under the often considerable pressures of earning a living he has never given way to the temptations of middlebrow literary good fellowship." Hynes noted that although "it is the criticism that has made his reputation," the best of Grigson's work "has been written in celebration of pictures, of places, of artists, of moments of vision, of the star that the black seeds make in a halved pear." More than one critic commented on a "Grigson paradox," as Valentine Cunningham termed it in the *Times Literary Supplement*. Cunningham cited the "mix of literary naturalist and nature-watching poet-critic," while another *Times Literary Supplement* contributor, after listing the natural history topics common to Grigson's essays, commented: "It seems strange that this Geoffrey Grigson should live in the same skin with the writer of sharp reviews and often sharper letters to periodicals." Hynes expressed the hope that readers in the future would award more attention to the positive side of Grigson's work. "It is a sad irony," Hynes concluded, "that because he has been so quick to attack and condemn others, he should not be recognized in his essential role, as one of the true celebrators of what is."

BIOGRAPHICAL/CRITICAL SOURCES:

BOOKS

Contemporary Literary Criticism, Gale, Volume 7, 1977; Volume 39, 1986.
Dictionary of Literary Biography, Volume 27: *Poets of Great Britain and Ireland, 1945-1960,* Gale, 1984.
Scarfe, Francis, *Auden and After,* Routledge, 1942.
Thwaite, Anthony, *Poetry Today, 1960-1973,* British Council, 1973.

PERIODICALS

Books Abroad, winter, 1967.
Book Week, December 19, 1965.
Book World, March 17, 1968.
Christian Science Monitor, November 30, 1967.
Economist, February 8, 1969.
Encounter, May, 1975.
Harper's, July, 1963.
Listener, November 16, 1967.
London Magazine, June, 1967; February/March, 1975.
New Review, February, 1975.
New Statesman, July 21, 1967; February 2, 1969; May 15, 1970; March 14, 1975.
New York Times Book Review, January 7, 1968.
Observer, June 18, 1967.
Poetry, April, 1970.
Review, September 3, 1970.
Saturday Review, November 13, 1965.
Spectator, June 14, 1968; August 2, 1975; December 18, 1976; December 1, 1982; September 22, 1984.
Times (London), October 23, 1980; November 4, 1982; December 16, 1982; October 27, 1983; January 24, 1985.
Times Literary Supplement, December 7, 1962; December 12, 1963; August 10, 1967; October 10, 1967; November 30, 1967; December 21, 1967; March 13, 1969; July 31, 1969;

December 4, 1969; September 4, 1970; November 30, 1970; February 4, 1972; June 1, 1973; April 19, 1974; July 25, 1975; November 10, 1978; September 12, 1980; January 16, 1981; May 28, 1982; October 22, 1982; February 11, 1983; December 14, 1984.

*　　*　　*

GRIMBLE, Reverend Charles James
See ELIOT, T(homas) S(tearns)

*　　*　　*

GRISHAM, John 1955-

PERSONAL: Born February 8, 1955, in Jonesboro, AR; son of a construction worker and a homemaker; married Renee Jones; children: Ty, Shea (daughter). *Education:* Received B.S. from Mississippi State and J.D. from University of Mississippi. *Religion:* Baptist.

ADDRESSES: Home—Oxford, MS. *Agent*—c/o Ellen Archer, Doubleday, 1540 Broadway, New York, NY 10036-4039

CAREER: Writer. Admitted to the bar in Mississippi, 1981; lawyer in private practice in Southaven, MS, 1981-90. Served in Mississippi House of Representatives, 1984-90.

WRITINGS:

NOVELS

A Time to Kill, Wynwood, 1989.
The Firm, Doubleday (New York City), 1991.
The Pelican Brief, Doubleday, 1992.
The Client, Doubleday, 1993.
John Grisham (collection), Dell (New York City), 1993.
The Chamber, Doubleday, 1994.
The Rainmaker, Doubleday, 1995.
The Runaway Jury, Doubleday (New York City), 1996.
The Partner, Doubleday, 1997.
The Street Lawyer, Doubleday, 1998.

MEDIA ADAPTATIONS: The Firm was adapted as a film directed by Sydney Pollack and starring Tom Cruise, Gene Hackman, and Jeanne Tripplehorn, for Paramount Pictures, 1993; *The Pelican Brief* was adapted as a film directed by Alan J. Pakula and starring Julia Roberts and Denzel Washington, 1994; *The Client* was adapted as a film directed by Joel Schumacher and starring Susan Sarandon and Tommy Lee Jones, 1994; *The Chamber* was adapted as a film directed by James Foley and starring Chris O'Donnell and Gene Hackman, 1996; *A Time to Kill* was adapted as a film directed by Joel Schumacher and starring Matthew McConaughey and Sandra Bullock, 1996; *The Rainmaker* was adapted as a film directed by Francis Ford Coppola and starring Matt Damon and Claire Danes, 1997.

SIDELIGHTS: When John Grisham began writing his first novel, he never dreamed that he would become one of America's bestselling novelists. Yet the appeal of his legal thrillers such as the *The Firm, The Pelican Brief,* and *The Client* has been so great that the reading public regularly buys millions of copies of his books, and nearly all of his novels have been turned into major motion pictures.

As a youth, Grisham had no dreams of becoming a writer, although he was an avid reader. His father traveled extensively in his job as a construction worker, and the Grisham family moved many times. Each time the family took up residence in a new town, Grisham would immediately go to the public library to get a library card. In 1967, the family moved to a more permanent home in Southaven, Mississippi. There Grisham enjoyed greater success in high school athletics than he did in English composition—a subject in which he earned a D grade. After high school graduation, he enrolled at Mississippi State University to study accounting, with the ambition of eventually becoming a tax lawyer. By the time he earned his law degree from the University of Mississippi, however, his interest had shifted to criminal law. Therefore, he returned to Southaven to establish a practice in that field.

Although his practice was successful, Grisham was not happy and grew restless. He switched to the more lucrative field of civil law and won many cases, but a sense of personal dissatisfaction remained. Hoping to somehow make a difference in the world, he entered politics with the aim of reforming his state's educational system. Running as a Democrat, he won a post in the state legislature; four years later, he was reelected. After a total of six years in public office, Grisham, convinced that he would never be able to cut through the red tape of government bureaucracy in his effort to improve Mississippi's educational system, resigned his post in 1990.

While working in the legislature, Grisham continued to run his law office. His first book, *A Time to Kill,* was inspired by a scene he saw one day in court in which a preadolescent girl testified against her rapist. "I never felt such emotion and human drama in my life," Grisham disclosed to *People.* "I became obsessed wondering what it would be like if the girl's father killed that rapist and was put on trial. I had to write it down."

Despite the limited initial success of *A Time to Kill,* Grisham was not discouraged from trying his hand at another novel. The second time around, he decided to follow guidelines set forth in a *Writer's Digest* article for plotting a suspense novel. The result was *The Firm,* the story of a corrupt Memphis-based law firm established by organized crime for purposes of shielding and falsifying earnings. Recruited to the practice is Mitchell McDeere, a promising Harvard law graduate who is overwhelmed by the company's apparent extravagance. After learning of his employers' uncompromising methods, including relentless surveillance of its employees and their families, McDeere grows increasingly alarmed—and curious. When his criminal bosses discover that McDeere has been indulging his curiosity, he becomes an instant target of both the firm and the authorities who are monitoring the firm's activities. American agents from both the Central Intelligence Agency and the Federal Bureau of Investigation pressure McDeere to function as a spy within the firm. When he runs afoul of the ostensible good guys, McDeere finds himself in seemingly endless danger.

Grisham was not as motivated when writing *The Firm* as he had been when composing *A Time to Kill,* but with his wife's encouragement he finished the book. Before he even began trying to sell the manuscript, he learned that someone had acquired a bootlegged copy of it and was willing to give him $600,000 to turn it into a movie script. Within two weeks, Doubleday, one of the many publishers that had previously rejected *A Time to Kill,* offered Grisham a contract.

Upon *The Firm*'s publication, several reviewers argued that Grisham had not attained a high art form, although it was generally conceded that he had put together a compelling, thrilling narrative. *Los Angeles Times Book Review* critic Charles Champlin wrote that the "character penetration is not deep, but the accelerating tempo of paranoia-driven events is wonderful." Chicago *Tribune Books* reviewer Bill Brashler offered similar praise, proclaiming that *The Firm* reads "like a whirlwind." The novel was listed on the *New York Times* bestseller list for nearly a year, and it sold approximately ten times as many copies as its predecessor. By the time the film version was released, there were more than seven million copies of *The Firm* in print. This amazing success gave Grisham the means he needed to build his dream house, quit his law practice, and devote himself entirely to writing.

In a mere one hundred days, Grisham wrote his follow-up to *The Firm.* Another legal thriller, *The Pelican Brief* tells the story of a brilliant, beautiful female law student named Darby Shaw. When two Supreme Court justices are murdered, Shaw postulates a theory as to why the crimes were committed. Just telling people about her idea makes her gravely vulnerable to the corrupt law firm responsible for the killings. Soon she is running for her life—all the while bravely continuing to investigate the conspiracy. In reviewing *The Pelican Brief,* some critics complained that Grisham had followed the premise of *The Firm* far too closely. John Skow reflected this opinion in his review for *Time*: "*The Pelican Brief* . . . is as close to its predecessor as you can get without running *The Firm* through the office copier."

In just six months, Grisham put together yet another bestseller entitled *The Client.* This legal thriller focuses on a young boy who, after learning a sinister secret, turns to a motherly lawyer for protection from both the mob and the FBI. Like *The Firm* and *The Pelican Brief,* the book drew lukewarm reviews but became a bestseller and a major motion picture. For a time in the spring of 1993, after *The Client* came out and *A Time to Kill* was republished, Grisham was in the rare and enviable position of having a book at the top of the hardcover bestseller list and books in the first, second, and third spots on the paperback bestseller list.

With his fifth novel, Grisham departed from his proven formula and proceeded at a more leisurely pace. He took a full nine months to write *The Chamber,* a book in which the "good guys" and "bad guys" are not as clearly defined as in his previous efforts. The novel tells the tale of Ku Klux Klansman Sam Cayhall, who is on death row for the murder of two young sons of a Jewish civil rights attorney. After languishing in prison for years, Cayhall is surprised by the arrival of his estranged grandson, Adam Hall. Hall, an attorney, sets out to reverse his grandfather's death sentence, even though he considers Sam to be the family demon.

The novel is a careful study of a family's history, an examination of the relationship between lawyer and client, and a description of life on death row. It is "a curiously rich milieu for a Grisham novel," according to *Entertainment Weekly* critic Mark Harris, "and it allows the author to do some of his best writing since [*A Time to Kill.*]" Skow credited Grisham with producing a thought-provoking treatise on the death penalty. In his *Time* review, Skow noted that *The Chamber* "has the pace and characters of a thriller, but little else to suggest that it was written by the glib and cheeky author of Grisham's legal entertainments. His tough first novel, the courtroom rouser *A Time to Kill,* is a closer match. . . . Grisham may not change opinions with this sane, civil book, and he may not even be trying to. What he does ask, very plainly, is an important question: Is this what you want?" A reviewer for the London *Sunday Times* stated that "Grisham may do without poetry, wit and style, and offer only the simplest characterisation. The young liberal lawyer may be colourless and the spooky old prisoner one-dimensional; but there is no doubt that this ex-lawyer knows how to tell a story." While this book was less obviously commercial than his previous three books, Grisham had little trouble selling the movie rights to *The Chamber* for a record fee. The movie, starring Chris O'Donnell and Gene Hackman, was released in 1996.

Grisham's 1995 novel, *The Rainmaker,* features a young lawyer, Rudy Baylor, recently graduated from law school, who finds himself desperate for a job when the small firm he had planned to work for is bought out by a large, prestigious Memphis firm that has no use for him. After going to work for Bruiser Stone, a shady lawyer with underworld clients, Baylor finds himself averting an FBI raid on Stone's firm while also trying to pursue a lawsuit brought by a terminally ill leukemia patient against an insurance company that has refused to pay for her treatment. While some reviewers again directed harsh criticism at Grisham for his "pedestrian prose" and "ridiculously implausible" plot (in the words of *New York Times* critic Michiko Kakutani), others praised the novel. Garry Abrams, for instance, writing in the *Los Angeles Times Book Review,* commended the author's "complex plotting," noting that "In his loping, plain prose, Grisham handles all his themes with admirable dexterity and clarity." The book was made into a motion picture starring Matt Damon and Claire Danes and released in 1997.

Grisham also garnered surprisingly warm critical comments for his next novel, 1996's *The Runaway Jury.* Set in a Mississippi gulf coast town, the novel features a legal showdown between several large tobacco companies—"Big Tobacco," in Grisham's parlance-and the widow of a man who died of lung cancer after smoking heavily for three decades. At issue in the trial are the makeup and actions of the jury. Big Tobacco hires the ruthless Rankin Fitch to influence the jury in subtle ways to ensure that it will acquit the tobacco companies of any wrongdoing, but Fitch finds himself challenged unexpectedly by a mysterious man, Nicholas Easter, who gets himself appointed to the jury. Along with his girlfriend, Marlee, Easter appears to have even greater influence over the actions of the jury than Fitch does. Writing in the *New York Times,* Christopher Lehmann-Haupt remarked that Grisham's "prose continues to be clunky, the dialogue merely adequate and the characters as unsubtle as pushpins." But Lehmann-Haupt also averred that "the plot's eventual outcome is far more entertainingly unpredictable" than Grisham's previous novels, and he declared that Grisham "for once . . . is telling a story of genuine significance."

Grisham continued his streak of phenomenally popular novels with 1997's *The Partner,* about a law-firm partner who fakes his own death and absconds with $90 million. In pursuit are his former partners and a shady defense contractor who had planned to split the millions, which were generated by a fraudulent claim. With the help of a mysterious Brazilian, Eva Miranda, the fugitive figures out an ingenious scheme to hide the money but is unable to avoid the pursuit of his enemies. Discussing his less-than-virtuous protagonist, Grisham told Mel Gussow of the *New York Times,* "I wanted to show that with money you can really manipulate the system. You can buy your way out of trouble." *Philadelphia Inquirer* reviewer Robert Drake called *The Partner* "a fine book,

wholly satisfying, and a superb example of a masterful storyteller's prowess captured at its peak."

Grisham's most recent book received the usual critical brickbats and begrudging concessions. "Mr. Moneybags takes on the street people in his latest novel," observed *Booklist* of 1998's *The Street Lawyer.* "Is there a moral here?" There are certainly moral questions raised in this novel about a Yale-educated lawyer who eschews the primrose legal path after he and his colleagues are taken hostage one day by a homeless Vietnam veteran. The journey taken by Michael Brock "from high-priced corporate suites to a free legal clinic in one of Washington, D.C.'s toughest neighborhoods" departs somewhat from Grisham's customary thriller formula. But in its pitting of an idealistic young attorney against powerful forces with wealth and prestige, it is typical of the novelist's work. While conceding it would undoubtedly top the best-seller lists, Michiko Kakutani of the *New York Times* called *The Street Lawyer* "a perfunctory brand-name novel with an unlikable hero, a slapdash plot and some truly awful prose." Writing in *USA Today,* Deirdre Donahue bemoaned Grisham's cliched characters, faulty plotting, and "merely adequate prose." But, she continued, "[h]e possesses that far more rare gift, the ability to hook a mass audience into his fictional world from the very first paragraph."

BIOGRAPHICAL/CRITICAL SOURCES:

BOOKS

Authors and Artists for Young Adults, Volume 14, Gale (Detroit), 1995, pp. 115-21.
Contemporary Literary Criticism, Volume 84, Gale, 1995, pp. 189-201.
Pringle, Mary Beth, *John Grisham: A Critical Companion,* Greenwood Press (Westport, CT), 1997.

PERIODICALS

Booklist, February 1, 1993, p. 954.
Christianity Today, October 3, 1994, p. 14.
Christian Science Monitor, March 5, 1993, p. 10.
Detroit News, May 25, 1994, p. 3D.
Entertainment Weekly, April 1, 1994, pp. 15-20; June 3, 1994, p. 48; July 15, 1994, p. 54; July 29, 1994, p. 23; June 7, 1996.
Forbes, August 30, 1993, p. 24.
Globe and Mail (Toronto), March 30, 1991, p. C6.
Los Angeles Times, April 13, 1997.
Los Angeles Times Book Review, March 10, 1991, p. 7; April 5, 1992, p. 6; April 4, 1993, p. 6; May 14, 1995, p. 8.
New Republic, August 2, 1993, p. 32; March 14, 1994, p. 32; August 22, 1994, p. 35.
Newsday, March 7, 1993.
New Statesman & Society, June 9, 1995, p. 35.
Newsweek, February 25, 1991, p. 63; March 16, 1992, p. 72; March 15, 1993, pp. 79-81; December 20, 1993, p. 121.
New York, August 1, 1994, pp. 52-53.
New Yorker, August 1, 1994, p. 16.
New York Times, March 5, 1993, p. C29; July 29, 1994, p. B10; April 19, 1995, pp. B1, B9; April 28, 1995, p. C33; May 23, 1996, p. C20; March 31, 1997, p. B1; February 10, 1998.
New York Times Book Review, March 24, 1991, p. 37; March 15, 1992, p. 9; October 18, 1992, p. 33; March 7, 1993, p. 18.
People Weekly, April 8, 1991, pp. 36-37; March 16, 1992, pp. 43-44; March 15, 1993, pp. 27-28; June 27, 1994, p. 24; August 1, 1994, p. 16.
Philadelphia Inquirer, March 23, 1997.

Publishers Weekly, February 22, 1992, pp. 70-71; May 30, 1994, p. 37; May 6, 1996, p. 71; February 10, 1997; January 19, 1998.

Saturday Evening Post, March 1997.

Southern Living, August, 1991, p. 58.

Sunday Times (London), June 12, 1994, p. 1.

Time, March 9, 1992, p. 70; March 8, 1993, p. 73; June 20, 1994, p. 67; August 1, 1994.

Tribune Books (Chicago), February 24, 1991, p. 6; September 8, 1991, p. 10; February 23, 1992, p. 4; February 28, 1993, p. 7.

USA Today, February 4, 1998.

Voice Literary Supplement, July-August, 1991, p. 7.

Wall Street Journal, March 12, 1993, p. A6.

West Coast Review of Books, June 15, 1989, p. 80.

*   *   *

GRUMBACH, Doris (Isaac) 1918-

PERSONAL: Born July 12, 1918, in New York, NY; daughter of Leonard William and Helen Isaac; married Leonard Grumbach (a professor of physiology), October 15, 1941 (divorced, 1972); children: Barbara, Jane, Elizabeth, Kathryn. *Education:* Washington Square College, A.B., 1939; Cornell University, M.A., 1940. *Politics:* Liberal. *Religion:* Episcopalian.

ADDRESSES: Home—Sargentville, ME. *Agent*—Maxine Groffsky, 2 Fifth Ave., New York, NY 10011.

CAREER: Writer. Metro-Goldwyn-Mayer, New York City, title writer, 1940-41; *Mademoiselle,* New York City, proofreader and copy editor, 1941-42; Time Inc., associate editor of *Architectural Forum,* 1942-43; Albany Academy for Girls, Albany, NY, English teacher, 1952-55; College of Saint Rose, Albany, instructor, 1955-58, assistant professor, 1958-60, associate professor, 1960-69, professor of English, 1969-73; *New Republic,* Washington, DC, literary editor, 1973-75; American University, Washington, DC, professor of American literature, 1975-85. Visiting University fellow, Empire State College, 1972-73; adjunct professor of English, University of Maryland, 1974-75. Literary critic; *Morning Edition,* National Public Radio, book reviewer, beginning 1982. Board member for National Book Critics Circle and PEN/Faulkner Award; judge for writing contests. *Military Service:* U.S. Navy, Women Accepted for Volunteer Emergency Service, 1941-43.

MEMBER: American Association of University Professors, PEN, Phi Beta Kappa.

WRITINGS:

The Spoil of the Flowers, Doubleday, 1962.
The Short Throat, the Tender Mouth, Doubleday, 1964.
The Company She Kept (biography), Coward, 1967.
Chamber Music, Dutton, 1979.
The Missing Person, Putnam, 1981.
The Ladies, Dutton, 1984.
The Magician's Girl, Macmillan, 1987.
Coming into the Endzone, Norton, 1991.
Extra Innings: A Memoir, Norton, 1993.
Fifty Days of Solitude, Beacon Press (Boston), 1994.
The Book of Knowledge: A Novel, Norton, 1995.
Life in a Day, Beacon Press, 1996.

Also author of introductions and forwards for books. Contributor to books, including *The Postconcilor Parish,* edited by James

O'Gara, Kennedy, 1967, and *Book Reviewing,* edited by Silvia E. Kameran, Writer, Inc., 1978. Columnist for *Critic,* 1960-64, and *National Catholic Reporter,* 1968–; author of nonfiction column for *New York Times Book Review,* 1976–, column, "Fine Print," for *Saturday Review,* 1977-78, and fiction column, *Chronicle of Higher Education,* 1979–. Contributing editor, *New Republic,* 1971-73; book reviewer for *MacNeil-Leher Newshour,* Public Broadcasting Service. Contributor of reviews and criticism to periodicals, including *New York Times Book Review, Chicago Tribune, Commonweal, Los Angeles Times, Nation, Washington Post, Washington Star,* and *New Republic.* Grumbach's works have been translated into foreign languages.

SIDELIGHTS: Doris Grumbach, a biographer and respected literary critic, is the author of several novels with historical, biographical, and autobiographical elements. Early in her career, Grumbach worked as a title writer, copy and associate editor, literary editor, and an English teacher; her career as a novelist did not begin until her early forties.

Her first two books, *The Spoil of the Flowers,* about student life in a boarding house, and *The Short Throat, the Tender Mouth,* about life on a college campus three months before Hitler's march on Poland, "were by a beginner at a time in my life when I no longer should have been a beginner," Grumbach relates in *Contemporary Authors Autobiography Series (CAAS).* "There are some good things, I believe, in both novels: had I much time ahead of me now, I would rewrite them and resubmit them for publication."

Grumbach's third book, *The Company She Kept,* is a literary biography of the acerbic novelist Mary McCarthy. This book became the subject of a threatened lawsuit before its publication and of a volatile critical debate after its release. *The Company She Kept* parallels events and characters in McCarthy's novels with those in her life. "The fiction of Mary McCarthy is autobiographical to an extraordinary degree, in the widest sense of autobiography," Grumbach explains in the foreword to the book. "In the case of Mary McCarthy there is only a faint line between what really happened to her, the people she knew and knows, including herself, and the characters in her fictions." To prepare the biography, Grumbach spent a year reading McCarthy's work and criticism of it and interviewed the author extensively at her Paris home. Difficulties with McCarthy arose, Grumbach says, when McCarthy, who suggested she read the galleys of the book to catch any factual errors, protested against some of the information Grumbach had included in the manuscript.

In a *New York Times Book Review* article on her dispute with McCarthy, Grumbach reports that McCarthy voluntarily provided her with intimate biographical details in conversation and in a detailed memorandum. McCarthy's anger over their inclusion therefore came as a surprise, says Grumbach. "I was unprepared for the fury of her response when she saw the galleys . . . and realized that I had used the autobiographical details she had, as she said, given me," comments Grumbach. "She had said, once, that it felt strange to have a book written about one, 'a book that includes you as a person, not just a critical analysis of your writings.' Now she insisted that the *curriculum vitae* had been sent to be 'drawn upon,' not used, although just how this was to be done continues to be a mystery to me. . . . [McCarthy's] feeling was that the tapes and her letters to me had been intended solely for 'your own enlightenment.'"

For all the attendant publicity, however, *The Company She Kept* was not well received by the literary establishment. Writes Stephanie Harrington in *Commonweal*: "To anyone who has read

The Company She Kept, . . . the newspaper stories that followed the book's publication must have seemed too preposterous to be anything but a desperate attempt by the publisher's publicity department to drum up business for a clinker." A *Times Literary Supplement* contributor, who describes *The Company She Kept* as "sparkily written and often critically sharp," feels that Grumbach falls short of her stated goal of "weaving one fabric of [the] diverse threads of McCarthy's biography and her fiction." Grumbach, says the reviewer, "never fully succeeds in dramatizing the complex interactions that go into such a process; [therefore, *The Company She Kept*] is likely to end up as required reading for gossips."

Ten years after publishing *The Company She Kept* and fifteen years after writing her novels, *The Short Throat, the Tender Mouth* and *The Spoil of the Flowers*, Grumbach returned to fiction. Her first novel after the hiatus was *Chamber Music*, written as the memoirs of ninety year-old Caroline MacLaren, widow of a famous composer and founder of an artists' colony in his memory. Released with a 20,000 copy first printing and a $20,000 promotional campaign, *Chamber Music* won the popular and critical acclaim that eluded Grumbach's earlier books. Peter Davison in the *Atlantic Monthly* calls the book "artful, distinctive, provocative, [and] compassionate." *Chamber Music*, writes Victoria Glendinning in the *Washington Post Book World*, "is a book of originality and distinction." *Chamber Music* is the story of "the chamber of one heart," says Grumbach's character Caroline MacLaren in the introduction to her memoirs.

The novel's plot revolves around the subjugation of Caroline to her husband Robert and to Robert's music. Their marriage is a cold and barren one, and *Chamber Music* charts its course through Robert's incestuous relationship with his mother, his homosexual affair with a student, and, finally, to his agonizing death in the tertiary stage of syphilis. Especially noted for its sensitive handling of its delicate subject matter and for its characterizations, *Chamber Music* is called by the *New York Times*'s John Leonard, "one of those rare novels for adults who listen." The characters in *Chamber Music*, Leonard continues, "are all stringed instruments. The music we hear occurs in the chamber of Caroline's heart. It is quite beautiful." With her third novel, Grumbach "makes us hear the difficult music of grace," says Nicholas Delbanco in the *New Republic*.

Although *Chamber Music*'s "revelations of sexuality are meant to shatter," as one *Publishers Weekly* contributor comments, and the passage on Robert's illness gives "a clinical description so simply precise, so elegantly loathsome, that it would do nicely either in a medical text or in a book on style," as Edith Milton observes in *Yale Review*, it is the contrast between *Chamber Music*'s action and its language that gives the novel its impact. While much of the material in *Chamber Music* is meant to shock, the language is genteel and full of Victorian phrases. "What gives the main part of this book its polish and flavor is the contrast between matter and manner," says Glendinning. "Clarity and elegance of style account . . . for the distinction of *Chamber Music*," writes Eleanor B. Wymard in *Commonweal*, and other critics have high praise for Grumbach's writing. A *Washington Post Book World* reviewer claims the book's language is "as direct and pure as a Hayden quartet," and Abigail McCarthy in *Commonweal* states that *Chamber Music* has "the classical form, clarity, and brilliance of a composition for strings." Because it is Caroline's story, the novel adopts her voice—a voice that is "slightly stilted, slightly vapid, of the genteel tradition," one *Atlantic* contributor observes. Asserts Milton: "The novel is wonderfully written in [Caroline's]

voice to evoke a time gone by, an era vanished. . . . The prose, understated, beautiful in its economies, supports a story of almost uncanny bleakness."

Franny Fuller, the protagonist of Grumbach's novel *The Missing Person*, is also patterned after an actual figure. Franny, a 1930s movie star and sex symbol, closely resembles actress Marilyn Monroe. Written as a series of vignettes interweaving the events of Franny's career with an ongoing commentary by a gossip columnist, *The Missing Person* traces the actress's life from her sad beginnings in Utica, New York, through her rise to stardom, and finally to her disappearance from both Hollywood and the public consciousness. "Here, with certain sympathetic changes, is quite visibly another tale about the sad life of Marilyn Monroe," observes the *New York Times*'s Herbert Mitgang. "Missing person," says Cynthia Propper Seton in the *Washington Post Book World*, refers to "this sense that one is all facade, that there is no self inside." Franny is supposed to serve as a prototype for all the "missing persons" who are, "above all, missing to themselves," claims Herbert Gold in the *New York Times Book Review*. "There seems evidence," Abigail McCarthy writes in *Commonweal*, "that Doris Grumbach may initially have thought of Franny Fuller's story as a feminist statement in that women like Franny whom America 'glorifies and elevates' are sex objects made larger than life. But if so, as often happens in the creative process, she has transcended the aim in the writing. The creatures of the Hollywood process she gives us, men as well as women, are all victims."

Grumbach switches her topic from the rise then demise of a 1930s starlet in *The Missing Person*, to the public ostracism then acceptance of two aristocratic lesbian lovers of the eighteenth century in her novel *The Ladies*. "Grumbach compellingly recreates the lives of two women who so defied convention and so baffled their contemporaries that they became celebrities," lauds Catharine R. Stimpson in the *New York Times Book Review*. The story relates Grumbach's concept of how Eleanor Butler and Sarah Ponsonby, two Irish aristocrats from the 1700s known as "the Ladies of Llangollen," shocked the community with their lesbian relationship but were eventually accepted and visited by such noteworthy individuals as Anna Seward, the Duke of Wellington, and Walter Scott. Stimpson notes the book "eloquently documents the existence of women who lived as they wished to, instead of as society expected them to."

As Grumbach relates, Lady Eleanor, feeling the lack of love from her parents because she wasn't a boy, becomes the boy in her behavior and dress. Always looking to fill her need for acceptance and love, Eleanor falls in love with the orphan, Sarah Ponsonby, who is being sexually harassed by her guardian. Eleanor attempts to rescue Sarah, but the two are caught before they get far. A second attempt prompts the families to allow the couple to leave together, but under the condition that Lady Eleanor is banned from Ireland forever. After a couple years of wandering, Eleanor and Sarah settle with a former servant and create their own haven in Wales. Eleanor and Sarah "seemed to each other to be divine survivors, well beyond the confines of social rules, two inhabitants of an ideal society. . . . They had uncovered a lost continent on which they could live, in harmony, quite alone and together," writes Grumbach in *The Ladies*. Eventually, visited by other aristocrats, they become more secure within the outer community, however, problems arise in their relationship as their greed and fame alters their lives.

The Ladies met with good reviews. Stimpson, while recognizing Grumbach's pattern of blurring biography and fiction, praises the book noting that "*The Ladies* is boldly imagined, [and] subtly crafted." Comparing Grumbach's work with the likes of Virginia Woolf and Charlotte Perkins Gillman, the *Washington Post Book World*'s Sandra Gilbert claims Grumbach has "recounted their story with grace and wit," and applauds "the sureness with which Grumbach accumulates small details about the lives of her protagonist and the tough but loving irony with which she portrays their idiosyncrasies."

The title for Grumbach's next novel, the *The Magician's Girl,* is borrowed from Sylvia Plath's poem "The Bee Meeting." In this story Grumbach writes about three women who were college roommates and grew up during the twenties and thirties. In episodic fashion, the stories of Minna, Liz, and Maud are related from their childhood to their sixties, and from their hopes and dreams to their reality. Pretty, shy Minna marries a doctor, has a son, and becomes a history professor. After surviving years in a loveless marriage, at the age of sixty she finally develops a loving relationship with a young man in his twenties. Not long after they meet and she experiences this fulfillment, though, she is killed in a car accident. Maud, the overweight and unattractive daughter of a nurse and army sergeant, marries a handsome man whom she eventually rejects, has twins whom she neglects, and spends most of her time writing poetry. Her poetry is good but she destroys it all, except for the copies she sends to Minna in her letters; she commits suicide before realizing the true success of her writings. Liz, the only survivor, lives with her partner in a lesbian relationship, achieving fame as a photographer, her subjects all freaks of one kind or another. Summarizing the book's theme, Anita Brookner in her review for the *Washington Post Book World,* states that the formulaic stories about these three women demonstrates "the way early beginnings mature into not very much, for despite the achievements that come with age, a sense of disillusion persists." Brookner asserts that Grumbach asks more questions about women's lives than she answers in her story, including the question, "Is that all?," and surmises that this may be more important than the answers. In conclusion, she praises *The Magician's Girl* as "a beautifully easy read, discreet and beguiling, and attractively low-key. It is an honorable addition to the annals of women's reading."

The reviews for *The Magician's Girl* were mixed. Several critics faulted Grumbach for too closely describing the lives of Sylvia Plath and Diane Arbus as the characters of Maud and Liz respectively. Other critics found her writing weak in definition and description. *Times Literary Supplement*'s Marianne Wiggins finds events "unlocated in time" and places "without a sense of period." She asserts that it is written "as if the text were a rehearsal for a talent contest," and considers this especially disconcerting since she regards Grumbach as the "master of the quick sketch" and points out that generally "when her narrative shifts to describing the specific, it soars." In contrast, Paula Deitz in the *New York Times Book Review* commends Grumbach's attention to detail in *The Magician's Girl.* She deems that the characters described "are all rich images, informed with the magic conveyed by the small details that reveal the forming of these lives."

Grumbach shares feelings, events, and remembrances of the year she turned seventy in her 1991 autobiography, *Coming into the End Zone: A Memoir.* "What is most delightful about *Coming into the End Zone*—[is] the wry, spry, resilient, candid recording of present happenings and suddenly remembered past happenings

which fill almost every page with anecdotes and reflections," exclaims *Washington Post Book World*'s Anthony Thwaite. Grumbach comments on a wide range of topics, including contemporary annoyances such as phrases like "the computer is down," the death of several friends from the complications of acquired immunodeficiency syndrome, her dislikes of travel, her move to rural Maine, her memories of being fired from the *New Republic,* and Mary McCarthy's last curt comment to her. "The best moments are the passages in which the author seems least to be writing for posterity, merely trying to capture herself on the page, moments when the need to maintain a public persona gives way to the vulnerability of the private person, sometimes even to the young girl still inside this old woman," declares Carol Anshaw in the Chicago *Tribune Books.* "The book that Ms. Grumbach intended as a confrontation with death winds up being a celebration of life," comments Noel Perrin in the *New York Times Book Review,* adding that "it is a deeply satisfying book." "Grumbach's reflections record—with honesty, fidelity, much important and unimportant detail, and with much grace and informal wit—her feelings of the time. I know no other book like it," hails Thwaite. He concludes, "This is a book to grow old with even before one is old. The best is yet to be."

Grumbach continues her reminiscences in *Extra Innings: A Memoir.* Reviewers disagree about how satisfactorily she presents her experiences. In *Washington Post Book World,* Diana O'Hehir defines a memoir as a grab bag and, directing her comments to Grumbach, writes: "I felt yours wasn't enough of a grab bag. Not enough gossip about people. Not enough detail about you, not enough specific detail about relationships, family." However, Kathleen Norris presents her view in the *New York Times Book Review* that the book is "more of a hodepodge" than *End Zone.* Norris maintains that "for all its recounting of ordinary events, *Extra Innings,* like *End Zone,* is a document still too rare in literary history, an account of a woman who has lived by words. Ms. Grumbach wittily chronicles the absurdities and ambiguities of the modern American writer's life."

In *The Book of Knowledge* Grumbach introduces four central characters as adolescents the summer before the stock market crash, then touches on each of their lives into adulthood, through the Great Depression and World War II. Two of the characters are a brother and sister who become intimate, sexually and emotionally, that summer. The other two are the vacationing son and daughter of a wealthy stockbroker, with whom the brother and sister become friends. All strive for selfhood in various fashions; and the two young men eventually have a homosexual relationship. Nina Mehta writes in the Chicago *Tribune Books* that "Grumbach cuts right to sexuality, condemning her main characters to lives stunted by their inability to deal honestly with their sexual feelings." According to Julia Markus of the *Los Angeles Times Book Review,* "The stories of [the four] and their families are told and interwoven with great irony, subtlety and beauty." Markus concludes that "with her masterful conciseness and with her own unique haunting force, Doris Grumbach has brilliantly delineated the tragedy of an entire generation."

But other reviewers fault Grumbach for not delving into the foursome. Grumbach makes "a lot of tendentious commentary about puberty and the chasteness of homosexual inclinations," points out Mehta, "but what's most disheartening . . . is the book's lack of insight." Mehta maintains that "by neglecting to ventilate her characters' lives with even a breeze of introspection, Grumbach gives them less personality, less psychological weight, than they deserve." Sara Maitland asserts in the *New York Times*

Book Review: "Ms. Grumbach prods at her four central characters with a sharp stick, but when they turn over, she withdraws her authorial attention in disgust." Maitland decries that the reader is "never shown the painful workings through of . . . personal choices we are *told* the characters have to endure."

BIOGRAPHICAL/CRITICAL SOURCES:

BOOKS

Contemporary Authors, Volume 9, Gale (Detroit), 1983.
Contemporary Authors Autobiography Series, Volume 2, Gale, 1985.
Contemporary Literary Criticism, Volume 22, Gale, 1980.

PERIODICALS

America, June 2, 1979.
American Spectator, January, 1982.
Atlantic Monthly, March, 1979.
Christian Science Monitor, February 26, 1987, p. 22.
Commonweal, October 6, 1967; June 22, 1979; January 15, 1982.
Library Journal, March 1, 1979.
Listener, August 9, 1979.
Los Angeles Times Book Review, July 16, 1995, p. 3.
Ms., April, 1979.
Nation, March 28, 1981, pp. 375-76.
National Review, June 8, 1979.
New Republic, March 10, 1979.
New Statesman, August 17, 1979; August 28, 1981.
Newsweek, March 19, 1979.
New Yorker, April 23, 1979.
New York Times, March 13, 1979; July 20, 1989.
New York Times Book Review, June 11, 1967; March 25, 1979; March 29, 1981, pp. 14-15; September 30, 1984, p. 12; February 1, 1987, p. 22; September 22, 1991; November 21, 1993, p. 11; June 25, 1995, p. 19.
Observer, August 12, 1979.
Publishers Weekly, January 15, 1979; February 13, 1981.
Spectator, August 11, 1979.
Time, April 9, 1979.
Times Literary Supplement, December 7, 1967; November 30, 1979; September 11, 1981; July 12, 1985; June 19, 1987, p. 669.
Tribune (Chicago), September 29, 1991; August 13, 1995, p. 6.
Washington Post Book World, March 18, 1979; February 10, 1980; April 5, 1981, pp. 9, 13; September 30, 1984, p. 7; January 4, 1987, pp. 3, 13; September 8, 1991; October 24, 1993, p. 5.
Yale Review, autumn, 1979.

*   *   *

GUARE, John 1938-

PERSONAL: Born February 5, 1938, in New York, NY; son of Edward and Helen Claire (Grady) Guare; married Adele Chatfield-Taylor (an artist), May 20, 1981. *Education:* Georgetown University, A.B., 1961; Yale University, M.F.A., 1963.

ADDRESSES: Home—New York, NY. *Agent*—R. Andrew Boose, One Dag Hammarskjold Plaza, New York, NY 10017.

CAREER: Playwright. Playwright-in-residence at New York Shakespeare festival, 1977; Yale University, New Haven, CT, adjunct professor of playwriting, 1978-81; visiting artist, Harvard University, 1990-91; fellow, Juilliard School, 1993-94; lecturer,

New York University and City College of New York. Member of Board of Directors, Municipal Arts Society of New York City. *Military service:* U.S. Air Force Reserve, 1963.

MEMBER: Authors League of America, Dramatists Guild (member of board of directors), Eugene O'Neill Playwrights' Conference (founding member).

AWARDS, HONORS: Obie Award, 1968, for *Muzeeka;* Obie Award as New York Drama Critics Most Promising Playwright, 1968-69, for *Cop-Out;* New York Drama Critics Circle Award for Best American Play, 1971, for *The House of Blue Leaves;* Outer Critics Circle Prize for playwriting, 1971; New York Drama Critics Circle Award for Best Musical of 1971-72, for *Two Gentlemen of Verona;* Antoinette Perry (Tony) Awards for Best Musical and for Best Libretto, 1972, for *Two Gentlemen of Verona;* Rockefeller grant in playwriting; Joseph Jefferson award for playwriting, 1977, for *Landscape of the Body;* Award of Merit, American Academy of Arts and Letters, 1981; New York Film Critics Award, Los Angeles Film Critics Award, National Society of Film Critics Award, Venice Film Festival Grand Prize, and Academy Award nomination for best original screenplay, all 1981, all for *Atlantic City;* New York Institute of the Humanities fellowship, 1982; named Literary Lion, New York Public Library, 1986; Rockefeller grant; honorary doctorate, Georgetown University, 1991.

WRITINGS:

PLAYS

Universe, first produced in New York, 1949.
Did You Write My Name in the Snow? first produced in New Haven, CT, 1962.
To Wally Pantoni, We Leave a Credenza, first produced in New York, 1964.
The Loveliest Afternoon of the Year [and] *Something I'll Tell You Tuesday* (both first produced off-off-Broadway at Cafe Cino, 1966), Dramatists Play Service, 1968.
Muzeeka and Other Plays: Cop-Out, Home Fires (includes *Muzeeka,* first produced in Waterford, CT, 1967, produced in New York, 1968, and *Cop-Out* and *Home Fires,* both first produced in Waterford, 1968, produced in New York, 1969), Grove, 1969.
(Contributor) John Lahr, editor, *Showcase I: Plays from the Eugene O'Neill Foundation,* Grove, 1969.
A Play by Brecht (a musical based on Bertolt Brecht's *The Exception the Rule;* music by Leonard Bernstein, lyrics by Stephen Sondheim), first produced on Broadway at Broadhurst Theatre, February 18, 1969.
Kissing Sweet [and] *A Day for Surprises: Two Short Plays* (*Kissing Sweet,* first produced on television, 1969; *A Day for Surprises,* first produced in London, 1971), Dramatists Play Service, 1970.
(Contributor) *Off-Broadway Plays,* Volume I, Penguin (London), 1970.
(With Milos Forman) *Taking Off* (screenplay; produced by Universal, 1971), New American Library, 1971.
The House of Blue Leaves (first produced off-Broadway at Truck and Warehouse Theatre, February 10, 1971, produced on Broadway at Plymouth Theatre, October, 1986), Viking, 1972.
(With Mel Shapiro and Galt MacDermot) *Two Gentlemen of Verona* (based on Shakespeare's play; produced in New York at Delacorte Theatre, July 22, 1971; produced on

Broadway at St. James Theatre, December 1, 1971), Holt, 1973.

Un Pape a New York, first produced in Paris at Gaiete-Montparnesse, 1972.

Marco Polo Sings a Solo (first produced in Nantucket, MA, at Cyrus Pierce Theatre, August 6, 1973, produced off-Broadway at New York Shakespeare Festival Public Theatre, January 12, 1977), Dramatists Play Service, 1977.

(With Harold Stone) *Optimism, or The Adventures of Candide* (based on Voltaire's novel), produced in Waterford at Eugene O'Neill Foundation Theatre, September, 1973.

Rich and Famous (first produced off-Broadway at Estelle Newman Public Theatre, February 19, 1976), Dramatists Play Service, 1977.

Landscape of the Body (first produced in Lake Forest, IL, at Academy Festival Theatre, 1977, produced off-Broadway at Shakespeare Festival Public Theatre, October 12, 1977), Dramatists Play Service, 1978.

Bosoms and Neglect (first produced off-Broadway at Longacre Theatre, May 3, 1979, revised version produced in New Haven at Yale Repertory Theatre, October, 1979, and off-Broadway at New York Theatre Workshop, April 8, 1986), Dramatists Play Service, 1979.

In Fireworks Lie Secret Codes, first produced off-Broadway at Mitzi E. Newhouse Theatre, March 5, 1981.

Atlantic City (screenplay), produced by Paramount Pictures, 1981.

Lydie Breeze (first play of a projected historical tetralogy), first produced in New York at American Place Theatre, February, 1982.

Gardenia (second play of a projected historical tetralogy; first produced in New York at Manhattan Theatre Club, April 28, 1982), Dramatists Play Service, 1982.

Three Exposures (collected plays, including *The House of Blue Leaves, Bosoms and Neglect,* and *Landscape of the Body*), Harcourt, 1982.

Hey, Stay a While, produced in Chicago, IL, at Goodman Theatre, 1984.

Women and Water (third play of a projected historical tetralogy), first produced in Washington, DC, at Arena Stage, November 29, 1985.

(With Wendy Wasserstein, David Mamet, Maria Irene Fornes, Michael Weller, Samm-Art Williams, and Spalding Gray) *Orchards* (seven one-act plays based on stories by Anton Chekhov), first produced in New York at Lucille Lortel Theatre, April 22, 1986.

Six Degrees of Separation (produced in New York at the Mitzi E. Newhouse Theater, June, 1990), Vintage, 1990.

Four Baboons Adoring the Sun, Dramatists Play Service (New York City), 1995.

The War Against the Kitchen Sink, Smith and Kraus, 1996.

Also author of preface for *From Ibsen: Workshop,* Da Capo Press, 1978.

OTHER

(Author of introduction) Dawn Powell, *The Locusts Have No King,* Yarrow Press, 1990.

(Author of preface) Jon R. Baitz, *The Substance of Fire and Other Plays,* Theatre Communications Group, Inc., 1991.

(Author of introduction) Chuck Close, *Chuck Close: Life and Work, 1988-1995,* Thames and Hudson (New York City), 1995.

John Guare, Smith and Kraus (Lyme, NH), 1996.

MEDIA ADAPTATIONS: Six Degrees of Separation was adapted as a motion picture in 1993, directed by Fred Schepis, starring Will Smith, Stockard Channing, and Donald Sutherland.

SIDELIGHTS: John Guare has been called "the great romantic poet of contemporary American theatre" by Richard Christiansen in the *Chicago Tribune,* as well as "the world's oldest living promising young playwright," a line from one of Guare's own plays, which he now regrets having mentioned to a literal-minded interviewer. "Whatever you say about John Guare's preeminence among major American dramatists, he is by far the funniest," states *Los Angeles Times* writer Lawrence Christon. "There is an antic, unpredictable, indirect quality to his people, who are so self-absorbed that they're almost dreamlike, and fairly impervious to the ruin they generate around them."

In *The House of Blue Leaves,* the play's protagonist is Artie, a zookeeper who yearns to sell his Tinpan Alley-type songs but instead must cope with an insane wife, a demanding girlfriend, and a son whose idea of rebellion is to kill the pope. Eventually, after one rejection too many, Artie kills his wife and retreats into a fantasy world. "This nightmarish farce appears to derive in part from Guare's relationship with his own parents; the play is autobiographical not only in inspiration but also in some of its details," Suzanne Dieckman contends in the *Dictionary of Literary Biography.* "[The son's] story of his childhood humiliation . . . for instance, Guare claims to be 'an exact word-for-word' report of [his] own experience." However dark the comedy, the playwright "is not simply a prankster," notes Harold Clurman in a *Nation* review. "What motivates him is scorn for the fraudulence of our way of life. In *The House of Blue Leaves,* he has been aroused by the obsession with big shots, 'personalities,' stars, the 'in' tribe. That is a way of saying that we no longer see people as human beings; we worship 'names.' The imbecile, the villainous, the irredeemably mediocre possess glamour . . . if they have been sufficiently publicized."

Bosoms and Neglect is another in Guare's stable of black comedies, in this case dealing with a blind, cancer-ridden octogenarian whose last days are spent in verbal duals with her son, a middle-aged man called Scooper. While *New York Times* critic Mel Gussow diagnoses the play as having "theatrical schizophrenia" in its disjointed two acts, the reviewer also finds that *Bosoms and Neglect* "is more interesting than many other current plays." "Beneath its quirky surface, [the work] tells us that unrequited love between children and parents is potentially more catastrophic than it is between lovers," Christon says in another *Los Angeles Times* article. "But it also shows us how no moral or message or insight is enough to maintain the godawful slipperiness of our emotional equilibrium. With Guare the line between insanity and reason flickers like a hairline cut on an old film. That's what makes his comedy so special."

In 1982, Guare left the realm of modern times to begin an historical tetralogy. The first three plays of the tetralogy encompass a period in America from post-Civil War times to the turn of the century, and examine the lives of a young woman, Lydie Breeze, and the three men who share her world. *Lydie Breeze, Gardenia,* and *Women and Water* are all set on Nantucket island, where the main characters attempt to form a utopian commune that disintegrates with jealousy and murder. "The imagery that runs through this frantic family history—disease, insanity, mutilation, death, decay, poisoned sex—is not new in [the author's] work, even though the period idiom is," Frank Rich points out in the *New York Times.* Rich has mixed reactions to Guare's efforts in *Lydie Breeze,* calling the play "a literate ambitious experiment" that nonetheless has "luminous and savage theatrical bits [floating] within a murky, incorporeal whole."

To a *New Yorker* critic, *Lydie Breeze* has "an elaborate plot and contains a great deal of whizzing, cometlike dialogue, but it also has within it a great stillness, an immense silence, which amounts to a statement of reverence. (The stillness makes the play, full of action though it is, something like a painting. After it is over, it lives on in one's imagination as if it were a single object—or, rather, a still space with objects in it, a tableau.)" *Newsweek's* Jack Kroll feels that Guare "has seized on the turn of the century as the pivotal moral moment in American history. He's taken the Ibsen-like themes of tainted blood and skelton-stuffed closets and turned them into a Yankee Doodle Deadly saga of broken promises. Because he's John Guare, he has also had a lot of fun doing this. The glory of Guare is his unabashed (or perhaps abashed) romanticism, his bifocal vision of the tragic and the absurd, his natural instinct for the theatrical. It may be that the true contemporary form of tragedy is one that triggers a laugh as its proper response—a new kind of laugh, a slapstick sob at the Strangelovian nature of our fate."

The events in *Gardenia* take place twenty years before those dramatized in *Lydia Breeze,* while *Women and Water* is set in an even earlier era, with Guare "trying to parallel the complex family saga with the Civil War itself," according to Gussow in his *New York Times* review. Gussow notes that "while it is intriguing to follow the continuing family chronicle . . . one cannot say that the journey has been overly enlightening, or that it has taken profitable advantage of [the author's] considerable talent as a playwright." Nevertheless, "even as the play makes its rocky crossing, there are moments that remind us of Mr. Guare's perceptive eye for physical detail . . . and for momentous emotional disturbances. . . . After three plays, Lydie remains dramatically elusive, as [Guare] continues to aspire to be a playwright as architect." While Christiansen's praise for *Women and Water* is likewise measured, the *Chicago Tribune* critic finds it "thrilling indeed to see an artist of Guare's stature paint on such a broad canvas, to reach for the surge and sweep of man's history in a production that calls for all-out theatrical effects."

Six Degrees of Separation was a critical and popular success when it opened in New York City in 1990. The title of the play refers to a scientific claim that it only takes six steps to link anyone on earth with anyone else genetically. Based on true events, the play features a white, wealthy New York society couple whose lives are disrupted by a gay black man falsely claiming to be the son of actor Sidney Poitier. Not until after the couple invites the man, Paul, into their home and lives do they realize that he is an imposter. By then, however, he has forever altered their perspectives on life. As *Newsweek* critic Jack Kroll notes, "Paul is a major creation: he's a figure of dizzying ambiguity, weirdly innocent, sexually seductive, socially unsophisticated, startlingly insightful." Ultimately, the play becomes a social commentary on how contemporary people are separated from one another on many different levels, from class and race to gender and sexual orientation.

Commenting in the *New York Times,* Frank Rich states that the author "transports the audience beyond the dailiness of journalistic storytelling to the magical reaches of the imagination." Clive Barnes, writing in the *New York Post,* remarks that Guare is unable to fully explain how Paul's scam works and thus is forced to "[fill] out his canvas with a brief, none too acceptable, tragi-

comic subplot." However, Barnes continues, "in the play's magnificent final phase, the emphasis is placed not on the how, but the why of the deception." Calling *Six Degrees of Separation* a "masterwork," Rich avers: "Among the many remarkable aspects of Mr. Guare's writing is the seamlessness of his imagery, characters and themes, as if this play had just erupted from his own imagination in one perfect piece."

"Guare forces a critical review of all those aspects of society which drive people to live in fantasy instead of being honest with themselves and with each other," Dieckman concludes. "If his plays sometimes seem bogged down with the weight of too many words, too many ideas, they are themselves an accurate reflection of contemporary life—bombarded from all directions with information, dreams, and conflicting demands."

BIOGRAPHICAL/CRITICAL SOURCES:

BOOKS

Contemporary Literary Criticism, Gale (Detroit), Volume 8, 1978; Volume 14, 1980; Volume 29, 1984; Volume 67, 1992.
Dasgupta, Guatam, *American Playwrights: A Critical Survey,* Volume I, Drama Book Specialists, 1981.
Dictionary of Literary Biography, Volume 7: *Twentieth-Century American Dramatists,* Gale, 1981.

PERIODICALS

Chicago Tribune, December 20, 1985.
Commonweal, May 8, 1992.
Entertainment Weekly, December 24, 1993.
Lear's, January, 1994, p. 10.
Los Angeles Magazine, March 1991.
Los Angeles Times, June 22, 1982; October 9, 1984; October 22, 1984; February 7, 1986; November 2, 1996.
Nation, March 1, 1971.
New Republic May 19, 1982; May 5, 1986.
Newsweek, February 14, 1977; May 14, 1979; February 1, 1982; June 25, 1990.
New Yorker, February 14, 1977; October 24, 1977; March 15, 1982.
New York Post, June 15, 1990.
New York Times, March 7, 1971; May 4, 1979; October 14, 1979; December 7, 1979; May 29, 1981; February 21, 1982; February 25, 1982; April 29, 1982; May 2, 1982; May 9, 1984; December 8, 1985; March 16, 1986; March 20, 1986; April 6, 1986; April 9, 1986; April 13, 1986; April 23, 1986; June 15, 1990; November 9, 1990.
Saturday Review, November 20, 1973.
Village Voice, April 24, 1974; February 14, 1977; May 14, 1979.
Washington Post, May 31, 1984; January 17, 1986.

*   *   *

GUEST, Judith (Ann) 1936-

PERSONAL: Born March 29, 1936, in Detroit, MI; daughter of Harry Reginald (a businessman) and Marion Aline (Nesbit) Guest; married husband, Larry (a data processing executive), August 22, 1958; children: Larry, John, Richard. *Education:* University of Michigan, B.A., 1958.

ADDRESSES: Home—4600 West 44th St., Edina, MN 55424. *Office*—c/o Viking/Penguin, 375 Hudson St., New York, NY 10014.

CAREER: Writer. Employed as teacher in public grade schools in Royal Oak, MI, 1964, Birmingham, MI, 1969, and Troy, MI, 1975.

MEMBER: Authors Guild, Authors League of America, P.E.N. American Center, Detroit Women Writers.

AWARDS, HONORS: Janet Heidinger Kafka Prize from University of Rochester, 1977, for *Ordinary People.*

WRITINGS:

NOVELS

Ordinary People (Book-of-the-Month Club selection), Viking, 1976.
Second Heaven (Book-of-the-Month Club selection), Viking, 1982.
The Mythic Family: An Essay, Milkweed, 1988.
(With Rebecca Hill) *Killing Time in St. Cloud,* Delacorte, 1988.
Errands, Ballantine, 1997.

Also author of a screenplay adaptation of *Second Heaven* and of three short stories by Carol Bly, entitled *Rachel River, Minnesota.* Contributor to periodicals, including *The Writer.*

MEDIA ADAPTATIONS: Ordinary People was filmed by Paramount in 1980, directed by Robert Redford, starring Mary Tyler Moore, Donald Sutherland, Timothy Hutton, Judd Hirsch, and Elizabeth McGovern; a stage version was published by Dramatic Publishing in 1983.

SIDELIGHTS: Judith Guest is a popular novelist who achieved startling success with *Ordinary People,* her first book. Contrary to custom, Guest sent the manuscript to Viking Press without a preceding letter of inquiry and without the usual plot synopsis and outline that many publishing houses require. The manuscript was read by an editorial assistant who liked it well enough to send Guest a note of encouragement and pass the story along to her superiors for a second reading. Months passed. Then, in the summer of 1975, when Guest was in the midst of moving from Michigan to Minnesota, came the word she'd been waiting for: Viking would be "honored" to publish *Ordinary People,* the first unsolicited manuscript they had accepted in twenty-six years. Guest's book went on to become not only a best-selling novel—selected by four book clubs, serialized in *Redbook,* and sold to Ballantine for paperback rights for $635,000—but also an award-winning film that captured the 1980 Oscar for best movie of the year. Since that time, Guest has published another novel, *Second Heaven,* which also deals with family relationships and problems of communication.

The story of a teenage boy's journey from the brink of suicide back to mental health, *Ordinary People* shows the way that unexpected tragedy can destroy even the most secure of families. Seventeen-year-old Conrad Jarrett, son of a well-to-do tax lawyer, appears to have everything: looks, brains, manners, and a good relationship with his family. But when he survives a boating accident that kills his older brother, Conrad sinks into a severe depression, losing touch with his parents, teachers, friends, and just about everyone else in the outside world. His attempt to kill himself by slashing his wrists awakens his father to the depth of his problems, but it also cuts Conrad off from his mother—a compulsive perfectionist who believes that his bloody suicide attempt was intended as a punishment for her. With the help of his father and an understanding analyst, Conrad slowly regains his equilibrium. "Above all," writes *New York Review of Books* contributor Michael Wood, "he comes to accept his mother's

apparent failure to forgive him for slashing his wrists, and his own failure to forgive her for not loving him more. It is true that she has now left his father, because he seemed to be cracking up under the strain of his concern for his son, but Conrad has learned 'that it is love, imperfect and unordered, that keeps them apart, even as it holds them somehow together.'"

"The form, the style of the novel dictate an ending more smooth than convincing," according to Melvin Maddocks in *Time.* "As a novelist who warns against the passion for safety and order that is no passion at all, Guest illustrates as well as describes the problem. She is neat and ordered, even at explaining that life is not neat and ordered." While *Newsweek*'s Walter Clemons agrees that *Ordinary People* "solves a little too patly some of the problems it raises," he also allows that "the feelings in the book are true and unforced. Guest has the valuable gift of making us like her characters; she has the rarer ability to move a toughened reviewer to tears." *Village Voice* contributor Irma Pascal Heldman also has high praise for the novel, writing that "Guest conveys with sensitivity a most private sense of life's personal experiences while respecting the reader's imagination and nurturing an aura of mystery. Without telling all, she illuminates the lives of 'ordinary people' with chilling insight."

Guest's insights into her male protagonist are particularly keen, according to several reviewers, including Lore Dickstein, who writes in the *New York Times Book Review:* "Guest portrays Conrad not only as if she has lived with him on a daily basis—which I sense may be true—but as if she has gotten into his head. The dialogue Conrad has with himself, his psychiatrist, his friends, his family, all rings true with adolescent anxiety. This is the small, hard kernel of brilliance in the novel." But while acknowledging that Guest's male characters are well-defined, several reviewers believe that Beth, the mother, is not fully developed. "The mother's point of view, even though she is foremost in the men's lives, is barely articulated," writes Dorothea D. Braginsky in *Psychology Today.* "We come to know her only in dialogue with her husband and son, and through their portrayals of her. For some reason Guest has given her no voice, no platform for expression. We never discover what conflicts, fears and aspirations exist behind her cool, controlled facade."

Guest herself has expressed similar reservations about the character, telling a *Detroit News* contributor that Beth is "pretty enigmatic in the novel. The reader might have been puzzled by her." But Guest also believes that Mary Tyler Moore's portrayal of Beth Jarrett in the film adaptation of the novel did much to clarify the character. "[Mary Tyler Moore] just knocks me out," Guest told John Blades in a *Chicago Tribune* interview. "She's a terrific actress, a very complex person, and she brought a complexity to the character that I wish I'd gotten into the book. I fought with that character for a long time, trying to get her to reveal herself, and I finally said this is the best I can do. When I saw Mary in the movie, I felt like she'd done it for me."

Guest was also pleased with the movie's ending, which was more inconclusive than the book's. "The more things get left open-ended the better," Guest told Blades. "If you tie everything into a neat little bow, people walk out of the theater and never give it another thought. If there's ambiguity, people think about it and talk about it." She believes director Robert Redford's sensitive presentation "leaves the viewer to his own conclusions," which is how it should be.

In 1982, Guest published *Second Heaven,* a novel that shares many of its predecessor's concerns. "Again, a damaged adolescent boy stands at the center of the story; again, the extent of his wounds will not be immediately apparent," notes Peter S. Prescott in *Newsweek.* "Again, two adults with problems of their own attempt to save the boy from cooperating in his own destruction." In an interview with former *Detroit Free Press* book editor Barbara Holliday, Guest reflects on her fascination with what she calls this "crucial" period known as adolescence: "It's period of time . . . where people are very vulnerable and often don't have much experience to draw on as far as human relationships go. At the same time they are making some pretty heavy decisions, not necessarily physical but psychological decisions about how they're going to relate to people and how they're going to shape their lives. It seems to me that if you don't have sane sensible people around you to help, there's great potential for making irrevocable mistakes."

The way that signals can be misinterpreted, leading to a breakdown in communication between people who may care deeply for one another, is a theme of both her novels and a topic she handles well, according to novelist Anne Tyler. "[Guest] has a remarkable ability to show the unspoken in human relationships— the emotions either hidden or expressed so haltingly that they might as well be hidden, the heroic self-control that others may perceive as icy indifference," Tyler writes in the *Detroit News.*

In *Second Heaven,* it is Gale Murray, abused son of a religiously fanatic father and an ineffectual mother, who hides his feelings behind a facade of apathy. After a brutal beating from his dad, Gale runs away from home, seeking shelter with Catherine (Cat) Holzmann, a recently divorced parent with problems of her own. When Gale's father tries to have his son institutionalized, Cat enlists the aid of Mike Atwood, a disenchanted lawyer, who is falling in love with Cat. He takes on the case largely as a favor to her. According to Norma Rosen in the *New York Times Book Review,* "Cat and Michael must transcend their personal griefs and limits in order to reach out for this rescue. In saving another's life they are on the way to saving their own."

Because of the story's clear delineation of good versus evil and its melodramatic courtroom conclusion, *Second Heaven* strikes some critics as contrived. "Everything in the book is so neat and polished; so precisely timed and calibrated," suggests *New York Times* reviewer Christopher Lehmann-Haupt, "the way the newly divorced people dovetail, conveniently providing a surrogate mother and a fatherly counselor for battered Gale Murray. . . . The reader continually gets the feeling that Mrs. Guest is working with plumb line and level and trowel to build her airtight perpendicular walls of plot development." Or, as Rosen puts it: "On the one hand there are the clear evils of control, rules, order. They are associated with inability to love, fanaticism, brutality. Clutter and lack of organization are good. . . . Yet in the context of the author's antineatness and anticontrol themes, the technique of the novel itself appears at times to be almost a subversion: the quick-march pace, the click-shot scenes, the sensible serviceable inner monologues unvaried in their rhythms."

While acknowledging the book's imperfections, Jonathan Yardley maintains in the *Washington Post* that "the virtues of *Second Heaven* are manifold, and far more consequential than its few flaws. . . . Neither contrivance nor familiarity can disguise the skill and, most particularly, the sensitivity with which Guest tells her story. She is an extraordinarily perceptive observer of the minutiae of domestic life, and she writes about them with humor and affection." Concludes *Chicago Tribune Book World* contributor Harry Mark Petrakis: "By compassionately exploring the

dilemmas in the lives of Michael, Catherine, and Gale, Judith Guest casts light on the problems we often endure in our own lives. That's what the art of storytelling and the craft of good writing are all about."

With *Errands,* Guest continues to examine the contemporary American family with adolescent children in crisis. The Browner family is introduced while on their way to their annual vacation. They are a likable, normal family except that Keith, the father, must begin chemotherapy as soon as they return. But the treatment is not successful; his wife, Annie, and three young children, Harry, Jimmy, and Julie, must carry on without him. Life without Keith is a struggle for each of them and they are each in a state of crisis when Jimmy has a dangerous accident that almost blinds him. But Jimmy's accident requires them to support each other and begins the rebuilding process for this troubled family. Writing in the *New York Times Book Review,* Meg Wolitzer admires the "natural cadences and rhythms" spoken by the children, but suggests that the adults "never fully come to life" and that overall "the novel, while appealing, seems slightly sketchy and meditative." On the other hand, Brad Hooper, in *Booklist,* notes that "Guest is perfectly realistic in her depictions of family situations; her characters act and react with absolute credibility." And Sheila M. Riley, in *Library Journal,* declares Errands "true, touching, and highly recommended."

BIOGRAPHICAL/CRITICAL SOURCES:

BOOKS

Contemporary Literary Criticism, Gale (Detroit), Volume 8, 1978; Volume 30, 1984.

PERIODICALS

Booklist, October 15, 1996, p. 379.
Chicago Tribune, November 4, 1980.
Chicago Tribune Book World, October 3, 1982.
Detroit Free Press, October 7, 1982.
Detroit News, September 26, 1982; October 20, 1982.
Library Journal, October 15, 1996, p. 90.
Ms., December, 1982.
Newsweek, July 12, 1976; October 4, 1982.
New Yorker, July 19, 1976; November 22, 1982.
New York Review of Books, June 10, 1976.
New York Times, July 16, 1976; October 22, 1982; January 24, 1997.
New York Times Book Review, July 18, 1976; October 3, 1982; January 12, 1997, p. 18.
Psychology Today, August, 1976.
Publishers Weekly, April 19, 1976.
Saturday Review, May 15, 1976.
Time, July 19, 1976; October 25, 1982.
Village Voice, July 19, 1976.
Washington Post, September 22, 1982.

*   *   *

GUILLEMIN, Jacques
  See SARTRE, Jean-Paul

*   *   *

GUT, Gom
  See SIMENON, Georges (Jacques Christian)

GUTERSON, David 1956-

PERSONAL: Born May 4, 1956, in Seattle, WA; son of Murray Bernard (a criminal attorney) and Shirley (Zak) Guterson; married Robin Ann Radwick, January 1, 1979; children: Taylor, Travis, Henry. *Education:* University of Washington, B.A., 1978, M.A., 1982.

ADDRESSES: Agent—Georges Borchardt, Inc., 136 East Fifty-seventh St., New York, NY 10020.

CAREER: High school English teacher in Bainbridge Island, WA, 1984–.

AWARDS: PEN/Faulkner Award, Pacific Northwest Bookseller's Award, and Abby Award nomination, all for *Snow Falling on Cedars.*

WRITINGS:

The Country Ahead of Us, the Country Behind (stories), Harper, 1989.
Family Matters: Why Homeschooling Makes Sense, Harcourt Brace Jovanovich (New York City), 1992.
Snow Falling on Cedars, Harcourt Brace (San Diego), 1994.

Contributor to periodicals, including *Harper's, Sports Illustrated,* and *Gray's Sporting Journal.*

SIDELIGHTS: In 1989 David Guterson made his publishing debut with a collection of short stories, *The Country Ahead of Us, The Country Behind.* As its title implies, the stories focus on characters at significant but often basic crossroads in their lives. *People Weekly*'s V. R. Peterson described the stories as being about moments of "lesser revelation," such as an old man confronting his mortality, or a man on a hunting trip with both his father and son, reflecting youth and age. Reviewers found the collection to be a respectable effort. *Boston Book Review* praised the stories as "poignant and thought provoking" and Peterson asserted that the reflection Guterson evokes in *The Country Ahead* "leads to moments of vivid understanding." However, when the book was re-released in 1996 after the commercial and critical success of Guterson's novel, *Snow Falling on Cedars,* the stories were deemed pale in comparison. When viewed alongside the more mature novel, this collection was evaluated as somewhat studied and inauthentic.

In addition to writing fiction, Guterson is an English teacher at a public high school in the state of Washington. In 1992 he wrote a nonfiction book about his experiences inside and outside of the educational system. Despite the fact that he himself teaches in a public school, he chose to school his three sons at home with the help of his wife. In *Family Matters: Why Homeschooling Makes Sense,* Guterson explains this choice and makes an argument for the social and intellectual advantages offered by homeschooling. Not only does he offer his own experiences and opinions, but he also provides well-documented answers to many basic questions about homeschooling. *Kirkus Reviews* evaluated the book as "a lite rate primer for anyone who wants to know more about alternatives to the schools."

Guterson is best known for his award-winning first novel, *Snow Falling on Cedars.* This novel, which tells the story of a murder trial set on a small Puget Sound island, transcends the genre of courtroom drama to comment intimately on race relations, war, love, and forgiveness. *Snow Falling on Cedars* is set in the 1950s and narrated mostly in flashback. The dead man, his accused murderer, and a local journalist who is involved in both the case itself and the lives of those involved, have all carried scars from their experiences in World War II back to their lives on the island. The grudge between the white victim and the Japanese-American accused are inflected with the racial animosity of the war, and a hidden interracial love affair proves to have a pivotal effect on the case's outcome. Susan Kennedy, writing for the *New York Times Book Review,* noted Guterson's extensive research and applauded the resulting work as "densely packed" and "multifaceted." *Booklist* described the novel as not only thematically complex, but also "compellingly suspenseful." A writer for *Kirkus Reviews* praised *Snow Falling on Cedars* for communicating "truths through detail." This critic wrote, "Justice and morality are proven to be intimately woven with beauty—the kind of awe and wonder that children feel for the world."

Guterson told *Contemporary Authors:* "I write because something inner and unconscious forces me to. That is the first compulsion. The second is one of ethical and moral duty. I feel responsible to tell stories that inspire readers to consider more deeply who they are."

BIOGRAPHICAL/CRITICAL SOURCES:

BOOKS

Contemporary Authors, Volume 132, Gale (Detroit), 1991.

PERIODICALS

Booklist, August 19, 1996.
Boston Book Review, September 1, 1996.
Kirkus Review, July 1, 1992; July 1, 1994.
New York Times Book Review, October 16, 1994.
People Weekly, May 27, 1996, p. 38.

*   *   *

GWENDOLYN
See BENNETT, (Enoch) Arnold